RAND McNALLY
14 x 21 INCH MAP OF
NORTH AMERICA

SCALE

Copyright by Rand McNally & Company, Chicago
Made in U. S. A.

REGIONAL AREAS OF THE UNITED STATES

1. THE NORTHEAST
2. THE SOUTH AND SOUTHERN HIGHLANDS
3. THE MIDWEST
4. THE SOUTHWEST
5. THE WEST
6. THE NORTHWEST

A Bibliography
of North American Folklore
and Folksong

This edition is limited to 1500 copies,
of which 1493 are for sale.

A Bibliography
of North American Folklore
and Folksong

by

CHARLES HAYWOOD

Queens College

NEW YORK

GREENBERG : PUBLISHER

Manufactured in The United States of America

To

FRANCES AND JOHNNY

Acknowledgments

The very nature of this work necessitated advice, guidance, and assistance from many individuals, institutions, and publishers. The number is legion. I extend my heartfelt appreciation and profound indebtedness to all of them. I wish it were possible to single out each one individually. I shall merely mention a few: Dr. George Herzog, for his invaluable advice and suggestions in the early stages of planning this work. His expect study, *Research in Primitive and Folk Music in The United States* (Bulletin No. 24 American Council of Learned Societies, Washington, D. C., 1936), first awakened in me a realization of the scope of the problem and the need for further investigation. Dr. Alfred L. Kroeber gave generously of his time with helpful suggestions and illuminating hints. His wise and judicious observations gave confidence and encouragement to one weighed down by doubt and indecision in the last phases of this work. I am very grateful to Dr. George Peter Murdock for his expert advice in the matter of Indian tribal location and distribution.

I owe a special debt to Dr. Gladys A. Reichard. Her enthusiasm, encouragement and many helpful suggestions after reading the manuscript helped me immeasurably in completing the work. I am equally indebted to Dr. James L. Mursell, Dr. Douglas Moore, Dr. Ryland Crary, Dr. Harold Rugg, and Dr. Howard A. Murphy for their advice in discussing the content and organization of the material.

During the arduous, heartless task of collecting material for the book I have often found encouragement in the unsolicited and generous advice from many folklore scholars of this country. I wish to single out two such eminent leaders in this field: Dr. Archer Taylor, who called my attention to a mine of folklore data available in the Catalogue Division of the library of New York University. I have only touched the surface of the million indexed cards contained there. I plan to return for a more thorough investigation. And Dr. Stith Thompson, whose suggestions on bibliographical data on the Indian folktale were most fruitful.

This work could never have been completed without the devoted, tireless, and courteous help of many librarians. One cannot possibly mention them all. To each one my deepest gratitude. Dr. Harold Spivacke, Chief of the Division of Music, and Dr. Duncan Emrich, Chief of the Folklore Section, of the Library of Congress were most helpful in placing the great collection of American folklore material at my disposal. What a wealth of untapped riches still needs to be carefully analyzed and catalogued! To these two gracious scholars and their assistants my profoundest appreciation.

I cannot thank too much the unflagging help I got from the New York Public Library. These hard working, enthusiastic librarians gave unstintingly of their time to help locate material and check data. A great many folksong items and rare Songsters were found in the American Collection of the Library. To its director and dear friend, Mr. John Tasker Howard, and Dr. Carlton Sprague Smith, Chief of the Music Division, and their able assistants, my sincerest thanks. My work in checking and examining folksong collections, arrangements and recordings was greatly facilitated by the enthusiastic help given me by Miss Gladys Chamberlain and her staff at the 58th Street Branch of the New York Public Library.

Invaluable help was given me by the Library and staff of Columbia University. My work would have been impossible without their generous cooperation. I roamed freely in the stacks amidst a veritable forest of Americana treasures. The librarian was always on hand helping to locate the item, and to solve many a bibliographical puzzle. Dr. Catharine Miller, head of the Music Library, was always ready with advice and valuable suggestions. To all these kind people my deepest appreciation.

I am indebted to Miss Nouvart Tashjian of the Cataloguing Division of the New York University Library for placing at my disposal the great many files of entries of American periodicals. I am also very grateful to my dear friends and colleagues, Mr. Morris Gelfand and Dr. Joseph H. Brewer and the members of the Queens College library for their untiring, yet ever-smiling, cooperation. The excellent library of the Museum of Natural History was of tremendous help. To its librarians, and Miss Bella Weitzner in particular, my warmest gratitude.

I also wish to thank the authors and publishers who have been most gracious in permitting me to reprint some material from their works: To J. Frank Dobie and the University of Texas Press for printing on the inside page of his splendid *Guide to Life and Literature of the Southwest* the following statement: "Not copyrighted. Anybody is welcome to help himself to any of it in any way." I did. This warm generosity is typical of the man to whom all students of American folklore, particularly the Southwest, are deeply indebted. To Henry Holt and Company for allowing me to reprint some items listed in the bibliography of *Mike Fink* by Walter Blair and Franklin J. Meine (1933). To the *Journal of American Folklore* and Gladys J. Haney for permission to use some entries from her very fine bibliographic study: "Paul Bunyan Twenty-five Years After," Vol. 55: 155–169, 1942. To Leslie Marshall, editor of the Swedenborg Press, for permission to quote a number of entries from Robert Price's excellent work: *John Chapman; A Bibliography of Johnny Appleseed* (1944). My gratitude to *Western Folklore* (formerly *California Folklore Quarterly*) for reprinting some items from its "Bibliography of California Folklore," which appeared in Vol. 2 (Nos. 1, 2, 3, 4), January, April, July, October, 1943. To Yale University Press and its author, Dr. George Peter Murdock, for permission to reproduce the "American Indian Tribal Map," and reprint some entries from the *Ethnographic Bibliography of North America* (1941).

To the many journals and periodicals, both here and abroad (*see* pp. 4–5; 753–54), whose articles, footnotes and bibliographies have provided the body of materials of this compendium my most profound gratitude and indebtedness.

My heartfelt thanks to my publisher, Jae Greenberg, whose patience and faith made this project possible. He believed in its worth and encouraged me to go on. And to all those associated with him my fullest appreciation. Especially to Elliott MacDowell, editor, whose helpful suggestions made the long, hard task easy. And to Miss Fay Travers, whose skill was not only manifested in setting up and seeing this book through the press, but in offering much wise counsel.

To Mrs. Katharine Hansson and Miss Hazel B. Whitcomb I owe a special debt of gratitude for their untiring effort, expert ability, and sustained devotion in preparing the index.

And, finally, I offer my profound indebtedness to my wife, Frances, who watched, waited patiently, and often wondered (who wouldn't, seeing a roomful of shoe boxes filled with 3 x 5 slips!). And yet, throughout these long, arduous years there was always that kind smile, and enlivening sense of humor at the right moment to fortify, stimulate, and encourage.

Although many gracious people have advised and guided me in this compilation, and much of its value is due to them, yet none of these is accountable for any of the shortcomings of this work. For all these I assume full responsibility.

Contents

BOOK ONE
THE AMERICAN PEOPLE NORTH OF MEXICO

BOOK TWO
THE AMERICAN INDIANS NORTH OF MEXICO

Introduction

In the fall of 1939 I introduced a course in American Folksong at Queens College. It was an attempt to present a panorama of American culture—from the colonial days to the present—as reflected in its folksongs and folk dances. The major historical epochs in the growth of American civilization were treated, the social background briefly discussed, and the corresponding folksongs performed. The official title in the catalogue reads: "The American Scene in Ballad and Song." A considerable change in the procedure and sequence of this course has taken place within the last few years. At the beginning, the main emphasis was on the folksongs; more recently there has been a marked interest among the students in our folklore. This has been particularly stimulated by the realization that there still exists a large body of folklore to be collected and that we need not necessarily live in far-off places to find it. A great many of the students have been gathering various folklore items in their own "neck of the woods." It was at first difficult to make students realize that there is still a rich storehouse of folklore and folksong awaiting the scrutinizing collector in a cosmopolitan city like New York. The students would not at first accept the idea that the folk who still sing "old countree" songs, recount "strange" folk tales, legends, and myths, still believe in "weird" superstitions, practice "old-fashioned" remedies, and engage in "exotic" customs, are not necessarily living in remote, inaccessible mountain regions, resembling the types often caricatured in the *New Yorker*. A few excursions in their own backyards (an area not frequently found in New York), or in their own apartment houses, have yielded surprising results to these skeptical New Yorkers.

However, a rather difficult situation arose when the students attempted to write their term papers on topics selected by themselves or suggested by the instructor. The difficulty was not in the body of material available—in the library at Queens College, and particularly in the various libraries of New York City, public and private—but rather in the lack of a scientifically compiled bibliography of all the various aspects of American folklore and folksongs, which the students could readily use. A few bibliographies were available, but their limited range became quite obvious. Not one, with the exception of the splendid annual bibliographies of Ralph S. Boggs in the March issues of the *Southern Folklore Quarterly*, begun in 1939, attempted to cover every phase of folklore and folksong. But, unfortunately, even these listings fail to mention musical arrangements and recordings. And if some bibliography[1] did include a fairly good selection of books, articles, and collections, it did not offer a comprehensive classification of the materials. Within the same limitation is the one edited by Lomax and Cowell.[2] Although it has the virtue of a regional classification, rather broadly divided into four divisions: "The North, The White South, The West, and The Negro South," the work makes no attempt at completeness. The purpose of the collections is clearly stated by the compilers: "Only a few of the most recent articles were included, since their inclusion would have made this a scholarly rather than

---

[1] "Bibliography" by Harold W. Thompson in: *American Ballads and Songs* by John and Alan Lomax. New York: The Macmillan Co., 1934 (pp. 613-621). Bibliographical Supplement in *Our Singing Country* by the same authors (1941) (pp. 405-510). Mainly on folksongs.

[2] Lomax, Alan, and Cowell, Sidney R. *American Folk Song and Folk Lore. A Regional Bibliography.* New York: Progressive Education Association, 1942. 59 pp.

a popular bibliography."[3] At best, this compilation is but a small fragment of the total, ever-increasing body of American folklore. Dr. George Herzog's listings of folklore data is mainly concerned with folk music,[4] and the very nature of the work precluded exhaustive treatment or thorough classification. Nevertheless, it is a highly informative and scholarly contribution. The general indexes of the *Journal of American Folklore* (1888-1926), the *American Anthropologist,* and the *Publications of the Modern Language Association* (1884-1935, 1936-1940), however useful, are by their very nature limited in scope and material. And none of these solved one of the major needs of folklore students, namely, to offer a "guide to the bulk of earlier work."[5]

It became increasingly obvious that there was no thorough bibliography of American folklore and folksong available, that there was no single compilation systematically organized and critically annotated. What was begun as a mere attempt to fill in the gaps of existing bibliographies in meeting the needs of my own students, eventually—that is after about ten years of study, compilation and classification—grew into the present work: a compendium of our vast traditional heritage in lore and song.

I had never suspected how formidable was the amount of materials that had been published in the field of American folklore and folksong. After some years of collecting the data, I found myself buried under an avalanche of some 40,000 items and still sadly aware that I had not covered everything, that many important items were omitted and that even some of the most obvious and most easily accessible had failed to catch my eye. But these are the inevitable bugbears and despairs of a bibliographer. By its very nature, no bibliography can be complete and definitive. All bibliographies could very justifiably have the descriptive adjective "tentative" added to the title.

The systematic scientific collection and study of American folklore and folksong began in the latter part of the last century with the founding of the American Folklore Society in 1888. It was stimulated largely by anthropologists in their work with primitive cultures.[6] The influence, efforts, and achievements of these scholars have borne fruitful results. What an amazing amount of work has been done in the last quarter of a century! The enthusiasm and labors of a few individuals have stimulated thousands of workers. What was yesterday special or extra-curricular work for the scholar of English or anthropology, has today become a full-time job for the specialist. A decade ago less than a handful of institutions of higher learning offered courses in American folklore and folksong. Today the list is imposing and ever-growing. Among the colleges and universities giving such courses, both undergraduate and graduate, we find: Chico State College, Calif., Columbia University, Cornell University, Franklin and Marshall College, Juilliard School of Music, Murray State College, Ky., Queens College, and the universities of Arizona, Arkansas, California, Cincinnati, Colorado, Indiana, Miami, New Mexico, North Carolina, and Wayne University. One institution has added a professorship in folklore and graduate courses leading to the Ph.D. degree.[7] The importance of this change and recognition of this important body of learning is, I believe, best illustrated by the establishment of a Folklore

---

[3] ibid, p. 2.

[4] Herzog, George. *Research in Primitive and Folk Music in the United States.* Washington, D. C.: American Council of Learned Societies, 1936. Bulletin No. 24. 97 pp.

[5] Halpert, H. "American Regional Folklore." *JAFL* 60: 355-366, 1947.

[6] The work of the Bureau of American Ethnology is of paramount importance in the study of American Indian culture, lore, and song, and in laying a solid foundation for the scientific study of folklore in this country.

[7] Indiana University—at present held by Dr. Stith Thompson, Dean of the Graduate School.

Section in the Library of Congress, as part of the Division of Music.[8] Not only is there a vast and yet unclassified amount of folklore material in the Archive of the Folklore Section of the Library of Congress, but various scholars with the help of their colleagues and students have been accumulating rich fruitful archives of regional lore and song. The recording machine has been a friendly aid in these endeavors. As an illustration of the great number of recordings of America in lore and song, the Folklore Section of the Library of Congress now[9] has about 40,000 songs on more than 10,000 disks. And field workers are adding to the Archive more material daily. In addition, we also witness the growth of new folklore societies with state and regional publications stimulating the study and collection of folklore. To get an idea of the tremendous enthusiasm and great productivity in the various fields of American lore going on at present, behold the number of scholars, students, and amateurs engaged in research projects in various aspects of folklore and folksong in the United States.[10] The list is indeed astonishing. One hundred and thirty individuals (and there are undoubtedly a great number that have not reported) have informed the American Folklore Society's Committee on Research in Folklore for 1947 that they were occupied with creative activity. Some were working on more than one project. The total number of projected studies and collections, covering every phase of folklore and folksong, was truly imposing. One was recording Spanish *corridos* in Arizona; another was collecting ballads and songs from the Pacific Northwest; another was completing for publication some Oneida tales; and another was compiling a book of Southern Illinois tales; one was finishing a volume on *Lore of the Lumberwoods*; one was compiling a bibliography of Michigan folklore; one was completing a comprehensive musical companion to F. J. Child's *The English and Scottish Popular Ballads*; while another folklorist was working on a checklist of North American folk-heroes and similar figures and still another was compiling a dictionary of proverbial sayings.

A far cry indeed from a statement made by a man long prominent in American musical life who, some years ago, wrote the following in his book of memoirs:[11] "In this country [America] we have no peasantry, and what slight remains of folk-songs and folk-dances we possess, apart from the music of the Negro, have only recently been dug out of the isolated mountain fastness of Kentucky and Tennessee. These are generally of British origin and cannot be considered as having been part and parcel of our national life. As against the rich subsoil of the folk-songs of Germany, Bohemia, Russia, France and Scotland, we can show but the thinnest artificial layer of music." Furthermore, the author of the above lines believed that the untutored folk were entirely incapable of a "refined and developed" art. That was, he stated, only possible through the skill, technique, and education of the great composers, who polished and refined these crude utterances, lifted them "upward and [the folksongs] became the possession and delight of the cultured classes."

Although Dr. Walter Damrosch traveled far over the land, bringing the finest compositions—symphonic, choral, and operatic—to many sections of the land, and to whom America will always owe a great debt of gratitude, yet he has sadly oblivious of the wealth and variety of the American folk song; and the little that he was aware of, he claimed, had been "created and carefully nurtured by a small educated class."

One can perhaps forgive the misconceptions of this venerable and well-loved

---

[8] The Archive of American Folksong was incorporated into the Folklore Section in 1946, with Duncan Emrich as chief.

[9] This introduction was first written in November, 1948.

[10] Halpert, H.: "Work in Progress: 1947." *JAFL* 61: 71-82, 1948.

[11] Damrosch, Walter, *My Musical Life*. New York: Charles Scribner's Sons, 1923. p. 323.

composer-conductor. Perhaps we might pose in his favor the extenuating circumstance that after all he was a product of European culture, tradition, and attitudes, which, until not so long ago, still considered the vast domain of America inhabited by "primitive savages," particularly in the arts. But how can we explain and justify the statement by a young music historian born and trained in this country, made in a book published in 1947?[12] "The United States has no national folk music," he declared. To support this pronouncement, he marshals the following reasons: "Because the country is young and because it is a nation of heterogeneous peoples. . . . There is no established nationalism as such in the United States. There is no indigenous American style. American music has no one style, but is rather a complexity of heterogeneous styles." Feeling somewhat uneasy, perhaps, that he has overstated his case, the author searches for some substitutes for what he considers our total lack of folk song expression. "Our absence of native folk music," he propounds, "is in part [!] supplied by (1) composed songs such as the Stephen Foster melodies, (2) cowboy songs, (3) American Indian music (of little influence on American music) and (4) Afro-American music, which has had the greatest influence upon American music in general." It would take much more than space allows to comment upon the misconception of American history, culture, institutions, and music displayed by the author of the above quotation.

Every statement he makes—that there is no nationalism in the United States, that there is no indigenous American style and no one American style (What country, pray, has one style? And what, furthermore, is style?), that there is no native folk music, etc.—shows clearly his failure to understand the meaning of folk song. He mentions, somewhat reluctantly and hesitantly, a number of categories of songs found in this country. But he fails to realize that these are products of the folk—expressions of their aspirations, hopes, joys, and struggles, composed by some individual whose identity has been lost and completely submerged in the people, and hence *are* folk songs. The author is literally surrounded by them and fails to notice their presence. That is indeed, a new type of musical consciousness. If some of our capable music historians would devote to the varied aspects of our American musical heritage but a fraction of the time they spend on the music of other cultures and periods (without in the least minimizing their significance and contribution), such misconceptions and distortions might be avoided.

The reason so much space has been devoted to discussing the opinions of Drs. Damrosch and Miller (and they, alas, are not the only ones) is because their remarks carry considerable weight and influence. Dr. Miller's *Outline of History of Music* is used by many high school and college students. Especially useful in memorizing basic facts and in preparing for examinations (more or less the purpose of the *College Outline Series*), the book leaves the students with erroneous information.

In the reports of the various members of the Folklore Research Committee[13] one demand is made perhaps more than any other: namely, the urgent need for a general comprehensive folklore bibliography. The worker in American Indian lore and music, whether it be of a particular culture area or tribe; the student of American folk tales, customs, superstitions or folk speech; those interested in the ethnic and foreign-language groups of America; the collectors of regional or state folklore and folksong; or those interested in folklore and song of the various occupations—all are anxious to have bibliographies of their particular discipline. In seeking to satisfy these various needs this volume was expanded to encompass all the areas and classifica-

---

[12] Miller, Hugh. *An Outline of the History of Music.* New York: Barnes & Noble, 1947. pp. 203-204.
[13] "Folklore Research in America." *JAFL* 60 (No. 238): 350-416, 1947.

tions of our folklore, including the North American Indians and all the people living north of Mexico.

The interest in our traditional heritage is not limited to our scholars and specialists only. American folklore and folksong have won widespread appeal—they have become "popular." Folk heroes and legendary figures, with appropriate folksong background (not too often, alas!), are seen on the screen, heard on the radio and in the theatre. Billy the Kid, Jesse James, Johnny Appleseed, Pecos Bill, and others have superseded the gangster heroes of yesterday. Musical plays such as "Oklahoma," "Dark of the Moon," "Sing Out, Sweet Land," "Bloomer Girl," "Annie Get Your Gun," and others—not to mention the great many folk plays written by some of our outstanding playwrights—are being performed in many sections of the country. Our composers are exploiting folk themes and folk characters for their musical compositions—vocal, instrumental, and dramatic. Even commercial advertising is finding our folklore profitable.

From the foregoing statements, one can readily surmise my general conception and meaning of folklore. It is the sum total *traditional* heritage of a people. And by "traditional" I do not mean only that of bygone days, of the dim past. I seek to include in it the heritage of yesterday and the changes, alterations, and accretions taking place today. While the great body of folklore is traditional, implying the past, one must not fail to recognize that many traditions are being made, or set in motion, and some even crystallized in our own day. To take but one example: speech. Our American speech is daily undergoing changes, additions, and transformations. The last war brought new words and expressions into our speech. These are vital elements of our folk patterns, and they must be recognized as such, a point H. L. Mencken emphasizes in his studies in the American language. Furthermore, tradition ought not be relegated entirely to oral transmission to make it legitimate folklore material. Much of our traditional lore has come to us, and still does originate, from written sources.

Folklore is not a *survival*, a museum piece, unaltered and fixed, merely gathering dust which the cultured and more advanced members of a later society purify and polish to make it presentable and understandable, but rather it is a vital *living* organism, still growing and developing, wherever people live, struggle, hope, make merry, despair, and die. Folklore is alive—in the country and city, among the rich and poor. It is a vivid panorama or cavalcade of man's life with his fellow men. Folklore, like the people who make it up, is not static; it is in constant flux, ever changing, ever creating and re-creating. "It is a lively, fluid, phenomenon."[14] It is dialectic as the social organism. "Folklore," observes one of our leading students of anthropology, is "concerned with the realities of life and not with the relics of the dead past."[15] Folklore is not an exclusive discipline; it is perhaps the most inclusive of all. "It calls upon," observes Herskovits, "history, ethnology, psychology, linguistics." For each of these shares and contributes in creating the vast heritage of folklore. This conception of the totality of human experience as being well within the province of folklore is eloquently expressed by Botkin.[16] "The essence of folklore is something that cannot be contained in a definition, but that grows upon one with folklore experience. Old songs, old stories, old sayings, old beliefs, customs, and practices—the mindskills and handskills that have been handed down so long that

---

[14] Davidson, Donald. *TFSB* 6 (No. 4) : 45, Dec. 1940.

[15] Herskovits, Melville J.: "Folklore After a Hundred Years, a Problem of Definition." *JAFL* 59 (No. 232) : 99, 1946.

[16] Botkin, B. A.: *A Treasury of American Folklore.* New York: Crown Publishers, 1944. p. xxi.

they seem to have a life of their own, a life that cannot be destroyed by print, but that constantly has to get back to the spoken word to be renewed; patterned by common experience; varied by individual repetition, inventive or forgetful; and cherished because somehow characteristic or expressive: all this, for want of a better word, is 'folklore'."

This conception of folklore has guided me in the compiling and arrangement of material for this bibliography. I have tried to make it all-inclusive rather than exclusive. Every book or article that casts some light on the traditional life of the American folk was welcome in this compilation. In addition to specialized books and articles, I have also examined, and, when of interest, indexed, personal diaries and letters, travel books, biographies, social and cultural histories, regional fiction, and regional cook books. From all of these and many other sources, I gathered a mine of information on the life, customs, manners, beliefs, folk speech, songs, dances, and tales of the people who helped build this great land—its roads, trains, canals, and homes— made its laws and institutions, and created what we know as the American way of life.

I may have erred occasionally on being too generous with my entries; for that I beg forgiveness and indulgence. And if I have overlooked some—of that I am sure— again I beg those who will use this reference work to call my attention to it, and the changes and corrections will be made in the next edition. My general criterion for including material in this bibliography, as well as my conception of what constitutes folklore, may be summed up in a conversation I had some time ago with Dean Stith Thompson. While we were discussing the general scheme, content, and classification of this work, I was asked whether I would include a book or an article on the building of log-cabins in the bibliography. My answer was that if the study dealt merely with measurements and piecing together of parts (the kind of literature accompanying a pre-fabricated log cabin, in which the only folklore was in the retention of the word "log-cabin"), I would hardly think it wise to include it in the bibliography. But if the author of the study told us not only how to put the parts together, but also how the trees were cut down, how the people lived, toiled, played, their manners of speech and dress, their beliefs and superstitions—if the author discussed but one of these items listed above, then unquestionably it belongs in a folklore bibliography.

The American people have become aware of their heritage. The work of the scholars, specialists, and enthusiasts has caught on. There is hardly a commercial publisher in America today that does not include some folklore or folksong books on its lists. The production and sale of folksong records in albums and individual titles go on apace. Recording companies pride themselves on the number of new pressings they make each month. The performers range the whole gamut from the imitation and pseudo-performer to the authentic native folk singer; from the simple, direct, and spontaneous performance to the artificially manipulated and vulgarized distortion. But, they all sell! Very often the public is unable to distinguish the real from the imitation. Indeed, folklore has gone commerical. Business sees in it tempting possibilities for lucrative ventures. Some students of folklore regard all this with grave concern and suspicion. They are disturbed by this over-popularization of a very strict academic and scientific discipline. Some even fear that folklore is being diverted to "propaganda purposes."[17]

All these fears are, I believe, greatly exaggerated. What we behold in the folk arts today is but the enthusiastic interest of a large section of the American people in a tremendously vital phase of their traditional heritage and culture. These so-called popularizations are the inevitable reactions and responses to a new discovery—joyful,

---

[17] J., T. G. *JAFL* 61 (No. 241): 311, 1948.

exalting, even if somewhat strained. In this light one can understand, if not wholly condone, Tin Pan Alley's exploitation of American folksong idiom, and particularly that based on Negro rhythm and melody, jazz and its derivatives, as well as the blues. All these musical expressions, although much different from their original melodic configurations, are being recognized as part of our folksong, and for these reasons they were included in this bibliography.

The general plan upon which the entries of Book One—*The American People North of Mexico*—of this bibliography have been catalogued is regional, ethnic, and occupational, followed by a section of miscellaneous categories. The decision in favor of a regional classification rather than one based upon the various folklore subdivisions was largely determined by educational needs. In a rather interesting manner, a number of teachers from the elementary schools, high schools, and colleges decided for me the type of classification they felt was best suited for their work. Through them I became convinced that if folklore and folksong are to have meaning and give pleasure as well as arouse a deep lasting affection for our cultural heritage, they must become part of our educational curriculum. There is hardly a subject in our courses of study, no matter on what educational level, that cannot be related to some aspect of folklore. The impact of this fundamental fact came upon me by the numerous letters I received in response to a radio program—"I Hear America Singing"—I presented on Station WQXR in the season 1937-1938. Those programs really started me on my quest for American lore and song. What was most revealing in the public response to these weekly broadcasts was the demand of many teachers for guidance in planning integrated educational programs through the utilization of folk material. They stressed the need for programs on the life and lore of their particular regions, states, and cities, in so far as they participated and shared in the general scheme of American civilization.

In selecting the regional divisions of the country, I have been largely guided by the study made by Odum and Moore.[18] However, in several instances some states were classified with other regions because it was felt that there were greater traditional affinities than those set up and discussed by these authors. First under the heading, *Folklore,* the country as a whole is treated, listing bibliographies, periodicals, serial publications, general studies. This is followed by entries under the various categories and subdivisions of folklore, such as folktales, legends, myths, beliefs: superstition, magic, witchcraft, folk medicine, weather lore, plant lore; customs: dress, ornaments, folk foods, games, dances; humor, proverbs, riddles, folk speech, place names, etc. The same detailed cataloguing is then done for each of the main regions of the United States. Each state within these regional areas, taken alphabetically, is then fully treated for all the categories enumerated above. All the folklore classifications in the country as a whole, in each region, and in each state are followed by corresponding sections on *Folksong.* Included in the latter are ballad and song studies and collections, children's nursery rhymes, games, and folk dances, as well as bibliographies and periodicals devoted to these special fields. Since the American folksong is so closely linked to the ballads and songs of England, Scotland, and Ireland (witness the monumental pioneering work of Professor Childs with the English and Scotch ballads), I have included selected listings of ballad and folksong studies, periodicals, collections, and arrangements and recordings of these people to afford the American students a ready list of important data for comparative study. This is far from being complete or exhaustive. No doubt a number of very important foreign publications

---

[18] Odum, Howard W., and Moore, Harry E. *American Regionalism.* A Cultural Historical Approach to National Integration. New York: Henry Holt and Company, 1938. 693 pp.

were overlooked. The same applies to the selected German and French studies found in this bibliography. See particularly the sections on the Pennsylvania-Germans and the French-Canadians.

In order to make us more fully aware how these folksongs have been part of our culture, the influence they have had and are having so widely upon our musical creativeness, I have included complete listings of musical arrangements—vocal and instrumental, solo and ensemble—from the simplest to the most elaborate stage spectacles; in all instances giving arranger's or composer's name, the publisher, and the resources needed for their performance. In addition, extensive cataloguing of recordings are given. An attempt was made to include records made and deposited in federal, regional, and state archives, as well as those manufactured by commercial companies, listing album collections as well as individual titles. I have tried to make each regional area, and every state within it, a complete bibliographical unit of all aspects of folklore and folksong material.

Under the *ethnic classification* I wished to emphasize the richness of our culture, the multiplicity of elements that make it up; a country of many peoples, beliefs, customs, traditions, and songs. The Negro is extensively examined and catalogued in folklore and folksong. A very large section is devoted to Negro religious and secular music. Under the latter heading, full recognition is given to their influences on American popular music—jazz and the blues, as well as minstrelsy. The folklore and folksong of the Creole Negro as well as a selection of those living in the West Indies are indexed. Appropriate emphasis is also given to the religious songs of the White folk, in a section under the heading *White Spirituals*. The Spanish Americans, the French Canadians, the Pennsylvania Germans, the Norwegians, the Swedes, the Jews, the Italians, etc.—all the non-English-speaking American groups find a place, in so far as their native folklore and folksong have been affected by life in the New World, in this bibliography.

Under *occupational classification* are listed all the working groups who, toiling together, not only built this land, but also created a fascinating and rich lore and song. In this section are found and analyzed the folklore and folksong, dances, games, musical arrangements, and recordings of the cowboys, the sailormen, the lumberjacks, the miners—49'ers, anthracite, bituminous, and others—and the railroad workers.

In the miscellaneous section I have listed entries dealing with a great many of our *folk characters*—"good, bad, and notorious." Davy Crockett, Paul Bunyan, Johnny Appleseed, Mike Fink, John Henry, Billy the Kid, Joe Margarac, and many others are classified there. Also studies and collections in lore and song of *Our Wars*— from '76 to World War II—are indexed. *The Shakers*, with their customs, beliefs, religious and secular songs, and dances are catalogued. A great many entries are devoted to the people of *Canada* and their folklore heritage, including a large section on the *French-Canadians*.

Book Two—*The American Indians North of Mexico*—is based on the major *culture area divisions*. I have been guided in this classification to a great extent by the studies of Wissler,[19] Kroeber,[20] and Murdock.[21] The following areas are used in this bibliography: the Northeast Woodland, the Southeastern, the Plains, the Plateau, the Great Basin, the California, the Southwest, the Northwest, the Mackenzie-Yukon, and

---

[19] Wissler, Clark. *Indians of the United States;* Four Centuries of Their History and Culture. New York: Doubleday, Doran and Co., 1940.

[20] Kroeber, A. L. *Cultural and Natural Areas of North America.* Berkeley, Cal.: University of California Press, 1939.

[21] Murdock, George Peter. *Ethnographic Bibliography of North America.* Yale Anthropological Studies, Vol. 1. New Haven: Publications for the Department of Anthropology, 1941.

the Arctic (Eskimo). While the names and geographic locations of each of the culture areas are fairly well recognized and established, the still puzzling problem is the exact location of some of the border-line tribes. To resolve this difficulty, I have in most instances used Wissler's (modified by Kroeber) classifications and Murdock's distribution and divisions, as found in his map.

After consideration of materials relating to the general character of the American Indians in lore—bibliographies, periodicals; myths, legends, folk tales; beliefs: religious practices, rituals and ceremonies, folk medicine, magic; customs, games, language,[22] folk literature, art; and music: including songs, dances, musical arrangements and recordings—each culture area and each tribe is taken up separately in alphabetic sequence, and entries in lore and music are classified under the same subdivisions as above. Thus, as in Part I, each culture area and each tribe presents a complete bibliography by itself.

In getting material for this bibliography, I examined the contents of books, studies, collections, monographs, periodicals, and serial publications on folklore and folksong available in many libraries in the country, or bibliographies and studies based on materials in these institutions. I have indexed the articles in our major folklore and anthropological journals from the first issues up to about *July, 1948*. Included among these, to mention a few, were the *Journal of American Folklore*, the *Publications of the Texas Folklore Society*, the *Western Quarterly*, the *New York Folklore Quarterly*, the *Southern Folklore Quarterly*, the *American Anthropologist*, and many others. I have also listed, and wherever possible examined the work of government, institutional, and individual archives and collections in the United States. Thus the materials on the subject of American folklore and folksong in the Library of Congress, as well as the invaluable collections in the Folklore Section of the Division of Music, have been investigated and listed. The publications of the Bureau of American Ethnology, with its many collections, bulletins, proceedings, and yearbooks on the American Indian, were examined and indexed. University publications such as the *California University Publications in Archaeology and Ethnology*, as well as those of Columbia University, Yale University, University of Arizona, University of New Mexico, University of Pennsylvania, and Washington University, were catalogued. Museum publications of the Peabody Museum, Museum of Natural History, Museum of the American Indian, and others have yielded a rich harvest. Journals such as *American Speech, Dialect Notes, American Antiquarian, Proceedings of the American Philosophical Society, Proceedings of the* [various] *Sessions of the International Congresses of Americanists*, and others, added many important valuable entries to this bibliography. Foreign books, monographs, periodicals, and serials have been checked and classified. Libraries such as those of the New York Public Library, Columbia University, Harvard University, New York University, with its amazing index file of over one million cards of all articles in journals published in this country from 1728 to 1870, have afforded much folklore data. State historical journals as well as regional periodicals, such as the *New England Quarterly* and the *Southwest Review*, to mention but two, are rich sources for the folklore bibliographer. One of the most invaluable sources of folklore information, from which I have drawn copiously, always deeply grateful that such materials were at hand, was the innumerable publications compiled, produced, and written by the Federal Writers' Project and Historical Records Survey of the Works Progress Administration. I consider those volumes, ranging the whole field of American culture, one of the major

---

[22] To maintain uniformity in classification with Book One I have kept the heading "speech" (meaning folk speech) in Book Two, the Indian section. However, I am fully aware that "language" would have been a much better and more inclusive term. I beg the readers to note this fact. In the cross reference in the Index this matter is clarified.

contributions to American folklore in this century. In addition, personal communications with leading scholars and research workers in American folklore and folksong have given many invaluable clues to articles, journals, and collections.

After ten years of involvement in the work of compiling this long list of entries, one simply had to come to the decisive moment—and stop. Certainly not because everything in this field had been examined and included, but simply because of the physical limitations of book publishing. Not to mention editorial and financial problems. For this and other reasons this book has taken much longer to see through the press than anticipated. For that, our deepest apology and regrets. I shall most eagerly welcome suggestions, corrections, and criticism. In future supplements and editions I hope to obviate the inevitable omissions in this work. Nevertheless, this bibliography attempts to present for the first time an over-all view of what Constance Rourke called "The Roots of American Culture." All the diverse elements and ramifications of our accumulated folk traditions are, I believe, for the first time brought together. This volume emphasizes the diversity of American culture and civilization. It shows up forcefully and dramatically that America is a complex of many cultural forces. Many peoples and traditions have contributed and added to make up the "American."

It is fervently hoped this work will prove to be an aid in research and study for the scholar and specialist, as well as for the interested layman. The historian of American culture, and comparative institutions, the musicologist, the ethnologist, the librarian, the composer and dramatist, the folksong enthusiast, the music arranger as well as the record collector, the movie and radio director—all these should find this guide to our traditions of great help. This compilation can also make, I believe, a significant contribution to our teachers. In planning programs in the school and community—musical, literary, dramatic, regional, ethnic, occupational—the bibliography can serve as a ready aid in choosing the proper materials, or at least in knowing what there is available. The integrated curriculum and course of study can become immeasurably enriched through the utilization of folklore and folksong. How much more meaningful the history or geography lesson can be with the help of folklore and folksong, wisely selected and intelligently introduced. The school or college orchestra, band, or choral group can now readily find the proper folksong compositions and arrangement best suited for performance. And this also applies to the dramatic organizations who will find in the section under Folk Plays a useful guide. Furthermore, the teachers, seeing the paucity of folklore items in their own regions, states, or towns, may inspire their students to do "field work," to go out and collect. Among other things it is an excellent way to know your fellow men—how they live and think. There is hardly a better way of getting closer to and more appreciative of our humblest folk. And that is a great lesson in democracy.

* * * *

Key to Abbreviations

A. Serial Publications

AA (Amer. Anthro.)—American Anthropologist, Menasha, Wisconsin.

AAFS-LC—Archive of American Folksong, Library of Congress, Washington, D. C.

AI (Amer. In.)—America Indígena, Organo Oficial del Instituto Indígenista Americano, Mexico, D. F.

AM (Amer. Mer.)—American Mercury, New York, N. Y.

Amer. Antiq.—American Antiquarian, Worcester, Mass.

Amer. Cath. Quart. Rev.—American Catholic Quarterly Review, Philadelphia, Pa.

Amer. Hist. Rev.—American Historical Review, New York, N. Y.; Lancaster, Pa.

Amer. Jour. Phil.—American Journal of Philology, New York, N. Y.

Amer. Jour. Phys. Anthro.—American Journal of Physical Anthropology, Washington, D. C.

Amer. Jour. Sociol.—American Journal of Sociology, Chicago University, Chicago, Ill.

Amer. Mus. Jour.—American Museum Journal, New York, N. Y.

Amer. Natur.—American Naturalist, Salem, Mass.

Amer. Notes Queries—American Notes and Queries, Philadelphia, Pa.

An. Soc. folk. Mexico (ASFM)—Anuario de la Sociedad folklórica de Mexico, Mexico, D. F.

Ann. Arch. Rep.—Annual Archaeological Report, being part of Appendix to the Report of the Minister of Education, Ontario, Toronto

Ann. N. Y. Acad. Sci.—Annals of the New York Academy of Science, New York, N. Y.

Ann. Rep. Bur. Amer. Ethnol.—Annual Report, Bureau of American Ethnology, Washington, D. C.

Ann. Rep. Can. Geol. Survey—Annual Reports of the Canada Geological and Natural History Survey, Ottawa

Ann. Rep. Regents Univ. N. Y.—Annual Reports of the Regents of the University of the State of New York, Albany, N. Y.

Ann. Rep. Regents Smithson. Inst.—Annual Reports of Board of Regents of the Smithsonian Institution, Washington, D. C.

Anthro. Papers Amer. Mus. Nat. Hist.—Anthropological Papers of the American Museum of Natural History, New York, N. Y.

Anthro. Records—Anthropological Records, Berkeley, University of California.

Anthro. Rec. Amer. Mus. Nat. Hist.—Anthropological Records of the American Museum of Natural History, New York, N. Y.

Arch. wissen. Kunde Russl.—Archiv für wissenschaftliche Kunde von Russland, Berlin.

Art and Arch.—Art and Archaeology, Baltimore, Md.

AS (Amer. Sp.)—American Speech, Columbia University Press, New York, N. Y.

BAE (Bur. Amer. Ethnol.)—Bureau of American Ethnology, Washington, D. C.

Bol. Asoc. folk. Argen. (BAFA)—Boletin de la Asociacion folklórica, Buenos Aires, Argentina.

BLAM (Bol. lat. amer. mus.)—Boletin latino-americano de música, Montevideo, Uruguay.

Bull. Amer. Mus. Nat. Hist—Bulletin of the American Museum of Natural History, New York, N. Y.

Bull. Arch. Soc. Del.—Bulletin of the Archaeological Society of Delaware, Wilmington.

Bull. Buf. Soc. Natur. Sci.—Bulletin of the Buffalo Society of Natural Sciences, Buffalo, N. Y.

Bull. Can. Dept. Mines—Bulletins and Annual Reports of the Canada Department of Mines, National Museum of Canada, Ottawa.

Bull. Free Mus. Sci. and Arts—Bulletin of the Free Museum of Science and Arts, University of Pennsylvania, Philadelphia.

Bull. Société d'Anthro.—Bulletin de la Société d'Anthropologie, Paris.

Bull. Tex. Arch. Ethnol. Soc.—Bulletin of the Texas Archaeological and Ethnological Society.

Bull. Tex. Arch. Paleon. Soc.—Bulletin of the Texas Archaeological and Paleontological Society, Abilene, Texas.

Bull. U. S. Nat. Mus.—Bulletin of the United States National Museum, Washington, D. C.

Bur. Amer. Ethnol. Bull.—Bureau of American Ethnology, Bulletin. Washington, D. C.

CFQ (Cal. Folk. Quart.)—California Folklore Quarterly (now changed to Western Quarterly). *See below,* Organ of the California Folklore Society, University of California Press, Berkeley, California.

Chicago Natur. Hist. Mus. Bull.—Chicago Natural History Museum Bulletin, Chicago, Ill.

Col. Univ. Contr. Anthro.—Columbia University Contributions to Anthropology, New York, N. Y.

Coll. Kans. State Hist. Soc.—Collections of the Kansas State Historical Society, Topeka, Kansas.

Coll. Mass. Hist. Soc.—Collections of the Massachusetts Historical Society, Cambridge, Mass.

Coll. Minn. Hist. Soc.—Collections of the Minnesota Historical Society, St. Paul.

Coll. N. Y. State Hist. Soc.—Collections of the New York Historical Society, New York, N. Y.

Coll. State Hist. Soc. Wis.—Collections of the State Historical Society of Wisconsin, Madison.

Contr. North Amer. Ethnol.—Contributions to North American Ethnology, Department of the Interior, United States Geographical and Geological Survey of the Rocky Mountain Region, Washington, D. C.

EA (Estud. afrocub.)—Estudios afrocubanos, Revista trimestral, Habana, Cuba.

Explor. Field Work Smithson. Inst.—Explorations and Field Work of the Smithsonian Institution, Washington, D. C.

FF (Folk. Fel.)—Folklore Fellows.

FFC (Folk. Fel. Com.)—Folklore Fellows Communications, Helsinki, Finland.

Field Mus. Natur. Hist.—Field Museum of Natural History, Department of Anthropology, Leaflets, Chicago.

FL (Folk-Lore)—Folk-Lore, Journal of the Folk Lore Society, London.

FLJ (Folk-Lore Jour.)—Folk-Lore Journal, predecessor of Folk-lore, London, 1883-89.

FSSNE (Folk Song Soc. North-East)—Folk Song Society of the North-East, Cambridge, Mass.

Flor. Hist. Soc. Quart.—Florida Historical Society Quarterly, Jacksonville, Florida.

Folk. Amer. (FA)—Folklore Americas.

Geog. Tidssk.—Geografisk Tidsskrift, Kjøbenhavn.

Geol. Surv. Can. Anthro. Serv.—Geological Survey of Canada, Anthropological Series, Ottawa.

HF (Hoos. Folk.)—Hoosier Folklore, Bloomington, Indiana.

HFB (Hoos. Folk. Bull.)—Hoosier Folklore Bulletin (changed to *Hoosier Folklore*), Bloomington, Indiana.

Hist. Mag.—Historical Magazine, Boston, N. Y.

Ind. Notes and Monogr.—Indian Notes and Monographs, Museum of the American Indian, Heye Foundation, New York, N. Y.

Inter. Archiv. Ethno.—Internationales Archiv für Ethnographie, Leiden.

Inter. Jour. Amer. Ling.—International Journal of American Linguistics, New York, N. Y.

Iowa Jour. Hist. and Pol.—Iowa Journal of History and Politics, Iowa City, Iowa.

JAFL (Jour. Amer. Folk.)—Journal of the American Folklore Society, New York, N. Y.

JEFDS (Jour. Eng. Folk Dance Soc.)—Journal of the English Folk Dance and Song Society, London, England.

Jour. Amer Geog. Soc.—Journal of the American Geographical Society, New York, N. Y.

Jour. Anthro. Inst. Gt. Brit.—Journal of the Royal Anthropological Institute of Great Britain and Ireland, London.

Jour. Ethnol. Soc.—Journal of the Ethnological Society, London.

Jour. Ill. State Arch. Soc.—Journal of the Illinois State Archaeological Society, Urbana, Ill.

Jour. Royal Geog. Soc.—Journal of the Royal Geographical Society, London.

Jour. Société Amer.—Journal de la Société des Americanistes, Paris.

Jour. Wash Acad. Sci.—Journal of the Washington Academy of Sciences, Washington, D. C.

Leaflets Mus. Amer. Indian—Leaflets of the Museum of the American Indian, Heye Foundation, New York, N. Y.

Medd. Grønl.—Meddelelser om Grønland, Kjøbenhavn.

Mem. Amer. Anthro. Assoc.—Memoirs of the American Anthropological Association, Lancaster, Pa.

Mem. Amer. Folk Soc. (MAFLS)—Memoirs of the American Folklore Society, Lancaster, Pa., etc.

Mem. Amer. Mus. Nat. Hist.—Memoirs of the American Museum of Natural History, New York, N. Y.

Mem. Amer. Philo. Soc.—Memoirs of the American Philosophical Society, Philadelphia, Pa.

Mem. Can. Dept. Mines—Memoirs of the Canada Department of Mines, Geological Survey, Ottawa.

M & L (Music Letters)—Music and Letters, London, England.

MLJ (Mod. Lang Jour.)—Modern Language Journal, St. Louis, Missouri.

MLN (Mod. Lang. Notes)—Modern Language Notes, Baltimore, Maryland.

MLR (Mod. Lang. Rev.)—Modern Language Review, Cambridge, England.

MM (Mod. Music)—Modern Music, New York, N. Y.

MQ (Music Quart.)—Musical Quarterly, New York, N. Y.

MSNC (Music Sup. Nat. Conf.)—Music Supervisors' National Conference, Chicago, Ill.

MTNA (Music Teach. Nat. Assoc.)—Music Teachers' National Association, Series, Pittsburgh, Pennsylvania.

Mus. Bull. Can. Dept. Mines—Museum Bulletins of the Canada Department of Mines, Geological Survey, Ottawa.

Mus. Jour.—Museum Journal, University of Pennsylvania, Philadelphia.

Nat. Ed. Assoc. Jour.—National Education Association Journal, Washington, D. C.

Nat. Hist.—Natural History, New York, N. Y.

n. s.—new series.

New Mex. Anthro.—New Mexico Anthropologist, Albuquerque, New Mexico.

New Mex. Hist. Rev.—New Mexico Historical Review, Santa Fe, New Mexico.

NYFQ (N. Y. Folk Quart.)—New York Folklore Quarterly, Albany, N. Y.

NYPL (N. Y. Pub. Lib.)—New York Public Library, New York City.

N. Y. State Mus. Bull.—New York State Museum Bulletin, Albany, N. Y

N. Y. U.—New York University.

o. s.—old series.

Ohio State Hist. Arch. Quart.—Ohio State Archaeological and Historical Quarterly, Columbus.

P (Palacio)—El Palacio, Sante Fe, New Mexico.

Papers Mich. Acad. Sci.—Papers of the Michigan Academy of Science, Arts and Letters, New York.

Peabody Mus. Papers—Peabody Museum Papers, Cambridge, Harvard University.

Penna. Arch.—Pennsylvania Archaeologist, Milton, Pa.

Pop. Sci. Month.—Popular Science Monthly, New York.

Proc. Amer. Antiq. Soc.—Proceedings of the American Antiquarian Society, Worcester, Mass.

Proc. Amer. Assoc. Adv. Sci.—Proceedings of the American Association for the Advancement of Science, Philadelphia, etc.

Proc. Amer. Philo. Soc.—Proceedings of the American Philosophical Society, Philadelphia.

Proc. Amer. Sci. Congr.—Proceedings of the American Scientific Congress, Washington, D. C.

Proc. Can. Inst.—Proceedings of the Canadian Institute, Toronto.

Proc. Ind. Acad. Sci.—Proceedings of the Indiana Academy of Science, Greencastle, Indiana.

Proc. Intern. Congr. Amer.—Proceedings of the Sessions of the International Congress of Americanists, Paris, etc.

Proc. Nat. Acad. Sci.—Proceedings of the National Academy of Science, Washington, D. C.

Proc. New Jersey Hist. Soc.—Proceedings of the New Jersey Historical Society, Newark.

Proc. Pac. Sci. Congr.—Proceedings of the Pacific Science Congress, Toronto, Canada.

Proc. Royal Can. Inst.—Proceedings of the Royal Canadian Institute, Toronto, Canada.

Proc. Trans. Nova Scotian Inst.—Proceedings and Transactions of the Nova Scotian Institute of Natural Science, Halifax, N. S.

Proc. Trans. Royal Soc. Can.—Proceedings and Transactions of the Royal Society of Canada, Ottawa.

Proc. U. S. Nat. Mus.—Proceedings of the United States National Museum, Washington, D. C.

Publ. Amer. Ethnol. Soc.—Publications of the American Ethnological Society, New York.

Publ. Amer. Sociol. Soc.—Publications of the American Sociological Society, Chicago.

Publ. Champl. Soc.—Publications of the Champlain Society, Toronto, Canada.

Publ. Flor. State Hist. Soc.—Publications of the Florida State Historical Society, Deland, Fla.

Publ. Miss. Hist. Soc.—Publications of the Mississippi Historical Society, Oxford, Miss.

Publ. Mod. Lang. Assoc. (PMLA)—Publications of the Modern Language Association of America, New York, N. Y.

Publ. Penn. Hist. Com.—Publications of the Pennsylvania Historical Commission, Philadelphia, Pa.

Publ. Phila. Anthro. Soc.—Publications of the Philadelphia Anthropological Society, Philadelphia, Pa.

Quart. Los Angeles County Mus.—Quarterly of the Los Angeles County Museum.

Reports of Explorations and Surveys—Reports of Explorations and Surveys to Ascertain the Most Practicable and Economical Route from the Mississippi River to the Pacific Ocean (33rd Congress, 2nd Session, H. R. Ex. Doc. 91). Washington, D. C.

Rep. U. S. Nat. Mus.—Reports of the United States National Museum, Washington, D. C.

Rev. Arquivo mun. São P. (RAMSP)—Revista do arquivo municipal, São Paulo, Brasil.

Rev. brasil. Rio Janeiro (RBRJ)—Revista brasileira. Rio de Janeiro.

Rev. mex. sociol. (RMS)—Revista mexicana de sociología. Instituto de investigaciones sociales, Universidad nacional de México, Mexico, D. F.

SFQ (South. Folk Quart.)—Southern Folklore Quarterly, Gainesville, Florida.

Smithson. Contr. Knowledge—Smithsonian Institution Contributions to Knowledge, Washington, D. C.

Smithson. Miscel. Coll. — Smithsonian Institution Miscellaneous Collections, Washington, D. C.

So. Workman—Southern Workman, Hampton, Va.

Soc. Publ. Amer. Music—Society for the Publication of American Music, New York, N. Y.

Southw. Hist. Quart.—Southwestern Historical Quarterly, Texas State Historical Association, Austin, Texas.

Southw. Jour. Anthro.—Southwestern Journal of Anthropology, Albuquerque, New Mexico.

SRCS (sus. rev. cul. sup.)—Sustanica, Revista de cultura superior, Tuscaman.

SRL (Sat. Rev. Lit.)—Saturday Review of Literature, New York, N. Y.

Stat. Etno. Mus.—Statens Etnografiska Museum, Smärre Medelanden, Stockholm.

SW (Southw. Mus.)—Southwestern Musician, Arlington, Texas.

TFSB (Ten. Folk. Soc. Bull.)—Tennessee Folksong Society Bulletin, Maryville, Tenn.

TFSP (Tex. Folk. Soc. Pub.)—Texas Folklore Society Publication, Austin, Texas.

Trans. Acad. Sci. St. Louis—Transactions of the Academy of Science of St. Louis, St. Louis, Missouri.

Trans. Amer. Ethnol. Soc.—Transactions of the American Ethnological Society, New York, N. Y.

Trans. Anthro. Soc. Wash.—Transactions of the Anthropological Society of Washington, D. C.

Trans. Coll. Amer. Antiq. Soc.—Transactions and Collections of the American Antiquarian Society, Worcester, Mass.

Trans. Ethnol. Soc.—Transactions of the Ethnological Society, London.

Trans. Free Mus. Sci. Art—Transactions of the Free Museum of Science and Art, University of Pennsylvania, Philadelphia.

Trans. Hist. Lit. Com. Amer. Philo. Soc.—Transactions of the Historical and Literary Committee of the American Philosophical Society, Philadelphia, Pa.

Trans. Kans. Acad. Sci.—Transactions of the Kansas Academy of Science, Topeka.

Trans. N. Y. Acad. Sci.—Transactions of the New York Academy of Science, New York, N. Y.

Trans. Rep. Nebr. State Hist. Soc.—Transactions and Reports of the Nebraska State Historical Society, Lincoln, Nebraska.

Trans. Royal Can. Inst.—Transactions of the Royal Canadian Institute, Toronto.

Univ. Cal. Publ. Arch. Ethnol.—University of California Publications in American Archaeology and Ethnology, Berkeley, California.

Univ. New Mex. Publ. Anthro.—University of New Mexico Publications in Anthropology, Albuquerque, New Mexico.

Univ. Penn. Mus. Anthro. Publ.—University of Pennsylvania Museum Anthropological Publications, Philadelphia.

Univ. Penn. Mus. Jour.—University of Pennsylvania Museum Journal, Philadelphia.

Univ. Wash. Publ. Anthro.—University of Washington Publications in Anthropology, Seattle.

Verhandl. Berl. Gesel. Anthro. Ethnol. Ur.—Verhandlungen der Berliner Gesellschaft für Anthropologie, Ethnologie und Urgeschichte, Berlin.

Wash. Histor. Quart.—Washington Historical Quarterly, Seattle.

WF (West Folk.)—Western Folklore (formerly *California Folklore Quarterly*), University of California Press, Berkeley, California.

Wis. Arch.—Wisconsin Archaeologist, Madison.

WP (Waman Puma)—Waman Puma, revista mensual de cultura folklore, Cuzco, Peru.

Yale Univ. Publ. Anthro.—Yale University Publications in Anthropology, New Haven, Conn.

Year. Publ. Mus. City Milwaukee—Yearbook of the Public Museum of the City of Milwaukee, Wisconsin.
Zeit. f. Ethno.—Zeitschrift für Ethnologie, Berlin, Germany.
Zeit. f. Musik—Zeitschrift für Musik, Leipzig, Germany.
Zeit. f. Rassen.—Zeitschrift für Rassenkunde, Stuttgart, Germany.
Zeit. f. vergleich. Musik.—Zeitschrift für vergleichende Muskiwissenschaft, Berlin, Germany.
Zeit. f. vergleich. Rechts.—Zeitschrift für vergleichende Rechtswissenschaft, Stuttgart, Germany.
Zeit. Gesel. f. Erd.—Zeitschrift der Gesellschaft für Erdkunde, Berlin, Germany.

B. Music Publishers

ABC..................ABC Music Corp., 799 Seventh Avenue, New York, N. Y.
Acme..................Acme Music Corp., 562 Fifth Avenue, New York, N. Y.
Alexander..................Alexander Perry Music Publishing, 1619 Broadway, New York, N. Y.
Alfred..................Alfred Music Co., Inc., 145 West 45th Street, New York, N. Y.
Algonquin..................Algonquin Music, Inc., 1650 Broadway, New York, N. Y.
Alliance..................Alliance Music Co., 1658 Broadway, New York, N. Y.
Alpha..................Alpha Music, Inc., 501 Madison Avenue, New York, N. Y.
American..................American Music, Inc., Portland, Oregon
American Music......American Music Publishing Co., 1695 Broadway, New York, N. Y.
Apollo..................Apollo Music Co., 301 West 41st Street, New York, N. Y.
Appleton..................Appleton Music Publications, Inc., Appleton, Wisconsin
Arch..................Arch Music Co., 1619 Broadway, New York, N. Y.
Argosy..................Argosy Music Corp., 1650 Broadway, New York, N. Y.
Ascher..................Ascher, Emil, Inc., 640 Fourth Avenue, New York, N. Y.
Associated..................Associated Music Publishers, Inc., 25 West 45th Street, New York, N. Y.
Augsburg..................Augsburg Publishing Co., 425 South 4th Street, Minneapolis, Minnesota
Axelrod..................Axelrod Publishing Company, Providence, Rhode Island
Beacon..................Beacon Music Co., 1619 Broadway, New York, N. Y.
Belwin..................Belwin, Inc., 43 West 23rd Street, New York, N. Y.
Berlin..................Berlin, Irving, Music Corp., 1650 Broadway, New York, N. Y.
Big Three..................Big Three, The, Music Corporation, 799 Seventh Avenue, New York, N. Y.
Birchard..................Birchard, C. C., & Company, 285 Columbus Avenue, Boston, Mass.
Boosey-Hawkes......Boosey-Hawkes-Belwin, Inc., 30 West 57th Street, New York, N. Y.
Boston..................Boston Music Company, 116 Boylston Street, Boston, Mass.
Bourne..................Bourne, Inc., 799 Seventh Avenue, New York 19, N. Y.
Breitkopf..................Breitkopf Publications, Inc., 25 West 45th Street, New York, N. Y.
Broadcast..................Broadcast Music, Inc., 580 Fifth Avenue, New York 19, N. Y.
Caesar..................Caesar, Irving, Publishers, 1619 Broadway, New York, N. Y.
Century..................Century Music Publishing Company, 47 West 63rd Street, New York, N. Y.
Chappell..................Chappell & Company, Inc., RKO Building, New York 20, N. Y.
Chart..................Chart Music Publishing House, Inc., 400 South State Street, Chicago 5, Ill.
Church..................Church, The John, Company, 1712 Chestnut Street, Philadelphia, Pa.
Church-Sunday......Church and Sunday School Music Publishing Ass'n, 124 North 15th Street, Philadelphia, Pa.
Circle..................Circle Music Publications, Inc., RKO Building, New York 20, N. Y.
Composers..................Composers Press, Inc., 853 Seventh Avenue, New York, N. Y.
Coolidge..................Coolidge Publishing Company, Lander, Wyoming
Consolidated..................Consolidated Music Publishers, Inc., 221 West 47th Street, New York, N. Y.
Cos Cob..................Cos Cob Press, Inc., 209 West 57th Street, New York, N. Y.
Crawford..................Crawford Music Corporation, RKO Building, New York, N. Y.
Cundy..................Cundy-Bettoney Company, Inc., Hyde Park, Boston, Mass.
Ditson..................Ditson, Oliver, Company, Inc., Theodore Presser Co., distributors, 1712 Chestnut Street, Philadelphia, Pa.
Donaldson..................Donaldson, Douglas & Gamble, Inc., 1619 Broadway, New York, N. Y.
Dorian..................Dorian Music Publishers, Inc., 119 West 57th Street, New York, N. Y.
Educational..................Educational Music Bureau, 30 East Adams Street, Chicago 3, Ill.
Edwards..................Edwards Music Co., 1619 Broadway, New York, N. Y.
Elkan-Vogel..................Elkan-Vogel Company, Inc., 1716 Sansom Street, Philadelphia 3, Pa.

Elkin	Elkin & Company, Ltd., London, England
Emerson	Emerson Music Publications, Inc., 725 Riverside Drive, New York, N. Y.
Encore	Encore Music Publications, Inc., 1674 Broadway, New York, N. Y.
Enterprise	Enterprise Music Corp., 1619 Broadway, New York, N. Y.
Exclusive	Exclusive Publications, Inc., 1619 Broadway, New York, N. Y.
Famous	Famous Music Corporation, 1619 Broadway, New York, N. Y.
Fillmore	Fillmore Music House, 528 Elm Street, Cincinnati, Ohio
C. Fischer	Fischer, Carl, Inc., 56 Cooper Square, New York, N. Y.
J. Fischer	Fischer, J., & Bro., 119 West 40th Street, New York 18, N. Y.
Fitzsimons	Fitzsimons, H. T., Company, 23 East Jackson Boulevard, Chicago, Ill.
Flammer	Flammer, Harold, Inc., 251 West 19th Street, New York 11, N. Y.
Foley	Foley, Charles, 67 West 44th Street, New York 18, N. Y.
Forster	Forster Music Publisher, Inc., 216 South Wabash Avenue, Chicago Ill.
Fox	Fox, Sam, Publishing Company, 1250 Sixth Avenue, New York, N. Y.
Frontier	Frontier Publishers, Evanston, Ill.
Galaxy	Galaxy Music Corporation, 50 West 24th Street, New York, N. Y.
Gamble	Gamble Hinged Music Company, 228 South Wabash Avenue, Chicago, Ill.
General	General Music Publishing Co., Inc., 400 Madison Avenue, New York, N. Y.
Gershwin	Gershwin, George, Publishing Co., RKO Building, New York, N. Y.
Gilbert	Gilbert, L. Wolfe, Music Publishing Company, 6912 Hollywood Boulevard, Hollywood, Calif.
Golden	Golden Gate Quartet Music Co., 420 Madison Avenue, New York, N. Y.
Gray	Gray, H. W., Company, 159 East 48th Street, New York, N. Y.
Guild	Guild Music Publishers, Inc., 25 Central Park West, New York, N. Y.
Hall	Hall & McCreary Company, 434 South Wabash Avenue, Chicago 5, Ill.
Handy	Handy Brothers Music Company, Inc., 1650 Broadway, New York, N. Y.
Handy, W. C.	Handy, W. C., 1650 Broadway, New York, N. Y.
Harcourt	Harcourt Brace & Company, Inc., 38 Madison Avenue, New York, N. Y.
Harms	Harms, T. B., Co., RKO Building, New York, N. Y.
Hatch	Hatch Music Company, 611 Washington Street, Boston, Mass.
Hinds	Hinds, Hayden & Eldredge, Inc., 5 Union Square, New York, N. Y.
Hoffman	Hoffman, Raymond A., 509 South Wabash Avenue, Chicago, Ill.
Horton	Horton Music Corp., 1619 Broadway, New York, N. Y.
Humphries	Humphries, Bruce, Inc., Boston, Mass.
Huntzinger	Huntzinger, 137 West 4th Street, Cincinnati, Ohio
Imperial	Imperial Music Publications, 1619 Broadway, New York, N. Y.
Jacobs	Jacobs, Walter, Inc., 799 Seventh Avenue, New York 19, N. Y.
Jefferson	Jefferson Music Co., 1619 Broadway, New York, N. Y.
Jenkins	Jenkins, J. W., Sons Music Company, 1217 Walnut Street, Kansas City.
Jewel	Jewel Music Publishing Company, 1674 Broadway, New York, N. Y.
Kalmar	Kalmar & Ruby Music Corporation, 6301 Sunset Boulevard, Hollywood, Calif.
Kammen	Kammen, J. & J., Music Co., 1619 Broadway, New York, N. Y.
Kay	Kay & Kay Music Publishing Corporation, 1658 Broadway, New York, N. Y.
Kjos	Neil A. Kjos Music Company, Chicago, Ill.
Knickerbocker	Knickerbocker Music Publishers, Inc., 1619 Broadway, New York, N. Y.
Leeds	Leeds Music Corporation, 1270 Sixth Avenue, New York, N. Y.
Lewis	Lewis Music Publishing Co., Inc., 240 West 55th Street, New York, N. Y.
Lorenz	Lorenz Publishing Company, Dayton, Ohio
Luckhardt	Luckhardt & Belder, 3 East 43rd Street, New York, N. Y.
McKinley	McKinley Music Company, Chicago, Ill.
McLaughlin	McLaughlin & Reilly Company, Boston, Mass.
Marks	Marks, Edward B., Music Corporation, RCA Building, New York, N. Y.
Master	Master Music Publishers, 1674 Broadway, New York, N. Y.
Mercury	Mercury Music Corp., 47 West 63rd Street, New York, N. Y.
Metro	Metro Music Co., 64 Second Avenue, New York, N. Y.
Miller	Miller, Bob, Inc., 1619 Broadway, New York, N. Y.
Mills	Mills Music, Inc., 1619 Broadway, New York 19, N. Y.
Missud	Missud, Jean M., Salem, Mass.

Morris.................Morris Music Company, 1023 Arch Street, Philadelphia, Pa.
Morris, Ed.............Morris, Edwin H., & Co., 1619 Broadway, New York, N. Y.
Movietone.............Movietone Music Corporation, 1250 Sixth Avenue, New York, N. Y.
Music................Music Library of Chicago, 1004 Lyon & Healy Building, Chicago, Ill.
Music Publ.............Music Publishers Holding Corporation, 619 West 45th Street, New York
                      19, N. Y.
Musicians..............Musicians Publishing Company, Los Angeles, Calif.
Mutual.................Mutual Music Society, Inc., 1270 Sixth Avenue, New York, N. Y.
National..............National Music Publishing Corp., 1841 Broadway, New York, N. Y.
New Music............New Music Edition, Box 2888, Hollywood Station, Los Angeles, Calif.
New Music Press.....New Music Press, Inc., 330 Park Avenue, New York, N. Y.
Novello...............Novello & Co., 159 East 48th Street, New York, N. Y.
Olman.................Olman Music Corporation, 1629 Broadway, New York, N. Y.
Omega................Omega Music Edition, 20 West 45th Street, New York, N. Y.
Original..............Original Music Publishing Co., 1650 Broadway, New York, N. Y.
Oxford................Oxford University Press, 114 Fifth Avenue, New York, N. Y.
Oxford Music.........Oxford Music Corp., 1619 Broadway, New York, N. Y.
Pagani................Pagani, O., & Bro., 289 Bleecker Street, New York 14, N. Y.
Paull.................Paull-Pioneer Music Corporation, 1657 Broadway, New York, N. Y.
Paxton...............Paxton Music, Inc., 1619 Broadway, New York, N. Y.
Presser...............Presser, Theodore, Company, 1712 Chestnut Street, Philadelphia, Pa.
Pro Art..............Pro Art Publications, 143 West Broadway, New York, N. Y.
Quincke...............Quincke, W. A., & Company, 430 South Broadway, Los Angeles, Calif.
Regent................Regent Music Corp., 1619 Broadway, New York, N. Y.
Remick...............Remick Music Corporation, 1250 Sixth Avenue, New York, N. Y.
Republic...............Republic Music Corp., 607 Fifth Avenue, New York, N. Y.
Rialto................Rialto Music Publishing Corp., 45 Astor Place, New York, N. Y.
Ricordi..............Ricordi, G., & Company, Inc., 12 West 45th Street, New York, N. Y.
Robbins...............Robbins, J. J., & Sons, Inc., 221 West 47th Street, New York 19, N. Y.
Robbins Music........Robbins Music Corp., 799 Seventh Avenue, New York, N. Y.
Rodheaver............Rodheaver Company, 28 East Jackson Boulevard, Chicago, Ill.
Rossiter..............Rossiter, Will, 173 West Madison Street, Chicago, Ill.
Royal.................Royal Music Corp., 1587 Broadway, New York, N. Y.
Santly................Santly-Joy, Inc., 1619 Broadway, New York, N. Y.
Saunders.............Saunders Publications, 5617 Hollywood Boulevard, Los Angeles, Calif.
Schirmer..............Schirmer, G., Inc., 3 East 43rd Street, New York, N. Y.
Schmidt, A. P..........Schmidt, A. P., Company, 120 Boylston Street, Boston, Mass.
Schmidt, P. A..........Schmidt, Paul A., Music Company, Minneapolis, Minnesota
Schroeder.............Schroeder & Gunther, Inc., 6 East 45th Street, New York, N. Y.
Schuster..............Schuster & Miller, Inc., 1619 Broadway, New York, N. Y.
Select................Select Music Publications, Inc., 1619 Broadway, New York, N. Y.
Shapiro...............Shapiro, Bernstein & Company, Inc., 1270 Sixth Avenue, New York, N. Y.
Sheldon-Mitchell.....Sheldon-Mitchell Publishing Corp., 200 West 34th Street, New York, N. Y.
Sherman..............Sherman, Clay & Company, Kearney and Sutter Streets, San Francisco,
                      Calif.
Silver Burdett........Silver Burdett Company, 45 East 17th Street, New York 3, N. Y.
Skidmore..............Skidmore Music Company, 1270 Sixth Avenue, New York, N. Y.
Southern.............Southern Music Publishing Company, Inc., 1619 Broadway, New York,
                      N. Y.
Sprague...............Sprague-Coleman, 66 West 55th Street, New York, N. Y.
Summy................Summy, Clayton F., Company, 429 South Wabash Avenue, Chicago, Ill.
Superior..............Superior Music, Inc., 1619 Broadway, New York, N. Y.
Supreme..............Supreme Music Corp., 1619 Broadway, New York, N. Y.
Twentieth.............Twentieth Century Music Corp., 799 Seventh Avenue, New York, N. Y.
Universal.............Universal Music Corp., 799 Seventh Avenue, New York, N. Y.
University............University Music Corp., 1650 Broadway, New York, N. Y.
Vogel.................Vogel, Jerry, Music Company, Inc., 114 West 44th Street, New York, N. Y.
Volkwein.............Volkwein's, Pittsburgh 22, Pa.
Wa-Wan...............Wa-Wan Press, Newton Center, Mass.

Weil...................Weil, Milton, Music Company, 54 West Randolph Street, Chicago, Ill.
White-Smith...........White-Smith Publishing Company, 40 Winchester Street, Boston, Mass.
Williams...............Williams, Clarence, Music Publishing Company, 145 West 45th Street,
                         New York, N. Y.
Willis....................Willis Music Company, 3 East 43rd Street, New York, N. Y.
Winston................Winston-Music Co., Inc., 190 Riverside Drive, New York, N. Y.
Winthrop Rogers.....Winthrop Rogers, Ltd., London, England
Witmark..................Witmark, M., & Sons, 488 Madison Avenue, New York, N. Y.
Wood........................Wood, B. F., Music Company, 88 St. Stephen Street, Boston, Mass.
Words....................Words & Music, Inc., 1619 Broadway, New York, N. Y.
World..................World Music, Inc., 607 Fifth Avenue, New York, N. Y.

C.   Records

AAFS-LC....Archive of American Folk Song,
            Library of Congress, Division
            of Music, Folklore Section
AL...............Aladdin
AP..............Apollo
BB..............Bluebird
BE...............Beacon
BI...............Bibletone
BN...............Bluenote
BR...............Brunswick
BW...........Black and White
CA...............Capitol
CH...........Champion
CO...........Columbia
COM...........Commodore
CR...............Crown
DE...............Decca
DEL...........Delta
DI...............Diamond
DISC...........Disc
EL...............Elite
GE...............General Electric
GL...............Globe
GR...............Gramophone (HMV)
HA...............Hargail

HRS.............Hot Record Society
JAZZ...........Jazz
KE...............Keynote
MA...............Majestic
ME...............Melotone
MER...........Mercury
MU...............Musicraft
OD...............Odeon
OK...............Okey
PA...............Paramount
PD...............Polydor
PE...............Perfect
PER...........Perfectaphone
PH...............Philharmonic
PI...............Pilotone
PIC...........Picture
SA...............Salabert
SI...............Silvertone
SO...............Sonora
TI...............Timely
UHCA.........United Hot Club of America
VI...............Victor
VM...........Victor Masterpiece Set
VO...............Vocalion

D.   Musical Terms

A...............Alto
a cap...........a cappella
accomp.......accompanied
B................Bass

Bar.............Baritone
Orch...........Orchestra
S...............Soprano
T...............Tenor

BOOK ONE

The American People
North of Mexico

Part One: General Bibliography

FOLKLORE

BIBLIOGRAPHIES

American Bibliography (1941–   ).
In: *Publications of the Modern Language Association of America.* Issued Quarterly.
In the first number of each year beginning in 1941—an excellent American bibliography is printed, containing a great deal of material on balladry, folklore, and folksong.

Andrews, H. A., and others
"Bibliography of Franz Boas." *AA* 45 (No. 3) Part 2:67–109, 1943.

Beers, Henry Putney
Bibliographies in American History: Guide to Materials For Research. New York: H. W. Wilson Co., 1938.

Belden, H. M.
Folklore Bibliography. Folklore arranged under the direction of Josephine V. Brower, Presented by the Literature Committee of the General Federation of Women's Clubs, 1913–1914. Minneapolis: The University Press, 1914. 14 pp.

Bibliography in each issue of *American Speech,* contains valuable data on books dealing with American speech and dialect. Vol. 1, 1926. Baltimore, Md.

Boggs, Ralph Steele
"Bibliography of American Folklore." Appears annually in the March issue of the *Southern Folklore Quarterly,* beginning with *SFQ* 2 (No. 1) 43–48, 1938, etc.

————.
"Folklore de las Americas." *BAFA* II No. 9–12, pp. 91–96, 1940.

————.
"Una bibliografía general del folklore." *FA* 3:9–12, 1943.
Some fifty titles suggested as a basis for any folklore library.

Boston Public Library
Finding List of Fairy Tales and Folk Stories in Books at the Branches of the Public Library of the City of Boston. Boston: The Trustees, 1908. 48 pp.

Charles, Dorothy; Joseph, Bea; and Loher, Ruth
Bibliographic Index 1938–   . *A Cumulative Bibliography of Bibliographies.* New York: H. W. Wilson Co., 1938.

Coan, Otis W., and Lillard, Richard G.
America in Fiction; An annotated list of novels that interpret aspects of life in the United States. Stanford University, Calif.: Stanford University Press, 1941. 180 pp.

Daugherty, D. H.
A Report on Publication and Research in Musicology and Allied Fields in the United States, 1932–1938. Compiled for the Committee on Musicology of the American Council of Learned Societies, Washington, D. C.: American Council of Learned Societies, 1938.

————; **Ellinwood, Leonard; Hill, Richard**
A Bibliography of Periodical Literature in Musicology and Allied Fields. Assembled for the Committee on Musicology of the American Council of Learned Societies. Washington, D. C.: American Council of Learned Societies, 1943. 150 pp. No. 2. October 1, 1939 to September 30, 1940. Section 4 (Ethnology), pp. 79–85, deals with North American and Latin American folklore and folksong.

Eastman, Mary Huse
Index to Fairy Tales, Myths and Legends. Supplement. Boston: F. W. Faxon Co., 1937. 566 pp.

Herzog, Elizabeth Greenbaum
General Index, American Anthropologist, Current anthropological literature, and Memoirs of the American Anthropological Association. 1929–1938. Menasha, Wisconsin: 1940, 122 pp., (AA42, No. 4 Part 3)

Herzog, George
Research in Primitive and Folk Music in the United States. American Council of Learned Societies, Bulletin No. 24, April 1936. Washington, D. C.: American Council of Learned Societies, 1936. 97 pp.

Index of FF Communications, arranged according to volume and author. Vol. I–XLVII. Helsinki: 1934. 23 pp.

Index to the Journal of American Folklore. Index to volumes 1–40 (1888–1927). American Folklore Society Memoirs, vol. 14. New York: Stechert & Co., 1930. 106 pp.

Lesser, Alexander
"Bibliography of American Folklore, 1915–1928." *JAFL* 41:1–60, 1928.

Lomax, Alan, and Cowell, Sidney Robertson
American Folksong and Folklore. A Regional Bibliography. New York: Progressive Education Association, 1942. 59 pp.

Long, Percy Waldron, ed.
Publications of the Modern Language Association of America. *Index 1–50, (1884–1935).* Menasha, Wisc.: Published by the Association, 1936. 240 pp.

————.
Modern Language Association of America. *Vol. 55, Index 1936–1940.* Menasha, Wisc.: Published by the Association, 1940.

Lowie, Robert H.
"Bibliography of Franz Boas in Folklore."
JAFL 57:65–69, 1944.

Parsons, Elsie Clews
"Bibliography of Elsie Clews Parsons (1898–
1941)." *JAFL* 56:48–56, 1943.

PMLA—Bibliographies 1924–.
The bibliographies ran for a number of years
in the *American Year Book.*

Powell, J. W.
"Folklore Bibliography." *JAFL* 15:203, 1902.

Russell, F.
"Bibliography of Folklore Publications." *JAFL*
17:209, 1904.

Sonnenschein, William Swan
A Bibliography of Mythology and Folklore;
being the sections relating to those subjects in
The Best Books and *The Reader's Guide.* I, pp.
101–130, 131–154. London: Swan Sonnenschein & Co., 1897.

Thomas, N. W., comp.
Bibliography of Folklore, 1905. Publications
of the Folklore Society LVII. London: Published for the Folklore Society by D. Nutt,
1906. xxxvi pp. Also 2 vols., 1906–7.

Thompson, Stith
Motif—index of Folk Literature. A classification of narrative elements in folktales, ballads,
myths, fables, medieval romances, exempla,
fabliaux, jest-books and local legends. Bloomington, Ind.: Indiana University Press, 1932–
36. 6 vols. in 3. Indiana University Studies,
Vol. XIX, June, September, 1932. Studies No.
96–97; Vol. XX, No. 100–101; Vol. XXI, No.
105–106; Vol. XXII, No. 108–110; Vol. XXIII,
No. 111–112; Vol. 1–5, contains classified lists;
Vol. 6, alphabetical index. Also in FFC.

United States Library of Congress
Folk-lore: a short list of books . . . June 13,
1928. Washington, D. C.: 1928. (Select list of
references, No. 1067).

White, Mary Catherine
"Folklore of the United States for Children: A
Selected Bibliography." *Publishers' Weekly*
110: 1584–1589, 1926. illus.

Wilson, T.
"Folklore Bibliography." *JAFL* 15:204, 1902.

SERIAL PUBLICATIONS

Alberta Folklore Quarterly.
Publication of the Folklore and Local History
Project. Edmonton: University of Alberta.

American Anthropologist.
Washington; New York; Lancaster, Pa., I
(1888) XI-(1898). New ser. I (1899) –

American Literature.
A journal of literary history, criticism and
bibliography. Durham, N. C.: No. 1, March
1929–.

American Philosophical Society.
Philadelphia. *Proceedings:* 1838–.

American Speech, Quarterly.
Baltimore, Md., 1925–.

*Bulletin of the Folk-Song Society of the North-
east.*
Cambridge, Mass., 1930–1937.

Bulletin of the Kentucky Folklore Society.
Western Kentucky State Teachers College.

California Folklore Quarterly.
Publication of the California Folklore Society
Vol. I, 1942– . Published for the California
Folklore Society by the University of Califor-
nia Press, Berkeley and Los Angeles. Changed
to *Western Folklore.*

Contributions to Folklore. Baylor University,
Waco, Texas: 1929. No. 1–3 in 1 volume. Plates.
No more published.

Dialect Notes.
American Dialect Society, New Haven, Conn.
1–6, 1980–1896 (suspended 1897–1899)–1939.

Folk-Lore.
A quarterly review of Myth, Tradition, Institution and Custom. Folklore Society, London I
(1878)–.

Folklore Fellows.
FF Communications, edited for the Folklore
Fellows, Vol. I, 1913. Hamina: Suomalaisen
Tiedeakatemian Kustantama, 1913—
Finnish folklore publication.

Folklore Institute of America.
First report: Summer institute of folklore,
Indiana University, June 29–Aug. 22, 1942.
Bloomington, Indiana, 1943. 16 pp.

Folklore Primer.
Published by the Folklore Committee. Alabama
Association of English.

Folklore Journal.
Folklore Society, London. 1–7, Jan. 1883, Dec.
1889. United with *Archaeological Review* to
form *Folk-Lore,* a quarterly review.

Folk-News.
Folk festival council of New York. No. 1–116,
June 1932–Sept. 15, 1937. Vol. 6–8, No. 4, Oct.
1937–Dec. 1939. Have not been consistent in
the numbering.

Folk-Say.
Oklahoma Folklore Society, Norman, Okla-
homa. 1–4, 1929–1932. Issued as the Society's
Publication No. 1.

Folk Song Society.
London. *Journal* 1–8 (No. 1–35) 1889/1904–
1927/1931.

Hoosier Folklore.
Indianapolis, Indiana: Hoosier Folklore Society, and Indiana Historical Bureau. March 1946–. Successor to the *Hoosier Folklore Bulletin* printed with the aid of the Indiana Historical Bureau.

Indiana University Folklore Series.
Bloomington, Indiana: No. 1, 1940–.

Illinois Folklore.
Southern Illinois Normal University, Carbondale, Ill.

Journal of American Folklore Society.
American Folklore Society, Philadelphia, Pa., 1888–.

Language.
Journal of the Linguistic Society of America. Edited by George Melville Bolling, Aurelio M. Espinosa, and Edward Sapir. Baltimore: The Waverly Press, Vol. I, No. 1, March 1925.

Memoirs of the Folklore Society.
Published by the American Folklore Society, Philadelphia. No. 1. 1894–.

Modern Philology.
Chicago University, Chicago. No. 1, June 1903.

New York Folklore Quarterly.
Publication of the New York Folklore Society, Ithaca, N. Y.: Cornell University Press. Vol. I, No. 1, Feb. 1945.

Notes and Queries for readers and writers, collectors and librarians. London. No. 1, 1849–. 1–145 1849–1923 and caption title 1924– as *Notes and Queries.* 1849–1924 also numbered in 13 series of 12 vols. each. Index: Each series has index. Still continued.

Publications of the Folklore Foundation.
Vassar College, Poughkeepsie, New York, 1922.

Publications of the Pennsylvania Folklore Society.
Pennsylvania German. Muhlenberg College, Pa.

Publications of the Texas Folklore Society.
Austin, Texas: University of Texas Vol. I (1916), Vol. II (1923), since then about a volume every year.

Southern Folklore Quarterly.
Publication of the Southeastern Folklore Society. University of Florida, Gainesville, Florida.

Southern Workman.
Hampton Normal and Agricultural Institute, Hampton, Va. 1–68 No. 7, 1872–July 1939.

Tennessee Folklore Society Bulletin.
Publication of the Tennessee Folklore Society. Susan B. Riley, Peabody College, Tennessee. 1936–.

The Folklorist.
Journal of the Chicago Folklore Society, Vol. I, July, 1892–October, 1893. No more published.

The French Folklore Bulletin.
Publication of the French Folklore Society, 320 West 86th Street, New York 24, N. Y.

The Musical Quarterly.
G. Schirmer, New York, 1915–.

Wisconsin Folktale Booklets.
Publication of the Wisconsin Folklore Society. State Historical Museum, Madison, Wisconsin.

Word-Lore, the folk magazine, a recorder of dialect, folksong, ballad, epigram, place-name, phrase and field-lore. Vol. 1–Jan./Feb. 1926– London: Folk Press Ltd., bi-monthly.

Word Study.
Springfield, Mass.: G. & C. Merriam Co., Vol. I, No. 1. Sept. 1925.

Words.
A periodical devoted to the study of the origin, history and etymology of English words. Los Angeles, Cal. No. 1, Oct. 1934–.

PUBLISHERS' SERIES

American Customs Series.
New York: The Vanguard Press.

American Guide Series.
Works Progress Administration, WPA Writers' Project. New York: Hastings House, and others.

Seaport Series.
New York: Doubleday and Co.
A series of volumes dealing with the main seaport cities and towns of America.

Society in America Series.
New York: E. P. Dutton and Co.

"Sovereign State" Series.
New York: Dodd, Mead and Co.

The American Adventure Series.
Chicago: Wheeler Publishing Co.

The "American Folkways" Series.
New York: Duell, Sloan and Pearce.

The "American Lakes" Series.
Indianapolis: Bobbs-Merrill Co.

The "American Mountain" Series.
New York: Vanguard Press.

The American Trails Series.
Jay Monaghan, editor. Indianapolis, Ind.: Bobbs-Merrill Co.

"The Rivers of America" Series.
New York: Farrar and Rinehart, and Rinehart and Company.

Visage of America Series.
New York: Hastings House.

FOLKLORE SOCIETIES

The American Folklore Society.
Founded 1888. Secretary-Treasurer, MacEdward Leach, University of Pennsylvania, Philadelphia 4, Pa.

California Folklore Society.
University of California, Berkeley, Cal.

Canadian Folklore Society.
Gustave Lanctot, Dominion Archives, Ottawa, Canada.

Colorado Folklore Society.
Organized at the Western Folklore Conference in Denver, July 11, 1947. Levette J. Davidson, President.

French Folklore Society.
320 West 86th Street, New York, N. Y.

Hoosier Folklore Society.
Indiana University, Bloomington, Indiana.

Illinois Folklore Society.
Southern Illinois Normal University, Carbondale, Ill.

Kentucky Folklore Society.
Western Kentucky State Teachers College.

Michigan Folklore Society.
Central Michigan College of Education.

New Mexico Folklore Society.
Albuquerque, New Mexico. First founded in 1931, reorganized in 1946.

New York Folklore Society.
New York State College for Teachers, Albany, New York.

North Carolina Folklore Society.
University of North Carolina, Chapel Hill, North Carolina.

Pennsylvania Folklore Society.
H. W. Shoemaker, Pres., Box 431, Altoona, Pa.

Pennsylvania German Folklore Society.
Muhlenberg College, Pa.

South Carolina Negro Folklore Guild.
J. Mason Brewer, Claflin University, South Carolina. 1944.

Southeastern Folklore Society.
University of Florida, Gainesville, Florida.

Tennessee Folklore Society.
Tennessee Polytechnic Institute, Cookesville, Tenn.

Texas Folklore Society.
University of Texas, Austin, Texas.

The Badger State Folklore Society.
Incorporated in March, 1947. Affiliated with the Wisconsin Historical Society.

Virginia Folklore Society.
Arthur K. Davis, Jr., University of Virginia, Charlottesville, Va.

West Virginia Folklore Society.
John Harrington Cox, West Virginia University, Morgantown, W. Va.

Wisconsin Folklore Society.
State Historical Museum, Madison, Wis.

Hand, Wayland D.
"North American Folklore Societies." *JAFL* 56:161–192, 1943.

————.
"North American Folklore Societies: A Supplement." *JAFL* 59:477–494, 1946.

GENERAL STUDIES

Andrée, Richard
Ethnographische Parallelen und Vergleiche. Stuttgart: J. Maier, 1878. 303 pp. Vol. II, 1889.

Barroso, Gustavo
Através dos Folk-lores. São Paulo, Comp.— Melhoramentos de S. Paulo. 1927. 196 pp. bibl.

Bastian, A.
Der Völkergedanke im Aufbau einer Wissenschaft vom Menschen, und seine Begründung auf Ethnologische Sammlungen. Berlin: Ferd. Dümmlers Verlagsbuchhandlung, 1881.

Bates, Ernest S.
"American Folklore." *Saturday Review of Literature* 2:913–914, 1926.

Beckwith, Martha Warren
Folklore in America, Its Scope and Method. Poughkeepsie, N. Y.: Vassar College. The Folklore Foundation. 1931. 76 pp. Publication of the Folklore Foundation, No. 11.

Benedict, Ruth
"Folklore." In: *Encyclopaedia of the Social Sciences.* New York: The Macmillan Co., 1931.

Bergen, Fanny D., and Newell, William W.
"Topics for Collection of Folklore." *JAFL* 4:151–158, 1891.
A working classification for folklorists.

Bethe, Erich
Märchen, Sage, Mythus. Leipzig: Quelle & Meyer. 1922. x, 131 pp.

Blinkenberg, Christian Sorensen
The Thunderweapon in Religion and Folklore; a study in comparative archaeology. Cambridge: University Press, 1911. xii, 122 pp., illus.

Boas, Franz
Mythology and Folklore. In: *General Anthropology*, edited by Franz Boas. (pp. 609–626). New York: D. C. Heath and Co., 1938.

Boggs, R. S.
"Clasificación del folklore." *FA* 4:1–8, 1944.
A guide to archivists and bibliographers.

———.
"El Folklore, definición, ciencia y arte." *ASFM*
3:7–16, 1942.

———.
Folklore; an outline for individual and group
study. Chapel Hill, N. C.: University of North
Carolina Press, 1929. 47 pp., Univ. of N. C.
Extension Bulletin, Vol. I, No. 6.

———.
"Folklore Begins to Play an Important Part."
The Pan American, 2 (No. 2):40–42. May,
1941.

———.
"Folklore democrático y cultura aristocrá-
tica." *FA* 2:17–20, 1942.
"With decadence of European aristocratic culture, New World nations are finding their true
nationalism, Panamericanism and artistic inspiration in the democratic tradition of their own folklore." (Boggs)

———.
"Folklore democrático y cultura aristocrá-
tica." *WP* (año 4) 3 (No. 16):13–16, 1944.

———.
"Folklore": Materials, Science, Art. *FA* 3:1–8,
(June) 1943.

———.
"Génesis de 'Folklore Americas'." *FA* 1941,
1 (No. 1):1–3.

———.
"Representation of National Folklore Societies
in the Americas in Folklore Americas." *FA* 1
(No. 1):3–4, 1941.

———.
"Valor práctico del folklore." *AI* 5:211–217,
1945.

Botkin, B. A.
"The Folk and the Individual: Their Creative
Reciprocity." *English Journal* (College edi-
tion) 27:121–135, 1938.

———.
Folklore as a Neglected Source of Social His-
tory. In: *The Cultural Approach to History*.
Caroline F. Ware, ed. New York: Columbia
University Press, 1940.

———.
A Treasury of American Folklore. Stories,
ballads and traditions of the people; ed. by
B. A. B., with a foreword by Carl Sandburg.
New York: Crown Publishers, xxviii, 1944. 932
pp., music.

Burne, Charlotte Sophia
The Handbook of Folklore. London: Published
for the Folk-lore Society by Sidgwich & Jackson, Ltd., 1914. x, 364 pp. new ed., rev. and
enl. Publication of the Folklore Society,
LXXIII.

Cabrera, Ana S.
Rutas de América, el folklore, la música, la
historia, leyenda, las costumbres. Buenos
Aires: Penser, Ltd. 1941. 242 pp., music.

Cadilla de Martínez, María
"El Folklore." *ASFM* 3:43–66, 1942 .

Câmara Casendo, Luís da
"Folklore nos Estados Unidos." *RAMSP*, año
VII, 76:276–279, 1941.

Casanowicz, I. M.
Parallels in the Cosmogonies of the Old World
and the New. In: *Holmes Anniversary Volume*,
pp. 44–52. Washington, D. C.: James W.
Bryant Press, 1916.

Clasificación del Folklore.
Ciudad Trujillo. La Nación. Universitad de
Santo Domingo. Facultad de filosofía. Sección
de lingüísta folklore, 2. 1944. 15 pp.

Cocchiara, Giuseppe
Folklore. Milano: Hoepli, 1927. x, 142 pp.
Manuali Hoepli.

Clough, Wilson O.
"Has American Folklore a Special Quality?"
SFQ 8:115–121, 1944.

"Constitution of the American Folklore Society."
JAFL 59:217–220, 1946.

Corso, Raffaele
Folklore: Storia — obietto — metodo — bibliografia. Roma: Casa editrice Leonardo da Vinci,
1923. viii, 148 pp., illus., bibl. Studi di etnografia e di folklore I.

Cox, Marian Roalfe
An Introduction to Folklore. London: David
Nutt, 1904. New and enlarged Edition.

Cox, Sir George W.
*An Introduction to the Science of Comparative
Mythology and Folklore.* London: C. Kegan
Paul and Company, 1881.

Davidson, Donald
"Current Attitudes Towards Folklore." *TFSB*
6:44–51, 1940.

Dobie, J. Frank
"Twenty Years an Editor." *TFSP* 18:7–12,
1943.
Discussion of American folklore by one of its
most enthusiastic and creative workers.

Dorson, Richard M.
"Historical Method and American Folklore."
Indiana History Bulletin 23 (No. 1):84–98,
1946.

Dunn, J. P.
"Misunderstood Mythology." *Americana*
17:180–185, 1923.

Eisenstädter, Julius
*Elmentargedanke und Übertragungtheorie in
der Völkerkunde.* Stuttgart: Streker & Schroeder, 1912. vii, 206 pp. (Studien und Forschungen zur Menschen und Völkerkunde...xi).
Studies in folklore and transmission of folktales.

Fiske, John
Myths and Myth-Makers. Old Tales and Superstitions Interpreted by Comparative Mythology. Boston: James R. Osgood and Co., 1874; Boston: Houghton Mifflin & Co., 1914. vi, 251 pp., illus.
Chapter I: The Origin of Folklore.

Fleure, Herbert John
"Archaeology and folk tradition." In: *British Academy,* London. Proceedings 1931 (pp. 369–390). (The Sir John Rhys Memorial lecture).

Frazer, Sir James George
Folklore in the Old Testament. Studies in Comparative Religion, Legend and Law. London: Macmillan and Co., Ltd., 1923.

————.
Garnered Sheaves; essays, addresses and reviews. London: Macmillan & Co., Ltd., 1931. xi, 538 pp.

Frobenius, Leo
Die Weltanschauung der Naturvölker. Weimar: E. Felber, 1898. xv, 427 pp.

Gamis, Manuel
"El material folklórico y el progreso social." *AI* 5:207–211, 1945.

Going, Charles Buxton
Folklore and Fairy Plays. Boston: Walter H. Baker Co., 1927. 245 pp.
Contains some tunes.

Goldenweiser, Alexander A.
"Folk-Psychology." *Psychological Bulletin* 9:373–380, 1912.

Gomme, Sir George Laurence
Ethnology in Folklore. New York: D. Appleton & Co., 1892. vii, 203 pp.

————.
Folklore as an Historical Science. with twenty-eight illustrations. London: Methuen & Co., 1908. xvi, 371 pp.
Contents: History and folklore—Materials and methods — Psychological conditions — Anthropological conditions—Sociological conditions—European conditions—Ethnological conditions.

————.
Folk-Lore Relics of Early Village Life. London: Elliot Stock, 1883. ix, 246 pp.

————.
The Handbook of Folklore. London: Publ. for the Folklore Society by D. Nutt, 1890. vii, 193 pp., bibl. (Publication of the Folklore Society XX.)

Guichot y Sierra, Alejandro
Noticia Histórica del Folklore; orígenes en todos los países hasta 1890 desarollo en España hasta 1921. Sevilla: Hijos de G. Alvarez, impresores, 1922. 256 pp.

Halliday, William Reginald
"Folklore." In: *Encyclopaedia Britannica,* Vol. 9, pp. 446–447, 1936. 14th edition.

————.
Folklore Studies, Ancient and Modern. London: Methuen and Co., 1924. xv, 172 pp.

Halpert, Herbert
"American Regional Folklore." *JAFL* 60: 355–366, 1947

Hamel, Frank
Transformation in Folklore and Fairytale. New York: Frederick A. Stokes and Co., 1915.

Hartland, Edwin Sidney
Folklore; what is it and what is the good of it. London: D. Nutt, 1904. 47 pp., 2nd ed., bibl. Popular studies in mythology, romance and folklore No. 2.

————.
Mythology and Folktales, their relation and interpretation. London: David Nutt, 1900. 53 pp. (Popular studies in mythology, romance and folklore No. 7.)

————.
The Legend of Perseus; a study of tradition in story, custom and belief. London: D. Nutt, 1894–96. 3 Vols., bibl. (Grimm Library. No. 2, 3, 5.)

Hasluck, Frederick William
Letters on Religion and Folklore. annotated by Margaret M. Hasluck. London: Luzac & Co., 1926. xi, 256 pp.

Hazlett, W. C.
Faiths and Folklore. A dictionary of national beliefs, superstitions and popular customs, past and current, with their classical and foreign analogies, described and illustrated. London: 1905. 2 Vols.
A standard work, alphabetically arranged. Based on Brand and Ellis. Much inferior.

Herskovits, Melville J.
"Folklore After a Hundred Years: A Problem in Definition." *JAFL* 59:89–100, 1946.

Hewett, Edgar Lee
"From Culture to Civilization." *El Palacio.* 59:133–142, 1942.

Hutton, J. H.
"Nature and Sources of Folk Belief." *Folklore* (London) 53:82–94, 1942.

Jackson, G. P.
"American Indifference to the Study of Folklore." *JAFL* 32:438–439, 1919.

Jones, Louis C.
Folklore as a Living Force. In: *People's Festival in a People's War:* Third Annual Folk Festival of the Catskills (30 pp., music, illus.) Camp Woodland, Inc.: Norman Studer, 4407 48 St., Long Island City, N. Y.

Klöpper, Clemens
Folklore in England and America. Dresden: C. A. Koch, 1899.

Kluckhohn, Clyde
"Myths and Rituals": a general theory. *Harvard Theological Review* 35:45–79, 1942.

Knortz, Karl
Amerikanischer Aberglaube der Gegenwart; ein Beitrag zur Volkskunde. Leipzig: Genstenberg, 1913.

—————.
Streifzüge auf dem Gebiete amerikanischer Volkskunde altes und neues. Leipzig: E. Wartigs verlag, E. Hoppe, 1902. 284 pp.
American folklore.

—————.
Zur Amerikanischen Volkskunde. Tübingen: H. Laupp'sche buchhandlung, 1905. 73 pp.

Knuchel, Eduard Fritz
Die Umwandlung in Kult, Magie und Rechtsbrauch. Basel, Schweiz: Gezellschaft für Volkskunde, 1919. viii, 116 pp., bibl.

Krappe, Alexander Haggerty
The Science of Folk-lore. London: Methuen, 1930. xxi, 344 pp., bibl.

Krohn, Kaarle
Die Folkloristische Arbeitsmethode. Begruendet von Julius Krohn und weitgefuehrt von Nordischen Forschern. Instituttet før Sammelignende Kulturforskning. Serie B: Skrifter, Band V. Oslo: H. Aschenhong and Co., 1926.

Lang, Andrew
The Origins of Religion and other Essays. London: Watts & Co., 1908. 128 pp., illus.
There is a chapter on "The Method of Folklore."

Langer, Susanne K.
Philosophy in a New Key. A Study in the Symbolism of Reason, Rite and Art. Cambridge, Mass.: Harvard University Press, 1942. 248 pp.
Chapt. VII—Life-Symbols: The Roots of Myth. Discussion of the origins of ritual and myth.

Leach, Maria, ed.
Folklore Dictionary. New York; Funk and Wagnalls, 1949. Vol. 1 (A-I), 531 pp.
This volume and Volume 2 will contain 5000 to 8000 entries besides 25 general articles.

Lethaby, W. R.
Architecture, Mysticism, and Myth. London: Percival and Co., 1892. 2nd ed.

Lewis, Charles B.
"The Part of the Folk in the Making of Folklore." *Folklore* (London) 46 (No. 1):37–75, 1935.

Liebrecht, Felix
Zur Volkskunde; alte und neue Aufsätze. Heilbronn: Gebr. Henninger, 1979. xvi, 522 pp.

Liestøl, Knut
The Comparative Study of Folklore at the Institute. In: *Four Introductory Lectures.* Quatre Conferences d'Inauguration. Vier Einleitungs-Vorlesungen. Instituttet før Sammenlignende Kulturforskning. Series A. Forlesninger Vol. I. Oslo: H. Aschenhong and Co., 1925.

Lindgren, E. J.
The Collection and Analysis of Folklore. In: *The Study of Society, Methods and Problems* edited by F. C. Bartlett, M. Ginsberg, E. J. Lindgren, and R. H. Thoreless. pp. (328ff). London: Kegan Paul, Trench, Trubner and Co., Ltd. 1939.

Loomis, C. Grant
"Legend and Folklore." *CFQ* 2:279–297, 1943.

Machlaclan, John Miller
"Folk Concepts in the Novels of Thomas Wolfe." *SFQ* 9 (No. 4):175–186, 1945.

Mackenzie, A. S.
The Evolution of Literature; a manual of comparative literature. New York: Crowell, 1911. xvi, 440 pp.

Malinowski, Bronislaw
The Dynamics of Culture Change. New Haven, Conn.: Yale University Press, 1945.

Marett, Robert Ranulph
Psychology and Folklore. London: Methuen and Co., Ltd., 1920. ix, 275 pp.

Mason, Otis T.
"The Natural History of Folklore." *JAFL* 4:97–105, 1891.
"My purpose is to inquire how the folklorist is to bring his work into line with that of other naturalists."

McDowell, L. L.
"A Background of Folklore." *TFSB* 2 (No. 1), 1936.

Muehlmann, Wilhelm
Methodik der Voelkerkunde. Stuttgart: Ferdinand Enke Verlag, 1938.
Methodology of folklore study.

Muelle, Jorge C.
"Campo y límites del folklore." *WP* (año 4) 3 (No. 16):40–45, 1944.
Defines folklore and attempts to give its place in its related fields of ethnography, sociology, archaeology and history.

Myres, John Linton
"Folkmemory." *Folklore* 37:12–34, 1926.

Newberry Library, Chicago
Religions: Philosophy of religion, folklore, ethnic religions. Chicago: The Newberry Library, 1925. x, 237 pp.

Newell, W. W.
"Additional Collection Essential to Correct Theory in Folklore and Mythology." *JAFL* 3:23–32, 1890.

—————.
"Folklore Studies and Folklore Societies." *JAFL* 8:231–242, 1895.

—————.
"Topics for Collection of Folklore." *JAFL* 4:151–158, 1891.

Northcote, W. T.
"Folklore." In: *Encyclopaedia Britannica*, Vol. 10. pp. 601–602, 1910. Eleventh Edition.

Nourry, Émile Dominique
Manuel de Folklore. Lettre-préface de S. Charlety. Paris: E. Nourry, 1936. 191 pp., bibl.

Nunez y Domínquez, José de J.
"Importancia del Folklore." *ASFM* (pub. 1943) 2:255–261, 1941.
Classification and definition of the materials of folklore.

Oesterley, William Oscar Emil
The Sacred Dance; a study in comparative folklore. Cambridge, Eng.: The University Press, 1923. x, 234 pp.

Ogburn, William Fielding
"The Folk-ways of a Scientific Sociology." *Scientific Monthly* 30:300–306, 1930.

Parsons, E. C.
Review: *The History of Ethnological Theory* by R. H. Lowie. *JAFL* 53:73–80, 1940.

Pereda Valdés, Ildefonso
"Folklore Vínculo de Unión de las Naciones Americanas." *WP* 3 (No. 15) 49–51, 1943.
Folklore as a means of democratic understanding, union and friendship.

Phillips, Henry, Jr.
"Primitive Man in Modern Beliefs." *JAFL* 3:60–63, 1890.
A poem expressing the significance of folklore.

Pizarro, L. Leopoldo
"La Metodolgía Etnológica Frente al Folklore." *La Apenión* (Santiago de Chile) p. 10, Oct. 29, 1944.
General discussion involving environmental factors.

Powell, J. W.
"The Lessons of Folklore." *AA* 2:1–37, 1900. n.s.

Ramos, Artur
"Estudios de Folklore"; o mito e o conto popular: as antigas teorias mitográficas; as teorias filológicas e alegóricas; as teorias físicas e astronomicas. *RBRJ* 3:(No. 6) 137–152; (No. 7) 170–174; (No. 8) 12–25; 1943.
Seeks to distinguish between folktale and myth.

Redfield, Robert
"La Sociedad Folk." *RMS* 4:13–41, 1942.

Reichard, Gladys A.
"American Folklore Society." *JAFL* 56:161–164, 1943.

————.
"Franz Boas and Folklore." *American Anthropologist Memoir Series* 61:52–57, 1943.

Róheim, Géza
Animism, Magic and the Divine King. London: Kegan Paul, Trench, Trubner and Co., Ltd., 1930. 390 pp.

————.
"Myth and Folk-Tale." *American Imago* 2 (No. 3):266–279, 1941.

————.
The Origin and Function of Culture. Nervous and Mental Disease, Monographs 69. New York: Nervous and Mental Disease Monographs 1943. 107 pp.
"An attempt to explain civilization or culture as manifestation of the Eros."

Rojas, Alfonso Villa
"Significada y valor práctico del folklore." *AI* 5:295–302, 1945.

Romero, Jesús C.
"Observaciones acerca del término folklore." *ASFM* 1:17–40, 1942.
Attempts at a definition.

Rourke, Constance
A Note on Folklore. In: *The Roots of American Culture and other Essays.* Edited with a preface by Van Wyck Brooks (pp. 238–250). New York: Harcourt, Brace and Co., 1942. 305 pp.

————.
The Roots of American Culture, and other Essays. Edited, with a preface by Van Wyck Brooks. New York: Harcourt, Brace and Company, 1942. xii, 305 pp.
"These fragments ... reveal the rich stores of tradition that lie behind us, the many streams of native character and feeling from which the Americans of the future will be able to draw." (Brooks)

Rowe, John H.
"Métodos y fines del estudio folkórico." *WP* (año 4), 3, (No. 16):21–28, 1944.
Discussion of how to collect, analyze, systematize folklore studies, etc.

Saintyves, Pierre
Introducción al Folklore; traducción del Dr. Santo S. Faré. Buenos Aires: Fontana, 1942. 42 pp. Asociación Folklórica Argentina, Cuaderno Folklórico, No. 6.

————.
Manuel de Folklore. Paris: E. Nourry, 1936.

Sayce, R. U.
"The Modern Study of Folklore." *Folklore* 47 (No. 2):171–182, 1936.

Sébillot, Paul
Le Folk-lore; littérature orale et ethnographie traditionelle. Paris: O. Doin et fils, 1913. xxii, 393 pp., bibl.

Skinner, Hubert Marshall, comp.
Readings in Folklore ... with readings from Standard Literature relating to the same. New York: American Book Company, 1893. 448 pp.

Smith, Marian W.
"Musings on Folklore." *JAFL* 57:70–72, 1944.

Stavenhagen, Kurt
Kritische Gänge in die Volkstheorie. Riga: Verlag der Akt.-ges, 1936. 119 pp., bibl.

Sumner, William Graham
Folkways; a study of the sociological importance of usages, manners, customs, mores, and morals. Boston: Ginn and Company, 1906. v, 692 pp., bibl. (pp. 655–670).

Taylor, Archer
"The Problems of Folklore." *JAFL* 59:101–107, 1946.

Thompson, Stith
"American Folklore After Fifty Years." *JAFL* 51:1–9, 1938.

———.
"Folklore and Literature." *PMLA* 55:866–874, 1940.

———.
"Folklore in America in the Years Ahead." *Folklore Institute of America.* First Report Summer Institute of Folklore, Indiana University, 16 pp., Bloomington, Indiana. Folklore Institute of America, 1943.

———.
"Folklore of the Americas": an opportunity and a challenge. *PASC* 82:245–251, 1942 (Anthrop. Sciences). (Proceedings of the 8th Amer. Scientific Congress held in Wash., D. C., May 10–18, 1940. Dep't of State, Wash., D. C.)

Thorndike, Lynn
History of Magic and Experimental Science During the First Thirteen Centuries of Our Era. New York: Columbia University Press, 1923–41. 6 Vols.

Tsanoff, Radoslav
"Folklore and Tradition in a Growing Society." *TFSP* 15:1–8, 1939.

U. S. Library of Congress. Division of Music. Folklore Section
Folklore Recordings: Folktales, Proverbs, Legends, Riddles, Nursery Rhymes and Children's Games, etc., deposited in the Folklore Section, Collected by institutions and individuals.

Vance, Lee J.
"Folk-Lore Study in America." *Popular Science Monthly* 43:586–590, 1893. (New York).

White, J. G.
"Collection of Folklore." *JAFL* 30:413–414, 1917.

Wilson, Gordon
Passing Institutions: A Series of Essays about Things We Used to Know. Cynthiana. Kentucky: Hobson Book Press, 1943. 207 pp., illus.

Wundt, Wilhelm
Elements of Folk Psychology, Outlines of a psychological history of the development of mankind. Translated by Edward Leroy Schaub. London and New York: The Macmillan Co., 1916. xxiii, 532 pp.

SPECIAL STUDIES

Arévalo, Pedro
"El Folklore en la Novela Americana." *Algo* (Trujillo, Peru) Oct., 1940, pp. 37–41.

Arnold, Doris Sanford
"Folklore in the Schools." A Tenth-Grade Tour. *NYFQ* 1 (No. 4):244–247, 1945.
An interesting and vital project carried on by students in Cranford (New Jersey) High School during 1944.

Barbeau, C. M.
"Field of European Folklore in America." *JAFL* 32:185–197, 1919.

Belden, H. M.
"Relation of Balladry to Folklore." *JAFL* 24:1–13, 1911.

Benedict, R. F.
"A Matter for the Field-Worker in Folklore." *JAFL* 36:104, 1923.

Bergen, F D., and Newell, William W.
"Topics for Collection of Folklore." *JAFL* 4:151–154, 1891.

Boas, Franz
Music and Folk-Lore. In: *General Anthropology,* pp. 609–626. Boston: D. C. Heath and Co., 1938.

Boggs, R. S.
"Folklore in the University Curricula in the United States." *SFQ* 4:93–109, 1940.

———.
The Development of Folklore in a University. In: *Studies in Language, and Literature,* edited with a foreword by George R. Coffman. (pp. 106–111). Chapel Hill, N. C.: University of North Carolina Press, 1945. viii, 344 pp.

Botkin, B. A.
Folk and Folklore. In: *Culture in the South,* pp. 570–594. Chapel Hill, N. C.: The University of North Carolina Press, 1935.

———.
Folklore as a Neglected Source of Social History. In: *The Cultural Approach to History,* edited for The American History Association by Caroline F. Ware (pp. 308-316). New York: Columbia University Press, 1940.

———.
"The folkness of the folk." *English Journal,* coll. ed. 26:461–469, 1932.
A discussion of the terms "folk" and "lore."

———.
"Folksay and Folklore." *AS* 6 (No. 6):404–406, 1931.

———.
"Folksay and Space. Their Genesis and Exodus." *Southwest Review* 20: 321–335, 1935.

———.
"WPA and Folklore Research: Bread and Song." *SFQ* 3:7–14, 1939.

Brewster, Paul G.
"Notes on Contributions of the Clergy to Folklore and Allied Fields." *SFQ* 7:173–186, 1943.

Chamberlain, Alexander Francis
The Child and Childhood in Folk-thought. (The child in primitive culture.) New York: Macmillan & Co., 1896. x, 464 pp., bibl.

Clough, W. O.
"Has American Folklore a Special Quality?" *SFQ* 8:115–121, 1944.

Cole, William E.
"Some Contributions of Folklore Studies to Social Planning." *TFSB* 8:2–4, 1942.

"Conference on Character and State of Studies in Folklore." *JAFL* 59:495–527, 1946.

Curtin, J.
"European Folklore in the United States." *JAFL* 2:56–59, 1889.

Davila, Victor M.
"Sentido humanista y trascendencia sociologica del folklore." *Lestras* (Lima) 2 cuatrimestre 242–251, 1943.

Dawkins, Richard MacGillivray
"Folklore and Literature." *Folklore* 40:14–36, 1929.

Dusenbury, Jean B.
"Folklore in the Schools." An Eleventh-Grade Unit. *NYFQ* 1:117, 1945.
Experience of a teacher in Saugerties High School, Saugerties, N. Y.

"English Folklore in America."
JAFL 31:4–72, 83–157, 167–169, 1918.

Fitton, Mary Louis
"College Folklore." *Hoosier Folklore Bulletin* 1:40–41, 1942.
Folklore items from Hanover College, Indiana.

Hankey, Rosalie
"Campus Folklore and California's 'Pedro'." *CFQ* 3:29–35, 1944.

Jansen, William Hugh
"Folklore Items from a Teacher's Handbook." *Hoosier Folklore Bulletin* 2:1–8, 1943.

Jones, Louis C.
"Folklore in the Schools. A Student Guide to Collecting Folklore." *NYFQ* 2, (No. 2):148–153, 1946.
An excellent guide for all collectors.

Lawrence, Dorothea Dix
Folklore Music Map of the United States. New York: Hagstrom Company, 1946.

Lomax, Alan
"The Documentary Record, A New Perspective in the Field of Folk History." Paper read at Seventh Annual Meeting of the *Southeastern Folklore Society*, Gainesville, Fla., February 14, 1942.

Marett, R. R.
Psychology and Folklore. London: Methuen Co., Ltd., 1920. 275 pp.

Maclachlan, J. M.
"Folk Concepts in the Novels of Thomas Wolfe." *SFQ* 9 (No. 4):175–186, 1945.

Newell, W. W.
"Individual and Collective Characteristics in Folklore." *JAFL* 19:1–15, 1906.

Pearce, J. E.
"Folk-Lore and Its Influence in Determining Institutions." *TFSP* 1:62–74, 1916.

Porter, Kenneth Wiggins
"The Business Man in American Folklore." *Bulletin of the Business Historical Society*, Nov., 1944.

Rickard, J. A.
"Suggestions for Collecting Folklore." *TFSB* 1 (No. 1): 4–12, 1935.

Riley, Susan B.
"The Teacher and the Folk Arts." *TFSB* 9:1–9, 1943.
Discussion of the advantages of teaching folklore in the schools.

Smith, Rebecca W.
"Finding Folk-Lorists." *TFSP* 8:155–159, 1930.
A teacher's experiment in encouraging her students to do original research in folklore. Altho it relates to her activities at Texas Christian University (1928–29), it is of actual interest to all teachers of American civilization.

Sweeney, Margaret
"New Lamps for Old." *The Indiana Teacher* (Indianapolis) 84: (No. 1) pp. 8, 28, 30, (Sept.) 1939.
Suggestions for use of folklore in high school teaching.

Thompson, Stith
"Folklore and Literature." *PMLA* 55:866–875, 1940.

Tsanoff, Radoslav A.
"Philosophy in Folklore." *TFSP* 14:145–154, 1938.

West, V.
Folklore in the Works of Mark Twain. Lincoln, Neb.: University of Nebraska Press, 1930.

GENERAL COLLECTIONS

American Folk Art.
The art of the common man in America, 1750–1900. New York: The Museum of Modern Art, 1932. bibliography pp. 47–52.

Bailey, Carolyn Sherwin
Pioneer Art in America. Illustrated by Grace Paull. New York: The Viking Press, 1945. 221 pp.
A series of delightful stories for younger readers on our early crafts and folkways.

Botkin, B. A., ed.
A Treasury of American Folklore. The Stories,
Legends, Tall Tales, Traditions, Ballads and
Songs of the American People. Foreword by
Carl Sandburg. New York: Crown Publishers,
1944. xxviii, 932 pp., music.

Brodin, Pierre
Le Roman Regionaliste Américain; Esquisse
d'une geographie morale et pittoresque des
États-Unis. Préface de M. Maurice-Edgar
Coindreau. Paris: G. P. Maisonneuve, 1937.
157 pp.

Carmer, Carl
America Sings. Stories and Songs of our Coun-
try's Growth. Music arranged by Edwin J.
Stringham. Illustrated in color by Elizabeth
Black Carmer. New York: Alfred A. Knopf,
1942. 243 pp., music.

————.
The Hurricane's Children. Tales From Your
Neck o' the Woods. New York: Farrar and
Rinehart, 1937.

Chamberlain, Samuel, ed.
Fair Is Our Land: The Portrait of America.
New York: Hastings House, 1942.
   In nearly 400 photographs, etchings, woodcuts,
   lithographs, the rich panorama of the American
   scene is enshrined.

De Voto, Bernard
Mark Twain's America. Illustrated by M. J.
Gallagher. Boston: Little Brown and Co., 1932.
353 pp.
   Discussion of Mike Fink in whom "as the demi-
   god of the rivers, Casanova, together with Paul
   Bunyan, merges into Thor." Newspaper humor
   of the Southwestern frontier.

Doren, Carl Van, and Carmer, Carl
American Scriptures. Illustrated with 48 Pic-
tures from Famous Collections. New York:
Boni and Gaer, 1946.
   A compendium of American traditions drawn
   from characters and events in our nation's past.

Emrich, Marion V., and Korson, George, eds.
Child Book of Folklore. Illustrated by John
O'Hara Cosgrave. New York: Dial Press, 1947.
xv, 240 pp.

Federal Writers' Project
*Manuscripts of the Federal Writers' Project
on American Folklore for the Various States.*
Deposited in the Folklore Section, Division
of Music, Library of Congress.
   A mine of information, much of it yet untapped.

Griffin, Grace Gardner
Writings on American History. Washington,
D. C.: Gov't Printing Office, 1906.

Haliburton, T. C., ed.
The Americans at Home; or, Byeways, Back-
woods, and Prairies, edited by the Author of
"Sam Slick" (T. C. Haliburton). London:
Hurst and Blackett, Publishers, 1854. 2 Vols.

Hazard, Lucy L.
The Frontier in American Literature. New
York: Crowell Press, 1927.

Kelling, Lucile
United States Mural. Chapel Hill, N. C.: University of North Carolina Press, 1940.
   Bibliographical material of the American Scene—
   fiction.

Koch, Frederick Henry, ed.
American Folk Plays. Introduction: "American folk drama in the Making." Illustrated
with photographs of the original production
of the plays; Foreword by Archibald Henderson. New York: D. Appleton-Century Co., 1939.
xlvi, 592 pp. illus., music.
   Written by students in playwriting at Chapel Hill
   and in summer courses—in some of our leading
   universities." Representative plays of most of
   the states and regions of this country.

Lord, Russell
Behold Our Land. Boston: Houghton Mifflin
Co., 1938.

Robertson, Archie
Slow Train to Yesterday. Boston: Houghton
Mifflin Co., 1945. 230 pp., illus.
   A lively discussion of "the almost abandoned, in-
   dependently owned, dinky short-line railroads
   and everything connected with them, including
   stories, jokes, personalities, customs—."

Rourke, Constance
The Roots of American Culture. Edited with
an introduction by Van Wyck Brooks. New
York: Harcourt, Brace, and Co., 1942. 305 pp.
   Includes an essay on "Early American Music," a
   note on folklore, and an observation on the effect
   of Indian beliefs in the supernatural on witch-
   hunting Salem.

Sandburg, Carl
The People, Yes. New York: Harcourt, Brace
and Co., 1936.
   "The book is mined out of the rock of American
   sayings and story telling—wise cracks, allusions,
   metaphors, proverbs, quotations, anecdotes, jokes,
   boners, bromides." (Botkin)

Skinner, Charles M.
Myths and Legends of Our Own Land. Philadelphia: J. B. Lippincott Co., 1896. 2 Vols.

Smith, Martha L.
Going to God's Country. Introduction by Dr.
Clara E. Krefting. Boston: The Christopher
Publishing House, 1941.
   Folksy observations and experiences in various
   states of the Union.

Stewart, George R.
Names on the Land, A Historical Account of
Place-Naming in the United States. New York:
Random House, 1945. 418 pp.
   A mine of information on life, character and
   events reflected thru place names.

Whale, Marcellus S.
The Old Types Pass. New York: Christopher
Publishing Co., 1925. v, 192 pp.
   Contains 25 tales and sketches, glossary of 1500
   words and 42 idioms, 5 songs with music, and 8
   illustrative sketches.

Woodward, W. E.
The Way Our People Lived. New York: E. P. Dutton and Co., 1944. 402 pp.
A history of the manners and customs of the American people over three centuries.

MYTHS AND LEGENDS

Babcock, W. H.
Legends of the New World. Boston: R. G. Badger, 1919. 155 pp.
Poems.

Bonner, Willard
"The Flying Dutchman of the Western World." *JAFL* 59:282–288, 1946.
"Anyone who reads the tales of Captain Kidd that flourished in the first half of the nineteenth century cannot help being struck by the recurrence in them of elements of romantic witchcraft quite beyond the simple eighteenth century concept of Kidd the ferocious pirate robber. Captain William Kidd in the nineteenth cenruty became the Flying Dutchman of the Western World."

Brady, Caroline
Legends of Ermanaric. Berkeley, Cal.: University of California Press, 1943. x, 341 pp.

Campbell, C. Macfie
Delusion and Belief. Cambridge, Mass.: Harvard University Press, 1926. 378 pp.
A discussion on the nature and function of myths and legends.

Cassirer, Ernst
Die Begriffsform im Mythischen Denken. Leipzig, Germany: B. G. Teubner, 1922.

Chase, Mary Ellen, and del Plaine, Frances
Tales and Legends: In: *The Art of Narration.* New York: Crofts, 1926. xiv, 494 pp. (pp. 139–156).

Cox, Sir George W.
An Introduction to the Science of Comparative Mythology and Folklore. London: C. Kegan Paul and Company, 1881.

Daanson, Edouard
Mythes et Légendes. Étude sur l'origine et l'évolution des croyances réligieuses par la comparaison des textes originaux. Bruxelles: Par Souscription, 1913. 417 pp., illus.

Danzel, Theodor Wilhelm
Die psychologischen Grundlagen der Mythologie. In: *Festschrift Meinhof,* (pp. 495–501). Hamburg, Germany: J. J. Augustin, 1927.

Deniker, J.
The Races of Man: an Outline of Anthropology and Ethnography, Chapter VI. London: Walter Scott, 1900. xxiii, 611 pp.

"Dissemination of Myths and Literary Types." *JAFL* 34:269–307, 1921.

Dobie, B. McK.
"Legends of the Supernatural." *TFSP* 3:137–143, 1918.

Dondore, Dorothy Anne
"The Children of Eve in America": Migration of an Ancient Legend. *SFQ* 3:223–229, 1939.

Drake, Samuel Adams
The Myths and Fables of To-Day. Illustrations by Frank T. Merrill. Boston: Lee and Shepard, 1900.

Ehrenreich, P.
Die allgemeine Mythologie und ihre Grundlagen. Leipzig: J. C. Hinrichs, 1910. vii, (I) 288 pp. Mythologische Bibliothek, hrsg. von der Gesellschaft für Vergleichende Mythenforschung. "Literaturverzeichnis." pp. 285–288.

Farnell, L. R.
The Value and the Methods of Mythologic Study. From the Proceedings of the British Academy, Volume IX. London: British Academy, 1919.

Frazer, Sir James George
Myths of the Origin of Fire. New York: The Macmillan Co., 1930. 238 pp.

Gray, Dr. Louis Herbert, ed.
The Mythology of All Races. Boston: Marshall Jones Co., 1916. 10 vols.

Hartland, E. S.
The Science of Fairy Tales, An inquiry into fairy mythology. London: W. Scott, 1891. viii, 372 pp. (half title: The Contemporary Science Series. Ed. by H. Ellis.) Bibliographical list of works referred to: pp. 353–365.

Hulme, F. Edward
Myth-Land. London: Sampson Low, Marston, 1886.

Hutchinson, Rev. H. N.
Prehistoric Man and Beast. New York: D. Appleton and Co., 1897.
Contains a good deal of folklore in Part I, Chapt. IV (pp. 84–106). Myths, Part II, Chapt. X (pp. 214–240).

Ingalls, Jeremy
Book of Legends. New York: Harcourt, Brace and Co., 1941.

Keightley, Thomas
The Fairy Mythology. Illustrative of the Romance and Superstition of Various Countries. Bohn's Antiquarian Library. London: H. G. Bohn, 1850.

Kluckhohn, Clyde
"Myths and Rituals: A General Theory." *Harvard Theological Review* 35:45–79, 1942.

Kroeber, A. L.
"Catch-Words in American Mythology." *JAFL* 21:222–227, 1908.

Lang, Andrew
Custom and Myth. London: Longmans, Green & Co., 1893. x, 312 pp., illus.

————.
Myth, Ritual and Religion. New York, London: Longmans, Green & Co., 1899. 2 v. (The Silver Library). First printing, Aug., 1887. New ed.

————.
The Origins of Religion and other Essays. London: Watts and Co., 1908. 128 pp., illus.

Langenhove, F. Van
The Growth of a Legend. New York: G. P. Putnam's Sons, 1916. 321 pp.
Discussion on the nature and function of myths and legends.

Langer, Susanne K.
Philosophy in a New Key. A Study in the Symbolism of Reason, Rite, and Art. Cambridge, Mass.: Harvard University Press, 1942.
Chapt. VII—Life-Symbols: The Roots of Myth. Discussion of the origins of ritual and myth.

Loomis, C. Grant
"Legend and Folklore." *CFQ* 2:279–297, 1943.

————.
"The Miracle of Ponderosity." *CFQ* 3:41–44, 1944.
Tradition of Saints' Legends.

MacDougall, Curtis Daniel
Hoaxes. New York: Macmillan Co., 1940. viii, 336 pp., front. pl.
Among the folkloric hoaxes treated by the author are mythical monsters (the hodag), historical myths (Parson Weems' cheery tree myth), tall stories and legendary heroes (Johnny Appleseed).

Mannhardt, Wilhelm
"Formation de Mythes dans les Temps Moderne." *Mélusine* 1:561–570, 1878.

Mechem, Kirke
The Mythical Jayhawk. Topeka, Kansas: Kansas State Printing Plant, 1944. 11 pp.

Minckwitz, Johannes
Illustriertes Taschenwoerterbuch der Mythologie aller Voelker. Leipzig: Arnoldosche Buchhandlung, 1870.
Myths of all peoples.

Mitford, Mary Russell
Lights and Shadows of American Life. London: H. Colburn and R. Bentley, 1832. 3 vols.
Contains some legends and tales, as well as an interesting portion (vol. 3) on "The Last of the Boatmen"—Mike Fink.

Newell, W. W.
"Ritual Regarded as the Dramatization of Myth." *JAFL* 7:248–249, 1894.

Olcott, William Tyler
Star Lore of All Ages; a collection of myths, legends, and facts concerning the constellations of the northern hemisphere. New York: G. P. Putnam's Sons, 1911. xxii, 453 pp.

Puckett, Newbell N.
"Religious Folk Beliefs of Whites and Negroes." *Journal of Negro History* 16:9–35, 1931.

Raglan, Fitz Roy Richard Somerset, baron
The Hero; a study in tradition, myth, and drama. New York: Oxford University Press, 1937. xi, 311 pp., bibl.

Reichard, G. A.
"Literary Types and Dissemination of Myths." *JAFL* 34:269–307, 1921.

Róheim, Géza
"Myth and Folk Tale." *American Imago* 2 (No. 3):266–279, 1941.

Skinner, Charles M.
American Myths and Legends. Philadelphia: J. B. Lippincott Co., 1903. 2 Vols.

Spence, Lewis
Outlines of Mythology. London: Watts, 1944. vii, 118 pp.

Swanton, J. R.
"Practical Aspects of the Study of Myth." *JAFL* 23:1–7, 1910.

Van Gennep, Arnold
La Formation des Légendes. Bibliothèque de Philosophie Scientifique. Paris: Ernest Flammarion, 1910. 326 pp.

————.
Religion, Moeurs et Légendes. Essais d'Ethnographie et de Linguistique. Paris: Mercure de France, 1909. 318 pp.

Virenda, Vandyopadhyaya
Dictionary of Superstitions and Mythology. Biren Bonnerjea, Trans. London: Folk Press, Ltd., 1927. 320 pp.

Voragine, Jacobus de
The Golden Legend. (Granger Ryan and Herlmut Ripperger, Trans.) New York: Longmans, Green and Co., 1941. 356 pp.

Young, Kimball
Stereotypes, Myths and Ideologies. In: *Social Psychology,* Chap. IX (pp. 189–221). New York: F. S. Crofts and Co., 1944. 578 pp.
"Examines the individual's inner activity, especially the world of meaning that is vital to our understanding of external conduct."

MAGIC—SUPERSTITION— WITCHCRAFT

See: New England and Mass., pp. 181–84, 202–05

BIBLIOGRAPHY

Black, George F.
List of Works in the New York Public Library Relating to Witchcraft in the United States. New York: Public Library, Nov., 1908.

Ellison, Saram R.
The Saram R. Ellison, M. D. Collection on Magic and Allied Arts, Magical Wands, and Models of Illusion. New York: 1906. 32 pp.

Slater, John Herbert
"Some Books on Magic." *Bibliographical Society Transactions* (London) 3:171–193, 1896.

————.
"Some Books on Magic." *Literary Collector* (New York) 8:135–146, 1904.

U. S. Library of Congress
A Short List of References on Superstitions. Washington, D. C. 1924. (Select list of references, No. 856). Division of Bibliography.

GENERAL STUDIES AND COLLECTIONS

Aurand, Monroe Jr.
The Realness of Witchcraft in America. Harrisburg, Pa.: Privately Printed, The Aurand Press, 1942. 32 pp.

Beardsley, Richard K., and Hankey, Rosalie
"A History of the Vanishing Hitchhiker." *CFQ* 1:303–337, 1942; 2:13–25, 1943.
The author claims that the vanishing hitchhiker is in essence a modern ghost story—"it may have drawn on older sources but it gained its individuality and began its spread only as a modern story, drawing on our own cultural scene."

Beauchamp, W. M., Bergen, F. D., and Newell, W. W.
"Current Superstitions Among English-Speaking Population of U. S. and Canada." *JAFL* 2:12–22, 1889.

Beckwith, M. W.
"Signs and Superstitions Collected Among American College Girls." *JAFL* 36:1–15, 1923.

Bergen, Fanny D, ed.
Current Superstitions. Collected from the oral tradition of English speaking folk. With notes, and an introduction by William Wells Newell. Memoirs of the American Folk Lore Society, vol. 4. Boston: Houghton Mifflin and Company, 1896. viii, 161 pp.
"Almost the entire body of this tradition belongs to the English stock; it is the English population which, together with the language, has imposed on other elements of American life its polity, society, ethics, and tradition" (page 1 of the introduction).

————.
"Witch Stories." *JAFL* 12:68–69, 1899.

————.
"Current Superstitions." *JAFL* 9:55–66, 1896; 12:55–63, 1899.

————.
"Quilt Patterns." *JAFL* 3:51–59, 1890.

Berry, Brewton
You and Superstition. Illustrations by L. Frederic Stephens. Columbia, Mo.: Lucas Brothers, 1940. 249 pp., illus.

Black, William George
"Players' Superstitions." *Folk-Lore* (London) 1:276–277, 1890.

Blakeman, R.
A Philosophical Essay on Credulity and Superstition: and also on animal fascination, or charming. New York: 1849.

Boulton, Richard
A Compleat History of Magick, Sorcery, and Witchcraft. London: Printed for E. Curll, J. Pemberton, and W. Taylor, 1715. 2 vols.
Vol. 2 includes "The Tryals of Several Witches at Salem in New England."

Bruce, H.
"Our Superstitions." *Outlook* 98:999–1006, 1911.

Budge, Sir E. A. Wallis
Amulets and Superstitions. London, New York: Oxford University Press, 1930. xxxiv, 543 pp.

Caldwell, Otis William, and Lundeen, G. E.
An Experimental Study of Superstitions and Other Unfounded Beliefs as Related to Certain Units of General Science. New York: Bureau of Publications, Teachers College, Columbia University, 1932. 138 pp., bibl.

"Child-stealing Witch Game."
JAFL 3:139–148, 315, 1890; 13:299–300, 1900.

Clodd, Edward
Magic in Names, and In Other Things. London: Chapman and Hall. Ltd., 1920. vii, 238 pp., bibl.

Colquhoun, John Campbell
A History of Magic, Witchcraft, and Animal Magnetism. London: Longman, Brown, Green and Longmans, 1851. 2 vols.

Conklin, Edmund S.
"Superstitious Belief and Practice Among College Students." *Amer. Jour. of Psychology* (Worcester) 30:83–102, 1919.

"Current Superstitions Among English-Speaking Population of the United States and Canada." *JAFL* 2:12–22; 105–112, 1889.

Daggett, J. S.
Superstition and the Dread Prophecies for 1881–1885. Albany, N. Y.: Published for the Author, 1881. 63 pp.

Daniels, Mrs. Cora Linn (Morrison)
Encyclopaedia of Superstitions, Folklore and the Occult Sciences of the World; a comprehensive library of human belief and practice in the mystries of life ... Editorial staff, Cora Linn Daniels ... and Prof. C. M. Stevans ... with more than one thousand eminent assistants. Chicago & Milwaukee: J. H. Yewdale and Sons Co., 1903. 3 vols., illus.

Dawson, Warren Royal
The Bridle of Pegasus; studies in magic, mythology and folklore. London: Methuen & Co., Ltd., 1930. xv, 203 pp., bibl.

Dean, John Candee
"Astronomical Superstitions." *Popular Science Monthly* 75: 469–478, 1909.

Deerforth, Daniel
Knock Wood! Superstitions Through the Ages. New York: Brentano's, 1928. 200 pp.

de Lys, Claudia
A Treasury of American Superstitions. New York: The Philosophical Library, 1948. 494 pp.
". . . a compendium of facts about superstitions with something of their history and rational explanations of their origin. Arranged by subject, well indexed, with each page crowded with interesting fact and commentary . . ." (Library Jrnl.)

Dixie, Raymond
The Boy Magician; a large number of the latest and best tricks carefully selected for the rising generation of conjurers. Boston: Lothrop, Lee & Shepard Co., 1922. 218 pp., illus.

Drake, Samuel Adams
The Myths and Fables of To-Day. Illustrations by Frank T. Merrill. Boston: Lee and Shepard, 1900.

Emine, Earle Edward
"Supplementary Study of Superstitious Belief Among College Students." *Journal of Psychology* (Mass.) 12:183, 1941.

Evans, E. P.
"Superstition and Crime." *Popular Science Monthly* 54:206–221, 1898.

Evans, Henry Ridgely
Adventures in Magic. New York: L. Rullman, 1927. 87 pp. illus.

————.
The Old and New Magic. Introduction Paul Carus. Chicago: The Open Court Publ. Co., 1909. xxxii, 517 pp., illus.

Fielding, William John
Strange Superstitions and Magical Practices. Philadelphia: The Blakiston Company, 1945. xiii, 273 pp.

Forsyth, J. S.
Demonologia; or, Natural Knowledge Revealed; being an exposé of ancient and modern superstitions, credulity, fantaticism and imposture, as connected with the doctrine, cabala, and jargon, of amulets, apparitions, astrology, charms, demonology . . . witchcraft, etc. London: J. Bumpus, 1827. xvi, 438 pp.

Frazer, Sir James George
The Devil's Advocate; a Plea for Superstition . . . London: Macmillan & Co., Ltd., 1927. xi, 186 pp. Rev. & enl.

————.
The Golden Bough; a study in magic and religion. New York and London: The Macmillan Company, 1894. 2 vols. Issued in 1911–1915 in 12 vols.; also issued in One Volume in 1922: xiv, 752 pp.

————.
"The Influence of Superstition on the Growth of Institutions." *Royal Institute of Great Britain. Proceedings* (London) 19:450–461, 1911.

————.
Psyche's Task, A Discourse Concerning the Influence of Superstition on the Growth of Institutions. London: Macmillan & Co., Ltd., 1909. ix, 84 pp.

Gleadow, Rupert
Magic and Divination. London: Faber and Faber, 1941. 308 pp., illus.

Goldsmith, Milton (Astra Cielo)
Signs, Omens and Superstitions. New York: G. Sully & Company, 1918. vii, 159 pp.

Graubard, Mark
"Some Contemporary Observations in Ancient Superstitions." *JAFL* 59:124–133, 1946.

Haddon, Alfred Cort
Magic and Fetishism. London: A. Constable & Company, 1910. viii, 98 pp., bibl.

Hall, Manly Palmer
Magic; a Treatise on Natural Occultism. Los Angeles, Calif.: Hall Publications, 1934. 46 pp., illus.

Halpert, Herbert
"Witchcraft Stories." *HFB* 2:9–10, 1943.

Hand, W. D.
"The Three Nephites." *American Notes and Queries* (N. Y.) 2:56-57, 1942.
Discussion of the U. S. variants of the Spectral Hitchhiker legend, which parallel Three Nephites.

Hartmann, Franz
Magic, White and Black; or, The Science of Finite and Infinite Life . . . London: G. Redway, 1888. xii, 324 pp., illus.

Hoffman, W.
"Popular Superstitions." *Pennsylvania-German Society. Proceedings* 5:70–81.

Holland, Clive
"Some Superstitions of Seafaring Folks." *Nautical Magazine* (London) 143:12–15, 1940.

Igglesden, Sir Charles
Those Superstitions. Foreword by Marjorie Bowen. London: Jarrolds, 1932. 240 pp.

James, George Wharton
"Witches and Witchcraft of the Present Day." *The Traveler,* April, 1899, p. 57.

Jones, William
Credulities Past and Present, including the sea and seamen, miners, amulets and talismans, rings, word and letter divination, numbers, trials, exorcising and blessing of animals, birds, eggs, and luck. London: Chatto and Windus, 1880. xii, 560 pp.

Kenney, Eudorus Catlin
Ghosts, Devils, Angels and Sun Gods. A Series of Essays Against Superstition. n.p.: The Author, 1891. 126 pp.

King, John H.
The Supernatural: Its Origin, Nature and Evolution. London: Williams and Norgate, 1892. 2 vols, bibl.

Kittredge, George Lyman
Witchcraft in Old and New England. Cambridge, Mass.: Harvard University Press. 1929.

Knortz, Karl
Amerikanischer Aberglaube der Gegenwart, ein Beitrag zur Volkskunde. Leipzig: T. Gerstenberg, 1913. 156 pp.
Superstition, folklore.

Knowlson, Thomas Sharper
The Origins of Popular Superstitions and Customs. London: T. W. Laurie, 1910. 242 pp.

Kunz, George Frederick
The Magic of Jewels and Charms. With 90 illustrations . . . Philadelphia: J. B. Lippincott Co., 1915. xv, 422 pp., illus.
Contents: Magic stones and electric gems. On meteorites, or celestial stones. Stones of healing. On the virtues of fabulous stones, concretions and fossils. Snake stones and bezoars. Angels and ministers of grace. On the religious use of various stones. Amulets; ancient, medieval and oriental. Amulets of primitive peoples and of modern times. Facts and fancies about precious stones.

Kurtz, Benjamin Putnam
Studies in the Marvellous. Berkeley: The University Press, 1910. 244 pp. University of California Publications in Modern Philology. V. I, No. 2.

Lawrence, Robert Means
The Magic of the Horseshoe; with other folklore notes. Boston: Houghton Mifflin Company, 1898. iv, 344 pp.
Contents: The magic of the horseshoe.— Fortune and luck.—The folklore of common salt.—The omens of sneezing.—Days of good and evil omen. Superstitions dealing with animals.—The luck of odd numbers.—Topical Index.

Lehmann, Alfred Georg Ludvig
Aberglaube und Zauberei von den ältesten Leiten an bis in die Gegenwart . . . Stuttgart: F. Enke, 1925. xvi, 752 pp., illus., bibl.
Superstition and magic from the earliest times to the present.

Loeb, Margery L.
"The Black Art." *Natural History* 29:396–409, 1929. illus.

Logan, J. D.
"The Thirteenth Guest. A Study of Popular Superstitions." *Canadian Magazine* (Toronto) 46:9–14, 1915.

Loing, J. M.
Notes in Superstition and Folklore, introduction by D. H. Edwards. Brechin: Advertiser Office, 1885. xv, 107 pp.

Lowndes, Marion
Ghosts That Still Walk. Illustrated by Warren Chappell. New York: Alfred A. Knopf, 1942. xiv, 147 pp.
"These restless spirits belong to the eastern half of the United States and may be conjured up in a dozen states whose outposts are marked by Maine, Missouri, Mississippi and the Carolina "Low Country." (C. Grant Loomis)

Miller, Roland M.
"Superstitions Among College Students." *Sociology and Social Research* (Los Angeles) 13:361–365, 1929.

Mitra, Sarat Chandra
"The Evolution of Superstition About Unlucky Days and Objects." *Anthropological Society of Bombay, Journal* 9:225–242, 1912.

Negelein, Julius von
Weltgeschichte des Aberglaubens. Berlin: W. de Gruyter & Co., 1931–35. 2 vols., bibl.
A world history of superstition.

Newham, William
Essay on Superstition, being an inquiry into the effects of physical influence on the mind, in the production of dreams, visions, ghosts, and other supernatural appearances. London: J. Hatchard & Son, 1830. xvi, 430 pp.

Peabody, E. P.
"Mark Twain's Ghost Story." *Minnesota History* 18 (No. 1) : 28–35, 1937.
A Nursery Tale of the Talking Eggs.

Perry, William James
The Origin of Magic and Religion. London: Methuen & Co., 1923. ix, 212 pp., bibl.

Poyntz, Albary, ed.
A World of Wonders, with anecdotes and opinions concerning popular superstitions. London: R. Bentley, 1845. xii, 361 pp.

Rabaud, Camille
Phénomènes Psychique et Superstitions Populaires. Castres: Bonnet, 1909. 77 pp.
Psychic phenomena and popular superstitions.

Read, Carveth
The Origin of Man and of His Superstitions. Cambridge, Eng.: University Press, 1920. xii, 350 pp.

Redfield, W. A.
"Superstitions and Folk Beliefs." *TFSB* 3:11–40, 1937.

Robinson, Charles Frederick
"Some Psychological Elements in Famous Superstitions." *Journal of Religions, Psychology and Education* (Worcester, Mass.) 1:248–267, 1905.

Róheim, Géza
Animism, Magic, and the Divine King. London: K. Paul, Trench, Trubner & Co., Ltd., 1930. xviii, 390 pp.

Schele De Vere, Maximilian
Modern Magic. New York: G. P. Putnam's Sons, 1873. 466 pp.

Scott, George Ryley
Man and His Illusions, a collection of unpalatables. London: L. Cole, 1944. 112 pp.

Scott-Stokes, Henry F.
Perseus; or, Of Dragons. New York: E. P. Dutton & Company, 1925. vii, 74 pp.

Seabrook, William Buehler
Witchcraft; its power in the world today. New York: Harcourt, Brace & Co., 1940. ix, 387 pp., illus.

Sener, Samuel Miller
"Local Superstitions." Lancaster County Historical Society. Historical Papers and Addresses (Lancaster, Pa.) 9 (No. 8):233–245, 1905.

Skeel, M. H.
"Version of Game of Child-Stealing Witch." *JAFL* 3:315, 1890.

Smith, Catharine Cook
In Defense of Magic; the meaning and use of symbol and rite. New York: L. MacVeagh, The Dial Press, 1930. x, 152 pp.

Sobel, Jacob
"Prejudices and Superstitions Met With in the Medical Inspection of School Children." *International Congress on School Hygiene, Transactions* (Buffalo) 4:78–88, 1914.

Stauffer, Francis Henry
The Queer, The Quaint, The Quizzical; a cabinet for the curious. Philadelphia: R. A. Tripple, 1882. 367 pp.

Stevens, Samuel Eugene
Science and Superstition. New York: Truth Seeker Co., 1913. 119 pp.

Summers, Montague
Witchcraft and Black Magic. With 24 illustrations. London: Rider & Co., Ltd., 1946. 228 pp., illus.

Thompson, Alfred
Magic and Mystery. A Popular History. London: W. Stewart & Co., Ltd., 1894. 127 pp.

Thompson, Charles John Samuel
The Hand of Destiny; the folk-lore and superstitions of everyday life. London: Rider & Co., 1932. 303 pp., illus.

————.
The Mysteries and Secrets of Magic. Philadelphia: J. B. Lippincott Co., 1928. xvii, 320 pp., illus., bibl.

Thorndike, Lynn
A History of Magic and Experimental Science. New York: The Macmillan Company, 1923–41. 6 vols.

Thurston, Herbert
Superstition: A Backward Glance Over Nineteen Centuries. London: The Centenary Press, 1933. 127 pp.

Trenchard, John
The Natural History of Superstition. London: 1709. 54 pp.

Turner, T.
"The Human Comedy in Folk Superstitions." *TFSP* 13:146–175, 1937.

Vidler, Alexander Roper
Magic and Religion. London: A. R. Mowbray & Co., Ltd., 1930. 32 pp.

Virenda, Vandyopadhyaya
Dictionary of Superstitions and Mythology. London: Folk Press, Ltd., 1927. 320 pp.

Warner, Irene E. Yote
"Black Magic and Voodooism in America." *Occult Review* (London) 21:21–26, 1915.

Waterman, Phillip F.
Story of Superstition. New York: Alfred A. Knopf, 1929. 307 pp., illus., bibl.

Woolsey, John Martin
The Whims of the Ages: the moon the mother of all things; the day of doom and the flight of the gods. New York: 1916. 120 pp.

Wright, Thomas
Narratives of Sorcery and Magic; from the most authentic sources. London: R. Bentley, 1851. 2 vols.

Yardley, Edward
The Supernatural in Romantic Fiction. London: Longmans, Green & Co., 1880. viii, 141 pp.

Yelvington, H.
Ghost Lore. San Antonio, Texas: Naylor, 1936.

CUSTOMS—CEREMONIES

Banier, l'Abbé and Le Mascrier, l'Abbé
Histoires Générale des Cérémonies, Moeurs, et Coûtumes Religieuses de Tous les Peuples du Monde, représentée en 243 figures dessinées de la main de Bernard Picard: avec des explications historiques & curieuses. Paris: Rollin fils, 1741. 7 vols., illus.
Vol. 7 deals with Religious Ceremonies of the Americans.

Bergen, F. D.
"Traditionary American Local Dishes." *JAFL* 13:65, 1900.

Bourke, John Gregory
Compilation of Notes and Memoranda bearing upon the use of human ordure and urine in rites of a religious or semi-religious character among various nations. Washington, D. C., 1888.

———.
Scatologic Rites of all Nations. A dissertation upon the employment of excrementation remedial agents in religion, therapeutic divination, witchcraft, love-philters, etc., in all parts of the globe. Based upon original notes and personal compilation from over one thousand authorities. Washington, D. C.: W. H. Lowdermilk & Co., 1891. x, 496 pp. bibl. (pp. 469–483).

Cesaresco, Countess Evelyn M.
Folklore on Stone. In: *International Folk-lore Association.* Papers read at Memphis, Atlanta, and Chicago. Chicago: 1896. 44 pp., illus.

Cutler, Harry Gardner, and L. W. Yaggy
Panorama of the Nations; or, Journeys among the families of men: a description of their homes, customs, habits, employments and beliefs; their cities, temples, monuments, literature and fine arts. Chicago: Star Publishing Company, 1892. xv, 1034 pp., illus.

Dally, Nicolas
Moeurs Usages et Coûtumes de Tous les Peuples du Monde; d'après des documents authentiques et les voyages les plus recents; publié par Auguste Wahlen. Bruxelles: Libraire Historique—Artistique. 1843–1844. 4 vols., illus.
Vol. 4 deals with Africa and America.

Depping, Georg Bernhard
Evening Entertainments; or, Delineations of the manners, and customs of the various nations, interspersed with geographical notices, historical and biographical anecdotes, and descriptions in natural history. Designed for the instruction and amusement of youth. London: Printed for N. Hailes, 1817. viii, 338 pp., illus.

Doran, John
Habits and Men, with remnants of record touching the makers of both. London: R. Bentley, 1855. vi, 417 pp.

Doten, Dana
The Art of Bundling: being an inquiry into the nature and origins of that curious but universal folk-custom, with an exposition of the rise and fall of bundling in the eastern part of N. America . . . drawings by Lee Brown Coye. Weston, Vt.: The Countryman Press and New York: Farrar and Rinehart, 1938. x, 190 pp., illus.

Funk, Wilfred John
"So You Think It's New;" drawings by Russell Sherman. New York: Funk & Wagnalls Company, 1937. x, 198 pp., illus.

Gist, Noel P.
"Secret Societies." A Cultural Study of Fraternalism in the United States. *University of Missouri Studies* 15:1–184, 1904.

Haire, Frances Hamilton
The American Costume Book. New York: A. S. Barnes and Co., 1934. 164 pp.

Haliburton, Robert Grant
New Materials for the History of Man, derived from a comparison of the calendars and festivals of nations . . . No. 1. The Festival of the Dead. Halifax, Nova Scotia: Printed Privately, 1863. Reprinted, Toronto: Royal Astronomical Society of Canada, 1920. 126 pp.

Hamerton, Philip Gilbert
Human Intercourse. London: Macmillan and Co., 1884. xviii, 391 pp.

Hamilton, T.
Men and Manners in America. Phila: Carey, Lea and Blanchard. 1883. 2 vols.

Hammerton, John Alexander, ed.
Manners & Customs of Mankind. London: The Amalgamated Press, Ltd; 1931–32. 3 vols. in 2.

Haskin, Frederic J.
Curious Customs. Washington, D. C.: The Evening Star—The Sunday Star, 1933. 31 pp.

Hedge, Mary Ann
Man; or Anecdotes National and Individual. An historic mélange for the amusement of youth. London: A. K. Newman & Co., 1822, 271 pp.

Hertz, Robert
Mélanges de Sociologie Réligieuse et Folklore . . . avec une préface d'Alice Robert Hertz. Paris: F. Alcan, 1928. xvi, 252 pp., illus.
Discusses among other things, funeral rites and ceremonies.

Hibben, Sheila
American Regional Cookery. Boston: Little, Brown and Company, 1946. 335 pp.
One can often get fairly good insight to a people by the type of food they eat.

Hoffman, David
Miscellaneous Thoughts on Men, Manners, and Things . . . Baltimore: Coale & Co., 1837. vi, 374 pp.

Hutchinson, W.
Customs of the World; a popular account of the manners, rites and ceremonies of men and women in all countries. With an introduction by A. C. Haddon and with contributions by eminent authorities. London: Hutchinson & Co., 1913. 2 vols.

Keane, Augustus Henry
The World's Peoples; a popular account of their bodily & mental characters, beliefs, traditions, political and social institutions . . . With 270 illustrations reproduced from original photographs. New York: G. P. Putnam's Sons, 1908. xii, 434 pp., illus.

Knowlson, T. S.
The Origin of Popular Superstitions, Customs and Ceremonies. London: T. W. Laurie, 1940. 242 pp.

Lang, Andrew
Custom and Myth. London: Longmans, Green & Co., 1893. x, 312 pp., illus.

Lévy-Bruhl, Lucien
La Morale et la Science des Moeurs. Paris: F. Alcan, 1909. 300 pp.

McKown, Harry Charles
Fools and Foolishness; illustrated by Margaret Whittemore. Topeka, Kan.: School Activity Publishing Co., 1943. 263 pp., illus.

Mallery, Garrick
Customs of Courtesy. Washington, D. C.; Judd and Detweiler Printers, 1890. 15 pp.

Michael, Dorothy Jean
"Grave Decoration." *TFSP* 18:129–136, 1943.
Discusses these customs among Negroes, Whites, Mexicans and Indians in Texas.

Morris, Charles
Home Life in All Lands. Philadelphia: J. B. Lippincott, 1909. Illus.

Newell, W. W.
"Primitive Marriage Customs as Preserved in the Games of Children." *JAFL* 5:70–71, 1892.

Parsons, Elsie Clews
Fear and Conventionality. New York: G. P. Putnam's Sons, 1914. xviii, 239 pp., bibl.
On the manners and customs of people.

Partridge, Bellamy, and Bettmann, Otto
As We Were: Family Life in America, 1850–1900. In text and pictures. New York: Whittlesey House, 1946.
Contains over 300 delightful illustrations. A rare combination of amusement and information.

Powell, Thomas
All Round the World; or, Scenes and Adventures in Every Land. Being a Geographical and Historical Encyclopedia, Illustrating the Manners and Customs . . . of the Several Nations. New York: United States Publishing Company, 1873. xv, 512 pp., illus.
Republished in 1889, with additional chapters, under the title: *Illustrated Home Book of the World's Great Nations.*

Puckle, Bertram S.
Funeral Customs: Their Origin and Development. New York: Frederick A. Stokes, 1926.

Rogers, E. G.
"Family Folk Fronts in Rime and Rhythm." *TFSB* 9:3–7, 1945.
"—A number of efforts in verse which relate to lovers, courtships, marriage, and the general ups and downs of life."

Royall, Mrs. Anne (Newport)
Sketches of History, Life, and Manners, in the United States, by a traveler. New Haven, Conn.: Printed for the Author, 1826. xiii, 392 pp.

Sartori, Paul
Sitte und Brauch. Teil 1-3. Leipzig: W. Heims, 1910–14. (Handbücher zur Volkskunde, Band 5–8.)

Skeat, Walter William
The Past at Our Door; or, The Old In the New Around Us. London: Macmillan and Co., 1912. xi, 198 pp., illus.
Contents: The story of our food.—The story of our dress.—The story of our homes.

Spencer, Herbert
Ceremonial Institutions; being part IV of the Principles of Sociology. New York: D. Appleton and Company, 1880. ii, 237 pp., bibl.

———.
Manners and Fashion. Humboldt Library, No. 28. 1882.

Stiles, Henry Reed
Bundling; its origin, progress, and decline in America. Albany: Knickerbocker Publishing Co., 1871. 138 pp.

Sumner, William Graham
Folkways; a study of the sociological importance of usages, manners, customs, mores and morals. Boston: Ginn & Company, 1906. vii, 692 pp., bibl.

Train, Arthur Kissam
The Story of Everyday Things. New York: Harper & Brothers, 1941. xi, 428 pp., illus.

Trollope, Mrs.
Domestic Manners of the Americans. New York: Dodd, Mead and Co., 1901.

Verrill, A. Hyatt
Strange Customs, Manners and Beliefs. Boston: L. C. Page and Company, 1946. 302 pp., illus.
The author deals mainly with primitive people,—large section devoted to the American Indian.

Voegelin, Erminie W.
"Diffusion of a New Folk Custom." *AA* 48 (No. 2):290–292, 1946.

W., J. P.
"The Coercion of Custom." *Scottish Review* 35:69–89, 1900.

Wakefield, Priscilla
Sketches of Human Manners, delineated in stories intended to illustrate the characters, religion, and singular customs, of the inhabitants of different parts of the world. Philadelphia: Johnson & Warner, 1811. 252 pp.

Walsh, William Shepard
Curiosities of Popular Customs. Philadelphia: J. B. Lippincott Co., 1898. 1,018 pp.

Watson, Lillian
The Customs of Mankind. With notes on modern etiquette and newest trend in entertainment . . . Illustrated. Garden City, N. Y.: N. Doubleday, 1924. xvii, 753 pp., bibl.

Wolff, Edwin Daniel
Why Do We Do It. New York: The Macaulay Company, 1929. 304 pp., illus.

Woodward, W. E.
The Way Our People Lived. New York: E. P. Dutton and Co., 1944. 402 pp.
A history of the manners and customs of the American people over three centuries.

FOLKTALES

BIBLIOGRAPHIES

Eastman, Mary Huse
Index to Fairy Tales, Myths and Legends.
Boston: The F. W. Faxon Co., 1937. 566 pp.

Olcott, Frances J., comp.
"Fairy Tales for Children." *Bibliography Bulletin*, No. 13. New York State Library, Albany. June 1898.

Parsons, Elsie Clews
Bibliography of the Folk Tale. In: *Folk-Lore of the Antilles, French, and English.* Memoirs of the American Folklore Society, vol. 26, Part III (pp. 1–12). New York: The American Folklore Society, 1943. 487 pp.

Thompson, Stith
Important Works on the Folktale. In: *The Folktale.* (pp. 463–466). New York: The Dryden Press, 1946. 510 pp.
An excellent bibliography. Although many entries do not deal specifically with the American folktale, the selection is indispensable for comparative study.

———, Aarne, Antti
The Types of the Folktales. A Classification and Bibliography. Helsingfors, 1928. (Folklore Fellows Communications 74).

STUDIES AND COLLECTIONS

Aarne, Antti, and Thompson, Stith
The Types of the Folk-Tale. FFC 74, Helsinki, 1928.

"Accumulative Tales."
JAFL 2:209–212, 1889; 13:228–229, 1900; 18:33–45, 1905; 33:34–42, 1920.

Armfield, Mrs. Ann Constance (Smedley)
Wonder Tales of the World. New York: Harcourt, Brace and Howe, 1920. 271 pp.

Bartlett, Frederic Charles
"Psychology in Relation to the Popular Story." *Folklore* 31:264–293, 1908 (London).

———.
"Some Experiments on the Reproduction of Folk Stories." *Folklore* 31:30–47, 1908.

Beatty, Arthur
"Ballad, Tale and Tradition." *PMLA* 29:473–498, 1914.

Bergen, F. D.
"English Folktales in America—Johnny Cake." *JAFL* 2:60–62, 1889.

———.
"Golden Bird." *JAFL* 13:231–232, 1900.

Best, Edwin J.
"Stars and Coffee Grounds." Text of an anecdote of fortune telling. *TFSB* 6:23–30, 1940.

Boas, Franz
The Development of Folk-Tales and Myths. In: *Race, Language and Culture* by Franz Boas (pp. 397–406) rep. 1916. New York: Macmillan Co., 1940.

Bolte, Johannes
Name und Merkmale des Märchens FF (Folklore Fellows) Communications No. 36. Helsinki: Suomalainen Tiedeakatemia, 1920. 42 pp.
Classification of tales.

Brueyre, Loys
"De l'origine des Contes." Paris: *Mélusine* 1: 235–239, 1878.

Carmer, Carl
The Hurricane's Children; Tales from Your Neck o' the Woods. Illustrated by Elizabeth Black Carmer. New York, Toronto: Farrar & Rhinehart, Inc., 1937. xvi, 175 pp. illus.

Chase, Mary Ellen, and del Plaine, Frances
Tales and Legends. In: *The Art of Narration.* New York: Crofts and Co., 1926. (pp. 139–156).

Chase, Richard
"Jack and the Giants." *SFQ* 1 (No. 1):35–43, 1937.
Folktale.

Christensen, Arthur
Motif et Thème; plan d'un dictionnaire des motifs de contes populaires, de légendes et de fables. Helsinki: Suomalainen Tiedeakatemia, 1925. 52 pp. FF (Folklore Fellows). Communications No. 59.
Folklore classification.

Clodd, Edward
Tom Tit Tot; an essay on savage philosophy in folk tale. London: Duckworth & Co., 1898. x, 249 pp.

Clough, Ben C
The American Imagination at Work. With an Introduction and Comments, New York: Alfred A. Knopf, 1947. 726 pp. illus.
More than 200 tall tales and folk tales ranging in time from Cotton Mather to John Hersey.

Clough, Wilson O.
"A Neglected American Myth-Man." *CFQ* 2:85–88, 1943.
The lore of "the Feller."

Clouston, William Alexander
Popular Tales and Fictions, their Migrations and Transformations. New York: Scribner and Welford, 1887. 2 Vols.

"Comparison of Egyptian Folktale with American Folktales."
JAFL 17:255–264, 1904.

Conant, L.
"English Folktales in America." *JAFL* 8:143–144, 1895.

Cooke, E. J.
"English Folktales in America." *JAFL* 12:126–130, 1899.

Cosquin, Emmanuel
Études Folkloriques. Recherches sur les migrations des Contes Populaires et leur point de départ. Paris, France: Edouard Champion, 1922.

Les Contes Populaires et Leur Origine; dernier état de la question. Bruxelles: Polleunis, 1895. 24 pp.

Cox, Marion Roalfe
An Introduction to Folk-lore. New York: C. Scribner's Sons. 1895. xv, 319 pp.

Crane, T. F.
"Diffusion of Popular Tales." *JAFL* 1:8–15, 1888.

Dacqué, Edgar
Urwelt; Sage und Menscheit; eine Naturhistorisch—Metaphysische Studie. München: Oldenburg, 1925. 366 pp., illus. notes.

Davidson, Levette J.
"Moron Stories." *SFQ* 7:101–104, 1943.

Dickason, David H.
"Swallowing Snake Eggs." *HFB* 2:22, 1943.

Dietrich, Albrecht
Über Wesen und Ziele der Volkskunde; Über vergleichende Sitten und Rechtsgeschichte. Leipzig: Teubner, 1902. 67 pp.
Studies in Comparative Folklore.

Dorson, Richard M.
"Just B'ars." *Appalachia:* (n.s.) 8; 183, 1942.
A variant of "The Bear Ate Me" folktale.

English Folklore in America.
"Folktales." *JAFL* 1:227–234, 1888; 2:60–63; 213–218, 1889; 3:291–295, 1896; 6:54–62, 1893; 8:143–144, 1895; 12:126–130, 1899; 31:78–82, 1918.

Espinosa, Aurelio M.
"A New Classification of the Fundamental Elements of the Tar-Baby Story on the Basis of Two Hundred and Sixty Seven Versions." *JAFL* 1:31–37, 1943.

"Notes on the Origin and History of the Tar-Baby Story." *JAFL* 43:129–225, 1930.

Field, Rachel Lyman
American Folk and Fairy Tales. Drawings by Margaret Freeman. New York: Charles Scribner's Sons, 1929.

Fleming, Rachel Mary
Ancient Tales from Many Lands: A Collection of Folk Stories. Introduction by H. J. Fleure. London: Benn Brothers, Ltd., 1922. 193 pp., bibl.

Fyleman, R.
Folk Tales from Many Lands. Philadelphia: W. B. Saunders Co., 1940.

Halpert, Herbert
"The Cante Fable in Decay." *SFQ* 5:191–200, 1941.

"The Devil and the Fiddle." *Hoosier Folklore Bulletin* 2:39–43, 1943.

"Folktales Collected in the Army." *CFQ* 3:115–120, 1944.

"Folktale and 'Wellerism' "—A Note. *SFQ* 7:75–76, 1943.
"The Wellerism describes a scene with such vividness that it is clearly brought home to us, although we may not be able to catch the full implications." (Archer Taylor)

Hayward, S.
"English Folktales in America." *JAFL* 3:292–295, 1890.

Hunt, R. D., and Ament, William Sheffield
Oxcart to Airplane. Los Angeles, San Francisco, etc.: Powell Publishing Co., 1929. 458 pp.

Johnson, Edna, and Scott, Carrie E.
Anthology of Children's Literature. Illustrated by N. C. Wyeth. Boston: Houghton Mifflin Co., 1935. xxix, 917 pp. index.
Contains—Mother Goose Rhymes and Nonsense Verse, Fables, Folktales (English, Scotch), Myths, American Indian Legends, Bibliographies after each section. Indian Bibliography (pp. 369–371).

Keary, Charles Francis
Mythologies and Folktales. In: *The Dawn of History: An Introduction to Pre-Historic Study.* New York: Charles Scribner's Sons, 1906. xii, 367 pp.

Kiefer, Emma E.
Albert Wesselski and Recent Folktale Theories. Bloomington, Indiana: Indiana University Publications, Folklore Series No. 3, 1947.
"A stimulating refresher in comparative folklore, a lucid, simple, yet full guide to European scholarship in the field." (Elaine L. Lewis)

Kittredge, G. L.
"English Folk Tales in America." *JAFL* 3:391–392, 1890.

Köhler, Reinhold
Aufsätze über Märchen und Volkslieder. Berlin: Weidmann, 1894. 152 pp., bibl.
Discussion of tales and folksongs.

Korn, Friedrich
Mythologie der Volkssagen und Volksmärchen; eine Darstellung ihrer genetischen Entwicklung. Stuttgart: Scheibe, 1848. xvi, 1078 pp.
Mythology and origins of folktales.

Kozumplik, William A.
"Seven and Nine Holes in Man." *SFQ* 5:1–25, 1941.

Lee, Frank Harold
Folk Tales of All Nations. London: George G. Harrap and Co., Ltd., 1931. 947 pp.

Loomis, C. Grant
"Folklore of the Uncorrupted Body." *JAFL* 48:374–378, 1935.

Macculloch, John Arnott
The Childhood of Fiction, a study of folktales and primitive thought. London: John Murray, 1905. xi, 509 pp., bibl.

McGuire, Robert Graham
"The Black Dog." *HFB* 2:21–22, 1943

McLeod, Grace Dean
Stories of the Land of Evangeline. Boston: D. Lathrop Co., 1891. xv, 366 pp., illus.

Morgan, William
"The Organization of a Story and a Tale." With a Preface by Alfred North Whitehead. *JAFL* 58:169–194, 1945.
The author attempts "to define and describe some of the physical and subjective processes in individuals and in groups, which are involved in the formation of a story and a folktale."

Newell, W. W.
"English Folktales in America." *JAFL* 1:227–234, 1888.

———.
"Theories of Diffusion of Folk Tales." *JAFL* 8:7–18, 1895.

Old Tayles Newlye Relayted.
Enryched With All Ancyente Embellyshments. London: The Leadenhall Press, 1883.

Panzer, Friedrich
Märchen, Sage und Dichtung. München: Beck, 1905. 56 pp.

Pearce, J. E.
Tales that Dead Men Tell. Anthropological Papers, Univ. of Texas. Vol. I, No. 1 (Bulletin, No. 3537), 123 pp. illus. Austin, Texas: University of Texas, 1931.

Róheim, Géza
"Myth and Folk Tale." *American Imago* 2 (No. 3):266–279, 1941.

Sawyer, Rush
The Way of a Story Teller. New York: Viking Press, 1942.

Starr, F.
"Page of Child Lore." *JAFL* 4:55, 1891.

Taylor, Archer
"Some Trends and Problems in Studies of the Folk Tale." *Studies in Philology* 37:1–25, (January) 1940.

Thompson, Stith
The Folktale. New York: The Dryden Press, 1947. 522 pp.
"In the present volume, the author gives a somewhat detailed account of most of the world's great folktales and tells what students know about them. The stories of the peasants of Europe and Asia are handled with some completeness and the author has also used his special interest in the American Indian tale to balance the treatment with a substantial discussion of the stories of a typical primitive culture." The book has also a most valuable and useful Index of Tale Types, an Index of Motifs, and a General Index.

———.
"The Modern Study of the Folktale." *ASFM* 3:17–24, 1942.

———.
The Transmission of Folk-Tales. In: *Gayley Anniversary Volume.* Berkeley: The University of California Press, 1922.

———.
"The Transmission of Folktales." *University of California Publications in Modern Philology* 11:131–136, 1922.

Urbas, Wilhelm
Über Sagen und Märchen. Triest: 1888. 22 pp.

Yearsley, Percival M.
The Folklore of Fairy Tale. London: Watts & Co., 1924.

Zelenin, D.
"The Genesis of the Fairy Tale." *Ethnos* 5 (Nos. 1 and 2):54–58, (Stockholm) 1940.

TALL TALES

See: Section on Humor, pp. 25–35.

Studies and Collections

Barnum, P. T.
Struggles and Triumphs; or *The Life of P. T. Barnum,* written by himself, edited, with an introduction by George S. Bryan. New York: Alfred A. Knopf, 1927. 2 vols.
Contains a number of tall tales.

Blair, Walter
Tall Tale America. A Legendary History of Our Humorous Heroes. Illustrated by Sgt. Glen Rounds. New York: Coward-McCann, 1944. 262 pp.
A dazzling galaxy of our folk heroes—from Paul Bunyan to Windwagon Smith.

———.
Native American Humor (1800–1900). New York: American Book Co., 1937.
Intro (1–162) is a survey of American humor, includes discussion of tall tales.

Blakeley, Jim, comp.
Tall Tales. Franklin, Ohio and Denver, Colorado: Eldridge Entertainment House, Inc., 1936.

Bontemps, Arna, and Conroy, Jack
The Fast Sooner Hound. Boston: Houghton Mifflin Co., 1942.
A tall tale from the early days of railroading.

Boyle, Virginia Frazer
Devil Tales. New York: Harper and Brothers, 1900.

Davidson, Levette Jay
"Moron Stories." *SFQ* 7:101–104, 1943.

Derby, George Horatio
Phoenixiana; or Sketches and Burlesques. New York: D. Appleton and Co., 1903. 332 pp.

Dorson, Richard M.
"Print and American Tall Tales." *CFQ* 4:207–215, 1945.

Goodspeed, Charles Eliot
Angling in America. Boston: Houghton Mifflin Co., 1939.
Good yarns and some good "fish" stories.

Gordon, George Keith
"Captain Kidd and His Treasure." *TFSP* 9:142–144, 1931.
Stories of treasure hunting.

Halpert, Herbert
"Liar's Club Tales." *HFB* 2:11–13, 1943.

Haworth, Peter, coll. and arr.
Rumors and Hoaxes; Classic Tales of Fraud and Deception. Oxford: B. Blackwell, 1928. xxii, 282 pp.
Tall Tales. Ancient Greek: Ulysses and the Cyclops. Latin: Lucius Apullius; Medieval: Thousand and One Nights, Abou Hassan the wag, the deceitful Steward, the adventures of an empress etc., German traditional: The roguery of Reynard the Fox, Till Eulenspiegel, Grimm's: The Musicians of Bremen, Margaret of Navarre, etc.

Hayeslip, Eleanor
"Sorting Our Tall Tales." *NYFQ* 1:83–87, 1945.
The method of classification used for the folklore archives of New York State College for teachers, Albany, N. Y.

Heaton, John Langdon
The Book of Lies. New York: The Morse Company, 1896.

Krapp, Samuel Lorenzo
The Bachelors, and other tales, founded on American Incidents and Character. New York: J. & W. Sandford, 1836. 216 pp.

Loomis, C. Grant
"The American Tall Tale and the Miraculous." *CFQ* 4:109–128, 1945.

Masterson, James R.
"Travelers' Tales of Colonial Natural History." *JAFL* 59:51–67; 174–188, 1946.
Amazing accounts!

Shay, Frank
"The Tall Tale in America." In: *Folk-Say, a Regional Miscellany.* 2:382–385, 1930.

Sherwood, Robert Edmund
Here We Are Again. Recollections of an Old Circus Clown. Indianapolis: Bobbs-Merrill Co., 1926.
Among other interesting items, contains a few tall tales.

Thomas, Lowell A.
Tall Stories. The Rise and Triumph of the Great American Whopper. Illustrations by Herb Roth. New York: Funk and Wagnalls Co., 1931. 245 pp.

HUMOR
STUDIES AND COLLECTIONS

Aaberg, Jean Littlejohn
Spare the Rod—A Primer of Proverbs for Parents to Ponder. Drawings by Joe Musial. Philadelphia: David McKay Company. 1944. 79 pp., illus.

Adams, O. F.
"Is American Humor Humorous?" *Outlook* 49:961–962, 1894, June 2. *Reply,* M. P. Pendleton 50:134–136, 1894, June 28.

American Comic Almanac, With Whims, Scraps and Oddities. V. I, 1833– . Boston: T. Green. etc., 1832– .

American Humor: Beecher, Hawthorne, Holmes, Irving, Longfellow, etc. New York: G. P. Putnam's Sons, 1909. xxix, 287 pp.

The American Jest Book: Containing a choice selection of jests, anecdotes, bon mots, stories, etc. Harrisburg: Printed for Mathew Carey, 1796–97. 2 vols.

The American Joe Miller. With humorous illustrations. Philadelphia: J. Harding, 1847. vii, 219 pp.

American Wit and Humor, by One Hundred of America's Leading Humorists; Introduction by Joel Chandler Harris, including world famous cartoons and caricatures. New York: The Review of Reviews Co., 1907. 5 vols., illus.

Aswell, James R.
Native American Humor. Illustrated by Leo Hershfield. New York: Harper & Bros., 1947. xiii, 396 pp., illus.

Avery, Samuel Putnam
The Book of 1,000 Comical Stories; an endless repast of fun . . . Bill of fare: comprising tales of humor, laughable anecdotes, etc. Merry songs for merry moments . . . Appropriately illustrated with 250 comic engravings . . . New York: Dick & Fitzgerald, 1859. 120 pp., illus.

The Harp of a Thousand Strings; or, Laughter for a Lifetime. Konceived, comp., and komically konkokted, by Spavery (pseud.) . . . aided, added, and abetted by over 200 kurious kutz, from original designs . . . The whole engraved by Avery, S. P. New York: Dick & Fitzgerald, 1858. v, 368 pp., illus.

Baldwin, Joseph G.
The Flush Times of Alabama and Mississippi. A series of sketches. New York: D. Appleton & Co., 1898. x, 330 pp., illus.

Baldwin, Oliver P., com.
Southern and South-Western Sketches. Fun, Sentiment and Adventure . . . Richmond: J. W. Randolph, 1852. 190 pp.

Bangs, John K.
The Booming of Acre Hill, and other Reminiscenses of Urban and Suburban Life. Illustrated by Gibson, C. D. New York: Harper & Bros., 1900. 265 pp.

New Waggings of Old Tales. By Two Wags. Illus. by Herford, Oliver. Boston: Ticknor and Company, 1888. ix, 165 pp., illus.

Peeps At People, Being Certain Papers from the Writings of Anne Warrington Witherup (pseud.) . . . with illustrations by Penfield, E. New York: Harper & Brothers, 1899. 184 pp., illus.

Barnum, Phineas T.
Funny Stories. New York: G. Routledge and Sons, limited, 1890. xvi, 374 pp.

Barr, James
The Humor of America . . . Illustrations by C. E. Brock. London: W. Scott Pub. Co., 1909. xiii, 462 pp., illus.

Batchelder, E.
A Romance of the Sea-Serpent, or, the Ichthyosaurus. Also, a collection of the . . . authorities, with letters from distinguished merchants and men of science. Cambridge: J. Bartlett, 1850. 172 pp.

Baughman, Ernest W.
" 'Little Moron' Stories." *HFB* 2:17–18, 1943.

Beadle's Dime Book of Fun . . . no. 1–3. New York: Beadle and Co., 1860–66. 3 nos., illus.
No. 3 contains: Jim Smiley's Frog, by Mark Twain, pp. 29–32.

Becker, May Lamberton, ed.
The Home Book of Laughter. New York: Dodd, Mead & Co., 1948. 299 pp.
An anthology culled from the works of diverse authors; includes thirty prose pieces: essays, short stories and chapters from novels.

Beecher, Henry W.
Beecher as a Humorist; Selections from the Published Works of Henry Ward Beecher, comp. by Eleanor Kirk . . . New York: Fords, Howard and Hulbert, 1887. viii, 213 pp.

Bell, William Hemphill
The Quiddities of an Alaskan Trip. Portland, Ore.: C. A. Steel & Co., 1873. 67 pp., illus.

Berger, Josef
Bowleg Bill, the Sea-Going Cowboy; or, Ship Ahoy & Let 'er Buck! Being the adventures of a Wyoming ranch-hand as recounted by the best-accredited liars' benches along the entire coast of Massachusetts in which new and valuable hints to the whaleman, fisherman, and young student of deep water navigation are freely given, along with a narrative of astonishing exploits among the creatures of the deep and the not-too-deep, including sparm whale, swordfish, blue shark, sea sarpint, mermaid, and skipper's wife as well as many others; recorded by Jeremiah Diggs . . . with charts and diagrams by Groper, W. New York: The Viking Press, 1938. 188 pp., illus.

Biddle, Anthony J. D.
Shantytown Sketches. Philadelphia: D. Biddle, 1897. 75 pp.

Blair, Walter
Horse Sense in American Humor: From Benjamin Franklin to Ogden Nash. Chicago: The University of Chicago Press, 1942. xi, 341 pp., bibl., illus., index.
"It is a knowledgeable and authoritative history of American risibility-raisers." (E. L. Tinker)

Native American Humor (1800-1900). New York: American Book Company, 1937., xvi, 573 pp., bibl., illus.
The various headings are: "The Requisites for 'American Humor'," "Beginnings (1775–1830)," "Down East Humor (1830–1867)," Humor of the Old Southwest (1830–1867)," "Literary Comedians (1855–1900)," "The Local Colorists (1868–1900)," and "Mark Twain."

"The Popularity of Nineteenth-Century American Humorists." *American Literature* (Durham, N. C.) 3:175–194, 1931.

Two Phases of American Humor. Durham, N. C., 1931. Distributed by University of Chicago Libraries, Chicago, Ill.
Contents: 1. Burlesques in nineteenth-century American Humor. 2. The Popularity nineteenth-century American humorists.

Bley, Fritz
"Vom Köstlichen Yankee-Humor." *Velhagen und Klasings Monatshefte* 30 (Bd. 2): 191–194, 1916.

Boatright, Mody C.
"Frontier Humor: Despairing or Buoyant." *Southwest Review* 27:320–334, 1942.

Bradley, William O'Connell
Stories and Speeches of William O. Bradley; with biographical sketch by Thatcher, M. H. Lexington, Ky.: Transylvania Printing Company, 1916. xxiii, 196 pp.

Bradshaw, William G., comp.
Stuff That Travels. Saratoga Springs, N. Y., 1921. 115 pp.

Brewster, Paul G.
"Old Wine in New Bottles." *HFB* 3:16–22, 1944.
A study of American jests and their place in and relation to folklore.

Briggs, Samuel, comp.
The Essays, Humor, and Poems of Nathaniel Ames, Father and Son, of Dedham, Massachusetts, from their Almanacks, 1726–1775, with notes and comments, by Sam. Briggs . . . Cleveland, O.: Short & Forman, 1891. 490 pp., illus.

Browne, Charles Farrar
The Complete Works of Artemus Ward. Biographical sketch by Melville D. Landau, "Eli Perkins." New York: G. W. Dillingham Co., 1898, 499 pp., illus. New edition with portrait by Geflowski. London: Chatto and Windus, 1899. 518 pp.

Artemus Ward, his Book. With many comic illustrations. New York: Carleton, 1862. x, 262 pp., illus.

Artemus Ward: His Works, complete (Four volumes in one) ; with fifty illustrations and a biographical sketch by Melville D. Landon ("Eli Perkins") New York: G. W. Carleton & Co., 1875. ix, 347 pp., illus.

Artemus Ward in London, and other Papers. With comic illustrations by Howard, J. H. New York: G. W. Carleton & Co., 1867. vi, 229 pp., illus.

Artemus Ward on Wimmin's Rites. 4 a Kollexshun box . . . Bath: T. B. Tabb, 186–. 8 pp.

Artemus Ward's Lecture. (As delivered at the Egyptian Hall, London.) Edited by his executors, Robertson, T. W. & Hingston, E. P. London: J. C. Hotten, 1869. viii, 213 pp. illus.

Artemus Ward's Lecture on the Mormons. Edited with a prefatory note by Hingston, E. P. . . . London: Chatto and Windus, 1882. 64 pp., illus.

Artemus Ward's Panorama. (As exhibited at the Egyptian Hall, London.) Edited by his executors, Robertson, T. W. and Hingston, E. P. With thirty-four illustrations. New York: G. W. Carleton, 1869. vii, 213 pp., illus.

Sandwiches, by Artemus Ward. New York: Carleton, 1870. 31 pp., illus.

Browne, Lewis Allen
Around the Clock with the Rounder; dissected into twenty-four timely segments along one day's journey on Father Time's primrose path that goes round and round and recklessly recorded by Lewis Allen. Boston: J. W. Luce & Co., 1910. 28 pp., illus.

Burdette, Robert Jones
Hawk-Eyes, by Burdette, R. J. (the "Burlington Hawkeye" Man) New York: G. W. Carleton & Co., 1879. xii, 319 pp., illus.

Burgess, Gelett
The Bromide and other Theories. New York: The Viking Press, 1933. v, 113 pp., illus.
    Contents: The Bromide Theory. Neo-Friendship. Why Men Hate Women. The Educated Heart.

The Purple Cow! San Francisco: W. Doxey, at the Sign of the Lark, 1899. 32 pp., illus.

Burton, W. E.
The Cyclopedia of Wit and Humor . . . New York: D. Appleton & Co., 1859. 2 vols.

The Yankee Among the Mermaids, and other Waggeries and Vagaries. Philadelphia: T. B. Peterson & Bros., 1843. 192 pp., illus.

Byrn, Marcus Lafayette
The Adventures of Fudge Fumble, or the Love Scrapes of his Whole Life. By David Rattlehead. Philadelphia: T. B. Peterson & Brothers, 1865. 232 pp., illus.

Cahill, Francis J.
Rare Bits of Humor, After-Dinner Stories, Convivial Toasts and Humorous Anecdotes, compiled and arranged by F. J. Cahill. New York: G. Sully and Co., 1906. 156 pp.

Call, William T.
Josh Hayseed in New York, edited by Wm. T. Call (Sprouts). Illustrated by Coultraus. New York: Excelsior Publishing House, 1887. 127 pp., illus.

Carey, Thomas J., comp.
Brudder Gardner's Stump Speeches and Comic Lectures. Containing some of the best hits of the leading Negro delineators of the present day . . . New York: Excelsior Publishing House, 1884, 151 pp.

Carleton, Henry Guy
The Thompson Street Poker Club, from "Life" . . . London: G. Routledge & Sons, 1884. 48 pp., illus.

Caudle, Job
J. Caudle's Dinner-Table Harangues. Revealed in self-defence, by the ghost of Mrs. Caudle. New York: E. Winchester, 1845. 32 pp.

Charles, Lucile Hoerr
"The Clown's Functions." *JAFL* 58:25–34, 1945.

Clemens, Samuel L., comp.
Men and Things; America's Best Funny Stories. New York: Harper & Bros., 1906. viii, 304 pp., illus.

Selections From American Humor. Leipzig: B. Tauchnitz, 1888. 287 pp.

Clouston, W. A.
Books of Noodles, stories of simpletons; or Fools and their follies. New York: A. C. Armstrong & Son, 1888. xx, 228 pp. (Half-title: The book-lovers' library, ed. by H. B. Wheatley.)

Coffin, Robert Barry
Matrimonial Infelicities with an Occasional Felicity, by Way of Contrast. By an irritable way. To which are added as being pertinent to the subject, My Neighbors, and Down in the Valley. By Barry Gray. New York: Hurd and Houghton, 1865. x, 269 pp.

Coffin, Roland F.
Archibald the Cat and other Sea Yarns by the Old Sailor "Out of the World" i.e. Roland F. Coffin. With illustrations by Church, F. S. New York: The World, 1878, 60 pp.

The Comic Almanac. v. I, 1835–1880. Philadelphia: M. Fithian, etc. Annually.

Corcoran, D.
Pickings from the Portfolio of the Reporter of the New Orleans "Picayune" . . . Philadelphia: T. B. Peterson & Bros., 1846. 216 pp., illus.

Corrothers, James D.
The Black Cat Club. Negro humor and folklore. Illustrated by J. K. Bryans. New York: Funk & Wagnalls Co., 1902. v, 264 pp., illus.

Cox, Palmer
Frontier Humor, in Verse, Prose, and Picture. Philadelphia: Edgewood Publishing Co., 1889. xiv, 517 pp., illus.

——. *Frontier Humor,* Some Rather Ludicrous Experiences that Befell Myself and My Acquaintances Among Frontier Characters Before I Made the Acquaintance of My Esteemed Friends "the Brownies." Philadelphia, Pa.: Hubbard Publishing Company, 1895. 343 pp., illus.

——. *Squibs of California; or, Every-Day Life Illustrated.* Hartford, Conn.: Mutual Publishing Co., 1874. xvi, 491 pp., illus.

Cozzens, Frederick S.
The Sayings of Dr. Bushwhacker, and other Learned Men . . . New York: A. Simpson & Co., 1867. 213 pp.

——. *Sayings, Wise and Otherwise* by the author of Sparrow-Grass Papers etc. With a brief introductory note and autobiographic sketch by Mitchell, Donald G. New York: American Book Exchange, 1880. xxvii, 265 pp.

——. *The Sparrowgrass Papers; or, Living in the Country.* Philadelphia: 1865.

Crockett, Albert S.
Ditties from a Ditty Bag and War-Time Memories. New York: S. L. Parsons & Co., 1922. 63 pp.

Crockett's Comic Almanac. No. 1, 1839. New York: Elton, 1838.
See: Crockett, pp. 693–98.

Crofton, F. B.
The Bewildered Querists and other Nonsense. New York: G. P. Putnam's Sons, 1875. 127 pp.

Cullinan, John M.
Sagebrush Sayin's, by the Sagebrush Sage. Bloomington, Ill.: The Sagebrush Press, 1930. 32 pp.

Curtiss, Frederick H.
The Berkshire News Comic Book and Dyspeptic's Guide to the Grave. Great Barrington, Mass.: Douglas Bros., 1890. 70 pp.

The Cynic's Calendar of Revised Wisdom . . . by Oliver Herford, Ethel Watts Mumford, Addison Mizner. 1903–06, 1908. San Francisco: P. Elder and M. Shepard, 1902–07.

Dallas, Mary K.
The Grinder Papers. Being the adventures of Miss Charity Grinder, wherein are detailed her numerous hair-breadth escapes and wonderful adventures while on a visit to New York from the country. New York: G. W. Carleton & Co., 1877. 339 pp.

Davidson, Levette J.
"Moron Stories." *SFQ* 7:101–104, 1943.

Davis, Charles A.
Letters of J. Downing, major, Downingville Militia. Second Brigade, to his old friend, Mr. Dwight, of the New York Daily Advertiser. New York: Harper & Bros., 1834. ix, 259 pp.

Davis, Robert
"Some Characteristics of Northern Vermont Wit." *Vermont Historical Society* Proc. Montpelier) 5:317–333, 1937. n.s.

De Cordova, Rafael J.
The Wit and Humor of the 70's edited by Julian de Cordova. Boston: B. Humphries, 1939. 207 pp. illus.
Contents: Miss Jones' wedding, no cards. Mrs. Smith's surprise party. Mrs. Slocum at the Italian Opera. "Young America." Mrs. Grundy. The law in re Midge vs. Pige.

De Leon, Thomas C.
Schooners that Bump on the Bar: an Automatic Tow from "Ships that Pass in the Night." . . . Mobile: Gossip Printing Company, 1894. 79 pp., illus.

——. *Society as I have Foundered it, or The Microscopic Metropolitan Menu-Manipulator Marvellously Money-Magnetized.* By Cad McBallastir. Translated from the anglomaniaque tongue into American . . . Mobile, Ala.: The Gossip Printing Company, 1890. x, 73 pp., illus.

Denison, Thomas S.
Pomes ov the Peepul, by a Syndicate of the Amalgamated Di'lect Forgers Union . . . Illustrated by Will B. Johnstone. Chicago: T. S. Denison, 1904. 127 pp., illus.

Derby, George H.
Phoenixiana; or, Sketches and Burlesques. By John Phoenix . . . New York: D. Appleton and Company, 1856. 274 pp., illus.

——. *The Squibob Papers.* By John Phoenix . . . With comic illustrations by the author. New York: Carleton, 1865. 247 pp., illus.

A Dialogue Between a Southern Delegate and his Spouse, on his Return from the Grand Continental Congress. A fragment Inscribed to the Married Ladies of America, by their most Sincere Affectionate Friend and Servant Mary V. V. Printed by J. Rivington in the year 1774. 11 pp.
> This tract, in verse, has been ascribed to Jefferson but since it is apparently a Tory satire on Congress, it is hardly likely that Jefferson had anything to do with it.

Diaz, Abby M.
The John Spicer Lectures. Boston: D. Lothrop Company, 1887. 99 pp.
> *Contents:* Christmas Tree. Knives. Swapping Clothes. Food. Money. Riding. Fourth of July. Crying. Sneaks. Manners. Boys.

Dick, William B.
Uncle Josh's Trunk-Full of Fun. A Portfolio of First Class Wit and Humor. New York: Dick & Fitzgerald, 1869. 64 pp. illus.

Dorson, Richard M.
Davy Crockett, American Comic Legend: selected and edited by Dorson, R. M. With a foreword by Jones, Howard M. New York: Printed at the Spiral Press for Rockland Editions, 1939. xxvi, 171 pp., illus.
> "Aids personal and bibliographical; A word on the Almanacs; Notes to frontier humor and legend," pp. 161–171.

———.
"Jonathan Draws the Long Bow." *New England Quarterly* 16:244–279, 1943.
> The New England tall tale.

Dougherty, Hugh
Hughie Dougherty's Oratorical Speaker . . . as delivered by this great Demosthenies of burnt cork . . . New York: Benedict Popular Publishing Co., 1884. 60 pp.

Downs, Elizabeth Crooks
"American Humor." *North Carolina Univ. Library. Library Extension Publ.* (Chapel Hill), Jan. 1938, pp. 1–45.

Doyle, Jefferson E. P.
Tar-Heel Tales in Vernacular Verse. Illustrated by Bonar. New York: M. Doolady, 1873. 69 pp.

The "Dundreary" Joke Book. Filled chock full with side-splitting stories, queer conceits, comical conundrums, dry droll dialogues and lots of jokes calculated to cause roars of hearth laughter. New York: R. M. De Witt, 1873. 60 pp., illus. (De Witt's Song and Joke Books No. 166)

Dunn, Bob
Knackknack, Featuring Enoch Knox. New York: Dell Publishing Co., Copyright by Whitman Publishing Co., Racine, Wisconsin, 1936.

Dunne, Finley Peter
Mr. Dooley in the Hearts of his Countrymen. Boston: Small, Maynard & Company, 1899. xi, 285 pp.

———.
Mr. Dooley's Opinions. New York: Harper & Brothers, 1901. vi, 212 pp.

———.
Mr. Dooley's Philosophy. Illustrated. New York: Harper & Brothers, 1900. 257 pp., illus.

Eaph, Uncle (Jacob Thompson Johnson)
Humorous Short Stories. Atlanta, Ga.: Jacob T. Johnson Publishing Co., 1928.

Elton, R. H.
Rough and Ready Jester, Being a funny collection of anecdotes, witticisms, and odd sayings . . . New York: C. P. Huestis, 1858. 108 pp., illus.

Elton's Comic All-My-Nack. 1833. New York: R. H. Elton, publisher. 1833–34.

Evans, A. A.
Aunt Nabby, her Rambles, her Adventures, and her Notions, by Mrs. Peleg Newsby . . . Boston: Cupples and Hurd, 1888. x, 274 pp.

Ferguson, J. de Lancey
"On Humor as One of the Fine Arts." *South Atlantic Quarterly* (Durham, N. C.), April 1939, pp. 177–186.

———.
"The Roots of American Humor." *The American Scholar* 4:41–49, 1935.

Field, Eugene
Culture's Garland; being Memoranda of the Gradual Rise of Literature, Art, Music and Society in Chicago, and other western ganglia, with an introduction by Hawthorne, Julian. Boston: Ticknor and Company, 1887. xiv, 325 pp., illus.

———.
A Little Book of Nonsense. Boston, Mass.: Mutual Book Co., 1901. 28 pp.

———.
Nonsense for Old and Young . . . illustrated by Frohn, J. C. Boston: H. A. Dickerman & Son, 1901. 58 pp., illus.

———.
The Tribune Primer. Illustrated by his son, Roswell F. Field. To which is added an "Auto-Analysis," written by Mr. Field in 1894, and published by Frank M. Morris, Chicago. Reprinted by permission. Chicago: The Reilly & Britton Co., 1916. 63 pp., illus.

Finn, Henry J.
American Comic Annual. Edited by Finn, H. J., and illustrated by Johnston, D. C. Boston: Richardson, Lord & Holbrook, 1831. 1 vol., illus.

Fischer, Henry W. H.
Abroad with Mark Twain and Eugene Field: tales they told to a fellow correspondent. New York: N. L. Brown, 1922. xxi, 246 pp.

Flashes and Sparks of Wit and Humor by our American Humorists, containing a selection of the most laughter-provoking witticisms, comicalities, Yankee drolleries, etc. . . . New York: M. J. Ivers & Co., 1880. 64 pp.

Foolish Almanack for the Year. 1906. Boston: 1905.

The "Fourth," 1854: Log of the Smoothing Iron. New York: W. H. Tinson, 1854. 20 pp.

Franklin, Benjamin
Satires and Bagatelles. Detroit: Fine Book Circle, 1937. 139 pp., illus.

French, Joseph L.
Sixty Years of American Humor: a Prose Anthology, edited by French, J. L. Boston: Little, Brown, and Company, 1924. x, 401 pp.

Friend, James E.
One Thousand Liars. A Political Romance. National City, Cal.: Record Publishing Co., 1893. 147 pp., illus.

Greeley, Horace
Horace Greeley's Jokes. Edited for Glory and Printed for Fun. New York: Published from the Office of the Journeymen Printer's Co-operative Association, 1872. 64 pp.

Hafen, Ann W.
"Frontier Humor." *Colorado Magazine* Sept., pp. 177–188, 1947.

Haliburton, Thomas Chandler
The Clockmaker; or, The Sayings and Doings of Samuel Slick, of Slickville . . . Philadelphia: Carey, Lea, and Blanchard, 1838. x, 179 pp.

———.
Judge Haliburton's Yankee Stories. Philadelphia: Lindsay-Blakiston, 1846. 2 vols.

———.
The Letter-Bag of the Great Western; or, Life in a Steamer . . . New York: W. H. Colyer, 1840. viii, 112 pp.

———.
Nature and Human Nature. . . . New York: Stringer & Townsend, 1855. xi, 336 pp.

———.
The Old Judge; or, Life in a Colony. New York: Stringer & Townsend, 1849. 239 pp.

———.
Sam Slick's Wise Saws and Modern Instances; or what he said, did, or invented. Philadelphia: Blanchard & Lea, 1853. xii, 291 pp.

———.
Traits of American Humor, by Native Authors. Ed. and adapted by the author of "Sam Slick," etc. . . . London: Colburn and Co., 1852. 3 vols.

Halpert, Herbert
"City Jests." *HFB* 2:19–20, 1943.

Hammett, Samuel
Piney Woods Tavern; or, Sam Slick in Texas. Philadelphia: T. B. Peterson and Brother, 1858. x, 309 pp.

Hancock, Ernest
"The Passing of the American Comic." *Bookman* 22: 78–84, 1905.

Harris, George W.
Sut Lovingood. Yarns Spun by a Nat'ral Born Durn'd Fool. Warped and Wove for Public Wear. New York: Dick & Fitzgerald, 1867. xv, 299 pp.

———.
Sut Lovingood Travels with Abe Lincoln. Introduction by Edd Winfield Parks. Chicago: Printed and Published by the Black Cat Press, 1937. 44 pp.

Hart, Fred
The Sazerac Lying Club. A Nevada Book. San Francisco: H. Keller & Co., 1878. 240 pp., illus.

Harte, Bret
Fac-simile of the Original Manuscript of the Heathen Chinee, as written for the Overland Monthly, together with the corrected letter press, as published in the issue of September, 1870. San Francisco: John H. Carmany & Co., 1871. 9 pp.

———.
The Lectures of Bret Harte. Compiled from various sources. To which is added "The Piracy of Bret Harte's Fables." By C. M. Kozlay. Brooklyn, New York: C. M. Kozlay, 1909. ix, 53 pp.

———.
Sketches of the Sixties, by Bret Harte and Mark Twain being forgotten material now collected for the first time from the Californian, 1864–67. San Francisco: J. Howell, 1926. xvi, 221 pp.

Haweis, Rev. Hugh R.
American Humorists. New York: J. B. Alden, 1883. 192 pp.
The author discusses the character of American humor as reflected in the works of Washington Irving, Oliver Wendell Holmes, James Russell Lowell, Artemus Ward, Mark Twain, and Bret Harte.

Hill, George H.
Hill's Yankee Story Teller's Own Book; and Reciter's Pocket Companion. Containing a choice collection of Yankee Stories and Negro Lectures . . . to which are added several entirely original: written expressly for this work. Philadelphia: Turner & Fisher, 1836. 47 pp.

Hobart, George V.
John Henry by Hugh McHugh. New York: G. W. Dillingham Co., 1901. 96 pp., illus.

Holliday, Carl
The Wit and Humor of Colonial Days (1607–1800.) Phila.: J. B. Lippincott Company, 1912. 319 pp., bibl.

Hooke, Charles W.
Col. Evans from Kentucky, and other humorous
sketches, by Howard Fielding. New York: The
Manhattan Therapeutic Co., 1898. 32 pp., illus.

Hooper, Johnson J.
Simon Suggs' Adventures and Travels. Comprising all the scenes, incidents and adventures
of his travels, in a series of sketches of his life;
with Widow Rugby's husband, and twenty-six
other humorous tales of Alabama. Being the
most laughable and side-splitting stories that
have appeared in print. With seventeen illustrations from original designs by Darley. Philadelphia: T. B. Peterson, 1858. viii, 169 pp.,
illus.

House, Boyce
Tall Talk from Texas . . . San Antonio, Tex.:
The Naylor Company, 1945. 104 pp., illus.

Howard, Leon
The Connecticut Wits. Chicago, Ill.: The University of Chicago Press, 1943. xiii, 453 pp.,
bibl.

Hubbard, Frank McKinney
Abe Martin's Brown County Almanack; a
volume of philosophy, incidents and scenes
direct from the Paw Paw Belt of Indiana.
Illustrated by the author. Indianapolis: Abe
Martin Publishing Co., 1910. 61 pp., illus.

————.
Back Country Folks. A new full year's accumu-
lation of the philosophy and sketches of Abe
Martin, Miss Fawn Lippincott . . . and others,
of Brown County, Indiana. Illustrations by
Francis Gallup. Indianapolis: A. Martin Publishing Co., 191–. 93 pp., illus. (Reprinted in
part from the *Indianapolis News.*)

————.
Comments of Abe Martin and his Neighbors,
and Several More or Less Helpful Essays Bearing Directly on a Variety of Important Matters.
Indianapolis: A. Martin Publishing Co., 1923.
86 pp. illus.

Hudson, Arthur Palmer, ed.
Humor of the Old Deep South. New York: The
Macmillian Co., 1936. xxiv, 548 pp., bibl.
Examples of prose and poetry.

Irving, Washington
*Diedrich Knickerbocker's A History of New
York;* edited with a critical introduction by
Stanley Williams and Tremaine McDowell.
New York: Harcourt, Brace and Company,
1927. lxxvii, 475 pp., illus.

————.
*A History of New York, from the Beginning
of the World to the End of the Dutch Dynasty.*
Containing, among many surprising and curi-
ous matters, the unutterable ponderings of
Walter the Doubter, the disastrous projects of
William, the Testy, and the chivalric achieve-
ments of Peter, the Headstrong—the three
Dutch governors of New Amsterdam; being
the only authentic history of the times that
ever hath been or ever will be published. New
York: Siegel-Cooper Co., 18—. 307 pp.

————.
Letters of Jonathan Oldstyle, gent., by the
author of the *Sketch Book.* With a biographical
notice. New York: Published by William H.
Clayton, 1824. x, 67 pp.

————.
*Salmagundi; or, the Whim-Whams and Opin-
ions of Launcelot Langstaff, esq.* . . . No. 6
March 20, 1807. New York: Published by D.
Longworth, 1807. 1 No. (issued from Jan.,
1807, to Jan., 1808 in twenty numbers, with
continuous paging; No. 6 has caption title.)

Jones, John
*Adventures of Col. Gracchus Vanderbomb, of
Sloughcreek, in pursuit of the Presidency:*
also, the exploits of Mr. Numerius Plutarch
Kipps, his private secretary. Philadelphia: A.
Hart, 1852. viii, 202 pp.

Jones, Joseph S.
*Life of Jefferson S. Batkins, member from
Cranberry Center.* Written by himself by the
author of the "Silver Spoon" . . . Boston: Loring, 1871. 496 pp.

Kempt, Robert, comp.
The American Joe Miller. A Collection of
Yankee Wit and Humor. London: Adams and
Francis, 1865.

Kettell, Samuel
Yankee Notions. A Medley. By Timo. Titter-
well, esq. . . . Boston: Otis, Broaders and Co.,
1838. xvi, 255 pp.

Lafayette Compagnie, Paris
*Yank Talk; a Review of A. E. F. Humor;
Trench and Billet.* Paris: Lafayette Cie., 1918.
32 pp., illus.

Landon, Melville de Lancey
Comical Hits by Famous Wits . . . comprising
wit, humor, pathos, ridicule, satire by Mark
Twain, Josh Billings, Burdette, Sweet, Perkins
. . . with the philosophy of wit and humor, by
Melville. Chicago: Thompson & Thomas, 1900.
615 pp., illus.

————.
*Thirty Years of Wit and Reminiscences of
Witty, Wise and Eloquent Men.* New York:
Casell Publishing Co., 1891. xi, 305 pp., illus.

————, and M. A. (Eli Perkins)
*Library of Wit and Humor by Mark Twain and
Others, With the Philosophy of Wit and Humor.*
Chicago: Thompson and Thomas, 1883. Copy-
right by L. W. Yaggy, and in 1898 by the Star
Publishing Co.

Leacock, Stephen Butler
The Greatest Pages of American Humor . . .
a study of the rise and development of humorous writings in America with selections from
the most notable of the humorists. Garden City,
N. Y.: Doubleday, Doran & Co., 1936. vii, 293
pp.

———.
Humor: Its Theory and Technique, with examples and samples; a book of discovery. New York: Dodd, Mead & Company, 1935. v, 268 pp.

———.
"The Psychology of American Humor." *McGill University Magazine* 6:55–75, 1907. (Montreal)

Lewis, Charles B.
Sawed-Off Sketches; Humorous and Pathetic. Comprising Army Stories, Camp Incidents, Domestic Sketches, American Fables, New Arithmetic, etc., etc., etc., New York: G. W. Carleton & Co., 1884. 324 pp., illus.

Lewis, Henry C.
The Swamp Doctor's Adventures in the Southwest. Containing the whole of the Louisiana Swamp Doctor; Streaks of Squatter Life; and Far-Western scenes; in a series of forty-two humorous southern and western sketches . . . with fourteen illustrations, from original design by Darley. Philadelphia: T. B. Peterson and Brothers, 1858. 2 vols. in 1, illus.

Lewis, Oscar
The Origin of the Celebrated Jumping Frog of Calaveras County. San Francisco: The Book Club of California, 1931.

Locke, David R.
Ekkoes from Kentucky. By Petroleum V. Nasby . . . Bein a perfect records uv the ups, downs and experiences uv the Dimocrisy, doorin the eventful year 1867, ez seen by a naturalized Kentuckian. Illustrated by Nast, Thomas. Boston: Lee and Shepard, 1868. 324 pp., illus.

———.
The Struggles (Social, Financial and Political) of Petroleum V. Nasby . . . Embracing his trials and troubles, ups and downs, rejoicings and wailings; likewise his views of men and things. Together with the lectures "Cussid be Canaan," "The Struggles of a Conservative with the Woman Question." and "In Search of a Man of Sin." With an introduction by Hon. Charles Sumner. Illustrated by Nast, Thomas . . . Boston: I. N. Richardson and Company, 1873. 720 pp., illus.

Lowell, James Russell
The Biglow Papers, Edited, with an introduction, notes, glossary, and copious index, by Homer Wilbur . . . Cambridge, Mass.: G. Nichols, 1848. xxxii, 163 pp.

McKinney, Harold
Book of Proverbs; Maxims and Sayings . . . synopsized, illustrated, modernized. Corpus Christi, Texas: 1933. 91 pp., illus.

Magazine of Wit, and American Harmonist. Containing a collection of the most admired anecdotes, and a variety of the best songs . . . composed in honour of the . . . victories gained during the late war . . . Philadelphia: M'Carty & Davis, 1821. 142 pp.

MacMinn, G. R.
" 'The Gentlemen from Pike' in Early California." *American Literature* (Durham, N. C.) 8:160–169, 1936.

Macrae, Rev. David
National Humor: Scottish, English, Irish, Welsh, Cockney, Highland, American. Illustrated in color and others. Paisley: A. Gardner, 1904. 321 pp.

Majors, C. L., comp.
World War Jokes, a compilation of after dinner stories and amusing anecdotes, all of which have a direct application to soldiers and sailors and servicemen of the World War period. Ramer, Tenn.: 1930. viii, 112 pp.

Marble, Annie
The Hartford Wits. New Haven: Published for the Tercentenary of the Yale University Press, 1936. 29 pp.

Massett, S. C.
American Humour, Drifting About, or, What Jeems Pipes of Pipeville Saw and Did. Illustrated by Mullen. New York: Carleton Co., 1863.

Masson, Thomas Lansing
Our American Humorists. New York: Moffat, Yard and Company, 1922. 448 pp.

Masterson, James Raymond
Tall Tales of Arkansaw. Boston: Chapman & Grimes, 1943. x, 443 pp., music, bibl. (pp. 396–425).

Mathews, Cornelius
The Motley Book: a Series of Tales and Sketches. By the late Ben Smith. Vol. 1 New York: J. Turney, 1838. 3 vols., illus.

Mathews, William
Wit and Humor: Their Use and Abuse. Chicago: S. C. Griggs and Company, 1888. vi, 397 pp.

Meine, Franklin J., ed.
Tall Tales of the Southwest: An anthology of southern and southwestern humor, 1830–1860. New York: A. A. Knopf, 1930. xxxii, 456 pp.

Meyers, M., and Knapp, J.
Thesaurus of Humor. New York; Crown Publ., 1946. 600 pp.

The Miner's Progress or, Scenes in the Life of a California Miner. Being a series of humorous illustrations of the "ups and downs" of a gold digger in pursuit of his "pile." Sacramento: Published at the Daily Union Office, 1853. 13 pp., illus.

More Yankee Drolleries. A second series of celebrated works by the best American humorists . . . With an introduction by Sala, G. A. London: J. C. Hotten, 1865. 618 pp.
    Contents: Artemus Ward—his travels. Hans Breitmann's ballads. The Professor at the breakfast table. The Biglow Papers. Second series. John Billings, his book of sayings.

National Comic Almanac . . . Published by an association of gentlemen. New York: 1837.

Neal, Joseph C.
Charcoal Sketches; or, Scenes in a Metropolis. Philadelphia: T. B. Peterson & Bros., 1846. 222 pp.

New American Comic All-i-make. 1 (No. 1 n.s.) 1842. New York: Elton, 1838–42.

Newell, Robert H.
The Cloven Foot; being an adaptation of the English novel "The Mystery of Edwin Drood" to American scenes, characters, customs, and nomenclature; by Orpheus C. Kerr. New York: 1870.

Nye, Edgar W.
Bill Nye and Boomerang; or, the Tale of a Meek-Eyed Mule, and some other Literary Gems. Chicago: Belford, Clark, & Co., 1881. v, 286 pp., illus.

Old Abe's Jokes, Fresh from Abraham's Bosom. Containing all his issues, excepting the "greenbacks" to call in some of which this work is issued. New York: T. R. Dawley, 1864. 135 pp.

Paige, Elbridge G.
Dow's Patent Sermons. Philadelphia: T. B. Peterson and Bros., 1857. 4 vols.

Peck, George W.
Peck's Bad Boy and His Pa. Chicago: W. B. Corkey Co., 1893. First and only complete edition.

Peery, Robert
Small Town Humor. Little Blue Book No. 1397, ed. by E. Haldeman-Julius. Gerard, Kansas: Haldeman-Julius Co., 1929.

Phillips, William Hamilton, ed.
Old Yarns Knit Together, by Jackson Slocum of New York. New York: Phillips & Osborne, 1882. 64 pp., illus.

Pickens, William
American Aesop; Negro and other Humor. Boston: The Jordan & More Press, 1926. xx, 183 pp.

Porter, William T.
Big Bear's Adventures and Travels. Containing the whole of the Big Bear of Arkansaw and Stray subjects, illustrative of characters and incidents in the South and South-West, in a series of sixty-eight southern and south-western sketches . . . With eighteen illustrations from original designs by Darley. Philadelphia: T. B. Peterson and Bros., 1858. xii, 181 pp., illus.

——————.
Colonel Thorpe's Scenes in Arkansaw. Philadelphia: T. B. Peterson & Bros., 1858. 2 vols. in 1, illus.

Read, James A.
Journey to the Gold Diggins by Jeremiah Saddlebags. Illustrated by J. A. & D. F. Read. New York: Stringer & Townsend, 185–. 62 pp., illus.

Rice, Dan
Dan Rice's Original Comic and Sentimental Poetic Effusions . . . Philadelphia: R. F. Simpson, 1860. 84 pp.

Riddell, John L.
Orrin Lindsay's Plan of Aerial Navigation, with a Narrative of his Explorations in the higher regions of the atmosphere, and his wonderful voyage round the moon! New Orleans: Rea's Power Press Office, 1847. 33 pp.

Robb, J. S.
Streaks of Squatter Life, and Far-West Scenes . . . Philadelphia: T. B. Peterson & Brothers, 1843. x, 187 pp., illus.

Rourke, Constance
American Humor: A Study of Our National Character. New York: Harcourt, Brace and Co., 1931. x, 324 pp., bibl.

Sandburg, Carl
Good Morning, America. New York: Harcourt, Brace and Co., 1928.
Abounds with American Stuff in language and humor and lore.

Schoeneman, Friedrich
"Amerikanischer Humor." *Germanisch-Romanische-Monatschrift* (Heidelberg) 8:152–164, 216–227, 1920.

Scott, John F., ed.
Brudder Bones' Book of Stump Speeches and Burlesque Orations, Also containing Humorous Lectures, Ethiopian Dialogues, Plantation Scenes, Negro Farces and Burlesques, Laughable Interludes, and Comic Recitations. Interspersed with Dutch, Irish, French and Yankee stories . . . New York: Dick & Fitzgerald, 1868. 184 pp.

Shaw, Henry W.
Josh Billings: His Works, Complete. (Four volumes in one.) With one hundred illustrations by Nast, T. and others, and a biographical introduction. New York: G. W. Carleton & Co., 1880. xxxii, 504 pp., illus.

——————.
Josh Billings Struggling With Things. New York: G. W. Carleton & Co., 1881. 24 pp., illus.

——————.
Josh Billings' Farmer's Allminax for the Year 1870. New York: G. W. Carleton & Co., 1870–78. 4 vols., illus.

——————.
Josh Billings' Trump Kards. Blue Glass Philosophy. With illustrations in natural history by F. S. Church. New York: G. W. Carleton & Co., 1877. 45 pp., illus.

——．
Old Probability, Perhaps Rain—Perhaps Not.
By Josh Billings. With 250 comic illustrations.
New York: G. W. Carleton & Co., 1879. 337 pp.,
illus.

——．
Selections from the Writings of Josh Billings,
or; Proverbial Philosophy of Wit and Humor.
Introduction by Carl Purlington Rollins . . .
Illustrations by Nast, T. Athens, Georgia: K.
De Renne, 1940. xii, 72 pp., illus.

Shillaber, Benjamin P.
Mrs. Partington's Carpet-Bag of Fun. With 150
engravings, from Designs by Darley, McLenan,
Leech, Phiz, Henning, Cruikshank, Hine, Doyle,
Tenniel, Goater, Crowquill, etc. New York:
Garrett & Co., 1855. vi, 300 pp., illus.

——．
Mrs. Partington's Ridicule. A collection of wit
and humor, which the old lady offers to her
friends. Boston: Thomes & Talbot, 1863. 100
pp.

——．
Partingtonian Patchwork. Blifkins the Martyr:
the domestic trials of a model husband. The
modern syntax: Dr. Spooner's experiences in
search of the delectable. Partington papers:
Strippings of the warm milk of human kindness. New and old dips from an unambitious
inkstand . . . Boston: Lee and Shepard, 1873.
360 pp., illus.

Shomer, Louis, ed.
Laughter for the Millions. The Drollest Wit,
The Funniest Gags, The Gayest Laughs, The
Merriest Humor, The Greatest Hilarity. New
York: Louellen Publishing Co., 1938.

Slick, Sam J.
Yankee Notions; or, The American Joe Miller.
London: Ball, Arnold and Co., Edinburgh:
Fraser and Crawford; Glasgow: John Robert-
son, 1839.

Smith, Charles H.
Bill Arp's Peace Papers. Illustrated by Matt
O'Brian. New York: G. W. Carleton and Co.,
1873. 271 pp.

——．
Bill Arp's Scrap Book; humor and philosophy.
Letters "pendente lite," letters historic, domes-
tic and pastoral. Illustrated by Moser. Atlanta,
Ga.: J. P. Harrison & Co., 1884. v. 405 pp.

——．
Bill Arp, So-Called. A side-show of the southern side of the war. Illustrated by M. A. Sullivan. New York: Metropolitan Record Office,
1866. 214 pp.

Smith, Seba
The Life and Writings of Major Jack Downing
of Downingville, away down east in the state
of Maine. Boston: Lilly, Wait, Colman, & Holden, 1833. xii, 260 pp., illus.

——．
My Thirty Years Out of the Senate. New York:
Oaksmith & Co., 1859. 458 pp., illus.

Stephens, H. L.
The Comic Natural History of the Human Race,
designed and illustrated by Stephens, H. L.
Philadelphia: S. Robinson, 1851. 216 pp., illus.

Stone, M. E.
A Book of American Prose Humor; being a
collection of humorous and witty tales . . .
composed by the best known American writers.
New York: Duffield & Co., 1907. ix, 249 pp.

Sweet, A. E.
Sketches from "Texas Siftings." By Sweet &
Knox. Illustrated by Caskie, W. H. New York:
Texas Siftings Publishing Company, 1882. viii,
228 pp., illus.

Swope, Pierce Edward
"Pennsylvania German Humor." *American-*
German Review (Phila.) Feb. 1940, pp. 7–8,
35.

Taliaferro, H. E.
Carolina Humor, Foreword by Jackson, D. K.
Richmond, Va.: The Dietz Press, 1939. viii, 87
pp., illus.

Tandy, Jeanette
Crackerbox Philosophers in American Humor
and Satire. New York: Columbia University
Press, 1925. 181 pp.

Taylor, A. K.
"Poets and Humorists of the American Press."
Inland Printer (Chicago) 33:382–383, 1904.

Thomas, L. J.
Tall Stories; the Rise and Triumph of the
Great American Whopper . . . illustrations by
Roth, H. New York: Funk & Wagnalls Com-
pany, 1931. xi, 245 pp., illus.

Thompson, Stith
"The Prehistoric Development of Satire."
TFSP 1:78–98, 1916.
　　Traced through survivals in our own culture and
　　through contemporary customs among. existing
　　savages and barbarians.

Tricoche, Georges Nestler
"Remarques sur les Types Populaires Crées
par la Litterature Comique Américaine." *Revue*
de la Littérature Comparée (Paris) 11:250–
261, 1931.
　　The popular type as created by American comic
　　writing.

Turner's Comic Almanack for 1838. Philadelphia: Turner & Fisher, 1837–38.

Twain, Mark (Samuel Clemens)
The Celebrated Jumping Frog of Calaveras
County, and Other Sketches. Edited by John
Paul. New York: C. H. Webb, Publisher, 1867.

How to Tell a Story and Other Essays. New York: Harper and Brothers, 1892, 1897, 1898, 1899; C. L. Webster & Co., 1892; The Century Co., 1898; The Cosmopolitan, 1898; Samuel E. Moffett, 1899; American Publishing Co., 1900. Autograph Edition, The Writings of Mark Twain. Vol., XXII, Hartford, Conn.—The American Publishing Co.

Umland, Rudolph
"The Demise of the Little Moron." *Esquire* 20 (No. 3) :32–33, 154–155, 1943.

Valentine, William
A Budget of Wit and Humour; or, Morsels of Mirth for the Melancholy . . . New York: Dick & Fitzgerald, 1859. 264 pp.

Watterson, Henry, ed.
Oddities in Southern Life and Character; illustrations by W. L. Sheppard and F. S. Church. Boston: Houghton Mifflin and Co., 1892. xii, 485 pp.

Webb, C. H.
St. Twel'mo; or, The Cuneiform Cyclopedist of Chattanooga . . . Old Saws from Modern Files. New York: The Author, 1867. 59 pp.

Weiss, Harry Bischoff
A Brief History of American Jest Books. New York: The New York Public Library, 1943. 19 pp.

White, E. B. and K. S.
A Subtreasury of American Humor. New York: Modern Library, 1948.

White, Edmund Valentine
Senegambian Sizzles; Negro Stories. Illustrated by Leta Mae Calhoun. Dallas: B. Upshaw and Co., 1945. 128 pp., illus.

Wilder, Marshall Pinckney, ed.
The Wit and Humor of America. New York: Funk & Wagnalls Co., 1911. 10 vols.

Wilkinson, C. W.
"Backwoods Humor." *Southwest Review* 24: 164–181, 1939.

Women and Things; America's Best Funny Stories. New York: Harper & Bros., 1906. vii, 307 pp., illus.

Wood, Ray
The American Mother Goose. New York: Frederick A. Stokes, 1940. 110 pp.

Works Progress Administration
Montanans' Golden Anniversary; Humorous History, Handbook and 1940 Almanac, compiled by the workers of the Writers' Program of the Works Projects Administration in the state of Montana. Sponsored by State Department of Agriculture, Labor and Industry, State of Montana. Helena, Mont: State Pub. Co. 1939. 127 pp., illus.

Yankee Drolleries. The most celebrated works of the best American humorists . . . London: J. C. Hotten, 1870. 540 pp.
Includes most representative works by Artemus Ward, Major Smith, Locke, Newell and Lowell.

Ybarra, Thomas Russell
Davy Jones' Yarns, and other Salted Songs; illustrated by Henry Mayer. New York: H. Holt and Co., 1908. 102 pp., illus.

FOLK PLAYS

STUDIES AND COLLECTIONS

Allison, Tempe E.
"A Folk Play Version of the 'Processus Belial' in America." *PMLA* 53 (No. 2) :622–624, 1938.

Brewster, Paul G.
"A Roman Game and Its Survival on Four Continents." *Classical Philology* 38:134–137, 1943.
A study of the game "How Many Horns?" mentioned by Petronius and still current and popular in Europe, Asia and the Americas.

Buchanan, Annabel Morris
The Function of a Folk Festival. In: *Southern Folklore,* University of Florida. Vol. I, No. 1, March, 1937.

Dorson, Richard M.
"The Yankee on the Stage—a folk hero of American Drama." *New England Quarterly* 13:467–493, 1940.

Folkplays for Contests.
Seven one-act plays by various authors. Chicago: T. S. Denison and Co., 1940.

Koch, Frederick Henry
American Folk Plays. Edited with an introduction, "American folk-drama in the Making" by F. H. Koch. Illustrated with photographs of the original production of the plays: Foreword by Archibald Henderson. New York: Appleton-Century Co., 1939.

Spicer, Dorothy Gladys
The Book of Festivals. New York: Woman's Press, 1937. 429 pp.

The Folk Festival Handbook.
A Practical Guide for Local Communities. Philadelphia: Evening Bulletin Folk Festival Association, 1944. 64 pp., illus. bibliography.

FOLK MEDICINE

STUDIES AND COLLECTIONS

Alvarez, Walter C.
"The Emergence of Modern Medicine from Ancient Folkways." *Annual Report Smithsonian Institution for 1937:* 409–430 (1938).

Bergen, Fanny D.
"Some Saliva Charms." *JAFL* 3:51–59, 1890.

Bertolet, John Marshall
Witch-Doctors and Their Deceptions. Philadelphia: 1899. 8 pp. (Reprint from: Philadelphia Monthly Medical Journal, Dec., 1899.)

Black, William George
Folk-Medicine; A Chapter in the History of Culture. London: E. Stock, 1883. ii, 228 pp. (Folklore Society Publication, vol. 12.)

Brinton, Daniel G.
"Folk-Lore of the Bones." *JAFL* 3:17–22, 1890.

Clarkson, Rosetta E.
Magic Gardens; a modern chronicle of herbs and savory seeds . . . illustrated from the old herbals and ancient gardening books; the illustrations are facsimiles of the original sources. New York: The Macmillan Company, 1939. xviii, 369 pp., illus.

Doering, J. Frederick
"Folk Remedies for Diverse Allergies." *JAFL* 57:140–141, 1944.
    Treats mainly with Hay Fever remedies.

Fletcher, Robert
The Witches Pharmacopoeia. Read before the Historical Club of the Johns Hopkins Hospital. April 13, 1896. Baltimore: The Friedenwald Co., 1896. 30 pp.

Kahn, Max
"Vulgar Specifics and Therapeutic Superstitions." *Popular Science Monthly* 83:81–96, 1913.

Kanner, Leo
Folklore of the Teeth. New York: The Macmillan Co., 1928. xiii, 316 pp., bibl. (pp. 299–312.)

Lawrence, Robert Means
The Magic of the Horseshoe; with other folklore notes. Boston: Houghton, Mifflin & Co., 1898. iv, 344 pp., front.
    Also discussion on the folklore of sneezing, salt, the luck of odd numbers, and animal lore.

Leyel, Hilda
The Magic of Herbs; A Modern Book of Secrets. London: J. Cape, 1926. 320 pp., bibl. (pp. 309–316.)

Lipsky, Abram
"Psychotherapy in Folk-Medicine." *Popular Science Monthly* 84:227–234, 1914.

McKenzie, Daniel
The Infancy of Medicine; an enquiry into the influence of folklore upon the evolution of scientific medicine. London: Macmillan and Co., 1927. xiii, 421 pp., bibl. (pp. 384–408.)

Miller, Wm. Marion
"A Cure for Cholera." *JAFL* 59:531, 1946.

Newman, L. F.
"Some Notes on the Nutmeg Graters Used in Folk Medicine." *Folk-Lore* (London) 54:334–337, 1943.

O'Dell, Ruth W.
"Signs and Superstitions." *TFSB* 10:1–6, 1944.
    Beliefs concerning fertility, cures, and others.

The Old Herb Doctor; His Secrets and Treatments; over 1,000 Recipes. The astounding corrective and recuperative value of flowers, herbs, barks and roots now an open book . . . Hammond, Ind.; Hammond Book Company, 1941. 200 pp., illus.

Passin, Herbert, and Bennett, John W.
Social Process and Dietary Change. In: *The Problem of Changing Food Habits.* A report of the Committee on Food Habits of the National Research Council, Washington, D. C. National Research Council Bulletin 108.

Pettigrew, Thomas Joseph
On Superstitions Connected with the History and Practice of Medicine and Surgery. London: J. Churchill, 1844. viii, 167 pp.

Pickard, Madge E., and Buley, R. Carlyle
The Midwest Pioneer: His Ills, Cures, and Doctors. Crawfordsville, Indiana: R. E. Banta, 1945. 399 pp., illus.
    "Although largely concerned with midwest America, the book presents a valid picture of medical belief and practice in general in the United States in the last century."

Rivers, William Halse R.
Medicine, Magic and Religion, . . . New York: Harcourt, Brace & Co., 1924. viii, 146 pp. (International Library of Psychology, Philosophy and Scientific Method.)

Rolletson, J. D.
"The Folklore of Children's Diseases." *Folk-Lore* 54:287–307, 1943.

Sounin, Leonie de
Magic in Herbs, with an introduction by Miriam Birdseye. New York: M. Barrows & Co., 1941. xvi, 208 pp., illus.

Stemplinger, Eduard
Antike und Moderne Volksmedizin. Leipzig: Dieterich'sche Verlagsbuchhandlung, 1925. 120 pp., bibl.
    Primitive and modern folk medicine.

True, R. H.
"Folk Materia-Medica." *JAFL* 14:105–114. 1901.

Vance, Lee J.
"Three Lessons in Rhabdomancy." *JAFL* 4:241–246, 1891.
    Divining rod lore.

Warner, H. E.
"Folk Remedies." *JAFL* 4:168, 1891.

Wilson, C. B.
"Notes on Folk Medicine." *JAFL* 21:68–73, 1908.

ANIMAL LORE

STUDIES AND COLLECTIONS

Bergen, Mrs. Fanny Dickerson
Animal and Plant Lore; collected from the oral tradition of English speaking folk—with an introduction by J. Y. Bergen. Boston: Houghton, Mifflin & Co., 1899. vii, 180 pp. American Folklore Society. Memoirs, V. 7.

Edgar, Marjorie
"Imaginary Animals of Northern Minnesota." *Minnesota History* 21:352–356, 1935.

Fenner, Phyllis R.
There Was a Horse: Folktales From Many Lands. New York: Alfred A. Knopf, 1941. x, 282 pp.
"The sixteen stories from many lands have their chief source of interest in a horse—not the prosaic beast of burden, nor even the star of the record books—but in a magic horse that one would neither sell for gold nor give as a gift to anyone." (T. G. James)

Graham, Gid
Animal Outlaws: Collection of Animal Stories. Collinsville, Oklahoma: Gid Graham, 1938.

Gubernatis, Angelo de
Zoological Mythology, or The Legends of Animals. London: Trübner and Co., 1872. 2 Vols.

Heather, J. P.
"Animal Beliefs." *Folklore* 52:18–34, 136–149, 198–223, 1941.

Hulme, F. E.
Natural History, Lore and Legend ... Examples of quaint and bygone beliefs from divers authorities, ancient and modern. London: 1895. viii, 350 pp., illus.

Krappe, Alexander Haggerty
"Guiding Animals." *JAFL* 55:228–246, 1942.

Poteet, Gibbons
"Jointsnake and Hoop Snake." *TFSP* 8:124–128, 1930.
Mighty interesting snake yarns.

Strecker, J. K.
"On the Origin of the Reptile Myth." *TFSP* 5:70–77, 1920.

PLANT LORE

STUDIES AND COLLECTIONS

Beals, Katharine (McMillan)
Flower Lore and Legend. New York: H. Holt & Co., 1917. iv, 245 pp.

Bergen, F. D.
"Popular American Plant Names." *JAFL* 5:89–106, 1892; 6:135–142, 1893; 7:89–104, 1894; 9:179–193, 1896; 10:49–54, 143–148, 1897; 11:221–230, 273–283, 1898.

Britten, James and Holland, R.
A Dictionary of English Plant-Names. London: Trübner & Co., 1886. xxviii, 618 pp. (English Dialect Society. Publications, no. 22, 26, 45, Series C. Original glossaries ix).

Brown, Charles Edward
Flower Lore, lore and legends of garden flowers. Madison, Wis.: C. E. Brown, 1938. ii pp.

Brown, O. P.
The Complete Herbalist; or, The People Their Own Physicians by the Use of Nature's Remedies; Showing the great curative properties of all herbs—how they should be prepared, under what influences selected,—etc. A new and plain system of hygienics. Jersey City: The Author, 1865. illus.

Dixon, Royal
"The Folk Lore of Plants." *Trend* 8:124–127, 1914.

Dowling, Alfred E. P. Raymond
"A Study in the Flora of the Holy Church." *Amer. Cath. Quar. Rev.* 27:452–475, 1902.

Folkard, Richard, Jr.
Plant Lore, Legends and Lyrics. Embracing the myths, traditions, superstitions and folklore of the plant kingdom. London: S. Low, Marston, Searle, and Rivington, 1884. xxiv, 610 pp., illus.

Friend, Hilderic
Flowers and Flower Lore. Troy, N. Y.: Nims and Knight, 1889. xvi, 704 pp., illus.

Giles, Dorothy
Singing Valleys, The Story of Corn. New York: Random House, 1940. 361 pp.
American history in terms of the role played by corn, a vital factor in our folk-lore history and culture.

Gordon, Elizabeth
Mother Earth's Children, the frolics of the fruits and vegetables. With illustrations by M. T. Ross. Chicago: P. F. Volland Co., 1914. 95 pp., illus.

Hinkson, Katharine, ed.
The Book of Flowers. London: Smith, Elder & Co., 1909. xii, 319 pp.

Hulme, Frederick Edward
Bards and Blossoms. London: M. Ward & Co., 1877. 232 pp., illus.

Karasz, Ilonka
Astrological Calendar for the Gardener, calculations and text by Peter Blaine. New York: American Artists Group, 1941. 32 pp., illus.

Kip, Abraham Lincoln
Animal and Plant Correspondences. New York: The Knickerbocker Press, 1902. 237 pp.

Laing, Ernest V.
"Trees in Myth and Legend." *Royal Scottish Arboricultural Soc. Transac.* 34: 195–209, 1920.

Nash, Elizabeth Todd
One Hundred and One Legends of Flowers.
Boston: The Christopher Publishing House,
1927. 340 pp., illus.

Oldmeadow, Katherine L.
The Folklore of Herbs. Birmingham, Eng.:
Cornish Brothers Limited, 1946. 72 pp.

Prior, Sophia
"Carnivorous Plants and The Man-eating
Tree." *Field Museum of Natural History
(Chicago) Botany Dept. Leaflet.* No. 23, pp.
1–20, 1939. illus., bibl.

Pullen, C.
"Rhyme for Divination by Means of Apple
Seeds." *JAFL* 2:71, 1889.

Roy, Satindra N.
"Some Trees and Herbs in Rituals and Folk-
lore." *Journal of Anthropological Society of
Bombay* 14:588–604, 1931.

Sheldon, Harriet T.
The Mythology of Flowers, and other tales,
retold from Bulfinche's Mythology. Chicago:
F. E. Compton and Co., 1919. 17 pp., illus.

Skinner, Charles M.
*Myths and Legends of Flowers, Trees, Fruits,
and Plants, in all Ages and in all Climes.*
Philadelphia: J. B. Lippincott Company, 1925.
ix, 301 pp., illus.

Thiselton-Dyer, Thomas Firminger
The Folk-lore of Plants. New York: D. Appleton & Co., 1889. 328 pp.

Quinn, Vernon (pseud. Capini Vequin)
Vegetables in the Garden and their Legends.
Illustrated by Louis Mansfield. Philadelphia:
J. B. Lippincott, 1942. 261 pp.

Tudury, Moran and Gale
"Folklore of the Farm." *Country Gentleman,*
March, 1944.

WEATHER, AND
MISCELLANEOUS LORE

STUDIES AND COLLECTIONS

Butler, A. W.
"Local Weather Lore." *American Meterologi-
cal Journal* 313–316, 1884.

Dexter, Edwin Grant
Weather Influences. An Empirical Study of the
Mental and Physiological Effects of Definite
Meteorological Conditions. With an Introduc-
tion by Cleveland Abbe. New York: The Mac-
millan Co., 1904.

Garriott, Edward Bennett
Weather Folk-Lore and Local Weather Signs.
U. S. Department of Agriculture Weather
Bureau, Bulletin No. 33. Washington, D. C.:
U. S. Gov't Printing Office, 1903.

Hagen, W. B., and Dunwoody, H. H.
Weather Proverbs. Signal Service Notes No. 9.
Washington, D. C.: U. S. Printing Office, 1883.

Harley, Timothy
Moon Lore. London: Swan, Sonnenschein, Le
Bas and Lowrey, 1885.

Inwards, R. (comp. & arranged)
Weather Lore: A collection of proverbs, sayings and rules concerning the weather. London: E. Stock, 1898. 3rd ed. xii, 233 pp. fold.
front. (rev. & augm.). "Bibliography of weather
lore": p. 207–212.

Jones, William
Finger-ring Lore; historical, legendary, and
anecdotal. London: Chatto & Windus, 1898.
xvi, 567 pp., illus.

Olcott, William Tyler
Sun Lore of All Ages. New York and London:
G. P. Putnam's Sons, 1914. 364 pp.

Peet, S. D.
Astronomical Symbols in America. In: *International folk-lore association.* Papers read at
Memphis, Atlanta and Chicago. Chicago: 1896.
44 pp., illus.

Scott, Oral E.
The Stars in Myth and Fact. Caldwell, Idaho:
Caxton Printers, 1942. 374 pp., illus.

Talman, Charles Fitzhugh
"The Vocabulary of Weather. Experiences in
Gathering Material toward a Meteorological
Dictionary." *Quarterly Journal of the Royal
Meteorological Society* 51:139–144, 1925.

Vance, L. J.
"Weather Lore." *JAFL* 4:166, 1891.

PROVERBS—RIDDLES

BIBLIOGRAPHY

Bernstein, Ignacy
Catalogue des livres parémiologiques . . .
Varsovie: 1900. 2 vols.

Bonser, Wilfred
Proverb Literature; a bibliography of works
relating to proverbs . . . compiled from ma-
terials left by the late T. A. Stephens. London:
W. Glaisher, 1930. xx, 496 pp. (Folk-Lore
Society Publications, v. 89.)
Also, vols. 90–95, 1930–1934.

Bristol, England. Public Libraries
The Stuckey Lean Collection, edited by Norris
Mathews. Bristol: Libraries Committee, 1903.
viii, 268 pp.

Brunet, G.
"Bibliographie des proverbes." *Le Bibliophile
Belge* (Bruxells) 9:233–240, 1851.

A Catalogue of Books of Proverbs, Sayings, Maxims, Apophthegms, Adages, and Similitudes, by ancient, intermediate, and modern authors. New York: W. Gowans, 1851. 16 pp.

García Moreno, Melchor
Catálogo Paremiológico de Melchor García Moreno. Madrid: Librería (García Moreno), 1918. 248 pp., illus.

Gratet-Duplessis, Pierre Alexandre
Bibliographie Parémiologique. Études bibliographiques et littéraires sur les ouvrages, fragments d'ouvrages et opuscules spécialment consacrés aux proverbes dans toutes les langues; ... Paris: Potier, 1847. viii, 520 pp.

Jente, Richard
"A Review of Proverb Literature Since 1920." Corona: *Studies in Celebration of the 80th Birthday of Samuel Singer* ... Durham, 1941. (pp. 23–44).

Nopitsch, C. C.
Literatur der Sprichwörter, ein Handbuch für Literärhistoriker Bibliographer und Bibliotheker. Nürnberg, 1822.

Stirling-Maxwell, William
An Essay Toward a Collection of Books Relating to Proverbs, Emblems, Apophthegms, Epitaph, and Ana, being a catalogue of these at Keir. London: Priv. Print., 1860. v, 244 pp.

Taylor, Archer
A Bibliography of Riddles. Helsinki: Suomalaisen tiedeakatemian, Academia scientarium fennica, 1939. 173 pp. FF Communcations no. 126.

——.
An Index to "The Proverb." Helsinki: Suomalaisen tiedeakatemian, Academia scientiarum fennica, 1934. 105 pp.
"The following list of proverbs came into existence as the basis of my book, *The Proverb.*" (pp. 102–105.)

——.
"An Introductory Bibliography for the Study of Proverbs." *Modern Philology* 30:195–210, 1933.

STUDIES AND COLLECTIONS

Adams, Samuel Hopkins, ed.
Who and What; a Book of Clues for the Clever. New York: Boni and Liveright, 1927. xix, 149 pp.
A collection of riddles.

Anderson, John Henry
The Ladies' Budget of Wit. Conundrums sent in to compete for the valuable service of silver ... presented by Professor Anderson ... on his great conundrum night ... Metropolitan Hall, February 6th, 1852. New York: Baker, Godwin & Co., 1852. 60 pp.

Apperson, George Latimer
English Proverbs and Proverbial Phrases; a historical dictionary. London: J. M. Dent and Sons, Ltd. 1929. ix, 721 pp.

Aunt Sue's Budget of Puzzles, a Collection of Riddles, Charades, Enigmas, etc. New York: T. W. Strong, 1859.

B., H. W.
"Proverbs, Old Saws, and Wellerisms." *AS* 14 (No. 1):51–52, 1939.

Baier, E. R.
"Don't Cross the Bridge." *American Notes and Queries* (N. Y.) 2:79, 1942.
A study of the proverb, its early occurrence and variants.

Bailey, Nathaniel
Divers Proverbs. New Haven: Yale University Press, 1917.

Barber, J. W.
The Handbook of Illustrated Proverbs. Comprising also a selection of approved proverbs of various actions and languages, ancient and modern. Interspersed with numerous engravings and descriptions, adopted for the use of all ages and classes of persons. New Haven: G. F. Tuttle, 1857.

Bechtel, John H.
Proverbs. Philadelphia: The Penn. Publishing Co., 1905.

Benham, Sir William Gurney
Benham's Book of Quotations, Proverbs and Household Words; a collection of quotations from British and American authors, with many thousands of proverbs, phrases, maxims and sayings, from all sources ... with full verbal and classified index. Completely revised and enlarged edition. London: Ward, Lock & Co., 1936. 1259 pp.

Blakeman, Elisha D.
Two Hundred Poetical Riddles. For the instruction and amusement of youth. New York: D. M. Bennett, 1875. 42 pp.

Bohn, Henry G.
A Hand-Book of Proverbs. London: G. Bell and Son, Ltd., 1915. xvi, 583 pp.

The Booke of Meery Riddles; together with proper questions, and witty prouerbs, to make pleasant pastime; no lesse usefull then behooefull for any young man, or child, to know if he be quick-witted, or no. London: Printed by T. C. for Michael Sparke ... 1629.

Bryant, M. M.
"Collecting Proverbs." *HFB* 3:36, 1944.

Bush, William Eldridge
1800 Selected Proverbs of the World, Ancient, Medieval and Modern. Boston: Meador Publishing Company, 1938. 152 pp.

"California Spanish Proverbs and Adages." *CFQ* 3:121–123, 1944.

Chamberlain, A. F.
"Race Character and Local Color in Proverbs."
JAFL 17:28–31, 1904.

Champion, Selwyn Gurney
Racial Proverbs. New York. The Macmillan Co., 1938. 767 pp.

Cowan, Frank
A Dictionary of Proverbs and Proverbial Phrases of the English Language, Relating to the Sea and Such Associated Subjects as Fish, Fishing . . . With notes, explanatory, historic, and etymologic. Greenesburgh, Pa.: The Oliver Publishing House, 1894. 144 pp.

Davidoff, Henry, coll.
A World Treasury of Proverbs. New York: Random House, 1946. 526 pp.
> Although the collector does give quite a large number of proverbs, it is not as rich and inclusive a selection as it should be.

Downey, William Scott
Proverbs. Boston, J. M. Hewes & Co., 1854. 104 pp.

Dunwoody, Henry Harrison Chase
Weather Proverbs. Washington, D. C.: U. S. Gov't Printing Office, 1883. 148 pp. (United States Signal Service. Signal Service Notes 9.)

Espinosa, Aurelio M.
"California Spanish Folklore Riddles." *CFQ* 3:293–298, 1944.

The Fashionable Puzzler; or, Book of Riddles. A collection of enigmas, charades, rebusses, anagrams, logogriphes and conundrums. Selected by an American lady. With remarks on riddles by the late Mrs. Barbould. New York: J. E. Betts, 1835. viii, 320 pp.

Frikell, Wiljalba
Book of Riddles and Five Hundred Home Amusements Containing a Choice and Curious Collection of Riddles, Charades, Enigmas . . . New York: Dick & Fitzgerald, 1868. 112 pp., illus.

Garth, Thomas Russell
The Psychology of Riddle Solution: An Experiment in Purposive Thinking. n.p. 1920. 18 pp.

Glover, Ellye Howell
"Dame Curtsey's Book of Guessing Contests."
Chicago: A. C. McClurg & Co., 1908. x, 138 pp.
> Contains a great number of riddles.

Gomme, George Laurance
Dialect, Proverbs, and World Lore. (Gentleman's Magazine Library.) Boston: Houghton, Mifflin and Co., 1884.

Greenway, Nellie, comp.
Fifteen Hundred Riddles. A choice collection. Comprising riddles, conundrums, charades, and curious epitaphs. New York: J. S. Ogilvie Pub. Co., 1904. 109 pp.

Hardie, Margaret
"Proverbs and Proverbial Expressions Current in the United States East of the Missouri and North of the Ohio Rivers." *AS* 4 (No. 6) 461–472, 1929.

Harris, Mabel Arundel
Riddles and Laughter; a book of fun for young folks. New York: G. Sully & Company, 1932. 176 pp.

Hearn, Lafcadio
Gombo Zhebes; Little Dictionary of Creole Proverbs, selected from six Creole dialects . . . and some brief remarks upon the Creole idioms of Louisiana. New York: W. H. Coleman, 1885. 42 pp.; bibl.

Howard, Clarence J.
Howard's Book of Conundrums and Riddles. New York: Dick & Fitzgerald, 1869. 162 pp.

Humphreys, William Jackson
"Some Weather Proverbs and Their Justification." *Popular Science Monthly* 78:428–444, 1911.

————.
Weather Proverbs and Paradoxes. Baltimore: Williams & Wilkins Company, 1923. viii, 125 pp.

Jente, Richard
"The American Proverb." *AS* 7 (No. 5):342–348, 1932.

————.
The Untilled Field of Proverbs. In: *Studies in Language and Literature.* Edited with a foreword by George R. Coffman (pp. 112–119). Chapel Hill, N. C.: University of North Carolina Press, 1945. viii, 344 pp.

Jordan, Charlotte Brewster
Sphinx Lore. A collection of original, literary ingenuities and historical recreations, interspersed with charades, anagrams, and diagram and jingle-puzzles. New York: E. P. Dutton and Company, 1897. 191 pp., illus.

Lawson, James Gilchrist
The World's Best Conundrums and Riddles of All Ages. New York: George H. Doran Company, 1924. xxvi, 338 pp.

————.
World's Best Proverbs and Maxims. New York: Doubleday Doran and Co., 1926.

Lean, Vincent Stuckey
Lean's Collectanea. Collections—of proverbs (English & foreign), folklore, and superstitions, also compilations towards dictionaries of proverbial phrases and words, old and disused. Bristol: J. W. Arrowsmith, 1902–04. 4 Vols. in 5.

Leland, Charles Godfrey
The Hundred Riddles of the Fairy Bellaria. London: T. F. Unwin, 1892. xii, 149 pp.

Magoon, Elias Lyman
Proverbs for the People: or, Illustrations of practical Godliness drawn from the Book of Wisdom. Boston: Gould, Kendall, and Lincoln, 1849. xii, 272 pp.

Marvin, Dwight Edwards
Curiosities in Proverbs. New York: G. P. Putnam's Sons, 1916.

Matthews, Brander
"American Aphorisms." *Harper's* 131:864–868, 1915.

McClure, James Baird
Entertaining Anecdotes from Every Available Source. Chicago: Rhodes & McClure, 1881. 248 pp.

Merryweather, L. W.
"Hell in American Speech." *AS* 6 (No. 6):433–435, 1931.
    Proverbs.

New Riddle Book. New York: M. Day, 1829. 17 pp., illus.

Ordway, Edith B.
The Handbook of Conundrums. New York: Sully and Kleinteich, 1913. xvii, 198 pp.

Proverbs for the Nursery. New York: McLoughlin Bros., 18–. 34 pp., illus.

Puzzlewit, Peter
Guess Again, or The Riddler's Oracle: A Choice Collection of Entertaining Riddles . . . New York: Mafis & Cornish, 184–. 34 pp.

Ray, John
A Compleat Collection of English Proverbs also the most celebrated proverbs of the Scotch, Italian, French, Spanish, and other languages. To which is added a collection of English words not generally used, with their meanings and original in two alphabetical catalogues; the one of each as are proper to the Northern, the other, to the Southern counties. London: Printed for W. Ottridge, by S. Bladon, 1768. Reprinted in 1857 under the editorship of R. Bohn.

Robertson, Greta
The Book of Conundrums. Cincinnati: Stewart & Kidd Company, 1921. 48 pp.

Schevill, Rudolph
"Some forms of the riddle question, and the exercise of the wits in popular fiction and formal literature." *California University Publications in Modern Philology* 2 (No. 3): 184–237, 1911.

Stevenson, Burton Egbert, ed.
The Home Book of Quotations, Classical and Modern. New York: Dodd, Mead and Co., 1934. 2,605 pp.

————.
The Home Book of Proverbs, Maxims, and Familiar Phrases. New York: The Macmillan Company, 1948. 2964 pp.
    A comprehensive one-volume edition. A historical and comparative study.

Swainson, Charles
A Handbook of Weather Folk-Lore; being, a collection of proverbial sayings in various languages relating to the weather, with explanatory and illustrative notes. Edinburgh: W. Blackwood & Sons, 1873. x, 275 pp.

Taylor, Archer
The Literary Riddle Before 1600. Berkeley, Calif.: University of California Press, 1948. 131 pp.

————.
The Proverb. Cambridge, Mass.: Harvard University Press, 1931. xi, 223 pp.
    "For the scholar's convenience I have compiled an index of the English, German, and Latin proverbs cited, and in it I have given references from works on the comparative study of proverbs . . ." Pref.

————.
"The Proverb, 'The Black Ox Has Not Trod on His Foot'." *Renaissance Lit. Philological Quarterly* 20:266–278, 1941.

————.
"Riddles Dealing with Family Relationships." *JAFL* 51:25–37, 1938.

Ward, S. H., and Watson, M. L.
The Green Guess Book. New York: Dodd, Mead & Co., 1897. vi, 111 pp.

Westermarch, Edward
"On the Study of Popular Sayings." *Nature* 122:701–703, 1928.

Whiting, B. J.
"Apperson's English Proverbs and Proverbial Phrases: Some Additions and Corrections." *JAFL* 61:44–48, 1948.

Willson, Frederick Newton
Paraphrased Proverbs. Princeton, N. J.: Graphics Room Ed., 1933. 55 pp.
    In Verse.

SPEECH

STUDIES AND COLLECTIONS

A., H. M.
"Names and Nicknames." *AS* 14 (No. 1):49–50, 1939.

Adkins, Nelson F.
"Early Americanisms." *AS* 8 (No. 1):75–76, 1933.

Aiken, Janet R.
"Levelling Dialects." *Bookman* 70:20–25, 1930.

Alexander, Henry
"American English." *Queens Quarterly* 44:169–175, 1937.
    A Review of Craigie's *Dictionary of American English,* and of Mencken's *American Language.*

————.
"A Sidelight on Eighteenth Century American English." *Queen's Quarterly* 31:173–181, 1923.

"Early American Pronunciation and Syntax." *AS* 1 (No. 3) :141–148, 1925.

"Is There An American Language?" *Queen's Quarterly* 34:191–202, 1926.

"The American Language." *Queen's Quarterly* 30:353–362, 1923.

Allvine, Glenden
Studio Lingo. In: *The Silver Screen*, by Roger Whately, Jack O'Donnell, and H. W. Hanemann, (pp. 241–268). Los Angeles, 1935.
The author lists about 375 terms used in the Hollywood studios.

Amend, Ottilie
"Theatrical Lingo." *AS* 3 (No. 1) :21–23, 1927.

"American Words."
Saturday Review of Literature. 13 (No. 12) :8, Jan. 18, 1936.

Ames, Joseph S., et al.
Nomenclature for Aeronautics. Compiled by the National Advisory Committee for Aeronautics. Report No. 240. Washington, D. C.: U. S. Government Printing Office, 1926. 77 pp.

Angel, Anne
"Golf Gab." *AS* 1 (No. 12) : 627–633, 1926.

Anonymous
"American English." *London Times Literary Supplement,* p. 40, 1926.

"American Slang." *Catholic World* 123:106–107, 1926.

"American Word-Crashing." *Literary Digest* 106:17, 1930.

"Aviators Speak a Language All Their Own." *Literary Digest* 97:73–74, 1928.

"Birth Pangs of Slang." *Literary Digest* 116:20, 1933.

"Broadcast English." *London Times,* Friday, July 27, 1928. p. 12.

"Collegians Have Language All Their Own." *Word-Study* 3:3–4, 1927.

"Common Speech of America." *Catholic World* 120:825–826, 1926.

"Dialect Areas of the United States." *School and Society* 30:319, 1929.

"Lunch-Wagon Slanguage." *World's Work* 61 (No. 2) :29, 1932.

"Mortuary Nomenclature." *Hygeia* (Chicago) : Nov. 1925, pp. 651.

"Radio English." *Saturday Review of Literature* 3:187, 1926.

"Slang in Evolution." *Literary Digest* 84:28–29, Feb., 1925.

"Slanguage, American Slang as it is To-Day." *Manchester Guardian Weekly* 21:228, 1929.

"Stabilizing Anglo-American Speech." *Literary Digest* 72:27–28, Jan., 1922.

"The American 'Ganguage'." *Literary Digest* 113:36, 1932.
The slang of Gangsters.

"The New American Language." *The Forum* 77:265–268, 1927.

"Undressing Adopted Words." *Literary Digest* 88:65, Jan. 9, 1926.

"Talk American." *Manchester Guardian Weekly* 29:116, August 11, 1933.

"Thieves' Thesaurus." *Literary Digest* 91:64–66, 1926.

Trade Names: A Compilation of Over 5000 Trade Names used by Electrical and Radio Manufacturers. New York: Gage Publishing Co., 1926. 60 pp.

"As she is spoke."
Daily Progress (Charlottesville, Virginia), May 21, 1937. p. 4.
An editorial on American dialects.

Askew, H., Maxwell, Herbert, et al.
"Surnames Derived from the Divisions of Time." *N&Q* 152:280, 319, 357, 393, 431, April 16 et seq., 1927.

Atherton, H. E., and Gregg, Darrell L.
"A Study of Dialect Differences." *AS* 4 (No. 3) :216–223, 1929.

Austin, Mary
The American Rhythm. New York: Harcourt, Brace and Co., 1923. viii, 155 pp.

Ayres, Harry Morgan
"The English Language in America." In: *The Cambridge History of American Literature.* ed. by Trent, Erskine, Sherman and Van Doren. New York: The Macmillan Co., 1917. Reprinted in 1 Vol. in 1945.
Includes discussion of changes in American speech, dialects, American tradition in speech and usage, sectional peculiarities and modern tendencies.

————, **and Greet, W. Cabell**
"American Speech Records at Columbia University." *AS* 5 (No. 5) :333–358, 1930.
   A great collection, covering the major dialects of the country.

Babbitt, E. H.
"College Words and Phrases." *Dialect Notes* 2 (Part 1) :1–70.

Baker, Sidney J.
"Influence of American Slang on Australia." *AS* 18:253–256, 1943.

Barker, Howard F.
"Queer Names." *AS* 6 (No. 2) :101–109, 1930.

————.
"Surnames in the United States." *American Mercury* 26:223–230, 1932.

Barkley, Dorothy
"Hospital Talk." *AS* 2 (No. 7) :312–314, 1927.

Barrère, A., and Leland, C. G.
A Dictionary of Slang, Jargon, and Cant. London: Ballantyne Press, 1889.

Bartlett, John Russell
Dictionary of Americanisms. New York: Bartlett and Welford, 1848. Boston: Little, Brown and Co., 1859. 2nd ed.

Beach, Joseph Warren
"The Native Style." *AS* 1 (No. 11) :576–583, 1926.

Beath, Paul Robert
"Aviation Lingo." *AS* 5 (No. 4) :289–290, 1930.

————.
"More Crook Words." *AS* 6 (No. 12) :131–134, 1930.

Beirne, Francis F.
"Newspaper English." *AS* 2 (No. 1) :8–12, 1927.

Benardete, Dolores
"Professorial Speech—New Style." *AS* 2 (No. 6) :259–269, 1927.

Bentley, Harold W.
"Linguistic Concoctions of the Soda Jerker." *AS* 11 (No. 7) :37–45, 1936.

Berkeley, Reginald
"English as She is Talkied." *Saturday Review*, No. 3940:638–639, May 2, 1931.

Bernstein, Herbert B.
"Fire Insurance Terminology." *AS* 1 (No. 10) :523–528, 1926.

Berrey, Lester V., and Van den Bark, Melvin
American Thesaurus of Slang. New York: Thos. Y. Crowell, 1945. 1231 pp.
   The world's most picturesque language fills this compendium of slang—the racetrack, army, navy, theatre, Broadway, Hollywood, hobo world, 100,000 entries.

————.
The American Thesaurus of Slang. Revised with a supplement of teens talk, jive jargon, and military slang. Introduction by Louise Pound. New York: Thomas Y. Crowell, 1947. 1231 pp.

Birss, John Howard
"Some Americanisms of a Hundred Years Ago." *AS* 7 (No. 2) :96–98, 1931.

Bisgaier, Paul
"Speech in the Post Office." *AS* 7 (No. 4) :278–279, 1932.

Bolinger, Dwight L.
"Among the New Words." *AS* 18:301–305, 1943.

Booth, Ernest
"The Language of the Underworld." *American Mercury* 14:78–81, 1928.

Botkin, B. A.
"An Anthology of Lizzie Labels." *AS* 7 (No. 1) :32–39, 1931.

————.
"Folk-Say and Folklore." *AS* 6 (No. 6) :404–406, 1931.
   The author explains his choice and meaning of the term "folk-say." He defines it as "literature about the folk as well as literature of the folk."

————.
"The Lore of the Lizzie Label." *AS* 6 (No. 2) :81–93, 1930.
   "The Lizzie labelists vie with one another in giving it picturesque and mirthful nicknames expressive of wily toughness, intractability, low degree, slowness, decrepitude, dilapidation, amorous promiscuity, and all-round cussedness." (B. A. B.)

Bowers, Fredson
"College Slang a Language All Its Own." *Literary Digest* 84:64–65, 1925.

Bowman, LeRoy E.
"The Terminology of Social Workers. Vogues in Social Work Terms." *AS* 1 (No. 9) :478–480, 1926.

Brackbill, Hervey
"Some Telegrapher's Terms." *AS* 4 (No. 4) :287–290, 1929.

Brogan, D. W.
"American Family Names." *Herald* (Glasgow), July 31, 1937.

Brown, Barbara
"Great American Slanguage." *Outlook* 156:417, 435, 1930.

Bryant, Margaret M.
"The People's Sayings." How You Can Help Record Them. *NYFQ* 1:50–56, 1945.
   An appeal and suggestion to the residents of New York State.

Buckhurst, Helen McM.
"Some Recent Americanisms in Standard Speech." *AS* 1 (No. 3) :159–160, 1925.

Burke, W. J.
"American Slang—Where to Find It. A Selected Reference List." *Wilson Bulletin* 8:220–221, 254, 1933.

————.
"The literature of slang. 1. Underworld cant and its subsidiaries." *Bulletin N. Y. Public Library* 40:1013–1022, Dec. 1936. 41:19–28, 113–124, 313–320, 681–695, 1937.
The history of the study of slang and cant with a thorough bibliography.

The Literature of Slang. With an introductory note by Eric Partridge. New York: New York Public Library, 1939.

Buxbaum, Katherine
"Mark Twain and American Dialect." *AS* 2 No. 5) :233, 1927.

Byington, Steven T., and Malone, Kemp
"What is Anglo-Saxon?" *AS* 5 (No. 2) :104–106, 1929.

C. P. M.
"Language of the Speakeasy." *AS* 6 (No. 2): 158–159, 1930.

————.
"The Charm of Slang." *Manchester Guardian Quarterly* 15:153, 1926.

Campbell, J. O.
"American English." *News Week* 3:4, Jan. 27, 1934.

Chamberlain, A. F.
"Algonkian Words in American English." *JAFL* 15:240–267, 1902.

Charmley, Beulah
"The Great Good Slang." *Modern Thinker* 6:22–26, 1935.

Colburn, Dorothy
"Newspaper Nomenclature." *AS* 2 (No. 5) :238–243, 1927.

Cole, Hilda
"Radio Slang." *Radioland*, March, 1935.

Collitz, Klara Hechtenberg
"Alliteration in American English." *AS* 7 (No. 3) :204–218, 1932.

————.
"Boost." *AS* 1 (No. 12) :661–672, 1926.
An extensive study of the origin and various uses of the word.

————.
"Nifty, Hefty, Natty, Snappy." *AS* 3 (No. 2) :119–128, 1927.

Compton, Nellie Jane
"Library Language." *AS* 2 (No. 2) :93–95, 1927.

Corruth, W. H.
"The Language Used to Domesticate Animals." *Dialect Notes* 1 (Part 6) :263–268.

Cottrell, W. F., and Montgomery, H. C.
"Glossary of Railroad Terms." *AS* 18:161–170, 1943.

Coues, R. W.
"Odd Terms in a Writer of Letters." *Dialect Notes* 6 (Part 1) :1–6, 1928.
From the letters of Susan Hale (1833–1910), sister of Edward Everett Hale.

Cowden, R. W.
"Slanging English Words." *English Journal* 14:697–706, 1925.

Craigie, Sir William A.
A Dictionary of American Language. Chicago: University of Chicago Press, 1944. 4 Vols.
A new language comes of age.

————.
"Americanisms." *Nation* 131:572, 1930.

————.
"An American Language." *Saturday Review of Literature* 7:614–615, 1931.
He contends "that the probability of a distinct American language is becoming constantly lessened."

————.
"The Study of American English." *Society for Pure English Tract No.* 32:199–219, 1927.

Creighton, Robert E.
"Jargon of Fistiana." *AS* 8 (No. 3) :34–39, 1933.
Lingo of the prize fighters.

Crespigny, Claude de
"American and English." *AS* 1 (No. 9) :490–494, 1926.

————.
"Peculiar Anglicizing." *AS* 1 (No. 10) :565–566, 1926.

Daggett, Windsor P.
"The Lineage of Speech." *Theatre Arts Monthly* 9:597–604, 1925.

Davidson, Levette Jay
"Auto-Tourist Talk." *AS* 9 (No. 2) :110–114, 1934.

————.
"Sugar Beet Language." *AS* 6 (No. 1) :10–15, 1930.

de Vere, M. Schele
Americanisms; The English of the New World. New York: Charles Scribner and Co., 1871.

Dickason, Frederick Garrett
"Two Centuries of American Common Tree-Names." *AS* 6 (No. 6) :411–424, 1931.

Dickson, Harris
Phrases of the People Recorded by Harris Dickson, Vicksburg, Mississippi. In: *American Stuff*, An Anthology of Prose and Verse, by members of the Federal Writers' Project. By the Guild's Committee for Federal Writers' Publications, Inc. New York: The Viking Press, 1937.

Dondore, Dorothy Anne
"Big Talk! The Flying, the Gabe, and the Frontier Boast." *AS* 6 (No. 1):45–55, 1930.
"For the student of language, however, no more interesting relationship is obvious than the habit of "Big Talk," the childishly naïve extolling of one's own prowess.

Eliason, Norman E.
"The language of the 'Buckeye'." *AS* 12 (No. 4):270–274, 1937.
Language of the cigar industry.

Emerson, Oliver Farrar
"Beguiling Words." *Dialect Notes* 5 (Part 4):91–96, 1921.
"These are words used in practical jokes upon the uninitiated in crafts, business houses, the army and navy, and doubtless in other relations." (The Author)

Eno, J. N.
"Irish Gaelic Clan Names and Family Names Abundant in America." *Americana* 21:415–425, 1927.

Ericson, Eston Everett
"Old-Fashioned Veterinary Terms." *AS* 12 (No. 2):160–161, 1937.
Picked up in Nebraska, but also heard in Montana, Maryland, Pennsylvania and North Carolina.

Erskine, John
"Do Americans Speak English." *The Nation* 120:410–411, April 15, 1925.

Ersine, Noel
Underworld and Prison Slang. Upland, Indiana: A. D. Freese & Son, 1935, 80 pp.

Farmer, John S.
Americanisms, Old and New. London: Privately Printed by T. Poulter and Sons, 1889.

————, and Henley, W. E.
Dictionary of Slang and Colloquial English. London: G. Routledge and Sons, Ltd., n.d.

Feather, William
"Anglicizing Americanisms." *AS* 1 (No. 4):269–270, 1926.

Finerty, James J.
'Criminalese,' *Slang Talk of Criminal.* Los Angeles: Published by the Author, P. O. Box 867, 1934.

Fischer, Walther
"Amerikanisches Englisch." In: *Handbuch der Amerikakunde*, Handbücher der Auslandskunde, Vol. 6. Frankfurt: M. Diesterweg, 1931.

Fitzpatrick, Robert J.
"Language of the Tobacco Market." *AS* 15: 132–136, 1940.

Forward, Kenneth
"Manners For Americans." *AS* 2 (No. 4):182–190, 1927.

Franz, W.
"Amerikanisches und britisches Englisch." In: *Festschrift Friedrich Kluge zum 70. Geburtstage.* (pp. 29–39). Berlin: Tübingen, 1926.

Fraser, G. M.
"Craft Surnames." *Word-Lore* 1:17–21, 1926.

Fuller, Norman
"Crook Argot." *AS* 3 (No. 3):254–255, 1928. Reprint from the *Denver Rocky Mountain News.*

Funk, Charles Earle
A Hog On Ice and Other Curious Expressions. New York: Harper and Bros., 1948.
"Dr. Funk, one of the lexicographical Funks, has traced the genealogy of several hundred of the picturesque expressions which spice our speech ... in an attempt to discover what they originally meant, how they reached their present meaning, who first used them and when ... This collection is not merely a holiday for those who like to play with words. Customs, beliefs and little snatches of history crop up on every page ... sidelights on our forebears ..." (John Wilson).

Gable, J. Harris
"American Stage-Hand Language." *AS* 4 (No. 1):67–70, 1928.

Gaffney, Wilbur
"Business English—Going and Coming." *AS* 1 (No. 7):447–449, 1926.

Gary, Lorena M.
"Anglo-American Altercation." *Overland Monthly* 93:5–6, 1935.

Geller, David
"Lingo of the Shoe Salesman." *AS* 9 (No. 4): 283–286, 1934.

Gepp, Edward
"Essex Speech in Some Dialects of the United States." *Essex Review* 31:97–104, 1922.

Gill, M. A.
Underworld Slang. Kansas City, Mo.: South Side Printing Co., 1929. 28 pp.

Gill, Robert S.
"Speech Tunes and the Alphabet." *AS* (No. 1):40–43, 1925.

"Glossary of Bookmakers' Slang."
Mr. (Exposed Pub. Co., 149 Madison Ave., N. Y. C.) 1, No. 4, pp. 128, 1938.

"Glossary of Farm Terms."
Pathfinder (Washington, D. C.): September 7, 1935, p. 9.

"Glossary of 'Tramp' Language."
AS 1 (No. 4):251, 1926.

Hall, L. B.
"English Origin of American Slang." *Morning Post* (London): Jan. 29, 1935.

Halliwell, James O.
A Dictionary of Archaic and Provincial Words. London: G. Routledge and Sons, Ltd., 1924.

Haney, John L.
"Our Agile American Accents." *AS* 1 (No. 7): 378–382, 1926.

Hanford, G. L.
"Metaphor and Simile in American Folk-Speech." *Dialect Notes* 5 (Part 5):149–180, 1922.
Addenda to the above Dialect Notes 5 (Part 7): 289–291, 1924 by B. Q. Morgan.

Hargan, James
"The psychology of prison language." *Journal of Abnormal and Social Psychology*, 30:359–365, 1935.

Harrison, Thomas Perrin
"Some Folk Words." *AS* 5 (No. 3):219–223, 1930.

Hayden, Marie Gladys
"Terms of Disparagement in American Dialect Speech." *Dialect Notes* 4 (Part 3):194–223, 1915.

Haydon, Broronlee
"Technique of the U. S. Slang." *Morning Post* (London), July 3, 1936.

Heck, Rev. Henry J.
"A Note on 'Annie Oakley'." *AS* 8 (No. 1): 76–78, 1933.

—————.
"Baseball Terminology." *AS* 5 (No. 4):279–280, 1930.

Hench, Atcheson L.
"From the Vocabulary of Automobile Thieves." *AS* 5 (No. 3):236–237, 1930.

Heyne, Paul
"Ueber den amerikanischen Sprachgebrauch." In: *Englisches Englisch* Part III (pp. 169–194). Freeburg: Bielefeld's Verlag, 1922. 2nd rev. ed.

Hicklin, Maurice
"Scribes Seek Snappy Synonyms." *AS* 6 (No. 2):110–122, 1930.
The language of literary critics.

Higginson, T. W.
"English Sources of American Dialect." *American Antiquarian Society*, Worcester, Mass., *Proceedings*, new series, vol. 4:159–166, 1938.

Hills, E. C.
"Exclamations in American Speech." *Dialect Notes* 5 (Part 7):253–284, 1924.

—————.
"Linguistic Substrata of American English." *AS* 4 (No. 6):431–433, 1929.

Hollister, Howard K.
"The Origin of a Dialect." *The Freeman* 7:376–377, 1923.

Hook, G. T.
"More Truck Driver Lingo." *Commercial Car Journal* (Phila.): June, 1938, pp. 26, 29, 60, 62; August, 1938, pp. 40, 42.

Hoops, Johannes
"Die amerikanische Sprache." *Englische Studien*, 57–318–319, 1923.

House, Dorothy E.
"Hospital Lingo." *AS* 13:227–229, 1938.

Huddle, Franklin P.
"Baseball Jargon." *AS* 18:103–111, 1943.

Hunter, E. R.
The American Colloquial Idiom: 1830–1860. Chicago: University of Chicago Press, 1925. Dissertation.

Irwin, Godfrey, ed.
American Tramp and Underworld Slang: words and phrases used by hoboes, tramps, migratory workers, etc., with tramp songs. With an essay on American slang in its relation to the English thieves' slang, by E. Partridge. London: Scholartis Press, 1931. 264 pp.

"Is There a Circus Slang?"
Book Buyer 3:26, May, 1937.
A bibliography of 10 articles discussing circus slang or jargon.

Jaeger, P. L.
"On English War-Slang." *Englische Studien* 60:272–299, 1926.

James, A. Lloyd
The Broadcast Word. London: Kegan Paul, Trench, Trubner, & Co., 1935. xii, 207 pp.

Jensen, Gerard E.
"Concerning the Use of Slang." *AS* 3 (No. 1): 12–13, 1927.

Johnson, Oakley Calvin
"Allusive Additions to the Vocabulary of English." *AS* 4 (No. 2):83–94, 1928.

Jones, Joe J.
"More Slang." *AS* 5 (No. 4):305, 1930.

Jones, L. S.
"The Value of Slang." *Star* (London), July 1, 1937.

Jones, P. J.
"American Jargon." *Daily Telegraph* (London), March 4, 1935.

Kane, Elisha K.
"The Jargon of the Underworld." *Dialect Notes* 5 (Part 10):433–467, 1927.

Kempton, J. H.
"Agronomic Jabberwocky." *Science*, 67:229–230, 1928.

Kennedy, Arthur G.
"Hothouse Words Versus Slang." *AS* 2 (No. 10):417–424, 1927.

Kenyon, John Samuel
American Pronunciation. Ann Arbor, Mich.: George Wahr, 1924.

—————.
"Some Notes on American R." *AS* 1 (No. 6): 329–339, 1926.

Klinghardt, H.
"Amerikanische Aussprache und Intonation." *Die Neueren Sprachen* 33:121–122, 1925.
American language and inflection.

Knight, George H.
"Conservatism in American Speech." *AS* 1 (No. 1):1–18, 1925.

Knortz, Karl
Amerikanische redensarten und volkesgebräuche... Mit dem anhang: Folkloristisches in Longfellow's *Evangeline*. Leipzig: Teutonia Verlag. 1907. 82 pp.

Krapp, George P.
"Irish English in America." *Catholic World* 122:680–682, 1926.

———.
"Is American English Archaic?" *Southwest Review* 12:292–303, 1927.

———.
The History of the English Language in America. New York: The Century Co., 1925. 2 vols.

———.
"The Psychology of Dialect Writing." *Bookman* 63:522–527, 1926.

Kuethe, J. Louis
"Modern Slang." *AS* 11 (No. 4):293–297, 1936.

———.
"Prison Parlance." *AS* 9 (No. 1):25–28, 1934.

Kurath, Hans
"The Origin of the Dialectical Differences in Spoken American English." *Modern Philology* 25:385–395, 1928.

"Labor's Language."
Literary Digest 123 (No. 16):7, 1937.

Larson, Cedric
"The Drinkers Dictionary." *AS* 12 (No. 2):87–92, 1937.

Laundry Age.
Laundry Dictionary: Terminology and Jargon of Commercial laundries, with a directory of the leading associations. Little Gold Business Book, No. 49. Stamford, Conn.: The Dahl Publishing Co., n.d. 48 pp.

Lawton, Sherman P.
Radio Speech. With an introduction by William P. Sandford and a short introductory essay by Henry A. Bellows. Boston: Expression Company, 1932. xxi, 450 pp.

Lee, Gretchen
"In Sporting Parlance." *AS* 1 (No. 7):369–370, 1926.

———.
"Trouper Talk." *AS* 1 (No. 1):36–38, 1925.
The Lingo of the theatre and dressing room.

Lindsay, Charles
"More Political Lingo." *AS* 2 (No. 10):443, 1927.

———.
"The Idiom of the Sheep Range." *AS* 6 (No. 5):355–359, 1931.

Lindsay, Vachel
"The Real American Language." *American Mercury* 13:257–265, 1928.

Littell, Robert
"Words and Idioms." *New Republic* 44:235–236, 1925.

Long, H. W. F.
"Dialect of the Schools." *Word-Lore* (London) 1:97–99, 1926.

Mabey, Richard A.
"The English of the Court Room: As Heard by the Shorthand Reporter." *AS* 1 (No. 4):264–268, 1926.

Macnamara, T. J.
"Can Dialect Survive." *Contemporary Review* 130:312–315, 1926.

Mallery, Richard D.
Our American Language. New York: Halcyon House, 1947. 276 pp.
According to reviewer Horace Reynolds, the book presents a rather "sketchy treatment of the American contribution to the fund of English words brought to these shores by our seed-folks."

Malone, Kemp
"American and Anglo-Saxon." *AS* 1 (No. 7):371–377, 1926.

Massey, W. B. A.
"The Divergence of American from English." *AS* 6 (No. 1):1–11, 1930.

Massingham, H. J.
"Country Speech." *Fortnightly Review* 136:774-783, 1931.

Masson, Thomas L.
"Speech, Common and Preferred. Word-Manufacture in the United States." *Century Magazine* 113:80–89, 1926.

Maurer, David W.
"Australian Rhyming Argot in the American Underworld." *AS* 19:183–195, 1944.
Pairs of words that express meaning of another word, which rhymes with the second of the pair.

———.
"Carnival Cant: A Glossary of Circus and Carnival Slang." *AS* 6 (No. 5):327–337, 1931.

———.
"Manuscript Glossaries of the American Vernacular. *AS* 17:193–195, 1942.
A review of some unpublished glossaries of vernacular terms, including criminal argots and the lingo of trampdom, the circus, certain of the crafts, and the army.

———.
"Prostitutes and Criminal Argots." *American Journal of Sociology* 44:546–550, 1939.

———.
"The Argot of the Confidence Men." *AS* 15:113–124, 1940.

———.
"The Argot of the Faro Bank." AS 18:3–11, 1943.

"The Argot of the Underworld." *AS* 2 (No. 2): 99–118, 1931.

"The Argot of the Underworld Narcotic Addict." *AS* 11 (No. 2):116–127; 179–192, 1936.

"The Lingo of the Good-People." *AS* 10 (No. 1):10–23, 1935.
Argot of the Underworld.

"Underworld Place Names." *AS* 15:340–342, 1940.

Mawson, D. O. S.
A Dictionary of Foreign Terms Found in the English and American Writing of Yesterday. New York: Crowell, 1935.

McClintock, Theodore
"English and American Sport Terms in German." *AS* 8 (No. 4):42–47, 1933.

McCormick, Elsie
"The American Slanguage." *St. Louis Post-Dispatch*, Sept. 20, 1925.

McDaniel, W. B.
"English and American Sport Terms Abroad." *AS* 3 (No. 5):436–437, 1928.

McDonald, P. B.
"Scientific Terms in American Speech." *AS* 2 (No. 2):67–70, 1927.

"Simplifying Engineering Terms." *AS* 3 (No. 6):481–484, 1928.

McPhee, M. C.
"College Slang." *AS* 3 (No. 2):131–133, 1927.

Mead, William Edward
"The American Dialect Dictionary." *PMLA* 29:225–235, 1914.

Meikeljohn, M. J. C.
"American English." *Spectator* (London) 138: 212–213, 1927.

Mellen, Ida
"Aquarium English." *AS* 3 (No. 6):460–463, 1928.

Mencken, H. L.
"English Terms for American Readers." *AS* 3 (No. 1):68–69, 1927.

The American Language. An Inquiry into the Development of English in the United States. New York: Alfred A. Knopf, 1937. xi and 769 pp. index, 4th edition enlarged.

The American Language. Supplement I: An Inquiry Into the Development of English in the United States. New York: Alfred A. Knopf, 1945. 744 pp.

The American Language. Supplement II. New York: Alfred A. Knopf, 1948. 890 pp.
This work follows the plan of the *First Supplement*. The latter presented material relating to the first six chapters of the original work (*The American Language.*), while Supplement II further discusses and adds new material for chapters seven to eleven, inclusive, The present volume deals with "The Pronunciation of American," "American Spelling," "The Common Speech," "Proper Names in America," and "American Slang."

Meredith, Mamie
"Inexpressibles, Unmentionables, Unwhisperables, and Other Verbal Delicacies of Mid-Nineteenth Century Americans." *AS* 5 (No. 4): 285–287, 1930.

Merryweather, L. W.
"Hell in American Speech." *AS* 6 (No. 6): 433–435, 1931.

Milburn, George
"Circus Words." *American Mercury* 24:351–354, 1931.

"Convicts' Jargon." *AS* 6 (No. 6):436–442, 1931.

"The Taxi Talk." In: *Folk-Say: A Regional Miscellany* 1:108–112, 1929.

Miller, Charles
"Furniture Lingo." *AS* 6 (No. 2): 125–128, 1930.

Moore, H. E.
"The American Language Crucible." *English Review* 40:226–232, 1925.

Moore, Ruth
"American Epitaphs and Tombstones." *AS* 6 (No. 7):383–390, 1926.

Morgan, B. Q.
"Simile and Metaphor in American Speech." *AS* 1 (No. 4):271–274, 1926.

Morris, Bernard
"The Lingo of Bus Drivers." *AS* 13:307–308, 1938.

Moss, Arnold
"Jewels from a Box Office. The Language of Show Business." *AS* 11 (No. 3):219–222, 1936.

Motherwell, Hiram
"The Language of Lobster Alley." *Bookman* 72:396–399, 1930.
The slang of theatrical people.

Mott, Gertrude
"What's Your Name." *Overland Monthly* 85: 175–177, 216–217, 1927. n.s.

Musser, B. F.
"A Study in American Slang." *Catholic World* 117:471–476, 1923.

Mutschmann, H. A.
A Glossary of Americanisms. Tartu-Dorpat, Estonia: K. Mattiesen, 1931. 72 pp.

Nieberg, George
"The American Slanguage." *Forum* 84:371–376, 1930.

Northup, Clark S.
Register of Bibliographies of the English Language and Literature. Cornell Studies in English. New Haven, Conn.: Yale University Press, 1925. 507 pp.

Nye, Russell B.
"A Musician's Word List." *AS* 12 (No. 1) : 45–48, 1937.
    Popular band and music lingo.

Oppenheimer, Reuben
"Legal Lingo." *AS* 2 (No. 2) :142–144, 1926.

"Our Own Language."
Railroad Men's Magazine, (June) 1930.

P. G. M.
"Race-Track Talk." *AS* 1 (No. 4) :292, 1926.

Parry, Albert
"Movie Talk." *AS* 3 (No. 5) :364–368, 1928.

Partridge, Eric
Slang, Today and Yesterday. London: Routledge, 1933. x, 476 pp.

Patten, Nathan van
"Organization of Source Materials for the Study of American English and American Dialects." *AS* 4 (No. 6) :425–429, 1929.

Paynter, Richard H.
"The Language of Drug Addicts." *AS* 4 (No. 1) :19–21, 1928.

Peterson, Martin S.
"Totemism in Boyhood Nicknames." *AS* 2 (No. 11) :476–477, 1927.

Phipson, E. A.
"British vs. American English." *Dialect Notes* 1 (Part 9) :428–430.

Pollack, F. Walter
"Courtship Slang." *AS* 2 (No. 4) : 202–203, 1927.

————.
"The Current Expansion of Slang." *AS* 2 (No. 2) :145–147, 1926.

Porter, Bernard H.
"Truck Driver Lingo." *AS* 17:102–105, 1942.

Pound, Louise
"American Euphemism for Dying, Death, and Burial." *AS* 11 (No. 3) :195–202, 1936.
    An Anthology.

————.
"Folklore and Dialect." *CFQ* 4:146–153, 1945.

————.
"Notes on the Vernacular." *The American Mercury* 3:233–237, 1924.

————.
"Research in American English." *AS* 5 (No. 5) :359–365, 1930.

————.
"Some Folk-Locutions." *AS* 17:247–251, 1942.

————.
"Spelling-Manipulation and Present-Day Advertising." *Dialect Notes* 5 (Part 6) :226–232, 1923.

————.
"The Jocularizing of French Words and Phrases in Present-Day American Speech." *Dialect Notes* 5 (Part 3) :77–79, 1920.

————.
"Vogue Affixes in Present-Day Word Coinage." *Dialect Notes* 5 (Part 1) :1–14, 1918.
    "Following is a list—not complete, of course—of contemporary coinages which exemplify the particular set of prefixes and endings now having especial popularity, and illustrate the present-day liking for novel verbal effect as an arrest to the attention." (The Author)

————.
"Word-Coinage and Modern Trade Names." *Dialect Notes* 4 (Part 1) :29–41, 1913.

Pound, Olivia
"Educational Lingo." *AS* 1 (No. 6) :311–314, 1926.

Powell, Francis T. S.
"Radio and the Language." *Commonweal* 9: 652–653, 1929.

Power William
"Americanisms." *Daily Record and Mail* (Glasgow), June 30, 1937.

Prenner, Manuel
"Slang Terms for Money." *AS* 4 (No. 5) :357–358, 1929.

R. S.
"American Slang in London." *AS* 3 (No. 2): 167, 1927.

Rainey, Lillian F.
"Old Words Made Over." *Century Magazine* 111:377–378, 1926.

Ramsaye, Terry
"Movie Jargon." *AS* 1 (No. 7) :357–362, 1926.

Read, Allen Walker
"British Recognition of American Speech in the Eighteenth Century." *Dialect Notes* 6 (Part 6) :313–334, 1933.

————.
"Dunglison's Glossary (1829–1830)." *Dialect Notes* 5 (Part 10) :422–432, 1927.
    Robley Dunglison (1798–1869) leading educator and medical doctor. He has often been called "by far the most voluminous and erudite author of his time in this country."

————.
"The Bear in American Speech." *AS* 10 (No. 3) :195–202, 1935.

————.
"The Comment of British Travelers on Early American Terms Relating to Agriculture." *Agricultural History* 7:99–109, 1933.

————.
"The Rationale of 'Podunk'." *AS* 14:98–108, 1939.
A discussion how this word came to be used as the designation for any small, out-of-the-way place.

Read, William A.
"Some Phases of American Pronunciation." *Journal of English and Germanic Philology* 22:217–244, 1923.

"Regional or Dialect Speech for Dramatic Purposes." *Theatre Arts Monthly*, February, 1931. p. 169.

Reuner, Brander de
"How English Names Trip American Tongues." *Literary Digest* 86:52, 56, 1925.

Reves, Haviland Ferguson
"What is Slang? A Survey of Opinion." *AS* 1 (No. 4):216–220, 1926.

Rockwell, Harold E.
"Color Stuff." *AS* 3 (No. 1):28–30, 1927.
Sport jargon.

————.
"Headline Words." *AS* 2 (No. 2):140–141, 1926.

Rose, Howard N., comp. and arr.
A Thesaurus of Slang. New York: The Macmillan Co., 1934. x, 120 pp.

Russell, E.
"Slang—face to face." *English Journal* (High School Edition) 23:740–744, Nov., 1934.

Russell, I. W.
" 'Highball' to Speed." *AS* 19:33–36, 1944.
Discussion of this American slang expression.

Russell, Jason Almus
"American Indian Metaphorical Expressions." *Words* 3:10–11, 1920.
49 figures of speech.

————.
"Colgate University Slang." *AS* 5 (No. 3):238–239, 1930.

Ryan, Quin A.
"Radio Speech, Proposing an Armistice in a War of Words." *Liberty* 5 (No. 8):79–82, 1928.

Samuels, V.
"Baseball Slang." *AS* 2 (No. 5):255–256, 1927.

Sandburg, Carl
The People, Yes. New York: Harcourt, Brace and Co., 1936.
American through and through.

Sanford, Winifred, and Jackson, Clyde
"Derrick Jargon." *Southwest Review* 19:265–278, 1934.

Saul, Vernon W. (Alias K. C. Slim)
"The Vocabulary of Bums." *AS* 4 (No. 5):337–346, 1929.

"Say it in American."
Morning Post (London), Sept. 11, 1936.

Schauffler, Robert H.
"Timesquarese." *Saturday Review of Literature* 1:817–818, 1925.

Schaupp, Zora
"Psychopathic English." *AS* 1 (No. 10):519–522, 1926.

Schorf, Carl
"Slang, Slogan and Song in American Politics." *Social Studies* 25:424–430, 1934.

Schultz, J. R.
"Chautauqua Notes." *AS* 9 (No. 3):232–234, 1934.

Scott, Fred Newton
"American Slang." *Society for Pure English Tract*, No. 24:118–127, 1926.

————.
"English and American Vernacular." *McNaught's Monthly* 3:144–145, 1925.
A short discussion of supreme importance.

Scott, Samuel M.
"The American Language." *Harvard Graduate's Magazine* 31:487–494, 1923.

Sheldon, E. S.
"What is a Dialect?" *Dialect Notes* 1 (Part 6):286–297.

Shewmake, Edwin F.
"Standards and Tendencies in American Speech." *South Atlantic Quarterly* 22:157–165, 1923.

Silver, R. G.
"A note of the vocabulary of strike-breakers." *Notes and Queries* 172:8, Jan. 2, 1937.

Simons, Hi
"A Prison Dictionary (Expurgated)." *AS* 8 (No. 3):22–33, 1933.

Skeffington, H. S.
" 'Irishing' the American Language." *Irish Press* (Dublin), Dec. 10, 1936.

Smith, C. Alphonso
"Dialect Writers." In: *The Cambridge History of American Literature*, ed. by Trent, W. P., Erskine, J., Sherman, S. P., and Doren, C. V. Vol. II (pp. 347–367). New York: The Macmillan Co., 1917. 3 Vols., Reprinted in 1 vol. edition in 1945.
The author discusses "Negro Dialect" in Joel Chandler Harris (Uncle Remus); in Virginia, Sea Islands, Louisiana; "Dialects of the Whites"; General Uniformity of American Speech, Western, New England, Southern, Middle West.

Smith, Charles Forster
"English as She is Spoke." *AS* 1 (No. 9):507–508, 1926.

Smith, Marian W.
"Cries of Derision—A Cultural Trait." *JAFL* 58:254–255, 1945.

Smith, Mr.
"Manhandled Americanisms." *Literary Digest International Book Review* 4:368, 1926.

Sobel, Bernard
"The Language of the Theatres." *Bookman* 69:148–151, 1929.

Spiller, Robert E.
"Cooper's Notes on Language." *AS* 4 (No. 4):294–300, 1929.

Sterck, Frank
"Slanguage." *The Ambrosian* 8:231–233, 1930.

Stewart, George R., Jr.
"Popular Names for the Mountain Sheep." *AS* 10 (No. 4):283–288, 1935.

Strachey, J. St. Loe
"Myth of An American Language." *Independent* 116:579, 587–588, 1926.

"Striking Lingo."
Word Study 12 (No. 4):4, Feb., 1937.
Strike-breaker's jargon.

Sutton, Vida Ravenscroft
"Radio and Speech." *AS* 8 (No. 1):10–12, 1933.

Svartengren, T. Hilding
"The Feminine Gender for Inanimate Things in Anglo-American." *AS* 3 (No. 2):83–113, 1927.

————.
"The Use of the Impersonal Gender for Inanimate Things." *Dialect Notes* 6 (Part 1):7–56, 1928.

"The Americanization of English."
Citizen (Ottawa): May 15, 1936.

The Slang Dictionary.
London: Chatto and Windus, 1922.

Thomas, W. H.
"The Decline and Decadence of Folk Metaphors." *TFSP* 2:14–17, 1923.

Thornton, Richard H.
An American Glossary. Being an attempt to Illustrate Certain Americanisms upon Historical Principles. Philadelphia: J. B. Lippincott Co., 1912. 2 Vols.

————.
"An American Glossary: A Specimen Passage." *Dialect Notes* 5 (Part 2):43–53, 1919.

————.
"Dialect Words in Old Newspapers." *Dialect Notes* 5 (Part 3):85, 1920.

————.
"Thornton's American Glossary." Being an Attempt to Illustrate Certain Americanisms Upon Historical Principles. Vol. III (Part 1): A-Dip. *Dialect Notes* 6 (Part 3):101–216, 1931. Part II: Dipping-Frog Pond; 6 (Part 4): 239–280, 1932. Part III: Front Office—half horse and half Alligator; 6 (Part 5):287–312, 1932. Part V: Horse shed, Johnny Cake; 6 (Part 7):369–384, 1933. Part III: Johnny—jump up—Longs and shorts; 6 (Part 8):392–416, 1933. Part VII: Long sauce—Nigger; 6 (Part 9):424–448, 1934. Part VIII: Nigger in the woodpile—Perique Persimmon—Puts and Calls; 6 (Part 10):456–480, 1935; 6 (Part 11):488–512, 1935. Parts X, XI: Put through—Slang: 6 (Parts 12 & 13):528–576, 1936. Part XII: Slang—whanger—spoils; 6 (Part 14): 600–616, 1937. Part XIII: Spook—under ditch; 6 (Part 15):624–648, 1937. Parts XIII–XVI: Spook-Yard, 6 (Parts 16 & 17):644–708, 1938.

Tibbals, Kate W.
"The Speech of Plain Friends. A Preliminary Survey." *AS* 1 (No. 4):193–209, 1926.

Trumbull, J. H.
"Words Derived from Indian Languages of North America." *Trans. Amer. Philo. Soc.* (Hartford), 1872.

Tunison, J. S.
"Newspaper Jargon." *Dialect Notes* 1 (Part 2): 84–100.

Tyson, Raymond
"A Guide to 'Variety'." *AS* 15:204–205, 1940.
Theatre lingo.

Voorhees, T. V.
"Slang." *Educational Review* 72:44–45, 1926.

W., I. S.
"American Uses of Animal Names Applied to Persons." *Notes and Queries* 169:363–367, 1935.

W. W.
"The Anglo-American Language." *New Statesman* 29:341–342, 1927.

Wade, Mark S.
"The American Language." *Canadian Magazine* 60:218–220, 1923.

Warnock, Elsie L.
"Terms of Approbation and Eulogy in American Dialect Speech." *Dialect Notes* 4 (Part 1): 13–25, 1913.

Wasson, Mildred
"Cockney American." *AS* 7 (No. 4):255–256, 1932.

Weber, Robert H.
"Smoker's Slang." *AS* 15:335–336, 1940.

Weekly, Ernest
"Americanism." *Quarterly Review* 247:140–154, 1926.

————.
Surnames. New York: E. P. Dutton and Co., 1927. Reprint.

Wellard, J. H.
"Some Observations on American Speech."
Nineteenth Century 117:374–384, 1935.

Wells, Whitney W.
"Drug Addicts Cant." *Dialect Notes* 5 (Part 6):246, 1923.

Wentworth, Harold
American Dialect Dictionary. New York: Thos. Y. Crowell Co., 1944. 752 pp.
 The vivid variations of Americanese—North, South, East, and West. 15,000 entries, and 60,000 quotations.

White, Charles
"English Origin of American Slang." *Morning Post* (London), Jan. 26, 1935.

White, Percy W.
"A Circus List." *AS* 1 (No. 4):282–283, 1926.

——————.
"More About the Language of the Lot." *AS* 3 (No. 5):413–415, 1928.
 Words and expressions in daily use around the circus and carnival lots.

——————.
"Stage Terms." *AS* 1 (No. 7):433–437, 1926.

Whitman, D. B.
"American Slang in England." *Manchester Guardian Weekly,* May 7, 1937, p. 374.

Whitman, Walt
"Slang in America." *The North American Review* 141: 435, 1885.

Wilstach, Frank J.
"Slang of Film Men." *New York Times,* March 11, 1928. p. 6.

Wimberly, Lowry Charles
"Spook English." *AS* 1 (No. 6):317–321, 1926.

Winship, G. P.
"Seventeenth Century Jottings." *Dialect Notes* 4 (Part 4):300–301, 1916.

Witman, Fred
"Jewelry Auction Jargon." *AS* 3 (No. 5):375–376, 1928.

Woods, Henry F.
American Sayings: Famous Phrases, Slogans, Aphorisms. New York: Duell, Sloan and Pearce, 1945. ix, 310 pp., bibl.
 Explains the origin and occasion of close to 300 popular phrases.

Woolf, Virginia, Wilson, E., et .al.
"American Language." *New Republic* 58:281–282, 335, 1929.

Work, James A.
"The American Slanguage." *Educational Review* 73:222–224, 1927.

Yeune, Herbert
"Prison Lingo." *AS* 2 (No. 6):280–282, 1927.

PLACE NAMES

STUDIES AND COLLECTIONS

Anonymous
"American Towns Bear Odd Names." *New York Times,* February 7, 1932. Sec. 2, p. 2.

——————.
"English Jawbreakers." *Literary Digest* 107: 19, 1930.
 On the pronunciation of English place-names.

——————.
"Titular Tour." *Atlantic Monthly* 154:639–640, 1934.
 Curious American place names.

Ashton, J. W.
"Some Folk Etymologies for Place Names." *JAFL* 57:139–140, 1944.

Atkinson, Rev. Canon
"The Progressive or Expansional Significance of Place Names." *Archaeological Journal (London)* 52 (Ser. 2 V. 2):253–265, 1895.

Baker, Marcus
Alaskan Geographic Names. U. S. Geological Survey. (21st Annual Report. Pt. 2), pp. 487–509, 1900.

Bayer, Henry G.
"French Names in Our Geography." *Romanic Review* 21:195–203, 1930.

Beecher, Willis Judson
"Geographical Names as Monuments of History." *Oneida Historical Society at Utica, Transactions.* No. 5, pp. 9–23, 1892.

Bell, Laura
"Some Geographical Names and Their Significance." *Geographical Society of Philadelphia. Bulletin* 18:31–34, 1920.

Berger, Vilhelm
Amerikanska Ortnamn af Svenskt Ursprung. New York: 1915. 12 pp.
 American place names of Swedish origin.

Blackie, C.
A Dictionary of Place-Names, Giving Their Derivations. With an Introduction by John Stuart Blackie. London: J. Murray, 1887. xxxix, 243 pp.

Boyd, Stephen G.
Indian Local Names with Their Interpretation. York, Pa.: The Author, 1885. x, 70 pp.

Brandsher, Earl L.
"Some Aspects of American Place-Names." *South Atlantic Quarterly.* (Durham, N. C.) 13: 174–188, 1914.

Byington, Steven T.
"On European and American River-Names." *AS* 2 (No. 10):425–428, 1927.

Caldwell, Norman W.
"Place Names and Place Name Study." *Arkansas Historical Quarterly.* 3:28–36, 1944.

Carey, Charles H.
"Some Early Maps and Myths," *Oregon Historical Quarterly*. 30:14–32, 1929.

Chrisman, L. H.
"The Romance of American Place Names." *Education* 50:173–178, 1929.

Clark, Ellery H.
"United States Place-Names Honoring the Navy." *United States Naval Institute. Proceedings*. (Annapolis) 1948, April, 453–455, illus.

Clarke, James Freeman
On Giving Names to Towns and Streets. Boston: Lockwood, Brooks & Co., 1880. 19 pp.

"Decisions of the U. S. Board on Geographical Names." *National Geographic Magazine*. 11: 478–480, 1900.

Errett, Russell
Indian Geographical Names. Cleveland: 1885. 51–59 pp.

Feipel, Louis N.
"American Place-Names." *AS* 1 (No. 2):78–91, 1925.

Field, David Dudley
Nomenclature of Cities and Towns in the United States. New York: M. B. Brown, 1885. 15 pp.

Flanagan, John T.
"An Early Discussion of Place Names." *AS* 14:157–159, 1939.

Gannett, Henry
American Names: A Guide to the Origin of Place Names in the U. S. Washington, D. C.: Public Affairs Press, 1947.

————.
The Origin of Certain Place-Names in the United States. U. S. Geological Survey, Bulletin No. 258. Washington, D. C.: U. S. Government Printing Office, 1905. iii, 280 pp., bibl.

Ganzenmüller, Konrad
Definitions of Geographical Names. With instructions for their correct pronunciation . . . New York: The Author, 1894.

Gatschet, Albert Samuel
Towns and Villages of the Creek Confederacy in the XVIII and XIX Centuries. Washington: Brown Printing Co., 1901.

Gemmill, William Nelson
Romantic America. Chicago: Jordan Publishing Company, 1926. iii, 143 pp.

Green, Samuel Abbott
Some Indian Names. Remarks on certain geographical names of Indian origin, at a meeting of the Massachusetts Historical Society, 1889. Boston: 1889. 3 pp.

Grinnell, George Bird
"Some Indian Stream Names." *AA* 15:327–331, 1913.

Harris, Clement Antrobus
"The Devil in Place-Names." *Chamber's Journal (London)* 13 (series 7):84–87, 1923.

Harshberger, John W.
"Geographical Names and Terms of Significance in Plant Geography and Ecology." *Geographical Society of Philadelphia Bulletin* 18: 100–107; 19:14–23, 45–50; 20:32–46, 1921–22. bibl.

Heck, Henry J.
"State Border Place-Names." *AS* 3 (No. 3): 186–190, 1928.

Heckewelder, John Gottlieb E.
Names, Given by the Lenni Lenape or Delaware Indians to Rivers, Streams, Places, & etc. in the Now States of Pennsylvania, New Jersey, Maryland and Virginia; and also names of chieftains and distinguished men of that nation; with their significations, and some biographical sketches . . . Philadelphia: J. Kay, Jr. and Co., 1833. 48 pp. Re-issued by *Pennsylvania German Folklore Society*, Vol. 5, No. 1, pp. 1–41, 1940.

Holt, Alfred Hubbard
American Place Names. New York: Thomas Y. Crowell Co., 1938. 222 pp., bibl. (pp. 221–222.)

Homburg, F.
"Names of Countries." *Journal of Geography, (Chicago)* 23:275–283, 1924.

Kelton, Dwight H.
Indian Names of Places Near the Great Lakes . . . Vol. I Detroit, Mich.: Detroit Free Press Printing Co., 1888. 55 pp.

Ker, Edmund Thomas
River and Lake Names in the United States. Their origins, meanings and historical associations. New York: Woodstock Publishing Co., 1911. 47 pp.

Kuehne, Oswald Robert
"Place Names in the United States as an Incentive to Foreign Language Study." *Modern Language Journal* 25:91–107, 1940.

Lawrence, Frederick W.
"The Origin of American State Names." *National Geographical Magazine* 38:105–143, 1920.

M. K. G. S.
"Aboriginal Names." *Southern Literary Messenger* 7:477–479, July 1841.
An article on the aboriginal names of the rivers, lakes, etc., in the United States containing lists of some, in which both the popular and cast-off Indian names are given.

Mallery, Richard D.
Our American Language. Garden City, N. C.: Halcyon House, 1947. xii, 276 pp.

"The Meaning of Indian Place Names." *Rhode Island Historical Society Collections* 22:33–38, 1929.

Maurer, David W.
"More Underworld Place-Names." *AS* 17:75–76, 1942.

Mawer, A.
Problems of Place-Name Study. Three Lectures at King's College. Cambridge, England: Cambridge University Press, 1929. 140 pp.

Mencken, Henry Louis
The American Language; An Inquiry into the Development of English in the United States. New York: A. A. Knopf, 1921. xvii, 492 pp., bibl. (pp. 427-457).

Meredith, Mamie
" 'Chicagonese,' Buffalonians', Manhattaniten', 'Omahogs,' and other name lore." *AS* 14:77–80, 1939.

———.
"Indian Place-Names as Viewed by a Scotch Noblewoman." *AS* 4 (No. 5):364–367, 1929.

———.
"Language Mixture in American Place-Names." *AS* 5 (No. 3):224–227, 1930.

———.
"Picturesque Town Names in America." *AS* 6 (No. 6):429–432, 1931.

Och, Joseph Tarcisius
Der deutschamerikanische Farmer; sein Anteil an der Eroberung und Kolonisation der Bundesdomäne der Ver. Staaten, ... Columbus, O.: The F. J. Heer Printing Co., 1913. xix, 248 pp., bibl.
Discussion of German-American place-names, pp. 228-235.

Phillips, W. Alison
"The Revolution in Place-Names." *Contemporary Review* 127:478–482, 1925.

Ramsay, James A.
"The Use of Place-Names in the Teaching of Geography." *Scottish Geographical Magazine (Edinburgh)* 29:429–432, 1913.

Read, Allen Walker
"Literary Place-Names." *The Palimpset* 9:450–457, 1928. (Iowa City).

———.
"The Basis of Correctness in the Pronunciation of Place-Names." *AS* 8 (No. 1):42–46, 1933.

Read, William A.
"Research in American Place-Names since 1928." *Zeitschrift für Ortsnamenforschung* 10:222–242, 1934.

Richmond, W. Edson
"Ballad Place Names." *JAFL* 59:263–267, 1946.

Sage, Evan T.
"Classical Place-Names in America." *AS* 4 (No. 4):261–271, 1929.

Salmon, Lucy M.
"Place-Names and Personal Names as Records of History." *AS* 2 (No. 5):228–232, 1927.

Scaife, Walter Bell
America: Its Geographic History 1492–1892; six lectures delivered to graduate students of the Johns Hopkins University; with a supplement entitled, "Was the Rio del Espiritu Santa of the Spanish Geographers the Mississippi?" ... Baltimore: The Johns Hopkins Press, 1892. 176 pp.

Sealock, Richard B.
"Place Names in Genealogy." *Indiana Historical Bulletin* 23 (No. 1):69–74, 1946.

Segourney, Mrs. Lydia H.
"Indian Names." *The Knickerbocker* 2:264–265, Oct. 1833.
"How can," asks the author, "the red men be forgotten while so many of our states, and territories, rivers, and lakes are designated by their names?"

Shankle, George Earle
American Nicknames: Their Origin and Significance. The T. H. Wilson Co. 1937. 599 pp.

———.
State Names, Flags, Seals, Songs, Birds, Flowers, and Other Symbols; a study based on historical documents giving the origin and significance of the state names, nicknames, mottoes, seals, flags, flowers, birds, songs, and descriptive comments on the capitol buildings and on some of the leading state histories, with facsimiles of the state flags and seals. New York: The H. W. Wilson Co., 1934. 512 pp., illus., bibl.

Sherwin, Reider T.
The Viking and the Red Man; the old Norse origin of the Algonquin language. New York: Funk & Wagnalls Co., 1946. 4 vols. bibl. (pp. 191–192).

Smith, Maurice G.
"American Indian Tribal Names." *AS* 5 (No. 2):114–117, 1929.

Spofford, Ainsworth Rand
"American Historical Nomenclature." *Amer. Hist. Assoc. Annual Rep.*, 1893, pp. 35–42.

Springer, O.
"Ortsnamen in der neuen Welt." *Germanisch-Romanische Monatsschrift.* (Heidelberg) 21:125–146, 1933.

Staples, Hamilton Barclay
"Origin of the Names of the States of the Union." *Amer. Antiq. Soc. Proc.* 1:366–383, 1881.

———.
Origin of the Names of the States of the Union. Worcester, Mass.: C. Hamilton, 1882. 25 pp.

Stewart, George R.
Names on the Land. A Historical Account of Place Naming in the United States. New York: Random House, 1945. 418 pp.
A mine of information on life, character, and events reflected in place names.

Swanson, Roy W.
"Scandinavian Place-Names in the American Dane Law." *Swedish-American Historical Bulletin* (St. Peter, Minn.) 2:6–17, 1929.

Tanner, H. S.
An Alphabetical Index to the Four Sheet Map of the United States. Philadelphia: Rackliff & Jones, 1836. v, 99 pp., illus.

Thalbitzer, William
"Eskimoiske stednavne fra Alaska og Grønland set i Arkaeologiens lys." *Geografisk Tidsskrift* (Kjøbenhaven.) : 35: 135–155, 1932. Bibl. (pp. 151–154).
English Summary (pp. 154–155).

The Editors
"Fun With Place Names." *AS* 14:134, 1939.

Tooker, William Wallace
"Algonquian Names of Some Mountains and Hills." *JAFL* 17:171–179, 1904.

Toomey, Noxon
Proper Names from the Muskhogean Languages. St. Louis, Mo.: Hervas Laboratories, 1917. 31 pp.

Trumbull, James Hammond
The Composition of Indian Geographical Names, Illustrated from the Algonkin Languages. Hartford: Case, Lockwood & Brainard, 1870. 51 pp.

United States Army Map Service. . . . *Geographical Names for Military Maps:* Army Map Service, Corps of Engineers. No. 126, (2nd edition) July 1945.

Von Engeln, Oscar Diedrich, and J. D. Urquhart
The Story Key to Geographic Names. New York: D. Appleton and Co. 1924. xiv, 379 pp., bibl.

Whitbeck, R. H.
"Geographic Names in the United States and the Stories They Tell." *National Geographic Magazine* 16: 100–104, 1905.

Whitney, Josiah Dwight
Names and Places; studies in geographical and topographical nomenclature. Cambridge, Mass.: University Press, 1888. 239 pp.

Wissler, Clark
"Names on the Land." *CFQ* 5 (No. 3) :302–304, 1946.

Wright, J. K.
"Study of Place-Names: Recent Work and Some Possibilities." *Geographical Review* 19: 140–144, 1929.

FOLKLORE OF ENGLAND

(A SELECTION)

BIBLIOGRAPHIES AND PERIODICALS

Chope, R. Pearse
Index to the Folk-lore in the Transactions of The Devonshire Association. Volumes I–LX. Exeter: Southwoods, 1929, 50 pp.

Folk-Lore.
A quarterly review of myth, tradition, institution and custom. Folk-lore Society, London. March, 1890.

Folk-Song Society, London.
United with English folk dance society to form English folk dance and song society. *Journal,* 1–8 (No. 1–35), 1889. 1904–27/31. *Report,* 1900–1931.

The Monthly Chronicle of North-Country Lore and Legend.
Periodical of Northumberland folklore. V. 1–5, 1887–1891. Newcastle-on-Tyne: Scott. 1887–91, 5 vols., illus.
No more published.

The Reliquary and illustrated archaeologist; a quarterly journal and review devoted to the study of the early pagan christian antiquities of Great Britain. Vol. 1. July, 1860. London: J. R. Smith, 1860–.
Absorbed the Illustrated Archaeologist, January, 1895.

Word-lore; the "folk" magazine. A recorder of dialect, folk song, ballad, epigram, place-name, phrase and field-lore. London. 1–3, Feb., 1926–1928.

GENERAL STUDIES AND COLLECTIONS

Addy, Sidney Oldall
Household Tales, with other traditional remains collected in the counties of York, Lincoln, Derby, and Nottingham. London: D. Nutt, 1895. xxxvi, 163 pp. music.

Apperson, George Latimer
English Proverbs and Proverbial Phrases. London: J. M. Dent and Sons, Ltd. 1929.

Atkinson, John Christopher
Forty Years in a Moorland Parish: reminiscences and researches in Danby in Cleveland. London and New York: Macmillan & Co., 1891. xv, 457 pp., 2nd ed.
English folklore.

Bailey, Harold
The Lost Language of London; a tale of King Cole founded on folklore, field-names, prehistoric hill figures and other documents. London: J. Cape, 1935. 287 pp. Illus.

Balfour, Mrs. Marie Clothilde, comp.
Examples of Printed Folklore Concerning Northumberland, coll. by M. C. Balfour, and edited by Northcote W. Thomas. London: Published for the Folklore Society by D. Nutt, 1904. xv, 180 pp., bibl.
Legends and Superstition.

Banks, Mrs. Mary Macleod
British Calendar Customs: Scotland with a preface by the Rev. J. A. MacCulloch. London: Published for the Folklore Society, W. Glaisher, Ltd., 1937, 3 volumes, illustrated, bibliography. (Publications of the Folklore Society CVIM).

Billson, Charles James
Leicestershire and Rutland. London: Published for the Folklore Society by D. Nutt, 1895. 153 pp., bibl. Publications of the Folklore Society XXXVII.
　Folklore in England—legends.

Blakeborough, Richard
The Land of Glory, and further grandfather's tales and legends of highwaymen and others. London: Richards, 1924. 268 pp., illus.
　Folklore of England.

——————.
Wit, Character, Folklore and Customs of the North Riding of Yorkshire; with a glossary of over 4,000 words and idioms now in use. London: H. Frowde, 1898. xi, 485 pp.

Bottrell, William
Traditions and Hearthsides Stories of West Cornwall. Penzance: Bearce, 1873. 298 pp., illus.

Brand, John
Brand's Popular Antiquities of Great Britian. Faiths and folklore; a dictionary of national beliefs, superstitions and popular customs, past and current, with their classical and foreign analogues described and illustrated. Forming a new edition of "The Popular Antiquities of Great Britian" by Brand and Ellis, largely extended, corrected, brought down to the present time, and now first alphabetically arranged, by W. Carew Hazlitt. London: Reeves and Turner, 1905. 2 vols., illus.

——————.
Observations on popular antiquities, chiefly illustrating the origin of our vulgar customs, ceremonies, and superstitions. With the additions of Sir Henry Ellis. London: Chatto and Windus, 1877. vi, 807 pp. new and rev. ed.

Brockett, John Trotter
A Glossary of North Country Words, with their etymology, and affinity to other languages; and occasional notices of local customs and popular supersitions. Newcastle-upon-Thyne: E. Charnley, 1846. 12 vols.

Burne, Charlotte Sophia
Shropshire Folk-Lore; a sheaf of gleanings. From the Collection of Georgina F. Jackson. London: Trubner, 1883–86. xiv, 663 pp., map. Issued in 3 parts.

——————.
The Handbook of Folk Lore. London: Published for the Folklore Society by Sidgwick & Jackson, Ltd., 1914. (V) x, 364 pp.

Courtney, M. A.
Cornish Feasts and Folk-lore. Penzance: Bearce, 1890. viii, 208 pp., Revised and reprinted from the Folk-lore Society Journals, 1886–1887.

Dexter, Thomas Francis George
Cornwall: the Land of the Gods. Truro, Cornwall: Jordan's Bookshop. London: C. A. Watts & Co., Ltd., 1932. 63 pp., illus., bibl.

Ehrentreich, Alfred, ed. and tr.
Englische Volksmärchen. Jena: E. Diederichs, 1938. 279 pp., bibl.
　English folktales from Cornwall, Wales and Scotland.

Ewen, C. L'Estrange
A History of Surnames of the British Isles. London: Kegan Paul, Trench, Trubner & Co., Ltd.; New York: The Macmillan Co., 1931. 528 pp.

Fleming, R. M.
Stories from the Early World; With an appendix by H. J. Fleure. London: Benn, 1922. 156 pp., bibl.

Fleure, Herbert John
Archaeology and Folk Tradition In: *Proceedings of the British Academy, Vol. XVII.* London, Great Britain: British Academy, 1932.

Folk-lore and Legends.
London: Gibbings, 1889. 4 Vols. Vol. 3—Scotland; Vol. 4—Ireland.

Friend, Hilderic
Flowers and Flower Lore. London: Swan Sonnenschein, Le Bas and Lowry, 1886. 3rd edition in one volume, illus., index, notes.

Gomme, Sir George Laurence, ed.
A Dictionary of British Folk-lore. London: D. Nutt, 1894–1898. 2 vols. Part I: *Traditional Games* by Alice Bertha Gomme.

——————.
British Folklore, Folk-Songs, and Singing Games. London: National Home-Reading Union, 1916. 31 pp., bibl.

——————.
Folklore Relics of Early Village Life. London: E. Stock, 1883. ix, 246 pp.

——————.
The Handbook of Folklore. London: Published for the Folklore Society by D. Nutt, 1890. vii, 193 pp., bibl.

Glyde, John, Jr., editor
The Norfolk Garland: A collection of the superstitious beliefs and practices, proverbs, curious customs, ballads and songs, of the people of Norfolk as well as anecdotes, illustrative of the genius or peculiarities of Norfolk celebrities. London: Jarrold and Sons, 1872, iv, 405 pp.

Groome (W. Wollaston)
"Suffolk Leechcraft." *Folk-Lore* (London) 6:117–127, 1895.

Gurdon, Lady Eveline Cammilla, comp.
Suffolk; Introduction by Edward Clodd. London: Published for the Folklore Society by D. Nutt, 1893. xv, 702 pp., bibl. Publications of the Folklore Society. XXXVII.
　Folktales and legends.

Gutch, Mrs. E., comp.
Examples of Printed Folklore Concerning Lincolnshire. London: Published for the Folklore Society by D. Nutt, 1908. xxiii, 437 pp. Publications of the Folklore Society LXIII.

————.
Examples of Printed Folklore Concerning the East Riding of Yorkshire. London: Published for the Folklore Society by D. Nutt, 1912. xvii, 235 pp. bibl. Publications of the Folklore Society LXIX.

Examples of Printed Folklore Concerning the North Riding of Yorkshire. London: Published for the Folklore Society by D. Nutt, 1901. xxxix, 447 pp. illus. bibl. Publications of the Folklore Society XLV.

Halliday, W. R.
Folklore Studies, Ancient and Modern. London: Methuen, 1924. xix, 172 pp.

Halliwell, James Orchard
The Nursery Rhymes of England; collected principally from oral tradition. London: T. Richards, 1842. viii, 192 pp. (Percy Society. Early English Poetry, vol. IV. Fifth edition, published in London and New York, F. Warne and Co., 1886. viii, 333 pp. with illustration by W. B. Scott.

————.
Popular Rhymes and Nursery Tales: A Sequel to the Nursery Rhymes of England. London: J. R. Smith, 1849. xi, 276 pp.

Hardwick, Charles
Traditions, Superstitions, and Folklore, (chiefly Lancashire and the north of England:) their affinity to others in widely-distributed localities; their eastern origin and mythical significance. Manchester: A. Ireland & Co. London: Simpkin, Marshall & Co., 1872. xix, 306 pp.

Harland, John
Lanchashire Folk-lore, illustrative of the superstitious beliefs and practices, local customs and usages of the people of the county Palatine. London: F. Warne and Company. New York: Scribner, 1867, xii, 308 pp.

Hartland, Edwin Sidney, ed.
English Fairy and Other Folktales. London: Walter Scott, 1890. xxiv, 282 pp.

————.
Mythology and Folktales; their relation and interpretation. London: D. Nutt, 1900. 53 pp. Popular studies in mythology, romance, and folklore No. 7.

————.
Gloucestershire. Edited with suggestions for the collection of the folk-lore of the country. London: Published for the Folk-lore Society by D. Nutt, 1892, 58 pp. Publications of the Folk-lore Society, XXXVII.

————.
The Science of the Fairytales. An Inquiry into Fairy Mythology. (The Contemporary Science Series). London: Walter Scott. New York: Charles Scribner's Sons, 1911.

Hazlitt, William Carew
English Proverbs and Proverbial Phrases. London: Reeves and Turner, 1907. xxx, 580 pp.

————.
Tales and Legends of National Origin, or Widely Current in England from Early Times, with critical introductions. London: 1892, xv, 486 pp.

Henderson, William
Notes on the Folklore of the Northern Counties of England and the Borders. A new edition with many additional notes. London: Published for the Folklore Society by W. Satchell, Peyton and Company, 1879, xvii, 391 pp. Publications for the Folklore Society II.

Heron-Allen, Edward
Barnacles in Nature and in Myth. London: Oxford University Press, 1928.

Hewett, Sarah
Nummits and Crummits: Devonshire customs, characteristics and folklore. London: 1900, vi, 219 pp.

Hole, Christina
English Folk-lore. New York: Charles Scribner's Sons, 1940. viii, 183 pp., illus., bibl.

————.
Haunted England, a survey of English ghost lore. Illustrated by John Farleigh. London: B. T. Batsford, Ltd., 1940. viii, 183 pp., illus., bibl.

————.
Witchcraft in England. Illustrated by Mervyn Peake. New York: Charles Scribner's Sons, 1947. 168 pp.
"In twelve compact chapters the book surveys the technique of magic, witchcraft in relation to religion, witches and their familiars, the rise of magic cults to the point of political significance, and the practice of divination." (Harry E. Wedeck)

Hope, Robert Charles
The Legendary Lore of the Holy Wells of England. Including Rivers, Lakes, Fountains and Springs. London: Elliot Stock, 1893, illus.

Hull, Eleanor
Folklore of the British Isles. with a preface by R. R. Marett. London: Methuen, 1928. xii, 318 pp. (Methuen's Anthropological Series).

Hunt, Robert
Popular Romances of the West of England; or Drolls, Traditions and Superstitions of Old Cornwall. London: 1871. 2 series in 1 vol., illus.

Jacobs, J., coll.
English Fairytales, (illustrated by John D. Batten). London: D. Nutt, 1898. xiv, II, 261 pp., front, pl. 3rd ed. rev.

More English Fairy Tales. London: David Nutt, 1894. xiv, 243 pp.

Johnson, Walter
Byways in British Archaeology. Cambridge: The University Press, 1912. xii, 529 pp., illus. Includes discussion of burial customs, folklore of the cardinal points, etc.

Kittredge, George Lyman
English Witchcraft and James the First; from Studies in the History of Religion presented to Crawford Howell Toy, by pupils, colleagues and friends. New York: The Macmillan Co., 1912. 65 pp.

Lyell, Thomas R. G.
Slang, Phrase and Idiom in Colloquial English and their Use. Tokyo: The Hokuseido Press, 1931. xxx, 764 pp.+54 pp.

Nance, Robert Morton
Folk-lore Recorded in the Cornish Language. Camborne: The Camborne Printing and Stationery Company, Led., 1923, 24 pp. Folklore of England.

Northall, G. F.
English Folk-Rhymes; a collection of traditional verses relating to places and persons, customs, superstitions, etc. London: K. Paul, Trench, Trubner & Co., 1892. xii, 565 pp., bibl.

Folk-phrases of Four Counties gathered from unpublished mss. and oral tradition. London: Frowde, 1894. 43 pp. (English Dialect Society, Publ. Vol. 73).

Ray, John
A Complete Collection of English Proverbs. Also the most celebrated proverbs of the Scotch, Italian, French, Spanish and other languages. To which is added a collection of English words not generally used. London: 1768. Reprinted in 1857, under the editorship of R. Bohn.

Ritson, Joseph, comp.
Fairy Tales, now first collected: to which are prefixed two dissertations: 1. On pygmies. 2. On fairies. London: Payne and Foss. 1831. vi, 207 pp.

Simpkins, John Ewart, comp.
Examples of Printed Folk-lore Concerning Fife, with some notes on Clackmannan, and Kinross-shires. Introduction by Robert Craig Maclagan, and an appendix from ms. Collections by David Rorie. London: Published for the Folk-lore Society by Sidgewick and Jackson, Ltd. 1914. xxxv, 419 pp., illus. (Publications of the Folk-lore Society, LXXI).

Smith, William, Rev.
Ancient Springs and Streams of the East Riding of Yorkshore: Their topography and traditions. London: Brown, 1923. 186 pp.

Stagg, John
The Minstrel of the North; or, Cumbrian Legends; being a poetical miscellany of legendary, Gothic and Romantic tales. Manchester: The Author, 1816. 352 pp.

Swainson, Charles
The Folklore and Provincial Names of British Birds. Publications of the Folklore Society VIII. London: Published for the Folklore Society by E. Stock, 1886. ii, 243 pp.

Thiselton-Dyer, Thomas Firminger
English Folk-lore. London: D. Bogue, 1880. viii, 290 pp., 2nd ed., rev.

Folk-lore of Women, as illustrated by legendary and traditional tales, folk-rhymes, proverbial sayings, superstitions, etc. London: E. Stock, 1905. xvii, 253 pp.

Tozer, Elias
Devonshire and Other Original Poems; with some account of ancient customs, superstitions, and traditions. Exeter: The Devon Weekly Times, 1873, 94 pp.

Udal, John Symonds
Dorsetshire Folk-lore, with a fore-say by the late William Barnes. Hertford: Stephen Austin & Sons, Ltd., 1922. xi, 406 pp.

Wimberly, Lowry Charles
Folklore in the English and Scottish Ballads. Chicago: University of Chicago Press, 1928. 466 pp.

Wright, Arthur Robinson
British Calendar Customs. Edited by T. E. Lones . . . with a preface by Professor S. H. Hooke. London: Published for the Folk-lore Society, W. Glaisher, Ltd., 1936–1940. 3 vols. (Publications of the Folklore Society CII, CVI).

English Folklore. London: Ernest Benn, Ltd., 1928. Sixpenny Library No. 33.

Wright, Mrs. E. M. (Lea)
Rustic Speech and Folk-lore. London: Milford, 1913. xx, 341 pp., bibl.

FOLKLORE OF SCOTLAND
(A SELECTION)

GENERAL STUDIES AND COLLECTIONS

Banks, Mary Macleod
British Calendar Customs: Scotland . . . With a preface by the Rev. Canon J. A. MacCulloch. London: Published for the Folk-lore Society, by W. Glaisher, Ltd., 1937–41. 3 vols. (Publications of the Folk-lore Society, 100, 104, 108.)
Contents: V. 1. Movable festivals. Harvest. March riding and wapynshaws. Wells. Fairs.— V. 2. The Seasons. The Quarters. Hogmanay. January to May.—V. 3. June to December. Christmas. The Yules.

British Calendar Customs: Orkney & Shetland. London: W. Glaisher . . . , 1946. xii, 110 pp., music. (Folk-Lore Society Publications, Vol. 112).

Barbour, John Gordon
Unique Traditions Chiefly of the West and South of Scotland. London: Hamilton, Adams & Co., 1886. 255 pp.

Black, George Fraser
Examples of Printed Folk-Lore Concerning the Orkney and Shetland Islands. London: Folk-Lore Society, 1903. xii, 277 pp. (Folk-Lore Society, Publications, Vol. 49).

Bryan, J. Jones, and Kerr, E.
"Folklore Objects from Argylshire" *Folk-Lore* (London) 5: 302–303, 1895.

Cameron, Isabel Edith
A Highland Chapbook. Stirling: E. Mackay, 1928. 133 pp.

Campbell, John Francis
Popular Tales of the West Highlands Orally Collected. With a translation. Edinburgh: Edmonston & Douglas, 1860–62. 4 vols. New edition. London: A. Gardner, 1890–93.

Campbell, John Gregorson
Clan Traditions and Popular Tales of the Western Highlands and Islands; Collected from oral sources by the late Rev. John Gregorson Campbell . . . Selected from the author's ms. remains and edited by Jessie Wallace and Duncan MacIsaac, with an introduction by Alfred Nutt . . . London: D. Nutt, 1895. xx, 150 pp., illus. (Waifs and Strays of Celtic Tradition. Argyllshire Series. No. V).

————.
Witchcraft & Second Sight in the Highlands & Islands of Scotland; Tales and Traditions Collected Entirely from Oral Sources . . . Glasgow: J. MacLehose and Sons, 1902. xii, 314 pp.

Campbell, J. L.
"Scottish Gaelic in Canada." *AS* 11 (No. 2): 128–136, 1936.

Chambers, Robert
Popular Rhymes, Fireside Stories, and Amusements of Scotland. Collected by the author of "Traditions of Edinburgh." Edinburgh: W. & R. Chambers, 1842. 76 pp.

————.
Scottish Jests and Anecdotes. To which are added, A Selection of choice English and Irish jests. Edinburgh: W. Tait, 1832. vii, 468 pp.

————.
Traditions of Edinburgh. Edinburgh: W. & C. Tait, 1825. 2 vols.

Cheviot, Andrew
Proverbs, Proverbial Expressions and Popular Rhymes of Scotland with introduction, notes, and parallel phrases. London: A. Gardner, 1896. xii, 434 pp.

Croker, Thomas Crofton
Fairy Legends and Traditions of the South of Ireland. London: J. Murray, 1825–28. 3 vols., illus., music.
Contents: Pt. 1. The Shefro. The Cluricaune.— The Banshee. The Phooka. Tierna na oge.— Pt. 2. The Merrow. The Dullahan. The Firdarrig. Treasure Legends. Rocks and Stones.—Pt. 3. The Elves in Ireland. The Elves in Scotland. On the Nature of the Elves. The Mabinogion and Fairy Legends of Wales.

Cromek, Robert Hartley
Remains of Nithsdale and Calloway Song: With Historical and Traditional Notices Relative to the Manners and Customs of the Peasantry . . . London: T. Cadell and W. Davies, 1810.
Contents: Introduction.—Sentimental Ballads.— Humorous Ballads.—Jacobite Ballads, 1715.— Jacobite Ballads, 1745.—Old Ballads and Fragments.—Appendix: Scottish Fames. A Specimen of the Tender Mercies of Claverhouse, from the Life of Alexander Peden. 'Taking the Beuk.' Description of the Stool of Repentance. History of Witchcraft . . . Character of the Scottish Lowland Fairies . . .

Denham, Michael Ailabie
The Denham Tracts. A Collection of Folklore. Edited by J. Hardy. London: D. Nutt, 1892–95. 2 vols. (Folklore Society Publications, Nos. 29, 35).

Dowman, James
"Superstitions of the Scot." *Westminster Review* (London) 153:61–72, 1900.

Driver, Helen
Tales of the Scottish Clans for Children (and Grown-Ups). Edinburgh: Grant & Murray, 1931. 224 pp., illus.

Edmondston, Rev. B., and Saxby, Jessie M. E.
The Home of a Naturalist. London: J. Nisbet & Co., 189-. 395 pp., illus.
Folklore of Shetland Islands.

Eno, J. N.
"Scottish Clans and Families Represented in America, and the Origin of Names." *Americana* 17:315–352, 1923.

Ferguson, James
"Old Scottish Epithets." *Chamber's Journal* (London) (Series 7.) 3:710–714, 1913.

Fergusson, R. M.
Rambles in the Far North. London: A. Gardner, 1884. vii, 266 pp.
Folklore data of the Northern Highlands.

Forbes, B. C.
499 Scottish Stories for the Price of 500. New York: B. C. Forbes Publishing Company, 1945. 216 pp.
"This pleasant little collection of Scottish tales is a typical variety of jestbook. It restricts its choice to a single theme, in this instance the reputed caution of the Scotch in money matters." (Archer Taylor)

Ford, Robert
Thistledown: A Book of Scotch Humour, Character, Folk-lore, Story & Anecdote. With illustrations by J. Duncan. New York: F. A. Stokes Co., 1891. 463 pp., illus.

Goodrich-Freer, A.
"More Folklore From the Hebrides." *Folk-Lore* (London) 13:29–62, 1902.

Gourie, Gilbert
'Shetland Folk-Lore: Further Tales." *Old-Lore Miscell. of Orkney, Caithness and Sutherland* (London) 5:16–20, 1912.

Grant, Anne (MacVicar)
Essays on the Superstitions of the Highlanders of Scotland . . . London: Longman, Hurst, Rees, Orme, and Brown, 1811. 2 vols.

Grant, Katharine (Whyte)
Myth, Tradition and Story from Western Argyll. Oban: The Oban Times Press, 1925. 112 pp., illus.

Gregor, Walter
"Further Report on Folk-lore in Scotland." *67th Report British Assoc. Adv. Science* (London) ; pp. 456–502, 1898.

———.
Kilns, Mills, Millers, Meal and Bread. London: D. Nutt, 1894. 39 pp.

———.
Notes on the Folk-Lore of the Northeast of Scotland. London: E. Stock, 1881. xii, 238 pp. (Folk-lore Society, Publications, No. 7).

Henderson, George
The Popular Rhymes, Sayings, and Proverbs of the County of Berwick; With illustrative notes . . . New Castle-on-Tyne: The Author, by W. S. Crow . . . 1856. viii, 184 pp.

Henderson, William
Notes on the Folk-lore of the Northern Counties of England and the Borders . . . London: W. Satchell, Peyton and Co., 1879. xvii, 391 pp. (Folk-lore Society Publications, No. 2).

Johnston, James B.
Place-Names of Scotland. London: Murray, 1934. 352 pp. New and Revised Edition.

Karutz, R.
"Eine schottische Rachepuppe." *Globus* 79: 110–11, 1901.

Kilgour, William T.
Lochaber in War and Peace; Being a Record of Historical Incidents, Legends, Traditions, and Folk-Lore . . . Paisley: A. Gardner, 1908. 346 pp., illus.

MacDiarmid, James
"Fragments of Breadalbane Folklore." *Gaelic Soc. of Inverness. Trans. Inverness.* 25:126–148; 26:31–59, 1907–1910.

———.
"Folklore of Breadalbane." *Gaelic Soc. of Inverness. Trans. Inverness* 26:136–156, 1910.

Macdonald, Sheila
"Old-World Survivals in Rossshire." *Folk-Lore* (London) 14:368–384, 1903.

Macfarlane, A. M.
"Sea Myths of the Hebrides." *Inverness Scientific Soc. and Field Club Trans.* 9:360–390, 1918–1925.

MacGregor, Alexander
Highland Superstitions; the druids, fairies, witchcraft, second-sight, hallow'een, sacred wells and locks, with several curious instances of Highland customs and beliefs—with a foreword on superstitions and their origin by Isabel Cameron. Stirling: E. Mackay, 1937. 86 pp., 5th edition.

Mackenzie, Donald Alexander
Scottish Folk-Lore and Folk Life; Studies in Race, Culture and Tradition. London: Blackie & Son Ltd., 1935. ix, 310 pp.

———.
Wonder Tales from Scottish Myth & Legend, with illustrations by John Duncan. London: Blackie & Son, Ltd. 1917. 224 pp., illus.

MacKinlay, James M.
Folklore of Scottish Lochs and Springs. Glasgow: W. Hodge & Co., 1893. xii, 364 pp., bibl.

Maclagan, Robert Craig
Evil Eye in the Western Highlands. London: D. Nutt, 1902. vii, 232 pp.

———.
"Ghost Lights of the West Highlands." *Folk-Lore* (London) 8:203–256, 1897.

———.
"Notes on Folklore Objects Collected in Argyleshire." *Folk-Lore* (London) 6:144–161, 1895.

———.
The Perth Incident of 1396 From a Folk-Lore Point of View. Edinburgh: William Blackwood & Sons, 1905. vii, 403 pp.

———.
Religio Scotia: Its Nature as Traceable in Scotic Saintly Tradition. Edinburgh: O Schulze & Co., 1909. viii, 233 pp.

Macleod, Fiona
"Sea-Magic and Running Water." *Contemporary Review* (London) 82:568–580, 1902.
Superstitious beliefs of Hebrides.

MacPhail, Malcolm
"Folklore from the Hebrides." *Folk-Lore* (London 7:400–404, 1898; 8:380–386, 1899; 9:84–93, 1900.

———.
"Traditions, Customs and Superstitions of the Lewis." (Hebrides) *Folk-Lore* (London) 6: 162–170, 1895.
Further remarks in Vol. 6, pp. 303–304.

McPherson, Joseph McKenzie
Primitive Beliefs in the North-east of Scotland. London: Longmans, Green & Co., 1929. xii, 310 pp., bibl.

Menmuir, Charles
"Folk-Lore in Scottish Ballad Poetry." *Scots Magazine* (London) 23:441–453, 1899.

Miller, Hugh
Scenes and Legends of the North of Scotland; or, The Traditional History of Cromarty. London: Nimmo, 1870. 487 pp., 14th ed.

Morrison, Norman
Hebridean Lore and Romance. Foreword by D. J. Macleod. Inverness: Printed at the "Highland News" Office, 1936. 238 pp.

Napier, James
Folk-lore; or, Superstitious Beliefs in the West of Scotland within this Century, with an appendix showing the probable relation of the modern festivals of Christmas, May Day, St. John's Day, and Hallowe'en, to ancient sun and fire worship. Paisley: Gardner, 1879. vii, 190 pp.

Nicholson, Edward W. B., ed.
Golspie; Contributions to its Folklore . . . London: D. Nutt, 1897. xv, 367 pp.
The materials were collected by a group of former pupils of the Golspie School.

Polson, Alexander
Our Highland Folklore Heritage. Dingwall: G. Souter; Inverness, The "Northern Chronicle" Office, 1926. vi, 167 pp.

Robertson, C. M.
"Folklore from the West of Ross-shire." *Gaelic Soc. of Inverness. Trans.* 26:262–299, 1910.

Rogers, Charles
Traits and Stories of the Scottish People. London: Houlston & Wright, 1867. xvi, 320 pp. (Binder's Title: *Folk Lore–Mythology–Tradition. Scotland.*)

Rorie, David
"Some Superstitions of the Fifeshire Fisher-Folk." *Folk-Lore* (London) 15:95–98, 1904.

Ross, Alexander
"Notes on Superstitions as to Burying Suicides in The Highlands." *Trans. Inverness Scientif. Soc. and Field Club.* 3:286–291, 1883–1888.

Saxby, Jessie M. E.
Birds of Omen in Shetland; with notes on the folklore of the raven and the owl, by W. A. Clouston. Privately Printed, 1893. 32 pp.

————.
Shetland Traditional Lore. Edinburgh: Grant & Murray, Ltd., 1932. 208 pp., illus.

Simpkins, John Ewart, comp.
Examples of Printed Folk-Lore Concerning Fife, With Some Notes on Clackmannan and Kinross-shires . . . London: Sidgwick & Jackson, 1914. xxxv, 419 pp., illus., bibl. (Folk-Lore Society Publications, vol. 71).

Simpson, Evelyn Blantyre
Folk Lore in Lowland Scotland. London: J. M. Dent & Co., 1908. vi, 236 pp.

Sinclair, George
Shetland Fireside Tales; or, The Hermit of Trosswickness. Edinburgh: Edinburgh Pub. Co., 1877. iv, 239 pp.

Spence, Lewis
"The Folklore of Edinburgh." *Nineteenth Century* (London) 102:88–97, 270–281, 1927.

Stewart, Rev. Alexander
'*Twixt Ben Nevis and Glencoe: The Natural History, Legends, and Folk-Lore of the West Highlands.* Edinburgh: W. Paterson, 1885. xv, 384 pp.

Teit, James A.
"Water-Beings in Shetlandic Folk-Lore, as Remembered by Shetlanders in British Columbia." *JAFL* 31:180–201, 1918.

Wilkie, James
Bygone Fife, from Culross to St. Andrews; Traditions, Legends, Folklore and Local History of "The Kingdom." Edinburgh: W. Blackwood & Sons, Ltd., 1931. xiv, 313 pp.

Wimberly, Lowry Charles
Folklore in the English & Scottish Ballads. Chicago: The University of Chicago Press, 1928. xiii, 465 pp., bibl.
"the present investigation relates to religion and magic, that is, to what is labeled 'superstition'."
—Foreword.

The Witch of Inverness and the Fairies of Tomnahurich. Inverness: J. Noble, 1891. 48 pp., illus.

FOLKLORE OF IRELAND

(A SELECTION)

PERIODICALS

Béaloideas; the journal of the Folklore of Ireland Society. Vol. I. 1927. Dublin: illus., plate, port. semi-annual.

Journal of the Irish Folk Song Society. Dublin: 1904.

GENERAL STUDIES AND COLLECTIONS

Andrews, Elizabeth
Ulster Folklore. New York: E. P. Dutton, Co., 1919. xiii, 121 pp., illus.

Argyll, John George
Adventures in Legend, being the last historic legends of the western Highlands. With numerous illustrations by Harrison Miller and Fairfax Muckley. Westminster, London: A. Constable & Co., 1898, xiv, 340 pp., illus.
Gaelic folklore.

Blake, R. Marley
"Folk-Lore with Some Account of the Ancient Gaelic Leeches and the State of the Art of Medicine in Ancient Erin." *County Louth Archaeological Soc. Jour.* (Dundalk) 4:217–225, 1919.

Campbell, John Francis
Popular Tales of the West Highlands, orally collected, with a translation by the late J. F. Campbell. New edition under the auspices of the Islay Association. Paiseley: Gardner, 1862–1890. 4 vols. illus. music, bibl.
Gaelic folklore.

Carbery, Mary
The Farm by Lough Gur; the story of Mary Fogarty (Sissie O'Brien) by Carbery, M.; with an introduction by Shane Leslie and decorations by Corsellis, E. London: Longmans, Green and Co., 1940. xix, 282 pp., illus.
"I . . . was trying to weave the notes, as I received them, into a continuous narrative, here and there filling inevitable gaps and supplying from history, folk-lore and other sources, certain passages which memory gave in shadowy form, or withheld."—Author's Message.

Cassidy, Patrick S.
The Borrowed Bride: a Fairy Love Legend of Donegal. Illustrated by Fred. Morgan, M., Lee, J. G., and others. New York: Holt Brothers, 1892. 255 pp., illus.

Coleman, Marguerite
"Coutumes et Superstitions d'Irlande." *Revue Mondiale.* 142:394:405, 1921.

Cooke, J.
"Notes on Irish Folklore from Connaught, collected chiefly in North Donegal." *Folk-Lore* (London) 7:299–301, 1896.

Croker, T. C.
Fairy Legends and Traditions of the South of Ireland. London: J. Murray, 1825–28. 3 vols. illus.
Contains music

————.
Killarney Legends; Arranged As a Guide to the Lakes. London: H. G. Bohn, 1853. xvi, 294 pp., illus. (Folk-Lore Mythology Tradition. Ireland.)

————.
Legends of the Lakes; or, Sayings and Doings at Killarney. Collected chiefly from the Manuscripts of R. Adolphus Lynch. London: J. Ebers and Co., 1829. 2 vols., illus., Contains music.

Cross, Tom Peete
"An Irish Folk-Tale." *JAFL* 23:419–428. 1910.

Cuchulain
Cuchulain of Muirthemne; the story of the Red Branch of Ulster; arranged and put into English by Lady Gregory. With a preface by W. B. Yeats. London: J. Murray, 1903. xix, 360 pp.
Irish folklore.

Curtin, Jeremiah, coll.
Hero-tales of Ireland. Illustrated by Maurice Day. London: Macmillan and Co., 1894. iii, 558 pp.

————.
Myths and Folk-lore of Ireland. Boston: Little, Brown and Co., 1890. vi, 345 pp.

Delargy, J.
The Gaelic Story-Teller; with some notes on Gaelic folk-tales. London: G. Cumberlege, 1945. 47 pp. (British Academy, London. The Sir John Rhys Memorial Lecture. 1945.) "From the Proceedings of the British Academy, Vol. xxxi."

Doherty, Thomas
"Some Notes on the Physique, Customs, and Superstitions of the Peasantry of Inneshowen, Co., Donegal." *Folk-Lore* (London) 1897. pp. 12–18.

Dottin, Georges
Contes et Légendes d'Irlande tr. du Gaélique. LeHarve: Edition de "LaProvince," 1901. 218 pp.
Irish tales and legends.

Flower, Robin
"Popular Science in Mediaeval Ireland." *Eriu* 9:61–67, 1921.

Franklin, D.
"Cliodhna the Queen of the Fairies of South Munster." *Journal Cork Historical & Archaeological Society* Ser. 2, Vol. 3:81–93, 1897.

Frost, William Henry
Fairies and Folk of Ireland. Illustrated by Sidney Richmond Burleigh. New York: Charles Scribner's Sons, 1900. xvi, 290 pp., illus.

Greene
"County Kildare Folk-Tales." from the Narration of Tom Daly, gardener at Millbrook *Journal County Kildare Archaeological Society* (Dublin) 3:254–259, 1901.

Gregory, Isabella Augusta (Persse) Lady
Gods and Fighting Men; the story of the Tuatha de Danaan, and of the Fianna of Ireland, arranged and put into English by Lady Gregory. With a preface by W. B. Yeats. London: J. Murray, 1904. xxviii, 476 pp.

————.
The Kiltarton History Book. London: T. F. Unwin, Ltd., 1926. viii, 155 pp.
Irish folklore, includes ballads and broadsides.

————.
"Living Legends of the Fianna." Edited by C. Hanbury-Williams. *Monthly Review.* 18 (No. 53):74–92, 1905.

————.
"Living Legends of the Saints." *Monthly Review.* Edited by C. Hanbury-Williams. 21 (No. 62):63–84, 1905.

Visions and Beliefs in the West of Ireland ... With two essays and notes by W. B. Yeats. New York: Putnam, 1920. 2 vols.

Greville-Nugent, Ermengarda
"A Visit to the Wise Woman of Lisclogher." *Nineteenth Century and After.* 54:955–965, 1903.

Haddon, A. C.
"A Batch of Irish Folk-Lore." *Folk-Lore* 4:349–364, 1893.

Henderson, George
Survivals in Belief Among the Celts. Glasgow: J. Maclehose and Sons, 1911. xi, 346 pp.

Hodgson, C. M.
"Folklore Collected in the Neighborhood of Currarevagh" and translated. *Journal Galway Archaeological and Historical Society* 3:17–33, 91–93, 154–165, 1903–04.

Hull, Eleanor
"The Black Pig of Kiltrustan." *Folklore* 29: 226–237, 1918.

"The Silver Bough in Irish Legend." *Folk-Lore* 12:431–445, 1902.

Hyde, Douglas
Beside the Fire; a collection of Irish—Gaelic folk stories. Edited and annotated by D. H., with additional notes by Alfred Nutt. London: D. Nutt, 1890. viii, 203 pp. Irish and English on opposite pages.

Joyce, Patrick Weston
Irish Local Names Explained. Dublin: Hodges, Figgis, and Co., Ltd.
Original Gaelic forms are given, the meanings of some six thousand places are explained, as well as their pronunciation.

Old Celtic Romances. Dublin: Hodges, Figgis, and Co., Ltd.
Thirteen of the most ancient Irish Romantic Tales are translated from the Gaelic.

The Origin and History of Irish Names of Places. Dublin: Hodges. Figgis, and Co., Ltd., 2 Vols.

Kennedy, Patrick
Bardic Stories of Ireland. Dublin: M'Glashan and Gill, 1871. xii, 321 pp.

Fictions of our Forefathers: Fion MacCamhail and his warriors. Dublin: M'Glashan, 1859. 82 pp. Reprinted from the Irish Quarterly Review, No. XXXV., Oct., 1859.

Legendary Fictions of the Irish Celts. London: Macmillan Co., 1866. xiv, 352 pp.

The Fireside Stories of Ireland. Dublin: M'Glashan, 1870. xii, 174 pp.

Larminie, William, ed. and tr.
West Irish Folk-tales and Romances. With introduction and notes, and appendix containing specimens of the Gaelic originals phonetically spelt. London: E. Stock, 1893. xxviii, 258 pp. (The Camden Library).

Lehmacher, Gustav
Heldenland: Keltische Sagen aus Ireland. Koln: Gehly, 1924. 111 pp.
Celtic tales from Ireland.

Lochlain, Colin O.
Irish Street Ballads. London: Constable and Co., 1939.

Lynd, Robert
Home Life in Ireland. With illustrations from photographs. London: Mills & Boon, Ltd., 1909. xii, 317 pp., illus.

McAnally, David Rice, Jr.
Irish Wonders; the ghosts, giants, pookas, demons, leprechawns, banshees, fairies, witches —popular tales as told by the people. Illustrated by H. R. Heaton. Boston: Houghton Mifflin and Co., 1888. xi, 218 pp.
Illustrated, with music.

M'Clintock, Letitia
"Some Superstitions of the Ulster Peasant." *Gentleman's Magazine* (London) 286:221–228, 1899.

McDonagh, Michael
"Irish Charms and Incantations for the Cure of Disease." *Occult Review* (London) 26:161–170, 1917.

MacDougall, James, ed.
Folk and Hero Tales. Introduction by Alfred Nutt, and three illustrations by E. Griset. London: D. Nutt, 1891. xxix, 311 pp.

Folktales and Fairy Lore in Gaelic and English, collected from oral tradition. Introduction and notes by Rev. George Calder. Edinburgh: J. Grant, 1910. xv, 328 pp.
Gaelic and English on opposite pages.

Mac Kay, John G.
More West Highland Tales; transcribed and translated from the original Gaelic by John G. MacKay. Edited by W. J. Watson, Donald Maclean, and H. J. Rose. Edinburgh: Published for the Scottish Anthropological and Folklore Society by Oliver and Boyd, 1940. Vol. 1.
Gaelic and English on opposite pages, contains subject index, and each tale is numbered referring its place in the Aarne-Thompson classification.

M'Kean, E. J.
"Irish Ghost-Lore." *Report and Proceedings Belfast National Historical and Philosophical Society* Session 1904–05: 32–36, 1905.

McManus, Seumas
In Chimney Corners. Merry tales of Irish folk-lore. Illustrated by Pamelia Colman Smith. New York: McClure, Phillips & Co., 1904. xii, 281 pp., illus.

Mahon, Michael P.
Ireland's Fairy Lore. Boston, Mass.: T. J. Flynn & Co., 1919. xv, 219 pp.

Marshall, John J.
Popular Rhymes and Sayings of Ireland. Series 1–2. Dungannon: Tyrone Printing Co., Ltd., 1924–26. 2 Nos.

Mason, Redfern
The Song Lore of Ireland; Erin's story in music and verse. New York: Wessels & Bissell Co., 1910. viii, 329 pp.

O'Connor, Norreys Jephson
Battles and Enchantments; retold from early Gaelic literature. London: Sands, 1924. x, 168 pp.

O'Fatharta, Donnal, coll.
Winter Amusements: or, Beside the Hearth in West Connaught; i.e. Tales, Poems, Songs, Riddles, etc. Baile-atha-Clath. Dublin: 1892. 144 pp.

O'Grady, Standish Hayes
Silva Gadelica (I-XXXI); a collection of tales in Irish with extracts illustrating persons and places. London: Williams and Norgate, 1892. 2 Vols.

O'Hanlon, John C.
"Irish Legendary Lore." *Archaeological International Folk-Lore Association* (Chicago) 1:348–359, 1898. (Congress World's Columbian Exposition.)

O'Rahilly, Thomas Francis, coll.
A Miscellany of Irish Proverbs. Dublin: The Talbot Press, Ltd., 1922. 174 pp.

O'Sheridan, Mary G.
Lays and Ranns from the Folk-Lore of the Gael. Chicago: 1920. 66 pp.

O'Súilleabhain, Seán
A Handbook of Irish Folklore; introductory note by Séamus O'Duilearga. Dublin: Published by the Educational Company of Ireland, Ltd., for the Folklore of Ireland Society, 1942. xxxi, 699 pp.

Omurethi
"County Kildare Folk-Lore about Animals, Reptiles, and Birds." *Journal County Kildare Archaeological Society* 3:179–1885, 1900.

Pim, Herbert Moore
A Short History of Celtic Philosophy. Notes by Prof. Eoin MacNeill. Dundalk: W. Tempest, 1920. 116 pp.

Read, D. H. Moutray
"Folklore and History in Ireland." *Folk Lore* 29:281–304, 1918.

"Some Characteristics of Irish Folklore." *Folk-Lore* 27:250–278, 1916.

Reynolds, James
Ghosts in Irish Houses. New York: Creative Age Press, 1947. 283 pp. illustrated.
> The author has traveled far and wide collecting tales and legends of haunted house and grove. A splendid collection poetically told.

Rhip, John
Celtic Folklore—Welsh and Manx. Oxford: 1901. 2 vols.

Ryan, Rev. John
Essays and Studies Presented to Professor Eoin Macneill . . . edited by Ryan, John. Dublin: The Sign of the Three Candles, 1940. xv, 593 pp., illus.
> Contents: Celtic Languages, Archaeology and Prehistory. Early and Medieval Irish History. Folklore.

Sébillot, Paul
Le Paganisme Contemporain Chez les Peuples Celto-Latins. Paris: O. Doin, 1908. xxvi, 378 pp., bibl.

Sheehan, Rev. Michael
Cnó Coilleadh Craobhaighe. The Irish of the People. Dublin: M. H. Gill & Son, Ltd., 1907. 111 pp., bibl.

Singleton, A. H.
"Dairy Folklore and other notes from Meath and Tipperary." *Folk-Lore* (London) 15: 457–462, 1904.

"Some Old Customs and Superstitions Yet Surviving in County Meath, Ireland." *Gentleman's Magazine* (London) 296:58–69, 1904.

Span, Reginald
"The Mysticism of Ireland." *Occult Review* (London) 25:93–98, 1917.

Squire, Charles
Celtic Myth and Legend, Poetry and Romance. With illustrations in colour and monochrome after paintings by J. H. F. Bacon and other artists. London: The Gresham Publishing Co., Ltd., 1905. xiv, 450 pp.

Stern, L. C.
"Das Märchen von Etain." *Zeitschrift für Celtische Philologie.* (Halle. a.s.) 5:522–534, 1905.

Stokes, Whitley
"The Death of Muirchertach macErca." *Review Celtique* (Paris) 23:395–437, 1902.

"The Songs of Buchet's House." *Review Celtique* (Paris) 25:18–39, 1904.

Wentz, W. Y. E.
The Fairy-Faith in Celtic Countries. London: Frowde, 1911. xxviii, 524 pp.

Westropp, Thomas J.
"A Folklore Survey of County Clare." Folk-Lore (London) 21:180–199, 338–349, 476–487; 22:49–60, 203–213, 332–341, 449–456; 23:88–94, 204–215, 1910–11.

————.
"Notes and Folklore from the Rennes copy of the 'Dindsenchas'." *Journal Royal Society of Antiquaries of Ireland* (Dublin) Ser. 5, Vol. 9:21–27, 1899.

————.
"A Study of thhe Folklore on the Coast of Connacht, Ireland." *Folk-Lore* (London) 29: 305–319; 32:101–123, 1918–1920.

Wilde, Jane Francesca Elgee
Ancient Cures, Charms and Usages of Ireland. Contributions to Irish Lore, by Lady Wilde. London: Ward and Downey, 1890. xi, 256 pp.

————.
Ancient Legends, Mystic Charms & Superstitions of Ireland; with sketches of the Irish past. Boston: Ticknor, 1902. xii, 347 pp.

Wood-Martin, W. G.
Traces of the Elder Faiths of Ireland; a folklore sketch; a handbook of Irish pre-Christian traditions. London: Longmans, Green, and Co., 1902. 2 vols., bibl.

Yeats, William Butler
"Away." *Fortnightly Review* (London) 77 (n.s. 71):726–740, 1902.
Many Irish peasants hold the superstition that people are often enchanted, or under the power of "the fairies" or "the others" and such people are said to be "away."

————.
Fairy and Folktales of the Irish Peasantry. London: W. Scott, and New York: T. Whittaker, 1888. xviii, 326 pp. (Reprinted by Boni & Liveright, N. Y., 1918.)

FOLKSONG

BIBLIOGRAPHIES

Bradley, Rush E.
Background Readings in Music. New York:
H. W. Wilson Company, 1938. 32 pp.
Contains a fairly good listing of American folk
song and dance bibliography.

Buchanan, Annabel Morris
American Folk Music. A Bibliography. Ithaca,
New York: National Federation of Music
Clubs, 1939.

Campbell, Olive Dame
The Southern Highlands; A Selected Bibliography. New York: Bulletin of the Russell
Sage Foundation Library, No. 39, 1920. (February).

Daugherty, D. H.
*A Bibliography of Periodical Literature in
Musicology and Allied Fields and a Record of
Graduate Theses Accepted.* No. 1: October 1,
1938–September 30, 1939. Washington, D. C.:
Compiled for the Committee on Musicology of
the American Council of Learned Societies,
1940.

————.
*A Report on Publications and Research in
Musicology and Allied Fields in the United
States, 1932–1938.* Washington, D. C.: Com-
piled for the Committee on Musicology of the
American Council of Learned Societies, 1938.

Folklore Musical.
Paris: *The Institute,* 1939. 2 volumes, include
bibliography.
Répertoire international des collection et centres
de documentation avec notices sur l'état actuel
des recherches dans les differents pays et references bibliographique.

Henry, Mellinger Edward
*A Bibliography for the Study of American
Folksongs,* with many titles of folksongs (and
titles that have to do with folksongs) from
other lands. London: The Mitre Press, 1937.
142 pp.
"This is not a scientific bibliography" (author's
prefatory note). The edition is limited to 750
copies.

Herzog, George
*Research in Primitive and Folk Music in The
United States.* Bulletin No. 24. Washington,
D. C.: American Council of Learned Societies,
1936. 97 pp.

Holmes, Thomas T., and Thayer, Gordon W.
*English Ballads and Songs in the John G.
White Collection of Folklore and Orientalia.*
Cleveland: At the Cleveland Public Library
and in the Library of Western University, 1931.

Howard, John Tasker
*Our American Music, Three Hundred Years
of It.* New York: Thomas Y. Crowell Company, 1939. 748 pp., illus., bibl. (pp. 683–684)
rev. ed.

Index to Authors and Subjects.
In: *The Musical Quarterly,* for vols. 1–10; New
York: G. Schirmer, Inc. (1915–1924).

Index to the Journal of American Folklore (vol.
1–40). In: *Memoirs of the American Folklore
Society,* vol. 14. New York: G. E. Stechert and
Company, 1930.

Index to the Musical Antiquary.
London (1900–1913). Chicago: Chicago Public Library Omnibus Project, 1941, illus. Federal Works Project— District No. 3.

Lesser, Alexander
"*Bibliography of American Folklore 1915–
1928.*" *JAFL* 41:1–60, 1928; pp. 37–47, 52–60.

"*List of Collectors and Persons* interested in the
Ballad and Folk Song field." *SFQ* 1 (No. 2):
61–73, 1937.

Lomax, Alan, and Cowell, Sidney Robertson
American Folk Song and Folklore, A Regional
Bibliography. New York: Progressive Educa-
tion Association, 1942. 59 pp. Service Center
Pamphlet No. 8.

Magriel, Paul David, comp.
A Bibliography of Dancing. New York: H. W.
Wilson Company, 1936. x, 229 pp. illus.
A list of books and articles on the dance and
related subjects.

Mattfeld, Julius, comp.
The Folk Music of the Western Hemisphere.
New York, 1925: Reprinted with additions,
from the Bulletin of the New York Public
Library, November and December, 1924. 74 pp.
A list of references in the New York Public
Library.

New York (City) Public Library.
*List of works in the New York Public Library
relating to folksongs, folk music, ballads, etc.*
New York: 1907, 40 pp. Reprinted from the
Bulletin, May, 1907.
English Songs and Ballads, pp. 7–14; United
States, pp. 37–40.

O'Brien, John
*Bibliography, Resource Material and Back-
ground Notes on Folk Song, Music and Dance.*
New York: New School for Social Research,
1934. 22 pp.

Payne, L. W., Jr.
"*Recent Research in Balladry and Folk Song.*"
TFSP 8:160–169, 1930.
A brief resumé of the chief publications in
balladry and folk song from 1921.

Scholes, Percy A.
A List of Books About Music in the English Language. London: Oxford University Press, 1940. 64 pp.

Sears, Minnie Earle, ed.
Song Index. An index to more than 12,000 songs in 177 song collections, comprising 262 volumes. New York: The H. W. Wilson Company, 1926. xxxii, 650 pp. Folk song bibliographies (xviii–xxvi).

Song Index Supplement. An index to more than 7000 songs in 104 song collections comprising 124 volumes. New York: The H. W. Wilson Company, 1934. xxxvii, 366 pp. Folk Song Collections (xxiii–xxviii).

Spivacke, Harold
"The Archives of American Folk Song in the Library of Congress." *SFQ* 1:31–36, 1938.

Taylor, Archer
"A Finding List of American Song." *SFQ* 3:17–25, 1937.
Just a sampling under letter "A."

Thompson, Harold W.
A Bibliography of American Folksongs. In: *American Ballads and Folk Songs,* coll. and comp. by John A. and Alan Lomax. (pp. 613–621). New York: The Macmillan Company, 1934.

Thompson, Stith
Motive—Index of Folk-Literature. Bloomington, Indiana: Indiana University, 1932–1935. Indiana University Studies, Numbers 96, 97, 100, 101, 105, 106, 107, 108, 109, 110, 111, 112; also issued as FF Communications Numbers 106–109, 116; 6 volumes.

United States Library of Congress. Music Division.
Copy of Typewritten Lists on American Folk Song Furnished by Oliver Strunk, Chief of Division of Music, Library of Congress. New York, 1936. 100 pp. (New York Public Library).

Check list of recorded songs in the English language in the Archive of American folksong to July, 1940. Alphabetical list with geographical index. Washington, D. C.: Library of Congress, Division of Music, 1942.

PERIODICALS

See: Periodicals under *Folklore,* pp. 4–5.

See *Periodicals* under individual *States, Regions,* and other *Subdivisions* of this Bibliography.

American Folk-Lore Society Memoirs.
New York: G. E. Stechert and Company, 1894. volume 1.

Belden, Henry Marvin
"Folk Song in America, some recent publications." *Modern Language Notes* 34 (No. 3): 139–145, 1919.

Bulletin of the Folksong Society of the Northeast.
Bulletin No. 1–12. Cambridge, Mass.: Powell Printing Co., 1930–37. Music.

California Folklore Quarterly.
Publication of the California Folklore Society, volume 1, 1942. Berkeley and Los Angeles: Published for the California Folklore Society by the University of California Press.

Bulletin of the Kentucky Folklore Society.
Western Kentucky: Western Kentucky State Teachers College.

Canadian Folklore Society.
Ottawa, Canada: Gustave Lanctot, Dominion Archives.

Etude: Music Magazine Monthly. Philadelphia, No. 1, October, 1883.

Folk-Lore Foundation Publications.
Poughkeepsie, New York: Vassar College, 1922–34. Martha Beckwith, editor, Vassar College.

Folk-Lore Primer.
Alabama: Published by the Folklore Committee Alabama Association of Teachers of English.

Folk News.
New York: Folk Festival Council, 222 Fourth Avenue, 1922.

Folk-Say: Edited by B. A. Botkin. Norman, Oklahoma: University of Oklahoma Press, 1930–1931.

Hoosier Folklore Bulletin.
Publication of the Hoosier Folklore Society. Bloomington, Indiana: Indiana University.

Journal of American Folklore, Quarterly No. 1, 1888. Menasha, Wisconsin: Published by the American Folklore Society.

Michigan Folklore Society.
Central Michigan: College of Education.

Musical Quarterly.
New York: G. Schrimer, Inc., 1915–.

New York Folklore Quarterly.
Publication of the New York Folklore Society. Ithaca: Cornell University Press.

North Carolina Folklore Society.
Chapel Hill, North Carolina; University of North Carolina.

Pennsylvania Folklore Society.
Altoona Pennsylvania: H. V. Shoemaker, Pres. Box 431.

Publications of the Pennsylvania Folklore Society.
Pennsylvania: Pennsylvania—German, Muhlenberg College.

Publications of the Texas Folklore Society.
Austin, Texas: University of Texas, volume 1 (1916), volumes II (1923), since then about about a volume every year.

Southern Folklore Quarterly.
Florida: Publication of the Southeastern Folklore Society, University of Florida.

Tennessee Folklore Society Bulletin.
Tennessee: Publication of the Tennessee Folklore Society, Susan B. Riley, Peabody College.

The French Folklore Bulletin.
Publication of the French Folklore Society, 320 West 86th Street, New York 24, New York.

Virginia Folklore Society.
Virginia: University of Virginia.

West Virginia Folklore Society.
West Virginia: West Virginia University.

Wisconsin Folktale Booklets.
Madison, Wisconsin: Publication of the Wisconsin Folklore Society, State Historical Museum.

GENERAL STUDIES

Aldrich, Richard
Folk Songs in America. In: *Musical Discourse,* pp. 56–72. New York: Oxford University Press, 1928, 305 pp.

"The American Folk Song."
The Spectator (London) 125:845–846, 1927.

"American Folk-Songs."
Nation 91:561–562, 1910.

"American Folk-Songs. Deplorable Lack of Typical Folk-Songs." *Music* 1 (No. 17):7, 1912.

"American-English Folksongs." (Cecil J. Sharp).
Musical Courier 77 (No. 9):37, Aug. 29, 1918.
Review and criticism.

Barry, Phillips
"American Folk Music." *SFQ* 1 (No. 2):29–49, 1937.

———.
"The Collection of Folk-Song." *JAFL* 27:77–78, 1915.

———.
"Das Volk Dichtet Nicht." *BFSSNE* 7:4, 1934.

———.
"Folk Music in America." *JAFL* 22:72–81, 1909.

———.
Folk Music in America. W.P.A. Federal Theatre Project. Publication No. 80S. Introduction by George Herzog. New York: National Service Bureau, 1939. 113 pp., Appendix, bibl.

———.
"Notes on the Ways of Folk Singers with Folk Tunes." *BFSSNE* 12:2–6, 1937.

———.
"The Origin of Folk Melodies." *JAFL* 23:440–445, 1910.

———.
"Some Aspects of Folk Song." *JAFL* 25:274–283, 1912.

———.
"Some Traditional Songs." *JAFL* 18:49–59, 1905.
Text and Music.

———.
"The Transmission of Folk-Song." *JAFL* 27:67–76, 1914.

Belden, Henry Marvin
"The Study of Folk Songs in America." *Modern Philology* 2:573–579, 1905.

Bellows, J. McClure
"America's National Music." *Opera Magazine* 3 (No. 8):13–14, 1916.

Birchard, C. C.
"American, A Treasure House of Folk Music." *Musician* 36:7, (September) 1931.

Boas, Franz
"Music and Folk-Lore." In: *General Anthropology:* 609–626. Boston: D. C. Heath and Company, 1938.

Boggs, Ralph Steele
"La recollección de la Musica folklorica en el Nuevo Mundo." *BLAM* 5:221–224, 1941 (published 1942).
"Brief statement of basic rules folkmusic collector would follow, on advantages of sound film and precise transcription, and on urgency of developing a standard system of classification" (Boggs).

Botkin, B. A.
"The Archive of American Folk-Song: Retrospect and Prospect." *Library of Congress Quarterly Journal* 2: (3 and 4) 61–69, 1945 (June).

Broadwood, Lucy E.
"English Folksong." *Monthly Journal of the International Musical Society* 6:497–499, 1905 (Leipzig).

Bronson, Bertrand H.
"Folksong and the Modes." *MQ* 32 (No. 1):37–49, 1946.

Cavendish, J. C.
"Folk Tunes as Materials for Music." *American Mercury* 4:79–82, 1925 (January).

"Cecil Sharp and American Folk Music." *Music Clubs Magazine* 14 (No. 4):17, March–April, 1935.

Clough, W. O.
"Has American Folklore A Special Quality." *SFQ* 8:115–121, 1944.

Combs, Josiah H.
"Dialect of the Folk-Song." *Dialect Notes* 4 (Part 5):311–318, 1916.

―――.
Folk-Songs du Midi des États-Unis. Paris VI: Les Presses Universitaires de France, Librarie, J. Gambrier, rue Danton, 1925.
A critical study in French of the folk-song and its status in America.

Crawford, Caroline
"The Drama of Life in the Lyrics of a Folk." *Nat'l. Educ. Assoc. Journ. of Proc.*, 1916, pp. 680.

Curtis-Burlin, Natalie
"Folk-Music of America." *Craftsman* 21:414–420, 1912.

Darkow, Martin
"Stephen Foster und das Amerikanische Volkslied." *Die Musik* 4 (No. 16):268–280, 1905.

Davis, Arthur Kyle, Jr.
"Some Recent Trends in the Field of Folk-Song." *SFQ* 1 (No. 2):19–25, 1937.

Dyson, G.
"The Place of Folk-Song in Music." In: *Cecil Sharp* by A. H. Fox-Strangways, Appendix A, pp. 213–216. London: Oxford University Press, 1933, 233 pp.

Elson, Louis Charles
"American Folk Song." *Musician* 17:816–817, 1912.

―――.
History of American Music. New York: The Macmillan Company, 1925. xiii, 423 pp., rev. ed., bibl.
Includes discussion of folk music.

Engel, Carl
An Introduction to the Study of National Music. Comprising Researches into Popular Songs, Traditions and Customs. London: Longmans, Green, Reader, and Dyer, 1866. x, 435 pp., bibl. (pp. 371–421).

―――.
"Review of: *American Ballads and Folksongs,* by John and Alan Lomax." *MQ* 21:107–112, 1935.

Farwell, Arthur
"The Relation of Folksong to American Musical Development." *Proceedings Music Teachers National Association*, pp. 197–205, 1907.

―――.
"The Influence of Folk Song upon Classical Music."—*International Quarterly* (Burlington, Vt.) 7:32–44, 1903.

Fawcett, Waldon
"Collecting American Versions of Old World Folk Songs." (Interview with C. Alphonso Smith.) *Musical America* 19 (No. 23):3, 1914.

Frankenstein, Alfred V.
"George Alley—a Study in Modern Folk-Lore." *Musical Courier* 104 (No. 16):6, April 16, 1932.

Fulling, Katherine Painter
"The Sacred Harpers: An American Phenomenon." *Musical America* 57 (No. 3):205, Feb. 10, 1937.

Gates, W. F.
"Wanted—Original National Music." *The Musician* 8:257, 1903.

Gilbert, Douglas
Lost Chords: The Diverting History of American Popular Songs. Garden City, New York: Doubleday Doran and Company, 1942, 377 pp.
The Song Hit Parade of Eighty Years, between 1860 and today. Text only. The influence of the folk permeate a lot of the material presented.

Gibbon, J. M.
"Meanings of Folk-Song Change Through The Ages." *Musician* 32:56, 1927 (December).

Gordon, Robert Winslow
"American Folksongs." *Caravan* (Washington, D. C.) 1, (No. 2):15–17, 1939.

―――.
Folk Songs of America. W.P.A. Federal Theatre Project. Publication No. 73-S. New York: National Service Bureau, 1938. Fifteen articles reprinted from *The New York Times*, 1927–1928.

Grainger, Percy.
"The Impress of Personality in Unwritten Music." *MQ* 1:416–435, 1915.

Grew, Sidney
"National Music and the Folk-Song." *MQ* 7:172–185, 1921.

Halpert, Herbert
"American Folk-Songs." *American Music Lover* 3, (No. 11):414–416, 1938 (March).

―――.
"Suggestions for the Collector." *HFB* 5 (No. 1):42–43, 1946.

―――.
"The folksinger speaks." *HFB* 3:29–35, 48–55, 1944.

Hazard, Lucy Lockwood
In Search of America. New York: Thomas Y. Crowell, 1930. xxv, 586 pp.
Part III is a discussion of folk song and folktale.

Heck, J. O.
"Folk Poetry and Folk Criticism." *JAFL* 40:1–77, 1928.

Herzog, George
"America's Heritage of Folk-Song." *Musical America* 59:6, 1939.
General introductory discussion.

Research in Primitive and Folk Music in the United States, a survey. Washington, D. C.: American Council of Learned Societies, 1936. IV, 97 pp. (American Council of Learned Societies, bulletin No. 24, April, 1936), bibl.

Holliday, Carl
"American Folk Songs." *Sewanee Review* 27: 139–150, 1919.

Howard, John Tasker
Our American Music, three hundred years of it. New York: Thomas Y. Crowell Co., 1939. 748 pp., illus., bibl. 2nd ed., rev. and enlarged. Chapter XV: Our Folk Music (pp. 404–462).

Our Contemporary Composers, American Music in the 20th Century. New York: Thomas Y. Crowell Company, 1943. 447 pp.
Includes discussion of Folk Song and racial expressions: from Indian sources, the Anglo-Saxon heritage, and Negro composers.

"Our Folk-Music and Its Probable Impress on American Music of the Future." Casual Remarks by Way of Survey. *MQ* 7:167–171, 1921.

"Our American Music. No. 29—Other Folk-Songs in America." *Voice of the Air* 2 No. 9): 6, 1930.

Howes, Frank
"Recent Work in Folk-Music." *Musical Association Proc.* (Leeds), 1937–1938, pp. 39–69.

Hudson, Arthur Palmer
Folk Songs of the Whites. In: *Culture of the South,* (pp. 519–547). Chapel Hill, North Carolina: University of North Carolina Press, 1935.
Discussion of old world ballads and songs.

Hull, A. E.
"Folk Element in Music." *Etude* 46:661–662, 1928.

Jackson, George P.
"America's Folk Songs." *Virginia Quarterly* 12:34–42, 1936.

"Why Does American Folk Music Spread So Slowly." *TFSB* 9:1–3, 1945.

Kidson, Frank, and Neal, Mary
English Folksong and Dance. Cambridge: Cambridge News Press, 1925. 178 pp. Music in text. Bibliography.

Kinscella, Hazel Gertrude
History Sings: Backgrounds of American Music. New York: The University Publication Company, 1940.

Knorr, R. M.
"Even Beethoven Took a Page from Our Musical Book. John Powell Sees American Folk Music as Mine of Material for Composers." *Musical America* 50 (No. 5) :8, March 10, 1930.

Lange, Francisco Curt
"Suma de las relaciones interamericanos en el campo de la música." *BLAM* 5:11–22, 1941 (published 1942).
"Excellent statement on music's part in development of a truly new world culture based on new world tradition, serving as foreword to this magnificent 638 page volume dedicated chiefly to U. S. A." (Boggs).

Lemmon, Blanche
"American folk-songs." *Etude* 58 (No. 4) :220, 274, 1940.

Leonard, F., and Sullivan, M.
"How People are Swayed by Song." *Etude* 57: 627–628, 1939 (October).

Lewis, Leo R.
"American Folksongs." *Etude* 24:769, 1906.

Lindsay, Charles
"The Nomenclature of the Popular Song." *AS* 3 (No. 5) :369–374, 1928.

Lloyd, A. L.
The Singing Englishman. An introduction to folksong. London: Worker's Music Association, Ltd. n.d. 69 pp., bibl.
A general discussion of the various types of folksongs.

"Library of Congress Making Collection of American Folk Songs." *Music Trades* 79 (No. 10) :14, Oct., 1931.

Lomax, Alan
"American Folk Music in Radio Broadcasts." *MTNA* Proceedings, Ser. 36:58–61, 1941.

"Archive of American Folk Song." *JAFL* 56: 59–61, 1943.
A summary of the Report of Alan Lomax, assistant in charge of the Archive of American Folk Song, prepared as part of the annual report of the Music Division of the Library Congress for the fiscal year 1941–1942. An extremely valuable summary of the doings of the Library and research work in various fields of American folk song.

"Folk Music of America." In: *Teacher's Manual and Classroom Guide for the American School of the Air.* New York: Columbia Broadcasting System, 1940–1941.

Lomax, John A.
Adventures of a Ballad Hunter. New York: The Macmillan Company, 1947. 302 pp. illus.
A life-time of experiences in collecting American folklore and folksongs by this country's outstanding collector. The folk singers he met and some of the songs (texts only) they sang.

Lummis, Charles F.
"New Mexican Folk-songs." *Cosmopolitan* 13: 720–729, 1892.
With music.

McGohan, H. M.
"Original American Folk Music." *Etude* 60: 527, 1942 (August).

MacIlwaine, H. C.
"The Educative Influence of Folk Music." *Universal Review* (London) 6:282–291, 1908.

MacLeish, Archibald
"Sound Laboratory in the Library of Congress." *The Caecilia* 68 (No. 6) :224–225, 1940.

M., J.
"Song Hunting in the Southern Mountains." *Musical Courier* 92 (No. 7) :45, Feb. 18, 1926.

Mark, J.
"Recollections of Folk-Musicians." *MQ* 16: 170–185, 1930.

Marks, Alfred T.
"Congress Library Collecting American Folk Songs." *Musical America* 51 (No. 13) :15, Aug., 1931.

Martin, H. F.
"Where Is Our National Music?" *Musical Digest* 10 (No. 3) :3, May 4, 1926.

Martinengo-Cesaresco, Countes E.
The Study of Folk Songs. London: G. Redway, 1886. xl., 395 pp.

Mason, Daniel Gregory
"Folk-Song and American Music." (A Plea for the Unpopular Point of View.) *MQ* 4:323–332, 1918.

Mason, Redfern
"American Folk-Music." *The Sackbut* 6 (No. 9) :237–239, 1926.

Mathews, W. S. B.
"Have We An American Folk Music?" *Violinist* 13 (No. 3) :21–22, 1912.

Metfessel, M.
"Collecting of Folksongs by Phonophotography." *Science* (n.s.) 67:28–31, 1928 (January).

Miles, Emma Bell
"Some Real American Music." *Harper's Monthly Magazine* 109:118–123, 1904.
Discussion of American folk song.

Modern Language Association of America
Popular Literature Section, Committee on Folksong. *Report of the Committee on Folksong of the Popular Literature Section of the Modern Language Association of America.* Gainesville, Fla.: The University of Florida in cooperation with the Southeastern Folklore Society, 1937. 73 pp. (Southern Folklore, quarterly, Vol. 1, No. 2, June, 1937.)

Morgan, A. L.
"Folk Music On the Air." *Etude* 58:158, 1940 (March).

"Music and Geography."
Musician 42:158, 1937 (September).

"Music and Nationalism."
Musician 44:14, 1939 (January).

Music of the New World.
Course 1, 2. Folkways in Music Handbooks. Volumes 1, 2, 3. New York: Southern Music Publishing Company (1619 Broadway) 1942–43–44.
Published for the National Broadcasting Company; Broadcast series of NBC Inter-American University of the Air. Bibliographies, record lists for each topic covered.

Newcomb, Mary
"Dixie Girl Assembles American Folk Songs." *Washington Post*, Sunday, Oct. 26, 1930.

Newell, W. W.
"Studies in Folk-Song and Popular Poetry." *JAFL* 8:94, 1897.
A review.

Newman, Ernest
"The Folk-Song Fallacy." *English Review* (London) 11:255–268, 1912.

Officer, H.
"Place of the Folk-Song in Modern Music." *Musician* 34:12, 1929 (October).

Payne, L. W., Jr.
"Recent Research in Balladry and Folk Songs." *TFSP* 8:160–169, 1930.
A brief resumé of the chief publications in balladry and folk song from 1921.

Pound, Louise
American Ballads and Songs. New York: Charles Scribner's Sons, 1922. xxxvi, 266 pp.

Powell, John
"How America Can Develop a National Music." *Etude* 45 (No. 5) :349–350, May, 1927.

———.
"Virginia Finds Her Folk-Music." *Musical Courier* 104 (No. 17) :6–7, 10, April 23, 1932.

Read, E. M. G.
"English Folk Songs in America." *Music Student London* 11 No. 8) :291–293, April, 1919.

Report of the Committee on Folksong of the Popular Literature Section of the Modern Language Association of America. *SFQ* 1 (No. 2) :1–73, 1937.
Gives a valuable list of collectors and persons interested in the ballad and folksong field. (pp. 61-73).

Roberts, Helen H.
"Suggestions to Field-Workers in Collecting Folk Music and Data About Instruments." *Journal of the Polynesian Society* 40 (No. 3) : 103–128, 1931.

Robinson, Frances
"Folk Music." *Current Literature* 30:350–351, 1901.

Root, Frederick W.
"Folk-Music." *Archives International Folk-Lore Association* 5:424–437, 1898. Chicago: Congress of the World's Columbian Exposition.

Sandburg, Carl
"Songs of the Old Frontiers. Words, Melodies With Essays." *The Country Gentleman,* April, 1927.

Scarborough, Dorothy
A Song Catcher in Southern Mountains: American Folk Songs of British Ancestry. New York: Columbia University Press, 1937. xvi, 476 pp., illus., music.

Schell, Otto
Das Volkslied. Leipzig: Heims, 1908. vii, 204 pp. (Handbücher zur volkskunde, III.)

Seeger, Charles
Folk Music as a Source of Social History. In: *The Cultural Approach to History* by Caroline F. Ware, ed. New York: Columbia University Press, 1940.

————.
"Importance to Cultural Understanding of Folk and Popular Music." *Musica viva* (organo oficial de la editorial cooperativa interamericana de compositores, Montevideo 1:3–5, 1942.

————.
"La Musica en los Estada Unidos." *BLAM* 5: 229–234, 1941.
Published 1942.

————.
"Oral and Written Traditions in the Americas." *Bulletin of the Pan-American Union* 79:290–293, 341–344, (May–June) 1945.
A discussion of the nature of folk-music.

Sharp, Cecil J.
English Folk-Song; Some Conclusions. London: Simpkin and Company, 1907. 143 pp.
Music in text.

Shearin, H. G.
"Kentucky Folk Songs." *Musical Monitor and World,* April 1914, pp. 212–223.

Siegmeister, Elie, ed.
The Music Lover's Handbook. New York: W. Morrow and Company, 1943. xiii, 817 pp., music.
The editor discusses folk songs and ballads in the section—"Fiddle Strings and Ballads."

Smith, E. C.
"Folk Song Exerts Universal Appeal." *Musician* 44:144, 1939 (September).

Smith, Reed
American Folksong. In: *International Encyclopedia of Music,* by Oscar Thompson, ed. New York: Dodd, Mead and Company, 1938.

"Songs of America."
Scholastic 32:9, 1938 (April 30).

"Songs of the U. S."
Time 33:46, 1939 (May 22).

Spofford, Ainsworth R.
"The Lyric Element in American History." *Columbia Historical Society Records,* vol. 7, 1904.

Stanley-Brown, Katherine (Oliver)
The Song Book of the American Spirit; illustrated by Rudolph Stanley-Brown. New York: Harper & Brothers, 1927. viii, 28 nos., illus.

Stegmeier, Henri
The Dance of Death in Folk-Song; With an Introduction on the Dance of Death. Chicago: The University of Chicago Libraries, 1939. iii, 231 pp.

Sternberg, Constantin
"National Music of the U.S.A." *Outlook* 85: 626, 1907.

————.
"What is American Music?" *Etude* 22:190, 1904.

Surette, Thomas Whitney
Syllabus of the Course of Five Lectures on National Music—Songs of the People. New York City: Education Department, 189–.

Taubman, Howard
"Our Folksongs." *New York Times Magazine:* 14–15, 1941 (June 8). Illustrated.

"The Study of Folk Songs in America."
Modern Philology 2:573–629, 1905.

Thomas, Jean
"The American Folk Song Festival." *AS* 10 (No. 1):36–37, 1935.

Tiersot, Julien
"Musical Ethnography in America." *The Musician* 12 (Nos. 2–3), 1907.

Tomás, Guillermo M.
Invincible America. The National Music of United States in Peace at War. Havana: "El Siglo XX," 1919, 205 pp., illus.
Instrumental and vocal concerts. Illustrated with photographic projections, engravings, historical comments, and musical examples.

Van Vechten, Carl
In the Garret. New York: Alfred A. Knopf, 1920.
Discusses American folksongs.

Walker, Conway
The Folk Song and Dance, and the voice as solo instrument. New York: The Caxton Institute, 1926. 101 pp.
Folk Songs of America (pp. 62–67).

West, S.
"Americans Want American Music!" interview with E. Siegmeister. *Etude* 62:28, 1944 (January).

Wheaton-Smith, Barbara
"Recorded Folksongs." *JAFL* 59:319–320, 1946.

Wheeler, Edith
"My Experience of Folk-Song Collecting."
Donahoe's Magazine 5:448–454, 1904, (Boston).

Williams, Alfred Mason
Studies in Folk-Song and Popular Poetry. With a prefatory note by Edward Clodd. London: E. Stock, 1895.

Williams, Iolo Aneurin
English Folk-Song and Dance. New York: Longmans, Green and Company, 1935. 200 pp. The English Heritage Series.

————.
"Notes on a Small Collection of Folk-Songs." *London Mercury* 4:35–47, 1921.

Williams, Ralph Vaughan
"Folk Song." In: *Encyclopaedia Britannica*, Vol. 9, pp. 447–448, 1936. 14th edition.

————.
National Music. New York: Oxford University Press, 1935. 146 pp.

Wilson, Katherine M.
Mint Sauce. Being Essays Chiefly on Music to Enlighten the Ignorant and Amuse the Enlightened. London: Peter Daires, 1927. 206 pp.
Chapter IV. Folk Song. A discussion of the general nature of folksong.

SPECIAL STUDIES

Anderson, Arthur Olaf
"Geography and Rhythm." *University of Arizona Bulletin* 8 (No. 8): *Fine Arts Bulletin* 2: Tucson, Arizona: 1935.
The musical influence of geographical location on rhythm.

Arlt, Gustave Otto
Status of Research in Folk Melodies. Chicago: The University of Chicago, 1929.
Master's Dissertation.

Barlow-Smith, Constance
"The Educational Value of the Folksong." In: *Journal of Proceedings and Addresses of the 48th Annual Meeting*, pp. 818–822. Boston, Mass.: National Education Association of the United States, July 2–8, 1910.

Bauer, Marion
"Contemporary trends in choral composition." *American Music Lover* 5 (No. 6):198–202, 1939.
The influence of folk music on choral writings.

Bayard, Samuel P.
"Aspects of Melodic Kinship and Variation in British-American Folk Tunes." In: *Papers Read at the International Congress of Musicology*. (pp. 122–130). New York: American Musicological Society, 1944.

Botkin, B. A.
"American Songs for American Children." *Music Educators Journal* 30 (3):24–25, 1944.
Words and music to Jenny Jenkins and John Henry, prepared by the M.E.N.C. Committee on Folk Music of the United States.
Continued in MEJ 30:4: 39, 1944.
Includes words and music for: Captain Jinks, Down in the Valley, My Lover is a Sailor Boy, and So Long, It's Been Good to Know You.
Continued in MEJ 30:5: 27, 1944.

Brands, Pearl Brown
"Music Popular at the Time of Lincoln." *Etude* 52 (No. 4):223–224, 1934. Illus.

Bronson, Bertrand H.
"Folksong and the Modes." *MQ* 32:37–49, 1946.

Buchanan, Annabel Morris
"Modal and Melodic Structure in Anglo-American Folk Music—A Neutral Mode." In: *Papers Read at the International Congress of Musicology*. New York: American Musicological Society, 1944. pp. 84–112.

Butterfield, Roger
"Folk Singer, John Jacob Niles Makes Rare Music from the Songs and Ballads of Early America." *Life* 15:57–60, 1943 (September 6).

Chase, Gilbert
"Folk Music on Records." *MJ* 6 (No. 1):15, 58–59, 1948.
A general discussion of the outstanding albums of American folksongs and dances.

Combs, Josiah H.
"Dialect of the Folk Song." *Dialect Notes* 4: 311–318, 1916.

Clark, Edgar Rogie
"Problems of Folk Song Interpretation." *Musical America* 68 (No. 4):37, 1948.
The element of simplicity and directness is emphasized. Avoid unnecessary embellishments in vocal delivery and in arrangements.

Davis, Arthur K. Jr.
"Four Articles." *University of Virginia News Letter:* April 1, 1931; February 1, 1932; November 15, 1934; March 1, 1935. University of Virginia, Virginia.

Erskine, John
"More Music in Small Towns." *Magazine Art* 31:264–265, 1938.

Ewen, David
"When We Were Musically Young." *American Mercury* 53:161–167, 1941.

Fillmore, J. C.
"Forms Spontaneously Assumed by Folk-Songs." *Illustrated Review of Reviews* 16:203–204, 1893 (August 12).

"Folk Songs in the Making."
Literary Digest 101:27, 1929 (April 13).

"Folk Songs in the White House." *Time* 37:57, 1941 (March).

Gary, R.
"Sentiment vs. Sentimentality." *Etude* 54:755–756, 1936.

Gomme, G. L.
"Songs of Labour." *Cornhill Magazine* (Smith, Elder and Company, London) 105: 646–659, 1912.

Guichard, Arthur de
"Need for American Folksongs as Basis for Musical Education." *Musical America* 17 (No. 4):22, 1912.

Halpert, Herbert
"Federal Theatre and Folksong." *SFQ* 2 (No. 2):81–87, 1938.

————.
"Folksong and the Dance." *American Music Lover* 4 (No. 2):51–53, 1938 (June).

————.
"The Popular Publication of Folk Songs." *American Music Lover* 2 (No. 8):247–248, 1936 (December).

————.
"Some American Folk Songs." *American Music Lover* 3 (No. 9):332–334, 1938 (January).

————.
"La techinca para la grabacion de Canciones folkloricas." *BLAM* 5:177–183, 1941 (published, 1942).

Hanson, Howard
"Music Made in America, Past and Future." *Musician* 45:138, 1940 (August).

Harris, Clement Antrobus
"Music in the World's Proverbs." *MQ* 19:382–393, 1933.
    The various instruments mentioned in proverbs; gives a comparative table of seventeen different instruments mentioned in proverbs.

Hart, William J.
Stories of Our National Songs. Boston: A. Wilde Company, 1942. 70 pp.

Hastings, W.
"Longfellow's Influence on Musical Composition." *Etude* 55:433–434, 1937 (July), illustrated.

Heck, J. O.
"Folk Poetry and Folk Criticism" *JAFL* 40:1–77, 1927.

Herzog, George
"Musical Typology in Folksong." *SFQ* 1:49–57, 1937.

————.
"The Study of Folksong in America." *SFQ* 2 (No. 2):59–65, 1938.

Hofmann, Charles
"United We Sing." *Junior Natural History Magazine* (New York) 21:11, March, 1945.
    Music, text and translation, etc., of one folksong each month from various regions.

Howard, John T.
"Native Elements in American Music." *American Scholar* 4:325–335, 1934.

Hubbard, William Lines
Popular Music. In: *The American History and Encyclopedia of Music.* Toledo, Ohio: Irving Squire, 1908, Vol. IV, pp. 71–99.

Hustvedt, S. B.
Ballad Books and Ballad Men. Raids and Rescues in Britain, America and the Scandinavian North, since 1800. Cambridge, Massachusetts: Harvard University Press, 1930.

Jackson, George Pullen
"Sing, Brother, Sing!" *TFSB* 9 (No. 4):1–3, 1945 (May).
    The flood of song cannot be stopped!

————.
"Some Enemies of Folk Music in America." In: *Papers Read at the International Congress of Musicology* (pp. 77–84). New York: American Musicological Society, 1944.

Justus, May
Mr. Songcatcher and Company. New York: Doubleday, Doran Company, 1940.

Kerby, M.
"Recapturing America's Folk Music." *Theatre Monthly* 53:44, 1931 (February).

"Keystone of Our Nation," homemade music, illustrated. *Etude* 58:77, 1940 (February).

Kinkeldey, Otto
"The Influence of Folk-Music on the Progress of Art." *MSNC* (9th Annual Meeting); 37–45, 1916.

————.
"The Influence of Folk Song Upon Artistic Practice." *MTNA* 10:273–287, 1915.

Knott, Sarah Gertrude
"I Hear America Singing," illustrated. *Survey Graphic* 28:229–235, 1939 (March).

————.
"The National Folk Festival—its Problems and Reasons." *SFQ* 3:117–124, 1939.

Kolisch, M.
"Nation Has Been Singing." *Independent* 114:701, 1925 (June).

Kolodin, Irving
"Folk Songs; Variations on a Theme." *Theatre Arts Monthly* 19:129–136, 1935 (Feb.).

Landowska, Wanda
"Discovering the Riches in Old Music," edited by D. Ewen. *Etude* 58:81–82, 1940 (February).

Le Massena, C. E.
"Challenge to American Musician." *Musician* 45:6, 1940.

Lomax, John A.
"Field Experiences with Recording Machines." *SFQ* I (No. 2):57–61, 1937.

—————.
"Some Types of American Folksong." *JAFL*
28:1–17, 1915.

Lyons, John Henry
Stories of our American Patriotic Songs. New
York: The Vanguard Press, 1942. 72 pp.

Mark, Jeffrey
"Recollections of Folk Musicians." *MQ* 16:
170–185, 1930.
   The author's experiences and reminiscences in
   the Southern Highlands.

Mason, Daniel Gregory
"Folk-songs in America—Mr. Howard Brock-
way's settings." *Arts and Decoration* (New
York) 14:122, 168, 1920.

McGill, Anna Blanche
"Irish Characteristics in our Old Song Sur-
vivals." *MQ* 18:106–120, 1932.
   Eleven tunes included.

Mead, Mrs. M. Janet Curler
Through the Year with American Music, A
collection of sketches and programs for groups
interested in presenting American music. Oxford, Ohio: The House Publication, 1941.

Mendel, Arthur
"What is American Music?" *Nation* 134:524,
1932.

Metfessel, M.
"Collecting of Folk-Songs by Phonophotography." *Science* (n.s.) 67:28–31, 1928 (January 13).

Miles, Emma Bell
"Some Real American Music." *Harper's Magazine* 99:118–123, 1904.

"Music Marches On."
Musician 44:178, 1939 (October).

Music of the New World.
   Handbook 1: 1942, 1943. Broadcast series of
   the Inter-American University of the Air. A
   public service feature of the National Broadcasting Company. (Research director and
   author of the handbook Gilbert Chase, Music
   Division, Library of Congress) 52 pp. New
   York: Published for the National Broadcasting Company by the Southern Music Publishing Company, Inc., 1942.

"Old Forgotten, far-off Things."
Literary Digest 113:17, 1932 (May 28).

"Our Unsung Idiom."
Literary Digest 88:31, 1926 (February 20).

Pound, Louise
The term "Communal." *PMLA* 39: 440–455,
1924.

Powell, John
"Value of Our Musical Tradition." Illustrated.
Magazine of Art 30:292–293, 1937 (May).

Pynn, N. A.
"American Music, what of it and why not?"
Musician 41:170, 1936 (Nov.).

Report of the Committee in Folksong of the
Popular Literature Section of the Modern
Language Association of America. *SFQ* 1 (No.
2) :1–73, 1937.

Robbins, L. H.
"Our History Written in Song." Illustrated.
New York Times Magazine: 16, 1941 (March
2).

Rosenfeld, Paul
"Folksong and Culture-Politics." *Modern
Music* 17 (No. 1) :18–24, 1939.
   The author compares contemporary increasing
   interest in folksongs in America with similar
   movements in the late 18th Cent. in Germany
   and in the 1860's in Russia.

"Second National Folk Song Festival."
Newsweek 5:20, 1935 (May 18).

Seeger, Charles
Folk Music as a Source of Social History. In:
The Cultural Approach to History, edited for
the American Historical Association by Caro-
line F. Ware, (pp. 316–324). New York:
Columbia University Press, 1940.

—————.
"Grass Roots For American Composers."
Modern Music 16 (No. 3) :143–149, 1939.

Simon, R. A.
"American Music Everywhere." *New Yorker*
16:66, 1940 (March 30).

"Songs We Used to Sing."
Atlantic Monthly 68:572–574, 1891.

Stegemeier, H.
The Dance of Death in Folk Song. Chicago:
University of Chicago Dissertations, 1939.

"The Guitar is the Natural Voice of America."
Guitarist 18 (No. 7) :24, 41, 1940. Illus.
   Includes general discussion of American folksong, with special emphasis on the guitar as an
   accompanying instrument.

"Thirty Years of Folk Songs," illustrated. *Newsweek* 17:61, 1941 (June 23).

Townsend, Arthur O.
*The American folk song and its influence on
the work of American Composers. Masters
Thesis:* University of California, 1939, unpublished.

"Types of American Folk Songs."
JAFL 28:1–17, 1915.

Vernon, Grenville
Yankee Doodle Doo. New York: Payson and
Clarke, Ltd., 1927. 165 pp., music.

Vernon, Lee
"Old Songs that Live." *Music* (Chicago) 18:
440–446, 1900.

Whittaker, W. Gillies
"The Folk-Music of North-Eastern England."
In: *Collected Essays* (pp. 1–65). London: Oxford University Press, 1940, 235 pp. Music in the text.

FOLKSONG COLLECTIONS
Texts Only

AMERICAN

Barnes, R. O.
I Hear America Singing. Introduction by Carl van Doren, Illustrations by Robert Lawson. Philadelphia: J. C. Winston Company, 1937.

Coyce, C. H., compiler
Good Old Songs. Martin, Tennessee: 1913.

The Encyclopedia of Popular Songs.
New York: cop. 1864.

Firth, C. H.
An American Garland. Ballads relating to America, 1563–1759, 1915. Oxford: B. H. Blackwell, 1915, xivii, 91 pp.

Ford, Worthington C.
Broadside Ballads, etc. Printed in Massachusetts, 1639–1800. Boston: Massachusetts Historical Society Collection, vol. LXXV, 1922.

————.
"The Isaiah Thomas Collection of Ballads."
Proceedings of the American Antiquarian Society. (N.S.) 33:44–122, 1924.
  List of Ballads in the Collection: 54–103, Broadsides, Ballads, etc. Printed in Massachusetts, 1639–1800.

Gordon, R. W.
Folksongs of America. Issued by Folk-song and folk-lore department. New York: National Service Bureau, 1938. III–IV, 110 pp. (National Service Bureau, Publication No. 73–75, Dec., 1938).

Jackson, George Stuyvesant
Early Songs of Uncle Sam (with introduction by Kenneth B. Murdock). Boston: B. Humphries, Inc., 1933. With music and illustrations 297, (1) p. front plates (1 double incl. music).
  "This study covers, roughly, songs contained in popular collections printed in the United States between 1825 and 1850. It is my belief that, with the exception of the Yankee Songster's pocket companion (1824), all the books fall within the period. . . . I have avoided dialect-songs."—editor's pref. With music. Bibl.: pp. 271–277.

Pound, Louise
American Ballads and Songs. New York: Charles Scribner's Sons, 1922.

Winslow, Ola E.
American Broadside Verse. From Imprints of the 17th and 18th Centuries. Selected and edited, with an introductory note. New Haven: Yale University Press, 1930. xxvi, 224 pp.

ENGLISH: A Selection

De Vaynes, Julia H. L.
The Kentish Garland. With additional notes, and pictorial illustrations by J. W. Ebsworth. Heroford: S. Austin and Sons, 1881, 2 vols.

Dixon, James H.
Ancient Poems, Ballads and Songs of the Peasantry of England. London: Percy Society Publications, Vol. 17, 1846..

Hazlitt, W. Carew, ed.
Remains of the Early Popular Poetry of England. London: J. R. Smith, 1864–1866, 4 volumes.

The Illustrated Book of English Songs.
From the 16th to the 19th century. London: Illustrated. London Library, 185–, iii-xvi, 336 pp.

Old English Songs from Various Sources.
With illustrations by Hugh Thomson and introduction by Austin Dobson. London: 1894.

Ramsay, Allan
The Tea-Table Miscellany: a collection of choice songs, Scots and English. Edinburgh: A. Donaldson, 1762, xxiv, 448 pp.

The Skylark.
Being an elegant collection of the best and newest songs in the English language. London: Vernon and Hood, 1800, xii, 300 pp.

Tegg's Comic Song Book.
Being an excellent collection of comic, laughable—and whimsical songs—the whole calculated to curl up the corners of the mouth, and cheer up the cockles of the heart, in these hard times. London: Thomas Tegg, 1818.

The Customs of London, otherwise called Arnold's Chronicle.
Containing among divers other matters, the original of the celebrated poem of the Nut-Brown Maid. Reprinted from the first edition, with additions included in the second. London: 1811.
  "This work is perhaps the most heterogeneous and multifarious miscellany that ever existed" (Warton).

The Universal Songster; or, Museum of Mirth: forming the most complete collection of ancient and modern songs in the English language—with index, front-piece, and twenty-nine woodcuts designed by G. and R. Cruikshank, and engraved by J. R. Marshall. London: Jones and Company, 183–, 3 volumes.

Williams, H., ed.
National Songs and Poetical Pieces. London: H. Hetherington, 1839. 84 pp.

The Wreath of Freedom; or Patriots Song Book, being a collection of songs in favour of public liberty. New Castle upon Tyne: J. Marshall, 1820. 40 pp.

SCOTCH: A Selection

The Blue Bell.
A Selection of Scottish Songs. Edinburgh:
J. Maclaran, 1851, 48 pp.

Burns, Robert
Burns' Popular Songs. Paisley: G. Caldwell
and Company (18–?), 24 pp.

Chambers, Robert
The Scottish Ballads: collected and illustrated
by Robert Chambers. Edinburgh: W. Tait,
1829. vii, 355 pp.

―――――.
The Scottish Songs: collected and illustrated
by Robert Chambers. Edinburgh: W. Tait,
1829. 2 vols.
No music, tunes indicated by title.

―――――.
The Songs of Scotland prior to Burns. With
the tunes. Edinburgh and London: W. and R.
Chambers, 1862. xviii, 462 pp.

Cunningham, Allan
The Songs of Scotland, ancient and modern,
with an introduction and notes, historical and
critical, and characters of the lyrical poets.
London: John Taylor, 1825, 4 volumes.
"Vigorous and intelligent critical opinion, and a
rich selection of poems." (Hustvedt).

Ramsay, Allan
The Tea-table Miscellany: A collection of
choice songs, Scots and English. Edinburgh:
A. Donaldson, 1762. xxxiv, 448 pp.

FOLKSONG COLLECTIONS:
With Music

GENERAL COLLECTIONS

Armitage, Marie Teresa
The Laural Unison Book, Teacher's edition;
Edited by M. Teresa Armitage. Boston: C. C.
Birchard Company, 1918.

Bantock, Granville, comp. and arr.
One Hundred Folk Songs of All Nations. Boston: O. Ditson Company. New York: C. H.
Ditson and Company, 1911, 175 pp., voice
and piano.

Botsford, Florence Hudson, ed.
Botsford Collection of Folk Songs, with Eng-
lish versions by American Poets, 3 volumes.
New York: G. Schirmer, Inc., 1930.

Brown, James Duff, and Moffat, Alfred
*Characteristic Songs and Dances of All Na-
tions.* Bayley and Ferguson, 1901, 24 pp.

Cartwright, Harriet Garton
Song Treasury. New York: The Macmillan
Company, 1920. v, 212 pp.
Folk songs of all nations, art songs, part songs,
national songs, Christmas songs and hymns.

Davison, G.
140 Folk Songs. London: T. A. Laurie, no date.

Deutsch, Leonard, coll. and arr.
A Treasury of the World's Finest Folk Song.
Songs of all nations. Accompanying text by
Claude Simpson. New York: Howell, Soskin,
1942. Illus.

Diller, Angela
When the World Was Young. Cincinnati:
Willis Music Company, 1921.
Folk Song music for piano.

Elson, Louis Charles, ed.
Folk Songs of Many Nations. New York: John
Church Company, 1905, 171 pp.

Folk Songs of Many Nations.
Cincinnati: The John Church Company, 1905,
171 pp., Voice and piano.

Glenn, Mabelle, ed.
Songs of Many Lands. Boston, New York, etc:
Ginn and Company, 1936, 192 pp.

Gluck, Alma, comp.
Folk Songs and Other Duets. New York: Ditson, 1909.

Gordon, Dorothy
Around the World in Song. New York: E. P.
Dutton and Company, Inc., 1928, 94 pp.

―――――.
Sing it Yourself. New York: E. P. Dutton and
Company, Inc., 1928, 82 pp.

Möller, Dr. Heinrich
Das Lied Der Völker. Eine Sammlung von
fremdländischen Volksliedern, ausgewählt,
übersetzt und mit benutzung der besten aus-
ländischen Quellen und Bearbeibungen von
H. M. Maintz: B. Schott's Sohne. n.d. 10 Bände.
Band 3: Englische und Nordamerikanische
volkslieder.

Reimann, Heinrich
Internationale Volksliederbuch, Eine Sammlung auslandische Volkslieder. Berlin: N. Sim-
rock, 1893, 3 volumes.
Scotch, English, Irish Songs included.

Sembrich, Marcella, ed.
My Favorite Folk Songs. Boston: Oliver Ditson Company, 1918, 138 pp. voice and piano.

Swan, Alfred J., ed.
Songs from Many Lands: 30 folk songs of
France, Scotland, Russia, Spain, and North
America. Arranged by celebrated composers
with new copyright translation by Helen Tay-
lor. London: Enoch and Sons, 1921, 62 pp.

BRITISH ISLES: A Selection

Boulton, Harold
Songs of the Four Nations: A collection of the
old songs of the people of England, Scotland,
Ireland, and Wales. Edited by H. B., the music
arranged by Arthur Somervell. London: J. B.
Cramer and Company, 1893, 270 pp.

Dime, S.
The Edinburgh Musical Miscellany: A collection of the most approved Scotch, English, and Irish Songs set to music. Edinburgh: 1792, 1793, 2 volumes, illustrated.

Gosset, Adelaide L. J., comp.
Lullabies of the Four Nations, a coronal of song with renderings from the Welsh and Gaelic. London: A. Maring, Ltd., 1915. xix, 278 pp.

Hadow, Sir William Henry
Songs of the British Isles. One Hundred National melodies selected and edited for the use of schools by W. H. Hadow. London: J. Curwen and Sons, 1903. 123 pp.
    Unison and part songs.

The Harmonist:
A select collection of ancient and modern catches, canons, epigrams, etc. Respectfully inscribed to the gentlemen of the Catch and Glee Clubs of Great Britain and Ireland. London: C. Wheatstone (C. A. 1800), 6 volumes in one, engraved music.

Kidson, Frank, and Shaw, Martin
Songs of Britain: A collection of one hundred English, Welsh, Scottish, and Irish National Songs, selected and edited by F. K. and M. S.; the tunes newly arranged with accompaniments for pianoforte by Martin Shaw. London: Boosey and Company, 1913, 200 pp.

Macmillan, Ernest
A Book of Songs; compiled for the entertainment and delight of English men and women everywhere, but especially for those at home and in Canada. New York: E. P. Dutton and Company, 1929. 180 pp.
    Published under the auspices of the National Council of Education.

The Masque.
A new and select collection of the best English, Scotch and Irish Songs. To which is added— A complete collection of toasts, sentiments, and hobnobs, now in vogue. A new edition with great addition. London: n.d. (ca. 1750).
    A miscellany of popular poetry from the middle of the 18th century, taken from ballad tradition—to the songs of contemporary opera successes of Handel and Arne.

The New Musical and Vocal Cabinet.
Comprising a selection of the most famous English, Scotch and Irish melodies, arranged for voice, violin, flute, etc. London: 1820, illustrated, with music.

Purdy, C. H.
The Songs of Wales. A complete collection of the vocal melodies of the principality, with the addition of the Welsh airs and part songs, the music edited by John Thomas, harpist to her Majesty, the Queen. London: no date.

A Selection of Scotch, English, Irish and Foreign Airs.
Adopted for the fife, violin, or German flute. Vol. II, dedicated to the Volunteers and Defense Bands of Great Britain, Ireland. Edinburgh: no date (ca. 1810). illustrated with music.

Shaw, Martin, and Kidson, Frank, eds.
Songs of Britain. A collection of one hundred English, Welsh, Scottish, and Irish National Songs. London: Boosey Edition: voice and piano.

Somervell, Arthur
Songs of the Four Nations. A collection of old songs of the people of England, Scotland, Ireland, and Wales, for the most part never before published. Edited by H. Boulton, music arranged by A. Somervell. London: J. B. Cramer and Company, 1893, viii, 270 pp.

Songs of England, Ireland and Scotland.
London: 1835, 2 volumes.

Spicker, Max
Songs of the British Isles; a collection of forty popular English, Irish, Scotch and Welsh Songs with piano accompaniment, compiled and edited by Max Spicker. New York: G. Schirmer, 1909, 93 pp.

The Vocal Magazine; or *British Songster's Miscellany,* containing all the English, Scotch and Irish Songs, Cantatas, Glees, Catches, Airs, Ballads, etc., deemed any way worthy of being transmitted to posterity. London: J. Harrison for J. Beu, 1778, in nine numbers, 1268 songs, 348 pp., and index of 11 pages with 16 engraved portraits.

Willan, Healey
Songs of the British Isles: arranged by Healey Willan. Boston: The Boston Music Company, 1928, 89 pp.

ENGLISH: A Selection

Aikin, J.
Essays on Song-Writing, with a collection of such English Songs as are most eminent for poetical merit. Warrington, England: J. Johnson, 1774, xiv, 286 pp.

Ashbee, C. R. and Janet E.
The Essex House Song Book, being a collection of songs formed for the singers of the Guild of handicrafts. London: The Essex House Press, 1903–05. 2 vols.
    Most of the melodies are unaccompanied.

Bantock, Granville, ed. and arr.
One Hundred Songs of England. Boston: Oliver Ditson Company, 1914, 204 pp.
    (The Musicians Library) Contains a number of folk songs from various counties, art songs, and airs from the English operas. Arranged for voice and piano.

Baring-Gould, Sabine
Songs of the West. London: Methuen, 1890, 1928.

————, and Sharp, Cecil J.
English Folk-Songs for Schools. Selected and Arranged by S. Baring-Gould and C. J. Sharp. London: J. Curwen and Sons, Ltd. 19–?

————, and Sheppard, Fleetwood H.
A Garland of Country Song. English folksongs with their traditional melodies. London: Methuen & Company, 1895, xi, 112 pp.

Barrett, William Alexander
English Folk-Songs. Collection, arranged with symphonies and accompaniments for pianoforte by William Alexander Barrett, for medium voice. London: Novello, Ewen and Company, (19–?), 95 pp.

The Billington; or, *Town and Country Songster;* containing words of 700 of the newest and most approved songs. London: 1790.

The Book of English Songs; from the sixteenth to the nineteenth century. London: Office of the National Illustrated Library, 1851, xiv, 320 pp., illus.

Bridge, Sir Frederick
The Old Cryes of London. London: Novello and Company, Ltd., 1921, 78 pp. Music in text.

Broadwood, Lucy E.
English Traditional Songs and Carols; Collected and edited with annotations and pianoforte accompaniments by Lucy E. Broadwood. London: Boosey and Company, 1908, 125 pp., voice and piano.

Chappell, William
A Collection of National English Airs; ancient song, ballad and dance tunes—harmonized by W. Crotch, G. A. Macfarren, and J. A. Wade. London: 1830–1840, 2 volumes.

————.
Old English Ditties, selected from William Chappell's "Popular Music of the Olden Time." With—the long ballads compressed, and—new works written by J. Oxenford and M. Macfarren. The symphonies and accompaniments by G. A. Macfarren. London: Chappell and Company, 189?, 2 vols.

————.
Old English Popular Music. A new edition, with preface and notes, and the earlier examples entirely revised by H. Ellis Wooldridge. London: Chappell and Company, 1893, 2 volumes.

————.
Popular Music of the Olden Time; A collection of ancient songs, ballads, and dance tunes, illustrative of the national music of England. Also a short account of the minstrels; the airs harmonized by G. A. Macfarren. London: 1859, 2 volumes.

Cornish, T. H.
British Melodies or Songs of the People. London: Smith, Elder & Company, 1821, viii, 131 pp.

Dalrymple, A.
A Collection of English Songs, with an appendix of original pieces. London. 1796.

Duncan, Edmonstoune
Lyrics from the Old Songbooks; collected and edited by E. Duncan. New York: Harcourt, Brace and Company, 1927, 64 pp.

Farnsworth, Charles Hubert, and Sharp, Cecil J.
Folk-Songs, Chanteys, and Singing Games. New York: The H. W. Gray Company, 1916. 111 pp.

Gomme, Alice Bertha
Children's Singing Games, with tunes to which they are sung. Illustrated by Winifred Smith. London: D. Nutt, 1894. 2 vols. illus.

Gordon, Dorothy
Sing it Yourself; collection of folk-songs from "The Young People's Concert Hour." Foreword by George H. Gartlan. New York: Dutton and Company, 1828, 82 pp.
    Contains some English folk tunes.

Hatton, John Liptrot
The Songs of England; A collection of English melodies, including the most popular traditional ditties, and the principal songs and ballads of the last three centuries, edited with new symphonies and accompaniments by J. L. Hatton. London: Boosey and Company, (19—). 2 volumes.

Jackson, Vincent
English Melodies from the 13th to the 18th Century. London: Dutton and Company, 1910.

Johnson, Noel
Three Folk Songs of Merrie England, edited by Milton Reynolds. Music arranged by Noel Johnson. London: Melton Reynolds, (19—), 3 songs for voice and piano.

Lawson, R.
The Ballads and Songs of Carrick, with nineteen musical illustrations, arranged for partsinging. Introductory notes. Paisley: J. R. Parlane, n.d., 30 pp.

Nicholson, Sydney Hugo
British Songs for British Boys; A collection of National Songs, designed for use of boys in schools and choirs; selected, arranged, and edited, with explanatory notes, by Sydney H. Nicholson, with a preface by J. G. Legge. London: Macmillan and Company, 1930, 220 pp.
    Contents: English Songs, Scottish Songs, Irish Songs, Welsh Songs, American and Plantation Songs, Sea Songs, Songs of Country Life, and Christmas Carols.

Old English Songs, A. D. 1250–1789. Morristown, New Jersey: "Bauner Steam Print," 18—, 11 pp.

Quilter, Roger
Old English Popular Songs. Boston: Boston Music Company, 1921. Solo voice and piano accompaniment.
  Contents: Three Poor Mariners, Drink to Me Only with Thine Eyes, Over the Mountains, The Jolly Mariner, Barbara Allen.

Ritson, Joseph
Ancient Songs from the Time of King Henry III, to the Revolution. Observations on the Minstrels. Dissertation on Ancient Songs and Music. London: 1790, illustrated.

———.
Pieces of Ancient Popular Poetry, from authentic manuscripts and old printed copies. London: W. Pickering, 1833, xvi, 172 pp. 2nd edition illustrated.

———
A Select Collection of English Songs, with their original airs, and a historical essay on the origin and progress of National Song. London: J. Johnson, 1783, 3 volumes, volume 3 contains music.

Reynardson, H. J. Birch
Popular Songs of Sussex. London: Stanley, Lucas Wehen and Company, (189—), 47 pp.

Rondelay; or, *The New Syrew;* A collection of choice songs. London: 1780, 292 pp.

Sawyer, F. E.
"Sussex Songs and Music." *Journal British Archaeological Association.* (London) 42: 306–327, 1886.

Scott, Harold
English Song Book; collected and edited with an introduction by Harold Scott. London: Chapman and Hall, Ltd., 1925, 149 pp.

Sharp, Cecil J.
English Folk-Carols, with pianoforte accompaniment and an introduction and notes; collected in various parts of England. London: Novello and Company, Ltd., 1911, 68 pp.

———.
Folk-Songs of England; edited by C. J. Sharp. London: Novello and Company, Ltd., 1908, 5 volumes in 2.
  Book I—Folk Songs from Dorset, coll. by H. E. D. Hammond.
  Book II—Folk Songs from the Eastern Countries, coll. by R. Vaughan Williams.
  Book III—Folk-Songs from Hampshire, coll. by George B. Gardiner.
  Book IV—Folk Songs from the various countries, coll. by C. J. Sharp.
  Book V—Folk Songs from Sussex, coll. by W. Percy Merrick.

———. coll. and arr.
Folk-Songs, Folk-Song Carols, Ballads, Pulling, and Capstan Chanteys. London: Novello and Company, Ltd., 1908, voice and piano.

———. ed. and arr.
One Hundred English Folksongs, with historical notes on the songs that are for voice (medium) and pianoforte. Boston: Oliver Ditson Company, 1916, xiv, 235 pp. (Musician's library).

———, and Williams, R. Vaughan
Folk-Songs from Somerset, collected and edited by C. J. Sharp and R. V. Williams. London: Novello and Company, Ltd., 1908, 6 volumes in 1. (Novello's School Songs.)

The Skylark, Being an elegant collection of the best and newest songs in the English language. London: J. Evans, 1791, 276 pp.

Stanford, Sir C. V.
The National Song Book; a complete collection of the folk songs, carols and rounds suggested by the Board of Education, (1905). Edited and arranged by C. V. Stanford. London: Boosey and Company, 1906, 236 pp.

Taillefer, N.
Rondeaus of the British Volunteers. London: S. Lucas, Weber and Company, 1878, 4th edition, vii, 118 pp.

Thomas, Vincent
Cryes of Olde London; arranged for voice and piano by V. Thomas. London: Goodwin and Tabb, Ltd., 1925.

The Thrush; a choice collection of the most admired popular songs, heroic, plaintive, sentimental, humorous, and bacchanalian. Arranged for the violin, flute, and voice. London: T. Tegg, 1827, 327 pp.

Whittaker, Wiseman, Wishart, eds.
The Clarendon Song Books. London: Oxford University Press, 1929.

Williams, Alfred
Folk-Songs of the Upper Thames; with an essay on folk-song activity in the upper Thames neighborhood, collected and edited by Alfred Williams. London: Duckworth, 1923, 306 pp.

Williams, Ralph Vaughan
Norfolk Rhapsody, No. 1; founded on folk-tunes, collected orally in Norfolk, and set as an orchestral piece. London: Oxford University Press, 1925, 40 pp.

Wilson, H. Lane
Old English Melodies. Words and Music arranged by H. L. Wilson. London: Boosey and Company, 1899, 119 pp.
  For solo, mixed quartet.

Wright, Thomas, ed.
Songs and Carols, from a MS. of the 15th century. London: Percy Society, 1847. Percy Society Publication No. 73.

SCOTCH: A Selection

Brown, Colin
The Thistle: A Miscellany of Scottish Song, with notes critical and historical. The melodies arranged in their natural modes; with an introduction, explaining the construction and characteristics of Scottish Music, the Principles, Laws, and Origin of Melody by Colin Brown, instrumental accompaniments and harmonies by James Merrylees. London: William Collins Sons and Company, no date, xxxv, 208 pp., glossary, voice and piano.

Burns, Robert
The Songs of Robert Burns, now first printed with the melodies for which they were written by James S. Dick. London: H. Frowde, 1903.

The Caledonian Musical Repository, A Selection of Esteemed Scottish Songs, adopted for the voice, violin, and German flute. London: B. Crosby and Company, 1806, 286 pp.

Campbell, Alexander, coll. and arr.
Albyn's Anthology. A select collection of the melodies and vocal poetry peculiar to Scotland and the Isles. The modern Scottish and English verses adopted to the Highland, Hebridean and Lowland melodies, written by Walter Scott and other living poets. Edinburgh: Oliver and Boyd, 1816–1818, 2 volumes.

Corri, Domenico
A New and Complete Collection of the Most Favourite Scots Songs; including a few English and Irish, with proper graces and ornaments peculiar to their character, likewise the new method of accompaniment of thorough bass. Edinburgh: Corri and Company (17—), 33 pp.

Cromek, Robert Hartley
Remains of Nithsdale and Galloway Song; with historical and traditional notices relative to the manners and customs of the peasantry. London: T. Cadell, 1810, viii, xxxii, 370 pp.

Crosby's Caledonian Musical Repository.
A choice selection of Esteemed Scottish Songs, adopted for the voice, violin, and German flute, with music, two title pages. London and Edinburgh: 1811, illustrated.

Cunningham, A.
The Songs of Scotland, ancient and modern; with an introduction and notes. London: J. Taylor, 1825, v, 4 volumes, without music.
Historical and critical and characters of the lyric poets.

Dixon, James Henry
Scottish Traditional Versions of Ancient Ballads. London: Percy Society, 1845, xvi, 108 pp.

Farmer, Henry George
Music in Mediaeval Scotland; with an introduction by Sir Richard R. Terry. London: William Reaves, (19—), 23 pp.

Favourite Scottish Songs.
London: Ascherberg, Hopwood, and Crew, Ltd., (19—), 40 pp., voice and piano.

Fraser, Marjory Kennedy, and Macleod, Kenneth
From the Hebrides; further gleanings of tale and song. Glasgow: Paterson's Publishers, Ltd., (19—), 131 pp.

Songs of the Hebrides; collected and arranged for voice and pianoforte. London: Boosey and Company, 1909, 1921, 3 volumes.

Twenty-four Selected Songs of the Hebrides, from volumes 1 and 2. Edited, translated and arranged for voice and pianoforte. London: Boosey and Company, 1914, 2 volumes in 1.

Gems of Scottish Songs. A Collection of Scottish Ballads. Arranged and compiled from the best sources and latest revivals of the author's works. London: Ditson Edition: voice and piano.

Graves, Alfred Perceval, editor
The Celtic Song Book; being representative folk songs of the six Celtic nations. London: Ernest Benn, Ltd., 1928, xix, 332 pp. music.

Hogg, James
The Jacobite Relics of Scotland; being the songs, airs, and legends, of the adherents to the House of Stuart; collected and illustrated by James Hogg. (Eltric Shepherd, pseud.) Edinburgh: Printed for William Blackwood and T. Cadell and W. Davies, 1819, 2 volumes.
Unharmonized melodies, historical notes on the songs.

Hopekirk, Helen
Seventy Scottish Songs. Boston: Oliver Ditson Company, 1905, 189 pp., voice and piano. The Musicians Library.

Jacobite Minstrelsy; with notes, illustrative of the text, and containing historical details in relation to the House of Stuart from 1640 to 1784. Glasgow: 1829.
A collection based on those of Ritson and Cunningham.

Johnson, James
The Scottish Musical Museum; consisting of six hundred songs, with proper basses for the pianoforte. Originally published by J. Johnson, and now accompanied with notes and illustrations of the lyric poetry and music of Scotland—by William Stenhouse. Edinburgh: W. Blackwood and Sons, 1839, 6 volumes.

Lawson, Malcolm
Songs of the North, gathered together from the Highlands and Lowlands of Scotland. Edited by A. C. Macleod and H. Boulton. The music arranged by M. Lawson. London: J. B. Cramer and Company, (189—), 2 volumes.

MacCunn, Hamish (arr.)
Songs and Ballads of Scotland; with pianoforte accompaniment. Glasgow: Paterson, Sons and Company, Ltd., (19—), 201 pp.

Macleod, A. C., and Boulton, Harold, eds.
Songs of the North; gathered together from the Highlands and Lowlands of Scotland, the music arranged by Malcolm Lawson. London: J. B. Cramer and Company, (19—), 3 volumes, 2 editions.

Marr, J. S.
Two Hundred and Twenty-Two Popular Scottish Songs with Music: The choicest melodies of Scotland, as sung by Wilson, Templeton, Mackay, and other popular vocalists. Glasgow: J. S. Marr, 1872, 138 pp.

Moffat, Alfred, arr.
Minstrelsy of Scotland. Scottish songs adapted to their traditional airs. London: Augener Edition: voice and piano.

Pittman, J., and Brown, Colin, eds.
The Songs of Scotland. A collection of One Hundred and Ninety Songs. The music edited by J. Pittman, and Colin Brown. The poetry edited (with notes) by Dr. Charles Mackay. London: Boosey and Company, 1877, 223 pp. Glossary.

Reid, John, comp.
Songs of Scotland; a selection by John Reid, with an essay by Fohn Foord. London: Boosey and Company, 1908, 259 pp.

Ritson, Joseph
Scottish Songs, with the musick and an historical essay. London: 1794, 2 volumes.

Swan, Alfred J., ed.
Songs from Many Lands; 30 folk songs of France, Scotland, Russia, Spain, and North America; arranged by celebrated composers with new copyright translations by Helen Taylor. London: Enoch and Sons, 1921. 62 pp.

Thomson, George
A Select Collection of Scottish Airs for Voice, with symphonies and accompaniments for pianoforte, violin and violin-cello by Pleyel, Kozeluch, and Haydn; with verses both Scottish and English, adapted to the airs, including upwards 100 new songs by Burns. London: T. Preston, 1803–1805, 4 volumes.

Thomson's Collection of the Songs of Burns, Sir Walter Scott, and other Poets, united to melodies of Scotland, with symphonies and accompaniments for the pianoforte by Pleyel, Haydn, Beethoven, etc. London: 1822–1825, 6 volumes in 2.

Whitelaw, Alexander
The Book of Scottish Song; collected and illustrated with historical and critical notices. London: Blackie and Son, 1845, xliii, 696 pp.

Whittaker, William Gillies
Selections reprinted from "North Countrie Ballads, Songs, and Pipe Tunes," edited and arranged by William Gillies Whittaker. London: J. Curwen and Sons, Ltd., 1921–1925.

Wilson, Dr. John
"The Folk Music of Scotland." *Musical Standard* 21:22–23, 1904. (London).

IRISH: A Selection

Alexander, Arthur
Four Irish Folksongs; freely arranged for piano, by Arthur Alexander. London: Oxford University Press, 1929, 9 pp.
    Contents: Nos. 728, 336, 335, 393, from the Petrie Collection.

Barry, J. M.
The Songs of Ireland. Dublin: J. Duffy, 1847, xxvi, 232 pp.

Bax, Arnold E., arr.
Irish Songs. London: Murdoch Edition: Voice and piano. 1922.
    Contents: "The Pigeons," "As I came over the grey, grey hills," "I heard a piper piping," "Across the door," "Beg," "Innish."

Brewer, Alfred Herbert
A Sprig of Shamrock; four old Irish airs for soprano or tenor voice with string quartet or pianoforte accompaniment; poems by F. W. Harvey; music adopted and arranged by Alfred Herbert Brewer. London: Novello and Company, 1925.

Bunting, E.
The Ancient Music of Ireland, to which is prefixed a dissertation on the Irish Harp and Harpers, including an account of the old melodies of Ireland, arranged for the pianoforte. Dublin: 1840.

Croker, T. Crofton, ed.
The Popular Songs of Ireland. London: 1839, xx, 340 pp., with introduction and notes.

Fisher, William Arms, ed.
Sixty Irish Songs. Boston: Oliver Ditson Company, 1915, 201 pp. (The Musicians Library), voice and piano.

Flood, William H. Grattan
A History of Irish Music. Dublin: Broune and Nolan, Ltd., 1905, 353 pp.

Fox, Charlotte Milligan
Annals of the Irish Harpers. London: Smith Elder and Company. 1911, 320 pp., illus.

Songs of the Irish Harpers; Collected and arranged for harp or piano (and voice). London: Bayley and Ferguson, 1910, 57 pp.

Graves, Alfred Perceval, editor
The Celtic Song Book; being representative folk songs of the six Celtic nations. London: Ernest Benn, Ltd., 1928. 332 pp., music.

The Irish Song Book, with original Irish airs. London: T. F. Unwin, 1895. xxv, 188 pp. (The New Irish Library.)

Harty, Hamilton
Songs of Ireland op. 18. London: Boosey Edition, No. 5947, voice and piano.
    Contents: "Lookin' back," "Dreaming," "Lullaby," "Grace for light," "Flame in the skies," "At Sea."

Hatton, J. L., and Molloy, J. L., eds.
Songs of Ireland. London: Boosey Edition: voice and piano, 245 pp.

Hannagan, Margaret, and Clandillon, Seamus, eds.
"*Londubh an Cairn,*" being Songs of the Irish Gaels in Staff and Sol-fa with English metrical translations. Dublin Cork: The Educational Company of Ireland, 1925, 150 pp.

Henebry, Richard
A Handbook of Irish Music. Dublin: Cork University Press, 1928, 325 pp., music in text.

Hughes, Herbert, ed.
Irish County Songs. London: Boosey Edition: voice and piano. 4 vols. 1909–1930.

Joyce, Patrick Weston
Ancient Irish Music. Containing One Hundred Airs never before published, and a number of Popular Songs. Dublin: Hodges, Figgis, and Co., Ltd.

―――.
Irish Peasant Songs in the English Language. With the old Irish airs: the words set to the music. Dublin: Hodges, Figgis, and Co., Ltd.

―――.
Irish Music and Song; A collection of songs in the Irish language, set to music. Edited for the "Society for the preservation of the Irish language." Dublin: M. H. Gill and Son, 1888, vi, 44 pp.

―――.
Old Irish Folk Music and Songs. A collection of 842 Irish airs and songs hitherto unpublished. Edited and annotated by P. W. Joyce. Language." Dublin: M. H. Gill and Son, 1888, 408 pp.

Lover, Samuel
Songs and Ballads; including those sung in his "Irish Evenings" and hitherto unpublished. New York: Wiley & Putnam, 1847, xiv, 224 pp.

Mason, Redfern
The Song-lore of Ireland; Erin's story in music and verse. New York: The Baker and Taylor Company, 1911, 321 pp., music in text.

Moffat, Alfred
The Minstrelsy of Ireland; 200 Irish songs adapted to their traditional airs—supplemented with historical notes by A. Moffat. London: Augener and Company, 1897, x, 346 pp.

Moore, Thomas
Moore's Irish Melodies; with symphonies and accompaniments by Sir John Stevenson, and characteristic works by Thomas Moore. Boston: P. Donahoe, no date, 199 pp.

O'Neill, Francis
Irish Folk Music, a fascinating hobby; with some account of Allied subjects including O'Farrell's treatise on the Irish or Union pipes and Tonhey's hints to amateur pipers. Chicago: The Regan Printing House, 1910, 359 pp.

Page, Nathaniel Clifford, ed.
Irish Songs: A collection of airs, old and new. New York: C. H. Ditson & Company, 1907, 124 pp.

Petrie, George, ed.
The Petrie Collection of the Ancient Music of Ireland. Arranged for the pianoforte. Dublin: Society for the Preservation and Publication of the Melodies of Ireland, 1855, vi, xxiv, 196 pp.

Rooney, Hubert E.
The Well-Known Songs of Ireland. Dublin: J. Duffy and Company, 1904, 85 pp.

The Shamrock; or Songs of Old Ireland. New York: Dick and Fitzgerald, 1862, 72 pp.

The Songs of Ireland; a collection of popular Irish airs—from the leading writers, new and old, including compositions of Moore, Lover, Molloy, and others, with accompaniments for the piano or organ. Boston: Oliver Ditson and Company, 1890. 121 pp.

Sparling, Henry Halliday, ed.
Irish Minstrelsy: being a selection of Irish songs, lyrics and ballads. London: W. Scott, 1887. xxvii, 516 pp.

Stanford, Sir Charles Villiers
Irish Songs and Ballads. The words by A. P. Graves. Music arranged by C. V. Stanford. London: Novello and Company, 1893, 125 pp.

―――.
A Sheaf of Songs from Leinster, op. 40. London: Stainer and Bell, Ltd., 1914, 27 pp. voice and piano.

―――.
Songs of Erin; a collection of fifty Irish Folk Songs. The words by A. P. Graves, and the music arranged by C. V. Stanford. London: Boosey and Company, 1901, 235 pp.

―――.
Songs of Old Ireland: A collection of fifty Irish melodies. The words by A. P. Graves, music arranged by C. V. Stanford. London: Boosey and Company, 1882, 135 pp.

AMERICAN

See: American Ballad Collections for More Complete List. pp. 118–20.

GENERAL COLLECTIONS:

Mainly for Voice and Piano,—
Some Unaccompanied.

America's Most Famous Songs.
New York: Leo Feist, Inc.
For voice and piano.

Bacon, Ernst
Along Unpaved Roads; Songs of a Lonesome People. A Collection of Eight American Folk Songs. Illustrations by Sotomayor. Philadelphia: Delkas Music Publishing Company, 1944, voice and piano.
Contents: Sourwood Mountain, Sucking Cider, Sinful Shoe, Careless Love, Common Bill, Midnight Special, De Boll Weevil, My Lulu.

Boni, Margaret Bradford, ed.
Fireside Book of Folk Songs. Arranged for voice and piano by Norman Lloyd. Illustrated by Alice and Martin Provensen. New York: Simon and Schuster, 1947, 323 pp.
A collection of 147 ballads, songs, chanteys, hymns, and spirituals culled from many sources and many countries,—a goodly representation from the United States. Not all are strictly speaking folk songs.

Botkin, B. A., ed.
A Treasury of American Folklore. The Stories, Legends, Tall Tales, Traditions, Ballads and Songs of the American People. Foreword by Carl Sandburg. New York: Crown Publishers, 1944.
  Contains words and tunes of 100 songs and ballads.

Breen, Mary J., and Lawson, Arthur
The Weekend Companion. New York: G. W. Stewart, 1940, xix, 372 pp., illus.
  Contains a number of songs, ballads and games.

Bowles, Paul
American Folk Songs. WPA Music Project. New York: WPA Arts Program, 1940. Voice and piano. Six songs.

————.
Twelve American Folk Songs. WPA Music Project. New York: Federal Works Agency, Works Projects Administration Arts Program, 1940. Voice and piano.

Burk, Cassie, Meierhoffer, Virginia, and Phillips, Claude Anderson
America's Musical Heritage. Illustrated by Milo Winter. Chicago: Laidlaw Brothers, 1942, 368 pp.
  Treated largely as a historical study for junior high school level, contains many folk tunes.

Carmer, Carl
America Sings: Stories and songs of our country's growth. Music arranged by Edwin J. Stringham, illustrated in color by Elizabeth Black Carmer. New York: Alfred A. Knopf, 1942.

————.
Songs of the Rivers of America. Music arranged by Dr. Albert Sirmay. New York: Farrar and Rinehart, 1943, xi, 196 pp.
  Words and music—for voice and piano.

Chase, Richard
Old Songs and Singing Games. Chapel Hill, North Carolina: University of North Carolina Press, 1938.

Coleman, Satis N., and Bregman, Adolph
Songs of American Folks. Illustrated by Alanson Hewes. New York: The John Day Company, 1943, 128 pp.
  Contains 47 songs arranged in nine groups, in simple arrangements for voice and piano.

Combs, Josiah H.
Folk Songs du Midi des États-Unis. Paris: Les Presses Universitaires de France, 1925.

Davison, Archibald T., Davis, Katherine K., and Kempf, Frederik W.
Songs of Freedom. Boston: Houghton Mifflin Co., 1942, 144 pp.
  Arranged for unison and mixed voices. Contains a number of folk tunes under headings: Songs of Occupations, Songs of the South, Spirituals, Chanteys, Cowboy Songs, Songs about special places and groups, Songs of Latin America, Songs of Canada, Hymns, etc.

Downes, Olin, and Siegmeister, Elie
A Treasury of American Song. New York: Alfred A. Knopf, 1943, 408 pp., 2nd ed., voice and piano.
  The songs range from Plymouth Rock to Broadway, 1940. "This collection is indispensable for any song-minded gatherings of America." (William Schuman).

Eckstorm, Mrs. Fannie (Hardy), and Smyth, Mary Winslow
Minstrelsy of Maine: folk-songs and ballads of the woods and the coast. Boston: Houghton Mifflin Company, 1927. xvi, 390 pp. bibl. (xi–xii).

Elson, Louis Charles, ed.
Folk Songs of Many Nations. Cincinnati: The John Church Co., 1905.

Ewen, David, ed.
Songs of America. A Cavalcade of Popular Songs. Arranged for Voice and Piano by Mischa and Wesley Portnoff. Chicago, Ill.: Ziff-Davis Publishing Co., 1947, 246 pp.
  A lot of commentary by the author that is diverting rather than significant. Many of the 58 "representative" tunes are not presented in complete version.

Finger, Charles Joseph
Frontier Ballads, heard and gathered by Charles J. Finger. Woodcuts by Paul Honoré. Garden City, N. Y.: Doubleday, Page & Co., 1927. 181 p., contains music.

Ford, Ira W.
Traditional Music of America. New York: E. P. Dutton & Co., Inc., 1940. 480 p.
  Melodies unaccompanied.

Foresman, Robert
Our Music in Story and Song. New York: American Book Company, 1947. 391 pp.
  Following a short, comprehensive history of the development of music, the book presents 250 songs of varied character: selections from great composers, spirituals, cowboy songs, hymns, community songs, and American favorites.

Frey, H., ed.
Robbins Mammoth Collection of American Songs. New York: Robbins Music Corporation, 1941.

Gardner, Emelyn Elizabeth
Ballads and Songs of Southern Michigan, collected and edited by Emelyn Elizabeth Gardner and Geraldine Jencks Chickering. Ann Arbor: The University of Michigan Press, 1939. xviii, 501 pp., unaccompanied melodies, bibl.

Gordon, R. W.
Folksongs of America. New York: National Service Bureau, 1938. III–IV, 110 pp. (National Service Bureau Publication No. 73–5, Dec., 1938). Issued by Folksong and Folklore Department.

Haufrecht, Herbert, comp. and ed.
Burl Ives—The Wayfaring Stranger. Twenty-one folk songs and ballads. New York: Leeds Music Corporation, 1945, 48 pp., voice and piano.
> The selection chosen from Burl Ives repertoire.

Hille, Waldemar, ed.
The People's Song Book. New York: Boni and Gaer, 1948. 128 pp.
> The first part, called "songs that helped build America," includes a number of old ballads, work songs, Negro spirituals and mountain tunes. Part two is called "World Freedom Songs" containing 21 Militant songs from 13 countries. Part Three entitled "American Trade Union Songs, "includes such songs as "The Scabs Crawl In," "Picket Line Priscilla," and others. Part four deals with American topical political songs, such as "Jim Crow," "The Talking Atomic Blues," etc. Some of the songs are arranged for piano or guitar, others for chorus.

Horn, Charles E.
National Melodies of America. The poetry of George P. Morris, Esq. Part I. New York: Davis and Horn, 1839. *Southern Literary Messenger* (Richmond, Va.) 5:770–773, 1839.

Hudson, Arthur Palmer
Folk Tunes from Mississippi. coll. by Arthur Palmer Hudson and ed. by George Herzog, Music Research department. National Play Bureau, Publication No. 25. New York: National Play Bureau. Works Progress Administration, Federal Theatre Project, 1937. xxii, 45 pp.
> Melodies without accompaniment.

Jackson, G. S.
Early Songs of Uncle Sam. Introduction by K. B. Murdock. Boston: B. Humphries, 1933.

Johnson, Margaret
Early American Songs; from the repertoire of the "Song Spinners"; arranged and edited with piano accompaniments and historical notes by Margaret and Travis Johnson. New York: Associated Music Publishers, Inc. vol. I. 1943, v., 64 p. vol. II, 1944.
> Melodies with piano accompaniment.

Jordan, Philip D., Kessler, Lillian
Songs of Yesterday; A Song Anthology of American Life. New York: Doubleday Doran, 1941. Voice and piano.

Landeck, Beatrice, comp.
Songs My True Love Sings. An Album of Immortal Love Songs for voice and piano or guitar. Piano settings by Charity Bailey. New York: E. B. Marks Music Corporation, 1946. 64 pp., illus.
> The Album consists mainly of ballads and lyric songs.

Linscott, Eloise Hubbard.
Folksongs of Old New England; coll. and ed. by Eloise Hubbard Linscott. With an introduction by James M. Carpenter. New York: The Macmillan Co., 1939. xxi, 337 p., with music, ref.

Loesser, Arthur, ed.
Humor in American Music. Arrangements by Alfred Kugel. Illustrated by Samuel M. Adler. New York: Howell, Soskin, Publishers, 1942, 315 pp., index, music (voice and piano).

Lomax, Alan; Seeger, Charles; and Crawford, Ruth
American Songs for American Children. Chicago: Music Educators National Conference, 1942.

Lomax, John Avery, and Alan
American Ballads and Folk Songs; coll. and compiled by John A. Lomax and Alan Lomax; with a foreword by George Lyman Kittredge. New York: The Macmillan Co. 1934. xxxix, 625 p., inc. music, bibl.

———.
Cowboy Songs and Other Frontier Ballads. coll. by John A. Lomax with an introduction by Barrett Wendell. New York: Macmillan, 1920. xiii, 44 p., contains music.

———.
Our Singing Country. A Second Volume of American Ballads and Folk Songs. Ruth Crawford Seeger, Music Editor. New York: The Macmillan Company, 1941, xxviii, 416 pp., bibl. music.

Luther, Frank
Americans and their Songs. New York: Harper Brothers, 1942. xiv, 323 p.
> 75 songs with piano accompaniment and 50 unaccompanied melodies. The Songs of America (1620–1900), a chronological list.

Maddy, Joseph E., and Miessner, W. Otto
All-American Song Book. New York: Robbins Music Corp., 1947.
> Contains 155 songs, for solo and choral singing.

Matteson, Maurice, coll. and arr.
American Folk Songs for Young Singers. Schirmer's American Folk Song Series, set 25. New York: G. Schirmer, Inc.: 1947, 102 pp.
> Arranged for chorus and piano.

McConathy, O., Beattie, J. W., and Morgan, R. V., editors
Music—Highways and Byways. New York: Silver Burdett Company, 1936, 252 pp., illus. music.
> Contains many folk songs of the world, including American folk songs and dances. Five Virginia folk songs arranged by John Powell.

McGill, Josephine
Folk-songs of the Kentucky Mountains. Twenty traditional ballads and other folk-songs, notated from the singing of the Kentucky mountain people and arranged with piano accompaniment by Josephine McGill. Introductory note by H. E. Krehbiel. New York: Boosey & Co., c. 1917. 106 p.
> Melodies with piano accompaniment.

Neely, Charles
Tales and Songs of Southern Illinois. collected by Charles Neely; edited with a foreword by John Webster Spargo. Menasha, Wis.: George Banta Publishing Co., 1938. xix, 270 p.
> Part of the songs accompanied by music.

Newell, William Wells, coll.
Games and Songs of American Children. New York: Harper and Brothers, 1893, 1903. New and Enlarged Edition.

Palmer, Mrs. Winthrop B.
American Songs For Children. New York: The Macmillan Company, 1931.
American folksongs from all sections: New England, The South, Negro Spirituals, The West, Indian, and American Play Songs.

Pendleton, Laura
A Child's Book of American Song. Cincinnati: Willis Music Company, 1931. Voice and piano.

Pound, Louise
American Ballads and Songs. New York: Charles Scribner's Sons, 1922.

Richardson, Mrs. Ethel (Park)
American Mountain Songs, compiled by Ethel Richardson, edited and arranged by Sigmund Spaeth. New York: Greenberg, 1927. 120 pp., music.

Russell, Sidney King
Songs for America. New York: The Fine Editions Press, 227 East 45th Street.

Sandburg, Carl
The American Songbag. New York: Harcourt Brace and Company, 1927, xvi, 495 pp.
The music is arranged for voice and piano.

Scarborough, Dorothy
A Song Catcher in Southern Mountains: American folksongs of British ancestry. New York: Columbia University Press, 1937. xvi, 476 p., music (unaccompanied melodies) p. 383–457.

Scott, Tom, ed. and arr.
Sing of America. Folk tunes collected and arranged by Tom Scott. Text by Joy Scott. Wood engravings by Bernard Brussel-Smith. New York: Thomas Y. Crowell, 1947. 83 pp.
This collection (35 tunes) "is on the polite-well-groomed side; it is slanted towards the children." (Horace Reynolds). Arranged for voice and piano.

Seeger, Charles, ed.
Resettlement Song Sheets. "A Series of American Songs to supplement and those rarely found in popular collections." Washington, D. C.: Special Skills Division of the Resettlement Administration, 1936–1937.

Sharp, Cecil James
American-English Folksongs, collected in the Southern Appalachians and arranged with pianoforte accompaniment by Cecil J. Sharp. First series. New York: G. Schirmer, c. 1918. 57 p.
6 ballads and 6 songs. Melodies with piano accompaniment.

English Folk-Songs from the Southern Appalachians, collected by Cecil J. Sharp. Comprising two hundred and seventy three songs and ballads with nine hundred and sixty tunes contributed by Olive Dame Campbell. Edited by Maud Karpeles. London: Oxford University Press, 1932. 2 vol., music, bibl.

Folk-Songs of English Origin, Collected in the Appalachian Mountains—with pianoforte accompaniment; first and second series. London: Novello and Company, Ltd., 1918, 1921. 2 volumes in 1.

Shay, Frank
My Pious Friends and Drunken Companions. New York: The Macaulay Company, 1927, 192 pp.
Early-day ballads, work songs and drinking songs.

Sherwin, Sterling
Songs of the Gold Miners, a golden collection of songs, as sung by and about the Forty-niners, by Sterling Sherwin and Louis Katzman, and an introduction by Beth Moore. With chord accompaniments for ukulele, tenor banjo, and guitar (also chord charts, with fingering for tenor banjo and guitar). New York: Carl Fisher, Inc., c. 1932. 48 p. Pub. No. 26191–48.
Words, melodies with piano accompaniment.

Siegmeister, Elie
Work and Sing, a Collection of the Songs that Built America, selected and arranged by Elie Siegmeister. A treasury of the American work songs of yesterday and today. With commentary, annotations and a critical biography. Illustrated by Julian Brazelton. New York: W. R. Scott, 1944. 96 pp., bibl. p. 95–96, with piano accompaniment.

Smith, Reed
American Anthology of Old World Ballads, compiled and edited by Reed Smith, settings by Hilton Rufty. New York: J. Fischer & Brothers, c. 1937. Publ. No. 7270–69, xxxii, 70 p., bibl.

Spaeth, Sigmund
Read 'em and Weep; the Songs You Forgot to Remember. Garden City, N. Y.: Doubleday, 1935. xiv, 267 pp. Music.

Weep Some More, My Lady. Garden City, N. Y.: Doubleday, Page & Co., 1927. xv, 268 pp. Music.

Stout, Earl Jonathan
Folklore from Iowa, collected and edited by Earl J. Stout. New York: The American Folklore Society, G. E. Stechert & Co., agents, 1936. x, 228 p.
Some of the songs with music (unaccompanied melodies).

Sturgis, Edith Barnes
Songs from the Hills of Vermont, sung by James and Mary Atwood and Aunt Jenny Knapp. Texts collected and edited by Edith B. Sturgis. Tunes collected and piano accompaniments arranged with historical notes by Robert Hughes. New York: G. Schirmer, c. 1919. Publ. No. 29137, ix, 57 p.
Melodies with piano accompaniment.

The American Musical Miscellany: A Collection of the Newest and Most Approved Songs, Set to Music. Northampton, Massachusetts: Printed by Andrew Wright for Daniel Wright and Company, 1798, 300 pp.

Thomas, Jean
Ballad Makin' in the Mountains of Kentucky; with music arranged by Walter Kob. New York: H. Holt & Co., 1939. xviii, 270 p.

Wheeler, Opal
Sing for America. Illus. by Gustaf Tenggren. New York: E. P. Dutton Co., 1947.
Music and verse of 24 folk tunes, with stories of their origin. For young readers and singers.

Wolfe, Jacques
American Songster. 17 American folksongs. New York: Carl Fischer and Co., 1947. Medium voice and piano.

Wyman, Loraine
Twenty Kentucky Mountain Songs. The words collected by Loraine Wyman, the melodies collected and piano accompaniments added by Howard Brockway. Boston: Oliver Ditson Co., c. 1920. Publ. No. 73480–115, 114 pp.
Melodies with piano accompaniment.

GENERAL COLLECTIONS: CHORAL

Armitage, Marie Teresa
Folk Songs and Art Songs for Intermediate Grades, Student's Edition. Boston: C. C. Birchard Company, 1924, The Laurel Music Series.

————, Dykema, Peter W.; Pitcher, Gladys; Stevens, David; and Vandevere, J. Hillian, editors
Our Land of Song—A Singing School. Boston: C. C. Birchard and Company, 1942. Illustrated by Martha Powell Setchell.
Delightfully well organized book for the elementary grades. Contains a number of American regional folk songs and dances.

Beattie, Breach, Glenn, Hesser, Goodell, Hall, and Wisenall, editors
The Golden Book of Favorite Songs. Chicago: Hall and McCreary, 1915, 1923, 128 pp.
"Most widely used assembly song book." Over 200 selections—many American folk songs, solo, SATB.

————.
The Gray Book of Favorite Songs. Chicago: Hall and McCreary Company, 1937 revised, 128 pp.
Especially designed for Junior and Senior High School assembly programs. Many folk songs for solo and choral performance.

Bowen, Cain, Goodell, Grant Osburn, and Woods, editors
Program Choruses, The Green Book. Chicago: Hall and McCreary Company.
Contains some mixed voice arrangements of folk songs.

Brown, Stanley K., editor
The Song Book of the American Spirit illustrated. New York: Harper & Bros. 1927. 28 pp., illus.

Canciones Pan Americanas; Songs of the Americas.
Published in collaboration with the Pan American Union, Washington, D. C. New York: Silver Burdett Comany, 1942.
Includes 3 folk songs of the U. S.

Carmer, Carl
America Sings. Stories and songs of our country's growth. Music arranged by Edwin J. Stringham. Illustrated in color by Elizabeth Black Carmer. New York: Alfred A. Knopf, 1942. 243 pp.

Chamberlain, D. B., and Harrington, K. P.
Songs of All the Colleges. New York: Hinds, Hayden and Eldredge, 1926.

Clark, Kenneth S.
The "Everybody Sing" Book. For Home, School and Community. New York: Paull-Pioneer Music Corporation, 1935.

Coleman, Satis N. and Bregman, Adolph
Songs of American Folks. New York: John Day Company, 1942.

Curtis, L. W., and others, editors
The Silver Book of Songs, for all grades. Chicago: Hall and McCreary Company.
A great number of folk songs in unison, two part, three part, and four part arrangement for young voices.

Damrosch, Frank
Folk-Songs and Part Songs, with preparatory exercises for choral classes. New York: G. Schirmer Company, 1896, xv, 80 pp.

Donovan, Richard
Fantasy on American Folk Ballads. New York: J. Fischer and Bro., 1940. (TTBB).
With accompaniment for piano—four hands. Content: "Farewell my Friends" (White Spiritual); "Old Bangum"; "In the Township of Danville I Courted My Love (Vt.)."

Dykema, P. W., Earhart, W., Dann, H., and McConathy, O., editors
Twice 55 Plus Community Songs. The New Brown Book. Enlarged to contain 175 songs and choruses with Responsive Readings. Boston: C. C. Birchard and Company, 1929. 176 number, solo, SATB.
Contains some folk songs.

————.
Twice 55 Community Songs. The New Green Book. Boston: C. C. Birchard and Company, 1930. 173 selections, solo and ensemble (SATB) arrangements.

Frey, Hugo, editor
America Sings, Community Song Book for Schools, Clubs, Assemblies, Camps, and Recreational groups. New York: Robbins Music Corporation, 1935.

——————.
Songs for America, for Schools, Assemblies, Music Clubs, and Social Groups. New York: Robbins Music Corporation, 1941.

Goldman, Richard Franko, editor
Seven Songs of the Early Republic. New York: Mercury Music Corporation, 1945. Settings by Carl Buchman.
    Contents: 1) Brother Soldiers, All Hail.
        2) Jefferson and Liberty.
        3) The Green Mt. Liberty.
        4) America, Commerce, and Freedom.
        5) For the Fourth of July.
        6) Washington.
        7) The Federal Constitution and Liberty Forever.

——————, **and Smith, Roger compilers and editors**
Landmarks of Early American Music, 1760–1800. New York: G. Schirmer, Inc., 1945.
    A Collection of Thirty-two Compositions, for orchestra, band, smaller instrumental groups, or mixed chorus.

Gordon, Edgar B., and others
The New Blue Book of Favorite Songs. Chicago: Hall and McCreary Company.
    Contains over 340 selections—including sea chanteys, old English tunes, Negro spirituals, war songs, etc., for mixed voices.

Harris, Roy, and Evanson, Jacob, editors
Singing Through the Ages. New York: American Book Company, 1940, 206 pp., solo voice and SATB, unaccompanied.
    Melodic and Harmonic Songs. Contains a number of American folk songs.

Jackson, George Pullen, coll. and ed.
Amercian Folk Music for High School and Other Choral Groups. Arranged by Charles Faulkner Bryan. Boston: C. C. Birchard and Company, 1947.
    Twenty-five songs. Choral arrangements, piano accompaniments.

Jameson, Gladys V., ed.
The School Glee Club. Chicago: Clayton F. Summy Company.
    Contains a good number of folk songs for mixed voices.

Landeck, Beatrice, compiler and editor
"Git on Board." New York: Edward B. Marks Music Corporation, 1944.
    Collection of Folk Songs, arranged for mixed voices. Introduction by Norman Studer. Vocal arrangements by Charity Bailey, Ernest Gold, Felix Guenther, J. Rosamond Johnson, and others.

Luther, Frank
Americans and Their Songs. New York: Harper and Brothers, 1942, 311 pp. illustrated.

Maddy, Joseph E., and Miessner, W. O., editors
All American Song Book. New York: Robbins Music Corporation, 1942, 144 pp. mixed voices.
    A Community Song Book for schools, homes, clubs, and community singing.

National Conference of Music Supervisors
I Hear America Singing. Boston: C. C. Birchard and Company, 1913.
    18 songs for community singing.

Oberndorfer, M. E. and A. E.
The New American Song Book. Chicago: Hall and McCreary Company, 1933, 160 pp.
    A collection of outstanding merit, used for American Unity Programs, for Americanization, and for Assembly. Arranged for mixed voices. Contains a large number of folk songs.

——————, **and Faulkner, A. S.**
Century of Progress in American Song. Chicago: Hall and McCreary Company, 1933.

O'Hara, Geoffrey
Golden Treasury Song Book. New York: Robbins Music Corp., 1947.
    154 Songs for 4 part choral singing.

Pierson, Underwood, and Perry, Lawrence
An American Frolic. Based on old American Folk Songs and Fiddle Tunes. Boston: C. C. Birchard and Company. 13 pp.
    Dramatic play with music—for school.

Siegmeister, Elie, comp. and arr.
Eight American Folksongs. New York: C. Fischer. SATB, a cap.

——————.
Songs of Early America, 1620–1830. New York: Edward B. Marks Corporation, 1944.
    Contains 16 songs for mixed voices—not all folk songs.

——————.
Work and Sing. New York: W. R. Scott, 96 pp., illustrated.
    A collection of the songs that built America. Selected and arranged by Elie Siegmeister; a treasury of American worksongs of yesterday and today, with commentary annotations and a critical bibliography; illustrated by Julian Brazelton.

Smith, F., Wilson, H. R., and Woods, G. H., editors
Songs We Sing. Chicago: Hall McCreary Company.
    For the classroom, the assembly, and all recreational gatherings. A good number of various American folk tunes for unison, two part and four part arrangement.

Stevens, D., and Dykema, P. W.
Sing! Boston: C. C. Birchard and Company, 1937, 144 pp. Decorations by M. B. Setchell.
    The All Purpose Song Book for Home; School; Community Choruses; Social Meetings and Festivities, with complete piano accompaniments. Solo and ensemble arrangements, includes a goodly number of folk songs, chanteys, spirituals, cowboy songs, etc.

357 Songs We Love to Sing.
    Chicago: Hall and McCreary Company, 1938. Songs for Every Purpose and Occasion for Home, School, and Assembly, Children's Songs, Cowboy and Mountain Songs. Stephen Foster, Folk Songs, Negro Spirituals; Plantation Songs, Rounds, Sea Songs and Chanteys, Singing Games.

Tobitt, Janet E.
Sing Together. New York: Girl Scouts, Inc., 1936, 96 pp. 14 West 49th Street.
Tunes, some with accompaniment, of folk songs and other melodies. Simple and easy range—for solo voice.

Twice 55 Community Songs: The Blue Book. Boston: C. C. Birchard and Company.

Twice 55 Community Songs, The Rose Book, For Women's Voices. Boston: C. C. Birchard and Company.

Twice 55 Games with Music, The Red Book. More than 110 singing games with directions. Boston: C. C. Birchard and Company.

Twice 55 Part Songs for Boys, The Orange Book. Boston: C. C. Birchard and Company.

Wheeler, Opal
Sing for America. Illustrated by Gustaf Tenggren. New York: E. P. Dutton, Inc., 1944, 127 pp., illustrated.
Stories and songs that have made America—not all are folk songs, piano—4 part voice arrangement.

Wilson, Harry Robert, editor and arranger
Ready Sing! New York: Emerson Books, Inc., 251 West 19th Street, choral.
A collection of American songs for group singing with music.

————.
Songs of the Hills and Plains. Early American Songs arranged for modern use. Chicago: Hall and McCreary Company.
Excellent collection and arrangements of American folk songs for home and classroom. Solo and ensemble.

————, and Christy, Van A., editors
The Modern Choral Hour. Chicago: Hall and McCreary Company.
The contents include choral arrangements of many folk tunes for two, three, or four part male and female voices and solo numbers.

Zanzig, Augustus D., editor
Singing America: Song and Chorus Book. Compiled, arranged, and edited for the National Recreation Association. Boston: C. C. Birchard and Company, 1940.
Fine collection of folk songs included, for solo and ensemble.

ARRANGEMENTS

————: Piano

American Sonata.
Siegmeister, E.: Marks: Piano.

American Symphonette.
Gould, Morton: Schirmer, transcribed for piano.

American Caprice. New York: Gould, Morton: G. Schirmer, Inc., for piano.

————: Violin, Cello

American Suite.
Cazden, Norman: Center: cello, piano.

Forty Folk Tunes.
Percy, C. A.: White-Smith: Violin and piano (easy).

————: Orchestra

List of American Orchestral Works
Recommended by WPA Music Project Conductor. Washington D. C.: July, 1941, WPA —1941.

An American Rhapsody.
Castelnuovo-Tedesco, Mario: MS: orchestra.

American Epic.
Morris, H.: MS: orchestra.

American Festival Overture.
Schuman, William: Schirmer: Orchestra.

American Rhapsody.
Grundman: Educational: Full Band.

American Holiday.
Siegmeister, E.: Music Guild: Orchestra.

American Overture.
Schlein, Irving: MS: Orchestra.

American Rhapsody.
Zimbalist, Efrem: MS: Orchestra.

American Suite.
Cadman, Charles W. Composers Press: Orchestra.

American Symphonette.
Gould, Morton: Schirmer: Symphony Orchestra.

American Symphonic Sketches.
Converse, Frederick S.: Birchard: orchestra.

American Symphony.
Antheil, George: Manuscript, 1921.

American Symphony.
Shure, Deane R.: New York: J. Fischer and Brothers.
The work is based on American folk music: Indian, English-American, and Negro.

Americana, op. 28.
Luening, Otto: MS: Orchestra.

Americana Suite.
Gruenberg, Louis: MS: Orchestra.

Americanese—suite on three early American pieces.
Maganini, Quinto: Musicus: Orchestra.

Early Americana—Suite.
Stoessel, A.: Birchard: Orchestra.

Epoch—A Choreographic Drama. In four American Phases. McKay, George F.: MS: Dance drama.

Folk Ryhthms of Today.
Harris, Roy: Mills: Symphony Orchestra.

Folk Song Symphony.
Harris, Roy. 1. The Girl I left behind me; 2. Western Cowboy; 3. Mountaineer Love Song; 4. Negro Symphony; 5. Johnny Comes Marching Home. New York: G. Schirmer, Inc., 1942 (revised), for chorus, orchestra, SATB.

From the American Folklore—Concert Overture.
Koutzen, Boris: MS: Orchestra.

From these States. Suite.
Bacon, Ernst: Associated Publishers: orchestra.

Overture on American Folk Themes.
Kleinsinger, George: Mills: Orchestra.

Sinfonietta Americana.
Wagner, Joseph F.: MS: Chamber Orchestra.

Three American Folk Songs.
Suite for small Orchestra. Kubik, Gail: Schirmer: Chamber Orchestra.

To America—Festival Overture.
Cowell, Henry D.: Broadcast: SATB, 2 orchestras:

RECORDS
See: Ballad Recordings, pp. 125-133.
Bibliographies

Chamberlain, Gladys E.
"A Record Bibliography." *Music Journal* 6 (No. 1) :30–31, 59–63, 1948.
An excellent selected bibliography of the literature on recorded music, including some folksong items.

Chase, Gilbert
"Folk Music on Records." *Music Journal* 6 (No. 1) :15, 58–59, 1948.
A general discussion of the outstanding albums of American folksongs and dances.

Check List of Anglo-American and other Folk Music on disks in the Archive of California, Department of Music, University of California, Berkeley, California, 1941.

Check List of Recorded Songs in the English language in the Archives of American Folksong to July, 1940. Library of Congress, Music Division. Washington, D. C.: 3 volumes I–216, II–456, III–138 pp., 1942, mimeo.

Collins, Dr. Fletcher, Jr.
Record Bibliography. North Carolina: Elon College.

Halpert, Herbert
"Some Recorded American Folksong." *American Music Lover* 2 (No. 7) :196–200, (November) 1936.

Lomax, Alan
List of American Folk Songs on Commercial Records in Report of the Committee of the Conference on Inter-American Relations in the field of music, William Berrien, Chairman. Washington, D. C.: Department of State, (September), 1940.

Mayer, David
"Folk Music on Records." *YMHA Bulletin* (New York City) 42:3, 1941. (February 14).

U. S. Library of Congress. Division of Music. Folklore Section.
Folk Music of the United States and Latin America. Combined Catalog of Phonograph Records. Washington, D. C.: 1948. 47 pp.
"This catalog lists 21 albums, 107 records, containing 341 titles, or all those issued by the Library of Congress since 1941. They have been selected as among the best and most representative of over 10,000 records in the collection of the Archive of American Folk Song." These albums contain songs and ballads, fiddle tunes, harmonica and banjo pieces, shanties, spirituals, work songs, blues, game songs, French ballads, Iroquois and Seneca songs, Sacred Harp songs, Miners' songs, etc.

Wheaton-Smith, Barbara
"Recorded Folksong." *JAFL* 59:319–320, 1946.

General Collections

A Collection of Ballads and Songs.
Burl Ives, vocal-guitar.   DE A–407
Content: The Fox; Dan Tucker; Erie Canal; Dublin City; Cockle-Shells; Lully-Too-Dum; Eddystone Light; Hullabaloo; Saturday Night; Aunt Rhody Nicodemus, Venezuela.

America's Favorite Songs I.
Bess Lomax, Butch Hawes, Pete Seeger, Tom Glazer,—Vocalists-guitar.   DISC–607
Contents: Down in the Valley; Casey Jones; Go Tell Aunt Nancy; The Cowboy's Lament; Buffalo Gals; Careless Love.

America's Favorite Songs. Vol. 2.
Cornelius Greenway's Smokey Mountaineers. 3–10".   DISC 633
Content: Lover's Farewell; Don't Let Your Sweet Love Die; Amelia Earhart's Last Flight; Dust on the Bible; Bully of the Town; Ragtime Annie.

American Folklore, Vols. 1, 2, 3.
John Jacob Niles, tenor, piano or dulcimer. 3–10", 1–12".   V–M–824

American Folk Songs.
Frank Luther, assisted by Zora Layman and Leonard Stokes, 34 songs, 10 sides. DE–A25

American Song Album.
Madrigal Singers, Lehman Engel, Conductor, 4 double disks.   CO–329

Early American Carols and Folksongs.
John Jacob Niles, vocal and dulcimer or piano. 4–10".   VM–718
Contents: Jesus, Jesus Rest Your Head; Down in the Forest; So Jesus the Saviour; Jesus the Christ Child is Born; The Cherry Tree; The Old Woman and the Pig; The Frog Went A-Courting.

Folk Music of the United States, 1942 Catalog of Phonograph Records.

Selected titles from the Archives of American Folk-Song, issued to January, 1943. Washington, D. C.: The Library of Congress, Reference Department, Division of Music, Recording Laboratory.

Contents: 6 Albums, edited by Alan Lomax.

Album I —Anglo-American Ballads

Album II —Anglo - American Shanties, Lyric Songs, Dance Tunes and Spirituals

Album III—Afro - American Spirituals, Work Songs, and Ballads

Album IV—Afro - American Blues and Game Songs

Album V —Bahaman Songs; Franch Ballads and Dance Tunes, Spanish Religious Songs and Game Songs.

Album VI—Songs from the Iroquois Longhouse, recorded and edited by William N. Fenton, Smithsonian Institute

Combined Catalogue Issued in 1948. Contains 21 volumes. In addition to above:

Album VII —Anglo-American Ballads.

Album VIII—Negro Work Songs and Calls.

Album IX —Play and Dance Songs and Tunes.

Album X —Negro Religious Songs and Services.

Album XI —Sacred Harp Singing

Album XII —Anglo-American Songs and Ballads.

Album XIV—Anglo-American Songs and Ballads.

Album XVI—Songs and Ballads of the Anthracite Miners.

Album XX —Anglo-American Songs and Ballads.

Album XXI— Anglo-American Songs and Ballads.

Folksay: American Ballads and Dances.

Woody Guthrie, Cisco Houston, Baldwin Hawes, Bess Lomax, Pete Seeger, Sonny Terry and Alec, Josh White and Leadbelly. 4–10″
A–75–10

Folk Songs.

Josh White, vocal-guitar. 3–10″.　　　A–358

Folk Songs and Ballads.

Susan Reed, with Irish Harp and Zither . . . 3–10″.　　　VM–1086

Contents: Venezuela; Go Away from my Window; Molly Malone; If I Had A Ribbon Bow; The Old Woman; The Ballad of Barberry Ellen; A Mighty Ship; Jenny Jenkins; My Love is Like a Red, Red Rose; The Soldier and the Lady.

Folk Songs and Ballads of America. Margaret Dodd Singers. Hargail Set.　　　HN–705

Folk Songs of America.

Almanac Singers. 3–10″.　　　G–21

Contents: The Dodger; Hard, Ain't It Hard; The State of Arkansaw; I Ride On Old Paint; House of the Rising Sun; Ground Hog!

Folk Songs of the Americas;

A collection of folk tunes taken from the book —*Singing America.* Vocalist, Elsie Houston, Alexandro Girallo, Federico Jimeno and mixed quartet. Instrumental accompaniment. 4–10″.
V–P55

Contents: El-a-noy (Pioneer) ; Lonesome Valley (White Spiritual) ; Shuckin' of the Corn (Tennessee) ; At the Gate of Heaven (New Mexico) ; To Bethelem Singing (Puerto Rico) ; Night Herding Song (Cowboy) ; Bouli's Ball (French Canadian) ; The Turtle Dove (English) ; La Cuisinere (French Canadian) ; Santa San Juanito (Ecuador) ; From Yon Mt. Verdant (Peru) ; Tutu Maramba (Brazilian) ; Que Lejos Estoy (Mexican) ; Vidalita (Argentine) ; Uy! Tara Lala (Mexican) ; Flowing River (Chile) ; Spring (Swedish) ; Little Grove, All In Green (Polish) ; Walking Song (Swiss) ; At Sunset (Finnish) ; Walking At Night (Czech) ; Vagabond's Song (Catalonian).

Minstrel Songs of the U. S. A.

Richard Dyer-Bennet, vocal-guitar. 4–10″.
VOX–632

Contents: "Along the Colorado Trail"; "The Racket's Around Blue Mountain Lake"; "The Quaker Lover"; "When Cockle Shells Turn Silver Bells"; "The Lass from the Low Country"; "Old Bangum"; "The Turkish Revery"; "Were You There."

Songs for Americans.

Earl Robinson with guitar.　　　TI–8

Contents: Jesse James; John Henry; Grey Goose; Abe Lincoln; Joe Hill; Horace Greeley; John Brown.

Street Cries.

American Ballad Singers—Siegmeister. In: *Two Centuries of American Folk Songs.* V–P41

Contents: Chimney Sweep (New Orleans) ; Blackberries (New Orleans) ; Charcoal (Springfield, Mo.).

The American Songbag.

Carl Sandburg—vocal, guitar. 4–10″. MU–11

The Songs of Early America.

(1620–1830). Compiled and Directed by Elie Siegmeister and his Singers.　　　BOST–ES1

Two Centuries of American Folk Songs.

American Ballad Singers—Siegmeister 3–10″.
V–P41

Contents: Poor Wayfaring Stranger (White Spiritual) ; Springfield Mt. (Nonsense ballad) ; Go To Sleep; Street Cries—Chimney Sweep & Blackberries (New Orleans) ; Strawberry (Brooklyn) ; Charcoal (Springfield, Mo.) ; Grandma Grunts; Kentucky Moonshiner; The Deaf Woman's Courtship; Pat Works on the Railway; Cotton-Picking Song; Upon De Mountain.

United States.

In the archives of Robert W. Gordon, Washington, D. C.

U. S. Library of Congress. Division of Music. Folklore Division.

Recordings in the Archive of American Folk Song. Field recordings in all aspects of American folksong, done by numerous workers and collectors, now (1948) totalling close to 10,000 records, and include some 35,000 songs, are deposited in the Archive of American Folk Song, Library of Congress, Music Division, Washington, D. C.

See: Check List of American Folk Song in the Archive of American Folk Song, 1940. 3 vols.

Wayfaring Stranger.
    Burl Ives, vocal-guitar.   OK–3
      Contents: Wee Cooper O'Fife; Riddle Song; The Cowboy's Lament; Tam Pierce; I Know Where I'm Going; I Know My Love; Peter Gray; Sweet Betsy from Pike; On Top of Old Smoky; Darlin' Corey; Leather Winged Bat; Cotton Eyed Joe.

Individual Titles

"Hand Me Down My Walking Cane."
    In: *American Folk Songs Album.* Luther; Layman; Stokes; guitar-fiddle-bass.   DE 25

"In the Baggage Coach Ahead."
    In: *American Folk Songs Album.* Luther; Layman; Stokes; guitar-fiddle-bass.   DE 25

"Letter Edged in Black."
    In: *American Folk Songs Album.* Luther; Layman; Stokes; guitar-fiddle-bass.   DE 25

"Maple on the Hill."
    In: *American Folk Songs Album.* Luther; Layman; Stokes; vocal-guitar-fiddle-bass.   DE 28

"My Horses Ain't Hungry."
    In: *American Folk Songs Album.* Luther; Layman; Stokes; guitar-fiddle-bass.   DE 25

"Nellie Bly."
    Massey and Westerners.   OK 06558

"Pass Around the Bottle."
    In: *American Folk Songs Album.* Luther; Layman; Stokes; guitar-fiddle-bass.   DE 25

"Put My Little Shoes Away."
    In: *American Folk Songs Album.* Luther; Layman; Stokes; guitar-fiddle-bass.   DE 25

"Seeing the Elephant."
    In: *Songs of Old California.* Luther; Layman and Century Quartet.   DE 49

"The Night is Serene."
    In: *Songs of Old California.* Luther; Layman and Century Quartet.   DE 49

"The White Hawk."
    In: *Songs of Old California.* Luther; Layman and Century Quartet.   DE 49

"When I Was Single."
    In: *American Folk Songs Album.* Luther; Layman; Stokes; guitar, fiddle-bass.   DE 25

"When the Roses Bloom Again."
    In: *American Folk Songs Album.* Luther; Layman; Stokes; vocal-guitar, fiddle-bass.   DE 25

THE BALLAD

THE BALLAD

BIBLIOGRAPHY

See: Folksong Bibliography; pp. 68–69.

Becker, M. L.
"Bibliography of Ballads." *Saturday Review of Literature* 5:657, March 3, 1928.

Broadsides, Ballads, etc. Printed in Massachusetts, 1639–1800.
Massachusetts Historical Society Collections, 75, 1922.
   A collection of 340 broadsides of English and Irish street ballads.

Child, Francis
Bibliography of Collection of Ballads. In: *English and Scottish Popular Ballads* (Volume V, pp. 455–468). Boston: Houghton Mifflin Company, 1892–1898.

Collins, Fletcher
"An aid in the discovery of folksongs; a list of finders for traditional ballads, songs, and play-parties in the Southeast." *SFQ* 5:235–250, 1941.

Collins, H. W.
An Analytical Index to the Ballad Entries, (1557–1709) in the Registers of the Company of Stationers of London. Chapel Hill, North Carolina: University of North Carolina Press, 1924.

Ford, W. C.
"The Isiah Thomas Collection of Ballads." *Proceedings of the American Antiquarian Society* n.s. 33:34–112.

Hustvedt, Sigurd B.
Ballad Books and Ballad Men. Cambridge: Harvard University Press, 1930.

————.
"A Melodic Index of Child's Ballad Tunes." *Publications of the University of California at Los Angeles in Languages and Literature* 1:51–78, 1936.

Lesser, Alexander
"Bibliography of American Folklore, 1915–1928." *JAFL 41:* 1–60, 1928.

Publications of the Ballad Society.
London: Hertford, 1868–1900, (1–38).

Rollins, Hyder E.
"Analytical Index to Ballad Entries (1557–1709) in the Registers of London." *Studies in Philology* 21:1–324, 1921.

GENERAL STUDIES

"Accumulative Rhymes." *JAFL* 18:37, 1905.

Allen, Philip S.
"Studies in Popular Poetry." Chicago: *Chicago University Decennial Publication,* No. 4, ser. 1, v. 7, 1902.

"Ancient Ballad."
N. and Q., (Second Series) :9:143.

"Anonymous Ballads."
N. and Q., (Third Series) :9, 143.

"Ballad Literature."
Living Age 254:253–254, July 27, 1907.

"Ballad Makers and Legislators."
N. and Q., (Third Series) :9:143.

"The Ballad of America."
Bookworld 1:103, 1898.

"Ballads."
Living Age 268:748–753, March 25, 1911.

"Ballads, Homiletic."
JAFL 29:191–192, 1916; 35:423, 425, 1922.

"Ballads in America."
Nation 98:128–129, February 5, 1914.

"Ballads Surviving in the U. S."
Department of Public Instruction of Va. Ballad Circular, January, 1916.

Barbour, F. M.
"Some Fusions in Missouri Ballads." *JAFL* 49:207–214, 1936.

Barry, Phillips
"American Ballads." *FSSNE* 6:10–18, 1933.

————.
"American Ballads." *JAFL* 25:188, 1912.

————.
"British Ballads (Old World Ballads in New England)." *FSSNE* 11:8–12, 1936.
   Old World ballads in N. E.: "The False Knight Upon the Road," "Bonnie Annie," "Alexander and Rosine," "Daniel Sullivan," "Patrick Sheehan."

————.
"British Ballads." *FSSNE* 12:8–11, 1937.
   Five examples of "secondary differentiation."

————.
"Child Ballads and Their Kin (New England)." *FSSNE* 3:6–11, 1931.
   Describes Old World ballad variants recorded—New England states: "Lord Banner," "Mary Hamilton," "John of Haselgreen," "Jack the Jolly Tar." Words and Music.

————.
"Communal Recreation." *FSSNE* 5:4–6, 1933.

————.
"An Essay on Tunes." *FSSNE* 5:3–6, 1933.

————.
"Garland of Ballads." *JAFL* 23:446–454, 1910.

————.
"Irish Come-All-Ye's." *JAFL* 22:374, 1909.

"Irish Folk-Song." *JAFL* 24:332–343, 1911.

The Music of the Ballads. In: *British Ballads from Maine, by Barry, Eckstorm, and Smyth,* pp. XXI–XXXVII. New Haven, Conn.: Yale University Press, 1929.

"Native Balladry in America." *JAFL* 22:364–373, 1909.

"Negro Folk Songs from Maine." *FSSNE* 8:13–16, 1934; 9:10–14, 1935; 10:21–24, 1935. Hymns and Ballads.

"New Ballad Texts." *JAFL* 24:344, 1911.

"Non-Child Ballads (Northeast and Canada)." *FSSNE* 3:14–17, 1931. Ballads of local origin, N. E. and eastern Canada.

"Some Traditional Songs." *JAFL* 53:49–59, 1905.

"The Psychopathology of Ballad-Singing." *FSSNE* 11:16–18, 1936.

"Traditional Ballads in New England." *JAFL* 53:123–138; 191–214; 291–304, 1905.

"The Transmission of Folk-Song." *JAFL* 27:67–76, 1914.

Beatty, Arthur
"Ballad, Tale and Tradition: A Study in Popular Literary Origins." *PMLA* 29 (NS 22) No. 4:473–498, 1914, bibliography.

"Ballad Variants." *JAFL* 20:154–156, 1907; 22:63–71, 1909.

"Some Ballad Variants and Songs." *JAFL* 22:63–71, 1909.

"Some New Ballad Variants." *JAFL* 20:154–156, 1910.

Beckwith, Martha W.
"The English Ballad in Jamaica: A Note Upon the Origins of the Ballad Form." *PMLA* 39:455–483, 1924. Musical examples.

Belden, H. M.
"Balladry in America." *JAFL* 25:1–23, 1912.

"Ballads and Songs Collected by the Missouri Folk Lore Society." *The University of Missouri Studies,* Vol. 15, No. 1, Columbia, Mo.: University of Missouri Press, 1940. 530 pp., bibl.

"Old Country Ballads in Missouri." *JAFL* 19:231–240, 281–299, 1906; 20:319–320, 1907; 23:429–431, 1910.

"Relation of Balladry to Folklore." *JAFL* 24:1–13, 1911.

"Three Old Ballads from Missouri." *JAFL* 23:429–431, 1910.

"The Vulgar Ballad." *The Sewanee Review* 19:213–227, 1911.

Bennett, W. C.
Shall We Have a National Ballad History for the English People? An Appeal to the Poets of England and America. Edinburgh: Henderson, Rait, and Fenton, 1868, 8 p.

Bowen, Edwin W.
"The Old English Ballad." *Sewanee Review 9:* 286–295, 1901.

Bradley, William Aspenwall
"Song-Ballets and Devil's Ditties." *Harper's Monthly Magazine* 130:901–914, 1914–1915.

Brandt, Alois
Zur Kritik der englischen Volksballaden. In: *Forschungen zur neueren Litteraturgeschichte,* pp. 51–75. Weimar: 1898.

Brewster, P. G.
Ballads and Songs of Indiana. (Indiana University Publications Folklore Series No. 1). Bloomington, Ind.: Indiana University, 1940.

"More Songs from Indiana." *SFQ* 4:175–203, 1940. Words only.

"More Indiana Ballads and Songs." *SFQ* 5:169–190, 1941.

"Traditional Ballads from Indiana." *JAFL* 48:295–318, 1935.

"Broadside Ballads."
The Times Literary Supplement. January 22, 1931, pp. 49–50.

Brockway, H.
"The Quest of the Lonesome Tunes." *MTNA, Papers of Proceedings* 14:59–67, 1919.

Bronson, Bertrand H.
"Folksong and the Modes." *MQ* 32 (No. 1): 37–49, 1946. Primarily with English Ballads.

"The Interdependence of Ballad Tunes and Texts." *CFQ* 3:185–207, 1944.

"Mrs. Brown and the Ballad." *CFQ* 4:129–140, 1945.

————.
"Professor Child's Ballad Tunes." *CFQ* 1:
185–200, 1942.
    Twenty-five musical illustrations.

Buchanan, Annabel Morris
Anglo-American Folk Music. In: *International
Cyclopedia of Music*, Oscar Thompson, ed.
New York: Dodd, Mead and Co., 1938.
    Comprehensive survey of Anglo-American folk
    music, with history, discussion, illustrations of
    each type, analyses of tunes and modes.

————.
"A Neutral Mode in Anglo-American Folk
Music." *SFQ* 4:77–92, 1940.

Carter, Isabel Gordon
"Some Songs and Ballads from Tennessee and
North Carolina." *JAFL* 46:22–51, 1933.
    Texts only.

Child, Francis James
*Child Memorial Volume Studies and Notes in
Philology and Literature, Vol. 5*, 1903.

Clawson, W. H.
"Ballad and Epic." *JAFL* 21:349–361, 1908.

Cleghorn, S. M.
"Shall We Have Ballads Again?" *Survey* 54:
491–492, August 1, 1925.

"Collecting American Ballads."
Newark Evening News, April 12, 1930.
    A review.

"Collecting Folk-Songs by Phonophotography."
Literary Digest 96:22–23, February 11, 1928.

Combs, J. H.
"Ballad from the Kentucky Mountains." *JAFL*
23:381–382, 1910.

Davidson, Thomas
"Professor Child's Ballad Book." *American
Journal of Philology* 5:466, 1909.

Davis, Arthur Kyle, Jr.
"On the Collecting and Editing of Ballads."
AS 5 (No. 6):452–455, 1930.

————.
"Some Problems of Ballad Publication." *MQ*
14:283–296, 1928.
    The author discusses five major problems: music
    publication, ribaldry, artificial geography, patrio-
    tism, and academic versus popular interest.

Doerflinger, William M.
"Ballads Are True, an Essay." Princeton, N. J.:
Argo, an Individual Review, November, 1930,
p. 5.

Dolph, Edward Arthur
"Ballads That Have Influenced Ballots." *New
York Times Magazine*, October 16, 1932, p. 19.

"The Dramatic Element in the Popular Ballad."
University of Cincinnati Studies, Ser. 11, 1:30–
31, 1905.

Eckstorm, Fannie Hardy
"The Ballad of Tradition." *FSSNE* No. 6, p. 19.
    A review of Professor Gordon Hall Gerould's
    book.

————.
"Local Rimes and Quatrains of the Northeast."
FSSNE 3:17–20, 1931.

————, and Barry, Phillips
"What is Tradition." *FSSNE* 1:2–3, 1930.
    A discussion of tradition—folk songs and the
    "ways" of the folk.

Eddy, M. O., and Tolman, A. H.
"Traditional Texts and Tunes." *JAFL* 35:335–
432, 1922.

Edmonds, Lila W.
"Songs from the Mountains of North Carolina."
JAFL 6:131–134, 1893.

"English Folk-Song in America."
Pittsburgh, Pa.: *Monthly Bulletin, Carnegie
Library*, January, 1918.

Entwistle, William J.
"Notations for Ballad Melodies." *PMLA* 55:
61–72, 1940.

Finlay, John
*Scottish Historical and Romantic Ballads,
Chiefly Ancient; with Remarks on the Early
State of Romantic Composition in Scotland.*
Edinburgh: A. Constable and Co., 1808, 2 vols.

Fluegel, Ewald
"Zur Chronologie der englischer Balladen."
Anglia 21:312–358, 1899. (Halle).
    Chronological Index to Child's "English and
    Scottish Ballads."

"Folk-Ballads in America."
London Times Literary Supplement, May 29,
1930.
    Criticism of "Traditional Ballads of Virginia."
    Edited by Arthur Kyle Davis, Jr.

Gayton, A. H.
"English Ballads and Indian Myths." *JAFL*
55:121–126, 1942.

Gerould, Gordon Hall
The Ballad of Tradition. New York: Oxford
University Press, 1932.

————.
"The Making of Ballads." *Modern Philology*
21:15–28, August, 1923.

Görbing, Friedrich
"Beispiele von realisierten Mythen in den
englischen und schottischen Balladen." *Anglia*
23:1–13, 1900.

Gordon, Philip
"The Music of the Ballads." *SFQ* 6:143–148,
1942.

Gordon, Robert W.
"Old Songs that Men Have Sung." *Adventure
Magazine*, a department from July 10, 1923 to
November, 1927.

Grahame, Pauline
"Some Songs of Long Ago." Iowa City, Iowa: *The Palimpsest*, March, 1929.

Gray, Marion Hunter
"The Flight of the Ballad." Terre Haute, Indiana: *Women's Department Club Bulletin;* part 1, February 17, 1930, p. 3; part 2, March 3, 1930, p. 2; part 3, March 10, 1930, p. 4.
Contains an original version of "Lamkin."

Gray, R. P.
"Balladry of New York State." *N. Y. Historical Society* (Albany):147–155. April, 1936.

Greig, Gavin
Last Leaves of Traditional Ballads and Ballad Airs. Aberdeen: The Buchan Club, 1925, ed. by Aleander Keith.
"A valuable reference book for the field worker who will find it of assistance in determining what ballads are likely to have survived in a particular locality." (Barry)

Gummere, Francis B.
Ballads. In: *Cambridge History of Literature,* vol. 11, ch. XVII, pp. 449–474. Cambridge: 1908.

———.
"The Ballad and Communal Poetry." Boston: *Studies and Notes in Philology and Literature,* 1896.

———.
"Ballad Origins." *Nation* 85:184, August 29, 1907.

———.
The Beginnings of Poetry. New York: Macmillan Co., 1901, 483 pp.
Study of ballad origins.

———.
"Primitive Poetry and the Ballad." *Modern Philology* 1:193–202, 1903.

———.
"Narrative in Popular Ballads." *Reader* 7:215–219, January, 1906.

———.
"Popular Ballad." *Nation* 85:122–123, August 8, 1907.
A review.

———.
"Primitive Poetry and the Ballad." *Modern Philology* 1:193–202, 373–390, 1903–1904.

Halpert, Herbert
"The Cante Fable in Decay." *SFQ* 5:191–200, 1941.

———.
"Some Ballads and Folk Songs from New Jersey." *JAFL* 52:52–69, 1939.

Hart, Walter Morris
"Ballad and Epic." *Studies and Notes in Philology and Literature* 9:1907.

———.
"Professor Child and the Ballad." *PMLA* 21 (New Series 14):755–808, 1906.
A thorough and scholarly discussion.

Hecht, Hans
"Neuere Literatur zur englisch-schottischers Balladendichtung." Leipzig: *Englische Studien* 36:370–384, 1906.

———.
"Schottische Balladensamler aus dem Kreise F. J. Childs." *Nachrichten von der Gesellschaft der Wissenschaften zu Göttingen,* Philologisch-Historische Klasse, pp. 407–426, 1930.
Discussion of Scottish ballads and the collectors.

Henderson, I. F.
The Ballad in Literature. Cambridge, Mass.: Harvard University Press, 1912.

Hendren, J. W.
A Study of Ballad Rhythm, with Special Reference to Ballad Music. (Princeton Studies in English, No. 14.) Princeton University Press, 1936.

Henry, Mellinger E.
Adventures of a Ballad Collector. Word Study. Springfield, Mass.: G. & C. Merriam Co., June, 1932.

———.
"Stray Fragments of Old." *New Jersey Journal of Education* 16, (No. 10):9, June, 1927.

———.
"The History of an American Folk-Song." *New Jersey Journal of Education* 53, (No. 8):10, April, 1929; 53, No. 9:9, May, 1929.

———.
"Two Ballad Fragments." *AS:* 1, (No. 4):247, January, 1926.

———.
"Where are the Folk-Songs and Ballads of New Jersey?" *New Jersey Journal of Education* 15, (No. 6): February, 1926.
Variants of the "Maid Freed from the Gallows," "Pretty Mohea," and "The Miner Boys" are printed.

Herzog, George
"Phillips Barry." *JAFL* 51:439–441, 1938.

Howard, John T.
Our American Music, Three Hundred Years of it. 2nd ed., rev. and enl. New York: Crowell and Co., 1939. Chapter XV: Our Folk Music. Part 3. Other Sources of Folk-Songs. P. 428–431.

Hudson, Arthur Palmer
"Ballets and Ballads." *AS* 5 (No. 1):86–88, 1929.

———.
Byron and the Ballad. In: *Studies in Language and Literature,* edited with a foreword by George R. Coffman. (pp. 216–230). Chapel Hill, N. C.: University of North Carolina Press, 1945. viii, 344 pp.

Folk-Songs of the Whites. In: *Culture in the South*, pp. 519–547. Chapel Hill, N. C.: University of North Carolina Press, 1935.
Discussion of old world ballads and songs.

Hustvedt, Sigurd B.
Ballad Books and Ballad Men: Raids and Rescues in Britain, America, and the Scandinavian North "Since 1800." Cambridge, Mass.: Harvard University Press, 1930.

James, Thelma G.
"The English and Scottish Popular Ballads of Francis T. Child." *JAFL* 46:51–69, 1933.

Johnston, Winifred
"Newspaper Balladry." *AS* 10 (No. 2):119–121, 1935.
"Like the ballad the modern newspaper is made up of material that, in the main, arouses emotional rather than intellectual excitement."

Ker, W. P.
On the History of the Ballads. In: *Form and Style in Poetry*, pp. 3–44. Lectures and notes, ed. by R. W. Chambers. London: The Macmillan Co., 1928. xv, 384 pp.

———.
"On the History of the Ballad." *Proceedings of the British Academy* 4:1910.

Kittredge, G. L., ed.
"Ballads and Rhymes from Kentucky." *JAFL* 20:251–277, 1907.

———.
"Ballads and Songs." *JAFL* 30:285–369, 1917.

———.
Introduction. In: *English and Scottish Popular Ballads*, by Sargent and Kittredge, pp. XI–XXXI. Boston and New York: 1904.

———.
"Notes to Songs Traditional in the United States." *JAFL* 29:156–179; 185–194, 1916.

———.
"Popular Ballad." *Atlantic Monthly* 101:276–278, February, 1908.

———.
"Various Ballads." *JAFL* 26:174–182, 1913.

Lambert, L. V.
"Ballads and the People." *Education* 28:146–153, November, 1907.

Lamson, Roy, Jr.
English Broadside Ballad Tunes of the 16th and 17th Centuries. In: *Papers Read at the International Congress of Musicology*, pp. 112–122. New York: American Musicological Society, 1944.

Lang, Andrew
"Notes on Ballad Origins." *Folk-Lore* 14:147–161, 1898.

———.
Ballads. In: *Encyclopaedia Britannica*, 11th ed.

"List of Collectors and Persons Interested in the Ballad and Folk Song Field." *SFQ* 1 (No. 2):61–73, 1937.

Lomax, John A.
"Adventures of a Ballad Hunter." *Southwest Review* 29:136–160, 1944.

———.
"Adventures of a Ballad Hunter." *TFSP* 19:9–20, 1944.
Gives vivid description of sermons of Negro preachers from Texas and North Carolina.

MacDonagh, Michael
The Ballads of the People. In: *Nineteenth Century and After*, v. 54, pp. 458–471. London: 1903.

McGill, Anna B.
"Irish Characteristics in Our Old Song-Survivals." *MQ* 18:106–119, 1932.

McGill, Josephine
"Old Ballad Burthens." *MQ* 4:293–306, 385–408, 1918.

Mackenzie, W. Roy
The Quest of the Ballad. Princeton, N. J.: Princeton University Press, 1919.

Martinengo, Countess Cesaresco
The Diffusion of Ballads. In: *Essays in the Study of Folk Songs*, pp. 171–196. London: J. M. Dent and Sons, Ltd. 1914. 295 pp., Everyman's Library.

Mather, Frank Jewett Otterburn, Jr.
"A Battle and Two Ballads." *The Sewanee Review* 12:385, 1904.

"Melody Hunters."
Time 30:48, December 27, 1939.
Illustrated.

Menmuir, Charles
"Folk-Lore in Scottish Ballad Poetry." *Scots Magazine* 23:441–453, 1899. (London).

Miles, Emma B.
"Some Real American Music." *Harper's Magazine* 109:118–123, 1904.

Miller, George Morey
The Dramatic Element in the Popular Ballad. Cincinnati, Ohio: University of Cincinnati Press, 1905. 5 app. (Univ. Studies of the Univ. of Cinc. Ser. II, v. I, No. I) Bibl.: pp. 57–59.
Appendices: A. The influence of dramatic folk customs on the origin and development of the modern drama. B. Lists of ballads altogether in dialogue or monologue, or beginning with dialogue or monologue.

"Modern Developments in Ballad Art."
Edinburgh Review 213:153–179, January, 1911.

Moore, J. R.
"The Influence of Transmission on the English Ballads." *Modern Language Review* 11:385–408, 1916.

Morton, A. L.
On the Nature of the Ballad. In: *Language of Men.* London: Cobbett Press, 1945.

Musick, Ruth Ann
"The Old Album of William A. Larkin." *JAFL* 60:201–251, 1947.
Forty-five Ballads found in Larkin's "Book of All Songs" are listed, mostly variants of traditional ballads.

Neely, Charles
"Four British Ballads in Southern Illinois." *JAFL* 52:75–81, 1939.

Newell, W. W.
"Old English Songs in American Versions." *JAFL* 5:325–326, 1892.

"Early American Ballads." *JAFL* 12:241–255, 1899; 13:105–122, 1900.

Norman, H. D.
"Native Wood Notes." *Atlantic* 138:771–775, December, 1926.

Northcote, Sydney
The Ballad in Music. New York: Oxford University Press, 1941. 124 pp.

O'Neill, Captain Francis
Irish Folk Music. Chicago: Lyon & Healy, 1910.

Irish Minstrels and Musicians. Chicago: Lyon & Healy, 1913.

Parsons, Elsie Clews
"A Few Ballads and Songs." *JAFL* 44:296–301, 1931.

"Ballads and Chanties Sung by May Hoisington." *JAFL* 44:296–301, 1931.

"Study of Variants." *JAFL* 33:87–90, 1920.

Payne, L. W., Jr.
"Recent Research in Balladry and Folk Songs." *TFSP* 8:160–169, 1930.

"Songs and Ballads—Grave and Gay." *TFSP* 6:209–237, 1927.

Pierce, Grade Adele
"In Old Ballad Days." *Chautauqua,* April, 1912.

Pike, R. E.
"Folk Songs from Pittsburgh, New Hampshire." *JAFL* 48:337–351, 1935.

"Poor Buckra Songs."
Atlantic Monthly 95:716–717, May, 1905.

Pound, Louise
American Ballads and Songs. New York: Charles Scribner's Sons, 1922.

Ballad. In: *Encyclopedia Britannica,* 14th ed., vol. 2, pp. 993–996, 1936.

"The Ballad and the Dance." *PMLA* 34:360–400, 1916.

"Beginnings of Poetry." *PMLA* 32 (NS 25) (No. 20) : 201–232, 1917.
Bibliography. A study in popular origins.

"The English Ballad and the Church." *PMLA* 35:161–188, 1920.

"The Ballad of Tradition." *Modern Language Notes,* February, 1933.
A review.

Folk-Song of Nebraska and the Central West: A Syllabus. Lincoln, Neb.: Nebraska Academy of Science Publications, Vol. 9, No. 3, 1915.

"Literary Anthologies and the Ballad." *SFQ* 6:127–141, 1942.

"Minstrelsy of Maine." *JAFL* 40:102, 1927.
A review.

"Mr. Bush on Ballads." *Literary Review* 3:758, June 9, 1923.

"New World Analogues of the English and Scottish Popular Ballads." *The Mid-West Quarterly* 3, (No. 3) :171.

"On the Dating of the English and Scottish Ballads." *PMLA* 47:10–16, 1932.

"Oral Literature." In: *The Cambridge History of American Literature* ed. by Trent, Erskine, Sherman and Van Doren. Vol. III, (pp. 502–517). New York: The Macmillan Co., 1917. 3 Vols. Reprinted in 1945 in 1 vol.
A general discussion of folk song and literature. Deals also with the English and Scottish traditional ballads, American ballads, Cowboy Songs, Game and Play-Party songs.

Poetic Origins and the Ballad. New York: The Macmillan Co., 1921.

"A Recent Theory of Ballad-Making." *PMLA* 44:622–631, 1929.
A Discussion of "The Gerould Theory of Ballad Origins."

"Sizing Our Ballads." *American Scholar* 5:360–366, 1936.

"The Term: 'Communal'." *PMLA* 39:440–454, 1924.
Discussion of the communal origins of poetry and song.

"Traditional Ballads in Nebraska." *JAFL* 26: 351–366, 1913.

Powell, John
"In the Lowlands Low." *SFQ* 1, (No. 1) :1–13, 1937.
"Provides a corrective for those who think loosely of our American music tradition as one observable in the highlands only." (Jackson)

Reid, S.
"Old Ballad Folk." *Independent* 71:1093–1098, November 16, 1911.

Report of "Talk on Ballads and Their Origin." Englewood, N. J.: Englewood Press, March 14, 1930, p. 7.

Richmond, W. Edson
"Ballad Place Names." *JAFL* 59:263–267, 1946.

Robbins, Russell Hope
"Burden in Carols." *Modern Language Notes* 58:16–22, 1942.

Rollins, Hyder E.
"Martin Parker, Ballad-Monger." *Modern Philology* 16:449, 1918.

"Notes on the Shirburn Ballads." *JAFL* 30: 283, 370–377, 1917.

Rourke, Constance
"Noble Sport of Ballad Hunting." *Nation* 139: 122, August 15, 1934.

Schaaf, I. M.
"Ground Hog Myth and its Origin." *JAFL* 34:323, 1921.

Schmidt, Wolfgang
"Amerikanische Volksballadenforschung." *Die Neueren Sprachen* 41:439–447, 1933.
The study of American ballads.

"Die Entwicklung der englisch-schottischen Volksballaden." *Anglia* 57:1–77, 113–207, 1933.

Sharp, Cecil J.
Introduction. In: *English Folk-Songs From the Southern Appalachians*, by Sharp and Karpeles, pp. XXI–XXXVII. London: Oxford University Press, 1932.

Shearin, Hubert G.
"British Ballads in the Cumberland Mountains." *Sewanee Review* 19:313–327, 1911.

Smith, C. Alphonso
"Ballads Surviving in the United States." *MQ* 2:109–129, 1916.

Smith, Reed
The Ballad in America. In: *South Carolina Ballads*. Cambridge, Mass.: Harvard University Press, 1928.

Ballad in Folk-Song. In: *South Carolina Ballads*, pp. 3–14. Cambridge, Mass.: Harvard University Press, 1928.

The Ballad in Literature. In: *South Carolina Ballads*, pp. 65–72. Cambridge, Mass.: Harvard University Press, 1928.

Ballads Surviving in America. In: *South Carolina Ballads*, pp. 169–174. Cambridge, Mass.: Harvard University Press, 1928.

Ballads Surviving in the United States. And Other Contributions. In: *Proceedings of the 19th International Congress of Americanists*, ed. by F. W. Hodge. Washington: 1917, illus.

"La Balada Tradicional." *BLAM* 5:275–284, 1941 (Pub. 1942).
Survival of English and Scottish ballads in U. S. A. and Canada, words and music of five. Selected bibl.

Communal Composition. In: *South Carolina Ballads*, pp. 15–36. Cambridge, Mass.: Harvard University Press, 1928.

Communal Transmission. In: *South Carolina Ballads*, pp. 37–54. Cambridge, Mass.: Harvard University Press, 1928.

"A Glance at the Ballad and Folk-Song Field." *SFQ* 1, (No. 2) :7–18, 1937.
Includes a list of the Child ballads in the U. S. and Canada.

South Carolina Ballads. Cambridge, Mass.: Harvard University Press, 1928. 174 pp., unaccompanied tunes.

The Road Downhill. In: *South Carolina Ballads*. Cambridge, Mass.: Harvard University Press, 1928.
A discussion of the effect of literacy on oral transmission.

"The Traditional Ballad in America." *JAFL* 47, (No. 183) :64, January–March, 1934.

"The Traditional Ballad in America." *SFQ* 1, (No. 1) :13–19, 1937.

Smyth, M. W.
"Northern Ballads." *Saturday Review of Literature* 10:368, 1933.

Snow, Wilbert
"Discoveries Down East ... British Ballads from Maine." *New York Herald-Tribune Books*, March 16, 1930.
A review.

"Laughter and Tears of American Ballads." *New York Herald Tribune Books*, Sunday, October 28, 1934.
Review of *American Ballads and Folksongs* by John A. and Alan Lomax.

"Songs (English) in American Versions."
JAFL 5:225–226, 1892.

Taylor, Archer
Edward and Sven i. Rosengärd, A Study in the Dissemination of a Ballad. Chicago: The University of Chicago Press, 1931. xi, 110 pp.

Tolman, A. H.
"Songs Traditional in the U. S." *JAFL* 29:155–197, 1916.

————, and Eddy, Mary O.
"Traditional Texts and Tunes." *JAFL* 35:335–342, 1932.

"Traditional English Ballads."
N. and Q. 3 (1st series): 49, 1893.

Whiting, B. J.
"Proverbial Material in the Popular Ballad."
JAFL 47:1–22, 1934.

"Why Despise the Ballad?"
Literary Digest 103:20, December 7, 1929.

Wilson, Edmund
"American Ballads and Their Collectors."
New Republic 47:168–170, June 30, 1926.

Wimberley, Lowry Charles
Death and Burial Lore in the English and Scottish Popular Ballads. Lincoln, Nebraska: University of Nebraska Studies in Language, Literature, and Criticism No. 8, 1927, 138 pp., bibl.

————.
Folklore in the English and Scottish Ballads. Chicago: University of Chicago Press, 1928, 466 pp.

SPECIAL STUDIES:

Individual Ballads

Listed Alphabetically

Cole, P. McA.
" 'Abigail Snow,' A Colonial Literary Ballad."
JAFL 14:140–142, 1901.

"Ah! No, No, I Never Will Marry."
N. and Q., (Third series), 8:77.

"Andy Bartin." *JAFL* 25:171–173, 1912.

Pound, Louise
"Baldy Green." *SFQ* 6:121–123, 1942.

Porter, Kenneth Wiggins
"Bangum the Boar Slayer and his Weapon."
JAFL 54:84–85, 1941.
American ballad variant of Child 18.

Barry, Phillips
"The Banks of the Gaspareaux." *FSSNE* 5:13–14, 1933.
Excellent. An old Maine woods song, going back to the square timber area.

"Barbara Allen." *JAFL* 6:132–133, 1893; 19:285–292; 1906; 20:256–257, 1907; 22:63–64, 1909; 26:352, 1913; 28:144, 1915; 29:160–162, 198, 1916; 30:317, 1917; 35:343, 1922; 39:97–102, 211–212, 1926.

Henry, Mellinger E.
"American Survivals of a Traditional Ballad."
New Jersey Journal of Education 16, (no. 6): 7, February 1927.
"Barbara Allen."

Millican, Charles B.
"A Georgia Version of 'Barbara Allen'." *JAFL* 42:303–305, 1929.

Steger, Stewart A., and Morrow, Loyal C.
"Barbara Ellen." *The University of Virginia Magazine,* 329–335, April 1913.

"Barbro Allen."
JAFL 6:132–133, 1893.
Music and text.

"The Battle of Roslin." Fought on the Plains of Roslin, 1303, and John Highlandman's Remarks on Glasgow. Glasgow: 1823, 8 pp.

Hendricks, Cecelia A.
"The Battle of Waterloo." *HFB* 4:21–24, 1945.

" 'Beautiful Katie' and the 'Gray Mare'."
JAFL 12:251–252, 1899; 30:325, 1917.

Herrick, Mrs. R. F.
"Two Traditional Songs. 1. 'Love's Impossibility' 2. 'Betsy Was a Lady Fair'." *JAFL* 19:130–132, 1906.

"The Bishop of Canterbury."
NYFQ 1:46–47, 1945.
A New York version belonging to the manuscript of Mr. Harry S. Douglass of Arcade in Wyoming County.

Gerould, Gordon Hall
"The Ballad of 'The Bitter Withy'." *PMLA* 23:141–168, 1908.

"A Black River Thaw."
NYFQ 1:107–108, 1945.
Text of a local ballad—in "the days of the Hartford coach."

"Blow, Ye Winds, Blow."
JAFL 18:49–50, 212–214, 1905.
Music and Text.

Flanders, Helen Hartness
" 'Blue Mountain Lake' " and " 'Barbara Allen'." *NYFQ* 2 (No. 1):52–58, 1946.
Two New York State versions, with tunes.

Watson, J. M.
"Ballad of 'Bold Dickie'." *JAFL* 8:256–257, 1895.

"Ballad of Bonny Hodge."
New England Magazine 12:475, 1895. n.s.

Henry, Mellinger E.
"Brian O'Lynn." *JAFL* 54:83–84, 1941.

"Brown Girl."
JAFL 18:295, 1905; 19:240, 1906; 20:254–255, 1907; 39:94, 1926.

Newton, Hilah Foote
"The Burning of the Phoenix." *NYFQ* 1:40–41, 1945.
Text of the historical ballad recounting the tragedy of the steamboat Phoenix in 1819, near Burlington, Vt.

Barry, Phillips
"The Burning of Henry K. Robinson's Camp at Ripogenns." *FSSNE* 12:20–21, 1937.
    A Maine ballad.

"By the Side of a Murmuring Stream."
New England Magazine 12:474, 1895. n.s.

"The Cambric Shirt."
JAFL 23:430–431, 1910; 26:174, 1913.

Barry, Phillips
"Cap Barnal." *FSSNE* 5:11, 1888.
    A variant of "The Two Constant Lovers."

————.
    "Captain Bunker." *FSSNE* 6:14–15, 1889.

"Captain Lovewell's Battle at Pigwacket."
New England Quarterly 9:380, 386, 1936.

"Captain Kidd."
N. and Q. 1, (Fifth Series) :375.

"Captain Ward and the Rainbow."
JAFL 18:137, 1905; 25:177–178, 1912; 30:332, 1917.

"Captain Wederburn's Courtship."
JAFL 23:377–378, 1910; 24:335–336, 1911; 29:157–158, 1916.

Barry, Phillips
"Caroline and Her Young Sailor Bred."
FSSNE 2:9–10, 1931. n.s.
    A variant resembling "The Gallant Hussar," and "Rosin the Bow." Recorded—Maine.

Eckstorm, Fannie H.
"Canady I O." *FSSNE* 6:10–13, 1933.

"Cherries and the Holy Family."
N. and Q. 9, (Fourth Series) :117, 210, 375.

" 'Cherry Tree:' Kentucky Mountain Ballad."
Golden Book 14:395, December 7, 1931.

Barry, Phillips
"The Cherry-Tree Carol." *FSSNE* 6:6–7, 1931.

Cutting, Edith E.
"The Cherry Tree Carol." *NYFQ* 1:48, 1945.
    A version of the famous song found in Elizabethtown, N. Y.

McGill, Josephine
"The Cherry-Tree Carol." *JAFL* 29:293, 1916.

"Cherry Tree Carol."
JAFL 29:293–294, 417, 1916; 30:297, 1917.

"Cherry-Tree Carol."
N. and Q. 12, (Fourth Series) :461, 494; 1 (Fifth Series) :15.

"Christmas Ballad."
N. and Q. 9, (First Series) :325.
    A variant of "The Ten Commandments."

Parker, Harrison
"The Clerk Colvill Mermaid." *JAFL* 60:265–285, 1947.
    The author disagrees with Samuel P. Bayard's hypothesis (*JAFL* 58, No. 228, 1945) that the banshee has modified the Scandinavian elf-woman into a mermaid, and that the "Johnny Collins" versions have been current in Irish tradition. Mr. Parker sets out to prove that the metamorphosis of the elf-woman into a mermaid came about in Shetland and Orkney, and that it had little to do with Irish Ballad tradition.

Barry, Phillips
"The Convict's Lament." *FSSNE* 6:18–19, 1931.

"The Crafty Farmer."
JAFL 23:451–452, 1910.

Barry, Phillips
"Ballad of the Cruel Brother." *JAFL* 28:300–301, 1915.

"The Cruel Brother."
JAFL 28:300–301, 1915; 29:93, 1916.

"The Cruel Miller."
Journal of the Folk-Song Society 7:23.

Karsten, Gustaf E.
"The Ballad of 'The Cruel Moor'." *Journal of Germanic Philology* 3:354–361, 1901. (Bloomington, Indiana.)

"The Cruel Mother."
JAFL 25:183–184, 1912; 30:293, 1917.

"Song of the Cuckoo."
N. and Q. 10, (First Series) :524; 11:38.

Herrick, R. F.
"Cupid's Arrow." *JAFL* 18:276, 1905.

"Daisy."
JAFL 2:288–290, 1890.
    Music and text.

"The Demon Lover."
JAFL 18:207–208, 1905; 20:257, 1907; 25:346, 1912.

Kittredge, G. L.
"The Ballad of the Den of Lions." *Modern Language Notes* 167–169, June 1911.

"Ballad of Dick and the Devil."
N. and Q. 1, (First Series) :172.

Flanagan, Margaret
"A Driller's Dream." *NYFQ* 1:88–98, 1945.
    One of the few ballads dealing with the folklore of the oil fields. Text only.

Barry, Phillips
"Earl Brand." *Modern Language Notes* 25:104.

"Earl Brand."
JAFL 28:152–154, 1915.

"Earl's Daughter."
N. and Q. 4, (Second Series) :7.

"Edward."
JAFL 39:93–94, 1926.

Schmidt, Erich
"Edward." In: *Forschungen zur neueren Litteraturgeschichte*, pp. 29–50. Weimar: 1898.

Bronson, Bertrand H.
" 'Edward, Edward,' a Scottish Ballad." *SFQ* 4:1–13, 1940.

————.
"A Footnote to 'Edward, Edward'." *SFQ* 4:159–161, 1940.

Lowrimore, Burton S.
"A California Version of 'Edward'." *CFQ* 5(No. 3):310–311, 1946.

Schmidt, Wolfgang
"Die Entwicklunsgeschichte der Edward-Ballade." *Anglia* 57:277–312, 1933.

Barry, Phillips
"Edward and Sven Rosengard." *FSSNE* 5:17–18, 1930.
A review.

"Young Edward."
JAFL 20:274, 1907.

"Elfin Knight."
JAFL 7:228–232, 1894; 18:49–51, 1905; 19:130, 1906.

Ralph, Julian
"The Transformation of Em Durham." *Harper's Monthly Magazine*, p. 272, July 1903.
A version of "Fair Margaret and Sweet William."

"Erlinton."
JAFL 23:447–448, 1910.

Barry, Phillips
"The Factory Girls' Come-All-Ye." *FSSNE* 2:12–13, 1931.
A Maine ballad. Insight into the economic plight of Lewiston factory girls in the middle of the 19th century. Words and melody.

————.
"Fair Charlotte." *FSSNE* 8:17–19, 1934.

————.
"Fair Florella." *AS* 3 (No. 6):441–447, 1928.

————.
"Fair Phoebe and her Dark-Eyed Sailor." *FSSNE* 6:8–10, 1933.
"One of a group of modern sophisticated ballads on the theme of "Hind Horn": the parted lovers, the shared father, the return of the man in disguise and the test of the woman's fidelity, with a close-up of Victorian domesticity." (Barry)

"Fair Janet." *JAFL* 7:253–256, 1894.

"Fair Margaret and False William." *JAFL* 19: 281–282, 1906; 28:154–155, 1915; 29:160, 1916; 30:302–304, 1917.

Barry, Phillips
"The Fall of the Pinkerton Mills." *FSSNE* 3:16–17, 1931.
A Massachusetts ballad. Words and tune.

"The False Knight." *JAFL* 29:334, 1916; 30: 285–286, 1917.

"False Lover Won Back." *Golden Book* 9:50, April 1929.

Moore, J. R.
"Missouri Variant of 'The False Lover Won Back'." *JAFL* 34:395–397, 1921.

"Fare Thee Well."
Journal of Folk Song Society 11:201.

"The Farmer's Curst Wife."
JAFL 19:298–299, 1906; 24:348–349, 1911; 30:329–332, 1917.

Beck, Earl Clifton
" 'The Farmer's Curst Wife,' (Child 278) in Michigan." *SFQ* 4:157–158, 1940.

Williams, Tyrrell
"The Origin of 'Frankie and Johnny'." *Missouri Historical Review* 34 (No. 2):292–293, 1940.

Mitcham, Mildred B.
"Another version of 'The Frog's Courting'." *HF* 5:85–92, 1946.

Barry, Phillips
"Fuller and Warren." *FSSNE* 8:12–13, 1934; 9:14–17, 1935.

" 'The George Aloe,' and 'The Sweepstake'." *JAFL* 18:134, 1905.

"George of Oxford."
JAFL 20:319–320, 1907.

"The Golden Vanitee"
N. and Q. 6, (Fifth Series):138; 8:260, 336, 438.

"Green Broomfield."
JAFL 24:14–15, 1911.

Belden, H. M.
"The Green Willow Tree." *PMLA* 33:363, 1918.

"The Gypsy Laddie."
JAFL 18:191–195, 1905; 19:294–295, 1906; 24:346–348, 1911; 25:173–177, 1912; 26:353, 1913; 30:323–325, 1917.
Many variants with music.

Kittredge, George L.
"Creative Art of the 'Hangman's Tree'." *JAFL* 19:22, 1906; 21:56, 1909.

"Heir of Linne."
JAFL 28:156–157, 1915.

"Henry Martin."
JAFL 18:135–136, 302–303, 1905; 30:327, 1916.
Music and text.

Barry, Phillips
"Henry K. Sawyer." *FSSNE* 9:17–22, 1935.
Maine—R. R. accident.

Percy, Thomas
"The Hermit of Warkworth," a *Northumberland Ballad.* Embellished with wood engravings by Nesbitt and Clenell, from designs by Thurston. London: A. Scholey, 1806, viii, 60 pp.

Nelles, W. R.
"Ballad of Hind Horn." *JAFL* 22:42–62, 1909.

"The House Carpenter."
JAFL 18:207–208, 1905; 19:295–297, 1906; 25:274–275, 1912; 26:330, 1913; 35:347–348, 1922.

"The Hunting of the Cheviot."
JAFL 18:294, 1905.

"I Am a Young Maiden Forsaken."
New England Magazine 12:473–474, 1895. n.s.

Eckstorm, Fannie H.
"The Indian Elopement." *FSSNE* 4:9–10, 1932.

Henry, Mellinger E.
"Jack Hall." *JAFL* 44:305, 1932.

——————.
"Jack Hall." *New Jersey Journal of Education* 9, (No. 7):8, March 1930.

"Jack Will Take the Ten."
New England Magazine 12:474, 1895. n.s.

Barry, Phillips
"The Jam on Gerry's Rock." *FSSNE* 10:18–20, 1935.
Words and music.

"James Harris."
JAFL 19:295–297, 1906; 20:257–258, 1907; 30:325–327, 1917
A variant of "The Demon Lover."

Barry, Phillips
"James Harris or the Daemon Lover." *FSSNE* 6:7–8, 1931.

"James Reilly."
N. and Q. 5, (Seventh Series):203, 274, 435.
A variant of "Willy Reilly."

Barry, Phillips
"Jane Was a Neighbor." *FSSNE* 2:6–8, 1931.
A variant of Child 170: "The Death of Queen Jane. Recorded in Kentucky. Text and tune.

"The Jealous Lover."
JAFL 25:10–11, 1912; 39:116–118, 1926.

"The Jew's Daughter."
JAFL 14:195–196, 1901; 15:195–196, 1902; 19:293–294, 1906; 29:163–166, 1916; 30:222, 1917; 35:344–345, 1922; 39:108–109, 212–213, 1926; 46:358–361, 1934.

Barry Phillips
"Jimmie Judges." *FSSNE* 10:20-21, 1935.
A Maine ballad.

Cox, John Harrington
"John Hardy." *JAFL* 32:505–520, 1919.

——————.
" 'The Yew Pine Mountains,, A 'John Hardy Ballad'." *AS* 2(No. 5):226–227, 1927.

Mulholland, C. C.
"Johnny and the Sairpent." *AS* 7(No. 3):238–239, 1932.
A variant of "Springfield Mountain," taken down from an old lady in Mills City, Pennsylvania. Text only.

Bayard, Samuel P.
"The 'Johnny Collins' Version of 'Lady Alice'." *JAFL* 58:73–103, 1945.
A brilliant piece of scholarly research. The author contends that this ballad is an offshoot of the ancient "Clerk Colvill" ballad. No music.

"The Jolly Patriot:" A *New Ballad.*
London: W. Webb, 1744, 7 pp.

"Judas."
PMLA 35:163, 165, 172, 178, 1920.

Baum, P. F.
"The English Ballad of Judas Iscariot." *PMLA* 31:181, 1916.

"Song of the Kid."
JAFL 11:209–212, 1898.

Newell, W. W.
" 'Song of the Kid,' (Passover), and an Equivalent from New England." *JAFL* 18:33–48, 1905.

Millican, Charles B.
"The Original of the Ballad, 'Kinge Arthur's Death,' in the Percy Folio MS." *PMLA* 96 (No. 40):1020–1024, 1931.

"The King's Dochters."
N. and Q. 1, (Eighth Series):372.

"King James and Brown."
PMLA 34:261, 1919.

"King John and the Bishop."
PMLA 46:1025, 1931.

Barry, Phillips
"King John and the Bishop." *JAFL* 21:57–59, 1908.

" 'The King of the Birds, or, The Lay of the Phoenix,' an Anglo-Saxon Song of the 10th or 11th Century."
Archaeologia 30:1899. (London).

"The Knight of Elle;" a *Scarce and Favorite Old Scotch Ballad.*
Glasgow: 182?, 8 pp.

"The Knight and the Shepherd's Daughter."
JAFL 22:377–378, 1909.

"Lady Alice."
JAFL 28:151–152, 1915; 30:317–318, 1917; 39:102–105, 1926.

"Lady Alice."
N. and Q. 1, (Second Series):418.

Gilchrist, Annie G.
"Note on the 'Lady Drest in Green' and other fragments of tragic ballads and folk-tales preserved amongst children." *Journal of the Folk Song Society*, 6:80–90.

"Lady Isabel and the Elf-Knight."
JAFL 18:132–133, 1905; 19:232, 1906; 22:65–66, 374–375, 1909; 23:374–377, 1910; 24:333–335, 344–345, 1911; 27:90–91, 1914; 28:148–149, 1915; 29:156, 1916; 30:286, 1917; 35:338–339, 1922.

Wimberly, Lowry Charles
"Two Traditional Ballads." *AS* 3(No. 2):114–118, 1927.
"Lady Isabel and the Elf-Knight," and "Young Hunting."

Allen, Mrs. E.
"The Lady in the West." *JAFL* 8:230, 1895.

"Lake Chemo."
FSSNE 7:14–16, 1934.

"Lamkin."
JAFL 13:118, 1900; 29:162–164, 1916; 30:318, 1917; 35:344, 1922.

"Lamkin."
N. and Q. 11, (Second Series):324, 392.
A variant of "Long Lankyn."

"Long Lankin."
N. and Q. 11, (Fourth Series):281, 379, 568.
A variant of "Lamkin."

Eckstorm, Fannie Hardy
"Two Maine Texts of 'Lamkin'." *JAFL* 52:70–74, 1939.

Henry, Mellinger E.
"An Old English Ballad Rare in America—'Lamkin'." *New Jersey Journal of Education* 19 (No. 1):9, 1929.

"The Lass of Rock Royal."
The Folk Lore Journal 7:31.

"Lass of Rock Royal."
JAFL 30:304–305, 1917.

"Leesome Brand."
PMLA 29:480n, 1914.

Schmitz, R. M.
"Leo Frank and Mary Phagan." *JAFL* 60:59–61, 1947.
Text only of a version from Joy May Creasy, a mountain lass from Kentucky. "The text itself shows the innocent migration of the story westward from the scenes of the original murder and trial of 1913 at Atlanta, Georgia."

Snyder, F. B.
"Leo Frank and Mary Phagan." *JAFL* 31:264–266, 1918.
A Georgia ballad.

Henry, Mellinger E.
"The Lexington Girl." *JAFL* 92:247–253, 1929.

"Little Cabin Boy."
JAFL 18:125–127, 1905.
Two versions, with music.

Henry, Mellinger E.
"Little Dicky Whigburn." *FSSNE* 3:15, 1932.

"Little Eleanor."
JAFL 18:128–130, 1905.

Henry, Mellinger E.
"Little Frankie." *New Jersey Journal of Education* 16 (No. 1):20, 1926.

Kirkland, Edwin C.
"The Effect of Oral Tradition on 'Robinhood' and 'Little John'." *SFQ* 4:15–21, 1940.

"Little Musgrave and Lady Barnard."
JAFL 23:371–374, 1910; 25:183, 1912; 30:309–317, 1917.

"Little Musgrove."
PMLA 39:455, 470–473, 1924.

"Lizzie Lindsay."
JAFL 35:345, 1922.

"Lord Bateman."
JAFL 20:251–252, 1907; 22:64–65, 1909; 26:353, 1913.

The Loving Ballad of Lord Bateman.
London: 1839, Illus. by George Cruikshank.

Parsons, Elsie Clews
"Lord Bateman." *JAFL* 41:585–588, 1928.
Bahamas.

"Young Beichan."
JAFL 17:209–211, 1904; 23:449–451, 1910; 30:294–297, 1917.
Variant of "Lord Bateman."

"Lord Lovell."
JAFL 18:291–293, 1905; 24:337, 1911; 26:353, 1913; 29:160, 1916; 35:342–343, 1922.
Verses, variants, with music.

"Lord Lovel."
N. and Q. 5 (Fourth Series):449, 521; 5 (Eleventh Series):330; 6:115, 171, 217, 296.

Ralph, Julian
"Lord Lovel." *Harper's Monthly Magazine*, July, 1903.

"Lord Lovel and Lady Nancy."
JAFL 19:283–285, 1906; 26:352, 1913.

"Lord Randal."
JAFL 13:115–116, 1900; 16:258–264, 1903; 18:195–207, 303–304, 1905; 22:376–377, 1909; 24:345–346, 1911; 29:157, 1916; 30:289–290, 1917; 35:339–340, 1922; 39:81–82, 1926.

"Lord Randal."
The Crimson Rambler, Tonkawa, Okla., 8 (No. 4).

Barry, Phillips
"Ballad of 'Lord Randal' in New England." *JAFL* 16:258–264, 1903.
Text and music.

Henry, Mellinger E.
"American Survival of a Traditional Ballad."
New Jersey Journal of Education 17 (No. 4):
11, 1927.
"Lord Randal."

"Oh Where d'ye go Courting, Sweet Nelson."
JAFL 18:198, 303–304, 1905.
A variant of "Lord Randal."

"Oh, Where Have You Been, Fair Elson, My Son?"
JAFL 16:263, 1903; 18:197, 1905.
A variant of "Lord Randal." Text and music.

"Oh, Where Have You Been, Sweet William, My Son?"
JAFL 18:196–197, 1905.
A variant of "Lord Randal." Text and music.

"Oh, Where Have You Been To, Teronto, My Son?"
JAFL 18:199, 1905.
A variant of "Lord Randal." Several versions with music.

"Oh, Where Have You Been, Tyrante, My Son?"
JAFL 18:201–207, 1905.
A variant of "Lord Randal." Several versions with music.

"Tyranty."
JAFL 16:264, 1903.
Text and music.

Miller, Edwin Shepard
"Nonsense and New Sense in 'Lord Thomas'."
SFQ 1:25–39, 1937.

"Lord Thomas and Fair Annet."
JAFL 18:128–130, 1905; 19:235–240, 1906;
20:254–258, 1907; 28:152, 1915; 29:159, 1916;
39:94–96, 1926.

"Lord Thomas and Fair Annet."
The Folk Lore Journal 7:33, 1889.

Barry, Phillips
"Lost Jimmie Whalen." *FSSNE* 11:4–7, 1936.
A Maine ballad.

Herrick, Mrs. R. F.
"Two Traditional Songs, 'Love's Impossibility,' and 'Betsy Was a Lady Fair'." *JAFL* 19:130–132, 1906.

Piper, Edwin Ford
"A Love-of-God Shave." *TFSP* 9:185–186, 1931.
A humorous song of the old English apprentice system. Text and melody.

The History of Tommy Potts; or, "The Lovers' Quarrell."
London: n. d., 24 pp.

Kittredge, G. L.
"The Ballad of Lovewell's Fight." In: *Bibliographical Essays: a Tribute to Wilberforce Eames.* Cambridge, Mass.: Harvard University Press, 1924, xix, 440 pp.

Barry, Phillips
"The Low River Shore." *FSSNE* 2:8–9, 1931.
A Maine variant of an old world ballad.

"Maid Freed from the Gallows."
JAFL 24:337, 1911; 26:175, 1913; 30:318–322, 1917; 39:105–106, 1926.

"The Maid Freed from the Gallows."
PMLA 39:475–476, 1924.

Francello, Elvira
"An Italian Version of 'Maid Freed From the Gallows'." *NYFQ* 2, (No. 2):138–140, 1946.

Krappe, Alexander Haggerty
"The Maid Freed from the Gallows." *Speculum* 16:236–241, 1941.

Smith, Reed
Five Hundred Years of "The Maid Freed from the Gallows." In: *South Carolina Ballads* (pp. 80–94). Cambridge, Mass.: Harvard University Press, 1928.

"Margaret and the Minister;" a True Tale. Soda Water.
Paisley: G. Caldwell, 182? 8 pp.

Kittredge, G. L.
"Note on the Song of 'Mary Blane'." *JAFL* 39:200, 1926.

Tolman, Albert H.
"'Mary Hamilton.' The Group Authorship of Ballads." *PMLA* 42:421–432, 1927.

Maloney, Thomas Vincent
"Mary Neil." *NYFQ* 1:99–100, 1945.
Text only. Version of "Charming Mary Neal," also bears resemblance to "Willie Riley."

"The Mermaid."
JAFL 18:136, 1905; 25:176–177, 1912; 26:175, 177, 1913; 30:333, 1917.
Variants and music.

Drew, Helen L.
"The Mermaid." *AS* 1(No. 4):293–294, 1926.
The author presents a Wyoming version: "The Three Sailor Boys."

Hull, Myra E.
"The Merman Lover" in Ballad and Song. In: *Studies in English in Honor of Raphael Dorman O'Leary and Selden Lincoln Whitcomb* ... Lawrence, Kansas: University of Kansas, 1940. (Kansas Univ. Publ. Humanistic Studies, Vol. vi, no. 4.

Barry, Phillips
"The Miami Lass." *FSSNE* 6:15–18, 1933.

"The Miller and His Three Sons."
N. and Q. 3 (Fourth Series):129.

"My Name Is Charles Guiteau."
NYFQ 1:49, 1945.
A New York version of the historical ballad recorded in Manlius, Onondaga County. The tune, not given, is claimed by the editor to be: "When the Work's All Done Next Fall."

Mooney, James
"My Pretty Little Pink." *JAFL* 11:104, 1898.

Hudson, Arthur Palmer
"A Ballad of the New Madrid Earthquake."
JAFL 60:147–150, 1947.
A song—"A Call to the People of Louisiana."
(text only)—giving dramatic account of the
Mississippi Valley earthquake of 1811–12, "and
moralizes upon its significance in divine econ-
omy."

"A Noble Dewell; or An Unmatchable Combate
Betwixt Sir William . . . and the Earl of
Southeast."
Scottish Historical Review 3:2–5, 1905. Glas-
gow).
A ballad describing a duel between James, earl
of Southeast, and Sir William Gray.

"The Nut Brown Maid."
JAFL 25:90, 1912.

Wright, Edward Theodore
*"The Nut-Browne Maid," from the Earliest
Edition of Arnold's Chronicle.* London: Picker-
ing, 1836.
"The text from *Arnold's Chronicle* is regarded as
the earliest and best version of the ballad."

Barry, Phillips, and Eckstorm, F. H.
"Olban, or, The White Captive." *BFSSNE*
8:19–24, 1934.
A fantastic ballad of Indian torture. Text and
music.

"Once There Were Two Ships."
JAFL 18:134, 1905.
Text and music.

Payne, L. W., Jr.
"One Evening As I Sat Courting." *TFSP*
2:6–8, 1923.
With music.

"Our Goodman."
JAFL 18:294–295, 1905; 19:166, 1907; 25:348,
1912.

"Our Gudeman Cam Home at E'en."
N. and Q. 154:233.

"The Outlandish Knight."
N. and Q. 3 (First Series):208; 1 (Fourth
Series):221, 344, 425, 543.
Discussion of ballad editing.

"Owl: of All the Brave Birds That Ever I See."
New England Magazine 12:473, 1895. n. s.

"Paul Jones."
N. and Q. 2 (Ninth Series):306, 353, 495.

Henry, Mellinger E.
" 'Pearl Bryant:' an Unpublished Variant of
an American Folk Song." *JAFL* 42:301–303,
1929.

"Peas, Beans, Oats and Barley."
Journal of Folk-Song Society 1:67.

Barry, Phillips
"Songs of the 'Pigwacket Fight'." *FSSNE* 5:
17, 1931. (continued from FSSNE No. 4.)

Eckstorm, Fannie H., and Barry, Phillips
"Songs of the Pigwacket Fight." *FSSNE*
9:3–9, 1932; 5:17–19, 1933; 6:3–4, 1933.
Versions of an early American border ballad.
(1725). Text and tune.

"Polly Oliver."
N. and Q. 12 (Third Series):229.

"Presbyterian Cat."
New England Magazine 12:475, 1895. n.s.

"Pretty Polly."
JAFL 12:248–249, 1899; 20:261–264, 1907.
A Blue Ridge ballad.

"Pretty Polly, She Mounted her Milk-White
Steed."
JAFL 18:132–133, 1905.
Text and Music.

"Ballad of Puir Mary Lee."
N. and Q. 4 (Second Series):8.

"Quaker's Wooing."
JAFL 18:55–56, 1905.
Two versions with music.

Wilson, Alexander
*"Rab and Ringan," a Tale. To Which is Added,
Verses Occasioned by Seeing Two Men Sawing
in Defiance of a Furious Storm.* Paisely: G.
Caldwell, 1827, 8 pp.
A Scotch ballad.

"Ram of Darby."
JAFL 18:51–54, 1905.
Several versions with music.

Belden, H. M.
"Ranordine, Rinordine, Rinor." *JAFL* 18:322,
1905.

"Popular Song in Missouri—'The Returned
Lover'." *Archiv für das Studium der neueren
Sprachen und Literaturen.* 120:62–71, 1908.

Kittredge, G. L.
"The Robber Maid." *JAFL* 39:214, 1926.

Gutch, John Mathew, (ed).
*A Lytell Qeste of "Robin Hode" With Other
Ancient and Modern Ballads and Songs Relating to this . . . Yeoman to Which is Prefixed
his History . . . Grounded Upon Other Documents Than Those Made Use of By His Former Biographer, "Mister Ritson."* With cuts
by F. W. Fairholt. London: Longman's, 1847,
2 vols.

*Historical Anecdotes of the Life of "Robin
Hood"; With a Collection of the Ancient
Poems, Songs and Ballads Relative to that
English Outlaw.* London: The Booksellers,
1846, viii, 256 pp.

Kirkland, Edwin C.
"The effect of oral tradition on 'Robin Hood
and Little John'." *SFQ* 4 (No. 1):15–21, 1940.
A discussion of texts and variants.

Malcolmson, Anne, ed.
Song of Robin Hood. Illustrated by Virginia Lee Burton. New York: Houghton Mifflin Co., 1947.
> The editor presents 15 variants, with music, of the ballad.

Ritson, Joseph
"Robin Hood." A Collection of All the Ancient Poems, Songs and Ballads, Now Extant, Relative to that Celebrated English Outlaw, to Which are Prefixed: Historical Anecdotes of His Life. With Woodcuts and Music. London: 1795, 2 vols.

"Robin Hood Ballad."
N. and Q. 8 (Third Series) :88, 158, 199, 257.

Pound, Louise
"American Text of 'Robin Hood and Little John'." *AS* 2 (No. 2) :75, 1927.
> First heard in Kentucky.

Wilson, E. L.
"Robin Hood and Little John." *JAFL* 23:432–434, 1910.

"Robin Hood and the Monk."
PMLA 35:165, 1920.

"Robin Hood and the Potter."
PMLA 35:165, 1920.

Hendricks, Cecilia Heunel
"Robin Tamson's Smiddy." *HFB* 3:55–57, 1944.
> Text only of this Scottish ballad from a Wisconsin informant.

"Robyn and Gandeleyn."
PMLA 35:164, 1920.

"St. Stephen and Herod."
PMLA 35:164, 178, 180, 1920.

"A Salt River Dirge."
Missouri Historical Review 34 (No. 3) :383–385, 1940.
> The ballad first appeared in the *Boon's Lick Times* of Nov. 14, 1840. Sung to the tune: "When Shall We Three Meet Again?"

Newton, Hilah Foote
"The Saltus Lament." *NYFQ* 1:42–43, 1945.
> A popular ballad recounting the adventures of the steamer "The Saltus" plying in Lake Champlain. The tune is: "Little Brown Jug."

Barry, Phillips
"Samuel Allen." *FSSNE* 9:17–22, 1935.
> A ballad of the Maine Lumberjacks.

"Samuel Hall."
N. and Q. 156:221, 257, 296.

Bronson, Bertrand H.
"Samuel Hall's Family Tree." *CFQ* 1:47–64, 1942.
> Words and Music.

"The Schooner Fred Dunbar." *FSSNE* 5:15–16, 1933.
> A favorite song about Penobscot Bay. Notes by Phillips Barry.

"The Shepherd's Daughter."
JAFL 22:383–384, 1909.

McGill, Josephine
"Sing All a Green Willow." *North American Review* 228:218–224, 1929.

"A Single Man of Twenty-Two."
N. and Q. 5 (Fourth Series) :382.

"The Ballad of Sir Andrew Barton."
N. and Q. 7 (Second Series) :316, 520.

Barry, Phillips
"Sir Hugh, or the Jew's Daughter." *FSSNE* 5:6, 1931.

"The Ballad of Sir Hugh."
N. and Q. 12:496; 1 (Second Series) :80, 121.

Steger, Stewart A., and Morrow, Loyal C.
"Sir Hugh, or, the Jew's Daughter." *The University of Virginia Magazine*, December, 1912.

Pound, Louise
"An American Text of 'Sir James the Rose'." *AS* 1 (No. 9) :481–483, 1926.

Ritter, Otto
"Zwei unbekannte Fassungen des 'Sir John Barleycorn'." *Anglia* 27:450–452, 1904. (Halle)

"Sir Lionel."
JAFL 19:235, 1906; 25:175, 176, 1912; 30:291, 1917.

"Sir Patrick Spence," All the Preserved Versions, Synoptically Reprinted From Child's Ballads for the Use of English Seminaries. Berlin: Mayer und Müller, 1904, folder.

Hand, Wayland D.
"Der Skonk Pole Cat." *JAFL* 58:258–259, 1945.
> Another version of the ballad. Text only.

Henry, Mellinger E.
"The Ballade of the Skunk." *JAFL* 57:281–282, 1944.
> Text only.

"Tale of the Skunks."
JAFL 7:253, 1894.

Barry, Phillips
"The Sons of North Britain." *JAFL* 26:183–184, 1913.

"Springfield Mountain."
JAFL 18:295–302, 1905.
> Several versions, with music.

Barry, Phillips
" 'Springfield Mountain': Materials for a Critical Study." *FSSNE* 7:4–5, 1934; 8:3–6, 1934; 9:8–10, 1935; 10:6–8, 1935; 11:13–15, 1936; 12:6–8, 1937.
> Discussion of different versions, conclusions, texts, and tunes. A Massachussetts ballad.

Damon, S. Foster
"Springfield Mountain." *JAFL* 59:531, 1946.
> "A Contemporary account of the Springfield Mountain tragedy as found in Joseph Fisk's versified *Ten Years Almanack*, 1761."

Henry, Mellinger E.
"Springfield Mountain." *FSSNE* 5:15, 1932.

Ireland, Irma T.
"Springfield Mountain." *Old Time New England* 32:1–8, 1941.
Discussion of history, sources, and variants.

Jordan, Philip D.
"A Further Note on 'Springfield Mountain'."
JAFL 52:118–119, 1939.

Barry, Phillips
"The Suffolk Miracle." *FSSNE* 5:7–10, 1932.

"Susannah Roger's Elegy on Jonathan Frye."
FSSNE 6:3–4, 1932.

"Sweet Trinity."
JAFL 16:259, 1903; 18:125–127, 1905; 23:381–382, 429–430, 1910; 30:330–331, 1917.

"Sweet William."
JAFL 16:259–260, 1903.
Text and music.

Newell, W. W.
"Ballad of 'Sweet William and Gentle Jenny'."
JAFL 7:252–255, 1894.

"Sweet William and Lady Margaret." *JAFL* 19:281–282, 1906; 35:340–342, 1922.

"Terence."
JAFL 16:261–262, 1903.
Text and music.

"There Was a Man Lived in the West, Bow Down, Bow Down." *JAFL* 18:130–132, 1905.
Two versions, with music.

Asbury, Samuel E.
"There Were Three (Two) Crows." *TFSP* 14:280–282, 1938.
Text and melody, as learned in North Carolina.

Neighbors, Alice Atkinson
"There Were Two Crows." *TFSP* 14:282–283, 1938.
Text and melody as sung in Indiana.

"The Three Rovers."
JAFL 22:154, 1907; 31:273, 1918.

"The Three Ravens."
N. and Q. 2 (Eighth Series) :69, 324, 437; 11 (Ninth Series) :485; 12:53.

Henry, Mellinger E.
"Thursday April." *FSSNE* 5:21, 1932.

Barry, Phillips
"Tittery Nan." *FSSNE* 6:13–14, 1933.

"Tom Cray." *FSSNE* 9:17–22, 1935.
A Maine Lumberjack ballad, Beave Brook.

The History of "Tommy Potts"; or "The Lovers' Quarrell."
London: n. d., 24 pp.

"A Trip to the Grand Banks."
FSSNE 4:16, 1932.
A Maine sea ballad.

"The Twa Bairns."
N. and Q. 11 (First Series) :88.
A variant of "The Bonnie Bairns."

"Twa Brothers."
JAFL 16:361, 1904; 29:158, 1916; 30:294–295, 1917.

Barry, Phillips
"The Two Brothers." *FSSNE* 5:6, 1933.

"The Twa Corbies."
N. and Q. 9 (Second Series) :143, 251.

"The Two Corbies."
JAFL 31:273, 1918.

"The Twa Sisters."
PMLA 29:478–479, 1914.

"The Two Sisters."
JAFL 18:130–132, 1905; 19:233–235, 1906; 30:286–289, 1917.

Barry, Phillips
"The Two Sisters." *FSSNE* 6:5–6, 1934.

" 'The Two Sisters': Prolegomena to a Critical Study." *FSSNE* 3:11–14, 1931.
A critical discussion of a traditional ballad. The author employs a three fold process of research: folklore background, origin of ballad as artistic expression, and re-creation of ballad in tradition.

Smelser, J. M.
"The 'Two Sisters' from Missouri." *JAFL* 44:295–296, 1931.

Taylor, Archer
"The English, Scottish, and American Version of the 'Twa Sisters,.'" *JAFL* 42:238–247, 1929.

"A 'Ballad of the Twelfth Day'."
PMLA 35:163, 1920.

Greg, W. W.
"A 'Ballad of the Twelfth Day'." *Modern Language Review* 8:64, 1913.

McGill, Josephine
"A Quaint Survival: 'The Twelve Apostles'."
MQ 16:186–190, 1930.
Music included.

Bond, Donald F.
"English Versions of the Carol of 'The Twelve Numbers'." *SFQ* 4:247–250, 1940.

Newell, William Wells
"The Carol of the Twelve Numbers." *JAFL* 9:215, 1891.

Taylor, Archer
"The Carol of the Twelve Numbers Once More." *SFQ* 4:161, 1940.

Yoffie, Leah Rachel Clara
"The Carol of the Twelve Numbers." *SFQ* 4:73–75, 1940.
The author suggests the ballad may be of Jewish origin.

Sutherland, Elihu Jasper
"Vance's Song." *SFQ* 4:251–254, 1940.
Text only.

"Villikins and His Dinah."
N. and Q. 12 (First Series):374; 8 (Seventh
Series):67, 94; 19 (Ninth Series):388; 1
(Thirteenth Series):173, 216, 233, 256, 318,
374, 437.

"Ballad of 'The Wars of France'."
N. and Q. 1 (First Series):445.

Wilson, A.
"*Watty and Meg*"; or, "*The Wife Reformed.*"
Owere True a Tale. Paisley: G. Caldwell and
Co., 18—, 8 pp.

"The Wee Brown Hen."
N. and Q. 7 (First Series):284.

"The Whummil Bore."
JAFL 20:155, 1908.

"The Wife Wrapt in Wether's Skin."
JAFL 19:298, 1906; 30:328–329, 1917; 39:
109, 1926.

"The Wild Colonial Boy."
N. and Q. 159:101.

"William and Margaret."
N. and Q. 12 (Fifth Series):151; 1 (Sixth
Series):502; 2:375.

Barry, Phillips
"William Carter, The Bensontown Homer."
JAFL 25:156, 1912.

————.
"Willie Leonard, or the Lake of Cold Finn."
FSSNE 8:10–11, 1934.

"Willy Reilly."
N. and Q. 8 (Fourth Series):418, 535.

"*The Wiltshire Ballads*"; or, *A New Song Composed by an Old Cavalier—(On the Refusal of
the Citizens of Salisbury to Sign a Petition in
Favor of the Exclusion Bill.)* London: 1680,
broadside.

Niles, J. J.
"Woman . . . in a Good Man's Mind." *Mentor*
18:12–15, March 1, 1930.

Barry, Phillips
"The Woody Queristers." *FSSNE* 12:19–20,
1937.
A whimsical quatrain ballad of Maine going back
to the 17th century.

————.
"The Wreck of the Schooner Medora."
FSSNE 11:19–20, 1936.
"An ode on the wreck of the schooner "Medora"
on the Great Lakes with the loss of all on board,
February 29, 1836." Words only.

Cox, John Harrington
"The Yew Pine Mountains, A John Hardy
Ballad." *AS* 2 (No. 5):226–227, 1927.

"Young Hunting."
JAFL 18:295, 1905; 20:252–253, 1907; 30:
297–304, 1917.

"Young Hunting."
The William and Mary Literary Magazine,
May, 1922.

COLLECTIONS

English Ballads:
A Selection

See: English Song Collections, pp. 78, 79–82.

Allingham, W.
The Ballad Book: A selection of the choicest
British Ballads. London: Macmillan and Com-
pany, 1898, xlviii, 398 pp., (Golden Treasury
Series).

Ancient Ballads; selected from Percy's collection,
with explanatory notes, from different authors,
for the use and entertainment of young persons.
London: Vernor, 1807. iv, 211 pp.

Ancient Historic Ballads.
New Castle: D. Alserhead and Sons, 1807, 236
pp., illustrated.

Anderson, W., collector
A Bunch of Gatherings, gleaned from the two
past generations, consisting of eight-page ballads, songs, tales, elegies, executions, etc.,
mostly poetical. Paisely: J. R. Parlane, 1860.

An Antidote Against Melancholy; compounded
of choice poems, jovial songs, merry ballads.
New York: Pratt Manufacturing Company,
1884, 123 pp.

Ashton, John
Modern Street Ballads. London: Chatto &
Windus, 1888. xvi, 405 pp. 56 illustrations,
without music.
Social, political, historical and humorous street
songs from the first half of the 19th century.

Ballads and Metrical Tales. Selected from Percy,
Ritson, Evans, Jamieson, Scott, etc. London:
J. Burns, 1845, 242 pp., illustrated.

Ballads and Romances.
New York: Charles Scribner's Sons, 1883.

Baring-Gould, Sabine
English Ministrelsie: A National Monument of
English Song. Edinburgh: 1895–1897, 8 vol-
umes in 7.

————.
Songs and Ballads of the West: A collection
made from the mouths of the people for voice
and pianoforte. London. 1892.

The Beauties of Ancient Poetry.
Intended as a companion to the beauties of
English poetry. London: E. Newbery, 1794.
xl, 204 pp.

The Bentley Ballads, comprising the Tipperary Hall Ballads, now first republished from "Bentley's Miscellany" 1846; with preface and notes by John Sheehan. London: 1869.

The Book of Ballads, ancient and modern, historical, traditional, and romantic. Illustrated with one hundred and twenty engravings. London: Bell and Daldy, 1875, 870 pp.

A Book of Favourite Modern Ballads.
Illustrated with fifty engravings by J. Evans from drawings by the first artists. London: W. Kent and Company, 1860, 167 pp.

Borrow, George, translator
Ballads of All Nations. Edited by R. B. Johnson, London. London: A. Rivers Ltd., 1927. xxiii, 342 pp.

The Boy's Book of Ballads.
Illustrated with sixteen engravings in wood from drawings by John Gilbert. London: Bell and Daldy, 1861, vii, 187 pp. New York: D. Appleton and Company, 1861, vii, 187 pp.

Broadwood, Lucy E., and Fuller-Maitland, John Alexander
English County Songs. Words and music. London: 1893. Arranged for voice and piano.

Chappel, W., editor
A Collection of National English Airs. Consisting of ancient song, ballad, and dance tunes, interspersed with remark and anecdote, and preceded by an essay on English minstrelsy. The airs harmonized by W. Gootch, G. A. Macfarren, and J. A. Wade. London: 1840, 2 volumes.

Popular Music of the Olden Time. A collection of ancient songs, ballads and dance tunes, illustrative of the national music of England. The whole of the airs harmonized by G. A. Macfarren. London: 1855, 2 volumes, illustrated.

Child, Francis James
The English and Scottish Ballads. Boston: Little, Brown and Company, 1860, 8 volumes, (British Poets).

The English and Scottish Popular Ballads. Boston: Houghton Mifflin and Company, 1882–1895, 10 parts in 5 volumes.

English and Scottish Popular Ballads. Edited from the collection of F. J. Child by A. C. Sargent and G. L. Kittredge. Boston: Houghton Mifflin and Company, 1904. xxxi, 730 pp., (Cambridge Edition of the Poets).

A Collection of Ballads.
Manchester: J. Swindells, 18–?

A Collection of Seventy-Nine Black-Letter Ballads and Broadsides, printed in the reign of Queen Elizabeth, between the years 1559 and 1597. Accompanies with an introduction and illustrative notes. London: J. Lilly, 1867, xxxvi, 319 pp.

Collier, John Payne
A Book of Roxburghe Ballads. London: Longman's, 1847, xxxii, 340 pp.

Old Ballads from Early Printed Copies of Rarity. London: Percy Society, 1840, xi, 131 pp.

Country Ballads; preserved by tradition. Pately Bridge: T. Thorp, 1869, 31 pp.

Dixon, J. H., editor
Ancient Poems, Ballads, and Songs of the Peasantry of England; taken down from oral recitation, and scarce publications. London: Percy Society, 1846. xv, 250 pp.

Doran, Dr., editor
The Bentley Ballads: A selection of the choicest ballads, songs, etc., attributed to Bentley's Miscellany. London: 1858.

Dyer, Sidney
Songs and Ballads. New York: Sheldon, Blakeman and Company, 1857, xv, 298 pp.

Ebsworth, J. W., editor
The Bagford Ballads; illustrating the last years of the Stuarts. Hartford: Ballad Society, 1878, Vols. 14–17, 20. 2 volumes.

"English folk songs in Canada."
JAFL 31:72–78, 130–133, 151–153, 158–179, 1918.

Evans, Thomas
Old Ballads, historical and narrative, with some modern date, collected from the rare copies and MSS., a new edition by R. H. Evans. London: 1810, 4 volumes.

Fluegel, Ewald
"Liedersammlungen des XVI Jahrhunderts, besonders aus der Zeit Heinrich's VIII." Anglia 12: 225–272, 585–597, 1889; 26: 94–285, 1903.

A Garland of Old Historical Ballads 1600–1752. The Aungervyle Society Publications, No. 5. Edinburgh: The Aungervyle Society, 1881, 20 pp.

Gaultier, Bon, editor
The Book of Ballads. Illustrated by Alfred Crowquill. London: W. S. Orr and Company, 1848, 152 pp. Edinburgh: 1859.
  Parodies in the style of old ballads, remarkable for the humorous use of the ancient models.

Gayton, William E., and Martin, Sir T.
The Book of Ballads. Edited by Bon Gaultier. Edinburgh: 1909, 18th edition.

Gerould, Gordon Hall
The Ballad of Tradition. London: Clarenden Press, 1932.

Goldsmith, Oliver, compiler
The Beauties of English Poesy. London: W. Griffin, 1767, 2 volumes.

Goodwin, James
Six Ballads with Burdens, from MS—in the library of Corpus Christi College, Cambridge. London: Percy Society, 1844, XII, 15 pp.

Goss, John, editor
Ballads of Britain. Introduction by Sir John Squire and decorations by J. Whitehead. London: John Lane, 1937, xx, 140 pp., tunes, texts and variants.

Graves, Robert
The English Ballad a short critical survey. London: E. Benn, Ltd., 1927. 139 pp.

Greig, Gavin, and Keith, Alexander
Last Leaves of Traditional Ballads and Ballad Airs. Aberdeen: University of Aberdeen, 1925.

Grosart, A. B., editor
The Towneley MSS. English Jacobite ballads, songs, and satires, etc. From the MSS. of Towneley Hall, Lancashire. Manchester: Privately printed, 1877, xxviii, 200 pp.

Gummere, Francis B.
Old English Ballads. Boston: Houghton Mifflin Company, 1897.

———.
The Popular Ballad. Boston. The Houghton Mifflin Company, 1907.

Hales, J. W., editor, and others
Bishop Percy's Folio Manuscript. Ballads and Romances. London: N. Trübner and Company, 1867–1868, 4 volumes.

Hall, Samuel Carter, editor
The Book of British Ballads. London: H. Jow, 1842–1845, 2 volumes. New York: Douglas, 1884, 153 pp. illustrated.
Contains 52 ballads, with an introduction to each ballad.

Halliwell, J. O., editor
The Early Naval Ballads of England. London: Percy Society, 1841, xii, 144 pp.

Hartshorne, C. H.
Ancient Metrical Tales. Printed chiefly from original sources. London: 1829.

Hayley, William
Ballads, founded on anecdotes relating to animals, with prints designed and engraved by William Blake. London: R. Phillips, 1805, 212 pp.

Hindley, Charles, editor
The Roxburghe Ballads. London: 1873 and 1874, 2 volumes, illustrated.

The Illustrated Book of English Songs from the 16th to the 19th century. London: n.d. illustrated.

Johnson, R. B.
Popular British Ballads, ancient and modern. London: J. M. Dent and Company, 1894, 4 volumes.

Kinloch, George Ritchie
The Ballad Book. Revised by Edmund Goldsmid. Edinburgh: 1891.

Kittredge, C. L., and Sargent, Helen Child
English and Scottish Popular Ballads. Boston: Houghton Mifflin and Company, 1904.

Langbridge, T.
Sent Back by the Angels, and other ballads of home and homely life. London: 1885.
"The characters in my ballads follow the speech which I have heard from the lips of my nurse, in what was then a pretty rural spot on the Staffordshire fringe of Birmingham ..."

Logan, W. H.
A Peddler's Pack of Ballads and Songs with illustrative notes. Edinburgh: Patterson, 1869, xv.

Mackay, Charles, editor
The Cavalier Songs and Ballads of England, from 1642–1684. London: The Percy Society, 1863.

———.
A Collection of Songs and Ballads, relative to the London prentices and trades and to the affairs of London generally. During the 14th, 15th, and 16th centuries. London: Percy Society, 1841. viii, 157 pp.

———.
The Songs and Ballads of the Cavaliers. London: C. Griffin and Company, 1864, viii, 310 pp.

Maclaren, Archibald
The Fairy Family: A series of ballads and metrical tales, illustrating the fairy mythology of Europe. London: Longmans, 1857, xv, 283 pp.

Moeran, E. J.
Six Folk Songs from Norfolk. Collected and arranged for voice and pianoforte by E. J. Moeran. London: Angener, Ltd., 1924, 27 pp., medium voice.

Moore, J. S.
The Pictorial Book of Ancient Ballad Poetry of Great Britain. To which are added, a selection of modern imitations, and some translations. London: H. Washbourne and Company, 1853, 871 pp., new edition.

Morley, Henry
The King and the Commons. Cavalier and Puritan Song, selected and arranged by Henry Morley. New York: (London printed), 1869. Voice and Piano.

Morton, Cora, ed.
Old Ballads. New York: American Book Company, 1917. 168 pp., illus., bibl.

Motherwell, William
Minstrelsy Ancient and Modern. London: Paisley's Edition, 1873. Voice and piano.

Niles, John J.
The Anglo-American Ballad Study Book. Containing eight ballads, current in tradition in the United States of America. New York: G. Schirmer.
(Schirmer's American Folk-Song Series 24) with the original Child texts and notes on variants and sources.

Old English Ballads.
A collection of favorite ballads of the olden time. London: Ward, Lock and Tyler, 1864, illustrated.
Short introductory notes on the origin of and the first appearance of each ballad.

Percy Society. Early English Poetry, ballads, and popular literature of the Middle Ages. Edited from original manuscripts and scarce publications. London: 1840–1852, 30 volumes.
An indispensable and inexhaustible source for the study of English folk song and balladry.

Percy, Thomas—Bishop of Dromore
Reliques of Ancient English Poetry. Consisting of old heroic ballads, songs, and other pieces of our poets (chiefly of the lyric kind). Together with some few of later date. London: J. Dodsley, 1767, many editions of this monumental work in England and America.

Philips, A.
A Collection of Old Ballads. Corrected from the best and most ancient copies extant, with introductions historical, critical, or humorous. London: J. Roberts, 1723–1725, 3 volumes.

Pictorial Penny Balladist.
London: J. C. Moore, 18–, 336 pp.

Prideaux, W. F.
"Ballads on the Coronation of King George II." *Notes and Queries 10 (ser. 9):* 121–122, 1902 (London).

Rimbault, E. F.
Old Ballads, illustrating the great frost of 1683–1684, and the fair on the River Thames. London: Percy Society, 1844, xxx, 38 pp.

Ritson, Joseph
Pieces of Ancient Popular Poetry. From authentic manuscripts and old printed copies. London: Talid T. Egerton, 1791. xiv, 152 pp.

————, editor
Robin Hood: A collection of all the ancient poems, songs, and ballads, now extant, relative to that celebrated English outlaw; to which are prefixed historical anecdotes of his life. London: C. Stocking, 1823. x, lxxiv, 240 pp.

————, and Goldsmid, E.
Ancient English Metrical Romances. Edinburgh: 1884, limited edition revised by E. Goldsmid, 3 volumes.

————, and Hazlitt, W. C.
Ancient Songs and Ballads. From the reign of King Henry II to the Revolution. London: 1877, 3rd edition revised by W. C. Hazlitt.

Roberts, John S.
The Legendary Ballads of England and Scotland. London: Chandos Classics, 1870.

Robson, John
Three Early English Metrical Romances. With an introduction and glossary. London: Camden Society, 1842. xlv, 132 pp.

Sargent, Helen Child, and Kittredge, George Lyman
English and Scottish Popular Ballads. From Child's collection. Introduction by Professor Kittredge. Boston: Houghton Mifflin Company, 1904.

Sharp, Cecil.
One Hundred English Folk Songs. Boston: Oliver Ditson Company, 1916, voice and piano.

————, and Marson, Charles L.
Folk Songs from Somerset. Gathered and edited in the pianoforte accompaniment. London: Simpkin and Company, Ltd., 1906, 3 series, xi, 82 pp.

Sharp, Sir Cuthbert
The Bishoprick Garland; or a collection of legends, songs, ballads, etc., belonging to the county of Durham. Sunderland: Hills and Company, 1906. v–viii, 84 pp.

Sheldon, F., editor
The Minstrelsy of the English Border. Being a collection of ballads, ancient, remodelled, and original, founded on well known border legends. London: Longmans, 1847. xxi, 432 pp.

Sidgwick, F., ed.
Legendary Ballads. Ballads and Lyrics of Love. Illustrated by Byam Shaw. New York: F. A. Stokes Company, 1908. xvi, 180 pp.

Simpson, Harold
A Century of Ballads—1810–1910. Their composers and singers. With introductory chapters on old ballads and ballad makers. London: Mills and Boom, 1910. xvii, 349 pp., illus.

Taylor, Deems
Traditional Airs. Newly harmonized by Deems Taylor, op. 15. New York: J. Fischer and Brothers, 1920, voice and piano.

Thompson, Henry, editor
Original Ballads of Living Authors. London: J. Masters, 1850, xiv, 256 pp.

Thornbury, Walter
Historical and Legendary Ballads and Songs. Illustrated by leading artists. Boston: W. F. Gill and Company, 1876. xxiii, 280 pp.

The Tournament and the Feast.
   Two early ballads printed from a MSS. preserved in the Public Library of the University of Cambridge. London: W. Pickering, 1836, xiv, 20, 22 pp.

Turner, J. W.
   The Minstrel's Gift. Containing songs and ballads; also melodies for the flute and violin. Boston: 1852.

Utterson, E. V., editor
   A Little Book of Ballads. Newport: Printed by Yelf and Company, 1836, 72 pp.

————.
   Select Pieces of Early Popular Poetry. Republished principally from early printed copies, in the black letter. London: Longman, 1817, 2 volumes.

Weitz, Guy
   Three Old English Songs. J. and W. Chester Ltd., voice and piano. (Repertoire Colignon) Contents: "Come, who'll buy primroses," "Molly's hoop," "Tom o' Bedlam."

Wilkins, W. Walker, editor
   Political Ballads of the Seventeenth and Eighteenth Centuries. London: Longman's, 1860, 2 volumes.

Williams, R. Vaughan
   Two English Folk-Songs. Arranged for voice and violin. London: Oxford University Press, 1935. 6, 3 pp.

————.
   Six English Folk-Songs. Arranged for piano and voice. London: Oxford University Press, 1935, 11 pp. Contents: "Robin Hood and the peddler," "The Ploughman," "One Man, two men," "The Brewer," "Rolling in the dew," "King William."

Wilson, H. Lane
   Old English Melodies. London: 1899, for voice and piano.

Wright, Thomas
   Political Ballads. Published in England during the Commonwealth. London: Percy Society, 1841, xvi, 268 pp.

————.
   The Political Songs of England. From the reign of John to that of Edward II. London: Camden Society, 1839, xviii, 408 pp. Camden Society Publication, vol. 6.

Scotch Ballads:
A Selection

See: Scotch Song Collections, pp. 79–80, 82–84.

Balfour, Sir James
   Ballads, and other fugitive poetical pieces, chiefly Scottish from the collections of Sir J. Balfour. Edinburgh: A. Lawrie and Company, 1834. ix, 42 pp.

Chambers, Robert
   The Romantic Scottish Ballads. Their epoch and authorship. n.p., 18–?, 46 pp.

————.
   The Scottish Ballads. Collected and illustrated. Edinburgh: W. Tait, 1829. vii, 399 pp.

Child, Francis James
   The English and Scottish Ballads. Boston: Little, Brown and Company, 1860, 8 volumes, (British Poets).

————.
   The English and Scottish Popular Ballads. Boston: Houghton Mifflin and Company, 1882–1895, 10 parts in 5 volumes.

————.
   English and Scottish Popular Ballads. Edited from the collection of F. J. Child by H. C. Sargent and G. L. Kittredge. Boston: Houghton Mifflin and Company, 1904. xxxi, 730 pp. (Cambridge Edition of the Poets.)

Clyne, N.
   The Romantic Scottish Ballads, and the Lady Wardlaw Heresy. Aberdeen: A. Brown and Company, 1859, 49 pp.

Gaultier, Bon
   The Book of Ballads. Edinburgh: Blackwood, 1870.

Gayton, William Edmonstone
   Ballads of Scotland. Edinburgh and London: W. Blackwood and Sons, 1858, 2 volumes.

Gilchrist, John
   A Collection of Ancient and Modern Ballads. Tales and songs with notes and observations. Edinburgh: W. Blackwood and Sons, 1815.

Herd, D., editor
   Ancient and Modern Scottish Songs. Heroic Ballads, etc., with memoir and illustrative notes by S. Gilpin. Edinburgh: 1870, 2 volumes. Reprint of the edition of 1776.

Hogg, James, collector
   Jacobite Relics of Scotland: The songs, airs and legends of the adherents to the House of Stuart. Paisley: J. R. Parlane, 1874.

Hopekirk, Helen
   Seventy Scottish Songs. Boston: Oliver Ditson Company, 1905, voice and piano, high, low voice.

The Illustrated Book of Scottish Songs. From the 16th to the 19th Centuries. London: n.d., illustrated.

Kinloch, George Ritchie, editor
   Ancient Scottish Ballads. Recovered from tradition, and never before published, with notes, historical and explanatory, and an appendix containing the airs of several of the ballads. London: 1827.

————.
   The Ballad Book. In: *Four Books of Choice Old Scottish Ballads,* M.D.CCCXXIII–M.DCCCXLIV. Edinburgh: Reprinted for private circulation, 1868.

Logan, W. H.
A Pedlar's Pack of Ballads and Songs. With illustrative notes. Edinburgh: W. Patterson, 1869. xiv, 479 pp.

Maidment, James
A New Book of Old Ballads. In: *Four Books of Choice Old Scottish Ballads.* (M.DCCCXXIII–M.DCCCXLIV) Edinburgh: Reprinted for private circulation, 1868, 4 parts in 1 volume.

————.
Scottish Ballads and Songs, historical and traditionary. Edinburgh: W. Patterson, 1868, 2 volumes.

M'Dowall, William
Among the Old Scotch Minstrels. Studying their ballads of war, love, social life, folk-lore, and fairyland. Edinburgh: D. Douglas, 1888. xi, 351 pp.

Motherwell, William
Minstrelsy, Ancient and Modern. With an historical introduction and notes. Glasgow: J. Wylie, 1827, iii, 390 pp. Boston: 1846, 2 volumes.

Murray, J. C.
The Ballads and Songs of Scotland. In view of their influence on the character of the people. London: 1874.

A North Country Garland.
In: *Four Books of Choice Old Scottish Ballads.* (M.DCCCXXIII-M.DCCCXLIV). Edinburgh: Reprinted for private circulation, 1868.

Ramsay, Allan
The Tea-table Miscellany. With a collection of choice songs, Scots and English. Edinburgh: A. Donaldson, 1762. xxxiv, 448 pp.

Respighi, Ottorino
Four Scottish Songs, for voice and piano, harmonized by Ottorino Respighi. New York: Universal Edition, 1925, 26 pp. German and English words.

Roberts, John S.
The Legendry Ballads of England and Scotland. London: Chandos Classics, 1870

Robson, J., editor
The Scottish Field. Manchester: Chetham Miscellanies, 1855. 1856. xv, 28 pp.

Scott, Sir Walter
Minstrelsy of the Scottish Border: Consisting of historical and romantic ballads, collected in the Southern counties of Scotland; with a few of modern date. London: T. Tegg, 1839. lxxiii, 559 pp.

Sharpe, Charles Kirkpatrick, editor
A Ballad Book; Edinburgh, 1823. In: *Four Books of Choice Old Scottish Ballads.* (M.D.-CCCXXIII–M.C.CCCXLIV). Edinburgh: Reprinted for private circulation, 1868.

Veitch, J.
The History and Poetry of the Scottish Border; their main features and relations. Edinburgh: 1884. 2nd new an enlarged edition.
Valuable critical discussion of the ballads.

Walker, Hugh
Popular Ballads. In: *Three Centuries of Scottish Literature.* Glasgow: J. MacLehose 1893, 2 volumes.

Irish Ballads:
A Selection

See: Irish Folk-Song Collections, pp. 79–80, 84–85.

Bunting, Edward
A General Collection of the Ancient Irish Music, containing a variety of admired airs never before published, and also the compositions of Conolan and Carolan; collected from the harpers of Ireland, and adapted for the pianoforte. Dublin: Hime, 1796?, iv, 26 pp. London: Preston, 1796?, iv, 36 pp. London: Clementi and Company, 1809, V.I.

Christie, W.
Traditional Ballad Airs. Edinburgh: 1876 and 1881.
"Christie's book ranks as a poetical, and not only musical, anthology."

Croker, Thomas Crofton, editor
The Historical Songs of Ireland, illustrative of the revolutionary struggle between James II and William III. London: Percy Society, 1841. viii, 139 pp.

————.
Popular Songs, illustrative of the French invasion of Ireland. London: T. Richards, 1845–1847. 4 parts in 1 volume, (The Percy Society).

Duffy, Charles Gavan
The Ballad Poetry of Ireland. Dublin: J. Duffy. 1845. xlviii, 252 pp.

Fitzgerald, John
"An Account of the Old Street Ballads of Cork (Ireland)." *Journal of the Cork Historical and Archaeological Society* 1: 63–71, 1892. (Cork).

Hardiman, J.
Irish Minstrelsy; or, Bardic remains of Ireland, with English poetical translations. London: J. Robins 1831, 2 volumes.

Harty, Hamilton, arr.
Three Irish Folk-Songs. London: Oxford University Press, 1929, 17 pp. voice and piano.

Joyce, Robert Dwyer
Ballads of Irish Chivalry. Edited, with annotations by P. W. Joyce. Dublin: Hodges, Figgis, and Co., Ltd.

Lover, Samuel, and others
The Book of Irish Ballads. Philadelphia: A. Winch, 1860, 72 pp.

——————.
Songs and Ballads, including these sung in
his "Irish Evenings" and hitherto unpublished.
New York: Wiley and Putnam, 1847, xiv,
224 pp.

MacCarthy, D. F.
The Book of Irish Ballads. Dublin: Duffy's
Library of Ireland, 1848, 21 pp.

O'Conor, Manus
*Com-All-Ye's and Ballads of Ireland, A Re-
pository of Ancient Irish Songs and Ballads.*
New York. 1901.

Stephens' Fenian Songster,
containing all the ballads and songs as sung
at the meetings of the Fenian Brotherhood.
New York: W. H. Murphy, 1866, 72 pp.

AMERICAN BALLADS

*See: American Song Collections, pp. 78–79,
85–94.*

American Patriotic Songs,
a carefully selected collection of the best and
most popular American national lyrics, words,
and music complete. Boston: Oliver Ditson
and Company, 1893, 88 pp.

Barry, Phillips
The Maine Songster. Cambridge, Mass.:
Powell Publishing Company, 1939.
Many of the tunes and texts are variants of old
world ballads.

——————, **and others**
British Ballads from Maine; the development
of popular songs with texts and airs by Phillips Barry, Fannie Hardy Eckstorm, and Mary
Winslow Smyth; versions of ballads included
in Professor F. J. Child's Collection. New
Haven: Yale University Press. London: H. Milford, Oxford University, 1929. xlvi, 535 pp.,
music.

Belden, Henry Marvin
*Ballads and Songs Collected by the Missouri
Folk-lore Society.* Columbia, Missouri: The
University of Missouri, 1940, xviii, 530 pp.,
some of the songs with music.

Botkin, B. A., editor
A Treasury of American Folklore, the stories,
legends, tall tales, traditions, ballads and songs
of the American people. Foreword by Carl
Sandburg. New York: Crown Publishers, 1944.
Contains words and tunes of 100 songs and ballads.

Campbell, Olive Dame, and Sharp, Cecil J.
*English Folk-Songs from the Southern Appa-
lachians.* New York and London: G. P. Putnam's Sons, 1917.

Carson, "Fidlin" John
A Remarkable Collection of Ballads and Songs.
Atlanta, Georgia: P. C. Brockman.

Chase, Richard, and Springfield, Lamar
Traditional Ballads, Songs, and Singing Games.
Chapel Hill, North Carolina: Institute of Folk
Music, University of North Carolina, 1935.

Coleman, Satis Narrona (Barton)
Songs of American Folks by Satis N. Coleman
and Adolph Bregman, illustrated by Alanson
Hewes. New York: The John Day Company,
1942, 128 pp.
"Original arrangements for voice with piano accompaniment, by Satis N. Coleman."

Combs, J. H.
Folk-songs du Midi des Etats-Unis par Josiah
H. Combs. Paris: Les Presses Universitaires
de France, 1925, 230 pp., bibliography (thesis).

Cox, John H.
Folk-Songs of the South. Cambridge, Massachusetts: Harvard University Press, 1925.

Creighton, Helen, coll.
Songs and Ballads from Nova Scotia. Toronto:
J. M. Dent & Sons, Ltd. 1933. 334 pp., unac-
comp. melodies.

Dean, M. C.
*The Flying Cloud, and 100 Other Time Songs
and Ballads.* Virginia, Minnesota, 1922.

Dobie, James Frank
Man, Bird, and Beast, edited by J. Frank Dobie.
Austin, Texas: Texas Folk-lore Society, 1930,
185 pp., illustrated (including music). Pub-
lications of the Texas Folk-lore Society Vol.
VIII.

——————.
Texas and Southwestern Lore, edited by
J. Frank Dobie. Austin, Texas: Published by
the Texas Folk-lore Society, 1927, 259 pp.,
illustrated (music). Publications of the Texas
Folk-lore Society, No. VI.

——————.
Tone The Bell Easy, edited by J. Frank Dobie.
Austin, Texas: Texas Folk-lore Society, 1932,
199 pp., (including music).
British Ballads in Texas, by Mabel Major: pp.
131–168.

Dodd, Margaret, ed.
Ballads and Folk Songs of America. New York:
Music Press, Inc. 1946.
Seven choral numbers arranged for mixed chorus.
Contents: "He's Gone Away," "Old Bangin',"
"Shuckin' of the Corn," "Per Spelmann," "The
WeeCooper of Five," "Sourwood Mountain," and
"A La Puerta del Cielo."

Downes, Olin, and Siegmeister, Elie
A Treasury of American Song; music arranged
by Elie Siegmeister. New York: Howell, Soskin and Company, 1940, 351 pp. 2nd ed. published by A. A. Knopf, 1943.

Eckstorm, Mrs. Fannie (Hardy)
Minstrelsy of Maine; folksongs and ballads of
the woods and the coast. Collected by Fannie
Hardy Eckstorm and Mary Winslow Smyth.
Boston: Houghton Mifflin Company, 1927, xvi,
390 pp., text and tunes.
List of books on American Folksongs—pp. xi–
xii.

Eddy, Mary Olive
Ballads and Songs from Ohio, collected and arranged by Mary O. Eddy, introduction by James Holly Hanford. New York: J. J. Augustin, 1939, xxvii, 330 pp., bibliography, unaccompanied melodies.

Finger, Charles Joseph
Frontier Ballads. Garden City, New York: Doubleday Page and Company, 1917, 181 pp.

Ford, Ira W.
Traditional Music of America. New York: E. P. Dutton & Co., Inc., 1940. 480 pp., melodies unaccompanied.

Gardner, E. E.
"Ballads" (from Michigan). *JAFL* 27:90–93, 1914.

————. **and Chickering, G. J.**
Ballads and Songs of Southern Michigan. Ann Arbor: University of Michigan Press, 1939.

Greenleaf, Elisabeth B.
Ballads and Sea Songs of Newfoundland. Cambridge, Mass.: Harvard Univ. Press, 1933. 395 pp., music.

Harris Collection of American Poetry.
Providence, Rhode Island: John Hay Library, Brown University.
An unrivalled collection of American sheets and early songbooks, including a complete set of the De Marsen broadsides, numbering several thousand sheets, and early Rhode Island and Massachusetts prints.

————.
Broadsides, Ballads, etc. Printed in Massachusetts 1639–1800. Boston: Massachusetts Historical Society, 1922, collection V, 75.

Haywood, Charles, ed. and arr.
The American Scene in Ballad and Song. New York: Greenberg: Publisher, c. 1950. illus., music: voice and piano.
The growth of American Civilization reflected in its folk songs. The narrative supplied by the voice of the people: diaries, letters and documents. Illustrated by old prints.

Hudson, Arthur Palmer
"Ballads and Songs from Mississippi." *JAFL* 29:93–194, 1915.

————.
Folksongs of Mississippi and their Background. Chapel Hill: University of North Carolina Press, 1936. xii, 321 pp., texts only.

————.
Folk Tunes from Mississippi. 2nd edition, edited by G. Herzog and H. Halpert, with preface by E. S. Woodward; W. P. A. Federal Theatre Project. New York: National Service Bureau, 1937, Publication No. 25.

Isaiah Thomas Collection of American Broadsides.
Worcester, Massachusetts: American Antiquarian Society, 1924, 302 pp. (without duplicates) 3 volumes.
This collection has been catalogued by Mr. Worthington C. Ford in a pamphlet published by the Society. Remarkably rich in Coverly prints.

Karpeles, Maud, collector and editor
Folk Songs from Newfoundland, pianoforte accompaniments by R. V. Williams, Clive Carey, Hubert J. Foss, Michael Mullinar. London: Oxford University Press, 1934.

Landeck, Beatrice, comp.
Songs My True Love Sings. An Album of Immortal Love Songs for voice and piano or guitar. Piano settings by Charity Bailey. New York: E. B. Marks Music Corporation, 1946. 64 pp., illus.
The album consists mainly of ballads and lyric songs.

Linscott, Eloise Hubbard
Folksongs of Old New England, collected and edited by Eloise Hubbard Linscott, with an introduction by James M. Carpenter. New York: The Macmillan Co., 1939. xxi, 337 pp., with music references.

Lomax, John Avery
Cowboy Songs and Other Frontier Ballads, collected by John A. Lomax, with an introduction by Barrett Wendell. New York: Macmillan Co., 1920. xiii, 414 pp., contains music.

————, **and Alan**
American Ballads and Folk Songs, collected and compiled by John A. Lomax, and Alan Lomax; with a foreword by George Lyman Kittredge. New York: The Macmillan Co., 1934. xxxix, 625 pp., includes music, bibl.

————.
Folk Songs: U. S. A. The 111 best American ballads. Music arrangements for piano and guitar by Charles and Ruth Seeger. New York: Duell, Sloan and Pearce, Inc., 1948, 384 pp.
The book "presents more than words and music—every section is introduced with a long and salty introduction, full of folk tales, and tall yarns, and incidents of the Lomaxes' collecting adventures. These introductions give the social settings and the local color for each of the songs and ballads. There are twelve chapters dealing with spirituals, Ballads of 'Hard Cases', Songs for Children, Work Songs, Cowboy Ditties, Love Songs, Dance Songs, War Ballads, Sailor's Chanteys, Lumberjack Ballads, Farmers' Tunes, Railroad songs."

————.
Our Singing Country; a second volume of American ballads and folksongs, collected and compiled by John A. Lomax and Alan Lomax; Ruth Crawford Seeger, music editor. New York: The Macmillan Co., 1941. xxxiv, 416 pp., bibl., unaccompanied melodies.

Luther, Frank
   Americans and Their Songs. New York: Harper & Brothers, 1942. xiv, 323 pp. 75 songs with piano accompaniment and 50 unaccompanied melodies. The songs of America (1620–1900) a chronological list.
   America's growth traced in a chronological arrangement of its songs.

Mackenzie, W. Roy
   Ballads and Sea Songs from Nova Scotia. Cambridge, 1928.

Morton, Cora, editor
   A Book of Old Ballads. New York, Cincinnati: American Book Company, 1917, 168 pp., illustrated, (map) bibliography p. 4.

Newell, William Wells
   "Early American Ballads." *JAFL 12:* 241–254, 1899; 13:105–122, 1900.

Niles, John J.
   The Anglo-American Ballad Study Book. Containing eight ballads, current in tradition in the United States of America. New York: G. Schirmer.
   (Schirmer's American Folk-Song Series 24.) With the original Child texts and notes on variants and sources.

Partridge Collection.
   American Broadsides of the nineteenth century bearing the imprints of J. Andress, H. Partridge, and J. Wrigley, presented by Mr. Horace Partridge to the Boston Public Library.

Pound, Louise
   American Ballads and Songs. New York: Charles Scribners' Sons, 1922.

Randolph, Vance
   The Ozarks. An American survival of primitive society. New York: The Vanguard Press, 1931, ix, 310 pp., music.

Richardson, Mrs. Ethel (Park)
   American Mountain Songs. Compiled by Ethel Richardson, edited and arranged by Sigmund Spaeth. New York: Greenberg, 1927. 120 pp., with music.

Sandburg, Carl
   The American Songbag. New York: Harcourt, Brace & Co., c. 1927. xxiii, 495 pp., contains music. "An American bookshelf of song": pp. xii–xiii.

Scarborough, Dorothy
   A Song Catcher in Southern Mountains; American folksongs of British ancestry. New York: Columbia University Press, 1937. xvi, 476 pp., music (Unaccompanied melodies) p. 383–457.

Sharp, Cecil James
   American-English Folksongs, collected in the Southern Appalachians, and arranged with pianoforte accompaniment by Cecil J. Sharp. First series. New York: G. Schirmer, c. 1918. 57 pp., 6 ballads and 6 songs, melodies with piano accompaniment, English words.

   —————.
   English Folksongs from the Southern Appalachians. Collected by Cecil J. Sharp. Comprising two hundred and seventy-three songs and ballads with nine hundred and sixty tunes, including thirty-nine tunes contributed by Olive Dame Campbell. Edited by Maud Karpeles. London: Oxford University Press, 1932. 2 vol., music, bibl.

Smith, Reed
   American Anthology of Old World Ballads. Compiled and edited by Reed Smith, settings by Hilton Rufty. New York: J. Fischer & Bro., c. 1937. Publ. No. J. F. & B. 7270–69. xxxii, 70 pp., bibl.

   —————.
   South Carolina Ballads. With a Study of the Traditional Ballad Today. Cambridge, Mass.: Harvard University Press, 1928. xi, 174 pp., music.

Tolman, Albert H.
   "Some Songs Traditional in the United States." *JAFL 29:* 155–197, 1916.

   —————, **and Eddy, Mary O.**
   "Traditional Texts and Tunes." *JAFL 35:* 335–432, 1922.

Wier, Albert E.
   Ballads the Whole World Sings. New York: D. Appleton and Company. 1917. 256 pp.

Wyman, L. and Brockway, H., coll. and arr.
   Lonesome Tunes. Folk-Songs from the Kentucky Mountains. New York: H. W. Gray Co., 1916.
   Arranged for voice and piano.

   —————.
   Twenty Kentucky Mountain Songs. Boston: Oliver Ditson Company, 1920.
   Arranged for voice and piano.

BALLAD ARRANGEMENTS
—————: *Unison*

"Billy Boy."
   Dunhill: Oxford: Unison.

"Caller Herrin'."
   Dunhill: Oxford: Descant.

"Ca' The Yowes."
   "Dunhill: Oxford: Descant.

"Farewell, Manchester."
   Prince Charles Stuart's Farewell in 1745.
   Dunhill: Oxford: Descant.

"The Farmer's Daughters."
   Whittaker: Oxford: Unison.

"Flowers in the Forest."
   Dunhill: Oxford: Descant.

"Flowers in the Valley."
   Whitehead: Carl Fischer: Unison.

"The Flowers O' The Forest."
Wiseman: Oxford: Unison.

"Girl I Left Behind Me."
Dunhill: Oxford: Descant.

"Gossip Joan—The Lincolnshire Poacher."
Whittaker: Oxford: Unison.

"Hey Johnnie Cope."
Wiseman: Oxford: Unison.

"How Should I Your True Love Know?"
Whittaker: Oxford: Descant.

"The Jolly Miller."
Dunhill: Oxford: Descant.

"The Laird O' Cockpen."
Wiseman: Oxford: Unison.

"Leezie Lindsay."
Dunhill: Oxford: Descant.

"The Lover's Farewell."
Dunhill: Oxford: Descant.

"The Piper of Dundee."
Dunhill: Oxford: Descant.

"Robin's Last Will."
Wiseman: Oxford: Unison.

"Saw Ye Nae My Peggy."
Greaves: Oxford: Unison.

"The Seeds of Love."
Northcote: Oxford: Descant.

"Wha'll be King but Charlie?"
Wiseman: Oxford: Unison.

"Wee Willie Gray."
Wiseman: Oxford: Unison.

"Wee Willie Winkie."
Robertson: Oxford: Unison.

"Yes, Sir."
Whittaker: Oxford: Descant.

"The Yorkshire Tike."
Carey-Whittaker: Oxford: Descant.

————: *Voice and Piano*

"An Old Folk Song."
Buchanan, Annabel Morris: J. Fischer.

"Ballad of Penn."
Gaul, Harvey: Galaxy: voice and piano.
N. Y. frontier.

"Barbara Allen."
Fischer, William Arms: Ditson: High, Med.
Voice.

"Come All Ye Fair and Tender Ladies."
Buchanan, Annabel Morris: J. Fischer.

"Lord Lovel."
J. C. J.: Ditson: voice and piano.

"The Sailor and Young Nancy."
Moeran, E. J.: Oxford University Press: voice
and piano.

"Searching for Lambs."
Goossens, Eugene: J. & W. Chester Ltd: voice
and piano.

"The Sprig of Thyme."
Grainger, Percy: Schirmer: High, Low voice.

"The Twa Corbies."
Ayres, Frederick: Schirmer: medium voice.

"The Twa Corbies."
Grainger, Percy: Schirmer: medium voice.
(arranged with 7 strings).

"Villikens and His Dinah."
Parry, John: Ditson: voice and piano.

————: *Female Voices*

"A Ballad to Queen Elizabeth of the Spanish
Armada."
Slater: Oxford: SA.

"All in a Garden Green."
Williams, Gerrard: Oxford: SA.

"Arise, Fair Maid."
Williams, Gerrard: Oxford: SA.

"A Ye Wakin', O!"
Whitehead: Oxford: SSA.

"An Old Man Came Courting Me."
Harwood: Oxford: SSA, with soprano solo.

"Barbara Allen."
Davis, Katherine K: Galaxy: SSA.

"Billy Boy."
Boston Music Co: SA.

"Billy Boy."
Treharne, B: Willis: SA.

"Black is the Color of My True Love's Hair."
Niles, John J.: Schirmer: SSA, soprano or
tenor solo a cappella.

"Braw, Braw, Lads."
Sneddon, James: Oxford: SA.

"Brother Green."
Buchanan A. M.: J. Fischer: SSA.

"Come All Ye Fair and Tender Ladies."
Buchanan, A. M.: J. Fischer: SSA.

"Come, All Ye Fair and Tender Ladies."
Boston Music Co.: SSA.

"Flora Macdonald's Lament."
Fox, George: Oxford: SSA.

"The Fox."
Boston Music Co.: SA.

"Ida Red."
Winstead: Witmark & Sons: SSA.

"I Wonder When I Shall be Married."
Boston Music Co.: SSA.

"In London Town."
Rootham: Oxford: SSA, a cappella.

"Jock O' Hazeldean."
Fox: Oxford: SSA.

"The Jolly Miller."
Dods: Oxford: SSA.

"A Ladie Gay."
Boston Music Co.: SSA.

"The Lass from the Low Countree."
Helm: Schirmer: SSAA, a cappella.

"Lonesome Dove."
Winstead, K.: Music Publishers Holding
Corp.: SSA.

"Lonesome Dove."
Winstead: Witmark & Sons: SSA.

"The Nightingale."
Brockway, H.: Gray: SSAA.

"Old Smokey."
Barthelson: I. Berlin: SSA.

"Red Rosey Bush."
Young-Breck: C. Fischer: SSA.

"Scottish Croon."
Whitehead: Oxford: SSA.

"Shepherd Kept Sheep."
Williams: Oxford: SA.

"Strawberry Fair."
Rix: Schirmer: SA.

"The Two Sisters."
Boston Music Co.: SSA.

"The White Cockade."
Diack: Oxford: SA.

"O, The Wraggle-Taggle Gipsies."
Rix: Schirmer: SSA, SA.

"O, The Wraggle-Taggle Gipsies."
Woodgate: Schirmer: SSA.

————: *Male Voices*

"An Acre of Land."
Williams, R. V.: Oxford: TTBB.

"Alas, To Whom Dare I Complain?"
Bartholomew: Schirmer: TTBB.

"As I Walked Out."
In: H. & M. Auditorium Series, No. 9. Grant-
Fishburn: Hall and McCreary: TTBB.

"Barbara Allen."
In: H. & M. Auditorium Series, No. 9. Grant-
Fishburn: Hall & McCreary: TTBB.

"The Boar's Head."
Bax, A.: Oxford: TTBB, a cappella.

"Corn Rigs."
Patterson: Oxford: TTBB.

"The Deil Cam' Fiddlin'."
Patterson: Oxford: TTB.

"Fantasy on American Folk Ballads."
Donovan, Richard F.: J. Fischer: TTBB, orchestra, or piano 4 hands.

"Flowers in the Valley."
Whitehead: Oxford: TTBB, a cappella.

"Grandma Grunts."
Bartholomew, M.: Schirmer: TTBB.
North Carolina ballad.

"Green Bottles."
Whittaker: Oxford: TBB, a cappella.

"Harry, the Tailor."
In: H. & M. Auditorium Series, No. 9. Grant-
Fishburn: Hall and McCreary: TTBB.

"High Barbary."
Hall, Arthur E.: Schirmer: TTBB.

"The Jolly Miller."
Trinkaus: Oxford: T(AT)TB.

"Lass O' Gowrie."
Durner: Oxford: TTBB, a cappella.

"My Johnny was a Shoemaker."
Bartholomew: Schirmer: TTBB.

"The Nightingale."
Brockway, Howard: H. W. Gray: TTBB.

"O, Good Ale."
Jacob, G.: Oxford: TTBB, a cappella.

"Old Maid's Song."
Brockway, Howard: H. W. Gray: TTBB.

"Seventeen Come Sunday."
Williams: Oxford: TBB.

"Sir Patrick Spence."
McBride, R. G.: MS: TTBB.

"Sound the Pibroch."
Robertson: Oxford: TTBB, a cappella

"Sweet Lillie."
Birchard: TTBB.

"There Was a Maid Went to the Mill."
Whittaker: Oxford: TBB, a cappella.

"Ten Green Bottles."
Warrell, A.: Oxford: TTBB, a cappella.

"Tobacco's but an Indian Weed."
Williams, R. V.: Oxford: TTBB, a cappella.

"Wee Cooper O' Fife."
Candlyn: Oxford: TTBB, a cappella.

"The Wee Town Clerk."
Roberton: Oxford: TTBB, a cappella.

"When I was Young and Single."
Kun, Ladislas: Ricordi: TTBB.

"World It Went Well With Me Then."
Williams, R. V.: Oxford: TTBB, a cappella.

————: *Mixed Voices*

"American Street Cries."
Siegmeister, E.: Carl Fischer: SATB.

"An Acre of Land."
Williams: Oxford: SATB, a cap.

"The Bailiff's Daughter of Islington."
Jacob: Oxford: SATB, a cap.

"Barbary Allen."
Treharne: Boston Music Co.: SATB.

"The Barkshire Tragedy," *and* "King Arthur Had Three Sons": Two Sets of Unaccompanied Choral Variations Upon English Folk Songs.
Boughton, R.: H. W. Gray: SATB.

"The Bashful Thames."
Purcell: Oxford: SATB, with Tenor or Soprano Solo.

"Behold, My Love, How Green the Groves."
Bainton: Oxford: SATB.

"The Boar's Head Carol."
Sargent: Oxford: SATB, a cap.

"Bonny Lighter Boy."
Foster: Oxford: SA(orMS)ATB, a cap.

"Brisk Young Sailor."
Morris, R. O.: Oxford: SSAATTBB, a cap.

"The Brisk Young Widow."
Warrell, A.: Oxford: SATB, a cap.

"Brother Green."
Brockway, H.: Gray: SSAATTBB, a cap.

"Brother Green."
Buchanan, A. M.: J. Fischer: SATB.

"Ca' the Yowes."
Candlyn: Oxford: SATB, with Alto and Baritone Solo, a cap.

"Ca' the Yowes."
Williams, R. V.: Oxford: SATB, and tenor solo.

"Come All Ye Fair and Tender Ladies."
Buchanan, A. M.: Fischer: SATB.

"Come, All Ye Fair and Tender Ladies."
Malin: Gamble Hinged: SSATBB.

"The Cuckoo."
Morris, R. O.: Oxford: SATB, a cap.

"Corn Rigs."
Burnett: Oxford: SATB.

"Dancing Maidens."
Boston Music: SATB.

"Dancing Maidens."
Treharne, B.: Willis: SSAB.

"The Deaf Woman's Courtship."
Siegmeister, E.: Carl Fischer: SATB, with alto and baritone solos, a cap.

"The Deil's Awa'."
Burnett: Oxford: SATB.

"Duncan Gray."
Bullock: Oxford: SATB.

"Duncan Gray."
Burnett: Oxford: SATB.

"Eppie Adair."
Bullock: Oxford: SATB.

"The Elf Knight."
Frost: Berlin: SATB.

"The False Young Man."
Malin: Gamble Hinged: SATB.

"Fantasie of Folk Songs."
James: Berlin: SATB.

"Far Over Yon Hills."
Foss: Oxford: SATB.

"Farewell, Nancy."
Foster, A.: Oxford: SSATB, a cap.

Five English Folk Songs.
Morris, R. O.: Novello and Co.: SSATB, a cappella.
  Contents: "Blow away the morning dew," "Cold blows the wind," "High Germany," "The Turtle Dove," "The Mare and the Fool."

"Flowers in the Valley."
Whitehead: Oxford: SATB, a cap.

"Frog Went Courtin'."
Niles, John J.: Schirmer: SSA. Soprano, tenor and baritone. (Or alto) solo, a cap.

"Go 'Way From My Window."
Niles, John J.: Schirmer: SSAATBB, soprano or tenor solo a cap.

"Gypsy Davy."
Treharne, B.: Willis: SATB, a cap.

"Gypsy Davy."
Boston, M.: SATB.

"Gypsy Laddie."
Malin: Gamble Hinged: SATB, soprano solo.

"The Gypsy Laddie."
Rufty, H.: Fischer: SATB, a cap.

"The Hebrew Children."
Buchanan, A. M.: J. Fischer: SATB.

"Henry Martyn."
Buchanan, A. M.: J. Fischer: SATB, a cap.

"He's Gone Away."
Lief, A.: Music Press: SSATBB.

"A Highland Lad."
Moodie: Oxford: SATB.

"The Inconstant Lover."
Malin: Gamble Hinged: SATB.

"I Will Give my Love an Apple."
Warrell, A.: Oxford: SATB, with baritone solo, a cap.

"Jenny Fair, Gentle Rosemarie."
Boston Music: SATB.

"John Barleycorn."
Demuth, H.: Oxford: SATB.

"John Dory."
Williams, R. V.: Oxford: SATB, a cap.

"Johnny I Hardly Knew."
Greaves: Oxford: SATB, a cap.

"The Keeper."
Malin: Boston Music Co.: SATB.

"Lady Isabel."
Frost: Berlin: SATB.

"Lady Margaret."
Boston Music: SAB.

"The Lawyer."
Morris, R. O.: Oxford: SSAATTBB, a cap.

"The Lincolnshire Poacher."
Whittaker: Oxford: SATB.

"The Little Family."
Treharne: Willis: SATB.

"Low Down in the Broom."
Warrell: Oxford: SATB, with Bar. solo, a cap.

"The Macgregor's Gathering."
Mansfield: Oxford: SATB, a cap.

"Make we Joy now in This Fest."
Walton: Oxford: SATB, a cap.

"My Tochter's the Jewel."
Rubbra: Oxford: SSATB, a cap.

"Oh, Mary Went A'Journeying."
Buchanan, A. M.: J. Fischer: SATB.

"The Nightingale."
Warrell: Oxford: SATB.

"Oh, No, John."
Nightingale, M.: Schirmer: SA(AT), Bar.

"Old Bangin."
Dodd, M.: Music Press: SATBB.

"Old Colony Times."
Siegmeister: C. Fischer: SATB, a cap.

"O Molly."
Kleinsinger: Berlin: SATB.

"O Rare Turpin."
Whittaker: Oxford: SATB, a cap.

"Per Spelmann."
Dodd, M.: Music Press: SSATBB.

"The Pretty Ploughing Boy."
Williams: Oxford: SATB, a cap.

"Rosemary and Thyme."
Powell: Birchard: SSAATTBB.

"The Rowan Tree."
Robertson: Oxford: SATB, a cap.

"Searching for Lambs."
Foster: Oxford: SA (orMS) ATB, a cap.

"Searching for Lambs."
Williams: Oxford: SATB, a cap.

"Seventeen come Sunday."
Morris: Oxford: SATB, a cap.

"Shepherd and his Fife."
Foster: Oxford: SATB, a cap.

"Soldier, Soldier."
Powell, John J.: Fischer: SATB, soprano and tenor solos, a cap.

"Sourwood Mountain."
Lief, A.: Music Press: SSATBB.

"Tarry Trousers."
Morris: Oxford: SATB, a cap.

"Ten Green Bottles."
Warrell: Oxford: SATB, a cap.

"Three Scottish Airs."
Mark: Stainer and Bell: mixed voices.

"To the Maypole Haste Away."
Randerson: Oxford: SATB, a cap.

"Sweet Willie."
Birchard: SATB.

"The True Lover's Farewell."
Malin: Gamble Hinged: SATB.

"The Wee Cooper of Five."
Lief, A.: Music Press: SATBB.

"With Jockey to the Fair."
Bullock: Oxford: SATB.

"The Wagoner's Lad."
Malin: Gamble Hinged: SATB, a cap.

"The Weak and Rambling One."
Powell, L.: Birchard: SAATBB.

"Wondrous Love."
Buchanan, A. M.: J. Fischer: SATB.

————————: *Piano*

America-Suite.
Schlein, Irving: MS: piano.

Americana—Five Mood Sketches Corn Cob, Indian Nocturne, Hillbilly, Night Sing, Music.
Gould, Morton: C. Fischer: Piano.

American Ballads.
Harris, Roy: C. Fischer: piano.
Contents: "Streets of Laredo," "Wayfaring Stranger," "The Bird," "Black is the Color of My True Love's Hair," "Cod Liver Ile."

Folk Song Fragments, op. 46.
Holst, Gustave: Oxford University Press.
Contents: Christmas day in the morning, O! I
hae seen the roses blow, The Shoemaker.

"Barbara Allen."
Bliss, James A.: J. Fischer: piano.

"Black is the Color of My True Love's Hair."
Harris, Roy: C. Fischer: piano.

"Lord Rendal."
Sowerby, Leo: Boston Music: piano.

"Old Gray Mare": Theme and Variation.
Britain, Radie: Halbreiter: piano.

"The Bird."
Harris, Roy: C. Fischer: piano.

——————: *Chamber Orchestra*

Beethoven, Ludwig Van
Schottische Lieder (Terzette, Duette und Soli);
mit Begleitung von Pianoforte, Violine and
Violonell—für den concertgebrauch herausge-
geben von Max Friedlaender. Leipzig: C. F.
Peters, 1890.

Blair, Fanny
Folk Song Fantasy. String Quartet, op. 28,
based on English American Folk tunes. New
York: Carl Fischer.

Bruch, Max
Fantasia on Scottish Folk Melodies, for violin
and piano, op. 46, edited by Theodore Spiering.
New York: Carl Fischer, 1916. 15 pp.

McEwen, John B.
Suite of Old National Dances, arranged for
String Quartet. London: Joseph Williams, Ltd.,
1924.

Rufty, Hilton
Suite in A, in folk tunes for violin, cello and
piano. New York: 1939.

Woodhouse, Charles (arranger)
Three Scottish Melodies; arranged for Cham-
ber Orchestra. London: Boosey and Hawkes,
Ltd., 1931. (Hawkes' School Series).

——————: *Orchestra*

Clifford, Hubert
A Kentish Suite, based on Kentish folk tunes.
London: Oxford University Press, 1936. for
small orchestra.

Mennin, Peter
Folk Overture.
Hargail: Orchestra.

Green, Ray
Casey Jones for piano and percussion orchestra. New York: New Music.

Milhaud, Darius
Opus Americana No. 2—ballet suite.
Elkan-Vogel: Orchestra.

Moore, Douglas
Overture on an American Tune.
MS; orchestra.

Shure, Deane R.
American Symphony, based on American Folk
music: Indian, English, American, Negro.
New York: J. Fischer and Brothers.

RECORDS

See: Recordings after each Region, State, *and*
after Section on American Characters.

Album Collections

American Ballads.
The Singing Sentinels ... 4–10".   SO–483
Contents: Desert Blue and Silver, Lonesome
Road, Colorado Trail, Down Mobile, Way Up
Yonder, Old Aunt Jeremiah, Dinah's in the
Kitchen, I told her that I loved her, Brass
Wagon, My Lawd what a mawnin,' Golden Slip-
pers, Long long ago, Hoosen Journey, Skip to
my Lou, Blue Tail Fly.

American Ballads.
John Jacob Niles, tenor-dulcimer. Vol. I.
                                           VM–604.

American Ballads.
John Jacob Niles, tenor-dulcimer. Vol. II.
4–10".   VM–718.

American Ballads.
John Jacob Niles, tenor-dulcimer. Vol. III.
3–10".   VM–846.

American Ballads and Folk Songs. vol. 2.
John Jacob Niles, vocal-dulcimer. 3–10".
                                           Disc 733
Contents: John Henry: Who Killed Cock Robin;
Frog went a courtin'; Lass from the Low Coun-
tree; Jack O'Diamonds; Go Away from my
Window.

American Folklore, Volume 3.
John Jacob Niles, vocal-dulcimer. 3–10" and
1–12"   Set M–V824
Contents: "You Got to Cross that Lonesome
Valley"; "The Lass from the Low Countree";
"Black is the Color of my True Love's Hair";
"Go 'way from my Window"; "One Morning in
May"; "The Wife of Usher's Well"; "The Death
of Queen Jane"; "Little Mattie Groves"; "In the
Baggage Coach Ahead"; "Old Dan Tucker";
"Billy Boy"; "Barbara Allen"; "I Was Born
4000 Years Ago"; "Ida Red"; "Bully of the
Town"; "Down in the Alley"; "Sourwood Moun-
tain"; "Buffalo Gals"; "Butcher Boy"; "East
Bound Train"; "Hand me Down my Walking
Cane"; "My Horses ain't Hungry"; "Little
Brown Jug"; "Pass Around the Bottle"; "Put
my Little Shoes Away"; "Boston Burglar"; "Skip
to my Loo"; "Little Rosewood Casket"; "Arkan-
sas Traveler"; "Pretty Polly"; "Maple on the
Hill"; "When I was Single"; "Blue-eyed Ellen";
"New River Train"; "Letter edged in Black";
"Goodbye my Lover, Goodbye".

American Folk Say; Ballads and Dances.
Asch–432

American Folk Songs Album.
Frank Luther, Zora Layman, Leonard Stokes, vocalists with guitar, fiddle and bass. 5–10".
DE–25
Contents: She'll be Coming 'round the mountain; When the roses bloom again; Can I sleep in your barn tonight?; Turkey in the Straw; Oh dem golden slippers; Rovin' Gambler.

Anglo-American Ballads, Album I.
Folk music of the United States, 1942, edited by Alan Lomax. Issued by the Library of Congress, Reference Department, Division of Music, Washington, D. C. 1943. Five records with Album. Sung by Mrs. Texas Gladden and recorded by Alan and Elizabeth Lomax. *In:* Album I: *Anglo-American Ballads, #AAF-S1A,* Library of Congress, Music Division, January, 1943. See also Albums 7, 12, 14, 16, 20 and 21.
Contents: The House Carpenter (Child no. 243); The Farmers Curst Wife (Child no. 278).

Anglo-American Ballads.
Album 7—Five Records. AAFS31, 32, 33, 34, 35. Edited by B. A. Botkin, Library of Congress.

Ballads.
Richard Dyer-Bennet, vocal-guitar 3–10".
Asch–461

Ballads and Folk Songs.
Richard Dyer-Bennet, vocal-guitar. K–108
Four British and Four American Ballads.

Ballads and Folk Songs Vol. 2.
Burl Ives, vocal-guitar. 4–10". DE–A431
Contents: Turtle Dove; The Devil's Nine Questions; No Wood Fire: Ten Thousand Miles; My Good Old Man; Po' Boy; I'm Sad and I'm Lonely; Cowboy's Lament.

Ballads and Songs.
Richard Dyer-Bennet, vocal-guitar. 4–10".
DE–A573
Contents: "The Devil and the Farmer's Bride"; "Eggs and Marrow Bone (The Old Woman)"; "The Willow Tree"; "Villikens and his Dinah"; "Swapping Song"; "The Old Man"; "Early One Morning"; "Greensleeves"; "Oh Sally My Dear."

Blue Ridge Ballads.
Texas Gladden and Hobart Smith. 3–10".
Disc 737
Contents: "House Carpenter"; "Devil and Farmer's Wife"; "Down in the Willow Garden"; "Poor Ellen Smith."

Burl Ives Album.
Burl Ives, Vocal-guitar. DE A–407
Contents: "Dublin City," "Cockle Shells," "Old Dan Tucker," "The Erie Canal," "The Eddystone Light," "Hullabaloo Belay," "Venezuela," "The Fox," "Lolly Too Dum," "Aunt Rhody," "Saturday Night," "Wake Nicodemus."

Carl Sandburg: Recital from—*"American Song-bag."*
Carl Sandburg, accompanying himself on the guitar. 4–10". MU–11
Contents: Gallows Song (Sam Hall); I ride on paint; Foggy, foggy dew; The horse named Bill; I'm sad and I'm lonely; Woven Spirituals; The good boy; Mamma have you heard the news? (Casey Jones.)

Child Ballads.
John Jacob Niles, vocal-dulcimer. 2–12".
Disc–665
Content: Edward, Barbara Allen, Marty Gowan.

Child Ballads from the Southern Highlands.
Cratis Williams, vocal guitar. 2–10". Disc 662

Early American Ballads.
John Jacob Niles, vocal-dulcimer. 4–10".
VM–604
Contents: Ballad of Barberry Ellen; Gypsey Laddie; I wonder as I wander; Lulle bullay (The Coventry Carol); My little Mohee; Seven joys of Mary.

Early American Carols and Folksongs.
John Jacob Niles, vocal-dulcimer. 4–12".
VM–718
Contents: Jesus, Jesus Rest your Head; When Jesus lived in Galilee; Down in Yon Forest; Jesus, The Christ is Born; See Jesus the Saviour; The Cherry Tree; Who killed Cock Robin; The Old Woman and the Pig; The Frog went Courting; The Carrion Crow.

Early American Folk Songs.
Bob Atcher, vocal-guitar. 4–10". CO–H6.
Contents: Barbara Allen; De Ladies' Man; Methodist Pie; Devilish Mary; Young Rogers the Miller; Old Smokey; The Hunters of Kentucky.

Elizabethan Love Songs.
Richard Dyer-Bennet, vocal-lute. 3–10".
Disc 609

Folk Songs and Ballads.
Susan Reed, soprano. Irish harp and zither. 3–10". Vol. I. VM–1086

Folk Songs and Ballads.
Susan Reed, soprano, Irish harp and zither. Vol. II. 3–10". VM–1107

Listen to Our Story. A Panorama of American Balladry. 4–10". Alan Lomax, ed. BR–1024
Contents: "Lady Gay"—Buell Kazee; "Derby Ram"—Bascom Lamar Lunsford; "Girl I Left Behind Me"—Dick Reinhart; "Pretty Polly"— Doc Boggs; "Death of John Henry"—Uncle Dave Macon; "Peck About My Saro Jane"— Uncle Dave Morton; "True Religion"—Rev. Clayburn; "Stackerlee"—Furry Lewis.

Olden Ballads.
Tom Glazer, voice-guitar. 3–10". KE–8137
Content: "The Sheeling Song," "Twelve Days of Christmas," "Green Sleeves," "Waly, Waly," "Hush Little Baby," "Sixteen Come Sunday," "Black-Eyed Susie," "Go Away from my Window," "Uncle Reuben," "Blow the Candle Out."

Old World Ballads in America.
Andrew Rowan Summers, accompanying himself on the dulcimer. 4–10". C–M408
Contents: The Cherry Tree Carol; Old Bangum; The Ballad of Mary Hamilton; The Hangman's Tree; The Two Sisters; Barbara Allen; Lady Gay.

Sing Out, Sweet Land.
Burl Ives, Alfred Drake, Chorus, and Orch. DE A–404
Includes: "Big Rock Candy Mountain," "Blue Tail Fly," "Little Mohee," "Wanderin!" "I Have Been A Good Boy," "Frankie and Johnny," "Rovin Gambler," "Casey Jones," "Street Cries."

Smoky Mountain Ballads.
Mainer-Morris, Carter Family; Uncle Dave Macon, and others. V–P70(27493–27497)
Contents: Riding on That Train Forty-Five; Darling Corey; The East Virginia Blues; Cumberland Mountain Deer Race; Intoxicated Rat; Chittlin' Cookin' Time in Chearham County; On a Cold Winter Night; Ida Red; Worried Man's Blues; Down in the Willow.

Sod-Buster Ballads: Folk Songs of America.
Sung by the Almanac Singers. GE–5018/20
Contents: The Dodger; The State of Arkansaw; I Ride on old Paint; House of the Rising Sun; Ground Hog; Hard, Ain't it Hard.

Sod Buster Ballads.
Pete Seeger, Woody Guthrie, and Millard Lampell. 3–10". COM–10

The Old American Folksongs.
Harp Singers. 2 records. MU–41
Contents: Poor Wayfaring Stranger; Old Ship of Zion; Frog Went-A-Courting; Sourwood Mountain; The Barnyard Song; On Springfield Mountain.

The Wayfaring Stranger; Two British and ten American Songs and Ballads. Sung by Burl Ives. 4–10". OK–Set K–3
Contents: American—Riddle Song; I Know Where I'm Going; I Know my Love; Cowboy's Lament; Leather-Winged Bat; Cotton-Eyed Joe; Darlin' Corey; Peter Gray; Sweet Betsy from Pike; On Top of Old Smoky.

Traditional Ballads.
Peter Pears, tenor and Benjamin Britten, piano. GR–DA 1873
Contents: "The Foggy Dew"; "The Ploughboy"; "Come You Not from Newcastle."

Two Centuries of American Folksongs.
Sung by the American Ballad Singers. V–P41
Contents: Poor Wayfaring Stranger; Springfield Mountain; The Deaf Woman's Courtship; Pat works on the Railway; Cotton Picking Song; Upon de Mountain; Street Cries; Kentucky Mountain; Grandma Grunts; Go to Sleepy.

Individual Ballads
Alphabetically Listed

"Adieu False Heart."
(Variant of "Barbary Allen") Arthur Smith Trio, guitars. BB–7651–A

"Always been a Rambler."
(Version of the Rich Old Farmer) Wade Mainer, Zeke Morris, vocal, guitar, and banjo. BB–16890B

"Angeline, the Baker."
Uncle Eck Dunford, vocal. V–40060–B

"Barbara Allen."
Brown and Orchestra OK–6049

"Barbara Allen."
Dadmun, vocalist V–4023

"Barbara Allen."
Luther, Layman, Stokes; vocal with guitar, fiddle and bass. In: *American Folk Songs Album.* De–25

"Barbara Allen."
Molly Malone, vocal and orchestra V–35710

"Ballad of Barberry Ellen."
John Jacob Niles, dulcimer. In: *Early American Ballads.* VM–604

"Barbara Allen."
Maxine Sullivan, vocal with John Kirby and Orchestra. Co–35710

"Barbara Allen."
A. R. Summers, vocal and dulcimer. In: *Old World Ballads in America.* CM–408

"Barbara Allen." (Child No. 84).
Sung by Rebecca Tarwater of Rockwood, Tennessee. Recorded in Washington, D. C., 1936 by Charles Seeger. In: Album I: *Anglo-American Ballads,* Washington, D. C. AAFS3B

"Barbara Allen."
Richard Dyer-Bennet, vocal-guitar Asch–461–1A

"Biggest Thing."
(Nonsense Ballad) Woody Guthrie, vocal-guitar Asch–432–3B

"Billy Boy."
Andrews Sisters, vocal trio De–2214

"Billy Boy."
Esmereldy and Frank Novak, and the Sourwood Mountain Boys. MU–300–B

"Billy Boy."
Frank Luther, vocal. De–2138

"Billy Boy."
Luther, Layman, Stokes; with guitar, fiddle and bass. In: *American Folk Songs Album.* De–25

"Black is the Color."
Burl Ives, vocal-guitar. Asch–345–2A

"Black is the Color of My True Love's Hair."
John Jacob Niles, tenor and dulcimer VM–824–3

"Blowin' Down This Road."
Woody Guthrie, vocal and guitar. In: *Dust Bowl Ballads*, volume I   V–P27

"Blue-eyed Ellen."
Luther, Layman, Stokes; with guitar, fiddle and bass. In: *American Folk Songs Album.*
De–25

"Blue Tail Fly."
Burl Ives, voice-guitar.   Asch–345

"Balakins. (Lamkin).
Sung by Mrs. Lena Bare Tarbyfill at Elk Park, North Carolina, 1939. In: Album VII: Library of Congress.   AAFS34A

"Bonnie Bay O'Biscay-O."
Hudson Valley Songs. Frank Warner, accompanied by ballad singers, instrumentalists.
Disc 8024

"Boston Burglar."
Luther, Layman, Stokes; vocals with guitar, fiddle and bass.   De–25

"Buckeyed Jim."
Burl Ives, vocal-guitar.   Asch–345–IA

"Bully of the Town."
Luther, Layman, Stokes; with guitar, fiddle and bass. In: *American Folk Songs Album.*
De–25

"Butcher Boy."
Luther, Layman, Stokes; with guitar, fiddle and bass. In: *American Folk Songs Album.*
De–25

"Careless Love."
Blind Boy Fuller; vocal and guitar. Vo–03457

"Careless Love."
Delmore Brothers, Alton and Rabon; vocal duet and guitar.   ..   BB–7436–B

"Careless Love."
Yale Glee Club. In: *Yale Glee Club.*
Co–36463
Set Co–79

"Casey Jones."
Riley Puckett, vocal and guitar.   Co–113–D

"Charles Guiteau."
Kelly Harrell, vocal.   V–20797–A

"Chittlin' Cookin' Time in Cheatham County."
Native Mountain Singers and instruments. In: *Smoky Mountain Ballads.*   V–P79

"Claude Allen."
Sung with guitar by Hobart Smith at Saltville, Virginia, 1942. In: Album VII: Library of Congress.   AAFS35A

"Cocaine Lil."
Madrigal Singers.   Co–4208–M

"Come You Not From Newcastle."
Pears, tenor, and Benjamin Britten, piano.
GR–DA 1873

"Cumberland Mountain Deer Race."
Uncle Dave Macon, vocal.   V–27494

"Cumberland Mountain Deer Race."
Uncle Dave Macon, vocal.   BB–7951–A

"Cumberland Mountain Deer Race."
Native Mountain Singers and Instruments. In: *Smoky Mountain Ballads.*   V–P79

"Danville Girl."
"Dock" Boggs; vocal.   Br–132

"Darby's Ram."
Bascom Lamar Lunsford; vocal.   Br–228

"Darlin' Cory."
Burl Ives, vocal and guitar. In: *Wayfaring Stranger.*   OK–6318

"Darling Cora."
B. F. Shelton, vocal and banjo. V–35838–A

"Darling Corey."
Monroe Brothers, Charles and Bill; vocals and guitar.   BB–6512–B

"Darling Corey."
Native Mountain Singers and instruments. In: *Smoky Mountain Ballads.*   V–P79

"Darling Corey."
Monroe Brothers.   V–27493

"Devil and Farmer's Wife."
Texas Gladden and Hobart Smith.   Disc 737

"Do Re Mi."
Woody Guthrie, vocal and guitar. In: *Dust Bowl Ballads*, Volume I.   V–P27

"Down in the Forest."
John Jacob Niles, vocal and dulcimer. In: *Early American Carols and Folk Songs.*
V–M718

"Down in the Valley."
Burl Ives, voice-guitar.   DE–8082

"Down in the Valley."
Luther, Layman and Stokes; with guitar, fiddle and bass. In: *American Folk Songs Album.*
DE–25

"Down in the Willow."
Wade Mainer, Zeke Morris; vocals.
BB–7298–B

"Down in the Willow."
Native Mountain Singers and instruments. In: *Smoky Mountain Ballads.*   V–P79

"Down in the Willow Garden."
Texas Gladden and Hobart Smith.   Disc 737

"Dusty Old Dust."
Woody Guthrie, vocal and guitar. In: *Dust Bowl Ballads*, Volume II.   V–P28

"Early One Morning."
Richard Dyer-Bennet, vocal-guitar. DE–A 573

"Eggs and Marrow Bone (The Old Woman)."
Richard Dyer-Bennet, vocal guitar. DE–A 573

"El-A-Noy."
Vocal and instrumental accompaniment. In:
Folk Songs of the Americas.   V–P55

"Engine One Forty-Three."
The Carter Family, vocals and guitar. (Version
of: The Wreck on the C and D). BB–6223–B

"Fate of Chris Lively and Wife."
Blind Alfred Reed, vocal and guitar.
V–21533–B

"Five Night's Experience."
Mustard and Gravy (Dixie's Fastest Combination), vocalist and guitars. BB–7905–A

"Fod" (Nonsense Song).
Sung with guitar and mandolin by Henry King
and Family at Visala, California, 1941. Recorded by Robert Sonkin. In: Album II: Recordings of American Folk Songs, Library of
Congress, 1943.   AAFS8B1

"Four Little White Doves."
Frank Luther, Zora Layman and Century H.
In: *Songs of Old California.*   De–49

"Fox Chase No. 2."
Henry Whittes, harmonica. BB–5259–B

"Frog Went A-Courtin'."
Nelson Eddy, baritone; and orchestra.
4316–M in Set VM–571

"Gallows Song."
Carl Sandburg, vocal and guitar. Mu–207–A

"Gently Johnny."
Richard Dyer-Bennet, vocal and guitar.
Asch 461–3B

"Good-bye, My Bonnie, Good-bye."
Carolina Tarhcals, fiddle, guitar and harmonica.   V–21193–B

"Goodbye, My Lover."
Luther, Layman and Stokes; with guitar,
fiddle and bass. In: *American Folk Songs
Album.*   De–25

"Go To Sleepy."
American Ballad Singers, Siegmeister. In:
Two Centuries of American Folk Songs.
V–P41

"Go 'way from My Window."
John Jacob Niles, tenor and piano. VM 824–4

"Grandma Grunts."
American Ballad Singers-Siegmeister In: *Two
Centuries of American Folk Songs.* V–P41

"Greensleeves."
Richard Dyer-Bennet, vocal-guitar. DE–A573

"Gypsy Laddie."
John Jacob Niles, vocal and dulcimer. In:
Early American Ballads.   VM–604

"Hansom' Winsome Johnny."
Libby Holman, vocalist, and Josh White,
guitar.   De–18306

"Henry Green."
Luther and Layman, vocalists.   DE–2931

"Henry Martin."
Burl Ives, vocal-guitar.   Asch 345–3B

"House Carpenter."
Texas Gladden and Hobart Smith. DISC 737

"I Am a Man on Constant Sorrow."
Emery Arthus; vocal and banjo. Vo–B5208

"Henry, Where You Been So Long?"
The Tobacco Tags; vocalists, guitars, mandolin.   BB–7912–A

"I Know my Love."
Burl Ives, vocal and guitar. In: *Wayfaring
Stranger.*   OK–6316

"I Know Where I'm Going."
Burl Ives, vocal and guitar. In: *Wayfaring
Stranger.*   OK–6316

"I'm Sad and I'm Lonely."
Carl Sandburg, vocal and guitar. In: Recital
from "American Songbag."   MC–11

"I Once Loved a Girl."
Richard Dyer-Bennet, vocal and guitar.
Asch 461–1B

"I Once Loved a Young Man."
J. E. Mainer's Mountaineers; vocal, guitar.
BB–7659–A

"Irene."
LeadBelly, voice accompanied by Sonny Terry,
Harmonica.   Asch 343

"I Wish I Was a Mole in the Ground."
Bascom Lamar Lunsford; vocal and banjo.
Br–219

"I Wish I Was a Single Girl Again."
Riley Puckett, vocal-guitar. BB–8083–B

"Jack O'Diamonds."
John Jacob Niles, tenor and dulcimer. V–2051

"Jennie Jenkins." (Dialog Song).
Sung with guitar and mandolin by Mr. and
Mrs. E. C. Ball at Rugby, Virginia, 1941. Recorded by Alan and Elizabeth Lomax. In:
Volume II: Recordings of American Folk
Songs, Library of Congress, 1943. AAFSA2

"Jesse James."
Riley Puckett, vocal-guitar.   CO–15033–D

"Joe Clark Steps Out."
An arrangement for orchestra by Charles G.
Vardell, Jr. Eastman-Rochester Symphony
Orchestra.   Co–2059

"John Hardy."
Buell Kazee, vocal.   Br–144

"John Hardy Was a Desperate Little Man."
The Carter Family, vocals and guitar.
BB–6033–B

"John Peel."
Associated Glee Songs.   V–19961

"John Peel."
Bob Crosby and orchestra.   De–1725

"John Peel" (Border Song).
Lambert Murphy, vocal.   V–4083

"Kentucky Moonshiner."
American Ballad Singers — Siegmeister. In:
Two Centuries of American Folk Songs. V–P41

"Kidderole."
Bascom Lamar Lunsford, vocal.   Br–230

"Knoxville Gal."
Lester McFarland and Robert A. Gardiner;
vocal duet, guitar and mandolin.   Vo–03601

"Lady Gay."
A. R. Summers, vocal. In: *Old World Ballads
in America.*   CM–408

"Lady of Carlisle."
Sung with guitar by Basil May at Salyersville,
Kentucky, 1937. In: *AAFS*, Library of Congress, 1943.   FM–1A

"Little Lulie." (Version of "Darlin' Corey".)
Dick Justice, vocal-guitar.   Br–336

"Little Lulie." (Version of "Darlin' Corey".)
Homer Briarhopper, vocal, guitar and mandolin.   De–5615

"Little Mattie Groves."
John Jacob Niles, vocal and dulcimer.
VM–824–7 & 8

"Little Rosewood Casket."
Luther, Layman, Stokes with guitar, fiddle and
bass. In: *American Folk Songs Album.* De–25

"Look On and Cry."
Wade Mainer and Sons of the Mountaineers.
BB–8120–B

"Lord Thomas and Fair Ellender."
Sung by Horton Barker at Chilhowie, Virginia,
1939. In: Album VII: Library of Congress.
AAFS33B

"Lost John."
Oliver Sims, harmonica.   Co–1513–D

"McKinley."
Riley Pluckett, vocal-guitar.   Co–15448–D

"Lulle Ballay." (Coventry Carol.)
John Jacob Niles, vocal and dulcimer. In:
Early American Ballads.   VM–604

"Molly Malone."
Maxine Sullivan, vocal with John Kirby and
His Orchestra.   Co–35710

"Mr. McKinley."
Homer Briarhopper; vocal, guitar and mandolin. Ballad on the death of McKinley.)
De–5588

"Mr. Johnny was a Shoemaker."
Yale Glee Club. In: *Yale Glee Club.*
Co–36462 Set Co–79

"My Little Mohee."
John Jacob Niles, vocal and dulcimer.
VM–604–2

"Mystery of the Dunbar's Child."
Richard (Rabbit) Brown; vocal-guitar.
V–35840–A

"Oh, dear what can the matter be."
Herbeck, vocal.   OK–5197

"Oh, dear what can the matter be."
Ella Logan, vocal.   BB–8057

"Oh Sally My Dear."
Richard Dyer-Bennet, vocal guitar.   DE–A573

"Old Bangum."
A. R. Summers, vocal and dulcimer. In: *Old
World Ballads in America.*   CM–408

"Old Bangum."
Richard Dyer-Bennet, vocal-guitar.   VOX–632.

"Old Kimball."
Sung by Mrs. Texas Gladden at Salem, Virginia, 1941. Recorded by Allen and Elizabeth
Lomax. In: Album I: *Anglo-American Ballads,*
Washington, D. C.   AAFS4A2

"Old Shoes and Leggins."
Uncle Eck Dunford, vocal.   V–40060–A

"Old Smoky."
Libby Holman, vocalist and Josh White, guitar.
De–18306

"Old Whisker Bill."
Buell Kazee, vocal and banjo.   Br–145–B

"O! Molly Dear, Go Ask Your Mother."
Kelly Harrell; vocal, fiddle and guitar (Version of "Drowsy Sleepers.")   V–20280–A

"O, no John."
Royal Dadmun, vocal.   V–4023

"On A Cold Winter Night."
Native Mountain Singers and instruments. In:
Smoky Mountain Ballads.   V–P79

"One Morning in May."
John Jacob Niles, vocal and piano.
VM–824–4

"One Morning in May."
Sung by Mrs. Texas Gladden at Salem, Virginia, 1941. Recorded by Alex and Elizabeth
Lomax. In: Album I: *Anglo-American Ballads,* Washington, D. C.   AAFS4B

"On Springfield Mountain."
The Old Harp Singers.   Mu–222–B

"On Top of Old Smoky."
Burl Ives, vocal-guitar. In: *Wayfaring Stranger,* OK–6317

"On Top of Old Smoky."
Esmereldy, soprano, Frank Novak and the Sourwood Mountain Boys. Mu–289–B

"The Ploughboy."
Peter Pears, tenor, and Benjamin Britten, piano. GR–DA 1873

"Poor Ellen Smith."
Texas Gladden and Hobart Smith. DISC 737

"Poor Lazarus." (Bad man ballad.)
Woody Guthrie, vocal-guitar. Asch 432–2B

"Pretty Boy."
Woody Guthrie, vocal-guitar. Asch–347

"Pretty Polly."
B. F. Shelton, vocal and banjo. V–35838–B

"Pretty Polly."
Sung with guitar by E. C. Ball at Rugby, Virginia, 1941. Recorded by Alan and Elizabeth Lomax. In: Album I: *Anglo-American Ballads,* Washington, D. C. AAFS3A

"Pretty Polly."
Sung with 5-String banjo by Pete Steele at Hamilton, Ohio, 1938. In: *FMIB,* Library of Congress, 1943.

"Pretty Polly."
'Dock' Boggs, banjo. Br–132

"Pretty Polly."
Luther, Layman, Stokes with guitar, fiddle and bass. In: *American Folk Songs Album.* De–25

"Ramblin' Gambler."
Dixon Brothers, vocal and guitars (Version of "The Rambling Boy.") BB–6809–I

"Riddle Song."
Burl Ives, vocal-guitar. In: *The Wayfaring Stranger.* OK–6315

"Riding on That Train Forty-Five."
Native Mountain Singers, and instruments. In: *Smoky Mountain Ballads.* V–P79

"Sally Let Your Bangs Hang Down."
Bill Cox and Cliff Hobbs, vocal duet and guitar. Pe–7–08–70

"Sammie, Where You Been So Long."
'Dock' Boggs, singer and 5 string banjo. Br–131–A

"Sanford Barnes."
Sung by I. G. Greer at Thomasville, Virginia with dulcimer by Mrs. I. G. Greer. Recorded at Greensboro, North Carolina, 1941. In: Album VII: Library of Congress. AAFS35A

"Single Girl."
The Carter Family, singers, guitar and auto-harp. Pe–7–04–53

"Sinking in the Lonesome Sea."
The Carter Family, singers, guitar and auto-harp. (Version of "The Golden Vanity"). Pe–7–12–63

"Sinking of the Titanic."
Richard (Rabbit) Brown, vocal-guitar. V–35840–B

"Soldier Won't You Marry Me?" (Humorous Song).
Sung with guitar by Russ Pike at Vislia, California, 1941. Recorded by Charles Todd and Robert Sonkin. In: Album II: Recordings of American Folk Songs, Library of Congress, 1943. AAFS8A1

"Sourwood Mountain."
Jeanne Behrend, piano (piano arrangement by Arthur Farwell). In: *Album of Piano Music by American Composers.* VM–764

"Sourwood Mountain."
Ralph Crane, baritone-orchestra. V–21751

"Springfield Mountain."
American Ballad Singers—Siegmeister. In: *Two Centuries of American Folk Songs.* V–P41

"Sugar Hill."
Dad Crockett, vocal, banjo. A version of "Old Joe Clark." BR–372

"Tam Pierce."
Burl Ives, vocal-guitar. In: *Wayfaring Stranger.* OK–6316

"Ten Thousand Miles." (Love Song).
Sung by Aunt Molly Jackson of Clay County, Kentucky. Recorded in New York, 1939, by Alan Lomax. In: Album II: *Recordings of American Folk Songs,* Library of Congress, 1943. AAFS7B

"The Bailiff's Daughter of Islington."
Lawrence Tibbett, baritone and piano accompaniment. Co–15549

"The Ballad of Mary Hamilton."
A. R. Summers accompanying self on dulcimer. In: *Old World Ballads in America.* CM–408

"The Barnyard Song."
Old Harp Singers of Nashville, Tennessee, unaccompanied. MC–222

"The Battle Ax and the Devil."
Bill Cox and Cliff Hobbs; vocal duet, and guitar. (Version of "The Farmer's Curst Wife"). Vo–04811

"The Blue Tail Fly."
Burl Ives, vocal-guitar. Asch–345–3A

"The Bold Soldier."
Burl Ives, voice and guitar. Asch–345

"The Boston Burglar."
Carl T. Sprague, vocal, fiddle, and guitar. V–20534–B

"The Boston Burglar."
Riley Puckett, vocal-guitar.   Co–15050–D

"The Cannon-Ball."
The Carter Family; vocal-guitar. (Version of
the "McKinley and Roosevelt" Ballad).
BB–6020–B

"The Carrion Crow."
John Jacob Niles, vocal and dulcimer. In:
Early American Carols and Folk Songs.
VM–718

"The Charleston Merchant."
Richard Dyer-Bennet, vocal-guitar.   K–519A

"The Cherry Tree."
John Jacob Niles, vocal and dulcimer. In:
Early American Carols and Folk Songs.
VM–718

"The Cherry Tree."
A. R. Summers accompanying self on dulcimer.
In: *Old World Ballads in America.*   CM–408

"The Deaf Woman's Courtship."
American Ballad Singers—Siegmeister. In:
Two Centuries of American Folk Songs. V–P41

"The Death of Dewey Lee."
The Carter Family; vocal-guitar.   Pe–17503

"The Death of Floyd Collins."
Red River Dave, Esmereldy, Dick Thomas,
Frank Novak, and the Sourwood Mountain
Boys.   Mu–286

"The Death of Queen Jane."
John Jacob Niles, vocal and dulcimer.
VM–824–6

"The Derby Ram."
Richard Dyer-Bennet, vocal-guitar.   K–517B

"The Devil and the Farmer's Wife."
Richard Dyer-Bennet, vocal-guitar.   DE–A573

"The Devil's Nine Questions." (Child No. 1).
Sung by Mrs. Texas Gladden at Salem, Vir-
ginia, 1941. Recorded by Alan and Elizabeth
Lomax. In: Album I: *Anglo-American Ballads,*
Washington, D. C.   AAFS4A1

"The Farmer's Curst Wife." (Child No. 278).
Sung by Horton Barker at Chilhowie, Virginia,
1939. Recorded by Herbert Halpert. In: Al-
bum I: *Anglo-American Ballads,* Catalog of
Phonograph Records, Library of Congress,
January 1943   AAFSIB

"The Fate of Talmadge Osborn."
Ernest Stoneman; vocal-guitar.   V–20672–B

"The Fiddling Soldier."
Bill Cox and Cliff Hobbs; vocalists and guitar.
(Version of "One Morning in May.")
Pe 7–08–70

"The Foggy Foggy Dew."
Burl Ives, vocal-guitar.   Asch 345–2A

"Foggy Foggy Dew."
Carl Sandburg, vocal and guitar.   Mu–208–A

"The Foggy-foggy Dew."
Peter Pears, tenor, and Benjamin Britten,
piano.   GR–DA 1873.

"The Four Marys."
Sung by Mrs. Texas Gladden at Salem, Virginia, 1941. In: Album VII: Library of Congress.   AAFS32B

"The Frog Went A-Courting."
John Jacob Niles, vocal and dulcimer. In:
Early American Carols and Folk Songs.
VM–718

"The Frog Went A-Courting."
Old Harp Singers of Nashville, Tennessee,
unaccompanied.   MU–222

"The Girl I Love, She Got Long Curly Hair."
John Estes, vocal.   BB–7849–B

"The Golden Vanity."
Richard Dyer-Bennet. Vocal-guitar. KE–517–A

"The Golden Willow Tree."
Part I and II. Sung with banjo by Justis Beg-
ley at Hazard, Kentucky, 1937. In: Album VII:
The Library of Congress.   AAFS31

"The Good Boy."
Carl Sandburg; vocal-guitar.   Mu–210–A

"The Gower Wassail Song."
Philip Tanner, unaccompanied.   CO–372M

"The Great Dust Storm."
Woody Guthrie, vocal-guitar. In: *Dust Bowl
Ballads, Volume II.*   V–P28

"The Gypsy Davy" (Child No. 200).
Sung with guitar by Woody Guthrie of Oke-
mah, Oklahoma. Recorded in Washington,
D. C., 1940 by Alan Lomax. In: Album I:
Anglo American Ballads, Library of Congress,
Music Division, 1943.   AAFS2A

"The Gypsy Laddie."
John Jacob Niles, tenor and dulcimer.
VM–604–I

"The Hangman's Tree."
A. R. Summers, vocal and dulcimer. In: *Old
World Ballads in America.*   CO–408

"The Highway Man."
Lestic; vocal-guitar.   DE–5559
  Version of "The Boston Burglar."

"The Horse Named Bill."
Carl Sandburg; vocal-guitar.   MU–208–B

"The House Carpenter."
Richard Dyer-Bennet, vocal-guitar KE–518–B

"The Intoxicated Rat."
Native Mountain Singers and instruments. In:
Smoky Mountain Ballads.   VI–P79

"The Jealous Lover of Lone Green Valley."
Vernon Dalhart; vocal, guitar and fiddle.
VI–19951–A

"The Kicking Mule."
John Evans; vocal-guitar.　　　　BR–237

"The Lady Gay."
Buell Kazee; vocal and banjo.　　BR–212
Version of "The Wife of Usher's Well."

"The Lass from the Low Countree."
John Jacob Niles, tenor and dulcimer.
VM–824–2

"The Lass from the Low Country."
Richard Dyer-Bennet, vocal-guitar.　VOX–632

"The Lincolnshire Poacher."
Richard Dyer-Bennet, vocal-guitar.　KE–517–B

"The Old Man."
Richard Dyer-Bennet, vocal-guitar.　DE–A573

"The Old Woman and the Pig."
John Jacob Niles, vocal and dulcimer. In:
Early American Carols and Folk Songs.
VM–718

"The Quaker Lover."
Richard Dyer-Bennet, vocal-guitar.　VOX–632

"The Rambling Boy."
Sung with banjo by Justus Begley at Hazard,
Kentucky, 1937. In: Album VII: Library of
Congress.　　　　　　　　　　AAFS31

"The Rich Farmer."
Sung by Mrs. Pearl Borusky at Antigo, Wisconsin, 1941. Recorded by Charles Daves. In:
Album I: *Anglo-American Ballads*, Washington, D. C.　　　　　　　　　　AAFS3B

"The Sow Took the Measles."
Burl Ives, vocal-guitar.　　　　ASCH–345

"The Spanish Merchant's Daughter."
Stoneman Family; guitar and harmonica.
VI–40206–A

"The Three Babes."
Sung by I. G. Greer of Thomasville, North
Carolina, with dulcimer by Mrs. I. G. Greer.
Recorded at Greensboro, North Carolina, 1941.
In: Album VII: Library of Congress.
AAFS34B

"The Three Ravens." Part I and II. Richard
Dyer-Bennet, vocal-guitar.　ASCH 461–2A–2B

"The Turtle Dove."
L. Engel, Madrigal Group.　　　CO–4167

"The Two Brothers."
Sung by Mrs. Texas Gladden at Salem, Virginia, 1941. In: Album VII: Library of Congress.　　　　　　　　　　　　AAFS32A

"The Two Sisters."
Sung by Horton Barker at Chilhowie, Virginia,
1931. In. Album VII: Library of Congress.
AAFS33A

"The Two Sisters."
A. R. Summers, vocal and dulcimer. In: *Old
World Ballads in America.*　　　CO–408

"The Wife of Usher's Well."
John Jacob Niles, vocal and dulcimer.
VM–824–5

"The Willow Tree."
Richard Dyer-Bennet, vocal-guitar.　DE–A573

"Three Night's Experience."
John Evans; vocal-guitar.　　　　BR–237

"Tom Joad."
Woody Guthrie; vocal-guitar. In: *Dust Bowl
Ballads, Volume I.*　　　　　　VI–P27

"Train Carry my Girl Back Home."
Wade Mainer, Zeke Morris; vocals and guitar.
BB–6890–A

"Travelin' Down the Road."
Uncle Dave Macon; vocal and banjo.
BB–7234–B

"Travelin' Man."
Virgil Childers; vocal and guitar. BB–7487–A

"Upon de Mountain."
American Ballads Singers—Seigmeister. In:
Two Centuries of American Folk Songs.
VI–P41

"Villikens and his Dinah."
Richard Dyer-Bennet, vocal-guitar.　DE–A 573

"Vigilante Man."
Woody Guthrie; vocal-guitar. In: *Dust Bowl
Ballads, Volume II.*　　　　　VI–P28

"Way up On Clinch Mountain."
Jilson Setters (J. W. Day) ; vocal, fiddle and
guitar.　　　　　　　　　　VI–21635–A

"Wee Cooper O'Fife."
Burl Ives, vocal-guitar. In: *The Wayfaring
Stranger.* Set K–3.　　　　　OK–6315

"We're Up Against It Now."
Uncle Dave Macon; vocal and banjo. VO–5009

"When I Was a Single Girl."
Lulu Belle and Scotty; vocal duet, instrumental
and guitar.　　　　　　　　VO–04772

"Who Killed Cock Robin."
John Jacob Niles, vocal-dulcimer. In: *Early
American Carols and Folk Songs.*　VM–718

"Who's That Knockin' at My Window?"
The Carter Family; vocal duet and guitar.
DE–5612

"Wild Bill Jones."
Wade Mainer and His Little Smilin' Rangers;
vocal, and various instrumental accompaniment.　　　　　　　　　　BB–7249–A

"Willie the Weeper."
Marc Williams, vocal-guitar.　　DE–5011

"Young Freda Bolt."
The Carter Family; vocal duet, guitar, and
autoharp.　　　　　　　　　DE–5612

"Young Henry Martin."
Philip Tanner, unaccompanied.　CO–372–M

THE FOLK DANCE

THE FOLK DANCE

BIBLIOGRAPHY

Carter, Harriet I.
Camping, a bibliography for the camp director, for the camp counselor, for the camp librarian. Chicago: Public Library Readers Bureau, 1942. 32 pp.

Collins, Fletcher
"An aid in the discovery of folk-songs." A list of finders for traditional ballads, songs, and play-parties in the Southeast. *SFQ* 5:235–250, 1941.

Magriel, Paul David, comp.
A Bibliography of Dancing. New York: H. W. Wilson Company, 1936. x, 299 pp., illus.
A list of books and articles on the Dance and related subjects. Includes a good section on folk and national dances.

PERIODICALS

Dance.
New York. I—Oct., 1923–.

Dance.
New York. vol. 1, no. 1. Jan.–Mar., 1940.

Dance.
East Stroudsburg, Pa., 1936–.

Dance Digest.
National Dance League, New York. I (Jan.) 1937–.

Dance Events.
New York. I (Nov.) 1932–Jan. 20, 1933.

Dance Magazine.
New York. vol. 1–17, no. 2. Nov., 1923–Dec., 1931.

Dance Observer.
New York. no. 1, Feb., 1934–.

Dance Review; the Magazine for Dancers everywhere. New York. Vol. 1-2, no. 2, May, 1919–March, 1920.

Dance World.
New York. Vol. 1–3, no. 7, 1930–Aug., 1932.

Dancer.
London. Vol. 1–5, no. 12, 1928–Dec., 1932.

Dancing Master.
Chicago. Vol. 144, no. 3, 1894–Dec., 1935.

Dancing Times.
London. 1–, 1894–1909. n.s. 1910.

English Dance and Song, the Magazine of the English Folk Dance and Song Society. V. 1, 1936. London. Bimonthly.

Journal of the English Folk Dance and Song Society. V. 1, 1932. London. Annual.

Promenade; American Square Dance Group. Vol. 1, no. 1, March, 1940–. New York: Margot Mayo, ed.

GENERAL STUDIES

Adams, Eleanore G.
"Folk Dance in the Rhythms Program; for high school boys and girls." *Journal of Health and Physical Education* 7:25–27, 58. (Jan.) 1936.

Alford, Violet, and Gallop, Rodney
The Traditional Dance. London: Methuen and Co., 1935.

Allen, F. L.
"When America Learned to Dance." *Scribner's* 102:11–17, (Sept.) 1937.

Allen, Willie Fay
"Ten Days of Work and Play at Brasstown." *Mountain Life and Work* 45 (No. 3):1930, October.

Andrews, Edward
"The Dance in Shaker Ritual." *Dance Index* 1:1942, January.

"Barn Dance Returns."
Recreation 31:471–476, 1937, bibliography.

Barry, Phillips
"Irish Come-All-Ye's." *JAFL* 22:374–388, 1909.

_____.
"Shaker Songs and Music." *FSSNE* 4:17–18, 1932.
Music and text illustrate the sacred dance of the Shakers.

Behre, H. E.
"Square Dancing on the Eastern Shore of Maryland." *SFQ* 9 (No. 4):213–222, 1945.

Belilajus, V. F.
"Folk Dancing in Chicago." *Recreation* 30:309, 1936. Illus.

_____.
"Why Folk Dancing." *Recreation* 30:538, 1937.

Blair, Kathryn
"Swing Your Partner." *JAFL* 40:96–99, 1927.

Botkin, B. A.
Folk Dances. In: *The American Play Party Song.* Lincoln, Neb.: The University Press, 1937.

Buchanan, Fannie R.
Folk Dances and How to Do Them.... Illustrated by Irma Camp Groff. Des Moines, Ia.: 1929.

Burchenal, Elizabeth
"Les danses populaires caractéristiques des États-Unis." *Art Populaire* 2:166–168, 1931. Paris. Institute de Cooperation Internationale.

"Reviving the Folk-Dance." *National Educ. Assn. Journal* 15:241, (Nov.) 1926.

Card, H. S.
"Public Interest in Folk Dancing." *Leisure* 3:27–28, 63, 1936. Illus.

Carpenter, Aileen
"Square Dancing in College." *Recreation* 32: 511–514, 538, 1938 (December) illustrated.

Cort, D.
"Swing your Partner." *Bookman* 65:642–644, 1927.

Craddock, J. R.
"The Cowboy Dance." *TFSP* 2:31–37.

Curtis, W. A.
"The Light Fantastic in the Central West. Country dances of many nationalities in Wisconsin." *Century* 73:570–579, 1907. Illus. (New York).

Cushman, Rebecca
Swing Your Mountain Gal. In: *Sketches of Life in the Southern Highlands.* Boston: Houghton Mifflin Company, 1934.

"Dance Steps Written Like Music."
Popular Science 135:95, (Sept.) 1939. Illus.

Davis, H. F.
"Square Dancing is Fun, but Teach an Easy one First." *Recreation* 33:629–30+, 1940 (February).

Douglas, E. A.
"Dance Captures America." *Magazine Art* 30:498–505, (Aug.) 1937. Illus.

Federal Writers' Project.
Square Dance. Chicago, Illinois: Writers' Project, WPA, Chicago Park District, 425 E. 14 St., 1940.

Finck, H. T.
"Folk Songs and Dances." *Nation* 101:669–670, (December 2) 1915.

Ford, Mr. and Mrs. Henry, assisted by Mr. and Mrs. Benjamin B. Lovett
Good Morning. Dearborn: The Dearborn Publishing Co., 1926.

Fox-Strangways, Arthur Henry
Folk-Dance in the Elementary School. In: *Cecil Sharp*, by H. Fox-Strangways, Appendix C, (pp. 218–220). (Quoted from Pamphlets No. 55 and No. 95 of the English Board of Education.) London: Oxford University Press, 1933. 233 pp.

French.
Prompter's Handbook. Boston: Oliver Ditson Co., 1893.

Gadd, May
"Folk Dance in America To-day." *Dance Observer*, p. 95, (October) 1937.

"Keeping Tradition Alive." *Dance Observer*, pp. 129-130, (Dec.) 1937.

"Pine Mountain Folk Art." *Dance Okemer:* 146, 1938 (December) illustrated.

"The Folk Dance as a Social Dance." *Dance Observer*, pp. 114–116, (Dec.) 1938.

Grayson, E. C.
"Country Dance Goes to Town." *New York Times Magazine:* 10, 1940 (March 31) illustrated.

Gunkler, O. H.
"Dance Drama in Kentucky." *Journal of Health and Physical Education* 7:157–159, 1936 (March).

Halpert, Herbert
"Folk-Song and the Dance." *American Music Lover* 4, (No. 2):51–53, (June) 1938.

Harrison, G. Harry
"The Square Dance—A Social Aid." *Recreation* 31:359–363, 1937, illustrated.

Hayden, Alice
"Modern Revival of the Folk Dance." *Research Quarterly of the American Physical Education Association* 7:27–41, May, 1936. (Ann Arbor, Michigan).

Hobbs, May Elliot
"English Folk Dancing in America." *Emerson Quarterly* 9:5–7, 12. (March) 1929. (Boston).

Hogan, William R.
"Dancing: Texas Amusements in the Republic of Texas." *Journal of Southern History:* 397–410, 1937.

Karpeles, Maud
"Some Additional Figures for Set-Running." *JEFDS* 2 (No. 3):1930.
American Square dance tunes.

"Square Dance Figures from Northern New York State." *JEFDS* 2 (No. 4):1931.

Kennedy, Douglas
"The American Big Set." *JEFDS* 3:140, 1937. (London).

Kopp, E. H.
The American Prompter and Guide to Etiquette. Cincinnati: John Church Company, 1896.

Kurtz, Homer H.
"Emerald Isle." *CFQ* 3:232–234, 1944.
Music, text and calls of this square dance from Indiana.

Lentz, Arthur
"Folk Dancing Here and There." *SFQ* 7:157–161, 1943.
General discussion and miscellany.

Lloyd, M.
"Instigation to the Dance." *Christian Science Monitor*, pp. 4–5, (October 7) 1936. Illus.
Striking performances of foreign ballets and native artists in U. S.

Lovett, Benjamin B.
"Special Dancing Through Old American Folk Dances." *Playground* 22:279, (Aug.) 1928.

M. M.
"Dance-Names New and Old." *AS* 7 (No. 5): 390, 1932.

McCabe, W. H.
"Music and Dance on a 17th Century College Stage." *MQ* 24:313–322, (July) 1938.

McDowell, L. L.
"Finding Folk Dances in Tennessee." *TFSB* 4:90–99, 1938.

————, and F. L.
Folk Dances of Tennessee: Old Play-Party Games of the Caney Fork Valley. Smithville, Tennessee: L. L. McDowell, 1938.

Maddocks, Durward
Swing Your Partner. A guide to modern country dancing. Brattleboro, Vt.: Stephen Daye Press, 1941. Illus.

Martin, John
"Dance Federation of Los Angeles." *N. Y. Times* X 10, (Feb. 20) 1938.
Discussion of dancers' organization on the West Coast.

————.
"Dance, Pioneer American Art." *North American* 244 (No. 2):231–250, 1937 (December).

Mayo, Margot
"Folk-dancing in Private Progressive Schools." *Dance Herald* 1:7, (Dec.) 1937. (New York).

————.
The American Square Dance. New York: Sentinel Books, 1948. 119 pp.

Meyerson, S., and Johnson, S.
Folk-dancing For Fun. Chicago: Meyerson, 1940.

Mitchell, N., and Mitchell, L.
"Dance Choir." *Theatre Arts Monthly* 23:72–75, 1939 (Jan.).

Mouvet, M.
"Choose Your Partners." *Colliers* 78: 5–6 Jl. 17, 1926.

Musick, Ruth Ann
"A Missouri Dance Call." *JAFL* 59:323–324, 1946.

Oliver, G.
"Modern Dance Program." *New Republic* 87: 244, (July 1) 1936.

Osborn, Mary Elizabeth
"Country Dance Calls from the Catskill Mountains." *AS* 3 (No. 2):142–145, 1927.

Owens, William A.
Dances: Texas. In: *Swing and Turn;* Texas Play-Party Games (pp. 13–23). Dallas, Texas: Tardy Publishing Company, 1936.

Parmelee, Patricia
"The Folk Dance." *Educational Dance* 1:6, (May) 1938.

Parrett, Vanita
"Cowboy Dance Calls." *TFSP* 18:115–125, 1943.
Texts of 12 square dance calls.

Peters, Nan
"The Ancestry of the Barn Dance." *American Dancer* 11:17, 38, 1938 (July), illustrated (New York).

"Pioneer Dance Calls."
Nebraska Folklore Pamphlets 22, 24 pp. 1939 (June) and 1939 (November). Nebraska: Federal Writers' Project.

Piper, Edwin Ford
"Quadrille Calls." *AS* 6 (No. 7):391–395, 1926.

Pledge, E. M.
"Folk Dancing, its Origins, Interest and Educational Value." *School*, pp. 887–890, (June) 1938. (Toronto).

Porter, Evelyn
Music Through the Dance. London: B. T. Batsford, 1937. 155 pp., illus., music.

Rogers, Frederick Rand
Dances—A Basic Educational Technique. New York: The Macmillan Co., 1941. 351 pp., illus.

Rohrbough, Lynn, ed.
Handy Country Dance Book. Part I: Longways and Circle Figures from New England, Midwest, and the South. Part II: Quadrilles. Part III: Square Dances of the Great Smoky Mts. Part IV: Favorite Square Dances, n.p., Delaware, 1941.

Ruoff, Franz
"Der Volkstanz und seine Literatur." *Die Musik* 28:590–592, 1936.
Folk dancing and books about it.

Sachs, Curt
World History of the Dance. New York: W. W. Norton and Co., 1937.

Sanders, J. O.
"Finding List of Southeastern Square Dance Figures." *SFQ* 6:263–275, 1942.
Contains also good bibliography.

————.
"Honor the Fiddler." *TFSP* 17:78–90, 1941.

Schell, John M.
Prompting. New York: Carl Fischer, 1890.

Schofield, Kenworth
"The Evolution of the Morris Dance." *English Dance and Song Magazine*, pp. 81–82, (May) 1938. (London).

Shaw, L.
"Let's Haul a Cowboy Dance. Illustrated."
Woman's Home Companion 66:108–109, 1939
(May).

Sinclair, Caroline B.
"Square Dance Figures of Tidewater, Virginia." *Journal of Health and Physical Education:* 407–410, 445–447, 1937 (September),
illustrated.

Syme, G. Jr.
"Music and the Dance." *Recreation* 29:3–41,
(Sept.) 1935.

Tolman, Beth
*How to Put On and Make Successful the
Country Dance Party.* Weston, Vermont: The
Countryman Press, 1938. 16 pp.

Torre, Mauro T.
"How Shall We Judge Folk Dance Contests."
Philippine Journal of Education 21:380–381,
1938.

Tshell, B.
"Episodes of Ranch Community Dances."
TFSP 5:104–106, 1920.

Wade, George W., and Jarman, H. E., compilers
The Corn Huskers Book of Old Time Dances,
showing how to "call" them and how to dance
them. Toronto, Canada: T. Burt, 1932.

Walker, Conway
The Folk Song and Dance. New York: The
Coxton Institute, 1926. Vol. 2. (Fundamentals
of Musical Art.)

White, Alice, and Tobitt, J. E.
Dramatized Ballads. Illustrated by Barbara
Danielsen. New York: Dutton, 1937. 192 pp.

Wilkinson, Winston
"Virginia Dance Tunes." *SFQ* 6:1–10, 1942.
Music of nine tunes.

Williams, Iolo A.
English Folk-Song and Dance. New York:
Longmans, Green and Co., 1935.

Winter, Marian Hannah
"Satire and Caricature in American Dancing."
Dance Observer 5:36, (March) 1938. Illus.

Young, Della I.
The Pioneer Dance. In: *Folk-Say, A Regional
Miscellany* (pp. 253–265). Norman, Oklahoma: University of Oklahoma Press, 1930.

COLLECTIONS—(Piano)

Boyd, Neva L., and Dunlavy, Tessie
Old Square Dances of America. Arranged for
piano. Chicago: H. T. Fitzsimons Company,
1925.

Brown, Florence (Warren), and Boyd, Neva L.
*Old English and American Games for School
and Playground,* by Florence Warren Brown
and Neva L. Boyd; harmonizing of music by
Gertrude Shoemaker. Chicago: Saul Bros.,
1915.

Brown, Marie Wilson
Incidental Dance Steps. Franklin, Ohio: Eldridge, 1925.
A useful book of dances.

Burchenal, Elizabeth
American Country Dances. Edited by Elizabeth
Burchenal. Piano arrangements by Emma
Howells Burchenal. Volume One contains
twenty-eight contradances, largely from the
New England States. New York: G. Schirmer,
1918.

————.
Folk Dances and Singing Games. New York:
G. Schirmer and Co., 1909–22.
Twenty-six folk dances of Norway, Sweden, Denmark, Russia, Bohemia, Hungary, Italy, England,
Scotland and Ireland, with the music, full directions for performance, and numerous illustrations.
Vol. II: Dances of the people, a second volume of
folk dances and singing games, containing 27
folk-dances from Belgium, Czecho-Slovakia, Denmark, England, Finland, France, Germany, Ireland, Lithuania, Poland, Portugal, Russia, Spain,
Sweden, and the United States. Vol. III: Folk
Dances from old homelands, a third volume of
folk dances and singing games from Belgium,
Czecho-Slovakia, Denmark, England, Finland,
France, Germany, Ireland, Lithuania, Poland,
Portugal, Russia, Spain, Sweden and the United
States. Piano arrangements by Emma Howells
Burchenal.

————.
"Les Danses Populaires Caracteristiques des
États-Unis." *Art Populaire* 2:166–168, 1931.
Institut de Cooperation Internationale, Paris.

Carpenter, Lucien O.
J. W. Pepper's Universal Dancing Master.
Containing full and complete descriptions of
every step and figure used in all the fashionable round, square, and fancy dances. Philadelphia, Pa.: J. W. Pepper, 1882. 36 pp., illus.
At head of top page: "A thoroughly practical
instructor."

Cazden, Norman
Five American Dances. New York: Music
Center.

Chalif, Louis Harvey
Folk Dances of Different Nations. New York
City: L. H. Chalif, 1926. 3 vols.

Coles, Alice M. Cowper
Old English Country Dance Steps. . . . English
Country Dances of the 17th Century. . . . Illustrated by diagrams and photographs. . . . London: J. Curwen & Sons, 1909. iv, 31 pp.

Cowell, Henry
Square Dance Tunes. New York: E. B. Marks
Corporation, arranged for piano.

Crampton, Charles Ward
The Folk Dance Book, for elementary schools,
classroom, playground, and gymnasium. New
York: A. S. Barnes and Company, 1909. ix,
81 pp.

Crawford, C.
Folk Dances and Games. New York: A. S. Barnes and Company, 1908. ix, 82 pp., front. With piano accompaniment.

"Dance Calls."
Nebraska Folklore Pamphlets 27 (series 3): continues in pamphlet 24, 1940 (April).

Dances of the People.
New York: G. Schirmer, 1933.

Dearmer, Percy, and Shaw, Martin
Song Time. London: J. Curwen and Sons, Ltd., 1915.

Dicks' Quadrille Call-Book.
New York: Fitzgerald Publishing Corp., 1878–1923.

Dunlavy, Tessie, and Boyd, N. L.
Old Square Dances of America. Chicago: Recreation Training School, 1925.

Durlacher, ed.
Honor Your Partner. 81 American Square, Circle, and Contra Dances, with complete instructions for doing them. New York: The Devin-Adair Co., 1949. 286 pp., illus., music (texts with piano accomp.).

Elsom, J. C., and Trilling, Blanche M.
Social Games and Group Dances. Philadelphia: J. B. Lippincott Co., 1919.

Familiar Dances: Jigs, Reels, Country Dance Tunes. Philadelphia: Presser Company, arranged for piano.

Fish, H. D.
Four and Twenty Blackbirds. Illustrated by Robert Lawson. New York: Frederick A. Stokes Co., 1937.

Folk Dances and Singing Games.
New York: G. Schirmer, 1933.

Folk Dances from Old Homelands.
New York: G. Schirmer, 1922.

Folk Dance Music.
New York: G. Schirmer, 1908.

Ford, Ira W.
Traditional Music of America. New York: E. P. Dutton and Co., 1940.

Foster, Arnold
Lancashire, Morris Dance Tunes edited by Maud Karpeles, pianoforte arrangements by Arnold Foster. London: Novello & Company, Ltd., 1930.

Fox, Grace I., and Merrill, Kathleen Gruppe
Folk Dancing in High School and College. Drawings by Charlotte St. John. New York: A. S. Barnes & Company, 1944. 89 pp.
   Music for piano, folk dances of many countries including some of America.

Frost, Helen, ed.
The Clog Dance Book. Introduction by Jesse F. Williams, piano arrangement by Ruth Garland. New York: A. S. Barnes & Company, 1921. Illustrated.

Gilbert, Henry F.
Three American Dances: Uncle Remus; Delphine; B'rer Rebbit. Boston: Boston Music Co., for piano.

Glass, Paul
Twenty American and Irish Fiddle Tunes. Works Projects Administration. New York: New York Public Library.

"Good Morning."
Music, Calls and Directions for Old Time Dancing as revised by Mr. & Mrs. Henry Ford. Dearborn, Michigan: 1941. Illustrated.

Greggerson, Herb.
Herb's Blue Bonnet Calls. El Paso, Texas: H. Greggerson, Box 3061, Station A.

Groos, K.
The Play of Man. Preface by J. Mark Baldwin. New York: D. Appleton and Company, 1901. ix, 412 pp.

Guenther, Felix
Swing Your Partner! American Square Dances, Reels and Jigs. Arranged for easy piano solo. New York: Mercury Music Corporation, 1944.
   Contains 14 selections.

Gulick, Luther Halsey
Folk and National Dances. New York: Russell Sage Foundation, 1908. 16 pp., illus. Department of Child Hygiene Pamphlets.

Harding's Collection of 200 Jigs, Reels and Country Dances. New York: Richmond-Robbins, Inc., 1929.

Herman, Michael
Folk Dances for All. New York: Barnes and Noble, 1947.
   Nineteen dances from as many nations, gives directions, photos by Gjon Mili, and drawings by Ben Stein, record list.

Hofer, Mari Ruef
All the World A-Dancing; a collection of folk dances of various nationalities, with historic comment and authentic descriptions of dance steps. Piano arrangements revised by Stella Roberts. Chicago: Clayton F. Summy Co., 1925. 69 pp.

————————, ed.
Polite and Social Dances. Chicago: Clayton F. Summy, arr. for the piano.
   Historical and period dances of all nations, with music, instruction, historical sketches. Section devoted to early American country dances.

Howe, Elias
Musical Omnibus. New York: F. Blume, 1863. 2 vols.

Hunt, Edgar H.
Fifty Old English Folk Dance Airs; for solo descant recorder. London: Schott, 1939. 16 pp., melodies only.

Karpeles, Maud
The Lancashire Morris Dance; containing a description of the Royton Morris Dance; collected and edited by Maud Karpeles. London: Novello and Company (19–?).

Kirkell, Miriam H., and Schaffnit, K.
Partners All—Places All! Forty-four Enjoyable Folk Dances for Everyone. Illustrated by Deirdre Baird. New York: E. P. Dutton & Co., 1949. Illus., music (piano & text), bibl., calls, and diagrams.

Lane, Eastwood
Five American Dances: The Crap Shooters; Around the Hall; A Gringo Tango; North of Boston, (Barn Dance) ; Pow Wow. New York: J. Fischer, for piano.

Levin, Mrs. Ida
Kentucky Square Dances, collected and arranged by Ida Levin. Louisville, Kentucky: Recreation Council, 1928.

Lovett, Benjamin B.
Good Morning. Dearborn, Michigan: The Dearborn Publishing Company, 1926.

Lunsford, Bascom Lamar, and Stephens, George Meyer
It's Fun to Square Dance: South Appalachian calls and figures. Asheville, North Carolina: Stephens Press, 1942. 16 pp.

Maddocks, Durward
Swing Your Partner. A guide to modern country dancing. Brattleboro, Vt.: Stephen Daye Press, 1941. Illus.

McDonald, Harl
Square Dances of the United States. Philadelphia: Presser Company, piano collection.

McNair, Ralph J.
Western Square Dances. Illustrated by Jack Downey Fitz Hugh. Denver, Colorado: Oran V. Siler, 1941. 126 pp.

Moses, Irene E. Phillips
Rhythmic Action, Plays and Dances. Springfield, Mass.: Milton Bradley Co., 1915.

O'Conor, Manus
Irish Come-All-Ye's. New York: Popular Publishing Co., 1901.

Old Familiar Dances. Piano collection. Boston: Oliver Ditson Co.

Old Time Dances.
New York: Paul Pioneer Co., 1940.

O'Neill, Captain Francis
O'Neills Irish Rose. Chicago: Lyon and Healy, 1915.

O'Neill's Music of Ireland. Chicago: Lyon and Healy, 1903.

"Pioneer Dance Calls."
Nebraska Folklore Pamphlets 22, 24 pp. Lincoln, Nebraska: Federal Writers' Project, June, 1939, November, 1939.

Playford, John
The English Dancing Master; or Plaine and Easie Rules for the Dancing of Country Dances, with the tunes to each dance. Reprinted from the London edition of 1651. Edition by H. Mellor and L. Bridgewater. London: 1933.

Porter, W. S., Heffer, Marjorie, and Heffer, Arthur B.
The Apted Book of Country Dances. Tunes arranged for the pianoforte by W. S. Porter. London: Stainer and Bell.
Twenty-four Country Dances from the last years of the 18th century, with tunes and instructions.

Powell, John
At the Fair: Sketches of American Fun (based on American folk themes), Hoochee-Coochee Dance, Circassian Beauty, Snake Charmer Merry-Go-Round, Clowns, Banjo-Picker. New York: G. Schirmer: For the piano.

Redler, C.
Learning to Dance. A Set of Quadrille. Boston: Oliver Ditson, 1844.

Reese, George G., and Beall, Thomas E.
Standard Call Book. Columbus, Ohio: Standard Dance Publishing Company, 1934. 331 West 2nd Avenue.

Rohrbough, Lynn
Handy Country Dance Book. Delaware, Ohio: Cooperative Recreation Service, 1941.
Country dances, quadrilles, mountain folk dances, favorite square dances.

Rollinson, T. H.
Favorite Reels, Jigs and Hornpipes. Boston: Oliver Ditson Company, piano collection.

Ryan, Grace L., coll.
Dances of our Pioneers. Music arrangements by Robert T. Benford. Illustrated by Brooks Emerson. New York: A. S. Barnes & Company, 1939.

Ryan, William Bradbury
Ryan's Mammoth Collection. New York: Elias Howe, 1883.

Seventy Good Old Dances.
Boston: Oliver Ditson Co.
Jigs, reels, hornpipes, country and Morris dances, etc. Piano collection.

Shambaugh, Mary Effie
Folk Dances for Boys and Girls. New York: A. S. Barnes and Co., 1929. 143 pp., illus., diagrs., bibl.
Contains the music for the dances.

Folk Festivals for Schools and Playgrounds, folk dances and melodies. Music arranged by Anna Pearl Allison. New York: A. S. Barnes and Co., 1932. xi, 155 pp., illus., bibl., music.

Sharp, Cecil J., and Butterworth, G.
The Country Dance Book. Part I: Containing a description of 18 traditional dances collected in country villages. Part II–IV: Containing 108 country dances from the English Dancing Master, 1650–1728. London: Novello and Co., Ltd., 1909–1916. 4 volumes.

Country Dance Book: Part V: Kentucky Running Set (Square Dances). New York: Novello & Company, Ltd.

—————.
The Morris Book. London: Novello & Company, 1912–1913. Five parts piano.

—————, and MacIlwaine, H. C.
The Morris Book: A History of Morris Dancing with a description of 11 dances as performed by the Morris Men of England. London: Novello Co., 1907. Illustrated, piano music.

Shaw, Lloyd
Cowboy Dances. Tunes arranged by Frederick Knorr. Caldwell, Idaho: The Caxton Printers, Ltd., 1939. 4th Printing, April, 1941.
> "The author transcribes the dances and music, analyses and classifies, and gives copious supplementary material. Each dance is carefully explained, and the whole is classified according to Types of Dances, Types of Western Squares, Symmetrical Dances, Round Dances, etc. There is an excellent chapter on 'The Calls'." (Blanche Evan)

Smith, L. L.
Old Time Dance Calls. Northboro, Iowa: n.d.

Snyder, Jack
Jack Snyder's Collection of 200 Favorite Jigs, Reels, Country and Folk Dances. New York: Jack Snyder Publishing Company, 1925.

Stanford, Sir Charles V.
Four Irish Dances; composed by C. V. S., arranged for piano by Percy Grainger. New York: J. Fischer and Bro., 1916.

Sym's Old Time Dances.
Jigs, Reels, Country Dances, for violin and piano, with calls endorsed by all leading authorities. New York: Vogel Music Company.

Ten Favorite Jigs.
Piano arrangement. Boston: Oliver Ditson Company.

Ten Favorite Country Dances.
Arranged for piano. Boston: Oliver Ditson Company.

Ten Favorite Hornpipes.
Piano collection. Boston: Oliver Ditson Company.

Ten Favorite Reels.
Arranged for piano. Boston: Oliver Ditson Company.

Three American Quadrilles.
Boston: Boston Music Company, 1926.

Tolman, Beth, and Page, Ruth
The Country Dance Book. Illustrated with drawings by F. W. P. Tolman. New York: Farrar and Rinehart, 1937. 191 pp., illus., music.
> The old fashioned square dance, its history, lore, variations and its callers. Complete and joyful instructions.

—————.
The Country Dance Book. Guilford, Vt.: The Contryman Press, 1937. Boston: E. C. Schirmer.

Unger, Ferdinand C.
Elssler Quadrilles. New York: 1840.

Wade, George, and Norman, Harry E.
Square Dances. Toronto, Canada: T. Burt & Company, 1937.

—————.
The Corn Huskers' Book of Old-Time Dances. Toronto, Canada: T. Burt and Co., Box 22, General Post Office. No music.

Wilson, Harry Robert, arr.
Sing-and-Dance. Folk Songs and Dances Including American Play-Party Games. Dance directions prepared by Beatrice A. Hunt; Music arranged by Harry Robert Wilson; Illustrations by Corina Melder-Collier. Chicago: Hall and McCreary, 1945. 80 pp. Voice and piano.

COLLECTIONS—(Violin and Piano)

Favorite Old Time Tunes.
Philadelphia: Presser. for violin and piano. Jigs, country dances, reels, hornpipes, etc. with traditional songs. Simple.

Glass, Paul, comp.
Twenty American and Irish Fiddle Tunes. Practical studies for violin classes. Works Project Administration Arts Program, 8 pp.

McGee, C. H., arr.
Old Time Jigs and Reels for the Violin. Boston: Oliver Ditson Company.

Mellie Dunham's Fifty Fiddlin' Dance Tunes.
New York: Carl Fischer.
> Mostly traditional (Maine).

Old Familiar Dances.
Boston: Oliver Ditson Co. For violin and piano.

Percy, Calvin A.
Forty Folk Tunes (Easy). Boston: White and Smith. For violin and piano.

Sym's Old Time Dances.
28 Traditional American Country Dances, Reels, Jigs, Square Dances. Boston: Haviland. Violin and piano.

White's Excelsior Collection of Jigs, Reels, and Hornpipes. New York: White-Smith, violin solo.

White's Unique Collection: Jigs, Reels, Hornpipes, etc. New York: White-Smith.

ARRANGEMENTS:
(Individual Titles)

—————: *Female Voices*

"Cindy."
Winstead, K.: Music Publishers Holding Corp.: SSA.

"Old Zip Coon" (Turkey in the Straw).
Boston Music Co.: SA.

"Pop! Goes the Weasel."
Grant-Schaefer, G. A.: Schmidt: SA, SSA.

"Pop! Goes the Weasel."
O'Shea, John: Witmark: SA.

"Turkey in the Straw."
Davis, Katherine K.: Galaxy: SA.

————: *Male Voices*

"Cindy."
Hall: Schirmer: TTBB.

"Cindy."
Malin: Gamble Hinged: TTBB.

"Pop! Goes the Weasel."
Kountz, Richard: Witmark: TBB, TTBB.

"The Arkansas Traveler."
Elmore: Ditson: TTBB. Four hand accompaniment.

"The Arkansas Traveler."
Stevens, David: Birchard: TTB.

"Turkey in the Straw."
Davis, Katherine K.: Galaxy: TB.

"Turkey in the Straw."
Kountz, Richard: Witmark: TTBB, TBB.

"Turkey in the Straw."
Schaeffer, W.: Witmark: TTBB.

————: *Mixed Voices*

"Cindy."
Wilson, H. R.: Hall & McCreary: SATB.

"Fiddler's Reel."
Howe, Mary: MS; alto or baritone solo, SATB, piano or orchestra.

"MacDonald's Farm."
Strickler, David: Schirmer: SATB, a cap.

"Mayday Dance" (Country Gardens).
Brant, Cyr de: J. Fischer & Bro.: SATB.

"Pop! Goes the Weasel."
Boston Music Co.: SATB.

"Pop! Goes the Weasel."
Kountz, Richard: Witmark: SAB, SATB.

"Pop! Goes the Weasel."
Martin: Hall & McCreary: SAB.

"Turkey in the Straw."
Kountz, Richard: Witmark: SATB.

"Turkey in the Straw."
Sanders, Robert L.: Carl Fischer: SATB accompaniment.

————: *Piano*

"The Arkansas Traveler."
Burg, Clarence: Composer's Music Corp.: Piano.

"Arkansas Traveler" (Concert Transcription).
Guion, David: Schirmer: Piano.

"Arkansas Traveler" (Concert Paraphrase).
MacDonald, Harl: Presser: Piano.

"Arkansas Traveler."
Pattison, L.: Schirmer: 2 pianos (4 hands).

"Country Gardens" (Handkerchief Dance).
Grainger, Percy A.: Schott & Co.: Piano.
English Morris Dance tune.

"Country Jig."
Guion, David: Schirmer: Piano.

"Country Jig in C Major."
Guion, D.: Schirmer: Piano (adv.).

"Country Jig" (D Major).
Guion, David: Schirmer: Piano.

"Fishers' Hornpipe" (Theme and Variation).
Grove, Charles: Ditson: Piano.

"Hobby in The Green."
Rufty, Hilton: Schirmer: Piano.

"Humoresque, Banjo Song."
Putnam, Eugene: Carl Fischer: Piano.

"Money Musk."
Sowerby, Leo: Birchard: Piano.

"Pioneer Dance" (From Suite: *In the South*).
Powell, John: Marthot: Piano.

"Pop! Goes the Weasel."
Grant-Schaefer, G. A.: Arthur P. Schmidt Co.: Piano.

"Quill Dance."
Putnam, Eugene: Carl Fischer: Piano.

"Sheep and Goat: 'Walkin' to the Pasture'."
Guion, David: Schirmer: Piano.

"Shepherd's Hey" (English Morris Dance Tune).
Grainger, Percy A.: Schirmer: Piano.
Uses four variations.

"Square Dance Tune."
Cowell, H.: E. B. Marks: Piano.

"The Leprechaun's Dance."
Grainger, Percy: J. Fischer & Bro.: Piano.

"Turkey in the Straw" (Concert transcription).
Guion, David: Schirmer: Piano.

"Turkey in the Straw."
Williams, J. M.: Boston Music Co.: Piano.

"The Girl I Left Behind Me."
Miller, W. B.: Ditson: Piano.

"The Irish Washerwoman" (Variation).
Grove, Charles: Ditson: Piano.

"The Irish Washerwoman" (Country Dance Tune).
Sowerby, L.: Schirmer: Piano (medium).

"The Irish Washerwoman" (Concert arrangement). Sowerby, Leo: Boston Music Co.: Piano.

"Turkey in the Straw."
Guion, D.: Schirmer: Piano (adv.).

"Turkey in the Straw." (From Way Down South).
Rasbach, O.: G. Schirmer: Piano (easy).

"Turkey in the Straw."
Weybright: Schirmer: Piano (2 pianos, 4 hands).

———: Piano: (4 Hands)

"Arkansas Traveler" (Concert paraphrase).
McDonald, Harl: Presser: Piano, 4 hands.

"Arkansas Traveler."
Orem, Preston Ware: Presser: Piano, 4 hands.

"Arkansas Traveler" (Free concert version).
Pattison, Lee: Schirmer: Two pianos, 4 hands.

"Natchez-in-the-Hill" (Three Virginia Country Dances).
Powell, John: Schirmer: Two pianos, four hands.

"Turkey in the Straw."
Orem, Preston Ware: Presser: Piano, four hands.

———: Violin and Piano

"Arkansas Traveler."
Maganini, Quinto: J. Fischer & Bro.: Violin and piano.

"Arkansas Traveler" (Concert transcription).
O'Hara, Geoffrey: J. Fischer & Bro.: Violin and piano.

"Arkansas Traveler" (op. 33, No. 6, Concert).
Vieuxtemps, Heinrich: White-Smith: Violin and piano.

"Fisher's Hornpipe."
Tracy, G. A.: White-Smith: Violin and piano.

"Natchez-on-the-Hill."
Powell, J.: Schirmer: Violin and piano.
Three Virginia Country Dances.

"Pop Goes the Weasel."
Kron, Louis-Saenger, Gustav: Carl Fischer: Violin and piano.

"Sailor's Hornpipe."
Tracy, G. A.: White-Smith: Violin and piano.

"Turkey in the Straw" (Concert version).
Manen, Juan: Carl Fischer: Violin and piano.

———: Organ

Familiar Dances: Reels, Jigs, etc.
Philadelphia: Presser Company.

Wilson, Mortimer
From Hickory and Cotton; 17 American Tunes (Arkansas Traveler, Country Dance, etc.) New York: Composers' Music Corporation.

———: Orchestra

"Arkansas Traveler."
Guion, D. W.: Schirmer: Orchestra (A. Schmid).

Collection of Hornpipes. Series I, II, III.
New York: Carl Fischer.

Collection of Hornpipes, Jigs, Reels and Clog Dances. Arranged by E. Fox, for small orchestra, additional 2nd clarinet and horns. New York: Carl Fischer.

Collection of Reels and Jigs.
Arranged by L. O. de Witt, revised by Seredy. New York: Carl Fischer.

Cowell, Henry
Old American Country Set. New York: Associated Publishers.

———.
Tales of Our Countryside. New York: Associated Publishers.

Gilbert, H. F. B.
Three American Dances. New York: Gray & Co.

"In Old Virginia" Overture (Southern Country Dance Themes).
Powell, John: Schirmer: Orchestra.

"Irish Washerwoman."
Sowerby, Leo: Boston Music Company: Orchestra.

McKay, George F.
Suite on Fiddlers' Tunes. New York: J. Fischer & Bros.

"Money Musk" (American Country Dance).
Sowerby, Leo: Birchard: Orchestra.

"Natchez-in-the-Hill."
(Three Virginia Country Dances.) Powell, John: Schirmer: Orchestra.

Old Familiar Dances.
Old Familiar dances for piano, violin and piano, mandolin and piano, flute or piccolo. Oliver Ditson Company.

Variations on the Theme—"Pop! Goes the Weasel." Cailliet, L.: Elkan-Vogel: Orchestra.

Powell, John
"At the Fair, Sketches of American Fun (Southern Tunes)." 1. Merry-Go-Round; 2. Circassian Beauty; 3. Hoochee-Coochee Dance. New York: G. Schirmer—full orchestra.

Quilter, Roger
Three English Dances for Small Orchestra Op. 11. London: Boosey & Company, 1910, 21 pp. Arranged for piano, four hands.

Reels, Hornpipes and Jigs.
Arranged by Paul de Ville. 100 traditional tunes: English, Scotch, Irish. Also: American selection: Arkansas Traveler, etc. New York: Carl Fischer.

Reels and Jiggs.
Arranged by G. H. Ross, for small orchestra, additional clarinet and horns. New York: Carl Fischer.

"Turkey in the Straw" (Transcription).
Guion, David: Schirmer: Orchestra.

"Turkey in the Straw, with Lamplighter's Hornpipe, Lardner's Reel." Lewis, W.: Carl Fischer: Orchestra.

————: *Chamber Orchestra*

"Arkansas Traveler."
Maganini, Quinto: J. Fischer & Bro.: Violin, piano, cello, and various combinations for school ensembles.

"Arkansas Traveler" (and other folk tunes).
McKay, George F.: Presser: Chamber orchestra.

"Arkansas Traveler" (Concert Transcription).
O'Hara, Geoffrey: J. Fischer & Bro.: Violin, cello, piano.

Cadman, Charles W.
American Suite. New York: Composer's Press: String Orchestra.
The third movement is based upon Southern mountain dance tunes.

"Folk Dance."
Bryan, Charles F.: MS: Chamber orchestra.

"Hobby-in-the-Green."
Rufty, Hilton: Schirmer: Various Combinations.

Kreutz, Arthur
American Dances. MS. Chamber Orchestra, 8 winds, strings.

McEwen, John B.
Suite of Old National Dances. Arranged for String Quartet. London: Joseph Williams, Ltd., 1924.
Group I: Country Dance (Old English) Two Scottish Dances; Strathspey, and Reel.

"Pop Goes the Weasel."
Sowerby, Leo: Fitzsimons: Chamber orchestra.

"Pop Goes the Weasel."
Sowerby, Leo: Fitzsimons Co.: Flute, oboe. clarinet, bassoon, horn.

"Sailor's Hornpipe."
Tuthill, Burnet C.: Carl Fischer: Wind Quintet.

"Turkey in the Straw."
Pochon, Alfred: Carl Fischer: String Quartet.

————: *Band*

"Arkansas Traveler."
Guion D. W.: Schirmer: Band (T. Clark).

Collection of Hornpipes.
Arranged by L. O. de Witt. New York: Carl Fischer.

Contra Dances.
Arranged by Paul de Ville. Includes: Hull's Victory, Hornpipe; McDonald's Virginia Reel, etc. New York: Carl Fischer.

Contra Dances and Hornpipes.
Arranged by L. O. de Witt. Nine traditional dances: Irish Washer-woman, Pop Goes the Weasel, etc. New York: Carl Fischer.

"Skip to My Lou."
Fred: Educational: Full Band.

Twelve English Country Dance Tunes.
Arranged by Gordon Jacob, from Cecil Sharp Collection. New York: Novello & Company. 3 sets—4 to a set. Great number of American origin.

Twelve Reels and Jigs.
Arranged by L. O. de Witt. New York: Carl Fischer.

"Turkey in the Straw."
Guion: Gamble Hinged: Band and piano.

"Turkey in the Straw."
Guion, David W. (Arr. by J. P. Sousa): Schirmer: Band.

Variations on the theme — "Pop! Goes the Weasel."
Cailliet, L.: Elkan-Vogel: Band.

————: *Various Instruments*

Old Familiar Dances: for piano, violin and piano, mandolin and piano, flute or piccolo. Boston: Oliver Ditson Co.

RECORDS

Album Collections

American Folk Dances.
In the Archive of the American Folk Dance, New York City.

American Square Dances.
Woodhull's Old Tyme Masters (Calls by Floyd C. Woodhull). 4–10″.   VI–36

Country Dances.
Ed Durlacher and the Top Hands. 4–10″.
SO–MS–479

Country Dances.
Reels, Squares, with and without calls by Tiny Clark and Mr. and Mrs. Sitter. 3–10″. Asch 344

Cowboy Square Dances.
Cooley's Buckle Busters   DE–226
Contents: Round the couple and swing when you meet; Chase that rabbit; Chase that squirrel; Bird in a cage; Three rail pen; Go through and swing; Boy around a boy; Girl around a girl; Lady round the lady; Gent solo.

Early American Dances.
As revived by Mr. and Mrs. Henry Ford.
Ford Orchestra 12–10".   A–213
Contents: 101–A—Plain Quadrille, Part I; 101–B—Plain Quadrille, Part II (without calls); 102–A—Standard Club Quadrille, Figure I; 102–B—Standard Club Quadrille, Figure II (with calls); 102–C—Standard Club Quadrille, Figure III; 102–D—Jigs and Reels (with calls); 107–A Heel and Toe Polka; 107–B—Rye Waltz; 108–A—Captain Jinks; 108–B—The Little Log Cabin in the Lane (Swinging Calls); 111–A—Blue Danube Waltz; 111–B—Tales from the Vienna Woods (Waltz); 113–A—Hull's Victory, Contre Dance; 113–B—Lady Walpole's Reel, Contre Dance (without calls); 114–A—Portland Fancy, Circle Quadrille; 114–B—A Good Mixer, Novelty March (with calls); 115–A—Quadrille, Medley of Hornpipes; 115–B—Standard Quadrille, Grape-vine Twist (without calls); 116–A—Ticknors Quadrille; 116–B—Quadrille, "Cub" Berdan's Favorite (without calls); 117–A—Virginia Reel, Contre Dance (with calls); 117–B—Barn Dance —Military Schottische; 118–A—Fireman's Dance, Circle Quadrille; 118–B—Money Musk, Contre Dance (without calls).

As revived by Mr. and Mrs. Henry Ford.
Ford Orchestra 8–10".   A–208
Contents: 103–A—Hungarian Varsovienne; 103–B—Old Southern Schottische; 104–A—Lancer's "Oriental," Figures I and II; 104–B—Lancer's "Oriental," Figures III and IV, without calls; 105–A—Lancer's "Oriental," Figures I and II; 105–B—Lancer's "Oriental," Figures III and IV (with calls); 106–A—Lancer's "Oriental," Figure V (without calls); 106–B—Lancer's "Oriental," Figure V (with calls); 109–A—Hinky-Dinky, Parlee-Voo; 109–B—Life on the Ocean Wave (Swinging Calls); 110–A—Badger Gavotte; 110–B—Varsovienne Waltz; 112–A—Black Cat Quadrille, Part I; 112–B—Black Cat Quadrille, Part II (without calls); 119–A—Lady Round the Lady (Singing call); 119–B—Fireman's Dance Circle Quadrille (with calls).

Fiddle Tunes.
A 1. The Last of Callahan.
  2. The Ways of the World.
  3. Glory in the Meeting House. Played on the fiddle by Luther Strong at Dales-burg, Kentucky, 1937. Recorded by Alan and Elizabeth Lomax. In: Album II: Recordings of American Folk Songs, Library on Congress, 1943.   AAFS9.

Fiddle Tunes.
1. Grub Springs.
2. Eighth of January.
3. Sally Goodin. Played on the fiddle by W. E. Claunch with guitar, at Guntown, Missis-sippi, 1939.
4. Cindy. Played on the fiddle and sung by W. E. Claunch, with guitar, at Guntown, Mississippi, 1939. Recorded by Herbert Halpert. In: Album I: Recordings of Ameri-can Folk Songs, Library of Congress, 1943.   *AAFS9B*

Five String Banjo Tunes.
1. Old Joe Clark.
2. Chilly Winds. Played by Wade Ward at Galax, Virginia, 1939. Recorded by Pete Seeger and Alan Lomax.
3. Cripple Creek. Played by Herbert Smoke at Winchester, Virginia, 1940. Recorded by Alan Lomax.
4. Coal Creek March. Played by Pete Steele at Hamilton, Ohio, 1935. Recorded by Alan and Elizabeth Lomax. In: Album II: Re-cordings of American Folk Songs, Library of Congress, 1943.   AAFS10.

Folk Dances.
Children Records.   PIC–Vol. 6.
Contents: Turkey in the Straw, Carousel, Take a Little Peek, The Kerry Dance, Shoo Fly Don't Bother Me, Mexican Hat Dance.

Honor Your Partner.
Ed. Durlacher. 3 Albums. (3-12" each). Devin-Adair Co.
A complete course in square dancing.

Jig Time Quadrille.
Chalmers Wood's Novelty Trio.   PA–F3344/6
Contents: Figure 1. Father O'Flynn; Rory O'More; Figure 2. Donnybrook; The Blackthorne Stick; Garry Owen; Figure 3. Biddy of Sligo; Pet of the Pipers; Figure 4. Irish Whiskey; Haste to the Wedding; Lannagan's Ball; Figure 5. The May Moon; Paddy Whack; Irish Washer-woman; Figure 6. Sorry to Part; Humours of Donnybrook; Rakes of Kildare; Biddy; Roaring Jenny; St. Patrick's Day (5 sides) and Scottish Waltz Medley; Wi' a hundred Pipers; Coming Thro' the Rye; Skye Boat Song; Ye Banks and Ye Braes; Wi' a hundred Pipers.

Longways Dances.
American Square Dance Group. 3–10".
    DE–275
Contents: Money Musk; Boston Fancy; Hull's Victory; The Tempest; Fireman's Dance; Vir-ginia Reel.

Maypole Dances.
Black Diamond Band.   GR–B3356/7.
Contents: Entry-Come lasses and lads; Double Plait—Now is the month of Maying; Panels—Drink to me only; Single Plait and Spider's Web—Merry Old England; Amo Amas-Amo amas; Two and one—British Grenadiers; Gypsy's tent—The Gypsy Loves; Threes-Lass of Richmond Hill; Spider's Web—Merry Old England; Single Plait—The Jolly Waggoner; Circling and Clown-ing—The May Queen; Exit—Begone dull care.

Medley of Reels.
Ford's Old Time Dance Orchestra.   VI–19964

More Old Time Dances.
Byron Wolfe and Orchestra.   Set DE–56
    DE–2651/5
Contents: Virginia Reel; Waltz Quadrille; Paul Jones; Princess Glide; Gavotte; Montana Dance and Waltz.

Morris Dances.
Folk Dance Band.   GR–B9296.
Contents: "Lads a Bunchun" and "Bean Setting."

Morris Dances.
Folk Dance Band.   GR–B9297.
    Contents: "Shepherd's Hey" and "Glorishears-Bampton Tradition."

Morris Dances.
Folk Dance Band.   GR–B9298.
    Contents: "Country Gardens" and "Bobbing Joe."

Morris Dances.
Folk Dance Octet.   CO-DB1795.
    Contents: "The 29th of May" ("Headington"), and "The Abram Circle Dance."

Mountain Frolic: Square Dances and Hoedowns from the Southern Mountains.
Uncle Dave Macon and his Fruit Jar Drinkers: The Crockett Family; Bradley Kincaid; Al Hopkins and his Buckle Busters; The Tennessee Ramblers. 4–10″.   BR–1025
    Contents: "Arkansas Traveler"; "Sourwood Mountain"; "Cindy"; "Old Joe Clark"; "Sugar Hill"; "Sail Away, Ladies"; "Black Eyed Susie"; "Sally Goodin"; "Sally in the Garden"; "Cluck Old Hen."

Old Time Fiddlin' Pieces.
Clayton McMichen.   DE–66

Play and Dance Songs and Tunes.
In: Album 1X: Five Records: *AAFS*41 (Dulcimer pieces), *AAFS*42 (Fiddle and banjo pieces), *AAFS*43, *AAFS*44, *AAFS*45 (Negro game songs), Library of Congress. Edited by B. A. Botkin.

Play Party Games—Square Dances.
Frank Luther, American Square Dance Orchestra.   DE–A–278
    Contents: Brown Jug; Oh Susanna; Skip to My Lou; Old Dan Tucker. .

Quadrilles (With Calls).
American Square Dance Group, Margot Mayo, Leader. Calls by Manny. 3–10″.   DE–A–277

Reels.
Scottish Country Dance Orchestra.
                  GR–B3556.
    Contents: Rachel Rae; High Road to Linton; Fight about the Fireside; Brown's Reel & Strathspeys; Money Musk; Braes o'Tullimut; Highland Whiskey.

Running Set.
American Square Dance Group, Margot Mayo, 3–10″   DE–274
    Contents: Hog-eyed Sally; Sally Goodin; Turkey Buzzard; Sugar in the Gourd; Old Granny Hare; Old Joe Clark; Soldier's Jog; Sugar in my Coffee; Leather Britches; Sourwood Mountain; Pigtown Fling.

Scottish Country Dances.
Chalmers Wood and his Scottish Dance Orchestra.   CO–DB1277
    Contents: "The Dashing White Sergeant" (Dashing White Sergeant and Miss Clementine Loughan) and "Strip the Willow" (Drops of Brandy; Frolicksome Paddy; I Have a Wife O' My Ain.)

Scottish Country Dances.
Highland Military Band.   CO–4055
    Contents: "Haymakers Reel," and "Cumberland Reel."

Scottish Country Dances.
Highland Military Band.   CO–4056
    Contents: "Flower of Edinburgh," and "Strip the Willow."

Scottish Solo Dances.
Highland Military Band.   CO–4752
    Contents: "Irish Jig" (Irish Washerwoman) and "Dutch Dance" (Wooden Shoes).

Scottish Solo Dances.
Highland Military Band.   CO–4753
    Contents: "Sailor's Hornpipe" (College Hornpipe) and "Toe Dance" (Pizzicato from "Sylvia" Ballet).

Six English Folk Dance Tunes.
The Folk Dance Octet, Arnold Foster, Conductor.   CO–M–394
Six Sides: 2 Morris Dances and 4 Country Dances.

Skye Eightsome Reel.
Scottish Country Dance Orchestra. GR–B3228
    Contents: Fairy Dance; Deil amang the Tailors; The Wing That Shakes; Speed the Plough.

Square Dance.
American Square Dance Group, Margot Mayo, Dir., with Manny (Calls). 3–10″   KE–130
    Contents: Chicken Reel, Double Chassez, Silent Couple, Preakness Quadrille, Sq. Dance Medley, The New Portland Fancy.

Square Dance Album.
Cactus Andy and the Texas Dandies BW–65

Square Dances.
Paul Hunt and his Rock Candy Mountaineers. 3–10″   Disc 631
    Contents: Rakes of Mallow, Rig a Jigjig, Golden Slippers, Little Brown Jug, Soldier's Joy, Lamplighter's Hornpipe.

Square Dances.
Al MacLeod's Country Dance Band with calls. 3–12″   DE–A–229

Square Dances.
Carson Robison and His Old Timers. Lawrence V. Loy, Dance Calls. 4–10″.   CO–47
    Contents: The First Two Ladies; Cross Over; Darling Nellie Gray; Buffalo Boy; Go 'Round the Outside; Oh Susanna; Dive for the Oyster (Part 1); Dive for the Oyster (Part 2); Little Brown Jug; Possum in the Simmon Tree.

Square Dances.
Carson Robison & His Pleasant Valley Boys; Calls by Lawrence V. Loy. 4–10″.   VI–8086
    Contents: Spanish Cavaliero, Irish Washwoman, Solomon Levi, Comin' Round the Mountain, Jingle Bells, Paddy Dear, Golden Slippers, Turkey in the Straw.

Square Dances.
With and without calls. Woodhull's Old Tyme Masters. 4–10″.   VI–C–36

Square Dances with Calls.
Ralph Page, the Singing Caller & His New England Orchestra. 3–10″.   DISC–630
    Contents: Disgusted Brides, Red River Valley, Odd Couple in the Center, Monadnock Muddle, Ladies' Whirlgig, Star the Ring.

Square Dances without Calls.
Paul Hunt, and his Rock Candy Mountaineers.
                        DISC–631
    Contents: Rakes of Mallow; Rig a Jigjig; Golden Slippers; Little Brown Jug; Soldier's Joy; Lamplighter's Hornpipe.

Strathspeys.
Chalmers Wood and his Scottish Dance Orchestra.   CO–DB1278
    Contents: "The Glasgow Highlanders" (Glasgow Highlanders and Jenny's Bawbee) and "Petronella" (Petronella; Chester Castle; The Persian Dance.)

Swing Your Partner.
Bill Dickinson's Tuxedo Colonels, Calls by Paul Conklin. 3–12″.   VI–C39
    Contents: Quadrille Fig; Hodge, No. 1 and 3 Pattern Dances; Buffalo Gal; Chase Your Partner; Darling Nelly Gray; Duck the Oyster; Lady 'Round the Lady; Life on the Ocean Wave.

Sword Dance Suite.
Folk Dance Orchestra.   GR–B8808
    Contents: Sleight's Sword Dance Tunes—Figures 1–4.

The Denman Quadrilles.
Harry Davidson and Orchestra. CO–DX1232/3

U. S. Library of Congress. Division of Music. Folklore Section.
    Fiddle Songs and Tunes. Michael Cruise, Tucson, Arizona.   AAFS–LC

———.
Fiddle Tunes, Square Dance Tunes, and Folk Recorded Songs in Kentucky by Margot Mayo Recording Project.   AAFS–LC

———.
Play and Dance Songs and Tunes. Album. 5 records—containing Dulcimer pieces (AAFS 41); Fiddle and banjo pieces (AAFS 42); Square Dances (AAFS 43); and AAFS 44; and Negro Game Songs (AAFS 45).
                      AAFS 41/45

———.
Recordings of Square Dance Calls, H. Edward Behre, Alexandria, Va., coll.   AAFS–LC

———.
Singing "Cindy" and Calling Square Dances.
                      AAFS–LC

Virginia Reels.
Victor Orchestra.   VI–20447
    Contents: Miss McCloud's Reel; Old Dan Tucker; Pop Goes the Weasel; Money Musk No. 1 and No. 2.

Individual Titles

"Ace of Diamonds."
Folk Dance Band.   GR–B2707

"Adson's Sarabande."
Folk Dance Orchestra.   GR–B8169

"A Devil's Dream."
Played by String Band: J. C. Fowler, Elie Buckner, and Alva Ruffner, with calling by S. C. Simon at Lubbock Texas, 1937. In: Album IX: Library of Congress   AAFS44A

"Alabama Gal."
Riley Puckett and Clayton McMichen, vocalist with fiddle and guitar.   CO–1191
    (A version of "Buffalo Gals").

"Althea."
National Military Band.   CO–DB1004

"Amarillis."
Folk Dance Octet.   CO–DB1796

"Animals A-Comin'."   CO–36464
    In: *Yale Glee Club.*   Set CO–79

"Argeers."
National Military Band.   CO–DB1004

"Arkansas Traveler."
Boston "Pops" Orchestra—Arthur Fiedler
                      VI–4502

"Arkansas Traveler."
Jimmy Dorsey and Orchestra.   DE–2363

"Arkansas Traveler."
In: *Frontier Ballads and Cowboy Songs.*
                      ASCH–410

"Arkansas Traveler."
Luther, Layman, Stokes, vocalists with guitar, fiddle and bass. In: *American Folk Songs Album.*   DE–25

"Arkansas Traveler."
Clayton McMichen, violin.   DE–2648

"Arkansas Traveler."
Byron Wolfe's Orchestra.   DE–2562

"Arkansas Traveler."
A Woodchopper and Square Dance Band.
                    OK–06296
    In: *Swing Your Partner.*   Set KE–2

"A Soldier's Joy."
Gid Tanner and his Skillet Lickers. BB–5658–A

"A Trip to Kilburn."
National Military Band.   CO–DB1003

"Back to Back."
Ed Durlacher and the Top Hands.
                    SO–MS479–8

"Barn Dance—Down South."
Harry Davidson and Orchestra.   CO–DX1177

"Barn Dance—Those Were the Days."
Harry Davidson and Orchestra.   CO–DX1265

"Beatin' up Sandy."
Al Hopkins and His Buckle Busters; banjo and guitar.   BR–182–A

"Beggar Boy."
National Folk Barn Dance Orchestra.
CO–DB 84

"Beggar Boy."
National Folk Dance Orchestra. CO–DB2244

"Bile dem Cabbage Down."
Played by E. C. Ball on the guitar and Blair
C. Ready on the mandolin, with singing by
E. C. Ball, at Rugby, Virginia, 1941. In: Album IX: Library of Congress. AAFS43A2

"Billie in the Low Ground."
Jilson Setters, J. W. Day; fiddle, guitar
VI–21417–B

"Bird in a Cage."
Cooley's Buckle Busters. In: *Cowboy Square Dances*. DE–226

"Blackberry Blossom."
Arthur Smith Trio; fiddle and guitars.
BB–5896–B

"Blackberry Quadrille."
Woodhull's Old Tyme Masters. VI–C36

"Black-eyed Susie."
Al Hopkins and his Buckle Busters; vocal, fiddle, banjo, and guitar. BR–175–B

"Black-eyed Susie."
Gid Tanner; fiddle, banjo and guitar (Square dance). CO–15283–D

"Black-Eyed Susie."
Riley Puckett; vocal, fiddle, banjo. CO–119–D

"Black Jack."
National Military Band. CO–DB1002

"Black Nag."
National Military Band. CO–5734

"Bonnets So Blue."
BBC Military Band. CO–5434

"Boston Fancy."
American Square Dance Group. In: *Longways Set*. DE–275

"Boy Around a Boy."
Cooley's Buckle Busters. In: *Cowboy Square Dances*. DE–226

"Brighton Camp."
National Military Band. CO–DB2246.

"Broom, the Bonny, Bonny Broom."
National Military Band. CO–DB1004

"Buffalo Gal."
Bill Dickinson's Tuxedo Colonels In: *Swing Your Partner*. VI–C34

"Buffalo Gals."
Luther, Layman, Stokes, with guitar, fiddle and bass. In: *American Folk Songs Album*.
DE–25

"Buffalo Gals."
Shorty McCoy BB–33–0511

"Bug in the Taters."
Al Hopkins and his Buckle Busters; vocal fiddle, banjo and guitar. BR–182–B

"Cailliet."
Variation on "Pop goes the Weasel." Boston "Pop" Orchestra—Arthur Fiedler VI–4397

"Callahan's Reel."
Fiddlin' Powers and Family; fiddle.
VI–19450–A

"Can I Sleep in Your Barn Tonight?"
Frank Luther; Zora Layman, Leonard Stokes, vocalists with guitar, fiddle and bass. In: *American Folk Songs Album*. DE–25

"Captain Jinx."
Woodhull's Old Tyme Masters. In: *Square Dances*. VI–C36

"Catching of Quails."
Folk Dance Orchestra. GR–B8169

"Chase that Rabbit."
Cooley's Buckle Busters. In: *Cowboy Square Dances*. DE–226

"Chase that Squirrel."
Cooley's Buckle Busters." In: *Cowboy Square Dances*. DE–226

"Chase Your Partner."
Bill Dickinson's Tuxedo Colonels In: *Swing Your Partner*. VI–C34

"Chestnut."
National Folk Dance Orchestra. CO–DB2250

"Chicken Reel."
Jimmy Dorsey and Orchestra. DE–1086

"Chicken Reel."
Joe Daniels and Hot Spots. DE–1677

"Childgrove."
Folk Dance Band. GR–C1265

"Chilly Winds" (Square Dance).
Played by Wallace Swann and his Cherokee String Band, with square dancing at Asheville Folk Festival, Asheville, North Carolina, 1941. In: Album II: Recordings of American Folk Songs, Library of Congress, 1941. AAFS10B

"Christchurch Bells."
Folk Dance Band. GR–C1264

"Christchurch Bells."
National Military Band. CO–DB2248

"Cinda."
Al Hopkins and his Buckle Busters; vocals with fiddle, banjo and guitar. BR–105A

"Cindy."
Frank Luther Singers. DE–A–311

"Cindy" (Country Dance).
Pete Seeger and Orchestra; vocal with banjo.
ASCH 432–4A

"Cindy."
Shorty McCoy. BB–33–0511

"Cindy."
Yale Glee Club. CO–6463

"Circassion Circle."
Morris Motors Band. CO–DB1673

"Circassian Circle."
National Folk Dance Orchestra. CO–DB1359

"Circassian Circle."
Scotch Country Dance Orchestra. GR–B2215

"Clap Dance."
Folk Dance Band. GR–B2708

"Cluck Old Hen."
Al Hopkins and his Buckle Busters; vocal
with fiddle, banjo and guitar. BR–175–A

"Cluck Old Hen" (Fiddle tune).
The Hill Billies. VO–B5020

"Cochin China."
Folk Dance Band. GR–B2707

"Community Lancers" (3 sides) and "Valse
Memories" (1 side).
Court Symphony Orchestra and Debroy Somers
Band. CO–5509/10

"Corn Rigs."
National Folk Dance Orchestra. CO–DB1594

"Country Jig" (David Guion), Jeanne Behrend,
piano. In: Album of Piano Music by American
Composers. VM–764

"Cotton Baggin'."
Gid Tanner and his Skillet Lickers.
CO–115404–D

"Cotton Patch." (Square Dance)
Gid Tanner and his Skillet Lickers.
BB–5591–A

"Country Gardens."
Victor Concert Orchestra. VI–20802

"Cripple Creek."
Fiddlin' Powers and Family. VI–19449–A

"Cripple Creek."
(from "From the Southern Mountain Suite"
by Lamar Stringfield.) National High School
Orchestra. VI–22095

"Cumberland Gap."
Gid Tanner and his Skillet Lickers.
CO–15303–D

"Cumberland Gap."
Riley Puckett; vocal with fiddle and banjo.
CO–245–D

"Cumberland Long Eight."
Folk Dance Orchestra. CO–DB1952

"Cumberland Square Eight."
Folk Dance Orchestra. CO–DB1953

"Dance All Night with the Bottle in My
Hand." Stripling Brothers; fiddle and guitar.
VO–5395

"Dargason."
Folk Dance Orchestra. GR–B8169

"Darling Nellie Gray."
Bill Dickinson's Tuxedo Colonels. In: Swing
your Partner. VI–C34

"Destiny Waltz."
Harry Davidson and Orchestra.
CO–DX1232/3

"Devil in the Kitchen."
Boston Pipe Band. DE–14007

"Devil's Dream."
Played on the dulcimer by Thomas Mann at
Ortonville, Iowa, 1937. In: Album IX: Library
of Congress. AAFS41B1

"Dick's Maggot."
National Folk Dance Orchestra.
CO–DB2244

"Did You Ever See a Lassie."
Victor Band. VI–21618

"Done Gone."
A. C. (Eck) Robertson; fiddle (Country
Dance). VI–19372–B

"Donkey On the Railroad Track."
The Hill Billies. VO–B5020

"Duck the Oyster."
Bill Dickinson's Tuxedo Colonels. In: Swing
Your Partner VI–C34

"Durang's Hornpipe."
Victor Orchestra. VI–20592

"Durham Reel."
National Folk Dance Orchestra.
CO–DB1359

"Eighth of January."
Dr. Humphrey Bate and his Possum Hunters;
instrumental. BR–239

"Epping Forest."
BBC Military Band. CO–5504

"Esperanzo-Barn Dance."
Harry Davidson and Orchestra.
CO–DX1240

"Fiddler's Dream."
Arthur Smith; fiddle and guitars.
BB–5843–A

"Fine Companion."
National Folk Dance Orchestra. CO–DB84

"Fireman's Dance."
American Square Dance Group. In: Longways Set DE–275

"Fire on the Mountain."
Gid Tanner and his Skillet Lickers.
CO–15115–D

"Fire on the Mountain."
Riley Puckett and Clayton McMichen; vocal, fiddle and guitar. CO–15185–D

"Flamborough Sword Dance."
BBC Military Band. CO–9800

"Flowers of Edinburgh."
Folk Dance Band. GR–C1264

"Flowers of Edinburgh."
Scotch Country Dance Orchestra.
GR–B2215

"Forked Deer."
Clinch Valley Boys; vocal with fiddle and guitar, banjo. CH–302–B

"Forked Deer."
Jilson Setters; fiddle and guitar.
VI–21407–A

"Forky Deer."
Uncle Am Stuart; fiddle and banjo.
VO–B14846

"Fourpence-Halfpenny-Farthing."
BBC Military Band. CO–5503

"Foursome Reel" (Moneymusk and the De'il Amang' the Tailors). Chalmers Wood and his Scottish Dance Orchestra. CO–DB1279

"Fox Chase."
Gid Tanner and his Skillet Lickers; instrumental. CO–15017–D

"French Reel."
Folk Dance Band. GR–B2711

"Frog Went A-Courting."
The Old Harp Singers. MU–222–A

"Galopede."
Folk Dance Band. GR–B9279

"Galopede."
Morris Motors Band. CO–DB1672

"Gathering Peascods."
BBC Military Band. CO–5504

"Gavotte."
Byron Wolfe and Orchestra. In: *More Old Time Dances.* DE–56

"Gent Solo."
Cooley's Buckle Busters. In: *Cowboy Square Dances.* DE–226

"George Washington."
Pope's Arkansas Mountaineers; Instrumental.
VI–21469–B

"Geud Man of Ballangigh."
National Folk Dance Orchestra.
CO–DB2242

"Girl Around a Girl."
Cooley's Buckle Busters. In: *Cowboy Square Dances.* DE–226

"Girls' Joy."
Folk Dance Band. GR–B2709

"Git Along."
Gid Tanner and his Skillet Lickers.
BB–5488–B

"Goddesses."
National Military Band. CO–DB574

"Goddesses."
National Military Band. CO–DB2246

"Goin' Up the Country."
Cliff and Roy; vocals with fiddle and guitar. (Version of "Old Dan Tucker")
CO(Dal–1290–1)

"Go Through and Swing."
Cooley's Buckle Busters. In: *Cowboy Square Dances.* DE–226

"Gov. Alf Taylor's Fox Chase."
The Hill Billies; vocalists with fiddle, guitar and banjo. VO–B5016

"Grand Old Duke."
Scotch Country Dance Orchestra.
GR–B2193

"Greenwich Park."
National Military Band. CO–DB1003

"Grey Eagle."
Uncle Am Stuart; fiddle and banjo.
VO–14839

"Grimstock."
National Folk Dance Orchestra.
CO–DB2250

"Haste to the Wedding."
BBC Military Band. CO–5434

"Haste to the Wedding."
National Folk Dance Orchestra.
CO–DB1360

"Haste to the Wedding, Off She Goes," Jig (Medley). Played on the dulcimer by Thomas Mann at Ortonville, Iowa, 1937. In: Album 1X: Library of Congress AAFS41A1

"Heartsease."
National Folk Dance Orchestra. CO–DB84

"Heartsease."
National Folk Dance Orchestra. CO–DB2244

"Heel and Toe Polka."
Ford's Old Time Dance Orchestra.
VI–19909

"Helston Furry Processional."
BBC Military Band. CO–9769

"Hey, Boys, Up We Go."
Folk Dance Band. GR–B9484

"Hey, Boys, Up We Go."
National Military Band. CO–5733

"Highland Fling." (The Keel Row and Braes o' Mar.)
Royal Air Force Band.   CO–DB476

"Highland Fling."
Scotch Country Dance. Orchestra.
   GR–B2193

"Hit and Miss."
National Folk Dance Orchestra.   CO–DB84

"Hog-eyed Sally."
American Square Dance Group. In: *Running Set.*   DE–274

"Hop About Ladies."
Oliver Sims; harmonica.   CO–17137–1

"Horseshow-Band."
Stripling Brothers; fiddle guitar and banjo.
   VO–5395

"Hull's Victory"
American Square Dance Group. In: *Longways Set.*   DE–275

"Hull's Victory."
Folk Dance Orchestra.   CO–DB1953

"Hunsdon House."
National Folk Dance Orchestra.
   CO–DB2241

"Hunt the Squirrel."
Folk Dance Band.   GR–B8685

"Hyde Park."
National Folk Dance Orchestra.
   CO–DB2250

"If All the World."
National Military Band.   CO–5734

"If All the World Were Paper."
Folk Dance Band.   GR–B9480

"Indian Queen."
BBC Military Band.   CO–9769

"Irish Washerwoman."
Played on the dulcimer by Thomas Mann at Ortonville, Iowa, 1937. In: Album 1X: Library of Congress.   AAFS41A2

"Irish Washerwoman."
Victor Concert Orchestra.   VI–22131

"Jamaica."
National Military Band.   CO–DB814

"Jenny Pluck Pears."
Folk Dance Band.   GR–B9483

"Jenny Pluck Pears."
Folk Dance Octet.   CO–DB1796

"Kirkby Sword Dance."
BBC Military Band.   CO–9800

"Lady of the Lake."
Victor Orchestra   VI–20592

"Lady 'round the Lady."
Bill Dickinson's Tuxedo Colonels. In: *Swing Your Partner.*   VI–C34

"Lady 'round the Lady."
Cooley's Buckle Busters. In: *Cowboy Square Dances.*   DE–226

"Lady Spellor."
Folk Dance Band.   GR–B2958

"Lancer's Quadrille."
American Square Dance Group.
   DE–15060–61

"Leather Britches."
American Square Dance Group. In: *Running Set.*   DE–274

"Lena" (Schottische).
International Novelty Quartet.   VI–20253

"Life on the Ocean Wave."
Bill Dickinson's Tuxedo Colonels. In: *Swing Your Partner.*   VI–C34

"Lightfoot Bill."
Woodchopper and Square Dance Band. In: *Swing Your Partner.*   OK–06299

"Lilli Burlero."
BBC Military Band.   CO–5503

"Little Brown Jug."
Frank Crumit, voice, orchestra.   VI–24092

"Little Brown Jug."
Kirby and Orchestra.   OK–5570

"Little Brown Jug."
Frank Luther and American Square Dance Orchestra. In: *Play Party Games — Square Dances.*   DE–A278

"Little Brown Jug."
Luther, Layman, Stokes, vocalists; with guitar, fiddle and bass. In: *American Folk Songs Album.*   DE–25

"Little Brown Jug."
Louisse Massey and Westerners.   OK–05425

"Liza Jane."
Riley Puckett; vocal, fiddle.   CO–15014–D

"Loolie Lou Skip to My Love."
Ed Durlacher and the Top Hands. (Circle Dance.)   SO–MS–479–6

"London is a Fine Town."
National Military Band.   CO–DB1002

"London is a Fine Town."
National Military Band.   CO–DB2243

"Long Eight."
Morris Motors Band.   CO–DB1674

"Long Eight."
National Dance Orchestra.   CO–DB1621

"Mage on a Spree."
Folk Dance Band.   GR–B9484

"Mage On a Spree."
National Military Band.　　　CO–5733

"Maid in the Moon."
National Folk Dance Orchestra.　CO–DB2250

"Maid's Morris."
National Military Band.　　　CO–DB814

"Merry, Merry Milkmaids."
Folk Dance Band.　　　GR–B8686

"Military Two Step—Uncle Sammy."
Harry Davidson and Orchestra.　CO–DX1185

"Mississippi Sawyer."
Played by String Band: J. C. Fowler, Elie
Buckner, and Alva Ruffner, with calling by
S. C. Simon, at Lubbock, Texas, 1937. In:
Album 1X: *Library of Congress.*　AAFS44B

"Money Musk."
American Square Dance Group. In: *Longways
Set.*　　　DE–275

"Money Musk."
Ford's Old Time Dance Orchestra.　VI–19964

"Montana Dance and Waltz."
Byron Wolfe and Orchestra. In: *More Old
Time Dances.*　　　DE–56

"Morpeth Rant."
Morris Motors Band.　　　CO–DB1673

"Morpeth Rant."
National Folk Dance Orchestra.　CO–DB1361

"Mountain March."
Folk Dance Band.　　　GR–B2708

"Mutual Love."
Folk Dance Band.　　　GR–B8733

"Mutual Love."
Folk Dance Band and Folk Dance Orchestra.
　　　GR–B9485

"My Lady Cullen."
Folk Dance Band and Folk Dance Orchestra.
　　　GR–B9485

"My Lady Cullen."
Folk Dance Orchestra.　　　GR–B4456

"My Love is But a Lassie'O."
Woodchopper and Square Dance Band. In:
Swing your Partner.　Set KE–2. OK–06299

"Nancy's Fancy."
Folk Dance Band.　　　GR–C1263

"Nancy's Fancy."
Played on the dulcimer by Thomas Mann at
Ortonville, Iowa, 1937. In: Album IX: *Library
of Congress.*　　　AAFS41B2

"Napoleon."
Folk Dance Band.　　　GR–B2710

"Naval Three Step-Blaze of Glory."
Harry Davidson and Orchestra.　CO–DX1211

"Naval Three Step–Here There and Everywhere.'
Harry Davidson and Orchestra. CO–DX1222

"Nellie Bly."
Ed Durlacher and the Top Hands.
　　　SO–MS479–1

"New Bo-Peep."
National Military Band.　　　CO–DB494

"Never Love Thee More."
National Folk Dance Orchestra.　CO–DB2242

"Newcastle."
BBC Military Band.　　　CO–5505

"Newcastle."
Folk Dance Band.　　　GR–B8687

"Northern Nancy."
National Folk Dance Orchestra.　CO–DB1593

"Norwich Long Dance."
Morris Motors Band.　　　CO–DB2257

"Nottingham Swing.'
Folk Dance Orchestra.　　　CO–DB1952

"Nottingham Swing."
National Folk Dance Orchestra.　CO–DB2261

"Number 111."
J. E. Mainer's Mountaineers; vocals, with
fiddle, guitars.　　　BB–6424–B

"Oaken Leaves."
Folk Dance Band and Folk Dance Orchestra.
　　　GR–B9481

"Oh, Fly Around my Pretty Little Miss."
Sung with banjo by O. L. Coffey of Shulls
Mills, North Carolina. In: Album **IX**: *Library
of Congress.*　　　AAFS42B3

"O Susanna."
Riley Puckett; vocal with banjo.
　　　CO–15014–D

"Oh, Susanna."
Frank Luther and American Square Dance
Orchestra. In: *Play Party Games–Square
Dances.*　　　DE–A278

"Oh, Susannah."
Woodhull's Old Tyme Masters." In: *Square
Dances.*　　　VI–C36

"Old Blue Sow."
Played by Enos Canoy on the fiddle, Tim
Canoy on the mandolin, and Lola Canoy on
the guitar at Magee, Mississippi, 1939. In:
Album IX: *Library of Congress.*　AAFS42AI

"Old Dan Tucker."
Frank Luther and American Square Dance
Orchestra. In: *Play Party Games–Square
Dances.*　　　DE–A278

"Old Dan Tucker."
Luther, Layman, Stokes; vocalists, with guitar,
fiddle and bass. In: *American Folk Songs
Album.*　　　DE–25

"Old Granny Hare."
American Square Dance Group. In: *Running Set*.   DE–274

"Old Joe Clark."
American Square Dance Group. In: *Running Set*.   DE–274

"Old Joe Clark."
Riley Puckett; vocal with fiddle and banjo.   CE–15033–D

"Old Liza Jane."
Uncle Am Stuart; fiddle, and banjo.   VO–A–14846

"Old Sally Brown."
Sung with banjo by Calvin Cole, assisted by Dan Tate, at Fancy Gap, Virginia, 1941. In: Album IX: *Library of Congress*.   AAFS42B2

"Old Zip Coon."
Victor Orchestra.   VI–20592

"Ole Rattler."
Cumberland Ridge Runners; vocal with fiddle and guitar.   PE–12914B

"One Eleven Special."
Curley Fox; with fiddle and guitar.   DE–5169

"On Sourwood Mountain."
The Old Harp Singers.   MU–222A

"Oranges and Lemons."
National Folk Dance Orchestra.   CO–DB2241

"Original Round Dance–La Rinka."
Harry Davidson and Orchestra.   CO–DX1202

"Parson's Farewell."
Folk Dance Band.   GR–B9483

"Parson's Farewell."
National Military Band.   CO–5733

"Patty on the Turnpike."
Fiddlin' Powers and Family.   VI–19450–B

"Paul Jones."
Byron Wolfe and orchestra. In: *More Old Time Dances*.   DE–56

"Petronella."
Scottish Dance Orchestra.   GR–B3555

"Picking Up Sticks."
BBC Military Band.   CO–5505

"Pigtown Fling."
American Square Dance Group. In: *Running Set*.   DE–274

"Pigtown Fling."
Played on the dulcimer by Thomas Mann at Ortonville, Iowa, 1937: In: Album IX: *Library of Congress*.   AAFS41A3

"Piper's Fancy."
National Folk Dance Orchestra.   CO–DB1621

"Plain Quadrille."
Ford's Old Time Dance Orchestra.   VI–35771

"Polka Mazurka-Violetta."
Harry Davidson and Orchestra.   CO–DX1280

"Polka—See Me Dance the Polka."
Harry Davidson and Orchestra.   CO–DX1179

"Pop Goes the Weasel."
Folk Dance Band.   GR–C1645

"Pop Goes the Weasel."
Merrymacs—vocal.   DE–1968

"Pop Goes the Weasel."
Victor Band.   VI–20151

"Pop Goes the Weasel."
Woodhull's Old Tyme Masters. In: *Square Dances*.   VI–C36

"Pore Little Mary Settin' in the Corner."
Sung with fiddle by Enos Canoy, with beating of straws by Jim F. Myers at Magee, Mississippi, 1939. In: Album IX: *Library of Congress*.   AAFS42A3

"Princess Glide."
Byron Wolfe and Orchestra. In: *More Old Time Dances*.   DE–56

"Progress Barn Dance—Her Golden Hair."
Harry Davidson and Orchestra.   CO–DX1191

Quadrilles (From Three Old American Quadrilles).
    Victor Orchestra.   VI–20638
    Contents: Chillicothe; Virginny Shore; O Susanna; Arkansas Traveler.

"Queen's Jig."
Folk Dance Band and Folk Dance Orchestra.   GR–B9482

"Queen's Jig."
Folk Dance Orchestra.   GR–B8170

"Red River Valley."
Ed Durlacher and the Top Hands.   SO–MS479–5

"Reel o' Tulloch."
Chalmers Wood and his Scottish Orchestra.   CO–DB1279

"Rhif Wyth."
National Folk Dance Orchestra.   CO–DB1623

"Rock and Rye Waltz."
Massey and the Westerners.   OK–05511

"Rock Island."
Buell Kazee; vocal and banjo.   BR–145–H

"Roll on the Ground."
Al Hopkins and his Buckle Busters; vocalists, banjo, fiddles and guitar.   BR–186–A

"Roll on the Ground."
Sung with 5 string banjo by Thaddeus C. Willingham at Gulfport, Mississippi, 1939. Recorded by Herbert Halpert. In: Volume II: Recordings of American Folk Songs, *Library of Congress*, 1943.   AAFS8B2

"Round Dance–Maxina." CO–DX1202

"Round that Couple."
Cooley's Buckle Busters. In: *Cowboy Square Dances.* DE–226

"Round the Couple and Swing when you Meet."
Cooley's Buckle Busters. In: *Cowboy Square Dances.* DE–226

"Row Well, Ye Mariners."
National Military Band. CO–DB494

"Row Well, Ye Mariners."
National Military Band. CO–DB2243

"Rufty-Tufty."
Folk Dance Band. GR–B2958

"Rufty–Tufty."
National Military Band. CO–5733

"Rye Waltz."
Byron Wolfe and Orchestra. DE–2090

"Rustic Schottische."
Cliff and Ray. OK–04204

"Sage Leaf."
Folk Dance Band. GR–C1265

"Sailor's Hornpipe" (Jack's the Lad).
Royal Air Force Band. CO–DB476

"Sally Ann."
Al Hopkins and his Buckle Busters, 5 string banjo and guitar. BR–105–B

"Sally Gooden."
American Square Dance Group. In: *Running Set.* DE–274

"Sally Goodin."
Played on the banjo by Justus Begley at Hazard, Kentucky, 1937. In: Album IX: *Library of Congress.* AAFS42B1

"Sally Goodin."
Played by Oscar Harper on the fiddle, Harman Clem on the guitar, Homer Peters on the banjo, and Ray Hanby on the bass viol with callings by Bob McClary, at Dallas Square Dance Club, Dallas, Texas, 1942. In: Album IX: *Library of Congress.* AAFS43B2

"Sallie Goodin."
Woodchopper and Square Dance Band. In: *Swing your Partner.* OK–06297

"Sallie Johnson and Sallie in the Low Ground."
A. C. (Eck) Robertson; fiddle (Country Dances). VI–19372–A

"Sanita Hill."
Ed Durlacher and the Top Hands. SO–MS479–4
Progressive Circle.

"Schottisch-Honeysuckle and the Bee."
Harry Davidson and Orchestra. CO–DX1179

"Scotch Cap."
Folk Dance Band and Folk Dance Orchestra. GR–B9481

"Scotch Cap."
Folk Dance Orchestra. GR–B4456

"Seaside Polka."
Ford's Old Time Dance Orchestra. VI–19909

"Sellenger's Round."
Folk Dance Band. GR–B8686

"Sellenger's Round."
National Military Band. CO–5734

"Shepherd's Hey"
Minneapolis Symphony Orchestra, Ormandy. VI–1666

"Shepherd's Holiday."
Folk Dance Band. GR–B9483

"Sir Roger de Coverly."
Royal Air Force Band. CO–DB476

"Skip to My Lou."
Elnora Crocket and the Cumberland Mountaineers; vocals with fiddle, guitar and banjo. CR–3188

"Skip to My Lou."
Frank Luther and American Square Dance Orchestra. In: *Play Party Games–Square Dances.* DE–A278

"Skip to My Lou."
Luther, Layman, Stokes, vocalists, with guitar, fiddle and bass. In: *American Folk Songs Album.* DE–25

"Skip to My Lou."
Uncle Eck Dunford; vocal with guitar, banjo, and fiddle. (Play Party Song.) VI–20938–A

"Soldier's Joy."
American Square Dance Group. In: *Running Set.* DE–274

"Soldier's Joy."
National Folk Dance Orchestra. CO–DB1593

"Soldier's Joy."
Played by Nashville Washboard Band (James Kelby on the Mandolin, Frank Dalton on the guitar, Tom Carroll on the tin can, and Therpolis Stokes on the washboard) at Nashville, Tennessee, 1941. In: Album IX: *Library of Congress.* AAFS43A1

"Soldier's Joy."
Victor Orchestra. VI–20592

"Soldier's Joy."
A. Woodchopper and Square Dance Band. In: *Swing your Partner.* OK–06297 KE–2

"Soldier's Joy."
Woodhull's Old Tyme Masters. In: *Square Dances.* VI–C36

"Sourwood Mountain."
American Square Dance Group. In: *Running Set.* DE–274

"Sourwood Mountain."
Luther, Layman, Stokes, vocalists with guitar, fiddle and bass. In: *American Folk Song Album.*   DE–25

"Sourwood Mountain."
Old Harp Singers of Nashville, Tennessee, unaccompanied.   MU–222

"Sourwood Mountain."
Riley Puckett; vocal with fiddle and banjo.   CO–245–D

"Speed the Plough."
Folk Dance Band.   GR–C1645

"Speed the Plough."
Morris Motors Band.   CO–DB1672

"St. Bernard Waltz."
Harry Davidson and Orchestra.   CO–DX1245/6

"Steam Boat."
Folk Dance Band.   GR–B8684

"Step and Fetch Her."
Folk Dance Orchestra.   CO–DB2258

"Stephanie Gavotte."
Harry Davidson and Orchestra.   CO–DX1265

"Strip the Willow."
Scottish Dance Orchestra.   GR–B3555

"Sugar in My Coffee."
American Square Dance Group. In: *Running Set.*   DE–274

"Sugar in the Gourd."
American Square Dance Group. In: *Running Set.*   DE–274

"Sugar in the Gourd."
Fiddlin' Powers and Family.   VI–19449–B

"Swedish Masquerade."
Folk Dance Band.   GR–B2711

"Sweet Kate."
National Military Band.   CO–DB494

"Tantoli."
Folk Dance Band.   GR–B2710

"Thady You Gander."
Folk Dance Band.   GR–B8732

"The Arcadian Lancers."
Harry Davidson and Orchestra.   CO–DX1245/6

"The Arkansas Traveler."
Gid Tanner and Puckett.   CO–15017–D

"The Barnyard Song."
The Old Harp Singers.   MU–222–B

"The Bishop."
National Folk Dance Orchestra.   CO–DB2256

"The Black Nag."
Folk Dance Band.   GR–B9480

"The Boatman."
Folk Dance Band and Folk Dance Orchestra.   GR–B9481

"The Boatman."
Folk Dance Orchestra.   GR–B4456

"The Bonny Breast-Knot."
National Folk Dance Orchestra.   CO–DB2260

"The Boston Two Step."
Harry Davidson and Orchestra.   CO–DX1191

"The Bow."
Folk Dance Band.   GR–B2709

"The Butterfly."
National Military Band.   CO–DB569

"The Comical Fellow."
Folk Dance Band.   GR–B8733

"The Comical Fellow."
Folk Dance Band and Folk Dance Orchestra.   GR–B9482

"The Dressed Ship."
National Folk Dance Orchestra.   CO–DB1622

"The First of April."
National Folk Dance Orchestra.   CO–DB1622

"The Girl Behind Me."
Woodhull's Old Tyme Masters.   VI–C36

"The Girl Behind Me."
Woodhull's Old Tyme Masters. In: *Square Dances.*   VI–C36

"The Girl I Left Behind Me."
Played by Oscar Harper on the fiddle, Herman Clem on the guitar, Homer Peters on the banjo, and Ray Hanby on the bass viol, with calling by Bob McClary, at Dallas Texas, 1942. In: Album IX: *Library of Congress.*   AAFS43B1

"The Highland Schottische."
Harry Davidson and Orchestra.   CO–DX1280

"The Ladbroke—Give Me A Little Cosy Corner."
Harry Davidson and Orchestra.   CO–DX1222

"The Lancers—Hearts of Oak Lancers."
Harry Davidson and Orchestra.   CO–DX1172/3

"The Last Waltz—The Pink Lady."
Harry Davidson and Orchestra.   CO–DX1211

"The Long Eight."
National Folk Dance.   CO–DB2251

"The Maid Peeped Out."
Folk Dance Band.   GR–B2958

"The Mary and Dorothy."
Folk Dance Orchestra.   GR–B4455

"The Merry Conceit."
National Military Band.   CO–DB1004

"The Merry Milk Maids."
English Orchestra.   CO–4615

"The Merry Merry Milkmaids."
Folk Dance Band. GR–B9484

"The Mock Hobby Horse."
National Military Band. CO–DB574

"The Mock Hobby Horse."
National Military Band. CO–DB2245

"The Old Mole."
English Orchestra. CO–4615

"The Old Mole."
Folk Dance Band. GR–B8687

"The Pleasures of the Town"
National Folk Dance Orchestra. CO–DB1359

"The Ribbon Dance."
Folk Dance Orchestra. GR–B4455

"The Round."
Folk Dance Orchestra. GR–B8170

"The Roving Cowboy."
Buell Kazee; vocal–banjo. BR–156

"The Spaniard."
National Folk Dance Orchestra. CO–DB1360

"The Tempest."
American Square Dance Group. In: Longways Set. DE–275

"The Tempest."
Folk Dance Band. GR–B8732

"The Train" (Harmonica Solo).
Played on one harmonica by Chub Parham,
with clogging, at Ashville Folk Festival, Ash-
ville, North Carolina, 1941. Recorded by Alan
Lomax. In: Album II: Recordings of American
Folk Songs, Library of Congress, 1941.
AAFS10B2

"The Twin Sisters."
National Folk Dance Orchestra. CO–DB1361

"The Veleta."
Harry Davidson and Orchestra. CO–DX1177

"The Way to Norwich."
Folk Dance Orchestra. CO–DB2254

"The Wearin' of the Green."
Woodhull's Old Tyme Masters. VI–V36

"The Welsh Reel."
National Folk Dance Orchestra. CO–DB1623

"Three Around Three."
National Folk Dance Orchestra. CO–DB1594

"Three Meet." (The Pleasures of Town).
National Military Band. CO–DB569

"Three Rail Pen."
Cooley's Buckle Busters. In: Cowboy Square
Dances. DE–226

"Tink-a-Tink."
Folk Dance Band. GR–C1263

"Triple Right and Left Four."
Woodhull's Old Tyme Masters. In: Square
Dances. VI–C36

"Turkey Buzzard."
American Square Dance Group. In: Running
Set. DE–274

"Turkey in Straw."
Alfredo Campoli, orchestra. VI–26600
Two Irish reels; Irish Jig.

"Turkey in Straw."
Andre Kostelanetz, orchestra. BB–8214

"Turkey in the Straw" (fiddle tune setting).
Victor Concert Orchestra—Bourdon. VI–22131

"Turkey in the Straw."
Frank Luther, Zora Layman, Leonard Stokes,
vocalists with guitar, fiddle and bass. In:
American Folk Songs Album. DE–25

"Turkey in the Straw."
Carson Robison and Orchestra. BB–11460

"Turkey in the Straw."
Victor Concert Orchestra. VI–22131

"Twin Sisters."
National Folk Dance Orchestra. CO–DB2252

"Uptown-Downtown."
Ed Durlacher and The Top Hands.
SO–MS479-3

"Valse Blue."
Harry Davidson and Orchestra. CO–DX1240

"Virginia Reel."
American Square Dance Group. In: Longways
Set. DE–275

"Virginia Reel."
Ford's Old Time Dance Orchestra. VI–35771

"Virginia Reel."
Byron Wolfe and orchestra. In: More Old
Time Dances. DE–56

"Walkin' uptown."
Woodchopper and Square Dance Band. In:
Swing your Partner. Set K-2 OK–06298

"Waltz Hesitation—Mighty Lak' a Rose."
Harry Davidson and Orchestra. CO–DX1185

"Waltz Quadrill."
Byron Wolfe and Orchestra. In: More Old
Time Dances. DE–56

"Waltz—The Druid's Prayer."
Harry Davidson and Orchestra.
CO–DX1172/3

"Wearin' of the Green."
Woodhull's Old Tyme Masters. In: Square
Dances. VI–C36

"We Won't Go Home Till Morning."
Folk Dance Band.   GR–B8684

"Where'd You Git Whiskey?"
Sung with fiddle by Enos Canoy with beating
of straws by Jim F. Myers, at Magee, Mississippi, 1939. In: Album IX: *Library of Congress*.   AAFS42A2

"Ye Old Rye Waltz."
Massey and the Westerners.   OK–05511

"Yorkshire Square Eight."
Morris Motors Band.   CO–DB1674

"Yorkshire Square Set."
Morris Motors Band.   CO–DB2257

"You Did It So Well."
Ed Durlacher and The Top Hands.
                                    SO–MS479–7

"Young America Hornpipe."
Victor Orchestra.   VI–20592

SONG GAMES

SONG GAMES

THE PLAY-PARTY
BIBLIOGRAPHY

Botkin, B. A.
Bibliography of the American Play-Party Song.
In: *The American Play Party Song*, with a collection of Oklahoma texts and tunes. (pp. 383–389). The University Studies of the University of Nebraska. Lincoln, Nebr.: The University of Nebraska Press, 1937. 37 (No. 1–4):400 pp., music.

Collins, Fletcher
"An Aid in the Discovery of Folk-songs; a list of finders for traditional ballads, songs and play parties in the Southeast." *SFQ* 5:235–250, 1941.

McLendon, Altha Lea
"A Finding List of Play-Party Games." *SFQ* 8:201–234, 1944.
   A reference list of 302 U. S. game titles.

Moore, Helen Ashworth
"Bibliography of Play Party." *TFSP* 13:335–336, 1937.

Payne, L. W., Jr.
"Finding List for Texas Play-Party Songs." *TFSP* 1:39–44, 1916.
   The author gives valuable suggestions to collectors of play-party songs.

GENERAL STUDIES

Ames, Mrs. L. D.
"The Missouri Play-Party." *JAFL* 24:295–318, 1911.

Atkins, Laura
"Some Play-Party Games of South Texas." *TFSP* 17:98–107, 1941.

Ball, Leona N.
"The Play-Party in Idaho." *JAFL* 44:1–26, 1931.

Botkin, B. A.
The American Play Party Song. The University Studies of the University of Nebraska. Lincoln, Nebr.: The University of Nebraska Press, 1937. 400 pp., music, bibl.

———.
"The Play-Party in Oklahoma." *TFSP* 7:7–25, 1928.

Campbell, Marie
"Play-Party Tunes and Fritter-Minded Ballads." *TFSB* 5:17–48, 1939.

Clark, Clarice
"Ballads of Smoky: Hymns and Party Play Songs of Kentucky Mountaineers—Their Texts and Tunes." *New York Times*, (August 25) 1929. pp. 7.

Douthitt, S. W.
"Play-Parties in Kentucky." *Letters* (The University of Kentucky) 3:30–38, 1930.

Dudley, R. E., and Payne, L. W., Jr.
"Texas Play-Party Song and Games." *TFSP* 1:7–35, 1916.
   The authors present texts only of forty-six games and songs.

Duncan, Ruby
"The Play-Party in Hamilton County (Texas)." *TFSB* 6:1–15, 1940.

"Eastern Illinois Play-Party Songs." *JAFL* 32:486–496, 1919.

Featherstone, Mae
"The Snap Party in Mills County (Texas)." *TFSP* 14:200–206, 1938.

Gardner, Emelyn E.
"Some Play-Party Games in Michigan." *JAFL* 33:91–133, 1920.

Gates, Helen
"Toodala" (Texas folk-dance). *TFSP* 17:91–97, 1941.

Hall, Joseph S.
"Some Party-Games of the Great Smoky Mountains." *JAFL* 54:68–71, 1941.

Hamilton, Goldie
"The Play Party in Northeast Missouri." *JAFL* 27:289–303, 1914.

Herzog, George
"Play-Party Song." *AS* 12 (No. 3):215–217, 1937.
   A Review of B. A. Botkin's *The American Play-*

J., B. S.
"The Gin-Around." *Godey's Lady's Book and Magazine* 89:61–64, 1874.

Jacobs, Adam
"Party Plays; Nature Dances of the Kentucky Hills." *Theatre Arts Magazine* 15:247–250, (March) 1931.

Mahan, Bruce E., and Grahame, Pauline
"Play-Party Games." *The Palimpset* (The State Historical Society of Iowa) 10:33–67, 1929.

McDowell, L. L.
"The Play-Party and Song." *TFSB* 9: (No. 4) 3–8, 1945.
   With musical examples. Good introductory article.

Moore, Helen Ashworth
"The Play-Party in Victoria County (Texas)." *TFSP* 13:300–336, 1937.
   With musical examples.
   Party Song.

Piper, Edwin Ford
"Some Play-Party Games of the Middle West."
JAFL 28:262–289, 1915.

"Play-Party Songs."
JAFL 34:111–120, 1921.

Randolph, Vance
"The Ozark Play-Party." *JAFL* 42:201–233, 1929.

――――――, and Clemens, Nancy
"Ozark Mountain Party-Games." *JAFL* 49: 199–207, 1936.

Richardson, Vivian
"The Singing Games Have Eternal Youth."
Dallas News, (April 1) 1928.
Discussion of Texas Play-Party.

Van Doren, Carl
"Some Play-Party Songs from Eastern Illinois."
JAFL 32:486–496, 1919.

Warnick, Florence
"Play-Party Songs in Western Maryland."
JAFL 54:162–166, 1941.
Words only of twelve songs.

Wedgewood, Harriet L.
"The Play-Party." *JAFL* 25:268–273, 1912.

Whiting, J. D.
"Game of Farmer and His Wife." *JAFL* 2:310, 1889.

COLLECTIONS

Botkin, Benjamin A.
The American Play-Party Song, with a collection of Oklahoma texts and tunes. Lincoln, Nebr.: University of Nebraska Press, 1937. 400 pp.

Collins, Fletcher, Jr.
Alamance Play-Party Songs and Singing Games. Elon College, North Carolina, 1940. Obtainable from the County Superintendent of Public Schools.

Durlacher, Ed
The Play Party Book: Singing Games for Children. With pictures by Arnold Edwin Bare. Music arranged by Ken MacDonald. New York: The Devin-Adair Co., 1945. Unpaged.
Contains thirty-seven singing games handed down from frontier frolics and from children's play. Directions for the dance given.

Ford, Ira W.
Traditional Music of America. New York: E. P. Dutton & Company, 1940.

Isham, C. S.
"Games of Danville, Virginia." *JAFL* 34:116–120, 1921.

McDowell, L. L., and F. L.
Folk Dances of Tennessee: Old Play Party Games of the Caney Fork Valley. Smithville, Tenn.: L. L. McDowell, 1938.

Wilson, Harry R., and Hunt, Beatrice A.
Sing-and-Dance. Folk-Songs and Dances Including American Play-Party Games. Dance Directions prepared by Beatrice A. Hunt; Music arranged by Harry Robert Wilson. Illustrations by Corina Melder-Collier. Chicago: Hall and McCreary, 1945. 80 pp., voice and piano.

Wolford, Leah Jackson
The Play-Party in Indiana. Indianapolis: Indiana Historical Commission, 1916. 120 pp., bibl., music.
A collection of folk-songs and games, with descriptive introduction and correlating notes.

CHILDREN'S SINGING GAMES AND PLAY RHYMES

SINGING GAMES

GENERAL STUDIES

Babcock, William Henry
"Carols and Child-Lore at the Capital." *Lippincott's Monthly Magazine* (Phila.) 38:320–342, 1886.

――――――.
"Games of Washington Children." *AA* 1:243–297, 1888.
Texts only.

Backus, Emma M.
"Song Games from Connecticut." *JAFL* 14: 295–299, 1901.

Barbeau, Charles Marius
Les Enfants Disent. Montreal: Editions Paysana, 1943. 90 pp.
Drawings and music.

Bergen, F. D.
"Pigments used by children in their play."
JAFL 8:151–153, 1895.

Berle, A. A.
"Terms in Playing Marbles." *Dialect Notes* 1 (Part 4) 220.

Bett, Henry
The Games of Children; Their Origin and History. London: Methuen & Co., Ltd., 1929. ix, 131 pp., bibl. (pp. 115–128).

Brewster, Paul G.
"Game-Songs from Southern Indiana." *JAFL* 49:243–263, 1936.

Brown, Florence, and Boyd, Neva L.
Old English and American Games for School and Playground. Chicago: FitzSimons, 1917.

Chamberlain, A.
"Folklore of Canadian Children." *JAFL* 8: 252, 1895.

Chase, Richard, ed.
Old Songs and Singing Games. Chapel Hill: University of North Carolina Press, 1938. xii, 52 pp., music.
Graded material for schools, suitable for children and adults.

Clark, A. M. L.
"Games of Children in Lancaster, Massachusetts." *JAFL* 10:325–326, 1897.

Columbia Broadcasting Company. American School of the Air.
Children's Rhymes and Game Songs. The First in the Series: "Well Springs of Music." Alan Lomax, Commentator. Saturday, March 1, 1941. MS.
Appropriate rhymes and music was used.

Combs, J. H., and Palmer, Rev. F. L.
"Marbles: A Word List." *Dialect Notes* 5 (Part 5):186–188, 1922.

Cox, John Harrington
"Singing Games." *SFQ* 6:183–261, 1942.
Descriptive music and verses of 40 from West Virginia.

Craddock, I. C.
"Tale of the Wild Cat, a Child's Game." *JAFL* 10:322–324, 1897.

Crawford, C.
Folk Dances and Games with piano accompaniment. New York: A. S. Barnes & Co., 1908. ix, 82 pp.

Culin, Stewart
"Street Games of Boys in Brooklyn, New York." *JAFL* 4:221–237, 1891.

Darby, Loraine
"Ring Games from Georgia." *JAFL* 30:218–221, 1917.

"Diffusion of Song-Games."
JAFL 6:96, 1893.

Douglas, Norman
London Street Games. London: The St. Catherine Press, 1916.

Farnsworth, C. H., and Sharp, Cecil J.
Folksongs, Chanteys, and Singing Games. New York: Gray Co., 1916.

Federal Writers' Project.
"Children's Singing Games." *Nebraska Folklore Pamphlets* 7. Lincoln, Nebraska: Federal Writers' Project, 1937 (June 1).

"Florida Song-Games."
JAFL 15:193–195, 1902.

Flowers, Paul
"Rhymes, Songs and Ditties." *TFSB* 10:7–9, 1944.
Texts only of dances and games.

Gilchrist, Anne G.
"Some English and Scottish Folk-Dances Surviving Amongst Children." *JEFDS* 4 (No. 2): 1931.
Music, and discussion of American variants.

Gomme, Alice Bertha
Children's Singing Games. London: David Nutt, 1894. 2 volumes.

————.
Old English Singing Games. London: George Allen, 1900.

————.
The Traditional Games of England, Scotland, and Ireland. With tunes, singing and rhymes, and methods of playing according to the variants extant and recorded in different parts of the Kingdom. Collected and annotated by A. B. Gomme. London: David Nutt, 1894 and 1898. 2 volumes.

Gomme, Sir George Lawrence
British Folk-Lore, Folk-Songs and Singing Games. London: National Homereading Union, 1916. 31 pp., bibl.

Grahame, Pauline
"School-Day Games." *The Palimpsest* (The State Historical Society of Iowa) 10:68–81, 1919.

Haavio, Elsa
The Game of Rich and Poor, a comparative study in traditional singing games. Helsinki: Suomakainen tiedeakatemia, 1932. 342 pp., bibl.

Halden, Ch.
"Chansons Populaires et Jeux Enfantines au Canada." *La Quinzaine* (Paris) 68:78–110, 1906.
Folk Songs and Children's Games in Canada.

Hall, Ida B.
"Pioneer Children's Games." *TFSP* 17:141–151, 1941.

Heck, Jean O.
"Folk Poetry and Folk Criticism as Illustrated by Cincinnati Children in their Singing Games." *JAFL* 40:1–77, 1927.

Henry, Mellinger E.
"Nursery Rhymes and Game Songs from Georgia." *JAFL* 47:334–340, 1934.

Hofer, Mari Ruef
Popular Folk Games and Dances. Chicago: A. Flanagan & Company, 1907.

————.
Children's Singing Games, Old and New. Chicago: A. Flanagan & Company, 1901.

Hornby, John
The Joyous Book of Singing Games. New York: The Macmillan Company, 1914.

Jeffries, Charles
"White Comanches." *TFSP* 19:117–125, 1944.
Texan children's sports.

Johnson, C. E.
Education by Plays and Games. New York: Ginn and Co., 1907.

Johnson, Edna, and Scott, Carrie E.
Anthology of Children's Literature. Illustrated by N. C. Wyeth. Boston: Houghton Mifflin Company, 1935. xxix, 917 pp.
Contains Mother Goose Rhymes, Nonsense Verse, Fables, Folktales, Legends, and bibliography after each section.

Jones, Joseph
"More on Marble Names and Games." *AS* 10 (No. 2):158–159, 1935.

Krehbiel, Henry Edward
"Southern Song Games," Articles No. 1–2. 1. How Florida "Crackers" dance without offence to their religious notions—Kissing games at Royal Courts and in rural communities. 2. Contributions from Washington and New Orleans, melody and variants of "The needle's eye." *Clippings from The New York Daily Tribune:* Sunday, July 27, and August 3, 1902.

La Salle, Dorothy
Play Activities for Elementary Schools. New York: A. S. Barnes and Co., 1929.

McDowell, Mrs. L. L.
"Games of Long Ago." *TFSB* 10 (No. 3) 1–4, 1944.
Verses and description of children's games, rhymes and riddles of Tennessee.

McGhee, Z.
"A Study in the Play Life of Some South Carolina Children." *Pedagogical Seminary* (Worcester) 7:457–478, 1900.

Newell, William Wells
Games and Songs of American Children. New York: Harper and Brothers, 1884, 1911. xii, 242 pp.
Some melodies are harmonized. Still among the best books on the subject.

————.
"Primitive Marriage Customs as Preserved in the Games of Children." *JAFL* 5:70–71, 1892.

Newton, Marion Bromley
Graded Games and Rhythmic Exercises for Primary Schools. New York: A. S. Barnes & Company, 1908.

Ovington, M.
"Dance-Rhyme of Children in Brooklyn, New York." *JAFL* 12:293–294, 1899.

Petrone, Lucille
"Children's Singing Games from the Newark, New Jersey Playgrounds." *National Recreation Association,* Miscellaneous Bulletin. 817, Nov., 1939.
4 singing games with texts and melodies.

Porter, Grace Cleveland
Negro Folk Singing Games and Folk Games of the Habitants. Traditional melodies and text transcribed by Author. London: J. Curwen & Sons, Ltd., 1914. xix, 35 pp., illus. Accompaniments by H. W. Loomis.

Pullen, C. L.
"A Rhyme for Divination by Means of Apple-Seeds." *JAFL* 2:71, 1889.

Pyrnelle, L. C.
"Florida Song-Games." *JAFL* 15:193–195, 1902.

Rural Recreation for Kentucky.
National Youth Administration for Kentucky, November, 1938.
Children's games.

Skeel, M. H.
"Version of Game of Child-Stealing Witch." *JAFL* 3:315, 1890.

Smith, Charles E.
Games and Game Leadership. New York: A. S. Barnes and Co., 1932.

Smith, Winifred
"A Modern Child's Game Rhymes." *JAFL* 39:82, 1926.

Social Plays, Games, Marches, Old Folk Dances, and Rhythmic Movements for Use in Indian Schools. Washington, D. C.: U. S. Government Printing Office, 1911.

Spenney, Susan D.
"Riddles and Ring-Games from Raleigh, North Carolina." *JAFL* 34:110–115, 1921.

Starr, F.
"Page of Child Lore." *JAFL* 4:55, 1891.

Stealey, Mary Catherine
"Singing Games from Clarksburg, West Virginia." *National Recreation Association, Miscellaneous Bulletin* 518, Oct., 1938.
Two singing games with texts, melodies and description of action.

Udal, J. S.
"Dorsetshire Children's Games." *Folk-Lore* (London) 7:202, 1889.

"Virginia Children's Song Games."
JAFL 3:288–290, 1890.

Walter, L. E.
Old English Singing Games. London: A. & C. Black, Ltd., 1926.

Whiting, J. D.
"Unprinted Game Song." *JAFL* 2:238, 1889.

Williams, Talcott
"A Game of Children in Philadelphia." *JAFL* 12:292, 1899.

Yoffie, Leah Rachel Clara
"Three Generations of Children's Singing Games in St. Louis." *JAFL* 60:1–51, 1947.
"This study . . . has shown that the children of fifty years ago played more of the traditional games of England than children do to-day. The influence of kindergarten and elementary school instruction on games and dances has helped to preserve some of these old games, but most of those which have not been sustained by this influence have died out and been forgotten. New song-games have taken their place, some being adaptations of the old ones, and other being creations growing out of a changed environment." (The author.)

Zuger, John A.
"Technical Terms in the Game of Marbles." *AS* 9 (No. 1):74–74, 1934.

COLLECTIONS

Bancroft, Jessie H.
Games for the Playground, Home, School and Gymnasium. New York: The Macmillan Co., 1937. Rev. and enl. ed. ix, 685 pp., front., illus., plates.
Includes songs with music.

Barnett, Cecille J.
Games, Rhythms, Dances. Oshkosh, Wisconsin: State Teachers College, 1941.

Beard, Daniel Carter
For Playground, Field and Forest: The Outdoor Handy Book. New York: Scribner's Sons, 1912. xvi, 496 pp., illus.

Brown, F. W., and Boyd, N. L.
Old English and American Games. Chicago: Saul Brothers, 1915.

Burchenal, Elizabeth
Folk Dances and Singing Games. New York: G. Schirmer and Co., 1909–22.
Twenty-six folk dances of Norway, Sweden, Denmark, Russia, Bohemia, Hungary, Italy, England, Scotland, and Ireland, with the music, full directions for performance, and numerous illustrations. Vol. II, Dances of the people, a second volume of folk dances and singing games, containing 27 folk-dances from Belgium, Czecho-Slovakia, Denmark, England, Finland, France, Germany, Ireland, Lithuania, Poland, Portugal, Russia, Spain, Sweden, and the United States. Vol III: Folk Dances from old homelands, a third volume of folk dances and singing games from Belgium, Czecho-Slovakia, Denmark, England, Finland, France, Germany, Ireland, Lithuania, Poland, Portugal, Russia, Spain, Sweden and the United States. Piano arrangements by Emma Howells Burchenal.

Chase, Richard
Old Songs and Singing Games. Chapel Hill, N. C.: University of North Carolina Press, 1938.

Children's Games.
Siegmeister, E.: MS: SATB, a cap.

Children's Singing Games.
Sets I–V, (books 198, 199, 227–9). London: Novello & Company, 1909–1912.

Elsom, James Claude, and Trilling, Blanche M.
Social Games and Group Dancing; a collection of games and dances suitable for community and social use. Introduction by Professor M. V. O'Shea. Philadelphia: J. B. Lippincott Co., 1927. 314 pp., 2nd ed., rev., and enl.
Contains music for the dances; bibl. pp. 305–309.

Farnsworth, C. H., and Sharp, Cecil J.
Folk Songs, Chanteys and Singing Games. New York: n.d. voice and piano.

Forsythe, Clarence
Old Songs for Young Americans. Harmonized by C. Forsythe, decorated by B. Ostertag. New York: Doubleday, Page and Co., 1901. 46 pp.
"Especially arranged for little piano players."

Gomme, Alice Bertha
Old English Singing Games. Dedicated to all children throughout Her Majesty's dominions. Illustrated by E. Harwood. London: G. Allan, 1900. 56 pp., illus.

————, coll.
The Traditional Games of England, Scotland and Ireland, with tunes, singing rhymes, and methods of playing according to the variants extant and recorded in different parts of the kingdom. London: D. Nutt, 1894–98. 2 vols., illus. (incl. music) bibl.
Contents: I. Accroshay-Nuts in May; II. Oats and Beans-Would you Know; together with a memoir on the study of children's games. Annotated.

Gosset, A. L. J.
Lullabys and Baby Songs. New York: 1900.

Hofer, Mari Ruef
Children's Singing Games, Old and New, for vacation schools, playgrounds, school-yards, kindergartens, and primary grades. Chicago: A. Flanagan Co., 1914. rev. and enl. ed.
Includes music.

Johns, Altona (Trent), arr.
Play Songs of the Deep South; illustrated by James A. Porter. Washington, D. C.: The Associated Publishers, 1944. 33 pp., illus.
With piano accompaniment, and directions for dancing.

Kidson, Frank, and Moffat, Alfred
Eighty Singing Games. London: Bayley and Ferguson, 1907.

Lovett, James D'Wolf
Old Boston Boys and the Games They Played. Boston: Privately Printed at the Riverside Press, 1906.

Marsh, Chester Geppert
Singing Games and Drills; for rural schools, playground, workers, and teachers. Illustrations from photographs by Edward Watson. New York: A. S. Barnes and Co., 1925. ix, 162 pp.
Contains music.

Newell, William Wells
Games and Songs of American Children. New York: Harper & Brothers, 1883, new and enlarged edition 1903.
Some of the melodies are harmonized.

North, Robert
Town and Country Games. Illustrated by Garry Mackenzie. New York: Thos. Y. Crowell Co., 1947. 224 pp.
Also includes singing games.

Potter, Edna
This Way and That; a book of singing games. Illustrated by the author. New York: Oxford University Press, 1930. 52 pp.

Quilter, Roger
A Children's Overture. Founded on Nursery Rhymes, op. 17. London: Chappell & Co., 1921. Based on traditional game songs and nursery rhymes; such as—"Boys and Girls, Come out to Play," "I Saw Three Ships Go Sailing By," "Sing a Song of Sixpence," "Over the Hills and Far Away," "A Frog He Would A-Wooing Go," and "Here We Go Round the Mulberry Bush." Also arranged for piano solo, and for band.

Russell, Martha Stockton
Swing, Swing, Play; How to Do It; Illustrated with fifty-eight folk songs. . . . New York: The Viking Press, 1938. 93 pp.
Arranged for voice and piano.

Songs for the Little Ones at Home.
New York: American Tract Society, 1884.

Sperling, Harry
The Playground Book. New York: A. S. Barnes and Co., 1929. vi, 105 pp., illus.
Includes music.

The Spanish American Song and Game Book.
New York: A. S. Barnes, 1942. 87 pp.
Spanish and English texts, some songs with music and directions.

Wessells, Katherine Tyler, ed. and arr.
Singing Games. Illustrated by Corinne Malvern. New York: Simon and Schuster, 1947. 42 pp.
17 games arranged for voice and piano with directions for the games. No. 40 of the little Golden Library.

Wier, Albert Ernest
Songs the Children Love to Sing. New York: D. Appleton & Company, 1916.

────────
The Book of a Thousand Songs. New York: D. Appleton and Co., 1918.

Wollaston, Mary A.
The Song Play Book; Singing games for children; edited by C. Ward Crampton. New York: A. S. Barnes and Co., 1917. vii, 61 pp.

Wood, Clement, and Goddard, Gloria
The Complete Book of Games. Illustrated with over one hundred diagrams. New York: Halcyon House, 1938. 894 pp.

PLAY RHYMES
A. Nursery Rhymes

GENERAL STUDIES

Bett, Henry
Nursery Rhymes and Tales; their origin and history. London: Methuen & Co., Ltd., 1924. ix, 130 pp.

Chambers, Robert
Popular Rhymes of Scotland. London: W. R. Chambers, 1870. viii, 400 pp.

Cole, Pamela McArthur
"Old Nursery Rhymes." *JAFL* 13:230–231, 1900.

Eckenstein, Lina
Comparative Studies in Nursery Rhymes. London: Duckworth & Co., 1906. vi, 231 pp., bibl.

Faithfull, R. C., et al.
"Nursery Rhymes and the English Language." *Spectator* (London) 137:684–685, 726, April 16 et seq. 1927.

Foley, Martha
"Mother Goose—The Inside Story! Nursery Rhymes Haven't Always Been so Innocent. Once They Were Dynamite." *New York Herald Tribune Magazine:* 17, 1941, September 14th.

Green, Percy B.
A History of Nursery Rhymes. London: Greening & Co., 1899. xvi, 195 pp.

Halliwell, J. O., editor
The Nursery Rhymes of England. Collected principally from oral tradition. London: Percy Society, 1842. viii, 192 pp.

Halsey, Rosalie Vrylina
Forgotten Books of the American Nursery; a history of the development of the American story-book. Boston: C. E. Goodspeed & Co., 1911. viii, 244 pp.

Henry, Mellinger E.
"Nursery Rhymes and Game-Songs from Georgia." *JAFL* 47:334–341, 1934.

Knapp, F. B.
"A Nursery Yarn." *JAFL* 8:327, 1895.

Newell, William Wells
"Nursery Rhymes from Maine." *JAFL* 4:269–270, 1891.

"Nursery Rhyme, English in Alabama." *JAFL* 32:399, 1919.

"Nursery Rhyme from Maine." *JAFL* 55:269–270, 1942.

"Nursery Rhyme, House That Jack Built." *JAFL* 11:202–212, 1898.

"Nursery Rhyme, Old New England." *JAFL* 13:230–231, 1900.

Perrault, Charles
Histories or Tales of Past Times Told by Mother Goose with Morals. Written in French by Perrault and Englished by G. M. Gent. Newly edited by J. Saxon Childers. London: The Nonesuch Press, 1925. 128 pp., illus.

Rolland, Eugene
Rimes et Jeux de L'enfance. Paris, Maisonneuve et Cie., 1883. iii, 395 pp.
Les Litteratures populaires de toutes les nations.—t. xiv.

Schultz, J. R.
"Nursery Rime Variants." *AS* 8 (No. 2):70, 1933.
Two interesting variants of "This Little Pig Went to the Market."

Whiting, J. D.
"Johnny Cake" (Nursery tale). *JAFL* 2:217–218, 1889.

———.
"Three Jolly Welshmen" (Nursery rhyme). *JAFL* 3:242–243, 1890.

Wilson, Marguerite Ivins
"Yours Till ———." *Utah Humanities Review* 1 (No. 3):245–260, 1947.
A study of children's autograph rhymes in Utah. The collection and examples have been contributed by students of the fifth, sixth, seventh and eighth grades in various parts of the state of Utah. A most fruitful and exciting field for further research and comparison.

COLLECTIONS

Bertail, Inez, ed. and arr.
Complete Nursery Song Book. Illustrated by Walt Kelly. New York: Lothrop, Lee and Shepard Co., 1947. 152 pp., illus.
A treasury of childhood rhymes and music. 170 songs, simple piano accompaniments, 200 full-color illustrations.

Betts, Ethel Franklin
Familiar Nursery Jingles, with illustrations in colors and in black and white. New York: Frederick A. Stokes Co., 1908. ix, 54 pp., illus.

Chambers, Robert
Popular Rhymes of Scotland. London: W. and R. Chambers, 1870. New and enl. ed. viii, 400 pp.
Children's songs and nursery rhymes.

Champlain, John Denison, and Bostwick, Arthur E.
The Young Folk's Cyclopoedia of Games and Sports. New York: Henry Holt & Company, 1890.
Traditional Games and Nursery Rhymes.

Cummins, Dorothy Berliner
Lullabies of Many Lands.... Illustrated by Nellie Farnam. New York: Harper & Brothers, 1941. 72 pp., illus.

Dykema, Peter W.
Fifty Nursery Songs and Games, Traditional Melodies. Phila: Presser and Co.

Elliot, J. W.
Mother Goose's Nursery Rhymes. Set to music by J. W. Elliot. New York: McLoughlin Brothers, 1890. 110 pp.

Fish, Helen D.
Four and Twenty Blackbirds—Nursery Rhymes of Yesterday. New York: Stokes, 1937.

Forbes, Edith Emerson, comp.
Favourites of a Nursery of Seventy Years Ago; and some of later date. Boston: Houghton Mifflin Company, 1916. ix, 620 pp., illus.

Fraser, Phyllis
Mother Goose. Illustrated by Miss Elliot. Little Golden Books. New York: Simon and Schuster, 1946. 42 pp.

Fyleman, Rose
Sugar and Spice—A Collection of Nursery Rhymes, New and Old. Illustrated by Janet Laura Scott. Racine, Wisconsin: Whitman Publishing Co., 1935. 61 pp.

———.
Widdy-Widdy-Wurkey, nursery rhymes from many lands. Pictures by Valery Carrick. Oxford: B. Blackwell, 1934. 70 pp., illus.

Gale, Leah, arr.
Nursery Songs. Illustrated by Corinne Malvern. New York: Simon and Schuster for Artists and Writers' Guild, Inc., 1942. 42 pp.
In the series: *The Little Golden Books.* Simple arrangements for voice and piano.

Graham, John
Traditional Nursery Rhymes. London: J. Curwen & Sons, Ltd., 1911.

Halliwell-Phillipps, James Orchard, ed.
The Nursery Rhymes of England, collected principally from oral tradition. London: Printed for the Percy Society by T. Richards, 1842. viii, 192 pp.

———.
Popular Rhymes and Nursery Tales, a sequel to the Nursery Rhymes of England. London: J. R. Smith, 1849. xi, 276 pp.

Hastings, Thomas
The Mother's Nursery Songs. New York: Haven, 1834. 72 pp., music.

Hofer, Mari Ruef
Old Tunes New Rimes and Games for Kindergarten and Primary Grades. Chicago: A. Flanagan Company, 1917. 30 pp., illus.
Contains music.

How, Louis
Nursery Rhymes of New York City. New York: Alfred A. Knopf, 1919. 71 pp.

Hunt, Evelyn
Music Time. New York: The Viking Press, 1947.
"A comprehensive critical collection of the best in modern nursery school music." (Virginia Kirkus.)

Johnstone, Arthur Edward
Ten Mother Goose Jingles. New York: Carl Fischer: Voice and piano.

Lang, Andrew
The Nursery Rhyme Book. Illustrated by L. Leslie Brooke. London: F. Warne and Co., 1898. 298 pp., illus.

Mason, M. H.
Nursery Rhymes and Country Songs. London: Metzler & Company, Ltd., 1878, 1908.

Montgomerie, Nora and William, eds.
Scottish Nursery Rhymes. London: The Hogarth Press, 1947. 151 pp., illus., music.

Mother Goose's Book of Nursery Rhymes and Songs. London: J. M. Dent & Sons, Ltd. New York: E. P. Dutton & Co., 1910. xx, 248 pp. (Everyman's Library).

Mother Goose's Nursery Rhymes, Tales and Jingles. London: Warne and Company, n.d.

Mother Goose Suite.
Guion, D.: Schirmer: orchestra.

Movrat, J. S.
The Second Book of Nursery Rhymes. London: n.d., illustrated. Voice and piano.

Northall, G. F.
English Folk Rhymes; a collection of traditional verses relating to places and persons, customs, superstitions, etc. London: K. Paul, Trench, Trübner and Co., 1892. xii, 565 pp.

Nursery Rhymes.
Illustrated by C. Lovat Fraser. New York: Alfred A. Knopf, 1946. 49 pp.
A new edition of an old favorite whose gay pictures aptly illustrate ageless rhymes.

Nursery Rhymes for Good Children, with xylographic embellishments. London: n.d. (ca. 1840).

Nursery Tales.
Illustrated by Masha. New York: Simon and Schuster, 1946.

Piper, Watty, ed.
Mother Goose Rhymes. Illustrated by Eulalie and Lois L. Lenski. New York: The Platt and Munk Co., 1932. Un-numb. pp.

Powell, Charles
The Poets in the Nursery. Introduction by John Drinkwater. London: John Lane Company, 1920. 79 pp.
Parodies of modern poets, pretended treatment of well known nursery rhymes.

Ride a Cock-Horse, and other nursery rhymes. Illustrated by Mervin Peake. London: Chatto and Windus, 1940. 28 pp., illus.

Rimbault, Edward F.
Nursery Rhymes. London: Cramer, Wood & Company, n.d.

Ritson, Joseph
Gammer Gurton's Garland or, The Nursery Parnassus. London, 1810. Reprinted 1866. 65 pp.

Salmon, Arthur L.
"Some Further Folk-Rhymes." *Gentleman's Magazine* (London) 290:614–620, 1901.

Sharp, Cecil J.
Nursery Songs from the Appalachian Mountains. Arranged with pianoforte accompaniment by Cecil J. Sharp, illustrated by Esther B. Mackinson, in silhouette. London: Novello & Company, cop. 1921–1923. 2 volumes.

——————.
Nursery Songs from the Southern Appalachians. London: Novello & Company.

Sweeney, James Johnson
Three Young Rats, and other rhymes. Drawings by Alexander Calder. New York: C. Valentin, 1944. xviii, 130 pp., illus.

The Margaret Tarrant Nursery Rhyme Book.
Illustrations by Margaret Tarrant. New York: E. P. Dutton Co., 1947.

The Real Mother Goose, Illustrated by Blanche Fisher Wright. Chicago: Rand McNally, 1946. 128 pp. new ed.

Tobitt, Janet Evelyn, comp.
Sing Me Your Song, O! New York: Janet E. Tobbitt, 1941. 64 pp. Unaccom. melodies.

Warner, Lorraine d'Oremieulx, coll.
A Kindergarten Book of Folk Songs. Boston: E. C. Schirmer, 1923. 70 pp.
Arranged for 1 voice and piano. *Contents:* 1. Mother Goose, her songs; 2. Songs of the Seasons; 3. Songs for Every day; 4. Dialogues, Games, and Street Calls; 5. Something About Geography; 6. Lullabies and Songs of Festival.

Wier, Albert Ernest
Songs the Children Love to Sing; a collection of more than three hundred songs for mothers and for children of all ages. Arranged for singing or playing. New York: D. Appleton and Company, 1916. 256 pp.

——————.
Songs to Sing to Children; Selected with additions by Albert E. Wier from *New Songs for New Voices,* edited by Louis Untermeyer, and Clara and David Mannes. New York: Harcourt, Brace and Co., 1935. 128 pp.

——————.
Young America's Music. New York: C. Scribner's Sons, 1939. 8 vols.
V. 1. contains cradle songs, nursery rhymes, and musical games; V. 3. folk songs, national songs; v. 5. carols.

Wood, Ray
Mother Goose in the Ozarks. Raywood, Texas: The Author, 1946. Unnumbered, illus.

——————.
The American Mother Goose. New York: Stokes, 1940. xviii, 110 pp.
Verse, game rhymes and counting-out rhymes of children.

PLAY RHYMES
B. Counting Out and Rope-Skipping Rhymes
GENERAL STUDIES

Ashton, J. W.
"Some Jump-Rope Rhymes from Iowa." *JAFL* 52:119–123, 1939.

Bolton, Henry Carrington
The Counting Out Rhymes of Children, their antiquity, origin, and wide distribution. A study in folk-lore. London: E. Stock, 1888. ix, 121 pp., bibl.

Brewster, Paul G.
"Rope-skipping, Counting-out and other Rhymes of Children." *SFQ* 3:173–185, 1939.

"Children's Incantations and Rhymes." *JAFL* 2:113–116, 1889.

"Counting-out Game Variants." *JAFL* 8:255–256, 1895.

"Counting-out Rhymes from New York." *JAFL* 27:325, 1914.

"Counting-out Rhymes from the Southern States." *JAFL* 32:377, 1919.

"Counting out Rhymes in Michigan." *JAFL* 31:521–536, 1918.

Crockett, Dolores N.
"Children's Rhymes from Michigan." *JAFL* 44:116, 1931.

Fife, Austin E.
"Rope Skipping Rhymes Collected at Greensboro, North Carolina." *JAFL* 59:321–322, 1946.

————.
"Two Variants of the 'Charlie Chaplin' Rhyme." *JAFL* 59:532, 1946.
Two Utah variants on the Rope Skipping Rhyme.

Gardner, Emelyn E.
"Some Counting-Out Rhymes in Michigan." *JAFL* 31:91, 1918.

Halpert, Herbert, Lt.
"Skipping Rhymes from Calgary, Alberta." *CFQ* 3:154–155, 1944.

Johnson, Frederick
"More Children Jumping Rhymes." *JAFL* 42:305–306, 1929.

Leon, Alice
"Variants of Counting-out Rhymes." *JAFL* 8:255–256, 1895.

Magill, Jessie A., E. G. H., and The Editor
"Double-Dutch." *The New York Times Magazine:* 15, 1946, April 28.
Three very delightful jump-rope jingles.

Maryott, Florence
"Nebraska Counting-Out Rhymes." *SFQ* 1 (No. 4):39–63, 1937.

McDowell, Kathleen F.
"Jump-Rope Jingles." *The New York Times Magazine:* 1946, April 14.

"Michigan Counting-Out Rhymes." *JAFL* 31:521–436, 1918.

Monroe, Will Seymour
"Counting-out Rhymes of Children." *AA* 6:46–51, 1904, n.s.

Nulton, Lucy
"Jump Rope Rhymes as Folk Literature." *JAFL* 61:53–67, 1948.

Park, Natalie and Helen
"Jump-Rope Rhymes." *CFQ* 1:377, 1942.
Texts of 5 from Berkeley, California.

Porter, Kenneth Wiggins
"Children's Songs and Rhymes of the Porter Family"; Robert Porter, 1828–1910; Ellis K. Porter, 1860–1936. *JAFL* 54:167–175, 1941.

"Rhode Island Counting-out Rhymes." *JAFL* 4:171, 1891.

Sone, Violet West
"Rope-jumping Rhymes." *TFSP* 78:195–199, 1943.

Speroni, Charles
"Some Rope-skipping Rhymes from Southern California." *CFQ* 1:245–252, 1942.

Stockbridge, F. P.
"Anglo-Cymric Score." (Rhode Island Counting-Out Rhyme). *JAFL* 4:171, 1891.

Thompson, D. W.
"Some Pennsylvania Rope-Jumping Rhymes." *JAFL* 47:383–386, 1934.

COLLECTIONS

Counting Rhymes.
Illustrated by Corinne Malvern. New York: Simon and Schuster, 1946.

Petersham, Maud and Mishka
The Rooster Crows: A Book of American Rhymes and Jingles. New York: The Macmillan Company, 1945. 65 pp., illus.
"Here are the counting-out rhymes, the words for the singing games and the rhymed riddles that American boys and girls have said and sung for generations" M.G.D.

Wood, Ray
Peckerwood Rhymes. Beaumont, Texas: Graystone, Press, 1938.
56 texts of children's songs and rhymes, no music.

RECORDS

Album Collections

Folk Songs.
Children Records.   PIC–Vol. 5
Contents: Blue Tail Fly, Funiculi Funicula, Erie Canal, Frère Jacques, Do You Ken John Peel, Oh Susanna.

Lullabies and Rounds.
Pete Seeger, vocal-guitar. 2–10″.   DISC–601

More Uncle Mac's Nursery Rhymes (From Mother Goose Nursery Rhymes.) Uncle Mac with Given Catley, Stanley Riley, the Greenbank Children's Choir and Orchestra.
                                        VI–BC 47
Contents: Boys and Girls Come Out to Play; The Grand Old Duke of York; A Frog He Would A-Wooing Go; Here We Go Looby-Loo; Dance to Your Daddy; Tom, He Was a Piper's Son; Twinkle, Twinkle Little Star; There Was a Little Man; Little Miss Muffett; Little Jack Horner; London Bridge is Falling Down; Mary, Mary, Quite Contrary; Here We Come 'Gathering Nuts in May; The Lion and the Unicorn; The Farmer's in the Dell; Lavender's Blue, Dilly, Dilly; Oh, What Have You Got for Dinner, Mrs. Bond?; Cock-Doodle-Doo; Pussy Cat, Pussy Cat; I Had a Little Nut Tree.

Mother Goose Nursery Rhymes.
Josephine Therese, Marilyn Miller and Bobby Hastings, and piano. VI–BC 33
Contents: Jack and Jill; There Was A Crooked Man; Three Blind Mice; Humpty Dumpty; Sing a Song of Sixpence; The North Wind Doth Blow; Tom, Tom the Piper's Son; Simple Simon; Little Miss Muffet; Mary Had a Little Lamb; Baa, Baa, Black Sheep; Hey Diddle Diddle; Twinkle, Twinkle Little Star; The King of France; Goosey Goosey Gander; Ding Dong Bell; Lucy Lockett; Little Boy Blue; Ride a Cock Horse; Little Tommy Tucker; Hickory Dickory Dock; Georgie Porgie; Old King Cole; See Saw, Margery Daw; Pussy Cat; Peas Porridge Hot; Lazy Mary; The Man in the Moon; Little Jack Horner.

Mother Goose Rhymes.
Frank Luther, vocal. DE–252/4

Mother Goose Songs.
Frank Luther, tenor, and orchestra. DE–CU100

Mother Goose Songs.
Earl Rogers. 2–10″. MU–RR1

Musical Tales Vol. III.
Vocalists and small orchestral ensemble. PIC
Contents: Old MacDonald Had a Farm; Polly Put the Kettle On; Three Blind Mice; We'll All Go A-Singing; Yankee Doodle; Doing the Honkey-Pokey.

Musical Tales.
Children Records. PIC–Vol. 4
Contents: Skip to My Lou, Three Little Kittens, Pop Goes the Weasel, Oh Dear! What Can the Matter Be?, A Frog Went A-Walking.

Noah's Ark—Zoological Tunes.
Henry Hall and B. B. C. Orchestra. 12″.
CO–7347M
Content: 12 old and new nursery rhymes.

Negro Children's Games, Lullabies and Ring Games.
1. "All Hid?" Sung by Hettie Godfrey at Livingston, Ala., 1940. 2. "Little Girl, Little Girl." 3. "Pullin' the Skiff." Led by Ora Dell Graham at Drew, Miss., 1940. 4. "Old Uncle Rabbit." 5. "Sea Lion Woman." Sung by Katherine and Christine Shipp at Byhalia, Miss., 1939. 6. "Ain't Gonna Ring No More." Sung by group at Kirby Industrial School, Atmore, Ala., 1934. 7. "Shortenin' Bread." Led by Ora Dell Graham at Drew, Miss., 1940. In: *Album 4, Library of Congress, Music Division,* 1943. AAFS20 A

Negro Lullabies and Ring Games.
1. "Poor Little Johnny." 2. "Go to Sleep." Sung by Harriet McClintock at Livingston, Ala., 1940. 3. "Rosie." Sung by Mr. and Mrs. Joe McDonald at Livingston, Ala., 1939. 4. "Gon' Knock John Booker to the Low Ground." 5. "Run, Nigger, Run." Sung by Moses (Clear Rock) Platt at Central State Farm, Sugarland, Tex., 1933. In: *Album 4, Library of Congress,* 1943. AAFS20 B

Nursery Days.
Woody Guthrie, vocal-guitar. 3–10″. DISC–605

Nursery Rhymes.
Frank Luther, tenor, and orchestra. DE–CU 101

Nursery Rhymes.
"Two Ton" Baker, vocal-piano. MER–4
Contents: 26 Nursery Rhymes including Baa Baa Black Sheep, Just Like Me, Humpty Dumpty, Little Bo Peep, etc.

Nursery Stories.
Craig McDonnell, vocalist, with introduction by Helen E. Meyers, at the Organ. VI–BC 49
Contents: Owl and the Pussy Cat; The Duck and the Kangaroo; Mr. and Mrs. Spikky Sparrow; The Broom, the Shovel, the Poker and the Tongs; The Jumblies; The Table and the Chair.

Nursery Work Songs.
Woody Guthrie, vocal-guitar. 5–10″. DISC–602

School Days.
Leadbelly, Pete Seeger, Charity Bailey, and Cisco Huston. 3–10″. DISC–604

Singing Games.
The Children Next Door, Madge Tucker, Director. VI–BC 29
Contents: Itiskit, Itasket; I'll give to You a Paper of Pins; London Bridge; Mulberry Bush; The Farmer in the Dell; Oats, Peas, Beans and Barley Grow.

Singing Games.
Victor Orchestra. VI–20806
Contents: London Bridge; Here We Go Round the Mulberry Bush; Soldier Boy; The Muffin Man.

Singing Games.
Victor Orchestra. VI–22759
Contents: Baa, Baa Black Sheep; the Big Gray Cat; Hippity Hop to the Barber Shop; Pussy Cat, Pussy Cat; Ten Little Indians; The Snail; Sally Go Round the Moon; A Hunting We Will Go.

Singing Games.
Victor Orchestra. VI–22760
Contents: Hickory Dickory Dock; Ride a Cock Horse; Yankee Doodle; Sing a Song of Sixpence; The Thread Follows the Needle.

Singing Games.
Victor Orchestra. VI–22761
Contents: Bean Porridge Hot; Dutch Coupler.

Songs and Singing Games.
Earl Rogers, tenor. 2–10″. MU–RR4

Songs for Children.
Erva Giles, soprano-piano. VI–20212

Songs for Children.
Ann Howard, soprano, with Myrtle C. Eaver, piano. VI–20621
Contents: Sing a Song of Sixpence; I Love Little Pussy; Pussy Cat, Pussy Cat; Dickory, Dickory Dock; Diddle, Diddle Dumpling; Wee Willie Winkie; Bean Porridge Hot; Three Little Mice; Jack and Jill; Feast of Lanterns.

Songs for Little People.
Lewis James, vocal-orchestra. 3–10″.
VI–22133/5

Songs to Grow On—Lullabies and Rounds.
Pete Seeger, and others. 2–10″.   DISC–601

32 Children's Songs.
Frank Luther, vocal.   DE–1003/5

Traditional Nursery Rhymes and Folk Songs.
Annette Blackwell, vocal-piano.   CO–DB 706

Uncle Mac's Nursery Rhymes.
Uncle Mac and Children's Chorus.   VI–Y3

U. S. Library of Congress. Division of Music.
Folklore Section.
Children's Songs. Gail and Deborah Owen.
AAFS–LC

————.
Colorado Singing Folk Songs, by Mischau
Children of Denver.   AAFS–LC

Individual Titles

"A Frog's Wooing."
Lewis James, vocal.   VI–22134

"Alphabet Song."
James Harkins.   BB–5102

"Alphabet Song."
Lewis James.   VI–22134

"Baa, Baa Black Sheep."
James Harkins.   BB–5270

"Baa, Baa Black Sheep."
Lewis James.   VI–22133

"Baa, Baa Black Sheep."
Josephine Therese, Marylin Miller and Bobby
Hastings.   V–BC–33

"Baa, Baa Black Sheep."
Uncle Mac's Album.   VI–BC–11

"Bimini Gal."
Sung and played by Nassau String Band at
Nassau, Bahamas, 1935. In: *Album 5, Library
of Congress,* 1943.   AAFS21 B3

"Calendar Song."
James Harkins.   BK–Z

"Ding Dong Dell."
In: *Uncle Mac's Nursery Rhymes.* Uncle Mac,
Children's Chorus and orchestra.   VI–BC 11

"Don't Lie Buddy" (Answer Back Song).
Josh White, Lead Belly, vocal-guitar.
ASCH–432–3A

"Fox Chase."
Played on the harmonica by Sanders Terry of
Durham, N. C. In: *Album 4,* Library of Con-
gress, 1943.   AAFS19 B

"Georgie Porgie."
James Harkins, vocal.   BB–5102

"Georgie Porgie."
Lewis James, vocal.   VI–22134

"Goosey, Goosey Gander."
James Harkins, vocal.   BK–3

"Goosey, Goosey Gander."
Josephine Therese, Marylin Miller, Bobby
Hastings.   V–BC 33

"Goosey, Goosey Gander."
Uncle Mac, Children's Chorus and Orchestra.
VI–BC 11

"Gwan Roun', Rabbit."
Sung by Anne Williams and group of Dundee,
Miss., 1942. In: *Album 9,* Library of Congress.
AAFS45 B3

"Hallie Rock" (Jumping Dance).
Sung with drum by group at Nassau, Bahamas,
1935. In: *Album 5, Library of Congress,* 1943.
AAFS21 B2

"Hey Diddle Diddle."
Mixed Quartet, piano.   BB–7851

"Hey Diddle Diddle."
Josephine Therese, Marylin Miller and Bobby
Hastings.   B–BC 33

"Hickory Dickory Dock."
Lewis James, vocal.   VI–22133

"Hickory Dickory Dock."
Josephine Therese, Marylin Miller, Bobby
Hastings.   VI–BC 33

"Hickory Dickory Dock."
In: Uncle Mac's Album.   VI–BC 11

"Humpty Dumpty."
James Harkins, vocal.   BB–5102

"Humpty Dumpty."
Lewis James, vocal.   VI–22134

"Humpty Dumpty."
Uncle Mac, Children's Chorus and Orchestra.
VI–BC 11

"I Don't Mind the Weather."
Sung by Jim Henry at State Penitentiary,
Parchman, Miss., 1937. In: *Album 4, Library
of Congress,* 1943.   AAFS16 A1

"Jack and Jill."
James Harkins, vocal.   BB–5102

"Jack and Jill."
Lewis James, vocal.   VI–22133

"Jack and Jill."
Josephine Therese, Marilyn Miller, Bobby
Hastings.   VI–BC 33

"Jack and Jill."
In: *Uncle Ned's Nursery Rhymes.*   VI–BC 11

"Jack Be Nimble."
Lewis James, vocal.   VI–22134

"Little Bo-Beep."
Lewis James, vocal.   VI–22133

"Little Bo-Beep."
Mixed Quartet, piano.   BB–7851

"Little Bo-Beep."
Josephine Therese, Marilyn Miller, Bobby
Harkins.   VI–BC 33

"Little Bo-Beep."
In Album: *Uncle Mac's Nursery Rhymes.*
Uncle Mac, Children's Chorus and Orchestra.
VI–BC 11

"Little Boy Blue."
Lewis James, vocal.   VI–22134

"Little Rosa Lee."
Sung by Eva Grace Boone and group at Brandon, Miss., 1937. In: *Album 9, Library of Congress.*   AAFS45 B2

"Little Sally Walker."
Sung by Eva Grace Boone and group at
Brandon, Miss., 1939. In: *Album 9, Library of
Congress.*   AAFS45 A2

"Little Tommy Tucker."
Clifford Johns.   BB–6159

"Little Tommy Tucker."
J. Therese, M. Miller and B. Hastings.
VI–BC 33

"London Bridge is Falling Down."
Lewis James, vocal.   VI–22133

"Lost John."
Played on the harmonica by Sanders Terry of
Durham, N. C. Recorded in New York in 1938
by Alan and Bess Lomax. In: *Album 4, Library
of Congress,* 1943.   AAFS19 A

"Mistress Mary."
James Harkins, vocal.   BB–5102

"Mistress Mary."
Lewis James, vocal.   VI–22134

"Old King Cole."
James Harkins, vocal.   BB–5102

"Old Lady Sittin' in the Dining Room."
Sung by Eva Grace Boone and group at
Brandon, Miss., 1939. In: *Album 9, Library of
Congress.*   AAFS45 2

"Old Mother Hubbard."
Clifford Johns, vocal.   BB–6159

"Polly, Put the Kettle On."
Lewis James, vocal.   VI–22134

"Polly, Put the Kettle On."
In: *Uncle Mac's Nursery Rhymes.* VI–BC 11

"Ride a Cock Horse."
Lewis James, vocal.   VI–22134

"Ride a Cock Horse."
J. Therese, M. Miller, B. Hastings, Miller.
VI–BC 33

"Ring a Ring of Roses."
James Harkins, vocal.   BK–2

"Ring a Ring of Roses."
In: *Uncle Mac's Nursery Rhymes.* VI–BC 11

"Robin Sing for Me."
Clifford Johns, vocal.   BB–6159

"Rock-a-Bye Baby."
Ruth Rodgers, soprano-orchestra.   VI–22617

"Sail, Gal" (Ring Game).
Led by Elizabeth Austin at Old Bight, Cat
Island, Bahamas, 1935. In: *Album 5, Library
of Congress,* 1943.   AAFS21 B1

"Satisfied."
Sung by Anne Williams and group of Dundee,
Miss., 1942. In: *Album 9, Library of Congress.*
AAFS45 B4

"See-Saw Margery Daw."
Mixed Quartet with piano.   BB–7851

"Simple Simon."
James Harkins.   BB–5102

"Sing a Song of Sixpence."
James Harkins.   BB–5102

"Sing a Song of Sixpence."
Lewis James, vocal.   VI–22134

"Sing a Song of Sixpence."
J. Therese, M. Miller and B. Hastings.
VI–BC 33

"Sing a Song of Sixpence."
In Album: *Uncle Mac's Nursery Rhymes.*
Uncle Mac, Children's Chorus and orchestra.
VI–BC 11

"Sissy in the Barn."
Sung by Eva Grace Boone and group at
Brandon, Miss., 1937. In: *Album 9, Library of
Congress.*   AAFS45 B1

"The Dog and the Cat."
Clifford Johns.   BB–6159

"The Farmer in the Dell" (Singing Game).
Victor Band.   VI–21618

"The Mulberry Bush."
In Album: *Uncle Mac's Nursery Rhymes.*
Uncle Mac; Children's Chorus and orchestra.
VI–BC 11

"Twinkle Little Star."
Mixed Quartet with piano.   BB–7851

"We're Goin' Around the Mountains."
Sung by Eva Grace Boone and group at
Brandon, Miss., 1937. In: *Album 9, Library of
Congress.*   AAFS45 A1

"Winnie the Pooh and Christopher Robin."
Frank Luther, vocal.   DE–1447/9

Part Two: Regional Bibliography

THE NORTHEAST

THE NORTHEAST

FOLKLORE

BIBLIOGRAPHY

A Bibliography of New England (a yearly compilation). In the March (No. 1) issues of *The New England Quarterly*. Has a section on: "Literature and Folklore."

Beach, R. F.
Outdoor New England: books on trails, woods, and mountains. New Haven: New England Trail Conference, 1936. 14 pp.

Boston Public Library.
The Prince Collection. A catalogue of books and manuscripts which formerly belonged to the Rev. Thomas Prince, and was by him bequeathed to the Old South Church, and is now deposited in the public library of the city of Boston. Boston: A. Mudge & Son, city printers, 1870. xvi, 160 pp. Part I (Americana) was issued separately in 1868.

Forbes, A. B.
"Bibliography of New England." *New England Quarterly* 12:181–195, (March) 1939.

Forbes, Mrs. Harriette (Merrifield)
New England Diaries, 1602–1800; a descriptive catalogue of diaries, orderly books and sea journals. Topsfield, Mass.: Perkins, 1923. viii, 439 pp.

Historical Records Survey, Mass.
Guide to the Manuscript Collections in the Worcester Historical Society. Prepared by the Historical Records Survey, Division of community service programs, works project administration. Boston, Mass.: The Historical Records Survey, 1941. iii, 54 pp.

Massachusetts Historical Society, Boston. Library.
Catalogue of Books in The Massachusetts Historical Library. Boston: Printed by S. Hall, No. 53, Cornhill, 1796.

Morrison, Hugh Alexander
Preliminary Check List of American Almanacs, 1639–1800. Washington, D. C.: U. S. Government Printing Office, 1907. 160 pp.

Nichols, Charles Lemuel
"Checklist of Maine, New Hampshire and Vermont Almanacs." *American Antiquarian Society, Proceedings,* 38:63–163, 1929, n.s.

Palmer, Waldo (comp.)
General Index to volumes I to X (1928–1937) of *The New England Quarterly.* An Historical Review of New England Life and Letters. Boston: The New England Quarterly, 1941. 224 pp.

Rochester, N. Y. Museum of Arts and Sciences.
Almanacs Now in Possession of the Rochester Museum of Arts and Sciences. Rochester, N. Y., 1935. 24 pp.

PERIODICALS

A Handbook of New England; an annual publication. No. 1. 1916– . Boston, P. E. Sargent.

Bulletin of the Folk Song Society of the Northeast. Cambridge, Mass., 1930–1937. (No. 1–12).

Bickerstaff, Isaac
The Rhode Island Almanack, for the Year of Our Lord Christ. . . . Providence, R. I. Printed and sold by Brown & Danforth.

Dickinson, Samuel N.
The Old American Comic Almanac, with Whims, Scraps and Oddities from the Land of Johnny Bull, Brother Jonathan and Mons. Nontongpaw. Boston. No. 1, 1839.

Leavitt's Farmer's Almanack, Improved, and Miscellaneous Year Book. . . . Calculations as to Latitude and Longitude, as to answer for all the New England States . . . by Dudley Leavitt. Concord, N. H.: From the Mirror Press of Russell & Davis, Printers, etc. 1797–

> *Title varies:* 1797– ; The New England Calendar, Almanack. The Scholar's Almanack and Farmer's Daily Register. The New England Almanack. Published on a new Principle. 18–22: Leavitt's Genuine, Improved New England Farmer's Almanack and Agricultural Register. 1823: Leavitt's Genuine, Improved New England Farmer's Almanack and Scholar's Diary. 1824–25: Leavitt's New England Farmer's Almanack. 1826– : Leavitt's Improved New England Scholar's Almanack. 1831–32: Leavitt's, The Improved Farmer's and Scholar's Almanack. 1833–39: Leavitt's, The New England Farmer's and Scholar's Almanack, on an Improved Plan. 1840–44: The New England Almanack, on an Improved Plan. 1845–47: The New England Farmer's Almanack, on an Improved Plan. 1848: Leavitt's Improved New England's Farmer's Almanack and Year Book. 1849: The Farmer's Almanack. 1850–75: Leavitt's Almanack and Miscellaneous Year Book. 1876– : Leavitt's Farmer's Almanack, Improved, and Miscellaneous Year Book.

Magazine of New England History. V. 1–3. Newport, R. I., 1891–1893.

New England Magazine; an illustrated monthly. Boston. 1–6, Jan. 1884–Oct. 1888; n.s. V. 1–56 No. 6, Sept. 1889–Mar. 1917.

Shaw, Henry Wheeler
Josh Billings' Farmer's Allminax, 1870—New York: G. W. Carlton, 1870—.
> Ceased publication about 1880.

The American Almanac and Repository of Useful Knowledge for—1830-1861. V. 1-32. Boston: Gray & Bowen, etc.—1829-1861. 32 vols.

The Farmers' Almanack, for the Year of our Lord, 1799: Being the Third Year after Bissextile, or Leap Year: and the Twenty Third of American Independence. Adapted to the District of Maine. Calculated for the Meridian of Portland. Lat. 43 deg. 43 min. North. But will answer for any of the Northern States. Printed at Portland, Me.: Baker & George, 1798. 36 pp.

The Farmers and Mechanics Almanac, for the Year of our Lord—New York: Moffat's Vegetable Life Pills and Phoenix Bitters.

The National Comic Almanac for the Year 1836, Calculated for Each State in the Union with Humorous Stories and Anecdotes. Mass.: Published by the President of the American Eating Club.

The New England Almanac, and Farmer's Friend. V. 1, 1860—New London, Bridgeport (1890-).

The New-England Farmer's Almanac, for the Year of the Christian Era—. Claremont, New Hampshire: The Claremont Manufacturing Co.

The New England Quarterly; an Historical Review of New England Life and Letters. V. 1, Jan. 1928—. Baltimore: The Williams & Wilkins Company.
Includes section "Bibliography."

The "New England River Series" Manchester, N. H.: Standard Book Co.

Thomas, Robert B.
The (Old) Farmer's Almanack, Calculated on a New and Improved Plan, for the Year of our Lord 1797—. Boston: Jenks Palmer & Co.

Thomas's Massachusetts, Connecticut, Rhode Island, New Hampshire & Vermont Almanack. 1797—. Worcester, Mass.: Printed for Isaiah Thomas.

Turner's Comick Almanack for 1840, Correctly Calculated for the Whole United States and Territories. Boston: James Fisher. New York and Philadelphia: Turner and Fisher.

Weatherwise's Almanack, for the Year of our Lord 1797. Printed at Boston, and sold by J. Boyle, C. Bingham, B. Larkin, Wm. Pelham, E. Larkin, J. Nancrede, J. West, J. Bumstead, and other Booksellers in Town and Country.

GENERAL STUDIES AND COLLECTIONS

Anon.
"Indian and Yankee." *American Penny Mag.* 1:610, Oct. 25, 1845.
An amusing anecdote emphasizing the ingenuity of the Yankee.

Ashley, Clifford W.
The Yankee Whaler. Boston: Houghton Mifflin Company, 1926.

Barnum, Phineas T.
Funny Stories. London: George Routledge and Sons, Ltd., 1890.

———
Struggles and Triumphs: or, Forty Years' Recollections of P. T. Barnum, written by Himself. Buffalo: Warren, Johnson & Co., 1873.
"The greatest and most 'practical wag' that ever came out of a country store was the Connecticut Yankee, P. T. Barnum." (B. A. Botkin.)

Beckett, Sylvester Breakmore
Guide Book of the Atlantic and St. Lawrence, and St. Lawrence and Atlantic railroads, including a full description of all the interesting features of the White Mountains, with illustrations from original sketches by C. E. Beckett, engraved on wood by Baker, Smith and Andrew Portland: Sanborn & Carter, 1853. vi, 180 pp., illus.

Bernard, John
Retrospections of America, 1797-1811. Edited from the Manuscripts by Mrs. Bayle Bernard. With an Introduction, Notes and Index, by Laurence Hutton and Brander Matthews. New York: Harper & Bros., 1886.

Botkin, B. A., ed.
A Treasury of New England Folklore. New York: Crown Publishers, 1947. xxvi, 960 pp., music.
The stories, legends, tall tales, traditions, and ballads of the salty, funloving Yankees; 500 stories and 50 songs (words and music).

Browne, G. W.
The River of Broken Waters: The Merrimac. (New England River Series). Illustrated by Frank Holland. Manchester, N. H.: Standard Book Co., 1920. 103 pp.
The romance, tradition, history, folklore, scenery, people, literature and industry of "the busiest river in the world."

Burnaby, Dr. Andrew
Travels Through The Middle Settlements in North America in the Years 1759 and 1760, with observations on the state of the Colonies. London: T. Payne, 1775. viii, 106 pp.
The author's travels extended from Virginia to New England.

Burnham, G. P.
Gleanings from the Portfolio of the "Young 'Un," A Series of Humorous Sketches. Boston: R. B. Fitts & Co., 1849.

Burt, Henry Martyn
Burt's Illustrated Guide of the Connecticut Valley, containing descriptions of Mount Holyoke, Mount Mansfield, White Mountains, Lake Memphremagog, Lake Willoughby, Montreal, Quebec, etc. Northampton: New England Publishing Co., 1867. vi, 281 pp., illus.

Calvin, E. E.
A Saga of the St. Lawrence: Timber and Shipping Through Three Generations. Boston: Bruce Humphries, Inc., 1945. 178 pp.

Chamberlain, Samuel
A Small House in the Sun; the visage of rural New England; photographs and comment. New York: Hastings House, 1936. 96 pp., illus.

————.
Beyond New England Thresholds, photographs and comment. New York: Hastings House, 1937. 95 pp., illus.

————.
Ever New England. Introduction by Donald Moffat. New York: Hastings House, 1947.
Although not strictly a folklore book, the 277 full-page photographs speak eloquently and nostalgically of the old traditions of the New England folk.

New England Doorways, photographs and comment. New York: Hastings House, 1939. 101 pp., illus.

————.
Open House in New England; with 217 photographs by the author. Brattleboro, Vt.: Stephen Daye Press, 1937. 191 pp., illus.

Chaplin, H. W.
Five Hundred Dollars, and other stories of New England life. Boston: Little, Brown and Co., 1887. 305 pp.

Colton, Joseph Hutchins
Colton's Traveler and Tourist Guide-Book Through New England and Middle States and the Canadas. Containing the routes and distances . . . by railroads, stage roads, canals, lakes and rivers; together with descriptions of the . . . states, and . . . principal cities, towns, and villages. New York: J. H. Colton, 1850. vii, 94 pp.

Corbett, John
The Lake Country. An annual of olden days in central New York. The land of gold. Rochester, N. Y.: Democrat and Chronicle Print, 1898. 161 pp., illus.
Traditions, legends (Finger Lakes, Indians) and customs.

Crandall, Arthur G.
New England Joke Lore, The Tonic of Yankee Humor. Philadelphia: F. A. Davis Company, 1922.

Currier, J. Mac N.
"Contributions to the Folklore of New England." JAFL 2:291–294, 1889; 4:253–256, 1891; 6:69–70, 1893.

Dame, Lawrence
New England Comes Back, with an Introduction by Stewart H. Holbrook. New York: Random House, 1940.

Dodge, Nathaniel Shatswell
Sketches of New England, or Memories of the Country, by John Carver, esquire (pseud.) justice of the peace and quorum. New York: E. French, 1842. vi, 286 pp.

Drake, Samuel Adams
A Book of New England Legends and Folklore. In Prose and Poetry. Illustrated by F. T. Merrill. Boston: Little, Brown and Co., 1901. xvi, 477 pp., illus.

————.
Nooks and Corners of the New England Coast. New York: Harper and Bros., 1875. 459 pp., illus.

Dwight, Timothy
Travels in New England and New York (1796–1815). New Haven Conn.: T. Dwight, 1821–22. 4 vols.

Early, Eleanor
An Island Patchwork; illus. by Virginia Grilley. Boston: Houghton, Mifflin Co., 1941. vii, 289 pp., illus., map.

————.
A New England Sampler. Boston: Waverly House, 1940. xii, 372 pp., incl. front., illus.

Eaton, E. M.
"Between Chores They Pegged Shoes; Little Shoemaker's Shops in New England Farmyards." *Christ. Science Monthly Magazine* p. 15, Nov. 14, 1942.

Federal Writers' Project
Here's New England! A guide to vacationland, written and compiled by members of the Federal Writers' Project of the Works Progress Administration in the New England States; sponsored by the New England council, Boston. Boston: Houghton Mifflin Co., 1939. vi, 122 pp. (American Guide Series).

————.
Living Lore of New England. Manuscripts of the Federal Writers' Project of the Works Progress Administration for the State of Connecticut.

————.
Manuscripts of the Federal Writers' Project of the Works Progress Administration for the various states. In Folklore Section, Library of Congress.

————.
The Berkshire Hills (American Guide Series) Compiled and written by Workers of the Federal Writers' Project of the Works Progress Administration for the State of Massachusetts. New York: Funk & Wagnalls Co., 1939.

U. S. One: Maine to Florida (American Guide Series) Compiled and Written by the Federal Writers' Project of the Works Progress Administration. With 30 photographs. New York: Modern Age Books, Inc., 1938.

Forbers, Allan, comp.
  Some Indian Events of New England. Boston: State Street Trust Co., 1934.
    A collection of interesting incidents in the lives of the early settlers of this country and the indians; with reproductions of rare prints.

————.
  Other Indian Events of New England. Boston: State Street Trust Co., In Commemoration of its Fiftieth Anniversary. 1941.
    A collection of interesting incidents in the lives of the early settlers and the Indians of this country; with reproductions of old prints and photographs. Vol. II.

Frost, Frances
  Village of Glass. New York: Farrar and Rinehart, 1942.
    A story of old men and old women in New England.

Gould, R. E.
  Yankee Storekeeper. New York: McGraw Hill and Company, 1945.
    Contains a lot of Northeast stuff.

Graham, Ramona
  Hills of New England. Wellesley, Mass.: The Author, 1946. 36 pp.

Hard, Walter
  The Connecticut. Illustrated by Douglas W. Gorsline. (American River Series). New York: Rinehart and Co. 1947. 310 pp.
    The book "is not so much a study of a body of water as it is of the people who dwell along its banks." (T. C. Chubb.)

Harlow, Alvin F.
  Steelways of New England. New York: Creative Age Press, 1946.

Henderson, H. W.
  A Loiterer in New England. New York: G. H. Doran and Co., 1919. 445 pp.

Hopkins, Mark
  Early Letters of Mark Hopkins, and others from his brothers and their mother. A picture of life in New England from 1770–1857. New York: The John Day Company, 1929. 365 pp., illus.

Humphrey, Zephine
  A Book of New England; illustrated by Thomas P. Robinson. New York: Howell, Soskin, 1947. 292 pp.

Huntington, Arria Sargent
  Under a Colonial Roof-Tree; fireside chronicles of early New England. Boston, Mass.: Houghton Mifflin & Co., 1891. 133 pp.
    "An especial purpose of the foregoing collection was to preserve the descriptions of life in his boyhood, taken from letters of the late Theodore G. Huntington." p. 131.

Johnson, Burges
  As Much As I Dare, A Personal Recollection. New York: Ives Washburn, Inc., 1944.
    Rich in gleanings of Yankee life, lore, anecdotes, humor, and speech.

Johnson, Clifton
  Highways and Byways of New England; including the states of Massachusetts, New Hampshire, Rhode Island, Connecticut, Vermont and Maine. New York: The Macmillan Co., 1915. xi, 299 pp.

————.
  New England, A Human Interest Geographical Reader. New York: The Macmillan Company, 1917.

————.
  New England and Its Neighbors. New York: The Macmillan Company. 1902.

Jones, Richard Franc
  Richard Baxter, a story of New England life of 1830 to 1840. Binghampton, N. Y.: Jones of Binghampton, 1904. xiv, 331 pp., illus.

Josselyn, John Gent.
  An Account of Two Voyages to New-England, Made during the years 1638, 1663. Boston: Published by William Veazie, 1865.

Kalm, Per
  Travels Into North America; Containing Its Natural History, and a Circumstancial Account of its Plantations and Agriculture in General, with the Civil, Ecclesiastical and Commercial State of the Country, the Manners of the Inhabitants, and Several Curious and Important Remarks on Various Subjects. Tr. into English by John Reinhold Forster. London: Printed for the Editor. 1770–1771. 3 vols.

Kendall, Edward Augustus
  Travels Through the Northern Parts of the United States, in the Years 1807 and 1808. New York: Printed and Published by I. Riley, 1809. 3 vols.

Kittredge, George Lyman
  The Old Farmer and His Almanack; being some observations on life and manners in New England a hundred years ago, suggested by reading the earlier numbers of Mr. Robert B. Thomas's Farmer's Almanack, together with extracts curious, instructive, and entertaining, as well as a variety of miscellaneous matter. Cambridge: Harvard University Press, 1920. xiv, 403 pp., illus.

Littlefield, Louise (Hall), comp.
  The Triad Anthology of New England Verse. Foreword by Angela Morgan. Portland, Me.: Falmouth Book House, 1938. 166 pp.

Loomis, C. Grant
  "Silvester Judd's New England Lore." *JAFL* 60: 151–158, 1947.
    The author finds in Judd's transcendental novel, *Margaret,* "a storehouse of early lore and language for the folklorist and linguist." Numerous passages are quoted.

Lunt, George, ed.
  Old New England Traits. New York: Hurd and Houghton, 1873. v, 244 pp.
    Reminiscences of old Newburyport.

Marlowe, George Francis
Coaching Roads of Old New England. Their
Inns and Taverns and Their Stories. Illustrations by the Author. New York: The Macmillan Co., 1945. 197 pp., illus.
"A curiosity shop of historical New England
bric-a-brac; and filled with a gentle anthology
of anecdote." (I. Mallet.)

———.
Churches of Old New England. Illustrated by
Samuel Chamberlain. New York: Macmillan
Co., 1947.
Also includes interesting folklore asides—grave-
stone inscriptions, local anecdotes and customs.

Marryat, Frederick Capt.
A Diary in America, with Remarks on Its
Institutions. Philadelphia: Carey & Hart, 1839.
3 vols.

Martineau, Harriet
Society in America. New York: Saunders and
Otley, 1837. 3 vols.

Melville, Herman
Moby Dick: or The Whale. Illustrated by
Rockwell Kent. New York: The Modern
Library, 1930. 823 pp., illus.
On many occasions we read of the seamen's
superstitions and beliefs in White Whales,
omens and legends.

Miles, Mark
"The Yankee." *The Mirror of the Philoma-
thean Society* (Phillips Academy of Andover)
5 (No. 3): 17, 1859.

Mitchell, Edwin Valentine
It's An Old New England Custom. Illustrated.
New York: The Vanguard Press, 1946. 277 pp.
Filled with interesting yarns, anecdotes, epi-
taphs, bundling, and other curoisae.

———.
The Horse & Buggy Age in New England.
New York: Coward-McCann, 1937.

Mixer, Knowlton
Old Houses of New England, with photographs.
New York: The Macmillan Co., 1927. **xx,**
346 pp., illus.

Mussey, June Barrows
Old New England, with hundreds of old engravings. New York: A. A. Wyn, 1946. 127
pp., illus.
The old prints speak eloquently of the lore and
traditions of the people.

———.
Yankee Life. New York: Alfred A. Knopf,
1947. 556 pp., with 93 reproductions of woodcuts and engravings.
New Englanders of three centuries speak for
themselves on how they made the Yankee way
of life—on sea and land, in pulpit, school and
shop. Mr. Mussey has compiled a delightful
anthology that brings to life the plain, everyday
New England of pre-Civil war times.

"New England Folklore" *JAFL* 2:219–294,
1889; 4:253–256, 1891; 6:59–70, 1893.

Parsons, Elsie Clews
Folk-Lore From the Cape Verde Islands. Vol.
15, Parts I and II, of the Memoirs of the
American Folk-Lore Society. Cambridge,
Mass.: Published by the American Folk-Lore
Society, 1923. 373 pp., 267 pp., bibl., tunes.
Part I consists of 133 Folk-Tales in English.
Part II consists of these tales in Portuguese,
(some with tunes), 183 proverbs and sayings (in
Portuguese and English), and 291 riddles. These
tales are from the Portuguese Negro immigrants
of the Cape Verde Islands. They are scattered
through eastern Massachusetts, Rhode Island
and the seaports of Connecticut.

Peattie, Roderick, ed.
The Friendly Mountains. New York: The
Vanguard Press, 1942. 340 pp., illus.
These comprise the Adirondacks of New York,
the White Mountains of New Hampshire, the
Green Mountains and Taconics of Vermont, with
a brief mention of Katahdin in Maine.

Powell, Lyman Pierson, ed.
Historic Towns of New England. New York:
G. P. Putnam's Sons, 1898. xxi, 599 pp., illus.

Prime, W. C.
Along New England Roads. New York: Harper & Brothers, 1892.

Quincy, Josiah
Figures of the Past, from the Leaves of Old
Journals; with an Introduction and Notes by
M. A. De Wolfe Howe. Boston: Little, Brown
and Company, 1926. First published in 1883;
re-issued in 1911.

Shepard, Odell
Pedlar's Progress, The Life of Bronson Alcott.
Boston: Little, Brown and Company, 1937.
Spicy asides and rich insight on Yankee char-
acter and mores.

Simpson, George
Information Roundup: A New Treasury of
Odd and Fascinating Knowledge. New York:
Harper and Brothers, 1948. 587 pp.
Among sundry matters the author also treats
superstitions, beliefs, and other folklore items.

Snow, Edward Rowe
Famous New England Lighthouses. Boston:
The Yankee Publishing Co., 1945. 457 pp.,
map, bibl.

———.
Romance of Boston Bay. Illustrated with old
prints. New York: Tudor Publishing Company, 1945.
Weird, fascinating, mysterious tales of New
England history, sea-lore, and adventure, covering everything from sea serpents to duels in old
castles.

Standard Oil Co. of New York
Historic Tours in Soconyland. New York:
Standard Oil Co. of New York, 1925. 7 pp.,
illus.
Include brief mention of legend, tradition, place
names, and description of cities, towns, and
roads.

Sweester, Moses Foster
Here and There in New England and Canada.
Boston: Passenger Department Boston and
Maine Railroad, 1889. 3 vols. in 1.
    Contents: All along shore. Among the moun-
    tains, lakes and streams.

The Laughing Philosopher: or Fun, Humour,
and Wit; Being a Collection of Choice Anecdotes, Many of Which, Never Before in Print,
Originated in or about "The Literary Emporium." Pittsburgh, Pa.: Published by Cook
and Schoyer. Louisville, Ky.: Maxwell, Cook
and Co., 1834.

The Story of a Father and Son or "Unscrewing
the Inscrutable." Cambridge, Mass.: Elliott
Addressing Machine Company.

Towne, Charles Hanson
Jogging Around New England. New York:
D. Appleton-Century Co., 1939.

Tozzer, Alfred M.
"The Boston and Cambridge Branches, American Folklore Society." *JAFL* 59: 483–484,
1946.

Tudor, William
Letters in the Eastern States. New York: Kirk
and Mercein, 1820. vi, 356 pp.

Verrill, Alpheus Hyatt
The Real Story of the Whaler: Whaling, past
and present. New York: D. Appleton and Co.,
1916. xv, 248 pp., illus.

Webster, Clarence M.
Town Meeting Country. (American Folkways
Series). New York: Duell, Sloan and Pearce,
1945. ix, 241 pp.
    The book is "historically accurate and liberally
    spiced with anecdotes and Yankee flavor." (H.
    S. Pearson.)

Wehman, Henry J.
Wehman's Idle Hours with the Humorists,
Brimful of Fun about Yankee Yarns, Western
Sports, Boarding House Hash, Rich College
Scraps, Wild Widows' Wit, and Tall Tales of
Sailors and Marines. New York: Henry J.
Wehman, n.d.

White, Rev. Henry
*The Early History of New England Illustrated
by Numerous Interesting Incidents.* Concord,
N. H.: S. Boyd, 1841. iv, 420 pp. bibl.

Wright, Richardson
Grandfather Was Queer. Early American Wags
and Eccentrics from Colonial Times to the
Civil War. Philadelphia: J. B. Lippincott Company, 1939.

——————.
Hawkers and Walkers in Early America, strolling peddlers, preachers, lawyers, doctors, players, and others, from the beginning to the
Civil War. With 68 illustrations from old
sources. Philadelphia: J. B. Lippincott Co.,
1927. 317 pp., bibl.

FOLKTALES—LEGENDS

Abbott, Katherine Mixer
Old Paths and Legends of New England. New
York: G. P. Putnam's Sons, 1903. 484 pp.,
illus.
    Saunterings over historic roads and glimpses of
    picturesque fields and old homesteads in Massa-
    chusetts, Rhode Island and New Hampshire.

Bartlett, John Henry
*The Legend of Ann Smith, a New England
Story in Verse.* Chicago: M. A. Donahue &
Company, 1931. 90 pp., illus.

Bonner, Willard Hallan
Pirate Laureate: The Life & Legends of Captain Kidd. New Brunswick, N. J.: Rutgers University Press, 1947.

Brown, Marshall
Wit and Humor, A Choice Collection. Chicago:
S. C. Griggs and Company, 1877.

Browne, George Waldo
Real Legends of New England. Illustrations
by Alexander Key. Chicago: A. Whitman &
Co., 1930. 264 pp., illus.

Carmer, Carl
The Hurricane's Children. Tales from Your
Neck o' the Woods. New York: Farrar &
Rinehart, 1937.

Dorson, Richard M.
"Jonathan Draws the Long Bow." *New England Quarterly* 16:244–279, 1943.
    Survey of New England literature and tall tales.

——————.
Jonathan Draws the Long Bow. Cambridge,
Mass.: Harvard University Press, 1946. viii,
274 pp.
    A collection of New England tall tales, Yankee
    yarns and local legends. Excellent bibliographical
    footnotes. "Note an the printed sources for New
    England folktales" (pp. 261–263).

——————.
"Just B'ars." *Appalachia* Dec. 1942, pp. 174–
187.
    Bear tales from New England.

——————.
New England Popular Tales and Legends.
Cambridge, Mass.: Harvard University Press,
1943.

Drake, Samuel Adams
*A Book of New England Legends and Folk-
lore in Prose and Poetry.* Illustrated by F. T.
Merrill. Boston: Roberts Bros., 1884, 1888.
461 pp. Boston: Little Brown and Co., 1910.
xvi, 477 pp. illus., plates.
    Extracts from writings of various authors.

——————.
The Myths and Fables of To-day.
Boston: Lee and Shepard, 1900.

Fenn, George Manville, ed.
The World of Wit and Humour, with over 200 illustrations. London: Cassell and Company, 1899. 2 vols.

Fisher's Comic Almanac for 1845. Boston: Published by James Fisher.

Forbes, Esther
Paul Revere & the World He Lived In. Boston: Houghton Mifflin Company, 1942.
　The legend of the famous ride further analyzed, as well as much on social life in Colonial New England.

Fuller, Edmund
Thesaurus of Anecdotes, A New Classified Collection of the Best Anecdotes from Ancient Times to the Present Day. New York: Crown Publishers, 1942.

Goodell, Charles L.
Black Tavern Tales, Stories of Old New England. Brooklyn: Willis McDonald & Co., 1932.

Goodspeed, Charles E., comp.
A Treasury of Fishing Stories. New York: A. S. Barnes and Co., 1946.

————.
Angling in America, Its Early History and Literature. Boston: Houghton Mifflin Company, 1939.

Gough, John B.
Brilliant Diamonds of Poetry and Prose. Comprising the Most Unique, Touching, Pithy, and Beautiful Literary Treasures..., edited by Rev. O. H. Tiffany. Boston: Union Publishing Company, 1893.

Graves, Merle Dixon
Bubblin's an' B'ilin's at the Center. Rutland, Vt.: The Tuttle Company, 1934. 212 pp., illus.

Haliburton, Thomas Chandler
Sam Slick. Edited with a Critical Estimate and a Bibliography by Ray Palmer Baker. New York: George H. Doran Company, 1923. 420 pp., illus., bibl.

————.
Sam Slick in Search of a Wife; or Wise Saws. New York: G. Munro, 1882.

————.
The Clockmaker; or, *The Sayings and Doings of Sam Slick, of Slickville.* Philadelphia: Carey, Lea, and Blanchard, 1836. 218 pp.

————.
Traits of American Humor, by Native Authors. London: Colburn and Co., 1852. 3 vols.

Hawthorne, Nathaniel
Legends of New England. Boston: J. R. Osgood and Company, 1877. 104 pp.
　Contents: The Gray Champion.—The Maypole of Merry Mount.—Endicott and the red cross.—Roger Malvin's burial.

Ives, Franklin Titus
Yankee Jumbles; or Chimney Corner Tales of the 19th Century Events, comprising subjects of Fact, Fun and Fiction. New York: Broadway Publishing Co., 1903. 390 pp.

Jewett, S. O.
Tales of New England (Riverside Aldine Series). Boston: Houghton Mifflin Co., 1891. 276 pp.

Johnson, Edward
The Wonder-Working Providence of Sion's Saviour in New England. Edited by J. Franklin Jameson. New York: C. Scribner's Sons, 1910. viii, 285 pp.

Kempt, Robert, comp.
The American Joe Miller: A Collection of Yankee Wit and Humour. London: Adams and Francis, 1865.

Kirkland, Frazar
Cyclopaedia of Commercial and Business Anecdotes. New York: D. Appleton and Co., 1864. 2 vols.

Leland, C. G.
Algonquian Legends of New England. Boston: Houghton Mifflin Co., 1884. 379 pp.
　Myths and folklore of the Merrimac, Passamaquoddy and Penobscot.

Loomis, C. Grant
"Jonathanisms; American Epigrammatic Hyperbole." *WF* 6 (No. 3) :211–227, 1947.
　"A Jonathanism is an integral element of tall-tale lore and is, perhaps, the initiating force behind the longer, exaggerated anecdote." (C. G. Loomis.)

Lowell, Amy
Legends. Boston: Houghton Mifflin Company, 1921. xiv, 259 pp.
　Contains also legends of New England.

Mather, Cotton
Magnalia Christi Americana; or, The Ecclesiastical History of New England, from Its First Planting, in the year 1620, unto the Year of Our Lord 1698, in Seven Books. Hartford, Conn.: Silas Andrus & Son, 1852.
　"The myth-making imagination" rides supreme on many pages of this work.

New England Folklore
The Devil and Tom Walker. The first Worcester Edition. Worcester, Mass.: F. P. Rice, Sold by Putnam, Davis and Co., 1896. 11 pp.

Parsons, E. C.
"Accumulative Tales Told by Cape Verde Islanders in New England." *JAFL* 33:34–42, 1920.

Perry, Clair Willard
New England's Buried Treasure. New York: Stephen Daye Press, 1946. 348 pp. (The American Cave Series.)

Price, Robert
"A Boyhood for Johnny Appleseed." *The New England Quarterly* 17 (No. 3) : 381–382, 391–393, 1944.
> The story of Appleseed's childhood in the Connecticut Valley.

————.
"New England Origins of Johnny Appleseed." *The New England Quarterly* 12:454–469, 1939.

Shaw, Henry Wheeler
Josh Billings on Ice, and Other Things. New York: Carleton, Publisher. London: S. Low, Son & Co., 1870.

Skinner, Charles M.
Tales of Puritan Land. In: *Tales and Legends of Our Own Land*, Vol. I (pp. 185–317). Philadelphia: J. B. Lippincott and Co., 1896.

Smith, Grace Partridge
"A Yankee Tale—Fact or Folksay?" *JAFL* 58:344–345, 1945.
> Variants of a tale first heard in Mass., but found also in other New England States.

Spofford, Harriet Elizabeth (Prescott)
New England Legends. Boston: J. R. Osgood and Co., 1871. 40 pp., illus.
> *Contents:* The true account of Captain Kidd.—Charlestown.—Salem.—Newburyport.—Dover.—Portsmouth.

Stowe, Harriet Beecher
Oldtown Folks and Sam Lawson's Fireside Stories. Boston: James R. Osgood, 1869.

Tandy, Jennette
Crackerbox Philosophers in American Humor and Satire. New York: Columbia University Press, 1937. xi, 181 pp.

Thomas, Lowell
Tall Stories, The Rise and Triumph of the Great American Whopper. New York: Funk & Wagnalls Company, 1931.

Tit-Bits of American Humor, Collected from Various Sources. New York and London: White and Allen, n.d.

Tit-Bits of Fun, for Jolly Mortals.
A Collection of Outrageous Jokes, Mirthful Stories, Witty Sayings and Exhilirating (!) Anecdotes. New York: G. Blackie & Co., 1874. 64 pp., illus.

Tryon, Henry H.
Fearsome Critters. Cornwall, New York: Idlewild Press, 1939.
> Stories of strange animals.

Tucker, T. W.
Waifs from the Way-Bills of an Old Expressman. Boston: Lee and Shepard, 1872.

Valentine, Dr. W.
Comic Metamorphoses, Being a Perfect Encyclopedia of Fun and Humor. New York: Dick and Fitzgerald, 1855.

Wheeler, Florence E.
"John Chapman's Line of Descent from Edward Chapman of Ipswich." *Ohio Archaeological and Historical Quarterly* 48:28–33, Jan. 1939.
> Further discussion of Johnny Appleseed's New England origins.

Whittier, John Greenleaf
Legends of New England. Hartford: Hammer & Phelps, 1831. iv, 142 pp.
> In prose and verse.

Williams, Leewin B., comp. and ed.
Master Book of Humorous Illustrations. Nashville: Abingdon-Cokesbury Press, 1938.

Witherspoon, Halliday (Nutter, William Herbert)
Liverpool Jarge. Boston: Square Rigger, 1933. 120 pp.
> Sailors' yarns and lingo.

SUPERSTITIONS—WITCHCRAFT

The Blue Laws of Connecticut, taken from the code of 1650 and the public records of the colony of Connecticut previous to 1655 . . . with an account of the persecution of witches and Quakers in New England, and some extracts from the Blue Laws of Virginia. New York: The Truth Seeker Co., 1920. 88 pp. illus.

Burr, George Lincoln
The Literature of Witchcraft. New York: G. P. Putnam's Sons, 1890. pp. 37–66. Reprinted from the *Papers of the American Historical Association,* vol. IV, pp. 235–266, 1890.

————.
Narratives of the Witchcraft Cases, 1648–1706. New York: C. Scribner's Sons, 1914. xviii, 467 pp.

————.
New England's Place in the History of Witchcraft. Worcester, Mass.: The Society, 1911. 35 pp.

Chamberlayne, Richard
Lithobolia; or, The Stone-Throwing Devil. Being an exact and true account (by way of journal) of the various actions of infernal spirits, or (devils incarnate) witches, or both; and the great disturbance and amazement they gave to George Walton's family, at a place call'd Great Island in the province of New-Hantshire (sic) in New England, chiefly in throwing about (by an invisible hand) stones, bricks, and brick-bats of all sizes, with several other things, as hammers, mauls, ironcrows, spits, and other domestick utensils, as came into their hellish minds, and this for the space of a quarter of a year . . . London: Printed and Are To Be Sold by E. Whitlock, 1698. 3–16 pp. Reprinted: Boston, 1924, In: Davis, W. G. "The Ancestry of Lydia Harmon," pp. 91–108.

Clarke, Helen Archibald
Longfellow's Country. New York: The Baker and Taylor Co., 1909. 252 pp.
> The author tells a number of witchcraft stories, and a chapter on the lore of Hiawatha.

Disosway, Ella Taylor
South Meadows, A tale of long ago. Philadelphia: Porter and Coates, 1874. v, 280 pp.

Drake, Samuel Gardner
Annals of Witchcraft in New England, and elsewhere in the United States, from their first settlement. Drawn up from unpublished and other well authenticated records of the alleged operations of witches and their instigator, the devil. Boston: W. E. Woodward, 1869. liii, 306 pp. (Half-title: Woodward's Historical Series No. VIII.)

——————.
The Witchcraft Delusion in New England; its Rise, Progress, and Termination, as exhibited by Dr. Cotton Mather, in The Wonders of the Invisible World. Roxbury, Mass.: Printed for W. E. Woodward, 1866. 3 vols. (Woodward's Historical Series. No. v–vii).

Gibson, Katharine
Nathaniel's Witch. New York: Longman's Green, 1941.
> The story of early New England—how Nathaniel met a witch and brought her to town on Christmas.

Gould, Lieut.-Com. R. T.
The Case for the Sea-Serpent. New York: G. P. Putnam's Sons, 1934.

Hale, John
A Modest Enquiry into the Nature of Witchcraft, and How Persons Guilty of that Crime May Be Convicted: and the Means Used for their Discovery Discussed, Both Negatively and Affirmatively, According to Scripture and Experience. Boston: B. Green and J. Allen, for B. Eliot, 1702. 176 pp.

Johnson, Clifton
What They Say in New England. A Book of Signs, Sayings, and Superstitions. Boston: Lee and Shepard, 1896.

Kittredge, George Lyman
Notes on Witchcraft. Worcester, Mass.: The Davis Press, 1907. 67 pp.
> Reprinted from the Proceedings of the American Antiquarian Society, Vol. XVII.

——————.
Witchcraft in Old and New England. Cambridge, Mass.: Harvard University Press, 1929.

Mather, Cotton
Strange Phenomena of New England: In the Seventeenth Century: including the "Salem Witchcraft," "1692." Collected and arranged for re-publication by Jones, Henry. New York: Piercy & Reed, 1846. iv, 54 pp.

Mather, Increase
Remarkable Providences Illustrative of the Earlier Days of American Colonisation. With introductory preface, by George Offor. London: J. R. Smith, 1856. xix, 262 pp.

Nevins, Winfield S.
Witchcraft in Salem Village in 1692, together with some account of other witchcraft prosecutions in New England and elsewhere. Salem, Mass.: North Shore Publishing Company; Boston, Lee and Shepard, 1892. 272 pp., illus.

Orians, G. Harrison
"New England Witchcraft in Fiction." *American Literature* 2:54–71, 1930.

Putnam, Allen
Witchcraft of New England explained by Modern Spiritualism. Boston: Colby and Rich, 1888. 482 pp., bibl.

Stetson, George R.
"The Animistic Vampire in New England." *AA* 9:1–14, 1896, o.s.

Summers, Montague
A Popular History of Witchcraft. New York: E. P. Dutton and Company, 1937. xvi, 276 pp.

The Linnean Society of Boston
Report of a Committee of the Linnean Society of New England relative to a large marine animal supposed to be a serpent, seen near Cape Ann, Massachusetts, in August 1817. Boston: published by Cummings and Hilliard, No. 1, Cornhill Univ. Press . . . Hillard and Metcalf, 1817. 52 pp.

Whittier, John Greenleaf
The Supernaturalism of New England. London: Wiley and Putnam, 1847. ix, 71 pp.

Willard, S.
Some Miscellany Observations on Our Present Debates Respecting Witchcrafts, in a dialogue between S & B. Philadelphia: Printed by William Bradford, for Hezekiah Usher, 1692. Boston: 1869. 24 pp.

Williams, Espy William H.
Witchcraft; or, The Witch of Salem. A Legend of Old New England. In Five Acts. New Orleans: E. A. Brandao & Co., 1886. 53 pp.

Winsor, Justin
The Literature of Witchcraft in New England. Worcester, Mass.: C. Hamilton, 1896. 25 pp.

BELIEFS—CUSTOMS—TRADITIONS

Alden, Timothy
A Collection of American Epitaphs and Inscriptions, with occasional notes. New York: S. Marks, printer, 1814. 5 vols.

An Opera Goer.
The Lorgnette: or, Studies of the Town. New York: Stringer & Townsend, 1851.

Backus, Mrs. E. M.
"New England Folk Beliefs in the Last Century." *JAFL* 45:501–502, 1932.

Bartlett, Arthur
"The Discovery of L. L. Bean." *The Saturday Evening Post* 219 (No. 24): 31, 92, 95, 97, Dec. 14, 1946.
"The Yankee ingenuity which thus produced the first leather-topped rubber shoes has also enabled Bean to develop many other items which had never occurred to more orthodox manufacturers."

Bliss, William Root
The Old Colony Town and Other Sketches. Boston: Houghton Mifflin and Co., 1893. 219 pp.
Deals mainly with social life, customs, and traditions. Has one chapter: "Old Colony Witch Stories."

Bowles, Ella Shannon
Homespun Handicrafts. Philadelphia: J. B. Lippincott Company, 1931.

Butler, Frances Anne
Journal. Philadelphia: Carey, Lea & Blanchard, 1835. 2 vols.

Butterworth, Hezekiah
In Old New England, The Romance of a Colonial Fireside. New York: D. Appleton and Company, 1895.

Carter, Robert
A Summer Cruise on the Coast of New England. Boston: Crosby and Nichols, 1864.

Chase, Mary Ellen
A Goodly Heritage. New York: Henry Holt and Company, 1932.

Claflin, Mary B.
Brampton Sketches, Old-Time New England Life. New York: T. Y. Crowell & Co., 1890.

Coffin, Robert P. Tristram
Mainstays of Maine. New York: The Macmillan Company, 1944.

Cole, P. McA.
"New England Funerals." *JAFL* 7:217–223, 1894.

————
"New England Weddings." *JAFL* 6:103–107, 1893.

Copeland, Jennie F.
Every Day but Sunday, The Romantic Age of New England Industry. Brattleboro, Vt.: Stephen Daye Press, 1936.

Crawford, Mary Caroline
Social Life in Old New England. Boston: Little, Brown and Co., 1914. xiii, 515 pp., front., plates, ports.
New England social life and customs.

Doten, Dana
The Art of Bundling: being an inquiry into the nature and origins of that curious but universal folk-custom, with an exposition of the rise and fall of bundling in the eastern part of N. America ... drawings by Lee Brown Coye. Weston, Vt.: The Countryman press and New York: Farrar and Rinehart, 1938. x, 190 pp., illus.

Drake, Samuel Adams
Our Colonial Homes. Boston: Lee and Shepard, 1894. 211 pp., illus.

Dwight, Timothy
Travels; in New England and New York. New Haven: T. Dwight, 1821–22. 4 vols.
Mainly on social customs and traditions.

Earle, Alice Morse
Child Life in Colonial Days, with many illustrations and photographs. New York: The Macmillan Company, 1899. xxi, 418 pp.

————
Colonial Dames and Good Wives. Boston: Houghton Mifflin & Company, 1895. 315 pp.

————
Costumes of Colonial Times. New York: C. Scribner's Sons, 1894. xiv, 264 pp.

————
Customs and Fashions in Old New England.. New York: Scribner's Sons, 1893. 387 pp., 4 pl.

————
Home Life in Colonial Days ... Illustrated by photographs, gathered by the author, of real things, works, and happenings of olden times. New York: The Macmillan Company, 1898. xvi, 470 pp.

————
Old-Time Gardens, Newly Set Forth. New York: The Macmillan Company, 1901.

————
"Old-Time Marriage Customs in New England." *JAFL* 6:97–102, 1893.

————
Stage-Coach and Tavern Days. New York: The Macmillan Company, 1900. xvi, 449 pp.

————
The Sabbath in Puritan New England. New York: Charles Scribner's Sons, 1891. vii, 335 pp.

Eggleston, Edward
"Some Curious Colonial Remedies." *American Historical Review* 5:199–206, 1900.

Felt, Joseph Barlon
The Customs of New England. Boston: Press of T. R. Marvin, 1853. 208 pp.
Contents: 1. Furniture or household appurtenances. 2. Fashions of dress.

Ford, E. E.
"Bride-Stealing in New England." *JAFL* 6:303–305, 1893.

Greene, Asa
The Life and Adventures of Dr. Dodimus Duckworth, A. N. Q., to which is added, The History of a Steam Doctor, by The Author of "A Yankee Among the Nullifiers." (Asa Greene). New York: Peter Hill, 1833. 2 vols.

Hanley, Miles L.
" 'Serenade' in New England." *AS* 8 (no. 2): 24–26, 1933.
A New England version of the Charivaria custom.

Harlow, Frederick Pease
The Making of a Sailor, or Sea Life Aboard a Yankee Square-Rigger. Publication Number 17 of The Marine Research Society. Salem, Mass.: The Marine Research Society, 1928.

Hendren, Joseph W.
"Epitaphs from Down East." *New England Quarterly* 11:524–540, 1938.
From gravestones of Puritan New England.

Hoagland, M. F.
"Notes on Old New England Customs." *JAFL* 6:301–303, 1893.

Hodges, N. D. C.
"Survival in New England of Foundation Sacrifice." *JAFL* 12:290–291, 1899.

Jones, Edward Franc
Richard Baxter, a story of New England life of 1830 to 1840. Binghampton, N. Y.: Jones of Binghampton, 1904. xiv, 331 pp.

"Josh Billings"
Old Probability, Perhaps Rain—Perhaps Not, with 250 Comic Illustrations. New York: G. W. Carleton & Co., 1875.

Larcom, Lucy
A New England Girlhood, outlined from memory. Boston: Houghton Mifflin Co., 1889. 274 pp.

Lawrence, Henry Wells
The Not-Quite Puritans; some genial follies and peculiar frailties of our revered New England ancestors. Boston: Little, Brown, and Co., 1928. x, 228 pp., bibl.

Lawrence, Robert Means
New England Colonial Life. Cambridge, Mass.: The Cosmos Press, inc., 1927. 276 pp.

Lesley, Mrs. Susan Inches (Lyman)
Recollections of My Mother, Mrs. Anne Jean Lyman of Northampton; being a picture of domestic and social life in New England in the first half of the nineteenth century. Boston: Houghton Mifflin and Co., 1899. vi, 505 pp.

Mitchell, Edwin Valentine
It's An Old New England Custom. Illustrated with quaint cuts. New York: Vanguard Press, 1946. 277 pp.

————.
The Horse and Buggy Days in New England. New York: Coward-McCann, 1937. viii, 232 pp.

Mussey, June Barrows
Yankee Life By Those Who Lived It. New York: Alfred A. Knopf, 1947. viii, 543 pp.
A collection of passages from the autobiographies of New Englanders, rich insight into early social life and customs.

Newell, William Wells
"Conjuring Rats." *JAFL* 5 (no. 16):23–24, 1892.
A New England belief that rats can be made to leave one's house by sending them a letter asking them to go to another place.

Rawson, Marion Nicholl
Little Old Mills. New York: E. P. Dutton & Co., 1935.

Sherwood, "Uncle" Bob
Hold Yer Hosses! The Elephants Are Coming. New York: The Macmillan Company, 1932.

Slater, George A.
The Hills of Home, American life pictured in New England in the last half of the nineteenth century. New York: Rudge, 1931. 48 pp.

Stiles, Henry Reed
Bundling; its origin, progress, and decline in America. Albany: Knickerbocker Publishing Co., 1871. 138 pp.

Trollope, Mrs. F. M.
Domestic Manners of the Americas. New York: Dodd, Mead and Co., 1901. 2 Vols.

Whipple, J. Rayner
"Old New England Weather Vanes." *Old-Time New England* 31:45–56, 1940.

Wolcott, Imogene B.
The Yankee Cook Book; an Anthology of Incomparable Recipes from the Six New England States and a Little Something About the People Whose Tradition for Good Eating is Herein Permanently Recorded... from the Files of Yankee Magazine and From Time Worn Recipe Books and Many Gracious Contributors; Decorations by Edwin Earl and Alanson B. Hewes. New York: Coward-McCann, 1939. xv, 398 pp., illus.
"What delighted me most in this book and what makes it a delightful piece of literature for anybody who is not interested in the details of cooking, are the yarns and anecdotes which are spread liberally throughout." (August P. Loring, Jr.)

SPEECH

Allen, Frederic D.
"Contributions to the New England Vocabulary." *Dialect Notes* 1 (Part I):18, 1890.

Ament, William S.
"Some Americanisms in Moby Dick." *AS* 7 (no. 5):365–367, 1932.

Ashley, C. W.
The Yankee Whaler. Boston: Houghton Mifflin Co., 1926.
Glossary of whaling terms on pp. 123–146.

Barnow, A. J.
"Echoes of the Pilgrim Fathers' Speech."
Mededeelingen der Koninklijke Academie van Wetenschappen, Afd. Letterkunde, Deel 55. Serie A. Nr. 6, pp. 139–189. Amsterdam, 1923.

Briggs, L. B. R.
"A Few New England Words." *Dialect Notes* 1 (Part 4) :209–211.

Bushnell, David I. Jr.
"New England Names." *AA* 13:235–239, 1911, n. s.

Colcord, Joanna Carver
Sea Language Comes Ashore. New York: Cornell Maritime Press, 1945.

Daniele, M. Grant
"New England Notes." *Dialect Notes* 1 (Part 4) :211–213.

De Vere, M. Schele
Americanism; The English of The New World. New York: Charles Scribner & Co., 1871.

England, Geo. A.
"The Real Dialect of Northern New England." *Writer's Monthly*, March, 1926.

Forbes, Harriette N.
New England Diaries, 1602–1800. A Descriptive Catalogue of Diaries, Orderly Books and Journals. Privately Printed, 1923. viii, 439 pp.

"Gay, Picturesque Language Along New England Coast." *Evening Transcript*, Aug. 11, 1937, p. 9.
  A collection of New Bedford, Mass.

Harris, Rachel S.
"New England Words for the Earthworm." *AS* 8 (no.4) : 12–17, 1933.

Hoar, George F.
The Obligations of New England to the County of Kent. A Paper Read before the American Antiquarian Society as a part of the Report of the Council, April 29, 1885. Worcester, Mass. Press of Charles Hamilton, 1885.

Killheffer, Marie
"A Comparison of the Dialect of 'The Bigelow Papers' with the Dialect of Four Yankee Plays." *AS* 3 (No. 3) :222–236, 1928.

Kurath, Hans
Linguistic Atlas of New England. Sponsored by the American Council of Learned Societies, and assisted by universities and colleges in New England. Providence, R. I.: Brown University, 1939–1943. xii, 240 pp., maps, diagrs. Linguistic Atlas of the United States.
  A bibliography of dialects and speech in the New England States.

"New England Words for the Seesaw." *AS* 8 (no. 2) :14–18, 1933.

————, and Long, P. W.
"Plans for a Survey of the Dialects of New England." *Dialect Notes* 6 (Part 2) :65–72, 1930.

Matthews, Albert
"Colonial and Early Pioneer Words" *Dialect Notes* 4 (Part 6) :375–385, 1917.

Matthews, William
"Early New England Words." *AS* 15:225–232, 1940.

McQuesten, Gertrude
"Yankee Twang-New England Dialect." *Emerson Quarterly*, March 1925. pp. 9–13.

Orbeck, Anders
Early New England Pronunciation As Reflected in Some Seventeenth Century Town Records of Eastern Massachusetts. Ann Arbor, Mich.: George Wahr, 1927, x, 148 pp.

Perrin, P. G.
"New England Provincialisms, 1818." *Dialect Notes* 5 (Part 9) :383–384, 1926.

Penzl, Herbert
"New England Terms for 'Poached Eggs'." *AS* 9 (No. 2) :90–95, 1934.

Pound, Louise
"The Dialect of Cooper's Leather-Stocking." *AS* 2 (No. 12) :479–488, 1927.
  In James Fenimore Cooper's Novels: *The Deerslayer, The Last of the Mohicans, The Pathfinder, The Pioneers,* and *The Prairie.*

Read, Allen Walker
"Bilingualism in the Middle Colonies." *AS* 12 (No. 2) :93–99, 1937.

"Two New England Lists of 1848." *Dialect Notes* 6 (Part 10) :452–454, 1935.

Schultz, John Ritchie
"Chautauqua Talk." *AS* 7 (No. 6) :405–411, 1932.

Sheldon, E. S.
"A New Englander's English and the English of London." *Dialect Notes* 1 (Part 2) :33–42.

Spies, Heinrich
Kultur und Sprache in neuen England. Leipzig: Teubner, 1928. xiv, 22 pp., zweite ergänzte Auflage.
  A study of culture and language in New England.

"Various Contributions." *Dialect Notes* 1 (Part 1) :22, 1890.

Wolfe, Julia W.
"Some New England Neologisms." *AS* 5 (No. 2) :134–136, 1929.

PLACE NAMES

Baylies, Francis
The Origin of Local and Other Names: a letter from Hon. Francis Baylies . . . to Hon. P. W. Leland . . . Brooklyn: 1879. 3 pp.

Bushnell, David, I. Jr.
"New England Names." *AA* 13:235–239, 1911.
n. s.

Lithgow, Douglas Robert
Dictionary of American Indian Place and Proper Names in New England; with many interpretations. Salem, Mass.: The Salem Press Co., 1909. xxi, 400 pp., bibl.
　　"List of Abnaki words (Maine and New Hampshire). List of Massachusetts, or Natick, Indian words, pp. 393–396.

Wright, Harry Andrew
"Some Vagaries in Connecticut Valley Indian Place-Names." *The New England Quarterly* Sept., 1939, pp. 535–544.

PROVERBS

Hardie, Margaret
"Proverbs and Proverbial Expressions Current in the United States East of the Missouri and North of the Ohio Rivers." *AS* 4(No. 6.): 461–472, 1929.
　　The author lists 225 proverbs.

FOLKSONG

PERIODICALS

Bulletin of the Folk Song Society of the Northeast. Phillips Barry, ed. Cambridge, Mass.: The Powell Publishing Co., 1930–1937.
　　Splendid articles on various aspects of ballad and songs.

Johnson, H. E.
"Early New England Periodicals Devoted to Music." *MQ* 26:153–161, (April) 1940.

GENERAL STUDIES

Barrows, M.
"Some Half-Forgotten New England Songs." *New England Magazine* 12:472–475, 1895.
n. s.

Barry, Phillips
"American Ballads (New England)." *FSSNE* 6:10–18, 1933.
　　Steeped in local origin and tradition of the northeast. Words and tunes. Also, observations on variants of "The Lass of Mohea."

————.
"Ballad of 'Lord Randal' in New England." *JAFL* 16:258–264, 1903.
　　Text and music.

————.
"British Ballads." *FSSNE* 11:8–12, 1936.

————.
"Child Ballads and Their Kin." *FSSNE* 3:6–11, 1931.

————.
"Non-Child Ballads." *FSSNE* 3:14–17, 1931.
　　Northeast and Canada.

————, and Eckstorm, F. H.
"Olban, or, The White Captive." *FSSNE* 8:19–24, 1934.
　　A fantastic ballad of Indian torture. Text and music.

————.
"Traditional Ballads in New England." *JAFL* 18:123–138, 191–214, 291–304, 1905.

Cole, P. Mc A.
"'Abigail Snow,' a Colonial Literary Ballad." *JAFL* 14:140–142, 1901.

Eckstorm, Fannie Hardy
"Folk-Song Society of the Northeast." *JAFL* 56:170–171, 1943.

————.
"Local Rimes and Quatrains of the Northeast." *FSSNE* 3:17–20, 1931.
　　Words and melody of local lore and events.

————.
"Who Was Pangus?" *New England Quarterly* 12:203–226, 1939.
　　A fascinating incident in New England lore, connected with Lovewell's famous fight.

Henry, Mellinger E.
"The Ballad of the Skunk." *JAFL* 57:281–282, 1944.
　　Text only.

Newell, W. W.
"'Passover Song of the Kid', and an equivalent from New England." *JAFL* 18:33–48, 1905. bibl.

"New England Ballads." *New England Quarterly* 1:587–588, 1928.

Scull, G. D.
"English Ballads About New England." *New England Historical and Genealogical Register* 36, 1882.

Smyth, M. W.
"Northern Ballads." *Saturday Review of Literature* 10:368 (December 23) 1933.

COLLECTIONS

See: American Folksong and Ballad Collections. pp. 78–79, 85–91, 118–20.

Allin, A. (pseud of Mrs. A. A. Curtis)
Home Ballads: A Book for New Englanders, in three parts. Boston: J. Monroe and Co., 1851. 238 pp.

Botkin, B. A.
Songs and Rhymes In: *A Treasury of New England Folklore.* Part Five, (pp. 835–914). New York: Crown Publishers, 1947. 934 pp.
　　A rich harvest of New England songs. Words and tunes (from various printed and recorded sources) of Songs of the Sea and the Woods; Hymns of Faith and Freedom, Ballads, Sea Songs and Chanteys, Lumberjack Songs and Ballads, Nursery and Humorous Songs, Game and Dance Songs. Rhymes and Jingles: Play Rhymes, and Rhymes for Occasions.

Jackson, George Pullen
Down East Spirituals, and Others of Olden Time; Three Hundred Songs Supplementary to the author's Spiritual Folk Songs of Early America. New York: J. J. Augustin, 1943. 296 pp. unaccomp. melodies, bibl. (pp. 284–287).
  The author considers New England to have been the source from which the white spirituals spread through the land.

Jordan, Philip D., and Kessler, Lillian
Songs of Yesterday, A Song Anthology of American Life. Garden City, N. Y.: Doubleday, Doran & Co., 1941.
  Facsimile reproductions; for voice and piano.

Linscott, Eloise Hubbard
Folksongs of Old New England, collected and edited by Eloise Hubbard Linscott. With an introduction by James M. Carpenter. New York: The Macmillan Co., 1939. xxi, 337 pp., with music references.

New England Songster. Portsmouth, N. H.: Nathaniel March and Co., 1932.

Ring, Lyle R.
New England Folk Songs. Boston: E. C. Schirmer Music Co., 1934.
  Arranged for voice and piano.

Stevens, David, arr.
Ten New England Folk Songs. New York: G. Schirmer, Inc.
  For unison and piano.

GAMES

See: Children's Games and Rhymes, pp. 161–68.

Newell, William Wells
Games and Songs of American Children. New York: Harper & Brothers, 1903. New and enl. ed.

ARRANGEMENTS

————: Piano

MacDowell, Edward
New England Idyls. New York: G. Schirmer.

————: Orchestra

A New England Overture. Alexander, Joseph: MS.

New England Symphony. (#2, in B flat minor, op. 33). Stillman-Kelley, E.: Schirmer: Orchestra.

RECORDS

Album Collections

"New England." In the Archive of the Folk Song Society of the Northeast, Cambridge, Mass.

The Folk Songs of New England. Earl Rogers, voice-piano. 3–10".   MU 68

Individual Titles

"Brookfield Murder." Earl Rogers, voice-piano.
                                   MU 68

"Cape Cod Girls." Earl Rogers, voice-piano.
                                   MU 68

"I Had A Little Nut Tree." Earl Rogers, voice-piano.   MU 68

"Our Good Man." Earl Rogers, voice-piano.
                                   MU 68

"The Ocean Burial." Earl Rogers, voice-piano.
                                   MU 68

"Old Man Who Lived In The Wood." Earl Rogers, voice-piano.   MU 68

"Woman All Skin And Bones." Earl Rogers, voice-piano.   MU 68

CONNECTICUT

FOLKLORE

BIBLIOGRAPHY

Bates, Albert Carlos
"Check List of Connecticut Almanacs, 1709–1850, with introduction and notes." *American Antiquarian Society, Proceedings,* 24:93–215, 1914. (Worcester, Mass.) n. s.

Fisher, Samuel Herbert
The Publications of Thomas Collier, Printer, 1784–1808. Litchfield, Conn.: The Litchfield Historical Society, 1933. xiii, 98 pp., illus.
  Valuable entries on Connecticut Almanacs.

Flagg, C. A.
Reference List on Connecticut Local History. New York State Library Bulletin No. 53. New York: State Library. Dec. 1900.

PERIODICALS

Bulletin of the Connecticut Historical Society. No. 1—Nov. 1934—Hartford.

The Connecticut Magazine. Devoted to Connecticut in its various phases of history, literature, scenic beauty, art, science, industry. v. 1–11; v. 12, No. 1–3; Jan. 1895–1908. Hartford, Conn.: The Connecticut Quarterly Company.

GENERAL STUDIES AND COLLECTIONS

Allis, Marguerite
Connecticut Trilogy, with Drawings by the Author. New York: G. P. Putnam's Sons, 1934.

Bacon, Edwin Munroe
The Connecticut River and Valley of the Connecticut; three hundred and fifty miles from mountain to sea; historical and descriptive. New York: G. P. Putnam's Sons, 1906. xx, 487 pp.

Barber, John Warner
City Guide to New Haven; being a pocket directory for citizens and strangers, to the prominent objects of interest within and around the city. New Haven: The Author, 1860. 36 pp.
  Local legend, story and anecdote.

——————.
Connecticut Historical Collections, containing a general collection of interesting facts, traditions, biographical sketches, anecdotes, etc., relating to the history and antiquities of every town in Connecticut, with geographical descriptions. Illustrated by 180 engravings. New Haven: The Author, 1836. viii, 560 pp.

Caulkins, Frances Manwaring
History of Norwich, Connecticut: From Its Possession by the Indians, to the Year 1866. Hartford, Conn.: Published by the Author, 1866.

Cross, Wilbur L.
Connecticut Yankee, An Autobiography. New Haven: Yale University Press, 1943.
  A full, rich life—replete with many incidents, anecdotes, and observation on New England traditions.

Federal Writers' Project
Connecticut, A Guide to its Roads, Lore, and People. American Guide Series. Written by Workers of the Federal Writers' Project of the Works Progress Administration for the State of Connecticut. Boston: Houghton Mifflin & Co., 1938. xxxiii, 593 pp., illus.

Hard, Walter R.
The Connecticut. Illustrated by Douglas W. Gorsline. (Rivers of America Series). New York: Rinehart and Co., 1947. x, 310 pp., bibl.

Higbee, Lillian M.
Bacchus of Windham and the Frog Fight. Willimantic, Conn.: Quality Print Shop, 1930. Illus.

Hooper, Marion
Life Along the Connecticut River, introduction by Charles Crane, text by Marion Hooper, photography by Lewis Brown, Ralph Day, Newell Green, R. D. and M. E. Snively and Cortland Luce. Brattleboro, Vt.: Stephen Day Press, 1939. 120 pp.

Johnson, Clifton
Historic Hampshire in The Connecticut Valley; happenings, in a charming old New England county from the time of the dinosaur down to about 1900 . . . 200 illustrations. Springfield, Mass.: Milton Bradley Co., 1932. 406 pp.

Nutting, Wallace
Connecticut Beautiful. Illustrated by the author with three hundred and four pictures covering all the counties in Connecticut. Framingham, Mass.: Old America Co., 1923. 301 pp.

Peters, Samuel
The Rev. Samuel Peters' LL.D. General History of Connecticut, from its first settlement under George Fenwick to its latest period of amity with Great Britain prior to the Revolution; Including a Description of the Country, and Many Curious and Interesting Anecdotes. With an Appendix, pointing out the Causes of the Rebellion in America Together with the Particular Part taken by the People of Connecticut in its Promotion. By a Gentleman of the Province. London: 1781. To which are Added, Additions to Appendix, Notes and Extracts from Letters, Verifying Many Important Statements Made by the Author.
New York: D. Appleton and Company, 1877. 285 pp.
  "Apparently Peters was determined to be interesting even to the extent of cracking credibility." (George Philip Krapp.)

Roberts, George Simon
Historic Towns of the Connecticut River Valley. Schenectady, N. Y.: Robson and Adee, 1906. vii, 494 pp., illus.

Shelton, Jane de Forest
The Salt-Box House; eighteenth century life in a New England hill town. New York: Charles Scribner, 1929. 302 pp., new ed.
  Old Shelton homestead in Ripton parish, Stratford, Conn.

Shepard, Odell
Connecticut; Past and Present. New York: Alfred A. Knopf, 1939. xix, 316 pp., illus.

——————, and Willard
Holdeast Gaines. New York: The Macmillan Company, 1946. 647 pp.
  "The book's most singing passages are reserved for the scenery and customs of Connecticut" (Herbert Lyons).

Sigourney, Mrs. Lydia Howard (Huntley)
Sketch of Connecticut, Forty Years Since. . . . Hartford: O. D. Cooke & Sons, 1824. 278 pp.
  "A descriptive prose work . . . tracing primitive habits and traditions, with some intermingling of fiction."

Smith, Chard Powers
The Housatonic. Puritan River. Illustrated by Armiss Landeck. (The Rivers of America Series.) New York: Rinehard and Company, 1946. 352 pp.

Smith, Helen Evertson
Colonial Days and Ways as Gathered from Family Papers. Decorations by T. Guernsey Moore. New York: The Century Co., 1900. viii, 376 pp.

Smith, Judge Martin H.
"Old Slave Days in Connecticut." *The Connecticut Magazine* 10(No. 1):113–114, Jan.–March, 1906.

Sterry, Iveagh Hunt, and Garrigus, William H.
They Found a Way, Connecticut's Restless People. Brattleboro, Vt.: Stephen Daye Press, 1938.

Taylor, John Metcalf
The Witchcraft Delusion in Colonial Connecticut, 1647–1697. New York: The Grafton Press, 1908. xv, 172 pp.

Todd, Charles Burr
In Olde Connecticut: Being a Record of Quaint, Curious and Romantic Happenings There in Colonial Times and Later. New York: The Grafton Press, 1906. x, 244 pp.

Wallace, John
Village Down East. Brattleboro, Vermont: Stephen Daye Press, 1943. 187 pp., 182 illus., 1 map.

Webster, Clarence M.
Town Meeting Country. (American Folkways Series.) New York: Duell, Sloan and Pearce, 1945. ix, 246 pp.
> The region dealt with is Eastern Connecticut and South Central Massachusetts. "This volume stands out for the success with which it views the developed culture of a region in its influences on the formation of local custom and local character." (J. W. Ashton.)

FOLKTALES—LEGENDS

Abbott, K. M.
Old Paths and Legends of New England (Connecticut Deerfield, Berkshire). New York: G. P. Putnam and Sons, 1907. 408 pp., illus.

Binney, Alice Stead
The Legend of Laddin's Rock. New York: Knickerbocker Press, 1902. v, 29 pp.

Clemons, W. Harry
"The Legends of Machimoodus." *The Connecticut Magazine* 7(No. 5):454, 1902–1903.
> A devil's tale.

Drake, Samuel Adams
Connecticut Legends. In: *A New England Book of Legends and Folklore in Prose and Poetry* (pp. 417–441). Boston: Little, Brown and Co., 1901. 47 pp., illus.

Humphreys, Colonel David
The Life & Heroic Exploits of Israel Putnam, Major-General in the Revolutionary War. New York: E. Strong, 1834. 190 pp., illus.
> Botkin (see: *Folklore of New England,* pp. 514–516) quotes an interesting tale—"Old Put's Wolf."

Weaver, William Lawton
The Battle of the Frogs, at Windham, 1758, with various accounts and three of the most popular ballads on the subject . . . Willimantic, Conn.: J. Walden, 1857.

SPEECH

Babbitt, E. H.
"Dialect of Western Connecticut." *Dialect Notes* 1(Part 7):338–343.

Fuller, M. Cordelia
"Word List from Danbury, Connecticut." *Dialect Notes* 6(Part 6):283–284, 1932.

Mathews, M. M.
"Humphrey's Glossary." *Dialect Notes* 5(Part 9):375–382, 1926.
> David Humphrey (1752–1818), a native of Connecticut, gained some reputation as a writer. In the back of one of his plays: *The Yankey in England,* appears a glossary, often referred to as the oldest glossary of Americanisms in existence, dating back to 1815.

Mead, W. E., and Chase, C. D.
"A Central Connecticut Word List." *Dialect Notes* 3(Part 1):1–25, 1905.

PLACE NAMES—WEATHER LORE

Backus, E. M.
"Weather-Signs from Connecticut." *JAFL* 8:26, 1895.

Dexter, Franklin Bowditch
"The History of Connecticut, as illustrated by the Names of Her Towns." In: *American Antiquarian Society,* (Worcester, Mass.) *Proceedings,* 1885. n. s, V. 3, pp. 421–448.

Turnbull, James Hammond
Indian Names of Places etc., in and on the Borders of Connecticut; with interpretations of some of them. Hartford: Case, Lockwood and Brainard Co., 1881. xi, 93 pp.

Wright, Harry Andrew
"Some Vagaries in Connecticut Valley Indian Place-Names." *New England Quarterly* 12:535–544, 1939.

FOLKSONG

GENERAL STUDIES

"A Black River Thaw."
> *NYFQ* 1:107–108, 1945.
> Text of a local ballad—"In the days of the Hartford Coach."

Henry, Mellinger Edward
"Brian O'Lynn." *JAFL* 54:83–84, 1941.
> A local ballad.

DELAWARE

FOLKLORE

BIBLIOGRAPHY

Hawkins, D. L.
A Checklist of Delaware Imprints Up to and Including 1800; a contribution to the history of printing in Delaware. (M. A. Thesis.) New York: Columbia University Library, 1928. xxxi, 74 pp.

PERIODICALS

Delaware Historical Society Papers. nos. 1–67; 1879–1922. n.s. 1–1927. Wilmington, The Historical Society.

GENERAL STUDIES AND COLLECTIONS

Canby, Henry Seidel
The Brandywine. (The Rivers of America Series.) Illustrated by Andrew Wyeth. New York: Farrar and Rinehart, 1941. 285 pp.

Federal Writers' Project
Delaware, a Guide to the First State. (American Guide Series.) Compiled and written by the Federal Writers' Project of the W.P.A. for the State of Delaware. New York: The Viking Press, 1938. xxv, 549 pp., illus. bibl.

————.
New Castle on the Delaware. Compiled by the Delaware Federal Writer's Project of the W.P.A. New Castle Historical Society, 1936.

Johnson, Amandus
The Swedish Settlements on the Delaware. Philadelphia: University of Pennsylvania Press, 1911.

Louhi, Evert Alexander
The Delaware Finns; or, the first permanent settlements in Pennsylvania, Delaware, West New Jersey and eastern part of Maryland. New York: The Humanity Press, 1925. 331 pp.

Wildes, Harry Emerson
The Delaware. Illustrated by Irwin D. Hoffman. (The Rivers of America Series.) New York: Farrar and Rinehart, 1940. x, 398 pp., illus., bibl.

FOLKTALES—LEGENDS

Bross, William
, *Legend of the Delaware;* an historical sketch of Tom Quick. To which is added the Winfield family; also, miscellaneous papers and articles. Chicago: Knight & Leonard Co., 1887. 195 pp.

MacMurray, Thomas J.
The Legend of the Delaware Valley, and Other Poems. Toronto: W. Briggs, 1887. viii, 132 pp.

Montgomery, Elizabeth
Reminiscences of Wilmington (Del.) in Familiar Village Tales, Ancient and New. Philadelphia: T. K. Collins, Jr., 1851.

Skinner, Charles M.
On and Near the Delaware. In: *Tales and Legends of our own Land.* Vol. I (pp. 143–185.) Philadelphia: J. B. Lippincott Co., 1896.

SPEECH

Greet, William Cabell
"Delmarva Speech." *AS* 8 (no. 4):56–63, 1933.

DISTRICT OF COLUMBIA
(Washington, D. C.)

FOLKLORE

GENERAL STUDIES AND COLLECTIONS

Ames, Mary (Clemmer)
Ten Years in Washington: or, Inside Life and Scenes in Our National Capital as a Woman Sees Them. Embracing a full account of the many marvels and interesting sights of Washington . . . Hartford, Conn.: Hartford Pub. Co., 1882, xxi, 608 pp., illus.

Andrews, Marietta
My Studio Window; Sketches of the Pageant of Washington Life. New York: E. P. Dutton & Co., 1928. xix, 450 pp., illus.
Observations and impressions during thirty-two years of life in the nation's capital.

Binckley, Mrs. John M.
"Some Reminiscences of Mrs. John M. Binckley in Washington. Edited by John B. Larner." *Columbia Histor. Soc. Records* (Washington) 29–30:343–353, 1928.

Chapin, Elizabeth (Moore)
American Court Gossip; or, Life at the National Capital. Marshalltown, Ia.: Chapin & Hartwell Bros., 1887. 269 pp.

Clark, Allen Culling
Life and Letters of Dolly Madison. Washington, D. C.: W. F. Roberts Co., 1914. 517 pp., illus.

Clay-Clopton, Virginia
A Belle of the Fifties; Memories of Mrs. Clay, of Alabama covering Social and Political Life in Washington and the South, 1853–1866 . . . Illustrated from contemporary portraits. New York: Doubleday, Page & Co., 1904. xxii, 386 pp.

Colman, Mrs. Edna Mary
Seventy-Five Years of White House Gossip; from Washington to Lincoln . . . Garden City, N. Y.: Doubleday, Page & Co., 1925. viii, 334 pp.

Crowninshield, Mary
Letters of Mary Boardman Crowninshield, 1815–1816. Cambridge: Printed at the Riverside Press, 1905. xiv, 82 pp.

Dahlgren, Madeleine
A Washington Winter. Boston: J. R. Osgood and Company, 1883. 247 pp.

————.
Etiquette of Social Life in Washington. Washington, D. C.: Mohun Bros., 1876. 51 pp. 4th ed.

Duffield, Isabel
Washington in the 90's; California Eyes Dazzled by the Brilliant Society of the Capitol (!) . . . San Francisco: Press of Overland Monthly, 1929. 118 pp., illus.

Ellet, Elizabeth Fries
The Court Circles of the Republic; or, The Beauties and Celebrities of the Nation; illustrating life and society under eighteen presidents . . . Hartford, Conn.: Hartford Publ. Co., 1869. xiv, 586 pp., illus.

Federal Writers' Project
Washington, City and Capital. (American Guide Series) Federal Writers' Project of the Works Progress Administration. Washington, D. C.: U. S. Gov't Printing Office, 1937.

Gerry, Elbridge
The Diary of Elbridge Gerry, Jr.; With a preface and footnotes by Claude G. Bowers, foreword by Annette Townsend. New York: Brentano's, 1927. xxv, 222 pp.
Includes an account of a journey on horseback from Massachusetts to Washington. The latter part of the diary treats of the social life of Washington during the Madison administration.

Gouverneur, Marian
As I Remember; Recollections of American Society during the Nineteenth Century. New York: D. Appleton and Co., 1911. 416 pp.

Hall, Florence Marion
Social Usages at Washington. New York: Harper & Bros., 1906. x, 165 pp.

Hobart, Jennie (Tuttle)
Memories. Paterson, N. J.: Priv. Print., 1930. 89 pp.

Lockwood, Mary Smith
Yesterdays in Washington. Rosslyn, Va.: Commonwealth Co., 1915. 2 vols.

Logan, Mrs.
Thirty Years in Washington; or, *Life and Scenes in Our National Capital* . . . Hartford: A. D. Worthington & Co., 1901. xxxii, 752 pp., illus.

Lomax, Elizabeth
Leaves from an Old Washington Diary, 1854–1863 . . . New York: Books, Inc., distributed by E. P. Dutton and Co., 1943. 256 pp.

Moore, Joseph West
Picturesque Washington: Pen and Pencil Sketches of its Scenery, History, Traditions, Public and Social Life . . . Providence: J. A. & R. A. Reid, 1887. 308 pp., illus.

O'Brien, Robert Lincoln
"Social Life at the White House." *Munsey's Magazine* 33:255–262, 1905.

Smith, Margaret
The Forty Years of Washington Society, Portrayed by the Family Letters of Mrs. Samuel Harrison Smith, from the collection of her grandson, J. Henley Smith; ed. by Gaillard Hunt . . . New York: C. Scribner's Sons, 1906. xii, 424 pp., illus.

Vincent, Elizabeth Kipp
In the Days of Lincoln; Girlhood Recollections and Personal Reminiscences of Life in Washington During the Civil War . . . Gardena, Cal.: Spanish Amer. Institute Press, 1924. 35 pp.

CHILDREN'S GAMES

Babcock, William Henry
"Carols and Child-lore at the Capital." *Lippincott's Monthly Magazine* 38:320–342, 1886. (Phila.)

————.
"Song-Games and Myth Dramas at Washington." *Lippincott's Monthly Magazine* (Phila.) 37:239–257, 1886.

PLACE NAMES

"Geographic Nomenclature of the District of Columbia. A Report." *AA* 6:29–52, 1893.

"Local Names." (Washington, D. C.) *JAFL* 1: 146–147, 1888.

MAINE

FOLKLORE

BIBLIOGRAPHY

Hall, D. B.
Reference List on Maine Local History. New York State Library Bulletin No. 63. Albany: State Library, June 1901.

Manuscripts Relating to the History of Maine. List 1–2. Index. The University of Maine Studies, Second Series No. 45. *The Maine Bulletin* 41:1–427, 1938; 42:1–261, 1939; 43:8–211, 1941. Index.

Noyes, Reginald Webb
A Bibliography of Maine Imprints to 1820. Stonington, Me.: Printed by Mrs. and Mr. R. W. Noyes, 1930. ix, 22 pp.

————.
A Guide to the Study of Maine Local History. New York: Columbia University Library, 1936. 87 numb.

Williamson, Joseph
A Bibliography of the State of Maine, from the earliest period to 1891. Portland, Maine: Thurston Press, 1896. 2 Vols. 738 pp., 669 pp.

PERIODICALS

Maine Historical Society. Collections. v. 1–10; 2d. ser. v. 1–10; 3d ser. v. 1–2. 1831–1906. Portland, The Society. *Proceedings.* 1899– .

Robinson, Daniel
The Maine Farmers' Almanac, for the Year of Our Lord ——. Hallowell, Maine: Masters, Smith & Co.

GENERAL STUDIES AND COLLECTIONS

Attwood, Stanley Bearce
The Length and Breadth of Maine. Augusta, Me.: Kennebec Journal Print Shop, 1946. xxiv, 279 pp., bibl.

Averill, Gerald.
Ridge Runner. Philadelphia, Pa.: J. B. Lippincott Co., 1948. 217 pp.
The author tells these stories "with the skill and technique of the deacon-seat narrator, and the book as a whole becomes a very personal thing in all the magnificence of deep-Maine wood story telling." (John Gould).

Barry, William E.
A Stroll Thru' the Past. Portland: The Southwest Press, 1933. vi, 93 pp., plates, map.

Beston, Henry
The St. Lawrence. (Rivers of America Series.) Illustrated by A. Y. Jackson. New York: Farrar and Rinehart, 1942. 274 pp.

Brooks, Annie Peabody
Ropes' Ends; Tradition, Legends, and Sketches of Old Kennebunkport and Vicinity. Illustrated. Kennebunkport, Me.: The Author, 1901. 236 pp., incl. front. pl.

Coffin, Robert P. Tristram
Kennebec: Cradle of Americans. (Rivers of America Series.) Illustrated by Mariland de Gogorza. New York: Farrar and Rinehart, 1937. x, 292 pp., illus.

————.
Maine Ballads. New York: The Macmillan Co., 1938. xiv, 106 pp.

————.
Yankee Coast. Written and Illustrated by R. P. Coffin, abetted by Peggy Coffin. New York: Macmillan Co., 1947. 333 pp., illus.

Collins, Charles W.
The Acadians of Madawaska, Maine. Boston: New England Catholic Historical Society, 1902.

Decrow, G.
"Folk-lore from Maine." *JAFL* 5:318–320, 1892.

Downing, Major Jack
The Life and Writings of Major Downing, of Downingville, Away Down East in the State of Maine, Written by Himself. Boston, Mass.: Lilly, Wait, Colman & Holden, 1834.

Drake, Samuel Adams
The Pine-Tree Coast. Boston: Estes & Lauriat, 1891. 396 pp.

Federal Writers' Project
Maine: A Guide "Down East." (American Guide Series.) By Workers of the Federal Writers' Project of the Works Progress Administration for the State of Maine. Boston: Houghton Mifflin and Co., 1937. xxvi, 476 pp., illus., bibl.

Hamlin, Helen
Nine Mile Bridge; Three years in the Maine woods. New York: W. W. Norton & Co., 1945. 233 pp., illus.

————.
Pine, Potatoes and People. Decorations by the author. New York: W. W. Norton and Co., 1948. 238 pp., illus.
A lively, folksy, conversational Maine commentary, capturing much of the people of Aroostook —their lives, their affairs, traditions and customs. A good portion is given to the isolated French-Canadian villages.

Holbrook, Stewart H.
Holy Old Mackinaw: a Natural History of the American Lumberjack. New York: The Macmillan Company, 1938. viii, 278 pp., bibl., logger's dictionary, pp. 258–265.

Jennison, Keith
The Maine Idea. Stories and pictures arranged by K. J. New York: Harcourt Brace and Co., 1943. 89 pp.
"It is simply a breath of Maine air and a brief visit with Maine folk."

Jones, Herbert G.
I Discover Maine, Little-Known Stories about a Well-Known State. Portland: The Machigonne Press, 1937.

Kimball, George Selwyn
Jay Gould Harmon with Maine Folks; a picture of life in the Maine woods. Boston: C. M. Clark Publishing Co., 1905. 442 pp.

MacDougall, Arthur R., Jr.
Where Flows the Kennebec. Illustrated by Milton C. Weiler. New York: Coward-McCann, 1947.
A delightful volume of stories . . . about Dad Dean, the lovable Maine guide who combines a potent mixture of fishing, philosophy and sharp Down East Humor.

"Maine Folklore." *JAFL* 5:318–320, 1892; 31: 272–273, 1918.

Meader, Stephen W.
Lumberjack. New York: Harcourt, Brace and Company, 1934.

Mitchell, Edwin Valentine
Maine Summer. Illustrations by Ruth Lepper. New York: Coward - McCann, 1939. 210 pp., illus.

Nason, Emma Huntington
Old Hallowell on the Kennebec. Augusta, Maine: Press of Burleigh and Flynt, 1909.

Noyes, Alfred
The Secret of Pookuck Island. New York: J. B. Lippincott Co., 1943. 183 pp.
A young boy's adventures on the Maine Coast. Glimpses of tradition and lore. Juvenile.

Nutting, Wallace
Maine Beautiful . . . a pictorial record covering all the counties of Maine with texts. Framingham, Mass.: Old America Co., 1924. 302 pp., illus.

Ogilvie, Elisabeth
The Ebbing Tide. New York: Thomas Y. Crowell Co., 1947.
A fast moving story of Maine Island life.

Peattie, Roderick, ed.
The Friendly Mountains. New York: Vanguard Press, 1942. 340 pp., illus.
Brief mention is made of Mt. Katahden of Maine.

Stephens, C. A.
My Folks in Maine. Norway, Maine: The Old Squire's Book Store, 1934. 304 pp.

Stowe, Harriet Beecher
The Pearl of Orr's Island, A Story of the Coast of.Maine. Boston: Houghton Mifflin and Company, 1891.

Sylvester, Herbert Milton
Maine Pioneer Settlements: Old York. Boston: W. B. Clarke Co., 1909.

Wallace, John
Village Down East. A Sketch Book. Brattleboro, Vt.: Stephen Daye Press, 1943. 184 pp., 182 illustrations.
Drawings capturing the spirit and .character of Maine people.

Wasson, George S.
Sailing Days on the Penobscot; The River and and Bay as they were in the old days with a record of the vessels built there. Compiled by Lincoln Colcord. Salem, Mass.: Marine Research Society, 1932. Illus.

Wilson, Charles Morrow
Aroostook: Our last frontier. Maine's picturesque potato empire. Illustrated with 32 photographs and 12 caricatures. Brattleboro, Vt.: Stephen Daye Press, 1937. 240 pp., illus.

Wilson, W. N.
Along the Maine Coast. New York: Whittlesey House, 1947.
A portfolio of paintings, some in full color, with text by Dorothy Mitchell. Mainly a guide, but affords interesting asides in folk life.

FOLKTALES—LEGENDS

Bishop, W. H.
"Fish and Men in the Maine Islands." *Harper's New Monthly Magazine* 61 (No. 364) :506–507, Sept. 1880.
The story of the *Haskell,* and the ghost crew.

Brooks, Noah
Tales of the Maine Coast. New York: C. Scribner's Sons, 1894. 271 pp.
Contents: Pansy Pegg—The Apparition of Jo Murch—The Hereditary Barn—The Phantom Sailor—The Honor of a Family—The Waif of Nautilus Island—A Century Ago.

Cox, William T.
Fearsome Creatures of the Lumberwoods, with a Few Desert and Mountain Beasts. Washington, D. C.: Judd & Detweiler, 1911.

Crankshaw, Mabel
Homespun Yarns of Maine. Philadelphia: Dorrance and Co., 1943.
Stories of the Maine Coast.

Farquar, Samuel T.
"The Tame Trout." *CFQ* 3:177–184, 1944.
A reprint in full of: "The tame trout and other fairy tales," narrated by Ed. Grant of Beaver Pond, Maine.

Jones, Rufus Matthew
Rufus Jones' Selected Stories of Native Maine Humor, edited by Nixon Orwin Rush. Worcester, Mass.: Clark University Library, 1945. 23 pp.

Maine Writers Research Club
Maine, Past and Present. Boston: D. C. Heath and Co., 1929. x, 321 pp., illus.
"Compilation of—stories of Maine towns and counties"—Pref.

Maule, Francis I., and Grant, Ed
The Tame Trout and Other Fairy Tales, narrated by Ed Grant of Beaver Pond, Maine, chronicled by Francis I. Maule of Philadelphia. Phillips: Maine Woods and Woodsman Print, 1904.

Ward, Artemus
"Maine in March." *Vanity Fair,* p. 181, April 20, 1861.

Whiting, B. J.
"Independent Origins: Maine and Morogoro." *JAFL* 6:85–86, 1947.
A folk tale of Revolutionary Days.

CUSTOMS—TRADITIONS

Chase, Mary Ellen
A Goodly Heritage. New York: Holt and Co., 1940. 298 pp.
An account, largely autobiographical of Maine seacoast life.

Coatsworth, Elizabeth Jane
Country Neighborhood, with decorations by Hildegard Woodward. New York: The Macmillan Co., 1944. 181 pp., illus.

————.
Maine Ways. New York: Macmillan Co., 1947.
Impressions and descriptions, country life and customs, conveys interesting information of the Maine folk.

Foster, Elizabeth
Dirigo Point. New York: Houghton Mifflin Co., 1944. 209 pp.
A novel full of rustic and homely details in a backwoods Maine Camp.

Gould, John
The House that Jacob Built. New York: William Morrow & Co., 1947. 256 pp.
A book of Maine ways and wayfaring, but particularly strong on speech and colloquialisms.

Graham, Elinor
Our Way Down East. New York: The Macmillan Co., 1943. 173 pp.
The author captures and vividly describes much of the Maine folkways and characters.

Rich, Louise (Dickinson)
Happy the Land. Philadelphia: J. B. Lippincott Co., 1946. 259 pp.

Richmond, Bernice
Winter Harbor. Decorations by John O'Hara Cosgrave. New York: H. Holt and Co., 1943. 211 pp., illus.

Steele, Thomas Sedgwick
Paddle and Portage, from Moosehead Lake to Aroostook River, Maine. Boston: Estes and Lauriat, 1882. 148 pp., illus.

SPEECH

Carr, Joseph William, and Chase, George Davis
"A Word List from Maine." I. *Dialect Notes* 3:239–251, 1907.

Chase, George Davis
"Maine Word-Lists"—More. *Dialect Notes* 4 (Part 2):151–153, 1914.

England, George Allan
"Rural Locutions of Maine and Northern New Hampshire." *Dialect Notes* 4(Part 2):67–83, 1914.

Estabrooke, Horace Melvyn
"A Word-List from Aroostook." *Dialect Notes* 3 (Part 5):407–418, 1909.

Gould, John
The House That Jacob Built. New York: William Morrow & Co., 1947. 256 pp.
　　Good on folk speech and colloquialism.

Greet, William Cabell
"A Record from Lubec, Maine, and Remarks on the Coastal Type." *AS* 6 (No. 6):397–403, 1931.

Hadlock, W. S., and Stimson, A. K.
"Traditional Cat Names." *JAFL* 59:529–530, 1946.
　　Heard by the authors in Islesford, Little Cranberry Island, near Mount Desert, Maine.

Leonard, Arthur N., and Chase, George D.
"Word-Lists from Maine." *Dialect Notes* 4 (Part 1):1–6, 1913.

Maxfield, Ezra Kempton
"Maine Dialect." *AS* 2 (No. 2):76–83, 1927.

————.
"Maine Word List." *Dialect Notes* 5 (Part 9): 385–390, 1926.

Morison, S. E.
"Notes from Maine." *AS* 4 (No. 5):356, 1929.

Perkins, Anne E.
"More Notes on Maine Dialect." *AS* 5 (No. 2): 118–131, 1929.

————.
"Vanishing Expressions of the Maine Coast." *AS* 3 (No. 2):134–141, 1927.

Shapleigh, F. E.
"Word-List from Maine." *Dialect Notes* 4 (Part 1):54–55, 1913.

Sheldon, Edward S.
"Some Specimens of a Canadian-French Dialect Spoken in Maine." *PMLA* 3:210–218, 1887.

PLACE NAMES

Brininstool, Earl Alonzo
"Indian Names in Maine." *JAFL* 18:316, 1905.

Eckstorm, Mrs. Fannie (Hardy)
Indian Place-Names of the Penobscot Valley and the Maine Coast. Orono, Me.: Printed at the University Press, 1941. xxix, 272 pp., bibl. (The University of Maine Studies, Second Series No. 55.)

————.
"The Indian Names of Two Maine Mountains" *New England Quar.* 9:132–142, 1936.

Greenleaf, Moses
Indian Place-Names; Indian Names of Some of the Streams, Islands, on the Penobscot and St. John Rivers in Maine. Taken from a letter from M. Greenleaf, esq., to Rev. Dr. Morse. New Haven: Priv. Prtd., 1903. 12 pp.

Hubbard, Lucius Lee
Indian Place-Names. In His Woods and Lakes of Maine. Boston: J. R. Osgood & Co., 1884. pp. 191–216.

————.
Some Indian Place-Names in Northern Maine, with explanations derived from the Indians, and a cross-index. Being a part of the appendix to "Woods and Lakes of Maine." Boston: J. R. Osgood and Co., 1884. pp. 192–216.

————.
Woods and Lakes of Maine; a trip from Moosehead Lake to New Brunswick in a birch-bark canoe, to which are added some Indian place-names and their meanings, now first published. ...New and original illustrations. Boston: J. R. Osgood and Co., 1884. xvi, 223 pp., illus.

Randel, William Pierce
"Town Names of York County, Maine." *New England Quarterly* 11:565–575, 1938.

Smith, Edgar Crosby
Moses Greenleaf, Maine's First Map-Maker. A biography: with letters, unpublished manuscripts and a reprint of Mr. Greenleaf's rare paper on Indian place names ... Bangor: The DeBurians, 1902. xviii, 166 pp.

FOLKSONG

GENERAL STUDIES AND COLLECTIONS

Barry, Phillips
"The Banks of the Gaspereaux." *FSSNE* 5:13–14, 1933.
　　An old Maine woods song, going back to the Square Timber Area.

————.
"The Burning of Henry K. Robinson's Camp at Ripogenns." *FSSNE* 12:20–21, 1937.

"Caroline and Her Young Sailor Bred."
FSSNE 2:9–10, 1931, n.s.
A variant, resembling "The Gallant Hussar" and "Rosin the Bow." Recorded in Maine.

"The Factory Girls' Come-All-Ye." *FSSNE* 2:12–13, 1931.
Insight into the economic plight of Lewiston factory girls in the middle of the 19th century. (Words and melody).

"Folk Songs of Mary Wyatt and Henry Green." *FSSNE* 12:14–18, 1937.

"Henry K. Sawyer." *FSSNE* 9:17–22, 1935.
Maine R. R. Accident.

"The Jam on Gerry's Rock." *FSSNE* 10:18–20, 1935.

"Jimmie Judges." *FSSNE* 10:20–21, 1935.
A Lumberman tragedy in the Bonshee River.

"Lost Jimmie Whalen." *FSSNE* 11:4–7, 1936.
Variants of a Maine ballad: four versions given, texts and tunes.

"The Low River Shore." *FSSNE* 2:8–9, 1931.
A Maine variant of an Old World ballad.

The Maine Woods Songster. Cambridge, Mass.: Powell, 1939. 102 pp.
Texts, tunes and analytical notes.

"Negro Folk Songs from Maine." *FSSNE* 8:13–16, 1934; 9:10–14, 1935; 10:21–24, 1935.

"Samuel Allen." *FSSNE* 9:17–22, 1935.
A ballad of the Maine lumberjacks.

"The Schooner Fred Dunbar." *FSSNE* 5:15–16, 1933.
A favorite song about Penobscot Bay.

"Tom Cray." *FSSNE* 9:17–22, 1935.
Maine, Beaver Brook, Lumberjack.

"The Woody Queristers." *FSSNE* 12:19–20, 1937.
A whimsical quatrain ballad going back to the 17th century.

————, Eckstorm, Fanny H., and Smyth, Mary W.
British Ballads from Maine; the development of popular songs with texts and airs, versions of ballads included in Professor F. J. Child's Collection. New Haven, Conn.: Yale University Press, 1929. xlvi, 535 pp., music (unaccomp. melodies), bibl. (pp. 497–502).

Day, Holman F.
Pine Tree Ballads: Rhymes, Stories of Un-planed Human Natur' up in Maine. Boston: Houghton Mifflin Co., 1902, illus.

"Discoveries Down East: British Ballads from Maine." *New York Herald Tribune Books,* (March 16) 1930. A review.

Eckstorm, Fannie Hardy
"Canady I O." *FSSNE* 6:10–13, 1933.
Words and tunes. Closely related to "Buffalo Skinners."

————.
"Two Maine Texts of 'Lamkin' " *JAFL* 52:70–74, 1939.

————, and Smyth, Mary Winslow
Minstrelsy of Maine: Folk-Songs and Ballads of the Woods and the Coast. Boston: Houghton Mifflin Company, 1927. xvi, 390 pp., bibl. (xi-xii)

"Folk-Song in Maine" *Portland Sunday Telegram and Sunday Press Herald,* (April 27) 1930. A review.

Gray, Roland Palmer
Songs and Ballads of the Maine Lumberjacks, with other songs from Maine, collected and edited by Roland Palmer Gray. Cambridge: Harvard University Press, 1924. xxi, 191 pp.

Pound, Louise
"Minstrelsey of Maine." *JAFL* 40:102, 1927. A Review.

"A Trip to the Grand Banks." *FSSNE* 4:15, 1932.
"A true picture of the fisherman's life, with its splendid sweep of rhythm and spirited melody, is of the 'old salt salty.' " (Barry.)

CHILDREN'S RHYMES

"Maine Nursery Rhymes." *JAFL* 4:269-270, 1891.

ARRANGEMENTS

————: *Piano*

Bauer, Marion
Letters from a Maine Farm. Seven Pieces for the Piano—Op. 9. New York: Composer's Music Corporation, 1924.
Inspired by Maine lore and legend. Includes: Legend of the Cascadilla.

MARYLAND

FOLKLORE

PERIODICALS

Maryland Historical Magazine. Baltimore. V. 1, 1906. Maryland Historical Society.

Maryland History Notes. Baltimore. V. 1, 1943. Maryland Historical Society. Quarterly.

GENERAL STUDIES AND COLLECTIONS

Alsop, George
A Character of the Province of Maryland.
Described in four distinct parts. Also a small
treatise on the wild naked Indians (or Susquehanokes) of Maryland . . . New ed. with an
introduction and copious historical notes, by
John Gilmary Shea. New York: W. Gowans,
1869. 125 pp.

Bergen, Fanny D.
"On the Eastern Shore." *JAFL* 2:295–300,
1889.
General folklore items.

Beverley-Giddings, A. R.
River of Rogues. New York: William Morrow
and Company, 1948. 378 pp.
"Using old records and legends of the Eastern
Shore, where he himself makes his home, Mr.
Beverley-Giddings has created a lively tale that
offers a particularly interesting picture of a way
of life in one part of the United States a century
and a quarter ago." (Mary Ross.)

Bullock, W. R.
"Collection of Maryland Folklore." *JAFL*
11:7–16, 1898.

Federal Writers' Project
Maryland, a Guide to the Old Time State.
(American Guide Series) Compiled and writ-
ten by the Federal Writers' Project of the
Works Progress Administration of the State
of Maryland. New York: Oxford University
Press, 1940. xxviii, 561 pp., bibl.

Fife, Austin E.
"Baltimore Branch, American Folklore Society" (Maryland Folklore Society). *JAFL*
59:481–483, 1946.

Footner, Hulbert
Rivers of the Eastern Shore: Seventeen Maryland Rivers Illustrated by Aaron Sopher.
(Rivers of America Series). New York: Farrar
and Rinehart, 1944. 375 pp.

Harbaugh, T. C.
Middletown Valley in Song and Story. No
Publisher, 1910. 173 pp.

Ingraham, Prentiss
Land of Legendary Lore. (Sketches of romance and reality on the eastern shore of
the Chesapeake.) Easton, Md.: Gazette Publishing House, 1898.

Kennedy, John Pendleton
Rob of the Bowl. New York: Putnam and
Co., 1856, rev. ed.

Lee, C.
"Negro Lore from Baltimore." *JAFL* 5:110–
112, 1892.

Speers, Mary Walker Finely
"Maryland and Virginia Folklore." *JAFL*
26:190–191, 1913.

White, Andrew
A Relation of Maryland. In: Hall, C.C. ed.:
Narrative of Early Maryland 1633–34, New
York: Charles Scribner's Sons, 1910. pp. 63–
112, First Ed., London, 1635.

Whitney, Annie Weston, and Bullock, Caroline Caufield
Folk-Lore from Maryland. Memoirs of the
American Folklore Society, vol. 18, New York:
The American Folklore Society, 1925. 239 pp.
A magnificent collection of every aspect of folk-
lore. What every state should have!

FOLKTALES—LEGENDS

Nyburg, Sidney Lauer
The Buried Rose: Legends of Old Baltimore.
New York: Alfred A. Knopf, 1932. x, 302 pp.

Parsons, E. C.
"Tales from Maryland and Pennsylvania."
JAFL 30:209–217, 1917.

Townsend, George Alfred
The Entailed Hat; or Patty Cannon's Times.
New York: Harper and Brothers, 1884.

MAGIC—SUPERSTITION

Dahlgren, Madeleine V.
South-Mountain Magic; A Narrative. Boston:
J. R. Osgood and Co., 1882. 218 pp.

Parke, Francis Neal
"Witchcraft in Maryland." *Maryland Historical
Magazine* 31: pp. 271–298, 1936.

Seip, E. C.
"Witch-Finding in Western Maryland." *JAFL*
14:39–44, 1901.

BELIEFS—CUSTOMS—TRADITIONS

Cook, Ebenezer
The Sot-Weed Factor: or, *A Voyage to Maryland.* A Satyr. In which is described the laws,
government, courts and constitutions of the
country; and also the buildings, feasts, fro-
licks, entertainments, and drunken humours
of the inhabitants of that part of America. In
burlesque verse. London: Printed and sold by
B. Bragg, 1708. 21 pp.

Byron, Gilbert
These Chesapeake Men. Dover, Del.: The
Author, Kings Highway, 1942.
Poems of the Chesapeake Bay Country.

Earle, Swepson
The Chesapeake Bay Country. Baltimore,
Md.: Thomsen-Ellis Co., 1923. 510 pp., bibl.

Thomas, J. W.
Chronicles of Colonial Maryland. Baltimore,
1900. 334 pp., illus.

Whitney, Annie Weston
"Items of Maryland Beliefs and Customs."
JAFL 12:273–274, 1899.

Wilstach, Paul
Tidewater Maryland. New York: Tudor Publishing Co., 1945. 383 pp.

FOLK MEDICINE

Wrenshall, L. H.
"Incantations and Popular Healing in Maryland, Pennsylvania." *JAFL* 15:268–274, 1902.

SPEECH

Kuethe, J. Louis
"Johns Hopkins Jargon." *AS* 7 (No. 5): 327–338, 1932.
A glossary college slang.

————.
"'Water' Terms in Maryland." *AS* 10(No. 2): 153–154, 1935.

McKinsey, Folger
"Colloquial Expression Indigenous to Maryland." *Baltimore Sun,* Dec. 5, 1938, p. 6, col. 8.

Read, Allen Walker
"Boucher's Linguistic Pastoral of Colonial Maryland." *Dialect Notes* 6(Part 7):337–360, 1933.
Additional comment: (pp. 360–363).

"Words from Maryland." *AS* 15:451–452, 1940.

Zimmerman, Rev. H. E.
"Word List from Maryland." *Dialect Notes* 4(Part 5):343, 1916.

PLACE NAMES

Heckewelder, J. G. E.
Names Given by the Lenni Lenape or Delaware Indians to Rivers, Streams, and Places in the now States of New Jersey, Pennsylvania, Maryland and Virginia, with their significations. Publications, Pennsylvania German Folklore Society, vol. 5(No. 1). Allentown, Pa.: Penn. German Folklore Society, 1940.

Kuethe, J. Louis
"A List of Maryland Mills, Taverns, Forges and Furnaces of 1795." *Maryland Historical Magazine* 31:155–169, 1936.

Marye, William Rose
"The Place-Names of Baltimore and Harford Counties." *Maryland Historical Mag.* 25:321–365, 1930.

FOLKSONG

DANCES

Behre, H. Edward
"Square Dancing on the Eastern Shore of Maryland." *SFQ* 9(No. 4):213–221, 1945.

Warnick, Florence
"Play Party Songs in Western Maryland." *JAFL* 54:162–166, 1941.
Words only of 12 songs.

————.
Play Party Songs in Western Maryland. Washington, D. C.: privately printed, 1942. 11 pp.

RECORDS

U. S. Library of Congress. Division of Music. Folklore Section.
Old English Ballads Recorded in Maryland, by Prof. MacEdward Leach and Prof. H. Beck. University of Pennsylvania Project. AAFS-LC.

MASSACHUSETTS
FOLKLORE
BIBLIOGRAPHY

Flagg, Charles Allcott
A Guide to Massachusetts Local History; being a bibliographic index to the literature of the towns, cities, and counties of the State including books, pamphlets, articles in periodicals and collected works, books in preparation, historical manuscripts, newspaper clippings, etc. Salem, Mass.: The Salem Press Co., 1907. ix, 256 pp.

Nichols, Charles Lemuel
Notes on the Almanacs of Massachusetts. Worcester, Mass.: The Society, 1912. 122 pp.

Paltsits, Victor Hugo
The Almanacs of Roger Sherman, 1750–1761. Containing also prose and poetical selections and a complete collection of the "Sayings" found in them . . . Worcester, Mass.: Davis Press, 1907. 48 pp.

PERIODICALS

Massachusetts Historical Society. Collections, V. 1, 1792—Cambridge, Mass.: The Massachusetts Historical Society. *Proceedings,* V. 1, 1791—

The Massachusetts Magazine, devoted to Massachusetts history, genealogy, biography. Quarterly V. 1, 1908—Salem, Mass.: The Salem Press Co.

GENERAL STUDIES AND COLLECTIONS

Atwood, Charles R.
Reminiscences of Taunton, In Ye Auld Lang Syne. Taunton: Republican Steam Printing Rooms, 1880. 266 pp.

Babson, John J.
History of the Town of Gloucester, Cape Ann. Gloucester: Procter Brothers, 1860. xi, 610 pp., illus., plates, fold map.
Including the Town of Rockport with notes and additional 1st and 2nd Series Gloucester: 1860–91.

Babson, Roger W., and Saville, Foster H.
Cape Ann, A Tourist Guide. Rockport, Mass.: Cape Ann Old Book Shop, 35 High Street, 1936. 118 pp.
Mentions numerous items of local folklore, connected with Dogtown, old houses and mills. Contains a fairly good bibliography of Cape Ann.

Bangs, Mary Rogers
Old Cape Cod; The Land, The Men, The Sea.
Boston: Houghton Mifflin Company, 1920.

Barber, John Warner
Historical Collections, being a general collection of interesting facts, traditions, biographical sketches, anecdotes, etc., relating to
the history and antiquities of every town in
Massachusetts, with geographical descriptions.
Illustrated by 200 engravings. Worcester: La-
zell, 1848. viii, 631 pp., illus.

Barry, John S.
*A Historical Sketch of the Town of Andover,
Mass., with Family Genealogies.* Boston:
Samuel G. Drake, 1853.

Bassett, Sara Ware
Heart's Haven. New York: Doubleday, Doran
and Co., 1944. 204 pp.
    The author brings the folksy flavor and authen-
    ticity to this novel of Cape Cod life and manners.

Bigelow, Ella A.
*Historical Reminiscences of the Early Times
in Marlborough, Massachusetts,* and Prominent
Events from 1860 to 1910, Including Brief
Allusions to Many Individuals and an Account
of the Celebration of the Two Hundred and
Fiftieth Anniversary of the Incorporation of the
Town. Marlborough, Mass.: Times Publishing
Co., 1910.

Bigelow, E. Victor
*A Narrative of the Town of Cohasset, Massa-
chusetts.* Cohasset: Published under the Auspices of the Committee on Town History, 1898.

Biglow, William
History of the Town of Natick, Mass., from
the Days of the Apostolic Eliot MDCL, to the
Present Time, MDCCCXXX. Boston: Marsh,
Capen & Lyon, 1830.

Brooks, Charles
*History of the Town of Medford, Middlesex
County, Massachusetts,* from its First Settle-
ment, in 1630, to the Present Time, 1855.
Boston: James M. Usher, 1855.

Brooks, Henry Mason
The Olden Time Series; gleanings, chiefly
from old newspapers of Boston and Salem,
Massachusetts, selected and arranged with
brief comments. Boston: Ticknor and Company, 1886. 6 vols., illus.
    Contents: 1. Curiosities of the old lottery. 2. The
    days of the spinning-wheel in New England. 3.
    New England Sunday. 4. Quaint and curious ad-
    vertisements, etc.

Chaffin, William L.
History of the Town of Easton. Cambridge,
Mass.: J. Wilson and Sons, Printers, 1886.
838 pp., illus.

Coffin, Joshua
*Sketch of the History of Newbury, Newbury-
port, and West Newbury, from 1635 to 1845.*
Boston: S. G. Drake, 1845. viii, 416 pp.

Connoly, James B.
The Book of the Gloucester Fisherman; illus.
by Henry O'Connor. New York: The John
Day Co., 1930. 303 pp., illus., plates.

Crafts, James M.
History of the Town of Whately, Mass. Including a Narrative of Leading Events from
the First Planting of Hatfield: 1661–1899, as
Revised and Enlarged, with Family Genealogies. Orange, Mass.: Printed for the Town
by D. L. Crandall, 1899.

Crosby, Everett Uberto
Nantucket in Print. Nantucket, Mass.: Printed
by the Inquirer and Mirror Press. 1946.
    Legends and early writings by missionaries and
    explorers.

Digges, Jeremiah, ed.
Cape Cod Pilot. Written with Editorial and
Research Assistance of the Members of the
Federal Writers' Project. American Guide
Series, Federal Writers' Project, Works Prog-
ress Administration for the State of Massa-
chusetts. Sponsored by Poor Richard Asso-
ciates. Provincetown and New York: Modern
Pilgrim Press and the Viking Press, 1937.
(bibl. pp. 390–391).

——.
In Great Waters, The Story of the Portuguese
Fishermen. New York: The Macmillan Com-
pany, 1941.

Early, Eleanor
And This Is Cape Cod! Boston: Houghton
Mifflin Company, 1936.

Eastman, Sophie E.
In Old South Hadley. Chicago: The Blakely
Printing Co., 1912.

Edwards, Agnes
The Romantic Shore. Salem, Mass.: The Salem
Press Company, 1915.

Emery, Sarah Anna, ed.
Reminiscences of a Nonagenarian. Newburyport, Mass.: William H. Huse & Co., 1879.

Esquemeling, Joseph
The History of the Buccaneers of America. Con-
taining detailed accounts of these Bold and
Daring Freebooters chiefly along the Spanish
Main, in the West Indies, and in the Great
South Sea. With some introductory notices of
piracies on the coast of New England in the
year 1724. Boston: 1851. illus.

Farmer, S. B.
"Folklore of Marblehead." *JAFL* 7:252–253,
1894.

Federal Writers' Project
A Historical Sketch of Auburn, Massachusetts,
From the Earliest Period to the Present Day,
with Brief Accounts of Early Settlers and
Prominent Citizens, written and compiled by
the Federal Writers' Project of the Works
Progress Administration for the State of Massachusetts. Sponsored by the Auburn Centennial Committee. 1937.

The Armenians in Massachusetts (American Guide Series) written and compiled by the Federal Writers' Project of the WPA for the State of Mass. Boston: American Historical Society, 1937.

The Berkshire Hills. (American Guide Series). Compiled and written by Members of the Federal Writers' Project of the Works Progress Administration for Massachusetts. Sponsored by the Berkshire Hills Conference, Inc. New York: Funk and Wagnalls Company, 1939. xiv, 368 pp., illus.

Massachusetts, a Guide to its Places and People (American Guide Series). Written and compiled by the Federal Writers' Project of the Works Progress Administration for the state of Mass. Boston: Houghton Mifflin Co., 1937. xxxvi, 675 pp., bibl.

Whaling Masters. (American Guide Series). Written and compiled by the Federal Writers' Project of the Works Progress Administration of Mass. New Bedford, Mass.: Reynolds Printing, 1938.

Frost, Elizabeth Hollister
This Side of Land: an Island Epic. New York: Coward-McCann, 1942.
The author uses old songs, proverbs, and bits of folk wisdom of the time—describing the daily life of the women and showing the insular psychology of the people of Nantucket.

Gookin, Warner Foote
Capawack, alias Martha's Vineyard. Edgarton, Mass.: Dukes County Historical Society, 1948. 58 pp.

Greylock, Godfrey (Joseph Edwards Adams Smith)
Taghconic; The Romance and Beauty of the Hills. Boston: Lee and Shepard, 1879. 381 pp. Description and travel, legends, customs in Berkshire County, Mass.

Haley, Nelson Cole
Whale Hunt: The Narrative of a Voyage by Nelson Cole Haley, Harpooner in the Ship Charles W. Morgan, 1849–53. New York: Ives Washburn, 1948. 304 pp.
"For a zestful New England boy there were the storms and gales, and a fine hurricane. There were also deserted anchorages, and isles with cannibals, English remittance men and muscular native belles. There were the hazardous search for whales, in open boat in mid-ocean; there were topographical and humane observations like a latter-day Defoe, with the saving grace of a clipped Cape Cod humor." (William Germain Dooley)

Halton, Edith Austin
For Those in Peril. New York: G. P. Putnam's Sons, 1943. 277 pp.
"A tale of Cape Cod Whalers it is Falmouth itself, with the smell of the sea and the salt marshes and the home-baked bread, with its courage and its prejudices, its gossips and unsung heroes." (Louise M. Field.)

Hine, C. G., coll.
The Story of Martha's Vineyard, from the Lips of Its Inhabitants, Newspaper Files and Those Who Have Visited Its Shores, Including Stray Notes on Local History and Industries. New York: Hine Brothers, 1908.

Historical Celebration of the Town of Brimfield, Hampden County, Mass., Wednesday, October 11, 1876, with the Historical Address of Rev. Charles M. Hyde, D.D., and Other Addresses, Letters, Documents, etc., Relating to the Early History of the Town. Published by Vote of the Town. Springfield, Mass.: The Clark W. Bryan Co., 1879.

Hobart, Benjamin
History of the Town of Abington, Plymouth County, Massachusetts, from Its First Settlement. Boston: T. H. Carter and Son, 1866.

Holberg, Ruth Langland
Tibby's Adventure. Illustrated by Phyllis N. Coté. New York: Doubleday, Doran and Co., 1944. 122 pp.
A story for young readers of adventure, lore and romance of Cape Ann fishermen.

Huntoon, Daniel T. V.
History of the Town of Canton, Norfolk County, Massachusetts. Published by the Town. Cambridge: John Wilson and Son, University Press, 1893.

Hyde, William
"Reminiscences of Danvers in the Forties and Fifties." *The Historical Collections of the Danvers Historical Society,* 5:8–9, 1917.

Kendrick, Fannie Shaw
The History of Buckland, 1775–1935, with Genealogies by Lucy Cutter Kellog. Buckland, Mass.: Published by the Town of Buckland Committee, 1937.

Kittredge, George Lyman, ed.
Letters of Samuel Lee and Samuel Sewall Relating to New England and the Indians. Cambridge: John Wilson and Son, University Press, 1912. (Reprinted from *The Publications of The Colonial Society of Massachusetts, Vol. XIV*).
In the writings of the Colonial fathers one finds much material on the beliefs, myths, traditions, legends and customs of the early settlers.

Kittredge, Henry Crocker
Cape Cod. Its People and Their History. Boston: Houghton Mifflin Company, 1930. xii, 330 pp., bibl.

Mooncussers of Cape Cod. Boston: Houghton Mifflin Company. 1937.

Leonard, Henry C.
Pigeon Cove and Vicinity. Boston: F. A. Searle, 1873. 193 pp.
Interesting bits of local lore and legend.

Lincoln, Joseph C.
The Bradshaws of Harness. New York: D. Appleton-Century Co., 1943. 380 pp.
The author evokes "the grubby, gossipy, salty hometown atmosphere of Cape Cod." (C. Brody.)

———.
Cape Cod Yesterdays. Paintings and drawings by Harved Brett. Garden City, N. Y.: Blue Ribbon Books, 1939. 286 pp.

Mackaye, Percy
Dogtown Common. New York: The Macmillan Co., 1921. 110 pp.
A long poem dealing with local lore and events.

Macy, William F., and Hussey Roland B.
The Nantucket Scrap Basket, Being a Collection of Characteristic Stories and Sayings of the People of the Town and Island of Nantucket, Massachusetts . . . Published for the benefit of "Sons and Daughters of Nantucket." Nantucket: The Inquirer and Mirror Press, 1916. xii, 183 pp.

Marquand, John P.
Lord Timothy Dexter of Newburyport, Mass. New York: Minton, Balch and Co., 1925. 378 pp.

Marshfield, 70°–40′ W: 42°–5′ N, The Autobiography of a Pilgrim Town, Being An Account of Three Hundred Years of a New England Town; Founded by the Pilgrims; Lived in and Developed by the Royalists; Adopted by Daniel Webster & Beloved by Many of the Ancestors of Those Who Today Make It Their Home, 1640–1940. Marshfield, Mass.: Marshfield Tercentenary Committee, 1940.

"Massachusetts Folklore." *JAFL* 7:252–263, 1894.

McIntire, E. C.
Picturesque Cape Ann. Gloucester, 1910.

Northend, Mary Harrod
Memories of Old Salem, Drawn from the Letters of a Great-Grandmother. New York: Moffat, Yard and Company, 1917.

Packard, Winthrop
Old Plymouth Trails. Boston: Small, Maynard & Company, 1920.
Besides telling much on customs, legends, and history, the author spins a number of good yarns.

Pease, Zephaniah W.
History of New Bedford. New York: The Lewis Historical Publishing Company, 1918. 3 vols.

Pringle, James Robert
History of the Town and City of Gloucester, Cape Ann, Mass. Gloucester, Mass.: The Author, 1892. 340 pp.

Reynard, Elizabeth
The Narrow Land; folk chronicles of Old Cape Cod. Boston: Houghton Mifflin Co., 1932. xi, 326 pp., illus., bibl.

Rich, Shebnah
Truro—Cape Cod, or Land Marks and Sea Marks. Boston: D. Lothrop and Company, 1884. Second ed. rev.

Roads, Samuel, Jr.
The History and Traditions of Marblehead. Marblehead: Press of N. Allen Lindsey & Co., 1897. 3rd ed.

Robinson, Francis Joseph George
Tragabigzanda or Cape Ann, an Informer. Boston: The Progressive Print, 1935. 32 pp.

Smith, Chard Powers
The Housatonic. Puritan River. Illustrated by Armiss Landeck. (The Rivers of America Series). New York: Rinehart and Company, 1946. 352 pp.

Smith, Joseph Edward
The History of Pittsfield, Berkshire County, Massachusetts. Boston: Lee and Shepard, 1869–76. 2 vols., illus.

———.
Taghonic; or Letters and Legends About Our Summer Home. Boston: Redding and Company, 1852. vi, 228 pp.

Snow, Edward Rowe
The Islands of Boston Harbor, Their History and Romance, 1626–1935. Andover, Mass.: The Andover Press, 1935.

———.
The Romance of Boston Bay. Boston: The Yankee Publishing Co., 1944.
Many legends and beliefs are included.

Solley, George Willis
Alluring Rockport, An Unspoiled New England Town on Cape Ann. Manchester by the Sea: North Shore Press, Inc., 1924.
An irregular, rocky shore with ledges and sandy coves; quarries haunted by artists; Campers in Bearskin Neck; Old Mansions built with Pirate's Gold, A Meeting House, fired on by the British in the War of 1812, "A Fighting Parson"; "A Deserted Village"; "A Witch House"; "A Likker Raid" of olden times; Quaint Stories of other days, A Mecca for Home-Lovers, Writers and Artists.

Swift, C. F., ed.
Genealogical Notes of Barnstable Families, Being a Reprint of the Amos Otis Papers, Originally Published in "The Barnstable Patriot," revised by C. F. Swift, Largely from Notes Made by the Author. Barnstable, Mass.: F. B. & F. P. Goss, 1888.

Tarbell, Arthur Wilson
Cape Cod Ahoy! A Travel Book for the Summer Visitor. Boston: A. T. Ramsay & Co., 1932.

The Westfield Jubilee: A Report of the Celebration at Westfield, Mass., on the Two Hundredth Anniversary of the Incorporation of the Town, October 6, 1869, with the Historical Address of the Hon. William G. Bates, and other Speeches and Poems of the Occasion, with an Appendix, Containing Historical Documents of Local Interest. Westfield, Mass.: Clark & Story, Publishers, 1870.

Thompson, Francis M.
A History of Greenfield, Shire Town of Franklin County, Massachusetts (1682–1900). Greenfield, Mass.: Press of T. Morey and Son, 1904.

Thompson, Harold W., ed.
The Last of the "Logan." The true adventures of Robert Coffin, Mariner, in the years 1854 to 1859. Ithaca, N. Y.: Cornell University Press, 1947.
A narrative of whaling and shipwreck, life among the Cannibals of Fiji; Escape to Sydney and the Bush, and the Australian Gold Rush. Valuable for its chronological table of American whaling from the primitive days of shore whaling at Nantucket, and for its fine bibliography on whaling.

Tibbetts, Fred W.
The Story of Gloucester, Massachusetts, permanently settled 1623. Gloucester: Clark the Printer, 1917. 52 p., illus.
An address prepared by Frederick W. Tibbetts and given before the convention of the Mass. State Fireman's Association at City Hall, Gloucester, Thursday afternoon, September 21, 1916.

Tourtellot, Arthur Bernon
The Charles. (Rivers of America Series). Illustrated by Ernest J. Donnelly. New York: Farrar and Rinehart, 1941. x, 356 pp., illus. bibl.

Tozzer, Alfred M.
"The Boston and Cambridge Branches, American Folklore Society." *JAFL* 59:483–484, 1946.

Traiper, Donald G., and others
Barnstable: Three Centuries of a Cape Cod Town. Maps by James F. McLaughlin. Sketches by Vernon Coleman. Illustrated with Photographs. Hyannis: F. B. and F. P. Goss, 1939. xiv, 500 pp.

Underwood, Francis H.
Quabbin, The Story of a Small Town, with Outlooks upon Puritan Life. Boston: Lee and Shepard, 1893. viii, 375 pp.
The story of Enfield, Mass.

Webster, Clarence M.
Town Meeting Country. (American Folkways Series). New York: Duell, Sloan and Pearce, 1945. ix, 246 pp.
The region dealt with is Eastern Connecticut and South Central Massachusetts. "This volume stands out for the success with which it views the developed culture of a region in its influences on the formation of local custom and local character." (J. W. Ashton.)

Webber, John S., Jr.
In and Around Cape Ann Gloucester, 1885. Printed at the Cape Ann Advertiser office. 97 pp. 1885.

Weymouth Historical Society
History of Weymouth, Massachusetts. Weymouth, Mass.: Weymouth Historical Society, 1923. 4 vols.

Wilson, H. B.
"Syrian Folklore Collected in Boston." *JAFL* 16:133–147, 1903.

FOLKTALES—LEGENDS

Allen, Joseph C.
Tales and Trails of Martha's Vineyard. Boston: Little, Brown and Company, 1938.

Austin, William
Peter Rugg, the Missing Man. In: *A Book of New England Legends and Folklore in Prose and Poetry* by Samuel Adams Drake. (pp. 90–105). Boston: Roberts Brothers, 1883.
A Massachusetts tale.

Brooks, Elbridge Streeter
Stories of the Old Bay State. New York: American Book Company, 1899. 284 pp., illus.

Coleman, John C.
Colonial Legends and Folklore . . . Albany: Order of the Founders and Patriots of America. New York Society, Publications, No. 24, 1910. 15 pp.

Converse, Parker Lindall
Legends of Woburn, Now First Written and Preserved in Collected Form. Woburn, Mass.: Printed for Subscribers Only, 1892.

Crosby, Everett Uberto
Nantucket in Print. Nantucket, Mass.: Printed by the Inquirer and Mirror Press.
Legends and early writings by missionaries and explorers.

Drake, Samuel Adams
Boston Legends. In: *A Book of New England Legends and Folklore in Prose and Poetry* (pp. 3–115). Boston: Little, Brown and Co., 1901. 477 pp., illus.

_____.
Cambridge Legends. In: *A Book of New England Legends and Folklore in Prose and Poetry* (pp. 115–128). Boston: Little, Brown and Co., 1901. 477 pp., illus.

_____.
Cape-Ann Legends. In: *A Book of New England Legends and Folklore in Prose and Poetry* (pp. 237–273). Boston: Little, Brown and Co., 1901. 477 pp., illus.

_____.
Hampton and Portsmouth Legends. In: *A Book of New England Legends and Folklore in Prose and Poetry* (pp. 319–345). Boston: Little, Brown and Co., 1901. 477 pp., illus.

_____.
Ipswich and Newbury Legends. In: *A Book of New England Legends and Folklore in Prose and Poetry* (pp. 273–315). Boston: Little, Brown and Co., 1901. 477 pp., illus.

_____.
Lynn and Nahant Legends. In: *A Book of New England Legends and Folklore in Prose and Poetry* (pp. 128–167). Boston: Little, Brown and Co., 1901. 477 pp., illus.

———.
Marblehead Legends. In: *A Book of New England Legends and Folklore in Prose and Poetry* (pp. 205–237). Boston: Little, Brown and Co., 1901. 447 pp., illus.

———.
Nantucket and other Legends. In: *A Book of New England Legends and Folklore in Prose and Poetry* (pp. 441–461). Boston: Little, Brown and Co., 1901. 477 pp., illus.

———.
Old Colony Legends. In: *A Book of New England Legends and Folklore in Prose and Poetry* (pp. 365–393). Boston: Little, Brown and Co., 1901. 477 pp., illus.

———.
Salem Legends. In: *A Book of New England Legends and Folklore in Prose and Poetry* (pp. 167–205). Boston: Little, Brown and Co., 1901. 477 pp., illus.

———.
York, Isles-of-Shoals, and Boon-Island Legends. In: *A Book of New England Legends and Folklore in Prose and Poetry* (pp. 345–365). Boston: Little, Brown and Co., 1901. 477 pp., illus.

Earle, Alice Morse
In Old Narragansett, Romances and Realities. New York: Charles Scribner's Sons, 1898. vii, 196 pp.

Emerson, William Andrew
Worcester Legends; Incidents, Anecdotes, Reminiscences, etc., Connected with the Early History of Worcester, Mass., and Vicinity. Worcester: Delholm & McKay Co., 1905. 61 pp., illus.

Federal Writers' Project
Old Newbury Tales. (An Historical Reader for Children.) Written and Compiled by the Federal Writers' Project of the Works Progress Administration for the State of Mass. Historical Society of Old Newbury, 1937.

Mann, Charles E.
In the Heart of Cape Ann, or the Story of Dogtown, with illus. by Catherine M. Follansbee. Gloucester, Mass.: Proctor Bros., 1896. 71 pp., illus., pl., maps.
An exhaustive study of the legends and ruins of Dogtown Common.

Needham, Walter
"Grandpa Was Quite a Fellow." *The Sat. Eve. Post.* 219 (No. 19):13, Nov. 9, 1946.
A tall tale.

Reynard, Elizabeth
The Narrow Land, Folk Chronicles of Old Cape Cod. Boston: Houghton Mifflin Company, 1934.

Smith, G. H.
"Legend of the Origin of Nantucket Island." *JAFL* 54:83, 1941.

Sullivan, John L.
Life and Reminiscences of a 19th Century Gladiator. Boston: Jas. A. Hearn & Co., 1892.
The story of the famous Boston-born pugilist, and the many legends that have grown about him.

Wyer, H. S., ed.
Spun-Yarn from Old Nantucket. Nantucket: The Inquirer and Mirror Press, 1914.

SUPERSTITIONS—WITCHCRAFT

Bibliography

Burr, George Lincoln
"The Literature of Witchcraft." *American Historical Assoc. Papers* 4:237–266, 1890.

———.
Narratives of the Witchcraft Cases, 1648–1706. New York: C. Scribner's Sons, 1914. xviii, 467 pp.

———.
"A Witch-Hunter in the Book-Shops." *Bibliographer* 1:431–446, 1902.

Holmes, Thomas James
Cotton Mather and his Writings on Witchcraft. Chicago: The University of Chicago Press, 1926.

Moore, George Henry
Bibliographical Notes on Witchcraft in Massachusetts. Worcester: The Author, 1888. 31 pp.

General Studies and Collections

Allen, Rowland Hussey
The New-England Tragedies in Prose. I. The Coming of the Quakers. II. The Witchcraft Delusion. Boston: Nichols and Noyes, 1869. 156 pp.

Beard, George M.
The Psychology of the Salem Witchcraft Excitement of 1692 and its Practical Applications to Our Own Times. New York: G. P. Putnam's Sons, 1882. xx, 112 pp., illus.

Benton, Rita
Franklin, and Other Plays. New York: The Writers Publishing Co., 1924. 229 pp.

Burr, George Lincoln
"The Literature of Witchcraft." *American Historical Assoc. Papers.* 4:237–266, 1890.

———.
"A Witch-Hunter in the Book-Shops." *Bibliographer* 1:431–446, 1902.

Calef, Robert
More Wonders of the Invisible World: or, the Wonders of the Invisible World displayed in five parts. Salem, Mass: William Carlton, 1796. 308 pp.
A revision of the London 1700 edition.

——————.
More Wonders of the Invisible World, or the Wonders of the Invisible World. Displayed ... To Which is Added a Postscript, Relating to a Book Entitled "The Life of Sir Wm. Phips." Printed in London, A. D., 1700. Reprinted in Salem: Cushing and Appleton, 1823. xv, 17–312 pp.

——————.
The Wonders of the Invisible World Displayed. Boston: T. Bedlington, 1828. xvi, 17–333 pp., illus.

Cavendish, Pauline Bradford
Ye Little Salem Maid, a story of witchcraft. Illustrated by E. W. D. Hamilton. Boston: Lamson, Wolffe & Co., 1898. ix, 321 pp.

Chamberlain, George Walter
"Sundry Documents Relating to Witchcraft in Massachusetts." *New England Historical and Genealogical Register* 70:65–69, 1916.

Coleman, John C.
Colonial Legends. An Address Delivered Before the New York Society of the Order of the Founders and Patriots of America ... January 20, 1910. Albany: The ... Society, 1910. 15 pp.

Connecticut Statutes
Blue (the) Laws of New Haven Colony, Usually Called Blue Laws of Connecticut; Quaker Laws of Plymouth and Massachusetts; Blue Laws of New York, Maryland, Virginia, and South Carolina. First Record of Connecticut; Interesting Extracts from Connecticut Records; Cases of Salem Witchcraft; Charges and Banishment of Rev. Roger Williams, etc. .... Compiled by Antiquarian (pseud. Royal Hinman.) Hartford: Case, Tiffany and Co., 1838. x, 13-336 pp.

"Curiosities of Puritan History. Witchcraft." *Putnam's Monthly Magazine* 2:249–259, 1853.

Davis, H. P.
Expose of Newburyport Eccentricities, Witches and Witchcraft. The Murdered Boy, and Apparition of the Charles-Street School-House. Newburyport, Mass.: 1873. 24 pp.

Dean, John Ward
Lithobolia; or, The Stone-Throwing Devil. Boston: 1889. 3 pp.

Derby, Caroline Rosina
Salem, a tale of the seventeenth century. New York: Harper & brothers, 1874. vi, 336 pp.

Dow, George Francis
"Witchcraft Records relating to Topsfield." *Topsfield Historical Society. Historical Collections.* (Topsfield, Mass.) 13:39–143, 1908.

Du Bois, Constance Goddard
Marthe Corey: A Tale of the Salem Witchcraft. Chicago: A. C. McClurg and Company, 1890. 314 pp.

Fiske, John
Witchcraft in Salem Village. Boston: Houghton Mifflin Co., 1923. 60 pp., illus.

Fowler, Samuel P.
An Account of the Life, Character, etc., of the Rev. Samuel Parris, of Salem Village, and of his Connection with the Witchcraft Delusion of 1692. Salem: W. Ives & G. Pease, 1857. 20 pp.

——————.
Salem Witchcraft: comprising More Wonders of the Invisible World, collected by Cotton Mather; together with notes and explanations, by Fowler, S. P. Boston: W. Veazie, 1865. xxi, 450 pp.

A Further Account of the Tryals of the New England Witches. With the Observations of a Person who was upon the Place several Days when the suspected Witches were first taken into Examination. To which is added, Cases concerning Witchcrafts and Evil Spirits personating Men. Written at the Request of the Ministers of New-England. By Increase Mather ... London: Printed for J. Dunton, 1693.

Gannon, Frederic Augustus
Witchcraft in Old Salem; the Delusion of 1692, The Recovery, The War, The Press. Salem: Salem Co., 1944. 16 pp., illus.

Gemmill, William Nelson
The Salem Witch Trials, a Chapter of New England History. Chicago: A. C. McClurg and Co., 1924. iii, 240 pp.

Goodell, Asher Cheney
Further Notes on the History of Witchcraft in Massachusetts ... Additional Evidence of the Passage of the Act of 1711, for Reversing the Attainders of the Witches; Also Affirming the Legality of the Special Court of Oyer and Terminer of 1692. Cambridge: J. Wilson & Son, 1884. 52 pp.

——————.
Reasons for Concluding that the Act of 1711, Reversing the Attainders of the Persons Convicted of Witchcraft in Massachusetts in the Year 1692, Became a Law. Being a reply to supplementary notes, etc., by George H. Moore. Cambridge: John Wilson & Son, 1884. 21 pp.

Green, Samuel Abbott
Groton in the Witchcraft Times. Cambridge: J. Wilson & Son, 1883. 29 pp.

Hammand, Esther Barstow
Road to Endor, illustrated by E. M. Simon, New York: Farrar & Rinehart, 1940. x, 434 pp.

Haraszti, Zoltan
"Cotton Mather and the Witchcraft Trials." *Boston Public Library* 15:179–184, 1940.

Holmes, Thomas James
Cotton Mather and His Writings on Witchcraft. Chicago: The University of Chicago Press, 1926.

Hutchinson, Francis

An Historical Essay Concerning Witchcraft. With observations upon matters of fact; tending to clear the texts of the Sacred Scriptures, and confute the vulgar errors about that point. And also two sermons: one in proof of the Christian religion; the other concerning good and evil angels. 2nd ed. London: Printed for R. Knaplock, 1720. 336 pp.

Hutchinson, Thomas

The Witchcraft Delusion of 1692. From an unpublished manuscript . . . in the Massachusetts archives; with notes by Poole, W. F. Boston: D. Clapp & Sons, 1870. 43 pp. Repr.: New-England Historical and Genealogical Register. Oct., 1870.

Kimball, Mrs. Henrietta D.

Witchcraft Illustrated. Witchcraft to be Understood. Facts, Theories and Incidents. With a Glance at Old and New Salem and its Historical Resources. Boston: G. A. Kimball, 1892. 135 pp., illus.

Lawson, Deodat

A Brief and True Narrative of Some Remarkable Passages Relating to Sundry Persons Afflicted by Witchcraft at Salem Village: which happened from the nineteenth of March, to the fifth of April, 1692. Boston: Printed for Benjamin Harris, 1692. Boston, 1936.

———•

Christ's Fidelity the Only Shield Against Satan's Malignity. Asserted in a Sermon delivered at Salem-Village, the 24 of March, 1692. Being Lecture Day there and a time of publick examination of some suspected for witchcraft. Boston: B. Harris, 1693. 79 pp.

Mather, Cotton

Late Memorable Providences Relating to Witchcrafts and Possessions, Clearly Manifesting, Not Only That There Are Witches, But That Good Men (As Well As Others) May Possibly Have Their Lives Shortened by Such Evil Instruments of Satan . . . London: Printed for T. Parkhurst, 1692. 144 pp.

———•

Memorable Providences, Relating to Witchcrafts and Possessions. A faithful account of many wonderful and surprising things, that have befallen several bewitched and possessed persons in New-England. Particularly, a narrative of the marvellous trouble and releef (sic) experienced by a pious family in Boston, very lately and sadly molested with evil spirits. Whereunto is added, a discourse delivered unto a congregation in Boston, on the occasion of that illustrious providence. Boston: R. Pierce, 1689.

The Wonders of the Invisible World: Being an Account of the Tryals of Several Uuitches (!), Lately Excuted (sic) in New-England: and of Several Remarkable Curiosities Therein Occurring. Together with, I. Observations upon the nature, the number, and the Operation of the Devils. II. A short narrative of a late outrage committed by a knot of witches in Swede-Land, very much resembling, and so far explaining, that under which New-England has laboured. III. Some councels directing a due improvement of the terrible things lately done by the unusual and amazing range of evil-spirits in New-England. IV. A brief discourse upon those temptations which are the more ordinary devices of Satan. Bostun (sic): J. Dunton, 1693. 106 pp.

Middlemore, Merell

"The Treatment of Bewitchment in a Puritan Community." *International Journal of Psycho-Analysis.* (London) 15:41–58, 1934.

Moore, George Henry

Final Notes on Witchcraft in Massachusetts: a Summary Vindication of the Laws and Liberties Concerning Attainders with Corruption of Blood . . . In reply to the "Reasons," etc. of Hon. Abner C. Goodell, Jr. New York: The Author, 1885. 120 pp.

———•

Notes on the History of Witchcraft in Massachusetts; With Illustrative Documents. Worcester, Mass.: C. Hamilton, 1883. 32 pp.

———•

Supplementary Notes on Witchcraft in Massachusetts: A Critical Examination of the Alleged Law of 1711 for Reversing the Attainders of the Witches of 1692. Cambridge: J. Wilson & Son, 1884. 25 pp.

Musick, J. R.

The Witch of Salem; or, Credulity Run Man . . . illustrations by Carter, F. A. New York: Funk & Wagnalls Company, 1893. viii, 392 pp., illus.

Nevins, Winfield Scott

Witchcraft in Salem Village in 1692, Together With Some Account of Other Witchcraft Prosecutions in New England and Elsewhere. Salem, Mass.: Northshore Publishing Co., 1892.

Newell, J. H.

"Superstitions of Irish Origin in Boston." *JAFL* 5:242–243, 1892.

O'Dwyer, George Francis

"Ann Glover, First Martyr to the Faith in New England." *U. S. Catholic Historical Soc. Historical Records and Studies* 15:70–78, 1921.

Perley, Martin Van Buren
A Short Sistory of the Salem Village Witch-craft Trials, illustrated by a verbatim report of the trial of Mrs. Elizabeth Howe: a memorial of her. Salem, Mass.: M. V. B. Perley, 1911. 76 pp.

————.
"Where the Salem 'Witches' were Hanged." *Essex Institute. Historical Collections* (Salem) 57:1–18, illus., 1921.

Peterson, Henry
Dulcibel; a tale of old Salem . . . illustrations by Howard Pyle. Philadelphia: The J. C. Winston Co., 1907. 402 pp., illus.

Poole, William Frederick
Cotton Mather and Salem Witchcraft. Boston: 1869. 63 pp.

Rahv, Philip
"The Dark Lady of Salem." *Partisan Review* 8:362–381, 1941.

Records of Salem Witchcraft, copied from the original documents. Roxbury, Mass.: for W. E. Woodward, 1864.

Sergeant, Philip Walsingham
Witches and Warlocks. London: Hutchinson and Co., Ltd., 1936. 290 pp., illus.

Springfield, Mass.
Testimony Against Hugh Parsons, Charged with Witchcraft, 1651, Taken Before William Pynchon, at Springfield. 53 pp.

Tapley, Charles Sutherland
Rebecca Nurse, Saint but Witch Victim. Boston: Marshall Jones Company, 1930. xiii, 105 pp., illus.

Thacher, James
An Essay on Demonology, Ghosts and Apparitions and Popular Superstitions. Also an account of the witchcraft delusion at Salem in 1692. Boston: Carter & Holmes, 1831. iv, 234 pp.

Towne, Mrs. Abbie W.
"William Towne, His Daughters, and the Witchcraft Delusions." In: *Topsfield Historical Society, Historical Collections* 1: pp. 12–14, 1895.

————, **and Marietta Clark**
"Topsfield in the Witchcraft Delusion." *Topsfield Historical Society. Historical Collections.* (Topsfield, Mass.) 13:23–38, 1908.

A True Account of the Tryals, Examinations, and Executions of Divers Witches, at Salem, in New England, for their bewitching of sundry people and cattel to death, and doing other great mischiefs, to the ruine of many people about them. With the strange circumstances that attended their enchantments: and their conversation with devils, and other infernal spirits. In a letter to a friend in London. London: Printed for J. Conners, 1693. 8 pp.

Upham, Mrs. Caroline E.
Salem Witchcraft in Outline. Salem: Salem Press Publishing & Printing Co., 1891. xiii. 161 pp., illus.

Upham, Charles W.
Lectures on Witchcraft, Comprising a History of the Delusion in Salem, in 1692. Boston: Carter & Hendee, 1832, vi, 300 pp.

————.
Salem Witchcraft, with an account of Salem Village, and a history of opinions on witchcraft and kindred subjects. Boston: Wiggin & Lunt, 1867. 2 vols. illus.

————.
Salem Witchcraft and Cotton Mather, a reply. Morrisania, N. Y.: 1869.

Young, Martin
The Devil's Legacy. To earth mortals. Being the keynote to black arts!! . . . with the most authentic history of Salem witchcraft! New York: M. Young, 18—. 96 pp.

CUSTOMS—TRADITIONS

Bliss, William Root
Colonial Times on Buzzard's Bay. Boston: Houghton Mifflin and Company, 1888.

Committee of the House
History of the Emblem of the Codfish in the Hall of the House of Representatives, Compiled by a Committee of the House. Boston: Wright and Potter Printing Co., 1895.

Crosby, Everett Uberto
Books and Baskets, Signs and Silver of Old-Time Nantucket. Nantucket, Mass.: Printed by the Inquirer and Mirror Press, 1940. 72 pp.

Dexter, Timothy
A Pickle for the Knowing Ones: or, *Plain Truths in a Homespun Dress.* Newburyport: Printed for the Author, 1805.

Drake, Samuel Adams
Historic Fields and Mansions of Middlesex. Boston: James R. Osgood and Co., 1874. xiv, 442 pp., illus.

————.
Old Boston Taverns and Tavern Clubs. New illustrated edition with an account of "Cole's inn," "The Baker's arms," and "Golden ball" by Walter K. Watkins; also a list of taverns, giving the names of the various owners of the property, from Miss Thwing's work on "The Inhabitants and estates of the town of Boston, 1630–1800," in the possession of the Massachusett's Historical Society. Boston: W. A. Butterfield, 1917. 124 pp., illus., maps.
Life and social customs.

————.
Old Landmarks and Historic Personnages of Boston. Boston: Little, Brown and Co., 1900. New and revised ed., xviii, 484 pp., illus.

Drew, Benjamin
Burial Hill, Plymouth, Mass.: Its monuments and gravestones numbered and briefly described, and the inscriptions and epitaphs thereon carefully copied. Plymouth, Mass.: D. W. Andrews, 1894. vii, 177 pp.

Farnham, Joseph E. C.
Brief Historical Data and Memories of My Boyhood Days in Nantucket. Providence: Joseph E. C. Farnham, 1923.

Freese, John Wesley
Historic Houses and Spots in Cambridge, Mass., and near-by Towns. Boston: Ginn and Co., 1898. viii, 144 pp.

Hazard, Caroline
Anchors of Tradition. New Haven, Conn.: Yale University Press, 1924. 242 pp.

Newell, W. W.
"Christmas Maskings in Boston." *JAFL* 9:178, 1896.

Palmer, Wilson
Reminiscences of Candia. Cambridge, Mass.: The Riverside Press, 1905.

Russell, William S.
Pilgrim Memorials, and Guide to Plymouth. Boston: Crosby, Nichols, Lee and Company, 1860.

Sargent, Winthrop
Letters of John Andrews, Esq., of Boston, 1772–1776, compiled and edited from the Original Mss., with an Introduction, by Winthrop Sargent. Cambridge: Press of John Wilson and Sons, 1866.
Much on the traditions and customs of the Bostonians of the eighteenth century.

Thwing, Annie Haven
The Crooked & Narrow Streets of the Town of Boston, 1630–1822. Boston: Marshall Jones Company, 1920.

Todd, Charles Burr
In Olde Massachusetts; sketches of old times and places during the early days of the Commonwealth. New York: The Grafton Press, 1907. viii, 253 pp.

Underwood, Francis H.
Quabbin, The Story of a Small Town, with Outlooks Upon Puritan Life. Boston: Lee and Shepard, 1893.

Vorse, Mary Heaton
Time and the Town, A Provincetown Chronicle. New York: The Dial Press, 1942.
An entertaining account and keenly appreciative insight into the life and manners and habits of the people of Provincetown.

PROVERBS—RIDDLES

Thurston, H. S.
"Riddles from Massachusetts." *JAFL* 18:182, 1905.

———.
"Sayings and Proverbs from Massachusetts." *JAFL* 19:122, 1906.

SPEECH

Adams, W. P.
"Nantucket Word-List." *Dialect Notes* 4 (Part 2):156–157, 1914.

Alexander, Henry
"The Language of the Salem Witchcraft Trials." *AS* 3 (No. 5):390–400, 1928.

Allen, F. S.
"Terms from Massachusetts, Connecticut and Florida." *Dialect Notes* 4 (Part 4):301–302, 1916.

Chase, George Davis
"Cape Cod Dialect" I, II. *Dialect Notes* 2 (Part 5):289–303; 2 (Part 6):423–429.

———.
"Cape Cod Dialect. Addenda." *Dialect Notes* 3 (Part 5):419–422, 1909.

Eckstorm, Fannie Hardy
"Pixilated," a Marblehead Word. *AS* 16:78–80, 1941.

James, Henry J.
"Notes on Cape Cod Dialect." *Dialect Notes* 5 (Part 7):286–288, 1924.

Macy, William F.
"More Nantucket Sayings." *Proceedings Nantucket Historical Association,* 41st Annual Meeting, 1935, pp. 27–29.

———, and Hussey, Roland B.
"Nantucket Word-List." *Dialect Notes* 4 (Part 5):332–337, 1916.

———.
The Nantucket Scrap Basket. Nantucket, Mass.: The Inquirer and Mirror Press.

Phillips, Mrs. Wendell B.
"Cape Cod-erisms." *Atlantic Monthly* 140:576, 1927.

Read, Allen Walker
"Nantucketisms of 1848." *AS* 10 (No. 1):38–42, 1935.

Rees, Byron J.
"Word-List-Chilmark Martha's Vineyard, Mass., 1917." *Dialect Notes* 5 (Part 1):15–17, 1918.

Rogers, Susan F.
"Colonial Cookery Terms." *Dialect Notes* 4 (Part 3):239–242, 1915.
The terms were taken from old recipes preserved in the family of Miss Rogers, and collected by her for use in the Chimney Corner Inn, the home of Deacon John Cooper, built in Cambridge in 1657.

Smith, Herbert W.
"Cape Cod Word-List." *Dialect Notes* 4 (Part 2):155–156, 1914.

"Notes from Cape Cod." *Dialect Notes* 4 (Part 4) :263–267, 1916.

"Addenda to the Cape Cod Lists, from Provincetown and Brewster, Mass." *Dialect Notes* 4 (Part 1) :55–58, 1913.

Taylor, Phoebe
"Lower Cape Cod Names and Pronunciation in Every Day Speech." *AS* 8 (No. 2) :78, 1933.

WEATHER LORE

Brooks, Henry Mason
"Salem Weather Sayings." *JAFL* 3:309–310, 1890.

PLACE NAMES

Barrows, Charles Henry
An Historical Address Delivered Before the Citizens of Springfield . . . with five appendices, viz: Meaning of Indian local names, the cartography of Springfield, Old place names of Springfield . . . Springfield, Mass.: Connecticut Valley Historical Society, 1916. 100 pp.

Federal Writers' Project
The Origin of Massachusetts Place Names of the State, Counties, Cities, and Towns, compiled by workers of the Writers' Project of the Work Projects Administration in Massachusetts. Sponsored by the State Librarian of the State of Massachusetts. New York: Harian Publications, 1941. vi, 55 pp.

Green, Samuel Abbott
The Town of Becket. Cambridge: 1890. 2 pp.

Harding, William B.
Origin of the Names of the Towns in Worcester County. Worcester: C. Jillson, 1883. 21 pp.

Horsford, Eben Norton
The Indian Names of Boston, and Their Meaning. Cambridge: J. Wilson & Son, 1886. 26 pp.

Kinnicutt, Lincoln Newton
Indian Names of Places in Plymouth, Middleborough, Lakeville and Carver, Plymouth County, Massachusetts. With interpretations of some of them. Worcester, Mass.: The Commonwealth Press, 1909. 64 pp.

Indian Names of Places in Worcester County Massachusetts, with interpretations of some of them. Worcester, Mass.: The Commonwealth Press, 1905. 59 pp.

FOLKSONG

GENERAL STUDIES AND COLLECTIONS

Barry, Phillips
"The Fall of the Pemberton Mills." *FSSNE* 3:16–17, 1931.
A ballad of the collapse of the Pemberton Mill, Lawrence, Monday, January 10, 1860. (Words and tune.)

"Springfield Mountain: Materials for a Critical Study." (Mass. Ballad.) *FSSNE* 7:4–5, 1934; 8:3–6, 1934; 9:8–10, 1935; 10:6–8, 1935; 11:13–15, 1936; 12:6–8, 1937.
Discussion of different versions, conclusions, texts and tunes.

Damon, S. Foster
"Springfield Mountain." *JAFL* 59:531, 1946.

Eckstorm, Fannie H.
"The Indian Elopement." *FSSNE* 4:9–10, 1932.
A Northeast account of an actual event, the melody variant of an old ballad—'The Turkish Lady.'

Ford, Worthington C.
Broadsides, Ballads, etc. Printed in Massachusetts, 1639–1800. Massachusetts Historical Society Collections, Vol. LXXV, (Boston), 1922.
Mr. Ford lists 3,423 broadsides printed in Massachusetts, with full titles, imprint and first two lines of poetical sheets, which are few, compared with the prose broadsides.

Ireland, I. T.
"Springfield Mountain." *Old Time New England* 32: (No. 8), July 1941.

Jordan, Philip D.
A further note on "Springfield Mountain." *JAFL* 52:118–119, 1939.

Procter, George H.
Fisherman's Ballads and Songs of the Sea. Gloucester: 1874.

"Springfield Mountain." *JAFL* 18:295–302, 1905.
Several versions, with music.

CHILDREN'S GAMES

Clark, A. M. L.
"Games of Children in Lancaster, Mass." *JAFL* 10:325–326, 1897.

Lovett, James D'Wolf
Old Boston Boys and Games They Played. Boston: Privately Printed at the Riverside Press, 1906.

ARRANGEMENTS

————: *Piano*

"Tanglewood Tales." Rolfe, W.: G. Schirmer.

NEW HAMPSHIRE

FOLKLORE

BIBLIOGRAPHY

Bent, Allan H.
Introduction to a Bibliography of the White Mountains. Boston: Houghton Mifflin Co., 1911.

Hammond, Otis G.
Check List of New Hampshire Local History. Concord, N. H.: New Hampshire Historical Society, 1925.

PERIODICALS

New Hampshire Historical Society. Collections.
v. 1, 1824– . Concord, N. H. *Proceedings.* v. 1,
1872– .

The Granite Monthly; a New Hampshire Magazine devoted to history, biography, literature,
and state progress. v. 1, 1877– . Concord,
N. H.: H. Metcalf, etc.

GENERAL STUDIES AND COLLECTIONS

Aldrich, Thomas Bailey
An Old Town by the Sea. Boston: Houghton
Mifflin Company, 1893. 128 pp.
Customs and way of life of the Portsmouth folks.

Anderson, John, and Morse, Stearns
The Book of the White Mountains. New York:
Minton, Balch and Co., 1930. 300 pp., illus.
An entertaining guide book, with occasional
asides into the folklore of the region.

Bowles, Ella (Shannen)
Let Me Show You New Hampshire. Introduc-
tion by Kenneth Roberts. New York: Alfred A.
Knopf, 1938. xvii, 338 pp.

Brewster, Charles W.
Rambles about Portsmouth. Sketches of Persons, Localities and Incidents of Two Centuries: Principally from Tradition and Unpublished Documents; with a Biographical Sketch
of the Author, Wm. H. Y. Hackett. Portsmouth,
N. H.: Lewis W. Brewster, 1869.

Browne, G. W.
The River of Broken Waters: The Merrimac.
(New England River Series.) Illustrated by
Frank Holland. Manchester, N. H.: Standard
Book Co., 1918. 103 pp., illus.
The romance, tradition, history, folklore, scenery,
people, literature and industry of "the busiest
river in the world."

Cannon, Le Grand, Jr.
Look to the Mountain. New York: Henry Holt
and Co., 1942.
An historical novel of New Hampshire during
the years just before the Revolution. Succeeds in
capturing the life and lore of the early pioneers.

Chase, Francis
*Gathered Sketches from the Early History of
New Hampshire and Vermont;* containing
vivid and interesting account of a great variety
of the adventures of our forefathers, and of
other incidents of olden time. Original and
selected. Claremont, N. H.: Tracy, Kenney and
Co., 1856. 215 pp.

Cook, Howard M.
Wayside Jottings, or Rambles Around the Old
Town of Concord, New Hampshire and Its
Suburbs. Concord, N. H.: Edson C. Eastman,
1910.

Crawford, Lucy, Wife of Ethan Allen
*History of the White Mountains from the First
Settlement of Upper Coos and Pequaket.*
White Hills, 1846.

Drake, Samuel Adams
*The Heart of the White Mountains, Their
Legend and Scenery.* New York: Harper &
Bros., 1881.

Early, Eleanor
Behold the White Mountains. Boston: Little,
Brown and Co., 1935. xiii, 219 pp.

Federal Writers' Project
Hands That Built New Hampshire. Compiled
by the Workers of the Writers' Project of the
Works Progress Administration for the State
of New Hampshire. Brattleboro, Vermont:
Stephen Daye Press, 1940.
Mainly on the arts and crafts of the New Hamp-
shire folk.

————.
New Hampshire, a Guide to the Granite State.
(American Guide Series). Written by Workers
of the Federal Writers' Project of the Works
Progress Administration for the State of New
Hampshire. Boston: Houghton Mifflin Co.,
1938.

————.
The Berkshire Hills. (American Guide Series.)
Compiled and Written by Members of the
Federal Writers' Project of the Works Progress
Administration for Massachusetts. Sponsored
by the Berkshire Hills Conference, Inc. New
York: Duell, Sloan and Pearce, 1939. xiv, 368
pp., illus.

Frost, Robert
New Hampshire. New York: Henry Holt and
Co., 1933.
A book of poems—steeped in the life, lore and
speech of the folks of the Granite state.

Hall, Joseph Fred
The Legend of Chocorua; a story of the hills
of New Hampshire. Norwood, Mass.: Printed
by Ambrose Bros., 1915. 23 pp.

Hayes, Lyman S.
*The Connecticut River Valley in Southern Ver-
mont and New Hampshire.* Rutland: The
Tuttle Co., 1929.

Jennison, Keith
New Hampshire Stories and Pictures. New
York: Harcourt, Brace and Co., 1944., illus.

Jones, Alice J.
In Dover on the Charles. A Contribution to
New England Folklore. Newport, R. I.: The
Milne Printery, 1906.

Kilbourne, Frederick Wilkinson
Chronicles of the White Mts. Boston, New
York: Houghton Mifflin Co., 1916. xxxii, 433
pp., front., plates, map.

King, Thomas Starr
*The White Hills: Their Legends, Landscape
and Poetry.* Boston: Crosby, Nichols & Co.,
1860. xv, 403 pp., illus. 60 illus. engraved by
Andrew.

Marble, Thomas Littlefield
Product of the Mills; a romance. Boston:
Humphries, 1935. 242 pp.

Peattie, Roderick, ed.
The Friendly Mountains. New York: The Vanguard Press, 1942. 340 pp., illus.
Discuss the history and lore of the White Mountains of New Hampshire.

Poole, Ernest
Great White Hills of New Hampshire. New
York: Doubleday Company, 1945.
Quite a bit on tall tales, anecdotes, and folk talk.

Prime, W. C.
Among the Northern Hills. New York: Harper
and Bros., 1895.

Rawson, Marion Nicholl
New Hampshire Borns A Town. New York: E.
P. Dutton & Co., 1942.

Shute, Henry A.
The Real Diary of a Real Boy. Chicago: The
Reilly & Lee Co., 1906.

————.
*"Sequil" or Things Which Ain't Finished in
the First.* Boston: The Everett Press, 1904.

Spaulding, John H.
Historical Relics of the White Mountains also
a concise White Mountain guide. Mt. Washington: J. R. Hitchcock, 1858. xi, 104 pp., reprinted in Boston: N. Noyes, 1885.

Thaxter, Celia
Among the Isles of Shoals. Boston: James R.
Osgood & Co., 1873. 184 pp.
Lives of the fishermen—their stories, tradition,
and beliefs.

————.
An Island of Garden, with Pictures and Illus-
trations by Childe Hassam. Boston: Houghton
Mifflin & Co., 1894. ix, 126 pp.

Weygandt, Cornelius
The Heart of New Hampshire. Things Held
Dear by Folks of the Old Stocks. Illustrated.
New York: G. P. Putnam's Sons, 1944. xvii, 210
pp.

————.
New Hampshire Neighbors. Country folks and
things in the White Hills. New York: Henry
Holt and Co., 1937., illus.

————.
November Rowen. A Late Harvest from the
Hills of New Hampshire. New York: D. Apple-
ton-Century Co., 1941.

Willey, Benjamin Glazier
History of the White Mountains; Together with
Many Interesting Anecdotes Illustrating Life
in the Backwoods . . . Illustrations by Fred-
erick Thompson. North Conway, N. H.: I. N.
Andrews, 1869. xii, 296 pp.

————.
Incidents in White Mountain History: Con-
taining Facts Relating to the Discovery and
Settlement of the Mountains, Indian History
and Traditions, a Minute and Authentic Ac-
count of the Destruction of the Willey Family,
Geology and Temperature of the Mountains;
Together with Numerous Anecdotes Illustrat-
ing Life in the Backwoods. Boston: Nathaniel
Noyes, 1856. xii, 321 pp.

FOLKTALES AND LEGENDS

Bisbee, E. E.
*White Mountain Scrap Book of Stories and
Legends of the Crystal Hills or White Moun-
tains of New Hampshire.* Lancaster, N. H.:
Bisbee Press, 1939.

Drake, Samuel Adams
The Heart of the White Mountains, their legend
and scenery. Illustration by W. Hamilton Gibson. New York: Harper and Bros., 1882. xii,
318 pp., maps.

————.
White Mountain and Other Legends. In: *A
Book of New England Legends and Folk Lore
in Prose and Poetry* (pp. 461–472). Boston:
Little, Brown and Co., 1901. 477 pp., illus.

English, J. S.
Indian Legends of the White Mountains. Boston: Rand Avery Supply Co., 1915.

**Gore, Mrs. Moody P. and Speare, Mrs. Guy E.
(comp.)**
New Hampshire Folk Tales. Plymouth, N. H.:
Federation of Women's Clubs, 1932. 265 pp.,
illus.
Varied and exciting collection of tales associated
with the different counties of the state.

————.
More New Hampshire Folk Tales. Plymouth,
N. H.: Mrs. Guy E. Speare, 1936. 287 pp.,
illus.

Harvey, Peter
*Reminiscences and Anecdotes of Daniel Web-
ster.* Boston: Little, Brown and Company, 1877.

Hawthorne, Nathaniel
The Snow Image; and other tales. ('The Great
Stone Face') with illustrations by Marcus
Waterman. New York: Hurd and Houghton,
1868. 31 pp. col. front., col. plates.

King, James Starr
*The White Hills: Their Legends, Landscape
and Poetry.* (White Mountains their descr. &
travels.) with 60 illus. engraved by Andrew,
from drawings by Wheelock. Boston: Crosby,
Nichols & Co., 1866. xv, 403 pp., front., illus.

Lord, C. C.
"Items and Incidents in Hopkinton." *The
Granite Monthly* 2:307, July 1879.
Two tall tales.

SPEECH

Carr, Joseph William
"A Word List from Hampstead, S. E. New Hampshire." *Dialect Notes* 3 (Part 3):179–204, 1907.

Crathern, Alice T.
"A Note on Some New Hampshire Colloquialisms." *AS* 6 (No. 2):151, 1930.

Greenough, C. N.
"Terms from S. E. New Hampshire." *Dialect Notes* 4 (Part 1):54, 1913.

Russell, Jason Almus
"Colloquial Expressions from Hillsborough County, New Hampshire." *AS* 5 (No. 5):418–420, 1930.

Wilner, Leo
"New Hampshire Word-List." *Dialect Notes* 4 (Part 2):153–155, 1914.

PLACE NAMES

Burt, Frank H.
"Nomenclature of the White Mountains." *Appalachia* 13:359–390, 1915.

———.
"The Nomenclature of the White Mountains." *Appalachian Mountain Club* 14:37–49, 261–280, Appalachia (Boston): 1918.

Farmer, John
A Catechism of the History of New-Hampshire, From its First Settlement to the Present Period; for the Use of Schools and Families. Concord: Hoag and Atwood, 1830. vi, 108 pp., illus.
Contains a list of the most considerable towns in New-Hampshire; their names and origins.

State Planning and Development Commission
Communities, Settlements, and Neighborhood Centers in the State of New Hampshire. An inventory prepared by the state planning and development commission. Concord: 1937. 5 pp.

FOLKSONG

GENERAL STUDIES

Jones, Joseph
"A Doleful Tragedie." *SFQ* 8:235–238, 1944.
Text only of a New Hampshire ballad.

Pike, Robert E.
"Amanda the Captive." *JAFL* 56:137–138, 1943.
A ballad recounting an incident supposed to have taken place along the upper Merrimac, in the general vicinity of Lincoln, New Hampshire. Text only.

———.
"Folk Songs from Pittsburgh, New Hampshire." *JAFL* 48:337–352, 1935.

CHILDREN'S GAMES

Halpert, Lt. Herbert
"Children's Game Rimes from New Hampshire." *JAFL* 58:349–351, 1945.
No tunes given.

ARRANGEMENTS
————: *Piano*

Bauer, Marion
From the New Hampshire Woods: Indian Pipes; Pine-Trees; White Birches; Three Preludettes. New York: G. Schirmer, for the piano.

NEW JERSEY

FOLKLORE

PERIODICALS

New Jersey Historical Society, Collections. 1, 1846– ; Documents. 1, 1880– ; Proceedings. 1, 1845– .

New Jersey Journal of Education. New Egypt, N. J., Newark. v. 1–20, No. 6. Oct. 1911–Feb. 1931.

GENERAL STUDIES AND COLLECTIONS

Beck, Henry Charlton
Fare to Midlands; forgotten towns of central New Jersey. New York: E. P. Dutton and Co., 1939.

———.
Forgotten Towns of New Jersey. New York: E. P. Dutton and Co., 1936. 278 pp.

———.
Jersey Genesis; The Story of the Mullica River. New Brunswick, N. J.: Rutgers University Press, 1945. xiv, 304 pp.
The author goes deep into the heart of Down Jersey—a country of wild legend and wilder truth.

———.
"New Jersey Folklore Society." *JAFL* 59:486–487, 1946.

Dolan, Marie B.
Folk-Lore in New Jersey. (thesis for degree Master of Arts deposited in Rutgers University Library.)

Federal Writers' Project
Matawan (1686–1936). Federal Writers' Project of the Works Progress Administration for the State of New Jersey. Keyport, N. J.: Brown Publ. and Print. Co., Inc., 1936.

———.
New Jersey, a Guide to its Present and Past. (American Guide Series). Compiled and Written by the Federal Writers' Project of the Works Progress Administration for the State of New Jersey. New York: The Viking Press, 1939. xxxii, 735 pp., illus., bibl.

The Swedes and Finns in New Jersey. (American Guide Series). Written and Illustrated by the Federal Writers' Project of the Works Progress Administration for the State of New Jersey. Bayonne, N. J.: Jersey Printing Co., 1938.

Society of Colonial Wars.
Historic Roadsides in New Jersey; a condensed description of the principal colonial and revolutionary landmarks in New Jersey. Plainfield, N. J.: W. L. Glenney, 1928. 115 pp.

Weygandt, Cornelius
Down Jersey; Folks and their Jobs, Pine Barrens, Salt Marsh and Sea Islands. New York: D. Appleton-Century Co., 1940. xii, 348 pp.

FOLKTALES—LEGENDS

Beck, Henry Charlton
"Renzie Down in Jersey." *NYFQ* 4 (No. 1):46–50, 1948.
Three tales about this remarkable preacher on horseback.

_____.
"The Jersey Devil and Other Legends of the Jersey Shore." *NYFQ* 3 (No. 2):102–106, 1947.

WITCHCRAFT

Nelson, T.
"Test for Witchcraft in New Jersey, 1730." *JAFL* 5:149–150, 1892.

PROVERBS—RIDDLES

Coad, Oral S.
"Proverb Collecting in New Jersey." *NYFQ* 3 (No. 4):320–322, 1947.
An appeal to New Jerseyites to bestir themselves and gather the proverbs of the Garden State.

Halpert, Herbert
"Negro Riddles Collected in New Jersey." *JAFL* 56:200–202, 1943.

SPEECH

Lee, F. B., and Skillman, W. J.
"Jerseyisms; Jerseyisms—Additions and Corrections." *Dialect Notes* 1 (Part 7):327–334; 1 (Part 8):382–383.

PLACE NAMES

Eno, Joel N.
"New Jersey County Names." *Mag. of History* 25:111–113, 1917.

_____.
Indian Words, Personal Names, and Place-Names in New Jersey. AA 4:183–192, 1902.

_____.
Personal Names of Indians of New Jersey: being a list of six hundred and fifty such names gleaned mostly from Indian deeds of the seventeenth century. Paterson: The Paterson History Club, 1904. 83 pp.

Federal Writers' Project
The Origin of New Jersey Place Names. Compiled by workers of the Writers' Program of the Work Projects Administration in the State of New Jersey. N. P.: 1939. bibl.

Heckewelder, J. G. E.
Names Given by the Lenni Lenape or Delaware Indians to Rivers, Streams and Places in the now states of New Jersey, Pennsylvania, Maryland and Virginia, with their significations. Publications, Pennsylvania German Folklore Society, Vol. 5 (No. 1). Allentown: Penn. German Folklore Society, 1940.

Nelson, William
The Indians of New Jersey, With Some Notice of Indian Place Names. Paterson: Press Publishing Company, 1894. 168 pp.

Vermeule, C. C.
"New Jersey, Some Early Place-Names." *Proceedings of the New Jersey Historical Society* 10:241–252, 1925; 11:151–160, 1926. n.s.

FOLKSONG

GENERAL STUDIES AND COLLECTIONS

Halpert, Herbert
"The Cante Fable in New Jersey." *JAFL* 55: 133–144, 1942.

_____.
"Some Ballads and Folk Songs from New Jersey." *JAFL* 52:52–69, 1939.

_____.
"The Piney Folk Singers, interviews, photos, and songs." *Direction* 2 (No. 5):4–6, 15, Sept. 1939. (Darien, Conn.)

Henry, Mellinger Edward
"Pearl Bryan." *JAFL* 56:139–140, 1943.
A new version of the famous ballad, from Leonia, New Jersey.

_____.
"Where are the Folk-Songs and Ballads of New Jersey." *New Jersey Journal of Education,* vol. 15, (No. 6), (Feb.) 1926.
Variants of the "Maid Freed from the Gallows," and "The Miner Boys" are printed.

Platt, Charles Edward
Ballads of New Jersey in the Revolution. Morristown, N. J.: The Jerseyman Print, 1886. vi, 167 pp., illus., texts only.

CHILDREN'S GAMES

Petrone, Lucille
"Children's Singing Games from Newark, New Jersey Playgrounds." *National Recreation Association,* Miscel. Bull. 817, Nov. 1939.
Four singing games with texts and melodies.

NEW YORK

See: The Shakers, pp. 732–36.

FOLKLORE

BIBLIOGRAPHY

Cornell University, Ithaca
Collection of Regional History. Report of the Curator. 1st. 1942–45. Ithaca, 1945. v.

Folklore of New York State. An archive of folklore of the Empire State, collected under the guidance of Dr. Louis C. Jones, now on permanent loan in the library of the Farmer's Museum, Cooperstown, N. Y.
> The material is indexed by counties, an index of collectors and the type of material they collected and an index of the informants. The organization within the collection is set up on a basis of subject classification.

New York Historical Society, Library.
Catalogue of the Books, Tracts, Newspapers, Maps, Charts, Views, Portraits, and Manuscripts in the library of the New York Historical Society. New York: Press of J. Seymour, 1813. vii, 139 pp.

———.
Survey of the Manuscript Collections in the New York Historical Society. New York: The New York Historical Society, 1941. v, 96 pp.

New York State. Library.
Annotated List of Principal Manuscripts in the New York State Library. Albany: University of the State of New York, 1899. 237 pp. (State Library Bulletin. History, No. 3, June, 1899.)

New York State Teachers College, Geneseo.
The Empire State Yesterday and Today; a selective bibliography on New York State compiled by the reading guidance classes of the State Teachers College at Geneseo, New York, under the direction of C. Elta Van Norman. Geneseo, N. Y.: State Teachers College, 1944. 54 pp.

Romantic New York State, a reading list of New York history, story, and legend. Distributed by Cornell's Department of Rural Sociology. Ithaca, N. Y.: Cornell University.

Severance, Frank Hayward
"The Story of Phiney's Western Almanack, with notes on other Calendars and Weather Forecasters of Buffalo." *Buffalo Historical Society,* Publications, 24:343–358, 1920.

Wall, Alexander James, comp.
A List of New York Almanacs, 1694–1850. New York Public Library, 1921. 122 pp.

PERIODICALS

New York Folklore Quarterly.
Publication of the New York Folklore Society. v. 1, 1945–   . Ithaca, N. Y.: Cornell University Press.

New York Historical Society.
Quarterly Bulletin. v. 1. April 1917. New York, The Society.

New York History.
Published quarterly by the New York State Historical Association. v. 1, Oct. 1919. Albany, N. Y.

GENERAL STUDIES AND COLLECTIONS

Bacon, Edgar Mayhen
The Hudson River from Ocean to Source. New York: G. P. Putnam's Sons, 1902. Illus.
> An historical and legendary account.

Ballard, Byron
Sociology of East Fishkill, Beekman, and Pawling, Dutchess County, New York, State of New York, Federal Writers' Project. In possession of Prof. Genevieve Lamson, Vassar College: Blodgett 21.
> Typewritten—contains much folklore, customs, humor, etc.

Beston, Henry
The St. Lawrence. (The Rivers of America Series.) Illustrated by A. Y. Jackson. New York: Farrar and Rinehart, 1942. xi, 274 pp., illus.
> "The Canadian Boat Song" (words and music), p. 265.

Botkin, B. A.
"Living Lore of the New York City Writers' Project." *NYFQ* 2 (No. 4):252–263, 1946.
> The work of the Writer's Project in gathering folklore among the inhabitants of New York. Various examples of lore given.

Bowen, Croswell
Great River of the Mountains: The Hudson. Introduction by Carl Carmer. Photographs and prose by Croswell Bowen. New York: Hastings House, 1941. 96 pp.
> "This is history made visual and magically come alive. It is the legendry 'of far off things and battles long ago.' It is the romance of the trades of yesterday and to-day. It is the adventure of geography. It is the balladry of the moon tide's struggle against the downrush of waters born in Thunder."—Intro.

Bryant, Margaret M.
"Folklore in the Schools: Folklore in College English Classes." *NYFQ* 2 (No. 4):286–296, 1946.

Carmer, Carl
Genesee Fever. New York: Farrar and Rinehart, 1941. 360 pp.
> Fiction—contains a lot of lore.

———.
The Hudson. Illustrated by Stow Wengenroth. (Rivers of America Series.) New York: Farrar and Rinehart, 1939. xii, 434 pp., illus., bibl. (pp. 408–421).

———.
Listen for a Lonesome Drum, A New York State Chronicle. New York: Farrar and Rinehart, 1936. 381 pp., illus.
> A mine of New York lore.

Carson, Russell M. L.
Peaks and People of the Adirondacks. Garden City: Doubleday, Doran and Co., 1928. 269 pp., illus.

Chamberlain, M. E.
"Folk-lore from Northern New York." *JAFL* 5:336–337, 1892.

Clark, T. Wood
The Bloody Mohawk. New York: The Macmillan Co., 1940.
A historical novel, using legend and tradition.

Cutting, Edith E.
Lore of an Adirondack County. Ithaca, N. Y.: Cornell University Press, 1943. 86 pp.
Folklore from Essex County, New York.

Donk, Emma C.
"Folklore in the Schools"; A Unit—Grades 9–12. *NYFQ* 1:186–188, 1945.

Drummond, Alexander M., and Gard, Robert E., eds.
The Lake Guns of Seneca and Cayuga, and Eight Other Plays of Upstate New York With an Introduction by Harold W. Thompson. Ithaca, N. Y.: Cornell University Press, 1945. 273 pp.
This book contains nine plays of upstate New York, full of humor and history, fantasy and folklore, romance and legends, taken from the past of an imaginative people.

Dwight, Timothy
Travels in New England and New York (1796–1815). New Haven, Conn.: T. Dwight, 1821–22. 4 vols.

Farmers' and Country Merchants' Almanac and Ready Reference Book. 1870. Containing Historical Sketches of the Counties of Albany, Rensselaer, Washington, Warren, Schenectady, Saratoga, Rutland, and Bennington; Together with Farmers' Names, Postal and Internal Revenue Matters, Valuable Receipts, Maxims, and Information Useful to Everybody. . . . Albany, N. Y.: C. Van Benthuysen & Sons, 1870. 207 pp.

Federal Writers' Project
Albany Guide: Past and Present. (American Guide Series.) Federal Writers' Project of the Works Progress Administration for the State of New York. Albany, N. Y.: 1938.

————.
Almanac for New Yorkers, 1938, 1939. Federal Writers' Project of the Works Progress Administration in the City of New York. New York: Modern Age Books, 1938.

————.
Dutchess County. (American Guide Series.) Compiled by the Workers of the Dutchess County Unit of the Federal Writers' Project of the Works Progress Administration in the State of New York. Philadelphia: William Penn Association, 1937.

————.
The Italians of New York. A Survey Prepared by Workers of the Federal Writers' Project of the Works Progress Administration in the City of New York. New York: Random House, 1938.

————.
New York, a Guide to the Empire State. (American Guide Series.) Compiled by Workers of the Federal Writers' Project of the Works Progress Administration in the State of New York. New York: Oxford University Press, 1940. xxxi, 782 pp., illus.

————.
New York Panorama. (American Guide Series.) A Comprehensive View of the Metropolis. Presented in a Series of Articles Prepared by the Federal Writers' Project of the Works Progress Administration in New York City. New York: Random House, 1938.

————.
Rochester and Monroe County. (American Guide Series.) Federal Writers' Project of the Works Progress Administration of the State of New York. New York: Scranton's, 1937.

Gardner, Emelyn Elizabeth
Folklore from the Schoharie Hills. Ann Arbor: University of Michigan Press, 1937. xv, 351 pp., illus., music, bibl. (pp. 322–331).

Harbaugh, T. C.
Middletown Valley in Song and Story. No Publ. 1910. 173 pp.

Headley, Rev. J. T.
Letters from the Backwoods and the Adirondacks. New York: John S. Taylor, 1850. 105 pp.

Hogner, Nils, and Scott, Guy
Cartoon Guide of New York. 100 cartoons and text, with large map. New York: J. J. Augustin, 1941.

Husted, Mary Irving
Hudson River Children. Boston, Mass.: Bruce Humphries, 1943. 73 pp.

Knickerbocker, Dietrich
A History of New York: From the beginning of the world to the end of the Dutch dynasty. New York: Inskeep and Bradford, 1809. Philadelphia: Bradford and Inskeep.
Containing, among many surprising and curious matters, the unutterable ponderings of *Walter the Doubter,* the disastrous projects of *William the Testy* and the chivalric achievements of *Peter the Headstrong,* the three Dutch governors of New Amsterdam.

Jones, Louis C.
"New York Folklore Society." *JAFL* 59:491–493, 1946.

————, **and Lowie, Robert H.**
"New York Branch, American Folklore Society." *JAFL* 59:489–491, 1946.
This article supplements Lowie's sketch, and considers data between 1893 and 1896.

McGoff, Parker (Paddy)
"Scenes of My Childhood." *NYFQ* 2(No. 4):
246–251, 1946.
Folklore reminiscences of South Brooklyn, N. Y.

Newton, Hilah Foote
"Horses and Steamboats on Champlain." *NFQ*
1:33–45, 1945.

Niles, Grace G.
The Hoosac Valley, Its Legend and Its History.
New York: G. P. Putnam's Sons, 1912. 584 pp.,
illus.

Peattie, Roderick, ed.
The Friendly Mountains. New York: The Vanguard Press, 1942. 340 pp., illus.
One of the ranges discussed are the Adirondacks
of New York.

Pound, Arthur
Lake Ontario. (The American Lakes Series.)
Indianapolis: Bobbs-Merrill Co., 1945. 384 pp.,
illus.
"Mr. Pound sketches its story from the day in
1615 when Etienne Brulé first saw the lake right
down to contemporary war boom in a volume
which successfully combines geology, history,
biography, statistics and folklore." (Carl Briden-
baugh.)

Reid, W. Max
The Mohawk Valley. New York: G. P. Putnam's Sons, 1901. 455 pp., illus.

———.
Story of Old Fort Johnson. New York: G. P.
Putnam's Sons, 1906. 455 pp., illus.

Smith, Agnes Scott
"The Dutch had a word for it." *NYFQ* 2 (No.
3):165–173, 1946.
Dutch folklore in the Hudson valley, near
Kingston.

Stanley, Edward
Thomas Forty. New York: Duell, Sloan and
Pearce, 1947.
A historical novel of Westchester and New York
City—lots of local color in the period of the
Revolution.

Studer, Norman
People's Festival in a People's War. Third
Annual Folk Festival of the Catskills; 1942.
New York: 4007—48th St., Long Island City,
1943. 22 pp.

———.
"Catskill Folk Festival." *NYFQ* 1:160–166,
1945.

———.
*Third Annual Folk Festival of the Catskills,
1942:* People's Festival in a People's War.
Long Island City, N. Y.: 1942. 28 pp., illus.

Sylvester, N. B.
*Historical Sketches of Northern New York and
the Adirondack Wilderness,* including traditions of the Indians, early explorers, pioneer
settlers. New York: 1877. 316 pp., illus.

**The New York Chapter, Appalachian Mountain
Club.**
In the Hudson Highlands. New York: 1945. ix,
265 pp.
A guide for hikers, but rich in legend, lore and
anecdote.

Thompson, Harold William
Body, Boots and Britches. Philadelphia: J. B.
Lippincott Co., 1940. 530 pp.

———.
"Folklore of the Empire State." *New York
History* 19:116–123, 1938.

Tomlinson, E. T.
Mystery of Ramapo Pass. Boston: Houghton
Mifflin Co., 1922.

Towne, Charles Hanson
Loafing Down Long Island. New York: Century Co., 1921. 212 pp., illus.

Van De Water, Frederic
Lake Champlain and Lake George. The American Lake Series. New York: Bobbs-Merrill
Company, 1946.
The Champlain-George waterway and valley,
its history, its people, and the lovely land are
here the subject of a truly notable work of
regional literature.

Walker, Barbara K.
"Folklore in the Schools, Collecting by Seventh
Graders." *NYFQ* 2(No. 3):228–236, 1946.
An interesting project by students of the seventh
grade in Cornwall resulting in the gathering of
items in Childlore, Folksay, Customs, Characters, Tales, and Ghost stories.

Watson, John Fanning
*Annals and Occurrences of New York City and
State, in the Olden Time;* being a collection
of memoirs, anecdotes, and incidents. Philadelphia: 1846. 390 pp., illus.

Way, Frederick, Jr.
The Allegheny. (The Rivers of America Se-
ries.) New York: Farrar and Rinehart, 1942.
Illus.

Weller, Ethelyn
North Collins Remembers. A Comprehensive
History of North Collins and Vicinity. Go-
wanda, N. Y.: Niagara Frontier Publishing
Co., 1941. 42 pp., illus.

Wildes, Harry Emerson
The Delaware. (The Rivers of America Series.)
Illustrated by Irwin D. Hoffman. New York:
Farrar and Rinehart, 1940. x, 398 pp.

Wilstach, Paul
Hudson River Landings. Indianapolis: Bobbs-
Merrill Co., 1933. 311 pp., illus.

**Zimm, Louise H., Corning, Rev. A. Elwood, and
others**
Southeastern New York. A History of the
Counties of Ulster, Dutchess, Orange, Rock-
land and Putnam. New York: Lewis Historical
Publishing Company, 1946. 3 vols., illus.

FOLKTALES—LEGENDS

Bellows, Arnold H.
"The Elm Tree Grave at Woodstock." *NYFQ* 2(No. 3):214–216, 1946.
"With this grave is connected a story in which history and legend are interwoven with a mysticism that borders upon the supernatural."

Bonner, Willard Hallam
"Hudson River Legends of Captain Kidd." *NYFQ* 2(No. 1):40–51, 1946.

————.
Pirate Laureate: The Life and Legends of Captain Kidd. New Brunswick, N. J.: Rutgers University Press, 1947. xvi, 239 pp.
"History, literature, legend and folklore all mesh very neatly in the myth that envelops Captain William Kidd of New York City, and the present work undertakes to analyze and separate those various elements of the myth." (Richard M. Dorson).

Bugbee, Willis Norton
Echoes from the North, A Collection of Legends, Yarns, and Sagas. Syracuse, N. Y.: Willis N. Bugbee Co., 1946. 168 pp.

Burnham, T. O. H. P.
The Forest Arcadia of Northern New York, Embracing a View of Its Mineral, Agricultural, and Timber Resources. Boston and New York, 1864.
Contains (pp. 176–186) the tale of the "Crusade of the Bell."

Coffin, Tristram
The Lost Gold Mine of the Hudson, by a Summer Visitor. New York: Knickerbocker Press, 1915. 64 pp.
A legend of Orange County.

Curtis, Blanche Densmore
The Legend of Sam's Point. Illustrated by Charles C. Curran. Cragsmoor, N. Y.: 1910. 11 pp., illus.
A poem describing a legend known in Ulster County.

Dengler, Dorothy
"Tales of Buried Treasure in Rochester." *NYFQ* 2(No. 3):174–181, 1946.

Dickason, David H.
"Swallowing Snake Eggs." *HFB* 2:22, 1943.
A New York version of this legend.

Dorson, Richard M.
"Mose the Far-famed and World-renowned." *American Literature* 15:288–300, 1943.
Mid 19th Century New York City legendary character.

————.
"Sam Patch—Bibliography." *NYFQ* 1:(No. 3) 151, 1945.

————.
"Sam Patch—Jumping Hero." *NYFQ* 1 (No. 3):133–151, 1945.

Dunham, Harvey L.
"French Louie." *NYFQ* 2(No. 3):182–190, 1946.
A delightful character of the woodlands in the West Canada Lakes.

Early, Eleanor
Adirondack Tales; decorations by Virginia Grilley. Boston: Little, Brown & Co., 1939. 247 pp., 5 p., illus.

Epps, Percy M. Van
"Andrew's Bank Deposit." *NYFQ* 1(No. 4): 221–223, 1945.
An interesting tale of a "bank" deposit of a farm lad in the Mohawk-Dutch hinterland.

Gallant, Samuel, and Shapiro, Irwin
"Two Urban Folk Tales." *NYFQ* 2(No. 4): 276–278, 1946.
Folktales heard in New York City.

Gilligan, Edmund
Strangers in the Vly. New York: Charles Scribner's Sons, 1941.
A modern legend of the Catskill Mountains.

Halpert, Herbert
"Aggressive Humor on the East Branch." *NYFQ* 2(No. 2):85–97, 1946.
The author presents twenty folk tales gathered on the East Branch of the Delaware River which drains the western slope of the Catskills.

————.
"John Darling, a New York Munchhausen." *JAFL* 57:97–107, 1944.

Hampton, Vernon Boyce
"Indians and Tavern Tales of Staten Island." *NYFQ* 4(No. 1):61–65, 1948.
According to the author the island was formerly inhabited by the Algonquin or Delaware Indians of the Lenni-Lenape nation. The island is also rich in local lore,—"tales of horror as well as of romance are told concerning some of the ancient homes of white men scattered here and there over our countryside."

Irving, Washington
A Legend of the Kaatskill Mountains. Illustrated with original designs by eminent artists. New York: G. P. Putnam and Sons, 1870. 32 pp., illus.

————.
The Legend of Sleepy Hollow. Boston: D. Estes & Company, 1900. 63 pp.

Jagendorf, M.
"John Darling References." *NYFQ* 3(No. 4): 329–330, 1947.

Ladu, C. E., and Eastman, E. R.
Growing Up in The Horse and Buggy Days. New York: Nesterman Publ. Co., 1943. 263 pp.
Up State tales of the "David Harum" Country.

Lee, John Wiltsee
Stories of the Hudson. New York: G. P. Putnam's Sons, 1871.

Legends and Poetry of the Hudson. New York: P. S. Wynkoop & Son, 1868. vii, 87 pp.

Lichtenthaeler, Frank E.
Storm Blown Seed of Schoharie. Pennsylvania German Folklore Society Publications. Vol. 9, pp. 1–105. Mühlenberg, Pa.: The Society, 1944.

Murray, W. H. H.
Adirondack Tales. Boston: Houghton-Mifflin Co., 1877.

Neal, Janice
"Wa'n't That Remarkable!" *NYFQ* 1(No. 4): 209–220, 1945.
Indian legends (Delawares, Mohawks, Oneidas) tales, remedies, songs (text only), riddles, anecdotes, epitaphs.

North, Nelson L.
Ask and Receive, Including Stories and Folklore of the Adirondack and Lake Champlain Region. Chicago: Scroll Publishing Co., 1901. 83 pp.

O'Beirne, James
"Una Ban: An Irish Song and Story." *NYFQ* 2(No. 4):269–272, 1946.
Irish folklore in New York City.

O'Hara, Edgar B.
"Si Brown and Big Dick, a couple of boys of New York State." *NYFQ* 2(No. 3):209–212, 1946.
Tales of two popular folk heroes of the Indian Lake country.

Pattison, Robert B.
"Matthias the Impostor." *NYFQ* 3(No. 2): 138–141, 1947.
"—as a zealous, religious fanatic, an impostor, a possible murderer, and a remarkable personality of his time, Robert Matthews is part of the history and folklore of Westchester County and of New York State."

Perry, Clay
"Cave Lore of the Taconics." *NYFQ* 3(No. 2): 107–115, 1947.
Stories and legends about Indian Oven Cave, Bentley's Cavern, and Boston Corner.

Popering, Edna Van, and Worth, Eloise
"Two Salt-Sea Tall Tales." *NYFQ* 2(No. 2): 141–142, 1946.
Tales of the Giant Oyster and the Sea Serpent.

Pryer, Charles
Legends, Traditions and Superstitions of Westchester . . . New York: The Knickerbocker Press, 1890. 74 pp.

Rogers, F. D.
Folk-Stories of the Northern Border. Clayton, N. Y.: Thousand Islands Publishing Co., 1897. 273 pp., illus.
Tales of Jefferson County, New York.

Searing, Annie Eliza
The Land of Rip Van Winkle; a Tour Through the Romantic Parts of the Catskills; its legends and traditions. Illustrations by Joseph Lauber, Charles Volkmar, and others . . . New York: G. P. Putnam's Sons, 1884. xii, 147 pp., illus.

Seldes, Gilbert
"A Messianic Murderer." In: *The Stammering Century.* New York: John Day Co., 1928.
The extraordinary story of "Matthias the Impostor."

Shaw, Edward Richard
Legends of Fire Island and the South Side . . . New York: Lovell, Coryell & Co., 1895. 212 pp., illus.

Skinner, Charles M.
The Hudson and Its Hills. In: *Myths and Legends of Our Own Land* (pp. 17–109). Vol. I. Philadelphia: J. B. Lippincott Co., 1896.

————.
The Isle of Manhattoes and Nearby. In: *Tales and Legends of Our Own Land* (pp. 109–139). Vol. I. Philadelphia: J. B. Lippincott Co., 1896.

Smith, Philip Henry
Legends of the Shawangunk (Shon-Gum) and Its Environs; including historical sketches, biographical notices, and thrilling border incidents and adventures relating to those portions of the counties of Orange, Ulster and Sullivan lying in the Shawangunk region. Illustrated by numerous engravings and pen sketches by the author. Pawling, N. Y.: Smith & Company, 1887. viii, 168 pp., illus.

Stone, William L.
Matthias and His Impostures; or, The Progress of Fanaticism, Illustrated in the Extraordinary Case of Robert Matthews and Some of His Disciples. New York: Harper Bros., 1835.

Tucker, O. J.
Legends on the Netherlands; to which are added some legends of Manhattan Island. New York: Concord Co-operative Printing Co., 1892. 185 pp.

Wagenen, Jared Van, Jr.
"The Huddleston Murder; A Schoharie County Tragedy." *NYFQ* 2(No. 1):5–14, 1946.

Walker, Warren
"The Beckwith Murder Case." *NYFQ* 2(No. 2):120–129, 1946.
The 'gruesome' details of a famous murder case "that has kept it the favorite folk tale of Columbia County."

Walter, George W.
"When the Bells Tolled." *NYFQ* 2(No. 2): 130–137, 1946.
"To my ears the sound (of bells) becomes the cry of a human voice, sometimes shouting in anger, sometimes gentle like a kind old lady in lavender and lace. Here are a few of the stories I have gathered in upstate New York—the stories the bells tolled." (G. W. W.)

Ward, Christopher
"Mr. Pierson and the New Messiah." *New Yorker,* Dec. 8, 1934.
More about "Matthias the Impostor."

Weller, Ethelyn
"Wild Animals of Southern Erie County."
NYFQ 4(No. 1):50–54, 1948.
Animal tales.

Witthoft, John
"A Snake Tale from Northern New York."
NYFQ 3(No. 2):134–137, 1947.

SUPERSTITIONS—WITCHCRAFT

Bailey, William S.
"The Kianton Spiritualists and Their River
Expedition." *Jamestown Post-Journal*, Nov. 11,
12, 1943.
The story of the voyage of the spirit directors
and their terrestrial workers of Harmonia from
the Allegheny to the Gulf of Mexico.

Barnes, G.
"Superstitions and Maxims from Dutchess
County." *JAFL* 36:16–22, 1923.

Carpenter, Edmund S.
"The Elixir Spring of Kiantone." *NYFQ* 2(No.
2):106–120, 1946.
A fascinating tale associated with the founding
of the Kiantone colony of the *Association of
Beneficents.*

Featherstonhaugh, Duane
"Ghosts of the Schenectady Area." *NYFQ* 3
(No. 2):115–124, 1947.

Fodor, Nandor
"Lycanthropy as a Psychic Mechanism." *JAFL*
58:310–316, 1945.
The author cites examples of New York patients
who observed this hallucination.

Gardner, Emelyn E.
"Two Ghost Stories." *JAFL* 58:155–156, 1945.

Hawley, Herbert J.
"The Sea Serpent of Silver Lake." *NYFQ* 2
(No. 3):191–196, 1946.
An exciting account of the strange "appearance"
of the Sea Serpent in Silver Lake, Wyoming
County—as recounted in the *Wyoming Times*,
July-September, 1855.

Jones, Louis C.
"Hitchhiking Ghosts in New York." *CFQ* 3:
284–292, 1944.
Discussion of 49 variants of this legend.

————.
Spooks of the Valley: Ghost Stories for boys
and girls. Illustrated by Erwin Austin. Boston:
Houghton Mifflin Company, 1948. 111 pp.
Ghost lore from the Upper Hudson Valley.
Among some of the famous spooks encountered
are Captain Kidd, the Horseman of Leeds, Miss
Wyatt, and others.

————.
"The Ghosts of New York: An Analytical
Study." *JAFL* 57:237–254, 1944.

Laidlaw, William K.
"Albany County Witch Lore." *NYFQ* 2 (No.
1):61–62, 1946.

McCadden, Helen M.
"Folklore in the Schools. Folk Beliefs: Current Report." *NYFQ* 3 (No. 4):330–340, 1947.
A great deal of superstitions still prevail among
second- and third-generation Americans.

O'Beirne, James
"The Ghostly Priest Who Says Mass, a Father
Matthew Version." *NYFQ* 2 (No. 3):212–214,
1946.
A Glens Falls' variant of the story about the
ghostly priest who returns from the dead to say
Masses for which he has been paid but which he
has been unable to say.

Shaw, James G.
"Union College Ghost." *NYFQ* 2 (No. 2):137–
138, 1946.
A story of Mohawk Valley.

Skeel, Mary H.
"Superstitions of Childhood on the Hudson
River." *JAFL* 2:148, 1889.

Sper, Felix
"Ghosts and Bricks." *Players Magazine* (Chey-
enne), Dec, 1943, p. 9, 14.
Historical folk dramas of New York State.

Webb, Wheaton P.
"Witches in The Cooper Country." *NYFQ*
1:5–20, 1945.

Willis, Alice
"Tales from a Mountain Homestead." *NYFQ*
3 (No. 4):302–312, 1947.
"The stories of witches, fairies, and other 'un-
cany critters' which they (Scotch-Irish and
Dutch) brought over from their homes in Europe
found fertile ground in the dark wooded regions
of the Catskills."

"Witchcraft in New York." *N. Y. Historical
Society Collections, Publication Fund Series*,
1869, pp. 273–276.

CUSTOMS—TRADITIONS

Adams, Samuel Hopkins
Canal Town. Chicago: Consolidated Book
Publishers, 1944. 471 pp.
A novel of a western New York Community, with
glimpses of its lore and customs, in the hey days
of the Erie Canal.

Earle, Alice Morse
Colonial Days in Old New York. New York: C.
Scribner's Sons, 1896. 312 pp.

Edmonds, Walter D.
The Wedding Journey. Boston: Little Brown
Co., 1947.
A novel of life and customs of New York, and
vivid descriptions of trips on the Erie Canal
from Schenectady to Buffalo.

Filkin, Francis
*Account Book of a Country Storekeeper in the
18th Century at Poughkeepsie;* records in
Dutch and English, preserved among the papers
in the office of the clerk of Dutchess County,
N. Y. Poughkeepsie: Vassar Brother's Institute, 1911. 122 pp.

"Funeral Customs in Mohawk Valley."
JAFL 2:70, 1889.

Grant, Mrs. Anne (Mac Vicar)
Memoirs of an American Lady, with sketches
of manners and scenes in America as they
existed previous to the Revolution; with unpublished letters and a memoir of Mrs. Grant
by James Grant Wilson. New York: Dodd,
Mead and Co., 1901. 2 vols., illus.

Harsford, C.
"Tradition of Shelter Island, N. Y." *JAFL*
12:43–44, 1899.

Porter, Marjorie Lansing
"The Fifteenth of Redford." *NYFQ* 2 (No.
3) :205–208, 1946.
    Description of an annual celebration by the
    French residents of Redford on the Saranac.

Potter, Charles Francis
"Round Went the Album." *NYFQ* 4 (No. 1) :
5–14, 1948.
    A delightful collection of autograph album verse
    —from young and old.

Thompson, Harold W.
"Epitaphs." *NYFQ* 3 (No. 4) :353–356, 1947.
    Eight epitaphs from the burial grounds in Coop-
    erstown, N. Y. The author presents five classi-
    fications of epitaphs, those containing a grim
    warning, stately rhetoric, a story, unconscious
    humor, and genuine poetry.

—————
"Epitaphs." *NYFQ* 4 (No. 1) :66–71, 1948.
    A number of very interesting epitaphs telling a
    story.

Tousey, Sanford
Dick and the Canal Boat. Garden City: Doubleday, Doran and Co., 1943. unpaged.
    A children's book of life in Canal Days on the
    Erie.

Van Rensselaer, Jeremias
*Correspondence of Jeremias Van Rensselaer,
1651–1674,* translated and edited by A. J. F.
Van Laer, archivist, Archives and History
division. Albany: The University of the State
of New York, 1932. 494 pp.

—————, **Mrs. Maria (Van Cortlandt)**
*Correspondence of Maria van Rensselaer,
1669–1689;* translated and edited by A. J. F.
van Laer. Albany: The University of the State
of New York, 1935. 206 pp.

Van Wagenen, Jared, Jr.
"The Passing Bell no Longer Tolls." *NYFQ*
3 (No. 4) :298–302, 1947.
    An old custom of tolling the church bells pro-
    claiming the passing of a member of the com-
    munity (a cross roads hamlet of east-central
    New York) to the Great Beyond.

Weller, Ethelyn
"Celebration of July 4, 1811." *NYFQ* 3 (No.
2) :141–144, 1947.
    How the early settlers in Erie County celebrated
    their national holiday.

WEATHER LORE—FARM LORE

Boughton, Audrey, comp.
"Weather Lore, Fall Quarter." *NYFQ* 1 (No.
4) :251–252, 1945.

—————.
"Weather Lore: Spring Quarter." *NYFQ* 1:
123, 1945.

—————.
"Weather Lore, Summer Quarter." *NYFQ*
1:189–190, 1945.

Boyer, Ruth A.
"Farm Lore: Insects, Animals and the
Weather." *NYFQ* 2 (No. 1) :74–76, 1946.

Relihan, Catherine, comp.
"Farm Lore. Herb Remedies." *NYFQ* 2 (No.
2) :156–158, 1946.
    The herb remedies were taken from the Folklore
    Archives of the New York State College for
    Teachers.

Travis, Phebe Allen
"Bird Lore of New York State." *NYFQ* 1 (No.
4) :197–204, 1945.

"Weather Lore: Winter Quarter."
NYFQ 1:60–62, 1945.
    A number of items from the Folklore Archives
    at the State College for Teachers, Albany, N. Y.

FOLK MEDICINE

Adams, Samuel Hopkins
"Our Forefathers Tackle An Epidemy—The
Cholera of 1832." *NYFQ* 3 (No. 2) :93–101,
1947.
    Amazing what the medical men concocted to
    combat the deadly scourge of cholera. The man-
    ner of dissemination of the disease was debated
    by the "meteorasts" and the "tellurists". . .
    "Quackeries flourished. . . . Cholera cures, herb-
    alist, floralist, and Thomsonian were hawked
    along turnpike and towpath by the itinerant med-
    ical shows."

Crandall, Samuel
"Folk Cures of New York State." *NYFQ* 1:
178–180, 1945.

Relihan, Catherine, (comp.)
"Farm Lore. Herb Remedies." *NYFQ* 2 (No.
2) :156–158, 1946.

Skeel, Mary H.
"Stick Doctoring." *JAFL* 4:165–166, 1891.
    Medicinal superstition of early settlers of the
    Hudson River.

Webb, Wheaton Phillips
"The Wart." *NYFQ* 2 (No. 2) :98–106, 1946.
    A delightful narrative in which many remedies
    for the removing of warts are prescribed.

PROVERBS

"Proverbs and Sayings."
NYFQ 2 (No. 3) :218–220, 1946.

SPEECH

Babbitt, E. H.
"The English of Lower Classes in New York and Vicinity." *Dialect Notes* 1 (Part 9):457–464.

Bowen, B. L.
"A Word List from Western New York." *Dialect Notes* 3 (Part 6):435–451. 1910.

Crowningshield, Gerald
"Dialect of Northeastern New York." *AS* 8 (No. 2):43–45, 1933.

Emerson, O. F.
"The Ithaca Dialect." *Dialect Notes* 1 (Part 3):85–173.

McConnell, Oviatt
"Slang as she is slung in Buffalo." *Times* (Buffalo), Jan. 10, 1937.

Monroe, B. S.
"Ithaca Local Circle Word List." *Dialect Notes* 1 (Part 8):395–400.

Northup, C. S.
"Word List from Cornell." *Dialect Notes* 1 (Part 9):411–427.

Palmer, F. L.
"Dialect Words from 'The Pioneers'." *Dialect Notes* 5 (Part 5):185–186, 1922.
This novel by Fenimore Cooper, describes conditions of 1793 in the New York region by Otsego Lake.

Russell, Jason Almus
"Colloquial Expressions from Madison County, New York." *AS* 5 (No. 2):151–153, 1929.

Shapleigh, Mrs. F. E.
"Word List from Roxbury, New York." *Dialect Notes* 4 (Part 1):54, 1913.

Shulters, J. R.
"Hop-field terms from Western New York." *Dialect Notes* 5 (Part 5):182–183, 1922.

Smith, Agnes Scott
"The Dutch had a word for it." *NYFQ* 2 (No. 3):165–173, 1946.
Dutch folklore in the Hudson Valley, near Kingston.

Thomas, C. K.
"Pronunciation in Upstate New York." *AS* 10 (No. 2):107–112; (No. 3):208–212; (No. 4):292–297, 1935; 11 (No. 1):68–77; (No. 2): 142–144; (No. 4):307–313, 1936; 12 (No. 2): 122–127, 1937.

————.
"Standards of Pronunciation in New York City." *Quarterly Journal of Speech* 21:265–266, 1935.

White, Henry Adelbert
"A Word List from Central New York." *Dialect Notes* 3 (Part 8): 564–569, 1912.

PLACE NAMES

Anon.
"Indian Names." *American Penny Magazine* 1:322, June 28, 1845.
An account of the progress made by the Committee appointed by the N. Y. Historical Society to make an aboriginal map of the state. The Society also attempted an interpretation of Indian names and place names.

Asher, George Michael
A Bibliographical and Historical Essay on the Dutch Books and Pamphlets to New-Netherland, and to the Dutch West-India Company and to its Possessions in Brazil, Angola, etc., as also on the maps, charts etc. of New-Netherland by N. I. Visscher and of the three existing views of New Amsterdam . . . Amsterdam: F. Muller, 1854–67. 1 vol., bibl.

————.
Indian Names in New York, with a Selection from Other States, and Some Onondaga Names of Plants. Fayetteville, N. Y.: H. C. Beahchamp, 1893. 148 pp.

Beauchamp, William Martin
Aboriginal Place Names of New York. New York State Museum Bulletin 108. Albany, N. Y.: State Education Department, 1907. 336 pp.

Benson, Egbert
Memoir on the Origin of Place Names Read Before the Historical Society of the State of New York, December 31, 1816. Jamaica: H. C. Sleight, 1825. 127 pp.

Bolton, Reginald Pelham
Aboriginal Place-Names of the County of Westchester. New York: n.p., 1942. 67 pp.

Davis, William Thompson
"Staten Island Names. Ye Olde Names and Nicknames." *Proc. of the Nat. Science Assoc. of Staten Island. Special No. 21,* 1896. pp. 20–76.

Eno, Joel N.
"New York County Names." *Mag. of History* 22:76–82, 127–130, 166–169; 23:11–15, 126–128, 1916.

Flick, Alexander Clarence
New York Place Names. New York: 1937. pp. 293–332, bibl.

Hale, Edward E.
"Dialectical Evidence in the Place-Names of Eastern New York." *AS* 5 (No. 2):154–167, 1929.

Hanford, Franklin
Name Sources of Townships of Monroe Co. Scottsville, N. Y.: n.p., 1930. 3 pp.
Clipps from "The Monroe Republican," Scottsville, N. Y.

————.
On the Origin of the Names of the Names of Places in Monroe County, New York. Scottsville, N. Y.: I. Van Hooser, 1911. 54 pp. (Scottsville Literary Society. Publications. No. 5.)

Maar, C.
"Origin of Classical Place-Names of Central New York." *New York State Historical Association Quarterly* 7:155–167, 1926.

"More Schoolhouses."
NYFQ 2 (No. 1):64–65, 1946.
Origin of place names, and that of schoolhouses.

Prince, J. Dyneley
"Forgotten Indian Place Names in the Adirondacks." *JAFL* 13:123–128, 1900.

Ruttenber, E. M.
Footprints of the Red Men. Newburgh, N. Y.: New York State Historical Association, 1906. 241 pp., illus.
Indian Geographical names in the Valley of the Hudson's River, the Valley of the Mohawk, and on the Delaware: their location and the probable meanings of some of them.

Schoolcraft, Henry R.
"Aboriginal Nomenclature." *The Knickerbocker* 58:109–112, 1861.
On the origin of the Indian names: Geneva, Neversink, Sing Sing, Manhattan, Croton, Poughkeepsie, etc.

————.
"Indian Names of the Islands in Bay of New York." *The Broadway Journal* 1:138–139, March 1, 1845.
An interesting historical survey of the changes of names various localities and rivers underwent since the coming of the white man.

————.
Report on the Aboriginal Names and Geographical Terminology of the State of New York. Part 1. – Valley of the Hudson. Made to the New York Historical Society . . . New York: The Author, 1845. 43 pp.

"Sources of Wyoming County Place Names." *Historical Wyoming* Nov., 1947. pp. 21–22.

Smith, Dorothy Guy
"Strange Names of School Districts." *NYFQ* 1:152–159, 1945.

Tooker, Wm. Wallace
"Indian Geographical Names on Long Island." *Brooklyn Daily Eagle Almanac* 1888, pp. 55–56; 1889, 25–26; 1890, 35–37.

————.
The Indian Names for Long Island. New York: F. P. Harper, 1901. 49 pp. (Algonquian Series, V. 4.)

————.
Indian Place-Names in East-Hampton Town, with Their Probably Significations. Sag. Harbor: J. H. Hunt, 1889. 10 pp.

————.
"Indian Place-Names on Long Island." *Brooklyn Daily Eagle Almanac* 1904. pp. 409–410.

Tuxedo Club
Report to the Exectutive Committee of the Tuxedo Club, from the Committee appointed to examine into the original historical names of the Tuxedo region; together with a copy of the manuscript map of this portion of New York and New Jersey, made for Washington in the years 1778–1779. New York: 1888. 7 pp.

Van Epps, Percy M.
"The Place Names of Glenville." *Glenville, N. Y. Historian. Report of Town Historian* No. 1:1–4, 1926.

FOLKSONG
GENERAL STUDIES

Albrecht, Henry F.
"Troy Street Cries." *NYFQ* 1 (No. 4):238, 1945.
Text only.

Barry, Phillips
"The Wreck of the Schooner Medora." (Great Lakes). *FSSNE* 11:19–20, 1936.

Bishop, Fern
"Songs My Grandmother Sang." *JAFL* 48:379–383, 1935.

Bowman, Frank
"A Ballad of Salmon River." *NYFQ* 3 (No. 2):145–148, 1947.
A ballad (text only) composed by Samuel Hardy, a local rhymster, describing an event that occurred in the town of Montague.

Cutting, Edith
"Peter Parrott and His Songs." *NYFQ* 3 (No. 2):124–133, 1947.
Texts, and melody sung by the informant who lives in Redford, Clinton County, New York.

Flanders, Helen Hartness
" 'Blue Mountain Lake' " and " 'Barbara Allen'." *NYFQ* 2 (No. 1):52–58, 1946.
New York State versions, with tunes.

Francello, Elvira
"An Italian Version of 'Maid Freed From the Gallows'." *NYFQ* 2 (No. 2):139–140, 1946.

Gray, R. P.
"Balladry of New York State." *New York Historical Society* (Albany) 147–155, April 1936.

Haufrecht, Herbert, and Cazden, Norman
"Music of the Catskills." *NYFQ* 4 (No. 1):32–46, 1948.
The authors recount their experiences in gathering folksongs in the Catskills. Some texts and tunes are given. An extensive list of vocal and instrumental music the authors collected is added.

Jones, Louis C.
"Henry Backus, the Saugerties Bard." *N. Y. History* (New York State Historical Association) 23:139–148, 1942.

" 'The Berlin Murder' Case in Folklore and Ballad." *New York History* 17:196–205, 1936.

Kimball, F. P.
"Old Songs Tell a Story of a Changing New York." *New York Times Magazine*, July 3, 1927.

Lewis, Elaine Lambert
"Folk Songs for the Seven Millions." *NYFQ* 1:57–59, 1945.
Discussion of the character and contributions made by the Brooklyn Public Library Folklore Broadcasts.

Mills, Dorothy, and Bishop, Morris
"Songs of Innocence." *The New Yorker* 13 (No. 39):32–42, 1937.
Sidewalk rhymes of New York. Tunes transcribed by Charles Seeger.

"My Name Is Charles Guiteau." *NYFQ* 1:49, 1945.
A New York version of the historical ballad recorded in Manlius, Onondaga County. The tune, not given, is claimed by the editor to be "When the Work's All Done Next Fall."

Newton, Hilah Foote
"The Saltus Lament." *NYFQ* 1:42–43, 1945.
A ballad of the adventures of the steamer "The Saltus" on Lake Champlain.

Smith, Carleton Sprague
"Folk Songs of Old New York." *Musical America* 59:7, 1939.
Discussion of popular urban songs that achieved folk status by historical process. No music.

Stimson, Anna K.
"Cries of Defiance and Derision, and Rhythmic Chants of West Side New York City, 1893–1903." *JAFL* 58:124–129, 1945.
Battle cries of New York children, thirty in number, tunes to three.

Studer, Norman
"Winter Folklore Conference." *NYFQ* 1:59–60, 1945.
The agenda of the conference in "The role of folklore in a democracy," held in New York City on March 10, 1945, is given.

————.
"The World is a Neighborhood." In: *4th Annual Folk Festival of the Catskills*, 1943. Camp Woodland, Phoenicia, New York. 32 Unnumbered pages.
Words and music of thirteen ballads and songs and two dances.

Thompson, Harold William
Body, Boots and Britches. Philadelphia: J. B. Lippincott Co., 1940. 530 pp.

COLLECTIONS

Bancker, Gerard
Unique Collection of Broadsides. Gathered by Gerard Bancker, provincial treasurer of New York, and to be sold for the estate of the late Jas. A. Bancker, New York. Embracing the largest collection of pre-revolutionary and revolutionary broadsides relating to New York City and state that has ever been offered for sale... to be sold... March 25th, 1898... Catalogue comp. and sale conducted by Stan. V. Henkels... Philadelphia, 1898... Facsimiles of the Broadsides—17. (Columbia University, N. Y.)

Haufrecht, Herbert
Folk Songs of the Catskills. New York: The Music Center, arr. for voice and piano.

How, Louis
Nursery Rhymes of New York City. New York: Alfred A. Knopf, 1919. 71 pp.

New York Cries in Rhyme.
New York: 1812.

Ring, Constance Varney, and others
Mid-Hudson Song and Verse. Poughkeepsie, N. Y.: Librarian's Office, Vassar College. 178 typewritten pages. Foreword by Pres. H. N. MacCrackens. Text and tunes given.

Ship, E. Richard
Inter Mountain Folk: Songs of Their Days and Ways. Casper: Casper Stationery Co., 1922. 113 pp.

CHILDREN'S RHYMES AND GAMES

Brewster, Paul G.
"Johnny on the Pony. A New York State Game." *NYFQ* 1 (No. 4):239–240, 1945.

"Countin-out Rhymes from New York." *JAFL* 27:325, 1914.

How, Louis
Nursery Rhymes of New York City. New York: Alfred A. Knopf, 1919. 71 pp.

Millard, Eugenia L.
"Sticks and Stones. Children's Teasing Rhymes." *NYFQ* 1:21–32, 1945.
Teasing, taunting and jeering rhymes gathered in various counties of the Empire State. A tune for one is given.

DANCES

Boetcher, Harriet
"Folklore in the Schools. A Handy Guide to Square Dances." *NYFQ* 2(No. 1):71–75, 1946.
Give list of dances, accompaniments and recordings.

Cazden, Norman
Dances from Woodland, op. 48, for piano. New York: The Music Center.

————.
Reels, Jigs and Squares: 200 Dance Tunes for Violin and Piano, op. 50. New York: The Music Center, 1945.

Karpeles, Maud
"Square Dance Figures From Northern New York State." *JEFDS* No. 4, Second Series, 1935.

ARRANGEMENTS:
(Individual Titles)

——————: *Voice and Piano*

"Ballad of Penn."
Gaul, Harvey B.: Galaxy.
A ballad of the New York frontier.

"Down by the Erie Canal."
Garrison, Frederick: E. B. Marks.

"The Erie Canal."
Bacon, Ernst: Carl Fisher.

——————: *Male Voices*

"The Erie Canal."
In: *H. & M. Auditorium Series No. 29.* Grant,
R. W.: Hall and McCreary: TTBB.

"The Erie Canal."
Pitcher, Gladys: Birchard (New York) : TTBB.

"The Erie Canal."
Scott, Tom: Words and Music Inc.: TTBB.
Fred Waring Glee Club Arrangement.

"The Erie Canal."
Treharne, B.: Boston Music Co.: TB.

"The Erie Canal."
Wilson: Hall and McCreary: TBB.

——————: *Piano*

Cazden, Norman
Dances from Woodland, op. 48. New York:
The Music Center.

Lane, Eastwood
Adirondack Sketches: The Old Guide Story;
Legend of the Lonesome Lake; Down Stream;
The Land of the Loon; A Dirge for Jo Indian;
Lumberjack Dance. New York: J. Fischer and
Bro., for piano.

Stage Work

Hudson River Legend-Ballet.
Wagner, J. W.: Marks.

RECORDS

Album Collections

Hudson Valley Songs.
Frank Warner, accompanied by ballad singers,
instrumentalist.   3-10", DISC 611
Content: Blue Mountain Lake; Tom More, In
the Days of '49; British Soldier; Montcalm &
Wolfe; Bonnie Bay O'Biscay-O; A Trip on the
Erie.

Middle Atlantic and the East (New York).
In the Archive of the Folklore Foundation,
Vassar College, New York.

**U. S. Library of Congress. Division of Music,
Folklore Section.**
New York Public Library Recording Project.
Music and Folklore from New York City Area.
AAFS–LC.

Individual Titles

"Blue Mountain Lake."
Hudson Valley Songs. Frank Warner, accom-
panied by ballad singers, instrumentalists.
DISC 8024

"British Soldier."
Hudson Valley Songs. Frank Warner, accom-
panied by ballad singers, instrumentalists.
DISC 8024

"Montcalm & Wolfe."
Hudson Valley Songs. Frank Warner, accom-
panied by ballad singers, instrumentalists.
DISC 8024

PENNSYLVANIA

See: Pennsylvania German, pp. 581–90.

FOLKLORE

PERIODICALS

Pennsylvania Folk-Lore Society, Publications,
V. 1, 1927– . Reading, Pa.: Reading Eagle
Press.

Pennsylvania History.
Official organ of the Pennsylvania Historical
Association. Quarterly. V. 1, 1934– . Phila-
delphia, Pa.: University of Philadelphia Press.

*The Pennsylvania Magazine of History and Biog-
raphy.* V. 1, 1877– . Philadelphia, The Historical Society of Pennsylvania.

BIBLIOGRAPHY

Armor, William Crawford
"Scotch-Irish Bibliography of Pennsylvania."
Scotch-Irish in America, Proceedings and
Addresses of the 8th Congress, pp. 253–289,
1896.
Arranged by county.

Beers, Henry Putney, comp.
"Pennsylvania Bibliographies". In: *Pennsylvania History* 2 (Nos. 2, 3, 4), 3 (No. 1), April
1935–January 1936.

Heckman, Oliver S., comp.
What To Read About Pennsylvania. Harrisburg: Dep't of Public Instruction, Pennsylvania Historical Commission, 1942. vi, 97 pp.

Pennsylvania Historical Commission.
Pennsylvania Bibliography; articles published
by societies belonging to the Pennsylvania
Federation of Historical Societies. Harrisburg,
1933. 102 pp. Bulletin No. 2 of the Pennsylvania Historical Commission.

Pittsburgh Carnegie Library.
Pennsylvania; a reading list for the use of
schools with special reference to Indian warfare and the local history of Pittsburgh. Pittsburgh: Carnegie Library, 1911. vi, 83 pp.

Sewickley, Pa., Public Library.
An Annotated Catalog of the Alexander C. Robinson Collection of Western Pennsylvania. Sewickley: Library Society of Sewickley, Pennsylvania, 1940. 229 pp.

GENERAL STUDIES AND COLLECTIONS

"Alleghanies Folklore."
JAFL 1:105–117, 1888.

Bonos, Arlene Helen
"Romany Rye of Philadelphia." *AA* 44:257–274, 1942.
Lore among the Gypsy tribes of Philadelphia.

Brinton, D. G.
"Reminiscences of Pennsylvania Folklore." *JAFL* 5:177–185, 1892.

Brush, Frederic
The Alleghanians. New York: The Blackshaw Press, 1940. 203 pp.
A narrative in verse and prose.

Coleman, J. Walter
The Molly Maguire Riots. Richmond, Va.: Garret and Massie, 1936.
The story and lore of the anthracite coal workers.

Federal Writers' Project
Erie, a Guide to the City and County. (American Guide Series). Erie County unit of the Federal Writers' Project of the Works Progress Administration of Pennsylvania. Philadelphia: William Penn Association, 1938.

————.
Pennsylvania, a Guide to the Keystone State. (American Guide Series). Written and Compiled by the Federal Writers' Project of the Works Progress Administration for the state of Pennsylvania. New York: Oxford University Press, 1940. xxxii, 660 pp., illus., bibl.

Hanna, Charles Augustus
Wilderness Trail or, The Ventures and Adventures of the Pennsylvania traders on the Allegheny post. New York: G. P. Putnam's Sons, 1911. 2 vols.

Hoffman, Charles Fenno
A Winter in the West. New York: Harper and Bros., 1835. 2 vols.
Narrative of a journey through Pennsylvania, the old Northwest, Missouri, Kentucky, Tennessee, and Virginia.

Huntley, George W.
Sinnamahone. Boston: Christopher Publishing House, 1945. 411 pp.
Deals with Pennsylvania lumbering.

Keyser, Naaman H., and Kain, C. Henry
History of Old Germantown. Philadelphia: Horace F. Mc Cahn, 1907.

Korson, George Gershon
Black Land; The way of life in the coal fields. (The Way of Life Series). Evanston, Ill.: Row, Peterson and Co., 1941. 72 pp.

————.
Coal Dust on the Fiddle. Songs and Stories of The Bituminous Industry. Philadelphia, Pa.: University of Pennsylvania Press, 1943. 460 pp., music, bibl.

————.
Minstrels of the Mine Patch. Songs and Stories of the Anthracite Industry. Philadelphia, Pa.: University of Pennsylvania Press, 1938. 332 pp., music, bibl.

————.
Pennsylvania Songs and Legends: A Folklore Anthology. Illustrated. Philadelphia, Pa.: University of Pennsylvania Press, 1949. 466 pp.
The first comprehensive collection of Pennsylvania folklore and folk music from colonial days to the present, chiefly from oral sources. Thirteen chapters by authorities in their respective fields. More than 100 folk songs and ballads with music; also tall tales, legends, Indian myths, anecdotes, place names, superstitions, etc.

Mitchell, Edwin Valentine
It's an Old Pennsylvania Custom. New York: Vanguard Press, 1946. 262 pp., illus.
In some fifteen chapters the author covers the ground from cave-dwelling to Philadelphia taverns, taking in on the way, pies, courtship, customs, the wearing of beards, musical manners . . . historical, domestic, culinary lore; Pennsylvania speech and sections on witchcraft, superstitions and magical practices.

Owens, F. G.
"Folklore from Buffalo Valley, Central Pennsylvania." *JAFL* 4:115–128, 1891.

Pastorius, Francis Daniel
"Description of Pennsylvania, 1700." (Translated from the original German by Lewis H. Weiss.) *Old South Leaflets* 4, No. 95, Boston, 1898.

Phillips, H., Jr.
"First Contribution to the Study of Folk-Lore of Philadelphia and Its Vicinity." *American Philosophical Society.* March 1888, pp. 159–170.

Searight, Thomas Brownfield
The Old Pike. A history of the National road, with incidents, accidents, and anecdotes thereon. Uniontown, Pa.: The Author, 1894. 384 pp., illus.

Shoemaker, Henry Wharton
Black Forest Souvenirs. Reading, Philadelphia: Bright Faust Printing Co., 1914. xix, 404 pp., illus.
Collected in Northern Pennsylvania.

————.
Eldorado Found, The Central Pennsylvania Highlands; a tourist's survey. Altoona, Pa.: Altoona Tribune Publishing Co., 1917. 143 pp., illus.
The region described comprises the counties of Clinton, Centre, Mifflin, Union, Lycoming, Cameron, and Snyder.

————.
A Forgotten People: the Pennsylvania Mountaineers, an address at the Women's Club, Bellefonte, Pa.: April 24, 1922. 4 pp.

————.
Gypsies and Gypsie Lore in the Pennsylvania Mountains; an address. Altoona, Pa.: Times Tribune Co., 1924. 13 pp., illus.

————.
Mountain Minstrelsy of Pennsylvania. Philadelphia: N. F. McGirr, 1931.

————.
"Pennsylvania Folklore Society." *JAFL* 56: 180–181, 1943.

Way, Frederick, Jr.
The Allegheny. (The Rivers of America Series.) Illus. by Henry C. Pitz. New York: Farrar & Rinehart, 1942. 280 pp., illus., bibl. (pp. 219–222).

Weygandt, Cornelius
The Blue Hills; Round and Discoveries in the Country Places of Pennsylvania. New York: Henry Holt and Co., Inc., 1936.

————.
Philadelphia Folks. New York: D. Appleton-Century Co., 1938. xx, 357 pp., illus.

Wildes, Harry Emerson
The Delaware. (The Rivers of America Series.) Illustrated by Irwin D. Hoffman. New York: Farrar and Rinehart, 1940.
"The Delaware is a symbol rather than a stream. It marks the place where cultures clashed, where peoples blended into true Americans, where a nation was born and where, by bitter battle, the United States was saved."

Wright, J. E., and Corbett, Doris S.
Pennsylvania. Pioneer Life in Western Pennsylvania. Pittsburgh: University of Pittsburgh, 1940. 251 pp., illus.

FOLKTALES—LEGENDS

Boker, George H.
"The Legends of the Hounds." *Lebanon County Historical Soc. Papers.* 3(No. 1):31–50, 1904.

Buck, William Joseph
Local Sketches and Legends Pertaining to Bucks and Montgomery Counties, Pennsylvania. Philadelphia: Printed for the Author, 1887. 340 pp.

Fauset, A. H.
"Tales and Riddles Collected in Philadelphia." *JAFL* 41:529–538, 1928.

Federal Writers' Project
Tales of Pioneer Pittsburgh. (American Guide Series.) Compiled and Written by the Workers of the Federal Writers' Project of the Works Progress Administration for the state of Pennsylvania. Philadelphia: Wm. Penn Association, 1937.

Halpert, Lt. Herbert
"Pennsylvania Fairylore and Folktales." *JAFL* 58:130–134, 1945.

Henning, David C.
"Tales of the Blue Mountains." *Historical Society of Schuylkil County, Pa. Publications* Vol. 3, 1911.

Herr, C. C.
"Lititz (Eastern Pennsylvania)." *JAFL* 8:308–312, 1895.

Newell, W. W.
"Tale of the Blue Mountains in Pennsylvania." *JAFL* 11:76–78, 1898.

Parsons, Elsie Clews
"Tales from Maryland and Pennsylvania." *JAFL* 30:209–217, 1917.

Potts, W. J.
"Marriage of a Widow in a Shift." *JAFL* 3: 314, 1890.
A folk tale of Philadelphia.

Riepel, Anna M.
"The Saga of Old Tug. Tall Tales from Northern Pennsylvania." *NYFQ* 4(No. 1): 54–60, 1948.

Shoemaker, Henry Wharton
Black Forest Souvenirs, collected in northern Pennsylvania. Reading, Pa.: Bright-Faust Printing Co., 1914. xix, 404 pp.
Legends of the West Branch Valley of the Susquehanna.

————.
In the Seven Mountains; legends collected in Central Pennsylvania. Reading, Pa.: The Bright Printing Co., 1913. xix, 433 pp., illus.
Contents: Invocation—Explanatory Preface—In the Seven Mountains—Dan Treaster's Nights—The Ghost—The Canoe—The Logan Brothers —Dorman Panther—The Token—Pipsisseway's Pine—Uncle Job—Swartzell Panther—A Modern Petrarch—The Thread—On the Ledge—The Indian Mound—Lynx of Indianville Gap— Turned to Stone— The Devil's Turnip Patch—Story of the Cannon Hole—The Ghostly Lights—The Old Fort—An Episode of '65 Flood—At the Gate of the Dead.

————.
Juanita Memories; legends collected in Central Pennsylvania. Philadelphia: J. J. McVey, 1916. xv, 395 pp., bibl.

————.
More Allegheny Episodes: Legends and traditions old and new. Gathered among the Pennsylvania mountains. Altoona, Pa.: Mountain City Press, Times Tribune Co., 1924. 2 vols.

————.
More Pennsylvania Mountain Stories. Reading, Pa.: The Bright Printing Co. xv, 405 pp.

————.
North American Mementos; legends and traditions gathered in northern Pennsylvania. Altoona, Pa.: The Times Tribune Publishing Co., 1920. 383 pp.

———. *Penn's Grandest Cavern;* The history, legends and description of Penn's Cave in Center County, Pennsylvania. Altoona, Pa.: Altoona Tribune Press, 1916. 94 pp., rev. ed., illus.

———. *Pennsylvania Mountain Stories.* Bradford, Pa.: Bradford Record Publishing Co., 1908. 89 pp.

———. *Some Stories of Old Deserted Houses in the Central Pennsylvania Mountains,* compiled from local sources. Altoona, Pa.: Times Tribune Co., 1931. 81 pp.

———. *South Mountain Sketches;* folk tales and legends collected in the mountains of southern Pennsylvania. Altoona, Pa.: Times Tribune Co., 1920. 332 pp., illus.

———. *Susquehanna Legends,* collected in Central Pennsylvania. Reading, Pa.: The Bright Printing Co., 1913. xviii, 389 pp., illus.

———. *Tales of the Bald Eagle Mountains in Central Pennsylvania.* Reading, Pa.: The Bright Printing Co., 1912. xx, 490 pp.

———. *The Indian Steps,* and other Pennsylvania Mountain Stories. Reading, Pa.: The Bright Printing Co., 1912. ix, 427 pp.

———. *True Stories of the Pennsylvania Mountains;* an address at the Story-telling League, May 2, 1923, Reading, Pa. Altoona, Pa.: Altoona Tribune Press, 1923. 10 pp.

"Two Pennsylvania Mountain Legends." *Publications of the Pennsylvania Folk-Lore Society* 1(No. 4)13–15, 1928.

Wild Life in Western Pennsylvania. New York: Composite Printing Co., 1903. vii, 83 pp.
The author includes a number of legends.

Stoker, A. F.
Indian History and Legends of Pennsylvania's Picturesque Playgrounds. Scranton, Pa.: International Textbook Co., 1936.

Western Pennsylvania Historical Survey.
Guidebook to Historic Places in Western Pennsylvania, compiled by the Western Pennsylvania Historical Survey. Pittsburgh: University of Pittsburgh Press, 1938. ix, 186 pp., bibl.

Wright, Caleb Earl
Legends of Bucks County. A Novel. Doylestown, Pa.: B. McGinty, 1887. 280 pp.

CUSTOMS—TRADITIONS

Anderson, Sherwood
Marching Men. New York: John Lane Co., 1917.
The author freely uses native lore.

Boyd, James
Roll River. New York: Charles Scribner's Sons, 1935.
Pennsylvania life in fiction.

Brush, Katherine
Don't Ever Leave Me. New York: Farrar and Rinehart, 1935.
A novel utilizing manners, customs, and lore.

Hare, Amory
Deep Country. New York: Charles Scribner's Sons, 1933.
Describes the social life in the country near Philadelphia.

Mitchell, Edwin Valentine
It's an Old Pennsylvania Custom. New York: Vanguard Press, 1946. 262 pp., illus.
In some fifteen chapters the author covers the ground from cave-dwellings to Philadelphia taverns, taking in on the way,—courtship, customs, the wearing of beards, musical manners—historical, domestic, culinary lore; Pennsylvania speech, and sections on witchcraft, superstitions and magical practices.

Munroe, Kirk
Derrick Sterling, a Story of the Mines. New York: Harper Bros., 1888.

Strawbridge, Ann West
Dawn After Danger. New York: Coward McCann, 1934.
A novel utilizing local lore.

Todd, C. B.
"Corpus Christi Festival at St. Mary's, Pa." *JAFL* 11:126–128, 1898.

Turnbull, Agnes
Remember the End. New York: The Macmillan Co., 1938.
A story of Western Pennsylvania.

MAGIC—SUPERSTITION—WITCHCRAFT

Aurand, Ammon Monroe, Jr.
An Account of the "Witch" Murder Trial, York, Pa., January 7–9, 1929. Commonwealth of Pennsylvania vs. John Blymyer, et al. Harrisburg, Pa.: Aurand Press, 1929. 31 pp.

Bayard, Samuel P.
"Witchcraft, Magic and Spirits on the Border of Pennsylvania and West Virginia." *JAFL* 51:47–59, 1938.

Bennett, J.
"Lackawanna Spooners." *Saturday Review of Literature* 5:108, Sept. 8, 1928.

Cowan, J. L.
"Welsh Superstitions from Pennsylvania." *JAFL* 15:131–132, 1902.

Crosby, J. R.
"Modern Witches of Pennsylvania." *JAFL* 40: 304–309, 1927.

Grumbine, E. L.
"Folklore and Superstitions; Beliefs of Lebanon County." *Lebanon County Historical Society. Papers.* 3:254–294, 1906.

Gummere, Amelia Mott
Witchcraft and Quakerism. A Study in Social History. Philadelphia: The Biddle Press, 1908. 69 pp., illus.

Rothschild, Zeta
"The Queer Side of Things—The Pennsylvania Witch-Murder." *Wide World* (London) 65 (No. 386): 163–167, 1930. illus.

Schweidler, A.
Mary Schweidler, the Amber Witch. The most interesting trial for Witchcraft ever known, printed from an imperfect manuscript by her father . . . New York: Wiley and Putnam, xi, 180 pp., 1845.

Sener, Samuel Miller
"Local Superstitions." *Lancaster County Historical Society. Historical Papers and Addresses.* 9(No. 8):233–245, 1905.

Shoemaker, Henry Wharton
"The Origins and Language of Central Pennsylvania Witchcraft." *Pennsylvania Folk-Lore Society*, Publications, Vol. 1, No. 2, Reading Eagle Press, Reading, 1927.

PROVERBS—RIDDLES

Fauset, A. H.
"Tales and Riddles Collected in Philadelphia." *JAFL* 41:529–538, 1928.

Shoemaker, Henry Wharton
"Scotch-Irish and English Proverbs from Central Pennsylvania." *Pennsylvania Folklore Society* Publications, No. 13. Altoona: Times-Tribune Co., 1931.

————.
Scotch-Irish and English Proverbs and Sayings of the West Branch Valley of Central Pennsylvania. An address by Henry Wharton Shoemaker at the Rotary Club, Milton, Pennsylvania, June 6, 1927. Reading: Reading Eagle Press, 1927. 24 pp.

SPEECH

Comfort, Anne Westar
"Some Peculiarities of Quaker Speech." *AS* 8(No. 1):12–14, 1933.

De Camp, L. Sprague
"Scranton Pronunciation." *AS* 15:368–372, 1940.

Heydrick, B. A.
"Pennsylvania Word-List." *Dialect Notes* 4 (Part 5):337–339, 1916.
Chiefly from Adams, York, Lancaster, Lebanon and Schuylkill Counties.

Maxfield, Ezra Kempton
"Quaker 'Thee' and Its History." *AS* 1(No. 12):638–644, 1926.

————.
"Quaker 'Thou' and 'Thee'." *AS* 4(No. 5): 359–361, 1929.

"The Speech of South-Western Pennsylvania." *AS* 7(No. 1):18–20, 1931.

Newlon, Claude M.
"Dialects on the Western Pennsylvania Frontier." *AS* 4(No. 2):104–110, 1928.

Pennypacker, Isaac R.
"The Quaker Origins." *AS* 2(No. 9):395–402, 1927.

Savage, Howard J.
"College Slang Words and Phrases from Bryn Mawr College." *Dialect Notes* 5(Part 5):139–148, 1922.

Shoemaker, Henry Wharton
"Old Time Words." *Pennsylvania Folklore Society Publication* No. 12. Altoona: Times-Tribune Press, 1930.

————.
Thirteen Hundred Old Time Words of British, Continental or Aboriginal Origins, still in use among the Pennsylvania Mountain People. Altoona, Pennsylvania: Times-Tribune Press, 1930. 75 pp.

Tucker, R. Whitney
"Linguistic Substrata in Pennsylvania and Elsewhere." *Language* 10:1–5, 1934.

————.
"Notes on the Philadelphia Dialect." *AS* 19: 37–42, 1945.

Zimmerman, H. E.
"Word List from Pennsylvania." *Dialect Notes* 1(Part 9):411–427.

FOLK MEDICINE

Hohman, Johann Georg
John George Hohman's Long Lost Friend; or, Book of Powwows. A collection of mysterious and invaluable arts and remedies; for man as well as animals; with many proofs of their virtue and efficacy in healing diseases, etc. . . Harrisburg, Pa.: The Aurand Press, 1930. 94 pp., illus.

Wrenshall, L. H.
"Incantations and Popular Healing in Maryland and Pennsylvania." *JAFL* 15:268–274, 1902.

PLACE NAMES

Donehoo, George P.
History of the Indian Villages and Place-Names in Pennsylvania. Harrisburg, Pa.: Author's Limited Edition, 1928. xiv, 290 pp.

————.
The Changing of Historic Place Names . . . with an introduction and glossary of some historic names changed or misspelled in Pennsylvania, by Henry W. Shoemaker . . . Published under the auspices of the Pennsylvania Alpine Club. Altoona, Pa.: Tribune Press, 1921. 14 pp.

Espenshade, A. Henry
Pennsylvania Place Names. Pennsylvania State College Studies in History and Political Science, No. 1. Pennsylvania State College., 1925. 375 pp.
It is arranged under three main heads: "State Counties and County Seats," "The Larger Towns," and "Villages and Townships." A Comprehensive study.

Hamilton, Hugh
Sir William Penn; His Proprietary Province and its Countries; Those of the Commonwealth of Pennsylvania, with the Chronology, Etymology, and Genealogy of the countries . . . Harrisburg: Press of Central Printing and Publishing House, 1920. 14 pp., illus.

Heckewelder, J. G. E.
Names Given by the Lenni Lenape or Delaware Indians to Rivers, Streams and Places in the now States of New Jersey, Pennsylvania, Maryland and Virginia, with their significations. Publications, Pennsylvania German Folklore Society, vol. 5(No. 1). Allentown, Pa.: Penn. German Folklore Society, 1940.

McKirdy, James
"Origin of the Names Given to the Counties in Pennsylvania." *Western Pennsylvania Historical Mag.* 8:37–58, 104–119, 159–174, 235–256, 1925.

MacReynolds, George
Place Names in Bucks County, Pennsylvania, alphabetically arranged in a historical narrative. Doylestown: The Bucks County Historical Society, 1942. viii, 474 pp., illus.

Prowell, George R. and Eno, J. N.
"Pennsylvania County Names." *Mag. of History* 19:231–238; 24:234–235, 1914–17.

Randel, William Pierce
"The Place Names of Tioga County, Penna." *AS* 14:181–191, 1939.

Shoemaker, Henry Wharton
Place Names and Altitudes of Pennsylvania Mountains. Altoona (Pa.): Times Tribune Press, 1923. 15 pp., illus.

Snyder, Charles Fisher
"Township Names of Old Northumberland County, Their Origin and Meaning." *Northumberland County Historical Society (Sunbury, Pa.) Proceedings and Addresses* 8:195–248, 1936.

FOLKSONG

GENERAL STUDIES AND COLLECTIONS

Bayard, Samuel Preston
Hill Country Tunes. Instrumental. Memoir 39. American Folklore Society. Phila.: American Folklore Society, 1944. viii, 96 pp., illus., 100 tunes.
Folk music of Western Pennsylvania.

_____.
"Unrecorded Folk Traditions in Pennsylvania." *Pennsylvania History* 12:1–14, 1945.
A study of songs and ballads.

Cowan, Frank
Southwestern Pennsylvania in Song and Story. With notes and illustrations. With an appendix: The battle ballads and other poems of Southwestern Pennsylvania. Greensburg, Pa.: The Author, 1878. vii, 424 pp.

Henry, Mellinger, E.
"Mountain Minstrelsy of Pennsylvania." *FSSNE* 4:18, 1930.
A review.

_____.
"Traditional Ballad of Pennsylvania." *Altoona Tribune* (Altoona, Pa.), Jan. 30, 1932, pp. 6.
A version of "Sir Hugh, or The Jew's Daughter."

Jackson, George Pullen
"Revolution in Pittsburgh." *TFSB* 12:1–6, May, 1946.

Kirkland, Edwin C.
"Welsh Folksongs." *TFSB* 9:1–7, 1943.
Words and music of four folksongs recorded from a student of Knoxville, Tenn., who got it from her mother, born in Pennsylvania.

Korson, George
Coal Dust on the Fiddle. Songs and Stories of the Bituminous Industry. Philadelphia: University of Penn. Press, 1943. 460 pp., music, bibl.

_____.
Minstrels of the Mine Patch. Songs and Stories of the Anthracite Industry. Philadelphia: University of Penn. Press, 1938. 332 pp., music, bibl.

_____.
Pennsylvania Folk Songs and Ballads. New York: F. H. Hitchcock, 1927. 196 pp.
Songs and ballads of the anthracite miners; a seam of folk lore which overran through Pennsylvania.

Le Mon, Melvin, arr.
The Miner Sings. A Collection of Folk Songs and Ballads of the Anthracite Miner. Introduction and Notes by George Korson. New York: J. Fischer & Bro., 1936. Arranged for Voice and Piano.

Pennsylvania Folk Songs and Ballads for School, Camp and Playground. Lewisburg, Pa.: Pennsylvania Folk Festival, Bushnell University, 1937.

Shoemaker, Henry Wharton
Mountain Minstrelsy of Pennsylvania, compiled by Henry W. Shoemaker, chairman Historical Commission of Pennsylvania, 1923-1930. Phila.: McGirr, 1931. 319 pp., rev. and enl.

North Pennsylvania Minstrelsy, as sung in the backwood settlements, hunting cabins and lumber camps in Northern Pennsylvania, 1840–1923. Altoona, Pa.: Altoona Tribune Co., 1919. Rev. and enl. new edition, 1923. 228 pp., illus. Texts only of a number of ballads and songs. A rich harvest.

——————.
"Origins of Pennsylvania Folk-Songs and Legends." *The Altoona Tribune* (Altoona, Pa.), June 6, 1930 (an editorial).

——————.
"Pennsylvania, the Mother of Folk Songs." *The Altoona Tribune* (Altoona, Pa.), June 3, 1930 (an editorial).

——————.
The Music and Musical Instruments of the Pennsylvania Mountaineers. Altoona, Pa.: Altoona Tribune Company, 1923. 10 pp.

CHILDREN'S GAMES

Thompson, D. W.
"Some Pennsylvania Rope-Jumping Rhymes." *JAFL* 47:383–386, 1934.

Williams, T.
"A Game of Children in Philadelphia." *JAFL* 12:292, 1899.

ARRANGEMENTS

——————: *Mixed Voices*

"Poor Wayfarin' Man O' Grief."
Gaul, Harvey B.: Galaxy: SATB, sop. solo.
A sacred folk hymn of the Penn-Ohio Border.

——————: *Orchestra*

Symphony No. 1 in E Minor—(Pennsylvania).
Cadman, Charles W.:MS:orchestra.

RHODE ISLAND

FOLKLORE

BIBLIOGRAPHY

Bartlett, John Russell
Bibliography of Rhode Island. A Catalogue of books and other publications relating to the State of Rhode Island, with notes, historical, biographical and critical. Printed by the order of the General Assembly. Providence: A. Anthony, 1864. iv, 287 pp.

Brigham, C. S.
Bibliography of the State of Rhode Island. In: *State of Rhode Island and Providence Plantations at the End of the Century....* Edward Field, ed.... Boston and Syracuse: The Mason Publishing Company, 1902. 3 vols.

Chapin, Howard Millar
"Check List of Rhode Island Almanacs, 1643–1850, with introduction and notes." *American Antiquarian Society, Proceedings*, 25:19–54, 1915. (Worcester, Mass.) n.s.

Rhode Island Imprints; a list of books, pamphlets, newspapers and broadsides printed at Newport, Providence, Warren, Rhode Island between 1727 and 1800. Providence: The Society, 1915. 88 pp., illus.

Tuttle Company
Books, Pamphlets Pertaining to Rhode Island. ... Offered for sale by the Tuttle Company. Rutland, Vt.: Rutland, Tuttle Co., 1932. 25 numb. Catalogue 109.

PERIODICALS

Arnold, James N., ed.
The Narragansett Historical Register, A magazine devoted to the antiquities, genealogy and historical matter illustrating the history of the Narragansett Country, or Southern Rhode Island. Hamilton, R. I.: Narragansett Historical Publishing Company, 1882.

Rhode Island History.
V. 1, 1942– . Providence, R. I. Quarterly. Publication of the Rhode Island Historical Society. *Collections.* 1827–1941; *Proceedings.* 1872–1914; *Publications.* 1893–1901.

GENERAL STUDIES AND COLLECTIONS

Bacon, E. M.
Narragansett Bay: Its Historical and Romantic Associations. Illustrated with fifty drawings by author, and with numerous photographs. New York and London: G. P. Putnam's Sons, 1904. 377 pp., illus.
Contains some Jonny-Cake Stories.

Baker, Virginia
Massasoit's Town Sowams in Pokanoket. Its History, Legends and Traditions. Warren, R. I.: The Author, 1894. 43 pp.

Brown, Mary Louise
Rhode Island in Verse. Providence: The Roger Williams Press, 1936. xiv, 244 pp.

Carpenter, Esther Bernon
South County Studies of some eighteenth century persons, places and conditions in that portion of Rhode Island called Narragansett. With an introduction by Caroline Hazard, compiled largely from letters now first published by Oliver Wendell Holmes. Boston: Printed for the Subscribers, 1924. xv, 296 pp.

Denison, Frederic
Westerly (Rhode Island) and Its Witnesses. For two hundred and fifty years, 1626–1876, including Charlestown, Hopkinton and Richmond, until their separate organization, with the principal points of their subsequent history. Providence: J. A. & R. A. Reid, 1878.

Earle, Alice Morse
In Old Narragansett; romances and realities. New York: C. Scribner's Sons, 1898. vii, 196 pp.

Federal Writers' Project
Rhode Island, a Guide to the Smallest State.
(American Guide Series). Compiled and written by the Federal Writers' Project of the Works Progress Administration for the State of Rhode Island. Boston: Houghton Mifflin Co., 1937. xxvi, 500 pp., illus., bibl.

Greene, Welcome Arnold
The Providence Plantations for Two Hundred and Fifty Years. An historical review of the foundation, rise and progress of the city of Providence ... also, sketches of the cities of Newport and Pawtucket, and the other towns of the state for which Providence is the commercial centre, together with an account of the celebration of the two hundred and fiftieth anniversary of the settlement of Providence, including the oration by Chief-Justice Thomas Durfee, list of organizations and societies participating and other matters connected therewith, being an historical souvenir of this occasion. Providence, R. I.: J. A. & R. A. Reid, 1886. 468 pp., illus.

Hazard, Caroline
Anchors of Tradition; a presentment of some little known facts and persons in a small corner of colonial New England called Narragansett, to which are added certain weavings of fancy from the thread of life upon the loom of time. New Haven, Conn.: Yale University Press, 1924. viii, 242 pp.
Contents: Studies—Ballads—Stories.

Narragansett Ballads with Songs and Lyrics.
Boston: Houghton Mifflin Co., 1894. v, 107 pp.
Poems—historical and traditional.

Thomas Hazard, son of Rob't., called College Tom. A study of life in Narragansett in the 18th century by his grandson's granddaughter. Boston: Houghton Mifflin Co., 1893. viii, 324 pp.

Hazard, Thomas Benjamin
Nailer Tom's Diary; otherwise the Journal of Thomas B. Hazard of Kingston, Rhode Island, 1778 to 1840, which includes observations on the weather, records of births, marriages and deaths, transactions by barter and money of varying value, preaching friends and neighborhood gossip. Printed as written and introduced by Caroline Hazard. Boston: The Merrymount Press, 1930. xxiv, 808 pp.

Hazard, Thomas Robinson
Recollections of Olden Times: Rowland Robinson of Narragansett and His Unfortunate Daughter. With genealogies of the Robinson, Hazard and Sweet families of Rhode Island. ... Also, a genealogical sketch of the Hazards of the middle states, by Willis P. Hazard. Newport, R. I.: J. P. Sanborn, 1879. 228 pp.

The Jonny-Cake Letters of "Shepherd Tom."
Providence, R. I.: Sidney S. Rider, 1880, 1882, 1888.

The Jonny-Cake Papers of "Shepherd Tom," together with Reminiscences of Narragansett schools of former days; with a biographical sketch and notes by Rowland Gibson Hazard; illustrated by Rudolph Ruzicka. Boston: Printed for the Subscribers, 1915. xix, 529 pp., illus.

Kimball, Gertrude Selwyn
Pictures of Rhode Island in the Past, 1642–1833, by Travelers and Observers. Providence, R. I.: Preston & Rounds Co., 1900. xiii, 175 pp.
Extracts from travelers' narratives, letters, diaries, etc.

Providence in Colonial Times, with an Introduction by J. Franklin Jameson. Boston: Houghton Mifflin Company, 1912. xxi, 392 pp.

Livermore, Rev. Samuel Truesdale
Block Island. I. A Map and Guide; II. A History. Hartford, Conn.: Press of the Case, Lockwood & Brainard Company, 1882. 125 pp.
Much of the material from the author's—*History of Block Island,* published in 1877.

Potter, E. R.
Early History of Narragansett. Providence: Marshall, Brown and Co., 1835. 316 pp.

Preston, Howard Willis
Rhode Island's Historic Background. State of Rhode Island and Providence Plantations, Rhode Island Tercentenary Commission. Providence: Remington Press, 1936. 62 pp., illus.

Tourtellot, Arthur Bernan
The Charles (The Rivers of America Series). ill. by Ernest J. Donnelly. New York: Farrar & Rinehart, Inc., 1941. x, 356 pp., illus., bibl. pp. 343–348.

FOLKTALES—LEGENDS

Dorson, Richard M.
"The Jonny-Cake Papers." *JAFL* 58:104–112, 1945.
In the Jonny-Cake Letters of "Shepherd Tom." Hazard presents "a rich harvest of diversified folk narratives," of the Narragansett Country.

Drake, Samuel Adams
Rhode Island Legends. In: *A Book of New England Legends and Folklore in Verse and Poetry* (pp. 393–417). Boston: Little, Brown and Co., 1901. 477 pp., illus.

Mitchell, Joseph
"Dragger Captain." *The New Yorker* 22 (No. 48):41–42, (Jan. 11) 1947.
Sea yarns from Block Island folk.

Munro, Wilfred Harold
Tales of an Old Sea Port; a general sketch of the history of Bristol, Rhode Island, including, incidentally, an account of the voyages of the Norsemen, so far as they may have been connected with Narragansett Bay: and personal narratives of some notable voyages accomplished by sailors from Mount Hope lands. Princeton, N. J.: Princeton University Press, 1917. 292 pp., illus.

Palmer, Henrietta Raymer, ed.
Rhode Island Tales; depicting social life during the Colonial, Revolutionary and Post-Revolutionary Era. New York: The Purdy Press, 1928, 181 pp., illus.
    Contains tales, legends, beliefs, and customs, told by various authors.

CUSTOMS—TRADITIONS

Carpenter, Esther Bernon
South County Studies of Some Eighteenth Century Persons, Places & Conditions in that Portion of Rhode Island Called Narragansett; with an introduction by Carolyn Hazard, compiled largely from letters now first published by Oliver Wendell Holmes. Boston: Printed for the Subscribers, 1924. xv, 296 pp.

Field, Edward
Early Habits and Customs and Old Landmarks. In: *State of Rhode Island and Providence Plantations at the End of the Century:* a history, illustrated with maps, facsimiles of old plates and paintings and photographs of ancient landmarks. Boston and Syracuse: The Mason Publishing Company, 1902. 3 vols.

Harris, Edward Doubleday
A Copy of the Old Epitaphs in the Burying Ground of Block Island, Rhode Island. Cambridge, Mass.: Press of J. Wilson & Son, 1883. 66 pp.

Middleton, Alcia Hopton
Life in Carolina and New England During the Nineteenth Century, as illustrated by reminiscences and letters of the Middleton family of Charleston, S. C., and of the De Wolf family of Bristol, Rhode Island. Bristol, R. I.: Privately Printed, 1929. xii, 233 pp., illus.
    De Wolf and Hopton legends.

Updegraff, Florence M.
Traveler's Candle. New York: Harcourt, Brace and Co., 1942.
    The story of a Quaker Family life in the Rhode Island Colony in 1680.

Weeden, William Babcock
Early Rhode Island, a Social History of the People. New York: The Grafton Press, 1910. x, 381 pp.

SPEECH

Simpson, Claude M.
"Early Rhode Island Pronunciation 1636–1700, as Reflected in Published Town Records." *Dialect Notes* 6 (Part 14) :579–582, 1937.

————.
"Lexical Notes from Rhode Island Town Records." *Dialect Notes* 6 (Parts 12 & 13): 517–527, 1936.

————.
The English Speech of Early Rhode Island, 1636–1700. Harvard Ph.D. dissertation, Cambridge: Harvard University, 1936.

PLACE NAMES

Brigham, Clarence Saunders
Seventeenth Century Place-Names of Providence Plantations, 1639–1700. Providence: n.p., 1903. 28 pp.

Parsons, Usher
Indian Names of Places in Rhode Island. Providence: Knowles, Anthony & Co. Printers, 1861. iv, 32 pp.

Rhode Island Historical Society
Harris Papers, with an introduction by Irving B. Richman and a calendar and notes by Clarence S. Brigham. Providence: Printed for the Society, 1902. 410 pp.
    "List of seventeenth century place-names in Providence Plantations, 1636–1700," compiled by Clarence S. Brigham: pp. 373–400.

Rider, Sidney Smith
The Lands of Rhode Island as They were Known to Caunounicus and Miantunnomu, when Roger Williams came in 1636. Providence: The Author, 1904. 297 pp., illus.

Trumbull, James Hammond
"Indian Local Names in Rhode Island." *Book Notes* (Providence, R. I.) 29 (No. 9) :65–68, 1912.

FOLKSONG
COLLECTIONS

Hazard, Caroline
Narragansett Ballads with Songs and Lyrics. Boston: Houghton Mifflin Co., 1894. 107 pp.

ARRANGEMENTS

————: *Female Voices*

"The Two Sisters."
    Treharne, Bryceson: Willis: SSA a cap.
    Rhode Island version of the old traditional ballad.

CHILDREN'S GAMES AND RHYMES

"Rhode Island Counting-Out Rhyme."
JAFL 4:171, 1891.

VERMONT
FOLKLORE
BIBLIOGRAPY

Gilman, Marcus Davis
The Bibliography of Vermont; or, A list of books and pamphlets relating in any way to the state. With biographical and other notes. Burlington, Vt.: Printed by the Free Press Association, 1897. vii, 349 pp.

Index to the Contents of the Vermont Historical Gazetteer, edited and published by Abbie M. Hemenway. Prepared under the direction of George W. Wing, State Librarian. Rutland, Vt.: The Tuttle Company, 1923. xii, 1118 pp.

Newton, Earle Williams
Index to the Proceedings of the Vermont Historical Society. New Series, Vols. 1–10. Montpelier: Vermont Historical Society, 1943. iv, 86 pp.

O'Gorman, J. Leo
"Journals of Early Travels in Vermont. A Bibliography." *Proceedings of the Vermont Historical Society* 8(No. 4):263–278, Dec. 1939.
"—from the earliest days up to 1830."

Tuttle, Charles E.
A Bibliography of Vermont. In: C. F. Libbie & Co. Auction Sale Catalogue, Nov. 18–21, 1919. pp. 131–214.

Whitney, E. Lee, comp.
"Index to the Vermonter, Vol. 1–17." Published by the Vermont Historical Society through the courtesy of the compiler. *Proceedings of the Vermont Historical Society* (1911–1912) pp. 115–162, 1913.

PERIODICALS

Proceedings. Vermont Historical Society. V. 1, 1861—. Montpelier, etc. *Collections.* V. 1–2, 1870–1871.

The Vermont Historical Gazetteer: a Magazine, Embracing a History of Each Town, Civil, Ecclesiastical, Biographical, and Military. Edited by Abbey Maria Hemenway. Burlington, Vt.: A. M. Hemenway, etc., etc., 1868–1891. 5 vols. Quarterly.

The Vermonter. White River Junction, Vt. V. 1, 1895—. A Monthly Magazine.

GENERAL STUDIES AND COLLECTIONS

Baker, Mary Eva
Folklore of Springfield, Springfield, Vt.: The Altrurian Club of Springfield, 1922. 177 pp., illus.

Carpenter, Ernest C.
The Boyhood Days of President Calvin Coolidge, or From The Green Mountains to The White House, Original Sketches of Plymouth Life. Rutland, Vt.: The Tuttle Company, 1925.

Chase, Francis, ed.
Gathered Sketches from the Early History of New Hampshire and Vermont; containing vivid and interesting account of a great variety of adventures of our forefathers, and of other incidents of olden time. Original and selected. Claremont, N. H.: Tracy, Kenney & Co., 1856. 215 pp.

Cleghorn, Sarah N.
A Turnpike Lady, Beartown, Vermont, 1768–1796. New York: Henry Holt and Co., 1907.
"Sarah Cleghorn is Vermont's most liberal spirit of recent decades a combination of lavender and old lace and dynamite."

Crane, Charles E.
Winter in Vermont. New York: Alfred A. Knopf, 1941.
Filled with accurate anecdote and lore.

Federal Writers' Project
Vermont, a Guide to the Green Mountain State (American Guide Series). Written by workers of the Federal Writers' Project of the Works Progress Administration for the State of Vermont. Boston: Houghton, Mifflin Co., 1937. xxi, 392 pp., illus., bibl.

Greene, Frank L.
Vermont, the Green Mountain State; Past, Present, Prospective. St. Albans: St. Albans Messenger Company Print, 1907. 80 pp.

Hard, Walter R.
A Mountain Township; with an Introduction by Dorothy Canfield Fisher. New York: Harcourt, Brace and Company, 1933. xx, 218 pp.

————.
Salt of Vermont. Brattleboro: The Stephen Daye Press, 1931. 96 pp.

————.
Vermont Valley. New York: Harcourt, Brace and Company, 1939. xii, 187 pp.
Character stories of Vermonters written in verse.

————.
Vermont Vintage. Brattleboro, Vt.: Stephen Daye Press, 1937. 94 pp.

————, **and Margaret**
This Is Vermont. Brattleboro, Vt.: Stephen Daye Press, 1936.

Hayes, Lyman S.
The Connecticut River Valley on Southern Vermont and New Hampshire. Rutland, Vermont: The Tuttle Co., 1929.

Jennison, Keith Warren
Vermont Is Where You Find It. Stories and Pictures. New York: Harcourt, Brace and Co., 1941. 118 pp., 57 pl.
Pictorial account of Vermont folkways with text.

Mussey, Barrons
Vermont Heritage. New York: A. A. Wyn, 1946.

Peattie, Roderick, ed.
The Friendly Mountain. New York: The Vanguard Press, 1942. 340 pp., illus.
Section of the book devoted to the history and ethnology of the Green Mountains and Taconics of Vermont.

Perkins, Nathan
A Narrative of a Tour Through the State of Vermont from April 27 to June 12, 1789. Woodstock, Vt.: The Elm Tree Press, 1920. 31 pp.

Pierce, Enid Crawford, and Flanders, Helen Hartness
Green Mountain Verse: An Anthology of Contemporary Vermont Poetry. New York: Farrar and Rinehart, 1944.

Robinson, Rowland E.
Centennial Edition of the Works of E. Robinson. Rutland: The Tuttle Co., 1934. 7 vols.
"The most original and autochthonous of nineteenth-century Vermont prose-writers."

——————.
Danvis Folks. Boston: Houghton Mifflin Company, 1894.

——————.
Sam Lovel's Camps, Uncle Lisha's Friends under Bark and Canvas. A Sequel to *Uncle Lisha's Shop.* New York: Forest and Stream Publishing Co., 1899.

——————.
Uncle Lisha's Outing. Boston: Houghton Mifflin and Company, 1897.

——————.
Uncle Lisha's Shop, Life in a Corner of Yankeeland. New York: Forest and Stream Publishing Co., 1902.

Taggard, Genevieve
A Part of Vermont. East Jamaica, Vt.: The River Press, 1945. 23 pp.
Poems of Vermont places and folk.

The Green Mountain Series.
Brattleboro: The Stephen Daye Press, 1931. 42 pp.
An anthology of Vermont verse; a book of Vermont biographies; a collection of Vermont ballads; and a miscellany of Vermont prose. Sponsored by the Committee on Vermont traditions and ideals of the Commission on County Life.

Thompson, Daniel P.
History of the Town of Montpelier, from the Time It Was First Chartered in 1781 to the Year 1860. Together with Biographical Sketches of Its Most Noted Deceased Citizens. Montpelier, Vt.: E. P. Walton, Printer, 1860.

Thompson, Zadock
History of Vermont, Natural, Civil and Statistical in Three Parts. Burlington, Vt.: The Author, 1853. 4 pts. in 1 vol., illus.

Tupper, Frederick, and Brown, Helen Tylor, eds.
Grandmother Tyler's Book: The Recollections of Mary Palmer Tyler. New York: G. P. Putnam's Sons, 1925.
This clear-eyed and disillusioned book has an interest that transcends geographical boundaries. It is the closest thing to Jane Austen that ever came out of this state."

FOLKTALES—LEGENDS

Allen, Ethan
A Narrative of Colonel Ethan Allen's Captivity, Containing His Voyages and Travels, Written by Himself; and now faithfully reprinted from the original edition; with an introductory note by John Pell, Esq., and illustrations by Will Crawford. New York: Printed for The Fort Ticonderoga Museum by R. W. Ellis, The Georgian Press, 1930. xvii, 134 pp. First ed. Philadelphia, 1779.

Davis, Robert
"Some Characteristics of Northern Vermont Wit." *Proceedings of the Vermont Historical Society* 5:322–323, Dec. 1937. N.S.

De Puy, Henry Walter
Ethan Allen and the Green Mountain Heroes of '76. With a Sketch of the Early History of Vermont. Buffalo: Phinney & Co., 1857. xvii, 428 pp.
Some of the legends that have grown about this hero are told.

Holbrook, Stewart H.
Ethan Allen. New York: The Macmillan Company, 1940.
The hero of the Green Mountain Boys and his legend.

Pell, John
Ethan Allen. Boston: Houghton, Mifflin Company, 1929.

CUSTOMS—TRADITIONS

Dean, Leon W.
Green Mountain Boy: Seth Warner. New York: Farrar and Rinehart, 1944. 242 pp.
A biography for boys about an officer in the Revolutionary army, using freely local traditions, customs, and speech.

Fisher, Dorothy Canfield
Tourists Accommodated. New York: Harcourt, Brace and Co., 1932.
A work of fiction using Vermont flavor.

Grelle, Leone Rice
Country Road. New York: The Macmillan Company, 1945. 83 pp.
Made up of nearly one hundred nature poems. "—many pages are full of local color and rich hints of a passing New England." (T. H. McNeal).

Humphrey, Zephine
The Beloved Community. New York: E. P. Dutton and Co., 1930.
A novel of Vermonters and local color.

Lee, John Parker
Uncommon Vermont. Rutland. Vermont: The Tuttle Co., 1926.

Lee, W. Storrs
Stagecoach North. New York: The Macmillan Co., 1941.
"This is an honest, extremely readable book about life in Middlebury, Vermont, during the first half-century of the American republic."

Peck, Theodora
Hester of the Grants. New York: Fox, Duffield and Co., 1905.
A novel, filled with the flavor of the Vermonters.

Thompson, Daniel P.
The Green Mountain Boys. Montpelier: E. P. Walton and Sons, 1893. 2 Vols.
A fictionalized romance.

Waller, Mary
The Woodcarver of 'Lympus. Boston: Little, Brown and Co., 1914.
A novel.

SPEECH

"Words from West Brattleboro, Vt."
Dialect Notes 3 (Part 6) :452–455, 1910.

FOLKSONG

BIBLIOGRAPHY

Flanders, Helen H.
"First Supplement to Index of Ballads and
Folk-Songs in the Archive of Vermont Folk-
Songs at Smiley Manse, Springfield, Ver-
mont." *Proceedings, Vermont Historical So-
ciety* 7:279–285, 1939.

————.
"Index of Ballads and Folk-Songs in the
Archive of Vermont Folk-Songs at Smiley
Manse, Springfield, Vermont." *Proceedings,
Vermont Historical Society*, 8:(No. 2) 214–
251, (June) 1940.

————.
"Index of Ballads and Folk-Songs in the
Archive of Vermont Folk-Songs at Smiley
Manse, Springfield, Vermont." *Proceedings,
Vermont Historical Society*, New Series, vol.
7 (No. 2), Vermont Historical Society, Brat-
tleboro, Vermont, (June) 1939.

GENERAL STUDIES AND COLLECTIONS

Flanders, Helen Hartness, ed.
A Garland of Green Mountain Song. Piano settings by Helen Norfleet. Published as part of
the Publication programme of the Committee
of Vermont Tradition and Ideals of the Vermont Commission on Country Life. Green
Mountain Pamphlets, No. 1. Boston: John
Worley Company, 1934. 86 pp.

————.
Country Songs of Vermont. Collected by H. H.
Flanders, with Piano Accompaniment by Helen
Norfleet. New York: G. Schirmer, Inc., 1937.
50 pp. (American Folk-Song Series, Set 19.)
Arranged for voice and piano.

————.
The New Green Mountain Songster; traditional folksongs of Vermont, collected, transcribed and edited by Helen Hartness Flanders,
Elizabeth Flanders Ballard, George Brown,
and Phillips Barry. New Haven: Yale University Press, 1939. xx, 278 pp. (unacc. melodies).

————.
"Prospecting for Folk Songs in Vermont."
Vermonter (White River Junction) 36:197–
200, 1931.

————.
"The Quest for Vermont Ballads." *Proceedings,
Vermont Historical Society* 7:53–72, 1939.

————.
"Three Vermont Ballads." *Proceedings, Vermont Historical Society* 7:99–107, 1939.

————, and Brown, George
Vermont Folk Songs and Ballads. Brattleboro,
Vt.: Stephen Daye Press, 1931. 256 pp.
Words and melodies.

Hanson, E. P., and Crichton, Kyle
"Music Round the Mountains, Vermont State
Symphony Orchestra." *Colliers* 104:10–111–,
(Dec. 30 1939. Illus.

Hughes, Robert, and Sturgis, Edith B.
Songs From the Hills of Vermont, sung by
James and Mary Atwood, and Aunt Jenny
Knapp. Texts collected and edited by Edith
B. Sturgis. Tunes collected and piano accom-
paniments arranged with historical notes, by
Robert Hughes. New York: G. Schirmer, 1919.
ix, 57 pp.
Arranged for voice and piano.

Newton, Hilah Foote
"The Burning of the Phoenix." *NYFQ* 1:40–
41, 1945.
Text of the historical ballad recounting the
tragedy of the Steamboat, The Phoenix, in 1819,
near Burlington, Vermont.

Smith, Grace Partridge
"The Frog's Courting." *JAFL* 52:125–127,
1939.
A Vermont variant.

Vermont Chap Book.
Middlebury, Vt.: Middlebury College Press,
1941.

RECORDS

Collections

"New England—Vermont."
In the *Archive of Vermont Folk-Songs* (Springfield, Vt.).

THE SOUTH AND SOUTHERN HIGHLANDS

THE SOUTH AND SOUTHERN HIGHLANDS

FOLKLORE

BIBLIOGRAPHIES

Agnew, Janet Margaret
A Southern Bibliography: fiction 1929–1938. Baton Rouge: Louisiana State University Library School. Bibliographical Series, No. 1. 63 pp.

Boyd, William K., and Brooks, Robert P.
History of the South: A Selected Bibliography and Syllabus, 1584–1876. Athens, Ga.: The McGregor Co., 1918.

Campbell, Olive Dame
"*The Southern Highlands:* A Selected Bibliography." *Bulletin of the Russell Sage Foundation Library.* New York: Feb., 1920. No. 39.

Meyer, H. H. B.
List of References on the Mountain Whites. U. S. Library of Congress, Division of Bibliography, No. 633, March 6, 1922.

PERIODICALS

Journal of Southern History. Southern Historical Association. Baton Rouge, Louisiana. February, 1935

See: Periodical and Journal Listing under the Various States.

Southern Folklore Quarterly. Alton C. Morris, University of Florida, Editor.

South Atlantic Quarterly. Duke University, Durham, North Carolina.

GENERAL STUDIES AND COLLECTIONS

Botkin, Benjamin A.
Folk-Say and Folk-Lore. In: *Culture in the South.* W. T. Couch, ed. (pp. 570–593). Chapel Hill: University of North Carolina Press, 1934.

Brown, Samuel R.
The Western Gazetteer; or emigrant's directory containing a geographical description of the western states and territories, viz., the states of Kentucky, Indiana, Louisiana, Ohio, Tennessee and Mississippi, and the territories of Illinois, Missouri, Alabama, Michigan and Northwestern. Auburn, N. Y.: H. C. Southwicks, 1817. 360 pp.

Brown, William Wells, M.D.
My Southern Home; or The South and Its People. Boston: A. G. Brown and Co., Publishers, 1880.

Burdette, Kay
Cookery of the Old South. Baytown, Texas: Author's Edition, 1941. 152 pp. New ed.

Byrd, Sam
Small Town South. Boston: Houghton Mifflin Co., 1942. 237 pp.
Life and people of a North Carolina village and a small Florida town. "An extraordinary picture of the decay of a civilization as it is expressed in the lives of individuals affected." (G. W. Johnson)

Carmer, Carl
Deep South. New York: Farrar and Rinehart, 1930. 83 pp.
Poems in Southern flavor and lore.

Carter, Hodding
The Lower Mississippi. (The Rivers of America Series.) Illustrated by John McCrady. New York: Farrar and Rinehart, 1943.
A study of the mighty Father of Waters from Cairo to New Orleans. It brings to the reader the gleam of sunlight on the armor of De Soto. The overtones of Indian character pitted against the volatile French temperament, and the romance of the great city port.

Cash, W. J.
The Mind of the South. New York: Alfred A. Knopf, 1941.
Civilization, temperament and folkways of the Southern States.

Coleman, Caroline S.
"Knights of the Pack: The Heyday of the Foot Peddler." *SFQ* 7:187–191, 1943.

Dahlgren, Madeleine
South Mountain Magic. A Narrative. Boston: J. R. Osgood & Co., 1882. 218 pp.

Daniels, Jonathan
A Southerner Discovers the South. New York: The Macmillan Co., 1938.

Davis, Julia
The Shenandoah. (The Rivers of America Series.) New York: Rinehart and Co., 1946. 374 pp., illus.
"This is a book about the peoples of the Valley, about all the stories, customs, heritage of one of America's most historic places." (N. K. Burger)

De Witt, Cornelius, and McNeer, Mary
The Story of the Southern Highlands. Lithographs by Cornelius De Witt, Text by May McNeer. New York: Harper and Bros., 1945. Unpaged.

Dick, Everett
The Dixie Frontier. New York: A. Knopf, 1948.
A vivid account of life on the Southern frontier down to the Civil War. It brings together scattered fragments of experiences, adventure and folklore.

Ericson, Eton Everett
"Folklore of Southern United States." *Folklore* (London) 49:167, 1938.

Fulton, Maurice Garland, ed.
Southern Life in Southern Literature; selections and representative prose and poetry. New York: Ginn and Co., 1917. xiv, 530 pp., illus., bibl. (pp. 528–530).

Gaines, Francis Pendleton
The Southern Plantation. New York: Columbia University Press, 1925.

Gilman, Mrs. Caroline
Recollections of a Southern Matron. Charleston S. C.: Walker, Richards and Co., 1837. viii, 268 pp.

Goodrich, Frances L.
Mountain Homespun. New Haven: Yale University Press, 1931.

Gordon, Caroline
The Women on the Porch. New York: Charles Scribner's Sons, 1944. 316 pp.
A novel rich in the traditions, life, speech, and folkways of the South.

Green, Paul
Out of the South. The life of a people in dramatic form. New York: Harper and Bros., 1939. xii, 577 pp.
Contents: The House of Connelly, The No 'Count boy, Saturday Night, The Field God, Quare Medicine, The Hot Iron, In Abraham's Bosom, Unto Such Glory, Supper for the Dead, Potter's Field, The Man Who Died at Twelve O'Clock, White' Dresses, Johnny Johnson, Hymn to the Rising Sun, The Lost Colony.

————.
The Field God, and *In Abraham's Bosom.* New York: R. M. McBride and Co., 1927. 317 pp.
Folk plays with music.

————.
The Highland Call. A Symphonic play of American history in two acts; with hymn tunes, folksongs, ballads, and dance. Chapel Hill, N. C.: The University of North Carolina Press, 1941. xix, 280 pp., plates.

Grumman, R. M.
"The Sixth Annual Meeting of the Southeastern Folklore Society." *SFQ* 5:134–135, 1941.

Hamer, B. D.
"Funeral Flowers for the Bride," a comedy of mountain people. *The Carolina Playbook,* 10 No. 3, 1937.

Harris, Bernice Kelly
Janey Jeems. Garden City, N. Y.: Doubleday, 1946. 306 pp.
"The locale is rather indefinitely the Southern Highlands.... By a sympathetic insight into strength of character and by concentrating on the vital interests of these characters, however, Mrs. Harris has written a novel that is effective and illustrates the way in which the folk culture of a region may be adapted to literary treatment." (J. W. Ashton.)

Higginson, Thomas Wentworth
Letters and Journals of Thomas Wentworth Higginson, 1846–1906. Edited by Mary Thatcher Higginson. Boston: Houghton Mifflin Co., 1925.

Holliday, Carl
A History of Southern Literature. New York: The Neole Publishing Co., 1906.

————.
Three Centuries of Southern Poetry (1607–1907). Nashville, Tenn.: Smith and Lamar, 1908.

Hudson, Arthur Palmer, ed.
Humor of the Deep South. New York: The Macmillan Co., 1936. xxiv, 548 pp.

Huth, Hans
Report on the Preservation of the Mountain Culture in Great Smoky Mountains National Park. Washington, D. C., U. S. Department of Interior, National Park Service, August 1941.

Jones, Virgil Carrington
The Hatfields and the Mc Coys. Chapel Hill: University of North Carolina Press, 1948.
The story that emerges in this action packed book proves even more fantastic than legend suggested it to be.

Justus, May
Bluebird, Fly Up! Philadelphia, Pa.: J. B. Lippincott Co., 1943. 187 pp.
A story of the folks who live in the Great Smokies. Juvenile.

Kephart, Horace
Our Southern Highlanders. New York: Outing Publishing Co., 1913, and Macmillan Co., 1922. 469 pp.
"An authoritative source in the characteristics, background, mode of living, and speech of the mountain people."

Kroll, Harry Harrison
The Rider on the Bronze Horse. Indianapolis: The Bobbs-Merrill Co., 1942.
A story that is alive with the ferment of a Southern community in a time of change.

Leighton, Clare
Southern Harvest. New York: The Macmillan Co., 1942. 157 pp., illus.
"The author catches the romance inherent in many Southern rural activities, such as cotton picking, tobacco-raising, hog-killing, sorghum-making, and corn-shucking." (J. H. Hankins.)

Lenski, Lois
Blue Ridge Billy. Illustrated by the author. New York: J. B. Lippincott Company, 1946. 203 pp.
"In this book, as in her two previous regional stories—*Bayou Suzette,* and *Strawberry Girl*—Lois Lenski gives a wealth of information about the folklore, customs and traditions of a colorful people. The dialect of the region is skillfully handled." (E. Hodges.)

Liddell, Viola Goode
With A Southern Accent. Norman, Oklahoma: University of Oklahoma Press, 1948.
An intimate story of Southern family life, with an accent on its customs, traditions, humor and speech.

Lumpkin, Grace
To Make My Bread. New York: Macaulay Co., 1932.

McDowell, Lela
Fiddles in the Cumberlands; Edited by Lela McDowell Blakenship. New York: Richard R. Smith, 1944. 310 pp.

> The diary and letters of a Tennessee girl during the Civil War.

McIlwaine, Shields
The Southern Poor White from Lubberland to Tobacco Road. Norman, Okla.: Oklahoma University Press, 1939. xxv, 274 pp., 3 pl., illus.

> An attempt "to tell the social story of the poorwhites and then to show its literary treatment in different periods."

Mackaye, Percy
The Gobbler of God. A Poem of the Southern Appalachians. Illustrated by Arvia Mackaye. New York: Longmans, Green and Company, 1928. xv, 91 pp., front., illus.

McNeer, May Yonge
The Story of the Southern Highlands. Illustrated by C. H. DeWitt. New York: Harper and Brothers, 1945. 33 pp.

> "The customs and superstitions that still prevail in the more remote regions give the story a curiously archaic flavor... The old songs and singing games are here, too." (M. G. D.)

Matthews, Etta Lane
Over the Blue Wall; illustrations by James Daugherty. Chapel Hill, N. C.: The University of North Carolina Press, 1937. xii, 328 pp.

Mooney, J.
"Folklore of the Carolina Mountains." *JAFL* 2:95–104, 1889.

Morris, Alton C.
"Southeastern Folklore Society." *JAFL* 56: 183–184, 1943.

Olmsted, Frederick L.
A Journey in the Seaboard Slave States. New York: Dix and Edwards, 1856. 723 pp.

Parker, Haywood
Folklore of the North Carolina Mountaineer. Asheville, N. C.: 1906.

Peattie, Roderick, ed.
The Great Smokies and the Blue Ridge. (Second volume in the American Mountain Series.) New York: Vanguard Press, 1945. 350 pp., illus.

> The contributors to this volume are Donald Culross Peattie, Alberta Pierson Hannum, Edward S. Drake, Ralph Erskine, Arthur Stupka, John Jacob Niles and Henry Sharp. "Here is a beautifully illustrated book about the leaf-fringed legends which haunt the Great Smokies and the Blue Ridge—about their history and geology and trees and flowers and their running brooks—about the unspoiled people." (Alfred Mynders.)

Preece, Harold, and Kraft, Celia
Dew on Jordan. New York: E. P. Dutton & Co., 1946. 221 pp.

> "From their cabin in the Cumberlands, the authors, both avid sect collectors, rambled far and near. They watched the dubious ecstasies of snake cults, and listened to the word as proclaimed by Holiness Sects, Disciples of Christ, Hardshell Baptists, and a score of others." (John Bicknell.)

Pyrnelle, Louis Clarke
Diddle, Dumps and Tot; or Plantation Child Life. New York: Harper and Bros., 1882. 1910.

Raine, James Watt
The Land of Saddle-bags; a study of the mountain people of Appalachia. New York: Published jointly by Council of Women for Home Missions and Missionary Education Movement of the U. S. and Canada, 1924. x, 260 pp.

Robertson, Ben.
Red Hills and Cotton: An Up-Country Memory. New York: Alfred A. Knopf, 1942. 296 pp.

> "Woven like an old quilt, this book gives a personal pattern of kinfolk by the Blue Ridge in Carolina—a picture of people and their ways." (Rosemary Benet.)

Roche, Emma Langdon
Historic Sketches of the South. New York: The Knickerbocker Press, 1914.

Royall, Anne (Newport)
The Black Book; or A Continuation of Travels in the United States. Washington, D. C.: Printed for the Author, 1828–29. 3 Vols.

———————.
Mrs. Royall's Southern Tour, or Second Series of the Black Book. Washington. D. C.: Printed for the Author, 1830–31. 3 Vols.

Saxon, Lyle
Father Mississippi. New York: Century Co., 1929.

Sheppard, Muriel E.
Cabins in the Laurel. With 128 full-page photographs by Bayard Wootten. Chapel Hill: The University of North Carolina Press, 1935.

Siler, Margaret R.
Cherokee Indian Lore, and Smoky Mt. Stories. Bryson City: Bryston City Times, N. C., 1938.

Smiley, P.
"Folklore from Virginia, South Carolina, Georgia, Alabama and Florida." *JAFL* 32: 357–383, 1919.

Street, James H.
Look Away: A Dixie Note Book. New York: The Viking Press, 1936.

The Intercoastal Waterway: Norfolk to Key West (American Guide Series). Compiled by the Federal Writers' Project of the Works Progress Administration. Washington, D. C.: U. S. Gov't. Printing Office, 1937.

The Ocean Highway: New Brunswick, New Jersey to Jacksonville, Florida. With 32 photographs (American Guide Series). Compiled and written by the Workers of the Federal Writers' Project of the Works Progress Administration. New York: Modern Age Books, 1938.

Thomas, Jean
Blue Ridge Country (American Folkways Series). New York: Duell, Sloan and Pearce, Inc. 1942.
Bounded roughly by the Ohio River on the north, the great Kanawha on the east, and the Tennessee on the south and west, it traverses parts of eight states whose center is the Cumberland Gap celebrated in song and story.

————.
"Feuds Die out but Feud Tales Persist Among the Southern Mountain Folk. Many of the Old Rancors Live only in Memory." *The New York Times Magazine* Nov. 26, 1933. p. 11.

————.
The Traipsin' Woman. New York: E. P. Dutton and Co., 1933.

Thornbough, Laura
The Great Smoky Mountains. New York: Thomas Y. Crowell Co., 1937.

Tyre, Nedra
Red Wine First, New York: Simon and Schuster, 1947. 208 pp.
A series of "deep South monologues" by persons on relief or old-age pensions. It captures the languages, social customs and folkways of the southern folk.

U. S. One: Maine to Florida (American Guide Series). Compiled and written by the Federal Writers' Project of the Works Progress Administration. Illustrated. New York: Modern Age Books, Inc., 1938.

"Virginia Blue Ridge Folklore."
JAFL 20:151–152, 1907.

Wade, John Donald
Southern Humor. In: *Culture in the South* (pp. 616–629). Chapel Hill: University of North Carolina Press, 1935.

Watterson, Henry
Oddities in Southern Life and Character; illus. by W. L. Sheppard & F. S. Church. Boston and New York: Houghton Mifflin & Co., 1900. xii, 485 pp.
An anthology with interpretive notes.

Wilson, Charles Morrow
Backwoods America. Chapel Hill, N. C.: University of North Carolina Press, 1934.

Wiltse, H. M.
"Southern Field of Folklore." *JAFL* 8:209–212, 1895.

FOLKTALES AND LEGENDS

Carter, I. G.
"Mountain White Folk-Lore; Tales from the Southern Blue Ridge." *JAFL* 38:340–374, 1925.

Chase, Richard
The Jack Tales. Folk Tales from the Southern Appalachians Collected and Retold by Richard Chase, with an Appendix by Herbert Halpert and Illustrations by Berkeley Williams, Jr. Boston: Houghton Mifflin Co., 1943. xiii, 202 pp.

Cooke, Mrs. Sarah Johnson
Bypaths in Dixie; folk tales of the South... with an introduction by Harry Stillwell Edwards, New York: E. P. Dutton & Co., 1911. 316 pp., illus.

Eggleston, George Cary
Joe Lambert's Ferry, with other stories of the frontier and early settlers. Boston: D. Lathrop and Company, 1883. 150 pp.
Includes tall tales and legends of the South.

Field, Rachel
American Folk and Fairy Tales. New York: Scribners and Sons, 1929. 302 pp.
Stories of the Southern Mountains are also included.

Green, Paul
Salvation on a String, and Other Stories of the South. New York: Harper and Brothers, 1946. 278 pp.
There are tales of backwoods wisdom, and backwoods superstition, and the Paul Bunyan legend of prowess, and others. The idiom and vernacular speak of the heritage of Elizabethan balladry.

Hendricks, W. C., ed.
Bundle of Troubles and Other Tarheel Tales. Compiled by the Workers of the Federal Writers' Program of the Works Progress Administration in the State of North Carolina. Durham, N. C.: Duke University Press, 1943. 206 pp., illus.

Herrick, R. F.
"Black Dog of the Blue Ridge." *JAFL* 20:151–152, 1907.

Mackaye, Percy
Tall Tales of the Kentucky Mountains; 12 tales told in mountain vernacular, by Solomon Shell, a legendary figure. New York: George H. Doran Co., 1926.

Malloy, J. Leavin's
"A legend of the Carolina Mountains." *The Carolina Playbook,* 10, No. 1, 1937.

Meine, Franklin J.
Tall Tales of the Southwest. An anthology of southern and southwestern humor, 1830–1860. New York: Alfred A. Knopf, 1930. xxxii, 456 pp., illus., bibl.

Rogers, E. G.
"Concerning the Nathan Forrest Legend." *TFSB* 4:32–63, 1938.

Wardle, H. N.
"Note on the Ground Hog Myth and its Origin." *JAFL* 32:521–522, 1919.

SUPERSTITIONS

Bacon, A. M., and Herron, Miss
"Conjuring and Conjure-Doctors in the Southern United States." *JAFL* 9:143–147; 224–226, 1896.

"Cumberland Mountain Superstitions." *JAFL* 12:131–135, 1899; 24:319–322, 1911.

Duncan, Hannibal G., and Winnie L.
"Superstitions and Sayings Among the Southern Highlanders." *JAFL* 42:233–238, 1929.

Shearin, H. G.
"Superstitions in the Cumberland Mountains." *JAFL* 24:319–322, 1911.

Wiltse, H. M.
"Mountain Superstitions of the South." *JAFL* 12:131–135, 1899.

FOLK MEDICINE

Bacon, A. M., and Herron, Miss
"Conjuring and Conjure-Doctors in the Southern United States." *JAFL* 9:143–147; 224–226, 1896.

Martin, Roxie
"Old Remedies Collected in the Blue Ridge Mountains." *JAFL* 60:184–185, 1947.

Yeats, Irene
"Conjures and Cures in the Novels of Julia Peterkin." *SFQ* 10:137–149, 1946.

RIDDLES

Carter, Isabel Gordon
"Mountains White Riddles," *JAFL* 47:76–81, 1934.

Hudson, Arthur Palmer
"Some Folk Riddles from the South." *South Atlantic Quarterly* (Duke University, Durham, North Carolina) 42:78–93, 1943.

SPEECH

Berrey, Lester V.
"Southern Mountain Dialect." *AS* 15:45–55, 1940.

C. G.
"Southern Mountain Accent." *AS* 9 (No. 3): 251, 1934.

Carpenter, Charles
"Variation in the Southern Mountain Dialect." *AS* 8 (No. 1):22–25, 1933.

Carson, W. P.
A Descriptive Study of Literary Dialect of the Southern Highlander. New York: Columbia University Press, 1926.

Chapman, Maristan
"American Speech as Practiced in Southern Highlands." *Century Magazine* 117:617–623, 1929.

Clark, J. D.
"Similes from the Folk Speech of the South." *SFQ* 4:119–133, 1940.

_____.
"Similes from the Folk Speech of the South: a Supplement to Wilstach's Compilations." *SFQ* 4:205–226, 1940.

Combs, Josiah H.
"A Word-List from the South." *Dialect Notes* 5 (Part 2):31–40, 1919.

_____.
"Old, Early and Elizabethan English in the Southern Mountains." *Dialect Notes* 4 (Part 4):283–297, 1916.

_____.
"The Language of the Southern Highlanders." *PMLA* 46: (No. 4) 1302–1323, (Dec.) 1931.

Dingus, L. R.
"Appalachian Mountain Words." *Dialect Notes* 5 (Part 10):468–471, 1927.
The list was compiled from *The Land of the Saddle Bags* by James Watt Raine.

Epler, Blanch N.
"A Bit of Elizabethan English." *National Geographic Magazine* 64:684–730, 1933.

Evans, Medford
"Southern Long 'I'." *AS* 10 (No. 3):188–190, 1935.

Greet, William Cabell
Southern Speech. In: *Culture in the South* (pp. 594–616). Chapel Hill: University of North Carolina Press, 1935.

Hall, Joseph Sargent
Phonetics of Great Smoky Mt. Speech. New York: King's Crown Press, 1942. 110 pp. American Speech, reprints and mimeographs, No. 4.

Hill, A. A.
"A Report of the Proposed Investigation of Southern Speech." *Dialect Notes* 6 (Part 9): 420–424, 1934.

Johnson, H. P.
"Who Lost the Southern R?" *AS* 3 (No. 5): 377–383, 1928.

Kephart, Horace
Our Southern Highlanders. New York: The Macmillan Co., 1922. 469 pp., new and enl. ed.
Has chapter on the Mountain Dialect.

Lenski, Lois
Blue Ridge Billy. Illustrated by the author. Philadelphia: J. B. Lippincott Co., 1946. 203 pp.
"All the people who make up Billy's world speak the idiom of the Southern Highlands—words that go back to the time of Chaucer."

Mackaye, Percy
Tall Tales of the Kentucky Mountains; 12 tales told in mountain vernacular by Solomon Shell, a legendary figure. New York: George H. Doran Co., 1928.

Morley, Margaret W.
The Carolina Mountains. New York: Houghton Mifflin Co., 1913. viii, 397 pp.
Has chapter entitled "The Speech of the Mountains."

Owens, Bess Alice
"Folk Speech of the Cumberlands." *AS* 7 (No. 2) :89–95, 1931.

Roscoe, Burton
"Southern Accent." *American Mercury* 11:73–75, 1927.

Sizer, Miriam M.
"Christian Names in the Blue Ridge of Virginia." *AS* 8 (No. 2) :34–37, 1933.

————.
"Surnames in Blue Ridge of Virginia." *AS* 12 (No. 4) :267–269, 1937.

Still, James A.
"Christian Names in the Cumberlands." *AS* 5 (No. 4) :306–307, 1930.

Walker, Ralph S.
"A Mountaineer Looks at his Speech: Specimens of Mountain Speech." *TFSB* 5:1–13, 1939.

Wheatley, Katharine E.
"Southern Standards." *AS* 9 (No. 1) :36–45, 1934.
A discussion of Southern dialect, inflection, and comparison with other regions.

Wilson, Charles M.
"Beefsteak When I'm Hungry." *Virginia Quarterly* 6:240–250, 1930.
Speech of the Southern Mountaineers.

————.
"Elizabethan America." *Atlantic Monthly* 144: 238–244, 1929.
On the speech and habits of the Southern Highlands, "Appalachia and Ozarkadia."

Wise, C. M.
"Southern American Dialect." *AS* 8 (No. 2) : 37–43, 1933.

Word-lists from the South.
Greensboro, N. C.: The American Dialect Society, 1944. 72 pp. Publication, No. 2, No. 3 (pp. 7–12) consists of comments for *word-lists from the South,* ed. by George P. Wilson.

PLACE NAMES

Fink, Paul M.
"Smoky Mountains History as told by Place-Names." *East Tennessee Historical Society Publ.* 6:4–11, 1934.

Still, James A.
"Place Names in the Cumberland Mountains." *AS* 5 (No. 2) :113, 1929.

CHILDREN'S RHYMES AND PLAY SONGS

Chase, Richard
Old Songs and Singing Games. Chapel Hill, N. C.: University of North Carolina Press, 1938.

"Counting-Out Rhymes from the Southern States." *JAFL* 32:377, 1919.

Trent-Johns, Altona
Play Songs of the Deep South. Washington, D. C.: Associated Publishers, Inc., 1947.
Fifteen game songs with music.

DANCES

Hall, Joseph S.
"Some Party-Games of the Great Smoky Mountains." *JAFL* 54:68–71, 1941.

FOLKSONG

BIBLIOGRAPHY

See: Section under *Folklore* above, and p. 237.

Campbell, Olive Dame
The Southern Highlands: A Selected Bibliography. Bulletin of the Russell Sage Foundation Library, No. 39. New York: February, 1920.

Collins, Fletcher
"An aid in the discovery of folk-songs; a list for finders of traditional ballads, songs and play parties in the Southeast." *SFQ* 5:235–250, 1941.

Shearin, H. G., and Combs, J. H.
A Syllabus of Kentucky Folk Songs. Lexington, Ky.: Transylvania Studies in English II, 1911.

PERIODICALS

See: Section under *Folklore* above, and p. 237.

Southern Folklore Quarterly.
Alton C. Morris, ed. University of Florida with Southeastern Folklore Society, Gainesville, Florida, 1937—

The Cumberland Empire.
Quarterly Review, published at Big Laurel, Virginia, Vol. 1, 1932. James Taylor Adams, editor.
Articles on folklore, folksongs and balladry.

GENERAL STUDIES

"Appalachian (Southern) Songs and Ballads." *JAFL* 29:198–202, 1916.

Barry, Phillips
"English Folk-Songs from the Southern Appalachians." A Review of Cecil J. Sharp's Collection, edited by Maud Karpeles. *FSSNE* 2(No. 6):20, 1932.

Bonner, Aletha
"Memorybook Pages of a Musical Pilgrim . . . III. 'I Hear America Singing'—In the South." *Etude* 55 (No. 1):10, Jan. 1937.

Bradley, W. A.
"Song Ballets and Devil's Ditties." *Harper's Magazine* 130:901–914, (May) 1915.
Contains the "Assassination of J. B. Marcum."

Brockway, Howard A.
"The Quest of the Lonesome Tunes." *MTNA* 14:59–68, 1919.

Campbell, John Charles
The Southern Highlander and his Homeland. New York: Russell Sage Foundation, 1921.

Campbell, Olive Dame
"Songs and Ballads of the Southern Mountains." *The Survey* 33:371–374, (Jan. 2) 1915. Illus.

Collins, Fletcher
"An aid in the discovery of folk-songs; a list for finders of traditional ballads, songs and play parties in the Southeast." *SFQ* 5:235–250, 1941.

Crichton, Kyle
"Thar's Gold in Them Hill-billies' Recording Hill-billy and Race Music." *Colliers* 101:24– , (April 30) 1938.

Davis, Arthur Kyle, Jr.
"English Folk Songs from the Southern Appalachians," and "Ballads and Sea Songs of Newfoundland." *MLN* pp. 102–106, (Feb.) 1935.
A review.

"Folk-Song in the South."
Living Age 282:27–33 (July 4), 1914.

Fuson, Henry Harvey
Ballads of Kentucky Highlands. London: The Mitre Press, 1931. 219 pp.

Gordon, R. W., comp.
"Folk-etchings; Songs of the Southern Mountaineers." *Forum* 80:474–475, 1928.

Harbison, Katherine
"In the Great and Lone Prairie." *SFQ* 2(No. 3), 1938.
Songs and ballads, with tunes, from Illinois, Ohio, and blue grass section of Kentucky.

Henry, Mellinger E.
"Ballads and Songs of the Southern Highland." *JAFL* 42:254–300, 1929.

————.
"Collecting Ballads in Southern Highlands." *New Jersey Educational Review* 8 (No. 5):14, (March–April) 1935.

————.
"Life in the Great Smoky National Park." *New Jersey Journal of Education*, (October) 1930, vol. 20, (No. 2).
Contains data on ballad collecting.

————.
"Still More Ballads and Folk Songs from the Southern Highlands." *The Charlotte Observer* (Charlotte, N. C.), a review by Phillips Russell, (Aug. 13), 1934.
New collection of folk ballads. New Jersey Teacher Records. Songs of Singing Harmon family.

————.
"Still More Ballads and Folk-Songs from the Southern Highlands." *JAFL* 45:1–176, 1932.

————.
"Teachers as Collectors of Folk Songs; American Survivals of the Popular Ballad; the Southern Highlands now practically their only home." *New Jersey Journal of Education* 15 (No. 7):6, (March) 1926.

————.
"The Southern Highlands." *New Jersey Journal of Education*, 19 (Nos. 3 and 4):10, (Dec.) 1929.
Some account of the home of the mountain singers.

Hite, G. C.
Mountain People and Their Songs. Beckley, W. Va.: The Author, 1939.

Horne, Dorothy Duerson
"An Inquiry into the Musical Background of the Folksongs of the Southern Mountains." *TFSB* 4:70–81, 1938.

Hudson, Arthur Palmer
Folk-Songs of the Whites. In: *Culture in the South*, ed. by W. T. Couch, pp. 519–547. Chapel Hill: The University of North Carolina Press, 1935.

————.
"Singing South." *Sewanee Review* 268–295, 1936.

Hume, Edgar Erskine
"The Slaughter of De La Bastic." *Americana* 34 (No. 4), 1940. Carlisle Barracks, Pa.: The American Historical Company.

Hutchinson, Percy
"The Balladry and Folkways of Kentucky Mountains." Review of *Devil's Ditties* by Jean Thomas. In: *The New York Times Book Review*, Jan. 31, 1932.

"Interest Widens in Songs of Folk Origin in the Southern Mountains." *Musician* 37:17 (March) 1932.

Iler, Charles A.
"Our Southern Folk Songs and the Music of the Future." *Musical Monitor* 7 (No. 7):307–308, March, 1918.

Jackson, George Pullen
"The Folk Celebrates a Centennial." *TFSB* 10 (No. 2):1–7, 1944.
On the spread of religious folk song and music in the South, and influence of B. F. White.

——————.
White Spirituals in the Southern Uplands; the story of the fasola folk, their songs, singings, and "buckwheat notes" by George Pullen Jackson. Chapel Hill: The University of North Carolina Press, 1933. xv, 344 pp., including music, bibl.

Jordan, David Starr
"Some Folk-Songs of the South." *California Illustrated Magazine* 1:52–53, 1891–92.
Words only.

Kephart, Horace
Our Southern Highlanders. New York: The Outing Publishing Co., 1913.

Kirkland, Winifred
"Mountain Music." *The Outlook* (N. Y.) 123:593, 1919.

"Liza Jane."
JAFL 6:131–132, 1893.
Text and music.

Martin, Harold H.
"Minstrel Man of the Appalachians., *Sat. Eve. Post* 220, No. 47 (May 22, 1948), pp. 30, 162, 164, 167.
"The wild, sweet, lonely tunes were dying out. That's why Bascom Lunsford went around singing and playing—and why you may be dancing the Georgia Rang-Tang, instead of the rumba."

McGill, Josephine
"Following Music in a Mountain Land." *MQ* 3:364–384, 1917.

——————.
"Sing All A Green Willow." *North American Review* 228:218–224, 1929.
Old World ballad surviving in the Kentucky hills.

"Mountain Minstrelsy."
Berea Quarterly (Berea, Ky.) 9 (No. 3):5–13, (April) 1905.

O'Dell, Ruth W.
"Moonshine in the Tennessee Mountains." *TFSB* 12:1–5, Sept., 1946.

Owens, Bess Alice
"Songs of the Cumberlands," *JAFL* 49:215–243, 1936.

P., H. F.
"Quaint 'Lonesome Tunes' Unearthed by Loraine Wyman and Howard Brockway." *Musical America* 24 (No. 19):2, 1916.

Peabody, C. and Rawn, I. N.
"More Songs From the Southern Appalachians." *JAFL* 29:198–202, 1916.

Perrow, E. C.
"Songs and Rhymes from the South." *JAFL* 25:137–155, 1912; 26:123–173, 1913; 28:129–190, 1915.

Petrau, Lawrence
"Mountain Tunes, a Neglected Feature of American Music." *"Peabody Bulletin"* (Balt., Md.) pp. 19–29, (May) 1932.

Pound, Louise
"Folk-Songs from the Southern Appalachians." *JAFL* 46:199–200, 1933.
A review.

"Pretty Polly."
JAFL 12:248–249, 1899; 20:261–264, 1907.
Blue Ridge Ballad.

Raine, James Watt
The Land of Saddle-Bags; a study of the mountain people of Appalachia. New York: Published jointly by the Council of Women for Home Missions and Missionary Education Movement of the U. S. and Canada, 1921.

Rawn, Isabel N. and Peabody, Charles
"More Songs and Ballads from the Southern Appalachians." *JAFL* 29:198–202, 1916.

Scarborough, Dorothy
"Preserve Our Mountain Music." *The Carolina Skyland* (Asheville, N. C.), (October) 1930.

——————.
A Song Catcher in Southern Mountains: American Folk Songs of British Ancestry. New York: Columbia University Press, 1937. xvi, 476 pp., illus., music.

Shearin, Hubert G.
"British Ballads in the Cumberland Mountains." *The Sewanee Review* 19:313–327, 1911 (July).

——————, and Combs, J. H.
A Syllabus of Kentucky Folk Songs. Lexington, Ky.: Transylvania Studies in English II, 1911.

Shoemaker, Henry W.
"Cade's Cove in the Southern Highlands." Altoona, Pa.: Altoona Tribune (April 13), 1931. (An editorial.)

——————.
"Great Smoky National Park." *Altoona Tribune*, March 28, 1931.
Contains ballad material.

Smith, A.
"Hill Billy Folk Music." *Etude* 51:154, (March) 1933.

Smith, Reed
"Traditional Ballads in the South." *JAFL* 27:55–56, 1914.

——————.
"Traditional Ballad in the South During 1914." *JAFL* 28:199–203, 1915.

"Songs and Ballads from the Southern Appalachians." *JAFL* 29:198–202, 1916.

"Songs Sung in the Southern Appalachians."
A review in *The Times Literary Supplement*,
p. 231, (April 4) 1935.

"Southern Secular Songs." *JAFL* 24:255–294,
351–396, 1911.

"The Shy Singers of the Southern Mountains."
The Jersey Journal, pp. 13, (August 16) 1934.

Sutton, Maude Minish
"Blue-Ridge Ballads Record Local History."
Musical America 48 (No. 25):5, 20, Oct. 6,
1928.

Stringfield, Lamar
"Music of the Carolina Mountains." *The Baton*
8(No. 4):708, Feb., 1929.

Thomas, D.
"That Traipsin' Woman; Jean Thomas, Origi-
nator of the American Folk-Song Festival."
Independent Woman 13:169, (June) 1934.

Thomas, Jean
Ballad Makin' in the Mountains of Kentucky.
New York: Henry Holt and Co., 1939. Music,
illus.

————.
Devil's Ditties. Being stories of the Kentucky
Mountain people, with the songs they sing.
Harmonization by Philip Gordon. Drawings
by Cyril Mullen. Chicago: W. Wilbur Hat-
field, 1931.

————.
"Jilson Setters, Singin' Fiddler of Lost Hope
Hollow." *AS* 8(No. 2):28–30, 1933.

————.
The Singin' Fiddler of Lost Hope Hollow. New
York: E. P. Dutton and Co., 1938. 242 pp.,
illus.
    This is the story of Jilson Setters, the blind
    mountaineer. The life and song of the Kentucky
    folk. Many ballads and songs (texts only) given.

————.
The Sun Shines Bright. New York: Prentice-
Hall, 1940. 275 pp.
    Author's experiences in the Southern Mts. with
    the people, their music, life, traditions, what she
    did, and how she organized the *Singin' Gather-
    ins.*

————.
"*When Singin' Comes In, Fightin' Goes Out.*"
Musical Digest 30(No. 3):8,31, 1948.
    Music brings peace to the feuding Hatfields and
    the McCoys.

Wilson, Charles Morrow
Backwoods America. Chapel Hill: The University of North Carolina Press, 1934.
    Contains a chapter entitled "Mountain Ballads."

Zolotov, M.
"Hillbilly Boom." *Saturday Evening Post* 216:
22–3-, (Feb. 12) 1944.
    Uncle Art Sotherly seeks out country music in
    the bayous, canebrakes and hills.

COLLECTIONS

See: Folk Song Collections on pp. 85–91.

Acuff Smoky Mountain Songs. Nashville, Tenn.:
Acuff-Rose Company.
    Arranged for voice and piano.

Baldwin, Lucy Harvie
Grandmother's Songs. New York: George G.
Baldwin, 1926.

Bradley, William Aspenwall
*Singing Carr and Other Song Ballads of the
Cumberlands.* New York: Alfred A. Knopf,
1918. viii, 29 pp.

Campbell, Olive A. Dame, and Sharp, C. J.
*English Folk-Songs From the Southern Appa-
lachians*, comprising 122 songs and ballads,
and 323 tunes, collected by Dame Olive A.
Campbell and Cecil J. Sharp, with an introduction and notes. New York: G. P. Putnam's
Sons, 1917.

Carter, Isabel Gordon
"Mountain White Ballads." *JAFL* 47(No.
183):76, 1934.

Chase, Richard
Old Songs and Singing Games. Chapel Hill:
University of North Carolina Press, 1938.

Cox, John Harrington
Folk Songs of the South. Cambridge: Harvard
University Press, 1925. 545 pp. (no music).

Davis, Joe
Folio of Hill Country Songs and Ballads. New
York: Joe Davis, 1658 Broadway.

Fuson, Harvey H.
Ballads of the Kentucky Highlands. London:
The Mitre Press, 1931.

Henry, Mellinger E.
Songs Sung in the Southern Appalachians.
London: The Mitre Press, 1934.

————.
Folk-Songs from the Southern Highlands. New
York: J. J. Augustin, 1939. xxvii, 460 pp.
    Many tunes included.

Keene, Hank
Hank Keene's Collection of Hill Billy Songs.
South Coventry, Conn.: Hank Keene Music
Co., 1932. 20 pp.
    Songs with piano accompaniments.

Kincaid, Bradley
*My Favorite Mountain Ballads and Old Time
Songs.* Prairie Farmer Radio Station. Chicago:
1928. Books 1, 2 and 3.

Lomax, John A. and Alan
American Ballads and Folk Songs. With a
foreword by George Lyman Kittredge. New
York: Macmillan Company, 1934. xv, 625 pp.,
bibl.
    One of the great collections by America's out-
    standing song collectors. Texts and tunes, and
    much valuable information.

————.
Our Singing Country; a second volume of American ballads and folk songs, collected and compiled by John A. Lomax and Alan Lomax. Ruth Crawford Seeger, music editor. New York: The Macmillan Co., 1941. xxxiv, 416 pp., unaccompanied melodies, bibl.
> All the Lomax volumes contain many songs of the Southern folk.

Lunsford, Bascom Lamar
Manuscript Collection of Folk-Songs and Ballads of the Southern Appalachians. Asheville, N. C.

————, **and Stringfield, Lamar**
30 and 1 Folk Tunes from the Southern Mountains. New York: Carl Fischer, Inc., 1929.
> Arranged for voice and piano.

McMeekin, I. M.
Melodies and Mountaineers. Boston: Stratford, 1921.

Meddy, Homer Basil, and Phillips, Loren
Ballads of Mountain and Prairie. Shelbyville, Ind.: Blue River Press, 1941. 32 pp.

Mountain Songs. Chicago: Belmont Music Company, 3411 W. Chicago Avenue, 1937.

Niles, John Jacob
Ballads, Carols and Tragic Legends from the Southern Appalachian Mountains. New York: G. Schirmer (Set 18).
> In simple arrangements for voice and piano.

————.
Ballads, Love-Songs, and Tragic Legends from the Southern Appalachian Mountains. New York: G. Schirmer (Set 20).
> In simple arrangements for voice and piano.

————.
More Songs of the Hill Folk; Ten Ballads and Tragic Legends from Kentucky, Virginia, Tennessee, North Carolina and Georgia. New York: G. Schirmer, 1936 (Set 17).
> For voice and piano.

————.
Seven Kentucky Mountain Songs. New York: G. Schirmer, Inc. (Set 8).

————.
Songs of the Hill Folk. Twelve Ballads from Kentucky, Virginia and North Carolina. New York: G. Schirmer (Set 14).

————.
Ten Christmas Carols from the Southern Appalachian Mountains. New York: G. Schirmer (Set 16).

Rawn, Isabel Nanton, and Peabody, Charles
"More Songs and Ballads from the Southern Appalachians." *JAFL* 29:198, 1916.

Richardson, Ethel Park, and Spaeth, Sigmund
American Mountain Songs. New York: Greenberg Publisher, 1927.
> In simple arrangements for voice and piano.

Robinson, Carson J.
Mountain Ballads and Old Time Songs. Chicago: M. M. Cole Publishing House, and New York: G. Schirmer, Inc.
> Arranged for Spanish guitar.

Scarborough, Dorothy
A Song-Catcher in Southern Mountains. Revised edition. Musical appendix by Elva Therman, corrected and completed. New York: Columbia University Press, 1938.
> American folk-songs of British ancestry.

Sharp, Cecil James
American - English Folk - Songs, collected in southern Appalachians, and arranged with pianoforte accompaniment by Cecil J. Sharp. New York: G. Schirmer, 1918. First Series. Second Series, 1921.

————.
English Folk-Songs from the Southern Appalachians; collected by Cecil J. Sharp; comprising two hundred and seventy songs and ballads with nine hundred and sixty-eight tunes, including thirty-nine tunes contributed by Olive Dame Campbell, edited by Maud Karpeles. London: Oxford University Press, 1932. 2 vols., bibl. (pp. 427–430).
> Tunes only. Volume I—consists of 122 songs and ballads and 323 tunes. Published by G. P. Putnam's Sons, New York, 1917. 341 pp.

————.
Folk-Songs of English Origin, collected in the Appalachian Mountains by Cecil J. Sharp, with piano accompaniment. London: Novello and Co., Ltd., 1921. Second Series.

Songs of Dixie; a collection of Camp Songs, Home Songs, Marching Songs, Plantation Songs, by favorite authors. Chicago: Fitz-Simmons, 1890. Voice and piano.

Weedon, Miss Howard
Songs of the Old South. New York: Doubleday, Page and Co., 1900.

Wier, A. E., ed.
Songs of the Sunny South. New York: Appleton-Century Co., 1929.

Wightman, Francis P.
Little Leather Breeches and Other Southern Rhymes. New York: Taylor and Co., 1899.

Wilson, Harry R.
Songs of the Hills and Plains. Chicago: Hall and McCreary, 1943.

Wyman, Loraine
Lonesome Tunes; folk songs from the Kentucky mountains, the words collected and edited by Loraine Wyman, the piano accompaniment by Howard Brockway. New York: The H. W. Gray Co., 1916.

————.
Twenty Kentucky Mountain Songs. The words collected by Loraine Wyman. The melodies collected and piano accompaniment added by Howard Brockway. Boston: O. Ditson Company, 1920.

Zeke Manners Hillbilly Songs. New York: Robbins Company. Voice and piano.

ARRANGEMENTS

See: Arrangements of American Folksongs and Ballads, pp. 91–92, and pp. 120–25.

(*Individual Songs and Ballads*)

──────: *Voice and Piano*

"Red Rosy Bush."
  Young, V.: Carl Fischer: voice and piano.

──────: *Female Voices*

"Crawdad Song."
  Wilson, H. R.: Hall and McCreary: SSA.

"Frog Went A-Courting."
  Brockway, H.: Gray: SSAA.

──────: *Male Voices*

"Frog Went A-Courting."
  Brockway, H.: H. W. Gray: TTBB.

"Grandma Grunts."
  Bartholomew: Schirmer: TTBB.

"Root, Hog or Die."
  Bingham, S.: H. W. Gray: TTBB.

"Sourwood Mountain."
  Bartholomew-Hall: Schirmer: TTBB.

"Sourwood Mountain."
  Hall, Arthur: Schirmer: TTBB.

"Weevily Wheat."
  Kuh, L.: Ricordi: TTBB.

──────: *Mixed Voices*

"Deaf Woman's Courtship."
  Siegmeister, E.: C. Fischer: SATB.

"Frog Went Courtin'."
  Niles, John J.: Schirmer: SATB, Sopr., Ten., and Bar. Soli. a cappella.

"Grandma Grunts."
  Siegmeister, E.: C. Fischer: SATB.

"He's Gone Away."
  Clokey, Joseph: C. Fischer: SATB.

"Immensity."
  Buchanan, A. M.: J. Fischer: SATB.

"I Wonder as I Wander."
  Niles-Horton: Schirmer: TTBB, with solo for medium voice.

"Jinny Jinkins."
  Clokey, Joseph: C. Fischer: SSATBB.

"Shuckin' of the Corn."
  Dodd, M.: Music Press: SSATBB.

"Sourwood Mountain."
  Brockway, H.: Gray: SSAATTBB.

"The Inconstant Lover."
  Malin, D.: Musical Research Society: SATB, a cap.

"The Nightingale."
  Warrell, A.: Oxford: SATB.

"The Nightingale."
  Warrell, Arthur S.: Willis: SATB, a cap.

"The Riddle Song."
  Warrell, A.: Oxford: SATB.

"The Wagoner's Lad."
  Malin: Gamble: SATB.

"Who's That A Callin'?"
  Cain: Hall and McCreary: SATB.

"Wondrous Love."
  Buchanan, A. M.: J. Fischer: SATB.

──────: *Piano*

"Sourwood Mountain."
  Farwell, A.: Schirmer: piano.

──────: *Chamber Music*

A Mountain Episode.
  Stringfield, L.: Baron: String Quartet.

"In a Log Cabin" (from Ten Modern Trios).
  Stringfield, Lamar: Carl Fischer: Chamber Music.
    Based on Southern Mountain themes, composed for flute or violin, 'cello, piano.

Mountain Dawn.
  Stringfield, L.: Musicus: flute, strings.

"Spoon River."
  Grainger, Percy: Schirmer: for six or more instruments.

"String Quartet."
  Gaul, Harvey B.: J. Fischer and Bro.: Chamber Music.
    Based on traditional Anglo-American tunes, ("Barbara Allen," "Sourwood Mountain," etc.)

──────: *Orchestra*

Appalachian Spring-Ballet Suite.
  Copland, Aaron: Boosey and Hawkes: Orchestra.

"Cripple Creek" (*From the Southern Mountain Suite*).
  Stringfield, Lamar: Carl Fischer: Symph. Orch.

From the Blue Ridge—Symphonic Sketches.
  Stringfield, L.: MS: Orchestra.

From the Southern Mountain Suite.
  Stringfield, Lamar: Carl Fischer: Symph. Orch.

Hill Billy.
  Gould, Morton: C. Fischer: Orchestra (large and small).

Moods of a Moonshiner—Symphonic Suite.
  Stringfield, L.: Baron: Orchestra.

Mountain Sketches.
  Stringfield, L.: C. Fischer: chamber group;
  violin, cello, piano.

Southern Nights Suite.
  Guion, David: Schirmer: orchestra.

————: *Band*

"Cripple Creek" *(From the Southern Mountain
  Suite).*
  Stringfield, Lamar: C. Fischer: Band.

Down South: American Sketch.
  Myddleton, Wm. H.: Schirmer: Band.

From the South—Overture. Issac-Lillya: Educational: Full band.

————: *Stage Work*

A Mirror for the Sky.
  Kubik, Gail: MS: folk opera, 22 acts, 15
  scenes.

Appalachian Spring—chamber ballet.
  Copland, Aaron: Boosey: ballet.

Down in the Valley.
  Weil, Kurt: Schirmer: Folk Opera (1948).
    The work is based on the well-known folk tune,
    "Down in the Valley," around which the whole
    is thematically developed. Other tunes included
    are: "Hop Up My Ladies," "Sourwood Moun-
    tain," "The Little Black Train," and "The Lone-
    some Dove." The librettist is Arnold Sundgaard.

A Tree on the Plains.
  Bacon, Ernst: Associated: opera.

Sourwood Mountain: an American Frolic based
  on old American folk-songs and fiddle tunes by
  Pierson Underwood and Lawrence Perry. Boston: C. C. Birchard, 1943.
    Consists of one act—about fifty minutes. Singing
    and dancing.

RECORDS

*See: Records—Collections and Individual Num-
  bers of American Folksongs and Ballads,
  pp. 92–94; and pp. 125–33.*

Collections

All Time Hits From the Hills. Eddy Arnold
  and the Tennessee Plowboys. VI–196.
    Contents: "Molly Darling," "The Prisoner's
    Song," "Seven Years with the Wrong Woman,"
    and others.

Blue Ridge Ballads. Texas Gladden and Hobart Smith. 3–10". DISC 737.
    Contents: "House Carpenter"; "Devil and Farm-
    er's Wife"; "Down in the Willow Garden"; "Poor
    Ellen Smith."

Child Ballads from the Southern Highlands.
  Cratis Williams, vocal guitar. 2–10". DISC 662.

*The Martins and The Coys: A Mountain Ballad
  Opera.* BBC
    A contemporary folktale made into an opera by
    Alan and Elizabeth Lomax. The recording was
    made under the direction of Roy Lockwood.
    Contemporary songs by Woody Guthrie and The
    Almanacs. Included in the cast are: Burl Ives,
    Pete Seeger, Arthur Smith, Lily May Pearson,
    Will Geer, Sonny Terry, and others.

*Mountain Frolic: Square Dances and Hoe-
  Downs from the Southern Mountains.* Uncle
  Dave Macon and his Fruit Jar Drinkers; The
  Crockett Family; Bradley Kincaid; Al Hop-
  kins and his Buckle Busters; The Tennessee
  Ramblers. 4–10". BR 1025.
    Contents: Arkansas Traveler; Sourwood Moun-
    tain; Cindy; Old Joe Clark; Sugar Hill; Sail
    Away, Ladies; Black Eyed Susie; Sally Goodin;
    Sally in the Garden; Cluck Old Hen.

Smoky Mountain Ballads. Mainer-Morris.
  VP–79.

The South. In the Archive of American Folk-
  Song, Library of Congress, Music Division
  (Wash., D. C.). AAFS–LC.

"The South: (Mountaineer Songs)." Collection of late Dorothy Scarborough. Columbia
  University, N. Y.

Individual Titles

"Cumberland Mountain Deer Race." Uncle Dave
  Macon. V27494.

"Ida Red." Acuff and Mountain Boys.
  OK–05359.

"Ida Red." In: *American Folk Songs Album,*
  Luther; Layman; Stokes (voc.) with guitar,
  fiddle and bass. D–25.

"Ida Red." In: *Smoky Mountain Ballads.* Native
  mountain singers and instruments. *VP–79.*

"Ida Red." Wills and Texas Playboys. OK-05079.

"She'll Be Comin' Round the Mountain." In:
  American Folk Songs Album. Frank Luther,
  Zora Layman; Leonard Stokes vocalist, with
  guitar, fiddle and bass. *DE–25.*

"She'll Be Comin' Round the Mountain." Tommy Tucker. OK–5553.

"Who's Gonna Shoe Your Pretty Little Feet?"
  Woody Guthrie, Cisco Houston (Vocal Guitars). ASCH 432–4B.

ALABAMA

FOLKLORE

BIBLIOGRAPHY

Duke University, Durham, N. C. Library
  *Checklist of Alabama Pamphlets in the Duke
  University Library.* Durham, 1942. 53 pp.

Ellison, Rhoda Coleman
A Checklist of Alabama Imprints, 1807–1870.
University, Ala.: University of Alabama Press,
1946. 151 pp.

Folklore. Alabama Association of Teachers of
English. Montevallo: Association of Teachers
of English, 1917.
Bibliography of folklore.

Owen, T. McA.
"Bibliography of Alabama." *American Historical Association. Annual Report,* 1897, pp.
777–1248.

PERIODICALS

The Alabama Historical Quarterly. Published
by the State Department of Archives and History. Vol. 1, 1930. Montgomery, Alabama. No
more published.

Publications of the Alabama Historical Society.
Miscellaneous Publications. vol. 1, 1900—.
Montgomery, Alabama. *Transactions,* 1898–
1904. Tuscaloosa, Ala.

GENERAL STUDIES AND COLLECTIONS

Agee, G. W.
Rube Burrow, King of Outlaws. Chicago: The
Henneberry Co., 1890.

Alabama, A Guide to the Deep South. (American Guide Series.) Compiled and written by
the Federal Writers' Program of the Works
Progress Administration for the State of Alabama. New York: Richard R. Smith, 1941.

Baldwin, Joseph G.
Flush Times in Alabama and Mississippi. San
Francisco: Sumner, Whitner and Co., 1883.
330 pp. New York: D. Appleton and Co., 1898.
330 pp. Americus, Ga.: The Americus Book
Co., 1908.

Carmer, Carl
Stars Fell on Alabama. Illus. by Cyrus LeRoy
Baldridge. New York: Farrar and Rinehart,
Inc., 1934. xiv, 294 pp., illus.

Coates, Robert M.
The Outlaw Years: The History of the Land
Pirates of the Natchez Trace. New York: The
Macaulay Co., 1930.

Gielow, Martha S.
Mammy's Reminiscences and Other Sketches.
New York: A. S. Barnes and Co., 1898.

Hobson, Anne
In Old Alabama; illus. by Carol McPherson.
New York: Doubleday, Page & Co., 1903. 237
pp., front pl.
Being the chronicles of Miss Mouse the little
black merchant. Ten dialect stories and song.

Hurston, Zora Neale
Mules and Men. Philadelphia: J. B. Lippincott
Co., 1935.

Kennedy, Stetson
Palmetto Country. (American Folkways Series). New York: Duell, Sloan and Pearce, 1942.
340 pp.
In the chapter "Stuff and Such," a great deal of
interesting folk material indigenous to the Southern land.

Kroll, Harry Harrison
Waters Over the Dam. Indianapolis: the Bobbs-
Merrill Co., 1944. 299 pp.
"This is distinctly a Southern book, in that every
word springs straight up from Southern earth."
(E. Welty.)

Lewis, Kate (Porter)
Alabama Folk Plays. Edited, with an introduc-
tion by Frederick H. Koch, illustrated with
photographs from the original production.
Chapel Hill, N. C.: The University of North
Carolina Press, 1943. xxi and 152 pp.

Royall, Mrs. Anne (Newport)
Letters from Alabama on Various Subjects, to
which is added an appendix, containing remarks on sundry members of the 20th and 21st
Congress, and other high characters at the seat
of Government. In one volume. Washington,
D. C.: Printed for the Author, 1830. 232 pp.

Smiley, P.
"Folklore from Virginia, South Carolina,
Georgia, Alabama and Florida." *JAFL* 32:
357–383, 1919.

Tartt, Ruby Pickens
"Richard, the Tall-Hearted, — Alabama
Sketches." *Southwest Review* 29:234–244, 1944.

Woodall, N. F.
"Old Signs in Alabama." *JAFL* 43:325–326,
1930.

Young, Martha
*Plantation Bird Legends and Uncle Remus
Stories.* New York: D. Appleton and Co., 1916.

SPEECH

Brooks, Cleanth, Jr.
*The Relation of the Alabama-Georgia Dialect
to the Provincial Dialects of Great Britain.*
Louisiana State University Studies. Diamond
Jubilee Publication, Study No. 20. Baton
Rouge: State University Press, 1935. 103 pp.

Payne. L. W., Jr.
"A Word-List from East Alabama." *Bulletin of
the University of Texas.* Austin, Texas Repre-
senative Series, No. 8, 1–3:279–391, 1909.

———.
"A Word-List from East Alabama." *Dialect
Notes* 3 (Part 4):279–328, 1908; 3 (Part 5):
343–391, 1909.

PLACE NAMES

Read. William A.
Indian Place Names in Alabama. Louisiana
State University Studies No. 29. Baton Rouge,
La.: Louisiana State University Press, 1937.
xvii, 84 pp. 2 maps.

Swanton, John R.
"Indian Place Names." *AS* 12 (No. 3):212–214, 1937.
    A few addenda and corrections of Prof. Read's *Indian Place Names in Alabama*.

FOLKSONG

STUDIES AND COLLECTIONS

Carmer, Carl
Stars Fell on Alabama. Illustrated by Cyrus LeRoy Baldridge. New York: Farrar and Rinehart, Inc., 1934. xiv, 294 pp.
    Contains Negro and other songs.

Hobson, Anne
In Old Alabama. New York: Doubleday, Page and Co., 1903. 6 pp., 237 pp., front pl.
    Contains a number of tunes accompanying the dialect stories.

Thomas, Margaret F.
Musical Alabama. Tuscaloosa: Weatherford Printing Company, 1925—vol. 1, 1936—vol. II, Montgomery: Paragan Press.

ARRANGEMENTS

———: *Mixed Voices*

"Fuguing Hymn." Buchanan, A. M.: J. Fischer: SATB.
    An Alabama tune.

ARKANSAS

FOLKLORE

BIBLIOGRAPHY

Allen, Albert Henry, ed.
Arkansas Imprints, 1821–1876. New York: Published for the Bibliographical Society of America by R. R. Bowker Co., 1947. xx, 236 pp.

Historical Records Survey.
Inventory of the County Archives of Arkansas. Prepared by the Historical Records Survey, Division of Women's and Professional and Service Projects, Works Progress Administration. Little Rock, Ark.: 1939.

———.
Union List of Arkansas Newspapers, 1819–1942. A partial inventory of Arkansas newspaper files available in offices of publishers, libraries and private collections in Arkansas. Prepared by the Historical Records Survey, Division of Community Service Program, Works Progress Administration. Little Rock, Ark.: 1942. 240 pp.

Matthews, J. P., and Jones, V. L.
Arkansas Books. Compiled by P. Matthews, and V. L. Jones. Fayetville, Ark.: University of Arkansas Bulletin, General Extension Service, Vol. 25 (No. 8), 1931.

PERIODICALS

Arkansas Historical Association. Publications. v.1–4. Fayetteville, Ark., etc. 1906–1917.

The Arkansas Historical Quarterly. v.1, March 1942. Fayetteville: The Arkansas Historical Association. 1942.

Arkansas Historical Review. v.1, no. 1–2. Feb. 1934. No more published.

GENERAL STUDIES AND COLLECTIONS

Allsopp, Frederick William
Albert Pike: A Biography. Little Rock, Arkansas: Parke-Harper Co., 1928.

———.
Folklore of Romantic Arkansas. Kansas City, Kansas: The Grolier Society, 1931. 2 vols., illus.

Arkansas, A Guide to the State. (American Guide Series). Compiled and written by the Federal Writers' Program of the Works Progress Administration of the State of Arkansas. New York: Hastings House, Publishers, 1941.

Beason, George D.
I Blew In From Arkansas. Chicago: Geo. D. Beason, Publisher, 1908.
    A trip of fun through Hoosierdom.

Blair, Walter
"Inquisitive Yankee Descendants in Arkansas." *AS* 14:11–22, 1939.
    "The custom of asking persistent questions of travelers was old at the time of David Crockett's exploits."

Carter, Hodding
The Lower Mississippi. (The Rivers of America Series.) Illustrated by John McCrady. New York: Farrar and Rinehart, 1942. x, 467 pp., illus.
    "The Old Cabin Home," words and music, pp. 441. Selected bibliography, pp. 443–451.

Clemens, Samuel L.
Life on the Mississippi. New York: Harper and Brothers, 1927.

Davis, Clyde Brion
The Arkansas. (The Rivers of America Series) illustrated by Donald McKay. New York: Farrar and Rinehart, Inc., 1940. 340 pp.

Edmonds, William H.
The Truth About Arkansas. St. Louis: Woodward & Tiernan Print. Co., 1895. 16 pp., illus.

Fletcher, John Gould
Arkansas. Chapel Hill, N. C.: The University of North Carolina Press, 1947. 421 pp.
    A panoramic, detailed story of the state. But it is also "filled with wild comic anecdotes, tall tales, tragic incidents, personalities, mysteries, symbolic forces, descriptions of time and place and person." (Marguerite Young.)

Foreman, Grant
Indians and Pioneers. New Haven: Yale University Press, 1930.

Guide to North Little Rock.
Industrial Center of Arkansas. Compiled and Written by the Federal Writers' Project of the Works Progress Administration of the State of Arkansas, 1938.

Harman, S. W.
Hell on the Border. Fort Smith: Phoenix Publishing Co., 1898. xiii, 714 pp., illus.
Exciting narrative of the reign of "Hanging Judge" Isaac C. Parker.

Hogue, Wayman
Back Yonder. New York: Minton, Balch and Co., 1932.

Jackson, Thomas W.
On a Slow Train Through Arkansaw. Chicago: T. W. Jackson Publishing Co., 1903. 96 pp., illus.
Funny railroad stories sayings of the Southern darkies—all the latest and best minstrel jokes of the day.

Knoop, Faith Yingling, and Grant, James R.
Arkansas Yesterday and To-Day. Chicago, Phila.: J. B. Lippincott Co., 1935. 350 pp., illus.

Medearis, Mary
Big Doc's Girl. Philadelphia: J. B. Lippincott Co., 1942.
A novel of the Arkansas countryside.

Nuttall, Thomas
A Journal of Travel Into the Arkansas Territory, During the Year 1819. With occasional observations on the manners of the aborigines. Illustrated by a map and other engravings. Philadelphia: T. H. Palmer, 1821. xii, 296 pp., illus.

Paine, Albert Bigelow
The Arkansas Bear; a tale of fanciful adventure told in song and story. Illustrated by Frank Ver Beck. New York: R. H. Russell, 1898. 118 pp., illus.

_____.
The Arkansas Bear; complete, being "The Arkansas Bear" and "The Arkansas Bear and Elsie"—told in song and story; illustrated by Frank Ver Beck. Philadelphia: Henry Altemus Company, 1929. 297 pp., illus., music.

Pope, William F.
Early Days in Arkansas. Little Rock, Arkansas: F. W. Allsopp, 1895. 330 pp.

Read, Opie
An Arkansas Planter. Chicago: Rand McNally and Co., 1896. 315 pp., illus.
Fiction—very revealing.

_____.
The Captain's Romance; or, Tales of the Backwoods. New York: F. T. Neely, 1896. 139 pp.
Imaginative tales of pioneer life and adventures, utilizing customs, traditions and lore of the pioneers.

_____.
Odd Folks. New York: F. T. Neely, 1897. 192 pp.

_____.
Opie Read in the Ozarks, Including many of the rich, rare, quaint, eccentric, ignorant and superstitious sayings of the natives of Missouri and Arkansas. Pictures by F. I. Wetherbee. Chicago: R. B. McKnight & Co., 1905. 96 pp., illus.

Simon, Charlie May
Straw in the Sun. New York: E. P. Dutton, 1945. 253 pp.
"The author has given us a quiet book, descriptive and interpretative of life in the Arkansas Ozarks. It is a book of subdued color, but with masterly contrasts of sunlight and shadow." (E. L. Saucier.)

Thanet, O.
"Folklore in Arkansas." *JAFL* 5:121–125, 1892.

The Big Bear of Arkansas, and Other Sketches. Illustrative of characters and incidents in the South and South-West. Philadelphia, Pa.: Carey and Hart, 1845.

Thorpe, T. B.
The Hive of the Bee Hunter. New York: D. Appleton and Co., 1854. 312 pp.
Chapter: "The Big Bear of Arkansas."

Wallace, Edward Tatum
Barington. New York: Simon and Schuster, 1945. 311 pp.
Kaleidoscope of An Arkansas Village. "The stories—swing from anecdote to contemporary folklore." (E. Evans.)

Wilson, Charles Morrow
Acres of Sky. New York: G. P. Putnam's Sons, 1930.

_____.
Backwoods America. Chapel Hill, N. C.: University of North Carolina Press, 1934. 209 pp., illus.

Wood, R.
Mother Goose in the Ozarks. Raywood, Texas: The Author; 1938.

FOLKTALES AND LEGENDS

Davis, Clyde Brion
"The Story of the 'Arkansas Traveler'." *Arkansas Gazette Centennial Edition,* No. 20, 1919, p. 26.

Eno, Clara B.
"Legends of Arkansas." *Arkansas Historical Quarterly* 2:32–38, 1943.

Masterson, James R.
Tall Tales of Arkansaw. Boston: Chapman and Grimes, 1943. xi, 443 pp., bibl., index, illus.
"This is not merely a collection of tall tales, but a carefully documented survey of the whole field of Arkansas humor." (Vance Randolph.)

Mercer, H. C.
"On the Track of the Arkansas Traveler." *The Century Magazine* 51:707–708, 1896.

"The Arkansas Traveler." *Hobbies*, The Magazine for Collectors, 41:106–107, 1936.

SPEECH

Blair, Walter
"Inquisitive Descendants in Arkansas." *AS* 14 (No. 1):11–22, 1939.
Characteristic colloquialisms in frontier days.

Carr, Joseph William
"A List of Words From Northwest Arkansas." *Dialect Notes* 2 (No. 6):416–422; 3:68–103, 1905; (No. 2):124–165, 1906; 3 (No. 3):205–238, 1907; 3 (No. 5): 392–406, 1909.

PLACE NAMES

Branner, John C.
"Some Old French Place Names in the State of Arkansas." *Modern Language Notes* 14:65–80, 1899.

FOLKSONG

GENERAL STUDIES AND COLLECTIONS

Cox, John Harrington, ed.
The Arkansas Traveler. In: *Folk Songs of the South,* pp. 503–505. Cambridge: Harvard University Press, 1925. 545 pp.

Garrison, Theodore
"The Native American Influence in Folksongs of Arkansas." *Arkansas Historical Quarterly* 6 (No. 2):165–179, 1947.

Harry Macarthy, the Arkansas Comedian; His Book of original songs, ballads and anecdotes, as presented by the author in his well known Personation Concerts. Indianapolis: State Sentinel Steam Printing Establishment, 1870.

Letzig, M. H.
"Music Forums, Little Rock, Arkansas." *Recreation* 33:269–272, 1939 (August), illus.

Masterson, James R.
Tall Tales of Arkansas. Boston: Chapman and Grimes, 1943, 443 pp.
"—an emanation compounded of slow trains, hound dogs, fiddle tunes, moonshine, chewin' terbaccer, and such uses like an exhalation from the swamps and mountains of Arkansas." (Horace Reynolds.)

Mercer, H. C.
"On the Track of the Arkansas Traveler." *Century Magazine* 51(NS29):707–712, 1896, musical illustrations.

Stackard, Sallie Walker
The History of Lawrence, Jackson, Independence and Stone Counties, Arkansas. Little Rock, Ark.: Arkansas Democrat Co., 1904. Chapt. VI (pp. 78–94): "Folk Songs of Arkansas," contains 33 texts. Includes 13 Civil War Songs, 8 game songs.

The Arkansas Traveller's Songster, containing the celebrated story of the Arkansas Traveller, with the music for violin and piano, and also an extensive and choice collection of new and popular comic and sentimental songs. New York: Dick and Fitzgerald, 1863.

Vineyard, Catherine Marshall
"The Arkansas Traveler." *TFSP 18:* 11–60, 1943.
Gives 18 versions, discusses origin of text and tunes—University of Texas M.A. Diss., 1942.

RECORDS

Collections

U. S. Library of Congress. Division of Music. Folklore Section.
Recordings of Folksongs Made in Arkansas. John Lomax, coll.   AAFS–LC

ARRANGEMENTS

————: *Mixed Voices*

"Arkansas Traveler."
Delaney, R.: Schirmer: descant unison.

"The Arkansas Traveler."
Stevens, D.: Birchard: TTB.

"Rosemary and Thyme."
Powell, L.: Birchard. SSAATTBB.

"The Weak and Rambling One."
Powell, L.: Birchard: SAATBB.

————: *Piano*

"Arkansas Traveler."
Burg, C.: Composers Music Corp. (N. Y.): Piano.

"The Arkansas Traveler and Rackinsac Waltz."
Cumming, William: Peters and Webster; Piano. (1847– Louisville).

"Arkansas Traveler."
Guion, D.: Schirmer: Piano. (advanced).

"Arkansas Traveler."
MacDonald, H.: Presser: Piano, Concert Paraphrase, also arr. for 4 hands.

"Arkansas Traveler."
Orem, P. W.: Presser: Piano (4 hands).

"Arkansas Traveler."
Pattison, L.: Schirmer: Two Pianos—4 hands. Concert version.

————: *Violin and Piano*

"Arkansas Traveler."
Maganini, Q.: J. Fischer: Violin and Piano.

"Arkansas Traveler."
O'Hara, G.: J. Fischer: Violin and Piano.

————: *Chamber Orchestra*

"Arkansas Traveler."
O'Hara, Geoffrey: J. Fischer: Chamber Group: Violin, or cello, piano.

"Arkansas Traveler," and other folk tunes. McKay, George F.: Presser: Chamber orchestra.

"Arkansas Traveler."
Maganini, Q.: J. Fischer: Chamber orchestra, and school ensembles.

————: *Symphony Orchestra*

McDonald, Harl
The Legend of the Arkansas Traveler. Philadelphia: Elkan-Vogel Company, 1946, for orchestra.

FLORIDA

FOLKLORE

BIBLIOGRAPHY

Frost, Pattie Porter
Preliminary Check list of Floridiana, 1500–1865, in the Libraries of Florida. Jacksonville, 1930. 16 pp. (From Florida Library Bulletin, vol. 2, no. 2, April 1930.)

Hanna, Alfred Jackson
Recommended Readings for the Florida Centennial. A standard guide to the best books on Florida, with helpful explanations and critical evaluations. Winter Park, Fla.: Union Catalog of Floridiana, 1945. 64 pp.

Historical Records Survey.
Guide to the Depositories of Manuscript Collections in the United States: Florida, Prepared by the Historical Records Survey . . . Works Progress Administration. Jacksonville. The Florida Historical Records Survey Project, 1940. 27 pp.

————.
Inventory of the County Archives of Florida. Prepared by the Historical Records Survey, State Archive Survey, Division of Women's and Professional Projects, Works Progress Administration. Jacksonville, Fla.: 1939.

Knauss, James Owen
Territorial Florida Journalism. Deland: The Florida State Historical Society, 1926. x, 250 pp.
A valuable list of early Florida newspapers and periodicals.

PERIODICALS

The Florida Historical Quarterly. v.1, 1908. Jacksonville. Quarterly. Suspended publication from July 1909 to July 1924 —.

Southern Folklore Quarterly. v.1, March 1937 —. Jacksonville, Fla.

Tequesta; the Journal of the Historical Association of Southern Florida. No. 1, March 1941 —. Coral Gables, Fla. Published as a Bulletin of the University of Florida.

GENERAL STUDIES AND COLLECTIONS

Anon.
"A Friend in Need." *Brother Jonathan* 3:47, Sept. 10, 1842.
An account of a man obtaining a divorce in Florida by return mail.

————.
"Glimpses of life in Florida during the Seminole War." *The Knickerbocker* 38:214, Sept. 1851.
Descriptive essay of life in St. Augustine, Florida, during the war between the U. S. Army and Seminole Indians. (1835–1842).

————.
"Domestic Miscellany." *Army and Navy Chronicle* 7:236, Oct. 11, 1838.
An account of a brilliant ball which was given in honor of Perry's victory on Lake Erie on Sept. 10, 1938 at the Florida House, Pensacola, Florida.

————.
"Domestic Miscellany. Summer Amusements." *Army and Navy Chronicle* 5:221, Oct. 5, 1837.
An account of an evening of entertainment given on board the U. S. Sloop-of-War Concord, which included a representation of "The Tragedy of Douglas."

Baker, Charles H.
Blood of the Lamb. New York: Rinehart & Co., 1946. 275 pp.
"—a regional novel, written from the inside out, with a fine eye for the sad yet garish color of the Florida Scrub, a fine ear for its heat-drugged speech, a fine understanding of the pellegra-ridden folk who inhabit it." (William Du Bois.)

Bartram, John
Diary of a Journey Through the Carolinas, Georgia and Florida, from July 1, 1765, to April 10, 1766. Annotated by Francis Harper. Philadelphia: The American Philosophical Society, 1942. iv, 120 pp., illus.

Beecher, Eunice White
Letters From Florida. New York: D. Appleton and Company, 1879. 85 pp., illus.

Byrd, Sam
Small Town South. Boston: Houghton Mifflin Co., 1942.
Life and people in a North Carolina village and small Florida town, "an extraordinary picture of the decay of civilization as it is expressed in the lives of individuals affected." (G. W. Johnson.)

Cabell, Branch, and Hanna, A. J.
The St. Johns: A Parade of Diversities. (Rivers of America Series). Illustrated by Doris Lee. New York: Farrar and Rinehart, 1943, 342 pp.
"It is as a masterpiece of tale-telling out of school that "The St. Johns" achieves immortality —and nowhere has the need been greater than in "The best-lied-about State in the Union." (Stetson Kennedy.)

Douglas, Marjory Stoneham
The Everglades. Illustrated by Robert Fink.
(Rivers of America Series.) New York: Rinehart Co., 1947. 406 pp.
"Her obvious excitement over the subject, an
unearthliness, strong rhythm, very little repetition and discursion, a compactness of natural
imagery that is dazzling and, above all, an organization and discipline that approach poetic form
... will unquestionably remain unique among the
Rivers of America series, unique in fact, in any
company." (John Hersey.)

Florida, a Guide to the Southermost State, (American Guide Series). Compiled and written by
the Federal Writers' Project of the W.P.A. of
the State of Florida. New York: Oxford University Press, 1939.

Friedman, Kenneth
Cartoon Guide of Florida. New York: J. J.
Augustin, 1941. 100 cartoons and text, with
large map.

Hanna, Alfred Jackson and Abbey, Kathryn
Lake Okeechobee. The American Lakes Series.
Indianapolis: The Bobbs-Merrill Co., 1948. 379
pp.
Not only a rich historical and geographical account, but delightful asides among strange and
bizarre people and stories.

Hulley, Lincoln
Florida the Beautiful. DeLand, Fla.: E. O.
Painter Publishing Co., 1925. 47 pp.
A book of poems—includes interesting informa-
tion on place names.

Huss, Veronica and Werner, Evelyn
"The Conchs of Riviera, Florida." *SFQ* 4:141–
151, 1940.

Kennedy, Stetson
"Náñigo in Florida." *SFQ* 4:153–156, 1940.

———.
Palmetto Country. (American Folkways Series). New York: Duell, Sloan and Pearce,
1942. 340 pp.
In the chapter "Stuff and Such" a great deal of
interesting folk material indigenous to the Southern land.

Matschat, Cecile Hulse
Suwanee River; strange green land. (American
River Series) illus. by Alexander Kay. New
York: Farrar & Rinehart, 1938. x, 296 pp.,
illus., incl. maps.
"Rivers and American folk" by Constance Lind-
say Skinner. Bibliography p. 283–288.

Pope, Edith
Colcorton. New York: Charles Scribner's Sons,
1944. 330 pp.
"Mrs. Pope's country is the coastal jungle around
St. Augustine.... Her characters are saltwater
crackers plus a strong dash of minorcen."
(William DuBois.)

Ramirez, Manuel D.
"Italian Folklore from Tampa, Florida." Introduction. *SFQ* 5:101–106, 1941.

Rawlings, Marjorie Kinnan
Cross Creek. With decorations by Edward
Shenton. New York: Charles Scribner's Sons,
1942. 368 pp.
The author catches the community of land and
people.

Seeing St. Augustine. (American Guide Series).
Compiled and written by the Federal Writers'
Project of the W.P.A. St. Augustine: The
Record Company, 1937.

Smiley, P.
"Folklore from Virginia, South Carolina,
Georgia, Alabama and Florida." *JAFL* 32:357–
383, 1919.

Stowe, Mrs. H. E.
Palmetto-Leaves. Boston: 1873. 321 pp., illus.

Verrill, Alpheus Hyatt
Romantic and Historic Florida. New York:
Dodd, Mead & Co., 1936. xvi, 291 pp., illus.

Von Hesse, Maxeda Ferguson
Inherit the Wind. New York: William Morrow
and Co., 1944, 282 pp.
Setting of Cracker portraits against Seminole
backgrounds.

MYTHS—FOLKTALES—SUPERSTITIONS

Doering, Frederick J.
"Legends from Canada, Indiana and Florida."
SFQ 2 (No. 4):213–220, 1938.

Judson, Edward Zane Carroll (Ned Buntline)
Matanzas, or a Brother's Revenge. A tale of
Florida. Boston: G. H. Williams, 1848. 100 pp.

Kennedy, Stetson
"Náñigo in Florida." *SFQ* 4:153–156, 1940.
African cult introduced from Cuba into Key
West and Tampa.

Olschki, Leonardo
"Ponce de Leon's Fountain of Youth": History
of a Geographic Myth. *Hispanic American Historical Review.* (Durham, N. C.: Duke U.) 21:
361–385, 1941.

Smith, G. H.
"Three Miami Tales." *JAFL* 52:194–208, 1939.

SPEECH

Allen, F. Sturges
"Florida Word List." *Dialect Notes* 4 (Part 5)
344–345, 1916.

PLACE-NAMES

Drew, F.
"Place Names of Indian Origin in Florida."
Florida Historical Society 6:197–205, 1928.

Read, William A.
*Florida Place-Names of Indian Origin and
Seminole Personal Names.* Baton Rouge, La.:
Louisiana State University Press, 1934. v, 83
pp.

FOLKSONG

GENERAL STUDIES

Morris, Alton C.
"Mrs. Griffin of Newbury." *SFQ* 8:133–198, 1944.
> Informant of a great Florida collection of folksongs and ballads.

RECORDS

"The South" (Florida).
In the archives of *University of Florida.* (Gainesville, Fla.)

ARRANGEMENTS

————: *Orchestra*

Natchez on the Hill.
Powell, John: Schirmer: orchestra.

GEORGIA

FOLKLORE

BIBLIOGRAPHY

Brooks, Robert Preston, comp.
A Preliminary Bibliography of Georgia History. Athens, Ga.: The McGregor Company, 1910. 46 pp.

Mackall, Leonard Leopold
The Wymberley Jones De Renne Georgia Library. Savannah, Ga.: Printed for the Society by Braid and Hutton, 1918. 26 pp.
> Another issue, greatly enlarged, was issued 3 vols. in 1931.

PERIODICALS

The Georgia Historical Quarterly. Published by the Georgia Historical Society, vol. 1, March 1917 —. Savannah, Georgia.

The Georgia Review. v.1, 1947 —. Athens: University of Georgia Press, 1947.

GENERAL STUDIES AND COLLECTIONS

Federal Writers' Project.
Augusta. (American Guide Series). Compiled and written by the Augusta Unit, Federal Writers' Project in Georgia, Works Progress Administration. Augusta, Georgia: Tidwell Printing Co., 1938.

————.
Dreams and Shadows: Survival Studies among the Georgia Coastal Negroes, compiled and written by the Savannah Unit, Federal Writers' Project in Georgia, Works Progress Administration. Athens, Georgia: University of Georgia Press, 1940.

————.
Georgia, a Guide to its Towns and Countryside. (American Guide Series). Compiled and written by workers of the Writers' Program of the Works Progress Administration in the State of Georgia. Athens, Georgia: The University of Georgia Press, 1940.

————.
Savannah. (American Guide Series). Compiled and written by the Savannah Unit of the Federal Writers' Project in Georgia of the Works Progress Administration. Savannah, Georgia: Review Printing Co., 1937.

Cheney, Brainard
River Rogue. Boston: Houghton Mifflin Company, 1942. 443 pp.
> The folklore of the raftsman—heroic and extravagant, covers the regions of the Oconee and Ocmulgee Rivers, which join together to form the Altamaha.

Clark, Richard H.
Memoirs of Judge Richard H. Clark, ed. by Lollie Belle Wylie. Atlanta, Ga.: Franklin Printing and Publishing Company, 1898. xii, 407 pp.

Felton, Rebecca
Country Life in Georgia in the Days of My Youth . . . Atlanta, Ga.: Printed by the Index Printing Company, 1919. 299 pp.

Graver, J. T.
"Forever and Ever." *Virginia Quarterly Review* 19:37–49, 1943.
> Social life and customs.

Harley, Timothy
Southward Ho! Notes of a Tour To and Through the State of Georgia in the Winter of 1885–6. London: S. Low, Marston, Searle & Rivington, 1886. vi, 198 pp., illus.

Henkle, Henrietta
Deep River. New York: Harcourt, Brace and Company, 1944. 381 pp.
> A novel of Georgia life.

Herring, John Lewis
Saturday Night Sketches; Stories of Old Wiregrass Georgia. Illustrated by Tom J. Nicholl. Boston: The Gorham Press. 1918. 303 pp., illus.

Kemble, Frances Anne
Journal of a Residence on a Georgia Plantation in 1838–39. New York: Harper & Brothers, 1863. 337 pp.

Kennedy, Stetson
Palmetto Country. (American Folkways Series). New York: Duell, Sloan and Pearce, 1942. xii, 340 pp.

Knight, Lucian Lamar
Georgia's Landmarks, Memorials and Legends. Atlanta, Ga.: Printed for the Author by the Byrd Printing Company, 1913–1914. 2 vols.

Leigh, Frances Butler
Ten Years on a Georgia Plantation Since the War. London: Bentley, 1883. xi, 347 pp.

Longstreet, Augustus Baldwin
Georgia Scenes. Augusta, Ga.: S. R. Sentinel
Office, 1835. 235 pp.
　Characters, incidents and traditions in the first
　half century of the Republic.

Lovell, Caroline Couper
The Golden Isles of Georgia. Boston: Little,
Brown and Company, 1932. viii, 300 pp., bibl.
　Much on social life and customs.

Moore, Francis
A Voyage to Georgia, Begun in the Year 1735.
Containing on account of the settling of the
town of Frederica, in the southern part of the
province; and a description of the soil, air,
birds, beasts, trees, rivers, islands, etc. . . .
London: 1744. (In: *Georgia Historical Society.
Collections.* Savannah, 1840, vol. 1, pp. 79–
152).

A New Voyage to Georgia. By a young gentleman. Giving an Account of his travels to South
Carolina, and part of North Carolina. To which
is added, A Curious Account of the Indians, by
an honorable person. And a poem to James
Oglethorpe, esq., on his arrival from Georgia.
London: Printed for J. Wilford, 1737. (In:
Georgia Historical Society. Collections. Savannah, 1842, v.2, pp. 37–66).
　A reprint of an extremely rare pamphlet. (The
　first edition was published in 1735).

Parsons, Elsie Clews
"Folk Lore from Georgia." *JAFL* 47:386–390,
1934.

Peeples, Edwin A.
Swing Low. Boston: Houghton Mifflin Co.,
1945. 293 pp.
　A novel of Negro and white types against a
　background of local mores and attitudes.

Powell, Arthur Gray
I Can Go Home Again. Chapel Hill: The University of North Carolina Press, 1943. viii, 301
pp.
　Reminiscences of life and manners.

Raper, Arthur
Tenants of the Almighty. New York: The Macmillan Co., 1943.
　The story of Greene County, Georgia, and how
　her people have lived on their farms and in the
　small towns.

Smiley, P.
"Folklore from Virginia, South Carolina,
Georgia, Alabama and Florida." *JAFL* 32:
357–383, 1919.

Steed, Hal
Georgia: Unfinished State. New York: Alfred
A. Knopf, 1942. 360 pp., photographs, map.
　A rapid cavalcade of the state, of the past and
　present, mostly the present; social, political,
　economic, and some insight and description of
　local color.

MYTHS—FOLKTALES—SUPERSTITIONS

Backus, E. M.
"Folktales from Georgia." *JAFL* 13:19–32,
1900.

Harper, Mass.
"Tales of the Okefinokee." *AS* 1 (No. 8):407–
420, 1926.
　Here in this isolated region in Georgia one still
　finds linguistic reminders of the Elizabethan era.

Harris, Joel Chandler
Stories of Georgia. New York: American Book
Co., 1896. 315 pp.

Jones, Charles Colcock
*Negro Myths from the Georgia Coast Told in
the Vernacular.* Boston: Houghton Mifflin and
Co., 1888.

Moore, R. A.
"Superstitions from Georgia." *JAFL* 5:230–
231; 1892; 7:305–309, 1894; 9:226–228, 1896.

Steiner, R.
"Observation on the Practice of Conjuring in
Georgia." *JAFL* 14:173–180, 1901.

————.
"Superstitions and Beliefs from Central
Georgia." *JAFL* 12:261–271, 1899.

Stroup, Thomas B.
"Two Folk Tales from South-Central Georgia."
SFQ Vol. 2 (No. 4): 207–212, 1938.

————.
"Another Southern Analogue to the Mak
Story." *SFQ* 3:5–6, 1939.

CHILDREN'S RHYMES AND GAMES

Darby, L.
"Ring Games from Georgia." *JAFL* 30:218–
221, 1917.

Henry, Mellinger E.
"Nursery Rhymes and Game-Songs from
Georgia." *JAFL* 47:334–341, 1934.

SPEECH

Combs, J. H.
"A Word-List from Georgia." *Dialect Notes*
5 (Part 5):183–184, 1922.

Mathews, M. M.
"Sherwood's Provincialisms." *Dialect Notes* 5
(Part 10):415–421, 1927.
　Rev. Adiel Sherwood (1791–1879), born in New
　York, and educated in New England, collected
　material for a *Gazetteer of the State of Georgia,*
　which appeared in 1827. The above list is taken
　from that edition.

FOLKSONG

GENERAL STUDIES

Backus, Emma M.
"Christmas Carols from Georgia." *JAFL* 12:
272, 1899.

Barrow, David C.
"A Georgia Corn-Shucking." *Century Magazine,* 24:873–878.

"Folk Music of Georgia." *MQ* 19:717–733,
(October) 1933.

"Georgia's Unwritten Airs." *Musical America* 19 (No. 20) :23, 1914.

Millican, Charles B.
"A Georgia Version of 'Barbara Allan'." *JAFL* 42:303–305, 1929.

Redfearn, S. F.
"Songs from Georgia." *JAFL* 34:121–124, 1921.

Snyder, F. B.
"Leo Frank and Mary Phagan" (Georgia Ballad). *JAFL* 31:264–266, 1918.

RECORDS

Collections

U. S. Library of Congress. Division of Music. Folklore Section.
Folk Music of the Okefinokee Swamp Region of Georgia. Frances Harper.   AAFS-LC

KENTUCKY

FOLKLORE

BIBLIOGRAPHIES

Historical Records Survey.
Inventory of the County Archives of Kentucky. Prepared by the Historical Records Survey, Division of Women's and Professional Projects, Works Progress Administration. Louisville, Ky.: 1937.

———.
Supplemental Checklist of Kentucky Imprints, 1788–1820, Including the original Kentucky Ledger, 1800-1854 . . . Louisville, Ky.: Historical Records Survey, . . . 1942. xii, 241 pp.

Jillson, Willard Rouse
Early Kentucky Literature, 1750–1840. Frankfort, Ky.: The Kentucky State Historical Society, 1931. 104 pp.

———.
Rare Kentucky Books: 1776–1926. Louisville, Ky.: The Standard Printing Co., 1939. 192 pp.
A check and finding list of scarce, fugitive, curious and interesting books and pamphlets with annotation and prices current appended.

Kentucky. University. Dept. of Library Science.
Books with Kentucky Background for High School Libraries. Lexington, Ky.: Department of Library Science, 1941.

List of Books Relating to Kentucky.
U. S. Library of Congress. Division of Bibliography. Washington, D. C.: U. S. Gov't. Printing Office, 1925.

McMurtie, Douglas C., and Allen, Albert H.
American Imprints Inventory. The Historical Records Survey Division of Women's and Professional Projects of the Works Progress Administration No. 5, Check List of *Kentucky Imprints 1787–1810.* Louisville, Ky.: The Historical Records Survey, 1939. No. 1, A Preliminary Check List of Mission Imprints. 1808–1850. Washington, D. C.: The Historical Survey, 1937.

Shearin, Hubert G., and Combs, Josiah H.
A Syllabus of Kentucky Folk-Songs, Transylvania University Studies in English II. Lexington, Ky.: Transylvania Printing Co., 1927.

PERIODICALS

Bulletin of the Kentucky Folklore Society, Lucy B. Thomas, Pres. Western Kentucky State Teachers College.

The Filson Club History Quarterly. v.1, 1926 ––. Louisville, Ky.: The Filson Club.

Register. Kentucky State Historical Society. v.1, 1903 ––. Frankfort, Ky. Quarterly.

GENERAL STUDIES AND COLLECTIONS

Barton, William E.
Kentucky Pine Knot. New York: 1924. 485 pp., 42 ill., plates.
A story of Kentucky life.

Campbell, Marie
Cloud Walking. Foreword by Alice V. Keliher. Illustrated by John A. Shelman, IIIrd. New York: Farrar and Rinehart, 1942. 272 pp.
The story of a Kentucky Mt. community—their life and lore.

———
"Survivals of Old Folk Drama in the Kentucky Mountains." *JAFL* 51:10–24, 1938.

Clark, Thomas D.
The Kentucky. (The Rivers of America Series). Illustrated by John A. Spelman. New York: Farrar and Rinehart, 1942.
It is the story of Boonesboro and of the Blue Grass Country where Kentuckians have developed a life which is in many ways unique in America.

Cobb, Irwin S.
Kentucky. (Cobb's America Guyed Books). Illustrated by John T. McCutcheon. New York: George H. Doran Co., 1924.

Coleman, John Winston
Slavery Times in Kentucky. Chapel Hill.: The University of North Carolina Press. 1940. xiv, 351 pp., illus., bibl.

Collins, Lewis
History of Kentucky: revised, enlarged, and brought down to the year 1874, by his son Richard Collins. Louisville, Ky.: R. H. Collins, 1877. 912 pp.

Combs, Josiah, H., ed.
All That's Kentucky, An Anthology of Poetry and Lore. Louisville: John P. Morton & Co., 1915. xxiv, 285 pp.

Davenport, Francis Garvin
Ante-Bellum Kentucky, A Social History, 1800–1860. Oxford, O.: The Mississippi Valley Press, 1943. xvii, 238 pp., bibl.

Duncan, Kunigunde, and Nikols, D. F.
Mentor Graham, The Man Who Taught Lincoln. Chicago: The University of Chicago Press, 1945. 724 pp.
"More than a life of a man, this book is a vivid picture of pioneer life in Kentucky, Indiana and Illinois, an entertaining study in folkways, superstitions, homey sayings, home-made customs, religious oddities, simple remedies, improvisations by a capable people in the wilderness."

Firestone, Clark B.
Sycamore Shores. New York: R. M. McBride and Co., 1936. 247 pp.
"Part of the material in this volume was first printed in the Cincinnati Time's Star."

Fox, John, Jr.
Blue Grass and Rhododendron; Out-Doors in Old Kentucky. New York: C. Scribner's Sons, 1901. x, 294 pp.
Much on the mountain folk—their customs, characters, beliefs and tales.

——————.
Hell Fer Sartain. New York: Charles Scribner's Sons, 1904.

Furman, Lucy
Quare Women. Concord, Mass.: Atlantic Monthly Press, 1923.

Hall, Eliza Calvert
The Land of Long Ago. Sketches of olden times in the rural districts of the Pennyrile. Boston: Little, Brown and Co., 1909.

Haney, William
The Mountain People of Kentucky. An Account of Present Conditions with the Attitude Toward Improvement. Cincinnati, O.: R. Clarke, 1906. 196 pp.

Harlow, Alvin F.
Weep No More, My Lady. New York: Whittlesy House, McGraw-Hill Book Co., 1942. illus.
"Of stories handed down and memories of his family, of wanderings from show-place to hinterland, of word-picture and record of local talk, Mr. Harlow has made an individual and delightful reconstruction of a commonwealth."

Hewlett, M. H.
Kentucky, In: *Extemporary Essays,* (pp. 232–236). London and New York: H. Milford, Oxford University Press, 1922. 256 pp.

Hulbert, Archer Butler
Boone's Wilderness Road. Cleveland, O.: The A. H. Clark Company, 1903. 207 pp.

Hutchinson, Percy
"The Balladry and Folkways of Kentucky Mountains." Review of *Devil's Ditties* by Jean Thomas. In: *New York Times Book Review,* Jan. 31, 1932.

Jillson, Willard Rouse
The Glory of the Hills. Frankfort, Ky.: Frankfort Garden Club, 1933.

Johnson, L. F.
Famous Kentucky Tragedies and Trials. Louisville, Kentucky: Baldwin Law Book Co., 1916.

Jones, John Beauchamp
Wild Western Scenes . . . The War-path: A narrative of adventures in the wilderness: with minute details of the captivity of sundry persons; amusing and perilous incidents during their abode in the wild woods; fearful battles with the Indians; ceremony of adoption into an Indian family, encounters with wild beasts and rattlesnakes, etc. Philadelphia: J. B. Lippincott & Co., 1865. 335 pp.

Kennedy, P.
"Minstrels of the Kentucky Hills; The Traipsin' Woman's Twelfth Annual American Folksong Festival." *Travel* 79:14–15, 1942.

Kentucky, a Guide to the Bluegrass State. (American Guide Series). Compiled and written by the Federal Writers' Project of the Works Progress Administration for the State of Kentucky. New York: Harcourt, Brace and Co., 1939.

Knight, Grant C.
James Lane Allen and the Genteel Tradition. Chapel Hill: University of North Carolina Press, 1935.

Lexington, and the Bluegrass Country. (American Guide Series). Compiled and written by the Federal Writers' Project of the Works Progress Administration for the State of Kentucky. Lexington, Kentucky: The Commercial Printing Co., Press, 1938.

Mackaye, Percy
Kentucky Mountain Fantasies. Three Short Plays for an Appalachian Theatre. Illustrations by Arvia Mackaye. New York: Longmans, Green and Company, 1928. xiv, 173 pp., front., illus.

——————.
This Fine Pretty World: A Comedy of the Kentucky Mountains. New York: The Macmillan Company, 1924. xxv, 197 pp.

McNemar, Richard
The Kentucky Revival; or, A Short History of the Late Extraordinary Outpouring of the Spirit of God in the Western States of America, Agreeably to Scripture Promise and Prophecies concerning the latter day: With a brief account of the entrance and progress of what the world calls *Shakerism* among the subjects of the late revival in Ohio and Kentucky. Cincinnati, Ohio: 1807. (Reprinted in Albany, 1808.)

Michaux, André
Journal of Travels into Kentucky, July 15, 1793–April 11, 1796. In: Thwaites, Reuben G., ed.: *Early Western Travels, 1748–1846.* 1904. vol. 3, pp. 25–104.

Ogden, George W.
Ogden's Letters from the West, 1821–1823. In: Thwaites, Reuben G., ed: *Early Western Travels, 1746–1846.* Cleveland, O., 1905. vol. 19, pp. 19–112.

Poole, Ernest
Nurses on Horseback. New York: The Macmillan Co., 1932. viii, 168 pp., illus.

Price, S. F.
"Kentucky Folklore." *JAFL* 14:30–38, 1901.

Ranck, George W.
Boonesborough; Its Founding, pioneer struggles, Indian experiences, Transylvania days and revolutionary annals. Felson Club Publications, No. 16. Louisville: J. P. Morton and Company, 1901. xi, 286 pp., plates, 2 port. (incl. front.) plans.

Rothert, O. A.
The Outlaws of Cave-in-Rock. Accounts of the famous highwaymen and river pirates who operated in pioneer days. Cleveland, Ohio: A. H. Clark Co., 1924.

Skinner, Constance Lindsay
Pioneers of the Old Southwest; A Chronicle of the Dark and Bloody Ground. New Haven: Yale University Press, 1921. xi, 304 pp., bibl.

Sutton, Margaret
Jemima, Daughter of Daniel Boone. New York: Charles Scribner's Sons, 1942.
    A story for young readers describing the life of the Kentucky pioneers.

Thomas, Jean
Ballad Makin' in the Mountains of Kentucky. With music arranged by Walter Kob. New York: Henry Holt and Company, 1939. xv, 270 pp., illus., music.

—————.
Big Sandy. New York: H. Holt and Co., 1940. 302 pp.
    On social life, customs, traditions and lore of the Kentucky folk. Discusses the Hatfield-McCoy feud.

—————.
Blue Ridge Country. (American Folkways). New York: Duell, Sloan and Pearce, 1942. x, 338 pp.
    Description of Kentucky Mountains, the people, customs, beliefs, feuds, games, songs, etc.

—————.
Devil's Ditties. Being stories of the Kentucky Mountain People by Jean Thomas, with the songs they sing. Harmonizations by Philip Gordon. Drawings by Cyril Mullen. Chicago: W. Wilbur Hatfield, 1931. 180 pp., illus., music.

Toulmin, Harry
The Western Country in 1793; Reports on Kentucky and Virginia. Ed. by Marion Tinling and Godfrey Davies. San Marino, Calif., 1948. xx, 141 pp.

Townsend, John Wilson
Three Kentucky Gentlemen of the Old Order. Frankfort, Ky.: The Roberts Printing Company, 1946. 51 pp.
    Contents: "The Mayor of Mississippi", "A Country Doctor of the Blue Grass", "Jim Roche, Raconteur".

Trout, Allan M.
"The Charm of Kentucky Folklore." *Filson Club History Quarterly* (Louisville), July 1947, pp. 179–196, illus.

Van Doren, Carl
Folklore in Kentucky, in *Roving Critic* (pp. 100–104). New York: Alfred A. Knopf, 1923. 262 pp.

Warren, Louis Austin
Louisville Lincoln Loop; A Day's Tour in "Old Kentucky." Louisville: The Standard Printing Company, 1922. 43 pp.

Wilson, Gordon
"Kentucky Folklore Society." *JAFL* 56:172–173, 1943.

FOLKTALES

Allen, James Lane
Flute and Violin. Collection of Kentucky tales and romances. New York: Harper and Brothers, 1891.

Bird, Robert Montgomery
Nick of the Woods, or Jibbenainosay. A Tale of Kentucky. Philadelphia: Carey, Lea and Blanchard, 1837.
    Reprinted in 1928 by Vanguard Press, New York, edited by Mark Van Doren.

Bradley, William Aspenwall
Old Christmas and Other Kentucky Tale in Verse. Boston: Houghton Mifflin Co., 1917. xi, 111 pp.

Campbell, Marie
"Cindy Gives Out Singing to her House." *TFSB* 3:76–96, 1937.

Childs, Alice
"The Red Rag Under the Churn: A Folk-Tale of the Kentucky Mountains." *AS* 5 (No. 2): 142–144, 1929.

Halpert, H.
"Family Tales of a Kentuckian." *HFB* 1:61–71, 1942.

Mackaye, Percy
Tall Tales of the Kentucky Mountains. New York: The Century Co., 1924. New York: George A. Doran, 1926. 185 pp., illus.
    Twelve tales told in mountain vernacular by Solomon Shell, a legendary figure.

—————.
Weathergoose—Woo! Illustrated by Arvia Mackaye. New York: Longmans, Green and Company, 1929. 189 pp., incl. front., illus., plates.
    Seven tales of the Kentucky Hills.

Mutzenberg, Charles G.
Kentucky's Famous Feuds and Tragedies; authentic history of the world famous Vendettas of the dark and bloody ground. New York: R. F. Feno and Co., 1917. 333 pp.

Stuart, Jesse
Beyond Dark Hills. New York: E. P. Dutton and Co., Inc., 1938.
    Contains humorous character and incident.

—————.
Head O'W-Hallow. 19 Stories about the mountain people of eastern Kentucky. New York: E. P. Dutton and Co., 1936.

—————.
Man With a Bull-Tongue Plow. New York: E. P. Dutton and Co., 1934. 361 pp.

—————.
Tales From The Plum Grove Hills. New York: E. P. Dutton and Company, 1946. 256 pp.

————.
Taps for Private Tussie. Illustrated by Thomas Benton. New York: E. P. Dutton and Co., 1943. 253 pp.
"It is an expanded folktale told through the mind of a growing boy. This novel has the laughter and sadness of mountain music." (William Du Bois.)

Thatcher, M. H.
Stories and Speeches of William O. Bradley with Biographical Sketch. Lexington, Ky.: Transylvania Printing Co., 1916.
Humor, anecdote, and folktale.

Truitt, Orlie Julian
Doin's at Sadieville. Covington, Ky.: Published by the Author, Pamphlet, P. O. Box 113, Ludlow Branch, 1943.
A series of strange stories of old Kentucky.

MAGIC—SUPERSTITION

Combs, Josiah H.
"Sympathetic Magic in the Kentucky Mountains." *JAFL* 27:328–330, 1914.

Thomas, Daniel L., and Lucy B.
Kentucky Superstitions. Princeton, N. J.: University Press, 1920. viii, 334 pp.
A compilation of almost 4,000 superstitions of every type.

SPEECH

Botkin, B. A.
"Folk Speech in the Kentucky Mountain Cycle of Percy Mackaye." *AS* 6 (No. 4):264–276, 1931.

Dunlap, Fayette
"A Tragedy of Surnames." *Dialect Notes* 4 (Part 1):7–8, 1913.
From Boyle County, Kentucky.

"Early English Slang Survivals in the Mountains of Kentucky." *Dialect Notes* 5 (Part 4):115–118, 1921.

Fruit, J. P.
"Kentucky Words." *Dialect Notes* 1 (Part 5): 230–234, 1890–96.

————.
"Kentucky Words and Phrases." *Dialect Notes* 1 (Part 2):63–69.

Hench, Atcheson L.
"Kentucky Pioneers," *AS* 12(No. 1):75–76, 1937.

Knott, Hon. J. Proctor
Duluth! Speech delivered by Hon. J. P. K. of Kentucky, delivered in the House of Representatives, on the St. Croix and Superior Land Grant, January 27, 1871.
A remarkable and humorous speech abounding in folksy idioms.

Shearin, Hubert G.
"An Eastern Kentucky Dialect Word-List." *Dialect Notes* 3 (Part 7):537–540, 1911.

Weeks, Abigail E.
"A Word-List from Barbourville, Ky." *Dialect Notes* 3(Part 6):456–547, 1910.

PLACE NAMES

Woods, Robert E.
Heroes of the War of 1812 For Whom Kentucky Counties are Named. Jeffersontown, Ky.: 1937. n.p.:1938. 1 vol (ms.) For voice and piano.

FOLKSONG

BIBLIOGRAPHY

Shearin, Hubert, and Combs, Josiah
A Syllabus of Kentucky Folk-Songs. Transylvania University Studies in English, Vol. II. Lexington, Ky.: Transylvania Printing Co., 1911.

GENERAL STUDIES AND COLLECTIONS

Barry, Phillips
"Jane was a Neighbor." *FSSNE* 2:6–8, 1931.
A variant of Child 170: "The Dead, Queen Jane," recorded in Kentucky. (Text and tune.)

Bradley, William Aspenwall
"Song-Ballets and Devil's Ditties." *Harper's Monthly Magazine* 130:901–914, 1914–15. illus.

Brockway, Howard
"Quest of the Lonesome Tunes." *Art World* 2:227–230, (June) 1917.

————.
"The Quest of the Lonesome Tunes." *Music Teacher's National Association Papers and Proceedings*, 14:59–67, 1920.

Campbell, Marie
"Liquor Ballads." *SFQ* 2:157–164, 1938.
An important series of ballads from the Kentucky Mountains. "Funeral Ballads" 3:107–115, 1939; "Feuding Ballads" 3:165–172, 1939.

"Cherry Tree": Kentucky Mountain Ballad. *Golden Book* 14:395, (Dec.) 1931.

Combs, Josiah H.
"Ballad from the Kentucky Mountains." *JAFL* 23:381–382, 1913.

Crichton, Kyle
"Thar's Gold in Them Hill-Billies Recording Hill Billy and Race Music." *Colliers* 101:24, (April 30) 1938.

Federal Music Project.
Songs Collected by Workers of the Federal Music Project of the Works Progress Administration in Boyd, Floyd and Rowan Counties, Kentucky. n.p.: 1938. 1 vol. (ms.).
Arranged for voice and piano.

"Folk Festivities Attended by 14,000. Sixth Annual Kentucky Event Sponsored by Folksong Society and WPA in Ashland." *Musical America* S6 (No. 13):27, Aug., 1936.

Harbison, Katherine
"In the Great and Lone Prairie." *SFQ* 2 (No. 3), (Sept.) 1938.
Songs and ballads with tunes from Illinois, Ohio, and Blue Grass Section of Kentucky.

Hay, John
Pike County Ballads. Illustrated by N. C. Wyeth. Boston: Houghton Mifflin Company, 1912. 45 pp.

Henry, Mellinger E.
"Devil's Ditties." *JAFL* 45:273, 1935.

————.
"The Lexington Girl." *JAFL* 42:247–253, 1929.

Hume, Edgar Erskine
"The Slaughter of De La Bastic." *Americana* 34 (No. 4). Carlisle Barracks, Pa.: The American Historical Company, 1940.

"Hunting the Lonesome Tune in the Wilds of Kentucky." *Current Opinion* 62:100–101, (Feb.) 1917.

Hutchinson, Percy
"The Balladry of Folk-Ways of Kentucky Mountaineers."
Review of *Devil's Ditties* by Jean Thomas, in *New York Times Book Review*, Jan. 31, 1932.

"Kentucky's Ancient Minstrel Wanders Afar from His Folks." *Lit. Digest*, 114:26–27, (Dec. 24) 1932.

"Kentucky Folksongs." *Musical Leader* 26 (No. 9):240, 1913.

"Kentucky Songs." *JAFL* 36:376–379, 1923.

Kittredge, George L., ed.
"Ballads and Rhymes from Kentucky." *JAFL* 20:251–277, 1907.

McGill, Josephine
" 'Sing all a Green Willow': Old World Ballads Surviving in the Kentucky Hills." *North Amer. Rev.* 288:218–224, (August) 1929.

"Notes From Pine Mountain Settlement School." *Pine Mountain, Harlan Co., Kentucky*, Vol. 7, (No. 1) (January) 1935.
Contains a few ballads, texts and tunes of Kentucky songs.

"Old Kentucky Ballads."
Berea Quarterly, 1901.

"Oversea Ballads in Kentucky Valleys."
Rev. of Reviews, 44:497–498, (October) 1911.

Schmitz, R. M.
"Leo Frank and Mary Phagan." *JAFL* 60:59–61, 1947.
Text only of a version from Joy May Creasy, a mountain lass from Kentucky. "The text itself shows the innocent migration of the story westward from the scenes of the original murder and trial of 1913 at Atlanta, Georgia."

Shearin, Hubert G.
"Kentucky Folk Songs." *Modern Language Review*, 6:513.

Snook, S.
"Hill Billy and River Songs at Their Source." *Etude* 58:513, (Aug.) 1940.

Sutherland, Elihu Jasper
"Vance's Song." *SFQ* 4:251–254, 1940.
Words only.

Thomas, Jean
Ballad Makin' in the Mountains of Kentucky. New York: Henry Colt and Co., 1939. Music, illus.

————.
Devil's Ditties. Being stories of the Kentucky Mountain People told by J. T., with the songs they sing. Harmonization by Philip Gordon. Drawings by Cyril Mullen. Chicago: W. Wilbur Hatfield, 1931.

————.
The Singin' Fiddler of Lost Hope Hollow. New York: E. P. Dutton & Co., 1938. 242 pp.

————.
The Singin' Gatherin'; Tunes from the Southern Appalachians. In collaboration with Joseph A. Leeder. New York: Silver, Burdett Co., 1939. xii, 113 pp., illus.

————.
Sun Shines Bright. New York: Prentice-Hall, 1940.

————.
The Traipsin' Woman. New York: E. P. Dutton & Co., 1933.

Treat, Asher E.
"Kentucky Folksongs in Northern Wisconsin." *JAFL* 52:1–51, 1939.
Fifty-six texts, with music.

Truitt, F.
"Songs from Kentucky." *JAFL* 36:376–379, 1923.

Voice of the Hills
"Traipsin' Woman is Rallying Kentucky Minstrels Again." *Newsweek* 2:24 (June 6) 1938.

ARRANGEMENTS

(Collections): Voice and Piano

Combs, Josiah, coll.
Folk Songs from the Kentucky Highlands. Piano accompaniments by Keith Mixson. Schirmer's American Folk Song Series, Set I. New York: G. Schirmer, Inc., 1939.

Fuson, Henry Harvey
Ballads of the Kentucky Highlands. London: The Mitre Press, 1931. 219 pp., without music.

McGill, Josephine
Folksongs of the Kentucky Mountains. Twenty traditional ballads and other folksongs, notated from the singing of the Kentucky mountain people and arranged with piano accompaniment by Josephine McGill. Introductory note by H. E. Krehbiel. New York: Boosey & Co., 1917. 106 pp., melodies with piano accompaniment, English words.

Niles, John J.
Seven Kentucky Mountain Songs. New York: G. Schirmer, 1929. Voice and piano.

Sulzer, E. G., ed.
Twenty-five Kentucky Folk Ballads. Lexington, Ky.: Transylvania Press, 1936.

Thomas, Jean
Ballad Makin' in the Mountains of Kentucky; with music arranged by Walter Kob. New York: H. Holt and Co., 1939. xviii, 270 pp.

Wheeler, Mary
Kentucky Mountain Folk-Songs; piano accompaniment by Clark Gregory Bridge, introduction by Edgar Stillman Kelley. Boston: The Boston Music Company, 1937.

Wyman, Loraine
Lonesome Tunes. Folksongs from the Kentucky mountains. The words collected and edited by Loraine Wyman, the pianoforte accompaniment by Howard Brockway. New York: Gray, 1916.

————.
Twenty Kentucky Mountain Songs. The words collected by Loraine Wyman, the melodies collected and piano accompaniments added by Howard Brockway. Boston: Oliver Ditson Co., c.1920. Publ. No. 73480–115. 114., pp., melodies with piano acompaniment.

————: *Female Voices*

"The Carrion Crow, or The Tailor and the Crow." Horton: Schirmer: SSA. Sopr. and Alto Soli, a cappella.

"The Frog in the Spring."
Niles, John J.: Schirmer: SSA, a cappella.

"I Wonder When I Shall be Married."
Cain: Boston Music Co.: SSA.

"Jack O' Diamonds."
Niles, John J.: Schirmer: SSAA. Tenor or Baritone Solo, a cappella.

"Old Smokey."
Barthelson: Irving Berlin: SSA.

"One Morning in May, or The Nightingale."
Niles-Horton: Schirmer: SAA. Soprano and Tenor Soli.

"The Little Family."
Malin, D.: Boston Music Co.: SA.

————: *Male Voices*

"Cindy."
Cain, N.: Boston Music Co.: TBB.

"Cindy."
Malin: Gamble Hinged: TTB.

"Cindy."
Malin, Don: Musical Research Society: TTAB, a cap.

"Oh, Miss 'Liza Jane."
Horton: Gamble Hinged: TTBB.

"Sourwood Mountain."
Malin: Gamble Hinged: TTBB.

"Sourwood Mountain."
Scott, Tom: Words and Music Inc.: TTBB. (Fred Waring Glee Club Arrangement.)

"The Ground Hog."
Cain, H.: Boston Music Company: TTBB.

"The Mountain Girl" (Kentucky's "Sourwood Mountain"). Manney: Broadcast Music, Inc.: TTBB.

————: *Mixed Voices*

"The Carrion Crow, or The Tailor and the Crow." Horton: Schirmer: SATB. Sopr. and Baritone Soli, a cappella.

"Cherry Tree Carol."
Cain, H.: Boston Music Co.: SATB.

"The Frog in the Spring."
Niles, John J.: Schirmer: SATB, a cappella,

"The Keeper."
Cain, H.: Boston Music Co.: SATB.

"The Little Family."
Treharne, B.: Willis: SATB.
A Kentucky Mountain Ballad.

"Kentucky Moonshiner."
Siegmeister, E.: C. Fischer: SATB, with Bar. Solo, a cappella.

"One Morning in May, or The Nightingale."
Niles-Norton: Schirmer: SATB. Soprano and Tenor Soli.

"Sourwood Mountain."
Malin: Gamble Hinged: SATB.

————: *Two Pianos—4 Hands*

"My Little Mohee."
Niles, John J.: G. Schirmer—2 pianos, 4 hands.

————: *Orchestra*

Kentucky Sonata.
Helm, Everett: MS: Violin and orchestra.

Ol' Kaintuck—Overture. De Lamarter, Eric: Music Publishers Holding Corp.
Based on Kentucky Mountain airs.

Say Paw—Rhapsody on Kentucky Mountain Folk Tunes. Holden, David J.: MS: Orchestra.

RECORDS

"The South" (Kentucky).
In the archives of the *American Folk Song Library of Congress, Music Division* (Washington, D. C.).

U. S. Library of Congress. Division of Music. Folklore Section.
Songs of Kentucky and Tennessee. Recording Project of Artus M. Moser. 28 records.
AAFS–LC.

LOUISIANA

FOLKLORE

See: Creole Folklore pp. 544–46.

BIBLIOGRAPHIES

Alabama University. Library.
A Bibliography of Louisiana. Books and Pamphlets in the T. P. Thompson Collection of the University of Alabama Library, comp. by Donald E. Thompson. University of Alabama Press, 1947. vii, 210 pp. (University of Alabama Studies, No. 2).

French, B. F.
Historical Collections of Louisiana. Report of Commissioner of Agriculture for 1870. Washington, D. C.: U. S. Gov't Printing Office, 1871.

Historical Records Survey.
Guide to Depositories of Manuscript Collections in Louisiana. Prepared by the Louisiana Historical Records Survey . . . WPA. University, La.: Dept. of Archives, 1941.

Index to a Collection of Americana Relating Principally to Louisiana Art and Miscellanea. New Orleans, La.: In the Private Library of T. P. Thompson, 1912. 203 pp.

Michaud, Marguerite
"L'Acadie dans la littérature." L'Action Nationale 29 (No. 4) :273–284, 1947.
A bibliographical article on Acadia and the Acadians.

McVoy, Mrs. Lizzie Carter, and Campbell, Ruth Bates
A Bibliography of Fiction by Louisianians and on Louisiana Subjects. Baton Rouge: Louisiana State University Press, 1935. 87 pp.

Thompson, Thomas Payne
Louisiana Writers Native and Resident, Including others whose books belong to a bibliography of that state, to which is added a list of artists . . . New Orleans, 1904. 64 pp.

Tinker, Edward Larocque
"Boimare, First and Still Foremost Bibliographer of Louisiana." Papers of the Bibliographical Society of America (Chicago) 24: Parts (1–2) :34–42, 1930.

PERIODICALS

The Louisiana Historical Quarterly. v.1, 1917 —. New Orleans, La.: The Louisiana Historical Society.

Proceedings of the Historical Society of East and West Baton Rouge. v.1–2, 1916–1918.

Publications of the Louisiana Historical Society. v.1 —. 1895–1919. New Orleans: Louisiana State Historical Society, 1895–1919.

GENERAL STUDIES AND COLLECTIONS

Bellamann, Henry
Sin and Magnolias. New York: Simon and Schuster, 1944. 281 pp.
"It is Louisiana with its swamps and miasma and the sweep of the Mississippi." (Rose Feld.)

Bossu, Jean Bernard
Travels Through That Part of North America Formerly Called Louisiana. (Translated from French by John P. Forster.) London, Eng.: T. Davies, 1771.

Cable, George Washington
Strange True Stories of Louisiana. London: K. Paul, Trench, 1890. ix, 350 pp.
Many folk tales, superstitions, and beliefs. Includes—"The 'haunted house' in Royall Street".

Charlevoix, Pierre F. X. de
History and General Description of New France. (Translated with notes by John Shea.) New York: J. G. Shea, 1866–1872. II vols.

Claudel, Calvin
"History of Louisiana Folklore Association." SFQ 8:11–21, 1944.
The work of Alcée Fortier, and of the association from 1892–1896.

————.
"New Orleans Branch, American Folklore Society (The Louisiana Folklore Association)." JAFL 59:488–489, 1946.

Eaton, Evelyn
The Sea is So Wide. New York: Harper and Brothers, 1943.
A novel of the deportation of the Acadians in 1755.

Fearn, Frances (Hewitt), ed.
Diary of a Refugee. Illustrated by Rosalie Urquart. New York: Moffat, Lord and Company, 1910. ix, 149 pp., illus.

Fortier, Alcée
"Bits of Louisiana Folk-Lore." PMLA 3:100–168, 1887.
Popular tales, song (text only) and proverbs in patois by the Creoles of Lower Louisiana.

————.
Louisiana; comprising sketches of counties, towns, events, institutions, and persons, arranged in cyclopedic form. In two volumes, with a supplementary volume of contemporary biography. Atlanta, Ga.: Southern Historical Association, 1909, 1914. 3 vols.

————.
Louisiana Studies; Literature, Customs and Dialects, History and Education. New Orleans: F. F. Housell and Brothers, 1894. vi, 307 pp.

Hearn, Lafcadio, and others
New Orleans. Historical Sketch; Book and Guide to New Orleans and Environs. Edited and compiled by several leading writers of the New Orleans Press. New York: W. H. Coleman, 1885. 324 pp., illus.
Exhaustive account of the traditions, historical legends and remarkable personalities of the Creole City.

Historical Records Survey.
County-Parish Boundaries in Louisiana. Prepared by the Historical Records Survey, Division of Professional and Service Projects, Works Progress Administration . . . New Orleans, La.: The Department of Archives, Louisiana State University, 1939. vi, 139 pp.
One gathers much on lore, customs and traditions of the folk inhabiting the counties.

Judson, Edward Zane Carroll (Ned Buntline)
The Mysteries and Miseries of New Orleans. New York: L. Ormsby, 1853. 104 pp.

Kane, Harnett T.
Deep Delta Country. (American Folkways Series.) New York: Duell, Sloan and Pearce, 1944. 283 pp.

———.
Natchez on the Mississippi. New York: William Morrow and Co., 1947. 373 pp., illus.
Replete with historical facts and incidents, as well as hearsay and local gossip.

———.
Plantation Parade; The grand manner in Louisiana. Illustrated with photographs by James H. Ricau and Chet Kellog, Guy F. Bernard, and others . . . New York: W. Morrow and Co., 1945. vi, 342 pp., illus., bibl.

Keyes, Frances Parkinson
Crescent Carnival. New York: Julian Messner, 1942.
A three generations novel about a Louisiana plantation family.

King, Grace Elizabeth
Balcony Stories. New York: The Century Co., 1893. 245 pp., illus. New York: The Macmillan Co., 1925. 296 pp., illus., plates.
Louisiana and New Orleans life and balcony stories.

———.
New Orleans: The Place and the People; with illustrations by Frances E. Jones. New York and London: Macmillan Co., 1895. xxi, 404 pp., illus., plates.

Laughlin, Clarence John
Ghosts Along the Mississippi, an essay in the poetic interpretation of Louisiana's plantation architecture. 100 photos by the author. New York: C. Scribner's Sons, 1948. 22 pp. 100 plates.

Lockwood, Myra
Free River. A Story of Old New Orleans. Illustrated by the author. New York: E. P. Dutton and Company, 1942. 255 pp.
The story of the city, thru Spanish and French rule. Occasional glimpses into lore and ceremonies.

Louisiana, a Guide to the State. (American Guide Series.) Compiled and written by the Federal Writers' Project of the Works Progress Administration. New York: Hastings House, Publishers, 1941.

McVoy, Lizzie Carter, ed.
Louisiana in the Short Story. Baton Rouge: Louisiana State University Press, 1940. xiii, 291 pp. Louisiana State University Studies No. 41.

Miller, Helen Topping
Wild Lilac. New York: D. Appleton-Century Co., 1943.
A modern romance in Louisiana.

New Orleans City Guide.
(American Guide Series.) Written and compiled by the Federal Writers' Project of the Works Progress Administration for the city of New Orleans. Boston: Houghton Mifflin Co., 1938.

O'Donnell, E. P.
Delta Country. (American Folkways Series.) New York: Duell, Sloan and Pearce, 1943.
The customs, traditions and lore of the many people who inhabit the state of Louisiana and of the legendary city of New Orleans.

Ott, Eleanore
Plantation Cookery of Old Louisiana. New Orleans, La.: Harmauson, 1938.

Parker, Maud May
Louisiana; A Pageant of Yesterday and Today. New Orleans: Hauser Printing Co., 1917. 65 pp.

Ripley, Eliza Moore
Social Life in Old New Orleans, Being Recollections of My Girlhood. New York: D. Appleton and Company, 1912. 331 pp.

Roberts, W. Adolphe
Lake Pontchartrain. Indianapolis: Bobbs-Merrill Company, 1946. 476 pp.
". . . if one likes good old French and Spanish colonial swashbuckling history, romance, and legend brought down to the present and projected into the future, 'Lake Ponchartrain' will provide some mighty fine reading matter." (Roark Bradford.)

Saxon, Lyle
Fabulous New Orleans. Illustrated by E. H. Suydam. New York, London: The Century Company, 1928. xii, 330 pp., illus.

———.
Old Louisiana. Illustrated by E. H. Suydam. New York, London: The Century Company, 1929. xvi, 388 pp., illus., bibl.

Stoddard, Amos
Sketches, Historical and Descriptive of Louisiana. Philadelphia: Published by Mathew Carey, A. Small . . . 1812. viii, 488 pp.

Sublette, C. M., and Kroll, Harry Harrison
Perilous Journey. Indianapolis: Bobbs-Merrill Co., 1943.
A tale of the Mississippi River and the Natchez Trace.

Tallant, Robert
Mardi Gras. Illustrated. New York: Doubleday and Co., 1947. 269 pp., bibl.
    The author tells the origins—historical and
    mythological—of the New Orleans Carnival. The
    story is enlivened with many anecdotes, songs
    and photographs.

"Tensas, Madison"
*Odd Leaves from the Life of a Louisiana
Swamp Doctor.* Philadelphia, Pa.: T. B. Peterson and Brothers, 1846. 203 pp., 6 original
illustrations by Darley.

MYTHS AND LEGENDS

Schertz, H. P.
Legends of Louisiana; the romance of the
royal oak. The brother of the Sultan. New
Orleans: The New Orleans Journal, 1922.

Strecker, J. K.
"Reptile Myths in Northwestern Louisiana."
TFSP 4:44–52, 1919.

FOLKTALES

Beazly, J.
"The Uneasy Ghost of Lafitte." *TFSP* 3:185–
188, 1918.

Bergen, F. D.
"Louisiana Ghost Story." *JAFL* 12:145–147,
1899.

Claudel, Calvin
"Golden Hair." *SFQ* 5:257–263, 1941.

————.
"Possum and Coon and the Law against Meat"
—A Louisiana Folktale.
    Paper read at seventh annual meeting of South-
    eastern Folklore Society, Gainsville, Fla., Feb.
    14, 1942.

Doering, J. Frederick
"Three White Hexes." *JAFL* 59:322–323, 1946.

Field, Rachel
American Folk and Fairy Tales. New York:
Charles Scribner's Sons, 1929. 302 pp.

Fortier, Alcée
"Four Louisiana Folktales." *JAFL* 19:123–
126, 1906.

————.
"Louisiana Nursery Tales." *JAFL* 1:140–145,
1888; 2:36–40, 1889.

Kerney, Ellen
"The Bogyman." *American Notes and Queries*
(N. Y.) 5:79, 1942.
    Notes on *Bras Soupé,* or Squier, New Orleans
    Negro outlaw, shot in 1834.

"Louisiana Folktales."
JAFL 7:317, 1894; 19:123–126, 1906.

Ray, M.
"Stories of Jean Sotk" (White Louisiana).
JAFL 21:364–365, 1908.

**Saxon, Lyle, Tallant, Robert, and Dreyer, Ed-
ward**
Gumbo Ya-Ya; A Collection of Louisiana
Folktales. Boston: Houghton Mifflin Co., 1945.
    "Here is folklore without pedantry, down-to-
    earth sociology, without pain or footnotes." (H.
    T. Kane.)

Tucker, Philip C.
"Le Loup Blanc of Bolivar's Peninsula." *TFSP*
7:62–68, 1928.
    The Peninsula which for three miles contains
    Galveston Bay, east of Galveston. A tale of the
    French Cajuns of Louisiana.

CUSTOMS AND SUPERSTITIONS

Fortier, Alcée
"Customs and Superstition in Louisiana."
JAFL 1:136–140, 1888.

Roberts, Hilda
"Louisiana Superstitions." *JAFL* 40:144–208,
1927.

PLACE NAMES

Read, William A.
"Indian Place-Names in Louisiana." *Louisiana
Historical Quarterly,* July 1928. 20 pp. Re-
print.

————.
Louisiana Place-Names of Indian Origin.
Louisiana State University and Agricultural
and Mechanical College. Bulletin, New Series,
Vol. 19. No. 2. 1927. xii, 72 pp.

Stanley, Marion E.
"Name-Lore from New Orleans." *AS* 2(No. 9):
412, 1927.

SPEECH

Bailey, Oran B.
"Glossary of Cafe Terms." *AS* 18:307–308,
1943.
    56 slang terms and meanings of food serving,
    used by waiters in east Texas and west Louisiana.

Ditchy, Jay Karl
Les Acadiens Louisinais et leur parler. Baltimore: Johns Hopkins Press, 1932.

Fortier, Alcée
"Acadians of Louisiana and Their Dialect."
PMLA 6(No. 1):64–94, 1889.

Geddes, James, Jr.
*A Study of an Acadian-French Dialect Spoken
on the North Shore of the Baie-des-Chaleurs.*
Halle: S. M. Niemeyer, 1908. xvii, 317 pp.
    Contains valuable bibliography to 1908.

Scanland, J. M.
"In the Land of Evangeline." *So. Workman*
40:231–237, 1911.
    Character and customs of the Acadians.

Hogrefe, Pearl
"Notes from Louisiana." *AS* 9(No. 1):79, 1934.
    Some French, English and Negro words found in
    Louisiana speech.

Hughes, Herbert L.
"Older English in Louisiana." *AS* 11(No. 4): 368–369, 1936.

Pearce, J. W.
"Notes from Louisiana." *Dialect Notes* 1 (Part 2):69–72.
On dialect.

Phillips, Hosea
Etude sur la parler de la paroisse. Evangéline (Louisiana). Paris: Droz, 1936. iv, 135 pp.

Riedel, E.
"New Orleans Word-List." *Dialect Notes* 4 (Part 4):268–270, 1916.

Routh, James
"Louisiana Gleanings (Word List)." *Dialect Notes* 5 (Part 6):243–245, 1923.

————.
"Word List from Louisiana." *Dialect Notes* 4 (Part 5):346–347, 1916.

Smith, Harley, and Phillips, Hosea
"The Influence of English on Louisiana 'Cajun' French in Evangeline Parish." *AS* 14:198–202, 1939.

FOLKSONG

See: Creole Folksong pp. 546–49.

GENERAL STUDIES AND COLLECTIONS

Brewster, Paul G.
"The Battle of New Orleans": an example of communal composition. *SFQ* I (No. 3):25–29, 1937.
Excellent for 1812 War.

Claudel, Calvin
Mr. Doering's "Songs the Cajuns Sing." *SFQ* 8:123–131, 1944.

Doering, J. F.
"Songs the Cajuns Sing." *SFQ* 7:193–201, 1943.
Texts (French) of eight folksongs and ballads.

Monroe, Mina
Bayou Ballads; Twelve Folksongs from Louisiana. Texts and music collected by Mina Monroe, edited with the collaboration of Kurt Schindler. New York: G. Schirmer, Inc. viii, 55 pp., music. (Voice and piano.)

Peterson, Mrs. Clara (Gottschalk)
Creole Songs from New Orleans in the Negro Dialect, set to music by Clara Gottschalk Peterson. New Orleans: L. Grunewald Co., Ltd c.1902. 20 pp., melodies with piano accompaniment, Creole dialect words, followed by English translation.

Whitfield, Irene Thérèse
Louisiana French Folk Songs. University, La.: Louisiana State University Press, 1939. xiv, 159 pp. With music (unaccompanied melodies), bibl.

MISSISSIPPI

FOLKLORE

BIBLIOGRAPHY

Department of Archives and History. Mississippi.
A Library of Mississippi History. Publications of the Mississippi Department of Archives and History, and Publications of the Mississippi Historical Society. Jackson, Miss., 1926. 19 pp.

Historical Records Survey
Inventory of the County Archives of Mississippi. Prepared by the Historical Records Survey, Division of Women's and Professional Projects, Works Progress Administration. Jackson, Miss.: 1937.

McMurtrie, Douglas Crawford
A Bibliography of Mississippi Imprints, 1798–1830. Beauvoir Community, Miss.: The Book Farm, 1945. 168 pp., bibl.

Owen, T. McA.
"Bibliography of Mississippi." *American Historical Association. Annual Report* 1:633–828, 1899.

PERIODICALS

The Journal of Mississippi History. vol. 1, 1939 —. Jackson, Miss.: Mississippi Historical Society.

Publications of the Mississippi Historical Society. vols. 1–14. Oxford, Miss., etc.: The Society, 1898–1914.

GENERAL STUDIES AND COLLECTIONS

Baldwin, Joseph G.
Flush Times in Alabama and Mississippi. San Francisco: Sumner, Whitney and Co., 1883, 330 pp. New York: D. Appleton and Co., 1893. 330 pp. Americus, Ga.: The American Book Co., 1908.

Carter, Hodding
The Lower Mississippi. (The Rivers of America Series). Illustrated by John McCrady. New York: Farrar and Rinehart, 1942. x, 467 pp., illus.
"The Old Cabin Home," words and music, pp. 441. Selected bibliography, pp. 443-451.

Clemens, Samuel (Mark Twain)
Life on the Mississippi. New York: Harper & Bros., 1908.

Cobb, J. C.
Mississippi Scenes. Philadelphia: 1851.

Cohn, David L.
Where I Was Born. Boston, Mass.: Houghton Mifflin Company, 1948. 380 pp.
Altho not strictly in the field of folklore, the book, a penetrating analysis of life in the Mississippi Delta, presents illuminating information on the customs and traditions of the Negro and white folks in that region.

Davis, Reuben
Recollections of Mississippi and Mississippians. Boston: Houghton Mifflin Co., 1891. vi, 446 pp.

Darden, John P.
The Secret of Success; or Family Affairs, a memoir in one volume. By a Mississippian. Cincinnati: W. Scott, 1853. viii, 364 pp.

Faulkner, William
Absalom, Absalom. New York: Random House, 1936.
The author makes use of old traditions, customs, and sayings.

Fulkerson, Horace Smith
Random Recollections of Early Days in Mississippi . . . Baton Rouge: Otto Claitor. 1937. xi, 158 pp.

Gay, Earl
Heaven is a Sunswept Hill. New York: Macmillan Co., 1943.
A novel of the farming people who live in the rich floodlands of the Lower Mississippi.

Hudson, Arthur Palmer
Humor of the Old Deep South. New York: Macmillan Co., 1936, xxiv, 548 pp.
Mostly about the folkways of Mississippi preachers, politicians, doctors, farmers, and Negroes.

———.
"Mississippi Folklore Society." JAFL 56:175–176, 1943.

———.
Specimens of Mississippi Folklore. Collected with the assistance of students and citizens of Mississippi and edited by Arthur Palmer Hudson. Published under the auspices of the Mississippi Folklore Society, 1928. Ann Arbor, Mich.: Mimeographed and Printed by Edwards Brothers, 1928. 6 pp. xx numb. 2–173 numb.

James, Alice, ed.
Mississippi Verse. Chapel Hill, N. C.: The University of North Carolina Press, 1934. xviii, 94 pp.

O'Donnell, E. P.
Delta Country. New York: Duell, Sloan and Pearce, 1943.
An American folkways book on the Mississippi Delta.

Mississipi, a Guide to the Magnolia State.
(American Guide Series). Written and compiled by the Federal Writers' Project of the Works Progress Administration. New York: The Viking Press, 1938. xxiv, 545 pp., illus., bibl.

Mississippi Gulf Coast.
(American Guide Series). Compiled and written by Federal Writers' Project of the Works Progress Administration, for the State of Miss. Gulfport, Miss.: Gulfport Printing Co., 1939.

Russell, Charles Edward
A-Rafting on the Mississip'. New York: The Century Co., 1928. xii, 357 pp., illus., music.

Russell, Irwin
Christmas-Night in the Quarters, and other poems. New York: Century Co., 1917.
With an introduction by Joel Chandler Harris, and an historical sketch by Maurice Garland Fulton.

Sublette, C. M., and Kroll, Harry Harrison
Perilous Journey. New York: The Bobbs-Merrill Co., 1943.
A tale of the Mississippi River and the Natchez Trace.

Sale, John B.
A Tree Named John. Chapel Hill: University of North Carolina Press, 1929.

Saxon, Lyle
Father Mississippi. New York: Century Co., 1929.

Street, James B.
Look Away: A Dixie Notebook. New York: Viking Press, 1936.

Young, Stark
Heaven Trees. New York: Charles Scribner's Sons, 1926.
A novel of life on a plantation "forty miles from Memphis by the carriage-road."

———.
River House. New York: Charles Scribner's Sons, 1929.
The scene is laid in Northwest Mississippi.

———.
So Red the Rose. New York: Charles Scribner's Sons, 1934.
A novel of life in the Natchez Area.

FOLKTALES

Halpert, Herbert
"Tales of a Mississippi Soldier." SFQ 103–114, 1944.

Hudson, Arthur Palmer, McCarter, Pete Kyle
"The Bell Witch of Tennessee and Mississippi." *JAFL* 47:22–45, 1934.

McDowell, Mrs. Katherine Sherwood Bonner
Dialect Tales. New York: Harper Brothers, 1883.

"Mississippi Negro Tales."
JAFL 40:213–303, 1927.

RIDDLES

Halpert, Herbert
"A Few Riddles." *HFB* 3:38, 1944.
From Texas and Mississippi.

PLACE NAMES

Benson, Carl
"Literary Gossip. On Certain Etymologies." *The Literary World* 7:457, Dec. 1850.
Excerpt from an article treating the different meanings given by the Indian for "Mississippi" and "Niagara".

FOLKSONG

STUDIES

Hudson, Arthur Palmer
"Ballads and Songs from Mississippi." *JAFL* 29:93–194, 1915.

———.
Folksongs of Mississippi and Their Background. Chapel Hill: The University of North Carolina Press, 1936. xii, 321 pp., no music.

———.
Folk Tunes from Mississippi, collected by Arthur Palmer Hudson and edited by George Herzog, Music Research Department. New York: National Play Bureau, Works Progress Administration, Federal Theatre Project, 1937. xxii, 45 pp. (National Play Bureau, publication No. 25).
Melodies without accompaniment, English words.

———.
Specimens of Mississippi Folk-Lore. Ann Arbor: Edwards Brothers, 1928.

Young, S.
"Ballads in Mississippi." *New Republic* 88: 229, (Sept. 30) 1936.

ARRANGEMENTS

————: *Piano*

Mississippi Suite.
Grofè, F.: Schirmer: piano.

RECORDS

Collections

U. S. Library of Congress. Division of Music. Folklore Section.
Mississippi Socio-Musical Study. Alan Lomax and Lewis Jones, in collaboration with Charles S. Johnson and John W. Work of Fisk University. 10–12", and 61–16" records. 1942.
AAFS–LC

NORTH CAROLINA

FOLKLORE

BIBLIOGRAPHY

Historical Commission
Handbook of County Records Deposited with the North Carolina Historical Commission . . . Raleigh: Edwards & Broughton Printing Co., 1925. 45 pp., illus.

Historical Records Survey
Guide to the Manuscript Collections in the Archives of the North Carolina Historical Commission. Prepared by the North Carolina Historical Records Survey Project, Division of Community Service Programs, Works Progress Administration. Raleigh: The North Carolina Historical Commission, 1942. v. 216 pp.

———.
The Historical Records of North Carolina. Prepared by the Historical Records Survey of the Works Progess Administration. Raleigh: The North Carolina Historical Commission, 1938.

———.
Inventory of the State Archives of North Carolina. Prepared by the North Carolina Historical Records Survey Project, . . . Work Projects Administration. Raleigh: The North Carolina Historical Records Survey Project, 1939.

Hussey, Minnie Middleton
North Carolina Folklore: A Bibliography compiled by Minnie Middleton Hussey, May, 1930. Issued by the North Carolina Library Commission, vol. 7 (No. 12) Sept. 1930, North Carolina College for Women, Greensboro, N. C.

McMurtrie, Douglas Crawford
"A Bibliography of North Carolina Imprints, 1761–1800." *North Carolina Historical Review* 13:47–86, 143–166, 219–254, 1936. illus.

Weeks, Stephen Beauregard
A Select Bibliography of North Carolina. List of books for schools, libraries and amateurs. Raleigh, N. C.: North Carolina Library Commission, 1913. 23 pp.

———.
The Weeks Collection of Caroliniana. Raleigh: E. M. Uzzell & Co., 1907. 31 pp.

PERIODICALS

The North Carolina Historical Review. vol. 1, 1924 —. Raleigh, North Carolina Historical Commission. Quarterly.

GENERAL STUDIES AND COLLECTIONS

Arthur, John Preston
Western North Carolina; a history (from 1730 to 1913). Raleigh, N. C.: Edwards & Broughton Printing Co., 1914. 710 pp. incl. ports.

Attmore, William
Journal of a Tour to North Carolina, 1787. Chapel Hill: The University, 1922.

Brickell, John
The Natural History of North Carolina. With an account of the trade, manners, and customs of the Christian and Indian inhabitants. Illustrated with copper-plates, whereon are curiously engraved the map of the country, several strange beasts, birds, fishes, snakes, insects, trees, and plants, etc. Dublin: Printed by James Carson, 1737. (Raleigh: Reprinted by authority of the Trustees of the Public Libraries, 1911). xiv, 417 pp., illus.

Brown, Frank C.
"North Carolina Folklore Society." *JAFL* 56: 178–179, 1943.

Cheshire, Joseph Blount
Nonnulla; Memories, Stories, Traditions, More or Less Authentic. Chapel Hill: The University of North Carolina Press, 1930. xviii, 255 pp. "A cross-section of North Carolina life."—Foreword.

Cobb, Lucy M.
"Drama in North Carolina." *Southern Literary Messenger* (Richmond, Va.) 2:228–235, 1940 (April).

Daniels, Jonathan
Tar Heels. A Portrait of North Carolina. New York: Dodd, Mead and Co., 1941.

Ericson, Eston Everett
"Folklore and Folkway in Tarboro." *Free Press* (1824–1850). *SFQ* 5:107–125, 1941.

Fletcher, Inglis
Lusty Wind for Carolina. Indianapolis: The Bobbs-Merrill Co., 1944. 509 pp. Fiction—North Carolinian life.

———.
Men of Albermarle. Indianapolis: The Bobbs-Merrill Company, 1942. 566 pp.

———.
Raleigh's Eden. Indianapolis: The Bobbs-Merrill Company, 1940. 662 pp.

Flinch, Robert
Folk Playmaking in North Carolina; a Survey. With a foreword "Strolling players in Eighteenth Century North Carolina," by Archibald Henderson. n.p.: 1941. xxxvi, 291 pp.

Harris, Mrs. Bernice (Kelly)
Folk Plays of Eastern Carolina. Edited with an introduction by Frederick H. Koch. Illustrated with photographs by Charles Farrell. Chapel Hill: The University of North Carolina Press, 1940. xix, 294 pp., music.

———.
Janey Jeems. New York: Doubleday and Company, 1946. 306 pp.
"Perhaps no writer has caught the idiom of rural Carolina more exactly than Mrs. Harris. Not only the dialogue but the narrative and descriptive passages make use of it." (Nash K. Burger.)

———.
Portulaca. New York: Doubleday, Doran and Company, 1941. iv, 335 pp.
"All her novels, of North Carolina life and folk, are as flavorful and folksy as a fried pork chop, as cool as fresh spring water drunk from a gourd dipper." (Nash K. Burger.)

———.
Sweet Beulah Land. New York: Doubleday, Doran and Co., 1943.
A novel of the North Carolina river country.

Henderson, Archibald
Twenty-Fifth Anniversary; The Carolina Playmakers. The Carolina Play-Book . . . Chapel Hill, 1943. 2 nos., illus.

Hussey, Minnie Middleton
"North Carolina Folklore." *The North Carolina Library* Bulletin, Vol. 7. No. 12, Sept., 1930.

Koch, Frederick Henry, ed.
Carolina Folk-Plays. With an introduction on making a folk theater. Illustrated from photographs of the original productions of the plays. Foreword by Paul Green. New York: H. Holt and Co., 1926–1941. First, second and third series.

———.
"Making a Native Folk Drama." *SFQ* Vol. 1 3:29–35, 1937.

Larkin, Thomas Oliver
Chapters in the Early Life of Thomas Oliver Larkin, Including His Experiences in the Carolinas and Building of the Larkin House at Monterey, from his original manuscripts edited and with an introduction and notes by Robert J. Parker . . . San Francisco, Cal.: California Historical Society, 1939. 77 pp.

Lawson, John
History of Carolina. London: T. Warner and Co., 1718.
Containing the exact description and natural history of the country; together with the present state thereof, and a journal of a thousand miles traveled through several nations of Indians, with account of their customs, etc.! Reprint: Raleigh, N. C., O. H. Perry and Co., 1860. 390 pp.

Lunsford, Bascom Lamar
"Folklore in North Carolina." *Cullowhee State Normal Bulletin,* Vol. 2, No. 4. January 1926. Cullowhee, N. C.

Mooney, J.
"Folklore of the Carolina Mountains." *JAFL* 2:95–104, 1889.

Morley, Margaret Warner
The Carolina Mountains. Boston: Houghton Mifflin Company, 1913. viii, 397 pp., illus.

North Carolina, A Guide to the Old North State (American Guide Series). Compiled and written by the Federal Writers' Project of the Federal Works Agency, WPA, for the State of North Carolina. Chapel Hill: University of North Carolina Press, 1939.

"North Carolina Folklore."
JAFL 32:384–393, 1919.

"North Carolina Mountain White Folklore."
JAFL 2:95–104, 1889; 20:241–250, 1907.

North Carolina. University. Carolina Playmakers.
Folk Plays of the Carolina Playmakers . . . Chapel Hill, N. C.: University of North Carolina, 1923. 2 parts.

———.
Original Folk-Plays of North Carolina. Chapel Hill, N. C.: University of North Carolina, 1923. illus.

———.
Drama In the South; the Carolina Playmakers Coming of Age. Chapel Hill, N. C.: 1940. 14 pp.

Parker, H.
"Folklore of the North Carolina Mountaineers." *JAFL* 20:241–250, 1907.

Parsons, Elsie Clews
"Notes on the Folklore of Guilford County, N. C." *JAFL* 30:201–208, 1917.

Rockwell, Ethel Theodora
Children of Old Carolina. An historical pageant of North Carolina for children. Chapel Hill: The University of North Carolina Press, 1925. 63 pp.

Schaw, Janet
Journal of a Lady of Quality, Being the Narrative of a Journey from Scotland to the West Indies, North Carolina and Portugal, in the Years 1774 to 1776 . . . New Haven: Yale University Press, 1921. 341 pp.

Shaffer, Edward Terry H.
Carolina Gardens. New York: Huntington Press, 1937.
"The history, romance, and tradition of many gardens of two states through more than two centuries."

Sharpe, Bill
Tar on My Heels, a press agent's notebook. Illus. Winston-Salem: The Tar Heels, 1946. 229 pp.

Sheppard, Muriel E.
Cabins in the Laurel. Chapel Hill: University of North Carolina Press, 1935.

"Skitt" (H. E. Taliaferro)
Fisher's River (North Carolina) Scenes and Characters. New York: Harper and Bros., 1859.

Sprunt, James
Chronicles of the Cape Fear River. Raleigh: Edwards and Broughton Printing Co., 1914.

Thornborough, Laura
The Great Smokey Mountains. New York: Thomas Y. Crowell Co., 1937.

Walser, Richard
North Carolina in the Short Story. Chapel Hill, N. C.: University of North Carolina Press, 1948.
Fifteen tales that portray the North Carolina scene.

Warner, Charles Dudley
On Horseback. A Tour in Virginia, North Carolina and Tennessee. With notes of travel in Mexico and California. Boston: Houghton Mifflin and Co., 1888. 331 pp.

Wilson, Peter Mitchell
Southern Exposure. Chapel Hill: The University of North Carolina Press, 1927. 197 pp.

Zeigler, Wilbur Gleason
The Heart of the Alleghanies; or Western North Carolina; comprising its topography, history, resources, people, narratives, incidents, and pictures of travel, adventures in hunting and fishing and legends of its wildernesses. Raleigh, N. C.: A. Williams & Co., 1883. 386 pp., illus.

FOLKTALES—LEGENDS

Albertson, Catherine Seyton
Legends of the Dunes of Dare . . . Raleigh, N. C.: Capital Printing Company, 1936. 22 pp., illus.
Includes a traditional account of the death of Theodosia Burr Alston.

———.
Roanoke Island in History and Legend. No place, no publisher, no date, 26 pp., 5 pl. 1st printing, March 1934, 2nd printing, August 1936, 3rd printing, June 1939.

———.
Wings Over Kill Devil, and Legends of the Dunes of Dare. No place, no publ., no date, 37 pp., 5 illus., 2 pl.

Boggs, Ralph Steele
"North Carolina Folktales Current in the 1820's." *JAFL* 47:269–289, 1934.

———.
"North Carolina White Folk Tales and Riddles." *JAFL* 47:289–329, 1934.

———.
"Running Down the Fool Killer." *TFSP* 14:169–173, 1938.

Chase, Richard
"Jack and the Fire Dragaman." *SFQ* 5:151–155, 1941.
A tale from Beech Creek.

———.
"Jack's Hunting Trip." *SFQ* 2 (No. 3):145–149, 1938.

———.
The Jack Tales: Told by R. M. Ward and His Kindred in the Beech Mountain Section of Western North Carolina and by other Descendants of Council Harmon (1803–1896) Elsewhere in the Southern Mountains with Three Tales from Wise County, Va. Set down from these sources and edited by Richard Chase. With an appendix compiled by Herbert Halpert. Illustrated by Berkeley Williams, Jr. Boston: Houghton Mifflin Co., 1943. xii, 201 pp.

———.
"The Lion and the Unicorn" (the Jack Tales, No. 2). *SFQ* 1 (No. 4):15–21, 1937.

———.
"The Origin of the Jack Tales." *SFQ* 3:187–191, 1939.

————, and Kay
"Jack and the Bean Tree." *SFQ* 2 (No. 4):
199–203, 1938.

————.
"Lucky Jack" the Jack Tales No. 5). *SFQ* 3:
21–24, 1939.

Cobb, Lucy M., and Hicks, Mary A.
Animal Tales from the Old North State. Illus.
by Inez Hogan. New York: E. P. Dutton and
Co., 1938. 200 pp.

Edmunds, Pocahontas Wight
*Land of Sand; Legends of the North Carolina
Coast.* Drawing by Mary Moreland Junkin.
Richmond, Va.: Garrett and Massie, 1941.
viii, 35 pp., illus.

Hendricks, W. C., ed.
Bundle of Troubles and Other Tarheel Tales.
By Workers of the Writers' Project of the
Works Projects Administration in the State
of North Carolina. Durham, N. C.: Duke Uni-
versity Press, 1943. ix, 206 pp.
  37 stories selected from 200 folk sources in
  North Carolina.

Heyward, Du Bose, and Allen, H.
Carolina Chansons. New York: The Macmil-
lan Co., 1922. 131 pp.
  Legends of the Low Country.

Parsons, Elsie Clews
"Tales from Guilford County, N. C." *JAFL*
30:168–200, 1917.

Sprunt, James
Tales and Traditions of the Lower Cape Fear.
Wilmington: Le Gwin Bros., 1896.

Taylor, George C.
"The Miller and the Devil." *TFSP* 14:251–252,
1938.
  A folk tale.

CUSTOMS, BELIEFS, WITCHCRAFT

Cross, T. P.
"Witchcraft in North Carolina." *Studies in
Philology* (University of North Carolina) 16:
217–287.

Ericson, Eston Everett
"Madstones in North Carolina." *Folklore* (London) 49:165–166, 1938.

Hoke, N. C.
"Folk Custom and Folk Belief in North Carolina." *JAFL* 5:113–120, 1892; 20:24, 1907.

McAtee, W. L.
"Bird Folklore from Roanoke Island, North
Carolina." *JAFL* 60:86–87, 1947.

RIDDLES

Boggs, Ralph S.
"North Carolina White Folk Tales and Riddles." *JAFL* 47:289–329, 1934.

Carter, Isabel Gordon
"Mountain White Riddles." *JAFL* 47:76–81,
1934.

Taylor, Archer
"A Riddle of Moving-Spring." *SFQ* 8:23–27,
1944.
  A North Carolinian riddle is related to its classical origin.

SPEECH

Buxbaum, Katherine
"Heard in North Carolina." *AS* 10(No. 2):156–
157, 1935.

Kephart, Horace
"A Word-List from the Mountains of Western
North Carolina." *Dialect Notes* 4(Part 6):407–
419, 1917.

Smith, C. Alphonso
"Dialect in Eastern Virginia and Western
North Carolina." *Dialect Notes* 4(Part 2):
167, 1914.

————.
"Word-List from North Carolina." *Dialect
Notes* 4(Part 5):343–344, 1916.

Steadman, J. M., Jr.
"North Carolina Word List." *Dialect Notes* 5
(Part 1):18–21, 1918.

Wilson, George P.
"Three North Carolina Letters Showing Occasional Spelling." *AS* 11(No. 3):223–226, 1936.

PLACE NAMES

Battle, Kemp Plummer
*The Names of the Counties of North Carolina
and The History Involved in Them.* Winston,
N. C.: W. A. Blair, 1888. 38 pp.

"Tar Heels." *AS* 1 (No. 6): 355, 1926.
  An explanation how North Carolina came to be
  called by that name.

Works Progress Administration.
*How They Began: the Story of North Carolina
County, Town, and Other Place Names,* compiled by workers of the WPA Writers' program of the Work projects administration in
the state of North Carolina. New York: Harian
Publ., 1941. 73 pp.

FOLKSONG
GENERAL STUDIES

Asbury, Samuel E.
"There Were Three (Two) Crows." *TFSP* 14:
280–282, 1938.
  Text and melody as learned in North Carolina.

Backus, Emma M.
"Early Songs from North Carolina." *JAFL* 14:
286–294, 1901.

Bascom, L. R.
"Ballads and Songs of Western North Carolina." *JAFL* 22:238–250, 1909.

Brown, Frank C.
"Ballad Literature in North Carolina." In: Reprint from Proceedings and Addresses of the *15th Annual Session of the Literary and Historical Association of North Carolina*, Dec. 1–2, 1914.

————.
"North Carolina Folk Songs, and Their Classification." In: Paper read at 7th Annual Meeting of the *Southeastern Folklore Society* (Gainesville, Fla.), Feb. 14, 1942.

Carter, Isabel Gordon
"Some Songs and Ballads from Tennessee and North Carolina." *JAFL* 46:22–51, 1933.
Text only.

Edmonds, L. W.
"Songs from the Mountains of North Carolina." *JAFL* 6:131–134, 1893.

Gray, M. H.
"Mount Mitchell Gives Up Treasure." In: *Women's Department Club Bulletin*, pp. 2 (Terre Haute, Ind.), Feb. 23, 1931.
An account of ballad collecting in North Carolina.

Henry, Mellinger E., and Matteson, Maurice
"Songs from North Carolina." *SFQ* 5:137–149, 1941.

Lomax, John A.
"Some Ballads of North Carolina." *North Carolina Booklet*, 2:26–42, 1911.

Lunsford, Bascom Lamar
"Folk-Lore in Western North Carolina." *Cullowhee State Normal Bulletin*, vol. 2 (No. 4), Jan. 1926. (Cullowhee, N. C.)

"North Carolina Mountain White Songs." *JAFL* 6:131–134, 1893; 14:286–294, 1901; 22:238–250, 1909.

Sheppard, Muriel Earley
Cabins in the Laurels. Chapel Hill: The University of North Carolina Press, 1935. 313 pp.

Stringfield, Lamar
"Music of the Carolina Mountains." *The Baton* 8 (No. 4):7–8, Feb., 1929.

GAMES—
CHILDREN'S RHYMES

Backus, Emma M.
"An Ancient Game of Courtship from North Carolina." *JAFL* 13:104, 1900.

Fife, Austin E.
"Rope Skipping Rhymes Collected at Greensboro, North Carolina." *JAFL* 59:321–322, 1946.

ARRANGEMENTS

Collections: Voice and Piano

Henry, Mellinger, E., and Matteson, Maurice
Twenty-Nine Beech Mountain Folk-Songs and Ballads, for voice and piano. New York: G. Schirmer, 1936. Set 15.

Bartholomew, Marshall, and Wetmore, Susannah
Mountain Songs of North Carolina. New York: G. Schirmer, Inc., 1926.
Arrangements for voice and piano.

Stringfield, Lamar
Eight North Carolina Mountain Ballads. New York: G. Schirmer, Inc.

————: *Unison*

"Grandma Grunts."
Bartholomew, M.: Schirmer: Unison.

"The Wedding of the Duck."
Bartholomew, M.: Schirmer: Unison.

————: *Female Voices*

"Billy Boy."
Treharne, Bryceson: Willis: SA.

"Down in the Forest."
Niles-Brant: Schirmer: SSA, a cap.

————: *Male Voices*

"Grandma Grunts."
Bartholomew, M.: Schirmer: TTBB, a cap.

"Sweet Willie."
Malin, D.: Birchard: TTBB.

————: *Mixed Voices*

"Down in the Forest."
Niles-Brant: Schirmer: SATB, a cap.

————: *Orchestra*

Carolina Suite.
Hier, Ethel Glenn: MS: Orchestra.

RECORDS

The South (North Carolina). Durham, N. C.: Duke University.

U. S. Library of Congress. Division of Music. Folklore Section.
North Carolina Folk Songs. Frank C. Brown, collector. 80 records.   AAFS–LC

SOUTH CAROLINA

FOLKLORE

Charleston Library Society.
A Catalogue of Portraits, Books, Pamphlets, Maps and Manuscripts Presented to the Charleston Library Society, May 12, 1906, by Hon. Wm. Ashmead Courtenay. Columbia, S. C.: Privately Printed, 1908. 148 pp.

Hendley, Kathryn
South Carolina Today; a selected bibliography. New York: 1936. iii, 17 numb. (Columbia University School of Library, typewritten).

Historical Records Survey.
Inventory of the County Archives of South Carolina. Prepared by the Historical Records Survey, Division of Women's and Professional Projects, Works Progress Administration. Columbia, S. C., 1937.

PERIODICALS

The South Carolina Historical and Genealogical Magazine. Published quarterly by the South Carolina Historical Society, I — Jan. 1900. Printed for the Society by Walker, Evans, and Cogswell Co., Charleston, S. C.

South Carolina Speech Bulletin. Published by South Carolina Speech Association. Ed., John Walker McCain, Winthrop College, Rock Hill, S. C. May 1939, I No. 1.

GENERAL STUDIES AND COLLECTIONS

Allan, Glenn
Little Sorrowful. New York: Samuel Curl, 1947. 256 pp.
"The people of Little Sorrowful-cracker-barrel philosophers, happy-go-lucky shad fishermen and their alternately nagging and loving wives, wild bucks and purty gals—are quaint, folksy and free-wheeling." (N. K. Burger.)

De Saussure, Mrs. Nancy (Bostick)
Old Plantation Days; being recollections of Southern life before the Civil War. New York: Duffield and Co., 1909. 123 pp.

Esterby, J. H.
The South Carolina Rice Plantation. Chicago: University of Chicago Press, 1945. 478 pp., map, index.

"Folk-Lore from St. Helena, South Carolina." *JAFL* 38:217, 1925.

Johnson, Guy B.
Folk Culture in St. Helena Island. Chapel Hill, N. C.: University of North Carolina Press, 1930.

Middleton, Alicia Hopton
Life in Carolina and New England During the Nineteenth Century, as illustrated by reminiscences and letters of the Middleton family of Charleston, South Carolina, and of the De Wolf family of Bristol, Rhode Island. Bristol, R. I.: Privately Printed, 1929. xii, 233 pp., illus.
De Wolf and Hopton legends.

Molloy, Robert
Charleston: A Gracious Heritage. Illustrated by E. H. Suydam. New York: D. Appleton-Century Company, 1947. 311 pp.
Although the material is presented in informal sequence, the author manages to get in a great deal of amusing lore and legend.

Mooney, J.
"Folklore of the Carolina Mountains." *JAFL* 2:95–104, 1889.

Palmetto Pioneers: Six Stories of Early South Carolinians. (American Guide Series.) Compiled by the Federal Writers' Project, of the Works Progress Administration. The Division of Adult Education, State Department of Education, South Carolina, 1937.

Neilson, Peter
The Life and Adventure of Zamba, an African Negro King, and His Experience of Slavery in South Carolina. Written by Himself. Corrected and arranged by Peter Neilson. London: Smith, Elder and Co., 1847. xx, 258 pp.

Pinckney, Josephine
Great Mischief. New York: The Viking Press, 1948. 247 pp.
A novel of Charleston life against a background of a mad, amusing procession of supernatural events, witchcraft, and magic.

Robertson, Ben
Red Hills and Cotton; An Up-Country Memory. New York: Alfred A. Knopf, 1942. 296 pp.
"Woven like an old quilt, the book gives a personal pattern of kinfolk, by the Blue Ridge in Carolina—a picture of people and their ways." (Rosemary Benet.)

————.
Travelers Rest. Clemson, S. C.: The Cottonfield Publishers, 1938.
His characters speak the folk speech of the natives.

Schoolcraft, Mary
The Black Gauntlet. A tale of plantation life in South Carolina. Philadelphia: J. B. Lippincott and Co., 1860. x, 569 pp.

Siler, Margaret R.
Cherokee Indian Lore, and Smoky Mt. Stories. Bryson City: Bryson City Times, N. C., 1938. Pamphlet.

Smiley, P.
"Folklore from Virginia, South Carolina, Georgia, Alabama, and Florida." *JAFL* 32: 357–383, 1919.

Smith, Alice Ravenel Huger
A Carolina Rice Plantation of the Fifties; 30 paintings in watercolour by Alice R. Huger Smith, narrative by Herbert Ravenell Sass, with chapters from the unpublished memoirs of D. E. Huger Smith. New York: W. Morrow and Company, 1936. xii, 97 pp.

Smith, Reed
"South Carolina Folklore Society." *JAFL* 56: 184–185, 1943.

Smythe, Augustine T., Sass, Herbert Ravenal, and others
The Carolina Low Country. New York: The Macmillan Co., 1931.
Narrative and description of Charleston plantation life, Negro life, Negro spirituals, words and music.

South Carolina, A Guide to the Palmetto State.
(American Guide Series.) Compiled by the
workers of the Federal Writers' Program of
the Works Projects Administration for the
State of South Carolina. New York: Oxford
U. Press, 1941.

Taylor, Rosser Howard
Ante-Bellum South Carolina; a Social and
Cultural History. Chapel Hill: The University
of North Carolina Press, 1942. ix, 201 pp.

Wauchope, George Armstrong
Writers of South Carolina. Columbia: The
State Co., 1910.

FOLKTALES—LEGENDS

Bennett, John
"Folktales from Old Charleston." *Yale Review* 32 (n.s.) 721–740, 1943.

————.
The Doctor to the Dead. Grotesque Legends
and Folk-Tales of Old Charleston. New York:
Rinehart and Company, 1946. xv, 260 pp.

————.
Madame Margot; a grotesque legend of old
Charleston. New York: The Century Co., 1921.
110 pp.

Lee, F. H., ed.
Folk Tales of All Nations. New York: Tudor
Publishing Company, 1946. 947 pp.
South Carolina Tales, pp. 106–111.

Parsons, Elsie Clews
Folk Tales of the Sea Islands, South Carolina.
Memoirs of the American Folklore Society, No.
16. Philadelphia: The American Folklore Society, 1923. 218 pp.

South Carolina Folk Tales: Stories of Animals
and Supernatural Beings. Compiled by workers of the Writers' Program of Works Progress
Administration. Bulletin of the University of
South Carolina. Columbia, S. C.: 1941. xi,
122 pp.
"The collection is composed of thirty-three animal stories recorded in the familiar 'Uncle
Remus,' type Negro and thirty-three stories of the
supernatural, nineteen of which are recorded in
this type dialect, six in standard English, and
those remaining partly in one and partly in the
other." (Adams.)

Stewart, S. E.
"Seven Folk Tales from the Sea Islands, S. C."
JAFL 32:394–396, 1919.

Taylor, George C.
"The Miller and the Devil." *TFSP* 14:251–252,
1938.
A folk tale.

SUPERSTITIONS—FOLK MEDICINE

Fitchett, E. H.
"Superstitions in South Carolina." *Crisis* 43:
360–361, 370, 1936.
A list of 40 health superstitions and sayings.

Hawkins, John
"Magical Medical Practice in South Carolina." *Popular Science Monthly* 70:165–174,
1907.

Waring, M. A.
"Superstitions from South Carolina." *JAFL* 8:
251–252, 1895.

PROVERBS—RIDDLES

Bradley, F. W.
"South Carolina Proverbs." *SFQ* I (No. 1):57–
104, 1937.

SPEECH

Parler, Mary Celestia
"Word List from Wedgefield, South Carolina."
Dialect Notes 6 (Part 2):79–85, 1930.

Primer, Sylvester
"Word-List from South Carolina." *Dialect
Notes* 1 (Part 2):57–59.
Mainly from Charleston.

Smith, Reed
"Gullah." *Bulletin No. 190, of the University
of South Carolina,* (Nov. 1) 1926. (Columbia,
S. C.)

"Word List from South Carolina." *Dialect Notes*
4 (Part 5): 344, 1916.
Terms noted from usage at Charleston.

PLACE NAMES

Federal Writers' Project
Palmetto Place Names. Compiled by workers
of the Writers' program of the Works Projects
Administration in the state of South Carolina.
Columbia: n.p., 1941. 158 pp., bibl.

CHILDREN'S GAMES

McGhee, Z.
"A Study in the Play Life of Some South Carolina Children." *Pedagogical Seminary* (Worcester) 7:451–478, 1900.

FOLKSONG

GENERAL STUDIES AND COLLECTIONS

Pound, Louise
"South Carolina Ballads." *JAFL* 42:76, 1929.
A review.

Smith, Reed, coll. and ed.
South Carolina Ballads, with a study of the
traditional ballad today. Cambridge: Harvard
University Press, 1928. x, 174 pp., music, bibl.

————.
The Traditional Ballad and Its South Carolina Survivals. Bulletin of the University of
South Carolina, No. 162. Columbia, S. C.: University of South Carolina, Extension Division,
1925. 124 pp., illus., music.

TENNESSEE

FOLKLORE

BIBLIOGRAPHY

Beasley, Gladys, comp.
Tennessee Through the Printed Page; a Classified List of Materials Relating to Tennessee for School Libraries, Rev. ed. Nashville, Tenn.: Nashville Public Schools, School Library Division, 1943. 32 pp.

Lawson McGhee Library. Knoxville, Tenn.
Calvin Morgan McClung Historical Collection of Books, Pamphlets, Manuscripts, Pictures and Maps Relating to Early Western Travel and the History and Genealogy of Tennessee and other Southern States. Presented to Lawson McGhee Library by Mrs. Calvin M. McClung. Knoxville, Tenn.: Knoxville Lithographing Co., 1921. 192 pp.

PERIODICALS

The American Historical Magazine and Tennessee Historical Society Quarterly. v. 1–9, Jan. 1896–Oct. 1904. Nashville, Tenn.

Tennessee Folklore Society Bulletin. 1–14 (1935–1943). Dorothy Horne, Editor.

Tennessee Historical Magazine. v. 1–9, March 1915–Jan. 1926. v. 10, 1937. Ser. 2, v. 1–3, Oct. 1930–Jan. 1937. Nashville, Tenn. 1915–1937.

Tennessee Historical Quarterly. v. 1–6; March 1942—Dec. 1947. Nashville.

GENERAL STUDIES AND COLLECTIONS

Allison, John
Dropped Stitches in Tennessee History. Nashville: Marshall and Bruce Co., 1897. 152 pp., front plates.

Buchanan, Annabel Morris
"A Folk Festival Above the Clouds." (White Top Folk Festival.) *Holland's Magazine,* Dallas, Texas, August, 1935.

Carr, John
Early Times in Middle Tennessee. Nashville: Published for E. Carr, by E. Stevenson and F. A. Owen, 1857.

Carter, Hodding
The Lower Mississippi. The Rivers of America Series. Illustrated by John McCrady. New York: Farrar and Rinehart, 1942. x, 467 pp., illus.
"The Old Cabin Home," words and music, pp. 441. Selected bibliography, pp. 443–451.

Davidson, Donald
The Tennessee. The Rivers of America Series. Illustrated by Mrs. Davidson. New York: Rinehart and Company, 1946.

Hallum, John
The Diary of an Old Lawyer; or Scenes Behind the Curtain. Nashville, Tenn.: Southwestern Publishing House, 18895. xxviii, 458 pp.

Hamilton, Harry
River Song. Indianapolis: Bobbs-Merrill, 1945. 242 pp.
A novel about Tennessee people—"it is a fresh treatment of a Southern locale in a healthy and refreshing manner." (Haldeen Braddy.)

Ingraham, Joseph Holt, ed.
The Sunny South; or, The Southerner at Home, Embracing Five Years' Experience of a Northern Governess in the Land of the Sugar and the Cotton. Philadelphia: G. G. Evans, 1860. 526 pp.

Kirkland, Edwin C.
"Tennessee Folklore Society." *JAFL* 56:185–186, 1943.

Lewis, T. M. N.
"Early Chapters of Tennessee." *TSFB* 8:27–53, 1942.

McIlwaine, Shields
Memphis Down in Dixie. New York: E. P. Dutton and Co., 1948. 400 pp.
The third volume of the *Society in America Series* is a mine of anecdote, romance and history.

Moffat, A.
"The Mountaineers of Middle Tennessee." *JAFL* 4:314–320, 1891.

Moore, John Trotwood
Old Mistis, and Other Songs and Stories from Tennessee. Nashville; Cokesbury Press, 1925. vii, 358 pp.

Read, Opie
The Waters of Caney Fork; a Romance of Tennessee. Chicago: Rand, McNally & Company, 1898. 287 pp.

Roark, Eldon
Memphis Bragabouts: Characters I Have Met. Drawings by F. L. Miller. New York: Whittlesey House, 1945. 224 pp., illus.

Scott, Evelyn
Background in Tennessee. New York: R. M. McBride and Co., 1937. 302 pp.

Tennessee, a Guide to the State. (American Guide Series.) Compiled and written by the Federal Writers' Project of the Works Progress Administration for the State of Tennessee. New York: The Viking Press, 1939.

Williams, Joseph S.
Old Times in West Tennessee. Reminiscences — Semi-Historic — of Pioneer Life and the Early Emigrant Settlers in the big Hatchie Country, by a Descendant of One of the First Settlers (Joseph S. Williams). Memphis: W. G. Cheeney, Printer and Publisher, 1873. As reported by a correspondent of *The Missouri Republican.*
Also contains Davy Crockett exploits.

Williams, Samuel Cole
Early Travels in the Tennessee Country, 1540–1800; with introductions, annotations and index. Johnson City, Tenn.: The Watauga Press, 1928. xi, 540 pp., illus.

FOLKTALES—LEGENDS

Anderson, Geneva
"Tennessee Tall Tales." *TFSB* 5:51–65, 1939.

Aswell, James R., and others
God Bless the Devil! Liars' Bench Tales, by James R. Aswell, Julia Willhart, Jennette Edwards, E. E. Miller, Lena E. Lipscomb of the Tennessee Writers' Project. Chapel Hill: University of North Carolina Press, 1940. xi, 254 pp., illus.

Bandy, Lewis David
"Witchcraft and Divination in Macon County." *TFSB* 9(No. 2):1–13, 1943.
Fourteen legends of witches and haunted houses.

Bell, Charles Bailey, M. D.
The Bell Witch, a Mysterious Spirit. Nashville: Lark Bindery, 1934. 228 pp.

Hudson, Arthur P., and McCarter, Pete Kyle
"The Bell Witch of Tennessee and Mississippi." *JAFL* 47:22–45, 1934.

Ingram, M. V.
An Authenticated History of the Famous Bell Witch. The Wonder of the 19th Century, and Unexplained Phenomenon of the Christian Era. The Mysterious Talking Goblin that Terrorized the West End of Robertson County, Tennessee, Tormenting John Bell to His Death. The Story of Betsy Bell, Her Lover and the Haunting Sphinx. Clarksville, Tenn.: W. P. Titus, 1894. 316 pp.

Miller, Edward
Sven, the Hundred Proof Irishman. In: *Manuscripts of the Federal Writers' Project of the Works Progress Administration for the State of Tennessee.*

Miller, Harriet Parks
The Bell Witch of Middle Tennessee. Clarksville, Tennessee. 1930.
A folk legend also known in Mississippi.

Moore, John Trotwood
Songs and Stories from Tennessee. Chicago: J. C. Bauer, 1897.

Parks, Edd Winfield
Long Hunter: The Story of Big-Foot Spencer. New York: Farrar and Rinehart and Co., 1942.
The hero of the Tennessee frontier whose exploits have become almost legendary.

Taylor, Robert L.
Echoes, Centennial and Other Notable Speeches, Lectures, and Stories. Nashville, Tenn.: S. B. Williamson and Co., 1899.
Abounds in humor.

BELIEFS AND SUPERSTITIONS

Anderson, U.
"A Comparative Study of Some of the Older Beliefs and Usages of East Tennessee." *TFSB* 3:1–7, 1937.

Carter, Roland D.
"Mountain Superstitions." *TFSB* 10:1–6, 1944.
Tennessee Mt. beliefs about the moon, bodily ills and cures.

Farr, T. J.
"Middle Tennessee Folk Beliefs Concerning Love and Marriage." *SFQ* 2(No. 3):165–174, 1938.

———.
"Riddles and Superstitions of Middle Tennessee." *JAFL* 48:318–337, 1935.

———.
"Tennessee Folk Belief Concerning Children." *JAFL* 52:112–116, 1939.

McGlasson, Cleo
"Superstitions and Folk Beliefs of Overton County." *TFSB* 7:(No. 2)13–27, 1941.

Wiltse, H. M.
"Superstitions of the South" (White). *JAFL* 14:204–208, 1901.

PROVERBS—RIDDLES

Blair, Marion E.
"The Prevalence of Older English Proverbs in Blount County, Tennessee." *TFSB* 4:1–24, 1938.

Carter, Isabel Gordon
"Mountain White Riddles." *JAFL* 47:76–81, 1934.

Farr, T. J.
"Riddles and Superstitions of Middle Tennessee." *JAFL* 48:318–337, 1935.

———.
"Riddles of Middle Tennessee." *TFSB* 1 (No. 3), 1935.

Redfield, W. A.
"A Collection of Middle Tennessee Riddles." *SFQ* 1(No. 3):35–51, 1937.

SPEECH

Bewley, Irene
"Picturesque Speech." *TFSB* 9:4, 1943.

Brown, Calvin S.
"Word List from Tennessee." *Dialect Notes* 4 (Part 5):345–346, 1916.

Darnell, H. J., and Rall, E. E., and others
"Terms from Tennessee." *Dialect Notes* 4 (Part 1):58, 1913.

Edson, H. A., and Fairchild, E. M.
"Tennessee Mountain Word-List." *Dialect Notes* 1(Part 8):370–377.

Farr, T. J.
"Folk Speech of Middle Tennessee." *AS* 11
(No. 3):275–276, 1936.

————.
"More Tennessee Expressions." *AS* 15:446–
448, 1940.

————.
"The Language of the Tennessee Mountain
Regions." *AS* 14:89–92, 1939.

Neitzel, Stuart
"Tennessee Expressions." *AS* 1(No. 4):373,
1936.

"Picturesque Speech." *TFSB* 10:10, 1944.

Pollard, Mary O.
"Terms from the Tennessee Mountains." *Dialect Notes* 4(Part 2):242–243, 1915.

Smith, Rebecca W.
"A Tennessean's Pronunciation in 1841." *AS*
9(No. 4):262–263, 1934.

PLACE NAMES

Fink, Paul M.
"Some East Tennessee Place Names." *TFSB*
7(Nos. 3–4):40–50, 1941.

McWhorter, A. W.
"Classical Place Names in Tennessee." *Word
Study* 9(No. 2):7–8, 1933.

FOLK MEDICINE

Carter, Roland D.
"Mountain Superstitions." *TFSB* 10:1–6, 1944.
Tennessee Mt. beliefs about the moon, bodily ills,
and cures.

Conwell, Edward L.
"Tennessee Remedies." *JAFL* 46:89–90, 1933.

Rogers, E. G.
Early Folk Medical Practices in Tennessee
Murfreesboro, Tenn.: Mid-South Publ. Co.,
1941. 67 pp.

FOODS

Old-Time Tennessee Recipes. New York: *Greenberg: Publisher,* 1946. 300 pp., illus.
337 recipes handed down from generation to
generation.

Pendleton, Charles S.
"Illicit Whiskey-Making." *TFSB* 12(No. 1):
1–16, 1946.

WEATHER LORE

Carter, Roland D.
"Mountain Superstitions." *TFSB* 10:1–6, 1944.
Tennessee Mt. beliefs about the moon, bodily
ills, and cures.

Wells, J. C.
"Weather and Moon Superstitions in Tennessee." *JAFL* 6:298–300, 1893.

FOLKSONG

GENERAL STUDIES AND COLLECTIONS

Anderson, Geneva
"A Collection of Ballads and Songs From East
Tennessee." *TFSB* 2(No. 3), 1936.

————.
"Additional English and Scottish Ballads
Found in East Tennessee." *TFSB* 8:59–78,
1942.
Texts only of fourteen ballads.

Cambiare, Celestin P.
East Tennessee and Western Virginia Mountain Ballads. London: Mitre Press, 1934.

Carter, Hodding
The Lower Mississippi. The Rivers of America Series. Illustrated by John McCrady. New
York: Farrar and Rinehart, 1942. x, 467, illus.
"The Old Cabin Home," words and music, pp.
441.

Carter, Isabel Gordon
"Some Songs and Ballads from Tennessee and
North Carolina." *JAFL* 46:22–51, 1933.
Texts only.

Crawford, Bruce
"Folk Music at White Top." *New Republic* 76:
74–75, (August 30) 1933.

"Dresbach."
"A Musical Tennessee Landlord." *Spirit of the
Times* 16:603, (Feb. 13) 1847.

Jackson, George Pullen
"Old Rabbit." *TFSB* 9(No. 3):3, 1943.
Words and music.

Kirkland, Edwin Capers
"A Check List of the Titles of Tennessee Folk-
songs." *JAFL* 59:423–476, 1946, bibl.
A splendid list. "This check list attempts for the
first time to assemble all the titles of the folk-
songs of Tennessee, which are found not only in
the obvious and well known collections, but also
in these and in sources that one would not ordi-
narily examine for Tennessee material."

————.
"Collecting Ballads and Folk-Songs in Tennessee." *TFSB* 2(No. 2), 1936.

————.
"'Sir Patrick Spens' Found in Tennessee."
SFQ 1 (No. 4):1–3, 1937.

————.
"The effect of oral tradition on 'Robin Hood
and Little John.'" *SFQ* 4:15–21, 1940.
Tennessee variants.

————.
"Welsh Folk-Songs." *TFSB* 9:1–7, 1943.
Words and music of four folksongs from a student of Knoxville, Tennessee, who got them from
her mother's home in Pennsylvania.

————, and M. N.
"Popular Ballads Recorded in Knoxville, Tennessee." *SFQ* 2(No. 2):65–81, 1938.

McDowell, L. L.
Memory Melodies; a collection of folksongs from middle Tennessee. Smithville, Tenn., 1947. 128 pp. Unaccomp. melodies.

———.
Tennessee Folk Songs. Delaware, Ohio: Cooperative Recreation Service, 1939.

Moore, John Trotwood
Songs and Stories from Tennessee. Chicago: J. C. Bauer, 1897.

Smith, C. E.
"Music from the Grass Roots." *Christian Science Monitor,* pp. 8–9, (March 8) 1941. Illus.

Steele, M.
"Mahomet Annexes White Top Mountain." *Musician* 40:9–10, (August) 1935.

Syford, Ethel C.
"A Tennessee Mountain Work Song." (Oh, My Paw He's Lost His Shoe.) *JAFL* 58:157, 1945.
Text only.

"Tennessee Folk-Songs." *JAFL* 27:255–266, 1914.

Wall, Mabelle S.
"Folk Music Echoes from White Top Mountain." *Tempo* 1(No. 10):21–23, (October) 1934.

CHILDREN'S GAMES

Lassiter, Robert
"Games We Played." *TFSB* 12(No. 1):17–22, 1945.

McDowell, Mrs. L. L.
"Games of Long Ago." *TFSB* 10(No. 3):1–4, 1944.
Verses and description of children's games, rimes and riddles of Tennessee.

ARRANGEMENTS

———: *Voice and Piano*

"Tennessee Mountain Morning Hymn."
Gaul, Harvey B.: Galaxy: Sop. Solo.
A folk hymn.

———: *Female Voices*

"Kemo Kimo."
In: H. & M. Auditorium Series, No. 50. Wilson, H. R.: Hall & McCreary: SSA.

"Lazarus."
Reynolds, Gerald: J. Fischer: SSAA.
Tennessee Mountain ballad hymn.

"Lulle-Lullay."
Niles-Brant: Schirmer: SSA, a cap.

———: *Male Voices*

"Kemo Kimo."
In: H. and M. Auditorium Series No. 44. Wilson, H. R. Hall and McCreary: TBB.

———: *Mixed Voices*

"Soldier, Won't You Marry Me?"
In: H. and M. Auditorium Series No. 37. Wilson, H. R.: Hall and McCreary; S-Bar.

"Tennessee Mountain Psalm."
Gaul, Harvey B.: Galaxy: SATB, Bar., Sop. Soli.
An adaptation from the ninety-third Psalm tune.

"The Monkey's Wedding."
C.: Boston Music Co.: SATB.

"The Monkey's Wedding."
Treharne, B.: Willis: SATB.
Humorous song.

———: *String Quartet*

Gaul, Harvey
Tennessee Devil Tunes. New York: J. Fischer and Bros., 1936. String Quartet.

RECORDS

"Who's Gonna Shoe Your Pretty Little Feet?"
Woody Guthrie, Cisco Houston, Vocal Guitar.
ASCH 423–4B

VIRGINIA

FOLKLORE

BIBLIOGRAPHIES

Cappon, Lester Jesse
Bibliography of Virginia Since 1865. University of Virginia: Institute for Research in the Social Sciences, 1930. 900 pp.

Hubbell, Jay Broadus
Virginia Life in Fiction. Dallas: 1922. 79 pp. Bibliography pp. 55–78.

"List of Works in the New York Public Library Relating to Virginia." *New York Public Library. Bulletin* 11:64–83, 99–125, 143–168, 1907.

Swem, Earl Gregg
A Bibliography of Virginia. Richmond: Davis Bottom, 1916–19. 3 parts. (Virginia State Library. Bull. v.8, no. 2–4; v.10, no. 1–4; v.12, no. 1–2)

———.
Virginia Historical Index. Roanoke, Va.: Stone Printing and Manufacturing Company, 1934–36. 2 vols.
Exhaustive and extremely valuable reference books.

Virginia University Library
The Byrd Library, a Collection of Virginiana, in the Library of Virginia, founded on the Alfred Henry Byrd gift; compiled by John S. Patton—with a prefatory note by Robert Lewis Harrison. Charlottesville: The University Press, 1914. 45 pp.

Wynne, Thomas Hicks
Catalogue of the . . . Library Collected by the Late Hon. Thomas H. Wynne, of Richmond, Va. . . . rich in works relating to the History of Virginia, and in the local history of . . . Richmond, Va., . . . Richmond: Richmond Dispatch Steam Presses, 1875. 158 pp.

PERIODICALS

Bulletin of the Virginia Folk-Lore Society. Nos. 1–12, 1913–1924. Arthur Kyle Davis, Jr. Archivist, University of Virginia, Charlottesville, Va.

The Cumberland Empire. v. 1, 1932—. Big Laurel, Va. Quarterly, 1932; Monthly. 1933.

The Virginia Almanack for the Year . . . By Robert Andrews. 1781–1792. Richmond: Printed and sold by J. Dixon & T. Nicolson.

The Virginia Almanack for the Year of our Lord, God . . . 1752–1778. Williamsburg: Printed and sold by William Hunter.

The Virginia Historical Magazine. v. 1, July, 1891—Jan. 1892. Quarterly. Richmond, Va.

The Virginia Magazine of History and Biography, Published Quarterly by the Virginia Historical Society. v. 1, 1893—. Richmond: The Society.

The Virginia Quarterly Review. Virginia University, Charlottesville. April 1925.

GENERAL STUDIES AND COLLECTIONS

Bacon, A. M., and Parsons, E. C.
"Folklore from Elizabeth City County, Virginia." *JAFL* 35:250–327, 1922.

Bagby, George William
The Old Virginia Gentleman, and Other Sketches. Edited with an introduction by Thomas Nelson Page. New York: Charles Scribner's Sons, 1910. 312 pp. Repr. 1911.

Buchanan, Annabel Morris
Adventures in Virginia Folkways, series of 8 articles. In: *Richmond Times Dispatch Sunday Magazine.* Richmond, Va.: May 24 to July 12, 1936.
　Survey of Virginia balladry, folksong, games, dances, sea chanties, folklore, etc., in authentic but popular style, no tunes.

Cabell, James Branch
Let Me Lie, Being in the Main an Ethnological Account of the Remarkable Commonwealth of Virginia and the Making of its History. New York: Farrar, Straus and Co., 1947. xvi, 286 pp.
　Has, among other interesting gleanings in the lore, manners and customs of the Virginians, a chapter—"Myths of the Old Dominion".

Cooke, John Esten
Stories of the Old Dominion, from the Settlement to the End of the Revolution. New York: Harper and Brothers, 1879. 337 pp.

Cordon, Armistead C.
In the Picturesque Shenandoah Valley. Richmond: Garrett and Massie, Inc., 1930.
　Reference to "Bessie Bell and Mary Gray," p. 102.

Davis, Arthur Kyle, Jr.
"Virginia Folklore Society." *JAFL* 56:187–189, 1943.

Federal Writers' Project
Virginia. (American Recreation Series). Compiled by the workers of the WPA Writers' project in the State of Virginia. Sponsored by the Virginia Conservation Commission. Northport, N. Y.: Bacon and Wieck, 1940. 35 pp.

————.
Virginia, a Guide to the Old Dominion State. (American Guide Series.) Compiled by the Workers of the Writers' Program of the W.P.A. in the State of Virginia. New York: Oxford University Press, 1940.

Harriot, Thomas
Narratives of the First English Plantation of Virginia. First printed at London in 1588, now reproduced after De Bry's illustrated edition printed at Frankfort in 1590, the illustrations having been designed in Virginia in 1585 by John White. London: B. Quaritch, 1893, vi, 111 pp. Reprinted with an introductory essay by Randolph G. Adams. Ann Arbor: Edward, 1931.

Hurst, Samuel Need
The Mountains Redeemed; The Romance of the Mountains, a True Story of Life and Love in Southwest Virginia. Interwoven with an exposition of her mountain life and the weird religion of the mountains, embracing scores of humorous, ridiculous, laughable, and tragic stories, episodes, and incidents, and the religious, moral, educational, industrial and political redemption of the mountains.—Illustrated by S. N. Hurst, Jr. Appalachia, Va.: Hurst and Company, 1929. xvii, 384 pp., illus.

Kibler, James Luther
Sketches of One Hundred and Thirty-Three Historic Virginia Landmarks from Cape Henry to Richmond. Richmond: Garret & Nassie, 1929. xi, 141 pp., illus.

Lee, F. W.
"Christmas in Virginia Before the War." *So. Workman* (Hampdon, Va.) 37:686–689, 1908.

————.
"Harvest Time in Old Virginia." *So. Workman* (Hampdon, Va.) 37:566–567, 1908.

Moffat, L. G., and Carrière, J. M.
"A Frenchman Visits Norfolk, Fredericksburg, and Orange County, 1816." *Virginia Magazine of History and Biography* 53 (Nos. 2 and 3): 1945.

Moore, Virginia
Virginia Is a State of Mind. New York: E. P. Dutton and Co., 1942.

Newton, M. M. P.
"Aunt Deborah Goes Visiting; a Sketch from Virginia Life." *JAFL* 4:354–356, 1891.

Niles, Blair
The James. From Iron Gate to the Sea. Rivers of America Series. Illustrated by Edward Shenton. New York: Farrar & Rinehart, 1945. 335 pp.

Nutting, Wallace
Virginia Beautiful. Illustrated by the author with over three hundred pictures of landscapes and dwellings. Garden City. N. Y.: Garden City Publishing Co., 1935. 262 pp., illus.

Patterson, Mrs. Bruce V., ed.
Guide Book of the Virginia Peninsula. Newport News, Va.: Franklin Printing Company, 1936. 94 pp., illus.

"Record of Grace Sherwood's Trial for Witchcraft, in 1705, in Princess Anne County, Virginia." *Virginia Historical Society Collections* 1:69–78, 1833.

Rothery, Agnes Edwards
New Roads in Old Virginia; with illustrations by Alice Acheson. Boston: Houghton Mifflin Company, 1929. viii, 223 pp., illus.

—————.
Virginia, The New Dominion. Illustrated by E. H. Suydam. New York: D. Appleton-Century Co., 1940. xiii, 368 pp., illus.

Royall, William Lawrence
Some Reminiscences. New York: Neale Publishing Co., 1909. 210 pp.

Smiley, P.
"Folklore from Virginia, South Carolina, Georgia, Alabama, and Florida. *JAFL* 32:357–383, 1919.

State Planters' Bank and Trust Co., Richmond, Va.
Roads of Romance in Virginia, From the Mountains to the Sea. Richmond, Va.: State Planters' Bank and Trust Co., 1931. 30 L., illus.

Strother, David Hunter
Virginia Illustrated: Containing a Visit to the Virginian Canaan, and the Adventures of Porte Crayon *(pseud.)* and His Cousins. New York: Harper & Bros., 1857. ix, 300 pp., illus.

Thorburn, Grant
Laurie Todd's Notes on Virginia: with a Chapter on Puritans, Witches and Friends. New York: The Author, 1848. 36 pp.

Verrill, Alpheus Hyatt
Romantic and Historic Virginia. New York: Dodd, Mead & Company, 1935. xvi, 242 pp., illus.

FOLKTALES AND LEGENDS

"Blue Ridge, Virginia Tales." *JAFL* 38:340–374, 1925.

Caperton, Helena Lefey
Legends of Virginia. Richmond: Garrett and Massie, 1931. 74 pp.

Chase, Richard
Jack Tales; told by R. M. Ward and his kindred in the Beech Mountain section of Western North Carolina and by other descendents of Council Harmon (1803–1896) elsewhere in the Southern Mountains; with three tales from Wise County, Virginia, set down from these sources and edited, appendix by Herbert Halpert. Boston, Mass.: Houghton Mifflin, 1943. xii, 201 pp.

Page, Rosewell
Hanover County; its history and legend. Richmond: Garrett and Massie, 1925. 153 pp.

Parsons, E. C.
"Tale and Song from Virginia." *JAFL* 34:125, 1921.

CUSTOMS AND TRADITIONS

Allan, Elizabeth Randolph
A March Past; Reminiscences . . . Richmond, Va.: The Dietz Press, 1938. xxx, 274 pp., illus.

Allan-Olney, Mary
The New Virginians, by the author of 'Junia', etc. Edinburgh: B. Blackwood and Sons. 1880. 2 vols.
An account of the experiences of an English family in Virginia after the Civil War.

Andrews, Marietta (Minnigerode)
Memoirs of a Poor Relation; Being the Story of a Post-War Southern Girl and Her Battle With Destiny. New York: E. P. Dutton & Company, 1927. xiv, 455 pp., illus.

Bagby, George William
The Old Virginian Gentleman and Other Sketches . . . New York: C. Scribner's Sons, 1911.
Much on customs and traditions.

Bradley, Arthur Granville
Other Days; Recollections of Rural England and Old Virginia. 1860–1880. London: Constable & Co., 1913. xi, 427 pp.

—————.
Sketches From Old Virginia. London: Macmillan & Co., 1897. ix, 284 pp., illus.

Bruce, Philip Alexander
Social Life of Virginia in the Seventeenth Century. An Inquiry into the origin of the higher planting class, together with an account of the habits, customs, and diversions of the people. Richmond, Va.: Whitted & Shepperson, 1907. 268 pp., bibl.

Bruce, William Cabell
Below the James; a Plantation Sketch. New York: The Neale Publishing Co., 1918. 157 pp.

Byrd, William
Another Secret Diary of William Byrd of Westover, 1739–1741, With Letters & Literary Exercises, 1696–1726. Edited by Maude H. Woodfin . . . Richmond, Va.: The Dietz Press, 1942. xiv, 490 pp.

——.
The Secret Diary of William Byrd of Westover, 1709–1712, edited by Louis B. Wright and Marion Tinling. Richmond, Va.: The Dietz Press, 1941. xxviii, 622 pp.

Claiborne, John Herbert
Seventy-Five Years in Old Virginia; with some account of the life of the author and some history of the people amongst whom his lot was cast,—their character, their condition, and their conduct before the war, during war and after the war. New York: Neale Publishing Company, 1904. xvi, 360 pp.

Conway, Moncure Daniel
Barons of the Potomack and the Rappahannock. New York: The Grolier Club, 1892. xvii, 290 pp., illus.

Cooke, John Esten
The Virginia Comedians; or, Old Days in the Old Dominion. New York: D. Appleton and Company, 1883. 2 vols.

Durand
A Huguenot Exile in Virginia; or, Voyages of a Frenchman Exiled for His Religion, With a Description of Virginia & Maryland; From the Hague Edition of 1687; with an introduction and notes by Gilbert Chinard. New York: Press of the Pioneers, 1934. 1889 pp., illus.

Earle, Swepson
The Chesapeake Bay Country. Baltimore, Md.: Thomsen-Ellis Company, 1923. 510 pp., illus., bibl.

Fithian, Philip Vickers
Journal & Letters of Philip Vickers Fithian, 1773–1774: A Plantation Tutor of the Old Dominion; edited with an introduction by Hunter Dickinson Farish. Williamsburg, Va.: Colonial Williamsburg, 1943. xiv, 323 pp., illus.
  Princeton University Press issued a two volume edition of Fithian's letters (1767–1774), 1934.

——.
"Journal of Philip Fithian Kept at Nomini Hall, Virginia, 1773–1774." *American Historical Review* 5:290–319, 1900.

Fordham, Elias Pym
Personal Narrative of Travels in Virginia, Maryland, Pennsylvania, Ohio, Indiana, Kentucky, and of a Residence in the Illinois Territory: 1817–1818 . . . Edited by F. A. Ogg. Cleveland: The A. H. Clark Co., 1906. 248 pp.

Goodwin, Maud (Wilder)
The Colonial Cavalier; or Southern Life Before the Revolution; illustrated by Harry Edwards. Boston: Little, Brown & Co., 1897. 316 pp., illus., bibl.

Hall, Granville Davisson
Old Gold. Chicago: The Mayer & Miller Co., 1907. 212 pp.
  On customs, beliefs, and folkways.

Hubbell, Jay Broadus
Virginia Life in Fiction. Dallas, 1922. 79 pp.

Jefferson, Thomas
Notes on the State of Virginia; Written in 1781, Somewhat Corrected and Enlarged in the Winter of 1782, For the Use of a Foreigner of Distinction, in Answer to Certain Queries Proposed by Him. Paris: 1785. 391 pp., illus.

Johnson, Brita Elizabeth
Maher-Shalal-Hash-Baz; or, Rural Life in Old Virginia. Claremont, Va.: S. Olson, 1923. 328 pp.
  A novel using local lore and customs.

Kennon, Elizabeth Beverly, and Sinclair, S. S. S.K.
"Kennon Letters." *Virginia Magazine* 31:185–206, 1923.

Long, Calista Cralle
Journal of Calista Cralle Long; a Diary of a Forty-Two Day Journey, Campbell Co., Va. to Union Co., Ky., Dec. 1836–Jan. 1837. Fayetteville, W. Va.: A. R. Long, 1940. 17 pp.

MacLeod, Anna Mary
The Washington Randolphs and Their Friends; Extracts from the Diary of a Lady of Old Virginia . . . Lynchburg, Va.: J. P. Bell Company, 1915. 189 pp.

McDonald, James
Life in Old Virginia. A description of Virginia, more particularly the Tidewater Section, together with many humorous stories. Edited by J. A. C. Chandler. Norfolk, Va.: The Old Virginia Publishing Co., 1907. vii, 374 pp.

Meade, Julian Rutherford
I Live in Virginia. New York: Longmans, Green and Co., 1935. x, 310 pp.

Mordecai, Samuel
Virginia, Especially Richmond, in By-Gone Days; with a glance at the present; being reminiscences and last words of an old citizen. Richmond: West & Johnson, 1860. xvi, 359 pp.

Orr, Lucinda
Journal of a Young Lady. 1782. Baltimore: J. Murphy and Company, 1871. 56 pp.

Osborne, Joseph Alexander
Williamsburg in Colonial Times. Incidents in the lives of the English colonists in Virginia during the 17th and 18th centuries, as revealed in old documents and files of the Virginia Gazette; introduction by Rev. W. A. R. Goodwin; Illustrated by Elmo Jones. Richmond, Va.: The Dietz Press, 1935. xxii, 196 pp., illus.

Page, Thomas Nelson
The Old Dominion, Her Making and Her Manners. New York: C. Scribner's Sons. 1908. ix, 394 pp.

————.
The Old South; Essays Social and Political. New York: C. Scribner's Sons. 1892. ix, 344 pp.
A great deal on social life and customs in Virginia.

————.
Social Life in Old Virginia Before the War. With illustrations by Misses Cowles. New York: C. Scribner's Sons, 1897. viii, 109 pp., illus.

Pleasants, Sally
Old Virginia Days and Ways . . . Menasha, Wis.: G. Banta Pub. Co., 1916. 165 pp.

Preston, Margaret Junkin
Aunt Dorothy; an Old Virginia Plantation Story. Illustrated. New York: A. D. F. Randolph and Co., 1890. 92 pp., illus.

Randolph, Mary
The Virginia Housewife: or, Methodical Cook. Stereotype ed., with amendments and additions. Baltimore: J. Plaskitt, 1836. xii, 180 pp.

Reniers, Perceval
The Springs of Virginia; Love, Life and Death at the Waters, 1775–1900. Chapel Hill: The University of North Carolina Press, 1941. x, 301 pp., illus., bibl.

Ritson, Anne
A Poetical Picture of America, Being Observations Made, During a Residence of Several Years, at Alexandria and Norfolk in Virginia; Illustrative of the manners and customs of the inhabitants: and interspersed with anecdotes arising from a general intercourse with society in that country, from the Year 1799 to 1807. London: Printed for the Author, 1809. 177 pp.

Rucker, Maude
West Virginia, Her Land, Her People, Her Traditions, Her Resources. New York: W. Neale, 1930. 237 pp., illus.

Selden, John Armistead
The Westover Journal of John A. Selden, esqr., 1858–1862, with an introduction and notes by John Spencer Bassett. Northampton, Mass.: Department of History. Smith College, 1921.

Squires, William Henry Tappey
The Days of Yester-Year in Colony and Commonwealth; A Sketch Book of Virginia. Portsmouth, Va.: Pointcraft Press, 1928. xvi, 301 pp.

Standard, Mary Newton
Colonial Virginia, Its People and Customs. Philadelphia: J. B. Lippincott Co., 1917.

Tucker, George (supposed author)
Letters from Virginia . . . Baltimore: Published by Fielding Lucas, jr., J. Robinson, Printer, 1816. viii, 220 pp.

Wardlaw, Georgia Dickinson
The Old and the Quaint in Virginia. Richmond, Va.: The Dietz Press, 1939. xii, 328 pp., illus.

Wecter, Dixon
The Saga of American Society; A Record of Social Aspiration, 1607–1937. New York: C. Scribner's Sons, 1937. xii, 504 pp., illus., bibl.

Wertenbaker, Thomas J.
Patrician and Plebian in Virginia; or, The Origin and Development of the Social Classes of the Old Dominion. Charlottesville, Va.: The Author, 1910. vi, 239 pp.

Williams, Rebecca
The Vanishing Virginian; with an introduction by Douglas Southall Freeman. New York: E. P. Dutton & Company, 1940. 277 pp.

Wilson, Goodridge
Smyth County History and Traditions. Kingsport, Tenn.: Kingsport Press, 1932. xi, 397 pp.

Wilstach, Paul
Potomac Landings. Photographs by Roger B. Whitman and Others. Garden City, N. Y.: Doubleday, Page & Company, 1921. xii, 376 pp.

————.
Tidewater Virginia. Indianapolis: The Bobbs-Merrill Company, 1929. 326 pp., illus.

RIDDLES

Hench, Atcheson L.
"To Come to Fetch Fire." *JAFL* 52:123–124, 1939.

SPEECH

Bell, W. H.
"A Better Speech for Virginians." *Virginia Journal of Education* 29:236, 1936.

Davis, Arthur Kyle, Jr., and Hill, Archibald A.
"Dialect Notes on Records of Folk Songs from Virginia." *AS* 8 (No. 4):52–56, 1933.

Dingus, L. R.
"A Word List from Virginia." *Dialect Notes* 4 (Part 3):177–193, 1915.

"Dramatic History of Albemarle is Reflected in Quaint Names." *Daily Progress* (Charlottesville, Va.) July 1, 1937, p. 7.

Gerard, William R.
"Some Virginia Indian Words." *AA* 7:222–250, 1905. n.s.

Green, B. W.
Word Book of Virginia Folk-Speech. Richmond: Privately Printed, 1912. 530 pp.
"—it is indispensable to the student of Virginia dialect, especially the dialect of the tidewater section." (C. Alphonso Smith)

Greet, William Cabell
"A Phonographic Expedition to Williamsburg, Virginia." *AS* 6 (No. 3) :161–172, 1931.

―――――, and Meloney, William Brown
"Two Notes on Virginia Speech." *AS* 6 (No. 2) :94–96, 1930.

Laubscher, G. G.
"Terms from Lynchburg, Virginia." *Dialect Notes* 4 (Part 4) :302, 1916.

Man, A. P., Jr.
"Virginia Word-List." *Dialect Notes* 4 (Part 2) :158–160, 1914.

McCutheon, J. Wilson
"Virginia Expressions." *AS* 11 (No. 4) :372–373, 1936.

Shewmake, Edwin F.
"Distinctive Virginia Pronunciation." *AS* 18: 33–38, 1943.

―――――.
English Pronunciation in Virginia. Richmond, Va.: Privately Printed, 1927. University of Virginia Dissertation (1920).

―――――.
"Laws of Pronunciation in Eastern Virginia." *Modern Language Notes* 40:489–492, 1925.

Smith, C. Alphonso
"Dialect in Eastern Virginia and Western North Carolina." *Dialect Notes* 4 (Part 2) : 167, 1914.

Tressider, Argus
"Notes on Virginia Speech." *AS* 16:112–120, 1941.

―――――.
"The Sounds of Virginia Speech." *AS* 18:261–272, 1943.

―――――.
"The Speech of the Shenandoah Valley." *AS* 12 (No. 4) :284–288, 1937.

Walsh, Chad.
"Transcription from Southwest Virginia." *AS* 12 (No. 1) :83, 1937.
    Phonetic transcription of a singing and speaking phonograph record made by a "hill-billy" artist.

Wyllie, John
"Short dictionary of slang, jargon, cant, and popular customs now or formerly current at the University of Virginia." *University of Virginia Alumni News* 24:80–81, 1936.

PLACE NAMES

Long, Charles Massie
Virginia Country Names. Two Hundred and Seventy Years of Virginia History. New York: Neale Publ. Co., 1908. 207 pp.

McJimsey, George Davis
"Topographic Terms in Virginia." *AS* 15:3–39, 149–180, 262–301, 381–420, 1940.

―――――.
Topographic Terms in Virginia. New York: Columbia University Press, 1940. 151 pp., bibl., (*AS* Reprints and Monographs. No. 3).

Robinson, Morgan Poitiaux
Virginia Counties: Those Resulting From Virginia Legislation. Richmond: D. Bottom, 1916. 283 pp., (Virginia. State Library. Bull. v.9, No. 1–3).

Tooker, William W.
"Meaning of Some Indian Names in Virginia." *William and Mary College Quarterly Historical Magazine* 14:62–64. Williamsburg, Va.: 1905.

―――――.
"Some More About Virginia Names." *AA* 7: 524–579, 1905. n.s.

―――――.
"The Powhatan Name for Virginia." *AA* 8: 23–28, 1906, n.s.

FOLKSONG

GENERAL STUDIES AND COLLECTIONS

Broadsides on Virginia, From the Originals in the British Museum and Bodleian Library, Oxford. Boston: 1926. 5 facsims. (*Americana Series;* photostat reproductions by the Massachusetts Historical Society, No. 173)
    Contents: "A Voyage to Virginia; or, The Valiant Soldier's Farewell to His Love"; "The Maydens of London's Brave Adventures"; "The Woman Outwitted"; "The Trappan'd Maiden; or, The Distressed Damsel"; "A Net for a Night-Raven".

Buchanan, Annabel Morris
Adventures in Virginia Folkways. Series of eight articles in Richmond Times Dispatch, Sunday Magazine. Richmond, Va.: (May 24–July 12,) 1936.
    Survey of Virginia balladry, folksong, games, dances, sea chanties, folklore, etc., in authentic but popular style.

―――――.
The Fourth Annual White Top Mountain Festival." *Music Clubs Magazine* 14 (No. 1) :19–20, Sept.–Oct. 1934.

―――――.
"White Top (Va.) Folk Festival." *Fischer Edition News* 11 (No. 1) :6–8, Jan.–Mar., 1935.

Chapell, Louise Watson
Folk-songs of Roanoke and the Albemarle. Morgantown, West Virginia: The Ballad Press, 1939, 203 pp., bibliography, unaccompanied melodies.

Combs, Josiah Henry
Folk-Songs du Midi des États Uni. Paris: Les Presses Universitaires de France, 1925. 230 pp. Bibliography at end of each chapter.

Cox, John Harrington
Folk-Songs from West Virginia. Boston, Mass.: Harvard University Library, Doctor's Dissertation.

———.
Folksongs, Mainly from West Virginia. Introductory essay and supplementary references by Herbert Halpert. Issued by Folksong and Folklore Department. New York: National Service Bureau, Works Progress Administration, Federal Theatre Project, 1939, viii, 88 pp. (National Service Bureau Publication No. 81–S), melodies without accompaniment, English words, 1939.

Davis, Arthur Kyle, Jr.
Traditional Ballads of Virginia. Collected under the auspices of the Virginia Folk-lore Society, edited by Arthur Kyle Davis, Jr. Cambridge, Mass.: Harvard University Press, 1929. xviii, 634 pp.
Ballad music—pp. 547–606. List of references—pp. 17–18.

"English Ballads Transplanted in Virginia."
New York Times Book Review Aug. 3, 1930. pp. 2.

Folk Songs to Sing. Compiled by the Virginia Writers' Project, illustrated by the Virginia Art Project, bound by the School Library Project. Harmonizations by the Virginia Music Project. Sponsored by the Virginia State Board of Education. Richmond, Va.: 1942 (mimeographed) 47 pp.

Jackson, George Pullen
"Ballad Art Revived at White Top Festival."
Musical America 54 (No. 14):8, Sept., 1934.

———.
"The White Top Mountain Folk Festival."
The Musical Leader 65 (No. 8):6, Aug. 24, 1933.

L., T. D.
"Folklore is the Theme of White Top Conference." *Musical America* 56 (No. 14):14, 17, Sept., 1936.

"Mountain Music Festival in Asheville." *Music Clubs Magazine* 14 (No. 1):20, Sept.–Oct. 1934.

Parsons, Elsie Clews
"Tale and Song from Virginia." *JAFL* 34:125, 1921.

Peyton, J. Lewis
History of Augusta County (Va.). Richmond, Va.: 1882. p. 106.
Reference to "Bessy Bell and Mary Gray."

Powell, John
"Virginia Finds Her Folk Music." *Musical Courier*, pp. 5, (April 23), 1932.

Speers, Mary Walker Finely
"Maryland and Virginia Folk-Lore." *JAFL* 26:190–191, 1913.

Virginia Folk-Lore Society. Popular Ballads of Virginia. Boston, Mass.: Harvard University Library, Typed Mss.

Waddell, Joseph A.
Annals of Augusta County (Va.). Richmond, Va.: 1886. pp. 362–364.
Quotation from "Bessy Bell and Mary Gray."

Wall, Mabelle S.
"Folk Music Echoes from White Top Mountain." *Tempo* 1 (No. 10): 21–23, Oct., 1934.

"White Top Folk Festival." *Musical America* 55 (No. 14):12, Sept. 1935.

DANCES

Wilkinson, Winston
"Virginia Dance Tunes." *SFQ* 6:1–10, 1942.
Music of nine tunes.

ARRANGEMENTS

———: *Voice and Piano*

Powell, John, arr.
Five Virginia Folk-Songs, for baritone, (separate or complete). Pretty Sally; The Two Brothers; The Deaf Woman's Courtship; At the Foot of Yonder Mountain; The Rich Old Lady. New York: J. Fischer and Bro., voice and piano.

———: *Female Voices*

"Come All Ye Fair and Tender Ladies." Treharne, B.: Willis: SSA.

"The Fox."
Treharne, B.: Willis: SA.

———: *Mixed Voices*

"Bangam and the Boar."
Treharne, B.: Willis: SATB, a cap.

———: *Piano*

Sonata Virgianesque.
Powell, John: Schirmer: violin, piano.

———: *Orchestra*

A Set of Three.
Powell, John: Schirmer: Symph. Orch.
Virginia folk airs.

At the Fair-Suite.
Powell, John: Schirmer: Chamber orchestra.

From a Loved Past.
Powell, John: Schirmer: Symph. Orch.
Second movement of a violin concerto, based on a Virginia folk tune.

In Old Virginia: Overture.
Powell, John: Schirmer: Symph. Orch.
Southern Country Dance Themes.

RECORDS

"The South" (Virginia).
In the *Archive of Virginia Folk-Lore Society*,
University of Virginia.

"The South" (Virginia and North Carolina).
From the Collection of the late Prof. Dorothy
S. Scarborough.

**U. S. Library of Congress. Division of Music.
Folklore Section.**
American Folksongs Collected in Virginia, by
Richard Chase.   AAFS–LC

WEST VIRGINIA

FOLKLORE

BIBLIOGRAPHY

Archives and History Department. West Virginia.
A Bibliography of West Virginia. Parts I and II. Compiled by Innis C. Davis, state archivist with the assistance of Emily Johnston, librarian, and other members of the staff of the Department of Archives and History. Charleston: Charleston Printing Co., 1939. 143 pp., 392 pp.

Historical Records Survey
Inventory of the County Archives of West Virginia. Prepared by the Historical Records Survey . . . Works Progress Administration. Charleston, W. Va.: The Historical Records Survey, 1937.

PERIODICALS

West Virginia History; Quarterly Magazine, v.1, 1939 — Charleston, W. Va. Issued by the Archives and History Department of West Virginia.

West Virginia Historical Magazine Quarterly. v.1–5, 1901–1905. Published by the West Virginia Historical and Antiquarian Society, Charleston, W. Va.

GENERAL STUDIES AND COLLECTIONS

Barnett, C. S.
Hill Country Wonders. In: *American Stuff;* An Anthology of Prose and Verse by members of the Federal Writers' Project, with sixteen prints by the Federal Art Project. (pp. 53–54). Copyright by the Guilds' Committee for Federal Writers' Publications, Inc. New York: The Viking Press, Inc., 1937.

Callahan, James Morton
History of the Making of Morgantown, West Virginia; a Type Study in Trans-Appalachian Local History. Morgantown, West Virginia: 1926. 330 pp.

Cox, John H.
"West Virginia Folk-Lore Society." *JAFL* 56: 189–190, 1943.

Federal Writers' Project
Folk Studies. Compiled and written by the workers of the Writers' Project, Works Progress Administration in West Virginia. Sponsored by the Education Department of West Virginia, 1940–1941.
Contents: No. 1, 2, 3, Smoke Hole and Its People, 1940; No. 4, My Memory Book, 1940; No. 5, Mountain State Tintypes, 1940; No. 6, Oceana and the Cook Family, 1940; No. 9, Pineville, Where Wyoming Trails Cross, 1940; No. 10, The Bulltown Country, 1940; No. 11, Of Stars and Bars, 1940; No. 12, Sutton-on-the-Elk, 1941.

West Virginia, a Guide to the Mountain State. (American Guide Series). Compiled by the Workers of the Writers' Program of the W.P.A. in the State of West Virginia. New York: Oxford University Press, 1941.

West Virginia. (American Recreation Series). Compiled by Workers of the W. P. A. Writers' Project in the State of West Virginia . . . Northport, N. Y.: Bacon & Wieck. 24 pp.

Historic and Scenic Markers Commission
West Virginia Historic and Scenic Highway Markers. Erected by the State of West Virginia . . . in cooperation with The Works Progress Administration . . . Charleston, W. Va.: Mathews Prg. & Litho. Co., 1937. 247 pp., illus.

Hughes, Josiah
Pioneer West Virginia. Charleston, W. Va.: The Author, 1932. 186 pp.
"Dim sidelights on pioneer families": (pp. 109–123).

Lambert, Oscar Doane
Camps and Firesides West of the Alleghenies. Charleston, W. Va.: West Virginia Publishing Co., 1941. 288 pp.
Much on frontier and pioneer life.

MacCorkle, William A.
The White Sulphur Springs; the Traditions, History, and Social Life of the Greenbrier White Sulphur Springs. New York: Neale Publishing Co., 1916. 410 pp.

Reniers, Perceval, and Ashton, Woodman
The Midland Trail Tour in West Virginia; Being also an account of the old stage coach days on the James River and Kanawha Turnpike. New York: Midland Publications Company, 1926. 31 pp., illus.

Royall, Mrs. Anne
Sketches of History, Life and Manners in the United States. By a Traveler. New Haven, Conn.: Printed for the author, 1826.
"One of America's first newspaperwomen here portrays the lives and customs of early West Virginia residents."

Rucker, Mrs. Maude A., comp.
West Virginia, Her Land, Her People, Her Traditions, Her Resources. New York: W. Neale, 1930.

Schaeffer, John Randolph
Over the Alleghenies by the Northwestern Turnpike, Now the Great Scenic Federal Highway. Strasburg, Va.: 1928. 144 pp., illus.

Thompson, R.
Webster County History-Folklore. From the Earliest Time to the Present. Illustrations, Woodcuts by Fred Thompson. Webster Spring, W. Va.: Star Printers, 1942. 200 pp., illus.

FOLKTALES

Montague, Margaret
Up Eel River. New York: The Macmillan Co., 1928. 225 pp., illus.
Monologues and tales of the West Virginia lumberman, includes tales of Tony Beaver and Paul Bunyan.

Musick, Ruth Ann
"A Snake Story from West Virginia." *JAFL* 60:301, 1947.

WITCHCRAFT

Bayard, Samuel P.
"Witchcraft magic and spirits on the border of Pennsylvania and West Virginia." *JAFL* 51: 47–59, 1938.

Cox, John Harrington, and Ghigo, Francis
"The Witch Bride." *SFQ* 7:203–209, 1943.

MOON LORE

Mockler, W. E.
"Moon Lore from West Virginia." *Folklore* (London) 50:310–314, 1939.

SPEECH

Axley, Lowry
"West Virginia Dialect." *AS* 3 (No. 6):456, 1928.

Pendleton, Paul E.
"How the Wood-Hicks Speak." *Dialect Notes* 6 (Part 2):86–89, 1930.
Observations made in Upshur County, West Virginia.

Woofter, Carey
"Dialect Words and Phrases from West-Central West Virginia." *AS* 2 (No. 8):347–367, 1927.

PLACE NAMES

Chrisman, Lewis H.
"The Origin of Place Names in West Virginia." *West Virginia History* 7 (No. 2):77–88, 1946.

Kenny, Hamill
"The Synthetic Place Names in West Virginia." *AS* 15:39–45, 1940.

———.
West Virginia Place Names. Piedmont, Va.: The Place Name Press, 1946. 768 pp.
Their origin and meaning including nomenclature of the streams and mountains.

FOLKSONG

GENERAL STUDIES AND COLLECTIONS

Cambiaire, Celestin Pierre
East Tennessee and Western Virginia Mountain Ballads. London: The Mitre Press, 1934.

Chappell, L. W.
Folk-Songs of Roanoke and the Albemarle. Morgantown, W. Va.: The Ballard Press, 1939.

Combs, Josiah Henry
Folk-Songs du Midi des États-Unis. Paris: Les Presses Universitaires de France, 1925. 230 pp.
Bibliography at the end of each chapter.

Cox, John Harrington
Folk-Songs, Mainly From West Virginia. Introductory essay and supplementary references by Herbert Halpert. American Folk-Song Publication #5. New York: National Service Bureau, 1939. xiv, 109 pp. melodies without accompaniment.

———.
Folk-Songs from West Virginia. Harvard University Library, Doctor's Dissertation.

Richardson, Anna Davis
"Old Songs from Clarksburg, W. Va. 1918." *JAFL* 32:497–504, 1919.

Wilson, Ann Scott
"Pearl Bryan." *SFQ* 3:15–19, 1939.

ARRANGEMENTS

———: *Choral*

"The Three Farmers."
Treharne, B.: Willis: SAAB, SATB.

THE OZARK MOUNTAINS

FOLKLORE

BIBLIOGRAPHY

Snyder, Robert McClure
Hahatonka in the Ozarks; Historical and Bibliographical Notes. Kansas City, Mo.: 1931. 30 pp.

PERIODICALS

Arcadian Life. Caddo Gap, Arkansas. 1933–1941. Monthly. Edited and published by Otto Ernest Rayburn.

Arcadian Magazine. Eminence, Missouri, 1931–1932. Monthly. Edited and published by Otto Ernest Rayburn.

Ozark Guide. Eureka Springs, Arkansas. Quarterly. 1943–. Otto Ernest Rayburn, editor.

Ozark Life. Kingston, Arkansas, 1925–1930, monthly. Edited and published by Otto Ernest Rayburn.

Rayburn's Ozark Guide 1:5, March–April, 1944.
Content: Ozark Bookshelf 11–14. Ozarkian
Lore and Logic 21–25. Otto Ernest Rayburn,
editor, Lonsdale, Ark.

GENERAL STUDIES AND COLLECTIONS

Arthur, George Clinton
Backwoodsmen, Daring Men of the Ozarks; a
true history of backwoodsmen of the Ozarks,
including the life of Nathaniel (Stub) Borders.
Boston: The Christopher Publishing House,
1940. 99 pp.

Barker, Catherine
Yesterday Today; life in the Ozarks. Caldwell,
Id.: The Caxton Printers, Ltd., 1941. 263 pp.

Bonnell, Clarence
The Illinois Ozarks. Harrisburg, Ill.: Register
Publishing Co., 1946. 150 pp.

Broadfoot, Lennis Leonard
Pioneers of the Ozarks; illustrated by the
author. Caldwell, Id.: The Caxton Printers,
Ltd., 1944. 195 pp., illus.
"Every picture...has been drawn...from life
sittings...The short stories are such as fell from
the lips of the sitters...and have been written
in their own native dialect." Pref.

Dorrance, Ward A.
Three Ozark Streams: Log of the Mocassin
and the Wilma. Richmond, Mo.: The Missour-
ian Press, 1937. 58 pp.
Contents: The Black River, The Jack's Fork, The
Current River.

Drygalski, Erich von
Amerikanische Landschaft; Entstehung und
Entwicklung in Einzelbildern. Ozarkland, von
Rudolf Schottenloher; Kanadische Prärie, von
Max Eichmeier; Florida, von Peter Berger;
Jamaica von A. Wilhelm Küchler; Seattle, von
Homer L. Seeger. Herausgegeben von Erich
von Drygaliski...Berlin: W. de Gruyter &
Co., 1936. viii, 532 pp., illus.
Essays on social, economic and cultural life in
America, including folkloristic asides.

Ellis, J. Breckenridge
The Little Fiddler of the Ozarks. Chicago:
Laird and Lee, 1913.

Hamilton, Mrs. Rose L.
*Fickle Fortune: A Romance of Life Among the
Ozarks.* New York: The Grafton Press, 1928.
254 pp.

Hauck, Louise Platt
Marise, a Story for Girls. Illustrated by Beth
Krebs Morris. Indianapolis: The Bobbs-Mer-
rill Company, 1929. 298 pp.
A Juvenile tale of two girls' experiences in the
Missouri Ozarks.

Hogue, Wayman
Back Yonder; An Ozark Chronicle: woodcuts
by Howard Simon. New York: Milton, Balch
and Co., 1932. x, 303 pp.
"Perhaps the best non-fictional book ever written
about the Ozark country; but there are not many
folk songs in it." (Vance Randolph.)

———.
"Ozark People." *Scribner's Magazine* 89:509–
520, 1931.

Howard, Guy
Walkin' Preacher of the Ozarks. New York:
Harper and Bros., 1945. 275 pp.
"It contains considerable interesting information
about the life and customs of the hills." (Pres-
cott.)

Lane, Rose Wilder
Hill-Billy. New York: Harper & Brothers,
1926.
Ozark life and manners, also contains nine folk
songs.

Luther, C. H.
An Ozark Scrapbook. Siloan Springs, Ark.:
Bar D Press, 1944. 96 pp.
A volume of prose and verse.

Lyon, Marguerite
And Green Grass Grows All Around ... with
illustrations by Ronald Bean. Indianapolis:
The Bobbs-Merrill Co., 1942. 307 pp., illus.

———.
Fresh from the Hills; illustrated by Lois
Fisher. Indianpolis: The Bobbs-Merrill Co.,
1945. 283 pp.

———.
Take to the Hills; a chronicle of the Ozarks.
...With illustrations by Ronald Bean. Indianapolis: The Bobbs-Merrill Co., 1941. 305 pp.,
illus.

McCanse, Ralph Alan
The Road to Hollister, a hill country pastoral.
Boston: R. G. Badger, 1931. 143 pp.
Told in verse.

Newburger, Gabriel F.
Ozark Anthology. Cedar Rapids, Ia.: The
Torch Press, 1938. 185 pp.
"Sketches...preserving the unique language and
customs of the Ozark people. They are written
in the valid dialect of the region." Pref.

Owen, Luella Agnes
Cave Regions of the Ozarks and Black Hills.
Cincinnati: The Editor Publishing Co., 1898.
228 pp.

Preston, John
Saucer Ears in the Ozarks. Coeur D'Alene,
Idaho: John Preston, 1102 N. Fifteenth St.,
1943. 300 pp.
A tale about a boy growing up in the Ozarks.

Randolph, Vance
From an Ozark Holler. New York: The Vanguard Press, 1933.

———, ed.
An Ozark Anthology. Stories and Sketches by
Charles J. Finger, Charlie May Simon, Charles
Morrow Wilson, Eleanor Risley, Rose O'Neill,
Thomas Hart Benton, Rose Wilder Lane, and
other Ozark Writers. Caldwell, Idaho: The
Caxton Printers, Ltd., 1940. 374 pp.

Ozark Mountain Folks. New York: Vanguard Press, 1932. ix, 279 pp., illus., music.

The Ozarks. An American Survival of Primitive Society. New York: Vanguard Press, 1931. ix, 310 pp.
Includes songs with music.

Rayburn, Otto Ernest
Ozark Country. (American Folkways Series). New York: Duell, Sloan and Pearce, 1942. ix, 352 pp.
A region rich in folklore, folksong and mountain tradition.

Reminiscent History of the Ozark Region. Chicago: Goodspeed Bros., 1894.

Riggle, Harry Lyons
Rhymes of the Ozark Hills. San Gabriel, Calif.: Brownville Press, 1944. 48 pp., illus.

Schultz, Gerard
Early History of the Northern Ozarks. Jefferson City, Mo.: Midland Printing Co., 1937. 192 pp., illus.

Sheehan, Murray
Half-Gods. New York: E. P. Dutton and Company, 1927. 467 pp.
A novel of the Ozarks.

Simon, Charlie May
Straw in the Sun. New York: E. P. Dutton, 1945. 253 pp.
"The author has given us a quiet book, descriptive and interpretative of life in the Arkansas Ozarks. It is a book of subdued color, but with masterly contrasts of sunlight and shadow." (E. L. Saucier.)

Sper, Felix
"Plays from the Ozarks." *SFQ* 8:239–248, 1944.

Spurlock, Pearl
Over the Ozark Trails in the Shepherd of the Hills Country.... Branson, Mo.: Printed by the White River Leader, 1936. 113 pp., illus.

Starr, Fred
Pebbles from the Ozarks. Siloan Springs, Ark.: Bar D Press, 1942. 55 pp.
Essays and anecdotes of the Ozark people.

Stern, Mrs. Elizabeth Gertrude (Levin)
Gambler's Wife. New York: The Macmillan Company, 1931. iv, 447 pp.
A novel of the Ozark Country.

Stribling, Thomas Sigismund
Backwater. New York: Doubleday, Doran and Company, 1930. 308 pp.
A novel of the Mississippi River settlements to the east of the Ozarks.

Wilson, Charles Morrow
Acres of Sky. New York: Putnam's Sons, 1930. vii, 340 pp.
A Tale of the War Eagle Creek region near Hog Eye, Arkansas.

Backwoods America; with illustrations by Bayard Wootten. Chapel Hill: University of North Carolina Press, 1935. 209 pp., illus.

FOLKTALES—LEGENDS

Buel, James W.
Legends of the Ozarks. St. Louis: W. S. Bryan, 1880. 110 pp., illus.

Moore, T.
Mysterious Tales and Legends of the Ozarks. Philadelphia: Dorrance and Co., Inc., 1938.

Randolph, Vance
From an Ozark Holler. Stories of the Ozark Mountain Folk. New York: Vanguard Press, 1933.

Vincent, J. W.
Tales of the Ozarks. Linn Creek, Mo.: Reveille Prtg. House, 1913. 16 pp.
Contents: The lover's leap; What Jack Carrender found; A game of cross purposes; A hunter hunted; The rise of '37; The unofficial quarantine; A backwood's Christmas dinner.

BELIEFS—SUPERSTITIONS

Randolph, Vance
"Folk Beliefs in the Ozark Mountains." *JAFL* 40:78–93, 1927.

"Ozark Superstitions." *JAFL* 46:1–22, 1933.

Ozark Superstitions. Decorations by Louis E. Jefferson. New York: Columbia University Press, 1947. viii, 367 pp., bibl.
"A veritable treasury of backwoods custom and belief. Here are gathered the thousands of magical beliefs that relate to Ozark farming, weather, household tasks, the medical care of people and their animals, water witches, ghosts, witchcraft, and individual destinies from birth to the grave. The author neglects no phase of hillbilly life in which magical thinking or practice plays a part." (Carl Withers.)

Read, Opie
Opie Read in The Ozarks. Including many of the rich, rare, quaint, eccentric, ignorant and superstitious sayings of the natives of Missouri and Arkansas. Pictures by F. I. Wetherbee, Chicago: R. B. McKnight & Co., 1905. 96 pp.; illus.

GAMES—RIDDLES

Randolph, Vance, and Clemens, Nancy
"Ozark Mountain Party-Games." *JAFL* 49: 199–207, 1936.

————, and Spradley, Isabel
"Ozark Mountain Riddles." *JAFL* 47:81–97, 1934.

————, and Taylor, Archer
"Riddles in the Ozarks." *SFQ* 8:1–10, 1944.
35 texts from Missouri and Arkansas.

SPEECH

Allison, Vernon C.
"On the Ozark Pronunciation of 'It'." *AS* 4 (No. 3) :205–206, 1929.

Randolph, Vance
"A Possible Source of Some Ozark Neologisms." *AS* 4 (No. 2) :116–117, 1928.

——————.
"A Third Ozark Word List." *AS* 5 (No. 1) :16–21, 1929.

——————.
"A Word-List from the Ozarks." *Dialect Notes* 5 (Part 9) :397–405, 1926.

——————.
"A Fourth Ozark World-List." *AS* 8 (No. 1) : 47–53, 1933.

——————.
"Is There An Ozark Dialect." *AS* 4 (No. 3) : 203–204, 1929.

——————.
"Literary Words in the Ozarks." *AS* 4 (No. 1) : 56–57, 1928.

——————.
"More Words from the Ozarks." *Dialect Notes* 5 (Part 10) :472–479, 1927.

——————.
"Recent Fiction and the Ozark Dialect." *AS* 6 (No. 6) :425–428, 1931.

——————.
"The Grammar of the Ozark Dialect." *AS* 3 (No. 1) :1–11, 1927.

——————.
"The Ozark Dialect in Fiction." *AS* 2 (No. 6) : 283–289, 1927.

——————.
"Verbal Modesty in the Ozarks." *Dialect Notes* (6 (Part 1) :57–64, 1928.

——————, **and Clemens, Nancy**
"A Fifth Ozark Word List." *AS* 11 (No. 4) : 314–318, 1936.

——————, **and Ingleman, Anna A.**
"Pronunciation in the Ozark Dialect." *AS* 3 (No. 5) :401–407, 1928.

——————, **and Sankee, Patti**
"Dialectical Survivals in the Ozarks." 1. Archaic Pronunciation; 2. Grammatical Peculiarities; 3. Archaic Vocabulary. *AS* 5 (No. 3) : 198–208, 1930; 5 (No. 4) :264–269, 1930; 5 (No. 5) :424–430, 1930.

——————, **and Spradley, Isabel**
"Quilt Names in the Ozarks." *AS* 8 (No. 1) : 33–36, 1933.

Wilt, Napier
"Ozark Words Again." *AS* 12 (No. 3) :234–235, 1937.

FOLKSONG

GENERAL STUDIES AND COLLECTIONS

Garrison, Theodore
Forty-Five Folk Songs Collected from Searcy County, Arkansas. M. A. thesis, University of Arkansas. Fayetville: University Library, 1944.
Forty-seven texts and thirty-two tunes.

——————.
"Some Survivals of British Balladry Among Ozark Folk Songs." *Arkansas Historical Quarterly* 5:246–262, 1946.
A discussion of Searcy County items.

Hummel, Lynn E.
Ozark Folk-Songs. M. A. thesis for the Music Department of the University of Missouri, 1936. MS. Columbia, Mo.: University Library.
Words and music of 116 songs.

Manerva Carolyn Shepherd Collection.
This collection contains manuscript copies of about fifty texts. Unpublished. In Mrs. Shepherds Home in Osceola, Missouri.

Manuscript Collection of Twenty Ballads Texts.
Collected by Walter E. Owen, who lived in Clinton, Henry County, Missouri, in 1861. Unpublished. The Owen Manuscript is kept in Mrs. Hartley C. Banks' house in Columbia.

Randolph, Vance
Ozark Folksongs, Vol. I, edited for the State Historical Society of Missouri. Columbia, Mo.: The State Historical Society of Missouri, 1946. 439 pp., music (unaccompanied melodies), bibl., illus.
Treats mainly with traditional ballads in the Ozarks.

——————.
Ozark Folksongs, Vol. II. Columbia, Mo.: State Historical Society of Missouri, 1948. 436 pp.
"Authoritatively annotated, it is a rich source book of Americana that brings together both the familiar and lesser-known songs and ballads of the South and West popularized in the Ozark region." (W. G. Tyrrell).

——————.
The Ozarks: An American survival of Primitive Society. New York: The Vanguard Press. 1931.
Contains some ballads.

——————.
Ozark Mountain Folks. New York: The Vanguard Press, 1902.
Contains a number of folk-songs.

——————, **and Emberson, Frances**
"The Collection of Folk Music in the Ozarks." *JAFL* 60:115–125, 1947.
General discussion and chronological account of research done by various folk song hunters in the Ozark Mountains.

——————, **and Spradley, Isabel**
"Ozark Mountain Ballads." *JAFL* 47:81, 1934.

Shell, Lilith
"Folk Songs, Mountain Entertainment." *Arkansas Gazette*, Little Rock, March 11, 1928. p. 16.
Twelve songs are printed, with comments.

Todd, Charles, and Sonkin, Robert
"Ballads of the Okies." *New York Times Magazine*, Nov. 17, 1940. pp. 3–4, 18.

Wilson, Charles Morrow
Backwoods America. Chapel Hill, N. C.: University of North Carolina Press, 1934.
The author presents 12 texts from the Arkansas Ozarks. However, the best songs were collected in the Appalachians.

CHILDREN'S RHYMES

Wood, Ray
Mother Goose in the Ozarks. Raywood, Texas: The Author, 1946. Unnumbered, illus.

————.
Peckerwood Rhymes. Beaumont, Texas: Graystone Press, 1938.
56 texts of children's songs and rhymes, no music.

ARRANGEMENTS

————: *Orchestra*

Ozarka.
Busch, Carl: Fitz Simmons: Symphony Orchestra.
The work on thematic material from the Ozark Mountain Region, Missouri.

Ozark Set.
Siegmeister, Elie: Marks: Orchestra.

Symphonic Rhapsody.
Forst, Rudolph: MS: Orchestra.
Based on two Ozark Mountain folk tunes.

RECORDS

Ozark.
Siegmeister. Minneapolis Symphony Orchestra. Mitropoulos   CO.–MX–262

U. S. Library of Congress. Division of Music. Folklore Section
Regional Survey of Ozark Folk Song. Vance Randolph, coll.   AAFS–LC

THE MIDWEST

THE MIDWEST

FOLKLORE

BIBLIOGRAPHY

Finley Collection on the History and Romance of the Northwest. Arranged Alphabetically by authors and Edward Caldwell. Galesburg, Ill.: Knox College, 1928, 1938.
> Contents: 1. The Narratives of the Early Settlers; 2. Reprints of Manuscript Archives; 3. The Narrative and Reports of the Early Jesuit Missionaries; 4. The Early History of New France, **Canada, and Louisiana; 5. The Later General** Histories of the Mississippi Valley; 6. Narratives of Early Travelers in the Pioneer Days; 7. Histories of the State of Illinois; 8. History of other Mississippi Valley States; 9. Early Guide Books and Gazetteers; 10. Early Periodicals and other Literary Work; 11. Historical Periodicals; 12. Historical Society and Club Publications; 13. Miscellaneous subjects: Indians, Religious History and Biography; 14. Maps; 15. Bibliographies.

Surrey, Nancy Maria (Miller), ed.
Calendar of Manuscripts in Paris Archives and Libraries Relating to the History of the Mississippi Valley to 1803. Washington, D. C.: Carnegie Institution of Washington, Dep't. of Historical Research, 1926–1928. 2 vols.

PERIODICALS

Central States Bulletin.
Knoxville, Tennessee. Madeline Kneberg, Sec'y-Treas., University of Tennessee. No. 1, Oct.–Nov., 1946.

Mid-America. Illinois Catholic Historical Society; Loyola University. Institute of Jesuit History. Chicago. V. 1, 1918–1934.

Midwest: A Magazine of God's Country. V. 1, 1914 to Oct., 1917. Lincoln, Neb., etc. 1914–1917.

Midwest Bookman; A Monthly Journal Devoted to the Interest of the Literature of the Middle West. Kansas City, Mo. V. 1–4, No. 1—1919–Aug., 1922.

Mid-West Story, A Regional Journal of the Old Northwest. Vincennes. V. 1–2 No. 10. Dec., 1931–Aug. 15, 1938.

Mid-West Quarterly.
Nebraska University. V. 1–5. Oct., 1913–July, 1918.

Mississippi Valley Historical Review.
Mississippi Valley Historical Association. Cedar Rapids, Ia.: Lincoln, Neb. V. 1, June, 1914. *Quarterly Proceedings.* V. 1, 1907—V. 15, 1924.

The Midwest; A Monthly of Literature, News and Opinion. Chicago: The Midwest, 1934. 1 vol. Sept.–Nov., 1934.

The Midwest; A Review. V. 1, Nov., 1936. Monthly. Minneapolis, 1936–1937.

The Midwest Review of Literature.
V. 1, 1933–. Waukegan, Ill. Monthly.

GENERAL STUDIES AND COLLECTIONS

"An Early Missouri River Journal. Introduction by G. J. G." *Mid-America* (Chicago) 2:236–254, 1931. n.s.

Anderson, A. M.
Fur Trappers of the Old West. Chicago: Wheeler Publishing Co., 1946.
> Exciting adventure story for younger readers of the exploits of Jim Bridger, Tom Fitzpatrick, Major Henry, Wolf Andrews, Tall Bear and Jed Smith.

Ashe, Thomas
Travels in America Performed in 1806, for the purpose of Exploring the Rivers Alleghany, Monongahela, Ohio, and Mississippi, and Ascertaining the Produce and Conditions of their Banks and Vicinity. London: R. Phillips, 1808. 3 vols.

Atwater, Caleb
The Writings of Caleb Atwater. Columbus: Published by the Author; Printed by Scott and Wright, 1833. 408 pp., illus.
> A description of things seen and discovered on a tour to Prairie du Chien, thence to Washington in 1829.

Baird, Robert
View of the Valley of the Mississippi; or, The Emigrant's and Traveller's Guide to the West. Philadelphia: H. S. Tanner, 1834. ix, 372 pp., illus.

Barber, John Warner, and Howe, Henry
All the Western States and Territories from the Alleghanies to the Pacific, and from the lakes to the gulf, containing their history from the earliest times ... the whole being illustrated by 240 engravings ... principally from drawings taken on the spot by the authors. Cincinnati: Howe's Subscription Book Concern, 1867. xi, 704 pp.

Beasley, Norman
Freighters of Fortune; The Story of the Great Lakes. New York: Harper & Bros., 1930.

Bishop, Nathaniel Holmes
Four Months in a Sneak-Box. A boat voyage of 2600 miles down the Ohio and Mississippi Rivers along the Gulf of Mexico. Boston: Lee and Shepard, 1879. xii, 322 pp., illus.

Blair, Walter A.
A Raft Pilot's Log; a History of the Great Rafting Industry on the Upper Mississippi, 1840–1915. Cleveland: The Arthur H. Clark Co., 1930. 328 pp., illus., bibl.

Blegen, Theodore C.
Grass Roots History. Minneapolis, Minn.: University of Minnesota Press, 1948. 266 pp.
"The author...plumps for history based upon the lives of humble folk, claiming that the experiences of ordinary men and women engaged in the routine affairs of daily life are as important to our knowledge of the past as the study of great political and economic movements." He argues strongly for the validity and usefulness of folklore material in historical study and evaluation.

Bradbury, John
Travels in the Interior of America, in the Years 1809, 1810, and 1811...London: Sherwood, Neely and Jones, 1819. xiv, 346 pp.

Bradford, William John Alden
Notes on the Northwest, or Valley of the Upper Mississippi. New York: Wiley and Putnam, 1846. vi, 302 pp.

Caldwell, Norman Ward
The French in the Mississippi Valley, 1740–1750. Urbana, Ill.: The University of Illinois Press, 1941. 133 pp., illus., bibl.

Carter, Hodding
Lower Mississippi. Illustrated by John McCrady. (Rivers of America Series). New York: Farrar & Rinehart, 1942. x, 467 pp., illus., bibl.
The author also includes the words and music of: "The Old Cabin Home," p. 441.

———.
Upper Mississippi: A Wilderness Saga; Illustrated by David and Lolita Granahan. (Rivers of America Series). New York: Farrar & Rinehart, 1937. x, 258 pp., illus.

Chambers, Julius
The Mississippi River and It's Wonderful Valley; twenty-seven hundred and seventy-five miles from source to sea, with 80 illustrations and maps. New York: G. P. Putnam's Sons, 1910. xvi, 308 pp.

Chittenden, Hiram Martin
History of Early Steamboat Navigation on the Missouri River. Life and Adventures of Joseph La Barge. New York: F. P. Harper, 1903. 2 vols., illus.

Clark, Thomas D.
"The American Backwoodsman in Popular Literature." *Indiana Historical Bulletin* 23 (No. 1):51–52, 1946.

Cole, Fay-Cooper
"Growth of Anthropology in the Midwest." *Central States Bulletin* 1:1–9, 1946.

Collins, John Sloan
Across the Plains in '64. Incidents of Early Days West of the Missouri River. Two Thousand Miles in an Open Boat From Fort Benton to Omaha. Omaha, Neb.: National Printing Co., 1904. 151 pp.

Colton, Joseph Hutchins
The Western Tourist and Emigrant's Guide, with a compendious gazetteer of the states of Ohio, Michigan, Indiana, Illinois, and Missouri and the territories of Wisconsin and Iowa; being an accurate and concise description of each state, territory and county....Also, describing all the principal stage routes, canals, rail-roads, and the distances between the towns. ...New York: J. H. Colton, 1839. vi, 180 pp., map.

Conclin, George
Conclin's New River Guide; or A Gazetteer of All the Towns, on the Western Waters: Containing sketches of the cities, towns, and countries...on the Ohio and Mississippi Rivers, and their principal tributaries...with their population...commerce, &c., &c., in 1848.... Cincinnati: G. Conclin, 1849. 128 pp., illus.

Davis, Clyde Brion
The Arkansas. (Rivers of America Series). Illustrated by Donald McKay. New York: Farrar and Rinehart, 1940.
"One of the most rambunctious of American rivers, one of the longest; at times it is one of the most treacherous and surely no American river has seen more varied or more incredible history in the making."

Deatherage, Charles P.
Steamboating on the Missouri River in the 'Sixties....Kansas City, Mo.: Alexander Printing Co., 1924. 39 pp., illus.

Devol, George H.
Forty Years a Gambler on the Mississippi. New York: George H. Devol, 1892. viii, 300 pp., 2nd ed.

Dondore, Dorothy Anne
The Prairie and the Making of Middle America. Cedar Rapids, Iowa: The Torch Press, 1926. xiii, 472 pp., bibl. (pp. 435–451).

Dorrance, Ward Allison
Where the Rivers Meet. New York: C. Scribner's Sons, 1939. 352 pp.

Faris, John Thompson
Seeing the Middle West...with frontispiece and 91 doubletone illustrations. Philadelphia: J. B. Lippincott Company, 1923. 253 pp.

Fearon, Henry Bradshaw
Sketches of America. A Narrative of Five Thousand Miles Through the Eastern and Western States of America....With remarks on Mr. Birkbeck's "Notes" and "Letters." London: Longman, Hurst, Rees, Orme and Brown, 1818. xi, 454 pp.

Federal Writers' Project
Mississippi Gulf Coast, Yesterday and To-Day, 1699–1939. Compiled and written by Federal Writers' Project in Mississippi...W. P. A. Gulfport, Miss.: Gulfport Printing Co., 1939. viii, 162 pp.

Firestone, Clark Barnaby
Flowing South. New York: R. M. McBride & Company, 1941. 263 pp., illus., bibl.

Flagg, Edmund
The Far West: or, A Tour Beyond the Moun-tains.... New York: Harper & Bros., 1838. 2 vols.

Flanagan, John T.
America is West. An Anthology of Midwestern Life and Literature. Minneapolis: University of Minnesota Press, 1945. vii, 677 pp.
"A Baedecker of Midwestern legend, history and literature."

Fleming, Andrew Magnus
Old Father Waters. Boston: Meador Publish-ing Company, 1936. 350 pp.
A work of fiction.

Flint, Timothy
Condensed Geography and History of the Western States, or the Mississippi Valley. Cincinnati: E. H. Flint, 1828. 2 vols.

———•

History and Geography of the Mississippi Val-ley. Cincinnati: E. H. Flint, L. R. Lincoln, 1852. Vol. II.

———•

Recollection of the Last Ten Years, Passed in Occasional Residences and Journeyings in the Valley of the Mississippi ... in a series of let-ters to the Rev. James Flint.... Boston: Cum-mings, Hilliard & Co., 1826. 395 pp.

Frederick, John T.
Out of the Midwest. New York: Whittlesey House, 1944. 405 pp.
A collection of stories by Midwestern writers. "It is as Midwestern as a watertower" (Oscar Cargill).

Freeman, Lewis Ransome
Waterways of Westward Wandering; Small Boat Voyages Down the Ohio, Missouri and Mississippi Rivers. New York: Dodd, Mead and Co., 1927. xii, 368 pp., illus.

Galloway, William Albert
Old Chillicothe; Shawnee and Pioneer History; Conflicts and Romances in the Northwest Ter-ritory. Xenia, O.: The Buckeye Press, 1934. xiii, 336 pp., bibl.

Gilman, Chandler Robbins
Life on the Lakes: Being Tales and Sketches Collected During a Trip to the Pictured Rocks of Lake Superior. New York: G. Dearborn, 1836. 2 vols.

Glover, John
"Westward Along the Boone's Lick Trail in 1826; the Diary of Colonel John Glover." *Missouri Historical Review* 39:184–199, 1945.

Hansen, Harry
Midwest Portraits; A Book of Friendships. New York: Harcourt, Brace and Company, 1923. 357 pp.
Contains a chapter —"Forgotten shrines and episodes."

Hanson, Joseph Mills
The Conquest of the Missouri; Being the Story of the Life and Exploits of Captain Grant Marsh. Chicago: A. C. McClurg & Co., 1909. xiv, 458 pp.

Hatcher, Harlan
Lake Erie. Indianapolis: The Bobbs-Merrill Co., 1945. 416 pp.
"The volume is a notable contribution to our regional literature." (George R. Stewart)

———•

The Great Lakes. New York: Oxford Univer-sity Press, 1945. 384 pp., illus.
A story with rich pageantry—Indian, lumber-jacks, military, etc.

Havighurst, Walter
Land of Promise: The Story of the Northwest Territory. New York: The Macmillan Com-pany, 1946. viii, 384 pp.
You penetrate the vast uncharted land with the first French missionaries and fur traders. You meet the furtive scouts and brave explorers. You follow the exploits of George Rogers Clark, of Johnny Appleseed, and tragic Tecumseh, and also hear the legends, anecdotes, and tales of the people.

Hawks, Francis Lister
The History of the Western States, Illustrated by Tales, Sketches and Anecdotes ... by Lam-bert Lilly, schoolmaster (pseud.) Boston: W. D. Ticknor, 1838. 156 pp., illus.

James, Uriah Pierson
James' River Guide: Containing descriptions of all the cities, towns, and principal objects of interest on the navigable waters of the Mississippi Valley.... Cincinnati: U. P. James, 1856. 128 pp., illus.

Johnson, Clifton
Highways and Byways of the Great Lakes. Illustrated by the author. (American Highways and Byways Series). New York: Macmillan Co., 1911. 328 pp.

———•

Highways and Byways of the Mississippi Val-ley. New York: The Macmillan Company, 1906. xiii, 287 pp., illus.

Jones, L. N., ed.
Midwest Prize Plays. Chicago: Dramatic Publ. Co., 1938.

Kingsford, William
Impressions of the West and South, during a six weeks' holiday. Toronto: A. H. Armour & Co., 1858. 83 pp.

Landon, Fred
Lake Huron. Indianapolis, Indiana: Bobbs-Merrill, 1944. 398 pp., bibl. notes, index, maps, photos.
The first volume in a new series—"The American Lakes."

Loomis, Chester A.
A Journey on Horseback Through the Great West in 1825. Bath, N. Y.: Plaindealer Press, 1890. 15 pp.

Ludwig, G. M.
The Influence of the Pennsylvania Dutch in the Middle West. Publications, Pennsylvania German Folklore Society, Vol. 10. Allentown, Pa.: Pennsylvania German Folklore Society, 1945.

Maitland, James
The Golden Northwest. Chicago: The Rollins Publishing Company, 1879. 112 pp., illus.

McClintock, Marshall
The Story of the Mississippi; pictures by C. H. Dewitt. New York: Harper & Bros., 1941. 39 pp., illus.

McMurry, Charles Alexander
Pioneer History Stories of the Mississippi Valley. . . . Bloomington, Ill.: Public School Publishing Co., 1894. 173 pp.

————.
Pioneers of the Mississippi Valley. New York: The Macmillan Company, 1905. xvii, 218 pp., illus.

Merrick, George Byron
Old Times on the Upper Mississippi; the Recollections of a Steamboat Pilot from 1854 to 1863. Cleveland: The A. H. Clark Company, 1909. 323 pp., illus.

Milburn, George
Black Jack Country. (American Folkways Series). New York: Duell, Sloan and Pearce Co., 1943.
A strip of country starting with Kansas City in the North and leaving off at Dallas in the South, taking in Southeastern Kansas, Southwestern Missouri, the Western edge of Arkansas, and a corner of Northeastern Texas, old fashioned American outlawry culminated. Here bootlegging and ballot-box stuffing were invented. Here the refinements of ordinary robbery, train and bank, were introduced for the first time in history.

Mondale, R. Lester
The Missouri Still Runs Wild. Kansas City, Mo.: Westport Publishing Co., 1943. 58 pp.

Moore, Nathaniel Fish
Diary; A Trip from New York to the Falls of St. Anthony in 1845 . . . Chicago: Pub. for the Newberry Library by the University of Chicago Press, 1946. xviii, 101 pp., illus., bibl.

Nute, Grace Lee
Lake Superior. (The American Lake Series). Indianapolis, Indiana: Bobbs-Merrill Co., 1944. 376 pp., bibl., map.

Parker, Amos Andrew
Trips to the West and Texas. Comprising a journey of eight thousand miles, through New York, Michigan, Illinois, Missouri, Louisiana and Texas, in the autumn and winter of 1834–5. Interspersed with anecdotes, incidents and observations. With a brief sketch of the Texian war. Concord, N. H.: W. White, 1836. iv, 380 pp., illus.

Petersen, William John
Steamboating on the Upper Mississippi, the waterway to Iowa; Some River History. Iowa City, Ia.: The State Historical Society of Iowa, 1937. 575 pp., bibl.

————, **ed.**
"The Log of the Henry M. Shreve to Fort Benton in 1869." *Mississippi Valley Historical Review* 31:537–578, 1945.

Pike, Zebulon Montgomery
Exploratory Travels Through the Western Territories of North America: Comprising a voyage from St. Louis, on the Mississippi, to the source of that river. . . . Performed in the years 1805, 1806, 1807 by order of the government of the United States. London: Longman, Hurst, Rees, Orme, and Brown, 1811. xx, 436 pp.

Quick, Herbert
Mississippi Steamboatin'; a History of Steamboating on the Mississippi and its Tributaries. New York: H. Holt and Company, 1926. xiv, 342 pp., illus., bibl.

Raine, Ralph L.
Literature of the Middle Western Frontier. New York: Columbia University Press, 1925.

Regan, John
The Western Wilds of America; or, Backwoods and Prairies; and Scenes in the Valley of the Mississippi. . . . Edinburgh: J. Menzies and W. P. Nimo, 1859. vii, 408 pp., illus.

Rosskam, Edwin
Towboat River. New York: Duell, Sloan and Pearce, 1948. 295 pp., illus.

Saxon, Lyle
Father Mississippi. New York: D. Appleton-Century Co., 1943. xi, 427 pp., illus., bibl.

Schoolcraft, Henry Rowe
Journal of a Tour Into the Interior of Missouri and Arkansaw . . . in 1818 and 1819. London: 1821.

————.
Travels in the Central Portions of the Mississippi Valley; Comprising observations on its mineral geography, internal resources and aboriginal population. . . . New York: Collins and Hannay, 1825. iv, 459 pp., illus.

Shields, Joseph Dunbar
Natchez: Its Early History. Louisville, Ky.: J. P. Morton & Company, 1930. 274 pp.

The Culture of the Middle West.
Appleton, Wis.: Lawrence College, 1944. 72 pp.
Lectures of the Lawrence College faculty on geology, history, politics, literature and art.

Thorp, Joseph
Early Days in the West. Along the Missouri One Hundred Years Ago. Liberty, Mo.: Gilmer, 1924. 94 pp.

Thwaites, Reuben Gold
Early Western Travels, 1746–1846. A series of annotated reprints of the best and rarest contemporary volumes of travel, descriptive of the aborigines, and social and economic conditions in the middle and far West, during the period of early American settlement.... Cleveland, O.: The A. H. Clark Company, 1904–07. 32 vols.
A mine of information on many aspects of American and Indian lore.

Tixier, Victor
Tixier's Travels on the Osage Prairies, edited by John F. McDermott.... Norman: University of Oklahoma Press, 1940. xv, 309 pp.

Van Tramp, John C.
Prairie and Rocky Mountain Adventures; or, Life in the West. To which is added a view of the states and territorial regions of our Western empire; embracing history, statistics, and geography, and descriptions of the chief cities of the West. Columbus, O.: Segner & Condit, 1870. viii, 775 pp., illus.

Vestal, Stanley
Short Grass Country. (American Folkways Series.) New York: Duell, Sloan and Pearce, 1942.
A land of colorful history and lusty life which stretches from Wichita almost to Denver—the land of buffalo hunts, tornadoes, oil, county-seats wars—the range of Coronado, Buffalo Bill, and Wyatt Earp.

Wells, William Franklin
Western Scenery; or, Land and River, Hill and Dale, in the Mississippi Valley... lithographed from original sketches.... Cincinnati, O.: O. Onken, 1851. 52 pp., illus.

West, Victor Royce
Folklore in the Works of Mark Twain. University of Nebraska Studies in Language, Literature and Criticism, No. 10. Lincoln, Nebr.: University Press, 1930. 81 pp.
"In this study Mississippi Valley folklore has been given major consideration."

Wild, J. C.
The Valley of the Mississippi; Illustrated in a Series of Views. Edited by Lewis Foulk Thomas. Painted and lithographed by J. C. Wild. Accompanied with historical descriptions.... St. Louis, Mo.: Chambers and Knapp, 1841. vi, 145 pp., illus.

Wilson, Charles Morrow
Backwoods America; with illustrations by Bayard Wootten. Chapel Hill: The University of North Carolina Press, 1934. 209 pp.

Wimberly, Lowry C., ed.
Mid-Country. Introduction by B. A. Botkin. Lincoln, Nebraska: University of Nebraska Press, 1945. 510 pp. Distributed by Crowell Publishers, N. Y.

FOLKTALES—LEGENDS—MYTHS

Conroy, Jack, ed.
Midland Humor. A Harvest of Fun and Folklore. New York: A. A. Wyn, 1947.

Judson, Katharine Berry, ed.
Myths and Legends of the Mississippi Valley and the Great Lakes. Chicago: A. C. McClurg & Co., 1914. xiv, 215 pp.

Thomas, George Francis
Legends of the Land of Lakes, or History, traditions, and mysteries, gleaned from years of experience among the pioneers, voyageurs and Indians; with descriptive accounts of the many natural curiosities met with from Lake Huron to the Columbia River. And the meaning and derivation of names and rivers, lakes, towns, etc., of the Northwest. Chicago: G. F. Thomas, 1884. Illus.

Thompson, Stith
"The Folktale in the Middle West." *HFB* 1:39, 1942.

Thompson, William F.
"Frontier Tall Talk." *AS* 9 (No. 3):187–199, 1934.

CUSTOMS

Buley, R. C.
"Mid-West Social and Cultural History." *Mississippi Valley Historical Review* 28:481–510, 1937.
Contains much material of interest to folklorist.

Burman, Ben Lucien
Big River to Cross; Mississippi Life Today; drawings by Alice Caddy. New York: The John Day Company, 1940. 294 pp., illus.

Deedes, Henry
Sketches of the South and West; or, Ten Months' Residence in the United States. Edinburgh: W. Blackwood and Sons, 1869. vi, 170 pp.

Drury, John
Historic Midwest Houses. Minneapolis: University of Minnesota Press, 1947.
"Here is the personal side of Midwestern history as revealed by the picturesque homes of its famous and colorful men and women. 141 photographs combine with the text to form a record of some of the most treasured examples of native American architecture."

Ellet, Elizabeth Fries L.
Pioneer Women of the West. New York: C. Scribner, 1852. xi, 434 pp.
Much on the manners and customs of the old Northwest.

———.
Summer Rambles in the West. New York: J. C. Riker, 1853. viii, 268 pp.
A narrative of a trip from Buffalo through Michigan, Illinois and Minnesota.

Emerson, F. V.
"Life Along a Graded River." *American Geographical Society Bulletin* (New York) 44:
674–681, 761–768, 1913.

Hall, James
Letters from the West; Containing sketches of
scenery, manners and customs; and anecdotes
connected with the first settlements of the
Western sections of the United States. London:
H. Colburn, 1828. vi, 385 pp.

———.
Notes on the Western States; Containing
descriptive sketches of their soil, climate, resources, and scenery. Philadelphia: H. Hall,
1838. xxiii, 304 pp.

———.
*The Romance of Western History; or Sketches
of History, Life and Manners in the West.*
Cincinnati: Applegate and Co., 1857. iv, 420
pp.

Hoffman, C. F.
A Winter in the West. By a New Yorker. New
York: Harper & Bros., 1835. 2 vols.
   Letters descriptive of Chicago and vicinity in
   1833–34.

Kinzie, Juliette Augusta Magill
Wau-Bun; or, Early Days in the Northwest.
London: S. Low, Son & Co., 1856. xii, 498 pp.,
illus.
   Life and manners in the old Northwest.

Meeker, Nathan Cook
*Life in the West; or, Stories of the Mississippi
Valley.* New York: S. R. Wells, 1868. vi, 360
pp.

Milburn, Rev. W. H.
*The Pioneer Preachers and People of the
Mississippi Valley.* New York: Derby and
Jackson, 1860. xii, 465 pp.

Nicholson, Meredith
The Valley of Democracy. With illustrations
by Walter Tittle. New York: C. Scribner's Sons,
1918. x, 284 pp., illus.
   Deals with social, cultural and political life in
   the Mississippi Valley. The first part is entitled:
   "The Folks and their Folksiness."

North, Sterling
"Midwestern Salt." *Mademoiselle* Sept., 1943.
p. 152.

Ohler, Clara May
Frontier Life in the Old Northwest. New Haven,
Conn.: 1908. (pp. 297–314), illus.

Peltz, Eduard
Das Mississippi-Gesenke. Mit besonderer rück-
sicht auf besiedelungsverhältnisse.... Leipzig:
F. Fleischer, 1871. vi, 58 pp.
   Life among the Colonists in the Mississippi
   Valley.

Sealsfield, Charles (Charles Postel)
The Americans As They Are; Described in a
Tour Through the Valley of the Mississippi.
London: Hurst, Chance & Co., 1828. vi, 218 pp.

Young, John A.
"Traveling to the Middle West in 1838." *Annals of Iowa* 19 (Ser. 3):139–145, 1933.

FOLK MEDICINE

Pickard, Madge E., and Buley, R. Carlyle
*The Midwest Pioneer, His Ills, Cures, and
Doctor.* Crawfordsville, Indiana: R. E. Banta,
1945. 339 pp., illus., bibl., index.

Pound, Louise
"Snake Lore in the Central West." *The Prairie
Schooner* 1, No. 2, April, 1927.

SPEECH

Burnham, Josephine M.
"Some Observations on Middle-Western
Speech." *Dialect Notes* 5 (Part 9):391–396,
1926.

J., B. D.
"Mid-Western Speech." *AS* 8 (No. 3):75, 1933.

McDermott, John Francis
"French Surnames in the Mississippi Valley."
AS 9 (No. 1):28–30, 1934.

Meyer, A. W.
"Some German-Americanisms from the Middle
West." *AS* 2 (No. 2):134, 1926.

Parmenter, C. E., and Treviño, S. N.
"The Length of the Sounds of a Middle West-
erner." *AS* 10 (No. 3):129–133, 1935.

Pound, Louise
"American Indefinite Names." *AS* 6 (No. 4):
257–259, 1931.
   The list is for the Central Western Region.

———.
"Intentional Mispronunciation in the Central
West." *Dialect Notes* 5 (Part 5):133–138, 1922.

Prescott, Russell T.
"Middlewestern Farm English." *AS* 12 (No.
2):102–107, 1937.

Quick, Herbert
Vandemark's Folly. Indianapolis: The Bobbs-
Merrill Co., 1922. 477 pp.
   "On the whole the student of linguistics will find,
   we believe, in these novels of Herbert Quick an
   accurate and fairly comprehensive illustration of
   the speech of the Middle West of a past generation or two, with its many colloquialisms and its
   intermingling of bits of the dialect of the various
   older parts of the country, as well as its coloring
   imparted to it by an injection of various foreign
   elements." (A.G.K.)

———.
One Man's Life; An Autobiography. Indianapolis: The Bobbs-Merrill Co., 1925. 408 pp.

———.
The Invisible Woman. Indianapolis: The
Bobbs-Merrill Co., 1924. 488 pp.

Russell, Jason Almus
"Erie Canal Colloquial Expressions." *AS* 6
(No. 2):97–100, 1930.

Thompson, William F.
"Frontier Tall Talk." *AS* 9 (No. 3):187–199, 1934.

Wilson, C. W.
"Backwood's Language." *Scholastic* 26:8–9, 1935.

FOLKSONG

GENERAL STUDIES AND COLLECTIONS

Combs, Josiah H.
Folk-Songs du Midi des États-Unis. Paris: Libraire J. Gambier, 1925.

Harbison, Katherine
"In the Great Meadow and the Lone Prairie." *SFQ* 2:149–157, 1938.

Pound, Louise
"Folk Songs of Nebraska and the Central West." A Syllabus. *Nebraska Academy of Science,* (Lincoln), Publications Vol. 9, (No. 3), 1915.

RECORDS

The Middle West: Mainly Nebraska. In the State University of Iowa, Iowa City.

ILLINOIS

FOLKLORE

BIBLIOGRAPHY

Beck, Lewis Caleb
A Gazetteer of the States of Illinois and Missouri; containing a general view of each state, a general view of their counties, and a particular description of their towns, villages, rivers, &c., &c. With a map, and other engravings. Albany: C. R. and G. Webster, 1823. vii, 352 pp., illus.

Buck, Solon Justus
Travel and Description, 1765–1865, Together With A List of County Histories, Atlases, and Biographical Collections and A List of Territorial and State Laws.... Springfield, Ill.: The Trustees of the Illinois State Historical Library, 1914. ix, 514 pp.

Federal Writers' Project
Selected Bibliography; Illinois, Chicago, and Its Environs; Federal Writers' Project, Illinois, Works Progress Administration.... Chicago, 1937. ii, 58 pp. (American Guide Series).

Historical Records Survey
Inventory of the County Archives of Illinois. Prepared by the Historical Records Survey.... Works Progress Administration ... No. 1. Chicago: The Historical Records Survey, 1937–. Illus., bibl.

————.
Inventory of the State Archives of Illinois.... Prepared by the Illinois Historical Records Survey, Division of Community Service Programs. Works Progress Administration. Chicago: Illinois Historical Records Survey... 1942. Illus.

Sager, Juliet G.
General Index to Collections, Journals, Publications, 1899–1928. Quincy, Ill.: The Royal Printing Co., 1930. 95 pp.

PERIODICALS

Illinois Folklore.
Quarterly published by the Illinois Folklore Society. No. 1—October, 1947.

Illinois State Historical Society. Journal. Springfield. V. 1, April, 1908–. *Papers,* in Illinois History and Transactions... 1937–. Supersedes its *Publications.* 1900–1936.

GENERAL STUDIES AND COLLECTIONS

Ade, George
Stories of the Streets and of the Town, In: *The Chicago Record, 1893–1900.* Illustrated by John T. McCutcheon and others, edited with an introduction by Franklin J. Meine. Chicago: The Caxton Club, 1941. xxx, 278 pp., illus., bibl.

Conroy, Jack
"Chicago Industrial Folklore." In: *Manuscripts of the Federal Writers' Project* of the Works Progress Administration for the State of Illinois.

Davidson, Alexander, and Struve, Bernard
History of Illinois from 1673–1884. Springfield, Ill.: H. W. Rokker, 1884. 1040 pp.

Federal Writers' Project
Galena Guide. (American Guide Series). Compiled and Written by the Federal Writers' Project (Illinois) Works Progress Administration. City of Galena: 1937.

————.
Illinois: Chicago and its Environs. (American Guide Series). Federal Writers' Project, Illinois Works Progress Administration. Chicago: 1937.

————.
Illinois: A Descriptive and Historical Guide. (American Guide Series). Compiled and Written by the Works Progress Administration for the State of Illinois. Chicago: A. C. McClurg and Co., 1939. xxii, 687 pp., illus., bibl.

Folk-Plays for Contests; Seven One-Act Plays by Various Authors. Chicago: T. S. Denison & Co., 1940. 139 pp.

Gray, James
The Illinois. (Rivers of America Series). Illustrated by Aaron Bohrod. New York: Farrar and Rinehart, 1940. x, 355 pp., bibl.

Hand, Wayland D.
"Chicago Folk-lore Society." *JAFL* 56:168–170, 1943.

Hansen, Harry
The Chicago. (Rivers of America Series). New York: Farrar and Rinehart, 1942.

Havighurst, Walter
Upper Mississippi. (American River Series). Illustrated by David and Lolita Granahan. New York: Farrar and Rinehart, 1937.

Hyatt, Harry Middleton
Folklore from Adams County, Illinois. New York: Alma Egan Hyatt Foundation, 1935. xvi, 723 pp., maps.

Masters, Edgar Lee
The Sangamon. (Rivers of America Series). Illustrated by Lynd Ward. New York: Farrar and Rinehart, 1942. 258 pp.

Quaife, Milo Milton
Checagou; from Indian Wigwam to Modern City, 1673–1935. Chicago: The University of Chicago Press, 1933. ix, 212 pp.

————.
Pictures of Illinois One Hundred Years Ago. (The Lakeside Classics). Chicago: R. R. Donnelly and Sons Co., 1918.

FOLKTALES—LEGENDS

Conroy, Jack
Slappy Hooper, World's Biggest, Fastest, and Bestest Sign Painter. In: *Chicago Industrial Folklore.* Manuscripts of the Federal Writers' Project of the Works Progress Administration for the State of Illinois.
A legend of an extraordinary craftsman.

Federal Writers' Project
Illinois Historical Anecdotes. Compiled by the Workers of the Writers' Program of the Works Projects Administration in the State of Illinois. ... Chicago, Ill.: 1940. 93 ff.
  Contents: From Geysers to Oats, From Industries to Wedding Bells, From Iron Rails to Fire Dancers.

————.
Stories from Illinois History; compiled by the Workers of the Writers' Program of the Works Projects Administration in the State of Illinois. ... Chicago, Ill.: 1941. 92 pp.

Harris, Jesse W.
"Myths and Legends from Southern Illinois." *HF* 5 (No. 1):14–20, 1946.

————.
"Substituting for the Off Ox." *JAFL* 60:298–299, 1947.
  Three Southern Illinois versions of this humorous yarn are given.

————.
"The Catskin Legend in Southern Illinois." *JAFL* 58:301–302, 1945.

Jansen, William Hugh
"Lore of the Tankbuilders." *HFB* 3:27–29, 1944.
  Tales from a steel town, East Chicago, Indiana.

Neely, Charles, and Spargo, John Webster
Tales and Songs of Southern Illinois. Menasha, Wis.: George Banta, 1938.

Reed, Earl H.
Tales of a Vanishing River. Illustrated by the author. New York: John Lane Company, 1920. 266 pp.
  Tales of the Kankakee River, Illinois.

Smith, Grace Partridge
"European Origin of an Illinois Tale." *SFQ* 6:89–94, 1942.

————.
"Tall Tales from Southern Illinois." *SFQ* 7: 145–147, 1943.

CUSTOMS—BELIEFS

Allison, Lelah
"Folk Beliefs Regarding Weather in Southeastern Illinois." *JAFL* 61:68–70, 1948.

Bonnell, Clarence
The Illinois Ozarks. Harrisburg, Ill.: Register Publishing Co., 1946. 150 pp.

Bromme, Traugott
Missouri and Illinois. Taschenbuch für Einwanderer und Freunde der Länder—und Völkerkunde.... Baltimore, Md.: C. Scheld & Co., 1835. 41 pp.

Brown, Charles Edward
Scenic and Historic Illinois; Guide to One Thousand Features of Scenic, Historic and Curious Interest in Illinois.... Arranged by Cities and Villages. Madison, Wis.: C. E. Brown, 1928. 40 pp.

Buckingham, J. H.
Illinois As Lincoln Knew It; a Boston reporter's record of a trip in 1847, edited by Harry E. Pratt... Springfield, Ill.: 1938. 84 pp., illus.

Ballance, Charles
"Journal." *Illinois State Historical Society, Journal* 30:70–84, 1937 (Springfield).
  Description of social life and customs in the middle of the 19th Century.

Birkbeck, Morris
Letters from Illinois. London: Taylor & Hessey, 1818. xv, 114 pp.

Carter, C. C.
"Frontier Sketches." *Illinois State Historical Society, Journal* (Springfield) 32:51–70, 206–230, 1939.

Cobbett, William
A Year's Residence in the United States of America... In Three Parts. London: J. M. Cobbett, 1822. vi, 360 pp.
  In the second part the author discusses the customs of the people.

Farnham, E. W.
Life in Prairie Land. New York: Harper & Bros., 1846. xii, 408 pp.

Federal Writers' Project
Pioneer Days in Illinois. Compiled by the Workers of the Writers' Program of the Work Projects Administration in the State of Illinois. Chicago, Ill.: 1940. 78 pp.
　Contents: Pioneer Days in Illinois, From Mules to Lotus Time, From Fences to Dan Cupid.

Flagg, Edmund
　...*Flagg's The Far West, 1836–1837....* In: *Early Western Travels, 1748–1846.* Cleveland, O.: 1906. V. 26, pp. 21–370; V. 27, pp. 13–121.

　—————.
　The Far West; or, A Tour Beyond the Mountains. Embracing Outlines of Western Life and Scenery; Sketches of the Prairies, Rivers, Ancient Mounds, Early Settlements of the French, etc. New York: Harper & Bros., 1838. 2 vols.

Flagg, Gershom
Pioneer Letters of Gershom Flagg; ed. with introduction and notes by Solon J. Buck.... Springfield, Ill.: Illinois State Journal Co., 1912. 47 pp.

Flower, Richard
Flower's Letters from the Illinois—January 18, 1820–May 7, 1821.... In: *Early Western Travels, 1748–1846.* Cleveland, O.: V. 10, pp. 111–169, 1904.

Fordham (Elias Pym)
Personal Narrative of Travels in Virginia, Maryland, Pennsylvania, Ohio, Indiana, Kentucky and of a Residence in the Illinois Territory: 1817–1818.... Edited by F. A. Ogg. Cleveland: The A. H. Clark Co., 1906. 248 pp.

Grierson, Francis
The Valley of Shadows; Recollections of the Lincoln Country, 1858–1863. Boston: Houghton Mifflin Company, 1909. viii, 278 pp.

Hyater, Earl W.
"Wanderings in the West in 1839." *Illinois State Historical Society, Journal* (Springfield) 33:389–411, 1940.

Illinois in 1837; a sketch descriptive of the situation, boundaries, face of the country... also, suggestions to emigrants, sketches of the counties, cities and principal towns of the state... to which are appended the Letters from the Rambler in the West. Philadelphia: S. A. Michell, 1837. viii, 143 pp.

Illinois Poets; foreword by Glenn Ward Dresbach; edited by the House of Henry Harrison, Publisher. New York: 1935. 208 pp.
　An anthology of 64 poets.

Johnson, Charles Beneulyn
"Every Day Life in Illinois Near the Middle of the Nineteenth Century." *Illinois State Historical Society, Trans.* 13:44–53, 1914.

　—————.
Illinois in the Fifties; or, A Decade of Development, 1851–1860. Champaign, Ill.: Flanigan-Pearson Co., 1918. 175 pp.

Lenz, T. W.
Reise Nach Saint Louis am Missisippi.... Weimar: B. F. Voigt, 1838. xii, 251 pp.
　Impressions of a trip to St. Louis on the Missisippi River.

Masters, Edgar Lee
Illinois Poems. Prairie City, Ill.: The Press of J. A. Decker, 1941. 66 pp.

Norlin, E. T.
"Present-day Superstitions at La Harpe, Ill.", survivals in a community of English origin. *JAFL* 31:202–215, 1918.

Oliver, William
Eight Months in Illinois, with Information to Immigrants.... Chicago: W. M. Hill, 1924. 260 pp.

Passin, Herbert, and Bennett, John W.
"Changing Agricultural Magic in Southern Illinois": a Systematic Analysis of Folk-urban Transition. *Social Forces* 22:98–106, 1943.

Patterson, Robert W.
Early Society in Southern Illinois. Chicago: Fergus Print Co., 1881. 34 pp.

Quaife, Milo Milton, ed.
Pictures of Illinois, One Hundred Years Ago. Chicago: R. R. Donnelley & Sons Co., 1918. xxiii, 186 pp.
　Contents: Historical Introduction; Observations of an English Immigrant in 1817, by M. Birkbeck; A Tour in Southern Illinois in 1822, by W. N. Blane; A Journey Up the Illinois River in 1821, by H. R. Schoolcraft.

Roberts, Daniel Arthur
Illinois Vignettes. Chicago: Litho by Rapid Copy Service, 1943. 85 pp., illus.
　A book of poems.

Smelser, Marshall
"Material Customs in the Territory of Illinois." *Illinois State Historical Society, Journal* (Springfield) 29:5–41, 1936.

Snyder, J. F.
"The Old French Towns of Illinois in 1839." *Illinois State Historical Society, Journal* (Springfield) 36:345–367, 1943. Illus.

Stevens, Frank Everett
James Watson Webb's Trip Across Illinois in 1822. Sycamore, Ill.: Sycamore Tribune Print, 1924. 16 pp.

Waller, Elbert
Illinois Pioneer Days. Litchfield, Ill.: E. B. Lewis, 1918. 80 pp., illus.

Wilkey, Major Walter (pseud.)
Western Emigration. Narrative of a Tour to, & One Year's Residence in "Edensburgh," (Illinois) by Major Walter Wilkey (pseud.), an honest yeoman of Mooseboro', State of Maine. A more humorous and interesting "Traveler's Guide to the West," was never before published, and by which it will be perceived that the famous "Maine-Pine-Swamp Speculation," has been completely outdone! ... New York: G. Claiborne, and Others, 1839.

Woods, John
*Two Years' Residence in the Settlement on
the English Prairie, in the Illinois Country* ...
a description of the principal towns ... with
the habits and customs of the back-woodsmen.
London: Longman, Hurst, Rees, Orme and
Brown, 1822. 310 pp., illus.

SPEECH

Allison, Lelah
"Folk Speech from Southeastern Illinois." *HF*
5:93–102, 1946.

Curtiss, Mrs. Laura C.
"Expressions Heard from Chicago People of
New England Antecedents." *Dialect Notes* 3
(Part 6) :458, 1910.

"Olympia Pioneer."
In: *The Bangor Mercury* of 1845. Cited by
Thornton in *American Glossary*, Vol. 2, pp.
974, 1912,—on Illinois slang.

Rice, W. O.
"The Pioneer Dialect of Southern Illinois."
Dialect Notes 2 (Part 4) :225–249.

PLACE NAMES

Barge, W. D., and Caldwell, N. W.
"Illinois Place-Names." *Journal of the Illinois
State Historical Society* 29:189–311, 1936.

Stennett, W. H.
*A History of the Origin of the Place Names
Connected with the Chicago and Northwestern
and Chicago, St. Paul, Minneapolis and Omaha
Railways.* Chicago: 1908. 201 pp., illus., maps.

FOLKSONG

GENERAL STUDIES AND COLLECTIONS

Allison, Lelah
"The Maud Wreck." *SFQ* 5:37–38, 1941.
Words and music of this Illinois ballad, based on
a train wreck near Maud, Illinois, 1904.

Harbison, Katherine
"In the Great and Lone Prairie." *SFQ* 2 (No.
3), (Sept.) 1938.
Songs and ballads with tunes from Illinois, Ohio,
and Blue Grass section of Kentucky.

Longini, Muriel Davis
"Folksongs of Chicago Negroes." *JAFL* 52:
96–111, 1939.

McIntosh, David S.
"Southern Illinois Folksongs." *Illinois State
Historical Society, Journal* 31:297–322, 1938.
Music.

Neely, Charles
"Four British Ballads in Southern Illinois."
JAFL 52:75–81, 1939.

————.
Tales and Songs of Southern Illinois, collected
by Charles Neely; edited with a foreword by
John Webster Spargo. Menasha, Wis.: George
Banta Publishing Co., 1938. xix, 270 pp., part
of the songs accompanied by music.

INDIANA

FOLKLORE

BIBLIOGRAPHY

Historical Records Survey.
Inventory of County Archives of Indiana. Pre-
pared by the Historical Records Survey. Works
Progress Administration. Indianapolis: Indiana
Historical Bureau, 1937. Bibl. included.

Indiana Historical Bureau.
*Publications of the Indiana Historical Bureau
and the Indiana Historical Society.* Indianapolis, 1940. (pp. 187–200).

PERIODICALS

Hoosier Folklore Bulletin. V. 1, 1942–. Bloomington, Indiana University. Changed to
Hoosier Folklore.

Indiana Historical Collections.
V. 1, 1916–. Indianapolis, 1916–1922.

Indiana Historical Society.
Publications. V. 1, 1895–1944. Indianapolis.

Indiana History Bulletin.
V. 1, 1923–. Indianapolis: Indiana Historical
Bureau. Monthly.

Indiana Magazine of History.
V. 1, 1905–. Indianapolis: G. S. Gottman, etc.
1905–. Quarterly.

Indiana University Publications.
Folklore Series. No. I—1940. Indiana University, Bloomington, Ind., illus., music.

GENERAL STUDIES AND COLLECTIONS

Bond, Richmond P.
"Animal Comparisons in Indiana." *AS* 2 (No.
1) :42–58, 1926.

Bynner, Witter
Indian Earth. New York: A. A. Knopf, 1929.
ix–xvi, 77 pp.

Clark, Thomas D.
"The American Backwoodsman in Popular
Portraiture." *Indiana Magazine of History* 42:
1–28, 1946.

Ehamann, Bess V.
Back Trails of Indiana. New York: Horizon
House, 1944. 207 pp.
A narrative of family and community life during
pioneer days on the Ohio River in Southern
Indiana.

Esarey, Logan
The Indiana Home. Crawfordsville, Indiana:
R. E. Banta, 1943. ii, 108 pp.
Local history and some folklore.

Federal Writers' Project.
Indiana, a Guide to the Hoosier State. (American Guide Series). Compiled and written by
the workers of the Writers' Program of the
Works Projects Administration of the State of
Indiana. New York: Oxford University Press,
1941.

Halpert, Herbert, and Robinson, Emma
" 'Oregon' Smith, an Indiana Folk Hero." *SFQ*
6:163–168, 1942.

Harmeyer, Alice J.
"More Folklore from Smithville, Indiana."
HFB 4:15–18, 1945.

Holaday, Eileen
"Folklore from Smithville, Indiana." *HFB* 4:
10–15, 1945.

Martin, John Bartlow
Indiana: An Interpretation. New York: Alfred
A. Knopf, 1947. 300 pp., map.
    One man's interpretation of "the Hoosier char-
acter, the Hoosier thought, and the Hoosier way
of living."

Power, Richard Lyle
"The Hoosier as an American Folk Type."
Indiana Magazine of History (Indianapolis)
38:107–122, 1942.

Trowbridge, C. C.
Mearmear Traditions, edited by Vernon Kin-
ietz. Ann Arbor, Mich.: University of Michigan
Press, 1938.

Thompson, Stith
"Hoosier Folklore Society." *JAFL* 56:171–172,
1943.

Tullis, C. O.
"Folklore from Kankakee Valley." *HFB* 4:24–
25, 1945.

Wilson, William Edward
The Wabash. Illustrated by John De Martelly.
(The Rivers of America). New York: Farrar
and Rinehart, 1940. xi, 339 pp., illus., bibl.

FOLKTALES—LEGENDS

Baughman, Ernest W.
"Bobby Hayes, Quarry Worker." *HFB* 1:75–
77, 1942.
    Legendary hero of Indiana.

————.
"The Cadaver Arm." *HFB* 4:30–31, 1945.
    Legend.

————, and Holaday, Clayton A.
"Tall Tales and 'Sells' from Indiana University
Students." *HFB* 3:59–70, 1944.

Brewster, Paul G.
"Folktales from Indiana and Missouri." *Folklore* (London) 50:294–310, 1939.

Doering, Frederick J.
"Legends from Canada, Indiana and Florida."
SFQ 2 (No. 4):213–220, 1938.

Federal Writers' Project
Hoosier Tall Stories; compiled and written by
the Federal Writers' Project in Indiana. Works
Progress Administration. Indianapolis, 1937.
31 pp.

Halpert, H.
"Indiana Folktales. *HFB* 1:3–34, 1942.
    34 tales, comparative notes and bibl.

————.
"Indiana Storyteller." *HFB* 1:43–61, 1942.

————.
"Liar's Club Tales." *HFB* 2:11–13, 1943.

————.
"Witchcraft Stories: an Indiana Witch." *HFB*
2:10, 1943.

————, and Mitchell, C. B., and Dickason,
D. H.
"Folktales from Indiana University Students."
HFB 1:85–97, 1942.

Hartikka, H. D.
"Tales Collected from Indiana University Students." *HF* 5:71–82, 1946.

Hendricks, Cecilia Hennel
"Robin Tamson's Smiddy." *HFB* 3:55–57,
1944.

Jansen, William Hugh
"Bill Waltz, A Hoosier Character." *HFB* 5
(No. 1):38–39, 1946.

————.
"Folklore Items from a Teacher's Notebook."
HFB 2:1–8, 1943.
    Texts of tales from Indiana University Students,
with notes.

————.
"Tall Tales from a Steel Town." *HFB* 1:41–
42, 78–81, 1942.
    East Chicago, Indiana.

Miller, William Marion
"Another Phantom Hitchhiker Story." *HFB* 5
(No. 1): 40–41, 1946.

O'Bryant, Jean
"Indiana Folktales." *Folio,* a quarterly of
Indiana writing (Indiana University, Bloom-
ington) 6 (No. 3):40–42, 1941.

Sweeney, Margaret
"Tales and Legends Collected by Jefferson-
ville Students." *HFB* 3:39–48, 1944.

CUSTOMS

Billings, William Becker
A State Is Born. Indianapolis: Margaret Billings, 1944. 18 pp.
    A poem.

Bowman, Heath
Hoosier; illustrated from photographs by the
author. Indianapolis: The Bobbs-Merrill Co.,
1944. 360 pp., bibl.

Burns, Lee
Life in Old Vincennes. Indianapolis: Printed
for the Society, 1929. *Indiana Historical Society, Publications. V. 8, No. 9.*

Chamberlain, Ebenezer Mattoon
"Journal of Ebenezer Mattoon Chamberlain,
1832–5. A diary of a journey from Maine to
Indiana, together with a description of the
villages and cities, flora and fauna of the
country, manners and customs of the pioneers."
Indiana Magazine of History 15:233–259, 1919.

Cockrum, William
Pioneer History of Indiana, Including Stories, Incidents and Customs of the Early Settlers. Oakland City, Ind.: Press of Oakland City Journal, 1907. 638 pp.

Dean, Thomas
Journal of Thomas Dean. A Voyage to Indiana in 1817. Ed. by John Candee Dean. Annotated by Randle C. Dean. Indianapolis: C. E. Pauley & Co., 1918. 345 pp. (Indiana State Historical Society, Publications). V. 6, No. 2.

Dreiser, Theodore
A Hoosier Holiday. With illustrations by Franklin Booth. New York: J. Lane Co., 1916. 513 pp., illus.

Esarey, Logan
The Indiana Home. Crawfordsville, Ind.: R. E. Banta, 1943. 108 pp.

Fordham (Elias Pym)
Personal Narrative of Travels in Virginia, Maryland, Pennsylvania, Ohio, Indiana, Kentucky, and a Residence in the Illinois Territory. 1817–1818. Edited by F. A. Ogg. Cleveland: The A. H. Clark Co., 1906. 248 pp.

Harper, Samuel Alain
A Hoosier Tramp. Chicago: The Prairie Club, 1928. 151 pp.

Lindley, Harlow, ed.
Indiana As Seen by Early Travelers; a collection of reprints from books of travel, letters and diaries prior to 1830. Indianapolis: Indiana Historical Commission, 1916. 596 pp.

Parr, Enoch
"Memoir of Enoch Parr, 1808–1851." *Indiana Magazine of History* 22:371–453, 1928.

Parsons, John
A Tour Through Indiana in 1840; the Diary of John Parsons of Petersburgh, Virginia; edited by Kate Milner Rabb. New York: R. M. McBride & Co., 1920. 391 pp.

Power, Richard Lyle
"The Hoosier as an American Folk-Type." *Indiana Magazine of History.* (Bloomington) 38:107–122, 1942.

Pratt, Sarah (Smith)
The Old Crop in Indiana; Drawings by Helen Humphreys, Josephine Hollingsworth. Indianapolis: The Pratt Poster Co., 1928. 271 pp., illus.

Satterthwaite, Myrtillus N.
Hoosier Courtships in the Horse and Buggy Days. Greenfield, Ind.: Wm. Mitchell Printing Co., 1943. 234 pp.

Smith, Oliver Hampton
Early Indiana Trials: And Sketches. Reminiscences by Hon. O. H. Smith. Cincinnati: Moore, Wilstach, Keys & Co., 1858. 640 pp.

Smith, William C.
Indiana Miscellany: consisting of sketches of Indian life, the early settlement, customs, and hardship of the people. Cincinnati: Pub. by Poe & Hitchcock, 1867. 304 pp.

Turpie, David
Sketches of My Own Times. Indianapolis: Bobs-Merrill Co., 1903. 387 pp.

Wood, Aaron
Sketches of Things and Peoples in Indiana. Indianapolis: J. M. Olcott, 1883. 48 pp.

BELIEFS—FOLK MEDICINE

Brewster, Paul G.
"Folk Beliefs and Practices from Southern Indiana." *HFB* 2:23–38, 1943.
Discusses 250 beliefs.

————.
"Folk Cures and Preventions from Southern Indiana." *SFQ* 3:33–43, 1939.

Tullis, C. O.
"Folk Beliefs from Mt. Ayr High School." *HFB* 5 (No. 1):35–36, 1946.

PROVERBS—RIDDLES

Brewster, Paul G.
"Folk Sayings from Indiana." *AS* 14: 261–269, 1939.
Proverbs, idioms and 'sayings'.

————.
"Riddles from Southern Indiana." *SFQ* 3:93–105, 1939.

Green, Marjory Titus
"Proverbs from Greene County, Indiana." *HFB* 4:1–10, 1945.

SPEECH

Bloom, Margaret
"Eggleston's Notes on Hoosier Dialect." *AS* 9 (No. 4):319–320, 1934.

Bond, Richmond
"Animal Comparisons in Indiana." *AS* 2 (No. 1):42–58, 1927.

Brewster, Paul G.
"Folk sayings from Indiana." *AS* 14:261–268, 1939.

————.
"More Indiana Sayings." *AS* 16:21–25, 1941.

————.
"Names of Indiana Quilt Patterns." *CFQ* 3:61, 1944.
Fifty-five names from Southern Indiana.

————.
"Still Another Batch of Indiana Sayings." *AS* 19:155–156, 1944.
About sixty phrases heard in Southern Indiana.

Brown, Rollo Walter
"A Word-List from Western Indiana." *Dialect Notes* 3 (Part 8):570–593, 1912.

Dunn, Jacob Piatt
The Word Hoosier. Indianapolis: Bobbs-Merrill Co., 1907. 37 pp. (Indiana Hist. Soc. Publ. V. 4, No. 2).

Gibbens, V. E.
"Notes on Indiana Speech." *AS* 19:204–206, 1944.

Hanley, O. W.
"Dialect Words from Southern Indiana." *Dialect Notes* 3 (Part 2):113–123, 1906.

Markwardt, A. H.
"Folkspeech in Indiana and Adjacent States." *Indiana Historical Bulletin* 17:120–140, 1940.

McAtee, W. L.
Rural Dialect of Grand County, Indiana, in the 90's. Privately printed, 1942. 81 pp., supplement 10 pp.

Short, O. D.
"Origin of the Term 'Hoosier'." *Indiana Magazine of History* 25:101–103, 1929.

PLACE NAMES

Brewster, Paul G.
"Additional Observations on Indiana Place-Names." *HFB* 3:74–76, 1944.

"A Glance at Some Indiana Place-Names." *HFB* 2:14–16, 1943.

Dunn, Jacob Piatt
True Indian Stories, with Glossary of Indiana Indian Names. Indianapolis: Sentinel Printing Company, 1908.

Ellis, Horace
"Indiana's Map of Patriots." *National Republic* 20:8–9, 1932.
Discussion of place-names selected because of the popularity of famous men.

Guernsey, E.
Indiana; the Influence of the Indian upon its History,—with Indian and French names for natural and cultural locations. Indianapolis, Ind.: Conservation Department. Publication No. 122, 1933.

FOLKSONG

GENERAL STUDIES AND COLLECTIONS

Barry, Phillips
"Fuller and Warren." *FSSNE* 8:12–13, 1934; 9:14–17, 1935.
A tragical ballad dealing with the fatal consequences of a fickle maid's "two-timing." The event took place in 1820. Melody in *FSSNE* 9—p. 1 (1935).

Brewster, Paul G.
Ballads and Songs of Indiana. Indiana University Publications, Folklore Series No. 1. Bloomington: Indiana University, 1940.

"Folk Songs from Indiana." *SFQ* 3:201–222, 1939.
Words only, except 25.

"Indiana's Representation in the Archive of American Folksong." *HFB* 4:25–29, 1945.

"More Indiana Ballads and Songs." *SFQ* 5:169–190, 1941.

"More Songs from Indiana." *SFQ* 4:175–203, 1940.

"Some Folk-Songs from Indiana." *JAFL* 57:282–287, 1944.
Text only of seven ballads: "The Dumb Wife," "The Spinning Wheel," "Untitled," "Kidd and the Bacon," "Young Men and Maidens," "Allan Water," "The Death of Floyd Collins."

"Traditional Ballads from Indiana." *JAFL* 48:295–318, 1935.

Doering, J. Frederick
"Folksongs of the Corn Belt." *JAFL* 57:72–76, 1944.
Text only to five songs.

Halpert, Herbert
"A Group of Indiana Folksongs." *HFB* 3:1–15, 1944.
Text only of twelve songs and ballads.

Neighbors, Alice Atkinson
"There Were Two Crows." *TFSP* 14:282–283, 1938.
Text and melody as sung in Indiana.

Willets, Jane
"Five Folksongs from Richmond, Indiana." *HF* 5 (No. 1):21–28, 1946.

Wolford, Leah Jackson
The Play Party in Indiana; a collection of folksongs and games, with descriptive introduction and correlating notes. Indianapolis: Indiana: Historical Commission, 1916. 120 pp., music, bibl.

GAMES

Brewster, Paul G.
"Game-Songs from Southern Indiana." *JAFL* 49:243–263, 1936.

"Some Unusual Forms of 'Hopscotch'." *SFQ* 9 (No. 4):229–231, 1945.

Wolford, Leah Jackson
The Play Party in Indiana; a collection of folksongs and games, with descriptive introduction and correlating notes. Indianapolis: Indiana Historical Commission, 1916. 120 pp., music, bibl.

DANCE

Kurtz, Homer H.
"Emerald Isle." *CFQ* 3:232–234, 1944.
Music, text and calls of this square dance.

Wolford, Leah Jackson
The Play Party in Indiana; a collection of folksongs and games, with descriptive introduction and correlating notes. Indianapolis: Indiana Historical Commission, 1916. 120 pp., music, bibl.

RECORDS

U. S. Library of Congress. Division of Music. Folklore Section.
Recorded Folk Songs of Old Vincennes, Indiana. Capt. Van Netter, coll.　　　AAFS–LC

IOWA

FOLKLORE

BIBLIOGRAPHY

Cook, Luella E.
"Histories of Iowa Counties." *Iowa Journal of History and Politics* 36:115–151, 1938.

Historical Records Survey.
Inventory of the County Archives of Iowa. Prepared by the Historical Records Survey.... Works Progress Administration. Des Moines, Ia.: The Historical Records Survey, 1938. Bibl. included.

PERIODICALS

Annals of Iowa.
V. 1, 1863. Iowa City, 1863–1915. It had some changes in title.

Iowa Journal of History and Politics.
V. 1, 1903–15, 1917. Iowa City, Ia.: The State Historical Society of Iowa.

Palimpsest.
V. 1, July, 1920–. Iowa City: The State Historical Society of Iowa. Monthly.

GENERAL STUDIES AND COLLECTIONS

Christensen, Thomas Peter, ed.
Sagas of the Hawkeyes,—Being Stories and Incidents of Early Iowa. Iowa City, Ia.: The Mercer Printing Co., 1945. 84 pp.
"Stories from old newspapers, local histories and biographies"—Foreword.

Dondore, Dorothy Ann
The Prairie and the Making of Middle America: Four Centuries of Description. Cedar Rapids, Iowa: Torch Press, 1926.

Federal Writers' Project.
Guide to Cedar Rapids and Northeast Iowa. Compiled and written by the Federal Writers' Project of the Works Progress Administration of the State of Iowa. Cedar Rapids, Iowa: Laurance Press, 1937.

————.
Guide to Dubuque. (American Guide Series). Compiled and written by the Federal Writers' Project of the Works Progress Administration of the State of Iowa. Dubuque, Iowa: The Hoermann Press, 1937.

————.
Iowa, a Guide to the Hawkeye State. (American Guide Series). Compiled and written by the Federal Writers' Project of the Works Progress Administration of the State of Iowa. New York: The Viking Press, 1938. xxviii, 583 pp., illus., bibl.

Glass, Remley J.
Iowa and Counties of Iowa and Something of Their Origin and Histories. Mason City, Ia.: Klipto Loose Leaf Company, 1940.

Havighurst, Walter
Upper Mississippi. (American River Series). Illustrated by David and Lolita Granahan. New York: Farrar and Rinehart, 1937.

Iowa Authors and Artists.
Prairie Gold, by Iowa Authors and Artists. Jacket and frontispiece by J. N. Darling; decorations by Harriet Macy and Louise Orwig. Chicago: The Reilly & Britton Co., 1917. 352 pp., illus.

Lea, Albert Miller
The Book That Gave to Iowa Its Name; A Reprint. Iowa City, Ia.: The State Historical Society of Iowa, 1935. vi, 53 pp.
"The reprint...follows the original, page for page, line for line, and in type as nearly as possible like the original in size and style." First published in Philadelpha: H. S. Tanner, 1836.

Mott, Frank Luther
Literature of Pioneer Life in Iowa; (With a partially annotated bibliography). Iowa City, Iowa: The State Historical Society of Iowa, 1923. 89 pp.

Quick, Herbert
The Hawkeye, The Invisible Woman, Vandemark's Folly. Indianapolis: Bobbs-Merrill, 1923. 477 pp.
Trilogy on Iowa life, manners and tradition.

Robeson, George F.
"Justice in Early Iowa." *The Palimpset* 5 (No. 3) 105, 1924.

Rouse, Clara B.
Iowa Leaves.... Chicago: Illinois Printing and Binding Co., 1891. 451 pp., illus.

Stong, Phil
Hawkeyes: A Biography of the State of Iowa. New York: Dodd, Mead and Company, 1940. ix, 300 pp. (Sovereign States Series).

Stout, Earl J., coll. and ed.
Folklore from Iowa. Memoirs of the American Folklore Society, vol. 29. New York: G. E. Stechert & Co., 1936. x, 228 pp., music.
Content: Ballads and Folk Songs, Current Beliefs, Cures, Household Lore.

Suckow, Ruth
Country People. New York: Alfred A. Knopf, 1924.
A novel using a great deal of local lore and customs.

Van Vechten, Carl
In the Garret. New York: Alfred A. Knopf, 1920. 347 pp.
Music—Addresses, Essays, Lectures.

FOLKTALES—LEGENDS

Aurner, Clarence Ray
Iowa Stories. Iowa City, Ia.: Clio Press, 1921–23. 3 vols., illus.

French, Alice (Octave Thaner)
Stories of a Western Town. New York: Charles Scribner and Sons, 1893.

Musick, Ruth Ann
"Iowa Student Tales." *HF* 5:103–110, 1946.

Ruth, Edith, and Petersen, W. J.
True Tales of Iowa. Mason City, Ia.: Yelland and Hanes, 1932. xiv, 364 pp.

Sigmund, Jay G.
Wapsipinicon Tales. Cedar Rapids, Iowa: Prairie Publishing Co., 1927.
Poems.

Weippert, G. M.
"Legends of Iowa." *JAFL* 2:287–290, 1889.

CUSTOMS

Chapin, Lon F.
Early Days in Iowa. Pasadena, Calif.: Southwest Publishing Co., 1931. xiv, 226 pp.

Clement, Jesse
"Gleanings from the Note Book of the Itinerating Editor." *Iowa Journal of History and Politics* 38:282–305, 1940.
Social life and customs in the early 19th Century.

Cole, Cyrenus
A History of the People of Iowa. Cedar Rapids, Ia.: The Torch Press, 1921. xiv, 572 pp., illus.

Fleming, Andrew Magnus
Iowa Pioneers. Boston: Meador Publishing Company, 1933. 344 pp.

Garland, Hamlin
Iowa, O Iowa! Iowa City: Clio Press, 1935. viii, 58 pp.
A book of poems.

Ivins, Virginia (Wilcox)
Yesterdays; Reminiscences of Long Ago. Illustrations by William N. S. Ivins. Keokuk, 191-. 107 pp., illus.

Jordan, Philip D.
"A Prairie Tour in 1850." *Palimpsest* 22:213–224, 1941.

Macbride, Thomas Huston
In Cabins and Sod-Houses. Iowa City: State Historical Society of Iowa, 1928. xv, 368 pp.
Social and cultural life, with the habits and traditions, of the founders of the state.

Mason, Charles
Life and Letters of Charles Mason, Chief Justice of Iowa.... Washington, D. C.: 1939. 12 vols.

Morris, Emmet L., ed.
Iowa Today, "Where the Tall Corn Grows." Marquette, Ia.: 1931. 219 pp., illus.

Parker, George Frederick
Iowa Pioneer Foundations. Iowa City, Ia.: The State Historical Society of Iowa, 1940. 2 vols.

Parker, Nathan Howe
The Iowa Handbook, for 1850–57. Boston: J. P. Jowett & Co., 1856–7. 2 vols.

Petersen, William John
"Iowa in 1835." *Palimpset* 16:87–102, 1935.

————.
Iowa: The Rivers of Her Valleys. Iowa City, Ia.: The State Historical Society of Iowa, 1941. 581 pp., illus., bibl. (pp. 323–361).

Plumbe, John
Sketches of Iowa and Wisconsin, Taken During a Residence of Three Years in Those Territories. St. Louis: Chambers, Harris & Knapp, 1839. 103 pp.

Swisher, Jacob Armstrong
"Iowa in 1844." *Palimpset* (Iowa City) 25:141–155, 1944.

————.
"Some Historic Sites in Iowa." *Iowa Journal of History and Politics* 32:195–259, 1934.

Tuttle, Charles Richard
An Illustrated History of the State of Iowa, being a complete civil, political and military history of the state from its exploration down to 1875.... With historical and descriptive sketches of each county... embracing interesting narratives of pioneer life.... Chicago: R. S. Peale & Company, 1876. 732 pp., illus.

RIDDLES

McCollum, Catharine Ann, and Porter, Kenneth Wiggins
"Winter Evenings in Iowa, 1873–1880." *JAFL* 56:97–113, 1943.
Riddles, games and songs. Text by C. A. McCollum. Edited and annotated by K. W. Porter.

SPEECH

Buxbaum, Katherine
"Some Iowa Locutions." *AS* 4 (No. 4):302–304, 1929.

Mott, Frank Luther
"A Word-List from Pioneer Iowa and an Inquiry into Iowa Dialect Origins." *Philological Quarterly* 1:202–221, 304–310, 1922.
Good bibliography included.

————.
"The Pronunciation of the Word Iowa." *Iowa Journal of History and Politics* 23:355–362, 1925.

Read, Allen Walker
" 'Liberty' in Iowa." *AS* 6 (No. 5):360–367, 1931.

PLACE NAMES

Fitzpatrick, T. J.
"The Place-Names of Appanoose County, Iowa." *AS* 3 (No. 1):39–66, 1927.

——.
"The Place-Names of Des Moines County, Iowa." *Annals of Iowa* 21 (Ser. 3): 56–73, 127–140, 535–552, 604–640, 1937, bibl.

——.
"The Place-Names of Van Buren County, Iowa." *Annals of Iowa* 18 (Ser. 3): 12–41, 87–116, 1931. bibl.

Hills, Leon C.
History and Legends of Place Names in Iowa. Illus. (The Meaning of Our Map.) Omaha: Omaha School Supply Co., 1937. 78 pp., incl. front., bibliography, p. 5–6.

Read, Allen Walker
"Observations on Iowa Place-Names." *AS* 5 (No. 1):27–44, 1929.

——.
"Literary Place Names." *Palimpsest* 9: 450–457, 1928.

Shambaugh, Benj. F.
"The Naming of Iowa." *Palimpsest* 16:81–86, 1935.

FOLKSONG

GENERAL STUDIES AND COLLECTIONS

McCollum Catharine Ann, and Porter, Kenneth Wiggins
"Winter Evenings in Iowa, 1873–1880." *JAFL* 56:97–113, 1943.

Original Songs of the Old Settlers Quartette of Jefferson County, Ia. Fairfield, Iowa: 1918.

Stout, Earl Jonathan
Folklore from Iowa, collected and edited by Earl J. Stout. New York: The American Folklore Society, G. E. Stechert and Co., Agents, 1936. x, 228 pp.
Some of the songs with music. (Unaccompanied Melodies.)

Van Vechten, Carl
In a Garret. New York: Alfred A. Knopf, 1920. Contains the "Folk-Songs of Iowa," p. 73–.

——.
The Folksongs of Iowa. In: *Sacred and Profane Memories.* New York: A. A. Knopf, 1932. viii, 230 pp., illus., bibl.

GAMES—CHILDREN'S RHYMES

Ashton, J. W.
"Some Jump Rope Rhymes from Iowa." *JAFL* 52:119–123, 1939.

McCollum Catharine Ann, and Porter, Kenneth Wiggins
"Winter Evenings in Iowa, 1873–1880." *JAFL* 56:97–113, 1943.

RECORDS

U. S. Library of Congress. Division of Music. Folklore Section.
Religious Songs of Iowa. 16–12" records.
AAFS–LC

KANSAS

FOLKLORE

BIBLIOGRAPHY

Green, Charles R.
Books and Pamphlets Relating to Kansas. Lyndon, Kan.: 1901. 17 pp.

Historical Records Survey.
Inventory of the County Archives of Kansas. Prepared by the Historical Records Survey.... Works Progress Administration. Topeka, Kan.: The Historical Records Survey, 1937.

Kansas State Historical Society.
A List of Books Indispensable to a Knowledge of Kansas History and Literature.... Topeka, Kan.: W. R. Smith, 1916. 16 pp.

PERIODICALS

Kansas State Historical Society, Transactions.
V. 1, 1881—Vol. 17, 1928. Topeka, 1881–1928. Superseded by the Kansas Historical Quarterly. *Publications.* V. 1–3, 1886–1930.

The Kansas Historical Quarterly.
V. 1, Nov., 1931. Topeka, Kan.: Kansas State Historical Society, 1931–.

GENERAL STUDIES AND COLLECTIONS

Cobb, Irwin S.
Kansas; with illustrations by John T. McCutcheon. New York: George H. Doran Company, 1924. vii, 61 pp.

Federal Writers' Project.
Kansas, a Guide to the Sun Flower State. (American Guide Series). Compiled and written by the Federal Writers' Project of the Works Progress Administration for the State of Kansas. New York: The Viking Press, 1939. xviii, 538 pp., illus., bibl.

Greene, Max
The Kanzas Region: Forest, Prairie, Desert, Mountain, Vale and River.... Incidents of Travel.... New York: Fowler & Wells, 1856. viii, 192 pp.

Hayes, Charles Edward
The Four Winds. New York: The Macmillan Co., 1942. 379 pp.
A grim tale of a Kansas farm family.

Henry, Stuart
Conquering our Great American Plains. New York: E. P. Dutton and Co., 1930. 395 pp.
"A picture of Abilene, Kansas when it was at the end of the Chisholm Trail." (Dobie).

Howe, E. W.
Venture in Common Sense. Made up chiefly of extracts from E. W. Howe's Monthly. The Free Lance Books II. New York: Alfred A. Knopf, 1919.

Humphrey, Mary A.
The Squatter Sovereign; or, Kansas in the 50's. A life picture of the early settlement of the debatable ground. Chicago: Coburn & Newman Pub. Co., 1883. 354 pp., illus.

Ise, John
Sod and Stubble: The Story of a Kansas Homestead. New York: Wilson Erickson, Inc., 1936. 326 pp., illus.
An account of the author's parents' lives.

McCormick, Fannie
A Kansas Farm, or The Promised Land. New York: John B. Alden, Publisher, 1891.

McNeal, T. A.
When Kansas Was Young. New York: Macmillan Co., 1922.
"Episodes and characters of Plains Country." (Dobie).

Phifer, Lincoln
The Dramas of Kansas. Girard, Kan.: L. Phifer, 1915. 192 pp.

Pitzer, Robert Clairborne
Three Frontiers; Memories and a Portrait of Henry Littleton Pitzer, as Recorded by his Son, Robert Clairborne Pitzer. Muscatine, Iowa: The Prairie Press, 1938.

Ropes, Hannah Anderson
Six Months in Kansas. By a Lady. Boston: J. P. Jewett & Co., 1856. 213 pp.
A series of letters.

Snow, Florence L.
Pictures On My Wall. Lawrence: University of Kansas Press, 1945. 161 pp., illus.
"This book of memorabilia touches upon interesting items of folk history and folklore." (E. E. Leisy).

Streeter, Benjamin
The Kaw: The Heart of a Nation. (American River Series). Illustrated by Isabel Bate and Harold Black. New York: Farrar and Rinehart, 1941. ix, 371 pp., illus., bibl.

Walter, George
History of Kanzas, Also, Information Regarding Routes, Laws, &c. &c. ... New York: N. Y. Kanzas League, 1854. 59 pp.

Whittemore, Margaret
Sketchbook of Kansas Landmarks. Illustrated by the Author. Topeka, Kan.: The College Press, 1936. 125 pp., illus.

Youngman, W. E.
Gleanings from Western Prairies. Cambridge: Jones & Pigott, 1882. xv, 214 pp.

FOLKTALES—LEGENDS

Green, Charles Ransley
Tales and Traditions of the Marias des Cygnes Valley. From Arvonia to Quenemo, in Osage Co., Kan. ... Olathe, Kan.: 1914. 92 pp., illus.

Malin, James Claude
John Brown and the Legend of Fifty-Six. Philadelphia: The American Philosophical Society, 1942. xii, 794 pp., bibl.

Stevenson, Anna B.
A Sunflower Sheaf; Stories and Anecdotes of the Early and Later Days of the Sunflower State. New York: The Exposition Press, 1946. 327 pp., bibl.

CUSTOMS

Crawford, Samuel J.
Kansas in the Sixties. Chicago: A. C. McClurg & Co., 1911. xvii, 441 pp.

Delbee, Cora
"The Fourth of July in Early Kansas." *The Kansas Historical Quarterly* 8:115–139, 1939.

Ebbutt, P. G.
Emigrant Life in Kansas. London: Swan, Sonnenscheim & Co., 1886. viii, 237 pp.

Eldridge, S. W.
Recollections of Early Days in Kansas. Topeka, Kansas State Historical Society, Publications, Vol. 2, 1920.

Isely, Bliss
Early Days in Kansas. Wichita: Eagle Press, 1927. 152 pp., illus.

Landes, Kenneth Knight
Scenic Kansas. Topeka, Kansas: Kansas State Printing Plant, 1936. 55 pp., illus.

Lindsay, Nicholas Vachel
Adventures While Preaching the Gospel of Beauty. New York: M. Kennerley, 1914. 186 pp.

McNamara, John
Three Years on the Kansas Border. By a Clergyman of the Episcopal Church. ... New York: Miller, Orton & Mulligan, 1856. viii, 240 pp.

Stephens, Kate
Life at Laurel Town in Anglo-Saxon Kansas. Lawrence: Alumni Association of the University of Kansas, 1920. 251 pp.
"Corn Song"—words and music, pp. 152–154.

Streeter, Floyd Benjamin
Prairie Trails & Cow Towns; with illustrations from old prints. Boston: Chapman & Grimes, 1936. 236 pp., illus., bibl.

Western Border Life; or, What Fanny Hunter Saw and Heard in Kanzas and Missouri. New York: Derby & Jackson, 1856. xii, 408 pp.

FOLK MEDICINE

Davenport, G. C.
"Folk Cures from Kansas." *JAFL* 11:129–132, 1898.

SPEECH

Howe, E. W.
Country Town Sayings; a Collection of Paragraphs from the Atchison Globe. Topeka, Kansas: Crane and Co., 1911.

Pingry, Carl, and Randolph, Vance
"Kansas University Slang." *AS* 3 (No. 3):218–221, 1928.

Randolph, Vance
"Wet Words in Kansas." *AS* 4 (No. 5):385–389, 1929.

Ruppenthal, J. C.
"A Word-List from Kansas." *Dialect Notes* 4 (Part 2):101–114, 1914; 4 (Part 5):319–331, 1916.

"Jottings from Kansas." *Dialect Notes* 5 (Part 6):245–246, 1923.

PLACE NAMES

Hay, R.
"Kaw and Kansas: A Monograph on the Name of the State." *Transactions of the Kansas State Historical Society* 9:521–526, 1906.

Scheffer, Theo. H.
"Geographical Names in Ottawa County." *Kansas Historical Quarterly* 3:227–245, 1934.

FOLKSONG
GENERAL STUDIES

Hull, Myra E.
"Kansas Play-Party Songs." *Kansas Historical Quarterly* 7:258–286, 1938. Music.

Reinbach, Edna, comp.
Music and Musicians in Kansas. Topeka: Kansas State Historical Society, 1930. Bibl.

Porter, Kenneth Wiggins
"Kansas Song." *JAFL* 60:299–301, 1947.
A popular frontier ballad (text only given) of which many versions and variants existed.

Pound, Louise
American Ballads and Songs. New York: Charles Scribner's Sons, 1922.
Contains a number of ballads and songs from Kansas.

MICHIGAN
FOLKLORE

See: Folklore and Song of the Lumberjack, pp. 630–34.

BIBLIOGRAPHY

Historical Records Survey.
Guide to Manuscript Collections in Michigan. ... Prepared by the Michigan Historical Records Survey Project ... Works Progress Administration. Detroit: Michigan Historical Records Survey Project, 1941.

Inventory of the County Archives of Michigan. Prepared by the Historical Records Survey, Works Progress Administration. Detroit, Mich.: The Historical Records Survey, 1937. Bibl.

Michigan Library Commissioners, Board of.
Books on Folklore and Legend in Summer Library School Collection. N.p.: 1912. 3 pp.

"Michigan, Through Three Centuries." A Guide to an Exhibition of Books, Maps, Manuscripts in the William L. Clements Library." *Michigan Univ. Wm. L. Clements Library of American History, Bulletin,* No. 27, pp. 1–20, 1927.

Streeter, Floyd Benjamin
Michigan Bibliography. A partial catalogue of books, maps, manuscripts and miscellaneous materials relating to the resources, development and history of Michigan from the earliest times to July 1, 1917.... Lansing, Mich.: Michigan Historical Commission, 1921. 2 vols.

PERIODICALS

Michigan Historical Commission Bulletin. No. 1, 1913—No. 18, 1944. Lansing, Mich. *Collections.* V. 1, 1874—V. 39, 1929.

Michigan History Magazine.
V. 1, 1917–. Lansing: Official Organ of the Michigan Historical Commission and the Michigan State Historical Society. Quarterly.

Publications in Michigan Academy of Arts and Science, Proceedings. Evelyn E. Gardner, Chairman, of Michigan Folklore Society.

GENERAL STUDIES AND COLLECTIONS

Brock, Emma L.
Then Came Adventure. New York: Alfred A. Knopf, 1941. 184 pp.
A children's book using folklore of the Michigan woods.

Dorson, Richard M.
"Folk Tradition of the Upper Peninsula." *Michigan History,* March, 1947, pp. 48–65.

Federal Writers' Project.
Michigan, a Guide to the Wolverine State. (American Guide Series). Written and compiled by the Federal Writers' Project of the Works Progress Administration for the State of Mich. New York: Oxford University Press, 1941.

Michigan's Upper Peninsula—Its Places and People.... Compiled by Workers of the Writers' Program of the Works Projects Administration in the State of Michigan. Lansing: 1940. 23 pp.

Hedrick, U. P.
The Land of the Crooked Tree. New York: Oxford University Press, 1948. 350 pp.
A colection of essays on various aspects of pioneer life in the woods (northern tip of the southern peninsula). Pleasant, flavorsome, folksy reading.

Jones, Bertrand L.
"Folklore in Michigan." *Kalamazoo Normal Record* 4:297–302, 1914.

Lewis, Janet
The Invasion. New York: Harcourt, Brace and Co., 1932.
A novel in which the traditions, beliefs, and customs are integral with the characters and plot.

McCartney, Eugene Stock
"Folklore Heirlooms." *Michigan Acad. of Science, Arts and Letters* 16:105–210, 1932. Illus., bibl.

Schoolcraft, Henry Rowe
"Discourse delivered before the Historical Society of Michigan." In: *Historical and Scientific Sketches of Michigan.* Detroit: 1834. pp. 51–109.

Stevens, James
The Saginaw Paul Bunyan. New York: Alfred A. Knopf, 1932.

Walton, Ivan H.
"Michigan Folklore Society." *JAFL* 56:174–175, 1943.

White, Stewart Edward
Blazed Trail. New York: Doubleday, Doran, 1902.
The author used a great deal of Michigan lore.

————.
Riverman. New York: Doubleday, Doran, 1908.
A novel of Michigan life and customs.

FOLKTALES—LEGENDS—MYTHS

Bald, F. Clever
"Some Myths About Michigan." *Michigan Historical Commission. Michigan History Magazine* 28:595–609, 1944.

Dorson, Richard M.
"Dialect Stories of the Upper Peninsula: A New Form of American Folklore." *JAFL* 61: 113–151, 1948.
Includes French, Finnish, Cornish, Swedish and Italian; and various dialect jokes.

————.
"The Lynching of the McDonald Boys." *Am. Mercury* 46:698–703, June, 1948.
An historical legend that happened at Menominee, Michigan, in 1881. Gives also ballad text.

Hamlin, Marie Caroline Watson
Legends of Le Détroit. Illustrated by Isabella Stewart. Detroit: T. Nourse, 1884. 317 pp., illus.
Legends and stories of the French in Detroit.

Kane, Grace Franks
Myths and Legends of the Mackinacs and Lake Region. Cincinnati, Ohio: Editor Publ. Co., 1897.

Littlejohn, F. J.
Legends of Michigan and the Old Northwest. Allegan: Northwestern Bible and Publ. Co., 1875.

Martin, John Bartlow
Call It North Country: The Story of Upper Michigan. New York: Alfred A. Knopf, 1944. 281 pp., illus., maps.
The author includes many forgotten tall tales and yarns.

Reed, Earl H.
Sketches in Duneland. New York: J. Lane Co., 1918. 281 pp., illus.
The author includes a number of old tales and legends.

BELIEFS—SUPERSTITIONS

McGuire, Robert Graham
"The Black Dog." *HFB* 2:21, 1943.
The black dog as augur of death, from Detroit, Michigan.

"Michigan Miner's Superstition."
JAFL 13:226, 1900.

CUSTOMS

Gray, Anna Brockway
"Letters From Long Ago." *Michigan Historical Commission. Michigan History Magazine* 13: 469–491; 15:459–480; 18:150–160; 20:185–212, 1929–1936.

Hazelton, George H.
"Reminiscences of Seventeen Years Residence in Michigan, 1836–1853." *Michigan Pioneer and Hist. Soc. Coll.* 21:370–418, 1894.

Kirkland, Caroline Matilda S.
A New Home—Who'll Follow? or, Glimpses of Western Life. New York: C. S. Francis, 1841. iv, 298 pp.

Lewis, Ferris E.
Then and Now in Michigan. Illustrated by Norma M. Schram. Hillsdale, Mich.: Hillsdale School Supply Co., 1944. vii, 170 pp., illus., bibl.

Plumb, Ralph Gordon
Lake Michigan. Manitowoc, Wis.: Brandt Printing and Binding Co., 1941. 208 pp.

Smith, Joshua Toulmin
Journal in America; 1837–1838, edited with an introduction and notes by Floyd Benjamin Streeter. Metuchen, N. J.: C. F. Heartman, 1925. 54 pp.

Storrow, Samuel Appleton
Narrative of a Tour in the Northwest in 1817. N.p., 1818. 39 pp.

Swan, Lansing B.
Journal of a Trip to Michigan in 1841. Rochester: G. P. Humphrey, 1904. 54 pp.

SPEECH—PLACE NAMES

Dustin, Fred
"Some Place-Names Around Saginaw." *Michigan Historical Magazine* 12:729–739, 1928.

————.
"Isle Royale Place Names". *Michigan History* 30 (No. 4): 681-722, 1946. illus.

Foster, Theodore G.
"Place Names of Ingham County". *Michigan Historical Commission. Michigan History Magazine* 26:480–517, 1942.

Fox, George R.
"Place Names of Berrien Co., Michigan." *Michigan Historical Monthly* 8:6–35, 1924.

————.
"Place Names of Cass County." *Michigan History* 27:463–491, 1943.

Hamilton, Charlotte
"Chippewa County Place Names." *Michigan History* 27:638–643, 1943.

Veltman, Peter
"Dutch Survivals in Holland, Michigan." *AS* 15:80–84, 1940.

FOLKSONG

See: Songs of the Lumberjacks, pp. 632–34.

GENERAL STUDIES AND COLLECTIONS

Beck, Earl Clifton
Songs of the Michigan Lumberjacks. Ann Arbor: University of Michigan Press, 1942. 296 pp., contains unaccompanied tunes.

————.
" 'The Farmer's Curst Wife' (Child 278) in Michigan." *SFQ* 4:157–158, 1940.

Carpenter, Margaret
"Whitewashing Song Sung by a Painter of English Ancestry in Wixom, Michigan." *JAFL* 51:107, 1938.

Gardner, Emelyn Elizabeth
"Ballads." *JAFL* 27:90–93, 1914.

————.
Ballads and Songs of Southern Michigan; coll. and ed. by Emelyn Elizabeth Gardner and Geraldine Jencks Chickering. Ann Arbor: The University of Michigan Press, 1939. xviii, 501 pp., unacc. melodies, bibl., illus.

Halpert, Herbert
"A Michigan Lumberjack Singer." *HFB* 1:81–84, 1942.

Johnson, Arli Kolehmainen
"Michigan Folklore: Finnish Labor Songs from Northern Michigan." *Michigan History* 31 (No. 3):331–344, 1947.
Texts only: Songs of the sharecroppers, IWW's and hoboes.

CHILDREN RHYMES

"Counting Out Rhymes in Michigan." *JAFL* 31:521–536, 1918.

Crockett, Dolores N.
"Children's Rhymes from Michigan." *JAFL* 44:116, 1931.

GAMES

Gardner, E. E.
"Play Party Games in Michigan." *JAFL* 33:91–133, 1920.

MINNESOTA

FOLKLORE

See: Section on Norwegian-American, p. 580.

BIBLIOGRAPHY

Historical Records Survey.
Inventory of the Archives of Minnesota. Historical Records Survey. Works Progress Administration. Saint Paul: The Historical Records Survey, 1937.

Loehr, Rodney C., ed.
Minnesota Farmers' Diaries.... With an introduction and notes. Saint Paul: The Minnesota Historical Society, 1939. ix, 247 pp.

Nute, Grace Lee, comp.
Guide to the Personal Papers in the Manuscript Collections of the Minnesota Historical Society. Saint Paul: The Minnesota Historical Society, 1935. x, 146 pp.

Williams, John Fletcher
"Bibliography of Minnesota." *Minnesota Historical Society. Collections* (St. Paul) 3:13–75, 1880.

————.
Bibliography of Minnesota. Previous to 1870. St. Paul: Office of Press Printing Co., 1870. 65 pp.

PERIODICALS

Minnesota History.
Minnesota Historical Society, S. Paul. V. 1, February, 1915. V. 1–5 as *Minnesota Historical Bulletin.*

Minnesota Historical Society. Annals. 1851–1856. St. Paul. *Collections* 1872–1920.

GENERAL STUDIES AND COLLECTIONS

Bishop, Harriet E.
Minnesota; Then and Now. St. Paul: D. D. Merrill, Randall & Co., 1869. 100 pp., illus.

Blegen, Theodore Christian
Minnesota, Its History and Its People; a study outline with topics and references... with the assistance of Lewis Beeson. Minneapolis: The University of Minnesota Press, 1937. viii, 237 pp.

Bond, John Wesley
Minnesota and Its Resources; to which are appended camp-fire sketches, or, notes of a trip from St. Paul to Pembina and Selkirk settlement on the Red River of the North. New York: Redfield, 1853. 364 pp.

Brainerd, C. N.
"Minnesota as Seen by Travelers. A New Yorker in the Great West, 1867." *Minnesota History* 12:43–64, 1931.

Carney, Mary Vance
Minnesota, the Star of the North. Boston: D. C. Heath & Co., 1918. xvii, 249 pp., bibl., illus.

Featherstonhaugh, George William
A Canoe Voyage up the Minnay Sotar (Minnesota) River.... London: R. Bentley, 1847. 2 vols.

Federal Writers' Project.
Minnesota, a State Guide. (American Guide Series). Compiled and written by the Federal Writers' Project of the Works Progress Administration. New York: The Viking Press, 1938.

_____.
St. Cloud Guide, The Granite City. Written and compiled by the Federal Writers' Project of the Works Progress Administration for the State of Minnesota. St. Cloud, Minnesota: 1936.

Folsom, William Henry Carman
Fifty Years in the Northwest. With an introduction and appendix containing reminiscences, incidents and notes. Edited by E. E. Edwards. St. Paul: Pioneer Press Company, 1888. xliii, 763 pp., illus.

Hankins, C.
Dakota Land; or, the Beauty of St. Paul. An Original Illustrated, Historic and Romantic Work on Minnesota, and the Great North-West. New York: Hankins & Son, 1869. 425 pp., illus.

Havighurst, Walter
Upper Mississippi. (American River Series). Illustrated by David and Lolita Granahan. New York: Farrar and Rinehart, 1937.

Johnson, John S.
Minnesota, En Kortfattet Historie Av Nordmaendenes Bebyggelse Av Staten, deres gjøremaal, foreninger oglivsvilkaar, med avsnit om den Norske kirkes historie.... Saint Paul: McGill-Warner Co., 1914. 322 pp., illus.
The Norwegians in Minnesota, in connection with the Minnesota-Norway Centennial Exposition.

League of Minnesota Poets.
Minnesota Skyline; Anthology of Poems About Minnesota. Carmen Nelson, editor. Minneapolis: The League of Minnesota Poets, 1944. 141 pp.

Le Sueur, Meridel
North Star Country. (American Folkways Series). New York: Duell, Sloan and Pearce, 1946. viii, 327 pp.
The story of Minnesota, Wisconsin and the western shores of the Great Lakes.... "This is the living history of the making of a country...."

_____.
"Notes on North Country Folkways." *Minnesota History* 25:215–223, 1944.

Marryat, Frederick
"Minnesota As Seen By Travelers. Captain Marryat In Minnesota, 1838." *Minnesota History* 6:168–184, 1925.

Mayer, Francis Blackwell
With Pen and Pencil On the Frontier in 1851; The Diary and Sketches of F. B. M.... Saint Paul: The Minnesota Historical Society, 1932. xii, 214 pp., illus.

Neill, Edward Duffield
"The French Voyageurs to Minnesota during the Seventeenth Century...." *Minnesota Historical Society, Coll.* 1:17–36, 1872.

Nisbeth, Hugo
"Minnesota As Seen By Travelers. A Swedish Visitor in the Early Seventies. Chapters from the Author's Two Years in America." *Minnesota History* 8:386–421, 1927.

Nute, Grace Lee
The Voyageur's Highway, Minnesota's Border Lake Land. St. Paul: The Minnesota Historical Society, 1941. xiii, 113 pp., illus., bibl.
Includes songs with music.

O'Connell, Donald
The North Star State in Pictures. St. Paul: Publ. by the Itaska Press for the Minnesota Historical Society, 1946. 60 pp., illus.

Owens, John P.
"Minneosta as Seen by Travelers. Up the Minnesota Valley to Fort Ridgely in 1853." *Minnesota History* 11:161–184, 1930.

Schilplin, Maude C., ed.
Minnesota Verse, An Anthology. St. Cloud, Minn.: The Times Publishing Company, 1934. xxxvi, 268 pp., bibl.

Schoolcraft, Henry Rowe
"A Memoir on the History and Physical Geography of Minesota." *Minnesota Historical Society* 6:108–132, 1872.

Sickels, Alice L.
Around the World in St. Paul. Minneapolis: University of Minnesota Press, 1945. 262 pp., illus., index.

Stevens, John Harrington
Personal Recollections of Minnesota and Its People.... Minneapolis, Minn.: 1890. 432 pp.

Thompson, Stith
"Folklore and Minnesota History." *Minnesota History* 26:97–105, 1945.

FOLKTALES—LEGENDS

Flandrau, Charles E.
The History of Minesota and Tales of the Frontier. St. Paul: E. W. Porter, 1900. vii, 408 pp.

Potter, Merle
101 Best Stories of Minnesota. Indianapolis: 1931. xvi, 301 pp., illus.

Taylor, Archer
"Old World Tale from Minnesota." *JAFL* 31: 555, 1918.

CUSTOMS—BELIEFS

Cannon, Cornelia J.
Red Rust. Boston: Little, Brown and Co., 1928.
A novel of Minnesota life, customs and tradition.

Edgar, Marjorie
"Finnish Charmer from Minnesota." *JAFL* 47:381–383, 1934.

————.
"Imaginary Animals of Northern Minnesota." *Minnesota History* 21:352–356, 1935.

Ellet, Elizabeth Fries
Summer Rambles in the West. New York: J. C. Riker, 1853. viii, 268 pp.

Farrar, J. Maurice
Five Years in Minnesota. Sketches of Life in a Western State. London: S. Low, Marston, Searle & Rivington, 1880. xiv, 269 pp.

Ford, Antoinette Elizabeth
My Minnesota. Chicago: Lyons and Carnahan, 1929. 416 pp., illus.

Lewis, Sinclair
Main Street. The Story of Carol Kennicott. New York: Harcourt, Brace and Howe, 1921.

Lindquist, Maude Lucille, and Clark, J. W.
Early Days and Ways in the Old Northwest. New York: C. Scribner's Sons, 1937. x, 295 pp.

McLeod, Martin
"Diary." *Minnesota Historical Society. History Bulletin* 4:351–439, 1922.

McNally, William J.
House of Vanished Splender. New York: G. P. Putnam and Co., 1931.
Mainly concerned with historical incidents.

Ostenso, Martha
O River, Remember. New York: Dodd, Mead Co., 1943. 393 pp.
A novel of frontier days in the Red River Valley.

Painter, Clara Searle
Minnesota Grows Up. Illustrations by Jane McCarthy. Minneapolis: The University of Minnesota Press, 1936. 144 pp., illus., bibl., music.

Raeder, Ole Munch
America in the Forties; the letters of Ole Munch Raeder, translated and edited by Gunnar J. Malmin. Minneapolis: Pub. for the Norwegian-American Historical Association by the University of Minnesota Press, 1929. xxi, 244 pp.

Richards, Carmen, and Breen, Genevieve
Minnesota Writers. A collection of Autobiographical Stories by Minnesota Prose Writers. Minneapolis: The Lund Press, 1945. 204 pp.

Rolvaag, Ole E.
Peder Victorious. New York: Harper and Brothers, 1929.
Adventures of Prairie Pioneers, begun in South Dakota in the novel "Giants of the Earth."

Russell, Morris Craw
Uncle Dudley's Odd Hours; Western Sketches, Straws of Humor.... Lake City, Minn.: "The Home Printery," 1904. 256 pp.

Sibley, H. H.
"Description of Minnesota." *Collections of the Minnesota Historical Society* 1:37–42, 1872.

Summer Saunterings in the Land of Lakes.... By a St. Paul newspaper man. St. Paul: Brown & Treacy, 1882. 40 pp., illus.

SPEECH

Klaeber, Fr.
"A Word-List from Minnesota." *Dialect Notes* 4 (Part 1):9–12, 1913.

PLACE NAMES

Culkin, William E.
North Shore Place Names, with maps and illustrations. St. Paul, Minn.: Scott-Mitchell Publishing Co., 1931. xi, 95 pp., illus.
"This treatise undertakes to give the origin of the place names along the North Shore of Lake Superior between Fond du Lac in Duluth on the southwest and the Pigeon river at the Canadian boundary on the northeast". pp. 13–14.

Gilfillan, Rev. Joseph Alexander
Minnesota Geographical Names Derived from the Chippewa Language. St. Paul Minn.: 1887. pp. 451–476. (Minnesota Geological and Natural Survey. Annual Report No. 15).

Stennett, W. H.
A History of the Origin of the Place Names Connected with the Chicago and Northwestern and Chicago, St. Paul, Minneapolis and Omaha Railways. Chicago: 1908. 201 pp., map., illus.

Upham, Warren
Minnesota Geographic Names, Their Origin and Historic Significance. St. Paul: Minnesota Historical Society, 1920. viii, 735 pp. (Collections of the Minnesota Historical Society, Vol. XVII.)

Williamson, A. W.
"Minnesota Geographical Names Derived from the Dakota Language, with some that are obsolete." *Geologic and Natural History Survey of Minnesota,* 13th Annual Report, St. Paul, 1885.

FOLKSONG

See: Songs of the Lumberjacks, pp. 632–34.

GENERAL STUDIES AND COLLECTIONS

Dean, M. C.
Flying Cloud and One Hundred and Fifty Other Old Time Songs and Ballads. Virginia, Minnesota: The Quickprint, n.d.

Nute, Grace Lee
The Voyageur's Highway, Minnesota's Border Lake Land. St. Paul: The Minnesota Historical Society, 1941. xiii, 113 pp., illus., bibl., music.

MISSOURI

FOLKLORE

BIBLIOGRAPHY

Conard, Howard Lewis, ed.
Encyclopedia of the History of Missouri, a compendium of history and biography for ready reference. New York: The Southern History Company, 1901. 6 vols.
Bibliography of Missouri: Vol. 1, pp. 215–270.

Historical Records Survey.
Inventory of the County Archives of Missouri. Prepared by the Historical Records Survey. Works Progress Administration. St. Louis, Mo.: The Historical Records Survey, 1937.

Sampson, F. A.
"Bibliography of Books of Travel in Missouri." *Missouri Historical Review* 6:64–81, 1912.

United States. Library of Congress. Division of Bibliography.
List of Books on the History of Missouri. . . . Jan. 20, 1925. Washington, D. C., 1925. (Select list of references, No. 896).

PERIODICALS

Missouri Historical Review.
State Historical Society of Missouri, Columbia, Mo. V. 1, Oct., 1906–. Quarterly.

Missouri Historical Society. Collections. V. 1, 1880–. St. Louis, Mo.

GENERAL STUDIES AND COLLECTIONS

Beck, Lewis Caleb
A Gazetteer of the States of Illinois and Missouri; containing a general view of each state, a general view of their counties, and a particular description of their towns, villages, rivers, &c., &c. . . . Albany: Printed by C. R. and G. Webster, 1823. vii, 352 pp., illus.

Belden, H. M.
"Missouri Folklore Society." *JAFL* 56:176–177, 1943.

Buel, James W.
The Border Outlaws: An authentic and thrilling history of the most noted bandits of ancient and modern times; The Younger brothers, Jesse and Frank James, and their comrades in crime. St. Louis: Historical Publ. Co., 1881. 148 pp., illus.

Craig, James H.
Kettle Drums and Tom Toms. Illustrated by Monte Crews. Kansas City, Mo.: Burton Publishing Co., 1928. 323 pp.
A novel of Missouri country life.

Dacus, Joseph A.
Illustrated Lives and Adventures of Frank and Jesse James and the Younger Brothers, the noted Western Outlaws. St. Louis: N. D. Thompson and C., 1881.

De Voto, Bernard Augustine
Mark Twain's America. Boston: Little, Brown and Co., 1932.

Doneghy, Dagmar
The Border; a Missouri Saga. New York: W. Morrow & Co., 1931. 343 pp.
A novel utilizing incidents and lore of the Missourians.

Dorrance, Ward Allison
The Sundowners. New York: Charles Scribner's Sons, 1942. 343 pp.
A novel of Missouri farm life on the banks of the "big muddy." An intimate portrayal of American folkways and robust characters.

————————.
The Survival of French in the Old District of Sainte Genevieve. Columbia, Mo.: The University of Missouri Studies, Vol. 10, No. 2, April 1, 1935. Illus., music, bibl.

————————.
Those Ozark Streams; Log of the Mocassin and the Wilma. Richmond, Mo.: The Missourian Press, 1937.

————————.
We're from Missouri. Frontispiece by Thomas Hart Benton. Richmond, Mo.: The Missourian Press, 1938. 97 pp.
Consists of short stories and sketches.

————————.
Where the Rivers Meet. New York: Charles Scribner's Sons, 1939.

Edwards, John L.
Notes Guerrillas, or, The Warfare of the Border. St. Louis: Bryan, Brand and Co., 1887. 488 pp., illus.

Ellis, J. Breckenridge
The Little Fiddler of the Ozarks. Chicago: Laird and Lee, 1913.

Elsea, Albert F., and Moss, Neil
Our Missouri. New York: The Macmillan Company, 1939. x, 352 pp., illus., bibl.

Evans, James N., Keith, A. Wendell, M.D.
Autobiography of Samuel S. Hildebrand the Renowned Missouri "Bushwacker," and Unconquerable Rob Roy of America. Jefferson City, Mo.: State Times Book and Job Printing House, 1870. 312 pp., illus.

Federal Writers' Project.
Missouri, a Guide to the "Show Me" State. (American Guide Series). Written and compiled by the Federal Writers' Project of the Works Progress Administration for the State of Missouri. New York: Duell, Sloan and Pearce, 1941.

Flagg, Edmund
The Far West; or, A Tour Beyond the Mountains. Embracing outlines of Western life and scenery; sketches of the prairies, rivers, ancient mounds, early settlements of the French, etc.... New York: Harper & Bros., 1838. 2 vols.

Grubb, Marion
"Missourian Arcady." *Commonweal* 24:525–526, 1936.
Customs, language and history of the French in the old Sainte Genevieve District of Missouri.

Hannum, Anna Pachall, ed.
A Quaker Forty-Niner; The Adventures of Charles Edward Pancoast in the American Frontier. Forword by John Bach McMaster. Philadelphia: University of Pennsylvania Press, 1930.

Herklotz, Hildegard Rose
"Jayhawkers in Missouri, 1858–1863." *Missouri Historical Review* 17:266–284, 505–513; 18:64–101, 1923–1924.

Lindsay, Nicholas Vachel
Adventures While Preaching the Gospel of Beauty. New York: M. Kennerley, 1914. 186 pp.

Marsh, Susan Louis (Cotton), and Vannest, Charles Garrett
Missouri Anthology. Boston: The Christopher Publishing House, 1932. viii, 128 pp.

"Missouriana."
Missouri Historical Review 30:162–178, 1936.

Montieth, John
Parson Brooks: A Plumb Powerful Hardshell. St. Louis, Mo.: O. H. P. Applegate, 1884.

Morris, Lucille
Bald Knobbers. Caldwell, Idaho: The Caxton Printers, Ltd., 1939. 253 pp., illus.

Neihardt, John G.
The River and I. New York: G. P. Putnam's Sons, 1910. ix, 325 pp.

O'Hanlon, Rev. John
Life and Scenery in Missouri. Reminiscences of a Missionary Priest. Dublin: J. Duffy & Co., Ltd., 1890. xii, 292 pp.

Schiavo, Giovanni Ermenegildo
The Italians in Missouri. Chicago: The Italian American Publishing Co., 1929. 216 pp., illus.

Schoolcraft, Henry Rowe
A View of the Lead Mines of Missouri. New York: C. Wiley and Co., 1819. 299 pp.

————.
Summary Narrative of an Exploratory Expedition to the Sources of the Missouri River in 1820. Philadelphia: Lippincott, Grambo and Co., 1855. 596 pp.

Schultz, Gerard
Early History of the Northern Ozarks. Jefferson City, Mo.: Midland Printing Co., 1937. 192 pp., illus.

Spotts, Carle Brooks
The Development of Fiction in the Missouri Frontier (1830–1860). Columbia, Mo.: 1935. 70 pp.

Stevens, Walter Barlow
Missourians One Hundred Years Ago.... Columbia, Mo.: The State Historical Society of Missouri..., 1917. 48 pp.

————.
"The Missourian." *Missouri Historical Review* 17:117–129, 1923.

Tuck, Clyde Edwin
The Bald Knobbers; a Romantic and Historical Novel. Indianapolis: B. F. Bower and Co., 1910.

Vestal, Stanley
The Missouri. (Rivers of America Series). Illustrated by Getlar Smith. New York: Farrar and Rinehart, 1945. x, 368 pp., illus., bibl. (pp. 349–354).

Weeks, Raymond
The Hound-Tuner of Callaway. New York: Columbia University Press, 1927.

Wetmore, Alphonso
Gazetteer of the State of Missouri.... To which is added an appendix, containing frontier sketches. St. Louis: C. Keemle, 1837. xvi, 382 pp.

Wilson, Charles Morrow
Backwoods America. Chapel Hill, N. C.: University of North Carolina Press, 1935. 209 pp., illus.

Wright, Harold Bell
The Calling of Dan Matthews. New York: A. L. Burt Co., 1909.

————.
The Shepherd of the Hills. New York: A. L. Burt Co., 1907.

Younger, Cole
The Story of Cole Younger. By Himself. Chicago: Press of the Henneberry Co., 1903. 123 pp., illus.

FOLKTALES—LEGENDS

Brewster, Paul G.
"Folktales from Indiana and Missouri." *Folk-Lore* (London) 50:294–310, 1939.

Carrière, Joseph Medard, ed.
Tales from the French Folklore of Missouri. Evanston and Chicago: Northwestern University, 1937. viii, 354 pp., illus., music.

Collins, Earl
Folktales of Missouri. Boston: Christopher Publishing Co., 1935. 133 pp.

Hauck, Louise Platt
Missouri Yesterdays: Stories of the Romantic Days of Missouri. Kansas City, Mo.: Burton Publishing Co., 1920. 207 pp.

"Legends of 'Jim Johnson'."
Missouri Historical Quarterly Review 34:581–582.

Miller, William Marion
"La Guignolée in Southeast Missouri." *French Folklore Bulletin* 4 (No. 21):61–64, 1945.

Moore, T.
Mysterious Tales and Legends of the Ozarks. Philadelphia: Derrance and Co., Inc., 1938.

Musick, John Roy
Stories of Missouri. New York: The American Book Co., 1897. 288 pp.

Musik, Ruth Ann, and Ashton, John W.
Folklore From In And Near Kirksville, Missouri. Phila., Pa.: The Folklore Society, c. 1950.

Yoffie, L. R.
"Yiddish Folk Stories and Songs in St. Louis." St. Louis: *Washington University Record* 5:20–22, 1910.

CUSTOMS

Beck, W. G.
"Survivals of Old Marriage Customs Among the Low Germans of West Missouri." *JAFL* 21:60–67, 1908.

Berthold, Eugénie
Glimpses of Creole Life in Old St. Louis. St. Louis: Missouri Historical Society, 1933. 28 pp.

Bryan, William Smith
A History of the Pioneer Families of Missouri, with numerous sketches, anecdotes, adventures, etc., relating to early days in Missouri. . . . St. Louis, Mo.: Bryan, Brand & Co., 1876. 528 pp., illus.

Clark, Thomas D.
"Manners and Humors of the American Frontier." *Missouri Historical Review,* 35 (Oct., 1940):3–24. St. Louis, 1940.

Cozine, June
Missouri History Depicted Through Food Customs. Maryville, Mo.: State Teachers College. *The Northwest Missouri State Teachers College Studies.* Vol. 8, No. 1, 1944.

Crittenden, Henry Huston
The Crittenden Memoirs. New York: G. P. Putnam's Sons, 1936. xv, 542 pp., illus.
Particularly valuable for information on the "James Gang."

Dickey, Lily Ann
"The Pastimes of Missourians before 1900." *Missouri Historical Review* 37:134–149, 1943.

Houck, Louis
Memorial Sketches of Pioneers and Early Residents of Southeast Missouri. Cape Girardeau: Naeter Bros., 1915. 135 pp.

Mackay, James
Extracts from Capt. McKay's Journal—and Others. . . . Madison, Wis.: State Historical Society of Wisconsin, Proceedings, 1915. pp. 185–210.

Owen, Mary Alicia
"Social Customs and Usages in Missouri During the Last Century." *Missouri Historical Review* 15:176–190, 1920.

Park, Eleanora, and Morrow, Kate S.
Women of the Mansion, Missouri, 1821–1936. Jefferson City, Mo.: The Midland Printing Company, 1936. vi, 435 pp.
"Story . . . of the Executive mansions and of the domestic and social life and interesting experiences of the women and children who dwelt therein." Foreword.

Shoemaker, Floyd Calvin
Missouri—Heir of Southern Tradition and Individuality. Columbia: State Historical Society of Missouri, 1942.

White, John Barber
The Missouri Merchant One Hundred Years Ago. Columbia: State Historical Society of Missouri, 1919. 23 pp.

Zimmermann, Eduard
"Travel Into Missouri in October, 1838." *Missouri Historical Review* 9:33–43, 1914.

SPEECH

Carrière, Joseph Medard
"Creole Dialect of Missouri." *AS* 14:109–119, 1939.

Carter, Virginia
"University of Missouri Slang." *AS* 6 (No. 3):203–206, 1931.

Crumb, D. S.
"The Dialect of Southeastern Missouri." *Dialect Notes* 2 (Part 5):304–337.

Emberson, Frances Guthrie
Mark Twain's Vocabulary; A General Survey. Columbia, Mo.: The University of Missouri Studies, Vol. 10 (No. 3):53 pp., 1935.

Ramsay, Robert L., and Emberson, Frances Guthrie
A Mark Twain Lexicon. Columbia, Mo.: The University of Missouri Studies, Vol. 13 (No. 1):278 pp., 1938.

Read, Allen Walker
"Pronunciation of the Word 'Missouri'." *AS* 8 (No. 4):22–36, 1933.

————.
"The Strategic Position of Missouri in Dialect Study." *Missouri Alumnus* 20:231–232, 1932.

PLACE NAMES—PROVERBS

Eaton, David W.
"How Missouri Counties, Towns and Streams Were Named." *Missouri Historical Review* 10:197–213, 263–287; 11:164–200, 330–347; 13:57–74, 1916–17.

Oevitch, J. P.
"Proverbial Comparisons of Oklahoma and Missouri." *HFB* 3:37, 1944.

Ramsay, R. L., and others
Introduction to a Survey of Missouri Place Names. Columbia, Mo.: The University of Missouri Studies. Vol. 9, No. 1, 1934. 124 pp., illus.

————.
"The Study of Missouri Place-Names at the University of Missouri." *Missouri Historical Review* 27:132–144, 1933.

Read, Allen W.
"Plans for the Study of Missouri Place-Names." *Missouri Historical Review* 22:237–241, 1928.

FOLKSONG

GENERAL STUDIES AND COLLECTIONS

Barbour, Frances M.
"Some Fusions in Missouri Ballads." *JAFL* 49:207–215, 1936.

Belden, Henry Marvin
A Partial List of Song-Ballads and Other Popular Poetry Known in Missouri. Columbia, Mo.: University of Missouri, 1910. 11 pp.
Lists 145 items, texts only.

————.
Ballads of the Meeks Murder in Missouri. Columbia: The University of Missouri, 1940. xviii, 530 pp. Some of the songs with music, (unaccompanied melodies).
Ballads and songs collected by the Missouri Folk-lore Society.

————.
Ballads and Songs Collected by the Missouri Folk-lore Society. In: *The University of Missouri Studies,* Vol. 15 (No. 1). Columbia, Mo.: University of Missouri Press, Jan. 1, 1940. 530 pp., music (unaccomp. melodies).

"Folk-Song in Missouri-Bedroom Window." *Archiv für das Studium der Neueren Sprachen und Literaturen.* 119:430–431, 1917.

————.
"Old County Ballads in Missouri." *JAFL* 19: 231–240, 281–299, 1905; 20:319–320, 1906.

————.
"Popular Song in Missouri.... 'The Returned Lover'." *Archiv für das Studium de Neueren Sprachen und Literaturen* 120:62–71, 1918.

————.
"Three Old Ballads from Missouri." *JAFL* 23: 429–431, 1908.

Collection of Missouri Folk Songs.
Collected in 1935 by Charles Van Ravenswaay, Director of the Missouri Historical Society, in the Fayette and Bonneville area of central Missouri. Contains the texts of some 200 folk songs. Unpublished. The manuscript is filed in the Jefferson Memorial Building, St. Louis, Missouri.

Dorrance, Ward Allison
The Survival of French in the Old District of Sainte Genevieve. The University of Missouri Studies, Vol. 10 (No. 2). Columbia: The University of Missouri, 1935. 133 pp., illus., music, bibl.

Hudson, Arthur Palmer
"A Ballad of the New Madrid Earthquake." *JAFL* 60:147–150, 1947.
A song—"A Call to the People of Louisiana." (text only)—giving dramatic account of the Mississippi Valley earthquake of 1811–12, "and moralizes upon its significance in divine economy."

McDonald, Grant
A Study of Selected Folk-Songs of Southern Missouri. Master's thesis. Music Department of the University of Iowa. MS. in the University Library, 1939.
Consists of 38 texts and thirty-seven tunes, a good representative collection.

"Missouri, Old Country Ballads." *JAFL* 19:231–240, 281–389, 1906; 20:319–320, 1907; 23: 429–431, 1910; 34:395–396, 1921.

Moore, J. R.
"Missouri Variant of 'The False Lover Won Back'." *JAFL* 34:395–397, 1921.

Musick, Ruth Ann
"Three Folksongs from Missouri." *HF* 5 (No. 1):29–34, 1946.

"National Folk Festival at St. Louis." *Music Clubs Magazine* 14(No. 1):20–21, Sept.-Oct. 1934.)

"National Folk-Festival To be Held in St. Louis, Mo." *Musical Courier* 108(No. 9):7, March 3, 1934.

Smelser, J. M.
The "Two Sisters" from Missouri. *JAFL* 44: 295–296, 1931.

Yoffie, Leah Rachel Clara
Yiddish Folk Stories and Songs in St. Louis. *Washington University Record* 5:20–22, 1910. St. Louis.

CHILDREN'S GAMES AND RHYMES

Joffie, Leah Rachel Clara
"Three Generations of Children's Singing Games in St. Louis." *JAFL* 60:1–52, 1947. An excellent comparative study. Texts only.

Wood, Ray
Mother Goose in the Ozarks. Raywood, Texas: The Author, 1938.

DANCE

Hamilton, Goldie
"The Play-Party in Northeast Missouri." *JAFL* 27:289–303, 1914.

Musick, Ruth Ann
"A Missouri Dance Call." *JAFL* 59:323–324, 1946.

ARRANGEMENTS

————: *Mixed Voices*

"The Deaf Old Woman."
Davis, Katherine K.: Galaxy: SATB. A Missouri variant.

NEBRASKA

FOLKLORE

BIBLIOGRAPHY

Berry, Myrtle D., comp.
"Local Nebraska History—A Bibliography." *Nebraska History* 26:104–115, 1945.

Historical Records Survey.
Inventory of the County Archives of Nebraska. Prepared by the Historical Records Survey. Works Progress Administration. Lincoln, Neb.: The Historical Records Survey, 1939. Bibl.

Omaha Public Library.
Nebraska; Material in the Omaha Public Library. Omaha, 1931. 21 pp., illus.

PERIODICALS

The Nebraska History Magazine.
Quarterly. Nebraska State Historical Society, Lincoln, 1918–. 1–7, 1918–1924, as Nebraska History and Record of Pioneer Days. 8–18, 1925–1937, V. 19, No. 4, O/D 1938 as Nebraska History Magazine. V. 8, Pt. 2—V. 10, Pt. 1, never published.

The Prairie Schooner.
V. 1, 1927–. Lincoln, Neb.: Quarterly.

GENERAL STUDIES AND COLLECTIONS

Cather, Willa
A Lost Lady. New York: Alfred A. Knopf, 1923. 173 pp.

————.
O Pioneer. Boston: Houghton Mifflin Co., 1913. 308 pp.

Condra, George Evert, and others
Nebraska Beautiful. Lincoln, Neb.: University of Nebraska Press, 1925. 116 pp., illus.

Ericson, Eston Everett
"Nebraska Folklore and Popular Sayings." *Folklore* (London) 49:148–153, 1938.

Federal Writers' Project.
Almanac For Nebraskans. Written and compiled by the Federal Writers' Project, W.P.A., State of Nebraska. Lincoln, Nebraska: Woodruff Printing Co., 1938.

————.
Lincoln City Guide. (American Guide Series). Federal Writers' Project, W.P.A. Lincoln, Nebraska: Woodruff Printing Co., 1937. 87 pp., illus., bibl.

————.
Nebraska, a Guide to the Cornhusker State. (American Guide Series). Compiled and written by the Federal Writers' Project of the W.P.A. for the State of Nebraska. New York: The Viking Press, 1939. xxiii, 424 pp., illus., bibl.

————.
Nebraska Folklore Pamphlets. Issued by the Federal Writers' Project in Nebraska in cooperation with the Nebraska Public Instruction Department. Lincoln, Nebraska, 1937–1938. Valuable material collected and mimeographed by the Federal Theatre Project, at Lincoln, Nebraska: No. 1. Cowboy Songs, (Part I), 1937; No. 2. Indian Place Legends, 1937; No. 3. Children's Singing Games, 1937; No. 4. Historical Legends, 1937; No. 5. Beath, P. R.-Febold Feboldson, (Part I), 1937; No. 6. Animal Legends, 1937; No. 7. Children's Games, 1937; No. 8. Beath, P. R.-Febold Feboldson (concl.) Antoine Barada, 1937; Nos. 9–10. Proverbs, Prophecies, Signs and Sayings, 1937; No. 11. Cowboy Songs, (Part II), 1937; No. 12. Indian Ghost Legends, 1937; No. 13. Tall Tales, 1938; No. 14. Place Name Stories, 1938; No. 15. Songs About Nebraska, 1938; No. 16. Ballads, 1938; No. 17. Nebraska Cattle Brands, 1938; No. 18. Nebraska Farmers' Alliance Songs of the 1890's, 1938, and others.

————.
Old Bellevue. (American Guide Series). Compiled and written by the Federal Writers' Project, W.P.A., State of Nebraska. Papillion, Nebraska: Papillion Times, 1937.

————.
Pioneer Recollections. *Nebraska Folklore Pamphlets 25.* Federal Writers' Project of Nebraska of the W.P.A. for the State of Nebraska. Lincoln, Nebraska: Jan., 1940.

Reminiscences of Dad Streeter. *Nebraska Folklore Pamphlets, No. 19.* Federal Writers' Project in Nebraska, Lincoln, Feb., 1939.
Deals with lore of the frontier, Southwest, and West.

Pound, Louise
"Nebraska Folklore and Ethnology Group." *JAFL* 56:17, 1943.

————.
"Old Nebraska Folk Customs." *Nebraska History* 28:3–31, 1947.

Sandoz, Mari
Old Jules. Boston: Little, Brown and Co., 1935. 424 pp., illus.

————.
Slogum House. Boston: Little, Brown and Co., 1937. 400 pp.
"A searing narrative told with dazzling vividness in the language of the frontier."

Sheldon, Addison E.
"Documents of Nebraska Life." *Nebraska State Historical Society Publications,* 1923.

————.
History and Stories of Nebraska. Chicago and Lincoln: The University Publishing Co., 1913. 306 pp., illus., maps.

————.
History, Old and New: History, Stories, Folklore. Lincoln: The University Publishing Company, 1937. x, 470 pp., illus.

————.
Nebraska, the Land and the People.... Chicago: The Lewis Publishing Company, 1931. 3 vols., illus., bibl.

Spence, Thomas H.
Westward Across Nebraska; drawings by Helen Church Tilden. Hastings, Neb.: Democrat Printing Company, 1939. 85 pp.
A book of poems using much local lore.

Whisenand, Emma (Boge)
This is Nebraska; drawings made from prints by Esther Boquest Boardman. Kansas City, Mo.: Burton Publishing Co., 1941. 150 pp., illus.

FOLKTALES—LEGENDS

Beath, Paul R.
Febold Feboldson: Tall Tales from the Great Plains. Illustrated by Lynn Trank. Lincoln: University of Nebraska Press, 1948. xi, 124 pp.
The amazing achievements of the "indomitable Swedish pioneer who surmounts any difficulty."

Federal Writers' Project.
Historical Legends. *Nebraska Folklore Pamphlets 4.* Nebraska Writers' Project in Nebraska, Lincoln, June 15, 1937.

————.
Legends of Febold Feboldson and Antoine Barada. *Nebraska Folklore Pamphlets 1 and 8.* Federal Writers' Project in Nebraska. Lincoln, Nebraska: July 1, 1937 and Sept. 15, 1937.

Pioneer Tales. *Nebraska Folklore Pamphlets 29.* Federal Writers' Project in Nebraska. Lincoln, Nebraska: July, 1940.

————.
Reminiscences of Dad Streeter. *Nebraska folklore pamphlets 19.* Federal Writers' Project in Lincoln, Nebraska: February, 1939.

————.
Tall Tales. *Nebraska Folklore Pamphlets 13.* Federal Writers' Project in Nebraska. Lincoln, Nebraska: July, 1938.

Mattes, Merrill J.
"Historic Sites in Missouri Valley Reservoir Areas." *Nebraska History* 28 (No. 3):161–175, 1947., illus.

Musick, Ruth Ann
"Miracle Man Steele." *Prairie Schooner* 20: Fall, 1946.
A tall tale and local legend.

Pound, Louise
"Nebraska Strong Men." *SFQ* 7:133–143, 1943.
Discusses literature of Febold Feboldson, Paul Bunyan, Antoine Barada, and Moses Stocking.

Sandoz, Mari
"Some Tall Tales of Nebraska." *Nebraska History* 24:57–58, 1943.

Wood, Asa Butler
Pioneer Tales of the North Platte Valley and Nebraska Panhandle; a miscellaneous collection of historical reference material, anecdotal and reminiscent.... Gering, Neb.: Courier Press, 1938. 288 pp., illus.

CUSTOMS

Beadle, Erastus Flavius
To Nebraska in '57, a Diary of Erastus F. Beadle. New York: The New York Public Library, 1923. 89 pp., illus.

Burkley, Francis Joseph
The Faded Frontier. Omaha, Neb.: Burkley Envelope and Printing Co., 1935. 436 pp., illus.
Life and happenings of early Nebraskan pioneer life.

Compendium of History, reminiscences and biography of Nebraska, embracing an account of early explorations, early settlement, Indian occupancy, Indian history and traditions.... Chicago: Alden Pub. Co., 1912. 1099 pp., illus.

Dale, Edward Everett
"Culture on the American Frontier." *Nebraska History* 26:75–90, 1945. Illus.

Daughters of the American Revolution. Nebraska.
Collection of Nebraska Pioneer Reminiscences, issued by the Nebraska Society of the Daughters of the American Revolution. Cedar Rapids, Ia.: The Torch Press, 1916. 361 pp., illus.

Federal Writers' Project.
Early Nebraska Cooking. *Nebraska Folklore Pamphlet 28.* Federal Writers' Project in Nebraska. Lincoln, May, 1940.

_____.

Nebraska Cattle Brands. (History, Process, Origin of Certain Brands). *Nebraska Folklore Pamphlet 17.* Federal Writers' Project in Nebraska. Lincoln, Nebraska, November, 1938.

_____.

Pioneer Schools. *Nebraska Folklore Pamphlets 30.* Federal Writers' Project in Nebraska. Lincoln, Nebraska: Dec., 1940.

Fulton, Frances I. Sims
To and Through Nebraska. By a Pennsylvania Girl. . . . Lincoln: Journal Company, 1884. 273 pp.

Meredith, Mamie
" 'Billing the Bridal Couple' in Pioneer Days." *AS* 8 (No. 2) :22–24, 1933.
A Nebraska custom of firing with an "unloaded" gun into a *shivaree* party.

Pound, Louise
"Old Nebraska Folk Customs." *Nebraska History* 28:3–31, 1947.

Simmons, Harry P.
Under the Kerosene Lamp; being the prairie pioneer's primer, with photographs by the author. York, Neb.: The Mechanical Arts Co., 1922. 223 pp., illus.

" 'Soft Drinks' of the Nebraska Pioneer." *AS* 7 (No. 5) :391–392, 1932.
Cooking "substitutes" of the frontier housewife.

Woolworth, James M.
Nebraska in 1857. Omaha City: N. T. C. C. Woolworth, 1857. 105 pp.

BELIEFS—SUPERSTITIONS

Cannell, Margaret
Signs, Omens, and Portents in Nebraska Folklore. Lincoln, Nebraska: University of Nebraska Studies in Language, Literature, and Criticism. No. 13, 1933. pp. 7–50, bibl.

Federal Writers' Project.
Pioneer Religion. *Nebraska Folklore Pamphlets, 26.* Federal Writers Project in Nebraska. Lincoln, Nebraska: February, 1940.

Pound, Louise
"Nebraska Rain Lore and Rain Making." *CFQ* 5:129–142, 1946.

PROVERBS

Federal Writers' Project.
Proverbs, Prophecies, Signs, and Sayings. Part I and II. *Nebraska Folklore Pamphlets 10, 11.* Federal Writers' Project in Nebraska. Lincoln, Nebraska: Oct. 1, 1937, and Oct. 15, 1937.

Snapp, Emma Louise
Proverbial Lore in Nebraska. Lincoln, Nebraska: University of Nebraska Studies in Language, Literature, and Criticism, 1933. pp. 53–112, bibl.

FOLK MEDICINE

Black, Pauline Monette
Nebraska Folk Cures. Lincoln, Nebraska: University of Nebraska, 1935. Studies in Language, Literature, and Criticism. *No. 15.* 49 pp., bibl.

SPEECH

Burwell, M. A.
"Expressions from Boyd County, Nebraska." *AS* 6 (No. 3) :230–231, 1931.

Cannell, Margaret
"Indian Personal Names from the Nebraska and Dakota Regions." *AS* 10 (No. 3) :184–187, 1935.

Grill, Emma V.
"More Nebraska Sandhill Talk." *AS* 8 (No. 1) :80, 1933.

Meredith, Mamie
"Squaw Patch, Squaw Corn, Calico Corn, Yankee Corn, Tea Wheat, Sandy Wheat." *AS* 7 (No. 6) :420–422, 1932.
Descriptive speech of Nebraska farmer.

Pound, Louise
"A Second Word List from Nebraska." *Dialect Notes* 3 (Part 7) :541–549, 1911; 4 (Part 4) : 271–282, 1916.

_____.

"Dialect Speech in Nebraska." *Dialect Notes* 3 (Part 7) :55–67, 1905.

Van den Bark, Melvin
"Nebraska Cow Talk." *AS* 5 (No. 1) :52–76, 1929.

_____.

"Nebraska Pioneer English." *AS* 6 (No. 4) : 237–252; 7 (No. 1) :1–17, 1931; 7 (No. 3) : 161–171, 1932; 8 (No. 4) :48–52, 1933.

_____.

"Nebraska Sandhill Talk." *AS* 4 (No. 2) :125–133, 1928.

PLACE NAMES

Federal Writers' Project.
Origin of Nebraska Place Names. Compiled by the Federal Writers' Project. Works Progress Administration, State of Nebraska. . . . Lincoln, Neb.: Stephenson School Supply Co., 1938. 28 pp.

_____.

Place Name Stories. *Nebraska Folklore Pamphlets 14.* Federal Writers' Project in Nebraska. Lincoln, Nebraska: August, 1938.

Fitzpatrick, Lillian Linder
Nebraska Place-Names. University of Nebraska Studies in Language, Literature and Criticism No. 6. Lincoln, Neb.: The University Press, 1925. 166 pp.

Link, John T.
Toponomy of Nebraska. Lincoln, Nebraska: University of Nebraska, 1933. 186 pp.

———.
The Origin of the Place-Names of Nebraska." *Nebraska Geological Survey Bulletin* Ser. 2 (No. 7), 186 pp., 1933. bibl.

Pangle, Mary Ellen
"Place-Names in Nebraska." *Jour. of Amer. Hist.* 26:177–188, 1932.

FOLKSONG

GENERAL STUDIES AND COLLECTIONS

Dale, Edward Everett
"Culture on the American Frontier." *Nebraska History* 26:75–90, 1945.

Federal Writers' Project.
Ballads of Nebraska. *Nebraska Folklore Pamphlets 16.* Federal Writers' Project of Nebraska. Lincoln, Neb.: (Oct.) 1938.

———.
Nebraska Farmers' Alliance Songs of the 1890's (Words only, by known composers). *Nebraska Folklore Pamphlets 18 and 20.* Federal Writers' Project in Nebraska, (Lincoln). December, 1938; May, 1939.

———.
Songs About Nebraska. *Nebraska Folklore Pamphlets 15.* Federal Writers' Project in Nebraska, (Lincoln). September, 1938.

Kirkland, Edwin C.
"University faculty folk songs." *TFSB* 4 (No. 3):33–41, 1940.
    Texts and tunes of six songs, chiefly from Nebraska.

Pound, Louise
American Ballads and Songs. New York: Charles Scribner's Sons, 1922.

———.
"A Nebraska Folk-Song." *Folk Lore* 30:113. (London).

———.
Folk-Songs of Nebraska and the Central West: A Syllabus. Nebraska Academy of Science Publications, Vol. 10 (No. 3). Lincoln, Neb.: 1915.

———.
"Traditional Ballads in Nebraska." *JAFL* 26: 351–366, 1913.

CHILDREN'S GAMES

Federal Writers' Project.
Children's Singing Games. *Nebraska Folklore Pamphlets.* Federal Writers' Project in Nebraska. Lincoln, Nebraska: June 1, 1937.

DANCES

Federal Writers' Project.
Dance Calls. *Nebraska Folklore Pamphlets 27.* Series 3. (Continues Pamphlet 24). Lincoln, Nebraska: April, 1940.

———.
Pioneer Dance Calls. *Nebraska Folklore Pamphlets 22 and 24.* Federal Writers' Project in Nebraska, June, 1939; November, 1939.

RECORDS

The Middle West: Mainly Nebraska. Iowa City: The State University of Iowa.

OHIO

FOLKLORE

BIBLIOGRAPHY

Historical Records Survey.
Inventory of the County Archives of Ohio. Prepared by the Historical Records Survey. Works Progress Administration. Columbus, O.: The Historical Records Survey, 1937. Bibl.

Thomson, Peter Gibson
A Bibliography of the State of Ohio. Being a catalogue of the books and pamphlets relating to the history of the state. With collations and bibliographical and critical notes,... Cincinnati: The Author, 1880. vi, 436 pp.

———.
Catalogue of Books Relating to the State of Ohio, the West, and Northwest. Cincinnati: The Author, 1890. 108 pp.

PERIODICALS

Historical Society of Northwestern Ohio. Quarterly Bulletin. V. 1, 1929–. Toledo, O.

Ohio State Archaeological and Historical Quarterly. V. 1, 1887–. Columbus, O.

GENERAL STUDIES AND COLLECTIONS

Bond, Beverly W., Jr.
The Civilization of the Old Northwest. New York: The Macmillan Co., 1934.

Bromfield, Louis
Pleasant Valley. New York: Harper and Bros., 1945. 321 pp.
    "The book is enlivened by romantic digressions, retellings of the legends of Johnny Appleseed and the lost Dauphin, and sketches of local character" (Orville Prescott).

Federal Writers' Project.
Chillochothe and Ross County, Ohio. (American Guide Series). Compiled and written by Workers of the Federal Writers' Project of the Works Progress Administration for the State of Ohio. The Northwest Territory Committee, 1938.

———.
Lima and Allen County, a Guide. (American Guide Series). Federal Writers' Project of the Works Progress Administration for the State of Ohio, 1931.

———.
Martin's Ferry Sesquecentennial. (American Guide Series). Federal Writers' Project, W.P.A. in Ohio. Martin's Ferry Sesquecentennial Committee, 1937.

———.
The Beautiful River. Compiled by Workers of the Writers' Program of the Works Projects Administration in the State of Ohio.... Cincinnati, O.: Wiesen-Hart Press, 1940. 40 pp., illus.

———.
The Cincinnati Guide. (American Guide Series). Illustrated. Compiled by Workers of the Writers' Project of the Works Progress Administration. Cincinnati: The Viesen-Hart Press, 1943. 570 pp.

———.
The Ohio Guide. (American Guide Series). Compiled by Workers of the Federal Writers' Project of the Works Progress Administration in the State of Ohio. New York: Oxford University Press, 1940.

———.
Zanesville and Muskingum County. (American Guide Series). Federal Writers' Project of the Works Progress Administration in the State of Ohio. Zanesville Chamber of Commerce, 1937.

Firestone, Clark B.
Sycamore Shores. New York: R. M. McBride and Company, 1936. xi, 247 pp., illus., bibl. (pp. 241–247).
"A book full of charm and rhythm in which he explores the tributaries of the Ohio." (H. Reynolds).

Fisher, Dorothy Canfield
The Deepening Stream. New York: Harcourt, Brace and Co., 1930.
A novel.

Harris, Adah Glasener
Clipped Wings. Philadelphia: Dorrance and Co., 1943. 320 pp.
The saga of five generations of an Ohio family.

Howe, Henry
Historical Collections of Ohio; containing a collection of the most interesting facts, traditions, biographical sketches, anecdotes, etc., relating to its general and local history; with descriptions of its counties, principal towns and villages.... Cincinnati: Derby, Bradley & Co., 1847. 581 pp., illus.

———.
Historical Collections of Ohio. An encyclopedia of the state ... illustrated by about 700 engravings, contrasting the Ohio of 1846 with 1886–90.... Cincinnati: C. J. Krehbiel & Co., 1907. 2 vols., illus.

Lossing, Benson John
A Pictorial Description of Ohio. New York: Ensign & Thayer, 1850. 131 pp., illus.

Richter, Conrad
The Fields. New York: Alfred A. Knopf, 1946. 288 pp.
"This book (a novel), in its pungent, simple language and its unpretentious narrative charm is alive with the atmosphere of forest and clearing of the early northwest territory." (Alfred Butterfield).

Shafer, Claude
Cartoon Guide of Ohio. 100 Cartoons and text, large map in flap. New York: J. J. Augustin, 1941.

Thayer, Gordon W.
"Cincinnati Branch, American Folklore Society." *JAFL* 59:484–485, 1946.

FOLKTALES—LEGENDS

Howells, William Dean
Stories of Ohio. New York: American Book Co., 1897. 287 pp.

Miller, William Marion
"A Boundary Moving Ghost." *NYFQ* 1:105–106, 1945.
Heard by the author in eastern Darke County, Ohio.

———.
"A Modern Atrocity Story." *JAFL* 58:156–157, 1945.
Picked up in an industrial town in Southwestern Ohio.

———.
"A Threshing Ring in Southern Ohio." *HFB* 5 (No. 1):3–13, 1946.

———.
"How to Become a Witch." *JAFL* 57:280, 1944.
A "recipe" given by a descendant of one of the original French settlers in eastern Darke County, Ohio.

———.
"The Snake Dilemma." *JAFL* 53:217–218, 1940.

CUSTOMS

Abdy, Harry Bennett
On the Ohio; Illustrations by Rowena Meeks Abdy—the "Painter Lady"—from sketches, etc., made during the voyage. New York: Dodd, Mead and Co., 1919. xiv, 300 pp., illus.

Anderson, Sherwood
Tar,—A Mid-West Childhood. New York: Boni and Liveright, 1926.
All his writings molded in traditions, manners and custom of the American folk.

———.
Winesburg, Ohio. New York: Viking Press, 1927.
Fiction—folk characters and manners permeate every page.

Freeman, Lewis Ransome
Waterways of Westward Wanderings; Small Boat Voyages down the Ohio, Missouri and Mississippi Rivers. New York: Dodd, Mead and Co., 1927. xii, 368 pp., illus.

Hatcher, Harlan Henthorne
The Buckeye Country; a Pageant of Ohio. New York: H. C. Kinsey & Company, 1940. xiii, 325 pp., illus., bibl.

Howells, William Cooper
Recollections of Life in Ohio, from 1813 to 1840. With an introduction by his son W. D. Howells. Cincinnati: R. Clarke & Co., 1895. 207 pp.

Howells, William Dean
My Year in a Log Cabin. New York: Harper & Brothers, 1893. 62 pp.

————.
The Leatherwood God. New York: The Century Co., 1916.
A novel.

Jones, Nelson Edwards
The Squirrel Hunters of Ohio; or, Glimpses of Pioneer Life. Cincinnati: The T. R. Clarke Co., 1898. vii, 363 pp., illus.

Packard, Silas Sadler
My Recollections of Ohio. New York: The Ohio Society of New York, 1890. 26 pp.

Thwaites, Reuben Gold
Afloat on the Ohio. An Historical pilgrimage of a thousand miles in a skiff, from Redstone to Cairo. Chicago: Way & Williams, 1897. xiv, 334 pp.

Volz, Joseph Albert
Rambles in Ohio. Carthagena, O.: The Messenger Press, 1935. viii, 187 pp., illus.

Venable, William Henry
A Buckeye Boyhood. Cincinnati: Robert Clarke Company, 1911. 190 pp.

Welker, Martin
Farm Life in Central Ohio Sixty Years Ago. Cleveland, 1895. Reprinted from Western Reserve Historical Society, V. 4.

SPEECH

Bolwell, Robert
"College Slang Words and Phrases." *Dialect Notes* 4 (Part 3):231–238, 1915.
From students of Western Reserve University.

Hart, J. M.
"Notes from Cincinnati." *Dialect Notes* 1 (Part 2):60–63.

Kenyon, John S.
"Word List from Western Reserve." *Dialect Notes* 4 (Part 6):386–404, 1917.
The words represent the dialect of the Connecticut Western Reserve of Northeastern Ohio.

Parry, W. H.
"Dialect Peculiarities in Southeastern Ohio." *Dialect Notes* 4 (Part 5):339–342, 1916.

PLACE NAMES

Martin, Mrs. Maria Ewing
Ohio, 1803–1903. "*Origin of its Place Names*" Cleveland: Sayers Print Co., 1903. 16 pp.

Torrey, Volta
"Cleveland Name-Lore." *AS* 3 (No. 2):164, 1927.

FOLKSONG

GENERAL STUDIES AND COLLECTIONS

Anderson, George K.
"Two Ballads from 19th Century Ohio." *JAFL* 51:38–46, 1938.

Eddy, Mary O., coll. and arr.
Ballads and Songs from Ohio. New York: J. J. Augustin, 1939. xxvii, 330 pp., music, illus.

Galbreath, C. B.
"Song Writers of Ohio. Benjamin Russell Hanby, Author of 'Darling Nelly Gray'." *Ohio Archaeological and Historical Quarterly* 14:180–215, 1905.

Harbison, Katherine
"In the Great and Lone Prairie." *SFQ* 2 (No. 3), 1938.
Songs and ballads with tunes from Illinois, Ohio, and Blue Grass Section of Kentucky.

Henry, Mellinger E.
"Pearl Bryant." *JAFL* 42:301–303, 1929.
An unpublished variant of an American Folksong.

DANCE

Kurtz, Homer H.
"Emerald Isle." *CFQ* 3:232–234, 1944.
Music, text and calls of a square dance current in western Ohio and Indiana.

WISCONSIN

FOLKLORE

See: Norwegian-American Folklore and Folksong. p. 580.

BIBLIOGRAPHY

Historical Records Survey.
Inventory of the City Archives of Wisconsin, ... Prepared by the Wisconsin Historical Records Survey. Works Progress Administration.... Madison, Wis.: The Wisconsin Historical Records Survey, 1941–42. 2 vols.

————.
Inventory of the County Archives of Wisconsin. Prepared by the Historical Records Survey. Works Progress Administration. Madison, Wis.: The Historical Records Survey, 1937. Bibl.

Legler, Henry Eduard
Narratives of Early Wisconsin Travellers, Prior to 1800. Madison: State Historical Society of Wisconsin, 1906. (pp. 157–193).

Smith, Alice E.
Guide to the Manuscripts of the Wisconsin Historical Society. Madison: State Historical Society of Wisconsin, 1944. xiv, 290 pp., illus.

Thwaites, Reuben Gold, ed.
Descriptive List of Manuscript Collections of the State Historical Society of Wisconsin, together with reports on other collections of manuscript material for American History in adjacent states. Madison: The Society, 1906. viii, 197 pp.

PERIODICALS

Wisconsin State Historical Society. Studies. V. 1, 1916–. Madison, Wis.

The Wisconsin Magazine of History. V. 1, 1917–. Menasha, Wis.

GENERAL STUDIES AND COLLECTIONS

Bartlett, William W.
History, Tradition and Adventure in the Chippewa Valley. Chippewa Falls, Wis.: The Chippewa Printery, 1929. 244 pp., illus.

————.
Loggin Camp Diversion and Humor. In: *History, Tradition and Adventure in The Chippewa Valley.* (pp. 232–236). Chippewa Falls, Wis.: The Chippewa Printery, 1929.

Brown, Charles E.
"Wisconsin Folklore Society." *JAFL* 56:190–191, 1943.

————.
Scenic and Historic Wisconsin. Guide to one thousand features of scenic, historic, and curious interest in Wisconsin. . . . Madison, Wis., 1930. 29 pp.

————, ed.
Wisconsin Folktale Booklets. Madison, Wis.: University of Wisconsin.

Christensen, T. P.
"Danish Settlement in Wisconsin." *Wisconsin Magazine of History* 12:19–40, 1928.

Copeland, Louis Albert
"The Cornish in Southwest Wisconsin." *Wisconsin Historical Collections* 15:301–334, 1898.

Davis, Susan B.
Wisconsin Lore for Boys and Girls. Eau Claire, Wis.: E. M. Hale & Co., 1931. xv, 283 pp., illus.

Derleth, August William
The Wisconsin, River of a Thousand Isles. (Rivers of America Series.) Illustrated by John Steuart Curry. New York: Farrar & Rinehart, 1942. xi, 366 pp., illus., bibl.

Dickinson, Thomas H., ed.
Wisconsin Plays I, II. New York: B. W. Huebsch, 1914, 1918.

Dondna, Edgar
"Wisconsin Writers." *Wisconsin Blue Book:* 71–80, 1927.

Federal Writers' Project.
Wisconsin, A Guide to the Badger State. (American Guide Series.) Compiled by the Workers of the Writers' Program of the Works Progress Administration of the State of Wisconsin. New York: Duell, Sloan and Pearce, 1941.

Folsom, William Henry Carman
Fifty Years in the Northwest. With an introduction and appendix containing reminiscences, incidents, and notes. St. Paul: Pioneer Press Company, 1888. xliii, 763 pp., illus.

Gray, James
Pine, Stream & Prairie; Wisconsin and Minnesota in Profile. New York: A. A. Knopf, 1945. xi, 312 pp., illus.

Grignon, Augustin
"Seventy-two Years' Recollections of Wisconsin." *Wisconsin State Hist. Soc. Coll.* 3:195–295, 1857.

Havighurst, Walter
Upper Mississippi. (American River Series.) Illustrated by David and Lolita Granahan. New York: Farrar and Rinehart, Inc., 1937.

Hebberd, Stephen Southrick
History of Wisconsin under Dominion of France. Madison, Wis.: Midland Pub. Co., 1890. 178 pp.

Heffner, R. M. S.
German Settlements in Wisconsin. In: *Conference in Non-English Speech in the United States,* Ann Arbor, Mich., August 2–3, 1940. Washington, D. C.: Bulletin of the American Council of Learned Societies, 1942. No. 34, pp. 581–669.

Holmes, Fred L.
Alluring Wisconsin; the historic glamor and natural loveliness of an American commonwealth. Milwaukee, Wis.: Hale and Co., 1937. 480 pp.
With map and plates from original photographs.

————.
Badger Saints and Sinners; foreword by Hamlin Garland; drawings by Ozzie Johnson. Milwaukee: E. M. Hale and Company, 1939. 570 pp., illus.

Howe, Henry
The Diary of a Circuit Rider; Excerpts from the notes of Henry Howe, made while traveling in Southern Wisconsin between the years 1864 and 1868, . . . edited by Jesse Howe Nebelthau; illustrated by Dorothy Kurtzman Phelps. Minneapolis: The Voyageur Press, 1933. xiii, 144 pp., illus.

Giegold, Georg
Aus dem Urwald. Erzählungen, Skizzen und Gedichte. Kenosha, Wis.: Deutschen Druck- und Verlags-Geshäfte, 1898. 120 pp., illus.
Stories, sketches and poems of travels in Wisconsin.

Kinzie, Juliette Augusta (Magill)
Wau-bun, the 'Early Day' in the Northwest.
New York: Derby and Jackson, 1856. 498 pp.

Le Sueur, Meridel
North Star Country. New York: Duell, Stran, and Pearce, Inc., 1945. 327 pp., illus. index.

Ludloff, Karl
Amerikanische Reisebilder. Skizzen über der Staat Wisconsin. Milwaukee: Brueker & Ludloff, 1881. 124 pp.
Impressions of and experiences in Wisconsin.

Nelligan, John E.
"The Life of a Lumberman." *Wisconsin Magazine of History* 13:3–65; 131–185, 1929. Vol. 13:241–304, 1930.

Rounds, Charles Ralph
Wisconsin Authors and Their Works. Madison, Wis.: Parker Educational Co., 1918. 400 pp.

Schlytter, Leslie Evan
The Tall Brothers. New York: D. Appleton-Century Company, 1941. 449 pp.
More than passing observations into life and customs and struggles of a Wisconsin lumbering town.

Thwaites, Reuben Gold
Down Historic Waterways; six hundred miles of canoeing upon Illinois and Wisconsin rivers. Chicago: A. C. McClurg & Co., 1902. 300 pp., illus.

Titus, William A.
Wisconsin Writers; Sketches and studies. Chicago, 1930. xi, 433 pp.

Wisconsin Rural Plays; prize-winning rural plays in the original play writing contests conducted by the Wisconsin Dramatic Guild. Chicago: The Dramatic Publishing Company, 1931. 131 pp.

FOLKTALES—LEGENDS

Brown, Charles E.
"Johnny McGorry and the red stocking." *HFB* 2:20–21, 1943.

———.
Lake Mendota, pre-history, history and legends. The Wisconsin Archaeological Society. Madison, Wis.: Democrat Printing Co., 1933. 7 pp., illus.

———.
"A Wisconsin Endless Tale." *HFB* 2:20–21, 1943.

Cole, Harry Ellsworth
Baraboo, Dells, and Devil's Lake Region; scenery, archaeology, Indian legends, and local history briefly treated. . . . Baraboo, Wis.: Baraboo News Publishing Co., 1921. 95 pp., illus.

Stagecoach and Tavern Tales of the Old Northwest. Edited by Louise Phelps Kellog. Cleveland: The Arthur H. Clark Co., 1930. 376 pp.

Holand, Hjalmar Rued
Old Peninsula Days; Tales and Sketches of the Door County Peninsula. Ephraim, Wis.: Pioneer Publishing Co., 1925. 244 pp., illus.

Kearney, Luke Silvester
The Hodag, and other Tales of Logging Camps. Wausau, Wisconsin: The Author, 1938. 158 pp.

Thomas, George Francis
Legends of the Land of Lakes, or History, Traditions and Mysteries, Gleaned from Years of Experience Among the Pioneers, Voyageurs, and Indians; with descriptive accounts of the many natural curiosities met with from Lake Huron to the Columbia River. And the meaning and derivation of names of rivers, lakes, towns, etc., of the Northwest. . . . Chicago: G. F. Thomas, 1884. Illus.

Tutt, Clara Little
Badger Tales. Chicago: Dallas, Lyons and Carnahan, 1940. vi, 200 pp., illus.

CUSTOMS

Brown, Stirling Wilson
In the Limestone Valley. Pen Pictures of Early Days in Wisconsin. n.p.: 1900. viii, 214 pp.

Davis, Susan Burdick
Our Wisconsin, A Pageant. Milwaukee: E. M. Hale and Company, 1934. 48 pp., illus.

Folsom, William Henry Carman
Fifty Years in the Northwest. With an introduction and appendix containing reminiscences, incidents, and notes. . . . St. Paul Pioneer Press Company, 1888. xliii, 763 pp., illus.

Fox, Dorothea M.
Pedalling to Adventure. Cedar Rapids, Ia.: The Torch Press, 1940. 138 pp., illus., bibl.

Holmes, Frederick Lionel
Old World Wisconsin: Around Europe in the Badger State. Illustrated with photographs, and sketches by Max Fernekes. Eau Claire, Wis.: E. M. Hale and Co., 1944. 368 pp., illus.

Kartak, Mollie Maurer
"Memories of My Childhood." *Wisconsin Magazine of History.* 10:417–423, 1926–27.

Krueger, Lillian
"Social Life in Wisconsin; Pre-Territorial Through the Mid-Sixties." *Wisconsin Magazine of History.* 22:312–328, 396–426, 1939.

Lacher, J. H. A.
"The Taverns and Stages of Early Wisconsin." *Wisconsin State Historical Society. Proc.* 1914-1915, pp. 118-167.

Marryat, Frederick
"An English Officer's Description of Wisconsin in 1837." *Wisconsin State Historical Society Collections* 14: 137–154, 1898.
From the author's *Diary in America.*

Nelligan, John E.
"The Life of a Lumberman." *Wisconsin Magazine of History.* 13:3–65, 131–185, 241–304, 1929.

Steele, James William
Summer Days in the Lake Country. Chicago: Milwaukee & St. Paul Railway Pass. Dept., 1901. 73 pp.

Verwyst, Chrysostom
Reminiscences of a Pioneer Missionary. Madison: The Society, 1916. (pp. 147-185).

Wisconsin State Historical Society.
Four Episodes in Wisconsin Pioneering. Madison: The Society, 1912. (pp. 181-218).
Pioneer life, customs and manners, and hardships.

PLACE NAMES

Cassidy, Frederic G.
The Place-Names of Dane County, Wisconsin. Foreword by Robert L. Ramsay. Publication of the American Dialect Society Number 7. 1947.

Cole, Harry Ellsworth
Baraboo and Other Place Names in Sauk County, Wisconsin. Baraboo: The Baraboo News Publishing Co., 1912. 50 pp.

Federal Writers' Project
Wisconsin Indian Place Legends. Folklore. Federal Writers' Project, Madison, Wis.: 1936. 50 pp.

SPEECH

Savage, Howard J.
"Word List from Southwestern Wisconsin." *Dialect Notes* 5(Part 6):233–240, 1923.

FOLKSONG

STUDIES

Hendricks, Cecilia Heunel
"Robin Tamson's Smiddy." *HFB* 3:55–57, 1944.
Text only of this Scottish ballad from a Wisconsin informant.

DANCES

Curtis, W. A.
"The Light Fantastic in the Central West. Country Dances of Many Nationalities in Wisconsin." *Century Magazine,* 73:570–579, 1907. illus.

RECORDS

U. S. Library of Congress. Division of Music. Folklore Section.
Folkmusic of Wisconsin. Prof. Leland A. Coon. Recording Project.　　　　　　　AAFS–LC

THE SOUTHWEST

THE SOUTHWEST

See: The Spanish-American, pp. 593–606; and The Cowboy, pp. 610–27.

FOLKLORE

BIBLIOGRAPHY

A Guide to the Literature of the Southwest. Albuquerque: Inter Americana Bibliographies, No. 2, 1942.

Bloom, Lansing B.
Comprehensive Index to New Mexico Historical Review. v. 1-15, 1926-1940. Albuquerque: Historical Society of New Mexico and University of New Mexico, 1941.

Coan, Charles Florus, comp.
Bibliography of the Southwest. Albuquerque, 1927. 35 pp.

Davidson, L. J., and Bostick, P.
The Literature of the Rocky Mountain West 1803-1903. Caldwell, Idaho: The Caxton Printers Ltd., 1939.

Dobie, J. Frank, ed., and comp.
Guide to Life and Literature of the Southwest. Austin, Texas: The University of Texas Press. Special Printing for University Press in Dallas, Southern Methodist University, 1943. 111 pp., illus.
A Bibliographical Handbook divided into thirty-three headings with introductory observations.

Hazard, Lucy Lockwood
The Frontier in American Literature. New York: Thomas Y. Crowell Co., 1927.

Lomax, Alan, and Cowell, Sidney R.
American Folk Song and Folk Lore. A Regional Bibliography. New York: Progressive Education Association, 221 W. 57th St., N. Y. C.
Liberal as to what folklore comprises, and lists well-selected collection of titles of all sorts of books pertaining to the Southwest.

Major, Mabel; Smith, Rebecca W., and Pearce, T. M.
Southwest Heritage: A Literary History with Bibliography. Albuquerque: University of New Mexico Press, 1938.
Mainly fiction, poetry, drama, etc.

Pearce, Thomas M.
Southwest Heritage, A Literary History and Bibliography. Albuquerque, 1938.

Rader, Jesse Lee
South of Forty, from the Mississippi to the Rio Grande, A Bibliography. Norman: University of Olahoma Press, 1947. xi, 336 pp.

Rogers, John William
Finding Literature on the Texas Plains; with a representative bibliography of books on the Southwest by J. Frank Dobie. Dallas, Tex.: The Southwest Press, 1931. 57 pp.

Rusk, Ralph Leslie
The Literature of the Middle Western Frontier. New York: Columbia University Press, 1925.

Saunders, Lyle, comp.
A Guide to Materials Bearing on Cultural Relations in New Mexico. Albuquerque, New Mexico: The University of New Mexico Press, 1944. 528 pp.
A comprehensive bibliography—including a number of entries on folklore and folksong of the Spanish-speaking population, the Indians; Pueblos, Navahos and Apaches, and the American frontier.

Tucker, Mary
Books of the Southwest. New York: J. J. Augustin, 1937. 105 pp.
A general bibliography: Deals with Indians of the Southwest. Spain in the Southwest, American pioneer history, the Southwest Country, The Southwest in Literature.
"Better in Indians and the Spanish period than in Anglo-American Culture." (Dobie).

Wagner, Henry Raup
A List of Books Relating to the South-West, in Spanish, and printed during the Colonial Period. Santiago, Chile: La Imprenta Diener, 1917. 43 pp.

———,
The Plains and the Rockies. Came out in 1920-1921. Revised and extended by Charles L. Camp. San Francisco: Grabhorn Press, 1937 (reprinted).
"A contribution to the bibliography of original narratives of travel and adventure, 1800-1865."

———,
The Spanish Southwest, 1542-1794; an annotated bibliography. Albuquerque: The Quivira Society, 1937. 2 vols.

PERIODICALS

El Palacio. v. 1, 1918—. Santa Fe, N. M. Monthly (Irregular). Published by the Museum of New Mexico and the School of American Research.

Southwestern Lore; official publication of the Colorado Archaeological Society. v. 1, 1935—. Gunnison, Colo. Quarterly.

The Masterkey. v. 1, 1927—. Los Angeles, Published eight times a year by the Southwest Museum. Illus.

The Southwest Bulletin. v. 1, no. 1-3 (July, 1926-March 1927). Los Angeles, 1926-27. 1 vol.

The Southwestern Historical Quarterly. v. 1, 1897—. Austin, Tex.: The Texas State Historical Association.

The Southwest Review. Texas University. Southern Methodist University, Austin; Dallas, Texas. June 1915—. 1-9 as *Texas Review.*

GENERAL STUDIES AND COLLECTIONS

Alter, J. Cecil
James Bridger. Salt Lake City, Utah: Shepard Book Co., 1925. 546 pp., illus., bibl.
  Contains number of versions of the Hugh Glass Bear Story. James Bridger, trapper, frontiersman, scout and guide: a historical narrative. . . . With which is incorporated a verbatum copy, annotated, of James Bridger, a biographical sketch, by Maj. Gen. Grenville M. Dodge . . . Salt Lake City, Utah.

Armer, Laura
Southwest. Illustrated from paintings by the author. London: Longmans, Green and Co., 1935. xiii, 224 pp., illus.

Arnold, Elliott
Blood Brother. New York: Duell, Sloan and Pearce, 1947. 558 pp.
  His two most important figures in the book are an Indian and a White man, the Apache Chieftain Cochise and the American General Oliver Otis Howard. Cochise was the greatest of all the Apache leaders in their struggle to survive against American treachery, cruelty, and deceit . . . no one will finish the book without a deeper understanding of the background of Southwestern life." (T. M. Pearce).

Austin, Mary
The Flock. Illustrated by E. B. Smith. Boston: Houghton Mifflin Co., 1906. 266 pp.
  The author skilfully weaves folklore into her romances.

————,
Lost Borders. New York and London: Harper and Bros., 1909. 208 pp.
  Fiction.

————,
One Smoke Stories. Boston and New York: Houghton Mifflin Co., 1934. 294 pp., illus.
  Fiction.

————,
"Folk Plays of the Southwest." *Theatre Arts Monthly* 17:599-610. August 1933.

Bailey, Philip A.
Golden Mirages. New York: The Macmillan Co., 1941. xvii, 353 pp.
  "An authoritative book on the legends, tall tales, customs, languages and manners of the wild region stretching from San Diego on the west to Maricopa and Pima Counties (Arizona) on the east and centering in the area around the Salton Sea.

Becker, May
Golden Tales of the Southwest, decorations by Lois Lenski. New York: Dodd, Mead & Company, 1939. xiii, 265 pp., illus.
  Short stories, some use folklore.

Blake, Forrester
Riding the Mustang Trail. New York: C. Scribner's Sons, 1935. 5 p.l., 261 pp., front, plates, ports.
  An account of a trail drive of wild horses from New Mexico to Oklahoma.

Botkin, Benjamin Albert, ed.
The Southwest Scene, An anthology of Regional Verse. Oklahoma City: The Economy Co., 1931. xi, 115 pp.
  Collection of poetry.

Boynton, Percy H.
The Rediscovery of the Frontier. Chicago: University of Chicago Press, 1931.

Burns, Walter Noble
Tombstone; an Iliad of the Southwest. Garden City, N. Y.: Doubleday Doran and Co., 1927.

Callison, John J.
Bill Jones of Paradise Valley. His Life and Adventures for Over Forty Years in the Great Southwest. He was a Pioneer in the Days of the Buffalo, The Wild Indian, The Oklahoma Boomer, The Cowboy and the Outlaw. Kingfisher, Oklahoma: J. J. Callison, 1914.

Campbell, T. J.
Pioneer Priests of North America. New York: The American Press, 1911.

Casey, P. R., ed.
Southwestern Lore in Poetry. Gunnison, Colorado: Colorado Archaeological Society, Inc., 1943.

Cather, Willa
Death Comes for the Archbishop. New York: Alfred A. Knopf, 1932. 303 pp.
  "Best known novel concerned with the Southwest." (Dobie).

Cattermole, E. G.
Famous Frontiersmen Pioneers and Scouts. Tarrytown, N. Y.: W. Abbot, 1926., 544 pp.
  Adventure tales and anecdotes.

Clark, Thomas D.
The Rampaging Frontier. Indianapolis: The Bobbs-Merrill Co., 1939.
  "Historical picturization and analysis, fortified by incidents and tales of 'Varmints,' 'Liars,' 'Quarter Horses,' Fiddlin', 'Foolin' with Gals,' etc." (Dobie).

Clemens, Jeremiah
Mustang Gray. Philadelphia: J. B. Lippincott and Co., 1858. 296 pp.

Cole, Jackson
The Valley of Revenge. New York: Arcadia House, 1944. 256 pp.
  A western yarn about a Robin Hood of the Southwest.

Corbin, Alice
The Sun Turns West. Santa Fe, N. Mex.: 1933. 72 pp., illus.

Corle, Edwin
Desert Country. (American Folkways Series). New York: Duell, Sloan and Pearce, 1941. viii, 357 pp.
  Desert Country stretches from the Mexican Border to the ghost towns of Nevada, from the Mojave to the Grand Canyon. It is a strange and dramatic country.

————, *Listen, Bright Angel.* New York: Duell, Sloan and Pearce, 1946. viii, 312 pp., illus.
A dramatic narrative and guide of the Southwest. But the main emphasis is upon the Grand Canyon spectacle of Colorado; with the narrative many bits of folklore are given.

Cutbirth, Ruby Nichols
Ed Nichols Rode a Horse. Dallas: Texas Folklore Society and University Press, 1943, x, 134 pp.

Dobie, J. Frank
Coronado's Children. Garden City, N. Y.: Garden City Publ. Co., Inc., 1934. 367 pp., music.

————, *Folklore of the Southwest.* In: *Chronicles of Oklahoma,* Oklahoma Historical Society, Vol. 2, No. 3, Sept. 1924.

————, ed.
Southwestern Lore. Publications of the Texas Folk-Lore Society Number IX. Dallas: The Southwest Press. 1931. 198 pp.

————, *Tongues of the Monte.* Garden City, N. Y.: Doubleday, Doran and Co., 1935.

————, *Vaquero of the Brush Country.* Dallas: Southwest Press, 1929.

Dondore, Dorothy Anne
The Prairie and the Making of Middle America. Cedar Rapids, Iowa: The Torch Press, 1926.

Duffus, R. L.
The Santa Fé Trail. New York: Longmans, 1930. Bibl.
"Best work on the subject." (Dobie)

Edgarton, Lucille Selk
Pillars of Gold. New York: Alfred A. Knopf, 1941.
An adventure filled novel, with excursions into local lore and character.

Editors of Look Magazine
The Santa Trail. New York: Random House, 1946. 267 pp., illus.
". . . Nothing is left out. Color is there. Atmosphere is there. . . . And you have a vivid sense of the immense movement as a whole." (S. Burt).

Finger, Charles Joseph
The Distant Prize. A book about rovers, rangers, and rascals, decorations by Henry Pitz. New York: D. Appleton Century Co., 1935. ix, 330 pp., illus.

Foreman, Grant
Indians & Pioneers; the story of the American Southwest before 1830. New Haven: Yale University Press, 1930. xvi, 348 pp., bibl.

————, *Pioneer Days in the Early Southwest.* Cleveland: The Arthur H. Clark Company, 1926. 349 pp., bibl.

Gardiner, D. K.
Snow Water. New York: Doubleday, Doran and Co., 1939.

Garrard, Lewis H.
Nah-Toyah and the Taos Trail (1850). Oklahoma City: Harlow Publ. Co., 1927. 320 pp., illus.
"Has reading list prepared by Stanley Vestal." (Dobie).

Geiser, Samuel Wood
"Southwestern Sittings." 1. William Douglas Walbach. *Southwest Review* 29:291-297, 1944.

Greer, Hilton R.
Voices of the Southwest. New York: The Macmillan Co., 1923. 207 pp.
An anthology of Texas Poetry.

Gregg, Josiah
Commerce of the Prairies: or the Journal of a Santa Fé Trail Trader. New York: H. G. Langley, 1844.

————, *Diary and Letters of Josiah Gregg, Southwestern Enterprises, 1840-1847.* Ed. by Maurice Garland Fulton. Norman, Oklahoma: University of Oklahoma Press, 1941.

————, *Scenes and Incidents in the Western Prairies:* During Eight Expeditions, and Including a Residence of Nearly Nine Years in Northern Mexico. Philadelphia: J. W. Moore, 1857. 2 vols., illus.

Hafen, LeRoy R.
The Overland Mail 1849-1869. Cleveland: The A. H. Clark Co., 1926. 361 pp.

Harris, George W.
Sut Lovingood. New York: Dick and Fitzgerald, 1867. 299 pp.

Hobbs, James
Wild Life in the Far West; personal adventures of a border mountain man. Comprising hunting and trapping adventures with Kit Carson and others; captivity and life among the Comanches; . . . desperate combats with Apaches, grizzly bears, etc., etc. Hartford: Wiley, Waterman & Eaton, 1873. 488 pp., illus.

Holden, W. C.
Rollie Burns or an Account of the Ranching Industry on the South Plains. Dallas, Texas: The Southwest Press, 1932.

Holling, Holling C.
Tree on the Trail. New York: Houghton Mifflin Co., 1942.
The history of the Southwest is told as a cottonwood tree on the Santa Fe Trail.

Hooper, J. J.
Adventures of Captain Simon Suggs. Philadelphia: T. B. Peterson and Bros., 1 cop. 1846. 201 pp.

Ickes, Anna
Mesa Land; the history and romance of the American Southwest. Boston: Houghton Mifflin Company, 1933. ix, 235 pp., illus.

Irving, Washington
A Tour on the Prairies. Philadelphia: Lea & Blanchard, 1835. xv, 274 pp.

Janvier, Thomas Allibone
Santa Fe's Partner. New York & London: Harper & Brothers., 1907. 236 pp.

Kluckhohn, Clyde
To the Foot of the Rainbow; a tale of twenty-five hundred miles of wandering on horseback through the Southwest enchanted land. New York: The Century Co., 1927. xiii, 276 pp.

Kupper, Winnifred Thalman
"Folk Characters and the Sheep Industry." *TFSP* 15: 85-118, 1939.

————————,
The Golden Hoof: The Story of the Sheep of the Southwest. New York: Alfred A. Knopf, 1945. xi, 203 pp., bibl.
"It includes many other facts, and a wealth of lore." (Stanley Walker).

Lanham, Edwin
Thunder on the Earth. New York: Harcourt, Brace and Co., 1941. 570 pp.

Laut, Agnes Christina
Romance of the Rails. New York: R. G. McBride & Co., 1929. 2 vols.

————————,
Through Our Unknown Southwest, the wonderland of the United States . . . the home of the cliff dweller and the Hopi, the forest ranger and the Navajo, the lure of the painted desert. New York: McBride, Nast & Co., 1913. xxx, 271 pp., illus.

Lewis, Willy Newbury
Between Sun and Sod. Clarindon, Texas: Clarindon Press, 1938.

Long, Haniel
Piñon Country (American Folkways Series.) New York: Duell, Sloan and Pearce, 1941. xi, 327 pp.
Canyons, caverns, walking red rains, great rock-like ships, and covered wagons are part of the Piñon Country of the Southwest whose people include the Navajo, Mormon, Pueblos, and Spanish American.

Lummis, Charles Fletcher
A New Mexico David, and Other Stories and Sketches of the Southwest. New York: Charles Scribner's Sons, 1891. ix, 271 pp., illus.

————————,
Mesa, Canyon, and Pueblo; our wonderland of the Southwest, its marvels of nature, its pageant of earth building, its strange people: its centuried romance. Illustrated with nearly 100 rare photographs. New York: The Century Company, 1925. xvi, 517 pp., illus.
Based on the author's "Some Strange Corners of Our Country." Bibl. pp. 485-495.

————————,
Some Strange Corners of Our Country; the Wonderland of the Southwest. New York: The Century Company, 1903. xi, 270 pp., illus.

Major, Mabel, and Smith, Rebecca W.
The Southwest in Literature; An Anthology for High Schools. New York: The Macmillan Company, 1929. xvii, 370 pp., illus.

Man, Bird and Beast. Publ. Texas Folklore Society, Austin, Texas, 1927. J. Frank Dobie, ed.

McCarty, John L.
Maverick Town. The Story of Old Tascosa. Illustrated with photographs and drawings by Harold D. Brighee. Norman: University of Oklahoma Press, 1946. 277 pp.
"In digging out the story of old Tascosa with such scrupulous care and in laying a wreath on its Dusty grave, Mr. McCarty has made a solid contribution to Southwestern history." (Stanley Walker).

McCoy, Joseph G.
Historic Sketches of the Cattle Trade of the West and Southwest. Kansas City, Mo.: Ramsey, Millett and Hudson, 1874, 427 pp., illus. Reprinted—Washington, D. C., 1932.

Mersfelder, L. C. (Larry)
Cowboy-Fisherman-Hunter. Kansas City, Mo.: Brown-White-Lowell Press, 1941.
True stories of the American Southwest.

Mills, Enos A.
The Grizzly, Our Greatest Wild Animal. Boston: Houghton Mifflin Co., 1919. 288 pp.
"He saw much and wrote vividly." (Dobie).

Munk, Joseph Amasa
Southwest Sketches. New York: G. P. Putnam's Sons, 1920. xi, 311 pp., illus.
History, tradition, legend and custom form part of the life seen and recorded.

Nelson, William Hamilton
Twelve Wonders of the Western World. San Francisco: Danner Publishing Co., 1934. 108 pp., illus.

Parsons, Elsie Clews
"Relations Between Ethnology and Archaeology in the Southwest." *American Antiquity* 5: 214-220, 1940.

Pattie, James Ohio
The Hunters of Kentucky; or, The Trials and Toils of Trappers and Traders, during an Expedition to the Rocky Mountains, New Mexico, and California . . . New York: W. H. Graham, 1847. 100 pp.

Pearce, Thomas M., and Hendon, Telfair
America in the Southwest: A Regional Anthology. Albuquerque: University of New Mexico Press, 1933. xxvi, 346 pp.
————————, and Thomason, A. P., eds.
Southwesterners Write. The Southwest in Stories and Articles by Thirty-two Contributors. Albuquerque, N. M.: The University of New Mexico Press, 1946. ix, 365 pp., illus.

Perry, George Sessions, ed.
Roundup Time. A Collection of Southwestern Writing. New York: Whittlesey House, 1943. xvi, 384 pp.

Pike, James
Scout and Ranger, Princeton, N. J.: Princeton University Press, 1932. First published in 1865.

Postel, Charles (Charles Sealsfield or Francis Hardman, pseudonyms)
The Cabin Book. New York: J. Winchester, 1844. 155 pp.

Prudden, Theophil Mitchell
On the Great American Plateau. Wanderings Among the canyons and buttes, in the land of the cliff-dwellers and the Indians of to-day. Illustrated by Edward Leaming. New York: G. P. Putnam's Sons, 1906. viii, 243 pp., illus.

Raine, James Watt
The Land of Saddle-Bags; a study of the mountain people of Appalachia. Published jointly by Council of Women for Home Missions and Missionary Education movement of the U. S. and Canada. N. Y., 1924. x, 260 pp., music.

Reid, John C.
Reid's Tramp; or, A Journal of the Incidents of Ten Months Travel Through Texas, New Mexico, Arizona, Sonora, and California . . . Selma, Alabama: Printed at the Book and Job Office of John Hardy & Co., 1858. 237 pp.

Rhodes, Eugene Manlove
The Hired Man on Horseback. Boston: Houghton Mifflin Company, 1938. 263 pp.
Poetry of the Southwest.

Rideing, William Henry
A Saddle in the Wild West . . . New York: D. Appleton and Company, 1879. 165 pp.

Rister, Carl C.
Southern Plainsmen. Norman, Oklahoma: University of Oklahoma Press, 1938. Bibl.

Roberts, Edward
With the Invader: Glimpses of the Southwest. San Francisco: S. Carson & Co., 1885. 156 pp., illus.

Rogers, John Williams, Witherspoon, Kathleen, and Acheson, Sam
Three Southwest Plays. Dallas, Texas: Southwest Review, 1942.

Ruess, Everett
On Desert Trails, with introduction by Hugh Lacy, and foreword by Randall Henderson. El Centro, Calif.: Desert Magazine Press, 1940. 72 pp., illus.

Shedd, John Cutler
Desert Lore. Los Angeles: J. R. Miller, 1931. 47 pp., illus.
Poems of the Southwest country.

Stover, Elizabeth Matchett
Son-of-a-Gun Stew, A Sampling of the Southwest; foreword by John William Rogers, illustrations by Harold D. Bugbee, Dallas: University Press, Southern Methodist University, 1945. x, 216 pp., illus.

Sweet, Alex E., and Knox, J. Armoy
On a Mexican Mustang. Through Texas from the Gulf to the Rio Grande. London: 1883. Later edited in Hartford, Conn., 1887. 672 pp., illus.

Thane, Eric
High Border Country (American Folkways Series.) New York: Duell, Sloan and Pearce, 1942.
Indigenous material, colorful, dramatic, these tales of mountain men, of redskins, of prospectors, of soldiers, vigilants, Chinese, cowboys, outlaws, copper barons, of farmers, herders, some good, some bad, some notorious.

Thomas, Alfred Barnaby
Forgotten Frontiers. Norman: Oklahoma University Press, 1932. 420 pp.

Thorpe, Thomas Bangs
The Hive of the Bee-Hunter. New York: D. Appleton & Co., 1854. 312 pp.

Townshend, Richard Baxter
The Tenderfoot in New Mexico. New York: Dodd, Mead & Co., 1924. ix, 257 pp.

————,
Last Memories of a Tenderfoot. London: J. Lane, 1926. xi, 270 pp., illus.

Vestal, Stanley
Fandango. Boston and New York: Houghton Mifflin Co., 1927. 66 pp.
Poetry of the Southwest.

————,
The Old Santa Fé Trail. Boston: Houghton Mifflin Co., 1939.

Waters, Frank
The Colorado; illustrated by Nicolai Fechin; maps by George Annand. (Rivers of America Series.) New York: Rinehart & Company, 1946. xii, 400 pp., illus., bibl.

Webber, Charles Wilkins
The Hunter-Naturalist or Wild Scenes and Wild Hunters. Phila.: Lippincott, Grambo & Co., 1852. 610 pp.

————,
The Romance of Forest and Prairie Life: Narratives of Perilous Adventures and Wild Hunting Scenes. London: H. Vizetelly, 1853. 239 pp.

White, Stewart Edward
Arizona Nights. New York: The McClure Co., 1907. 351 pp., illus.

Whiting, Lillian
The Land of Enchantment; from Pike's Peak to the Pacific . . . Boston: Little, Brown and Company, 1909. xii, 347 pp., illus.

Wilson, Charles Morrow
Backwoods America. Chapel Hill: University of North Carolina Press, 1935.

Woodhull, Frost
"Folk-Lore Shooting." *TFSP* 9: 1-14, 1931.
 A chronicle of incredible deeds. But who says
 you've got to believe them!

Wooten, Mattie Lloyd
Women Tell the Story of the Southwest. San
Antonio: Naylor Co., 1940.
 An Anthology.

Wynn, A.
"Pioneer Folkways." *TFSP* 13:190–238, 1937.

Yauger, Fay
Planter's Charm. Dallas: The Kaleidograph
Press, 1935. 78 pp.
 Poetry of the Southwest.

FOLKTALES—LEGENDS—MYTHS

Arnold, Oren
Wild Life—the Southwest. Dallas: Banks
Upshaw and Co., 1936.
 "Chapters on various characteristic animals and
 plants." (Dobie).

Bailey, Philip A.
Golden Mirages. The story of the lost Pegleg
mine, the legendary three gold buttes and
yarns of and by those who know the desert.
New York: The Macmillan Company, 1940.
xvii, 353 pp., illus., bibl.

Barclay, Lillian Elizabeth
"The Coyote: animal and folk character."
TFSP 14: 36-103, 1938.

Becker, Mary L.
Golden Tales of the Southwest. New York:
Dodd, Mead and Co., 1939.
 "The best anthology of Southwestern narratives."
 (Dobie).

Blair, Walter
Native American Humor (1800-1900). New
York: American Book Co., 1937. ix, 549 pp.,
illus., index, bibl.

Boatright, Mody C.
"Comic Exempla of the Pioneer Pulpit." *TFSP*
14: 155-168, 1938.

————,
"Frontier Humor: Despairing or Buoyant?"
Southwest Review, Vol. 27, Spring 1942.

Botkin, B. A.
Tall Talk and Tall Tales of the Southwest.
In: *The New Mexico Candle,* New Mexico
Normal University, Las Vegas, New Mexico,
June 28, 1933.

Calvin, Ross
River of the Sun; Stories of the Storied Gila.
Albuquerque, N. M.: University of New Mex-
ico Press, 1946. xix, 159 pp., illus.

De Huff, Elizabeth
Tay Tay's Tales. New York: Harcourt, Brace
and Co., 1922.

Dobie, James Frank
Apache Gold and Yaqui Silver; Illustrated by
Tom Lea. Boston: Little Brown and Com-
pany, 1939. xvii, 366 pp., illus.
 Legends of mines and hidden treasures.

————,
Coronado's Children; tales of lost mines and
buried treasures of the Southwest. Illustrated
by Ben Carlton Mead. Dallas, Tex.: The
Southwest Press, 1930. xiv, 367 pp., illus., bibl.
pp. 343-359.)

————,
"Legends of Buried Treasure and Lost Mines."
TFSP 3: 3-19, 28, 48, 51-56, 60-61, 64-66, 80,
95-98, 1924.

————,
"Legends of the Southwest." *Country Gentle-
man,* Nov. 1925, Jan., Mar., Aug., Oct., 1926,
July, 1927.

————,
On the Open Range. Dallas: The Southwest
Press, 1931. 312 pp., illus.
 Chapter III is on "Bars and Bar Hunters."

————,
"Rattlesnake Lore." *Holland's Magazine* (Dallas, Texas), Sept., 1926.

————,
Spur-Of-The-Cock. Texas. Folklore Society
Publications, No. XI. Austin, Tex.: Texas Folk-
lore Society, 1933. 112 pp., illus., music.
 Tales and legends of the Southwest.

————,
Tone the Bell Easy. Austin, Texas: **Texas**
Folklore Society, 1932. 199 pp.

————,
Tongues of the Monte. Dallas: University
Press, 1942. Also Garden City, N. Y.: Double-
day Doran and Co., Inc., 1935. 301 pp., illus.
 Chapters "Juan Oso," and "Under the Sign of
 Ursa Major"—deals with Bear Stories.

————, **Boatright, Mody C. and Ransom,**
Harry H., eds.
Coyote Wisdom. Texas Folklore Publications,
No. 14. Austin: Texas Folklore Society, 1938.
300 pp.

Donoghue, David
"Myths in Oil Finding." *TFSP* 9:45-47, 1931.

Ferguson, Robert G.
*Camp Fire Tales of Lost Mines and Hidden
Treasure.* Tucson, Ariz.: 1937. 35 pp.

Geiser, Samuel Wood
"100 Lashes for a Good Man." *The Southwest
Review,* 30(4): 374-376, Summer, 1945.

Goodwyn, Frank
The Magic of Limping John. A Story of the
Mexican Border Country. New York: Farrar
and Rinehart, 1944. 275 pp., illus.

Hittell, Theodore H.
The Adventures of John Capen Adams. New York: Charles Scribner's Sons, reprinted 1926. 373 pp. (First published in 1860).
  Wonderful grizzlie bear stories.

Judson, Katharine Berry
Myths and Legends of California and the Old Southwest. Chicago: A. C. McClurg & Co., 1912. xvi, 193 pp.

Laughlin, Edward Douglas
The Yaqui Gold. San Antonio, Texas: The Naylor Company, 1943. 80 pp.
  The story of the Yaqui Gold Country in Texas.

Littlejohn, E. G.
"Lost Gold of the Llano Country." *TFSP* 3: 20-23, 1918.

Marshall, James
Santa Fe. New York: Random House, 1945. 465 pp., index, illus.
  "A boisterous account of one of the most amazing feats in our history . . . (with) tales as tall as the Rockies. . . ."

McCrackin, Josephine
Overland Tales. San Francisco: A. L. Bancroft & Co., 1877. xi, 383 pp.
  Historical and legendary.

McKee, L. V., and Summers, P. A.
Dusty Desert Tales. Caldwell, Idaho: Caxton, Printers Ltd., 1941.

Meine, Franklin Julius, ed.
Tall Tales of the Southwest. An anthology of Southern and Southwestern Humor 1830-1860. New York: Alfred A. Knopf, 1930. xxxii, 456 pp., bibl.
  "A well edited and well selected anthology with appendices affording a guide to the whole field of early Southern humor and realism." (Dobie).

Miller, Joaquin
True Bear Stories. Chicago: Rand, McNally, 1900. 259 pp.

Mitchell, John D.
Lost Mines of the Great Southwest. Phoenix, Arizona: Journal Co., 1933. 174 pp.

Morris, Ann Axtell
Digging in the Southwest. Garden City, N. Y.: Doubleday, Doran and Co., 1933.

Morrison, F.
"Don José—the love mad López." *CFQ* 1: 369-371, 1942.
  Legendary figure of Southwestern U. S.

Moses, Leon Denny
"Five Legends of the Southwest." *TFSP* 10: 71-81, 1932.

Peck, Leigh
Don Coyote. Illustrated by Virginia Lee Burton. Boston: Houghton Mifflin Co., 1942. 78 pp.

Smith, Walter Vernon
Tales of the Spanish Southwest, stories of the Spanish Rule in California, New Mexico, Arizona and Texas . . . New York: H. Holt and Company, 1934. xi, 181 pp., illus.

Stretcher, J. K.
"Reptiles of the South and Southwest in Folklore." *TFSP* 5:56–59, 1920.

Vestal, Stanley
Big Foot Wallace. Boston: Houghton Mifflin Co., 1942.
  A great character in Texan pioneer life whose deeds have become legend and lore of the Southwest and of Texas in particular.

————,
Dobe Walls, A Story of Kit Carson's Southwest. Boston: Houghton Mifflin Co., 1929., 314 pp.
  Excellent characterization of the Plains Indians.

————,
"The Saga of the Cob Pipe." *The Southwest Review,* 30(4): 354-356, Summer, 1945.

Weadock, Jack
Dust of the Desert; Plain Tales of the Desert and Border. New York: Appleton-Century Co., 1936.

Webber, Charles Wilkins
Tales of the Southern Border. Philadelphia: J. B. Lippincott & Co., 1856. 400 pp., illus.

Whittaker, M. L.
Pathbreakers and Pioneers of the Pueblo Region. Pueblo: Franklin Press, 1917.

Wooten, Mattie Lloyd, comp.
Women Tell the Story of the Southwest. San Antonio, Tex.: The Naylor Company, 1940. xvii, 394 pp.

Yelvington, Henry
Ghost Lore. A collection of tales the author heard in Texas, Mexico, Oklahoma City, and other places. San Antonio, Texas: The Naylor Co., 1936.

CUSTOMS—BELIEFS

Austin, Mary
The Land of Little Rain. Boston: Houghton Mifflin Company, 1904. xi, 280 pp., illus.

Baker, Ray Stannard
"The Great Southwest." *Century Magazine* 64: 1-15, 213-225, 360-373, 535-54, 1902.

Bush, I. J.
Gringo Doctor. Caldwell, Idaho: Caxton Printers, 1939.
  "Dr. Bush represented frontier medicine and surgery on both sides of the Rio Grande. Living at El Paso, he was for a time with the Maderistas in the revolution against Diaz." (Dobie).

Campa, Arthur Leon
The Spanish Religious Theatre in the Southwest. Albuquerque: University of New Mexico, 1934. Language Series, Vol. 5, Nos. 1 and 2.

Cole, M. R.
Los Pastores. A Mexican Play of the Nativity. With illustrations and music. Memoirs of the American Folklore Society, vol. 9. Boston: Houghton Mifflin & Co., 1907. xxxi, 234 pp., music.

Curtis, William Eleroy
A Summer Scamper, along the old Santa Fé Trail and Through the Gorges of Colorado to Zion. Chicago: Inter-Ocean Publishing Co., 1883. 113 pp.

Cutbirth, Ruby Nichols
Ed Nichols Rode a Horse. Austin, Texas: The Texas Folklore Society, and University Press in Dallas, 1943.
"It reflects the social and economic life, manners and customs of a people carving out of a wilderness, a new life." (Carlton).

De Huff, Elizabeth
Taytay's Memories. New York: Harcourt, Brace and Co., 1924.

Dick, Everett
The Sod House Frontier. New York: D. Appleton-Century Co., 1937.

————,
Vanguards of the Frontier. New York: D. Appleton-Century Co., 1941.

Dobie, J. F.
"Weather Wisdom of the Texas-Mexican Border." *TFSP* 2: 87-99, 1917.

Eickemeyer, Rudolf
Letters from the Southwest. Illustrated by E. W. Deming. New York: J. J. Little & Co., 1894. 111 pp.

Fergusson, Erna
Our Southwest . . . New York: A. A. Knopf, 1940. 376 pp., illus.

Fergusson, Harvey
Home in the West. New York: Duell, Sloan and Pearce, 1945. 247 pp.
A fascinating biography of life in the Southwest at the turn of the century.

Gregg, Josiah
Commerce of the Prairies, or the Journal of a Santa Fé Trader, during eight expeditions across the Great Western Prairies, and a residence of nearly nine years in Northern Mexico. New York: H. G. Langley, 1845. 2 vols., illus.

Hand, Wayland D.
"Quilt Patterns." *CFQ* 3:151-152, 1944.
Reproductions of those advertised by Stearns and Foster, Cincinnati, Ohio.

Hart, John A.
Pioneer Days in the Southwest from 1850-1879. Guthrie, Okla.: The State Capitol Co., 1909. 320 pp.
"Much on frontier ways of living." (Dobie). Contributions by Charles Goodnight, Emanuel Dubbs, John A. Hart, etc.

Horgan, Paul
The Common Heart. New York: Harper and Bros., 1942.
A finely wrought novel having the Southwest as its background.

Hulbert, Archer Butler
Southwest on the Torquoise Trail; the first diaries on the road to Santa Fe, edited with bibliographical resumé, 1810-1825. . . . Colorado Springs, Denver: The Denver Public Library, 1933. xiv, 301 pp., illus.

Ingraham, Joseph Holt
The South-west. By a Yankee. New York: Harper & Brothers, 1835. 2 vols.

Leigh, William R.
The Western Pony. New York: Huntington Press, 1933. 116 pp., illus. by William R. Leigh.
An account of mustangs and Indian ponies.

Lewis, Henry Clay
The Swamp Doctor's Adventures in the South-West. Containing the whole of the Louisiana swamp doctor; streaks of squatter life; and far-western scenes; in a series of forty-two humorous Southern and Western sketches . . . With fourteen illustrations from original designs by Darley. Philadelphia: T. B. Peterson and Brothers, 1858. 2 vols. in 1.

Magoffin, Susan
Down the Santa Fé Trail Into Mexico; the diary of Susan Shelby Magoffin . . . New Haven: Yale University Press, 1926. xxv, 294 pp., illus., bibl.

Mora, Joaquin
Trail Dust and Saddle Leather. New York: Charles Scribner's Sons, 1946.
"Although Mr. Mora adds little to the lore and history of the range, he has much to say that will be useful to the student of Western and Southwestern customs." (Stanley Walker).

Osgood, Ernest Staples
The Day of the Cattleman. Minneapolis: The University of Minneosta Press, 1929. x, 283 pp., maps, bibl.

Pearson, Edmund
Dime Novels. Boston: Little Brown and Co., 1929. 280 pp.
Fictionalized, but authentic glimpse of life in the Southwest.

Pierson, Rev. Hamilton W.
In the Brush; or Old-Time Social, Political and Religious Life in the Southwest. New York: D. Appleton and Co., 1881. 321 pp., illus.

Prentis, Noble L.
South-Western Letters. Topeka, Kan.: Kansas Publishing House, 1882. 133 pp.

Rak, Mary Kidder
A Cowman's Wife. Boston: Houghton Mifflin Co., 1934.
"The realities of life as experienced by a woman from the outside on a small Arizona ranch." (Dobie).

Richards, Clarice E.
A Tenderfoot Bride. New York and Chicago: Fleming H. Revell Co., 1920. 226 pp.

Richardson, Albert Deane
Beyond the Mississippi. Hartford, Conn.: American Publishing Co., 1867. xvi, 572 pp.
From the great river to the great ocean. Life and adventure on the prairies, mountains and the Pacific coast, 1857-1867.

Seward, Anna
"California in the Eighties, As Pictured in the Letters of Anna Seward." *California Historical Society Quarterly* 16: 291-303; 17: 28-40, 1937.

Steele, James W.
Frontier Army Sketches. Chicago: Jansen, McClurg & Co., 1883. 329 pp.

Stewart, Elinor P.
Letters of a Woman Homesteader. Boston: Houghton Mifflin Co., 1914.

Thompson, William Tappan
Major Jones's Courtship; illus. by Darley. Philadelphia: Carey & Hart, 1844. 200 pp.

White, Owen P.
A Frontier Mother. New York: Minton, Balch and Co., 1929. 101 pp.

Wooten, Mattie Lloyd, ed.
Women Tell the Story of the Southwest. San Antonio, Tex.: The Naylor Company, 1940. xvii, 394 pp.

SPEECH

Hyacinth, Socrates
"South-Western Slang." *The Overland Monthly* 3(No. 2):125, 1869. Devoted to the Development of the Country Entered—1869, by John H. Carmany. San Francisco: A. Roman and Co., 1869.

Pearce, Thomas M.
"The English Language in the Southwest." *New Mexico Historical Review* 7: 210-232, 1932.

——————,
"The Southwestern Word Box." *New Mexico Quarterly* 2: 263-268, 340-344, 1932.

FOLKSONG

See: Folksong of the Spanish-American, pp. 601-6; Songs of the Cowboys, pp. 617-27.

STUDIES

Koehler, E. B.
"Our Musical Beginnings in the Southwest." *Etude* 59:7-, 1941.

Spell, Lota M.
The Contribution of the Southwest to American Music. Texas Federation of Music Clubs. Survey and discussion.

RECORDS

"The Old Chisholm Trail": Songs of the American Southwest. Kansas Boys, Tony Kraber. Ke-104.
Contents: The Old Chisholn Trail; Green Grow the Lilacs; Whiskey, Rye Whiskey; The Tenderfoot; Blood on the Saddle; The Boll Weevil Song; The Next Big River.

ARIZONA

See: Spanish-American Folklore and Folksong, pp. 593–606.

FOLKLORE

BIBLIOGRAPHY

A Bibliography of Arizona Folklore is being compiled by the newly created Committee of Arizona University to study folklore in the State. Dr. A. O. Andersen, Dean of the College of Fine Arts. 1944.

Alliot, Hector
Bibliography of Arizona; being the record of literature collected by Joseph Amosa Munk, and donated by him to the Southwest Museum of Los Angeles, Calif. (Folklore, Music and Indian bibl.) Los Angeles: The Southwest Museum, 1914.

Historical Records Survey
Inventory of the County Archives of Arizona. Prepared by the Historical Records Survey, Works Progress Administration. Phoenix, Ariz.: The Historical Records Survey, 1938.

Lutrell, Estelle
A Bibliographical List of Books, Pamphlets and Articles on Arizona in the University of Arizona Library. Tucson, Ariz.: Press of the Arizona Daily Star, 1913. 60 pp. (Library Bibliography, No. 1).

Munk, Joseph Amasa
Bibliography of Arizona Books, Pamphlets and Periodicals in the Library of Dr. J. A. Munk. Los Angeles, Calif.: 1900. 28 pp. Second edition in 1908 issued under title: *Arizona Bibliography.*

PERIODICALS

Arizona Historical Review; A Quarterly. v. 1, 1928/29—. Phoenix, Ariz.

Arizona Quarterly. Critical Journal of Literature, History, and Folklore devoted to the interpretation of life and culture of the Western States. University of Arizona.

Hall, Dick Wick (Editor and Miner)
Salome Sun—Monthly Magazine, published in Salome, Arizona. Replete with Arizona and Southwest lore and speech, 1921. See: Vol. 1 (Nos. 2, 3, 4) 1921; Vol. II (No. 1) 1922; Vol. III (No. 1, 2) 1923; Vol. IV (No. 2) 1924; Vol. V (No. 1) 1925; Vol. VII (No. 11) 1927.

GENERAL STUDIES AND COLLECTIONS

Arizona University
Opportunities in Arizona Folklore. In: Arizona University Bulletin, Vol. XVI, No. 1, January 1, 1945. General Bulletin No. 9. Tucson: University of Arizona, 1945. 55 pp., bibl.

Bailey, Philip A.
Golden Mirages. New York: The Macmillan Co., 1941. 353 pp.
"An authoritative book on the legends, tall tales, customs, language, and manners of the wild region stretching from San Diego in the West to Maricopa and Pima countries (Arizona) on the east and centering in the area around the Salton tree." (D. Emrich).

Bancroft, Hubert Howe
History of Arizona and New Mexico, 1530-1888. San Francisco, Cal.: The History Co., 1889. 829 pp.

Boyer, Mary G., ed.
Arizona in Literature, a collection of the best writings of Arizona authors from early Spanish days to the present time. Glendale, Calif.: The Arthur H. Clark Co., 1934. 574 pp., illus.

Browne, John Ross
Adventures in the Apache Country: A Tour Through Arizona and Sonora . . . London: S. Low, Son, and Marston, 1869. 535 pp., illus.

Burns, Walter Noble
Tombstone; an Iliad of the Southwest. New York: Doubleday, Page and Co., 1927. ix, 388 pp.
The authentic and thrilling story of the old boom town of Tombstone, Arizona, with its two-gun outlaws, gamblers, Indian fighters, and sheriffs.

Cipriano, Padre
The Old Santa Fé Trail Across Arizona. Los Angeles: Press of the West Coast Magazine, 1913. 48 pp., illus.

Colt, Clem
Coyote Song. New York: Samuel Curl, 1947.
A novel of the Arizona territory in 1890.

Coolidge, D.
Arizona Cowboys. New York: E. P. Dutton and Co., 1938.

Corle, Edwin
Desert Country (American Folkways). New York: Duell, Sloan & Pearce, 1941. viii, 357 pp.

Federal Writers' Project
Arizona, A State Guide. (American Guide Series). Compiled and written by the Federal Writers' Project of the Works Progress Administration for the State of Arizona. New York: Hasting House, Publishers, 1940.

————,
Mission San Xavier del Bac, Arizona; a descriptive and historical guide, compiled by workers of the Writers' Program of the Works Progress Administration . . . New York: Hastings House, 1940. 57 pp., illus., bibl. (American Guide Series).

Forrest, Earle R.
Arizona's Dark and Bloody Ground. Caldwell, Idaho: Caxton Printer's Ltd., 1936.
Graham-Tewksbury feud.

Gillmore, Frances, and others
"Opportunities in Arizona Folklore." *Arizona Univ. General Bull.* (Tucson) No. 9, pp. 1-55, 1945.

Golden, Frank Alfred, ed.
The March of the Mormon Battalion. New York: Century Co., 1928.

Gregory, Herbert E.
"The Navajo Country." *American Geographical Society, Bulletin* 47: 561-577, 652-672, 1915.

Harris, William Richard
By Path and Trail. Salt Lake City: Press of the Intermountain Catholic, 1908. xi, 225 pp.
Comments on Indians (Yaquis, Digger), mountaineers, and traders—social conditions, customs, tales, and beliefs.

Humphrey, Zephine
Cactus Forest. New York: E. P. Dutton & Co., 1938. 245 pp.

Inman, Henry
The Old Santa Fe Trail. Topeka: Crane & Co., 1916. xvi, 493 pp.

James, George Wharton
A Little Journey to New Mexico and Arizona; Strange Places and Peoples in our Southwestern Land. Chicago: A. Flanagan Company, 1930. 270 pp., illus.

King, Frank
Wranglin' the Past. Los Angeles, Calif.: The Author, 1935.

Knibbs, Henry Herbert
Saddle Songs and Other Verse. Boston: Houghton Mifflin Co., 1916.

Lake, Stuart N.
Wyatt Earp, Frontier Marshall. Boston: Houghton Mifflin, 1931.

Manning, Reg
Cartoon Guide to Arizona. One hundred cartoons with text, with an oversized map of Arizona. New York: J. J. Augustin, 1941.

Monnet, Paul
"The Land of the Hopis." *Overland Monthly* 55: 206-215, 1915.

Munk, Joseph Amasa
Arizona Sketches. New York: The Grafton Press, 1905. ix, 230 pp., illus.

Nelson, William Hamilton
Alluring Arizona; being a series of connected sketches of the youngest state in the American Union, and the oldest in the world. San Francisco: W. H. Nelson, 1927. xiii, 133 pp.

Rak, Mary Kidder
Border Patrol. Boston: Houghton Mifflin and Company, 1938.

Spicer, Edward H.
Pascua: A Yaqui Village in Arizona. Chicago: University of Chicago Press, 1940. 319 pp., illus.

White, Stewart Edward
Arizona Nights. New York: The McClure Co., 1907. 351 pp., illus.

FOLKTALES—LEGENDS

Arnold, Oren
Superstition's Gold; the romantic history of hidden treasure in the Superstition mountain with its famous Lost Dutchman mine, including Indian Legends. Phoenix, Ariz.: The Arizona Printers, 1934. 32 pp.

Storm, Barry
Trail of the Lost Dutchman. An authentic story of the fabulous Lost Dutchman and of other originally Spanish mines in the Superstition mountains of Arizona. Phoenix, Ariz.: Goldwaters, 1939. 115 pp., illus.

CUSTOMS—BELIEFS

Brown, James Cabell
Calabazas; or, Amusing Recollections of an Arizona "City." San Francisco: Valleau & Peterson, 1892. 251 pp., illus.

Hughes, Dan de Lara
South From Tombstone, a Life Story. London: Methuen & Co., Ltd., 1938. v, 311 pp.

Lockwood, Francis Cummings
Arizona Characters. Los Angeles: The Times-Mirror Press, 1928. xiv, 230 pp., illus.

————,
"Pioneers: 1854 to 1864." *Arizona Historical Review* 5:55-61, 135-140, 276-333, 327-332, 1932.

————,
Pioneer Days in Arizona, from the Spanish Occupation to Statehood. New York: The Macmillan Co., 1932. xvi, 387 pp., illus., bibl. (pp. 345-367).

————,
Life in Old Tucson. Los Angeles: The Ward Richie Press, 1943.

Murdock, John Roberts
Arizona Characters in Silhouette. Arizona State Teachers College, Tempe. Bulletin, General Series, No. 9, 1933. 100 pp., illus.

Rak, Mary Kidder
A Cowman's Wife. Boston: Houghton Mifflin Co., 1934.
"The realities of life as experienced by a woman from the outside on a small Arizona ranch." (Dobie).

————,
Mountain Cattle. Boston: Houghton Mifflin, 1936.
Life on a small Arizona ranch.

Sloan, Richard E.
Memories of an Arizona Judge. Stanford, Calif.: Stanford University Press, 1932. xii, 250 pp.

Summerhayes, Martha
Vanished Arizona; Recollections of My Army Life. Philadelphia: J. B. Lippincott Co., 1908. 269 pp., illus.

SPEECH

Man, A. P., Jr.
"Word-List from Arizona." *Dialect Notes* 4 (Part 2):164–165, 1914.

PLACE NAMES

Barnes, Will C.
"Arizona Place Names." *Arizona University. General Bulletin* 6(No. 2): 1-503, 1935. Bibl. (pp. 502-503).

————,
"Arizona Place Names." *Arizona Historical Review* 5: 286-301, 1933.

Lloyd, Elwood
Arizonology; A compilation of more than two thousand names found on the maps of Arizona, together with information concerning their meaning, history, and many other interesting facts about this wonderful state. Flagstaff, Arizona: The Coconino Sun, 1933. 92 pp.

FOLKSONG

See: Spanish-American Folksong, pp. 601–6.

RECORDS

U. S. Library of Congress. Division of Music. Folklore Section.
Collection of Arizona Folklore. University of Arizona Recording Project, under the direction of Frances Gillmor.   AAFS-LC

NEW MEXICO

See: Folklore and Folksong of the Southwest, pp. 328–36; Folklore and Folksong of the Spanish-Americans, pp. 593–606.

FOLKLORE
BIBLIOGRAPHY

Bancroft, Hubert Howe
Bibliography of Early New Mexican History. In: *History of Arizona and New Mexico 1503-1888.* (pp. 19-26). San Francisco: History Company, 1889.

Bloom, Lansing B.
*Comprehensive Index to New Mexico Histori-
cal Review.* v. 1-15, 1926-1940. Albuquerque:
Historical Society of New Mexico and University of New Mexico, 1941.

Saunders, Lyle, comp.
*A Guide to Materials Bearing on Cultural
Relations in New Mexico.* Albuquerque, New
Mexico: The University of New Mexico Press,
1944. 528 pp.
  A comprehensive bibliography—including a
number of entries on folklore and folksong of
the Spanish-speaking population, the Indians;
Pueblos, Navahos and Apaches, and the Ameri-
can frontier.

Winship, George Parker
"A List of Books Useful to the Student on
the Coronado Expedition." 14th Annual Report, Bureau of American Ethnology, pp.
599-613. Washington, D. C.: U. S. Gov't.
Printing Office, 1896.

PERIODICALS

The New Mexico Historical Review. v. 1, 1926—.
Santa Fe, N. M. Quarterly.

GENERAL STUDIES AND COLLECTIONS

Austin, Mary
The Land of Journey's Ending, with illustra-
tions by John E. Jackson. New York: The
Century Co., 1924. ix, 459 pp., illus.

———,
The Land of Little Rain. Boston & New York:
Houghton Mifflin Co., 1904. 280 pp., illus.
  A work of fiction—rich in lore.

Boyd, E.
Saints and Saint Makers of New Mexico.
Santa Fe, N. M.: Laboratory of Anthropology,
1946. vi, 139 pp., bibl.

Bright, Robert
The Life and Death of Little Jo. Garden City,
New York: Doubleday, Doran, 1944. 216 pp.,
illus.
  A story of an ancient Spanish-American com-
munity not far from the Colorado border in the
State of New Mexico—"it has sincerity, a rue-
ful humor and an indolent charm." (John
Chamberlain).

Calvin, Ross
Sky Determines. New York: The Macmillan
Co., 1934.
  "In New Mexico whatever is both old and pecu-
liar appears upon examination to have a con-
nection with the arid climate." (Dobie).

Campa, Arthur L.
"New Mexico Folklore Society." *JAFL* 56:
178, 1943.

Carr, Harry
The West Is Still Wild, romance of the present and the past; with illustrations by Charles
H. Owens. Boston: Houghton Mifflin Company,
1932. iv, 257 pp., illus.

Cather, Willa
Death Comes for the Archbishop. New York:
Alfred A. Knopf, 1927. 303 pp.
  "Classical historical fiction on New Mexico."
(Dobie).

Davis, William Watts H.
The Spanish Conquest of New Mexico. Doylestown, Pa.: "Democrat", 1886. 32 pp.

Dobie, J. Frank
Coronado's Children. Dallas, Texas: The
Southwest Press, 1930. 367 pp., illus.

French, William John
*Some Recollections of a Western Ranchman,
New Mexico, 1883-1899.* London: Methuen
& Co., Ltd., 1927. vi, 283 pp.

Goodwyn, Frank
The Magic of Limping John. A Story of the
Mexican Border Country. New York: Farrar
and Rinehart, 1944. 275 pp., illus.

Hall, D. J.
Enchanted Sand; a New Mexican Pilgrimage.
London: Methuen & Co., Ltd., 1932. vii, 242
pp., illus.

Henderson, Alice Corbin
The Torquoise Trail. An Anthology of New
Mexico Poetry. Boston: Houghton Mifflin Co.,
1928.

Hewett, E. L., and Fisher, R. G.
Mission Monuments of New Mexico. Albu-
querque: University of New Mexico Press,
1934. 269 pp., 65 illus. (5th Handbook of
Archaeological History—School of American
Research.)

James, George Wharton
A Little Journey to New Mexico and Arizona;
strange places and peoples in our southwestern
land. Chicago: A. Flanagan Company, 1930.
270 pp., illus.

Janvier, Thomas Allibone
Stories of Old New Spain. New York: D. Ap-
pleton and Company, 1898. 326 pp.
  Fiction—using folklore background.

Laughlin, Ruth
Caballeros. Caldwell, Idaho: Caxton Printers,
Ltd., 1945. (reprint).
  ". . . A complete Baedeker of the City of Santa
Fe, with chapters on its Spanish folkways, his-
tory, songs, plays, crafts, etc. (Elaine L. Lewis).

Lindsay, Nicholas Vachel
*Adventures While Preaching the Gospel of
Beauty.* New York: M. Kennerley, 1914.
186 pp.

Lucero-White, Aurora, comp. and ed.
The Folklore of New Mexico, Vol. I. Santa
Fe: Seton Village Press, 1941. 49 pp., illus.
  The volume contains romances, corridos, cuen-
tos, proverbios, dichos, adivinanzas.

Lummis, Charles F.
The Land of Poco Tiempo. New York: Charles
Scribner's Sons, 1893 and 1906, 1925. xii,
310 pp., illus.

McKenna, James A.
Black Range Tales; Chronicling Sixty Years
of Life and Adventures in the Southwest . . .
Introduction by Shane Leslie; illustrated with
numerous woodcuts by Howard Simon. New
York: Wilson-Erickson, 1936. xiv, 300 pp.,
illus.

Pearce, Thomas M., and Hall, James
Cartoon Guide of New Mexico. 100 Cartoons
and text, large map in flap. New York: J. J.
Augustin, 1939. 107 pp., illus.

Powers, Stephen
Afoot and Alone; a walk from sea to sea, by
the Southern route. Adventures and Observations in Southern California, New Mexico.
Arizona, Texas, etc. Hartford, Conn.: Columbian Book Co., 1872. xvi, 327 pp., illus.

Tedlock, E. W., Jr.
"New Mexico Folklore Society." *JAFL* 59:
487-488, 1946.

Townshend, Richard Baxter
The Tenderfoot in New Mexico. New York:
Dodd, Mead & Co., 1924. ix, 257 pp., illus.

————.
Last Memories of a Tenderfoot. London: J.
Lane, 1926. xi, 270 pp., illus.

Twitchell, Ralph Emerson, comp. and ed.
Old Santa Fe, The Story of New Mexico's
Ancient Capital. Santa Fe: Santa Fe New
Mexican Publ. Corp., 1925.

Wallace, Susan Arnold E.
The Land of the Pueblos. New York: J. B.
Alden, 1888. 285 pp., illus.

FOLKTALES—LEGENDS

Applegate, Frank G.
Native Tales of New Mexico. Introduction
by Mary Austin, illustrated in color by author.
London & Philadelphia: J. B. Lippincott Co.,
1932. 263 pp.

Barker, Ruth Laughlin
"New Mexico Witch Tales." *TFSP* 10:62-70,
1932.

Campa, Arthur L.
New Mexico Folk Tales. Albuquerque, N. M.:
University of New Mexico, 1930.

Dobie, J. Frank
Apache Gold and Yaqui Silver. Boston: Little,
Brown and Co., 1939. 366 pp., illus.
Tales from Mexico and New Mexico.

Espinosa, José Manuel
Spanish Folk-Tales from New Mexico. Mem-
oir of the Amer-Folklore Society, No. 30.
Phila.: Amer-Folklore Society, 1937.

Le Noir, Phil
"The Hermit of Las Vegas." *TFSP* 10:124-126,
1932.
A strange and real character!

Lummis, Charles Fletcher
The King of the Broncos, and other stories
of New Mexico. New York: Charles Scribner's Sons, 1897. ix, 254 pp.

————,
The Enchanted Burro, stories of New Mexico
and South America. Chicago: Way and Williams, 1897. 277 pp., illus.

Morrison, Frederic
"Tales from Southern California and New
Mexico." *CFQ* 2:121-127, 1943.

CUSTOMS—BELIEFS

Campa, Arthur L.
Los Comanches, A New Mexican Folk Drama.
Albuquerque: University of New Mexico,
Bulletin 376, 1942.

————,
"The New Mexican Spanish Folktheater." *SFQ*
5:127-131, 1941.

Cleaveland, Agnes Morley
No Life for A Lady. Boston: Houghton, Mifflin Co., 1941.
"Bright, witty, penetrating, anecdotal. Best account of frontier life from woman's point of
view yet published. New Mexico is the setting,
towards the turns of the century." (Dobie).

Davis, William Watts Hart
El Gringo, or New Mexico and Her People.
New York: Harpers and Bros., 1857. Santa
Fe: (Reprinted) The Rydal Press, 1938.
332 pp.
"Excellent on manners and customs." (Dobie)

Ellison, Edith Nicholl
The Desert and the Rose. Boston: The Corn-
hill Company, 1921. 215 pp., illus.
Farm life and lore.

Ellison, Samuel
"Memoir of a Kentuckian in New Mexico,
1848-1884, by J. Manuel Espinosa." *Historical
Society of New Mexico, Publications No. 45.*
Santa Fe, N. M., 13 pp.

Englekirk, John E.
"Notes on the Repertoire of the New Mexican
Spanish Folktheater." *SFQ* 4: 227-237, 1940.

Federal Writers' Projects
Calendar of Annual Events in New Mexico
(American Guide Series) Written and Compiled by Federal Writers' Project, Illustrated
by the Federal Art Project of New Mexico.
Santa Fe, N. M.: The Santa Fe Civic League,
1937.

————,
New Mexico, a Guide to the Colorful State.
(American Guide Series). Compiled by the
Workers of the Federal Writers' Project of
the Works Progress Administration in the
State of New Mexico. New York: Hastings
House, 1940. xxxvii, 458 pp., illus., bibl.

Ferguson, Harvey
Home in the West. New York: Duell, Sloan and Pearce, 1944. 247 pp.
The first chapters give an intimate picture of life in New Mexico in the early days.

————,
Rio Grande. New York: Alfred A. Knopf, 1933. x, 296 pp., illus.
"The drama and evolution of human life in New Mexico." (Dobie).

Fulton, Maurice G., and Horgan, Paul, eds.
New Mexico's Own Chronicle. Dallas: B. Upshaw & Co., 1937. 3p. xxiv, 372 pp., illus.
Three races in the writings of four hundred years. Selections from writers dealing with New Mexico.

Horgan, Paul
Far from Cibola. New York: Harper and Bros., 1938. 163 pp.
Fiction—Life in New Mexico.

————,
The Return of the Weed. New York: Harper and Bros., 1936. 197 pp.
Fiction—Short stories.

Hoyt, Henry F.
A Frontier Doctor. Boston: Houghton Mifflin Co., 1929. 260 pp.
"Texas Panhandle and New Mexico during Billy the Kid days." (Dobie).

Hurt, Wesley R.
"Witchcraft in New Mexico." *Palacio*, April 1940, pp. 73-83.

James, George Wharton
New Mexico, the Land of the Delight-Makers. Boston: The Page Company, 1920. v-xvii, 469 pp., illus.

Keleher, William Aloysius
The Fabulous Frontier; Twelve New Mexico Items. Santa Fe, N. M.: The Rydal Press, 1945. ix, 317 pp., illus.
Historical events and characters—frontier life, customs and manners.

Martin, Curtis
The Hills of Home. Boston: Houghton Mifflin Co., 1944. 185 pp.
"I remember tales of local life in a small New Mexican town."

Pattie, James O.
Personal Narrative. Cincinnati: E. H. Flint, 1830. 300 pp.
Exciting narrative of life and character in New Mexico and California.

Poe, Sophie A.
Buckboard Days. Edited by Eugene Cunningham. Caldwell, Idaho: Caxton Printers, 1936.
"Mrs. Poe was there—New Mexico." (Dobie).

Rael, Juan B.
"New Mexican Spanish Feasts." *CFQ* 1: 83-90, 1942.

Rhodes, Mae D.
The Hired Man on Horseback. Boston: Houghton Mifflin Co., 1938.
"Biography of Eugene Manlove Rhodes, but also autobiography of the woman who ranched with 'Gene.'" (Dobie).

Wilder, Mitchell A., and Breitenbach, Edgar
Santos: the religious folk art of New Mexico; texts and photographs by ——, with a foreword by Rudolph A. Gerken. Colorado Springs, Colo.: Taylor Museum of the Colorado Springs fine arts center. 1943.

SPEECH—PROVERBS

Pearce, Thomas M.
"New Mexican Folk Etymologies." *P* 50: 229-234, 1943.

————,
"The English Proverb in New Mexico." *CFQ* 5(No. 4): 350-354, 1946.

PLACE NAMES

Harrington, J. P.
"Old Indian Geographical Names Around Santa Fe, New Mexico." *Amer. Anthropologist* 22: 341-359, 1920.

FOLKSONG

See: Spanish-American Folksong, pp. 601–06.

RECORDS

U. S. Library of Congress. Division of Music. Folklore Section.
Folksong of New Mexico. Recorded by Dean J. D. Robb of the University of New Mexico.
AAFS-LC

OKLAHOMA

FOLKLORE

BIBLIOGRAPHY

Historical Records Survey
Inventory of the County Archives of Oklahoma. Prepared by the Historical Records Survey. Works Progress Administration. Oklahoma City, Okla.: The Historical Records Survey. 1937.

PERIODICALS

Chronicles of Oklahoma. v. 1, 1921—. Oklahoma Historical Society, Oklahoma City, Okla.

GENERAL STUDIES AND COLLECTIONS

Botkin, Benjamin Albert
Folk Say: A Regional Miscellany. Norman, Okla.: The University of Oklahoma Press, 1929-1932.

————,
"Oklahoma Folklore Society." *JAFL* 56:179-180, 1943.

Caldwell, M.
"Gleanings from Byways of Oklahoma Folklore." *Chronicles of Oklahoma* 4:45-49, Oklahoma City, 1926.

Coldiron, Daisy Lemon
Songs of Oklahoma; drawings by John Shelby Metcalf. Dallas, Tex.: The Kaleidograph Press, 1935. xiii, 132 pp.
Poems of places, people, and events.

Collins, Hubert E.
Warpath and Cattle Trail; Illustrated by Paul Brown. New York: W. Morrow and Co., 1928. 296 pp.
"The pageant of trail life as it passed by a stage stand in Oklahoma. Autobiographical." (Dobie).

Callison, John J.
Bill Jones of Paradise Valley, Oklahoma. His Life and Adventures for Over Forty Years in the Great Southwest. He was a Pioneer in the Days of the Buffalo, The Wild Indian, The Oklahoma Boomer, The Cowboy and The Outlaw. Kingfisher, Oklahoma: J. J. Callison, 1914.

Debo, Angie
Prairie City, The Story of an American Community. New York: Alfred A. Knopf, 1944. xiv, 260 pp., illus.
The story of a small community from its settlement on the Oklahoma land run of 1889 to the present.

Federal Writers' Project
Oklahoma, a Guide to the Sooner State. (American Guide Series). Writers' Program of the Works Progress Administration in the State of Oklahoma. Norman: The University of Oklahoma Press, 1941. xxvi, 442 pp., illus., bibl.

Fox, Norman A.
Thorson of Thunder Gulch. New York: Dodd, Mead and Co., 1945. 215 pp.
A story of Old Oklahoma.

James, Marquis
The Cherokee Strip. New York: The Viking Press, 1945. 350 pp.
An autobiography that fills the pages "with the tangy special flavor of the American tall story."

Kidd, Robert Lee
Oklahoma, Past and Present: brief sketches of men and events in Oklahoma history from Coronado to the Present. Oklahoma City, Okla.: Frontier Publishing Co., 1939. 86 pp., illus., bibl.

Miller, Freeman Edwin
Oklahoma, and Other Poems. Buffalo: C. W. Moulton, 1895. vii, 126 pp.

Nix, Evett Dumas
Oklahombres, Particularly the Wilder Ones. . . . St. Louis, 1929. xix, 280 pp., illus.
A gallery of characters—outlaws.

Ridings, Sam P.
The Chisholm Trail. Guthrie, Oklahoma: Cooperative Publ. Co., 1936.

FOLKTALES—LEGENDS

The Last Run, Kay County, Oklahoma, 1893. Stories Assembled by the Ponca City Chapter of the Daughters of the American Revolution. Ponca City: The Courier Printing Co., 1939.

Thompson, Jim
"Snake" Magee and the Rotary Boiler. In: *Manuscripts of the Federal Writers' Project of the Works Progress Administration for the State of Oklahoma.*
A story of drillers commonly called "snakes."

CUSTOMS

Collings, Ellsworth
The 101 Ranch . . . Norman: University of Oklahoma Press, 1937. xiv, 249 pp., illus.

Conover, George W.
Sixty Years in Southwest Oklahoma; or, The Autobiography of George W. Conover, with some thrilling incidents of Indian life in Oklahoma and Texas . . . Anadarko, Okla.: N. T. Plummer, 1927. iii, 129 pp., illus.

Gardner, James H.
"One Hundred Years Ago in the Region of Tulsa." *Chronicles of Oklahoma* 11:765-785, 1933, illus.

Gould, Charles Newton
Travels Through Oklahoma. Oklahoma City: Harlow Publishing Company, 1928. 174 pp., illus.

Hicks, Elijah
"The Journal of Elijah Hicks." *Chronicles of Oklahoma* 13: 68-99, 1935.

Irving, Washington
A Tour on the Prairies. Paris: A. and W. Galignani and Co., 1835. x, 199 pp.

Jaros, Samuel
The Story of Oklahoma, as told by Winne & Winne, Wichita, Kansas. New York: S. Jaros, 1902. 40 pp., illus.

Morrison, W. B.
"A Journey Across Oklahoma Ninety Years Ago." *Chronicles of Oklahoma* 4:333-337, 1926.

Nuttall, Thomas
A Journal of Travel Into the Arkansas Territory, During the Year 1819. With occasional observations on the manners of the aborigenes. Illustrated . . . Phila.: T. H. Palmer, 1821. viii, 296 pp., illus.
A journey from Philadelphia down the Ohio and Mississippi Rivers to the Arkansas; thence across Arkansas to the interior of the modern Oklahoma; returning via the Arkansas and Mississippi Rivers, and then to New Orleans.

Tilghman, Zoe A.
Outlaw Days; a true history of early-day Oklahoma characters . . . Oklahoma City: Harlow Publishing Company, 1926. iii, 138 pp., illus.

FOLK MEDICINE

Smith, Walter R.
"Northwestern Oklahoma Folk Cures." *TFSP* 8:74-85, 1930.

PROVERBS

Oevitch, J. P.
"Proverbial Comparisons from Oklahoma and Missouri." *HFB* 3:37, 1944.

PLACE NAMES

Gould, Charles N.
Oklahoma Place Names. Norman, Oklahoma: University of Oklahoma Press, 1933. 146 pp.

"Origin of County Names in Oklahoma." *Chronicles of Oklahoma* 2: 75-82, 1924.

Wright, Muriel H.
"Some Geographic Names of French Origin in Oklahoma." *The Chronicles of Oklahoma* 7:188-193, 1929.

FOLKSONG

STUDIES

"American Music in Oklahoma." *Musician* 43:143, 1938.

Moore, Ethel Perry
An Experiment in Collecting and Classifying the Folk-Songs Sung in Oklahoma. (In MS). Norman, Okla.: University of Oklahoma Library, 1926.

DANCES

Botkin, Benjamin Albert
The American Play-Party Song, with a collection of Oklahoma texts and tunes. Lincoln, Nebr.: University of Nebraska, 1937.

ARRANGEMENTS

Stage Work

Rodgers, Richard and Hammerstein, Oscar 2nd
Oklahoma. New York: Random House, 1945. 146 pp.
  The text of the highly successful musical play. Captures the folk spirit successfully thru song, dance, costume, setting and speech.

TEXAS

See: Folklore and Folksong of the Spanish-Americans, pp. 593–606; and Folklore and Song of the Cowboy, pp. 610–27.

FOLKLORE

BIBLIOGRAPHY

Agatha, Sister M.
Texas Prose Writings; a reader's digest. Foreword by Leonides Warren Payne, Jr. Dallas: Banks Upshaw & Co., 1936. xx, 168 pp., illus.

Barnes, Florence Elberta
Texas Writers of Today; foreword by Robert Adger Law. Dallas, Tex.: Tardy Publishing Co., 1935.

Carroll, H. Bailey
Texas County Histories; A Bibliography. Foreword by Walter Prescott Webb. Austin: Texas State Historical Association, 1943. xxxii, 200 pp.

Dobie, James Frank
A Corner Forever Texas. Austin, 1938. 8 pp. Extract from *The Alcalde,* April 1938.

————,
Guide to Life and Literature of the Southwest, with a few observations. Austin, Texas: The University of Texas Press, 1943. 111 pp., illus.

Dykes, J. C.
"Dime Novel Texas; or, The Sub-Literature of the Lone Star State." *Southwestern Historical Quarterly* 49(No. 3): 327-340.

Gammel's Book Store
Catalogue of Books and Pamphlets Relating to Texas. (Collections of A. C. De Con and H. P. N. Gammel) 1000 volumes. Austin, Tex.: Gammel Book Co., 1897. 30 pp.

Historical Records Survey
Inventory of the County Archives of Texas. Prepared by the Historical Records Survey. Works Progress Administration. San Antonio. Tex.: Historical Records Survey, 1937.

Payne, L. W.
A Survey of Texas Literature. Chicago: Rand McNally & Co., 1928.

Raines, Cadwell Walton
A Bibliography of Texas. A descriptive list of books, pamphlets, and documents relating to Texas in print and manuscript since 1536. Austin, Texas: Gammel Book Co., 1896. xvi, 268 pp.

U. S. Library of Congress
Texas Centennial Exhibition, Held at the Library of Congress, Washington, D. C., December 15, 1945-April 15, 1946. Washington: U. S. Gov't Printing Office, 1946. iii, 54 pp.

————,
Texas: A Bibliographical List. Washington, D. C., 29 pp. (Select List of References, No. 1100).

Whitmore & Smith, comp.
Check-List of Books On and About Texas and the Great Southwest, and other Works. Dallas, Tex.: Whitmore & Smith, 1935. 28 pp., illus.

Young, Stark, ed.
Treasury of Life and Literature. New York: Charles Scribner's Sons, 1937.
  "Represents the Texas part of the Southwest." Since then about a volume every year.

PERIODICALS

Contributions to Folk-Lore Nos. 1-3. Waco, Texas: *Baylor University*, 1929, in 1 volume, plates, no more published.

Frontier Times. v. 1, 1926—. Bandera, Texas. Monthly.

Historical Publications, Series 1—, 1940—. Waco, Tex.: Baylor University Press.

Panhandle-Plains Historical Review. v. 1, 1928—. Canyon, Texas. Annual.

Range Life Series. Austin, Texas, 1942—. Published by the Texas Folklore Society.

Southwest Review. v. 1, 1915—. Dallas, Tex. Quarterly.

Texas Folklore Society Publications. Austin, Texas: J. F. Dobie, Editor, etc. I (1916); II (1923).
 Since then about a volume every year.

Texas Review. See: Southwest Review.

Texas State Historical Association. Quarterly, 42 vols. (1940). Austin, Texas: 1898. vols. XVI to XLII titled *Southwestern Historical Quarterly.*

The Southwestern Historical Quarterly. v. 1, 1897—. Austin, Tex.: The Texas State Historical Association.

GENERAL STUDIES AND COLLECTIONS

Averitt, William
 Stories and Poems of Western Texas. New York: J. B. Alden, 1890. 123 pp.

Baker, DeWitt Clinton
 A Texas Scrap-Book. Made up of the history, biography, and miscellany of Texas and its people. New York: A. S. Barnes and Company, 1875. xii, 657 pp., illus.

Baker, Karle Wilson
 Star of the Wilderness. New York: Coward Mc Cann, Inc., 1942. 508 pp.
 Fiction: on Texas before the Revolution against Mexico.

Banks, C. Stanley, and McMillan, Grace Taylor
 The Texas Reader: An Anthology of Romantic History, biography, legends, folklore, and epic stories of the Lone Star State. San Antonio, Texas: The Naylor Co. 1947. 291 pp.

Barnes, Leola Christie
 Silver Century . . . San Antonio, Tex.: The Naylor Company, 1936. xiii, 65 pp., illus.
 Poems in honor of the Texas centennial.

Beaty, John O., and others
 Texas Poems. Dallas, Tex.: Dealey and Lowe, 1936. 105 pp.

Bechdolt, Frederick Ritchie
 Tales of Old Timers. New York, London: The Century Co., 1924. 367 pp., 6 plates.
 "Forceful retelling of the story of the Mier Expedition and of other activities of the 'fighting Texans.'"

Benedict, Carl Peters
 A Tenderfoot Kid in Gyp Water. Austin, Texas: Texas Folklore Society, 1943. 115 pp., illus.

Benedict, H. Y. , and Lomax, J. A.
 The Book of Texas, Garden City N. Y.: Doubleday, Page & Co., 1916. xxiii, 448 pp., illus.

Blake, R. B.
 "Rose and his story of the Alamo, III: a vindication of Rose and his story." *TFSP* 15: 27-41, 1939.

Boatright, Mody C.
 "More About 'Hell in Texas.'" *TFSP* 19. 134-138, 1944.

————, **and Day, Donald, eds.**
 Backwoods to Border. Texas Folk-Lore Society Publications, Number XVIII. Austin, Texas: Texas Folk-Lore Society and University Press in Dallas, 1943. xv, 235 pp.

————, **eds.**
 From Hell to Breakfast. Texas Folk-Lore Society Publications, Number XIX, J. Frank Dobie, General Editor. Austin, Texas: Texas Folk-Lore Society and University Press in Dallas, 1944. x, 215 pp., drawings, index.

Boyle, Lois F.
 Texas Legacy. San Antonio, Texas: Naylor Company, 1935. Collection of Poetry.

Bracht, Viktor
 Texas in 1848; translated from the German by Charles Frank Schmidt. San Antonio, Tex.: The Naylor Printing Company, 1931. xxiv, 223 pp., illus., bibl.

Burleson, Rufus C.
 Life and Writings of Rufus C. Burleson. Waco, Tex.: 1901. 887 pp.
 "The autobiographical part of this amorphously arranged volume is a social document of the first rank." (Dobie).

Cranfiel, J. B.
 Chronicle, A Story of a Life in Texas. New York: Fleming H. Revell Co., 1916. 496 pp.

Cunningham, Eugene
 Triggernometry, a Gallery of Gunfighters. New York: The Press of the Pioneers, Inc., 1934. xvii, 441 pp., illus.

Cutbirth, Ruby Nichols
 Ed Nichols Rode a Horse. Dallas, Texas: Texas Folk-Lore Society and University Press, 1943. x, 134 pp.

David, Robert D.
 Malcolm Campbell, Sheriff. Casper, Wyoming: Wyomingana, inc., 1932.
 "Much of the 'Johnson County War' between cowmen and thieving masters." (Dobie).

Day, Donald
Big Country: Texas. (American Folkways Series.) New York: Duell, Sloan and Pearce, 1947. x, 326 pp.
"Here are the fundamentals of the Texas tradition . . . The humorous anecdotes are well above the level of the exasperating tall tale which has only its primitive exaggeration to excuse it." (G. Louis Joughin).

Dixon, Samuel Houston
Romance and Tragedy of Texas History. Houston: Texas Historical Publishing Co., 1924.

Dobie, James Frank
"Rose and His Story of the Alamo, I: The line that Travis drew." *TFSP* 15: 9-16, 1939.

————,
The Book of Texas. New York: The Grolier Society, 1929.

————,
Coffee in the Gourd. Austin, Texas: Texas Folk-Lore Society, 1935. 110 pp., music.

————,
The Flavor of Texas. Dallas, Texas: Dealey & Lowe, 1936. 287 pp., illus.

————,
Folklore in Texas. Austin, Tex.: University of Texas, Bulletin 2245, Dec. 1, 1922.

————,
Foller De Drinkin' Gou'd. Texas Folk-Lore Society Publications, Number VII. Austin, Texas: Texas Folk-Lore Society, 1928. 201 pp.

————,
"Texas Folk-Lore Society." *JAFL* 56: 186-187, 1943.

————,
Tone the Bell Easy. Texas Folk-Lore Society Publications, Number X. Austin, Texas: Texas Folk-Lore Society, 1932. 199 pp.

————,
Spur-of-the-Cock. Texas Folk-Lore Society Publications, Number XI. Austin, Texas: Texas Folk-Lore Society, 1933. 112 pp.

————,
A Vaquero of the Brush Country. Dallas: Publ. of the Texas Folk Lore Society, 1929. xv, 314 pp., illus.

————, **and Boatright, Mody C., eds.**
Straight Texas. Texas Folk-Lore Society Publications, Number XIII. Austin, Texas: Texas Folk-Lore Society, 1937. 348 pp.

————, **Boatright, Mody C., Ransom, Harry H. eds.**
In The Shadow of History. Texas Folk-Lore Society Publications, Number XV. Austin, Texas: Texas Folk-Lore Society, 1939. 186 pp.

————,
Texian Stomping Grounds. Texas Folk-Lore Society Publications, Number XVII. Austin, Texas: Texas Folk-Lore Society, 1941. 162 pp.

Domenech, Abbe Emmanuel H.
Missionary Adventures in Texas and Mexico. London: 1858.
"Delightful folklore." (Dobie).

Douglas, Claude Leroy
Famous Texas Feuds. Dallas, Tex.: The Turner Co., 1936. v, 173 pp.

Duval, John C.
The Adventures of Big-Foot Wallace, the Texas Ranger and Hunter. Macon, Ga.: J. W. Burke and Co. 1885. (Reprinted Austin, Texas, 1921; Austin, 1935.)

Evans, Will Franklin
Border Skylines; fifty years of "tallying out" on the Bloys round-up ground. Dallas, Texas: Published for the Bloys camp meeting association by C. Baugh, 1940. 587 pp.
"Chronicles of the men and women—cow people and cow country—responsible for the best known camp meeting held annually, Texas has ever had." (Dobie).

Farber, James
Those Texans; Illustrations by John H. Mc Clelland. San Antonio, Tex.: The Naylor Company, 1945. xi, 171 pp., illus.
It contains stories and anecdotes of events throughout the whole range of Texas history.

Federal Writers' Project
Texas, a Guide to the Lone Star State. (American Guide Series). Compiled by the Workers of the Writers' Program of the Works Progress Administration in the State of Texas. New York: Hastings House, 1940., illus., bibl.

Fergusson, Harvey
Rio Grande. New York: Alfred A. Knopf, 1933. 296 pp.
"His chapter on 'The Prairie Man' is a pungent interpretation of Josiah Gregg." (Dobie).

Foreman, L. L.
The Road to San Jacinto. New York: E. P. Dutton & Co., 1943. 285 pp.
Against the background of the Texas war for Independence, he has written a lively, colorful tale in which the reader glimpses most of the leading figures and main events of that brief but fruitful struggle. One meets "Colonel" Davy Crockett, that fabulous mixture of demagogue, man of the world, and deadly backwoods fighter, whose exploits reached climax at the Alamo.

Graham, Philip, ed.
Early Texas Verse, Collected from the original newspapers. Austin, Tex.: The Steck Co., 1936. xv, 131 pp.

Green, Thomas Jefferson
Journal of the Texan Expedition Against Mier. Austin, Texas: The Steck Co., 1936. First printed in 1845.
"Green was one of the leaders of the Mier Expedition." (Dobie).

Greer, Hilton Ross
Voices of the Southwest; a book of Texan verse. New York: Macmillan Co., 1923. xx, 207 pp.

Hammer, Laura V.
Short Grass and Long Horns. Norman, Oklahoma: University of Oklahoma Press, 1943. 269 pp., illus.
The author has assembled stories of men and women who had a part in early Panhandle history.

Harper, Jack and Newbern
Odd Texas. Dallas: B. Upshaw and Company, 1936. 122 pp., illus.
Flavored with humorous and spicy anecdotes.

Hogner, Dorothy Childs
South to Padre; illustrated by Nils Hogner. Boston: Lothrop, Lee and Shepard Company, 1936. 232 pp., illus.

Holley, Mary Austin
Texas. Observations, historical, geographical and descriptive, in a series of letters, written during a visit to Austin's colony with a view to a permanent settlement in that country, in the autumn of 1831. Baltimore: Armstrong & Plaskitt, 1833. 167 pp.

House, Boyce
Texas, Proud and Loud, illustrated by Winston Croslin. San Antonio, Tex.: The Naylor Company, 1945. 104 pp., illus.
The humorous side of the Texans.

Houston, Margaret Bell
Magic Valley. New York, London: D. Appleton Co., Inc., 1934. viii, 310 pp.

Hunt, Lenoir
Bluebonnets and Blood; the Romance of "Tejas." Houston, Tex.: Texas Books, 1938. xv, 433 pp., illus., bibl.

Hunter, John Marvin, comp.
The Trail Drivers of Texas. San Antonio: Jackson Printing Co., 1920. 2 Vols., 498 pp., illus.

Jarvis, Ida (Van Zandt)
Texas Poems. Nashville, Tenn.: Gospel Advocate Publishing Co., 1893. 90 pp.

Jennings, Napoleon Augustus
A Texas Ranger. Foreword by J. Frank Dobie. Dallas, Texas: Southwest Press, 1930. xv, 287 pp.

Johnson, Siddie Joe
Texas, The Land of the Tejas. New York: Random House, 1943. 55 pp., illus.

Lanham, Edwin Moultrie
The Wind Blew West. New York: Longmans, Green & Co., 1935. Maps.

Law, Robert Adger
"History of the Folk-Lore Society of Texas." *TFSP* 1: 3-7, 1916.

Lomax, John A.
"Unexplored Treasures of Texas Folk-Lore." *TFSP* 1: 96-102, 1916.
A challenge to students and investigators of Texan Lore.

Lowrie, Samuel Harman
Culture Conflict in Texas, 1821-1835. New York: Columbia University Press, 1932.
Spanish-American culture contacts.

Lubbock, Francis Richard
Six Decades in Texas, or Memoirs of Francis Richard Lubbock, Governor of Texas in wartime, 1861-63. A personal experience in business, war and politics, ed. by C. W. Raines. Austin: B. C. Jones & Co., 1900. xvi, 685 pp., illus., plates, ports.

McDaniel, H. F. and Taylor, N. A.
The Coming Empire, or 2000 Miles in Texas on Horseback. New York: A. S. Barnes & Co., 1877. Dallas, Texas: Reprinted, Turner Co., 1936. 389 pp.

Martin, Jack
Border Boss. San Antonio, Texas: The Naylor Co., 1942.
Biography of Capt. John R. Hughes, and a great deal about the Texas Rangers.

Menn, Alfred E.
"Let's Go to Texas;" A Historical and Descriptive Book of Texas. Austin, Tex.: Firm Foundation Publishing House, 1936. 138 pp., illus.

Mills, William W.
Forty Years at El Paso, 1858-1898; recollections of war, politics, adventure, events, narratives, sketches, etc. Chicago: W. B. Conkey, 1901. 166 pp.

Mogoffin, Susan Shelby
Down the Santa Fe Trail. New Haven, Conn.: Yale University Press, 1926.

Molyneaux, Peter
The Romantic Story of Texas. New York: The Cordova Press, 1936. x, 463 pp.

Montgomery, Whitney
The Road to Texas. Dallas, Texas: The Kaleidograph Press, 1940.
Southwestern Poetry.

Myers, John Myers
The Alamo. New York: E. P. Dutton and Co. 1948. 240 pp.
"The essence of Mr. Myers' book lies in two sections: Biographical sketches of the four main participants of the battle: Bowie, Travis, Crockett and Santa Ana: and a day-by-day account of the siege . . . (it tells) one of the best known stories from America's past." (J. Frank Dobie).

Olmstead, Frederick Law
A Journey Through Texas, or A Saddle Trip in the Southwestern Frontier; with a statistical appendix. New York: J. Low, Son & Co., 1857. xxxiv, 516 pp., map.

Parker, Wylie Apton
Here Is Texas; a Sourcebook of Centennial Program Material. San Antonio: The Naylor Company, 1936. vi, 75 pp., illus., bibl.

Pentecost, George E.
Song of the Winter Garden. San Antonio.
Tex.: The Naylor Company, 1940. 78 pp.
A book of poems about Texas scenes and Texas
people.

Perry, George Sessions
Hold Autumn in Your Hand. New York: The
Viking Press, 1941. 249 pp.
Fiction of a Texas farm hand.

——————,
Texas: A World in Itself; illustrated by Arthur
Fuller. New York: Whittlesey House, 1942.
xi, 293 pp., illus.

——————,
Walls Rise Up. New York: Doubleday Doran
& Co., 1939. 236 pp.
"A kind of Crock of Gold both whimsical and
earthy—laid on the Brazos River."

Pilgrim, Thomas (pseud. for Arthur Morecamp)
Live Boys; or *Charley and Nasho in Texas.*
Boston: Lee and Shepard, and New York:
C. T. Dillingham, 1879. 308 pp.

Philips, Shine
*Big Spring: The Casual Biography of a
Prairie Town.* Drawings by Jerry Bywaters.
New York: Prentice-Hall, 1942. 231 pp.
The story of a town as one man sees it and re-
members its past.

Plenn, Jaime Harrysson
Saddle in the Sky; the Lone Star State. Illustrated by Agnes Lilienberg Muench. Indianapolis: The Bobbs-Merrill Company, 1940.
287 pp., illus.

Randolph, John Hayward
Texas Brags. Illustrated by Mark Storm.
Houston: 1945. 62 pp., illus.

Rogers, John William, and Dobie, J. Frank
Finding Literature on the Texas Plains. Dallas: Southwest Press, 1931. 57 pp.

Rollins, Hyder E.
"O. Henry's Texas." *Texas Review* 4: 295-
307, 1919.

Smith, Henry
"Reminiscenes." In: *Southwestern Historical
Quarterly,* Vol. XIV: 24–73, 1910. Austin:
Texas State Historical Association.

Smythe, Henry
Historical Sketch of Parker Country, Texas.
St. Louis: L. C. Lavat, 1877. vii, 476 pp.
"One of various good county histories replete
with fighting." (Dobie).

Sowell, Andrew Jackson
*Early Settlers and Indian Fighters of South-
west Texas.* Austin, Texas: B. C. Jones &
Co., 1900. viii, 844 pp.

——————,
Rangers and Pioneers of Texas: A concise
account of the early settlements, hardships,
massacres, battles, and wars by which Texas
was rescued from the rule of the savage, and
consecrated to the empire of civilization. San
Antonio, Texas: Shepard Bros. & Co., 1844.
411 pp.
"A book down to bedrock." (Dobie).

Stapp, William P.
The Prisoners of Perote, 1845. Austin, Texas:
The Steck Co., 1936. Reprint.
"Journal of one of the Mier men who drew
a white bean." (Dobie).

Sweet, Alex E., and Knox, J. Armoy
*On a Mexican Mustang Through Texas from
the Gulf to the Rio Grande.* London: Chatto
& Windus, 1884. 672 pp., illus. Reprinted in
Hartford, Conn., 1887.

Thomason, John W.
Lone Star Preacher. New York: Charles
Scribner's Sons, 1941.
"Story of the Texas chaplain who carried a Bible
in one hand and a captain's sword in the other
through the Civil War." (Dobie).

Thompkins, Walter A.
Texas Tumbleweed. New York: Phoenix Press,
1943. 256 pp.
The story of a dangerous pilgrimage to the West
to claim a mine.

Thompson, Stith
Round the Levee. Publications of the Texas
Folk-lore Society, No. 1., 1916. Austin, Tex.:
Texas Folk-lore Society, 1935. 111 pp., re-
printed.

Upton, Elsie
"The Austin Hill Folk." *TFSP* 7: 40-48, 1941.

Vern, Jules Adolphe
Ballades du Texas. Houston, Tex.: Édition
du "Bayou", 1937. 59 pp., illus.
Texan poems.

Waugh, Julia Nott
Castroville and Henry Castro. San Antonio,
Texas: Standard Printing Co., 1934.
"Best written monograph dealing with any aspect
of Texas history that I have read." (Dobie).

Webb, W. Prescott
"Miscellany of Texas Folk-Lore." *TFSP* 2:
38-49, 1923.

——————,
"Notes on the Folk-Lore of Texas." *JAFL* 28:
290-299, 1915.

White, Owen Payne
Lead and Likker. New York: Minton, Balch
& Company, 1932. vii, 274 pp.
Contents: Five El Paso worthies—Salt of the
earth (Charles Howard).—Jack Hays.—Buckets
of blood (William Clarke Quantrill).—Reminis-
cences of Texas divines.—Henry Plummer.— Big
foot Wallace.—John Glanton.— Fred Patterson.
—Belle Starr.—Hendry Brown.—Chris Evans.—
Ben Thompson.—The art of drink on the border.

——————,
Texas, An Informal Biography. New York:
G. P. Putnam's Sons, 1945. ix, 268 pp., illus.

Winter, Nevin, O.
Texas—The Marvelous. The State of the
Six Flags. New York: Garden City Publish-
ing Co., 1939. 336 pp.

Worrell, John
A Diamond in the Rough; embracing anecdote,
biography, romance and history. Indianapolis:
W. B. Burford, 1906. 282 pp.
Sketches of Houston, the Texan War.

FOLKTALES—LEGENDS

"Bibliography of Texas Legends." In: *Legends of Texas*—edited by J. Frank Dobie. Publications of the Texas Folk-Lore Society, Number III. (pp. 256-260). Austin, Texas: Texas Folk-Lore Society, 1924.

Arrewood, Charles F.
"Well done, liar." *TFSP* 18: 79-88, 1943.
Six tall tales, two ghost stories, and proverbial sayings current in Texas.

Atkinson, Mary Jordan, and Dobie, J. Frank
"Pioneer Folk Tales." *TFSP* 7: 69-77, 1928.

Barns, Florence Elberta
"Strap Buckner of the Texas Frontier." *TFSP* 8: 129-151, 1930.
The author gives the historical background and the legends.

Barrera, Genoveva
"How the Burro Tricked the Buzzard." *TFSP* 17: 115-117, 1941.

Barton, Henry W.
"Sand Storm Yarns." *TFSP* 14: 266-267, 1938.
Tall yarns.

Beazley, Julia
"The Uneasy Ghost of Lafitte." *TFSP* 3: 185-189, 1924.

Bertillon, L. D.
"Lost Lead Mine on the Brazos, King County." *TFSP* 3: 77-78, 1924.

————,
"Steinheimer's Millions." *TFSP* 3: 91-95, 1924.
Buried treasure.

————,
"The Lobo Girl of Devil's River." *TFSP* 13: 79-95, 1937.

Blackwell, John William
"Will-O-the-Wisp of the Esperanza." *TFSP* 17:118-119, 1941.

Blittersdorf, Louise von
"Buried Treasure Legends of Milam County." *TFSP* 3:99-103, 1924.

————,
"Irish Fairies in Texas." *TFSP* 13:185-189, 1937.

Bludworth, G. T.
"The Texas Pecan; The Man in the Moon." *TFSP* 7:79-80, 1928.
A tale heard in Throckmorton County.

Boatright, Mody C.
Tall Tales from Texas. Dallas, Texas: The Southwest Press, 1934.

————,
"The Tall Tale in Texas." *South Atlantic Quarterly* (Durham, N. C.) 30:271-279, 1931.

Bolton, P.
"Texas Tall Tales." *Life* 15:11-12, Nov. 1, 1943.

Bryan, Frank
"On the Jefferson Road." *TFSP* 17:1-25, 1941.
Legend after the Civil War.

Callan, Austin
"Lover's Leap At Santa Anna." *TFSP* 3:169-171, 1924.

Chambers, Cornelia
"The Adventures of Little Audrey." *TFSP* 13: 106-110, 1937.
An American humorous character.

Chapman, Iva
Twelve Legendary Stories of Texas. Illustrations by Warren Hunter. San Antonio, Tex.: The Naylor Company, 1940. viii, 79 pp., illus.

Craddock, John R.
"The Corn Thief—A Folk Anecdote." *TFSP* 7:78, 1928.
Heard in Dickens County.

————,
"The Headless Squatter." *TFSP* 3:135-137, 1924.
Legend of the supernatural.

————,
"The Legend of Stampede Mesa." *TFSP* 3:111-115, 1924.
Legend of the supernatural.

————,
"Legends of the Supernatural." *TFSP* 3:111-114, 135-136, 1918.

————,
"The Waiting Woman." *TFSP* 3:167-169, 1924.
Lover's legend.

Crockett, David
Colonel Crockett's Exploits and Adventures in Texas. The narrative brought down from the death of Col. Crockett to the battle of San Jacinto, by an eye-witness. Philadelphia: T. K. and P. G. Collins, 1836. 216 pp., front.

————,
A Narrative of the Life of David Crockett, of the State of Tennessee. Written by himself. American Edition printed at Philadelphia: E. L. Carey & A. Hart, and London: T. Lombard, 1834. 113 pp.

De Zavala, Adina
History and Legends of the Alamo and Other Missions in and around San Antonio. San Antonio: 1917.

Deaver, J. M.
"Fishback Yarns from the Sulphurs." *TFSP* 7:42-44, 1928.
The "Sulphurs" includes all the territory in northeast Texas drained by the Sulphur River, and lying between Big Cypress Creek and Red River.

Dobie, Bertha McKee
"The Death Bell of the Brazos." *TFSP* 3:141-143, 1924.
Legend of the supernatural.

—————,
"The Legend of the Salt Marshes." *TFSP* 3: 143, 1924.

—————,
"Mysterious Music in the San Bernard River." *TFSP* 3:137-141, 1924.
Legend of the supernatural.

Dobie, J. Frank
"An Inquiry into the Sources of Treasure Legends of Texas." *TFSP* 3:3-12, 1924.

—————,
"A Preface on Authentic Liars." In: *Tall Tales from Texas* by Mody C. Boatright. Dallas, Texas: The Southwest Press, 1934.

—————,
"Antonette's Leap: The Legend of Mount Bonnell." *TFSP* 3:171-179, 1924.
Lover's legend.

—————,
"How Dollars Turned into Bumble Bees, and Other Legends." *TFSP* 3:52-57, 1924.
Legend of buried treasure.

—————,
"Legendary Spanish Forts Down the Nueces." *TFSP* 3:43-49, 1924.
Legends of lost treasure.

—————,
"The Nigger Gold Mine of the Big Bend." *TFSP* 3:64-67, 1924.

—————,
"The Roadrunner in Fact and Folklore." *TFSP* 15:146-174, 1939.

—————,
"The Battlefields of Palo Alto and Resaca de la Palma." *TFSP* 3:51-52, 1924.
Legends of buried treasure.

—————,
"The Hole of Gold Near Wichita Falls." *TFSP* 3:80-81, 1924.
Legend of buried treasure.

—————,
"The Silver Ledge on the Frio." *TFSP* 3:60-62, 1924.
Legend of buried treasure.

—————,
"The Snively Legend." *TFSP* 3:95-99, 1924.
Legend of buried treasure.

—————,
"Treasure Legends of McMullen County." *TFSP* 3:28-43, 1924.

—————,
"Where El Dorado is." *Southwest Review:* Spring Number, 1927.

—————, ed.
Legends of Texas. Austin, Texas: Texas Folk-Lore Society, 1924. 279 pp.
Contents: Legends of Buried Treasure and Gold Mines; Legends of the Supernatural; Legends of Lovers; Legendary Origins of Texas Flowers; Names and Streams; Miscellaneous Legends. Illustrations. Bibliography.

—————, Boatright, Mody C., and Ransom, H. H., eds.
Coyote Wisdom. Texas Folk-Lore Society Publications, Number XIV. Austin, Texas: Texas Folk-Lore Society, 1938. 300 pp., illus.

—————,
Mustangs and Cow Horses. Texas Folk-Lore Society Publications, Number XVI. Austin, Texas: Texas Folk-Lore Society, 1940. 429 pp.
"The object of this book is not to present writers, but represent horses — mustangs and ranch horses." (The Editors).

Dodson, Ruth
"The Ghost Nun." *TFSP* 18:137-139, 1943.
Three versions of the vanishing hitchhiker legend from Texas.

Eckert, Flora
"Lover's Leap in Kimble County." *TFSP* 3: 163-167, 1924.

Eddins, A. W.
"Anecdotes from Brazos Bottoms." *TFSP* 13: 86-105, 1937.

—————,
"Brazos Bottom Philosophy." *TFSP* 2:50-51, 1923.
Two tales.

—————,
"How Sandy Got His Meat: a Negro tale from Brazos Bottoms." *TFSP* 1:47-49, 1916.

—————,
"The First Corn Crop in Texas." *TFSP* 3:236-237, 1924.

Emory, A. M.
Told at Tuxedo. New York and London: G. P. Putnam's Sons, 1887. 145 pp.
Romantic tales and legends.

Estill, Julia
"Grandfather Wiley and His Dream." *TFSP* 9:130-132, 1931.
Treasure hunting in Gillespie County.

—————,
"Lost Mines of the Llano and San Saba." *TFSP* 3:24-28, 1924.
Legends of buried treasure.

—————,
"The Enchanted Rock in Llano Country." *TFSP* 3:153-159, 1924.
A Legend of lovers.

Featherstone, Mae
"Silver Dreams and Copper Plates." *TFSP* 13:258-269, 1937.
Texas lore of gold and silver mines.

Gates, Sue
"Windy Yesterdays." *TFSP* 14:264-266, 1938.
Tall tales.

Gay, J. Leeper
"The Accursed Gold in the Santa Anna Mountains." *TFSP* 3:78-80, 1924.
Legend of buried treasure.

Gould, John
"Pie-Biter." *TFSP* 14:185-191, 1938.
The legendary prowess of Jim Baker.

Gunter, Lillian
"Buried Treasure Legends of Cooke County."
TFSP 3:81-84, 1924.

Hamer, Marcelle Lively
"Anecdotes as Side Lights to Texas History."
TFSP 15:59-74, 1939.

Hammett, Samuel A.
Piney Woods Tavern; or Sam Slick in Texas.
Philadelphia: J. B. Peterson & Bros., 1858.
309 pp.

Heimsath, Charles H.
"The Mysterious Woman in Blue." *TFSP* 3:
132-135, 1924.
Legend of the supernatural.

Hinsdale, Laura
Legends of the Gulf Coast. Biloxi, Miss.: Daily
Herald, 1913. 49 pp.

Hoole, W. Stanley
Sam Slick in Texas. San Antonio, Texas: The
Naylor Co., 1945. 78 pp. bibl.
Deals with the author of "Sam Slick," Samuel
Adams Hammett—reflects the life and humor
of the early frontier.

House, Boyce
Tall Tales from Texas. Illustrated by William
Kresse, "Hollywood" drawings by Vic Le May.
San Antonio, Tex.: The Naylor Company, 1945.
104 pp., illus.

Hughs, Fannie May
*Legends of Texas Rivers and Sagas of The
Lone Star State;* an historical interpretation of
the folklore together with the part played by
the old landmarks in modern industrial development. Dallas, Tex.: Mathis, Van Nort & Co.,
1937. xvi, 252 pp., illus.

Hunter, J. Marvin
"Mysterious Gold Mine of the Guadalupe
Mountains." *TFSP* 3:67-72, 1924.
Legend of buried treasure.

————,
"Roy Bean As Coroner." *TFSP* 14:254-256,
1938.

Kincaid, Edgar B.
"Lost Mine Near Sabinal." *TFSP* 3:62-64,
1924.
Legend of buried treasure.

Laughlin, Edward Douglas
The Yaqui Gold. San Antonio, Texas: The
Naylor Co., 1943. 80 pp.
The Story of the Yaqui Gold Country in Texas.

Lave, Edith C.
"The Legend of Cheetwah." *TFSP* 3:130-132,
1924.
Supernatural.

Leisy, Ernest E.
"Jesse Holmes, the 'Fool Killer'." *TFSP* 8:
152-154, 1930.

Littlejohn, E. G.
"Life and Legends of Lafitte the Pirate." *TFSP*
3:179-185, 1924.

————,
"Lost Gold of the Llano Country." *TFSP* 3:
12-20, 1924.
Legend of buried treasure and lost mines.

Looscan, Adele B.
"The Woman of the Western Star: a Legend
of the Rangers." *TFSP* 3:115-118, 1924.

Martin, Roscoe
"The Treasure Cannon of the Neches." *TFSP*
3:84-89, 1924.

Mathes, C. H.
"Jeff Howell's Buryin'." *TFSP* 6:19-22, 1940.

McKenna, James A.
Black Range Tales. New York: Wilson-Erick-
son, Inc., 1936.
"Reminiscences of prospecting life." (Dobie).

Morris, J. W.
"The Pirate Ship of the San Bernard: a Legend of Theodosia Burr Allston." *TFSP* 3:191-
197, 1924.

Moses, Louise von Blittersdorf
"Irish Fairies in Texas." *TFSP* 13:185-189,
1937.

Munroe, Kirk
With Crockett and Bowie; or, Fighting for the
Lone-Star Flag; a Tale of Texas. Illustrated
by V. Perard. New York: C. Scribner's Sons,
1897. vi, 347 pp., illus.

"Old Texans Talk." *Southwest Review* 29:117-
120, 1943.
Five anecdotes.

"Paisano Tracks." *TFSP* 18:140-150, 1943.
Legends and tales from Texas.

Parks, Etta
"Big Sam and de Golden Chariot." *TFSP* 19:
29-35, 1944.

Parks, H. B.
"Buried in Bexar County." *TFSP* 9:133-142,
1931.
Yarns about treasure hunting.

————,
"Razorbacks." *TFSP* 9:15-26, 1931.
Hog yarns heard in East Texas.

Payne, L. W., Jr.
"Francesca: A Legend of Old Fort Stockton."
TFSP 3:157-159, 1924.
Legend of lovers.

————,
"The Wagon-Load of Silver in Clear Fork
Creek." *TFSP* 3:103-104, 1924.
Legend of buried treasure.

Pearce, James Edwin
Tales That Dead Men Tell. Austin, Texas:
The University Press, 1935. 118 pp.

Penn, A. W.
"Tall Tales for the Tenderfeet." *TFSP* 7:38-41, 1928.

Perry, George Sessions
Hackberry Cavalier. New York: Viking Press, 1944. 246 pp.
Yarn and tall tales of Texan people and places.

Platter, Lynne Wooten
"The Toe Wiggled." *TFSP* 14: 256-259, 1938.
A tall tale.

Potter, Fannie Cora
Texas in History—Story—Legend. Dallas, Tex.: The South-West Press, 1933. viii, 220 pp., illus.

Pounds, Jimmie, III
"Hugo: The Giant Unkillable Bull Frog." *TFSP* 14:262-263, 1938.
A tall tale.

Ransom, Nancy R.
Texas Wild Flower Legends. Dallas, Tex.: the Kaleidograph Press, 1933. 119 pp., illus.

Ratchford, Fannie E.
"Legend Making on the Concho." *TFSP* 14: 174-184, 938.

————,
"Moro's Gold." *TFSP* 3:104-111, 1924.
Legend of buried treasure.

————,
"Native Treasure Talk up the Frio." *TFSP* 3:57-60, 1924.

Scudday, Roy
"The Musical Snake." *TFSP* 19:162-164, 1944.
A tall tale.

Sears, Edward S.
"The low down on Jim Bowie." *TFSP* 19:175-199, 1944.

Sherrill, R. E.
"Lost Copper Mines and Spanish Gold, Haskell County." *TFSP* 3:72-77, 1924.
Legends of buried treasure.

Sims, Dunny
"Moron Jokes." *TFSP* 19:155-161, 1944.
The author shows the relation of these jokes to "traditional patterns of numbskull folktales popular especially in Northern Europe."

Sjolander, John P.
"Rhymes of Galveston Bay." *TFSP* 3:143-153, 1924.
Legends of the supernatural.

Smedley, Betty
"Legends of Wichita County." *TFSP* 8:117-123, 1930.

Smith, M., and Eddins, A. W.
"Wise Saws from Texas." *TFSP* 13:239-244, 1937.

Smith, Mrs. L. G.
"A True Story of Buried Gold." *TFSP* 14-259-261, 1938.

Spratt, J. S.
"Lover's Retreat and Lovers' Retreat, Palo Pinto." *TFSP* 3:159-163, 1924.

Strecker, John K.
"Folk-Lore Relating to Texas Birds." *TFSP* 7:25-37, 1928.

Sutherland, Mary A.
"The Dream Woman and the White Rose Bush." *TFSP* 3:89-91, 1924.
Legend of buried treasure.

————,
"Treasure Chest on the Nueces." *TFSP* 3-49 51, 1924.

Swisher, Bella French
"How the Water Lilies Came to the San Marcos River." *TFSP* 3:200-201, 1924.
A legend of the origin of Texas flowers.

Taylor, N. A.
"The Devil and Strap Buckner." *TFSP* 3:118-130, 1924.
Legend of the supernatural.

Tracy, M. W.
"Roy Bean: Law West of the Pecos." *TFSP* 13:111-119, 1937.

Tevis, Dean
Texana; a pictorial history of Texas. San Antonio, Tex.: The Naylor Company, 1936. 142 pp., illus.
Humorous anecdotes.

Vestal, Stanley
Big-Foot Wallace. Boston, Mass.: Houghton Mifflin Co., 1942.
A great character in Texan pioneer life whose deeds have become legend and lore of the Southwest and of Texas in particular.

Webb, J. O.
"Lafitte Lore." *TFSP* 3:189-191, 1924.

Webb, W. Prescott
"The White Steed and the Prairies." *TFSP* 3:223-226, 1924.
Miscellaneous Legends.

————,
"Wild-horse Stories of Southwest Texas." *TFSP* 1:58-61, 1916.

Woods, Dee
"Panther Yarns." *TFSP* 19:126-133, 1944.

Zuber, W. P.
"Inventing Stories about the Alamo." *TFSP* 15:42-47, 1939.

————,
"Rose and his Story of the Alamo II: An escape from the Alamo." *TFSP* 15:17-27, 1939.

CUSTOMS—BELIEFS—SUPERSTITIONS

Adams, Andy
A Texas Matchmaker. Illustrated by Boyd Smith. Boston: Houghton Mifflin Co., 1904. 355 pp.

Allen, John Taylor
Early Pioneer Days in Texas. Dallas, Tex.:
Wilkinson Printing Co., 1918. 267 pp., illus.
Contains poems, pp. 185-267.

Allen, William M.
Five Years in the West; or How an inexperi-
enced young man finds his occupation. With
reminiscences and sketches of real life. By a
Texas preacher. Nashville, Tenn.: Southern
Methodist Publishing House, 1884. 211 pp.

Allen, Winnie, and C. W.
Pioneering in Texas; true stories of the early
days. Illustrated by Pauline B. Adams. Dallas,
Tex.: The Southern Publishing Co., 1935. 290
pp., illus.

Arrington, Alfred W.
Rangers and Regulators of the Tanaha; or
Life among the lawless. New York: R. M.
De Witt, 1856.

A Visit to Texas: Being the journal of a traveler through those parts most interesting to
American settlers. With description of scenery,
habits, etc., etc. New York: Goodrich & Wiley,
1834. iv, 264 pp.

Banta, William
Twenty-Seven Years on the Texas Frontier.
Bandera, Texas: Frontier Times, 1933. First
printed in 1893.

Barker, Eugene Campbell
The Life of Stephen F. Austin, 1793-1836,
founder of Texas. Nashville, Dallas: Cokesbury
Press, 1925. v-xv, 551 pp.
Contains some interesting historical data and
social customs.

————,
The Austin Papers. Washington, D. C.: U. S.
Government Printing Office, 1924-1928. 3 vols.
"Four volumes of sources for any theme—social
history connected with colonial Texas." (Dobie).

Barry, James Buckner
A Texas Ranger and Frontiersman; the days
of Buck Barry in Texas, 1845-1906, ed. by
James K. Greer. Dallas, Tex.: The Southwest
Press, 1932. xi, 254 pp., illus.
Reminiscences of frontier life.

Beazley, Julia
"The Black Cat of Cole'd Plantation." *TFSP*
13:182-184, 1937.
Superstitious beliefs.

Bertillon, L. D.
"The Horn Worshipers." *TFSP* 3:230-233,
1924.

Boatright, Mody C.
"Backwoods Belles." *TFSP* 18:61-78, 1943.

————,
"Comic Exempla of the Pioneer Pulpit." *TFSP*
14:155-168, 1938.

————,
Gil Morgan: Minstrel of the Oil Fields. Austin,
Tex.: Texas Folklore Society Publications 20,
1945. xii, 104 pp., illus.

————,
"Law and Laughter on the Frontier." *The
Southwest Review* 30(2):175-181, Winter 1945.

Bogusch, E. R.
"Superstitions of Bexar County." *TFSP* 5:
112-125, 1920.

Bourke, J. G.
"Folk-foods of the Rio Grande Valley and of
Northern Mexico." *JAFL* 8:41-71, 1895.

Bracht, Viktor
Texas in 1848. Translation by C. F. Schmidt.
San Antonio, Texas: Naylor Printing Co., 1931.
"Better on natural resources than on human in-
habitants; a German book of the '40's." (Dobie).

Braddy, Haldeen
"East Texas Hunting Windies." *SFQ* 9(No. 4):
187-189, 1945.

————,
"The Spook Of Sulphur Springs, Texas." *JAFL*
59:317-319, 1946.

Carl, Prince of Solons-Braunfels
Texas, 1844-1845. Houston, Texas: Anson
Jones Press, 1936.

Cazneau, William Leslie
Eagle Pass; or, Life on the Border. New York:
G. P. Putnam & Co., 1852. viii, 188 pp.

Chabot, Frederick C.
The Perote Prisoners. San Antonio, Texas:
Naylor Co., 1934.
"Annotated diaries of Texas prisoners in Mex-
ico." (Dobie).

Chalk, Sam L.
"Early Experience in the Abilene Country."
West Texas Historical Association Yearbook
(Abilene) 4:93-104, 1928.

Coolidge, D.
Texas Cowboys. New York: E. P. Dutton &
Co., 1937.

"Courtship and Marriage in the Rio Grande
Valley." *JAFL* 9:104-107, 1896.

Cox, C. C.
"Reminiscences." In: *Southwestern Historical
Quarterly*, Vol. VI. Austin: Texas State Histor-
ical Association, 1926.
Diary edited by M. E. Martin. Overland journeys
to the Pacific. From Texas to California in 1849.

Crowell, Evelyn Miller
Texas Childhood. Dallas, Texas: The Kaleidograph Press, 1941.

Daughters of the American Revolution
Historic Costumes and Furnishings, Presented
by Texas Society, Daughters of American Revolution to Texas State College for Women.
Temple, Tex.: American Printing Co., 1940.
75 pp., illus.
"This collection has as its center of interest the
gowns of the wives of the presidents and governors of Texas."

Denison, George Stanton
"Some Letters of George Stanton Denison, 1854-1866: Observations of a Yankee on Conditions in Louisiana and Texas." Edited by James A. Padgett. *Louisiana Historical Quarterly* 23:1132-1240, 1940. Bibl.

Dewees, William B.
Letters From An Early Settler of Texas. Louisville, Ky.: New Albany Tribune Printer, 1858. viii, 312 pp.

Dickey, Jeston, and Roselle, B. L.
Pageants and Plays of Pioneers, Commemorating the Centennial of Texas. Illustrated by Arthur Mathis, Jr. San Antonio, Tex.: Carleton Printing Co., 1935. 162 pp., illus., bibl.

Dobie, Bertha McKee
"The Ghosts of Lake Jackson." *TFSP* 7:135-136, 1928.
Recounted by the Negro, Old Alf.

Dobie, J. Frank
The Flavor of Texas. Dallas, Tex.: Dealey & Lowe, 1936. 287 pp., illus.
Includes chapters on Bean, Green, Duval, Kendall, and other famous Texan characters.

————,
"The Pacing White Mustang." *American Mercury*, Dec., 1927.

————,
"The Tournament in Texas." *TFLS* 5:93-103, 1920.

————,
"Weather Wisdom of the Texas-Mexican Border." *TFSP* 2:87-99, 1917.

Douglas, Claude Leroy
Cattle Kings of Texas. Dallas, Tex.: C. Baugh, 1939. xiv, 376 pp., illus.

Duval, John Crittenden
Early Times in Texas . . . Illustrated by Jerry Bywaters. Dallas: Tardy Publishing Co., 1936. xxiv, 284 pp., illus.

Estill, J.
"Customs Among the German Descendants of Gillespie County (Texas)." *TFSP* 2:67-74, 1917.

Falconer, Thomas
"Notes of a Journey Through Texas and New Mexico, in the years 1841 and 1842." *Royal Geographical Society of London, Journal* 13:199-226, 1843.

Featherstone, Mae
"The Threshing Crew." *TFSP* 19:167-174, 1944.
Harvest customs in Mills County.

Fenley, Florence
Oldtimers: Their Own Stories, Southwest Texas, mostly ranch life. Uvalde, Texas: The Hornby Press, 1939. 254 pp.

Flack, Captain
The Texas Ranger, or Real Life in the Backwoods. London: Darton & Co., 1866. 319 pp.

Forney, John Wien
What I Saw in Texas. Philadelphia: Ringwalt & Brown, 1872. 92 pp., illus.

Gambrill, Herbert Pickens
Mirabeau Lamar. Dallas: Southwest Press, 1934, xvi, 317 pp.
"Sprightly biography of a frontiersman." (Dobie).

Gay, Beatrice Grady
Into The Setting Sun. Santa Anna, Texas: Published by Author, 1936.
"Coleman County scenes and characters, dominated by ranger character." (Dobie).

Gillett, James B.
Six Years with the Texas Rangers, 1875-1881. Austin, Texas: Van Baeckmann-Jones Co., 1921. 332 pp. Reprinted Yale University Press, 1925.
"A bully narrative anywhere." (Dobie).

————, **and Driggs, H. R.**
The Texas Ranger; the story of the Southwestern frontier. Illustrated with drawings. Yonkers-on-Hudson, New York: World Book Co., 1927. xiii, 218 pp., illus.
The life story of Captain Gillett—spiced with many interesting folklore items.

Greer, James Kimmins
Buck Barry. Dallas: 1932.
Life and exploits of the Texas rangers.

————,
Grand Prairie. Dallas, Tex.: Tardy Publishing Co., 1935. 284 pp., illus.
A great deal on the customs of the pioneers in Texas between 1850 and 1890.

Guerra, Fermina
"Rancho Buena Vista: its ways of life and traditions." *TFSP* 17:59-77, 1941.

Hall, David
"Witching For Water With the Bible." *TFSP* 13:176-181, 1937.

Hanscom, Otho Anne
Parade of the Pioneers . . . Illustrated. Dallas, Tex.: Tardy Publishing Co., 1935. xi, 266 pp., illus.
Incidents in Texan history—pioneer life, customs and traditions.

Harris, Mrs. Dilue
"Reminiscences." In: *Southwestern Historical Quarterly*, Vols. IV and VII. Austin: Texas State Historical Association, 1901.

Hogan, William Ransom
"Amusements in the Republic of Texas." *Journal of Southern History* 3:397-421, 1937.

Holden, W. C.
Alkali Trails. Dallas, Texas: The Southwest Press, 1930. 253 pp., illus.
"Pioneer life—West Texas." (Dobie).

Holley, Mary Austin
Texas—in a Series of Letters. Baltimore, 1835. reprinted under the title, *Letters of an American Traveler*, ed. by Mattie Austin Hatcher. Austin, Texas: The Steck Co., 1935. viii, 410 pp.

Holt, Roy
"Frijoles." *TFSP* 17: 49-58, 1941.
Popular Texas folk food.

House, Boyce
I Give You Texas. An indispensable guidebook for centennial visitors and vade-mecum for after luncheon orators. Dallas, Tex.: Dealey and Lowe, 1936. 83 pp., illus.

Hoyt, Henry F.
A Frontier Doctor. Boston, Mass.: Houghton Mifflin Co., 1929. 260 pp.
"Texas Panhandle and New Mexico during Billy the Kid days." (Dobie).

Jackson, George
Sixty Years in Texas. Dallas, Tex.: Wilkinson Co., 1908. 384 pp., illus.

Jackson, Mattie
The Rising and Setting of the Lone Star Republic. San Antonio, 1926. 268 pp., illus.

Kirtley, Guy
" 'Hoping-Out' in Texas." *TFSP* 17:26-32, 1941.
"The customs of neighbors exchanging work and enjoying each others company on such occasions as syrup making, hog killing, quilting, canning, erecting buildings and wakes."

Kittrell, Norman G.
Governors Who Have Been and Other Public Men of Texas. Houston, Texas: Dealy, Adex, Elgin Co., 1921. 301 pp.
"Many lawyer anecdotes." (Dobie).

Krey, Laura (Smith)
And Tell of Time. Boston: Houghton Mifflin Co., 1938. xi, 712 pp.
A work of fiction of the Brazos River Country of lower Texas.

————,
On the Long Tide. Boston: Houghton Mifflin Co., 1940. 642 pp., illus.
Fiction of the Colonial days of Texas.

Lamar Papers. Dallas: Texas State Library, J. F. Warley Directory Company, 1908. 6 vols.
"Six volumes of scrappy source material on Texas history and life." (Dobie).

Linn, John J.
Reminiscences of Fifty Years in Texas. Austin, Texas: The Steck Company, 1936. 369 pp., illus. (First published in 1883.)
"Mixture of personal, narrative, and historical notes, written with energy." (Dobie).

Lockhart, John W.
Sixty Years on the Brazos . . . Los Angeles: Press of Dunn Bros., 1930. 336 pp., illus.

Matthews, Sallie Reynolds
Interwoven. Houston: Anson Jones Press, 1936.
"Ranch life on the Texas frontier as a refined and intelligent woman saw it." (Dobie).

Maverick, Mary A. (Adams)
Memoirs. San Antonio, Texas: Alamo Printing Co., 1921. 136 pp.
"Mrs. Maverick's husband, Sam Maverick, was among the citizens of San Antonio haled off to Mexico as a prisoner in 1842." (Dobie).

Morgan, Ruth
"The Crafts of Early Texas." *The Southwest Review* 30: (2): 155-160, Winter, 1945.

Paine, Albert Bigelow
Captain Bill McDonald; a story of frontier reform. New York: J. J. Little & Ives Co., 1909. 448 pp., illus.
One of the great Texan rangers.

Parker, Amos Andrew
Trip to the West and Texas. Comprising a journey of eight thousand miles, through New York, Michigan, Illinois, Missouri, Louisiana and Texas, in the autumn and winter of 1834-5. Interspersed with anecdotes, incidents and observations . . . Concord, N. H.: W. White, 1836. iv, 380 pp., illus.

Pickrell, Annie Doom
Pioneer Women in Texas. Austin, Tex.: The E. L. Steck Company, 1929. 474 pp.

Porter, William S. (Henry, O.)
Heart of the West. Garden City, New York: Doubleday, Page & Co., for Review of Reviews Co., 1919. 313 pp.
"Interpretative stories of the Texas range life." (Dobie).

Powers, Stephen
Afoot and Alone; a walk from Sea to Sea, by the Southern route. Adventures and observations in Southern California, New Mexico, Arizona, Texas, etc. Hartford, Conn.: Columbia Book Co., 1872. xvi, 327 pp., illus.

Raht, Carlysle Graham
The Romance of Davis Mountains and Big Bend Country; a history . . . drawings by Waldo Williams. El Paso: The Raht Book Company, 1919. 381 pp., illus.
Includes observations on customs, manners, and pioneer life.

Rankin, Melinda
Texas in 1850. Boston: Damrell & Moore. 1850. 199 pp.

Raymond, Dora Neill
Captain Lee Hall of Texas. Norman, Oklahoma: University of Oklahoma Press, 1940.
"Excellent work." (Dobie).

Reid, Samuel C.
Scouting Expeditions of the Texas Rangers. Austin, Texas: The Steck Co., 1936. First printed in 1859.
"Texas Rangers in Mexican War." (Dobie).

Roberts, Mrs. Dan W.
Rangers and Sovereignty. San Antonio, Texas: Wood Printing and Engraving Co., 1914. 190 pp.

————,
A Woman's Reminiscences of Six Years in Camp with the Texas Rangers. Austin, Texas: Van Boeckmann-Jones Co., 1928. 64 pp.

Rye, Edgar
The Quirt and the Spur; Vanishing Shadows of the Texas Frontier. Chicago: W. B. Conkey Company, 1909. 363 pp., illus.

Santleben, August
A Texas Pioneer; early staging and overland freighting days on the frontiers of Texas and Mexico. Edited by I. D. Affleck. New York: Neale Publishing Co., 1910. 321 pp.

Scarborough, Dorothy
The Wind. New York: Harper & Bros., 1925. 337 pp.
Fiction—Texas life.

Schmitz, Joseph
"Impressions of Texas in 1860." *The Southwestern Historical Quarterly* 42: 334-350, 1939.

———,
Thus They Lived; Social life in the Republic of Texas. San Antonio, Tex.: The Naylor Company, 1935. vi, 141 pp., bibl.

Scott, F. J.
"Customs and Superstitions Among Texas Mexicans on the Rio Grande Border." *TFSP* 2: 75-84, 1917.

Shipman, Alice Jack
Taming the Big Bend; a history of the extreme Western portion of Texas from Fort Clark to El Paso. Austin, Tex.: Von Boeckmann-Jones Co., 1926. viii, 215 pp., illus.
"Sketches of pioneer citizens and places of historical interest"—also customs, manners, and traditions.

Simmons, Frank
"The Wart Doctor." *TFSP* 14: 192-194, 1938.
About the devil and his doings.

Siringo, Charles A.
A Texas Cow-boy; or, *Fifteen Years on the Hurricane Deck of a Spanish Pony.* Taken from real life. Chicago: M. Umbdenstock & Co., 1885. xii, 316 pp., illus.

———,
Riata and Spurs. Introduced by Gifford Pinchot. New York and Boston: Houghton Mifflin Co., 1912. (repr. 1919, 1927.) xiv, 276 pp.

Smith, L. Walden
Saddle Up. San Antonio, Tex.: The Naylor Company, 1937. 276 pp., illus.
A personal narrative of ranch life in McMullen County, Texas.

Smithwick, Noah
The Evolutions of a State; or Recollections of Old Texas Days. Austin, Texas: The Steck Company, 1935. 354 pp., music. First printed in 1900 by Gammel Book Co.
"Best of all books dealing with life in early Texas. Bully reading." (Dobie).

Sonnichsen, Charles L.
"Mexican Spooks from El Paso." *TSFP* 13: 120-129, 1937.

Sowell, Andrew Jackson
Early Settlers and Indian Fighters of Southwest Texas. Facts gathered from survivors of frontier days. Austin, Texas: B. C. Jones and Co., 1900. viii, 844 pp., illus.

———,
Rangers and Pioneers of Texas. With a concise account of the early settlements, hardships, massacres, battles and wars, by which Texas was rescued from the savage and consecrated to the empire of civilization. San Antonio, Texas: Shepard Bros. & Co., 1884. 411 pp.
"A book down to bedrock." (Dobie).

Steagall, Archie
"The Voodoo Man of the Brazos." *TFSP* 17: 113-114, 1941.
The Witchcraft exploits of Negro Moe Green of Wharton.

Stevens, Walter Barlow
Through Texas. A Series of Interesting Letters by (a) Special Correspondent of the St. Louis Globe Democrat. St. Louis: 1892. 108 pp., illus.

Stiff, Edward
A New History of Texas; Being a Narration of the Adventures of the author in Texas, and a description of the soil, climate, productions, minerals, towns, bays, harbors, rivers, institutions, and manners and customs of the inhabitants of that country . . . Cincinnati: Published by G. Conclin, 1847. 246 pp., illus.

Sweet, Alex E., and Knox, J. A.
On a Mexican Mustang Through Texas, from the Gulf to the Rio Grande. Hartford, Conn.: S. S. Scranton & Company, 1883. 672 pp., illus.
Humorous satire.

Taylor, Rose McLaury
The Saddle and the Plow. Maryland: The Bobbs-Merrill Co., 1942.
A story which conveys the flavor of the land, the time, and the people in the Texas plains in the Eighties.

Thomas, Robert Harper, ed.
Journalists' Letters Descriptive of Texas and Mexico. Mechanisburg, Pa,: Farmers' Friend Print, 1888. 149 pp., illus.

Turner, Tressa
"The Human Comedy in Folk Superstitions." *TFSP* 13: 146-175, 1937.

Van Demark, Harry
A Texas Ranger: A play of the great Southwest in three acts. Philadelphia: Penn Publ. Co., 1919. 67 pp., illus.

Webb, Walter Prescott
The Texas Rangers; drawings by Lonnie Rees. New York and Boston: Houghton, Mifflin & Co., 1935. 583 pp., bibl.

Walker, Virginia
"Pie suppers in East Texas." *TFSP* 17: 33–34. 1941.

Williams, J. W.
"Robson's Journey Through West Texas in 1879." *West Texas Historical Association Year Book* (Abilene) 20: 109–124. 1944.

Willrich, Georg
Erinnerungen aus Texas. Warheit und Dichtung. Aufgezeichhet während der Unter-
suchungshaft zu Harnover. Leipzig: C. E.
Kollmann, 1854. 3 vols.
    Reminiscences of a stay in Texas.

Wright, John and W.
Recollections of Western Texas; descriptive
and narrative . . . 1852-55. Interspersed with
illustrative anecdotes. London: W. & F. G.
Cash, 1857. 88 pp.

Wright, Solomon Alexander
*My Rambles as East Texas Cowboy, Hunter,
Fisherman, Tie-Cutter.* Austin, Texas: Texas
Folklore Society ("Range Life Series"), 1942.
xii, 159 pp.

Wynn, Afton
Pioneer Folk Ways. TFSP 13: 190-238, 1937.
    Mainly with the folk of Parker County, Texas.

PROVERBS—RIDDLES

Atkinson, M. J.
"Familiar Sayings of Old-Time Texans." *TFSP*
5: 78-92, 1920.

Halpert, Herbert
"A Few Riddles." *HFB* 3: 38, 1944.
    Five given from Texas and Mississippi.

Smith, Mrs. Morgan, and Eddins, A. W.
"Wise Saws from Texas." *TFSP* 13: 239-244,
1937.
    Sayings and proverbs.

FOLK MEDICINE

Day, Donald
"Leaves of mesquite grass." *TFSP* 19: 63-81,
1944.

Guinn, Leon
"Home remedies from Scurry County." *TFSP*
14: 268, 1938.

Hatfield, Sadie
"Folklore of Texas plants." *TFSP* 18: 157-162,
1943.
    Texan plants used as cures, food, drink, cosmetics,
    etc.

Lewis, Gabe
"Old-Time Remedies from Madison County."
TFSP 14: 267-268, 1938.

Nixon, Pat Ireland
A Century of Medicine in San Antonio.
San Antonio, Texas: Published by the Author,
1936.
    "Rich in information, diverting in anecdote, and
    tonic in philosophy." (Dobie).

Red, Mrs. George P.
The Medicine Man in Texas. Houston, Texas:
Standard Printing & Lithographing Co., 1930.
344 pp.

Simmons, Frank
"The Wart Doctor." *TFSP* 14: 192-194, 1938.

Woodhull, Frost
"Ranch Remedies." *TFSP* 8: 9-73, 1930.
    A very interesting list of "Pharmacopoeia Tex-
    ana"—for animals and human beings.

PLACE NAMES

Dienst, Alex
"The Naming of Metheglin Creek." *TFSP*
3: 208-209, 1924.

Dobie, J. Frank
"Bibliography of Texas Place Names." *TFSP*
13: 70-78, 1937.

————.
"How the Brazos River Got Its Name." *TFSP*
3: 209-218, 1924.

————,
"Stories in Texas Names; iv. Prolonged
Shadows." *Southwest Review* 21: 411-417,
1936.

————,
"Stories in Texas Place Names." *TFSP*
13: 1-78, 1937.

————,
Straight Texas . . . Austin, Tex.: Texas Folklore Society, 1937. 348 pp., illus. (music) bibl.,
(Texas Folklore Society. Publications. No.
xiii).

Fullmore, Zachary Taylor
*The History and Geography of Texas as Told
in County Names* . . . Austin: Press of E. L.
Steck, 1915. ix, 312 pp., illus. (Revised in
1926.)

Hill, Frank P.
"Plains Names." *Panhandle-Plains Historical
Review* (Canyon, Texas) 10: 36-47, 1937.
bibl.

Littlejohn, E. G.
"How the Brazos and the Colorado Originated."
TFSP 3: 218-223, 1924.

Massengill, Fred I.
*Texas Towns; Origin of Name and Location
of Each of the 2,148 Post Offices in Texas.*
An interesting compilation of nomenclature
running the whole gamut of human interest
and sympathies, including religion, history,
sports, ranch life, and personalities all properly classified for your convenience, entertainment and to add to the sum total of useful
knowledge. Terrell, Tex.: n.p., 1936. 222 pp.

Morgan, Paul
*Texas Ballads, Legends of Texas Names and
Origins in Ballad Form.* Dallas, Texas: Tardy
Publishing Co., 1934. 173 pp.

Payne, L. W., Jr.
"How Medicine Mounds of Hardeman County
Got Their Names." *TFSP* 3: 207-208, 1924.

————,
"Indian Bluff on Canadian River." *TFSP*
3: 205-207, 1924.
    Legend in name.

"Place-Names." *West Texas Historical and Scientific Society. Publ.* (Alpine, Tex.) No. 8: 18-22, 1938.

Raht, Carlysle Graham
The Romance of Davis Mountains and the Big Bend Country. El Paso, Texas: The Raht Books Co., 1919. 381 pp.

Smith, Victor J.
"How Dead Horse Canyon Got Its Name." *TFSP* 3: 209, 1924.

Strecker, John K.
Animals and Streams: A contribution to the study of Texas Folk Names. Waco, Texas: Baylor University, 1929. (Contributions to folklore, number 2.)
Discussion and Alphabetic treatment of stream names derived from Texas fauna.

SPEECH

Bailey, Oran B.
"Glossary of Café Terms." *AS* 18: 307-308, 1943.
56 slang terms and meanings of food serving, used by waiters in east Texas and west Louisiana.

Berry, Edward
"Sawmill Talk (East Texas)" *AS* 3 (No. 1): 24-25, 1927.

Bourke, J. G.
"Language and folk-usage of the Rio Grande Valley." *JAFL* 9: 81-115, 1896.

Braddy, Haldeen
"Tall Talk of the Texas Trans-Pecos." *AS* 15: 220-222, 1940.

Bryson, Artemisia Baer
"Homely Words in Texas." *AS* 9 (No. 1): 70-71, 1934.

———,
"Some Texas Dialect Words." *AS* 4 (No. 4): 330-331, 1929.

Buckner, Mary Dale
"Ranch Diction of the Texas Panhandle." *AS* 8 (No. 1): 25-32, 1933.

Crow, C. L.
"Word List from Texas." *Dialect Notes* 1 (Part 9): 411-427; (Part 5): 347-348, 1916.

Eddins, A. W.
"The State Industrial School Boy's Slang." *TFSP* 1: 44-46, 1916.
Taken from some students of the State Juvenile Training School.

Hall, David
"Folk Names of Texas Cacti." *TFSP* 11: 90-93, 1933.

Littlejohn, E. G.
"The Holy Spring of Father Margil at Nacogdoches." *TFSP* 3: 204-205, 1924.
Legend of name.

O'Quinn, Trueman E.
"Colloquialisms Along the Sabine." *TFSP* 13: 245-249, 1937.
Words and expressions found in the Sabine River Country.

Rollins, Hyder E.
"A West Texas Word List." *Dialect Notes* 4 (Part 3): 224-230, 1 1915.

Stanley, Oma
"The Speech of East Texas." *AS* 11 (no. 1): 3-36; 11 (no. 2): 145-166; 11 (no. 3): 232-251; 11 (no. 4): 327-355, 1936; 16: 3-16, 1941.
Good bibliography included.

FOLKSONG
GENERAL STUDIES AND COLLECTIONS

Allan, Francis D.
Lone Star Ballads. Galveston: 1874.
Frontier and Confederate Songs.

Dobie, J. Frank
"More Ballads and Songs of the Frontier Folk." *TFSP* 7:155-180, 1928.
Text and tunes of a number of songs: historical songs, and cowboy songs.

———,
"Texas-Mexican Border Broadsides." *JAFL* 36: 185-191, 1923.

Hogan, W. R.
"Amusements in the Republic of Texas." *Journal of Southern History* 3: 397-421, 1937.
Popular songs and other folk-lore matter.

Kittle, T. L.
"Folk music of the Upper Rio Grande." *Southwest Review* 30: 192-195, 1945.

Major, Mabel
"British Ballads in Texas." *TFSP* 10: 131-168, 1932.
Presents ballads of supernatural, love ballads, ballads of the sea, and humorous ballads. Texts and tunes.

Morgan, Paul A.
Texas Ballads: Legends of Texas Names and Origins, in Ballads Form. Dallas: Tardy Publishing Company, 1934. 183 pp.

Neighbors, Alice Atkinson
"Old Obadiah" and "My Juanita." *TFSP* 13:250-257, 1937.
Words and tunes.

Owens, William A.
Texas Folk Songs. Doctoral Thesis, University of Iowa, June, 1941.

Pan American Union, Music Division
14 Traditional Spanish Songs from Texas, transcribed by Gustavo Duran from recordings made in Texas, 1934-1939, by John A., Ruby T., and Alan Lomax, with an original drawing by Antonio Rodríguez Luna. Washington, D. C.: Music Division, Pan American Union, 1924. vi, 20 pp.
Unaccompanied melodies.

Payne, L. W., Jr.
"One Evening as I Sat Courting." *Texas Folk-lore Society Publications* (Austin), (No. 2) pp. 6-7, 1923.

———,
"The Frog's Courting." *TFSP* 5:5-48, 1926.
Texas version.

Peabody, C.
Texas Version of "The White Captive." *JAFL* 25: 169-170, 1912.

Sjolander, J. P.
"Rhymes of Galveston Bay." *TFSP* 3:143-149, 1924.

Smithwick, Noah
The Evolution of a State or Recollections of Old Texas Days. Austin, Texas: Gammel Book Co., 1900. 354 pp., incl. music.

"Songs from Texas."
Time 37:36, (March 24), 1941.

Speck, Ernest
"The Song of Little Llano." *TFSP* 19: 155-156, 1944.
Text only of a song about hog stealers.

Texas Centennial Celebrations . . .
Songs Texas Sings; Centennial Edition for Schools; Compiled for Public Schools Division of the Texas Department of Publicity for Centennial Celebrations. Dallas, Tex.: Turner Co., 1936. 31 pp., illus.
Arranged for four mixed voices (SATB).

Webb, W. Prescott
"Miscellany of Texas Folk-Lore." *TFSP* 2: 38-49, 1923.
Contains texts of Hobo Songs, Railroad Songs, Slum Songs, Cowboy Songs, Negro Songs, and Stories, but no music.

———,
"Notes on Folk Lore of Texas." *JAFL* 28:290-299, 1915.
Five secular songs.

NURSERY RHYMES AND GAMES

Alexander, Frances
Mother Goose on Rio Grande. Dallas, Texas: Banks Upshaw, 1944. 101 pp.

Romberg, Annie
"Fighting a Nest of Bumblebees, an Almost Forgotten Thrilling Sport." *TFSP* 18: 151-156, 1943.
Boy's sport in Texas.

DANCES

Atkins, Laura
"Some Play Party Games of South Texas." *TFSP* 17: 98-107, 1941.

Da Silva, Owen
Mission Music in California. A collection of old California Mission hymns, and masses, transcribed and edited by Rev. Owen de Silva. Accompaniments and chirography by Arthur M. Bienbar. Mission sketches by Paul A. Moore, with an introduction by the Hon. John Steven McGroarty. Los Angeles: W. F. Lewis, 1941.

Duncan, Ruby
"The Play Party in Hamilton County." *TFSB* 6: 1-15, 1940.

Gates, Helen
"Toodala." *TFSP* 17:91-97, 1941.
Texan folk dance.

Owens, William A.
Swing and Turn: Texas Play-Party Games. Special edition for the Texas Folklore Society. Dallas: Tardy Publishing Company, 1936. xxxiii, 117 pp., music, bibl.

Payne, L. W., Jr.
Finding List of Texas Play-Party Songs. Texas Folk-lore Society Publications, Austin, Texas, 1916. (No. 1) pp. 35-38.

RECORDS

U. S. Library of Congress. Division of Music. Folklore Section.
Collection of Folklore and Folkmusic in the Austin Area.   AAFS-LC.

ARRANGEMENTS

See: Cowboy Songs, pp. 617-27.

(Individual Titles)

———: *Voice and Piano*

"McCaffie's Confession."
Fox, Oscar J.: Schirmer: voice and piano.

"Texas Cowboy's Lament."
Fox, Oscar J.: C. Fischer: voice and piano.

THE WEST

THE WEST

See: The Cowboy, pp. 610–27; The '49ers, pp. 636–43.

FOLKLORE
BIBLIOGRAPHY

American Art Association, New York
Americana, Historical Broadsides, Books, Tracts of the Colonies, Revolutionary War, etc.; unusual collection of early almanacs and newspapers: rare items relating to pioneer days in California, Oregon and other Western states . . .
New York: American Art Association, 1923. 198 pp.

Bay, Jens Christian
A Handful of Western Books. Cedar Rapids, Ia.: The Torch Press, 1935. 44 pp.

————,
A Second Handful of Western Books. Cedar Rapids, Ia.: The Torch Press, 1936. 56 pp.

————,
A Third Handful of Western Books. Cedar Rapids, Ia.: The Torch Press, 1937. 58 pp.

Davidson, Levette J.
Rocky Mountain Life in Literature. A Descriptive Bibliography. Denver: University of Denver Book Store, 1936. 25 pp.

————————, and Boswick, P.
The Literature of the Rocky Mountains West. Caldwell, Idaho: Caxton Printers, 1939. bibl.

Dellenbaugh, Frederick Samuel
Books by American Travellers and Explorers from 1846 to 1900. New York: G. P. Putnam's Sons, 1920. (pp. 131-170, 681-728).
Reprinted from *Cambridge History of American Literature,* Vol. 3, Chapter 14.

Rader, Jessie L.
South of Forty: from the Mississippi to the Rio Grande, A Bibliography. Norman, Oklahoma: University of Oklahoma Press, 1947. xi, 336 pp.

Turner, Frederick Jackson
List of References on the History of the West. Cambridge, Mass.: Harvard University Press, 1913. 129 pp.

Wagner, Henry Raup
The Plains and the Rockies; a bibliography of original narratives of travel and adventure, 1800-1865. Revised and extended by Charles L. Camp. San Francisco: Grabhorn Press, 1937. 299 pp.

Winther, Oscar Osburn
The Trans-Mississippi West: A Guide to Its Periodical Literature, (1811-1938). Bloomington, Ind.: Indiana University, 1942. xv, 263 pp.

PERIODICALS

Out West. A Magazine of the Old Pacific and the New. (Formerly *The Land of Sunshine.)* V.1, 1894—Los Angeles, Cal. Vol. 1-15 have title: *Land of Sunshine.*

Overland Monthly. Devoted to the Development of the Country. V.1, 1868—San Francisco.

GENERAL STUDIES AND COLLECTIONS

Ackley, Richard Thomas
"Across the Plains in 1858." *Utah Historical Quarterly* 9: 190—228, 1941.

Altrocchi, Julia (Cooley)
The Old California Trail: Traces in Folklore and Furrow. Illustrated from photographs by the author. Caldwell, Idaho: The Caxton Printers, Ltd., 1945. 327 pp., illus., bibl., index.

Atwood, Wallace W.
The Rocky Mountains. (The American Mountain Series.) New York: Vanguard Press, 1946.

Banning, William, and Banning, Geo. Hugh
Six Horses. New York: The Century Co., 1930. 410 pp., illus., bibl.
"A combination of history and autobiography. Routes to and in California; much of Texas. Excellent on drivers, travelers, stations, 'pass the mustard, please.' " (Dobie).

Barber, John Warner, and Howe, H.
All the Western States and Territories, from the Alleghanies to the Pacific, and from the Lakes to the Gulf, containing their history from the earliest times, with local history, incidents of pioneer life . . . Cincinnati: Howe's Subscription Book Concern, 1867. xi, 733 pp.

Beadle, John Hanson
The Undeveloped West, or Five Years in the Territories. A complete history of the region between the Mississippi and the Pacific. Philadelphia: National Publishing Co., 1873.
Its resources, climate, inhabitants, natural curiosities, etc. Life and adventure on prairies, mountains and Pacific Coast.

————,
Western Wilds, and the Men Who Redeem Them; an authentic narrative, embracing an account of seven years' travel and adventure in the Far West. Detroit: J. C. Chilton, 1877. xvi, 628 pp.

Bechdolt, Frederick Ritchie
Giants of the Old West. New York: The Century Co., 1930. 245 pp., illus.
Contents: John Colter.—Ashley and His Young Men. —Stephen Fuller Austin. —The Alamo Had None. —William Becknell. —James Pattie. — Brigham Young. —John Augustus Sutter. — Alexander Majors. —Charles Goodnight.

Bond, Fred
*Westward How? Through the Scenic West.
How, Where and When to Go, What to See,
and How to Shoot It.* San Francisco: Camera
Craft Publishing Company, 1947. 324 pp.,
illus.
"By the West, the author means the national
parks, principal cities, and other scenic attrac-
tions in Arizona, California, Colorado, Idaho,
Montana, Nevada, New Mexico, Oregon, South
Dakota, Utah, Washington, Wyoming and Western Canada: and let it be said now that he
knows his West as few people do." (Hector Lee).

Branch, Edward Douglas
*Westward; the Romance of the American
Frontier.* Woodcuts by Lucina S. Wakefield.
New York: D. Appleton and Company, 1930.
ix, 626 pp., illus.

Bronson, Edgar Beecher
The Vanguard: A Tale of the Old Frontier.
Told from the notes of Clark B. Stocking, who
for fifty years fought in the forefront of the
firing line. New York: 1913.
From *The Cavalier*, New York, June 7, 14, 21,
28, 1913.

Bryant, Edwin
Rocky Mountain Adventures. New York: Hurst
and Co., 1885. 452 pp.

Carleton, Lieut. J. Henry
The Prairie Logbooks. Edited with an intro-
duction by Louis Pelzer. Chicago, Ill.: The
Caxton Club, 350 East 22nd St. 1944. 295 pp.
An account of the dragoon campaigns to the
Pawnee villages in 1844 and the Rocky Mts. in
1845.

Carvalho, S.
Incidents and Adventure in the Far West;
with Col. Fremont's last expedition across the
Rocky Mountains: Including Three Months
Residence in Utah . . . New York: Derby &
Jackson, 1857. xv, 380 pp.

Chapman, Arthur
*Out Where the West Begins, and other West-
ern Verses.* Boston: Houghton Mifflin Company, 1917. ix, 90 pp.

Chittenden, Hiram Martin
The American Fur Trade of the Far West.
New York: R. R. Wilson, Inc., 1935. 2 Vols.
Anecdotes, hunting tales, characters.

Clampitt, John W.
Echoes from the Rocky Mountains; Reminiscences and thrilling incidents of the romantic and golden age of the great West . . .
Chicago: Belford, Clarke & Co., 1889. xvi,
671 pp., illus.

Codman, John
*The Round Trip by Way of Panama, Through
California, Nevada, Utah, Idaho, and Colorado* . . . New York: G. P. Putnam's Sons,
1879. xiii, 331 pp.

Cole, F. R.
"Western Wanderings." *Cape Quarterly Review*
(Cape Town) 1: 207-226, 1881.

Coleman, Rufus Arthur, ed.
The Golden West in Story and Verse. New
York and London: Harper and Bros., 1933.
442 pp.
Folk poems.

Collier, Wm. R., and Westrate, Edwin
Dave Cooke of the Rockies. New York: Rufus
Rockwell Wilson, 1936.

Conard, Howard Louis
"Uncle Dick" Wooton, the pioneer frontiersman of the Rocky Mountain Region. . . .
Chicago: W. E. Dibble & Co., 1890. viii, 473
pp., illus.

Coolidge, Dane
Fighting Men of the West . . . illustrated with
halftones. New York: E. P. Dutton & Co.,
1932. 343 pp., illus.

————,
Death Valley Prospectors. New York: E. P.
Dutton and Co., Inc., 1937., 178 pp.

Corle, Edwin
Desert Country (American Folkways). New
York: Duell, Sloan and Pearce, 1941.

Cox, James
My Native Land. The United States: its
wonders, its beauties, and its people; with
descriptive notes, character sketches, folklore,
traditions, legends and history . . . St. Louis:
Blair Publishing Co., 1895. 400 pp., illus.

Crawford, John Wallace
The Poet Scout. Being a Selection of Incidental
and Illustrative Verses and Songs. San Francisco: H. Keller & Co., 1879. xx, 208 pp.,
illus.

Cronau, Rudolf
Im Wilden Western. Eine Künstlerfahrt durch
die Prairien und Felsengebirge der Union.
Mit Illustrationen. Braunschweig: O. Löbecke,
1890. vi, 383 pp.
Impressions of Western life and sights.

Dale, Edward Everett
"Culture on the American Frontier." *Nebraska
History* 26: 75-90, 1945. Illus.

Dana, Richard Henry
Two Years Before the Mast. New York: Literary Guild of America, 1931. 483 pp.
Customs, social life, tales of adventures, superstition, terms. "It is the classic of the hide and
follow trade of California." (Dobie).

Davidson, Levette Jay
"Rocky Mountain Folklore." *SFQ* 5: 205-219,
1941.

Drannan, William F.
*Thirty-One Years on the Plains and in the
Mountains.* Chicago: Rhodes and McClure
Publishing Co., 1900. 586 pp.
Trapper and guide tales, characters.

Driggs, Howard R.
Westward America. New York: Somerset Books, 1947.

Drumheller, Daniel Mont
"Uncle Dan" Drumheller Tells Thrills of Western Trails in 1854. Spokane: Inland-American Printing Co., 1925. 131 pp.

Erskine, Mrs. Gladys (Shaw)
Broncho Charlie, A Saga of the Saddle. New York: Thomas Y. Cromwell Co., 1934. 316 pp.

Fergusson, Harvey
Wolf Song. New York: Alfred A. Knopf, 1927. "Graphic historical novel of Mountain Men." (Dobie).

Finch, R.
Plays of the American West. New York: Greenberg Publisher, 1947. 247 pp.

Finger, Charles Joseph
Foot-Loose in the West, being the account of a journey to Colorado and California and other Western states; with sketches made on route by Helen Finger. New York: W. Morrow and Company, 1932. viii, 302 pp., illus.

Forbes, Stuart Falconer
Trail Sketches: World Pictures of the West. Boston: the Christopher Publishing House, 1925. 116 pp.
Poems of Western life and traditions.

Fulton, Robert Lardin
Epic of the Overland. San Francisco: A. M. Robertson, 1924. 109 pp.

Ganson, Eve
Desert Mavericks. Santa Barbara, Calif.: Wallace Hebberd, 1928. Illus.

Gardner, Raymond Hatfield (Arizona Bill)
The Old West. Adventures of Arizona Bill. In collaboration with B. H. Monroe. Illustrated by Grady Sowell. San Antonio, Texas: The Taylor Co., 1944. 308 pp.
A highly fictitious narrative, in which the author is to have been with Custer, Wild Bill Hickok, Buffalo Bill, Deadwood Dick, Calamity Jane, The Earps, Doc Holliday, Tom Horn, Belle Starr, the James brothers, Billy the Kid, Pat Garrett, and others. The author knew them all!

Gerould, Katharine
The Aristocratic West. New York: Harper & Brothers, 1925. 200 pp., illus.
Contents: The Aristocratic West. —Salt Lake: The City of Saints. —Our Northwestern States. —New Mexico, and the backwash of Spain. — Reno. —San Francisco revisited.

Gibson, A. H.
Tales from the West. Cincinnati: Editor Publishing Co., 1900. 151 pp.
Not folktales, but they include folklore material.

Gilfillan, Archer B.
Sheep. Boston: Little, Brown and Co., 1928.

Glassock, Carl Burgess
Bandits and the Southern Pacific. New York: Frederick A. Stokes Co., 1929. 294 pp.

Golder, Frank Alfred, ed.
The March of the Mormon Battalion from Council Bluffs to California. New York and London: The Century Co., 1928. 295 pp.

Gottschall, A. H.
The Experience of a Rover, from Maine to California and from British America to the Gulf, Without a Purse. Marietta, Pa.: The Author, 1876. 52 pp.

Graham, William Oran
The West; A Collection of Verses Expressing the Spirit of the West. Kansas City, Mo.: W. O. Graham, 1916. 38 pp.

Grant, Blanche C.
When Old Trails Were New; The Story of Taos. New York: The Press of the Pioneers Inc., 1934. 344 pp.

Loomis, C. Grant
"The Western Man." CFQ 5 (No. 3): 309, 1946.
Reprint of a poem recounting the amazing exploits of a "Western Man," first appeared in *Golden Era* 24 (No. 17): 3, 1876.

Gray, Arthur Amos
Men Who Built the West. Caldwell, Idaho: The Caxton Printers, Ltd., 1945. 220 pp., 62 illus.
The book "is a solid contribution to the juvenile literature of its subject." (J. B. Virtue).

Greenwood, Annie (Pike)
The Sagebrush Folks. New York, London: D. Appleton Century Co., Inc., 1934 xi. 483 pp.

Greer, James K.
Bois d'Arc to Barbed Wire. Dallas: Dealey and Lowe, 1936. 427 pp., illus.
Of mustangs and cow-ponies.

Gregg, Josiah
Commerce of the Prairie: or the Journal of a Santa Fe Trader, during eight expeditions across the great western prairies and a residence of nearly nine years in Northern Mexico. (Illus. with maps.) New York & London: J. W. Moore, 1844. II vols.

Greve, Alice Wheeler
Shadow on the Plains. Portland, Ore.: Binfords and North, 1945. 272 pp.
A story of the Old Oregon Trail—combines Western adventure, romance and horror, with interesting historical fact.

Grinnell, George Bird
Beyond the Old Frontier. New York: Charles Scribner's Sons, 1913. 374 pp.

——————,
Trails of the Pathfinders. New York: Charles Scribner's Sons, 1911. x, 460 pp., illus.
Journeys of Alexander Henry, Jonathan Carver, Alexander Mackenzie, Lewis and Clark, Zebulon M. Pike, Alexander Henry (the younger), Ross Cox, Samuel Parker, Thomas J. Farnham and Frémont.

―――――,
When Buffalo Ran. New Haven: Yale University Press. 1920.

Grissom, Irene Welch
Verses of the New West; with illustrations by Glen H. Spurgeon. Caldwell, Id.: The Caston Printers, Ltd., 1931. viii, 102 pp., illus.

Hendricks, George David
The Bad Man of the West. Drawings by Frank Anthony Stanush. San Antonio, Texas: The Naylor Co., 1941. xv, 310 pp., bibl. (pp. 293-298).

Hill, J. L.
The End of the Cattle Trail. Long Beach, Calif.: G. W. Moyle Publ. Co., May, 1924. 120 pp.

Horan, Jack
Poems of the West; illustrated by Leo Beauleaurie. Great Falls, Mont.: Call Printing Co. 1929. 56 pp.

Howe, Henry
The Great West; containing narratives of the most important and interesting events in Western history—remarkable individual adventures—sketches of frontier life . . . New York: G. F. Tuttle, 1858. xi, 576 pp., illus.

Hubbs, James
Wild Life in the Far West. San Francisco: A. L. Bancroft and Co., 1874.
Adventure, anecdotes, tall tales.

Hufford, David Andrew
Death Valley: Swamper Skis Traditional Lore: Why, When, How? Los Angeles: D. A. Hufford and Co., 1902. 43 pp.
Desert tales, tradition, superstition.

Irving, Washington
The Adventures of Captain Bonneville Astoria issued under the title of *The Discovery of the Oregon Trail,* illuminative material by Philip Ashton Rollins. Adventures of Capt. Bonneville (in the Rocky Mountains and West). New York: G. Putnam, 1850, 1851, 1868, and many subsequent editions.

―――――.
The Rocky Mountains: or, Scenes, Incidents, and Adventures in the Far West; digested from The Journal of Capt. B. L. E. Bonneville—and illustrated from various sources. Philadelphia: Carey, Lea and Blanchard, 1837. 2 Vols.

―――――,
The Western Journals of Washington Irving. Edited and annotated by John Francis McDermott. Illustrations, Maps. Norman, Okla.: University of Oklahoma Press., 1944. 201 pp.
The American and Exploration Travel Series. Tho the author does not identify himself with Western life, he nevertheless records interesting bits of Western and Indian lore.

Ivins, Virginia
Pen Pictures of Early Western Days. Illustrations by Wm. S. Ivins. Keokuk, Ia.: 1905. 157 pp., illus.

James, Will
Cow Country. New York: Scribner's Sons, 1931.

Jones, John Beauchamp
Wild Western Scenes; a narrative of adventure in the Western wilderness . . . Illustrated with sixteen engravings from original designs. Philadelphia: Grambo & Co., 1852. 263 pp., illus.

Jones, Theodore Elden
Leaves from an Argonaut's Note Book. San Francisco: The Whitaker and Roy Co., Inc., 1905. 304 pp.
Pioneer tales, customs, beliefs, legend.

Judson, Edward Zane Carroll (Ned Buntline)
Norwood or *Life on the Prairie.* New York: W. F. Burgess, 1850. 75 pp.

Kent, Henry Brainard
Graphic Sketches of the West. Chicago: R. R. Donnellery & Sons, 1890. 254 pp., illus.

Kingsley, Rose Georgina
South by West; or, Winter in the Rocky Mountains and Spring in Mexico. Edited with a preface by the Rev. Charles Kingsley. London: W. Isbister & Co., 1874. xvii, 411 pp., illus.

Knibbs, Henry Herbert
Riders of the Stars; A Book of Western Verse. Boston: Houghton Mifflin Company, 1916. v, 81 pp.

Lambourne, Alfred
The Old Journey; Reminiscences of Pioneer Days. Salt Lake City: G. Q. Cannon & Sons Co., 1897. 53 pp., illus.

Landon, Melville D. (Eli Perkins)
Eli Perkins, Thirty Years of Wit, and Reminiscences of Witty, Wise and Eloquent Men. New York: Cassell Publishing Co., 1891.

Laut, A. C.
The Story of the Trapper. New York: D. Appleton and Co., 1902. 248 pp., Illus.
"A popular survey, emphasizing types and characters." (Dobie).

Lee, Bourke
Death Valley Men. New York: The Macmillan Co., 1932. 319 pp.
Characters, anecdotes, tales, lost mines.

Leigh, William R.
The Western Pony. New York: The Huntington Press, 1933.
"One of the most beautiful books ever printed on the west; beautiful illustrations: illuminating text." (Dobie).

Le Noir, Phil
Rhymes of the Wild and Wooly. Santa Fe, N. M.: New Mexico Publ. Co., 1920. 23 pp.

Leonard, Zenas
Narrative of the Adventures of Zenas Leonard . . . edited by Milo Milton Quaife. Chicago: The Lakeside Press, 1934. xxiv, 278 pp.

Lesley, L. B.
Uncle Sam's Camels. Edited by Burt Lewis. Cambridge: Harvard University Press, 1929.

Lewis, Alfred Henry (Dan Quin)
Wolfville Days. New York: Frederick A. Stokes Co., 1897. 337 pp., illus.

Linderman, Frank Bird
On a Passing Frontier. New York: Charles Scribner's Sons, 1920.

Linford, Velma
Wyoming: Frontier State. Denver, Colorado: The Old West Publishing Co., 1947.
Includes a great deal of Western folk material.

Lowe, Percival Green
Five Years a Dragoon ('49 to '54) and Other Adventures of the Great Plains. Kansas City, Mo.: The F. Hudson Publishing Co., 1906. 417 pp., illus.

Lummis, Charles Fletcher
A Tramp Across the Continent. New York: C. Scribner's Sons, 1892. xiii, 270 pp.

Magoffin, Susan Shelby
Down the Santa Fe Trail. New Haven, Conn.: Yale University Press, 1926.
"Delectable diary." (Dobie).

Majors, Alexander
Seventy Years on the Frontier. Chicago: New York: Rand, McNally and Co., 1893. 325 pp., illus.

Marcy, Randolph Barnes
Border Reminiscences. New York; Harper & Brothers, 1872. ix, 396 pp., illus.

————,
Thirty Years of Army Life on the Border. Comprising descriptions of the Indian nomads of the plains; explorations of new territory; a trip across the Rocky Mountains in the winter . . . incidents in the life of different frontier men, etc., etc., . . . With numerous illustrations. New York: Harper & Brothers, 1866. xvi, 442 pp., illus.

Maule, Harry Edward
Great Tales of the American West . . . New York: The Modern Library, 1945. xvii, 361 pp.
A selection of fictional tales by various authors on life, incidents, and manners of the Western pioneers.

————,
"Scherzo on a Six-Gun." *New York Times Book Review,* May 6, 1945. pp. 5.
An article on the writing of the western fiction.

McCoy, Joseph G.
Historic Sketches of the Trade of the West and Southwest. Kansas City, Mo.: Ramsey, Millett and Hudson, 1874. 427 pp., illus. (reprinted, Wash., D. C., 1932.)

McCracken, Harold
Frederick Remington: Artist of the Old West. Philadelphia: J. Lippincott Co., 1947, 157 pp., illus.
"A great deal of the Old West, as a way of life, survives in Remington's drawings, paintings and sculpture. But only early in his work will you find the physical aspect of the West itself, as you will find it, for example, in Alfred Miller's paintings." (Dale L. Morgan).

McGroarty, John Stephen
Just California and Songs Along the Way. Los Angeles: The Times-Mirror Company, 1903. 63 pp.
Poems of the Californians.

McNeer, May Yonge
The Story of the Great Plains. Lithographs by C. H. DeWitt. New York: Distributed by Harper and Brothers for Artists and Writers Guild, 1943. Unpaged.
In the series of regional picture books for young readers.

Mills, Enos Abijah
The Rocky Mountain Wonderland. Boston: Houghton Mifflin Co., 1915. xiii, 362 pp., illus., map.

Minturn, William
Travels West. London: S. Tinsley, 1877. 396 pp.

Monaghan, Jay
Last of the Bad Men. Indianapolis: Bobbs-Merrill Company, 1946. 293 pp.
"Out of the biography of Tom Horn emerges a cunning, nerveless figure; a man either born without conscience or so brutalized by his earlier experiences that his conscience had atrophied." (Ernest Haycox).

Moore, J. M.
West. Wichita Falls, Texas: Lovelace Bookstore, 1935.

Morgan, Dale L.
The Humboldt, Highroad of the West. (The Rivers of America Series.) Illustrated by Arnold Blanch. New York: Farrar and Rinehart, 1943. 374 pp.

Nelson, John L.
The Colorado: Desert River. (The Rivers of America Series). Illustrated by Tora Selander Nelson. New York: Farrar and Rinehart, 1942.
"The Colorado, half recluse, half challenger, has created the greatest wonder of the world—Grand Canyon."

Nevins, Allan
Fremont, Pathmaker of the West. New York: D. Appleton-Century Co., Inc., 1939.

Northall, W. K., ed.
Life and Recollections of Yankee Hill: together with Anecdotes and Incidents of His Travels. New York: Published for Mrs. Cordelia Hill, by W. F. Burgess, 1850.

O'Byrne, John
"Pikes Peak or Bust," and Historical Sketches of the Wild West. Colorado Springs, 1922. 141 pp., illus.

Paden, Irene D.
The Wake of the Prairie Schooner. New York: The Macmillan Co., 1943. xix, 514 pp., pen and ink drawings, map, bibl., index.
"For a person who wants to know how the trail (The Oregon and California Trail) looks today, it is the best available document." (Wilbur Schramm).

Palmer, Fanny
Sonnets of California. New York: The Purdy Press, 1927. 35 pp.

Parkman, Francis
The Oregon Trail; sketches of prairie and Rocky-Mountain Life. Edited by Charles H. J. Douglas. New York: The Macmillan Co., 1928. xxi, 362 pp., map.

Perkins, Charles Elliott
The Pinto Horse; illustrations by Edward Borein and a foreword by Owen Winter. Santa Barbara, Calif.: Fisher & Skofield; 1937. 76 pp., illus.

Poe, Sophie A.
Buckboard Days. (ed. by Eugene Cunningham). Caldwell, Idaho: The Caxton Printers, 1936.

Porter, Lavinia Honeyman
By Ox Team to California; A Narrative of Crossing the Plains in 1860. Oakland, Cal.: Oakland Enquirer Publishing Co., 1910. xi, 139 pp.

Powers, Alfred, ed.
Buffalo Adventures on the Western Plains: Fifty Pictures from Old Prints. Portland, Ore.: Binfords and Mort, 1946. 66 pp.

Read, George Willis
A Pioneer of 1850 . . . The Record of a Journey Overland from Independence, Missouri, to Hanktown (Placerville), California, in the spring of 1850 . . . Illustrated from old prints. Boston: Little, Brown and Company, 1927. xxvi, 185 pp., illus.

Remington, Frederic
Crooked Trails. Illustrated by the author. New York: Harper & Bros., 1898. vi, 151 pp., illus.
———,
Pony Tracks. New York: Harper and Brothers, 1895. 269 pp., illus.

Rhodes, Eugene Manlove
West is West. New York: H. K. Fly and Co., 1917. 304 pp.

Richardson, Albert D.
Beyond the Mississippi From the Great River to the Great Ocean; Life and Adventure on the Prairies, Mountains, and Pacific Coast—1857-1867. Hartford, Conn.: American Publishing Co., 1867.

Robb, John S. (Solitaire)
Streaks of Squatter Life, and Far West Scenes; a series of humorous sketches descriptive of incidents and characters in the wild west. Phila.: Carey & Hart, 1847. 187 pp., illus.

Robinson, Phil
Sinners and Saints. A Tour Across the States, and Round Them; With Three Months Among the Mormons. Boston: Roberts Bros., 1883. x, 370 pp.

Root, Frank, and Connelley, W. E.
The Overland Stage to California. Topeka, Kansas: Crane and Co., 1901. 630 pp., illus.

Ross, William Wilson
10,000 Miles by Land and Sea. Toronto: J. Campbell & Son, 1876. viii, 284 pp.
———,
Roundup. Dallas, Texas: Arew Arnold, Banks Upshaw and Co., 1937.
"A collection of western stories, poems and articles for young people."

Rowse, A. L.
West Country Stories. New York: The Macmillan Company, 1947. vii, 222 pp.

Rusling, James Fowler
The Great West and Pacific Coast; or, Fifteen thousand miles by stage coach, ambulance, horseback, railroad, and steamer. . . among Indians, Mormons, miners and Mexicans. . . New York: Sheldon & Co., 1877. xx, 215 pp., illus.

Russell, Charles Marion
Good Medicine. Memories of the Real West, with an introduction by Will Rogers, and a biographical sketch by Nancy C. Russell. Garden City, N. Y.: Garden City Publ. Co., 1936.
———,
Studies of Western Life, With descriptions by Granville Stuart. New York: The Albertype Co., 1890. 12 plates.
———,
Trails Plowed Under. Garden City, New York: Doubleday, Page and Co., 1927.

Ruxton, George Frederick A.
Life in the Far West. Edinburgh: W. Blackwood and Sons, 1849. xvi, 312 pp.
Reprinted in 1915 by Nuting Publishing Co., N. Y., under title: *In The Old West.*

Sage, Rufus B.
Rocky Mountain Life; or Startling Scenes and Perilous Adventures in the Far West, During an Expedition of Three Years. Boston: Wentworth & Company, 1857. xiv, 363 pp., illus.

Santee, Ross
Men and Horses. New York and Lond.: The Century Co., 1926. Illus., 268 pp.

Schaeffer, Mrs. Mary T.
Old Indian Trails; incidents of camp and trail life, covering two years' experience through the Rocky Mountains of Canada. With 100 illustrations from photographs by the author and Mary W. Adams and a map. New York: G. P. Putnam's Sons, 1911. xiv, 364 pp., illus.

Seymour, Silas
Incidents of a Trip Through the Great Platte Valley to the Rocky Mountains and Laramie Plains in the Fall of 1866. New York: D. Van Nostrand, 1867. 130 pp.

Shoenberger, John H.
From Great Lakes to the Pacific; Pioneering the Wilderness in 1875. Illustrations by Ralph Pereida. San Antonio, Tex.: The Naylor Company, 1934. xvi, 211 pp., illus.

Snelling, William Joseph
Tales of Travels West of the Mississippi . . . With map and numerous engravings. Boston: Gray and Bowen, 1830. xvi, 162 pp., illus.

Sperry, Armstrong
Wagons Westward. Chicago, Philadelphia: John C. Winston Co., 1936. ix, 276 pp.

Steele, David McConnell
Going Abroad Overland; Studies of Places and People in the Far West. New York: G. P. Putnam's Sons, 1917. x, 197 pp.

Stegner, Wallace
Mormon Country. (American Folkways Series). New York: Duell, Sloan and Pearce and Co., 1942.
The myths and legends of the Mormons, their folkways and great leaders. It is the Saga of a great-people who played a magnificent part in the building of the West.

Stevens, Thomas Wood
Westward Under Vega. New York: Covici-Friede, 1938. 143 pp.
A narrative poem.

Stimson, Alexander Lovett
History of the Express Companies: and the Origin of the American Railroads. New York: No publisher, 1858.

Stoddard, Charles Augustus
Beyond the Rockies. New York: Charles Scribner's Sons, 1894. 214 pp.
Place names, tall stories, adventure tales, customs, social life.

Stong, Phil
Horses and Americans. New York: Frederick A. Stokes Co., 1939.

Targ, William, ed.
The American West. A Treasury of Stories, Legends, Narratives, Songs and Ballads of the American West, edited with an introduction by W. T. Cleveland and New York: The World Publishing Company, 1946. xii, 596 pp., illus.

Terrell, John Upton
Plume Rouge. New York: The Viking Press. 1942.
A novel of the westward movement in America of the men and women who early followed the trail of Lewis and Clark.

Thane, Eric
High Border Country. (American Folkways Series). New York: Duell, Sloan and Pearce Inc., 1942.
Indigenous material, colorful, dramatic, these tales of mountain men, of redskins, of prospectors, of soldiers, vigilantes, Chinese, cowboys, outlaws, copper barons, of farmers, herders, some good, some bad, some notorious.

————,
The Great West. Containing Narratives of the Most Important and Interesting Events in Western History—Remarkable Individual Adventures—Sketches of Frontier Life—Description of Natural Curiosities: To Which Is Appended Historical and Descriptive Sketches of Oregon, New Mexico, Texas, Minnesota, Utah, California, Washington, Nebraska, Kansas, etc., etc., etc. New York: George F. Tuttle, 1857; Cincinnati: Henry Howe.
Among other things, tells some anecdotes of Mike Fink.

Thomas, D. K.
Wild Life in the Rocky Mountains; or, The Lost Million Dollar Gold Mine. Illustrated by Alice Moseley and M. Reynolds. A true story of actual experiences in the Wild West. n. p.: C. E. Thomas Pub. Co., 1917. 221 pp., illus.

Twain, Mark
Roughing It. Hartford, Conn.: The American Publishing Co., 1899. 591 pp.
Roughing It comes nearer catching the energy, the youthfulness, the booming optimism, the recklessness, the lust for the illimitable in Western life than any other book." (Dobie).

Vaughn, Robert
Then and Now; or, Thirty-Six Years in the Rockies. Personal reminiscences . . . Minneapolis: Tribune Printing Co., 1900. 461 pp.

Vestal, Stanley
Fandango; Ballads of the Old West. Boston: Houghton Mifflin Co., 1927. 66 pp.
"A tale of Mountain Men in Taos— as fine a ballad as America has produced." (Dobie).

————,
Mountain Men. Boston: Houghton Mifflin Co., 1937. x, 296 pp., illus., bibl.

————,
Short Grass Country. (The American Folkways). New York: Duell, Sloan & Pearce, 1941. x, 304 pp.

————,
"The Histrionic West." *Space* 1 (No. 2): 13-16, 1934.

————, *The Missouri*. (Rivers of America Series). Illustrated by Gerblar Smith. New York: Farrar and Rinehart, 1945. 368 pp.
The romance of the "Big Muddy."

Walsh, C. C.
Early Days of the Western Range, a Pastoral Narrative. Boston: Sherman, French & Company, 1917. 81 pp., illus.
Poems of western life.

Welles, Alonzo Merritt
Reminiscent Ramblings. Illustrations by the author. Denver, Col.: The W. F. Robinson Printing Co., 1905. 459 pp., illus.

Webb, Walter Prescott
The Great Plains. Boston: Houghton Mifflin Co., 1931. xv, 525 pp., illus., bibl.
"No other work on the plains country goes so meatily into causes and effects." (Dobie).

Weekes, Mary
The Last Buffalo Hunter. New York: Thos. Nelson and Sons, 1939.
"Canada—but buffalo hunters were pretty much the same everywhere." (Dobie).

Weller, Earle Vonard
Ballads of Eldorado . . . with decorations by Barse Miller. San Francisco: The Book Club of California, 1940. x, 46 pp., illus.
Contents: The period of Spain and Mexico. — The days of Forty-Nine. —San Francisco.

Wellman, Paul I.
Death on the Prairie. The Thirty Years' Struggle for the Western Plains. New York: The Macmillan Co., 1934, 298 pp.. illus.

————, *The Bowl of Brass.* Philadelphia: J. B. Lippincott Co., 1944.
A dramatic novel of the days when men fought to convert the old cattle-empires into farming land.

West, Ray B., Jr., ed.
The Rocky Mountain Reader. New York: E. P. Dutton and Co., 1946. 436 pp.
Verse and prose by writers dealing with regional plot and background. The states included are Idaho, Wyoming, Montana, Nevada, Utah and Colorado. Among the writers one finds the names of Bernard de Voto, Wallace Stegner, Edwin Dorlo, Vardis Fisher and others.

————, *Western Prose and Poetry.* New York: Rufus A. Coleman, Harper and Brothers, 1932.
"Themes common to the Southwest."

White, Stewart Edward
Long Rifle and Ranchero. Garden City, N. Y.: Doubleday, Doran and Co., 1933.
"Fiction that is historic."

————, *Rawhide.* In: *Arizona Nights.* New York: Grosset and Dunlap, 1907. 351 pp., illus.
This story—"I rank first on the western theme, because it utilizes folk motifs about rawhide with such skill." (Dobie).

————, *The Last Frontier. Part 1: the Forty-Niners,* by Stewart Edward White. *Part 2: The Passing of the Frontier,* by Emerson Hough. New Haven: Yale University Press, 1918. vii, 273 pp., iii, 181 pp.

————, *The Westerners.* New York: Doubleday, Doran and Co., 1917. 344 pp.

Whiting, Lillian
The Land of Enchantment, From Pike's Peak to the Pacific . . . With illustrations from photographs. Boston: Little, Brown, and Company, 1904. xii, 347 pp.

Widney, Joseph Pomeroy
The Lure of the Land; an Idyll of the Pacific. Los Angeles, Cal.: Pacific Publishing Co., 1932. 194 pp.
Poems of the Californians.

Wilkey, Major Walter
Western Emigration, Narrative of a Tour to, and One Year's Residence in "Edensburgh" (Illinois), by Major Walter Wilkey, an Honest Yoeman of Mooseboro', State of Maine—New York: G. Claiborne, and others, Publishers, 1893.
Reprinted 1914 by William Abbott as Extra No. 28 of *The Magazine of History With Notes and Queries.*

Wright, W. H.
The Grizzly Bear. New York: Charles Scribner's sons, 1928.
"Best work ever written on the grizzly." (Dobie).

Wriston, Jennie Amelia
A Pioneer's Odyssey. Menasha, Wis.: George Banta Publishing Company, 1943. xii, 92 pp.

Yale University Library
William Robertson Coe Collection of Western Americana.
Described "as the finest collection of such source material east of the Rocky Mountains." Consists of original diaries, manuscripts, letters, photographs, newspapers, etc., etc. "The collection covers the period beginning with the Spanish exploration of Juan Pérez and Fray Tomas in 1774, which included British Columbia and parts of Washington and Oregon. It ends about 1890."

FOLKTALES—LEGENDS

Barclay, Lillian Elizabeth
"The Coyote: Animal and Folk Character." *TFSP* 14:36-104, 1938.
Coyote wisdom.

Bontemps, Arna, and Conroy, Jack
The Fast Sooner Hound. Boston: Houghton Mifflin, 1942.
A tall tale from the early days of railroading.

Borland, Hal
"The Magnetic West." *The New York Times Book Review,* Aug. 15, 1943.
Discussion of "The Log of the Cowboy," and other stories of Andy Adams.

Branch, D.
"Buffalo Lore and Boudin Blanc." *TFSP* 5: 126-136, 1920.

Browne, Charles F.
Artemus Ward: His Travels. New York: Carleton Publisher, 1866.

Carr, Harry
The West is Still Wild. Romance of the Past and Present. Boston: Houghton Mifflin, 1932. Anecdotes and short stories.

Clark, Howard D.
Lost Mines of the Old West. Buena Park, Cal.: Ghost Town Press, 1946. 64 pp.

Clifford, Josephine (Mrs. McCrackin)
Overland Tales. Philadelphia: Claxton, Remsen and Haffelfinger, 1877. 282 pp.

Coe, Urling C.
Frontier Doctor. New York: The Macmillan Co., 1939. 264 pp., illus.
"Lusty autobiography full of characters and anecdotes." (Dobie).

Cox, William T.
Fearsome Creatures of the Lumberwoods. With a Few Desert and Mountain Beasts. Washington, D. C.: Press of Judd and Detweiler, Inc. 1910.
Animal tales.

Davidson, Levette J.
"Western Campfire Tales." *CFQ* 2:177-190, 1943.

——————, and Blake, Forrester
Rocky Mountain Tales. Norman, Oklahoma: University of Oklahoma Press, 1947. 302 pp.
"Exhaustively the authors have searched through the works of those who recorded indiscriminately the fact and fiction of the building of the Rocky Mountain culture and economy, through copies of newspaper files of early and recent years, even in the oral lore of old timers, for the gems of unadorned fiction which constitute the essence of the folktale . . . (a book of) compelling reading and sound scholarship." (Austin E. Fife).

Dobie, J. Frank
The Longhorns. Boston: Little, Brown and Co., 1941. xiii, 388 pp.

——————,
"The Pacing of the White Mustang." *American Mercury*, Dec. 1927.

——————,
Tales of the Mustangs. Dallas: The Book Club of Texas, 1936. Illus.

Evans, Estwick
A Pedestrious Tour, of four thousand miles through the Western States and territories during the winter and spring of 1818. Interspersed with brief reflections upon a great variety of topics. Concord, N. H.: Printed by Joseph C. Spear, 1819. 256 pp.
Among the author's "variety of topics" Mike Fink also appears.

Finger, Charles Joseph
Frontier Ballads; Woodcuts by Paul Honoré. Garden City, N. Y.: Doubleday, Page & Co., 1927. 181 pp.

——————,
In Lawless Lands. New York: M. Kennerley, 1924. 292 pp.

Hall, James
Legends of the West: Sketches illustrative of the habits, occupations, privations, adventures and sport of the pioneers of the West. Cincinnati: R. Clarke & Co., 1869. xvi, 435 pp.
Contents: Harpe's Head. The backwoodsman. The divining rod. The Seventh Son. The missionaries. The Indian wife's lament. A legend of Carondelet. The intestate. Michael de Coucy. The emigrants. The barrack-master's daughter. The isle of the yellow sands.

Inman, Henry
Tales of the Trail; Short Stories of Western Life. Topeka, Kan.: Crane & Company, 1898. viii, 280 pp., illus.
Mainly historical,—some legendary.

Irving, Washington
Astoria; or Anecdotes of an enterprise beyond the Rocky Mountains. Philadelphia: Carey, Lea and Blanchard, 1836.

Jaeger, Edmund C.
Denizens of the Desert. Boston, Mifflin Co., 1922.
" 'Don Coyote', the roadrunner, and other characteristic animals."

Judson, Katharine Berry
Myths and Legends of the Great Plains. Chicago: A. C. Mc Clurg & Co., 1913. 204 pp.

Maxwell, William Audley
Crossing the Plains, Days of '57. San Francisco: Sunset Publishing House, 1915. 179 pp.
Pioneer anecdotes, transportation stories.

McClure's Magazine
Tales from McClure's: The West. London: Doubleday & Mc Clure Co., 1898. 195 pp., illus.

Page, Elizabeth
Wagons West. New York: Farrar and Rinehart, Inc., 1930. 361 pp.
Covered wagon and pioneer tales.

Peck, Leigh
Don Coyote. Boston: Houghton Mifflin Co., 1941.
For young readers.

Santschi, R. J.
Doodlebugs and Mysteries of Treasure Hunting. Oak Park, Ill.: Century Press, 1941. 156 pp.

——————,
Treasure Trails: The Book of Lost Mines and Buried Treasure. Glen Ellyn, Illinois: Century Press, 1942. enlarged edition, 183 pp.
The stories are laid in Africa, Abyssinia, the United States, especially in the West.

Sutton, Fred E., and MacDonald, A. B.
Hands Up! Stories of the Six-Gun Fighters of the Old West. Indianapolis: Bobbs-Merrill Co., 1927.
Contains a few cowboy songs.

Walterhouse, Roger Rilus
Bret Harte, Joaquin Miller, and the Western Local Color Story: a Study in the Origins of Popular Fiction. Chicago: University of Chicago Libraries, 1939. ii, 89 pp.

Wear, George W.
Scraps. Boston: Meador Publishing Company, 1934. 156 pp.
Anecdotes of western life and character.

CUSTOMS—BELIEFS—SUPERSTITIONS

Adams, W. H. Davenport
The Hunter and the Trapper of North America: from the French of Benedict Revoil. London: Nelson & Sons, 1874. 393 pp., illus.
Tales of the Ranger.

Ayer, I. Winslow
Life in the Wilds of America, and Wonders of the West in and Beyond the Bounds of Civilization. . . Grand Rapids, Mich.: The Central Publishing Company, 1880. 528 pp., illus.

Baldwin, James
In My Youth; From the Posthumous Papers of Robert Dudley. Indianapolis: Bobbs-Merrill Co., 1914. 493 pp.

Bandel, Eugene
Frontier Life in the Army. . . . edited by Ralph P. Bieber. Glendale, Calif.: The Arthur H. Clark Co., 1932. 330 pp., illus.

Barrows, William
The United States of Yesterday and of To-Morrow. Boston: Roberts Bros., 1888. viii, 432 pp.

Batty, Joseph
Over the Wilds to California; or, Eight Years From Home. Edited by Rev. John Simpson. Leeds: J. Parrott, 1867. 64 pp.

Beaugrand, Honoré
Six Mois dans les Montagnes—Rocheuses. Colorado—Utah—Nouveau-Mexique . . . Avec une préface de Louis Fréchette. Montréal: Granger Frères, 1890. 323 pp., illus.
Experiences and observations of life, customs and traditions in the Rocky Mountains.

Bechdolt, Frederick Ritchie
When the West Was Young. New York: The Century Co., 1922. 319 pp.
Social life, customs, tales.

Bell, Horace
On the Old West Coast: being further reminiscences of a ranger: Maj. Horace Bell. (Lanier Bartlett ed). New York: W. Morrow & Co., 1930. xiv, 336 pp., front., illus.
"Story of pioneer justice that resides more in folk anecdotes than in chroniclings."

————,
Reminiscences of a Ranger, or Early Times in California. Los Angeles: Yarnell, Coystile and Mathes, Printers, 1881, 457 pp.

Biddle, Ellen (McGowan)
Reminiscences of a Soldier's Wife. Philadelphia: J. B. Lippincott Company, 1907. 256 pp., illus.

Bishop, Isabella Lucy
A Lady's Life in the Rocky Mountains. New York: G. P. Putnam's Sons, 1879-80. xii, 296 pp., illus.

Boatright, Mody C.
"Law and Laughter on the Frontier." *The Southwest Review,* 30 (No. 2): 175-181, 1945.

Booth, George
Frontier Folk. New York: A. S. Barnes and Co., 1880. 26 pp.

Bowles, Samuel
Across the Continent: A Summer's Journey to the Rocky Mountains, the Mormons, and the Pacific States, with Speaker Colfax Springfield, Mass.: S. Bowles & Co., 1865. xix, 438 pp.

Bostwick, Arthur Elmore
The Different West, as seen by a transplanted Easterner. Chicago: A. C. Mc Clurg & Co., 1913. 184 pp.

Bowman, Anne
The Bear Hunters of the Rocky Mountains. Boston: Crosby and Nickals, 1863., 474 pp.

Briggs, Lloyd Vernon
California and the West, 1881, and Later. Boston: Wright and Potter Printing Company, 1931. xiv, 214 pp., illus.
A personal narrative in diary form.

Browning, Mesbach
Forty-Four Years of the Life of a Hunter. Philadelphia: J. B. Lippincott Co., 1928.
"Prodigal on bear and deer." (Dobie).

Buckskin Mose
Buckskin Mose, or Life From the Lakes to the Pacific. New York: Henry L. Hinton, 1873. 285 pp., illus.

Callahan, Genevieve A.
Sunset All-Western Foods; How to Cook Them, How to Serve Them. San Francisco: Lane Publishing Company, 1947.

Chaffin, Lorah B.
Sons of the West. Caldwell, Idaho: The Caxton Printers, 1941.
Historical and biographical sketches of early Wyoming.

Chalfant, Willie Arthur
Death Valley; the Facts. London: H. Milford, Oxford University Press, 1936. 160 pp.
Desert tales, superstitions.

Chapman, Arthur
The Pony Express. New York: G. P. Putnam's sons, 1932.

Colberg, Paul
Als fahrender Musikant in Californien; Eleb-
nisse und Abenteuer eines Deutschen . . .
Dresden: E. Haendcke, 1907. 216 pp.
  Adventures of a German musician in California
  —social life, customs and traditions.

Conner, A. Palmer
The Romance of the Ranches. Los Angeles:
Tith Insurance and Trust Co., n.d., 44 pp.
  Legend and tradition of the great land of giants.

Crawford, Charles Howard
*Scenes of Earlier Days in Crossing the Plains
to Oregon, and Experiences of Western Life.*
Petaluma, Cal.: J. T. Studdert, Book and Job
Printer, 1898. 186 pp., illus.

Dall, Caroline
My First Holiday; or, Letters Home from
Colorado, Utah, and California. Boston: Rob-
erts Bros., 1881. 450 pp.

Detling, Retta
*Sketches of Travel and Experiences Amidst
Western Scenes.* Shoreham, Vt., 1894. 90 pp.

Dick, Everett N.
The Sod House Frontier. New York: D. Appleton-Century Co., 1937.

———,
Vanguards of the Frontier; a Social History
of the Northern Plains and Rocky Mountains
from the Earliest White Contacts to the Coming of the Homemaker. New York: D. Appleton-Century Company, 1941. xvi, 574 pp., bibl.

Dickenson, Luella
*Reminiscenes of a Trip Across the Plains in
1846 and Early Days in California.* San Francisco: The Whitaker & Ray Company, 1904.

Dickson, Albert Jerome
Covered Wagon Days; a journey across the
plains in the sixties. Cleveland: The Arthur
A. Clark Co., 1929. 287 pp., illus.

Dobie, J. Frank
Pistols, Poker and Petite Mademoiselle in a
Stagecoach. In: *The Flavor of Texas.* Dallas:
Dealey and Lowe, 1936. 2877 pp., illus.

Dozier, Melville
"Reminiscences." *Historical Society of Southern California. Annual Publ.* (Los Angeles)
15 (part 4): 65-111, 1933.

Ellet, Elizabeth Fries
Summer Rambles in the West. New York:
J. C. Riker, 1853. 268 pp.

Farquar, Samuel T.
"The Use of Hard Money in the West." *CFQ*
8:149-150, 1944.
  How silver and gold, rather than paper currency,
  became traditional in the West.

Ferris, Warren Angus
Life in the Rocky Mountains. A Diary of the
Wanderings on the Sources of the Rivers
Missouri, and Colorado, from February, 1830,
to November, 1835. St. Louis: 1843-44. 56 pp.

Finley, Rev. James Bradley
Autobiography of Rev. James B. Finley; or,
Pioneer Life in the West. Edited by W. P.
Strickland. Cincinnati: Methodist Book Con-
cern, 1855. 455 pp., illus.

Fitzgerald, Oscar Penn
California Sketches. Nashville, Tenn.: Pub.
House of the M. E. Church, South, 1889. 208
pp.

Flack, Captain
The Texas Ranger, or Real Life in the Backwoods. London: Darton and Co., 1866. 319 pp.
  Also under the title: *A Hunter's Experience in
  the Southern States of America.*

Frederick, J. V.
Ben Holladay, the Stage Coach King. Glen-
dale, Calif.: Arthur H. Clark and Co., 1940.
Bibl.

Fulton, Maurice G., ed.
Diary and Leters of Josiah Gregg. Norman,
Okla.: University of Oklahoma Press, 1941.

Gerstäcker, Friedrich Wilhelm C.
Scenes of Life in California . . . San Francisco: J. Howell, 1942, xiii, 188 pp.

———,
Wild Sports—the Far West. London: G.
Routledge and Co., 1854. 396 pp., illus.
  "Nothing better on the backwoods life—the
  Mississippi Valley." (Dobie).

Gradet, Roger
Images du Far-West. 250 Illustrations et
Textes. Paris: Rieder, 1937. 172 pp., illus.
  On the life and manners of the Western folk.

Grey, William
A Picture of Pioneer Times in California . . .
with anecdotes and stories taken from real
life. San Francisco: W. M. Hinton & Co.,
1881. vii, 677 pp.

Hafen, LeRoy R., ed.
*Overland Routes to the Gold Fields, 1859,
From Contemporary Diaries.* Glendale, Cal.:
The Arthur H. Clark Co., 1942. 320 pp., illus.

———,
The Overland Mail. Cleveland: The A. H.
Clark Co., 1926. 361 pp.

———, **and Young, Francis Marion**
Fort Laramie and the Pageant of the West.
Glendale: Author, H. Clark Co., 1938. 429
pp., illus.

Haley, J. Evetts
Charles Goodnight, Cowman and Plainsman.
Boston: Houghton, Mifflin Co., 1936. 435 pp.,
illus.
  Remarkable observations in buffalo hunting.

Hamilton, William T.
My Sixty Years on the Plains. New York:
Forest and Stream Publishing Co., 1905. 244
pp.

Hanson, Joseph Mills
The Conquest of the Missouri. New York:
Rinehart and Company, 1946. 458 pp., illus.
   A fascinating story, with many interesting asides
   on the people and their customs,—of Captain
   Marsh, the man who named the 'Big Muddy.'"

Harte, Francis Bret
M'liss, an Idyll of Red Mountain. New York:
De Witt Publishing Co., 1873.
   Customs, social life.

————,
Sketches of the Sixties. San Francisco: Howell
Publishing Co., 1929.
   Characters, customs.

Haycox, Ernest
Action by Night. Indianapolis: Little, Brown
and Co., 1943.
   A novel of the Great Plains—from the Missouri
   to the Cascades, from the Rio Grande to Great
   Falls.

Hayes, Benjamin Ignatius
Pioneer Notes from the Diaries of Judge Benjamin Hayes: 1849-1875. Los Angeles: Privately printed, 1929. 307 pp.

Howe, Edgar Watson
Plain People. New York: Dodd, Mead & Company, 1929. 317 pp.

Irving, Washington
*Adventures of Captain Bonneville; or, Scenes
Beyond the Rocky Mountains of the Far West.*
London: R. Bentley, 1837. 3 vols.

Jaeger, Edmund Carroll
Denizens of the Desert. Boston: Houghton,
Mifflin Co., 1922. xiv, 299 pp.
   Superstitions, desert tales.

Judson, Edward Zane Carroll (Ned Buntline)
Norwood or Life on the Prairie. New York: W.
F. Burgess, 1850. 75 pp.

King, Frank Marion
*Longhorn Trail Drivers; Being a True Story
of the Cattle Drives of Long Ago . . .* Los
Angeles: Printed by Haynes Corporation, 1940.
xiii, 272 pp., illus.

————,
Pioneer Western Empire Builders, a true story
of the men and women of pioneer days . . .
profusely illustrated, including an original
illustration by Charles M. Russell. Pasadena,
Calif.: Trail's End. Publishing Co., 1946. 383
pp., illus.

Kirkland, Caroline M. S.
Forest Life. By the author of "A New Home."
New York: C. S. Francis & Co., 1842. 2 vols.

Lewis, Meriwether, and Clark, W.
*History of the Expedition Under the Command
of Captains Lewis and Clark, to the Sources
of the Missouri, Thence Across the Rocky
Mountains and down the river Columbia to
the Pacific Ocean.* Performed during the years
1804-5-6. By order of the government of the
United States. . . . Philadelphia: Bradford
and Inskeep, 1814. 2 vols.
   Numerous subsequent editions, with additional
   material, have appeared.

Leyburn, James Graham
Frontier Folkways. London: H. Milford, Oxford University Press, 1935. 29 pp.
   Frontier and pioneer life, manners, customs.

Lilienthal, Jesse
Gambler's Wife, the Life of Melinda Jenkins.
New York: Houghton, Mifflin Co., 1933.
   Life and customs on the frontier.

Lippincott, Sara Jane
New Life in New Lands: Notes of Travel.
New York: J. B. Ford and Co., 1873. vi,
413 pp.

Mann, E. B.
Gunsmoke Trail. New York: William Morrow, 1942. 279 pp.
   A western fiction filled with authentic life of the
   cow country of the old days.

Majors, Alexander
Seventy Years on the Frontier; Alexander
Majors' Memoirs of a lifetime on the border;
with a preface by "Buffalo Bill" (General
W. F. Cody) ed. by Colonel Prentiss Ingraham. Chicago: Rand, McNally & Company,
1893. 325 pp., illus.

McMurry, Charles Alexander
*Pioneers of the Rocky Mountains and the
West.* New York: The Macmillan Company,
1906. x, 248 pp., illus.

Meyer, Robert, Jr.
"Calendar of Western Folk Events." *Western Folklore* 7:56, 1948.

Mora, Jo
Trail Dust and Saddle Leather. New York:
Charles Scribner's Sons, 1946.
   "Although Mr. Mora adds little to the lore
   and history of the range, he has much to say
   that will be useful to the student of Western
   and Southwestern customs." (Stanley Walker).

Muir, John
Steep Trails. Edited by William Frederick
Badé. Boston: Houghton Mifflin Co., 1918. ix,
389 pp.
   A rich harvest of many observations of Western
   life—the people, the towns, the woodlands and
   mountains.

Olden, Sarah Emilia
Little Slants at Western Life; a notebook
of travel and reflection. New York: H. Vinal,
Ltd., 1927. 245 pp., bibl.
   General observations on life, customs, and Indians.

Parker, Paul M.
"Along the Dirty Plate Route." *CFQ* 3:16-20,
1944.
   The adventures of Henry Miller in California,
   Oregon and Nevada.

Parkman, Francis, Jr.
The California and Oregon Trail; Being
Sketches of Prairie and Rocky Mountain Life.
New York. G. P. Putnam, 1849. 448 pp., illus.

Pattie, James Ohio
The Hunters of Kentucky; or, The Trials and Toils of Trappers and Traders During an Expedition to the Rocky Mountains, New Mexico, and California. New York: W. H. Graham, 1847. 100 pp.

Postel, Charles (Charles Sealsfield or Francis Hardman, pseudonyms)
Frontier Life. New York: C. M. Saxton, 1859, 376 pp.

Ranahan, Thomas
The Overland Stage and Pony Express. Chicago: Privately printed, 1927.

Reid, Mayne
The Scalp Hunters. London: G. Routledge and Sons, 1892. 158 pp.
"Some deep-dyed pictures of Mountain men." (Dobie).

Richardson, Albert Deane
Beyond the Mississippi: From the Great River to the Great Ocean. Life and Adventures on the Prairies, Mountains and Pacific Coast . . . 1857-1867. Hartford, Conn.: American Publishing Co., 1867. xvi, 572 pp., illus.

Roe, Frances M. A.
Army Letters from an Officer's Wife, 1871-1888. Illustrated from contemporary photographs. New York: D. Appleton and Co., 1909. x, 387 pp., illus.

Santee, Ross
Sleepy Black. New York: Farrar and Rinehart, 1933.
Story of a horse for younger readers—Much about life and customs of the West.

Smith, Mary
Miss Smith Crosses the Plains. Edited by Dorothy Gardiner, 24 pp.
A diary in the form of a letter to her sister Mattie.

Stewart, Catharine
New Homes in the West. Nashville: Cameron and Fall, 1843. iv, 198 pp.

Strubberg, Friedrich Armand
The Backwoodsman; or, Life on the Indian Frontier . . . London: J. Maxwell and Co., 1864. iv, 428 pp., illus.

Sutley, Zachary Taylor
The Last Frontier. New York: The Macmillan Company, 1930. vi, 350 pp.
Life, customs and manners in the far West.

Swisher, James
How I Know, or, Sixteen Years' Eventful Experience. An authentic narrative, embracing a brief record of serious and severe service on the battle-fields of the South; a detailed account of hazardous enterprises . . . on the western frontier. Cincinnati, O.: The Author, 1880. x, 384 pp., illus.

Thwaites, Reuben Gold
Early Western Travels, 1748-1846; a series of annotated reprints of some of the best and rarest contemporary volumes of travel, descriptive of the aborigines and social and economic conditions in the middle and far West, during the period of early American settlement, edited with notes, introductions, index, etc. . . . Cleveland, O.: The A. H. Clark Company, 1904-07. 32 vols., illus.
An invaluable source for social life, customs and traditions, as well as historical data of early America and its people.

Twitchell, Ralph Emerson
Old Santa Fe. Santa Fe: Santa Fe New Mexican Publishing Corp., 1925. 488 pp.
Characters, customs.

Voelker, Frederic E.
"The Mountain Men and Their Part in the Opening of the West." *Missouri Historical Society Bulletin,* July 1947, pp. 151-162.

Waescher, Giesbert
Der Reiter von Chicago; ein Ritt durch den wilden Westen von Chicago nach San Franzisco, unter Indianern, Cowboys, Farmenn (sic) und Farbigen; selbsterlebtes . . . Minden in Westfalen: W. Köhler, 1924. 144 pp., illus.
An account of a trip from Chicago to San Francisco. Valuable information on customs, traditions and social life in the West.

Waters, Frank
Midas of the Rockies; Biography of Winfield Scott Sratton, millionaire miner. New York: Covici Friede, 1937.

Williams, Joel Strother
A Missourian in the Far West; or, The World as Seen by a Stranger. Carrollton, Mo.: Democrat Printing Company, 1906. viii, 72 pp.

Wilson, Rufus Rockwell
Out of the West. Illustrations by Sidney E. Fletcher. New York: The Press of the Pioneers, 1933. 452 pp., illus.

SPEECH

Adams, Ramon F.
Western Words. A Dictionary of the Range, Cow Camp and Trail. Norman, Okla.: University of Oklahoma Press, 1944. 182 pp.

Adkins, Nelson F.
"A Study of John G. Neihardt's Song of Three Friends." *AS* 3 (No. 4): 276-290, 1928.

Hale, Edward E.
"Geographical Terms in the Far West." *Dialect Notes* 6 (Part 6): 216-234, 1932.

Kessler, Heinrich
Der Verwendung de Mundart bei Bret Harte." In: *Beiträge Zur Erforschung der Sprache und Kultur Englands und Amerikas* von Wilhelm Horn, Vol. V. pp. 181-262. Breslau, 1928.
A minute discussion and examination of the dialect literature produced by Bret Harte.

McCarthy, Don
Language of the Mos Shorn-Western Terms.
Billings, Mont.: Montana Gazette Printing
Company, 1936. 24 pp.

McCoy, Colonel Tim
" 'Rough Rider, Bronco Buster, Rancher and
authority on the Indian sign language.' A
dictionary for dudes." *Harper's Bazaar*, June
1936, pp. 79, 141-144.
"Forty terms well known to Westerners defined."

Mullen, Kate
"Westernisms." *AS* 1 (No. 3:) 149-153, 1925.

Pardoe, T. E.
"Some Studies of Rocky Mountain Dialects."
Quarterly Journal of Speech 21: 345-355, 1935.

Pound, Louise
"Peter Funk, The Pedigree of a Westernism."
AS 4 (No. 3) :183-186, 1928.
The imaginary, mythical purchaser of goods that
fail to bring anticipated prices.

Raine, James W.
"The Speech of the Land of Saddle Bags."
Quarterly Journal of Speech Education 10:
230-237. 1924.

Schultz, J. R.
"Feature of Colorado Life as seen by Bayard
Taylor." *Colorado Magazine* 12: 161-168, 1935.
"A study of differences on Western speech as
illustrated in the contrast of Colorado terms with
those of California."

PLACE NAMES

Farquar, Francis P.
Place Names of the High Sierra. Publications of the Sierra Club, No. 62. San Francisco: Published by the Sierra Club, 1926. x,
128 pp.

Hale, Edward E.
"Geographical Terms in the Far West." *Dialect Notes* 6 (part 4) : 217-234, 1932.

Waterman, T. T.
"The Geographical Names Used by Indians of
the Pacific Coast." *Geographical Review* 12:
175-194, 1922.

FOLKSONG

See: Cowboy Songs, pp. 617-27; American
Characters, pp. 708-14.

GENERAL STUDIES AND COLLECTIONS

Dale, Edward Everett
"Culture on the American Frontier." *Ne-
braska History* 26:75-90, 1945. Illus.
Discussion of songs included.

Davidson, Levette Jay
"Songs of the Rocky Mountain Frontier." *CFQ*
2:89-112, 1943.
Texts only: Pike's Peak Parodies; Spanish
songs; Bull whackers and Stage Coach Drivers
songs; Cowboy songs and Christmas Carols.

Pound, Louise
"Some Texts of Western Songs." *SFQ* 3:25-
32, 1939.

CALIFORNIA

See: Lore and Song of the 49'ers., pp. 636-43;
The Cowboys, pp. 610-27; The Spanish-Americans, pp. 593-606.

FOLKLORE

BIBLIOGRAPHY

American Art Association, New York
*Tracts of the Colonies, Revolutionary War,
Americana, Historical Broadsides, Books,*
etc.; unusual collection of early almanacs and
newspapers; . . . many of which are the
property of Mr. H. C. Holmes, of San Francisco. New York: American Art Association,
1923. 198 pp.

"Bibliography of California Folklore." *CFQ*
2:63-70; 169-175; 245-251; 347-352; 1943.
Originally undertaken by the Southern California Writer's Project of the W.P.A. The material
was completed, verified and topical index prepared by Prof. Gustave O. Arlt of U.C.L.A.

Cowan, Robert Ernest, and Robert Granniss
*A Bibliography of the History of California,
1510-1930.* San Francisco: J. H. Nash, 1933.
3 vols.

Coy, Owen C.
Guide to the County Archives of California.
Sacramento: California State Printing Office,
1919. ix, 622 pp.

De Witt, Frederic M.
California Index Cards. A bibliography of the
history and literature of that part of the west
coast of North America known as California,
from the earliest period to the present . . .
Series 1-23. Oakland, Cal.: De Witt & Snelling, 1915–.

Gaer, Joseph, ed.
Bibliography of California Literature; Fiction
of the Gold-Rush Period; Drama of the Gold-
Rush Period; Poetry of the Gold-Rush Period. San Francisco, 1935. 123 pp., illus.
(California Relief Administration . . . Monograph, No. 8).

Hanna, Phil Townsend
Libros Californianos; or, Five Feet of California Books. Los Angeles: J. Zeitlin, Primavera Press, 1931. 74 pp.

Historical Records Survey
Inventory of the County Archives of California.
Prepared by the Historical Records . . .Works
Progress Administration. San Francisco, Cal.:
The Historical Records Survey, 1937.

Redlands, Cal. A. K. Smiley Public Library
*A List of Books in the A. K. Smiley Public
Library, Redlands, California, Relating to
California.* October 1914. n.p. 1914. 15 pp.

Society of California Pioneers, San Francisco
A List of Items in the Library and Museum of the Society of California Pioneers. San Francisco, 1931. 6 pp.

Wagner, Henry Raup
"The Templeton Crocker Collection of Californiana." *California Historical Society Quarterly* 19:79-85, 1940.

Works Progress Administration
Bibliography of California Fiction, Poetry and Drama in Three Volumes . . . Produced on a Works progress administration project, administrative project . . . Oakland, Cal., 1938. 3 vols.

PERIODICALS

California Folklore Quarterly. Published by the California Folklore Society. Berkeley and Los Angeles: University of California Press, Vol. 1, No. 1, Jan. 1942. Changed to *Western Folklore.*

California Life. v. 1, 1925—. Pasadena, Cal.: California Life, Inc., semi-monthly.

California Historical Society Quarterly. v. 1, 1922—. San Francisco.

California History Nugget. California State Historical Association, Berkeley. V. 1-2, No. 2—January-November 1924. n. s. V. 2, October 1928—. n. s. V. 1 not published. Suspended May 1931—March 1934.
Devoted to the story of the Golden West.

Historical Society of Southern California Publications. Quarterly. Los Angeles, Calif. V. 1, 1884—. Volume numbering begins with 2, 1891; V. 2, pt. 2, never issued.

Land of Sunshine; Out West; Los Angeles, California. Out West 1-51 June 1894—Apr. 1923. 1-15, 894—Dec. 90 as *Land of Sunshine.* Suspended May to Nov. 1910. Merged into *Overland Monthly.*

Out West Magazine, Los Angeles, Calif. V. 1-51, June 1894—April 1923. 1-15 1894—Dec. 1901 as *Land of Sunshine.* May-November 1910 suspended, merged into *Overland Monthly.* 33-40 also as New Series, V. 1-8.

Overland Monthly and Out West Magazines, San Francisco. V. 1-15 July 1868—December 1875. Series 2, 1-93, No. 4, 1883—July 1935. Suspended 1876—1882; February 1933; September 1934—February, May 1935, never published. Numbering irregular.

Quarterly of the Society of California Pioneers. V. 1, 1924—. San Francisco: Published by Order of the Board of Directors, 1924.

The Golden West. V. 1, 1919—V. 7, 1925 Los Angeles: C. E. Stokes, 1919-1925. Semi-monthly.

The Grizzly Bear. V. 1, 1908-1932. Los Angeles, etc.: Grizzly Bear Publishing Company, 1908-1932.

The Pioneer: or, California Monthly Magazine. V. 1-4; Jan. 1854-Dec. 1855. San Francisco, Cal.: Le Count and Strong, etc., 1854-1855.

Touring Topics. Automobile Club of Southern California, Los Angeles. V. 1, 1909—. 1-25, 1909-1933 as *Touring Topics.*

GENERAL STUDIES AND COLLECTIONS

Alger, Horatio, Jr.
Joe's Luck; or, *A Boy's Adventures in California.* New York: A. L. Burt, 1887.

Altrocchi, Julia Cooley
"Folklore of the Old California Trail." *CFQ* 3:1-11, 1944.

————,
The Old California Trail: Traces in Folklore and Furrow. Caldwell, Idaho: The Caxton Printers, 1945. 327 pp.

Anonymous
"John Bidwell." *The Grizzly Bear* 1:25—, (October) 1907.

Atherton, Gertrude
Golden Gate Country. (American Folkways.) New York: Duell, Sloan and Pearce, 1945. xi, 256 pp., bibl.

————,
California, an Intimate History. Illustrated. New York: Boni and Liveright, 1927. x, 356 pp., illus.

————,
The Splendid Idle Forties; Stories of Old California . . . with illustrations by Harrison Fisher. New York: The Macmillan Company, 1902. vii, 389 pp.
Rich in romance and legend of the Mexicans and others in California.

Atkinson, Fred William
Argonauts of 1769. Watsonville, California: Pajaronian Press, 1936. 166 pp.
Anecdotes, tales, customs.

Ayers, James J.
Gold and Sunshine Reminiscences of Early California; illustrations from the collection of Charles B. Turrill. Boston: R. G. Badger, 1922. xiv, 359 pp., illus.

Bailey, Paul D.
Sam Brannan and the California Mormons. Los Angeles: Westernlove Press, 1943.
Story of the Mormons in early California history.

————,
The Gay Saint. Hollywood, Calif.: Murray and Gee, 1944. 301 pp.
The incredible adventures of Sam Brannan the man who became California's first millionaire, in the Gold-Dust days.

Baird, Mabel
" 'Pony Bob' and His Comrades of the Pony Express." *Overland Monthly* 64: 598-, 1932.

Baker, George H.
"Records of a California Residence." *Society of California Pioneers. Quarterly* (San Francisco) 8: 39-70, 1931. Illus.

Bancroft, Hubert Howe
California Inter Pocula. San Francisco: The History Co., 1888. v-vi, 828 pp. The works of H. H. Bancroft, Vol. XXXV.

————,
California Pastoral; 1769-1848. San Francisco: The History Co., 1888. vi, 808 pp. bibl. (pp. 751-792.) The works of H. H. Bancroft, Vol. XXXIV.

Barker, Charles Albro, ed.
Memoirs of Elisha Oscar Crosby. Reminiscences of California and Guatemala from 1849 to 1864. San Marino, Calif.: The Huntington Library, 1945. xxvi, 119 pp., illus., index.

Bechdolt, Fred R.
"Death Valley, Strange Pocket in the Sierras." *Arrowhead Magazine* 2:1-, 1906 (June).

Beckwourth, James P.
The Life and Adventures of James P. Beckwourth. New York: Alfred A. Knopf, 1931. 405 pp.
Tall tales, anecdotes, adventure.

Beechey, Frederick William
Narrative of a Voyage to the Pacific and Bering's Strait in the Years 1825-26-27-28. Philadelphia: Carey and Lea, 1832. 493 pp.

Beers, George A.
Vasquez; or The Hunted Bandits of the San Joaquin. New York: R. M. DeWitt, 1875. 141 pp.

Bell, Horace
On the Old West Coast. New York: W. Morrow and Co., 1930. 336 pp., illus.
Social life, customs, superstition, tall tales, characters, trials, fakes, fads, lost mines.

————,
Reminiscences of a Ranger; or Early Times in Southern California. The foreword is written by Arthur M. Ellis and the illustrations are by James S. Bordrero. Santa Barbara: W. Hebberd, 1927. 490 pp., illus.

Bidwell, John
A Journey to California. San Francisco: J. H. Nash, 1937. 48 pp.

————,
"Early California Reminiscences." *Out West* 20: 76-78, 182-188, 285-287, 377-379, 467-468, 559-562; 21: 79-80, 193-195, 1904.

Blanco, Antonio Fierro de
The Journey of the Flame. Boston: Houghton Mifflin Company, 1933.
"Bully and flavorsome; the Californias." (Dobie).

Bonsal, Stephen
Edward Fitzgerald Beale, a Pioneer in the Path of Empire. New York and London: G. P. Putnam's Sons, 1912. 312 pp.

Bolton, Herbert Eugene
Anza's California Expeditions. Berkeley: University of California Press, 1930. 5 Vols.

Bowman, Mary
Bowman's Scrapbook: 1887-1914. Los Angeles: Los Angeles Public Library, 1914. 5 Vols.
Bandits, characters, tales, anecdotes, social life, customs.

Bradley, Glen Danford
The Story of the Pony Express. Chicago: A. C. McClurg Co., 1913.

Brewer, William Henry
Up and Down California in 1860-1864 . . . With a preface by Russell H. Chittenden. New Haven: Yale University Press; London: H. Milford, Oxford University Press, 1930. xxx, 601 pp., illus.

Browne, John Ross
Crusoe's Island. New York: Harper and Brothers, 1864. 436 pp.
Adventure tales of the early days.

Bryant, Edwin
What I Saw in California; being the journal of a tour, by the emigrant route and south pass of the Rocky Mountains, across the continent of North America . . . and through California, in the years 1846, 1847 . . . New York: D. Appleton & Co., 1849. 480 pp.

Burleigh, George Shepard
Signal Fires on the Trail of a Pathfinder. New York: Dayton and Burdick, 1856. 162 pp.
Folk poem.

Burnett, Peter Hardeman
Recollections and Opinions of an Old Pioneer. New York: D. Appleton and Co., 1880. xiii, 448 pp.

Camp, William Martin
San Francisco: Port of Gold. (Seaport Series). Illustrated. New York: Doubleday and Co., 1948. 518 pp.
Regional lore, customs and incidents fill its many pages.

Carr, Harry
Los Angeles, City of Dreams. New York and London: D. Appleton-Century Co., Inc., 1935. 403 pp.
Customs, social and civic life, tall tales, anecdotes.

Carter, Charles Franklin
The Missions of Nueva California, a historical sketch, illustrated from drawings by the author. San Francisco: The Whithaker and Ray Co., 1900. xv, 189 pp.

Caughey, John Walton
California. New York: Prentice-Hall, 1940.
xiv, 680 pp.
  Has a good bibliography (pp. 607-649).

Chase, Joseph Smeaton
California Coast Trails. Boston and New York:
Houghton, Mifflin Co., 1913. 326 pp.

Chickering, Allen L.
"Bandits, Borax and Bears. A Trip to Searles
Lake in 1874." *California Historical Society,
Quarterly* 17: 99-117, 1938.

Clealand, Robert Glass
A History of California, the American Period:
New York: The Macmillan Co., 1922. 512 pp.
  Customs, social life, legend, characters.

————,
California in our Times: 1900-1940. New York:
Alfred A. Knopf, 1947.
  The whole story of one of the most vivid phe-
  nomena of American life: the spectacular growth
  of California in our century.

————,
From Wilderness to Empire. New York: Alfred A. Knopf, 1947. 388 pp.
  A history of California from its discovery in
  1542, through its days as a Mexican colony, the
  gold rush, and almost virtual control by the
  Central Pacific Railroad, to the beginning of a
  new era in 1900.

————,
Pathfinders. Los Angeles: Powell Publishing Co., 1929. 452 pp.

Clyman, James
"His Diaries and Reminiscences." *California
Historical Society Quarterly.* 4:105-141, 272-
283, 307-360; 5:44-84, 109-138, 255-282, 378-
401; 6:58-68, 1925-1927.

————,
*James Clyman, American Frontiersman, 1792-
1881;* the adventures of a trapper and covered wagon emigrant as told in his own reminiscences and diaries; edited by Charles L.
Camp. San Francisco, Cal.: California Historical Society,, 1928. 247 pp., illus.

Colburn, Mrs. Frona Eunice Wait (Smith)
The Kingship of Mt. Lassen. San Francisco:
Nemo Publishing Co., 1922. 69 pp.
  Myth, legend, place names, characters.

Colton, Walter
Three Years in California: 1846-1849. Cin-
cinnati: H. W. Derby and Co., 1851. 456 pp.
  Customs, social life, characters, tales.

Cone, Mary
Two Years in California. Chicago: S. C. Griggs
and Co., 1876. 238 pp.
  Place names, social life, customs, characters.

Cowan, Robert Ernest
Forgotten Characters of Old San Francisco.
Los Angeles: The Ward Ritchie Press, 1938.
65 pp.
  Tales of odd characters.

Coy, Owen Cochran
The Great Trek. San Francisco and Los An-
geles: Powell Publishing Co., 1931. 349 pp.
  Characters, place names, superstition.

Coyner, David H.
The Lost Trappers. New York: Hurst and Co.,
1892. 225 pp.

Crossby-Batt, Jil Lillie Emma
The Last of the California Rangers. New York
and London: Funk and Wagnalls, 1928.
299 pp.

Dana, Julian
The Sacramento: River of Gold. (American
River Series). Illustrated by John O'Hara
Cosgrave. New York: Farrar and Rinehart,
1939. 294 pp., illus.

Davis, Carlyle Channing
The True Story of Ramona. New York: Dodge
Publishing Co., 1914. 265 pp.
  Southern California lore.

Davis, John Francis
California, Romantic and Resourceful. San
Francisco: A. M. Robertson, 1914. 80 pp.
  Weather lore, characters.

Dellenbaugh, Frederick Samuel
Fremont and '49: The story of a remarkable
career and its relation to the exploration and
development of our western terrritory, especially California. New York: G. P. Putnam's
Sons, 1914. 547 pp.

Dixon, William Hipworth
White Conquest. London: Chatto and Windus,
1876. 2 Vols.

Drury, Aubrey
California, an Intimate Guide. New York and
London: Harper and Brothers, 1939. 592 pp.

Dumas, Alexandre
A Gil Blas in California. Los Angeles: The
Primavera Press, 1933. 170 pp.
  Tall stories, customs, social life.

"Early California History." *Land of Sunshine*
(Los Angeles), 14:486-496, 1901.
  A translation into English of Don Miguel Costanso's account of the expeditions of 1769 and
  the first European settlements in California.

Eldredge, Z. Skinner
The Beginnings of San Francisco. San Francisco: Z. S. Eldredge, 1912. 2 vols.

Ellerby, Rose Lucile
Tales of California Yesterdays . . . illustra-
tions by Howard Willard. Los Angeles, Cal.:
W. T. Potter, 1916. 205 pp., illus.
  Fiction using local color, customs, and legends.

Engelhardt, Zephyrin
The Franciscans in California. Harbor Springs,
Mich.: Holy Childhood Indian School. 1897.
516 pp.

Evans, Albert S.
A La California; or, Sketches of Life in the Golden State: 1849-1872. San Francisco: A. L. Bancroft & Co., 1873. 379 pp., illus.
Place names, legends, superstition, anecdotes, social life, customs.

Fairfield, Asa Merrill
Fairfield's Pioneer History of Lassen County, California. San Francisco: H. S. Crocker Co., 1916. 506 pp.
Characters, legends, pioneer tales.

Federal Writers' Project
A History of the Ranchos in San Diego County. San Diego: Union Title Insurance and Trust Co., 1939, 86 pp.
Customs, social life, legend, practice.

————,
California; A Guide to the Golden State, compiled and written by the Federal Writers' Project of the Works Progress Administration for the State of California . . . New York: Hastings House, 1939. xxxi, 713 pp., illus., bibl.

————,
Los Angeles: A Guide. New York: Hastings House, 1940.
Place names, customs, legends.

————,
San Diego: A California City. San Diego Historical Society, 1937. 138 pp.
Place names, legend, customs.

————,
San Francisco Bay Area: A Guide. New York: Hastings House, 1940.
Place names, customs, legends.

Fisher, Anne B.
The Salinas, Upside-Down River. (Rivers of America Series.) Illustrated by Walter K. Fisher. New York: Farrar and Rinehart, 1945. 316 pp.
"It has genuine local quality." (George R. Stewart).

Forbes, Alexander
California: A History of Upper and Lower California. San Francisco: J. H. Nast, 1937. 229 pp.
Place names, characters, customs.

Giffen, Guy J.
"Notes on Some Lesser California Desperadoes." *Westways* 27: 22-, 1937 (May).

Gill, William
California Letters of William Gill: Edited by Eva Turner Clark. New York: Downs Printing Co., 1922.
Pioneer tales, ancdotes.

Graves, Jackson Alpheus
My Seventy Years in California: 1857-1927. Los Angeles: The Times and Mirror Press, 1927. 478 pp.
Customs, anecdotes, legends, civic and social life.

Green, Julia Boynton
This Enchanting Coast; Verse on California Themes. Los Angeles: The Times-Mirror Press, 1928. 63 pp.

Griffin, John S.
A Doctor Comes to California; The Diary of John S. Griffin, M. D. San Francisco, Calif.: California Historical Society, 1943. 97 pp.
A Journal of a doctor's experiences on the old Santa Fe and Gila trail.

Grigsby, Russell C.
From the Backwoods of Old Tuolumne. Stockton, Calif.: The author, 108 E. Weber Ave., 1943. 154 pp., illus.
Consists of 40 of the author's columns, and illustrated with 38 photos.

H., E. M.
Ranch Life in California. London: W. H. Allen and Co., 1886. 171 pp.
Customs, social life.

Habberton, John
Romance of California Life; Illustrated by Pacific Slope Stories, Thrilling, Pathetic and Humorous. New York: Baker, Pratt & Co., 1880. 502 pp., illus.

Hafen, Leroy R.
The Overland Mail, 1849-69. Cleveland: Arthur H. Clark, 1926.

Haskins, C. W.
Argonauts of California. New York: Fords, Howard and Hulbert, 1890. 501 pp.
Customs, social life, characters, anecdotes.

Hawthorne, Hildegarde
California's Missions, Their Romance and Beauty. Illustrated by E. H. Suydam. New York: D. Appleton-Century Co., 1943. 229 pp.
She writes history with a salty and commonsensible manner.

Hazard, Caroline
The Golden State; a semi-centennial collection of California verse written from 1889 to 1939. Santa Barbara, Cal.: The Schauer Printing Studio, 1939. 39 pp.

Henshall, John A.
"A Bandit of the Golden Age." *Overland Monthly* 53: 313-, 1925.

————,
"Tales of the Early California Bandits." *Overland Monthly* 53: 403, 1925.

Hildrup, Hesse S.
The Missions of California and the Old Southwest. Chicago: A. C. McClurg and Co., 1907. 100 pp., illus.

Hittell, Theodore Henry
Adventures of James Capen Adams. New York: Charles Scribner's Sons, 1911, 373 pp.
Early-day hunting tales, tall stories.

Huntington Library, San Marino, Calif.
California From Legendary Island to Statehood; an exhibition at the Huntington Library. San Marino, 1933. 27 pp., illus.

Hutton, William Rich
California, 1847-1852. San Marino, Calif.:
The Huntington Library, 1942. 56 plates.
His drawings, reproduced from originals in the
Huntington Library, with an Introduction by
Willard O. Waters.

———,
Glances at California, 1849-1853. San Marino,
Calif.: The Huntington Library, 1942, 86 pp.
Diaries and letters of William Rich Hutton,
surveyer, with a brief memoir and notes by
Willard O. Waters.

Jackson, Joseph Henry
*Continent's End: A Collection of California
Writing.* New York: Whittlesey House, 1944.
415 pp.

Jacobson, Pauline
City of the Golden 'Fifties. Berkeley and
Los Angeles: University of California Press,
1941. xvi, 290 pp.
The story and lore of San Francisco.

James, George Wharton
California, Romantic and Beautiful. Boston:
The Page Co., 1914. 433 pp.

———,
Heroes of California. Boston: Little, Brown
Co., 1910. 515 pp.

———,
In and Out of the Old Missions of California:
An Historical and Pictorial Account of the
Franciscan Missions. Boston: Little, Brown
and Co., 1905. 392 pp., illus.

Judson, Edward Zane Carroll (Ned Buntline)
Red Dick, the Tiger of California. New York:
Street & Smith, 1890. 210 pp.

Kahn, Jules
Histoires Californiennes (1866-1875.) Préface du Suzanne Teissier. Paris; Sansot, 1925.
230 pp.
Historic and folk tales.

Kanderdine, Thaddeus S.
*A California Tramp and Later Footprints; or,
Life on the Plains and in the Golden State
Thirty Years Ago.* Philadelphia: Press of
Globe Printing House, 1888. 415 pp.
Folk drama, stage, theater tales.

Keeler, Charles Augustus
Sequoia Sonnets. Berkeley, Calif.: Pub. at the
Sign of the Live Oak, 1919. 113 pp.

Keffer, Frank McCleunan
History of the San Fernando Valley. Glendale,
California: Stillman Printing Co., 1934. 329
pp.
Local legend, customs, characters.

Kentt, Ernest
The Crimson Trail of Joaquin Murieta. Los
Angeles: Wetzel Publishing Co., 1928. 215 pp.

Kip, W. I.
The Crimson Trail of Joaquin Murieta, Los
Monthly 2: 401-, 1885.

Kirchhoff, Theodor
"Norton the First." *Society of California Pioneers Quarterly,* 5 (No. 4): 205-, 1928.

Layne, Joseph Gregg
"Three Notorious Bandits." *California Historical Society Quarterly* 13: 327-, 1934.

Lyman, George D.
Ralston's Ring. California Plunders the Com-
stock Lode. New York: Charles Scribners'
Sons. 1937.

Mackey, Margaret Gilbert
Cities in the Sun. Los Angeles: Goodwin Press,
1938. 181 pp., illus.
The story and lore of Los Angeles.

MacMullen, Jerry
Paddle-Wheel Days in California. Illustrated
by the author. Palo Alto, Calif.: Stanford
University Press, 1945. 157 pp.
"A fascinating book for anyone interested in
California or in steamboats—an outstanding ex-
ample of how local history should be written."
(George R. Stewart).

Majors, Alexander
Seventy Years on the Frontier. Chicago and
New York: Rand McNally and Co., 1893.
325 pp.
Anecdotes, frontier life.

Marryat, Francis Samuel
Mountains and Molehills. New York: Harper
and Brothers, 1855. 393 pp.
Tales of early days.

Maxwell, Hu
Idylls of the Golden Shore. New York: G. P.
Putnam's Sons, 1889. viii, 233 pp.

Mayo, Morrow
Los Angeles. New York: A. A. Knopf Co.,
1933.
Social life, sports, games, tall tales, anecdotes.

McCue, James
Twenty-one Years in California. San Fran-
cisco: Privately printed, 1878.
Tales of the stagecoach days.

McGlashan, Charles Fayette
History of the Donner Party. Sacramento:
H. S. Crocker Co., Printers, 1902. 261 pp.

McGroarty, John Stephen
California, Its History and Romance. Los
Angeles: Grafton Publishing Co., 1911. 393 pp.

———,
California of the South. Chicago, Los Angeles,
etc.: S. J. Clarke Publishing Co., Inc., 1933-
1935. 5 Vols.

McKinstry, George, Jr.
*Thrilling and Tragic Journal While on a
Journey Over-land to California: 1846-47.*
West Hoboken, New Jersey: Biber, 1917.
Story of Donner tragedy.

McLeer, Mary
The Story of California. Lithographs by C. H.
DeWitt. New York: Harper and Brothers,
1944. unpaged.
A rich and colorful cavalcade of California's
characters and events.

McWilliams, Carey
Southern California Country: An Island on the Land (American Folkways Series.) New York: Duell, Sloan, and Pearce, 1946. xiii, 387 pp.
Although the work is mainly a socio-economic study, the author nevertheless includes a great deal of the folklore background. "All the tales of the famous and forgotten characters— are arrayed by Mr. McWilliams." (Alan Cranston).

Meriwether, Lee
The Tramp at Home. New York: Harper and Brothers, 1889. 296 pp.
California conditions, local tales, customs, social life.

Merrill, Olin S.
Mysterious Scott, the Monte Cristo of Death Valley. Chicago: privately printed, 1906.

Merwin, Henry Childs
The Life of Bret Harte. Boston: Houghton, Mifflin Co., 1911. 362 pp.
Pioneer characters and tales.

Miller, Max
Harbor of the Sun; The Story of the port of San Diego. New York: Doubleday, Doran and Co., 1940.

Moody, Alan
Sleep in the Sun. Illustrated by Edwin Earle. Boston: Houghton Mifflin Co., 1945. 137 pp.
A novel presenting a "series of engaging incidents offering the warm flavor of life in the canyon." (Theodore Pratt).

Mooso, Josiah
The Life of Josiah Mooso. Winfield, Kansas: Telegram, 1888.

Morrison, Gouverneur Merion
Junipero Serra, Padre Pioneer. Santa Barbara, Calif.: Denton-Coogan, 1934.
Characters, place names, beliefs.

Mortimer, Charles
Life and Career of the Most Skillful and Noted Criminal of His Day—Charles Flin of Mass. Sacramento: Record, 1873.

Newmark, Harris
Sixty Years in Southern California—1853-1913; edited by Maurice H. and Marco R. Newmark. New York: The Knickerbocker Press, 1926. xxxiii, 732 pp., 172 illustrations, 2nd ed. rev.

North, A. W.
The Mother of California. San Francisco: P. Elder & Co., 1908.

Norton, Henry Kittredge
The Story of California, From the Earliest Days to the Present. Chicago: A. C. McClurg and Co., 1913. 390 pp.
Crime, social life, customs, trials, humor.

Older, Cora Miranda
California Missions and Their Romances; foreword by Herbert E. Bolton, preface by R. L. Duffus. New York: Coward McCann, 1938. xxiv, 314 pp., illus.

Older, Fremont
My Own Story. New York: The Macmillan Co., 1926. 340 pp.

Parkinson, Jessie Heaton
Adventuring in California, Yesterday, Today, and Day Before Yesterday; With Memoirs of Bret Harte's "Tennessee." San Francisco: Harr Wagner Publishing Co., 1921. xxv, 120 pp., illus.
Place names, social life, customs.

Pattie, James O.
Personal Narrative. Cincinnati: A. H. Flint, 1838. 300 pp.

Paz, Ireneo
Life and Adventure of the Celebrated Bandit Joaquin Murieta, His Exploits in the State of California. Translated by Francis P. Belle. Chicago: Regan Publishing Corp., 1925. 174 pp.

Peattie, Roderick W.
The Pacific Coast Ranges. (American Mountain Series.) New York: Vanguard Press, 1946. illus., maps.

————,
The Sierra Nevadas: The Range of Light. Introduction by Donald Culross Peattie. Illus. New York: The Vanguard Press, 1947. 398 pp.
Not much on folklore but a bit on the fringe in Idwal Jones' chapter.

Pennoyer, Albert Sheldon, ed.
This Was California; a collection of woodcuts and engravings reminiscent of historical events, human achievements and trivialities from pioneer days to the gay nineties. New York: G. P. Putnam's Sons, 1938. 224 pp., illus.

Peixotto, Ernest Clifford
Romantic California. New York: C. Scribner's Sons, 1927. 272 pp.
Legend, folk drama, mystery plays, early-day terms, social life, wedding and christening celebrations and customs.

Potter, David M., ed
Trail to California. The Overland Journal of Vincent Geiger and Wakeman Bryerly. New Haven: Yale University Press, 1945. lxviii, 200 pp., bibl.

Powell, E. Alexander
Gentlemen Rovers. New York: C. Scribner's Sons, 1913. 245 pp.
Tales of the early-day uprisings in California.

Putnam, George Palmer
Death Valley and Its Country. (American Folkways Series.) New York: Duell, Sloan and Pearce, 1946.
Another notable contribution in the American Folkways Series. All the legends, tales, characters come to life again.

Rensch, Hero Eugene
Historic Spots in California; the Southern Counties; with an introduction by Robert Glass Cleland. Stanford University, Cal.: Stanford University Press, 1932. xvii, 267 pp.

———,
Historic Spots in California: Valley and Sierra Counties; with an introduction by Robert Glass Cleland. Stanford University, Cal.: Stanford University Press, 1933. xxiii, 597 pp.

Revere, Joseph Warren
Keel and Saddle: A Retrospect of Forty Years of Military and Naval Service. Boston: J. R. Osgood and Company, 1873. xiii, 360 pp.

Richman, Irving Berdine
California Under Spain and Mexico: 1535-1847. Boston and New York: Houghton Mifflin Co., 1911. 541 pp.
Social life, customs, characters, trials.

Ridge, John Rolland
History of Joaquin Murieta. Hollister, Calif.: Evening Free Lance, 1927. 84 pp.

Rider, Fremont
Rider's California. New York: The Macmillan Co., 1925. 667 pp.
Place names, legend, characters.

Riesenberg, Felix, Jr.
Golden Gate: The Story of San Francisco Harbor. New York: A. A. Knopf, 1940.

Root, Frank Albert, and Connelley, William Elsey
The Overland Stage to California. Topeka, Kansas: The authors, 1901. 630 pp.

Royce, Josiah
California, From the Conquest of 1846 to the Second Vigilance Committee in San Francisco. Boston and New York: Houghton Mifflin and Co., 1886. 513 pp.

Ryan, William R.
Personal Adventure in Upper and Lower California in 1848-49. With the author's experience of the mines. Illustrated by twenty-three drawings. London: W. Shoberl, 1850. 2 vols.

Sands, Frank
A Pastoral Prince; the History and Reminiscences of J. W. Cooper. Santa Barbara, Calif.: no publisher, 1893. 190 pp.
Pioneer tales, customs, practices, characters.

Saunders, Charles Francis
Finding the Worthwhile in California. New York: R. M. McBride and Co., 1923. 229 pp.
Place and mountain names, local legend, plant lore, local tales and legends, tradition, social life.

———,
Southern Sierras of California. Boston: Houghton Mifflin Co., 1923. 367 pp.
Place and mountain names, local legend, plant lore, local legends and tales, tradition, social life. life.

———,
With Flower and Trees in California. New York: R. M. McBride and Co., 1914.
Place and mountain names, local legend, plant lore, local tales and legends, tradition, social life.

Sawyer, Eugene Taylor
The Life and Career of Tiburcio Vasquez. San Francisco: Bacon and Co., Printers, 1875. 48 pp.

Scherer, James Augustin Brown
Lion of the Vigilantes. Indianapolis: The Bobbs, Merrill Co., 1939. 335 pp.
Early-day characters, place names, customs, social life, crime, law and law enforcement.

Sexton, Ella
Stories of California. New York and London: The Macmillan Co., 1912. 211 pp.
Tall stories, local legends, customs, social life, tradition.

Shaw, David Augustus
El Dorado; or California as seen by a Pioneer, 1850-1900. Los Angeles, Cal.: B. B. Baumgardt and Company, 1900. vii, 313 pp., illus.

Shay, John C.
Twenty Years in the Backwoods of California. Boston: The Roxburgh Publishing Co., Inc., 1923. 142 pp.
Crime, early-day trappers and pioneer tales.

Sherman, Edwin Allen
The Life of Admiral John Drake Sloat. Oakland, Calif.: Carruth and Carruth, Printers, 1902. 258 pp.

Shuck, Oscar Tully
The California Scrapbook; A Repository of Useful Information and Select Reading . . . San Francisco and New York: H. H. Bancroft and Co., 1869. 704 pp., illus.
Folk poems, tales, anecdotes . . . "mainly culled from the various newspapers and periodicals of the Pacific coast."

Smith, Charles W.
Journal of a Trip to California: Across the continent from Weston, Mo., to Weber Creek, Calif., in the summer of 1850. Edited with an introduction and notes, by R. W. G. Vail. New York: The Cadmus Book Shop, 1920. 79 pp.

Smith, Henry N.
"The Western Hero in the Dime Novel". *Southwest Review* 33:378–384, 1948.

Soule, Frank
The Annals of San Francisco. New York and San Francisco: D. Appleton and Co., 1855. 824 pp.
Local tales, and characters.

Spalding, William Andrew
History and Reminiscences of Los Angeles City and County. Los Angeles: J. R. Finnell and Sons Publishing Co., 1931. 4 vols.

Spears, John Randolph
Illustrated Sketches of Death Valley and other Borax Deserts of the Pacific Coast. Chicago and New York: Rand McNally and Co., 1892. 226 pp.
Superstitions, desert tales, and adventure.

Swift, Thomas P.
Pen Pictures of California. Pasadena, Cal.:
Post Printing & Binding Co., 1926. 67 pp.
Poems, descriptive of the state, places, and
people.

Tinkham, George Henry
California Men and Events: Time 1769-1890.
Stockton, Calif: Printed by the Record Pub-
lishing Co., 1915. 330 pp.

Tuthill, Franklin
The History of California. San Francisco:
H. H. Bancroft and Co., 1886. 657 pp.
Place names, social life, customs, characters.

Van Brunt, Jessie
California Missions, painted and described
by the author. Los Angeles, Cal.: Wetzel Publishing Co., 1932. 5 pp., mounted plates.

Wagstaff, Alexander E.
Life of David S. Terry, presenting an authentic, impartial and vivid history of his eventual
life and tragic death. San Francisco; Continental Publishing Company, 1892. xvi, 526 pp.,
illus.

Walker, Franklin Dickerson
San Francisco's Literary Frontier. New York:
Alfred A. Knopf, 1939. 400 pp.

Warren, Charles Sumner
History of Santa Monica. Santa Monica, Calif.:
Cawston Publishing Co., 1934.
Place names, legend, customs.

Wells, C.
Three Years Wanderings in California. New
York: no publisher given, 1859.
Customs, social life, characters, adventure.

White, Stewart Edward
*The Story of California: Gold, The Gray
Dawn, The Rose Dawn.* Garden City, N. Y.:
Doubleday, Page & Company, 1927. 1204 pp.,
illus.

————,
Old California in Picture and Story. Illustrated
in color and black and white from contemporary prints. Garden City, N. Y.: Doubleday,
Doran & Company, 1937. xii, 122 pp.

Willard, Charles Dwight
The Herald's History of Los Angeles City.
Los Angeles: Kingsley-Barnes and Neuner Co.,
1901. 365 pp.
Marriage—customs, place names.

Wilson, John Albert
History of Los Angeles County, California.
Oakland, Calif.: Thompson and West, 1880.
192 pp.

Wilson, Neill Compton
*Silver Stampede; the Career of Death Valley's
Hell-Camp, Old Panamint.* New York: The
Macmillan Co., 1937. 319 pp.
Terms, superstition, characters, crime, methods
of justice, mining tales.

Winther, Oscar Osburn
*Express and Stage Coach Days in California
from the Gold Rush to the Civil War.* London:
H. Milford, Oxford University Press, 1936.
197 pp.

Wise, Henry Augustus
*Los Gringos: or, An Inside View of Mexico
and California* . . . New York: Baker and
Scribner, 1849. xvi, 453 pp.

Wood, R. E.
Life and Confessions of James Gilbert Jenkins.
San Francisco: Allen and Wood, 1864.
Stories of characters and crime, insight on
social life and modes.

Yerrington, J. A.
"Stories of Hank Monk." *Sunset* Vol. 12,
(No. 1) 24-, 1903 (Nov.)
Tales of the stagecoach days.

Young, John Philip
*San Francisco; A History of the Pacific Coast
Metropolis.* San Francisco and Chicago: S. J.
Clarke Publishing Co., 1912. 2 Vols.
Local practices, characters.

FOLKTALES—LEGENDS

Altrocchi, Rudolph
"The Wild Girl of the Santa Barbara Channel
Islands." *CFQ* 3: 59-60, 1944.
A legend.

Armstrong, Maurice McNeil
In the Shadow of San Juan. Los Angeles:
Pueblo Pub. Co., 1910. 207 pp.

Atherton, Gertrude
Golden Gate Country (American Folkways).
New York: Duell, Sloan and Pearce, 1945.
256 pp.
A chronicle of the generations that have grown
in Golden Gate Country. She examines a number of current legends.

Bell, Horace
On the Old West Coast. New York: Morrow,
1930.
"A golden treasury of anecdotes." (Dobie).

Caldwell, George Walter
*Ghost Stories of the California Missions and
Rhymes of the Gypsy Trail.* Hollywood, Cal.:
G. W. Caldwell, 1939. 188 pp., illus.

————,
Legends of San Francisco. San Francisco:
Phillips and Von Orden Co., 1919. 91 pp.
A collection of poems.

Carillo, Adolfo
Cuentos Californianos. Los Angeles: 191—.
96 pp., illus.

Chalfant, W. A.
Tales of the Pioneers. Stanford University,
Calif.: Stanford University Press, 1943.
Chronicles of the California-Nevada border in
the early days.

Claudel, Calvin
"Tales from San Diego." *CFQ* 2: 113-120, 1943.
    The author states that although these tales are not truly Californian, they do represent the spread of tales into different areas through the shifting and moving about of people, especially as seen in wartime.

Cloud, Roy W.
On the Trails of Yesterday, California Stories. Illustrated by Ray Bethers. San Francisco: Harr Wagner Publishing Company, 1931. xxii, 219 pp., illus.

Cuentos de California. Los Angeles: 1904. 77 pp.
    California tales by various authors.

Dangel, R.
"Bear and Fawns." *JAFL* 42:307-308, 1929.

Ellerby, Rose Lucile
Tales of California Yesterdays. Los Angeles: W. T. Potter, 1916. 205 pp.
    Legends, customs, characters.

Elias, Sol P.
Stories of the Stanislaus. Modisto, California: privately printed, 1924.
    Local tales, legends, traditions.

Evertsen, Laura
"Simon Galavis, a Legend." *Historical Society of Southern California Publications* 7:31-.

Federal Writers' Project
The Old West: Pioneer tales of San Bernardino County. Compiled by the Federal Writers' Project of the WPA of California. San Bernardino: The Sun Co., 1940.
    Folktales and legends.

Figel, Phil
"Legend of the Six Sisters." *The Grizzly Bear* p. 2-, 1914 (Dec.)

Fitzgerald, O. A.
"Millions or Myths." *Touring Topics* p. 26—, 1927 (July).
    Lost Mines.

Forbes, A. S. C.
Mission Tales in the Days of the Dons . . . with nine full illustrations and decorative drawings by Langdon Smith. Chicago: A. C. McClurg & Co., 1909. 343 pp., illus.

Gayton, A. H.
"Areal Affiliations of California Folktales." *AA* 37 (No. 4): 582-599, 1935.

Goodwyn, Frank
The Magic of Limping John. New York: Farrar and Rinehart, 1944. 275 pp., illus.

Guinn, James Miller
"The Myth of Gold Lake." *The Grizzly Bear* p. 58—, 1907 (Nov.)

————,
"Myth of Gold Lake." *Historical Society of Southern California Publications* 6:82-6, 1903.

Halpert, Herbert
"Lola: A Folk Tale." *CFQ* 3: 153-154, 1944.

Hand, Wayland D.
"White Liver." *JAFL* 59:323, 1946.

Hankey, Rosalie
"California Ghosts." *CFQ* 1:155-177, 1942.

————,
"Campus Folklore and California's 'Pedro.'" *CFQ* 3:29-35, 1944.
    Origin of Student Shout on University Campuses.

Hanna, Phil Townsend
Libros Californianos: or 5 Feet of California Books. Los Angeles: Ji Zeitlin, Primavera Press, 1931. 74 pp.
    California tales.

Harriman, Alice
"Bells of Ramona's County." *Touring Topics* 25:44, 1929.

————,
"The First Bell Rung in California." *Touring Topics* 25:44—, 1929 (July).

————,
"The Miserere of San Luis Rey." *Touring Topics* 25:36—, 1929 (Sept.)

Harte, Bret
The Bell Ringer of Angels and other Legendary Tales of California. Boston: Houghton, Mifflin & Co., 1894. 334 pp.

————,
The Adventure of Padre Vicente. Berkeley, California: W. and E. Bentley, 1939.
    Legend of old San Francisco.

Hawthorne, Hildegard
Romantic Cities in California. Illustrated by E. H. Suydam. New York; London: D. E. Appleton-Century Co., 1939. xvii, 456 pp., illus.
    Local and sectional tales.

Johnson, Philip
"In Quest of the Lost Breyfogle." *Touring Topics* p. 18—, 1929 (Feb.)
    Lost mines.

Judson, Katharine Berry
Myths and Legends of California and the Old Southwest. Chicago. A. C. McClurg & Co.,, 1912, xvi, 193 pp.

Kirkman, George Wycherley
"Piracy on the Pacific." *Touring Topics* p. 14—, 1927 (Oct.)
    Pirate tales.

Kistler, Jessie
Tales Told by the Mission Bells. Los Angeles: Research Publishing Co., 1947. 239 pp.

Wagner, H. R.
"Quivira, a Mythical California City." *California Historical Society Quarterly* 3: 262—, 1924.

Lowrimore, Burton
"Six California Tales." *CFQ* 4:154-157, 1945.

Mabie, Hamilton Wright, ed.
Folk Tales. Garden City, New York: Nelson, Doubleday, Inc., 1927. 215 pp.

Manly, William Lewis
Death Valley in '49. San Jose, California: Pacific Tree and Vine Co., 1894. 498 pp.
Tales of a desert tragedy.

Massett, Stephen C.
"Drifting About, or What Jeems Pipes of Pipesville Saw and Did. New York: Carlton, 1863.
Humorous tales.

Morrison, Frederick
"Lola: a folktale." *CFQ* 3:153-154, 1944.

————,
"Tales from Southern California and New Mexico." *CFQ* 2:121-127, 1943.

Munk, Joseph Amasa
Activities of a Life-Time. Los Angeles: Times-Mirror Press, 1924. 221 pp.
Pioneer anecdotes.

Newcomb, R.
The Old Mission Churches and Historic Houses of California. Philadelphia and London: J. P. Lippencott Co., 1925. 379 pp.
Mission tales, legends and tradition.

Neihardt, John Gneisenau
The Splendid Wayfaring. New York: The MacMillan Co., 1920. 290 pp.
Tales of early-day guides.

Plowman, Gisela J.
"Pedro-ing at California." *CFQ* 3:277-283, 1944.

Shannon, Monica
California Fairy Tales. Garden City, New York: Doubleday Page and Co., 1926. 298 pp.

————,
Eyes for the Dark. Garden City, New York: Doubleday Page and Co., 1928. 311 pp.
Fairy tales.

Smeaton, B. H.
"The Siegal Rock Ghost." *CFQ* 3:234-235, 1944.
A haunted house in Berkeley, California.

Steele, James
Old California Days. Chicago: Belford, Clarke Co., 1889. 227 pp.
Legends and stories of mission life, Spanish-California terms.

Stephenson, Terry E.
"The Santa Ana Wind." *CFQ* 2:35-40, 1943.

————,
Shadow of Old Saddleback. Santa Ana, Calif.: Press of the Santa Ana High School and Junior College, 1931. 209 pp.

Townsend, Juliana
Seven Sprays and a Golden Poppy. Los Angeles: Times-Mirror Printing and Binding House, 1919. 31 pp.
Tales in poetry and song.

Voiles, Jane
"Genoese Folkways in a California Mining Camp." *CFQ* 3:212-216, 1944.

Walsh, Marie T.
The Mission Bells of California. San Francisco: Harr Wagner Publishing Co., 1934. 327 pp.
Mission bell legend and tales.

CUSTOMS—BELIEFS—SUPERSTITIONS

Anonymous
"Old California Days." *Land of Sunshine* 7:239—, 1900.

Bancroft, Hubert Howe
Popular Tribunals. San Francisco: The History Co., 1887. 2 Vols., illus.

Bandini, Helen Elliot
History of California. New York: American Book Co., 1908. 302 pp.
Social and political life, and much on customs and traditions.

Barrows, H. D.
"An Early California Romance." *The Grizzly Bear* 8:7—, (April) 1914.

Bary, Helen Valeska
The Course of Empire. New York: Coward-McCann, Inc., 1931. 368 pp.
Frontier and pioneer life.

Barry, Theodore A.
Men and Memories of San Francisco in the Spring of '50. San Francisco: A. L. Bancroft and Co., 1873. 296 pp.
Characters, social life, customs.

Bates, Mrs. B. D.
Incidents on Land and Water, or Four Years on the Pacific Coast. Boston: Joseph French and Co., 1857.
Anecdotes, customs, social life, adventure.

Bell, Horace
On the Old West Coast. New York: W. Morrow and Co., 1930. 336 pp., illus.
"Social History by Anecdote. California." (Dobie).

Benton, Joseph Augustine
The California Pilgrim. San Francisco: Marvin and Hitchcock, 1853. 261 pp.
Social life, customs.

Bidwell, John
"Address of John Bidwell, an Account of My Experiences and Observations in California, and Its Inhabitants, Their Occupations, Government and So Forth." *Society of California Pioneers Quarterly* 3:9-45, 1926. illus.

Boehmer, Fritz
"Experiences of My Early Life in California." *Society of California Quarterly* 4:87-103, 1927.

Bogardus, Emory Stephen
Southern California, Center of Culture. Los Angeles: University of Southern California Press, 1938. 84 pp.
Festivals, feast days, superstition, social life transportation.

Brown, John Henry
Reminiscences and Incidents of Early Days of San Francisco: 1845-50. San Francisco: The Grabhorn Press, 1933. 138 pp.
Social and civic life.

Bynum, Lindley, ed.
"The Record Book of the Rancho Santa Ana del Chino." *Historical Society of Southern California,* 1934, pp. 1-55.

Cale, George M.
My Early Days in Los Angeles. Los Angeles: privately printed, 1930.
Customs, social life and civic life.

Carmany, John H., and Cyrus W.
California Miscellany, (Vol. IV). San Francisco: Towne and Bacon, 1861.

Chambliss, William H.
Chambliss Diary. New York: Chambliss and Co., 1895.
Social life, customs and anecdotes.

Champagnac, Jean Baptiste Joseph
Le Jeune Voyageur en Californie; récits intructifs et moraux offrant des détails curieux sur cette région de l'Amerique et sur les coutumes, usages et moeurs de ses habitants. Paris: P. C. Lehuby, 1852. 248 pp., illus.
Includes observations on customs, traditions and dress.

Church, Andrew Smith
"Memoirs of Andrew S. Church." *Society of California Pioneers Quarterly* 3:154-201, 1926, illus.

Cox, Palmer
Squibs of California, or *Every Day Life;* Illustrated. Hartford, Conn.: Mutual Publishing Co., 1874. 491 pp.

Coy, Owen C.
"Paper Towns and Easy Money." *American Historical Association, Pacific Coast Branch, Proceedings.* 1928, pp. 103-125.

Coyne, Joseph Stirling
Cockneys in California. In One Act. New York: M. Douglas, 1851. 19 pp.

Cross, Ira B.
"California and Hard Money." *CFQ* 4:270-277, 1945.

Dana, Julian
The Man Who Built San Francisco. New York: The Macmillan Co., 1936. 397 pp.

Dargity, Dale
"The Social Life of California: 1840-1860." *The Grizzly Bear* p. 3—, 1930 (July).

Delano, Alonzo
Old Block's Sketch Book, or, Tales of California Life. Sacramento: Anthony and Co., 1856. 78 pp.
Social life, customs, entertainment, characters.

De Rupert, A. E. D.
Californians and Mormons. New York: J. W. Lovell, 1881. 181 pp.
Social life, customs.

Dexter, A. Hersey
Early Days in California. Denver: Tribune-Republicans Press, 1886. 214 pp.
Social life, customs, characters.

Dickenson, Luella
Reminiscences of a Trip Across the Plains in 1846 and Early Days in California. San Francisco: The Whitaker & Ray Co., 1904. 117 pp., illus.

Drake, Samuel Adams
The Young Vigilantes; A Story of California Life in the Fifties. Illustrated by L. J. Bridgman. Boston: Lee and Shepard, 1904. 284 pp.

Dressler, Albert
California's Pioneer Circus. San Francisco: H. S. Crocker Co., Inc., 1926. 98 pp.
Early day entertainment, characters.

Dryry, R. Sheldon
The Startling and Thrilling Narrative of the Dark and Terrible Deeds of Henry Madison and His Associate and Accomplice, Miss Ellen Stevens. Cincinnati: Barclay & Co., 1857.

Farley, Charles Andrews
"The Moral Aspect of California; a Thanksgiving Sermon of 1850." *California Historical Society Quarterly* 19:299-307, 1940.

Filcher, Joseph Adams
Untold Tales of California. San Francisco: privately printed, 1903.
Social life, customs.

Fisher, Anne
Cathedral in the Sun. New York: Carlyle House, 1940. viii, 408 pp.
A novel of the San Carlos Borromeo mission.

Forbes, Robert Bennet
Personal Reminiscences. Boston: Little, Brown & Co., 1892. 412 pp.

Frankenstein, Alfred
"California Localisms." *CFQ* 2:41-42, 1943.

Gay, Frederick A.
Sketches of California. An account of the life, manners and customs of the inhabitants . . . Also interesting information in relation to the canchalagua, a Californian plant of rare medicinal virtues. New York: 1848. (Reprinted, Tarrytown, N. Y.: W. Abbatt, 1925).

Griffin, John S.
A Doctor Comes to California; The Diary of John S. Griffin, M.D. San Francisco, Calif.: California Historical Society, 1943. 97 pp.
A Journal of a doctor's experiences on the old Santa Fe and Gila River trail in 1846 and 1847 with an introduction and notes by George Walcott Ames Jr.

Gudde, Erwin Gustav
Sutter's Own Story. New York: Putnam's Sons, 1936.
Customs, social life.

H, E. M.
Ranch Life in California. London: W. H. Alben and Co., 1886. 171 pp.

Harlan, Jacob Wright
California, '46 to '88. San Francisco: The Bancroft Co., 1888. 242 pp.
Customs, characters.

Hayden, Dorothea
These Pioneers. Los Angeles: 1938. 287 pp.

Hayes, Benjamin Ignatius
Pioneer Notes from the Diaries of Judge Benjamin Hayes, 1849-1875. Los Angeles: Private Printing, 1929. xi, 307 pp., illus.

Hollingsworth, John McHenry
"Journal of John McHenry Hollingsworth." *California Historical Society Quarterly* 1:238—, 1922.

Huffman, O. H.
History of Five California Counties. Chicago: Lewis Publishing Co., 1892.
Local customs, characters.

Hutton, William Rich
Glances at California, 1847-1853. Diaries and Letters . . . with a brief memoir and notes by Willard O. Waters. San Marino: The Huntington Library, 1942. xx, 86 pp., bibl.

Ingersoll, Luther A.
Ingersoll's Century Annals of San Bernardino County: 1769-1904. Los Angeles: L. A. Ingersoll, 1904. 887 pp.
Characters, customs, belief.

Johnson, Philip
"A River Upside Down." *Touring Topics* p. 26—, 1929 (Nov.).
Superstition.

Kabberton, John
Some Folks. New York: Derby Brothers, 1877. 502 pp.
Tales of early day life, customs.

Kip, William Ingraham
The Early Days of My Episcopate. New York: T. Whittaker, 1892. x, 263 pp.

Knight, Maria
"Early Days in San Francisco." *Overland Monthly*, 30:252, 1914.

Knoche, Johann Eduard
"The Autobiography of Johann Eduard Knoche." *Society of California Pioneers Quarterly* 2:215-232, 1925.

Lelièvre, Matthieu
Un Missionaire en Californie (1849-1856); aventures et travaux du Rév. William Taylor. Paris: Bureau de la Société des Traités Religieux, 1870. 428 pp.
The adventures of a Methodist missionary in California in the gold-rush. Much on social life, customs and manners.

Letts, John M.
A Pictorial View of California; including a description of the Panama and Nicaragua routes, with information and advice interesting to all, particularly those who intend to visit the Golden region. By a returned Californian. New York: H. Bill, 1853. vii, 224 pp., illus.

Lindley, Walter, and Widney, J. P.
California of the South. New York: D. Appleton and Co., 1888. 377 pp.
Climate, customs, beliefs.

Lummis, Charles Fletcher
"Mr. Eayrs of Boston." *Out West Magazine*, 30:159, February, 1909.

Lynch, James
With Stevenson in California. No publisher given, 1896. 65 pp.
Tales of early-day California life, customs and manners.

MacDonald, W. Colt
California Caballero. New York: Covici-Friede, 1936. 314 pp.
Fiction, customs, social life.

Mackey, Margaret Gilbert
Los Angeles Proper and Improper. Los Angeles: Goodwin Press, 1938. 181 pp.
Social habits, customs.

Madison, James
"California's Pioneer Circus." *California Historical Society Quarterly* 6:98—, 1927.

Marye, George Thomas
From '49 to '83 in California and Nevada. San Francisco: A. M. Robertson, 1923. 212 pp.
Social life, customs.

McGowan, Edward
Narrative of Edward McGowan. San Francisco: Privately Printed, 1857. 240 pp.

McMullen, Jerry
Paddle-Wheel Days in California. Stanford University, California: Stanford University Press, 1944. 157 pp.
A history of the river steamboats in California in the late 19th Century.

Meads, S. P.
Glimpses of the Wet Past in Northern California. Berkeley, Calif.: Sather Gate Book Shop, n. d.
Early day morals.

Mulford, Prentice
"California Culinary Experiences." *Overland Monthly*, 2:556, 1884.

———,
Prentice Mulford's Story; or, Life By Land and Sea; A Personal Narrative. With a preface and conclusion by A. E. Waite. London: W. Rider and Son, Ltd., 1913. x, 297 pp.

Murgotten, Alexander Philip
"Pioneer Publisher Tells of the Early Days." *The Grizzly Bear* 6:3—, (March) 1912.

Mylar, Isaac L.
Early Days at the Mission San Juan Bautista.
Wattsonville, Calif.: Evening Pajaronian,
1929. 195 pp.
Local social life, custom, practice.

Nevins, Allan
Fremont, Pathfinder of the West. New York:
D. Appleton-Century Co., 1939. 649 pp.
General insight and observations on customs
and manners of the Californians.

————,
Fremont, the West's Greatest Adventurer.
New York: Harper Brothers, 1928. 2 Vols.

Newmark, Harris
Sixty Years in Southern California. Boston:
Houghton, Mifflin Co., 1930. 744 pp.

Nunes, Joseph A.
Fast Folks; or the Early Days in California.
Philadelphia: Barnard and Jones Printers,
1861. 95 pp.
Folk drama, social life.

Packman, Ana Bégué
Early California Hospitality; the cookery customs of Spanish California, with authentic
recipes and menus of the period. Glendale,
Calif.: The Arthur H. Clark Co., 1938. 182 pp.,
illus.

Palmer, John Williamson
*The New and the Old; or, California and India
in Romantic Aspects.* With thirteen illustrations, engraved by A. V. S. Anthony . . . New
York: Rudd & Carleton. 1859. xiv. 433 pp.,
illus.

Peters, Harry Twyford
California on Stone. Garden City, New York:
Doubleday and Doran Co., Inc., 1935. 227 pp.
Early-day customs in pictures and script.

Phillips, Catherine Coffin
*Cornelius Cole, Pioneer and United States
Senator.* San Francisco: no publisher, 1929.
Early-day characters, customs, practices.

————,
*Portsmouth Plaza, The Cradle of San Fran-
cisco.* San Francisco: J. H. Nash, 1932. 464 pp.
Social life, commercial practices, entertainment,
advertisement.

Phillips, Grace Darling
Far Peoples. Chicago: University of Chicago
Press, 1929. 274 pp.
Customs, beliefs, practice.

Pond, William Chauncey
*Gospel Pioneering, Reminiscences of Early
Congregationalism in California.* Oberlin,
Ohio: The News Printing Co., 1921. 191 pp.
Beliefs, practices.

Powers, Laura Bride
Old Monterey; California's Adobe Capital.
San Francisco: San Carlos Press, 1934. 299 pp.
Social and civic life, customs, legends of the
first capital.

Pumphrey, Margaret Blanche
Under Three Flags. Caldwell, Idaho: The
Caston Printers Ltd., 1939. 293 pp.
Customs, social life, practice.

Quigley, Hugh
*The Irish Race in California and on the Paci-
fic Coast.* San Francisco: A Roman and Co.,
1878. 548 pp.

Quinn, James M.
"Pioneer Ads and Advertisers." *Historical
Society of Southern California Publications,* 5:
295-, 1894.

————,
"Pioneer Courts and Judges of California."
*Historical Society of Southern California Pub-
lications,* 8: 174-, 1897.

Réau, Antatolie Cécile
*La Société Californienne de 1850 d'après Bret
Harte.* Paris: Ollier-Henry, 1921. 367 pp.
Life in California as reflected in the works of
Bret Harte.

Reppert, Sierra
"The Record of California's Greatest Criminal." *The Grizzly Bear* 3:1, (July) 1909.

Robinson, Alfred
Life in California Before the Conquest. San
Francisco: private press of Thomas C. Rus-
sell, 1925. 316 pp.
Medicine, terms, characters, customs, social life.

Rodman, Willoughby
*History of Bench and Bar of Southern Cali-
fornia.* Los Angeles: W. J. Porter, 1909. 267
pp.
Legal lore, court practice.

Rosevelt, Hilda
"Feminine Philanthropy." *Overland Monthly*
5: 181-, 1892.

Royce, Josiah
"Provincialism, Based Upon a Study of Early
Conditions in California." *Putnam's Magazine,*
1909, pp. 232-240.

Ryder, David Warren
"Stage Coach Days." *Sunset* 59 (No. 3) 16—,
1907 (Sept.).

Sanchez, Nellie Van de Grift
"Keeper of the Keys." *Touring Topics* 25:
24-, 1929 (Jan.).

————,
Spanish Arcadia. Los Angeles: Powell Publishing Company, 1929. 413 pp., illus., bibl.

Schoonover, Thomas J.
*The Life and Times of General John A.
Sutter.* Sacramento, Calif.: Press of Bullock-
Carpenter Printing Co., 1907. 312 pp.
Tall stories, customs, practices.

Shinn, Charles Howard
Graphic Description of Pacific Coast Outlaws.
San Francisco: R. R. Patterson, 188-(?).

Shippey, Lee
It's an Old California Custom. With contemporary illustrations. (American Customs Series). New York: The Vanguard Press, 1948. 292 pp.
"The book is a readable and often interesting rewrite of California's more superficial historical aspects, gathered from 'scores of source books' and 'friends who are veritable geysers of knowledge.'" (Courtenay Terrett).

Smith, Mrs. Sarah Hathaway (Bixby)
Adobe Days. Cedar Rapids, Iowa: The Torch Press, 1925. 208 pp.
Custom, social life.

Smith, Rollin Carrol
Postmarked Vermont and California, 1862-1864, edited by Fannie Smith Spurling, with drawings by Rollin C. Ayres. Rutland, Vt.: The Tuttle Publishing Co., 1940. 202 pp., illus.
Letters of Rollin C. Smith written while he was living in California and letters written to him by his father, Orlin Smith of Pittsford, Vermont.

Smythe, William Ellsworth
History of San Diego: 1542-1907. San Diego: The History Co., 1907. 736 pp.
Much on local custom, social life.

Sooy, Louise Pinkney
Early California Customs: 1769-1847 London: H. Milford, Oxford University Press, 1932. 136 pp.

Speroni, Charles
"The Observance of St. Joseph's Day Among the Sicilians of Southern California." *SFQ* 4:135-139. 1940.

Steele, James
Old California Days. Chicago: Morrill & Co., 1892. viii, 272 pp., illus.

Stewart, William Frank
Last of the Filibusters, or Recollections of the Siege of Rivas. Sacramento: H. Shipley and Co., 1857. 85 pp.
Early day practice, customs.

Sutter, John Augustus
The Diary of Johann August Sutter. San Francisco: The Grabhorn Press, 1932. 56 pp.
Customs, social life.

Swasey, William F.
The Early Days and Men of California. Oakland, Calif., New York, etc.: Pacific Press Publishing Co., 1891. 406 pp.
Early-day characters, customs.

Taylor, Benjamin Franklin
Between the Gates. Chicago: S. C. Griggs and Co., 1878. 292 pp.
Curious litigation, early day legal procedure.

Taylor, William
California Life Illustrated. New York: Carlton and Porter, 1867. 391 pp., illus.
Social life, customs, characters, habits, beliefs.

Thomas, William Henry
On Land and Sea, or, California in the Years 1843, 44, and 45. Boston: De Wolfe, Fiske and Co., 1884. 351 pp.
Pioneer characters, customs, social life.

——————,
Reminiscences of a Pioneer. San Francisco: privately printed, 1912.
Pioneer and frontier life.

Triplett, Frank
Conquering the Wilderness; or, New Pictorial History of the Life and Times of the Pioneer Heroes and Heroines of America. New York: N. D. Thompson Publishing Co., 1888. xxxix, 742 pp., illus.

Truman, Benjamin Cummings
Semi-Tropical California: Its Climate, Healthfulness, Productivity and Scenery. San Francisco: A. L. Bancroft and Co., 1874, 204 pp.
Weather lore.

Ver Mehr, Jean Leonhard Henri Corneille
Checkered Life: In the Old and New World. San Francisco: A. L. Bancroft and Co., 1887. 476 pp.

Wells, Evelyn
Champagne Days in San Francisco. New York, London: D. Appleton-Century Co., Inc., 1939. 284 pp.
Social life, customs.

——————,
Fremont Older. New York, London: D. Appleton-Century Co., Inc., 1936. 407 pp.

White, William Francis (Grey, William, pseud.)
A Picture of Pioneer Times in California. San Francisco: W. N. Hinton and Co., 1881. 677 pp.
Characters, social life, customs, lawlessness, beliefs.

Williams, Mary Floyd
History of the San Francisco Committee of Vigilance of 1851. Berkeley, Calif.: University of California Press, 1921. 543 pp.

Wolcott, Marjorie Tisdale
Pioneer Notes from the Diaries of Judge Benjamin Hayes. Los Angeles: privately printed, 1929.
Customs, social life, crime, court procedure.

Woods, Rev. James
Recollections of Pioneer Work in California. San Francisco: J. Winterburn & Co., 1878. 260 pp.

Woods, Samuel D.
Lights and Shadows of Life on the Pacific Coast. New York: Funk and Wagnalls Co., 1910. 474 pp.
Customs, social life.

Woon, Basil Dillon
San Francisco and the Golden Empire. New York: H. Smith and R. Hoss, 1935. 407 pp.
Much valuable information on customs, social life.

Workman, Boyle
Boyle Workman's the City that Grew, as Told to Caroline Walker. Los Angeles: The Southland Publishing Co., 1935.
Customs, social life, celebrations, crime, law enforcement, characters, legends, beliefs, superstitions, costumes.

Wright, Corrine King
Cold Embers. Los Angeles: Wetzel Publishing Co., 1931.
Social life, customs.

FOLK MEDICINE

Anonymous
"Medicine." *Hutchin's California Magazine* 1: 257-, 1856 (Dec.).

Guinn, James M.
"Some Historic Fads and Fakes." *Historical Society of Southern California Publications* 6: 148-.

Holder, Charles Frederick
The Channel Islands of California. Chicago: A. C. McClurg and Co., 1910. 397 pp.
Superstition, legendary medicine, early-day sports.

Lyman, George D., M.D.
"The First Native Born California Physician." *California Historical Society Quarterly* 4:284-,

———,
"The Scalpel Under Three Flags." *California Historical Society Quartely* 4:142-.

O'Leary, A.
A Year in California, and a Contest with her Quacks. St. Louis, Mo.: privately printed, 1888.

Praslow, Dr. J.
The State of California, a Medico-Geographical Account. Translated by Frederick C. Cordes. San Francisco: J. J. Newbegin, 1939.

Tyson, James Lawrence
Diary of a Physician in California. Philadelphia: G. S. Appleton, 1850. 92 pp.

SPEECH

"A Word List from California."
Dialect Notes 5(Part 4):109-114, 1921.
General words, local words, occupational words, student's terms, underworld terms, grocery, flower terms, animal and automobile.

Bryant, Margaret M.
"Saying the Masses." *SFQ* 10:129-136, 1946.

Chrétien, C. D.
"Brontling." *CFQ* 1:96-97, 1942.
A folkspeech of Boonville, California.

Grant, Rena V.
"The Localized Vocabulary of California Verse." *CFQ* 1:253-290, 1942.

Hildebrand, J. R.
"California's Coastal Red-Wood Region." *National Geographic Magazine* 75:134-184, 1939.
Mention of local words and phrases.

Hills, E. C.
"New Words in California." *Modern Language Notes* 38:187-188, 1923.

Lloyd, Elwood
Californology. Hollywood: Hartwell Publishing Co., 1930.
Floating language.

Warnock, Elsie
"Terms of Disparagement in the Dialect Speech of High School Pupils in California and New Mexico." *Dialect Notes* 5 (Part 2): 60-73, 1919.

PLACE NAMES

Anonymous
"California Names, a Gazeteer." *Westways* Vol. 31, serially, Jan. to July, 1939.

———,
"Stories behind California's Place Names." *California Historical Nugget* 1:39-43, 59-66, 79-87, 1924.

Bailey, G. E.
"The History, Origin and Meaning of Some California Towns and Places." *Overland Monthly* 44: 89-93; 199-204, 1904.

Bowman, J. N.
"The Meaning of the name Sonoma.'" *CFQ* 5(No. 3):300-302, 1946.

Brown, Charles
"Early Events." *Society of California Pioneers Quarterly* Vol. 7, 1:35—,
Place names, characters, anecdotes, weather lore.

Bunnell, Lafayette H.
Origin of Names in the Yosemite Valley. Sacramento: J. D. Young, Supt-State Prig. 1890.

Drake, C. M.
California Names and Their Literal Meaning. Los Angeles: Jones Book and Printing Co., 1893. 80 pp.

Farquhar, Francis Peloubet
Place Names of the High Sierra. San Francisco: Sierra Club, 1926. x, 128 pp.

———,
"Place Names of the High Sierra." *Sierra Club Bulletin* 11:380-407, 1923. (San Francisco).

Forbes, A. S. C.
California Landmarks and Missions. Los Angeles: privately printed, 1925.
Place names, legend and tradition.

Gudde, Erwin G.
"The Solution of the Islay Problem." *CFQ* 5 (No. 3):298-299, 1946.
Islay Creek in San Francisco.

———,
1,000 California Place Names. Their Origin and Meaning. Berkeley and Los Angeles; University of California Press, 1947. vii, 96 pp.

Hanna, Phil Townsend
"Some Early Geographical Conceptions of California." *Touring Topics* p. 22-, 1925 (Sept.).

—————,
The Dictionary of California Land Names.
Los Angeles: The Automobile Club of South-
ern California, 1946. xxi, 360 pp.

Hill, Archibald A.
"California Place-Names from the Spanish."
AS 7 (no. 4): 317-318, 1932.

Jones, Joseph
"Street-Names of Palo Alto, California." *AS*
7(no. 4): 273-277, 1932.

King, E. R., comp.
*Handbook of Historical Landmarks of Cali-
fornia.* Los Angeles: privately printed by E.
R. King, 1938. 155 pp.

Kroeber, Alfred Louis
California Place Names of Indian Origin.
Berkeley: University of California Press, 1916.
69 pp.

Lovejoy, Ora A.
"A Study of Southern California Place Names."
*Historical Society of Southern California Pub-
lications* 11:44-, 1900.

McNary, Mrs. Laura Kelly
California Spanish and Indian Place Names,
their pronunciation, meaning and location.
Los Angeles: Wetzel Publishing Co., 1931.
77 pp.

Marshall, Martha L.
*A Pronouncing Dictionary of California Names
in English and Spanish.* San Francisco, Calif.:
The French Book Store, 1925. 40 pp.

Moreno, Henry Manuel
*Moreno's Dictionary of Spanish-Named Cali-
fornia Cities and Towns . . .* Chicago: M. A.
Donohue Co., 1916. 95 pp.

Mott, Gertrude (Mrs. Frank K.)
A Handbook for Californiacs. A Key to Mean-
ing and Pronunciation of Spanish and Indian
Place Names. With foreword by Herbert E.
Bolton. San Francisco: Harr Wagner Publish-
ing Co., 1926. xii, 104 pp.

Olonsted, F. L.
"Place Names for California." *Landscape
Architect* 13:40-42, 1922.

Palou, Francisco
Historic Memoirs of New California. Berke-
ley: University of California Press, 1926. 4
Vols.

Quinn, James M.
"Some California Place Names." *Historical
Society of Southern California Publications,*
7: 39-, 1896.

Sanchez, Nellie Van De Grift
"Origin of California." *Motor Land* 33: 9,
1933.

—————,
*Spanish and Indian Place Names of California,
Their Meaning and Their Romance.* San Fran-
cisco: A. M. Robertson, 1914. 445 pp.

Shafer, Robert
"The Pronunciation of Spanish Place Names
in California." *AS* 17: 239-246, 1942.

Southern, May Hazel
*Our Storied Landmarks, Shasta County, Cali-
fornia.* Redding, California: Privately Printed,
1942. 100 pp.

Spalding, Phebe Estelle
Patron Saints of California: Franciscan Series.
No. 1-3. Claremont, Cal.: Saunders Studio
Press, 1934—35. 3 Nos., illus.

—————,
*Patron Saints of California: the Virgin Se-
ries.* No. 1-2. Claremont, Cal.: Saunders
Studio Press, 1934. 2 Nos., illus.

Stewart, George R.
"The Nomenclature of Stream-Forks on the
West Slope of Sierra Nevada." *AS* 14: 191-
198, 1939.

Tensch, Hero Eugene
Historic Spots in California. London: H. Milford, Oxford University Press, 1933. 2 Vols.

Valejo, M. G.
*Report on Derivation and Definition of the
Names of Several Counties in California.* San
Jose, Calif.: H. H. Robinson, State Printer,
1850. 16 pp.

Van Tuyle, Bert
Know Your California. Los Angeles: Wallace
Press, n.d.

Waterman, Thomas Talbot
"The Geographical Names Used by the Indians of the Pacific Coast." *Geographical Review* 12:175-194, 1922. illus.

—————,
Yurok Geography. Berkeley: University of
California Press, 1920. 314 pp., bibl.

Wells, Harry L.
California Names; Over 2500 Place Names,
Individual Names, Words and Phrases in Common Use in the Golden State, Spelled, Pro-
nounced, Defined, and Explained. Los Angeles: Kellaway-Ide-Jones Co., 1934. 94 pp.,
illus.

Wyatt, Roscoe D.
*Names and Places of Interest in San Mateo
County with Pronunciation, History and Tra-
ditions.* Redwood City, Calif.: San Mateo
County Title Co. . . . 1936. 30 pp., illus.

PROVERBS

Adams, Owen S.
Proverbial Comparisons from California."
CFQ 5(No. 4): 334-338, 1946.

FOLKSONG

See: Spanish American Folksongs, pp. 601-06;
Songs of the '49ers, pp, 642-43; Songs of the
Cowboys, pp. 617-27.

BIBLIOGRAPHY

"Bibliography of California Folklore and Folk-song." *CFQ* 2:63-70; 169-175; 245-251; 347-352, 1943.

Robertson, Sidney H., ed.
Check List of California Songs. Berkeley: University of California, Department of Music, Folk Music Project, Work Projects Administration. 1940. 160 pp.

GENERAL STUDIES AND COLLECTIONS

Alverson, Mrs. Rosana Margaret
Sixty Years of California Song. San Francisco: Sunset Publishing House, 1913. 275 pp.

Appleton, D. E., compiler and arranger
California Songster: A selection of local and other popular songs, giving a sketch of the ups and downs of a California life. San Francisco: Noisy Carriers Book and Stationery Company, 1855. vi, 56 pp.

Arnold, F. W.
Festivals and Plays for Children. Cincinnati: Willis Music Company, 1921.

Bronson, B. H.
"Where Is Mah Good Old Man." *CFQ* 2: 44-45, 1943.
Text of a song.

"California's Half Century. Two Argonaut Songs." *Land of Sunshine* 13:165.

da Silva, Rev. Owen, ed.
Mission Music of California. A collection of Old California mission hymns and masses. Accompaniments and chirography by Arthur M. Bienbar. Mission sektches by Paul A. Moore. With an introduction by John Steven McGroarty. Los Angeles, Cal.: Warren F. Lewis, 1941. xv, 132 pp., bibl., illus., music.

Earle, Henry Edmond
"An Old Time Collector: Reminiscences of Charles F. Lummis." *CFQ* 1: 179-183, 1942.
His work in collecting Spanish folksongs in California.

Hague, Eleanor
"California Songs, III." *Masterkey* 2(no. 3): 89-93, 1937.

——————,
"When the Dons and Their Damsels Danced." *Westways* 27: 18-, 1935 (October).
Folk dance.

Handy, W. J.
"Some Early California Songs." *Out West* (Los Angeles) 29: 430-437, 1908.

Lengyel, Cornel, editor
A San Francisco Songster 1849-1939. In: " History of Music in San Francisco." San Francisco: Works Progress Administration, 1939.

Lowrimore, Burton S.
"A California Version of 'Edward.'" *CFQ* 5 (No. 3):310-311, 1946.

Rodriguez, Jose
Music and Dance of California, compiled by W. J. Perlman. Hollywood, California: Bureau of Musical Research.

Southern, May Hazel
"To Sally Stubbs, Down East by Phebe", and "To Phebe Out West from Sally." *CFQ* 2: 151-152, 1943.
Texts only to two ballads of California in middle of 19th century.

Stone, John A.
Put's Golden Songster, Containing the largest and most popular collection of California songs ever published by the author of "Put's Original California Songster." Entered according to Act of Congress in the year 1858, by John A. Stone, in the Clerk's Office of the District Court of the United States for the Northern District of California. San Francisco: D. E. Appleton and Company, 1858.

CHILDREN'S GAMES AND DANCES

Speroni, Charles
"Some rope-skipping rhymes from Southern California." *CFQ* 1: 245-252, 1942.

The Homer H. Kurtz Collection of Fiddler's Tunes consists of 563 pieces of music: 68 Hornpipes, 112 Jigs, 164 Reels, 75 Waltzes, 26 Schottisches, 11 Polkas, 23 Marches, 12 Clogs, 7 Flings, 43 Songs. 2 Cakewalks. 19 Two-Steps, and 1 Minuet. *CFQ* 3: 160, 1944.

ARRANGEMENTS

Voice and Piano

——————,

Lummis, Charles Fletcher
Spanish Songs of Old California, collected and translated by Charles F. Lummis. Pianoforte accompaniments by Arthur Farwell. Los Angeles: Chas. F. Lummis, 1923. 35 pp.
Melodies with piano accompaniment, Spanish and English words.

McCoy, William I.
Folk Songs of the Spanish California. San Francisco: Sherman, 1926.
Arrangements for voice and piano.

Ross, Gertrude, and Hague, Eleanor
Early Spanish Californian Folk Songs. New York: J. Fischer and Brothers.
Voice and piano, 5 songs.

Orchestra

——————,

Converse, Frederick S.
California - Festival Orchestra. New York: Birchard.

Maganini, Quinto
"Tuolomne—A California Rhapsody." New York: Musicus: Trumpet and Orchestra.

Partch, Harry
San Francisco Newsboy Cries. Ms. (Instruments built by the composer on a 43-tone-to-the octave scale.)

Still, William Grant
Old California. New York: Carl Fischer: Symphony Orchestra.

RECORDS

Studies

Cowell, Sidney Robertson
"The Recording of Folk Music in California." CFQ 1 (No. 1): 7-24, 1942.

Collections

Songs of Old California. Frank Luther, Zora Layman, Century Quartet. De-49.

U. S. Library of Congress. Division of Music. Folklore Section.
Folklore and Folksong from Informants in the Southern California Area. University of California at Los Angeles Recording Project, under direction of Prof. Wayland D. Hand.
AAFS-LC.

Watkins, F. E.
Spanish-California Folk Songs recorded by Charles Fletcher Lummis. ms. 1942.

Individual Titles

"A Teamster's Song." Frank Luther; Zora Layman and Century Quartet. De-49.

"Jackson." Frank Luther, Zora Layman and Century Quartet. De-49.

COLORADO

FOLKLORE

BIBLIOGRAPHY

Campbell, Vera
Myths and Legends of Colorado, a Bibliography. Greely, Colorado State Teachers College. 1924. 12 pp.

Historical Records Survey
Inventory of County Archives of Colorado. Prepared by the Historical Records Survey. Works Progress Administration. Denver, Colo.: The Historical Records Survey, 1938. bibl.

PERIODICALS

The Colorado Magazine. V. 1, 1923-. Published by the State Historical Society of Colorado. Denver.

GENERAL STUDIES AND COLLECTIONS

Brigham, Lillian, comp.
Colorado Travelore, a Pocket Guide; romance of its trails, railroads, highways, and airways. Denver: The Peerless Printing Co., 1943. xxxii, 502 pp., illus.

Clark, Charles M.
A Trip to Pike's Peak and Notes By the Way . . . being descriptive of incidents and accidents that attended the pilgrimage . . . Chicago: S. P. Rounds' Steam Book and Job Printing House, 1861. vii, 134 pp., illus.

Cody, Colonel W.
An Autobiography of Buffalo Bill. New York: The Cosmopolitan Book Co., 1910.

D. A. R. (Sarah Platt Decker Chapter, Darango, Colorado)
Pioneers of San Juan Country. Colorado Springs: Out West Publishing Co., 1942. 192 pp.

Davidson, Levette Jay
"Colorado Folklore." The Colorado Magazine 18 (No. 1): 1-13, 1941.

————,
"Pikes Peak Prevaricator." Colorado Magazine (State Historical Society, Denver, Colorado) 20 (No. 6): 216-225, 1943.

————,
"Pioneer Preachers of the Rockies." Iliff Review, 1:56-64, 1944.

DeQuille, Dan
The Big Bonanza. Introduction by Oscar Lewis. Illustrations from the 1876 edition. New York: Alfred A. Knopf, 1947. 488 pp.
The story of the discovery and development of the fabulous Comstock lode, and of the epic of Virginia City. An American classic.

Duvall, Laura S.
Colorado in Verse & Picture . . . 1916-1928. Denver: Welch-Haffner Printing Company, 1928. 206 pp., illus.

Federal Writers' Project
Colorado, a Guide to the Highest State. (American Guide Series). Compiled by the workers of the Writers' Program of the Work Project Administration of the State of Colorado. New York: Hastings House, 1941. xxxiii, 511 pp., illus., bibl.

————,
Colorado Ghost Towns: A Picture Record With Texts of the Early Gold and Silver Mining Camps. (American Guide Series). New York: Hastings House, 1946, illus.

————,
Death Valley (American Guide Series). Written and compiled by the Federal Writer's Project of the Works Progress Administration of Northern California. Boston: Houghton Mifflin Co., 1939.

Fuller, A.
Peak and Prairie. From a Colorado Sketch Book. New York: G. P. Putnam's Sons, 1894. 391 pp.

Garland, Hamlin
They of the High Trails. New York, Harper Bros., 1916.

Hafen, LeRoy R., and Ann W.
Colorado, a Story of the State and Its People. Denver, Col.: The Old West Publishing Co., 1943. 436 pp., illus.

Ives, Ronald L.
"Folklore of Easter Middle Park, Colorado." *JAFL* 54:24-43, 1941.

James, George Wharton
The Wonders of the Colorado Desert. Boston: Little, Brown Co., 1906. 2 Vols.
Desert tales, lost mines.

Lavender, David Sievert
One Man's West; line drawings by William Arthur Smith. Garden City, N. Y.: Doubleday, Doran & Co., 1943. vi, 298 pp., illus.

Monroe, Arthur Worley
San Juan Silver; dedicated to the pioneers of Western Colorado and to the memory of Chief Ouray and Chipeta. Historical tales of the silvery San Juan and western Colorado. Grand Junction, Colo.: Grand Junction Sentinel, 1940. ix, 250 pp.

North, Mary Remsen
Down the Colorado, By a Lone Girl Scout with an introduction by Frederick S. Dellenbaugh . . . with 31 illustrations. New York: G. P. Putnam's Sons, 1930. xiii, 164 pp., illus.
Contains—"Cowboy Song" with music, pp. 152.

Pritchett, Lulita Crawford
The Shining Mountains: A story of pioneer Colorado. Illustrated by Sanford Tously. Chicago, Ill.: Albert Whitman and Co., 1939.

Rockwell, Wilson
New Frontier; Saga of the North Folk; illustrations by Josephine McKittrick. Denver, Colo.: The World Press, 1938. xvi, 215 pp., illus., bibl.

Ruxton, G. A.
Adventures in Mexico and the Rocky Mountains. London: Murray 1847.

Sabin, E. L.
Kit Carson Days. Chicago: A. C. McClurg, 1914.

Smith, Honora De Busk
"Cowboy Lore in Colorado." *TFSP* 9:27-44, 1931.
Deals with Clay Allison, known "killer"; and just yarns.

Willard, Henry
The Past and Present of the Pike's Peak Gold Regions. Reprinted from the edition of 1860, with introduction and notes by Le Roy R. Hafen . . . Princeton: Princeton University Press, 1932. xv, 186 pp.

Walsh, Richard and Salsbury, M. S.
The Making of Buffalo Bill. Indianapolis: Bobbs Merrill, 1938.

Willison, George F.
Here They Dug the Gold. New York: Reynal and Hitchcock, 1946.
The dramatic action-packed days of the Pike's Peak Gold Rush, and the dauntless pioneers who found wealth, disaster, and adventure in the Western Hills.

Wright, J. W.
Colorado in Color and Song, color reproductions from photographs. Verse by J. W. W., F. H. Mayer, and others. Denver: F. S. Thayer, 1899. 26 pp., illus.

FOLKTALES—LEGENDS—MYTHS

Bancroft, Caroline
"Lost Mine Legends of Colorado." *CFQ* 2: 253-263, 1943.

Bancroft, George, Jr.
"Industrial Page Series of Lost Mine Series." *Rocky Mountain News,* Jan.-July, 1914.

Bigney, T.
A Month With the Muses. Colorado Tales and Legends of the earlier days, in verse and some fugitive rhyming lines. Pueblo, Colo.: T. O. Bigney, 1875. 130 pp.

Boyer, Warren E.
Vanishing Trails of Romance; Legendary and Historical Tales and Events Gleaned Along the Moccasin-Winged Trails of Aztec and Indian, and the Blazed Trails of Explorer and Pioneer Settler in Enchanting Colorado . . . Denver, Col.: Great West Publishers, 1923. 94 pp., illus.

Breakenridge, William
Helldorado. Boston: Houghton Mifflin, 1928.

Hill, Alice Polk
Tales of the Colorado Pioneers. Denver: Pierson & Gardner, 1884. 319 pp.

Kay, Eleanor
"Lost Mines and Buried Gold." *New Mexico Magazine* 13(No. 9), 1935 (Sept.)

Mecum, Laura T.
Pike's Peak, Yesterday and Today; Stories and Legends Concerning the Region of the Monarch of the Plains. Colorado Springs: 1926. 72 pp., illus.

CUSTOMS—BELIEFS

Ashley, Susan Riley
"Reminiscences of Colorado in the Early 'Sixties.'" *Colorado Magazine* 13: 219-230, 1936.

Barney, Libeus
Early-Day Letters from Auraria (now Denver), Written by Libeus Barney to the "Bennington Banner," Bennington, Vermont, 1859-1860. Denver: A. J. Ludditt Press, 1860. 88 pp.
Letters reminiscent of pioneer days in the West."

Byrne, Bernard James
A Frontier Army Surgeon; an authentic description of Colorado in the eighties. Cranford, N. J.: Allen Printing Co., 1935. 160 pp.

Ellis, Anne
The Life of an Ordinary Woman. Boston: Houghton Mifflin Co., 1929.
Colorado country and town.

Hafen, LeRoy R., ed.
Colorado Gold Rush; contemporary letters and reports, 1858-1859. Glendale, Calif.: The Arthur H. Clark Company, 1941. 386 pp., illus. (The Southwest Historical Series, X.)

Hill, Emma Shepard, comp.
Foundation Stones. Denver, Colo.: E. S. Hill, 1926. 243 pp., illus.
Life of the pioneers, their habits and customs.

Leckenby, Charles Harmon, comp.
The Tread of Pioneers . . . Some highlights in the dramatic and colorful history of northwestern Colorado. Steamboat Springs, Col.: The Pilot Press, 1945. 206 pp., illus.

Lewis, Edward J.
"Diary of a Pike's Peak Gold Seeker in 1860." *Colorado Magazine* 14: 201-219; 15: 20-33, 1937-1938.

Lewis, Oscar
Silver Kings. Illustrated. New York: Alfred A. Knopf, 1946.
The fabulous story of the four Irish immigrants, Mackay, Fair, Flood and O'Brien, who make themselves multimillionaires and lords of the famous Nevada Comstock mines.

Londoner, Wolfe
"Western Experiences and Colorado Mining Camps." *Colorado Magazine* 6: 65-72, 1929.

Rockwell, Wilson
New Frontier; Saga of the North Folk; illustrations by Josephine McKittrick. Denver, Col.: The World Press, 1938. xvi, 215 pp., illus., bibl.

Stanton, Irving Wallace
Sixty Years in Colorado; reminiscences and reflections of a pioneer in 1860 . . . Denver, Col.: 1922. 320 pp., illus.

Thomas, C. S.
"An Argonaut of the Roaring Fork." *Colorado Magazine* 7: 205-216, 1930, illus.

Willison, George Findlay
Here They Dug the Gold. New York: Brentano's, 1931. xiii, 299 pp., illus.
Adventures of gold diggings in Colorado—customs, traditions, and humor.

PLACE NAMES

Davidson, Levette, J., and Koehler, Olga Hazel
"The Naming of Colorado's Towns and Cities." *AS* 7(No. 3):180-187, 1932. Bibl.

Hafen, LeRoy R.
"Colorado Cities—Their Founding and the Origin of their Names." *Colorado Magazine* 9: 170-183, 1932.

——,
"The Counties of Colorado: A History of their Creation and the Origin of their Names." *Colorado Magazine* 8:48-60, 1931.

Federal Writers' Project
"The Names of Colorado Towns, Prepared by the Colorado Writers' Project." *The Colorado Magazine* 17(No. 1): 28-36, 81-94, 125-143, 189-197, 221-229; 18:24-36, 59-71, 142-156, 227-239; 19: 17-29, 73-78, 110-114, 141-153, 175-184, 219-235; 20: 26-36, 71-76, 108-118, 1940.

Paxson, Frederick Logan
"The County Boundaries of Colorado." *The University of Colorado Studies* 3: 197-215, 1906.

Richie, Eleanor L.
"Spanish Place Names in Colorado." *AS* 10 (No. 2): 88-92, 1935.

Trager, George L.
"Some Spanish Place Names of Colorado." *AS* 10(No. 3): 203-207, 1935.

SPEECH

Jones, Joseph
"Cabin Names from Colorado." *AS* 11(No. 3): 276-278, 1936.

Schultz, J. R.
"Features of Colorado Life as seen by Bayyard Taylor." *Colorado Magazine* 12:161-168, 1935.
"A study of differences in Western speech as illustrated in the contrast of Colorado terms with those of California."

FOLKSONG

STUDIES

Davidson, Levette J.
"Songs of the Rocky Mountain Frontier." *CFQ* 2: 89-112, 1943.
Survey of folk and popular songs of the 1850's and 1860's in Colorado. Words only.

Grant, Alexander, comp.
University of Colorado Song Book. Boulder, Colo.: University of Colorado, 1928. 96 pp.
Arranged for 4 voices, or for 1 voice with piano accomp.

Meinhardt, W.
Musical History of Colorado. Editor, E. B. Pathorne, no imprint.

NEVADA

FOLKLORE

BIBLIOGRAPHY

Historical Records Survey
Inventory of the County Archives of Nevada. Prepared by the Historical Records Survey. Works Progress Administration. Reno, Nev.: The Historical Records Survey, 1937.

GENERAL STUDIES AND COLLECTIONS

Brewer, William Henry
Up and Down California in 1860–1864; a journal . . . New Haven: Yale University Press, 1930. xxx, 601 pp., illus.

Buck, Franklin Augustus
A Yankee Trader in the Gold Rush, letters compiled by Katherine A. White. Boston: Houghton Mifflin Company, 1930. viii, 294 pp., illus.

Clemens, Samuel L. (Mark Twain)
Roughing It. Hartford: American Publishing Co., 1871.

Federal Writers' Project
Nevada, a Guide to the Silver State. (American Guide Series). Compiled by Workers of the Writers' Project of the Works Progress Administration in the State of Nevada. Portland, Oregon: Binford and Mort, 1940.

Goodwin, Charles Carroll
As I Remember Them. Salt Lake City, Utah: Salt Lake Commercial Club, 1913. 360 pp.
Reminiscences of Nevada pioneer life.

Lillard, Richard G.
Desert Challenge: An Interpretation of Nevada. (The American Scene Series). New York: Alfred A. Knopf, 1942. viii, 388 pp., illus., bibl.
The story of Nevada illustrated with photographs. More of history and reportage than lore, but still of interest to folklorists, excellent picture of mining camps, old and new, with many good stories.

————,
"Evolution of the Washoe Zephyr." *AS* 18: 257-260, 1943.
Tale of the strange behavior of this violent desert wind of west Nevada.

Lyman, George D.
Ralston's Ring: California Plunders the Comstock Lode. New York: Charles Scribner's Sons, 1937.

Mack, Effie Mona, and Byrd, Wall Sawyer
Our State: Nevada. Caldwell Id.: The Caxton Printers, Ltd., 1946. 323 pp., illus., bibl.

Martin, Anne
"Nevada, Beautiful Desert of Buried Hopes." *Nation* 115:88-92, 1922.

Marye, George T., Jr.
From '49 to '83 in California and Nevada. Chapters from the Life of George Thomas Marye, a Pioneer of '49 (by his Son). San Francisco: A. M. Robertson and Co., 1923.

Mathews, Mary McNair
Ten Years in Nevada: or, Life on the Pacific Coast. Buffalo: Baker, Jones & Co., 1880. 343 pp., illus.

Merrill, Orin S.
"Mysterious Scott," the Monte Cristo of Death Valley, and tracks of a tenderfoot . . . Chicago O. S. Merrill, 1906. 210 pp., illus.
Much lore on mining, customs and beliefs.

Morgan, Dale L.
The Humboldt, Highroad of the West. Illustrated by Arnold Blanch. (The Rivers of America). New York: Farrar & Rinehart, 1943. x, 374 pp., illus., bibl. (pp. 355-365).

Scrugham, James Graves, ed.
Nevada; A Narrative of the Conquest of a Frontier Land; comprising the story of her people from the dawn of history to the present time. Chicago: The American Historical Society, 1935. 3 vols., illus.

Wright, William
The Big Bonanza; an authentic account of the discovery, history, and working of the world-renowned Comstock lode of Nevada . . . adventures connected with mining, the Indians, and the country; amusing stories, experiences, anecdotes, etc., etc. . . . Introduction by Oscar Lewis. New York: A. A. Knopf, 1947. xli, 439 pp., illus.

FOLKTALES

Chalfant, W. A.
Tales of the Pioneers. Palo Alto: Stanford University Press, 1942. xi, 129 pp.
The population of this region—Panamint, Bodie, Pioche, and Mammoth—consists largely of a backwater from the Nevada mines.

Hart, Fred W.
The Sazerac Lying Club. A Nevada Book. San Francisco: Henry Keller and Co., 1878.

Loomis, C. Grant
"Harte's Tall Tales from Nevada." *CFQ* 4: 216-238, 1945.

FOLKSONG

See: Folksong of the West, p. 373; Songs of the Cowboy, pp. 617-27.

UTAH

FOLKLORE

BIBLIOGRAPHY

"A Regional Bibliography," appears in each quarterly issue of the *Utah Humanities Review.*
Besides listing books and periodicals on general regional subjects, it also lists materials having direct reference to folklore and folksong.

Historical Records Survey
Inventory of the County Archives of Utah. Prepared by the Historical Records Survey. Works Progress Administration. Ogden, Utah: The Historical Records Survey, 1937.

Lee, Hector, comp.
A Bibliography of the Archives of the Utah Humanities Research Foundation 1944—47. Bulletin, University of Utah. vol. 38, no. 9, Dec. 1947. 41 pp.
"The materials collected by the Foundation are housed at the library of the University of Utah, where they can be readily consulted. Cataloguing has been based on a classification of five types of materials: (1) loose-leafed, unbound manuscripts and typescripts, (2) books and other bound matter, (3) microfilm, (4) photostats and photographs, and (5) phonograph records" (Editor s introduction).
The archive contains an extensive folklore section under the following headings: Anecdote, Divination, Customs, Games, Ghost Stories, Holidays, Hunting Stories, Legends, Medicine, Mining Lore, Monsters, Music, Nicknames, Outlaws, Place Names, River Lore, Supernatural Occurrences, Superstitions and Weather Lore.

Winther, Oscar Osburn
Mormons—A Bibliography. In: *The Trans-Mississippi West: A Guide to its Periodical Literature (1811-1938).* Bloomington University Publications, Social Science Series 3 (pp. 126-130). Bloomington, Ind.: Indiana University Bookstore.

PERIODICALS

Utah Historical Quarterly. V. 1, 1928—. Salt Lake City, Utah: Utah State Historical Society.

Utah Humanities Review. A Regional Quarterly. Vol I, No. 1, January 1947.— Hector Lee, editor. Published at the University of Utah by the Utah Humanities Research Foundation.

GENERAL STUDIES AND COLLECTIONS

Anderson, A. M.
Fur Trappers of the Old West Chicago: Wheeler Publishing Co., 1946, 252 pp.
The thrilling adventures of the fearless and daring Jim Bridger, and his men.

Anonymous
Mormons. The Mormons have stepped down and out of celestial government; the American Indians have stepped up and into celestial government, 4 pages. No publ., n.d.

Bailey, Paul D.
For This My Glory. Los Angeles: Westernlore Press, 1943.
A novel of Mormon life.

————,
Gay Saint. Hollywood: Murray and Gee, 1944.
A novel based on the life of Sam Brannan.

————,
Sam Brannan and the California Mormons. Los Angeles: Westernlore Press, 1943.
Story of the Mormons in early California history.

Bancroft, Hubert H.
History of Utah. San Francisco: The History co., 1889.

Birney, Hoffman
Zealots of Zion; drawings by Charles Hargens. Philadelphia: The Penn Publishing Company, 1931. 317 pp., illus., bibl.

Brodie, Fawn M.
No Man Knows My History: The Life of Joseph Smith. New York: Alfred A. Knopf, Inc., 1945. 476 pp., illus.
The life of the founder of Mormonism.

Bryant, V. E. B.
Between the Covers of the Book of Mormon. Independence, Mo.: Herald Publ., 1945.

Burton, Richard F.
The City of the Saints. London: Longman, Green, Longman and Roberts, 1861.

Carle, C.
Listen, Bright Angel. New York: Duell, Sloane, and Pearce, 1946.
A book on Mormon life, leaders, and traditions.

Creer, Leland Hargrave
The Founding of an Empire: The Exploration and Colonization of Utah, 1776-1856. Salt Lake City, Utah: Bookcraft, 1947. 454 pp.
Nearly half of the book is devoted to events prior to 1847, the year when the Mormon pioneers first arrived. A great deal is given to the Indians, Mexicans, and the pathfinders, the mountain men—Roubidoux, Bridger, Ogden, Sablette, Smith, Goodyear and others. The second half of the book is given to a historical study of Mormons and Mormonism.

Culmsee, C., ed.
Utah Sings. Provo, Utah: Brigham Young University Press, 1945.
Poems by Utah authors.

Daughters of the Utah Pioneers. Salt Lake City: Daughters of the Utah Pioneers. A series of books dealing with the people, places, and ideas that went into the State of Utah. Some of the titles: *Builders of Uintah: A History of Uintah County,* 1948. *Echoes of Yesterday: A History of Summit County,* 1947. *Heart Throbs of the West,* Vol. 8, 1947. *History of Juab County,* 1948. *Memories That Live: A History of Utah County,* 1948. *Tales of a Triumphant People: History of Salt Lake County,* 1847-1900, 1947. *These Our Fathers: A History of Sanpete County,* 1948. *Thru the Years: A History of Sevier County,* 1948.

De Voto, Bernard
The Chariot of Fire. New York: The Macmillan Co., 1926.
A work of fiction.

Donan, Patrick
Utah: A Peep Into a Mountain-Walled Treasury of the Gods. Buffalo, N. Y.: Matthews, Northrup Co., 1891. 96 pp.

Federal Writers' Project
Utah, a Guide to the State (American Guide Series). Compiled by Workers of the Writers' Program of the Works Progress Administration for the State of Utah. New York: Hastings House, 1941.

Elsensohn, Sister Alfreda
Pioneer Days in Idaho County. Vol. I. Caldwell, Idaho: The Caxton Printers, 1947. xx, 527 pp., bibl., index, and 2 maps.

Out of a careful selection of materials the author has woven a rich tapestry of early historic life, customs, traditions, legends, anecdotes, place names, and bizarre characters in one of the largest counties in the state of Idaho.

Ertz, Susan
The Proselyte. New York: D. Appelton-Century Co., Inc., 1933.
A novel of Utah and Mormon life.

Ferris, Benjamin G.
Utah and the Mormons. New York: Harper and Bros., 1854.

Ferron, Richard M.
"Legendary Mining Men in Eastern Utah." *Utah Human. Rev.* 2 (No. 4): 381–382, 1948.

The author discusses Dave Brittin, Kale Rhodes, and the colorful Finn Britt.

Fife, Austin and Mrs.
Private Mormon Folklore Collection.

"It consists at present (1948) of thirteen volumes of notes on all phases of Mormon folklore including stenographic and phonographic transcriptions of several hundred interviews, excerpts from private journals, letters, student compositions, family histories and other manuscript sources, and copies of obscure published desiderata from newspapers, local publications, and other literature." (Austin E. Fife).

Fisher, Vardis
Children of God, New York: Harper & Bros., 1939.
A novel.

Greenwood, Annie Pike
The Sagebrush Folks. New York: D. Appleton-Century Co., Inc., 1934. 438 pp.

Gunnison, Lieut. John Williams
The Mormons, or Latter-Day Saints in the Valley of the Great Salt Lake. A History of the Mormons. Phila., Pa.: J. B. Lippincott Co., 1856. 168 pp.

Hand, Wayland D.
"Folklore from Utah's Silver Mining Camps." *JAFL* 55:132—161, 1942.

Hanks, N. C.
Men of the Rockies. Heber City, Utah: The author, 1945.

Harmer, Mabel
Story of the Mormon Pioneers. Salt Lake City: Deseret News Press, 1943.

Hickman, W. A.
Brigham's Destroying Angel, ed. with notes by J. H. Beadle. New York: George A. Crofutt Co., 1872.

Hinkley, Helen
The Mountains Are Mine. New York: Vanguard Press, Inc., 1946. 394 pp.

"Mrs. Hinkley is admittedly a good story teller and has carefully avoided most of the historical cliches of Mormon fiction, while at the same time including a well detailed account of a unique type of life. Mormon history and folkways are the subjects for great literature." (Moyle Q. Rice).

Irving, Washington
Adventures of Captain Bonneville in the Rocky Mountains and Far West. New York: G. P. Putnam's Sons, 1849. 428 pp. First edited in 1837.

James, George Wharton
Utah, The Land of Blossoming Valleys; the story of its desert wastes . . . of the origin, development, and beliefs of the Mormon Church . . . Boston: The Page Company, 1922. xix, 371 pp., illus.

Johnson, H. C.
Scenic Guide to Utah. Susanville, California: Scenic Guides, Box 288, 1947.

Kelly, Charles
Salt Desert Trails. Salt Lake City: Western Printing Co., 1930. 178 pp.

———,
Outlaw Trails. Salt Lake City: Western Printing Co., 1938. 337 pp.

Lee, Hector
"Let's Preserve Our Local Culture." *Utah Educational Review* 39:172, 1946.

McGavin, E. Cecil
Nauvoo the Beautiful. Salt Lake City: Stevens and Wallis, Inc., 1946. 354 pp., illus.

A dramatic story of the accomplishments of the early Mormons who built this beautiful town on the Mississippi River in Southern Illinois. They erected—out of a swampy, fever infested area— "one of the largest and most progressive cities in the upper river basin." The book is flavored by human interest stories gleaned from unpublished diaries, letters, and biographies of early Mormon leaders.

Morgan, Dale Lowell
The Great Salt Lake. Indianapolis: The Bobbs, Merrill & Co., 1947. 432 pp., illus.

A highly documented study of Utah history—of its people, their lives and achievements. A Lake Series Volume.

Muench, Josef
Salt Lake City. New York: Hastings House, 1947. illus. (Visage of America Series.)

Olson, Edmund T.
Utah; A Romance of Pioneer Days, with historical accounts or turbulent scenes incident to the adjustments of social and political differences between the Latter-day Saints and the government of the United Sates . . . profusely illustrated with rare, antique and modern pictures. Salt Lake City, Utah: The Author, 1931. xix, 345 pp.

Reagan, Albert B.
"Forts Roubidoux and Kit Carson in Northeastern Utah." *New Mexico Historical Quarterly:* 121-132, April, 1935.

Snell, George Dixon
Root, Hog and Die. Caldwell, Idaho: The Caxton Printers, Ltd., 1936.
A work of fiction.

Stegner, Wallace
Mormon Country. American Folkways Series. New York: Duell, Sloan & Pearce, Inc., 1942. x, 362 pp., index.
The myths and legends of the Mormons, their folkways, and great leaders.

————,
"Mormon Trees—Lombardy Poplars." *Scholastic,* 46:18, April 23, 1945.

Stinhouse, Mrs. T. B. H.
Tell It All: The story of a life's experience in Mormonism. Including a full account of the Mountain Meadows Massacre, and of the life, confession and execution of Bishop John D. Lee. London: S. Low, Marston, Searle and Rivington, 1882.

Stokes, Jeremiah
The Soul's Fire. Los Angeles: Sutton House, 1936.

Whipple, Maurine
This is the Place: Utah. New York: Alfred A. Knopf, 1945. 222 pp., illus.
Places in Utah, pictures and commentary.

————,
The Giant Joshua. Boston: Houghton Mifflin Company, 1941.
A regional novel containing much folklore data, particularly medical and local lore.

FOLKTALES—LEGENDS

Allen, D. R.
"The Alta Legend." *Utah Magazine* 8:19, April 1946.

Durham, L. Marsden
" 'Thus Saith the Lord'—A Tale of the 'Underground'—1887." *Utah Humanities Review* (No. 4) : 347-354, 1947.
A humorous tale of a Mormon family, rich in speech idioms and 'folksy' expressions.

Fife, Austin E.
"Popular Legends of the Mormons." *CFQ* 1: 105-127, 1942.

————,
"The Bear Lake Monsters." *Utah Humanities Review* 2 (No. 2) : 99-106, 1948.
"The story teller's imagination was as common a trait among our pioneer ancestors as was apostolic insistence upon veracity. Thanks to them we possess in Deseret today a rich and varied fabric of local legends, of which one of the most picturesque is that of the Bear Lake Monsters."

————,
"The Legend of the Three Nephites among the Mormons." *JAFL* 53:1-49, 1940.

————,
"Legends of Latter-Day Saints." In: *Regional American Folklore,* ed. by Stith Thompson. To be published.

"Flint Singer Returns to the Underworld." *Desert Magazine* 10:15-17, May, 1947.
A Utah character and legend.

Hand, Wayland D.
"The Three Nephites in Popular Tradition." *SFQ* 2:123-129, 1938.

Hunter, Milton R.
Utah Indian Stories. Springville, Utah: Art City Publishing Co., 1946, illus.
Besides information on Indian and white relationship, customs and traditions, a number of tales are included.

Jeffcott, Vernon
"Tales of Pioche." *Utah Humanities Review* 2 (No. 2) :192-193, 1948.
Stories of early mining days in Pioche, Nevada.

Lee, Hector
The Three Nephites. Dissertation submitted for Ph.D. Degree, University of New Mexico, 1946. MS.

————, **and Folland, Harold**
"Legend of Butch Cassidy." *Legend* 2:7, June 1946.

Smith, Ruby K.
"Legend of the Tribe of Very Much Wind." *Improvement Era* 49:17, 93, 155, 1946.

Stegner, Wallace
"I Dreamed I Saw Joe Hill Last Night." *Pacific Spectator* 1:184, 1947.

CUSTOMS—BELIEFS

Cannon, M. Hamlin
"Angels and Spirits in Mormon Doctrine." *CFQ* 4:343-350, 1945.

Carlton, A. B.
The Wonderlands of the Wild West, with Sketches of the Mormons. n.p.: 1891. viii, 346 pp., illus.

Codman, John
The Mormon Country. A Summer with the "Latter-Day Saints." New York: United States Publishing Company, 1874. 225 pp., illus.

Driggs, Howard R.
Ben, the Wagon Boy. Drawings by Perry Driggs. Salt Lake City: Deseret Book Co., 1944.
Chapters of Utah history, life and manners.

Earl, Mrs. Angie
Angie Earl's Treasured Lion House Recipes.
Salt Lake City, Utah: Bookcraft, 1947. 106 pp.
A cookbook of unusual traditional recipes. "Between red-checked cover simulating the calico tablecloths of the Utah pioneers, Mrs. Angie Earl, long-time cateress at the social center now maintained in historic Lion House in Salt Lake City has collected and assembled the 'patterns' for ninety culinary masterpieces as a 1947 Centennial contribution." (Lila M. Canavan).

Ekman, Beatrice K.
"Pioneer Cookery." *Relief Society Magazine* 34:311, May, 1947.

Ferris, Benjamin G.
Utah and the Mormons . . . From personal observation during a six months' residence at Great Salt Lake City. New York: Harper & Bros., 1854. xii, 347 pp.

Fife, Austin E.
"Folk Belief and Mormon Cultural Autonomy." *JAFL* 61:19-30, 1948.
The article also lists very important bibliographical data on the Mormon theme.

Lyman, Amy B.
"Pioneer Stories and Incidents." *Relief Society Magazine* 34:245, 178, 1947.

Remy, J., and Benchley, J.
A Journey to Great Salt Lake City, with a sketch of the history, religion, and customs of the Mormons, and an introduction in the religious movement in the United States. London: W. Jeffs, 1861. 2 vols.

Russell, Osborne
Journal of a Trapper, 1834-1843. Boise, Idaho: Syms-York Co., Inc., 1921. 149 pp.

Scowcroft, Richard
Children of the Covenant. Boston: Houghton, Mifflin Co., 1945. 292 pp.
A Mormon novel of the changes brought on a Mormon community by new socio-economic forces.

Sorensen, Virginia
On This Star. New York: Reynal and Hitchcock, 1946. 275 pp.
A novel of a Utah valley. It contains rich background in local history, local lore and customs. "Woven carefully into the texture of her book are such things as baptisms for the dead, temple marriage, family reunions (with their inevitable group portraits), community self-dependence, funerals, folk-songs, conversions, migrations, and now-outlawed plural marriage." (Edward F. Chapman).

Toponce, Alexander
Reminiscences of Alexander Toponce, Pioneer, 1839-1923. Ogden, Utah: Century Printing Co., 1923. 248 pp., illus.

Walkup, Fairfax Proudfit
"The Sunbonnet Woman—Fashions in Utah Pioneer Costume." *Utah Humanities Review* 1 (No. 3):201-222, July 1947.

This article is based on materials gathered by the Utah Pioneer Costume and Manners Project, recording pioneer dress from the period 1845-1875. "Garments and accessories are measured, analyzed, and photographed; detailed records (including photographs) are kept on data cards, which are to be filed in the archives of the University of Utah, where they will be available for study."

FOLK MEDICINE

Baker, Pearl, and Wilcox, Ruth
"Folk Remedies in Early Green River." *Utah Humanities Review* 2(No. 2):191-192, 1948.

Mays, Joy S., and Tassoni, Joseph P.
"Home Remedies." *Utah Humanities Review* 1 (No. 2):187, 1947.
Taken from diaries in the archives of the Utah Humanities Research Foundation: cures for whooping cough, worms, rheumatism, and itch.

Noall, Claire
"Superstitions, Customs, and Prescriptions of Mormon Midwives." *CFQ* 3:102-114, 1944.
Description of their use of herbs and cures in childbirth.

————,
"Mormon Midwives." *Utah Historical Quarterly* 10:84-144, 1942.

SPEECH—PLACE NAMES

Bero, John A.
"Utah Place Names." *Utah Humanities Review* 2:79-80, 1947.
Curiously, very few, only five, cities in Utah derive their names from the *Book of Mormon*.

Federal Writers' Project
Origins of Utah Place Names. Compiled and written by Utah Federal Writers' Project, Works Progress Administration. Salt Lake City, Utah: n.p., 1938. 36 pp., illus., Second Edition (American Guide Series).

Frisby, Leah R., and Lee, Hector
"The Deseret Readers." *Utah Humanities Review* 1(No. 3):240-244, 1947.

Ivins, S. S.
"The Deseret Alphabet." *Utah Humanities Review* 1(No. 3):223-239, 1947.
"The pure Adamic language" and alphabet devised by the early Mormon in search for a language reform with their belief in the restoration of the biblical "ancient order of things." The word "deseret" means a "honey bee," which became their symbol of industry.

Jenson, Andrew
"Origin of Western Geographical Names. Associated with the History of the 'Mormon' People." *Utah Genealogical and Historical Mag.* (Salt Lake City) 10:6-16, 81-85, 120-128, 181-190; 11:34-40, 82-91, 141-144, 170-177; 12:41-48, 1920-21.

Utah University
The Deseret First Book, by the Regents of the Deseret University. Salt Lake City: 1868. 36 pp., illus.

—————,
The Deseret Second Book, by the Regents of
the Deseret University, 1868. 72 pp., illus.

PROVERBS

Polve, Adella
"Utah Folksay." *Utah Humanities Review* 1
(No. 3):300-301, 1947.
A list of proverbs common in various parts of
the state.

FOLKSONG

BIBLIOGRAPHY

Utah Folk Songs. Studies and collections in the
Archives of the Utah Humanities Research
Foundation, University of Utah. *See:* Bulletin,
vol. 38, no. 9, Dec. 1947, p. 11.
Classified under three headings: "Mormon Folk
Songs," "Pioneer Songs," and "The Mormon
Car."

STUDIES

Anderson, Mrs. Matilda Foster
"The Mormon Car." *Utah Humanities Review*
1(No. 2):187-188, 1947.
A song, to the tune of "John Brown's Body"
sung by Mormon pioneers as they crossed the
plains to Utah in 1858.

Davidson, Levette J.
"Mormon Songs." *JAFL* 58:273-300, 1945.
Discussion and classification, no tunes given.

Fife, Austin E.
"The Mormon Car." *Utah Humanities Review*
1(No. 3):298-299, 1947.
The text of a Mormon ballad. The tune (not
given) is "Jeannette and Jeanot."

—————, and **Fife, Alta S.**
"Folk Songs of Mormon Inspiration." *WF*
6:42-52, 1947.

Gates, Susa Young
"How Utah's Pioneers Carried Music Across
the Rockies." *Musical America* 23:3 (Nov. 20),
1904.
The author was a daughter of Brigham Young.

Hubbard, Lester A.
"Songs and Ballads of the Utah Pioneers."
Utah Humanities Review 1:74-96, 1947.
Songs popular with the Mormons—from the
serious to the comic. Many variants of 'Old
Country Ballads' are included. Texts only.

Ivins, S. S.
"Another Mormon Song: The Reformation."
Utah Humanities Review 1(No. 2):185-186,
1947.
Text of a song popular in the '50's of the 19th
Century. Text only, the tune to which it was
sung was "Rosa May."

Wheelwright, Lorin F., ed.
Art Division Source Book. Basic materials on
music, drama, art, pageantry, Parades for the
Utah Centennial, 1847-1947. Salt Lake City:
Utah Centennial Commission, 1947. 224 pp.
mimeo.

Very useful section on folk music: "Music and
Pioneer Migration" provides words and music to
a variety of period songs: the emigrant crossing
from Europe, the trek across the plains, the
handcart days, the home in the valley, the
United Order, the Utah War, the coming of the
railroad; and includes vignettes of "The Singing
Bowler Family," "Ballo, the Little Bandleader
of Zion," "A Dying Minstrel," together with
specific suggestions for their use. (William
Mulder).

COLLECTIONS

Daughters of Utah Pioneers, comp.
Pioneer Songs. Music arranged by Alfred M.
Durham. Salt Lake City, Utah: Daughters of
Utah Pioneers, 1932. 278 pp.
Collection of songs used by the pioneers en
route to and in the early settlements of the
West. Also songs inspired and composed by
the pioneers in memory of their experiences.

Briegel, George F.
44 Old Time Mormon and Far West Songs.
New York: 1933.

Lyon, John
The Harp of Zion. Linden: T. C. Armstrong,
1853. 225 pp.
Contains early Mormon hymns.

Pioneer Songs (of the Mormons). Salt Lake
City: n.d. 1 sheet, 5 illus.

*Sacred Hymns and Spiritual Songs for the
Church of Jesus Christ of Latter-Day Saints.*
Salt Lake City, Utah: 1883.

The Bee-Hive Songster. Salt Lake City, Utah:
1868.
The booklet is the work of a Welsh proselyte
who signed himself "Ieuan."

Utah Centennial Commission
Utah Centennial Commission. Source Book,
Arts Division. Salt Lake City, 1946. (Mimeo.)

Utah Sings. Edited by Harrison R. Merrill and
Elsie Talmadge Brandley. Provo, Utah: Utah
Academy of Sciences, Arts and Letters, 1935.
Wild West. n.p.: C. E. Thomas Pub. Co.,
1917. 221 pp., illus.

CHILDREN'S RHYMES

Wilson, Marguerite Ivins
"Yours Till—: A Study of Children's Auto-
graph Rhymes in Utah." *Utah Humanities
Review* 3:245-260, 1947.

RECORDS

**U. S. Library of Congress. Division of Music.
Folklore Section.**
*Phonograph Transcriptions of Mormon Folk
Songs and Oral Lore,* made by Dr. and Mrs.
Austin E. Fife of Occidental College, Los
Angeles, California.

—————.
*Recording Project—Mormon Songs, Ballads
and Legends in Utah.* 87 Records. AAFS-LC

WYOMING

FOLKLORE

BIBLIOGRAPHY

Becker, M. L.
"Readers Guide; Novels of Wyoming and Montana." *Saturday Review of Literature* 9:227, Nov. 5, 1932.

Hebard, Grace Raymond, comp.
History and Romance of Wyoming; a guide to book titles and historic places . . . Laramie, Wyo.: 1928. 2 pp.

Historical Records Survey
Inventory of the Archives of Wyoming. Prepared by The Historical Records Survey. Works Progress Adminsitration. Cheyenne. Wyo.: The Historical Records Survey, 1938.

Wheeler, Eva Floy
A Bibliography of Wyoming Writers. Laramie: University of Wyoming, 1939. University of Wyoming Publications, Vol. 6, No. 2:11-37.

PERIODICALS

Wyoming. Historical Department. Annals. Periodical published in 10 vols. titled consecutively: *Quarterly Bulletin,* 2 vols., 1923-4; Annals, vols. 3-9, 1925-34; vols. 10-11, 1938-9; Annals and Eight Biennial Reports, vol. 10, No. 1, January, 1938.

Wyoming Historical Society.
Collections. v. 1, 1897—. Cheyenne. *Miscellanies.* v. 1, 1919—. Laramie, Wyo.: The Laramie Republican Company.

GENERAL STUDIES AND COLLECTIONS

Burt, Struthers
Powder River; Let 'er Buck. (American River Series.) Illustrated by Rose Santee. New York: Farrar and Rinehart, Inc., 1938. xi, 389 pp., illus., bibl.

Chaffin, Lorah B.
Sons of the West. Caldwell, Idaho: The Caxton Printers, 1941.
Historical and biographical sketches of early Wyoming.

Ermine, Will
The Drifting Kid. New York: Doubleday Company, 1947.
A Western story from Wyoming.

Federal Writers' Project
Wyoming, a Guide to Its History, Highways, and People. (American Guide Series.) Compiled by Workers of the Writers' Program of the W.P.A. in the State of Wyoming. New York: Oxford University Press, 1941.

Guernsey, C. A.
Wyoming Cowboy Days. New York: G. P. Putnam's Sons, 1936. 288 pp., illus.

Hafen, LeRoy., and Ghent, William J.
Broken Hand, Chief of the Mountain Men. Denver, Colo.: Old West Publishing Co., 1931. 316 pp.
Life and exploits of Thomas Fitzpatrick.

————, and Young, Francis Marion
Fort Laramie and the Pageant of the West. Glendale: Arthur H. Clark Co., 1938. 429 pp., illus.

Linford, Velma
Wyoming: Frontier State. Denver, Colorado: The Old West Publishing Co., 1947. 428 pp.
Includes a great deal of Western folk material.

McPherren, Ida
Trail's End. Boston, Mass.: Manthorne and Burack, 1943. 322 pp.
A story of pioneering days in Wyoming.

Mokler, Alfred J.
History of Natrona County, Wyoming, 1888-1922. Chicago: R. R. Donnelly & Sons, Co., 1922. 477 pp., map, illus.
True portrayals of the yesterdays of a new country and a typical frontier town of the middle west. Fortunes and misfortunes, tragedies and comedies, struggles and triumphs of the pioneers.

Rollinson, John K.
Pony Trails in Wyoming. Caldwell, Idaho: Caxton Printers, Ltd., 1941.

Spring, Agnes W.
Caspar Collins. New York: Columbia University Press, 1927. 187 pp., illus.
Indian fighter of the 60's.

Trenholm, Virginia Cole
Footprints on the Frontier; Saga of the Laramie region of Wyoming. Douglas, Wyo.: Douglas Enterprise Co., 1945. 384 pp., illus., bibl.

————, and Corley, Maurine
Wyoming Pageant. Casper, Wyoming: Prairie Publishing Company, 1946. 291 pp., illus., maps and teaching aids.
A history of the state—its adventurous pioneers—Jim Bridger among them, conflict with the Indians (a chapter is devoted to their customs and legends), interesting details on fur-trading and trapper trails, and the tribulations of the covered wagon caravans. Many observations on legends, place names and customs.

CUSTOMS—BELIEFS

Carrington, Margaret Irvin
Ab-sa-ra-ka, Home of the Crows: being the experience of an officer's wife on the plains . . Philadelphia: J. B. Lippincott & Co., 1868. xii, 284 pp., illus.

Hough, Donald
Show Above Town. New York: W. W. Norton & Co., 1943. 282 pp.

Stewart, Elinore Pruitt
Letters of a Woman Homesteader. With illustrations by N. C. Wyeth. Boston: Houghton Mifflin Co., 1914. vii, 281 pp., illus.
Description of ranch life in Southwestern Wyoming.

Talbot, Ethelbert
My People of the Plains. New York: Harper & Bros., 1906. x, 264 pp., illus.

Walker, Tacetta B.
Stories of Early Days in Wyoming; Big Horn Basin. Casper, Wy.: Prairie Publishing Company, 1936. 271 pp., illus., bibl.

SPEECH

Bruner, Helen, and Francis, Frances
"A Short Word List from Wyoming." *Dialect Notes* 3(Part 7):550-551, 1911.

Clough, Wilson O.
"Note on Dialect in the Uinta Mountains of Wyoming." *AS* 11(No. 2):190-192, 1936.

Cook, Dorothy
"More Yellowstone Lingo." *AS* 10(No. 1): 75-76, 1935.

PLACE NAMES

Clough, Wilson O.
"Some Wyoming Place Names." *SFQ* 7: 1013, 1943.

"Wyoming Place Names." *Annals of Wyoming* 14: 158-161, 227-239; 15: 85-90, 1942.

FOLKSONG

See: Folksongs of the West, p. 373; Songs of the Cowboys, pp. 617-27.

THE NORTHWEST

THE NORTHWEST

See: Lore and Songs of the Lumberjacks, pp. 630-34; Paul Bunyan, pp. 689-92.

FOLKLORE

BIBLIOGRAPHY

Appleton, John Bargate, comp.
The Pacific Northwest: a selected bibliography, 1930-1939. Portland, Oregon: Northwest Regional Council, 1930. 455 pp.

Guillén y Tato, Julio Fernando
Repertorio de los m.sss., cartas, planos y dibujus relativos a las Californias, existentes en este museo. Madrid, 1932. 127 pp., illus.
A bibliography of the Pacific coast.

Inland Empire Council of Teachers of English.
Northwest Books, reports of the Committee on books of the Inland Empire Council of Teachers of English, 1942; review of over 1100 books, selected magazine bibliography. Portland, Ore.: Binfords & Mort, 1942. 356 pp.

Judson, Katherine Berry
Pacific Northwest: a brief descriptive list of books, with suggested outline for study. Seattle: Seattle Public Library, 1910. 12 pp.

————.
"Collecting Pacific Northwest Americana." *Pacific Northwest Quarterly.* 30:67–76, 1939. Bibl.

————.
Check-list of Books and Pamphlets relating to the history of the Pacific Northwest to be found in representative libraries of that region. Olympia, Wash.: E. L. Boardman, 1909. 191 pp.

————.
Pacific Northwest Americana. A check list of Books, and Pamphlets Relative to the Pacific Northwest. New York: H. W. Wilson Co., 1921. xi, 329 pp. Second and rev. ed.

Rockwood, Eleanor Ruth
Books on the Pacific Northwest for Small Libraries. New York: The H. W. Wilson Co., 1923. 55 pp.

Smith, Charles Wesley
A Union List of Manuscripts in Libraries of the Pacific Northwest. Seattle: University of Washington Press, 1931. 57 pp.

Subject Index to the History of the Pacific Northwest and Alaska. As found in the United States Government Documents, Congressional Series, in the American State Papers and in other Documents, 1789-1881. Prepared by Katharine B. Judson, for the Seattle Public Library. Olympia: Washington State Library, 1913.

PERIODICALS

Northwest Magazine. V. 1, 1883—. V. 18, 1903 St. Paul, Minn. Monthly.

The Northwest. V. 1, 1942—. St. Paul, Minn.

Western Magazine. V. 1, 1925—. St. Paul, Minn. Monthly.

GENERAL STUDIES AND COLLECTIONS

Barneby, William Henry
Life and Labor in the Far, Far West: being notes of a tour in the western states, British Columbia, Manitoba, and the Northwest Territory. London: Cassell & Company, 1884. xvi, 432 pp.

Barrows, John R.
Ubet. Caldwell, Idaho: Caxton Printers Ltd., 1934.

Binns, Archie
The Timber Beast. New York: Charles Scribners' Sons, 1944.
A novel of the adventure, romance of loggers and logging in the Pacific Northwest today.

Blankenship, Russell
And There Were Men. New York: Alfred A. Knopf, 1942. 301 pp.
A picture of the men who molded the Pacific Northwest. Essays on a Motley Crew: Squaw men, Tough guys, Preachers, Indians and Such.

Brackenridge, Henry Marie
Journal of a Voyage Up the River Missouri; performed in Eighteen Hundred and Eleven. ...Baltimore: Coale and Maxwell..., 1816. viii, 246 pp.

Bradford, William John Alden
Notes on the Northwest, or Valley of the Upper Mississippi. New York: Wiley & Putnam, 1846. vi, 302 pp.

Brady, Cyrus Townsend
Northwestern Fights and Fighters; illus. with original drawings, maps and photographs. New York: The McClure Co., 1907. xxv, 373 pp., illus.

Briggs, Harold Edward
Frontiers of the Northwest. A History of the Upper Missouri Valley. New York: D. Appleton-Century, 1940. xiv, 629 pp., illus., bibl.

Bronson, Edgar Beecher
Cowboy Life on the Western Plains; the Reminiscences of a Ranchman. New York: Grosset & Dunlap, 1910. 369 pp.

Calkins, Frank Welles
Frontier Sketches. Chicago: M. A. Donohue & Co., 189–. 134 pp., illus.

Case, Robert Ormond and Victoria
Last Mountains. The Story of the Cascades.
New York: Doubleday, Doran and Co., 1945.
236 pp.
    The author limits the study to Oregon and Washington. Rather lightly treated.

Chittick, Victor L. O., ed.
Northwest Harvest: a Regional Stocktaking.
New York: The Macmillan Co. 1948. 226 pp.
    Includes a discussion by James Stevens of the role of folklore in a changing industrial society. A valuable contribution.

Coues, Elliott
History of the Expedition Under Lewis and Clarke, to the sources of the Missouri River, thence across the Rocky Mountains and down the Columbia River to the Pacific Ocean, performed during the years 1804–5–6, maps, illustrations. New York: 1893. IV vols.

—————.
New Light on the Early History of the Greater Northwest. The manuscript journals of Alexander Henry, fur trader of the Northwest Company, and of David Thompson, official geographer and explorer of the same company, 1799–1814. Exploration and adventure among the Indians on the Red, Saskatchewan, Missouri, and Columbia Rivers. New York: 1897. III vols.

—————.
The Expeditions of Zebulon Montgomery Pike to Headwaters of the Mississippi River, during the years 1805–6–7. (With copious, critical commentary, memoir of Pike, new map and other illustrations and index.) New York: 1895. III vols.

Destler, Chester McArthur
"Diary of a Journey Into the Valleys of the Red River of the North and the Upper Missouri." *Mississippi Valley Historical Review.* (Cedar Rapids), pp. 425–442, 1946.

Dye, Eva (Emery)
McLoughlin and Old Oregon; a chronicle.
Chicago: A. C. McClurg & Co., 1913. viii, 381 pp.

Edwards, William Seymour
In to the Yukon. Cincinnati: The R. Clarke Company, 1905. xii, 335 pp., illus.

Ernst, Alice Henson
High Country; Four Plays of the Pacific Northwest. Portland: The Metropolitan Press, 1935. Foreword by Edith J. R. Isaacs, illus. by Constance Cole, xv, 208 pp.

Federal Writers' Project.
The Oregon Trail: the Missouri River to the Pacific Ocean. Compiled and written by the Federal Writers' Project of the Works Progress Administration. . . . New York: Hastings House, 1939. xii, illus., bibl.

Flandrau, Grace C.
Frontier Days Along the Upper Missouri. St. Paul, Minn.: 1927. 40 pp.

Fountain, Paul
The Great Northwest and the Great Lake Region of North America. London: Longmans, Green and Co., 1904. viii, 355 pp.

Galloway, William A.
Old Chillicothe. Shawnee and Pioneer History. Conflicts and Romances in the Northwest Territory. Xenia, Ohio: Buckeye Press, 1934.

Gillham, Charles Edward
Raw North; illustrated by Bob Hines. New York: A. S. Barnes and Company, 1947. xvi, 275 pp., illus.

Godwin, George Stanley
Vancouver; a Life, 1757–1798. London: P. Allan, 1930. xi, 308 pp., illus.

Holbrook, Stewart Hall, ed.
Promised Land; A Collection of Northwest Writing. New York: Whittlesey House, 1945. xviii, 408 pp.

Irving, Washington
Astoria, or Anecdotes of an Enterprise Beyond the Rocky Mountains. Philadelphia: Carey, Lea & Blanchard, 1836. 2 vols.

Johnson, Richard Byron
Very Far West Indeed. A few rough experiences on the Northwest Pacific coast. London: Sampson, Low, Marston, Low & Searle, 1872. vi, 280 pp., illus.

Jones, Edward Gardner, ed.
The Oregonian's Handbook of the Pacific Northwest. Portland: The Oregonian Publishing Co., 1894. 631 pp., illus.

Laut, Agnes Christina
The Overland Trail; the Epic Path of the Pioneers to Oregon . . . with forty-nine illustrations. . . . New York: Frederick A. Stokes Company, 1929. xx, 358 pp., illus.

Linderman, Frank Bird
On A Passing Frontier. New York: Charles Scribner's Sons, 1920.

Mandat-Grancey, Edmond, baron de
Cow-Boys and Colonels; Narrative of a journey across the prairie and over the Black Hills of Dakota. . . . New York: E. P. Dutton and Co., 1887. 364 pp., illus.

Meacham, Walter E.
Bonneville the Bold, the story of his adventures and explorations in the old Oregon country. . . . Portland, Ore.: 1934. 47 pp., map.

Meeker, Ezra
The Busy Life of Eighty-Five Years of Ezra Meeker. Ventures and Adventures . . . The Oregon Trail. . . . Seattle, Wash.: The Author, 1916. xii, 399 pp., illus.

Merriam, Harold Guy, ed.
Northwest Verse, An Anthology. Caldwell, Id.: The Caxton Printers, Ltd., 1931. 355 pp.
    Contains verse produced in the last twelve or fifteen years in the States of Montana, Idaho, Oregon and Washington.

Morrow, Honoré Willsie
On To Oregon! The Story of a Pioneer Boy.
New York: W. Morrow and Company, 1926.
247 pp., illus.

Morton, Arthur S.
Under Western Skies, being a series of pen-
pictures of the Canadian West in early fur
trade times. Toronto: T. Nelson & Sons, Ltd.,
1937. 232 pp., illus.

Murphy, John Mortimer
*Rambles in North-Western America from the
Pacific Ocean to the Rocky Mountains....*
London: Chapman & Hall, 1879. xii, 364 pp.

Nelson, William Hamilton
Twelve Wonders of the Western World. San
Francisco, Calif.: Danner Publ. Co., 1934.
108 pp., illus.

North Dakota University.
The Book of A Pageant of the Northwest,
written in collaboration by eighteen undergraduate members of the Sock and Buskin Society,
University of North Dakota under the direction
of Professor Frederick H. Koch.... Grand
Forks: Times-Herald Publishing Co., 1914. 80
pp., illus.

Nute, Grace Lee
The Voyageur. New York: D. Appleton-Cen-
tury Co., 1931. 289 pp., illus., maps, bibl.
The most complete study of the Voyageur and
his place in the history of the Northwest. Both
French and English texts of Voyageur Songs.

Paden, Irene
The Wake of the Prairie Schooner, illustrated
by the author. New York: The Macmillan
Company, 1943. xix, 514 pp., illus.

Page, Elizabeth
Wagons West; a story of the Oregon Trail.
New York: Farrar & Rinehart, 1930. xiv, 361
pp., illus., bibl.
Narrative of the overland journey of Henry Page
to California in 1849, based upon his letters to
his wife.

Parkman, Francis
The Oregon Trail. New York: The Limited
Editions Club, 1943. Chicago: John C. Winston
Co., 1931. 388 pp. Illus. First published 1849.

Patterson, W. G.
"'Calamity Jane'—A Heroine of the Wild
West." *Wide World Magazine* (London) 11:
450–457, 1903.

Ross, Nancy Wilson
Farthest Reach. New York: Alfred A. Knopf,
1941.
The author captures the unique flavor of the
Pacific Northwest.

Rucker, Maude
The Oregon Trail and Some Of Its Blazers.
New York: W. Neale, 1930. 293 pp., illus.
Contents: The Name Oregon; Settlement of
Oregon; The Oregon Pioneers of 1843; Jesse
Applegate, by Joseph Schafer; A Day With the

Cow Column, by Jesse Applegate; Recollections
of My Boyhood, by Jesse Applegate; Letters of
Jesse Applegate; Lindsay Applegate's Reminiscences; Herrick's Account of Jesse Applegate.

Russell, Osborne
*Journal of a Trapper; or, Nine Years in the
Rocky Mountains, 1834–1843;* being a general
description of the country, climate, rivers,
lakes, mountains, etc., and a view of the life
of a hunter in those regions. Boise, Id.: Syms-
York Company, 1921. xviii, 149 pp.

Smedley, William
Across the Plains of '62. Denver, 1916. 56 pp.,
illus.

Stoddard, Charles Warren
Over the Rocky Mountains to Alaska. St. Louis,
Mo.: B. Herder, 1914. 168 pp.

Terrell, John Upton
Plume Rouge, A Novel of the Pathfinders. New
York: The Viking Press, 1942. 498 pp.

Victor, Frances
The River of the West. Life and Adventure in
the Rocky Mountains and Oregon; embracing
events in the life-time of a mountain-man and
pioneer.... Also, a description of the country.
... San Francisco, Calif.: R. J. Trumbull &
Co., 1870. 602 pp., illus.

West, Ray B., ed.
Rocky Mountain Reader. New York: E. P.
Dutton Co., 1946. 463 pp.
"—This collection again demonstrates that the
use of regional history, customs, attitudes, character types, etc., gives an attractive flavor to the
work of an author, but that his revelations and
understandings need to go deeper if he expects
to make a lasting contribution to literature."
(Levette J. Davidson.)

Wheeler, Olin D.
Indianland and Wonderland.... A region of
the wonderful phenomena, reached by the
Northern Pacific Railroad. St. Paul: Northern
Pacific R. R., 1894. 108 pp.

FOLKTALES

Cole, Harry Ellsworth
*Stage Coach and Tavern Tales of the Old
Northwest. ....* Cleveland: The Arthur H.
Clark Company, 1930. 376 pp., illus.

Dawson, Charles
*Pioneer Tales of the Oregon Trail and of Jef-
ferson County.* Topeka: Crane & Company,
1912. Illus.

Mallet, Thierry
Plain Tales of the North. New York: G. P.
Putnam's Sons, 1926. 136 pp.

Pounds, Jimmie
"Hugo: the Giant Unkillable Frog; and Paul
Bunyan: oil man." *TFSP* 14:262–264, 1938.

Snelling, William Joseph
Tales of the Northwest, edited by John T.
Flanagan. Minneapolis: University of Min-
neapolis Press, 1936.

Young, Egerton Ryerson
Stories from Indian Wigwams and Northern Campfires. Toronto: W. Briggs; London: C. H. Kelly, 1893. 293 pp., illus.

MYTHS—LEGENDS

Gordon, Hanford Lennox
Legends of the Northwest. Containing: Prelude—The Mississippi. The feast of the Virgins, a legend of the Dakotas. Winona, a legend of the Dakotas. The legend of the falls, a legend of the Dakotas. The sea gull, the Ojibwa legend of the Pictured Rocks of Lake Superior. Minnetonka. St. Paul, Minn.: The St. Paul Book and Stationery Co., 1881. viii, 143 pp., illus.

Judson, Katharine Berry
Myths and Legends of the Pacific Northwest; especially of Washington and Oregon. Chicago: A. C. McClurg & Co., 1910. xvi, 144 pp., with 50 illus.

Lyman, William Denison
The Columbia River; its history, its myths, its scenery, its commerce. New York: Knickerbocker Press, 1909. x, 409 pp., illus.

Thomas, George Francis
Legends of the Land of Lakes, or History, traditions and mysteries, gleaned from years of experience among the pioneers, voyageurs and Indians; with descriptive accounts of the many natural curiosities met with from Lake Huron to the Columbia River. And the meaning and derivation of names of rivers, lakes, towns, etc. of the Northwest. Chicago: G. F. Thomas, 1884. Illus.

Winther, Oscar O.
The Great Northwest. New York: Alfred A. Knopf, 1947.
"A history which takes into full account social and folk phenomena. Provides factual background for fur trade, settling, stage-coach and paddle-wheel eras, for lumbering, steel and irrigation days. Authoritative and lively." (Elaine L. Lewis.)

CUSTOMS

Adams, Harriet L.
A Woman's Journeyings in the New Northwest. Cleveland, O.: B-P. Print. Co., 1892. 180 pp.

Colby, Elbridge
"Through the Northwest in Pioneer Times." *Overland Monthly* (San Francisco) 65:73–81, 1915.
A discussion of Theodore Winthrop's *Canoe and Saddle.* Description of life and manners in the Old Northwest.

Douthit, Mary Osborn, ed.
The Souvenir of Western Women. Portland, Ore.: Anderson & Duniway Company, 1905. 216 pp., illus.
"A complex picture of the works of and pioneer experiences of the women of the Pacific Northwest—the "Old Oregon" country—from the time of woman's first appearance in those unexplored wilds to the present day."—Pref.

France, G. W.
The Struggles for the Life and Home in the Northwest. By a pioneer homebuilder, 1865–1889. New York: I. Goldmann, 1890. 608 pp.

Johnstone, C.
Winter and Summer Excursions in Canada. London: Digby, Long & Co., 1894. xv, 213 pp., illus.

Jones, Nard
Scarlet Petticoat. New York: Dodd, Mead & Company, 1941. 303 pp., bibl.
A novel of the Pacific Northwest.

Patterson, Raymond Albert
"Uncle Rufus" and "Ma." The story of a summer jaunt, with their friends, in the new Northwest. New York: 1882. 67 pp.

Seton, Grace
A Woman Tenderfoot. Over One hundred and fifty illustrations. New York: Doubleday, Page and Co., 1900. 361 pp., illus.

Thane, Eric
High Border Country. (American Folkways.) New York: Duell, Sloan & Pearce, 1942. ix, 335 pp.

Winthrop, Theodore
The Canoe and the Saddle, Adventures Among the Northwestern Rivers and Forests; and, Isthmiana. Boston: Ticknor and Fields, 1863. 375 pp.

SPEECH

Garrett, Robert M.
"A Word List from the Northwest." *Dialect Notes* 5 (Part 2):54–59, 1919; 5 (Parts): 80–84, 1920.

Harvey, Bartle T.
"A Word-List from the Northwest." *Dialect Notes* 4(Part 1):26–28, 1913.

————.
"Addenda to the Word List from the Northwest." *Dialect Notes* 4(Part 2):162–164, 1914.

Lehman, Benjamin H.
"A Word-List from Northwestern United States." *Dialect Notes* 5(Part 1):22–29, 1918.

————.
"Additional Words from the Northwest." *Dialect Notes* 5(Part 5):181, 1922.

Petersen, Sarah Christine
"Yellowstone Park Language." *AS* 7 (No. 1): 221–23, 1931.

PLACE NAMES

Sylvester, A. H.
"Place-naming in the Northwest." *AS* 18:241–252, 1943.
Especially in the forest service.

FOLKSONG

BIBLIOGRAPHY

Appleton, John Bargate, comp.
The Pacific Northwest: A Selected Bibliography, 1930–1939. Portland, Ore.: Northwest Regional Council, 1939. 455 pp.

STUDIES

Howay, F. W.
"Memorandum on the Ballads of the Northwest Fur Trade." *New England Quarterly* 1: 71-79, 1928.

"The Northwestern Man." *FSSNE* 4:13-14, 1932.
A ballad based on historical fact, June 1791.

Maier, G.
"Inspiration from the Northwest." *Etude* 57: 513-, (Sept.) 1939.

ARRANGEMENTS

————: *Orchestra*

Inch, Herbert R.
Northwest Overture. Philadelphia: Elkan-Vogel.

Saar, Louis
From the Mountain Kingdom of the Great Northwest.—Suite. New York: Luckhardt & Belder. For Symphony Orchestra.

IDAHO

FOLKLORE

BIBLIOGRAPHY

Historical Records Survey.
Inventory of the County Archives of Idaho. Prepared by the Historical Records Survey. Works Progress Administration. Boise, Idaho: The Historical Records Survey, 1937. Bibl.

PERIODICALS

Idaho State Historical Society. Bulletin. V. 1, 1908–. Boise.

GENERAL STUDIES AND COLLECTIONS

Bailey, Robert G.
River of No Return (the great Salmon river of Idaho) a century of central Idaho and Washington history and development; together with the wars, customs, myths, and legends of the Nez Perce Indians. Lewiston, Id.: Bailey-Blake Printing Co., 1935. xxiv, 515 pp., illus.

Defenbach, Byron
Idaho; the place and its people; a history of the gem state from prehistoric to present days. Chicago: The American Historical Society, 1933. 3 vols., illus., bibl.

Donaldson, Thomas Corwin
Idaho of Yesterday. Caldwell, Id.: The Caxton Printers, Ltd., 1941. 406 pp., illus.

Federal Writers' Project.
Idaho, a Guide in Word and Picture. Compiled and written by the Federal Writers' Project of the Works Progress Administration. Caldwell, Idaho: The Caxton Printers Ltd. 1937. 431 pp., illus., bibl.

————.

Idaho Lore. (American Guide Series). Written and Compiled by the Federal Writers' Project of the Works Progress Administration, Vardis Fisher, State Director. Copyright, 1939 by George H. Curtis, Secretary of State for the State of Idaho. Caldwell, Idaho: The Caxton Printers Ltd., 1939. 256 pp., illus.
A mine of folklore, legends, folktales, beliefs, cures, etc.

————.

The Idaho Encyclopedia. Compiled by the Federal Writers' Project of the Works Progress Administration. Vardis Fisher, state director. Caldwell, Idaho: The Caxton Printers Ltd., 1938. 452 pp., bibl. (pp. 433–442), illus.

————.

Tours in Eastern Idaho. (American Guide Series). The American Guide Project, a Federal Writers' Project, Works Progress Administration. Washington, D. C.: U. S. Gov't Printing Office, 1937.

Goulder, William Armmistead
Reminiscences: Incidents in the Life of a Pioneer in Oregon and Idaho. Boise, Id.: T. Regan, 1909. 376 pp.

Greenwood, Mrs. Annie Pike
The Sagebrush Folks. New York and London: D. Appleton-Century Co., Inc., 1934. xi, 483 pp.

McGeorge, Alice Sutton
Kamaiwea: The Coeur D'Alene. Kansas City, Mo.: Burton Publishing Co., 1939.
A tale of the Idaho gold rush.

Sabin, Edwin L.
Kit Carson Days. Chicago: A. C. McClurg and Co., 1914. 669 pp., illus., bibl.
"a work long standard, rich on rendezvous, bears, and many other associated subjects. Bibliography." (Dobie.)

Shupe, Verna Irene
The Argonauts and Pioneers. Pocatello, Id.: Graves and Potter, Tribune Press, 1931. 65 pp., illus.
The first edition in 1916—was entitled, *Forty-Niner's Diary.*

Talbot, Ethelbert
My People of the Plains. New York: Harper & Bros., 1906. x, 264 pp., illus.

Walgamott, Charles Shirley
Reminiscences of Early Days; a series of historical sketches and happenings in the early days of Snake River Valley. Twin Falls, Id.: 1926. 2 vols., illus.

————. *Six Decades Back*. Illustrated by R. H. Hall. Caldwell, Id.: The Caxton Printers, Ltd., 1936. 358 pp., illus.

Most of the material had previously appeared in the author's *Reminiscences of Early Days*.

FOLKTALES

Bruneau, Lyda Hoffman
Stories of Idaho, with illustrations depicting life in the state of Idaho from pioneer days to the present time. Lewiston, Id.: R. G. Bailey Printing Co., 1940. 95 pp., illus.

Gillilan, James David
Trail Tales. New York and Cincinnati: The Abingdon Press, 1915. 182 pp.

Tales "tall and broad," in *Idaho Lore* (pp. 113–140), Federal Writers' Project of the W.P.A. Caldwell, Idaho: The Caxton Printers, Ltd., 1939.

SPEECH

Jensen, Paul
"Desert Rats' World-List from Eastern Idaho." *AS* 7 (No. 2):119–123, 1931.

Kernan, Henry S.
"Idaho Lumberjack Nicknames." *CFQ* 4:239–243, 1945.

PLACE NAMES

Koch, Elers
"Geographic Names of Western Montana, Northern Idaho." *Oregon Histor. Quar.*, March, 1948. pp. 50–62.

Rees, John E.
Idaho Chronology, Nomenclature, Bibliography. Chicago: W. B. Conkey Company, 1918. 125 pp.

FOLKSONG

DANCES

Ball, Leona N.
"The Play Party in Idaho." *JAFL* 44:1–26, 1931.

CHILDREN'S RHYMES

Maloney, Violetta G.
"Jumping Rope Rhymes from Burley, Idaho." *HFB* 3 (No. 1):24–25, 1944.

MONTANA

FOLKLORE

BIBLIOGRAPHY

Becker, M. L.
" 'Reader's Guide': Novels of Wyoming and Montana." *Saturday Rev. of Lit.* 9: 227, Nov. 5, 1932.

Davies, John Francis
Montana Literature; Review and Comments. Butte, Mont.: 1914. 5 pp. (Typewritten).

Historical Records Survey.
Inventory of the County Archives of Montana. Prepared by the Historical Records Survey. Works Progress Administration. Missoula, Mont.: The Historical Records Survey, 1939.

PERIODICALS

Historical Society of Montana. Bulletin. No. 1, 1907–1908. Helena, Mont.

GENERAL STUDIES AND COLLECTIONS

Aikman, Duncan
Calamity Jane and the Lady Wildcats. New York: Blue Ribbon Books, 1937.

Barnett, Grace, and Olive
The Mystery of Yogo Creek. New York: Oxford University Press, 1944. 160 pp.

Adventure on a Montana ranch. Juvenile.

Binney, Hoffman
Vigilantes, a chronicle of the rise and fall of the Plummer gang of outlaws in and about Virginia City, Montana, in the early '60's; drawings by Charles Hargens. Philadelphia: The Penn Publishing Co., 1929. 346 pp., illus.

Burt, Struthers
Powder River; Let 'er Buck. (American River Series.) Illustrated by Rose Santee. New York: Farrar and Rinehart, Inc., 1938. xi, 389 pp., illus., bibl.

Dimsdale, Thomas Josiah
The Vigilantes of Montana; or, Popular Justice in the Rocky Mountains; being a correct and impartial narrative of the chase, capture, trial and execution of Henry Plummer's road agent band . . . the whole being interspersed with sketches of life in the mining camps of the "Far West." Virginia City, Mont.: T. E. Castle and C. W. Bank, 1921. 276 pp., illus.

Federal Writers' Project.
Copper Camp. Compiled and written by the Federal Writers' Project of the Works Progress Administration for the State of Montana. Illustrated. New York: Hastings House, 1939. 308 pp.

The exciting story and adventures of the growth of Butte.

————. *Montana; a Profile in Pictures,* sponsored by Montanans incorporated, compiled by workers of the Writers' program of the Works Progress Administration in the State of Montana. New York: Fleming Publishing Company, 1941. 58 pp., illus.

————. *Montana, a State Guide Book.* (American Guide Series.) Compiled and written by the Federal Writers' Project of the Works Progress Administration for the State of Montana. New York: The Viking Press, 1939. xxiii, 430 pp. illus., bibl.

Haycox, Ernest
Bugles in the Afternoon. Boston: Little, Brown and Co., 1944. 306 pp.
A novel.

Howard, Joseph Kinsey
Montana: High, Wide and Handsome. New Haven, Conn.: Yale University Press, 1943. vi, 347 pp., index, bibl.
"By means of description, stories of peoples and events, pertinent comment, and the marshalling of facts, the author presents in chronological order the periods of Montana's development." (L. J. Davidson.)

————, ed.
Montana Margins. New Haven, Conn.: Yale University Press, 1946. xviii, 527 pp.
"These tales do not tell what people say: they show what people do, and actions here certainly speak louder than words. Here are the folk in action that has been traditional from the early days of our country, but set in a new world, Montana. Raciness gives the whole book its authenticity and the folklorist his interest." (H. G. Merriam.)

Norton, Harry J.
Wonder-Land Illustrated; or, Horseback Rides Through the Yellowstone National Park. Virginia City, Mont.: H. J. Norton, 1874. 132 pp.

Price, Con
Trails I Rode. Illustrations by Charlie Russell. Pasadena, Calif.: Trails End Publishing Co., 1947.
Reminiscences of a Montana cowboy.

Raymer, Robert George
Montana, the Land and the People. . . . Chicago: The Lewis Publishing Company, 1930. 3 vols., illus.

Rollins, Philip Ashton
Gone Haywire, Two Tenderfoots on the Montana Cattle Range in 1886. New York: Charles Scribner's Sons, 1939.

Russell, Charles M.
Good Medicine. Memories of the Real West. With an introduction by Will Rogers, and a biographical sketch by Nancy C. Russell. Garden City, N. Y.: Garden City Publ. Co., 1936.

Upham, Hiram D.
"Upham Letters from the Upper Missouri." *Montana. State University. Historical Reprints. Sources of Northwest History.* Missoula, 1933. No. 19, pp. 1–9.

FOLKTALES

Halpert, Lt. Herbert
"Montana Cowboy Folktales." *CFQ* 4:244-254, 1945.

"Montana Folkways." *Frontier and Midland* (Missoula) 18:17–23, 1937.
A chapter from the Montana state guide.

CUSTOMS

Alderson, Nannie G., and Smith, Helena Huntington
A Bride Goes West. New York: Farrar and Rinehart, 1942.
Life in Montana in the 80's.

Brinig, Myron
Singerman. New York: Farrar and Rinehart Inc., 1929. 446 pp.
A novel of Montana life.

————.
Wide Open Town. New York: Farrar and Rinehart Inc., 1931. 306 pp.

Call, Hughie
Golden Fleece. Boston: Houghton Mifflin Co., 1942.
Montana life in the early 20th century—a glimpse into habits and customs.

Hubbard, Margaret Ann
Lone Boy. New York: Macmillan Co., 1944. 259 pp.
A story for young readers of the Montana gold rush.

Maerdian, O.
Pioneer Ranching in Central Montana, from . . . letters . . . written in 1882–1883. *Montana State University. Missoula. Historical Reprints.* No. 10, 1930.

Mathews, Alfred E.
Pencil Sketches of Montana. New York: The Author, 1868. 95 pp., illus.

Nelson, Bruce Opie
Land of the Dacotahs. Minneapolis: University of Minnesota Press, 1946. 354 pp., illus.

Vaughn, Robert
Then and Now; or, Thirty-Six Years in the Rockies. Personal reminiscences . . . of the first pioneers of the state of Montana. Minneapolis: Tribune Printing Co., 1900. 461 pp.

Walker, Mary Richardson
The Diary of Mary Richardson Walker, June 10–Dec. 21, 1838. *Montana. State University. Missoula. Historical Reprints.* No. 15, 1931.

Walker, Mildred
Winter Wheat. New York: Harcourt, Brace and Co., 1944. 306 pp.
A regional novel that captures the spirit and life of the people.

SPEECH

Hayden, Marie Gladys
"A Word List from Montana." *Dialect Notes* 4(Part 2):243–245, 1915.

PLACE NAMES

"Geographical Names of Western Montana, Northern Idaho." *Oregon Hist. Quar.*, March 1948. pp. 50–62.

FOLKSONG

RECORDS

U. S. Library of Congress. Division of Music. Folklore Section.
Irish Songs Recorded in Butte, Montana. Wayland D. Hand, coll.   AAFS-LC.

NORTH DAKOTA

FOLKLORE

BIBLIOGRAPHY

Historical Records Survey.
Inventory of the Archives of North Dakota. Prepared by the Historical Records Survey. Works Progress Administration. Bismarck, N. D.: The Historical Records Survey, 1938. Bibl.

PERIODICALS

North Dakota Historical Quarterly. v. 1, 1926–Bismarck, N. D.
Published by the North Dakota State Historical Society.

North Dakota State Historical Society. Bulletin. No. 1, 1917–. Bismarck, N. D.

GENERAL STUDIES AND COLLECTIONS

Bercovici, Konrad
On New Shores. New York: Century Co., 1925.
Contains chapters on French settlements at Wild Rice, N. D., and on the Russo-Germans in N. D.

Boyer, John
Emigrants. New York: Century Co., 1925.

Collins, Mary Brynton
The Checkered Years. Caldwell, Idaho: The Caxton Printers, Ltd., 1937.
A novel.

Craig, Wallace
"North Dakota Life: Plant, Animals, and Human." *American Geographical Society. Bulletin* 40:321–332, 401–415, 1908.

Crawford, Lewis F.
Badlands and Bronco Trails. Bismark: Capital Book Co., 1922. 114 pp., illus.
Adventures of the Amazing Ben Arnold Conner.

Custer, Elisabeth B.
"Boots and Saddles," or, Life in Dakota with General Custer. New York: Harper and Bros., 1885. 312 pp., map and portrait.

Donan, Patrick
The Land of the Golden Grain. North Dakota. ...Home for the Homeless. Chicago: C. R. Brodix, 1883. 70 pp.

Federal Writers' Project.
North Dakota, a Guide to the Northern Prairie State. (American Guide Series.) Federal Writers' Project of the Works Progress Administration for the State of North Dakota. Fargo, N. D.: Knight Printing Co., 1938. xx, 371 pp., illus., bibl. (pp. 345–360).

Feikema, Feike
The Golden Bowl. St. Paul: The Webb Publishing Co., 1944. 226 pp.
"He has gathered in this novel the full harvest of his observations for this regional story of the Dakota Dust bowl." (Andrea Parke.)

Foley, James W.
Prairie Breezes. Boston: R. B. Badger, 1905.
A book of verse.

Garland, Hamlin
The Moccasin Ranch. New York: Harpers and Bros., 1909.
A novel in which folklore plays a considerable part.

"Journal of the Atkinson-O'Fallon Expedition Edited by Russell Reid and Clell G. Gannon." *North Dakota Historical Quarterly* 4:5–56, 1929.

Mynadier, H. E.
"The Journal of H. E. Mynadier. A Boat Trip from Fort Union to Omaha in 1860." *North Dakota Historical Quarterly* 1:41–51, 1927.

Nelson, Bruce
Land of the Dacotahs. Minneapolis: University of Minnesota Press, 1946. 354 pp., illus.
The wonderful legends and fabulous history of the last remaining outpost of the "Wild West."

Palmer, Bertha Rachel
Beauty Spots in North Dakota. Boston: R. G. Badger, 1928. 266 pp., illus.

Putnam, Grace Brown, and Ackerman, A., eds.
North Dakota Singing. New York: The Paebar Company, 1936. 252 pp.
An anthology of North Dakota poetry.

Quarley, Carlton C.
"Pioneer Norwegian Settlements in North Dakota." *North Dakota Historical Quarterly* 5:14–37, 1930.

Reese, John B.
Some Pioneers and Pilgrims on the Dakota, or From the Ox Team to the Aeroplane. Mitchell: The Author, 1920. 94 pp., illus.

Rowbotham, Francis Jameson
A Trip to Prairie Land: Being a glance at the shady side of emigration. In two parts: Part I. The Life on the Prairie. Part II. The Farming Prospects of Northern Dakota. London: S. Low, Marston, Searle & Rivington, 1885. xii, 243 pp.

Tallent, Annie D.
The Black Hills, the Last Hunting Ground of the Dakotas. St. Louis: Nixon, 1899. 713 pp., illus.

Van Ostrand, Ferdinand A.
"Diary of Ferdinand A. Van Ostrand." *North Dakota Historical Quarterly* (Bismarck) 9:219–242; 10:3–46, 83–124, 1942.

Vestal, Stanley
Mountain Men. Boston: Houghton Mifflin Co., 1937. 296 pp., illus.

CUSTOMS

Blegen, John H.
"A Missionary Journey on the Dakota Prairies in 1886." *North Dakota Historical Quarterly* (Grand Forks) 1:16–29, 1927.

Briggs, William Marlowe
Dakota in the Morning. New York: Farrar and Rinehart, 1942. 277 pp.
A plain, homespun story of everyday life in the Dakota Territory of the Eighties and Nineties.

Dayton, Edson Carr
Dakota Days, May, 1886–August, 1898. Hartford: Privately Printed, 1937. 128 pp.

Rolvaag, O. E.
Giants in the Earth. New York: Harpers and Bros., 1924.

————.
Peder Victorious. New York: Harpers and Bros., 1921.
A sequel to Giants in the Earth.

Taylor, Joseph Henry
Sketches of Frontier and Indian Lives in the Upper Missouri and Great Plains. Bound with Kaleidoscopic Lives. Valley City: E. P. Getchall, 1932.

Torrey, E. C.
Early Days in Dakota. Minneapolis: Farnham Printing and Stationery Co., 1925.

Towne, Arthur E.
Old Prairie Days. Otsego, Mich.: The Otsego Union Press, 1942.
Reminiscences of life in the Dakota Territory in the Eighties.

Trinka, Zena Irma
North Dakota of Today. St. Paul: L. F. Dow Co., 1920. xix, 259 pp., illus.

Waldo, Edna La Moore
Dakota, Scenes from Pioneer Days in the Dakotas. Caldwell, Idaho: Caxton Printers, Ltd., 1936. 459 pp.

Williams, Mary A.
Fifty Pioneer Mothers of McLean County, North Dakota. Washburn, N. D.: Washburn Leader, 1932. 200 pp., illus.

SPEECH

Stefansson, Vilhjalmur
"English Loan-Names Used in the Icelandic Colony of North Dakota." *Dialect Notes* 2 (Part 5) 1903.

PLACE NAMES

Reid, Russell
"Name Origins of North Dakota Cities, Towns and Counties."*North Dakota History* 13 (No.3): 118–143, 1946.
Continued in subsequent numbers.

OREGON
FOLKLORE
BIBLIOGRAPHY

Historical Records Survey.
Guide to the Manuscript Collections of the Oregon Historical Society. Prepared by the Oregon Historical Records Survey. Works Progress Administration. Portland, Ore.: The Oregon Historical Records Survey, 1940. ii, 133 pp.

————.
Inventory of the County Archives of Oregon. Prepared by the Historical Records Survey. Works Progress Administration. Portland, Ore.: The Historical Records Survey, 1939.

PERIODICALS

Oregon Historical Society Quarterly.
V. 1, 1900–. Salem.

GENERAL STUDIES AND COLLECTIONS

Adams, William L.
Oregon As It Is; its present and future, by a resident for twenty-five years, being a reply to inquirers. Portland, Ore.: "Bulletin" Steam Book and Job Printing Rooms, 1873. 61 pp.

Allen, A. J., comp.
Ten Years in Oregon. Travels and Adventures of Dr. E. White and Lady, west of the Rocky Mountains. . . . Ithaca, N. Y.: Press of Andrus, Gauntlett & Co., 1850. xvi, 430 pp.

Anderson, Eva Greenslit, and Cullins, Dean
Stories of Oregon, illustrated by Paul Keller. Lincoln, Neb.: The University Publishing Co., 1943. 256 pp., illus.

Barzee, C. Louis
Oregon in the Making. (Oregon Folkways, 1860–90). Salem, Oregon: Statesmen Publ. Co., 1936.

Carey, Charles H.
"Theodore Talbot Journals, 1843, 1849–52." *Oregon Historical Society. Quarterly* (Eugene) 30:326–338, 1929.

Damon, Samuel Chenery
A Trip from the Sandwich Islands to Lower Oregon, and Upper California; or, Thirty Leaves selected from "Our Log-Book." Honolulu, Oahu: H. I. Printed at the Polynesian Office, 1923. 86 pp.

Denny, Emily Inez
Blazing the Way; or, True Stories, Songs and Sketches of Puget Sound and other Pioneers; with illustrations by the author, and from authentic photographs. Seattle: Rainier Printing Co., 1909. 503 pp., illus.

Dobbs, Caroline
Men of Champoeg; a record of the lives of the pioneers who founded the Oregon government. Portland, Ore.: Metropolitan Press, 1932. 218 pp., illus., bibl.

Dye, Eva Emery
The Soul of America, An Oregon Iliad. New York: The Press of the Pioneers, Inc., 1934.

Elliot, T. C.
"The Mysterious Oregon." *Washington Historical Quarterly* 22:289–292, 1931.

Farnham, Thomas Jefferson
Life, Adventures and Travels in California, and, Travels in Oregon, (from authentic sources). New York: Sheldon, Lampart, 1855. iv, 468 pp.

————.
Travels in the Great Western Prairies, the Anahuac and Rocky Mountains, and in the Oregon Territory. Poughkeepsie: Killey and Lossing, 1851. 197 pp.

Federal Writers' Project.
Oregon, End of the Trail. (American Guide Series.) Compiled by the Workers of the Federal Writers' Project of the Works Progress Administration of the State of Oregon. Rutland: Binfords and Mort, 1940.

————.
The Rainbow of the Years. A Pageant compiled by workers of the Writers' Program of the Works Projects Administration in the State of Oregon.... Portland, 1940. 27 pp.

Gatschet, A. S.
"Oregonian Folk Lore." *JAFL* 4:139–142, 1891.

Greve, Alice Wheeler
Shadow on the Plains. Portland, Ore.: Binfords & Mort, 1944. 272 pp.
A novel of the wagon train of 1847 and the Whitman mission.

Harkness, Ione B.
"Basque Settlements in Oregon." *Oregon Historical Quarterly* 34:273–275, 1933.

Hastings, Lansford Warren
Emigrants' Guide to Oregon and California. Princeton: Princeton University Press, 1932. 157 pp.
Among other things, contains numerous items on weather lore.

Hedrick, Helen
The Blood Remembers. New York: Alfred A. Knopf, 1941. 288 pp.
A regional novel of the Klamath Country. Good insight into white and Indian customs.

Irving, Washington
Astoria, or Anecdotes of an Enterprise Beyond the Rocky Mountains. Philadelphia: Carey, Lea & Blanchard, 1836. 2 vols.

James, Thomas Horton
Rambles in the United States and Canada During the Year 1845, With a Short Account of Oregon.... London: S. Clarke, 1846. viii, 259 pp.

Johnston, Overton, and Winter, Wm. H.
Routes Across the Rocky Mountains ... of the Emigration of 1843.... Princeton: Princeton University Press, 1932. xix, 199 pp. Reprinted from the edition of 1846.

Lee, Daniel, and Frost, J. H.
Ten Years in Oregon. New York: J. Collord, 1844. 344 pp.

Lockley, Fred
Oregon Folks. New York: The Knickerbocker Press, 1927. vii, 220 pp.

————.
Oregon Trail Blazers. New York: The Knickerbocker Press, 1929. v, 369 pp.

————.
Oregon's Yesterdays. New York: The Knickerbocker Press, 1928. v, 350 pp.

Meeker, Ezra
The Busy Life of Eighty-Five Years of Ezra Meeker. Ventures and Adventures.... The Oregon Trail.... Seattle, Wash.: The Author, 1916. xii, 399 pp., illus.

Minto, John
Rhymes of Early Life in Oregon and Historical and Biographical Facts, by John Minto, a pioneer of 1844. Salem, Ore.: Statesman Publishing Co., 1915. 80 pp., illus.

Nash, Wallis
Oregon: There and Back in 1877. London: Macmillan & Co., 1878. xviii, 285 pp., illus.

Paden, Irene D.
The Wake of the Prairie Schooner. New York: The Macmillan Co., 1943. xix, 514 pp., pen and ink drawings, maps, bibliography, index.
"The book is a rich piece of human experience and historical reconstruction—(of the Oregon Trail)" (Wilbur Schramm.)

Pratt, Alice Day
A Homesteader's Portfolio. New York: The Macmillan Company, 1922. vi, 181 pp.

Ross, Nancy Wilson
Farthest Reach; Oregon & Washington. New York: Alfred A. Knopf, 1941. xiv, 359 pp., illus., bibl.

Thornton, Jessy Quinn
Oregon and California in 1848. With an appendix, including recent and authentic information on the subject of the gold mines of California.... New York: Harper & Bros., 1849. 2 vols., illus.

Warre, Henry James
Sketches in North America and the Oregon Territory. London: Dickinson & Co., 1849. 5 pp., illus.

Woods, John B., and Rogers, Nelson S.
Your Oregon, Yesterday, Today, and Tomorrow; a study of the physical environment and of the people in it. Portland, Ore.: Northwest Regional Council, 1942. 219 pp., illus.

FOLKTALES

Dawson, Charles
Pioneer Tales of the Oregon Trail and of the Jefferson County. Topeka: Crane & Co., 1912. xv, 488 pp.

CUSTOMS

Applegate, Jesse
A Day With the Cow Column in 1843. Recollections of My Boyhood. Oregon Pioneer of 1843.... Chicago: Caxton Club, 1934. xvii, 207 pp.

Banks, Louis Albert
An Oregon Boyhood. Boston: Lee and Shepard, 1898. 173 pp., illus.

Barzee, Clark Louis
Oregon in the Making; 60's to Gay 90's. Illustrated by P. J. Rennings. Salem, Ore.: Statesman Publishing Co., 1936. 140 pp., illus.

Clarke, S. A.
Pioneer Days of Oregon History. Portland: J. K. Gill Co., 1905. 2 vols., illus.

Cole, George E.
Early Oregon. Jottings of Personal Recollections of a Pioneer of 1850. Spokane: Shaw & Borden Co., 1905. 95 pp.

Dye, Eva
The Soul of America; an Oregon Illiad. New York: The Press of the Pioneers, 1934. vi, 366 pp.

Geer, Theodore T.
Fifty Years in Oregon; Experiences, observations, and commentaries upon men, measures and customs in pioneer days and later times. New York: Neale Pub. Co., 1912. 356 pp.

Judson, Katharine Berry
Early Days in Old Oregon. Chicago: A. C. McClurg & Co., 1916. 263 pp., illus., bibl.

Kennedy, George W.
The Pioneer Campfire, in Four Parts: With the Emigrants on the Great Plains, With the Settlers in the Log Cabin Homes, With the Hunters and Miners, With the Preachers on the Trails, at Camp Meetings and in Log Cabins; Anecdotes, Adventures and Reminiscences. Portland, Ore.: Clarke-Kundret Printing Co., 1914. 240 pp., illus.

Lovejoy, Asa Lawrence
"Lovejoy's Pioneer Narrative, 1842–48...."
Oregon Historical Quarterly 31:237–260, 1930.

McArthur, Harriet
Recollections of the Rickreall. Portland, Ore.: Press of Koke-Chapman Co., 1930. 24 pp.

Miller, James D.
"Early Oregon Scenes: A Pioneer Narrative."
Oregon Historical Quarterly 31:55–68, 160, 180, 275–284, 1930.

Traill, Catharine Parr Strickland
Canada and the Oregon. The backwoods of Canada: being letters from the wife of an emigrant officer illustrative of the domestic economy of British America. London: M. A. Natali, 1846. viii, 351 pp., illus.

SPEECH

Cannell, Margaret
"Indian Personal Names from the Nebraska and Dakota Regions." *AS* 10 (No. 3):184–187, 1935.

Elliot, T. C.
"The Chinook Wind. Origin of the Term."
Oregon Historical Quarterly 33:243–249, 1932.

Hausen, T. Josephine
"Wallowa County, Oregon, Expressions." *AS* 6 (No. 3):229–230, 1931.

Pearce, Helen
"Folk Sayings in a Pioneer Family of Western Oregon." *CFQ* 5:229–242, 1946.

PLACE NAMES

Elliot, T. C.
"Jonathan Carver's Source for the Name Oregon." *Oregon Historical Society Quarterly* 23:53–69, 1922.

————.
"The Strange Case of Jonathan Carver and the Name Oregon." *Oregon Historical Society Quarterly* 21:341–368, 1926.

Holman, Frederick V.
"Oregon County Names." *Mag. of History* 13:119–122, 1911.

Lewis, William S.
"Some Notes and Observations on the Origin and Evolution of the Name Oregon as Applied to the River of the West." *Washington Historical Quarterly* 17:218–222, 1927.

McArthur, Lewis A.
Oregon Geographic Names. Portland, Oregon: Privately Published, 1928. xii, 450 pp.

————.
"Oregon Geographic Names." *Oregon Historical Quarterly* 26:309–423, 1925; 27:295–366, 412–447, 1926; 28:65–110, 163–224, 1927.
Supplementary to the above: 27:131–191, 225–264, 412–447; 28:281–306; 29:211–213; 43:299–317; 44:1–18, 176–218, 286–312, 339–360; 45:42–74, 1926–43.

"Place Names and Their Origin."
U. S. Works Progress Administration, Oregon Oddities. May 15, 1940. pp. 1–4, bibl.

FOLKSONG

See: Folksongs of the Northwest, p. 408.

COLLECTIONS

Denny, Emily Inez
Blazing the Way; or True Stories, Songs and Sketches of Puget Sound and other Pioneers; with illustrations by the author and from authentic photographs. Seattle: Rainier Printing Co., 1909. 503 pp.

Oregon University.
Songs of Our Oregon. Eugene: University of Oregon Cooperative Store, 1929. 37 pp.
For 1 voice, or 4 voices, with piano accomp.

SOUTH DAKOTA

FOLKLORE

BIBLIOGRAPHY

Federal Writers' Project.
A Selected List of South Dakota Books, compiled by volunteer workers of the South Dakota Writers' Project, Works Progress Administration and of the South Dakota Library Association. Pierre: South Dakota Library Association, 1943. vii, 36 pp.

Historical Records Survey.
Inventory of the County Archives of South Dakota. Prepared by the Historical Records Survey. Works Progress Administration. Rapid City, S. D.: The Historical Records Survey, 1937.

South Dakota, Department of History.
South Dakota Historical Collections Compiled by the State Historical Society. Vol. 1–18. A valuable series; a volume issued every two years.

PERIODICALS

South Dakota Historical Review.
V. 1–2. Oct., 1935–July, 1937. Pierre, S. D. Quarterly.

GENERAL STUDIES AND COLLECTIONS

Aikman, Duncan
Calamity Jane, and the Other Lady Wildcats. New York: Henry Holt and Co., 1927. 347 pp., illus.

Boyles, Kate, and Virgil D.
The Homesteaders. Chicago: McClurg, 1909. 346 pp., illus.
Fiction—makes use of history and lore.

Briggs, William Marlowe
Dakota in the Morning. New York: Farrar and Rinehart, 1942.

Burleigh, B. W., and Wenzlaff, G. G.
A Book of Dakota Rhymes. Yankton: Yankton Printing Co., 1907. 168 pp.

Carr, Robert V.
Black Hills Ballads. Denver: Reed Publicity Co., 1902. 175 pp., front.
A work of fiction.

Clark, Badger
Skylines and Wood Smoke. Custer: Chronicle Shop, 1935. 73 pp.

_____.
Spike. Boston: Badger, 1925. 215 pp., illus.

Connelley, William Elsey
Wild Bill and His Era. (The Life of James Butler "Wild Bill" Hickok.) New York: Press of the Pioneers, 1933. 229 pp., illus.

Coursey, O. W.
Wild Bill (James Butler Hickok). Mitchell: Educator Supply Co., 1924. 80 pp., illus.

Custer, Mrs. Elizabeth Bacon
"Boots and Saddles," or, Life in Dakota with General Custer. New York: Harper Bros., 1885. 312 pp., illus.

Disbrow, Edward Delavan
The Man Without a Gun. Boston: Chapman & Grimes, 1936. 96 pp.
"True stories of life in the Dakotas in the early nineties."

Federal Writers' Project.
Custer State Park, in the Black Hills of South Dakota. (American Guide Series.) Federal Writers' Project of the Works Progress Administration for the State of South Dakota. The Custer State Park Board, 1938.

_____.
Hamlin Garland, Memorial Dedication. Pierre: Federal Writers' Project, 1936. 12 pp.

_____.
MSS (Manuscripts). Pierre and Custer, South Dakota Writers' League, 1936–37, 8 issues, illus.

_____.
Pioneer Mitchell. (American Guide Series.) A Brochure compiled by the Federal Writers' Project, Works Progress Administration for the state of South Dakota. The Parents Teachers Association, Mitchell, S. D., 1938.

_____.
South Dakota, Guide. (American Guide Series.) Federal Writers' Project of the Works Progress Administration for the state of South Dakota. Pierre: State Publishing Co., 1938. Bibl. (pp. 425–435).

Garland, Hamlin
A Daughter of the Middle Border. New York: Macmillan Co., 1921.

_____.
Prairie Folks. New York: The Macmillan Co., 1899.

Gessner, Robert
Broken Arrow. New York: Farrar and Rinehart, 1933. 280 pp.
A work of fiction.

Hueston, Ethel
Calamity Jane. Indianapolis: Bobbs-Merrill Co., 1937.

Hunkins, Ralph Valentine
South Dakota, Its Past, Present, and Future. New York: The Macmillan Company, 1932. viii, 312 pp., illus., bibl.

Lane, Rose Wilder
Let the Hurricane Roar. New York: Longmans, Green and Co., 1933. 152 pp.
   A novel using folklore background.

Marsh, Elias J.
"Journal ... Account of a Steamboat Trip on the Missouri River, May–August, 1859." *South Dakota Historical Review* 1:79–125, 1936. Illus.

Price, Sam Goodale
Black Hills, the Land of Legend; illustrated by Charlotte Gutshall and drawings. ... Los Angeles: De Vorss & Co., 1935. 139 pp., illus.

Stokes, George W.
Deadwood Gold. History of early gold mining in the northern Beach Hills. Yonkers-on-Hudson: World Book Co., 1926. 163 pp., illus.

Torrey, Edwin C.
Early Days in Dakota. Minneapolis: Farnham Printing and Stationery Co., 1925. 289 pp.

White, Stewart Edward
Gold. Garden City: Doubleday, Doran and Co., 1913. 449 pp.

————.
The Westerners. New York: Doubleday Doran and Co., 1917. 344 pp., front.

Wilstach, Frank J.
Wild Bill Hickok; the Prince of Pistoleers. Garden City: Doubleday Doran and Co., 1928. 304 pp., illus.

FOLKTALES

Federal Writers' Project.
Sodbusters, Tales of Southeastern South Dakota. (American Guide Series.) Written and illustrated by the workers of the Federal Writers' Project, Works Progress Administration. Alexandria: South Dakota Writers' League, 1938. 27 pp., illus.

————.
Unfinished Histories: Tales of Aberdeen and Brown County. Written by workers of the Federal Writers' Project, Works Progress Administration in South Dakota. ... Mitchell: South Dakota Writers' League, 1938. 58 pp., illus.

Lowe, Barrett
Heroes and Hero Tales of South Dakota. Minneapolis: Hale, 1931. 196 pp., illus.

SPEECH

Sebastian, Hugh
"Agricultural College Slang in South Dakota." *AS* I1 (No. 3):278–280, 1936.

PLACE NAMES

Federal Writers' Project.
South Dakota Place-Names. Compiled by workers of the Writers' Program of the Works Progress Administration in the State of South Dakota. ... Vermillion: Univ. of South Dakota, 1940. 689 pp.
   Contents: Lake Names; River and Creek Names; Mountains, Valleys, and other Natural Features; Historic Sites, Parks and other Features; Gold Mines and Ghost Towns.

FOLKSONG
COLLECTIONS

Carr, Robert Van
Black Hills Ballads. Denver, Col.: The Reed Publishing Co., 1902. 175 pp., front.

WASHINGTON
FOLKLORE
BIBLIOGRAPHY

Hassell, Susan Whitcomb
A Hundred and Sixty Books by Washington Authors. Everett Haskell Press, 1916. 40 pp.

Pollard, Lancaster
"Check List of Washington Authors." *Pacific Northwest Quarterly*, Jan., 1940. Vol. 31.

GENERAL STUDIES AND COLLECTIONS

Atwood, Albert
Glimpses in Pioneer Life on Puget Sound. Seattle: Denny-Coryell Co., 1903. 483 pp., illus.

Binns, Archie
The Roaring Land. New York: Robert M. McBride and Co., 1942.
   A history and description of the State of Washington.

Blankenship, George E.
Lights and Shades of Pioneer Life on Puget Sound, by a Native Son. Olympia, Wash.: 1923. 90 pp.

Clark, William S.
"Pioneer Experience in Walla Walla." *Washington Historical Quarterly* 24:9–24, 1933.

Denny, Emily Inez
Blazing the Way; or, True Stories, Songs, and Sketches of Puget Sound and other Pioneers; with illustrations by the author. ... Seattle: Rainier Printing Co., 1909. 503 pp., illus.

————, ed.
Pioneer Days on Puget Sound. Seattle: Alice Harriman Co., 1908. 21 pp.

Federal Writers' Project.
Washington, a Guide to the Evergreen State. (American Guide Series.) Compiled by the Federal Writers' Program of the Works Progress Administration in the State of Washington. Portland, Oregon: Binfords & Mort, 1941. xxx, 687 pp., illus., bibl. (pp. 644–653.)

_____.
Told by Pioneers. . . . Tales of Frontier Life as Told by Those Who Remember the Days of the Territory and Early Statehood of Washington. Olympia: 1937–38. 3 vols., illus.

Ferbrache, James A.
A Legend of the Kootenai Trail, Spokane, Wash.: Art Printing Co., 1921. 115 pp., illus. A poem.

Goddard, John W.
Washington, the Evergreen State, Yesterday, Today, Tomorrow. New York: C. Scribner's Sons, 1942. 311 pp., illus., bibl.

Griffin, John A.
"Washington Thirty Years Ago." *Washington Historical Quarterly.* 7:133–135, 1916.

Hunter, George
Reminiscences of an Old Timer. A recital of the actual events, incidents, trials . . . of a pioneer, hunter, miner, and scout of the Pacific Northwest, together with his later experiences. . . . The several Indian wars, anecdotes, etc. Battle Creek, Mich.: Review and Herald, 1888. xxv, 508 pp., illus.

Lee, Aaron
From the Atlantic to the Pacific; reminiscences of pioneer life and travels across the continent, from New England to the Pacific Ocean, by an old soldier. . . . Seattle: Metropolitan Press, 1915. 190 pp., illus.

Leighton, Caroline C.
Life at Puget Sound, with sketches of travel in Washington Territory, British Columbia, Oregon and California. 1865–1881. Boston: Lee and Shepard, 1884. ix, 258 pp.

Winthrop, Theodore
The Canoe and the Saddle; or, Klalam and Klickitat. Tacoma: John E. Williams, 1913. 332 pp., illus.

FOLKTALES—LEGENDS

Blankenship, Mrs. George E.
Tillicum Tales of Thurston County. Olympia, Wash.: 1916. 392 pp., plates.
    Early history of Thurston County, Washington, together with biographies and reminiscences of those identified with pioneer days.

Ranck, Glenn N.
Legends and Traditions of Northwest History. Vancouver, Wash.: American Printing and Stationery Company, 1914. 152 pp., illus.

SPEECH

Williams, G.
"Logger-Talk." *Washington University. Chapbooks* No. 41, 1930.

PLACE NAMES

Eels, M.
"Aboriginal Geographic Names in the State of Washington." *AA* 5:27–35, 1892.

Bowman, J. N.
"Washington Nomenclature. A Study." *Wash. Hist. Quar.* 1:5–13, 1906.

Meany, Edmond S.
Origin of Washington Geographic Names. Seattle: University of Washington, 1923. ix, 357 pp. Appeared in *Washington Historical Quarterly.* Vols. 8–13, 1917–1923.

Oliphant, J. Orin
"Notes on Early Settlements and on Geographic Names of Eastern Washington." *Wash. Hist. Quar.* 22:172–202, 1931.

Smith, Charles Wesley
"The Naming of Counties in the State of Washington." *Wash. State University Bulletin.* Univ. Studies No. 6, 1913. 15 pp.

FOLKSONG

Denny, Emily Inez
Blazing the Way; or, True Stories, Songs and Sketches of Puget Sound and other Pioneers; with illustrations by the author. . . . Seattle: Rainier Printing Company, 1909. 503 pp., illus.

ALASKA

FOLKLORE

BIBLIOGRAPHY

Wickersham, James
Alaskan Literature, a Bibliography of 1724–1924. Fairbanks, Alaska: Alaska Agricultural College and School of Mines, 1927.
    Contains the titles of all Histories, Travels, Voyages, Newspapers, Periodicals, Public Documents, etc. Printed in English, Russian, German, French, Spanish, etc. relating to, descriptive of, or published in Russia, America, or Alaska, from 1724 to and including 1924.

GENERAL STUDIES AND COLLECTIONS

Allan, A. A.
Gold, Men and Dogs. New York: G. P. Putnam's Sons, 1931. vii, 337 pp., illus.

Badlam, Alexander
The Wonders of Alaska. With illustrations and maps. San Francisco: The Bancroft Company, 1890. vii, 152 pp., illus.

Ballou, M. M.
The New Eldorado: A Summer Journey to Alaska. Boston: Houghton Mifflin Company, 1889. xi, 352 pp.

Barbeau, Chares Marius
Alaska Beckons. Illustrated by Arthur Price. Caldwell, Id.: The Caxton Printers, 1947. 343 pp., illus., bibl.

Broke, Horatio George
With Sock and Stock in Alaska. London: Longmans, Green & Co., 1891. xi, 158 pp.

Brower, Charles D.
Fifty Years Below Zero; A lifetime of adventure in the far North. . . . New York: Dodd, Mead & Company, 1942. x, 310 pp., illus.

Burr, Agnes Rush
Alaska, Our Beautiful Northland of Opportunity. Boston: Page Co., 1919. xii, 428 pp.

Craig, Lulu Alice
Glimpses of Sunshine and Shade in the Far North; or, My Travels in the Land of the Midnight Sun. Cincinnati: The Editor Publishing Co., 1900. ix, 123 pp.

Dall, William Healy
Alaska and its Resources. Boston: Lee and Shepard, 1870. 627 pp., bibl. (595–609).

Dow, Peter
Alaska, America's Northern Wonderland. Hot Springs, Ark.: 1927. 128 pp.

Federal Writers' Project.
Alaska, Last American Frontier. (American Guide Series.) Compiled by the Federal Writers' Program of the Works Progress Administration in Alaska. Merle Colby, ed. New York: The Macmillan Company, 1939.

Freuchen, Peter
It's All Adventure. New York: Farrar & Rinehart, 1938. vi, 508 pp., illus.

Gerrish, Theodore
Life in the World's Wonderland. . . . A graphic description of the great Northwest, from St. Paul, Minnesota, to the land of the midnight sun. . . . Biddeford, Maine: Press of the Biddeford Journal, 1887. 421 pp., illus.

Gillham, Charles Edward
Raw North. Illustrated by Bob Hines. New York: A. S. Barnes and Company, 1947. xvi, 275 pp., illus.
"Ice Worm Song"—words and melody, pp. 62–63.

Henderson, Alice Palmer
The Rainbow's End: Alaska. Chicago: H. S. Stone & Co., 1898. 296 pp., illus.

Hubbard, Bernard Rosecrans
Mush, You Malemutes. New York: The American Press, 1932. xiv, 179 pp., illus.
Stories by "The Glacier priest," rich in lore as well as natural phenomena.

Keithahn, Edward L.
Monuments in Cedar. Ketchikan, Alaska: Roy Anderson, 1945. 160 pp., illus.

Margeson, Charles Anson
Experiences of Gold Hunters in Alaska. Hornesville, N. Y.: The Author, 1899. 297 pp., illus.

Muir, John
Travels in Alaska. Boston: Houghton Mifflin Company, 1915. ix, 326 pp., illus.

Noonan, Dominic A.
Alaska, the Land of Now. Seattle, Wash.: Sherman Printing Co., 1921. 134 pp.
A book of poems.

Seppala, Leonhard
Seppala, Alaskan Dog Driver. Boston: Little, Brown and Company, 1930. vi, 295 pp., illus.
Contents: Prologue by Elizabeth M. Ricker.— Seppala Tells His Story.

Spurr, Josiah Edward
Through the Yukon Gold Diggings: A narrative of personal travels. Boston: Eastern Publishing Company, 1900. 276 pp., illus.

Stefansson, Evelyn
Here is Alaska, with a foreword by Vilhjalmur Stefansson, with photographs by Frederick Machetanz and others. New York: C. Scribner's Sons, 1943. 154 pp., illus.

Stuck, Hudson
Ten Thousand Miles with a Dog Sled; a narrative of winter travel in interior Alaska. New York: C. Scribner's Sons, 1916. xxii, 420 pp., illus.

Van Valin, William B.
Eskimoland Speaks. Caldwell, Id.: The Caxton Printers Ltd., 1941. 242 pp., illus.

Wardman, George
A Trip to Alaska, a narrative of what was seen and heard during a summer cruise in Alaskan waters. Boston: Lee & Shepard, 1885. 237 pp.

Whymper, Frederick
Travel and Adventure in the Territory of Alaska. New York: Harper & Bros., 1869. xviii, 353 pp.

Wickersham, James
Old Yukon; Tales, Trails, Trials. Washington, D. C.: Washington Law Book Company, 1938. xi, 514 pp., illus.

Williamson, Thames Ross
Far North Country. (American Folkways). New York: Duell, Sloan & Pearce, 1944. xi, 236 pp.

Willoughby, Florance
Alaskans All. Boston: Houghton Mifflin Company, 1933. x, 234 pp., illus.
On characters—their deeds and wonders. Some incredible.

———————
Alaska Holiday. Boston: Little Brown and Company, 1940. 295 pp., illus.

———————
Gentlemen Unafraid. New York: G. P. Putnam's Sons, 1928. xiii, 285 pp., illus.

CUSTOMS

Bell, William Hemphill
The Quiddities of an Alaskan Trip. Portland, Ore.: C. A. Steel & Co., 1873. 67 pp., illus.
Humorous incidents and characters.

Chase, Will H.
The Sourdough Pot. Kansas City, Mo.: Burton Publishing Co., 1943. 206 pp.
A story of the Alaska Gold Rush in the nineties. Touches on customs and manners.

Cryan, R. W. W.
"Diary Jottings in Alaska." *Westminster Review* (London) 153:557–566, 1900.

Davis, Mary Lee
Sourdough Gold, the Log of a Yukon Adventure. Boston: W. A. Wilde Company, 1933. 351 pp., illus.

——————.
We Are Alaskans. Illustrated by author's photographs and sketches by Olaus J. Murie. Boston: W. A. Wilde Company, 1931. xi, 335 pp., illus.

Fitz, Frances Ella
Lady Sourdough.... New York: The Macmillan Company, 1941. 319 pp., illus.

Helmericks, Constance
We Live in Alaska. Boston: Little, Brown and Company, 1944. 266 pp.

Kendrick, Sylvester J.
Chilkoot Pass, and Songs of Alaska. Los Angeles: Coast Printing Company, 1926. 61 pp.
A book of poems, of places, customs and beliefs."

Lawing, Nellie
Alaska Nellie. Seattle, Wash.: Seattle Printing and Publishing Company, 1940. 201 pp., illus.
Her adventurous life against a background of the customs, beliefs, and traditions of the people.

Reynolds, Henry Derr
Kladawah. New York: H. D. Reynolds & Co., 1917. 24 pp., illus.
Alaskan life in poems.

Simonson, Sigurd Jay
Among the Sourdoughs. New York: Fortuny's, 1939. 153 pp.

Sullivan, May Kellog
A Woman Who Went to Alaska. Boston: J. H. Earle & Company, 1902. 392 pp., illus.

Wiedemann, Thomas
Cheechako Into Sourdough. Portland, Ore.: Binfords & Mort, 1942. 296 pp.
Adventures, and observations on customs, manners, and gold mining.

Willard, Caroline McCoy
Life in Alaska. Letters of Mrs. Eugene S. Willard.... Philadelphia: Presbyterian Board of Publication, 1884. 384 pp., illus.

Wright, Julia McNair
Among the Alaskans. Philadelphia: Presbyterian Board of Publication, 1883. 351 pp.

PLACE NAMES

Clark, J. D., and De Camp, L. S.
"Some Alaskan Place Names." *AS* 15:60–62, 1940.

CANADA

CANADA

FOLKLORE

See: French-Canadian Folklore, pp. 565-69.

PERIODICALS

Alberta Folklore Quarterly.
Vol. I, March, 1945. Edmonton, Alberta: University of Alberta, Canada.

Canadian.
Toronto. Vol. 1–91, No. 4. March, 1893–April, 1939. 1893–Jan., 1925, appeared as: *Canadian Magazine of Politics, Science, Art and Literature.* August, 1895–July, 1937: *Canadian Magazine. Index:* Vol. 1–25, 1893–1905 in vol. 25.

Canadian Historical Review.
Toronto. Vol. 1, 1920–. Supersedes *Review of Historical Publications Relating to Canada. Index:* 1–10, 1920–1929.

Queens Quarterly.
Kingston, No. 1, July, 1893–.
Published by Alumni and Friends of *Queens University.*

GENERAL STUDIES AND COLLECTIONS

"Alberta Folklore Project."
School and Society 57:699–700, 1943.

Barbeau, C. Marius
"Canadian-English Folklore." *JAFL* 31:1–3, 1918.

―――――.
The Kingdom of Saguenay. Toronto: The Macmillan Co., 1936. 167 pp.
Folklore of St. Lawrence.

Beston, Henry
The St. Lawrence. (The Rivers of America Series). Illustrated by A. Y. Jackson. New York: Farrar & Rinehart, Inc., 1942. 274 pp.
The river, its voyageurs, its fur trade, its folklore, its missionaries, its Catholicism, its French-Indian intercourse, its chansons, its fisheries, its little French farms. Farther east its Montagnais Algonquin Indians.

Bleakney, F. E.
"Folklore from Ottawa and Vicinity." *JAFL* 31:158–169, 1918.

Boyle, D.
"Canadian Folklore." *JAFL* 11:159–165, 1898.

Brown, George William, ed.
Readings in Canadian History, Original Sources from Canada's Living Past. ... From the Discovery of America to British North America at the End of the Eighteenth Century. Toronto: J. M. Dent & Sons, Ltd., 1940. xii, 378 pp., illus., music, bibl.

Campbell, Grace
Thorn-Apple Tree. New York: Duell, Sloan & Pearce, Inc., 1943.
A novel of Scottish-Canadians in Ontario a century ago.

"Canadian Negro folklore."
JAFL 38:621, 1925.

"Canadian English folklore."
JAFL 11:159–161, 1898; 31:1–3, 1918.

Chamberlain, A.
"Folklore of Canadian Children." *JAFL* 8: 252, 1895.

Chase, Eliza Brown
In Quest of the Quaint. Illustrations by the writer, from water color and pencil sketches. Philadelphia: Ferris & Leach, 1902. viii, 253 pp., illus.

Comeau, Napoleon Alexander
Life and Sport on the North Shore of the Lower St. Lawrence and Gulf, containing chapters on salmon fishing, trapping, and folk-lore of the Montaignais Indians and tales of adventure on the fringe of the Labrador Peninsula. Quebec: Daily Telegraph Printing House, 1909. 440 pp., plates, front., ports.

Devine, P. K.
Folklore of Newfoundland. St. John's, Newfoundland: Robinson & Co., 1937.

Duncan, Dorothy
Bluenose: A Portrait of Nova Scotia. New York: Harper & Bros., 1942. 273 pp.
A vivid portrayal of the blend of two cultures—the Acadians and Scotch-English.

"English Canadian folklore from Ontario."
JAFL 31:4–82, 1918.

"English folklore collected in counties of Oxford and Waterloo, Ontario." *JAFL* 31:135–153, 1918.

"English folklore collected at Roebuck, Greenville County, Ontario." *JAFL* 31:154–157, 1918.

"English folklore from Ottawa and vicinity."
JAFL 31:158–169, 1918.

Fauset, Arthur Huff
"Folklore from the Half-Breeds in Nova Scotia." *JAFL* 38:300–315, 1925.

―――――.
Folklore from Nova Scotia. Memoirs of the American Folklore Society, vol. 24. New York: G. E. Stechert & Co., 1931. xxii, 204 pp.
Content: Folk Tales, Ballads and Songs (no music), Game Songs and Counting-Out Rhymes, Nursery Rhymes and other verses, Riddle Tales and Riddles, Folk Notions.

Fraser, Sister St. Thomas of the Angels
"Folklore of Nova Scotia." *Catholic Truth Society of Canada*, 1931.

Gard, Robert E.
"The Alberta Folklore and Local History Project." *JAFL* 59:480–481, 1946.

Godsell, Philip H.
"Stage Steamer and Pack Train." *Alberta Folklore Quarterly* 2:72–77, June, 1946.

Greenough, William Parker
Canadian Folk Life and Folklore. New York: G. H. Richmond, 1897. xii, 199 pp.

Patterson, G.
"Folklore of Newfoundland." *JAFL* 8:285–290, 1895; 10:214–215, 1897.

Pritchett, John Perry
The Red River Valley, 1811–1849. A Regional Study. New Haven, Conn.: Yale University Press, 1942. 295 pp.
> The relations of Canada and the United States. This volume covers the colonization of the Red River Valley, the early years when it attracted the attention of French, English, Canadians, and Americans.... Touches on the life, habits and background of the different peoples inhabiting the region. More of an historical survey.

Sallans, G. Herbert
Little Man. Boston: Bruce Humphries, 1942. 420 pp.
> A striking novel of Canada and her people.

Shaw, B. M. H.
"The Vanishing Folklore of Nova Scotia." *Dalhousie Review* 3:342–349, 1923.

Waugh, F. W.
"Canadian folklore from Ontario." *JAFL* 31:4–82, 1918.

Wintemberg, W. J.
"Some Items of Negro Canadian Folklore." *JAFL* 38:621, 1925.

———.
"Folklore from Grey County, Ontario." *JAFL* 31:83–124, 1918.

———.
"Folklore Collected in the Counties of Oxford and Waterloo." *JAFL* 31:135–153, 1918.

———.
"Folklore Collected at Roeback, Grenville County, Ontario." *JAFL* 31:154–157, 1918.

———.
"Folklore Collected in Toronto and Vicinity." *JAFL* 31:125–134, 1918.

FOLKTALES—MYTHS—LEGENDS

Abrams, William Amos, ed.
The Merry Devil of Edmonton. Durham, N. C.: Duke University Press, 1942. 290 pp., bibl., index, 2 plates.
> Contains reprint of the Life and Death of the Merry Devil of Edmonton, by T. B., 1631.

Borrett, William C.
Tales Told Under the Old Town Clock. Halifax, Nova Scotia: The Imperial Publishing Co., 1943.
> Twenty-five stories from Nova Scotia's history.

Cree, Charles Clay
"Legend of Creation." *Alberta Folklore Quarterly* 2:69–71, June, 1946.

Doering, Frederick J.
"Legends from Canada, Indiana and Florida." *SFQ* 2 (No. 4):213–220, 1938.

Fraser, C. A.
"Scottish Myths from Ontario." *JAFL* 6:185–198, 1893.

Gard, Robert E.
Johnny Chinook. Tall Tales and True from the Canadian West. Introduction by Donald Cameron. Illustrations by Walter Phillips, R.C.A. New York: Longmans, Green & Co., 1945, 360 pp.
> The stories for the most part fall into the same classification as do the tales of the West and Southwest of the United States.... But some of the folk characters are peculiarly of Western Canada.

———.
"Alberta's Wild Bill Hickock." *Alberta Folklore Quarterly* 2:62–65, June, 1946.

Hooke, Hilda M.
Thunder in the Mountains: Legends of Canada. Toronto: Oxford University Press, 1948. 223 pp.

Johnson, Emily Pauline
Legends of Vancouver. Vancouver, B. C.: Saturday Sunset Presses, 1913. xvii, 138 pp., illus.

Judson, Katharine Berry, ed.
Myths and Legends of British North America. Chicago: A. C. McClurg & Co., 1917. 211 pp.

Le Moine, Sir James MacPherson
The Legends of the St. Lawrence, told during a cruise of the yatch (!) Hirondelle from Montreal to Gaspe. Quebec: C. E. Holiwell, 1898. 203 pp., illus.

Skinner, Charles Montgomery
Myths and Legends Beyond our Borders. Philadelphia: J. B. Lippincott Co., 1899. 319 pp.
> Folklore of Canada and Mexico.

Smyth, Fred J.
Tales of the Kootenays, with historical sketches by the author and others. Cranbrook, B. C.: Printed in the Office of the Courier, 1938. 205 pp., illus.

CUSTOMS—BELIEFS—SUPERSTITIONS

Beauchamp, W. M., Bergen F. D., Newell, W. W.
"Current superstitions among English-speaking population of United States and Canada." *JAFL* 2:12–22, 105–112, 1889.

Doering, J. Frederick
"More Folk Customs from Western Ontario."
JAFL 58:150–155, 1945.

——————, and Eileen Elita
"Some Western Ontario Beliefs and Practices."
JAFL 51:60–68, 1938.

"English folklore in Canada, Superstitions."
JAFL 2:12–122, 105–112, 1889; 8:285–290,
1895; 10:214–215, 1897; 31:135–157, 1918.

Holland, Clive
"Some Superstitions of Seafaring Folks." *Nautical Magazine* (London) 143:12–15, 1940.

Jamison, C. V.
"Signs and Omens from Nova Scotia." *JAFL*
6:38, 1893.

Teit, J. A.
"Water Beings in Shetlandic Folklore as remembered by Shetlanders in British Columbia." *JAFL* 31:180–201, 1918.

Waghorne, A. C.
"Christmas Customs in Newfoundland." *JAFL*
6:63, 1893.

"Death Signs and Weather Signs from Newfoundland and Labrador." *JAFL* 13:297–299,
1900.

Whittle, W.
"Christmas 'Fools' and 'Mummers' in Newfoundland." *JAFL* 6:63–65, 1893.

RIDDLES

Greenleaf, Elizabeth B.
"Riddles of Newfoundland." *The Marshall
Review,* 1 (No. 3):5–20, 1938. (Marshall College, Huntington, West Va.)

SPEECH

Ahrend, Evelyn R.
"Ontario Speech." *AS* 9 (No. 2):136–139,
1934.

Chamberlain, A. F.
"Dialect Research in Canada." *Dialect Notes*
1 (Part 2):43–56.

De Witt, Marguerite E.
Americanadian Euphonetic Notes. New York:
The Author, 1924.

"Our Americanadian Problems of the Spoken
Word." *AS* 1 (No. 3):170–180, 1925.

Emeneau, M. B.
"The Dialect of Lunenburg, Nova Scotia."
Language 2:140–147, 1935.

England, George Allan
"Newfoundland Dialect Items." *Dialect Notes*
5 (Part 8):322–346, 1925.

Evans, Mary S.
"Terms from the Labrador Coast." *AS* 6 (No.
1):56–58, 1930.

Greenleaf, Elisabeth Bristol
"Newfoundland Words." *AS* 6 (No. 4):306,
1931.

McLay, W. S. W.
"A Note on Canadian English." *AS* 5 (No. 4):
328–329, 1930.

Mott, Lewis F.
"Canadian Word List." *Dialect Notes* 4 (Part
5):332, 1916.
  Collected at St. Johns, Newfoundland.

Munroe, Helen C.
"Montreal English." *AS* 5 (No. 1):21, 1929.

Patterson, G.
"Dialect of the People of Newfoundland."
JAFL 8:27–40, 1895; 9:19–37, 1896; 10:203–
210, 1897.

"Notes on the Dialect of the People of Newfoundland." *Proceedings and Transactions of
the Nova Scotian Institute of Natural Science*
9:44–78, 1896.

Strong, William Duncan
"More Labrador Survivals." *AS* 6 (No. 4):
290–291, 1931.

Tweedie, W. M.
"British Maritime Provinces Word-List." *Dialect Notes* 1 (Part 8):377–381.

PLACE NAMES
(Includes French Canada)

Anderson, William Patrick
Place Names on Anticosti Island, Que. Ottawa:
F. A. Acland, 1922. 15 pp. Map.

Armstrong, G. H.
*The Origin and Meaning of Place Names in
Canada.* Toronto: The Macmillan Co. of
Canada, Ltd., 1930. vii, 312 pp.

Baker, Edna
Prairie Place Names. Toronto: The Ryerson
Press, 1928. 28 pp., illus.

Boas, Franz
Geographical Names of the Kwakiutl Indians.
New York: Columbia University Press, 1934.
83 pp.

Bell, Charles N.
*Some Historical Names and Places of the
Canadian Northwest.* Winnipeg: Manitoba
Free Press Print, 1885. 8 p.

Bremmer, Benjamin
*Tales of Abegweit (Prince Edward Island)
Containing Historical, Biographical and Humorous Sketches and Selections.* With an appendix of place-names in Prince Edward Island
with their origins or meanings. Charlottetown,
P.E.I.: Irwin Printing Company, Ltd., 1936.
xiv, 132 pp., illus.

Brown, Thomas J.
Place-Names of the Province of Nova Scotia.
North Sidney, N. S.: 1922. 158 pp.

Canada. Geographic Board.
Place Names of Alberta. Published for the Geographic Board by the Department of the Interior. Ottawa: F. A. Acland, 1928. 138 pp. Map.

———.
Report. . .. Containing All Decisions. 1st, 1898–. Ottawa.
    Includes various special reports on the origin of place names, and other appendices.

Charbonneau, Louis
"Toponymie de la Province d'Ontario." *Société Historique du Nouvel-Ontario, Documents Historique.* (Sudbury) No. 1:33–42, 1942.

Deschênes, E. B.
"L'Apport de Cartier et de Jean Alfonse dans L'Onomastique de la Gaspésie." *Recherches Historiques* (Levis, Que.) 40:410–430, 1934.

———.
"Essai de Toponymie Gaspésienne." *Recherches Historiques* (Québec) 42:148–173, 200–215, 1936.

Douglas, R.
Meaning of Canadian City Names. By R. Douglas. . .. Ottawa: F. A. Acland, 1922. 21 pp.

———.
Place-Names on Magdalen Islands, Quebec. Ottawa: F. A. Acland, 1922. 11 pp., illus.

———.
Place-Names of Prince Edward Island, with Meanings. Ottawa: F. A. Acland, 1925. 55 pp.

———.
"The Place Names of Canada." *Scottish Geographical Magazine, (Edinburgh)* 36:154–157, 1920.

Duff, Louis Blake
The Romance of Our Place-Names; a series of eight radio addresses, Feb. 20 to April 10, 1934. Station CKTB, St. Catharines. . .. Fort Erie, Ont.: The Review Co., 1934. 22 pp.

Frame, Elizabeth
A List of Micmac Names of Places, Rivers, etc., in Nova Scotia. Cambridge: J. Wilson & Son, 1892. 12 pp.

Ganong, W. F.
"An Organization of the Scientific Investigation of Indian Place-Nomenclature of the Maritime Provinces of Canada." *Royal Society of Canada. Proc. and Transac. Ottawa,* 1913–14. Series 3, vol. 5 section 2, pp. 179–193; vol. 6, section 2, pp. 179–199; vol. 7, section 2, pp. 81–106; vol. 8, section 2, pp. 259–293.

———.
"Crucial Maps in the Early Cartography and Place-Nomenclature of the Atlantic Coast of Canada, VIII." *Royal Society of Canada Transactions. (Montreal).* 30 (ser. 3, sec. 2):109–129, 1936.

———.
Monographs of the Place-Nomenclature, Cartography, Historic Sites, Boundaries and Settlement—Origins of the Province of New Brunswick, with a supplement thereto, and a plan for a general history of the province. Ottawa: Royal Society of Canada. Transactions, 1895–1906.

———.
"The Origin of the East-Canadian Place-Names Gaspé, Blomidon, and Bras d'Or." *Royal Society of Canada. Proc. and Transac. Ottawa,* 1928. Series 3, vol. 22, section 2, pp. 249–270.

———.
"The Origin of the Major Canadian Place-Names Fundy and Miramichi." *Transactions of the Royal Society of Canada* Ser. 3, vol. 20, sec. II, pp. 15–35, 1926.

Gardiner, Herbert Fairbairn
Nothing But Names. An inquiry into the origin of the names of the counties and townships of Ontario. Toronto: G. N. Morang & Co., 1899. 561 pp.

Geographic Board. Department of the Interior.
Geographical Names of the Province of Quebec. Quebec. Department of Lands and Forests, 1926. viii, 158 pp.
    Issued also in French, in 1921.

———.
Place-Names of Alberta. Quebec: Department of Lands and Forests, 1928.

———.
Place Names of Manitoba. Ottawa: J. O. Patenaude, 1933. 95 pp.

Johnson, George
"Place Names of Canada," *Ottawa Literary and Scientific Society Transactions.* 1898. No. 1, pp. 24–62.

Johnson, Henry Smith
Norfolk Place Names. Simcoe, Ont.: Pearce Publishing Co., 1934. 15 pp., illus.

Johnston, Albert J.
Lambton County Names and Places. Sarnia: Lambton County Council, 1925. 55 pp., illus.

Keenleyside, H. L.
"Place-Names of Newfoundland." *Canadian Geographical Journal.* (Montreal) 29:255–267, 1944. Illus.

Lewis, Ella N.
East Elgin Place Names. Ontario: Sutherland Press, Ltd., 1935. 25 pp., illus.

Miller, Émile
"Laurentie, Laurentides, Laurentin et Laurentien," *Pays Laurentien, (Montreal)* 1:268–273. 1916.

Moore, William F.
Indian Place Names in Ontario. Toronto: The Macmillan Company of Canada. Ltd.. 1930. 48 pp.

Pacifique, Père
Études Historiques et Géographiques. Ristigouche, Co. Bonaventure, P. Q., Canada: L'Auteur, 1935. 321 pp., illus.

Pelland, Alfred
Vastes Champs Offerts à La Colonisation et à L'Industrie. La Gaspésie... esquisse historique, ses ressources, ses progrès et son avenir. Québec: Ministre de la Colonisation, des Mines et des Pêcheries, 1914. 276 pp., illus., bibl.

Prowse, George Robert Farrar
Exploration of the Gulf of St. Lawrence, 1499–1525. Winnipeg, 1929. (2 parts in one volume), charts.

Rand, Silas Tertius
Micmac Place-Names in the Maritime Provinces and Gaspé Peninsula Recorded between 1852 and 1890. Ottawa: Surveyor General's Office, 1919. 116 pp.

Robinson, Percy J.
"On the Derivation of Certain Place-Names in the Georgian Bay." *Royal Canadian Institute. Transactions.* (Toronto) 10:127–129, 1915.

————.
"Some of Cartier's Place-Names, 1535–1536." *Canadian Historical Review* (Toronto) 26: 401–405, 1945.

Rouilliard, Eugène
"Les Noms Géographiques dans Québec." *Nouvelle France* (Québec) 12:515–520, 1913.

————.
Noms Géographiques de la Province de Québec et des Provinces Maritimes, Empruntés aux Langues Sauvages. Québec: É. Marcotte, 1906. 110 pp., illus.

. . . *Noms Sauvages Étymologie.* . . . Québec: E. Marcotte, 1905. 17 pp.

Rousseau, Jacques
"La Toponymie de l'Ile aux Coudres." *Sociétés de Géographie de Québec et de Montréal. Bulletin.* (Québec) 1942, Oct., pp. 89–100; Nov., pp. 106–114; Dec., pp. 121–127. Illus., bibl.

Roy, Pierre-Georges
Les Noms Géographiques de la Province de Québec. Lévis, 1906. 514 pp.

Taylor, Isaac
Words & Places; Illustrations of History, Ethnology and Geography. London: J. M. Dent & Sons, Ltd., 1911. xx, 467 pp.

Tyrrell, Joseph Burr
Algonquian Indian Names of Places in Northern Canada. Toronto: The University Press, 1915. 231 pp.

Walbran, John T.
British Columbia Coast Names, 1592–1906; to which are added a few names in adjacent United States territory; their origin and history, with map and illustrations. Ottawa: Govt. Printing Bureau, 1909. 546 pp., illus.

Whitcher, A. H.
"Geographical Nomenclature," *Proceedings of the D. L. S. Association, 1893;* pp. 67–72.

White, James
"Place-Names in the Rocky Mountains Between the 49th Parallel and the Athabaska River." *Royal Society of Canada. Transactions.* (Ottawa) 10 (ser. 3, sec. 2):501–535, 1917.

————.
Place-Names in the Thousand Islands. Ottawa: Govt. Printing Bureau, 1910. 7 pp.

Wintemberg, W. J.
"The Crimean War and Some Place-Names of Canada." *Transactions of the Royal Society of Canada.* (ser. 3), 21 (sec. 2):71–79, 1927.

Wood, William Charles Henry
Place-Names of Quebec. Montreal, 1922. 20 pp.

CHILDREN'S GAMES AND RHYMES

"English Folklore in Canada,—Child Rhymes and Games." *JAFL* 8:252–255, 1895.

Halpert, Herbert
"Skipping Rhymes from Calgary, Alberta." *CFQ* 3:154–155, 1944.
Texts only.

FOLKSONG

See: American Folksong and Ballad Studies and Collections, pp. 68-133.

BIBLIOGRAPHY

The Canadian Federation of Music Teachers Associations.
A List of Canadian Music. Toronto: Oxford University Press, 1946. 23 pp.
A great many compositions and arrangements listed are of folk origin. *Contents:* Piano solos, piano duets, two pianos, violin and piano, cello and piano, viola and piano, flute, organ, concertos and orchestral, chamber music; songs and choral compositions. List of Canadian composers and publishers.

GENERAL STUDIES AND COLLECTIONS

"A Trip to the Grand Banks." *FSSNE* 4:16, 1932.
A true picture of fisherman's life.

"Balladry of the Newfoundland Coast." A Review of "Ballads and Sea Songs of Newfoundland." *New York Times Book Review* 5, 1933 (April 9).

Barry, Phillips
"Songs and Traditions of the Meramichi." *FSSNE* 10:15–17, 1935.
Deals with the calamitous forest fires of October, 1825 in New Brunswick.

————.
"Songs and Traditions of the Meramichi." *FSSNE* 11:21–23, 1936.
Ballads of the famous Meramichi (Eastern Canada) fire which occurred in 1825 words and music: different version.

—————.
"The Bold Northwestern Man." *FSSNE* 10: 17–18, 1935.
"A tragedy of Queen Charlotte Island" (words and music).

—————.
"The Lightning Flash." *FSSNE* 3:14–15, 1931.
A non-Child ballad of Nova-Scotia.

—————.
"The Sons of North Britain." *JAFL* 26:183–184, 1913.
Discussion of English folk-songs in Nova-Scotia.

Bleakney, F. Eileen
"Folk-Lore from Ottawa and Vicinity." *JAFL* 31:158, 1918.

Botsford, Florence Hudson
Songs of the Americas, from the Botsford Collection of Folksongs. New York: G. Schirmer Inc., 1940. 106 pp.
Contains a number of Canadian songs, for voice and piano.

"Canadian English Folk Songs."
JAFL 31:170–179, 1918.

Creighton, Helen, coll.
Songs and Ballads From Nova Scotia. Toronto: J. M. Dent and Sons, Ltd., 1932. xxii, 334 pp., bibl., unaccompanied melodies.

—————, and Senior, Doreen H.
Twelve Folksongs from Nova Scotia. London: Novello, 1940. 41 pp., voice and piano.

Doerflinger, William
"Cruising for Ballads in Nova Scotia." *Canadian Geographical Journal* 16 (No. 2):91–97, 1938.

Doering, J. F.
"Donald Monroe, a Canadian Version of a Scottish Folksong." *JAFL* 55:170–174, 1942.
Text only—from Ontario.

Eckstorm, Fannie H.
"Canady I-O." *FSSNE* 6:10–13, 1933.

Emerson, Frederick R.
Newfoundland Folk Music. In: *The Book of Newfoundland*, Vol. I, (pp. 234–238). Edited by J. R. Smallwood. St. John's: Newfoundland Book Publishers, 1937.

"English Folk Songs in Canada."
JAFL 31:72–78, 130–133, 151–153, 158–179, 1918.

Fauset, Arthur Huff
Folk-lore from Nova Scotia. Memoir of the American Folklore Society, No. 24. Philadelphia: American Folklore Society, 1931.
Numerous ballads and songs included.

Fraser, A.
"The Gaelic Folk-Songs of Canada." *Transactions of the Royal Society of Canada* 60, sec. 2:49–60, 1903 (Ottawa).

Gibbon, J. Murray
Canadian Folk Songs (Old and New). Selected and translated by O'Hara, Geoffrey, and O'Brien, Oscar. New York: E. P. Dutton and Company, 1927, 1941.

Greenleaf, Elisabeth Bristol, coll. and ed.
Ballads and Sea Songs of Newfoundland. Music recorded in the field by Grace Yarrow Mansfield. Cambridge, Mass.: Harvard University Press, 1933. 395 pp., unaccompanied melodies.
Also contains music to a number of dances (quadrilles, cotillions, jigs, and step dances).

Greenough, William Parker
Canadian Folklife and Folklore. New York: G. H. Richmond, 1897. xii, 199 pp., illus., music.

"Irish Songs in Canada."
JAFL 31:162–167, 1918.

Karpeles, Maud, coll. and ed.
Folk Songs from Newfoundland with pianoforte accompaniments by R. Vaughan Williams, Olive Carey, Hubert Foss, and Michael Mullinger. London: Oxford University Press, 1934, 2 vols. 14 ballads and 16 songs.
Arranged for voice and piano.

Kempf, P.
"Treasure Trove of Melody in Canada's Folk-Songs." *Musician* 32:14–15, 1927 (July).

Mackenzie, W. Roy
Ballads and Sea Songs from Nova Scotia. Boston: Harvard University Press, 1928. xxxvii, 421 pp.

—————.
"Ballads from Nova Scotia." *JAFL* 23:371–380, 1910; 25:182–187, 1912.

—————.
"Ballad Singing in Nova Scotia." *JAFL* 22:327–331, 1909.

—————.
The Quest of the Ballad. Princeton, New Jersey: Princeton University Press, 1919.

Macmillan, Ernest
A Book of Songs. Compiled for the entertainment and delight of English men and women everywhere, especially for those at home and in Canada. New York: E. P. Dutton and Co., 1929. xii, 180 pp.
Arranged for one, and four voices, with piano accompaniment.

—————.
"Music in Canada." *Ontario Literary Review* 24:386–396, 1940.
Has valuable bibliography.

McLennan, William
Songs of Old Canada. Dawson Brothers, 1886.

Murphy, James
Songs and Ballads of Newfoundland—Ancient and Modern. St. John's, N'fld.: 1902. 90 pp.

Stewart, George
"Popular Songs of Old Canada." *Living Age* 28 (ser. 7):162–167, 1905.

——.
"Popular Songs of Old Canada." *Monthly Review* 19:64–75, 1905 (London).

RECORDS
Collections

U. S. Library of Congress. Division of Music. Folklore Section.
Helen Creighton Recording Project in Nova Scotia. 44–12″.   AAFS–LC.

Part Three: Ethnic Bibliography

THE NEGRO

THE NEGRO

FOLKLORE
BIBLIOGRAPHIES

See: Bibliography of American Folklore, pp. 3–4.

Corrado, Gini, ed.
Bibliografia Sulla Demografia delle Popolazioni Primitive. Commissione per lo Studio della Demografia della Popolazioni Primitive, Rome. 1938. 830 pp.
　Section on Negro (pp. 311–368).

Du Bois, W. E. B., Johnson, Guy B., and others
Encyclopedia of the Negro, preparatory volume with reference lists and reports. Introduction by Anson Phelps Stokes. New York: The Phelps-Stokes Fund, Inc., 1945. 207 pp.

Funkhouser, Myrtle
"Folklore of the American Negro." *Bulletin of Bibliography* (Boston) 16:28–29, 49–51, 72–73, 108–110, 136–137, 159–160, 1937–1939.

Lesser, Alexander
"Bibliography of American Folklore," 1915–1928. *JAFL* 41:47–52, 1928.
　Lists a number of items on Negro folklore, pp. 47–52.

The Negro: A Selected Bibliography.
The New York City Public Library, 1935.

Work, Monroe Nathan
Bibliography of the Negro in Africa and America. New York: H. W. Wilson Co., 1928.

PERIODICALS

See: Folklore Periodicals, pp. 4–5.

Journal of Negro History.
Association for the study of Negro life and history. Lancaster, Pa., Washington, D. C., V. 1. 1916– .

Negro History Bulletin.
Association for the study of Negro life and history. Washington, D. C.: No. 1, October 1937– .

Negro Quarterly.
1942–1943. New York: Negro Publication Society of America.

Negro Story; a Magazine for all Americans. Chicago, V. 1. 1944.

Negro Year Book, an annual encyclopedia of the Negro. V. 1. 1912. Tuskegee Institute, Ala., Negro Year Book Publishing Co. No editions were published for 1920/21, 1923/24, 1927/28–1929/30.

Southern Workman.
V. 1. 1900. Hampton, Va. Discontinued with V. 68, No. 7, July 1939.

The Negro Handbook.
1942–1947. New York: W. Malliet and Co. Florence Murray, ed.

GENERAL STUDIES AND COLLECTIONS

Adams, Edward C. L.
Nigger to Nigger. New York: Charles Scribner's Sons, 1928. xii, 270 pp.

—————.
Potee's Gold, a drama of Negro life near the big Congaree swamp. Columbus, S. C.: The State Company, 1929. 49 pp., illus.

Ballowe, Hewitt Leonard
The Lawd Saying the Same. Introduction by Donald Joseph. Illus. Baton Rouge, La.: Louisiana State University, 1947. xvi, 254 pp.
　It has the quality of a folk history of the Negro sugar plantation worker. The 24 tales touch on customs and beliefs of the Negro filled with authentic descriptions and colloquialisms.

Beasley, Delilah Liontium
The Negro Trail Blazers of California. Los Angeles: Times Mirror Printing and Binding House, 1919. 317 pp.

Bergen, F. D.
"Uncle Remus and Folklore." *Outlook* 48: 427–428, 1893 (Sept. 2).

Blackburn, M. J.
Folklore from Mammy Days. Boston: Walter H. Baker Co., 1924. ix, 105 pp.

Botkin, B. A.
A Treasury of American Folklore. Stories, ballads, and traditions of the people. New York: Crown Publishers, 1944. 932 pp.
　Contains many Negro folklore items, tales, legends, myths, etc.

—————.
Folk-Say and Folk-Lore. In: *Culture in the South,* by W. T. Couch, ed., pp. 570–593. Chapel Hill, N. C.: University of North Carolina Press, 1934.

—————.
Lay My Burden Down. A Folk History of Slavery. Chicago: University of Chicago Press, 1945. xxi, 286 pp., illus.
　"The Negro's own story of bondage and emancipation, told in proud, bitter and fervent words by over two thousand former slaves."

Botume, Elizabeth Hyde
First Days Amongst the Contrabands. Boston: Lee and Shephard, 1893. 286 pp.
　Life and lore of the Gullah of the Carolina Coast.

Brewer, J. Mason
"South Carolina Negro Folklore Guild." *JAFL* 59:493–494, 1946.

—————.
"Afro-American Folklore." *JAFL* 60:377–383, 1947.

Brown, Sterling
Negro in American Fiction. Washington: Associates in Negro Folk Education, 1937.

Cade, John B.
"Out of the Mouths of Ex-Slaves." *Journal of Negro History* July, 1935.

Calverton, Victor F., ed.
Anthology of American Negro Literature. New York: The Modern Library, 1929. xii, 535 pp.
Many of the essays, articles, and poems deal with Negro customs, traditions, beliefs, folktales, and dialect.

"Canadian Negro Folklore."
JAFL 38:621, 1925.

Christensen, Mrs. Abigail M. H.
Afro-American Folk Lore, Told Round Cabin Fires on the Sea Islands of South Carolina. Boston: Houghton Mifflin Co., 1898. xiv, 116 pp.
18 fables.

Cohn, David L.
God Shakes Creation. New York: Harper & Bros., 1935.

Collection of Slave Narratives.
Based on interviews with former slaves. In: *Microfilm,* Library of Congress.
Described and illustrated by B. A. Botkin in the Library of Congress *Quarterly Journal of Current Acquisitions,* Nov., 1944.

Cross, T. P.
"Folklore from the Southern States (Negro)." *JAFL* 22:251–255, 1909.

Crum, Mason
Gullah: Negro Life in the Carolina Sea Islands. Durham, N. C.: Duke University Press, 1940. xv, 351 pp., bibl. (pp. 345–351).
Lot of folklore material—customs, songs, dialect, food, and other interesting data.

Culbertson, E. H.
Color in Court: A Play of Negro life in 1 Act. New York: French, 1933.

Davis, Henry C.
"Negro Folk-Lore in South Carolina." *JAFL* 27:241–254, 1917.

Davis, M. E. N.
"Louisiana Folklore" (Negro). *JAFL* 18:251–252, 1905.

Deming, Clarence
By Ways of Nature and Life. New York: G. P. Putnam's Sons, 1884.

Dobie, James Frank, ed.
Follow de Drinkin' Gou'd. Austin. Texas: Published by the Texas Folklore Society, 1928. 201 pp., illus., music.
Part III, pp. 81–144 deals with Negro folklore and folksongs.

Drew, Benjamin
The North-Side of Slavery. The Refugee: or The Narratives of Fugitive Slaves in Canada, Related by Themselves, with an account of the history and condition of the colored population of Upper Canada. Boston: J. P. Jewett and Co.; New York: Sheldon, Lamport and Blakeman, 1856. xii, 387 pp.
Experiences of ex-slaves recounted in their own words.

Drums and Shadows: Survival Studies Among the Georgia Coastal Negros. Foreword by Guy B. Johnson, photographs by Muriel and Malcolm Bell, Jr. Savannah University, Georgia Writers' Project, W.P.A. Athens, Ga.: University of Georgia Press, 1940. 274 pp.
This work is oriented toward the problem of African heritages in this country.

Duncan, E. G.
Big Road Walker. New York: Frederick A. Stokes Co., 1940.

Edmonds, Randolph
Six Plays for a Negro Theatre. Boston: Baker, Walter H. & Co., 1934. Foreword by Frederick H. Koch. 155 pp.

Embree, Edwin Rogers
Brown America, The Story of a New Race. New York: The Viking Press, 1931. vi, 311 pp.

Emerson, William Canfield
Stories and Spirituals of the Negro Slave. Boston: R. G. Badger, 1930. 79 pp.
Includes music.

Eppse, Mere R.
The Negro, Too, in American History. Nashville, Tennessee: National Publication Society, 1943. P. O. Box 445. 591 pp.

Fauset, Arthur Huff
Black Gods of the Metropolis. Publications of the Philadelphia Anthropological Society No. 8, 126 pp., 4 illus., bibl. Philadelphia: University of Pennsylvania Press, 1944.
A descriptive and analytical study of various Negro cults in some major cities in the U.S.

Featherstonhaugh, George William
Excursion Through the Slave States. London: J. Murray, 1844. 2 Vols.
"Superb on manners and folk ways." (Dobie)

Fitchett, E. H.
"Traditions of the Free Negro in Charleston, South Carolina." *Journal of Negro History* 25:139–152, 1940.

"Folklore from St. Helena, South Carolina."
JAFL 38:217–238, 1925.

Ford, Theodore P.
God Wills the Negro. Chicago, Ill.: The Geographical Institute Press, 1939.
An anthropological and geographical restoration of the best history of the American Negro people, being in part a theological interpretation of Egyptian and Ethiopian backgrounds. Compiled from ancient and modern sources, with a special chapter on eight Negro spirituals.

Frazier, E. F.
Traditions and Patterns of Negro Family Life
in the United States. In: *Race and Culture
Contacts*, by E. B. Reuter, pp. 191–207. New
York: 1934.

**Gordon, Armistead Churchill, and
Page, Thomas Nelson**
Befo' de War; echoes in Negro dialect. New
York: C. Scribner's Sons, 1888. vi, 131 pp.
A collection of poems.

Green, Paul
Lonesome Road. New York: Robert M. Mc-
Bride, 1926.

Grissom, Mary Allen
The Negro Sings a New Heaven. Chapel Hill:
The University of North Carolina Press, 1930.
101 pp., music.

Harris, Joel Chandler
Free Joe and Other Georgian Sketches. New
York: C. Scribner's Sons, 1887. 236 pp.

*The Tar-Baby, and Other Rhymes by Uncle
Remus.* New York: D. Appleton and Company,
1904. 189 pp., illus.

Uncle Remus and His Friends. Boston and
New York: Houghton Mifflin and Company,
1892. 357 pp.
Old plantation stories, songs, and ballads, with
sketches of Negro character.

Uncle Remus, His Songs and His Sayings; the
folk-lore of old plantation. New York: D.
Appleton and Company, 1881. 231 pp., illus.
New ed. rev. and ed. with one hundred and
twelve illustrations by A. B. Frost. 1917. xxi,
265 pp.

Herskovits, Melville J.
"African Gods and Catholic Saints in New
World Negro Belief." *AA* 39:635–643, 1937.

Freudian Mechanisms in Primitive Negro
Psychology. In: *Essays Presented to Charles
Gabriel Seligman*, pp. 75–84. London: Rout-
ledge Co., Ltd., 1934.

"Some Next Steps in the Study of Negro
Folklore." *JAFL* 56:1–7, 1943.

"The Ancestry of the American Negro." *The
American Scholar* 8:84–94, 1938–1939.

The Myth of the Negro Past. New York:
Harper & Bro., 1941. 374 pp., bibl. (pp. 341–
355).
Chapter VIII: The Contemporary Scene: Language and the arts, discussion of the African
survival in Negro music.

"What Has Africa Given America?" *The New
Republic* 84:92–94, 1935.

Heyward, Du Bose
Mamba's Daughters. New York: Doubleday,
Doran & Co., 1929. 344 pp.

Porgy. New York: George H. Doran, 1925.
196 pp.
Rich in Charleston Negro lore, speech and slang.

Higginson, Thomas Wentworth
Army Life in a Black Regiment. Boston:
Fields, Osgood and Co., 1870. 294 pp.
Chapter IX deals with Negro spirituals.

Holland, Rupert Sargent, ed.
*Letters and Diary of Laura M. Towne, Written
from the Sea Islands of South Carolina, 1862–
1884.* Cambridge, Mass.: Harvard University
Press, 1912. 310 pp.

Hurston, Zora Neale
"High John de Conquer"; Negro folklore
offers solace to sufferers. *American Mercury*
57:450–8, Oct., 1943.

Jonah's Gourd Vine. Philadelphia: J. B. Lippincott, 1934.

Mules and Men. Introduction by Franz Boas.
Ten illustrations by Miguel Covarrubias.
Phila.: J. B. Lippincott Company, 1935. 342
pp.
Deals with Negro folk lore, Voodooism, Negro
tales and songs from Florida and Louisiana.
Songs, pp. 309–331.

Johnson, Charles S.
Shadow of the Plantation. Chicago, Ill.: The
University of Chicago Press, 1934. xiv, 214 pp.
Narrative of old slaves of Macon County, Ala-
bama, shedding much light on customs, tradi-
tions and beliefs of Negroes.

Johnson, Georgia Douglas
Plumes, a Folk Tragedy. New York: Samuel
French, Publisher, 1927.

Johnson, Guy B.
Folk Culture in St. Helena Island. Chapel
Hill: University of North Carolina Press, 1930.
xi, 183 pp., music, bibl.
The work deals with the superstitions, tales,
riddles, rhymes, games and proverbs of the Gullah living in St. Helena. Discusses the folk songs,
the spirituals in particular; a part is devoted to
the Gullah dialect.

Johnson, James Weldon
God's Trombones. New York: The Viking
Press, 1927. 56 pp., illus.
Seven Negro Sermons in Verse, Drawings by
Aaron Douglas.

The Book of American Negro Poetry. New
York: Harcourt Brace & Co., 1922. 217 pp.

Johnston, Harry H., Sir
The Negro in the New World. London: Methuen and Co., Ltd., 1910. 499 pp.
An historical survey of the Negro in the New World. The author's attitude and prejudice are summed up in the following paragraph: "For many thousand years he has been a relatively idle creature as compared to the industrious European or Asiatic; who, when not in slavery to each other, were the slaves of ambition, of art, of science, of gluttony, of lust, and of religion. In other words, they *worked*. The Negro became constitutionally so lazy, and he thought out very few problems for himself, and every now and then borrowed ideas from the Caucasian who impinged on his territories in Northern Africa." (p. xi of the Introduction).

Jones, Raymond J.
A Comparative Study of Religious Cult Behavior Among Negroes with Special Reference to Emotional Group Conditioning Factors. Washington, D. C.: Howard University Studies in the Social Sciences, Vol. II, No. 2, 1939.

Kennedy, Robert Emmet
Black Cameos. Decorations by Edward Larocque Tinker. New York: A. & C. Boni, 1924. xxv, 210 pp.
"Verbal transcriptions of Negro life in southern Louisiana." Introd.

Kennedy, Stetson
Palmetto Country. (Amercan Folkways Series). New York: Duell, Sloan & Pearce Co., 1942. 340 pp.
In the chapter "Stuff and Such"—a great deal of interesting folk material indigenous to the Southern land.

Law, Robert Adger
"Notes on Some Recent Treatments of Negro Folk Lore." *TFSP* 7:140–144, 1928.
Discusses C. L. Adam's: "Congaree Sketches."

Lawson, H. J.
Negro in American Drama. Urbana, Ill.: University of Illinois, 1939.

Lee, C.
"Negro Lore from Baltimore." *JAFL* 5:110–112, 1892.

Leighton, Clare
Southern Harvest. New York: Macmillan Co.. 157 pp., 1942.

Lind, J. E.
"Phylogenetic Elements in the Psychoses of the Negro." *Psychoanalytic Review* 4:303–332, 1917.

Linton, William James
Poetry of America; selections from one hundred American poets from 1776 to 1876. With an introductory review of colonial poetry, and some specimens of Negro melody. London: G. Bell, 1876, xlii, 387 pp., music.

Locke, Alain Le Roy, and Gregory, Montgomery, eds.
Plays of Negro Life; a source book of native American drama. Decorations and illustrations by Aaron Douglas. New York: Harper and Bros., 1927. 430 pp., bibl.

The Negro in America. Chicago: American Library Association, 1933.

The New Negro; an Interpretation. Book decoration and portraits by Winold Reiss. New York: A. and C. Boni, 1925. xviii, 446 pp., ills., bibl. (pp. 415–446), music.

Lomax, John A.
"Adventures of a Ballad Hunter." *TFSP* 19:9–20, 1944.
Describes Negro sermons by preachers of Texas and North Carolina.

McDowell, Tremaine
"The Negro in the Southern Novel Prior to 1850." *Journal of English and Germanic Philology* 25:455–473, 1926.

Mikell, I. Jenkins
Rumbling of the Chariot Wheels. Columbia, S. C.: The State Co., 1923. 273 pp.
Lore of the Gullah.

Moderwell, Hiram Kelly
"The Epic of the Black Man." *New Republic* (N. Y.) 12:154–155, 1917.

Murray, D.
"Negro Genius." *JAFL* 18:319–321, 1905.

Negro Caravan.
New York: Dryden Press, 1942. 1082 pp.
Selected and edited by Sterling A. Brown, Howard University, Arthur P. Davis, Virginia Union University and Ulysses Lee, Lincoln University. "Folk literature," pp. 412–491.

Odum, Howard W.
Rainbow Round My Shoulder. Indianapolis: The Bobbs-Merrill Co., 1928.

Social and Mental Traits of the Negro. New York: Columbia University Press, 1910. 302 pp.
Research into the conditions of the Negro race in Southern towns; a study of race traits, tendencies and prospects. (*Studies in History, Economics, and Public Law,* vol. 37, no. 3).

Ortiz Roderigo, Néstor R.
"El folklore negro en la literatura norte-americana." *Nosotros* (Buenos Aires) 6: (No. 65) 150–157, 1941.

Ott, Eleanore
Plantation Cookery of Old Louisiana. New Orleans: Harmanson, 1938.

Owen, Nicholas
Journal of a Slave-dealer. London: G. Routledge & Sons, Ltd., 1930. 120 pp., illus.
"A view of some remarkable incidents in the life of Nicholas Owen on the coast of Africa and America from the year 1746 to the year 1757." Edited with an introd. by Eveline Martin.

Parsons, Elsie Clews
Folk-Lore of the Sea Islands, South Carolina. Memoirs of the American Folklore Society, Vol. 16. Cambridge, Mass.: The American Folklore Society, 1923. xxx, 217 pp., music, bibl.

————.
"Folklore from Aiken, South Carolina."
(Negro). *JAFL* 34:1–39. 1921.

————.
"Joel Chandler Harris and Negro Folklore."
Dial (May 17) 1919.

Peeples, Edwin A.
Swing Low. Boston: Houghton Mifflin Co.,
1945. 293 pp.
A novel dealing with white and Negro types
faithfully drawn presenting rich insight into the
people's attitudes.

Pendleton, N.
"Negro Folklore and Witchcraft in the South."
JAFL 3:201–207, 1890.

Peterkin, Julia Mood
Green Thursday. New York: Alfred A. Knopf,
1924. 188 pp.

————.
Roll, Jordan Roll. New York: R. O. Ballou,
1933. 341 pp.
The text by Julia Peterkin, the photographic
studies by Doris Ulmann. Rich in lore, dialect
and tradition of Negro and plantation life.

————.
Scarlet Sister Mary. Indianapolis: Bobbs-
Merrill Co., 1928.
Rich in life of the South,—its people, customs,
traditions, and folkspeech.

Pipes, James
Ziba. Decoration by Edith Mahier. Norman,
Okla.: University of Oklahoma Press, 1943.
188 pp.
"The author assimilated the picturesque and poetic language and flaming imagination of Negroes
from saw mills, cotton plantations, levee camps,
and cane farms,—these poems have caught the
magical word-sense and the rich music of the
Negro improvisations." (William Rose Benet)

Porter, James A.
Modern Negro Art. New York: Dryden Press,
1944. 272 pp., illus.
A history and criticism of Negro art in America.

Powdermaker, Hortense
After Freedom. New York: The Viking Press,
1939.
The author studies the problem of acculturation
in a rural Negro community in Mississippi.

Puckette, Clara Childs
Old Mitt Laughs Last. Boston: Bobbs-Merrill
Co., 1944. Illus.
A novel that has caught the speech inflections
and the folk characteristics of the Gullahs.

Ramos, Arthur
As Culturas Negras no Novo Mundo. Rio de
Janeiro: Civilização Brasileira, S/A, 1937. 399
pp., illus.
Negroes in America—folklore, social life and
customs.

————.
O Negro nos Estados Unidos. In: *Brasil-Esta-
dos.* pp. 323–326. Rio de Janeiro: Ed. Diáriode
notícias, 1939.
Discussion of Negro folklore.

Ravenel, H. W.
"Recollections of Southern Plantation Life."
Edited by Marjorie S. Mendenhall. *Yale Review* 25:748–787, 1936.
"A document written in Feb., 1876. Along with
his description of the habits, customs, and superstitions of South Carolina Negroes, the author
cites much of their vocabulary."

Redpath, James
*The Roving Editor; or Talks with Slaves in
the Southern States.* New York: A. B. Burdick, 1859. xvi, 349 pp.
The author, according to B. A. Botkin, used the
editorialized interview, "which means conversations into a narrative and descriptive commentary, sprinkled with dialect and exhortation."

Rice, James Henry
Glories of the Carolina Coast. Columbus, S. C.:
R. L. Bryan Company, 1936. xiv, 211 pp.
About the Gullah,—life, traditions and lore.

Richardson, Willis
Plays and Pageants from the Life of the Negro.
Washington, D. C.: The Associated Publishers,
Inc., 1930.

Rourke, Constance
Traditions for a Negro Literature. In: *The
Roots of American Culture, and Other Essays,*
(pp. 262–274). New York: Harcourt, Brace &
Co., 1942. 308 pp. Edited with a preface by
Van Wyck Brooks.
The author believes that the traditions of a
Negro literature exist for the most part in frag-
mentary songs and brief tales.

Roussève, Charles Barthelemy
The Negro in Louisiana; aspects of his history and his literature. New Orleans: The
Xavier University Press, 1937. xvii, 212 pp.,
illus., music.

Rowe, G. C.
"The Negroes of the Sea Islands." *Southern
Workman* 29:709–715, 1900.

Russell, Sir William Howard
My Diary North and South. Boston: T. O. H.
P. Burnham, 1863.

Rutledge, Archibald
Days Off in Dixie. New York: Doubleday, Page
and Co., 1924.

————.
Heart of the South. Columbia, S. C.: The
State Co., 1924.

————.
Old Plantation Days. New York: Frederick A.
Stokes Co., 1921.

————.
Plantation Game Trails. Boston: Houghton
Mifflin Co., 1921.

————.
Tom and I on the Old Plantation. New York:
Frederick A. Stokes Co., 1918.

Sale, John B.
The Tree Named John; with twenty-five silhouettes by Joseph Cranston Jones. Chapel
Hill: The University of North Carolina Press,
1929. xii, 151 pp., illus.

Sass, Herbert Ravenal
Adventures in Green Places. New York: Minton, Balch and Co., 1926.

————.
The Way of the Wild. New York: Minton, Balch and Co., 1925.

Saxon, Lyle
Fabulous New Orleans. Illustrated by E. H. Suydam. New York: Appleton-Century Co., 1939. New ed.

————.
Father Mississippi. New York: Century Company, 1929.

Scarborough, Dorothy
From a Southern Porch. New York: G. P. Putnam's Sons, 1919. ix, 318 pp.
A novel, rich in lore and song.

————.
In the Land of Cotton. New York: The Macmillan Co., 1923. x, 370.

Singer, Caroline, and Baldridge, Cyrus Le Roy
White Africans and Black. New York: W. W. Norton & Co., 1929.

Smith, William S.
Life at the South; or, "Uncle Tom's Cabin" as it is. Being narratives, scenes, and incidents in the real "life of the lowly." Buffalo: G. H. Derby & Co., 1852. vi, 519 pp., illus.
Social life and customs.

Smythe, Augustine T., Sass, Herbert R., and others
The Carolina Low Country. New York: Macmillan, 1931.
Narrative and description of Charleston plantation life, Negro life, Negro spirituals, words and music.

Spaulding, H. G.
"Under the Palmetto." *Continental Monthly* 4: 188–203, 1863.

Speck, F. G.
"The Negroes and the Creek Nation." *Southern Workman* 37:106–110, 1908.

Speers, M. W. F.
"Maryland and Virginia Folklore" (Negro). *JAFL* 23:435–439, 1910; 25:284–286, 1912; 26:190–191, 1913.

Still, William
The Underground Rail Road: A Record of Facts, Authentic Narratives, Letters, etc., Narrating the Hardships, Hair-breadth Escapes and Death Struggles of the Slaves in Their Efforts for Freedom, as Related by Themselves and Others, or Witnessed by the Author; together with sketches of some of the larger stockholders and most liberal advisers of the road. Illustrated with 70 fine engravings by Bensell, Schell, and others, and portraits from photographs from life. Philadelphia, Pa.: People's Publishing Co., 1879. 780 pp., rev. ed.

Stoney, Samuel G., and Shelby, Gertrude Mathews
Black Genesis. New York: The Macmillan Co., 1930. 192 pp., illus.

Talley, Thomas Washington
Negro Folk Rhymes, Wise and Otherwise. New York: Macmillan Co., 1922. xii, 347 pp., music.

The Negro in Virginia. New Hastings, New York: Virginia State Writers' Program, Works Progress Administration, 1940.

Thompson, Stith
Round the Levee. Austin, Texas: Texas Folklore Society, 1935. 111 pp. (Publications of the Texas Folklore Society, No. 1, 1916.)

Turner, L. M.
'Bout Cullud Folkses. New York: Henry Harrison, Publ., 1938.

Weeden, Miss Howard
Songs of the Old South; verses and drawings by Howard Weeden. New York: Doubleday, Page & Co., 1900. xii, 94 pp., illus.
Poems illustrating social life, beliefs, and traditions of the Negro.

Whaley, Marcellus S.
The Old Types Pass—Gullah Sketches of the Carolina Sea Islands. Boston: Christopher Publishing House, 1925.

Williams, Rev. John G.
De Ole Plantation. Charleston, S. C.: Walter, Evans & Cogswell Co., Printers, 1896. xi, 67 pp.

Wintemberg, W. J.
"Some Items of Negro Canadian Folklore." *JAFL* 38:621, 1925.

Woofter, Thomas Jackson
Black Yeomanry; life on St. Helena Island. New York: H. Holt Company, 1930. x, 291 pp., illus.

MYTHS—LEGENDS

Bennett, John
The Doctor to the Dead. Grotesque Legends and Folk-Tales of Old Charleston. New York: Rinehart and Company, 1946. xv, 260 pp.
The author includes three stories in the Gullah dialect.

Carneiro, Edison
Religioes Negras; notas de etnografia religiosa. Rio de Janeiro: Civilizacao brasileira S. A. 1936. 180 pp., illus.
Symbolism and myth in Negro religious practices.

Chamberlain, A. F.
"Negro Creation Legend." *JAFL* 3:302, 1890.

Davenport, Frederick Morgan
Primitive Traits in Religious Revivals; a study in mental and social evolution. New York. London: The Macmillan Co., 1906. xii, 323 pp.

Drums and Shadows; Survival studies among
the Georgia Coastal Negroes. Savannah unit,
Georgia Writers' Project, WPA, foreword by
Guy B. Johnson, photographs by Muriel and
Malcom Bell. Athens, Georgia: University of
Georgia Press, 1940.

Harris, Joel Chandler
Nights with Uncle Remus; myths and legends
of the old plantation. Boston: T. R. Osgood
and Company, 1883. xxxvi, 416 pp.

————.
*Uncle Remus: being legends of the old plan-
tation.* Illustrations by Fritz Eichenberg.
Mount Vernon, New York: The Peter Pauper
Press, 1937. 135 pp.

————.
*The Uncle Remus . . . book from Joel Chan-
dler Harris, retold by Miriam Blanton Huber.*
Illustrations by A. B. Frost. New York: D. Appleton-Century Company, Inc., 1935. viii, 151
pp.

————.
Uncle Remus, His Songs and Sayings. New
and revised edition, with 112 illus. by A. B.
Frost. New York: D. Appleton and Company,
1908. xxi, 265 pp.
Many editions of this work have been issued.
Deals with legends and stories of animals, Negro
songs, legends of the old plantation, and plantation proverbs.

Herskovits, Melville J.
"African Gods and Catholic Saints in New
World Negro Belief." *AA* 39:635–643, 1937.

————.
The Myth of the Negro Past. New York: Harper & Brothers, 1941. 374 pp.

Jamison, C. V.
"Louisana (Negro) Legend Concerning Will-o'-
the-Wisp." *JAFL* 18:250, 1905.

Jones, Charles Colcock
*Negro Myths from the Georgia Coast Told in
the Vernacular.* Boston: Houghton Mifflin Co.,
1888. Reprinted by the State Co., 1925. 192
pp., 61 fables, 8 page glossary.

Oertel, H.
"Notes on six Negro myths from the Georgia
coast." *JAFL* 2:309, 1889.

Smith, Nathan Ryno
Legends of the South. By somebody who wants
to be considered nobody. Baltimore: Steam
Press of W. K. Boyle, 1869. 70 pp.
Contents: 1. Legend of the White Sulphur. 2.
Legend of the White Sulphur. 3. Legend of Sweet
Spring. 4. Legend of the Mammoth Cave. 5.
Legend of the Hot Springs of Virginia.

Young, Martha
Plantation Bird Legends. Illus. by J. M.
Condé. New York and London: D. Appleton
& Co., 1916. 249 pp.

FOLKTALES
Bibliography

See: Folktale Bibliographies, p. 22.

"Bibliography of Negro Tales."
JAFL 30:170, 1917.

General Studies and Collections

Adams, Edward C.
Congaree Sketches. Intro. by Paul Green.
Chapel Hill: The University of North Caro-
lina Press, 1927. xvii, 116 pp.
Scenes from Negro life in the swamps of the
Congaree and tales by Tad and Scip of heaven
and hell with other miscellany.

"Alabama Negro Tales."
JAFL 32:373–374, 1919; 40:213–303, 1927.

Backus, E. M.
"Negro Tales from Georgia." *JAFL* 25:125,
126, 128–136, 1912.

————.
"Tales of the Rabbit from Georgia Negroes."
JAFL 12:108–115, 1899.

Bennett, John
The Doctor to the Dead. Grotesque Legends
and Folk-Tales of Old Charleston. New York:
Rinehart and Company, 1946. xv, 260 pp.
The author includes three stories in the Gullah
dialect.

Botkin, B. A.
Lay My Burden Down. Chicago: University of
Chicago Press, 1945. xxi, 286 pp.
The 280 narratives comprising the ingredients
of this volume "throw light on the aspects of the
American slave system as a moral order, rather
than an economic one. The documents selected
for inclusion in the volume substantiate the fact
that the slave developed within the system a set
of attitudes, sentiments, and conducts which were
complimentary to those of the master; both
groups strove to reach the maximum satisfaction
of their desires according to their own status;
each set up the objectives that it wished to
achieve and each sought to attain these goals in
its own way." (J. Mason Brewer).

Bradford, Roark
Ol' King David an' the Philistine Boys. New
York: Harper & Bros., 1930. vi, 227 pp., illus.
A second volume of 'hilariously' delightful Negro
biblical stories.

————.
Ol' Man Adam an' His Chillun'. New York:
Harper & Bros., 1928. xxiv, 264 pp., illus.
A collection of Negro biblical interperations.
"Green Pastures" is based on these tales.

————.
This Side of Jordan. New York: Harper &
Bros., 1929. 255 pp., illus.
"Something of the hot blood, the uncurbed pas-
sions, the frank immorality of these colored folk,
whom he has known all his life, has seeped its
way into his tale." (The Milwaukee Journal.)

———, and Connolly, Marc
Green Pastures. Ol' Man Adam an' His Chillun. New York: Farrar & Rinehart, Inc., 1930. xvi, 173 pp.

Branner, J. C.
How and Why Stories. New York: H. Holt & Co., 1921. xi, 104 pp., illus.

Brewer, J. Mason
Humorous Folk Tales of the South Carolina Negro. Publications of the South Carolina Negro Folklore Guild, No. 1. Orangeburg, South Carolina: South Carolina Negro Folklore Guild, 1945. xxi, 64 pp.

———.
"Juneteenth." Illustrated by Tom B. Smith. *TFSP* 10:9–54, 1932.
Tales gathered from Texan Negroes.

Brown, William Norman
"The Tar-Baby Story at Home." *Scientific Monthly* 15:228–234, September, 1922.

Carroll, Walter
"De Lost John; a Negro Play of Piedmont, Carolina." *Carolina Playbook* (Chapel Hill) 15:69–75, 1942. illus.

Cobb, Lucy M., and Hicks, Mary A.
"Negro Folktales." *TFSP* 17:108–112, 1941.

———.
"Why Brer Buzzard Vomits." *SFQ* 2 (No. 4): 203–206, 1938.

Cole, Helen Rosemary
"Why is Mistletoe." *JAFL* 59:528–529, 1946.
A Negro story heard in Dallas, Texas.

Connolly, Marc
The Green Pastures, a fable suggested by Roark Bradford's southern sketches, "O'l Man Adam an' His Chillun'." New York: Farrar and Rinehart, 1930. xvi, 173 pp.
Attempts "to present certain aspects of a living religion in the terms of its believers—thousands of Negroes in the deep South." (Intro., p. xv).

Coomaraswamy, Ananda K.
"A Note on the Stickfast Motif." *JAFL* 57: 128–132, 1944.
The author attempts to show that the Stickfast Story, with or without the Tar-baby element, may well have been pre-Buddhist before it was Buddhist and Jaina, and that it could have originated in India.

Cox, J. H.
"Negro Tales from West Virginia." *JAFL* 47: 334–341, 1934.

Crimmins, Martin L.
"Mr. Possum and Mr. Coon." *TFSP* 9:165–166, 1931.
Negro tale.

Cross, T. P.
"Folklore from the Southern States" (Negro). *JAFL* 22:251–255, 1909.

Davis, H. C.
"Negro Folklore in South Carolina." *JAFL* 27:241–254, 1914.

Davis, M. E. M.
"Louisiana Folklore" (Negro). *JAFL* 18:251–252, 1905.

Drums and Shadows; Survival studies among the Georgia Coastal Negroes. W.P.A. Writers' Program, Georgia. Foreword by Guy B. Johnson. Athens, Georgia: University of Georgia Press, 1940.

Eddius, A. W.
"Brazos Bottom Philosophy." *TFSP* 9:153–164, 1931.
Negro anecdotes.

———.
"How Sandy Got his Meat: A Negro tale from Brazos Bottoms." *TFSP* 1:47–49, 1916.

Emmons, Martha
"Cats and the Occult." *TFSP* 11:94–100, 1933.
Negro tales of the evil connected with cats.

———.
"Confidences from Old Nacogdoches (Texas)." *TFSP* 7:119–134, 1928.
Negro superstitions and tales.

———.
"Dyin' Easy." *TFSP* 10:55–61, 1932.
Negro tales of death and ghosts.

Fauset, A. H.
"Negro folk-tales from the South (Alabama, Mississippi, Louisiana)." *JAFL* 40:213–303, 1927.

"Florida Negro Tales."
JAFL 30:222–227, 1917; 32:374, 1919.

Goldsborough, Edmund K.
Ole Man an' Ole Miss. Washington, D. C.: National Publishing Co., 1900. 219 pp., illus.
Dialect stories and anecdotes illustrating the Eastern Shore Negroes.

Gonzales, Ambrose Elliott
Laguerre, a Gascon of the Black Border. Columbia, S. C.: The State Co., 1924. xvi, 318 pp.
This, and the succeeding items by the author are Gullah tales.

———.
The Black Border; Gullah Stories of the Carolina Coast (with a glossary). Columbia, S. C.: The State Company, 1922. 348 pp.

———.
The Captain; stories of the black border. Columbia, S. C.: The State Co., 1924. xvi, 384 pp.

———.
With Aesop along the Black Border. Columbia, S. C.: The State Co., 1924. xiv, 298 pp.

Harris, Joel Chandler
Daddy Jake the Runaway, and Short Stories Told After Dark, by "Uncle Remus," Joel Chandler Harris. New York: The Century Company, 1889. 145 pp.

———.
Stories from Uncle Remus. Edited by Mrs. J. C. Harris; with the A. B. Frost illustrations. New York: The Saalfield Publishing Company, 1934. 34 pp.

————.

Tales from Uncle Remus. Illustrated by Milo Winter. Boston: Houghton Mifflin Company, 1935. xv, 61 pp.

————.

The Tar-Baby, and Other Rhymes of Uncle Remus. With illustrations in color by A. B. Frost and E. W. Kemble. New York: D. Appleton and Company, 1904. xiv, 189 pp.

————.

Told by Uncle Remus; new stories of the old plantation. Illustrations by A. B. Frost, J. M. Condé, and Frank Verbeck. New York: Grosset and Dunlap, 1936. 295 pp.

————.

Uncle Remus and Brer Rabbit. New York: F. A. Stokes Company, 1907. 63 pp.

————.

Uncle Remus and His Friends; old plantation stories, songs and ballads, with sketches of Negro character. Illustrations by A. B. Frost. Boston: Houghton Mifflin Company, 1892. xv, 357 pp.

————.

Uncle Remus and the Little Boy. Illustrations by J. M. Condé. Boston: Small, Maynard and Company, 1910. xi, 173 pp.

————.

Uncle Remus, His Songs and Sayings. New and revised edition, with 112 illustrations by A. B. Frost. New York: D. Appleton and Company, 1895. xxi, 265 pp.

————.

Uncle Remus Returns. Illustrations by A. B. Frost, and J. M. Condé. Boston: Houghton Mifflin Company, 1918. v, 174 pp.

Harvey, Emily N.
"A Brer Rabbit Story." *JAFL* 32:443–444, 1919.

Hendricks, W. C.
Bundle of Troubles and Other Tarheel Tales. Durham, North Carolina: Duke University Press, 1944. 206 pp.
    "Written in real dialect, they deal with ghosts, haunts, whang doodles, witches, smart 'critters', 'Champeen terbacker chawers', Negro preachers, and others . . ." (C. L. Snyder).

Heyward, Mrs. Jane Sereven
Brown Jacket. Columbia, S. C.: The State Co., 1923. 64 pp.
    Contains 12 Gullah stories.

Hobson, Anne
In Old Alabama; being the chronicle of Miss Mouse, the little black merchant, by Anne Hobson; illustrated by Carol Mac Pherson. New York: Doubleday Page & Co., 1903.

Hurston, Zora Neale
Mules and Men. Phila.: J. B. Lippincott Co., 1935.
    Pp. 122–137, passim deals with "Big Lies" as told by Florida Negroes.

Johnston, W. P.
"Two Negro Tales (Louisiana)." *JAFL* 9:194–198, 1896.

Lee, F. H., ed.
Folk Tales of All Nations. New York: Tudor Publishing Company, 1946. 947 pp.
    Negro tales, pp. 112–119.

Leitner, E. H.
"Negro Tales from Georgia." *JAFL* 25:125–136, 1912.

"Louisiana Negro Tales."
JAFL 9:194–198, 1896; 18:250, 1905; 40:213–303, 1927.

McBryde, John McLaren
Brer Rabbit in the Folk-Tales of the Negro and Other Races. Sewanee, Tenn.: The University Press at the University of the South, 1911. 24 pp., bibl.

McIlhenny, E. A.
"Trubble, brudder alligator, trouble." *TFSP* 14:135–144, 1938.

McLennan, M.
"Origin of the cat; a Negro tale." *JAFL* 9:71, 1896.

Milne-Horne, M. P.
Mama's Black Nurse Stories. Edinburgh and London: 1890.

"Mississippi Negro Tales."
JAFL 40:213–303, 1927.

Mitchell, Mrs. Minnie Belle
Gay Moon Tales. Indianapolis: The Bobbs Merrill Co., 1926. 169 pp., illus. by Will Vawter.

O'Connor, Kate Stoner
"How Mr. Polecat Got His Scent." *TFSP* 7:137–138, 1928.
    Tale told by an old Negro man.

Odum, Howard W.
Cold Blue Moon, Black Ulysses Afar Off. Indianapolis: The Bobbs-Merrill Company, 1931.
    Negro folk tales.

Owen, Mary Alicia
"Ole Rabbit An' De Dawg He Stole." *JAFL* 3:135–138, 1890.
    Negro folktale.

————.

Voodoo Tales. As Told Among the Negroes of the Southwest; coll. from original sources by T. A. Owen, introd. by C. G. Leland, illus. by A. Owen and Louis Wain. New York: G. P. Putnam's Sons, 1893. xv, 310 pp., illus.

Parsons, Elsie Clews
Folk Tales of the Sea Islands, South Carolina. Memoirs of the American Folklore Society, No. 16. Philadelphia: American Folklore Society, 1923.

————.

"Joel Chandler Harris and Negro Folklore:" Review of *Uncle Remus Returns,* by J. C. Harris. *Dial* 64:491–493, 1919.

————.
"Provenience of Certain Negro Folk-Tales, Playing Dead Twice in the Road." *Folk-Lore* 28:408–414, 1917 (London).

————.
"Provenience of Certain Negro Folk-Tales, II. The Password." *Folk-Lore* 29:206–218, 1917 (London).

————.
"The Provenience of Certain Folk-Tales, III. Tar Baby." *Folk-Lore* 30:227–234, 1919 (London).

————.
"The Provenience of Certain Negro Folk-Tales, IV. Missing Tongues." *Folk-Lore* 32:194–201, 1921 (London).

————.
"The Provenience of Certain Negro Folk-Tales, V. The House Keeper." *Folk-Lore* 34:363–370, 1923 (London).

————.
"Tales from Guilford County, North Carolina." *JAFL* 30:168–200, 1917.

————.
"Ten Folk Tales from Cape Verde Islands." *JAFL* 30:230–238, 1917.

Rhame, John M.
"Flaming Youth." *AS* 8 (No. 3):39–43, 1933.
A story in Gullah dialect.

Robb, Bernard
Welcum Hinges; with a foreword by Alexander William Armour, and an introduction by Thomas Lomax Hunter. Gravure illustrations by Woodi Ishmael. New York: E. P. Dutton & Co., 1942. 215 pp.
Plantation folktales and sayings in the Negro dialect and idiom of "Uncle Woodson," at Gay Mont, the Robb estate in Caroline county, Va.

Royal, A.
"I'se sho nuff lucky." *TFSP* 13:137–145, 1937.

Sale, John B.
The Tree Named John, with 22 silhouettes by Joseph Cranston Jones. Chapel Hill: The University of North Carolina Press, 1929. 151 pp., illus., plates.

Schoolcraft, Mrs. Henry R.
The Black Gauntlet: A Tale of Plantation Life in South Carolina. Philadelphia: J. B. Lippincott and Co., 1860. 569 pp.

Simms, William Gilmore
The Wigwam and the Cabin. New York: Wiley and Putnam, 1845. 2 Vols.
Contains a number of Gullah tales.

Smiley, Portia
"Folk-lore from Virginia, South Carolina, Georgia, Alabama and Florida." *JAFL* 32:357–383, 1913.

South Carolina Folk Tales.
Compiled by workers of the Writers' Program of Work Projects Administration. Columbia, South Carolina: Bulletin of the University of South Carolina, 122 pp., 1940.
Contains 33 animal stories recorded in Negro dialect, and 33 stories of the supernatural, 19 of which are recorded in this type dialect.

Stewart, S. E.
"Seven folk tales from the Sea Islands, South Carolina." *JAFL* 32:394–396, 1919.

Stoney, Samuel Gaillard
Black Genesis; a chronicle. Illustrations by Martha Bensley Bruére. New York: The Macmillan Co., 1930. xxix, 192 pp. Illus.
"Tales of the Gullah Negroes of the Carolina low country, told in the Gullah dialect."

Taylor, Helen Louise, and Wolcott, R.
"Items from New Castle, Delaware." *JAFL* 51:92–94, 1938.

Throop, Palmer A.
"De Pot Song." *TFSP* 7:139, 1928.
Negro folktale from Texas.

Vann, Wilham H.
"Two Negro Folktales." *TFSP* 18:172–180, 1943.

Whiting, Helen Adele
Negro Folk Tales. Washington, D. C.: Associated Publishers, Inc., 1947.
Ten African and America stories for grades I to III.

————.
Negro Folk Tales for Pupils in the Primary Grades. Washington: The Associated Press, 1938.

Young, Martha
Plantation Bird Legends and Uncle Remus Stories. New York: D. Appleton & Co., 1916. 249 pp.

BELIEFS—CUSTOMS—SUPERSTITIONS

Adams, George C. S.
"Rattlesnake Eye." *SFQ* 2 (No. 1):37–39, 1938.

Bolton, H. C.
"Decoration of Graves of Negroes in South Carolina." *JAFL* 4:2–4, 1891.

Burt, W. C.
"The Baptist Ox." *JAFL* 34:397–398, 1921.

Cohn, David Lewis
God Shakes Creation. New York: Harper & Bros., 1935. xvi, 299 pp., illus.
Social life and customs of the Mississippi delta Negroes.

Dixwell, J.
"Mourning Customs of Negroes." *JAFL* 21:365, 1908.

Drums and Shadows; Survival Studies among the Georgia Coastal Negroes. Savannah Unit, Georgia Writers' Project, WPA. Athens, Georgia: University of Georgia Press, 1940.

Emmons, Martha
"Confidences from Old Nacogdoches (Texas)." *TFSP* 7:119–134, 1928.
     Negro superstitions and tales.

―――――.
"Cats and the Occult." *TFSP* 11:94–100, 1933.
     Negro tales of the evil connected with cats.

―――――.
"Dyin' Easy." *TFSP* 10:55–61, 1932.
     Negro tales of death and ghosts. One has tune and text: "Jesus Gonna Make Up My Dyin Baid."

Farrow, Stephen S.
Faith, Fancies and Fetich. New York: The Macmillan Co., 1926.

Faulk, John H.
"The Life of Christ in ten acts; a religious drama." *TFSP* 17:126–140, 1941.

Fauset, Arthur Huff
Black Gods of the Metropolis; Negro religious cults of the Urban North. Phila., Pa.: University of Pennsylvania Press, 1944. x, 126 pp.
     "A study of five Negro religious cults in the Philadelphia of today." (Pref.).

Gist, Noel P.
"Secret Societies," a cultural study of fraternalism in the United States. *University of Missouri Studies* 15:1–184, 1904.

Hendrix, W. S.
"The Hell-Hounds." *TFSP* 1:75–77, 1916.
     Negro belief in Hell-Story heard by the author in Sylacuaga, Alabama.

Jones, Raymond Julius
A Comparative Study of Religious Cult Behavior Among Negroes, with special reference to emotional group conditioning factors. Washington, D. C.: Publ. by the Graduate School for the Division of Social Sciences, Howard University, 1939. v, 125 pp. (The Howard University Studies in The Social Sciences, Vol. II, No. 2).

Kane, H. P.
"Reception by the Dead (Negro)." *JAFL* 5:148, 1892.

Lake, Mary Daggert
"Superstitions about Cotton." *TFSP* 9:145–152, 1931.
     Recounted by the colored students of I. M. Terrell High School of Fort Worth, Texas.

Lee, F. W.
"Christmas in Virginia before the War." *Southern Workman* (Hampton, Va.) 37:686–689, 1908.

―――――.
"Harvest Time in Old Virginia." *Southern Workman* (Hampton, Va.) 37:566–567, 1908.

Lomax, Ruby Terrill
"Negro Baptizing." *TFSP* 19:1–8, 1944.
     Rituals practiced in southern United States.

"Louisiana Negro Superstitions." *JAFL* 18:229–230, 1905.

Mays, Benjamin Elijah
The Negro's God as Reflected in his Literature. Lithographs by James L. Wells. Boston: Chapman and Grimes, 1938. viii, 296 pp., bibl.

―――――, and **Nicholson, Joseph Williamson**
The Negro's Church. New York: Institute of Social and Religious Research, 321 pp., 1933.
     Negro beliefs.

Michael, Dorothy Jean
"Grave Decoration." *TFSP* 18:129–136, 1943.
     Describes these customs among Negroes, whites, Mexicans, and Indians in Texas.

"Negro superstition concerning the violin." *JAFL* 8:329–330, 1892.

"Negro wakes in Los Angeles." *CFQ* 3:326–328, 1944.
     Four are described.

Newell, W. W.
"Negro superstitions of European origin." *JAFL* 12:294–295, 1899.

―――――.
"Plantation Courtship." *JAFL* 8:106, 1895.

"Patience Pennington" (Mrs. Elizabeth W. Allston Pringle)
A Woman Rice Planter. New York: The Macmillan Co., 1913. 447 pp.
     Customs and traditions of the Gullah.

Puckett, Newbell Niles
Folk Beliefs of the Southern Negro. Chapel Hill: The University of North Carolina Press. London: H. Milford, 1926. 644 pp., plates, bibl.
     An extensive and detailed study,—invaluable.

―――――.
"Religious Folk Beliefs of Whites and Negroes." *Journal of Negro History* 16:9–35, 1931.

Royal, Aylett
"I's Sho' Nuff Lucky." *TFSP* 13:137–145, 1937.
     Negro Mammy's tales of superstitions.

Seale, Lea, and Marianna
"Easter Rock: a Louisiana Negro Ceremony." *JAFL* 55:212–218, 1942.
     Easter festival among Negroes of Concordia Parish, Louisiana. Includes words only of songs.

Showers, S.
"Weddin' and Buryin' in the Black Belt." *New England Magazine* 18:478–483, 1898, n.s.

Steiner, R.
"Seeking Jesus, a religious rite of Negroes in Georgia." *JAFL* 14:172, 1901.

―――――.
"Sol Lockhart's call (Negro superstitions, Georgia)." *JAFL* 13:67–70, 1900.

————.
"Superstitions and beliefs from Central Georgia." *JAFL* 12:261–271, 1899.

Thomas, Daniel Lindsey
Kentucky Superstitions. Princeton, N. J.: Princeton University Press, 1920. 334 pp.

Waring, M. A.
"Mortuary Customs and Beliefs of South Carolina Negroes." *JAFL* 7:318–319, 1894.

Williamson, G.
"Superstitions from Louisiana." *JAFL* 18:229–230, 1905.

WITCHCRAFT

Culin, S.
"Negro sorcery in the United States." *JAFL* 3:281–287, 1890.

Dana, M.
"Voodoo, its effect on the Negro race." *Metropolitan Magazine* 27:529–538, 1908. (New York).

Gittings, Victoria
"What Williams Saw." *JAFL* 58:135–137, 1945.
The adventures of William Aquila of Frederick County, Maryland, with the supernatural.

Hall, J. A.
"Negro Conjuring and Tricking." *JAFL* 10:241–243, 1897.

Haskell, J. A.
"Sacrificial Offerings Among North Carolina Negroes." *JAFL* 4:267–269, 1891.

Hurston, Zora
"Voodoo in America." *JAFL* 44:317–418, 1931.

Kennedy, Stetson
Palmetto Country (American Folkways Series). New York: Duell, Sloan & Pearce Co., 1942. 340 pp.
In the chapter 'Black Magic' the author describes transplanted voodoo and conjure practices.

Minor, M. W.
"How to Keep off Witches." *JAFL* 11:176, 1898..

Owen, Mary Alicia
Voodoo Tales, as told among the Negroes of the Southwest . . . collected from original sources. Introduction by Charles Godfrey Leland; illustrated by Juliette A. Owen and Louis Wain. New York: G. P. Putnam's Sons, 1893. xv. Published in London the same year, under title: *Old Rabbit, the Voodoo, and other Sorcerers.*

Pendleton, L.
"Negro Folklore and Witchcraft in the South." *JAFL* 3:201–207, 1890.

Steagall, Archie
"The voodoo man of the Brazos (The Witchcraft exploits of Negro Moe Green of Wharton)." *TFSP* 17:113–114, 1941.

Tallant, Robert
Voodoo in New Orleans. New York: The Macmillan Company, 1946. 247 pp.
"The author has explored the mysteries of Voodoo in New Orleans—from its first manifestation in slavery times, as a primitive, obscene African religion to the present." (N. K. Burger)

Tartt, Ruby Pickens
"Carrie Dyke's Midwife." *TFSP* 19:21–28, 1944.
This Negro midwife relates her beliefs of witchcraft.

PROVERBS—RIDDLES

Brewer, J. Mason
"Old-Time Negro Proverbs." *TFSP* 11:101–105, 1933.

Davidoff, Henry, coll.
A World Treasury of Proverbs. New York: Random House, 1946. 526 pp.
"Mr. Davidoff has dug up some fresh and savory American Negro proverbs." (Horace Gregory)

Halpert, Herbert
"Negro Riddles Collected in New Jersey." *JAFL* 56:200–202, 1943.

Harris, Joel Chandler
Uncle Remus, His Songs and Sayings. New and revised edition, with 112 illus. by A. B. Frost. New York: D. Appleton and Company, 1908. xxxi, 265 pp.
Many proverbs of Negro and plantation life.

"Louisiana Negro Riddles."
JAFL 35:105–115, 1922.

Malone, Kemp
"Negro Proverbs from Maryland." *AS* 4 (No. 4):285, 1929.

Perkins, A. E.
"Riddles from Negro Children in New Orleans." *JAFL* 35:105–115, 1922.

FOLK MEDICINE

See: Sections on Beliefs—Customs—Superstition and Witchcraft.

Cameron, Vivian K.
Folk-Beliefs Pertaining to Health of the Southern Negro. Evanston, Illinois: Northwestern University, unpublished Master's thesis, 1930.

Packwood, L. H. C.
"Cure for an aching tooth (Negro, Va.)." *JAFL* 13:66–67, 1900.

SPEECH

Barker, Howard F.
"The Family Names of American Negroes." *AS* 14:163–175, 1939.

Barnett, A. G.
"Colonial Survivals in Bush-Negro Speech." *AS* 7 (No. 6):393–397, 1932.

Benardete, Dolores
"Eloise." *AS* 7 (No. 5) :349–364, 1932.
A comprehensive discussion of a Negro woman's
speech living in Brooklyn.

Bennett, John
"Gullah: A Negro Patois." *The South Atlantic
Quarterly* pp. 332–347, 1908; pp. 39–52, 1909.

Billups, Edgar P.
"Some Principles for the Representation of
Negro Dialect in Fiction." *Texas Review* 8:99–
123, 1923.

Campbell, Killis
"Poe's treatment of the Negro and of the Negro
dialect." *University of Texas Studies in English* 16:107–114, July 1936.

Chappell, Naomi C.
"Negro Names." *AS* 4 (No. 4) :272–275, 1929.

Flowers, Paul
"Picturesque Speech." *TFSB* 10:9–10, 1944.
Explanations of expression 'bo-dollar', 'silver dol-
lar', used by Negroes in the South.

Heriford, Merle
"Slang Among Nebraska Negroes." *AS* 13:
316–317, 1938.

Hibbard, Addison
"Aesop in Negro Dialect." *AS* 1 (No. 9) :495–
499, 1926.

Holmes, Urban T.
"A Study in Negro Onomastics." *AS* 5 (No.
6) :463–467, 1930.
Fanciful and ornate naming of children.

Hucks, J. Jenkins
*Plantation Negro Sayings on the Coast of
South Carolina in Their Own Vernacular.*
Georgetown, S. C.: Charles W. Rouse, 1899.
Pamphlet.

Hudson, A. P.
"Some curious Negro names." *SFQ* 2:179–193,
1938.

Kane, Elisha K.
"The Negro Dialects Along the Savannah
River." *Dialect Notes* 5 (Part 8) :354–367,
1925.

Krapp, George Philip
"The English of the Negro." *The American
Mercury* 2:190–195, 1924.

Lockwood, J. Palmer
Darkey Sermons from Charleston County. Co-
lumbia, S. C.: The State Co., 1925. 45 pp.
Three sermons in Gullah.

Lomax, Ruby Terrill
"Negro Nicknames." *TFSP* 18:163–171, 1943.
Cites from 2 to 3 hundred different types.

McDowell, Tremaine
"Notes on Negro Dialect in the American Novel
to 1821." *AS* 5 (No. 4) :291–296, 1930.

"The Use of Negro Dialect by Harriet Beecher
Stowe." *AS* (No. 5) :322–326, 1931.

Mencken, H. L.
"Designations for Colored Folk." *AS* 19:161–
174, 1944.
Discusses the use of black, Negro, Nigger, coon,
and other such words.

Meredith, Mamie
"Negro Patois and its Humor." *AS* 6 (No. 5) :
317–321, 1931.

Newton, Mary Mann-Page
"Aunt Deborah Goes Visiting, A Sketch from
Virginia Life." *JAFL* 4:354–356, 1891.
Negro speech and character.

"Objecting to the Negro Dialect." *Literary Digest*
(New York) 53:1253, 1916.

Purcell, J. M.
"Mrs. Stowe's Vocabulary." *AS* 13:230–231,
1938.
Valuable lexical notes on words she uses, especially on some not found in any dictionary.

Sebastian, Hugh
"Negro Slang in Lincoln University." *AS* 9
(No. 4) :287–290, 1934.

Seidelman, Morton
"Survivals in Negro Vocabulary." *AS* 12 (No.
3) :231–232, 1937.

Smith, C. A.
Diallect Writers. In: *The Cambridge History of
American Literature*, Vol. 2:347–366, 1926.

Smith, Reed
Gullah. Bulletin of the University of South
Carolina, No. 190. Columbia, S. C.: The University Press, 1926. 45 pp.
"—a thorough and informative study which attempts a history of the dialect and of the literature of the dialect, and presents an analysis of it,
with numerous examples."

Stanley, Oma
"Negro speech of East Texas." *AS* 16:3–16,
1941.

Van Patten, Nathan
"The Vocabulary of the American Negro as Set
Forth in Contemporary Literature." *AS* 7 (No.
1) :24–31, 1931.

Whaley, Marcellus Seabrook
The Old Type Pass; Gullah sketches of the
Carolina Sea Islands. Illustrated by Edna Reed
Whaley. Boston: The Christopher Publishing
House, 1925. 192 pp., music.

Whitney, Annie Weston
"Die los' ell an' yard." *JAFL* 10:293–298, 1897.
Discussion of the phrase in Negro speech and
lore.

Wilkinson, Lupton A.
"Gullah vs. Grammar." *North American Review* 236:539–542, 1933.
On the primitive and grammarless simplicity of
the Gullah Negro dialect.

Williams, Rev. John G.
De Old Plantation. Reprint by Walker, Evans
and Cogswell Co., of material originally appearing in: *Charleston News and Courier* and *Sunday News*, 1896. 68 pp.
The "Brudder Coteny's Sermons."

Wise, C. M.
"Negro Dialect." *Quarterly Journal of Speech*
19:522–528, 1933.

FOLKSONG

See: Section on Minstrelsy, pp. 522-41

BIBLIOGRAPHY

*See: Bibliography of American Folk Song,
pp.68-69.*
"Bibliography of Negro Folk Songs." *JAFL* 24:
393–394, 1911.

Damon, Samuel F.
"The Negro in Early American Songsters."
Papers of the Bibliographical Society of America. (Chicago) 28 (Part 2):132–163, 1934.

Henry, Mellinger Edward
*A Bibliography for the Study of American
Folk-Songs, with many titles of folk-songs
(and titles that have to do with folk-songs)
from other lands.* London: The Mitre Press,
1937. 142 p.

Howard, John Tasker
Our American Music. Three Hundred Years of
it. New York: Thomas Y. Crowell Company.
1939. 749 pp., illus. bibl. (pp. 680–683) rev. ed.

Mattfeld, Julius, comp.
Folk Music of the Western Hemisphere. New
York, N. Y.: Public Library, 1925.

"Negro Folk Songs in American Folk Music in
Africa." *Negro Yearbook 1937–1938.* (Tuskegee Institute). pp. 482–487, 1937.

New York Public Library
*List of Books in the New York Public Library
Relating to Folk-Song, Folk Music, Ballads,
etc.* New York: Public Library Bulletin, May,
1907. 40 pp. American Negro, pp. 28.

The Negro. A Selected Bibliography. New York,
N. Y.: Public Library, 1935.

Thompson, H. W.
Bibliography of American Folk Songs. In:
American Ballads and Folk Songs, by J. A.
Lomax and Alan Lomax, pp. 613–621. New
York: The Macmillan Co., 1934.

Varley, Douglas H.
"African Native Music, an annotated Bibliography." *Royal Empire Society Bibliographies*
(London), No. 8, 1936.
New World Entries, pp. 86 ff.

White, Newman Ivey
Bibliography of Negro Folk Songs. In: *American Negro Folk Songs.* (pp. 469–480). Cambridge, Mass.: Harvard University Press, 1928.
x, 501 pp., music.

Work, Monroe N.
*A Bibliography of the Negro in Africa and
America.* New York: H. W. Wilson Company,
1928.
Contains 17,000 references, a number of them
dealing with folksong.

———.
The Negro Year Book, 1931—. Alabama: Tuskegee Institute.
Contains "The Negro in Music."

PERIODICALS

See: Folksong Periodicals, pp. 69-70.

Negro Music Journal.
A Monthly devoted to the educational interest
of the Negro in Music. Washington, D. C. 1–2
(Nos. 1–15). Sept. 1902–Nov. 1903.

GENERAL STUDIES

Allen, G.
"Negro's Contribution to American Music."
Current History 26:245–249, (May) 1927.

Ames, Russell
"Art in Negro Folk Song." *JAFL* 56:241–255,
1943.
The author contradicts and strongly condemns
the position taken by a number of students of
folklore that the Negro folksong is the expression of a backward and illiterate people.

Armstrong, Orland Kay
*Old Mass's People and Old Time Slaves Tell
Their Story.* Indianapolis: Bobbs-Merrill Company, 1931.
Contains a few Negro songs.

"Art from the Cabin Door."
Outlook 141:268–269, (Oct. 21), 1925.

Backus, E. M.
"Cradle Songs of Negroes in North Carolina."
JAFL 7:310, 1895.

Bales, Mary Virginia
"Some Negro Folk Songs of Texas." *TFSP* 7:
85–113, 1928.

Barrett, Harris
Negro Folk Songs. Hampton, Va.: Press of
Hampton Normal and Agricultural Institute,
1912.

Barry, Phillips
"Negro Folk Songs from Maine." *FSSNE* 8:
13–16, 1934; 9:10–14, 1935; 10:21–24, 1935.
In the last group the author also includes Hymns
and Ballads.

Barstow, M.
"Singers in a Weary Lan'." *World Outlook*
(Oct.) 1919.

Barton, W. E.
"Hymns of the Slave and the Freedman." *New
England Magazine* 19:609–624, 1899. n.s.
Music in text.

———.
"Old Plantation Hymns." *New England Magazine* 19:443–456, 1898.
Music in text.

———.
Old Plantation Hymns. A collection of hitherto
unpublished melodies of the slave and the
freedman, with historical and descriptive notes.
Boston Lamson, Wolffe and Company, 1899.

——————.
"Recent Negro Melodies." *New England Magazine* 19:707–719, 1899. n.s.

Bass, Robert Duncan
"Negro Songs from Pedee Country." *JAFL* 44:418–437, 1931.

Bergen, Mrs. F. D.
"On the Eastern Shore." *JAFL* 2:296–298, 1889.
Two fragments, with a brief discussion of the Negroes of the eastern shore of Maryland.

"Black Art Inspires White Artists." *Literary Digest* 81:30, (May 31) 1924.

"Black Music—and Its Future Transmutation into Real Art." *Our Opinion* 63:26–27, (July) 1917.

"Black Voices."
Nation 119:278, (September 17), 1924.

Brawler, Benjamin
The Negro Genius. New York: Dodd, Mead and Company, 1937.

Brown, Francis J., and Roucek, Joseph S.
Racial and National Mementos. New York: Prentice-Hall, 1937.

Brown, John Mason
"Songs of the Slave." *Lippincott's* 2:617–623, 1868.

Cable, George W.
"Creole Slave Songs." *Century Magazine* 9:807, 1886.

Cameron, Ian
"Negro Songs." *Musical Times* (London) 63:431–432, 1913.

"Canning Negro Melodies."
Literary Digest 52:1556, (May 27), 1916.

Carlyle, N. T.
"Old Time Darkey Plantation Melodies." *TFSP* 5:137–143, 1921.

Carter, Isabel Gordon
"On the Trail of Negro Folk-Songs." "The Negro and His Songs." *JAFL* 87:623, (a review) 1925.

Chauvet, Stephen
Musique Nègre. Considerations, tecnique instruments de musique (92 fig.) recueil de 118 airs notés. Paris: Société d'éditions Géographiques Maritimes et Coloniales, 1929.

Christensen, Mrs. Abigail M. Holmes
"Spirituals and 'Shouts' of Southern Negroes." *JAFL* 7:154–155, 1894.

Cox, John Harrington
Folk Songs of the South, collected under the auspices of the West Virginia Folklore Society. Folk tunes edited by Lydia Hinkel. Cambridge, Mass.: Harvard University Press, 1925. xxxi, 545 pp., music.

Crichton, Kyle
"Thar's Gold in them Hill-Billies Recording Hill Billy and Race Music." *Colliers* 101: 24 (April 30), 1938. illus.

Curtis-Burlin, Natalie
"Again the Negro." *Poetry* (Chicago), pp. 147–151, (Dec.) 1917.

——————.
"A Plea for Our Native Art." *MQ* 6:175–178, 1920.

——————.
"Black Singers and Players." *MQ* 5:499–504, 1919.

——————.
"Negro Music at Birth." *MQ* 5:86–89, 1919.

——————.
"The Negro's Contribution to the Music of America, the Larger Opportunity of the Colored Man of Today." *Craftsman* (New York) 23:660–669, 1913.

Damon, Samuel Foster
"The Negro in Early American Songsters." *Papers of the Bibliographical Society of America* (Chicago) 28 (Part 2):132–163, 1934. bibl. pp. 154–163.

Dobie, J. Frank, ed.
Follow de Drinkin' Gou'd. Austin, Texas: Published by the Texas Folklore Society, 1928. 201 pp. (Publications of the Texas Folklore Society No. VII). Illus., music, bibl.

——————.
Tone the Bell Easy. Publications of the Texas Folklore Society, *No. X.* Austin, Texas: Texas Folklore Society, 1932. 199 pp. Illus., music.

Duncan, Todd
"The Role of the Negro in American Music." In: *Who is Who in Music.* 1941 Edition. (pp. 568–569). Chicago: Lee Stern Press, 1940.

Ende, A. von
"Die Musik der amerikanischen Neger." *Die Musik* (Berlin) 5 (Heft 24):368–375, 1906.
Analysis of the ethnic and musical characteristics of American Negro music.

Engel, Carl
An Introduction to the Study of National Music, comprising researches into popular songs, traditions and customs. London: Longmans, Green, Reader and Dyer, 1866.
Includes discussion of African music, fugitive references to the American Negro.

Ferrero, F.
"La Musica dei Negri Americani." *Rivista Musicale Italiana,* (Torino) 13:393–436, 1906.
Music of the American Negro.

Fletcher, John Gould
"Negro Folk-Poetry." *Nation* (London) 20:763–764, 1922.

"Folk-Songs in the Making."
Literary Digest 101:27, (April 13), 1929.

Furness, Clifton Joseph
"Communal Music Among Arabians and Negroes." *MQ* 16:38–52, 1930.

Gagnon, Ernest
"Les Sauvages de l'Amérique et l'Art Musical." *Proceedings of the 15th Session of the International Congress of Americanists,* (Quebec) 1:179–189, 1906.
 Christian Mission influences on Negro song and text.

Gálvez, Zoila
"Una Melodía Negra." *EA* 6:23–26, 1940. (Published 1942).
 "Finds same African Negro melodic base in Brasilian Negro Xangó, Afro-Cuban religious melody and Tennessee Mountain White hymn." (Boggs).

Goldstein, Walter
"The Natural Harmonic and Rhythmic Sense of the Negro." *Music Teachers' National Association Proceedings* (Hartford), Series 12: 29–39, 1918.

Gordon, R. W.
"Lyrics Collected from the Folk-Songs of Georgia Negroes." *Golden Book* 8:194–196, Aug. 1928.

——.
"Old Songs That Men Have Sung." *Adventure Magazine,* July 10, 1923 to Nov. 1927.

——, ed.
"Palmettos; Folk-Songs of Georgia Negroes." *Golden Book* 9:76–77, May 1929.

Graham, Alice
"Original Plantation Melodies as One Rarely Hears Them." *Etude* (Phila.) 40:744, 1922.

Grant, Frances
"Negro Patriotism and Negro Music." *Outlook* (New York), 121:343–347, 1919.

Grissom, Mary Allen
The Negro Sings a New Heaven. Chapel Hill: University of North Carolina Press, 1930.

Guial, E. L.
"Among Negro Singers." *Lakeside* 11:421.
 Discussion and songs.

——.
"Among the Sable Singers." *Western Monthly* (Chicago) 11:421–426, 1869.

Handy, W. C.
"A Panorama of Negro Music." In: *Who Is Who in Music* 1941 Edition. (pp. 566–567). Chicago: Lee Stern Press, 1940.

——.
Negro Authors and Composers of the United States. New York: Handy Brothers Music Company, Inc., 1937.

Hare, Maud Cuney
"The Drum in Africa, The Use of Music by a Primitive People." *Musical Observer,* (July) 1918.

——.
Negro Musicians and their Music. Washington, D. C.: The Associated Publishers, Inc., 1936. (pp. 64–112.)

Harris, Joel Chandler
"Plantation Music." *Critic,* (New York) 3: 505–506, 1883.

Harrison, R. C.
"The Negro as Interpreter of His Own Folk-Songs." *TFSP* 5:144–153, 1921.

Henry, Mellinger E.
"Negro Songs from Georgia." *JAFL* 44:437–447, 1931.

Herskovits, Melville J.
"El estudio de la Música Negra en el hemisférío Occidental." *BLAM* 5:133–142, 1941. (Published 1942).
 Stresses the importance of African survivals in American Negro music.

——.
The Myth of the Negro Past. New York: Harper and Brothers, 1941. 374 pp., bibl. (pp. 341–355).
 Chapter VIII: The Contemporary Scene: Language and Arts. Discussion of the African survival in Negro music.

Hichens, W.
"Music, a Triumph of African Art." *Art and Archaeology* 33:36–41, (Jan.) 1932.

"Higher Music of American Negroes."
Literary Digest, (October 5), 1912.

Hobson, Anne
In Old Alabama; being the Chronicles of Miss Mouse, the little black merchant. Illustrated by Carol McPherson. New York: Doubleday, Page and Co., 1903. 237 pp.
 Negro Plantation songs, (pp. 157–237).

Holliday, Carl
Three Centuries of Southern Poetry. Nashville, Tenn., and Dallas, Tex.: Publishing House of M. E. Church, South, Smith and Lamar, 1908. 267 pp.
 "Plantation Melodies," pp. 107–111, texts only.

Holzknecht, R. J.
"Some Negro Song Variants from Louisville, Kentucky." *JAFL* 41:558–578, 1928.

Hornbostel, Erich M. von
"African Negro Music." *Africa, Journal of the International Institute of African Languages and Cultures,* pp. 30–62, (Jan.) 1928.
 Excellent. It casts light on relation of Negro American to African influences. Author claims that American Negro adapted himself to new environment, and to the new musical idioms. "Negro slaves in America, and their descendants, abandoning their original musical style, have adapted themselves to their white masters and produced a new kind of folk music in that style. This shows how readily the Negro abandons his own style of music for that of the European." See: *JAFL* 41:172–174, 1928. (Sapir—review of "Negro Spirituals").

————.
African Negro Music. London: Oxford University Press, 1928. Reprinted from *Africa*, Vol. 1, (No. 1).

————.
"American Negro Songs." *International Review of Missions* 15:748–753.

Howard, John Tasker, Jr.
"Capturing the Spirit of the Real Negro Music; first accurate recordings by Natalie Curtis Burlin of Negro part singing." *The Musician* (New York), 24 (No. 3):13–41, 1919. illus.

————.
Our American Music, Three Hundred Years of it. New York: Crowell and Company, 1939. 2nd ed. rev. and enl.
      Chapter XV: Our Folk Music. Part 2: Negro Music, pp. 415–428.

————.
"Rambling 'Round in Music Land." *The Musician* 29, (June) 1924.

Howe, M. A. D.
"Song of Charleston." *Atlantic Monthly* 146: 108–111, July 1930.

Howe, R .Wilson
"The Negro and His Songs." *So. Workman* (Hampton, Va.) 51:381–383, 1922.

Hubbard, William Lines
Negro Music and Negro Minstrelsy. In: *The American History and Encyclopedia of Music*. Vol. 4:49–70. Toledo: Irving Squire, 1908.

Hurston, Zora Neale
Mules and Men, with an introduction by Franz Boas. Philadelphia, London: J. B. Lippincott Co., 1935. 342 pp., illus., by Miguel Covarrubias.
      Songs, with music, pp. 309–331.

"In the Driftway."
Nation 131:245, (Sept. 3) 1930.

Jenks, F. H., and Kidson, C.
Negro Music of the United States. In: *Grove's Dictionary of Music and Musicians*, edited by J. A. Fuller Maitland, Vol. 3:359–362. London: The Macmillan Company, 1907.

Johnson, Guy B.
Negro Folk Songs. In: *Culture in the South*, (pp. 547–570). Chapel Hill: University of North Carolina Press, 1935.
      Discussion of the various types of Negro songs found in the South.

Johnson, James Weldon
The Book of American Negro Poetry, chosen and edited with an essay on the Negro's creative genius. New York: Harcourt Brace and Company, 1922.

————.
"National Negro Anthem." *Missionary Review of the World* 59:300, (June) 1936.

————.
"National Negro Anthem: 'Lift Ev'ry Voice and Sing'." *World Tomorrow* 12:257, 1929.

————.
"Negro Folk Songs and Spirituals." *Mentor* 17:50–52, (Feb.) 1929.

————.
Introduction. In: *Book of American Negro Spirituals*. Vol. 1 (pp. 11–50). New York: Viking Press, 1926, 2 Vols. for voice and piano. Music arr. by R. Johnson.
      James W. Johnson argues strongly for the African origins of Negro music.

Kennedy, R. Emmet
"Poetic and Melodic Gifts of the Negro." *Etude* 41:159–160, (March) 1923.

Kerlin, Robert Thomas
"Canticles of Love and Woe." *So. Workman* (Hampton, Va.) 50:62–64, 1921.
      Negro spirituals.

————.
Negro Poets and Their Poems. Washington, D. C.: Associated Publishers, 1923.

Kingsley, Walter
"Enigmatic Folk Songs of the Southern Underworld." *Current Opinion* 67:165, 1919 (New York).

Kirby, Percival R.
"A Study of Negro Harmony." *MQ* 16:404–414, 1930.
      Music in the text.

Krehbiel, Henry Edward
Afro-American Folk Songs. A Study in Racial and National Music. New York: G. Schirmer, 1914.
      The author contends that the African musical elements and background are the dominant characteristics in the music of the American Negro.

————.
Folk Music Studies. Slave songs in America. Their origin and characteristics; growth of interest in them; the literature of the subject. A series of articles in "The New York Tribune," New York, 1899.

————.
"Lafcadio Hearn and Congo Music." *The Musician* (Boston) 11:544–545, 1906.

Laubenstein, Paul Fritz
"Race Values in Aframerican Music." *MQ* 16: 378–404, 1930.

Lemmermann, Karl
"Improvised Negro Songs." *New Republic* (New York) 13:214–215, 1917.

Linton, William James
Poetry of America; selections from one hundred American poets from 1776 to 1876. With an introductory review of Colonial poetry, and some specimens of Negro melody. London: G. Bell, 1878.

Locke, Alain Le Roy
The Negro in America. Chicago: American Library Association, 1933.

————, **comp.**
A Decade of Negro Self Expression. With a foreword by Howard A. Odum. Charlottsville, Va.: 1928.

————.
The Negro and His Music. Washington, D. C.: The Associates in Negro Folk Education, 1936. 142 pp.
"Reading references" at end of each chapter; "Record Illustrations" at the end of most chapters.

————.
The New Negro; an Interpretation. New York: A. and C. Boni, 1925.
Contains a chapter on Negro music, composers, and interpreters.

————.
"Toward a Critique of Negro Music." *Opportunity Magazine* (Nov. and Dec.) 1934.

Logan, William Augustus
"Song Gleaning Among the Cabins." *The Musician* 44:122, (July) 1939.

Lomax, John Avery
"Self-Pity in Negro Folk-Songs." *Nation* 105: 141–145, (Aug. 9) 1917.

————.
"Some Types of American Folk-Songs." *JAFL* 28:1–17, 1915.

————, **and Alan**
Negro Folk Songs as Sung by Lead Belly. New York: The Macmillan Company, 1936. xiv, 242 pp. music (unaccompanied melodies).
Introductory essay on the life of Lead Belly, touching on the place of Negro music in American culture after the Civil War.

Longini, Muriel Davis
"Folksongs of Chicago Negroes." *JAFL* 52:96–111, 1939.

Ludlow, Helen Wilhelmina
Its Story and Its Songs: Tuskegee Normal and Industrial School for Training Colored Teachers, at Tuskegee, Alabama. Edited by Helen W. Ludlow. Hampton, Va.: Normal School Press, 1884.

Marsh, J. B. T.
The Story of the Jubilee Singers; with their songs. London: Hodder and Stoughton, 1876.

McKim, J.
"A Letter on Negro Singing." *Dwight's Journal of Music* (Boston), (Nov. 8), 1862.

————.
"Negro Songs." *Dwight's Journal of Music* (Boston), (Aug. 9), 1862.

Meikleham, R.
"Negro Ballad" (Virginia). *JAFL* 6:300–301, 1893.

Metfessel, Milton
Phonophotography in Folk Music, American Negro Songs in New Notation. With an introduction by Carl E. Seashore. The University of North Carolina, Social Study Series. Chapel Hill: The University of North Carolina Press, 1928. 181 pp., bibl.

Miller, George A.
"Sounding a New Note of Freedom in Negro Music." *Musical America* 36 (No. 8):9, 1922 (New York).

Milling, Chapman J.
"Delia Holmes—A Neglected Negro Ballad." *SFQ* 1, (No. 4):3–9, 1937.

Moderwell, Hiram Kelley
"The Epic of the Black Man." *New Republic* (New York) 12:154–155, 1917.

Montague, J. Harold
A Historical Survey of Negro Music and Musicians and their Influence on Twentieth Century Music. Master's Thesis. Syracuse University (New York) (unpublished), 1939.

Murphy, E. F.
"Black Music." *Catholic World* 130:687–692, 1930.

Murphy, Jeannette Robinson
"Gawd Bless Dem Yankees." *Century* (New York) 56, (new series) 34:797–798, 1898.

————.
"Must the True Negro Music Become Obsolete?" *Kunkle's Musical Review,* (St. Louis) 30, (No. 305):10, 1905.

————.
"The Survival of African Music in America." *Popular Science Monthly* (New York) 55:660–672, (Sept.) 1899.

————.
"The True Negro Music and Its Decline." *Independent,* (New York), 55:1723–1730, (July 23), 1903.

Nathanson, Y. S.
"Musical Ability of the Negro." *Annals of the American Academy* 140:186–190, (Nov.) 1928.

"Negro Folk Songs: Acclaimed America's Musical Treasure." *Musical America,* (Aug. 3) 1918.

Negro Folk Songs in America (and) Folk Music in Africa. In: *The Negro Year Book* (Tuskegee Institute, Tuskegee, Alabama) *1937–1938.*

"Negro Melodies and National Music." *Music Review* 2:514–516, 1893.

"Negro Minstrelsy, Ancient and Modern." *Putnam's Monthly* 5:72–79, (Jan.) 1855.

"Negro Music in America." *Playground* 23:234–235, (July) 1929.

"Negro Music in the Land of Freedom." *Outlook* 106:611–612, (March 21) 1914.

"Negro Songs."
JAFL 24:394–396, 1911.

"Negro Songs, Indian and Negro in Music."
Literary Digest, (June 29) 1912.

"Negro's Contribution to American Art."
Literary Digest 55:25–26, (Oct. 20), 1917.

Nelson, Rose K., and Cole, Mrs. Dorothy Jane (Lowenhaupt)
The Negro's Contribution to Music in America.
Publications, No. N–4. New York: Service Bureau for Intercultural Education, 1941. rev. ed.

Niles, A.
"Ballads, Songs and Snatches; Columbia Race Records." *Bookman* 67:422–424, 1928.

Niles, John Jacob
"Shout, Coon, Shout!" *MQ* 16:516–530, 1930.

―――――.
"White Pioneers and Black." *MQ* 18:60–76, 1932.
　　The character of the Negro and his music.

Norman, H. D.
"Native Wood Notes." *Atlantic* 138:771–775, (Dec.) 1926.

O'Connell, L.
"The Folk-Songs of Afro-America." *The Musician* (Boston) 11:503–504, 1906.

Odum, Anna Kranz
"Negro Folk Songs from Tennessee." *JAFL* 27:255–265, 1914.

Odum, Howard W.
"Down the Lonesome Road." *Country Gentleman* 79:18–19, (May) 1926.

―――――.
"Folk Song and Folk Poetry as Found in the Secular Songs of the Southern Negroes." *JAFL* 24:255–294, 351–396, 1911.

―――――, and Johnson, Guy B.
The Negro and His Songs. Chapel Hill: The University of North Carolina Press, 1925.

Peabody, Charles
"Notes on Negro Music." *JAFL* 16:148–152, 1903.

Pearce, G. Wilfred
"Negroes and Negro Melodies." A letter in The New York Sun, Feb. 15, 1894.

"Percy Grainger's Tribute to the Music of American Negro." *Current Opinion* (New York) 59:100–101, 1915.

Pereda Valdés, Ildefonso
Línea de color. Santiago de Chile: Ed. Ercilla, 1938. 248 pp.
　　Includes a discussion of Negro music in the U. S., pp. 68–76.

Perrow, E. C.
"Songs and Rhymes from the South." *JAFL* 25:137–155, 1912; 26:123–173, 1913; 28:129–190, 1915.
　　Six of the melodies are Negro.

Perry, Edward G.
Negro Creative Musicians. In: *Negro Anthology,* edited by Nancy Cunard, (pp. 356–359). London, 1934.

Pike, Gustavus R.
The Jubilee Singers and Their Campaign for Twenty Thousand Dollars. London: Hodder and Stoughton, 1873; Boston: Lee and Shepherd, 1873.

―――――.
The Singing Campaign for Ten Thousand Pounds, or *The Jubilee Singers in Great Britain.* London: Hodder and Stoughton, 1874.

"Plantation Songs."
So. Workman (Hampton, Va.) 29–32:35–37, 41–42, 45–46, 48–50, 1900–1921.

Pratt, Waldo Selden, and Boyd, Charles N.
Negro Music. In: *Grove's Dictionary of Music and Musicians.* New York: Macmillan American Supplement, 1920. vi, 307 pp.

"Recent Contributions to the Study of Negro Songs." *Social Forces* 4:788–792 (June) 1926.

Redfearn, S. F.
"Songs from Georgia." *JAFL* 34:121–124, 1921.

"Review of: *American Negro Folksongs* by Newman L. White." *American Literature* 1:106, 1929.

Scarborough, Dorothy
A Song Catcher in Southern Mountains: American Folk Songs of British Ancestry. New York: Columbia University Press, 1937. xvi, 476 pp., illus., music.

―――――.
From a Southern Porch. New York: G. P. Putnam's Sons, 1919. ix, 318 pp.
　　Contains some original Negro songs.

―――――.
On the Trail of Negro Folk-Songs, assisted by Ola Lee Gulledge. Cambridge, Mass.: Harvard University Press, 1925. 289 pp., illus., music.

Seale, Lea and Marianna
"Easter Rock: A Louisiana Negro Ceremony." *JAFL* 55:212–218, 1942.
　　Easter festival among Negroes of Concordia Parish, Louisiana. Includes words only of songs.

Searchinger, Cesar
The Folk Elements in American Music. In: *The Art of Music* (New York), Vol. 4, pp. 277–330, 1915.

Seashore, Carl E.
"Three New Approaches to the Study of Negro Music." *Annals of the American Academy* 140:191–192, (Nov.) 1928.

Singleton, Esther
États-Unis d'Amérique. In: *Encyclopédie de la Musique et Dictionaire du Conservatoire* (Paris), (Partie 1):3245–3332, 1921.

Smith, Joseph Hutchinson
"Folk-Songs of the American Negro." *Sewanee Review* 32:206.

————.
"Sig Negro Folk-Songs." *TFSP* 7:113–119, 1928.
Music and texts.

Smythe, A. T., and others
The Carolina Low-Country. New York: The Macmillan Company, 1932.
Section on Negro culture and music.

"Songs of Protest."
Time 27:51, 1936, June 15.

"Songs from the Heart of the American Negro."
New York Times Book Review, (October 18) 1925. (a review).

Spaulding, H. G.
"Under the Palmetto." *Continental Monthly* 4:188–203, 1863 (New York).

Speers, M. W. F.
"Negro Songs and Folk-Lore." *JAFL* 23:435–439, 1910.

Spence, M. E.
"The Jubilee of Jubilees at Fisk University." *Southern Workman* (Hampton, Va.) 51:73–80, 1922.

Stanley, May
"Foundation for Negro Music of the Future." *Musical America*, (July 6) 1918.

Steward, T. G.
"Negro Imagery." *New Republic* 12:248.

Talley, Thomas W.
Negro Folk Rhymes, Wise and Otherwise. New York: The Macmillan Company, 1922.
Contains eleven tunes.

Thomas, Will H.
Some Current Folk-Songs of the Negro. Austin, Tex.: Published by the Texas Folklore Society, 1936. 13 pp.

Thompson, Stith, ed.
Round the Levee. Publications of the Texas Folklore Society, No. 1, 1916. Austin, Texas: Texas Folklore Society, 1935. 111 pp.

Tiersot, Julien
La Musique Chez Les Peuples Indigènes de L'Amérique du Nord. (États-Unis et Canada). Paris: Libraire Fitchbacker, n.d., 93 pp., bibl., music.
The brochure is a reprint of an article that appeared in the organ of the International Society of Music, vol. 11, no. 2. The author discusses the general musical characteristics of Indian music, giving representative examples of various tribes. He also includes a discussion, with examples, of Negro music.

Tonsor, Johann
"Negro Music." *Music* (Chicago) 11:119–122, 1892–1893.

Trux, J. J.
"Negro Minstrelsy (Ancient and Modern)." *Putnam's Monthly* 5:73, (January) 1855.

Tupper, V. G.
"Plantation Echoes; a Negro Folk Music-Drama, as given each year in Charleston, South Carolina." *Etude* 55:153, (March) 1937.

U. S. Library of Congress
Seventy-Five Years of Freedom; Commemoration of the 75th Anniversary of the Proclamation of the 13th Amendment to the Constitution of the United States. The Library of Congress. Washington, D. C.: U. S. Government Printing Office, 1943. 108 pp.
Discussion of contributions and achievements in Negro art, music and literature.

Van Deusen, John G.
The Black Man in White America. Washington, D. C.: Associated Publishers, 1938.

Van Vechten, Carl
"The Songs of the Negro." *The New York Herald-Tribune Books*. (A Review), (October 25), 1925.

Walker, Conway
The Folk Song and Dance. New York: The Caxton Institute, 1926.
Fundamentals of Musical Art, volume 2, 101 pages; Negro Spirituals and Songs, pages 67–69.

Waterman, Richard A.
"'Hot' Rhythm in Negro Music." *Journal of the American Musicological Society* 1 (No. 1):24–38, 1948.
"This paper represents an attempt to characterize this rhythmic style in objective terms by isolating its major components, to summarize the history of its spread from Africa into various portions of the Americas from the standpoint of the dynamics of musical diffusion, and to indicate by means of a brief analysis of musical rhythms of a West Indian island the essential homogeneity of the style." (The author.)

White, Clarence Cameron
"Musical Genius of the American Negro." *Etude* 42:305–306, (May) 1924.

————.
"Negro Music a Contribution to the National Music of America." *Musical Observer* (New York) 18, (No. 11): 18–19; 19: (No. 1):16–17; (No. 2):50–51; (No. 3):13, 1919–1920.

————.
Negro's Gift to American Music. In: *Anthology of American Negro Literature*, edited by V. F. Calverton, pp. 267–277. New York: The Modern Library, 1929.

White, Newman Ivey
American Negro Folk Songs. Cambridge, Mass.: Harvard University Press, 1928. x, 501 pp., contains music bibliography (pp. 469–480).
A detailed critical analysis and discussion of all the aspects of Negro folk song.

————.
"Racial Traits in the Negro Songs." *Sewanee Review* (Sewanee, Tenn.) 28:396–404, 1920.

————.
"The White Man in the Woodpile. Some Influences on Negro Secular Folk Songs." *AS* 4 (No. 3):207–215, 1929.

Whiting, H. A. J.
Negro Art, Music and Rhyme for Young Folks.
Washington, D. C.: The Associated Publishers,
1938.

Williams, Emily Harper
"The Emancipation of Negro Music." *Musical
America*, (Jan. 5) 1918.

Wilson, H. J.
"The Negro and Music." *Outlook*, (Dec. 1)
1906.

Work, John Wesley
"Negro Folk Song." *Opportunity*, (October)
1923.

————.
"The Music of the Negro." *MSNC* (12th Meeting):42–47, 1919.

Work, Monroe N.
"Some Parellelisms in the Development of
Africans and Other Races." *Southern Workman*
(Hampton, Va.) 36:106–111, 1907.
    Contains musical examples.

————.
"The Spirit of Negro Poetry." *Southern Workman* (Hampton, Va.) 37:73–77, 1908.

COLLECTIONS

*See: American Folksong and Ballad Collections,
pp. 85-90, and pp. 118-20, and Negro Spirituals
Collections, pp. 457-61.*

Allen, William Francis
Slave Songs of the United States. New York: A.
Simpson and Company, 1867.
    Contains 136 songs, including seven Creole
    songs.

Armitage, Marie Teresa
*Folk Songs and Art Songs for Intermediate
Grades.* Student's Edition. Boston: C. C. Birch-
ard and Company, 1924.

————.
The Laurel Unison Book. Teacher's Edition.
Boston: C. C. Birchard and Company, 1918.

**Armstrong, Mrs. Mary Frances (Morgan), and
Ludlow, Helen Wilhelmina**
Hampton and Its Students. By Two of Its
Teachers. With fifty cabin and plantation songs,
arranged by Thomas P. Fenner. New York: G.
P. Putnam's Sons, 1874.

Barrett, Harris
Negro Folk Songs. Hampton, Va.: Press of the
Hampton Normal and Agricultural Institute,
1912. 10 pp.

Barton, W. E.
Old Plantation Hymns. A collection of hitherto
unpublished melodies of the slave and the freedman, with historical and descriptive notes. Boston: Lamson, Wolffe and Company, 1889.

Blades, William C.
*Negro Poems, Melodies, Plantation Pieces,
Camp Meeting Songs, etc.* Boston: R. G. Badger,
1921. v, 168 pp.
    Texts only.

Bond, Carrie Jacobs
Old Melodies of the South. Compiled by Carrie
Jacobs Bond. Transcribed by March Gillon
and Oliver Chalifoux. Chicago: The Bond Shop,
Carrie Jacobs Bond and Sons, 1918. 39 pp.

Botsford, Florence Hudson, comp. and ed.
*Folk Songs of Many Peoples with English
Versions by American Poets.* Compiled and
edited by Florence Hudson Botsford. New York:
The Women's Press, 1921–1922. 3 vols.
    Ten Negro songs in Vol. 2, pp. 32–50.

Brown, James Duff
*Characteristic Songs and Dances of All Na-
tions.* Edited with historical notes and a bibliography by J. D. Brown. The music arranged for
the pianoforte by Alfred Moffat. London: Bayley and Ferguson, 1901.

Burleigh, Harry T.
Negro Folk Songs. New York: Ricordi Company, 1921. 4 vols. Voice and piano.

————.
Plantation Melodies Old and New. New York:
G. Schirmer, 1901.

Coleridge-Taylor, S.
Twenty-four Negro Melodies. Transcribed by
S. Coleridge-Taylor. Introduction by Booker T.
Washington. Boston: Oliver Ditson and Com-
pany, 1905.

Curtis-Burlin, Natalie
Hampton Series: Negro Folk Songs, Nos. 6716,
6726, 6756, 6766. Recorded by Natalie Curtis-
Burlin in Four Books. Books 1–2: Spirituals;
Books 3–4: Work-and-Play Songs. New York:
G. Schirmer Inc., 1918–1919.
    For solo and choral performance.

Downes, Olin, and Siegmeister, Elie
A Treasury of American Song, by Olin Downes
and Elie Siegmeister. New York: Howell, Soskin & Co., 1940. 351 pp., piano accompaniment, music arranged by Elie Siegmeister.
    Has a good selection of Negro songs.

Farwell, Arthur
Folk Songs of the West and South. Negro,
Cowboy and Spanish Californian. Harmonized
by Arthur Farwell. Newton Center, Mass.: The
Wa-Wan Press, 1905.

————.
From Mesa and Plain Indian. Cowboy and
Negro Sketches for pianoforte by Arthur Far-
well. The Wa-Wan Series of American Compo-
sitions, Vol. 4, No. 28. Newton Center, Mass.:
The Wa-Wan Press, 1905. pp. 1.

Fenner, Thomas P.
*Cabin and Plantation Songs as Sung by the
Hampton Students;* arranged by Thomas P.
Fenner, Frederick G. Rathbun, and Miss Bessie
Cleveland, third edition, enlarged by the addi-
tion of 44 songs. New York: G. P. Putnam's
Sons, 1901. 166 pp. first ed., Hampton, Va.,
1874.

Finger, Charles J., comp.
Frontier Ballads. Woodcuts by Paul Honoré.
Garden City, N. Y.: Doubleday, Page and Co.,
181 pp.
　Nine Negro songs.

Gellert, Lawrence, and Siegmeister, Elie
Negro Songs of Protest. New York: Carl Fischer, 1936.

————.
Negro Songs of Protest. Negro Anthology made
by Nancy Cunard, 1931–1933, London 1934, pp.
366–367; reprinted from the *New Masses*
November 1930, January 1931, May 1932.

Grant-Schaefer, G. A.
Songs From the South, adapted and arranged
with pianoforte accompaniments. Boston: A. P.
Schmidt Company, 1925.

Hallowell, Emily, ed.
Calhoun Plantation Songs, Sung by the Students at the Calhoun Colored School. Collected
and edited by Emily Hallowell. Boston: C. W.
Thompson Company, 1907.

Johnson, J. Rosamond
Rolling Along in Song. New York: Viking
Press, 1937. Arranged for voice and piano.
　A cavalcade of Negro song.

Kennedy, R. Emmett
Black Cameos. New York: Dodd, Mead and
Company, 1924. 210 pp., illus.
　Contains twenty songs, mainly religious.

————.
Mellows. New York: Dodd, Mead and Company, 1925.
　Collection—arranged for voice and piano. Work
　songs, street cries and spirituals.

————.
More Mellows. New York: Dodd, Mead and
Company, 1931. Arranged for voice and piano.

Lomax, John A., and Alan
American Ballads and Folk Songs. New York:
The Macmillan Company, 1934.
　A rich harvest, as in all the Lomax collections,
　of Negro folksongs: spirituals, social songs, game
　songs, courting songs, blues, etc.

————.
Our Singing Country. New York: The Macmillan Co., 1941. Unaccomp. tunes.

————.
Folk Song: U. S. A. The 111 best American
ballads. Music arrangements for piano (or
guitar) and voice by Charles and Ruth Seeger.
New York: Duell, Sloan and Pearce, Inc., 1948.
384 pp.

Macy, James C.
Jubilee and Plantation Songs. Characteristic
favorites, as sung by the Hampton students,
Jubilee Singers, Fisk University students, and
other concert companies. Also a number of new
and pleasing selections. Boston: O. Ditson and
Company, 1887.

Marsh, J. B. T.
The Story of the Jubilee Singers, with their
songs. (London, Boston, etc. 1877, etc., 1892
pp. Other editions by G. D. Pike, and T. F.
Seward, partly with different titles; all refer
to the songs of the Jubilee Singers of Fisk University.) Boston: Houghton, Osgood and Company, 1880.

McDowell, L. L.
Songs of the Old Camp Ground. Ann Arbor,
Mich.: Edwards Bros., 1937.
　Texts and tunes.

Mees, Arthur, arr.
Six Authentic Negro Melodies. Arranged for
the Mendelssohn Glee Club by Arthur Mees.
New York: Mendelssohn Glee Club, 1899. 27
pp.

Milligan, Harold Vincent
Camp Meeting. Boston: A. P. Schmidt Company, 1924.

Mitchell, Mrs. M. L.
Songs of the Confederacy and Plantation Melodies. Cincinnati: The George B. Jennings Company, 1901.

Monroe, Mina
Bayou Ballads; Twelve Folksongs from Louisiana. Texts and music collected by Mina Monroe, edited with the collaboration of Kurt
Schindler. New York: G. Schirmer, Inc., 1921.
viii, 55 pp., melodies with piano accompaniments, French, Negro dialect, English words.

Noble, Gilford Clifford
The Most Popular Plantation Songs. New
York: Hinds, Noble and Eldridge, 1911.

Parrish, Lydia
Slave Work Songs of the Georgia Sea Islands.
New York: Creative Age Press, 1942. xxxi,
256 pp., bibl.

Peterson, Mrs. Clara (Gottschalk)
*Creole Songs from New Orleans in the Negro
Dialect.* Set to music by Clara Gottschalk
Peterson. New Orleans: L. Grunewald Co.,
Ltd., 1902. 20 pp.
　Melodies with piano accompaniment. Creole
　dialect words, followed by English translation.

Sandburg, Carl
The American Songbag. New York: Harcourt,
Brace & Co., 1927. xxiii, 495 pp.
　A good representation of spirituals, work songs,
　lyric songs, and blues.

Sawyer, J. J.
Jubilee Songs and Plantation Melodies. Nashville: Colored Concert Company, H. B. Theatle, Proprietor, 1884.

Scarborough, Dorothy
On the Trail of the Negro Folk Songs. Cambridge, Mass.: Harvard University Press, 1925.

Seward, Theodore Freylinghuysen
*Jubilee Songs as Sung by the Jubilee Singers
of Fisk University* (Nashville, Tenn.). New
York: Bigelow and Main, 1872.

————, and White, George L.
Jubilee Songs: as Sung by the Jubilee Singers. (Part I–II, enlarged). New York: Bigelow and Main, 1884. 2 vols.

Siegmeister, Elie
Work & sing, a collection of the songs that built America, selected and arranged by Elie Siegmeister; a treasury of the American work songs of yesterday and today. With commentary, annotations, and a critical biography. Illustrated by Julian Brazelton. New York: W. R. Scott, 1944. 96 pp., bibl. pp. 95–96, with piano accompaniment.

Smith, N. Clark
Favorite Folk-Melodies as Sung by Tuskegee Students. Wichita, Kans.: The Author, 1914.

Spaeth, Sigmund
Read 'Em and Weep; the Songs You Forgot to Remember. Garden City, N. Y.: Doubleday, 1935. xiv, 267 pp., music.

————.
Weep Some More, My Lady. Garden City, N. Y.: Doubleday, Page & Co., 1927. xv, 268 pp., music.

Stuart, Ruth McEnery
Plantation Songs, and other verses. Illustrated by E. W. Kemble. New York: D. Appleton and Co., 1916. vii, 135 pp.
  A book of poems capturing the rhythm, flavor and life of the Negro.

The Negro Singer's Own Book.
Phila.: Turner and Fisher.

Tiersot, J. B. E.
Chansons Nègres: 1. Chansons des anciennes Colonies françaises; 2. Chansons de Nègres d'Amérique. Paris: Heugel et Cie, 1933.
  A study of French-Canadian and Negro music.

Turner, Harriet
Folk-Songs of the American Negro. Boston: The Boston Music Company, 1925.

Twenty-Two Years' Work of the Hampton Normal and Agricultural Institute. Hampton, Va.: Hampton Normal School Press, 1893.
  Has "Songs of Two Races" at end.

White, Clarence Cameron
Negro Folk Melodies. Phila.: Presser, 1927.

White, Newman I.
American Negro Folk Songs. Cambridge: Harvard University Press, 1928. 501 pp., music, bibl.
  Includes fifteen tunes representing different types of Negro song. Chapter II: Religious song; Chapters IV, V: Social songs; Chapters VII, VIII, IX: Labor songs; Chapter XI: Recent events; Chapter XIII: Race Consciousness; Chapter XIV: Blues and miscellaneous songs.

Wier, Albert Ernest
Songs of the Sunny South, containing more than two hundred songs redolent of plantation and minstrel ditties, Negro spirituals, Stephen Foster's ballads and songs. Arranged for singing and playing. New York: D. Appleton and Company, 1929. 256 pp.

Williams, Nancy Middleton
Melody in Ebony; little stories in verse and folk ballads from tales of the old southern plantation Negro. Arkansas: Hot Springs National Park, 1944. 28 pp., illus.

Wood, Clement
Negro Songs, an Anthology. Girard, Kan.: Haldeman-Julius Company, 1924.

Work, Frederick J.
Folk-Songs of the American Negro. Nashville: Fisk University Press, 1915.

————.
New Jubilee Songs as Sung by the Fisk Jubilee Singers of Fisk University. Collected and harmonized by F. J. Work. Nashville, Tenn.: Fisk University, 1902.

————.
Some American Negro Folk Songs. Boston: A. P. Schmidt Co., 1909.

Work, John Wesley
Folk Songs of the American Negro. Nashville, Tenn.: Press of Fisk University, 1915.

————.
American Negro Songs; a comprehensive collection of 230 folk-songs, religious and secular. New York: Howell, Soskin and Company, 1940. vii, 259 pp., bibl.
  Mainly in choral arrangement.

RECORDS

GENERAL COLLECTIONS

Anthology of Negro Folk Songs.
  Leadbelly, vocal-Guitar. 3–12". DISC 680

United States (Negro).
  Collection of late Dorothy Scarborough, Columbia University, New York City.

United States (Negro-Secular Songs).
  In Archive of American Folk Song, Library of Congress, Music Division, Washington, D. C.

United States (Negro-Georgia and Florida).
  In Archive of Library of Congress, Music Division, Washington, D. C.

United States (Negro—Sound Films and Graph Recordings of Southern Negro Singing). In: University of California, Los Angeles.

THE NEGRO — SPIRITUALS

SPIRITUALS

BIBLIOGRAPHY

"American Negro Music."
The International Review of Missions 15:748–753, 1926.
A review of books on spirituals and Negro folk-songs.

Index to Negro Spirituals.
Cleveland: Public Library, 1937. Does not give publishers or date of publications or keys.
A cross index of thirty popular collections. Lists the books, where each is found, lists variants. It is not an exhausting compilation.

Index of Negro Spirituals.
Washington, D. C.: Library of Congress. (To appear.)

New York Public Library
List of Books in the New York Public Library Relating to Folk-Song, Folk Music, Ballads, etc. New York: Public Library Bulletin, (May) 1907. 40 pp.
American Negro, pp. 28.

GENERAL STUDIES

See: American Folksong and Ballad Studies and Collections, pp. 85-90, and pp. 118-120.

"American Negro Music."
The International Review of Missions 15:748–753, 1926.
A review of books on spirituals and Negro folk-songs.

Andreu, Enrique
Los "Spirituals Negro Songs" y au acción etnico-social. *Estudios Afrocubanos*, 1937. 1:76–91. (A lecture delivered before the Society of Afrocuban Studies in Havana, March 29, 1937.)
Jazz and blue music and their relations with the spirituals of the North American Negro. Origin, development, and function of the spiritual, in the life of the North American Negro today.

Arrowood, M. D., and Hamilton, T. H.
"Nine Negro Spirituals, 1850–1861, from Lower South Carolina." *JAFL* 41:579–585, 1928.
Texts and tunes.

Asbury, Samuel E., and Meyer, Henry E.
"Old-Time White Camp-Meeting Spiritual." *TFSP* 10:169–185, 1932.

Backus, Emma M.
"Christmas Carols from Georgia." *JAFL* 12:272, 1899.
Two songs.

————.
"Negro Hymns from Georgia." *JAFL* 10:116, 202, 264, 1897; 11:22, 1898; 26:374–376, 1913.

————.
"Negro Songs from North Carolina." *JAFL* 11:60, 1898.

Bales, Mary Virginia
"Some Negro Folk-Songs of Texas." *TFSP* 7:85–112, 1928.
Contains Spirituals (with music); Love Songs and Songs of Home Life; Work Songs and Songs of Field Life; Negro Songs about the Negro; Dance Songs and Game Songs, and Miscellaneous Songs (with music).

Barragan, M.
"Putting the Spirit into the Spirituals." *Etude* 49:95, (February) 1931.

Barrett, W. A.
"Negro Hymnology." *Musical Times* (London) 15:559–561, 1871–1872.

Barrow, David C.
"A Georgia Corn-schucking." *Century Magazine* (New York) 24: (new series II) 872–878, 1882.

Barton, W. E.
"Hymns of Negroes." *New England Magazine* 19:669 et seq.; 707 et. seq.
A number of songs with some musical notations and discussions.

"Blight of Jazz and the Spirituals."
Literary Digest 105:20, (April 12) 1930.

Carlson, A. D.
"Negro Spirituals at Our Own Firesides." *Better Homes and Gardens* 10:16, (July) 1932.

Carlyle, N. T.
"Old Time Darky Plantation Melodies." *TFSP* 5:137–143, 1921.

Chirgwin, A. M.
"Vogue of the Negro Spirituals." *Edinburgh Review* 247:57–74, (Jan.) 1928.

Christensen, Mrs. Abigail M. Homes
"Spirituals and Shouts of Southern Negroes." *JAFL* 7:154–155, 1894.

Clothier, Agnes E.
"Two Negro Spirituals from Georgia." *JAFL* 55:98, 1942.

Cox, John Harrington
Folk Songs of the South. Cambridge: Harvard University Press, 1925. xxi, 545 pp., music.

Curtis-Burlin, Mrs. Natalie
"Negro Music at Birth." *MQ* 5:86–89, 1919.

————.
"The Negro's Contribution to the Music of America." *The Craftsman* 23:660–669, 1913.

Deming, Clarence
By-Ways of Nature and Life. New York and London: G. P. Putnam's Sons, 1884. 383 pp.

"Desecration of Spirituals."
Southern Workman (Hampton, Va.) 51:501–503, 1922.

Dobie, James Frank, ed.
Follow de Drinkin' Gou'd. Publications of Texas Folk-Lore Society, No. 7. Austin, Texas: Published by the Texas Folk-Lore Society, 1928. 201 pp., illus., music.
Part III, pp. 81–144, deals with Negro folklore and folksongs.

"Done Yo' See de Chariot Ridin' on de Clouds?" *JAFL* 9:210, 1896.

DuBois, William Edward Burghardt
The Souls of Black Folk; Essays and Sketches. Chicago: A. C. McClurg and Company, 1903. 264 pp.
Chapter 14: "The Sorrow Songs."

Elzy, Ruby
"Spirit of the Spirituals." *Etude* 61:495–496, (Aug.) 1943.

Emerson, William C.
Stories and Spirituals of the Negro Slaves. Boston: Richard G. Badger, The Gorham Press, 1930. 79 pp.

Emmons, Martha
"Walk Around My Bedside." *TFSP* 13:130–136, 1937.
Two spirituals of Death's visitation—with music.

———.
"Dyin' Easy." *TFSP* 10:55–61, 1922.
"Even as death itself may be foretold, so dyin' 'easy' or 'hard' may be prognosticated." Contains music and text of "Jesus Gonna Make Up My Dyin' Baid," containing the phrase "tone the bell easy."   .

Engel, Carl
"Negro Spirituals." *MQ* 12:299–314, 1926.

"Enigmatic Folk-Songs of the Southern Underworld." *Current Opinion* (New York) 17:165–166, 1919.

Fisher, William Arms
"Swing Low, Sweet Chariot: The Romance of a Famous Spiritual." *Etude* 50:536 (August) 1932.

Ford, Theodore P.
God Wills the Negro; an anthropological and geographical restoration of the lost history of the American Negro people, being in part a theological interpretation of Egyptian and Ethiopian backgrounds. Compiled from ancient and modern sources, with a special chapter on eight Negro spirituals. Chicago: The Geographical Institute Press, 1939.

Garnett, L. A.
"Spirituals." *Outlook* 130:589, (April 12) 1922.

Gaul, Harvey Bartlett
"Negro Spirituals." *New Musical Review,* (New York) 17:147–151, 1918.

Graham, Alice
"Original Plantation Melodies as One Rarely Hears Them." *Etude* 40, 1922.
An account of Negro singing at Columbus, Miss.

Grant, Frances
"Negro Patriotism and Negro Music." How the old "spirituals" have been used at Tennessee School, Hampton and Tuskegee to promote Americanization. *Outlook* (New York) 121:343–347, 1919. Illus.

Grissom, Mary Allen
The Negro Sings a New Heaven. Chapel Hill: The University of North Carolina Press, 1930. 101 pp.
Songs with music.

Haskell, M. A.
"Negro Spirituals." *Century Magazine* 36:577–581, 1899. n.s.
Songs with musical notation. See also ibid., Vol. 14, p. 263, for eleven songs.

Higginson, Thomas Wentworth
Army Life in a Black Regiment. Boston: Fields, Osgood and Company, 1870. 296 pp.
Chapter IX is on Negro spirituals.

———.
"Hymns of Negroes." *Atlantic* 19:685 et seq. (June) 1867.
Thirty-six religious and two secular songs, musical notation.

———.
"Negro Spirituals." *Atlantic Monthly* (Boston) 19:685–694, 1867.

Hilarion, Sister Mary
"Negro Spiritual." *Catholic World* 143:80–84, (April) 1936.

Hobson, Anne
In Old Alabama, being the Chronicles of Miss Mouse, the little black merchant. New York: Doubleday, Page and Company, 1903. 237 pp., illus.
Words of 54 spirituals and Negro songs, pp. 157–237.

Holliday, Carl
Three Centuries of Southern Poetry. Nashville, Tenn., and Dallas, Tex.: Publishing House of the M. E. Church, South, Smith and Lamar, Agents, 1908. 267 pp.
"Plantation Melodies," pp. 107–111, texts only.

Hurston, Zora Neale
Mules and Men, with an introduction by Franz Boas. Philadelphia, London: J. B. Lippincott Company, 1935. 342 pp., illus.
Negro songs with music, pp. 309–331.

———.
Spirituals and Neo-Spirituals. In: *Negro Anthology,* edited by Nancy Cunard, (pp. 359–361). London, 1934.

Jackson, George Pullen
"The Genesis of the Negro Spiritual." *American Mercury* 26:243–248, 1932.

White and Negro Spirituals. Their Life Span and Kinship. Tracing 200 Years of Untrammeled Song Making and Singing Among Our Country Folk, with 116 Songs as Sung by Both Races. New York: J. J. Augustin, 1943. xiii, 349 pp., appendices, bibl., index, photos, music.
>An impressive array of proof that the white spiritual folksong was the basis and origin of the Negro spiritual, and that the latter had no African origin.

Jackson, M.
"On the Interpretation of Negro Spirituals." *Etude* 52:486, (August) 1934.

"Jesus Gonna Make Up My Dyin' Baid."
In: *Dyin' Easy* by Martha Emmons. *TFSP* 10:60–61, 1932.
>Text and melody of this spiritual.

Johnson, Guy Benton
Folk Culture on St. Helena Island, South Carolina. Chapel Hill: The University of North Carolina Press, 1930. 183 pp., includes music.

————.
John Henry; tracking down a Negro legend. Chapel Hill: The University of North Carolina Press, 1929. 155 pp., includes music.

————.
Negro Folk Songs. In: *Culture in the South,* by W. T. Couch, pp. 547–569. Chapel Hill: University of North Carolina Press, 1934.

————.
"The Negro Spiritual: A Problem in Anthropology." *AA* 32:569–570, 1930. n.s.

Johnson, James Weldon
"National Negro Anthem: Lift Ev'ry Voice and Sing." *Work Tomorrow* 12:257, (June) 1929.

————.
"Negro Folk-Songs and Spirituals." *Mentor* 17:50–52, (February) 1929.

Kerby, M.
"Warning Against Over-refinement of the Negro Spiritual." *Musician* 33:9, (July) 1928.

Kerlin, Robert Thomas
"Canticles of Love and Woe: Negro Spirituals." *So. Workman* (Hampton, Va.) 1:62–64, 1921.

Locke, Alain
Spirituals. In: *75 Years of Freedom.* Commemoration of the 75th Anniversary of the Proclamation of the 13th Amendment to the United States. Washington, D. C.: Library of Congress, 1943. vi, 108 pp.

————.
The Spirituals. In: *The New Negro.* New York: Boni, 1925.

Logan, W. A.
"Song Gleaning Among the Cabins," Collecting Negro Spirituals. *Musician* 44:122, (July) 1939.

Lorenz, Edmund Simon
The American Spirituals and Gospel Songs. In: *Practical Church Music,* pp. 91–112. New York: F. H. Revell Company, 1909.
>A discussion of purposes, methods and plans.

————.
The American Spiritual. In: *Church Music; What a Minister Should Know About,* pp. 314–327. New York: F. H. Revell Company, 1923.

McIlhenny, E. A.
Befo' de War Spirituals. Boston: Christopher, 1933.

MacTaggart, E.
"I Saw a Spiritual Born." *Etude* 58:236, (April) 1940.

Moreland, J. R.
"De Promise Lan'." *Catholic World* 133:435 (July) 1931.

————.
"Doomsday: Negro Spirituals." *Catholic World* 130:438, (January) 1930.

Moss, Carleton
"Spirituals to Swing." *New Theatre Magazine* Vol. 1. 1939. (London).

Murphy, E. F.
"Black Music." *Catholic World* 130:687–692, (March) 1930.

"Negro Hymn of the Day of Judgment."
JAFL 9:210, 1896.

"Negro Spiritual."
Etude 41:678 (Oct.) 1924.

"Negro Spiritual."
Literary Digest 98:34, (September 22) 1928.

"Negro Spiritual Contest in Columbus, Ga."
Playground 20:90–92 (May) 1926; 20:605–606, (February) 1927.

"Negro Spirituals."
Living Age, April 2, 1921.

Niles, Abbe
"Rediscovering the Spirituals." *Nation* 123:598–600, (December 8) 1925.

Niles, John J.
"Shout, Coon, Shout!" *MQ* 16:516–530, 1930.
>The author discusses the origin and various types of coon-shouting.

Odum, A. K.
"Negro Folk Songs from Tennessee." *JAFL* 27:255–266, 1914.

Odum, Howard W.
"Ain't Gwine Drive My God No More." *JAFL* 26:374–376, 1913.

————.
"Religious Folk-Songs of the Southern Negroes." *American Journal of Religious Psychology and Education* 3:265–365, 1908–1909.

———.
"Swing Low, Sweet Chariot." *Country Gentlemen*, pp. 18–19, 49–59, (March) 1926.

———, and Johnson, Guy B.
The Negro and His Songs. Chapel Hill: The University of North Carolina Press, 1925. 306 pp.
> Chapters 2, 3 and 4 deal with religious songs,— many texts included.

O'Sheel, S.
"Two Spirituals." *Commonweal* 9:480, (February 27) 1929.

Owen, May West
"Negroes Spirituals: Their Origin, Development and Place in American Folk-Song." *Musician Observer* (New York) 19, (No. 12):12–13, 1920.

Parks, H. B.
"Follow the Drinking Gourd." *TFSP* 7:81–84, 1928.
> A story of anti-slavery days, of escape of slaves to the North and Peg Leg Joe. Music given.

Parrish, Lydia
"Plantation Songs of Our Old Negro Slaves; With Scores." *Country Life* 69:50–54, (Dec.) 1935. illus.

Parsons, Elsie Clews
"From Spirituals to Vaudeville." *JAFL* 35:331, 1922.

Perkins, A. E.
"Negro Spirituals From the Far South." *JAFL* 35:223–249, 1922.

"Poetry and Eloquence of the Negro Preacher."
The New York Times Book Review, (June 19), 1927.

Pound, Louise
"Ancestry of a Negro-Spiritual." *Modern Language Notes* 33:442–444, (Feb.) 1933.
> The author traces the Negro spiritual: "Weeping Mary" to a Methodist revival hymn.

"Preserving the Negro Spiritual." *Musician* 34: 13, (June), 1929.

Proctor, H. H.
"The Theology of the Songs of the Southern Slaves." *Southern Workman* 36:584–592, 652–656, (Nov. and Dec.) 1907.

Smith, Nicolas Joseph Hutchinson
"Six New Negro Folk-Songs with Music." *TFSP* 7:113–118, 1928.
> "De Hammah Keeps A-Ringin'"; "John Hardy"; "Come in Town," (a song of definite African origin); "Abraham"; "O Bud!".

Smith, Reed
Gullah. Columbia, S. C.: University of South Carolina Press, Bulletin 190, 1926. 45 pp.
> The dialect of the Negroes of the Coast and Sea Islands; some spirituals.

Smythe, Augustine T.; Sass, Herbert Ravenel; Huger, Alfred; Ravenel, Beatrice; Waring, Thomas R.; Rutledge, Archibald; Pickney, Josephine; Heyward, Du Bose; Hutson, Katherine C.; and Gordon, Robert W.
The Caroline Low Country. New York: The Macmillan Company, 1931.
> Contains "The Negro Spiritual," pp. 191–222 and "Spirituals," pp. 223–327.

Speers, Mary Walker Finley
"I Wz Dere Win He Walked in Galilee." *JAFL* 26:190–191, 1913.
> Maryland and Virginia folklore. Camp-meeting hymn.

"Spirituals and Race Relations."
Christian Century 48:230–231, (Feb. 18) 1931.

Talbot, Edith Armstrong
"True Religion in Negro Hymns." *Southern Workman* (Hampton, Va.) 51:213–216, 260–264, 334–339, 1922.

Terrell, Clemmie S.
"Spirituals from Alabama." *JAFL* 43:322–324, 1930.

Thurman, Howard
Deep River: An Interpretation of Negro Spirituals. Oakland, Calif.: Mills College, Eucalyptus Press, 1946. 39 pp.

———.
The Negro Spiritual Speaks of Life and Death. New York: Harper and Brothers, 1947. 55 pp.

Turner, Lucille P.
"Negro Spirituals in the Making." *MQ* 17:480–485, 1931.

White, James Cameron
"The Story of the Negro Spiritual 'Nobody Knows the Trouble I've Seen'." *Musical Observer* (New York) 23, (No. 6) 1924.

Willet, N. L.
"Spirituals on St. Helena." *New York Times* (a letter), Nov. 30, 1928.

Work, John Wesley
"Plantation Meistersinger; Alabama State Sacred Harp Shape-Note Singing Convention." *MQ* 27:97–106, 1941.

Work, Monroe N.
"The Negro in Music." *Negro Year Book, 1931–1932*, (Tuskegee Institute), pp. 439.

COLLECTIONS

Abbott, Francis H.
Eight Negro Songs (from Bedford Co., Virginia). Collected by Francis H. Abbott. Edited by Alfred J. Swan. New York: Enoch and Sons, 1923. 47 pp. Voice and piano.

Allen, William Francis
Slave Songs of the United States. New York: P. Smith, 1929. 115 pp. Choral.

Armstrong, Mrs. Frances (Morgan)
Hampton and His Students, with 50 cabin and plantation songs, arranged by Thomas P. Fenner. New York: G. P. Putnam's Sons, 1874. 255 pp., illus.
Songs (with music), pp. 171–255.

Ballanta (Taylor), Nicholas George Julius
Saint Helena Island Spirituals. Recorded and transcribed at Penn Normal, Industrial and Agricultural School, St. Helena Island, Beaufort County, South Carolina. New York: G. Schirmer, Inc., 1925. 93 pp.

Barrett, Harris
Negro Folk Songs. Hampton, Va.: Press of the Hampton Normal and Agricultural Institute, 1912. 10 pp.

Barton, William Eleazar
Old Plantation Hymns; a collection of hitherto unpublished melodies of the Slave and the Freedman, with historical and descriptive notes. Boston: Lamson, Wolffe and Company, 1899. Reprinted from *New England Magazine* for December, 1898, and January and February 1899. 45 pp.

Benedict, Helen Dymond
Belair Plantation Melodies. Eight Negro folksongs collected from Belair Plantation in Louisiana. Cincinnati, Ohio: The Willis Music Company, 1924. 17 pp.

Bolton, Dorothy G., ed.
Old Songs Hymnal; words and melodies from the State of Georgia. Music arranged by Harry T. Burleigh. New York, London: The Century Company, 1929. 208 pp.

Bowdon, Rosario
Negro Songs. New York: Flammer. 8 songs arranged for mixed (SATB) voices, also with orchestra or piano accompaniment.

Botsford, Florence Hudson, comp, and ed.
Folk Songs of Many Peoples, with English versions by American poets. New York: G. Schirmer and The Woman's Press, 1921–1922. 3 vols.
There are ten American Negro Songs, volume 2, pp. 32–50.

Brown, Lawrence
Spirituals. London: Schott and Company, 1923. 19 pp.
Contains five numbers, for voice and piano.

Burleigh, Harry Thacker
Negro Folk Tunes. New York: G. Ricordi and Company, 1921. Voice and piano.

————.
Negro Spirituals Arranged for Solo Voice. New York: G. Ricordi and Company, 1917–1924. 43 numbers, each a separate song, in folio. Voice and piano.

Christy, Edwin P.
Christy's Plantation Melodies. Philadelphia, New York, etc.: Fisher and Brother, 1851. 71 pp.
Some religious songs included.

Clark, F. A.
Twelve Negro Spirituals for Men's Voices. Phila.: Theodore Presser, 1937.

Clarke, B. M. P.
Collection of Negro Spirituals for Mixed Voices. New York: Hardy Brothers Music Company, Inc.

Cohen, Lily Young
Lost Spirituals. Thirty-six illustrations by Kenneth K. Pointer, and forty-one plates of musical compositions, as composed by Negroes and set down in music by the author. New York: W. Neale, 1928. xxi, 743 pp., illus.

Cooper, Thomas (Bishop)
The African Pilgrim Hymns. London: Bertraud, 1820.

Crowley, J. A.
Three Negro Spirituals. Boston: White-Smith, for male voices.

Curtis-Burlin, Mrs. Natalie
Hampton Series Negro Folk-Songs, recorded by N. C. Burlin. New York and Boston: G. Schirmer, 1918–1919. 4 vol. Arranged for male (TTBB) voices.

————, ed.
Songs and Tales from the Dark Continent, recorded from the singing and the sayings of C. Kamba Simango and M. Madikane Cele, by Natalie Curtis. New York, Boston: G. Schirmer, 1920. Choral and percussion.
Highly informative material on African music, and valuable for rhythmic and melodic comparisons with that of the American Negro.

Dann, Hollis
Fifty-Eight Spirituals for Choral Use. Harmonized by Harvey Worthington Loomis. Boston: C. C. Birchard and Company, 1924. 61 pp. Arranged for male (TTBB) voices, and mixed (SATB) voices.

————.
Twenty-One Spirituals. Boston: Birchard. Arranged for mixed (SATB) voices.

Dett, R. Nathanial
Negro Spirituals, Arranged for Solo Voice. Cincinnati: John Church Company, 1919. Voice and piano.

————.
Negro Spirituals. Cincinnati: John Church, 1919. 3 vols. Arranged for Solo, and SATB.

————.
Religious Folk Songs of the Negro as Sung at Hampton Institute. Hampton, Va.: Hampton Institute, 1927. xxvii, 236 pp.
Choral arrangement.

————.
The Dett Collections of Negro Spirituals. Dett, R. N.: Hall and McCreary: SATB.
Four books. First group (H. & M. Series No. 13) contains 28 tunes; Second group (H. & M. Series No. 14) contains 15 tunes; Third group (H. & M. Series No. 15) contains 17 tunes; Fourth group (H. & M. Series No. 16) contains 14 tunes.

Diton, Carl, ed.
Thirty-Six South Carolina Spirituals. Collected and Harmonized by Carl Diton for Church, Concert and general use. New York: G. Schirmer, 1930. 54 pp.
Solo, and choral, with accompaniment.

Farwell, Arthur
Folk-Songs of the West and South. Negro, Cowboy and Spanish Californian. Harmonized by A. Farwell. The Wa-Wan Series of American Compositions, Vol. 4, No. 27. Newton Center, Mass.: The Wa-Wan Press, 1905. iv, 11 pp. Voice and piano.

_____.
Two Negro Spirituals. Newton Center, Mass.: Wa-Wan Press, 1905.

Fenner, Thomas P.
Cabin and Plantation Songs, as sung by the Hampton Students, arranged by Thomas P. Fenner, Frederick G. Rathbun, and Miss Bessie Cleveland. 3rd ed., enl. by the addition of 44 songs. New York: G. P. Putnam's Sons, 1901. 166 pp.

_____.
Religious Folk Songs of the American Negro. Hampton, Va.: Hampton Institute Press, 1924.

_____.
Religious Folk Songs of the Negro as Sung on the Plantations. New edition. Arranged by the Musical Directors of the Hampton Normal and Agricultural Institute from the Original Editions by Thomas P. Fenner. Hampton, Va.: The Institute Press, 1909. 178 pp.

_____.
Religious Songs of the Negro as Sung on the Plantations. New edition. Hampton, Va.: Hampton Press, 1918. 2nd edition, 1921. 180 pp. Contains 145 songs.

Finn, Elizabeth M., comp.
Songs, Shouts, Stunts ... 2d ed. with additional material. Philadelphia: The Judson Press, 1929. 199 pp.
"Religious Songs," (pp. 1–41) have musical accompaniments.

Fisher, William Arms
Seventy Negro Spirituals, edited by William Arms Fisher. Boston and New York: Oliver Ditson and Company (The Musician's Library) 1926. 112 pp. Voice and piano.

_____, and Others
Ten Negro Spirituals, arranged by William Arms Fisher, Harvey B. Gaul, J. Rosamund Johnson, Charles Fonteyne Manney. New York: Oliver Ditson and Company, 1925. 32 pp.

Frey, Hugo
A Collection of 25 Selected Famous Negro Spirituals, Transcribed and arranged by Hugo Frey. New York: Robbins-Engel, Inc., 1924. 47 pp.

Friedenthal, Albert
Musik, Tanz und Dichtung bei den Kreolen Amerikas. Berlin: Wilmersdorf, H. Schnippel, 1913. 328 pp.
Negro folksong and dances, mainly from South America.

Gaul, Harvey B.
Nine Negro Spirituals. New York: The H. W. Gray Company, 1918. 25 pp. Arranged for voice and piano.

_____.
Negro Spirituals. Boston: Oliver Ditson and Company, 1923–1924. 6 vols., 6 songs.

Gellert, Lawrence, comp.
Me and My Captain. New York: Hours Press, 1939.
A collection of 24 songs for voice and piano.

Gillette, James R.
Three Negro Spirituals for the Organ. New York: J. Fisher and Bro.

Goodell, Walter
Forty-Two Popular Spirituals. H. and M. Auditorium Series, No. 45. Chicago: Hall and McCreary; SATB.

Gruenberg, Louis
Negro Spirituals. New York: Universal. Voice and piano.
Five numbers—freely transcribed for medium voice and piano.

Guion, David W.
Two Darkey Songs. New York: G. Schirmer, 1918. Voice and piano.

_____.
Darkey Spirituals, Collected and arranged by David W. Guion. New York: M. Witmark and Sons, 1918. 12 nos. in one volume.

Hallowell, Emily
Calhoun Plantation Songs. Boston: C. W. Thompson and Company, 1907. 74 pp. Illus. Contains 69 songs for male voices (TTBB).

Handy, W. C.
Collection of Negro Spirituals. New York: Handy Brothers Music Company, Inc., 1938.

Harris, Roy
Medley from the Sunny South. New York: G. Schirmer, Inc., 1945.
Medley of a Foster melody, and spirituals; arranged for mixed voices (SATB).

Jackson, Marylou
Negro Spirituals and Hymns. New York: J. Fisher and Brother.
Contains 25 numbers for female (SSA) voices.

Jesseye, Eva A.
My Spirituals. New York: Robbins-Engel, Inc., 1927. 81 pp.
Sixteen songs for voice and piano.

Johnson, Hall
Green Pasture Spirituals. New York: Farrar and Rinehart, and Carl Fischer, 1930.
Twenty-five spirituals for voice and piano.

Johnson, J. Rosamond
Album of Negro Spirituals. New York: E. B.
Marks: voice and piano.
Twenty-six of the most popular spirituals.

———.
Rolling Along in Song. A Chronological Sur-
vey of American Negro Music. New York:
Viking Press, 1937. Voice and piano.
With 87 arrangements of Negro Songs, including
Ring Shouts, Spirituals, Work Songs, Plantation
Ballads, Chain-Gang, Jail House, and Minstrel
Songs, Street Cries, and Blues.

———.
Sixteen New Negro Spirituals. New York:
Handy Brothers Music Company, 1939

———.
Utica Jubilee Singers Spirituals. Boston:
Oliver Ditson Company, 1930.
Arranged for male (TTBB) voices.

Johnson, James Weldon, and J. R.
The Book of American Negro Spirituals. Edi-
ted with an introduction by James W. Johnson.
Musical arrangements by J. Rosamund John-
son. Additional numbers by Lawrence Brown.
New York: The Viking Press, 1925.

———.
The Second Book of Negro Spirituals. Edited
with an introduction by James Weldon Johnson. Musical arrangements by J. Rosamund
Johnson. New York: The Viking Press, 1926.

———.
Books of American Negro Spirituals. New
York: The Viking Press, 1940. 2 vols. in one.

Jubilee and Plantation Songs: Characteristic
Favorites, as sung by the Hampton Singers,
Jubilee Singers, Fisk University Students and
other concert companies.

Kennedy, R. Emmett
Mellows: A Chronicle of Unknown Singers.
New York: Albert and Charles Boni, 1925.

———.
More Mellows. New York: Dodd, Mead and
Company, 1931.
Contains unharmonized spirituals, ballets without
music, harmonized spirituals and harmonized
folksongs.

Lamkin, Marjorie, and Hall, Wendell
Southern Songs and Spirituals, with Piano
and Ukelele accompaniment. Chicago: Foster
Music Publisher, Inc., 235 South Wabash
Avenue.

McIlhenny, E. A.
Befo' de War Spirituals; words and melodies.
Boston: The Christopher Publishing House,
1933.

Moton, Robert R.
*Religious Folk-Songs of the Negro as Sung on
the Plantation.* Fourth edition. Hampton, Va.:
Hampton Institute Press, 1909.

Negro Spirituals.
St. Louis, Mo.: The Woman's Auxiliary Presbyterian Church, U. S., 270–277 Field Building.

Newton, Ernest
Twelve Negro Spiritual Songs. London: F.
Pitman Hart and Company, Ltd., 1925.

Niles, John J.
Impressions of a Negro Camp-Meeting. New
York: Carl Fischer. Voice and piano.
8 traditional tunes.

———.
Seven Negro Exaltations. New York: G.
Schirmer. Voice and piano.

Noble, Gilford Clifford
The Most Popular Plantation Songs. New
York: Hinds, Hayden and Eldridge, 1911.

Parrish, Lydia
Slave Songs of the Georgia Sea Islands. Music
transcribed by E. Churchill, and R. MacGimsey. Introduction by Olin Downes. New York:
Creative Age Books, 1942. Illus., and music.

Payne, J., ed.
Negro Spirituals. New York: Edward Schu-
berth and Company, 1939.

Pike, G. D.
The Jubilee Singers and Their Campaign.
Boston: 1873. With musical appendix.
This book is one of the earliest collections of
Negro spirituals.

———.
*The Singing Campaign for 10,000 Pounds, or,
The Jubilee Singers in Great Britain.* With an
appendix containing Slave Songs. New York:
1875. Rev. ed.

Rodeheaver, H. A.
Rodeheaver's Negro Spirituals. Chicago: The
Rodeheaver Company, 1923.

———.
Rodeheaver's Plantation Melodies. Chicago:
The Rodeheaver Company, 1916.

Seward, Theodore Frelinghuysen
Jubilee Songs: as sung by the Jubilee Singers
of Fisk University, Nashville, Tennessee, under
the auspices of the American Missionary Association. New York: Biglow, Main and Co.,
1872.
Twenty-four songs, for mixed voices (SATB).

Smith, N. Clark
*New Jubilee Songs for Quartet, Choir or
Chorus, Concert, Church and Home.* Chicago:
Smith Jubilee Music Company, 1906.

———.
New Plantation Melodies, as sung by the
Tuskegee Institute Quartette. Tuskegee Insti-
tute, 1909.

Stickles, William
*Spirituals. Time Honored Songs of the Negro
People.* New York: Hansen Music Publishing
Co., 1947.
Arranged for female, male, and mixed voices.

Still, William Grant, arr.
Twelve Negro Spirituals. New York: Handy Brothers Music Company, 1937. 2 vols.
Contains twelve complete spirituals, words and music, and twelve stories depicting Negro life at the time. These spirituals were inspired by Ruby Berkeley Goodwin. Illustrated by Albert Barbelli.

Taylor, Marshall W.
A Collection of Revival Hymns and Plantation Melodies. Cincinnati, 1883.

Thomas, Edna
Negro Spirituals. Arranged by Edna Thomas. London: Keith Prowse and Company, Ltd., 1924. 6 vols.

White, Clarence C.
Bandana Sketches. Four Negro Spirituals. New York: C. Fischer. Arranged for violin and piano.

————.
Concert Paraphrases of Traditional Negro Melodies. New York: C. Fischer. Arranged for violin and piano.

————.
From the Cotton Fields, Op. 18. New York: C. Fischer. Arranged for violin and piano.

————.
Forty Negro Spirituals. Philadelphia: Presser, 1927. Choral.

Wilson, Mortimer
From the Hickory and Cotton (American Tunes). New York: Composers Music Corp.
Spirituals and other southern tunes arranged for the organ.

Work, Frederick J.
Folk Songs of the American Negroes. Nashville, Tenn.: The Institute Press, 1907.
91 spirituals—SATB.

————.
New Jubilee Songs, as Sung by the Fisk Jubilee Singers of Fisk University. Nashville, Tenn.: Fisk University, 1902.
47 songs, arranged for mixed (SATB) voices.

Work, John W.
American Negro Songs and Spirituals. New York: Crown Publishers, 1940.
230 Songs: Spirituals, Blues, Work Songs, Hollers, Jubilees and Social Songs. Four part arrangements.

ARRANGEMENTS

Individual Titles

————: *Unison*

"Balm In Gilead."
Burleigh, H. T.: Ricordi.

"By and By."
Burleigh, H. T.: Ricordi.

"Hard Trial."
Burleigh, H. T.: Ricordi.

"Oh, Didn't It Rain."
Burleigh, H. T.: Ricordi.

"Oh, Peter, Go Ring-a Dem Bells."
Burleigh, H. T.: Ricordi.

"Outshines the Sun."
Rhodes: Birchard.

————: *Voice and Piano*

"Ain't Goin' to Study War No More."
Burleigh, H. T.: Ricordi.

"A Little Wheel A-Rollin' In My Heart."
Grant-Schaefer, G. A.: Schmidt.

"A Man Goin' 'Round Takin' Names."
Dett, R. N.: Church.

"Backslidin'."
Meyer, L. R.: FitzSimons.

"Balm in Gilead."
Burleigh, H. T.: Ricordi.

"Bear the Burden."
White, C. C.: C. Fischer.

"Black Sheep, Where You Left You' Lamb."
Manney, C. F.: Ditson.

"Blow Your Trumpet, Gabriel."
Grant-Schaefer, G. A.: Ditson.

"Bone Come A-Knittin'."
Wolfe, J.: Flammer.

"Brother, Please Don't Let This Harvest Pass."
Powell-Kearon: Jenkins.

"By and By."
Burleigh, H. T.: Ricordi.

"Calvary (Never Said a Mumblin' Word)."
Grant-Schaefer, G. A.: Ditson.

"Carry Me Home."
Thomas, L.: Schirmer.

"Couldn't Hear Nobody Pray."
Burleigh, H. T.: Ricordi.

"Deep River."
Burleigh, H. T.: Ricordi.

"Deep River."
Fischer, W. A.: Ditson.

"De Gospel Train."
Burleigh, H. T.: Ricordi.

"De Moon's A-Goin' Down."
Grant-Schaefer, G. A.: Schmidt.

"De New-Born Boy" (Christmas).
Gaul, H. B.: Ditson.

"De Ol' Ark's A-Moverin'."
Guion, D.: Schirmer.

"Dey Can't Catch Me for to Bury Me."
Meyer, L. R.: FitzSimons.

"Didn't My Lord Deliver Daniel?"
Burleigh, H. T.: Ricordi.

"Don't Be Weary, Traveler."
Fisher, W. A.: Oliver Ditson.

"Don't Leave Me, Lawd."
Reddick, W.: Ricordi.

"Don't You Weep When I'm Gone."
Burleigh, H. T.: Ricordi.

"Don' Yuh Let Nobody Turn Yuh Roun'."
Grant-Schaefer, G. A.: Schmidt.

"Down by the Ribber Side."
White, C. C.: Carl Fischer.

"Down the Rivah."
MacGimsey, R.: Carl Fischer.

"Ev'ry Time I Feel the Spirit."
Burleigh, H. T.: Ricordi.

"Every Time I Feel the Spirit."
Fisher, W. A.: Ditson.

"Follow Me."
Dett, R. N.: Church.

"Give Me Jesus."
Burleigh, H. T.: Ricordi.

"Go Down in the Lonesome Valley."
Burleigh, H. T.: Ricordi.

"Go Down Moses."
Burleigh, H. T.: Ricordi.

"Goin' to Shout."
Manney, C. F.: Ditson.

"Go Tell it on the Mountains."
Gaul, Harvey B.: Ditson.

"Great Gittin' Up Mornin'."
Brown, L.: Associated.

"Hail the Crown."
Robinson, A.: Ditson.

"Hard Trials."
Burleigh, H. T.: Ricordi.

"Has Anybody Seen My Lord."
Manney, C. F.: Ditson.

"Heav'n Heav'n."
Burleigh, H. T.: Ricordi.

"He's Just De Same Today."
Burleigh, H. T.: Ricordi.

"He's the Lily of the Valley."
Fisher, W. A.: Ditson.

"His Name So Sweet."
Johnson, H.: C. Fischer.

"Honor! Honor!"
Johnson, H.: C. Fischer.

"I Cannot Stay Here By Myself."
Johnson, H.: C. Fischer.

"I Don't Feel No-Ways Tired."
Burleigh, H. T.: Ricordi.

"I Don't Want to Stay Hyeh No Longer."
Wells, J. B.: Boston.

"I Got a Home In-a Dat Rock."
Burleigh, H. T.: Ricordi.

"I Heard of a City Called Heaven."
Johnson, H.: Robbins.

"I Know de Lord's Laid His Hands on Me."
Burleigh, H. T.: Ricordi.

"I Love Mary."
Reddick, W.: Ricordi.

"I'm A-Goin' To See My Friends Again."
Dett, R. N.: John Church.

"I'm All Wore Out A-Tollin' Fo' De Lawd."
Gaines, S. R.: Ditson.

"I'm A-Rolling."
Fisher, W. A.: Ditson.

"I'm A-Wand'rin'" (Old Slave Song).
Gaines, S. R.: Ditson.

"I'm Going Home."
White, C. C.: C. Fischer.

"I'm Goin' to Tell God All My Troubles."
Brown, C.: Associated.

"I'm So Glad Trouble Don't Last Always."
Dett, R. N.: Church.

"I'm Troubled in Mind."
Fisher, W. A.: Ditson.

"In Dat Day."
Heilman, W. C.: Ditson.

"Is Massa Goin' to Sell Us Tomorrow?"
Fisher, W. A.: Ditson.

"I Stood on de Ribber ob Jordan."
Burleigh, H. T.: Ricordi.

"I've Been in de Storm So Long."
Burleigh, H. T.: Ricordi.

"I Want To Be Ready."
Burleigh, H. T.: Ricordi.

"John's Gone Down On De Island."
Burleigh, H. T.: Ricordi.

"Jonah and the Whale."
McGimsey, Robert: C. Fischer.

"Joshua Fit de Battle Ob Jericho."
Burleigh, H. T.: Ricordi.

"Keep A-Inchin' Along."
Grant-Schaefer, G. A.: Schmidt.

"Land Uv Degradashun."
MacGimsey, R.: C. Fischer.

"Let Us Cheer The Weary Traveler."
Burleigh, H. T.: Ricordi.

"Listen To De Lambs."
Fisher, W. A.: Ditson.

"Listen To Yo' Gyarden Angel."
Spalding, Albert: C. Fischer.

"Little David."
Smith, D.: Fillmore.

"Little David, Play On Yo' Harp."
Burleigh, H. T.: Ricordi.

"Little David, Play On Your Harp."
Grant-Schaefer, G. A.: Schmidt.

"Little Door Opened In Heaven."
Meyer, L. R.: FitzSimons.

"Little Wheels A-Turnin' In My Heart."
Fisher, W. A.: Ditson.

"Lord, I Want To Be."
Wille, S.: Galaxy.

"My Brudder's Died And Gone To Hebben."
Gaines, S. R.: Ditson.

"My Father Took A Light."
Manney, C. F.: Ditson.

"My Good Lord Done Been Here."
Johnson, H.: C. Fischer.

"My Lord What A Morning."
Burleigh, H. T.: Ricordi.

"My Lord, What A Morning."
Dawson, W. L. FitzSimons.

"My Way's Cloudy."
Burleigh, H. T.: Ricordi.

"New Born Again."
Heilman, W. C.: Ditson.

"Noah's Ark."
Grant-Schaefer, G. A.: Schmidt.

"Nobody Knows De Trouble I've Seen."
Burleigh, H. T.: Ricordi.

"Nobody Knows De Trouble I See."
Johnson, J. R.: Ditson.

"Nobody Knows De Trouble I've Seen."
White, C. C.: Carl Fischer.

"No More."
Brown, L.: Associated.

"Oh, Brothers, You'll Be Called On."
Stewart, H. E.: Ditson.

"Oh Didn't It Rain."
Burleigh, H. T.: Ricordi.

"Oh! The Land I Am Bound For."
Dett, R. N.: John Church.

"Oh! Wasn't Dat A Wide Ribber."
Burleigh, H. T.: Ricordi.

"Oh, When I Get To Heaven."
Manney, C. F.: Ditson.

"O, Lord, I Done Done."
Boatner, E.: Ditson.

"On A Hill" (Lullaby).
Beach, H. A. A.: Schmidt.

"O Rocks, Don't Fall On Me."
Burleigh, H. T.: Ricordi.

"Poor Me."
Dett, R. N.: John Church.

"Praise God, I'm Satisfied."
Guion, D.: Schirmer.
Based on Negro Spiritual.

"Promise' Land" (A Hallelujah Song).
Burleigh, H. T.: Ricordi.

"Ride On, King Jesus."
Burleigh, H. T.: Ricordi.

"Ride On, King Jesus."
Gaul, H. B.: Ditson.

"Roofs."
McGimsey, Robert: C. Fischer.

"Run To Jesus."
Burleigh, H. T.: Ditson.

"Sail Over Yonder."
Grant-Schaefer, G. A.: Ditson.

"Scandalize My Name."
Burleigh, H. T.: Ricordi.

"Shadrack."
McGimsey, Robert: C. Fischer.

"Shout Yo' Glory."
Guion, D.: Schirmer.

"Sin."
Manney, C. F.: Ditson.

"Sinner Please Doan Let Dis Harves' Pass."
Burleigh, H. T.: Ricordi.

"Sit Down."
Hayes, R.: Ricordi.

"Sit Down, Servant, Sit Down."
Dett, R. N.: Schirmer.

"Somebody's Knockin' At The Door."
Fisher, W. A.: Ditson.

"Somebody's Knockin' At Your Door."
Dett, R. N.: Church.

"Sometimes I Feel Like A Motherless Child."
Burleigh, H. T.: Ricordi.

"Sometimes I Feel Like A Motherless Child."
Fisher, W. A.: Oliver Ditson.

"Sometimes I Feel Like I Wanna Go Home."
Fisher, W. A.: Ditson.

"Standin' In De Need O' Prayer."
Reddick: Boston.

"Stan' Still, Jordan."
Burleigh, H. T.: Ricordi.

"Stay In De Field, O Warrior."
Mitchell, H.: Boston.

"Steal Away."
Brown, L.: Winthrop.

"Steal Away."
Burleigh, H. T.: Ricordi.

"Steal Away."
Fisher, W. A.: Ditson.

"Steal Away."
Johnson, H.: C. Fischer.

"Steal Away."
Manney, C. F.: Ditson.

"Sweet Little Jesus Boy."
McGimsey, R.: C. Fischer.

"Swing Low, Sweet Chariot."
Antrim, D. K.: C. Fischer.

"Swing Low, Sweet Chariot."
Fischer, W. A.: Ditson.

"Swing Low, Sweet Chariot."
Reddick, W.: J. Fischer.

"Swing Low, Sweet Chariot."
Rogers, J. H.: Ditson.

"Take My Mother Home."
Johnson, H.: C. Fischer.

"The Crucifixion."
Fisher, W. M.: Ditson.

"The Little Angel Band."
Grant-Schaefer, G. A.: Schmidt.

"There's A Meetin' Here Tonight."
Burleigh, H. T.: Ditson.

"The Song of the Contrabands" ("O Let My
People Go"). Lockwood-Raker: Horace Waters: 1861. 7 pp.

"Thunderin', Wonderin'."
McGimsey, R.: C. Fischer.

" 'Tis Me O Lord."
Burleigh, H. T.: Ricordi.

"Travelin' To The Grave."
Reddick, W.: J. Fischer.

"Trouble."
McGimsey, R.: C. Fischer.

"Wade In De Water."
Boatner, E.: Ditson.

"Wade In De Water."
Burleigh, H. T.: Ricordi.

"Walk In Jerusalem Jus' Like John."
Powell-Keanton: Jenkins Sons.

"Walk Together, Children."
Johnson, J. R.: Ditson.

"Weepin' Mary."
Burleigh, H. T.: Ricordi.

"Weepin' Mary."
Thomas, L.: Schirmer.

"Were You There."
Burleigh, H. T.: Ricordi.

"Were You There."
Manney, C. F.: Ditson.

"What A Tryin' Time."
Fisher, W. A.: Ditson.

"When The Lord Called Moses."
Manney, C. F.: Ditson.

"Witness."
Johnson, H.: C. Fischer.

"You May Bury Me In De Eas'."
Burleigh, H. T.: Ricordi.

"Zion Hallelujah."
Dett, R. N.: John Church.

————: Female Voices

"Behold That Star."
Burleigh, H. T.: Ricordi: SSA, accomp.

"By and By."
Burleigh, H. T.: Ricordi: SSA.

"Can't Stay Away."
Cain, Noble: Gamble Hinged: SSA.

"De Blin' Man Stood In the Road."
Burleigh, H. T.: Ricordi: SSA.

"Deep River."
Burleigh-Taylor: Ricordi: SA, SSA.

"Deep River."
Clokey, J. W.: J. Fischer: SSA.

"Deep River."
Work, J. W.: Whitmark: SA, SSAA.

"De Gospel Train."
Burleigh, H. T.: Ricordi: SA.

"De Gospel Train."
Christy: Hall and McCreary: SSA.

"Done Paid My Vow To The Lord."
Dett, R. N.: Presser: SSA.

"Ezekiel Saw De Wheel."
Burleigh, H. T.: Ricordi: SSA.

"Go Down Moses."
Burleigh-MacCarthy: Ricordi: SA.

"Go Down Moses."
Burleigh-Page: Ricordi: SSA.

"Heaven, Heaven."
Burleigh, H. T.: Ricordi: SA, SSA.

"Hew Down the Tree."
Dett, N.: Hall and McCreary: SSAA.

"His Name So Sweet."
Johnson, Hall: C. Fischer: SSA.

"Honor! Honor!"
Johnson, H.: C. Fischer: SSA.

"I Couldn't Hear Nobody Pray."
Carpenter, L.: Witmark: SSAA.

"I Couldn't Hear Nobody Pray."
Gaul, H. B.: J. Fischer: SSAA.

"I Don't Feel Noways Tired."
Burleigh, H. T.: Ricordi: SSA.

"I'm A-Wanderin'."
White-Smith: Gaines, S. R.: SSA, SSAA.

"I'm Gwine To Sing In De Heavenly Choir."
Milligan, H. V.: Schmidt: SSAA.

"I'm So Glad Trouble Don't Last Always."
Dett, R. N.: Presser: SSA.

"I'm So Glad Trouble Don't Last Always."
Niles-Horton: Schirmer: SSA, Sopr. Solo, a cap.

"I'se Mighty Tired."
Cain, Noble: Flammer: SSA, accomp.

"I Want To Be Ready."
Burleigh, H. T.: Ricordi: SSA.

"I Will Pray."
Carpenter, L.: Witmark: SSAA.

"Jesus Is Risen" (Easter Spiritual).
Gaul, H. B.: Ditson: SSA.

"Jesus The Christ Is Born."
Talmadge: Schirmer: SSAA, a cap.

"Jesus Walked This Lonesome Valley."
Dawson: Gamble Hinged: SSA.

"Keep On Prayin' To The Lord."
Booth, G.: Schirmer: SSS.

"Let Us Cheer The Weary Traveler."
Luvaas: Birchard: SSA.

"Listen to the Lambs."
Dett-Harris: Schirmer: SSAA.

"Little Wheel A-Turnin'."
In: H. & M. Auditorium Series, No. 50. Wilson, H. R.: Hall and McCreary: SSA.

"My Home Is Over Jordan."
Ambrose, P.: Schmidt: SSA.

"My Way's Cloudy."
Burleigh, H. T.: Ricordi: SSA.

"Nobody Knows the Trouble I See."
Bornschein, F.: J. Fischer: SSA.

"Nobody Knows De Trouble I've Seen."
Burleigh, H. T.: Ricordi: SSA.

"Nobody Knows De Trouble I See."
Clokey, J. W.: J. Fischer: SSA.

"Nobody Knows De Trouble I've Seen."
Zamecnick: C. Fischer: SA.

"Oh, Didn't It Rain."
Burleigh, H. T.: Ricordi: SSA.

"Oh, Peter, Go Ring-a Dem Bells."
Burleigh, H. T.: Ricordi: SSA.

"Oh, When I Get To Heaven."
Manney, C. F.: Ditson: SSA.

"O Lawd, Look Down."
Huntley, F. H.: Schirmer: SSA.

"O Lord, Have Mercy On Me."
Burleigh-Taylor, D.: Ricordi: SA, SAA.

"Outshines the Sun."
Rhodes: Birchard: SSA, SA.

"Rain."
Ambrose, P.: Schmidt: SSA.

"Rain."
Turner, H. M.: Schmidt: SSA.

"Sinner, Please Don't Let Dis Harves' Pass."
Burleigh, H. T.: Ricordi: SSA.

"Somebody's Knocking At Your Door."
Dett, R. N.: Presser: SSA.

"Sometimes I Feel Like A Motherless Child."
Burleigh, H. T.: Ricordi: SSA.

"Soon I'm Goin' Home."
Lester, Wm.: J. Fischer: SSA(A).

"So's I Can Write My Home."
Cain, Noble: Flammer: SSA, accompanied.

"Steal Away."
Johnson, H.: C. Fischer: SSA.

"Swing Low, Sweet Chariot."
Burleigh, H. T.: Ricordi: SSA, SA.

"Swing Low, Sweet Chariot."
Carpenter, L.: Witmark: SSAA.

"Swing Low, Sweet Chariot."
Huntley, F. H.: Schirmer: SSA.

"Swing Low, Sweet Chariot."
Macklin: Boston: SSA.

"Swing Low, Sweet Chariot."
Montague, J. H.: Witmark: SA, SSAA.

"Swing Low, Sweet Chariot."
Reddick, W.: J. Fischer: SSA.

"Swing Low, Sweet Chariot."
Trinkhaus, G. J.: Witmark: SA.

"The Man in White."
Burleigh, H. T.: Ricordi: SA.

"There's A Meeting Here To-night."
Dett, R. N.: Presser, SSA.

" 'Tis Me, O Lord."
Burleigh, H. T.: Ricordi: SA.

"Wade In De Water."
    Burleigh-Taylor, D.: Ricordi: SA, SSA.

"Wasn't That a Mighty Day."
    Work, J. W.: J. Fischer: SSA.

"Wasn't That a Wide River."
    Cain, N.: Flammer: SSA.

"Weepin' Mary."
    Burleigh, H. T.: Ricordi: SSA.

"Were You There?"
    Burleigh, H. T.: Ricordi: SSA, SA.

"Were You There?"
    Manney, C. F.: Ditson: SSA.

"You Goin' to Reap."
    Burleigh, H. T.: Ricordi: SA, SSA.

————: *Male Voices*

"And I Ain't Got Weary Yet."
    Lieurance, T.: Presser: TTBB.

"Bear De Burden."
    White-Brower: C. Fischer: TTBB, a cap.

"Blow, Gabriel."
    White, C. C.: C. Fischer: TTBB.

"Bones Come A-Knittin'."
    Bartholomew, M.: Schirmer: TTBB.

"Climbin' De Mountain."
    Bird, R.: Gray: TTBB.

"Couldn't Heah Nobody Pray."
    Bartholmew, M.: Schirmer: TTBB (Ten. Sol).

"Couldn't Hear Nobody Pray."
    Curtis-Burlin: Schirmer: TTBB.

"De Animals A-Comin'."
    Bartholomew: Schirmer: TTBB.

"Deep River."
    Burleigh, H. T.: Ricordi: TTBB.

"Deep River."
    Cain, N.: Ditson: TTBB.

"Deep River."
    Work, J. W.: Witmark: TTBB.

"De Gospel Train."
    Burleigh, H. T.: Ricordi: TTBB.

"De Ol' Ark's A-Moverin'."
    Guion-Deis: Schirmer: TTBB.

"De Wind Blow Over My Shoulder."
    Bartholomew: Schirmer: TTBB.

"Didn't My Lord Deliver Daniel."
    Russell, A.: J. Fischer: TTBB.

"Down By the Ribber Side."
    White, C. C.: J. Fischer: TTBB.

"Down By the Ribber Side."
    White-Brower: C. Fischer: TTBB.

"Down to De Rivah."
    Gimsey-Willoughby: C. Fischer: TTBB.

"Ezekiel Saw De Wheel."
    Burleigh, H. T.: Ricordi: TTBB.

"Freedom Train."
    Siegmeister, E.: MS: TTBB, piano.

"General Roll Call."
    Crowley, J. A.: White-Smith: TTBB.

"Gettin' Ready."
    Adams, R.: Presser: TTB.

"Go Down Moses."
    Burleigh, H. T.: Ricordi: TTBB.

"Go Down Moses."
    Dixon, D.: Hall & McCreary: TTBB, with treble trio.

"Go Down Moses."
    Gaul, H. B.: J. Fischer: TTBB.

"Go Down, Moses."
    Huntley, F. H.: Schirmer: TTBB.

"Going Home to Live With God."
    Work, J. W.: J. Fischer: TTBB.

"Goin' to Shout."
    Manney, C. F.: Ditson: TTBB.

"Goin' to Shout All Over God's Heab'n."
    Peery, R. B.: Presser, TTBB.

"Good News, Chariot's Comin'!"
    Curtis-Burlin, N.: Schirmer: TTBB.

"Good News From Heaven."
    Whitford, H.: J. Fischer: TTBB.

"Gospel Ship."
    Scott, T.: Words and Music, Inc.: TTBB. Fred Waring Glee Club arrangement.

"Heaven Bells."
    McKay, G. F.: Hall & McCreary: TTBB.

"Heaven, Heaven."
    Burleigh, H. T.: Ricordi: TTBB.

"He Never Said a Mumbling Word."
    Work, J. W.: Presser: TTBB.

"His Name Is So Sweet."
    Johnson, H.: C. Fischer: TTBB, a cap.

"Honor! Honor!"
    Johnson, H.: C. Fischer: TTBB, a cap.

"Humble."
    Bartholomew, M.: Schirmer: TTBB.

Hymn of Freedom. From Negro Spiritual: "O Ride On, Jesus." Curtis-Burlin, N.: Schirmer: TTBB.

"I Couldn't Hear Nobody Pray."
    Gaul, H. B.: J. Fischer: TTBB.

"I Got Shoes."
    Bartholomew, M.: Schirmer: TTBB.

"I'll Hear the Trumpet Sound."
Huntley, F. H.: Shirmer: TTBB.

"I Love Mary."
Reddick, W.: Ricordi: TTBB.

"I'm All Wore Out A-Toilin' Fo' De Lawd."
Gaines, S. R.: Ditson: TTBB.

"I'm A-Wanderin' " (Slave Song).
Gaines, S. R.: White-Smith: TTBB.

"I'm Goin' Home."
White-Brower: C. Fischer: TTBB.

"I'm Gwine to Sing In De Heavenly Choir."
Milligan, H. V.: Schmidt: TTBB.

"I'm Not Weary Yet."
Gest, E.: Presser: TTBB.

"I'm So Glad Trouble Don't Last Always."
Jones, G. J.: Witmark: TTBB.

"I'm Troubled In Mind."
Russell, A.: J. Fischer: TTBB.

"I Saw De Light."
Pitcher, G.: Birchard: TTBB.

"It's Me."
Huntley, F. H.: FitzSimons: TTBB.

"Jesus On the Water Side."
Aschenbrenner, W.: FitzSimons: TTTBBB.

"Jesus Walked This Lonesome Valley."
Dawson: Gamble Hinged: TTBB (Bar. Solo).

"Joshua Fit the Battle of Jericho."
Cain, N.: Boston Music Co.: TB.

"Joshua Fit De Battle Ob Jericho."
Gaul, H. E.: J. Fischer: TTBB.

"Keep In The Middle Of The Road."
Bartholomew, M.: Schirmer: TTBB.

"King Jesus Is A-Listenin'."
Dawson, W. L.: FitzSimons: TTBB.

"Lawd, I Cannot Stay Away."
Bartholomew, M.: Schirmer: TTBB.

"Let My People Go."
Scott, T.: Words and Music Co., Inc.: TTBB.
Fred Waring Glee Club arrangement.

"Listen to the Lambs."
Dett, N.: Schirmer: TTBB.

"Little David, Play On Your Harp."
Hanke, H.: J. Fischer: TTBB.

"Little Wheel A-Turnin'."
In: H. & M. Auditorium Series, No. 44. Wilson,
H. R.: Hall & McCreary: TBB.

"Live Humble."
Irwin, M.: White-Smith: TTBB.

"Lord, I Want To Be."
Wille, S.: Galaxy: TTBB.

"Lord, I Want Two Wings."
White, C. C.: J. Fischer: TTBB.

"Lord, I Want Two Wings."
White, C. C.: C. Fischer: TTTBBB.

"My Lord, What A Morning."
Work, J. W.: Presser: TTBB.

"Nobody Knows the Trouble I've Seen."
In: H. & M. Auditorium Series, No. 48. Andersen, A. O.: Hall & McCreary: TBB.

"Nobody Knows de Trouble I've Seen."
Burleigh, H. T.: Ricordi: TTBB.

"Nobody Knows the Trouble I've Seen."
In: H. & M. Auditorium Series, No. 22. Grant,
R. W.: Hall and McCreary: TTBB.

"Nobody Knows the Trouble I've Seen."
Olds, W. B.: Hall and McCreary: TTBB, with
treble trio, and tenor or baritone solo.

"Nobody Knows De Trouble I See."
Pitcher, G.: Birchard: TTBB.

"Nobody Knows the Trouble I See."
Treharne, B.: Willis: TTBB.

"Nobody Knows De Trouble I've Seen."
White-Brower: C. Fischer: TTBB.

"Oh, De Lan' I Am Bound For."
Delmore-Howorth: Gamble Hinged: TTBB.

"Oh My Lawd What Shall I Do?"
Guion, David: Schirmer: TTBB.

"Oh, Peter, Go Ring-a Dem Bells."
Burleigh, H. T.: Ricordi: TTBB.

"O Lawd, Look Down."
Huntley, F. H.: Schirmer: TTBB.

"Old Ark's A-Moverin'."
Bartholomew, M.: Schirmer: TTBB.

"Ol' Gray Robe."
Huntley, F. H.: Schirmer: TTBB.

"O Lord, Have Mercy On Me."
Burleigh, H. T.: Ricordi: TTBB.

"On Mah Way to Heaven."
Strickland, L.: J. Fischer: TTBB.

"Peter On the Sea."
Crowley, J. A.: White-Smith: TTBB.

"Po' Ol' Lazarus."
Work, J. W.: J. Fischer: TTBB.

"Promise' Lan'."
Burleigh, H. T.: Ricordi: TTBB.

"Ready When He Comes."
Bartholomew, M.: Schirmer: TTBB.

"Religion Is A Fortune."
Loomis, H. W.: Birchard: TTBB.

"Religion Is A Fortune."
Stoessel, A.: Birchard: TTBB (also with
piano, strings and harp.)

"Ride On."
Crowley, J. A.: White-Smith: TTBB.

"Ride On, Moses."
Zeiner, E. J. A.: Schirmer: TTBB.

"Rise Up, Shepherds, and Follow."
Dett, R. N.: J. Fischer: TTBB.

"Roll, Jord'n, Roll."
Newell, R.: J. Fischer: TTBB.

"Roll Jordan."
Bartholomew, M.: Schirmer: TTBB.

"Scandalize My Name."
Pitcher, G.: Birchard: TTBB.

"Set Down, Servant."
Scott, T.: Words and Music, Inc.: TTBB.
Fred Waring Glee Club arrangement.

"Sittin' Down Beside of the Lamb."
Work, J. W.: Presser: TTBB.

"Some Folks Say."
Huntley, F. H.: Schirmer: TTBB.

"Soon I'm Goin' Home."
Lester, W.: J. Fischer: TTBB.

"Standin' In De Need O' Prayer."
Bartholomew, M.: Schirmer: TTBB.

"Standin' In De Need of Prayer."
Peery, R. R.: Presser: TTBB.

"Stand the Storm."
Work, J. W.: J. Fischer: TTBB.

"Steal Away."
In: H. & M. Auditorium Series, No. 48. Andersen, A. O.: Hall and McCreary: TBB.

"Steal Away."
Bartholomew, M.: Schirmer: TTBB.

"Steal Away."
Johnson, H.: C. Fischer: TTBB, a cap.

"Steal Away."
Newell, R.: J. Fischer: TTBB.

"Steal Away."
Scott, T.: Words and Music, Inc.: TTBB.
Fred Waring Glee Club arrangement.

"Steal Away."
Stoessel, A.: Birchard: TTBB (also with piano,
strings and harp).

"Swing Low, Sweet Chariot."
Bartholomew, M.: Schirmer: TTBBB (Bass
Solo).

"Swing Low, Sweet Chariot."
Burleigh, H. T.: Ricordi: TTBB.

"Swing Low, Sweet Chariot."
Gaul, H. E.: Gray: TTBB.

"Swing Low, Sweet Chariot."
Huntley, F. H.: Schirmer: TTBB.

"Swing Low, Sweet Chariot."
Peery, R. R.: Presser: TTBB.

"Swing Low, Sweet Chariot."
Reddick, W.: J. Fischer: TTBB.

"Swing Low, Sweet Chariot."
Scott, T.: Words and Music, Inc., TTBB.
Fred Waring Glee Club arrangement.

"Swing Low, Sweet Chariot."
Stoessel, A.: Birchard: TTBB (also with piano,
strings and harp).

"Swing Low, Sweet Chariot."
Trinkhaus, G. J.: Witmark: TTBB.

"The Battle of Jericho."
Bartholomew, M.: Schirmer: TTBB.

"The Crucifixion."
Harling, F.: Ricordi: TTBB.

"The Man In White."
Burleigh, H. T.: Ricordi: TB.

"They Led My Lord Away Yet."
Lewis, H. M.: Galaxy: TTBB.

"'Tis Me, O Lord."
Burleigh, H. T.: Ricordi: TTBB.

"Travelin' To De Grave."
Reddick, W.: J. Fischer: TTBB.

"Wade In De Water."
Burleigh, H. T.: Ricordi: TTBB.

"Wade In De Water."
Hall, A.: Schirmer: TTBB.

"Wasn't That a Mighty Day."
Work, J. W.: J. Fischer: TTBB.

"Were You There."
Burleigh, H. T.: Ricordi: TTBB.

"Were You There."
Scott, T.: Words and Music, Inc.: TTBB.
Fred Waring Glee Club arrangement.

————: Mixed Voices

"Adam in the Garden."
Binder, A. W.: Elkan-Vogel: SATB.

"Ain't Dat Good News."
Milligan, H. V.: Schmidt: SATB.

"Ain't Gonna Study War No More."
Milligan, H. V.: Schmidt: SATB.

"Am-a That Good News."
Dawson, William L.: MS: SATB, a cap.

"A Medley of Negro Spirituals."
Treharne, B.: G. Schirmer: SATB, a cap.

"And I Ain't Got Weary Yet."
Lieurance, T.: Presser: SATB.

"An' He Never Spoke A Mumblin' Word."
Diton, C.: Schirmer: SATB.

"And He Never Said A Mumblin' Word."
Krone, M.: Neil Kjos: SATB.

"At the Beautiful Gate."
Diton, C.: Schirmer: SSATB.

"A Wheel In A Wheel."
Loomis, H. W.: Birchard: SATB.

"Babylon is Fallen."
Cain, N.: Flammer: SATB, a cap.

"Bear De Burden."
White, C. C.: C. Fischer: SATB.

"Be Ready When My Jesus Comes."
Milligan, H. V.: Schmidt: SATB.

"Bles' My Soul An' Gone Away."
Cain, N.: Flammer: SATB, a cap.

"By and By."
Cain, N.: Gamble Hinged: SATB.

"Camp Meeting."
Milligan, H. V.: Schmidt: SATB.

"Can't Stay Away."
Cain, N.: Gamble Hinged: SSAATTBB.

"Chilly Water."
Cain, N.: Harold Flammer: SATB, a cap.

"A City Called Heaven."
Christy: Schirmer: SATB.

"City Called Heaven."
Kemmer, G. W.: Ricordi: SATB.

"Come Along, O Sinner."
Lester, W.: J. Fischer: SATB.

"Come On Sinner, Come."
Gaines, S. R.: Ditson: SSAATTBB.

"Couldn't Hear Nobody Pray."
Burleigh, H. T.: Ricordi: SATB.

"Couldn't Hear Nobody Pray."
Cain, N.: Schirmer: SSAATTBB.

"Couldn't Hear Nobody Pray."
Goodell: Hall and McCreary: SATB, a cap.

"Cross it for Yourself."
Clokey, J. W.: J. Fischer: SATB.

"Daniel In the Lion's Den."
Loomis, H. W.: Birchard: SATB.

"De Angel Gabriel."
Cain, N.: Gamble Hinged: SSAATTBB.

"Deep River."
Burleigh, H. T.: Schirmer: SATB.

"Deep River."
Dett, N.: Hall and McCreary: SATB, arr. as a
Motet.

"Deep River."
Diton, C.: Schirmer: SATB.

"Deep River."
Fisher, W. A.: Ditson: SATB.

"Deep River."
Mitchell: Birchard: SATB.

"Deep River."
Robertson, Sir H.: FitzSimons: SATB.

"De Gospel Train."
Burleigh, H. T.: Ricordi: SATB.

"Didn't My Lord Deliver Daniel."
Burleigh, H. T.: Schirmer: SATB.

"Didn't My Lord Deliver Daniel."
Wilson: Hall and McCreary: SATB.

"Dig My Grave."
Burleigh, H. T.: Schirmer: SATB.

"Don't Be Weary, Traveler."
Bron-Wright: Birchard: SSAATB, ten. solo.

"Don't Be Weary, Traveler."
Burleigh, H. T.: Ricordi: SATB.

"Don't Be Weary, Traveler."
Dett, R. N.: Presser: SSATBB, a cap.

"Don't Be Weary, Traveler."
Jackson, E. A.: Gray: SATB.

"Don't You Weep No More, Mary."
Dett, R. N.: Schirmer: SATB.

"Down By the Ribber Side."
White, C. C.: C. Fischer: SATB.

"Down In Yon Forest."
Niles-De Brant: Schirmer: SATB.

"Dust, Dust and Ashes."
Dett, N.: Hall and McCreary: SATB, arranged
as a Motet.

"Ev'ry Time I Feel the Spirit."
Burleigh, H. T.: Ricordi: SATB.

"Every Time I Feel the Spirit."
Diton, C.: Schirmer: SATB.

"Every Time I Feel the Spirit."
Fisher, W. A.: Ditson: SATB.

"Ezekiel Saw De Wheel."
Burleigh, H. T.: Ricordi: SATB.

"Ezekiel Saw De Wheel."
Cain, N.: Gamble Hinged: SSAATTBB.

"Father Abraham."
Burleigh, H. T.: Schirmer: SATB.

"Father Abraham."
Treharne, B.: Boston Music Company: SATB.

"Father Abraham."
Treharne, B.: Willis: SSAATTBB, (8 pts.)

"Fearin' of the Judgement Day."
Swift, F. F.: Associated: SATB.

"For the Beauty of the Earth."
Work, J. W.: J. Fisher: SATB.

"Gently, Lord, O Gently Lead Us."
Dett, R. N.: John Church: SATB.

"Glory to that New-born King."
Work, J. W.: Presser: SSATTBB.

"Go Down, Moses."
Burleigh-Page: Ricordi: SATB.

"Go Down, Moses."
Cain, N.: Schirmer: SATB.

"Go Down, Moses."
Gaul, H. B.: J. Fischer: SATB.

"Go, Down, Moses."
Jackson, E. A.: Gray: SATB.

"Go Down, Moses."
Kemmer, G. W.: Ricordi: SATB.

"Go Down, Moses."
Wheelwright, L.: Witmark: SATB, piano accomp., orchestra available.

"Go Down Moses."
In: H. & M. Auditorium Series, No. 37. Wilson, H. R.: Hall and McCreary: S. Bar.

"God Saves His Chillun."
Lester, W.: J. Fischer: SATB.

"God Tole Hezykiah."
Binder, A. W.: Elkan-Vogel: SATB.

"Going Home to Live with God."
Work, J. W.: J. Fischer: SATB.

"Gonna Join De Heavenly Choir."
Cain, N.: Harold Flammer: SATB, a cap.

"Got-a My Soul Baptized."
Rhodes: Birchard: SATB.

"Go Tell it on de Mountains."
Burleigh, H. T.: Ricordi: SATB.

"Great Day."
White, C. C.: C. Fischer: SSAATTBB, a cap.

"Hail the Crown."
Bron-Wright: Birchard: SSATB.

"Hear De Lamb A-Crying."
Burleigh, H. T.: Ricordi: SATB.

"Hear Me Pray."
Bron-Wright: Birchard: SATB, ten. solo.

"Heaven, Heaven."
Burleigh, H. T.: Ricordi: SATB.

"He's Gone Away."
Siegmeister, E.: Ditson: SATB.

"He's the Lily of the Valley."
Fisher, W. A.: Ditson: SATB.

"His Name So Sweet."
Johnson, H.: C. Fischer: SATBB, a cap.

"Hold the Wind."
Milligan, H. V.: Schmidt: SATB.

"Honor! Honor!"
Johnson, H.: C. Fischer: SATBB, a cap.

"I Couldn't Hear Nobody Pray."
Gaul, H. B.: J. Fischer: SATB.

"I Got Religion."
Cain, N.: Schirmer: SATB.

"I Know I Have Another Building."
White, C. C.: Presser: SATB.

"I Know the Lord's Laid His Hands On Me."
Milligan, H. V.: Schmidt: SATB.

"I'll Never Turn Back No More."
Dett, R. N.: J. Fischer: SATB.

"I'm A-Rolling."
Burleigh, H. T.: Ricordi: SATB.

"I'm A-Wanderin'."
Gaines, S. R.: White-Smith: SATB.

"I'm Goin' Home."
White, C. C.: C. Fischer: SATB, a cap.

"I'm Gwine ter Wait."
Clark, F. A.: Presser: SATB.

"I'm Gwine to Sing in de Heavenly Choir."
Milligan, H. V.: Schmidt: SATB.

"I'm So Glad Trouble Don't Last Always."
Jones, G. J.: Witmark: SATB.

"I'm So Glad Trouble Don't Last Always."
Niles-Horton: Schirmer: SATB, Ten. Solo, a cap.

"I'm Troubled In Mind."
Fisher, W. A.: Ditson: SATB.

"In That Great Gettin' Up Morning."
Cain, N.: Gamble Hinged: SSAATTBB.

"I Saw De Light."
Pitcher, G.: Birchard: SATB.

"Ise Comin' Lord to You."
Britain, Radie: Clayton Summy: SATB.

"It's Me, O Lord."
Klemm, G.: Witmark: SATB.

"I Wanna Be Ready."
Miller, J.: Galaxy: SATB.

"I Want to be Ready."
Cain, N.: Gamble Hinged: SSAATTBB.

"I Want to be Ready."
Goodell: Hall and McCreary: SATB, a cap.

"I Wish I'se In Heaven Settin' Down."
Bron-Wright: Birchard: SSATBB.

"Jacob's Ladder."
Loomis, H. W.: Birchard: SATB.

"Jericho."
In: H. & M. Auditorium Series, No. 52. Sheehan, R.: Hall and McCreary: SATB (or boys' voices).

"Jesus Born in Bethlea."
Buchanan, A. M.: J. Fischer: SATB.

"Jesus is a Rock in a Weary Lan'."
Work, J. W.: Presser: SATB.

"Jesus is Risen."
Gaul, H. E.: Ditson: SATB.

"Jesus, Jesus, Rest Your Head."
Niles-Warrell: Schirmer: SATB.

"Jesus On the Water Side."
Aschenbrenner, W.: FitzSimons: SATB.

"Jesus the Christ is Born."
Niles-Warrell: Schirmer: SATB, a cap.

"Jesus the Christ is Born."
Warrell: Schirmer: SSAATTBB, a cap.

"Jesus Walked This Lonesome Valley."
Dawson: Gamble Hinged: SATB.

"Joshua Fit the Battle of Jericho."
Christy: Hall and McCreary: SATB, Div.

"Joshua Fit de Battle of Jericho."
Gaul, H. B.: J. Fischer: SATB.

"Joshua Fit de Battle ob Jericho."
Montague, J. H.: Witmark: SATB.

"Joshua Fit the Battle of Jericho."
Strickling-Webster: Associated: SATB.

"Judgment Day."
Manney, C. F.: Ditson: SSATBB.

"Keep on Prayin' to the Lord."
Booth, G.: Schirmer: SATBB.

"King Jesus is A-listenin'."
Dawson, Wm. L.: FitzSimons: SATB.

"Let Us Cheer the Weary Traveler."
Burleigh, H. T.: Ricordi: SATB.

"Let Us Cheer the Weary Traveler."
Dett, R. N.: Presser: SSATBB.

"Listen to the Lambs."
Dett, R. N.: Schirmer: SSAATTBB, SAB.

"Little David, Play On Your Harp."
Diton, C.: Schirmer: SSATB.

"Little David, Play On Yo' Harp."
Lewis, H. M.: J. Fischer: SATB.

"Little David, Play On Yo' Harp."
Reddick, W.: Witmark: SATB.

"Little David, Play On Yo' Harp."
Wilson, H. R.: Hall and McCreary: SAB; SSAATTBB.

"Mary Wore Three Links of Chain."
Clokey, J. W.: J. Fischer: SATB.

"My Home is Over Jordan."
Grant-Schaefer, G. A.: Schmidt: SATB.

"My Lord Says He's Gwine to Rain Down Fire."
Johnson, J. R.: Ditson: SATB.

"My Lord, What Morning."
Burleigh, H. T.: Ricordi: SATB.

"My Lord, What a Morning."
Dawson, Wm. L.: FitzSimons: SATB.

"My Way's Cloudy."
Dett, N.: Hall and McCreary: SATB, arr. as a Motet.

"Nobody Knows De Trouble I've Seen."
Burleigh, H. T.: Ricordi: SATB.

"Nobody Knows de Trouble I See."
Manney, C. F.: Ditson: SATB.

"Nobody Knows De Trouble I've Seen."
White, C. C.: C. Fischer: SATB.

"O Hear the Lambs A-crying."
Dett, R. N.: Presser: SATB.

"Oh, John."
Reynolds: Schirmer: SATB.

"Oh, Mary, Don't You Weep."
Dett, R. N.: Birchard: SATB.

"Oh, Mary, Doncha Weep."
Johnson, M. and T.: Hall and McCreary: SSATB.

"Oh, Mary, Don't You Weep."
Nightingale, M.: Schirmer: SA (AT), Bar. Solo.

"Oh, Mary Went A-Journeying."
Buchanan, A. M.: J. Fischer: SATB.

"Oh, Po' Little Jesus."
James, P.: Schirmer: SATB.

"Oh, Rise An' Shine."
Kemmer, G. W.: Ricordi: SATB.

"Oh, What a Beautiful City."
Boatner, E.: Schirmer: SSATBB.

"Ole Ark's A-Moverin'."
Cain, Noble: Harold Flammer: TTBB.

"O Lord, Send the Fire."
Cain, N.: Hall and McCreary: SATB-Div.

"On Canaan's Shore."
Loomis, H. W.: Birchard: SATB.

"On That Sabbath Morn."
Dett, N.: Hall and McCreary: SATB.

"O Lawd, Look Down."
Huntley, F. H.: Schirmer: SATB.

"Old Plantation Days."
Page, N. C.: White: SATB, and orchestra.

"O Ride On, Jesus, Hymn of Freedom."
Curtis-Burlin, N.: Schirmer: SSATBB.

"Outshines the Sun."
Rhodes: Birchard: SATB.

"Peter, Go Ring Dem Bells."
Cain, N.: Harold Flemmer: SATB, a cap.

"Poor Mourner's Got a Home At Last."
Diton, C.: Schirmer: SATB.

"Prayin' An' A Moanin'."
Utterback, M. W.: Witmark: SATB.

"Religion is a Fortune."
Loomis, H. W.: Birchard: SATB.

"Ride On, King Jesus."
Smith, R. A.: C. Fischer: SSAATTBB, a cap.

"Rise Up, Shepherds, and Follow."
Dett, R. N.: J. Fischer: SATB.

"Rise Up, Shepherd, and Foller."
Kemmer, G. W.: Ricordi: SATB.

"Roll Dat Ol' Chariot Along."
Reddick, W.: Witmark: SATB.

"Roll De Ol' Chariot Along."
Howorth, W.: Gamble Hinged: SATB.

"Roll, Jordan, Roll."
Cain, N.: Hall and McCreary: SATB-Div., a cap.

"Roun' De Glory Manger."
James, P.: Schirmer: SATB, Sop. Solo.

"Shouting Sun."
McCollin, F.: Presser: SATB.

"Sinner, Please Don't Let Dis Harves' Pass."
Burleigh, H. T.: Ricordi: SATB.

"Sinner, Please Don't Let This Harvest Pass."
Howorth: Gamble Hinged: SATB.

"Sinner, Please Don't Let This Harvest Pass."
Montague, J. H.: Witmark: SATB.

"Sinner, Please Don't Let This Harvest Pass."
White, C. C.: Presser: SSAATTBB.

"Somebody's Knocking At Your Door."
Dett, R. N.: Presser, SATB.

"Somebody's Knockin' At Yo' Door."
Reddick, W.: Witmark: SATB.

"Sometimes I Feel Like A Motherless Child."
Christy, Van A.: Schirmer: SATB.

"Sometimes I Feel Like A Motherless Child."
Fisher, W. A.: Ditson: SATB.

"Son of Man."
White, C. C.: C. Fischer: SATB.

"Soon I'm Goin' Home."
Lester, W.: J. Fischer: SATB.

"So Sad."
Burleigh, H. T.: Schirmer: SATB.

"Spirit Ob De Lord Done Fell."
Cain, N.: Gamble Hinged: SSAATTBB.

"Stan' Ready."
Cain, N.: Gamble Hinged: SSAATTBB.

"Steal Away."
Bron-Wright: Birchard: SSATBB.

"Steal Away."
Burleigh, H. T.: Ricordi: SATB.

"Steal Away."
Johnson, H.: C. Fischer: SATTBB.

"Steal Away."
Kemmer, G. W.: Ricordi: SATB.

"Steal Away."
Lynn, George: Mills: SATB, a cap.

"Steal Away to Jesus."
Fisher, W. A.: Ditson: SATB.

"Sweet Jesus, Guide My Feet."
Meeker, E.: Associated: SATB.

"Swing Low, Sweet Chariot."
Bron-Wright: Birchard: SATB.

"Swing Low, Sweet Chariot."
Burleigh, H. T.: Ricordi: SATB.

"Swing Low, Sweet Chariot."
Cain, N.: FitzSimons: SATB.

"Swing Low, Sweet Chariot."
Cain: Hall and McCreary: SATB, a cap.

"Swing Low, Sweet Chariot."
Diton, C.: Presser: SATB.

"Swing Low, Sweet Chariot."
Fisher, W. A.: Ditson: SATB.

"Swing Low, Sweet Chariot."
Huguelet, A.: C. Fischer: SATB.

"Swing Low, Sweet Chariot."
Huntley, F. H.: Schirmer: SATB.

"Swing Low, Sweet Chariot."
Reddick, Wm.: J. Fischer: SATB.

"Swing Low, Sweet Chariot."
Smith, R. A.: C. Fischer: SATB, a cap.

"Swing Low, Sweet Chariot."
Trinkhaus, G. J.: Witmark: SAB, SATB.

"Tell Bruddah 'Lijah."
Treharne, B.: Boston Music Co.: SATB.

"Tell Brudder 'Lijah."
Treharne, B.: Willis: SSAATTBB.

"The Chariot Jubilee."
Dett, R. N.: Presser: SATB, Motet based on Negro spiritual.

"The Crucifixion."
Kemmer, G. W.: Ricordi: SSAATTBB.

"The Crucifixion."
Robertson, H. S.: Carl Fischer: SATB.

"The Hebrew Children."
Buchanan, A. M.: J. Fischer: SATB.

"The Little Angel Band."
Grant-Schaefer: Schmidt: SATB.

"The Little Light O' Mine."
Work, J. W.: Galaxy: SATB.

"There's A Man Goin' Roun'."
Kleinsinger: Berlin: SATB.

"The Story of Norah."
Niles-Harris: Schirmer: SSAATTBB.

"This Train."
Binder, A. W.: Elkan-Vogel: SATB.

"Travelin' To De Grave."
Reddick, Wm.: J. Fischer: SAB.

"Wade In the Water."
Cain, N.: Schirmer: SATB.

"Walk Together Chillun."
Cain, N.: Gamble Hinged: SATB.

"Walk Together Children."
Johnson, J. R.: Ditson: SATB.

"Wasn't That a Mighty Day?"
Dett, R. N.: Schirmer: SATB.

"Wasn't That a Mighty Day?"
Work, J. W.: J. Fischer: SATB.

"Wasn't That a Wide River?"
Cain, N.: Harold Flammer: SATB, a cap.

" 'Way Over Jordan."
Cain, N.: Harold Flammer: SATB, a cap.

"Weeping Mary."
Dett, R. N.: J. Fischer: SATB.

"Were You There?"
Burleigh, H. T.: Ricordi: SATB.

"When Your Lamp Burns Down."
Robertson, H. S.: C. Fischer: SATB.

"Where You Goin', Poor Sinner?"
Milligan, H. V.: Schmidt: SATB.

"Wide River."
White, C. C.: C. Fischer: SATB, a cap.

"Who Did Swallow Jonah."
Protheroe, D.: Ditson: SATB.

"Who's That Callin'?"
Clark, F. A.: Presser: SATB.

" 'Zek'll Saw De Wheel."
Clokey, J. W.: J. Fischer: SATB.

————————: Piano

Coleridge-Taylor, Samuel
Twenty-Four Negro Melodies. Opus 59, with a preface by Booker T. Washington. Boston: O. Ditson Company; New York: C. H. Ditson and Company, 1905. 127 pp. (The Musician's Library, Vol. XVII.)

————————.
Six Negro Melodies. Boston: O. Ditson Company.

"Deep River."
Kohlmann, C.: Presser.

MacDowell, Edward
Woodland Sketches, op. 51 #7 "From Uncle Remus." London: Elkin and Company, Ltd.

White, Clarence C.
Bandana Sketches: Four Negro Spirituals. Arranged for piano by Arthur Friedheim. New York: Carl Fischer.
Contents: Chant. Nobody Knows de Trouble I've Seen; Lament. I'm Troubled in Mind; Slave Song. Many Thousand Gone; Negro Dance. Sometimes I Feel Like a Motherless Child.

————————.
Spiritual, Opus 18, No. 3. New York: C. Fischer.

————————: Two Pianos

"Death, Ain't Yuh Got No Shame."
Triggs, H.: Schirmer.

"Deep River."
Simmons, H.: Axelrod Publishing.

Powell, John
Rhapsody Négre. Arranged from orchestral score by Edwin Hughes. New York: Schirmer.

————————: Organ

"Deep River."
In: Three Negro Spirituals. Gillette, J. R.: J. Fischer Bro.

"Deep River."
Kemmer, G. W.: Schirmer.
Complete title: Organ Prelude on the Negro Spiritual "Deep River."

"Deep River."
In: From the Hickory and Cotton. 17 American Tunes. Wilson, M.: Composers Music Corp.

From the Hickory and Cotton.
Wilson, Mortimer: Composers.
Spirituals and other southern tunes.

"Keep Me From Sinking Down."
Diton, C.: Schirmer.

"Nobody Knows de Trouble I See."
In: Three Negro Spirituals. Gillette, J. R.: J. Fischer and Bro.

"Nobody Knows de Trouble I Seen."
Kohlmann, C.: Presser.

"Nobody Knows de Trouble I've Seen."
White-Nelson: C. Fischer.

"Swing Low, Sweet Chariot."
Diton, C.: Schirmer: Organ, Transcription, Op. 2.

"Swing Low, Sweet Chariot."
Lemore, E. H.: Presser.

"The Angels Done Changed My Name."
In: Three Negro Spirituals. Gillette, J. R.: J. Fischer and Bro.

Three Negro Spirituals.
Gillette, James R.: J. Fischer.

————————: Violin and Piano

"Ain't It A Sin To Steal On Sunday."
In: Outlandish Suite. Dyer, S.: J. Fischer.

"Cabin Song."
White, C. C.: C. Fischer.

"Deep River."
Ambrosio, W. F.: C. Fischer.

"Go Down, Moses" (Paraphrased as Levee Dance). White, C. C.: C. Fischer.

"I'm Troubled in Mind."
In: *Bandana Sketches*. White, C. C.: C. Fischer.

"Many Thousand Gone."
White, C. C.: C. Fischer.

"Nobody Knows de Trouble I've Seen."
In: *Bandana Sketches*. White, C. C.: C. Fischer.

"On the Bayou."
White, C. C.: C. Fischer.

Plantation Melodies.
Powell, M.: C. Fischer.
Includes Negro tunes and Foster songs.

"Somebody's Knockin' At Your Door" (Paraphrased as Pilgrim Song). White, C. C.: C. Fischer.

"Sometimes I Feel Like A Motherless Child" (Dance). White, C. C.: C. Fischer.

"Spiritual."
White, C. C.: C. Fischer.

"Swing Low, Sweet Chariot" (Paraphrased as Plantation Song). White, C. C.: C. Fischer.

—————: *String Quartet*

"Deep River."
Pochon, A.: C. Fischer.

"Go Down, Moses."
Pochon, A.: C. Fischer.

String Quartet on Negro Themes, op. 19.
Mason, Daniel G.: SPAM.

String Quartet on Negro Themes.
McDonald, H.: MS.

"Swing Low, Sweet Chariot."
Pochon, A.: C. Fischer.

—————: *Chamber Orchestra*

American Suite.
Cadman, Charles W.: Composer's Press: String Orchestra.
The second movement is a free development of material from Negro spirituals.

"Deep River."
Trinkhaus, G.: Witmark: Brass Quartet.

"Dum-a-lum," Variation on a Negro Spiritual.
Morris, H.: MS: Orchestra for eleven instruments.

Five Negro Spirituals.
Benjamin, Arthur, and Primose, W.: C. Fischer.
Contents: I'm Travelin' to the Grave; March On; Gwine to Ride up in the Chariot; I'll Hear the Trumpet Sound; Rise, Mourners.

From a Negro Melody.
Stringfield, L.: MS: Chamber orchestra.

"Go Down, Moses."
Gould, M.: Mills Music: String Orchestra.

"Gwine To Ride Up In The Chariot."
In: *Five Negro Spirituals*. Benjamin, A.: C. Fischer: Chamber group, violin, piano, or cello.

"I'll Hear The Trumpet Sound."
In: *Five Negro Spirituals*. Benjamin, A.: C. Fischer: Violin, cello or piano.

"I'm Travelin' to the Grave."
In: *Five Negro Spirituals*. Benjamin, A.: C. Fischer: Violin, cello or piano.

"March On."
In: *Five Negro Spirituals*. Benjamin, A.: C. Fischer: Violin, piano or cello.

"Nobody Knows the Trouble I've Seen."
Gould, M.: Mills Music: String Orchestra.

"Rise, Mourners."
In: *Five Negro Spirituals*. Benjamin, A.: C. Fischer: Violin, cello or piano.

Scherzo. From Afro-American Symphony reduced for small orchestra. Still, Wm. Grant: J. Fischer and Bro.

"Sometimes I Feel Like A Motherless Child."
Gould, M.: Mills Music: String Orchestra.

"Swing Low, Sweet Chariot."
Gould, M.: Mills Music: String Orchestra.

—————: *Orchestra*

Afro-American Symphony.
Still, William S.: J. Fischer.

American Symphony (Based on American Folk Music: Indian, English-American Negro.)
Shure, Deane R.: J. Fischer and Bro.

A Negro Parade (Based on Negro Folk Music).
Stringfield, Lamar: J. Fischer and Bro.

A Negro Rhapsody.
Goldmark, Rubin: Universal.

Appalachia. Variationen uber ein altes sklavenlied mit schlusschor für grosses orchester.
Delius, Frederick: Berlin, Harmonie, 1906.
Variations on a spiritual for orchestra and chorus.

Bandana Sketches. Four Negro Spirituals, Opus 12. White, Clarence C.: C. Fischer.

"Bear the Burden."
White, C. C.: C. Fischer.

Comedy Overture on Negro Themes.
Gilbert, Henry, F. B.: Gray.

Concert Paraphrases of Traditional Negro Melodies. White, C. C.: C. Fischer.

Darker America.
Still, Wm. Grant: Birchard.

"Dum-A-Lum." Variations on a Negro Spiritual.
Morris, H.: MS: Chamber orchestra.

Fantasy on American Folk Tune.
Stringham, E. J.: MS: violin, orchestra.

From the Cotton Fields, Op. 18,
White, C. C.: C. Fischer.

"I'm Going Home."
White, C. C.: C. Fischer.

"I'm Troubled in Mind."
In: Bandana Sketches. White, C. C.: C. Fischer.

"Listen to the Lambs."
Dett, R. N.: MS: Fantasia for Violin and Orchestra.

"Many Thousand Gone."
In: Bandana Sketches. White, C. C.: C. Fischer.

Negro Folk Symphony, No. 1.
Dawson, William Levi: MS: orchestra.

Negro Rhapsody.
Gilbert, Henry, F. B.: Gray.

"Nobody Knows de Trouble I've Seen."
In: Bandana Sketches. White, C. C.: C. Fischer.

Orchestral Variations on "Deep River" and "Water Boy." Herrmann, Bernard: MS.

Overture on Negro Themes.
Dunn, James P.: J. Fischer.

Pages from Negro History.
Still, W. G.: C. Fischer: School orchestra.

Plain-Chant for America.
Still, W. G.: J. Fischer: Baritone, orchestra, organ.

Port Royal, 1861.
McKay, George F.: MS: String orchestra. Suite on Negro Folksongs.

Rhapsodie Négre.
Powell, John: Schirmer: Piano and orch.

"Sheep and Goat Walkin' to the Pasture."
Guion, D.: Schirmer.

"Sometimes I Feel Like A Motherless Child."
(Negro Dance). *In:* Bandana Sketches. White, C. C.: C. Fischer.

Spirituals.
Gould, Morton: Mills: Orchestra.

Symphonic Rhapsody.
Kramer, A. Walter: C. Fischer: Orchestra and violin.

"There's a Great Day Comin'."—Variations.
McKay, George F.: MS: orchestra.

"Wilderness Road."
Siegmeister, E.: Leeds: Orchestra.

—————: *Band*

Bandana Sketches. Four Negro Spirituals, Op. 12.
White, Clarence C.: C. Fischer.

"Cabin Songs."
White-Lake: C. Fischer.

"Swing Low, Sweet Chariot."
Bennett: Gamble Hinged: 4B flat clarinets.

"Wilderness Road."
Siegmeister, E.: Leeds: Band.

—————: *Oratorio*

The Ordering of Moses.
Dett, R. Nathaniel: J. Fischer and Bro. Based on Scripture and Negro folklore.

RECORDS
Album Collections

American Spirituals.
Kenneth Spencer, vocal-piano. 4–10".
SO–MS 478

Bible Tales.
Golden Gate Quartet. VP 61

Spirituals Transcribed for Chamber Orchestra— by Adolf Busch. Busch Chamber Players.
CO–MM 764

Deep River Boys.
Spirituals and Jubilees. PI–118

Folk Songs.
Josh White, vocal-guitar. 3–10". ASCH 358

Golden Gate Spirituals.
Golden Gate Quartet. 4–10". CO–145
Contents: "I will be home again," "Jezebel," "Blind Barnabus," "Joshua Fit," "Wade in the Water," "Swing Low," "No Restricted Signs," "God's Gonna Cut You Down."

Gospel Songs.
Sister Rosetta Tharpe. 4–10". DE–A 527

Jubilee Spirituals.
Bibletone Jubileers. 3–10". BI–SP
Contents: Run On, Travelin', Shoes, Gospel Train, Ezekiel Saw the Wheel, Old Ship of Zion, Didn't It Rain.

Negro Religious Songs and Services.
Edited by B. A. Botkin. *In: Album 10,* Nos. AAFS46, 47, 48, 49, 50. Library of Congress.

Negro Spirituals.
Dorothy Maynor, soprano-male choir. VM–879
Contents: I Couldn't Hear Nobody Pray; Were You There?; Nobody Knows the Trouble I've Seen; In Dat Great Gittin' Up Morning; Rise Up, Shepherd, an' Foller; Old-Time Religion; Steal Away to Jesus; Go Tell It On De Mountain.

Negro Spirituals.
Jane Pickens, Soprano-piano. CO–35580

Negro Spirituals.
Paul Robeson, bass and piano. 4–10".
CO -MM 610

"Quartet in G Minor" (on Negro Themes by Daniel Gregory Mason, op. 19). Coolidge String Quartet. VM–894

Songs and Spirituals.
Marian Anderson, contralto-piano. 4–10".
VM–986
Contains, besides art songs, the spirituals: "My Soul's Been Anchored in the Lord"; "Hard Trials"; and "Dere's No Hiddin' Place Down Dere."

Spirituals.
Camp Meetin' Choir with Deacon Tom Foger and Sister Bernice Dobson. 3–10". DI–D4
Contents: Anyhow, I'm Gonna Walk Right On, If I Can Just Make It, Working on the Building, Lord Search My Heart, Don't Wonder About Him.

Spirituals. Deep South Songs.
Thrasher Wonders and Two Gospel Keys. 3–10" DISC–658

Three Spirituals.
Hall Johnson Chorus. VI–36020

Tuskegee Institute Choir.
William Dawson, Director. COSMO–2001

U. S. Library of Congress. Division of Music. Folklore Section
Collection of Negro Religious Songs, Sermons, etc. Hampton Institute Duplicating Project. 100 Records. AAFS–LC

——————.
Folk Religion of the Negro. John Faulk, Rosenwald Fellow. 132 Records (1942).
AAFS–LC

United States (Negro).
In the Archive of the Library of Congress, Music Division (See List, issued 1948).

United States (Negro-Spirituals).
Collection of Mr. Edward P. Jennings, New York City.

United States (Negro).
East of Mississippi and below Washington, D. C. Lawrence Gellert, New York City.

United States (Negro-Spirituals).
In: American Museum of Natural History, New York.

United States (Negro-St. Helena, South Carolina). In: University of North Carolina, Chapel Hill, North Carolina.

United States (Negro, Sea Islands—Georgia and South Carolina). Mrs. Maxfield Parrish, Windsor, Vermont.

United States (Negro, Sea Islands—South Carolina and Georgia). In: Fisk University, Nashville, Tenn.

Wings Over Jordan—Eight Negro Spirituals.
Wings Over Jordan Choir, Worth Kramer, Conductor. Rev. Glenn T. Settle, Narrator.
VM–499

Individual Titles

"Ain't No Grave Can Hold My Body Down."
Sung by Bozie Sturdivant at Silent Grove Baptist Church, Clarksdale, Miss., 1942. In: *Album 10,* No. AAFS47A, Library of Congress.

"All God's Chillun Got Shoes."
The Charioteers. CO–8468

"Amazing Grace."
Rev. Nathan Smith and his Burning Bush Congregation. DE–7494

"Anyhow."
Golden Gate Quartet. OK–6238

"Arise and Shine."
Lonnie McIntorsh, vocal. VI–21411–A

"At the Gate of Heaven."
In: *Folk Songs of the Americas.* Vocal and instrumental accompaniment. VP–55

"Babylon Is Falling Down."
Rev. F. W. McGee, sermon and congregation.
VI–21090–B

"Battle of Jericho."
In: Album—*Yale Glee Club*—Set C–79.
CO–36464

"Black Diamond Express to Hell."
Rev. A. Nix and Congregation. (Negro Sermon.) ME–M12545

"Black Sheep, Where You Left You' Lamb."
Kenneth Spencer, vocal-piano. SO–MS478–8

"Blind Old Barnabus."
Thrasher Wonders. DISC–163

"Bones, Bones, Bones."
Golden Gate Quartet. CO–36937

"Bye and Bye."
Hall Johnson Choir. VI–4460

"Can't Help from Crying Sometimes."
Joshua White, vocal-guitar. PE–0285

"Can't No Grave Hold My Body Down."
Two Gospel Keys. AP–137

"Certainly Lord."
Sung by Dock Reed and Vera Hall at Livingston, Alabama, 1940. In: *Album 10,* No. AAFS47 B2, Library of Congress.

"Charity."
The Two Gospel Keys. DISC–152

"Choose Your Seat and Set Down."
Sung by Dock and Henry Reed, and Vera Hall, at Livingston, Ala., 1937. In: *Album 3,* No. AAFS11 A2, Recordings of American Folk Songs, Washington, D. C., 1943.

"City Called Heaven."
Marian Anderson, contralto. VI–8958

"City Called Heaven."
Camilla Williams, soprano, and piano.
VI–10–1425

"City Called Heaven."
Kenneth Spencer, vocal-piano. SO–MS478–5

"City Called Heaven."
Robert Weede, baritone with piano accompaniment. CO–17293–D

"Come On Ezekiel Let's Go 'Round the Wall."
Mitchell's Christian Singers.　　　VO–03016

"Couldn't Hear Nobody Pray."
Wings Over Jordan Choir.　　　VM–499–4

"Couldn't Hear Nobody Pray."
In: Album—*Yale Glee Club.*　　CO–36464

"Count Out the Angels."
Mitchell's Christian Singers.　　　VO–03016

"Deep River."
Add-A-Part: Virginia Duffey, pianist.
　　　　　　　　　　　　　　　CO–45101

"Deep River."
Frances Alda, Soprano, male quartette.
　　　　　　　　　　　　　　　VI–1268

"Deep River."
Marian Anderson, Contralto-piano.　VI–2032

"Deep River."
Behrend-Kelberine, piano duo.　　VI–1999

"Deep River" (arr. Burleigh-Jacchia).
Boston "Pops" Orchestra, Fiedler.　VI–4428

"Deep River."
In Album: *12 Favorite American Songs.* Nelson Eddy, baritone-piano.　　VM–C–27

"Deep River."
Flonzaley String Quartet.　　　VI–1276

"Deep River."
Gould String Orchestra.　　　DE–18204

"Deep River."
Kenneth Spencer, vocal-piano.　SO–MS478–3

"Deep River."
Vocal Ensemble.　　　　　　　PH–116–A

"Deep River."
Wings Over Jordan Choir.　　　VM–499–5

"De Ole Ark A-Moverin' Along."
In Album: *Favorite Negro Spirituals.* Hampton Institute Quartet.　　　　VMC–35

"Dere's A Man Goin' 'Roun' Takin' Names."
Paul Robeson, bass-piano.　　　VI–25809

"Der's No Hidin' Place."
Marian Anderson, contralto-piano.　VI–7552

"Didn't My Lord Deliver Daniel."
Paul Robeson, bass-piano.　　　VI–25809

"Do Lord Remember Me Good."
Golden Eagles Gospel Singers.　　DE–7313

"Do, Lord, Remember Me."
Sung with banjo by Jimmie Strothers and Joe Lee at State Farm, Virginia, 1936. In: *Album 10,* Record No. AAFS46 A1, Library of Congress.

"Don't Stay Away."
Wings Over Jordan Choir.　　　VM–499–3

"Do You Call That Religion."
Birmingham Jubilee Singers.　　CO–14163D

"Down on Me."
Sung by Dock Reed at Livingston, Alabama, 1940. In: *Album 10,* No. AAFS47 B1, Library of Congress.

"Dry Bones."
The Carolinians.　　　　　　　BB–7917–A

"Dry Bones."
Thrasher Wonders.　　　　　　Disc–5028

"Ev'ry Time I Feel De Spirit."
Marian Anderson, contralto-piano.　VI–2032

"Every Time I Feel De Spirit."
Fisk Jubilee Singers.　　　　　CO–562D

"Every Time I Feel De Spirit."
John Charles Thomas, baritone-orchestra.
　　　　　　　　　　　　　　　VI–2163

"Ezekiel Saw the Wheel."
Fisk Jubilee Singers.　　　　　CO–818D

"Ezekiel Saw De Wheel."
In Album: *Favorite Negro Spirituals.* Hampton Institute Quartet.　　　　VMC–35

"Famine In the Land."
Mitchell's Christian Singers.　　OK–06117

"Fire Down Yonder."
Heavenly Gospel Singers.　　　BB–7212–A

"From Jerusalem to Jericho."
Lulu Belle and Scotty.　　　　OK–05958

"Funeral Train."
Rev. J. M. Gates, Preacher and Congregation.
　　　　　　　BB–5111–B; VI–20217–B

"Getting Ready to Leave This World."
Chuck Wagon Gang.　　　　　OK–05782

"Glory."
Sonny Terry, Alek, Woody Guthrie, Cisco Houston.　　　　　　　　ASCH–432–2A

"God Don't Never Change."
Blind Willie Johnson, vocal-guitar.
　　　　　　　　　　　　　CO–149579–D

"Go Down Moses."
Add-a-part: Accompaniment for voice, Virginia Duffey, pianist.　　　　VI–45108

"Go Down Moses."
Hall Johnson Choir.　　　　　VI–4553

"Go Down Moses."
In Album: *Swing Low.* Hampton Institute Quartet; Charles Flax, baritone.　V–P78

"Go Down Moses."
Southern Male Quartet.　　　CO–8479

"Go Down Moses."
Kenneth Spencer, vocal-piano　SO–MS478–7

"Go Down Moses."
Tuskegee Quartet.　　　　　　VI–20518

"God's Gonna Separate the Wheat from the Chaff." Blind Joe Taggard, vocal-guitar.
ME–M12544

"Goin' to Ride Up In De Chariot."
Paul Robeson, Lawrence Brown.   VI–26251

"Goin' to Ride Up In De Chariot."
Kenneth Spencer, vocal-piano.   SO–MS–478–2

"Goin' to Shout All Over God's Heaven."
In Album: *Favorite Negro Spirituals*. Hampton Institute Quartet.   MC–35

"Go Tell It On De Mountain."
In: *Negro Spirituals*. Dorothy Maynor, piano-male choir.   VM–879

"Go Where I Send Thee."
Mitchell Christian Singers.   OK–06117

"Hand in the Test of Judgment."
Golden Gate Quartet.   BB–7376

"Handwriting On the Wall."
Sung by Dock and Henry Reed and Vera Hall, at Livingston, Ala., 1937. In: *Album 3*, No. AAFS11 A3, Recordings of American Folk Songs, Washington, D. C., 1943.

"Happy Am I."
Elder Lightfoot, Solomon Michaux.   VI–24607

"Hard Trials."
Marian Anderson, contralto-piano   VI–7552

"Hear De Lambs A-Cryin'."
Roland Hayes, tenor-piano.   CO–69812D

"Hear De Lam's A'Cryin'."
Kenneth Spencer, vocal-piano.   SO–MS478–2

"Heav'n, Heav'n."
Marian Anderson, contralto-piano.   RO–1765

"Heaven, Heaven."
Vocal Ensemble.   PH–116–A

"He Never Said A Mumblin' Word."
Golden Gate Quartet.   OK–6529

"Holy Babe—Parts I and II."
Sung by Keeley Pace, Aaron Brown, Joe Green, Matthew Johnson, and Paul Hayes at Cumins State Farm, Gould, Arkansas, 1942. In: *Album 10*, No. AAFS49 A and B. Library of Congress.

"Home In That Rock."
Birmingham Jubilee Singers.   CO–14163D

"Honor! Honor!"
Charles Holland, tenor-piano.   VI–4556

"House Done Built Without Hands."
Sung by Joe Lee at State Farm, Virginia, 1936. In: *Album 10*, No. AAFS46 A2. Library of Congress.

"How Long."
Lead Belly, voice, accompanied by Sonny Terry, harmonica.   ASCH–343

"How Much I Owe."
Lonnie McIntosh, vocal-guitar.   VI–21411–B

"I Am the True Vine."
Blind Gary, vocal-guitar.   PE–5–12–66

"I Can't Stay Away."
Marian Anderson, contralto-piano.   VI–1966

"I Can't Stay Here By Myself."
Hall Johnson Choir.   VI–4547

"I Couldn't Hear Nobody Pray."
Dixie Jubilee Singers.   BR–2773

"I Couldn't Hear Nobody Pray."
In: *Negro Spirituals*. Dorothy Maynor, soprano-male choir.   VM–879

"I Don't Feel No-ways Tired."
Marian Anderson, contralto-piano.   VI–1982

"I Got a Mule."
Hall Johnson Choir.   VI–4497

"I Heard the Preachin' of the Elders."
Birmingham Jubilee Singers.   CO–14345

"I Heard Zion Moan."
Golden Gate Quartet.   BB–7962

"I Know A City Called Heaven."
Hall Johnson Choir.   VI–4497

"I Know I Got Religion."
Rev. J. M. Gates, Preacher and Congregation.
BB–5111–A; VI–20217–A

"I Know Lord Laid His Hands On Me."
Marian Anderson, contralto-piano.   VI–1896

"I'll Be Rested."
Roosevelt Graves and Brother, vocal-guitar.
PE–6–11–74

"I'll See the Sign of Judgement."
Brother George and Singers.   OK–05261

"I Love Traveling."
The Two Gospel Keys.   DISC–153

"I'm In His Care."
The Charioteers.   CO–35741

"I'm In His Care."
Gospel Singers.   BB–7212–A

"In Bright Mansions Above."
In Album: *Favorite Negro Spirituals*. Hampton Institute Quartet.   Set MC–35

"In Dat Great Gittin' Up Morning."
In: *Negro Spirituals*. Dorothy Maynor, soprano-male choir.   UM–879

"In New Jerusalem."
Sung with harmonica by Turner Junior Johnson at Clarksdale, Miss., 1942. In: *Album 10*, No. AAFS50 B1. Library of Congress.

"I've Been 'Buked."
Heavenly Gospel Singers.   BB–18047–B

"I've Found a Hiding Place."
Chuck Wagon Gang.   OK–05782

"I Want To Be Ready."
In Album: *Favorite Negro Spirituals*. Hampton Institute Quartet. MC–35

"I Want To Go Home."
Roland Hayes, Tenor-piano. CO–17275D

"I Wish My Mother Was On That Train."
Blind Joe and Emma Taggard, vocal-guitar.
VO–1063–A

"Jerusalem."
Paul Robeson, bass-piano. VI–27348

"Jes' Gone 'Long."
In Album: *Favorite Negro Spirituals*. Hampton Institute Quartet. MC–35

"Jesus Goin' to Make Up My Dying Bed."
Mitchell's Christian Singers. CO–04357

"Jesus Gonna Make Up My Dying Bed."
Joshua White, vocal-guitar. PE–0258

"Jesus I Love You."
Thrasher Wonders. DISC–159

"Jesus Is a Holy Man."
Brother George and Sanctified Singers.
OK–05670

"Jesus Is A Rock In A Weary Land."
The Charioteers. CO–35787

"Jesus Is A Rock In a Weary Land."
Southern Male Quartet. CO–8479

"Jesus Is Everything To Me."
Mitchell's Christian Singers. OK–05995

"Jesus Is Gonna Shake My Righteous Hand."
Biddleville Quintette. CH–50035B

"Jesus Met the Woman at the Well."
Two Gospel Keys. AP–137

"Jesus Will Make It All Right."
Edward W. Claybourne, vocal-guitar.
VO–A1093

"Job."
Golden Gate Jubilee Quartet. BB–7376A

"Job."
In Album: *Bible Tales*, Set V–P61. Golden Gate Quartet. BB–7376

"John, the Revelator."
In Album: *Bible Tales*. Golden Gate Quartet.
VI–P61

"John, the Revelator."
Golden Gate Jubilee Quartet. BB–7631–A

"John Wrote the Revelation."
Heavenly Gospel Singers. BB–6708–A

"John Wrote the Revelations."
Gold Star Quartet. PE–6–12–51

"Jonah."
Thrasher Wonders. DISC–160

"Jonah."
Golden Gate Jubilee Quartet. BB–7154–A

"Jonah and the Whale."
In Album: *Bible Tales*. Golden Gate Quartet.
VI–P61

"Joshua Fit De Battle of Jericho."
Hall Johnson Choir. VI–4460

"Joshua Fit the Battle of Jericho."
Kenneth Spencer, vocal-piano. SO–MS478–6

"Joshua Fit De Battle of Jericho."
Eleanor Steele, soprano; Hall Clovis, tenor-piano. PD–561140

"Joshua Fit the Battle of Jericho."
Josh White, vocal-guitar. ASCH 358–1A

"Keep Inching Along."
In Album: *Swing Low*. Hampton Institute Quartet, Charles Flax, baritone. VI–P78

"Lay Down Late."
Paul Robeson, Lawrence Brown. VI–26251

"Lead Me To That Rock."
Mitchell's Christian Singers. OK–05948

"Lead Me to the Rock."
Sung by Wash Dennis and Charlie Sims, at State Penitentiary, Parchman, Miss., 1936. In: *Album 3*, No. AAFS12 A. Recordings of American Folk Songs, Washington, D. C., 1943.

"Let That Lie Alone."
Edward W. Claybourne, vocal-guitar. VO–1903

"Let Us Break Bread Together."
Marian Anderson, contralto-piano. VI–10–1040

"Lit'l Boy" (Christ in the Temple Before the Scribes). Roland Hayes, tenor-piano.
CO–17275D

"Little David."
Fisk Jubilee Singers. CO–818D

"Little David."
Eleanor Steele, soprano; Hall Clovis, tenor-piano. PD–561140

"Little David Play On Your Harp."
In Album: *Favorite Negro Spirituals*. Hampton Institute Quartet. VMC–35

"Little David, Play On Yo' Harp."
Kenneth Spencer, vocal-piano. SO–MS478–8

"Lonesome Valley."
In: *Folk Songs of the Americas*. Vocal and instrumental accompaniment. VI–P55

"Lord, I Can't Stay Away."
Marian Anderson, contralto. VI–8958

"Lord, I Can't Turn Back."
Mitchell's Christian Singers. OK–03024

"Lord, I Want to Die Easy."
Joshua White, vocal-guitar. PE–0285

"Mary an' Martha."
In Album: *Favorite Negro Spirituals.* Hampton Institute Quartet. VMC–35

"Meet Me In Jerusalem."
Sung with harmonica by Turner Junior Johnson at Clarksdale, Miss., 1942. In: *Album 10,* No. AAFS50 A1. Library of Congress.

"Moses Smote the Waters."
Golden Gate Quartet. CO–36937

"Motherless Child."
Golden Gate Quartet. BB–7463

"Motherless Child."
Joshua White, vocal-guitar. PE–0258

"Motherless Child."
Thrasher Wonders. DISC–154

"Motherless Children."
Josh White, vocal-guitar. ASCH–358–1B

"Motherless Children."
Joshua White, guitar; Wilson Myers, bass. MU–250

"My Father Is a Husband Man."
Joshua White, vocal-guitar. PE–0311

"My Lord Heard Jerusalem When She Moaned."
Heavenly Gospel Singers. BB–6708–B

"My Lord, I'm Trampin'."
Mitchell's Christian Singers. DE–04122

"My Lord is Writing."
Golden Gate Quartet. BB–7804

"My Lord, What A Morning."
In Album: *Swing Low.* Hampton Institute Quartet; Charles Flax, baritone. VI–P78

"My Poor Mother Died A-Shouting."
Mitchell's Christian Singers, male quartet, unaccompanied. CO–416M; DE–04720

"My Soul's Been Anchored in the Lord."
Marian Anderson, contralto-piano. VI–7552

"My Time Ain't Long."
Mitchell's Christian Singers. DE–04122

"New Dry Bones."
Heavenly Gospel Singers. BB–6057–A

"Noah."
Golden Gate Quartet. BB–7962

"Nobody Knows the Trouble I've Seen."
Add-a-part: Accompanied for voice, Virginia Duffey, pianist. VI–45108

"Nobody Knows the Trouble I've Seen."
Mildred Bailey, voice-piano. CO–35348

"Nobody Knows the Trouble I've Seen."
Boston "Pops" Orchestra, Fiedler. VI–4428

"Nobody Knows De Trouble I've Seen."
Hampton Institute Quartet. VI–27473

"Nobody Knows the Trouble I've Seen."
In: *Negro Spirituals.* Dorothy Maynor, soprano-male choir. VM–879

"Nobody Knows the Trouble I See."
Robert Merrill, baritone and orchestra. VI–10–1427

"Nobody Knows De Trouble I've Seen."
Vocal Ensemble. PH–116B

"No More."
Paul Robeson, bass-piano. VI–26289

"No Stranger Now."
Brother George and Sanctified Singers. OK–05670

"Oh, Death."
Pattan and Lee, vocal-guitar. VO–02904

"Oh, the Lamb of God, the Lord Done Sanctified Me." Sung by Joe Lee at State Farm, Virginia, 1936. In: *Album 10,* No. AAFS46 A3. Library of Congress.

"Oh, What A Beautiful City."
Marian Anderson, contralto-piano. VI–10–1040

"Oh, What a Beautiful City."
Camilla Williams, soprano-piano. VI–10–1425

"Old-Time Religion."
Vocal Ensemble. PH–116–B

"Ole-Time Religon."
In Album: *Favorite Negro Spirituals.* Hampton Institute Quartet. MC–35

"Old-Time Religion."
In: *Negro Spirituals.* Dorothy Maynor, soprano-male choir. VM–879

"Old-Time Religion."
Tuskegee Quartet. VI–20519

"O Lord, Don't 'Low Me to Beat 'Em" (Negro Holler). Sung by Willie Williams at State Penitentiary, Richmond, Va., 1936. In: Library of Congress, 1943. FM–2 B

"On Ma Journey."
Paul Robeson, baritone. VI–20013

"Plenty Good Room."
Roland Hayes, tenor-piano. CO–69812D

"Preacher and the Bear."
In Album: *Bible Tales.* Golden Gate Quartet. VI–P61

"Reign Massa Jesus."
In Album: *Favorite Negro Spirituals.* Hampton Institute Quartet. VMC–35

"Rise Up, Shepherd, an' Foller."
In: *Negro Spirituals.* Dorothy Maynor, soprano-male choir. VM–879

"River, Stay 'Way from My Door."
Paul Robeson, bass-piano. VI–22889

"Rock My Soul."
Golden Gate Quartet.   BB–7804

"Rock My Soul."
Mitchell's Christian Singers.   DE–04720

"Rock My Soul in the Bosom of Abraham."
Wings Over Jordan Choir.   VM–499–1

"Roll, Jordan Roll."
Dixie Jubilee Singers.   BR–2773

"Roll, Jordan, Roll."
Vocal Ensemble.   PH–116–B

" 'Round 'Bout de Mountain."
Roland Hayes, tenor-piano.   CO–17178D

"Run Li'l Chillun."
Hall Johnson Choir.   VI–4547

"Run, Old Jeremiah" (Negro Shout).
Sung by Joe Washington Brown, and Austin
Coleman at Jennings, Louisiana, 1934. In:
Album 3, No. AAFS12 B. Recordings of Amer-
ican Folk Songs, Washington, D. C., 1943.

"Samson."
In Album: Bible Tales. Golden Gate Quartet.
                                        VI–P61

"Shine Like A Star in the Morning."
Sung by Joe Lee at State Farm, Virginia, 1936.
In: Album 10, No. AAFS46 B2. Library of
Congress.

"Sometimes I Feel Like A Motherless Child."
Marian Anderson, contralto-piano.
                            RO–1765; VI–1982

"Sometimes I Feel Like A Motherless Child."
Paul Robeson, baritone.   VI–20013

"Sometimes I Feel Like a Motherless Child."
Sarah Vaughan, vocalist.   MU–525

"Sometimes I Feel Like a Motherless Child."
Wings Over Jordan Choir.   VM–499–2

"Standing By the Bedside."
Mitchell's Christian Singers, male quartet-
unaccompanied.   CO–416M

"Standin' in the Need of Prayer."
The Mullen Sisters with Tony Mottola and his
orchestra.   VI–P194

"Steal Away to Jesus."
Fisk Jubilee Singers.   CO–562D

"Steal Away."
Hampton Institute Quartet.   VI–27470

"Steal Away to Jesus."
In: Negro Spirituals. Dorothy Maynor, unacc.
male choir.   VM–879

"Steal Away."
Paul Robeson, baritone-piano.   VI–19742

"Steal Away to Jesus."
The Charioteers.   CO–35787 CO–8459

"Steal Away to Jesus."
Tuskegee Quartet.   VI–20519

"Steal Away."
Sung with harmonica by Turner Junior John-
son, at Clarksdale, Miss., 1942. In: Album 10,
No. AAFS50 B2. Library of Congress.

"Sweet Turtle Dove."
Wings Over Jordan Choir.   VM–499–8

"Swing Low" (Grand Old Spirituals).
Hampton Institute Quartet. BB–27470–27473

"Swing Low, Sweet Chariot."
Bing Crosby, vocal-orchestra.   DE–1819

"Swing Low, Sweet Chariot."
Eleanor Steele, soprano; Hall Clovis, tenor-
piano.   PD–561140

"Swing Low, Sweet Chariot."
"Fats" Waller, piano.   VI–27458

"Swing Low, Sweet Chariot."
In Album: Swing Low. Hampton Institute
Quartet, Charles Flax, baritone.   VP–78

"Swing Low, Sweet Chariot."
John Charles Thomas, baritone-orchestra.
                                        VI–2168

"Swing Low, Sweet Chariot."
Paul Robeson, bass-piano.   CO–B8973

"Swing Low, Sweet Chariot."
The Charioteers.   CO–8468

"Swing Low, Sweet Chariot."
Tommy Dorsey's Orchestra.   VI–36399

"Swing Low, Sweet Chariot."
Vocal Ensemble.   PH–116–A

"Take My Hand and Lead Me On."
Gospel Light Jubilee Singers.   BB–8049–B

"Take My Hand."
Mitchell's Christian Singers.   OK–06081

"Take Your Burden to the Lord."
Blind Willie Jackson and Brother, vocal-gui-
tars-harmonica-piano.   CR–3325

"Telephone to Glory."
Blind Willie Jackson and Brother, vocal-gui-
tars-harmonica-piano.   CR–3325

"That's Why Darkies Were Born."
Paul Robeson, bass-piano.   CO–B8973

"The Blind Ploughman."
Paul Robeson, voice-piano.   VI–27348

"The Blood-Strained Banders" (The Blood
Stained Bandits). Sung with 4-string banjo by
Jimmie Strothers at State Farms, Virginia,
1936. In: Album 3, No. AAFS12 A2. Record-
ings of American Folk Songs, Washington,
D. C., 1943.

"The Day is Past and Gone."
Biddleville Quintette.   CH–50035A

"The Gospel Train is Comin'."
Edward W. Claybourne, vocal-guitar. VO–1982

"The Lord's Supper."
Rev. Nathan Smith's Burning Bush Congregation, Negro Preacher and Congregation.
DE–7148

"The Man of Calvary" (Easter Day Service).
Spoken by Sin-Killer Griffin, with Congregational responses and singing, at Darrington State Farm, Sandy Point, Texas, 1934. In: *Album 10*, No. AAFS48 A. Library of Congress.

"The New Buryin' Ground."
Sung by Willie Williams and group at State Penitentiary, Richmond, Virginia, 1936. In: *Album 3*, No. AAFS11 B. Recordings of American Folk Songs, Washington, D. C., 1943.

"The Old Ark's A'Moverin'."
Wings Over Jordan Choir. VM–499–7

"There's A Man Goin 'Roun' Takin' Names."
Kenneth Spencer, vocal-piano. SO–MS478–6

"There's A Man Goin' Around Takin' Names."
Joshua White, vocal-guitar. PE–0264

"There's No Hiding Place Down There."
Lulu Belle and Scotty. OK–05958

"There's No Hiding Place Down There."
In Album: *Swing Low*. Hampton Institute Quartet, Charles Flax, baritone. PE–0311

"The Storm is Passing Over."
Blind Joe Taggard, vocal-guitar. ME–12544

"This Heart of Mine."
Joshua White, vocal-guitar. PE–0311

"This Old World Is In A Bad Condition."
Heavenly Gospel Singers. BB–7301–A

"This is the Way We Mourn."
Thrasher Wonders. DISC–5028

" 'Tis Me."
In Album: *Swing Low*. Hampton Institute Quartet, Charles Flax, baritone. VI–P78

"Tone the Bell."
Golden Eagles Gospel Singers. DE–7314

"Trampin'."
Marian Anderson, contralto-piano. VI–1896

"Travelin' Shoes."
Golden Gate Quartet. BB–7463

"Trouble About My Mother."
Patton and Lee, vocals-guitar. VO–02904

"Trouble So Hard."
Sung by Dock and Henry Reed and Vera Hall at Livingston, Alabama, 1937. In: *Album 3*, No. AAFS11 A1. Recordings of American Folk Songs, Washington, D. C., 1943.

"Trying to Get Ready."
Wings Over Jordan Choir. VM–499–5

"Twelve Gates to the City."
Blind Gary, vocal-guitar. PE–7–04–55

"Walk Together Chillun."
Hall Johnson Choir. VI–4460

"Want to Go to Heaven When I Die."
In Album: *Favorite Negro Spirituals*. Hampton Institute Quartet. VMC–35

"Wasn't That A Mighty Storm" (Service).
Sung by Sin-Killer Griffin and Congregation at Darrington State Farm, Sandy Point, Texas, 1934. In: *Album 10*, No. AAFS48 B. Library of Congress.

"We Are Almost Down to the Shore."
Sung with banjo by Jimmie Strothers at State Farm, Va., 1936. In: *Album 10*, No. AAFS46 B1. Library of Congress.

"Were You There."
Marian Anderson, contralto-piano. VI–1966

"Were You There."
Richard Crooks, tenor-orchestra. VI–11–8814

"Were You There."
Roland Hayes, tenor-piano. CO–69812D

"Were You There."
In: *Negro Spirituals*. Dorothy Maynor, soprano-male choir. VM–879

"Were You There."
Paul Robeson, baritone-piano. VI–19742

"Were You There."
Southern Male Quartet. CO–35718

"When Death Come Creepin' In Your Room."
Golden Eagles Gospel Singers. DE–7313

"When I Lay My Burden Down."
Sung with harmonica by Turner Junior Johnson at Clarksdale, Miss., 1942. In: *Album 10*, No. AAFS50 A2. Library of Congress.

"Where Are You Runnin' Sinner?"
Birmingham Jubilee Singers. CO–14163D

"Woke Up This Morning."
Roosevelt Graves and Brother, vocal-guitar.
PE–6–11–74

"Woven Spirituals."
Carl Sandburg, vocal-guitar. MU–209–B

"You Got to Cross that Lonesome Valley."
John Jacob Niles, tenor-dulcimer. VM–824–1

"Your Enemy Cannot Harm You."
Edward W. Claybourne, vocal. VO–1082

"You're Tired, Chile."
Roland Hayes, tenor-piano. CO–17275D

THE NEGRO — WORK SONGS, SOCIAL SONGS

THE NEGRO—WORK SONGS, SOCIAL SONGS

WORK SONGS

See: American Folksong and Ballad Collections, pp. 85-90, and pp. 118-20.

GENERAL STUDIES

Barrow, David C.
"A Georgia Corn-Shucking." *Century* 24:873–878, 1882 (New York). n.s. v. 2.

D., C. W.
"Contraband Singing." *Dwight's Journal of Music* 19:182, 1861, (Boston).

Engel, C.
"Views and Reviews"; Negro folk songs as sung by Lead Belly. *MQ* 23:388–395, 1937, (July).

Gilbert, A. K.
"Aunt Sukey's Apocalypse." *Literary Digest* 96:32, 1928, (March 31).

Kingsley, Walter
"Engimatic Folk Songs of the Southern Underworld." *Current Opinion* 67:165–166. 1919, (New York).

Lemmermann, K.
"Improvised Negro Songs." *New Republic* 13:214–215, 1917 (December 22).

Lomax, Alan
Reels and Work Songs. In: *75 Years of Freedom.* Commemoration of the 75th anniversary of the Proclamation of the 13th Amendment to the U. S. Washington, D. C.: Library of Congress, 1943. vi, 108 pp.

Lomax, John A.
"Sinful Songs of the Southern Negro." *MQ* 20:177–187, 1934 (April).

————, and Alan
Negro Folk Songs as Sung by Lead Belly. Musical notation by George Herzog. New York: Macmillan Company, 1936. 242 pp.

Niles, John J.
"Singing Soldiers." *Scribners Monthly* 80:662–670, 1926 (Dec.); 81:90–95, 1927 (Jan.).
Great deal of material on the songs of the Negro soldiers in World War I.

Odum, Howard W., and Johnson, Guy B.
Negro Workaday Songs. Chapel Hill: The University of North Carolina Press, 1928. London: H. Milford, Oxford University Press, 1926. 278 pp.

————.
"Negro Workaday Songs." *Scholastic* 32:20, 1938, March 5.

Ortíz Roderigo, Nestor R.
"El Negro Norteamericana y sus cantos de labor." *SRCS* 2 (7–8):552–560.

Seitz, D. C.
"Ballads of the Bad; colored chain gangs chansons." *Outlook* 143:478, 1926, (August 4).

Thomas, G.
"Some Texas Negro Work Songs." *TFSP* 5:154–180, 1921.

"Track-lining Chantey."
Atlantic Monthly 146:281, 1930 (August).
Words and music.

Wheeler, Mary
Steamboatin' Days; Folk Songs of the River Packet Era. Baton Rouge, La.: Louisiana State University Press, 1944. x, 121 pp., unaccompanied melodies.

COLLECTIONS

See: American Folksong and Ballad Collections, pp. 85-90, and pp. 118-20.

Gellert, Lawrence, and Adomian, Lan
Me and My Captain. New York: Hours Press, 1939. 255 Fifth Avenue.
Negro songs of protest,—contains 24 numbers, arranged for voice and piano.

Leiding, Harriette Kershaw
Street Cries of an Old Southern City. Charleston, North Carolina: The Daggett Printing Company, 1910.

Lomax, John A., and Alan
Negro Folk Songs as Sung by Lead Belly. New York: The Macmillan Company, 1936. xiv, 242 pp., music.

Odum, Howard W., and Johnson, Guy B.
Negro Workaday Songs. Chapel Hill: University of North Carolina Press, 1926. 278 pp., music.

Siegmeister, Elie, ed.
Work and Sing. Bennington, Vermont: William R. Scott, 1944. Music.
Arranged for four parts.

Wheeler, Mary, comp.
Roustabout Songs: A Collection of Ohio River Valley Songs, arranged by William J. Reddick. Voice and piano. New York: Remick Music Corporation, 1939.

Work, John W.
American Negro Songs and Spirituals. 230 Songs, Spirituals, Blues, Work Songs, Hollers, Jubilees and Social Songs. New York: Crown Publishers, 1940.

ARRANGEMENTS:

Individual Titles

————: *Voice and Piano*

"Hammer Song."
Brown, Lawrence: Associated.

"Water Boy."
Robinson, A.: Winthrop.

"Workin, Workin."
McGimsey, Robert: C. Fischer.

—————: *Female Voices*

"Ida Red."
Winstead, K.: Music Publishing Holding Corp.: SSA.

"Water Boy."
Robinson, A.: Boston Music Co.: SSAA.

—————: *Male Voices*

"Ballad of the Boll Weevil."
Loomis, E.: Birchard: TTBB.

"Chain Gang Song."
Howe, Mary: Schirmer: TTBB. With orchestral accompaniment.

"Check-a-Hank."
Repper, C.: Birchard: TTBB.

"Cotton-Pickin' Song."
Curtis-Burlin, N.: Schirmer: TTBB.

"Gwine to Alabamy."
Siegmeister, E.: C. Fischer: TTB, a cap.

"Levee Song."
In: *H. and M. Auditorium Series, No. 48.* Andersen, A. O.: Hall & McCreary: TBB.

"Water Boy."
Bornschein, F.: C. Fischer: Unison.

"Water Boy."
Osgood, H. O.: Ricordi: TTBB.

"Water Boy."
Pitcher, Gladys: Birchard: TTBB.

"Water Boy."
Robinson, A.: Boston Music Company: TTBB.

—————: *Mixed Voices*

"Chain Gang Song."
Howe, Mary: Schirmer: SATB with orchestra.

"Cotton-Picking Song."
Siegmeister, E.: C. Fischer: SATB.

"Music in the Mine."
Dett, R. N.: Schirmer: SATB.

"Water Boy."
Robinson, A.: G. Schirmer: SATB, Soprano Solo, a cap.

—————: *Orchestra*

"Can'tcha Line 'Em."
Still, W. G.: MS: orchestra.

RECORDS

Album Collections

Negro Sinful Songs.
Lead Belly, vocal-guitar. 5–10".   MU–41

Negro Work Songs and Calls.
Edited by B. A. Botkin. In: *Album 8:* Five Records: AAFS36, 37, 38, 39, 40. Library of Congress.

Songs by Lead Belly.
Lead Belly, vocal-guitar; Sonny Terry and harmonica. 3–10".   ASCH–A343

The Midnight Special and Old Southern Prison Songs. Lead Belly and Golden Gate Quartet. 3–10".   Set V–P50
Contents: Midnight Special; Ham an' Eggs; Grey Goose, Stewball; Pick A Bale of Cotton; Alabama Bound.

Work Songs of the U.S.A.
As sung by Lead Belly with his 12-string guitar. 3–10".   DISC–735

Individual Titles

"Ain't Goin' Down to the Well No Mo'."
Lead Belly, vocal-guitar.   MU–224

"Ain't No More Cane On This Brazos."
Sung by Ernest Williams and group at Central State Farm, Sugarland, Texas, 1933. In: *Album 3,* No. AAFS13 A. Recordings of American Folk Songs, Washington, D. C., 1943.

"Ain't You Glad."
Lead Belly, vocal-guitar; Sonny Terry, harmonica.   ASCH–343–2A

"Alabama Bound."
Lead Belly and Golden Gate Quartet. VI–27268

"Alabamy Bound."
Joe Daniels and His Hot Shots in Drumnasticks.   DE–1854

"Altoona Freight Wreck."
Red River Dave, Esmereldy, Dick Thomas, Frank Novak, and the Sourwood Mountain Boys.   MU–288

"Arwhoolie" (Cornfield Holler).
Sung by Thomas J. Marshall at Edwards, Miss., 1939. In: *Album 8,* No. AAFS37 A1. Library of Congress.

"Behind the Stone Wall."
Carter Family, vocal-guitar-autoharp.   PE–6–03–1

"Black Betty."
Lead Belly, vocal-guitar.   MU–224

"Chain Gang Boun'."
Joshua White and His Carolinians. CO–35559

"Charleston (S. C.) Street Cries."
Negro Fish, Flower and Vegetable Hucksters. 10".   SPS–1

"Come On, Boys, and Let's Go to Huntin'."
Sung by Henry Truvillion at Burkeville, Texas, 1940. In: *Album 8,* No. AAFS37 B2. Library of Congress.

"Cotton Picker's Congregation."
Ambros Orchestra.   DE–1526

"Cotton-Picking Song."
In: *Two Centuries of American Folk Songs.*
American Ballad Singers, Siegmeister. VI–P41

"Cryin' Who? Cryin' You!"
Joshua White and His Carolinians.   CO–35561

"Diamond Joe" (Holler).
Sung by Charlie Butler at State Penitentiary,
Parchman, Miss., 1937. In: *Album 4,* No.
AAFS16 A2. Recordings of American Folk
Songs, Washington, D. C., 1943.

"Every Mail Day."
Kenneth Spencer, vocal-piano.   SO–MS478–4

"Fannin' Street."
Lead Belly, vocal-guitar.   MU–225

"Frankie and Albert."
In: *American Negro Sinful Songs.* Set MC–31.
Huddie Ledbetter, acc. himself on guitar. 10″.
MC–223

"Gallows Song."
In: *Recital from "American Songbag."* Carl
Sandburg, vocal-guitar.   MC–11

"Go Down, Old Hannah."
Sung by James (Iron Head) Baker, Will
Crosby, R. D. Allen, and Mose (Clear Rock)
Platt at Central State Farm, Sugarland, Texas,
1933. In: *Album 8,* No. AAFS38 B. Library of
Congress.

"Go Down Old Hannah."
Lead Belly, vocal-guitar.   MU–224

"Goin' Home, Boys."
Joshua White, and His Carolinians.   CO–35560

"Green Corn."
Lead Belly, vocal-guitar.   MU–225

"Grey Goose."
Lead Belly and Golden Gate Quartet. VI–27267

"Grey Goose."
In: *Songs for Americans.* Earl Robinson with
guitar.   TI–Set 8

"Ham an' Eggs."
Lead Belly and Golden Gate Quartet. VI–27266

"Hammer, Ring."
Sung by Jesse Bradley and group at State
Penitentiary, Huntville, Texas, 1934. In: *Al-
bum 8,* No. AAFS39 A. Library of Congress.

"Hard Times."
Joshua White, guitar; Wilson Myers, bass.
MU–249

"Heaving the Lead Line."
Called by Sam Hazel at Greenville, Miss., 1939.
In: *Album 8,* No. AAFS36 B1. Library of
Congress.

"Howell's Railroad."
J. H. Howell, harmonica solo. Imitation of Railroad.   BL–7162–A

"I'm Going to Leland."
Sung by Frank Jordan and group at State
Penitentiary, Parchman, Miss., 1936. In: *Album 3,* No. AAFS14 A2. Recordings of American Folk Songs, Washington, D. C., 1943.

"I Wonder What's the Matter."
Sung by "Lightning" and group at Dorrington
State Farm, Sandy Point, Texas, 1934. In:
Album 8, No. AAFS39 B. Library of Congress.

"Jack O'Diamonds."
J. J. Niles, vocal-dulcimer.   VI–2051

"Jack O'Diamonds."
Vocal group.   PA–12373–A

"Jerry."
Josh White, vocal-guitar.   ASCH–358–3B

"Jerry" (Lord, Dis Timber Got to Roll).
Joshua White and His Carolinians. CO–35562

"Joe the Grinder" (Holler).
Sung by Irvin Lorory at Cumins State Farm,
Gould, Ark., 1939. In: *Album 4,* No. AAFS16
A3. Recordings of American Folk Songs,
Washington, D. C., 1943.

"Jumpin' Judy."
Sung by Allen Prothero at State Penitentiary,
Nashville, Tenn., 1933. In: *Album 3,* No.
AAFS14 B1. Recordings of American Folk
Songs, Washington, D. C., 1943.

"Jumpin' Judy."
Sung by Kelly Pace and group at Cumins State
Farm, Gould, Ark., 1934. In: *Album 3,* No.
AAFS13 B2. Recordings of American Folk
Songs, Washington, D. C., 1943.

"Long Hot Summer Days."
Sung by Clyde Hill and group at Clemens
State Farm, Brazoria, 1939. In: *Album 3,* No.
AAFS13 A2. Recordings of American Folk
Songs, Washington, D. C., 1943.

"Long John."
Sung by "Lightning" and group at Darrington
State Prison Farm, Sandy Point, Tex., 1934.
In: *Album 3,* No. AAFS13 B1. Recordings of
American Folk Songs, Washington, D. C., 1943.

"Look Down That Long, Lonesome Road."
Sung by group at State (Reid) Farm, Boykin,
S. C., 1934. In: *Album 3,* No. AAFS14 B2. Re-
cordings of American Folk Songs, Washington,
D. C., 1943.

"Looky, Looky Yonder."
Lead Belly, vocal-guitar.   MU–224

"Mealtime Call."
Called by Thomas J. Marshall at Edwards,
Miss., 1939. In: *Album 8,* No. AAFS37 A4.
Library of Congress.

"Mississippi Sounding Calls: I–II."
Called by Joe Shores at Greenville, N. C., 1939.
In: *Album 8,* No. AAFS36 B2 and 3. Library
of Congress.

"Monday, Tuesday, Wednesday."
Joshua White, guitar; Wilson Myers, bass.
MU–249

"New Prisoner's Song."
'Dock' Boggs, vocal-banjo.　　BR–133–B

"Nine Foot Shovel."
Joshua White and His Carolinians.　CO–35559

"Old Rattler."
Sung by Mose (Clear Rock) Platt and James (Iron Head) Baker at Central State Farm, Sugarland, Texas, 1934. In: *Album 8*, No. AAFS38 A. Library of Congress.

"On A Monday."
Lead Belly, vocal-guitar; Sonny Terry, harmonica.　　ASCH–343–3A

"Pick a Bale of Cotton."
Lead Belly, and Golden Gate Quartet.
VI–27268

"Poor Howard."
Lead Belly, vocal-guitar.　　MU–225

"Possum Was An Evil Thing."
Sung by Henry Truvillion at Burkeville, Texas, 1940. In: *Album 8*, No. AAFS37 B1. Library of Congress.

"Prison Bound."
Joshua White, guitar; Wilson Myers, bass.
MU–248

"Quittin' Time Songs: I–II."
Sung by Samuel Brooks at Edwards, Miss., 1939. In: *Album 8*, No. AAFS37 A2–3. Library of Congress.

"Roll 'Im On Down" (Bahaman Launching Song). Sung by David Pryor and group of Andros Island men at Nassau. In: *Album 8*, No. AAFS40 A. Library of Congress.

"Rosie."
Sung by Jeff Webb and group at State Penitentiary, Parchman, Miss., 1937. In: *Album 3*, No. AAFS14 A. Recordings of American Folk Songs, Washington, D. C., 1943.

"Rovin' Gambler."
In: *American Folk Songs Album*. Frank Luther, Zora Layman, Leonard Stokes, vocal-guitar-fiddle-bass.　　DE–25

"Stacker Lee."
Woody Guthrie, vocal-guitar.　ASCH–347

"Stewball."
Lead Belly and Golden Gate Quartet. VI–27267

"Sugar Baby."
'Dock' Boggs, vocal-banjo.　　BR–118A

"The Boll Weevil."
Lead Belly, vocal-guitar.　　MU–226

"The Boll Weevil Song."
Tony Kraber, vocal-guitar.　　KE–507A

"The Grey Goose."
Sung by James (Iron Head) Baker, and group at Central State Farm, Sugarland, Texas, 1934. In: *Album 3*, No. AAFS15 A. Recordings of American Folk Songs, Washington, D. C., 1943.

"The Rock Island Line."
Sung by Kelly Pace, Charlie Porter, L. T. Edwards, Willie Hubbard, Luther Williams, Napoleon Cooper, Albert Pate, and Willie Lee Jones, at Cumins State Farm, Gould, Arkansas, 1934. In: *Album 8*, No. AAFS40 A. Library of Congress.

"Told My Cap'n."
Joshua White and His Carolinians.　CO–35562

"Trouble."
Josh White, vocal-guitar.　　ASCH–358–3A

"Trouble."
Joshua White, and His Carolinians.　CO–35560

"Water Boy."
Nelson Eddy, baritone-orchestra.　CO–17329–D

"Water Boy."
Kenneth Spencer, vocal-piano.　SO–MS478–1

"Water Boy."
The Charioteers.　　CO–8459

"Water Boy."
Waller, organ.　　VI–27460

"Work All De Summer."
Paul Robeson, bass-piano.　　VI–25809

"Yellow Woman's Door Bell."
Lead Belly, vocal-guitar.　　MU–224

SOCIAL SONGS—LYRIC SONGS— THE DANCE

See: General Studies and Collections of American Folksongs, Ballads and Negro Folksongs. pp. 85-90; pp. 118-20; and pp. 450-52.

GENERAL STUDIES

Backus, E. M.
"Cradle Songs of Negroes in North Carolina." *JAFL* 7:310, 1895.

Bales, Mary Virginia
"Some Negro Folk Songs of Texas." *TFSP* 7: 85–113.

Barry, Phillips
"Negro Folk Songs from Maine." *FSSNE* 8: 13–16, 1934; 9:10–14, 1935; 10:21–24, 1935.
　In the last group are also included hymns and ballads.

Bass, Robert Duncan
"Negro Songs from Pedee Country." *JAFL* 44: 418–437, 1931.

Bergen, Mrs. F. D.
"On the Eastern Shore." *JAFL* 2:296–298, 1889.
　Two fragments, with a brief discussion of the Negroes of the eastern shore of Maryland.

Christensen, A. M. H.
"Spirituals and 'Shouts' of Southern Negroes."
JAFL 7:154–155, 1894.

Gordon, R. W.
"Lyrics Collected from the Folk-Songs of
Georgia Negroes." *Golden Book* 8:194–196,
Aug., 1928.

————, ed.
"Palmettos; Folk-Songs of Georgia Negroes."
Golden Book 9:76–77, May, 1929.

Guial, E. L.
"Among the Sable Singers." *The Western
Monthly* (Lakeside Monthly, Chicago) 2:421–
426, 1869.

Henry, Mellinger E.
"Negro Songs from Georgia." *JAFL* 44:437–
447, 1931.

Holzknecht, R. J.
"Some Negro Song Variants from Louisville."
JAFL 41:558, 1928.

Howe, M. A. D.
"Song of Charleston." *Atlantic Monthly* 146:
108–111, July 1930.

Johnson, Guy B.
Negro Folk Songs. In: *Culture in the South,*
(pp. 547–570). Chapel Hill: University of
North Carolina Press, 1935.
> Discussion of the various types of Negro songs
> found in the South.

Johnson, James Weldon
"Negro Folk Songs and Spirituals." *Mentor*
17:50–52, Feb. 1929.

Lemmermann, Karl
"Improvised Negro Songs." *New Republic* 13:
214–215, 1917.

Levinson, A.
"Negro Dance." *Theatre Arts Monthly* 11:282–
293, 1927. April.

Longini, Muriel Davis
"Folksongs of Chicago Negroes." *JAFL* 52:
96–111, 1939.

Niles, John J.
"Shout, Coon, Shout!" *MQ* 16:516–530, 1930.

Odum, Anna Kranz
"Negro Folk Songs from Tennessee." *JAFL* 27:
255–265, 1914.

Odum, Howard W.
"Folk Song and Folk Poetry as Found in the
Secular Songs of the Southern Negroes."
JAFL 24:255–294, 351–396, 1911.

————, and Johnson, Guy B.
The Negro and His Songs. Chapel Hill: The
University of North Carolina Press, 1925.
> Lengthy discussion of social and lyric songs.

Scarborough, Dorothy
On the Trail of Negro Folk-Songs. Cambridge,
Mass.: Harvard University Press, 1925.

Spaulding, H. G.
"Under the Palmetto." *Continental Monthly*
4:188–203, 1863 (New York).

White, Newman I.
American Negro Folk Songs. Cambridge,
Mass.: Harvard University Press, 1928. x, 501
pp., music, bibl.
> A number of chapters in this excellent study deal
> with social songs and dance.

————.
"The White Man in the Woodpile. Some Influ-
ences on Negro Secular Folk Songs." *AS* 4
(No. 3):207–215, 1929.

COLLECTIONS

Benedict, Helen Dymond
Belair Plantation Melodies. New Orleans, La.:
Helen D. Benedict, 1924. 17 pp.

Hobson, Anne
In Old Alabama. New York: Doubleday, Page
& Co., 1903. 237 pp.
> Ten dialect stories and songs.

Parrish, Lydia
Slave Songs of the Georgia Sea Islands. New
York: Creative Age Publishing Company, 1942.
Illus., music.

Scherpf, John C.
African Quadrilles, selected from the most admired Negro melodies and arranged for the
pianoforte by John C. Scherpf. Set. I. New
York: E. Riley, cop. 1844.

Williams, Charles A.
"Cotton Needs Pickin'," *Characteristic Negro
Folk Dances.* Norfolk, Virginia: Guide Publish-
ing Company, 1928.

Work, John, editor
American Negro Songs and Spirituals. 230
Songs— Spirituals, Blues, Work Songs, Hollers,
Jubilees and Social Songs. New York: Crown
Publishers, 1940.

ARRANGEMENTS:

Individual Titles

————: *Voice and Piano*

"Oh! Rock me, Julie."
Burleigh, H. T.: Ricordi.

"Shortnin' Bread."
Eckstein, M.: Carl Fischer.

"Shortnin' Bread."
Wolfe, Jacques: Flammer.

Simon Legree—A Negro Sermon. (Text Vachel
Lindsay). Alter, Martha: MS: For baritone,
two pianos.

————: *Piano*

"Short'nin' Bread."
Wolfe-Hopkins: Schirmer: 2 pianos, 4 hands.

"Plantation Dance."
Wright, N. L.: Schirmer.

————: *Female Voices*

"Short'nin' Bread."
Wilson, H. R.: Hall & McCreary: SSAA.

————: *Mixed Voices*

"All the Pretty Little Horses."
Binder, A. W.: Elkan-Vogel: SATB.
Lullaby.

————: *Orchestra*

A Deserted Plantation Suite.
Still, William G.: Robbins.

American Jubilee Overture.
Wagner, Joseph F.: MS.

A Negro Parade—Symphonic Patrol.
Stringfield, L.: J. Fischer.

Charleston Rhapsody.
Bennett, Robert R.: MS (1926) for orchestra.

Chorale and Fugue in Jazz.
Gould, Morton: C. Fischer.

Comedy Overture on Negro Themes.
Gilbert, Henry F. B.: Gray.

Concerto in F.
Gershwin, George: Harms: Piano and orchestra.

Creation.
Gruenberg, Louis: Universal: baritone, and 8 instruments.

Daniel Jazz.
Gruenberg, Louis: Universal: tenor, and 8 instruments.

Jazz Poem.
Thompson, Randall: C. Fischer: Piano, orchestra.

Jazz-Suite.
Gruenberg, Louis: Cos. Cob: Orchestra.

Jazz Symphony.
Antheil, George: Manuscript, 1925.

Jazzettes.
Gruenberg, Louis: MS: string orchestra.

"Juba Dance" (from *In the Bottoms.*)
Dett, R. N.: Summy: orchestra.

Kaintuck.
Still, W. G.: MS: Piano, orchestra.

"Negro Episode" (from *Two Episodes for Orchestra.*) Gilbert, Henry F. B.: Gray: Orchestra.

Negro Rhapsody.
Gilbert, Henry F. B.: Gray.

Negro Rhapsody.
Goldmark, Rubin; Associated.

Negro Rhapsody.
Stokowski, Leopold: MS.

Plantation Overture.
Weaver, Paul: MS.

Second Rhapsody.
Gershwin, G.: New World: Piano and orchestra.

The Black Man Dances—Suite.
Still, W. G.: MS.

New Orleans Mardi Gras. Overture. (Based on Negro dance tunes). Wilson, Mortimer: New York: Schirmer.

————: *Stage Work*

A Southern Interlude.
Still, W. G.: MS: opera, 2 acts.

Emperor Jones.
Gruenberg, Louis: Cos Cob: opera.

Lenox Avenue—ballet.
Still, W. G.: J. Fischer: Stage Work, chorus, orchestra, ballet, soloists.

Porgy and Bess.
Gershwin, George: Birchard: folk opera.

RECORDS

See: Negro Record Songs Albums and Individual Titles, pp. 475-82, 485-87, 499-520.

Individual Titles

"Shortenin' Bread."
Andrews Sisters, vocal trio.　　DE–1744

"Shor'nin Bread."
Conrad Thibault, baritone-orchestra. VI–24404

"Shortenin' Bread."
Clayton McMichen, fiddlin' solo.　　DE–2647

"The Gallis Pole."
In: *American Negro Sinful Songs.* Set MC–31.
Huddie Ledbetter, vocal-guitar.　　MC–227

CHILDREN'S RHYMES AND GAMES
GENERAL STUDIES

Backus, E. M.
"Cradle Songs of Negroes in North Carolina."
JAFL 7:310, 1895.

Clarke, Mary Olmstead
"Song Games of Negro Children in Virginia."
JAFL 3:288–290, 1890.

Darby, Loraine
"Ring Games from Georgia." *JAFL* 30:218–221, 1917.

Krehbiel, Henry Edward
"Southern Song Games." *New York Tribune:*
1902, July 27, and August 4.

Perkins, A. E.
"Riddles from Negro Children in New Orleans." *JAFL* 35:105–115, 1922.

Perrow, E. C.
"Rhymes from the South." *JAFL* 25:137–155, 1912; 26:123–173, 1913; 28:129–203, 1915.

Talley, Thomas W.
Negro Folk Rhymes, Wise and Otherwise. New York: The Macmillan Company, 1922.
Contains eleven tunes.

Whiting, H. A. J.
Negro Art, Music and Rhyme for Young Folks. Washington, D. C.: The Associated Publishers, 1938.

COLLECTIONS

Porter, Grace Cleveland
Negro Folk Singing Games and Folk Games of the Habitants. Traditional melodies and text transcribed by Grace Cleveland Porter. Accompaniments by Harvey Worthington Loomis. London: J. Currier & Sons, Ltd., 1914.

Trent-Johns, Altona
Play Songs of the Deep South. Illustrated by James A. Porter. Washington, D. C.: The Associated Publishers, Inc., 1945. 33 pp.
Words and music (piano) of singing games played by Negro children in the South.

Whiting, H. A. J.
Negro Art, Music and Rhyme for Young Folks. Washington, D. C.: The Associated Publishers, 1938.

RECORDS

Album Collections

Negro Children's Games.
1. "All Hid?" Sung by Hettie Godfrey at Livingston, Ala., 1940; 2. "Little Girl, Little Girl"; 3. "Pullin' the Skiff." Led by Ora Dell Graham at Drew, Miss., 1940; 4. "Old Uncle Rabbit"; 5. "Sea Lion Woman." Sung by Katherine and Christine Shipp at Byhalia, Miss., 1939; 6. "Ain't Gonna Ring No More." Sung by group at Kirby Industrial School, Atmore, Ala., 1934; 7. "Shortenin' Bread." Led by Ora Dell Graham at Drew, Miss., 1940. In: *Album 4*, No. AAFS20 A. Library of Congress, Music Division, 1943.

Negro Lullabies and Ring Games.
1. "Poor Little Johnny"; 2. "Go to Sleep." Sung by Harriet McClintock at Livingston, Ala., 1940; 3. "Rosie." Sung by Mr. and Mrs. Joe McDonald at Livingston, Ala., 1939; 4. "Gon' Knock John Booker to the Low Ground"; 5. "Run, Nigger, Run." Sung by Moses (Clear Rock) Platt at Central State Farm, Sugarland, Tex., 1933. In: *Album 4*, No. AAFS20 B. Library of Congress, 1943.

United States, Negro (Religious and Game Songs). Collection of Late Dorothy Scarborough, Columbia University, New York City.

Individual Titles

"All Around the Maypole."
Sung by Eva Grace Boone and group at Brandon, Miss., 1939. In: *Album 9*, No. AAFS45 A4. Library of Congress.

"Bimini Gal."
Sung and played by Nassau String Band at Nassau, Bahamas, 1935. In: *Album 5*, No. AAFS21 B3. Library of Congress, 1943.

"Don't Lie Buddy" (Answer Back Song).
Josh White, Lead Belly, vocal-guitars.
ASCH–432–3A

"Fox Chase."
Played in the harmonica by Sanders Terry of Durham, N. C. In: *Album 4*, No. AAFS19 B. Library of Congress, 1943.

"Gwan Roun', Rabbit."
Sung by Anne Williams and group of Dundee, Miss., 1942. In: *Album 9*, No. AAFS45 B3. Library of Congress.

"Hallie Rock" (Jumping Dance).
Sung with drum by group at Nassau, Bahamas, 1935. In: *Album 5*, No. AAFS21 B2. Library of Congress, 1943.

"I Don't Mind the Weather."
Sung by Jim Henry at State Penitentiary, Parchman, Miss., 1937. In: *Album 4*, No. AAFS16 A1. Recordings of American Folk Songs, Washington, D. C., 1943.

"Little Rosa Lee."
Sung by Eva Grace Boone and group at Brandon, Miss., 1937. In: *Album 9*, No. AAFS45 B2. Library of Congress.

"Little Sally Walker."
Sung by Eva Grace Boone and group at Brandon, Miss., 1939. In: *Album 9*, No. AAFS45 A2. Library of Congress.

"Lost John."
Played on the harmonica by Sanders Terry of Durham, N. C. Recorded in New York in 1938 by Alan and Bess Lomax. In: *Album 4*, No. AAFS19 A. Washington, D. C., 1943.

"Old Lady Sittin' in the Dining Room."
Sung by Eva Grace Boone and group at Brandon, Miss., 1939. In: *Album 9*, No. AAFS45 A2. Library of Congress.

"Riddle Song."
Josh White, vocal-guitar. KE–8138

"Sail, Gal" (Ring Game).
Led by Elizabeth Austin at Old Bight, Cat Island, Bahamas, 1935. In: *Album 5*, No. AAFS21 B1. Library of Congress, 1943.

"Satisfied."
Sung by Anne Williams and group of Dundee, Miss., 1942. In: *Album 9*, No. AAFS45 B4. Library of Congress.

"Sissy in the Barn."
Sung by Eva Grace Boone and group at Brandon, Miss., 1937. In: *Album 9*, No. AAFS45 B1. Library of Congress.

"We're Goin' Around the Mountains."
Sung by Eva Grace Boone and group at Brandon, Miss., 1937. In: *Album 9*, No. AAFS45 A1. Library of Congress.

THE NEGRO — BLUES

THE NEGRO — BLUES

BLUES and JAZZ
(A Selection)
BIBLIOGRAPHY

Ganfield, Jane
Books and Periodical Articles on Jazz in America from 1926–1932. Bibliography. School of Library Service, Columbia University, June 6, 1933. (mimeo.)

Handy, W. C.
Bibliography. In: *Father of the Blues,* pp. 305–308. New York: The Macmillan Company, 1941.

PERIODICALS, SERIALS

Jazz Information.
V. 1, 1939. Weekly. New York.

Jazz Magazine.
V. 1, 1942. Forest Hills, N. Y. Edited by Robert Thiele and Dann Priest.

Melody; the Magazine of Words and Music.
V. 1, 1935—. New York: Engel-Van Wiseman, Inc.

Miller, Paul Eduard
Down Beat's Yearbook of Swing. Introduction by Fletcher Henderson. Chicago: Down Beat Publishing Co., 1939. 183 pp., illus., music., bibl. Published in 1943 under title: *Miller's Yearbook of Popular Music.*

Miller's Yearbook of Popular Music. Chicago: PEM Publications, 1943. viii, 195 pp.
Contents: Biographies—How to Listen to Hot Music—Record Valuations.

Esquire's ... Jazz Book. 1944. New York: A. S. Barnes & Company, etc., 1943. Editor: 1944. Paul Eduard Miller.
Contains valuable information on doings in jazz, music and musicians and discography.

Esquire's 1945 Jazz Book. Introduction by Arnold Gingrich. New York: A. S. Barnes & Company, 1945. xi, 256 pp.

Esquire's 1946 Jazz Book. New York: Smith and Durrell, 1946.

Swing, the Guide to Modern Music.
V. 1, 1938. Detroit: Cats Meow Publishing Company.

The Baton; setting the tempo of modern music. Monthly. V. 1, March, 1941. Detroit.

The Dominant. Orchestra Monthly.
V. 1, 1920. New York: Dominant Publishing Company.

GENERAL STUDIES

Adorno, T. W.
"On Popular Music." *Studies in Philosophy and Social Science* (N. Y.) 9:17–48, 1941.
Emphasis on psychological factors.

Andreu, Enrique
"Nos 'Spiritual Negro Songs' y su acción etnico-social." *Estudios Afrocubanos* 1:76–91, 1937.

"A Negro Explains Jazz."
Literary Digest 4:28–29, 1919.

Antrim, Doron Kemp, ed.
Paul Whiteman, Jimmy Dorsey, Rudy Vallee. Freddie Rich ... give their secrets of dance band success.... New York: Famous Stars Publishing Co., 1936. 87 pp., illus.

"Tin Pan Avenue." *Scribner's* 99:74–76, Feb., 1936.

Armstrong, Louis
Swing That Music, with an introduction by Rudy Vallee. Music section edited by Horace Gerlach, with special example of swing music contributed by Benny Goodman, Tommy Dorsey.... New York: Longmans, Green and Co., 1936. xii, 136 pp.

Arntzenius, L. M. G.
Amerikaansche Kunstindrukken. Amsterdam: A. de Lange, 1927. 190 pp., illus.
Among other musical matters the author also discusses Negro music and jazz.

Austin, Cecil
"Jazz."
Music and Letters (London) 6:256–268, 1925.
Includes music.

Baresel, Alfred
Das Jazz-Buch; Anleitung zum Spielen, Improvisieren und Komponieren moderner Tanzstücke mit besonderer Berücksichtigung des Klaviers.... Leipzig: J. H. Zimmermann, 1926. 34 pp., illus., music.
A guide to method and style of jazz composing.

Das Neue Jazzbuch; ein praktisches Handbuch für Musiker, Komponisten, Arrangeure, Tänzer und Freunde der Jazzmusik, mit 40 Notenbeispielen. Leipzig: W. Zimmermann, 1929. 98 pp., music.
A jazz handbook for musicians, composers, arrangers, dancers and friends of jazz music.

Beeler, B.
"New Light on Jazz." *Etude* 55:406, 1937 (June).

Bergman, L.
"Swinging the Classics." *New York Times Magazine:* January 14, 1940. p. 17, illus.

Bernhard, Paul
Jazz, eine Musikalische Zeitfrage. Mit noten-beigaben. München: Delphin-Verlag, 1927. 109 pp., music.

Berry, R. E.
"Home of the Blues, Beale St. Memphis." *N. Y. Times Magazine:* May 5, 1940. pp. 21.

"Bessie's Blues."
Time 30:38, 1937 (November 22).

Blesh, Rudy
Shining Trumpets. New York: Alfred A. Knopf, 1946. xvi, 365 pp. List of records (pp. 362-365).
A concise history of jazz from the early days to modern times.

———.
This is Jazz; a series of lectures at the San Francisco Museum of Art. San Francisco: Privately Printed, 1943. 36 pp.

Biddle, Mark
"Jazz in the School Music Program." *School Musician* (N. Y.), April 1942, pp. 10–11.

"Blight of Jazz and the Spirituals."
Literary Digest 105:20, 1930 (April 12).

"Blues!"
Etude 45:434, 1927 (June).

Bolgen, Kaare A.
"An Analysis of the Jazz Idiom." *Music Teachers Review* 11:3–9, 1941 (New York).

Bond, Frederick Weldon
The Negro and the Drama; the direct and indirect contribution which the American Negro has made to drama and the legitimate stage, with the underlying conditions responsible. Washington, D. C.: The Associated Publishers, 1940. x, 213 pp., bibl. (pp. 202–208).

Bragaglia, Anton Giuglio
Jazzband. Milano: Edizioni "Corbaccio," 1929. 291 pp., illus.

Brown, Sterling A.
"Blues, Ballads and Social Songs." In: *75 Years of Freedom.* Commemoration of the 75th Anniversary of the Proclamation of the 13th Amendment to the U. S. (pp. 17–25). Washington, D. C.: Library of Congress, 1943. vi, 108 pp.

———.
"The Blues as Folk Poetry." In: *Folk-Say,* edited by B. A. Botkin. Norman, Okla.: Oklahoma University Press, 1930.

Burley, Dan
Dan Burley's Original Handbook of Harlem Jive. Illustrations by Melvin Tapley. Foreword by Earl Conrad. New York: The Author, 1944. 157 pp., illus.
"Here is a true native son of the Negro-American language, or the Negro transformation of the English language. Here is the idiom transmitted and transfused, extracted and distilled, absorbed and reflected." The Foreword, pp. 3.

Cadman, B. M.
"Hot and Hybrid." *Etude* 57:374, 1939 (June).

Calloway, Cab
Cab Calloway's Cat-alogue. New York: Mills Artists, 1938.
About 150 'Harlemese' or 'jive' terms listed and defined, more than half relating directly to swing music.

Cesana, Otto, and Holloway, Marion
"Jazz is American, you snob—and vastly overrated." *Musical Digest* 30 (No. 2):12–14, 13–31, 1948.
Two opposing views presented.

Chatelain, Amy
"Une forme d'art moderne. 'The Jazz-music'." *Wissen und Leben. Neue Schweizer Rundschau. Nouvelle Revue Suisse.* Zurich. Vol. 20, No. 10, pp. 966–972, 1927.

Clarke, E.
"Where Does American Musical Composition Stand?" *Etude* 53:704, 1935 (December).

Coeuroy, André
Le Jazz. Paris: C. Aveline, 1926. 150 pp.

———.
Panorama de la Musique Contemporaine.... Paris: Kra, 1928. 230 pp.
Includes chapter on "Folksong and Jazz."

Condon, Eddie
We Called it Music. Narration by Thomas Sugrue. New York: Henry Holt and Co., 1947. 341 pp.
A story of the growth of jazz. Contains an excellent appendix, compiled by John Swingle, listing the Chicago bands and Eddie Condon on records.

Cons, C. L.
"Jargon of Jazz." *American Mercury* 38, supplement X, May 1936.

Copland, Aaron
"Jazz Structure and Influence." *Modern Music* 4:9–14, 1927.
Includes music.

Dexter, Dave
Jazz Cavalcade, the Inside Story of Jazz. With a foreword by Orson Welles. New York: Criterion, 1946. xi, 258 pp., bibl. (pp. 238–246).

Dickerson, Reed
"Hot Music." *Harpers* 172:567–575, 1936.

"Dissonance Turns Tragic."
Musician 47:10, 1942 (January).

Dodge, Roger Pryor
"Harpsichords and Jazz Trumpets." *Hound and Horn* (Camden, N. J.) 7:587–608, 1934.

Egg, Bernhard
Jazz-Fremdwörterbuch. Leipzig: W. Ehrler & Co., 1927. 47 pp.
A lexicon of jazz lingo.

Ellis, Norman
Instrumentation and Arranging for the Radio and Dance Orchestra. New York: Roell Publications, 1936. xxviii, 209 pp., music.

Engel, Carl
"Jazz: a Musical Discussion." *Atlantic Monthly* 130:182, 1922.

Ewen, David
Men of Popular Music. New York: Ziff-Davis Publishing Co., 1944. 213 pp., bibl., list of recordings.

Feather, L.
"Tempo di Jazz." *Musician* 46:113, 129, 144, 162, 1941. (June–October).

Ferguson, O.
"Man with the Blues in his Heart." *New Republic* 91:277–279, 1937 (July 14).

————.
"Young Man with a Horn." *New Republic* 87:354, 1936 (July 29).

Fleischmann, Hugo R.
"The first jazz opera and operetta." *Chesterian* (London) 9:152–155, 1928.

Frankenstein, Alfred V.
Syncopating Saxophones. Chicago: R. O. Ballou, 1925. 103 pp., illus.

Gardner, Carl E.
"Ragging and Jazzing." *Metronome* (N. Y.) 35 (No. 10):35, 1919.

Gilbert, Douglas
Lost Chords; the Diverting Story of American Popular Songs. Garden City: Doubleday, Doran & Co., 1942. xii, 377 pp.

Gilbert, Will G.
...*Jazzmuziek;* inleidung tot de Volksmuziek der Noord-Amerikaansche Negers. 's-Gravenhage: J. P. Kruseman, 1939. 116 pp., music.

Giles, R. Y.
"Jazz Comes of Age." *Scholastic* 27:7–8, 1935 (October 19). Illus.

Goffin, Robert
Au Frontières du Jazz. Préface de Pierre Mac-Orlan. Illustrée de 60 photographies. Paris: Editions du Sagittaire, 1932. 256 pp.

————.
Jazz, from the Congo to the Metropolitan; introduction by Arnold Gingrich. Garden City, N. Y.: Doubleday, Doran & Co., 1944. xii, 254 pp., bibl. (pp. 249–254).

————.
La Nouvelle-Orléans, Capitale du Jazz. New York: Editions de la Maison Française, 1946. 269 pp.

————.
"Where Jazz Was Born." *Pageant* (N. Y.), Feb. pp. 93–96, 1945.

Goldberg, Isaac
George Gershwin, a Study in American Music. New York: Simon & Schuster, 1931. 305 pp., illus., music.

————.
Tin Pan Alley; A Chronicle of the American Popular Music Racket. New York: The John Day Co., 1930. xi, 341 pp., illus., music.

Gombosi, Otto Johannes
"The Pedigree of the Blues." *MTNA*, Proc., ser. 40:382–389, 1946.

Goodman, Benny
"Jam Session." *Pictorial Review* 39:15, 1938 (May). Illus.

————, **and Kolodin, Irving**
The Kingdom of Swing. New York: Stackpole Sons, 1939. 265 pp.

Greene, Maude
"The Background of the Beale Street Blues." *TFSB* 7:1–10, 1941.

Hagin, B. H.
"Music." *Nation* 148:653–654, 1939 (June 3).

Handy, William C., ed.
Blues: An Anthology, with an introduction by Abbe Niles; illustratioins by Miguel Covarrubias. New York: A. & C. Boni, 1926. 180 pp., illus., music.

————.
Collection of Blues. Words and music complete.... New York: Robbins-Engel, Inc., 1925. 36 pp. Voice and piano.
    Contents: Aunt Hagar's Blues, Beale Street Blues, Darktown Reveille, Joe Turner Blues, Ole Miss Blues, St. Louis Blues, Sundown Blues, The Basement Blues, Yellow Dog Blues.

————.
Father of the Blues. New York: The Macmillan Company, 1941.
    (Bibliography of compositions, arrangements, books, 305–308.)

————.
"The Birth of the Blues." *Victor Record Review* (Camden, N. J.), Sept. 1941, pp. 12–14, 16.

————.
"The Heart of the Blues." *Etude* 58 (No. 3):152, 193, 211, 1940.

Harap, Louis
"The Case for Hot Jazz." *MQ* 27:47–61, 1941.

Hart, James D.
"Jazz Jargon." *AS* 7 (No. 4):241–254, 1932.

Harvey, H.
"It's Swing"—with glossary of swing terms, illustrated. *Delineator* 129:10–11, 1936 (November).

Hill, Edward Burlingame
"Jazz." *Harvard Graduates' Mag.* (Boston) 34:362–365, 1926.

Hobson, Wilder
American Jazz Music. New York: W. W. Norton Company, 1939. 230 pp., illus.
    Includes music ("Yellow Dog Blues," pp. 64, 67; "Thirty Records," pp. 177–217).

Hoerée, Arthur
"Le Jazz." *Revue Musicale* (Paris) 8:213–241, 1928.

——————.
"Le Jazz et Son Influence Sur La Musique d'Aujourd'hui." *Menestrel* (Paris) 91:361–363, 1929.

——————.
"Le Jazz et la Musique d'Aujourd'hui." *Cahiers de Belgique* (Bruxelles) 2:108–111, 1929.

Howe, Martin
Blue Jazz. Bristol: The Perpetua Press, 1934. 33 pp.

Hughes, L.
"Out of work; Love again Blues." *Poetry* 56: 20–21, 1940 (April).

"In Praise of Jazz."
Irish Monthly (Dublin) 62:133–143, 1934.

"Jazz Analyzed."
Commonweal 30:220–23, 1939 (April 28).

"Jazz Origin Again Discovered."
Music Trade Review (N. Y.) 68 (No. 24):32–33, 1919.

"Jazz Symphony."
Time 30:44–45, 1937 (December 20).

Johnson, Guy B.
"Double Meanings in the Popular Negro Blues." *Journal of Abnormal and Social Psychology*, April, 1927.

Johnson, James Weldon
Black Manhattan. New York: Alfred Knopf, 1930.
Includes discussion of blues, its origin and significance in Negro life and American culture (pp. 74–103).

Jones, Max
Balladeer for America. In: *Folk: Review of People's Music.* London: 1945. Part 1, pp. 27–32.
A discussion of Josh White, his singing and the songs.

Kallen, Horace Meyer
Swing as Surrealist Music. In: *Art and Freedom*, by H. M. Kallen, (pp. 831–834). New York: Duell, Sloan & Pearce, 1942.

Kaufman, H. L.
"From Ragtime to Swing"; Short History of Popular Music. *Scholastic* 32:29–30, 1938 (April 30).

Kempf, P., Jr.
"Striking the Blue Note in Music." *Musician* 34:29, 1929 (August).

Koebner, Franz Wolfgang
Jazz und Shimmy; Brevier der Neuesten Tänze. Berlin: Dr. Eysler & Co., 1921. 122 pp., illus.

Kolodin, Irving
"What About Swing." *Parents Magazine* 14: 18–19, 1939 (August). Illus.

Kool, Jaap
"The Triumph of the Jungle." *Littell's Living Age* 324:338–343, 1924.

Kristensen, Sven Moller
Jazzen og dens Problemer. København: Athenaeum, 1946. 120 pp., illus.

Lambert, Constant
"Jazz." *Life and Letters* (London) 1:124–131, 1928.

Lang, Iain
Background of the Blues. London: Worker's Music Association, Ltd., 1943. 55 pp.

Lange, Arthur
Arranging for the Modern Dance Orchestra. New York: Robbins Music Corp., 1927. x, 238 pp., music.

Lapham, Claude
Scoring for the Modern Band. London: I. Pitman & Sons, Ltd., 1937. xi, 164 pp., music.

Lastrucci, Carlo L.
"The Professional Dance Musician." *Journal of Musicology* 3:168–172, 1941.

Lee, George
Beale Street, Where the Blues Began; with foreword by W. C. Handy. New York: R. O. Ballou, 1934. 296 pp.

Levin, A. F.
"Swing Glories in its Humble Origin." *Musician* 44:66, 1939 (April).

——————.
"Swing Marches On." *Musician* 44:219, 1939 (December).

Levinson, Andre
"The Negro Dance Under European Eyes." *Theatre Arts Monthly* 11:282–293, 1927. Illus.

Little, Arthur W.
From Harlem to the Rhine. New York: Covici, Friede, 1936. (pp. 108–125).

Lloyd, Llewelyn C.
"Jazz and the Modern Spirit." *Monthly Musical Record* (London) 56:327–328, 1926.

Locke, Alain Le Roy
The Negro and His Music. Washington, D. C.: The Associates in Negro Folk Education, 1936. 142 pp.
References at end of each chapter, and "recorded illustrations."

Marks, Edward Bennet
They All Had Glamour, From the Swedish Nightingale to the Naked Lady. New York: J. Messner, 1944. xii, 448 pp., illus.

——————.
They All Sang, From Tony Pastor to Rudy Vallée, as told to Abbott J. Liebling. New York: The Viking Press, 1934. xi, 321 pp., illus., music.

Martin, D.
"Origin of Boogie-Woogie." *Etude* 59:445, 1941 (July).

Martin, John
"Inquiry Into Boogie Woogie." *N. Y. Times Magazine:* 18, 1944 (July 16).

Martinez Andrade, Roberto
"La musica de 'jazz' y 'swing'." *Haz; Revista Nacional del S.E.U.* (Madrid), Abril 1945, pp. 35–36, illus.

Mellers, W. H.
"Searchlight on Tin Pan Alley." *Scrutiny* (Cambridge) 8:390–405, 1940.

Mendl, Robert William S.
The Apeal of Jazz. London: P. Allan & Co., Ltd., 1927. vii, 186 pp., music.

Mezzrow, Milton "Mezz," and Wolfe, Bernard
Really the Blues. New York: Random House, 1946. 388 pp.
The authors "have given us a multi-sided book which is technically, psychologically, and historically interesting."

Mila, Massimo
"Jazz Hot." Pan (Milano), 1 Gennaio, pp. 84–96, 1935.

Milhaud, Darius
Études. Paris: C. Aveline, 1927. 100 pp.
Has a chapter: "L'évolution du jazz-band et de la musique des Nègres d'Amérique du Nord."

———.
"Jazz Band and Negro Music." *Living Age* 323: 169–173, 1924 (October 18).

Miller, Glenn
Glenn Miller's Method for Orchestral Arranging. New York: Mutual Music Society, 1943. 116 pp., music.

Mooser, R. Aloys
"Le Jazz et la Musique." *Dissonances* (Genève) 16 (No. 3–4):41–46, 1943.

Mosher, J.
"Swing Band is Born." *Collier's* 103:17, 1939 (May 20). Illus.

Mougin, Stéphane
"La Musique de Jazz." *Nouvelle Revue* (Paris) 113 (Ser. 4):288–296, 1931.

Moynahan, J. H. S.
"Ragtime to Swing." *Saturday Evening Post* 209:406, 1937 (February 13). Illus.

Nelson, Stanley Rupert
All About Jazz; with a foreword by Jack Hylton. London: Heath, Cranton, Ltd., 1934. 190 pp., illus.

Nicholas, E. J., and Werner, W. L.
"Hot Jazz Jargon." *Vanity Fair,* Nov. 1935.

Niles, Abbe
"Blue Notes." *New Republic* 45:292–293, 1926 (February 3).

Nye, R. B.
"Musician's Word List." *AS* 12:45–48, 1937. Swing dance terms.

"On Swinging Spirituals."
Current History 50:52, 1939 (July).

Osgood, Henry Osborne
"Jazz." *AS* 1 (No. 10):513–518, 1926.
Discussion of the origin of the word.

———.
So This Is Jazz. Boston: Little, Brown and Company, 1926. viii, 258 pp.

———.
"The Anatomy of Jazz." *American Mercury* 7 (No. 28), April, 1926.

Panassie, Hugues
Hot Jazz; the Guide to Swing Music. Translated by Lyle and Eleanor Dowling. New York: Witmark & Sons, 1936. xvi, 363 pp.
"Appendix: List of records" (pp. 297–356).

———.
La Musique de Jazz et le Swing. Paris: Corrêa, 1945. 172 pp.
Includes a record list, pp. 161–169.

———.
The Real Jazz: Translated from the French by Anne Sorelle Williams, and adapted for American publication by Charles Edward Smith. New York: Smith and Durrell, 1942. xiv, 326 pp.
List of records, pp. 237–326.

Patterson, Frank
"Jazz—The National Anthem?" *Musical Courier* 84 (No. 18):18, (No. 19):6, 1922.

Poldowski
"The Influence of Jazz." *Chesterian* (London) 9:10–12, 1927.

Ramsey, Frederick, Jr., and Smith, Charles Edward, eds.
Jazzmen. With 32 pages of illustrations. New York: Harcourt, Brace & Company, 1939. xv, 360 pp.

Redeker, Hans
"De Jazz Als Cultureel Symptoom." *Criterium* (Amsterdam), Nr. 3–4, pp. 105–116, 1946.

Rottweiler, Hektor
"Über Jazz." *Zeitschrift für Sozialforschung.* (Paris) 5:235–259, 1936.

Reynolds, Quentin
"Rhythm Man." Bob MacGimsey. *Colliers* 103: 22, 1939 (May 13). Illus.

Rosenthal, George S., ed.
Jazzways. New York: Greenberg: Publisher, 1947. 120 pp., illus.
A Collection of articles on various aspects of Jazz by leaders in this field. List of collector's items included.

Sargent, Norman and Tom
"Negro-American Music, or the Origin of Jazz." *Musical Times* (London) 72:653–655, 751–752, 847–848, 1931.

Sargent, Winthrop
Jazz: Hot and Hybrid. New York: Arrow Editions, 1939. 234 pp., illus., music.
> The author attempts a scientific analysis of its background and developments. Contains many musical illustrations and a good bibliography, (pp. 225–229).

Scarborough, Dorothy
"The Blues as Folksongs." *TFSP* 2:52–66, 1917.
> Also gives the music to one song.

Schonemann, A. C. E.
"Jazzing Up Our Musical Terms." *AS* 1 (No. 9):500–501, 1926.

Schwerké, Irving
King Jazz and David (Jazz et David, Rois). Twenty-seven studies on music and modern musicians, of which the studies on jazz and American composers are in French and English, the others in English.... Preface by Léon Vallas. Paris: Privately printed for the author, by Les Presses Modernes, 1927. x, 259 pp.

Secor, E. A.
"Just What Really is Swing Music?" *Etude* 58:240, 1940 (April).

Seiber, Mátyás
"Rhythmic Freedom in Jazz." *The Music Review* 6:89–94, 1945.

Seldes, Gilbert Vivian
The Seven Lively Arts. New York: Harper & Brothers, 1924. x, 398 pp., illus.

Smith, Charles Edward
"Swing." *New Republic* 94:39–41, 1938 (February 16).

—————.
"New Orleans Style, by C. E. Smith and William Russell." *Modern Music* 18:235–241, 1941.

"Soldier-Man Blues from Somewhere in France." *Literary Digest* 93:50–52, 1927 (June 18).

Spaeth, Sigmund
"Dixie, Harlem and Tin Pan Alley, Who Writes Negro Music and How?" *Scribner's* 99: 23–26, 1936 (January).

Specht, Paul L.
How They Become Name Bands; The Modern Technique of a Danceband Maestro. New York: Fine Arts Publications, 1941. 175 pp., illus.
> A chapter on—"Jazz Phantasy."

Spelberg, E. D.
"Jazz." *Smidse* (Arnhem) 3:264–272, 1927.

Spencer, Onah
"First Blue Disc Was Made by Mamie Smith." *Down Beat* (Chicago), June 15, p. 8, 1941. Illus.

"Spirituals to Swing."
Time 32:23, 1939 (June 2). Illus.

"Stale Bread's Sadness Gave Jazz to the World." *Literary Digest* 61 (No. 4):47–48, 1919.

"Swing is on its way, but up or down?" *Newsweek* 12:26, 1938 (July 25).

Taubman, H.
"Swing and Mozart Too." *N. Y. Times Magazine:* December 29, 1939. pp. 74, illus.

Taylor, Nicholas G.
"Jazz Music and Its Relation to African Music." *Musical Courier* 84 (No. 22) 7, 1922.

"The Language of the Jitterbug." *Better English* 2 (No. 5):51, 1938.

Thompson, Virgil
"Jazz." *American Mercury* 2:465–467, 1924.

—————.
"Swing Music." *Modern Music,* May–June, 1936, pp. 12–17.

Toledano, Ralph de
"Autobiography in Tone." *SRL* 31 (No. 5):47, 1948.
> The story of Ferdinand "Jelly Roll" Morton whose music is "accepted as a cornerstone in the structure of jazz. He carried within his mind and heart the lively rhythms of the New Orleans tenderloin, the poignant emotion of his people, the slow melancholy of the Bayou country and the metabolic patter of congo-square. In his piano style he could combine the rolling thump of the barrelhouse and delicacy of Creole quadrille, the solid syncopation of the African drum-beat and the shimmer of the *tangana*, the full-throated blues and the tinkle of ragtime."

—————.
Frontiers of Jazz; foreword by Milton Gabler. New York: O. Durrell, 1947. xiv, 178 pp.

"Tom-Tom Beat in Harlem."
M'walimu Festival chorus Revives the Negro's African Heritage. *Newsweek* 13:37, 1939 (April 3). Illus.

"To Replace Ragtime." *Literary Digest* 46:641, 1913 (March 22).

Ulanov, Barry
"Jazz of this quarter." *View* (N. Y.), Oct., 1944, pp. 97–99, illus.

Vallée, Rudy
Vagabond Dreams Come True. New York: E. P. Dutton & Co., 1930. xiii, 262 pp.

Van Vechten, Carl
"The Blues." *Vanity Fair* (Aug.) 1925; (March) 1926.

Webb, H. Brook
"The Slang of Jazz." *AS* 12 (No. 3):179–184, 1937.

Weirick, Paul
Dance Arranging; a guide to scoring music for the American dance orchestra. New York: Witmark Educational Publications, 1934. x, 142 pp., music.

"Where the Word 'Jazz' Started."
Music Trade Review 68 (No. 18) :50, 1919.

Whiteman, Paul
An Experiment in Modern Music. Aeolian Hall, New York, February 12, 1924. 12 pp., illus.
> Programme of a concert given by Paul Whiteman and his Palais Royal Orchestra, assisted by Zes Confrey and George Gershwin, with new compositions for the occasion by Victor Herbert and George Gershwin.

──────.
"New Concepts in Present Day Music." Edited by J. F. Cooke. *Etude* 57:227+, 1939 (April).

──────.
"This Thing Called Jazz." *Rotarian* 54:346, 1939 (June). Illus.

──────, and Lieber, Leslie
How To Be A Bandleader. New York: R. M. McBride & Company, 1941. 144 pp., illus.
"List of records," pp. 141–144.

──────, and McBride, Mary Margaret
Jazz. New York: J. H. Sears & Co., 1926. 298 pp., illus.

Wilson, E.
"Shanty-boy Ballads and Blues." *New Republic* 47:227–229, 1926 (July 14).

Witmark, Isidore
The Story of the House of Witmark: From Ragtime to Swingtime. New York: L. Furman, 1939. xvii, 480 pp., illus.

Woollcott, Alexander
The Story of Irving Berlin, with 16 illustrations, portrait by Neysa McMein. New York: G. P. Putnam's Sons, 1925. viii, 237 pp.

BLUES COMPOSITIONS
(A Selection)

See: General Collections of: American Folksongs, pp. 85-90; American Ballads, pp. 118-20; and Negro Folksongs, pp. 450-52.

Bacon, Ernst, and Luening, Otto
Coal Scuttle Blues. New York: Associated Music Publishers, 1944. 2 pianos.

Braham, Philip
Limehouse Blues. New York: 1924. Voice and piano.

Coppola, Piero
Deux Danses Symphoniques Pour Grand Orchestre. Paris: A. Ledue, 1930. 33 pp.

Decruck, Fernande
Complainte de Dinah, pour Saxophone, alto E^b, et piano. Paris: Les Editions de Paris, 1934. 238 pp.

──────.
Red in Blues, pour trompette B^b, et piano. Paris: Les Editions de Paris, 1934.

Elwell, Herbert
Blue Symphony. For Medium Voice and String Quartet. MS.

Garriguenc, R.
N. O. Rhapsody, for Saxaphone, E^b Alto, and Piano. Paris: Les Editions de Paris, 1934.

Gershwin, George
George Gershwin's Song-Book. Alajalov, illustrator. New York: Random House, 1932. xi, 167 pp.
Arranged for voice and piano.

──────.
George Gershwin's Song-Book; special piano arrangements edited and revised by Herman Wasserman. New York: Simon and Schuster, 1941. 126 pp.

──────.
Rhapsody in Blue. New York: Harms: For piano and orchestra.

Grofé, Ferde
Three Shades of Blue. Leonia, N. J., 1927.
Contents: Indigo, Alice Blue, Heliotrope.

Handy, William C.
Blues: An Anthology edited by W. C. Handy, with an Introduction by Abbe Niles. Illustrations by Covarrubias. New York: A. & C. Boni, 1926. 180 pp., illus., music.

──────.
Collection of Blues. Words and music complete. ... New York: Robbins-Engel, 1925. 36 pp.

Kern, Jerome David
"Left All Alone Blues," fox-trot from the musical play *The Night Boat.* Piano, violins (1 & 2), cello, bass, flute, clarinet, trombone, etc. New York: T. B. Harms Co., 1920. 11 parts.

La Rocca, D. J.
Barnyard Blues, jazz fox-trot for orchestra.... New York: L. Feist, 1917. 15 parts.

Moross, Jerome
Those Everlasting Blues. For Chamber Orchestra. MS.

Nancarrow, Conlon
Toccata for Piano and *Violin. Prelude and Blues* for *Piano.* Los Angeles, 1938. 12 pp. In: *New Music*, Vol. 11 (No. 2).

Price, Sammy
Five Boogie Woogie and *Blues Piano Solos....* Transcribed by Frank Paparelli. New York: Leeds Music Corp., 1943. 20 pp.

Tansman, Alexandre
Sonatine Transatlantique, en Trois Parties.... Fox-trot; Spiritual et Blues; Charleston.... Pour Piano Seul. Paris: A. Leduc, 1930. 12 pp.

Williams, Clarence
The "Boogie Woogie" Blues Folio; First "Boogie-Woogie" tunes of Clarence Williams, George Thomas, and Charles "Cow Cow" Davenport. With annotations by Clarence Williams. New York: C. Williams Publ. Co., 1940. 24 pp.
A collection for voice and piano.

Yaucey, Jim
Five Boogie Woogie and Blues Piano Solos....
New York: Leeds Music Corp., 1943. 24 pp.

RECORDS (BLUES)

Bibliography

Delaunay, Charles
Hot Discography. 1938 Edition, printed in France. New York: Commodore Record Company, Inc., 1943. 382 pp.
Exhaustive catalogue of "Hot Jazz" recordings.

Lomax, Alan
"List of American Folk Songs on Commercial Records." In: *Report of the Committee of the Conference on Inter-American Relations in the Field of Music.* William Berrien, Chairman. Department of State, Washington, D. C., September, 1940.
"A selected list of 320 records, classified and critically described, includes records of most styles of contemporary folk song—'hillbilly', 'Negro blues', 'yodeling', 'holiness'—and lots of more old-fashioned pieces." (Alan Lomax.)

Panassie, Hughes
"List of Records." In: *Hot Jazz:* The Guide to Swing Music. Translated by Lyle and Eleanor Dowling, (pp. 297–356). New York: Witmark & Sons, 1936. 363 pp.

Rosenthal, George S., ed.
"Bibliography: List of Collector's Items." In: *Jazzways.* New York: Greenberg: Publisher, 1947. 120 pp.

Sargent, Winthrop
"Bibliography of Jazz." In: *Jazz: Hot and Hybrid.* New York: Arrow Editions, 1939. 234 pp.

Smith, Charles Edward
The Jazz Record Book.... New York: Smith & Durell, 1942. xiv, 515 pp., illus., music.
"A selected bibliography of books and periodicals," pp. 509–510. "Index of bands and other recording units," pp. 511–515.

Wolff, Charles
Disques. Répertoire Méthodique du Phonographe. Préface de Pierre Mac Orlan. Paris: Éditions Pièrre Roger, 1932. 579 pp.
A general catalogue of records, with an extensive listing of jazz and dance records, (pp. 478–519). A supplement was issued in 1934. 48 pp.

Album Collections

Blues, Part 1, 2 & 3.
Illinois Jacquet, "Shorty" Nadine, Les Paul, etc.   DISC–6024–6025

Blues.
Lonnie Johnson, vocal-guitar, with John Davis, piano. 3–10".   DISC–710
Contents: Solid Blues; Rocks in My Bed; Drifting Along Blues; In Love Again; Blues in My Soul; Blues for Everybody.

Blues.
Brownie McGhee.   DISC–727
Contents: Just Me and My Dog; Lonesome Blues; Go On; Secret Tojo Blues; The Way I Feel; Pawnshop.

Blues.
Josh White, Nora Lee King, Jack Dupree, May Lou Williams, Sonny Terry, and Woody Guthrie.   ASCH–550

Blues with Stella Brooks.
With Frank Newton, Sidney Becket and Joe Sullivan's group. 3–10".   DISC–620
Contents: West End Blues; As Long As I Live; St. Louis Blues; Jazz Me Blues; I'm A Little Piece of Leather; I'll Never Be the Same.

Brunswick Collectors Series, Vol. I.
King Oliver.   BR–1022
Contents: "Black Snake Blues," "Willie the Weeper," "Aunt Hagar's Blues," "Speakeasy Blues," "Sugar Foot Stump," "Snag It No. 2," "Somedy's Sweetheart," "Too Bad."

Brunswick Collectors Series, Vol. II.
Red Nichols and His Five Pennies.   BR–1019
Contents: "Ida," "Avalon," "Washboard Blues."

Hot Jazz Classics.
Bessie Smith, Empress of the Blues. 4–10".
                    CO–31

Jazz at the Philharmonic.
Vol. 1, 2, 3, 4, 5.   DISC

Josh White Sings.
Josh White, vocal-guitar. 2–12".   DISC–661
Contents: Women Blues—Dupree; Mean Mistreatin' Woman; Baby, Baby; Miss Otis Regrets.

Low Down Blues.
Kid Rena's Jazz Band.   DEL–801/803

Low Down Blues.
Ernestine Washington with Bunk Johnson Band. 2–10".   DISC–712
Contents: The Lord Will Make A Way Somehow; Where Could I Go; God's Amazing Grace.

Midnight Special.
Leadbelly, Woody Guthrie and Cisco Huston. 3–10".   DISC–726

Singin' the Blues.
Louis Armstrong and his Hot Six; Mildred Bailey with the Ellis Larkins Trio; Jack Teagarden's Big Eight; Ethel Waters with the Herman Chittison Trio.   VP–192
Contents: Blues for Yesterday; Blues in the South; That Ain't Right; I Don't Want to Miss Mississippi; St. Louis Blues; Blues after Blues; Blues after Hours; Careless Love; Blues in My Heart.

Songs by Josh White.
Vocal-guitar. 3–10".   ASCH–348

Southern Exposure: An Album of Jim Crow Blues. Joshua White, vocal-guitar.   KE–107

The Birth of the Blues.
The Dixieland Jazz Group of "NBC's Chamber Music Society of Lower Basin Street," Cond. Henry Levine with Lena Horne, Vocalist.
VP–82
  Contents: St. Louis Blues; Memphis Blues; Beale Street Blues; Joe Turner Blues; Aunt Hagar's Blues; East St. Louis Blues; Careless Love Blues; John Henry Blues.

The Birth of the Blues.
An Album of W. C. Handy Music Dixieland Jazz Group of NBC's Chamber Music Society of Lower Basin Street.   VP–62

The Blues: Parts I–IV.
Meade Lux Lewis, piano.   BN–8/9

The History of Jazz.
In Four Albums: Vol. I—The Solid South, CE16; Vol. II—The Golden Era, CE17; Vol. III—Then Came Swing, CE18; Vol. IV—This Modern Age, CE19.   CE 16–19

The Saga of Mr. Jelly Lord.
Recordings of Jelly Roll Morton, from 1895–1916. 12 Albums. 45–12″.   CI–XJM1–90
Alan Lomax writes an exhaustive introductory essay and explanation.

Women Blues.
Josh White, vocal-guitar. 2–12″.   DISC–681

Individual Titles

"Aberdeen Mississippi Blues."
Bukka White, vocal, with guitar and washboard.   OK–05743

"Achin' Heated Blues."
Willie (The Lion) Smith, and His Cubs.
DE–1503

"After Hour Blues."
Frank Newton Quintet.   BN–14

"Ain'tcha Tired of Makin' Me Blue."
Chet Atkins and his Colorado Mountain Boys.
VI–20–2587

"Ain't Gonna Be Treated This Way."
Woody Guthrie and Cisco Houston with guitars.
In: *Blues*—Album.   ASCH–550

"Alabama Bound."
Lead Belly, and Golden Gate Quartet.
VI–27268

"Alberta."
Lead Belly, vocal with guitar.   BB–8559

"All Out and Down."
Huddie Ledbetter, vocal-guitar.   ME–0314

"Amen."
Woody Herman and His Orchestra.   DE–18346

"And One Two Blues."
Joe Smith, trumpet.   CO–36281

"Andy's Blues."
Joe Sullivan, piano.   CO–540

"Another Man Done Gone."
Sung by Vera Hall at Livingston, Alabama, 1940. In: Album IV: Library of Congress, Washington, D. C., 1943.   AAFS16 B1

"Arkansas Blues."
Teddy Grace, and Ensemble.   DE–2602

"Apex Blues."
Louis Armstrong Band.   BR–500196

"Apex Blues."
Jimmie Noone's Apex Club Orchestra. VO–1207

"At the Jazz Band Ball."
Wingy Manone's Dixieland Band, and others.
CA–CE 16

"Aunt Hagar's Blues."
Dixieland Jazz Group.   VI–27544

"Aunt Hagar's Blues."
The Dunning Sisters, vocalists.   CA–BD7

"Aunt Hagar's Blues."
Ted Lewis Band.   CO–CB64

"Aunt Hagar's Blues."
Paul Whiteman and His Orchestra.   DE–2145

"B. and O. Blues."
Pete Johnson, piano.   SO–12006

"Baby Baby."
Libby Holman, vocalist and Josh White, guitar.
DE–18304

"Baby Doll."
Bessie Smith, vocalist.   CO–35674

"Bachelor Blues."
Teddy Bunn, vocal-guitar.   BN–503

"Back Bay Blues."
New Friends of Rhythm.   VI–26315

"Back Log Blues."
The Florida Kid (Ernest Blunt), vocal with piano and bass.   BB–8680

"Back to Johnson City."
J. E. Mainer's Mountaineers; singer, guitar.
BB–7845–A

"Back Water Blues."
Josh White, vocal-guitar.   DE–23582

"Bad Housing Blues."
Josh White, vocal-guitar.   KE–515B

"Bad Luck and Trouble."
Walter Davis; singer, guitar, piano. BB–8107–B

"Barney's Bounce."
Nappy La Mare's Louisiana Levee Loungers, and others.   CA–CE 16

"Basie Blues."
Count Basie and His Orchestra.   CO–36601

"Basin Street Blues."
Louis Armstrong and His Savoy Ballroom Five.
OK–8690

"Basin Street Blues."
Milt Herth. DE–1134

"Basin Street Blues."
J. C. Higginbotham Quintet. BB–N 7

"Basin Street Blues."
Paul Laval and His Woodwindy Ten. VI–27304

"Basin Street Blues."
The Mullen Sisters with Tony Mottola.
VI–P194

"Basin Street Blues."
Louisiana Rhythm Kings. VO–15828

"Basin Street Blues."
Wingy Mannone and His Orchestra. BB–6411

"Basin Street Blues."
Port of Harlem Seven. BB–N7

"Basin Street Blues."
Fats Waller on the Ivories. VP–109

"Beale Street Blues."
Lang-Venuti All Star Orchestra. CO–108

"Beale Street Blues."
Guy Lombardo and His Orchestra. DE–4371

"Beale Street Blues."
Wingy Mannone and His Orchestra. BB–10401

"Beale Street Blues."
Jelly Roll Morton and His Red Hot Peppers.
BB–10252

"Beale Street Blues."
Jack Teagarden and His Orchestra. CO–35323

"Bear Mash Blues."
Erskine Hawkins, trumpet; Lee Meyer Stanfield, string bass. BB–30–0813

"Bear Trap Blues."
Jimmy Yaucey, piano. OK–05490

"Becky Deem, She Was a Gambling Gal."
Huddie Ledbetter; vocal-guitar. ME–60455

"Beer Garden Blues."
Clarence Williams and his Orchestra. OK–2541

"Beggar's Blues."
Sonny Greer and His Memphis Men.
CO–1868D

"Betty and Dupree."
Teddy Grace, and Ensemble. DE–2602

"Biffhy Blues."
Henry Allen and His Orchestra. RCA Reissue

"Big Boy Blues."
Bill Coleman and His Orchestra. VI–26223

"Big Boy Blues."
Billy Kyle and His Swing Club Band. OK–3815

"Big Chump Blues."
Jimmy Smith and His Sepians. DE–8591

"Bill Coleman Blues."
Bill Coleman, trumpet, with Django Remhardt,
guitar. VI–27318

"Big Four Blues."
Leroy Carr, vocal with Strappy Blackwell,
guitar. BB–7970

"Big House Blues."
Duke Ellington and His Cotton Club Orchestra.
CO–35682

"Bill Street Blues."
Bill Coleman Orchestra. Swing 21

"Billie's Blues."
Billie Holiday, and Band. OK–3288

"Birth of the Blues."
Benny Goodman and His Orchestra. CO–36359

"Black and Blue."
Louis Armstrong and orchestra. (HJC).
CO–38052

"Black Evil Blues."
Alice Moore, vocal, with instrumental accompaniment. DE–7028

"Black Panther Blues."
Sonny Boy Williamson. BB–34–0701

"Black Pony Blues."
Arthur "Big Boy" Crudup. VI–20–2793

"Blood Hound Blues."
Victoris Spivey, accompanied by Henry Allen,
Jr., J. C. Higginbotham, Charlie Holmer, Will
Johnson, Pop Foster. BB–8619

"Blowing the Blues."
Sonny Terry, vocal, with harmonica. OK–5684

"Blue."
Benny Goodman's Boys: 1920. BR–3975

"Blue."
Earl Hines and His Orchestra. DE–714

"Blue Again."
Ted Straeter and his orchestra. DE–24054

"Blue and Worried Man."
Blind Boy Fuller, vocal, with guitar, and Sonny
Boy Terry, harmonica. OK–05440

"Blue As I Can Be."
Tommy McClennan, singer, guitar and bass.
BB–34–0706

"Bluebird Sentimental."
Count Basie and His Orchestra. DE–1965

"Blue Blazes."
Jimmy Lunceford and His Orchestra. OK–4667

"Blue Blue."
Bessie Smith, with novelty accompaniment.
CO–14611

"Blue Champagne."
Martin's Orchestra. BB–11256

"Blue Feelin'."
Duke Ellington and His Orchestra.   VI–24521

"Blue Light Blues."
Benny Carter and His Orchestra.   VI–26221

"Blue Lou."
All Star Band.   VI–26144

"Blue Nights."
Earl Hines and His Orchestra.   BB–6744

"Blue Rain."
Glenn Miller and Orchestra.   VI–20–1536

"Blue Rain."
Bea Wain, vocal, orchestra.   VI–30–0816

"Blue Ramble."
Duke Ellington and His Orchestra.   CO–35834

"Blue Reefer Blues."
Richard M. Jones and His Jazz Wizards.
                                                        DE–7061

"Blue Rhythm Fantasy."
Gene Krupa and Orchestra.   OK–5627

"Blue River."
Jack Teagarden and His Orchestra.   DE–4071

"Blue Sonata."
Sonny Burke and Orchestra.   OK–5813

"Bluer Than Bluer Than Blue."
The Four Blues, vocalists.   DE–8637

"Blues."
A Jam Session at Victor. Bunny Berigan,
trumpet; Tommy Dorsey, trombone; Fats
Waller, piano; Dick McDonough, guitar;
George Wettling, drums.   VI–25559

"Blues."
Count Basie and Orchestra.   OK–5862

"Blues."
Bunny Berigan and His Blue Boys.   DE–18116

"Blues."
J. C. Higginbotham, trombone.   CO–36011

"Blues."
From *American Concertette* by Morton Gould.
José Iturbi, pianist.   VI–10–1127

"Blues."
Lonnie Johnson, vocal-guitar.   DISC–5060

"Blues."
Ted Lewis and His Orchestra, Sophie Tucker,
vocalist.   CO–36299

"Blues."
Sung with guitar by "Little Brother" at Texas
State Penitentiary, Huntsville, Texas, 1934. In:
Album IV: Library of Congress, Washington,
D. C., 1943.   AAFS17B2

"Blues."
Pastor's Orchestra.   BB–11168

"Blues."
Artie Shaw and His New Music.   VI–27411

"Blues A Poppin'."
Cootie Williams and his Rug Cutters. OK–5618

"Blues at Blue Note."
Edmond Hall's Blue Note Jazz Men.   BN–28

"Blues At High Noon."
Snub Mosely and His Orchestra.   DE–8614

"Blues at Midnight."
Ernie Fields and Orchestra.   OK–5344

"Blues At Midnight."
Helen Proctor, vocal, with orchestral accompaniment.   DE–7666

"Blues Downstairs."
Woody Herman and His Orchestra.   DE–2508

"Blues for Everybody."
Lonnie Johnson, vocal-guitar and piano.
                                                        DISC–710

"Blues for Norman." 1 & 2.
Lester Young, Howard McGhee, etc.
                                                        DISC–2001

"Blues for Tommy."
Port of Harlem Seven.   BB–N7

"Blues Galore."
Johnny Dodds and His Chicago Boys. DE–7413

"Blues Got Me."
Garland Wilson.   Swing 19

"Blues in B Flat."
Hazel Scott, piano.   DE–18340

"Blues in B Minor."
Garland Wilson, piano.   BR–500222

"Blues in C Sharp Minor."
Teddy Wilson and His Orchestra.   CO–36274

"Blues in Disguise."
Mezz Mezzrow and His Orchestra.   VI–25636

"Blues in E-Flat."
Red Norvo and His Swing Octet.   CO–3079D

"Blues Interlude."
Chocolate Dandies.   DE–18255

"Blues In The Air."
Sidney Bechet and His New Orleans Feet-
warmers.   VI–20–1510

"Blues in the Groove."
Jimmy Lunceford and His Orchestra. OK–5395

"Blues in the Night."
Bing Crosby, vocalist and orchestra. DE–4183

"Blues in the Night."
Judy Garland, vocalist and orchestra. DE–4081

"Blues in the Night."
Benny Goodman and his Sextet.   OK–6553

"Blues in the Night."
Woody Herman Orchestra.   DE–4030

"Blues in the Night."
Harry James and His Orchestra.   CO–36500

"Blues in the Night."
Guy Lombardo Orchestra.   DE–4177

"Blues in the Night."
Jimmie Lunceford Orchestra.   DE–4125

"Blues in the Night."
Alec Templeton, piano.   DE–18271

"Blues in the Night."
Joe Turner, vocalist and orchestra.   DE–7885

"Blues in Thirds."
Sidney Bechet and His New Orleans Feet-
warmers.   VI–27204

"Blues in Thirds."
Earl Hines, piano.   HRS 21

"Blues Krieg."
Gene Krupa and Orchestra.   OK–5909

"Blues of Bechet."
Sidney Bechet (One Man Band).   VI–27485

"Blues of Israel."
Gene Krupa and His Chicagoans.   DE–18114

"Blues in My Soul."
Lonnie Johnson, vocal-guitar and piano.
                                  DISC–710

"Blues My Girl Friend Taught Me."
Raymond Scott and His Orchestra. CO–35980

"Blues on Parade."
Woody Herman and His Orchestra.   DE–3501

"Blues on the Down Beat."
Pete Johnson, piano.   DE–25264

"Blues Petite."
John Kirby and Orchestra.   OK–5805

"Blues to the Lonely."
Jack Teagarden and His Orchestra. DE–3642

"Blues Upstairs."
Woody Herman and His Orchestra.   DE–2508

"Blues With A Feelin'."
Duke Ellington and His Kentucky Club Orchestra.   CO–35955

"Blues Without Words."
Teddy Bunn, vocal and guitar.   BN–504

"Bluest Blues."
Ted Daffan.   OK–6719

"Bluin' The Blues."
Original Dixieland Jazz Band.   RCA Reissue

"Bluin' The Blues."
New Orleans Rhythm Kings.   DE–464

"Bluin' The Blues."
Muggsy Spanier and his Ragtime Band.
                                  BB–10719

"Boll Weevil Blues."
Kokomo Arnold; singer, guitar.   DE–7191

"Boll Weevil Blues."
Sung by Vera Hall at Livingston, Alabama,
1940. In: Album IV: Library of Congress,
Washington, D. C., 1943.   ASFS 16 B2

"Boogie Woogie Blues."
Albert Ammons, piano.   BN–2

"Boogie Woogie in Blue."
Harry (The Hipster) Gibson at Piano. MU–64

"Boogie Woogie in St. Louis Blues."
Earl Hines and His Orchestra.   BB–10674

"Boogie Woogie Woman."
Robert Petway, singer with instrumental accompaniment.   BB–8987

"Born to be Blue."
Mel Tormé, Sonny Burke and Orchestra.
                                  MU–397

"Bridewell Blues."
Nolan Welch, vocal, with Louis Armstrong
cornet, and Richard M. James, piano. OK–8372

"Broken Heart Blues."
Sonny Boy Williamson.   BB–9031

"Brownskin Blues."
Dick Justice, vocal, guitar.   BR–336

"Brussels Blue."
J. Wiener, piano.   CO–13047

"Buddy Bolden's Blues."
Jelly Roll Morton, piano.   GE–4003

"Bull Fiddle Blues."
Johnny Dodds and His Chicago Footwarmers.
                                  CO–35681

"Bull Frog Blues."
Charles Pierce and His Orchestra. UHCA 1–2

"Bumble Bee."
Memphis Minnie McCoy; singer, guitar, piano.
                                  VO–1476

"Bundle of Blues."
Duke Ellington and His Orchestra. CO–35836

"Buss Robinson's Blues."
Pete Johnson, piano.   SO–12006

"BVD Blues."
Roosevelt Sykes and his original Honey Dip-
pers.   VI–20–2658

"Bye Bye Blues."
Yank Rachell.   BB–34–0715

" 'C' Blues."
Barney Bigard and His Orchestra. BB–11581

"Cafe Society Blues."
Count Basie and His Rhythm Section. CO–101

"Cake Walking Babies."
Bessie Smith, vocalist.   CO–35673

"Caliope Blues."
Woody Herman and His Orchestra.   DE–3500

"Canal Street Blues."
Red Allen and His Orchestra.   DE–18092

"Canal Street Blues."
King Oliver's Creole Jazz Band.   UHCA 67–68

"Cannonball Blues."
Carter Family, vocal-guitar.   PE–7–05–55
(Ballad of McKinley and Roosevelt.)

"Cannon- Ball Blues."
Jelly Roll Morton and His Red Hot Peppers.
                                    BB–10254

"Can't Read, Can't Write, Gonna Buy Me A
Telephone." Pete Brown and His Band.
                                    DE–8625

"Careless Love."
Lulu Jackson; singer, guitar.   VO–1193

"Careless Love Blues."
Josh White, guitar, vocal.   ASCH–550–1B

"Casbah Blues."
Woody Herman and His Orchestra.   DE–2582

"Case Of The Blues."
"Snub" Mosely's Band.   DE–8626

"Caution Blues."
Earl Hines, piano.   CO–35876

"Celeste Blues."
Meade Lux Lewis, celeste.   DE–819

"Chain Gang Blues."
Kokomo Arnold; singer, guitar.   DE–7069

"Charity Blues."
Gene Gillmore, vocal, with piano, guitar and
washboard.   DE–7671

"Chimes Blues."
Cow Cow Davenport; fiddle, barrelhouse piano.
                                    PA–12800

"Chimes Blues."
King Oliver's Creole Jazz Band.   UHCA 67–68

"Chimes in Blues."
Earl Hines piano.   HRS 21

"Choo Choo Blues."
Skelton Brothers.   DE–6071

"Coal Cart Blues."
Louis Armstrong and His Orchestra. DE–18091

"Coal Cart Blues."
Clarence Williams' Blue Five.   OK–8245

"Cold In Hand Blues."
Bessie Smith, and members of Fletcher Henderson's Orchestra.   CO–35672

"Collector Man Blues."
Walter Roland, guitar, piano.   PE–0293

"Come On Over to My House."
Jay McShann's Kansas City Stompers.
                                    CA–10030

"Confessin' the Blues."
Walter Brown—Jay McShann.   AL

"Confessin' The Blues."
Jay McShann and His Orchestra.   DE–8859

"Cotton Choppin' Blues."
Big Bill Broonzy, vocal with guitar and piano.
                                    OK–05149

"Cotton Mill Blues."
Lester (The Highway Man), guitar, hill billy.
                                    DE–5559

"Cotton Patch Blues."
Tommy McClennan, vocal with guitar. BB–8408

"Cotton Pickin' Blues."
Robert Petway.   BB–9036

"Countin' The Blues."
Ma Rainey, and Her Georgia Jazz Band.
                                    UHCA 83–84

"Countless Blues."
The Kansas City Six.   CO–509

"Country Blues."
"Dock' Boggs; vocal-banjo.   BR–131B

"Country Blues."
Sung with guitar by McKinley Morganfield at
Stovall, Mississippi, 1941. In: Album IV: Li-
brary of Congress, Washington, D. C., 1943.
                                    AAFS18A

"Country Rag."
Played on the guitar by Smith Casey at Clem-
ens State Farm, Brazoria, Texas, 1939. In:
Album IV: Library of Congress, Washington,
D. C.,1943.   AAFS17A2

"Cow Cow Blues."
Cow Cow Davenport, piano.   VI–01198

"Cow Cow Blues."
Freddie Slack and His Orchestra.   CA–102

"Cow Cow Blues."
Sam Price and His Texas Blusicians. DE–7732

"Cow Cow Blues."
Bob Zurke and His Delta Rhythm Band.
                                    VI–26646

"Crawfish Blues."
Leadbelly, Eddie Miller's Quartet and others.
                                    CA–CE16

"Crescendo in Blue."
Duke Ellington and His Orchestra. CO–36125

"Cross Road Blues."
Robert Johnson; singer, guitar.   PE–7–0581

"Crow Jane Blues."
Julius Daniels; singer, 2 guitars. VI–21065–A

"Crying Mother Blues."
Red Nelson, vocal, with Cripple Clarence
Lofton, piano.   DE–7171

"C.W.A. Blues."
Walter Roland; singer, guitar, piano. PE–0293

"D. B. Blues."
Helen Humes and Lester Young.　AL

"A Touch of Blue."
Joes Thomas' Big Six.　HRS 1016

"Dallas Blues."
Woody Herman and His Orchestra.　DE–2629

"Dallas Blues."
Ted Lewis and His Orchestra.　CO–35684

"Davenport Blues."
Bix and His Rhythm Jugglers.　HRS–22

"Davenport Blues."
Adrian Rollins and His Orchestra.　DE–359

"Daybreak Blues."
J. C. Higginbotham Quintet.　BN–501

"Daybreak Blues."
Frank Newton Quintet.　BN–501

"Dead Man Blues."
Jelly Roll Morton and His Red Hot Peppers.
RCA Reissue

"Dead Man's Blues."
Georgia White, vocal, piano and guitar.
DE–7534

"Death Letter Blues."
Ida Cox and Her All Star Band.　OK–05336

"Death Letter Blues."
Jimmy Yaucey, piano.　BB–8630

"Deceitful Blues."
Texas Alexander; vocal-guitar.　VO–02912

"Dee Blues."
Jimmy Harrison, Trombone.　CO–36008

" 'Deed I Do."
Jack Teagarden's Chicagoans.　CA–10027

"Deep Blue Sea Blues."
Tommy McClennan, singer with instrumental
accompaniment.　BB–9005

"Deep Creek."
Jelly Roll and His Red Peppers.　RCA Reissue

"Deep River Blues."
Piccadilly Revel Band.　CO–4614

"Deep River Blues."
Riviera Palace Orch.　PER–3138

"Deep Sea Blues."
Ida Cox and Her All Star Band.　OK–05336

"Deep Water Blues."
Jazz Gillum.　VI–34–0709

"Defense Blues."
Leadbelly, Brownie McGhee, Pop Foster and
Willie-the-Lion-Smith.　DISC–5085

"Defense Factory Blues."
Josh White, vocal-guitar.　KE–516B

"De Kalb Blues."
Lead Belly, vocal, with guitar.　MU–226

"Deliver Me To Tennessee."
Gene Krupa and His Orchestra.　CO–36591

"Deliver Me To Tennessee."
Woody Herman and His Orchestra.　DE–18346

"Delta Land Blues."
Skeets Tolbert and His Orchestra.　DE–8608

"Depot Blues."
Charlie Lincoln; vocal-guitar.　CO–14420–D

"Dexter Blues."
Jay McShann.　DE–8583

"Dicky Wells Blues."
Bill Coleman, trumpet and Django Reinhardt,
guitar.　VI–27318

"Dicky Wells Blues."
Dicky Wells and His Orchestra.　VI–27318

"Did You Ever Love a Woman."
Josh White with Edmond Hall, vocal with
orchestra.　DE–23475

"Diminuendo in Blue."
Duke Ellington and His Orchestra.　CO–36125

"Dinah's Blues."
Paul Laval and His Woodwindy Ten.　VI–27303

"Dipper Mouth Blues."
Glenn Miller and Orchestra.　OK–5131

"Dipper Mouth Blues."
Muggsy Spanier and his Ragtime Band.
BB–10506

"District Attorney Blues."
Bukka White, vocal with guitar and Washboard.　OK–05683

"Diving Duck Blues."
John Estes; vocal, guitar, piano, mandolin.
BB–17677–A

"D Natural Blues."
Fletcher Henderson and His Orchestra.
CO–1543D

"Doctor Blues."
Walter Davis, vocal and piano.　BB–8367

"Doctor Blues."
Luis Russell and His Orchestra.　OK–8766

"Doggin' Man Blues."
Andy Kirk and his orchestra and Bea Booze.
DE–48073

"Dog House Blues."
St. Louis Jimmy.　VI–20–2650

"Dogtown Blues."
Bob Crosby and His Orchestra.　DE–15038

"Don't Deal With The Devil."
Tampa Red, vocal, with guitar, piano and bass.
BB–8991

"Don't You Love Your Daddy No More?"
Lead Belly, vocal-guitar.　　　BB–8550

"Downhearted Blues."
Mildred Bailey and Her Alley Cats.　DE–18109

"Downright Disgusted Blues."
Wingy Mannone and His Orchestra. BB–10296

"Do You Dig My Jive."
Sam Price and His Texas Blusicians. DE–8575

"Down and Out Blues."
Kokomo Arnold; vocal-guitar.　　DE–7163

"Down South Blues."
"Dock" Boggs; vocal-banjo.　　BR–118–B

"Down South Blues."
Jazz Gillum, singer with instrumental accompaniment.　　　　　　　　　BB–9004

"Down to Steamboat Tennessee."
Lee Wiley.　　　　　　　　COM–1507

"Draftin' Blues."
Count Basie and Orchestra.　　OK–5897

"Dream Blues."
Johnny Hodges and Orchestra.　OK–5353

"Drifting Along Blues."
Lonnie Johnson, vocal-guitar and piano.
　　　　　　　　　　　　DISC–710

"Dupree Blues."
Count Basie and His Rhythm.　　DE–3071

"Dupree Blues."
Woody Herman and His Orchestra.　DE–3500

"Dupree Blues."
Georgia White; vocal, guitar, piano. DE–7100

"Eagle Rock Rag."
Eddie Miller's Quartet, and others.　CA–CE 16

"Early Mornin' Blues."
Albert Ammons and His Rhythm Kings.
　　　　　　　　　　　　DE–975

"East Chicago Blues."
Little Brother, piano.　　　　BB–10177

"East St. Louis Blues."
Chamber Music Society of Lower Basin Street
and Dixieland Jazz Group.　　VP–82

"East St. Louis Blues."
Faber Smith, vocal, with Jimmy Yaucey, piano.
　　　　　　　　　　　　OK–05464

"East Virginia Blues."
Carter Family.　　　　　　VI–27494

"Easy Rider."
Lead Belly, vocal-guitar.　　BB–8570

"Easy Rider Blues."
Georgia White, vocal, with piano and guitar.
　　　　　　　　　　　　DE–7135

"Eddie's Blues."
Eddie South, violin.　　　　VI–26222

"Edmond Hall Blues."
Edmond Hall Celeste Quartet.　　BN–18

"Empty Bed Blues."
Bessie Smith and members of Fletcher Henderson's Orchestra.　　　　　CO–35675

"Empty Bed Blues."
Vocal Blues with instrumental accompaniment.
Bessie Smith; Charles Green, trombone; Porter Gramger, piano.　　　　CO–31–8

"Everybody Loves Somebody Blues."
New Orleans Rhythm Kings.　　BB–10956

"Everyday Blues."
Dorothy Donigan, piano solo.　BB–8979

"Evil Blues."
Count Basie and His Orchestra.　DE–2922

"Evil Blues."
Washboard Sam and His Washboard Band.
　　　　　　　　　　　　BB–8997

"Evil Hearted Man."
Josh White, vocal-guitar.　　KE–8138

"Evolution Blues."
Cousin Joe and Sam Price Trio.　DE–48061

"Fairy Tale Blues."
Little Bill Gaither, vocal with piano and bass.
　　　　　　　　　　　　DE–7812

"Fare Thee Well."
Libby Holman, vocalist and Josh White, guitar.
　　　　　　　　　　　　DE–18304

"Farewell Blues."
Count Basie and His Rhythm Section. CO–101

"Farewell Blues."
Lang-Venuti All Star Orchestra.　UHCA–106

"Farewell Blues."
Woody Herman and His Orchestra.　DE–2582

"Farewell Blues."
Wingy Mannone and His Orchestra. BB–10401

"Feet Draggin' Blues."
Harry James and His Orchestra.　CO–35227

"Fifty-Fifty Blues."
Louis Armstrong and his all stars. VI–20–2530

"Five O'Clock Blues."
Jimmy Yaucey, piano.　　　VI–26590

"Five Point Blues."
Bob Crosby and His Orchestra.　DE–2108

"Five Point Blues."
Yank Lawson and trumpet.　　DE–25298

"Flea On Me."
Bo Carter; vocal, guitar, fiddle, folk guitar.
　　　　　　　　　　　　BB–B–6695

"Flood Water Blues."
Lonnie Johnson, vocal-guitar.　DE–7397

"Floyd's Guitar Blues."
Andy Kirk and His Orchestra.　DE–2483

"Four Day Worry Blues."
Huddie Ledbetter; vocal-guitar.   ME–0315

"Forty-Four Whistle Blues."
Sonny Terry, vocal and harmonica.   OK–5684

"Freight Train Blues."
Roy Acuff and His Smoky Mountain Boys.
OK–4466

"Freight Train Blues."
Trixie Smith, and band.   DE–7489

"Friendless Blues."
Big Bill Broonzy, vocal with guitar and piano.
BB–5535

"Friendless Blues."
Tampa Red and Georgia Tom; vocal, 2 guitars,
piano, banjo.   VO–1491

"From Now On."
Jazz Gillum.   BB–9034

"From 20 to 44."
Lonnie Johnson, vocalist with instrumental accompaniment.   BB–8980

"Gamblin' Charley."
Charlie Lincoln; singer, guitar.   CO–14420–B

"Georgia Hound Blues."
Tampa Red and Georgia Tom; 2 guitars, knife
guitar.   PE–7–01–67

"Get Along Home, Cindy."
Lulu Belle and Scotty; duet, fiddle, 5 string
banjo, guitar.   PE–6–03–59

"Get Along Home, Cindy."
Bascom Lamar Lunsford; singer, 5 string
banjo.   BR–228

"G. I. Blues."
Duke Henderson with Tiny Webb Trio. GL–108

"Gibing Blues."
Champion Jack Dupree, vocal, with piano and
bass.   OK–06104

"Gin Mill Blues."
Erskine Hawkins and His Orchestra. BB–10409

"Give It Up Daddy Blues."
Albennie Jones and Sam Price and his Trio.
DE–48069

"Goin' Home."
Tommy Dorsey and Orchestra.   VI–25600

"Goin' to Chicago Blues."
Count Basie and His Orchestra.   OK–6244

"Goin' To Chicago Blues."
Joe Turner with Freddie Slack Trio. DE–4093

"Gonna Buy Me A Telephone."
Pete Brown and His Band.   DE–8625

"Gonna Hit the Highway."
Washboard Sam and His Washboard Band.
BB–8997

"Goodbye Blues."
The Chocolate Dandies: 1930.   CO–35679

"Good Dues Blues."
Dizzy Gillespie and His Orchestra.   MU–399

"Good Feeling Blues."
Blind Boy Fuller, vocal with guitar, and Sonny
Boy Terry, harmonica.   OK–06231

"Good Gal Blues."
Johnny Hodges and Orchestra.   OK–5170

"Good Morning Blues."
Count Basie and His Orchestra.   DE–1446

"Good Morning Blues."
Lead Belly, voice, accompanied by Sonny
Terry, harmonica.   ASCH–343

"Good Mornin' Blues."
Libby Holman, vocalist and Josh White, guitar.
DE–18305

"Good Morning Blues."
The Kansas City Six.   CO–511

"Good Morning Schoolgirl."
Sonny Boy Williamson; singer, harmonica,
guitar.   BB–7059–A

"Good Times Blues."
Ramblin' Thomas; vocal-guitar.   PA–12752

"Got No Blues."
Louis Armstrong and Hot Five.   OK–3204

"Got To Reap What You Sow."
Tampa Red; vocal-guitar.   VO–1404

"Grabbin Blues."
Freddie Johnson and Arthur Briggs.
BR–500263

"Grand Piano Blues."
Earl Hines and His Orchestra.   BB–6744

"Graveyard Blues."
Teddy Grace, and Ensemble.   DE–2606

"Graveyard Blues."
Georgia White, vocal, with piano and guitar.
DE–7135

"Gravier Street Blues."
Johnny Dodds and His Orchestra.   DE–18094

"Green Grass Blues."
Big Bill Broonzy, vocal, with guitar and piano.
OK–06242

"Grinder Man Blues."
Memphis Slim, vocal, with piano and bass.
BB–8584

"Ground Hog Blues."
Sonny Boy Williamson.   BB–9031

"Gulf Coast Blues."
Teddy Grace, and Ensemble.   DE–2605

"Gut Bucket Blues."
Louis Armstrong and his Hot Five. CO–36152

"Hangover Blues."
Alix Commbelle and Orchestra.   Swing 11

"Hard Times Blues."
Ida Cox and Her All Star Band.   OK–05298

"Hard Times Blues."
Josh White, vocal-guitar.   KE–516A

"Harlem Blues."
J. Wiener, piano.   CO–LF–37

"Harlem Flat Blues."
Duke Ellington.   BR–500248

"Harlem Gin Blues."
Sam Price and His Texas Blusicians. DE–8609

"Harmonica Blues."
Sonny Terry, vocal, with harmonica. OK–5453

"Harmony Blues."
Mary Lou Williams and Her Kansas Seven.
                                   DE–18122

"Harvard Blues."
Count Basie and His Orchestra.   OK–6564

"Hell Hound on My Trail."
Robert Johnson; vocal-guitar.   VO–03623

"Hello Baby."
Walter Davis, singer with piano.   BB–8998

"Hersal Blues."
Hersal Thomas, piano.   OK–8227

"He's A Jelly-Roll Baker."
Lonnie Johnson, Blues Singer, with piano,
guitar, and bass.   BB–9006–A

"He's My Man."
Kausar Katie, singer with instrumental accompaniment.   BB–8999

"Hesitating Blues."
Muggsy Spanier and His Ragtimers. DE–4271

"Higginbotham Blues."
J. C. Higginbotham and His Six Hicks.
                                   CO–36011

"Higginbotham Blues."
Benny Morton and His Orchestra.   CO–36011

"High Society."
Nappy La Mare's Louisiana Levee Loungers,
and others.   CA–CE–16

"High Society Blues."
Mound City Blue Blowers.   DE–1274

"Highway 49."
Joe Williams.   BB–9025

"Highway 51."
Curtis Jones; vocal, piano, guitar, drum.
                                   VO–03990

"Hittin' The Bottle Stomp."
Mississippi Jook Bank; piano, guitar, tambour-
ine, kazoo, barrelhouse.   PE–139

"Hollow Log Blues."
Robert Petway, vocal with instrumental accompaniment.   BB–8987

"Home Again Blues."
Jungle Band.   BR–500140

"Honey Chile."
The Four Blues, vocalists.   DE–8637

"Hong Kong Blues."
Hoagy Carmichael, playing, singing, and
whistling his own composition.   DE–18395

"Honky Tonk Train Blues."
Meade "Lux" Lewis, piano.   DE–25263

"Honky Tonk Train Blues."
Charlie Spand, piano.   SI–65101

"Honky Tonk Train Blues."
Jess Stacy, piano.   DE–18110

"Hootie's Blues."
Jay McShann and His Orchestra.   DE–8859

"Hot Club Blues."
Dicky Wells and Orchestra.   Swing 3

"House of David Blues."
Fletcher Henderson Orch.   BR–500191

"Hour of Plenty Blues."
Pee Wee Russell's Rhythmaken.   HRS–1001

"House Rent Blues."
Clarence Williams' Blue Five.   OK–8171

"How Could I Be So Mean."
Lonnie Johnson, vocal-guitar.   DISC–5061

"How Long."
Lead Belly, vocal and guitar, Sonny Terry,
harmonica.   ASCH–343–1B

"How Long Blues."
Wingy Mannone and His Orchestra. BB–10749

"How Long, How Long Blues."
Count Basie and His Rhythm.   DE–2355

"I Be's Troubled."
Sung with guitar by McKinley Morganfield
Stovall, Mississippi, 1941. In: Album IV: Li-
brary of Congress, Washington, D. C., 1943.
                                   AAFS18B

"I Can't Quit That Man."
Ida Cox and Her All Star Orchestra. OK–6405

"Ida Red."
Tanner's Skilled Lickers.   VI–27496

"I Feel All Right."
Walter Davis, singer with piano.   BB–8998

"If I Didn't Love You."
Bea Booze, vocalist with instrumental accompaniment.   DE–8629

"I Get the Blues at Bedtime."
Washboard Sam.   VI–34–0710

"I Got a Right to be Blue."
Tampa Red, vocal, guitar, piano and bass.
BB–8991

"I Gotta Right to Sing the Blues."
Louis Armstrong. GR–6942

"I Gotta Right to Sing the Blues."
Billie Holiday, and Band. CO–527

"I Gotta Right to Sing the Blues."
Lena Horne. VI–27818

"I Gotta Right to Sing the Blues."
Jack Teagarden and His Orchestra. OK–6272

"I Have A Place to Go."
Lil Green, vocalist with instrumental accompaniment. BB–8985

"I Have to Go."
Sonny Boy Williamson, vocalist with instrumental accompaniment. BB–8992

"I'll Get You Off My Mind."
Big Joe and His Rhythm. BB–8986

"I Lost My Sugar In Salt Lake City Blues."
Johnny Mercer. CA–122

"I Love to George Brown So Slow."
Bea Booze, vocalist with instrumental accompaniment. DE–8629

"I'm A Steady Rollin' Man."
Robert Johnson; vocal-guitar. PE–7–12–76

"I'm Gonna Leave You On The Outskirts of Town." Jazz Gillum. BB–9042

"I'm Gonna Move To The Outskirts of Town."
Count Basie and His Orchestra. CO–36601

"I'm Gonna Move To The Outskirts of Town."
Louis Jordan and His Tympany Five. DE–8593

"I'm Gonna Move To The Outskirts of Town."
Jimmie Lunceford and His Orchestra.
DE–18325

"I'm in Love with Love."
Lonnie Johnson, vocal-guitar. DISC–5060

"I'm in the Mood for Love."
Red Nichols and His Pennies. CA–10029

"I'm Lonesome."
The Three Bits of Rhythm. DE–8572

"I'm On My Last Go-Round."
Hudy Leadbelly, with guitar. BB–8981

"Im Prayin' Humble."
Bob Crosby and His Orchestra. DE–2210

"I'm Sad and I'm Lonely."
Carl Sandburg, vocal-guitar. MU–209–A

"I'm Talkin' 'Bout You."
Memphis Minnie (Minnie McCoy) singer, guitar, piano. VO–1476

"I'm Wasting My Time On You."
Lil Green. BB–9010

"Immigration Blues."
Duke Ellington and His Kentucky Club Orchestra. VO–1077

"Inflation Blues."
Louis Jordan Tympany Five. DE–24381

"Indiana Blues."
Jerry Wayne. BE–100

"In the House Blues."
Bessie Smith, with novelty accompaniment.
CO–14611

"Irene."
Lead Belly, vocal-guitar. ASCH–343–2B

"It Ain't No Lie."
Big Joe and His Rhythm. BB–8986

"It Is The Gold."
Buddy Johnson. DE–8523

"It's A Blue World."
Tommy Reynolds and Orchestra. OK–5317

"It's A Cryin' Pity."
Tommy McClennan, vocalist with instrumental accompaniment. BB–9005

"It Was Only A Dream."
Bob Crosby and His Orchestra. DE–4137

"I've Been Treated Wrong."
Washboard Sam and His Washboard Band.
BB–9007

"I've Got Too Many Blues."
Mabel Robinson with Sam Price's Blusicians.
DE–8601

"I've Had The Blues So Long."
Woody Herman and His Orchestra. DE–770

"I Wonder Who's Boogienin' My Woogie Now."
Buddy Johnson and His Band. DE–8611

"Jab Blues."
Wesley Wallace, Jabo Williams, piano. TI–3

"Jazz It Blues."
New Orleans Rhythm Kings: 1934. DE–162

"Jazz Me Blues."
Bix and His Gang. CO–36156

"Jazz Me Blues."
Stella Brooks. DISC–620

"Jazz Me Blues."
The Cellar Boys (Teschemacher's Chicagoans).
UHCA–61–62

"Jazz Me Blues."
Larry Clinton and Orchestra. VI–20–2637

"Jazz Me Blues."
Clinton's Bluebird Orchestra. BB–11240

"Jazz Me Blues."
Dorsey Brothers Orchestra. CO–36064

"Jazz Me Blues."
Gene Krupa and His Chicagoans. DE–18115

"Jazz Me Blues."
Ted Lewis and His Orchestra.   DE–4272

"Jazz Me Blues."
Jimmy MacPartland and His Orchestra.
DE–18042

"Jazz Me Blues."
Wingy Mannone and His Orchestra. BB–7198

"Jazz Me Blues."
Charles Pierce and His Orchestra.
UHCA–71–72

"Jazz Me Blues."
The Wolverines (Bix Beiderbecke, cornet and others).   HRS–25

"Jealous Hearted Blues."
Ma Rainey, and Howard Scott, Charlie Green, Don Redman.   UHCA–85–86

"Jealous Woman Blues."
Little Bill Gaither, vocal with piano and bass.
OK–06044

"Jelly Bean Blues."
Ma Rainey and Her Georgia Jazz Band.
UHCA–83–84

"Jelly Jelly."
Josh White, vocal-guitar.   DE–23582

"Jess Stacy Blues."
Jess Stacy and All His Stars.   ASCH–350–2

"Jet Black Woman."
Pinewood Tom (Joshua White); vocal-guitar.
PE–5–12–51

"Jigg Saw Puzzle Blues."
Joe Venuti & Eddie Lang's Blue Five. CO–1229

"Jim Crow Train Blues."
Josh White, vocal-guitar.   KE–515A

"Jimtown Blues."
Will Bradley and His Orchestra.   CO–35376

"Jimtown Blues."
Ben Pollack and His Orchestra.   CO–36235

"Joe Louis and John Henry Blues."
Sonny Boy Williamson, vocal with instrumental accompaniment.   BB–8403

"Joe Turner Blues."
Dixieland Jazz Group.   VI–27543

"John Henry Blues."
Dixieland Jazz Group.   VI–27545

"Jumpin' Down Blues."
Big Joe Turner, vocal with Willie Smith, piano.
DE–7827

"Jump Steady Blues."
Pine Top Smith, piano.   CO–65–66

"Jump Steady Blues."
Montana Taylor, piano.   CO–65–66

"Junction Blues."
Erskine Hawkins and His Orchestra. BB–10790

"Jungle Blues."
Benny Goodman's Boys.   BR–500201

"Jungle Blues."
Ted Lewis.   CO–14176

"Jungle Blues."
Jelly Roll Morton and His Red Hot Peppers.
BB–10256

"Just For You Blues."
Teddy Wilson Quintet.   MU–316

"Katy Fly."
Elijah Jones; vocal, guitar, mandolin.
BB–7616–B

"Katy Lee Blues."
Yank Rachell.   BB–34–0715

"Keep What You Got."
Lonnie Johnson, vocal-guitar.   DISC–5062

"Keystone Blues."
Jimmy Noone and His Orchestra.   DE–18095

"Kind Hearted Woman."
Robert Johnson, vocal-guitar.   PE–7–03–56

"Kind Lover Blues."
Arthur "Big Boy" Crudup.   VI–20–2793

"Last Goodbye Blues."
Art Tatum and His Band.   DE–8536

"Last Mile Blues."
Ida Cos and Her All Star Orchestra. OK–6405

"Laughing Boy Blues."
Woody Herman and His Orchestra.   DE–1801

"Left A Good Deal in Mobile."
Josh White with Edmond Hall, vocal and orchestra.   DE–23475

"Let Your Money Talk."
Kokomo Arnold, vocal-guitar.   DE–7191

"Limehouse Blues."
Sidney Bechet and His New Orleans Feet-warmers.   VI–27600

"Limehouse Blues."
Larry Clinton and His Orchestra.   VI–26523

"Limehouse Blues."
Duke Ellington and His Orchestra.   VI–22743

"Limehouse Blues."
Benny Goodman and His Sextet.   OK–6486

"Limehouse Blues."
Fletcher Henderson and His Orchestra. DE–157

"Limehouse Blues."
Ted Lewis.   CO–14274

"Limehouse Blues."
Quintet of the Hot Club France.   DE–2304

"Limehouse Blues."
Reisman Orchestra.   VI–27435

"Livery Stable Blues."
Fletcher Henderson and His Orchestra.
CO–1002D

"Livery Stable Blues."
Muggsy Spanier and His Ragtime Band.
BB–10518

"Londella Blues."
Yank Rachell, singer with instrumental accompaniment.
BB–8993

"Lonely Boy Blues."
Jay McShann and His Orchestra.
DE–4787

"Lonesome Blues."
Sidney Bechet and His New Orleans Feetwarmers.
BN–13

"Lonesome Blues."
Brownie McGhee.
DISC–727

"Lonesome Day Blues."
Jesse James, vocal with piano.
DE–7213

"Lonesome Man Blues."
Harry (Freddie) Shayne, vocal with piano.
DE–7663

"Lonesome Road."
Tommy Dorsey and Orchestra.
VI–26508

"Lonesome Train."
Blind Sonny Terry, harmonica and voice; accompanied by Woody Guthrie, guitar.
ASCH–550

"Lonesome Valley Blues."
Texas Alexander, vocal-guitar.
VO–02876

"Lonesome Weary Blues."
Bertha Chippie Hill, Louis Armstrong and Richard M. Jones.
OK–8453

"Lorenzo's Blues."
Omer Simeon Trio.
DISC–6001

"Lost Your Head Blues."
Bessie Smith, and members of Fletcher Henderson's Orchestra.
CO–35674

"Louise."
Blind Boy Fuller, vocal-guitar.
VO–03408

"Louise, Louise Blues."
Big Bill Broomzy, vocal-guitar, piano, banjo.
ME–7-08–65

"Louise, Louise Blues."
Bob Crosby and His Orchestra.
DE–2032

"Lover's Lane Blues."
Washboard Sam and His Washboard Band.
BB–9007

"Lovesick Blues."
Betha Chippie Hill, Louis Armstrong and Richard M. Jones.
OK–8453

"Lovin' Mama Blues."
Albert Ammonds, Meade Lux Lewis and Pete Johnson, pianists.
OK–5186

"Low Down Blues."
Teddy Grace, and Ensemble.
DE–2604

"Lowland Blues."
Red Nichols and Orchestra.
OK–5676

"Lulu's Mood."
Wingy Manone's Dixieland Band, and others.
CA–CE–16

"Mad About Him, Sad Without Him, How Can I Be Glad Without Him Blues." Jerry Wald and His Orchestra.
DE–4345

"Mad About Him, Sad Without Him, How Can I Be Glad Without Him Blues." Dinah Shore.
VI–27940

"Mad Without Her, Sad Without Her, How Can I Be Glad Without Her Blues." Delta Rhythm Boys.
DE–4266

"Magnolia Blues."
Santo Pecora and His Back Room Boys.
CO–36159

"Mama Blues."
Salty Homes and His Brown Country Boys.
DE–46116

"Mama Long and Tall."
Erskine Butterfield and Blue Boys.
DE–8596

"Mama, Mama Blues."
Louis Jordan and His Tympany Five.
DE–8627

"Mamie's Blues."
Jelly Roll Morton, piano.
GE–4001

"Mandy Lee Blues."
King Oliver's Creole Jazz Band.
UHCA–69–70

"Married Woman Blues."
Sleepy John Estes, vocal, with guitar and harmonica.
DE–7289

"Me and My Chauffeur."
Mabel Robinson with Sam Price's Blusicians.
DE–8601

"Me and My Chauffeur Blues."
Memphis Minnie.
OK–6288

"Me and My Dog Blues."
Blind Boy Fuller, vocal, with guitar, and Sonny Boy Terry, harmonica.
OK–05933

"Mean Acting Mama."
Elijah Jones, vocal-guitar, mandolin, harmonica.
BB–7616–A

"Mean and Evil Woman."
Tampa Red.
BB–9024

"Mean Mama Blues."
Charles Mitchell.
VI–33–0508

"Mean Old Bed Bug Blues."
The Rhythmakers.
UHCA–105

"Mean Old 'Frisco Blues."
Arthur "Big Boy" Crudup.
VI–20–2659

"Mecca Flat Blues."
Albert Ammons, piano. SO–12001

"Mellow Blues."
Jimmy Yancey, piano. VI–26591

"Memphis Blues."
Ambrose and His Orchestra. DE–660

"Memphis Blues."
Chamber Music Society of Lower Basin Street
and Dixieland Jazz Group. VP–82

"Memphis Blues."
Will Bradley and Orchestra. OK–5130

"Memphis Blues."
Fletcher Henderson's Orchestra. DE–158

"Memphis Blues."
Milt Herth. DE–1183

"Memphis Blues."
Harry James. CO–36713

"Memphis Blues."
Guy Lombardo and His Orchestra. DE–4077

"Memphis Blues."
Midnight Trio. DISC–6010

"Memphis Blues."
Dinah Shore, vocalist. VP–139

"Michigan Water Blues."
Jelly Roll Morton, piano. GE–4002

"Mighty Blues."
Port of Harlem Jazzmen. BB–N3

"Mile Pound Hammer Is Too Heavy."
Monroe Brothers (Charles and Bill); vocals,
guitar, mandolin. BB–6422–B

"Milk Cow Blues."
Bob Crosby and His Orchestra. DE–1962

"Milk Cow Blues."
John Estes; vocal-guitar, piano, mandolin.
BB–7677–B

"Minuet in Blues."
Barney Bigard and Orchestra. OK–5378

"Mississippi River Blues."
Big Bill Broonzy, vocal with guitar and piano.
BB–5535

"Mississippi Valley Blues."
Gene Autry, vocalist and guitar. OK–2991

"Mistreated."
Harlem Leonard and His Orchestra. BB–11544

"Mitchell Blues."
J. E. Mainer's Mountaineers. BB–7845

"Moaning Blues" (Bloodhound Blues).
Victoria Spivey and group. BB–8619

"Moanin' the Blues."
Baron Lee. BR–500193

"Mobile Blues."
Wade's Moulin Rouge Orchestra. PA–20295

"Mobile Blues."
Boyd Senter, clarinet, etc. OD–165335

"Mobile Bay Blues."
Rex Stewart and His Orchestra. BB–11057

"Money Blues."
Fletcher Henderson and His Orchestra.
CO–35669

"Monkey Face Blues."
St. Louis Jimmy, with Instr. Accomp.
VI–20–2598

"Mood Indigo."
Sonny Greet and the Duke's Men. CA–10028

"Moonshine Woman Blues."
Doctor Clayton. BB–9021

"Mound Bayou."
Pete Brown and His Band. DE–8613

"Mournful Serenade."
Jelly Roll and His Red Hot Peppers. BB–8515

"Mournin' Blues."
Bob Crosby and His Orchestra. DE–2482

"Mr. Freddie Blues."
Meade "Lux" Lewis, piano and solo.
BR–A–505–053

"Mr. Freddie Blues."
Mary Lou Williams, piano. DE–2797

"Muddy River Blues."
Jack Teagarden and His Orchestra. CO–35297

"Muggin' The Blues."
Richard M. Jones and His Jazz Wizards.
DE–7064

"Mule Face Blues."
King Oliver and His Orchestra. BB–6778

"Mule Skinner Blues."
Woody Guthrie, Cisco Houston, and Pete Seeger—vocal, guitar and banjo. ASCH–432–1A

"My Big Money—Blues."
Jazz Gillum, singer with orchestral accompaniment. BB–34–0707

"My Black Name Blues."
Sonny Boy Williamson, singer with instrumental accompaniment. BB–8992

"My Favorite Blues."
Benny Carter and His Orchestra. BB–11288

"My First Love Blues."
Tampa Red. BB–34–0700

"My Inspiration."
Bob Crosby and His Orchestra. DE–2209

"My Last Love."
Lonnie Johnson, vocal-guitar. DISC–5061

"My Own Blues."
Doctor Clayton, vocalist with instrumental accompaniment. BB–9003

"Navy Blues."
The Seven "Hot" Air Men.　　　CO–CB–53

"New Lost Train Blues."
J. E. Mainer's Mountaineers; fiddle, mandolin,
2 guitars.　　　BB–6424–A

"New Orleans Blues."
Blue Lou Barker's Band.　　　DE–7538

"New Orleans Hop Scop Blues."
Jimmy Noone and His Orchestra.　　DE–18095

"New Someday Baby."
Sleepy John Estes; vocal-guitar.　　DE–7473

"New St. Louis Blues."
Ted Lewis.　　　CO–4088

"New St. Louis Blues."
Boyd Senter, clarinet.　　　OD–165090

"The New St. Louis Blues."
J. Wiener, piano.　　　CO–13024

"New Stranger Blues."
Tampa Red and Georgia Tom; 2 guitars.
　　　PE–7–01–67

"New Way of Livin' Blues."
Ramblin' Thomas; vocal-guitar.　　PA–12752

"Night Shift Blues."
Edmond Hall's Blue Note Jazz Men.　BN–29

"Night Watchman Blues."
Big Bill.　　　OK–6705

"1941 Blues."
Little Bill Gaither, vocal with piano and bass.
　　　OK–06044

"No Blues At All."
John Kirby and His Orchestra.　　VI–27926

"No Friend Blues."
Jazz Gillum.　　　BB–9034

"No More Ball and Chain."
Pinewood Tom (Joshua White); vocal-guitar.
　　　PE–6–05–51

"No More Lovers."
Arthur "Big Boy" Crudup, with Instr. accomp.
　　　VI–20–2565

"Nothin' But The Blues."
Gene Gifford and His Orchestra.　　BB–10704

"Nothing But Blues."
St. Louis Jimmy.　　　VI–34–0718

"No Use of Worryin'."
"Roosevelt" Antrim; vocal-guitar.　　BB–7475

"Off Time Blues."
Earl Hines, piano.　　　HRS–19

"Oh Baby."
Blues Singer with Instrumental Accompaniment.　　　OK–6739

"Old Man Blues."
Sidney Bechet and His New Orleans Feet-
warmers.　　　VI–26663

"Old Man Blues."
Duke Ellington and His Cotton Club Orchestra.
　　　BB–6450

"Old Man Blues."
Harlem Footwarmers.　　　OK–8869

"Old Quaker Blues."
Jimmy Yancy, piano　　　OK–05490

"One and Two Blues."
Mound City Blue Blowers.　　　CO–36281

"One Woman's Man."
Jay McShann and His Orchestra.　　DE–8607

"Original Chinese Blues."
Boyd Senter and His Centerpedes.　OD–165577

"Original Mr. Freddie Blues."
Harry (Freddie) Shayne, vocal, with piano.
　　　DE–7663

"Original Jelly Roll Blues."
Jelly Roll Morton and His Red Hot Peppers.
　　　BB–10255

"Overwork Blues."
Etta Jones with Luther Henderson Orchestra.

"Papa, Mam's All Alone Blues."
Margaret Johnson and Clarence Williams Blue
Five.　　　OK–8185

"Parchman Farm Blues."
Bukka White, vocal, with guitar and washboard.　　　OK–05683

"Pastel Blue."
John Kirby and His Orchestra.　　DE–2367

"PDQ Blues."
Fletcher Henderson and His Orchestra.
　　　CO–1002D

"Pearl Harbor Blues."
Doctor Clayton, vocalist with instrumental accompaniment.　　　BB–9003

"Perdido Street Blues."
Louis Armstrong and His Orchestra. DE–18090

"Perdido Street Blues."
New Orleans Wanderers.　　　UHCA–15–16

"Pete's Blues."
Pete Johnson, piano.　　　SO–12005

"Piano Boogie."
Dorothy Donigan, piano.　　　BB–8979

"Piney Brown Blues."
Pete Johnson and His Boogie Woogie Boys.
　　　DE–18121

"Pinetop's Blues."
Pine Top Smith—Boogie Woogie Piano.
　　　BB–1002

"Please Mr. Johnson."
Buddy Johnson. DE–8507

"Pleasin' Man Blues."
Helen Humes and Lester Young. AL–

"Plow Hand Blues."
Big Bill Broonzy, vocal with guitar and piano.
OK–05452

"Poor Boy Blues."
St. Louis Jimmy. BB–9040

"Poor Man's Blues."
Bessie Smith, and novelty accompaniment.
CO–14399

"Port of Harlem Blues."
Frank Newton Quartet. BN–14

"Potato Head Blues."
Louis Armstrong and His Savoy Ballroom Five.
CO–35660

"Pounding Heart Blues."
Sidney Bechet's Quintet. BN–6

"Pounding Heart Blues."
Port of Harlem Jazzmen. BN–6

"Prayin' The Blues."
Dorsey Brothers Orchestra. CO–36063

"Preachin' The Blues."
Bessie Smith, accompanied by Joe Smith, Charlie Green, Fletcher Henderson and James P. Johnson. CO–35842

"Profoundly Blue."
Edmond Hall Celeste Quartet. BN–17

"Project Highway."
Sonny Boy Williamson; vocal, harmonica, guitar. BB–7302–B

"Put 'Em Down Blues."
Louis Armstrong and His Hot Five. CO–59–60

"Ragging the Scale Blues."
Joe Venuti and His New Yorkers. OD–238122

"Railroad Blues."
Cow Cow Davenport, piano. DE–7462

"Railroad Blues."
Trixie Smith, and Fletcher Henderson's Orchestra. CO–81–82

"Rainy Day Blues."
Yank Rachell, singer with instrumental accompaniment. BB–8993

"Rainy Day Blues."
Big Joe Turner, vocal, with Willie Smith, piano.
DE–7824

"Rambler's Blues."
Lonnie Johnson, vocalist. BB–34–0708

"Ramblin' On My Mind."
Robert Johnson; vocal-guitar. PE–7–05–81

"Ramblin' With That Woman."
Washboard Sam and His Washboard Band.
VI–20–2606

"Really The Blues."
Tommy Ladnier and His Orchestra. BB–10089

"Red Onion Blues."
Johnny Dodds and His Orchestra. DE–18094

"Red River Blues."
Jay McShann. DE–8595

"Red River Blues."
Laura Smith; vocal-piano. VI–20945–B

"Rent Party Blues."
Johnny Hodges and Orchestra. OK–5100

"Revolutionary Blues."
Mezz Mezzrow and His Orchestra. BB–10088

"Rhapsody in Blue."
Glenn Miller. VI–20–1529

"Rich Man's Blues."
Dinah Washington, Lucky Thompson, and His All Stars. AP–374

"Richmond Blues."
Julius Daniels; vocal, banjo. VI–21065–B

"Ride, Red, Ride."
Lucky Millinder and His Orchestra. DE–4146

"River Bed Blues."
Woody Herman and His Orchestra. DE–2629

"Riverside Blues."
Alice Moore, vocal, with instrumental accompaniment. DE–7028

"Riverside Blues."
King Oliver's Jazz Band. OK–40034

"Roberta."
Lead Belly, vocal-guitar. BB–8709

"Rock Island Line."
Leadbelly, the Zutty Singleton Creole Trio and Band, and others. CA–CE–16

"Rocking the Blues."
Count Basie and His Orchestra. OK–6010

"Rocking The Blues."
Port of Harlem Jazzmen. BN–3

"Rocks in My Bed."
Joe Turner with Freddie Slack Trio. DE–4093

"Rocky Mountain Blues."
Duke Ellington and His Cotton Club Orchestra.
CO–35682

"Rocky Mountain Blues."
Fletcher Henderson and His Orchestra.
CO–970D

"Roll Dem Bones."
Jazz Gillum, instr. accomp. VI–20–2580

"Roll Me, Baby."
Tommy McClennan, singer with instrumental accompaniment. BB–34–0706

"Room Rent Blues."
King Oliver's Jazz Band. OK–8148

"Rounder's Luck."
Homer Callahan; vocal-guitar.   ME–6–02–59

"Royal Garden Blues."
Count Basie and His Rhythm Section. CO–101

"Royal Garden Blues."
Bix Beiderbecke and New Orleans Lucky.
CO–35664

"Royal Garden Blues."
Bob Crosby and His Orchestra.   DE–3339

"Royal Garden Blues."
Tommy Dorsey and His Orchestra.   VI–25326

"Royal Garden Blues."
Edmond Hall's Blue Note Jazz Men.   BN–29

"Royal Garden Blues."
John Kirby and Orchestra.   OK–5187

"Royal Garden Blues."
Ted Lewis and His Orchestra.   CO–35684

"Royal Garden Blues."
Wingy Mannone and His Orchestra. BB–10331

"Royal Garden Blues."
Mezz Mezrow and His Orchestra.   BB–10087

"Royal Garden Blues."
Red Nichols and His Pennies.   CA–10029

"Royal Garden Blues."
Zutty Singleton and His Band.   DE–465

"Royal Garden Blues."
The Wolverines (Bix Beiderbecke, Cornet and
others).   HRS–26

"Sail On Little Girl, Sail On."
Lead Belly, vocal with guitar.   BB–8550

"Salty Mama Blues."
Joe Marsala and His Delta Four.   GE–1717

"San."
Paul Whiteman's Orchestra.   CA–10026

"San Antonio Blues."
Big Bill, vocal-guitar.   CO–38070

"Santa Claus Blues."
Clarence Williams' Blue Five.   OK–8245

"Satanic Blues."
Bud Freeman and His Summe Cum Laude
Orchestra.   DE–2781

"Saturday Night Blues."
Sidney Bechet and His New Orleans Feet-
warmers.   BN–502

"Seaman's Blues."
Ernest Tubb, with Instr. accom.   DE–46119

"Secret Tojo Blues."
Brownie McGhee.   DISC–727

"See See Rider Blues."
Bea Booze, vocal.   DE–48055

"Serenade in Blue."
Benny Goodman and His Orchestra. CO–36622

"Shaking the Blues Away."
Tampa Blue Band.   PA–3460

"Shaking the Blues Away."
Paul Whiteman.   GR–5647

"She's A Solid Old Killer."
Tampa Red, with instr. accom.   VI–20–2597

"She Wanted To Sell My Monkey."
Tampa Red.   BB–9024

"Shipwreck Blues."
Bessie Smith, with novelty accompaniment.
CO–14663

"Shorty George."
Sung with guitar by Smith Casey at Clemens
State Farm, Brazoria, Texas, 1939. In: Album
IV: Library of Congress, Washington, D. C.,
1943.   AAFS17B1

"Sidewalk Blues."
Jelly Roll Morton and His Red Hot Peppers.
RCA Reissue

"Silicosis Is Killin' Me."
Pinewood Tom (Joshua White); vocal-guitar.
PE–6–05–51

"Singin' The Blues."
Bobby Hackett and Orchestra.   OK–5493

"Singin' The Blues."
Lionel Hampton and His Orchestra. VI–26557

"Singin' The Blues."
Frankie Trumbauer.   OD–165093

"Sister Kate."
Barney Bigard, Eddie Miller's Quartet, and
others.   CA–CE–16

"Skunk Hollow Blues."
Johnny Hodges and Orchestra.   OK–5533

"Sleepy Man Blues."
Bukka White, vocal, with guitar and washboard.   OK–05743

"Sloppy Drunk Blues."
Washboard Rhythm Kings.   BB–8164

"Slow and Easy Blues."
Jimmy Yaucey, piano.   VI–26591

"Slow Drag."
Cow Cow Davenport; piano.   PA–12800

"Slow 'Em Down Blues."
Art Hodes and His Chicagoans.   BN–506

"Smokehouse Blues."
Jelly Roll Morton and His Red Hot Peppers.
BB–8372

"Smokehouse Blues."
Omer Simeon, Earl Hines, Claude Roberts,
Wallace Bishop.   BR–7109

"Sobbin' Blues."
Bunny Berigan and His Orchestra.   VI–26116

"Society Blues."
Kid Org: Spikes Pods of Pepper Orchestra.
Nordskog–3009

"S.O.L. Blues."
Louis Armstrong and His Savoy Ballroom Five.
CO–35661

"Solid Blues."
Lonnie Johnson, vocal-guitar and piano.
DISC–710

"Someday, Baby."
Joe Williams.   BB–9025

"Some Day Blues."
Pete Johnson Blues Trio.   BN–11

"Southern Casey Jones."
Jesse James; vocal, piano.   DE–7213

"Southern Exposure."
Joshua White, vocal-guitar.   KE–514

"Special Agent."
Sleepy John Estes; vocal-guitar.   DE–7491

"Spike Driver Blues."
Miss. John Hurt; vocal-guitar.   OK–8692

"Stack O'Lee Blues."
Johnny Dodds and His Chicago Boys. DE–1676

"Stars Fell on Alabama."
Jack Teagarden's Chicagoans.   CA–10027

"St. James Infirmary."
Josh White, vocal-guitar.   ASCH–358–2A

"St. James Infirmary Blues."
Artie Shaw and His Orchestra, vocal and
trumpet solo by "Hot Lips" Page.   VI–27895

"St. Louis Blues."
Albert Ammons, piano.   SO–12002

"St. Louis Blues."
Louis Armstrong.   OD–165975

"St. Louis Blues."
Stella Brooks.   DISC–620

"St. Louis Blues."
Chamber Music Society of Lower Basin Street
and Dixieland Jazz Group. In: *Birth of Blues.*
VP–82

"St. Louis Blues."
Dorsey Brothers Orchestra.   DE–119

"St. Louis Blues."
W. C. Handy.   EL–5039

"St. Louis Blues."
John Kirby and His Orchestra.   VI–27926

"St. Louis Blues."
Meade Lux Lewis, piano.   SI–12002

"St. Louis Blues."
Guy Lombardo and His Orchestra. DE–2478

"St. Louis Blues."
Vincent Lopez Orchestra.   BR–5056

"St. Louis Blues."
Emmet Miller, vocal.   OD–165415

"St. Louis Blues."
Django Reinhardt, guitar and solo. SWING 7

"St. Louis Blues."
Maxine Sullivan, vocal with Claude Thornhill
and band.   VI–25895 DE–4154 CO–36341

"St. Louis Blues."
Art Tatum, piano.   DE–8550

"St. Louis Blues."
Paul Whiteman Orchestra.   KE–5149

"St. Louis Blues."
Mary Lou Williams and her Chosen Five.
ASCH–450–1004

"St. Louis Woman Blues."
St. Louis Jimmy.   BB–9040

"St. Peter Blues."
Nolan Welch, vocal, with Louis Armstrong
cornet, and Richard M. James, piano. OK–8372

"Steel Guitar Blues."
Roy Acuff and his Smoky Mountain Boys.
OK–4376

"Stingaree Blues."
King Oliver and His Orchestra.   BB–10707

"Stones in My Passway."
Robert Johnson; Negro singer, guitar, traces
of voodoo.   VO–3723

"Stormy Monday Blues."
Earl Hines and His Orchestra.   BB–11567

"Streamline Blues."
Johnnie Temple, vocal, with orchestral accompaniment.   DE–7660

"Street Wallein' Blues."
Washboard Rhythm Kings; vocals, washboard
band.   BB–8155–A

"Sue Cow."
Bo Carter; vocal-guitar.   BB–B–6695

"Suitcase Blues."
Hersal Thomas, piano.   OK–8227

"Swinging the Blues."
Count Basie and His Orchestra.   DE–1880

"Tailspin Blues."
Mound City Blue Blowers.   BB–10209

"Talking About My Time."
Pinewood Tom (Joshua White) and B. Moss:
Duet, 2 guitars.   ME–5–11–59

"T.B. Blues."
Lead Belly, vocal-guitar.   BB–8559

"T.B. Blues."
Josh White, vocal-guitar.   ASCH–550–1A

"T.B. Blues."
Sonny Boy Williamson, vocal with instrumental
accompaniment.   BB–8333

"T-Bone Blues."
Les Hite and His Orchestra. BB–11210

"Tailgate Ramble."
Wingy Manone's Dixieland Band, and others.
CA–CE–16

"Tailspin Blues."
Mound City Blue Blowers. GR–6951

"Tell Me, Mama."
Jazz Gillum, vocal, with instrumental accompaniment. BB–34–0707

"Tell Me Why."
Lonnie Johnson, vocal-guitar. DISC–5060

"Tell Me Your Blues."
Jimmie Lytell and His Dixieland Seven.
BE–106

"Terraplane Blues."
Robert Johnson, vocal, with guitar. VO–03416

"Terrible Blues."
Clarence Williams Red Onion Jazz Babies.
VI–31

"Texas Blues."
Foy Willing and His Riders of the Purple Sage.
CA–162

"Texas Moaner Blues."
Clarence Williams' Blue Five. OK–8171

"That Ain't Right."
King Cole Trio. BB–8630

"That's The Blues Old Man."
Johnny Hodges and His Orchestra. BB–1117

"The Basement Blues."
Andy Kirk, band. BR–500124

"The Big Eight Blues."
Jack Teagarden's Big Eight. HRS–2007

"The Birth of the Blues."
Marlene Fingerle and Arthur Schutt. DE–24037

"The Birth of the Blues."
Vincent Lopez. BR–5056

"The Birth of the Blues."
Jack Smith, vocal. GR–5247

"The Blues."
Artie Shaw and His New Music. OK–4401

"The Blues."
All Star Band. VI–26144

"The Blues in My Flat."
Benny Goodman Quartet. VI–26044

"The Blues My Baby Gave to Me."
Frank Newton and His Orchestra. BB–10216

"The Blues in Your Flat."
Benny Goodman Quartet. VI–26044

"The Blues What Am."
Jazz Gillum, Blues Singer, with instr. accomp.
VI–20–2580

"The Bourgeois Blues."
Lead Belly, vocal with guitar. MU–227

"The Cannon Ball."
Pete Brown and His Band. DE–8625

"The 'C' Jam Blues."
Duke Ellington, Solos by Ray Nance. VI–27856

"The East Virginia Blues."
Carter Family; vocals, guitar, oboes.
PE–13153–B; BB–5650–B

"The East Virginia Blues."
In: Smoky Mountain Ballads. Native Mountain Singers and Instruments. VP–79

"The Good Old Hometown Blues."
Boyce's Harlem Serenaders. DE–8602

"The Heartsick Blues."
Buchanan Brothers and the Georgia Catamounts. VI–20–2553

"The Last Call."
Lonnie Johnson, vocalist with instrumental accompaniment. BB–8980

"The Last Fair Deal Going Down."
Robert Johnson; Negro singer, guitar.
PE–7–04–60

"The Little Boy Blues."
High Martin, and Sandra Deel, and chorus and orch. DE–24373

"The Lonesome Road."
Armstrong and Orchestra. OK–3026

"The Mooche."
Sonny Greer and the Duke's Men. CA–10028

"The New Confessin' Blues."
Jay McShann. DE–8595

"The N.R.A. Blues."
Bill Cox and Cliff Hobbs; vocal duet, guitar.
PE–13090

"The Red Cross Store Blues."
Lead Belly, vocal-guitar. BB–8709

"Things About Coming My Way."
Tampa Red and Georgia Tom; vocals, guitars.
VO–1637

"Thirsty Mama Blues."
Hot Lips Page Trio. BB–8981

"32–20 Blues."
Robert Johnson; vocal-guitar. PE–7–04–60

"Three Ball Blues."
Blind Boy Fuller, vocal, with guitar, and Sonny Boy Terry, harmonica. OK–05440

"Thriller Blues."
Clarence Williams Blue Five. BB–11368

"Timbrook Blues."
Jib Byrd; vocal-guitar. PA–12997

"Times Square Blues.
Clarence Profit Trio. DE–8503

"Tin Roof Blues."
Charlie Barnet and His Orchestra.   BB–10131

"Tin Roof Blues."
Tommy Dorsey and His Orchestra.   VI–26105

"Tin Roof Blues."
Art Hodes' Blue Three.   SI–102

"Tin Roof Blues."
Sherry Magee and Dixielanders.   OK–5281

"Tin Roof Blues."
New Orleans Rhythm Kings.   UHCA–87–88

"Tip Easy Blues."
Jones and Collins Astoria Hot Eight. BB–10952

"Tishomingo Blues."
Henry Busse and His Orchestra.   DE–4325

"Tishomingo Blues."
Duke Ellington.   BR–500245

"TNT Blues."
Fletcher Henderson and His Orchestra.
CO–509D

"Toddlin' Blues."
Bix and His Rhythm Jugglers.   HRS–23

"Tonky Blues."
Maurice Rocco, piano.   DE–8523

"Too Evil to Cry."
Champion Jack Dupre, piano-vocal.
ASCH–550–2B

"Train Fare Blues."
Arthur "Big Boy" Crudup.   VI–20–2565

"Training Camp Blues."
Roosevelt Sykes.   OK–6709

"Transportation Blues."
Charlie Trout's Melody Artists.   CO–4479

"Trixie Blues."
Trixie Smith, and band.   DE–7469

"Trouble in Mind."
Jay McShann's Kansas City Stompers.
CA–10030

"Trumpet Blues."
Harry James, trumpet and orchestra. CO–36549

"Trumpet Blues."
Korn Kobblers.   EL–5041

"Twin City Blues."
Woody Herman and His Orchestra. DE–1801

"Two Faced Man."
Jimmie Lytell and His Dixieland Seven.
BE–106

"219 Blues."
Louis Armstrong and His Orchestra. DE–18090

"Two White Horses."
Sung with guitar by Smith Casey at Clemens
State Farm, Brazoria, Texas, 1939. In: Album
IV: Washington, D. C., 1943.   AAFS17A1

"Uncle Bud."
Tampa Red and Georgia Tom; vocals-guitars.
VO–1263

"Uncle Sam Says Blues."
Joshua White, vocal-guitar.   KE–514

"Unfair Lovers."
Little Eddie Boyd.   VI–20–2555

"Unfortunate Blues."
The Champ Music of L. Welk.   OK–5803

"Unlucky Woman."
Pete Brown and His Band.   DE–8613

"Until My Baby Comes Home."
Nora Lee King, accompanied by Mary Lou
Williams.   ASCH–550

"Until My Baby Comes Home Blues."
Mary Lou Williams—Nora Lee King, piano
and vocal.   ASCH–550–2A

"Uptown Blues."
Jimmie Lunceford and Orchestra.   OK–5362

"Varsity Yale Blues."
Piccadilly Revels Band.   CO–4641

"Vicksburg Blues."
Leroy Carr, vocal, with Scrappy Blackell, guitar.   BB–7970

"Wabash Blues."
Louis Panico, band.   BR–8710

"Wabash Blues."
Boyd Senter, clarinet, etc.   OD–165283

"Wailing Blues."
The Cellar Boys.   HRS–3

"Walking Blues."
Dinah Washington, with Lucky Thompson, and
His All Stars.   AP–374

"Wake Up Cold In Hand."
Jazz Gillum.   BB–9042

"Wanderin' Blues."
Charlie Barnet and His Orchestra.   BB–10721

"Wang Wang Blues."
Jungle Band.   BR–500140

"Wang Wang Blues."
Paul Whiteman's Orchestra.   CA–10026

"War Time Blues."
Sonny Boy Williamson, vocal with instrumental
accompaniment.   BB–8580

"Washboard Blues."
Glen Gray and Casa Loma Orchestra with
Hoagy Carmichael, vocal.   DE–2397

"Weary Blues."
Johnny Dodds, Black Bottom Stompers.
VO–15632

"Weary Blues."
Tommy Dorsey and His Orchestra.   VI–26054

"Weary Blues."
Dorsey Brothers Orchestra. DE–15013

"Weary Blues."
Erskine Hawkins and His Orchestra. BB–7839

"Weary Blues."
Tommy Ladnier and His Orchestra. BB–10086

"Weary Blues."
Kid Rena's Jazz Band. DELTA–807/806

"Weary Land Blues."
J. C. Higginbotham Quintet. BN–501

"Weary Land Blues."
Frank Newton Quintet. BN–501

"Weatherbeaten Blues."
Teddy Weatherford, piano and solo. SWING 5

"Wee Baby Blues."
Art Tatum and His Band. DE–8526

"Welfare Blues."
Speckled Red, piano. BB–8069

"West End Blues."
Louis Armstrong (trumpet) and Earl Hines (piano). CO–36377

"West End Blues."
Louis Armstrong and His Hot Five. OK–3204

"West End Blues."
Stella Brooks. DISC–620

"West End Blues."
Jelly Roll Morton and His New Orleans Jazz-men. BB–10442

"West End Blues."
Cootie Williams and His Rug Cutters. OK–6370

"What-Cha-Call-'Em Blues."
Fletcher Henderson and His Orchestra. CO–35668

"What Did I Do To Be So Black and Blue."
Mugsy Spanier and His Ragtime Band. BB–10682

"Whatcha Going to Do."
Josh White, vocal-guitar. KE-8138

"What Every Woman Knows."
Etta Jones with Luther Henderson and His Orch. VI–20–2564

"What is the Matter Now?"
Skeets Tolbert and his Gentlemen of Living, with Jean Eldridge. DE–8631

"When I Get to Thinkin'."
Blues Singer with piano, drums, and guitar. OK–6739

"When the Sun Goes Down."
Libby Holman, vocalist and Josh White, guitar. DE–18305

"When the Sun Goes Down."
Pinewood Tom (Joshua White), vocal-guitar. PE–5–12–51

"When They Play Them Blues."
Frankie (Half Pint) Jaxon. DE–7742

"When You Feel Low Down."
Lonnie Johnson (Blues Singer), with piano, guitar and bass. BB–9006–B

"Whistler's Blues."
Milton Orent—Frank Roth Orch. DISC–6067

"Whistling Blues."
Meade Lux Lewis, whistling and piano accompaniment. BB–10175

"Why Don't You Do Right?"
Benny Goodman and His Orchestra. CO–36652

"Why I Love You."
Lonnie Johnson, vocal-guitar. DISC–5062

"Why Should I Be Blue."
Tennessee Ramblers. BB–8984

"Wild Man Blues."
Louis Armstrong's Original Washboard Beaters. PA–3492

"Wild Man Blues."
Sidney Bechet and His New Orleans Feet-warmers. VI–26640

"Wild Man Blues."
Johnny Dodds and His Chicago Boys. DE–2111

"Wild Man Blues."
Johnny Dodd's Black Bottom Stompers. BR–3567

"Wild Man Blues."
Jelly Roll Morton and His Red Hot Peppers. BB–10256

"Wild Man Blues."
Jimmie Noone Orch. BR–500165

"Willow Tree."
Mildred Bailey and Her Alley Cats. DE–18108

"Willow Tree Blues."
Sonny Boy Williamson. VI–20–2623

"Winin' Boy Blues."
Jelly Roll Morton, piano. GE–4004

"Winin' Boy Blues."
Jelly Roll Morton and His New Orleans Jazz-men. BB–10429

"Wolverine Blues."
Chicago Jazz Classics: Goodman, Miller, Freeman, Sullivan. BB–1007

"Wolverine Blues."
Bob Crosby and His Orchestra. DE–3340

"Wolverine Blues."
Jelly Roll Morton Trio. BB–10258

"Wolverine Blues."
Jack Teagarden and His Orchestra. CO–35297

"Workingman Blues."
King Oliver's Jazz Band. OK–40034

"Workingman's Blues."
Brownie McGhee (Blind Fuller No. 2).
OK–6698

"Worried Blues."
Lead Belly, vocal-guitar. BB–8570

"Worried Blues."
Carter Family, vocal-guitar. PE–7–05–55

"Worried Life Blues."
Andy Kirk and His Cloud of Joy. DE–4381

"Worried Man Blues."
In: *Smoky Mountain Ballads*. Native Mountain
Singers and Instruments. VP–79

"W.P.A. Blues."
Bigg Bill Broomzy, vocal, guitar, piano, banjo.
PE–6–08–61

"Yellow Dog Blues."
Eddie Condon's Chicago Rhythm Kings.
BR–500315

"Yellow Dog Blues."
Art Hodes and His Chicagoans. BN–505

"Yellow Dog Blues."
The Rhythmakers. UHCA–107

"You Can't Lose-A Me Cholly."
Lead Belly, vocal-guitar. BB–8750

"You Don't Know My Mind Blues."
Teddy Grace, and Ensemble. DE–2605

"You Got Me To The Place."
Lil Green. BB–9010

"You Got to Love the Gal."
Little Eddie Boyd. VI–20–2555.

"You'll Get Them Blues."
Buddy Johnson and His Band. DE–8611

"Young Woman's Blues."
Bessie Smith, and members of Fletcher Henderson's Orchestra. CO–35673

"You've Been A Good Ole Wagon."
Bessie Smith, vocalist. CO–35672

THE NEGRO—MINSTRELSY

BIBLIOGRAPHY

Boston Public Library
The Allen A. Brown Collection of Books on the Stage.

Buffalo Public Library. Grosvenor Library
Collections on Negro Minstrelsy.
An extensive collection of material on the subject.

Damon, Samuel F.
"The Negro in Early American Songsters." *Papers of the Bibliographical Society of America* (Chicago) 28 (Part 2): 132–163, 1934.

Gordon, Robert Winslow
Chronological List of Songsters, 1760–1875. Washington, D. C.: Library of Congress, Music Division.

Louisville (Ky.) Free Public Library. Colored Department
Some Books and Pamphlets, Music, Magazines and Newspapers by Negro Writers, Composers and Editors in the Colored Department of the Louisville Free Public Library. Louisville, Ky., 1921. 11 pp.

National Recreation Association
Music Composed by Negroes. New York: 192–. 7 pp. Typewritten Community Service, No. 168a.

New York Public Library
The Folk Music of the Western Hemisphere; a list of references in the New York Public Library. Compiled and annotated by Julius Mattfeld. New York: 1924. pp. 799–830, 864–889.

New York Public Library. Main Branch
Theatre Collection.
A vast amount of material—books,—newspapers, clippings, programs, etc. on all aspects of the American theatre. Excellent collection of minstrel plays and songsters.

New York Public Library. 135th Street Branch
The Negro; a selected bibliography compiled by the 135th Street Branch Library, situated in Negro Harlem.... New York: The New York Public Library, 1930. 14 pp.
In 1935, a new list (the third) was compiled, 21 pp., illus. In 1940, a fourth list was made, of 19 pp., illus.

Sonneck, Oscar G. T., and Upton, William T.
List of Songsters. In: *A Bibliography of Early Secular American Music,* (18th Century). (pp. 533–535). Washington, D. C.: The Library of Congress, (Music Division), 1945. 617 pp.

Thorpe, Alice Louise
American Songsters of the Eighteenth Century. Providence, R. I.: Brown University.

Wittke, Carl
"Bibliography of Minstrelsy." In: *Tambo and Bones.* Durham, N. C.: Duke University Press, 1930.
Actually the bibliography is not listed in that manner. It runs through the volume in the footnotes. Altogether it makes up a splendid list—books, articles, and newspapers, as well as songsters.

Work, Monroe Nathan, comp.
A Bibliography of the Negro in Africa and America. New York: The H. W. Wilson Co., 1928. xxi, 698 pp.

GENERAL STUDIES

Anon
Negro Minstrelsy, the Old Fashioned Troupes. Boston: 189–.
This account, a most valuable one, is found in the *Allen A. Brown Collection of Books on the Stage,* Boston Public Library.

Asbury, Herbert
"The Old-Time Gangs of New York." *American Mercury,* August, 1927. pp. 478–486.

Bacon, L. I.
"Banjo's Ringin', Darkies Singin'." *Christian Science Monitor:* 4, (January 24) 1942, illustrated.

Ballantine, W. E.
"Christy Minstrelsy: its Origin and Development in America and England." *English Illus. Magazine* 4:43–52, 1909 (London). illus.

"Banjo and Bones (Negro Minstrels)."
Saturday Review of Politics, Literature, Science and Art. (London) 57:739–740, 1884.

Barnes, Edwin N. C.
Near Immortals? Stephen Foster, Edward MacDowell, Victor Herbert.... Washington, D. C.: Music Education Publications, 1940. 48 pp.

"Beginnings of Negro Minstrelsy."
Sun (N. Y.). Vol. 58, Jan. 30, 1918. p. 6, col. 3. An editorial.

"Black Stephen Foster" (Bland).
Time 34:44, (August 21) 1939.

Bowman, J. G.
"Singer to Pioneers." Stephen Foster. *Atlantic Monthly* 156:83–88, (July) 1935.

Branen, Jeffrey T., and Johnson, Frederick G.
How to Stage a Minstrel Show; a manual for the amateur burnt cork director. Illustrated by Harlan Tarbell. Chicago: T. S. Denison & Co., 1921. 65 pp., illus.

Brown, T. Allston
"Early History of Negro Minstrelsy." *New York Clipper* 61:24, May–August, 1913.

————.
History of the American Stage. Containing biographical sketches of every member of the profession that has appeared on the American stage, from 1733 to 1870. New York: Dick & Fitzgerald, 1870. 421 pp.

————.
History of the New York Stage from the First Performance in 1732 to 1901. New York: Dodd, Mead and Co., 1903. 3 vols.

————.
"The Origin of Minstrelsy." In: *Fun in Black* by Charles H. Day. New York: R. M. DeWitt, 1874. 70 pp., illus.

Bullivant, Cecil H.
Home Fun. New York: Dodge Publishing Co., 1910. 549 pp., illus.

Burnett, J. G.
"National Elements in Stephen Foster Art." *South Atlantic Quarterly* 21:322–326, 1922. (Durham, North Carolina).

Carlton, Albert
The Business End of a Minstrel Show. New York: M. Whitmark & Sons, 1906. 41 pp.

Clapp, Henry Austin
Reminiscences of a Dramatic Critic, with an essay on the art of Henry Irving. Boston: Houghton Mifflin and Co., 1902. viii, 241 pp.
  It has a chapter on: "Spectacle, farce, melodrama, and minstrelsy fifty years ago."

Clark, Thomas D.
"My Old Kentucky Home in Retrospect." *Filson Club History Quarterly.* (Louisville), April, pp. 104–116, 1948.

Courtright, William
The Complete Minstrel Guide, containing gags, jokes, parodies, speeches, farces and full directions for a complete minstrel show. Chicago: The Dramatic Publ. Co., 1901. 137 pp.

Cravens, K.
"Birth of Sweet Adeline." *Etude* 60:138+, (February) 1942.

Crawford, Mary Caroline
The Romance of the American Theatre. Boston: Little, Brown and Co., 1913. xiv, 407 pp.

Crosby, Agnes Foster
"The Man Who Wrote 'Old Folks at Home'." *Bookman* 38:615–617, 1914.

Damon, Samuel F.
"The Negro in Early American Songsters." *Papers of the Bibliographical Society of America* (Chicago) 28. (Part 2):132–163, 1934.

Darkow, Martin
"Stephen C. Foster und das amerikanische Volklied." *Die Musik* 4 (Heft 16):268–280, 1904 (Berlin).

Davidge, William Pleater
Footlight Flashes New York: American News Company, 1866. xii, 274 pp., illus.

Davis, Albert W.
"Past Days of Minstrelsy, Variety, Circus and Side Show." *Americana* 7:529–547, 1912.

Day, Charles H.
"Fun in Black." *Harper's Magazine* (New York), 1874, pp. 16, 42.

————.
Fun in Black; or, Sketches of Minstrel Life. New York: R. M. De Witt, 1874. 70 pp., illus.

De Voto, Bernard
"Stephen Foster Songs." *Harper* 183:109–112, (June) 1941.

Dick's Ethiopian Scenes, Variety Sketches and Stump Speeches. New York: Dick & Fitzgerald, 1879.

Dick's Stump Speeches and Minstrel Jokes. New York: Dick & Fitzgerald, 1889.

Dimmick, Ruth Crosby
Our Theatres To-Day and Yesterday. Beginning of the drama on Manhattan island and the troublous days of early managers and players, with anecdotal account of the growth of the amusement industry. Stories and personal sketches of men and women connected with famous houses in a bygone era, as well as the present. From 1732 to 1913. New York: The H. K. Fly Company, 1913. 97 pp., illus.

Dondore, Dorothy Anne
The Prairie and the Making of Middle America. Cedar Rapids, Iowa: The Torch Press, 1928. 483 pp.

Dumont, Frank
Burnt Cork; or, The Amateur Minstrel. A collection of humorous speeches, end men's jokes, conundrums, recitations and farces.... New York: De Witt, 1881.

————.
Frank Dumont's Minstrel Joke book. New York: De Witt, 1898.

————.
The Whitmark Amateur Minstrel Guide and Burnt Cork Encyclopedia. New York: M. Whitmark & Sons, 1899. vii, 149 pp., illus.

Eaton, Walter P.
"Negro Minstrels." *The American Scholar:* (March) 1935.

Field, Al Griffith
"History of American Minstrelsy." *The Kit Kat* (Columbus, O.) 8 (No. 2).

————.
Watch Yourself Go By. Columbus, O.: Printed by Spohr & Glenn, 1912. 593 pp., illus.

Foster, Morrison
Extracts from the Scrapbook of Foster.... n.p., n.d. 332 f.
  Typewritten reproductions of newspaper clippings . . . from the original. (In New York Public Library).

——————.
My Brother Stephen. Indianapolis: Privately Printed, 1932. 55 pp.

Francis and Day's "Jokelets," as Performed by the Mohawk, Moore and Burgess' Minstrels. New York: n.d.

Fuller, Hiram
Belle Brittan on Tour, at Newport, and Here and There. New York: Derby & Jackson, 1858. xii, 359 pp.

Gaines, Francis Pendleton
The Southern Plantation: A Study in the Development and Accuracy of a Tradition. New York: Columbia University Press, 1925. viii, 245 pp.

Galbreath, Charles Burleigh
Daniel Decatur Emmett, author of "Dixie." Columbus, O.: Press of F. J. Heer, 1904. 66 pp., illus.

Goldberg, Isaac
Tin Pan Alley; A Chronicle of the American Popular Music Racket. New York: The John Day Company, 1930. xi, 341 pp., illus., music.

Gombosi, Otto Johannes
"Stephen Foster and 'Gregory Walker'." *MQ* 30:133–146, 1944.

Gough, John B.
Sunlight and Shadows, or Gleanings from My Life Work. Comprising personal experiences and opinions, anecdotes, incidents, and reminiscences.... Hartford: A. D. Worthington and Co., 1881. xxii, 542 pp.

Greenwood, I. J.
The Circus: Its Origin and Growth Prior to 1835. New York: Dunlop Society, 1898.

Habberton, J.
"The World's Greatest Song Writer." *Literary Era,* June, 1901 (Philadelphia).

Hare, Walter Ben
The Minstrel Encyclopedia. Boston: Walter H. Baker Company, 1921. 222 pp., illus., music.

Harris, Joel Chandler
"Negro Plantation Music and Banjo." *Critic* 3:505–534.

Haverly, Jack
Negro Minstrels, A Complete Guide to Negro Minstrelsy. Chicago: F. J. Drake & Company, 1902. 129 pp.

Haywood, Charles
James A. Bland: Prince of the Colored Song Writers. Flushing, N. Y.: Flushing Historical Society, 1944. 8 pp.
The life and work of Bland, and his place in American minstrelsy.

Hodges, Fletcher
A Pittsburgh Composer and His Memorial. Pittsburgh: The Historical Society of Western Pennsylvania, 1938. 32 pp.

Homby, B. R.
"Oldtimer Remembered, Darling Nelly Gray." *Time* 39:48, (March 23), 1942.

Hornblow, Arthur
A History of the Theatre in America from Its Beginnings to the Present Time. Philadelphia: J. B. Lippincott Company, 1919. 2 vols.

Howard, John Tasker
Stephen Foster, America's Troubadour. New York: Thomas Y. Crowell Co., 1934. xiii, 445 pp., illus., bibl. (pp. 402–429).

——————.
"The Literature on Stephen Foster." *Notes* (Washington, D. C.) 1 (No. 2): March, 1944.

Hutton, Laurence
"The Negro on the Stage." *Harper's Magazine* 79:133–134, 1889 (June).

Ireland, Joseph Norton
Records of the New York Stage from 1750 to 1860. New York: T. H. Morrell, 1866–67. 2 vols.

Jackson, George Pullen
"Stephen Foster's Debt to American Folk-Song." *MQ* 22:154–169, 1936.

James, Edward
The Amateur Negro Minstrel Guide. New York: Dick & Fitzgerald, 1880.

Jennings, J. J.
Theatrical and Circus Life; or Secrets of the Stage, Greenroom and Sawdust Arena. St. Louis: Sun Publishing Co., 1882. 608 pp., illus.

K., F. J.
"Semi-centennial of the death of Stephen Foster." *Musical America* 19 (No. 6):9, 1913.

Keeler, Ralph
"Three Years as a Negro Minstrel." *Atlantic Monthly* 24:71–85, 1869.

——————.
Vagabond Adventures. Boston: Fields, Osgood & Co., 1872. viii, 274 pp.

Kendall, John Smith
"New Orleans' Negro Minstrels." *Louisiana Historical Quarterly,* January, 1947. pp. 128–148. (New Orleans).

King, Mrs. A. T.
"Some Facts About Stephen Collins Foster." *Musical Courier* 79 (No. 7):16, 1919.

Langworthy, Helen
The Theatre in the Lower Valley of Ohio, 1797-1860. M. A. Thesis. State University of Iowa, 1926.

Lawrence, John E.
Dixie Minstrel First-Part; a complete routine for the circle. Chicago: T. S. Denison & Co., 1924. 37 pp.
Words of songs only.

Leavitt, M. B.
Fifty Years of Theatrical Management. With reproductions of over 500 photographs. New York: Broadway Publishing Co., 1912. xxii, 735 pp., illus.

Leman, Walter Moore
Memories of an Old Actor. San Francisco: A. Roman Co., 1886. xv, 406 pp.

Lilly, Josiah Kirby
Foster Hall; a reminder of the life and work of Stephen Collins Foster, 1826–1864. Indianapolis: The Author, 1932. 7 pp.

Logan, Olive
"The Ancestry of Brudder Bones." *Harper's Magazine* 58:692.

Ludlow, Noah Miller
Dramatic Life As I Found It; A record of personal experience; with an account of the rise and progress of the drama in the West and South, with anecdotes and biographical sketches of the principal actors and actresses who have at times appeared upon the stage in the Mississippi valley. St. Louis: G. I. Jones and Company, 1880. xix, 733 pp.

McCleary, A. L.
" 'My Old Kentucky Home,' an 85 Year Old Folk Song, and Something of its History." *Etude* 57:299, (May) 1937. Illustrated.

McDevitt, W.
"Old Refrain, 'Swanee River'." *Hobbies* 45:245, (March) 1940.

————.
"Those Good Old Time Songs!, But Who Wrote Them?" *Hobbies* 45:22–23, (April) 1940.

MacGowan, Robert
The Significance of Stephen Collins Foster. Indianapolis: Priv. Print., 1932. 25 pp.

Mackay, Charles
Life and Liberty in America, or, Sketches of a Tour in the United States and Canada in 1857–8. New York: Harper & Brothers, 1859. viii, 413 pp.

Mahan, Bruce E., and Grahame, Pauline
"The Past at Play." *The Palimpsest,* February, 1929.

Marks, Edward Bennet
They All Had Glamour, from the Swedish Nightingale to the Naked Lady. New York: J. Messner, 1944. xii, 448 pp., illus.

————.
They All Sang, From Tony Pastor to Rudy Vallée, as told to Abbott J. Liebling. New York: The Viking Press, 1934. xi, 321 pp., illus., music.

Matthews, Brander
"Banjo and Bones." *Saturday Review (London),* June 7, 1884.

————.
"The Rise and Fall of Negro Minstrelsy." *Scribner's Magazine* 57:754–759, 1915 (June).

May, Earl Chapin
"George R. Guy." *New York Herald Tribune,* July 14, 1929.
About a distinguished minstrel, who together with his six sons formed the famous "Guy Brothers Mighty Minstrels".

————.
"The Good Old Minstrel Days." *The Elks Magazine,* Dec., 1927. pp. 48–52. Illus.

Miller, Kelly
"The Negro Stephen Foster." (James A. Bland). *Etude* 57:431–432+, (July) 1939.

Milligan, Harold Vincent
"Stephen C. Foster." *MTNA,* Ser. 12, pp. 66–72, 1918.

————.
Stephen Collins Foster; A Biography of America's Folksong Composer. New York: G. Schirmer, 1920. viii, 116 pp.

Minstrel Gags and End Men's Handbook. New York: Dick and Fitzgerald, n.d.

"Minstrel Men." *Sun (N. Y.),* vol. 85, Jan. 23, 1918. p. 6, col. 5–6.
Letters from readers relating to old Negro minstrel troupes: San Francisco, Kelly & Leon, Billy Bernard, etc.

Moody, Richard
"Negro Minstrels." *Quarterly Journal of Speech* 30:321–328, 1944.

Murray, Elsie
Stephen Foster at Athens; his first compositions.... Athens, Pa.: Tioga Point Museum, 1941.

Nevin, R. P.
"Stephen C. Foster and Negro Minstrelsy." *Atlantic Monthly* 20:608–616, 1867.

Newcomb, Bobby
Bobby Newcomb's Guide to the Minstrel Stage. New York: De Witt, 1871.

————.
"Tambo": His Jokes and Funny Sayings. With which is incorporated—"Hints to the Amateur Minstrel." New York: De Witt, 1892. 60 pp.

Niles, Abbe
"Ballads, Songs, and Snatches: Columbia Race Records." *Bookman* 67:422–424, (June) 1928.

Niles, John J.
"Shout, Coon, Shout!" *MQ* 16:516–530, 1930.

Oberndorfer, Anne S. F.
"Life and Songs of Stephen C. Foster." *American Collector* 2:391–393, 1926.

"Obituary, Not Eulogistic."
N. Y. Musical Review and Choral Advocate 5 (No. 5): 418-419, 44, 1854; 6 (14-15), 1855.

Odell, George C. D.
Annals of the New York Stage. New York: Columbia University Press, 1927—. Vol. 1.
Vol. I (to 1798) . . . to Vol. XIV (1888–1891) of the series are filled with many valuable references to Negro minstrelsy. Invaluable sources.

Origin of Negro Minstrelsy and the Birth of Emmett's "Dixie." Mt. Vernon, Ohio: Christian Music Publishing Company.

Paskman, Dailey, and Spaeth, Sigmund
"Gentlemen, Be Seated!" A Parade of Old-Time Minstrels. Foreword by Daniel Frohman; profusely illustrated from old prints and photographs, and with complete music for voice and piano. Garden City, N. Y.: Doubleday Doran & Company, 1928. xvii, 247 pp., illus.

"Passing of the Minstrels."
The Literary Digest, August 16, 1919, pp.28–29.
Written on the occasion of the dissolution of the minstrel partnership between Primrose and Dockstader.

Phelps, H. P.
Players of a Century: A Record of the Albany State. Including notices of prominent actors who have appeared in America. Albany: J. McDonough, 1880. x, 424 pp.

Powell, Herbert Preston
The World's Best Book of Minstrelsy. Illustrated by Charles Clark, for producing. . . . Philadelphia: The Penn Publishing Co., 1926. 319 pp., illus.

Purdy, Claire Lee
He Heard America Sing; the Story of Stephen Foster. Illustrated. New York: Julian Messner, 1940. x, 236 pp., music.

Pyper, George D.
The Romance of an Old Playhouse. Salt Lake City, Utah: The Seagull Press, 1928. 343 pp.
The story of the Salt Lake theatre.

Quinn, Arthur Hobson
A History of the American Drama, from the beginning to the Civil War. New York: Harper & Brothers, 1923. xv, 486 pp., bibl.

———.
A History of the American Drama, from the Civil War to the present day. New York: Harper & Brothers, 1927. 2 vols.

Ramsey, F., and Smith, Charles E.
Jazzmen. New York: Harcourt, Brace & Company, 1939.

Reynolds, H.
Minstrel Memories. The Story of Burnt Cork Minstrelsy in Great Britain from 1863 to 1927. London: A. Rivers, Ltd., 1928. 255 pp., plates, ports.
Many of the "monarchs of American minstrelsy" pass across the pages of this informative volume.

Rice, Edw. Le Roy
Monarchs of Minstrelsy from "Daddy" Rice to Date. New York: Kenney Publishing Company, 1911. 366 pp., illus.

Rossiter, H.
How to Put on a Minstrel Show. Chicago: 1931. (With music).

Rothenberg, Irvin W.
"Stephen Collins Foster, his life and his music." *Northumberland County Historical Society, Proc.* 12:152–165, 1942.

Sawyer, Eugene T.
"Old-Time Minstrels of San Francisco Recollections of a Pioneer." *Overland Monthly* (San Francisco) 81:5–7, Oct., 1923. Illus.

Smith, Earl Hobson
Stephen Foster; or, Weep No More My Lady; a biographical play on the life of Stephen Collins Foster, father of American Folk Songs. Knoxville, Tenn.: The Foster Players, 1935. 67 pp.

Smith, Solomon Franklin
The Theatrical Apprenticeship and Anecdotal Recollections of Sol Smith. . . . Comprising a sketch of the first seven years of his professional life; together with some adventures in after years. Philadelphia: Carey & Hart, 1846. 215 pp., illus.

———.
The Theatrical Journey—Work and Anecdotical Recollections of Sol Smith. . . . Philadelphia: T. B. Peterson, 1854. 254 pp.

Spaeth, Sigmund
Barber Shop Ballads and How to Sing Them. New York: Prentice-Hall, 1940.

———.
Read 'Em and Weep. New York: Doubleday, Page & Company, 1927.

———.
Weep Some More, My Lady. New York: Doubleday, Page & Company, 1927.

Spinney, Frank Oakman
"A New Hampshire Minstrel Tours the Coast. Rhodolphus Hall and His Letters." *California Historical Soc. Quart.* (San Francisco) 20: 243–258, 1941.

Spitzer, Marian
"The Lay of the Last Minstrel." *The Saturday Evening Post,* March 7, 1925. pp. 12 ff.

Stone, Henry Dickinson
Personal Recollections of the Drama; or Theatrical Reminiscences. . . . Albany: C. Van Benthuysen & Sons, 1873. xii, 316 pp.

Strang, Lewis Clinton
Players and Plays of the Last Quarter Century; an historical summary of causes and a critical review of conditions existing in the American Theatre at the close of the nineteenth century. Boston: L. C. Page & Company, 1903. 2 vols.

The American Minstrel.
Providence, Rhode Island: L. D. Chapin, semimonthly.

Tompkins, Eugene
History of the Boston Theatre, 1854–1901....
Boston: Houghton Mifflin Co., 1908. xv, 550 pp.

Townsend, Charles
Negro Minstrels; with Endmen's Jokes, gags, speeches, etc.; full instructions for getting up darky entertainment. Chicago: T. S. Denison, 1891. iv, 76 pp.

Towse, John Rankin
Sixty Years of the Theatre—An Old Critic's Memoirs. New York: Century Company, 1916.

Trux, J. J.
"Negro Minstrelsy, (Ancient and Modern)."
Putnam's Monthly 5:72–79, (Jan.) 1855.

Walker, Kent
Staging the Amateur Minstrel Show. Boston: Walter H. Baker Company, 1931. 96 pp., illus.

Walters, Raymond W.
Stephen Foster: Youth's Golden Gleam; A sketch of his life and background in Cincinnati, 1846–1850. Princeton, N. J.: Princeton University Press, 1936.

Wemyss, Francis Courtney
Theatrical Biography of Eminent Actors and Authors. New York: W. Taylor & Co., 1852.

———.
Theatrical Biography, or the Life of an Actor and Manager. Glasgow: 1848.

———.
Twenty-Six Years of the Life of an Actor and Manager.... New York: Burgess, Stringer & Co., 1847. 2 vols.

———.
Wemyss' Chronology of the American Stage, from 1752 to 1852. New York: W. Taylor & Co., 1852. 191 pp.

Werner, Morris Robert
Barnum. New York: Harcourt, Brace and Co., 1926. vii, 381 pp., bibl.

"West Virginia Minstrels."
JAFL 32:358–363, 1919.

"When Minstrelsy Was in Flower."
International Musician (Newark), May, 1941.
p. 26.

White, Newman I.
"The White Man in the Woodpile." *AS* 4 (No. 3): 210, 1929.
The author discusses the influence of white composers and their music upon Negro minstrelsy.

Wilson, Francis
Francis Wilson's Life of Himself. Boston: Houghton Mifflin Company, 1924. ix, 463 pp.

Wittke, Carl Frederick
Tambo and Bones; a History of the American Minstrel Stage. Durham, N. C.: Duke University Press, 1930. ix, 269 pp., bibliographical footnotes.
A scholarly study of the history and development of Negro minstrelsy as part of American social history.

Wood, William B.
Personal Recollections of the Stage, embracing notices of actors, authors, and auditors, during a period of forty years. Philadelphia: H. C. Baird, 1855. xxi, 477 pp.

Wright, R. L.
Hawkers and Walkers. Philadelphia: Lippincott & Company, 1934.

COLLECTIONS—SONGSTERS
(Minstrel and Others)

See: Negro Song Collections, pp. 450-52; Negro Spirituals, pp. 457-61.

Abecco, Rapfael
Sig'r R. Abecco's Sentimental Songster. Eureka Theatre, San Francisco. San Francisco: D. E. Appleton & Co., 1864. 60 pp. (No music).

A Choice Collection of Popular Music, including a variety of miscellaneous reading matter, interesting to the people. Albany: C. Van Benthuysen, 1859. 32 pp.
Unaccompanied melodies.

Ain't You Awful Songster. Containing a full collection of the most popular songs, as sung by the leading artists of the present time. New York: A. J. Fisher, 1874. 60 pp. (Dime Song Books. No. 39).
Words only.

Albain, W.
50 Songs As Sung By The Colored Opera Troupe. Music and words, written, composed, and arranged by W. Albain. London: Davidson, 18—. 34 pp. (Davidson's Universal Melodist).

Allan, Francis D.
Allan's Lone Star Ballads. A Collection of Southern Patriotic Songs, made during Confederate Times. Galveston, Texas: J. D. Sawyer, 1874. iv, 222 pp.
Texts only, some of the tunes indicated.

American Dime Song Book. Philadelphia: cop. 1860.

American Mock-Bird; or, Cabinet of Anacreon, being a Selection of the Most Elegant and Fashionable Songs; Sung in the Anacreontic and Philharmonic Societies, and in most genteel circles, with a Number of Choice Masonic Songs and Sentiments. New York: Published by David Longworth, at the Shakespeare Gallery, No. 11, Park, 1801. 258 pp.

Austin, Nat
Nat. Austin's Comic and Sentimental Song Book. The whole comp. and arr. by Nat Austin, the Shakesperian clown & ballad singer. Boston: 186–. 24 pp.

Barnello's Voodoo Incantations or How to Eat Fire. New York: n.d.

Barney Brallaghan's Collection of Irish Songs. Containing all the queer, quizzical, quaint, comic and sentimental songs, as sung by Powers, Collins, Hudson and Barney Williams. New York: n.d.

Beadle's Dime Military Song Book and Songs of the War. A collection of national and patriotic songs. New York: Beadle and Co., 1864. iv, 76 pp.

Beadle's Dime Union Song Book. No. 1–15. Comprising new and popular patriotic songs for the times. New York: Beadle and Co., 1859–1864.

Beadle, Publishers
The New Dolly Varden Songster, containing the latest, comic and sentimental copyright songs. Written by the best ballad writers of the day. New York: Beadle and Adams, 1872. 64 pp.
Without music.

Bennetts', The Kitchen Domestic Songster. New York: A. J. Fisher, 1877. 60 pp. (Dime Song Books. No. 138.)
Words only.

J. S. Berry's Comic Song Book. New York: De Witt, 1863.

"Big Thing on Ice" Songster. New York: R. M. De Witt, 1869. 128 pp. (De Witt's ten cent songsters, No. 5.)
Words only.

Bigelow, M. A.
The Northern Harp. Containing Songs from St. Lawrence and Forest Melodies. Auburn: 1852.

Birch, Billy
Billy Birch's Ethiopian Melodist. New York: 1862.

Black Diamond Songster. Illustrated with woodcuts. New York: Turner and Fisher, n.d.

Bland, James
James A. Bland's De Golden Wedding Songster. New York: New York Popular Publishing Co., 1880. 64 pp. (The Favorite Dime Song Book, No. 114.)
Words only.

Bobbing Around Songster. Philadelphia: Fisher & Brother, 1851. 252 pp.
Words only.

Bob Branigan's Funny But Very True Songster. New York: 1887.

Bobby Newcomb's San Francisco Minstrels' Songster. New York: De Witt, 1868.

Bolton, Sarah (Knowles)
Facts and Songs for the People. Prepared especially for use in the Blaine and Logan Campaign. Cleveland, O.: C. E. Bolton, 1884. 48 pp., illus.
Contains a few tunes.

Boosey's Musical Cabinet. A collection of standard and popular vocal and pianoforte music ... No. 4. Twenty songs of the Christy's Minstrels with choruses and pianoforte accompaniments. London: Boosey & Sons, 18—.

Brower, Frank
Frank Brower's Black Diamond Songster and Ebony Jester. Containing a choice selection of new and original songs, stump speeches, pathetic ballads, jokes, specimens of Ethiopian oratory, Negro dialogues, plantation scenes, witticisms, etc., etc., never before published, as sung and delivered by Frank Brower. New York: Dick & Fitzgerald, 1863. 72 pp.
Words only, tunes of most songs indicated by title.

Brown, Harry
Harry Brown's Moonlight Walk Songster, containing all the latest comic and sentimental songs of the day, sung in America and Gt. Britain. New York: Ornum & Co., 187–. 69 pp.
Words only.

Brown, William Wells
The Anti-Slavery Harp: A Collection of Songs for Anti-Slavery Meetings . . . Boston: B. Marsh, 1851. 46 pp., illus.
Words only, most tunes indicated by title.

Brown University Library
Series of Old American Songs, reproduced in facsimile from original or early editions in the Harris Collection of American poetry and plays, Brown University, with brief annotations by S. Foster Damon, curator. Providence, R. I.: Brown University Library, 1936. 50 facsim.

Bryant's Essence of Old Virginny, containing all the new fashionable laughable Negro songs, as sung by the celebrated Bryant's Minstrels. New York: Robert M. De Witt, 1857. Illus.

Dan Bryant's "Shoo Fly" Songster. New York: Robert M. DeWitt, 1869.

Bryer, David E.
The Harrison Campaign Songster. Logansport, Ind.: The Home Music Co., 1892. 32 pp.
Most of the songs for 4 voices; Some tunes indicated by title.

Bunker Hill Songster. Containing National and Patriotic Songs, as sung by the principal vocalists. New York: Murphy, Printer and Publisher, 1850. 34 pp., illus.
Words only.

Burgess, Cool
Cool Burgess', Oh! Don't Get Weary Children Songster; containing the latest collections of the most popular songs of the day . . . New York: A. J. Fisher, 1877. 59 pp. (Dime Song Books, No. 126).
Words only, except for tune of "Slavery Days."

———.
Cool Burgess' I'll Be Gay Songster. Containing a fine collection of this great artist's best songs, as sung by him in all the principal theatres of the United States and Canada . . . New York: New York Popular Publishing Co., 1880. 64 pp. (The Favorite Dime Song Book, No. 122).
Words only.

Burleigh, H. T., ed.
Negro Minstrel Melodies. A Collection of twenty-one songs. Preface by W. J. Henderson. New York: G. Schirmer, Inc., 1909. 52 pp.
Arranged for voice and piano.

Byron, Thomas F.
Republican Club Campaign Book for 1888; thirty rousing songs written to popular airs . . . Chicago: Protection Publication Company, 1888.
Words only—tunes indicated.

Campbell, M. C.
Wood's Minstrels' Songs, containing a selection of the most popular choruses, quartettes, glees, trios, duetts, songs, parodies, burlesques, etc. Also, funny stories, satrical jokes, quaint sayings, conundrums, repartees, etc., as told by the celebrated E. Horn. At Wood's Minstrel Hall. The whole revised and corrected by M. Campbell. New York: Dick & Fitzgerald, 1855. 74 pp., illus.
Tunes indicated for most songs; five numbers with tunes.

————.
Wood's New Plantation Melodies, containing a selection of the most popular choruses, quartettes, glees, trios, duets, songs, parodies, burlesques, etc. Also, funny stories, satirical jokes, quaint sayings, conundrums, repartees, etc., as told by the celebrated E. Horn, at Wood's Minstrel Hall. The whole rev. and corr. by M. Campbell . . . New York: Dick & Fitzgerald, 1855. iv, 66 pp.
Words only.

Carncross and Sharpley's Minstrel.
Philadelphia: 1860.

Carroll, William J.
William Carroll's Comic Banjo Songster. Containing a large and vast collection of original songs written, composed, and sung by this leading . . . banjo artist . . . together with a collection of the latest and most popular songs of the period . . . New York: New York Popular Publishing Co., 1883. 60 pp. (The Favorite Dime Song Book, No. 248). 60 pp.
Words only.

Chaff, Gumbo (pseudonym)
The Ethiopian Glee Book, containing the songs sung by the Christy Minstrels with many popular Negro melodies in four parts, arranged for quartet clubs. Boston: Howe, 1848. 111 pp., music.

Charley Monroe's Clown Song Book.
Lancaster: 1867.

Charles Konollman's Barney McCoy, or Come to My Arms, Norah Darling Songster. New York: n.d.

Child, Francis James
War-Songs for Freemen. Dedicated to the Army of the United States: and especially to the 2d, 15th, and 20th Regiments of Massachusetts Volunteers . . . and to the 43d, 44th, and 45th Regiments . . . Boston: Ticknor & Fields, 1863. 56 pp., music.

Christy, Edwin Pearce
Christy's Plantation Melodies, No. 5. The only authorized edition of genuine Christy's songs as sung at Christy's Opera House, published under the authority of E. P. Christy, originator of Ethiopian Minstrels, and the first to harmonize Negro melodies. New York: Fischer & Brothers, 1851–1853. 3 vols.

Christy, E. Byron, and W. E.
Christy's New Songster and Black Joker, containing all the most popular and original songs, choruses, stump speeches, witticisms, jokes, etc. as sung and delivered by the world-renowned Christy's Minstrels at their opera house. Compiled and arranged by E. B. Christy and William E. Christy. New York: Dick & Fitzgerald, 1868. 72 pp.

Christy, George N.
Christy's Essence of Old Kentucky. Containing a choice collection of new and popular songs, interludes, dialogues, funny speeches, darkey jokes and plantation wit. New York: Dick & Fitzgerald, 1862. 72 pp.

————, **and White, Charles**
Christy's and White's Ethiopian Melodies. Containing two hundred and ninety-one of the best and most popular and approved Ethiopian melodies ever written. Being the largest and most complete collection ever published. Comprising the Melodeon Song Book; Plantation Melodies; Ethiopian Song Book; Serenader's Song Book, and Christy and Wood's New Song Books . . . Philadelphia: T. B. Peterson & Brothers, 1854. 434 pp., illus.
Words only.

Christy's Bones and Banjo Melodist. Being a collection of the most popular, fashionable patriotic Ethiopian comic and humorous songs, speeches, etc. . . . New York: Dick and Fitzgerald, 1867.

Christy's Minstrel Songs. Books 1, 3–5, 7. London: Boosey & Co., 1900. (Boosey's Musical Cabinet. Vocal series, No. 4 & 75, 26 & 70, 27, 71, 88 & 91, 148).

Christy's Panorama Songster. Containing the songs as sung by the Christy, Campbell, Pierce's Minstrels and Sable Brothers. Illustrated with woodcuts. New York: W. H. Murphy, 1857. 136 pp., illus.
Words only.

Civis, George W.
Songs for the Great Campaign of 1860; comprising a choice collection of original and selected solos, glees, choruses, etc., etc., from the best authors. New York: Published at the Tribune Office, 1860. 118 pp., music.

Clark, George M., arr. and comp.
"Drifting With the Tide" Song Book. Montpelier, Vt.: 1872. 24 pp.
Words only, except for three songs.

————.
Original and Selected Comic and Sentimental Songs. Montpelier, Vt.: Argus and Patriot Printing House, 1871. 24 pp.
Words only.

Clark, George Washington
The Harp of Freedom. New York: Miller, Orton & Mulligan. Boston: J. P. Jewett & Co., and by the Author, Rochester, N. Y.: 1856. iv, 335 pp.
Some with music; others, tunes indicated.

The Library Minstrel. New York: Leavitt & Alden. Boston: Saxton & Miles, etc. . . . 1844. iv, 184 pp.
For 2 to 4 voices unaccompanied.

Clark and Williams' Pullman Car Songster. New York: n.d.

Comus, (The God of Laughter)
The Feast of Wit, or, Frolic of Laughter; containing the most admired anecdotes and songs. Philadelphia: E. T. Scott, 1821. iv, 144 pp.

Conroy, John
Conroy's Grand Duke Opera House Songster. New York: John Conroy, 1875. 64 pp.

Converse, Frank B., comp. and arr.
Frank Converse's "Old Cremona" Songster; containing a choice and popular collection of banjo songs, stump speeches, sentimental ballads, comic songs, comic quartettes, walk arounds, songs and dances, etc., etc. With music . . . New York: Dick & Fitzgerald, 1863. 72 pp.
Unaccompanied melodies.

Cotton, Benjamin
Ben Cotton's Own Songster. San Francisco: D. E. Appleton & Company, 1864. 64 pp.

Crockett's Free-and-Easy Song Book.
Comic, sentimental, amatory, sporting, African, Scotch, Irish, Western and Texian, national, military, naval and anacreontic: A new collection of the most popular stage songs . . . and also of favorite dinner & parlour songs. Together with glees, duets, recitations and medleys. Philadelphia: Kay & Troutman. Pittsburgh: C. H. Kay, 1846. 319 pp., illus.
Words only.

Cummings, Amos J.
The Sun's Greely Campaign Songster. New York: The Sun, 1872. Music.
Campaign against Grant.

Lilly Dale Songster.
Philadelphia: Fisher & Brother, 1854. 66 pp.
Words only.

Dana, Mrs. Mary S. B.
The Temperance Lyre. A collection of original songs arranged and adapted to the most popular music of the day. New York: 1842.

Davidson, George Henry, ed.
Songs of the Christy Minstrels, the whole of the music and words. London: Music Publishing Co., 18—. 30 pp.

50 Songs, Music and Words, Sung by the Ethiopians at Canterbury Hall. London: Music Publishing Co., 18—. 33 pp.

De Le Ree, Peter
The American Republican Songster . . . New York: Published and for sale at the office of the New York Citizen, and at American Star House, 1844. 24 pp.
Words only.

Frank Depro's Too-Too Wilde Songster.
Contains all of his latest and original songs, as sung by him nightly with Buckley and Morris' Minstrels. New York: 1882.

De Susannah, and Thick Lip, Melodist.
New York: T. W. Strong, 1850. 94 pp., illus.
Words only.

Devere, Sam
Sam Dever's Combination Songster. Containing the latest collections of original and irresistibly funny Deitcher and other character sketches and comic songs . . . New York: A. J. Fisher, 1876. 60 pp. (Dime Song Books, No. 95).
Words only.

De Witt's Forget-Me-Not Songster. (Irish). New York: 1872.

De Witt's Forget-Me-Not Songster. (Sentimental). New York: 1872.

Ditson, Oliver, Company
The Home Melodist; a collection of songs and ballads, words and music. Boston: O. Ditson & Co., 1859. 96 pp.

Dixey's Songster.
Illustrated with woodcuts. Philadelphia: Winch, 1860.

Dixon, George Washington
Dixon's (The Celebrated Buffo Singer) Oddities. A glorious collection of nerve working, side cracking, care destroying, mouth tormenting songs; as sung by Mr. G. Dixon, at New York, Philadelphia, Boston, Baltimore and New Orleans Theatres, with shouts of applause. Including the new national song, composed and sung on the day of the celebration of the French Revolution; to which is added an ode, written by Mr. S. Woodworth, for the same occasion. Ithaca, N. Y.: Mack, Andrus & Co., 1846. 36 pp.
Words only.

Downey's Peter Napoleon Campana, Old Sport Songster . . . New York: Popular Publishing Co., 1879. 64 pp. (The Favorite Dime Song Book, No. 25).
Words only.

Jack Downing's Song Book, containing a selection of about 200 songs, many of which are new. Dedicated to President Andrew Jackson. By Jack Downing, M.D.M. First edition, illustrated with woodcuts. Providence: 1835.

Dumont, Frank, comp. and arr.
Lew Benedict's "Far West" Song Book, containing the songs, ballads and plantation songs of the famous Duprez & Benedict's gigantic minstrels. With a biography of the prince comedian Lew Benedict. Philadelphia: Merrihew & Son, 1871. 32 pp.
Words only.

Duncan Sisters. Down In The Meadows Songster. Containing a collection of the ... songs of the day, among which will be found ... "Down in the Meadows", "Naughty Cousin Joe", etc. New York: A. J. Fisher, 1878. 60 pp. (Dime Song Books, No. 156.)
Words only, except for tune of "Do Not Turn Me From Your Door."

Elliott, George H.
Francis & Day's Album of G. H. Elliott's Popular Songs. Together with a critical appreciation and biographical sketch by Charles Wilmott. London: Francis, Day & Hunter, 1910. 49 pp., illus.
With piano accompaniment; melody also in tonic sol-fa notation.

Elton's Out-and-Out Comic Songster. New York: 1938. 140 pp.
Words only.

Emmet, Joseph K.
J. K. Emmet's Love of the Shamrock Songster. Containing ... Emmet's Original Popular Songs, as sung by him ... in his Original Creation of "Fritz in Ireland." ... New York: A. J. Fisher, 1882. 60 pp. (Dime Song Books, No. 323).
Words only, except for tune of "Real Jam."

Engel, Jennie
Jennie Engel's Favorite Songs... Songs... sung by Miss Jennie Engel ... New York: A. J. Fisher; Baltimore: T. H. Denison & Co., 1873. 60 pp. (Dime Song Books, No. 28).
Words only.

Ethiopian Serenaders
Music of the Ethiopian Serenaders, nine songs and a set of Cotillions. Philadelphia: E. Ferrett & Co., 1845. 16 pp.
Songs with piano accompaniment.

Family Guide: Poems and songs of Byron, Moore and Burns. Philadelphia: Desmond & Co., 1878–82. 2 vols.

Oscar Farland's Songster. New York: 1876.

Fenian Brotherhood of America
Stephens' Fenian Songster. Containing all the heart-stirring and patriotic ballads and songs, as sung at the meetings of the Fenian Brotherhood. New York: W. H. Murphy, 1866. 72 pp., illus.

Florence, William Jermyn
Songs of the Florences: Comprising the Original Melodies of Those Distinguished Delineators of the Irish Boy and Yankee Girl. New York: Dick & Fitzgerald, 1860. 62 pp.
Words only.

Foley & Sheffer's Big Pound Cake Songster. A mammoth collection of Negro melodies. New York: A. J. Fisher, 1878. 60 pp. (Dime Song Books, No. 172).
Words only.

Foley & Sheffer's Oh! Oh! I'll Meet You Songster. Containing: "Oh! Oh! I'll Meet You"; "Hop Along, Sister Mary," etc. New York: Popular Publishing Company, 1879. 64 pp. (The Favorite Dime Song Book, No. 35).
Words only.

Formosa Songster, a complete miscellany of the most favorite songs. New York: Fisher & Denison, 1869. vi, 118 pp.
Words only.

Foster, John
John Foster's Great Barnum and London Circus Songster. New York: Popular Publishing Company, 1880. 32 pp. (The Favorite Dime Song Book, No. 145).
Words only.

Foster, Stephen Collins
(Complete Works) Songs, Compositions and Arrangements ... Produced by Foster Hall ... Indianapolis, Ind. Priv. Print. by J. K. Lilly, 1933. 1 vol. (32 pp.) and 229 pieces in 3 boxes.

Memories of Stephen Foster: Album of 16 songs. New York: E. B. Marks, arranged for voice and piano.

Stephen C. Foster's Forgotten Songs. Album of 10 songs, includes: Nancy's by My Side, Where Is Thy Spirit Mary, etc. New York: Edward B. Marks, arranged for voice and piano.

The Melodies of Stephen C. Foster. Pittsburgh: T. M. Walker, 1909. 307 pp.

Fox, Charles
Charley Fox's Dime Songster and Minstrel's Companion. Philadelphia: Turner & Fisher, 1860.

Charley Fox's Ethiopian Songster. Philadelphia: Turner & Fisher, 1858.

Charley Fox's Minstrel's Companion. Philadelphia: Turner & Fisher.

Charley Fox's Sable Songster. Containing many of the best banjo songs, jokes, and gems of wit. Composed by that favorite Ethiopian comedian, C. H. Fox. Selected and arranged by Eurastix Bust (pseud. of Charles H. Fox). New York: F. A. Brady, 1859. vi, 82 pp., illus.
Words only.

Garfield and Arthur Campaign Song Book, 1880. Washington: Published by the Republican Congressional Committee, 1880. 24 pp.
Melodies, accompanied, and some indicated by title.

Golden Rule.
Cincinnati: 1872.

Grigg's Southern and Western Songster; being a choice collection of the most fashionable songs, many of which are original. New edition, greatly enlarged. Philadelphia: Griggs & Elliot, 1835. xviii, 324 pp. First printed in 1826.
Words only, some tunes indicated by title.

Gorton, Joseph
Gorton's Original New Orleans Minstrel Songster. Containing many new and popular songs, recitations and musical sketches, as done by this company. New York: Popular Publishing Company, 1883. 59 pp.
Words only, except for the tunes of five songs.

Grosh, Aaron Burt
Temperance Pocket Companion; containing a choice collection of temperance hymns, songs, odes, glees, duetts, choruses, etc. Music arranged by W. L. Seaton . . . Utica: B. S. Merrell, 1852. 160 pp.

———.
Washingtonian Pocket Companion: containing a choice collection of temperance hymns, songs, odes, glees, duets, choruses, etc. . . . Utica: B. S. Merrell, 1845. 160 pp.

Gus Shaw's Comic Song and Recitation Book.
New York: Dick & Fitzgerald, 1860. v, 61 pp., illus.

Handy Andy's Budget of Songs.
New York: W. H. Murphy, 185–. 96 pp.
Words only, some tunes indicated by title.

Hare, W. Ben
The Minstrel Encyclopedia. Boston: 1921.

Harrigan, Edward
Harrigan & Braham's "The Last of the Hogans" Songster, containing all the songs sung in their new theatre . . . in their latest success, "The Last of the Hogans," as well as the songs of "Reilly and the 400" . . . New York: Benedict Popular Publishing Co., 1891, 28 pp.
Words only.

———.
Harrigan & Braham's The Major Songs. New York: H. J. Wehman, 1894.
Words only.

———.
Harrigan & Braham's Songs from "Reilly and the 400." . . . Also . . . a collection of the latest popular songs of the day. New York: The Benedict Popular Publishing Co., 1890. 28 pp.
Words only.

———.
Harrigan & Braham's Songs as sung in "The Woolen Stocking," "The Leather Patch." "The Mulligan Guards' Ball," "McSorley's Inflation," "Reilly and the 400." Chicago: H. J. Wehman, 1893.
Words only.

———.
Harrigan & Braham's Notoriety Songs. New York: H. J. Wehman, 1894.
Words only.

———.
Harrigan and Hart's Mulligan Guard's Surprise Songster. New York: A. J. Fisher, 1880.

———.
Harrigan & Hart's Slavery Days Songster. Containing a complete collection of the latest and best hits of the season. New York: A. J. Fisher, 1877. 60 pp. (Dime Song Books, No. 112).
Words only, except for tune of "Slavery Days."

Harrington, George
Christy's and White's Ethiopian Melodies. Philadelphia: Turner & Fisher, 1854.

Harris Collection of American Poetry.
Providence, R. I.: John Hay Library, Brown University.
An unrivalled collection of American sheet music and early songbooks.

Harrison Melodies. Original and selected . . .
Boston: Weeks, Jordan and Co., 1840. 72 pp.
Words only.

Harrison, William Bristow
Harrison's Comic Songster; being a choice collection of rare and original songs, as sung by Mr. Harrison . . . New York: Dick & Fitzgerald, 1862. 70 pp.

Hart, Bob
Bob Hart's Plantation Songster; being a collection of new, fashionable, patriotic, Ethiopian, comic and humorous songs, together with the celebrated stump-speech, "Dat's What's de Matter," and numerous comic recitations as sung and delivered by Bob Hart. New York: Dick & Fitzgerald, 1862. 72 pp. (Dick & Fitzgerald Dime Song Books).
Words only.

Harvest of Minstrel Songs.
Boston: White, Smith & Co., 1884. 176 pp.
Arranged for voice, chorus with piano accompaniment.

Haverly's Minstrels
Haverly's American-European Mastadon Minstrels . . . (Haverly's Songster) . . . Buffalo: The Courier Company Show Printers, 1888. 48 pp.
Words only.

Hayes and Wheeler Campaign Song Book, for the Centennial Year, containing over sixty original songs, adapted to popular melodies. New York: American News Company, 1876. iv, 72 pp.
Words only.

Haywood, Charles, ed. and arr.
A Collection of the Most Popular Songs of James A. Bland, compiled, edited and arranged for voice and piano by Charles Haywood, with an introductory essay: "James A. Bland, and the Place of the Negro in American Minstrelsy." New York: E. B. Marks and Co., 1946. 84 pp., illus., music.

Hengler, Thomas M.
T. M. Hengler's Fun in the Kitchen Songster.
Containing a full collection of the above un-
equalled song and dance artist . . . New York:
A. J. Fisher, 1875. 60 pp. (Dime Song Books,
No. 62).
Words only, some tunes indicated by title.

Herbert, Sidney
The Young Volunteer Campaign Melodist. Designed for the use of Bands of Hope, and all
other juvenile reform organizations. Boston:
J. M. Usher, 1864. 47 pp.

Her Own Boy Jack Songster, containing a collection of Mr. J. F. Mitchell's latest successes,
together with a selection of the choicest songs
of the day. New York: 1886.

Hickok, John Hoyt
The Social Lyrist: A collection of sentimental,
patriotic and pious songs, set to music, arranged for one, two and three voices. Harrisburg: W. O. Hickok, 1840. 144 pp.
Shape—note notation.

Hill, Mabel Wood
*Songs from "Calliope," or "The Vocal Enchant-
ress."* An unexpurgated miscellany, written
down for the first time. Providence, Rhode Island: Axelrod Publishing Company, 1940. 40
pp., voice and piano.

Hooper, Osman Castle
The Harrison Log Cabin Song Book of 1840.
Revised for the Campaign of 1888, with numer-
ous new songs to patriotic airs . . . Columbus,
O.: A. H. Smythe, 1888. 63 pp.

Howe, Elias J.
The Ethiopian Glee Book; containing the songs
sung by the Christy Minstrels, with many other
popular Negro melodies in four parts, arranged for quartet clubs, by Gumbo Chaff,
A.M.A. First Banjo Player to the King of
Congo. Boston: E. Howe, 1848–50. 4 vols. in 1.

Hubbard, Stephen
The Temperance Melodist; consisting of glees,
songs and pieces; arranged and adapted expressly for the use of "Temperance Watchman," "Sons of Temperance" Societies, and for
social and family circles throughout the Union.
With music to each song. Boston: O. Ditson,
1852.

The New Temperance Melodist; consisting of
glees, songs and pieces . . . Boston: O Ditson
& Co., 1859. 152 pp.

Hulbert, F. Randolph
Wandering Strains from the Lyre of the North.
A collection of songs and ballads. New York:
C. C. Childs, 1850. 52 pp.

Humorous and Sentimental Songs, as sung
throughout the United States by Hamlin's
Wizard Oil Concert Troupes in their open air
advertising concerts . . . Chicago: Hamlin's
Wizard Oil Co., 1884. 24 pp.

Hutchinson, John Wallace
Hutchinson's Republican Songster, for the
campaign of 1860. New York: O. Hutchinson,
1860. iv, 72 pp.
Words only.

Hutchinson Family
The Granite Songster; comprising songs of
the Hutchinson Family, without the music.
Boston: A. B. Hutchinson. New York: Charles
Holt, Jr., 1847. 69 pp.

*I'm Going to Have My Name Above the Door
Songster.* New York: 1887.

*I'm the Ghost of John James Christopher Benja-
min Binns' Songster.* New York: n.d., with
music.

Jeannette and Jeannot Songster, by the widow
Machree. New York: Marsh, n.d.

Johnson & Bruno's Tom Big Bee Bay Songster.
Containing . . . "Tom Big Bee Bay," "Just From
Arkansaw," etc. New York: Popular Publish-
ing Co., 1878. 64 pp. (The Favorite Dime Song
Book, No. 10).
Words only.

Johnson's New Comic Songs.
San Francisco: D. E. Appleton & Company,
1863. iv, 56 pp.

Johnson's Original Comic Songs.
San Francisco: D. E. Appleton & Company,
1864. 64 pp.

Jolly John Nash's Our Boys Songster.
New York: A. J. Fisher, 1876.

Kemp, Robert H.
*Father Kemp's Old Folks' Sacred and Popular
Songs.* Boston: Commercial Prtg. House, 1863.
12 pp.
Words only.

Kennedy, John
The American Songster, containing a choice
selection of about one hundred and fifty modern and popular songs . . . Baltimore: J. Kennedy, 1835. 256 pp. First printed in 1829.
Words only.

Kennedy, William
William Kennedy's Union Song Book. Com-
piled and arranged by William Kennedy, the
celebrated clown and comic singer. Brooklyn:
Brooklyn Times Print, 1866. 15 pp.
Words only.

King's Choice Selection of English Songs. Consisting of funny, droll, comical, serious, jovial,
tragical, whimsical, laughable, sentimentale,
pathetical, curious, and humorous songs. In:
*Dixon's (The Celebrated Buffo Singer) Oddi-
ties.* Ithaca, N. Y.: Mack, Andrus & Co., 1846.
36 pp.
Words only.

Kirkwood, L. J.
*Illustrated Sewing Primer with Songs and
Music.* New York: 1883.

Joe Lang's Old Aunt Jemima Songster. Containing a full list of the most popular songs of the day . . . New York: A. J. Fisher, 1873. vi, 116 pp. (A. J. Fisher's Ten Cent Publ. Song Books, No. 45).
Words only.

Leavitt's Song Book.
Consisting of songs sung by the Green Mountain Minstrels at their popular concerts. Montpelier, Vermont: 1868.

Leonard, Silas W.
The National Temperance Songster . . . Louisville: Morton & Griswold, 1854. 256 pp.

Lester and Allen's Ledger of Originalities Songster. New York: 1880.

Lincoln Campaign Songster.
For the use of clubs, containing all the most popular songs. Philadelphia: Mason and Company, 1864.

Lind-Goldschmidt, Jenny Maria
The Jenny Lind Melodist. Containing the Sweedish (sic) ballads, melodies & operatic gems as sung by Mad'lle Jenny Lind. New York: W. H. Murphy, 1853.
Words only.

Lingard, William Horace
William H. Lingard's On the Beach at Long Branch Song Book. Containing all his original songs, and a complete collection of the songs sung by the great and inimitable impersonator, William Horace Lingard. New York: Dick & Fitzgerald, 1868. 124 pp.
Words only, except for a few tunes.

Little Fisher-Maiden Songster.
New York: 1887.

Lloyd
Ethiopian Song Book. London: 1847.

Log Cabin Song Book.
New York: 1840.

Long, Sam
Sam Long's Comic Song Book . . . Containing a selection of the songs sung by him in all the Eastern and Western cities, with unbounded applause. n.p., 188–. 32 pp., illus.

Macaulay, Stewart, arr.
Songs of Kunkel's Nightingale Opera Troupe. A selection of the songs of the company. Baltimore: J. T. Ford, 1854. vi, 52 pp., illus.

Mademoiselle Alberta's Darling Little Ell Songster. New York: 1886.

Marsh's Selection, or Singing for the Million. New York: Richard Marsh, 1854. 3 vols. in 1.

Martz, Dick
Martz's Song Book. Boston: W. H. Piper, 187–. 16 pp.
Words only.

May, Fred
Fred May's Comic Irish Songster; containing all the most popular Irish comic songs, as sung by Fred May and J. H. Ogden. New York: Dick & Fitzgerald, 1862. 74 pp.
Words only, some tunes indicated by title.

———.
The Frisky Irish Songster; a collection of gay, rollicking, comic and eccentric songs . . . New York: Dick & Fitzgerald, 1862. iv, 72 pp.
Words only, tunes of most songs indicated by title.

James McAvoy's Waiting, Waiting, Waiting Songster. New York: 1873.

McCarty, William
Songs, Odes and Other Poems on National Subjects, compiled from various sources. Philadelphia: W. McCarty, 1842.

Minstrel Folio: A collection of new and popular minstrel songs, as sung by leading minstrels all over the country. New York: A. Saalfield, 1885. 196 pp.
For voice, chorus and piano accompaniment.

Minstrel Songs, old and new; a collection of world-wide famous minstrel and plantation songs, including the most popular of the celebrated Foster melodies arranged with pianoforte accompaniment. Boston: Oliver Ditson Co., 1882. 215 pp.
For voice with piano accomp. Chorus of each song arranged for SATB.

Miss St. George Hussey's "The Ship that Brought Me Over" Songster. New York: 1870.

Mock-Bird; consisting of a complete collection of the most admired American and English songs, ballads, glees, etc., which have been sung with applause at the public theatres. Also some of the best and most favorite Scotch, Irish and Welsh songs, together with a curious collection of original toasts and sentiments, used in the most polite circles, including a variety of scarce old songs, not to be found in any other collection. Baltimore: Warner & Hanna, 1805. 104 pp.
Words only.

Moore, Thomas
Tom Moore's Irish Melodies Songster. New York: Dick & Fitzgerald, 1863.

Morris, Billy
Billy Morris' Songs, as sung at Morris Bros., Pell and Trowbridge's Opera House. Boston: G. D. Russell and Co., 1864. 60 pp., illus.
Words only.

Morris, George Pope, comp.
American Melodies; containing a single selection from the production of two hundred writers. Illustrations designed and engraved by L. P. Clover, Jr. New York: Linen and Fennell, 1841. 286 pp.
Texts only.

Murphy, John E.
Murphy and Mack's Autograph Album Writer;
containing over 350 choice selections of the
very best verses, suitable for autograph albums,
birthdays, and valentines; also containing the
poetry of love. New York: A. J. Fisher, 1888.

*Murphy & Mack's Dan McCarty's Party Song-
ster.* Containing the latest and best collection
of songs, as sung by the above artists . . . New
York: New York Popular Publishing Co.,
1881. 58 pp.

Murphy and Mack's Rafferty Blues Songster,
containing the best songs ever published, all
new . . . New York: A. J. Fisher, 1880. 60 pp.
(Dime Song Books, No. 233).
Words only, except for tune "The Auld Scotch
Songs."

*Myles Morris' The Flag with the Harp on the
Green Songster.* New York: 1887.

National "Campaigner." Marching songs, Republican clubs. Philadelphia: D. T. Limerick
& Co., 1894. 31 pp.

*National Republican Grant and Wilson Cam-
paign Song Book.* Portrait of Grant on Cover.
Washington, D. C.: Union Republican Congressional Committee, 1872.

Naval Songster, or Columbian Naval Melody.
Boston: 1813.

Nigger Melodies: Being the entire and complete
work of Ethiopian songs extant. New York:
18—.

Noble, Gilford Clifford, comp.
The Most Popular Plantation Songs. New
York: Hinds, Noble and Eldredge, 1911. 108
pp.
Most of the songs arranged by SATB.

Offord, William
Comic Sentimental Songbook, containing a
collection of rare and original songs. Brooklyn,
New York: W. Offord, 1865. 72 pp.
Words only, some tunes indicated by title.

Ogden, John H.
The Charley O'Malley Irish Comic Songster.
Containing . . . humorous and sentimental Irish
songs, together with funny recitations, as sung
and given by J. H. Ogden . . . New York: Dick
& Fitzgerald, 1862. 72 pp.
Words only.

Old Plantation Songster.
Philadelphia: Fisher & Bro., 1850. 64 pp.
Words only.

Old Uncle Ned Songster.
Philadelphia: Fisher & Bro., 1852. 121 pp.
Words only.

Original Clay Songs: Humorous and sentimental.
Designed to inculcate just political sentiments,
to suit the present political crisis, and to advocate the claims of Henry Clay to the highest
honors his country can bestow. Cincinnati:
Philomath, Union Co., Ind., 1842. 16 pp.
Words only, tunes indicated by title.

Pastor, Tony
Tony Pastor's Bowery Songster. New York:
Dick & Fitzgerald, 1872.

Tony Pastor's Comic Songster. n.p., 1864. 72
pp.
Words only, some tunes indicated by title.

Tony Pastor's "444" Combination Songster.
Embracing all the new comic and Irish lyrics
as sung by that celebrated vocalist and comedian. New York: Dick & Fitzgerald, 1864. 72
pp.
Words only, tunes indicated by title.

Tony Pastor's Great Sensation Songster. n.p.,
1864. 72 pp.
Words only, tunes indicated by title.

Tony Pastor's New Comic Irish Songster. n.p.,
1864. 72 pp.
Words only, most tunes indicated by title.

Tony Pastor's New Union Song Book. New
York: Dick & Fitzgerald, 1862. 72 pp.
Words only, most tunes indicated by title.

Tony Pastor's Opera House Songster: A collection of original comic songs, local lyrics, and
burlesque ovations. New York: Dick & Fitzgerald, 1865.

Tony Pastor's "Own" Comic Vocalist: Being a
collection of orginal comic songs sung by the
celebrated comic singer and jester, Tony Pastor. Compiled by John F. Poole. New York:
Dick & Fitzgerald, 1863. 72 pp.
Words only.

Phillips, Augustus G.
Gus Phillips' "Oofty Gooft" Songster. Containing one of the most complete collections of this
great Dutch comique's best songs and recitations as performed by him in all the principal
theatres throughout the United States . . . New
York: N. Y. Popular Publishing Co., 1880. 63
pp. (The Favorite Dime Song Book, No. 75).
Words only.

Pixley, Annie
Annie Pixley's Songster, containing the great-
est collection of this popular favorite's songs
ever published . . . New York: N. Y. Variety
Publishing Co., 1886. 24 pp.
Words only.

Plantation Lullabies.
Hamilton, Ont.: Duncan Lithograph Co., 188–.
51 pp.
Words only, except for 13 songs preceding p. 5.
These were sung by the Famous Canadian Jubi-
lee Singers Male Quartette.

Pop Goes the Weasel Songster.
Philadelphia: Fisher & Bro., 1853. 44 pp.
Words only.

Punch and Judy, Ventriloquism, and Comic Songs. New York: Dick & Fitzgerald, 1882.

Rial, Jay
"I am Coming Back Again." Jay Rial's Ideal Uncle Tom's Cabin Song Book. San Francisco: Francis Valentine & Co., 1883. 24 pp.
Words only.

Robinson, Dr.
Pacific Song Book (California Songster). San Francisco: D. E. Appleton & Co., 1854.

Rooney, Patrick
Pat Rooney's Clarabel Magee Songster. Containing a grand collection of Mr. Rooney's own original productions as sung by him all over the world . . . New York: A. J. Fisher, 1882. 60 pp. (Dime Song Books, No. 324).
Words only, tunes indicated by title.

Russell, Sol Smith
Sol Smith Russell's Character Vocalist, containing the character songs of the inimitable American humorist and protean character delineator. New York: Dick & Fitzgerald, 1869. 72 pp.
Words only.

Rentz Santley's Lovely Venus Songster. New York: 1884.

Saucy Kate, and Jeannette and Jeannot Songster. Philadelphia: Fisher & Bro., 1849. 48 pp.
Words only.

Scanlan, William James
Wm. J. Scanlan's Peggy O'More Songster. Containing all the popular songs sung by this great artist in . . . 'Shane-na-lawn.' New York: W. J. A. Lieder, 1885. 64 pp. (Dime Song Books, No. 375).
Words only.

"Schneider" Free and Easy Songster. New York: R. M. DeWitt, 1869. 128 pp. (DeWitt's Ten Cent Songsters, n.s., No. 7).
Words only.

Sentimental Songs for the Lady's Songster. Philadelphia: Fisher & Bro., 1852. 113 pp.
Words only.

Shamrock Four's Smart Little Bit of a Man Songster . . . New York: N. Y. Popular Publishing Co., 1882. 60 pp. (The Favorite Dime Song Book, No. 213).
Words only.

Shaw, Frederick T.
Fred. Shaw's Dime American Songster, containing a selection of comic songs, composed and sung by Fred. Shaw . . . New York: F. A. Brady, 1859. 77 pp.
Words only.

"Shoo, Fly, Don't Bodder Me" Songster, containing the gems of popular melodies . . . New York: Fisher & Denison, 1871. vi, 113 pp.
Words only.

Smith, William H.
Campaign Songs of 1888. St. Clair, Mich.: W. H. Smith, 1888. 24 pp.
Words only, tunes indicated by title.

Songs of Love and Beauty. Philadelphia: Fisher & Bro., 1851. 236 pp.
Words only.

Squatter Sovereignty. Complete and only songster. New York: N. Y. Popular Publishing Co., 1890. 16 pp.
Words only.

Stearns, John Newton
Band of Hope Songster: A collection of temperance songs . . . New York: National Temperance Soc., 1889. 63 pp.

Stone, John A.
Put's Golden Songster. Containing the largest and most popular collection of California songs ever published . . . San Francisco: D. E. Appleton & Co., 1858. 64 pp.
Words only, tunes indicated by title.

————.
Put's Original California Songster; detailing the hopes, trials, and joys of a miner's life. San Francisco: D. E. Appleton & Company, 1868.
Contains many texts and tunes of the '49ers.

Surridge, J. H.
The Original Christy Minstrel Song Book: Containing all the new songs as sung only by the Christys. New York: 1865. 19 pp.
Words only. Historical sketch of Christy's minstrels, p. 2.

Sykes, L. Fayette
Garfield and Arthur Campaign Song Book, 1880. New York: Pub. by Republican Central Campaign Club, 1880. 24 pp.
Words only, some tunes indicated by title.

Taylor, M.
The Gold Digger's Song Book. Marysville: Marysville Daily Herald, 1856.

Thayer, Ambrose A.
Morris Brothers, Pell & Trowbridge's Songs. Boston: Published at Russell's Music Store, 1860. iv, 48 pp.
Includes tunes to half the songs.

The Acme Haversack of Song and Patriotic Eloquence. Old War Songs and G. A. R. and patriotic. Syracuse, N. Y., 1894. 159 pp.

The Aeolian Harp and Singer's Nonpariel (sic!). A collection of the most fashionable sentimental songs. New York: G. W. & S. Turney, 185–. 255 pp.

The Aeolian Harp, or Songster's Cabinet; being a selection of the most popular songs and recitations, patriotic, sentimental, humorous, etc. Philadelphia: S. Hart and Son, 1829. 124 pp.

The Amateur's Song Book. Boston: 1843.

The American Big 4's Latest Songster.
New York: n.d.

The American Minstrel.
Cincinnati: 1837.

The American Naval and Patriotic Songster, as
sung in various places of amusement in honor
of Hull, Jones, Decatur, Perry, Bainbridge,
Lawrence, etc. Baltimore: P. N. Wood, 1836.

The American Songster; containing a choice se-
lection of eighty-three songs; including Tyrone
Power's favourite songs. Philadelphia: W. A.
Leary, 1845. 189 pp., without the music.

The American Star: Being a choice collection of
the most approved patriotic and other songs.
Together with many original ones, never before published. Philadelphia: M. Carey & Son,
1817. 215 pp.
Without the music, tunes indicated by title.

The Arkansas Traveller's Songster; containing
the celebrated story of the Arkansas traveller,
with the music for violin or piano, and also an
extensive and choice collection of new and
popular comic and sentimental songs. New
York: Dick and Fitzgerald, 1864. 71 pp.

The Banner Songster. A choice collection of new
and popular songs; together with many old
favorites. New York: The American News Co.,
1865. viii, 100 pp.
Words only.

The Big Sunflower Songster.
New York: DeWitt, 1868.

The Black-Bird, consisting of a complete collection of the most admired modern songs. New
York: Evert Duyckinck, G. Bunce Print., 1812.
140 pp.
Words only.

The Bold Soldier Boy Songster.
Philadelphia: Fisher & Brothers, 1848. 48 pp.,
illus.
Words only.

The Bonny Bunch of Roses Songster, containing
songs and ballads as sung . . . throughout the
United States and Great Britain. New York:
Orhum & Co., 1871. 67 pp.
Words only.

The Book of Popular Songs, being a compendium
of the best sentimental, comic, Negro, Irish,
Scotch, national, patriotic, military, naval, social, convivial and pathetic songs, ballads and
melodies, as sung by the most celebrated opera
and ballad singers, Negro minstrels and comic
vocalists of the day. Philadelphia: W. P. Hazard, 1864. 320 pp.
Includes tunes of 17 songs; tunes of many other
songs indicated.

*The Book of 1000 and One Songs, or Songs for
the Millions.* New York: 1846.

The Camp Fire Songster.
New York: Dick & Fitzgerald, 1862. 70 pp.
Words only; tunes indicated by title.

*The "Champagne Charlie" and "Coil Oil Tommy"
Songster.* San Francisco: D. E. Appleton &
Company, 1868. iv, 64 pp.

The Christy Minstrel Album, containing 52 of
the most popular songs with music. New York:
1861.

The Clown's Song Book; a collection of the very
latest songs as sung by C. L. Fowler, clown,
comic vocalist, Ethiopian comedian and pan-
tomimist. Burlington: 1868.

The Columbia Harmonist; containing the newest
and much admired naval and patriotic songs;
as well as great variety of fashionable, sentimental and other polite songs; together with
most of those elegant odes, occasioned by the
recent successes of our American heroes. Philadelphia: Thomas Simpson, 1814.

The Columbian Sentinel.
Boston: 1818.

The Dayton's Old Age vs. Youth Songster . . .
New York: New York Popular Publishing Co.,
1880. 64 pp. (The Favorite Dime Song Book,
No. 88).
Words only.

The Dime Melodist: Comprising the music and
words of the new and most popular songs and
ballads, by J. R. Thomas, W. V. Wallace,
Stephen Glover, . . . and other eminent composers. New York: I. P. Beadle, 1859. iv, 72 pp.
Unaccompanied melodies.

The Dockstaders' T'Shovel Songster.
New York: Popular Publishing Co., 1880. 64
pp. (The Favorite Dime Song Book, No. 67).
Words only.

The Elfin Star Songster, containing all the popular songs of the day, as sung by Little Ettie,
and Harvey Blodgett. Hartford, Conn.: G. L.
Coburn, 1873. 32 pp.
Words only.

The Encyclopedia of Popular Songs.
New York: 1864.

The Eolian Songster, a choice collection of the
most popular, sentimental, patriotic, naval, and
comic songs. Cincinnati: U. P. James, 1832. ix,
252 pp.
Words only, except for 13 songs in shape—note
notation.

The Erin-Go-Bragh Songster, containing a fine
selection of sentimental songs, including all of
Moore's Irish Melodies. New York: P. J.
Kenedy, 1874. vi, 180 pp.
Words only.

The Feast of Wit, or, a collection of choice
anecdotes, bon mots, etc. with a few much admired patriotic, naval and jovial songs. Exeter:
Published by Abel Brown. C. Norris, Printer,
1825. 64 pp.
Words only.

The Flag of Our Union Songster. A collection of patriotic union and naval songs, original and selected, from the best authors, and adapted to the times. Philadelphia: A. Winch, 1861. iv, 72 pp.
Words only, some tunes indicated.

The Forget-Me-Not Songster, containing a choice collection of old ballad songs as sung by our grandmothers. Embellished with numerous engravings. New York: Nafis and Cornish, 1842. viii, 256 pp., illus.
Words only.

The Freedman's Bureau Book of Songs. New York: Hilton & Company, n.d., 110 pp.

The Freemen's Glee Book; a collection of songs, glees and ballads with music. Published under the auspices of the Central Fremont and Dayton Glee Club of the City of New York and dedicated to all who, cherishing Republican liberty consider freedom worth a song. Edited by Henry Camp. New York: Miller, Orton & Hulligan, 1856.

The Genevieve De Brabant Songster. New York: DeWitt, 1869.
Some tunes included.

The Goose Hangs High Songster. Philadelphia: M. M. DeWitt, 1866.

The Granite Songster; comprising the songs of the Hutchinson family. Boston: A. B. Hutchinson, 1847. 69 pp.
Words only.

The Grant Campaign Songster. New York: DeWitt, 1868.

The Great "Kickapoo" Indian Camp Songs; as rendered this season by the popular comedians Frank Clayton, G. E. Ellwood, Colby and Allen, Dr. Higgins, Tom Adams, Barney Chambers, etc. New York: 1885.

The Great Milburn's "Good as Gold" Songster. New York: 1870.

The Guiding Star Songster. Comprising the most popular songs of the day. Songs of war, songs of sentiment, songs of humor, songs of the olden time. New York: The American News Co., 1865. viii, 100 pp., illus. (The "American" Series.)

The Harrison Medal Minstrel. Philadelphia: 1840.

The Hayes Illustrated Campaign Song & Joke Book. New York: The American News Co., 1876. 46 pp., illus.
Words only, tunes indicated by title.

The Horace Greeley Campaign Songster. New York: G. Munro, 1872. 64 pp., illus.
Words only, tunes indicated by title.

The Hutchinsons Family Book of Poetry; containing sixty-seven of their most popular songs. Boston: S. Chison, 1858. 69 pp.

The Jolly Miller Songster. Published exclusively for the edification of The Ancient and Honourable Guild of Right Worthy Millers. Minneapolis: The Northwestern Miller, 1905. 48 pp.
Words only.

The Kentucky Minstrel and Jersey Warbler: being a choice selection of coon melodies. Philadelphia: Robinson and Peterson, 1844. 64 pp., illus.
Words only, tunes indicated by title.

The Lady Washington Temperance Songster. N.p., 183-. 242 pp.
Words only, tunes indicated by title.

The Language of Fowers, and How to Grow Flowers, Fruit, etc. Songster. New York: 1882.

The Lanigan Ball Comic Songster; containing a choice collection of Irish songs, Dutch songs, burlesque speeches, scraps of fun, and popular comic songs, as sung by Tony Pastor, J. C. Stewart, and other comic vocalists. New York: Dick and Fitzgerald, 1863. 72 pp.
Words only, tunes indicated by title.

The Little 'Ah Sid' Songster. New York: Dick & Fitzgerald, 1875.

The Little American Songster, containing a choice collection of modern and popular songs, as sung by Jefferson, Cowell, Horn, Miss Fisher, Miss Kelly, etc., etc., etc. New York: Nafis & Cornish, 184-. 250 pp.
Words only.

The Little Mac Songster; containing a splendid collection of entirely new and original patriotic, convivial, comic, gay and rollicking camp songs; interspersed with comic speeches, recitations and bits of camp wit. New York: Dick & Fitzgerald, 1862. 72 pp.

The Log Cabin Song-Book. A collection of popular and patriotic songs, respectfully dedicated to the friends of Harrison and Tyler . . . New York: Log Cabin Office, 1840. 72 pp.
Words only, tunes indicated by title.

The Love and Sentimental Songster. A choice collection of popular, love and sentimental songs by Stephen C. Foster, and others. New York: Dick & Fitzgerald, 1862. 72 pp.
Words only.

The Lovers' Forget-Me-Not and Songs of Beauty. A choice collection of sentimental, comic and temperance songs with all the late Negro melodies. Philadelphia: 1847.

The Maid of the Mill Songster. New York: 1887.

The Mary Taylor Melodist, or, one hundred and twenty choice gems of the operas. New York: T. W. Strong, 1845. 96 pp.
Words only. Contains 77 patriotic and popular songs.

The Moss Rose Songster.
Philadelphia: Fisher & Bro., 185–. 46 pp., illus.
Words only.

The Musical Gift.
Albany, N. Y.: Weed, Parsons & Co., 1859. 16 pp.
Unaccompanied melodies.

The Musical Repertory. A selection of the most approved ancient and modern songs. In four parts. Published and sold at the Hallowell Bookstore, sign of the Bible. By Ezekiel Goodale. Augusta: Printed by Peter Edes, 1811. 209 pp.
Words only, some tunes indicated by title.

The National Four Rick Rack Songster.
New York: 1879.

The National Minstrel; embracing a collection of the most popular and approved national, patriotic, moral, love, sentimental, comic and Negro songs. Buffalo: 1858.

The National Songster; containing a choice collection of patriotic, comic, Irish, Negro and sentimental songs. Embellished with 60 engravings. New York: March, 1858.

The Negro Forget-Me-Not Songster.
Philadelphia: Fisher & Brother, 18—.

The Negro Melodist: Containing a great variety of the most popular airs, songs, and melodies, comic, humorous, sentimental, and patriotic. Cincinnati: U. P. James, 186–. 66 pp.
Words only.

The Negro Minstrel; containing a choice selection of the most popular Negro songs. No. 1. Glasgow: 1850. 24 pp.
Words only.

The Negro Singers' Own Book.
Philadelphia: Turner and Fisher, n.d.

The New Haven Whig Song Book, prepared for the New Haven County Mass Convention, Thursday, Oct. 8, 1840. New Haven: Whig Gen. Con., 1840. 21 pp.
Words only.

The New Song Book, containing a choice collection of the most popular songs, glees, choruses, extravaganzas, etc., many of which have never been published . . . Hartford: S. Andrus and Son, 1851. vi, 126 pp., illus.
Words only.

The Nightingale, or, Musical Companion, being a collection of entertaining songs. New York: Printed and sold by Smith and Forman, at the Franklin Juvenile Bookstores . . . , 1814. 72 pp.
Words only.

The Nightingale; or, The Jenny Lind Songster: devoted to the publication of all the choicest songs sung by Jenny Lind, and other celebrated vocalists. Together with the most popular songs, duets, glees, catches, etc., of the age; with appropriate music adapted to the voice, flute, violin and piano . . . New York: Stringer & Townsend, 1850.

The Nightingale Songster; or Lyrics of Love and Humor, containing a choice collection of songs of the affections, and embracing all the most popular and fashionable comic, convivial, moral, sentimental, and patriotic songs. New York: Dick and Fitzgerald, 1863. 72 pp.
Words only.

The Northern and Eastern Songster; a choice collection of fashionable songs. Engraved frontpiece. Boston: Charles Gaylord, 1835. 312 pp.
Words only.

The Original Novelty 4 Songster.
New York: N. Y. Popular Publishing Co., 1886. 16 pp. (The Favorite Dime Song Book, No. 206).
Words only.

The Parlour Song Book. A choice and well-selected collection of the most popular sentimental, patriotic, naval, and comic songs. New York: Leavitt and Allen, 1850. 160 pp.
Words only.

The People's Favorite Songster; containing a choice collection of sentimental, comic, naval, pirate, ballad, fireman's and Negro songs. With engravings. Philadelphia and New York: Fisher & Bro., 1842.

The People's Free-And-Easy Songster: A choice collection of comic, sentimental, amatory, sporting, Irish, Scotch, African, military, naval and patriotic songs . . . New York: W. H. Murphy, 1846. 256 pp., illus.
Words only.

The Rough and Ready Songster; embellished with twenty-five engravings, illustrative of the American victories in Mexico. By an American officer. New York: Nafis & Cornish, 1848. 250 pp.
Words only, some tunes indicated by title.

The Sailor's Companion; being a collection of the most favorite songs now in vogue. New York: Leavitt and Allen, 1857.

The Sailor's Song Book, or Music of the Forecastle; containing patriotic, nautical, naval, moral and temperance songs; adapted to popular and familiar tunes. Music arranged in 2 parts by Uncle Sam. Boston: Kidder & Wright, 1842.

The Scotch Lassie Jean Songster.
Containing one of the grandest collections of songs ever before published. New York: N. Y. Popular Publishing Co., 1880. 64 pp.
Words only.

The Serenader's Own Book; containing a choice collection of new and popular songs, ballads, etc. With woodcuts. New York: Marsh, 1840.

The Shamrock; or Songs of Old Ireland. A choice collection of sentimental, comic, convivial, political, and patriotic songs of Erina. New York: Dick & Fitzgerald, 1862. 72 pp.
Words only, some tunes indicated by title.

The Singer's Geni; being a superior collection of the most admired, sentimental songs of the present day. Illustrated with many woodcuts. Philadelphia: 1845.

The Singer's Own Book; a well-selected collection of the most popular sentimental, amatory, patriotic, naval and comic songs. Philadelphia: Key and Biddle, 1832. 320 pp.
Words only.

The Songster's Museum: A new and choice collection of popular songs, selected from the best authors. New York: Johnstone and Van Norden, 1824. 72 pp.
Words only.

The Souvenir Minstrel, or, Singer's Remember Me. A choice collection of the most admired songs, duets, glees, choruses, etc., as sung by Messrs. Braham, Sinclair, Incledon, and others . . . With all the new songs. Philadelphia: J. B. Perry, 1842. 256 pp.
Words only.

The Sport's Own Songster. A collection of choice, rich and spicy songs and ballads. New York: G. Blackie & Co., 1874. 32 pp.
Words only.

The Stars and Stripes Songster No. 2.
New York: DeWitt, n.d.

The Union Song Book; containing the best and most popular national and patriotic songs, new and old. Philadelphia: Lee & Walker, 1861.

The United States Songster. A choice selection of about one hundred and seventy of the most popular songs: including nearly all the songs contained in *The American Songster* . . . and a number of new and original songs, written expressly for this work. Cincinnati: U. P. James, 1836. 223 pp., illus.
Words only, except for tune "Settin on a Rail."

The Universal Songster; a new collection of the most fashionable, popular, sentimental, comic, patriotic and naval songs. Together with catches, glees, etc. New York: J. H. Turney, 1832. 243 pp.

The Vocal Annual, or Singer's Own Book.
Boston: Hill, 1832. With woodcut.

The Vocal Lyre; a choice selection of the most popular, sentimental, patriotic and comic songs, of the present time. Newark, N. J.: B. Olds, 1852. viii, 148 pp.

The Washington Temperance Song Book: A collection of temperance songs set to music, arranged for 1, 2 and 3 voices. By a Washingtonian. Harrisburg: Hickok and Cantine; Philadelphia: Smith and Peck, 1842.

The Whig Song Book.
Columbus: I. N. Whiting, 1840. 108 pp.

The Wide-Awake Vocalist; or, Rail Splitters' Song Book, words and music for the Republican Campaign of 1860. Embracing a great variety of songs, solos, duets and choruses, arranged for piano or melodeon . . . New York: E. A. Daggett, 1860. 64 pp.

The Yankee Doodle Songster: A collection of national songs, comic and patriotic. Philadelphia: Winch, 1861. With woodcuts.

Thompson, David, and K., comp.
Songs That Mother Used to Sing; an anthology of the best-loved songs, together with brief comment about the inspired poets who wrote the words and, wherever possible, something of how the songs came to be written . . . Chicago: A. C. McClurg & Co., 1931. 135 pp.

Tippecanoe Song Book: A collection of log cabin and patriotic melodies . . . Philadelphia, 1840.

Touch the Elbow Songster; containing all the new and popular patriotic army songs. New York: Dick & Fitzgerald, 1862. 72 pp.
Words only, except for one tune—"Comrades, touch the Elbow."

Troubadour Songster . . .
N.P., 1883. 8 pp.
Words only.

Uncle Ned Songster.
Philadelphia: Fisher & Brothers, 18—.

Uncle True Songster.
Philadelphia: Fisher & Bro., 1850. 148 pp.
Words only.

Unsworth, James
Unsworth's Burnt Cork Lyrics. Consisting of all his popular and original songs, etc. etc. Embracing, also, the latest novelties in Ethiopian delineation. Ed. and comp. by J. H. Collins. With photographic illustrations by Fredericks. New York: R. M. DeWitt, 1859. vi, 72 pp., illus.
Words only.

U. S. Library of Congress. Music Division.
Catalogue of First Editions of Stephen C. Foster, by Walter R. Whittlesey, and O. G. Sonneck. Washington: U. S. Gov't Printing Office, 1915. 79 pp.

Wait For the Wagon and Katy Darling Songster.
N.p., 1851. 48 pp.
Words only, most tunes indicated by title.

Ward and Lynch's Invitation Songster.
New York: n.d.

Wehman Brothers
Good Old-Time Songs . . . New York: 1910-1916. 4 vols. in 2.
Words only. *Contents:* No. 1–177 songs; No. 2–174 songs; No. 3–173 songs; No. 4–166 songs.

Six Hundred and Seventeen Irish Songs and Ballads. New York: Wehman Bros., 190-. 124 pp.
Words only.

Wesley Brothers Long and Short of It Songster. New York: n.d.

Wesley Brothers Two Extremes Songster: Containing a full collection of these two eccentric Negro delineators of wit and song. New York: 1875.

Whaley, M. S.
The Old Types Pass Songster. Boston: 1925.

Wheatley & Traynor's Dublin Boys Songster . . . New York: N. Y. Popular Publishing Co., 1883. 60 pp. (The Favorite Dime Book Song Book).
Words only, except for four songs.

When the Band Begins to Play Songster, containing . . . songs and ballads as sung in theatres and concert-rooms throughout the United States and Great Britain. New York: Ornum & Co., 1872. 68 pp.
Words only.

Whig Songs for 1844.
New York: Greely and McElrath, 1844. 16 pp.

White, Charles
White's New Book of Plantation Melodies. Philadelphia: T. B. Preston and Brothers, 18—. 70 pp., illus.

————.
White's New Illustrated Melodeon Song Book. New York: 1848.

Widdows, Frederick
Blaine and Logan Campaign Song Book. N. Y.: Republican National Committee, 1884. 50 pp., illus.
With tunes, in part accompanied, or indicated by title.

Wier, Albert Ernest, comp.
Songs of the Sunny South, containing more than two hundred songs redolent of plantation and minstrel days, including plantation and minstrel ditties, Negro spirituals, Stephen Foster ballads and songs, arranged for singing and playing . . . New York: D. Appleton and Co., 1929. 256 pp.

Wightman, Francis P., comp.
Little Leather Breeches and Other Southern Rhymes; being a number of folk-lore, songs, Negro rhymes, street-venders' cries, etc., gathered from various parts of the South. New York: Taylor and Company, 1899.

Wilson, John
Words of the Songs of Mr. Wilson's Entertainment. New York: G. F. Nesbitt, 1849. 16 pp.

Woodworth, Samuel
Melodies, duets, trios, songs, and ballads, pastoral, amatory, sentimental, patriotic, religious, and miscellaneous. Together with metrical epistles, tales, and recitations. 2nd ed., comprising many late productions never before published. New York: Elliot and Palmer, 1830. 288 pp. First ed. publ. in 1826. N. Y.: James M. Campbell.
No music, some tunes indicated.

Wood's Minstrel Songs; containing a selection of the most popular choruses, quartettes, glees, trios, duets, songs as told by the celebrated R. Horn. The whole revised and corrected by M. Campbell, acting manager of Wood's Minstrels. New York: Dick and Fitzgerald, 1855.
With music and woodcuts.

Wood's New Plantation Melodies . . . New York: Dick & Fitzgerald, 18—.

Works Progress Administration
A San Francisco Songster, 1849–1939. History of Music in San Francisco Project W.P.A. Lengyel, Cornel, editor. San Francisco: W.P.A. History of Music Project, 1939. Vol. 2, 208 pp., music, bibl., appendices (A–K).
A treasury of San Francisco life in song.

Young, Martha
Plantation Songs for My Lady's Banjo and other Negro Lyrics and Monologues by E. Shepperd (pseud.); with pictures from life by J. W. Otts. New York: R. H. Russell, 1901. 150 pp.

Young Republican Campaign Song Book.
Compiled by Henry Camp for the campaign of 1888. New York: 1888.
Contains some of the tunes.

THE NEGRO — CREOLE

See: Louisiana Folklore and Folksong, pp. 262-65.

FOLKLORE

PERIODICALS

La cypière, organe du Cercle français du Southwestern Louisiana Institute (Lafayette, La.). 1941, I, No. 1; 1942, II, No. 1. Mimeo.
Texts of tales on Jean-Sot and Ti-Jean sans peur, in French and notes on Louisiana French vocabulary.

Mélusine; recueil de mythologie littérature populaire, traditions et usages. t. 1–11; 1878-1910/12. Paris: Libraire Viaut, 1878–1912.
French folklore magazine, no more published. Contained some articles on French-American lore.

GENERAL STUDIES AND COLLECTIONS

Asbury, Herbert
The French Quarter. New York: Alfred A. Knopf, 1936.

Bronsard, James F.
Louisiana Creole Dialect. Baton Rouge, La.: Louisiana State University Press, 1942. xiv, 134 pp., bibl.
56 pages are devoted to the folklore of the French speaking Negroes of Southern Louisiana. It includes proverbs, medical formulas, superstitions, poetry and folktales.

Cable, George W.
The Creoles of Louisiana. New York: Charles Scribner's Sons, 1884.

Chapin, Kate
Bayou Folk. Boston and New York: Houghton Mifflin & Co., 1894. 313 pp.
Twenty-three short stories.

Coleman, Edward M., ed.
Creole Voices: Poems in French by Free Men of Color. Washington, D. C.: Associated Publishers, 1946. 130 pp.

Deiler, John Hanno
The Settlement of the German Coast of Louisiana and the Creoles of German Descent. Philadelphia: Americana Germanica Press, 1909.

Dorrance, Ward Allison
The Survival of French in the Old District of Sainte Genevieve, Missouri. University of Missouri: University of Missouri Studies, Vol. 10, No. 2.

Fortier, Alcée
"A Few Words about the Creoles of Louisiana." An address delivered at the Ninth Annual Convention of the Louisiana Educational Association. Boston: Printed at the Truth Book and Job office, 1892. 11 pp. On cover: Louisiana, Dep't of Education Part of Circular 9, Series 1.

"Bits of Louisiana Folklore." *Transactions and Proceedings of the Modern Language Association of America* 3:125–132, 1887.

"Bits of Louisiana Folk-Lore." *PMLA* 3:100-168, 1887.
Popular tales, songs (text only) and proverbs in patois by the Creoles of Lower Louisiana.

Louisiana Studies, Literature, Customs and Dialects, History and Education. New Orleans: F. F. Hausel and Brother, 1894. vi, 307 pp.

Freyss, Jean-Paul, and Dawson, Jeannine
"The French Folklore Society." *JAFL* 59:485-486, 1946.

Hearn, Lafcadio
Creole Sketches edited by Charles Woodward Hutson, with illustrations by the author. Boston: Houghton Mifflin Company, 1924. First published in 1895.

"Letters of a Poet to a Musician." *The Critic* 48:309–318, 1906 (New Rochelle, New York).

The Writing of Lafcadio Hearn. Large paper edition. Boston: Houghton Mifflin Company, 1922. 3 vols.

Hurston, Zora Neale
Mules and Men. Philadelphia: J. B. Lippincott Co., 1935.

Jarreau, Lafayette
Creole Folklore of Pointe Coupée Parish. M. A. Thesis, unpublished. Louisiana State University, 1930.

Kane, Harnett T.
The Bayous of Louisiana. Illustrated by Tilden Landry, photos. New York: William Morrow and Co., 1943.
The author tells of sharecroppers in fur, terrapin hunts, shrimp trawling and other occupations, he captures the tang of speech and folk character of the people.

Lafargue, André
"Louisiana Linguistic and Folklore Backgrounds." *Louisiana Historical Quarterly* 24:744–75, 1941.

Lanusse, Armand
Creole Voices; poems in French by free men of color, first published in 1845, edited by Edward M. Coleman. Washington, D. C.: The Associated Publishers, 1945. xcvi, 130 pp.

Saxon, Lyle
Fabulous New Orleans. Illustrated by E. H. Suydam. New York: Appleton-Century Co., 1939. new ed.

FOLKTALES—LEGENDS

Brueyre, Loys
"Contes Créoles." *Mélusine* (Paris) 1:43–46, 1878.

Claudel, Calvin
"Four Tales from the French Folklore of Louisiana." *SFQ* 9 (No. 4):191–208, 1945.

————.
"Some Creole Folktales." *Iconograph* (New Orleans, La.), No. 2, March 1941. No pagination.

————.
"Study of Two French Tales from Louisiana." *SFQ* 7:223–231, 1943.

————.
"Three Tales from the French Folklore of Louisiana." *JAFL* 1:38–44, 1943.

————, and Carrière, Joseph M.
"Snow Bella": a tale from the French folklore of Louisiana. Collected by C.A.C., and edited by J.M.C. *SFQ* 6:153–162, 1942.

Fortier, Alcée, coll. and ed.
Louisiana Folk-Tales. In French Dialect and English translation. Memoirs of the American Folklore Society, vol. 2. Boston: Houghton Mifflin and Company, 1895. xi, 122 pp.
Content: Animal Tales, Märchen, Appendix, includes *The Tar Baby.*

Hewitt, Leonard Ballowe
The Lawd Sayin' the Same. Negro Folk Tales of the Creole Country. University, La.: Louisiana State University Press, 1947. xvi, 254 pp., illus.

Lavigne, Jeanne de
Ghost Stories of Old New Orleans. Illustrated by Charles Richards. New York: Rinehart and Company, 1946. 374 pp.
From haunted streets and ghost-ridden mansions come these legends and tales.

Lee, F. H., ed.
Folk Tales of All Nations. New York: Tudor Publishing Company, 1946. 947 pp.
Louisiana (Creole) Tales, pp. 89–91.

Saucier, Corinne Leila
Ul Vieux Garçon. Louisiana Folk Tales and Songs in French Dialects with Linguistic Notes. M. A. Thesis. George Peabody College, No. 1. 13 pp. 1923.

Saxon, Lyle; Dreyer, Edward; and Tallant, Robert
Gumbo-Ya-Ya. A Collection of Louisiana Folk Tales. Material gathered by the workers of the W.P.A. Louisiana Writers' project. Boston: Houghton Mifflin & Co., 1945. 581 pp., illus.

Thériot, Marie and Lehaye, Marie
"Legend of Foolish John." *SFQ* 7:153–156, 1943.
Three folktales from Louisiana French.

Thompson, Ray M.
The Land of Lafitte the Pirate. Photographs by Eugene Delcroix. Drawings by Tildne Landry. New Orleans, La.: Jefferson Parish Yearly Review, 435 Metairie Road, 1944. 128 pp.
A history in words and pictures of the Louisiana Bayouland of Jean Lafitte.

Trappey, Adams Shelby Holmes
Creole Folklore in Phonetic Transcription. M. A. Thesis, unpublished, Louisiana State University, May 6, 1916.
Collection from New Iberia Parish, La.

CUSTOMS AND SUPERSTITIONS

Fortier, Alcée
"Customs and Superstitions in Louisiana." *JAFL* 1:136–140, 1888.

Lavergne, Remi
A Phonetic Transcription of the Creole Negro's Medical Treatments, Superstitions and Folklore in the Parish Coupée. M. A. Thesis, unpublished, Louisiana State University, 1930.

Tallant, Robert
Voodoo in New Orleans. New York: Macmillan Co., 1946. viii, 247 pp.

PROVERBS

"Creole Proverbs."
JAFL 9:38–42, 1896.

Hearn, Lafcadio
Gombo Zhebes. New York: W. H. Coleman, 1885. v, 42 pp.
Little dictionary of Creole proverbs, selected from six Creole dialects. Translated into French and into English, with notes, complete index to subjects and some brief remarks upon the Creole idioms of Louisiana.

SPEECH

Bronssard, James F.
Louisiana Creole Dialect. Baton Rouge, La.: Louisiana State University Press, 1942. xiv, 134 pp., bibl.
56 pages are devoted to the folklore of the French speaking Negroes of Southern Louisiana. It includes proverbs, medical formulas, superstitions, poetry and folktales.

Carrière, J. M.
"Creole Dialect of Missouri." *AS* 14:109–119, 1939.

Faine, Jules
Philologie Créole. Port-au-Prince, Haiti: 1936.

Fortier, Edward J.
"Non-English Writings: French." In: *The Cambridge History of American Literature,* ed. by Trent, Erskine, Sherman and Van Doren. Vol. III (pp. 590–598). New York: The Macmillan Co., 1917. 3 Vols. Reprinted in 1 vol. in 1945.
Discussion of Louisiana French literature and language.

Lafargue, André
"Louisiana Linguistic and Folklore Backgrounds." *Louisiana Historical Quarterly* 24: 744–755, 1941.

Lane, G. S.
"Notes on Louisiana-French." *Language* 10: 323–333, Dec. 1934; 11:5–16, March 1935.

Northup, C. S.
"A Bibliography of the English and French Languages in America." *Dialect Notes* 2(Part 3):151–178, 1899.

Read, William A.
"Creole and 'Cajun'." *AS* 1(No. 9):483, 1926.
A definition and differentiation of these two often misunderstood terms.

————.
Louisiana French. Louisiana State University Studies No. 5. Baton Rouge, La.: University Press, 1931. xxiv, 253 pp.
"Full of valuable material especially on words" (Mencken). Excellent bibliography.

Routh, James; Becker, E. O., and others
"Terms from Louisiana." *Dialect Notes* 4 (Part 6):420–431, 1917.
Terms from New Orleans, De Soto Parish, Bird Names and Animal Names.

St. Martin, Thad
"Cajuns." *Yale Review* 26:859–862, 1937.

Tinker, Edward Larocque
"Gumbo, the Creole dialect of Louisiana, together with a bibliography." *Proceedings American Antiquarian Society* 45:101–142, 1935.

————.
Les Écrits de Lange Française au XIXième Siècle. Essais Biographiques et Bibliographiques. Paris: Libraire Ancienne Honoré Champion, 1932. 502 pp.

————.
"Louisiana Gumbo." *Yale Review* 21:566–579, 1932.
Gumbo is the French dialect of the Negroes of New Orleans and vicinity.

Wartburg, Walther Von.
Atlas of Louisiana French. In: *Conference on non-English Speech in the United States,* Ann Arbor, Michigan, August 2–3, 1940. Bulletin of the American Council of Learned Societies (Washington, D. C.) 1942, No. 34. pp. 581–669.

FOODS

Coleman, William H.
La Cuisine Créole; a Collection of Culinary Recipes. New York: Coleman, 1885.
Attributed to Lafcadio Hearn

Cooper, Virginia M.
Creole Kitchen Cook Book. San Antonio, Texas: Naylor, 1941. 233 pp.

Eustis, Celestine
Cooking in Old Creole Days. New York: Russell, 1903.

James, Virginia E.
"La Creole" Cook Book. Memphis: Van Fleet-Mansfield, 1892.

CREOLE—OUTSIDE OF LOUISIANA
MISCELLANEOUS

Bates, W. C.
"Creole Folklore from Jamaica." *JAFL* 9:38–42, 121–126, 1896.

Carrière, Joseph M.
"Creole Dialect of Missouri." *AS* 14:109–119, 1939.

Collins, Charles W.
The Acadians of Madawaska, Maine. Boston: New England Catholic Historical Society, 1902.

Comhaire-Sylvain, S.
"Creole Tales from Haiti"; Creole and English Texts. *JAFL* 50:292–295, 1937.
Musical examples and bibliography.

Faine, Jules
Le Créole dans l'univers; études comparatives des parlers français-créoles. Port-au-Prince, Haïtï: Imprimerie de l'état, 1939. Vol. 1, bibl.

Hearn, Lafcadio
Two Years in the French West Indies. New York: Harper and Brothers, 1890.
In the Appendix are found Creole melodies and 4 songs.

Newell, W. W.
"Creole Folklore from Jamaica." *JAFL* 9:126–128, 1896.

FOLKSONG
GENERAL STUDIES

Cable, George W.
"Creole Slave Songs." *Century Magazine* 31 (No. 6):807–828, 1886 (April).

————.
"The Dance in Place Congo." *Century Magazine* 21:517–532, 1886.

Fortier, Alcée
"Bits of Louisiana Folk-lore." *PMLA* 3:100–168, 1887.
Popular tales, songs (text only) and proverbs in patois by the Creoles of lower Louisiana.

————.
Louisiana Folk Tales. Memoirs of the American Folk-lore Society, Volume II. New York: G. E. Stechert, 1895, for the American Folklore Society.
The author mentions a number of songs.

Hare, Maud Cuney
"Folk Music of the Creoles." *Musical Observer* 19(No. 9–10):16–18; (No. 11):12–14; 1920.

Hurston, Zora Neale
Mules and Men. Philadelphia: J. B. Lippincott Company, 1935.

Krehbiel, Henry E.
Afro American Folk Songs: A Study in racial and national music. New York: G. Schirmer, 1914.
Chapters 10 and 11 deal with Creole folk music.

Le Jeune, Emilie
"Creole Folk Songs." *Louisiana Historical Quarterly* 2:454–462, 1919.

————.
"Creole Songs." *Musical Observer* 19 (No. 3): 1920.

————.
"Creole Songs." *Music Teachers National Association, Proceedings* 12:23–28, 1918 (Hartford, Connecticut).

McMaster, Ann H.
Creole Songs. In: *The International Encyclopedia of Music and Musicians,* Oscar Thompson, editor. pp. 601–602. New York: The Macmillan Co., 1939.

Peterson, Clara Gottschalk
Creole Songs from New Orleans in the Negro Dialect. New Orleans: Grunewald, 1902.

Sadler, Cora
Creole Songs. Ann Arbor: University of Michigan, (Master's Thesis), 1939 (unpub.).

Singleton, Esther
États-Unis d'Amérique. In: *Encyclopédie de la Musique et Dictionnaire du Conservatoire.* Music Créole.
Contain 9 tunes.

Specht, Will
"Has the Creole a Music of His Own." *Musical America* 48 (No. 15):5, 22, 25, July 28, 1928.

Tomayo, D.
"Refranes Criollos." *Archivos del Folklore Cubano* 1:225–227.

Whitfield, Irene Thérèse
Louisiana French Folksongs. Romance Language Series, No. 1. Baton Rouge: Louisiana State University Press, 1939.

COLLECTIONS

See: American Folksong and Ballad Collections, pp. 85-90, 118-20.

Allen, William Francis
Slave Songs of the United States. 136 songs, including seven Creole songs. New York: A. Simpson & Company, 1867.

Armitage, Maria T.
Folk Songs and Art Songs for Intermediate Grades. Boston: C. C. Birchard, 1924.
Contains 2 Creole songs.

Botsford, Florence H.
Botsford Collection of Folk Songs. New York: G. Schirmer, 1930.
Volume I contains 2 Creole songs.

Cable, George W.
"Creole Slave Songs." *Century Magazine* 31: 807–828, 1886.
A number of songs with music.

Friedenthal, Albert
Die Volksmusik der Kreolen Amerikas. Berlin: Schlesinger, 1911 (Die Stimmen der Völker).

————.
Musik, Tanz und Dichtung bei der Kreolen Amerikas. Berlin-Wilmersdorf: H. Schnippel, 1913.

Hare, Maud Cuney
Six Creole Folk Songs with original Creole and translated English text by Maude Cuney Hare. Six songs for medium voice with piano accompaniment. New York: Carl Fischer, 1921.

Lomax, John A., and Alan
American Ballads and Folk Songs. New York: Macmillan Company, 1935.
Has 7 Creole songs.

————.
Our Singing Country. A Second Volume of American Ballads and Folk Songs. New York: The Macmillan Company, 1941.
Contains 7 Creole tunes and text (pp. 180–194).

Monroe, Mina
Bayou Ballads; twelve folk-songs from Louisiana. Texts and music collected by Mina Monroe, ed. with the collaboration of Kurt Schindler. New York: G. Schirmer, 1921. viii, 55 pp., music (voice and piano).

Nickerson, Camille, arranger
Five Creole Songs: 1. Chere, Mo Lemme Toi; 2. Lizette, To Quitte la Plaine; 3. Danse, Conni Coine; 4. Fois Do Do; 5. Michien Bainjo. Boston Music Company, 1942. Voice and piano.

Peterson, Clara Gottschalk
Creole Songs—From New Orleans. New Orleas: L. Gruenwald Company, 1902.

Pound, Louise
American Ballads and Songs. New York: Scribner's and Son, 1922.

Tiersot, Julien
Chanson des Négres d'Amérique. Paris: Heugel & Cie, 1933.

Whitfield, Irene Thérèse
Louisiana French Folk Songs. Baton Rouge: Louisiana State University Press, 1939 (Romance Language Series, No. 1).

ARRANGEMENTS (Individual Titles)

————: *Voice and Piano*

"Ah, Suzette, Chere." (from Bayou Ballads). Monroe, Nina: Schirmer: voice and piano.

"Musieu Bainjo."
Grant-Schaefer: Schmidt: voice and piano.

————: *Female Voices*

"Ay, Ay, Ay" ("Alas!").
Pitcher, Gladys: Birchard: SSA.

"March Along Grenadiers." (En Avant Grenadiers). C.: Boston Music Co.: SA.

"En Avan', Grenadie."
Reynolds, Gerald: C. Fischer: SSA.

"March Along, Grenadiers." (En Avan', Grenadie). Treharne, Bryceson: Willis: SA.

"Mister Bainjo."
Boston Music Co.: SA.

"Mister Bainjo."
Treharne, Bryceson: Willis: SA.

"Onward March, Grenadiers." (En Avan', Grenadie). Reynolds, Gerald: J. Fischer: SSAA.

"Poor Lolotte."
Boston Music Co.: SA.

"Poor Lolotte."
Treharne, Bryceson: Willis: SSA.

————: *Male Voices*

"Ay, Ay, Ay."
Stickles: Huntzinger: TTBB.

————: *Mixed Voices*

"Ay, Ay Ay."
Pitcher, Gladys: Birchard: SATB.

"Ay, Ay, Ay."
Stickles: Huntzinger: SATB.

"Mister Banjo."
Burleigh, H. T.: Ricordi: SATB.

————: *Piano*

"Ay, Ay, Ay, Serenata Criolla."
Garland, A.: Presser: piano.

"Le bannier, chanson négre."
Gottchalk, Louis Moreau: Les fils de B. Schott:
piano.

————: *Orchestra*

Creole Suite.
Broekhoven, John Avon: J. Fischer: orchestra
(for full or small orchestra).

Dance in the Place Congo.
Gilbert, Henry F. B.: orchestra.

Louisiana Symphony.
Janssen, Werner: MS: Orchestra.

————: *Stage Work*

A Bayou Legend.
Still, W. G.: MS: opera, 3 acts.

RECORDS

Album-Collections

Bayou Ballads of the Louisiana Plantations.
Marguerite Castellanos-Taggart, Soprano, with
Edna McLaughlin, piano. 3–10". VM 728

Creole (Louisiana French).
Archive of American Folk Song, Library of
Congress, Music Division, Washington, D. C.

Creole (Louisiana).
Howard University, Washington, D. C.

Creole Folk Songs.
Mabel Hobson, Soprano-piano. VI–25838
Contents: En avant Grenadiers; Ah, Suzette,
Chere; Z'Amours Marianne; Pauv' Piti Mom'zelle
Zizi.

Creole Songs.
Adelaide Van Wey, contralto, and Robert N.
Hill, piano. 3–10". Disc–629
Contents: Compere Lapin; Tan 'siro e' dou;
Aine, de, trois; Caroline; La Maison Denise;
Salangadou; Chere mo l'aime toi; Papa va
peche; Go 'way Cat; Morceau piment; Aurore
Pradere. *Also:* Street Cries; Watermelon, Char-
coal, Shrimpy, Chimney Sweep, Devil Crab, Blue-
berries, Sweet Oranges.

Individual Titles

Acadian Songs and Dance Tunes.
Played on the fiddle by Wayne Perry at Crowley, La. In: *Album 5,* Record No. AAFS23 A1,
2, Library of Congress.
Content: Acadian Waltz; Acadian Blues.

"Ah, Suzette, Chère."
M. Castellano-Taggart, Soprano. VM–728–5

"Ah, Suzette, Cheri."
Mabel Hobson, Soprano-piano. VI–25838

"Ay, Ay, Ay."
Glen Gray and Casa Loma Orchestra. DE–2437

"Ay, Ay, Ay."
Harry Horlick and Orchestra. DE–2154

"Ay, Ay, Ay."
Tito Schipa, vocal-orchestra. VI–6601

"Blues Nigres."
Cleoma Falcon, vocal-accordian DE–17004

"Cajun Love Song."
The Zutty Singleton Creole Trio, and others.
CA–CE 16

"Cane Field."
In: *Bayou Ballads of the Louisiana Planta-
tions.* M. Castellanos-Taggart, soprano-piano.
VM–728

"Clementine."
M. Castellanos-Taggart, soprano. VM–728–4

"Dansez Codaine."
M. Castellanos-Taggart, soprano. VM–728–3

"En Avant Grenadiers."
Mabel Hobson, soprano-piano.　　　VI–25838

"En Avant, Grenadiers."
Marguerite Castellanos-Taggart, soprano.
　　　　　　　　　　　　　　　VM–728–2

"Gué-Gué Zolingaire."
M. Castellanos-Taggart, soprano.　　VM–728–5

"If I Had My Way, I'd Tear the Building Down.
God Don't Never Change" (Cajun). Vocalist-
piano.　　　　　　　　　　　CO 14343–D

"Joe Férail."
Sung with fiddle by Joe Segura at Del Cham-
bre, La. In: *Album 5*, Record No. AAFS23, B2,
Library of Congress, 1943.

"Le Plus Jeune des Trois" (Acadian).
Sung by Julien Hofpauir at New Iberia, La.
In: *Album 5*, Record No. AAFS22 A, Library
of Congress, 1943.

"Les Clefs de la Prison" (Acadian).
Sung by Elida Hofpauir at New Iberia, La.,
1934. In: *Album 5*, Record No. AAFS22 B2,
Library of Congress, 1943.

"Micheu Banjo."
Roland Hayes, tenor, with piano accompaniment.　　　　　　　　　　　DE–17294–D

"O Chère 'Tite Fille."
Sung with accordian by Ogdel Carrier at
Angola, La. In: *Album 5*, Record No. AAFS23
B1, Library of Congress.

"Pauv' piti Mom'zelle Zizi."
Mabel Hobson, soprano-piano.　　　VI–25838

"Pauv' Piti Mom'zelle Zizi."
M. Castellanos-Taggart, soprano.　VM–728–3

"Petite Fille à Albert Moreau."
Sung with fiddle by Joe Segura at Del Cham-
bre, La. In: *Album 5*, Record No. AAFS23 A3,
Library of Congress, 1943.

"Sept Ans Sur Mer" (Acadian).
Sung by Elida Hofpauir and her sister at New
Iberia, La., 1934. In: *Album 5*, Record No.
AAFS22 B1, Library of Congress, 1943.

"Suzanne, Suzanne, Jolie Femme."
Marguerite Castellanos-Taggart, soprano.
　　　　　　　　　　　　　　　VM–728–2

"Ta Oblis De Vernier" (Cajun).
Happy Fats and Rayne-Bo Rambler, vocal-
string band.　　　　　　　　　BB 2042–B

"Tan Patate La Tchuite."
Marguerite Castellanos-Taggart, soprano.
　　　　　　　　　　　　　　　VM–728–1

"Vous T'E in Morico."
M. Castellanos-Taggart, soprano.　VM–728–4

"Z'Amours Marianne."
Mabel Hobson, soprano-piano.　　　VI–25838

"Z'Amours Marianne."
Marguerite Castellanos-Taggart, soprano.
　　　　　　　　　　　　　　　VM–728–1

"Zelim to Quitte La Plaine."
M. Castellanos-Taggart, soprano.　VM–728–6

"Zozo Mokeur."
M. Castellanos-Taggart, soprano.　VM–728–6

THE NEGRO — WEST INDIES

THE NEGRO — WEST INDIES
(A Selection)

FOLKLORE

GENERAL STUDIES AND COLLECTIONS

Aimes, Hubert H. S.
"African Institutions in America." *JAFL* 18: 15–32, 1905.

Andrade, Manuel J.
Folklore from the Dominican Republic. Memoirs of the American Folklore Society, No. 23. Philadelphia: American Folklore Society, 1931.

Beckwith, Martha Warren
Black Roadways, A Study of Jamaican Folklife. Chapel Hill: University of North Carolina Press. 1929. xvii, 233 pp. (*See:* Review by M. J. Herskovits, *JAFL* 43:332–338, 1930.)

———.
Jamaica Anansi Stories. With Music Recorded in the field by Helen Roberts. Memoirs of the American Folklore Society, vol. 17. New York: The American Folklore Society, 1924. xi, 295 pp., music.
> Contains Animal Stories, Sorcery Tales, Modern European Stories, Songs and Dances, and Riddles. The stories were collected from Negro storytellers.

———.
Jamaica Folklore. With music recorded in the field by Helen H. Roberts. Memoirs of the American Folklore Society, vol. 21. New York: G. E. Stechert & Co., 1928. 332 pp., illus., music, bibl.
> *Contents:* Folk Games of Jamaica, Christmas Mummings in Jamaica, Jamaica Proverbs, and Notes in Jamaican Ethnobotany.

Blackburn, Mary Johnson
Folklore from Mammy Days. Boston: Walter H. Baker Co., 1924. ix, 105 pp., music (pp.93-105).

Blake, Edith
"The Maroons of Jamaica." *North American Review* 167:558–568, 1898 (New York).

Bowman, Laura, and Le Roy, Antoine
The Voice of Haiti; original native ceremonial songs, voodoo chants, drum beats, stories of traditions, etc. New York: Clarence Williams Music Publishing Co., 1938.
> Includes 32 native ceremonial songs and voodoo chants.

Bridges, George Wilson
The Annals of Jamaica. London: J. Murray, 1828. 2 vols.

Clavel, M.
"Items of Folklore from Bahama Negroes." *JAFL* 17:36–38, 1904.

Comhaire-Sylvain, Suzanne
A Propos du Vocabulaire des Croyances Paysannes. Port-au-Prince, Haiti, 1938. 12 pp.
> A glossary of folk beliefs.

———.
Études Haïtiennes. Port-au-Prince, Haiti: L'Auteur: 1939.
> Studies in Haitian folklore.

Denis, L., and Duvalier, F.
"La Civilisation Haïtienne." *Revue Anthropologique* 46 (Nos. 10–12) :353–373, 1936.

Edwards, Bryan
Observations on the Disposition, Character, Manners, and Habits of Life, of the Maroon Negroes of the Island of Jamaica; and a detail of the origin, progress, and termination of the late war between those people and the white people. In his: *Historical Survey of the Island of Saint Domingo.* London: J. Stockdale, 1801. xix, 443 pp., illus.

———.
The History, Civil and Commercial, of the British Colonies in the West Indies . . . London: Printed for J. Stockdale, 1793–94. 2 vols.

Finlay, H. H.
"Folklore from Eleuthera, Bahamas." *JAFL* 38:293–299, 1925.

"Folk-lore of the Negroes of Jamaica."
Folk Lore (London) 15:87–94, 206–215, 1904.

Gardner, William James
History of Jamaica, from its discovery by Christopher Columbus to the year 1872.... Sketches of the manners, habits and customs of all classes of its inhabitants . . . London: E. Stock, 1873, viii, 512 pp.

Goeje, Claudius Henricus de
"Beiträge zur Völkerkunde von Surinam." *Internationales Archiv für Ethnographie* 19:1–34, 1910 (Leiden).
> Studies in Surinam folklore; music and tunes included.

Herskovits, Melville J.
Life in a Haitian Valley. New York: London: A. Knopf, 1937. xxx, 350 pp., plates, diagrams.
> Study of native life in the valley of Mirebalais.

———, and Frances S.
Rebel Destiny; among the Bush Negroes of Dutch Guiana. New York: Whittlesey House, 1934. 366 pp.

———.
Surinam Folk-Lore: with transcriptions of Surinam Songs and musicological analysis, by Dr. M. Kolinski. New York: Columbia University Press, 1936. xx, 766 pp. xxxvii pl.
> *Contents:* 1. Notes on the culture of the Paramaribo Negro. 2. Stories, riddles, proverbs, and dreams. 3. Music, bibl.

———.
Trinidad Village. New York: Alfred A. Knopf, 1947. viii, 351 pp., xxv pp., bibl.

Hickeringill, Edmund
Jamaica Viewed: with All the Ports, Harbours, and their Several Soundings, Towns, and Settlements Thereunto Belongings, with the Nature of its Climate, Fruitfulnesse of the Soile, and Its Suitableness to English Complexions. London: 1661. 2nd ed.

Hurston, Zora Neale
Tell My Horse. Philadelphia: J. B. Lippincott Co., 1938. 301 pp., illus.
Social life, traditions and beliefs of the Haitians.

Jacob, Kléber Georges
Contribution à l'Étude de l'Homme Haïtien, au service de l'histoire ethno-sociale de l'ethnie haïtienne. Port-au-Prince, Haïti: Imprimerie de l'État, 1946. 208 pp., bibl.

Jekyll, W.
Jamaican Song and Story. Publication of the Folk-lore Society, 55. London: D. Nutt, 1907. xxxviii, 288 pp., illus., music.
Annancy stories, digging sings, ring tunes, and dancing tunes, collected and edited by Walter Jekyll: with an introduction by Alice Werner, and appendices on traces of African melody in Jamaica by C. S. Meyers, and on English airs and motifs in Jamaica, by Lucy E. Broadwood.

Johnson, J. H.
"Folklore from Antigua, British West Indies." *JAFL* 34:40–88, 1921.

Kahn, Morton Charles
Djuka, the Bush Negroes of Dutch Guiana, with an Introduction by Blair Niles, and a foreword by Clark Wissler. New York: The Viking Press, 1931. xxiv, 233 pp., illus., bibl.

Leslie, Charles
A New and Exact Account of Jamaica, wherein the antient and present state of that colony, its importance to Great Britain, laws, trade, manners and religion, together with the most remarkable and curious animals, plants, trees, etc., are described: with a particular account of the sacrifices, libations, etc. at this day in use among the negroes. Edinburgh: R. Fleming, 1740. ii, 376 pp.

Lewis, Matthew Gregory
Journal of a West India Proprietor (1815–'17) Kept During a Residence in the Island of Jamaica, edited with an Introduction by Mona Wilson. London: G. Routledge & Sons, Ltd., 1929. vi, 356 pp. First issued in 1834.

Leyburn, James Graham
The Haitian People. New Haven: Yale University Press, 1942. 342 pp., bibl. (pp. 322–336).
Many references to the dance, besides much information of general folklore value.

Livingstone, William Pringle
Black Jamaica; a Study in Evolution. London: S. Low, Marston and Company, 1899. 298 pp., illus.

Loederer, Richard A.
Voodoo Fire in Haiti. Translated by Desmond Ivo Vesey, with illustrations by the author. New York: Doubleday, Doran & Company, 1935. viii, 274 pp.

Long, Edward
The History of Jamaica: or, General Survey of the Antient and Modern State of that Island. London: T. Lowndess, 1774. 3 vols. illus.

Mars, Jean Price
Ainsi Parla l'Oncle . . . ; Essais d'Ethnographie. Port-au-Prince: Imprimerie de Compiègne, 1928. iv, 243 pp., illus., music, bibl.
Folklore of Haiti, with many references, and examples, to music and dance.

———.
Formation Ethnique, Folk-Lore et Culture du People Haitien. Port-au-Prince: Val'cin, 1939. iv, 151 pp., bibl.

Marsden, Peter
An Account of the Island of Jamaica, with reflections on the treatment of the slaves . . . Newcastle: 1788.

Ogilby, John
America; Being the Latest and Most Accurate Description of the New World; containing the original of the inhabitants, and the remarkable voyage thither . . . Their habits, customs, manners, and religions. Their plants, beasts, birds, and serpents . . . London: Printed by the author, 1671. 674 pp., illus.

Panhuys, L. C. van, jonkheer
"Folklore in Nederlandsch West Indie." *West—Indische Gids* ('s–Gravenhage) 14:124–130, 1932.

Parsons, Elsie Clews
"Barbados Folklore." *JAFL* 38:267–292, 1925.

———.
"Bermuda Folklore." *JAFL* 38:239–266, 1925.

———.
Folk-Lore of the Antilles, French and English. Part I (1933); II (1936); III (1942). Memoirs of the American Folklore Society. Vol. 26. New York: American Folklore Society, 1943.

———.
Folklore from the Cape Verde Islands. Parts I, II. Vol. 15 of the Memoirs of the American Folklore Society. Cambridge, Mass.: American Folklore Society, 1923. 373 pp., 267 pp., bibl., music.
Although located near the shores of Massachusetts and Rhode Island the culture of the people, and their lore, is closely linked with many of their Latin-American neighbors.

———.
"Spirituals and other Folklore from the Bahamas." *JAFL* 41:453–525, 1928.

Phillippo, James Mursell
Jamaica: Its Past and Present State. London: J. Snow, 1843. xvi, 487 pp., illus.

Pim, Bedford Clapperton Trevelyan
The Negro and Jamaica. Read before the Anthropological Society of London, February 1,
1866. London: Trübner & Co., 1866. vii, 72 pp.

Powles, Louis Ditson
The Land of the Pink Pearl; or, Recollections
of Life in the Bahamas. London: S. Low,
Marston, Searle & Rivington, 1888. xi, 321 pp.

Prince, Nancy (Gardener)
The West Indies; being a description of the
island, progress of Christianity, education, and
liberty among the colored population generally.
Boston: Dow & Jackson, 1841. 15 pp.
>   Deals mainly with Jamaica.

Rampini, Charles
Letters from Jamaica; the Land of Streams and
Woods. Edinburgh: Edmonston and Douglas,
1873. 182 pp., illus.

Renny, Robert
An History of Jamaica. With observations on
the climate, scenery, trade, productions, negroes, slave trade, diseases of Europeans, customs, manners and dispositions of the inhabitants. London: J. Cawthorn, 1807. xx, 333 pp.

Saint Quentin, Auguste
Introduction à l'Histoire de Cayenne. Antibes:
J. Marchand, 1872. 208 pp.
>   History of French Guiana. The author devotes
>   a portion to the folklore and music of the natives.

Seabrook, William B.
The Magic Island. New York: Harcourt, Brace
& Co., 1929. x, 336 pp., illus., music.
>   The author touches on many aspects of Haitian
>   folklore and music.

Senior, Bernard Martin
*Jamaica As It Is, As It Was, and As It May
Be . . .* with a faithful detail of the manners,
customs and habits of the colonists . . . London: T. Hurst, 1835. vii, 313 pp.

Sloane, Sir Hans, M.D.
*A Voyage to the Islands Madera, Barbadoes,
Nieves, S. Christopher and Jamaica,* with the
Natural History of the Herbs and Trees, Four-
footed Beasts, Fishes, Birds, Insects, Reptiles.
London: 1707, 1725. 2 vols., illus.

Steedman, Mabel
Unknown to the World, Haiti. London: Hurst
and Blackett, Ltd., 1939. 287 pp.

Stewart, John
An Account of Jamaica, and Its Inhabitants.
By a gentleman long resident in the West
Indies. London: Longman, Hurst, Rees and
Orme, 1808. xii, 305 pp.

Thoby-Marcelin, Philippe, and Marcelin, Pierre
Canapé-Vert. Translated by Edward Larocque
Tinker. New York: Farrar & Rinehart, 1944.
xxvii, 225 pp., illus.
>   A fictionalized account of Haitian life; rich in
>   folk beliefs, customs and traditions.

——————.
The Beast of the Haitian Hills. New York:
Rinehart and Company, 1946. 210 pp.
>   The book abounds in elaborate voodoo rituals,
>   tales, fables and proverbs of the Haitians.

Vandercook, John W.
Black Majesty. New York: Harper & Bros.,
1928. 202 pp., illus., bibl.

——————.
Tom-Tom, with Illustrations from photo-
graphs taken by the author and others. New
York: Harper & Bros., 1926. xvi, 258 pp.
>   Life and manners in Dutch Guiana.

Williams, Cyrnic R.
*A Tour Through the Island of Jamaica from
the Western to the Eastern End . . . in 1823.*
London: 1827.

Williams, Eric
The Negro in the Caribbean. Washington,
D. C.: The Associates in Negro Folk Educa-
tion, 1942. 119 pp., bibl.

Williams, Joseph John
Psychic Phenomena in Jamaica. New York:
The Dial Press, 1934. 309 pp., bibl. (pp. 286–
299).
>   Social life, customs, beliefs in the supernatural,
>   magic and witchcraft treated.

Woodson, Carter G.
"Life in a Haitian Valley." *Journal Negro
History* 22:366–369, 1937.
>   Review of the book.

FOLKTALES—LEGENDS

Belpre, Pura
The Tiger and the Rabbit, and Other Tales.
Illustrated by Kay Peterson Parker. Boston:
Houghton Mifflin & Company, 1946. 118 pp.
>   Fifteen well told tales of Puerto Rico.

Cleare, W. T.
"Four Folk Tales from Fortune Island, Bahamas." *JAFL* 30:228–229, 1917.

Comhaire-Sylvain, Suzanne
Contes du Pays d'Haiti. Port-au-Prince, Haiti:
1938. 43 pp.
>   A number of Haitian folk tales.

——————.
"Creole Tales from Haiti." *JAFL* 51:219–346,
1938.
>   The author includes a number of melodies of
>   ballad songs.

——————.
Les Contes Haïtiens. Paris: Imprimerie de
Meester, 1937. 2 vols. in 1. Illus., bibl.
>   A study of Haitian folk tales.

Courlander, Harold
Haiti Singing. Chapel Hill: The University of
North Carolina Press, 1939. xii, 273 pp.
>   The music and lore of the Haitians, with numer-
>   ous musical examples.

—————.
Uncle Bouqui of Haiti. New York: William Morrow and Co., 1942.
> Humorous tales about two folk heroes of the mountains of Haiti,—for younger readers.

Edwards, Charles L.
Bahama Songs and Stories. A Contribution to Folk-Lore. Memoirs of the American Folk-Lore Society, vol. 3. Boston: Houghton Mifflin and Company, 1895. 111 pp., music, illus.
> Contains 40 songs and 38 stories.

—————.
"Tales from Bahama Folk-lore." *JAFL* 4:47–54, 247–252, 1891.

Meade, Florence O.
"Folk Tales from the Virgin Islands." *JAFL* 45:363–373, 1932.

Milne-Home, Mary Pamela
Mamma's Black Nurse Stories: West Indian Folk-Lore. Edinburgh and London: William Blackwood and Sons, 1890. xii, 131 pp.

Parsons, Elsie Clews
Folk-Tales of Andros Island, Bahamas. Memoirs of the American Folklore Society, vol. 13. Lancaster, Pa.: The American Folklore Society, 1918. xvii, 167 pp., music, bibl.

—————.
Folk-Lore of the Antilles, French and English. Part I, 1933; Part II, 1936; Part III, 1942. Memoirs of the American Folklore Society, No. 26. Philadelphia: American Folklore Society, 1933–1942.

—————.
"Jamaica Folk Stories." *JAFL* 35: 328–330, 1922.

—————.
"Ten Folk Tales from the Cape Verde Islands." *JAFL* 30: 230–238, 1917.

—————.
"A West Indian Tale." *JAFL* 32: 442–443, 1919.

Roberts, Helen H.
"Three Jamaican Folk Stories." *JAFL* 35: 328–329, 1922.

St. Johnston, Sir Thomas Reginald
A West Indian Pepper Pot; or, Thirteen 'Quashie' Stories, with coloured illustrations by Eva Wilkin. London: P. Allan & Co., Ltd., 1928. xiii, 209 pp.

Simpson, George Eaton
"Traditional Tales from Northern Haiti." *JAFL* 56: 255–266, 1943.

—————, **and Cineas, J.B.**
"Folktales of Haitian Heroes." *JAFL* 54: 176–185, 1941.
> 19 legends in English about Henri Christophe, 2 about Toussaint Louverture, and 2 about Dessalines.

Smith, Pamela Coleman
Annancy Stories. New York: R. H. Russell, 1899. 79 pp., illus.

—————.
"Two Negro stories from Jamaica." *JAFL* 9: 278, 1896.

Stoddard, Florence J.
As Old as the Moon. Cuban Legends of the Antilles. New York: Doubleday, Page & Co., 1909. xxv, 205 pp., illus.

Tremblay, J., and Mercure, G.
"Anecdotes de la Côte-Nord, de Portneuf et de Wright." *JAFL* 33: 259–272, 1920.

Trowbridge, Ada Wilson
"Negro Customs and Folk Stories of Jamaica." *JAFL* 9: 279–287, 1896.

CUSTOMS—BELIEFS—SUPERSTITIONS

Banbury, Thomas
Jamaica Superstitions, or the Obeah Book. A complete treatise of the absurdities believed in by the people of the island. Jamaica: M. C. de Souza, 1894. 43 pp.

Beckwith, Martha Warren
Christmas Mummings in Jamaica. Poughkeepsie: Vassar College Folklore Publications, No. 2; 46 pp. 1923.
> Music recorded in the field by Helen H. Roberts.

—————.
Christmas Mummings in Jamaica. In: *Jamaica Folk-Lore.* Memoir of the American Folklore Society, vol. 21, pp. 1–67; music, illus. New York: The American Folklore Society, 1928.
> Reprint of the above publication.

—————.
The Hussay Festival in Jamaica. Publications of the Folk-Lore Foundation of Vassar College, No. 4, Poughkeepsie, 1924. 17 pp.

Belisario, I. M.
Sketches of Character in Illustration of the Habits, Occupations and Costumes of the Negro Population in the Island of Jamaica, drawn after Nature, and in Lithography. Kingston: 1837.

Bolton, H. Carrington
"Gombay,—A Festal Rite of Bermuda Negroes; and Some of their Songs." *JAFL* 3: 222–226, 1890.

Booy, T. de
"Certain West Indian Superstitions Pertaining to Celts." *JAFL* 28: 78–83, 1915.

Cannon, Walter Bradford
"Voodoo Death." *AA* 44: 169–181, 1942.

Carmichael, A. C.
Domestic Manners and Social Condition of the White, Coloured, and Negro Population of the West Indies. London: Whittaker, Treacher and Co., 1833. 2 vols.

Dana, M.
"Voodoo, its effect on the Negro race." *Metropolitan Magazine* (New York) 27: 529–538, 1908.

Dorsainvil, J. C.
Vodou et Névrose. Port-au-Prince, Haiti: Imprimée La Presse, 1931.

Junker, L.
"De Godsdienst der Boschnegers." *West-Indische Gids.* 's-Gravenhage, 1925. Jaarg. 7, pp. 81–95, 127–137, 153–164.
Religious rites among the Bush Negroes.

———.
"De Godsdienst der Boschnegers." *Onze Aarde.* Amsterdam, 1934. Jaarg. 7, pp. 331–336, illus., map.

Mars, Jean Price
Une Étape de l'évolution Haïtienne. Port-au-Prince, Haïti: Impr. "La Presse," 1929. viii, 208 pp.
Contains a section on religious beliefs, and ceremonialism.

Newell, William W.
"Myths of Voodoo Worship and Child Sacrifice in Haiti." *JAFL* 1: 16–30, 1888.

Owen, Mary A.
"Among the Voodoos," London: *Proceedings of the International Folklore Congress of 1891–1892,* 1893. pp. 313–26.

Panhuys, L. C. van, jonkheer
About the Ornamentation in Use by Savage Tribes in Dutch Guiana, and Its Meaning. 's-Gravenhage, 1904. pp. 619–621.
Excerpt from Proc. Int. Congr. of American. 13, 1902 (U.S.).

———.
"The Trafe Superstition in Surinam." *Proceedings of the 21st International Congress of Americanists* 1:182–185, 1924.

Parsons, Elsie Clews
"Spirit Cult in Haiti." *Journal de la Société des Américanistes de Paris* 20: 159–179, 1928.

Rigaud, Odette M.
"The Feasting of the Gods in Haitian Vodu." *Primitive Man* 19 (Nos. 1 and 2): 1–58, 1946.

Rouse, I.
"Some Evidence Concerning the Origin of West Indian Pottery-Making." *AA* 42: 77–80, 1940.

Sherlock, B. M.
"Custom and Superstition in Jamaica." *Empire Review* (London): November, 1924.

Simpson, George Eaton
"Four Vodun Ceremonies." *JAFL* 59: 154–167, 1946. Illus.

———.
"Haitian Magic." *Social Forces* (Baltimore) 19: 95–100, 1940.

———.
"Sexual and Familial Institutions in Northern Haiti." *AA* 44: 655–674, 1942.

———.
"The Belief System of Haitian Vodun." *AA* 47 (No. 1): 35–59, 1945.

———.
"The Vodun Service in Northern Haiti." *AA* 42 (No. 2): 236–254, 1940.
Description of the nature and character of the ritual. Discussion of the musical part—vocal and instrumental.

———.
"Two Vodun-Related Ceremonies." *JAFL* 61: 49–52, 1948.

Sullivan, Caroline
The Jamaica Cookery Book. Three hundred and sixty-four simple cookery recipes and household hints . . . Kingston, Jamaica: A. W. Gardner & Co., 1893. xii, 90 pp.

Tench, M. F. A.
"West Indian Folklore, The Zombi." *Folklore* 25: 370–371, 1914 (London).

Trowbridge, Ada Wilson
"Negro Customs and Folk Stories of Jamaica." *JAFL* 9: 279–287, 1896.

Williams, Joseph John
Psychic Phenomena of Jamaica. New York: The Dial Press, 1934. 309 pp., bibl.
Superstitions, witchcraft and magic in native rites.

———.
Voodoos and Obeahs: Phases of West India Witchcraft. New York: L. Mac Veagh, Dial Press, 1932. xix, 257 pp., bibl. (pp. 237–248).

PROVERBS—RIDDLES

Anderson, I., and Cundall, F.
Jamaican Negro Proverbs and sayings collected and classified according to subjects. Kingston, Jamaica: The Institute of Jamaica, 1910. vii, 48 pp.

Armbrister, H.
"Proverbs from Abaco, Bahamas." *JAFL* 30: 274, 1917.

Bates, William C.
"Creole Folk-lore from Jamaica. I. Proverbs." *JAFL* 9: 38–42, 1895.

Beckwith, Martha W.
"Jamaica Proverbs." *Vassar College Folklore Publication* No. 6, 6; 137.

———.
Jamaica Proverbs. In: *Jamaica Folk-lore.* Memoir of the American Folklore Society, vol. 21, pp. 5–137, bibl. New York: The American Folklore Society, 1928.

Franck, Harry A.
"Jamaica Proverbs." *Dialect Notes* 5 (Part 4): 98–108, 1921.

Grant, Cyril F.
"Negro Proverbs Collected in Jamaica." *Folk-Lore* (London) 28: 315–317, 1917.

Ivey, J. W.
"The wisdom of the Haitian peasant, or some Haitian proverbs considered." *Journal of Negro History* 26: 485–498, 1941.

Parsons, Elsie Clews
"Proverbs from Barbados and the Bahamas." *JAFL* 43: 324–325, 1930.

————.
"Riddles and Proverbs from the Bahama Islands." *JAFL* 32: 439–441, 1919.

————.
"Riddles from the Andros Islands." *JAFL* 30: 275–277, 1917.

Speirs, James
The Proverbs of British Guiana. Demerara: 1902.

FOLK MEDICINE

Barham, Henry
Hortus Americanus: Containing an account of the trees, shrubs and other vegetable productions of South America and the West-India Islands, and particularly of the Island of Jamaica....To which are added a Linnaean Index . . . Kingston, Jamaica: A. Aikman, printer, 1794. 212 pp.
"...curious and useful observations, respecting their uses in medicine, diet, and mechanics."

Beckford, William
A Descriptive Account of the Island of Jamaica. . . . London: Printed for T. and J. Egerton, 1790. 2 vols.

Beckwith, Martha W.
"Ethnobotany of the Jamaica Negro." *Vassar College Folklore Publication* No. 8: 47 pp.

————.
Plant Medicines. In: *Jamaica Folk-Lore.* Memoir of the American Folklore Society, Vol. 21, pp. 1–47, bibl., notes. New York: The American Folklore Society, 1928.

Blome, Richard
Extracts From a Description of the Island of Jamaica . . . London: Richard Blome, 1678. Reprinted by W. W. Anderson, New York, Kingston and London, 1851.

Dancer, Thomas
The Medical Assistant, or, Jamaica Practice of Physic, Designed Chiefly for the Use of Families and Plantations. London and Kingston: D. Douglas & W. Aikman, 1819.

Fawcett, William, and Rendle, A. B.
Flora of Jamaica; containing descriptions of the flowering plants from the island. London: British Museum of Natural History. Vol. I: 1910–1926. Illus.
The authors cite numerous examples of ethnobotany.

Gosse, Philip Henry
A Naturalist's Sojurn in Jamaica. Assisted by Richard Hill. London: Longmans, Brown, Green and Longmans, 1851. xxiv, 508 pp.

Steggerda, M.
"Plants of Jamaica Used by Natives for Medicinal Purposes." *AA* 31: 431–434, 1929. n.s.

GAMES—PLAYS

Beckwith, Martha W.
Folk Games of Jamaica. Vassar College Folklore Publication No. 1, 79 pp. 1922 (Poughkeepsie). Music recorded in the field by Helen H. Roberts.

Hurston, Zora
"Dance Songs and Games from the Bahamas." *JAFL* 43: 294–313, 1930.

Williams, Alfred M.
"Miracle Play in the West Indies." *JAFL* 9: 117–120, 1896.

SPEECH

Ayres, Harry Morgan
"Bermudian English." *AS* 8(No. 1): 3–10, 1933.

Comhaire-Sylvain, Suzanne
Le Créole Haïtien: Morphologie et Syntaxe. Wettern, Belgium: Imprimerie De Meester: Port-au-Prince, Haiti: L'Auteur, 1936. 180 pp.
A study of Creole dialects.

Munro, Helen L.
"West Indian English." *AS* 2 (No. 4): 201, 1927.

Whitehead, Henry S.
"Negro Dialect of the Virgin Islands." *AS* 7 (No. 3): 175–179, 1932.

FOLKSONG

GENERAL STUDIES AND COLLECTIONS

Beckwith, Martha Warren
Christmas Mummings in Jamaica; with music recorded in the field by Helen H. Roberts. Poughkeepsie, New York: Vassar College, 1923.

————.
Jamaican Folk-Lore; with music recorded in the field by Helen H. Roberts. Memoir of the American Folklore Society, No. 21. Philadelphia: American Folklore Society, 1929. 137 pp., bibl., notes.
Many musical examples in sections on Folk-Games and Christmas-Mummings.

————.
The Hussay Festival in Jamaica. Publication of the Folklore Foundation No. 4. Poughkeepsie, New York: 1924.

————.
"The English Ballad in Jamaica: A Note Upon the Origin of the Ballad Form." *MLA* 39: 455–483, 1924.

Bowman, Laura
The Voice of Haiti. New York: Clarence Williams Music Publishing Company, 1938.
Includes 32 native ceremonial songs and Voodoo chants.

Brady, Leona
"A West Indian Ballad from Harlem." *NYFQ* 2 (No. 4) : 266–268, 1946.
A historical ballad—"Queen Mary," with music.

Broadwood, Lucy E.
English Airs and Motifs in Jamaica. In: Walter Jekyll, *Jamaican Songs and Story,* (pp. 285–288). London: D. Nutt, 1907.

Castellanos, Israel
Instrumentos musicales de los afrocubanos. Habana: Imprenta "El siglo xx," 1927. 40 pp.
A study of Afro-Cuban musical instruments.

Chase, Gilbert
"Some Notes on Afro-Cuban Music and Dancing." *The Inter-American* (Washington, D. C.) 1 (No. 8) : 32–33, Dec., 1942.

Clark, Edgard Rogie
Moment Musical; ten selected articles. Fort Valley, Ga.: Department of Music, Fort Valley State College, 1940. 24 pp.

Courlander, Harold
Haiti Singing. Chapel Hill: The University of North Carolina Press, 1939. xii, 273 pp., including music, bibl.
Thorough discussion of music, instruments, rituals of the Haitian people.

——————.
"Haiti's Political Folksongs." *Opportunity* 19: 114–118, 1941.

——————.
"Musical Instruments of Cuba." *MQ* 28 (No. 2) : 227–240, April, 1942.
Particularly in reference to the Afro-Cuban cults.

——————.
"Musical Instruments of Haiti." *MQ* 27 (No. 3) : 371–383, 1941.

——————.
"Profane Songs of the Haitian People." *Journal of Negro History* 27: 320–344, 1942, (Washington, D. C.).

Cramer, Louise
"Songs of West Indian Negroes in the Canal Zone." *CFQ* 5: 243–272, 1946.
Words only.

Dawson, Warrington
"La caractère spécial de la musique Nègre en Amérique." *Société des Américanistes Journal.* n.s. 24: 273–286, 1932 (Paris).

Edwards, Charles L.
Bahama Songs and Stories; With Music. Memoirs of the American Folklore Society No. 3. Philadelphia: American Folklore Society, 1895.

——————.
"Tales from Bahama Folk-lore." *JAFL* 4: 47–54, 247–252, 1891.
Musical examples included.

Espinet, Charles S., and Pitts, Harry
Land of the Calypso; origin and development of Trinidad folksong. Port of Spain, Trinidad: B. W. I. Guardian Commercial Printery, 1944. 74 pp., illus., music.

Focke, Hendrik Charles
De Surinaamsche Negermuzik. Bijdragen tot de bevordering van de kennis der Nederlandsch West-Indsche Koloniën. Haarlem: A. C. Kruseman, 1855–1858. 2 vols.
A study of Negro music in Surinam. Musical examples in Vol. 2.

García Agüero, Salvador
Presenca africana na música nacional de Cuba. In: *Congresso Afro-Brasileiro,* (pp. 305–321). Rio de Janeiro: Civilização Brasileira s/a, 1940.

García Caturla, Alejandro
"Posibilidades sinfónicas de la musica afrocubana." *Musicalia* 2 (No. 7) : 15-17, 1929 (Havana).
Discussion of orchestral utilization of Afro-Cuban music.

Garrison, Lucy (McKim)
"Songs of the Port Royal 'Contrabands'." *Dwight's Journal of Music* 221: 254–255, 1862 (Boston).

Hearn, Lafcadio
Two Years in the French West Indies. New York: Harper and Brothers, 1890.
In the appendix are found Creole melodies and 4 songs.

Herskovits, Melville J., and Frances S.
Suriname Folk-Lore; with transcriptions of Suriname Songs and musiological analysis, by Dr. M. Kolinski. New York: Columbia University Press, 1936. xx, 766 pp.

Hurston, Zora Neale
Tell My Horse. Philadelphia: J. B. Lippincott Company, 1938. 301 pp.
"Songs of worship to voodoo gods," words and music, pp. 279–301.

Jekyll, Walter, coll. and ed.
Jamaican Song and Story: Annancy stories, digging sings, ring tunes, and dancing tunes. Introduction by Aline Werner; appendices on "Traces of African Melodies in Jamaica," by C. S. Meyers, and on "English Airs and Motifs in Jamaica," by Lucy E. Broadwood. London: D. Nutt, 1907.
Publication of the Folklore Society Vol. 55.

Krehbiel, Henry Edward
"Lafcadio Hearn and Congo Music." *The Musician* (Boston) 11: 544–545, 1906.

Lachatañeré, Rómulo
"Conga y afrocubanismo de exportación." *Norte* 2 (No. 3) : 30–31, Dec., 1941. (Revista Continental, N. Y.).
The corruption and distortion of native indigenous musical forms in the export market.

——————.
Oh,¡¡ mío Yemaya!! Manzanillo, Cuba: Editorial "El Arte," 1938. 214 pp.
Ritual songs of the Yorubá Negroes.

Lomax, Alan
"Haitian Journey." *Southwest Review* 23 (No. 2): 125–147, 1938.
The author's experiences while on a recording expedition in Haiti.

McKay, Claude
Songs of Jamaica with an introduction by Walter Jekyll. Kingston, Jamaica: A. W. Gardner Company, 1912.

Martín, Juan Luis
"Los tambores sagrados del ñañiguismo. Cosas de Afro-America." *Orbe* 1:28–29, 1931 (Havana).
The sacred drums in Afro-Cuban ritual.

Merwin, B. W.
"A Voodoo Drum from Haiti." *Museum Journal* 8: 123–125, 1917. (University of Pennsylvania, Philadelphia).

Meyers, Charles Samuel
Traces of African Melody in Jamaica. In: *Song and Story* by Walter Jekyll (pp. 278–285). London: D. Nutt, 1907.

Nicoleau, B. A., and Jaegerhuber, Werner A.
Six Concert Pieces Based on Voodoo Songs. Canez, Haiti.

Ortiz, Fernando
"Afro-Cuban Music." *Inter-American Quarterly* 1 (No. 3):66–74, 1939.
"Afro-Cuban music represents the fruitful blend between the musical innovations of various white people of Europe on one hand, and on the other the music of distinct and clearly differentiated groups of Negroes who covered almost an entire continent."

———.
La "clave" xilofónica de la musical cubana. Habana: Tipografía Molina y cía., 1935. 44 pp.

———.
"De la música afrocubano." *Universidad de Habana* 1: 111–125, 1934.
On Afro-Cuban music.

———.
"El estudio de la música afrocubano." *Musicalia* 1 (No. 4): 115–119, 1928; 1 (No. 5): 169–174, 1929.

———.
"La música sagrada de los negros Yurubá en Cuba." *Ultra* 3 (No. 13): 77–86, 1937 (July) (Havana), illus.
See also, the same author's article in *Estudios Afrocubanos* (Habana) 2: 89–104, 1928.

Panhuys, L. C.
"Les Chansons et la Musique de la Guyane Néerlandaise." *Journal de la Société des Américanistes* 9: 27–29, 1912. n.s. (Paris).
Songs and music of Dutch Guiana.

Parsons, Elsie Clews
"Spirituals from the American Colony of Samana Bay, Santo Domingo." *JAFL* 41: 525–529, 1928.

Quevedo, Raymond
Victory Calypsoes; popular compositions by the leading calypso artists of Trinidad. Port-of-Spain: Trinidad Publishing Co., 1944. 31 pp., illus.
Words only.

Reynolds, Quentin
"Jungle Dance." *Collier's,* Nov. 27, 1937. pp. 12, 45–47.
A discussion of the place of African elements in Cuban dance and ritual.

Roberts, Helen H.
"A Study of Folksong Variants Based on Field Work in Jamaica." *JAFL* 38: 149–216, 1925.

———.
"Lullabies in Jamaica." *JAFL* 41: 588–592, 1928.

———.
"Possible Survivals of African Song in Jamaica." *MQ* 12: 340–348, 1926.

———.
"Some Drum and Drum Rhythms of Jamaica." *Natural History* 24: 241–251, 1924. (New York).

Salazar, Adolfo
"El movimiento africanista en la música de arte cubana." *Estudios afrocubanos* 2: 3–18, 1938.
The role of Negro African elements in Cuban art music.

Sánchez de Fuentes, Eduardo
Influencia de los ritmos africanos en nuestro cancionero. In: *Las Bellas Artes en Cuba,* Carbonell y Rivero, José Manuel, ed. (pp. 155–202). Habana: 1928.
A study of African, as well as Spanish elements and influences in Cuban music.

White, C. C.
"Musical Pilgrimage to Haiti, the Island of Beauty, Mystery and Rhythm." *Etude* 47 (No. 7): 505–506, 1929 (July).

CHILDREN'S GAMES AND RHYMES

Beckwith, Martha Warren
Folk Games of Jamaica. In: *Jamaica Folk-Lore.* Memoir of the American Folk-Lore Society, Vol. 21, (pp. 5–95), music, illus. New York: The American Folklore Society, 1928.

Roberts, Helen H.
"Lullabies in Jamaica." *JAFL* 41: 588–592, 1928.

Parsons, Elsie Clews
"Ring Games and Jingles in Barbados." *JAFL* 43: 326–329, 1930.

DANCE

Leaf, Earl
Isles of Rhythm. Foreword by Katherine Dunham. New York: A. S. Barnes and Co., 1948. 211 pp. illus.
Altho it's not authoritative from the historical of anthropological aspects, the author succeeds in providing a number of excellent photographs on many West Indian customs and traditions, particularly Haitian dances, rituals and ceremonies.

Hurston, Zora
"Dance Songs and Games from the Bahamas." *JAFL* 43:294–313, 1930.

Simpson, George Eaton
"Peasant Songs and Dances of Northern Haiti." *Journal of Negro History* 25:203–215, 1940 (Washington, D. C.).

ARRANGEMENTS
————: *Voice and Piano*

McKay, Claude
Songs from Jamaica. London: Augener, Ltd., 1912. 11 pp.

Patterson, Massie, comp.
Calypso Songs of the West Indies. Free transcription by Maurice Baron. New York: M. Baron Co., 1943. 25 pp.
  Arranged for voice and piano.

Saunders, Max, and Evans, Hall
The Edric Connor Collection of West Indian Spirituals and Folk Tunes. New York: Boosey and Hawkes, 1945.
  Arranged for voice and piano, 8 songs.

Tiersot, Julien
Chansons Nègres,—Recueillies, Traduites et Harmonisées. Paris: Heugel, 1933. 94 pp.
  Includes Haitian songs.

————: *Piano*

Elie, Justin
Ancient Mountain Legends. 1. The Echo; 2. Homesickness; 3. Nocturne. New York: Carl Fischer.

————.
Indian Dance and Ritual. New York: Boosey and Hawkes.

————.
Méringues Populaires Haitiennes. Arrangées et harmonisées pour piano. New York: 1920.

"Prayer at Eventide."
Elie, Justin: Carl Fischer.

"Rumba."
Elie, Justin: Boosey & Hawkes.

"Tropical Dance."
Elie, Justin: Carl Fischer.

————: *Violin*

"Haytian Legend."
Elie, Justin: Carl Fischer.

————: *Orchestra*

Elie, Justin
Babylon: Suite of four orchestral sketches. New York: Carl Fischer.

————.
Kiskaya, Aboriginal Suite, in 4 movements. New York: Carl Fischer.

————.
Prayer at Eventide, Isma-O! Firefly Fancies (caprice). New York: Carl Fischer.

————.
Rumba, Indian Dance and Ritual. New York: Boosey & Hawkes.

Hammond, Richard
West Indian Dances. New York: MS.

RECORDS
Collections

Antilles, Barbados.
  Collection of late Dr. Elsie C. Parsons, Harrison, New York.

Bahama Islands.
  In Archive of American Folk Song Library of Congress, Music Division, Washington, D. C.

Calypso—Vol. I. Modern.
  3–10". DISC–614
    Contents: Tie Tongue Baby; Harlem Brown; Yankee Dollar; Nora the War is Over; New York Subway; Always Marry A Pretty Woman.

Calypso—Vol. II. Standard.
  3–10". DISC–628
    Contents: Donkey Wants Water; Matilda; Out the Fire; Dorothy; Small Island; Sly Monologue.

Calypso—Vol. III.
  Lord Invader (vocal) with Felix and his Internationals. 2–10". DISC–640
    Contents: Good Mada Made Us All; Cousin Family; Pound Your Planting in the Mortar; Mary Ann.

Cuban Cult Music.
  Recorded on location by Harold Courlander. 3–10". DISC–131

"Dig My Grave."
  Led by David Pryor and Henry Lundy at Nassau, Bahamas, 1935. In: Album V: (Library of Congress). AAFS21 A1

Folk Music of Haiti.
  Recorded on location by Harold Courlander. 4–10". DISC–142

U. S. Library of Congress. Division of Music. Folklore Section.
  Bahaman Spirituals. David Pryor of Nassau and Hebron Labor Camp, Hebron Md., with guitar. AAFS-LC

————.
  Haitian Folk Songs. Lise Paret Limardo. AAFS-LC

West Indies.
  Collection of Miss Katherine Dunham, New York.

THE NON-ENGLISH SPEAKING GROUPS

THE NON-ENGLISH SPEAKING GROUPS

FOLKLORE AND FOLKSONG
GENERAL STUDIES AND COLLECTIONS

Alland, Alexander
American Counterpoint. New York: John Day, 1944.
> Excellent photographs and a good text describe the lives of the Chinese, English, Welsh, French and Scotch, the Jews, the Italians...and all the rest of us who call ourselves Americans.

Bercovici, Konrad
On New Shores. New York: Century Company, 1925.
> Contains chapters on French Settlement at Wild Rice, North Dakota, and on the Russo-Germans in North Dakota.

Bowers, David F., ed.
Foreign Influences in American Life. Essays and Critical Bibliographies. Princeton: Princeton University Press, 1944. 254 pp.

Park, Robert Ezra, and Miller, Herbert A.
Old World Traits Transplanted. New York and London: Harper and Bros., 1921. 307 pp.

Post, Louis F.
"English of the Melting Pot." *The Freeman* 7:464–466, 490–493, 512–514, 537–539, 560–562, 1923.

"Progress Reports of Committee" of the popular literature section of the Modern Language Association, on folklore of non-English speaking groups. *SFQ* 6:170–172, 1942.

Shaw, Harry, and Davis, Ruth, eds.
Americans One and All. New York: Harper and Bros., 1947. xviii, 320 pp.
> "The main purpose of the editors in bringing these stories together is to show the common humanity of all Americans regardless of color, religion or nationality . . . this book makes to a better understanding of ethnic minority." (Paul J. Campisi)

"Some of our Immigrants."
Nat. Geographical Magazine (Wash., D. C.) 18:317–334, 1907.
> Excellent collection of photographs.

Spicer, Dorothy Gladys
Folk Festivals in the Foreign Community. New York: The Woman's Press, 1923. 152 pp.

U. S. Library of Congress. Division of Music. Folklore Section.
Traditional American Folklore and Folksongs of Minority Groups in Wisconsin, collected by Prof. Leland Coon of the School of Music, University of Wisconsin.   AAFS–LC

Wittke, Carl
We Who Build America: The Saga of the Immigrant. New York: Prentice Hall, 1939.
> Discusses the contributions of the various nationalities.

ARMENIAN
FOLKLORE

Edwards, G. D.
"Items of Armenian Folklore Collected in Boston." *JAFL* 12:97–107, 1899.

Federal Writers' Project
The Armenians in Massachusetts. (American Guide Series). Written and compiled by the Federal Writers' Project of the W. P. A. for the State of Massachusetts. Boston: The Armenian Historical Society, 1937.

Hoogasian, Susie, and Gardner, Emelyn E.
"Armenian Folktales from Detroit." (Collected by S. H. and ed. by E. E. G.) *JAFL* 57:161–180, 1944.
> Nine tales.

CHINESE
FOLKLORE

Asbury, Herbert
The Barbary Coast. New York: Alfred A. Knopf, 1933. 319 pp.
> Chinese customs.

"Chinese in Boston."
JAFL 5:321–324, 1892.

"Chinese Legend of Rip Van Winkle."
JAFL 2:70–71, 1889.

Culin, Stewart
"The Gambling Games of the Chinese in America." University of Pennsylvania, *Publications in Philology and Literature,* No. 14, 1891.

"Customs of Chinese in America."
JAFL 3:191–200, 1890.

Densmore, G. B.
The Chinese in California. San Francisco: Pattit and Russ, 1880. 122 pp.
> Chinese-California customs, beliefs, social life, superstitions.

"Funeral Ceremonies of Chinese in America."
JAFL 1:239–240, 1888.

Genthe, Arnold
Pictures of Old Chinatown. New York: Moffett, Yard and Company, 1909.
> Chinese customs.

Gong, Eng Ying
Tong War. New York: N. L. Brown, 1930. 287 pp.
> Chinese social life.

Hoy, William J.
"Chinatown Devises Its Own Street Names." *CFQ* 2:71–75, 1943.
> Folkways of San Francisco's Chinatown. Place names.

The Chinese Six Companies: A short general historical resume of its origin, function and importance in the life of the California Chinese. San Francisco: Chinese Consolidated Benevolent Association, 1942. 33 pp.

Lee, Jon
"Some Chinese Customs and Beliefs in California." *CFQ* 2:191–204, 1943.

————.
"Tragedy of the Seventh Day." *CFQ* 1:337–357, 1942.
Chinese New Year Festival, as celebrated in San Francisco bay area, California.

Loomis, A. W.
"Holiday in the Chinese Quarter." *Overland Monthly* 2:144–153, 1869.
Chinese customs in California.

————.
"Medical Arts in the Chinese Quarter." (California). *Overland Monthly* 7:496, 1871.
Folk-Medicine.

MacKenzie, Donald Alexander
Myths of China and Japan. London: The Gresham Publishing Co., Lts., 1923. 404 pp.
Chinese-Japanese California myths, legends.

Mencken, H. L.
Chinese Language in America. In: *The American Language,* by H. L. M., pp. 688–691. New York: Alfred A. Knopf, 1937. 4th ed., rev. and enl.

Wang, Joseph
"The Bill Collector." A Chinese Ghost Tale from New York City. *NYFQ* 1 (No. 4):231–232, 1945.

Wood, Willard
"A New Years Celebration in China Town." *Sunset* 2 (No. 1):59 pp., (May) 1903.
Chinese celebration.

FOLKSONG

Jacobs, A. Gertrude, comp.
The Chinese-American Song and Game Book. Illustrations by Chas. Chin Chen. Music by Virginia and Richard Mather. Text romanization by Ching L. Hsu, Chinese characters by Yun Hsia. New York: A. S. Barnes and Company, 1944. 96 pp.

CZECH AND SLAVONIC

FOLKLORE

Adamic, Louis
"The Yugoslav Language in America." *American Mercury* 12:319–321, 1927.

Dudek, J. B.
"Czech-American Names." *Czechoslovak Student Life* 18 (No. 6):4–10, 1928. (Lisle, Illinois.)

————.
"Czech Influence Upon the American Vocabulary." *Student Life* 18:6–19, 1928.

————.
"Czech Surnames in America." *American Mercury* (Nov.) 1925.

————.
"The Americanization of Czech Given-Names." *AS* 1:18–23 (Oct.) 1925.

————.
"The Americanization of Czech Surnames." *AS* 1:161–167 (Dec.) 1925.

————.
"The Bohemian Language in America." Part I, II. *AS* 2:299–312; 466–473, (April) 1927; (Aug.) 1927.

————.
"The Czech Language in America." *American Mercury* (June) 1925.

Manning, Clarence
"American-Slavonic." *AS* 11 (No. 4):370–371, 1936.

Senn, Alfred
"Einiges aus der Sprache der Amerika-Litauer." *Studi Baltici* (Rome) II, 1932.
A comprehensive study of the changes undergone by Lithuanian in America.

Wells, H. B.
"Slavonic-English Transliterations." *AS* 2 (No. 12):492–494, 1927.

DANISH

FOLKLORE

Christensen, T. P.
"Danish Settlement in Wisconsin." *Wisconsin Magazine of History* 12:19–40, 1928.

FINNISH

FOLKLORE

Edgar, Marjorie
"Finnish Charmer from Minnesota." *JAFL* 47:381–383, 1934.

Federal Writers' Project
The Swedes and Finns in New Jersey (American Guide Series). Written and illustrated by Federal Writers' Project of the W. P. A., State of New Jersey. Bayonne, N. J.: Jersey Printing Co., 1938.

Kolehmainen, John Ilmari
"Finnish Surnames in America." *AS* 14 (No. 1):33–38, 1939.

Mencken, H. L.
The Finnish Language in Amercia. In: *The American Language*, by H. L. M., pp. 675–680. New York: Alfred A. Knopf, 1937. 4th ed., rev. and enl.

U. S. Library of Congress. Division of Music. Folklore Section.
Materials in the Detroit, Michigan, area, particularly Finnish items. Wayne University Recording Project, under the direction of Professor Thelma G. James. AAFS–LC

FOLKSONG

Edgar, Marjorie
"Finnish Charms and Folk-Songs in Minnesota." *Minnesota History* pp. 406–410, 1936.

————.
"Old Finnish Folk Songs In Minnesota." *MTNA* (Ser. 40):137–142, 1946.

Johnson, Arli Kohelmainen
"Michigan Folklore: Finnish Labor Songs from Northern Michigan." *Michigan History* 31 (No. 3):331–344, 1947.
Texts only, songs of the sharecroppers, IWW's and hoboes.

FRENCH CANADIAN

See: Canada, pp. 422-28.

FOLKLORE
BIBLIOGRAPHY

Geddes, James
Bibliographical Outline of French-Canadian Literature. In: *The Papers of the Bibliographical Society of America.* v. 8 (No. 1–2):7–42. Chicago, Illinois: 1914.

————.
Bibliographie du parler français au Canada. Catalogue analytique des ouvrages traitant de la langue français au Canada, dressé par James Geddes et Ajoutor Rivard. Paris: H. Champion: Quebec: E. Marcotte, 1906. 99 pp. (Publications de la Societeté du parler français au Canada.)

Lesser, Alexander
"Bibliography of French Canadian Folklore, 1915–1928." *JAFL* 41:45–47, 1928.

PERIODICALS

Alberta Folklore Quarterly.
Publication of the Folklore and local History Project. Edmonton: University of Alberta.

Canada Français.
Société du parler français au Canada. Quebec. No., 1918–. Formed by the Union of *Parler Français* and *Nouvelle France.* Index: vols. 1–4, 1918–1920 in 4 vols.

Canadian Magazine.
Toronto. 1–91, No. 4, March, 1893–April, 1939. 1893—January, 1925 as Canadian Magazine of polotics, science, art and literature. August, 1895–July, 1937 as Canadian Magazine.

Le Canada Français.
Université Laval, Quebec. 1–4, 1888–1891.

Le Foyer Canadien; recueil littéraire et historique. Québec. 1–4, 1863–1866.

Le Parler Français.
Société du parler Français au Canada, Québec. 1–16, Sept., 1902–1918. 1–12, 1902–Aug., 1914, as Bulletin du parler francais au Canada. United with Nouvelle-France to form Canada français.

Les Archives de folklore: Recueil semestriel de traditions françaises d'Amerique. No. 1 (Publications de L'Université Laval). Montreal: Editions Fides, 1946.
A new review. The purpose, as stated by the director, is devoted to the study of the "folklore of the French of America, in its present state, its European origins, its creations, its relations with Indian and Anglo-Saxon civilization, its alterations and in its undeniable character of ethnic indicator."

Revue Canadienne.
Montreal. 1–80, 1864–1922. 17–23 also as n.s. V. 1–7. 24–28 as series 3, V. 1–7. 54–80 as n.s. V. 1–27. Suspended 1880.

Revue des traditions populaires; recueil mensuel de mythologie, litterature orale, ethnographie traditionelle et art popularie t. 1–34, 1886–1919. Paris: E. LeChevalier, 1886–1919. 34 in 26 vols., illus.

Revue d'ethnographie et des traditions populaires. 1–9 année; 1920–1928. Paris: Société Française d'ethnographie, 1920–1928. Quarterly. No more published.

Royal Society of Canada.
French name: Société Royale du Canada. Proceedings of Transactions, Ottawa; Montreal. 1–12, 1882–1894. Series 2, V. 1–12, 1895–1906. Series 3, V. 1+, 1907+.

Société Historique de Montréal.
Veillées du bon Vieux Temps a la Bibliothèque Saint-Sulpue à Montréal, les 18 Mars. et 24 Avril, 1919, sous les auspices de la Société Historique de Montréal et de la Société de Folklore d'Amérique. Montreal: Ducharme, 1920. 102 pp.

GENERAL STUDIES AND COLLECTIONS

Barbeau, Charles Marius
"L'étude de nos traditions orales." *Revue Canadienne* 21:24–33, 1917.

————.
"Le folklore Canadien-Français." *Royal Society of Canada, Proceedings and Transactions* 9 (1):449–481, 1915.

————.
Les Rêves des Chasseurs. Montreal: Editieus Beachmin, 1942. 117 pp.

————.
"Les traditiones orales française au Canada." *Le Parler Français* 15:300–318, 1917.

————.
"Notes sur la facétie des trois rêves." *JAFL* 32:178–180, 1919.

————.
Quebec, Where Ancient France Lingers; illustrations by Marjorie Borden. Toronto: The Macmillan Company, 1936. 173 pp., illus., music.

————.
Romancero du Canada. Toronto: Macmillan's in Canada, 1937. 254 pp.

————.
Saintes Arbisanes: I—Les Brodeuses. Cahiers d'Art Arca. Montreal, Canada: Editions Fides, 1944. ii, 116 pp., illus., bibl.
The work of the Ursalines among the "petites filles sauvagesses"—the Indian girls.

———.
Saintes Artisanes, II—Mille Petites Adresses.
Montreal: Éditions Lumen, 1946. 216 pp.
    Musical texts and analyses.

———.
The Arts of French Canada. In: *The Arts of
French Canada, 1616–1870.* Detroit: Detroit
Institute of Arts, 1946. 52 pp.
    Catalogue of an exhibit, with a preface by E. P.
    Richardson.

———.
"The Folklore Movement in Canada." *JAFL*
56:166–168, 1943.

———.
The Kingdom of Saguenay. Toronto: The Macmillan Co., 1936. 167 pp.
    Folklore of St. Lawrence.

———, and Massicotte, E-Z.
Veillées du Bon Vieux Temps. Montreal: G.
Ducharme, 1919.

Beaugrand, H.
"Lutins in the Province of Quebec." *JAFL* 5:
327–328, 1892.

Beers, W. George
"The Canadian Mecca." *Century Magazine*
24:1–6, 1882. (n.s. V. 2).

Beston, Henry
The St. Lawrence. (The Rivers of America
Series). Illus. by A. Y. Jackson. New York:
Farrar and Rinehart, 1942. 274 pp.
    "The river, its voyaguers, its fur trade, its folk-
    lore, its missionaries, its Catholicism, its French-
    Indian intercourse, its chansons, its fisheries, its
    little French farms. Farther east its Montagnais
    Algonquin Indians."

Bleakney, F. Eileen
"Folklore from Ottawa and Vicinity." *JAFL*
31:158–169, 1918.

Boyle, D.
"Canadian Folklore." *JAFL* 11:159–165, 1898.

Cather, Willa
Shadows in the Rock. New York: Alfred A.
Knopf, 1931. 280 pp.
    A novel of life in Quebec.

Chamberlain, A. F.
"Folklore of Canadian Children." Illustrations
by Ethel Seath. *Canadian Magazine:* 61:197–
202, 1923.

De Celles, A.
"Jours d'autre fois à Ottawa." *Royal Society
Canada, Proceedings and Transactions* 18 (1):
149–153, 1924.

Ducharme, Jacques
The Shadows of the Trees. New York: Harper
and Bros., 1943.
    The story of a French-Canadian in New England.

Duncan, Dorothy
Bluenose: A Portrait of Nova Scotia. New
York: Harper & Bros., 1942. 273 pp.
    A vivid portrayal of the blend of two cultures—
    the Acadians and Scotch-English.

Ernest-Beatrix, frère
*Humour, Légendes, Aventures; Histoires Cana-
diènnes.* Montréal: A. Lévesque, 1932. 158 pp.,
illus.

Federal Writers' Project
"French-Canadian Folklore." *Manuscripts of
the Federal Writers' Project of the Works
Progress Administration for the State of Rhode
Island.* Woonsocket, Rhode Island.

"French-Canadian Folklore."
JAFL 33:346–366, 1920.

Gibbon, John Murray
Canadian Mosaic. London: Dent and Company,
1941.

Greenough, William Parker
Canadian Folk-life and Folk-lore. New York:
G. H. Richmond, 1897. xii, 199 pp.

Kingman, Lee
Pierre Pidgeon. Illustrated by Arnold Edwin
Bare. Boston: Houghton Mifflin Co., 1944.
    Book story and pictures convey the atmosphere
    of the *Gaspé Country,* for children.

Lacourcière, Luc
"La Langue et le Folklore." *Canada Français*
33:1–14, 1946.

———.
"Les Études de Folklore Français au Canada."
Culture 6:3–9, 1945 (Quebec).

Nute, Grace Lee
The Voyageur. New York: D. Appleton-Century, 1931. vii, 289 pp., illus., maps, bibl.,
music.
    The most complete study of the Voyageur and
    his place in the history of the Northwest.

———.
The Voyageur's Highway, Minnesota's Border
Lake Land. St. Paul: The Minnesota Historical
Society, 1941. viii, 133 pp., illus., music, bibl.

Rose, E. H., and H. J.
"Quebec Folklore Notes, IV." *Folk-Lore* 25:
251–252.

Vestal, Stanley
King of the Fur Traders; the deeds and devil-
try of Pierre Esprit Radisson. Boston: Houghton Mifflin Co., 1940. x, 326 pp., bibl.

Wintemberg, W. J.
"Items of French Canadian Folklore." *JAFL*
21:362–363, 1908.

FOLKTALES—LEGENDS

Barbeau, C. Marius
"Anecdotes de Gaspé, de la Beauce et Témis-
couata." *JAFL* 33:173–258, 1920.

———.
"Blanche comme la neige." *Le Parler Français*
16:263–264, 1918.

———.
"Canadian Folklore: Folk Tales." *French Folk
lore Bulletin* 24:87–90, 1946.

"Canadian Folklore, III." *French Folklore Bulletin* 4 (No. 27) :159–166, 1946.

"Chansons et rondes de la Prairie." *JAFL* 33: 334–343, 1920.

"Contes populaires Canadiens." *JAFL* 29:1–136, 1916; 30:1–140, 1917; 32:112–167, 1919.

"Folklore Canadien, Les Orpheline." *Le Parler Français* 16:225–226, 1918.

"How the Raven Stole the Sun." *Transactions of the Royal Society of Canada*, 3me serie, 38:59–69, 1944, 8 plates. (Ottawa).

"La Belle-Jarretierè-Verte Conte Populaire Canadien." *Le Parler Français* 15:8–19, 1917.

"La Macaronée de Michel Morin, une autre version canadienne." *JAFL* 33:370–372, 1920.

"Les Métamorphoses dans les contes Populaires Canadiens." *Société Royale du Canada. Memoir.* (Ottawa). Série 3, vol. 10, pp. 143–160, 1916.

"Les trésors en fouis, d'apres la tradition Canadienne." *L'Almanach du Peuple* (Montreal) pp. 308–314, 1920.

————, and Daviault, Pierre
"Contes populaires Canadiens; 7 Série." *JAFL* 53:89–190, 1940.

Bolduc, E.
"Une conte de la Beauce. Dom Jean." *JAFL* 29:137–140, 1916.

"Canadian's Habitants' Legends." *JAFL* 19:341–342, 1906.

Cloutier, J. E.-A.
"Anecdotes populaires du Canada. III. Anecdotes de l'Islet." *JAFL* 33:273–294, 1920.

"French Canadian Folk Lore and Folk Tales: Anécdote Populaires." *JAFL* 33:273–294, 1920.

"French Canadian Folk Tales."
JAFL 17:265–267, 1904; 19:341–342, 1906; 29:1–151, 1916; 30:1–157, 1917; 32:90–167, 1919; 33:370–373, 1920; 36:205–271, 1923; 39:371–449, 1926.

Gagnon, A.
"La facétie des 'Trois rèves'; une autre version Canadienne." *JAFL* 33:373, 1920.

Garvin, Amelia Beers
Légendes du Saint-Laurent; illustrations de Chas. W. Simpson.... Montréal: 1925. 47 pp., illus.

Hooke, Hilda Mary
Thunder in the Mountains. Legends of Canada. New York: Oxford University Press, 1948. 223 pp.

Lambert, A.
"Contes populaires Canadiens." *JAFL* 36: 205–217, 1923.

Lanctot, G.
"Contes populaires Canadiens." *JAFL* 36:205–272, 1923.

————.
"Contes populaires Canadiens: Contes de Quebec." *JAFL* 39:371–449, 1926.

————.
"Contes populaires Canadiens, Sixieme Serie." *JAFL* 44:225–317, 1931.

"Fables, Contes et Formules." *JAFL* 29:141–151, 1916.

Maine, Dal
"Ghost Stories of Old Canada." *Winnipeg Free Press* (Magazine Section) June 18, 1938. et. seq.

Melcançon, C.
"Légendes de Percé." *Royal Society of Canada. Transactions and Proceedings* 16 (No. 1) :113–120, 1918.

Mercure, G., and Tremblay, J.
"Anecdotes Populaires du Canada, (première série). II. Anecdotes de la côte-nord, de Portneuf, et de Wright. *JAFL* 33:259–272, 1920.

Montal, L.
"L'adieu de la Grise, Conte Canadien." *Le Parler Français* 13:217–222, 1915.

Morin, V.
"Facéties et Contes Canadiens." *JAFL* 30:141–157, 1917.

Paré, A.
"Legendes de L'Isle-aux-Grues. I. Le Petit-Bonhomme sans tête." *Le Parler Français,* 16:109–114, 1918.

Petitot, Émile
La femme aux métaux. Meaux: E. Marguerith-Dupré, 1888. 24 pp.

Prud'homme, L. A.
"Quelques légendes du Nord-Ouest." *Royal Society of Canada, Proceedings and Transactions 18* (No. 1) :131–147, 1924.

Robert, F.
"Essai sur les contes Canadiens." *Le Canade Français:* 6:265–302, 1923.

Roquebrune, R. de
"Les Contes populaires du Canada." *Le Monde Nouveau: Le Canada Numero Special,* (Paris) 1923. pp. 30–35.

Roy, Pierre-Georges
"Les Légendes Canadiennes." *Cahiers des Dix* (Montréal) No. 2, pp. 45–92, 1937.

Shaw, B. M. H.
"The Vanishing Folklore of Nova Scotia."
Dalhousie Review 3:342–349.

Skinner, C. M.
"Three Wishes; a Quaint Legend of the
Canadian Habitants." *JAFL* 19:341–342, 1906.

Smith, Philip Henry
Acadia. A Lost Chapter in American History.
Pawling, N. Y.: The Author, 1884. 381 pp.,
illus.
    The author, besides presenting an historical ac-
count, narrates a number of legends (pp. 319–
368).

Taschereau-Fortier, Marie C. A.
L'Ogre de Niagara; illustrations d'Arline
Généreux. Montréal: A. Lévesque, 1933. 110
pp., illus.
    Tales and legends. *Contents:* L'ogre de Niagara;
La Sirène des Milles-Isles; Le Sorcier du Sague-
nay; Les sept géants des montagnes Rocheuses;
La légende de la mer Bleue; Le géant des
marches de pierre.

Tremblay, J.
"La Vente de la poule noire. Anecdote Canadien." *Royal Society of Canada; Proceedings
and Transactions 13* (No. 1) :87–94, 1919.

Tremblay, M.
"Contes Populaires Canadiens. Contes de Chicoutimi et de la malbaie." *JAFL* 32:101–112,
1919.

Wallace, Paul A. W.
Baptiste Larocque; legends of French Canada.
Toronto: The Musson Book Co., 1923. vii, 129
pp.

Wintemberg, W. J.
"French Canadian Folk Tales." *JAFL* 17:265–
268, 1904.

CUSTOMS—BELIEFS—SUPERSTITIONS

Dewey, A. Gordon
"Famous Canadian Trials. Sorcery and Sacri-
lege in Old Montreal." *Canadian Magazine*
(Toronto) 46:52–54, 1915.
    An account of the trial and sentence of François
Charles Flavart de Beaufort, guilty of magic,
sorcery and sacrilege.

"French Canadian Folk Lore and Folk Tales:
Customs (Christmas)." *JAFL* 14:59–60, 1901.

Hamlin, Helen
Pine, Potatoes and People. Decorations by
the author. New York: W. W. Norton and
Co., 1948. 238 pp.
    Captures the lives and traditions of the people
of Aroostook. A good portion is given to the
isolated French-Canadian villages.

Leeson, A. M.
"Certain Canadian Superstitions." *JAFL* 10:
76–78, 1897.

Massicotte, E.-Z.
"Croyances et dictons populaires des environs
de Trois Rivières." *JAFL* 32:168–175, 1919.

——————.
"Une noce populaire il y a cinquante ans."
*Royal Society of Canada, Proceedings and
Transactions* 17 (No. 1) 25–31, 1923.

FOLK MEDICINE

Lanctot, G.
"Fables, Contes et Formules." *JAFL* 29:141–
151, 1916.

Massicotte, E.-Z.
"Les remèdes d'autrefois." *JAFL* 32:176–178,
1919.

PROVERBS

Rivard, A.
"A propos de proverbs." *Le Canada-français,*
4:400–407, 1921.

SPEECH

Barbeau, Charles Marius
"Blason," géographie et généalogie populaires
de Québec. *JAFL* 33:346–366, 1920.

Chamberlain, A. F.
"Dialect Research in Canada." *Dialect Notes*
1, (Part 2) 1890.
    Contains a bibliography to 1890.

——————.
"The Vocabulary of Canadian French." *Proceedings of the 15th Session of the International Congress of Americanists,* 1:21–31 pp.,
1906.

Chartier, Emile
"The So-Called French Canadian Patois."
Queen's Quarterly 39:240–249, 1932.
    The French of the *habitant.*

Desilets, A.
"Le parler populaire au Canada-français." *Le
Canada-français,* 10:369–382, 1927.

Dionne, N.-É.
Le Parler populaire des Canadiens. Français
ou lexique des Canadianismes, acadianismes,
angliesmes, américanismes, mots anglais les
plus en usage au sein des familles canadiennes
et acadiennes françaises comprenant environ
15,000 mots et expressions. Préface par M.
Raoul de la Grasserie. Quebec: Laflamme et
Proulx, 1909. xxxiv, 671 pp.

Elliott, A. Marshall
"Contributions to a History of the French
Language in Canada." *American Journal of
Philology* 6, (Part 2) :1885.

——————.
"Speech Mixture in French Canada." *Ameri-
can Journal of Philology* 7, (Part 2) :1886; 81,
(Parts 2 and 3) :1887; 10, (Part 2) :1889.

Geddes, James
"American-French Dialect Comparison." Balti-
more, 1898.
    Reprinted from *Modern Language Notes,* vol. XII–
XIII. Bibl. p. 24.

Canadian French. The Language of the past decade, 1890–1900, with a retrospect of the causes that have produced them. Erlangen: Junge & Sohn, 1902. 66 pp.

Haden, Ernest F.
"French Speaking Areas of Canada." *Conference on non-English Speech in the United States*, (Ann Arbor, Mich.) August 2–3, 1940. Washington, D. C.: Bulletin of the American Council of Learned Societies, 1942. Vol. 34, pp. 581–669.

Lacourcière, Lue
"La Langue et le Folklore." *Canada Français* 33:1–14, 1946.

Maheux, G.
"Les noms populaires des insects au Canada." *Le Canada-français*, 2:307–317, 1919.

Pousland, Edward
Étude Sémantique de l'angliclsme dans le parler franco-américan de Salem (Nouvelle Angleterre). Paris: E. Droz, 1933. 310 pp.
"A study of the Anglicisms forming an integral part of the language of the French-Canadian Colony of Salem."

Rivard, A.
"Les dialects français dans le parler Franco-Canadien." *Proceedings of the 15th Session of the International Congress of Americanists*, (Quebec) 1:3–21, 1906.

Sheldon, Edward S.
"Some Specimens of a Canadian French Dialect Spoken in Maine." *PMLA* 3:210–218, 1887.

FOLKSONG

BIBLIOGRAPHY

The Canadian Federation of Music Teachers Association
A List of Canadian Music. Toronto: Oxford University Press, 1946. 23 pp.
Includes many arrangements of French-Canadian folksongs and dances.

GENERAL STUDIES

Barbeau, C. Marius
"Canadian-English Folk Songs." *JAFL* 31: 170–179, 1918.

———.
"Canadian Folk Songs." *University of Toronto Quarterly*. Jan., 1947. pp. 183–187.

———.
"Canadian Folk Songs as a National Heritage." *The Canadian Nation*, (Feb.) 1928.

———.
"Chansons et rondes de la Prairie." *JAFL* 33: 334–343, 1920.

———.
"Deux de Nos plus Belles Chansons." *Revue Trimestrielle Canadienne*, pp. 424–439, (Dec.) 1932.

"French and Indian Motifs in the Music." *Yearbook of the Arts in Canada*, 1928–1929. pp. 125–132.

———.
"Folk Songs." *JAFL* 31:170–179, 1918.

———.
"Folk Songs of French Canada." *Music and Letters:* 13:168–182, 1932.

———.
"Folk Songs of Old Quebec." *National Museum of Canada. Bulletin*. 75. 72 pp., illus., bibl.

———.
"French Canadian Folk-Songs." *MQ* 29:122–137, 1943.
Nine tunes, with text: Historical and musical background given.

———.
"How Folk-Songs Traveled." *Music and Letters* 15:1934.

———.
"Les Chants Populaires du Canada." *Revue de l'Amérique Latine* 7:119–122.

———.
"Modalité dans nos mélodies populaires." *Mémoires de la Société Royale du Canada*, 3rd Serie 38:15–25, 1944. (Ottawa), illus.
Discussion of scales and intervals in French-Canadian folksongs.

———, and Massicotte, E. Z.
"Chants Populaires du Canada." *JAFL* 23:1–89, 1919.
44 melodies and commentary.

———, and Sapir, Edward
Folk Songs of French Canada. New Haven: Yale University Press, 1925. xxii, 216 pp.

Barry, Phillips
"The Collection of Folk Song." *JAFL* 27:77–78, 1914.
Has 3 Canadian tunes.

Beck, E. C.
"Ze Skunk." *JAFL* 57:211–212, 1944.
A French-Canadian verse circulating in the lumberwoods.

Bélanger, Jeanine
"La loisse épique dans nos Chansons." *Extrait de Culture* (33 rue de 1 Alverne, Quebec) 4: 48–54, 1943.

Une Corde Oubliée de Notre Lyre. Ottawa, Société Royale du Canada, 1942. 24 pp.

Bleakney, F. Eileen
"Folklore from Ottawa and Vicinity." *JAFL* 31:158–169, 1918.
Contains 11 tunes.

Bridle, Augustus
"Composers Among Us." *Yearbook of the Arts in Canada, 1928–1929*. pp. 135–140.

Canadian Folk Song and Handicraft Festival.
General and daily programs. Chateau Fronte-
nac. Quebec, 1927, 1928, 1930.
Song texts given.

"Chansons of Old French Canada."
Canadian Magazine 61:197–202, (June) 1923.

Complin, Margaret
Pierre Falcon's "Chanson de la Grenouille."
Royal Society of Canada, Ottawa. Transactions.
33 (ser. 3, sec. 2) :49–58 pp., 1939.

Delamarre, Mariel Jean (Brunhes)
"Les Vielles Chansons Populaires Françaises
au Pays de Québec." *Correspondant.* 313 (n.s.
277) :208–223, 1928.

de Montigny, Louvigny
Le Bouquet de Mélusine. Montreal and New
York: Louis Carrier et Cie., 1928.
Contains a number of song texts recorded by
Marius Barbeau.

D'Harcourt, Marguerite Bedard
"La Chanson française au Canada." *Revue
Musicale,* numéro spécial (La Musique dans
les pays latins), pp. 82–97, Feb.–Mar., 1940.
Music.
Discussion of Barbeaus' Collection of French-
Canadian folk songs in the National Museum of
Ottawa (6,700 texts, 4,000 melodies).

Fraser, Alexander
"The Gallic Folk-Songs of Canada." *Royal
Society of Canada, Proceedings,* (Ottawa)
Series 9, Section 2, 1903.

"French-Canadian Folk-Songs."
JAFL 30:137–140, 1917; 32:1–89, 1917; 33:
321–345, 1920.

Greenough, William Parker
Canadian Folk-Life and Folk-Lore. New York:
George H. Richmond, 1897. xii, 199 pp.
Discussion of French-Canadian songs, pp. 129–
146.

Halden, Charles
"Chansons Populaires et Jeux Enfantins au
Canada." *La Quinzaine.* (Paris) 68:78–110,
1906.
Folk Songs and children's games in Canada.

Lanctot, G., and Barbeau, M.
"Chansons et Rondes de Laprairie." *JAFL* 33:
336–345, 1920.
11 texts and tunes included.

La Rue, F. A. H.
"Les chansons populaires et historiques du
Canada." *Le Foyer Canadien* 1:321–384, 1863.
Contains 7 songs and commentaries.

Lewis, J .O.
"Twelve Habitant Songs, with Words and
Music." *Canadian Magazine* (Toronto) 59:
182–199, (July) 1922.
Translated from the original French with histori-
cal notes.

MacMillan, J. R.
"Music in Canada." *Ontario Library Review*
24:386–396, 1940. Bibl.

Massicotte, Eduard Z., and Barbeau, C. M.
"Chants Populaires du Canada." *JAFL* 32:1–
89, 1919.
Contains 44 tunes, and 17 variants.

Meloche, Amé
"La Chanson Canadienne." *Culture,* (Quebec)
4:240–248, 1943.
A review of various publications on the French-
Canadian song by different authors that have ap-
peared within the last ten years.

Morin, L. P.
"Les Chansons Populaires du Canada." *Le
Monde Nouveau* (Paris), Le Canada Numero
Special, pp. 23–29, 1923.

Morin, Victor
"La Chanson Canadienne." *Royal Society of
Canada. Proceedings and Transactions.* 21
(ser. 3, sec. 1) :161–205, (Ottawa) 1927.

————.
La Chanson Canadienne. Origines, évolution,
épanouissement. Toronto: The University of
Toronto Press, 1928. 53 pp.

Nute, Grace Lee
The Voyageur. New York: D. Appleton-Cen-
tury, 1931. 289 pp., illus., maps, bibl.
The most complete study of the Voyageur and
his place in the history of the Northwest. Both
French and English texts of Voyageur Songs.

————.
Voyageur Songs. In: *The Voyageur* by Grace
Lee Nute. (pp. 103–155). New York: D. Ap-
pleton & Co., 1931. viii, 288 pp., illus.
Includes 16 tunes and texts.

Prud'homme, Louis Arthur
"French-Canadian Folk-Song." Translated and
summarized by Florence Randal Livesay.
Canadian Magazine (Toronto) 56:53–59, 1920.
Illus.

"Quelques Chants Populaires du Canada."
Revue de l'Amérique Latine 7:155–157.

Renault, Raoul
"French-Canadian Songs." *Le Courier du
Livre* (Quebec) 4:281–290; 327–338, 1900.

Roberts, Helen H.
"Folk-Songs of French Canada." *JAFL* 38:420,
1925.

Sapir, Edward
"French-Canadian Folk-Songs." *Poetry* (Chicago) 16:175–185, 1920.

Songs of Old Canada, a concert program. Association of Canadian Clubs, with introduction
by Marius Barbeau and Graham Spry. Quebec,
1928.

Stewart, George
"Popular Songs of Old Canada." *Monthly Review* (London) 19:64–75, 1904.

"The French-Canadian Folk-Song."
The Art of Music (New York) Vol. 5:374–376,
1915. National Society of Music.

"Three Folk-Songs of French Canada," *Queen's Quarterly,* (Kingston, Ca.) 19:286–290, 1922. Translations by Edward Sapir.

Waugh, F. W.
"Canadian Folk-Lore from Ontario." *JAFL* 31:4–82, 1918.
Contains 3 tunes.

Wood, William
"Footnotes to Canadian Folk-Songs." *Royal Society of Canada, Proceedings* (Ottawa) Series 2, section 2, 2:77–125, 1896.

Wyman, Loraine
"Songs from Percé." *JAFL* 33:321–335, 1920.
Contains 16 tunes, with French text.

COLLECTIONS

Allaire, Uldéric S.
Le Chansonnier Canadien. Pour l'école et le foyer, contenant au delà de 180 chansons. . . . Montreal: Beauchemin Limitée, 1931. 172 pp.
Contains French words with tunes.

Anselme, Père et Daniel, Frère, O. F. M. Cap.
Chansons d'Aeadie. Folklore: Premiere Serie. Preface par M, Marius Barbeau. Montreal: La Reparation, 1942. 60 pp.
Words and music. These songs are from Chetecamp, at Cap-Breton.

Back, G.
Collection of Canadian Airs. With symphonic accompaniments by Ed. Knight. London: 1823.

Barbeau, C. Marius
Alouette; Nouveau recueil de chansons populaires avec mélodies, choisies dans le répertoire du Musée National du Canada-(Collection Humanitias; Publiée sous le patronage de la Faculté des Lettres Université de Montréal). Montréal; Editions Lumen, 1946. 217 pp.
Words and tunes, followed by analytical commentary, and a list of variants.

————.
Folk Songs of Old Quebec. Song translated by Regina Lenore Schoolman. Illustrated by Arthus Lismer. Bulletin 75, Anthropological Series No. 16. 1935. National Museum of Canada, Department of Mines. 72 pp. bibl., illus.
15 songs, with text, variants, annotations and bibliography.

————.
Le Soldat Canadien Chante. Ottawa: Service de Guerre de la Légion Canadienne, 1940. 40 pp., illus.
Tunes with French words.

————.
Les Enfants Disent. Montreal: Editions Paysana, 1943. 90 pp.
Drawings and music.

————.
Romancero du Canada. Toronto: The Macmillan Company of Canada, Ltd. 1937. 254 pp. Also published at Montreal by Editions Beauchemin.
The accompaniments by M. Béclard-d'Harcourt.

————, ed.
Veillées du bon Vieux Temp. Montreal: G. Ducharme, 1919.
Words and tunes.

————, England, P., and Willan, Healy
Chanson Canadienne. Boston: Boston Music Company, 1929. 2 vols.
For voice and piano.

————, Lismer, Arthur and Bourinot, Arthur
Come a Singing! Canadian Folk-Songs. (National Museum of Canada; Bulletin no. 107; Anthropological Series no. 26.) Ottawa: Department of Mines and Resources. 1937. vi, 59 pp.

————, and Sapir, Edward
Folk Songs of French Canada. New Haven: Yale University Press, 1925.
Includes texts and tunes.

Berry, Cecelia Ray, ed.
Folk Songs of Old Vincennes. Chicago: H. T. Fitzimmons, 1946. 95 pp.
French texts collected by Anna C. Flynn; English versions by Frederic Burget and Libushka Bartusek. Introduction and notes by Joseph M. Carrière; melodies collected and harmonized by Cecelia Ray Berry.

Blaquière, Arthur
Répertoire du Petit Septuor de la Bonne Chanson. Folklore Canadien. Arrangement d'Arthur Blaquière. Montreal: Chez l'Auteur (3839 rue Botoel Notre-Dame de Grace). 10 pp.

Botsford, Florence Hudson, comp. and ed.
Folk Songs of Many Peoples. With English versions by American poets. New York: G. Schirmer, vol. 2, pp. 96-106.
French-Canadian Songs for voice and piano.

Brown, James Duff
Characteristic Songs and Dances of all Nations. Edited with historical notes and bibliography by James Duff Brown. The music arranged for the pianoforte by Alfred Moffat. London: Bayley & Ferguson, 1901. pp. 200-202.

Burpee, Lawrence Johnstone, comp.
Songs of French Canada, Toronto: The Musson Book Co., 1909. 87 pp.

Burque, François Xavier
Chansonnier Canadien-Francais. Recueil de chansons populaires, chansons nouvelles et vieilles chansons restaurées, par l'abeé F. X. Burque (musique par Mme. J. B. Duplain). Quebec: Imprimerie-Nationale, 1921. xvii, 283 pp.
French words. Tunes only.

Canadian Folk Song and Handicrafts Festival, under the auspices of the National Museum of Canada, Château Frontenac, Quebec, May 20-22, 1927. Quebec: 1927. 32 pp., illus.
Includes 8 folk songs, 3 with piano accompaniments. French or English and French words.

Canciones Panamericanas: Songs of the Americas. Published in collaboration with the Pan American Union, Washington, D. C. New York: Silver Burdett Company, 1942.
Includes two Canadian songs.

Creighton, Helen, coll.
Songs and Ballads from Nova Scotia. Toronto: J. M. Dent & Sons, Ltd., 1933. 334 pp., music.

French Songs of Old Canada.
Translation and illustrations. London: Wm. Heinemann, 1904.

Gadbois, Abbé Charles-Émile
La Bonne Chanson. Première année (1 a 50); deuxième année (51 à 100); troisième année (101 à 150); quatrième année (151 à 200); cinquième année (201 à 250). Série des Jeunes (25 Chansons). Saint-Hyacinthe: Seminaire de Saint-Hyacienthe 1937-1941.
Words and music.

Gagnon, Ernest
Chansons Populaires du Canada. Recueillies et publiées avec annotations. Québec: R. Morgan, 1880. xvii, 350 pp., music.
French words and tunes of each song with descriptive notes, 106 melodies. Many subsequent editions.

————, and Gibbon, J. Murray
Canadian Folk Songs, Old and New. Toronto: J. M. Dent & Sons, 1927.

Gascione, Margaret
Chansons of Old French Canada. Illustrations by Ethel Seath. Introduction by Marius Barbeau. Quebec: Chateau Frontenac, Canadian Pacific Railway Co., 1929. iv, 31 pp., illus.
11 songs—arranged for voice and piano; French words.

Gauthier, Conrad
40 *Chansons d'Autrefois.* (Mélodies et paroles.) Montréal: Thérien Frères, Limitée, 1932. 84 pp.
Tunes and French words.

Gibbon, John Murray, comp.
Canadian Folk-Songs, Old and New, Selected and Arranged by Murray J. Gibbon, Harmonization by Geoffrey O'Hara and Oscar O'Brien; decorations by Frank H. Johnston. New York: E.P. Dutton & Co., 1927. xxii, 105 pp., illus.
English and French words; music for one voice, with piano accompaniments.

Grant-Schaefer, George Alfred
French-Canadian Songs. For medium voice. Texts in English and French. Also published separately. Boston: Arthur P. Schmidt Co., 1925. 32 pp.
Arranged for voice and piano.

————.
Piano Solos, based on *French Canadian Melodies.* Boston: Arthur P. Shmidt.
Contents: "The Mill" (J'entends le Moulin); "Blow, Wind, Blow" (V'la l'bon vent); "The Crystal Streamlet" (A la Claire Fontaine); "The Bird at the Fountain" (a la Voletto); "On the Lumber Raft" (En roulant ma Boule) "O Canada!"

Greenleaf, Elisabeth B.
Ballads and Sea Songs of New Foundland. Cambridge, Mass.: Harvard University Press, 1933. 395 pp., music.

Greig, Gavin
Folk-Song of the North-East. Peterhead, 1914.

Jameson, R. P., and Heacox, A. E.
Chants de France. New York: D. C. Heath, 1922.
Arranged for voice and piano. Contains French-Canadian songs.

Knight, Edward
Canadian Airs, collected by Lieutenant Back, R. N. during the late Arctic expedition under Captain Franklin, with symphonies and accompaniments by Edward Knight, Jr. The words by George Soane, Esq. A. B. London: J. Power, 1823.

La Liberté, Alfred
Recueil de Chants Populaires du Canada. Paris: Max Eschig & Cie., 1926. 24 pp.
12 songs arranged for voice and piano, contains French words.

Mackenzie, W. Roy
Ballads and Sea Songs from Nova Scotia. Cambridge: Harvard University Press. 1928.

McLennan, William
Songs of Old Canada. Montreal: Dawson Bros., 1886. 83 pp.

MacMillan, Sir Ernest
A Book of Songs. Compiled for the Entertainment and Delight of the English men and women everywhere, but especially for those at Home and in Canada. New York: E. P. Dutton, 1929. Published under the Auspices of the National Council of Education.

————.
Four Canadian Chansons. Arranged for male voices. Boston: Boston Music Co.   **TTBB**

————, ed.
Twenty-One Folk Songs of French Canada. Music for voice and piano arranged by Achille Fortier, Alfred Laliberté, Oscar O'Brien, Leo Smith, and Ernest MacMillan. Introduction and English translation by J. Murray Gibbon. Ontario, Canada: The Frederick Harris Company, 1928. 53 pp.

Mélodies Populaire du Folklore Étranger. 2e Serie. 1er Fascicule—Pays de Langue Française: Belgique-Canada Suisse. Paris: Au Ménestrel, Heugel. Anthologie du Chant Scolaire.

Montigny, Louvigny Testard de
Le Bouquet de Mélusine. Scenes de folklore représentées au Festival de Québec, Mai 1928. Montréal: L. Carrier & Cⁱᵉ, 1928. 112 pp.

Myrand, Ernest
Noëls Anciens de la Nouvelle-France, Quebec: Laflamme & Proulx, 1907. 323 pp.
Contains music of some of the carols.

O'Hara, Geoffrey
Seven Songs of Old Quebec; with translations by J. Murray Gibbons and Geoffrey O'Hara. Boston: White-Smith Music Pub. Co., 1927. 22 pp.
Music arranged for 1 to 3 voices with piano accompaniment. *Contents:* 1. Gay la la; 2. Marianne wanders to the mill; 3. On, roll on, my ball I roll on; 4. Whence, O shepherd maiden?; 5. Now the winter's come to stay; 6. I have culled a rose; 7. Paddling along.

Porter, Grace Cleveland
Negro Folk Singing Games and Folk Games for the Habitants. London: J. Currier and Sons, 1914. xix, 35 pp.
Old French folk singing games, with French and English texts. Music and directions.

Préseault, Abbé Ernest
Chante. Nouvelles Chansons Canadiennes. Première Série. Melodies adapted to the text of various Canadian authors; harmonization by Rev. Fr. R. C. Lariviére, C. S. V. Hull: Les Éditions l'Éclair, 1939. 12 pp.

Prévost, P. E., arr.
Chansons Canadiennes. Paroles et musique par nos Canadiens. . . . harmonisées par P. E. Prévost. Illustrée par J. C. Franchère. Montreal: 1907. 113 pp.
Arranged for voice and piano, French text.

R. R., P. P. Jesuites, coll.
Les Chansons du Vieux Quebec. Harmonized by M. Eudore Piché. Montreal: Libraire Beauchemin, 1939. 224 pp.

Robertson, William Graham
French Songs of Old Canada; with translations. London: W. Heinemann, 1904. 32 pp., illus.
Tunes and French text.

Saar, Louis Victor
A Cycle of Canadian Folk Songs, New York: Carl Fischer. Arranged for female and mixed voices. SSA, SATB.

Sapir, E., and Barbeau, C. M.
Folk Songs of French Canada. New Haven: Yale University Press, 1925.

Somervell, Arthur, arr.
Twelve Ancient French-Canadian Folk-Songs. Collected orally by C. Marius Barbeau, English translations by Harold Boulton. London: Boosey & Co., 1927. 39 pp.
French and English words; music for 1 voice with piano acc.

The Latin American Song Book.
Complete with piano accompaniment. Boston: Ginn and Company, 1942.
Also French-American songs of Louisiana and French-Canadian songs. Arranged for voice and piano.

Tiersot, Julien, comp. and arr.
Forty-four French and Canadian Folk Songs. New York: G. Schirmer, 1910. v. 118 pp.
Arranged for voice and piano.

Tremblay, Amédée, arr.
Dix-huit Chansons Populaires du Canada. Ottawa: J. L. Orme et Fils, 1902. 35 pp.
18 songs arranged for voice and piano. French texts only.

Turcotte, Joseph Gers, ed.
Chansons Canadiennes, Vieux Chants de France, Noëls Populaires. Le Trois Rivières: P. H. Marineau, 1932. 131 pp., illus.
Arranged for 3, 4 & 5 voices (mixed), a cappella.

Vuillermoz, Émile, ed.
Chansons Populaires, Françaises et Canadiennes, Paris: A. Z. Mathot, 1910. 40 pp.
Music for 1 voice with piano acc. No. 1–3 have French and German words; No. 4–7, French only. *Contents:* 1. La belle Françoise; 2. Une perdriole; 3. Caecilia; 4. Bourrée de Chapdes Beaufort; 5. Les trois princesses; 6. Jardin d'amour; 7. Ronde des filles de Quimperlé.

Whitehead, Alfred E.
French Canadian Folk Songs. London: Oxford University Press. Arranged for mixed voices, a cappella.

Willan, Healey
Chansons Canadiennes-French Canadian Folk Songs. Collected by M. Barbeau; translated by Paul England. Ontario: Frederick Harris Company. 2 vols. For voice and piano.

ARRANGEMENTS:
(Individual Titles)

————: *Voice and Piano*

"Blanche comme la Neige."
Whitefield, B.: Schirmer.

"Cette Aimable Tourterelle."
Whitefield, B.: Schirmer.

"Down to the Crystal Streamlet."
Grant-Schaefer, G. A.: Schmidt.

"Gai lon la."
In: Marcella Sembrich. "My Favorite Folk-Songs." (Boston, 1918). arranged by C. F. Manney.

"I Hear the Millwheel."
Grant-Schaefer, G. A.: Schmidt.

"In All the Country 'Round."
Whitehead, A.: C. Fischer: Unison, (with descant).

"Isabeau Went A-Walking."
Whitehead, A.: C. Fischer: Unison (with descant)

"Je Ne Veux Pas Me Marier."
Whitefield, B.: Schirmer.

"Red River Boat Song."
Grant-Schaefer, G. A.: Schmidt.

"Sainte Marguerite."
Grant-Schaefer, G. A.: Schmidt.

"St. Lawrence Boat Song."
Grant-Schaefer, G. A.: Schmidt.

"The Nightingale's Song."
Grant-Schaefer, G. A.: Schmidt.

——————: *Female Voices*

"At the Clear Fountain."
Saar, L. V.: C. Fischer: SSA.

"En Roulant Ma Boule."
Hill, M. W.: Birchard: SSA.

"French Canadian Folk Song."
Hill, M. Wood: Birchard: SSAA

"Gay is the Rose."
Saar, L. V.: C. Fischer: SSA.

"In All the Country 'Round."
Saar, L. V.: C. Fischer: SSA.

"Je ne Suis Si Vilaine."
Hill, M. W.: Birchard: SSA.

"Mademoiselle, Will You Dance with Me?"
Branscombe, G.: Galaxy: SSA.

"Nanette."
Whitehead, A.: Schmidt: SA.

"O Fly, Little Swallow."
Whitehead, A.: Schmidt: SA.

"Pillon Suit la Chandelle."
Hill, M. W.: Birchard: SSA.

"Pledge the Canadian Maiden."
Saar, L. V.: C. Fischer: SSA.

"Sainte Marguerite."
Hill, M. W.: Birchard: SSA.

"Song of the Voyageur."
Helfer, W.: C. Fischer: SSAA.

"The Jolly Hunter."
Treharne, B.: Willis: SA.
Has English and French texts.

"Whence, O Shepherd Maiden?"
Anderson, W. H.: Galaxy: SSAA.

"Whence, O Shepherd Maiden?"
Saar, L. V.: C. Fischer: SSA.

——————: *Male Voices*

"Alouette."
In: H. & M. Auditorium Series No. 48. Andersen, A. O.: Hall and McCreary: TBB.

"Alouette."
Homier: C. Fisher: TTBB a cap.

"Song of the Voyageur."
Helfer, W.: C. Fischer: TTBB.

"Whence, O Shepherd Maiden?"
Anderson, W. H.: Galaxy: TTBB.

—————— *Mixed Voices*

"At the Clear Fountain."
Saar, L. V.: C. Fischer: SATB.

"Dear Love Whom I Adore."
Binchois: C. Fischer: SATB, a cap.

"Farewell Until We Meet Again."
Binchois: C. Fischer: SATB, a cap.

"Gay is the Rose."
Saar, L. V.: C. Fischer: SATB.

"In All the Country 'Round."
Saar, L. V.: C. Fischer: SATB.

"Nay, Thou Dost Displease Me."
Binchois: C. Fischer: SATB, a cap.

"Pledge the Canadian Maiden."
Saar, L. V.: C. Fischer: SATB.

"Song of the Voyageur."
Helfer, Walter: C. Fischer: SATB and Orchestra.

"The Maiden at the Spring."
Treharne, B.: Willis: SATB, a cap.
Has English and French texts.

"Whence, O Shepherd Maiden?"
Saar, L. V.: C. Fischer: SATB.

——————: *Piano*

"Blow, Wind, Blow" (V'la l'bon vent).
Grant-Schaefer, G. A.: Schmidt.

"O Canada!"
Grant-Schaefer, G. A.: Schmidt.

"On the Lumber Raft" (En Roulant ma Boule).
Grant-Schaefer, G. A.: Schmidt.

"The Bird at the Fountain" (A La Voletta).
Grant-Schaefer, G. A.: Schmidt.

"The Crystal Streamlet" A la Clair Fontaine).
Grant-Schaefer, G. A.: Schmidt.

"The Mill Wheel" (J'entends le Moulin).
Grant-Schaefer, G. A.: Schmidt.

——————: *Cello*

"Suite Canadienne."
Jacquet, H. M.: Birchard: Cello and Piano.

——————: *Violin*

"Suite Canadienne."
Jacquet, H. M.: Birchard.
Contents: "A La Claire Fontaine"; "Nostalgie"; "Une Bonne Histoire!"

Chamber Group

Jacquet, H. M.
Suite Canadienne. Boston: Birchard Music Co.: String Trio.

Pargeter, W.
String Quartet in G Major. Phila.: Oliver Ditson Co.

————: Orchestra

Brant, Henry
Variations on a Canadian Theme. MS.–Orchestra.

Helfer, Walter
Symphony on Canadian Airs. MS.–for full orchestra.

MacMillan, Ernest
Six Bergerettes from Lower Canada. Collected by Barbeau, Marius. London: Oxford University Press: Arranged for Chamber Orchestra. Suitable for Stage Presentation. Oboe, Viola, 'Cello, Harp and Voice.

————.
Two Sketches for String Quartet on French Canadian Folk Songs. London: Oxford University Press.
Contents: 1. Notre Seigneur; 2. Saint Malo.

Stage Work

Willan, Healy
L'Ordre de Bon Temp. (The Order of Good Cheer.) Ontario: Frederick Harris Company.
A Ballad Opera, based on French-Canadian folk songs. Libretto by Louvigny de Montigny. English translation by J. Murray Gibbons. Folk songs recorded by Marius Barbeau.

RECORDS

U. S. Library of Congress. Division of Music. Folklore Division.
French Acadian Songs, Indian Songs and Copper Eskimo Songs. Mme. Juliette Gaultier de la Verendrye, with zither and drum.
AAFS–LC

GERMAN

(Outside of Pennsylvania)

FOLKLORE

Bek, W. G.
"Survivals of Old Marriage Customs Among the Low Germans of West Missouri." *JAFL* 21:60–67, 1908.

Benardette, Dolores
"Immigrant Speech-Austrian Style." *AS* 5 (No. 1) :1–5, 1929.

Deiler, John Hanno
The Settlement of the German Coast of Louisiana and the Creole of German Descent. Philadelphia: Americana Germanica Press, 1909.

Estill, J.
"Customs among the German Descendants of Gillespie County (Texas)." *TFSP* 2:67–74, 1917.

Hays, H. M.
"On the German Dialect Spoken in the Valley of Virginia." *Dialect Notes* 3 (Part 4) :263–278, 1908.

Heffner, R. M. S.
German Settlements in Wisconsin. In: *Conference in Non-English Speech in the United States,* Ann Arbor, Mich., August 2–3, 1940. Washington, D. C.: Bulletin of the American Council of Learned Societies, 1942, No. 34, pp. 581–669.

Johnson, F. C.
Count Zinzendorf and the Moravian and Indian Occupancy of the Wyoming Valley, 1742–1763. In: *Proceedings and Collections of the Wyoming Historical and Geological Society, 1902–3.* pp. 119–182. Wilkes-Barre: 1904.

Lacher, J. H. A.
The German Element in Wisconsin. Published for the Benefit of the Salomon Brothers Memorial Fund by Muehlenberg Unit 36. Milwaukee: Steuben Society of America, 1925. 60 pp.
Includes discussion of place names, pp. 6–8, 47–49.

Meyer, A. W.
"Some German-Americanisms from the Middle West." *AS* 2 (No. 2) :134, 1926.

Prince, J. Dyneley
"The Jersey Dutch Dialect." *Dialect Notes* 3, (Part 6) 1910.

Wintemberg, W. J.
"German-Canadian Folklore." *Paper and Records,* Ontario Hist. Society 3:86–96, 1901. (Toronto).

————.
"German Folktales Collected in Canada." *JAFL* 19:241–244. 1906.

————.
"Items of German Canadian Folklore." *JAFL* 12:45–50, 1899.

GREEK

FOLKLORE

Doering, Eileen Elita
"A Charm of the Gulf of Mexico Sponge Fishers." *JAFL* 52:123, 1939.

————.
"Folk Customs and Beliefs of Greek Sponge Fishers of Florida." *SFQ* 7:105–107, 1943.

Lee, Dorothy D.
"Folklore of the Greeks in America." *Folk-Lore* (London) 47:294–310, 1936.

————.
"Greek Tales of Priests and Priestwife." *JAFL* 60:163–167, 1947.
Nine tales collected in the greater Boston area, in 1934 and 1937.

London, Sotiros S.
"American Greek." *AS* pp. 307, (March) 1926.

Macarthur, John R.
Ancient Greece in Modern America. Caldwell, Idaho: The Caxton Printers, 1943. 395 pp.
A discussion of the manifestation of Greek culture in the United States, with an interpretation of the classic legends.

Papanikolas, Helen Zeese
"The Fortress and the Prison." *Utah Humanities Review* 1 (No. 2) :134–146, 1947.
Customs, traditions, legends and songs (texts only) of Greek immigrants in a Utah community.

Sontos, Sotiros S.
"American Greek." *AS* 1 (No. 6) :307–310, 1926.

GYPSY

FOLKLORE

Bonos, Arlene Helen
"Romany Rye of Philadelphia" (Lore among four gypsy tribes of Philadelphia). *AA* 44: 251–274, 1942.

Shoemaker, H. W.
Gypsies and Gypsy Lore in the Pennsylvania Mountains. Altoona, Pa.: 1924.

HUNGARIAN

FOLKLORE

Halpert, Herbert
"Hungarian Lying-Contest Tales About America." *NYFQ* 1 No. 4) :236, 1945.

Mencken, H. L.
The Hungarian Language in America. In: *The American Language,* by H. L. M., pp. 680–682. New York: Alfred A. Knopf, 1937. 4th ed., rev. and enl.

FOLKSONG

Ware, Helen
"The American-Hungarian Folk-Song." *MQ* 2:434–441, 1916.
3 tunes given.

ITALIAN
FOLKLORE

Ciarlantini, Franco
Incontro Col Nord America. Milan: 1929.
Interesting examples of Italian-American speech.

Federal Writers' Project.
The Italians of New York: A survey prepared by workers of the Federal Writers' Project of the W. P. A., in the City of New York. New York: Random House, 1938.

Ferrazzano, Carlo
Poesie. Bologna: 1897: 5th ed., 1912.
Author of many *Macchiete Coloniali* (character sketches) using Italo-American speech patterns.

Fucilla, Joseph G.
"Anglicization of Italian Surnames in the United States." *AS* 18:26–32, 1943.

Garofalo, Alexander J.
"The Oven of the Seven Montelli." *NYFQ* 2 (No. 4) :272–275, 1946.
A tale of the supernatural told by an Italian resident of New York City.

Hoffman, Dan G.
"Stregas, Ghosts and Werewolves." *NYFQ* 3 (No. 4) :325–328, 1947.
Anecdotes of Italians of Causano, a small village between Rome and Naples, told by a Brooklyn informant whose parents and neighbors come from the other side.

Mangione, Jerre
Mount Allegro. Boston: Houghton Mifflin Co., 1942. 292 pp., illus.
A study of the Sicilian-Americans of Rochester. Contains lots of folklore material.

Pagano, Jo.
Golden Wedding. New York: Random House, 1943.
A chronicle of an Italian-American family.

Ramirez, Manuel D.
"Italian Folklore from Tampa, Florida." *SFQ* 5:101–106, 1941.

Rossetti, Carlo
"Americanismi." *Quaderni di Cultura Linguistica* 11. Milan: Le Lingue Estere, 1937.
Americanisms gathered from authors such as: Sinclair Lewis, O'Henry, John Dos Passos.

Rossi, Adolfo
Un Italiano in America. Treviso: 1907.
On Italian-American speech.

Sarfatti, M. G.
"L'Americano come lo si parla." *Nuova Autologia* 376:416–434, 1934.
American as spoken.

Schiavo, Giovanni Ermenegildo
The Italians in Missouri. Chicago: The Italian American Publishing Co., 1929. 216 pp., illus.

Speroni, Charles
"The Observance of St. Joseph's Day among the Sicilians of Southern California." *SFQ* 4: 135–139, 1940.

Trop, Sylvia
"An Italian Rip Van Winkle. The Story of Arigo." *NYFQ* 1:101–105, 1945.

Turano, Anthony M.
"The Speech of Little Italy." *American Mercury* 26:356–359, 1932.

Vaughan, Herbert H.
"Italian and its Dialects as Spoken in the United States." *AS* 1 (No. 7) :431–435, 1926.

———
"Italian Dialects in the United States, II." *AS* 2 (No. 1) :13–18, 1927.

Voiles, Jane
"Genoese Folkways in a California Mining Camp." *CFQ* 3:212–216, 1944.

Zallio, A. G.
"Piedmontese Dialects in the United States." *AS* 2:501–505, (Sept.) 1927.

JAPANESE
FOLKLORE

Brown, Frederick W.
"Anglicized Japanese." *Quarterly Journal of Speech Education* 13:15–23, 1927.

Crocker, Lionel
"The Impact of English on Japanese." *English Journal,* (College Edition) 17:228–294, 1928.

Ichikawa, Sanki
"English Influence on Japanese." *Studies in English Literature* 8 (No. 2) :165–208, 1928. (Tokyo).

Radin, Paul, ed.
"Folktales of Japan As Told in California." *JAFL* 59:289–308, 1946.

FOLKSONG

Hofmann, Charles
"Japanese Folksongs in New York City." *JAFL* 59:325–326, 1946.

JEWISH
BIBLIOGRAPHY

Rosenbach, Abraham Simon W., comp.
An American Jewish Bibliography, Being a list of books and pamphlets by Jews or relating to them, printed in the United States from the establishment of the press in the colonies until 1850. Baltimore: American Jewish Historical Society, 1926. xvii, 500 pp.

Schneider, Rebecca
Bibliography of Jewish Life in the Fiction of America and England. Albany: New York State Library School, 1916. 2 pp.

FOLKLORE

"American Yiddish."
American Mercury 7:205–207.

"American Yiddish."
The Nation 124:435–436.

Arbeter Vitzen.
Collected by a "nudnick" (a "pest"). New York: Hebrew Publishing Co., 1927.
Worker's jokes and humorous tales.

Aurand, A. M.
Little Known Facts about the Ritual of the Jews, and the esoteric folklore of the Pennsylvania-Germans. Harrisburg, Pa.: Aurand Press, 1939.

Ausubel, Nathan, ed.
A Treasury of Jewish Folklore. New York: Crown Publisher, 1948. 800 pp., music.
The stories, traditions, legends, humor, wisdom, and folksongs of the Jewish people. Altho the major portion of the volume deals with "Old World" folklore, a number of interesting examples are included showing the effect of American culture upon Jewish lore.

Brody, Alter
"Yiddish in American Fiction." *American Mercury* 7:205–207, 1926.

Buchwald, Nathaniel
"Non-English Writing: Yiddish." In: *The Cambridge History of American Literature* ed. by Trent, Erskine, Sherman, and Van Doren. Vol. III, (pp. 598–609). New York: The Macmillan Co., 1917. 3 Vols. Reprinted in 1 vol. in 1945.
Also includes discussion of Yiddish-American language forms and patterns as well as major Jewish writers and writings in America.

Der Amerikaner Vitzling.
New York: Hebrew Publishing Co., 1926.
"The American Humorist."—a collection of humorous tales and anecdotes.

Gideon, Henry
From the Cradle to the Chuppe. Boston: The A. P. Schmidt Co., 1923.

Gold, Mike
Jews Without Money; Woodcuts by Howard Simon. New York: H. Liveright, 1930. v, 309 pp., plates.
Autobiographical notes on life in New York's east-side. Mentions many old beliefs, traditions and superstitions.

"Jewish Folk Life in America."
JAFL 29:412–417, 1916.

Krauss, F. S.
"Jewish Folk Life in America." *JAFL* 7:72–75, 1894.

Levenson, Sammy
Meet The Folks. A Session of American Jewish Humor. New York: The Citadel Press, 1948.

Mendelssohn, S. F.
The Jew Laughs. Chicago: L. M. Stein, 1935. 222 pp.

Olswanger, Immanuel
Royte Pomerantsen. New York: Schochten Books, 1947.
A collection of humorous tales in Yiddish, many of them still current in New York's Jewish circles.

Richman, Jacob
Laughs From Jewish Lore. New York: Funk & Wagnalls Co., 1926. xxv, 372 pp.

Rothenberg, Julius G.
"Some American Idioms from the Yiddish." *AS* 18:43–48, 1943.

Shpall, Leo
"A Jewish Agricultural Colony in Louisiana." *Louisiana Historical Quarterly* 20:821–831, 1937.

Sonkin, Robert
"In Re 'Jewish Dialect and New York Dialect'." *AS* 8 (No. 1) :78–79, 1933.

Teitelbaum, Elsa
An Anthology of Jewish Humor. Edited by Abraham Burnstein. New York: Pardes Publishing House, 1946. 462 pp.
A collection of Jewish humor, anecdotes, parables and proverbs.

Thomas, C. K.
"Jewish Dialect and New York Dialect." *AS* 7 (No. 5) :321–326, 1932.

——————.
"More on New York Jewish Dialect." *AS* 8 (No. 3) :80–81, 1933.

Vaxer, Menashe
"Folklore of Jewish Communities."
The Jewish Landsmanschaften (In Yiddish), edited by Isaac E. Rontch and prepared by the Jewish Writers' Group of the Federal Writers' Project in New York City, 1938.

Wells, H. B.
"Notes on Yiddish." *AS* 4 (No. 1) :58–66, 1928.

Wolfe, George
"Notes on American Yiddish." *American Mercury* 29:473–479, 1933.

Yoffie, L. R.
"Yiddish Folk Stories and Songs in St. Louis." *Washington University Record* (St. Louis) 5: 20–22, 1920.

——————.
"Yiddish Proverbs, Sayings, etc. from St. Louis, Mo." *JAFL* 33:134–165, 1920.

FOLKSONG

Rubin, Ruth
Private Collection of 200 Texts of Songs, and 125 Tunes. New York City.
> *Contents:* Love songs, work songs, cradle songs, children's songs, songs of the underworld, holiday songs, war and pogrom songs. The collection also includes Palestinian, Soviet and World War II songs; as well as 25 Chassidic "Nigunim" (tunes) with and without words, and 11 "Badkhonische" (religious) songs, and wedding tunes. Half of the collection is in notebooks and half on discs.

—————.
"Yiddish Folksongs in New York City." *NYFQ* 2 (No. 1) :15–23, 1946.
> Discusses different types of folksongs still heard among the Jewish population of New York City. The author gives the text, but no tunes, to quite a few of these.

Yoffie, L. R.
"Yiddish Folk Stories and Songs in St. Louis." *Washington University Record* (St. Louis) 5: 20–22, 1910.

NORWEGIAN

FOLKLORE

Blegen, Theodore C.
Grass Roots History. Minneapolis, Minn.: University of Minnesota Press, 1948. 266 pp.
> "Being especially familiar with the Norwegian immigrants to the Middle West, Dean Blegen illustrates his thesis by numerous references to their pioneer ballads, diaries, early newspaper advertisements, letters sent by the settlers back to their native Norway and a mass of similar (and largely unpublished) data." (Leo Gurko)

Borgwardt, Elisabeth
Das skandinavische Element in amerikanischer Roman. Griefwald: Adler, 1936. 115 pp.
> The Scandinavian element in the American novel.

Bojer, John
Emigrants. New York: Century Co., 1925.
> A novel, rich in traditions, customs and beliefs.

Flaten, Nils
"Notes on American-Norwegian with a Vocabulary." *Dialect Notes* 2 (Part 2) :115–126, 1902.

Flom, George T.
"English Elements in Norse Dialects of Utica, Wisconsin." *Dialect Notes* 2 (Part 4) :257–268.

—————.
"English Loanwords in American Norwegian— as Spoken in the Koshkonong Settlement, Wisconsin." *AS* 1 (No. 10) :541–558, 1926.

—————.
"On the Phonology of English Loan Words in the Norwegian Dialects of Koshkonong in Wisconsin." In: *Studier Tilagnade Axel Kock* (pp. 178–189). Lund, Sweden, 1926.

Forbes, Kathryn
Mama's Bank Account. New York: Harcourt and Brace Co., 1943.
> The story of the Americanization of a Norwegian family.

Haugen, Einar
"Scandinavian." *Conference on non-English Speech in the United States,* (Ann Arbor, Mich.) Aug. 2–3, 1940. Washington, D. C.: Bulletin of the American Council of Learned Societies, 1942. 34:581–669.

Kimmerle, M. M.
"Norwegian-American Surnames in Transition." *AS* 17:158–165, 1942.

Mattison, M.
"Norsk Novelties." *AS* 9 (No. 2) :152, 1934.

Quarley, Carlton C.
"Pioneer Norwegian Settlements in North Dakota." *North Dakota Historical Quarterly* 5:14–37, 1935.

Rolvaag, Ella Valborg
"Norwegian Folk Narrative in America." *Norwegian-American Historical Association: Studies and Records* 12:33–59, 1941.

Rolvaag, O. E.
Giants in the Earth. New York: Harper and Bros., 1924.
> Norwegian lore is a rich mine in his novels.

—————.
Peder Victorious. New York: Harper and Bros., 1921.
> A sequel to *Giants in the Earth.*

Simley, Anne
"A Study of Norwegian Dialect in Minnesota." *AS* 5 (No. 6) :469–474, 1930.

Stefansson, V.
"English Loan-Nouns Used in the Icelandic Colony of North Dakota." *Dialect Notes* 2 (Part 5) :354–362.

White, George Le Roy
Scandinavian Names in American Fiction. Philadelphia: University of Pennsylvania Press, 1937.

U. S. Library of Congress. Division of Music. Folklore Section.
Four Norwegian Folk Tales. Read by Mrs. Gudrun Thorne-Thomsen, from her book: *East o' the Sun and West o' the Moon.* June 12, 1943. 1–16" record. AAFS–LC

FOLKSONG

Blegen, Theodore C., and Rand, Martin B.
Norwegian Emigrant Songs and Ballads. Songs Harmonized by Gerald J. Malmeir. Minneapolis: University of Minnesota Press, 1937.
> Collection contains 60 songs of old and new world origin.

Haugen, Einar
"Norwegian Emigrant Songs and Ballads." *JAFL* 51:69–75, 1938.

PENNSYLVANIA GERMAN

PENNSYLVANIA GERMAN

GERMAN FOLKLORE
A Selection
BIBLIOGRAPHY

Bellmann, Herbert
Bibliographie der deutschen Volkskunde. In: *Deutsche Volkskunde*, by Adolph Spamer, vol. 2. Berlin: Bibliographische Institut A. G., 1935. 2nd. ed.

Hoffman-Krayer, Eduard von
Volkskundliche Bibliographie, im Auftrage des Verbandes Deutscher Vereine für Volkskunde. Strassburg und Berlin: 1917–1924.

Lautenschlager, Friedrich
Bibliographische Hilfsmittel Oberrheinischer Volkstum Forschung. In: *Oberdeutsche Zeitschrift für Volkskunde*, Jahrg. 8:178–183, 1934.

Meier, John
Deutsche und Niederlandische Volkspoesie. Strassburg: K. J. Trübner, 1909.
A bibliography. "This is out of date, but still standard in many ways." (W. D. Hand).

PERIODICALS

Volkskundliche Zeitschriftenschau. Leipzig: No. 1, 1905—.

Wiener Zeitschrift für Volkskunde. Wien 1, 1917—.
Organ des Vereines für Osterreichische Volkskunde in Wien.

GENERAL STUDIES AND COLLECTIONS

Bach, Adolf
Deutsche Volkskunde, ihre Wege, Ergebnisse und Aufgaben; eine Einführung. Leipzig: S. Hirzel, 1937. xx, 530 pp., illus.
General discussion of the problems, aims of German folklore.

Bächtold-Stäubli, Hanns, and Hoffman-Krayer, Eduard von, eds.
Handwörterbuch des deutschen Aberglaubens. Berlin: W. de Gruyter & Co., 1927–1942. 10 vols., bibl., vol. 1, (pp. xv–lvvi)
"This is a monumental dictionary of superstitions. Nothing remotely approaches it in any language." (W. D. Hand).

Bechstein, Ludwig
Deutsches Sagenbuch. Leipzig: G. Wigand, 1853. xxiv, 813 pp., illus., music.
German legends.

Blumml, E. K.
Quellen und Forschungen zur deutschen Volkskunde. Bd. 1–8. Wein: Ludwig, 1908. 8 vols. in 2. Contains music.
Source studies of German folklore.

Böckel, Otto
Die deutsche Volkssage. Leipzig: Teubner, 1914. iv, 122 pp.
German tales and legends.

Bolte, Johannes
Name und Merkmale des Märchens. Helsinki: Suomalainen Tiedeakatemia, 1920. 42 pp. (FF Communications No. 36.)

————.
Zeugnisse zur Geschichte der Märchen. Helsinki: Suomalainen Tiedeakatemia, 1921. 71 pp. (FF Communications, No. 39.)

————. **and Polivka, George**
Ammerkungen zu den Kinder und Hausmärchen der Brüder Grimm. Leipzig: 1913–1932. 5 Vols.
Critical discussion of Brothers Grimm's Fairy Tales.

Brouner, F. J.
Von deutscher Sitt und Art. Volksitten und Volksbräuche in Bayern und den angrenzenden Gebieten. München: 1908. viii, 360 pp., illus.
German customs.

Eichblatt, Hermann
Deutscher Sagenschatz. Leipzig: H. Eichblatt, 1921–1925. 10 vols.
A comprehensive compendium of German legends.

Erich, Oswald Adolf
Wörterbuch der deutschen Volkskunde. Leipzig: A. Kröner, 1936. vii, 864 pp., illus. Kröners Taschenausgabe. bd. 127/128.
Lexicon of German folklore.

Germat, V.v., and Mackensen, L.
Quellen zur deutchen Volksunde. Berlin: De Gruyter, 1927–.
Source studies of German folklore.

Harmjanz, Heinrich
Die deutschen Feuersegen und ihre Varianten in Nord und Osteuropa; ein Beitrag zur vergleichenden Segensforschung. Helsinki: Suomalaisen Tiedeakatemian, 1932. 102 pp., bibl. FF (Folklore fellows) Communications No. 103.
A study of fire in religion and folklore.

————.
Volk, Mensch und Ding; erkenntniskritische Untersuchungen zur volkskundlichen Begriffsbildung. Königsberg: Ost-Europa Verlag, 1936. 182 pp.

————.**and Rohr, Erich**
Atlas der deutschen Volkskunde. Leipzig: Hirzel, 1937–1939.
Issued in portfolio. An atlas of German folklore.

Hepding, Hugo
Volkskundliche Ernte. Giessen: Von Munchowsche Universitätsdruckerei Otto Kindt, 1938. 273 pp.
Illustrations; music.

Jungbauer, Gustav
Geschichte der deutschen Volkskunde. Prag: Im Buchhandel durch die J. G. Calvesche Universitätsbuchhandlung in Prag, 1931. 193 pp.
History of German folklore.

Kläger, Emil
Legenden und Maerchen unserer Zeit. Wien: Wolf, 1917. 135 pp., plates.
Contemporary legends and tales.

Köhler, Reinhold
Aufsätze über Märchen und Volkslieder. Berlin: 1894.
Studies on folktales and folksongs.

————.
Kleinere Schriften. Weimar: Johannes Bolte, 1898–1900. 3 vols., illus.
Studies in the folktale, narrative poetry of the Middle Ages, and word lore.

Knortz, Karl
Die deutschen Volkslieder und Märchen. Zwei Vorträge. Zürich: Verlags-Magazin (J. Schabelitz), 1889. 117 pp.
German folksongs and folktales. Includes discussion and translation of "Ballads and Songs of Yorkshire."

Krappe, Alexander Haggerty
Études de mythologie et de folklore Germaniques. Paris: Leroux, 1928. viii, 189 pp., illus., bibl.
German mythology and folklore.

Kunzig, Johannes
Schwarzwald Sagen. Jena: Diederichs, 1930. x, 382 pp., illus.
Legends of the Black Forest.

Krohn, Kaarle
Die folkloristische Arbeitsmethode. Oslo: H. Aschenhoug & Co., 1926. 167 pp. Institutet før Sammenlignende Kulturførskning. Ser. B, Skrifter V.
Method of folklore study and research.

————.
Mann und Fuchs: drei vergleichende Märchenstudien. Commentationes variae in memoriam actorum CCL annorum edidit universitatis Helsingforsiensis, Nos. 3 and 4. Helsinki: 1891.

Leyen, Friedrich von der
Lesebuch der deutschen Volksmärchen. Berlin: Junker und Dünnhaupt, 1934. viii, 192 pp., bibl.
German folktales: variants printed in parallel columns, mostly on folded leaves.

————.
Lesebuch der deutschen Volkssage. Berlin: Junker und Dünnhaupt, 1933. ix, 191 pp., bibl.
Collection of German legends and epic tales.

————.
Das Reich deutscher Volksdichtung: Märchen, Sage, Legende, Zauberspruch, Rätsel und Volkslied. Berlin: Deutsche Buchgemeinschaft, 1935. 330 pp., bibl., music.
A collection of German folklore and folksong.

————.
Die schönsten Märchen der Weltliteratur, die unsere Jugend kennen sollte. Illustriert. Berlin: R. Bong, 1924. 2 vols., illus.
A selection of folktales from many countries.

Meier, John
Deutsche Volkskunde, in besondere zum Gebrauch der Volkschullehrer. Berlin: Gruyter, 1926. 344 pp., bibl.
German folklore for schools.

————.
Deutsche Volkslieder. Berlin: Jünker und Dünnhaupt, 1935–.
"It contains the best technical features of Grundtvig and Child, and pioneers the presentation of musical data on a broad and conclusive scale." (W. D. Hand).

————.
Grundriss der deutschen Volkskunde. Strassburg: Trübner, 1917. (Trübner's bibliothek. 6.)

———— (Festschrift)
Volkskundliche Gaben. Berlin and Leipzig: W. de Gruyter & Co., 1934. viii, 314 pp., illus., music, bibl.
Various articles on different aspects of German and comparative folklore.

Meyer, Elard Hugo
Deutsche Volkskunde. Strassburg: K. J. Trübner, 1898. viii, 362 pp., illus.

Müller, Erwin
Psychologie des deutschen Volkmärchens. München: J. Kösel & F. Pustet, 1928. xii, 160 pp.
Psychology of the German folktale.

Naumann, Hans
Grundzüge der deutschen Volkskunde. Leipzig: Quelle, 1922. 158 pp., illus.
Source studies of German folklore.

Neckel, Gustav
Vermischte Sagen. Leipzig: P. Reclam, jun., 1936. 294 pp.
Collection of legends.

————.
Vom Altertum zum Mittelalter. Leipzig: P. Reclam, jun., 1935. 302 pp.
A general collection of German folklore from ancient times to the Middle Ages.

Pessler, Wilhelm
Handbuch der deutschen Volkskunde. Potsdam: Akademische Verlagsgesellschaft Athenaion, 1934–1938. Published in 37 parts, 1935–1938.
Handbook of German folklore.

Riehl, W. H.
Die Volkskunde als Wissenschaft, mit einem
Verlagsbericht: "Zwölf Jahre Arbeit für die
deutsche Volkskunde." Berlin: Stubenrauch,
1935. 103 pp., illus.
Folklore as a science.

Rumpf, Max
Religiöse Volkskunde. Stuttgart: Kohlhammer,
1933. xv, 475 pp., illus.
Religious lore.

Sartori, Paul
Sitte und Brauch. Leipzig: W. Heims, 1910–
1914. 3 vols.
Custom and usage.

Seiler, Friedrich
Deutsche Sprichwörterkunde. München: Beck,
1922. x, 457 pp., bibl. (pp. 35–66).
Study of proverbs.

Singer, Samuel
Sprichwörter des Mittelalters. I. Von den
Anfangen bis ins 12. Jahrhundert. Bern: Herbert Lang and Cie. 1944, 1946, 1947. 3 vols.
viii, 198, 204, 162 pp.
In the words of Richard Jente it is the most
significant and valuable investigation of medieval
proverb lore.

Spamer, Adolf, ed.
Die deutsche Volkskunde. Leipzig: Biblio-
graphisches Institut A. G., 1935. 2 vols., illus.,
music, plates.
A series of articles on German and comparative
folklore.

Spiess, Karl
Das deutsche Volksmärchen. Leipzig: Tuebner,
1917. iv, 124 pp.
The German folktale.

Thimme, Adolf
Das Märchen. Leipzig: Heims, 1909. vi, 201
pp., bibl.
A study of the folk tale.

Wander, Karl Friedrich, ed.
Deutsches Sprichwörter-Lexicon. Ein Haus-
schatz für das deutsche Volk. Leipzig: F. A.
Brockhaus, 1867–1880. 5 vols.
Proverbs.

Weinhold, Karl (Festschrift)
Beitrage zur Volkskunde ... dargebracht im
Namen der schlesischen Gesellschaft für Volks-
kunde. Breslau: W. Koebner, 1896. v, 245 pp.
A series of scholarly studies on German and
comparative aspects of folklore.

Wesselski, Albert
Märchen des Mittelalters. Berlin: H. Stubenrauch, 1925. xxiii, 271 pp.

Winter, Leo
Die deutsche Schatzsage. Wattenscheid: Busch,
1925. 95 pp., bibl.
Lovers' legends.

Wossildo, Richard (Festschrift)
Volkskundliche Beiträge. Neumünster: Karl
Wachholtz verlag, 1939. viii, 188 pp., illus.,
music, maps.
A series of papers on various aspects of folklore.

Wuttke, Adolf
Die deutsche Volksaberglaube der Gegenwart.
3. bearbeitung von Elard Hugo Meyer. Berlin:
Wiegandt & Greiben, 1900. xvi, 535 pp.
German superstitions.

Zaunert, Paul
Deutsche Märchen seit Grimm. Jena: Diede-
richs, 1919–1923. 2 vols.
The German folktale since Grimm.

—————.
Deutsche Natursagen. Jena: Diederichs, 1921.
Vol. 1.
Nature legends.

PENNSYLVANIA GERMAN
FOLKLORE
BIBLIOGRAPHY

Riccardi, Saro John
Pennsylvania Dutch Folk Art and Architecture.
A Selective Annotated Bibliography. New
York: Public Library, 1942., 15 pp.

PERIODICALS

American-German Review; A Monthly Magazine, New York. Vol. 1, nos. 1–3, 1898–1899.

American-German Review. (Carl Schurz Memorial Foundation, Inc.). Philadelphia. Vol. 1,
Sept. 1934–.

German American Annals. (German American
Historical Society; National German American
Alliance; Union of Old German Students in
America; Deutscher Pionier-Verein) New
York, Philadelphia, Vol. 1–21, 1897. 1919.
Vol. 1–4, as *Americana Germanica.* vols. 5–21
also as n.s. vol. 1–17.

Journal of English and Germanic Philology.
Urbana, Ill. V. 1, 1897. 1–4, 1897–1902 as
Journal of Germanic Philology.

*Pennsylvania-German Society. Proceedings and
Addresses.* Lancaster. V. 1, 1891– .

*Pennsylvania-German Folklore Society, Proceed-
ings.* Allentown, Pa. No. 1, 1940– . *Publications,* Vol. 1, 1936– .

*Publications of the Pennsylvania Folklore So-
ciety.* Vol. 1, 1928– . H. H. Richard, Muhlenberg College, Chairman.

GENERAL STUDIES AND COLLECTIONS

Bachman, C. G.
The Old Order Amish of Lancaster County.
In: *Proceedings and Addresses of the Penn.
Germ. Society,* No. 49, 1941.

Barba, P. A.
Lewis Miller, Pennsylvania German Folk Artist. Publications, Pennsylvania German Folklore Society, Vol. 4 (No. 3). Allentown, Pa.: Penn. German Folklore Society, 1939.

Connor, W. L.
The Folk Culture of the Pennsylvania Germans: Its Value in Modern Education. Publications, Pennsylvania German Folklore Society, Vol. 5 (No. 4). Allentown, Pa.: Penn. German Folklore Society, 1940.

Die Wahre Separation, oder die Wiedergeburt, dargestelt in geistreichen und erbaulichen Versammlung's Reden und Betrachtungen, besonders auf das gegenwartege Zeitalter anwendbar. Gehalten an die Gemeinde in Jahre 1830. Zoar, Ohio: 1856. 2574 pp., 3 vol. quarto.
Spiritual and devotional lectures presented in the Congregation at the Zoar Community. Contains a great many curious theories of life, present and future.

Faust, Albert Bernhardt
The German Element in the United States, with special reference to its political, moral, social, and educational influences. Boston: Houghton Mifflin Company, 1909. 2 vols., illus., bibl. (v. 2, pp. 477–652).

Federal Writers' Project
Pennsylvania, a Guide to the Keystone State. (American Guide Series). Writers' Project of the WPA in Pennsylvania. New York: Oxford University Press, 1940.

Fries, Adelaide L., ed.
Records of the Moravians in North Carolina. Raleigh, N. C.: Historical Commission 1922, Vol. 1; 1925, Vol. 2; 1926, Vol. 3; 1930, Vol. 4.

Gibbons, Phebe H.
"Pennsylvania Dutch," and Other Essays. Philadelphia: J. B. Lippincott and Co., 1872. vii, 207 pp.
Contents: "Pennsylvania Dutch"—An Amish Meeting—Swiss Exiles—The Dunker love-feast —A friend—Cousin Jemima.

Graeff, Arthur D.
The Pennsylvania Germans in Ontario, Canada. In: *Pennsylvania German Folklore Society.* Publ. 2:3–80, 1946.

Hand, Wayland D.
"German-American Folklore." *JAFL* 60:360–372, 1947.

Hark, Ann
The Story of the Pennsylvania Dutch. Lithographs by C. H. DeWitt. New York: Harper and Bros., 1943., unpaged.

Hiss, Philip Hauson
Netherlands America. New York: Duell, Sloan and Pearce, 1943.
A study of the Dutch territories in the West.

Hoffman, W. J.
"Folklore of the Pennsylvania Germans." *JAFL* 1:123–135, 1888; 2:23–35, 191–202, 1889.

Jordan, Mildred
Apple in the Attic: A Pennsylvania legend. New York: Alfred A. Knopf, 1942.
"It has definitely the charm of legend, founded on the real and earthy environment of a Pennsylvania Dutch farm, rich in the scent of things growing, harvested, and marketed." (Beatrice Sherman.)

The Shoo-Fly Pie. New York: Alfred A. Knopf, 1944. 118 pp., illus.
A fictionalized account of the homely experiences of a Pennsylvania-Dutch family and children.

Kauffman, Henry
Pennsylvania Dutch. American Folk Art. New York: American Studio Books, 1946. 136 pp.
". . . this is a serious, worthy and helpful book."

Kemp, A. F.
The Pennsylvania German Versammlinge. Publications, Pennsylvania German Folklore Society, Vol. 9. Allentown, Pa.: Penn. German Folklore Society, 1944.
A study of various Pennsylvania German societies.

Keyser, Naaman H., and Kain, C. Henry, etc.
History of Old Germantown. Philadelphia: Horace F. McCahn, 1907.

Knortz, Karl
Amerikanische Lebensbilder — Skizzen und Tagebuchblätter. Zurich: Verlags-Magazin (J. Schabelitz), 1884. 208 pp.
German American customs and lore.

Deutsche in America. Leipzig: C. L. Hirschfeld, 1906. 48 pp.
The Germans in the U. S.

Nachklänge germanischen Glaubens und Brauchs in America; ein Beitrag zur Volkskunde. Halle: S. H. Peter, 1903, 122 pp.
German lore in America.

Krick, Richard
Examples of Pennsylvania Dutch (German) Folk Art. Philadelphia: Carl Schurz Memorial Foundation, 1943. 14 pp.

Kriebel, Howard Wiegner
The Schwenkfelders in Pennsylvania. Lancaster, Pa.: The Society, 1904.

Kuhns, Oscar
The German and Swiss Settlements of Colonial Pennsylvania. Harrisburg, Pennsylvania: The Aurand Press, 1946. 268 pp.

Lichten, Frances
Folk Art of Rural Pennsylvania. New York: Charles Scribner's Sons, 1946. xiv, 276 pp., with thirteen full page frontispieces, three tail pieces, three hundred and eight illustrations in black and white, and thirty-four illustrations in color.
"The book is excellent not only as a record of folk arts and crafts, but also as an illustrated history of the mores of the Pennsylvania Germans. The meticulous presentation of facts and the lavish use of examples make it a distinguished contribution to regional lore." (F. P. Walkup.)

Mann, H. M., Johnson, E. E. S., and others
Pennsylvania German Historical and Art Collections in Various Museums. Publications, Pennsylvania German Folklore Society, Vol. 7. Allentown, Pa.: Penn. German Folklore Society, 1943.
Museums and societies covered are: The Bucks County, The Schwenkfelder, The Pennsylvania State, The Berks County, The Hershey.

Metz, Christian
Historische Beschreibung der wahren Inspiration's Gemeinschaft, wie sie bestanden und sich fortgepflanzt, hat, und was von den wichtigen Ereignissen noch ausgefunden werden kann, besonders wie sie in den Jahren 1817 und 1818 und so fort wieder durch den Geist Gottes in neuen Werkzeugen aufgewecht worden, und was seit der Zeit in und mit dieser Gemeinde und deren herzugekommenen Gliedern wichtiges vorgefallen. Amana, Iowa: 1818.
Historical description of the True Inspiration's Community.

Owens, F. G.
"Folk-Lore From Buffalo Valley, Central Pennsylvania." *JAFL* 4:115–128, 1891.

Pastorius, Francis Daniel
Description of Pennsylvania, 1700. (Translated from the original German by Lewis H. Weiss.) In: *Old South Leaflets* (general ser.). Vol. 4, No. 95, Boston, 1898.

"Pennsylvania Germans" (Moravians). *JAFL* 8:308–312, 1895.

Reichard, H. H.
Pennsylvania-German Verse: An Anthology. In: Proceedings and Addresses of the *Pennsylvania-German Society,* No. 48. Lancaster: 1940.

Robacker, Earl F.
Pennsylvania Dutch Stuff: A guide to country antiques. Philadelphia: University of Pennsylvania Press, 1944. 163 pp., 15 illus.

————.
Pennsylvania German Literature. Changing trends from 1683 to 1942. Philadelphia: University of Pa. Press, 1943.
A survey covering 3 types of writing—High German, English and dialect.

Rosenberger, Jesse Leonard
The Pennsylvania Germans. Chicago: University of Chicago Press, 1923.

Shenk, John B., and Rice, Charles S.
Meet the Amish. New Brunswick, N. J.: Rutgers University Press, 1947. Illus.
A pictorial visit with the Pennsylvania Dutch. Contains 200 photographs, good text, and a fine glossary of expressions and colloquialisms.

Storr, F.
"Pennsylvania German Lore." *JAFL* 4:321–326, 1891.

Stoudt, John Baer
The Folk-lore of the Pennsylvania Germans. A paper read before the Pennsylvania German Society at the annual meeting, York, Pa., October 14, 1910. Philadelphia: Campbell, 1916. 155 pp., illus.

————.
"The Folklore of the Pennsylvania Germans." *Pennsylvania German Society Proceedings* 23, supplement, 1915. Reprinted 1916.

Stoudt, John Joseph
Consider the Lilies How They Grow; an interpretation of the symbolism of Pennsylvania German art. Allentown, Pa.: Schlechter's, 1937. 333 pp., illus. (Pennsylvania German Folklore Society, V. 2.)

The Pennsylvania German Folklore Society. Vol. I (Miscellaneous papers). Allentown, Pa.: Schlechter's, 1936.
Annual Memorial Volume 1933.

The Pennsylvania German Folklore Society. Volume 7. Fogelsville, Pennsylvania: Pennsylvania German Folklore Society, 1944. 170 pp.

Wallower, Lucille
Chooky. Philadelphia: David McKay Co., 1943.
A story for young readers, of Pennsylvania Dutch children and a baby chick.

Weygandt, Cornelius
Philadelphia Folks. New York: D. Appleton-Century Co., 1938. xx, 357 pp., illus.

————.
The Dutch Country. New York: D. Appleton-Century Co., 1939. xx, 352 pp.
Folks and treasures in the Red Hills of Pennsylvania.

————.
The Red Hills; a Record of Good Days, Outdoors and In, with Things Pennsylvania Dutch. Philadelphia: University of Pennsylvania Press, 1929.

Wood, Ralph, ed.
The Pennsylvania Germans. Princeton, N. J.: Princeton University Press, 1942. viii, 299 pp., illus., bibl.
A series of papers by various authors on the life and culture of the Pennsylvania Germans.

Ziegler, Samuel H.
"Pennsylvania German Folklore Society." *JAFL* 56:181–183, 1943.

FOLKTALES—LEGENDS

Aurand, Ammon Monroe, Jr.
Aurand's Collection of Pennsylvania German Stories and Poems. Beaver Springs, Pa.: A. M. Aurand and Son, 1916. 128 pp.

Brendle, Thomas Royce, ed. and tr.
Pennsylvania German Folktales, legends, once-upon-a-time stories, maxims, and sayings spoken in the dialect popularly known as Pennsylvania Dutch. Norristown, Pa.: Pennsylvania German Society, 1944. 238 pp. In: *Pennsylvania German Society.* Proceedings and addresses. Oct. 17, 1941. Vol. L.

Jordan, Mildred
Apple in the Attic: A Pennsylvania Legend. New York: Alfred A. Knopf, 1942.
"It has definitely the charm of legend founded on the real and earthy environment of a Pennsylvania Dutch farm, rich in the scent of things growing, harvested, and marketed." (Beatrice Sherman.)

Laux, James B.
Brother Albrecht's Secret Chamber. A Legend of the Ancient Moravian Sun Inn of Bethlehem, Pennsylvania. Lititz, Penna.: Express Printing Co., 1914. 62 pp.

"The Pennsylvania-German Legend." *AS* 2(No. 11):459–460, 1927.

CUSTOMS—TRADITIONS

Aurand, Ammon Monroe, Jr.
America's Greatest Indoor Sport: Two-in-a-Bed; or, *The Super-Specialist's Handbook on Bundling with the Pennsylvania Dutch.* Including "Ben" Franklin's advice on marriage. Harrisburg, Pa.: The Aurand Press, 1930. 45 pp.

————.
Little Known Facts About Bundling in the New World. Harrisburg, Pa.: The Aurand Press, 1938. 31 pp., illus.

————.
Little Known Facts About the Amish and the Mennonites; a study of the social customs and habits of Pennsylvania's "plain people." Harrisburg, Pa.: The Aurand Press, 1938. 30 pp.

————.
Little Known Facts About the Ritual of the Jews and the Esoteric Folklore of the Pennsylvania-Germans. An impartial examination into everyday beliefs and practices of the Pennsylvania-Germans, diligently compared with an English interpretation of the Jewish ritual, or, the religious customs and ceremonies of the Jews used in their public worship and private devotions, published in London in 1753; now voluminously annotated with illuminating references. Harrisburg, Pa.: The Aurand Press, 108 pp.

Beckel, C. E.
Early Marriage Customs of the Moravian Congregation in Bethlehem, Pennsylvania. Publication of the Pennsylvania German Folklore Society, No. 3 (2). Allentown, Pa.: Penn. German Folklore Society, 1938.

Estill, Julia
"Customs Among the German Descendants of Gillespie County." *TFSP* 2:67–74, 1923.

Fogel, E. M.
Of Months and Days. Publications, Pennsylvania German Folklore Society, Vol. 5 (No. 3). Allentown, Pa.: Penn. German Folklore Society, 1940.

————.
Twelvetide. Publications, Pennsylvania German Folklore Society, Vol. 6 (No. 5). Allentown, Pa.: Penn. German Folklore Society, 1941.
Christmas lore and customs.

Iobst, C. F.
En Quart Millich Un En Halb Beint Raahm, a Pennsylvania German Comedy. Publications, Pennsylvania German Folklore Society, Vol. 4 (No. 1). Allentown, Pa.: Penn. German Folklore Society, 1939.

Knauss, James Owen
Social Conditions Among the Pennsylvania Germans in the Eighteenth Century, as Revealed in German Newspapers Published in America. Lancaster, Pa.: New Era Publishing Co., 1922. x, 217 pp., bibl.

Landis, H. K.
Conestoga Wagons and Their Ornamental Ironing. Publications of the Pennsylvania German Folklore Society, Vol. 3 (No. 4). Allentown, Pa.: Penn. German Folklore Society, 1938.

Martin, Helen Reimensnyder
Barnabetta. New York: Century Co., 1914.
A novel of lore and manners of the Penna.-Dutch.

Mitchell, Edwin Valentine
It's an Old Pennsylvania Custom. New York: Vanguard Press, 1946. 262 pp., illus.
In some fifteen chapters the author covers the ground from cave-dwelling to Philadelphia taverns, taking in, on the way,—pies, courtship, customs, the wearing of beards, musical manners . . . historical, domestic, culinary lores; Pennsylvania speech and sections on witchcraft, superstitions and magical practices.

Myers, R. E.
The Moravian Christmas Putz. Publications, Pennsylvania German Folklore Society, Vol. 6 (No. 3). Allentown, Pa.: Penn. German Folklore Society, 1941.
Christmas customs.

Nitzsche, G. E.
The Christmas Putz of the Pennsylvania Germans. Publications, Pennsylvania German Folklore Society, Vol. 6 (No. 1). Allentown, Pa.: Penn. German Folklore Society, 1941.
Customs of Christmas tree decoration.

Nock, Albert Joy
"Utopia in Pennsylvania; The Amish." *Atlantic Monthly* 167:478–484, 1941.
Amish customs, folk literature.

Reichard, H. H., ed.
The Christmas Poetry of the "Pennsylvania Dutch." Publications, Pennsylvania German Folklore Society, Vol. 6 (No. 4). Allentown, Pa.: Penn. German Folklore Society, 1941.

Rominger, C. H.
Early Christmases in Bethlehem, Pennsylvania. Publications, Pennsylvania German Folklore Society, Vol. 6 (No. 2). Allentown, Pa.: Penn. German Folklore Society, 1941.

Sampson, Mrs. S., and Hayes, F. C.
"Quaker Wedding Ceremony." *SFQ* 7:211–212,
1943.

Schantz, F. J.
Domestic Life and Characteristics of the Penn-
sylvania-German Pioneer. In: *Proceedings and
Addresses of the Pennsylvania-German Society*.
Vol. 7, Pt. 6. Lancaster, Pa., 1900.

Schwamp, J. E.
An Account of the Manners of the German
Inhabitants in Pennsylvania. In: *Proceedings
and Addresses of the Pennsylvania German
Society*, Vol. 7, Pt. 21, 1910. Lancaster, Pa.

**Smith, Edward C., and Thompson, Virginia
Van Horn**
Traditionally Pennsylvania Dutch. New York:
Hastings House, 1946. 81 pp.
Charming and faithful account of the traditions
and customs of the early Pennsylvania settlers.
A delightful collection of full page original
drawings and many vignettes.

Stenifeldt, Berenice
The Amish of Lancaster County. Lancaster,
Pa.: Conestoga Publ. Co., 1943. 35 pp.
A brief account of some of the life and customs
of the Amish.

BELIEFS—SUPERSTITIONS—
WITCHCRAFT

Aurand, A. Monroe, Jr.
*Popular Home Remedies and Superstitions of
the Pennsylvania Germans*. Harrisburg, Pa.:
Aurand Press, 1941. 32 pp.

————.

The Realness of Witchcraft in America. With
special references to the Pennsylvania Germans
and the conflict of Science vs. old time beliefs
and customs. Harrisburg, Pa.: Aurand Press,
1942. 32 pp.

Fogel, Edwin Miller
*Beliefs and Superstitions of the Pennsylvania
Germans*. Philadelphia: American Germania
Press, 1915. 387 pp.

Hark, Ann
*Hex Marks the Spot, in the Pennsylvania
Dutch Country*. Philadelphia: J. B. Lippincott
Co., 1938.

Heizmann, Louis J.
"Are Barn Signs Hex Marks." *Historical Review of Berks County* (Reading, Pa.) October,
1946, pp. 11–14, illus.

Lick, David E., and Brendle, Thomas R.
"Plant Names and Plant Lore Among the
Pennsylvania Germans." *Pennsylvania German
Soc. Proc.* 33(Part 3):1–300, 1922. Illus.,
bibl.

Neifert, William N.
"Witchcraft." *Pennsylvania-German* (East
Greenville, Pa.) 9:114–121, 1908.

Rupp, W. J.
Bird Name and Bird Lore. In: *Proceedings and
Addresses of the Penn. Germ. Society*. No. 52,
1946.

Stark, Johann Friedrich
*Taegliches Hand-Buch in Guten und Boesen
Tagen*—welchem noch ein Taegliches Gebet—
Buechlein fuer SCHWANGERE, GEBAER-
ENDE UND UNFRUCHBARES beygefueget
ist Aufsneue durchgesehen von J. J. Stark.
Carlisle, Pa.: Moser and Peters, 1825. Illus.
Daily prayerbook for good and evil days; also
prayers for pregnant, and sterile women.

Wood, Ralph C.
"Life, Death, and Poetry As Seen by the Pennsylvania Dutch." *Monatshefte für deutschen
Unterricht* (University of Wisconsin, Madison)
37:453–465, (Nov.) 1945.

Williamson, Thomas Ross
D is For Dutch; a Last Regional Novel. New
York: Harcourt, Brace and Co., 1934.
Describes the Pennsylvania Dutch farmers, their
beliefs and superstitions.

FOLK MEDICINE

Aurand, Ammon Monroe, Jr.
*Popular Home Remedies and Superstitions of
the Pennsylvania Germans*. Harrisburg, Pa.:
Aurand Press, 1941. 32 pp.

————.

"*The Pow-Wow Book*; a treatise on the art of
healing by prayer" and "laying on of hands,"
etc., practiced by the Pennsylvania-Germans
and others; testimonials; remarkable recover-
ies; popular superstitions; etc., including an
account of the famous "witch" murder trial,
at York, Pa. Containing also the complete collection of remedies and cures in John George
Hohman's "Pow-wows, or Long Lost Friend";
in popular use since 1820. Harrisburg, Pa.:
The Aurand Press, 1929. x, 85 pp.; xi, 64 pp.

Brendle, Thomas R., and Unger, Claude W.
*Folk Medicine of the Pennsylvania Germans,
the Non-Cult Cures*. Proceedings and Addresses
of the Pennsylvania German Society No. 45.
Morristown, 1935.

Brown, C. F.
"Long-Hidden Friend." *JAFL* 17:89–152, 1904.
A charm-book and the good it can bring.

Doering, Frederick J.
"Pennsylvania German Folk Medicine in
Waterloo County, Ontario." *JAFL* 49:181–194,
1936.

————.

"Note on the dyeing of halb Leinich among
the Pennsylvania Dutch of Ontario." *JAFL*
52:124–125, 1939.

White, E. G.
"Folk-Medicine Among Pennsylvania Germans." *JAFL* 10:78–79, 1897.

RIDDLES

Stoudt, John Baer
"Pennsylvania-German Riddles and Nursery Rhymes." *JAFL* 19:113, 1906.

SPEECH

Allen, W. H.
"Pennsylvania-Dutch Word List." *Dialect Notes* 4 (Part 2):157–158, 1914.

Aurand, Ammon Monroe, Jr., coll. and ed.
Pennsylvania-German Dialect Stories and Poems. Harrisburg, Pa.: The Aurand Press, 1939. 24 pp.

————.
Quaint Idioms and Expressions of the Pennsylvania Germans. A collection of curious phrases and terms employed by groups of Americans numbering into the millions, that truly flavor their English. Harrisburg, Pa.: Aurand Press, 1939. 32 pp.

Bickel, Paul J.
"Note on Pennsylvania German." *AS* 5(No. 4):283–284, 1930.

Birmelin, John
Gezwitscher, a Book of Pennsylvania German Verse. Pennsylvania German Folklore Society, Publication No. 3 (1). Allentown, Pa.: Penn. German Folklore Society, 1938.

Buffington, Albert F.
English Loan Words in Pennsylvania German. In: *Studies in Honor of John Albrecht Walz* (pp. 66–85). Lancaster, Pa.: 1941.

————.
"Pennsylvania German." *AS* 14:276–287, 1939.

Follin, Maynard D.
"Pennsylvania Dutch." *AS* 4(No. 6):455–460, 1929.

Frey, John William
The German Dialect of Eastern York County, Pennsylvania. Urbana, Ill.: University of Illinois, 1941.

Haldemann, S. S.
Pennsylvania-Dutch: A dialect of South German with an infusion of English. Philadelphia: Reformed Church Publication Board, 1872. viii, 69 pp.

Harbaugh, Henry
Harbaugh's Harfe. Gedichte in Pennsylvanisch-deutscher Mundart. Philadelphia: Reformed Church Publication Board, 1902. 120 pp.
Poems in Pennsylvania-German dialect.

Hark, Rev. J. M.
Ein Hondfull Färsh; experiments in Pennsylvania-German verse with an Introduction on the Capability of the Pennsylvania-German for Poetic Expression. *Pennsylvania-German Society,* Proceedings and Addresses, Vol. 10, 1900. 31 pp. Lancaster.

Heydrick, B. A.
"Pennsylvania Word-List." *Dialect Notes* 4 (Part 5):337–339, 1916.
Chiefly from Adams, York, Lancaster, Lebanon and Schuylkill Counties.

Horne, A. R.
Pennsylvania-German Manual, for pronouncing, speaking and writing English. Kutztown, Pa.: Urick and Gehring, 1875. 171 pp., illus.

Kloss, Heinz
"Die Pennsylvaniadeutsche Literatur." *Akademie Zur Wissenschaftlichen Forschung Zur Pflege des Deutschtums,* Mitteilungen (Munich). Heft 4:230–272, 1931.

Kurath, Hans
Pennsylvania German. In: *Conference in Non-English Speech in the U. S.* Ann Arbor, Michigan, Aug. 2–3, 1940. Bulletin of the American Council of Learned Societies (Washington, D. C.), 1942. No. 34, pp. 581–669.

Lacher, J. H. A.
"The Language of the Pennsylvania German Gypsies." *AS* 1(No. 11):584–588, 1926.

Lambert, Marcus B.
A Dictionary of the Non-English Words of the Pennsylvania-German Dialect. Philadelphia: Wm. J. Campbell, 1924. 224 pp.

Learned, Marion Dexter
"The Pennsylvania-German Dialect." *American Journal of Philology* 9:1888; 10:1889.

Lins, James C.
Common Sense Pennsylvania German Dictionary.... Containing all the Pennsylvania-German words in common use. Reading, Pa.: J. C. Lins, 1895. 170 pp.

Logeman, H.
"Low-Dutch Elements in English." *Neophilologus* 16:31–46, 103–116, 1930.

Miller, Daniel, ed.
Pennsylvania-German. A collection of Pennsylvania-German productions in poetry and prose. Reading, Pa.: D. Miller, 1903–1911, 2 vols., illus.
Emphasizes speech.

Page, Eugene R.
"English in the Pennsylvania German Area." *AS* 12(No. 3):203–206, 1937.

Pennypacker, Samuel W.
"The Early Literature of the Pennsylvania Germans." *Proceedings of the Pennsylvania German Society.* Vol. 2, 1893; reprinted 1907.

Prince, J. Dyneley
"The Jersey Dutch Dialect." *Dialect Notes* 3 (Part 6):459–484, 1910.

Rauch, E.
Pennsylvania-Dutch Handbook. Mauch Chunk, Pa.: E. H. Rauch, 1879. viii, 238 pp.

Reed, Carroll
"Gender of English Loan Words in Pennsylvania German." *AS* 17:25–29, 1942.

Reichard, Harry Hess, ed.
Pennsylvania German Verse; an Anthology of Representative Selections in the German Dialect popularly known as Pennsylvania Dutch, with an Introduction. Norristown, Pa.: Pennsylvania German Society, 1940. xxxii, 299 pp.

————.
The Christmas Poetry of the "Pennsylvania Dutch." Publications, Pennsylvania German Folklore Society, Vol. 6 (No. 4). Allentown, Pa.: Penn. German Folklore Society, 1941.

Robacker, Earl Francis
Pennsylvania German Literature; Changing Trends from 1683 to 1942. Philadelphia: University of Pennsylvania Press, 1943. x, 217 pp., bibl. (pp. 189–202).

Savage, Howard J.
"Pennsylvania-German English." *AS* 12(No. 4):323–324, 1937.

Sebeok, Thomas A.
"German Travellers and Language in America." *AS* 18:279–282, 1943.

Seifert, Lester W. J.
Lexical Differences Between Four Pennsylvania German Regions. *Pennsylvania-German Folklore Society Publications,* 2:155–169, 1946.

Shoemaker, Alfred Lewis
Studies on the Pennsylvania German Dialect of the Amish Community in Arthur, Illinois. Urbana, Ill.: University of Illinois, 1940. 8 pp. (Abstract).

Shoemaker, Henry W.
"The Language of the Pennsylvania German Gypsies." *AS* 1:584–587, (Aug.) 1926.

————.
The Tree Language of the Pennsylvania German Gypsies. An address at the Clio Club, Williamsport, Pa., Dec. 2, 1925. Reading, Pa.: Reading Eagle Press, 1925. 16 pp.

Smyth, A. H.
"Teutonic Folk Names in America." *JAFL* 3:14–15, 1890.

Springer, Otto
"Study of the Pennsylvania German Dialect." *Journal of English and Germanic Philology* 42:1–39, 1943.
Excellent bibliography.

Stone, Ruth M.
"German Influence Upon English." *AS* 8 (No. 2):77, 1933.

Struble, George G.
"The English of the Pennsylvania Germans." *AS* 10 (No. 3):163–172, 1935.

Troxell, William S., ("Pumpernickle Bill")
Aus Pennsylfawnia; An Anthology of Translations into the Pennsylvania German Dialect. Philadelphia: University of Pennsylvania Press, 1938. xiii, 47 pp.

Werner, W. L.
"English Words in the Pennsylvania-German Dialect." *AS* 6 (No. 2):123–124, 1930.

Wollenweber, L. A.
Gemälde Aus Dem Pennsylvanischen Volks-leben; Schilderungen und Aufsätze in poetischer und prosaischer Form, in Mundart der Deutsch-Pennsylvanier. Cyklus 1. Philadelphia und Leipzig, 1869. 143 pp.
Description of life and customs among the Pennsylvania German told in their dialect.

FOLKSONG

BIBLIOGRAPHY

Ray, Alber G., and David, Hans T.
A Catalogue of Music by American Moravians (1742–1842). Bethlehem, Pa.: Moravian Seminary and College for Women, 1938.

PERIODICALS

Pennsylvania German Society Proceedings. Pennsylvania German Society. Allentown, Pa.: Schlechter's, 1891–1930.

Publications of the Pennsylvania Folklore Society. Muhlenberg College, H. H. Reichard, Chairman.

GENERAL STUDIES AND COLLECTIONS

Ausbund, das ist: Etliche schöne Christliche lieder, Wie sie in dem Gefangniss zu Bassau in dem schloss von den Schweizer Brudern und von andern rechtglaubigen Christen hin und her gedichtet worden. Allen und jeden Christen, Welchen Religion sie seyen, unpartheyisch fast Nützlich Nebst einem Anhang von 6 Liedern. Lancaster: Gedrückt bey Johann Bär, 1834. 6th edition.
There were many editions in Europe of this Amish tune book from the 16th Century on.

"Dancing for Flax by Pennsylvania Germans." *JAFL* 1:134, 1888.

Drummond, Robert R.
Early German Music in Philadelphia. New York: D. Appleton & Co., 1910.

Etter, Russell C.
"Extemporaneous Hymn-making among the Pennsylvania Dutch." *JAFL* 44:302–305, 1931.

Fisher, A. L.
Kurzweil un Zeitfertreib odder; Pennsylfaanish deutsche Folks-Lieder. Penn'a: Fischer Brüder, 1882. 187 pp.

Jackson, George Pullen
"The American Amish Sing Medieval Folk Tunes Today." *SFQ* 10:151–158. 1946.

————.
"The Strange Music of the Old Order Amish."
MQ 31:275–288, 1945.
    The author traces the comparison between the
    Amish tunes and the Old German folk melodies,
    and also shows the number of Amish songs re-
    lated to American folk melodies.

Pennsylvania Folk Festival
Pennsylvania Folk Songs and Ballads for
School, Camp and Playground. Foreword by
George Korson. Lewisburg, Pa.: Penn. Folk
Festival at Bucknell University, 1937. 131 pp.
    Arranged for voice and piano.

"Pennsylvania German Cradle Songs."
JAFL 19:119–120, 1906.

Sammlung Auerlesener Geistlicher Lieder, zum
gemeinschftlichen Gesang und eigenen Gebrauch in Christlichen Familien. Zoar, Ohio:
1867. 169 pp.
    Collection of Selected Sacred Hymns used in the
    Zoar Community.

Stoudt, John Baer
Folk-Lore of Pennsylvania Germans. Philadelphia: Campbell, 1916. 155 pp., illus.
    Contains two chapters on ballads.

Umble, John
"The Old Order Amish, their Hymns and
Hymn Tunes." *JAFL* 52:82–95, 1939.

Wayland, John W.
"Joseph Funk, Father of Song in Northern
Virginia." *Pennsylvania German* 22 (No. 10),
(Oct.) 1911.

Yoder, Joseph W.
Amische Lieder. Huntingdon, Pa.: Yoder Publishing Company, 1942. 1944 pp.
    Songs of the Old Order Amisch.

CHILDREN'S GAMES AND RHYMES

Brewster, Paul G.
"Traces of Ancient German Law in a German
Game-Song." *SFQ* 2 (No. 3), 1938.

Stoudt, John Baer
"Pennsylvania German Riddles and Nursery
Rhymes." *JAFL* 19:113, 1906.

DANCES

" 'Dancing' for Flax by Pennsylvania Germans."
JAFL 1:134, 1888.

Panabaker, D. N.
"Pastimes Among the Pennsylvania Dutch in
Waterloo." In: *Annual Report of the Waterloo
Historical Society* 19:246– , 1931.

RECORDS

Collections

The East and Middle Atlantic States.
Pennsylvania Dutch Songs. New York City: In
the Archive of Columbia University Library
Collection.

POLISH

FOLKLORE

De Angeli, Marguerite
Up the Hill. New York: Doubleday, Doran and Co., 1943. 88 pp.
A sympathetic, warm-hearted little story for young readers, of a Polish-American family in Pennsylvania.

Lane, Ralph
"Poland Is Not Yet Lost." *AS* 15:208–210, 1940.
Idiomatic expressions and colloquialisms.

Mencken, H. L.
The Polish Language in America. In: *The American Language,* by H. L. M., pp. 672–675. New York: Alfred A. Knopf, 1937. 4th ed., rev. and enl.

U. S. Library of Congress. Division of Music. Folklore Section.
Speech, Traditions, Legends and Folksongs of Polish Groups in Wisconsin. Collected by Prof. Edmund Zawacki and Miss Harriet Pawlowska of the Department of Slavic Languages, University of Wisconsin. 59 records.
AAFS–LC

"Wayne University Project to Record Polish Culture." *Michigan History Magazine* (Michigan Historical Commission, Lansing) 26: (No. 3) 407–408, 1942.

Wright, Betty Jane
"The Orange County Onion Harvest Festivals." *NYFQ* 2 (No. 3):197–204, 1946.
"Good citizens, good neighbors, and good farmers, our Polish friends have shown by their Festivals that they are also proud of their heritage and their folklore and of the chance to bring it to us in all its color and beauty."

FOLKSONG

Barry, Phillips
"Polish Ballad: Trzy Siostry. (The Three Sisters)." *FSSNE* 10:2–5, 1935.

PORTUGUESE

FOLKLORE

Digges, Jeremiah
In Great Waters, The Story of the Portuguese Fishermen. New York: The Macmillan Company, 1941. xix, 282 pp.
The story, including customs, lore and traditions of these fishermen living on the shores of Newfoundland and New England.

Lang, Henry R.
"The Portuguese Element in New England." *JAFL* 5 (No. 16):9–18, 1892.
Includes references to music—vocal and dance.

Parsons, Elsie Clews
Folk-Lore From the Cape Verde Islands. Vol. 15, Parts I and II of the Memoirs of the American Folklore Society. Cambridge, Mass.: American Folklore Society, 1923. 373 pp., 267 pp., bibl., tunes.
Part I consists of 133 Folktales in English. Part II consists of these tales in Portuguese (some with tunes), 183 proverbs and sayings (in Portuguese and English), and 291 riddles.

FOLKSONG

Hare, Maud Cuney
"Portuguese Folk Songs from Provincetown." *MQ* 14, (No. 1):35–53, 1928.
Texts and tunes of 14 melodies.

Lang, Henry R.
"The Portuguese Element in New England." *JAFL* 5 (No. 16): 9–18, 1892.
Folk song texts given, dancing also discussed.

RUSSIAN

FOLKLORE

C., G. D.
"Russian Words in Kansas." *Dialect Notes* 4 (Part 2):161–162, 1914.

Clark, Sydney Aylmer
Gold Tapestries of California. New York: R. M. McBride and Co., 1937. 315 pp.
Russian-California social life and customs.

Revyuk, Emil
The Ukranian Language in America. In: *The American Language,* by H. L. Mencken, pp. 664–667. New York: Alfred A. Knopf, 1937. 4th ed. rev. and enl.

Trager, George L.
"Slavic-Speaking Groups." *Conference on non-English Speech in the United States,* (Ann Arbor, Mich.) Aug. 2–3, 1940. Washington, D. C.: Bulletin of the American Council of Learned Societies, 1942. 34:581–669.

Wells, H. B.
"The Russian Language in the United States." *American Mercury* 25:448–451, 1932.

SPANISH-AMERICAN

See: The Southwest, pp. 328–58.

FOLKLORE

BIBLIOGRAPHY

Ashby, Eleanor, comp.
Spain and Spanish America in the Libraries of the University of California. A Catalogue. Berkeley, California: The Bancroft Library, 1930. 2 vols.

Bloom, Lansing B.
Comprehensive Index to New Mexico Historical Review. v. 1-15, 1926-1940. Albuquerque: Historical Society of New Mexico and University of New Mexico, 1941.

Bogardus, Emory S.
The Mexican Immigrants—An annotated bibliography. Los Angeles, California: Council on International Relations, 1929.

Boggs, Ralph Steele
Bibliography of Latin American Folklore. New York: H. W. Wilson & Co., 1940.

————,
Index of Spanish Folktales. Chicago: University of Chicago, 1930. FFC 90.

Campa, Arthur L.
A Bibliography of Spanish Folk-Lore in New Mexico. Albuquerque: University of New Mexico, 1930. *Language Series*, Vol. 2, No. 3.

Dobie, J. Frank
Guide to Life and Literature of the Southwest. With a few observations. Austin, Tex.: The University of Texas Press, 1943. 111 pp., illus.

Espinosa, Aurelio M.
"Field of Spanish Folklore in America." *SFQ* 5: 29-35, 1941.

Herzog, George
Research in Primitive and Folk Music in the United States. American Council of Learned Societies, Bull. 24. Wash.: 1936. 97 pp.

Honke, Lewis, ed.
Handbook of Latin American Studies, 1936— Cambridge: Harvard University Press.
These yearly bibliographies contain extensive items in folklore, music, ceremonials, legends, etc.

Jones, C. K.
A Bibliography of Latin American Bibliographies. Revised and enlarged by the author with the assistance of James A. Granier. The Library of Congress, Hispanic Foundation. Washington, D.C.: U.S. Gov't. Printing Office, 1942. 2nd ed.

Lesser, Arthur
"Bibliography of Spanish American Folklore, 1915-1928." *JAFL* 41:37-45, 1928.

Lomax, Alan, and Cowell, Sidney R.
American Folksong and Folklore; A Regional Bibliography. New York: Progressive Education Association, 1942. 97 pp.

Nichols, Madaline Wallis, ed.
A Bibliographical Guide to Materials on American-Spanish. edited for the Committee on Latin American Studies of the American Council of Learned Societies. Cambridge, Mass.: Harvard University Press, 1941. 114 pp.

Tucker, Mary
Books of the Southwest. New York: J. J. Augustin, **1937.**
A general bibliography: deals with the Indians of the Southwest, Spain in the Southwest, American pioneer history, the Southwest Country, the Southwest in Literature.

Wagner, Henry R.
The Spanish Southwest: 1542-1794. Albuquerque: The Quivira Society, 1937. 2 **parts.** An annotated bibliography.

GENERAL STUDIES AND COLLECTIONS

Allen, M. E. L.
Franciscan Missions. Los Angeles: Privately printed, 1912.
Folk art.

Austin, Mary
"Folk Plays of the Southwest." *Theatre Arts Monthly* 17: 599-610, (August) 1933.

————,
One Smoke Stories, Boston: Houghton Mifflin Co., 1934. xiv, 294 pp.
"Short narratives of the characteristic among Spanish-speaking New Mexicans" (Dobie)

Bandelier, Adolph Francis Alphonse
The Gilded Man (El Dorado) and other pictures of the Spanish occupancy of America. New York: D. Appleton and Co., 1893. iv, 302 pp.
"The dream of El Dorado" (Dobie)

Barker, Ruth Laughlin
Caballeros. New York: Appleton, Century Co., 1931.
"Fine and readable rendition of New Mexicans and Santa Fe." (Dobie)

Beals, Carlton
Mexican Maze. Philadelphia and London: J. B. Lippincott Co., 1931. 369 pp.

Blackmar, F. W.
Spanish Colonization in the Southwest. Baltimore: Johns Hopkins University, 1890.

Boggs, Ralph Steele
"El folklore Español en el Nuevo Mundo."
BAFA, 3, (No. 1-2): 8-10, 1940.
   Spanish folklore in the new world.

————,
"Spanish Folklore from Tampa, Florida."
SFQ 1 (no. 3): 1-13, 1917.

————
"Spanish Folklore in America; Folklore in
Pan Americanism; Latin American Folklore
Awaits Conquistadores." University of Miami:
Hispanic American Studies 1:122-165, 1940.
   Three lectures delivered at the Hispanic-Ameri-
can Institute in 1939.

Bourne, E. G.
Spain in America. New York: Harper Brothers,
1904.

Bright, Robert
The Life and Death of Little Jo. Garden
City, New York: Doubleday, Doran, 1944.
216 pp., illus.
   A novel of a New Mexican village, incidents
filled with old legends and use of witchcraft.

Byers, Samuel Hawkins Marshall
*The Bells of Capistrano and Other Romances
of the Spanish Days in California.* Los Angeles: The Grafton Publishing Co., 1916.
96 pp.

Carter, Charles Franklin
Stories of the Old Missions of California.
San Francisco: P. Elder and Co., 1917. 184
pp.
   Folk art.

Chapman, Charles Edward
The Founding of Spanish California. New
York: The Macmillan Co., 1916. 485 pp.

Clinch, Bryan James
California and Its Missions. San Francisco:
The Whitaker and Ray Co., Inc., 1914. 2 vols.

Davis, William Watts Hart
El Gringo; or New Mexico and Her People.
New York: The Rydal Press, 1938. 332 pp.

Denis, Mrs. Alberta Johnston
Spanish Alta California. New York: The Macmillan Co., 1927. 537 pp.

Engelhardt, Fr. Z.
Mission San Juan Bautista. Santa Barbara:
Schauer Printing Press, 1931.
   Contains examples of early Spanish melodies.

Espinosa, Aurelio M.
"Field of Spanish Folklore in America." *SFQ*
5: 29-35, 1941.
   Good bibliography.

————
"New Mexican Spanish Folklore." *JAFL* 23:
395-418, 1910; 24: 397-444, 1911; 26: 97-
122, 1913; 27: 105-147, 1914; 28: 204-206,
319-352, 1915; 29: 505-535, 1916.

————.
"Spanish-American Folklore." *JAFL* 60: 373-
377, 1947.

————,
"Spanish Folklore in New Mexico." *The
New Mexico Historical Review* (Santa Fe)
5 (no. 2): 135-155, 1926.

————, and J. M.
"The Texans." *New Mexico Quarterly Review* 13: 299-308, 1943.
   A New Mexican Spanish folk play of the middle
of the 19th century.

Fergusson, Harvey
The Blood of the Conquerors. New York:
Modern Age Books, Inc., 1937.
   A romantic tale of the Southwest where the
culture of Spanish America comes in dramatic
conflict with the new civilization from the north.
Also discusses the rites of the penitentes.

Foster, G.
M. Sierra Populaca. Berkeley and Los Angeles: University of California Press, 1945.

Freire-Marreco, B.
"New Mexican-Spanish Folklore." *JAFL* 29:
536-546, 1916.

Fulton, Maurice Garland
New Mexico's Own Chronicle; three races in
the writings of four hundred years, adapted
and edited by Maurice Garland Fulton and
Paul Horgan. Dallas: B. Upshaw and Co.,
1937. xviii, 155 pp., xxv, 372 pp., illus., bibl.

Garcis, Francisco Tomás
Hermengildo: On the Trail of a Spanish
pioneer. New York: J. P. Harper, 1900.
2 vols.

Garfías, Carlota
"Mexican Folklore Collected in New York
City." *JAFL* 51: 83-91, 1938.

Goy, Mrs. Antoinette Guernsey
Calle de Alvarado. Monterey, California: The
Monterey Trader Press, Feb., 1936.
   Legend, customs, traditions.

Hewett, Edgar L., and Fisher, Reginald
Mission Monuments in New Mexico. Albuquerque: University of New Mexico Press,
1944. 269 pp.

Hildrup, Jesse S.
*The Missions of California and the Old South-
west.* Chicago: A. C. McClurg & Co., 1907.
100 pp., illus.

Jackson, Helen Maria (Fisk)
*Father Junipero and the Mission Indians of
California.* Boston: Little, Brown Co., 1902.
159 pp.

————,
Glimpses of California and the Missions. Bos-
ton: Little, Brown Co., 1902. 292 pp.
   Tales and traditions.

Jaramillo, Cleofas M.
Shadows of the Past (Sombras del Pasado).
Illustrated by the author. Sante Fe: Seton
College Press, 1941. 115 pp., illus.

Kane, Harnett T.
The Bayous of Louisiana. New York: William
Morrow & Co., 1943.
He also speaks of the Spanish settlement of
Delacroix in St. Bernard Parish.

Keniston, Hayward
Spanish in the U. S. In: *Conference in non-
English speech in the United States,* Ann
Arbor, Michigan, Aug. 2-3, 1940. Bulletin of
the American Council of Learned Societies
(Wash. D.C.) 1942, No. 34, pp. 581-669.

Kibbe, P. R.
Latin Americans in Texas. New Mexico Uni-
versity. Inter-American Affairs School. Inter-
American Studies, No. 3. Albuquerque, 1946.

Laughlin, Ruth
Caballeros. Caldwell, Idaho: Caxton Printers,
Ltd., 1945. 418 pp., illus.
"—a complete Baedeker of the City of Santa Fe,
with chapters on its Spanish folkways history,
songs, plays, crafts, etc. (Elaine L. Lewis)

Long, Haniel
Piñon Country: (American Folkways Series).
New York: Duell, Sloan and Pearce, 1941.

Lowery, W.
*The Spanish Settlements within the Borders
of the United States.* New York: G. B. Putnam's Sons, 1901.

Lowrie, Samuel Harman
Culture Conflict in Texas: 1821-1835. New
York: Columbia University Press, 1932.
Spanish and American Culture Contacts.

Lucero-White, Aurora
The Folklore of New Mexico. Santa Fe, N.M.:
Seton Institute, Box 830, 1941. Vol. 1.
Contents: romances, corridos, cuentos, proverb-
ios, adivinanzas.

Luhan, Mabel Dodge
Winter in Taos. New York: Harcourt, Brace
and Company, 1935. viii, 237 pp., illus.

Lummis, Charles F.
"Catching Our Archaeology Alive." *Outwest*
22: 35-45, 1905.
"La Noche Esta Serena," (with harmonization
by Arthur Farwell).

————,
Flowers of our Lost Romance. Boston: Hough-
ton, Mifflin Co., 1929. 288 pp.
"Humanistic essays on Spanish contributions to
Southwestern civilization." (Dobie)

————,
The Land of Poco Tiempo. New York: C.
Scribner's Sons, 1893. 310 pp., illus.

Mendoza, Vicente T.
*El Apólogo Español en la Producción Folk-
lórica de México.* Universidad (Mexico, D.F.)
1938. Vol. No. 27. pp. 11-19.

————,
"Un ejemplo de romance de relación en
México; el casamiento del Ruilta Coche."
*Anales del Instituto de investigaciones esté-
ticas de la Universidad Nacional de México,*
1937, ano I, vol. I, No. I, pp. 15-27.

New Mexican-Spanish Folklore. *JAFL:* 23:
395-418, 1910; 26: 97-122, 1913; 27: 105-118,
1914; 28: 204-206, 1915.

Ortíz, P. A.
*Contribución al estudio de la civilización his-
pánica en el oeste de los Estados Unidos;*
(tesis para el título de doctor en filosofía y
letras.) México, D.F.: Universidad Nacional
autónoma de México, Facultad de filosofía y
letras, 1941. 116 pp. Mimeo.
Spanish civilization in the American West.

O'Sullivan, St. John
Little Chapters about San Juan Capistrano.
San Juan Capistrano, Calif: privately printed,
1912, 32 pp.
Legend, tradition, custom, social life.

Otero, Nina
Old Spain in our Southwest. New York:
Harcourt, Brace and Co., 1936.

Palóu, Francisco
*Life and Apostolic Labors of the Venerable
Father Junipero Serra.* Pasadena: C. W.
James, 1913. 338 pp.
A great deal of folklore, including customs,
beliefs, place names, and legends.

Peixotto, Ernest Clifford
Our Hispanic Southwest. Illustrations by the
author. New York: C. Scribner's Sons. 1916.
xx, 245 pp., illus.

Richman, I. B.
California Under Spain and Mexico. Boston:
Houghton Mifflin & Co., 1911.

Sanchez, George Isidore
Forgotten People; a Study of New Mexicans.
Albuquerque, N. M.: The University of New
Mexico Press, 1940. viii, 98 pp., illus.

Sanchez, Nellie Van De Grift
Spanish Arcada. San Francisco and Los
Angles: Powell Publishing Co., 1928.
Superstitions, odd beliefs, proverbs, medicine,
family and social life, customs.

Saunders, Charles Francis
The California Padres and Their Mission.
New York: Houghton, Mifflin Co., 1915.

Schinhan, Jan Philip
"Spanish Folklore from Tampa, Florida, VI:
Folksongs." *SFQ* 3: 129-163, 1939.

Stoddard, Charles Warren
In the Footprints of the Padres. San Fran-
cisco: A. M. Robertson, 1902. 335 pp.
Place names, legend, discovery tales.

Stone, Mary R. Van, and Sims, E. R.
"Canto Del Nino Perdido." *TFSP* 11: 48-89, 1933.
An old New Mexican folk play that originated about three centuries ago; gives five tunes.

Thomas, Alfred Barnaby
Forgotten Frontiers. Norman: Oklahoma University Press, 1932. 420 pp.

Winterburn, Rose Viola
The Spanish in the Southwest. New York: American Book Company, 1903. 224 pp., illus.

Zunser, Helen
"A New Mexican Village." *JAFL* 48: 125-179, 1935.

FOLKTALES—LEGENDS

Applegate, Frank Guy
Native Tales of New Mexico; Introduction by Mary Austin; with illustrations in color by the author. Philadelphia: J. B. Lippincott Company, 1932. 263 pp., illus.

Boggs, Ralph S.
Index of Spanish Folk Tales. FF Communications no. 90. Helsinki: 1930.

————,
"Spanish Folklore from Tampa, Florida. Una Ledi de Naso." *SFQ* I (No. 4): 9-15, 1937.

————,
"Spanish Folklore from Tampa, Florida (No. V) Folktales." SFQ 2 (No. 2): 87-107, 1938.

Campa, Arthur L.
New Mexico Folk Tales. Albuquerque: University of New Mexico, 1930.

Claudel, Calvin A.
"Spanish Folktales from Delacroix, Louisiana." *JAFL* 58: 209-224, 1945.

————,
"Three Spanish Folktales." *CFQ* 3: 21-28, 1944.

Cohen, Mildred
"Cuerpo Sin Alma." *TFSP* 14: 241-250, 1938.

De Huff, Elizabeth Willis
"The Metamorphosis of a Folk Tale." *TFSP* 12: 122-134, 1935.
A New Mexican Spanish folk tale, and how it came to be.

De Zavala, Adina
History and Legends of the Alamo and Other Missions in and Around San Antonio. San Antonio, 1917.

Dobie, J. Frank
Apache Gold and Yaqui Silver. Boston: Little, Brown and Co., 1939.
Legends of lost mines and money in Mexico and New Mexico.

————,
"Tale of the Two Companions." *TFSP* 19: 36-41, 1944.

Elder, David Paul
The Old Spanish Missions of California. San Francisco: P. Elder and Co., 1913. 89 pp.
Mission tales, legends and tradition.

Espinosa, Aurelio M.
"Comparative Notes on New Mexican and Mexican Spanish Folktales." *JAFL* 27: 211-231, 1914.

————,
"Hispanic Versions of the Tale of the Corpse Many Times 'Killed.' " *JAFL* 49: 181-193, 1936.

————,
"Spanish Folktales from California." *Hispania* 23: 121-144, 1940.

Espinosa, José Manuel
Spanish Folk Tales from New Mexico. Memoirs of the American Folklore Society, vol. 30. New York: G. E. Stechert and Co., 1937. xix, 222 pp., bibl.
Contents: Magic Tales, Religious Tales, Picaresque Tales, Romantic Tales, Short Tales and Anecdotes, Animal Tales.

————,
"The Legend of Sierra Azul." *New Mexico Historical Review* 9: 113-158, 1934, Bibl.

Gayton, A. H.
"Areal Affiliations of California Folktales." *AA* 37: 582-599, 1935.

Gonzáles, Jovita
"Among My Tales." *TFSP* 10: 99-108, 1932.
Folk tales of the Texas-Mexican border.

————,
"Tales and Songs of the Texas-Mexicans." *TFSP* 8: 86-116, 1930.

Goodwyn, Frank
"Folk-Lore of the King Ranch Mexicans." *TFSP* 9: 48-62, 1931.

————,
The Magic of Limping John, a Story of the Mexican Border Country, with illustrations by Grace Greenwood. New York: Farrar & Rinehart, 1944. 275 pp., illus.

Hallenbeck, Cleve, and Williams, Juanita
Legends of the Spanish Southwest. Glendale, California: The Arthur H. Clark Co., 1928. 342 pp., illus., bibl.

Harte, Bret
The Right Eye of the Commander, a New Year Legend of Spanish California. Garnished by Hans and served up savorily from the hand presses of Wilder & Ellen Bentley, Berkeley, 1937. 12 pp., illus.

House, Boyce
Roundup of Texas Humor. San Antonio, Tex.: The Naylor Company, 1949. xii, 308 pp.

Kincaid, Edgar B.
"The Mexican Pastor." *TFSP* 9: 63-68, 1931.
Lore of the Mexican shepherds.

Lummis, Charles Fletcher
A New Mexico David; and other stories and sketches of the Southwest. New York: C. Scribner's Sons, 1891. ix, 217 pp.

"Mexican and New Mexican Spanish Folk Tales." *JAFL* 27: 211-231, 1914.

Rael, Juan B.
"Cuentos Españoles de Colorado y de Nuevo Méjico." *JAFL* 52: 227-323, 1939.

———,
"Cuentos Españoles de Colorado y de Nuevo Méjico (Secunda Serie)." *JAFL* 55:1-94, 1942.

Saunders, Charles Francis
Capistrano Nights. New York: R. M. McBride & Co., 1930. 202 pp.
Folk tales and legends.

Schivendener, Normal, and Tibbels, Averil
Legends and Dances of Old New Mexico. New York: A. S. Barnes, 1934.

Shumard, Malnor
"Mexican Folk Escapades and Tales." *TFSP* 14: 234-240, 1938.

Storm, Dan
"The Pastor and the Serpent." *TFSP* 15: 122-133, 1939.

Sullivan, J.
"Spanish Folktale Recorded in the First Mesa, Arizona in 1885." *JAFL* 34: 221, 1921.

Sutherland, Mrs. Mary A.
"Pedro and Pancho." *TFSP* 2: 85-86 1923.
Two sketches of the border Mexicans.

Taylor, Hugh McGehee
"The Little White Dog." *TFSP* 12: 201-210, 1935.
A Texan *Ranchero* story.

Whatley, W. A.
"Mexican Münchausen." *TFSP* 19: 42-56, 1944.
Spanish folktales from Texas.

CUSTOMS—BELIEFS—SUPERSTITIONS

Anderson, L. I.
Art of the Silversmith in Mexico. New York: Wittenborn, 1941. 2 Vol.

Barker, Ruth Laughlin
Caballeros. New York: Appleton-Century Co., 1931.
Gives an excellent treatment of the Penitentes, pp. 215-226.

Bolton, Herbert E.
The Padre on Horseback. San Francisco: The Sonora Press, 1932.
"Life of the great Jesuit missionary Kino." (Dobie) Religious life and mores.

Bourke, John G.
"The Folk-Foods of the Rio Grande Valley and of Northern Mexico." *TFSP* 9: 85-117, 1931.

———,
"Miracle Play of the Rio Grande." *JAFL* 6: 89-95, 1893.

Campa, Arthur L.
Los Comanches, a New Mexican Folk Drama. Albuquerque: University of New Mexico Press, 1942, 43 pp. University of New Mexico bulletin, No. 376, Language Series, Vol. 7, No. 1.

———,
"The New Mexican Spanish Folktheater." *SFQ* 5: 127-131, 1941.

———,
The Spanish Religious Theatre in the Southwest. Albuquerque: University of New Mexico, 1934. Language Series, Vol. 5, Nos. 1 and 2.

"Courtship and Marriage in the Rio Grande Valley." *JAFL* 9: 104-107, 1896.

Crichton, Kyle S.
Law and Order, Ltd.; the rowsing life of Elfego Baca of New Mexico. Santa Fe, N. M.: New Mexican Publishing Corporation, 1928. viii, 219 pp., illus.

Dobie, J. Frank
"Weather Wisdom of the Texas-Mexican Border." *TFSP* 2: 87-99, 1923.

Englekirk, John Eugene
"Notes on the Repertoire of the New Mexican Spanish Folk-theater." *SFQ* 4 (No. 4): 227-237, 1940.

Espinosa, Aurelio M.
Los Comanches. New Mexico University Language Series. V. 1, No. 1. Albuquerque, N. M., 1907.

Field, Maria Antonia
Chimes of Mission Bells. San Francisco: The Philopolis Press, 1914. 79 pp.
Mission-bell tales, legends.

"Fiestas in New Mexico; San Ysidro's Day in Cordova; San Antonio's Day." *El Palacio* 48: 239-245, 1941.

Fisher, Reginald
"Notes on the relation of the Franciscans to the Penitentes." *El Palacio*, 48: 263-271, 1941. (Santa Fe, N. M.)

Foster, G.
M. Sierra Populaca. Berkeley and Los Angeles: University of California Press, 1945.
Folklore and beliefs.

Foster, Mira M.
"Social Life and Customs in Spanish Mexican California." *The Grizzly Bear*, 1918, p. 3-, (Aug).

Gerrard, Lewis Hector
Wah-to-Yah & the Taos Trail; prairie travel and scalp dances, with a look at los rancherosa from muleback and the Rocky Mountain campfire.... A new introduction by Carl I. Wheat, and illustrations from blocks designed and cut by Mallette Dean. San Francisco: The Grabhorn Press, 1936. 289 pp., illus.

Hurt, Wesley R.
"Spanish American Superstitions." *El Palacio* 47: 193-201, 1940.

―――,
"Witchcraft in New Mexico." *El Palacio* 57: 193-201, 1940.

Hauptmann, O. H.
"Spanish Folklore from Tampa, Florida: (No. IV) Superstitions" *SFQ* 2 (No. I): 11-31, 1938.

―――,
"Spanish Folklore from Tampa, Florida, No. VII: Witchcraft." *SFQ* 3: 197-200, 1939.

Henderson, Alice Corbin
Brothers of Light, The Penitentes of the Southwest. New York: Harcourt, Brace & Co., 1937.

Holway, Mrs. Mary Gordon
Art of the Old World in New Spain and the Mission Days of Alta California. San Francisco: A. M. Robertson, 1922. 122 pp.

Hopkins, Harry C.
History of San Diego, its Pueblo Lands and Water. San Diego, California: City Printing Co., 1929. 358 pp.

Humphrey, Norman D.
"Some Dietary and Health Practices of Detroit Mexicans." *JAFL* 58: 255-258, 1945.

James, George Wharton
In and out of the Old Missions of California. Boston: Little, Brown Co., 1927. 392 pp.
Tradition, folk art.

Jordan, David Starr
The Story of the Innumerable Company, and Other Sketches. San Francisco: The Whitaker and Kay Co., Inc., 1896. 294 pp.
Tales of customs, social life and practice at the missions.

Kubler, George
The Religious Architecture of New Mexico In the Colonial Period and Since the American Occupation. Colorado Springs: The Tayler Museum, 1940. 143 pp. illus.

Laughlin, Ruth
Caballeros; illustrations by Norma van Sweringen. New York: D. Appleton & Company, 1931. 379 pp., illus.

Lucero-White, Aurora
New Mexican Folklore; Coloquio de los Pastores. (music by Alejandro Flores. Santa Fe, N. M.: Santa Fe Press, 1940.
An old Christmas folk play.

Lummis, Charles Fletcher
The Land of Poco Tiempo. New York: Charles Scribner's Sons, 1893. 310 pp., illus.
Also deals with the Mexican Penitentes of New Mexico and Colorado.

―――,
The Spanish Pioneers. New York: A. C. McClurg & Co., 1918. 292 pp.
Spanish-California traits, customs, beliefs, practices.

Means, Florence Crannell
Teresita of the Valley. Boston: Houghton Mifflin Co., 1944. 166 pp.
A story for young readers, captures the spirit and life of the Spanish Americans in New Mexico.

Milford, Stanley J.
"A San Juan Burial." *El Palacio* 47:233-242, 1940.

Miller, Max
Harbor of the Sun: The Story of the Port of San Diego. New York: Doubleday, Doran & Co., 1940.

Moody, Alan
Sleep in the Sun. Boston: Houghton Mifflin Company, 1945. 137 pp., illus.
"It is a rather slight collection of sketches depicting a tiny Mexican community inhabiting one of the little canyons that run down toward the ocean from the Southern California coast range—it is a pleasant piece of California local color—." (Lionel Stevenson)

Newcomb, Rexford
Spanish Colonial Architecture in the United States. New York: J. J. Augustin, 1937. 39 pp.

Otero, Nina
Old Spain in Our Southwest; Illustrations by Aileen Nusbaum. New York: Harcourt, Brace and Company, 1936. ix, 192 pp., illus.
Customs, legends and folktales.

Parsons, Elsie Clews
"Fiesta of Sant' Ana, New Mexico." *Scientific Monthly* 16: 177-183, 1923.

Politi, Leo
Pedro, the Angel of Olvera Street. Illustrated by the author. New York: Charles Scribner's Sons, 1946. Unpaged.
In text, pictures, and music the author has captured the reverence and gaiety of the Mexican traditional celebration of Christmas. Olvera St. in Los Angeles.

Rael, Juan B.
"New Mexican Spanish Feasts." *CFQ* 1: 83-90, 1942.
Discusses the porciúcula of Aug. 2, Christmas, Epiphany, Holy Week, Sts. Anthony, John, James, Ann, and wedding ceremonies.

―――,
"The Theme of the Theft of Food by Playing Godfather in New Mexican Folklore." *Hispania* 20: 231-234, 1937.

Scholes, France V.
"Civil Government and Society in New Mexico in the Seventeenth Century." *New Mexico Historical Review* 10: 71-111, 1935.

Scott, Florence Johnson
"Customs and Superstitions Among Texas Mexicans on the Rio Grande Border." *TFSP* 2: 75-84, 1923.

Shippey, Lee
Folks You Should Know. Sierra Madre Calif.: Sierra Madre Press, 1930.
Discussion of customs and traditions, and dances.

Smith, Honora De Busk
"Mexican Plazas Along the River of Souls." *TFSP* 9: 69-84, 1931.
Rites, rituals and lore.

Sonnichsen, C. L.
"Mexican Spooks from El Paso." *TFSP* 13: 120-129, 1937.

"Spanish-American Baptismal Customs." Compiled by workers of the Writers' Program of the WPA in the State of New Mexico. *El Palacio* 49: 59-61, 1942.

"Spanish-American Wedding Customs." Compiled by workers of the Writers' Program of the Work Projects Administration in the State of New Mexico. *El Palacio* 49: 1-6, 1942.

"Spanish Fiestas in New Mexico." *El Palacio* 51: 101-106, 1944.

Storm, Dan
"The Little Animals of Mexico *El Coyote*, the *Doves*, and the *Dogs*." *TFSP* 14: 8-36, 1938.

Tingley, Elbert R.
Poco Loco. Sketches of New Mexican Life. Blair, Neb.: Danish Lutheran Publishing House, 1900. 94 pp.

Watkins, Frances E.
"A Bridal Chest of Spanish Times." *Masterkey* 18: 13-14, 1944.
Wooden handicraft of the Spanish Southwest.

Wilder, Mitchell A., and Breitenbach, Edgar
Santos, the Religious Folk Art of New Mexico. Foreword by Rudolph A. Gerken. Colorado Springs, Colorado: Taylor Museum of the Colorado Springs fine arts Center; Marchbanks Press, New York, 1943.

Williams, Arthur Durword
Spanish American Furniture. Milwaukee, Wisconsin: Brace, 1941.

Zavala, Silvio Arturo
The Spanish Colonization of America. Phila.: University of Pennsylvania Press, 1943.

Zeehandelaar, F. J.
"La Fiesta de Los Angeles." *Arrowhead Magazine* 1: 1-, 1906 (Feb).

FOLK MEDICINE

Berdau, Emil
"Der Mond in Volksmedizin, Sitte und Gebrauchen der Mexicanischen Grenzbewohnerschaft des südlichen Texas." *Globus (Braunschweig)* 88: 381-384, 1905.
Moon lore and medical practices.

Bourke, J. G.
"Popular Medicine Customs and Superstitions of the Rio Grande." *JAFL* 7: 119-146, 1894.

Nolen, Oran Warder
"Some Odd Mexican Customs." *TFSP* 19: 57-59, 1944.
Folk cures and remedies of Mexicans in Texas.

PROVERBS—RIDDLES

"California Spanish Proverbs and Adages." *CFQ* 3: 121-123, 1944.
Collected by the Editors from a note book in the possession of an aged lady in Los Angeles.

Campa, A. L.
Sayings and Riddles in New Mexico. New Mexico University Language Series, V. 6, No. 2. Albuquerque, N. M., 1937.

Espinosa, Aurelio
"California Spanish Folklore Riddles." *CFQ* 3: 293-298, 1944.

Rickard, J. A.
"Riddles of Texas Mexican Children." *TFSP* 18: 181-187, 1943.

Turbeville, Kay
"Proverbs of Spanish California." *Westways* 26:25 1934. (Mar).

SPEECH

Austin, Mary
"Geographical Terms from the Spanish." *AS* 8 (no. 3) : 7-10, 1933.

————,
"New Mexican Spanish." *Saturday Review of Literature* 7:930, 1931.
The author includes a small glossary of Spanish words current in the Southwest.

Bentley, Harold W.
A Dictionary of Spanish Terms in English; with special reference to the Southwest. New York: Columbia University Press, 1932. x, 243 pp.
"Reveals the Spanish-Mexican influence on life in the Southwest; it also guides to books in English that reflect this influence." (Dobie)

Bourke, J. G.
"Language and Folk-Usage of the Rio Grande Valley." *JAFL* 9: 81-115, 1896.

Crook, Alice M.
"Old-Time New Mexican Usages." *TFSP* 12: 184-189, 1935.

El Español en Méjico, los Estados Unidos, y la América Central. Trabajos de E. C. Hills, F. Semeleder, C. Carroll Marden, M. G. Revilla, A. R. Nykl, K. Lentzner, C. Gagini and R. Cuervo, with notes and studies by Pedro Henriquez Ureña. Buenos Aires, Impr. de la Universidad de Buenos Aires, 1938.
"An indespensable reference work for the Hispano American philologist, with many items of interest to the folklorist, especially in folk-speech." (Boggs)

Espinosa, Aurelio M.
Speech-Mixture in New Mexico. In: *The Pacific Ocean in History*, edited by H. M. Stephens and H. E. Bolton. New York: The Macmillan Company, 1917.

————,
Studies in New Mexican Spanish. New Mexico University Language Series, V. 1, No. 2, Albuquerque, N. M., 1909.

————,
"The Language of the Cuentos Populares Espanoles." *Language* (Sept.) 1927; (June) 1928.

————,
"The Spanish Language in New Mexico and Southern Colorado." *Publications of the Historical Society of New Mexico*, No. 16 (May) 1911.
The author has published many scholarly studies in Spanish on the above topic. For bibliography see: Mencken: *The American Language* (New York, 1937), pp. 647.

Hills, E. C.
"New Mexican Spanish." *PMLA* 21 (New Series 14): 706-755, 1906.

James, Earle K.
"Spanish Waning Cultural Influence Over Hispanic-America." *AS* 1 (No. 12): 645-649, 1926.

Kany, C. E.
"American-Spanish *amalaya* to express a wish." *Hispanic Review* 11: 333-337, 1943.

————,
"Impersonal *dizque* and its variants in American Spanish." *Hispanic Review* 12: 168-177, 1944.

————,
"Temporal Conjunction *a lo que* and its congeners in American Spanish." *Hispanic Review* 11: 131-142, 1943.

Kerchville, F. M., Comp.
A Preliminary Glossary of New Mexican Spanish . . . Some Semantic and Philological Facts of the Spanish Spoken in Chilili, New Mexico. New Mexico University Language Series, V. 5, No. 3. Albuquerque, N. M., 1934.

McKinstry, H. E.
"The American Language in New Mexico." *American Mercury* (March) 1930.

Mott, Gertrude
Handbook of Californians. San Francisco: Harr Wagner Publishing Co., 1926.
Spanish-California words and terms and their meaning.

Northrop, Stuart A.
"Terms from the Spanish." *AS* 12 (no. 1): 79-81, 1937.

Tallichet, H.
"A Contribution toward a Vocabulary of Spanish and American Words Used in Texas", A Vocabulary of Spanish and Mexican Words Used in Texas; Addenda to the Vocabulary of Spanish and Mexican Words Used in Texas." *Dialect Notes* 1 (Part 4): 185-195; 1 (Part 5): 243-253; 1 (Part 7): 324-326.

Tomás, T. Navarro
Linguistic Atlas of Spain and the Spanish of the Americas. In: *Conference of non-English speech in the United States*, Ann Arbor, Mich. Aug. 2-3, 1940. Bulletin of the American Council of Learned Societies (Wash., D. C.) 1942, No. 34, pp. 581-669.

Trager, George L.
"Spanish and English Loan Words in Taos." *International Journal of American Linguistics* (Indiana University, Bloomington, Indiana) 10: 144-158, 1944.

————, **and Valdez, Genevieve**
"English in Colorado Spanish." *AS* 12 (No. 1): 34-44, 1937.

Ward, Hortense Warner
"Ear Marks." *TFSP* 19: 106-116, 1944, 36 fig. Spanish Terms used in various ear marking.

————,
"Indian Sign on the Spaniards' Cattle." *TFSP* 19: 94-105, 1944, 51 fig.
Human figure designs used as cattle brands in Southwestern U.S.A.

Wesley, Howard D.
"Ranchero Sayings of the Border." *TFSP* 12: 211-220, 1935.

PLACE NAMES

Forrest, Earle Robert
Missions and Pueblos of the Old Southwest. Cleveland: The Arthur H. Clark Co., 1929. 386 pp.
Place names, conquest tales.

McNary, Laura K.
California Spanish and Indian Place Names; their pronunciation, meaning and location. Los Angeles: Wetzel Publishing Co., 1931. 77 pp.

Richie, Eleanor L.
"Spanish Place Names in Colorado." *AS* 10 (No. 2): 88-92, 1935.

Sanchez, Nellie Van De Grift
Spanish and Indian Place Names In California. San Francisco: A. M. Robertson, 1922.

Shafer, Robert
"The Pronunciations of Spanish Place Names in California." *AS* 17: 239-247, 1942.

Trager, George L.
"Some Spanish Place Names of Colorado." *AS* 10 (No. 3): 203-207, 1935.

FOLKSONG

BIBLIOGRAPHY

Campa, Arthur Leon
A Bibliography of Spanish Folklore in New Mexico. The University of New Mexico Bulletin, Language Series 5, 2, (No. 3). Albuquerque, N. M.: University of New Mexico, 1930. 28 pp.

Chase, Gilbert
A Guide to Latin American Music. The Library of Congress. Music Division. Washington, D. C.: U. S. Gov't. Printing Office, 1944. 274. pp.
An excellent bibliography. Spanish-American music, pp. 220-229.

———,
Bibliography of Latin American Folk Music. Washington, D. C.: The Library of Congress, Division of Music, 1942. U. S.-Spanish-Mexican folk music, pp. 117-128.

———,
Partial List of Latin American Music Obtainable in the United States, with a supplementary list of books and a selective list of phonograph records. Compiled by Gilbert Chase, Music Director, Library of Congress. Its Music Series, No. 1. Reproduced from typewritten copy. Washington, D. C.: Music Division, Pan American Union, 1941.
Includes "collections of Latin-American folk music," and a selective list of recordings of Latin American folk and popular music.

Herzog, George
Research in Primitive and Folk Music in The United States. American Council of Learned Societies, Bulletin No. 24. Washington, D. C.: Executive Offices, 1936. 97 pp.
Lists general collections and studies, pp. 84-85.

Lomax, Alan, and Cowell, Sidney Robertson
American Folksong and Folklore; A Regional Bibliography. New York: Progressive Education Association, 1942. 59 pp.
Section 10, deals with Spanish-American folklore and folksong, pp. 49-52.

GENERAL STUDIES

Atkinson, William C.
"The Chronology of Spanish Ballad Origins." *Modern Language Review* 32: 44-61, 1937.

Blackmar, Frank W.
Spanish Institutions of the Southwest. Baltimore: John Hopkins Press, 1891. 353 pp. illus.

Boatright, Mody C., ed.
Mexican Border Ballads and Other Lore. Austin, Texas: Folklore Society, 1946. 140 pp., some tunes.

Boggs, Ralph S.
"Spanish folklore in America; Folklore in Pan-Americanism; Latin America Folklore awaits Conquistadores." *The University of Miami, Hispanic-American Studies,* 1: 122-165, 1940.

Bourke, John G.
The Miracle Play of the Rio Grande. JAFL 5: 89-95, 1893.
A discussion of *Los Pastores.*

Campa, Arthur L.
Spanish Folk-Poetry in New Mexico. Albuquerque, New Mexico: The University of New Mexico Press, 1946. 224 pp. bibl.
Historical and comparative study; discusses the romance, the corrido, the decima, and the cancion.

———,
Spanish Religions Folk Theatre in the Southwest. The University of New Mexico Bulletin, Language Series, Vol. 5, (No. 1). Albuquerque: New Mexico University Press, 1934. 71 pp.

———,
Spanish Folksongs in New Mexico. New York: Columbia University, Ph.D. Thesis, 1940

———,
The Spanish Folk-Song in the Southwest. The University of New Mexico Bulletin, Modern Language Series 4, (No. 1). Albuquerque: New Mexico University Press, 1933.

Cole, M. R. ed.
Los Pastores: A Mexican Play of the Nativity. Memoirs of the American Folklore Society, No. 9. Boston: Houghton Mifflin and Company, 1907. 234 pp., illus., music and text.

Cowell, Sidney Robertson
"The Recordings of Folk Music in California." *CFQ* 1 (No. 1): 7-23, 1942.

Curtis, F. S., Jr.
"Spanish Songs of New Mexico" *TFSP* 4: 18-29, 1925.
Texts and tunes of 8 songs.

Da Silva, Rev. Owen, ed.
Mission Music of California. A Collection of Old California Mission Hymns and Masses. Accompaniments and Chirography Arthur M. Bienbar. Mission sketches by Paul A. Moore. With an introduction by John Steven Mc Groarty. Los Angeles, Cal.: Warren F. Lewis, 1941. xv, 132 pp. bibl., illus., music.

Dobie, Frank J. ed.
"Spanish Folk-Songs of New Mexico." *TFSP.* No. 4, 1925.

———,
"La Canción del Rancho de los Olmos." *JAFL* 36:192-195, 1923.

———,
"Texas-Mexican Border Broadside." *JAFL* 36: 185-191, 1923.

———,
"Versos of the Texas Vaqueros." *TFSP* 4: 30-43, 1925.
Texts and tunes of three ballads and one love song.

Elliot, Gilbert, Jr.
"Our Musical Kinship with the Spaniards." *MQ* 8 (No. 3): 413-418, 1922.

Engelhardt, Fr. Zephyrin
Mission San Juan Bautista. Santa Barbara: Schauer Printing Press, 1931.
Contains examples of early Spanish melodies.

———,
Santa Barbara Mission. San Francisco: James H. Barry Co., 1923. 470 pp.

Espinel, Luisa, comp.
"Canciones de mi padre; Spanish folksongs from Southern Arizona." *Arizona University. General Bull.* No. 10, pp. 4-56, 1946.
Includes music.

Espinosa, Aurelio Macedonio
"An Extraordinary Example of Spanish Ballad Tradition in New Mexico." Reprinted from *Stanford Studies in Language and Literature,* pp. 28-34, 1941.

———,
España en nuevo Méjico. New York: Allyn and Bacon, 1937. 73 pp. illus.
Contains a few songs and dances with tunes.

———,
"Los Romances Tradicionales en California." *Homenaje a Menéndez Pidal* Vol. I:299-313, 1925. (Madrid).

———,
"New Mexican-Spanish 'Coplas Populares.'" *Hispania* 18: 135-150, 1935.

———,
"Otro romance español tradicional." *Revista Bimestral de la Universidad de los Andes* (Menda, Venezuela) 2: 121-127, 1938.

———,
"Romancero Nuevo Mejicano." *Revue Hispanique* (Paris) 33, (No. 84):446-560, 1915; 40, (No. 97):215-227, 1917; 41-678-679, 1918.
Includes words and tunes of 9 ballads.

———,
"The Field of Spanish Folklore in America." *SFQ* 5 (No. 1): 29-35, 1941.
Discusses popular and traditional ballads and folk music.

———,
Traditional Ballads From Andalucía. In: *Flügel Memorial Volume.* Stanford University, Calif., 1916. pp. 106-107.
The Spanish ballads under discussion were collected in California.

———,
"Traditional Ballads in New Mexico." *Hispania* 15 (No. 2): March, 1932.

Fillmore, John Comfort, arr.
"El Borrachito" (The Tipsy Fellow). *Land of Sunhsine,* 14(4): 318-319, 1901.

Freire-Marreco, Barbara
"New Mexican Spanish Folklore." *JAFL* 29, (No. 114):536-546, 1916.
Wonderful examples of traditional Spanish ballads.

Garfías, Carlota
"Mexican folklore collected in New York City." *JAFL* 51: 83-91, 1938.
Includes 4 tunes.

Garrett, Eudora
"Mexican folkmusic." *El Palacio* 46:133-136, 1939.

Gonzáles, Jovita
"Folklore of the Texas Mexican Vaquero." *TFSP* 6: 7-22, 1927.
Texts only of 3 Mexican folk songs.

———,
"Tales and Songs of the Texas-Mexicans." *TFSP* 8: 84-116, 1930.
Tunes to five of the songs.

Goodwyn, Frank
"Folk-lore of the King Ranch Mexicans." *TFSP* 9:48-62, 1931.
Contains melody to one of the long corridos, "El Toro Moro."

Grandoff, Victor C.
"Folklore Notes about the Minorcans of old St. Augustine, Florida." *Revista Inter-Americana.* (University of Florida, Gainesville, Fla.) 1:31-34, 1940.

Hague, Eleanor
"California Songs, III." *Masterkey* II, (No. 3): 89-93, 1937.

———,
Latin-American Music: Past and Present. Santa Ana, Calif: The Fine Arts Press, 98 pp., illus., bibl.
Contains musical examples, and discussion of Mission Music and early music in California.

———,
Spanish-American Folk-Songs
Memoirs of the American Folklore Society, Vol. X. Lancaster, Pa.: The Folklore Society, 1917. 111 pp., bibl., unaccompanied melodies.
Many of the tunes were collected in Southern California, Arizona, Lower California, and Los Angeles.

———,
"Spanish-American Folk Songs." *JAFL* 24 (No. 93) 323-331, 1911.
Texts (Spanish) and melodies of 15 songs.

———,
"Spanish Songs from Southern California." *JAFL* 27 (No. 105): 331-332, 1914.

Hatcher, M. A.
"A Texas Border Ballad." *TFSP* 5: 49-55, 1921.

Kennedy, Stetson
"Cantantes Callejeros y La Cucaracha." *SFQ* 6:149-151, 1942.
Spanish words only of the Cucaracha sung by street singers of Key West and Tampa, Fla.

Koehler, Erna Buchel
"Our Musical Beginnings in the Southwest." *Etude* 59 (No. 1) 7: 64-65, 1941.

Knox, M.
"Sheperd Sings Folk Songs in New Mexico." *Etude* 57:70, (Jan.) 1939. illus.

Lomax, John A.
"Two Songs of the Mexican Cowboys from the Rio Grande Border." *JAFL* 28, (No. 110) 378-388, 1915.
Texts only.

Lucero-White, Aurora
New Mexican Folklore; coloquio de los pastore (Old Christmas Folk Play). Music by Alejandro Flores. Santa Fe, N. M.: Santa Fe Press, 1940.

Lummis, Charles Fletcher
"A New Mexican Folk-Song." *Land of Sunshine* 14:318-319, 1901.
Spanish and English text with music of *El Borrachito.* Arranged by J. C. Fillmore.

————,
"Catching our Archaeology Alive." *Out-West* 22: 35-45, 1905.
Discussion of collecting Spanish folksongs in the Southwest. Contains the song *La Hoche Esta Serena,* with harmonization by Arthur Farwell.

————,
The Land of Poco Tiempo. New York: Charles Scribner's Sons, 1925. 310 pp., illus.
Includes twelve New Mexico folk tunes.

McGill, Anne Blanche
"Old Mission Music." *MQ* 24: 186-193, 1938.

McMaster, Ann H.
Spanish Folksong in America. In: *The International Cyclopedia of Music and Musicians,* Oscar Thompson, ed., pp. 604-605. New York: 1939.

Meching, W. H.
"Songs and Stories from the Southern Atlantic Coastal Region of Mexico." *JAFL* 29:547-548, 1916.

Menéndez Pidal, Ramón
"Los Romances Tradicionales en America." *Cultura Espanola,* 1906. Madrid.

"Mexican-Texas Border Broadsides." *JAFL* 36: 185-191, 1923.

Mora, Joaquin
"Songs the Vaqueros Sing." *TFSP* 9: 118-123, 1931.
5 songs; words and melodies.

Morley, S. G.
"Spanish Ballad Problems." *University of California, Publications in Modern Philology* (Berkeley) Vol. 13, (No. 2); 207-228, 1925.

Rael, Juan B.
"New Mexican Wedding Songs." *SFQ* 4, (No. 2): 55-72, 1940.
Text (in Spanish) and one melody.

Report of the Committee of the Conference on Inter-American Relations in the Field of Music. William Berrien, Chairman. Washington, D. C.: September 3, 1940.

Ribera, Julián
"Para la historia de la Música popular." *Boletín de la Real Academia de la historia* 90:47-65, 192.
Discussion of Eleanor Hague's *Spanish-American Folksongs.*

Sandburg, Carl
"Spanish folksongs of New Mexico." *El Palacio* 21: 205-207.

Shaver, Lillie Terrell
"Spanish Mission Music." *Musical Observer* 19 (No. 4): 11, 1920.

————,
"Spanish Mission Music." *Papers and Proceedings of the Music Teachers National Association.* 40 Annual. Hartford, Conn., 1919.

Sister Joan of Arc
Catholic Musicians in Texas. San Antonio. Tex.: Our Lady of the Lake College, 1936. 64 pp.

————,
"Mission Music of the Southwest." *Catholic Choirmaster* 26 (No. 3): 102-104, (Sept. 13), 1940.

"Some California Songs." *The Masterkey* 8, (No. 1): 15-18, 1943; 8, (No. 4):115-117, 1943.

Spell, Lota M.
"Las canciones Populares Hispano-Americanas en los Estados Unidos." *BLAM* 5:200-206, 1941.
General observations.

————,
Music in Texas. Austin, Tex: 1936. 157 pp. illus.
Includes 10 Spanish American Songs.

————,
Music Teaching in New Mexico. Santa Fe: El Palacio Press, 1927. 12 pp.

Spizzy, Mabel Seeds, and Kinscella, Hazel Gertrude
La Fiesta; a unit of early California songs and dances. Lincoln: The University Publishing Co. 1939. 45 pp., music.
Dance routines included.

Taylor, Paul S.
"Songs of the Mexican Migration." *TFSP* 12: 221-245, 1935.
Songs by Mexican immigrants to the U.S. A most interesting collection with music. Also songs of the effects of the depression.

"Three Spanish-American Folk Songs from New Mexico." *Bulletin of the Pan American Union* 75, (No. 5):297-299, 1941.
> Music, text and directions of three singing games.

Van Stone, Mary R., ed.
Los Pastores; excerpts from an old Christmas play of the Southwest as given annually by the Griego family, Santa Fe, New Mexico. Cleveland. Gates Press, 1933. 44 pp. illus., music.

————, and Sims, E. R.
"Canto del niño perdido." *TFSP* 11: 48-89, 1933.
> Five tunes, with text of an old new Mexican religious play.

Watkins, Frances E.
"He said it with music."—Spanish-California folk songs recorded by Charles F. Lummis. *CFQ* 1 (No. 4): 359-367, 1942.

Weller, Rev. Philip T.
"Early Church Music in the United States" *The Caecilia* 46, No. 8, Sept. 1939.

Whatley, W. A.
"A Mexican Popular Ballad." *TESP* 4: 10-17, 1920.

Wood, B. D.
"A Mexican Border Ballad." *TFSP* 1: 55-58, 1916.

COLLECTIONS

Canciones Panamericanas. Songs of the Americas. Published in collaboration with the Pan-American Union, Washington, D. C. New York: Silver Burdett Company, 1942.

Da Silva, Owen Francis
Mission Music of California. A collection of old California Mission Hymns and Masses. Los Angeles: Warren F. Lewis, 1941. 132 pp., music.

Dickinson, Charles A., comp.
Las Posadas. Claremont, Calif.: Padua Hills Theatre, 1935. 16 pp., illus.
> Mexican Christmas songs, arranged for voice and piano.

Farwell, Arthur
Folk Songs of the West and South. Negro, Cowboy, and Spanish California. Arranged by A. Farwell. The Wa-Wan Series of American Composition, Vol. 4, No. 27. Newton Center, Mass.: The Wa-Wan Press, 1905. 4, 11 p.

————,
Two Spanish-Californian Songs. New York: Schirmer: Voice and piano.

Garrett, Eudora
Guitar Method, with guitar arrangements of Spanish-American Folk Songs of New Mexico. Albuquerque, N. M.: Works Progress Administration Music Project, 1939.
> 9 Spanish songs.

Hague, Eleanor
Early Spanish-California Folk Songs. New York: Carl Fischer, 1922.
> Arranged for voice and piano.

————, coll.
Spanish-American Folk-Songs. Memoirs of the American Folklore Society, Vol. 9. Lancaster, Pa.: The American Folklore Society, 1917. 111 pp., music, bibl.
> Contains 95 songs. Some from the southwest, the majority from Mexico, and some from Costa Rica and Cuba.

Luce, Allena
Canciones Populares. Boston: Silver, Burdett and Company, 1921.

Lummis, Charles Fletcher
Spanish Songs of Old California. Collected and translated by Charles F. Lummis. Pianoforte accompaniments by Arthur Farwell. Los Angeles: Chas. F. Lummis, 1923. 35 pp. Also published in New York by G. Schirmer.
> Melodies with piano accompaniment, Spanish and English words.

McCoy, William J.
Folk Songs of the Spanish Californians. San Francisco: Sherman, Clay and Company, 1926. 31 pp.
> Arranged for voice and piano. 10 songs.

Miller, Emily Maverick
Four Mexican Songs. Austin, Texas: 1917. 9 pp.
> Arranged for voice and piano.

Music of the Gold Rush Era. History of Music Project. Prepared with the assistance of the W. P. A. of California. History of Music in San Francisco Series, Vol. 1. San Francisco: 1939. 212 pp., illus., music.

Pan American Union, Music Division
14 Traditional Spanish Songs from Texas, transcribed by Gustavo Duran from recordings made in Texas, 1934-1939, by John A., Ruby T. and Alan Lomax, with an original drawing by Antonio Rodríguez Luna. Washington, D. C.: Music Division, Pan American Union, 1942. vi, 20 pp., unaccompanied melodies.

Ryan, Helen Chandler, Supervisor
Spanish American Folk Songs of New Mexico. Albuquerque, N. M.: Federal Music Project, Work Projects Administration, 1940.

————.
Spanish American Folk Songs of New Mexico. Introduction by A. L. Campa and Helen C. Ryan. Works Progress Administration. Federal Music Project, Units No. 1, No. 2 and 3. New Mexico: 1936-1937.
> Arranged for voice and piano. 13 songs. Unit 2 consists of 18 songs; unit 3 consists of 14 songs.

The Latin American Song Book. Published in cooperation with the Music Division of the Pan American Union. New York: Ginn & Co. 1942.
> Arranged for voice and piano, some for two voices.

The Spanish American Song and Game Book.
New York: A. S. Barnes, 1942. 87 pp.
Spanish and English texts, some songs with music and directions.

Van der Voort, Antoni
Old Spanish Songs, as sung by Sra. da. María Jimeno de Arata. Santa Barbara, Calif.: Santa Barbara Music Shop, 1928.
Arranged for voice and piano.

Van Stone, Mary R.
Spanish Folks Songs of New Mexico. Chicago: R. F. Seymour, 1926. Voice and piano.

CHILDREN'S RHYMES AND GAMES

Espinosa, Aurelio M.
"New Mexico Spanish Folklore. X. Children's Games. XI. Nursery Rhymes and Children's Songs." *JAFL* 29, (No. 114): 505-535, 1916.

Ryan, Helen Chandler, Supervisor
Spanish-American Singing Games of New Mexico. Albuquerque, N. M.: New Mexico Music and Writers' Projects Work Progress Administration, 1940.

Schinhan, Jan Philip
"Spanish folklore from Tampa, Florida. VI. Folksongs." *SFQ* 3: 129-163, 1939.
Music and texts of children's singing games.

Federal Music Project
Spanish-American Singing Games of New Mexico. Work Projects Administration. WPA Music Project Unit No. 3. Revised 1940. Santa Fe; 1940. 27 pp. (music).
Arranged for voice and piano, and directions for games.

————,
The Spanish-American Song and Game Book . . . Compiled by Workers of the Writers' Program, Music Program, and Art Program of the WPA in the State of New Mexico . . . New York: A. S. Barnes and Company, 1942. xv, 87 pp., illus.
Includes music (melodies with piano accompaniment), and description of the games and songs in Spanish and English.

The Spanish-American Song and Game Book.
New York: A. S. Barnes, 1942. 87 pp.
Spanish and English texts, some songs with music and directions.

"Three Spanish-American Folk Songs from New Mexico." *Bulletin of the Pan American Union* 75 (No. 5): 297-299, 1941.
Music, text and directions of three singing games.

DANCES

Brewster, Meta Sedillo
Mexican and New Mexican Folk Dances. Albuquerque: University of New Mexico Press, 1937.

"Folk Dances in Mexico." *Bulletin, Pan American Union* 73:96-99, (Feb.) 1939. illus.

Lucero-White, Aurora, ed.
Folk Dances of the Spanish Colonials of New Mexico. Music transcribed by E. Hanskins; patterns and description of dances by H. Mareau. Santa Fe, N. M.: Box 1200, 1937; and Examiner Publishing Company, 1940.

Schivendener, Normal, and Tibbels, Averil
Legends and Dances of Old New Mexico. New York: A. S. Barnes, 1934.

Shafter, Mary Severance
American Indian and Other Folk-Dances for Schools, Pageants, and Playgrounds. Music arranged by Josephine Condon. New York: A. S. Barnes & Co., 1927. 77 pp., illus., music.

Shambaugh, Mary Effie
Folk Festivals for Schools and Playgrounds. Folk dances and melodies. Music arranged by Anna Pearl Allison. New York: A. S. Barnes & Co., 1932. 155 pp., illus., music.

Shippey, Lee
Folks You Should Know. Sierra Madre, Calif: Sierra Madre Press, 1930.
Includes discussion of folk dances and mission customs.

ARRANGEMENTS

(Individual Titles)

————: *Voice and Piano*

Spizzy, Mabel Seeds, and Kinscella, Hazel Gertrude
La Fiesta: A Unit of Early California Songs and Dances. Lincoln, Neb.: The University Publishing Co., 1939. 45 pp., music.
Dance routines included.

"Angel of Love."
Lummis, C. F.: Fillmore (Los Angeles): Voice and piano.

"El Carbonero."
Lummis, C. F.: Fillmore (Los Angeles): Voice and piano.

"La Calandria."
Lummis, C. F.: Fillmore (Los Angeles): Voice and piano.

"The Old Man."
Lummis, C. F.: Fillmore (Los Angeles): Voice and piano.

————: *Choral*

"A La Puerta del Cielo."
Dodd, M.: Music Press: SATBB.

"Little Dove."
Robb, J.: Associated: SATB.

————: *Orchestra*

Sante Fe Tipica.
Mares, Pablo: C. Fischer: Orchestra.
Consists of 12 numbers based on folksongs and dances of new and old Mexico.

RECORDS
Bibliography

Chase, Gilbert, comp.
Partial List of Latin American Music Obtainable in the United States, with a supplementary list of books and a selective list of phonograph records. Washington, D. C.: Music Division, Pan American Union, Music Series No. 1, (March) 1941.

The Charles F. Lummis Collection of Spanish California and Indian songs in the Southwest Museum. Los Angeles.

Collections

Songs from El Niño Perdido.
Sung by Ricardo Archuleta at Cerro, New Mexico.
In: *Album 5, Record No.*   AAFS24B, Library of Congress, 1943.

El Tecolote (Spanish-American Ring Game).
Sung by Ricardo Achuleta at Cerro, New Mexico.
In: *Album 5, Record No.*   AAFS25A1, Library of Congress, 1943.

Songs from Los Pastores.
Sung by Franquilino Miranda and group at Catulla, Tex.
In: *Album 5,* Record No.   AAFS24A, Library of Congress, 1943.

Spanish-American Records.
In Archive of American Folk Song, Library of Congress, Music Division, Washington, D. C.

Spanish American Records.
Recorded by Eleanor Hague, California.

Spanish-American (New Mexico).
In the Archive of the New Mexico Folk Lore Society, University of New Mexico, Albuquerque, N. M.

Spanish-American (Texas).
From "Los Pastores," Mexican Religious play. Peabody Museum, Harvard University, Cambridge, Mass.

The Charles F. Lummis Collection of Spanish California and Indian Songs in the Southwest Museum, Los Angeles.
Has 350 Spanish California songs.

U. S. Library of Congress. Division of Music. Folklore Section.
Mexican Border Songs South of San Antonio, Texas. 25 Records.   AAFS–LC

Watkins, F. E.
Spanish-California Folk Songs, recorded by Charles Fletcher Lummis.   MS. 1942

SWEDISH AND SWISS

FOLKLORE

Anderson, Nancy Mae
Swede Homestead. Caldwell, Idaho: The Caxton Printers, 1942.
The story of the Swedish pioneer in the American Northwest.

Beath, Paul R.
Febold Feboldson: Tall Tales from the Great Plains. Illustrated by Lynn Trank. Lincoln: University of Nebraska Press, 1948. xi, 124 pp.
The amazing achievements of the "indomitable Swedish pioneer who surmounts any difficulty."

Beckman, Robert
"Notes on Swedish American." *AS* 3 (No. 6): 448–450, 1928.

—————.
"Swedish-American 'I Bane'." *AS* 3 (No. 6): 464–465, 1928.

Berg, Ruben Gustafsson
Svenskan in Amerika. Stockholm. P. A. Norstedt & Söners Förlag, 1904.

Berger, V.
Svensk-Amerikanska Spraket i America. Student foreningen Smaskrifter No. 87. Stockholm: 1900.
Swedish-American speech changes.

De Angeli, Marguerite
Elin's America. Illustrated in color and in black and white. New York: Doubleday, Doran and Company, 1941.
A book for young readers, giving a delightful account of Swedish pioneers, in the founding of New Sweden on the banks of the Delaware in the Sixteen Forties.

Deen, J. L., and others
A Swedish-English Vocabulary for Foresters. New Haven, Conn.: Yale University School of Forestry. Bulletin No. 40. 1935. 83 pp.

Federal Writers' Project
The Swedes and Finns in New Jersey (American Guide Series). Written and illustrated by Federal Writers' Project of the W. P. A., State of New Jersey. Bayonne, N. J.: Jersey Printing Co., 1938.

Hand, Wayland D.
"Schweizer Schwingen: Swiss Wrestling in California." *CFQ* 2:77–84, 1943.

Holter, Thorvald E.
"Twenty Idioms Illustrating the Influence of Swedish on English." *AS* 6 (No. 3):216–217, 1931.

Johnson, Amandus
The Swedish Settlements on the Delaware. Philadelphia: University of Pennsylvania, 1911. II vols.

Senn, Alfred
"Swiss Dialects in America." *Conference on non-English Speech in the United States.* (Ann Arbor, Mich.) Aug. 2–3, 1940. Washington, D. C.: Bulletin of the American Council of Learned Societies, 1942. No. 34, pp. 581–669.

Swanson, Roy W.
"The Swedish Surname in America." *AS* 3 (No. 6):468–477, 1928.

Zetterstrand, E. A.
"Engelskans Inflytande pa Svenska Spraket i America." *Ungdomsvanen* (Stockholm), (June, July, Aug.) 1904.
The English spoken by Swedes in America.

FOLKSONG

Barry, Phillips
"Swedish Ballad: De Two Systrarna (The two Sisters)." *FSSNE* 7:14, 1934.

Umble, John
"The Old Order of Amish, their Hymns and Hymn Tunes." *JAFL* 52:82–95, 1939.
Amish were Swiss-German immigrants who came to Pennsylvania in Colonial times.

SYRIAN

FOLKLORE

Wilson, H. B.
"Syrian Folklore Collected in Boston." *JAFL* 16:133–147, 1903.

Part Four: Occupational Bibliography

THE COWBOY

THE COWBOY

See: The Southwest, pp. 328-58, The West, pp. 360-401.

FOLKLORE

BIBLIOGRAPHY

Branch, E. Douglas
The Cowboy and His Interpreters. New York: D. Appleton Co., 1926. 277 pp.
"Useful bibliography on range matters." (Dobie)

GENERAL STUDIES AND COLLECTIONS

Abbott, E. C., and Smith, Helena Huntington
We Pointed them North. New York: Farrar and Rinehart, 1939.

Adams, Andy
Cattle Brands. Boston: Houghton Mifflin Co., 1906. 316 pp.

————.
Cowman. Boston: Houghton Mifflin Co., 1907. 384 pp.

————.
Reed Anthony. Boston: Houghton Mifflin Co., 1907. 384 pp.

————.
The Log of a Cowboy. Boston: Houghton Mifflin Co., 1903.
A novel—"every page illuminated by an easy intimacy with the life."

————.
The Outlet; Illustrated by E. Boyd Smith. Boston: Houghton Mifflin Co., 1905. 371 pp., 6 col. plates.

————.
The Ranch on the Beaver; Illustrations by Edward Borein. Boston: Houghton Mifflin Co., 1927. 307 pp.
Juvenile story of cowboy life.

————.
Wells Brother; Illustrations by Erwin E. Smith. Boston: Houghton Mifflin Co., 1911. 356 pp.
Juvenile story of cowboy life.

Adams, Ramon F.
"Cowboys Bendin' an Elbow." *The Southwest Review,* 30 (No. 4) :329–334, Summer, 1945.

Aldridge, Reginald
Ranch Notes. New York: Longmans, Green & Co., 1884. 227 pp.

Alldredge, Eugene Perry
Cowboys and Coyotes. Nashville: Marshall & Bruce Co., 1945. v, 184 pp., illus.

Allen, Jules Verne
Cowboy Lore. San Antonio, Texas: The Naylor Printing Co., 1933.
Historical backgrounds, famous songs, glossary of cowboy words.

Arnold, Oren, and Hale, J. P.
Hot Irons. New York: Macmillan Co., 1940.
"Technique and lore of cattle brands." (Dobie)

Barnard, Evan G. ("Parson")
A Rider of the Cherokee Strip. Boston: Houghton Mifflin Company, 1936.
"Rich in little incidents and Cowboy humor." (Dobie)

Barnes, Will C.
Apaches and Longhorns. Los Angeles, California: The Ward Ritchie Press, 1941.

Benedict, Carl Peters
Tenderfoot Kid On Gyp Water. Dallas, Texas: University Press, 1943. xviii, 115 pp. (Range Life Series).

Benton, Frank
Cowboy Life on a Sidetrack; being an extremely humorous and sarcastic story of the trials and tribulations endured by a party of stockmen making a shipment from the West to the East. Illustrated by E. A. Filleau. Denver: The Western Stories Syndicate, 1903. 207 pp., incl. pls. ports.

Benton, Jesse James
Cow by the Tail; introduction by Richard Summers. Boston: Houghton Mifflin Co., 1943. 225 pp.
An exciting personal account of cowboys and settlers. The heroes of the West parade through these pages.

Blake, Forrester
Riding the Mustang Trail; an account of a trail drive of wild horses from New Mexico to Oklahoma. New York: C. Scribner's Sons, 1935. 261 pp.

Blake, R. B.
"Traditional Nacogdoches." *TFSP* 14:195–199, 1938.

Bosworth, Allan R.
Sancho of the Long, Long Ago. Illustrated by Robert Frankenberg. New York: Doubleday and Co., 1947. 206 pp.
For young readers about Texan cowboy life, manners, songs, jokes and action.

Brininstool, Earl Alonzo
Trail Dust of a Maverick. Introduction by Robert A. Burdette. New York: Dodd, Mead and Co., 1914. 249 pp.
A book of poems.

Bronson, Edgar Beecher
Cowboy Life on the Western Plains. New York: Grosset & Dunlap Pub., 1910. 369 pp.

————.
Reminiscences of a Ranchman. Chicago: A. C. McClurg & Co., 1910. 369 pp., rev. ed.

The Red Blooded Horses of the Frontier. New York: G. H. Doran Co., 1910. 341 pp.

Burton, Harley True
A History of the J. A. Ranch. Austin, Texas: Press of Von Boeckmann-Jones Co., 1928. 147 pp.
"Facts about one of the greatest ranches of Texas and its founder." (Dobie)

Call, Hughie
Golden Fleece. Boston: Houghton Mifflin Co., 1942.

Canton, Frank M.
Frontier Trails; edited by E. E. Dole. Boston: Houghton Mifflin Co., 1930.

Clark, Charles Badger
Sun and Saddle Leather, including "Grass Grown Trails,' and New Poems. Illustrations from Photographs by L. A. Huffman. Boston: R. G. Badger, 1920. xxix, 221pp.
Cowboy verse.

Clark, N. M.
"God's Roundup: Texas Cowboys' Camp Meeting 53 Years Old." *Saturday Evening Post* 215:28, 1943. (March)

Clay, John
My Life on the Range. Chicago: Privately Printed, 1924.

Clealand, Robert Glass
The Castle on a Thousand Hills. San Marino, California: Huntington Library, 1941.
"On Spanish-Mexican ranching in California." (Dobie)

Cleaveland, Agnes Morley
No Life for a Lady. Boston: Houghton Mifflin Co., 1941.
Range life from a woman's point of view. Setting is New Mexico.

Coleman, Rufus A., ed.
The Golden West in Story and Verse. New York: Harper & Bros., 1932.

Collings, Ellsworth
The 101 Ranch. Norman, Oklahoma: University of Oklahoma Press, 1937.
"The 101 Ranch Wild West Show is emphasized in this book." (Dobie)

Cook, James H.
Fifty Years on the Old Frontier. New Haven: Yale University Press, 1923. 291 pp.

Coolidge, Dane
Arizona Cowboys. New York: E. P. Dutton & Co., 1938. 160 pp., illus.

Fighting Men of the West. New York: E. P. Dutton & Co., 1932. 343 pp., illus.

Old California Cowboys. New York: E. P. Dutton & Co., 1939. 158 pp., illus.
Lists a number of Corridos, pp. 114–128.

Texas Cowboys. New York: E. P. Dutton & Co., 1937. 162 pp., illus.

Coze, Paul
Rodeos de Cow-Boys et les Jeux du Lasso. Paris: Société-Française de Librarie, 1934. 177 pp.

Crawford, Lewis F.
Badlands and Bronco Trails. Bismark, North Dakota: Capital Book Co., 1926.
Adventures of the amazing Ben Arnold Connor.

Rekindling Campfires. Bismark, North Dakota: Capital Book Co., 1926. 324 pp.

Crouch, C. J.
"On the Old Cattle Trails." *National Republic* (Washington, D. C.) 18:19–21, March, 1931.

Culley, John
Cattle, Horses, and Men. Los Angeles: The Ward Ritchie Press, 1940.
"Much about noted Bell Ranch of New Mexico." (Dobie)

Dacus, Joseph A.
Illustrated Lives and Adventures of Frank and Jesse James, and the Younger Brother, the noted western outlaws. St. Louis: N. D. Thompson & Co., 1881.

Dawson, Peter
Trail Boss. New York: Dodd, Mead & Co., 1943.
"A tale that bristles with lively action, tense situations, excitement and suspense." (G. W. Harris)

DeWolff, J. H.
Pawnee Bill (Major Gordon W. Lillie), his experiences and adventures on the western plains; or, From the Saddle of a "cowboy and ranger" to the chair of a "bank president." Pawnee: Pawnee Bill's Historic Wild West Company, 1902. 108 pp., illus.
Interesting data also included on Geronimo, Custer, the western pony express, and the cowboy.

Denhardt, Robert Moorman
The Horse of the Americas. With a foreword by J. Frank Dobie. Illustrated. Norman, Okla.: University of Oklahoma Press, 1948. 208 pp.
Interwoven with the complex genealogy of our equine family to its present descendants one finds here a great deal of the customs and history of the North and South American cowboys.

Dobie, J. Frank
The Longhorns. Boston: Little, Brown & Co., 1941. xiii, 388 pp.
"It should be required reading for all who wish to develop more than a superficial appreciation of cowboy songs and cattle lore." (Levette J. Davidson)

Tales of the Mustang. Illustrations by Jerry Bywaters. Dallas: The Book Club of Texas, 1936. 89 pp., illus.
Legends and stories of horses, and cowboy lore.

——————.
Tongues of the Monte. Garden City, New York: Doubleday, Doran & Co., 1935.

A Vaquero of the Brush Country, partly from the reminiscences of John Young. Dallas, Texas: The Southwest Press, 1929. xv, 314 pp., bibli.

——————, Boatright, Mody C., and Ransom, H., eds.
Coyote Wisdom; Texas Folk Lore Publications, No. 14. Austin, Texas: Texas Folklore Society, 1938. 300 pp., illus., music.

——————.
Mustangs and Cow Horses. Texas Folklore Society Publications 16. Austin, Tex.: Texas Folklore Society, 1940.
Compilation of thirty-seven articles by various authors. "Half of book is made up of first-hand narratives of old-time mustangers; the remainder is a collection of stories of horses and historical and topical essays." (Dobie)

Evans, W. F.
Border Skyline. Dallas, Texas: C. Bough, 1940.

Favour, Alpheas H.
Old Bill Williams. Mountain Man. Chapel Hill: University of New York Press, 1936.

Field, Peter
Powder Valley Vengeance. New York: William Morrow & Co., 1943.
"Here is another lively and dusty yarn detailing certain new exploits of Powder Valley's famous two of trouble shooters: Pat Stevens, Sharpshooters Sam Sloan and big one-eyed Ezra." (G. W. Harris)

Finger, Charles Joseph
Life of Barnum; the man who lured the herd. Girard, Kansas: Haldeman-Julius Co., 1924. 96 pp.

Foley, James W.
Prairie Breezes. Boston: R. B. Badger, 1905.
A book of cowboy verse.

Forrest, E. R.
Arizona's Dark and Bloody Ground. Caldwell, Idaho: Caxton Press, 1936.
"War between sheepmen and cattlemen." (Dobie)

French, William
Some Recollections of a Western Ranchman. New York: Frederick A. Stokes, 1928. 283 pp.

Gana, Walter
The Trail Boss. Boston: Houghton Mifflin Co., 1937.
"Faithful fiction."

Garrison, Myrtle
Romance and History of California Ranchos. San Francisco: Harr Wagner Publishing Co., 1935. 206 pp.

Garst, Shannon
Cowboy Boots. Illustrated by Charles Hargins. New York: Abingdon-Cokesbury Press, 1947. 191 pp.
"Happy combination of lively story and interesting information in ranch life." A juvenile.

González, Jovita
"Folk-Lore of the Texas-Mexican Vaquero." *TFSP* 6:7–23, 1934.
Tales, legends and songs.

Goodwyn, Frank
"At a Branding Roundup." *TFSP* 18:103–114, 1943.
Detailed description of customs and practices in catching and throwing cattle in Texas.

Griggs, N. K.
Lyrics of the Lariat. Chicago: Fleming H. Revell, 1893.
Rich in cowboy lore and speech.

Guernsey, Charles
Wyoming Cowboy Days. New York: G. P. Putnam's Sons, 1936. 288 pp., illus.

Haley, Jo Evetts
Charles Goodnight, Cowman and Plainsman. Illustrated by H. Bugbee. Boston: Houghton Mifflin Co., 1936. viii, 485 pp., illus., bibl.
"This biography, taken from the long list of books about "Cowboys and Range Life," well represent the fighting code of the range." (Dobie)

Halsell, H. H.
Cowboys and Cattleland. Lubbock, Texas: The Author, 1937.

Hankins, R. M.
Lonesome River Justice. Philadelphia: Macrae-Smith Co., 1943.
"Life of the old gun-toting West. He writes of it convincingly and cleverly with gusto and sly humor." (G. W. Harris)

Hanson, Joseph M.
Frontier Ballads. Chicago: A. C. McClurg Co., 1910.

Harper, M. T., and G. D.
Old Ranches. Dallas, Texas: Regional Press, Inc., 1936.

Hastings, Frank S.
A Ranchman's Recollections. Chicago: The Breeder's Gazette, 1921. 235 pp.
"His story of 'Grandpa' is the best story that has been written of a cowboy's horse." (Dobie)

Holden, W. C.
Rollie Burns. Dallas, Texas: The Southwest Press, 1932. 243 pp.
Biography of a plains cowman.

Holling, Holling Clancy
The Book of the Cowboys. Illustrated by H. C. and Lucile Holling. New York: The Platt & Munk Co., 1936. 126 pp.

Horan, J.
Burnt Leather. Boston: The Christopher House, 1937. viii, 105 pp.
A book of poems.

Hosmer, P.
"Wild Horses and Hard Men." *St. Nicholas Magazine* (Columbus, O.) 58:110–113, Dec., 1930.

Hough, Emerson
The Story of the Cowboy. New York: D. Appleton-Century Co., 1936. x, 349 pp.

Inman, Henry
The Old Santa Fe Trail. New York: The Macmillan Co., 1897. xvi, 493 pp.

James, Will
All in the Day's Riding. New York: Charles Scribner's Sons, 1933. xiv, 251 pp., illus.

——.
Cowboy in the Making. New York: C. Scribner's Sons, 1937. 91 pp., illus.

——.
Cowboy Life in Texas or 27 yrs. a Maverick. Chicago: M. A. Donohue & Co., 1898. 213 pp.

——.
Cowboys North and South. New York: Charles Scribner's Sons, 1924. 217 pp., illus.

——.
Cow Country. New York: Charles Scribner's Sons, 1931. xii, 242 pp., illus.

——.
Flint Spears, Cowboy Rodeo Contestant. Illustrated.... New York: C. Scribner's Sons, 1938. xiv, 269 pp.

——.
Lone Cowboy. New York: Charles Scribner's Sons, 1930. x, 431 pp., illus.

——.
Smoky. New York: Charles Scribner's Sons, 1926. 310 pp., illus.
"Woven around horse heroes; with illustrations."

——.
Sun Up; Tales of the Cow Camps. New York: C. Scribner's Sons, 1931. 342 pp., illus.

——.
The American Cowboy. New York: Charles Scribner's Sons, 1942. 273 pp., illus.

——.
The Drifting Cowboy. New York, London: Charles Scribner's Sons, 1925. 241 pp., illus.

——.
Will James Cowboy Book. New York: Charles Scribner's Sons, 1938. 158 pp., illus.

Kent, W. H. B.
Range Rider. New York: The Macmillan Co., 1943. 193 pp.
A splendid fictionalized account of cowboy life and habits.

King, Frank M.
Wranglin' the Past. Los Angeles, California: Western Livestock Journal, 1935.

Knibbs, Henry Herbert
Riders of the Stars; a Book of Western Verse. Boston: Houghton Mifflin Company, 1916. v, 81 pp.

——.
Saddle Songs and other Verse. Boston: Houghton Mifflin Co., 1916.

Landon, Melville D. (Eli Perkins)
Eli Perkins, Thirty Years of Wit, and Reminiscences of Witty, Wise and Eloquent Men. New York: Cassell Publishing Co., 1891.

Lewis, Alfred Henry
Wolfville Days. New York: Frederick A. Stokes, 1902.

Lomax, John A.
Songs of the Cattle Trail and Cow Camp. New York: Macmillan Co., 1919.
An anthology of Cowboy and Western verse.

Long, Haniel
Piñon Country; (American Folkways Series). New York: Duell, Sloan & Pearce, 1941.

Longhead, Flora Haines
"The Old California Vaquero." *Land of Sunshine,* 5:109–119, 1898.

Mackay, Malcom S.
Cow Range and Hunting Trail; illustrated by Charles M. Russell. New York & London: G. P. Putnam's Sons, 1925. 243 pp., illus.

Mandat-Grancey, Edmond baron de
Cowboys and Colonels; Narrative of a journey across the prairie and over the Black Hills of Dakota,... New York: E. P. Dutton and Co., 1887. 364 pp., illus.

McCauley, James Emmet
A Stove-Up Cowboy's Story; (Range Life Series). Austin, Texas: Texas Folklore Society, 1943. xxii, 374 pp.

McCoy, Joseph G.
Historic Sketches of the Cattle Trade of the West and Southwest. Kansas City, Missouri: Ramsey, Millett & Hudson Co., 1874. 427 pp., illus.

McCracken, Harold
Frederic Remington: Artist of the Old West. Introduction by James Chillman, Jr. (with a bibliographical check list of Remington pictures and books.) Philadelphia, Pa.: J. B. Lippincott Co., 1947. 157 pp., 48 plates.
This remarkable painter-writer left a memorable gallery of Western life and characters, many of them reproduced in this book. As perhaps no other man, Remington "knew the West."

Mersfelder, L. C.
Cowboy - Fisherman - Hunter. Boston: Little, Brown and Co., 1941.

Miller, Lewis B.
Saddles and Lariats. Boston: D. Estes & Co., 1912. 285 pp.
"A fictional chronicle, based almost entirely on facts of a trail herd that tried to get to California in the 50's." (Dobie)

Moore, J. M.
West. Wichita Falls, Texas: Lovelace Bookstore, 1935.

Mora, Jo
Trail Dust and Saddle Leather. Illustrated by the author. New York: Charles Scribner's Sons, 1946. 246 pp.
"...The best thing in twenty-five years on the American cowboy and the tools of his trade." (H. Birney)

Nordyke, N. T.
"Boss of the Plains; Story Behind the Stetson." *Saturday Review of Literature* 25:18, May 16, 1942.

O'Keefe, R. W.
Cowboy Life. Reminiscences of an early life, early boyhood and experiences as a cowboy on a range, on the trail, as a manager of a ranch and the owner and operator in cattle. New York: Naylor Co., 1936. 244 pp., illus.

O'Neil, James B.
They Die But Once. New York: Knight Publications, Inc., 1935. 228 pp.
"Biographical narrative of a Tejano who vigorously swings a very big loop." (Dobie)

Osgood, Ernest Staples
The Day of the Cattleman.... Minneapolis: The University of Minnesota Press, 1929. x, 283 pp., illus., bibl. (pp. 259–268).

Payne, Stephen
Teen-Age Stories of the West. San Francisco: Lantern Press, 1948.

Perkins, Charles E.
The Phantom Bull. Boston: Houghton Mifflin Co., 1932. 70 pp., illus.
Fictional narrative.

————.
The Pinto Horse. Santa Barbara, California: W. Hebbord Co., 1927. 76 pp., illus.
Fictional narrative.

Perry, George Sessions
Roundup Time . . . New York: Whittlesey House, 1943. xvi, 384 pp.

Phillips, Paul C., ed.
Forty Years on the Frontier as seen in the Journals and Reminiscences of Granville Stuard. Cleveland: Arthur H. Clark Co., 1928.

Pioneer Settlement.
New York: American Geographical Society, 1932. 470 pp., illus.
Contributions by twenty-six authors.

Pound, Louise
"Joe Bowers Again." *SFQ* 3 (No. 3):13–17, 1937.

————.
"More Joe Bowers Lore." *SFQ* 2 (No. 3):131–135, 1938.

Price, Con
Trail I Rode. Illustrations by Charlie Russell. Pasadena, Calif.: Trails End Publishing Co., 1947.
Reminiscences of a Montana Cowboy.

Raine, James Watt
The Land of Saddle-Bags. New York: The Council of Women for Home Missions and Missionary Education Movement of the United States and Canada, 1924.

Raine, William McLeod, and Barnes, Will C.
Cattle. Garden City, New York: Doubleday, Doran Co., 1930. 340 pp.
Re-printed under title: *Cattle, Cowboys and Rangers.* Replete with the traditions, the lore, and characters of the cattle range.

Rak, Mary Kidder
A Cowman's Wife. Boston: Houghton Mifflin Co., 1934.
"The realities of life as experienced by a woman from the outside on a small Arizona ranch." (Dobie)

————.
Mountain Cattle. Boston: Houghton Mifflin Co., 1936.

Rhodes, Eugene Manlove
Good Men and True. New York: H. Holt & Co., 1910. 177 pp., illus.

————.
Once in the Saddle, and Paso por aqui. New York: Houghton Mifflin Co., 1927. 258 pp.

————.
Stepsons of Light. Boston: Houghton Mifflin Co., 1921. 317 pp.

Richards, Clarice E.
A Tenderfoot Bride. New York: Garden City Press, 1920.
"The telling has charm, warmth and nobility." (Dobie)

Richter, Conrad
The Sea of Grass. New York: Alfred A. Knopf, 1937.
"A poetic portrait in fiction of a big cowman." (Dobie)

Ridings, Sam P.
The Chisholm Trail. Medford, Oklahoma: The author, 1926. Guthrie, Oklahoma: Cooperative Publishing Co., 1936.
A history of the world's greatest cattle trail together with a description of the persons, a narrative of the events and reminiscences associated with the same. "A noble book, rich in anecdote and character." (Dobie)

Ripley, Thomas
They Died With Their Boots On. Garden City, N. Y.: Doubleday Doran and Co., 1935. 285 pp.
Deals mainly with John Wesley Hardin.

Robb, John S. (Solitaire)
Streaks of Squatter Life, and Far West Scenes; A Series of Humorous Sketches. Philadelphia: Carey & Hut Publishers, 1847. 187 pp., illus.
Descriptive of incidents and character in the wild West.

Rollins, Philip Ashton
The Cowboy. New York: Charles Scribner, 1936. 442 pp. Rev. and enl. ed.
"Text much enlarged as concerns branding, roping, etc., social customs, technical terms and old-time slang."

The Cowboy: His Characteristics, His Equipment, and His Part in the Development of the West. New York: Charles Scribner's Sons, 1922.

Rollinson, John K.
Hoofprints of a Cowboy and United States Ranger. Caldwell, Idaho: Caxton Printers, Ltd., 1941.

————.
Pony Trails in Wyoming. Caldwell, Idaho: Caxton Printers, Ltd., 1941.

————.
Wyoming Cattle Trails. Caldwell, Idaho: Caxton Printers, Ltd., 1948.
Recollections and general information on life, customs and traditions of cowboys and the cattle trails.

Romaine, F.
Whistling Bill. New York: Thomas Nelson & Sons, 1937.

Roosevelt, Theodore
"In Cowboy Land." *Century Magazine* 46, (No. 2), (June) 1893.

————.
Ranch Life and Hunting Trail. Philadelphia: Gebbie & Co., 1903. 295 pp.

Rush, Oscar
The Open Range: Bunk House Philosophy. Caldwell, Idaho: Caxton Printers, Ltd., 1936.

Russell, Charles M.
Good Medicine; illustrated letters of Ch. Russell with an introduction by Will Rogers and a biographical note by Nancy C. Russell. Garden City, N. Y.: Doubleday, Doran & Co., Inc., 1929. xii, 162 pp.

————.
More Rawhides... with illustrations by the author. Great Falls, Mont.: Montana Newspaper Association, 1925. 59 pp., illus.

————.
Rawhide Rawlins Stories; with illustrations by the author. Great Falls, Mont.: Montana Newspaper Association, 1921. 60 pp., illus.

————.
Trails Plowed Under; introduction by Will Rogers. Garden City, New York: Doubleday Page & Co., 1927. 211 pp., illus.
"He was a wonderful story teller, and most of his pictures tell stories." (Dobie)

Ruxton, G. F.
Life in the Far West. New York: Macmillan Co., 1915. (Reprint of edition of 1849.)

Santee, Ross
Cowboy. New York: Cosmopolitan Book Corp., 1928. 257 pp., illus.
"Passages in *Cowboy* combine reality and elemental melody in a way that no other range writer excepting Charles M. Russell has achieved." (Dobie)

————.
Men and Horses. New York: Century Co., 1926. 268 pp., illus.

Shawver, Lena, comp.
Chuck Wagon Wonder; and the Range Poems of Walt Cousins. New York: Naylor Co., 1939.

Siringo, Charles A.
A Lone Star Cowboy, being fifty years experience in the saddle as cowboy, detective and New Mexico ranger, on every cow trail in the wooly west. Santa Fe, N. M.: The Author, 1919. 290 pp., illus.

————.
A Cowboy Detective. . . . Chicago: W. B. Conkey Company, 1912. 519 pp., illus.

————.
A Texas Cowboy or Fifteen Years in the Hurricane Deck of the Spanish Cow Pony. Chicago: Rand McNally & Co., 1885. 347 pp.
"The first in time of all cowboy autobiographies and first, also, in plain rollickiness." (Dobie)

————.
Riata and Spurs. Boston: Houghton Mifflin Co,. 1927. xiv, 276 pp.

Smith, Helena Huntington, and Abbott, E. C.
We Pointed Them North. New York: Farrar & Rinehart, Inc., 1939. 281 pp., illus.
An outstanding memoir of an old time cowboy, Teddy Blue Abbott.

Smith, Honora De Busk
"Cowboy Lore in Colorado." *TFSP* 9:27–45, 1931.
A story about Clay Allison and other yarns.

Steedman, Charles J.
Bucking the Sagebrush. New York: G. P. Putnam's Sons, 1904. 270 pp., illus.

Stuart, Granville
Forty Years on the Frontier. Cleveland: The Arthur H. Clark Co., 1925. 2 vols.
"Nothing better on the cowboy has ever been written than the chapter entitled 'Cattle Business'. Vol. II." (Dobie)

"They Died With Their Boots On."
Literary Digest 114:32–3, December 3, 1932.

Thorp, Jack
"Banjo in Cow Camps." *Atlantic Monthly* 156:195–203.

————.
Pardner of the Wind. Caldwell, Idaho: Caxton Printers, Ltd., 1945.
"A 'must' book for folklorists in which this pioneer collector of cowboy songs just 'speaks' folklore—and humor and information—" (E. L. Lewis)

Torchiana, Henry A. W. van Coenen
California Gringos. San Francisco: P. Elder and Company, 1930. 281 pp., illus.

Tucker, Patrick T.
Riding the High Country; illustrated by Charles M. Russell. Caldwell, Idaho: Caxton Printers, Ltd., 1933.

Warren, Billy
Ride, Cowboy, Ride. Illustrated by the author. New York: Reynald and Hitchcock, 1946. 251 pp.
> This book tells all the details of a roundup, the branding of cattle, aces, and "bucking contests" and the jolly give and take of the range.

Wellman, Paul I.
The Trampling Herd. New York: Carrick & Evans, 1939.
> "An attempt to sum up the story of the cattle range in America." (Dobie)

Westermeier, Clifford P.
Man, Beast and Dust: The Story of Rodeo. Denver, Colo.: World Press, 1947.

White, Stewart Edward
Arizona Nights. New York: The McClure Co., 1907. 351 pp., illus.

Wister, Owen
The Virginian. New York: The Macmillan Co., 1902. 504 pp.
> "The classic of cowboy novels without cows." (Dobie)

Wright, Robert M.
Dodge City, Cowboy Capital. Wichita, Kansas: Wichita Eagle Press, 1913. 344 pp.

Wright, Solomon Alexander, and Dobie, J. F.
My Rambles as Last Texas Cowboy, Hunter, Fisherman, Tie-cutter by S. A. W. Introduction by J. F. Dobie. Austin, Texas: Texas Folklore Society, 1942. xii, 159 pp.

Young, Gordon Ray
Tall in the Saddle. Garden City, New York: Doubleday, Doran & Co., 1943.
> "Packed with lively action, gripping suspenses, vivid characterization, crisp dialogue and skillful writing, here is one western novel among a thousand." (G. W. Harris)

FOLKTALES—LEGENDS

Barnes, Will C.
Tales from the X-Bar Horse Camp. Chicago: Breeder's Gazette, 1920. 217 pp., illus.

Boatright, Mody C.
Tall Tales From Texas; illustrated by E. E. Keefer. Dallas, Texas: The Southwest Press, 1934. 100 pp., illus.

Chittick, Victor L. O., ed.
Ring-Tailed Roarers: Tall Tales of the American Frontier, 1830–60. Caldwell, Idaho: The Caxton Printers, 1941. 316 pp.

Dale, E. E.
Cow Country. Norman, Oklahoma: University of Oklahoma Press, 1942.
> "Bully tales and easy history." (Dobie)

Evans, J. M., ed.
Corral Full of Stories. El Paso, Texas: The Author, 1939.

Gillilan, James David
Trail Tales. New York: The Abingdon Press, 1915. 182 pp.

Halpert, Lt. Herbert
"Montana Cowboy Folk Tales." *CFQ* 4:244–254, 1945.

James, Will
Big Enough. Illustrations by the author. New York: C. Scribner's Sons, 314 pp., illus.
Legends and stories of horses.

The Dark Horse. New York: C. Scribner's Sons, 1939. xii, 306 pp., illus.

Horses I've Known. New York: C. Scribner's Sons, 1940. xv, 280 pp., illus.

Santee, Ross
"Tales the Cowpunchers Tell." *Travel* 59:16–194, August, 1932.

Smith, Honora De Busk
"Cowboy Lore in Colorado." *TFSP* 9:27–45, 1931.
> Yarns about Clay Allison and other characters—man and animal.

Streeter, Floyd B.
Prairie Trails and Cow Towns. Boston: Chapman and Grimes, 1936.

Sutton, Fred E., and MacDonald, A. B.
Hands Up! Stories of the Six-Gun Fighters of the Old West. Indianapolis: Bobbs-Merrill Co., 1927.

Webb, W. P.
"Wild Horse Stories of Southwest Texas." *TFSP* 1:58–61, 1916.

SPEECH

Adams, Ramon R.
Cowboy Lingo. Boston: Houghton Mifflin Co., 1936. 267 pp.
> "A dictionary of cowboy words, figures of speech, picturesque phraseology, slang, etc., with explanations of many factors peculiar to range life." (Dobie)

"Cowboy Speech." *AS* 3 (No. 2):168–169, 1927.

Western Words. A Dictionary of the Range, Cow Camp and Trail. Norman, Oklahoma: University of Oklahoma Press, 1944. 182 pp.

Allen, Jules Verne
Cowboy Lore. San Antonio, Texas: Naylor Printing Co., 1933.
> Contains a glossary of Cowboy words.

Braddy, Haldeen
"Cowboy Lingo of the Texas Big Bend." *Dialect Notes* 6 (Part 15):617–621, 1937.

————.
"Some Southwestern Cowboy Lingo." *AS* 12 (No. 2) :152, 1937.

D., M. W.
"Cow Range Talk." *AS* 15:452, 1940.

Meredith, Mamie
" 'Waddies' and 'Hoboes' of the Old West." *AS* 7 (No. 4) :257–260, 1932.
"Addressing a cowboy as *waddy* would be a recognition of his proficiency."

SONGS OF THE COWBOY

GENERAL STUDIES

"A Folk-Song of Recent Origin."
Literary Digest (New York) 48:985, 1914.

Allan's Lone Star Ballads.
Galveston: 1874.

Allen, Jules Verne
Cowboy Lore. San Antonio, Texas: Naylor Printing Co., 1933.
Historical backgrounds, famous songs, glossary of cowboy words.

Barnes, W. C.
"Cowboy and his Songs." *Saturday Evening Post,* 14–15, 122, 125, 128, (June 27) 1925.

Barry, Phillips
"The Cowboy's Lament." *FSSNE* 7:16–18, 1934.
Closely related in melody to "The Unfortunate Rake."

Busch, T.
"Ballads from America's Song Bag." *Scholastic* 27:7–84, (Nov. 2) 1935.

Butterfield, Roger
"Turkeys in the Straw." *SRL* 31 (No. 5):41, 56, 1948.
The author discusses a number of current "Western," hillbilly, and "Western" hillbilly recordings. "The great majority of these," says Butterfield, "are turkeys, and all of them are corny to a greater or less degree. But when it is done right, this kind of corn is mighty appealing."

Carlson, A. D.
"Cowboy Ballads at our own Firesides." *Better Home and Garden* 10:23+, (Nov.) 1931.

Charmley, B.
"American Cowboy Songs." *Education Magazine* 56:7–84, (Oct.) 1935.

Coolidge, D.
"Cowboy Songs." *Sunset* 29:503–510, (Nov.) 1912.

"Cowboy Songs and Ballads."
Poetry 10:255–259, (Aug.) 1917.

Craddock, John R.
"Songs the Cowboys Sing." *TFSP* 6:184–192, 1934.

Crouch, C. J.
"On the Old Cattle Trails." *National Republican* 18:19–21, (March) 1931.

Davidson, Levette Jay
"Home on the Range" again. *CFQ* 3:208–211, 1944.
A discussion of the conflicting evidence of the origin of this song.

————.
"Rocky Mountain Frontier Songs." *CFQ* 2:89–112, 1943.
Texts only.

Dobie, J. Frank
"Ballads and Songs of the Frontier Folk." *TFSP* 6:121–183, 1927; 7:154–180, 1928.

————.
"El Canción Del Rancho de los Olmos." *JAFL* 36:192–195, 1923.

————.
"More Ballads and Songs of the Frontier Folk." *TFSP* 7:155–180, 1928.

————.
"Ranch Mexicans: Vaqueros." *Survey* 66:167–170, (May) 1931.

————.
"Texas-Mexican Border Broadsides." *JAFL* 36:185, 1923.

————.
Texas and South-Western Lore. Texas Folk-Lore Society, No. 6. Austin, Texas: 1927. 259 pp., music.

————.
"The Cowboy and His Songs." *Texas Review* (Austin, Texas) 5:163–169, 1920.

————.
The Longhorns. Boston: Little, Brown and Company, 1941. 388 pp.
"It should be required reading for all who wish to develop more than a superficial appreciation of cowboy songs and cattle lore." (Levette J. Davidson)

Ellis, Annie Laurie
"Folk Music 'Oh, Bury Me Not on the Lone Prairie.' A Song of Texas Cowboys." *JAFL* 14:186, 1901.

————.
"Texan Cowboy Song." *JAFL* 27:237–239, 1914.

Federal Writers' Project
Cowboy Songs, Part I and II. Nebraska Folklore Pamphlets, I, II. Federal Writers' Project in Nebraska, Lincoln: May 15, 1937; Nov. 1, 1937.

"Fiddlin' Joe's Song Corral."
A Department in the *Wild West Weekly*—to preserve the old cowboy songs and frontier ballads.

"Four Cowboy Songs."
JAFL 26:185–188, 1913.

Fox, Oscar J.
"Outline of Paper on the Songs of the American Cowboy." MTNA 21:128–130, 1926.

Furlong, Charles Willington
Let Her Buck; a story of the passing of the old west. New York: G. P. Putnam's Sons, 1921.

Gaines, Newton
"Some Characteristics of Cowboy Songs." TFSP 7:145–154, 1928.
Discussion, with musical examples of "Git Along, Little Dogies"; "The Old Chisholm Trail"; "The Trail of '83"; "Rye Whiskey."

Haley, J. Evetts
"Cowboy Songs Again." TFSP 6:198–205, 1934.
Discussion and texts (no tunes).

Handy, W. J.
"Some Early California Songs." Outwest (Los Angeles) 29:430–437, 1908. illus.

Hastings, George E.
"Hell in Texas." TFSP 9:175–182, 1931.
Historical background of this tune. Text and melody given.

Hendren, J. W.
"An English Source of 'The Trail to Mexico'." TFSP 14:270–279, 1938.
The author shows the above tune is derived from "Early, Early, in the Spring." Explanatory discussion and tunes are given.

Howard, John T.
Our American Music, Three Hundred Years of It. New York: Crowell and Company, 1939. 2nd ed. rev. and enl.
Chapter XV: Our Folk Music. Part 3: Other Sources of Folk-Songs, pp. 431–432.

Isbell, B.
"Episodes at Ranch Community Dances." TFSP 5:104–106, 1920.

Kirchwey, Freda
"Birth of a Ballad; Note on a Cow-boy Minstrel." Century 110:21–25, (May) 1925.

Knibbs, Henry Herbert
Saddle Songs and Other Verse. Boston: Houghton Mifflin Company, 1922. vii, 101 pp.

Leisy, Ernest E.
"Oh, Bury Me Not." TFSP 9:183–184, 1931.
The author shows the relationship of this song to the once popular song "The Ocean Burial." Text only.

Lomax, John A.
"Cowboy Songs." In: Encyclopaedia Britannica, Vol. 9. pp. 448–449, 1936. 14th edition.

——————.
"Cowboy Songs and Other Frontier Ballads." Bookman (a review) 32:636–637, (Feb.) 1911.

——————.
"Cowboy Songs and Other Frontier Ballads." Dial (a review) 50:261–263, (April 1) 1911.

——————.
"Cowboy Songs of the Mexican Border." The Sewanee Review 19:1–18, (Jan.) 1911.

——————.
"'Home on the Range,' Story of a famous song." Scholastic 31:17 (Dec.11) 1937.

——————.
Hunting Cowboy Songs. In: Adventures of a Ballad Hunter, Chapter III. New York: The Macmillan Company, 1947.
5 tunes with texts.

——————.
"Some Types of American Folk-Songs." JAFL 28:1–17, 1915.

——————.
"Songs of Mexican Cowboys from the Rio Grande Border." JAFL 28:376–378, 1915.

——————.
"The Story of 'Good-Bye Old Paint'." Wild West Weekly, pp. 133–134, (Feb. 10) 1934.

——————.
"Two Songs of Mexican Cowboys from the Rio Grande Border." JAFL 28:376–378, 1915.

Lomax, Lilly (Lings)
"Trail Songs of the Cowpuncher." The Overland Monthly (San Francisco) 59:24–29, 1912.

Looscan, A. B.
"The Woman of the Western Star; A Legend of the Rangers." TFSP 3:115–117, 1918.

Metzger, B.
"Ukelele Cowboys." Sunset 68:22–23 (Jan.) 1927.

Moore, Arbie
"The Texas Cowboy." TFSP 6:196–198, 1934.
Text and tune.

Mora, Joaquin
"Songs the Vaqueros Sing." TFSP 9:118–124, 1931.

Niles, John J.
"White Pioneers and Black." MQ 18:60–75, (Jan.) 1932.

"Old Cowboy Ballads."
Literary Digest 53:701–702, (Sept. 16) 1916.

Peabody, Charles
"A Texas Version of 'The White Captive'." JAFL 25:169–170, 1912.

Pound, Louise
"Joe Bowers" Again. SFQ 1 (No. 3):13–17, 1937.

——————.
"Some Texts of Western Songs." SFQ 3:25–31, 1939.

——————.
"The Southwestern Cowboy Songs and the English and Scottish Popular Ballads." Modern Philology (Chicago) 11:195–207, 1913–1914.

Randolph, Vance
"Singing Cowboy." *JAFL* 14:274, 1901.
A review.

Reynolds, Quentin
"Singing in the Sun." *Colliers* 94:22+, (Nov. 10) 1934.

Riggs, Lynn
"High, Wide and Handsome." *Singing Cowboys;* a Book of Western Songs by Margaret Larkin. *Nation* pp. 674. (Dec. 16) 1931.
A review.

Sandburg, Carl
"Songs of the Old Frontier." *Country Gentlemen* (April) 1927.

Sires, Ina
"Songs of the Open Range." *TFSP* 6:192–196, 1934.
A statement of the author's purpose in collecting cowboy songs.

Siringo, Charles A.
The Song Companion of a Lone Star Cowboy; old favorite Cow-camp songs. Santa Fe, N. M.: The Author, 1919.

"Some Frontier Ballads That Are Fit to Print." *New York Times Book Review* p. 5, (Nov. 13) 1927.

Sutton, Fred E., and MacDonald, A. B.
Hands Up! Stories of the Six-Gun Fighters of the Old West. Indianapolis: Bobbs-Merrill Company, 1927.
Contains some cowboy tunes.

"The Dying Cowboy."
JAFL 1:114, 1888; 2:291, 1889; 4:325, 1891; 5:193, 1892.

Thorp, J.
"Banjo in Cow Camps." *Atlantic Monthly* 156:195–203.

White, John I.
"Rhyme on the Range." *AS* 2 (No. 10):440–442, 1927.
Discussion of rhyme-scheme found in cowboy songs.

Whitmire, Alice Gideon
"The Song of the Cowboy." In: *Who Is Who in Music,* 1941 Edition. pp. 564–565. Chicago: Lee Stern Press, 1940.

Will, G. F.
"Four Cowboy Songs." *JAFL* 26:185–188, 1913.

———.
"Songs of Western Cowboys." *JAFL* 22:256–261, 1909.

"'Young Lochinvar.' Musical prgoress in the west." *Etude* 56:355–356, (June) 1938. Illus.

COLLECTIONS

See: American Folksong and Ballad Collections, pp. 85-90, 118-20.

American Cowboy Songs.
Toronto: G. V. Thompson, 1944.

Arkansas Woodchoppers; Cowboy Songs with Yodel Arrangements. Chicago: M. M. Cole Publishing House, 1931.

Autry, Gene
Cowboy Songs of Ranch and Range. Milwaukee: Krueger, Dover Company, 1936. (new ed.)

———.
Rhymes of the Range. Evanston, Ill.: Frontier Publishers, 1933. For voice and piano.

Bingham, Seth, arr.
Five Cowboy Songs. New York: The H. W. Gray Company, 1930. Voice and piano.
Content: Days of '49; Root Hog or Die; The Dying Cowboy; Fuller and Warren; Dogie Song.

Botsford, Florence Hudson
Folk Song of Many People, with English versions by American poets. Compiled and edited by Florence Hudson Botsford. New York: The Women's Press, 1921–1922.

Briegel, George F.
Home on the Range: Cowboy Song Book. New York: Geo. F. Briegel, 1674 Broadway: Voice and piano.
Twenty-five Cowboy tunes. Out of this group only five are authentic folk tunes, the rest are composed imitations. The five are: Home on the Range; The Big Rock Candy Mountain; Goodbye Old Paint; The Big Corral, and Echo Canyon (Mormon Railroad Song).

Carr, Robert Van
Cowboy Lyrics. Chicago: W. B. Conkey Company, 1908. 182 pp. Reprinted in Boston: Small, Maynard & Co., 1912. xv, 229 pp., col. front.

Clark, Kenneth S.
The Cowboy Sings. New York: Paull Pioneer Music Company, 1932.
Traditional and modern tunes. Male quartet, piano, guitar, tenor banjo, ukelele.

———.
Cowboy Songs. New York: Paull-Pioneer Music Company, 1932.

Cowboy Ballads.
Portland, Ore.: American Music, Inc., 1940. Folio 5.
Containing twenty new songs, compiled with words and music. Guitar, Ukulele and Banjo Chords.

Don White's Folio of Western and Hill Country Songs. Portland, Ore.: American Music, Inc.

Durham, A. M.
Pioneer Songs. Salt Lake City: Daughters of Utah Pioneers, 1932.

Farwell, Arthur
Folk Songs of the West and South: Negro, Cowboy, and Spanish-Californian. Harmonized by A. Farwell. The Wa-Wan Series of American Compositions, Vol. 4, No. 27. Newton Centre, Mass.: The Wa-Wan Press, 1905.

From Mesa and Plain. Indian, Cowboy and Negro Sketches for pianoforte by Arthur Farwell. Wa-Wan Series of American Compositions, Vol. 4, No. 28. Newton Centre, Mass.: The Wa-Wan Press, 1905.

Finger, Charles J.
Frontier Ballads Heard and Gathered by Charles J. Finger. New York: Doubleday, Page and Company, 1927.

————.
Sailor Chanties and Cowboy Songs. "Little Blue Books," No. 301. Girard, Kans.: Haldeman-Julius.
Texts only.

Flanders, Helen H.
A Garland of Green Mountain Song. New York: Schirmer, 1934.

Fred Scott's Songs of the Open Road. Portland, Ore.: American Music, Inc.

Frey, Hugo, ed.
American Cowboy Songs. New York: Robbins Music Corp., 1936. enl. ed.

German, George B.
Cowboy Campfire Ballads, compiled and sung by George B. German. Yankton, S. D.: 1929. 38 pp., texts only.

Golden West Cowboys. Portland, Ore.: American Music, Inc. Folio No. 1.
General collection for voice and piano. Some of the tunes are not authentic.

Grant-Schaefer, G. A.
Cowboys at Play. Boston: Schmidt Company. A comedy of the plains for mixed voices. For Junior High School. Old tunes used. Time of performance forty minutes.

Hank, the Yodeling Ranger; Cowboy Songs. Toronto: G. V. Thompson, 1944.

Hanson, J. M.
Frontier Ballads. Chicago: A. C. McClurg and Company, 1910.

Klickman, F. H., and Sherwin, S.
Songs of the Saddle. New York: Sam Fox Publishing Company, 1933.

Larkin, Margaret, and Black, Helen
Singing Cowboy. New York: Alfred A. Knopf, 1931. 196 pp., illus.
Music arranged for voice and piano.

Lomax, John Avery
Cowboy Songs and Other Frontier Ballads, collected by John A. Lomax. With an introduction by Barrett Wendell. New York: Sturgis and Walton, 1910. xxvi, 191 pp.

————.
Cowboy Songs and Other Frontier Ballads. New York: The Macmillan Company, 1922.

Songs of the Cattle Trail and the Cow Camp. Foreword by William Lyon Phelps. New York: The Macmillan Company, 1919. xi, 189 pp.

————, **and Alan**
Cowboy Songs and Other Frontier Ballads. New York: The Macmillan Company, 1938. Revised and enlarged. Copyright 1910, 1916 and 1938. Edward N. Waters, music editor.
Texts and music.

Maddy, Homer Basil, and Phillips, Loren
Ballads of Mountain and Prairie. Shelbyville, Ind.: Blue River Press, 1941. 32 pp.

Riggs, Lynn
Cowboy Songs, Folk Songs and Ballads from "Green Grow the Lilacs." New York: Samuel French, 1932.

Sandburg, Carl
The American Songbag. New York: Harcourt, Brace & Company, 1927.
Section—"The Great Open Spaces"—contains 15 cowboy tunes. Voice and piano.

Siegmeister, Elie, and Downes, Olin
A Treasury of American Song. New York: Howell, Soskin & Co., 1940.
Section—"The Old Chizzum Trail."—contains 6 tunes, with accomp.

Sires, Ina, and Repper, C.
Songs of the Open Range. Boston: C. C. Birchard Company, 1928.

Siringo, Charles A.
The Song Companion of a Lone Star Cowboy; old favorite cow-camp songs. Sante Fe, N. M.: The Author, 1919. 42 pp.
Songs and music.

Sleepy Hollow Cowboys and Camp Girls. Portland, Ore.: American Music, Inc. Folio No. 1.

Songs of the Roundup Rangers: 25 Complete Cowboy Songs. New York: Vogel Music Company, 112 W. 44th Street. For voice and piano.

Thorp, N. Howard
Songs of the Cowboys, compiled by N. Howard Thorp ("Jack Thorp"). With an introduction by Alice Corbin Henderson. Boston: Houghton Mifflin Company, 1921. xxii, 184 pp.
No music.

White, John, and Shakley, George
The Lonesome Cowboy—Songs of the Plains and Hills. New York: George T. Worth and Company, 1930.
With chord accompaniment for Ukulele, Tenor Banjo and Guitar.

DANCES

Craddock, J. R.
"The Cowboy Dance." *TFSP* 2:31–37, 1917.

Parrett, Vanita
"Cowboy Dance Calls." *TFSP* 18:115–125, 1943.
Texts of a dozen square dance calls.

Scott, Roy S.
"The Cowboy Dance of the Northwest." *TFSP* 4:53–58, 1925.

Shaw, Lloyd
Cowboy Dances, a collection of Western square dances; with a foreword by Sherwood Anderson; appendix. Cowboy dance tunes arranged by Frederick Knorr. Caldwell, Idaho: Caxton Printers, 1939. (Fifth Printing, 1941) 397 pp., 144 pl. 89 diagrams, 35 musical numbers.
Excellent manual.

ARRANGEMENTS:
(Individual Titles)

―――――: *Voice and Piano*

"All Day on the Prairie."
Guion, D.: Schirmer.

"Come All Ye Jolly Cowboys."
Fox, O. J.: Carl Fischer: Voice and piano (high and low).

"Cowboy's Meditation."
Fox, O. J.: Schirmer.

"Cowboy's Meditation."
Guion, D.: Schirmer.

"Greer County."
Fox, O. J.: Carl Fischer.

"Home on the Range."
Eckstein, M.: Carl Fischer.

"Home on the Range."
Fox, O. J.: Schirmer.

"Home on the Range."
Guion, D.: Schirmer.

"Little Joe, the Wrangler."
Guion, D.: Schirmer.

"Lonesome Song of the Plains."
Guion, D.: Schirmer.

"McCaffie's Confession" Texas Frontier Ballad.
Fox, O. J.: Schirmer.

"McCaffie's Confession."
Guion, D.: Schirmer.

"O, Bury Me Not on the Lone Prairie."
Guion, D.: Carl Fischer.

"Old Paint."
Fox, O. J.: Carl Fischer.

"Ol' Paint."
Guion, D.: Schirmer.

"Ride, Cowboy, Ride."
Guion, D.: Schirmer.

"Rounded Up In Glory."
Fox, O. J.: Carl Fischer.

"Roy Bean." Texas Frontier Ballad.
Fox, O. J.: Schirmer.

"Roy Bean." Texas Frontier Ballad.
Guion, D.: Schirmer.

"Sail Away for the Rio Grande."
Fox, O. J.: Schirmer.

"Sail Away for the Rio Grande."
Guion, D.: Schirmer.

"Sam Bass."
Fox, O. J.: Carl Fischer.

"Texas Cowboy's Last Song."
Fox, O. J.: Carl Fischer.

"The Bold Vaquero."
Guion, D.: Schirmer.

"The Cowboy's Dream."
Guion, D.: Schirmer.

"The Cowboy's Lament" ("O, Bury Me Not").
Fox, O. J.: Schirmer.

"The Cowboy's Last Song."
Fox, O. J.: Carl Fischer: Voice and piano (high and low).

"The Hell-Bound Train."
Weston, P.: Schirmer.

"The Lone Prairie."
Farwell, A.: Schirmer.

"The Old Chisholm Trail."
Fox, O. J.: Carl Fischer.

"When the Work's All Done This Fall."
Guion, D.: Carl Fischer.

"Whoopie Ti Yi Yo."
Fox, O. J.: Carl Fischer.

―――――: *Female Voices*

"All Day on the Prairie."
Guion, David: Schirmer: SA (boy's voices).

"Home on the Range."
Lester, W.: Gamble Hinged: SSA.

"Oh, Bury Me Not on the Lone Prairie."
Finney, Ross Lee: Volkwein: SSAA.

"Whoopie Ti Yi Yo."
Treharne, B.: Boston Music Co.: SSA.

―――――: *Male Voices*

"All Day on the Prairie."
Guion-Riegger: Schirmer: TB, TTB, TTBB.

"All Day on the Prairie."
Guion-Treharne: Schirmer: TB, TTB, TTBB.

"Five Cowboy Songs."
Bingham, S.: H. W. Gray: TTBB.

"Git Along, Little Dogies."
In: H. & M. Auditorium Series, No. 48. Andersen, A. O.: Hall & McCreary: TBB.

"Git Along, Little Dogies."
Kun, L.: Ricordi: TTBB.

"Good-bye Ol' Paint."
Wilson, H. R.: Hall and McCreary: TBB.

"Greatest Miracle of All."
Guion, David: Schirmer: TTBB.

"Home on the Range."
In: H. & M. Auditorium Series, No. 48. Andersen, A. O.: Hall and McCreary: TBB.

"Home on the Range."
Fox-Page: Fischer: TTBB.

"Home on the Range."
In: H. & M. Auditorium Series, No. 9. Grant-Fishburn: Hall and McCreary: TTBB.

"Home on the Range."
Guion-Riegger: Schirmer: TB, TTB.

"Home on the Range."
Kun, L. Ricordi: TTBB.

"Home on the Range."
Lester: Gamble Hinged: TB.

"Home on the Range."
Tidmarsh: Birchard: TTBB.

"Lonesome Song of the Plains."
Guion, David: Schirmer: TTBB.

"Oh, Bury Me Not on the Lone Prairie."
Finney, Ross Lee: Volkwein: TTBB.

"Old Paint."
Fox, O. J.: Carl Fischer: TTBB.

"Red River Valley."
Scott, T.: Words and Music, Inc.: TTBB.
Fred Waring Glee Club Arrangement.

"Ride, Cowboy, Ride!"
Guion-Downing: Schirmer: TB, TTB, TTBB.

"Rounded Up in Glory."
Fox, O. J.: Carl Fischer: TTBB.

"Texas May I Never Wander."
Guion, David: Schirmer: TTBB.

"The Bold Vaquero."
Guion-Treharne: Schirmer: TTB.

"The Cowboy's Dream."
Guion, D.: Schirmer: TTBB.

"The Cowboy's Lament."
Fox, O. J.: Schirmer: TTBB.

"The Dogie Song."
Treharne: Boston Music Co.: TBB.

"The Dying Cowboy."
Bingham, S.: H. W. Gray: TTBB.

"The Little Old Sod Shanty."
Treharne, B.: Willis: TTB.

"The Trail to Santa Fe."
A Song of the Old Southwest. Baldwin, R. L.: Schirmer: TTBB.

————: *Mixed Voices*

"Cowboy's Lament."
Binder, A. W.: Elkan-Vogel: SATB.

"Greatest Miracle of All."
Guion, David: Schirmer: SATB.

"Home on the Range."
Guion-Riegger: Schirmer: SATB.

"Home on the Range."
Guion-Wagner: Schirmer: SSAATBB.

"Home on the Range."
Nightingale, M.: G. Schirmer: SATB.

"Lonesome Song of the Plain."
Guion, David: Schirmer: SATB.

"Night Herding Song."
Wilson, H. R.: Hall and McCreary: SATB-Div.

"Old Joe Clark."
Kleinsinger, G.: Associated: SATB.

"Ol' Paint."
Guion, David: Schirmer: SATB.

"Poor Lonesome Cowboy."
Grant-Schaefer, G. A.: Schmidt: SATB.
Junior High School.

"Rattlesnake."
Grant-Schaefer, G. A.: Schmidt: SATB.
Junior High School.

"Rounded Up In Glory."
Fox, O. J.: C. Fischer: SATB, with Bar. Solo.

"Texas May I Never Wander."
Guion, David: Schirmer: SATB.

"The Cowboy's Dream."
Guion, David: Schirmer: SATB.

"The Cowboy's Dream."
Guion-Treharne: Schirmer: SAB.

"The Dogies."
Treharne, B.: Willis: SAB.

"The Dying Cowboy."
In: H. & M. Auditorium Series, No. 21. Sheehan, R.: Hall and McCreary: Boy's voices, SATB.

"The Lone Prairie."
Wilson, H. R.: Hall and McCreary: SATB, Bar. Solo.

"The Mule."
Grant-Schaefer, G. A.: Schmidt: SATB.
Junior High School.

"The Old Chisholm Trail."
Clokey, J.: J. Fischer and Bro.: SSATBB.

"The Sunset Trail."
Cadman, Charles W.: White Smith: SATB.

"Western Star."
Delaney, Robert M.: MS: 5 part chorus, orchestra.

"Whoopee Ti Yi Yo."
In: H. & M. Auditorium Series, No. 10. Sheehan, R.: Hall and McCreary: SA Bar. (changing voices.)

—————: *Piano*

"Fuller and Warren."
Brodsky-Triggs: J. Fischer: 2 Pianos, 4 hands.

"Home on the Range."
Wallis: Schirmer: Piano (easy).

"Streets of Laredo."
Harris, Roy: C. Fischer: Piano.

—————: *String Quartet*

Kurtz, Edward
From the West-Suite. String Quartet. MS.

—————: *Orchestra*

Copland, Aaron
Billy the Kid—Suite from the Ballet. New
York: Boosey and Hawkes.

—————.
Four Dance Episodes from "Rodeo." Buckaroo
Holiday, Corral Nocturne, Saturday Night
Waltz, Hoe-Down. New York: Boosey and
Hawkes, for full orchestra.

—————.
Hoe-Down (from Rodeo). New York: Boosey
and Hawkes: String Orchestra.

—————.
*"Prairie Night and Celebration Dance" (from
Billy the Kid).* New York: Boosey and Hawkes:
Chamber Orchestra.

Gillis, Don
Cowtown-Suite. MS.

—————.
"Prairie Poem." MS.

Goldmark, Rubin
Call of the Plains. G. Schirmer.

Helfer, Walter
"Old Paint"—Symphonic Sketch. MS. for full
orchestra.

"Home on the Range."
Monger, H.: Theodore Presser Co.

Jones, Charles
Cowboy Song. New York: C. Fischer. For oboe
solo, percussion, and strings.

Kleinsinger, George
A Western Rhapsody. New York: E. B. Marks.
Full Orchestra and piano.
Based on Western Cowboy folksongs.

Maganini, Quinto
"Moonlight on the Painted Desert," from
Western Sketches. New York: Musicus.

McKay, George F.
Fantasy on Western Folksong. New York:
Boosey and Hawkes.
Chamber Orchestra—10 instruments.

—————.
Variants on a Texas Tune. MS.—for Chamber
Orchestra, 14 instruments.

Shepherd, Arthur
Horizons. Four Western Pieces. New York:
Birchard.

Siegmeister, Elie
Prairie Legend. New York: Leeds Music Corp.

—————.
Western Suite. New York: Leeds Music Corp.

—————: *Band*

"Home on the Range."
Monger, H. S.: Theodore Presser Co.

"Little Joe the Wrangler."
Hill: Educational: Full Band.

"Prairie Legend."
Siegmeister, E.: Leeds: Band.

Stage Work

Copland, Aaron
Billy the Kid—Ballet. New York: Boosey and
Hawkes. Woodwind by twos, orchestra.

—————.
Rodeo-Ballet. New York: Boosey and Hawkes,
woodwind by twos, orchestra.

Guion, David
Cowboy Production and Dance. MS. Stage
Presentation.

RECORDS

Album Collections

American Cowboy Classics.
Dick Thomas, baritone, and Frank Novak and
the Sourwood Mountain Boys. 4–10". MU–63

Cowboy.
In Archive of American Folk Song, Library of
Congress, Music Division, Washington, D. C.

Cowboy (Texas).
In Archive of American Folk Song, Library of
Congress, Music Division, Washington, D. C.

Cowboy Favorites.
Tex Ritter, voice-guitar. 4–10". CA–8141
Contents: "San Antonio Rose," "Try Me One
More Time," "Boll Weevil," "Rounded up in
Glory," "Blood on the Saddle," "The Chisholm
Trail," "Bad Brahma Bull," "Rye Whiskey."

Cowboy Songs.
Cisco Huston, vocal-guitar. 3–10". DISC–608
Contents: Blue Yodel No. 2; Drunken Rat;
Roving Gambler; Philadelphia Lawyer; Tying a
Knot in the Devil's Tail; Willy My Darling.

Cowboy Songs.
  The Ranch Boys.   DE–65
    Contents: Cowboy's Dream; Strawberry Roan; The Chisholm Trail; The Yellow Rose of Texas; Clementine; Little Ah Sid; Little Old Sod Shanty on the Claim; Goodbye Old Paint; Buffalo Gals; Cowboy Dance, Git Along Little Dogies; Little Joe the Wrangler; Bury Me Not on the Prairie; Cowboy's Lament; Cowboy Jack; Red River Valley; Big Corral; Sweet Bobby from Pike; Home on the Range.

Frontier Ballads and Cowboy Songs.
  Bill Bender, Clayton McMichon and a country dance orchestra.   ASCH–410
    Contents: Sam Hall; I Was Born 10,000 Years Ago; Old Joe Clark; Arkansas Traveler; Sweet Betsy from Pike; Mustang Grey; Jesse James and Buffalo Skinners.

Home on the Range.
  A Collection of Cowboy Songs.   DE–1427/9

Mexican Cowboy Songs.
  Los Rancheros.   DE–A276 (18208–12)

Songs of the West.
  Red River David, vocal-guitar.   SO–464
    Contents: Is the Range Still Open; Old Faithful; Wagon Trail; Red River Valley; The Last Round Up; Empty Saddles; Take Me Back to My Boots and Saddle; Home On the Range.

The Old Chisholm Trail (American Southwest).
  Tony Kraber acc. self on guitar. 3–10". KE–104
    Contents: The Old Chisholm Trail; Green Grow the Lilacs; Whiskey, Rye Whiskey; The Tenderfoot; Blood on the Saddle; The Boll Weevil Song; The Next Big River.

U. S. Library of Congress. Division of Music. Folklore Section.
  Cowboy Songs, Ranchers' Reminiscences, Square Dances, Fiddle Tunes, Negro Work Songs, Game Songs, Blues and Spitirituals. John A. Lomax, Aug.– Sept., 1942. AAFS–LC

——————.

  Recordings of Cowboy Songs Made in Texas by John A. Lomax.   AAFS–LC

Individual Titles

"A Cowboy's Lament."
  Burl Ives, voice-guitar.   DE–8082

"Abalone."
  In: *Songs of Old California.* F. Luther, Z. Layman and Century Quartet.   DE–49

"Adelita."
  In: *Songs of Old California.* Frank Luther; Zora Layman and Century Quartet.   DE–49

"Alla en el Rancho Grande."
  T. Dorsey and his Clambake Seven.   VI–26370

"Along the Santa Fe Trail."
  Dick Jurgens and Orchestra.   OK–5858

"Beaver Creek."
  The Prairie Ramblers.   OK–05892

"Beyond the Cloud."
  Rangers Quartet.   OK–06569

"Big Corral."
  Frank Luther and Trio.   DE–1428

"Big Corral."
  Ranch Boys—vocal trio.   DE–2646

"Billy the Kid."
  Vernon Dalhart, vocal-guitar.   BR–100

"Blood on the Saddle."
  Tony Kraber, vocal-guitar.   KE–506B

"Buffalo Skinners."
  In: *Frontier Ballads and Cowboy Songs.*
                         ASCH–410

"Bury Me Not on the Prairie."
  Ranch Boys, vocal.   DE–2645

"Bury Me Not on the Lone Prairie."
  Carl T. Sprague.   VI–20122

"Bury Me Not on the Lone Prairie."
  Dick Thomas, Frank Novak and the Sourwood Mountain Boys.   MU–299

"By the Lake Where Drooped the Willow."
  F. Luther and Z. Layman.   DE–2431

"Carry Me Back to the Lone Prairie."
  James Melton, tenor-piano.   VI–25185

"Chisholm Trail."
  Frank Luther and Trio.   DE–1428

"Cielite Lindo."
  In: *Songs of Old California.* Frank Luther, Zora Layman and Century Quartet.   DE–49

"Cowboy Dance."
  Ranch Boys, vocal.   DE–2644

"Cowboy's Dream."
  Carl T. Sprague.   VI–20122

"Cowboy Jack."
  Callahan Bros., vocals.   OK–03171

"Cowboy Jack."
  Esmereldy and Dick Thomas, Frank Novak and the Sourwood Mountain Boys.   MU–298–B

"Cowboy Jack."
  Ranch Boys, vocal.   DE–2645

"Cowboy Serenade."
  Millers Orchestra.   BB–11235

"Cowboy's Lament."
  Burl Ives, vocal-guitar.   DE–A431

"Cowboy's Lament."
  In Album: *The Wayfaring Stranger,* Set K–3. Burl Ives, vocal-guitar.   OK–6315, DE–A431

"Cowboy's Lament."
  Ranch Boys, vocal.   DE–2645

"Cowboy's Meditation."
  Luther and Trio, vocal.   DE–1427

"Cripple Creek."
Light Crust Doughboys. OK–05653

"Death Valley."
Blind Boy Fuller, vocal. OK–03420

"En el Rancho Grande" (Mexican Cowboy).
Cugat's Orchestra. VI–24673

"Girl I Left Behind Me."
Orville Knapp and Orchestra. DE–554

"Girl I Left Behind Me."
Frank Luther and Trio, vocal. DE–1428

"Girl I Left Behind Me."
Waller's Rhythm Group. UN–25116

"Goodbye Old Paint."
"Tex" Ritter, vocal-guitar. ME–12903

"Goodnight, Little Sweetheart."
Bob Wills and Texas Playboys. OK–06530

"Green Grow the Lilacs."
Tony Kraber, vocal-guitar. KE–505B

"Sam Hill."
In: *Frontier Ballads and Cowboy Songs*. Bill Bender, Clayton McMichon and Dance Orchestra. ASCH–410

"Headin' for That Land of Gold."
Montana Slim, the Yodeling Cowboy. BB–8983

"Home on the Range."
Jules Allen, vocal. VI–21627

"Home on the Range."
In Album: *Cowboy Songs*. Bing Crosby and Orchestra. DE–69

"Home on the Range."
Gould String Orchestra. DE–18206

"Home on the Range."
In Album: *Home on the Range*. Frank Luther and Trio, instrumental accompaniment. DE–1427

"Home on the Range."
Emile Renan, baritone; Lydia Mason, accompanist. CO–36134

"Home on the Range."
John Charles Thomas, baritone-piano. VI–1525

"Home on the Range."
Dick Thomas, Frank Novak and the Sourwood Mountain Boys. MU–301–A

"I Ain't Got No Home In This World Anymore."
Guthrie, vocal. VI–26624

"I'm Building a Home."
Acuff and Mountain Boys. OK–05403

"I'm Thinking Tonite of My Blue Eyes."
Atcher, vocal. OK–05134

"I Ride An Old Paint."
Carl Sandburg, vocal-guitar. MU–207–B

"I Was Born 4,000 Years Ago."
In: *American Folk Songs Album*. Luther; Layman, Stokes, vocal-guitar-fiddle-bass. DE–25

"I Was Born 10,000 Years Ago."
In: *Frontier Ballads and Cowboy Songs*. Bill Bender, Clayton McMichon, and Dance Orchestra. ASCH–410

"Jesse James."
In: *Frontier Ballads and Cowboy Songs*. Bill Bender, Clayton McMichon, and Dance Orchestra. ASCH–410

"Jesse James."
Riley Pluckett, vocal-guitar. CO–15033–D

"John Hardy."
Buell Kazee, vocal. BR–144

"John Hardy Was a Desperate Little Man."
The Carter Family, vocals and guitar. BB–6033–B

"Last Round-Up."
Ranch Boys, vocal trio. DE–5017

"Last Roundup."
Dick Thomas with Frank Novak and the Sourwood Mountain Boys. MU–300

"Little Dogies."
Dick Devall of Reed, Okla. In: *Anglo-American Songs and Ballads*. Album 20. AAFS–100

"Little Old Shanty on the Claim."
Ranch Boys, vocal. DE–2643

"Mustang Grey."
In: *Frontier Ballads and Cowboy Songs*. Bill Bender, Clayton McMichon and Dance Orchestra. ASCH–410

"My Sweetheart's A Cowboy."
Dick Devall of Reed, Okla. In: *Anglo-American Songs and Ballads*. Album 20. AAFS–100

"New Dry Bones."
Mitchell's Christian Singers. OK–03024

"Night Herding Song."
In: *Folk Songs of the Americas*. Vocal and instrumental accompaniment. VI–P55

"Old Chisholm Trail."
Jenkins, vocal. VI–24546

"Old Chisholm Trail."
"Mac" and His Haywire Orchestra. VI–21421

"Old Chisholm Trail."
Dick Thomas, Frank Novak and the Sourwood Mountain Boys. MU–299–A

"Old Chisholm Trail."
Marc Williams, vocal-guitar. DE–5106

"Ole Faithful."
R. Fox Band. DE–326

"Ole Faithful."
Ranch Boys, vocal trio. DE–5061

"Old Joe Clark."
In: *Frontier Ballads and Cowboy Songs*. Bill Bender, Clayton McMichon, and Dance Orchestra.   ASCH–410

"Old Joe Clark."
Frank Luther Singers.   DE–23248

"Peter Gray."
In Album: *Wayfaring Stranger*, K–3. Burl Ives, vocal-guitar.   OK–6317

"Prairieland Lullaby."
Spivak and Orchestra.   OK–6036

"Ramblin' Cowboy."
Carson Robinson, vocal.   VI–33–0509

"Red River Valley."
"Mac" and His Haywire Orchestra.   VI–21421

"Red River Valley."
Dick Thomas, Frank Novak and the Sourwood Mountain Boys.   MU–301–B

"Red Whiskey."
Dick Devall of Reed, Okla. In: *Anglo-American Songs and Ballads*. Album 20. AAFS–100

"Ridin' Down That Old Texas Trail."
The Westerners, vocal.   OK–05740

"Ridin' High."
Massey and Westerners.   OK–06502

"Rye Whiskey."
Montana Slim and The Big Hole Bronco Busters.   VI–20–2561

"Rye Whiskey, Rye Whiskey."
"Tex" Ritter, vocal-guitar.   ME–12664

"Sioux Indians."
Marc Williams, vocal-guitar.   DE–5011

"Sittin' By the Old Corral."
Montana Slim, vocal-guitar.   VI–33–0510

"Smoky Mountain Rag."
Acuff and Mountain Boys.   OK–05450

"Strawberry Roan."
Frank Luther and Trio, vocal.   DE–1429

"Strawberry Roan."
Ranch Boys, vocal trio.   DE–2642

"Sweet Betsey from Pike."
In Album: *Wayfaring Stranger*, K–3. Burl Ives, vocal-guitar.   OK–6317

"Sweet Betsy from Pike."
In: *Frontier Ballads and Cowboy Songs*. Bill Bender, Clayton McMichon and Country Dance Orchestra.   ASCH–410

"Sweet Betsy from Pike."
In: *Songs of Old California*. F. Luther, Z. Layman and Century Quartet.   DE–49

"Take Me Back to Col-ler-ran-da Fer to Stay."
Chuck Wagon Gang.   OK–02983

"Take Me Back to my Boots and Saddle."
John Charles Thomas, Baritone.   VI–Y313

"Take Me Back to My Boots and Saddle."
Dick Thomas, Frank Novak and the Sourwood Mountain Boys.   MU–298–A

"The Cowboy's Dream."
William and Cowboys.   DE–03892

"The Cowboy's Lament."
Ken Maynard, guitar.   CO–2310–D

"The Dying Cowboy."
Dick Devall of Reed Oklahoma. In: *Anglo-American Songs and Ballads*. Album 20.
                                 AAFS–100

"The Hammock."
In: *Songs of Old California*. Frank Luther, Zora Layman and Century Quartet.   DE–49

"The Horse Named Bill."
In: *Recital from "American Songbag."* Carl Sandburg, vocal-guitar.   MU–11

"The Kansas Boys."
Tony Kraber, vocal-guitar.   KE–507B

"The Last Round-Up."
Gene Autry, vocal-guitar.   OK–04485

"The Last Round Up."
Bing Crosby and Orchestra.   OK–2879

"The Last Round Up."
Dick Thomas, Frank Novak and The Sourwood Mountain Boys.   MU–300–A

"The Lone Star Trail."
Ken Maynard, guitar.   CO–2310–D

"The Mail Must Go Through."
Roy Rogers, vocal.   OK–04840

"The Next Big River."
Tony Kraber, vocal-guitar.   KE–507B

"The Old Chisholm Trail."
Tony Kraber, vocal-guitar.   KE–505A

"The Sioux Indians."
Sung by Alex Moore at Austin, Texas, 1940. Recorded by John A., and Bess Lomax. In: *Album 1*, Anglo-American Ballads, Library of Congress—Recordings, 1942.   AAFS5–B

"The Tenderfoot."
Tony Kraber, vocal-guitar.   KE–506B

"The Wheel of the Wagon is Broken."
Patsy Montana, vocal.   OK–04518

"The Zebra Dun."
Tex Fletcher, vocal-guitar.   DE–5302

"They Cut Down the Old Pine Tree."
F. Luther and vocal trio.   DE–5009

"Trail to Mexico."
F. Luther and vocal trio.   DE–1429

"Utah Carroll."
Cartwright Brothers, vocal-guitar.
CO–15410–D

"West of Rainbow Trail."
Montana Slim, the Yodeling Cowboy. BB–8983

"When Its Springtime in the Rockies."
Gene Autry, vocal-guitar. OK–03448

"When the White Azaleas Start Blooming."
Swift Jewel Cowboys. OK–04737

"Whiskey, Rye Whiskey."
Tony Kraber, vocal-guitar. KE–506A

"Whoopee-ti-yi-yo" (Git Along, Little Dogies).
Jenkens, vocal. VI–24546

"Whoopee Ti Yi Yo."
John White (The Lonesome Cowboy), vocal-guitar. PE–12712–B

"Zebra Dun."
F. Luther and vocal trio. DE–1428

THE LUMBERJACK

THE LUMBERJACK

See: Paul Bunyan in *American Characters,* pp. 689-92.

FOLKLORE

GENERAL STUDIES AND COLLECTIONS

Averill, Gerald
Ridge Runner. Philadelphia, Pa.: J. B. Lippincott Co., 1948. 217 pp.
The author tells these stories "With the skill and technique of the deacon-seat narrator, and the book as a whole becomes a very personal thing in all the magnificence of deep-Maine wood story telling." (John Gould).

Bartlett, Stanley Foss
Beyond the Sowdyhunk, with illustrations by the author. Portland, Me.: Falmouth Book House, 1937. 164 pp., illus.
A collection of short stories dealing with life and customs of the lumbermen of Maine.

Bartlett, William W.
Logging Camp Diversion and Humor. In: *History, Tradition and Adventure in the Chippewa Valley,* (pp. 232–236.) Chippewa Falls, Wis.: The Chippewa Printer, 1929.

Beck, Earl Clifton
Lore of the Lumber Camps. Detroit, Mich.: University of Michigan Press, 1949. xii, 348 pp.

Belding, George Angus
Tales from the Presque Isle Woods. New York: The Exposition Press, 1946. 124 pp.
Poems of life and lore of the lumberjacks.

Blair, Walter A.
A Raft Pilot's Log; a History of the Great Rafting Industry on the Upper Mississippi, 1840–1915. Cleveland: The Arthur H. Clark Co., 1930. 328 pp., illus., bibl.

Brown, A. A.
Lumbering on the Cumberland, a Romance Taken from Life. Cincinnati: The Lumber Worker Company, 1887. 136 pp., illus.

Buchanan, Iva L.
"Lumbering and Logging in the Puget Sound Region in Territorial Days." *Pacific Northwest Quarterly* (Seattle) 27:34–53, 1936.

Colvin, Addison Beecher
Lumbermen "Lew"; a story of fact, fancy and fiction, by Harvester Hiram (pseud.). Glenns Falls, N. Y.: Glenns Falls Publishing Co., 1918. 117 pp.

Conklin, Edwin P.
"Logging on Puget Sound, as Illustrated in the Lives of Sol Simpson and Mark E. Reed." *Americana* (Somerville) 29:256–283, 1935.

Cox, William T.
Fearsome Creatures of the Lumberwoods, with a Few Desert and Mountain Beasts. Washington, D. C.: Press of Judd and Detweiler, Inc., 1910.

Curl, Mervin James
"Fact and Fable of the Life of the Northern Woodsmen." *Stone & Webster Journal* (Boston) 24:200–210, 1919.

Durant, Edward W.
"Lumbering and Steamboating on the St. Croix River." *Minnesota Historical Society, Collections.* 10 (pt. 2):645–675, 1905.

Folsom, William Henry Carman
"History of Lumbering in the St. Croix Valley, with Biographical Sketches." *Minnesota Historical Society. Collections (St. Paul)* 9:291–324, 1901.

Fraser, Joshua
Shanty, Forest and River Life in the Backwoods of Canada. By the author of "Three Months Among the Moose." Montreal: J. Lovell & Son, 1883. 361 pp., illus.

Giroux, Télesphore
Anciens Chantiers du St.-Meurice. Les Trois-Rivières, Quebec: Les Éditions du Bien Public, 1935. 131 pp., illus.
Life, work, traditions of the chantymen of Quebec.

Glover, W. H.
"Lumber Rafting on the Wisconsin River." *Wisconsin Magazine of History* 25:155–177, 308–324, 1941. Bibl.

Grainger, M. Allerdale
Woodsmen of the West. Illustrated. London: E. Arnold, 1906. ix, 206 pp., illus.
Life and lore of the lumbermen of the Canadian west.

Handy, Ray DeWitt
Paul Bunyan and His Big Blue Ox; Stories and Pictures of the Lumberjack Hero of American Folklore. Chicago: Rand, McNally & Co., 1937. 64 pp., illus.

Havighurst, Walter
Upper Mississippi. A Wilderness Saga. New York: Farrar & Rinehart, 1937. 258 pp.
Part I is called: "The Epic of Lumber."

Holbrook, Stewart H.
Holy Old Mackinaw; Natural History of the American Lumberjack. New York: Macmillan Co., 1938. viii, 278 pp., bibl.
Stories of the lumberjacks in Maine, in the Middle West, and in the Pacific Northwest. Logger talk (pp. 258–265).

————.
Iron Brew; a Century of American Ore and Steel. New York: The Macmillan Co., 1940. viii, 352 pp.

——————.
"Lumberjacks Saturday Night." *American Mercury*, 56:331–337. (March) 1943.

Holmes, Fred L.
Alluring Wisconsin. Milwaukee: E. M. Hale & Co., 1937. 480 pp., with map and plates from original photographs.

Holter, Anton M.
"Pioneer Lumbering in Montana, edited by Margaret E. Parsons." *Frontier* (Missoula) 8:196–209, 1928.

Hosmer, Paul
Now We're Loggin'. Portland, Ore., Metropolitan Press, 1930. 210 pp.

Huntley, George William
Sinnemahone, a Story of Great Trees and Powerful Men. Boston: The Christopher Publishing Co., 1945. 411 pp.
Lumbering and the Chanteyman's life in the Pennsylvania woods.

K., J. H.
"Tall Tales of Tall Timber." *Survey* 54:408, 1925.

Kane, Grace Frank
Myths and Legends of Mackinacs and Lake Region. Cincinnati: Editor Publishing Company, 1897.

Kearney, Luke Sylvester
The Hodag, and other Tales of the Logging Camps. Wausau, Wisconsin: n.p., 1928. 158 pp.
A group of tales of the golden lumbering days.

Kirk, William
Norsk Nightingale. Being the Lyrics of a "Lumberyak." Boston: Small, Maynard & Company, 1916. viii, 66 pp.
Poetry. First published in 1905.

Larson, Agnes W.
"On the Trail of the Woodsman in Minnesota." *Minnesota History* 13:349–366, 1932.

Leech, Carl A.
"Lumbering Days." *Michigan Historical Commission. Michigan History Magazine* (Lansing) 18:135–142, 1934.

Lepine, Paul
The Life Story of a Lumberjack, The Hardships, Fights, Loves and Adventures of a Wanderer from Coast to Coast, the true story of Paul Lepine written by himself. n.p., 1924. 164 pp.

L'Heureux, Eugène
Le Problème des Chantiers. Chicoutimi: 1927. 31 pp.
Life, customs and manners, and social conditions of the Canadian lumbermen of Quebec.

McCormick, Dell
Tall Timber Tales. Caldwell, Idaho: The Caxton Printers, Ltd., 1939. 146 pp.

Meader, Stephen W.
Lumberjack. New York: Harcourt, Brace and Company, 1934.

Meyer, Marie E.
"Rafting on the Mississippi." *Palimpset* 8:121–131, 1927.

Milburn, George
The Hobo's Hornbook; a repertory for a gutter jongleur; decorations by William Siegel. New York: I. Washburn, 1930. xxi, 295 pp., illus., music.

Montague, Margaret
Up Eel River. New York: The Macmillan Co., 1928. 225 pp.
Monologues and tales of a West Virginia lumberman, includes legends of *Tony Beaver* and *Paul Bunyan*.

Nelligan, John E.
"The Life of a Lumberman." *Wisconsin Magazine of History* 13:3–65, 131–185, 241–304, 1929.

Nute, Grace Lee
The Voyageur; illustrations by Carl W. Bertsch. New York: D. Appleton and Company, 1931. viii, 288 pp., illus., bibl.
Includes songs with music.

Raney, William F.
"Pine Lumbering in Wisconsin." *Wisconsin Magazine of History* 19:71–90, 1935.

Rounds, Glen
Lumbercamp. New York: Holiday House, 1937. 117 pp.

Russell, Charles Edward
A-Rafting in the Mississip'. New York: The Century Co., 1928. vii, 357 pp., illus., 4 tunes.

Schlytter, Leslie Evan
The Tall Brothers. New York: D. Appleton-Century Company, 1941. 449 pp.
A novel of a Wisconsin lumbering town—the habits and lore of the struggling lumberjacks.

Springer, John S.
Forest Life and Forest Trees. Comprising winter-life among the loggers, and wild-wood adventure. With descriptions of lumbering operations on the various rivers of Maine and New Brunswick. New York: Harper & Bros., 1851. xii, 259 pp., illus., plates.

Stevens, James
"Last of the Shanty Boys: Paddy Dunn." *Amer. Mer.* 60: 725–31, June, 1945.

——————.
The Saginaw Paul Bunyan. New York: Alfred A. Knopf, 1932.

Stoveken, Ruth
"The Pine Lumberjacks in Wisconsin." *Wisconsin Magazine of History*, March, 1947, pp. 322–334. Illus.

Thompson, George S.
Up to Date; or, The Life of a Lumberman.
n.p.: 1895. 126 pp., illus.
Custom and traditions of Canadian lumbermen.

Thwing, Eugene
The Red-Keggers. Illustrations by W. Herbert
Dunton. New York: The Book-lover Press,
1903. 429 pp.

Tonkin, Joseph Dudley
The Last Raft. Harrisburg, Pa.: The Author,
1940. 145 pp., illus.
The rafting industry, and life of the lumbermen
in the West branch of the Susquehanna River.

Turner, J. M.
"Rafting on the Mississippi." *Wisconsin Magazine of History.* 23:163–176, 313–327, 430, 438;
24:56–65, 1939–1940.

Vinette, Bruno
"Early Lumbering on the Chippewa." *Wisconsin Magazine of History* 9:442–447, 1926.

Wadsworth, Wallace Carter
Paul Bunyan and His Great Blue Ox; Illustrated by Will Crawford. New York: Doubleday, Doran & Company, 1939. 238 pp.

Ward, Willis C.
"Reminiscences of Michigan's Logging Days."
*Michigan Historical Commission. Michigan
History Magazine* (Lansing) 20:301–312, 1936.

Warren, George Henry
*The Pioneer Woodsman As He Is Related to
Lumbering in the Northwest.* Minneapolis:
Press of Hahn & Harmon Company, 1914. 184
pp., illus.

White, Stewart Edward
The Blazed Trail. New York: Doubleday, Page
and Co., 1925.

White, William Allen
Court of Boyville. New York: Doubleday &
McClure Co., 1899. xx, 358 pp., illus.

Whiteshield, C. F.
Cloverland Echoes. Marquette, Mich.: Printed
by Guelff Printing Co., 1923. 58 pp., illus.
Poems.

Wisconsin River Lumber Rafting. I. Lumber
rafting on Wisconsin River (1849–50), by S.
A. Sherman. II. Personal experiences of a Wisconsin River raftsman (1868), by C. C. Lincoln. Madison: State Historical Society of Wisconsin, 1911. 189 pp., illus.

Wood, Leslie C.
Rafting on the Delaware River. Livingston
Manor, N. Y.: Livingston Manor Times, 1934.
270 pp.

SPEECH

Clark, J. W.
"Lumberjack Lingo." *AS* 7 (No. 1):47–53,
1931.

Holbrook, Stewart H.
"A loggers' dictionary and compendium of
useful knowledge." In: *Holy Old Mackinaw;* a
Natural History of the American Lumberjack.
New York: The Macmillan Company, 1938.
viii, 278 pp.

Kernan, Henry S.
"Idaho Lumberjack Nicknames." *CFQ* 4:239–
243, 1945.

Morrison, J. W.
"Lumberjack Rhetoric. The Terse and Picturesque Language of the Lumber Woods."
American Forests and Forest Life 30:722–
724, 1924.

Stevens, James
"Logger Talk." *AS* 1 (No. 3):135–140, 1925.

Williams, Guy
Logger Talk. University of Washington Chapbooks, No. 41. Seattle: University of Washington Bookstore, 1930.

SONGS OF THE LUMBERJACKS

See: American Folksong and Ballad Collections,
pp. 85-90, 118-20.

GENERAL STUDIES

Barry, Phillips
"Samuel Allen." *FSSNE* 9:17–22, 1935.
Maine Lumberjack.

──────.
"The Jam on Gerry's Rock." *FSSNE* 10:18–
20, 1935.
Words and music.

──────.
"Tom Gray." *FSSNE* 9:17–22, 1935.
Maine, Beave Brook, Lumberjack.

Beck, E. C.
"Lumberjack Ballads and Songs." *English
Journal* (College Edition) 21:52–58, 1932.

──────.
"Ze Skunk." *JAFL* 57:211–212, 1944.
A French-Canadian lumberjack verse circulating
in the lumberwoods of Michigan.

Bowman, James Cloyd
"Lumberjack Ballads." *Michigan Historical
Commission. Michigan History Magazine* 20:
231–245, 1936.

Eckstorm, Fannie H.
"Canady I O." *FSSNE* 6:10–13, 1933.

Gray, Roland Palmer
Songs and Ballads of the Maine Lumberjacks,
with other songs from Maine, collected and
edited by Roland Palmer Gray. Cambridge:
Harvard University Press, 1924. xxi, 191 pp.

Halpert, Herbert
"A Michigan Lumberjack Singer." *HFB* 1:81–84, 1942.

Holbrook, Stewart H.
Holy Old Mackinaw. A Natural History of the American Lumberjack. New York: The Macmillan Company, 1938.
Lists some of the well-known lumbermen songs.

Kane, Grace Franks
Myths and Legends of Mackinacs and Lake Region. Cincinnati: Editor Publishing Company, 1897.

Kearney, Luke Silvester
The Hodag, and Other Tales of Logging Camps. Wausau, Wisc: The Author, 1928. 158 pp.

Howard, John T.
Our American Music, Three Hundred Years Of It. New York: Crowell and Company, 1939. 2nd ed. rev. and enl.
Chapter XV: Our Folk Music. Part 3: Other Sources of Folk Songs, pp. 432–434.

White, S. E.
The Blazed Trail. New York: Doubleday, Page and Company, 1925.

Wilson, E.
"Shanty-Boy Ballads and Blues." *New Republic* 47:227–229, (July 14) 1926.

Wood, Ruth Elizabeth
"Songs and Ballads of the Maine Lumberjacks." *JAFL* 38:422, 1925.
A review.

COLLECTIONS

Barry, Phillips, ed.
The Main Woods Songster. Cambridge, Mass.: Powell Printing Company, 1939. 102 pp.
Texts, tunes, analytic notes.

———, Eckstorm, Fanny H., and Smyth, Mary W.
British Ballads from Maine. New Haven, Conn.: Yale University Press, 1929.
Contains many lumberjack tunes.

Beck, Earl Clifton
Songs of the Michigan Lumberjacks. Ann Arbor: University Press, 1942. xi, 296 pp., music, bibl., unaccompanied melodies, illus.

Creighton, Helen, coll.
Songs and Ballads From Nova Scotia. Toronto: J. M. Dent & Sons Ltd., 1933. 334 pp., illus., bibl., tunes and texts.
Contains a goodly number of lumberjack songs.

Day, Holman F.
Pine Tree Ballads: Rhymes, Stories of Unplanned Human Natur' up in Maine. Boston: Houghton Mifflin Company, 1902. Illus.

Dean, Michael C., comp.
The Flying Cloud and 150 Other Old Poems and Ballads. A Collection of Old Irish Songs, Songs of the Sea and Great Lakes, the Big Pine Woods, the Prize Ring and Others. Virginia, Minn.: The Quickprint, 1922.

Eckstorm, Fannie Hardy, and Smyth, Mary Winslow
Minstrelsy of Maine. Folk-Songs and Ballads of the Woods and the Coast. Boston: Houghton Mifflin Co., 1927. 390 pp.
Texts only. In part I. Songs of the Woods, the authors present a number of lumberjack songs, under the following classifications: The Oldest Woods Songs, Woods Songs of the Middle Period, and The Later Woods Songs.

Gardner, E. E., and Chickering, G. J., eds.
Ballads and Songs of Southern Michigan. Ann Arbor: University of Michigan Press, 1939. London: H. Milford, Oxford University Press. xviii, 501 pp., incl. front., illus.
Some of the songs with music (unaccomp.) "other songs sung in Michigan" (list of titles) pp. 477–483. Bibliography: pp. 491–494.

Gray, Roland Palmer
Songs and Ballads of the Maine Lumberjacks. With other songs from Maine. Coll. and ed. by Roland Palmer Gray. Cambridge: Harvard University Press, 1924. xxi, 191 pp.

Lomax, John A. and Alan
American Ballads and Folk-Songs. New York: The Macmillan Company, 1934.
Chapter XIX—The Shanty Boy (5 Songs).

———.
Folk Song U. S. A. New York: Duell, Sloan & Pearce, 1947.
Chapter VI—"Come All Ye Bold Fellers"—Contains lumberjack songs, Cowboy tunes, and miners' songs— arranged for voice and piano by Ruth and Charles Seeger.

———.
Our Singing Country. New York: The Macmillan Company, 1941.
Part III, Chapt. 2—"Lumberjacks and Teamsters," texts and tunes.

Mackenzie, W. Roy
Quest of the Ballad. Princeton, N. J.: Princeton University Press, 1906.

Pound, Louise
American Ballads and Songs. New York: Charles Scribner's Sons, 1922.

Rickaby, Franz Lee, coll. and ed.
Ballads and Songs of the Shanty-Boy. Cambridge, Mass.: Harvard University Press, 1926. xli, 244 pp., music.
Texts, and tunes (unaccompanied melodies).

Russell, P. R.
Shanty–Boy Songs. New York: John Wiley & Sons.

Sandburg, Carl
> *The American Songbag.* New York: Harcourt,
> Brace and Co., 1927.
>> Chapter on: "Lumberjacks, Loggers, and Shanty
>> boys"—tunes and words, some arranged for voice
>> and piano.

Sax, I. M.
> *Songs of the Lumberjacks.* New York: Mac-
> millan Company, 1927.

**Shoemaker, Henry W., French, J. C., and
Chatham, J. H.**
> *North Pennsylvania Minstrelsy,* as Sung in the
> Backwood Settlements, Hunting Cabins and
> Lumber Camps in the "Black Forest" of
> Pennsylvania, 1840–1910. Altoona, Pa.: Times
> Tribune Company, 1923. 228 pp., illus.

ARRANGEMENTS:
(Individual Titles)
————: *Male Voices*

"The Shanty Man's Life."
> Treharne, B.: Willis: TTB.

RECORDS
Collections

**U. S. Library of Congress. Division of Music.
Folklore Section.**
> *Helen Creighton Recording Project in Nova
> Scotia.*   AAFS–LC

Individual Titles

"Canaday."
> Earl Rogers, voice-piano.   MU–68

"Driving Saw Logs on the Plover."
> Pierre La Dieu, vocal.   CO–15278–D

"Jam On Jerry's Rock."
> Earl Rogers, voice-piano.   MU–68

"The Little Brown Bulls."
> Sung by Emery De Moyer at Rhinelander,
> Wisc., 1941. Recorded by Charles Draves. In:
> *Album 1*, Anglo-American Ballads, Washing-
> ton, D. C.   AAFS–5

"The Shanty Man's Life."
> Pierre La Dieu, vocal.   CO–15278–D

MINING AND MINERS

MINING AND MINERS

A. The Forty-Niners

FOLKLORE

See: Folklore of California, pp. 373-91.

BIBLIOGRAPHY

Gaer, Joseph, ed.
Bibliography of California Literature. Fiction of the Gold Rush Period. Drama of the Gold Rush Period. Poetry of the Gold Rush Period. *SERA* Project 2–F2–132. California Literary Research, 1930.

Wheat, Carl Irving
The Maps of the California Gold Region 1849–1857. San Francisco: 1942.
A biblio-cartography of an important decade.

Winther, Oscar Osburn
California Gold Rush. In: *The Trans-Mississippi West: A Guide to Its Periodical Literature* (1811–1938) (pp. 23–29). Indiana Univ. Publications, Social Science Series 3. Bloomington, Ind.: Indiana U. Bookstore.

GENERAL STUDIES AND COLLECTIONS

Allen, William Wallace, and Avery, R. B.
California Gold Book. San Francisco: Donahue and Henneberry, 1893. 439 pp.

Anonymous
California Gold Region. New York: F. M. Pratt, 1849. 48 pp.

Austed, David J.
The Gold Seeker's Manual. New York: D. Appleton, 1859.

Ayers, James J.
Gold and Sunshine. Boston: R. G. Badger, 1922. 359 pp.

Bailey, Paul
The Gay Saint. Hollywood, Calif.: Murray & Gee, 1944. 310 pp.
Adventures of Sam Brannan, the California gold dust millionaire.

Ball, Nicholas
The Pioneers of '49. Boston: Lee and Shepard, 1891. 288 pp.

Ballou, John
The Lady of the West; or The Goldseekers. Cincinnati: Author, 1855. 544 pp.

Bancroft, Hubert Howe
California Inter Pocula. A review of some classical abnormities. San Francisco: The History Company, 1888.
Deals with the period of the gold discoveries and early years of the American occupation.

Bayley, Charles
The Glory that was Gold. University of Denver, Central City Opera House Association, 1932.

Beals, Frank, L.
The Rush For Gold. Chicago: Wheeler Publishing Company, 1946. 252 pp.
"...an authentic and simply-told account of pioneer life."

Bennett, Horace
Bright Yellow Gold. Philadelphia: J. C. Waiston, 1935.

Bigham, Robert W.
California Gold-Field Scenes. Nashville: Southern Methodist Publishing House, 1886. 283 pp.

————.
California Gold-Field Scenes; selections from Quien-Sabe's Gold-Field Manuscripts. Introduction by A. G. Haygood. Nashville: Southern Methodist Publishing House, 1886. 283 pp.

Book Club of America. San Francisco.
A Camera in the Gold Rush. A series of photographs of Pacific coast towns, camps and mining operations of pioneer days, edited with texts, by Edith M. Coulter and Jeanne Van Nostrand. San Francisco: Book Club of California, 1946. 12 parts, mounted illus.

Borthwick, J. D.
The Gold Hunters; a first-hand picture of life in California mining camps in the early fifties. Edited by Horace Kephart. New York: Outing Publishing Company, 1927. 361 pp., illus.

————.
Three Years in California, 1815–54; with eight illustrations by the author. Edinburgh: W. Blackwood and Sons, 1857. vi, 384 pp.

Boyden, Seth
"Seth Boyden's Days in California 1849–'51. Extracts from his Diary." *New Jersey Historical Society. Proceedings* 12:309–318, 455–461; 13:70–76, 1927–28. n.s.

Bristol, Sherlock
The Pioneer Preacher. Chicago, New York: Fleming H. Revell Co., 1898. 336 pp.

Bronk, Mitchell
Discovering My Forty-Niner Father (A Paper read before the Photozetics Minister's Club of Philadelphia). Philadelphia: The Judson Press, 1942. 20 pp.

Brown, James Stephens
California Gold. Oakland: Pacific Press Publishing Co., 1894. 20 pp.

Bruff, J. Goldsborough
Gold Rush: The Journals of Drawings and Other Papers of J. Goldsborough Bruff, April 2, 1849—July 20, 1851, edited by Georgia Willis Read and Ruth Gaines. New York: Columbia University Press, 1949.

Buck, Franklin Augustus
A Yankee Trader in the Gold Rush: His Letters (1849–81). Boston and New York: Houghton, Mifflin Co., 1930. 294 pp., illus.

Buckbee, Edna Bryan
Pioneer Days in Angels Camp. Calif: Calaveras Californian, 1932. 80 pp.

Canfield, Chauncey de Leon
Diary of a Forty-Niner. Boston: Houghton Mifflin Company, 1920. xviii, 253 pp.
The diary "purported to be the experiences of Alfred T. Jackson, a pioneer miner who worked on Rock Creek, Nevada County, California." Preface, p. ix.

Cendrars, Blaise
Sutter's Gold. New York: Harper & Brothers, 1926. 179 pp., illus.

Chalfant, W. A.
Gold, Guns and Ghost Towns. Stanford, Cal.: Stanford University Press, 1947.

Chamberlain, Newell D.
The Call of Gold. Mariposa, Calif: Gazette Press, 1936.

Christman, Enos
One Man's Gold. New York: Whittlesey House, McGraw-Hill Book Co., 1930. 278 pp.

Clyman, James
James Clyman, American Frontiersman. San Francisco, California: Historical Society, 1928. 247 pp.

Coolidge, Dane
Silver and Gold; a story of luck and love in a Western mining camp. New York: E. P. Dutton & Co., 1919. vii, 260 pp.

Colton, Rev. Walter, U.S.N.
Three Years in California, 1846–1849. New York: A. S. Barnes and Company, 1850. 456 pp., illus.

Coy, Owen Cochran
Gold Days. San Francisco and Los Angeles: Powell Publishing Co., 1929. 381 pp.

Dane, G. Ezra, and Dane, Beatrice J.
Ghost Town. Ill. by Fred Ludekens. New York: Alfred A. Knopf, 1941. xx, 320 pp., illus.
A book "wherein is told much that is wonderful and tragic, and some that is hard to believe, about life during the gold rush and later in the town of Columbia in California's Mother Lode, as remembered by the oldest inhabitants and here for the first time set down."

Delano, Alonzo (Old Block)
Across the Plains and Among the Diggings; a reprint of the original edition with reproduction of numerous photographs taken by Louis Palenske and foreword and epilogue by Rufus Rockwell Wilson. New York: Wilson Erickson, Inc., 1936. xviii, 192 pp., illus.

The Miners' Progress; or Scenes in the Life of a California Miner. (A parody in the style of Pilgrims Progress). Sacramento: Published at the Union Office, 1853.

Pen-Knife Sketches; or Chips of the Old Block. Sacramento: Published at the Union Office, 1853. 112 pp., illus.
A series of original illustrated letters written by one of California's pioneer miners and dedicated to that class of her citizens by the author.

Dellenbaugh, Frederick
Fremont and '49. New York: G. P. Putman's Sons, 1914.
The story of a remarkable career and its relation to the exploration and development of our Western territory, especially California.

De Quincy, Thomas
Letters to a Young Man, and Other Papers. Boston: Ticknor, Reed and Fields, 1854. 300 pp.
Includes a chapter—"California and the Gold Mania."

Dickson, Albert Jerome
Covered Wagon Days. Cleveland: Arthur H. Clark Co., 1929. 287 pp., front, plates, ports., map.

Dietrich, Dr.
The German Emigrants; or Frederick Wohlgemuths' Voyage to California. Guben, Germany: Fechner, n.d.
Mining songs, tales, Characters.

Downie, William
Hunting for Gold. San Francisco: Press of the California Publishing Co., 1893. 407 pp.

Dumke, Glenn S., ed.
George W. B. Evans, Mexican Gold Trail, the Journal of a Forty-Niner. Preface by Robert Glass Cleland. San Farino, Calif.: The Huntington Library, 1945. 340 pp., illus., bibl., index.

Evans, George W. B.
Mexican Gold Trail: The Journal of a Forty-Niner. George W. B. Evans. Edited by Glenn S. Dumke. Preface by Robert Glass Cleland. San Marino, Cal.: The Huntington Library, 1945. xx, 340 pp., illus., bibl. note, appendix, index.
A mine of information on the travails, habits, customs and lore of the Forty-Niners.

Farish, Thomas Edwin
The Gold Hunters of California. Illustrated by F. I. Wetherbee. Chicago: M. A. Donohue & Co., 1904. 246 pp., illus.

Farwell, William Brigham
"Recollections of Gold Diggin's." *Society of California Pioneers Quarterly,* 1 (No. 1):17–, 1924.

Ferguson, Charles D.
The Experiences of a Forty-Niner. Cleveland: The Williams Publishing Co., 1888. 507 pp.

Ferguson, Robert G.
Camp Fire Tales of Lost Mines and Hidden Treasure. Tuscon, Ariz.: Author, 1937. 35 pp.

Foreman, Grant
Marcy and the Gold Seekers; the journal of
Captain R. B. Marcy, with an account of the
gold rush over the southern route. Norman,
Okla.: University of Oklahoma Press, 1939.
xiv, 433 pp.

Fulton, Robert Lardin
Epic of the Overland. San Francisco: A. M.
Robertson, 1924.

Gillia, William R.
Goldrush Days with Mark Twain. New York:
A & C Boni, 1930. 264 pp., illus.

Gold Rush: The Journals, Drawings, and other
papers of J. Goldsborough Bruff, Washington,
D. C., Captain, Washington City and California Mining Association. April 2, 1849–July
20, 1851. Edited by Georgia W. Read. 2 vols.
New York: Columbia University Press, 1943.

Glasscock, Carl Burgess
A Golden Highway. Indianapolis: Bobbs-Merrill Co., 1934. 333 pp.
    Scenes of history's greatest gold rush of yesterday
    and to-day.

──────.
Gold in Them Hills. Indianapolis: Bobbs-Merrill Co., 1932. 330 pp., illus.
    The story of the West's last wild mining days.

Greenleaf, Benjamin
The California Almanac for 1849. Repr. from
the copy in the Huntington Library, San
Marino, Calif., 1942.

Grembie, Marjorie
Gold of Ophir. New York: Doubleday Page,
1925.

Hafen, LeRoy R.
Colorado Gold Rush. Contemporary Letters
and Reports 1858–1859. *The Southwest His-
torical Series,* edited by Leroy R. Hafen. x.
Glendale, California: The Arthur H. Clark
Co., 1941.

──────, (ed.)
*Overland Routes to the Goldfields, 1859, from
Contemporary Diaries....* Glendale, Califor-
nia: The Arthur H. Clark Co., 1942.

Hale, Richard Lunt
The Log of Forty-Niner; journal of a voyage
from Newburyport to San Francisco in the
brig Gen'l. Worth, commanded by Captain
Samuel Walton, kept by Richard L. Hale...
edited by Carolyn Hale Russ. Boston: B. J.
Brimmer Company, 1923. 183 pp., illus.
    "Being the record of the adventures by sea and
    shore to the California gold fields and the Pacific
    Northwest, 1849–1854. Illustrated from original
    sketches by the author. Edited from original
    manuscripts, now for the first time published."

Hamilton, Marian
"California Gold-Rush English." *AS* 7 (No. 6):
423–433, 1932.

Hand, Wayland D.
"Californias Miners' Folklore: Above Ground,
Below Ground." *CFQ* 1:24–47, 127–155, 1942.

Hannum, Anna Paschall (ed.)
A Quaker Forty-Niner; The Adventures of
Charles Edward Pancoast on the American
Frontier. Foreword by John Bach McMaster.
Philadelphia: University of Pennsylvania
Press, 1930.

Helper, Hinton Rowan
The Land of Gold. Baltimore: Published for
the author by H. Taylor, 1855. 300 pp.

Howe, Octavius Thorndike
Argonauts of '49. Cambridge: Harvard University Press, 1923. 221 pp.

Hubbard, Margaret Ann
Lone Boy. New York: The Macmillan Company, 1944. 250 pp.
    A story for young readers of the Montana Gold
    Rush.

Hulbert, Archer Butler
*Forty-Niners, The Chronicle of the California
Trail.* Boston: Little, Brown & Co., 1931. 340
pp.

Hunter, George
Reminiscences of an Old Timer. San Francisco:
H. S. Crocker and Co., 1887. 454 pp.

Huntley, Sir Henry
California: Its Gold and Inhabitants. London:
T. C. Newby, 1856. 2 vols.

Ingalls, John
"California Letters of the Gold Rush Period."
American Antiquarian Society, Proceedings
47:145–182, 1937. n.s.

Jackson, Joseph Henry
*Anybody's Gold: The Story of California's
Mining Towns.* Illustrated by E. H. Suydam.
New York: D. Appleton-Century Co., 1941. xiv,
467 pp., illus., bibl.

──────, ed.
Gold Rush Album. 352 Pictures with text.
New York: Charles Scribner's Sons, 1949.
    "By a most congenial mating of pictures and
    words the book reviews the Gold Rush from
    exuberant beginning to domesticated and rather
    humdrum close." (Lloyd Haberly)

Jacobson, Pauline
City of the Golden 'Fifties. Berkeley: University of California Press, 1941.

Johnston, William Graham
Experiences of a Forty-Niner. Pittsburgh:
Privately printed, 1892. 392 pp.

Kelly, William
A Stroll Through the Diggings of California.
London: Simms and McIntyre, 1852. v, 240 pp.

Kip, Leonard
California Sketches, with Recollections of the Gold Mines. Introduction by Lyle H. Wright. Albany, N. Y.: E. H. Pease and Co., 1850. 57 pp.
An eye-witness account of the early days of the Gold-Rush, by a young New York lawyer.

Knower, Daniel
The Adventures of a Forty-Niner. An historic description of California, with events and ideas of San Francisco and its people in those early days. Albany: Weed-Parsons Prtg. Co., 1894. 200 pp., illus.

Lampson, Robin
Laughter Out of the Ground; a Novel in Cadence. New York: C. Scribner's Sons, 1935. xiii, 344 pp.
Poetry dealing with events and characters in the days of '49.

Lee, Edward Melvin
California Gold. Los Angeles: Tower-Lee Co. Inc., 1932. 94 pp.

Lewis, Oscar
Sea Routes to the Gold Fields. New York: Alfred A. Knopf, 1948.
The book is based on individual experiences drawn from diaries, journals and reminiscences.

Loring, Jules
West We Go. New York: G. P. Putnam's Sons, 1946.
A story for young readers of the adventures and excitement of the Gold Rush days of '49.

Lottritz, J. Martin
"Lore of Lost Mines." *New Mexico Magazine,* 15 (No. 10), (October, 1937), 12 pp.

Luper, David Rohrer
Argonauts of Forty-Nine. South Bend, Indiana: J. B. Stoll and Co., 1894. 146 pp.

Lyman, Albert
Journal of a Voyage to California and Life in the Gold Diggings. Hartford, Conn.: E. T. Pease; New York: Dexter and Brother, 1852. 192 pp.

Lyman, Chester Smith
Around the Horn to the Sandwich Islands and California. New Haven, Conn.: Yale University Press, 1924. 328 pp.

Lyman, George D.
John Marsh, Pioneer. New York: C. Scribner's Sons, 1930. 394 pp.

Manly, William Lewis
Death Valley in '49, Important chapter of California Pioneer History. The Autobiography of a Pioneer.... San Jose, Cal.: Pacific Tree and Vine Co., 1894. 498 pp. (Reprinted, Chicago: R. R. Donnelley & Sons Co., 1927.)

Mansfield, George C.
The Feather River in '49 and the Fifties. Oroville, Calif.: Register, 1924. 42 pp.

Marye, George T., Jr.
From '49 to '83 in California and Nevada. San Francisco: A. M. Robertson Co., 1923.
Chapters from the Life of George Thomas Marye, a Pioneer of '49 (by his son).

Massey, Ernest de.
A Frenchman In The Gold-Rush: The Journal of Ernest de Massey, argonaut of 1849, translated by Marguerite Eyer Wilbur. San Francisco: California Historical Society, 1927. xi, 183 pp., illus., maps.
Social life, customs, mining adventures, and mining tales.

M'Collum, William S.
California As I Saw It. Buffalo, N. Y.: G. H. Derby and Co., 1850. 72 pp.
Life, customs and practices in the mines.

McDonald, L. R. H.
Pacific Bank Handbook of California. San Francisco: Privately printed, no date.

McIlhany, Edward Washington
Recollections of a '49er. Kansas City: Hailman Printing Co., 1908. 212 pp.

McKenna, James A.
Black Range Tales. New York: Wilson-Erickson, Inc., 1936.

Mighels, Mrs. Ella Sterling (Clark)
Life and Letters of a Forty-Niner's Daughters. San Francisco: Harr Wagner Publishing Co., 1929. xvi, 371 pp.
Pioneer and forty-niner tales, anecdotes, folk music.

Miller, Joaquin
'49 The Gold-Seeker of the Sierras. New York: Funk & Wagnalls, 1884. viii, 148 pp.

The Miner's Progress; or Scenes in the Life of a California Miner. Being a series of humorous illustrations of the "ups and downs" of a gold digger in pursuit of his "pile". Sacramento: Published at the Daily Union Office, 1853. 13 pp., illus.

Moerenhout, Jacques Antoine
The Inside Story of the Gold Rush. San Francisco, California Historical Society, 1935. Transl. and edited from documents in the French Archives by Abraham P. Nasatir, in collaboration with George Ezra Dave, who wrote the introduction and conclusion. San Francisco: California Historical Society, 1935.

Monroe, Kirk
The Golden Days of '49. New York: Dodd, Mead & Co., 1899.

Montagu, Montagu
California Broadsides: Order of Fire. Envoy. The Project. The Departure. The Return. London: 1850. 16 pp.
Poems of the '49ers.

Morgan, Dale L., ed.
"Letters by Forty-Niners." *The Western Humanities Review* 3 (No. 2): 98–116, April 1949.

Paden, Irene D.
The Wake of the Prairie Schooner. New York:
The Macmillan Co., 1943. 514 pp.
    The greater portion of this book deals with the
    records and lore of the '49ers.

Pancoast, Charles Edward
The Quaker Forty-Niner. Philadelphia: University of Pennsylvania Press, 1930.

Parsons, George Frederic
*The Life and Adventures of James Wilson
Marshall.* Sacramento, Calif.: J. W. Marshall
and W. Burke, 1870. 188 pp. San Francisco:
G. Fields, 1935.

Patterson, Lawson B.
Twelve Years in the Mines of California. Cambridge, Mass.: Miles and Dillingham, 1862.
108 pp.

Paul, Rodman W.
California Gold: The Beginning of Mining in
the Far West. Cambridge, Mass.: Harvard University Press, 1947.
    A history of gold mining from 1848 to 1873.

Payson, George
Golden Dreams and Leaden Realities. New
York: G. P. Putnam & Co., 1853. 344 pp.

Peck, George Washington
Aurifodina; or Adventures in the Gold Region.
New York: Baker and Scribner, 1849. 103 pp.

Peters, Charles
*The Autobiography of Charles Peters, in 1915
the Oldest Pioneer Living in California, Who
Mined in the Days of '49. . . .* Sacramento, Cal.:
The La Grave Co., 1915. 231 pp., illus.

Potter, David M., ed.
The Trail to California. The Overland Journal
of Vincent Geiger and Wakeman Bryarly. New
Haven: Yale University Press, 1945.

**Reusch, H. E., and F. G., and Hoover, Mildred
Brooke**
*Historic Spots in California; Valley and Sierra
Counties.* Palo Alto: 1933.

Ritchie, Robert Welles
The Hell-Roarin' Forty-Niners. New York: J.
H. Sears & Co., 1928. 298 pp.

Rourke, Constance Mayfield
*Troopers of the Gold Coast or The Rise of
Lotta Crabtree.* New York: Harcourt, Brace &
Co., 1928. 262 pp.

Royce, Mrs. Sarah (Bayliss)
*Frontier Lady, Recollections of the Gold Rush
and Early California;* Edited by Ralph Henry
Gabriel. New Haven: Yale University Press;
London: H. Milford, Oxford University Press,
1932. 144 pp.

Russell, Thomas C., ed.
*The Shirley Letters from the California Mines;
1851–52.* San Francisco: Grabhorn Press, 1922.

Ryan, William Redmond
*Personal Adventures in Upper and Lower
California in 1848–49.* London: W. Shoberl,
1850. 2 vols.

Scherer, James Augustin Brown
*The Forty-Niner and the Story of the Golden
Teacaddy.* New York: Minton, Balch & Com-
pany, 1925. 127 pp., illus.

Schultz, James Willard
Gold Dust; with illustrations by Stockton Mulford. Boston: Houghton Mifflin Company, 1934.
243 pp.

Scott, Reva
Samuel Brannan and the Golden Fleece. New
York: The Macmillan Co., 1944. 462 pp.
    The amazing career of one of Joseph Smiths'
    apostles who set out to make a fortune in '49,
    sketched against a background of early Cali-
    fornia days.

Scott, William Anderson
The Wedge of Gold, or Achan in El Dorado.
San Francisco: Whittan, Towne & Co., 1855.
168 pp.
    Discourses delivered in Calvary Church, San
    Francisco also Philadelphia: Presbyterian Board
    of Publication (cop. 1855) 162 pp.

Senex
"San Francisco in 1849." *The Grizzly Bear*
pp. 20, 21, 1907 (Sept.)

Shaw, William
Golden Dreams and Waking Realities. London:
Smith Elder and Co., 1851. 316 pp.

Shay, John C.
Twenty Years in the Backwoods of California.
. . . Boston: The Roxburgh Publishing Co.,
1923. 142 pp.

Shinn, Charles Howard
*Mining Camps: A Study in Frontier Govern-
ment.* Introduction by Joseph Henry Jackson.
New York: Alfred A. Knopf, 1946. New ed.
First printed by C. Scribner's Sons in 1885.
    "A book of immense interest . . . tells the main
    story with directness, charm, a wealth of enter-
    taining anecdote and a genuine feeling." (Arthur
    Schlesinger, Jr.)

Smith, Niiima
Gold Stories of '49; by a Californian. Boston:
Copeland and Day, 1896. 52 pp.
    Poems depicting life and character of the gold
    rush days.

Spurr, George C.
The Land of Gold. Boston: A. Williams and
Co., 1881. 271 pp.

Stellman, Louis John
*Mother Lode, The Story of California's Gold
Rush.* San Francisco: Harr Wagner Publishing
Co., 1934. 304 pp.
    Place names, mining-camp tales, customs, social
    life, characters.

Stillman, J. D.
Seeking the Golden Fleece; a record of pioneer life in California; to which is annexed footprints of early navigators, other than Spanish, in California; with an account of the voyage of the schooner Dolphin. San Francisco: A. Roman & Co., 1877. 352 pp.

Strobridge, Idah Meacham
In Miners' Mirage-Land. Los Angeles: Baumgardt Publ. Co., 1904.

Stokes, George W.
Deadwood Gold. Yonkers-on-Hudson: World Book Co., 1926. 163 pp., illus.

Taber, Louise Eddy
California Gold Rush Days; Stories from the radio series.... San Francisco: Louise E. Taber, 1936. 3 nos., illus.

Twain, Mark (Samuel Langhorne Clemens)
Roughing It. New York. London: Harper Bros., 1903. 2 Vols. in 1.
Exciting narrative of the mining boom.

Upham, Samuel Curtis
Notes on a Voyage to California, via Cape Horn, Together with Scenes in El Dorado, in the Years 1849–50. Philadelphia: Privately printed, 1878. xxii, 594 pp., illus.
Also contains texts of current ballads.

Vizetelly, Henry
Four Months Among the Gold-Finders in Alta California; being the diary of an expedition from San Francisco to the gold districts. London: D. Bogue, 1849. xviii, 207 pp.
A fictitious narrative.

Watson, Editha L.
"Golden Phantoms: Tales of Lost Mines and Buried Treasure." *W. H. U. Syndicate Features,* Aug., 1935–December, 1936.

Webster, Kimball
A New England Forty-Niner. With an introduction and biographical sketch by George Waldo Brown. Illustrated by Frank Halland and others. Manchester, N. H.: Standard Book Company, 1917. vii, 240 pp., plates, 2 port.

Weight, Harold O.
"Ghost Town Miners." *Desert Magazine* 11:17, May, 1948.

————.
"Tim Cody's Lost Ledge." *Desert Magazine* 11:17, June, 1948.

Weld, John
The Pardners, A Novel of the California Gold Rush. New York: C. Scribner's Sons, 1941. 349 pp.

Wells, Evelyn, and Peterson, Harry G.
The 49'ers. New York: Doubleday & Co., 1949. 273 pp.
They tell the whole story: of the tortuous journeys by land and sea, how some made big strikes, and how many struck nothing, of great achievements and lawlessness. A valuable contribution to the gold rush centennial.

Wheat, Carl Irving
The Maps of the California Gold Region, 1848–1857, a bibliocartography of an important decade. San Francisco: The Grabhorn Press, 1942. xlii, 152 pp.

————.
Trailing of the Forty-Niners Through Death Valley. San Francisco: Taylor & Taylor, 1939. 37 pp., plates, maps.

White, Stewart Edward
The Forty-Niners, A Chronicle of Trail and El Dorado. New Haven: Yale University Press, 1918. ix, 273 pp., col. front.

————.
Gold. Garden City: Doubleday, Doran, 1913. 449 pp.

————.
The Story of California. Three Novels: *Gold, The Gray Dawn* and *The Rose Dawn.* New York: The Sun Dial Press, 1937.

Willard, James F.
The Gold Rush and Afterward. In: *Colorado; Short Studies of its Past and Present.* Boulder: University of Colorado Press, 1927.

Williams, Albert
'49 to '94. Respectfully inscribed to the native sons and daughters in tribute to our pioneer matrons. San Francisco: Upton Bros., 1894. 23 pp.
A book of poems.

Willison, George F.
Here They Dug the Gold. New York: Brentanos, 1931. Reprinted by Reynal and Hitchcock, 1946.
Authentic and dramatic chronicle of Colorado's early mining camp and bonanza kings.

Wiltsee, Ernest Abram
Gold Rush Steamers (of the Pacific). San Francisco: The Grabhorn Press, 1938. x, 367 pp., illus.

————.
The Pioneer Miner and the Pack Mule Express. San Francisco: California Historical Society, 1931. vii, 112 pp.

Works Project Administration.
Almanac for '49ers. Stanford University, Calif.: Delkin, 1938. 127 pp.

Wright, William (De Quille, Dan, pseud.)
History of the Big Bonanza. Hartford, Conn.: American Publishing Co., 1876. 569 pp., illus.

Young, Gordon Ray
Days of '49. New York: George H. Doran Company, 1925. 425 pp.
A novel with the life, customs, manners, and struggles of the gold seekers.

SONGS OF THE FORTY-NINERS

See: American Folksong and Ballad Collections, pp. 85-90, 118-20.

BIBLIOGRAPHY

Federal Writers' Project.
Bibliography of the Gold Rush, 1849. In: *Gold Rush Ballads, 1849. History of Music in San Francisco Series, Vol. II.* Works Progress Administration Northern California, San Francisco. Cornel Lengyel, editor, 1940.

GENERAL STUDIES AND COLLECTIONS

Baker, George H.
Miner's Life. Sacramento: Barker and Baker, 1854.

Black, Eleanora, and Robertson, Sidney, ed.
The Gold Rush Song Book. San Francisco, Cal.: The Colt Press, 1940. 55 pp., illus.
Texts and tunes.

Davidson, Levette Jay
"Rocky Mountain Frontier Songs." *CFQ* 2:89–112, 1943.
Texts only.

Drury, Wells
Three Pioneer Ballads. . . . San Francisco, 1931. 11 pp., illus.
"The versions here given are ... the most commonly heard in the mining-camps of California and Nevada." *Contents:* The Days of forty-nine, Baldy Green, Joe Bowers.

Emrich, Duncan
"Songs of the Western Miners." *CFQ* 1:213–232, 1942.
Mostly text, five with music.

Fitch, Anthony
Ballads of Western Mines and Others. New York: Cochrane Publishing Company, 1910. 60 pp., illus., front., plates.

Hulbert, A. B. coll.
Forty-Niners. Boston: Little, Brown and Company, 1932.

Lengyel, Cornel, ed.
Gold Rush Ballads: The Forty-Niners. A selection of ballads sung in San Francisco during the gold rush era (1849–1859). History of Music in San Francisco Series, Vol. II: A San Francisco Songster, Special School Edition. W. P. A. 1037. History of Music Project. San Francisco: W. P. A. of Northern California, 1940.

——————.
A San Francisco Songster, 1849–1939. History of Music in San Francisco Project, Works Progress Administration, San Francisco, 1939.

Lomax, John A. and Alan
American Ballads and Folk Songs. New York: The Macmillan Company, 1934.
Chapter XVIII—The Miner (3 songs).

Mighels, Mrs. Ella Sterling (Clark)
Life and Letters of a Forty-Niner's Daughter. San Francisco: Harr Wagner Publishing Company, 1929. 371 pp.
Tales, anecdotes and songs.

Put's Original California Songster, detailing the hopes, trials and joys of a Miner's life. San Francisco: D. E. Appleton and Company, 1868. vi, 32 pp.

Robinson, Dr.
Pacific Song Book (California Songster). San Francisco: D. E. Appleton & Co., 1854.

Sherwin, Sterling
Songs of the Gold Miners: A golden collection of songs, as sung by and about the Forty-Niners, by Sterling Sherwin and Louis Katzman and an introduction by Beth Moore. With chord accompaniments for ukulele, tenor banjo and guitar (also chord charts, with fingering for tenor banjo and guitar.) New York: Carl Fisher, Inc. c. 1932. Pub. No. 26191–48. 48 pp., English words, melodies with piano accompaniment.

Taylor, M.
The Gold Digger's Song Book. Marysville: Marysville Daily Herald, 1856.

"Untitled Songs from Miners' Melodies or Ditties from the Diggings." *Columbia Gazette,* (Nov. 6) 1852.

ARRANGEMENTS:
(Individual Titles)

——————: *Male Voices*

"Hoodah Day."
Bartholomew: Schirmer: TTBB.

——————: *Orchestra*

Eppert, Carl
The Argonauts of Forty-Nine, op. 35– A Symphonic Fantasy. MS.

Wilson, Mortimer
Overture—1849. MS.

Stage Work

Maganini, Quinto
The Argonauts—A California Tetralogy. An opera. New York: Musicus: For Dramatic cast, orchestra, and chorus.

RECORDS
Album—Collections

Songs of Old California.
Frank Luther, Zora Layman, with Century Quartet. Set DE–49 4–10".   DE–2472/5
Contents: On the Banks of the Sacramento; Sailing for San Francisco; Jackson; Cielito Lindo; The Night is Serene; Joe Bowers; Santy Ana; Adelita; Four Little White Doves; Linen Clothes; Seeing the Elephant; Hangtown Gals; The Hammock; A Teamster's Song; The White Hawk; Sweet Betsy from Pike; Little Ah Sid; Clementine; Abalone.

Individual Titles

"Clementine."
  In: *Songs of Old California*. F. Luther, Z. Layman and Century Quartet.   DE–49

"Days of Forty-Nine."
  Jules Allen, vocal.   VI–21627

"Hangtown Gals."
  In: *Songs of Old California*. Frank Luther, Zora Layman and Century Quartet.   DE–49

"Joe Bowers."
  In: *Songs of Old California*. Frank Luther, Zora Layman and Century Quartet.   DE–49

"Linen Clothes."
  In: *Songs of Old California*. Frank Luther, Zora Layman and Century Quartet.   DE–49

"Little Ah Sid."
  In: *Songs of Old California*. F. Luther, Z. Layman and Century Quartet.   DE–49

"On the Banks of the Sacramento."
  In: *Songs of Old California*. Frank Luther, Zora Layman and Century Quartet.   DE–49

"Sailing for San Francisco."
  In: *Songs of Old California*. Frank Luther, Zora Layman with Century Quartet.   DE–49

"Santa Ana."
  In: *Songs of Old California*. Frank Luther, Zora Layman and Century Quartet.   DE–49

"Tom More in the Days of '49."
  Hudson Valley Songs. Frank Warner, accompanied by ballad singers, instrumentalists.
          Disc–8024

B. ANTHRACITE, BITUMINOUS, AND OTHER MINING

FOLKLORE

GENERAL STUDIES AND COLLECTIONS

Adams, H. H.
"Doodlebugs and Doodlebuggers." *CFQ* 3:53–58, 1944.
> A term used in somewhat jocular contempt in oil parlance to denote any bogus mechanical instrument employed to divine the location of oil, or mineral deposits.

Adams, James Taylor
Death in the Dark: A Collection of Factual Ballads of American Mine Disasters. Big Laurel, Va.: Adams-Mullins Press, 1941. 120 pp.
> Twenty-three ballads (without music) of mines in Pennsylvania, Kentucky, Virginia, West Va., and Tennessee.

Anderson, Sherwood
Marching Men. New York: John Lane Co., 1917.
> A story of the Pennsylvania coal men and mines —fact, fiction and lore.

Bucklin, Mrs. Edna Bryan
The Saga of Old Tuolumni. New York: The Press of the Pioneers, Inc., 1935. 526 pp.

Coleman, J. Walter
The Molly Maguire Riots. Richmond, Va.: Garrett & Massie, 1936.
> A tragic chapter, filled with fact and lore, of the Pennsylvania Anthracite Miner.

Corle, Edwin
Coarse Gold. New York: E. P. Dutton & Co., 1942.
> A story of the revival of a Nevada mining town.

Dobie, J. Frank
Apache Gold and Yaqui Silver. Boston: Little, Brown & Co., 1939.
> Legendary tales of lost mines and buried treasure of the Southwest.

Federal Writers' Project.
Copper Camp. Compiled by the workers of the Writers' Projects Administration in the State of Montana. Illus. New York: Hastings House, 1943. 308 pp.
> The exciting adventures of copper mining in and the growth of Butte, Montana.

Hand, Wayland Debs
"Folklore from Utah's Silver Mining Camps." *JAFL* 54:132–161, 1941.

————.
"The Folklore, Customs, and Traditions of the Butte Miner." *CFQ* 5 (No. 1):1–27, 1946.

Jeffcott, Vernon
"Tales of Pioche." *Utah Humanities Review* 2 (No. 2):192–193, 1948.
> Stories of early mining days in Pioche, Nevada.

Korson, George Gershon
Black Land; the way of life in the coal fields. (The Way of Life Series). Evanston, Ill.: Row, Peterson and Co., 1941. 72 pp.

————.
Coal Dust on the Fiddle. Songs and stories of the Bituminous Industry. Philadelphia: University of Pennsylvania Press, 1943. xvi, 460 pp., illus., bibl., music.

————.
Minstrels of the Mine Patch. Songs and stories of the Anthracite Industry. Philadelphia: University of Pennsylvania Press, 1938. viii, 332 pp., illus., bibl., music.

————, ed.
Pennsylvania Songs and Legends: A Folklore Anthology. Introduction by the author. Philadelphia, Pa.: University of Pennsylvania Press, 1949. 466 pp., illus.
> Thirteen chapters by leading authorities in their respective fields. The editor discusses the lore and song of the Pennsylvania miners.

Lillard, Richard G.
Desert Challenge. (The American Scene Series.) New York: Alfred A. Knopf, 1942. 388 pp., illus. with photographs, map.
> The story of Nevada, also contains excellent picture of mining camps, old and new, with many good stories.

Lyman, George D.
Ralston's Ring. New York: Chas. Scribner's Sons, 1937.

————.
The Saga of the Comstock Lode. New York: Chas. Scribner's Sons, 1934.

"Michigan Miner's Superstition."
JAFL 13:226, 1900.

Munroe, Kirk
Derrick Sterling, A Story of the Mines. New York: Harper & Bros., 1888.
> Includes lore of the Pennsylvania miner.

Murdoch, Angus
Brown Copper. New York: The Macmillan Co., 1943.
> The story of the first United States mining boom.

Palais, Hyman
"Black Hill Miners' Folklore." *CFQ* 4:255–269, 1945.

Price, Sam Goodale
Black Hills, the Land of Legend. Los Angeles: De Voras, 1935.

Requa, Mack L.
Grubstake: A Study of Early Mining Days in Nevada, (c. 1874). New York: Charles Scribner's Sons, 1933.

Shinn, Charles H.
The Story of the Mine. New York: D. Appleton & Co., 1903. 272 pp.

Stone, Caroline R.
Inga of Porcupine Mine; Illus. by Ellen Simon. New York: Holiday House, 1942. 212 pp.
A children's story of a mining community of Northern Michigan. It pictures the life which the foreign-born of many nationalities are making for themselves in mining.

Strawbridge, Ann West
Dawn After Danger. New York: Coward-McCann, 1934.

Thomas, Jean
Ballad Makin' in the Mountains of Kentucky. New York: Henry Holt and Co., 1939. 270 pp.
Contains a number of miners' songs. Texts, and some tunes.

Wiley, Richard T.
Monongahela: The River and Its Region. Butler, Pa.: The Ziegler Company, 1937.

Wilson, Winifred Graham
"Miner's Superstitions." *Life and Letters Today,* 32:86–93, 1942.

Work Projects Administration.
Bituminous Coal Mining. Two volumes. Work Projects Administration. In Cooperation with United States Bureau of Mines. Philadelphia: 1939.

SPEECH

Davidson, Levette J.
"Mining Expressions Used in Colorado." *AS* 5 (No. 2):144–147, 1929.

Fay, A. H.
A Glossary of the Mining and Mineral Industry. Washington, D. C.: U. S. Government Printing Office, 1920. 754 pp. Bureau of Mines Bulletin No. 95.

Hand, Wayland D.
"Nicknames of Butte Miners." *CFQ* 5 (No. 3): 307–309, 1946.

Korson, George
"Anthracite Miners as Bards and Minstrels." *AS* 10 (No. 4):260–268, 1935.

————.

Glossary of Anthracite Technical and Colloquial Words and Phrases. In: *Minstrels of the Mine Patch,* (pp. 311–320). Philadelphia: University of Pennsylvania Press, 1938.

Lopushanksy, Joseph and Michael
"Mining Town Terms." *AS* 4 (No. 5):368–374, 1929.

Moore, Helen L.
"The Lingo of the Mining Camp." *AS* 2 (No. 2):86–88, 1927.

MINERS' SONGS

See: American Folksong and Ballad Collections, pp. 85-90, 118-20.

GENERAL STUDIES AND COLLECTIONS

Adams, James Taylor
Death in the Dark; a collection of factual ballads of American mine disasters; with a foreword and background stories by J. T. A. Big Laurel, Va.: Adams-Mullins Press, 1941.
Texts only.

"Ballads of Mine Regions Depict Life of the Workers. Rare bits of folklore in verse gathered in Pennsylvania are traced to their sources." *The New York World* Sept. 11, 1927.

Bennett, John
"Lackawanna Spooners." *Sat. Rev. of Lit.* 5:108, Sept. 8, 1928.
Marching song (words only) of workers loading coal boats—"from Harlem to Gowanus." Spooners, name applied to rapid professional handlers of the shovel.

Emrich, Duncan
"Casey Jones" and Other Ballads of the Mining West; with Illustrations by Bob Cormack. Denver, Colo.: Author's Edition, (1615 Grant St.) 1942. 16 pp.

————.

"Mining Songs." *SFQ* 6:103–106, 1942.
Words and music of "Cousin Jack" and "Casey Jones" and words only of "Liberty Engine Co. #1 from Nevada."

————.

"Songs of the Western Miner." *CFQ* 1:213–232, 1942.
Mostly text; five tunes given.

Evans, R. A.
"Coal Cracker's Song." *New Republic* 90:41, (Feb. 17) 1937. Illus.

Fitch, Anthony
Ballads of Western Mines and Others. New York: Cochrane Publishing Company, 1910. 60 pp., illus., front., plates.

Hand, Wayland D.
"California Miners' Folklore: Above Ground." *CFQ* 1:24–47, 1942.

————.

"California Miners' Folklore: Below Ground." *CFQ* 1:127–155, 1942.

Korson, George Gershon
Coal Dust on the Fiddle: Songs and Stories of the Bituminous Industry. Phila.: University of Pennsylvania Press, 1943. xvi, 460 pp., music, illus.

————.

Minstrels of the Mine Patch; Songs and Stories of the Anthracite Industry. Philadelphia: University of Pennsylvania Press, 1938. xii, 332 pp. Unaccompanied melodies, bibl.

————.
Songs and Ballads of the Anthracite Miner;
a seam of folklore which once ran through life
in the hard coal fields of Pennsylvania, gath-
ered and ed. by George G. Korson. New
York: F. H. Hitchcock, 1927. xxviii, 196 p.
This work first appeared in the United Mine
Worker's Journal.

————, ed.
*Pennsylvania Songs and Legends: A Folklore
Anthology.* Introduction by the author. Philadelphia: University of Pennsylvania Press,
1949. 466 pp., illus.
Contains more than 100 folk songs and ballads
with music, a number of these of the miners.

Le Mon, Melville, and Korson, George
The Miner Sings. New York: J. Fischer and
Bro., 1937.
Arranged for voice and piano.

Lomax, John A. and Alan
Our Singing Country. New York: The Macmillan Company, 1941.
Part III, Chapt. 5—"Miners' Songs," texts and
tunes.

Shoemaker, Henry W., comp.
Mountain Minstrelsy of Pennsylvania. Philadelphia: Newman F. McGirr, 1931. 319 pp.
3rd ed., rev. and enl.
Texts only—a rich harvest. Includes songs of the
lumberjacks, miners, canalers, wagoners, as well
as old country ballads and songs.

————.
North Pennsylvania Minstrelsy. As sung in the
Backwoods Settlements, Hunting Cabins and
Lumber Camps in the "Black Forest" of Penn-
sylvania, 1840–1923. Altoona, Pa.: Times Trib-
une Company, 1923. 228 pp.
Texts only, except for two tunes, pp. 44–45.

————.
"Songs of Mine Disasters." *Altoona Tribune*
Nov. 3, 1930.
An editorial.

Smith, Grace Partridge
"The Miner's Chant." *CFQ* 2:221–223, 1943.
Words and music of a bituminous miner's song.
(from Iowa.)

RECORDS

Album—Collections

*Songs and Ballads of the Anthracite Miners.
Album 16.* Recorded and edited by George
Korson. U. S. Library of Congress. Folklore
Section. 5 records.　　　　　AAFS–76/80

The East and Middle Atlantic States. Pennsylvania Anthracite Miners. George S. Korson,
Lewisburg, Pa.

**U. S. Library of Congress. Division of Music.
Folklore Section.**
Songs of the Pennsylvania Coal Miners. Re-
corded by George Korson.　　　AAFS–LC

Individual Titles

"A Celebrated Workingman."
Daniel Walsh at Centralia, Pa. In: *Album 16.
Songs and Ballads of the Anthracite Miners.*
Library of Congress.　　　　　AAFS–78

"Boys On the Hill"—Hornpipe: Fiddle Tune.
Played on the fiddle by James Muldowney of
Pottsville, Pa., in the Newkirk Tunnel Mine,
Tamaqua, Pa. In: *Album 16. Songs and Bal-
lads of the Anthracite Miners.* Library of
Congress.　　　　　AAFS–77

"Down, Down, Down."
William E. Keating at Pottsville, Pa. In: *Al-
bum 16. Songs and Ballads of the Anthracite
Miners.* Library of Congress.　　AAFS–76

"Down in a Coal Mine."
Morgan Jones at Wilkes-Barre, Pa. In: *Album
16. Songs and Ballads of the Anthracite Miners.*
Library of Congress.　　　　　AAFS–80

"John J. Curtis."
Andrew Rada at Shenandoah, Pa. In: *Album
16. Songs and Ballads of the Anthracite
Miners.* Library of Congress.　　AAFS–78

"Me Johnny Mitchell Man."
Jerry Byrne at Buck Run, Pa. In: *Album 16.
Songs and Ballads of the Anthracite Miners.*
Library of Congress.　　　　　AAFS–77

"On Johnny Mitchell's Train."
Jerry Byrne at Buck Run, Pa. In: *Album 16.
Songs and Ballads of the Anthracite Miners.*
Library of Congress.　　　　　AAFS–77

"Pay Day at Coal Creek" (Lament on a Mine
Disaster). Sung with 5-string banjo by Pete
Steele at Hamilton, Ohio, 1938. Recorded by
Alan and Elizabeth Lomax. In: *Album 2,* Re-
cordings of American Folk Songs, Library of
Congress, 1943.　　　　　AAFS6–B

"Rolling on the Rye Grass"—Reel: Fiddle Tune.
Played on the fiddle by James Muldowney in
the Newkirk Tunnel Mine, Tamaqua, Pa. In:
*Album 16. Songs and Ballads of the Anthracite
Miners.* Library of Congress.　　AAFS–77

"The Avondale Mine Disaster."
John J. Quinn at Wilkes-Barre, Pa. In: *Album
16. Songs and Ballads of the Anthracite
Miners.* Library of Congress.　　AAFS–76

"The Miner's Doom."
Daniel Walsh at Centralia, Pa. In: *Album 16.
Songs and Ballads of the Anthracite Miners.*
Library of Congress.　　　　　AAFS–79

"The Old Miner's Refrain."
Daniel Walsh at Centralia, Pa. In: *Album 16.
Songs and Ballads of the Anthracite Miners.*
Library of Congress.　　　　　AAFS–78

"The Shoofly."
Daniel Walsh at Centralia, Pa. In: *Album 16.
Songs and Ballads of the Anthracite Miners.*
Library of Congress.　　　　　AAFS–80

"Union Man."
Albert Morgan in the Newkirk Tunnel Mine,
Tamaqua, Pa. In: *Album 16. Songs and Bal-
lads of the Anthracite Miners.* Library of
Congress.   AAFS–79

"When the Breaker Starts Full Time."
Jerry Byrne at Buck Run, Pa. In: *Album 16.
Songs and Ballads of the Anthracite Miners.*
Library of Congress.   AAFS–79

C. Oil Drilling

FOLKLORE

GENERAL STUDIES AND COLLECTIONS

Adams, H. H.
"Doodlebugs and Doodlebuggers." *CFQ* 3:53–
58, 1944.
 Old beliefs describing methods of locating oil.

Boatright, Mody C.
Gil Morgan: Minstrel of the Oil Fields. Austin,
Tex.: Texas Folklore Society Publications 20,
1945. xii, 104 pp., illus.

Donoghue, David
"Myths in Oil Finding." *TFSP* 9:45–47, 1931.

House, Boyce
Oil Boom. Caldwell, Idaho: Caxton Printers,
1941.
 "This book gives the best picture of the gushing
 days of oil, money and humanity." (Dobie)

———.
Were You in Ranger? Dallas, Tex.: Tardy
Publishing Co., Inc., 1935. 210 pp.

Lanham, Edwin
Thunder in the Earth. New York: Harcourt,
Brace & Co., 1941. 570 pp.
 Fictionalized tale of oil.

SPEECH

Dignowity, Hartman
"Nicknames in Texas Oil Fields." *TFSP* 6:
98–101, 1927.

McTee, A. R.
"Oil Field Diction." *TFSP* 4:64–68, 1925.

Northup, Clark S.
"Oilfield Workers: The Language of the Oil
Wells." *Dialect Notes* 2 (parts 5 and 6), 1903–
1904.

———.
"The Language of the Oil Wells" I and II.
Dialect Notes 2 (Part 5):338–346; 2 (Part 6):
373–393. New York, Pennsylvania and West
Virginia.

Pond, Frederick R.
"Language of the California Oil Fields." *AS* 7
(No. 4):261–272, 1932.

Sawey, Orlan L.
"Pipe Line Diction." *TFSP* 18:200–204, 1943.

Stevens, Helen K.
"Oil Field Expressions." *AS* 12 (No. 2):153–
154, 1937.

Winfrey, James W.
"Oil patch talk." *TFSP* 19:139–148, 1944.
 Expressions used by oil workers in Gulf Coast of
 Texas.

THE RAILROADER

THE RAILROADER

FOLKLORE

BIBLIOGRAPHY

Donovan, Frank P., Jr.
The Railroad in Literature. Boston: The Railway and Locomotive Historical Society, Inc., 1940.
Contains a very good bibliography.

GENERAL STUDIES AND COLLECTIONS

Bontemps, Arna, and Conroy, Jack
The Fast Sooner Hound. Boston: Houghton Mifflin, 1942.
A tall tale from the early days of railroading.

Bromley, Joseph
Clear the Tracks! New York: Whittlesey House, 1943.
Written by a retired engineer who rode the old Black River Line and the Lackawanna. "The book is full of swift narrative, humor, and slang." (H. W. Thompson)

Cunningham, Frank
Big Dan. The Story of a Colorful Railroadeer. Salt Lake City: Deseret News Press, 1946. 350 pp.
"History, adventure and the romance of the rails are skillfully blended in the story, for wherever Big Dan happened to be, things seemed to happen. It is filled with the color of plantation life, stirring incidents of the Civil War and Confederate Army, amusing anecdote of the mountaineers of Kentucky and the Indians of the Southwest, thrilling adventures of railroading in Colorado and Utah in pioneer days. (E. A. West)

Donovan, Frank P., Jr.
The Railroad in Literature. Boston: The Railway and Locomotive Historical Society, Inc., 1940.
An exhaustive survey and bibliography.

Estes, George
The Rawhide Railroad. Canby, Oregon: Publishing House of the Clackmas County News, 1916.
"This is a story of a remarkable steam railroad actually constructed and successfully operated in the beautiful Walla Walla Valley many years ago." (Estes)

Hubbard, Freeman H.
Railroad Avenue; Great Stories and Legends of American Railroading. New York: Whittlesey House, 1945. 374 pp., illus.
The great characters of railroad fame—true and legendary, come to life in these pages, as well as the lusty tales of their deeds are recounted.

SPEECH

Anonymous
"A Glossary of Pullman Service Terms." *The Pullman News* 1:137, Sept., 1922.

Batie, Russell V.
"Railroad Lingo." *AS* 9 (No. 1):73–74, 1934.

Cottrell, W. F., and Montgomery, H. C.
"Glossary of Railroad Terms." *AS* 18:161–170, 1943.

Guiterman, Arthur
"Pullman Ode." *New Yorker* 13 (No. 6):69, 1937.

Harper, Robert S.
"Railroad Slang." *Writer's Digest,* pp. 40–42, 64, May, 1931.
Condensed from the *Railroad Man's Magazine.*

Hubbard, Freeman H.
Vocabulary of Railroad Lingo. In: *Railroad Avenue;* Great Stories and Legends of American Railroading, (pp. 331–367). New York: Whittlesey House, 1945.

Jones, Grover
"Railroad Lingo. A Study in Dialect—With an Essay on the Language of the Rails." *Bookman* 69:324–327, 1929.

Learned, Mrs. Walter
"The Dialect of Railway Employees." *JAFL* 4:175–176, 1891.
As heard on the New York, New Haven, and Hartford Railroads.

Loomis, Charles P.
"Lineman's English." *AS* 1 (No. 12):659–660, 1926.

Pollack, F. Walter
"The Sins of the Railroad Period." *AS* 2 (No. 5):247–248, 1927.
Deals with abbreviations and shortenings of railroad lines and terms.

Schultz, J. R.
"Railroad Terms." *AS* 12 (No. 2):154, 1937.

Sidney, F. H.
"Railroad Terms." *Dialect Notes* 4 (Part 5):355–357, 1916.

RAILROAD SONGS

See: American Folksong and Ballad Collections, pp. 85-90, 118-20.

GENERAL STUDIES AND COLLECTIONS

Alderson, William
On the wobbly "Casey Jones" and other songs. *CFQ* 1:373–376, 1942.
Gives also notes on "Joe Hill."

"Casey Jones." *Louisville Times,* March 4, 1911.
Establishes the historic facts in Jones's last midnight **run.**

"Casey Jones."

Words and music recounting the last great ride of this engineer are found in many song collections, besides those mentioned below. In addition one may add the following authors and books:

Delaney's Song Book, p. 58 (words only) NYPL; Downes, O., Treasury of American Song, pp. 264–266, voice and piano; Geller, Famous Songs, p. 231; Loesser, Humor in American Song, p. 208; Neely, Tales and Songs of Southern Illinois, pp. 167–171; Odum, Negro and His Songs, p. 207 (words); Odum, Negro Workaday Songs, p. 126; Popular Songs, Ser. 2, 1909 (NYPL); Pound, L., American Ballads, p. 133; Rebel Song Book, ILGWU, p. 58; Scarborough, D., On the Trail of the Negro Folk Song, p. 249; Shay, F., My Pious Friends, p 35; Spaeth, S., Reed 'em & Weep, p. 119; Sherwin, Railroad Songs of Yesterday, p. 4; Songs of the People, Workers Library, N Y., p. 12; Song Hit Folio, N. Y., vol. 1, no 3, p. 4 (NYPL); Song Hits, N. Y., vol. 1, Bk. 15, p. 8 (NYPL); IWW Songs, Industrial Workers of the World, Chicago, Ill., 1919, p. 38; More Rebel Songs for Sixpence, London, (Lansbury's Labour Weekly), p. 7; and others.

Donovan, Frank P., Jr.
The Railroad in Literature. Railway and Locomotive Historical Society, Inc. Boston: Harvard Business School, 1940.
Contains a discussion and listing of railroad songs.

Guthrie, Woody
"Songs of the Migration Trails." Direction 3:6–7, 1940.

Hubbard, Freeman H.
Railroad Avenue; Great Stories and Legends of American Railroading. New York: Whittlesey House, 1946. 374 pp., illus.
"...Casey Jones, 'Jawn' Henry, the Andrews Raid, Long John Simpkins, Jesse James, Kate Shelley, the Johnstown Flood, Harry McClintock, and some wonderful 'raildogs'." (Elaine L. Lewis). Texts only.

Lomax, John A. and Alan
American Ballads and Folk Songs. New York: The Macmillan Company, 1934.
Chapter I—Working on the Railroad, contains 17 songs, most of these with tunes.

————.
Our Singing Country. New York: The Macmillan Company, 1941.
Part III, Chapt. 4—"Railroaders and Hobos," texts and tunes.

Sandburg, Carl
The American Songbag. New York: Harcourt, Brace and Co., 1927.
Chapter on— "Railroad and Work Gangs."

Sherwin, Sterling, and McClintock, Harry K.
Railroad Songs of Yesterday. New York: Shapiro, Bernstein and Co., 1943.
For voice and piano. Contains among other well-known tunes, "Casey Jones," "I've Been Working on the Railroad," "Where Do You Work-a, John?" "Daddy's the Engineer," "The Runaway Train."

ARRANGEMENTS:
(Individual Titles)

————: Voice and Piano

"Casey Jones."
Kennedy, R. Emmet: In: The American Songbag, by Carl Sandburg, pp. 366–367. N. Y.: Harcourt, Brace & Co., 1927.

"Casey Jones."
Newton, Eddie: South. Calif. Music Co.: Voice and piano.

"Casey Jones."
Seeger, Ruth and Charles: In: Folk Song: U. S. A., by John and Alan Lomax, p. 248. N. Y.: Duell, Sloan & Pearce, 1947.

"Mama Have You Heard the News?"
(Casey Jones). Gilbert, Harry M.: In: The American Songbag, by Carl Sandburg, (pp. 368–369). N. Y.: Harcourt, Brace & Co., 1927.

————: Male Voices

"Railroad Chant."
Scott, Tom: Words & Music, Inc.: TTBB. Fred Waring Glee Club Arrangement.

RECORDS

"East Bound Train."
In: American Folk Songs Album. Luther; Layman; Stokes, vocal-guitar-fiddle-bass.   DE–25

"Mama Have You Heard the News." (Casey Jones). Carl Sandburg, vocal-guitar.
MU–210–B

"Midnight Special."
In: "The Midnight Special" and old Southern Prison Songs. Lead Belly and Golden Gate Quartet.   VI–P50

"New River Train."
In: American Folk Songs Album. Luther; Layman; Stokes; guitar-fiddle-bass.   DE–25

"900 Miles" (R. R. Song).
Woody Guthrie, Cisco Houston, Goodwin Hawes, Bess Lomax, instrumental-hot fiddle.
ASCH–432–1B

"Pat Works On the Railway."
In: Two Centuries of American Folk Songs. American Ballad Singers, Siegmeister. VI–P41

"Railroad Bill."
Riley Puckett; white singer. Negro bad man ballad.   CO–15040–D

"Riding on That Train Forty-Five."
Mainer, Morris, Ledford.   VI–27493

"The Midnight Special."
Lead Belly, and Golden Gate Quartet.
VI–27266

"The Wreck on the C & O Road."
Bradley Kincaid; vocal and guitar. CH–45098

"Track-Lining Song."
Sung by Allen Prothero at State Penitentiary,
Nashville, Tenn., 1933. In: *Album 8*, Library
of Congress. AAFS40–B

"Train."
Josh White, vocal-guitar. ASCH–358–2B

"Train Special."
Walter Hurdt, harmonic solo. Imitation of
Railroad. BL–8063–B

"Tramping Ties."
Called by Henry Truvillion at Wiergate, Texas,
1940. In: *Album 8*, Library of Congress.
AAFS36–A2

"Unloading Rails."
Called by Henry Truvillion at Wiergate, Texas,
1940. In: *Album 8*, Library of Congress.
AAFS36–A1

**U. S. Library of Congress. Division of Music.
Folklore Section.**
Railroad Songs. L. P. Temple, Washington,
D. C., coll. AAFS–LC

————.
*Mexican Folksongs Recorded at the Pennsyl-
vania Railroad Camp*. Charles Seeger, coll.
AAFS–LC

THE SEA — SAILORMEN — AND RIVER BOATMEN

THE SEA — SAILORMEN — AND RIVER BOATMEN

FOLKLORE

BIBLIOGRAPHY

Lewis, Charles Lee
Books of the Sea. An Introduction to Nautical Literature. Annapolis, Md.: United States Naval Institute, 1943. 318 pp.

PERIODICAL

Sea Lore; for all who love the sea & ships. V. 1, 1935–. Vancouver, B. C.: Bimonthly.

GENERAL STUDIES AND COLLECTIONS

An Old Salt.
Jack's Kit, or Saturday Night in the Forecastle. New York: Bunce & Brother.

Ashley, Clifford W.
The Yankee Whaler; intro. by Robert Cushman Murphy. Boston: Houghton, Mifflin Co., 1926. xxiv, 379 pp., incl. ill. plates.

Bayly, George
Sea-life Sixty Years Ago, a record of adventures which led up to the discovery of the relics of the long-missing expedition commanded by the Comte de la Perouse. London: K. Paul, Trench & Co., 1885. viii, 224 pp.

Beckett, W. N. T.
A Few Naval Customs, Expressions, Traditions and Superstitions. Portsmouth, England: Gieves, 1931. 92 pp.

Bell, Frederick Jackson
Room to Swing a Cat; Being Some Tales of the Old Navy. New York: Longmans, Green & Co., 1938. 272 pp., illus.

Blair, Walter, and Meine, Franklin J.
Mike Fink, King of the Mississippi Keelboatmen. New York: Holt, 1933. 283 pp., illus., bibl.

Brooks, Maud D.
"Rafting on the Allegheny." *NYFQ* 1 (No. 4): 224–230, 1945.

Chapelle, Howard Irving
The Baltimore Clipper; its origin and development. Salem, Mass.: The Marine Research Society, 1930. xii, 192 pp., illus.

—————.
The History of American Sailing Ships. New York: W. W. Norton & Co., 1935. xvii, 400 pp., illus., bibl.

Chatterton, E. Keble
Sailing the Seas. London: Chapman and Hall, 1931.

Cheney, Brainard
River Rouge. Boston: Houghton Mifflin, 1942. 443 pp.
"What Mr. Cheney doesn't know and doesn't set down about the life, customs, river lore and language (foul) of the raftsmen can hardly be worth knowing or recording." (Orville Prescott)

Chittenden (Hiram Martin)
History of Early Steamboat Navigation on the Missouri River. Life and Adventures of Joseph La Barge. New York: F. P. Harper, 1903. 2 vols., illus.
The life and adventures of the famous Missouri River pilot. "The best book ever written about steamboatin' on an American river."

Church, Albert Cook
Whale Ships and Whaling. New York: W. W. Norton and Co., 1938. 179 pp., illus.
"Author and publisher are to be congratulated for producing one of the finest books of New England maritime literature." (S.E.M.)

Clark, Arthur Hamilton
The Clipper Ship Era, New York: G. P. Putnams Sons, 1910. xii, 404 pp., illus.
An epitome of famous American and British Clipper ships, their owners, builders, and crews, 1843–1869.

Clark, Joseph G.
Lights and Shadows of Sailor Life as Exemplified in Fifteen Years' Experience, including the more thrilling events of the U. S. exploring expedition. Boston: J. Putnam, 1847. xii, 324 pp.

Cleveland, Richard Jeffry
Voyages of a Merchant Navigator in the Days That are Past. New York: Harper and Brothers, 1886. 245 pp.

Conrad, Joseph
The Mirror of the Sea: Memories and Impressions. Garden City, New York: Doubleday, Page and Company, 1921.

Culver, Henry B.
The Book of Old Ships and Something of their Evolution and Romance. Wherein will be found drawings and descriptions of many varieties of vessels, both long and round, showing their development from most remote times; the portraiture of their progress, their garnishments, etc., etc., etc., together with divers dissertations upon the *Origins of Shipping;* also an Appendix wherein will be discovered to the *inquisitive* much information appertaining to the Ancient Uses and *customs of the sea,* and mariners. Illustrated in lime and color with a variety of original designs of shipping compiled from authentic sources. Drawn by Gordon Grant. New York: Garden City Publishing Co., 1924. 306 pp., illus.

Dana, Richard Henry, Jr.
Two Years Before the Mast. New York: Houghton Mifflin Co., 1911.
> One of America's great classics of sea life; rich in customs, traditions, and beliefs.

Daniel, Hawthorne
The Clipper Ship. Illustrated by Frank J. Rigney. New York: Dodd Mead and Company, 1928. 277 pp., illus.

Dayton, Fred Erving
Steamboat Days. Illustrated by John Wolcott Adams. New York: Tudor Publishing Company, 1939. 436 pp.
> A saga of the development of Steamboat Navigaiton in America—from the early Long Island Steamers, across the New England waters to the Great Lakes, the Western River steamboats, the Atlantic Coast lines—the whole American network is richly told.

Deatherage, Charles P.
Steamboating on the Missouri River in the Sixties. ... Kansas City, Mo.: Alexander Printing Co., 1924. 39 pp., illus.

Derleth, August
The Wisconsin. (Rivers of America Series). Illus. by John Stewart Curry. New York: Farrar & Rinehart, 1942. 336 pp.
> The complex panorama is viewed from Sauk City.

Digges, Jeremiah
Bowleg Bill, The Sea-Going Cowboy, or Ship Ahoy & Let Er Buck! New York: The Viking Press, 1938.

————.
In Great Waters, The Story of the Portuguese Fishermen. New York: The Macmillan Company, 1941.

Durant, Edward W.
"Lumbering and Steamboating on the St. Croix River." *Minnesota Historical Society Collections* 10 (Pt. 2):645–675, 1905.

Federal Writers' Project.
Whaling Masters. (American Guide Series). Compiled and written by the Federal Writers' Project of the WPA of Mass. New Bedford, Mass.: Reynolds Printing, 1938.

Ferguson, Robert
Arctic Harpooner: A Voyage on the Schooner Abbie Bradford, 1878–1879. Edited by Leslie Dalrymple Stàer. Philadelphia: University of Pennsylvania Press, 1938. x, 216 pp.
> An interesting chapter in whaling and lore of the Arctic.

Firestone, Clark B.
Flowing South. New York: Robert M. McBride and Company, 1941. 263 pp.
> The author is concerned with all customs of Steamboat travel; rich in lore and anecdote of the Upper and Lower Mississippi.

Freeman, Lewis Ransome
Waterways of Westward Wandering; Small Boat Voyages Down the Ohio, Missouri and Mississippi Rivers. New York: Dodd, Mead and Co., 1927. xii, 368 pp., illus.

Haley, Nelson Cole
Whale Hunt: The Narrative of a Voyage by Nelson Cole Haley, Harpooner in the Ship Charles W. Morgan, 1849–53. New York: Ives Washburn, 1948. 304 pp.
> "For a zestful New England boy there were the storms and gales, and a fine hurricane. There were also deserted anchorages, and isles with cannibals, English remittance men and muscular native belles. There was the hazardous search for whales, in open boat in mid-ocean; there were topographical and humane observations like a latter-day Defoe, with the saving grace of a clipped Cape Cod Humor." (William Germain Dooley)

Hall, Captain Basil, R.N.
Fragments of Voyages and Travels. London: Edward Mixon, 1846.

Hanson, Joseph Mills
The Conquest of the Missouri. New York: Rinehart and Company, 1946. 458 pp., illus.
> A fascinating story, with many interesting asides on the people and their customs,—of Captain Marsh, the man who named the "Big Muddy."

Hereford, Robert A.
Old Man River. Illus. by Lee Conrey and Daniel R. Bishop. Caldwell, Idaho: The Caxton Printers, 1943. 301 pp.
> The story and adventures of Louis Rosché, who spent seventy-five years on the Mississippi and Missouri Rivers.

Jackson, Orton Porter, and Evans, F. E.
The New Book of American Ships. New York: Frederick A. Stokes Co., 1926. vi, 428 pp., illus.

Johnson, Capt., and Mrs. Irving
Westward Bound in The Schooner Yankee. New York: W. W. Norton & Company, 1936. viii, 348 pp., illus.

Judson, Edward Zane Carroll (Ned Buntline)
The Black Avenger of the Spanish Main. A thrilling story of the Buccaneer times. New York: S. French, 1847. 100 pp.

————.
Clarence Rhett, or The Cruise of a Privateer. An American sea story. New York: F. A. Brady, 1866. 78 pp.

————.
Cruisings, Afloat and Ashore, From the Private Log of Ned Buntline. Sketches of land and sea, humorous and pathetic, tragical and comical. New York: R. Craighead, 1848. 102 pp., illus.

Laing, Alexander
Clipper Ship Men. New York: Duell, Sloan and Pearce, 1944. 279 pp.

————.
The Sea Witch. New York: Murray Hill Books, 1944. 487 pp.
> A narrative of the experiences of Capt. Roger Murray and others in an American clipper ship during the years 1846 and 1856. New ed. illustrated by Gordon Grant.

Lamsley, Arthur
Sea Lure, with a foreword by the Right Hon. Lord Runciman and eleven illustrations by William Fyffe. London: Heath, Cranton Ltd., 1935. 184 pp., illus.

Lewis, Charles Lee
Books of the Sea. An Introduction to Nautical Literature. Annapolis, Md.: United States Naval Institute, 1943. 318 pp.
> An excellent discussion of the literature and bibliography of the sea.

Long, Stephen Harriman
Voyage in a Six-Oared Skiff to the Falls of Saint Anthony in 1817. . . . Philadelphia: H. B. Ashmead, 1860. 87 pp.

Loomis, Alfred F.
Ranging the Maine Coast. Illustrated by Edward A. Wilson. New York: W. W. Norton & Company, 1939. 274 pp., illus.

Lorentz, Pare
The River. New York: Stackpole Sons, 1938. 64 pp., illus.

Low, Gorham P.
The Sea Made Men, the story of a Gloucester lad, presented by Roger Babson, edited by Elizabeth L. Alling. New York: Fleming H. Revell Co., 1937. 280 pp.
> "The memoirs of . . . a Gloucester sea captain, Gorham P. Low."—p. 10.

Lubboch, Alfred Basil
The Down Easters: American Deep-Water Sailing Ships, 1869–1929. Boston: C. E. Lauriat Company, 1929. xvi, 285 pp.

McKay, Richard Cornelius
Some Famous Sailing Ships and Their Builder, Donald McKay. New York: G. Putnam's Sons, 1928. xxvii, 395 pp.

MacMechan, Archibald McKellar
Sagas of the Sea. London: J. M. Dent & Sons, Ltd., 1923. 156 pp., illus.
Sea lore of Nova Scotia.

————.
There Go the Ships. Toronto: McClelland and Stewart, Ltd., 1928. 293 pp.
Life and lore of Canadian seamen and ships.

MacMullen, Jerry
Paddle-Wheel Days in California. Illustrated by the author. Palo Alto, Calif.: Stanford University Press, 1945. 157 pp.
> A fascinating book for anyone interested either in California or in steamboats.

Masefield, John
Sea Life in Nelson's Time. New York: The Macmillan Company, 1925.

Melville, Herman
Moby Dick, or the Whale. New York: Harper & Bros., 1851. xxiii, 634 pp.

Merchants and Miners Transportation Co.
Tales of the Coast. Stories of life and high adventure in old days along the Atlantic seaboard and a brief history of the Merchants and Miners Transportation Co., Baltimore: The Read-Taylor Press, 1927. 63 pp., illus.

Merrick, George Byron
Old Times on the Upper Mississippi, the Recollections of a Steamboat Pilot from 1854 to 1863. Cleveland: The A. H. Clark Company, 1909. 323 pp., illus.

Mitchell, Joseph
"Dragger Captain." *The New Yorker* 22 (No. 48) 41–42, (Jan. 11) 1947.

Newton, Hilah Foote
"Horses and Steamboats on Champlain." *NYFQ:* 1:33–45, 1945.

Neihardt, John G.
The River and I. New York and London: G. P. Putnam's Sons, 1910.

Neville, Morgan
"The Last of the Boatmen." *The Western Souvenir,* 1829.

Nordhoff, Charles
Sailor Life on a Man of War. New York: Dodd, Mead & Co., 1881. 363 pp., illus.

Paden, Irene D.
The Wake of the Prairie Schooner. New York: Macmillan, 1943. xix, 514 pp., drawings, maps, bibl., index.

Patterson, John Edward
Sea-Pie; Being Some Minor Reminiscences and Tales of Other Men . . . with a title-page, and two drawings by J. Gridley Withycombe. London: M. Goschen, Ltd., 1915. xviii, 340 pp.

————.
The Lure of the Sea. New York: G. H. Doran Company, 1912. 102 pp.
Told in verse.

————.
The Sea's Anthology; From the Earliest Times Down to the Middle of the 19th Century; edited with notes, introduction and appendix. New York: George H. Doran Company, 1913. xxxvi, 383 pp.

Petersen, William John
Steamboating on the Upper Mississippi, the Waterway to Iowa; Some River History. Iowa City, Ia.: The State Historical Society of Iowa, 1937. 575 pp., bibl.

Pinckney, Pauline A.
American Figureheads and Their Carvers. New York: W. W. Norton & Company, 1940. 223 pp., illus., bibl.
The story and lore of the figureheads on ships.

Procter, George H.
The Fishermen's Memorial and Record Book,
containing a list of vessels and their crews,
lost from the port of Gloucester from the year
1830 to October 1, 1873,—including those lost
on the gale of August 24, 1873. It also contains
valuable statistics of the fishing business, off-
hand sketches, big trips, tales of narrow escapes, maritime poetry, and other matters of
interest to those toilers of the sea. Gloucester,
Mass.: Procter Brothers, 1873. iv, 172 pp., illus.

Quick, Herbert
Mississippi Steamboatin'; a History of Steamboating on the Mississippi and its Tributaries.
New York: H. Holt and Company, 1926. xiv,
342 pp., illus., bibl.

Reynard, Elizabeth
The Narrow Land. Boston: Houghton, Mifflin
Co., 1934.
Good yarns of the sea.

Rice, Cale Young
A Sea-Lover's Scrip. London: Hodder and
Stoughton, 1925. xi, 122 pp.
An earlier edition appeared as: *Sea Poems.*

Robinson, Charles Napier
The British Tar in Fact and Fiction. The
poetry, pathos, and humor of the sailor's life.
Introd. by John Leyland. Good prints. London
and New York: Harper & Brothers, 1909. ix–
xxiii, 520 pp., illus.

Rogers, Stanley Reginald Harry
Sea Lore, Illustrated by the Author. London:
G. G. Harrap & Co., Ltd., 1929. 261 pp.

———.
Ships and Sailors; Tales of the Sea. Illustrated
by the author. Boston: Little, Brown and Company, 1928. 303 pp., illus.

———.
Tales of the Fore-An-Aft, Illustrated by the
author. London: G. G. Harrap & Company,
Ltd., 1935. 263 pp., illus.

———.
The Book of the Sailing Ships, with one hun-
dred illustrations by the author. London: G. G.
Harrap & Company, Ltd., 1931. 281 pp., illus.

Rosskam, Edwin and Louise
Towboat River. Illustrated. New York: Duell,
Sloan and Pearce, 1948. 295 pp.
"All those who love the inland waters can be
thankful that this record of the river as it is today
was made by a couple imaginative enough to
understand river life, thoughtful enough to
describe it truthfully." (Horace Reynolds.)

Rowe, William Hutchinson
Shipbuilding Days in Casco Bay 1727–1890;
being footnotes to the Maritime history of
Maine. Yarmouth, Me.: The Author, 1929. xii,
222 pp.

Russell, Charles E.
A-Rafting on the Mississippi. New York: The
Century Co., 1928. xii, 357 pp., illus., music.
The adventures and hardihood of the keel-boat-
men.

Saxon, Lyle
Father Mississippi. New York: D. Appleton-
Century Co., 1943. xi, 427 pp., illus., bibl.

Shay, Frank
Iron Men and Wooden Ships. New York:
Doubleday, Doran & Co., 1924.

———.
Mary Read; the pirate wench. London: Hurst
& Blackett, Ltd., 1934. 286 pp.

Sébillot, Paul
Le Folklore des pecheurs. Paris: J. Maisonneuve, 1901. xii, 389 pp., bibl.
Of great value and interest for comparative study
purposes.

Smith, Cicely Fox
A Book of Famous Ships. Illustrations by Phil
Smith. Boston: Houghton Mifflin Company,
1924. vi, 181 pp.

———.
A Sea Chest; an Anthology of Ships and Sailormen. London: Methuen & Co., Ltd., 1927. viii,
716 pp.
Verse and prose.

———.
Sailor Town Days. Illustrated by Phil W.
Smith. London: Methuen & Co., Ltd., 1923. vi,
182 pp.

———.
Ships and Folks. London: E. Mathews, 1920.
78 pp.

———.
Adventures and Perils; being extracts from the
100 year-old Mariner's Chronicles and other
sources descriptive of shipwrecks and adventures at sea. London: M. Joseph, Ltd., 1936.
448 pp.

Sprague, Francis William
*Barnstable and Yarmouth Sea Captains and
Ship Owners;* list of sailings from New England to San Francisco. Boston: Privately
printed by T. R. Marvin & Son, 1913. 52 pp.

Swan, Oliver G., ed.
Deep Water Days. A Collection. Philadelphia:
McCrea, Smith Company, 1929.

Tisdale, Lieu
Three Years Behind the Guns, the true chroni-
cles of a "diddy box." New York: The Century
Co., 1908. 293 pp., illus.

Twain, Mark
Life in the Mississippi. Boston: H. O. Houghton & Co., 1883; and James R. Osgood & Co.,
1883.
Life and adventures of the raftsmen.

Verrill, A. Hyatt
The Real Story of the Whaler; Whaling, Past
and Present. New York: D. Appleton & Co.,
1916. xv, 248 pp.

Wallace, Frederick William
A Deepwater Yarn. . . . Stamford, Conn.: 1912.
24 pp., illus. (Shipmate Series No. 2.)

————————.
In the Wake of the Wind-ships, notes, records and biographies pertaining to the square-rigged merchant marine of British North America. New York: G. Sully & Co., 1927. xii, 282 pp., illus.

Ward, Edward W.
The Wooden World. London: Society for Nautical Research, 41 Westcombe Park Road, London, S. E. 3, Edwin Chappell, 1929. First published in London, 1707.

Wasson, George S.
Sailing Days on the Penobscot: The River and Bay as they were in the old days with a record of the vessels built there. Compiled by Lincoln Colcord, illustrated. Salem, Massachusetts: Marine Research Society, 1932. xiv, 465 pp., plates.

Waters, Frank
Eight Bells, Sailors. Snug Harbor Yarns and Ballads. New York: 1927.

Wells, Theodore
Narrative of the Life and Adventures of Capt. Theodore Wells of Wells, Me., giving a minute account of his voyages and the places visited. Biddeford: J. E. Butler & Co., 1874. 204 pp.

Wheeler, Mary
Steamboatin' Days. Baton Rouge, La.: Louisiana State University Press, 1944. 121 pp., 11 illus., music, index of songs.
Folksongs of the River packet era.

White, Stewart Edward
Blazed Trail. New York: Doubleday, Doran, 1902.

————————.
Riverman. New York: Doubleday, Doran, 1908.

Willard, Benjamin J.
Captain Ben's Book, a record of the things which happened to Capt. Benjamin J. Willard, pilot and stevedore, during some sixty years on sea and land, as related by himself. Portland, Me.: Lakeside Press, Printers, 1895. 204 pp., illus.

Williamson, W. M., ed.
Cornell's Sea Packet. New York: Cornell Maritime Press, 1941.

Witherspoon, Halliday (Nutter, William Herbert)
Liverpool Jarge, Yarns. Boston: Square Rigger Co., 1933. 120 pp.
Sailors' yarns and lingo.

Yexley, Lionel
Our Fighting Sea Men. London: Stanley Paul and Company, 1911.

FOLKTALES—LEGENDS

Chevalier, Henri Émile
Legends of the Sea. 39 Men for One Woman: An Episode of the Colonization of Canada.... New York: J. Bradburn, 1862. x, 310 pp.

Coffin, Captain R. F.
The Sea; An Old Sailor's Yarns. New York: 1884. 139 pp.

Edmonds, Walter D.
Mostly Canallers. (Collected Stories.) Boston: Little, Brown and Co., 1934. vii, 467 pp.

Popering, Edna Van, and Worth, Eloise
"Two Salt-Tea Tall Tales." *NYFQ* 2 (No. 2): 141–142, 1946.
Tales of the Giant Oyster and the Sea Serpent.

Waters, Frank
Eight Bells, Sailors' Snug Harbor Yarns and Ballads, with drawings by Robert Fawcett and a foreword by Joseph C. Lincoln. New York: D. Appleton & Company, 1927. xi, 151 pp., illus.
American sea life in prose and verse.

CUSTOMS—TRADITIONS—SUPERSTITIONS

Alden, Carroll Storrs, and Earle, Captain Ralph
Makers of Naval Tradition. Boston: Ginn and Company, 1925.

Arnold-Foster, D., Rear Admiral, R. N.
The Ways of the Navy. London and Melbourne: Ward, Loch and Company, 1932.

Bassett, Fletcher Stewart
Legends and Superstitions of the Sea and Sailors, in All Lands and at All Times. Chicago: Clarke & Co., 1885. 505 pp., illus.

Beckett, W. N. T., Commander, R. N.
A Few Naval Customs, Expressions, Traditions, and Superstitions. Portsmouth, England: Gieves, Ltd., 1931. 87 pp. 2nd ed.

Bishop, W. H.
"Fish and Men in the Maine Islands." *Harper's New Monthly Magazine* 61 (No. 364):506–507, Sept., 1880.
The story of the *Haskell* and the ghost crew.

Holland, Clive
"Some Superstitions of Sea-faring Folks." *Nautical Magazine* (London) 143:12–15, 1940.

Lovette, Leland P.
Naval Customs: Traditions and Usage. Annapolis, Md.: United States Naval Institute, 1939. xv, 404 pp., illus., bibl., music.

Lowry, R. G.
The Origin of Some Naval Terms and Customs. London: Sampson Low, Marston and Company, Ltd. 1930. ix, 102 pp.

McElroy, John William
"Seafaring in Seventeenth Century in New England." *New England Quarterly* 8:331–364, 1935.

Rapport, Dr. Angelo S.
Superstitions of Sailors. London: Stanley Paul Company, Ltd., 1928.

Wells, Rear Admiral Gerard, R.N.
Naval Customs and Traditions. London: Philip Alan, 1930.

SPEECH

Ageton, A. A.
"Annapolis, Cradle of the Navy." *National Geographic Magazine* 69:789–801, 1936.
Naval terms used by the students.

Anonymous
"Sea Lingo Passing on Modern Liners." *New York Times,* January 31, 1932. Sec. 2, p. 8.

Ashley, C. W.
The Yankee Whaler. Boston: Houghton Mifflin Company, 1926.
Glossary of Whaling Terms, (pp. 123–146).

Batchelder, Samuel F.
"Some Sea Terms in Land Speech." *New England Quarterly* 2:625–653, 1929.

Brackbill, Hervey
"Midshipman Jargon." *AS* 3 (No. 6):451–455, 1928.

Carr, Dorothy
"Some Annapolis Slang." *AS* 14–76–77, 1939.

Chase, George Davis
"Sea-Terms That Have Come Ashore." *New England Quarterly* 14:272–291, 1941.

Colcord, Joanna Carver
Sea Language Comes Ashore. New York: Cornell Maritime Press, 1945. 213 pp.
A rich collection of the expressions of maritime origin which have become figures of speech for shore.

————.
"Sea Terms Ashore." *Yachting* 58:32, 82, Dec., 1935.

Croucher, E. J.
"Sailor Words." *Word-Lore* 3:61–63, (April) 1928.

Denham, Edward
"Expressions, Chiefly of Whalers, Noted at New Bedford, Mass." *Dialect Notes* 4 (Part 3): 240–242, 1915.

Ferguson, Otis
"Vocabulary for Lakes, Deep Seas and Inland Waters." *AS* 19:103–111, 1944.
Picturesque sailors' speech.

Fraser, Edward, and Gibbons, John
Soldier and Sailor Words and Phrases. London: Routledge and Sons, 1925; New York: E. P. Dutton and Sons.

Goddard, L. F.
"Slang." *Daily Herald* (London): Aug. 4, 1936.
A brief vocabulary of the argot of English sailors.

Harvey, Bartle T.
"Navy Slang." *Dialect Notes* 4 (Part 2):150–151, 1914.

Healey, Jack
"Fo'c'sle Lingo." *AS* 3 (No. 4):345–346, 1928.

Jones, Claude E.
"A Note on Sailor Slang." *AS* 10 (No. 1):78–79, 1935.

"Language of the Sea."
AS 2 (No. 1):65, 1927.

Maurer, David W.
"Schoonerisms. Some Speech-Peculiarities of the North-Atlantic Fishermen." *AS* 5 (No. 5): 387–395, 1930.

Misfeldt, Orlo
"Argot of the Sea." *AS* 15:450–452, 1940.

"Navy Terms." *AS* 1 (No. 6):354–355, 1926.

Olds, Nathaniel S.
"Square-Rigger Relics in American Speech." *Atlantic Monthly* 150:383–384, 1932.

Richardson, C. B. W.
"Elegy for a Dying Tongue. Notes on the Language of the Sea." *Scribner's Magazine* 98:26, 67–68, 102–103, 121, 137–138, 179; 169; 106, 1935.

Smith, Logan Pearsall
English Sea Terms. In: *Words and Idioms. Studies in the English Language.* Chapter I. Boston: Houghton Mifflin Co., 1925. xi, 300 pp.

Sternbeck, Alfred
"Sea-Lore and Sea-Slang." *Neuphilologische Monatschrift* 3:113–133, 1931.

Wasson, George S.
"Our Heritage of Old Sea Terms." *AS* 4 (No. 5):377–383, 1929.

Westcott, Allan
"Sea Words on Shore Duty." *United States Naval Institute Proceedings* 52 (No. 7), July, 1926. 9 pp.

SEA SONGS:

Sea Shanties, Songs of the River Boatmen, and the Great Lakes

See: American Folksong and Ballad Collections, pp. 85-90, 118-20.

BIBLIOGRAPHY

Ford, Worthington Chauncey
Broadsides, Ballads &c. Printed in Massachusetts, 1639–1800. Vol. 75, Publications of the Massachusetts Historical Society, 1922.
A check-list of all prose and poetical broadsides found in twenty-five of the best libraries.

Neeser, Robert W., comp.
Bibliography of Books Dealing with American Naval Songs. In: *American Naval Songs and Ballads,* (pp. 359–361). New Haven: Yale University Press, 1938.

GENERAL STUDIES

"A Trip to the Grand Banks."
FSSNE 4:16, 1932.
Maine sea ballad.

Barry, Phillips
"The Schooner Fred Dunbar." *FSSNE* (No. 5), p. 15, 1933.

———.
"The Wreck of the Schooner Medora." *FSSNE* 11:19–20, 1936.
"An Ode on the wreck of the Schoooner Medora on the Great Lakes with the loss of all on board, February 29, 1836." Words only.

Bone, D. W.
Capstan Bars. New York: Harcourt, Brace and Company, 1932.

Colcord, Joanna C.
Songs of American Sailormen. With an introduction by Lincoln Colcord. New York: W. W. Norton & Company, 1938. 212 pp., illus., music.
A new, rev. ed. of "Roll and Go, Songs of American Sailormen," first published in 1924 by Bobbs-Merrill Co., Indianapolis. Still the best collection.

Finger, Charles J.
Sailor Chanties and Cowboy Songs. "Little Blue Books" No. 301. Girard, Kans.: Haldeman-Julius.

Firth, C. H., ed.
Naval Songs and Ballads. London: Publications of the Navy Records Society, Vol. XXXIII, 1908.

Fuller, W. G.
"Bells are Ringing, Sailors Singing." *Survey* 37:454–455, (Jan. 20) 1917.

Hatfield, James Taft
"Some Nineteenth Century Shanties." *JAFL* 59:108–113, 1946.
Texts and tunes to 12 shanties.

Hutchison, Percy A.
"Sailor's Chanties." *JAFL* 19:16–28, 1906.

———.
"Whaling the Capstan Bars." *New York Times Magazine* p. 4, (March 20) 1932.
A review of "Capstan Bars" by David Bone.

Jacobson, Pauline
"Chanteys Sung to the Rhythm of the Pumps." San Francisco: *The Evening Bulletin*, (May 27) 1916.

MacGill, Patrick
Songs of the Dead End. London: The Year Book Press, 1913. viii, 17 pp.

MacKenzie, W. Roy
"Ballads from Nova Scotia." *JAFL* 22:327–331, 1909.

Neeser, Robert W.
American Naval Songs and Ballads. New Haven: Yale University Press, 1938.

Newton, Hilah Foote
"The Saltus Lament." *NYFQ* 1:42–43, 1945.
A popular ballad recounting the adventures of the steamer "The Saltus" playing in Lake Champlain. The tune is "Little Brown Jug."

Parsons, Elsie Clews
"Ballads and Chanties Sung by May Hoisington." *JAFL* 44:296–301, **1931.**

Powell, John
"In the Lowlands Low." *SFQ* 1:1–12, 1937.
A sea shantey.

Reynolds, H.
"All Gone, Cap'n! Songs of the River." *Christian Science Monitor Magazine*, p. 8–9, (Nov. 14) 1942.

Russell, Charles Edward
A-Rafting on the Mississippi. New York: The Century Company, 1928.
Contains numerous raftsman tunes and texts.

Saunders, William
"Sailor Songs and Songs of the Sea." *MQ* 14: 339–358, 1928.
The author includes a number of texts but no tunes.

Shay, Frank
Iron Men and Wooden Ships. New York: Doubleday, Doran and Company, 1925.

Snook, S.
"Hill Billy and River Songs at Their Source." *Etude* 58:513+, (Aug.) 1940.

Thomas, Jean
Ballad Makin' in the Mountains of Kentucky. New York: Henry Holt and Company, 1939. 270 pp.
A chapter on "Chanteys." Texts and accompanied tunes.

Williams, Alfred Mason
"American Sea Songs." *Atlantic Monthly* 69: 489–501, 1892.

———.
"American Sea Songs" in: *Studies in Folk-Song and Popular Poetry.* Boston: Houghton Mifflin and Company, 1894. (pp. 1–36).
Vivid discussion of Sea Shanties of the songs of the full-rigged American clipper ships.

Wilson, E. A.
Blow High, Blow Low. New York: American Artists Group, 1941.

———, **Edmund**
"Shanty-Boy Ballads and Blues." *New Republic* 47:227–229, (July 14) 1926.

Ybarra, Thomas Russell
Davy Jones' Yarns and Other Salted Songs; illustrated by Henry Mayer. New York: H. Holt and Co., 1908. 102 pp., illus.

COLLECTIONS

Adams, Estelle Davenport
Sea Song and River Rhyme from Chaucer to Tennyson; selected and edited by Estelle Davenport Adams; with a new poem by Algernon Charles Swinburne, with twelve etchings. London: G. Redway, 1887. xxxii, 324 pp.

Allen, Gardner W.
Naval Songs and Ballads. Worcester, Mass.: American Antiquarian Society, 1926. 17 pp.

American Patriotic and Comic Modern Songs: Commemoration of Naval Victories, etc. Newburyport: Gilman, 1814–1816.

Barnes, James, ed.
Ships and Sailors; Being a collection of songs of the sea as sung by men who sail it; with numerous illustrations by Rufus F. Zogbaum. New York: Frederick A. Stokes Company, 1898. 124 pp.

Bartholomew, Marshall
Three Chanteys. New York: Schirmer: for male voices.

Bell, Frederick J.
Room to Swing a Cat. New York: Longmans, Green Company, 1938.

Bone, David W.
Capstan Bars. New York: Harcourt, Brace and Company, 1932.
Rich in folklore, many tunes included, glossary.

Bradford, J., and Fagge, A.
Old Sea Chanties. London: Metzler and Company, Ltd., 1904. 17 pp.

Bruce, Charles, comp. and arr.
Poems, Songs and Ballads of the Sea, and Celebrated Discoverers, Battles, Shipwrecks, and Incidents, illustrative of life on the Sea. London and Edinburgh: William P. Nimmo, 1878. 399 pp., 8 vols., illus.

Clemens, R.
Manavilins; A Muster of Sea Songs, as distinguished from Shanties. London: Heath, Cranton, Ltd. (n.d.)

Carmer, Carl Lamson
Songs of the Rivers of America, edited by Carl Carmer; music arranged by Dr. Albert Sirmay. Voice and piano. New York: Farrar and Rinehart, Inc., 1942. xi, 196 pp.
To accompany the series—*The Rivers of America.*

Colcord, J. C.
Songs of the American Sailormen. New York: W. W. Norton and Company, Inc., 1938. 212 pp., illus.
A revised edition (with new material) of "Roll and Go," (1924). Many tunes included. One of the best.

————.
Roll and Go, Songs of American Sailormen. Indianapolis: Bobbs-Merrill Company, 1924.

Columbia's Naval Triumphs. New York: 1813.

Dean, Michael C., comp.
The Flying Cloud and 150 Other Old Poems and Ballads. A Collection of Old Irish Songs, Songs of the Sea and Great Lakes, the Big Pine Woods, the Prize Ring and Others. Virginia, Minn.: The Quickprint, 1922.

Dougherty, Celius
Five Sea Shanties. New York: G. Schirmer, 1947. Arranged for voice and piano.
Contents: Rio Grande; Blow, Ye Winds; Cross the Western Ocean; Mobile Bay; Shenandoah.

Dunstan, R.
Sea Shanties. Yorkshire: Schofield and Sims, Ltd., 1939.

Eckstorm, Fannie Hardy, and Smyth, Mary Winslow
Minstrelsy of Maine: Folk-Songs and Ballads of the Woods and the Coast. Boston: Houghton Mifflin Company, 1927. 390 pp.
Texts only. Part II—Songs of the Sea and Shore, with the following subdivisions (with many seasongs given in each), Deep-Sea Songs, Chanteys, Pirate Songs, Mournful Songs (on the loss of ships and men of the sea), Coastwise Songs, and Songs of the Pioneers.

Emerich, Albert G., ed.
Songs for People; comprising natural, patriotic, sentimental, comic and naval songs. Philadelphia: J. and J. T. Gibon, 1849. Boston: O. Ditson and Company, 1852.

English Shanties and English Songs. London: J. Curwen and Sons, Ltd., 19—. Voice and piano.

Farnsworth, C. H., and Sharp, C. J.
Folk-Songs, Chanteys, and Singing Games. New York: Novello and Company, 1916. Arranged for voice and piano.

Finger, Charles J.
Sailor Chanties and Cowboy Songs. "Little Blue Books" No. 301. Girard, Kans.: Haldeman-Julius.

Freneau, Philip
Poems on Various Subjects, but Chiefly of the American War of Independence. London: J. R. Smith, 1861. xxii, 362 pp.

Frothingham, Robert
Songs of the Sea and Sailors' Chanteys. Boston: Houghton Mifflin Company, 1904.

Gillepsy, Edward, comp.
The Columbian Naval Songster. New York: 1813.

Goodell, Walter
Chanteys and Songs of the Sea. H. & M. Auditorium Series No. 41. Chicago: Hall and McCreary: SATB.
Contains 19 folk chanteys.

Grace, Harvey, and Shaw, Geoffrey and Martin
Sea Songs, Vol. II, Part I—of the Motherland Song Book. London: Stainer and Bell: SATB. 12 numbers.

Greenleaf, Elizabeth Bristol
Ballads and Sea Songs of New Foundland. Cambridge, Mass.: Harvard University Press, 1933. xliv. 395 pp., many tunes, illus.

Halliwell, J. O., ed.
The Early Naval Ballads of England. London: Percy Society, 1841. xii, 144 pp.

Holland, Edwin C.
Odes, Naval Songs, and Other Occasional Poems. Charleston, S. C.: 1813.

Horton, D. P., ed.
Naval Songs. New York: 1889.

Jackson, George S.
Early Songs of Uncle Sam. Boston: Houghton Mifflin Company, 1933.
Contains some naval songs.

Jack Tar's Songster.
Phila.: Fisher and Bro., 184–.

Kennedy, John
The American Songster. Containing a choice selection of about one hundred and fifty modern and popular songs. Baltimore: 1836. 256 pp.

King, Stanton H.
King's Book of Chanties. Boston: Oliver Ditson Company, 1918.
Voice and piano.

Lawson, C. C. P.
Naval Ballads and Sea Songs. London: Peter Davies, Ltd., 1933.

Lomax, John A., and Alan
American Ballads and Folk Songs. New York: The Macmillan Company, 1934.
Chapter XX—The Erie Canal, (8 songs); Chapter XXI—The Great Lakes, (1 song); Chapter XXII—Sailors and Sea Fights, (17 songs).

———.
Folk Song: U. S. A. New York: Duell, Sloan & Pearce, 1947.
Chapter V—"Blow, Boys, Blow," (8 songs).

———.
Our Singing Country. New York: The Macmillan Company, 1941.
Part III, Chapt. I—"Soldiers and Sailors"—texts and tunes.

Luce, Stephen B., Rear-Admiral, U. S. Navy, comp.
Naval Songs; a collection of original, selected and traditional Sea Songs, Songs of Sailors and Shanties. Compiled by Stephen B. Luce, Rear-Admiral, U. S. Navy. New York: Wm. A. Pond and Company, 1908. 2nd edition revised, 230 pp., illus.

Mackenzie, W. Roy
Ballads and Sea Songs from Nova Scotia. Cambridge, Mass.: Harvard University Press, 1928. 421 pp.

Marine Corp Song Book.
Issued by the Navy Department. Washington, D. C.: U. S. Government Printing Office, 1919. 96 pp.

Masefield, John
A Sailor's Garland. New York: The Macmillan Company, 1928.

McCarthy, Wm.
Songs, Odes and Other Poems on National Subjects. Philadelphia: W. McCarthy, 1842.

McPhee, Colin
Sea Shanty Suite. New York: Kalmus. Arranged for Baritone Solo, Men's Chorus in Unison, 2 pianos, and tympani.

Moore, Frank
Songs and Ballads of the American Revolution. New York: D. Appleton & Company, 1856. 324 pp.

National Songster; or a collection of the most admired patriotic songs on the brilliant victories achieved by the naval and military heroes of the U. S. A. Hagerstown: John Grut and Daniel May, 1814.

Naval Songster, or Columbian Naval Melody. Boston: 1813.

Navy Song Book.
Issued by the Navy Department. Washington, D. C.: U. S. Government Printing Office, 1919. 98 pp.

Neeser, Robert W., ed
American Naval Songs and Ballads. New York: Yale University Press, 1938. xviii, 372 pp., illus., bibl.
An excellent collection.

Niles, John J., and Moore, Douglas
Songs My Mother Never Taught Me. New York: Macaulay Company, 1929. 227 pp.

Nye, Pearl R.
Songs of the Ohio Canal. Akron, Ohio, 1938. Continuous roll, without pagination. Microfilm (L. C.—Music Division).

Ocean Songster.
Philadelphia: Fisher and Bro., 185–?

Pattee, Fred Lewis, ed.
The Poems of Philip Freneau, Poet of the American Revolution. Princeton, N. J.: 1902–1907. 2 vols.

Patterson, J. E.
The Sea's Anthology from the Earliest Times down to the Middle of the Nineteenth Century. New York: George H. Doran, 1913.

Patriotic and Naval Songster.
Philadelphia: 1898.

Procter Bros.
Fisherman's Ballads and Songs of the Sea. Gloucester: Procter Bros., 1874.

Rogers, Cameron, and Wilson, Edward
Full and By, being a collection of verses by persons of quality in praise of drinking . . . with prefaces by Don Marquis and Christopher Morley. New York. Doubleday, Page and Co., 1925. xxx, 153 pp., illus.

Sailor's Songster.
Philadelphia: Fisher and Bro., 184–.

Salty Sea Songs and Chanteys. 71 Songs of the Sea. New York: Leeds Music Corp. Voice and piano.

Sampson, John
The Seven Seas Shanty Book: Containing 42 sea shanties and songs, collected and recollected by John Sampson; arranged for piano by S. Taylor Harris, with a foreword by John Masefield. London: Boosey and Company, Ltd., 1927. 69 pp.

Sandburg, Carl
The American Songbag. New York: Harcourt, Brace & Co., 1927.
    Chapters on—"Great Lakes and Erie Canal," and "Sailormen," texts and tunes, most of them arranged for voice and piano.

Sharp, Cecil James
English Folk-Chanteys; with pianoforte accompaniment. Introduction and notes collected by C. J. Sharp. New York: The H. W. Gray Company, 1930. 75 pp.

————.
English Folk Shanteys. London: Simpkin, Marshall, Hamilton, Kent and Company, 1914, and Barnicott and Pearce, 1932.

————, coll. and arr.
Pulling and Capstan Chanteys. London: Novello and Company, Ltd., 1923. Voice and piano.

Shay, Frank
Deep Sea Chanties: Old Sea Songs. London: William Jeinemann, 1925.

————.
American Sea Songs and Chanteys, From the Days of Iron Men and Wooden Ships. New York: W. W. Norton Co., 1948. illus., music.

————.
Iron Men and Wooden Ships: Deep Sea Chanties. New York: Doubleday, Page and Company, 1926.

————.
A Little Book of Vagabond Songs; poems of the hills and sea, with etchings by Philip Kappel. New York: Harper & Bros., 1931. xviii, 60 pp.

Siegmeister, Elie, and Downes, Olin
A Treasury of American Song. New York: Howell, Soskin & Co., 1940.
    Chapter 3—"Thar She Blows"—songs of sailormen, arr. for voice and piano.

Simpson, Edward
Yarnlets. New York: G. P. Putnam's Sons, 1934.

Smith, Cicely Fox, ed.
A Book of Shanties. London: Methuen & Company, Ltd., 1927. 93 pp.

————.
Full Sail: More Sea Songs and Ballads. Illustrated by Phil W. Smith. Boston: Houghton Mifflin Co., 1926. vii, 119 pp.

————.
Rovings. Sea Songs and Ballads. London: Methuen & Co., Ltd. 1921. Illus.

————.
Sailor Town: Sea Songs and Ballads. New York: George H. Doran Co., 1919. ix, 136 pp.

————.
Sea Songs and Ballads, 1917–22. London: Methuen & Co., Ltd., 1923. vi, 136 pp.
    Contents: Sea Songs and Ballads, 1922. *Rovings,* 1921. From *Ships and Folks,* 1920. From *Rhymes of the Red Ensign,* 1919. From *Small Craft,* 1917.

————.
Small Craft Sailor Ballads and Chantys. New York: George H. Doran Co., 1919. 157 pp.

Smith, Laura Alexandrine
The Music of the Waters. A collection of the Sailors' Chanties, or working Songs of the Sea, of all maritime nations. Boatmen's fisher-, men's, and rowing songs, and water legends. London: K. Paul, Trench & Co., 1888. xxxv, 360 pp.

Soldiers' and Sailors' Patriotic Songs. New York: Loyal Publication Society, 1864.

Songs, Ballads, etc. Bound up for Preservation, to show what articles of this kind are in vogue with the Vulgar at this time, 1814.
    Purchased from a Ballad Printer and Seller in Boston, 1813. Presented to the Society by Isaiah Thomas, August, 1814.

Songs: Naval, Patriotic and Miscellaneous. New York: 1818.

Sprackling, Nelson
Clipper Ship Days. Sea Chanties. New York: Carl Fischer. Voice and piano.

Stone, Christopher
Sea Songs and Ballads. London: Oxford University Press, 1906.

Terry, Richard R.
Salt Sea Ballads. London: J. Curwen and Sons, 1930.

————.
The Shanty Book. 2 Parts. London: J. Curwen and Sons, 1921.
    Excellent introduction by Sir Walter Runciman on background and folklore of Sea Songs. The accompaniments are exemplary. 30 Shanties in Part I, and 35 in Part II.

The American Muse: or, Songster's Companion. New York: 1814.

The American Naval and Patriotic Songster, as sung in various places of amusement in honor of Hull, Jones, Decatur, Perry, Bainbridge, Lawrence, etc. Baltimore: P. N. Wood, 1831.

The American Patriotic Song Book. Philadelphia: 1816.

The American Song Book. New York and Boston: 1815.

The American Songster. New York: N. C. Nafis, 1839.

The American Star.
Richmond: 1817. 180 pp., 2nd ed.

The Book of Navy Songs; collected and edited by the Trident Society of the U. S. Naval Academy at Annapolis, Maryland. Garden City, N. Y.: Doubleday, Page and Company, 1926. 200 pp.

The Cabin-Boy and Forecastle Sailor's Delight, by an American Tar. New York: 1817.

The Chelsea Song Book. New York: Minton, Balch.

The Columbian Harmonist; selection of sentimental, patriotic and other songs. New York: 1814.

The Columbian Naval Melody.
Boston: 1813.

The Eagle and the Harp; a collection of patriotic and humorous songs and odes. Baltimore: 1812.

The Forecastle Songster.
New York: Richard Mash, 1847.

The Lafayette Songster.
Danville, Vt.: 1829.

The Modern Songster.
Baltimore, 1816. Second Baltimore Edition.

The Naval Songster; being a collection of naval victories and other excellent songs. Charlestown: 1815. 16 pp.

The Naval Temple.
Boston: 1816.

The New American Singer's Own Book. A choice selection of the most popular, sentimental, patriotic, naval and comic songs. Philadelphia: John B. Perry, 1845.

The Parlour Song Book; a choice and well-selected collection of the most popular, sentimental, patriotic, naval and comic songs. New York: Leavitt and Allen, 18—.

The People's Free and Easy Songster. A choice collection of comic, sentimental, amatory, sporting, Irish, Scotch, African, military, naval and patriotic songs. New York: Wm. H. Murphy, 18—.

The Sailor's Companion; or Songs of the Sea. Consisting of a well-selected collection of naval songs. New York: Leavitt and Allen, 1857.

The Sailor's Song Book, or Music of the Forecastle; containing patriotic, nautical, naval, moral and temperance songs, adapted to popular and familiar tunes, by Uncle Sam. Music arranged in two parts. Boston: Kidder and Wright, 1842.

The Singer's Own Book; a well-selected collection of the most popular, sentimental, patriotic, naval and comic songs. Philadelphia: Key, Mickele and Biddle, 1832. New York: Leavitt and Allen, 1851.

The Songster's Companion. Appendix, songs of late war with Great Britain. Brattleborough: 1815.

The Universal Songster.
New York: Solomon Kind, 1829.

The Trident Society of the U. S. N.
The Book of Navy Songs. New York: Doubleday, Page and Co.
Over 100 songs from "Anchors Aweigh" to "Zamboanga."

Tozer, Ferris, arr.
Sailors Songs or Chanties. The words by Frederick J. Davis, R. N. R. The music composed and arranged upon Traditional Sailor airs by Ferris Tozer. London: Boosey and Hawkes. Voice and piano.

Waters, Frank
Eight Bells. Sailors' Snug Harbor Yarns and Ballads. New York: D. Appleton and Company, 1927. xi, 151 pp.

Whall, W. B.
Sea Songs and Shanties, the songs harmonized by R. H. Whall and Ernest Reeves. London: Brown, Son and Ferguson, 1930. Voice and piano.

Wheeler, Mary
Steamboatin' Days. Folk Songs of the River Packet Era. Baton Rouge, La.: Louisiana State University Press. 121 pp.
Contents: Work Songs, Songs of the Boats, Soundings, Spirituals, Songs of Meditation, Love Songs, Dance Songs, Songs of Lawlessness. Index. Tunes.

Williams, R. Vaughan
Sea Songs and Shanties. Vols. III and IV: The Motherland Song Book. London: Stainer and Bell: SATB.

Wilson, James Jefferson, comp.
A National Song Book; being a collection of patriotic, martial and naval songs and odes, principally of American composition. Compiled by James Jefferson Wilson. Trenton: 1813.

ARRANGEMENTS
————: *Voice and Piano*

"Sail Away for the Rio Grande."
Fox, O. J.: Schirmer.

"Sail Away for the Rio Grande."
Guion, D.: G. Schirmer: Voice and piano (high and low).

"Shallow Brown."
Grainger, P.: Schirmer: Solo or 2 voices.

"The Mermaid."
Dunhill: Oxford: Descant.

"What Shall We Do With A Drunken Sailor?"
Guion, D.: Schirmer.

————: *Female Voices*

"Blow the Man Down."
McKay: Gamble Hinged: SSA.

————: *Male Voices*

"A-Roving."
Bartholomew, M.: Schirmer: TTBB.

"As Off to the South'ard We Go."
Bartholomew, M.: Schirmer: TTBB.

"Away to Rio."
Bartholomew, M.: Schirmer: TTBB.

"Blow the Man Down."
In: H. & M. Auditorium Series, No. 48. Andersen, A. O.: Hall & McCreary: TBB.

"Blow the Man Down."
In: H. & M. Auditorium Series No. 9. Grant-Fishburn: Hall and McCreary: TTBB.

"Blow the Man Down."
McKay: Gamble Hinged: TB.

"Boat Song."
Treharne, B.: Willis: TTB, TBB.

"Down Among the Dead Men."
Cobleigh: Schirmer: TTBB.

"Eight Bells."
Bartholomew, M.: Schirmer: TTBB.

"Eight Bells."
In: H. & M. Auditorium Series, No. 29. Grant, R. W.: Hall and McCreary: TTBB.

"Erie Canal."
Bartholomew, M.: Schirmer: TTBB, accomp.

"Haul Away Joe."
Scott, T.: Words and Music: TTBB.
Fred Waring Glee Club Arrangement.

"High Barbary."
Bartholomew-Hall: Schirmer: TTBB.

"High Barbary."
Hall: Schirmer: TTBB.

"Hoodah Day."
Bartholomew, M.: Schirmer: TTBB.

"Johnny, Come Down to Hilo."
Winslow, P.: Clayton F. Summy: TTBB.

"Medly of Sea Chanteys."
Andrews, M.: Ricordi: TTBB, a cap.

"Mobile Bay."
Bartholomew, M.: Schirmer: TTBB.

"Old Man Noah."
Bartholomew, M.: Schirmer: TTBB.

"Reuben Ranzo."
In: H. & M. Auditorium Series No. 9. Grant-Fishburn: Hall & McCreary: TTBB.

"Sail Away for the Rio Grande."
Guion, David: Schirmer: TTBB.

"Sea Shanty Suite."
McPhee, C.: Kalmus: Bar. Solo, Men's Chorus in Unison, 2 pianos, tympani.

"Shenandoah."
Bartholomew, M.: Schirmer: TTBB.

"Song of the Mississippi Boatmen."
Work, J. W.: J. Fischer and Bro.: TTBB.

"Ten Thousand Miles Away."
Winslow, P.: Clayton F. Summy: TTBB.

"The Erie Canal."
Pitcher, G.: Birchard: TTBB.

"The High Barbaree."
Winslow, P.: Clayton F. Summy: TTBB.

"What Shall We Do With a Drunken Sailor."
Bartholomew, M.: Schirmer: TTBB.

"What Shall We Do With a Drunken Sailor?"
Guion, David: Witmark: TTBB.

————: *Mixed Voices*

"A New Wind A-Blowin'."
Siegmeister, E.: Musette: SATB.

"Away to Rio."
Christy: Hall and McCreary: SAB.

"Blow the Man Down."
Harris, Roy: C. Fischer: SATB.
Free improvisation, also with orchestral accompaniment.

"Cape Cod Chantey."
Bowers, R. L.: John Church: SATB.

"Cape Cod Chantey."
Pitcher, G.: Birchard: SATB.

"Dollar and Half a Day" (Capstan Chanty).
Grainger, P.: Schirmer: SATB.

"High Barbary."
Christy: Schirmer: SATB.

"Johnny, Come Down to Hilo."
Whitehead, A.: H. W. Gray: SATB.

"Missouri."
Toye, Geoffrey: Boosey and Hawkes: SATB.

"Reuben Ranzo."
Treharne, B.: Birchard: SATB.

"Rio Grande."
Dyrssen: Birchard: SATB.

"Santo Anno."
Buchanan, A. M.: J. Fischer and Bro.: SATB.

"Shallow Brown."
Grainger, P.: Schirmer: SATB. Solo or unison chorus, version with piano or small orchestra of various instruments.

"Shenandoah."
Bartholomew, M.: Schirmer: SATB, a cap.

"Shenandoah."
Christy, V. A.: Schirmer: SATB.

"The Coast of High Barbary."
   Pitcher, G.: Birchard: SATB.

"What Shall We Do With a Drunken Sailor."
   Candlyn, T. F. H.: Galaxy: SATB.

"Whiskey Johnny."
   Dyrssen: H. W. Gray: SATB.

——————: *Piano*

"The Chantyman's March."
   Sousa, J. P.: C. Fischer.

——————: *Orchestra*

Bowles, Paul
   Yankee Clipper. MS. For ballet and full
   orchestra.

Harris, Roy
   Blow the Man Down. New York: Carl Fischer,
   1946.
      Arranged for SATB, contralto and baritone
      solos, and symphonic orchestra. A free improviza-
      tion.

Kubik, Gail
   The Erie Canal. New York: G. Schirmer, 1946.
   For full orchestra.

McPhee, Colin
   Sea Shanty Suite. New York: E. F. Kalmus.
   Arranged for male chorus, baritone solo, 2
   pianos, and 2 sets of tympani.

RECORDS

Album—Collections

Deep Sea Chanties and Whaling Ballads. Woody
Guthrie, Lee Hays, Millard Lampell, and Pete
Seeger. 3–10".   COM–11
   Contents: Blow, Ye Winds, Heigh-ho, Haul Away
   Joe, Blow the Man Down, The Golden Vanity,
   Away Rio, House of the Rising Sun.

Deep Sea Shanties and Whaling Ballads.
The Almanac Singers. 3–10".   GE–G20

Roustabout Songs. A Collection of Ohio River
Valley Songs. Conrad Thibault, baritone, and
orchestra. 3–10".   DE–451
   Contents: Alberta; Let Yo' Hair Hang Low;
   Cap'n Jim Reese Said; John Gilbert; Ohio River,
   She's So Deep and Wide; I'm Wukkin' My Way
   Back Home; Ain't Got No Place to Hang my
   Haid; The Hanging of Devil Winston.

Sea Chanties.
   John Goss, and chorus.   H.M.V.
   Contents: Early in the Morning; Shenandoah;
   What Shall We Do with a Drunken Sailor;
   Clear de Track; Billy Boy; Hanging Johnny;
   Fire Down Below.

Sea Chanties.
   Leonard Warren, baritone; Orchestra and
   Chorus.   VI–MO–1186
   Contents: Blow the Man Down; Rio Grande;
   The Drummer and the Cook; Shenandoah; Haul
   Away; Joe; Low Lands; The Drunken Sailor;
   A Rovin'.

Sea Shanties.
   John Goss, Cathedral Male Quartet and Piano.
                                         G–B2646
   Contents: Rio Grande, Billy Boy, Shenandoah.

Sea Shanties: A Medley.
   The Georgian Singers.   CO–DX–1047
   Contents: A-roving; Shenandoah; What Shall
   We Do with a Drunken Sailor; Rio Grande;
   Boney was a Warrior; Hullabaloo Balay (Shal-
   low Brown) ; Haul Away; Fire Down Below.

Songs of American Sailormen.
   Mordy Bauman, baritone-piano.   MU–75
   Contents: Rio Grande; Home, Dearie, Home;
   The Codfish Shanty; Shenandoah; A-Roving; The
   Drunken Sailor; Blow the Man Down; Haul
   Away Joe; The Constitution and the Guerriere;
   Can't You Dance the Polka; Galloping Randy
   Dandy O'; Whiskey Johnny.

Songs of the Sea.
   Royal Naval Singers.   CO–DX–862
   Contents: Billy Boy; Johnny Come Down to
   Hilo; Blow the Man Down; Whiskey Johnny;
   Sally Brown; Let the Bulgine Run; Blow My
   Bully Boys.

**U. S. Library of Congress. Division of Music.
Folklore Section.**
   *Helen Creighton Recording Project in Nova
   Scotia.*   AAFS–LC
   ——————.
   Sea Chanteys and Canal Songs.   AAFS–LC
   ——————.
   *William M. Doerflinger Collection of Sea
   Songs,* by Captain Patrick Tayleur. AAFS–LC

Individual Titles

"A Trip on the Erie."
   Hudson Valley Songs. Frank Warner, accompanied by ballad singers, instrumentalists.
                                         DISC–8024

"Anchors Aweigh."
   All Star Collegians.   OK–0445

"A-Roving."
   Narration with Singing. In: Album: *Songs
   under the Sails.*   VI–BC8

"Away Rio."
   The Almanac Singers.   GE–5017–A

"Away for Rio."
   Ralph Crane, baritone-orchestra.   VI–21750

"Away to Rio."
   Yale Glee Club. In: *Yale Glee Club.*
                               C–36462; Set C–79

"Barnacle Bill, the Sailor."
   Vocal by Billy Costello.   DE–1573

"Barnacle Bill, the Sailor."
   Vocal by Frank Luther.   DE–151

"Battleship Connecticut."
   Victor Symphony Band.   VI–21935

"Billy Boy."
   Ralph Crane, baritone-orchestra.   VI–21751

"Billy Boy."
Oscar Natzke, bass chorus and orch.
CO–DB2177

"Billy Boy."
Royal Naval Singers. CO–DX862

"Blow the Man Down."
Almanac Singers. GE–5016–A

"Blow, my Bully Boys."
Royal Naval Singers. In: *Songs of the Sea.*
CO–DX862

"Blow the Man Down."
Ralph Crane, baritone-orchestra. VI–21751

"Blow the Man Down."
Oscar Natzke, bass, chorus and orch.
CO–DB2167

"Blow the Man Down."
Narration with singing. In: *Songs under the Sails.* VI–BC8

"Blow the Man Down."
Earl Rogers, voice-piano. MU–68

"Blow Ye Winds High-O."
Almanac Singers. GE–5015

"Boney."
Narration with Singing. In: *Songs under the Sails.* VI–BC–8

"Bowline" (Negro Sea Chanty).
Sung by David Pryor and Henry Lundy at Nasau, Bahama, 1935. In: *Album V:* Library of Congress, 1943. AAFS–21A3

"Coast of High Barbary."
Almanac Singers. GE–5017–B

"Early in the Morning."
Narration with Singing. In: *Songs under the Sails.* VI–BC–8

"E-r-i-e."
Luther and Layman, vocalists. DE–2430

"Fire down Below."
Narration with Singing. In: *Songs under the Sails.* VI–BC–8

"Fisherman's Chantie."
Bobby Breen, vocalist. DE–2353

"Good-bye Fare You Well."
Narration with singing. In: *Songs under the Sails.* VI–BC–8

"Haul Away Joe."
Almanac Singers. GE–5015–B

"Haul Away, my Rosy."
Sung by J. M. (Sailor Dad) Hunt of Marion, Virginia. Recorded in Washington, D. C. by Alan Lomax, 1941. In: *Album II:* Library of Congress. AAFSA₂

"Hullabaloo Belay."
Richard Dyer-Bennet. KE–519–B

"Hullabaloo Balay" (Shallow Brown).
Oscar Natzke, bass, chorus and orch.
CI–DB2167

"Johnny Come Down to Hilo."
Royal Naval Singers. CO–DX8622

"Leave Her, Johnny."
Narration With Singing. In: *Songs under the Sails.* VI–BC–8

"Let the Bulgine Run."
Royal Naval Singers. In: *Songs of the Sea.*
CO–DX862

"Low Bridge, Everybody Down" (Erie Canal).
Luther and Layman, vocalists. DE–2430

"Out where the Big Ships Go By."
Oscar Natzke, bass, chorus and orch.
CO–DB2177

"Paul Jones."
Hofner and San Antonians. OK–06184

"Rio Grande."
Narration with Singing. In: *Songs under the Sails.* VI–BC–8

"Rose, Rose and up she Rose."
Engel Lund, soprano and piano. In: *Folk Songs of Many Lands.* MC–1128; Set MC–39

"Round the Bay of Mexico" (Negro Sea Chanty).
Sung by Pryor and Henry Lundy, at Nassau, Bahamas, 1935. In: *Album V:* Library of Congress, 1943. AAFS21A2

"Rye Whiskey, Rye Whiskey."
Tex Ritter, vocal-piano. OK–04911

"Rio Grande."
Oscar Natzke, bass, chorus and orch.
CO–DB2177

"Sailor Boy-Polka."
(Army Rookie Polka). Louise Massey and Westerners. OK–06042

"Sally Brown."
Sung by J. M. (Sailor Dad) Hunt of Marion, Virginia. Recorded in Washington, D. C., 1941 by Alan Lomax. In: *Album II:* Library of Congress, 1943. AAF6A1

"Sally Brown."
Royal Naval Singers. In: *Songs of the Sea.*
CO–DX862

"Santy Anna."
Narration with Singing. In: *Songs under the Sails.* VI–BC–8

"Shenandoah."
Oscar Natzke, bass, chorus and orch.
CO–DB2167

"Shenandoah."
Paul Robeson, bass and piano. GE–B8438

"Shenandoah."
Narration with Singing. In: *Songs under the Sails*. VI–BC–8

"Shenandoah."
Yale Glee Club. In: *Yale Glee Club*.
CO–36462; Set CO–79

"Salty Dog, Hey, Hey, Hey."
Allen Brothers. OK–02818

"Talking Sailor."
Woody Guthrie, voice and guitar. ASCH–347

"Ten Thousand Miles Away."
Narration with Singing. In: *Songs under the Sails*. VI–BC–8

"The Dom Pedro."
Narration with Singing. In: *Songs under the Sails*. VI–BC–8

"The Drunken Sailor" (New England version of an old Sea Chanty). Richard Dyer-Bennett, Lute Singer. KE–108

"The Drunken Sailor."
Oscar Natzke, bass, chorus and orch.
CO–DB2177

"The Golden Vanity."
Almanac Singers. GE–5016–B

"The Roving Sailor."
Engel Lund, soprano, piano. In: *Folk Songs of Many Lands*. MC–1128; Set MC–39

"The Stately Southerner."
Narration with Singing. In: *Songs under the Sails*. VI–BC–8

"What Shall we do with a Drunken Sailor."
Richard Dyer-Bennett. KE–519–B

"Whiskey Johnny."
Royal Naval Singers. In: *Songs of the Sea*.
CO–DX862

"Whiskey, Rye Whiskey."
Tony Kraber, vocal-guitar. KE–104

THE HOBO AND THE INDUSTRIAL WORKER

THE HOBO AND THE INDUSTRIAL WORKER

FOLKLORE

GENERAL STUDIES AND COLLECTIONS

Anderson, Nels
The Hobo: The Sociology of the Homeless Man. Chicago: The University of Chicago Press, 1923.

Davidson, Levette Jay
"Jack Leonard." *CFQ* 2:46, 1943.
Six quatrains of this hobo poem, words only.

Guthrie, Woody
Bound for Glory. Illustrated and sketched by the author. New York: E. P. Dutton & Co., 1943. 428 pp.
This book "is an eloquent piece of writing, wild as a train whistle in the mountains, a sumptuous picture of fighting, carousing, singing, laughing migratory America." (Horace Gregory)

"Hobo Hegemony." *Literary Digest* 123 (No. 15): 10–12, 1937.
Contains hobo lingo.

"Hobo Origin." *Literary Digest* 123 (No. 12): 27, 1937.
Suggests origin in "hello, bo."

Holbrook, Stewart H.
"Wobbly Talk." *American Mercury* 7:62–65, 1926.

Irwin, Godfrey, ed.
American Tramp and Underworld Slang: words and phrases used by hoboes, tramps, migratory workers, etc., with tramp songs. With an essay on American slang in its relation to the English Thieves' slang, by E. Partridge. London: Scholartis Press, 1931. 264 pp.
The chapter on Tramp songs gives the texts of 28 songs.

Klein, Nicholas
"Hobo Lingo." *AS* 1(No. 12):650–653, 1926.

Martin, Charles
"Hobogenesis." *North American Review* 243: 52–63, 1937.

Meredith, Mamie
" 'Waddies' and 'Hoboes' of the Old West." *AS* 7(No. 4):257–260, 1932.
"...addressing a cowboy as 'waddy' would be a recognition of his proficiency."

Milburn, George, comp.
The Hobo's Hornbook; a repertory for a gutter jongleur . . . decorations by William Siegel. New York: I. Washburn, 1930. xxi, 295 pp., illus., music.

Oliver, Robert T.
"Junglese." *AS* 7(No. 5):339–341, 1932.
A discussion of the classification of the various types of the "Brotherhood"—Knights of the Road.

Parker, Paul P.
"Along the Dirty Plate Route." *CFQ* 3:16–20, 1944.

Reitman, B. L.
"Dingbats and Hoboes." *Life* 3(No. 17):6, Oct. 1937.

Samolar, Charlie
"The Argot of the Vagabond." *AS* 2(No. 9): 385–392, 1927.

Sidney, F. H.
"Hobo Cant." *Dialect Notes* 5(Part 2):41–42, 1919.

Walden, Wayne,
"Crumbs." In: *Manuscripts of the Federal Writers' Project of the Works Progress Administration* in New York City.
A little anecdote about The Wobblies.

FOLKSONG

GENERAL STUDIES AND COLLECTIONS

"Death of Floyd Collins." *American Mercury* 42:297, Nov., 1937.

8 Union Songs of the Almanacs.
New York: New Theatre League, 1941.
Most of the texts by Almanac Singers, based on traditional tunes, sacred and secular.

Farmer's Alliance Songs of the 1890's.
Lincoln: Nebraska Federal Writers' Project, Works Progress Administration. Nos. 18 and 20.

Hille, Waldemar
The People's Song Book. New York: Boni & Gaer, 1948, 128 pp. 100 Songs, words and piano accompaniments.
"The third section of 'Union Songs,' is the labor organizer set to music."

Horton, Zilphia, comp. and ed.
Labor Songs. Atlanta Ga.: Southeastern Regional Office, Textile Workers Union of America, 1939. 64 pp. Texts only.
Contents: Old Favorite Tunes, Union Hymns, Songs for the Picket Line, Company Union Songs, Marching Songs, Spirituals, Popular Songs, Rounds, Funeral Song.

Industrial Workers of the World
I. W. W. Songs. Songs of Life—from the Mine, Mill, Factory, and Shop. Chicago: Industrial Workers of the World, 1926. 64 pp., illus.
Words only, many tunes indicated. Many editions of this collection.

International Ladies' Garment Workers' Union
Everybody Sings. New York: Educational Dep't., I. L. G. W. U., 1942. 48 pp., illus.
Words only, tunes indicated.

Irwin, Godfrey
American Tramp and Underworld Slang;
words and phrases used by hoboes, tramps,
migratory workers and those on the fringes
of society, with their uses and origins, with
a number of tramp songs. . . . London: E.
Partridge, Ltd., at the Scholaris Press, 1931.
263 pp.
"Songs of the Junglurs and Drag," (without
music), pp. 199–252.

Knibbs, Henry Herbert
Songs of the Outlands: Ballads of the Hoboes
and Other Verse. Boston: Houghton Mifflin
Company, 1914. v, 73 pp., illus.

Milburn, George
The Hobo's Hornbook. A Repertory for a
Gutter Jongleur. Collected and annotated by
George Milburn. New York: Ives Washburn,
1930. 295 pp.
A few tunes also included.

Porter, John E.
"Wobbly and Other Songs." *CFQ* 2:42–44,
1943.
Texts and variants in other sources of "The
Hobo's Last Lament."

Rebel Song Book.
New York: Rand School Press, 1935.

Rome, Harold J.
"Lyrics for Labor." *Fortune* 17:28, March
1933.

Sing Out Brother.
Highlander Folk School, Monteagle, Tenn.

Songs for America.
New York: Workers' Library Publication, Box
148, Station D, New York, 1935.

"Songs of the Times." *Time* 39:41, Feb. 9, 1942.

Tallmadge, James D.
Labor Songs. Chicago: IWW Publishing Company, 1886.

Todd, Charles, and Sonkin, Robert
"Ballads of the Okies." *N. Y. Times Magazine,*
November 17, 1940.

UAW-CIO Sings.
UAW-CIO Education Department, 28 West
Warren St., Detroit 1, Michigan

Wimberly, L. C.
"Hard Times Singing." *American Mercury*
32:197–202, June 1934.

Workers' Song Books, Nos. 1 and 2.
New York: Workers' Music League, 1935.

"Workers' Songs." *Survey* 23:503, October, 1934.

RECORDS

Album—Collections

Dust Bowl Ballads.
Woddy Guthrie, vocal-guitar

Vol. 1. Tom Joad; Do Re Mi; Blowin' Down
this Road. 3–10" V–P27

Vol. 2. The Great Dust Storm; Dusty Old Dust;
Vigilante Man. 3–10" V–P28

Roll the Union On.
Tropical Ballads. Pete Seeger, Lee Hays,
Baldwin Hawes. 3–10" DISC–370

Individual Titles

"Biggest Thing in the World."
Woody Guthrie, voice-guitar ASCH 347

"Blowin' Down This Road."
Woody Guthrie, vocal-guitar V–P27

"Coolee Dam."
Woody Guthrie, voice-guitar ASCH 347

"Do Re Mi."
Woddy Guthrie, vocal-guitar V–P27

"Down in Tennessee Valley." (Hobo Song)
Emery Arthur, vocal-banjo VO B–5208

"Dusty Old Dust."
Woody Guthrie, vocal-guitar. V–P28

"Hobo's Last Ride."
Buell Kazee, vocal-banjo BR 330

"The Gallis Pole."
Lead Belly, voice-guitar MU 227

"The Great Dust Storm."
Woody Guthrie, vocal-guitar. V–P28

"Tom Joad"
Woody Guthrie; vocal-guitar In: *Dust Bowl
Ballads, Volume I* V–P27

"Vigilante Man"
Woody Guthrie; vocal-guitar In: *Dust Bowl
Ballads, Volume II* V–P28

Part Five: Miscellaneous Bibliography

AMERICAN CHARACTERS

AMERICAN CHARACTERS
"Good, Bad and Notorious" in Lore and Song

See: Folktales, pp. 22-5, Humor, pp. 25-35, The Southwest, pp. 328-58.

FOLKLORE
GENERAL STUDIES AND COLLECTIONS

Bechdolt, Frederich R.
Tales of the Old-Timers. New York: The Century Co., 1924. 367 pp.
"Stories of 'The Warriors of the Pecos' (Billy the Kid and the troubles on John Chisum's ranch-empire), of Butch Cassidy and his Wild Bunch in their Wyoming hide-outs, of the way frontier Texans fought Mexicans and Comanches over the open range." (Dobie)

Blair, Walter
Tall Tale America, a legendary history of our humorous heroes. New York: Coward-McCann, 1944. ix, 262 pp.

Blankenship, Russell
And There Were Men. New York: Alfred A. Knopf, 1942. 301 pp.
A picture of the men who molded the Pacific Northwest. Essays on a motley crew: squaw men, tough guys, preachers, Indians and such.

Boatright, Mody C.
"Backwoods Belles." *TFSP* 18:61–78, 1943. illus.
A strange gallery of women, among them—Lottie Ritchers, Sally Ann Thunder Crockett, Bets Undergrove, Jerusha Stubbs, Betsey Buzzard, Florinda Fury, Sal Fungus, Zipporina, Katy Goodgrit, Nancy Bowers, Sal Fink, Sappina Wing, Judy Coon, Grace Peabody, Katy Whippoween.

Botkin, Ben
A Treasury of American Folklore. New York: Crown Publishers, 1944.
Part I: Heroes and Boasters: 1. Backwoods Boasters (Davy Crockett, Mike Fink) ; 2. Pseudo Bad Men; 3. Killers (Wild Bill Hickok, Billy the Kid, Jesse James, Quantrell, Sam Bass, Stackalee; 4. Free Lances (Roy Bean, Buffalo Bill, Big Foot Wallace) ; 5. Miracle Men (Pecos Bill, Old Stormalong, Bowleg Bill, Paul Bunyan, Febold Feboldson, John Henry, Casey Jones, Joe Magarac) ; 6. Patron Saints (Honest Abe, Johnny Appleseed).

Buel, James W.
The Border Outlaws. An authentic and thrilling history of the most noted bandits of ancient and modern times; The Younger brothers, Jesse and Frank James, and their comrades in crime. St. Louis: Historical Publishing Co., 1881. 148 pp., illus.

Canton, Frank M.
Frontier Trails. Boston: Houghton Mifflin Co., 1930.

Carmer, Carl
America Sings. Stories and Songs of our Country's Growing. New York: Alfred A. Knopf, 1942. 243 pp., illus., music.
The major portion of the book taken up with tales of America's folk heroes: Mr. Sims and Henry, Ethan Crawford, Stormalong, Ichabod Paddock, John Darling, Philetus Bumpus, Philip Babb, Anthony the Trumpeter, Oregon Smith, Mike Fink, Johnny Appleseed, Davy Crockett, Jim Higgins, Joe Magerac, Annie Christmas, Bill Cropper, Tony Beaver, Daniel Boone, De Knee-High Man, Brer Rabbit, John Henry, Spadebread, The Virginian Grant, Wild Bill Corlett, Pecos Bill, Big Foot Wallace, and Paul Bunyan.

The Hurricane's Children. New York: Farrar and Rinehart, 1937. 175 pp.
Deals with the best known American folk heroes: Mike Fink, Davy Crockett, Old Stormalong, Pecos Bill, Kemp Morgan, Strap Buckner, Tony Beaver, John Henry, also Ocean-Born Mary, Annie Christmas, and Febold Feboldson.

Casey, Robert J.
The Black Hills and Their Incredible Characters. Indianapolis: Bobbs-Merrill Co., 1949.
From the first opening of the hills to whites and the gold rush of 1874, the author describes the history of the region thru the stories of Custer, Wild Bill, Calamity Jane, and many others.

Cattermole, E. G.
Famous Frontiersmen, Pioneers and Scouts; the Vanguards of American Civilization.... Chicago: M. A. Donohue & Co., 188–. xvi, 540 pp., illus.
In the gallery of characters one encounters Daniel Boone, Simon Girty, Simon Kenton, Davy Crockett, Kit Carson, Buffalo Bill, Texas Jack, and many others.

Cody, William Frederick (Buffalo Bill)
Story of the Wild West and Camp-Fire Chats, by Buffalo Bill. A full and complete history of the renowned pioneer quartette, Boone, Crockett, Carson, and Buffalo Bill.... Philadelphia: Historical Publishing Co., 1888. xvi, 766 pp., illus.

Coolidge, Dane
Fighting Men of the West. New York: E. P. Dutton and Co., 1932.

Cunningham, Eugene
Triggernometry. Caldwell, Idaho: Caxton Printers Ltd., 1934. Bibl.
"Excellent survey of codes and characters. Written by a man of intelligence and knowledge." (Dobie)

Daugherty, James, ed.
Their Weight in Wildcats. Boston: Houghton Mifflin Co., 1936. 188 pp.

Dobie, J. Frank
The Flavor of Texas. Dallas, Tex.: Dealey &
Lowe, 1936. 287 pp., illus.
> Includes chapters on Bean, Green, Duval, Ken-
> dall, and other famous Texan characters.

————.
Southwestern Lore. Publications of the Texas
Folk-Lore Society, No. IX. Dallas, Tex.: The
Southwest Press, 1931. 198 pp.
> A great many of American characters parade
> through the pages of this volume.

Dorson, Richard M.
"America's Comic Demigods." *American
Scholar* 10:389–401, 1941.

Edwards, John N.
*Notes Guerrillas, or, The Warfare of the
Border.* St. Louis: Bryan, Brand and Co., 1887.
488 pp., illus.

Field, Rachel
American Folk and Fairy Tales. New York:
Charles Scribners Sons, 1929.
> Includes tales of American characters.

Finger, Charles
The Distant Prize; A Book About Rovers,
Rangers, and Rascals. New York: D. Appleton-
Century Co., 1935. ix, 330 pp., illus.

Gardner, Raymond Hatfield (Arizona Bill)
The Old West. Adventures of Arizona Bill. In
collaboration with B. H. Monroe. Illustrated
by Grady Sowell. San Antonio, Texas: The
Naylor Co., 1944. 308 pp.
> A highly fictitious narrative, in which the author
> claims to have been with Custer, Wild Bill
> Hickok, Buffalo Bill, Deadwood Dick, Calamity
> Jane, the Earps, Doc Holliday, Tom Horn, Belle
> Starr, the James Brothers, Billy the Kid, Pat
> Garrett, and others. The author knew them all!

Hendricks, George David
The Bad Man of the West. Drawings by Frank
Anthony Stannush. San Antonio, Texas: The
Naylor Company, 1941. xv, 310 pp., bibl. (pp.
293–298).

Hough, Emerson
The Story of the Outlaw. New York: Grossett
and Dunlap, 1907. 401 pp.

Hubbard, Freeman H.
Railroad Avenue: Great Stories and Legends of
American Railroading. New York: Whittlesey
House, 1946. 374 pp., illus.
> Much information on Casey Jones, "Jawn" Henry,
> the Andrews Raid, Long John Simpkins, Jesse
> James, Kate Shelley, the Johnstown Flood, Harry
> McClintock, and some wonderful "raildogs."

Kelly, Charles
Outlaw Trails. Salt Lake City: Western Printing Co., 1938. 337 pp.

Kelsey, D. M.
Our Pioneer Heroes, and Their Daring Deeds.
The lives and famous exploits of De Soto,
Champlain, La Salle, Smith, Standish, Boone,
Kenton, Brady, Crockett, Bowie, Houston,
Carson, Harney, Custer, California Joe, Wild
Bill, Buffalo Bill, Miles, Crook, and other hero
explorers, renowned frontier fighters, and cele-
brated early settlers of America, from the
earliest times to the present. Philadelphia: G.
O. Pelton, 1883. xviii, 578 pp., illus.

Le Noir, Phil
Rhymes of the Wild and Wooly West. Santa
Fe, N. M.: New Mexico Publishing Corpora-
tion, 1920. 23 pp.
> A book of poems, some dealing with desperadoes.

Malcolmson, Anne
Yankee Doodle's Cousin. Illustrated by Robert
McCloskey. Boston: Houghton Mifflin Co.,
1941.
> An excellent compilation of chief American char-
> acters found in the East, the South, the Missis-
> sippi Valley and the West.

McHugh, Vincent
Caleb Catlum's America. Harrisburg, Pa.:
Stackpole Sons, 1936.

Lockwood, Francis Cummings
Arizona Characters. Los Angeles: Times-Mirror, 1928. xiv, 230 pp., illus.

Mercer, A. S.
Banditti of the Plains. Cheyenne, Wyoming:
1894. Reprinted by the Grabhorn Press, California, 1935. 136 pp., illus.

Myers, John Myers
The Alamo. New York: E. P. Dutton and Co.,
1948. 240 pp.
> "The essence of Mr. Myers' book lies in two
> sections: Biographical sketches of the four main
> participants of the battle: Bowie, Travis, Crockett
> and Santa Ana; and a day-by-day account of the
> siege ... (it tells) one of the best known stories
> from America's past." (J. Frank Dobie)

Miller, Olive Beaupré
Heroes, Outlaws and Funny Fellows. Illustrated by Richard Bennett. New York: Doubleday, Doran and Co., 1939. 332 pp.
> *Contents:* Captain Kidd and his Buried Treasure;
> Lord Timothy Dexter, First Lord of "Americay";
> Old Stormalong; When Witches Rode Broom-
> sticks; Dutch Adventures in old New York;
> Christmas in Bethlehem, Penna.; Old Johnny
> Appleseed; Mike Fink and the Outlaws of Cave-
> in-Rock; A Twelfth-Night Prank in Cahokia;
> etc.

Perry, Frances M., and Beebe, K.
Four American Pioneers—D. Boone, D. Crock-
ett, G. R. Clark, Kit Carson. A Book for Young
Americans. New York: Werner School Book
Co., 1900. 255 pp., illus.

Raine, William McLeod
Famous Sheriffs and Western Outlaws. Garden
City, N. Y.: Doubleday, Doran and Co., 1929.

————.
Guns of the Frontier. Boston: Houghton Mifflin Co., 1940.

Ray, Clarence E.
Famous American Scouts. Lives of Daniel
Boone, Kit Carson, Davy Crockett, Wild Bill,
and others.... Chicago: J. Rogan and Co.,
1920. 189 pp.

Sabin, Edwin Le Grand
Wild Men of the Wild West. New York:
Thomas Y. Crowell Co., 1929. 363 pp.

Seaver, Edwin, ed.
Pageant of American Humor. Cleveland, O.:
The World Publishing Co., 1949.

Shay, Frank
Drawn from the Wood: Consolations in Words
and Music for Pious Friends and Drunken
Companions. New York: The Macmillan Co.,
1927.

——————.
Here's Audacity! American Legendary Heroes.
New York: The Macmillan Co., 1930. 256 pp.
Delightful sketches of Paul Bunyan, Old Storm-
along, Kemp Morgan, Casey Jones, Peco Bill,
Tony Beaver and John Henry.

——————.
More Pious Friends and Drunken Companions.
Illustrated by John Held, Jr. New York: The
Macaulay Co., 1928.
Includes music—tunes only.

——————.
My Pious Friends and Drunken Companions.
Illustrated by John Held, Jr. New York: The
Macaulay Co., 1927. Music.

——————.
The Pious Friends and Drunken Companions.
Illustrated by John Held, Jr. New York: The
Macaulay Co., 1936. 190 pp., illus.
This book is a combination of these two classics
of conviviality: *My Pious Friends and Drunken
Companions,* and *More Drunken Friends and
Pious Companions.*

Skinner, Constance L.
Pioneers of the Old Southwest; a chronicle of
the dark and bloody ground. New Haven: Yale
University Press, 1921. xi, 304 pp.

Sowell, Andrew Jackson
History of Fort Bend County, containing
biographical sketches of many noted characters. Houston, Tex.: W. H. Coyle and Co.,
1904. xii, 373 pp., illus.

——————.
Rangers and Pioneers of Texas. ... San Antonio, Tex.: Shepard Bros. & Co., 1884. 411 pp.,
illus.

Sparks, Jared
Makers of American History. ... New York:
The University Society, 1905. 176 pp.

Stevenson, Philip
Handicraft. In: *Folk Say, a Regional Miscel-
lany,* Vol. 2, pp. 322–323, 1930.
Discussion of meaning and status of Anglo-
American art, and our folk heroes.

Thane, Eric
High Border Country. (American Folkways
Series). New York: Duell, Sloan and Pearce,
1942.
Indigenous material, colorful and dramatic. These
tales of mountain men, redskins, prospectors,
soldiers, vigilantes, Chinese, cowboys, outlaws,
copper barons, farmers, heroes, some good, some
bad, some notorious.

The Great West: Containing Narratives of the
Most Important and Interesting Events in
Western History,—Remarkable Individual Ad-
ventures,—Sketches of Frontier Life—Descrip-
tion of Natural Curiosities: To Which Is Ap-
pended Historical and Descriptive Sketches of
Oregon, New Mexico, Texas, Minnesota, Utah,
California, Washington, Nebraska, Kansas,
Etc., Etc., Etc. New York: George F. Tuttle,
1857; Cincinnati: Henry Howe, 1857.

Trent, William P.
"A Retrospect of American Humor." *Century
Magazine,* 1901, pp. 45–64.

Vestal, Stanley
Mountain Men. Boston: Houghton Mifflin Co.,
1937. x, 296 pp., bibl.

Webber, Charles Wilkins
*Historical and Revolutionary Incidents of the
Early Settlers of the United States.* ... Phila-
delphia: D. Rulison, 1861. 416 pp.

——————.
The Romance of Forest and Prairie Life: Nar-
ratives of Perilous Adventures & Wild Hunting
Scenes. London: H. Vizetelly, 1853. 239 pp.

Woodhull, Frost
"Folklore Shooting." *TFSP* 9:5–14, 1931.
A gallery of American bad men pass in review.

CLAY ALLISON

Buffum, George T.
*Smith of Bear City and Other Frontier
Sketches.* New York: The Grafton Press, 1906.
Has a chapter—"The Evolution of Clay Allison."

Clark, O. S.
Clay Allison of the Washita, first a cowman
and then an extinguisher of bad men. Recol-
lections of Colorado, New Mexico, and the
Texas panhandle, reminiscences of a '79er.
Attica, Ind.: G. M. Williams, 1920. 38 pp.

Fulton, Maurice G.
"Clay Allison." *Southwest Review* 15 (No. 2):
192–215, 1931.

Lake, Stuart N.
Wyatt Earp: Frontier Marshall. Boston:
Houghton Mifflin Co., 1931. pp. 176–184.
Facts of Allison's collision with peace officers of
Dodge City.

Lewis, Alfred Henry
The Sunset Trail. New York: A. S. Barnes &
Co., 1905. x, 393 pp., illus.
Has chapter on the doings and on "The Intuitions
of Mr. Allison."

Siringo, Charles A.
Riata and Spurs. Boston: Houghton Mifflin Co.,
On pp. 175–180, are some tales of Clay Allison.
1927. xiv, 276 pp., rev. ed.

Smith, Honora De Busk
"Cowboy Lore in Colorado." *TFSP* 9:27–44,
1931.
  Also talks about "Clay Allison—The Famous
Killer."

JOHNNY APPLESEED

BIBLIOGRAPHY

Edwards, Everett E.
"References on Johnny Appleseed." *Agricultural Library Notes* 2:270–279, 1936.
  An annotated list.

"Johnny Appleseed Bibliography."
The Helper 78:25–27, June 16, 1926.

Odhner, Carl Theophilus
Annals of the New Church 1:200, 229, 250, 265,
295, 451, 533–534, 1904. (Academy of the New
Church: Bryn Athyn, Penna.)

Price, Robert
John Chapman; a bibliography of "Johnny
Appleseed" in American history, literature and
folklore. Paterson, N. J.: The Swedenborg
Press, 1944. vi, 40 pp.
  An excellent bibliography. *Contents:* 1. Bibliography; 2. References Chiefly Biographical; 3.
Johnny Appleseed in Story and Art; 4. Miscellaneous References; 5. Monuments and Other
Memorials; 6. Important Collections Relating to
John Chapman. Each of the above major subdivisions has numerous subheadings.

Wenn, Florence
"Index of Historical Articles in Indiana Newspapers 1909–1911." *Indiana Magazine of History* vols. 5, 6, 7, 1909–1911.

GENERAL STUDIES AND COLLECTIONS

Adams, Bob
"God's Planter." In: *Rude Rural Rhymes.*
New York: The Macmillan Co., 1925. p. 43.
  A poem.

Allsopp, Fred W.
Folklore of Romantic Arkansas. New York:
The Grolier Society, 1931. vol. 2, pp. 271–274.

"An Angel in Each Apple."
The Helper 85:2–6, 1930.

"An Important Character in Indiana's Early
Horticulture." *Indiana Farmer* 68:2, Nov. 1,
1913.

Anish, Clara L.
Apples in the Orchard. Radio Play. Performed
April 13, 1943. Board of Education program,
WSAI, Cincinnati, Ohio. MS.

"Apple Blossoms."
New York Times, May 16, 1943.
  An editorial.

"Arbor Day Is His Day."
The Target 94:4, May 5, 1934.

Atkinson, Eleanor
Johnny Appleseed, The Romance of the Sower.
. . . New York: Harper & Bros., 1915. 341 pp.,
illus.
  A novel based on his life, adventures, and legendary powers.

Austin, Mrs. Helen V.
"Johnny Appleseed, the Pioneer Pomologist of
the West." *Indiana Horticultural Society,
Trans.* 22:35–40, 1882.

Bailey, Carolyn Sherwin
"Lost in the Apple Cave." In: *Children of the
Handicrafts,* pp. 136–145. New York: The
Viking Press, 1935.

Baughman, A. G.
"Pioneer Men and Women of Ohio." *The Firelands Pioneer* 12:415–416, 1899. n.s.

Baughman, A. J.
"Historical Sketch of the Life and Work of
Johnny Appleseed." *The Firelands Pioneer* 13:
702–711, 1900. n.s.

Beard, Dan
Do It Yourself; a Book of the Big Outdoors,
pp. 89–95. Phila.: J. B. Lippincott & Co., 1925.
  The story of Johnny Appleseed for young readers.

————.
"Johnny Appleseed, the Good Turn Scout."
World Review 4:189, April 23, 1928.

Benét, Laura
"Johnny Appleseed's Trail." *Christian Science
Monitor,* Oct. 25, 1939.

Benét, Rosemary and Stephen Vincent
"Johnny Appleseed." In: *A Book of Americans.*
New York: Farrar & Rinehart, 1933. (pp. 47–
49).
  A poem.

Berrell, Howard A.
"Apples and Apples." *Iowa State Horticultural
Society, Report* 40:283–288, 1905.

"Biography of Johnny Appleseed."
Indiana Farmer 76:6–7, 1916.

Black, F. A.
"Johnny Appleseed. Historical Cachet Collectors Will Learn Interesting Highlights." *Covers*
3:6–7, Feb., 1941.

Black, J. R.
"Johnny Appleseed." *Nebraska Horticulture*
1:9–11, Nov., 1911.

Blair, J. C.
"Some Midwest Contributions to American
Pomology." *Iowa State Horticultural Society
Report* 55:223, 1930.
  The wonder deeds of Johnny Appleseed.

Boner, S. H.
"Life of Johnnie Appleseed." *Green's Fruit
Grower* 34:20, Dec., 1914.

Bonham, Martha E.
"Johnny Appleseed, Father of American Orchards." *Forward* 59:5, 14–15, May 18, 1940.

Botkin, B. A., ed.
A Treasury of American Folklore.... New York: Crown Publishing Co., 1944. pp. 255–256, 261–270.

"Brands Johnny Appleseed Tale History's Bunk." *Chicago Daily Tribune*, April 11, 1936.

Bromfield, Louis
Pleasant Valley. New York: Harper Bros., 1945. 321 pp.
"—the book is enlivened by romantic digressions, retellings of the legends of *Johnny Appleseed* and the lost Dauphin, and sketches of local character." (Orville Prescott)

———.
The Farm. New York: Harper & Bros., 1933. References to John Chapman, pp. 103–105.

Brown, H. Clark
Appleseed Johnny (A Poetic Drama of Pioneer Days). A dramatization of the life-story of Jonathan Chapman, the Johnny Appleseed of pioneer traditions, by Donald Thistle (pseud.) Cover design by Howard A. Mather.... Charles City, Ia.: The Torrence Printing Company, 1927. 54 pp., illus.

"By One Who Knew Him."
The Helper 78:6–10, 1926

C., H. W.
"Johnny Appleseed." *Rural New Yorker* 74:592, April 17, 1915.

Carmer, Carl
Johnny Appleseed: Old Brass Wagon. In: *America Sings*, pp. 94–99. New York: Alfred A. Knopf, 1942.

———.
The Hurricane's Children. New York: Farrar & Rinehart, 1937. 175 pp.

Castilo, Iantha
"A Folk Tale of Johnny Appleseed." *Missouri Historical Review* 19:622–629, 1925.

Catherwood, Mary Hartwell
Lazarre. Indianapolis: Bowen, Merrill Co., 1901.
John Chapman appears in this novel.

Chapin, Henry
The Adventures of Johnny Appleseed; illustrations by James Daugherty. New York: Coward-McCann, 1930. vii, 244 pp., illus.
A fictional account of his life and deeds.

Child, Lydia Maria
"Apple-Seed John." In: *History of Ashland County, Ohio,* by George William Hill. Cleveland: Williams Bros., 1880. p. 187.
Poem, reprinted in numerous anthologies.

Church of The New Jerusalem Library
John Chapman Collection. Cincinnati, Ohio: The Church of New Jerusalem Library.

Colby, Merle
All Ye People. New York: The Viking Press, 1931.
John Chapman appears as one of the characters in this novel.

Cunningham, J. O.
"John Chapman, Itinerant Nurseryman." In: *Cyclopedia of American Agriculture,* L. H. Bailey, ed., Vol. iv, pp. 561–562. New York: The Macmillan Co., 1912.

Curry, Mabel Stuart
"Johnny Appleseed's Grave." *Sentinel* (Fort Wayne, Ind.), Aug. 28, 1937.
A poem.

Curtis, R. I.
"John Chapman, alias, 'Johnny Appleseed'." *Ohio Pomological Society Trans, 1859,* pp. 68–69.

Daugherty, James
Their Weight in Wildcats. Boston: Houghton Mifflin Co., 1936. (pp. 21–30).

Davis, Florence Boyce
"Johnny Appleseed." *American Girl* 22:20–21, Oct., 1939.
A poem.

Dent, Floyd
"The Northwest Ordinance—Johnny Appleseed, Major County Benefactor." *News-Journal* (Mansfield, Ohio), April 26, 1938.

"Diamonds in Granite; Johnny Appleseed and His Mission." *Granite State Magazine* 1:215–218, May, 1906.

Dodds, Gilbert F.
"Eccentric Characters in Ohio History." *Dispatch* (Columbus, Ohio), March 7, 1937.

Douglas, Emily Taft
Appleseed Farm. Illustrated by Anne Vaughan. New York: Abingdon-Cokesbury Press, 1948. 128 pp.
The story of Johnny Appleseed's wonder deeds and goodwill adventures for young readers.

Douglass, Benjamin Wallace
"When Chapman Walked the Wilderness." *Country Home* 60:9, July, 1936.
A poem.

Duff, William A.
Johnny Appleseed. An American History Dramalogue. School of the Air Program of the Ohio Department of Education, Ashland, Ohio. Broadcast by the WEAO players of Ohio State University over WLW, Cincinnati, April 22, 1929.

———.
Johnny Appleseed, an Ohio Hero; Patron Saint of American Orchards. Ashland, Ohio: 1914. 10 pp.

———.
"Spirit of Service, the Work of Our Patron Saint of American Orchards." *Press* (Ashland, Ohio), Jan. 27, 1915.

————.
The Heart of Johnny Appleseed. In: *Little Stories of Old Sandusky*. Ashland, Ohio: 1921.

Du Puy, William Atherton
"St. John Appleseed." *Coronet* 1:9–13, April, 1937. (Reprinted in *Reader's Digest*, June, 1937, pp. 60–62.

Ellis, Homer C.
Pioneer Life of the Firelands. Norwalk, Ohio: 1939.

Emry, D. F.
"Johnny Appleseed." *Missouri State Horticultural Society, Annual Report* 33:12–13, 1890.

Erichsen, H.
"Johnny Appleseed; the Humble Record of John Chapman, Apostle of Apple-Growing." *Western Fruit Grower* 15:278–279, Sept., 1904.

Fast, Howard
"Tarry a While." *The Elks Magazine* 17:4–7, 42–44, May, 1939.
A short story.

————.
The Tall Hunter. Illustrated by Rafaello Busoni. New York: Harper & Bros., 1943. 103 pp.
A poetically told story for the young of that strange half-mythical Johnny Appleseed.

Federal Writers' Project
Connecticut. A Guide to Its Roads, Lore and People. Boston: Houghton Mifflin Co., 1938. p. 471.

————.
Indiana. A Guide to the Hoosier State. New York: Oxford University Press, 1941. p. 122.

————.
Tales of Pioneer Pittsburgh. Philadelphia: William Penn Association, 1937. (pp. 3–6.)

————.
The Ohio Guide. New York: Oxford University Press, 1940. pp. 82, 289, 291, 481–482, 498–499, 524, 567.

Flanders, W. R.
"A Review of John Chapman (Johnny Appleseed) in the Mid-West." *Kansas State Horticultural Society, Biennial Report* 37:137–140, 1922–23.

Freeland, Isabelle Virginia
"The Adventures of Brave Heart and Laughing Eyes to the Land of Johnny Appleseed." Cleveland, O., *Plain Dealer*, Aug. 26, 1917.

Frost, Frances
"American Ghost." *New York Herald Tribune*, Aug. 21, 1943.
A poem.

————.
Johnny Appleseed. In: *Legends of the United States*. (pp. 154–161). New York: Whittlesey House, 1943.

Gates, Arnold Francis
Song of the Leaves; Quest of Johnny Appleseed. West Leisenring, Pa.: Griglak Printery, 1940. 13 pp.

Gates, Josephine Scribner
"Johnny Appleseed." In: *A Character Book for 4th Grade*, Curtis G. Gentry, ed., p. 16. New York: C. Heath, 1929.

"Gentle Johnny Appleseed."
Missouri State Horticultural Society, Annual Report 43:218–224, 1922–23.

Glines, W. M.
Johnny Appleseed by One Who Knew Him. From original manuscripts edited by W. Paddock. Columbus, O.: 1922.

Gordon, Ruth Winslow
A Spray of Apple Blossoms. Georgetown, Ohio: 1935.

————.
"Apple Blossom Time." *Ohio Farmer* 177:261, April 25, 1936.

Goulder, Grace
"The Buckeye State's First Orchardist." *Cleveland Plain Dealer*, Oct. 13, 1940.

H., T. S.
"A Leaf in the History of Pomology at the West." *The Magazine of Horticulture* 12:132–135, April, 1846.
Robert Price considers this one of the earliest accounts of John Chapman.

Haley, W. D.
"Johnny Appleseed—A Pioneer Hero." *Harper's Monthly Magazine* 43:830–836, Nov., 1871.
"One of the most important of early accounts, basic to much of later popular belief." (Robert Price)

Harper, Robert C.
Trumpet in the Wilderness. New York: M. S. Mill Co., 1940.
Fiction. Chapman appears as one of the protagonists.

Harris, Robert C., comp.
Johnny Appleseed. Mimeographed booklet containing news articles, genealogical and biographical data . . . Fort Wayne, Ind.: Johnny Appleseed Memorial Commission, 1936.

————.
"Johnny Appleseed Source Book." *Old Fort News* (Fort Wayne) 9 (No. 1–2): 5–10, 1946. Illus.

Hatcher, Harlan
"The Literary Fourth Dimension." *English Journal* 27:459–460, 1938.

————, **and others**
Johnny Appleseed, a Voice in the Wilderness; the story of the pioneer John Chapman. Centennial tribute. Paterson, N. J.: The Swedenborg Press, 1945. iv, 74 pp., bibl.
Contents: Foreword, by Harlan Hatcher; Johnny Appleseed in American folklore and literature, by Robert Price; The arts salute Johnny Appleseed, by Florence Murdoch; The religion of Johnny Appleseed, by J. W. Stockwell; The story of Johnny Appleseed, by Ophia D. Smith; Modern interest in Johnny Appleseed, by J. W. Stockwell; The American pioneer, a poem by J. W. Stockwell.

"Hats Off to Johnny Appleseed." *Apple World* 1:17, June, 1914.

Havighurst, Walter
The Quiet Shore. New York: The Macmillan Co., 1937.
A novel in which Chapman plays a part.

"Here Is News Straight From Heaven For You." *The Helper* 78:2–3, 1926.

"Here's Some New Facts on the Only Johnny Appleseed." *Journal* (Mansfield, Ohio), Jan. 18, 1926.

"Here's the History of Johnny Appleseed." *American Forestry* 26:117, Feb., 1920.

Hillis, Newell Dwight
The Quest of John Chapman. The Story of a Forgotten Hero. New York: The Macmillan Co., 1904. xiii, 349 pp.
A work of fiction.

Himrod, James Lattimore
Johnny Appleseed; the true story of Jonathan Chapman, 1775–1846, by the grandson of one who knew him well. Chicago: Chicago Historical Society, 1926. 28 pp., illus., bibl.

"Honor Johnny Appleseed." *Florist's Review* 59:140–141, 142, Nov. 4, 1926.

Hottes, A. C.
"Johnny Appleseed, Father of Orchards." *Better Homes and Gardens* 11:100, May, 1934.

"How Johnny Appleseed Made the Earth Fruitful." *Literary Digest* 97:46–48, April 28, 1928.

Hunter, W. H.
"The Pathfinders of Jefferson County." *Ohio Archaeological and Historical Society Publications* 6:290, 293, 1898.

"Interesting History of America's Apple Pioneer." *American Fruits* 23:146, 148, June, 1916.

James, Alice Archer Sewall
The Torch. A Pageant of Light. Based on the early history of Urbana. Urbana, Ohio, 1922.

John Chapman Collection.
Leominster, Mass., Public Library.

"John Chapman or Johnny Appleseed." *Old Fort News* (Allen County-Fort Wayne Historical Society) 1:7–8, 1936.

"Johnny Appleseed." *Better Homes and Gardens* 10:40, 100, April, 1932.

"Johnny Appleseed."
Evening Telegraph (Bucyrus, Ohio), Oct. 17, 1912.

"Johnny Appleseed." *Green's Fruit Grower and Home Companion* 26:12, March, 1906.

Johnny Appleseed. In: *Home Life,* 110th Anniversary Edition, issued by First Federal Savings and Loan Association, Minneapolis, Minn.

"Johnny Appleseed." *Journal* (Providence, R. I.), Oct. 1, 1925.
An editorial.

"Johnny Appleseed." *Michigan History Magazine* 25:366–367, 1941.

"Johnny Appleseed." *New Church Messenger* 45:10, 1882.

"Johnny Appleseed." *New Jerusalem Messenger* 36:56, 58, 1879.

Johnny Appleseed. Radio play. Vacation Ventures Program, WLOK, Dayton, Ohio, Aug. 11, 1941. MS.

Johnny Appleseed. Radio play. Cavalcade of America, NBC, May 25, 1936. MS.

"Johnny Appleseed." *Youth's Companion* 99:299, April 30, 1925.

"Johnny Appleseed, a Pioneer Benefactor." *Palladium—Item Advertiser* (Richmond, Ind.), Dec. 13, 1940.

"Johnny Appleseed Again." *New York Times,* April 19, 1938.
An editorial.

"Johnny Appleseed and His Big Work." *Times-Gazette* (Ashland, Ohio), Jan. 15, 1918.

"Johnny Appleseed and His Wonderful Achievements." *Green's Fruit Grower and Home Companion* 27:3, July, 1907.

"Johnny Appleseed and His Work." *The Rural New-Yorker* 74:704, May 15, 1915.

"Johnny Appleseed by One Who Knew Him." *The Helper* 72:6–9, 1923.

"Johnny Appleseed by One Who Knew Him." *The Helper* 101:7, 1938.

"Johnnie Appleseed Gatherer and Scatterer of Seed." *Noble County Leader* (Caldwell, Ohio), Aug. 13, 1942.

"Johnny Appleseed Gave Ohio Medicinal Herbs." *Ohio State Horticultural Society Report 1921* 54:59, 1921.

"Johnny Appleseed—Hoosier Conservationist." *Outdoor Indiana* 10:8–9, 13, Jan., 1944.

Johnny Appleseed Memorial Commission.
John Chapman Collection. Fort Wayne, Ind.: The Johnny Appleseed Memorial Commission.

"Johnny Appleseed of Legend Really Existed, Data Show." *Sunday Star* (Washington, D. C.), May 10, 1936.

"Johnny Appleseed, or John Chapman." *Times* (Willard, Ohio), Aug. 25, 1910.

"Johnny Appleseed Was Real Character." *Press* (Pittsburgh, Pa.) June 23, 1937.

Johnson, Davis Ben
"Johnnie Appleseed." In: *Hills of Ohio and Other Poems*. Wauseon, Ohio.: 1936. (pp. 69–70).

Johnson, P.
"Johnny Appleseed Was No Myth." *Purdue Agriculturist* 35:3, Oct., 1940.

Kerley, Richard
"Johnny Appleseed." *Times-Star* (Cincinnati, Ohio), April 25, 1940.

Levenberg, Lawrence F.
"Johnny Appleseed, Pioneer Orchard Builder." *Star* (Indianapolis, Ind.), Feb. 6, 1927.

Karn, Oma
"A Soldier of Peace." *Our Young People*, Jan. 12, 1918.

Keazer, Pauline
"Lincoln Meets Johnny Appleseed." *The Grade Teacher* 57:28, 69, Feb., 1940.
A play for children.

Kellogg, Elizabeth R.
"Blossoms in the Wilderness: In Memory of John Chapman, 1775–1847." *Cincinnati Times-Star*, May 5, 1928.
A poem.

Langdon, William Chauncy
The Pageant of Indiana. Indianapolis: Hollenbeck Press, 1916. (pp. 47–55).
Contains—"St. Francis of the Orchards"—a play.

————.
"The Prayer of John Chapman." In: *Foundation Day Ceremonial for Indiana University*, p. 5. Bloomington, Ind., 1920.

Langtry, Rosa A.
"A Visit to the Grave of Johnny Appleseed." *Indiana History Bulletin* 4:218–220, 1927.

Laughlin, Clara E.
So You're Seeing New England. Boston: Little, Brown and Co., 1940. p. 63.

Legler, Mary Ferguson
"Johnny Appleseed Came This Way." *Columbus, O., Dispatch*, Sept. 8, 1944.
A poem.

"Leominster Claims Appleseed. Subject of Thousand Legends." *Sunday-Telegram* (Worcester, Mass.), May 22, 1938.

Lindsay, Vachel
Collected Poems. New York: The Macmillan Co., 1927.
Contains many Johnny Appleseed poems, such as: "The Fairy from the Appleseed," "How Johnny Walked Alone in the Jungle of Heaven," "Johnny Appleseed's Old Age," "Johnny Appleseed's Hymn to the Sun," etc.

————.
Johnny Appleseed and Other Poems. New York: The Macmillan Co., 1928.

————.
"Song for American Children in Praise of Johnny Appleseed." *Spectator* 126: 651–652, May 21, 1921.

————.
The Golden Book of Springfield. New York: The Macmillan Co., 1920.
A novel in which John Chapman plays a vital part.

MacDougall, Curtis Daniel
Hoaxes. New York: Macmillan Company, 1940. viii, 336 pp., front. pl.
"Among the folkloric hoaxes treated by the author are mythical monsters (The Lodge), historical myths (Parson's Weems' Cherry Tree Myth), tall stories, and legendary heroes (Johnny Appleseed).

M'Gaw, Rev. James F.
Philip Seymour; or, Pioneer Life in Richland County, Ohio. Mansfield, Ohio: 1857.
A novel.

McLachlan, J. B.
"Johnny Appleseed." *New Church Review* 32:302–307, 1925.

McMeekin, Clark
Reckon with the River. New York: D. Appleton-Century Co., 1941.
Fiction, with Chapman as one of the characters.

McMeekin, Isabel McLennan
Journey Cake. New York: Julian Messner, 1942.
A story of Johnny Appleseed for children.

————.
Thanks to Johnny Appleseed. A play in three acts. New York: Samuel French, 1929.

Malcolmson, Anne
"Johnny Appleseed," In: *Yankee Doodle's Cousins*, pp. 119–128. Boston: Houghton Mifflin Co., 1941.

Martin, Gertrude H.
"Johnny Appleseed." *Cincinnati, O., Enquirer*, May 15, 1944.
A poem.

————.
Johnny Appleseed and the Indians. In: *Plays and Ceremonies for Girl Scouts*. New York: Girl Scouts of America.

Martzolff, Clement L.
Fifty Stories from Ohio History. Columbus, Ohio: Ohio Education Publishing Company, 1921. (pp. 166–172).

Masters, Edgar Lee
"Johnny Appleseed." In: *Toward the Gulf*, pp. 42–45. New York: The Macmillan Co., 1918.
A poem.

Miller, Ethel Hull
Out of the Roaring Loom. Greenville, Pa.: Gold Seal Publications, 1936.
Fiction, with Chapman in the cast.

Miller, Olive Beaupré
"Old Johnny Appleseed." In: *Heroes, Outlaws and Funny Fellows of American Popular Tales*, pp. 73–82. New York: Doubleday, Doran & Co., 1939.

Miller, Wilhelm
"Johnny Appleseed." In: *Standard Cyclopedia of Horticulture*, L. H. Bailey, ed., Vol. II, pp. 1563–1564. New York: The Macmillan Co., 1925.

Miner, Virginia Scott
"Johnny Appleseed Song." *Talaria, a Quarterly of Poetry*. (Cincinnati, Ohio), June, 1944.
A poem.

Minn, Mrs. Elizabeth
"Fire Lands Reminiscences." *The Firelands Pioneer* 1:47, 1859.

Moore, Anne Carroll
"Johnny Appleseed." *New York Herald Tribune Books*, March 16, 1930.

Needham, Caroline F.
"Apple-Seed John." In: *Working Together*, Andrew W. Edson and Mary E. Laing, eds., pp. 71–77. New York: Benj. H. Sanborn & Co., 1925.

Nolen, Mrs. E. W.
Cowhide Trunk. New York: Oxford University Press, 1941. (pp. 72–82).
The author tells the story and adventures of Johnny Appleseed—for young readers.

Ohio Archaeological and Historical Society Museum Library
John Chapman Collection. Columbus, Ohio: Ohio Archaeological and Historical Society Museum Library.

"Ohio Owes Much to Johnny Appleseed Who Brought Trees and Herbs to the State." *Enquirer* (Cincinnati, Ohio), June 27, 1936.

Onstott, Anna Long
"John Chapman, Pioneer Nurseryman and Missionary, 1774–1845." *New-Church Messenger* 162:308–309, 1942.

————.
"The Story of Johnny Appleseed." *Children's Activities* 10:4–5, April, 1944.

————, and Stunz, Arthur N.
"John Chapman—'Johnny Appleseed', 1774–1845." *Men's Garden Clubs of America Year Book 1943*, pp. 38–42.

"Orchard Apostle."
New York Herald Tribune, May 11, 1944.
An editorial.

Paddock, W.
"The Story of Johnnie Appleseed." *Fruits and Gardens* 25:12, 15, Feb., 1927.

Page, Meredith
Johnny Appleseed; an Original Radio Script. The Ohio School of the Air; a production of the Radio Workshop, Ohio State University. Columbus, 1936. 29 pp.

Parker, Beryl, and Harris, Julia M.
Exploring New Fields. Boston: Houghton Mifflin Co., 1938. (pp. 327-329, 330–342).
The story retold for children.

Parson, Don
"Johnny Appleseed." *Paulding, O., Democrat*, Jan. 12, 1939.
A poem.

Peacock, N. D.
"Johnny Appleseed." *Purdue Agriculturist* 13: 336, April, 1919.

Peattie, Donald Culross
"John Chapman." In: *Dictionary of American Biography*, Vol. 4, pp. 17–18. New York: Charles Scribner's Sons, 1930.

Peck, Elizabeth
"Johnny Appleseed Comes." In: *American Frontier*, p. 96. New York: Doubleday, Doran & Co., 1937.
A poem.

Perry, Ernstine
Patron Saint of American Apple Orchards—Johnny Appleseed in the Pioneer Valley. In: *Johnny Appleseed Cookbook*, Springfield, Mass., 1941.

Pershing, Henry A.
"Johnny Appleseed and His Time." *Democrat* (Paulding, Ohio), Jan. 12, 1939.
A series of articles, beginning in the above issue.

————.
Johnny Appleseed and His Time, an historical romance; with illustrations from photographs, woodcuts, scenes of his wanderings, his autograhp, with many other interesting pictures. . . . Strasburg, Va.: Shenandoah Publishing House, 1930. xx, 379 pp., illus.

————.
"Queer John Chapman, Early Tree Planter." *Tribune* (South Bend, Ind.), Dec. 18, 1927.

"Pioneer Fort Wayne Women Knew Johnny Appleseed." *News-Sentinel* (Fort Wayne, Ind.), Nov. 6, 1926.

"Pioneer Incidents in the Life of Susan A. Wilbor, of Milan." *The Firelands Pioneer* 12:93, 1876.

"Pioneer Life in Huron County." *The Firelands Pioneer* 5:126, 1888. n.s.

Price, Robert
"A Boyhood for Johnny Appleseed." *New England Quarterly* 17:381–393, 1944.
The story of Appleseed's childhood in the Connecticut valley.

————.
Johnny Appleseed in American Folklore and Literature. In: *Johnny Appleseed, A Voice in the Wilderness*. . . . Centennial Tribute by Harlan Hatcher and others. . . . Paterson, N. J.: The Swedenborg Press, 1945.

————.
"New England Origins of Johnny Appleseed." *New England Quarterly* 12:454–469, 1939.

Randall, E. O.
"Johnny Appleseed Addendum." *Ohio Archaeological and Historical Society Publications* 9:313–317, 1901.

——.
"Pocket Book of Appleseed Johnny." *Ohio Archaeological and Historical Society Publications* 9:256–257, 1902.

"Recollections of Jonathan Chapman, a Primitive New-Churchman." *New Church Repository* 5:354–355, 1852.

Resneck, Daniel
"Patron Saint of All Orchards Spent Life Fulfilling New Year's Resolution to Become Apple Missionary." *Sunday Star* (Indianapolis, Ind.), Jan. 10, 1937.

Rice, Alonzo
"Johnny Appleseed." *Indiana Farmer* 65:10, Jan. 22, 1910.

Rice, Rosella
Johnny Appleseed. In: *History of the Ashland County Pioneer Historical Society*, pp. 57–99, 165–173. Ashland, Ohio: Brethren Publishing House, 1888.

Richardson, M. W.
"Tribute to Johnny Appleseed." *Fruit Grower* 27:310, June 1, 1916.

Roebuck, Wesley S.
"Outline of Facts Related to the Burial Place of John Chapman." *Ohio State Archaeological and Historical Quarterly* 52:276–284, 1943. Illus.

Sandburg, Carl
The People, Yes. New York: Harcourt Brace & Co., 1936. p. 231.

Savage, F. S., Jr.
"John Chapman, the Man Walked with God." Leominster, Mass., *Daily Enterprise*, March 17, 1938.
A poem.

Schoenfeld, Bernhard C.
Johnny Appleseed. Radio Play. Kate Smith Hour. 1940. MS.
The author discusses this play in *Scholastic Magazine*, Sept. 16, 1940. p. 17.

Schumann, Mary
My Blood and My Treasure. New York: Dial Press, 1941.
A novel.

Sherman, Daniel
"Reminiscences." *The Firelands Pioneer* 5:99, 1864.

Sickels, E. R.
School Bell Rings. New York: Charles Scribner's Sons, 1942. (pp. 113–122).
Appleseed's adventures told to children.

Smart, Charles Allen
"The Return of Johnny Appleseed." *Harper's Magazine* 179:233–234, 1939.

Smith, E. R.
Johnny Appleseed, a Pioneer Orchardist. Indiana Apple Show Commission, 1916. 7 pp.

Smith, Mrs. R. R.
Seedlings. In: *Plays for Spring and Summer Holidays*, A. P. Sanford, ed., (pp. 77–92). New York: Dodd, Mead & Co., 1938.

Smock, William
"All Have Heard, Few Know Story of Johnny Appleseed." *Tribune* (Mansfield, Ohio), May 20, 1939.

Snider, Denton J. ("Theophilus Middling")
Johnny Appleseed's Rhymes. St. Louis, Mo.: Sigma Publishing Co., 1894.

——.
The Freeburghers. St. Louis: Sigma Publishing Co., 1889.
A novel.

Snyder, Miles J.
"More About Johnny Appleseed." *Green's Fruit Grower and Home Companion* 28:15, June, 1908.

Speed, James
Johnny Appleseed. In: *Ten Outdoor Men*, pp. 110–124. New York: D. C. Heath, 1929.

Stern, R. B.
Johnny Appleseed. In: *Neighborhood Entertainments*, p. 185. New York: Sturgis & Walton, 1916.

Sterry, I. H., and Garrigus, W. H.
They Found a Way: Connecticut's Restless People. Brattleboro, Vt.: Stephen Daye Press, 1938. pp. 13, 328–329.

Stevens, Henry Bailey
Johnny Appleseed and Paul Bunyan; a play of American folklore in three acts with prologue. Boston: W. H. Baker, 1930. 92 pp.

——.
"Johnny Appleseed Was a Yankee." *The New Hampshire Troubadour* 7:3–5, 1937.

Stockwell, John W.
"On the Trail of Johnny Appleseed." *New Church Messenger* 161 (Part I):267–268; (Part II):283–284, 1941.

Sundgaard, Arnold, and Connolly, Marc
Everywhere I Roam. A Play. Unpublished.
Produced at the National Theatre, New York, Dec. 29, 1938.

Tafel, Leonard I.
"Johnny Appleseed." *New-Church Messenger* 161:10–13, 1931.

——.
"The Best Tramp." *Commercial Gazette* (Cincinnati, Ohio), Aug. 8, 1891.

"The Good That Men Do Lives After Them." *The Helper* 78:18–25, 1926.

"The History of Johnny Appleseed." *Florida Grower* 26:14, April 3, 1920.

"The Johnny Appleseed Club." *The Helper* 78: 12–17, 1926.

"The Planting of Johnny Appleseed." *Apple Specialist* 2:7, Dec., 1905.

The Story of Johnny Appleseed. Dreams of Yesteryear. Mimeographed booklet issued by the Johnny Appleseed Week Committee. Mansfield, Ohio, September 26, 1941.

"The Story of Johnny Appleseed." *Indiana Farmer* 61:3, June 30, 1906.

"The Story of Johnny Appleseed." *Journal News* (Evansville, Ind.), April 10, 1910.

"The Story of Johnny Appleseed." *Maryland Fruit Grower* 7:5–6, Aug., 1937; 4–5, Oct., 1937.

Thompson, Edith Osborne
"A Journey that Lasted a Lifetime." *The Target* 97:4, April 10, 1937.
A poem and editorial.

Turner, Nancy Byrd
"Rhyme of Johnny Appleseed." *Child Life*, Aug. 28, 1937.

Van Natter, Francis Marion
"The Appleseed Evangelist." *National Republic* 23:6–7, 32, Nov., 1935.

Venable, William H.
"Johnny Appleseed." In: *Poems of American History*, p. 234. Boston: Houghton Mifflin Co., 1908.

Watson, Elmo Scott
"Johnny Appleseed, Patron Saint of Arbor Day." *Twice a Week News* (Charles City, Iowa), April 22, 1927.

Way, Farer
"Saint Johnny Appleseed." *The Buckeye Bugle* 2:4, Jan., 1932.

Wayland, John Walter
History Stories for Primary Grades. New York: The Macmillan Co., 1919. (p. 46).

Webster, H. H., and Polkingham, A. R.
Johnny Appleseed. In: *What the World Eats*, pp. 13–15. Boston: Houghton Mifflin Co., 1938.

Wecter, Dixon
The Hero in America. New York: Charles Scribner's Sons, 1941. (pp. 193–198).

Weller, Arthur
"Paul Revere of the West." *National Republic* 20:19–20, July, 1932.

Wheeler, Col. Edward
"Fire Lands Reminiscences." *The Fire Lands Pioneer* 2:37, 1859.

Wheeler, Florence E.
"John Chapman." *Leominster 200th Anniversary*, June 2–8, 1940. (pp. 15–17). Souvenir Brochure Issued by the City of Leominster, Mass., 1940.

————.
"John Chapman's Line of Descent from Edward Chapman of Ipswich." Introduction by Robert Price. *Ohio Archaeological and Historical Quarterly* 48:28–33, 1939.
"The definitive study of John Chapman's family origins, carefully documented from original records and reputable genealogical studies." (Robert Price)

Williams, B. Y.
"Song for the Apple Orchard." *Classmate* 49:3, Oct., 1942.

Williams, E. G. C.
"Johnny Appleseed." *Men's Garden Clubs of America Year Book 1940*, pp. 12–13.

Williams, J. H.
"Did You Know." *Reflector-Herald* (Norwalk, Ohio), June 21, 1940.

Wright, Richardson
Grandfather Was Queer, Early American Ways and Eccentrics from Colonial Times to the Civil War. Philadelphia: J. B. Lippincott, 1939. (pp. 234–236).

————.
Hawkers and Walkers in Early America. Philadelphia: J. B. Lippincott Co., 1927. (pp. 214–215).

"Yessir, Johnny Appleseed Was a Real Fellow." *Prairie Farmer*, Feb. 20, 1943.

Zorbaugh, C. I.
"Ballad of Johnny Appleseed." *The Buckeye Bugle* 2:4, Jan., 1932.

ARKANSAS TRAVELER

See: Folklore and Folksong of Arkansas, pp. 249-52.

Allsopp, Fred W.
Rimeries. Little Rock, Ark.: Central Printing Co., 1926. 206 pp.
Version of the "Arkansas Traveler" in rhyme: "The Arkansas Traveler and the turn of the tune (An old prose story retold and expanded in rhyme)."

Hogue, Wayman
Back Yonder, An Ozark Chronicle. New York: Minton, Balch and Co., 1932. 303 pp.
Discussion of the Arkansas Traveler, (pp. 164–168).

Knoop, Faith Yingling, and Grant, James R.
Arkansas Yesterday and Today. Chicago, Philadelphia: J. B. Lippincott Co., 1935. 350 pp., illus.
Story of the Arkansas Traveler, (pp. 228–229).

Masterson, James R.
Tall Tales of Arkansas. Boston: Houghton Mifflin Co., 1943.

Mercer, H. C.
"On the Track of 'The Arkansas Traveler'." *Century Magazine* 51:707–712, 1895–96.

Pope, William F.
Early Days in Arkansas. Little Rock: F. W. Allsopp, 1895. 330 pp.
　　Version of the Arkansas Traveler (pp. 325–330).

Vineyard, Catherine Marshall
"The Arkansas Traveler." *TFSP* 18:11–60, 1943.

LITTLE AUDREY

Chambers, Cornelia
"The Adventures of Little Audrey." *TFSP* 13: 106–110, 1937.
　　An American humorous character sometimes parading as "Little Emma" or "Little Gertrude."

JIM BAKER

Gould, John
"Pie-biter (Jim Baker)." *TFSP* 14:185–191, 1938.

ANTOINE BARADA

"Barada, Antoine."
Nebraska Folklore Pamphlets, No. 8, pt. 2, pp. 9–11, Sept. 15, 1937.

Pound, Louise
Antoine Barada. In: *Nebraska Strong Men.* *SFQ* 7:133–143, 1943.

RUBE BARROW

Agee, G. W.
Rube Barrow, King of Outlaws. Chicago: The Henneberry Co., 1890.

SAM BASS

Gard, Wayne
Sam Bass. Boston: Houghton Mifflin Co., 1936.

Raine, William M., and Barnes, Will C.
Cattle, Cowboys and Rangers. New York: Grosset & Dunlap, 1930. (pp. 137, 139.)

Webb, W. P.
"The Legend of Sam Bass." *TFSP* 3:226–230, 1924.

ROY BEAN and PECOS BILL

Bell, Horace
On the Old West Coast; Being Further Reminiscences of a Ranger. Edited by Lanier Bartlett. New York: W. Morrow and Company, 1930. xiv, 236 pp., illus.
　　Contains anecdotal reminiscences of Roy Bean.

――――――.
Reminiscences of a Ranger; or Early Times in Southern California. Los Angeles: Yarnell, Caystile & Mathes, Printers, 1881. 457 pp.
　　Contains anecdotes of Roy Bean.

Bowman, James Cloyd
Pecos Bill, Chicago: Whitman and Co., 1937. 296 pp.
　　"The best and most characteristic representation of the broad humor of America."

Carmer, Carl
America Sings. Stories and Songs of our Country's Growing. New York: Alfred A. Knopf, 1942. 243 pp., illus., music. (pp. 220–228).

Fiske, I.
"Pecos Bill, Cyclone Buster." *American Mercury* 48:403–407, (Dec.) 1939.

Hunter, J. Marvin
"Roy Bean As Coroner." *TFSP* 14:254–256, 1938.

Lloyd, Everett
Law West of the Pecos. San Antonio, Texas: The University Press, 1931. 168 pp., illus.

Lomax, John A.
"Stop-Over at Abilene." *Southwest Review* 25 (No. 4):407–418, 1940.
　　A variant on a Roy Bean story.

McDaniel, Ruel
Vinegarroon, The Saga of Judge Roy Bean, "*Law West of the Pecos.*" Kingsport, Tenn.: Southern Publishers, 1936. 143 pp.

O'Reilly, Edward
"The Saga of Pecos Bill." *Century Magazine* 106:827–833, 1923.

Peck, Leigh
Pecos Bill and Lightning. Illustrated by Kurt Wiese. Boston: Houghton Mifflin Co., 1940. 67 pp.
　　A children's book.

Sonnichsen, C. L.
Roy Bean, Law West of the Pecos. Illustrated from photographs. New York: The Macmillan Co., 1943. 309 pp.
　　"The chief virtue of a full length book about Roy Bean is that it gives opportunity to appraise the magnitude of the old boy's fraud." (Hal Boland)

Tracy, M. W.
"Roy Bean: Law West of the Pecos." *TFSP* 13:111–119, 1937.

Twitchell, R. E. comp. and ed.
Old Santa Fe. The Story of New Mexico's Ancient Capital. Santa Fe: Santa Fe New Mexican Publishing Corp., 1925.
　　On pp. 348–350, we find a variant of a Roy Bean episode.

TONY BEAVER

Brown, Charles E.
Paul Bunyan and Tony Beaver Tales. Madison, Wis.: The Author, 1930. 18 pp.

Montague, Margaret
"The World's Funny Bone." *Atlantic Monthly* 140:327–336, 1927.
　　Adventure of Paul Bunyan and Tony Beaver.

――――――.
Up Eel River. New York: The Macmillan Co., 1928. 225 pp.
　　Monologue and tales of a West Virginia lumberman, includes legends of Tony Beaver and Paul Bunyan.

BECKWOURTH

Bonner, T. C., ed.
Life and Adventures of James P. Beckwourth.
Introduction by Bernard deVoto. New York:
Alfred A. Knopf, 1931. Repr. of the edition of
1856.
> Life story and tall tales of a great frontiersman,
> the "damn'dest liar" in the mountain.

BOWLEG BILL

Digges, Jeremiah
Bowleg Bill, the Sea-Going Cowboy, or Ship
Ahoy and Let 'Er Buck. New York: The
Viking Press, 1938.

BUFFALO BILL

Beals, Frank L.
Buffalo Bill. Chicago: Wheeler Publishing Co.,
1943.

Buffalo Bill (William Cody)
The Adventures of Buffalo Bill. New York:
Harper and Bros., 1927.

————.
An Autobiography of Buffalo Bill. New York:
Cosmopolitan Book Co., 1910.

————.
Story of the Wild West and Camp-Fire Chats,
by Buffalo Bill (Hon. W. F. Cody). A full and
complete history of the renowned pioneer
quartette, Boone, Crockett, Carson and Buffalo
Bill.... Philadelphia: Historical Publishing
Co., 1888. xvi, 766 pp., illus.

**Cody, Louisa Frederici (in collaboration with
Courtney Riley Cooper.)**
Memories of Buffalo Bill. New York, London:
D. Appleton & Co., 1919. 325 pp., illus.

Judson, Edward Zane Carroll (Ned Buntline)
Buffalo Bill. New York: International Book
Company, 1886. 314 pp., illus.

————.
Buffalo Bill's Best Shot. New York: Street and
Smith, 1890. 188 pp.

————.
Buffalo Bill's Last Victory; or Dove Eye, The
Lodge Queen. New York: Street and Smith,
1890. 191 pp.

Raine, William M., and Barnes, Will C.
Cattle, Cowboys and Rangers. New York:
Grosset & Dunlap, 1930. (p. 120).

Vestal, Stanley
Short Grass Country. (American Folkways
Series). New York: Duell, Sloan, and Pearce,
1942.
> The land of buffalo hunts, tornado, oil, county-
> seats wars, the range of Buffalo Bill and Wyatt
> Earp.

Walsh, Richard J.
The Making of Buffalo Bill. Indianapolis: The
Bobbs-Merrill Co., 1928.

Wetmore, Mrs. Helen
Buffalo Bill. Duluth: The Duluth Press Printing Co., 1900.

WHISTLING BILL

Romaine, F.
Whistling Bill. New York: Thomas Nelson and
Sons, 1937.

BILLY THE KID

Burns, Walter Noble
The Saga of Billy the Kid. New York: Doubleday, Page and Co., 1925. 256 pp.
> Issued as Penguin Book 1942. The true life story
> of the most notorious gunman of the Southwest.

Coe, George W.
Frontier Fighter. Boston: Houghton Mifflin Co.,
1934.
> "the autobiography of one of Billy the Kid's men
> as recorded by Nan Hillary Harrison." (Dobie)

Corle, Edwin
Mojave. New York: Liveright, 1934. 272 pp.
> Has chapter: "The Ghost of Billy the Kid."

Dobie, J. Frank
Billy the Kid Interpreted. In: *A Vaquero of
the Brush Country,* Chapters V, VI, XII. Dallas,
Texas: The Southwest Press, 1929. 314 pp.,
illus.

Fulton, Maurice Garland, ed.
*Pat F. Garrett's Authentic Life of Billy the
Kid.* New York: The Macmillan Co., 1927.
xxviii, 233 pp.

Garrett, Pat F.
The Authentic Life of Billy the Kid, the noted
desperado of the Southwest, whose deeds of
daring and blood made his name a terror in
New Mexico, Arizona and Northern Mexico.
. . . Santa Fe, N. M.: New Mexico Printing
and Publishing Co., 1882. 137 pp., illus.

Hoyt, Henry F.
A Frontier Doctor. Boston: Houghton Mifflin
Co., 1929. 260 pp.
> "Texas Panhandle and New Mexico during Billy
> the Kid days." (Dobie)

Raine, William M., and Barnes, Will C.
Cattle, Cowboys and Rangers. New York:
Grosset & Dunlap, 1930. (pp. 163, 169).

Rascoe, Burton
Belle Starr, "The Bandit Queen." New York:
Random House, 1941. viii, 340 pp., illus.
> Contains lore of Billy the Kid.

Siringo, Charles A.
History of "Billy the Kid." The leading spirit
in the bloody Lincoln County, New Mexico,
war. Santa Fe, N. M.: The Author, 1920. 142
pp.

DANIEL BOONE

BIBLIOGRAPHY

Jillson, Willard Rouse
Bibliography. In: *The Boone Narrative.* Louisville, Ky.: Standard Printing Co., 1932. 16 pp.

Miner, William Harvey
Daniel Boone. Contribution toward a bibliography of writing concerning Daniel Boone. New York: Dibdin Club, 1901. ix, 32 pp., illus.

GENERAL STUDIES AND COLLECTIONS

Alvord, Clarence Walworth
"The Daniel Boone Myth." *Illinois State Historical Society Journal* 19:16–30, 1926.

Bennett, Emerson
Ella Barnwell; a historical romance of border life in Kentucky, in the time of Daniel Boone. Cincinnati: U. P. James, 1868. 112 pp.

Bogart, William Henry
Daniel Boone, and the Hunters of Kentucky. Auburn: Miller, Orton & Mulligan, 1854.

Bruce, Henry A. B.
Daniel Boone and the Wilderness Road. New York: The Macmillan Co., 1910. xiii, 349 pp.

Bryan, Daniel
The Mountain Muse; comprising the Adventures of Daniel Boone; and the power of virtuous and refined beauty. Harrisonburg: Davidson & Bourne, 1813. 252 pp.

Ellis, Edward Sylvester
The Life and Times of Col. Daniel Boone, the Hunter of Kentucky. New York: Beadle and Co., 1861.

Filson, John
The Adventures of Colonel Daniel Boon, one of the first settlers at Kentucke.... Norwich, Conn.: Printed by John Trumbull, 1785. 24 pp.

Flint, Timothy
Biographical Memoir of Daniel Boone, the first settler of Kentucky: interspersed with incidents in the early annals of the country. Cincinnati: G. Conclin, 1840. 252 pp., illus.

Forbes-Lindsay, Charles H. A.
Daniel Boone, Backwoodsman. With illustrations by Frank McKernan. Philadelphia: J. B. Lippincott Co., 1908. v, 319 pp.

Frost, John
Heroes and Hunters of the West.... Philadelphia: H. C. Peck & T. Bliss, 1858. vii, 300 pp., illus.

Hale, Dr. John P.
Daniel Boone: Some Facts and Incidents Not Hitherto Published. Wheeling, Va.: L. Baker & Co., 1883. 18 pp.

Hartley, Cecil B.
Life of Daniel Boone, the Great Western Hunter and Pioneer. Comprising an account of his early history, his daring and remarkable career as the first settler of Kentucky.... To which is added his autobiography complete as dictated by himself.... Philadelphia: J. E. Potter, 1865. 351 pp.

Hawks, Francis Lister
The Adventures of Daniel Boone, the Kentucky Rifleman.... New York: D. Appleton & Co., 1844. 174 pp.

Henderson, Daniel MacIntyre
Boone of the Wilderness; a tale of pioneer adventure and achievement in "the dark and bloody ground." New York: E. P. Dutton & Company, 1921. iii, 207 pp.

Hill, George Canning
Daniel Boone, the Pioneer of Kentucky. A biography. New York: R. Worthington, 1884. viii, 262 pp., illus.

Hulbert, Archer Butler
Boone's Wilderness Road. Cleveland, Ohio: A. H. Clark Co., 1903. 207 pp. (Historic Highways of America. Vol. 6.)

I., Y.
"Social and Savage Life—Daniel Boon." *New Monthly Magazine and Literary Journal* (London) 8:519–526, 1823.

Jillson, Willard Rouse
Daniel Boone in Kentucky (A Story). Frankfort, Ky.: The State Journal Co., 1939. 20 pp.

————.
The Boone Narrative; the story of the origin and discovery coupled with the reproduction in facsimile of a rare item of early Kentuckiana, to which is appended a sketch of Boone and a bibliography of 238 titles.... Louisville, Ky.: Standard Printing Company, 1932. 16 pp., illus.

Jones, John Beauchamp
Wild Western Scenes: Narrative of Adventures in the Western Wilderness.... Wherein the exploits of Daniel Boone, the great American pioneer, are particularly described. Philadelphia: Grigg, Elliot & Co., 1849. xi, 270 pp., illus.

Kellog, Louise Phelps
"The Fame of Daniel Boone." *Kentucky State Historical Society Register* 32:187–198, 1934.

King, Roy T.
"Portraits of Daniel Boone." *Missouri Historical Review* 33:171–183, 1939.

Kottenkamp, Franz Justus
Die ersten Amerikaner im Westen. Daniel Boone und seine Gefährten.... Stuttgart: Schmidt & Spring, 1858. xii, 540 pp.
Adventures and exploits of Boone.

Lesquereux, Leo
"Daniel Boone and the Kentucky Character in 1855; a letter from America . . ." *Filson Club History Quarterly* (Louisville, Ky.) 15:209–226, 1941.

Marschall, Phyllis
Daniel Boone Blazed a Trail. In: *Plays of Story and Legend,* by A. P. Sanford, comp., pp. 99–134. New York: 1937.

Metcalf, Samuel Lytler
A Collection of Some of the Most Interesting Narratives of Indian Warfare in the West, containing an account of the adventures of Colonel Daniel Boone. . . . Lexington, Ky.: W. G. Hunt, 1821. iv, 270 pp.

Miner, William Harvey
Daniel Boone. Contribution toward a bibliography of writing concerning Daniel Boone. New York: Dibdin Club, 1901. ix, 32 pp., illus.

Norton, Frank Henry
The Days of Daniel Boone; a Romance of "The Dark and Bloody Ground." New York: New York Publishing Co., 1883. 406 pp.

Perry, Frances M., and Beebe, K.
Four American Pioneers—D. Boone, D. Crockett, G. R. Clark, Kit Carson. A Book for Young Americans. New York: Werner School Book Co., 1900. 255 pp., illus.

Rojanovsky, Fedor
Daniel Boone; Historic Adventures of an American Hunter among the Indians; lithographs in color by F. Rojanovsky. Edited by Esther Averill and Lila Stanley. London: Faber & Faber, Ltd., 1931.

Seymour, Flora Warren
Daniel Boone, Pioneer; illustrated by F. E. Shares. New York: The Century Co., 1931. xi, 206 pp., illus.

Shoemaker, Floyd C.
"Daniel Boone." *Missouri Historical Review* 21:208–214, 1926–27.

Stoudt, John Joseph
"Daniel and Squire Boone—a study in Historical Symbolism." *Pennsylvania History* 3:27–40, 1936.

Sweetser, Kate Dickinson
Ten Great Adventurers. Illustrated by George Alfred Williams. New York: Harper & Bros., 1915. 280 pp.
Contains a chapter on Daniel Boone.

Thwaites, Reuben Gold
Daniel Boone. New York: D. Appleton & Company, 1903. xv, 257 pp.

White, Edward Joseph
Daniel Boone; a patriotic drama in five acts. n.p.: 1923. 26 pp.

White, Stewart Edward
Daniel Boone, Wilderness Scout; illustrated by Remington Schuyler. Garden City, N. Y.: Doubleday, Page & Company, 1922. 308 pp.

Wilson, Samuel M.
"Daniel Boone, 1734–1934." *History Quarterly* (Louisville, Ky.) 8:183–204, 1934.

JOE BOWERS

Pound, Louise
"Joe Bowers Again." *SFQ* 3 (No. 3):13–17, 1937.

————.
"More 'Joe Bowers' Lore." *SFQ* 2 (No. 3):131–135, 1938.

JIM BOWIE

See: Davy Crockett, pp. 693-98.

Elfer, Maurice
Madam Candelaria, Unsung Heroine of the Alamo . . . wounded while trying to protect dying Bowie. Houston, Tex.: The Rein Company, 1933.

Ellis, E. S.
The Life and Adventures of Colonel Crockett. . . . New York: Beadle & Co., 1861.

Munroe, Kirk
With Crockett and Bowie; or, Fighting for the Lone-Star Flag. A Tale of Texas. . . . New York: C. Scribner's Sons, 1897. 347 pp.

Rohrbough, Edward G.
"How Jim Bowie Died." *TFSP* 15:48–58, 1939.

Sears, Edward S.
"The Low Down on Jim Bowie." *TFSP* 19:175–199, 1944.

JIM BRIDGER

Alter, J. Cecil
James Bridger: Trapper, Frontiersman, Scout and Guide. Salt Lake City: Shepherd Book Co., 1925.

Anderson, A. M.
Fur Trappers of the Old West. Chicago: Wheeler Publishing Co., 1946. 252 pp.
The thrilling adventures of the fearless and daring Jim Bridger, and his men.

Davidson, Levette Jay
"Colorado Folklore." *The Colorado Magazine* 18:4–7, 1941.
Discussion of Jim Bridger.

Trenholm, Virginia Cole, and Corley, Maurine
Wyoming Pageant. Casper, Wyoming: Prairie Publishing Company, 1946. 291 pp., illus., maps and teaching aids.
A history of the state—its adventurous pioneers—Jim Bridger among them, conflict with the Indians (a chapter is devoted their customs and legends), interesting details on fur-trading and trapper trails, and the tribulations of the covered wagon caravans. Many observations on legends, place names and customs.

Vestal, Stanley
  Jim Bridger: Mountain Man. New York: William Morrow and Company, 1946. 333 pp.
    "On the whole he has adequately set the scene for his hero's adventures and has honestly appraised the great guide's historical stature." (J. K. Howard)

STRAP BUCKNER

Barker, Eugene C.
  The Life of Stephen F. Austin, founder of Texas 1793–1836. . . . Nashville, Dallas: Cokesbury Press, 1925. xv, 551 pp., bibl.
    See also author's edition of the *Austin Papers,* Vol. I, pt. 1 and 2.

Barns, Florence Elberta
  "Strap Buckner of the Texas Frontier." *TFSP* 8:129–152, 1930.

_____.
  "Strap Buckner Again." *TFSP* 10:127–130, 1932.
    Some more amazing deeds of this amazing character.

Kuykendall, J. H.
  "Reminiscenses of Early Texans." *Texas State Historical Association. Quarterly* 6:236–253.

Lotto, F.
  Fayette County, Her History and Her People. Schulenberg, Tex.: The Author, 1902. xvi, 424 pp. (pp. 86–95).

McDaniel, H. F. and Taylor, N. A.
  The Devil and Strap Buckner. In: *The Coming Empire or Two Thousand Years in Texas on Horseback.* (pp. 49–73). New York: A. S. Barnes & Co., 1877.
    A Texas devil tale.

Taylor, N. A.
  "The Devil and Strap Buckner." *TFSP* 3:118–129, 1918.

PAUL BUNYAN

BIBLIOGRAPHY

Felton, Harold V.
  Bibliography of Paul Bunyan. In: *Legends of Paul Bunyan.* New York: Alfred Knopf, 1947. 418 pp., illus.
    A comprehensive bibliography of all writing, music, drama, painting, or sculpture on the legendary hero.

Halpert, Herbert
  "A Note on Haney's Bibliography of Paul Bunyan." *JAFL* 56:57–59, 1943.

Haney, Gladys J.
  "Paul Bunyan Represented in Art: A Bibliography." *JAFL* 55:163–164, 1942.

_____.
  "Paul Bunyan Twenty-Five Years After." *JAFL* 55:155–169, 1942.
    Excellent bibliography in all matters pertaining to Bunyan.

Hartshorn, Mellor
  Bibliography. In: *Paul Bunyan: A Study in Folk Literature.* Los Angeles, Calif.: Occidental College, 1934.

GENERAL STUDIES AND COLLECTIONS

Allen, William N.
  The Round River Drive. In: *Poetry Out of Wisconsin.* Edited by August Derleth and Raymond E. F. Larson, (pp. 16–20). New York: Henry Harrison, 1937.

Alvord, Thomas G., Jr.
  Paul Bunyan: A Legendary Hero of the Northwoods. New York: Boni, 1935. 111 pp.
    A book of poems.

_____.
  Paul Bunyan and Resinous Rhymes of the Northwoods. New York: Derrydale Press, 1934. 137 pp., illus.
    A book of poems.

Ames, Carleton C.
  "Paul Bunyan—Myth or Hoax?" *Minnesota History* 20:55–58, 1940.

Bartlett, Wm. W.
  Logging Camp Diversion and Humor. In: *History, Tradition and Adventure in the Chippewa Valley,* (pp. 232–236). Chippewa Falls, Wis.: The Chippewa Printery, 1929.

Beck, Earl Clifton
  Songs of the Michigan Lumberjacks. Ann Arbor, Mich.: University of Michigan Press, 1941. (pp. 248–260, 283, 284–290): in Appendix—Tall Tales from the Northwoods.

Botkin, Ben
  Paul Bunyan. In: *A Treasury of American Folklore,* (pp. 204–227). New York: Crown Publishers, 1944.

Bowman, James Cloyd
  The Adventures of Paul Bunyan. New York: The Century Co., 1927. 286 pp.
    Written especially for children. Paul is "the boy with a big heart," who comes to free the forests from their long bondage.

_____.
  "The Paul Bunyan Yarns." *Michigan History Magazine* 25:25–28, 1941.

Brooks, John Lee
  Paul Bunyan: Oil Man. In: *Follow de Drinkin' Gou'd.* TFSP 7:45–54, 1928.

Brown, Charles E.
  American Folklore: Paul Bunyan Tales. Madison, Wis.: The Author, 1926. 192 pp.

_____.
  Flapjacks from Paul Bunyan's Cook Shanty. Madison, Wis.: State Historical Society, 1941. 4 pp.

_____.
  Paul Bunyan: American Hercules. Madison, Wis.: The Author, 1937. 8 pp.

———.
Paul Bunyan and Tony Beaver Tales; tall yarns of the prince of American lumberjacks and of his Southern cousin, Tony Beaver, as told in the logging camps in the North and South. Madison, Wis.: C. E. Brown, 1930. 18 pp.

———.
Paul Bunyan Natural History. Describing the Wild Animals, Birds, Reptiles and Fish of the Big Woods About Paul Bunyan's Old Time Logging Camps, Habitat and Habits of the Flitterick, Gumberoo, Hangdown, Hidebehind, Hodag, Luferlang, Rumptifusel, Silver Cat, Shagamaw, Goofus Bird, Hoop Snake, Whirling Fish and Others. Madison, Wisconsin: C. E. Brown, 1935.

Brown, Theodore Ted
"Christmas On the Big Onion." *Wisconsin Octopus* 15:93–94, 1933.

Carmer, Carl
Paul Bunyan: The Shantyman's Life. In: *America Sings,* (pp. 236–241), illus. New York: Alfred A. Knopf, 1942.

Carpenter, Margarete
"Paul Bunyan: Oil Man." *TFSP* 14:263–264, 1938.

Charters, W. W.
"Paul Bunyan in 1910." *JAFL* 57:188–189, 1944.
The author claims that in 1910 appeared the first written account of Bunyan's exploits.

Chase, Stuart
"Paul Bunyan." *New Republic* 43:186–187, 1925.
A review of Steven's *Paul Bunyan.*

Conkle, Ellsworth P.
Paul and the Blue Ox. Austin, Texas: The Author, Department of Drama, University of Texas, Ms. 1934.
A play in eight scenes.

Davenport, Samuel R.
Sky River Drive. In: *Midwest Prize Plays,* edited by L. H. Jones, (pp. 68–86). Chicago: Dramatic Publishing Co., 1938.

Davis, Elrick B.
"Paul Bunyan Talk." *AS* 17:217–226, 1942.

Davis, M. L.
"Tall Tales; James Stevens of Paul Bunyan Fame." *Sunset* 62:16, May, 1929.

Dobie, J. Frank
"Paul Bunyan." *Nation* 121:237–238, 1925.
A criticism of Steven's and Shepard's Books.

Dorson, Richard M.
"America's Comic Demigod." *American Scholar* 10:389–401, 1941.

Ericksen, Mabel N.
The Ballad of Paul Bunyan. Bemidje, Minn.: The Author, 1939. 8 pp.
Told in verse.

Federal Writers' Project
Oregon—End of the Trail. Compiled and written by the Federal Writers' Project of the Works Progress Administration for the State of Oregon. Portland, Oregon: Bindfords, 1940.
Deals with some of the legendary deeds of Paul and Babe.

Felton, Harold V., ed.
Legends of Paul Bunyan. Illustrated by Richard Bennett. New York: Alfred A. Knopf, 1947. 418 pp., illus., bibl.
The editor has compiled a comprehensive collection of Bunyan stories from printed sources, to which he has added a bibliography of all writing, music, drama, painting and sculpture pertaining to them.

Field, Rachel
American Folk and Fairy Tales. New York: Charles Scribners Sons, 1929.

Finger, Charles J.
A Paul Bunyan Geography. York, Pa.: Maple Press, 1931. 39 pp.

Frost, Robert
Paul's Wife. In: *New Hampshire,* (pp. 44–48). New York: Henry Holt and Co., 1933.
"Told with the poet's usual grace and power."

Garland, Acel
Pipeline Days and Paul Bunyan. In: *Follow de Drinkin' Gou'd TFSP* 7:55–61, 1928.

Green, Paul
Salvation on a String, and Other Stories of the South. New York: Harper and Bros., 1946. 278 pp.
Contains a story of Paul Bunyan's legendary prowess.

Halpert, Herbert
"A Note on Haney's Bibliography of Paul Bunyan." *JAFL* 56:57–59, 1943.

Handy, R. D.
Paul Bunyan and His Blue Ox. Chicago: Rand, McNally, 1937. 64 pp.

Hartshorn, Mellor
Paul Bunyan: A Study in Folk Literature. Los Angeles, Calif.: Occidental College, 1934. 218 pp.
An M. A. Thesis. Good bibliography.

Hopkins, Bert
"Paul Bunyan, Only True American Myth." *The Wisconsin Magazine* 1:32–33, 1933.

James, Martin
"A Story About Paul Bunyan." *Jack and Jill* 2:4–9, 1940.

Jones, Edward R.
Bunyan's Progress. Madison, Wis.: Mrs. Edward Jones, 1929. 76 pp.

———.
Paul Bunyan, Preface, Prose, Etc. Madison, Wis.: Mrs. Edward Jones, 1930. 32 pp.

Jones, Louis C.
"Paul Bunyan is Back." *New York Times Magazine* 90:5, August 24, 1941.
A poem.

Langerock, Hubert
"The Wonderful Life and Deeds of Paul Bunyan." *Century Magazine* 106:23–33, 1923.

Langhead, W. B.
The Marvelous Exploits of Paul Bunyan. In: *In Our Times* (Source Readers in American History No. 5), (pp. 285–293). New York: The Macmillan Co., 1927.

———.
Paul Bunyan and His Big Blue Ox. Westwood, Calif.: Red River Lumber Co., 1940. 40 pp.

Leighton, Louise
I Hear Paul Bunyan. In: *Poetry Out of Wisconsin.* Edited by August Derleth and Raymond E. F. Larson. New York: Henry Harrison, 1937. 170 pp.

Littell, Robert
"Paul Bunyan." *New Republic* 41:234, 1925.
Review of Shepard's book.

Mallock, Douglas
"Paul Bunyan." *The American Lumberman* (Chicago, Ill.) 2032:33, 1914.

Martin, Wayne
"Paul Bunyan on the Water Pipeline." *Folk-Say* (Regional Miscellany) 1:50–63, 1929.

McCormick, Dell
Paul Bunyan Swings His Ax. Caldwell, Idaho: The Caxton Printers Ltd., 1936. 111 pp.

McDonald, James J.
Paul Bunyan and the Blue Ox. In: *Wisconsin Blue Book*, (pp. 113–128). Madison, Wis.: Democrat Printing Co., 1931.

McDonald, Marian
The Legends of Paul Bunyan. Madison, Wis.: University of Wisconsin, 1928. 75 pp.

MacKaye, Percy
"A Homer of the Logging Camp." *Bookman* 59:473–474, 1925.
Review of Steven's and Shepard's books.

Miller, Olive Beaupré
Big Paul Bunyan and His Blue Ox, Babe, and Paul Bunyan Goes West. In: *Heroes, Outlaws, and Funny Fellows*, (pp. 200–212, 314–332) New York: Doubleday, Doran Co., 1939.

Montague, Margaret
"The World's Funny Bone." *Atlantic Monthly* 140:327–336, 1927.
A humorous tale of Paul Bunyan and Tony Beaver.

———.
Up Eel River. New York: The Macmillan Co., 1928. 220 pp.
Monologues and tales of a West Virginia lumberman, includes legends of Tony Beaver and Paul Bunyan.

Morrissette, Pat
Paul Bunyan: An American Symbol. In: *Folk-Say*, The Land is Ours, (Edited by B. A. Botkin) 4:274–294, 1932.
In verse: "An attempt to crystallize in one personality derived from American folklore the characteristics of the American people."

Owen, Ray S.
"Paul Bunyan, The Surveyor Extraordinary." *Wisconsin Engineer* 34:91, 1929.

"Paul Bunyan."
Encyclopedia Brittanica 14th Edition 4:393, 1929.

"The Paul Bunyan Tales."
Minnesota History 21:176–178, 1940.

Peck, Leigh
Pecos Bill Meets Paul Bunyan and Starts a New Ranch. In: *Pecos Bill and Lightining*, (pp. 26–36). Boston: Houghton Mifflin Co., 1940. 67 pp., illus.

Pound, Louise
"Nebraska Strong Men." *SFQ* 7:133–143, 1943.
Includes discussion of Paul Bunyan literature.

Pounds, Jimmie
"Hugo: The Giant Unkillable Frog; and Paul Bunyan: Oil Man." *TFSP* 14:262–264, 1938.

Quaife, M. M.
"Reprints of an Article on Bunyan." *Minnesota History* 21:296–298, 1940.

Red River Lumber Co.,
The Marvelous Exploits of Paul Bunyan. Minneapolis, Minn.: 1922. 25 pp., illus.

Rounds, Glenn
How Paul Bunyan Lost a Cutting Crew in Kansas and Built the Biggest Dragline Ever Built. In: *Lumbercamp*, (pp. 72–73). New York: Holiday House, 1937.

———.
Ol' Paul, The Mighty Logger. New York: Holiday House, 1936. 288 pp., illus.

Rourke, Constance
American Humor. New York: Harcourt, Brace and Co., 1931. (pp. 233).

———.
"The Making of an Epic." *Sat. Rev. of Lit.* 2:81, 1925.
Review of Steven's and Shepard's books.

———.
"Paul Bunyan—Lumberjack." *New Republic* 23:176–179, 1920.

Sandburg, Carl
The People, Yes. New York: Harcourt, Brace and Co., 1936.
"The book is not only a magnificent example of the literary use of folklore, but also for the large number of folktales given."

Shepard, Esther
Paul Bunyan. Illustrated by Rockwell Kent. New York: Harcourt, Brace and Co., 1924. Rep. 1941. 233 pp., illus.
Stories of our great legendary character collected from lumbermen in the Northwest.

———.
Paul Bunyan. Seattle, Wash.: The McNeil Press, 1924. 235 pp.

————.
Paul Bunyan's Cornstalk. In: *Golden Tales of Our America*. By May L. Becker, (pp. 301–310). New York: Dodd Mead Co., 1929.

Shepard, Eugene S., and Karretta G.
Paul Bunyan—His Camp and Wife. Tomahawk, Wis.: Osborne Press, 1929. 97 pp.
A book of poems.

————.
"Round River Drive." *Wisconsin State Journal* Feb. 24, 1929.
Told in verse.

Sherman, Stuart
Paul Bunyan and the Blue Ox. In: *The Main Stream*, (pp. 71–79). New York: Charles Scribner's Sons, 1927.

Stevens, Henry Bailey
Johnny Appleseed and Paul Bunyan. Boston: Baker Publishing Co., 1931. 92 pp.
A Play in three acts and prologue.

Stevens, J.
"The Black Duck Dinner." *American Mercury* 2:161–169, 1924.

————.
Paul Bunyan. New York: Alfred A. Knopf, 1925. 245 pp., illus.

————.
"Paul Bunyan Stories." *Sat. Rev. of Lit.* 2:30, 1926.
A reply to Bate's criticism of his book.

————.
Paul Bunyan. New York: Alfred A. Knopf, 1925. 245 pp.

————.
The Saginaw Paul Bunyan. New York: Alfred A. Knopf, 1932. 261 pp.

————.
"When Rivers Were Young and Wild." *Woman's Home Companion* 58:26–27, 1931.

Stewart, K. Bernice, and Watt, Homer A.
"Legends of Paul Bunyan, Lumberjack." *Transactions of the Wisconsin Academy of Sciences, Arts, and Letters*, 18:639–651, 1916.

Stokes, Richard L.
Paul Bunyan: A Folk-Comedy in Three Acts. New York: G. Putnam and Sons, 1932. 102 pp.

————.
"Review of Paul Bunyan by R. L. Stokes." *Nation* 136:71, 1933.

Tabor, Edward O., and Thompson, Stith
"Paul Bunyan in 1910." *JAFL* 59:134–135, 1946.

Thompson, Harold W.
Body, Boots and Britches. Philadelphia: L. B. Lippincott Co., 1940. (pp. 129–131).

"Traditional Ceremonies in the U. S.: Return of Paul Bunyan." *Reader's Digest* 36:87, 1940.

Turney, Ida V.
A New Literary Type, With Special References to the Tales of Paul Bunyan. Ph.D. Thesis—University of Oregon.

————.
Paul Bunyan Comes West. Eugene, Oregon: University of Oregon Press, 1919. 34 pp.

————.
Paul Bunyan Comes West. Boston: Houghton Mifflin Co., 1928.

————.
Paul Bunyan Marches On. Portland, Oregon: Bindfords, 1942.

————.
Paul Bunyan, the Work Giant. Portland, Oregon: Bindfords, 1941. 80 pp.

Untermeyer, Louis
The Wonderful Adventures of Paul Bunyan. Retold by Louis Untermeyer. With illustrations by Everett Gee Jackson. New York: The Heritage Press, 1946. 131 pp.

Van Doren, Carl
The American Novel: 1789–1939. (pp. 270–291). New York: The Macmillan Co., 1940.

————.
"Document and Work of Art." *Century Magazine* 110:242–244, 1925.
Review of Steven's and Shepard's books.

————.
Paul Bunyan Goes West. In: *The Roving Critic*, (pp. 105–107). New York: Alfred A. Knopf, 1925.

Watt, Homer A.
Paul Bunyan Provides for His Crew. In: *The Rise of Realism*, by Louis Wann, ed., (pp. 270–273). New York: The Macmillan Co., 1933.

————.
The Rise of Realism. Edited by Louis Wann. New York: The Macmillan Co., 1933.
Discussion of Bunyan's place in American folklore (p. 779).

Wadsworth, Wallace C.
Paul Bunyan and His Great Ox. New York: Doubleday-Page, 1926. 238 pp.

Yates, Paul C.
Paul Bunyan in North Dakota. El Campo, Texas: El Campo Citizen's Press, 1937. 49 pp.
A narrative poem.

KIT CARSON
BIBLIOGRAPHY

Smith, Henry Nash
"Kit Carson in Books." *Southwest Review* 28:164–190, 1943.

GENERAL STUDIES AND COLLECTIONS

Abbott, John Stevens Cabot
Christopher Carson, Known As Kit Carson. New York: Dodd, Mead and Co., 1915. ix, 348 pp.

Adams, Capt. J. F. C.
The Fighting Trapper, or, Kit Carson to the Rescue. New York: Beadles and Adam's Dime Library, 1879. Reissued 1901.

Aiken, Albert W.
Kit Carson King of Guides. New York: Beadle's Boy's Library of Sport, 1884.
Story and adventure.

Beals, Frank L.
Kit Carson. Chicago: Wheeler Publishing Co., 1941.

Bourdett, Charles
The Life and Advent of Christopher Carson, the celebrated Rocky Mountain hunter, trapper, and guide. . . . Philadelphia: G. G. Evans, 1861. 374 pp.

Brewerton, G. D.
Overland With Kit Carson. New York: Coward McCann, Inc., 1930. 301 pp., illus.

Campbell, W. S.
Kit Carson, the Happy Warrior of the Old West. Boston: Houghton Mifflin Co., 1928.

Carson, Kit
Kit Carson's Life and Adventures from Facts Narrated by Himself. Hartford, Conn.: Dustin, Filman and Co., 1873. 604 pp., illus.
See: Milo Milton Quaife's edition, published in Chicago by Donnelley & Sons Co., 1935. 192 pp.

Cody, William Frederick
Story of the Wild West, and Camp Fire Chats. . . . Philadelphia: Historical Publishing Company, 1888. xvi, 766 pp.

Ellis, Edward Sylvester
Life and Times of Christopher (Kit) Carson, hunter, trapper, guide, Indian agent and Colonel, U. S. A. New York: New York Publishing Company, 1904. 260 pp.

Fergusson, Harvey
Wolf Song. New York and London: Alfred A. Knopf, 1927. 206 pp.
Of the mountain men of Kit Carson's time.

Fulton, Reed
Mocassin Trail, the story of a boy who took the trail with Carson. Illustrated by Ernest Walker. Garden City, N. Y.: Doubleday, Doran, 1929. x, 308 pp., illus.

Harbaugh, Thomas C.
Kiowa Charley, The White Mustanger, or, Rocky Mountain Kit's Last Scalp Hunt. New York: Beadle's Half Dime Library, 1879. 123 pp.

Hough, Emerson
The Way of the West, and the lives of three early Americans—Boone, Crockett, Carson; illustrated by Frederic Remington. Indianapolis: The Bobbs-Merrill Co., 1903. 446 pp.

Peters, De Witt Clinton
Kit Carson's Life and Adventures. Cincinnati, Ohio: Queen City Publishing Co., 1874. 604 pp.
Early-day scout and guide tales, characters.

Ray, Clarence E.
Famous American Scouts. Lives of Daniel Boone, Kit Carson, Davy Crockett, Wild Bill and others. . . . Chicago: J. Rogan and Co., 1920. 189 pp.

Reagan, Albert B.
"Forts Robidoux, and Kit Carson in Northwestern Utah." *New Mexico Historical Quarterly,* April, 1935, pp. 121–132.

Sabin, Edwin Legrand
Kit Carson Days, 1809–1868; illustrated by more than 100 half-tones, mostly from old and rare sources. Chicago: A. C. McClurg & Co., 1914. xiv, 669 pp., illus., bibl.
"a work long standard, rich on rendezvous, bears, and many other associated subjects." (Dobie)

Smith, Henry Nash
"Kit Carson in Books." *Southwest Review* 28: 164–190, 1943.
A literary and critical study of the Kit Carson exploits and legends as interpreted by various writers.

Vestal, Stanley
"Dobe Walls," A Story of Kit Carson's Southwest. Boston: Houghton Mifflin Co., 1929. 314 pp.

―――――――.
Kit Carson, the Happy Warrior of the Old West. Boston: Houghton Mifflin Co., 1928. xii, 297 pp.

DAVY CROCKETT

Abbott, John Stevens Cabot
David Crockett, His Life and Adventures. New York: Dodd and Mead, 1874. viii, 350 pp.

Allen, Charles Fletcher
David Crockett, Scout, Small Boy, Pilgrim, Mountaineer, Soldier, Bear Hunter, and Congressman, Defender of the Alamo. Philadelphia: J. B. Lippincott and Co., 1911. 308 pp.

"Anecdotes of Davy Crockett."
In: *Twenty-Five Cents of Nonsense;* or The Treasure Box of Unconsidered Trifles. Philadelphia, New York, and Boston: Fisher and Bros., (184–?).

Armstrong, A. B.
"How Crockett Defeated Huntsman." *TFSP* 18:147–148, 1943.

―――――――.
"An Oath With Reservations." *TFSP* 18:148, 1943.

Audobon, James
Ornithological Biography. Edinburgh: 1831–39. Vols. I, II, III.
Sheds light on Crockett's life in Tennessee.

―――――――.
The Viviparous Quadrupeds of North America. New York: J. J. Audobon, 1849–1854. 2 vols.

Beals, Frank L.
Davy Crockett. Chicago: Wheeler Publishing Company, 1941.

Blair, Walter
"Six Davy Crocketts." *Southwest Review* 25: 443–462, 1940.

Boatright, Mody C.
"Backwoods Belles." *TFSP* 18:61–78, 1943.

Brady, Cyrus Townsend
"David Crockett and the Most Desperate Defense in American History." *McClure's Magazine* 18:252–261, 1902.

Carmer, Carl
Confab With Crockett. New York: 194–. Writers' War Board. War Scripts, No. 5. Radio Drama. Also published in *Plays of Democracy*, M. G., ed., pp. 107–115. New York: 1944.

Cattermole, E. G.
Famous Frontiersmen, Pioneers and Scouts; the Romance of American History; thrilling narratives of renowned adventurers, explorers, heroes, trappers, scouts and Indian fighters. Tarrytown, N. Y.: W. Abbatt, 1926. xvi, 544 pp., illus.

Cody, William Frederick
Story of the Wild West and Camp-Fire Chats, by Buffalo Bill (Hon. W. F. Cody). A full and complete history of the renowned pioneer quartette, Boone, Crockett, Carson and Buffalo Bill. . . . Philadelphia: Historical Publishing Co., 1888. xvi, 766 pp., illus.

Crockett, David
An Account of Col. Crockett's Tour to the North and Down East, in the year of Our Lord one thousand eight hundred and thirty-four. His object being to examine the grand manufacturing establishments of the country; and also to find out the condition of its Literature and morals, the extent of its commerce, and the practical operation of "The Experiment." Written by himself. Philadelphia: E. L. Carey and A. Hart, 1835. 234 pp.

Address of Mr. Crockett, to the Voters of the Ninth Congressional District of the State of Tennessee. Washington: Printed by Gales and Seaton, 1829. 13 pp.

A Narrative of the Life of David Crockett, of the state of Tennessee. Written by himself. Philadelphia: E. L. Cary and A. Hart, 1834. vi, 113 pp.

Col. Crockett's Exploits and Adventures in Texas; written by himself. The narrative brought down from the death of Col. Crockett to the battle of San Jacinto by an eye witness. Philadelphia: T. K. and P. A. Collins, 1836. viii, 216 pp.
"A pseudo-autobiography; the preface purports to be written by an Alex. J. Dumas, who claims that he received the Crockett manuscript from a Charles T. Beale, who wrote the final chapter. The work is generally ascribed to Richard Penn Smith. cf. Sabin, *Amer. Bibl.*, v. 20, p. 471; Burton's Gentleman's Magazine, Phila. 1839, v. 5, pp. 119–121. *Dict. Amer. Biog.*"

David Crockett's Circular, to the citizens and voters of the Ninth Congressional district of the state of Tennessee. Washingon: 1831. 16 pp.

Life of Col. David Crockett, Written by Himself. Comprising his early life, hunting adventures, service under General Jackson in the Creek war, electioneering speeches, career in Congress, triumphal tour in northern states and services in the Texan war. To which is added, an account of Colonel Crockett's glorious death at the Alamo, while fighting in defence of Texas independence. Philadelphia: G. G. Evans, 1860. 405 pp., illus.
There were numerous editions of this work, with some changes in the title. Thus, *Life of David Crockett, the Original Humorist and Irrepressible Backwoodsman* . . . was published in Philadelphia by Porter & Coates, in 1865. However, with the exception of the first three and last paragraphs pages 239–405 are a reproduction of *Col. Crockett's Exploits and Adventures in Texas. . . . Written by Himself.* Philadelphia: T. K. and P. G. Collins, 1836. This was finished by Charles T. Beale, and ed. by Alex. J. Dumas.

Pictorial Life and Adventures of Davy Crockett. . . . Written by himself . . . with engravings from original designs. Philadelphia: T. B. Peterson & Brothers, 1852.

The Adventures of Davy Crockett; Told Mostly by Himself; with illustrations by John W. Thomason, Jr. New York, London: C. Scribner's Sons, 1934. ix, 258 pp.

The Autobiography of David Crockett. With an introduction by Hamlin Garland. New York: C. Scribner's Sons, 1923. 328 pp.

The Sayings of Davy Crockett in His Own Language, by Larry Mills. Dallas: Pioneer Press, 1938. 37 pp., illus.

Register of Debates in Congress. Vols. IV, V, VI, X, XI. Washington, D. C., 1827, 1828, 1829, 1830, 1834, 1835.
"Admit the intrusion of another hand; none the less if these speeches are read against the background of current debate their highly individual flavor becomes unmistakable at once. They are eager, positive, ardent, not too well ordered; and the turn of language is close in both rhythm and tone to that of the "Narrative." (Constance Rourke)

Davy Crockett's Vow; or His Last Shot for Vengeance. The Five Cent Wide Awake Library, No. 729. Frank Tousey, Publisher.

Crowell, Chester T.
"Davy Crockett." *American Mercury* 4:109–115, 1925.

Davis, James D.
History of the City of Memphis. Memphis, Tenn.: 1873.

Dead Game, or Davy Crockett's Double, by an Old Scout, *Pluck and Luck Weekly.* No. 412.

Dizance, Frank
Davy Crockett. Edinburgh: 1873. A play. In manuscript, N. Y. P. L.

Dorson, Richard Mercer, ed.
Davy Crockett, American Comic Legend. Foreword by Howard Mumford Jones. New York: Printed at the Spiral Press for Rockland Editions, 1939. xxvi, 171 pp., illus.
Anecdotes and woodcuts selected from the Crockett's Almanacs (1835–1856).

————.
"Davy Crockett and the Heroic Age." *SFQ* 6:95–103, 1942.

Elfer, Maurice
Madam Candelaria, Unsung Heroine of the Alamo. Including a personal account of the faithful woman who, staying in the mission when the battle raged and the doomed men sold their lives dearly as possible, obeyed Sam Houston's trust and was wounded by Mexican bayonets while trying to protect dying Bowie. Houston, Tex.: The Rein Company, 1933. 23 pp.
Includes an account of the death of David Crockett.

Ellis, E. S.
The Life and Adventures of Colonel Crockett. Embracing his career as hunter, soldier and Congressman.... New York: Beadle & Co., 1861. viii, 96 pp.
A new edition, much enlarged, was issued by H. T. Coates & Co., in Philadelphia, 1884. viii, 271 pp. New material on Sam Houston, Santa Ana, Rezin P., and Colonel James Bowie.

"Exploits of Davy Crockett."
In: *Mince Pie for the Million.* Philadelphia and New York: Turner and Fisher, 1846.

Flint, Timothy
Recollections of the Last Ten Years. New York: Cummings, Hilliard & Co., 1932.

Foster, Austin P.
"David Crockett." *Tennessee Historical Magazine* 9:166–177, 1925.

French, Mrs. J. Stewart, and Armstrong, Zella
The Crockett Family and Connecting Lines. Bristol, Tenn.: 1928.

Guild, Joseph C.
Old Times in Tennessee. Nashville: 1878.

Hall, Claude V.
"Early Days in Red River County." *Bulletin of the East Texas State Teachers College,* June, 1931.
Deals mainly with Crockett's journey into northeast Texas.

Hamilton, Elisabeth, ed.
How They Started; Nine famous men begin their careers. New York: Harcourt, Brace and Company, 1937. vi, 286 pp.
Selections from *Davy Crockett,* by Constance Rourke.

Haywood, John
The Civil and Political History of Tennessee. Nashville: Methodist Episcopal Church, 1891. 518 pp.

Hunter, J. Marvin
"Crockett's Colorful Career Ended in Texas." *Frontier Times* (Bandera) 15:139–140, 1938.

"Interview with Mrs. Clark."
The Dallas *Morning News,* Jan. 6, 1894.
She describes her meeting with Crockett.

La Salle, Charles E.
The Texan Trailer, or Davy Crockett's Last Bear Hunt. New York: Beadle's Dime Novels, No. 231.

Little, Lucius P.
Ben Hardin, His Times and Contemporaries. Louisville, Ky.: Courier Journal Job Printing Co., 1887.
Further light on Davy Crockett.

Mayer, Edwin Justus
Sunrise in My Pocket; or, The Last Days of Davy Crockett, an American Saga. New York: J. Messner, 1941. 245 pp.
A drama.

McIntyre, John Thomas
In Texas With Davy Crockett. Illustrations by John A. Huybers. Philadelphia: The Penn Publishing Company, 1914. 208 pp., illus.

McNeil, Everett
In Texas With Davy Crockett; a story of the Texas War of Independence. New York: E. P. Dutton & Company, 1908. xii, 398 pp.

Meine, Franklin J.
Tall Tales of the Southwest. An Anthology of Southern and Southwestern Humor. New York: Alfred A. Knopf, 1930. xxxii, 456 pp.

Milhous, John Philip
Davy Crockett, Half Horse, Half Alligator.... In: *American Folk Plays,* F. H. Koch, ed. (pp. 29–58). New York: 1939.

Moore, John Trotwood, and Foster, Austin P.
Tennessee, the Volunteer State. Chicago: The S. J. Clarke Publishing Company, 1923. 4 vols.

Munroe, Kirk
With Crockett and Bowie; or, Fighting for the Lone-Star Flag. A Tale of Texas. Illustrated by V. Perard. New York: C. Scribner's Sons, 1897. vi, 347 pp., illus.

Perry, F. M.
The Story of David Crockett For Young Readers. New York: Werner School Book Co., 1900. 64 pp.

————, and Beebe, K.
Four American Pioneers. D. Boone, D. Crockett, G. R. Clark, Kit Carson. A Book for young Americans. New York: Werner School Book Co., 1900. 255 pp., illus.

Phelan, James
History of Tennessee. The Making of a State. Boston: Houghton Mifflin Company, 1888. vi, 478 pp.

Porter, Kenneth W.
"Davy Crockett and John Horse: A Possible Origin of the Coonskin Story." *American Literature* 15 (No. 1):10–15, 1943.

Randolph, Vance
Ozark Mountain Folks. New York: Vanguard Press, 1932.
　　Contains ten Crockett tall tales of hunting and shooting.

Reavis, Jessie
"Who Jilted Davy Crockett." *TFSP* 18:148–149, 1943.

Roche, James Jeffrey
The Story of the Filibusters. To which is added the life of Colonel David Crockett. London: T. F. Unwin, 1891. xiii, 373 pp.

Rourke, Constance
Davy Crockett; illustrated by James MacDonald. New York: Harcourt, Brace and Co., 1934. xiii, 276 pp., bibl.
　　Finest scholarly work on this subject. Very valuable discussion of Crockett sources and bibliographical material.

————.
"Davy Crockett; Forgotten Facts and Legends." *Southwest Review* 19:149–161, 1934.

Seitz, Don Carlos
Uncommon Americans, Pencil Portraits of Men and Women Who Have Broken the Rules. Indianapolis: The Bobbs-Merrill Company, 1925. 328 pp., illus.

Sketches and Eccentricities of Col. David Crockett of West Tennessee. New York: J. & J. Harper, 1833. vii, 209 pp.
　　The author was unknown to Crockett, who wrote his *Narrative* to correct the wrong impressions produced by this publication.

Skinner, Constance Lindsay
Pioneers of the Old Southwest. A Chronicle of the Dark and Bloody Ground. New Haven: Yale University Press, 1922. xi, 304 pp., bibl.

Shapiro, Irwin
Yankee Thunder: The Legendary Life of Davy Crockett. Illustrated by James Daugherty. New York: Julian Messner, 1944. 205 pp., illus., bibl.

"The Lion of the West."
In: *The Beginnings of American English,* by M. M. Mathews (pp. 116–117). Chicago: The Chicago University Press, 1931.

Williams, Joseph S.
Old Time in West Tennessee. Reminiscences; semi-historic—of Pioneer Life and the Early Emigrant Settlers in the big Hatchie Country, by a Descendant of one of the First Settlers (Joseph S. Williams). Memphis: W. G. Cheeney, Printer and Publisher, 1873. As reported by a correspondent of *The Missouri Republican.*
　　Also contains Davy Crockett exploits.

Williams, Samuel Cole
Beginnings of West Tennessee in the Land of the Chickasaws, 1541–1841. Johnson City, Tenn.: 1930.

————.
Early Travels in the Tennessee Country, 1540–1800. Johnson City, Tenn.: 1928.

CROCKETT ALMANACS

Davy Crockett's Almanac, of Wild Sports of the West, and Life in the Backwoods. Calculated for all the States in the Union. Nashville: Snag and Sawyer, 1835. *Go ahead!*

Davy Crockett's Almanack, of Wild Sports in the West, and Life in the Backwoods. Calculated for all the States in the Union. Vol. I, No. 2. Nashville: Published for the Author, 1836. *Crockett's Method of Wading the Mississippi. Go ahead!*

Crockett's Yaller Flower Almanac. Go ahead! Snooks, no danger her going off! The Ringtail Roarer! Ripsnorter. Circumflustercated Grinner's Guide! Snagsville, Salt River: New York: Published by Boon Crockett and Squire Downing, Skunk's Misery, Down East. Elton, 1836.

Davy Crockett's Almanack, of Wild Sports in the West, Life in the Backwoods, & Sketches of Texas. O Kentucky! The Hunters of Kentucky!! Nashville: Published by the Heirs of Col. Crockett. Vol. I, No. 3, 1837. *Go ahead!*

Crockett's Texas Oldmanick. New York, Philadelphia: Turner & Fisher, 1837. *"Crockett goes a-head, though dead." Millions for Texas! But not a cent for taxes!!! With comic engravings of all the principal events of Texas.*

Davy Crockett's Almanack, of Wild Sports in the West, Life in the Backwoods, Sketches of Texas, and rows on the Mississippi. Nashville: Published by the heirs of Col. Crockett, 1838. *Go ahead!*

Crockett's Comic Almanac. Vol. I, No. 2. New York: Elton, 1839. *She's a little 'un, But she's a good 'un.*

Crockett's Awlmanaxe for 1839. New York: Turner & Fisher. No. 1.

The Crockett Almanac. Containing Adventures, Exploits, Sprees, & Scrapes in the West, & Life and Manners in the Backwoods. Vol. II, No. 1. Nashville: Published by Ben Harding, 1839. *An Unexpected Ride on the Horns of an Elk. Go ahead!*

The Crockett Almanac, Containing Adventures, Exploits, Sprees, & Scrapes in the West, & Life and Manners in the Backwoods. Vol. II, No. 2. Nashville: Published by Ben Harding, 1840. *Crockett scared by an Owl. Go ahead!!*

Crockett's Comic Almanack. Albany: A. Skinflint, 1840.

The Crockett Almanac, Containing Adventures, Exploits, Sprees, & Scrapes in the West, & Life and Manners in the Backwoods. Vol. 2, No. 3. Nashville: Published by Ben Harding, 1841. *Tussel [sic] with a Bear. Go ahead!*

The Crockett Almanac: Containing Sprees and Scrapes in the West, Life and Manners in the Backwoods; and Exploits and Adventures on the Praries [sic]. Correct Astronomical Calculations for every part of the United States, Territories, and Canada. Boston: J. Fisher, 1841. *A Squabble in the Mud. Go ahead.*

Crockett's Harrison Almanac for 1841. New York: Elton, 1841.

Ben Hardin's Crockett Almanac. With Correct Astronomical Calculations; for each State in the Union—Territories and Canada. Rows—Sprees and Scrapes in the West; Life and Manners in the Backwoods: and Terrible Adventures on the Ocean. New York: Turner & Fisher, 1842. *Go ahead!*

Ben Hardin's Crockett Almanac. Correct Astronomical Calculations; for each State in the Union—Territories and Canada. Rows—Sprees and Scrapes in the West: Life and Manners in the Backwoods: and Terrible Adventures on the Ocean. Baltimore: Turner, 1842. *Ben Hardin on a Raft. Go ahead!*

Crockett Comic Almanac. Worser Gotham. New York: Published by Doleful Serious, and sold at 98 Nassau, and 18 Division Streets. 1842. New Series, No. 1. *Lots of Funny Fun.*

Crockett Almanac. Improved Edition: Containing Real Stories. Boston: S. N. Dickinson, 1842.

Fisher's Crockett Almanac.
Edited by Ben Hardin. Calendar for the Whole Country. With Rows, Sprees, and Scrapes in the West: Life and Manners in the Backwoods: Terrible Battles and Adventures on Sea and Land. New York: Turner & Fisher, 1843.
I leave this rule for others when I'm dead,
Be always sure you're right, then go ahead.

Davy Crockett's Almanac. Life and Manners in the Backwoods: Terrible Battles and Adventures of Border Life: with Rows, Sprees, and Scrapes in the West. New York: Turner & Fisher, 1844.

Davy Crockett's Almanac. Life and Manners in the Backwoods: Terrible Battles and Adventures of Border Life: with Rows, Sprees, and Scrapes in the West. For Eastern, Northern and Middle States. Boston: James Fisher, 1844.
I leave this rule for others when I'm dead,
Be always sure you're right, then go ahead.

Davy Crockett's Almanac. Calendars correct for the entire Union, the territories, Texas, and the British Provinces. Boston: James Fisher, 1845.

Davy Crockett's Almanac.
Calendars correct for the entire Union, the Territories, Texas, and British Provinces. Philadelphia: Turner & Fisher, 1845.
I always leave this rule when I'm dead
Be always sure you're right, then go ahead.

Crockett's Almanac. Scenes in River Life, Feats on the Lakes, Manners in the Back Woods, Adventures in Texas, &c., &c. Calendar calculations for the whole union. Boston: James Fisher, 1846.

Crockett's Almanac. Scenes in River Life, Feats on the Lakes, Manners in the Back Woods, Adventures in Texas, &c., &c. Philadelphia: Turner & Fisher, 1846. *Crockett's wonderful escape up Niagara Falls, on his Pet Alligator.*

Crockett's Almanac. Scenes in River Life, Feats on the Lakes, Manners in the Back Woods, Adventures in Texas, &c., &c. Calendar calculated for the whole union. Baltimore: J. B. Keller, 1846.

Davy Crockett's Almanac: Daring Adventures in the Back Woods; Wonderful Scenes in River Life; Manners of Warfare in the West; Feats on the Prairie, in Texas & Oregon. Calendar Calculations, correct for the whole United States. New York: Turner & Fisher, 1847.
I leave this rule for others when I'm dead,
Be always sure you're right, then go ahead.

Davy Crockett's Almanac. Daring Adventures in the Back Woods: Wonderful Scenes in River Life; Manners of Warfare in the West; Feats on the Prairies, in Texas and Oregon. Boston: James Fisher, 1847.

Crockett's Almanac. Calculated for the whole United States. Philadelphia: Turner & Fisher, 1848.

Crockett's Almanac. Calculated for the whole United States. Boston: James Fisher, 1848. *The Birth of Crockett.*
I leave this rule for others when I'm dead,
Be always sure you're right, then go ahead.

Crockett Almanac. Calendar calculated for the whole United States. Philadelphia: Turner & Fisher, 1849.

Crockett Almanac.
Boston: James Fisher, 1849.

Crockett's Almanac, Containing Rows, Sprees, and Scrapes in the West; Life and Manners in the Backwoods, Adventures on the Ocean, &c. New York: Fisher & Brothers, 1850.

Crockett's Almanac. Containing Rows, Sprees, and Scrapes in the West; Life and Manners in the Backwoods. Adventures on the Ocean, &c. Philadelphia: R. Magee, 1850.

Crockett's Almanac. Containing Life, Manners and Adventures in the Backwoods, and Rows, Sprees, and Scrapes on the Western Waters. Philadelphia: Fisher & Brother, 1851.

Crockett Almanac, containing Life, Manners and Adventures in the Back Woods, and Rows, Sprees, and Scrapes on the Western Waters. With Handsome Illustrations. Boston: G. W. Cottrell & Co., 1852.
I leave this rule for others when I'm dead,
Be always sure you're right, then go ahead.

Crockett Almanac, Containing Life, Manners, and Adventures in the Back Woods, and Rows, Sprees, and Scrapes on the Western Waters. With Handsome Illustrations. Philadelphia: Fisher & Brother, 1852, 1853, 1854.

Crockett Almanac, Containing Life, Manners, and Adventures in the Backwoods, and Rows, Sprees, and Scrapes on the Western Waters. New York: Philip J. Cozans, 1854.

Crockett Almanac. Boston: G. W. Cottrell & Co., 1855.

Crockett Almanac. Philadelphia: Fisher & Brother, 1855.

Crockett Almanac. New York: Philip J. Cozans, 1856.

Crockett Almanac. Philadelphia: Fisher & Brother, 1856.

GENERAL CUSTER

Brill, Charles J.
Conquest of the Southern Plains; uncensored narrative of the battle of Washita and Custer's Southern Campaign. Oklahoma City: Golden Saga Publishers, 1938. 323 pp., illus., bibl.

Brininstool, Earl Alonzo
A Trooper with Custer, and Other Historic Incidents of the Battle of the Little Big Horn. Columbus, Ohio: The Hunter-Trader-Trapper Co., 1925. "The Frontier Series," Vol. I.

Custer, Mrs. Elizabeth Bacon
"Boots and Saddles,' or Life in Dakota with General Custer. New York: Harper and Bros., 1885. 312 pp., illus.

————.
Following the Guidon. New York: Harper & Bros., 1890. xx, 341 pp., music.

————.
General Custer at the Battle of the Little Big Horn, June 25, 1876. New York: Printed, Not Published, 1897.

————,
The Boy General; Story of the Life of Major General George A. Custer.... New York: C. Scribners, 1901. x, 204 pp.

————.
Tenting on the Plains; or, General Custer in Kansas and Texas. New York: C. L. Webster & Co., 1889. xiii, 702 pp.

Custer, George Armstrong
My Life on the Plains; or, Personal Experiences with Indians. New York: Sheldon & Co., 1874. 256 pp., illus.

Cyclorama of General Custer's Last Fight. Boston: Cyclorama Co., 1889.
An account of the Battles of the Little Big Horn with biographies of Custer and Chief Gall, and an interview with Sitting Bull.

Garst, Shannon
Custer: Fighter of the Plains. Illustrated by Harve Stein. New York: Julian Messner, 1944. 174 pp.
A colorful biography for younger readers.

Godfrey, Captain E. S.
"Custer's Last Battle." *Century Magazine,* Jan., 1892. 29 pp.

Graham, William Alexander
The Story of the Little Big Horn,—Custer's Last Fight. Harrisburg, Pa.: Military Services Publishing Co., 1945. xii, 178 pp.

Haycox, Ernest
Bugles in the Afternoon. Boston: Little, Brown and Co., 1944. 306 pp.
A novel dealing with the adventures of Gen. George Armstrong Custer.

Hunt, Frazier
Custer; the Last of the Cavaliers. New York: Cosmopolitan, 1928. 209 pp., illus.

Luce, Edward S.
Keogh, Comanche and Custer. Dedham, Mass.: The Author, 1939. xviii, 127 pp., illus.

Roe, Charles Francis
Custer's Last Battle on the Little Big Horn.... Illustrated by photographs, maps, and drawings. New York: R. Bruce, 1927. 40 pp., illus.

Van de Water, Frederick F.
Glory-Hunter. Indianapolis: Bobbs-Merrill Co., 1934.
Biography of General Custer.

Walker, J. E.
Campaigns of General Custer in the Northwest, and Final Surrender of Sitting Bull. London: Jenkins, 1881.

JOHN DARLING

Halpert, Herbert
"John Darling, A New York Munchhausen."
JAFL 57:97–107, 1944.

Jagendorf, M.
"John Darling References." *NYFQ* 3 (No. 4):
329–330, 1947.

Thompson, Harold W.
Body, Boots and Britches. Philadelphia: J. B.
Lippincott Co., 1940.

> Chapt. 6, 11, 12, have tales and discussions of
> local folk heroes of New York: John Darling,
> Bill Greenfield, Joe Call, Cal Corey, "Boney"
> Quillan, and others.

WYATT EARP

Lake, Stuart N.
Wyatt Earp, Frontier Marshall. Boston: Houghton Mifflin Co., 1931. 392 pp.

> "Best written of all bad man biographies."
> (Dobie)

Raine, William M., and Barnes, Will C.
Cattle, Cowboys and Rangers. New York:
Grosset & Dunlap, 1930. (pp. 208, 210).

Vestal, Stanley
Short Grass Country. (American Folkways
Series). New York: Duell, Sloan and Pearce,
1942.

> A land of colorful history and lusty life which
> stretches from Wichita almost to Denver—the
> land of buffalo hunts, tornadoes, oil, county-seats,
> wars—the range of Coronado, Buffalo Bill and
> Wyatt Earp.

MOSES EVANS

Day, Donald
"Moses Evans: The Wild Man of the Woods."
TFSP 18:89–104, 1943.

> Texan colorful figure.

FEOBOLDSON

Beath, Paul R.
"Feobold Feoboldson." *Nebraska Folklore
Pamphlets* 5:1–12, July 1, 1937; 8:1:1–8,
Sept. 15, 1937.

————.
*Febold Feboldson: Tall Tales from the Great
Plains.* Lincoln: University of Nebraska Press,
1948. xi, 124 pp.

> The amazing achievements of the "indomitable
> Swedish pioneer who surmounts any difficulty."

Botkin, Ben
Febold Feboldson. In: *A Treasury of Ameri-
can Folklore,* (pp. 227–230). New York:
Crown Publishers, 1944.

MIKE FINK

BIBLIOGRAPHY

"Bibliography of Mike Fink."
In: *Mike Fink, King of Mississippi Keelboatmen* by Walter Blair and Franklin J. Meine
(pp. 269–283). New York: Henry Holt and
Co., 1933. 283 pp., illus.

GENERAL STUDIES AND COLLECTIONS

Adkins, Nelson F.
"A Study of John G. Neihardt's Song of Three
Friends." *AS* 3 (No. 4): 276–290, 1928.

Alter, J. Cecil
James Bridger: Trapper, Frontiersman, Scout
and Guide. Salt Lake City: Shepherd Book
Co., 1925.

Ambler, Charles Henry
*A History of Transportation in the Ohio Val-
ley.* Glendale, Calif.: Arthur H. Clark Co.,
1931. (pp. 53–58.)

An Old Tale for the New Year, or, *Mike Fink.*
New York: J. A. Anderson, 1928.

Anon
"Lige Shattuck's Reminiscences of Mike Fink."
In: *St. Louis Reveille,* Feb. 28, 1848.

Ashe, Thomas
Travels in America Performed in 1806. London: R. Phillips, 1808. 3 Vols.

Audobon, John J.
*Delineations of American Scenery and Char-
acter.* New York: G. D. Baker and Co., 1926.
pp. 23–28; 56–63.

Baird, Robert
View of the Valley of the Mississippi; or The
Emigrants' and Travellers' Guide to the West.
Philadelphia: H. J. Tanner, 1834.

Bannon, Henry T.
Stories Old and Often Told, Being Chronicles
of Scioto County, Ohio. Baltimore: Waverly
Press, 1927. (pp. 116–118.)

Bechdolt, Frederick R.
Giants of the Old West. New York: Century
Co., 1930. (pp. 32–34.)

Bennett, Emerson
Mike Fink: A Legend of the Ohio. Cincinnati:
Robinson and Jones, 1848. 102 pp.

————.
Mike Fink, A Story of the Ohio. In: *The
Great West.* Cincinnati: Holland and Jones,
1847.

Bird, Robert Montgomery
Nick of the Woods, or the Jibbenaisosay. A
Tale of Kentucky. Philadelphia: Lea and
Blanchard, 1837. 2 Vols.

Blair, Walter, and Meine, Franklin
Mike Fink, King of Mississippi Keelboatmen.
New York: Henry Holt and Co., 1933. xiv, 283
pp. bibl. (pp. 269–283.)

Brackenridge, Henry M.
Journal of a Voyage Up the River Missouri,
performed in 1811. Baltimore: Coale and Maxwell, 1815. viii, 247 pp. (pp. 11–15.)

Bradley, James H.
"Descriptions of the Keelboats and Mackinaw
Boats used in Early Days on the Upper
Missouri." *Montana Historical Society* 9:140–
141, 1923.

————.
"Sketch of the Fur Trade of the Upper Mis-
souri River." *Contributions to the Historical
Society of Montana* 1923. pp. 320–324.
The death of Mike Fink.

Branch, Edward Douglas
Westward. A romance of the American Frontier. Woodcuts by Lucina Smith Wakefield.
New York: D. Appleton and Co., 1930. ix,
626 pp.

Brother Jonathan 2:342–344, 1842.
The incident of the disgraced Scalp-lock
described.

Carson, W. Wallace
"Early River Transportation." *The Mississippi
Valley Historical Review* June, 1920, Vol. 7,
pp. 26–38.

Cassedy, Ben
The History of Louisville, from its earliest set-
tlement till the year 1852. Louisville: Hull and
Brother, 1852. 255 pp. (pp. 75–79.)

Chicago Literary Budget.
Vol. 2, No. 49, December 9, 1854. Biographical
Sketch of Emerson Bennett, pp. 385–6, also
reveals first appearance of the novel, "Mike
Fink."

Chittenden, H. M.
The American Fur Trade in the Far West. New
York: Francis P. Harper, 1902. Vol. 4, pp.
707–712.

————.
*History of Early Steamboat Navigation on the
Missouri River.* New York: Francis P. Harper,
1903.

Churchill, Winston
The Crossing. Illustrations by Sydney Adam-
son and Lilian Bayliss. New York, London:
The Macmillan Co., 1904. vii, 598 pp.

Cist, Charles
The Last of the Girtys. In: *The Cincinnati
Miscellany* (January, 1845). Cincinnati, Rob-
inson and Jones, 1846. pp. 125–126.

Clemens, Samuel L.
Life on the Mississippi. Boston: Osgood, 1883.

Coates, Robert M.
The Outlaw Years. New York: The Macaulay
Co., 1930. (pp. 111–113.)

Craig, Neville B.
The History of Pittsburgh. New edition, with
introduction and notes by George T. Fleming.
Pittsburgh: J. R. Weldin Co., 1917. xxiv, 310
pp.

Crockett Almanac (1838).
Nashville: Published by the heirs of Col.
Crockett.
Contains story of "Mike, the Ohio Boatman,"
and a woodcut showing Mike Fink with shot-gun
laid over his arm, standing at tiller of Keel-boat.

Crockett Almanac 1840.
Nashville: Published by Ben Harding, Crockett
Vol. 11, No. 2, illus., woodcut.
Shooting match described.

Crocket Almanac, 1851.
Philadelphia, New York and Boston: Fisher
and Brother.
Contains: Mike Fink Trying to Save Mrs.
Crockett and an article on Hands of Celebrated
Gougers, including Mike Fink.

Crockett Almanac, 1852.
Philadelphia, New York, Boston and Balti-
more: Fisher and Brother.
Contains: Mike Fink's Treat to the Indians;
Mike Hunting a Moose; Bravery of Mike Fink's
Wife.

Crockett Almanac, 1853.
Philadelphia, New York, Boston and Balti-
more: Fisher and Brother.
Contains: The Celebrated Mike Fink Attacked
by a Wolf While Fishing in the Mississippi; Sal
Fink's Victory Over an Old Bear and Cubs; Mike
Fink Killing a Wolf with His Fists.

Crockett Almanac, 1854.
New York: Philip J. Cozans.
Contains: Mike Fink's View of a Steamboat; Sal
Fink, the Mississippi Screamer; How to Escape
a Bear; Mike Fink's Idea of a Gymnastic School.

Crockett, David
The Autobiography of David Crockett. Edited
by Hamlin Garland. New York: Charles Scribner's Sons, 1923.

Cuming, Fortescue
Sketches of a Tour to the Western Country
through the states of Ohio and Kentucky.
Pittsburgh: Cramer, Spear and Eichbaum,
1810. viii, 504 pp.

Cumings, Samuel
*The Western Pilot, Containing Charts of the
Ohio River and of the Mississippi.* Accom-
panied with directions for Navigating the same.
Cincinnati: Neg. Guilford, 1829. Reprinted
1832 and 1834.

Dahlinger, C. W.
Pittsburgh, a Sketch of its Early Social Life.
New York: G. Putnam Sons, 1916.

Dale, H. C.
The Ashley-Smith Explorations. The Discovery of a Central Route to the Pacific, 1822–1829. Cleveland: Arthur H. Clark Co., 1918.

" 'De Grachia' the Old Bear of Tironga Bayou, Arkansas." *Spirit of the Times,* 1847. Feb. 13, 1847. Vol. 16.
Mentions Mike Fink as a great hunter.

De la Hunt, T. J.
"A Holiday Gift Book from out of the West in 1829." *The Courier* (Evansville, Indiana), Dec. 1, 1918.

DeVoto, Bernard
Mark Twain's America. Boston: Little, Brown and Co., 1932. (pp. 60, 92, 241.)

Dick, Everett
The Story of the Frontier. New York: D. Appleton-Century Co., 1941. 574 pp., illus.
Mike Fink, the boaster—"all man, save what is wildcat and lightning." (pp. 164-165).

Dickson, Harris
"River Boom." *Colliers,* (May 9) 1931. pp. 75–77.

———.
"When New Orleans Was Young." *Colliers,* (April 4) 1931. p. 25.

Dondore, Dorothy A.
The Prairie and the Making of Middle America. Cedar Rapids: The Torch Press, 1926. pp. 234, 401, 447.

Dunbar, Seymour
A History of Travel in America. Indianapolis: Bobbs-Merrill, 1915. Vol. 1, pp. 288–92.

Edwards, Richard, and Hopewell M.
"Edwards Great West and Her Commercial Metropolis, Embracing a General View of the West, and a complete History of St. Louis." *Edward's Monthly* (St. Louis) 1860. p. 591.

Epler, William
"Some Personal Recollections of Peter Cartwright." *Illinois State Historical Society Journal* 13:379, 1920.

Evans, Estwick
A Pedestrious Tour, of four thousand miles through the Western States and territories during the winter and spring of 1818. Interspersed with brief reflections upon a great variety of topics. Concord, N. H.: Printed by Joseph C. Spear, 1819. 256 pp.
Among the author's "variety of topics" Mike Fink also appears.

Field, Joseph M.
"The Death of Mike Fink." *St. Louis Reveille* Oct. 21, 1844.

———.
The Drama in Pokerville; "The Bench and Bar of Jurytown" and other stories. By "Everpoint" (J. M. Field—of the St. Louis Reveille). With light illustrations by F. O. C. Darley. Phila.: Carey and Hart, 1847. 200 pp.
"The Death of Mike Fink" (pp. 177–183).

———.
"Mike Fink, the Last of the Boatmen." *St. Louis Reveille* June 14 and June 21, 1847.

Finley, James B.
Autobiography of Rev. James B. Finley, or Pioneers Life in the West. Edited by W. P. Strickland. Cincinnati: Printed for the Methodist Book Concern, 1854. pp. 309, 327–329.

Flint, James
Letters from America. Containing observations on the climate and agriculture of the western states, the manners of the people, the prospects of emigrants. Edinburgh: W. C. Trait, 1822. p. 86, viii, 330 pp.

Flint, Timothy
The First White Man of the West, or The Life and Exploits of Settler of Kentucky. Cincinnati: H. M. Rulison, 1856.

———.
Recollections of the Last Ten Years. Boston: Cummings, Hilliard and Co., 1826. 395 pp.

Freeman, Lewis R.
Waterways of Westward Wandering. New York: Dodd, Mead and Co., pp. 118–121, 168–173.

Gabriel, Ralph Henry
The Lure of the Frontier. New Haven: Yale University Press, 1929. (p. 160.)

Gould, Emerson W.
Fifty Years on the Mississippi: or Gould's History of River Navigation. St. Louis: Nixon-Jones Printing Co., 1889. pp. 41, 56–59, 65.

Grant, Helen Hardie
Peter Cartwright: Pioneer. New York: The Abingdon Press, 1931. (pp. 115–116, 149–150.)

Griswold, Rufus Wilmot
The Prose Writers of America. With a survey of the history, condition and prospects of American Literature. Philadelphia: Carey and Hart, 1847. 552 pp.
On Morgan Neville.

Grunbie, Sydney
Frontiers and the Fur Trade. New York: John Day Co., 1929.

Haliburton, T. C. ed.
Traits of American Humor by Native Authors. London, Coburn and Co., 1852. iii. (pp. 79–87.)
Deacon Smith's Bull detailed.

Hall, James
Letters From the West. London: Colburn and Co., 1828. vi, 385 pp. (pp. 90–94.)

———.
Statistics of the West, at the Close of the Year 1836. Cincinnati: J. A. James and Co., 1837. p. 220.

———.
The West: Its Commerce and Navigation. Cincinnati: H. W. Derby and Co., 1848, vii, 328 pp. (p. 112.)

Hazard, Lucy L.
The American Picaresque, in the Trans-Mississippi West. Boulder: University of Colorado, 1930. (pp. 195–217.)

————.
The Frontier in American Literature. Philadelphia: Crowell Press, 1927. (pp. 127–133.)

Hopewell, Menra
Legends of the Missouri and Mississippi. London: Ward and Tyler, 1874. (pp. 372–378.)

Hough, Emerson
The Covered Wagon. New York: D. Appleton and Co., 1922. 378 pp., p. 281.

Howe, Henry
The Great West. New York and Cincinnati: 1847. 2 Vols., Vol. I. (pp. 245–255.)

————.
Historical Collections of Ohio, 1847. Reprinted frequently up to 1902.
Vol. 1:321–322, contains a talk with a veteran Riverman—Captain John Fink, and Mike Fink.

Hulbert, Archer B.
The Ohio River; a Course of Empire. New York, and London: G. P. Putnam's Sons, 1906. xiv, 378 pp. (pp. 211–216.)

————.
The Paths of Inland Commerce. New Haven: Yale University Press, 1921. (pp. 63–64.)

————.
Waterways of Westward Expansion, The Ohio River and Its Tributaries. Cleveland: The A. H. Clark Co., 1903.

Kaine, Hiram
Mike Fink, in *The Cincinnati Miscellany, or, Antiquities of the West.* Cincinnati: Robinson and Jones, Oct., 1845, 1846. (pp. 31–32.)

"K" Correspondence
The Cincinnati Miscellany. February, 1845. pp. 156–157.

Keyes, James
Pioneers of Scioto County. Being a Short Biographical Sketch of Some of the First Settlers of Scioto County, Ohio. Portsmouth, Ohio: 1880. 121 pp. (pp. 3–4.)

Knox, Thomas W.
Underground, or, Life Below the Surface. Incidents and accidents beyond the light of day: Startling adventures in all parts of the world. Mines and the mode of working them. Under currents of society; gambling and its horrors. Hartford: J. B. Burr and Hyde; Chicago: J. B. Burr, Hyde and Co., 1873.

Leahy, Ethel C.
Who's Who on the Ohio River and Tributaries. Cincinnati: E. C. Leahy Publ. Co., 1931. (pp. 66–74.)

Lloyd, James T.
Lloyd's Steamboat Directory. Cincinnati: James T. Lloyd and Co., 1856. (pp. 35–38.)

Longstreet, Augustus B.
Georgia Scenes, Augusta, 1835. New York: Harper and Bros., 1840.

McClung, John Alexander
Sketches of Western Adventure. Louisville, Ky.: R. H. Collins and Co., 1879. xxix, 398 pp.

McKnight, Charles
Our Western Border One Hundred Years Ago. Philadelphia: J. C. McCurdy and Co., 1875.

Meine, Franklin Julius, and Blair, Walter
Mike Fink, King of Mississippi Keelboatmen. New York: Henry Holt and Co., 1933. xiv, 283 pp. bibl. (pp. 269–283.)

Mike Fink.
In: *Cincinnati: 1848.* Revised Edition. Cincinnati: V. P. James, 1852.

"Mike Fink."
Missouri Intelligences, Sept. 4, 1829.

"Mike Fink, The Last of the Boatmen."
The Western Monthly Review, July, 1829. pp. 15–19, Cincinnati: E. H. Flint.

Milburn, William Henry
Ten Years of Preacher Life. New York: Derby and Jackson. x, 363 pp. (pp. 216–222.)
Remembrances of the Mississippi.

Mississippi: Palladium.
Holly Springs, Miss.: June 6, 1851. p. 4.
The story of Deacon Smith's Bull.

Mitford, Mary Russell
Lights and Shadows of American Life. London: H. Colburn and R. Bentley, 1832. 3 vols.
Contains some legends and tales, as well as an interesting portion (vol. 3) on "The Last of the boatmen"—Mike Fink.

Monette, J. W.
History of the Discovery and Settlement of the Valley of the Mississippi. New York: Harper and Bros., 1846. Vol. II, Chapt. 1, Sec. 2.

Musick, John R.
Stories of Missouri. New York: American Book Co., 1897. (pp. 86–88.)

Neihardt, John G.
The Splendid Wayfaring. New York: The Macmillan Co., 1920.

————.
The Song of Three Friends. New York: The Macmillan Company, 1919. xv, 126 pp.

Neville, Morgan
The Last of the Boatmen. In: *The Western Souvenir,* A Christmas and New Year's Gift for 1829. Edited by James Hall. Cincinnati: N. and G. Guilford, 1829.

Ogg, Frederick Austin
The Old Northwest. New Haven: Yale University Press, 1919. (p. 114.)

Perrin, William Henry
"Western River Navigation a Century Ago."
Magazine of Western History 12:340–345, 1890.

————, Battle, J. H. and Kniffin, C.
Kentucky, a History of the State. Louisville and Chicago: F. A. Battery and Co., 1888, 8th edition, pp. 234–235.

Popular Biography. Vol. 1 (No. 1): November, 1929.
The life and doings of Mike Fink mentioned.

Porter, William T.
"Mike Fink's Death." *The Spirit of the Times* (New York): July 9, 1842. pp. 217.

Quick, Herbert, and Edward
Mississippi Steambotin'. A History of Steamboating on the Mississippi and its Tributaries. New York: Henry Holt and Co., 1926.

Richardson, Albert D.
Beyond the Mississippi. Hartford: American Publ. Co., 1867.

Riegel, Robert E.
America Moves West. New York: Henry Holt and Co., 1930. (p. 165.)

Robb, John S. (Solitaire)
"Trimming a Darky's Heel." *St. Louis Reveille* Jan. 25, 1847.

Rothert, Otto A.
The Outlaws in Cave-in-Rock. Cleveland: Arthur H. Clark Co., 1924.

Rourke, Constance
American Humour. A Study of the National Character. New York: Harcourt, Brace and Co., 1931. (pp. 53–55, 65, 152, 310.)

Rozier, Firman A.
Rozier's History of the Early Settlements of the Mississippi Valley. St. Louis: Pierrot and Son, 1890. (p. 64.)

Rusk, Ralph L.
Literature of the Middle Western Frontier. New York: Columbia University Press, 1925. Vol. I, pp. 73, 275, 306.

Sabin, Edwin L.
Wild Men of the Wild West. New York: Thomas Y. Crowell Co., 1929. (pp. 59–67.)

Sandburg, Carl
Abraham Lincoln: The Prairie Years. New York: Harcourt, Brace and Co., 1926, 2 Vols. (Vol. I, pp. 78–79.)

Saxon, Lyle
Father Mississippi. New York: Century Co., 1927. (pp. 137–138.)

Scharf, Thomas J.
History of St. Louis and County. Philadelphia: H. Evans and Co., 1883.

Shields, Joseph Dunbar
Natchez, Its Early History. Louisville: John P. Morton and Co., 1930. (pp. 261–263.)
Describes the incident of the disgraced scalp-lock.

Simms, William Gilmore
Transatlantic Tales. Sketches, and Legends by Various American Authors. Collected and arranged by Gilmore Simms. London: N. Bruce, 1842. (pp. 60–65.)
The incident of the disgraced scalp-lock.

Smith, Jackson, and Sublette
Record Book containing copies of letters from Indian agents and others, to the superintendent of Indian Affairs at St. Louis, from Sept. 10, 1830, to April 1, 1932. Vol. 32.
Official Report of Mike Fink's Death.

Solitaire (John S. Robb)
"Trimming a Darky's Heel." *The Saint Louis Weekly Reveille* 3 (No. 29): 1147. 1847. (Jan. 25.)
One of Mike's amazing exploits with his gun, and his encounter with a French Magistrate.

Spencer, Thomas Edwin
The Story of Old St. Louis. St. Louis: St. Louis Pageant Assn., 1914.

Spirit of the Times, Feb. 13, 1847. p. 605.
The incident of the trimming of a darky's heel.

Spirit of the Times, March 22, 1851. p. 52.
Deacon Smith's Bull discussed.

Spirit of the Times, April 15, 1848. p. 89.
Shattuck's reminiscences of Mike Fink.

Stevens, Walter B.
Missouri, the Center State, 1821–1915. Chicago: J. J. Clarke Publ. Co., 1915. (pp. 707–708, 712–713.)

St. Louis Republican, July 16, 1823.
Newspaper story of Fink's death.

Strickland, W. P.
The Pioneers of the West, or, Life in the Woods. New York: Carlton and Phillips, 1856. 403 pp., p. 197.

———— (Ed.)
Peter Cartwright, the Backwoods Preacher: An Autobiography. London, 1858.

"The Flatboatmen of the West."
The Cincinnati Miscellany 2:332–334, 1846.
The incident of the disgraced scalp-lock described.

"The Last of Mike Fink."
Louisville Journal Dec. 25, 1844.

The Western Boatman, a Periodical devoted to Navigation. Cincinnati: June, 1848. (p. 129.)
The story of the last of the Girtys.

Thorpe, T. B.
"Remembrances of the Mississippi."
Harper's Magazine 12:25–41, (Dec.) 1855.

————.
The Hive of the Bee Hunter. New York: Appleton Co., 1854. (p. 163.)
Discussion of Mike Fink, and the incident of the disgraced scalp-lock.

————. *The Mysteries of the Backwoods*. Phila., Pa.: 1846. (pp. 118.)
The incident of the disgraced scalp-lock.

Tripplett, Frank
Conquering the Wilderness. Chicago and New York: The Werner Co., 1895.

Turner, Frederick Jackson
The Frontier in American History. New York: Henry Holt and Co., 1921. 375 pp.

Van Buren, A de Puy
Jottings of a Year's Sojourn in the South, or, First Impressions of the Country and Its People. Battle Creek, Mich.: 1859. (pp. 312–314.)
Autobiography of Rev. James B. Finley.

Van Tramp, John C.
Prairie and Rocky Mountain Adventures, or, Life in the New West. Columbus, Ohio: Gilmore and Segner, 1867. 649 pp., (p. 95.)
Remembrances of the Mississippi.

Venable, W. H.
Beginnings of Literary Culture in the Ohio Valley. Cincinnati: R. Clarke and Co., 1891. (p. 228.)

Vestal, Stanley
Kit Carson, the Happy Warrior of the Old West. Boston: Houghton Mifflin Co., 1928.

"Western Citizen (Paris, Kentucky)."
Wisconsin Historical Society. Draper Mss. 29 cc. 45–46.
Description of Mike Fink's end.

Winsor, Justin
The Westward Movement. Boston: Houghton Mifflin Co., 1899.

NATHAN BEDFORD FORREST

Rogers, E. G.
"Concerning the Nathan Bedford Forrest Legend." *TFSB* 4:32–63, 1938.

HUGH GLASS

Neihardt, John G.
The Song of Hugh Glass. New York: The Macmillan Co., 1915.
"An epic in vigorous verse of the West's most famous man—and bear story.

Ruxton, George F.
Wild Life in the Rocky Mountains. New York: Outing Publ. Co., 1916. 303 pp.
Contains other version of the Hugh Glass story.

MUSTANG GRAY

Dobie, J. Frank
"Mustang Gray: Fact, Tradition and Song." *TFSP* 10: 109–123, 1932.
A character who operated mostly in Southwest Texas.

BOBBY HAYES

Baughman, Ernest W.
"Bobby Hays, Quarry Worker." *HFB* 1:75–77, 1942.
Legendary hero of Indiana.

JOHN HENRY

Bowman, James Cloyd
John Henry. Illustrated by Roy La Grove. Chicago: Albert Whitman Co., 1942.

Bradford, Roark
John Henry. Woodcuts by J. J. Lankes. New York: Harper and Bros., 1931. 225 pp., illus.

————.
John Henry, a play with music. Music composed by Jacques Wolfe. With eight stage sets designed for the play by Albert Johnson. New York: Harper and Bros., 1939, illus., music.

Chappell, Louis W.
John Henry, A Folk-Lore Study. Jena: Frommansche Verlag, Walter Biedermann, 1933. 144 pp., illus.

Hendricks, W. C.
John Henry of the Cape Fear. In: *Bundle of Troubles and Other Tarheel Tales*. Durham, N. C.: Duke University Press, 1944.

Hobart, George
John Henry. New York: G. W. Dillingham Co., 1901. 96 pp., illus.

Hubbard, Freeman H.
The Mighty Jawn Henry. In: *Railroad Avenue*, (pp. 58–65). New York: McGraw-Hill Book Co., 1945.

Johnson, Guy B.
"John Henry, a brief appreciative discussion of the John Henry Legend." *Southern Workman* April, 1927. pp. 158–160.

————.
John Henry; a Negro Folk Legend. In: *Ebony and Topaz*. New York: Opportunity Publ. Co., National Urban League, 1927.

————.
John Henry: Tracking Down a Negro Legend. Chapel Hill, N. C.: University of North Carolina Press, 1929. 155 pp., bibl.
Contains music, and a list of recordings.

Redwine, Newton
"John Henry." *The Beattyville Enterprise*, Beattyville, Ky., Feb. 1, 1929.

Shapiro, Irwin
John Henry and the Double Jointed Steam Drill. Illustrated by James Daugherty. New York: Julian Messner, Unpaged.

WILD BILL HICKOK

Botkin, Ben
Wild Bill. In: *A Treasury of American Folklore*, (pp. 72–93). New York: Crown Publishers, 1944.

Connelley, William Elsey
Wild Bill and His Era. New York: Press of the Pioneers, 1933. 229 pp., illus.
The Life of James Butler "Wild Bill" Hickok.

Coursey, O. W.
Wild Bill (James Butler Hickok). Mitchell: Education Supply Co., 1924. 80 pp., illus.

Gard, Robert E.
"Alberta's Wild Bill Hickok." *Alberta Folklore Quarterly.* 2:62–65, June, 1946.

Nichols, George Ward
"Wild Bill" (Hickok). *Harper's New Monthly Magazine* 34:273–285, 1867.

Raine, William M., and Barnes, Will C.
Cattle, Cowboys and Rangers. New York: Grosset & Dunlap, 1930. (pp. 103, 105, 106.)

"Wild Bill Hickok." *The Nebraska History Magazine,* Vol. X (April–June), 1927.
Devoted to "Wild Bill Hickok" and contains very good bibliography.

Wilstach, Frank J.
Wild Bill Hickok, The Prince of Pistoelers. New York: Doubleday, Page and Co., 1926. 304 pp., illus.

JESSE HOLMES

Boggs, Ralph S.
"Running down the Fool Killer." *TFSP* 14: 169–173, 1938.
More data on Jesse Holmes.

Leisy, Ernest E.
"Jesse Holmes, the Fool Killer." *TFSP* 8:152–156, 1930.

Southern Literary Messenger. 1862. p. 693.

CALAMITY JANE

Aikman, Duncan
Calamity Jane, and the Other Lady Wildcats. New York: Henry Holt, 1927. 347 pp., illus., and Blue Ribbon Books, 1937.

Hueston, Ethel
Calamity Jane. Indianapolis: Bobbs-Merrill, 1937.

JESSE JAMES

Botkin, Ben
Jesse James. In: *A Treasury of American Folklore,* (pp. 107–113). New York: Crown Publishers, 1944.

Buel, James W.
The Border Outlaws. An authentic and thrilling history of the most noted bandits of ancient and modern times, the Younger brothers, Jesse and Frank James, and their comrades in crime. St. Louis: Historical Publ. Co., 1881. 148 pp., illus.

Dacus, Joseph A.
Illustrated Lives and Adventures of Frank and Jesse James, and the Younger Brothers, The Noted Western Outlaws. St. Louis: N. D. Thompson and Co., 1881.

Gannett, Lewis
Sweet Land, illustrated by Ruth Chrisman Gannett. Garden City, N. Y.: The Sundial Press, 1934. viii, 237 pp., illus.
The story of a month's holiday exploring America by automobile, gathered in the author's column in the N. Y. Herald Tribune entitled "Books and Things."

Hubbard, Freeman H.
"And They Laid Jesse James in His Grave." In: *Railroad Avenue,* (pp. 105–124). New York: McGraw-Hill Book Company, 1945.

Love, Robertus
The Rise and Fall of Jesse James. New York: G. P. Putnam's Sons, 1926. 446 pp.

Triplett, Frank
The Life, Times, and Treacherous Death of Jesse James. The only correct and authorized edition. The facts and incidents dictated by Mrs. Jesse James, and Mrs. Zerelda Samuel, his mother. St. Louis, Chicago: J. H. Chambers and Co., 1882. 416 pp., illus.

CASEY JONES

Alderson, William
"On the Wobbley "Casey Jones" and other Songs" *CFQ* 1:373–376, 1942.
Gives also notes on Joe Hill, and 4 stanzas of 50,000 Lumberjacks from Idaho.

Botkin, Ben
Casey Jones. In: *A Treasury of American Folklore,* (pp. 241–246). New York: Crown Publishers, 1944.

Casey Jones, Engineer.
In: *Erie Railroad Magazine* 24 (No. 2) :13, 44, 1928. (April) See also Vol. 28.

Hathaway, Laurence J.
"The Epic Ride of Casey Jones." The engineer sped throughout the flaming hills to perilous Death Gulch Trestle." *Esquire* 23 (No. 5) :75, 1945.
A semi-fictionalized narration of Casey Jones' exploits.

Hubbard, Freeman H.
Casey Jones's Trip to the Promised Land. In: *Railroad Avenue,* (pp. 5–24). New York: McGraw-Hill Book Company, 1945.

Shapiro, Irwin
Casey Jones and Locomotive No. 638. New York: Julian Messner, 1944. Unpaged.
A story based on the song about that brave engineer Casey Jones, with illustrations by Donald McKay.

CAPTAIN KIDD

Bonner, Willard H.
Pirate Laureate: The Life and Legends of Captain Kidd. New Brunswick, N. J.: Rutgers University Press, 1947. 239 pp., bibl.

Spofford, Harriet E.
The True Account of Captain Kidd. In: *New England Legends.* Boston: J. R. Osgood & Co., 1871. 40 pp., illus.

LAFITTE, THE PIRATE

Beazley, Julia
"The Uneasy Ghost of Lafitte." *TFSP* 3:185–189, 1924.

Littlejohn, E. G.
"Life and Legends of Lafitte the Pirate." *TFSP* 3:179–185, 1924.

Thompson, Ray M.
The Land of Lafitte the Pirate. Photographs by Eugene Delcroix. Drawings by Tildne Landry. New Orleans, La.: Jefferson Parish Yearly Review, 435 Metairie Road, 1944. 128 pp.
A history in words and pictures of the Louisiana Bayouland of Jean Lafitte.

Webb, J. O.
"Lafitte Lore." *TFSP* 3:189–191, 1924.

LOPEZ

Morrison, Frederick
"Don José, The Love Mad Lopez." *CFQ* 1:369–371, 1942.
Legendary figure of Southwestern U. S.

JOE MAGARAC

Botkin, Ben
The Saga of Joe Magarac: Steelman. In: *A Treasury of American Folklore,* (pp. 246–254). New York: Crown Publishers, 1944.

Carmer, Carl
Joe Magerac: Down In a Coal Mine. In: *America Sings,* (pp. 116–124). New York: Alfred A. Knopf, 1942.

Francis, Owen
"Joe Magarac: Steelman." *Scribner's Magazine* 90 (No. 5):505–511, 1931.

O'Reilly, Edward
"Joe Magarac." *The Century Magazine* 106:827–833, 1923.

DAN MATTHEWS

Wright, Harold Bell
The Calling of Dan Matthews. New York: A. L. Bart Co., 1909.

KLONDIKE MIKE

Denison, Merrill
Klondike Mike: An Alaskan Odyssey. Illustrated. End paper maps. New York: William Morron and Co., 1943. 393 pp.
"Here is a parade of incredible human beings who played roles in the Alaskan gold fantasy, from such heart-warming characters as Jimmie the Goat, to such abandoned ones as Diamond-tooth Gertie and Mary the Pig—and standing before his vivid picture is Klondike Mike Mahoney, 6 ft. 2, red-headed, and with heart and strength for three men."

GIB MORGAN

Boatright, Moody C.
Gib Morgan: Minstrel of the Oil Fields. Austin, Tex.: Texas Folklore Society Publications 20, 1945. xii, 104 pp., illus.

OLD NEWT

Land, Myrtle Sloan
"Old Newt, the Practical Joker." *TFSP* 19:149–154, 1944.

EMPEROR NORTON

Lane, Allen Stanley
Emperor Norton, the Mad Monarch of America. Caldwell, Idaho: The Caxton Printers, Ltd., 1939. 286 pp.

ANNIE OAKLEY

Holbrook, Stewart
Little Annie Oakley and Other Rugged People. New York: The Macmillan Company, 1948. 239 pp.
"A collection of anecdotal sketches, of curious personages, it is written with the speed and conversational raciness of a man who forever is imagining himself in the presence of open-mouthed listeners." (Lloyd Lewis). The gallery of characters, besides Little Annie, consists of Calamity Jane, the boozy strumpet of Deadwood; Big Fred Hewlett, the two-fisted bartender and museum man of the Northwest; Ned Buntline, creator of the dime novel and of Buffalo Bill; Ed Schiefflin, the miner who named Tombstone; Joe Knowles, the original "Nature Man," Okay Fuller, the king of the "bull cooks" in the logging country; Little Luke Short, the wistful gambler and killer of boastful gamblers; Gilbert Patten, the gentle hack who created the Homeric Frank Merriwell; Kit Carson, the iron man of the mountain men; Henry Macloy, the neolithic corporal of the A.E.F.; and Jim Turnow, the mad Tarzan of the Northwest.

JUDGE PARKER

Botkin, Ben
Judge Isaac Parker. In: *A Treasury of American Folklore,* p. 132, 147. New York: Crown Publishers, 1944.

Harman, S. W.
Hell on the Border. (The reign of "Hanging Judge" Isaac C. Parker.) Fort Smith, Arizona: Phoenix Publ. Co., 1898. xiii, 714 pp.

SAM PATCH

BIBLIOGRAPHY

Dorson, Richard M.
"Sam Patch—Bibliography." *NYFQ* 1 (3): 151, 1945.

GENERAL STUDIES AND COLLECTIONS

Botkin, Ben
Sam Patch. In: *A Treasury of New England Folklore,* (pp. 4, 221). New York: Crown Publishers, 1947.

Clauson, James Earl
These Plantations, foreword by Sevelton Brown, and illus. by Milton Halladay and Paule Loring. Providence: Printed by the Roger Williams Press, E. A. Johnson Co., 1937. iii, 119 pp. maps.
"The tales, sketches, essays... which make up this volume have been chosen from a much larger number written for, and published in, the Evening Bulletin of Providence under the heading "These Plantations."—Foreword. Experiences of Sam Patch (pp. 70–72).

Dorson, Richard M.
"Sam Patch, Jumping Hero." *NYFQ* 1 (No. 3):133–151, 1945.

Finn, Henry J. (ed.)
American Comic Annual. Illus. by D. C. Johnson. Boston: Richardson, Lord & Holbrook, 1831. (pp. 216–220), front, illus.

Foreman, Edward R. (ed.)
Centennial History of Rochester, N. Y. Rochester: 1931. iv. pp. 79. 1. front illus., plates, ports, maps. col. coat of arms. (Lettered on cover: The Rochester historical society. Publication fund series.) vol. 4 compiled and edited by Ed. R. Foreman, city historian, under direction of the Board of trustees of the Rochester Public Library, Charles Hastings Wiltsie, President and Mayor Charles S. Owen.

Grieve, Robert
An Illustrated History of Pawtucket, Central Falls, and Vicinity. Pawtucket: 1897, (pp. 101–101).

Haliburton, Thomas Chandler
Sam Slick, the Clockmaker, or the sayings and doings of Sam Slick of Slickville. Philadelphia: Carey, Lea & Blanchard, 1837.

Hawthorne, Nathaniel
Rochester. In: *Tales, Sketches, and Other Papers,* (pp. 17–18). Boston and New York: Houghton, Mifflin and Company, 1883.

Howells, William Dean
Their Wedding Journey, illus. by Augustus Hoppin. Boston: J. R. Osgood & Co., 1872. (pp. 119–126), 287 pp., illus.

Kelley, Jonathan F.
Dan Marble: A Biographical Sketch. New York: 1851, (pp. 88, 91, 93–94).

Longwell, Charles P.
Historic Totowa Falls: and vicinity in art, literature, events; (pen drawing by Author). Paterson, N. J.: Call Printing & Publishing Co., 1942. (pp. 36–40).

Parker, Jenny M.
Rochester: A Story Historical. Rochester: Scranton, Wetmore & Co., 1884. viii, 412 pp. front., illus., (pp. 184–191).

UNCLE REMUS

Field, Rachel
American Folk and Fairy Tales. New York: Charles Scribner's Sons, 1929.
Includes tale of Uncle Remus.

Gerber, A.
"Uncle Remus Traced to the Old World." *JAFL* 6:245–257, 1893.

Harris, Joel Chandler
Uncle Remus and His Friends. New York: D. Appleton-Century Co., 1892.

————.
Uncle Remus, His Songs and His Sayings. Illustrated by A. B. Frost. New York: D. Appleton-Century Co., 1938. 256 pp. new and revised edition, first publ. 1880.

Parsons, Elsie C.
"Joel Chandler Harris and Negro Folklore." Review of *Uncle Remus Returns* by J. C. Harris. *Dial* 64:491–493, 1919.

OREGON SMITH

Carmer, Carl
Oregon Smith: Old Dan Tucker. In: *America Sings,* (pp. 76–84). New York: Alfred A. Knopf, 1942.

Halpert, H., and Robinson, Emma
"Oregon" Smith, an Indiana folk Hero." *SFQ* 6:163–168, 1942.

Jansen, William Hugh
"More on "Oregon" Smith." *HFB* 3:73–74, 1944.

BIG FOOT SPENCER

Parks, Edd Winfield
Long Hunter: The Story of Big Foot Spencer. New York: Farrar and Rinehart, 1942.
The hero of the Tennessee frontier whose exploits have become almost legendary.

STACKALEE

Botkin, B. A.
Stackalee. In: *A Treasury of American Folklore*, (pp. 122–131). New York: Crown Publishers, 1944.

Spencer, Onah L.
"Stackalee." *Direction* 4 (No. 5):14–17, 1941.

ROARING RALPH STACKPOLE

Bird, Robert Montgomery
Nick of the Woods, the Jibbenainosay; the wandering demon of the forest, and the howl of the red man. New York: Turner and Fisher, 186–, 36 pp., illus.
The adventures of Roaring Ralph Stackpole, "rascally horse thief and stentorian braggart."

Botkin, B. A.
Ralph Stackpole. In: *A Treasury of American Folklore*, pp. 4, 12. New York: Crown Publishers, 1944.

BELLE STARR

Rascoe, Burton
Belle Starr, "The Bandit Queen." New York: Random House, 1941. viii, 340 pp. front. plates, ports.
Contains lore of Billy the Kid. The true story of the romantic and exciting career of the daring and glamorous lady famed in legend and story throughout the West.... The true facts about the dastardly deeds and the come-uppance of such Dick Turpins, Robin Hoods, and Rini Rinaldos as the Youngers, the Jameses, the Daltons, the Starrs, the Doolins and the Jenningses. The real story with court records and contemporary newspaper accounts and testimony of old Lesters, here and there in the Southwest. Bibl. (pp. 299–336.)

MOSES STOCKING

Pound, Louise
Moses Stocking. In: *Nebraska Strong Men.* SFQ 7:133–143, 1943.

STORMALONG

Botkin, B. A.
Stormalong. In: *A Treasury of American Folklore*, pp. 178, 185, 247, 834. New York: Crown Publishers, 1944.

Carmer, Carl
Stormalong. In: *America Sings.* (pp. 28–36). New York: Alfred A. Knopf, 1942.

Shay, Frank
Here's Audacity! American Legendary Heroes. New York: The Macaulay Co., 1930. (pp. 17–31).

Shapiro, Irwin
How Old Stormalong Captured Moch a Dick. Illustrated by Donald McKay. New York: Julian Meissner, Inc., 1942. 48 pp.

DAD STREETER

"Reminiscences of Dad Streeter."
Nebraska Folklore Pamphlet 19. Federal Writers' Project in Nebraska (Lincoln) Feb., 1939.

SIMON SUGG

Botkin, B. A.
Simon Sugg. In: *A Treasury of American Folklore*, p. 3. New York: Crown Publishers, 1944.

Hooper, Johnson Jones
Simon Suggs' Adventures. Americus, Ga.: The Americus Book Co., 1928.

BIG FOOT WALLACE

Botkin, B. A.
"Big Foot" Wallace. In: *A Treasury of American Folklore*, pp. 133, 157–174, 323, 560. New York: Crown Publishers, 1944.

Carmer, Carl
Big-Foot Wallace: Texas Rangers. In: *America Sings*, (pp. 228–236). New York: Alfred A. Knopf, 1942.

Duval, John C.
The Adventures of Big-Foot Wallace, the Texas Ranger and Hunter. Philadelphia: Claxton, Remsen and Haffelfinger, Macon, Ga.: J. W. Burke and Co., 1870. 309 pp.

Vestal, Stanley
Big Foot Wallace. Boston: Houghton Mifflin Co., 1942.
A great character in Texan pioneer life whose deeds have become legend and lore of the Southwest and in Texas in particular.

THE YOUNGER BROTHERS

Botkin, B. A.
Younger Boys. In: *A Treasury of American Folklore*, p. 71. New York: Crown Publishers, 1944.

Dacus, Joseph A.
Illustrated Lives and Adventures of Frank and Jesse James, and the Younger Brothers, the Noted Western Outlaws. St. Louis: N. D. Thompson and Co., 1881.

Younger, Cole
The Story of Cole Younger, By Himself. Chicago: Press of the Henneberry Co., 1903. 123 pp., illus.

SONGS OF AMERICAN CHARACTERS

GENERAL COLLECTIONS

See: American Folksong and Ballad Collections, pp. 85-90, 118-20.

Finger, Charles J.
Frontier Ballads. Garden City, N. Y.: Doubleday, Page and Company, 1927.
Music and text. Includes many desperado tunes.

Shay, Frank
Drawn from the Wood: Consolidations in Words and Music for Pious Friends and Drunken Companions. New York: The Macmillan Company, 1927.

———.
More Pious Friends and Drunken Companions. Illustrated by John Held, Jr. New York: The Macauley Company, 1928. 190 pp., music-tunes only.

———.
My Pious Friends and Drunken Companions. Illustrated by John Held, Jr. New York: The Macauley Company, 1927. Music.

———.
The Pious Friends and Drunken Companions of Conviviality: My Pious Friends and Drunken Companions, and More Drunken Friends and Pious Companions. Illustrated by John Held, Jr. New York: The Macaulay Company. 1936. 190 pp., illus., music-tunes only.
This book is a combination of these two classics.

Sherwin, Sterling, and Powell, Harry A.
Bad Man Songs of the Wild and Wooly West; with an introduction by Peggy Walton. Cleveland: S. Fox Pub. Co., 1933. 46 pp.
Arranged for voice and piano, also with chords for ukulele, guitar, banjo. A good representative collection.

JOHNNY APPLESEED
ARRANGEMENTS
(None of these are folk tunes.)
———: *Voice and Piano*

Siegmeister, Elie
"Johnny Appleseed." In: *Treasury of American Song,* ed. by Olin Downes and Elie Siegmeister. New York: Alfred A. Knopf, 1943.
Arranged for voice and piano, set to the poem of Rosemary and Stephen Vincent Benét. The tune is not a folksong. It is an original song.

Wolfe, Jacques
"Johnny Appleseed." New York: C. Fischer: Voice & piano.
Not really a folk song, but a delightful original setting to the text of Merrick F. McCarthy.

———: *Mixed Voices*

Gaul, Harvey B.
Old Johnny Appleseed. Cantata for Treble Voices. Boston: C. C. Birchard & Co., 1926.

Kettering, Eunice Lea
Johnny Appleseed. Choral Arrangement, based on Vachel Lindsay's "In Praise of Johnny Appleseed." MS.

Kubik, Gail
"In Praise of Johnny Appleseed." For baritone, SATB, and full orchestra. MS.

———: *Orchestra*

Manton, Robert W.
Incidental Music for H. B. Steven's Johnny Appleseed and Paul Bunyan. Boston: Baker, 1931.

———: *Stage Work*

Loomis, Harvey Worthington, and Stevens, David
Johnny Appleseed. Operetta in One Act for Children. Cincinnati: Willis Music Co., 1925.

SAM BASS
ARRANGEMENTS
———: *Voice and Piano*

"Sam Bass."
Fox, O. J.: Carl Fischer.

ROY BEAN
ARRANGEMENTS
———: *Voice and Piano*

"Roy Bean. Texas Frontier Ballad."
Fox, O. J.: Schirmer.

"Roy Bean. Texas Frontier Ballad."
Guion, D.: Schirmer.

PAUL BUNYAN
ARRANGEMENTS
———: *Choral*

James, Dorothy
Paul Bunyan. Baritone Solo, Youth Chorus, and Orchestra. MS.

Siegmeister, Elie
"Paul Bunyan." MS: TTBB, piano.

———: *Orchestra*

Bergsma, William
Paul Bunyan, a Ballet for Puppets and Solo Dancers. Rochester, N. Y.: The Composer, MS.
Also arranged as a suite for school orchestra, and published by Carl Fischer, N. Y. C.

Howland, Russell
"Babe, the Blue Ox." Ann Arbor, Michigan. MS.
A March, first performed at the University of Wisconsin Paul Bunyan Homecoming in 1935.

Kreutz, Arthur
Paul Bunyan. New York: C. Fischer: Orchestra.

———.
"Winter of the Blue Snow," from Paul Bunyan. New York: C. Fischer: Orchestra.

Manton, Robert W.
Incidental Music for H. B. Steven's Johnny Appleseed and Paul Bunyan. Boston: Baker, 1931.

Moross, Jerome
"Paul Bunyan, an American Saga."
First performed by Charles Wiedman, in New York, 1935. MS in possession of Mr. Weidman.

Rich, John K., Grant, Allan, and Maddy, J. E.
Paul Bunyan—A Legend of the North Woods. New York: Chappell, 1940.
A Suite in four movements for orchestra and chorus.

————————: *Stage Work*

Britten, Benjamin
Paul Bunyan. An opera. New York: Boosey and Hawkes, Ltd.

KIT CARSON
ARRANGEMENTS
————————: *Mixed Voices*

Protheroe, Daniel
Kit Carson, the Story of a Pioneer, Cantata for baritone solo, chorus (SAB). Text by Frederick A. Martin. Boston: Willis.

DAVY CROCKETT
STUDIES
Beazley, Julia
"The Ballad of Davy Crockett." In: *Texas and Southwestern Lore,* edited by J. Frank Dobie. *TFSP* 6:205–206, 1927.
Text and tune.

The National Songster: Embellished with Twenty-five Splendid Engravings. Illustrative of the American Victories in Mexico. By an American Officer. New York, n.d.
Contains a number of Crockett songs (texts only).

ARRANGEMENTS
————————: *Orchestra*

Ryder, T. P.
David Crockett March. Boston: White and Smith Company, 1874.

Moross, Jerome
The Eccentricities of Davy Crockett. Choral, baritone, mixed chorus, orchestra, MS. This work is also composed as a ballet.

FRANKIE AND JOHNNY
ARRANGEMENTS
————————: *Voice and Piano*

"Frankie and Albert."
In: *The American Songbag,* by Carl Sandburg, p. 76–. New York: Harcourt, Brace and Co.
With piano accompaniment.

Frankie and Johnny (Song).
The saga of Frankie & Johnny, beautifully engraved by John Held, Jr. New York: W. V. McKee, 1930. 49 pp., illus.

"Frankie and Johnny."
Kendrick, Merle T.: Voice, piano, and ukelele.

"Frankie and Johnny."
Rodgers, Jimmie: Voice, piano, and ukelele.

Frankie and Johnnie. All Star Motion Picture. The song was printed by H. Engel, N. Y., 1934.

"Frankie and Johnnie."
In: "Old Songs Men Have Sung," by Robert W. Gordon. *Adventure,* August 20, 1923, May 10, 1925.

"Frankie and Johnnie." Melody and text. In *My Pious Friends and Drunken Companions,* by Frank Shay, p. 65. New York.

"Frankie and Johnnie." Melody and text. In: *Read 'Em and Weep,* by Sigmund Spaeth, p. 34. New York: Doubleday, Page & Co., 1926.

"Frankie Blues."
In: *The American Songbag,* by Carl Sandburg, p. 82. New York: Harcourt Brace and Co., 1927.

Frey, Hugo, arr.
"Frankie and Johnny." New York: Robbins Music Corp., 1933.
Vocal with piano accompaniment, and ukelele arrangement.

"Josie." In: *The American Songbag,* by Carl Sandburg, p. 84. New York: Harcourt Brace & Co., 1927.
A variant of Frankie and Johnny.

Krouse, H. Sylvester, arr.
"Frankie and Johnny." New York: E. B. Marks Music Corp., 1933.
Vocal, with piano accompaniment, and ukelele arrangement.

Leighton, Harry, arr.
"Frankie and Johnny, or, You'll Miss Me in the Days to Come." New York: T. Taylor, 1912.
Vocal, with piano accompaniment.

Marvin, Frankie
Frankie and Johnny Marvin Folio of Down Home Songs.
Vocal, piano, and guitar accomp.

Potter, Harold
"Frankie and Johnny." Philadelphia, Pa.: Morris Music Co., 1935.
Vocal, with piano accomp.

"Sadie." In: *The American Songbag,* by Carl Sandburg, p. 86. New York: Harcourt Brace & Co., 1927.

————————: *Choral*

"Frankie and Johnny."
Clokey, Joseph W.: TTBB(2), a cap.

"Frankie and Johnny."
Clokey, Joseph W.: SSATTB, a cap.

————: *Orchestra*

Dale, Jimmy
"Frankie and Johnny (You'll Miss Me in the Days to Come)." Fox trot by Leighton Bros. and Ren Shields, arranged for orchestra by Jimmy Dale. New York: Shapiro, Bernstein & Co., 1935.

————: *Stage Work*

Bonner, Eugene MacDonald
Frankie and Johnnie—Opera Comique. MS., for small orchestra.

Huston, John
Frankie and Johnny; illustrated by Covarrubias. New York: A. & C. Boni, 1930. 160 pp., illus.
An adaptation for the stage of the song "Frankie and Johnny," based on the many versions which Mr. Huston has discovered throughout the country. Twenty of these versions appear at the back of the book, with a note on the St. Louis one, "Frankie and Albert," which is the most authentic.

Kubik, Gail
Frankie and Johnnie—Ballet Sequence. MS. for Dance band and vocalist.

Moross, J.
Frankie and Johnny—Ballet. Stage Work, for Women's Trio and Orchestra. Chappell Publishing Co., New York.

Schimmerling, Hans
Frankie and Johnny, op. 39. Conception and construction by Bogia Horska. 1940. 34 pp.
Vocal, with pantomine.

JOHN HENRY

STUDIES

"A Fragment of 'John Hardy' from Kentucky." *Berea Quarterly,* p. 26, (October) 1910.

Bascom, Louise Rand
"Ballads and Songs of Western North Carolina." *JAFL* 22:247–249, 1909.
One variant of 'John Hardy', also mention of 'John Henry' as being sung in the mountains of North Carolina.

Campbell, Olive Dame, and Sharp, Cecil J.
English Folk-Songs from the Southern Appalachians. New York: G. P. Putnam's Sons, 1917.
No. 87 is a variant of 'John Hardy' with music.

Cox, John H.
Folk-Songs of the South. Boston, Mass.: Harvard University Press, 1925.
Discussion of 'John Hardy' on pages 175–188. Nine variants of 'John Hardy', one of which is 'John Henry'.

————.
"John Hardy." *JAFL* 32:505–520, 1919.
Five variants of 'John Hardy'.

————.
"The Yew Pine Mountain." *AS:* 226–227, (February) 1927.
The Henry-Hardy problem mentioned incidentally, Cox indicating that he has revised his earlier opinion. One new variant of 'John Hardy'.

Handy, W. C.
Blues. New York: Albert and Charles Boni, 1926.
Part of "John Henry Blues," pp. 138, based on a folk version of the hammer song.

Lomax, John A.
"Some Types of American Folk-Song." *JAFL* 18:14, 1905.
An excellent variant of 'John Henry' reported to have been heard in Kentucky and West Virginia.

Johnson, Guy B.
Ebony and Topaz—"John Henry": A Negro Legend. New York: Opportunity Publishing Company, National Urban League, 1927. Charles S. Johnson, editor.
A general discussion of the legend. One variant of the ballad, one of the hammer song, with tunes.

————, and Odum, Howard W.
Negro Workday Songs. Chapel Hill: University of North Carolina Press, 1926.
Chapter XIII is entitled "John Henry: Epic of the Negro Workingman." Eleven southern variants of the ballad, four hammer songs with general discussion. A tune on page 248.

Perrow, E. C.
"Songs and Rhymes from the South." *JAFL* 26:123–173, 1913.
Four hammer songs, one with tune, and one ballad, pp. 163–165, from Mississippi, Tennessee, Kentucky and Indiana.

Sandburg, Carl
"Songs of the Old Frontiers." *Country Gentleman,* (April) 1927.
Contains one "John Henry" ballad with music.

Scarborough, Dorothy
On the Trail of Negro Folk-Songs. Cambridge, Mass.: Harvard University Press, 1925. pp. 218–222.
Six hammer songs, one tune, brief comments on 'John Henry' whom the author appears to identify with 'John Hardy'.

Tally, Thomas W.
Negro Folk Rhymes. New York: The Macmillan Company, 1922.
One variant of 'John Henry' on page 105.

White, Newman I.
American Negro Folk-Songs. Cambridge, Mass.: Harvard University Press, 1928.
Three "John Henry" ballad variants, several hammer song types, one tune.

ARRANGEMENTS

————: *Voice and Piano*

Sandburg, Carl
The American Songbag. New York: Harcourt, Brace and Company, 1927.
> A twelve stanza variant of "John Henry" appears on pages 24–25. The tune is the same as that in "Country Gentleman," April, 1927. Other "John Henry" references in this book are: "Drivin' Steel, page 150; "If I Die a Railroad Man," page 362; "Ever Since Uncle John Henry Been Dead," page 376; "My Old Hammah," page 457.

"John Henry."
> Johnson, H.: C. Fischer: Voice and piano.

————: *Mixed Voices*

"John Henry."
> Niles-Groff: Schirmer: SSAATTBB, Ten. Solo, a cap.

"John Henry."
> Siegmeister, E.: Carl Fischer: SATB with Ten. solo.

Curtis-Burlin, Natalie
Negro Folk-Songs, Hampton Series. New York: G. Schirmer, 1918–1919.
> In Vol. IV—an arrangement of SATB.

————: *Orchestra*

Copland, Aaron
John Henry—Railroad Ballad. Arranged for Chamber Orchestra, MS.

Stringfield, Lamar
The Legend of John Henry—Symphonic Ballad. New York: J. Fischer: for full orchestra.

————: *Stage Work*

Bradford, Roark
John Henry, a play with music. Music comprised by Jacques Wolfe with eight stage sets designed for the play, by Albert Johnson. New York: Harper and Bros., 1939. Illus., music.

JESSE JAMES

STUDIES

"Jesse James." In: *The American Songbag,* by Carl Sandburg, pp. 420–421. New York: Harcourt Brace and Co., 1926. Arranged for voice and piano.

Norville, Josephine
"Songs of Jesse James." *AS* 5 (No. 3):256–257, 1930.

CASEY JONES

STUDIES AND COLLECTIONS

Alderson, William
"On the wobbly 'Casey Jones' and other songs." *CFQ* 1:373–376, 1942.
> Gives also notes on "Joe Hill" and four stanzas of "50,000 Lumberjacks from Idaho."

Emrich, Duncan
'Casey Jones' and Other Ballads of the Mining West; with illustrations by Bob Cormack. Denver, Colo.: Author's Edition, (1615 Grant Street), 1942. 16 pp.

————.
"Mining Songs." *SFQ* 6:103–106, 1942.
> Words and music of 'Cousin Jack' and 'Casey Jones' and words only of 'Liberty Engine Co. #1 from Nevada'.

ARRANGEMENTS

————: *Voice and Piano*

"Casey Jones."
> Kugel, Alfred. In: *Humor in American Song,* Arthur Loesser, ed. (pp. 208–209). New York: Howell, Soskin, Publ., 1942.

"Casey Jones."
> Newton, E.: Southern California Music Co.

————: *Orchestra*

"Casey Jones."
> Green, R.: New Music Co.: For piano and percussion orchestra.

"Three Inventories of Casey Jones."
> Green, Ray: MS: Piano and orchestra.

BILLY THE KID

ARRANGEMENTS

————: *Orchestra*

Copland, Aaron
Billy the Kid—Suite from the Ballet. New York: Boosey and Hawkes—for Orchestra.

UNCLE REMUS

ARRANGEMENTS

————: *Piano*

Gilbert, Henry F.
"Uncle Remus." In: *Three American Dances.* Boston: Boston Music Company.

Grant-Schaefer, G. A.
"Uncle Remus." New York: Schirmer: Piano (Med.)

MacDowell, Edward
Woodland Sketches, Op. 51, #7. From "Uncle Remus." London: Elkin and Company, Ltd.

RECORDS

————: *Individual Titles*

"Abe Lincoln."
> In: *Songs for Americans.* Earl Robinson, guitar.   TI—8

"Billy the Kid."
Vernon Dalhart, vocal-guitar. BR–100

"Casey Jones."
Alfred Drake. In: *Sing Out Sweet Land.*
DE–404

"Southern Casey Jones."
Jesse James, vocal-guitar. DE–7213

"Casey Jones."
André Kostelanetz, orchestra. BB–8233

"Casey Jones."
Riley Puckett, vocal and guitar. CO–113–D

"Casey Jones."
Vernon Dalhart, vocal-guitar. VI–20502

"Casey Jones."
Wolfe's Orchestra. DE–2562

"Mamma Have You Heard the News" (Casey Jones). In: *Recital from "American Songbag."*
Carl Sandburg, vocal-guitar. MU–11

"Frankie and Albert."
Lead Belly, vocal-guitar. MU–223

"Frankie and Johnny."
Alfred Drake. In: *Sing Out Sweet Land.*
DE–404

"Frankie and Johnny."
Guy Lombardo and His Royal Canadians.
DE–24288

"Jesse James."
In: *Frontier Ballads and Cowboy Songs.* Bill Bender, Clayton McMichon, and Dance Orchestra. ASCH–410

"Jesse James."
In: *Songs for Americans.* Earl Robinson, guitar. TI–8

"Jesse James."
Riley Puckett, vocal-guitar. CO–15033

"Sam Hall."
In: *Frontier Ballads and Cowboy Songs.* Bill Bender, Clayton McMichon, and Dance Orchestra. ASCH–410

"John Brown."
In: *Songs for Americans.* Earl Robinson, guitar. TI–8

"Death of John Henry."
Uncle Dave Macon, In: *Listen to Our Story.*
BR–1024

"John Hardy."
Eva Davis, solo-banjo. CO–167–D

"John Henry."
Sung by Arthur Bell at Cummins State Farm, Gould, Ark., 1939. In: *Album 3,* Recordings of American Folk Songs, Washington, D. C., 1943. AAFS15–B

"John Henry."
Richard Dyer-Bennet, vocal-guitar.
ASCH–461–3A

"John Henry."
Lead Belly, guitar-vocal; Sonny Terry, harmonica. ASCH–343–3B

"John Henry."
Salty Holmes and his Brown Country Boys.
DE–46116

"John Henry."
John Jacob Niles, tenor-dulcimer. V–2051

"John Henry."
John J. Niles. DISC–733

"John Henry."
Riley Puckett, vocal. CO–140031–D

"John Henry."
In: *Songs for Americans.* Earl Robinson, guitar. TI–8

"John Henry."
Spencer Trio: Billy Kyle, piano; Buster Bailey, clarinet; O'Neil Spencer, drums.
DE–63779

"John Henry."
Gid Tanner and Riley Puckett. CO–15019–D

"John Henry." (The Steel Driving Man).
Gid Tanner and His Skillet Lickers.
CO–15142–D

"John Henry."
Henry Thomas ("Ragtime Texas"), voice-whistling-guitar. VO–A–1094

"John Henry."
Josh White, vocal-guitar. KE–8138

"John Henry Was a Little Boy."
J. E. Mainer's Mountaineer's vocal-banjo-guitar. BB–6629–B

"John Henry Blues."
Earl Johnson and His Dixie Entertainers, vocal-fiddle-guitar-banjo. OK–45101

"John Henry Blues."
Dixieland Jazz Group. VI–27545

"John Henry Blues."
Vocal-guitar. CO–15019–D

"John Henry Blues."
Vocal-guitar. SI–3662

"Death of John Henry." (Steel Drivin' Man).
Uncle Dave Macon, voice-piano; Sam McGee, guitar. BR–112–A

"Death of John Henry."
Welby Toomey, same as Jennets.   SI–6005–A

"New John Henry Blues."
Bob and Joe Shelton and C. Fox, vocal-fiddle-banjo-guitar.   DE–5173

"The Nine Found Hammer."
Al Hopkins and His Buckle Busters. BR–177–A

"Joe Hill."
In: *Songs for Americans*. Earl Robinson, guitar.   TI–8

"Stack O'Lee Blues."
Johnny Dodds and His Chicago Boys. DE–1676

"Stacker Lee."
Woody Guthrie, vocal-guitar.   ASCH–347

"Stackerlee."
Furry Lewis.   BR–1024

Uncle Remus.
Norman Gordon. 2–10″.   VI–Y328

Uncle Remus Stories.
Sterling Holloway. 3–10″.   DE–A521

OUR WARS—FROM '76 TO WORLD WAR II

OUR WARS—FROM '76 TO WORLD WAR II

FOLKLORE

GENERAL STUDIES:
1776–1945

Coggeshall, George
History of American Privateers and Letters of Marque, during the war with England in the years 1812, '13, '14. Interspersed with several naval battles between American and British ships-of-war. New York: The Author, 1856. liv, 438 pp., front. pl.

Majors, C. L., comp.
World War Jokes, a compilation of after dinner stories and amusing anecdotes, all of which have a direct application to soldiers and sailors and servicemen of the World War period. Ramer, Tenn.: 1930. viii, 112 pp.

Matthews, William, and Wecter, Dixon
Our Soldiers Speak; 1775–1918. Boston: Little, Brown and Co., 1943. 365 pp.

Ribeiro, Joaquim
"Folklore de Guerra." *RBRJ:* 3; No. 6, pp. 153–171, 1943.
Diffusion and fusion of diverse folklore among soldiers of various cultures.

Sandoz, Mari
Tom-Walker. New York: Dial Press, 1947.
A chronicle of three generations of war veterans, —full of folklore of Civil War, World War I and and II periods. "The ways, the speech, the minutiae of daily life are vigorously reproduced."

SPEECH

Beukema, Herman
"West Point and the Gray-Clad Corps." *National Geographic Magazine* 69:777–789, 1936.
Terms used by the students.

Billman, J. I.
"Army Words." *AS* 1 (No. 10):564–565, 1926.

Colby, Elbridge
"Rhetoric in the Army." *AS* 1 (No. 4):221–225, 1926.

———.
"Soldier Speech." *AS* 11 (No. 1):50–63, 1936.

Garber, M. B.
A Modern Military Dictionary. Washington, D. C.: Published by the Author, 1936.

Fraser, Edward, and Gibbons, John
Soldier and Sailor Words and Phrases. London: Routledge and Sons, 1925.

Keeley, Mary Paxton
"A. E. F. English." *AS* 5 (No. 5):372–386, 1930.

McCartney, Eugene S.
"Additions to a Volume on the Slang and the Idioms of the World War." *Papers of the Michigan Academy of Sciences, Arts and Letters* 10:273–337, 1929.

McDavid, R. I.
"A Citadel Glossary." *AS* 14 (No. 1):23–32, 1939.
Cadet vernacular at the Citadel Military Academy of South Carolina.

Mencken, H. L.
"Some Words of Civil War Days." *AS* 10 (No. 4): 288, 1935.

Partridge, Eric
"Soldiers' Slang." *Quarterly Review* 256:347–359, 1931.

"The Army Has A Word For It."
Better English 2 (No. 6):50–51, 63, 1939.

"The Language of Hell."
Manchester Guardian Weekly 34:428, May 29, 1936.
"The American Colonial troops from New York and Rhode Island during the French and Indian War were reported to have been extremely profane."

"West Point Slang in 1878."
NYFQ 2 (No. 1):63–64, 1946.

SONGS OF OUR WARS

See: American Folksong and Ballad Collections, pp. 85-90, 118-120, American Songsters, pp. 527-541.

GENERAL STUDIES AND COLLECTIONS:
1776-1945

Boynton, Percy H.
"Patriotic Songs and Hymns." In: *The Cambridge History of American Literature* ed. by Trent, Erskine, Sherman and Van Doren. Vol. III (pp. 492–502). New York: The Macmillan Co., 1917. 3 vols. Reprinted in 1 vol. 1945.
The author discusses Songs from *Yankee Doodle* to *Over There* of World War I.

Browne, C. A.
The Story of Our National Ballads. New York: Crowell, 1931. 327 pp. rev. and enl.

Bunker Hill Songster. Containing National and Patriotic Songs. As sung by the Principal Vocalists. Woodcuts. Boston: Murphy, Printer and Publisher, Franklin Book Store, 184–. 34 pp.

Butler, Frances M.
"War Songs." *Lippincott's Magazine* 62:411–414, 1898.

Camp, F. B.
American Soldier Ballads. Los Angeles: G. Rice & Sons, 1917. xiii, 124 pp.

Converse, C. C.
"American War-Songs." *American Art Journal* 84:107–109, 1904.

————.
"American War Songs." *Open Court* 14:111–113, 1900.
Words only.

Croseley, Joseph W., arr.
The Book of Navy Songs. Collected by the Trident Literary Society of the United States Naval Academy. New York: Doubleday, Page and Company.

Dadmon, J. W., and Fuller, Arthur B.
Army and Navy Melodies. Boston: 1862.

Dolph, Edward Arthur, ed.
"Sound Off!" Soldier Songs from the Revolution to World War II. Music arranged by Philip Egner, illustrated by Lawrence Schick. New York: Farrar & Rinehart, 1942. xiii, 621 pp.
Songs are arranged for voice and piano. One of the best collections.

Eggleston, George Cary, ed.
American War Ballads and Lyrics; a collection of the songs and ballads of the Colonial Wars, the Revolution, the War of 1812–15, the War with Mexico, and the Civil War. New York: G. P. Putnam's Sons, 1889. 2 vols., illus.

Firth, C. H.
"Naval Songs and Ballads." *Navy Record Society* (English Navy) 1908.

Gus Williams' Camp-Fire Songster, a collection of Popular Patriotic Songs. New York: c. 1862. 70 pp.

Harrison Medal Minstrel; comprising a collection of the most popular and patriotic songs, illustrative of the enthusiastic feelings of a grateful but power-ridden people towards the gallant defender of their country. The Hero, the Patriot, the Farmer, the Statesman, and Philanthropist. 32 mo., original wrappers. Philadelphia: Grigg and Elliott. 192 pp.

Lawson, C. C. P.
Naval Ballads and Sea-Songs. London: Peter Davies, Ltd., 1933.

MacGill, P.
Soldier Songs. New York: E. P. Dutton Co., 1917. 120 pp.

Moore, Frank, ed.
Songs of the Soldiers. New York: G. P. Putnam, 1864. xv, 318 pp. The Red, White, and Blue Series.

Most Popular Songs of Patriotism. Chicago: Hinds, Hayden and Eldridge, 1916.

Oliver Ditson Company
American Patriotic Songs. Boston: Oliver Ditson Co., 1893. 88 pp.

Our National War Songs.
Cleveland: Brainard, 1884.

Petersen, C. S.
"Music of Marching Men up to 1865." *Etude* 56:361–362, (June) 1938.

Rimbault, Edward F.
"American National Songs." *Leisure Hour* 25: 90–92, 1876.
With music.

Scollard, C.
Ballads of American Bravery. The Silver Series of English and American Classics. New York: 1900.

Songs of the Soldiers and Sailors, U. S.
Washington, D. C.: 1917.

The American Sailor's Songster.
New York: P. J. Cozzans.

Uncle Sam's Naval and Patriotic Songster.
New York: P. J. Cozans, n.d.

Revolutionary War

General Studies and Collections

Allen, G. W.
"Naval Songs and Ballads." *Proceedings of the American Antiquarian Society* (N. S.) 35: 64–78.

Barney, S. E.
Songs of the Revolution: A paper read before the General David Humphrey Branch of the Connecticut Society of the Sons of the American Revolution. New Haven: 1893. 45 pp.

"A Camp Song of 1775 at Boston." *New England Historical and Genealogical Register, II,* 1857.

Fisher, William Arms
The Music that Washington Knew. Boston: Oliver Ditson Company, 1931. 44 pp.
Numerous musical examples included, and some tunes.

Goldman, Richard Franko, and Smith, Roger
Patriotic and Historical Music. In: *Landmarks of Early American Music,* 1760–1800, by Richard Franko Goldman and Roger Smith. New York: Schirmer: SATB.

Granville, Henry
"Songs of the Revolution." *Bachelor of Arts* 3:207–214, 1896.
Texts only.

Halliwell-Phillipps, James Orchard, coll. and ed.
The Early Naval Ballads of England. London: C. Richards, 1841. xii, 144 pp. (Percy Society—Early English Poetry, vol. II).

Howard, John Tasker, ed.
The Music of George Washington's Time. Washington, D. C.: Washington Building, 1931. 34 pp.
Numerous musical examples given.

Jackson, George Stuyvesant
Early Songs of Uncle Sam, with an introduction by Kenneth B. Murdock. Boston: Bruce Humphries, Inc., 1933. 297 pp., no music.

Kidson, Frank
"Some Guesses About 'Yankee Doodle'." *MQ* 3:98–103, 1917.

Loesser, Arthur, ed.
Humor in American Song. Music arranged by Alfred Kugel. New York: Howell, Soskin, Publ., 1942.
> Section—"Revolutionary Songs," contains 5 songs—voice and piano.

Mabie, Hamilton W.
"War-Songs of the Revolution." *Outlook* 59: 573–579, 1898.
> Without music.

Moore, Frank, ed.
Songs and Ballads of the American Revolution. Illustrated by the author. New York: D. Appleton & Company, 1856. xii, 394 pp. Reprinted in 1905, by Hurst & Co.
> Texts only.

National Songster, or, A Collection of the Most Admired Patriotic Songs on the Brilliant Victories, etc. Hagerstown: Gruber and May, 1814.

"Naval Songs and Ballads."
Blackwood 183:887–890, (June) 1908.

Neeser, Robert W.
American Naval Songs and Ballads. New Haven: Yale University Press, 1938.
> Texts only.

Newcomb, Lydia Bolles
"Songs and Ballads of the Revolution." *New England Magazine* 13 (n.s.):501–513, 1895–1896.
> Includes melodies.

"Paul Jones."
N. & Q. Ninth Series, 2:306, 353, 495.

Perry, Rob Roy, and Martens, Frederick H.
Great Days of the American Revolution. Phila.: Theodore Presser Co., SATB.
> Battles commemorated: Bunker Hill, 1775; Trenton, 1776; Saratoga, 1777; Flamborough Head, 1778; Stony Point, 1779; King's Mountain, 1780; Yorktown, 1781, and New York, 1783.

Platt, Charles Edward
Ballads of New Jersey in the Revolution. Morristown, N. J.: The Jerseyman Print, 1886. vi, 167 pp., illus., texts only.

Raymond, George Lansing
Ballads of the Revolution, and Other Poems. New York: G. P. Putnam's Sons, 1887. 194 pp.

"Revolutionary Poetry. Teaships. A New Song (to the Plaintive Tune of 'Hosier's Ghost')." *New England Historical and Genealogical Register* 11:337,1857.

Songs of the Revolution—Songs of the Late War —Naval and Military Victories—and Patriotic Odes. New York: Wilson and Co., 1844. Broadside.
> Contains the words of 25 popular songs of the American Revolution and the War of 1812. Also, with music, "Ode to Science" . . . arranged expressly for the 'Brother Jonathan,' for three or four voices." On verso, illustrations of Revolutionary scenes, portraits of generals, prose sketches, etc.

Stone, W. L.
Ballads and Poems relating to the Burgoyne Campaign. Albany, N. Y.: J. Munsell's Sons, 1893. 359 pp.

The American Naval and Patriotic Songster; as sung at various places of amusement in honor of Hull, Jones, Decatur. Perry, Bainbridge, Lawrence and etc., "Don't Give Up the Ship." By - - - -, plates, 32 mo. original cloth and title label, pp. 256. Baltimore: 1836.

The Eagle and the Harp; a collection of patriotic and humorous songs and odes. Baltimore: 1812.

War of 1812

General Studies

Brewster, Paul G.
"The Battle of New Orleans." *SFQ* 1, (No. 3): 25–29, 1937.
> An example of communal composition. The War of 1812.

Pearson, John C.
"Balladry of 1812." *NYFQ* 2 (No. 1):60, 1946.
> A six line jingle with obvious reference to the war of 1812.

War with Mexico

General Studies and Collections

McCarty, William, comp.
National Songs, Ballads, and Other Patriotic Poetry, Chiefly Relating to the War of 1846. Philadelphia: W. McCarty, 1852.

The Rough and Ready Songster: Embellished with twenty-five splendid engravings, illustrative of the American Victories in Mexico. By an American Officer. New York: Nafis and Cornish, Publisher, 1848. vi, 250 pp.
> Words only, some tunes indicated by title.

The Civil War

General Studies and Collections

Allan, Francis D.
Allan's Lone Star Ballads. A Collection of Southern Patriotic songs, made during the Confederate times. Galveston, Tex.: J. D. Sawyer, 1874. iv, 222 pp.
> Texts only, some of the tunes indicated.

Beadle's Dime Song Book, No. 11.
New York: Beadle and Company, 1863.

Beadle's Dime Songs for the War.
New York: Beadle and Company, 1861. 40 pp.

Browne, F. F., ed.
Bugle-Echoes: A collection of poems of the Civil War, Northern and Southern. New York: White, Stokes and Allen, 1886. x, 336 pp.

Child, Francis James
War-Songs for Freemen. Dedicated to the Army of the United States: and especially to the 2d, 15th, and 20th Regiments of Massachusetts Volunteers... and to the 43d, 44th, and 45th Regiments.... Boston: Ticknor & Fields, 1863. 56 pp., music.

Dolph, Edward Arthur
"The Singing Soldiers of the Sixties." *New York Times Magazine,* p. 9, (May 26) 1929.

Ellinger, Esther Parker
The Southern War Poetry of the Civil War. Philadelphia: Diss. University of Pennsylvania, 1918.

Jones, S. B.
Twenty Favorite Songs for the Grand Army of the Republic. Omaha: Republican Publishing and Printing House, 1882. 32 pp.

"Just Before the Battle, Mother."
N. & Q. Tenth Series, 4:208.

Mason, Miss E. V.
The Southern Poems of the War. Collected and arranged by Miss E. V. M. Baltimore: J. Murphy and Company, 1867. 456 pp.

Moore, Frank
Anecdotes, Poetry and Incidents of the War: North and South. New York: Publication Office, Bible House, J. Porteous, 1867. 560 pp.

———.
Personal and Political Ballads. New York: George P. Putnam, 1864. 368 pp.
"This volume contains a selection from the best Political and Personal Ballads that have appeared since the commencement of the present Rebellion. They have been gathered from various sources, Rebel as well as National, and are presented to the reader without note or comment." (F. M.)

———, coll.
Rebel Rhymes and Rhapsodies. New York: G. P. Putnam, 1864.

———, ed.
Songs and Ballads of the Southern People, 1861–1865. New York: D. Appleton & Company, 1886. 324 pp.

———.
Songs of the Soldiers. New York: G. P. Putnam, 1864. xv, 318 pp.

———, coll.
The Civil War in Song and Story: 1860–1865. New York: P. F. Collier, 1889. 500 pp.

———.
The Songs and Ballads of the Southern People. New York: D. Appleton and Co., 1886. 317 pp. Words only.

Mitchell, Mrs. M. L.
Songs of the Confederacy and Plantation Melodies. Cincinnati: The Geo. B. Jennnings Company, 1901.

Murphy, Jeannette Robinson
"Gawd Bless Dem Yankees!" *Century* (New York) 56:797–798, 1898. New series. Vol. 34.

Oliver Ditson Company
War Songs for Anniversaries and Gatherings of Soldiers, to which is added a selection of songs and hymns for Memorial Day. The choruses of all the songs are arranged for male voices. Boston: Oliver Ditson Co., 1883. 96 pp.

Our National War Songs.
Grand Old War Songs, Battle Songs, National Hymns, Memorial Hymns, Decoration Day Songs, Quartettes, etc. With accompaniment for piano or organ. Chicago: S. Brainard Sons Co., 1892. 224 pp.

Pearson, E. W.
The War of Rebellion in Song and Story. A Patriotic Historical Memorial Exercise for Public Schools. Concord, N. H.: Republican Press Association, 1894. 29 pp.
Tunes arranged for voice and piano, and chorus.

Richardson, Mrs. H. G.
"Buy Me a Milking Pail" and songs of the Civil War. *JAFL* 32:497–504, 1919.

Soldiers' and Sailors' Patriotic Songs.
New York: Published by the Loyal Publication Society of 1864, (May) 1864. v, pp. 19.

Songs of the Civil War, and Other Songs and Poems, mostly published in Boston. 8 Broadsides. New York: Public Library.

Stackard, Sallie Walker
The History of Lawrence, Jackson, Independence and Stone Counties, Arkansas. Little Rock, Ark.: Arkansas Democrat Co., 1904.
Chapter VI (pp. 78–94): "Folk Songs of Arkansas," contains 33 texts. Includes 13 Civil War Songs, 8 game songs.

Staton, Kate E.
Old Southern Songs of the Period of the Confederacy. The Dixie Trophy Collection. New York: Samuel French, Publisher, 1926. 146 pp. Words only.

Stone, James
"War Music and War Psychology in the Civil War." *Journal of Abnormal Psychology,* 36 (No. 4) (Oct.) 1941.

The Acme Haversack of Song and Patriotic Eloquence. Old War Songs and G. A. R. and Patriotic. Syracuse, N. Y.: 1894. 159 pp.

Thomas, Jean
Ballad Makin' in the Mountains of Kentucky.
New York: Henry Holt and Company, 1939.
270 pp.
  Contains texts and tunes of Civil War days.

Uncle Sam's Army Songster.
Indianapolis: 1862.

Uncle Sam's Naval and Patriotic Songster.
New York: P. J. Cozans.

War Lyrics and Songs of the South.
London: 1866.

War Songs of the Blue and the Gray, as sung by
the brave soldiers of the Union and Confederate Armies in camp, on the march, and in
garrison; with a preface by Prof. Henry L.
Williams.... New York: Hurst & Co., 1905.
215 pp.
  Words only.

Wharton, Henry Marvin
*War Songs and Poems of the Southern Con-
federacy, 1861–1865.* Collected and retold with
personal reminiscences of the war by H. M. W.
Philadelphia: 1904. 421 pp.

When the Band Begins to Play. Songster.
New York: De Witt & Co., 1872.

White, R. G.
*Poetry, Lyrical, Narrative, and Satirical of the
Civil War.* New York: The American News
Company, 1866. xii, 334 pp.

Williams, Alfred M.
"Folk Songs of the Civil War." *JAFL* 5:265–
283, 1892.

————.
Folk Songs of the Civil War. In: *Studies in
Folk-Song and Popular Poetry*, (pp. 36–71.)
Boston: Houghton Mifflin Company, 1894.

" 'Yankee Boys'—Civil War Ballad."
JAFL 46:36–37, 1933.

World War I

General Studies and Collections

"Ballads in the South During 1914."
JAFL 28:199–203, 1925.

Cary, M. B.
"Mademoiselle from Armentieres." *JAFL* 47:
369–376, 1934.

Densmore, Frances
"Songs of the Indian Soldiers During the
World War." *MQ* 20:419–425, (October) 1939.

Dolph, Edward Arthur
"The Songs the A. E. F. Used to Sing."
New York Times Magazine, p. 8, (No. 10)
1929.

Eiselen, M. R.
"Campaign Ballads." *Review of Reviews* 94:
60–61, (Oct.) 1936.

Garay, M. B., Jr.
"Mademoiselle from Armentieres." *JAFL* 47:
369–376, 1934.

Hench, Atcheson L.
"Communal Composition of Ballads in the
A. E. F." *JAFL* 34:386–389, 1921.

Loesser, Arthur, ed.
Humor in American Song. Music arranged by
Alfred Kugel. New York: Howell, Soskin,
Publ., 1942.
  Section—"You're In the Army Now"—contains
  13 songs, arranged for voice and piano.

Niles, John J.
"Singing Soldiers." *Scribners* 80:662–670,
(Dec.) 1926; (Jan.) 1927.

————.
Singing Soldiers. New York: Charles Scribners
Sons, 1927.

————.
"Woman—On a Good Man's Mind." *Mentor*
18:12–15, (March) 1930.

————, **Moore, Douglas S., and
Wallgreen, A. A.**
The Songs My Mother Never Taught Me.
New York: Macauley Company, 1929.
  Songs of World War I.

Parsons, Elsie Clews
"War Verses." *JAFL* 47:395, 1934.

Pound, Louise
"Hinkie Dinkie Parlevous." *JAFL* 36:202–203,
1923.

"Soldier Man Blues from Somewhere in France."
Literary Digest 93:50–52, (June 18) 1927.

United States Training Camp Activities.
Army Song Book.... Issued by the War Department Commission on Training Camp Activities and compiled with the assistance of
the National Committee on Army and Navy
Camp Music. Washington, 1918. 90 pp., illus.
  Unaccompanied melodies.

York, Dorothea
Mud and Stars. New York: Holt and Company,
1931.

World War II

Folklore

General Studies

Underwood, Agnes Nolan
"Folklore from G. I. Joe." *NYFQ* 3 (No. 4):
285–297, 1947.
  The ubiquitous Kilroy, the "identical twins"
  Clem and Smoe, the characteristics of Pots.
  Snafu (army) and MacGillicuddy pass in parade.
  Also, the special, and oft unprintable, vocabulary
  is treated, as well as foods. The author also discusses various army and navy songs (texts only),
  and a few superstitions, and bad luck omens are
  mentioned.

Folktales—Speech

Davidson, Bill
Tall Tales They Tell In The Services. Edited by B. D. Illustrated by Barney Tobey. New York: Thomas Y. Crowell, 1943. 75 pp.

Halpert, Herbert
"Folktales Collected in the Army." *CFQ* 3: 115–120, 1944.
Mainly of the tall tale type.

Miller, Wm. Marion
"Two Stories from World War II." *JAFL* 59: 198, 1946.

Roulier, Joseph B.
"Service Lore: Army Vocabulary." *NYFQ* 4 (No. 1):15:32, 1948.
The author discusses a number of forms of speech peculiar to soldiers in World War II.

WORLD WAR II

Songs

Studies and Collections

Arlt, Gustave O., and Harris, Chandler
"Songs of the Services." *CFQ* 3:36–40, 1944.
Text only—of World War II.

Palmer, Edgar A., ed.
G. I. Songs. Written, Composed, or Collected by "The Men in the Service." Illustrations by A. Loederer and Kurt Werth. New York: Sheridan House, 1944. 252 pp.
Texts and many tunes.

ARRANGEMENTS

(Individual Titles)

————: Female Voices

"When Johnny Comes Marching Home."
Martin, F.: Hall and McCreary: SSAA.

————: Male Voices

"There Was an Old Soldier" (Humorous).
Treharne, B.: Willis: TTB.

"The Song of the Contrabands, 'O, Let My People Go'." Lockwood-Raker: Horace Waters, 1861: TTBB.

"When Johnny Comes Marching Home."
Mead, G.: Galaxy: TTBB.

————: Mixed Voices

"Father Abraham."
Treharne: Boston Music Company: SATB.

"When Johnny Comes Marching Home."
Harris, R.: Schirmer: SATB.

"When Johnny Comes Marching Home."
Lambert, L.: Carl Fischer: SATB.

"When Johnny Comes Marching Home."
Lambert-Rosenberg: Witmark: SATB, a cap.

"When Johnny Comes Marching Home."
Lambert-Wilhousky: C. Fischer: SATB.

"When Johnny Comes Marching Home."
Wilson, H. R.: C. Fischer: SATB.

————: Orchestra

Gould, Morton
Symphony on Marching Tunes. MS. Civil War Tunes. *Includes:* When Johnny Comes Marching Home; Tramp, Tramp, Tramp; Tenting To-Night; Just Before the Battle, Mother.

Harris, Roy
When Johnny Comes Marching Home. New York: G. Schirmer. For full orchestra.

Seredy, J. S.
Around the Campfires. Selection of American Soldier Songs—Civil War. New York: C. Fischer.

————: Band and Woodwind Ensemble

"When Johnny Comes Marching Home."
Variations, Op. 9. Tuthill, B. C.: Galaxy: Woodwind quintet, piano.

"When Johnny Comes Marching Home."
Yoder, P.: Robbins Music Corp.

————: Organ

"When Johnny Comes Marching Home."
Lemare, E. H.: H. W. Gray.

RECORDS

Album—Collections

Anthology of Revolutionary, Civil War and Other American Songs. Madrigal Singers, Piano. Lehman Engel, Director. CM–329

Ballads of the American Revolution and the War of 1812. John and Lucy Allison, Sawyer's Minutemen. VI–P11
Contents: Free America; Unhappy Boston; The White Cockade; Yankee Doodle; The Boston Tea Tax; The Chieftain's Bride; The Bombardment of Bristol, R. I.; The Ballad of Bunker Hill; The Death of Warren; Johnny Has Gone For a Soldier; Riflemen's Song at Bennington; The Capture of Major André; Nathan Hale; Cornwallis Country Dance; The Constitution and the Guerriere; Hey Betty Martin; Hunters of Kentucky; Ye Parliament of England.

Patriotic Songs of America.
Popular Music Series Albums. VI–P24

Songs of the North—In the War Between the States, 1861–1865. Sung by Frank Luther, Zora Layman, with the Century Quartet. DE–46

Songs of the South—in the War Between the States, 1861–1865. Sung by Frank Luther, Zora Layman with the Century Quartet. DE–45

U. S. Library of Congress. Division of Music. Folklore Section.
Ballads and Songs of the American Wars in the Archive of American Folksongs. AAFS–LC
See: *Check List of American Folksongs* in the Archives, L. C. Music Division, 1940. 3 vols.

Recordings of Convalescent Soldiers Songs, recorded by Mrs. Ivalee Hobden, ARC, Barnes General Hospital, Vancouver, Washington. 3 records.   AAFS–LC

Soldiers' Songs of World War II, recorded by Alan Lomax.   AAFS–LC

Individual Titles

"A Life on the Vicksburg Bluff."
In: *Songs of the South.* F. Luther and Z. Layman, with Century Quartet.   DE–45

"All Quiet Along the Potomac Tonight."
In: *Songs of the South.* F. Luther and Z. Layman with Century Quartet.   DE–45

"Ballad of Bunker Hill."
In Album: *Ballads of American Revolution and War of 1812,* Set V–P11.   VI–26460

"Battle Cry of Freedom."
In: *Songs of the North.* F. Luther and Z. Layman with Century Quartet.   DE–46

"Battle Cry of Freedom."
Victor Male Chorus.   VI–35844

"Benny Havens, Oh!"
Luther and Layman.   DE–2432

"Bombardment of Bristol, R. I."
In Album: *Ballads of American Revolution and War of 1812,* V–P11.   VI–26459

"Bonnie Eloise."
In: *Songs of the South.* F. Luther and Z. Layman with Century Quartet.   DE–45

"Boston Tea Tax."
In Album: *Ballads of American Revolution and War of 1812,* V–P11.   VI–26458

"Capture of Burgoyne."
F. Luther, vocal.   DE–2431

"Capture of Major André."
In Album: *Ballads of American Revolution and War of 1812,* Set V–P11.   VI–26461

"Cheer, Boys, Cheer."
In: *Songs of the South.* F. Luther and Z. Layman with Century Quartet.   DE–45

"Chieftain's Pride."
In Album: *Ballads of American Revolution and War of 1812,* Set V–P11.   VI–26459

"Columbia, the Gem of the Ocean."
In: *Songs of the North.* Luther; Layman; Century Quartet.   DE–46

"Cornwallis' Country Dance."
In Album: *Ballads of American Revolution and War of 1812,* V–P11.   VI–26461

"Death of Warren."
In Album: *Ballads of American Revolution and War of 1812,* Set V–P11.   VI–26460

"Dixie."
Decca Band, Lyn Murray Chorus.   DE–1793

"Drill, Ye Tarriers, Drill."
Earl Robinson, guitar.   TI–804

"Eating Goober Peas."
In: *Songs of the South.* F. Luther and Z. Layman with Century Quartet.   DE–45

"Ever of Thee I'm Fondly Dreaming."
In: *Songs of the South.* F. Luther and Z. Layman with Century Quartet.   DE–45

"Father Abraham."
In: *Songs of the North.* F. Luther and Z. Layman with Century Quartet.   DE–46

"Free America."
In Album: *Ballads of American Revolution and War of 1812,* Set V–P11.   VI–26458

"Goodbye Mamma, I'm Off to Yokahama."
Teddy Powell, Frankie Masters.   OK–

"Grafted Into the Army."
In: *Songs of the North.* F. Luther and Z. Layman with Century Quartet.   DE–46

"Hard Crackers Come Again No More."
In: *Songs of the North.* F. Luther and Z. Layman with Century Quartet.   DE–46

"Here's Your Mule."
In: *Songs of the South.* F. Luther and Z. Layman with Century Quartet.   DE–45

"Hinky Dinky Parley Voo (Part 1)."
Sweet Violet Boys.   OK–03281

"Hunters of Kentucky."
In Album: *Ballads of American Revolution and War of 1812,* Set V–P11.   VI–26462

"Hy Betty Martin."
In Album: *Ballads of American Revolution and War of 1812,* Set V–P11.   VI–26462

"Johnny Has Gone For A Soldier."
In Album: *Ballads of American Revolution and War of 1182,* Set V–P11.   VI–26460

"Just After the Battle."
In: *Songs of the North.* Luther; Layman with Century Quartet.   DE–46

"Just Before the Battle, Mother."
In: *Songs of the North.* Luther; Layman with Century Quartet.   DE–46

"Just Before the Battle Mother."
Victor Male Chorus.   VI–35844

"K-K-Katy."
Victor Male Chorus.   VI–35937

"Lilly Dale."
In: *Songs of the South*. F. Luther and Z. Layman with Century Quartet.   DE–45

"Lorena."
In: *Songs of the South*. F. Luther and Z. Layman with Century Quartet.   DE–45

"Mademoiselle From Armentieres."
Victor Male Chorus.   VI–35937

"Marching Along."
In: *Songs in the North*. F. Luther and Z. Layman with Century Quartet.   DE–46

"Marching Through Georgia."
Victor Male Chorus.   VI–35844

"My Maryland."
In: *Songs of the South*. Frank Luther and Zora Layman with Century Quartet.   DE–45

"Nathan Hale."
In Album: *Ballads of American Revolution and War of 1812*, Set V–P11.   VI–26461

"Oh Wrap the Flag Around Me Boys."
In: *Songs of the North*. Luther; Layman; Century Quartet.   DE–46

"Over There Medley."
American Legion Officers Band.   VI–24433

"Riflemen's Song at Bennington."
In Album: *Ballads of American Revolution and War of 1812*, Set V–P11.   VI–26460

"Rose of Alabama."
In: *Songs of the South*. F. Luther and Z. Layman with Century Quartet.   DE–45

"Rose of No-Man's Land."
Victor Male Chorus.   VI–35937

"Sleeping for the Flag."
In: *Songs of the North*. Luther, Layman, Century Quartet.   DE–46

"Stonewall Jackson's Requiem."
In: *Songs of the South*. F. Luther and Z. Layman with Century Quartet.   DE–45

"Stonewall Jackson's Way."
In: *Songs of the South*. F. Luther and Z. Layman wtih Century Quartet.   DE–45

"Tenting Tonight."
Victor Male Chorus.   VI–35844

"Tenting Tonight on the Old Camp Ground."
In: *Songs of the North*. Luther; Layman with Century Quartet.   DE–46

"The Battle Hymn of the Republic."
In: *Songs of the North*. Luther; Layman; Century Quartet.   DE–46

"The Battle Hymn of the Republic."
Lawrence Tibbett, baritone-orchestra. VI–4433

"The Bonnie Blue Flag."
In: *Songs of the South*. Frank Luther, Zora Layman with Century Quartet.   DE–45

"The Cavaliers of Dixie."
In: *Songs of the South*. F. Luther, Z. Layman with Century Quartet.   DE–45

"The Constitution and Guerriere."
In Album: *Ballads of American Revolution and War of 1812*, Set V–P11.   VI–26462

"The Dying Volunteer."
In: *Songs of the North*. Luther, Layman with Century Quartet.   DE–46

"The Faded Coat of Blue."
In: *Songs of the North*. Luther; Layman; Century Quartet.   DE–46

"The Marines' Hymn."
Tony Pastor.   BB–1

"The Old Grey Mare."
Victor Male Chorus.   VI–35937

"The Vacant Chair."
In: *Songs of the North*. Luther; Layman; Century Quartet.   DE–46

"The Vacant Chair."
Victor Male Choir.   VI–35844

"300,000 More."
In: *Songs of the North*. F. Luther; Z. Layman, with Century.   DE–46

"Tramp, Tramp, Tramp."
In: *Songs of the North*. Luther; Layman; Century Quartet.   DE–46

"Tramp, Tramp, Tramp."
Victor Male Chorus.   VI–35844

"Unhappy Boston."
In Album: *Ballads of American Revolution and War of 1812*, Set V–P11.   VI–26458

"We Are Coming."
In: *Songs in the North*. F. Luther; Z. Layman with Century Quartet.   DE–46

"When Johnny Comes Marching Home."
Hoff and Orchestra.   OK–6450

"When Johnny Comes Marching Home."
In: *Songs of the North*. Luther; Layman with Century Quartet.   DE–46

"When Johnny Comes Marching Home."
Overture, Roy Harris; Minneapolis Symphony, Ormandy.   VI–8629

"When Johnny Comes Marching Home."
Victor Male Chorus.   VI–35844

"When the Cruel War Is Over."
In: *Songs of the South*. F. Luther; Z. Layman with Century Quartet.   DE–45

"When the Roll is Called."
Peerless Quartet, male.   VI–22945

"When the Yanks Go Marching In."
    Woody Guthrie, voice-guitar.   ASCH–347

"White Cockade."
    In Album: *Ballads of American Revolution
    and War of 1812*, Set V–P11.   VI–26458

"Who Will Care for Mother Now."
    In: *Songs of the South*. F. Luther; Z. Layman
    with Century Quartet.   DE–45

"Yankee Doodle."
    In Album: *Ballads of American Revolution
    and War of 1812*, Set V–P11.   VI–26458

"Yankee Doodle."
    Decca Band, Lyn Murray Chorus.   DE–1793

"Ye Parliament of England."
    In Album: *Ballads of American Revolution and
    War of 1812*, Set V–P11. John and Lucy Alli-
    son.   VI–26462

THE SHAKERS

THE SHAKERS

FOLKLORE

BIBLIOGRAPHY

MacLean, John Patterson
Bibliography of Shaker Literature, with an introductory study of the writings and publications pertaining to Ohio believers. Columbus, Ohio: 1905. 71 pp.

————.
"The Kentucky Revival and its Influence on the Miami Valley." *Ohio Archaeological and Historical Society,* Publications, 12:281–286, 1903., illus.

New York Public Library.
List of Works in the New York Public Library Relating to Shakers. New York, 1904. 10 pp. Reprinted from Bulletin, Nov. 1904.

Winter, Esther C., comp.
Shaker Literature in the Grosvenor Library; a bibliography. Buffalo: The Grosvenor Library, 1940. 119 pp. (Grosvenor Library Bulletin, Vol. 22, No. 4, June, 1940.)

GENERAL STUDIES

A Brief Exposition of the Established Principles and Regulations of the United Society of Believers Called Shakers. New York: 1851. 30 pp. The same, Watervliet, Ohio, 1832; The same Canterbury, N. H., 1843.

A Concise Answer to the General Inquiry Who or What are the Shakers. Union Village, Ohio: 1823 (First printing). Enfield, N. H.: Albion Chase, Printer, 1825, 14 pp., Reprinted.

A Holy, Sacred, and Divine Roll and Book, from the Lord God of Heaven to the Inhabitants of Earth. Revealed in the United Society at New Lebanon, County of Columbia, State of New York, U. S. A. Received by the Church of this Communion, and published in Union with the same. Canterbury, N. H.: 1843. 412 pp.

A Juvenile Guide, or Manual of Good Manners, consisting of Counsels, Instructions, and Rules of Deportment for the Young, by Lovers of Youth. Canterbury, N. H.: United Society, 1844. 137 pp. 2 parts.

A List of Different Tribes of Indians and From the World of Spirits Who Came to Learn the Way of God, of Mother's Children on Earth. Wisdom's Valley (Watervliet) South House, Oct. 26, 1842.

A Memorial Remonstrating against a certain Act of the Legislature of Kentucky entitled an Act to Regulate Civil Proceedings against certain Communities having Property in Common, and declaring that it shall and may be lawful to commence and prosecute suits, obtain decrees, and have execution against any of the Communities of People called Shakers without naming or designating the individuals or serving process on them otherwise than by fixing a Subpoena on the door of their Meeting house, etc. Harrodsburg, Ky.: Union Office, 1830. 8 pp.

A Return of departed spirits of the highest characters of distinction, as well as the indiscriminate of all notions, into the bodies of the "Shakers," in "United Society of Believers" in the second advent of the Messiah. By an associate of the Society. Philadelphia: 1843.

A Revelation of the Extraordinary Visitation of Departed Spirits and Distinguished Men and Women of all nations, and their manifestations Through the Living Bodies of the "Shakers." By a guest of the "Community" near Watervliet, N. Y. Philadelphia: 1869.

A Revision and Confirmation of the Social Compact of the United Society called Shakers, at Pleasant Hill, Kentucky. Harrodsburg, Ky.: Order of the Church, 1830. 12 pp.

A Shaker Broadside.
"Advice to Children in Behavior at Table." *NYFQ* 1(No. 4):233–236, 1945.

A Summary View of the Millennial Church, or United Society of Believers, comprising the Rise, Progress, and Practical Order of the Society, together with the general Principles of Their Faith and Testimony. Albany: C. Van Benthuysen, 1848. 384 pp. 2nd ed., rev. and enlarged. First printed in 1823.

Account of Some of the Proceedings of the Legislatures of the States of Kentucky and New Hampshire. 1823, etc., in Relation to the People called Shakers. New York: 1846. 103 pp. (reprint).

An Address to the State of Ohio.
Protesting against a certain Clause of the Militia enacted by the Legislature. Lebanon, Ohio: Office of the Farmer, 1818. 24 pp.

Andrews, Edward Deming
The Gift to the Simple. New York: J. J. Augustin, 1940. 170 pp., illus., music, bibl.
The work reveals "the nature of the most compelling and important motive in the Shaker's life, his religion, with its outward manifestations of song, music and devotional exercise in community worship." (Bayard.)

————., and Faith
Shaker Furniture, the craftsmanship of an American communal sect; photographs by William F. Winter. New Haven: Yale University Press, 1937. xi, 133 pp., bibl. (pp. 121–126).

726

————.
The Community Industries of the Shakers.
Albany: The University of the State of New York. 1932. 322 pp., illus., bibl.

B., A. B., and Evans, F. W.
Shakerism, the Possibility of the Race. Being Letters of A. B. B. and Elder F. W. Evans. Lebanon, Ohio: Office of the Shaker, 1872. 14 pp.

Bates, Barnabas
Peculiarities of the Shakers, described in a series of letters from Lebanon Springs, in the year 1832, containing an account of the origin, worship, and doctrines of the Shakers' Society by a visitor. New York: Porter, 1832. 116 pp.

Bates, Paulina
The Divine Book of Holy and Eternal Wisdom, revealing the Word of God, out of whose mouth goeth a Sharp Sword. Written by Paulina Bates, at Watervliet, N. Y., United States of North America; including other Illustrations and Testimonies arranged and prepared for the Press at New Lebanon, N. Y. Canterbury, N. Y.: United Society Called Shakers, 1849. 718 pp.

Bishop, Rufus, comp., revised by Wells, Seth Y.
Testimonies of the life, character, revelations and doctrines of our ever blessed Mother Ann Lee, and the elders with her; Through whom the word of eternal life was opened in this day of Christ's second appearing. Hancock, 1816.

Blinn, Henry C.
The Manifestation of Spiritualism Among the Shakers 1837–1847. East Canterbury, N. H.: 1899.

Brown, Thomas
An Account of the People Called Shakers. Their faith, doctrines, and practice, exemplified in the life, conversations, and experience of the author during the time he belonged to the society. To which is affixed a history of their use and progress to the present day. Cornwall, Orange County, N. Y. and Troy, N. Y.: Parker and Bliss, 1812. xii, 372 pp.

Carmer, Carl
Truth Shall Spring Out of the Earth. In: *Listen For a Lonesome Drum,* (pp. 115–221). New York: Blue Ribbon Books, 1940. 381 pp., illus.

Chapman, Eunice
An additional account of the conduct of the Shakers in the case of Eunice Chapman and her children. Albany: 1818. 82 pp.

Chase, Daryl
The Early Shakers; an Experiment in Religious Communism. Chicago: University of Chicago Library, 1936. 22 pp.

Dow, Edward French
A Portrait of the Millenial Church of Shakers. Orono, Me.: Printed at the University Press, 1931. 52 pp., bibl. University of Maine Studies, Second Series, No. 19.

Dunlavy, John
The Manifesto; or, A declaration of the doctrine and practice of the Church of Christ. New York: 1847. vii, 486 pp.

————.
The Nature and Character of the True Church of Christ proved by Plain Evidences, and showing whereby it may be known and distinguished from all others. New York: George W. Wood, 1850. 93 pp.

————.
Plain Evidences by which the Nature and Character of the True Church of Christ may be known and distinguished from all others. Taken from a work entitled "The Manifesto, or a Declaration of the Doctrines and Practice of the Church of Christ." Pleasant Hill, Ky.: 1818. Albany, N. Y.: Hoffman and White, 1834. 120 pp.

Condition of Society and its only Hope in obeying the Everlasting Gospel, as now developing among Believers in Christ's Second Appearance. Union Village, Ohio: Day Star Office, 1847. 121 pp.

Dyer, Joseph
A Compendium Narrative, Elucidating the Character, Disposition and Conduct of Mary Dyer, from the Time of her Marriage, in 1799, till she left the Society called Shakers in 1815, etc. By her Husband, Joseph Dyer. To which is Annexed a Remonstrance against the Testimony and Application of the said Mary for Legislative Interference. Concord, N. H.: Isaac Hill, for the Author, 1818. 90 pp.

Dyer, Mary
A Brief Statement of the Sufferings of Mary Dyer, occasioned by the Society called Shakers. Written by herself. To which is added Affidavits and Certificates. Also a Declaration from their Own Publication. Concord, N. H.: 1818. 35 pp.

————.
A Portraiture of Shakerism, exhibiting a general view of their character and conduct, from the first appearance of Ann Lee in New England, down to the present time. Concord, N. H.: 1822.

————.
The Rise and Progress of the Serpent, from the Garden of Eden to the Present Day, with a Disclosure of Shakerism, etc.; Also the Life and Sufferings of the Author, who was Mary Dyer, but now is Mary Marshall. Concord, N. H.: 1847.

Eads, H. L.
Shaker Sermons: scripto-rational. Containing the substance of Shaker theology. Together with replies and criticisms logically and clearly set forth. Shakers, N. Y.: The Shaker Manifesto, 1879. 222 pp.

Eells, Rev. Myron
Letters in Regard to the Shakers of Puget Sound, quoted at length in the chapter on that subject. Works by the same author referred to in the same chapter and in the tribal synopsis accompanying the chapter on the Nez Perce war, are "History of Indian Missions on the Pacific Coast," and "Ten Years of Missionary Work Among the Indians at Skakomish, Washington Territory, 1874–1884." Boston: Congregational Sunday School and Publishing Society, 1886. xii, 271 pp., illus. 2 pl. (Incl. front) 2 port.

Elkins, Hervey
Fifteen Years in the Senior Order of Shakers: a Narrative of Facts Concerning that Singular People. Hanover, N. H.: Dartmouth Press, 1853. 136 pp.

Evans, Frederick William
Ann Lee, the Founder of the Shakers. A Biography, with Memoirs of her Companions. Also a Compendium of the Origin, History, Principles, Rules and Regulations, Government and Doctrines of the United Society of Believers in Christ's Second Appearing. London: J. Burns. New York: D. Appleton and Co., 1859.

———.
Autobiography of a Shaker, and Revelation of the Apocalypse. New York: American News Co., 1869. 162 pp., Appendix.

———.
Religious Communism. A lecture by F. W. Evans (Shaker), of Mount Lebanon, Columbia Co., New York, U. S. A., delivered in St. Geore's Hall, London, Sunday evening, August 6th, 1871; with Introductory Remarks by the Chairman of the Meeting, Mr. Hepworth Dixon. Also some Account of the Extent of the Shaker Communities, and a Narrative of the Visit of Elder Evans to England. An abstract of a Lecture by Rev. J. M. Peebles, and his testimony in regard to Shakers.

———.
Shaker Communism, or Tests of Divine Inspiration, The Second Christian or Gentile Pentecostal Church, as exemplified by Seventy Communities of Shakers in America. London: James Burns, 1871. 120 pp.

———.
Shaker's Compendium of the Origin, History, Principles, Rules and Regulations, Government and Doctrines of the United Society of Christ's Second Appearing, with Biographies of Ann Lee, William Lee, James Whittaker, J. Hocknell, J. Meacham, and Lucy Wright. New York: D. Appleton and Co., 1859. 189 pp.

———.
A Short Treatise on the Second Appearing of Christ in and through the Order of the Female. New London, N. Y. and Boston: 1853. 24 pp.

———.
Tests of Divine Inspiration, or the Rudimental Principles by which True and False Revelation in all Eras of the World can be Unerringly Discriminated. New Lebanon: 1853. 128 pp.

———.
The Universal Church. Shakers, N. Y.: 1872. 16 pp., (Office of the Shaker).

Extract from an unpublished manuscript on Shaker history, giving an accurate description of their songs, dances, marches, visions, visits to the spirit land, etc., by an eyewitness. Boston: 1850.

General Rules of the United Society, and Summary Articles of Mutual Agreement and Release, Ratified and Confirmed by the Society at Watervliet, Montgomery County, Ohio, January 1833. Watervliet, Ohio: Union Office, 1833, 7 pp.
Also contains the signatures of members.

Gibson, Marywebb
Shakerism in Kentucky, founded by Ann Lee. Cynthiana, Ky.: The Hobson Press, 1942. ix, 141 pp.

Greeley, Horace
A Sabbath with the Shakers. In: *The Knickerbocker, or N. Y. Monthly Magazine,* 11:1838, N. Y.

Green, Calvin, and Wells, Seth Y.
A Summary View of the Millennial Church, or United Society of Believers (commonly called Shakers). Comprising the rise, progress and practical order of the Society; together with the general principles of their faith and testimony. Albany, N. Y.: 1823.

———.
Brief Exposition of the Established Principles and Regulations of the United Society of Believers called Shakers. New York: 1851. 30 pp.

Haskell, R.
The Musical Expositor. New York: 1847.
Music, customs and lore of the Shakers.

Haskett, William J.
Shakerism Unmasked, or the History of the Shakers; including a form politic of their government as Councils, Orders, Gifts, with and exposition of the Five Orders of Shakerism, and Ann Lee's grand foundation vision, in sealed pages with some extracts from their private hymns which have never appeared in public. Pittsfield, Mass.: 1828.

Holloway, Emory
Walt Whitman's Visit to the Shakers with Whitman's Notebook Containing his description and observations of the Shaker group at Mt. Lebanon. In: *The Colophon,* First Issue, Spring, 1930. Part 13. New York: 1933.

Howells, William Dean
Three Villages. Boston: J. R. Osgood & Co., 1884. 198 pp.
   Contents: Lexington, Mass.—Shirley, Mass,—Gnadenhütten, Ohio.

Improved Shaker Washing-Machine, etc. Manufactured and for sale by the United Society of Shakers. Shaker Village, N. H.: 12 pp., (n.d.)

Investigator; or a Defense of the Order, Government, and Economy of the United Society called Shakers against sundry charges and Legislative Proceedings. Addressed to the Political World by the Society of Believers at Pleasant Hill, Kentucky. Lexington, Ky.: Smith and Palmer, 1828. 57 pp.

Lamson, David R.
Two Years' Experience Among the Shakers: being a description of the manners and customs of that people, the nature and policy of their government. Their marvellous intercourse with the Spiritual World, the object and uses of confession, their inquisition, in short, a condensed view of Shakerism as it is. West Boylson, Mass.: 1848.

Leonard, William
A Discourse of the Orders and Propriety of Divine Inspiration and Revelation, showing the Necessity Thereof in all Ages to Know the Will of God. Also, a Discourse on the Second Appearing of Christ in and Through the Order of the Female. And a Discourse on the Propriety and Necessity of a United Inheritance in all Things in order to Support a true Christian Community. Harvard, Mass.: The United Society, 1853. 88 pp.

Leslie, Ann George
Dancing Saints. New York: Doubleday, Doran and Co., 1943. 307 pp.
   "The pages are alive with the atmosphere of Shaker life, with its religious fervor, its isolation from the outside world, its essential integrity." (Rose Feld).

Lomas, George Albert, Shaker
The Life of Christ is the End of the World. Watervliet, Ohio: 1869. 16 pp.

——————.
Plain Talks Upon Practical Religion. Being Candid Answers to Earnest Inquiries. Watervliet, N. Y.: 1873. 24 pp.

Lossing, Benson J.
"The Shakers at Lebanon, N. Y." *Harper's Monthly Magazine* 15:164, July 1857.

Mace, Fayette
Familiar Dialogues on Shakerism; in which the Principles of the United Society are illustrated and defended. Portland: Charles Day and Co., Printers, 1838. 120 pp.

MacLean, J. P.
A Sketch of the Life and Labors of Richard McNemar. Franklin, Ohio: 1905. 67 pp., bibl.

McNemar, Richard
The Kentucky Revival; or a Short History of the late Extraordinary Outpouring of the Spirit of God in the Western States of America, agreeably to Scripture Promises and Prophecies concerning the Latter Day, with a brief Account of the Entrance and Purposes of what the World call Shakerism, among the subjects of the late Revival in Ohio and Kentucky. Presented to the *True Zion Traveler* as a Memorial of the Wilderness Journey. New York: Reprinted by Edward O. Jenkins, 1846. 156 pp.
   The Preface is dated "Turtle Creek, 1807."

Melcher, Mrs. Marguerite (Fellows)
The Shaker Adventure. Princeton, N. J.: Princeton University Press, 1941. ix, 319 pp., bibl. (pp. 294–301).

Neal, Julia
By Their Fruits; the Story of Shakerism in South Union, Kentucky. Chapel Hill, N. C.: University of North Carolina Press, 1947. 279 pp., illus., bibl.

Nordhoff, Charles
The Communistic Societies of the United States. From Personal Visit and Observation: Including detailed accounts of the: Economists, Zoarites, Shakers, the Amana, Oneida, Bethel, Aurora, Icarian, and other Existing Societies, Their Religious Creeds, Social Practices, Numbers, Industries, and Present Condition. New York: Harper and Bros., 1875. 439 pp., illus., bibl.

——————.
The Shakers. In: *The Communistic Societies of the United States* (pp. 117–232). From Personal Visit and Observation. With illustration. New York: Harper and Bros., 1875. 439 pp.

O'Brien, Harriet Ellen
Lost Utopias; a brief description of three quests for happiness, Alcott's museum, rescued from oblivion, recorded and preserved by Clara Endicott Sears on Prospect Hill in the old township of Harvard, Massachusetts. Boston: P. Walton, 1929. 62 pp., illus.

One Hundredth Anniversary of the Organization of the Shaker Church. October 18, 1893. Enfield, N. H., 36 pp.

Pelham, R. W., ed.
Shakers: A Correspondence between Mary F. C., of Mount Holly City, and a Shaker Sister, Sarah L., of Union Village. Union Village, Ohio: 1868. 24 pp.

Philanthropos
A Brief Illustration of the Principles of War and Peace, showing the ruinous Policy of the former and the superior Efficacy of the latter, for National Protection and Defense, clearly manifested by their practical operations and opposite Effects upon Nations, Kingdoms, and People. Albany. Packard and Van Benthuysen, 1831. 112 pp.

Prescott, James J.
The Social Evil. North Union, Ohio: 1870. 14 pp.

Public Discourse delivered in Substance at Union Village, Ohio. August 1823. 36 pp.

Rathbone, Valentine (Minister of the Gospel)
A Brief Account of a Religious Scheme taught and propagated by a member of Europeans who lately lived in a place called Nisquenia, in the State of New York, but now residing in Harvard, Commonwealth of Massachusetts commonly called Shaking Quakers—To which is added a Dialogue between George the Third of Great Britain and his minister, giving an account of the late London mob, and the original of the Sect called Shakers. The whole being a discovery of the wicked machinations of the principal enemies of America. Worcester, 1782.
Considered the earliest printed mention of the Shakers.

————.
Some Brief Hints of a Religious Scheme Taught and Propagated by a Number of Europeans, living in a Place called Nisquenia, in the state of New York. Norwich, Conn.: 1871.

Respect and Veneration due from Youth to Age. New Bedford: 1870. 15 pp.

Robinson, Charles Edson
A Concise History of the United Society of Believers, called Shakers. East Canterbury, N. H.: 1893. ix, 134 pp., illus.

Rourke, Constance
The Shakers. In: *The Roots of American Culture and Other Essays* (pp. 195–237). Edited with a preface by Van Wyck Brooks. New York: Harcourt, Brace and Co., 1942. 305 pp.

Sears, C. E., comp.
Gleanings from Old Shaker Journals. Boston: Houghton Mifflin Co., 1916. xiii, 298 pp.

Smith, Col. James (of Kentucky)
Shakerism Detected, a Pamphlet Examined and Confuted in Five Propositions. Lebanon, Ohio and Lexington, Ky.: Richard McNemar, 1811. 12 pp. Reprinted by Request, Watervliet, Ohio, May 2, 1883. 12 pp.

Social Gathering Dialogue between Six Sisters of the North Family of Shakers. Mount Lebanon, New York. Albany: 1873. 18 pp.

Some Lines in Verse About Shakers, Not Published by Authority of the Society so called. New York: William Taylor and Co., No. 2, Astor House, 1846. 56 pp.

Stewart, Philemon
Holy, Sacred and Divine Roll and Book, from the Lord God of Heaven to the Inhabitants on Earth, Revealed in the United Society at New Lebanon. Canterbury, N. H.: The Society, 1843. 2 parts, 402 pp.

Taylor, Amos
A Narrative of the Strange Principles, Conduct and Character of the People known by the Name of Shakers. Worcester: 1782.

Testimonies Concerning the Character and Ministry of Mother Ann Lee and the First Witnesses of the Gospel of Christ's Second Appearance, given by some of the aged Brethren and Sisters of the United Society; including a few sketches of their own Religious Experiences approved by the Church. Albany: Packard and Van Benthuysen, 1872. 178 pp.

Testimony of Christ's Second Appearing exemplified by the Principles and Practice of the Church of Christ. History of the Progressive Work of God, extending from the Creation of Man to the Harvest, Comprising the Four Great Dispensations now consummating in the Millennial Church. Antichrist's Kingdom or Churches, contrasted with the Church of Christ's First and Second Appearing, the Kingdom of the God of Heaven. Lebanon, Ohio: United States Society called Shakers, 1808.

The Constitution of the United Society of Believers Called Shakers. Containing sundry Covenants and Articles of Agreement definitive of the Legal Grounds of the Institution. Watervliet, Ohio: 1833. 16 pp.
Contains several forms of the Church Covenant, from 1810 down to 1833.

The Higher Law of Spiritual Progression. Albany: 1868. 32 pp.

The Memorial of the Society of People of Canterbury, in the County of Rockingham, and Enfield in the County of Grafton, Commonly called Shakers. (No date—about 1818. 13 pp.)

The Original Shaker Communities in New England. The Plumer Papers, Frank Sanborn, ed. In: *The New England Magazine,* (New Series). Vol. 22, 1900.

The Shaker Society Against Gass and Banta.
No date, 8 pp. (Brief of a case in Kentucky).

The Testimony of Christ's Second Appearing; containing a general statement of all Things pertaining to the Faith and Practice of the Church of God in this Latter Day. Published in Union by the Order of the Ministry. Lebanon, Ohio: John 'Clean, office of *The Western Star,* 1808. 681 pp. 2nd edition, corrected and improved, Albany: 1810. 660 pp. 3rd edition, corrected and improved, Union Village, Ohio: B. Fisher and A. Burnett, Printers, 1823. 621 pp.

Van Sweringen Company, Cleveland.
Peaceful Shaker Village. Cleveland: The Van Sweringen Co., 1927. 23 pp., illus.

Warder, W. S.
Brief Sketch of the Religious Society of People called Shakers. London: 1818. 16 pp.

Weeks, Estella T.
"Shakerism in Indiana." *HFB* 4(No. 4):59–85, 1945.

Wells, S. Y.
Testimonies Concerning the Character and Ministry of Mother Ann Lee, and the first witnesses of the gospel of Christ's second appearing, given by some of the aged brethren and sisters of the United Society, including a few sketches of their own religious experience. Albany, N. Y.: 1827. 178 pp.

West, Arthur T.
"Reminiscences of Life in a Shaker Village." *New England Quarterly* 11:343–360, 1938.

White, Anna, and Taylor, Leila
Shakerism: its Meaning and Message. Embracing an Historical Account, Statement of Belief and Spiritual Experience of the Church from its Rise to the Present Day. Columbus, Ohio. 1905.

Whitely, John (of Shirley Village, Mass.)
A Shaker's Answer to the Oft-repeated Question "What would become of the world if all should become Shakers?" Boston: 1874. 32 pp.

Wickliffe, Robert
The Shakers: Speech of Robert Wickliffe in the Senate of Kentucky, January, 1831, On a Bill to Repeal an Act of the General Assembly of the State of Kentucky, entitled an Act to Regulate Civil Proceedings against certain Communities having Property in Common. Frankfort, Ky.: 1832. 32 pp.

Youngs, Benjamin S., Darrow, David, and Meacham, John
The Testimony of Christ's Second Appearing, containing a general statement of all things pertaining to the faith and practice of the church of God in this latter day.... Lebanon, Ohio: 1808. 4th ed. Albany, N. Y.: Published by the United Society, 1856.

Youngs, Isaac N.
A Concise View of the Church of God and of Christ, on Earth, Having its foundation in the faith of Christ's first and second appearing. New Lebanon: 1856.

FOLK MEDICINE

Catalogue of Medicinal Plants, Barks, Roots, Seeds, Flowers, and Select Powders, with Their Therapeutic Qualities, and Botanical Names, also Pure Vegetable Extracts, prepared in vacuo; Ointments, Inspissated Juices, Essential Oils, Double distilled and Fragrant Waters, etc., raised, prepared, and put up in the most careful manner by the United Society of Shakers at Mount Lebanon, N. Y. First established in 1800, being the oldest of the kind in the country. Albany: 1873. 58 pp.

FOLKSONG

GENERAL STUDIES AND COLLECTIONS

A Collection of Millenial Hymns.
Adapted to the present Order of the Church. Canterbury, N. H.: The United Society, 1847. 200 pp.

A Sacred Repository of Anthems and Hymns for devotional Worship and Praise. Canterbury, N. H.: 1852. 222 pp.

A Short Abridgement of the Rules of Music, with lessons for exercise, and a few observations for new beginners. New Lebanon: The Society, 1843. 40 pp. (reprinted 1846).

Andrews, Edwards D.
"The Dance in Shaker Ritual." *Dance Index I:* (Jan.) 1942.

————.
The Gift to be Simple: Songs, Dances and Rituals of the American Shakers. New York: J. J. Augustin, 1940. 170 pp., music, illus., bibl.

Barry, Phillips
"Notes on the Songs and Music of the Shakers." *FSSNE* 1:5–7, 1930.
P. B. claims that the source of a good part of Shaker music is British folk music.

————.
"Shaker Songs and Music." *FSSNE* 4:17–18, 1932.
Music and text illustrated. The sacred dance of the Shakers.

Extract from an unpublished manuscript on Shaker history, giving an accurate description of their songs, dances, marches, visions, visits to the spirit land, etc., By an eye-witness. Boston: 1850.

Haskell, R.
The Musical Expositor. New York: 1847.
Music, customs and lore of the Shakers.

Held, Conrad C., arr.
Fifteen Shaker Songs, with a preface by Edward D. Andrews. New York: G. Schirmer, 1944. 31 pp.
Arranged for voice and piano.

McNemar, Richard
A Selection of Hymns and Poems; for the use of believers. Collected from sundry authors. Watervliet, Ohio: 1833. 180 pp.

Millennial Praises, containing a collection of Gospel hymns, in four parts, adapted to the day of Christ's second appearing, composed for the use of His people. Hancock: Josiah Tallcott, Jr., 1813. viii, 288 pp.

Philos, Harmonaie
A Selection of Hymns and Poems for the Use of Believers; collected from sundry authors. Watervliet, Ohio: The Society, 1833. 186 pp.

Shaker Music. Inspirational hymns and melodies illustrative of the resurrection, life and testimony of the Shakers. Albany: 1875. (Revised ed. 1884, N. Y. imprint.)

Youngs, Isaac N., and Buckingham, D. A.
A Treatise on Music; agreeably to the Plan established and adopted at New Lebanon and Watervliet, New York, 1840.

WHITE SPIRITUALS

WHITE SPIRITUALS

See: American Folksong Collections, pp. 85-90; American Ballad Collections, pp. 118-20; Music of the Shakers, pp. 731-32; Negro Spirituals, pp. 454-61; Music of the Pennsylvania-Germans, pp. 590-91.

BIBLIOGRAPHY

Jackson, George Pullen
Bibliography of British and American Books containing Religious Folk Songs. In: *White and Negro Spirituals*, Their Life Span and Kinship. Tracing 200 years of untrammeled song making and singing among our country folk, with 116 songs as sung by both races, by George Pullen Jackson (pp. 296–301). New York: J. J. Augustin, 1943. 349 pp., illus., music, bibl.

Metcalf, Frank Johnson
American Psalmody; or, Titles of Books, Containing Tunes Printed in America from 1721–1820. New York: C. F. Heartman, 1917. 54 pp.

Warrington, James
Short Titles of Books Relating to or Illustrating the History and Practice of Psalmody in the United States, 1620–1820. Philadelphia: Priv. Print., 1898. 2 pp., 96 numb.

GENERAL STUDIES

Adams, Mrs. Crosby
Studies in Hymnology. Richmond, Va.: Onward Press.

Adkins, Nelson F.
"A Note on the Bibliography of Stephen Foster." *N. & Q.* (N. Y.) 163:331–332, 1932.
Refers to Horace Water's use of Stephen Foster Melodies in a Hymnal as early as 1860.

Asbury, Samuel E., and Meyer, Henry E.
"Old-Time White Camp-Meeting Spirituals." *TFSP* 10:169–185, 1932.
Interesting historical background, with ten spirituals in four part harmony by Meyer.

Babcock, William Henry
"Carols and Child-Lore at the Capital." *Lippincotts Monthly Magazine* (Philadelphia), 38:320–342, 1886.

Backus, E. M.
"Christmas Carols from Georgia." *JAFL* 12:272, 1899.

Barclay, Robert
The Inner Life of the Religious Societies of the Commonwealth; considered principally with reference to the influence of church organization on the spread of Christianity. London: 1876.

Barry, Phillips
"Notes on the Songs and Music of the Shakers." *FSSNE* 1:5–7, 1930.

———.
"Shaker Songs and Music." *FSSNE* 4:17–18, 1932.
Music and text illustrate the Sacred Dance of the Shakers.

Benson, Louis F.
The English Hymn. Philadelphia: President Board of Publication, 1915.
An historical survey of the whole subject of English hymnology.

Buchanan, Annabel Morris
American Folk Hymnody. In: *International Encyclopedia of Music,* edited by Oscar Thompson. New York: Dodd, Mead and Company, 1938.
A comprehensive study and analysis, with musical illustrations.

———.
"The Cherry Tree Carol (Christmas)." *Richmond Times Dispatch Sunday Magazine,* (Dec. 20), 1936.
Discussion.

———.
"June Meetin'." In Series of Articles: *Adventure in Virginia Folkway, Richmond Times Dispatch Sunday Magazine* (Richmond, Va.), (June 7) 1936.

Chase, Richard
"Blessings of Mary (The Seven Joys of Mary)." *JAFL* 48:4, 1935.
Discussion of traditional versions in Kentucky and North Carolina.

Cutting, Edith
"The Joys of Mary." *NYFQ* 3 (No. 4):323–324, 1947.
A New York version (text only) of "The Cherry Tree Carol."

Davidson, Donald
"The Sacred Harp in the Land of Eden." *Virginia Quarterly Review,* (University of Virginia, Charlottsville, Va.), (April) 1934.

———.
"White Spirituals and Their Historian." *Sewanee Review,* (University of the South Sewanee, Tenn.) 51:589–598, 1943.

———.
"White Spirituals; the Choral Music of the South." *American Scholar* 4:460–473, 1935.

Eddy, Mary O.
"Some Early American Hymns." *SFQ* 7:119–129, 1943.
Words and music of eleven early hymnals of Pennsylvania and Ohio.

Fisher, William Arms
Ye Olde New England Psalm-Tunes: 1620–1820. Boston: Oliver Ditson, 1930.
Historical discussion with musical examples.

Foote, Henry Wilder
Three Centuries of American Hymnody. Cambridge: Harvard University Press, 1940. xxii, 418 pp.

Fulling, K. P.
"Singers of the Soil." *Etude* 57:501–502, (Aug.) 1939. Illus.
   Story of buckwheat or shape notes.

"Future American Hymnology."
Musician 40:7, (June) 1935.

Gilchrist, Anne G.
"The Folk Element in Early Revival Hymns and Tunes." *Journal of the English Folk-Lore Society* 8:61–95, 1938.
   Critical discussion, tunes and texts.

Haskell, R.
The Musical Expositor. New York: 1847.
   Music, custom and lore of the Shakers.

Horne, Dorothy
"Dyadic Harmony in the Sacred Harp." *SFQ* 9 (No. 4):209–212, 1945.

———.
"Shape-Note Hymnals and the Art of Music of Early America." *SFQ* 5:251–256, 1941.

Howard, John Tasker
Hymns as Folk Songs. In: *Our American Music,* pp. 143. New York: Thomas Y. Crowell Company, 1939. 748 pp., rev. ed., bibl.

"Hymn from Maine."
Time 29:74–78, (May 24) 1937.

"Hymns from Home; Festival of American Music, Hamburg, Germany." *Commonweal* 14:172–, 1931.

Jackson, George Pullen
"America's Folksongs." *The Virginia Quarterly Review* 12:34–42, January, 1936.

———.
"Buckwheat Notes." *MQ* 19 (No. 4):1933.

———.
"Did Spiritual Folksongs Develop in the Northeast?" *SFQ* 3:1–3, 1939.

———.
Down-East Spirituals, and Others; Three hundred songs supplementary to the author's Spiritual Folksongs of Early America. New York: J. J. Augustin, 1943. 296 pp., music, bibl.

———.
"Early American Religious Folk Songs." *MTNA, Proceeding, 1934.* pp. 74–80.

———.
"Old-Time Country Singing." *SFQ* 1 (No. 1): 21–29, 1937.

———.
Spiritual Folksongs of Early America; two hundred and fifty tunes and texts, with an introduction and notes, collected and edited by George Pullen Jackson. New York: J. J. Augustin, 1937. 254 pp., music (unaccompanied melodies), bibl.

———.
"The Old Time Religion as a Folk Religion." (c.1740–1840.) *TFSB* 7 (No. 3–4):30–39, 1941.

———.
White Spirituals in the Southern Uplands, The Story of the Fasola Folk, their songs, singings, and "buckwheat notes" by George Pullen Jackson. Chapel Hill: The University of North Carolina Press, 1933. xv, 344 pp., music, bibl.

Lloyd, A. L.
"The Origin of Spirituals." *Keynote* (London), Spring pp. 4–8, 1946. Illus.

Long, Edwin McKean
Illustrated History of Hymns and Their Authors. Facts and incidents of the origin, authors, sentiments, and singing of hymns. Philadelphia: J. L. Landis & Co., 1882. vii, 558 pp.

Lorenz, Edmund Simon
The American Spiritual. In: *Church Music,* by E. S. Lorenz. New York: F. H. Revell, 1923.

Macdougal, Hamilton C.
Early New England Psalmody. An Historical Appreciation 1620–1820. Brattleboro, Vt.: Stephen Daye Press, 1940.

Metcalf, Frank J.
American Writers and Compilers of Sacred Music. New York: Abingdon Press, 1925.
   Good for historical background of early New England Hymn writers.

Nathan, Hans
"Career of a Revival Hymn." *SFQ* 7:89–100, 1943.
   Words and music, and discussion of "Old Church Yard."

Ninde, Edward S.
The Story of the American Hymn. Cincinnati: The Abingdon Press, 1921. 429 pp.

"On 'White Spirituals'."
Fisher Edition News. 10 (No. 2):1–4, May–Nov., 1934.

Powell, John
Introduction. In: *Twelve Folk Hymns from the Old Shape Note Hymnbooks and From Oral Tradition,* by Hilton Rufty, Annabel Buchanan, and John Powell. New York: J. Fischer and Bro., 1934.
   Discussion of utilization of folk-music idiom in sacred tunes.

Pratt, Waldo Selden
The Music of the Pilgrims. Boston: Oliver Ditson Company, 1921.
   General historical discussion with musical examples.

Robertson, Mary W.
"Religious Folk Songs of America." *Music Clubs Magazine* 13 (No. 3):27, Jan.–Feb., 1934.

Robertson, Mrs. H.
"Romance of the Folk Hymn." *Musician* 39:15 (October) 1934.

Scarborough, Dorothy
"Religious Songs of the Rural Mountain South."
A review of *White Spirituals in the Southern Uplands*. New York Times Book Review, (March 5), 1933. pp. 2.

Stebbins, George Coles
George C. Stebbins: Reminiscences and Gospel Hymn Stories, with an Introduction by Charles H. Gabriel. New York: George H. Doran Company, 1924. xxii, 327 pp.
Contains music.

Stevenson, Arthur Linwood
The Story of Southern Hymnology. Salem, Va.: A. L. Stevenson; Roanoke, Va.: Printed by the Stone Printing and Manufacturing Co., 1931. vi, 187 pp., bibl.

Thomas, Jean
Hymn Making. In: *Ballad Makin' in the Mountains of Kentucky*. (pp. 197–231). New York: Henry Holt and Company, 1930.
Texts and accompanied tunes.

Tillett, Wilbur F.
The Hymns and Hymn Writers of the Church. Nashville, Tenn.: Smith and Lamar, 1911.

Umble, John
"The Old Order of Amish, their Hymns and Hymn Tunes." *JAFL* 52:82–95, 1939.

Westman, R.
"Lord's Fiddle." *Etude* 59:315+, (May) 1941.

"White Spirituals of the Southern Uplands."
A review in the *London Times Literary Supplement*, 1933.

COLLECTIONS

A Choice Selection of Hymns and Spiritual Songs Designed for Camp Meetings. Montpelier, Vt.: 1827. 3rd ed.

Aldrich, Jonathan
The Sacred Lyre; a new collection of hymns and tunes; for social and family worship. Boston: Graves and Young, 1864. 632 pp.

Allen, Chester G., and Sherwin, W. F.
The Victory: A new collection of sacred and secular music comprising a great variety of tunes, anthems, glees. New York: Biglow & Main, 1869. 400 pp.
Words with music—SATB.

Alline, Henry
Hymns and Spiritual Songs. (Free Will Baptists). Stonyport, Conn.: 1802.

Andrews, William; Barclay, H., and Ogilvie, J.
The Order for Morning and Evening Prayer and Administration of the Sacraments and Some Other Offices of the Church. Together with a Collection of Prayers and Some Sentences of the Holy Scriptures. New York: W. Weyman and Hugh Gaine, 1769.

A New Selection of Hymns and Spiritual Songs ... for ... Camp Meetings. Woodstock, Vt.: 1832.

A Pocket Hymn Book. Designed as a constant companion for the pious. Collected from various authors. (Methodist). Wilmington: Published by Mathew R. Lockerman, in Market Street. Joseph Jones, Printer, 1806. 28th ed., 291 pp., without music.

Auld, Alexander
The Ohio Harmonist. Psalm & Hymn Tunes ... and a Supplement of Temperance Songs, also the Rudiments of Music. Enl. ed. Columbus, O.: Riely, 1856. 236 pp.

Baird, Thomas Dickson
Science of Praise; or, An Illustration of the Nature and Design of Sacred Psalmody. Zanesville, Ohio: Putnam & Clark, 1816. ix, 108 pp.

Ballanta, Nicholas G. J.
St. Helena Island Spirituals. New York: G. Schirmer, Inc., 1925.

Ballou, Silas
New Hymns, on Various Subjects. Newbury, Vt.: Printed by Nathaniel Coverly, 1797. 184 pp.

Barnes, L. B.
The Congregational Harp. A collection of hymn tunes, sentences, and chants ... for congregational uses, and social religious meetings. Boston: O. Ditson, 1856. 244 pp.
Words with music for SATB.

Beecher, Henry Ward
Plymouth Collection. Plymouth, Mass.: 1855–1856.

Belknap, Daniel
The Evangelical Harmony ... To which is prefixed, A Concise Introduction to the Grounds of Music. Boston: I. Thomas and E. T. Andrews, 1800. vi, 79 pp.

————.
The Middlesex Collection of Sacred Harmony. Boston: I. Thomas and E. T. Andrews, 1802. iv, 111 pp.

————.
Sacred Poetry. Consisting of Psalms and Hymns, adapted to Christian devotion, in public and private.... New edition, with additional hymns. Boston: Thomas and Andrews, and West and Blake, 1812. 276 pp.

Bell, Geo. A., and Hubert, P. M.
Hymns of Praise with Tunes. Biglow & Main, 1884.

Benedict, David
The Pawtucket Collection of Conference Hymns for Social Worship, Selected and Original. (Baptist). Providence: I. H. Cady, 1842. 8th ed. 203 pp., without music.

Benham, Asabel
Federal Harmony; containing in a familiar manner, the rudiments of psalmody; together with a collection of church music (most of which is entirely new). Middletown, Conn.: Printed by M. H. Woodward, 1795. 64 pp.

Benjamin, Jonathan
Harmonia Coelestis: A Collection of Church Music. Northampton: Andrew Wright, 1799. 80 pp.

Benson, Louis F.
The English Hymn. Philadelphia: The Presbyterian Board of Publication, 1915.

Bentley, William
A Collection of Psalms and Hymns for Public Worship. Boston: Rowe & Hooper, 1814. 144 pp.

Blessner, Gustave
Flora Sacra; a new collection of church music ... for singing schools, seminaries, private schools, private circles, and musical conventions. New York: S. T. Gordon, 1864. 208 pp.

Billups, Edward W.
The Sweet Songster. Kentucky: 1854.

Bonar, Horatius
The Bible Hymn Book. New York: R. Carter & Bros., 1853. 381 pp.

————.
Hymns of Faith and Hope. New York: R. Carter and Bros., 1867. 375 pp.

Bourne, Hugh
A Collection of Hymns for Camp Meetings (Primitive Methodists). Bemersley near Tunstall, England: 1822.

————.
A Collection of Hymns and Spiritual Songs for the Use of the (English) Primitive Methodists Generally Called Ranters. Pocklington: 1809.

————.
Large Hymn Book for the Use of the Primitive Methodists. Bemersley near Tunstall, England: 1825.

Boyd, James M.
Virginia Sacred Musical Repository. Winchester: 1818.

Braadus, Andrew
The Dover Selection of Spiritual Songs (Baptist) : 1828.

Bradbury, William Batchelder
The Jubilee: An Extensive Collection of Church Music for the Choir.... New edition. Boston: O. Ditson & Co., 1858. 384 pp.

————.
Golden Chain of Sabbath School Melodies. New York: Ivison, Phinney & Co., 1861. 127 pp.

————, and Main, S.
Cottage Melodies; a hymn and tune book for prayer and social meetings and home circle. New York: Carlton & Porter, 1864. iv, 320 pp.

Bramely, H. R., and Stainer, J.
Christmas Carols, New and Old. London: n.d. (ca. 1870).

Brooks, Philip
Christmas Songs and Easter Carols. London: 1903. Illus.

Brown, Alling
The Musical Cabinet; a collection of sacred music, comprising a great variety of psalm and hymn tunes. New Haven: Durrie & Peck, 1831. xix, 230 pp.

Buchanan, Annabel Morris
Choral Arrangements of White Spirituals and Folk Hymns. New York: J. Fischer and Brother, 1935–1936.

————.
Folk Hymns of America. New York: J. Fischer and Brothers, 1938.

Bullen, A. H.
A Christmas Garland. Carols and poems from the 15th Century, to the present time. London: 1885.

Buzzell, John, and Liby, Elias
Psalms, Hymns and Spiritual Songs. Kennebunk, Maine: 1823.

Caldwell, William, comp.
Union Harmony. Maryville, Tenn.: 1837.

Carden, Allen D.
The Missouri Harmony: or a collection of psalm and hymn tunes, and anthems, from eminent authors: with an introduction to the grounds and rudiments of music. Cincinnati: E. Morgan and Son, 1837.

————.
United States Harmony. Nashville: 1829.

————; Rogers, Samuel J., Moore, F., and Green, J., comp.
Western Harmony. Nashville: 1824.

Carrell, James P., and Clayton, Joe S., comp.
Virginia Harmony. Lebanon, Virginia: Printed in Winchester, Virginia, 1831.

Cayce, Elder C. H., ed.
The Good Old Songs. (Primitive Baptists). Thornton, Ark.: Cayce Publishing Company, 1913.
    Fasola notation.

Cennick, John
Sacred Hymns for the Use of Religious Societies, Generally Composed in Dialogues. Bristol, England: **1741.**

Chandler, Warren A.
Great Revivals and the Great Republic. Nashville: 1904.

Collins, T. K., comp.
Timbrel of Zion. Philadelphia: 1854.

Cooper, W. M., ed.
Sacred Harp. Dothan, Alabama: 1902. An enlarged edition of the 1844 Sacred Harp.

Daily, Elder J. R., ed.
Primitive Baptist Hymn and Tune Book. Madisonville, Ky.: J. D. Shain, 1902, 1918.
Fasola notation. Includes many folk hynms.

Dassey, William
The Choice. South Carolina: Printed in Philadelphia for Dassey, 1830. 3rd ed.

Davis, R.
Hymns Composed on Several Subjects and Divers Occasions. Boston: 1741. 6th ed.

Davison, Ananias, comp.
Kentucky Harmony. Rockingham County, Virginia: Printed in Harrisonburg, Virginia, 1815; second edition, 1817; fourth edition, 1821; fifth edition, 1826.

————.
Supplement to the Kentucky Harmony. Rockingham County, Virginia: Printed in Harrisonburg, Virginia: 1820.

Dearmer, Percy; Williams, R. Vaughan, and Shaw, Martin
The Oxford Book of Carols. London: Oxford University Press, 1931.

DeWitt, M. B., ed.
Bible Songs. Nashville: 1865.

Douthit, S. "Doc"
The Zion Traveller. Madisonville, Tenn.: 1835.

Dow, Peggy
A Collection of Camp Meeting Hymns. Philadelphia: 1816. 2nd ed.

Ely, Seth
Sacred Music. Germantown, Penna.: 1822.

Family Hymns. American Tract Society: 1833. 304 hymns.

Fenner, Thomas P.
Cabin and Plantation Songs, as Sung by Hampton Students. New York: G. P. Putnam and Sons, 1901. vi, 166 pp.
Includes a few songs "From Indian and Other Nationalities."

Funk, Joseph, comp.
Choral Music. Harrisonburg, Virginia: 1816.

————, comp.
Genuine Church Music. Mountain Valley, Va.: Printed in Winchester, Virginia, 1832.

Gambold, John
A Collection of Hymns of the Children of God. (For the English Moravians). London: 1754.

G., E. E.
Old English Carols Set to Music. Traditional and original. London: n.d.

Gillington, Alice E., coll. and ed.
Old Christmas Carols of the Southern Counties. London: J. Curwen and Sons, Ltd., 1910. 24 pp. Arranged for medium voice.

Gibson, S. A., and Harker, F. F.
Old Christmas Carols. Traditional melodies, newly arranged and harmonized. New York. n.d.

Glas, John
Christian Songs. Edinburgh: 1749. Reprinted in Provincetown, Rhode Island, 1787.

Golden Wreath, for the month of Mary; composed of daily considerations on the triple crown of Our Blessed Lady's joys, sorrows and glories; with examples and hymns set to music. Notre Dame, Ind.: The Ave Maria Press, 1938. vii, 232 pp.

Greeve, Richard Leighton, ed.
The Early English Carols. Oxford: The Clarendon Press, 1935. 461 pp., bibl. (pp. 325–350).

Harrod, John
Social and Camp Meeting Songs. Baltimore, Md.: 1817.

Harvey, Miss
Hymns and Spiritual Songs on Different Subjects. (Baptist). Hudson, N. Y.: Ashbel Stoddard, 1806.

Hastings, Thomas, and Mason, Lowell
Spiritual Songs for Social Worship. Adapted to the use of families and private circles in seasons of revivals to missionary meetings, to the monthly concert, and to other occasions of special interest. Utica, N. Y.: Hasting & Tracy & W. Williams, 1832.

————.
Sacred Songs for Family and Social Worship. New York: American Tract Society, 1855.

————, and Bradbury, William B.
The New York Choralist: ...Psalm & Hymn Tunes. New York: Newman, 1847. 352 pp.

————, and Warriner, Solomon
Musica Sacra; or Sprinfield & Utica Collections United: ...Utica: William Williams, 1819. 280 pp.

Hauser, William, comp.
Hesperian Harp. Wadley, Ga.: Printed in Philadelphia, 1848.

————, and Turner, Benjamin, comp.
Olive Leaf. Wadley, Ga.: Printed in Philadelphia, 1878.

Hayden, Amos Sutton
Introduction to Sacred Music. Pittsburgh: 1835.

Hendrickson, George, comp.
Union Harmony. Mountain Valley, Virginia: 1848.

Henry, George W.
The Golden Harp or Camp Meeting Hymns,
old and new, set to music. Auburn: W. T.
Moses, 1855.

Hickok, J. H., and Fleming, G.
Evangelical Music. Carlisle, Pa.: 1832.

Hill, Rowland
A Collection of Psalms and Hymns. London:
1783.

Hill, Uri K.
Vermont Harmony. Northampton, Mass.: 1801.

Hillman, Joseph, comp.
The Revivalist. Troy, New York: 1868. Revised
and enlarged edition printed in Albany, New
York, 1872.

Himes, Joshua V.
Millennial Harp (Adventist). Boston: 1843.

Himes, Paul, and Wilson, Jonathan
A Selection of Hymns from the Best Authors;
by elders Paul Himes and Jonathan Wilson.
(Methodists and Baptists). Greenfield, Mass.:
Printed by Ansel Phelps, 1817. Reg. 1816. 324
pp., without music.

Holden, Oliver
*The Union Harmony, or Universal Collection
of Sacred Music.* 2 vols. in 1. Boston: Isaiah
Thomas & Ebenezer T. Andrews, 1793. 295 pp.

Holyoke, Samuel
The Christian Harmonist. Salem, Mass.: 1804.

————.
*The Columbian Repository of Sacred Har-
mony....* Exeter, N. H.: Henry Ranlet, 1809.
440 pp.

Hymns and Spiritual Songs: Setting forth the
sufferings of Christ at his birth. Life and death
upon the cross. With the manifold benefits and
blessings that flow to believers therefrom.
Penrith: A. Bell, n.d., 16 pp.

*Hymns and Spiritual Songs for the Use of
Christians.* Eighth edition, revised, corrected
and enlarged, containing, in addition to those
heretofore published, a copious selection from
the best modern authors, and several original
hymns. Baltimore: Printed and sold by Warner
and Hanna, 1806, 280 pp., without music.

Ingalls, Jeremiah
Christian Harmony or Songster's Companion.
Exeter, New Hampshire: 1805.

Jackson, George Pullen, ed.
Down-East Spirituals and Others; Three hun-
dred songs supplementary to the author's spir-
itual folk-songs of early America. New York:
J. J. Augustin, 1943. 296 pp., illus., bibl.
Melodies and texts.

————.
Spiritual Folk-Songs of Early America; two
hundred and fifty tunes and texts, with an introduction and notes. New York: J. J. Augustin,
1937. x, 254 pp., illus., music, bibl.

————.
The Story of the Sacred Harp, 1844–1944.
Nashville: Vanderbilt University Press, 1944.
46 pp., illus.
A bibliographical history with comment and dis-
cussion of the music.

————.
White and Negro Spirituals; their life span
and kinship, tracing two hundred years of untrammeled song making and singing among our
country folk, with 116 songs, as sung by both
races. New York: J. J. Augustin, 1943. xiii, 349
pp., illus., music.

————.
White Spirituals in the Southern Uplands; the
story of the fasola folk, their songs, singings,
and "buckwheat notes." Chapel Hill: The University of North Carolina Press, 1933. xv, 444
pp., illus., music, bibl.

Jackson, John B., comp.
Knoxville Harmony. Madisonville, Tenn.: 1838.

James, Joe S., ed.
Original Sacred Harp. Atlanta, Ga: 1911.

————.
Union Harp and History of Songs. Douglas-
ville, Ga.: 1909.

Jocelyn, N., and S. S., comp.
Zion's Harp. District of Connecticut: 1824.
Issued as a companion to Nettleton's *Village
Hymns.* 33 pages of tunes.

Johnson, Alexander
The Tennessee Harmony. 1820. Preface of 2nd
edition dated "West Tennessee, Oct. 9th, 1920."

Johnson, Andrew W., comp.
Western Psalmodist. Cornersville, Tenn.:
Printed in Nashville, Tenn., 1853.

Jones, Abner
The Melody of the Heart. (Baptist-Christian).
Boston: 1804.

Laus Deo! The Worcester Collection of Sacred
Harmony. Boston: Isaiah Thomas, 1792.
152 pp.

Leavitt, Joshua, comp.
The Christian Lyre. New York: 1830.

Leslie, C. E.
The Sabbath School Queen. Pond: 1879.
126 pp.

Lewis, Freeman
The Beauties of Harmony. Pittsburgh: 1813.
4th ed., 1820.

Lightwood, James Thomas
Hymn-Tunes and Their Story. London: 1905.

Lloyd, Benjamin
The Primitive Hymns; spiritual songs, and
sacred poems, regularly selected, classified and
set in order, and adapted to social singing and
all occasions of divine worship. (Primitive
Baptist). Temple, Tex.: Published for the
Proprietress, Mrs. M. E. Atkins, 1906. xxii, 554
pp.

Long, Edwin McKean
The Revival Harp. Hymns and music adapted to his "Protracted Meeting Series" of Illustrated Sermons, and Seasons of Revival. Philadelphia: J. L. Landis, 1872.

Lorenz, Edmund Simon
American Spirituals and Gospel Songs. In: *Practical Church Music.* New York: F. H. Revell, 1909.

————, and Baltzell, I.
Songs of Grace. Dayton, Ohio: United Brethren Publishing House, 1879.

Lyon, John
The Harp of Zion. London: T. C. Armstrong, 1853. 225 pp.
    Contains early Mormon hymns.

Madan, Martin
A Collection of Psalms and Hymns. London: 1760.

Manly, Basil
Manly's Choice: A New Selection of Approved Hymns for Baptist Churches. Louisville, Ky.: Baptist Book Concern, 1891.

Mansfield, Rev. D. H.
The American Vocalist. Tunes, Anthems, Sentences & Hymns. In Three Parts. Boston: Wm. J. Reynolds, 1849. 360 pp.

Mason, Lowell
Carmina Sacra: or, Boston Collection of Church Music; comprising the most popular psalm and hymn tunes in general use. Boston: J. H. Wilkins & R. B. Carter, 1841.

————.
Carmina Sacra Enlarged. The American Tune Book: A complete collection of the tunes which are widely popular in America. Boston: Oliver Ditson & Company, 1869.

————.
Chapel Hymns: A selection of hymns, with appropriate tunes; adapted to vestry or other social religious meetings. Boston: T. R. Marvin, 1842.

————.
Choral Harmony: Being a selection of the most approved anthems, choruses, and other pieces of sacred music; suitable for singing societies, concerts, and various public occasions. Boston: Richardson & Lord, 1828.

————.
Juvenile Psalmist; or, The Child's Introduction to Sacred Music. Prepared at the request of the "Boston Sabbath School Union." Boston: Richardson, Lord and Holbrook, 1829.

————.
Fifty-Nine Select Psalm and Hymn Tunes, for public or private worship. Boston: Wilkins, Carter & Co., 1849.

————.
Lyra Sacra: Consisting of anthems, motetts, sentences, chants, etc. Original and selected: most of which are short, easy of performance and appropriate to the common and various occasions of public worship. Boston: Richardson, Lord and Holbrook, 1832.

————.
Mason's Hand-Book of Psalmody; a collection of ancient and modern psalm and hymn tunes, chants and short anthems, for public worship and family use; arranged for four voices. London: Houlston & Stoneham, 1852(?).

————.
Musical Service of the Protestant Episcopal Church. Boston: J. H. Wilkins and R. B. Carter, 1843.

————.
Occasional Psalm and Hymn Tunes, Selected and Original. Boston: Melvin Lord, 1836.

————.
Periodical Psalmody; consisting of original selected church music. Boston: Kidder & Wright, 1842.

————.
Sabbath School Songs; or Hymns and Music Suitable for Sabbath Schools. Boston: Massachusetts Sabbath School Society, 1834.

————.
Select Chants, Doxologies, etc. Adapted to the Use of the Protestant Episcopal Church in the United States of America. Boston: Richardson and Lord, 1824.

————.
Sentences, or Short Anthems, Hymn Tunes, and Chants, Appropriate to Various Occasions of Public Worship. Boston: Carter, Hendee and Company, 1834.

————.
Songs of Asaph; consisting of original psalm and hymn tunes, chants, and anthems. Boston: A. B. Kidder, 1843.

————.
The Boston Academy's Collection of Church Music: Consisting of the most popular psalm and hymn tunes, anthems, sentences, etc., old and new. Boston: Carter, Hendee & Co., 1835.

————.
The Boston Anthem Book; being a selection of anthems, collects motetts, and other set pieces. Boston: J. H. Wilkins & R. B. Carter, and Jenks & Palmer, 1839.

————.
The Boston Collection of Anthems, Choruses, etc. With a separate accompaniment for the organ. Boston: Carter, Hendee & Company, 1834.

————.

The Boston Handel and Haydn Society Collection of Church Music; being a selection of the most approved psalm and hymn tunes; together with many beautiful extracts from the works of Haydn, Mozart, Beethoven, and other eminent modern composers. Never before published in this country: The whole harmonized for three and four voices, with a figured bass for the organ and pianoforte. Circulated for public worship or private devotion. Boston: Richardson and Lord, 1822.

————.

The Choir; or Union Collection of Church Music, consisting of a great variety of psalm and hymn tunes, anthems, etc. Original and selected, including many beautiful subjects from the works of Haydn, Mozart, Cherubini, etc. Boston: Carter, Hendee and Company, 1832.

————.

The Choralist: A collection of sacred music, consisting of psalm and hymn tunes, chants, and anthems. Boston: 1847.

————.

The Hallelujah; a book for the service in the house of the Lord... to which is prefixed *The Singing School:* A manual for classes in vocal music. New York: Mason Brothers, 1854.

————.

The Modern Psalmist; a collection of church music, comprising the most popular psalm and hymn tunes and occasional pieces in general use.... The whole constituting a body of church music probably as extensive and complete as was ever issued. Boston: J. H. Wilkins and R. B. Carter, 1839.

————.

The New Carmina Sacra: or Boston Collection of Church Music. Boston: Wilkins, Carter & Co., 1850.

————.

The Sabbath School Harp; being a selection of tunes and hymns, adapted to the wants of Sabbath schools, families, and social meetings. Boston: Massachusetts Sabbath School Society, 1837.

————, **and Greene, David**
Church Psalmody: A Collection of Psalms and Hymns, adapted to public worship. Boston: Perkins & Marvin, 1931.

————.

Manual of Christian Psalmody; a collection of psalms and hymns, for public worship. Boston: Perkins & Marvin, 1832.

————, **and Babcock, Rufus, Jr.**
Union Hymns: Adapted to social meetings and family worship. Selected from *Church Psalmody,* with additional hymns. Boston: Perkins, Marvin & Co., 1834.

————, **and Ives, E., Jr.**
Juvenile Lyre; or Hymns and Songs, Religious, Moral, and Cheerful, Set to Appropriate Music, for the use of primary and common schools. Boston: Richardson, Lord & Holbrook, 1831.

————, **and Mason, William**
Asaph, or The Choir Book: A collection of vocal music, sacred and secular, for choirs, singing schools, musical societies and conventions, and social and religious assemblies. New York: Mason Brothers, 1861.

————.

The Hymnist; a collection of sacred music, original and selected. Boston: Tappan, Whittemore & Mason, 1849.

————, **and Mason, Timothy**
The Harp: A Collection of Choice Sacred Music; derived from the compositions of about one hundred eminent German, Swiss, Italian, French, English, and other European musicians; also original tunes by German, English and American authors. Cincinnati: Truman & Smith, 1841.

————.

The Sacred Harp or Eclectic Harmony: A new collection of church music, consisting of psalm and hymn tunes, anthems, sentences and chants, old, new and original. Cincinnati: Truman and Smith, 1835. Many subsequent editions appeared. It was continued with *The Sacred Harp: or Beauties of Church Music,* 1841; *Mason's Sacred Harp,* 1846, etc.

————, **Park, Edwards A., and Phelps, Austin**
The Sabbath Hymn and Tune Book for the Service of Song in the House of the Lord. New York: Mason Brothers, 1859.

————.

The New Sabbath Hymn and Tune Book for the Service of Song in the House of Lord. Boston: Ditson & Co., 1866.

————, **and Webb, George J.**
Cantica Laudis, or The American Book of Church Music: Being chiefly a selection of chaste and elegant melodies... for choirs and singing schools. New York: Mason and Law, 1850.

————.

Sacred Melodies, composed and arranged as solos, duets, trios, quartettes, etc., with an accompaniment for the pianoforte. Boston: Carter, Hendee & Company, 1833.

————.

The National Psalmist; a collection of the most popular and useful psalm and hymn tunes. Boston: Tappan, Whittemore and Mason, 1848.

————.

The Psaltery, a New Collection of Church Music, consisting of psalm and hymn tunes, chants, and anthems; being one of the most complete music books for church choirs, congregations, singing schools, and societies ever published. Boston: Wilkins, Carter & Company, 1845.

McAnnally, David R.
The Western Harp; a collection of social and revival hymns. St. Louis: 1855.

McCurry, John G., comp.
Social Harp. Andersonville, Ga.: Printed in Philadelphia, 1855.

McDowell, Lucien L.
Songs of the Old Camp Ground. Genuine Religious Folk Songs of the Tennessee Hill Country. Ann Arbor, Mich.: Edwards Bros., 1937. 85 pp., illus.
    Contains traditional rote songs, traditional song refrains, old hymns, and historical and descriptive notes.

Medley, Samuel
Hymns. (Baptist). Liverpool: 1801.

Mercer, Jesse, comp.
"Mercer's Cluster."—Popular designation for *The Cluster* of Spiritual Songs, Divine Hymns and Social Poems. Augusta, Ga.: 1817.

————.
The Cluster of Spiritual Songs. Georgia: Printed in Philadelphia for Mercer of Powelton, Georgia, 1823.

Merrill, A. D., and Brown, W. C.
The Wesleyan Harp. (Methodist). Boston: 1834. 2nd ed.

Messinger, Ruth Ellis
Christian Hymns of the First Three Centuries. Pamphlet. New York: Hymn Society of America.

Metcalf, Frank J.
Stories of Hymn Tunes. New York: Abingdon Press, 1928.

Metcalf, Samuel L.
The Kentucky Harmonist. Cincinnati: 1817.

Meyers, Levi C.
Manual of Sacred Music. Harrisonburg, Va.: 1853.

Miller, W. E.
David's Harp. London: 1805.
    Methodist musical propaganda deplores "indecorous style of music brought over from America."

Mintz, David B.
Collection of Hymns and Spiritual Songs. (Methodist). Newbern, N. C.: 1806.

————.
Spiritual Song Book. (Methodist). Halifax, N. C.: 1805.

Moore, William, comp.
Columbian Harmony. Wilson County, Tenn.: Printed in Cincinnati, 1825.

Nason, Elias
A Selection of Sacred Songs; for the use of schools, academies, and the social circle. Newburyport: M. H. Sargent, 1850. 111 pp.

The New Chorister. . . . M. E. Hymn Book. Philadelphia: Thomas Stokes, 1851. 64 pp.

Newton, John, and Cowper, William
Olney Hymns in Three Books. London: 1779.

Niles, John Jacob
Ballads, Carols, and Tragic Legends from the Southern Appalachian Mountains. New York: Schirmer, Inc., Set 18.

————.
Ten Christmas Carols from the Southern Appalachian Mountains. New York: Schirmer, Inc., Set 16.

O'Kelley, James
Hymns and Spiritual Songs Designed for the Use of Christians (Methodist-Christian). Raleigh, N. C.: 1816.

Palmer, James W.
The Western Harmonic Companion. Lexington: Printed in Cincinnati for Palmer, 1826.

Parkinson, William
A Selection of Hymns and Spiritual Songs. (Baptist). New York: 1809.

Peak, John
A New Collection of Hymns and Spiritual Songs. (Baptist). Windsor, Mass.: 1793. 3rd ed.

Perkins, W. O. and H. S.
The Nightingale; a choice collection of Songs, Chants & Hymns, for the Use of Juvenile Classes, Public Schools, and Seminaries. Boston: Oliver Ditson, 1860. 216 pp.

————.
The Starry Crown of Sunday School Melodies. New York: Pond, 1869. 160 pp.

Pious Songs. Social Prayer, Closet and Camp Meeting Hymns & Choruses. Baltimore, 1838. 467 pp.

Powell, John, Rufty, Hilton, and Buchanan, Annabel Morris
Twelve Folk Hymns from the Old Shape Note Hymnbooks and from Oral Tradition. New York: J. Fischer and Brother, 1934.

Relly, James and John
Christian Hymns, Poems and Spiritual Songs, Sacred to the praise of God, our Saviour. Burlington, N. J.: Reprinted by Isaac Collins in Market Street, 1776. 236 pp.
    American editions used by Universalists.

Revival Hymns and Tunes.
New York: 1858.

Rickert, E., coll. and arr.
Ancient English Christmas Carols. 1400–1700. London: 1928. Illus.

Rippon, John
A Selection of Hymns. London: 1787.

Sandys, William
Christmas Carols, Ancient and Modern. Including the most popular in the west of England, and the airs to which they are sung,— with an introduction and notes. London: 1833.

Scudder, M. L.
Wesleyan Psalmist: 1842.

Seagrave, Robert
Hymns for Christian Worship: 1742. 4th ed. 1748.

Sharp, Cecil J., and Karpeles, Maud
English Folk Songs from the Southern Appalachians. London: Oxford Press, 1932. 2 vols. Contain a number of carols.

Silva, Owen da
Mission Music of California: a collection of old California Mission hymns and masses. Los Angeles: 1941.

Smith, Elias
A Collection of Hymns for the Use of Christians (Baptist-Christian). Portland: Published and sold at the Herald Printing Office and Bookstore, Columbienrow. John P. Colcord, Printer, 1811. 4th ed.

————, **and Jones, Abner**
Hymns, Original and Selected, for the Use of Christians. Boston: Nathan Foster, 1810. 4th ed., 324 pp., without music.

Smith, Henry
Church Harmony. Chambersburg, Penna.: 1834. (German supplement by Heinrich Schmidt entitled *Kirchen-Harmonie*).

Smith, Joshua
Divine Hymns or Spiritual Songs, for the use of religious assemblies and private Christians: being formerly a collection by Joshua Smith and others. (Baptist.) Norwich, Conn.: Printed and sold by Sterry and Porter, 1803. 11th edition with additions and alterations.

Snow, Eliza R.
Poems, Religious, Historical and Political. Liverpool: 1856.
Contains many songs and hymns.

Snyder, William B., and Chappell, W. B.
The Western Lyre. Printed in Cincinnati, 1861.

The Southern Zion's Songster. Comp. by the Editor of the N. Carolina Christian Advocate. Raleigh: 1864. 128 pp.

Southland Spirituals. Atlanta Ga.: Commission on Interacial Cooperation.

Spense, R.
A Collection of Psalms and Hymns. York, England: 1781.

Steffey, J. W.
The Valley Harmonist. Winchester, Va.: 1836.

Swan, M. L., ed.
The New Harp of Columbia. Original Publication in 1867. A reprint of *Harp of Columbia,* 1848. Nashville, Tenn.: 1921. Obtainable from L. D. Schultz, 1126 Eleanor Street, Knoxville, Tenn.

Swan, W. H., and M. L., comp.
Harp of Columbia. Knoxville, Tenn.: 1848.

Terry, Esekiel
Hymns and Spiritual Songs, a New Edition. East Windsor, N. H.: 1816.

The Boston Collection of Sacred and Devotional Hymns: Intended to accommodate Christians on special and stated occasions. (Baptist.) Boston: Manning and Loring, 1808. xii, 324 pp.

The Camp Meeting Chorister. Philadelphia: 1830.

The New Book of Temperance Melodies. Philadelphia, New York, Boston and Baltimore: Fisher and Brothers, 185–. Woodcuts, original printed wrappers, 95 pp. unnumbered.

The New Hymn and Tune Book. Nashville: Southern Methodist Publishing House, 1880.

The New Jersey Harmony. Philadelphia: John McCullock, 1797.

The Original Sacred Harp. Haleyville, Alabama: 1936. Denson Revision.

The Oxford Book of Carols. London: 1943. Pocket ed.

The Young Convert's Companion. Boston: 1806.

Tillett, Wilbur F.
The Hymns and Writers of the Church. Nashville, Tenn.: Smith and Lamar, 1911.
General discussion.

Walker, William
The Southern Harmony and Musical Companion. Printed in New Haven, 1835. Philadelphia: E. W. Miller, 1847–1854. Reproduced in facsimile by the Federal Writers' Project of Kentucky, Works Progress Administration. New York: Hastings House, 1939.

————.
The Christian Harmony. Original edition, Spartansburg, S. C.: 1866. Revised edition by E. W. Miller, Philadelphia, 1901.
Fasola notation.

————, **comp.**
Southern Harmony. Spartansburg, S. C.: Printed in New Haven, Connecticut, 1835.

————.
Southern and Western Pocket Harmonist. Spartansburg, S. C.: Printed in Philadelphia, 1846.

Wesley, John
A Collection of Psalms and Hymns. Charleston,
S. C.: Lewis Timothy, 1737. 3rd edition, 1741.

————, **and Charles**
Hymns and Sacred Poems. Philadelphia:
Andrew and William Bradford, 1740.
"and sold for the benefit of the poor in Georgia."

White, B. F., and King, E. J.
Original Sacred Harp. Atlanta, Ga.: United
Harp Musical Association, 1911. (Reprint of
the Sacred Harp of 1844.)
The only hymnal published in the original four-
shape notation. "One of the finest collections of
folk hymns ever published."

Wiatt, Solomon
*Impartial Selection of Hymns and Spiritual
Songs* (Methodist Camp Meeting). Phila-
delphia: 1809.

Winchell, R.
*The Baptist Songster or Divine Songs for Con-
ference Meetings.* Withersfield, 1829.

Woodbury, I. B.
The Day-Spring; or, Union Collection of Songs
for the Sanctuary. New York: F. J. Huntington, 1859. 352 pp.

————.
The Dulcimer; or, the New York Collection of
Sacred Music. New York: F. J. Huntington,
1850. 352 pp.

————.
The Thanksgiving. A Collection of Music.
New York: F. J. Huntington, 1857. 352 pp.

Wright, Theodore, ed.
Songs and Carols. Printed from a Manuscript
in the Sloane Collection in the British Museum.
London: Pickering, 1836.
A reprint of twenty songs and carols from the
15th Century.

Zion's Songster; or a collection of hymns and
spiritual songs usually sung at Camp meetings.
Compiled by Thomas Mason, 10th edition. New
York: 1838.

ARRANGEMENTS

(Individual Titles)

————: *Unison*

"Our Prayer" (Based on Traditional Folk Tune).
Kinscella, H. G.: J. Fischer and Bro.: Unison.

"The Robin and the Thorn."
Niles: Schirmer: Unison.

————: *Voice and Piano*

"I Wonder As I Wander."
Niles, John J.: Schirmer.

"Poor Wayfaring Stranger."
Brown, L.: Associated: Voice and piano.

————: *Female Voices*

"Down in Yon Forest" (Christmas).
Niles, J. J.: Schirmer: SA, SSA. Mountain
Carol, North Carolina.

"I Wonder As I Wander."
Niles, J. J.: Schirmer: SSAA, Sopr. solo, a cap.

"I Wonder As I Wander."
Niles-Horton: Schirmer: SSA.

"Jesus the Christ is Born" (Christmas Carol).
Talmadge: Schirmer: SSAA, a cap.

"Lazarus."
Reynolds, G.: J. Fischer and Bro.: SSAA.
Tennessee Mountain ballad hymn.

"Lulle, Lullay."
Niles, J. J.: Schirmer: SSA.
Tennessee Carol.

"On the First Day of Christmas" (The Twelve
Days of Christmas). Goldsworthy: H. W. Gray:
SSA.

"Our Prayer."
Kinscella, H. G.: J. Fischer and Bro.: SA,
SSA, SSAA.

"Poor Wayfaring Stranger."
Jackson-Gatwood: J. Fischer and Bro.: SSA.

"Poor Wayfaring Stranger."
Scott: Lyon and Healy: SSA.

"Poor Wayfaring Stranger."
Wilson, H. R.: Hall and McCreary: SSA.

"Sing Me the Virgin Mary."
Niles-Horton: Schirmer: SSA, Sopr. solo, a cap.

"The Carol of the Birds."
Horton: Schirmer: SA, SSA, Sopr. Solo, a cap.

"The King Shall Come When Morning Dawns."
Niles, J. J.: Schirmer: SAA, a cap.

"The Promised Land."
Moore-Gilbert: Ricordi: SSA.

"The Seven Joys of Mary."
Talmadge: Schirmer: SSAA, a cap.

"The Story of Noah."
Niles-Harris: Schirmer: SSAA.

"Twelve Days of Christmas."
Saar, L. V.: E. C. Schirmer: SSA, Double
Chorus, Solo.

"When Jesus Lived in Galilee" (Christmas
Carol). Niles: Schirmer: SSA, with Children's
Unison Chorus, or Sopr. solo, a cap.

————: *Male Voices*

"Boundless Mercy."
Rufty, H.: J. Fischer and Bro.: TTBB.

"Choral Episode from the Evangel of the New
World." Thompson, V. D.: Presser: TTBB.
> Based on early American hymns: Paralytic,
> Russia; Pisgah; Pleading Savior; Oh, He's
> Taken My Feet from the Mire and the Clay.

"Down in Yon Forest."
Niles, J.: Schirmer: TB.

"I Am a Poor Wayfaring Stranger."
Scott, T.: Words and Music, Inc.: TTBB.
> Fred Waring Glee Club Arrangement.

"I Saw Three Ships."
Malin, Donald: Birchard: TTBB.

"I Wonder As I Wander."
Niles-Horton: Schirmer: TTBB, Medium Solo,
a cappella.

"Jesus Born in Bethlea."
Buchanan, A. M.: J. Fischer and Bro.: TTBB.

"Our Prayer."
Kinscella, H. G.: J. Fischer and Bro.: TTBB,
TTB, TBB.
> Based on traditional tune.

"Poor Wayfarin' Man O' Grief."
Gaul, Harvey B.: Galaxy: TTBB, Sop. solo.
> A sacred hymn tune of the Penn-Ohio border.

"Poor Wayfaring Stranger."
Jackson-Gatwood: J. Fischer and Bro.: TTBB.

"Tennessee Mountain Psalm."
Gaul, Harvey B.: Galaxy: Bar. Sop. Solo.
> Adaptation of 93rd Psalm tune.

"The Carol of the Birds."
Horton: Schirmer: TB.

"The King Shall Come When Morning Dawns."
Niles, J. J.: Schirmer: TTBB, a cap.

"The Little Family."
Treharne, B.: Willis: TTBB.
> Ballad Hymn of Kentucky.

"The Old Ship of Zion."
Gatwood, E. J.: J. Fischer and Bro.: TTBB.

"The Promised Land."
Moore-Gilbert: Ricordi: TTBB.

"The Story of Noah."
Niles-Harris: Schirmer: TTBB.

————: *Mixed Voices*

"Alabama" (Fuguing Hymn).
Buchanan, A. M.: J. Fischer and Bro.: SATB.

"And the Trees Do Moan" (Christmas).
Gaul, H. B.: Ditson: SATB.
> A Kentucky carol.

"Boundless Mercy."
Rufty, H.: J. Fischer and Bro.: SATB.

Cantata on Appalachian Christmas Carols.
Holden, David J.: MS: Mezzo Soprano Solo,
Female voices, organ or piano.

"Choral Episodes from the Evangel of the New
World." Thompson, V. D.: Presser and Co.:
SATB.
> Based on early American folk hymns.

"Curtains of Light."
Strong: Hall & McCreary: SATB.

Five Christmas Carols of Old England.
Content: "In Bethlehem", "Christmas Eve",
"Shepherd's Watch", "The Golden Carol".
Kingsley, G.: Oxford: SATB.

"Folk Hymns."
Powell, John: J. Fischer: SATB.

"Immensity."
Buchanan, A. M.: J. Fischer and Bro.: SATB.

"I Saw Three Ships."
Crawford, Louise: White-Smith: SATB.
> Christmas Carol.

"I Wonder As I Wander."
Niles-Horton: Schirmer: SATB, Sopr. or Ten.
Solo, a cappella.

"Jesus Ahatonhia (Jesus is Born)."
Brébeuf, (McGlinchee): Schirmer: SATB.

"Jesus Born in Bethlea."
Buchanan, A. M.: J. Fischer and Bro.: SATB.

"Jesus, Jesus, Rest Your Head" (Christmas
Carol). Niles-Warrell: Schirmer: SATB, a cap.

"Jesus the Christ is Born."
Niles: Schirmer: SATB.

"Jesus the Christ is Born."
Niles-Warrell: Schirmer: SATB, (full chorus).

"Lulle Lullay."
Niles-DeBrant: Schirmer: SATB, a cap.

"New Jordan" (Fuguing Hymn).
Buchanan, A. M.: J. Fischer and Bro.: SATB.

"O Jesus, My Savior."
Buchanan, A. M.: J. Fischer and Bro.: SATB.

"Our Prayer."
Kinscella, Hazel G.: J. Fischer and Bro.:
SATB, SAB.

"Parting Friends."
Binder, A. W.: Elkan-Vogel: SATB.

"Poor Wayfarin' Man O' Grief."
Gaul, Harvey B.: Galaxy: Sop. solo, SATB.
> A sacred folk hymn of the Penn-Ohio border.

"Poor Wayfaring Stranger."
Jackson-Gatwood: J. Fischer and Bro.: SATB.

"Poor Wayfaring Stranger."
Siegmeister, E.: C. Fischer: SATB, Ten. Solo,
a cap.

Psalm Tunes, Hymns and Chorales.
(Part 1a, Nos. 1–10, 1b, Nos 11–18). Goldman-
Smith: Schirmer: SATB.
> From *Landmarks of Early American Music:*
> *1760–1800*, by Richard Franko Goldman and
> Roger Smith.

"Retirement."
Buchanan, A. M.: J. Fischer and Bro.: SATB.

"See Jesus the Savior."
Niles: Schirmer: SATB, a cap.

"Sing We the Virgin Mary" (Folk Carol).
Niles-Norton: Schirmer: SATB.

"Tennessee Mountain Morning Hymn."
Gaul, Harvey, B.: Galaxy: Sop. solo, SATB.

"Tennessee Mountain Psalm."
Gaul, Harvey B.: Galaxy: Bar. and Sop. solo, SATB.

"The Babe of Bethlehem."
Powell, J.: J. Fischer and Bro.: SATB, a cap.
Traditional South.

"The Carol of the Angels."
Niles, John J.: Schirmer: SATB, a cap.

"The Carol of the Birds."
Horton: Schirmer: SSATB. Sopr. solo, a cap.

"The Female Convict."
Buchanan, A. M.: J. Fischer and Bro.: SATB.
A ballad hymn.

"The Hebrew Children."
Buchanan, A. M.: J. Fischer and Bro.: SATB.

"The King Shall Come When Morning Dawns."
Niles, John J.: Schirmer: SSAATTBB, a cap.

"The Little Family."
Treharne, B.: Willis: SATB.
A Kentucky ballad hymn.

"The Morning Trumpet."
Dalton, Sydney: J. Fischer and Bro.: SATB.

"The Old Ship of Zion."
Gatwood, E. J.: J. Fischer and Bro.: SATB.

"The Promised Land."
Burleigh, H. T.: Ricordi: SATB.

"The Seven Good Joys of Mercy."
Saar, L. V.: Carl Fischer: SATB.

"The Story of Noah."
Niles-Harris: Schirmer: SSAATTBB.

"When Jesus Lived in Galilee" (Christmas Carol). Niles: Schirmer: SATB, with children's unison chorus or Sopr. Solo, a cap.

"While Shepherds Watched Their Flocks."
Warrell, A.: Oxford: SATB, a cap.

"Wondrous Love."
Buchanan, A. M.: J. Fischer and Bro.: SATB.
Southern folk hymn.

——————: Piano

"Wayfaring Stranger."
Harris, Roy: C. Fischer: piano.

——————: Orchestra

Symphony on a Hymn Tune.
Thomson, Virgil: MS: Orchestra.

"Three Gospel Hymns."
Helm, Everett: Boosey and Hawkes: Orchestra.

"Two Preludes on Southern Folk Hymn Tunes."
Lewis, H. Merrils: MS: Chamber orchestra.

White Spiritual Symphony.
Bryan, Charles F.: MS: Orchestra.

RECORDS

Album—Collections

Christmas Hymns and Carols.
RCA Victor Chorale, Robert Shaw, Cond. 4–10".   VM–1077
Includes a number of white spirituals and hymns.

Early American Carols and Folksongs.
John Jacob Niles, vocal-dulcimer, 4–12".
VM–718

Religious and Worldly American Folk Songs.
The Old Harp Singers, of Nashville, Tenn. 2–10".   MU–41

Sacred Harp Singing.
Edited by George Pullen Jackson. In: Album 11, AAFS51 (hymns); AAFS52 (fuguing songs); AAFS53 (fuguing songs); AAFS54 (fuguing songs); and AAFS55 (anthems). Library of Congress.

The Seven Joys of Mary. Early American Carols.
John Jacob Niles, tenor-dulcimer. 3–10".
DISC–732
Contents: The Seven Joys of Mary; Matthew, Mark, Luke and John; I Wonder as I Wander; The Little Liking; The Carol of the Birds; The Carol of the Angels.

The Wayfaring Stranger.
Burl Ives, vocal-guitar.   ASCH–345

U. S. Library of Congress. Division of Music. Folklore Section.
Primitive Baptist Hymns and Other Folk Songs. Sung at the Home of Mr. and Mrs. L. L. McDowell, 1942.   AAFS–LC

————.
Sacred Harp Songs. Sung at the 37th Annual Session of the Alabama Sacred Harp Singing Convention, August, 1942.   AAFS–LC

Individual Titles

"Ballstown."
Led by Ernestine Tipton of Birmingham, Ala. In: Album 11, Library of Congress.
AAFS53 B1

"Cuba."
Alabama Sacred Singers, vocal   CO–15349-D

"David's Lamentation."
Led by Howard Denson of Tuscaloosa, Ala. In: Album 11, Library of Congress.   AAFS55 B1

"Edom."
Led by Mrs. Delilah Denson Posey of Birmingham, Ala. In: Album 11, Library of Congress.
AAFS53 B2

"Evening Shade."
Led by Euna Vee Denson Nail of Birmingham, Ala. In: *Album 11*, Library of Congress.
AAFS53 A2

"Fillmore."
Led by Ernestine Tipton of Birmingham, Ala. In: *Album 11*, Library of Congress.
AAFS54 A1

"God Gave Noah the Rainbow Sign."
Carter Family, vocal-guitar.   PE–6–11–59

"Heavenly Vision."
Led by Paine Denson of Birmingham, Ala. In: *Album 11*, Library of Congress.   AAFS55A

"I'm A-Gonna Change My Way."
Delmore Brothers, vocal-guitar.   BB–6349–A

"I Wonder As I Wander."
John J. Niles, tenor-dulcimer.   VM–604–3

"I Wonder As I Wander."
Gladys Swarthout, Mezzo Soprano, Orchestra.
VI–10–1181

"Jesus, Jesus Rest Your Head."
In: *Early American Carols and Folk Songs*.
John J. Niles, vocal-dulcimer.   VM–718

"Jesus, the Christ is Born."
In: *Early American Carols and Folk Songs*.
John J. Niles, vocal-dulcimer.   VM–718

"Little Black Train."
Carter Family, vocal-guitar.   PE–7–07–62

"Lonesome Valley."
Carter Family, vocal-guitar.   PE–7–07–62

"Lover of the Lord."
Led by L. P. Odem of St. Joseph, Tenn. In: *Album 11*, Library of Congress.   AAFS51 B2

"Lulle Lullay (The Coventry Carol)."
John J. Niles, tenor-dulcimer.   VM–604–4

"Mear."
Led by Paine Denson of Birmingham, Ala. In: *Album 11*, Library of Congress.   AAFS51 A2

"Milford."
Led by Mrs. M. L. Mann of Opelika, Ala. In: *Album 11*, Library of Congress.   AAFS52 B2

"Mission."
Led by A. Margus Cagle of Atlanta, Ga. In: *Album 11*, Library of Congress.   AAFS54 B1

"Montgomery."
Led by Mrs. Delilah Denson Posey of Birmingham, Ala. In: *Album 11*, Library of Congress.
AAFS52 A1

"Mountain Dew."
Bascom Lamar Lunsford, vocal-banjo. BR–219

"Mount Zion."
Led by Mrs. Maude Moncrief of Birmingham, Ala. In: *Album 11*, Library of Congress.
AAFS52 B1

"My Long Journey Home."
Monroe Brothers, vocal-guitar-mandolin.
BB–6422–A

"Northfield."
Led by Paine Denson of Birmingham, Ala. In: *Album 11*, Library of Congress.   AAFS52 A2

"Old Ship of Zion."
Silvertone Jubilee Quartet.   OK–05515

"On My Way to Canaan's Land."
Carter Family, vocal-guitar.   BB–8167–A

"On the Rock Where Moses Stood."
Carter Family, vocal-guitar.   PE–6–11–59

"Po' Ol' Laz'rus."
Yale Glee Club.   CO–36463

"Poor Wayfaring Stranger."
In: *Two Centuries of American Folk Songs*.
American Ballad Singers. Siegmeister. VP–41

"Poor Wayfaring Stranger."
Burl Ives, vocal-guitar.   ASCH–345–1A

"Poor Wayfaring Stranger."
The Old Harp Singers.   MU–221A

"Religion is a Fortune."
Alabama Sacred Singers, vocal.   CO–15349–D

"Rocky Road."
Alabama Sacred Singers.   CO–15274–1

"Sardis."
Led by Dock Owen of Sand Mountain, Marshall Co., Ala. In: *Album 11*, Library of Congress.   AAFS54 A2

"Seven Joys of Mary."
In: *Early American Ballads*. J. J. Niles, tenor-dulcimer.   VM–604

"Sherburne."
Led by R. M. Hornsby by Clay Co., Ala. In: *Album 11*, Library of Congress.   AAFS55 B2

"So Jesus the Saviour."
In: *Early American Carols and Folk Songs*.
J. J. Niles, vocal-dulcimer.   VM–718

"Stratfield."
Led by John M. Dye of Birmingham, Ala. In: *Album 11*, Library of Congress.   AAFS53 A1

"The Little Dove."
Sung by Aunt Molly Jackson of Clay County, Kentucky. Recorded in New York, 1939, by Alan Lomax. In: *Album 2*. Recordings of American Folk Songs, Library of Congress, 1943.
AAFS7 A

"The Old Ship of Zion."
The Old Harp Singers. MU–221 B

"The Seven Joys of Mary."
John J. Niles, tenor-dulcimer. VM–604–5–6

"Vain World Adieu."
Led by A. Marcus Cagle of Atlanta, Ga. In:
Album 11, Library of Congress. AAFS54 B2

"Wayfaring Stranger."
Burl Ives, voice-guitar. ASCH–345

"Wayfaring Stranger."
Frank Luther Singers. DE–A–311

"When Jesus Lived in Galilee."
In: *Early American Carols and Folk Songs.* J.
J. Niles, vocal-dulcimer. VM–718

"Windham."
Led by Owen of Sand Mountain, Marshall Co.,
Ala. In: *Album 11*, Library of Congress.
AAFS51 A1

"Wondrous Love."
Led by Lee Wells of Jasper, Ala. In: *Album
11*, Library of Congress. AAFS51 B1

"Woven Spirituals."
In: *Recital from "American Songbag."* Carl
Sandburg, vocal-guitar. MU–11

"You Got to Cross that Lonesome Valley."
In: *American Folk Lore.* Vol. 3. J. J. Niles,
vocal-dulcimer. VM–824

"You've Got to Walk in that Lonesome Valley."
Monroe Brothers, vocal-guitar-mandolin.
BB–6477–A

BOOK TWO

The American Indians
North of Mexico

Part One: General Bibliography

BIBLIOGRAPHY OF FOLKLORE AND MUSIC OF
THE AMERICAN INDIANS NORTH OF MEXICO

FOLKLORE

See: Bibliography and Serial Publications, under Folklore, Book I, pp. 3-5.

BIBLIOGRAPHY

Andrews, H. A., and others
"Bibliography of Franz Boas." *AA* 45 (No. 3): 67–109, 1943.

Bancroft, Hubert Howe
The Native Races of the Pacific States of North America. San Francisco: A. L. Bancroft & Co., 1874–75. 5 vols., illus., bibl.
    Contents: 1. Wild Tribes. 2. Civilized Nations. 3. Myths and Languages. 4. Antiquities. 5. Primitive History.

Barber, Edwin Atlee
Papers, Pamphlets and Books, Scientific, Historical and Genealogical. Philadelphia: 1893. 8 pp.

Bibliography.
List of Publications of the Bureau of American Ethnology, with index to authors and titles. Revised to June 30, 1937. Washington, D. C.: U. S. Government Printing Office, 1937.

"Bibliography of American Archaeology." *AA* 38:411–413, 1936. (Part of article—"Man's Antiquity—North America," by Edgar B. Howard.)

"Bibliography of North American Indian Mythology." *JAFL* 18:111–172, 1905.

Boas, Franz
"Bibliography of Franz Boas." *Boas Anniversary Volume.* In Columbia University, Psychology Library, it is brought up to date 1945.

Boew, John Otis
"A Selected Bibliography of American Indian Archaeology East of the Rocky Mountains." *Papers of the Excavation Club* 2, No. 1, 90 pp. Cambridge, 1943.

Boggs, Ralph Steele
"Bibliography of American Folklore." *SFQ* 2 (No. 1):43–48, 1938, etc.
    Appears annually in the March issue of the *Southern Folklore Quarterly.*

Brinton, Daniel Garrison
A Record of Study in Aboriginal American Languages. Media, Pa.: Printed for Private Distribution, 1898. 24 pp.
    A bibliography of the writer's own writings.

Brittin, L. H.
Notices and Descriptions of Books Published or Occurring for Sale, During the Year 1903, dealing with the North and South American Indians. New York: 1903. 77 pp. (NYPL).

Brooklyn Institute of Arts and Sciences. Museum.
Miscellaneous Collection of Book Lists and Descriptive Labels Relating to the Language, Arts and Customs of the American Indians.... Brooklyn, N. Y.: 1906–07. 45 pp.

Butler, Ruth Lapham, comp.
A Check List of Manuscripts in the Edward E. Ayer Collection. Chicago: The Newberry Library, 1937. vii, 222 pp., index.
    "Among the North American folklore items in the Check List of direct concern to the folklorist are the following: No. 367, Manibojou Stories, collected by Herman Haupt Jr., 20 pp. TS. No. 689, John Howard Payne, Papers concerning the Cherokees, 172 pp. Vol. I, II, Notes, 273 pp. Vol. IV "Letters to Payne" from John Ross, D. S. Butrick and others, 1826-1840; notes concerning the origin of the Indians and the ethnology of the Cherokees, 619 pp.; No. 715, Émile Fortune Stanislaus Joseph Petitot, Chants indiens du Canada Nord Ouest recueillis, classés et notés par Émile Petitot . . . 1889. 18 pp.; No. 719, Henry E. Phillips, When the First Ship Landed in Alaska, according to Thlinget tradition Sitka (1922). Note A. P. Kashevaroff. 6 pp T.S.; No. 773, (Daniel D. Rogers) A Schedule and Catalogue of Some Indian Receipts and Cures together with the receipts . . . 144 pp.; No. 814, R. V. D. Smith. An Ojibway Tale. 10 pp. Many other manuscripts . . . are concerned with speeches by Indian representatives, Indian place names and other aspects of folklore." (E. W. Voegelin)

Chamberlain, A. F.
"Periodical Literature." *JAFL* 23:41–170, 1911. bibl.

Conover, H. F.
A Selected List of Books on the Indians of North America. United States Library of Congress, Division of Bibliography. Washington, D. C.: The Library, 1939. 25 pp.

Culin, Stewart
Bibliography of Daniel F. Brinton, M. D. Philadelphia. 1900. 28 pp.
    "Reprinted from American Philosophical Society Memorial Volume, 1900, pp. 42-67."

Dennis, Elizabeth G.
The Indians of America; a reference list for schools and libraries. Boston: F. W. Faxon Co., 1928. xiv, 67 pp.

Denver. Art Museum. Indian Art Department.
A Guide to Articles on the American Indians In Serial Publications. Part I—Denver: 1934.

Drake, Samuel Gardner
Catalogue of the Private Library of S. G. Drake. . . . Chiefly Relating to Antiquities . . . and Biography of America, and in an Especial Manner to the Indians. . . . Boston: S. G. Drake, 1845. 80 pp.

Eames, Wilberforce
Periodicals. In: *Handbook of American Indians.* Vol. II, (pp. 232–234). Bureau of American Ethnology, Bulletin 30. Washington, D. C.: U. S. Government Printing Office, 1910.

——————.
Rare Americana Relating to the American Indians; being a portion of the library of Wilberforce Eames, with a few choice duplicates from the New York Public Library. New York: The Anderson Auction Co., 1910–15. 4 parts in 1 vol. (NYPL).

Edwards, Everett E.
"Agriculture of the American Indian." A classified list of annotated historical references with an introduction. U. S. Dep't of Agriculture Library. *Bibliographical Contributions* 23 (Ed. 2) Washington, D. C., June 1933.

——————, and Rasmussen, Wayne D.
A Bibliography on the Agriculture of the American Indians. U. S. Department of Agriculture, Miscel. Publ. 447. Washington, D. C., 1942.

Field, Thomas Warren, comp.
An Essay Towards an Indian Bibliography. Being a catalogue of books, relating to the history, antiquities, languages, customs, religion, wars, literature, and origin of the American Indians, in the library of Thomas W. Field. With bibliographical and historical notes, and synopses of the contents of some of the works least known. New York: Scribner, Armstrong, and Co., 1873. iv, 430 pp.

Gaines, Ruth, comp.
"Books on Indians–1929." *Indian Notes* 7:207–236, 1930.

Gayton, A. H.
"Bibliography of Folklore of the American Indian." *JAFL* 48:287–293, 1935.
(Found at end of article: "The Orpheus Myth in North America.")

General Index, American Anthropologist.
Current Anthropological literature, and memoirs of the American Anthropological Association, 1888–1928. National Research Council. Division of Anthropology and Psychology and Phillips Academy, Andover Mass, by Alfred Vincent Kidder. With the aid of Mrs. Marion Hale Britten and Mrs. Ida S. Chadwick. Menasha, Wis.: 1930. 193 pp., issued as V. 32 No. 3, pt. 2 of the American Anthropologist.

Geuthner, Paul (Antiquarian Booksellers, Paris)
Americana Bibliographie. Périodiques. Congrès. Découverte. Cartographie. Voyages. Missions Ecclésiastiques. Les Indiens. Les Esquimaux. Linguistique Américaine. Colonisation. Histoire Politique et Economique. Paris: G. Geuthner, 1914. 48 pp. (Catalogue 59).

Griffin, Grace Gardner
Writings on American History. Washington, D. C.: Gov't Printing Office, 1906.

Henkels, Stanislaus Vincent
Rare American History, being the library of a well-known Philadelphia collector, comprising an extensive collection of works on the North American Indians. . . . Philadelphia; 1910. iv, 182 pp. (NYPL).

Herzog, Elizabeth
General Index, American Anthropologist, Current Anthropological literature, and Memoirs of the American Anthropological Association. 1929–1938. Menasha, Wis.: 90 pp. Issued as American Anthropologist, Vol. 42, No. 4, Part 3.

Herzog, George
Research in Primitive and Folk Music in the United States, a Survey. American Council of Learned Societies, bulletin no. 24, April, 1936. Washington, D. C.: American Council of Learned Societies, 1936. iv, 97 pp., bibl.

Hodge, Frederick Webb, ed.
Bibliography of the American Indian. In: *Handbook of the American Indian, North of Mexico.* Vol. II (1179–1221). Bureau of American Ethnology, No. 30. Washington, D. C.: U. S. Gov't. Printing Office, 1910.

Huston, M.
"What to read on the American Indians, with annotations." *Missionary Review of the World.* (New York) 55: 461–463, July 1932.

Index to Early American Periodical Literature, 1728–1870. U. S. Work Projects Administration. The list of periodicals indexed by the W. P. A. 665–97–3–33. Sponsored by New York City, Board of Education, New York University English department, and the New York University libraries. New York: 1940.
Lists 351 periodicals. Contents indexed, consisting of more than one million cards. New York University, Washington Square, New York City. Particularly valuable for Indian lore.

Index to the Publications in American Archaeology and Ethnology. Berkeley, California. Vol 1–26, 1903–1929.

Lesser, Alexander
Bibliography of American Folklore, 1915-1928." *JAFL* 41:1–60, 1928.
The American Indian (pp. 2-36).

List of Publications of the Bureau of American Ethnology. With Index to Authors and Titles. Washington, D. C.: U. S. Gov't Printing Office, 1937. Revised to June 1937.

List of Publications of the Museum of the American Indian, Heye Foundation. Indian Notes and Monographs, No. 49. New York: Museum of the American Indian, Heye Foundation, 1946. 32 pp. Eighth Edition, fourth printing.
A series of publications relating to the American aborigines.

Littlefield, George Emery
Catalogue of Books and Pamphlets Relating to the American Indians. Boston: G. E. Littlefield, 1883. 24 pp.

Lowie, Robert H.
"Bibliography of Franz Boas in Folklore." *JAFL* 57:65–69, 1944.

McIlwraith, T. F., comp.
"Bibliography of Ethnology, Anthropology and Archaeology." *Canadian Historical Review* (Toronto).
Yearly bibliographies published in the March issue. Very extensive and valuable.

Miner, William Harvey
George Catlin: a short memoir of the man, with an annotated bibliography of his writings. New York: 1901. Excerpt from: *Literary Collector.* 3:23–27, 78–83, 1901.

Monroe, Helen, comp.
Classified List of Smithsonian Publications Available for Distribution, June 26, 1939. Washington, D. C.: The Smithsonian Institution, 1939. 35 pp.
Contains Section on Anthropology (Archaeology, Ethnology, and Philology), and Art.

Murdock, George Peter
Ethnographic Bibliography of North America. New Haven: Published for the Dep't. of Anthropology, Yale University, by the Yale University Press, 1941. xvi, 168 pp. (Yale Anthropological Studies, Vol. 1).

Museum Book Store, London
Catalogue of Rare Books, Pamphlets and Prints Relating to the History, Antiquities, Languages, Customs, Religion, Wars, Folklore, Literature, and the Origin of the Indians of America.... London: 1908. 56 pp.

Newberry Library, Chicago
A Check List of Manuscripts in the Edward E. Ayer Collection, compiled by Ruth Lapham Butler. Chicago: The Newberry Library, 1937. viii, 295 pp.

———.
Notes on the Historical Source Material in the Ayer Collection on the North American Indian, presented by Edward E. Ayer to the Newberry Library. Chicago: The Newberry Library, 1927. 8 pp.

New York Public Library
List of Works in the New York Public Library Relating to Folk Song, Folk Music Ballads, Etc. New York: Public Library Bulletin, May 1907. 40 pp.
American Indian (pp. 22-23).

Nijhoff, Martinus (The Hague)
Choix de Livres sur les Indigènes de l'Amérique; offerts aux prix marqués. . . . Le Haye: 191–. 43 pp.

Parsons, Elsie Clews
"Bibliography of Elsie Clews Parsons (1898-1941)." *JAFL* 56:48–56, 1943.

Riverside, Cal. Public Library
Indians. List of Books in the Library. Riverside, 1916. 29 pp. (Bulletin, no. 136).

Rivet, Paul
Bibliography Américaniste. Paris: Au Siège de la Société., 1927. 2 vols.

Russell, F.
"Bibliography of Folklore Publications." *JAFL* 17:209, 1904.

Samson, William H.
Important Collection of Americana from the library of W. H. Samson . . . including many rare Indian items, State and County histories, early Western New York books.... New York: Anderson Auction Company, 1911. vi, 80 pp. (NYPL).

Schoolcraft, Henry Rowe
Archives of Aboriginal Knowledge. Containing all the original papers laid before Congress respecting the Indian tribes of the United States. See: *Information Respecting the History, Conditions and Prospects of the Indian Tribes of the United States.* Illustrated by S. Eastman. Published by authority of Congress. Philadelphia: Lippincott, Grambo and Co., 1860. 6 v.

———.
A Bibliographical Catalogue of Books, translations of the Scriptures, and other publications in the Indian tongues of the United States, with brief critical notices. Washington, D. C.: C. Alexander, 1849.

Spofford, Amsworth R.
"Rare Books Relating to the American Indians." *AA* 3:270–286, 1901. n. s.

Thomas, N. W., comp.
Bibliography of Anthropology and Folklore. Containing works published within the British Empire. 1st, 2nd annual issue; 1906–1907. London: Published for the Joint Committee of the Royal Anthropological and Folklore Society, 1907–1908. Folklore Society Publications V. 57.

Thomas, William I.
Source Book for Social Origins. Ethnological Materials, Psychological Standpoints, Classified and Annotated. Bibliographies for the Interpretation of Savage Society. Chicago: University of Chicago Press. London: T. Fisher Unwin, 1909. 932 pp.

U. S. Bureau of American Ethnology.
Circular of Information regarding Indian popular names. Washington, D. C.: U. S. Government Printing Office, 1926. 8 pp.
Books on folk-lore, myths and legends (pp. 5-8).

————.
List of Publications of the Bureau of American Ethnology with index to authors and titles. Washington, D. C.: Gov't. Printing Office, 1906. 31 pp.

U. S. Library of Congress. Division of Bibliography.
List of Books on Indians in North America. August 4, 1932. Washington, 1932. 13 pp. (Select List of References No. 1252).

————.
A Selected List of Books on the Indians of North America. Compiled by Helen F. Conover. . . . Feb. 6, 1939. Washington, 1939. 25 pp. (Select List of References, No. 1440).

U. S. Office of Indian Affairs.
Bibliography of Indian Stories for young folks. Phoenix, Ariz.: Phoenix Indian School, 1929. 37 pp. Bulletin No. 13, 1929. Department of Interior.

Wellesley College Library.
Catalogue of Works in Alcove of North American Languages. Wellesley College, 1887. Boston: F. Wood, 1887. 69 pp.

White, Mary Catherine
"Folklore of the United States for Young Children: A Selected Bibliography." *Publishers' Weekly* (New York). 110:1584–1589, 1926. Illus.

Winsor, Justin
Bibliography of Aboriginal America. . . . In: *Narrative and Critical History of America.* Boston: Houghton Mifflin Co., 1884–89. pp. 413–444.
Contents: Bibliography of Aboriginal America. —The Comprehensive Treatises on American Antiquities. — Bibliographical Notes on American Linguistics.—Bibliographical Notes on the Myths and Religions of America.—Archaeological Museums and Periodicals.

SERIAL PUBLICATIONS

American Anthropologist.
Washington, New York, Lancaster, Pa., I(1888)–XI(1898), New Ser. I(1899)—.

American Antiquarian.
A quarterly journal devoted to the interests of collectors of autographs, paper money, portraints, etc. New York, 1–5, 1870–1889.

American Antiquarian and Oriental Journal.
Cleveland; Chicago: Vols. 1–36, no. 1, April 1878–Jan. 1914. Vol. 1–2, no. 1—as *American Antiquarian;* a quarterly journal devoted to early American history, ethnology, and archaeology.

American Antiquarian Society. Worcester, Mass.
Bulletin No. 1–6, July 19, 1913–January 5, 1917. *Proceedings.* No. 1–75, 1812–1849. *Proceedings* at the annual meetings. May 31, 1843–April 28, 1880. N. S. Vol. 1–1880. Suspended 1844–1848. Index: Partial Index 1812–1880, 1880–1903. *Transactions and Collections:* Nos. 1–12, 1820–1911. No. 1–7, 1820–1885, as *Archaeologia Americana.*

American Antiquity; a quarterly review of American Archaeology. (Society for American Archaeology.) Menasha, Wisconsin: I, July 1935.

American Ethnological Society, New York.
Bulletin. No. 1, Sept. 1860–Jan., 1861. Memoirs. *See:* American Anthropological Association Memoirs. *Monographs.* No. 1, 1940. *Publications,* No. 1, 1907. *Transactions* (New York). Vol. 1–3, 1845–1853.

American Naturalist.
Boston; New York. V. 1, March 1867.

Annals of Archaeology and Anthropology.
Institute of Archaeology, Liverpool. V. 1, 1908. Suspended October, 1916–1919.

Annual Archaeological Report.
Ontario (Geological Survey) 1886–. *Anthropological Division:* Summary Report. 1910–1913.

Anthropological Institute of Great Britain and Ireland. See: Royal..........................London: Journal 1871; 28 also as n.s. V. 1.

Anthropological Records.
Publications of the University of California. Berkeley, Cal.: No. 1, 1937–.

Archaeology and Ethnology.
Salt Lake City: University of Utah.

British Association for the Advancement of Science. London. *Reports:* Nos 1–108, 1831–1938. No mettings held 1917–1918.

Bulletin, National Museum of Canada.
Ottawa. No. 1. Oct. 23, 1913–.

Catholic University Anthropological Series.
Washington, D. C. No. 1, 1930–.

Columbia University Contributions to Anthropology. New York. Vol. 1, 1910–.

Contributions to North American Ethnology.
Vol. I–VII, IX. Ed. by J. W. Powell. Washington, D. C.: Govt. Print. Off., 1877–93. 8 vols. in 9. After 1879 published under supervision of Bureau of American Ethnology.

El Palacio.
School of American Research; Museum of New Mexico; Archaeological Society of New Mexico. Santa Fe, New Mexico I(1913)–.

Folk-lore.
A quarterly review of myth, tradition, and custom, being the transactions of the Folk-lore Society, and incorporating the Archaeological Review and the Folk-lore Journal. London: The Folk-lore Society, V. 1, 1890 (March).

Folk-lore Fellows.
Copenhagen Publications. Northern series. 1–3, 1904–1908; (N. S.) No. 3 pt. 1–2, 1917–21.

Heye Foundation: Museum of the American Indian, New York. Has Various Series: *Contributions* I(1913)–. *Indian Notes* I(1924)–. *Indian Notes and Monographs* I(1919)–. *Miscellaneous Series* I(1920)–. *Leaflets* I(1919)–.

Indian Miscellany.
Smithsonian Institution. Bureau of Ethnology. Indian Miscellany. Quarto Series. Washington: Library of the Bureau of Ethnology.

Indiana Historical Society.
Prehistory Research Series. V. 1, 1937–. Indianapolis.

International Journal of American Linguistics.
Bloomington, Indiana: Indiana University. Founded by Franz Boas in 1917. Resumed publication, Oct. 1944. C. F. Voegelin, editor.

Journal of American Folklore.
Vol. 1, April, 1888. Boston and New York: Houghton, Mifflin and Company, 1888–1910; Lancaster, Pa. and New York: The American Folklore Society, 1911–.

Language.
Journal of the Linguistic Society of America. Edited by George Melville Bolling, Aurelio M. Espinosa, and Edward Sapir. Baltimore: The Waverly Press, Vol. I, No. 1, March 1925.

Man.
(Royal Anthropological Institute of Great Britain and Ireland.) London: No. 1, 1901–. No. 1 issued as a supplement to the Institute's Journal. Index with the Journal.

Memoirs of the *American Anthropological Association.* Lancaster, Pa.: Menasha, Wis., V. 1–6. (No. 4 (No. 1–28) June 1905–Oct. 1919; No. 29, 1923–. V. 1, No. 1 has cover title: Memoirs of the Anthropological and Ethnological Societies. No. 42 issued as supplement to *American Anthropologist.*

Natural History.
See: *American Museum of Natural History.* American Museum Novitates. 1921.

Panamerican Union, Washington, D. C.
Bulletin I(1893) in English also in Spanish, Portuguese, and French. Since July 1911. Panamerican Bookshelf I(1938). Correo, lists, current events of cultural importance.

Peabody Museum of American Archaeology and Ethnology.
Cambridge, Mass.: Harvard University. Archaeological and Ethnological papers. I (1888)–, Memoirs I (1896)–.

Primitive Man.
Catholic Anthropological Conference, Washington, D. C. No. 1, 1928–. Index: 1–10.

Proceedings of the International Congress of Americanists.
1st Session, Nancy, 1875–.

Royal Society of Canada.
French name: Société Royal du Canada. *Proceedings and Transactions.* Ottawa; Montreal. 1–12, 1882–1894. S. 2 vol. 1–12, 1895–1906. 53 vol. i, 1907–.

Smithsonian Institution.
Washington, D. C. *Annual Report* to the Board of Regents, I (1846)–. *Smithsonian Contributions to Knowledge* I (1862)–. *Bureau of American Ethnology* I (1881)–. (Annual Report to the Secretary). *Bulletin of the Bureau of American Ethnology,* No. 1 (1887).

Société des Américanistes de Paris.
Paris, France. *Journal* I (1895)–. II (1904). New ser. I (1903–1904)–.
Contains excellent and comprehensive annual bibliographies.

Southwest Museum Leaflets.
The Southwest Museum. Highland Park, Los Angeles, California.

The American Indian, Carl Carmer, editor.
American Association on Indian Affairs, Inc. 381-4th Ave., New York 16, N. Y.

The Masterkey.
May 1927–. Los Angeles, Calif.: The Southwest Museum, (bi-monthly 1927–1931, irregular).

The Old West Series.
No. 1, 1933–. Denver: J. Van Male, 1933.

The Wisconsin Archaeologist.
Milwaukee: The Wisconsin Archaeologist Society. 1901–1937. 37 vols., illus.

University of California Publication in American Archaeology and Ethnology.
Berkeley: The University Press, No. 1, 1903–.

Yale University Publications in Anthropology.
No. 1–32. New Haven: Yale University Press. 1936–1945.

Zeitschrift für Ethnologie.
Berliner Gesellschaft für Anthropologie, Ethnologie und Urgeschichte. Berlin I (1869)–.

GENERAL STUDIES AND COLLECTIONS

Abbott, Arthur Platts
A Loving People. Bayonne, N. J.: Jersey Printing Co., 1931. xi, 147 pp., illus.

Adair, James (trader with the Indians)
The History of the American Indians; particularly those nations adjoining to the Mississippi, East and West Florida, Georgia, South and North Carolina, and Virginia: containing an account of their origin, language, manners, religious and civil customs, laws, form of government, punishments, conduct in war and domestic life, their habits, diet, agriculture, manufactures, diseases and methods of cure . . . with observations on former historians, the conduct of colony governors, superintendents, missionaries, etc. Also an appendix containing a description of the Floridas, and the Mississippi lands, with their productions—the benefits of colonizing georgiana, and civilizing the Indians—and the way to make all the colonies more valuable to the mother country. London: Printed for E. and C. Dilly, 1775. 464 pp., front.

Adair's History of the American Indians, edited under the auspices of the National society of the colonial dames of America in Tennessee, by Samuel Cole Williams. Johnson City: The Watanga Press, 1930. xxxviii, 508 pp.

Alcott, Frances Jenkins
The Red Indian Fairy Book. For the Children's Own Reading and for Story Tellers. Illustrated by Frederick Richardson. Boston: Houghton Mifflin Co., 1917. 338 pp.

Amsden, Charles
"America's Earliest Man." *The Masterkey* 18: (No. 1) :5–12, 1944.

Anon.
"American Indians and Civilization." *Monthly Literary Miscellany* 4:185–187, April 1851 (NYU).
An article dealing with the life of American Indians, lamenting the fact that they almost ceased to be objects of interest, etc.

"Chronicle." *Niles' Weekly Register* 16: April–Aug. 1819; 17: Sept., Nov., Dec., 1819; 17: Jan., April, 1820; 18: April, June, July, Aug., 1820 (NYU).
Items on various aspects of Indian life.

"Ethnological Sketch of the North American Indians." *The American Quarterly Register and Magazine* 1:169–177, May, 1848 (NYU).
An article on the history, character, conditions, and prospects of the United States.

"Indians of America." *Merry's Museum* 4:72–78, Sept. 1842.
General discussion on food, fishing, hunting, houses, dress, children, education, traditions and superstitions.

"Items of Interest." *Nile's Weekly Register* 33:276, Dec. 29, 1827; 35:41–42, Sept. 13, 1828; 35:144, Oct. 25, 1828; 35:160, Nov. 1, 1828; 35:192, Nov. 15, 1828 (NYU).
Observations and notes on Indian beliefs, traditions, customs, and ceremonies.

"Miscellaneous Paragraphs." *The Port-Folio* 4 (ser. 5) :468, Aug., 1817 (NYU).
On the origin of the North American Indians—on a curious discovery made by M. Julius Von Klaproth.

"North American Indians." *Southern Literary Messenger* 6:190–192, March 1840.
A descriptive account of the family names, government, military service, writing, music, and poetry, and other interesting information on Indian tribes.

"Review." *The North American Review* 45:34–59, July, 1837 (NYU).
A review of *Inquiries Respecting the History and Languages of the North American Tribes.* Detroit, 1823.

"Review of *Information Respecting the History, Condition and Prospects of the Indian Tribes of the United States;* collected and prepared under the direction of the Bureau of Indian Affairs, per Act of Congress, March 3, 1947." *De Bow's Review* 7:68–76, July, 1854 (NYU).
A review of Henry R. Schoolcraft's book.

"The American Aborigenes." *Niles' Weekly Register* 40:185–187, Nov., 1818 (NYU).
An essay on the fast disappearing Indians, the various tribes, their original habits, etc.

"The Indians." *Niles' Weekly Register* 47:205, Nov. 29, 1834 (NYU).
Descriptive account of the conditions of certain tribes of Indians throughout the United States.

Avebury, John Lubbock
The Origin of Civilisation and the Primitive Condition of Man. Mental and Social Condition of Savages. London: Longmans, Green, and Co., 1870. xx, 426 pp., illus.

Bandelier, A. F.
"Kin and Clan." *New Mexico Historical Review* 8(No. 3) :165–175, July 1933.
Reprint of lecture dated 1882.

Barbeau, Marius
En Quête de Connaissances Anthropologiques dans L'Amérique du Nord Depuis 1911. A l'usage exclusif des étudiants. Archives de folklore, Université Laval, 1945, 82 pp., mimeo.

————, and Melvin, Grace
The Indian Speaks. Caldwell, Idaho: The Caxton Printers, 1943.

Barrett, Stephen Melvil
Sociology of the American Indians. Kansas City, Mo.: Burton Publishing Company, 1946. 142 pp., illus.

Barton, Benj. Smith
New Views of the Origin of the Tribes and Nations of America. Philadelphia: Printed for Author by John Bioren, 1797. xii, cix, 83 pp.

Beach, William Wallace, ed.
The Indian Miscellany; containing papers on the history, antiquities, arts, languages, religions, traditions and superstitions of the American aborigenes; with a description of their domestic life, manners, customs, traits, amusements and exploits. . . . Albany: J. Munsell, 1877. viii, 490 pp., illus.

Beals, Ralph L.
The Emergence of an American Culture. In: *The Civilization of the Americas*, pp. 27–58. Berkeley, Cal.: University of California Press, 1939.

Beckwith, Martha Warren
Folklore in America. Publications of the Folklore Foundation 11, Vassar College, Poughkeepsie, 1931.

Benedict, Ruth
"Configurations of Culture in North America." *AA* 34:1–27, 1932. n.s.

Benezet, Anthony
Some Observations on the Situation, Disposition, and Character of the Indian Natives of This Continent. Philadelphia: Joseph Crukshank, 1784. v, 59 pp.

Besauri, Carlos
"El Psicoanálisis y la Etnología." *AI* 4:265–273, 1944.
Description of the use of psychoanalysis in the study of culture.

Bissell, B. H.
The American Indian in English Literature of the 18th Century. Yale Studies in English, No. 68. New Haven: Yale University Press, 1925. ix, 229 pp.

Boas, Franz
"America and the Old World." *Proc. Inter. Congr. Amer.* 21:21–28, 1925.

————.
"Ethnological Problems in Canada." *Journ. Anthro. Inst. Gt. Brit.* 40:529–539, 1910.

————.
"The Half-Blood Indian." *Popular Science Monthly* (New York) 45:761–770, 1894.

————.
"The History of the American Race." *Annals N. Y. Academy Sci.* 21:177–183, 1912.

————.
"Mind of Primitive Man." *JAFL* 14:1–11, 1901.

————.
Race, Language and Culture. New York: The Macmillan Co., 1940.

————.
Relationships Between North-West America and North-East Asia. In: *The American Aborigenes*, Diamond Jenness, ed., pp. 355–370. Toronto: 1933.

————.
"Romance Folklore among American Indians." *Romanic Review* 16:199–207, 1925.

————.
"Traits of Primitive Culture." *JAFL* 17:243–254, 1904.

Bower, Reuben Edward
The Unreached Indian; a treatise on Indian life and Indian Missions. Kansas City, Mo.: Central Board of Foreign Missions, 1920. 124 pp., illus., music.

Boyd, Robert K.
The Real Indian; some notes on the real character of the American Indian of the Northern frontier. Eau Claire, Wis.: Herges Printing Co., 1926. 16 pp.

Brand, Donald D.
"The Status of Anthropology in the Western United States." *New Mexico Anthropologist* 2 (No. 1):4–16, 1937.

————, et al.
"Symposium on Prehistoric Agriculture." *Bulletin, University of New Mexico, Anthropological Series* 1 (No. 5) 1936.

————, and Harvey, Fred E., eds.
So Live the Works of Men; Seventieth Anniversary Volume Honoring Edgar Lee Hewett. Albuquerque: University of New Mexico Press, 1939. 366 pp., illus.
Essays on archaeology, ethnology, anthropology, music, etc., etc.

Brinton, Daniel Garrison
Essays of an Americanist. I. Ethnologic and Archaeologic. II. Mythology and Folklore. III. Graphic Systems and Literature. IV. Linguistic. Philadelphia: Porter & Coates, 1890. xii, 489 pp., illus.

————.
The American Race: a linguistic classification of the native tribes of North and South America. Philadelphia: D. McKay, 1891. 17–329 pp., ix–xvi, 2 pl.

Brownell, Charles De Wolf
The Indian Races of North and South America. Comprising an account of the principal Aboriginal races; a description of their customs, mythology, and religious ceremonies—etc., with hand colored plates. New York: H. E. and S. S. Scranton, 1854. 640 pp. Boston: H. Wentworth, and Cincinnati: G. W. I. Miller, 1855.

Cambell, John
"Asiatic Tribes in North America." *Canadian Inst. Proc. new series*, Vol. 1; 171–206. Toronto: 1884.

Carli, Giovanni Rinaldo
Delle Lettere Americane.... Milano: Nell' Imperial Monistero di S. Ambrogio Maggiore, 1786. 4 vols.
A discussion of the origin, political organization, military systems, religious life, crafts, customs and manners, etc. of the American Indians.

Cass, Lewis
"Indians of North America." *North American Review* 22:53–119, 1826.

————.
Inquiries Respecting the History, Traditions, Languages, Manners, Customs, Religion, etc. of the Indians living within the United States. Detroit: Sheldon & Reed, 1823. 64 pp.

Catlin, George
"Catlin's Letters on the North American Indians." *New World* 3:387–388, Dec. 18, 1841 (NYU).
Extracts from the above giving a brief biography and describing various adventures among the Indians.

————.
"Mr. Catlin." *American Turf Register and Sporting Magazine* 7 (No. 12):554–561, Aug., 1836 (NYU).
Letter to the Editor of the "Evening Star", N. Y., concerning his exhibit of Indian scenes in Pittsburgh, giving his reasons for slighting New York, and telling him an Indian story.

Chamberlain, Alexander Francis
"North American Indian." *Encyclopedia Britannica* pp. 452–482. Cambridge, England: At the University Press, 1910. 11th Edition.

————.
"The Contributions of the American Indian to Civilization." *Proceedings of the American Antiquarian Society* (Worcester) 16:91–126, 1903. n.s.

Charlevoix, Pierre François Xavier de
Journal of a Voyage to North America. Undertaken by order of the French King. Containing the geographical description and natural history of that country, particularly Canada. Together with an account of the customs, characters, religion, manners and traditions of the original inhabitants . . . London: R. and J. Dodsley, 1761. 2 vols.

Christensen, Thomas P.
The Historic Trail of the American Indians. Cedar Rapids, Iowa: Laurance Press Co., 1933. 193 pp.

Chronicles of the North American Savages.
Vol. I, May, 1835. No. 1. Monthly. Cincinnati: T. H. Shreve and Co., 1835. Conducted by Isaac Galland.
Contains an account of the dealings of the first English Colonists with the Indians of Virginia; also of the Black-Hawk War. Includes vocabularies of the "Sawkee and Mus-quaw-kee Indian tongue" and an "Essay on the Chippewa language."

Clark, William Philo
The Indian Sign Language, with brief explanatory notes, etc., and a description of some of the peculiar laws, customs, myths, superstitions, ways of living, code of peace and war signals of our aborigines. Phila., Pa.: L. R. Hamersly and Co., 1885. 443 pp.

Condition of the Indian Tribes.
Report of the joint special committee appointed under joint resolution of March 3, 1865; with an appendix. Washington, D. C.: U. S. Gov't Printing Office, 1867.

Cook, James, and Ring, James
A Voyage to the Pacific Ocean, undertaken by the command of His Majesty for making discoveries in the northern hemisphere, to determine the position and extent of the west side of North America; its distance from Asia; and the practicability of a northern passage to Europe in the years 1776, 1777, 1778, 1779 and 1780. ("Cooks' Third Voyage.") London: W. A. Strahan, 1784.

Crawford, John
History of the Indian Archipelago. Edinburgh: A. Constable & Co., 1820. 3 vol.

Culin, Stewart
"Retrospect of the Folk-Lore of the Columbian Exposition." *JAFL* 7:51–59, 1894.

Curtis, Edward S.
The North American Indian. Being a Series of Volumes Picturing and Describing the Indian of the United States and Alaska. Written, Illustrated and Published by Edward S. Curtis. Edited by Frederick Webb Hodge. Foreword by Theodore Roosevelt. In 20 volumes. Seattle, Wash.: E. S. Curtis, 1907–1930. Illus., music.

Curtis, Natalie
The Indian's Book; an offering by the American Indians of Indian lore, musical and narrative, to form a record of the songs and legends of their race, recorded and edited by Natalie Curtis; illustrations from photographs and from original drawings by Indians. New York: Harper and Bros., 1907. xxx, 572 pp., illus., music.

Daugherty, G. H.
"Differentiation of Indian Cultures According to Geographical Atlas." *Open Court* 41:288–305.

————.
"The Indian Reveals his Character." *Open Court* 40:596–609.

Davis, Emily C.
Ancient Americans, the Archaeological Story of Two Continents. New York: Henry Holt and Co., 1931. 311 pp., illus.

Debo, Angie
The Road to Disappearance. Civilization of the American Indian. Norman: University of Oklahoma Press, 1941.

Dellenbaugh, Frederick S.
The North-Americans of Yesterday. A Comparative Study of North-American Indian Life, Customs, and Products, on the Theory of the Ethnic Unity of the Race. New York: G. P. Putnam's Sons, 1906.

Deloria, Ella Cara
Speaking of Indians. . . . New York: Friendship Press, 1944. x, 163 pp.

del Rio, Pablo Martinez
Los Origenes Americanos. Mexico: Porrua Hermanos, 1936. 277 pp., illus.

Dixon, Joseph K.
The Vanishing Race. The last great Indian Council, a record in picture and story. . . . The volume is illustrated with eighty photographs of Indian chiefs and Indian Life. Garden City: Doubleday, Page and Co., 1913. xviii, 231 pp., illus.

Dixon, Roland Burrage
The Building of Cultures. New York: Charles Scribner's Sons, 1928. x, 312 pp., illus., maps.

————.
"The Independence of the Culture of the American Indian." *Science* 35:46–55, 1912. n.s.

Drake, Samuel Gardner
Book of the Indians of North America. . . . Boston: Antiquarian Bookstore, 1841. xii, 696 pp.
Other editions—earlier and later—of this book were issued.

Duflot de Mofras, Eugene
Exploration du Territoire de l'Orégon, des Californies, et de la Mer Vermeille. Paris: A. Bernard, 1844. 2 vols., illus., bibl.

Eastman, Charles Alexander
Old Indian Days. New York: The McClure Co., 1907. 279 pp.

————.
The Soul of the Indian. Boston: Houghton Mifflin and Co., 1911. 170 pp.

————.
Wigwam Evenings. Sioux Folktales. New York: Cadmus Books, 1940. xvi, 253 pp., illus., reprint.

Edgeworth, Maria
Forgive and Forget. Also Stories of the Indians. Brookfield: E. and G. Merriam, 1830. 36 pp.

Eggan, Fred, ed.
Social Anthropology of North American Tribes. Essays in Social Organization, Law and Religion. Presented to Professor A. R. Radcliffe-Brown Upon the Occasion of His Accepting the Chair of Social Anthropology at Oxford University. Chicago: University of Chicago Press, 1937. 455 pp.

Ellis, Edward Sylvester
Indian Wars of the United States. Chicago: Kenyon, 1902. 484 pp., illus.

————.
True Stories of the American Indians. Philadelphia: 1905. viii 240 pp., illus.

Ellis, George Edward
"The Red Indian of North America in Contact With the French and English.". . . In: *Narrative and Critical History of America,* Wisor, Justin, ed. Boston: Houghton Mifflin Co., 1889. pp. 283–328.

————.
The Red Man and the White Man. Boston: Little, Brown and Company, 1882. 642 pp.

Embree, Edwin
Indians of the Americas, Historical Pageant. Illustrations by Howard Grieg. Boston: Houghton Mifflin Co., 1939. xi, 260 pp.

Emerson, Caroline D.
Indian Hunting Grounds. Drawings by Remington Schuyler. New York: Frederick A. Stokes and Co., 1938. Illus.
Children story of life habits of different tribes.

"Ethnology and Ethnography."
In: *Encyclopaedia Britannica,* Vol. 9. pp. 849–851, 1910. 11th edition.

Farrand, Livingstone
The Basis of American History. New York: Harper & Bros., 1904. xviii, 303 pp., bibl.

Fewkes, J. W., Fletcher, Alice C., Dixon, Roland B., and others
"The Problems of the Unity or Plurality and the Probable Place of Origin of the America Aborigines." *AA* 14:1–60, 1912. n.s.
Of particular reference to this work are the articles by Fewkes (p. 1-4); Fletcher (p. 37-43); Dixon (p. 57-60).

Figgins, J. D.
"A Further Contribution to the Antiquity of Man in America." *Proceedings of the Colorado Museum of Natural History* 12, (No. 2) 8 pp., illus. Denver, 1933, Denver, 1939.

Flanagan, John T.
"A Pioneer in Indian Folklore: James Athearn Jones, 1791–1854." *New England Quarterly* 12:443–453, 1939.

Fletcher, Alice C.
Indian Story and Song from North America. Boston: Small, Maynard and Company, 1900. 126 pp.

Francis, Francis
Saddle and Moccasin. London: Chapman and Hall, Ltd., 1887. xi, 322 pp.

Franklin, Benjamin
"Remarks Concerning the Savages of North America." *Republic of Letters* 1:195, 1836 (NYU).

Frazer, Sir James George
Anthologia Anthropologica. The Native races of America; a copious selection of passages for the study of social anthropology, from the manuscript notebooks of Sir James George Frazer. . . . Arranged and edited from the mss. by Robert Angus Downie. London: P. Lund, Humphries & Co., Ltd., 1939. ix, 351 pp.

————.
The Native Races of America. R. A. Downie, ed. London: 1939. 350 pp.

————.
Questions on the Customs, Beliefs and Languages of Savages. Cambridge, Eng.: University Press, 1910. 51 pp.

Friederici, G.
"Die Ethnographie in den 'Documentos Ineditos del Archivo de Indias'." *Globus* 90:287–289, 303–306, 1906.

————.
"Die Frage der vorkulumbischen Einwanderung nach America." *Zeit. Völker. Soz.* 5: 348–352, 1929.

Frost, John
Thrilling Adventures Among the Indians. Philadelphia: J. W. Bradley, Boston: L. P. Crown and Co., 1854. 512 pp.

Gallatin, Albert
A Synopsis of the Indian Tribes in North America. Transactions and Collections American Antiquarian Society Archaelogia Americana, Vol. 2. Cambridge, Mass., 1836.

Garland, Hamlin
Book of the American Indians. New York: Harpers and Bros., 1923.

Gennep, Arnold van
Religions, Moeurs et Légendes: essais d'ethnographie et de linguistique. Paris: Société du Mercure de France, 1908. 318 pp.
Ethnographic and linguistic essays on religious beliefs, customs and legends.

Gessner, Robert
Massacre, A Survey of Today's American Indian. New York: Cape and Smith, 1931. 418 pp., illus.

Gibbs, George
Instructions for Research Relative to the Ethnology and Philology of America. Washington, D. C.: Smithsonian Institution, 1863. 51 pp. (Smithsonian Miscellaneous Collections, 160.)

Gladfelter, Katherine Eleanor
Many Moons Ago and Now, a Course on the North American Indians for junior boys and girls. New York: Friendship Press, 1932. 157 pp., illus., music.

Goldenweiser, A. A.
"Social Organizations of the Indians of North America." *JAFL* 27:411–436, 1914.

Gomme, Sir George Laurence
Ethnology in Folklore. New York: D. Appleton and Co., 1892. vii, 203 pp.
(*Half-title:* Modern Science Series, ed. by J. Lubback).

Goodrich, Samuel Griswold
Lives of Celebrated American Indians. . . . Boston: Rand and Mann, 1849. iv, 315 pp., illus.

Gorges, Ferdinando
America Painted to the Life. The true history of the Spaniards proceedings in the conquests of the Indians, and of their civil wars among themselves. . . . Declaring the forms of their government, policies, religions, manners, customs, military discipline. . . . London: Printed for Nath. Brook at the Angel in Cornhil, 1659. 4 pts. in 1 vol.

Graves, C. S.
Before the White Man Came. Yreaha, Calif.: Siskiyon news, 1934.

Gray, G. W.
New World Picture. Boston: 1936. 402 pp.

Greene, J.
"Indian Traditions." *So. Workman* (Hampton, Va.) 38:691–692, 1910.

Gridley, Marion E.
Indians of Yesterday. Illustrated by Lone Wolf. Sponsored by the Indian Council Fire. Chicago, New York: M. A. Donahue and Co., 1940. 63 pp.
A story for young readers of life, habits and tradiions.

Grinnel, George Bird
The Story of the Indian. New York: D. Appleton and Co., 1905. 270 pp.

————.
The Indians of To-day. Illustrated with full page portraits of living persons. Chicago: H. S. Stone & Co., 1900. 185 pp., illus.

Haberly, Lloyd
Pursuit of the Horizon, a Life of George Catlin. New York: The Macmillan Company, 1948. 239 pp., illus.
A life of the amazing artist who set out to paint all American Indian tribes, "and almost did it."

Harper, Allan G.
Las Tierras de los Indios en los Estados Unidos. Washington, D. C.: Dep't of Interior, 1943. 54 pp.

Hartland, Edwin Sidney
Primitive Society. London: Methuen and Co., Ltd., 1921. 180 pp.
Chapt. xi—pp. 145-156: deals with the Indians North of Mexico.

Hatt, Gudmund
"North American and Eurasian Culture Connections." *Proc. Pac. Sci. Congr.* 5(Part 4): 2755–2765, 1933.

Heckwelder, Henry
"Indian Nations." *Memoirs, Historical Society,* (Pennsylvania) Vol. 12, 1881.

Henshaw, Henry W.
"Who Are the American Indians?" *AA* 2:193–214, 1889.

Heriot, G.
Travels Through the Canadas. London: R. Phillips, 1807. xii, 602 pp.

Hernández de Alba, Gregorio
"Lo indígena como expresión. Americana." *AI* 4:223–225, 1944.
Discussion of the widespread similarities of New World Indians.

Herskovits, Melville J.
Acculturation: The Study of Culture Contacts. New York: J. J. Augustin, 1938.

———.
Freudian Mechanisms in Primitive Society: *In: Essays Presented to C. G. Seligman,* pp. 75–84. London: 1934.

Hewitt, J. N. B.
Tribe. In: *Handbook of American Indians.* Vol. II, pp. 814–819. Bureau of American Ethnology, Bulletin 30. Washington, D. C.: U. S. Government Printing Office, 1910.
"Among the North American Indians a tribe is a body of persons who are bound together by ties of consanguinity and affinity and by certain esoteric ideas or concepts derived from their philosophy concerning the genesis and preservation of the environing cosmos, and who by means of these kinship ties are thus socially, politically, and religiously organized through a variety of ritualistic, and governmental, and other institutions, and who dwell together occupying a definite territorial area and who speak a common language and dialect."

Holling, Holling Clancy
The Book of Indians. Illustrated by H. C. and Lucile Holling. New York: The Platt and Munk Co., 1935. 125 pp.
An exciting book for young readers.

Hodge, Frederick Webb
Handbook of American Indians North of Mexico. Bulletin #30, Bureau of American Ethnology, Smithsonian Institution, Washington, D. C. Pt. 1–1907, Pt. 2–1910. Reprinted 1913.
Contains articles on all aspects of Indian folklore.

Holmes, William Henry
"Areas of American Culture Characterization Tentatively Outlined As An Aid in the Study of Antiquities." *AA* 413–447, 1914. ns.

———.
Handbook of Aboriginal American Antiquities. Part I Introductory: The lithic industries. Bulletin #60. Bureau of American Ethnology. Smithsonian Institution, Washington, D. C., 1919.

———.
Popular Fallacies. In: *Handbook of American Indians.* Vol. II, (pp. 282–286). Bureau of American Ethnology, Bulletin 30. Washington, D. C.: U. S. Government Printing Office, 1910.

———.
"Some Problems of the American Race." *AA* 12:149–182, 1910. n.s.

Holmes Anniversary Volume; Anthropological Essays presented to William Henry Holmes.... Washington: J. W. Bryan Press, 1916. vii, 499 pp., illus., bibl. (pp. 491-99).
A great collection of essays by representative authorities on all aspects of Indian archaeology, linguistics, ethnology, folklore, music, etc., etc.

Hooton, E. A.
Racial Types in America and Their Relations to Old World Types. In: *The American Aborigenes,* Diamond Jenness, ed., (pp.131–163). Toronto: 1933.

Hopkins, William John
The Indian Book. Boston: Houghton Mifflin and Co., 1911. viii, 239 pp., illus.
A collection of Mandan stories.

Hough, W.
"The Bison as a Factor in Ancient American Culture History." *Scientific Monthly* (New York) 30:315–319, 1930.

Howard, E. B.
"An Outline of the Problem of Man's Antiquity in North America." *AA* 38:394–413, 1936. n.s.

———.
"Evidence of Early Man in North America." *Mus. Jour* 24:61–158, 1935.

Howells, William White
The Heathens. New York: Doubleday & Co., 1948. 306 pp.
A study of primitive religion. "Primitive religion is semilogical and not mere make-believe,—it is an expansion of the whole world of reality."

———.
The Origin of American Indian Race Types. In: *The Maya and Their Neighbors,* (pp.3–9). New York: D. Appleton Co., 1940.

Hrdlicka, Ales
Anthropology in North America. Washington, D. C.: Gov't Printing Office, 1915.

———.
"The Coming of Man from Asia in the Light of Recent Discoveries." *Annual Reports, Smithson. Inst.,* pp. 463–470, 1935.

———.
"The People of the Main American Cultures." *Proc. Amer. Philo. Soc.* 65:157–160, 1926.

Hulbert, W.
Indian Americans. New York: Friendship Press, 1932. 161 pp., illus.

Humfreville, J. Lee
Twenty Years Among Our Hostile Indians.
New York: Hunter and Co., 1903. Illus.
Describing the characteristics, customs, habits,
religion, marriages, dances and battles of the wild
Indians in their natural state, together with the
entrance of civilization through their hunting
grounds.

Humphrey, Norman Daymond
"On Assimilation and Acculturation." *Psychiatry* 6 (No. 4) :343–345, 1943.

Huntington, Ellsworth
*The Red Man's Continent; A Chronicle of
Aboriginal America.* New Haven: Yale University Press, 1921. xii, 183 pp.

Jackson, Helen Maria Hunt
A Century of Dishonor. A sketch of the U. S.
Government's dealings with some of the Indian
Tribes, etc. Boston: Roberts Brothers, 1885.
514 pp. New ed.

James, George Wharton
*What the White Race May Learn From the
Indians.* Chicago: Fisher and Co., 1908. 269 pp.

Jenness, Diamond, ed.
The American Aborigines. Toronto: Univ. of
Toronto Press, 1933. 396 pp.

————.
"The Indian Background of Canadian History."
Bull. Can. Dep't Mines. 86:1–46, 1937.

————.
"Indians of Canada." *Bull. Can. Dep't. Mines*
65:1–446, 1932.

————.
The Prehistory of the Canadian Indians. In:
Custom Is King. L. H. D. Buxton, ed., (pp. 61–
84). London: 1936.

Jones, J. E.
Traditions of the North American Indians.
London: 1830. 3 vols.

Kenton, Edna
The Indians of North America: from the Jesuit
Relations and Allied Documents (Thwaites
Edition). New York: Harcourt, Brace and Co.,
1927.

King, John Edward
Folk-lore of the North American Indians, from
the Jesuit Relations' (1611–1637), 34 pp.
Manchester Literary and Philosophical Society.
Memoirs and Proceedings V. 46, 1902. (Manchester.)

Kingston, William Henry Giles
Adventures Among the Indians. Chicago: Belford, Clarke & Co., 1884. [v]–vi, 252 pp., illus.

Kluckhohn, Clyde
"Bronislaw Malinowski 1884–1942." *JAFL* 56:
208–219, 1943.
A critical evaluation of the man and his work.

————.
"Some Reflections on the Method and Theory
of the Kulturkreislehre." *AA* 38:157–196, 1936.

Krickeberg, W.
"Beiträge zur Frage der alten Kulturgeschichtlichen Beziehungen zwischen Nord-
und Südamerika." *Zeitschrift für Etnologie* 66
(Nos. 4–6) :287–373, 1934.
On the cultural relations between North and
South America.

————.
Die Völker Nord-und Mittel-Amerikas. In:
Illustrierte Völkerkunde, G. Buschan, ed. Vol.
I, pp. 64–217. Stuttgart: Strecker und
Schröder, 2 vols., illus., bibl. 1922–26.

Kroeber, A. L.
*Cultural and Natural Areas of Native North
America.* University of California Publications
in American Archaeology and Ethnology 39.
Berkeley: University of California Press, 1939.
242 pp., illus.
A detailed study and analysis of culture and environment in the North American Indian.

————.
"Cultural Relations Between North and South
America." *Proc. Inter. Congr. Amer.* 23:5–22,
1928.

————.
"Culture Element Distributions: III Area and
Climax." *University of California Publications
in American Archaeology and Ethnology* 37
(No. 3) 1936. Berkeley: The University Press,
1936.

————.
"Culture Elements Distributions: XV: Salt,
Dogs, Tobacco." *Anthropological Records* 6
(No. 1). Berkeley: University of California
Press, 1941.

————.
"Native American Population." *AA* 36:1–25,
1934. n.s.

————.
"The Morals of Uncivilized People." *AA* 12:
437–481, 1910. n.s.

————, **Benedict, Ruth, Emeneau, Murray
B., Herskovits, Mellville J., Reichard, Gladys A.,
and Mason, J. Alden**
"Franz Boas." *AA* 45 (No. 3) Part 2, 1943.
A memorial to a great student of human culture.

La Farge, Oliver, ed.
The Changing Indian. Norman: University of
Oklahoma Press, 1942.

————.
As Long as the Grass Shall Grow. New York:
Longmans, Green and Co., 1940. 140 pp.

Lamkin, Nina B., and Jagendorf, M.
Around America with the Indian. New York:
Samuel French, 1935.
A book for boys and girls about Indian legends
made into plays—Indian Village Life, Ceremonials, Dance, Music, Games.

Laufer, Berthold
Archaeology and Folklore. *In:* Farrington,
Oliver C.—*Physical Properties and Origin.*
Geology Leaflet No. 8, Field Museum of Natural History, Chicago. Chicago: Field Museum,
1927.

Leach, Maria, ed.
Folklore Dictionary. New York: Funk and Wagnalls, 1949. Vol. 1 (A-I), 531 pp.
With volume 2 it will contain 5000 to 8000 entries, besides 25 general articles.

Lehmann, W.
"Die Frage Völkerkundliche Beziehungen zwischen der Südsee und Amerika." *Orientalische Literaturzeitung* 33:321–340, 1930.

Lesser, Alexander
"Kinship Origins in the Light of Some Distributions." *AA* 31:710–730, 1929. n.s.

Leupp, Francis E.
In Red Man's Land; a Study of the American Indian. New York: F. H. Revell Co., 1914. 161 pp., illus.

————.
The Indian and His Problem. New York: Charles Scribner's Sons, 1910. 369 pp.

Lindquist, G. E. E.
Red Man in the United States. An intimate study of the social, economic and religious life of the American Indian, made under the direction of G. E. E. Lindquist with a foreword by Chas. H. Burke. New York: Geo. H. Doran, 1923. xxviii, 461 pp., front., illus., plates, ports, maps.

Linguistic Families of the Indian Tribes, North of Mexico, with Provisional List of the Principal Tribal Names and Synonyms. Publication of Bureau of American Ethnology. Smithsonian Institution, Washington, D. C., 1885.

Linton, Ralph, ed.
Acculturation in Seven Indian Tribes. New York: D. Appleton-Century Co., 1940. 526 pp.
Contents: The *Puyallup*—M. W. Smith; *White Knife Shoshoni*—J. J. Harris; *Southern Ute* (Basin)—M. K. Opler; *Northern Arapaho* (Plains)— H. Elkin; *The Fox* (North East)—H. F. Joffe; *Alkatcho Carrier* (Plateau)—I. Goldman; *The San Ildefonso*—W. Whitman.

————.
Crops, Soils, and Culture. In: *The Maya and Their Neighbors,* (pp. 32–40). New York: 1940.

————.
"The Significance of Certain Traits in North American Maize Culture." *AA* 26:345–349, 1924. n.s.

Lips, Julius Ernst
"Ethnopolitics and the Indian." *The Commonweal* 21 (No. 20):562–564, March 15, 1935.

————.
The Savage Hits Back. Introduction by Bronislaw Malinowski. Translated from German by Vincent Benson. New Haven: Yale University Press, 1937. xxxi, 254 pp.

Lloyd, J. William
Aw-Aw-Tam Indian Nights. Westfield, N. J.: The Lloyd Group, 1911.

Lowie, Robert H.
"American Culture History." *AA* 42:409–428, 1940. n.s.

————.
"The Matrilineal Complex." In: *University of California Publications in American Archaeology and Ethnology* 16 (No. 2):29–45, 1919. Berkeley: University of Calif. Press, 1919–1920.

Mallery, Garrick
"Pictographs of the North American Indians." *4th Annual Report: Bureau of American Ethnology,* 1882–1883, pp. 13–254, pls. I-LXXXIII, figs. 1–209. Washington, D. C.: U. S. Gov't Printing Office, 1886.
Northwestern rock carvings, materials upon which pictographs are made, totemic, religious, customs, tribal history, etc.

Martin, Paul S., Quimby, George I., and Collier Donald
Indians Before Columbus. Chicago: University of Chicago Press, 1947. 582 pp., illus., and charts, glossary.
The authors have succeeded in systematizing a huge mass of data into one of the most useful books on North America archaeology. . . . It also comments on the various theories that have been advanced to explain the origin of the American Indian, and some of the fallacious if not absurd beliefs concerning his way of life." (Carling Malouf).

Maximilian, Prince Alex
Voyage en l'Amérique du Nord. Paris: 1843.

Macleod, William Christie
The American Indian Frontier. London: Kegan Paul, Trench, Trubner and Co., Ltd., 1928.
Also discussion on various ceremonies, rites, etc.

————.
"On the Southwest Asiatic Origins of American Culture." *AA* 31:554–560, 1929. n.s.

Malinowski, Bronislaw
The Dynamics of Culture Change. New Haven: Yale University Press, 1945.

Marett, Robert Ranulph
Psychology and Folklore. London: Methuen & Co., Ltd., 1920. ix, 275 pp.

Matthews, W.
"Study of Ethics Among the Lower Races." *JAFL* 12:1–9, 1899.

McCown, T. D.
"The Antiquity of Man in the New World." *American Antiquity* 6:203–213, 1914.

McCreight, M. I.
The Wigwam: Puffs From the Peace Pipe. Du Bois, Pa.: M. I. McCreight, 1944. 58 pp.
Sketches of famous Indian Warriors.

McGee, W. J., and Thomas, C.
Prehistoric North America. In: *The History of North America.* F. N. Thorpe, ed. Vol. 19. Philadelphia: 1905. 428 pp.

McIntosh, John
Origin of the North American Indians; With a faithful description of their manners and customs. New York: Nafis & Cornish, 1843. xxxv, 345 pp., illus.

Mackay, J. E.
Indian Notes. Toronto: 1930.

McKenney, Thomas Loraine
Memoirs, Official and Personal.... New York: Paine and Burgess, 1846. 2 vols. in 1.

—————, **and Hall, James**
The Indian Tribes of North America, with Biographical Sketches and Anecdotes of the Principal Chiefs. New Edition, edited by Frederick Webb Hodge, Bushnell, David I, Jr. Edinburgh: John Grant, 1933–34. 3 Vols. Illustrated with 123 full-page Plates (chiefly from the Indian Gallery, formerly in the War Department at Washington). Photogravure Portraits, and two maps. Vol. III has an introduction by H. J. Braunholtz. First published in 1836–44. Philadelphia: E. C. Biddle. 3 vols.
Many subsequent editions of this work were published.

McLaughlin, Major James
My Friend the Indian. Boston: Houghton Mifflin Co., 1910.

MacLeod, W. C.
The American .Indian Frontier. New York: 1928. 598 pp.

McNicol, Donald Monroe
The Amerindians.... New York: Frederick A. Stokes Co., 1937. xix, 341 pp., bibl.

Meggers, Betty J.
"Recent Trends in American Ethnology". *AA* 48:176–214, 1946. n.s. Bibl.

Merriam, C. Hart
The Dawn of the World. Cleveland: The Arthur H. Clark Co., 1910.

Merrill, Rufus
150 Stories About Indians. Concord: N. H., R. Merrill, 1853. xiv, 192 pp., illus.

Miner, William Harvey
The American Indians North of Mexico. Cambridge, Eng.: University Press, 1917. x, 169 pp., bibl.

Mitra, Panchanan
A History of American Anthropology. Calcutta: University of Calcutta, 1933. x, 239 pp., bibl. (pp. 213–234).

Moncrieff, Ascott Robert H.
The Men of the Backwoods; true stories and sketches of the Indians and the Indian fighters. Illustrated by C. O. Murray. London: Griffith & Farran, 1880. 488 pp., illus.

Mooney, J.
"The Aboriginal Population of America North of Mexico." *Smithson. Inst. Misc. Coll.* 80 (Part 7):1–40, 1928.

Moorehead, Warren K.
American Indians in the United States. The present condition of the American Indian, his political history, and other topics; a plea for justice. Andover, Mass.: Andover Press, 1914. 440 pp., illus., plates, port.

—————.
"The Problem of the Red Paint People." *Holmes Anniversary Volume,* pp. 359–365, Washington, D. C., 1916.

Morse, Rev. Jedidah
A Report to the Secretary of War of the United States on Indian Affairs, comprising a narrative of a tour performed in the summer of 1820, under a commission from the President of the United States, for the purpose of ascertaining, for the use of government, the actual state of the Indian tribes in our country, etc. New Haven: S. Converse, 1822. 400 pp., front., port., fold. map.

Nelson, A. W.
Those Who Came First. La Grande, Oregon: The Author, 1934.

Newell, W. W.
"Additional Collection Essential to Correct Theory in Folk-Lore and Mythology." *JAFL* 3:23–32, 1890.

—————.
"Necessity of Collecting Traditions of Native Races." *JAFL* 1:162–163, 1888.

Nieuwenhuis, A. W.
Die Dualistische Kultur in Amerika. Ihre Enstehung in Südamerica, Verbreitung und Ethoschung ihren Elemente in Nordamerika, Sonderstellung im Mittelamerika. *Internationale Archiv für Ethnographie* 32 suppl. Leiden: E. J. Brill, Ltd., 1933. 147 pp.
On the duality of the roots of American culture.

Nordenskiöld, E.
"The American Indian as an Inventor." *Jour. Anthr. Inst. Gt. Brit.* 59:273–311, 1929.

—————.
"En Jämforelse Mellan Indiankulturen i Södra Sydamerika och i Nordamerika." *Ymer* 26: 298–315, 1926.

Nuttall, Z.
"The Fundamental Principles of Old and New World Civilizations." Peabody Museum Papers (Archaeological and Ethnological Papers of the Peabody Museum, Harvard Univ. Cambridge) Vol. 2, 575 pp., 1901.

Olson, Roland L.
"Clan and Moiety in Native America." *University of Californic Publications in Amercan Archaeology and Ethnology* 33 (No. 4):351–422, 1933.

Palmer, Rose Amelia, comp.
The North American Indians; an account of the American Indians north of Mexico, compiled from the original sources. New York: *Smithsonian Institute Series. Vol. 4, 1929.* 309 pp., *illus bibl.*

Parsons, Elsie Clews, ed.
American Indian Life, by Several of Its Students. Illustrated by Grant La Farge. New York: B. W. Huebsch and Company, 1922. iv, 419 pp., plates (part. col.) map.

Parsons, Talcott
"The Kinship System of the Contemporary United States." *AA* 45:22–39, 1943. n.s.

Pattie, James O.
The Personal Narrative of J. O. Pattie of Kentucky, during an expedition from St. Louis through the vast regions between that place and the Pacific Ocean, and thence back through the city of Mexico and Vera Cruz. Cincinnati: E. H. Flint, 1833. xi, 300 pp., 5 pl.

Payne, E. J.
History of the New World Called America. Oxford: At the Clarendon Press, 1892. 2 vols.
Book II—Aboriginal America

Payon, José Garcia
"Genesis del indio americano y origen de las culturas aborigenes de americanos." *Anales del Museo Nacional de Arqueologies, Historia y Ethnografia.* Epoca 5a 1 (No. 3):423–466, 1934.

Peet, Stephen Denison
Prehistoric America. Chicago: Office of the American Antiquarian, 1890–1905. 5 vols.
Vol. I—Prehistoric America.

———.
The North American Indians. In: *United States of America.* N. S. Shaler, ed. Vol. I, pp. 190–272. New York: D. Appleton and Co., 1894. 2 vols.

Pericot y Garcia, Luis
"La America indígena: el Hombre Americano; los Pueblos de America." *Historia de America y de los Pueblos Americanos.* Vol. I, 727 pp., illus. Barcelona: Salbat Editores, S. A., 1936.
The first of a series of twenty-three volumes dealing with aboriginal cultures and history of the Americas.
In the second part of volume, "The Peoples of America"—gives a rapid survey of the various tribes, linguistic affiliations, physical characteristics, myths, etc.

Phillips, Henry, Jr.
"Primitive Man in Modern Beliefs." *JAFL* 3: 60–63, 1890.
A poem expressing the significance of folklore.

Pizarro, L. Leopoldo
"La Metodolgía ethnológica frente al folklore." *La Opinión* (Santiago de Chile) p. 10, Act 29, 1944.
Discussion of the perspective and role of folklore in relation to environmental factors.

Powell, J. W.
"Indian Linguistic Families of America North of Mexico." *7th Annual Report, Bureau of Ethnology,* 1885–1886, pp. 7–139, 1 map. Washington, D. C.: U. S. Gov't Printing Office, 1891.
Nomenclature of linguistic families, literature relating to the classification of Indian families, Indian tribes sedentary population, tribal lands, etc. Linguistic families.

———.
"On Limitations to the Use of Some Anthropological Data." *1st Annual Report Bureau of American Ethnology* pp. 73–83. 1879–1880. Washington, D. C.: U. S. Gov't Printing Office, 1881.

———.
Outlines of the Philosophy of the North American Indians: Read before the American Geographical Society, at Chickering Hall, Dec. 29, 1876. New York: D. Taylor, 1877.

———.
"The Lessons of Folklore." *AA* 2:1–37, 1900. n.s.

Radin, Paul
"History of Ethnological Theories." *AA* 31:9–33, 1929. n.s.

———.
Primitive Man as Philosopher. Foreword by John Dewey. London and New York: D. Appleton and Company, 1927. xviii, 402 pp.

———.
"The Genetic Relationship of the North American Indian Languages." *University of California Publications in American Archaeology and Ethnology* 14 (No. 5):489–502, 1919. Berkeley: University of California Press, 1918–1919.

———.
"The Method and Theory of Ethnology." *AA* 36:315–316, 1934. n.s.

———.
The Method and Theory of Ethnology: An Essay in Criticism. New York: McGraw-Hill, 1933. 278 pp.

———.
The Story of the American Indian. New York: Boni and Liveright Co., 1927. xiv, 371 pp., incl. coll front., illus. pl.

Ratzel, Friedrich
The History of Mankind. London: The Macmillan Co., 1897. 3 vols., illus.

Reichard, Gladys
"Franz Boas and Folklore." *AA* 45:52–57, 1943.

Reid, Mayne
Odd People. Being a Popular Description of Singular Races of Man. Boston: Ticknor & Fields, 1861. 461 pp., illus.

Renaud, E. B.
"L'antiquité de l'homme dans l'Amérique du Nord." *L'Anthropologie* 38:23–50, 1928.

———.
"The Influence of Food on Indian Culture." *Social Forces* (Chapel Hill) 10:97–101, 1934.

Rhode, Halla, and Coon, Bessie
American Indian Life. San Francisco: Des Mones, University Press, 1939.

Rowe, John H.
"Métodos y fines del estudio folklorico." *WP* (año 4) 3 (No. 16):21–28, 1944.
Discussion of how to collect, analyze, systematize folklore studies, etc.

Salomon, Julian Harris
The Book of Indian Crafts and Indian Lore. New York and London: Harper Bros., 1928. 418 pp., illus.
Maps showing distribution of tribes, customs and legends. Music pp. 297-327.

Sanford, David A.
Indian Topics; or Experiences in Indian Missions, with Selection from Various Sources. New York: Broadway Publishing Co., 1911. 108 pp.

Sapir, E.
"Time Perspective in Aboriginal American Culture, a Study in Method." *Canada Geological Survey, Anthropological Series Memoir 90* (No. 13) 1916. 87 pp.

Sapper, K.
"Die Kulturzustand der Indianer vor der Berührung mit den Europäern und in der Gegenwart." *Proc. Inter. Congr. Amer.* 24: 73–96, 1930.

Schmidt, W.
Die altstämme Nordamerikas. In: *Festschrift Eduard Seler,* pp. 471–502. Stuttgart: 1922.

Schoolcraft, Henry Rowe
Algic Society. Constitution of the Algic Society, instituted March 28, 1832. Detroit: Cleveland and Sawyer, 1833. 23 pp.

————.
"Ethnological Sketch of the North American Indians." *American Quarterly Register and Magazine* (Philadelphia) 1:169–177, 1848.

————.
Historical and Statistical Information Respecting the History, Condition, and Prospects of the Indian Tribes of the United States. Collected and prepared under the direction of the Bureau of Indian Affairs. Published by the authority of Congress. Philadelphia: J. B. Lippincott, 1851–1857. xxviii, 25–756 pp., front., illus., plates (part. col.) ports. (part. col.)

————.
History of the Indian Tribes of the United States. Published by order of Congress under the direction of the Department of the Interior, Indian Bureau. Philadelphia: J. B. Lippincott and Co., 1860. xxviii, 756 pp.

————.
Information Respecting the History, Condition and Prospects of the Indian Tribes of the United States.... Illustrated by S. Eastman. Philadelphia: Lippincott, Grambo & Co., 1851–57. 6 vols., illus.

————.
Onéota, or Characteristics of the Red Race of America.... New York: Wiley & Putnam, 1845. vi, 512 pp., illus.
Originally issued, 1844–45, in eight numbers... bearing title: *Onéota, or The Red Race of America....* Afterwards issued under various titles: *The Red Race of America; The Indian in His Wigwam; The American Indians; Western Scenes and Reminiscences....*

————.
Personal memoirs of a residence of 30 years with the Indian tribes on the American frontier. Philadelphia: Lippincott, Grambo and Co., 1851. 703 pp.

————.
Plan for the Investigation of American Ethnology, to include the facts derived from other parts of the globe and the eventual formation of a museum of antiquities and the peculiar fabrics of nations; and also the collection of a library of the philology of the world, manuscript and printed. Submitted to the Board of Regents of the Smithsonian Institution at their first meeting at Washington, September, 1846. New York: Jenkins, 1846. 13 pp.

————.
The American Indians. Their history, condition and prospects. Buffalo: George H. Derby and Co., 1851. 495 pp.

————.
The Indian in his Wigwam, or Characteristics of the Red Race of America from Original Notes and Manuscripts. Buffalo: Derby and Hewson, 1848. 416 pp.

————.
The Indian Tribes of the United States: Their history, antiquities, customs, religion, arts, language, traditions, oral legends, and myths. Ed. by Francis S. Drake. Philadelphia: J. B. Lippincott & Co., 1884. 2 vols., illus.
An abridgment of the author's *Information Respecting the History, Condition and Prospects of the Indian Tribes of the United States,* with additional notes by the editor.

Schuricht, Herrmann
Mythus, Sagen und Geschichte Alt-Amerikas als Lehrmittel in amerikanischen Schulen. Vortrag, gehalten vor dem 13. deutsch-amerikanischen Lehrertag zu Buffalo, N. Y., am 26. Juli 1882. Milwaukee, Wis.: Druck von Doerflinger Book & Publishing Co., 1882. 15 pp.
Myths, tales and legends as teaching materials in American schools.

Sears, P. B.
"The Archaeology of Environment in Eastern North America." *AA* 34:610–622, 1932. n.s.

Seymour, Flora W.
The Indians To-Day. Chicago: Benj. H. Sanborn Co., 1927.

Slight, Benjamin
Indian Researches; or, Facts Concerning the North American Indians; including notices of their present state of improvement, in their social, civil, and religious condition.... Montreal: J. E. L. Miller, 1844. ix, 179 pp., illus.

Smith, Walter Brown
The Lost Red Paint People of Maine, a few things we think we know about them and more that we know we don't. Bar Harbor, 1930. 43 pp., illus. (Lafayette National Park Museum, Bulletin II.)

Smith, William
Some Account of the North-America Indians; their genius, character, customs, and dispositions toward the French and English nations. ... London: R. Griffiths, 1754. viii, 68 pp.
  Contains the speech of a Creek-Indian; a letter from an Indian maid of the Mohawks; Indian songs of peace; and an American fable.

Squier, E. L.
Children of the Twilight, folktales of Indian tribes. New York: 1926.
  Twana: 1-30, 138-167; Diegueño: 31-54; Pueblo-Apache: 55-79; Havasupai: 80-107; Hopi Eagle Dance: 108-137; Kit-Sap: 168-200; Tlingit: 201-257.

Stanford, E.
Compendium of Geography and Travel. London: 1878-1885. 6 vols.

Stanley, J. M.
"Portraits of North American Indians." *Smithson. Inst. Misc. Coll.* 2 (Part 3):1-76, 1852.

Starr, Frederick
American Indians. Boston: D. C. Heath & Co., 1898. x, 242 pp., illus.

Steward, Julian H.
"Acculturation and the Indian Problem." *America Indígena* 3 (No.4):323-328, Mexico, D.F. 1943.

Stratton, Ella
Wild Life Among the Red Men; containing a full account of their customs, traits of character, superstitions, modes of warfare, traditions, etc.... Philadelphia; National Publishing Co., 1910. xiii, 269 pp., illus.

Strong, James C.
Wah-Kee-Nah and Her People: The curious customs, traditions, and legends of the North American Indians. New York: G. P. Putnam's Sons, 1893.

Stubbs, Addison Woodward
The Indian Princess Me-nung-gah, and other poems. Boston: R. G. Badger, 1912. 152 pp.

Swanton, John R.
Social Organization. In: *Handbook of American Indians.* Vol. II, pp. 608-612. Bibl. Bureau of American Ethnology, Bulletin 30. Washington, D. C.: U. S. Government Printing Office, 1910.

————, and Dixon, Roland B.
"Primitive American History." *AA* 16:376-413, 1914. n.s.

The Travels of Capts. Lewis & Clarke ... containing an account of the Indian tribes, who inhabit the western part of the continent unexplored, and unknown before. With copious delineations of the manners, customs, religion, &c. of the Indians.... Philadelphia: Hubbard Lester, 1809. xii, 300 pp.

Thomas, Cyrus
The Indians of North America in Historic Times. In: *The History of North America,* G. C. Lee, ed., Vol. 2, 461 pp. Philadelphia: 1903.

Thompson, Stith
Motif-Index of Folk-Literature; A Classification of Narrative Elements in Folk-Tales, Ballads, Myths, Fables, Medieval Romances, Exempla, Fabliaux, Jest-Books, and Local Legends. 6 vols. F. F. Communications Nos. 106-109, 116, 117. Helsinki, 1932-36. (Also Indiana University Studies Nos. 96-97, 100, 101, 105-106, 108-110, 111-112. Bloomington, Indiana, 1932-36.)

True, Webster P.
The First Hundred Years of the Smithsonian Institution, 1846-1946. Washington, D. C.: The Smithsonian Institution, 1946. viii, 64 pp.

Trust, Estelle
Songs of the Lost Red Tribes. Shreveport: The Author, 1941. 10 pp.

Turner, G.
Traits of Indian Character; as generally applicable to the aborigines of North America. Philadelphia: Key & Biddle, 1836. 2 vols.

Tylor, Edward Burnett
Primitive Culture: Researches into the Development of mythology, philosophy, religion, art and custom. London: J. Murray, 1871. 2 vols.

University of California Anthropological Records.
Culture Element Distributions. Parts 1-24. Cal.: University of California Press, 1935-43. University of California Anthropological Records, v. 1, no. 1-7; v. 4, no. 1-2; v. 6, no. 1, 3-4; v. 7, no. 1-2, v. 8, no. 1-2, 4., bibl.
  Contents: Part 1. The Structure of California Indian Culture, by Stanislaw Klimek; Part 2. Yana, by E. W. Gifford and Stanislaw Klimek; Part 3. Area and Climax, by A. L. Kroeber; Part 4. Pomo, by E. W. Gifford and A. L Kroeber; Part 5. Southern California, by Philip Drucker; Part 6. Southern Sierra Nevada, by H. E. Driver; Part 7. Oregon Coast, by H. G. Barnett; Part 8. The Reliabiilty of Culture Element Data, by H. E. Driver; Part 9. Gulf of Georgia Salish, by H. G. Barnett; Part 10. Northwest California, by H. E. Driver; Part 11. Tribes Surveyed, by A. L. Kroeber; Part 12. Apache-Pueblo, by E. W. Gifford; Part 13. Nevada Shoshoni, by J. H. Steward; Part 15. Salt, Dogs, Tobacco, by A. L. Kroeber; Part 17. Yuman-Piman, by Philip

Drucker; Part 18. Ute-Southern Paiute, by O. C. Stewart; Part 19. Central California Coast, by J. P. Harrington; Part 20. Northeast California, by E. W. Voegelin; Part 21. Round Valley, by Frank Essene; Part 22. Plateau, by V. F. Ray; Part 23. Northern and Gosiute Shoshoni, by J. H. Steward; Part 24. Central Sierra, by B. W. Aginsky.

Unkalunt, A.
Earth Speaks. New York: Fleming H. Revell Co., 1940.

Vance, Lee James
"Folk-Lore Study in America." *Popular Science Monthly* 43:586–598, Sept., 1893.

Verrill, Alpheus Hyatt
Old Civilizations of the New World. Indianapolis: The Bobbs-Merrill Company, 1929. viii, 393 pp., bibl., music.

Waitz, Theodor
Die Indianer Nordamerica's. Leipzig: F. Fleischer, 1865. x, 180 pp.

Wake, C. S.
"American Origins." *American Antiquity* 26: 105–115, 1904.

―――――.
"Asiatic Ideas Among the American Indians." *American Antiquity* 27:153–162, 189–196, 1905.

Watson, Henry Clay
Nights in a Block-House; or, Sketches of Border Life: Embracing adventures among the Indians, feats of the wild hunters, and exploits of Boone, Brady, Kenton, Whetzel, Fleehart, and other border heroes of the west. Philadelphia: J. B. Lippincott & Co., 1856. 448 pp., illus.

Whipple, Lieut. A. W.
Report Upon the Indian Tribes. (Thomas Ewbank and Prof. Wm. Turner.) From U. S. Topographical Engineers, Bureau of Explorations. Washington, D. C.: 1855.

White, Leslie A.
"Morgan's Attitude Toward Religion and Science." *AA* 46:218–231, 1944. n.s.

Williams, Samuel Cole, ed.
Adair's History of the American Indians. Edited under the Auspices of the National Society of the Colonial Dames of America in Tenn. Johnson City: Watanga Press, 1930. 508 pp., map, originally published in 1775.

Williams, Thomas Benton
The Soul of the Red Man. Oklahoma City: The Author, 1937.

Williamson, Peter
The Travels of Peter Williamson, Among the different nations and tribes of savage Indians in America; with an account of their principles of religious, civil, and military; their genius, strength, ideas of a deity, and notions of the creation; with everything remarkable concerning their manners, customs, employments, diversions. . . . Edinburgh: R. Fleming . . ., 1768. viii, 184 pp.

Winsor, Justin
Narrative and Critical History of America. Boston: Houghton Mifflin and Co., 1884–1889. 8 vols., illus.
Vol. I—aboriginal America.

Wise, Jennings C.
Red Man in the New World Drama: A politico.legal study, with a pageantry of American Indian History. Washington, D. C.: F. Roberts Company, 1931. 628 pp.

Wissler, Clark
"Ethnic Types and Isolation." *Science* 23:147–149, 1906. n.s.

―――――.
Ethnological Diversity in America and Its Significance. In: *The American Aborigenes,* Diamond Jenness, ed., (pp. 65–216). Toronto: 1933.

―――――.
Indian Cavalcade; or, Life on the old-time Indian reservation. New York: Sheridan House, 1938. 351 pp.

―――――.
Indians of the United States. New York: Doubleday Doran and Co., 1940. 319 pp., illus.

―――――.
"Material Cultures of the North American Indians." *AA* 16:447–508, 1914. n.s.

―――――.
The American Indian. An Introduction to the Anthropology of the new world. New York: Oxford University Press, 1938. 3rd ed. 466 pp., illus., bibl., map.

―――――.
"The Psychological Aspects of the Culture-Environment Relation." *AA* 14:217–226, 1912. n.s.

―――――.
The Relation of Nature to Man in Aboriginal America. New York: Oxford Univ. Press, 1926. xx, 248 pp., bibl.
Lectures on the distribution of American Indian traits, aboriginal geography and ecology.

―――――, and others
Adventures in the Wilderness. New Haven: Yale University Press, 1925. 369 pp., illus. (The Pageant of America, vol. I.)

Wood, Norman B.
Lives of Famous Indian Chiefs from Cotachiqui, the Indian Princess, and Powhatan; down to and including chief Joseph and Geronimo. Aurora, Ill.: American Indian Historical Publishing Co., 1906. 771 pp., illus.

Woodbury, George and Edna T.
Differences Between Certain of the North American Indian Tribes. Denver: State Historical Society of Colorado, 37 pp., 1932.

Woods, C. A.
"A Criticism of Wissler's North American Culture Areas." *AA* 36:517–523, 1934. n.s.

Zeisberger, David
"History of Northern American Indians. Edited by Archer Butler Hulbert and William Nathaniel Schwarze." In: *Ohio Archaeology and Historical Quarterly* 19 (Nos. 1 and 2). Columbus, Ohio: Published by the Society Office, 1910. 189 pp.

MYTHS AND MYTHOLOGY

See: Beliefs—Witchcraft—Magic, pp. 771-77; Folktales—Legends, pp. 777-86.

STUDIES AND COLLECTIONS

Alexander, Hartley Burr
God's Drum and Other Cycles from Indian Lore. Illustrations by Anders John Hangseth. New York: E. P. Dutton and Company, 1927. ix, 231 pp.
Original poems utilizing themes from Indian legends.

———.

L'art et la philosophie des Indiens de l'Amérique du Nord; Série de conférences faites a la Sorbonne aux mois d'Avril et de Mai 1925, précédée d'une préface par A. van Gennep et illustrée de 5 planches en couleurs et de 21 en noir. Paris: E. Leroux, 1926. 118 pp., xxvi pl. (part col.)
Discussion of religion and myths of the North American Indians.

———.

Manito Masks; dramatizations with music of American Indian spirit legends. New York: E. P. Dutton & Co., 1925.

———.

North American Mythology. Boston: Marshall Jones Company, 1916. xxiv, 325 pp., illustrated, map, bibl. (pp. 313–325).
The author presents, in the words of Franz Boas, "A useful summary of the vast and rapidly increasing body of myths that is being collected by students of anthropology." The book is vol. X of the series *The Mythology of All Races*, edited by Louis Herbert Gray, in 13 volumes.

———.

The Religious Spirit of the American Indian, as shown in the development of his religious rites and customs. Chicago: The Open Court Publishing Company, 1910. 51 pp., illus.

———.

"The Rain Cloud in Indian Myth." *El Palacio* 21:314–319.

Anon.
"Some Account of Indian Theology." *American Museum* 10:233, Nov., 1791.

Boas, Franz
Mythology and Folklore. In: *General Anthropology*, edited by Franz Boas, pp. 609–626. New York: D. C. Heath and Co., 1938.

———.

"Mythology and Folk-Tales of the North American Indians." *JAFL* 27:374–410, 1914.

———.

Mythology and Folk-Tales of the North American Indians. In: *Race, Language and Culture* by Franz Boas, pp. 451–490. New York: The Macmillan Co., 1940.

———.

"The Development of Folk-Tales and Myths." *Scientific Monthly* 3:335–342, 1916.

———.

The Development of Folk-Tales and Myths. In: *Race, Language and Culture* by Franz Boas, pp. 397–406, reprinted, 1916. New York: The Macmillan Co., 1940.

———.

The Growth of Indian Mythologies. In: *Race, Language and Culture* by Franz Boas, pp. 425–436. New York: The Macmillan Co., 1940.

———.

"The Growth of Indian Mythologies." In: *Thomas, William Isaac: Source Book for Social Origins.* Boston: R. G. Badger, pp. 1925.

———.

"The Mythologies of the Indians." *International Quarterly* (N. Y.) 11:327–342, 12:157–173, 1905.

Brinton, Daniel Garrison
American Hero-Myths. A Study of the Native Religions of the Western Continent. Philadelphia: H. C. Watts & Co., 1882. vii–xvi, 251 pp.

———.

"The Myths of Manibozho and Ioskeha," *Historical Magazine*, July, 1867. 3–6 pp. Morrisania, N. Y.

———.

The Myths of the New World. A Treatise on the Symbolism and Mythology of the Red Race of America. New York: Leypoldt and Holt, 1868. viii, 307 pp. Philadelphia: D. McKay, 1896. 3rd ed. rev., xii, 360 pp.

———.

Mythology and Folk-Lore. In: *Essays of an Americanist* (pp. 101–193). Philadelphia: Porter and Coates, 1890, 489 pp., illustrated.

———.

"Myths of the New World." *JAFL* 14:184, 1901.

———.

Nagualism. A Study in Native American Folk-Lore and History. Philadelphia: MacCalla & Company, 1894. 65 pp.

Brown, Charles Edward
Winabozho; Hero-God of the Indians of the Old Northwest. Myths, legends and stories.... Madison, 1944.

Caldwell, George Walter
Rainbow Stories and Indian Myths. Illustrated by Jane Jefferson Flippen. San Francisco: Phillips & Van Orden Co., 1919. 117 pp., illus.

Chamberlain, A. F.
"Mythology of Indian Stocks North of Mexico." *JAFL* 18:111–122, 1905.

Charencey, Hyacinthe de, comte
Le Fils de la Vierge. Havre: Impr. Lepelletier, 1879. 28 p.
A study in myths.

————.
L'Orphée Américain. Caen: C. Valin fils, 1892. 16 pp.

Connelley, William Elsey
Indian Myths, illustrated by Wm. Wallace Clarke. New York, Chicago: Rand McNally & Co., 1928. xiv, 167 pp.

Cornyn, John Hubert
Indian Hero Tales; wonder stories of the first Americans. Boston, Mass.: Little, Brown & Co., 1921. 248 pp.

Cowles, Julia Darrow
Indian Nature Myths, with illustrations by Dorothy Dulin. Chicago: A. Flanagan Co., 128 pp., front., illus.

Curtin, Jeremiah
Creation Myths of Primitive America, in relation to the religious history and mental development of mankind. Boston: Little Brown and Co., 1898. xxxix, 222 pp.

Dangel, Richard
"Gibt es normannische Einflüsse auf den Mythos der nordamerikanischen Indianer?" *Anthropologische Gesellschaft in Wien, Mitteil.* 57:44–50, 1927. Bibl.
The author seeks to find Norman influences on the myths of the North-American Indians.

————.
"Kice-Manito, der 'Grosse Geist'." *Baessler-Archiv* (Berlin) 17:155–171, 1934.
The Great Spirit—Kice Manito

————.
"Mythen vom Ursprung des Todes bei der Indianem Nordamerikas." *Mitteilungen der Anthropologischen Gesellschaft in Wien*, 58: 341–374, 1928.
Indian myths on the origin of death.

Demetracopoulou, D.
"The Loon Woman Myth: A Study in Synthesis." *JAFL* 46:101–129, 1933.

"Dissemination of Myths and Literary Types." *JAFL* 34:269–307, 1921.

Dorsey, J. O.
"Modern Additions to Indian Myths and Indian Thunder Superstitions." *JAFL* 6:232–233, 1893.

Eells, Myron
"The Thunder Bird." *AA* 2:329–336, 1889.

Ehrenreich, Paul
Die allgemeine Mythologie und ihre ethnologischen Grundlagen. Leipzig, 1910.

Emerson, Ellen Russell
Indian Myths; or Legends, Traditions, and symbols of the Aborigines of America, Compared with Those of Other Countries Including Hindustan, Egypt, Persia, Assyria, and China. Boston: James R. Osgood and Company, 1884. xviii, 677 pp.

Forlong, Gen. J. G. R.
River of Life, or Sources and Streams of the Faiths of Man in all Lands. London: Turnbull & Spears, 1883. II vols.

Frazer, Sir James George
Myths of the Origin of Fire. London: Macmillan and Co., Ltd., 1930. vii, 238 pp. Bibliographical footnotes.

Gaylord
"A Summer in Georgia. Indian Myth—The Story of the 'Trysting Rock'." *Holden's Dollar Magazine* 8:101–103, Sept., 1851.

Gayton, A. H.
"English Ballads and Indian Myths." *JAFL* 55:126–133, 1942.

————.
"The Orpheus Myth in North America." *JAFL* 48:263–295, 1935.

George, Amara
Mythen und Sagen der Indianer Amerika's.... Düsseldorf: Arnz & Comp, 1856. 63 pp.

Gray, Louis Herbert, ed.
The Mythology of All Races. Boston: Marshall Jones Co., 1916–1932. XIII vols., illus.

H. F. S.
"Spider Myths of the American Indians." *Natural History* 21:382–385.

Hallowell, A. Irving
"Myth, Culture and Personality." *AA* 49:544–546, 1947.

Hartland, Edwin Sidney
Mythology and Folktales. Their relation and interpretation. London: D. Nutt, 1900. 53 pp.

Hewitt, J. F.
History of the Worship of Ia or Yah, The All-Wise Fish-Sun God, as told in the Mythology of the American Indians, Scandinavians, etc. In: *The Ruling Races of Pre-historic Times in India*, Vol. II. Westminster: Archibald Constable and Co., 1894.

Hewitt, J. N. B.
Mythology of the North American Indians. In: *Handbook of the American Indians North of Mexico*, F. W. Hodge, editor. V. 1, pp. 964–972. Washington, D. C.: 1907.

Hough, Walter
"Fire Origin in Myths of the World." *Proceedings of the 20th Session of the International Congresses of Americanists* 1:179–184, 1924.

Judson, Katharine B.
Old Crow and His Friends. Animal adventures based upon Indian myths. Boston: Little, Brown and Co., 1918.

Keary, C. F.
Mythologies and Folktales. In: *The Dawn of History:* An Introduction to Prehistoric Study. Chapter XI. London: Mozley and Smith, 1878.

Kluckhohn, Clyde
"Myths and Rituals: A General Theory." *The Harvard Theological Review* 35 (No. 1):45–79, 1942.

Knortz, Karl
Mythologie und Civilisation der nordamerikanischen Indianer. Leipzig: P. Frohberg, 1882. 76 pp.
Folklore of the North American Indians.

Koppers, W.
"Der Hund in der Mythologie der zirkumpazifischen Völker." *Wiener Beiträge zur Kulturgeschichte und Linguistic* 1:359–399, 1930.

Kunike, H.
"Der Coyote in der amerikanischen Mythologie." *Mexico Antiquo* (Mexico) 2:194–201, 1924.

————.
"Zur Astralmythologie der Nordamerikanischen Indianer." *Inter. Archiv. Ethno.* 27:1–29, 55–78, 107–134, 1926.

Lang, Andrew
Custom and Myth. New York: Longmans, Green and Co., 1910. 312 pp.

————.
Modern Mythology. London: Longmans, Green and Company, 1897. xxiv, 212 pp.

————.
Myth, Ritual and Religion. London: Longmans, Green and Co., 1887. 2 vols.

Langer, Susanne K.
Philosophy in a New Key. A Study in the Symbolism of Reason, Rite and Art. Cambridge, Mass.: Harvard University Press, 1942.
Chap. VII: Life, Symbols: The Roots of Myth.

Lenders, E. W.
"Mythe des 'Wah-ru-hap-ah-rar' oder des heiligen Kriegskeulenbundels." *Zeitschrift für Ethnologie.* (Berlin) Jahrg. 46, p. 404–420, 1914. Illus.
Myth of the holy war-bundle.

Lowie, Robert H.
"Catch Words for Mythological Motives." *JAFL* 21:24–27, 1908.

————.
Myths and Traditions of the Crow Indians. New York: The Trustees, 1918. 308 pp., Bibl. 305–306. (Anthropological papers of the American Museum of Natural History, vol. xxv, part 1.)

————.
"Test Theme in North American Mythology." *JAFL* 21:97–148, 1908.

Luomala, Katherine
"Oceania, American Indian and African Myths of Snaring the Sun." *Bernice P. Bishop Museum Bulletin* 168. Honolulu, 1940. 58 pp.

Mackenzie, Donald Alexander
Myths of Pre-Columbian America. (Half-title: Myth and Legend in Literature and Art.) London: The Gresham Publishing Company, 1924. iii–xiv, 351 pp., col. front, plates (1 fold), fold. map.

McClintock, Walter
"The Thunderbird Myth." *Masterkey* 15:164–168, 1941; 16:16–18, 1942.

Malinowski, B.
Myth in Primitive Psychology. New York: W. W. Norton and Co., 1926. 94 pp. The New Science Series, edited by C. K. Ogden. Vol. I.

Matthews, Washington
"Some Illustrations Between Myth and Ceremony." *Memoirs of the International Congress of Anthropology* (pp. 246–251). Chicago, 1894.

Molina-Téllez, Féliz
El Cielo en la mitologiá americana. Buenos Aires: Emecé Editores, 1944. 99 pp., illus.
The heaven in American mythology.

Morris, Cora
Stories from Mythology: North America. Boston: Marshall Jones Company, 1924. xi, 173 pp., col. front., plates. Bibl. (pp. 170–173).

Newell, W. W.
"Ritual Regarded as the Dramatization of Myth." *JAFL* 7:248–249, 1894.

Palmer, Rose A.
"Myths and Legends." In: *The North American* ... Chapt. viii. Vol. iv, Smithsonian Scientific Series. Washington, D. C., 1929.

Parker, Arthur Caswell
American Indian Freemasonry. Albany, N. Y.: Buffalo Consistory, 1919. 36 pp., illus.
A study in religion and mythology.

Peet, Stephen Denison
Myths and Symbols, or Aboriginal Religions in America. Chicago: Office of the American Antiquarian, 1905. xvi, 444 pp.

Pettazzoni, Raffaele
The Chain of Arrows: The diffusion of a mythical motive. London: Folklore Society Publications, XXXV, 151 pp.

Powell, J. W.
"Sketch of the Mythology of the North American Indians." *1st Annual Report*, Bureau of American Ethnology pp. 19–52, 1879–1880. Washington, D. C.: U. S. Gov't Printing Office, 1881.
Analysis of philosophic mythology and the correlation between mythology and philosophy plus actual Indian myths.

Radin, Paul
Literary Aspects of North American Mythology. Ottawa: Gov. Prtg. Bureau, 1915. 51 pp., Geological Survey. Museum Bull. Anthropological Series No. 16.

Reichard, Gladys A.
"Literary Types and Dissemination of Myths." *JAFL* 34:269–307, 1921.

Sarat, Chandra Nitra
"The Bear in Asiatic and American Ritual." *Journal of the Asiatic Society of Bombay* 7:467–.

Skinner, Charles Montgomery
American Myths and Legends. Philadelphia: J. B. Lippincott Co., 1903. 2 vols., illus.

————.
Myths and Legends of our Own Land. Philadelphia: J. B. Lippincott Co., 1896. 2 vols.

Smith, De Cost
Indian Experiences. Illustrations by the author, with drawings and photographs. Caldwell, Idaho: The Caxton Printers Ltd., 1943. 388 pp., illus., bibl.
The chapters on Indian myths and legends are unusually discriminating. His experiences range from the Great Sioux Reservation to the Crows, Cheyennes and Shoshones and to the N. Y. Iroquois.

Smith, Louise M.
The Indian Story of the Creation and Flood; being the First of the Myths and Legends of Colorado done into tales by Louise M. Smith. Illustrated by Robert L. Paley. Denver: 1906. 23 pp., illus.

Spence, L.
Myths of the North American Indians. Color plates by James Jack. New York: T. Y. Crowell Company, 1914. xii, 392 pp., incl. map, col. front, 35 pl. (31 col.).

Swanton, J. R.
"Concordance of American Myths and Beliefs." *JAFL* 20:220–222, 1907.

————.
"Practical Aspects of the Study of Myth." *JAFL* 23:1–7, 1910.

Thompson, Stith
Creation Myths. In: *The Folktale.* Part 3, Chapt. II, pp. 303–319. New York: The Dryden Press, 1947. 522 pp.
Discussion and examples of the myths among the Indians of the Southwest, California, the Eskimo, Northeast Woodland, Iroquois, Central Woodland, North Pacific Coast, and other areas.

Waters, Clement, and Erskine, Clara
A Handbook of Legendary and Mythological Art, with descriptive illustrations. Boston: J. R. Osgood and Company, 1883. xii, 575 pp., illus.

Wetherell, Caroline
A North American Indian Record, to Prove the Indubitable Existence of the Behemoth. With some observations to Christians of all Denominations, on the Perfect Truth and Analogy of the Book of Books, the Holy Bible. Dublin: J. Porteus, 1843. 16 pp.

Wilson, Gilbert L.
Indian Hero Tales. New York: American Book Co., 1916. 203 pp., illus.

————.
Myths of the Red Children. Boston: Ginn and Co., 1907. 154 pp., illus.

Wood, Charles Erskine Scott
A Book of Tales. Being Some Myths of the North American Indian. New York: The Vanguard Press, 1929.

Wundt, Wilhelm
Völkerpsychologie. Mythus und Religion. Vol. II. Leipzig, 1905.

BELIEFS—WITCHCRAFT—MAGIC

See: Myths and Mythology, pp. 768-71; Customs, pp. 786-94, Folk Medicine, pp. 803-06.

Aitken, B.
"Temperament in Native American Religion." *Journ. Anthro. Inst. Gt. Brit.* 60:363–387, 1930.

Anon.
"American Indians." *The Telescope* 1:138–139, Jan. 2, 1825.
A narrative on the religious beliefs of the Indians as contrasted with the Whites.

————.
"Credulity." *Niles' Weekly Register* 33:145–146, Nov. 3, 1827.
An editorial on the superstitious beliefs among the American Indians.

————.
"Indian Burial Place." *Dwight's American Magazine* 3:504, Aug. 6, 1847.
Description of ceremonies and beliefs connected with burying the dead. Illustrated.

————.
"Indian Journal." *Niles' Weekly Register* 71:82–83, Oct. 10, 1846.
Impressions of an Indian funeral ceremony, and accompanying rites.

————.
"Indian Paradise." *New World* 3:201, Sept. 25, 1841.
A brief account of the doctrines of life beyond the grave.

————.
"Indian Superstition." *New World* 1:159, Aug. 8, 1840.
A superstition based on the remarkable powers of a bird who sings from nightfall to daybreak, at the grave of a great Indian chief.

————.
"Indian Superstitions." *De Bow's Review* 16: 128–129, Feb. 1854.

————.
"Indians." *The American Magazine of Knowledge* 3:79, Nov., 1836.
Comments on the Indian's belief in the "Great Spirit."

————.
"The Busk." *Niles' Weekly Register* 25:169, Nov. 15, 1823.
A description of the religious ceremony of the Creek Indians, with corn, which, when fully ripe, expiates all sins and offences, except murder.

Armstrong, Perry A.
The Piasa; or, The Devil Among the Indians. Morris, Ill.: E. B. Fletcher, 1887. 48 pp., illus.

"Aspects of American Shaman."
JAFL 21:1–12, 1908.

Barber, Bernard
"Acculturation and Messianic Movements." *American Sociological Review* 6:—Oct., 1941.

————.
"A Socio-Cultural Interpretation of the Peyote Cult." *AA* 43:673–675, 1941.
The author tries to prove that the Ghost Dance and the Peyote Cult may in part be understood as alternative responses to a similar socio-cultural constellation.

Barrett, S. A.
"Indian Opinions of the Earthquake of April, 1906." *JAFL* 19:324–325, 1906.

Bayliss, C. K.
"Witchcraft Notes." *JAFL* 21:363, 1908.

Benedict, Ruth F.
The Concept of the Guardian Spirit in North America. Memoirs of the American Anthropological Association. No. 29, New York: Columbia University Press, 1923. 97 pp.

Ball, Sidney H.
"The Mining of Gems and Ornamental Stones by American Indians." *Anthropological Papers*, Nos. 13–18, Washington, D. C., Bureau of American Ethnology, Bulletin No. 128, 1941.

Bergen, Fanny D.
"American Indian Legends and Beliefs About the Squirrel and Chipmunk." *JAFL* 9:48–54, 1896.

————.
Annimal and Plant Lore. With Index of superstition in Vols. IV & VII of Memoirs of the American Folklore Society. Memoirs of the American Folklore Society No. 7. Philadelphia: American Folklore Society, 1899.

"Bibliography of Totemism."
JAFL 23:288–292, 1910.

"Bibliography of White Dog Sacrifice."
JAFL 1:103, 1888.

Blumensohn, Jules
"The Fast Among North American Indians." *AA* 35:451–469, 1933. n. s.

Boas, Franz
Prayer. In: *Handbook of American Indians* Vol. II. (pp. 303–304). Bureau of American Ethnology, Bulletin 30. Washington, D. C.: U. S. Government Printing Office, 1910.

————.
Religion. In: *Handbook of American Indians* Vol. II, pp. 365–371. Bibl. Bureau of American Ethnology, Bulletin 30. Washington, D. C.: U. S. Government Printing Office, 1910.

————.
Soul. In: *Handbook of American Indians* Vol. II, pp. 617–618. Bureau of American Ethnology, Bulletin 30. Washington, D. C.: U. S. Government Printing Office, 1910.

————.
The Idea of the Future Life Among Primitive Tribes. In: *Race, Language and Culture* by Franz Boas pp. 596–607, reprint (1922). New York: The Macmillan Co., 1940.

————.
"The Origin of Death." *JAFL* 30:486–491, 1917.

————.
The Origin of Totemism. In: *Race, Language and Culture* by Franz Boas pp. 316–323, reprint (1910). New York: The Macmillan Co., 1940.

Bonnejera, B.
"Hunting Superstitions of the American Aborigines." *Internationale Archiv für Ethnographie* (Leiden) 32:167–184, 1934.

Bourke, John Gregory
Compilation of Notes and Memoranda bearing upon the use of human ordure and urine in rites of a religious or semi-religious character among various nations. Washington, D. C. 1888.

————.
"Sacred Hunts of the American Indians." *Proceedings of the 8th Session of the International Congress of Americanists* (Paris) pp. 357–368, 1890.

————.
Scatologic Rites of all Nations. A dissertation upon the employment of excrementation remedial agents in religion, therapeutic divination, witchcraft, love-philters, etc., in all parts of the globe. Based upon original notes and personal compilation from over one thousand authorities. Washington, D. C.: W. H. Lowdermilk & Co., 1891. x, 496 pp. bibl. (pp. 469–483).

Brinton, Daniel Garrison
Religions of Primitive Peoples. New York: G.
P. Putnam's Sons. 1897. xiv, 264 pp.
American lectures in the history of religions,
2nd series, 1896–1897.

—————.
"The Origin of Sacred Numbers." *AA* 7:168–
174, 1894.

—————.
The Religious Sentiment, Its Source and Aim
a contribution to the science and philosophy
of religion. New York: Henry Holt and Co.,
1876. ix, 284 pp.

Budge, Sir Ernest Alfred T. W.
Amulets and Superstitions; the original text
with translations and descriptions of a long
series of Egyptian, Sumerian, Assyrian, Hebrew, Christian, Gnostic and Muslim amulets
and talismans, and magical figures, with chapters on the evil eye, the origin of amulets,
etc. . . . London: Oxford University Press, 1930.
xxxix, 543 pp., illus.

Bushnell, David I., Jr.
"The Various Uses of Buffalo Hair by the
North American Indians." *AA* 11:401–426,
1909. n. s.

Casanowicz, I. M.
"Parallels in the Cosmogonies of the Old World
and the New." *Holmes Anniversary Volume*,
pp. 44–52, Washington, D. C.: J. W. Bryan
Press, 1916.

Catlin, George
"Faith of the Indians." *The Musical Visitor*
3:59, Nov. 7, 1842.
An account of the beliefs of the Western tribes
in a future state, as prophesied by a chief.

Chamberlain, A. F.
"American Indian Legends and Beliefs About
the Squirrel and Chipmunk." *JAFL* 9:48–54,
1896.

—————.
"Primitive Nature Study", *Canadian Institute,
Transac.* 6:313–344, (Toronto), 1899.

Colbert, Edwin H.
"The Association of Man with Extinct Mam-
mals in the Western Hemisphere." *Proceedings
8 American Scientific Congress* 2:17–29, 1942.
(Wash., D. C.)

Conard, E. L. M.
"Les Idées des Indiens Algonquins Relatives
á la vie d'outre-tombe." *Revue de l'Histoire
des Religions* 42:1–95, 1900.
Beliefs of the Algonquian Indians in after life.

Cunningham, C., ed.
Talking Stone. Being early American stories
told before the white man's day on this continent by the Indians and Eskimos. Illustrated
by Richard Floethe. New York: Alfred A.
Knopf, 1939. 316 pp.

Cushing, Frank Hamilton
"Observations Relative to the Origin of the
Fylflot or Swastika." *AA* 334–338, 1907. n.s.

Dangel, R.
"Kice-Manito der "grosse Geist." *Baessler
Archiv* 17:155–171, 1934.

Deursen, A. Van
Der Heilbringer. Gronwigen: J. B. Wolters,
1931. 395 pp.
General discussion of Shamanism, religion and
magic among American Indians North of Mexico.
Well documented, excellent as source book.

Dixon, R. B.
"Aspects of the American Shaman." *JAFL*
21:1–12, 1908.

—————.
"Color-Symbolism of the Cardinal Points."
JAFL 12:10–16, 1897.

Dorman, Rushton M.
The Origin of Primitive Superstitions and
their development into worship of spirits and
the doctrine of spiritual agency among the
aborigines of America. Phila. Pa.: J. B. Lippincott, 1881. 398 pp.

Dorsey, J. O.
"Indian Doctrine of Souls." *JAFL* 6:298, 1893.

Eddy, Thomas M.
"The 'Walum–Olum or, Bark Record." *The
Ladies Repository.* 15: 269–272, May 1855.
A discussion and translation of the belief among
some Indian tribes of the formation of the world,
which closely parallels the account in the Holy
Scriptures.

Emerson, Ellen Russell
"The Book of the Dead and Rain Ceremonials."
AA 7:233–260, 1894., o.s.

Fergusson, E.
"Perpetual Pagans." *Scribner's Magazine* 92:
293—5, November, 1932.

Fewkes, J. Walter
Shrines. In:*Handbook of American Indians.*
Vol. II, pp. 558–559. Bibl. Bureau of American
Ethnology, Bulletin 30. Washington, D. C.:
U. S. Government Printing Office, 1910.

Fletcher, Alice Cunningham
"Prayers Voiced in Ancient America." *Art
and Archaeology* (Washington, D. C.) 9:73-75.

Frazer, Sir James George
The Fear of the Dead in Primitive Religion;
lectures delivered on the William Wyse foundation at Trinity College, Cambridge. London:
Macmillan and Co., Ltd., 1933–36, 3 vols.

—————.
*Totemica; A Supplement to Totemism and
Exogamy.* London: The Macmillan Co., 1937.
xii, 518 pp.
"From Australia, the classical land of Totemism,
the book leads through Melanesia to New Guinea,
thence to India and Africa and finally to America,
from which our first knowledge of the name and
institution of Totemism was derived."

————.
Totemism and Exogamy, a treatise on certain early forms of superstition and society. London: Macmillan and Co., Ltd. 1910. 4 vols.

Gatschet, A. S.
"Water-Monsters of American Aborigines." *JAFL* 12:255–260, 1899.

Goldenweiser, Alexander A.
"The Method of Investigating Totemism." *Anthropos* (10–11):256–623, 1915–1916.
For further studies in Totemism: see Bibliography of A. A. Goldenweiser in *AA* 43: 254–255, 1941.

————.
"The Origin of Totemism." *AA* 14:600–608, 1912. n. s.

Hadfield, P.
The Savage and His Totem. London: Allenson and Co., Ltd., 1938.
Chapt. VIII: The Diffusion of Totemism in America.

Haeckel, Josef
"Pseudo-Totemismus." *Mitteilungsblatt der Gesellschaft für Völkerkunde* 8:31–42, 1938. (Leipzig).

————.
"Zum Problem des Individual Totemismus in Nordamerika." *Internationales Archiv für Ethnographie* 35(Nos. 1–3):14–22, 1938.

Hall, N. P.
"Mystery of the Thunderbird." *Overland* US 87:109–10, April 1929.

Hallowell, Alfred Irving
Bear Ceremonialism in the Nothern Hemisphere. Philadelphia: University of Pennsylvania Press, 1926. 175 pp., bibl: pp. 163–175.

Harrington, M. R.
"The Thunderbird Costumes." *Masterkey* 20 (No. 6):195–196, 1946.

Henry, Alexander
"Religious Opinion of Indians." *The American Pioneer* 2:45, Jan. 1843.
Ideas on the hereafter.

Hewitt, J. N. B.
Adoption. In:*Handbook of the American Indian North of Mexico,* F. W. Hodge, editor. 1:15–16. Bureau of American Ethnology, Bulletin 30. Washington, D. C.: U. S. Government Printing Office, 1907.

————, and Swanton, John R.
Kinship. In:*Handbook of the American Indians North of Mexico,* F. W. Hodge, editor. 1:692–696. Bureau of American Ethnology, Bulletin 30. Washington, D. C.: U. S. Government Printing Office, 1907.

Hough, Walter
Poisons. In: *Handbook of American Indians.* Vol. II, (pp. 273–274). Bureau of American Ethnology, Bulletin 30. Washington, D. C.: U. S. Government Printing Office, 1910.

————.
Prayer Sticks In: *Handbook of American Indians.* Vol. II, (pp. 304). Bureau of American Ethnology, Bulletin 30. Washington, D. C.: U. S. Government Printing Office, 1910.

————.
"The Bison as a Factor in Ancient American Culture History." *Scientific Monthly* 30:315–319, 1930.

Howells, William
The Heathens. Primitive Man and His Religion. New York: Doubleday and Company, 1948. 306 pp., illus.

Jaeger, E.
"Indian V and Thunder God." *Nature Magazine* 35:469, Nov. 1942.

Jarvis, S. F.
"A Discourse on the Religion of the Indian Tribes of North America." *Coll. N. Y. Hist. Soc.* 3:181–268, 1821.

Jouvenceau, A.
"Indian Superstitions." *The Catholic Pioneer,* Jan. 1906, p. 15.

Kunz, George Frederick
Folklore of Precious Stones. Reprint Memoirs of the International Congress of Anthropology. pp. 267–281. Chicago, n. d.

Lang, Andrew
Magic and Religion. London: Longmans, Green and Co., 1901. x, 316 pp.

————.
The Making of Religion. London: Longmans, Green and Co., 1900. xxii, 355 pp.

————.
The Origin of Religion and Other Essays. London: Watts & Co., 1908. 128 pp., illus.

————.
The Secret of the Totem. London: Longmans, Green and Co., 1905. x, 215 pp.

Lee, D. Demetracoupoulou
"Some Indian Texts Dealing with the Supernatural." *Review of Religion,* pp. 404–411, May, 1941.

Leh, Leonard L.
"The Shaman in Aboriginal American Society." *University of Colorado Studies* 20 (No. 4): 199–263. Boulder, Colorado, Aug. 1934.

Lesser, Alexander
"Superstition." *Journal of Philosophy* 28 (No. 23):617–628, Nov. 5, 1931.

Leuba, James H.
"The Varieties, Classification, and Origin of Magic." *AA* 14:350–415, 1912. n. s.

Lincoln, Jackson Steward
The Dream in Primitive Cultures. London: Cresset Press, 1935. 359 pp., illus.

Loeb, Edwin M.
"Tribal Initiations and Secret Societies." *University of California Publications in American Archaeology and Ethnology.* 25:249–288, 1929. Berkeley: The University Press.

Lowie, Robert H.
"A New Conception of Totemism." *AA* 13:189–208, 1911. n. s.

———.
"Ceremonialism in North America." *AA* 16: 602–631, 1914. n.s. (Bibliography pp. 629–631).

MacCurdy, G. G.
"The Cult of the Ax." In: *Holmes Anniversary Volume.* . . . Washington: J. W. Bryan, 1916.

MacLeod, W. C.
"Child Sacrifice in North America." *Jour. Société Amér.* 23:127–137, 1931. n.s.

———.
"The Distribution and Process of Suttee in North America." *AA* 33:209–215, 1931. n. s.

———.
"The Distribution of Secondary Cremation and the Drinking of Ashes." *AA* 32:576–577, 1930. n. s.

———.
"The Nature, Origin and Linkages of the Rite of Hook-Swinging: with special reference to North America." *Anthropos* 29(Nos. 1–2):1–38, 1939.

Maitra, Susilkumar
"Religion and Magic: Being an Examination of the Views of Frazer, Marett, Leuba and Swanton." *Journal, Dep't of Letters,* University of Calcutta 27, 1935.

Marshall, Frederick
Curiosities of Ceremonies. London: 1880.

Martin, W. B.
"Religious Ideas of American Indians." *Catholic University Bulletin* (Wash.) 10:35–68, 225–243, 1904.

Matthews, Washington
Magic. In: *Handbook of the American Indians North of Mexico,* F. W. Hodge, editor. 1:783–785. Bureau of American Ethnology, Bulletin 30. Washington, D. C.: U. S. Government Printing Office, 1907.

———.
"Study of Ceremony." *JAFL* 10:257–263, 1897.

———.
"Treatment of Ailing Gods." *JAFL* 14:20–23, 1901.

Mooney, James
Prophets. In: *Handbook of American Indians.* Vol. II, pp. 309–310. Bureau of American Ethnology, Bulletin 30. Washington, D. C.: U. S. Government Printing Office, 1910.

———.
The Ghost-Dance Religion. *14th Annual Report: Bureau of American Ethnology,* 1892–1893. pp. 653–1101, pls. LXXXV–CXXII, figs. 56–104. Washington, D. C.: U. S. Gov't Printing Office, 1896.

———.
"The Mescal Plant Ceremony." *Therapeutic Gazette,* 3rd Series, Vol. 12, 1896.

Moore, Clarence B.
"Aboriginal Urn Burial in the U. S." *AA* 6: 660–670, 1904. n.s.

Mueller, J. G.
Geschichte der amerikanischen Urreligionen. Basel: Schweighauserische Verlagsbuchhandlung, 1867. vii, 706 pp.

Newell, W. W.
"Indian Messiah." *JAFL* 4:106, 1891.

Nieuwenhuis, A. W.
"The Difference Between the Conceptions of Soul(Animus) and Spirit(Spiritus) among the American Indians." *Proceedings of the 21st Session of the International Congress of Americanists* 1:125–139, 1924.

Ohlmarks, A.
Studien zum Problem des Shamanismus. Lund: 1939. 395 pp.
Studies in Shamanism

Parsons, Elsie Clews
"Ceremonial Impatience." *Journal of Philosophy, Psychology and Scientific Methods* 15: 157–164, 1918.

———.
"Die Flucht auf den Baum." *Zeit. für Ethno.* (Berlin) 54:1–29, 1922.

Peet, Stephen D.
"Sabaenism or Sky Worship in America." *The American Antiquarian,* July, 1894. p. 217.

———.
"The Cross in America." *Amer. Antiq.* (Chicago) 10:292–315, 1888.

———.
"The Swastika and Fire-Worship in America." *Amer. Antiq.* (Chicago) 26:185–192, 1904.

Petrullo, Vincenzo
The Diabolic Root: A Study in Peyotism, the new Indian religion, among the Delawares. Philadelphia: University of Pennsylvania Press, the University Museum, 1934. x, 185 pp., bibl.

Radin, Paul
Monotheism Among Primitive Peoples. With a foreword by Israel Zangwill. London: G. Allen & Union Ltd., 1924. 69 pp., bibl.

———.
Primitive Man as Philosopher. Introduction by John Dewey. New York: D. Appleton Co., 1927. xviii, 402 pp.

Primitive Religion; Its Nature and Origin. New York: The Viking Press, 1937. x, 322 pp. bibl.

———. "Religion of the North American Indians." *JAFL* 27:335–373, 1914.

Reik, Theodore
Ritual: Psychoanalytic Studies. New York: Farrar and Straus, 1946. 367 pp.
Includes discussion of puberty rites among some Indian tribes: California, Mandan, Niska, Thompson Indians, and Wabenaki.

Róheim, Géza
Animism, Magic and the Divine King. London: K. Paul, Trench, Trubner and Co., Ltd., 1930. 390 pp.

Sarat, Chandra Nitra
"The Bear in the Asiatic and American Ritual." *Journal of the Asiatic Society of Bombay*, VII, 467.

Sargeant, Rev. John
"Letter to Rev. Isaac Hollis" (May 20, 1743, Boston). *The Christian History* 1:150–154, July 9 and 16, 1743.
Information on the religious beliefs among the Indians at Houssatounoc.

Schmidt, Wilhelm
Der Ursprung der Gottesidee. Eine historisch-kritische und positive Studie. Band V: Nachtrage zu den Religionen der Urvölker Amerikas, Asiens und Australiens. Munster in Westfalen: Aschendorffsche Verlagsbuchhandlung, 1934, 921 pp.
Considerable attention given to California tribes 389 pp.), the Salish (172 pp.), the Lenape and other Algonkins (773 pp.), to North American religion.

———. *High Gods in North America*. Oxford: Clavendon Press, 1933. 148 pp.

Schoolcraft, Henry R.
"Hobbomok." *The Knickerbocker* 57:539–542, May, 1861.
The Indian's version of the creation of the American continent, and some of their religious beliefs.

Sinclair, A. T.
"Tattooing of the North American Indians." *AA* 11:401, 1909. n.s.

Smith, J. B.
"Some Early Beliefs of Indians." *Redman* 3: 453–454, 1911.

Smith, Seba
"The Religion and Superstition of the North American Indians." *The Literary Emporium* 3:87–90, March, 1846.

———. "The Religion and Superstition of the North American Indians—No. II." *The Literary Emporium* 3:97–100, April, 1846.
Comments on the beliefs and religious ceremonies of the Chippewas, Sauks and Musquakies.

———. "The Religion and Superstition of the North American Indians, No. III, IV, V." *The Literary Emporium* 3:129–133; 170–174; 230–233, May, June, Aug., 1846.
Belief and ceremonies for the dead among the Hurons, Iroquois, and Chepewyans, also comments on their beliefs in immortality.

———. "The Religion and Superstition of the North American Indians. No. VI." *The Literary Emporium* 4:289–293, Oct., 1846.
Belief and manner of burying the dead among the Caraibs of the West India Islands; and religious speech of Red Jacket, chief of the Senecas, made to a missionary.

Speck, Franck G.
"Snake Folklore: The Snake Who Swallows Her Young." *JAFL* 36:298–300, 1923.

———. "Reptile Lore of the Northern Indians." *JAFL* 36:273–280, 1924.

———, and Moses, J.
"The Celestial Bear Comes Down to Earth." *Reading Public Museum Art Gallery Scientific Publications* 7. Reading, Pennsylvania: Reading Public Museum Art Gallery, 1945. 91 pp., illustrated.

Spinden, Herbert J.
Indian Symbolism. New York: Exposition of Indian Tribal Arts, Inc., 18 plates, 1931.

Starr, F.
"Folklore of Stone Tools." *JAFL* 4:21–28, 1891.

Stevenson, James
"Ceremonial of Hasjelti Dailjis and Mythical Sand Painting of the Navajo Indians." *Eighth Annual Report of the Bureau of Ethnology*. Smithsonian Institution, Washington, D. C., 1891. pp. 229–285. Washington, D. C.: U. S. Government Printing Office.

Steward, Julian H.
"The Ceremonial Buffoon of the American Indian." *Papers Michigan Academy of Science, Art and Letters*, 14:187–207, 1931.

"Superstitions of the Indians." *American Antiquity* 27:132–136, 1905.

Swanton, John R.
Ordeals. In: *Handbook of American Indians*. Vol. II, pp. 144–146. Bureau of American Ethnology, Bulletin 30. Washington, D. C.: U. S. Government Printing Office, 1910.

———. "Primitive Improvidence." *Journal of Philosophy, Psychology and Scientific Methods* 13: 371–374, 1916.

———. Sacrifice. In: *Handbook of American Indians*. Vol. II, pp. 402–407. Bibl. Bureau of American Ethnology, Bulletin 30. Washington, D. C.: U. S. Government Printing Office, 1910.

———.
Shamans and Priests. In: *Handbook of American Indians.* Vol. II, pp. 522–524. Bibl. Bureau of American Ethnology, Bulletin 30. Washington, D. C.: U. S. Government Printing Office, 1910.

———.
Taboo. In: *Handbook of American Indians.* Vol. II, 665–666. Bureau of American Ethnology, Bulletin 30. Washington, D. C.: U. S. Government Printing Office, 1910.
"Whether considered in its negative or in its positive aspect this term may be applied in North America to a number of regulations observed at definite periods of life, in connection with important undertakings, either by individuals or by considerable number of persons."

———.
Thunderbird. In: *Handbook of American Indians.* Vol. II, pp. 746–747. Bureau of American Ethnology, Bulletin 30. Washington, D. C.: U. S. Government Printing Office, 1910.
"The Thunderbird was naturally held in awe, and a person who had been struck by lightning and recovered became an efficient Shaman."

———.
Totem. In: *Handbook of American Indians.* Vol. II, pp. 787–795. Bibl. Bureau of American Ethnology, Bulletin 30. Washington, D. C.: U. S. Government Printing Office, 1910.
"It is the recognition, exploitation, and adjustment of the imaginary mystic relations of the individual or of the body of organized persons to the postulated *Orendas*, mystic powers, surrounding each of these units of native society."

———.
Witchcraft. In: *Handbook of American Indians.* Vol. II, pp. 965–966. Bureau of American Ethnology, Bulletin 30. Washington, D. C.: U. S. Government Printing Office, 1910.
"Witchcraft may be defined as the art of controlling the will and well-being of another person by supernatural or occult means, usually to his detriment. If Shamans possessed supernatural powers that could be exerted beneficially, it was naturally supposed that they might also be exerted with injurious results, and therefore where Shamanism was most highly developed the majority of supposed witches, or rather wizards, were Shamans."

———.
Symbolism. In: *Handbook of American Indians.* Vol. II, pp. 662–664. Bureau of American Ethnology, Bulletin 30. Washington, D. C.: U. S. Government Printing Office, 1910.
Symbolism is found particularly in art, ritual, and mythology.

Wagner, Gunther
"Entwicklung und Verbreitung des Peyote Cultes." *Baessler Archive* Vol. 15, 1932.
Development and spread of the Peyote Cult.

Wardle, H. N.
"The Scope of the Rite of Adoption in Aboriginal North America." *Publ. Phila. Anthro. Soc.* 1:211–219, 1937.

Webster, Hulton
Primitive Secret Societies. A Study in Early Politics and Religion. New York: The Macmillan Co., 1908. 227 pp.

White, R.
"The Great Mystery." *So. Workman* (Hampton, Va.) 37:679–681, 1908.

Wissler, Clark
"The Lore of the Demon Mask." *Natural History* (New York) 38:339–352, 1928.

Zeleinin, D. M.
"Zur Frage der Entwicklungs-Geschichte der primitiven Religionen." *Ethnos* 2 (No. 3):74–91, 1937.
On the origin of primitive religions.

FOLKTALES—LEGENDS

See: Myths and Mythology. pp. 768-771.

BIBLIOGRAPHY

"Bibliography of American Indian Tales." *JAFL* 27:50–54, 1914; 34:303–307, 1921.

Henderson, Alice Corbin
Bibliography of Indian Legends. In: *Indian Legends* . . . by Marion F. Washburne. . . . Chicago: Rand McNally Company, 1915. 144 pp., illus.

Thompson, Stith
Bibliography of works dealing with and containing North American Indian Tales. In: *Tales of the North American Indians.* (pp. 373–386). Cambridge, Mass.: Harvard University Press, 1929.

GENERAL STUDIES AND COLLECTIONS

Allanson, Winona Blanche
Indian Moons, illustrations by W. J. Wilwerding. Minneapolis, Minn.: Augsburg Publishing House, 1927. 63 pp.

Anderson, B. G.
Indian Sleep Man Tales. Caldwell, Idaho: Caxton Printers, Ltd., 1940.

Austin, Mary
"Aboriginal fiction; review of 'Tales of the North American Indian'." *Saturday Review of Literature* 6:597–9, Dec. 28, 1929.

———.
"One-Smoke Stories." *Golden Book* 12:37–8, 1930.

Bache, Richard Meade
American Wonderland. . . . Philadelphia: Claxton, Remsen, and Haffelfinger, 1871. viii, 258 pp.

Barbeau, Charles Marius, and Melvin, Grace, ed.
The Indian Speaks, Caldwell, Id.: The Caxton Printers, Ltd.; Toronto, Ont.: The Macmillan Company of Canada, Ltd., 1943. 117 pp., illus.

Barkholder, M.
Before the White Man Came; Indian Legends and Stories. Toronto, Can.: 1923.

Bartlett, F. C.
Psychology and the Folk Story. In: *Psychology and Primitive Culture*, Chapt. III, pp. 57–104. London: Cambridge Press, 1923.

——.
"Psychology in Relation to the Popular Story." *Folklore* 31:264–293.

Basel, Edmund
Indian Legends, and, Clyde Warwick. Farmingdale: Nazareth Trade School Prtg. Off., 1907. 46 pp.

Baum, P. F.
"The Three Dreams, or 'Dream Bread' Story." *JAFL* 30:378–410, 1917.

Bayliss, Clara Kern
A Treasury of Indian Tales. New York: Thomas Y. Crowell, 1921. vi, 120 pp.

Beach, S. B.
Escalala: An American Tale. Utica: W. Williams, 1824. ix, 109 pp.

——.
"Bear Story."
JAFL 39:450–459, 1926.

——.
"Bear, the Celestial."
JAFL 13:92–103, 1900.

Beauchamp, William Martin
"Indian Corn Stories and Customs," *JAFL* 11:195–202, 1898.

Beckett, S. B.
Hester, the Bride of the Islands: A Poem. Portland: Bailey & Noyes, 1860. vi, 336 pp.

Bemister, Margaret
Indian Legends: Stories of America before Columbus. New York: The Macmillan Co., 1914. 187 pp.

——.
Thirty Indian Legends. Toronto: Macmillan Co. of Canada, Ltd., 1912. 182 pp.

Beston, Henry
The Sons of Kai; The Story the Indians Told. New York: The Macmillan Co., 1926. 55 pp.

Boas, Franz
"Dissemination of Tales Among the Natives of North America." *JAFL* 4:13–20, 1891.

——.
Dissemination of Tales Among the Natives of North America. In: *Language, Race and Culture* by Franz Boas pp. 437–445, reprinted, 1891. New York: The Macmillan Co., 1940.

——.
"Mythology and Folk-Tales of the North American Indians." *JAFL* 27:374–410, 1914.

——.
"Romance Folk-lore Among American Indians," *Romanic Review*, 16:199–207, 1925. (New York.)

——.
"The Development of Folk-Tales and Myths." *Scientific Monthly* 3:335–342, 1916.

Borland, Hal G.
Rocky Mountain Tipi Tales, frontispiece by Esther M. Mattsson. Garden City, N. Y.: Doubleday, Page and Company, viii, 247 pp., 1924.

Borsari, Ferdinando
La Letteratura Degl' Indigeni Americani, Napoli: L. Pierro, 1888. 76 pp.
    Discusses Indian tales and legends.

Brayman, James O.
The Burning Village; and Other Indian Stories. Buffalo: Phinney & Co., 1859. 63 pp., illus.

Brill, Ethel Claire
The Boy Who Went to the East, and Other Indian Fairy Tales, illustrated by Hugh Spencer. New York: E. P. Dutton and Co., 1917. ix, 296 pp. incl. illus., plates. front.

Brown, William Edgar
Echoes of the Forest. American Indian Legends. Nwah-Ke-nah-go-zid (Ojibway Indian Name). Boston: R. G. Badger, 1918. 264 pp., bibl.

Buchanan, John A.
Indian Legends, and Other Poems. Souvenir edition of the Lewis and Clark Fair. San Francisco: Whitaker & Ray Co., 1905. 140 pp.

Burkholder, Mabel Grace
Before the White Man Came; Indian legends and stories . . . illustrated by C. M. Manly. . . . Toronto: McClelland & Stewart, 1923. 317 pp., illus.

Caldwell, George Walter
Rainbow Stories and Indian Myths. Illustrated by Jane Jefferson Flippen. San Francisco: Phillips & Van Orden Co., 1919. 117 pp., illus.

Chamberlain, A. F.
"Wisdom of the North American Indians in Speech and Legend." *Proc. Amer. Antiq. Soc.* 23:63–96, 1913. n.s.

Compton, M.
The American Indian Fairy Tales. New York: Dodd, Mead and Co., 1907.

Coolidge, Florence Claudine
Little Ugly Face, and Other Indian Tales, illustrated by Maud and Miska Petersham. New York: The Macmillan Company, 1929. vi, 181 pp., col. illus.

Clarke, Helen Archibald
Longfellow's Country. New York: The Baker and Taylor Company, 1909. 252 pp., illus.
    Contents: Along the coast of New England.— Under the shadow of Blomidon.—Idyls from history.—The New England tragedies.—The lore of Hiawatha.—In Cambridge.

Cornelison, J.
Weyekin Stories. Titwatit Weyekishnim. By Cornelison, J., missionary to the Umatillas. San Francisco, Cal.: E. L. Mackey & Co., 1911. 30 pp., illus.

Culbertson, Anne Virginia
At the Big House Where Aunt Nancy and Aunt 'Phrony Held forth on the Animal Folks, illustrated by E. Warde Blaisdell. Indianapolis: The Bobbs-Merrill Company, 1904. 348 pp., illus.

Curry, Rev. Erastus S.
The Pre-Historic Races of America and Other Lands as Disclosed Thru Indian Traditions Comprehending also the Origin of Matter . . . and astronomy solving the chronological problems, etc., etc. Christy, Mo.: The Author, 1903. Illus., vol. 1.

Curtis, Natalie, ed.
The Indians' Book; an offering by the American Indians of Indian lore, musical and narrative, to form a record of the songs and legends of their race, recorded and ed. by Natalie Curtis; illustrations from photographs and from original drawings by Indians. New York: Harper and Brothers, 1907. ix–xxx, 572 pp. With musical illustrations.

Deming, Therese (Osterheld)
Red Folk and White Folk; with numerous full-page colour-plates after paintings in watercolour, together with illustrations in black-and-white, by Edwin Willard Deming, and with Indian folk-lore stories for children by Therese O. Deming. New York: F. A. Stokes Co., 1902. 52 pp., illus.

Donaldson, Mrs. Ellen Miller
Little Papoose Listens; Illustrations Hildegard Lupprian. Springfield, Mass.: Milton Bradley Co., 1924. iii, 146 pp., front., plates.

" 'Dream-bread' Story."
JAFL 30:378–410, 1917; 34:327–328, 1921.

Eastman, E. G.
Indian Legends Retold. Boston: Little, Brown and Co., 1919. xi, 161 pp., illus.

Field, Rachel
American Folk and Fairy Tales. New York: Charles Scribner's Sons, 1929. 302 pp.

Fife, Austin E.
"Detachable Members." *Utah Humanities Review* 1 (No. 2):186, 1947.
A folk tale in which a foreman, to get work done by the Indian construction in his absence, "detached" his eye, and left it to "keep an eye" so that there be no loitering.

Figueira, Gastón
"Leyenda del Maíz." *WP* 2:(Nos. 3–4) 26, Dec., 1941–Jan., 1942.
Traditions of the origin of corn.

Fisk, Gordon M.
Story of the Female Captive, and the Indian Leap, or Great Cove. Palmer, Mass.: Printed for M. Baldwin, the Blind Man. Merriam & Cooke's Press, 1844. 7 pp. (NYPL).

Fiske, W. A. A.
Indian Legends. Ithaca, N. Y.: Slingerland-Comstock Co., 1930.

Fletcher, Alice Cunningham
Indian Story and Song, from North America. Boston: Small, Maynard & Co., 1900. xiv, 126 pp., music.

Folk-Lore and Legends. North American Indian. Philadelphia: J. B. Lippincott Co., 1891. viii, 192 pp.

Gatschet, Albert Samuel
A Migration Legend of the Creek Indians, with a linguistic, historic and ethnographic introduction. Philadelphia: D. G. Brinton, 1884–88. 2 vols.

————.
"Water Monsters of American Aborigines." *JAFL* 12:255–260, 1899.

Gearhart, Ephraim Maclay
Skalalatoot Stories; a book of Real Indian "Bed Time Stories." Boston, Mass.: The Stratford Co., 1922. 70 pp.

Gelber, Adolf
Indianermaerchen; Manito und seine Leute, erzählt von Adolf Gelber, illustriert von Joseph Binder. Wien: Rikola-Verlag, 1921. 109 pp., illus.
Folktales.

Gher, Alphonso Moser
The Old Trail and the New; a tale of the Kittatinnies. Carlisle, Pa., n.p., 1909. 44 pp.

Gordon, Hanford Lennox
Indian Legends, & Other Poems. Salem: The Salem Press Company, 1910. viii, 405 pp.

Graves, Merle Dixon
Manitou and the Animals, an Indian Legend. Albany: L. L. Fuller, 1935. 48 pp., illus.

Greene, Richard Henry
Cannon Flashes and Pen Dashes. New York: W. H. Kelley & Company, 1866. 56 pp., 110 pp.
Poems of the Civil War, Followed by Moodus, an Indian Legend.

Gridley, M. E.
Indian Legends of American Scenes. With eleven full color illustrations; initial letters by Whirling Thunder. Chicago: M. A. Donahue and Co., 1939. 127 pp., illus.

Griffis, Joseph K.
Indian Story Circle Stories, by Chief Tahan. Burlington, Vt.: Free Press Printing Co., 1928. viii, 138 pp.

Grinnell, George Bird
Punishment of the Stingy and Other Indian Stories. New York: Harper and Brothers, 1901. x, 234 pp., illus.

Grossi, Vincenzo
Lingue, Letteratura e Tradizioni Popolari degl' Indigeni d'America. Part 1, Genova: A. Ciminago, 1890.
Language, litterature and traditions of the American Indians, mainly of the Eskimo.

Gunther, Erna
"Accretion in the Folktales of the American Indians." *Folk-Lore* 38:40–54, 1927.

H., R. S.
"Mental Traits of the Aborigines." *Southern Literary Messenger* 29:12–13, July, 1859.
A legend on the origin of Indian corn.

Hamilton, J. C.
"Stellar Legends of the American Indians." *Transaction of the Royal Astronomical Society.* Canada, 1905. pp. 47–50.

Hannay, James
The Maiden's Sacrifice. Saint John, N. B.: Strathmore Press, 1909. 7 pp.

Harrison, Amelia Williams
American Indian Fairy Tales; Snow Bird, the Water Tiger, etc. New York: Dodd, Mead & Co., 1907. 201 pp., illus.

Hartland, Edwin Sidney
Mythology and Folktales. Their Relation and Interpretation. London: D. Nutt, 1900. 53 pp.

Haury, Emil
"The Three-rings Continue to Tell Their Story." *The Kiva* 9 (No. 2):10–14. Tucson: Arizona State Museum, 1944.

Hawes, Barbara
Tales of the North American Indians, and Adventures of the Early Settlers in America. London: Longman, Brown, Green, and Longmans, 1844. xii, 362 pp.

Hoffman, Charles Fenno
Wild Scenes in the Forest and Prairie. With Sketches of American Life. New York: W. H. Colyer, 1843. 2 vols. in 1.

Horsford, Mary Gardiner
Indian Legends and Other Poems. New York: J. C. Derby, 1855. viii, 167 pp.

Hum-ishu-ma, Okinaqan Indian
Coyote Stories, edited and illustrated by Heister Dean Guie, with notes by L. V. McWhorter (Old Wolf) and a foreword by Chief Standing Bear. Caldwell, Id.: The Caxton Printers, 1933. 228 pp., illus.

Jacobsen, Norman
Minnie Totem; an Indian Legend; Story and Drawings.... New York: Melomime Publications, Inc., 1923. 24 pp., illus.

Johnson, E. B.
Animal Stories of the Indians. New York: Alfred A. Knopf, 1928. 155 pp.

Johnson, Edna, and Scott, Carrie E.
Anthology of Children's Literature. Illustrated by N. C. Wyeth. Boston: Houghton Mifflin Co., 1935. xxix, 917 pp.
A number of Indian tales, and a bibliography is included.

Judd, Mary Catherine, comp.
Wigwam Stories Told by North American Indians; with illustrations by Angel de Cora. Boston: Ginn & Company, 1915. ix, 278 pp., illus.
Contents: Pt. 1. Sketches of various tribes of North American Indians; Pt. 2. Traditions and Myths; Pt. 3. Stories recently told by Hiawatha and other heroes.

Kearney, W. D.
An Epic Poem entitled The Open Hand. An Indian Tale of Maine and New Brunswick, founded on historical facts and sustained by tradition. Presque Isle, Me.: First Printed by W. S. Gilman in 1864, and reprinted at Hartland, N. B., by F. H. Stevens, 1920. 58 pp.

Keary, C. F.
Mythologies and Folktales. In: *The Dawn of History:* An Introduction to Prehistoric Study. Chapter XI. London: Mozley and Smith, 1878.

Keppler, Emil Alexander Charles
With Tom Tom and Tomahawk. New York: A. G. Seiler & Company, 1902. 50 pp.

Kingston, W. H. G.
Adventures Among the Indians.... Illustrated. Chicago: Donohue, Henneberry & Co., 1890. 252 pp.
The same work as: *Anecdotes of the American Indians,* first published in 1844, which have been attributed, probably wrongly, both to John Lauris Blake and to Alexander Viets Blake. Also issued in 1861 under title—*The Boys' Book of Indian Battles and Adventures.*

Knortz, Karl
Märchen und Sagen der nord-amerikanischen Indianer. Jena: H. Costenoble, 1871. viii, 285 pp.
Tales and legends of the North-American Indians.

————.
Nokomis, Märchen und Sagen der nord-amerikanischen Indianer. Zurich: J. Schabelitz, 1887. 121 pp.
Folktales and legends of the North-American Indians.

Krickeberg, Walter
Indianermärchen aus Nordamerika. Jena: E. Diederichs, 1924. 419 pp., bibl.
North American Indian Folktales.

Knowles, James Sheridan
"An Indian Tradition." *The New York Mirror* 16:201, Dec. 22, 1838.

Kunike, H.
"Nordamerikanische Mondsagen." *Inter. Archiv Ethno.* 25:27–54, 1920.

Kutz, M. Jennie
Wah-ah-see, a Legend of the Sleeping Dew; and Other Poems. Chicago: S. S. Boyden, 1868. 200 pp.

Kyger, John Charles Fremont
No-wa-na; an Indian Tale Told in Verse. Chicago: Fremount Publishing Co., 1919. 136 pp., illus.

Laing, Mary Elizabeth
The Hero of the Longhouse; illustrated by David C. Lithgow. Yonkers-on-Hudson, N. Y.: World Book Company, 1920. xxv, 329 pp., illus.

Lamkin, Nina B., and Jagendorf, M. A.
Around America with the Indian; a book for boys and girls about Indian legends made into plays, Indian village life, ceremonials, dances, music, games; Indian music harmonized and original melodies written by Anne Church Collins, illustrated by Mary Ponton Gardner. New York: S. French, 1933. Illus., bibl., music.

Larned, William Trowbridge
American Indian Fairy Tales. Illustrated by John Roe. New York: P. F. Volland Co., 1921. 93 pp., col. illus. Reprinted by Wise Book Co., N. Y., 1936.
"With one exception, all the tales in this book are adapted from the legends collected by Henry R. Schoolcraft . . . and published in 1839 with the title "Algic Researches.""

Lee, F. H., ed.
Folk Tales of All Nations. New York: Tudor Publishing Company, 1946. 947 pp.
North American Indian Tales (pp. 63–84).

Lesueur, James W.
Indian Legends. Independence, Mo.: Zion's Printing and Publishing Company, 1928. 339 pp., illus.

Linderman, Frank Bird
Indian Old Man Stories; more sparks from War Eagle's Lodge-Fire. Illustrated by Charles M. Russell. New York: C. Scribner's Sons, 1920. xx, 169 pp., illus.

_____.
Indian Why Stories; Sparks from War Eagle's Lodge-Fire. Illustrated by Charles M. Russell, the cowboy artist. New York: C. Scribner's Sons, 1915. xvi, 236 pp., illus.

Littlejohn, Flavius Josephus
Legends of Michigan and the Old North West; or, A Cluster of Unpublished Waifs, Gleaned Along the Uncertain, Misty Line, Dividing Traditional from Historic Times. Allegan, Mich.: Northwestern Bible and Publishing Co., 1875. 566 pp.

Lybak, Johanna R. M.
Indian Legends. Illustrated by Alexander Key. Chicago. Lyons and Carnahan Publishers, 1925. xvi, 355 pp., illus. (Lettered on cover: *Long Ago Series.*)
New England States, pp. 3–73; Atlantic States, pp. 77–143; Mississippi Valley, pp. 147–255; Western States, pp. 257–349.

Mathews, Cornelius, comp.
The Enchanted Moccasins, and other Legends of the American Indians; compiled from original sources. New York: G. P. Putnam's Sons, 1877. vi, 388 pp., illus.
Originally issued as: *The Indian Fairy Book,* 1867.

_____.
Hiawatha, and other Legends of the Wigwams of the Red American Indians. Compiled from original sources. London: W. S. Sonnenschein & Co., 1882. vi, 344 pp., illus.
"They were originally compiled from the old tales and legends by the late Henry R. Schoolcraft, and are now re-interpreted and developed by the editor."—Pref.

McGregor, James Herman
Wigwam Smoke. Cynthiana, Ky.: The Hobson Book Press, 1945. xiii, 82 pp.

McKee, Louise
Dusty Desert Tales, by McKee, Louise and Summers, Richard, illustrated with photographs and with drawings by J. Powell Scott. Caldwell, Id.: The Caxton Printers, Ltd., 1941. 191 pp., illus.

Milling, Chapman J.
"Is the Serpent Tale an Indian Survival?" *SFQ* 1 (No. 1):43–57, 1937.

Mishnun, Virginia
The Indian's Dog. Washington, D. C.: Office of Indian Affairs, 1942. 53 pp., illus.
Legends and traditions.

Moody, Alan
Sleep in the Sun. Boston: Houghton Mifflin, 1945.

Morgan, William
"The Organization of a Story and a Tale." With a preface by Alfred North Whitehead. *JAFL* 58:169–194, 1945.
The author "attempts to define and describe some of the physical and subjective processes in individuals and in groups, which are involved in the formation of a story and a folktale."

Morrison, R.
Indian Legends Retold. Denver: T. A. Bagshaw Publ. Co., 1933. 23 pp., illus.

Norris, Philetus W.
The Calumet of the Coteau, and other Poetical Legends of the Border. Also a glossary of Indian Names, Words, and Western Provincialisms. Together with a guide-book of the Yellowstone National Park. Philadelphia: J. B. Lippincott & Co., 1884. 275 pp., illus.

North American Indian Fairy Tales.
London: Gibbins and Co., 1905.

Nutt, Alfred
"Irish Tales Among the Redskins." *Folk-Lore*
(London) 2:130, 1891.

Olcott, Frances Jenkins
The Red Indian Fairy Book; for the Children's
Own Reading and for Story-Tellers, with illus-
trations by Frederick Richardson. Boston:
Houghton Mifflin Co., 1917. xix, 338 pp., illus.

Osborn, Chase Salmon
Schoolcraft, Longfellow, Hiawatha, by Osborn,
Chase and Osborn, Stellanova. Lancaster, Pa.:
The Jacques Cattell Press, 1942. xix, 697 pp.,
illus. "Short Bibliography of the Chippewas":
pp. 82–85. "A Bibliography of Henry Rowe
Schoolcraft": pp. 624–653.
A study of the work of the student of Indian
mythology and of Longfellow's debt to him.

Parker, Arthur Caswell
Rumbling Wings. And Other Indian Tales.
Illustrated by Will Crawford. New York:
Doubleday, Doran and Co., 1928. xii, 279 pp.,
illus.

——————.
Skunny Wundy, and Other Indian Tales. Illus-
trated by Will Crawford. New York: George
H. Doran, 1926. 262 pp.

Pearce, J. E.
"Tales that Dead Man Tell." *Anthropological
Papers,* University of Texas. Vol. I, No. 1,
Bulletin No. 3537, 123 pp., illus. Austin, Texas:
University of Texas, 1935.

Peet, Stephen Denison
"The Piasa." *Amer. Antiq.,* Sept.–Oct., 1906.
pp. 262–265.
Legend of the Illinois Indians.

Phillips, Walter Shelley
Indian Tales for Little Folks. New York:
Platt and Munk Co., 1928. New ed.

——————.
Teepee Tales, by El Comancho (pseud.) pictures by Charles Livingstone Bull and El
Comancho. Chicago: The Reilly & Lee Co.,
1927. viii, 208 pp., illus.

——————.
Totem Tales. Indian Stories Indian Told, Gathered in the Pacific Northwest. Fully illustrated
by the author. Chicago: Star Publishing Co.,
1896. xvii, 326 pp., illus.

Priest, Josiah
*The Captivity and Sufferings of General Free-
gift Patchin of Blenheim, Schoharie County,
Among the Indians, under Brant, the Noted
Chief, during the Border Warfare in the Time
of the American Revolution,* now first published: with some account of the person and
character of Joseph Brant. Also, traits of
Mexican Tradition, Respecting the flood of
Noah, and the confusion of the ancient language. Albany: Packard, Hoffman and White,
1833. iv, 50 pp., illus.
Indian legends and tales of the Mohawk.

Reagan, Albert B.
The Sun God Moccasin Tales. Provo, Utah:
The Graham Printing Co., 1935.

Remington, Frederic
The Way of an Indian; written and illustrated
by F. Remington. New York: Fox, Duffield &
Co., 1906. 251 pp., illus.

Rhodes, William Henry
The Indian Gallows, and other poems. In two
parts. New York: E. Walter, 1846. 153 pp.
Contents: Part 1. The Indian Gallows. Part 2.
Theodosia, the Pirate's Prisoner, a tragedy. Mis-
cellaneous poems, relating chiefly to scenes in
Texas.

Roche, Ruth A.
Indian Legends. New York: Action Playbooks,
1944. 32 pp.

Sanborn, John Wentworth
Day-yu-da-gont; a poem, by John Wentworth
Sanborn . . . and the Hemlock-Bough House.
Seneca Indian Legends. Friendship, New
York: J. W. Sanborn, 1905. 18 pp.

Sanders, Helen Fitzgerald
Trails Through Western Woods. New York:
The Alice Harriman Co., 1910. x, 310 pp., illus.

Schoolcraft, Henry Rowe
Indian Fairy Book, from the Original Legends,
with eight illustrations in color by Florence
Choate and Elizabeth Curtis. New York: Frederick A. Stokes Company, 1916. vi, 303 pp.,
col. front., col. plates. First printed in New
York: Mason Brothers, 1856.

——————.
*The Myth of Hiawatha, and Other Oral Le-
gends, Mythologic and Allegoric, of the North
American Indians.* Philadelphia: J. B. Lippincott & Co., 1856. xxiv, 343 pp.
An earlier edition, New York, 1839, in two
volumes, appeared under title: *Algic Researches.*

——————.
Western Scenes and Reminiscences; together
with thrilling legends and traditions of the red
men of the forest. . . . Auburn, N. Y.: Derby &
Miller, 1853. v, 495 pp., illus.

Scott, R. G.
Indian Romances. Boston: Meador Publishing
Co., 1933. 141 pp., illus.

Severance, Mary Frances Harriman
Indian Legends of Minnesota. New York: D.
D. Merrill Co., 1893. 184 pp., illus.

Sexton, Bernard
Gray Wolf Stories; Indian Mystery Tales of
Coyote, Animals and Men, by Peter Gray Wolf
(pseud.) illustrated by Gwenyth Waugh. Caldwell, Id.: The Caxton Printers, Ltd., 1941. viii,
192 pp., illus., bibl.

Shoemaker, Henry Wharton
The Importance of Collecting Indian Legends,
an address before the 22nd Annual Convention
of the Keystone State Library Association at
Altoona, Pa., October 26, 1922. Altoona, Pa.:
Tribune Press, 1922. 7 pp.

Simmons, William Hayne
Onea; an Indian Tale. Charleston: J. B.
Stephens, printer, 1820. iv, 65 pp.

Skinner, Charles Montgomery
American Myths and Legends. Philadelphia:
J. B. Lippincott Co., 1903. 2 vols., illus.

Smalley, Donald
"The Logansport Telegraph and the Monster
of the Indian Lakes." *Indian Magazine of
History.* Sept., 1946. pp. 249–267.

Smith, L. R.
Fifty Indian Legends. Stories of curious ways
of Indian days. Illustrated by Mae H. Scan-
nell. Chicago: A. Albert Whitman and Co.,
1934. 128 pp., illus.

Squier, Emma-Lindsay
Children of the Twilight; Folk-Tales of Indian
Tribes. New York: Cosmopolitan Book Corpo-
ration, 1926. 257 pp.
  Contents: Brother of the Eagle. The Legend of
  the Champ Nuá. The Trembling God. The Land
  of the Red Gods. Why we dance the Eagle Dance.
  Ungrateful Gate. The White Totem. The Old
  Woman Who Talks with Foxes. Heavy Wings.

Stratton, F.
When the Storm God Rides. Tejas, and Other
Indian Legends. Illustrated by Berniece Bur-
rough. New York: Charles Scribner's Sons,
1936. x, 243 pp., illus.

*Tales, Traditions and Romance of Border and
Revolutionary Times. . . .* New York: Beadle
and Company, 1863. 64 pp.

Tanner, Dorothy
Legends from the Red Man's Forest. Chicago:
A. Flanagan, 1895. 128 pp., illus.

Teit, J. A.
"Story of the Bear." *JAFL* 39:450–459, 1926.

Thompson, Jeanette May
Over Indian and Animal Trails. With Eight
Illustrations in color by Paul Bransom. New
York: F. A. Stokes, 1918. ix, 263 pp., illus.

Thompson, Stith
"European Tales Among the North American
Indians." A Study in the Migration of Folk-
Tales. *Colorado College Publ. Language Series.*
(Colorado Springs 2:319–471, 1919. bibl.:
460–468.

———.
"The Indian Legend of Hiawatha." *Publ.
Modern Lang. Assoc.* 37:128–140, 1922.

———.
"Sunday School Stories Among Savages."
Texas Review 3:109–116, 1918.

———.
Tales of the North American Indians; selected
and annotated. Cambridge, Mass.: Harvard
University Press, 1929. xxiii, 386 pp., bibl.

———.
The Folktale. New York: The Dryden Press,
1947. 522 pp.
  In addition to a thoro and scholarly discussion
  of the nature and forms of the folktale, as well
  as a comparative study of the European and
  Asiatic folktale, the author gives a detailed account of the folktale of the North American Indian. Part 3, pp. 297–367.

———.
The Types of the Folk-Tale: Antti Aarne's
Verzeichnis der Märchen typen, translated and
enlarged. FF Communications No. 74, Helsinki,
1928.

Tuggle, Ruth Ashley
Indian Stories for Children. Illustrations by J.
Tuggle. La Grange, Ga.: 1907. 106 pp.

Unkalunt, Atalie
The Earth Speaks, by Princess Atalie. New
York, London: Fleming H. Revell Company,
1940. 223 pp., illus.

Voelker, Frederick E.
"The Piasa." *Illinois State Historical Soc.
Journal* 7:82–91, Springfield, Illinois: 1914.

Wade, Mary Hazelton
Indian Fairy Tales, as told to the Little
Children of the Wigwam. Pen and Ink Drawings by Sears Gallagher. Boston: W. A. Wilde,
1906. 240 pp., illus.

Wake, C. S.
"Legends of the American Indians." *American
Antiquity* 26:23–28, 1904.

———.
"Nihancan, the White Man." *American Antiquity* 26:225–231, 1904.

———.
"Traits of an Ancient Egyptian Folktale Com-
pared with Those of Aboriginal American
Tales." *JAFL* 17:255–264, 1904.

Warren, M. L. R.
*Manabozho, the Great White Rabbit, and
Other Indian Stories.* Chicago: Rand, McNally
and Company, 1918. 133 pp., incl. col. front.,
illus. col. pl.

Washburne, Marion F.
Indian Legends. With an introduction, sug-
gestions to teachers, and a bibliography by
Alice Corbin Henderson. Illustrated by Fred-
erick Richardson. Chicago: Rand McNally
Company, 1915. 144 pp., illus., col. pl.

Waterman, Thomas Talbot
*The Explanatory Element in the Folk-tales of
the North American Indians.* Boston: Houghton Mifflin & Co., 1914. 54 pp., bibl. (*JAFL*
27:1–54, 1914.)

Waters, Clement, and Erskine, Clara
*A Handbook of Legendary and Mythological
Art,* with descriptive illustrations. Boston: J. R.
Osgood and Company, 1883. xii, 575 pp., illus.

Webber, Samuel
Logan, an Indian Tale. Cambridge: Hilliard and Metcalf, 1821. vii, 53 pp.

Willoughby, Frederick Stanley Montgomery
The Indian Queen of Chenango: a poem in four cantos. By a student. Oxford: Printed by La F. Leal, 1844. 64 pp.

Wilstach, J. A.
The Battle Forest; a poem. New York: Press of American Banknote Co., 1890. 18 pp.

Wissler, Clark
"Star Legends Among the American Indians." *American Museum of Natural History Guide Leaflet Series No. 91.* New York: American Museum of Natural History, 1936. 29 pp.

Witman, Frederica K.
Legend of the Mound. Harrisburg: L. S. Hart, 1878. 39 pp. illus.

Wood, Charles E. S.
A Book of Tales; being some myths of the North American Indians. New York: The Vanguard Press, 1929. 165 pp.

Woodman, Jay Joshua
Indian Legends; being a choice collection of the best legends, stories and traditions as told by the warrior and the squaw to the papoose and showing how the young Indian of the olden time was educated. To which is added some personal narratives of Indian captivity as related by the unfortunate survivors. Boston, Mass.: The Stratford Company, 1924. 268 pp., illus.

Woods, C. L.
Kaw-Wau-Nita, and other poems. Stockton: D. H. Berdine, 1893. vi, 99 pp.

Wright, H. B.
Long Ago Told. Legends of the Papago Indians . . . Illustrated by Katherine F. Kitt. New York: D. Appleton-Century Co., 1929. xvii, 289 pp.

Wright, John Couchois
Crooked Tree. Indian Legends of Nothern Michigan. Harbor Springs, Mich.: C. F. Erwin, 1932. 143 pp., illus.

Pe-tah-se-ga, and other poems. N. P., 190—. 11 pp. illus.

Wynn, D.
Magic Kettle and Other Folk Stories of the North American Indians. London: George G. Harrap and Co., 1931.

Wysong, Thomas
The Rocks of Deer Creek, Hartford County, Maryland. Their Legends and History. Baltimore: A. J. Conlon, 1880. 123 pp., illus.

Zitkala-Sa
Old Indian Legends, retold by Zitkala-Sa. With illustrations by Angel De Cora. Boston: Ginn & Co., 1904. vii, 165 pp., illus.

ANECDOTES

Anecdotes of the American Indians, illustrating their eccentricities of character. By the author of "Evenings in Boston," "Ramon the Rover of Cuba," etc. New York: A. V. Blake, 1844. vi, 252 pp.

Anon.
"A Cunning Trick." *The New Yorker* 2:136, Nov. 19, 1836 (NYU).
A humorous anecdote.

"A Fair Business Transaction." *The New Yorker* 1:355 Aug. 27, 1836 (NYU).
Anecdote relating how an Indian named John Titus, of the Seneca tribe, forced a trader to pay the stipulated sum of five shillings for the logs he bought from the Indian.

"A Good Argument Against Imprisonment for Debt." *The Minerva* 1:115, July 20, 1822 (NYU).
An anecdote explaining an Osage Indian's philosophy regarding this "foolish" law.

"A Serious Question." *The American Pioneer* 1:224, July 1842 (NYU).
Anecdote of an Indian chief's remark on viewing a medal on which President Washington armed with a sword was depicted on one side, and an Indian burying a hatchet on the other side—asked—"Why does not the President bury his sword, too?"

"An Indian Anecdote." *Ladies Literary Cabinet* 6:126, Aug. 24, 1882 (NYU).
Humorous anecdote describing an Indian wrestling with his conscience.

"An Indian Joke." *The American Magazine of Knowledge* 3:232, March 1837 (NYU).
A joke of Governor "Jenks" of Rhode Island.

"An Indian's Illustration of Scripture." *Merry's Museum* 5:13, Jan. 1843 (NYU).

"Anecdote of the Pawnee Chief." *Weekly Visitor and Ladies Museum* 4:249–250, Feb. 16, 1822. n. s. (NYU).
Copied from Rev. Morse's report which in turn was taken from a journal of Capt. Bell of his expedition with Major Long to the foot of the Rocky Mountains in 1820.

"Bottled Thunder." *The Rover* 2:373, Nov. 23, 1844 (NYU).
An anecdote recounting how Indians reacted to an electric machine.

"Comic Anecdote." *The American Pioneer* 1:264, July 1842 (NYU).
An Indian's explanation of how one of their numbers became frozen to death.

"Conscience." *Pittsburg Recorder* 2:183, April 11, 1823 (NYU).
An anecdote of an honest Indian.

"Domestic Love—The Romance of a Savage Life." *Poughkeepsie Casket* 1:123, July 30, 1836 (NYU).
Anecdote of Black Hawk in his tour through the United States.

"Equality." *The American Pioneer* 2:362, Aug. 1843 (NYU).
An Indian chief's idea of equality.

"Honor Among the Indians." *Atkinson's Casket*, No. 2:89, Feb. 1833 (NYU).
An anecdote illustrating the reliability of an Indian's pledge.

"Honor Among Savages." *Parley's Magazine* 5:46–47, Feb. 1837 (NYU).
An anecdote involving General Scott and three Indian prisoners.

"Indian Affection." *The Telescope* 2:142-143, Feb. 4, 1826 (NYU).
A story of Blackfoot Indian devotion and help.

"Indian Anecdote." *American Museum* 2:594, Dec. 1787 (NYU).

"Indian Anecdote." *The Magnolia* 1:169, Feb. 22, 1834 (NYU).

"Indian Sagacity." *Collections of New Hampshire* 1:128, June 1, 1822 (NYU).

"Instance of the Sagacity of the American Indian." *New York Weekly Magazine* 1:129, Oct. 28, 1795 (NYU).
An anecdote.

"One of the Aborigenes." *Niles' Weekly Register* 69:194, Nov. 28, 1846 (NYU).
A humorous anecdote concerning a Penobscot Indian and the Attorney General of Maine.

"Reminiscences of Pittsburgh." *The Register of Pennsylvania* 7:348, May 28, 1831 (NYU).
Anecdote of an Indian who thought his squaw too beautiful, so bit off her nose, without remonstrance on her part, and other such items.

"Resistance to Pain." *Merry's Museum* 3:40, Feb. 1842 (NYU).
An anecdote of an Indian and a missionary.

"Self-Esteem." *The American Pioneer* 1:262, July 1842 (NYU).
Anecdote concerning an Indian's remark on a white man accosting him as "brother."

"Shenandoah, The Oneida Chief." *Ladies' Literary Cabinet* 5:188, April 20, 1822 (NYU).
Anecdotes, and specimens of eloquence.

"The Christian Indian." *The Evening Fire-Side* 1:311, Sept. 7, 1805 (NYU).
An incident showing the kindness and goodwill of an Indian towards his tormentors.

"The Christian Indian—An Anecdote." *The Christian's, Scholar's and Farmer's Magazine* 2:300, Aug. and Sept. 1790 (NYU).

"The Indian and Bear." *New York Mirror* 1:14, Aug. 9, 1823 (NYU).
An anecdote of an Indian's behavior towards the bear he had shot.

"The Seneca Indians." *Niles' Weekly Register* 37:19, Sept. 5, 1829 (NYU).
Anecdotes dealing with their chiefs, Hard Hickory, Comstock, and Seneca John.

Carver
"A Singular Instance of Parental Affection in a Navdowessie Woman." *The Rural Magazine, or Vermont Repository* 1:285–287, June 1795 (NYU).
An anecdote exemplifying Indian morals.

Crevecour, St. Jean De
"Indian Dreams." *Port-Folio* 3:103, June 4, 1843 (NYU).
Anecdote of the Indian interpretation of dreams, and, incidentally, satirizing the white man's wholesale appropriation of Indian territory.

Dorson, Richard M.
"Comic Indian Anecdotes." *SFQ* 10:113–138, 1946.

Drake, F. S.
"Honor." *The American Pioneer* 2:111, March 1835 (NYU).
An Indian Chief's idea of honor on meeting his own father in battle on the side of the enemy (the French).

Ellis, Edward Sylvester
True Stories of the American Indians, illustrated. . . . Philadelphia: 1905. viii, 240 pp.

Harsha, W. J.
"The Sense of Humor Among Indians." *So. Workman* (Va.) 39:504–505, 1910.

Hawes, Barbara
Tales of the North American Indians, and adventures of the early settlers in America. London: Longman, Brown, etc., 1844. xii, 362 pp.

Hildreth, S. P.
"Logan's Spring." *The American Pioneer* 1:114–115, March 1842 (NYU).
Anecdotes of Logan, characteristics of his magnanimity, and love of the white people.

Merrill, Rufus
150 Stories About Indians. Concord, N. H.: R. Merrill, 1853. xiv, 192 pp., illus.

Opler, Morris E.
"Humor and Wisdom of Some American Indian Tribes." *New Mexico Anthropologist* 3:3–10, Albuquerque, 1938.

Red Jacket
"Indian Logic." *The Weekly Register* 2:427–428, Aug. 29, 1812 (NYU).
An anecdote of this famous chief of the Seneca tribe.

Thompson, Pishey
Anecdotes of the North American Indians, and notices of the natural history of the immediate neighborhood of the city of Washington, United States. Boston: John Noble, 1857. 32 pp.

White, William
A Collection of Indian Anecdotes. Concord, N. H.: W. White, 1837. xiv, 192 pp., illus.

Wightman, H.
The Juvenile Polyanthos, or, Fireside Companion; being a selection of amusing stories. New York: Wightman & Wood, 1833. 108 pp.

CUSTOMS—MANNERS

See: Folk Poetry—Art—Drama, pp. 795-803.

Allen, G. M.
"Dogs of the American Aborigines." *Bulletin of the Museum of Comparative Zoology* 63: 431–517, 1920.

Allen, Zachariah
"The Conditions of Life, Habits, and Customs of the Native Indians of America . . ." *Rhode Island Historical Society. Proceedings.* pp. 97–151, 1880.

Anon.
"An Account of the North American Indians, their character, customs, etc. with some reflections on the state and government of the English colonies." *The American Magazine and Monthly Chronicle* 1 (No. 1):9–23, Oct., 1757 (NYU).

——————.
"An Ojibway Funeral." *American Penny Magazine* 2:161–163, April 18, 1846.
Description of a funeral ceremony for a child.

——————.
"American Indians." *American Penny Mag.* 1:321–322, June 28, 1845 (NYU).
Remarkable lack of feelings of humanity toward the Red Man by Americans. Also descriptions of the early life of the papoose, with illustrations.

——————.
"Characteristics of the American Indians." *Universal Asylum* 6:18, Jan., 1791 (NYU).

——————.
"Clam Bake," "Steamer," or "Bake-Out." *Niles' Weekly Register* 52:356, Aug. 5, 1837.
Description of the Indian feast associated with these names.

——————.
"Custom." *The American Pioneer* 2:57, Feb., 1843.
Description of an Indian custom in re-kindling a fire.

——————.
"Customs Among the Oregon Indians." *American Penny Magazine* 1:63, 1845.
Burial ceremony among the Chinook tribe.

——————.
"Customs and Manners of the American Indian." *The Minerva* 1:76, June 15, 1822.
Warfare customs among the Wyandottes and Iroquois.

——————.
"Customs and Peculiarities of the Indian." *Southern Literary Journal* 3:430–437, Dec., 1838.
General description of his religion beliefs, language peculiarities, eloquence, and tradition.

——————.
"Domestic Miscellany. The Indians—Their Situation and Future Destiny." *Army and Navy Chronicle* 2:310–311, Sept. 24, 1835 (NYU).

——————.
"Dress of an Indian Beau." *Atkinson's Casket,* No. 12:544, Dec., 1832.
Brief account and description of a young warrior's clothes.

——————.
"Extracts of a letter, dated—Washington, Kentucky, Sept. 3, 1791." *Gazette of the United States* 3:195, Oct. 15, 1791.
Among other things the author describes the mode of Indian burial, and customs associated with the ceremony.

——————.
"History of the Treatment of Prisoners Among the American Indians." *American Museum* 5:341–432, April, 1789 (NYU).
An account of the manner in which white prisoners are treated.

——————.
"How to Find Your Way Out of a Wood." *The New Yorker* 2:382, March 4, 1837 (NYU).
The Indian's amazing skill in finding his way out of the densest forests.

——————.
"Indian Clans." *Niles' Weekly Register* 36: 103, April 11, 1829.
Laws and customs regarding marriage, family and children.

——————.
"Indian Coquetry." *Select Reviews and Spirit of the F.M.* 5:69, Jan., 1811 (NYU).

——————.
"Indian Courtship." *New York Mirror* 2:362–363, June 11, 1825.
An account of an Indian brave's approach to the squaw he desires. He must prove his prowess as a hunter. He sends, via his mother, his choicest game. The squaw cooks it in her best manner and sends her brave choice morsels via her mother.

"Indian Customs." *New York Weekly Museum* 5:288, March 1, 1817.

"Indian Customs." *Niles' Weekly Register* 39:167–168, Oct. 30, 1830.
Description of a Creek religious custom.

"Indian Customs." *The National Era* 5:169, Oct., 1851.
An Indian wedding, and "Walking Thunder's" speech when a storm broke during the festivities.

"Indian Journal." *Niles' Weekly Register* 69:6, 25–26, 38, 51, 87, 134, 164, 179, 198, 210, 228, 274, 371, Sept. 6, 1845–Feb. 14, 1846 (NYU).
Various Indian items discussed—the finding of antiques, Canadian Indians, agricultural subjects, application of Choctaws and Cherokees for citizenship, fatal diseases, Pottawatomies, Sioux murderers, sale of Western lands, etc.

"Indian Justice." *Niles' Weekly Register* 34:379–380, Aug. 9, 1828.
Punishment of an Indian and Negro for killing a white man.

"Indian Notions." *Graham's American Monthly Magazine* 51:350, Oct., 1857.
His attitude towards the devil.

"Indian Slavery." *The National Register* 2:140–141, Oct. 26, 1816 (NYU).
An account of the torture practiced upon white captives by the Shawnee Indians, as related by Benjamin Powell, after five years a prisoner.

"Indian Story." *New York Mirror* 2:335, May 14, 1825.
An Indian describes the manner of wooing and winning a young maiden's heart.

"Indian Totem." *The American Magazine of Knowledge* 2:384, May, 1836.
Comments on the Indian's pride in his lineage.

"Indians. Lake Superior." *Niles' Weekly Register* 71:2–3, Sept. 5, 1846 (NYU).
Copy of letters date La Pointe, Aug. 5 and 7, 1846, containing a descriptive account of the Indian tribes and their mode of life.

"Indians of North America." *The American Magazine of Knowledge* 2:214–215, Jan., 1836.
Deals with religion, customs and manners.

"Jumping Rabbit's Story." *Merry's Museum* 6:20–22, 54–56, 65–68, 118–120, 140–143, 179–182, July–Dec., 1843.
A narrative giving a detailed account of games, festivities, hunting adventures among the Indians.

"Language Without Oaths." *Pougkeepsie Casket* 3:15, May 4, 1839 (NYU).
The author observes that Indians cannot swear in their vernacular.

"Mary May: The Newfoundland Indian." *The Knickerbocker* 23:5–23, June, 1844.
Habits and customs of the Newfoundland aborigenes, called "Red Indians."

"Mourning Among the Indian Women." *The Baltimore Literary Monument* 1:145, Dec., 1838.

"On the Mistaken Notions of a Certain Philosopher Respecting the Indian Character." *Universal Asylum* 8:110, Feb., 1792 (NYU).

"Portraits of the Aborigenes." *The New York Mirror* 13:71, Aug. 29, 1835 (NYU).
Announcement of a very splendid publication now in process, entitled the "Aboriginal Portfolio," which is a collection of lithographed and coloured portraits of the aboriginal inhabitants of the countries now held by the U.S. The artist is J. O. Lewis, who was appointed to take the portraits and costume of the various Indians.

"Scenes and Adventures in the Army, etc." *Southern Literary Messenger* 8:405–414, June, 1842 (NYU).
A descriptive account of Indians and life beyond the border by a Captain of United States Dragoons, also, his impressions of St. Louis and other cities nearby, their inhabitants, etc.

"Sketches of the Manners, Customs and History of the Indians of America." 11 Chapters. *Robert Merry's Museum* 1:116–119, 140–144, 181–187; 2:14–16, 54–60, 121–124, 135–137, 161–171, 1841.
While it deals mainly with the South and Central American Indians, the narrative is very informative in general social habits, traditions, and beliefs of many other tribes. Good illustrations.

"Strange Customs of Some of the Savage Nation." *Ladies' Literary Cabinet* 6:94, July 27, 1822.
Self-mutilation and torture among many tribes upon death or marriage in the family.

"The American Indians." *The American Review* 9:631, June, 1849 (NYU).
General observations on life and customs.

"The Indian Character." *Poughkeepsie Casket* 1:148, Sept. 10, 1836 (NYU).
Essay on the moral characteristics of the Indian, also a few specimens of their intellectual capacities in speeches from various chiefs.

————.
"The Indian Name of Logan." *Hazard's Register of Pennsylvania* 13:416: Dec. 28, 1833; 13: 94, 110–111, Feb. 8 and 15, 1834.
Origin of the celebrated name, also general discussion of Indian custom of interchanging names.

————.
"The Wild Fawn." *The Ariel* 3:10, May 16, 1829 (NYU).
A tale of the tragic love of the Indian girl Wild Fawn, with a history of Indian marriage and divorce customs.

————.
"Traits Of Indian Character." *Analectic Magazine* 3:145–146, Feb., 1814 (NYU).
Essay analyzing the character of the American Indian.

————.
"Traits of the American Indian Character." *Polyanthos* 2:176–178, June, 1806 (NYU).

B.
"An Account of the History, Manners, and Customs of the Indian Nations by the Rev. John Heckeweder." *Western Review and Miscellaneous Magazine* 1:65–74, Sept., 1819.

Bailey, Edgar Henry S.
"On the Delicacy of the Sense of Taste Among the Indians." *Kansas University Quarterly* 2 (No. 2):95–98, 1894.

Banier, M. l'Abbé, and Le Mascrier, M. l'Abbé
Histoire générale des cérémonies, moeurs, et coutumes religieuses sinées de la main de Bernard Picard: avec des explications historiques, & curieuses; par M. l'Abbé Banier . . . & par M. l'Abbé le Mascrier. Paris: Rollin Fils, 1741. 7 vols., illus.
Contents: V.1. Cérémonies religieuses des Juifs. Cérémonies religieuses des catholiques. V.2. Suite des cérémonies religieuses des catholiques. Memoirs historiques servant a l'histoire des inquisitions. V.3. Cérémonies religieuses des Grecs schismatiques. Cérémonies religieuses des chrétiens qui se sont donnés le nom de protestants, evangelistes et reformes. V.4. Suite des cérémonies religieuses des protestans. V.5. Cérémonies religieuses des Mahométans. Cérémonies religieuses des idolâtres. Cérémonies religieuses des idolâtres orientaux. V.6. Suite des cérémonies religieuses des idolâtres orientaux. V.7. Cérémonies religieuses des Americains. Cérémonies religieuses des peuples de l'Afrique.
Encyclopedic work on religious customs, manners, and ceremonies. Vol.7—treats the religious ceremonies of the American Indians.

Barbeau, C. Marius
"The Hooked Rug, Its Origin." Ottawa, Canada. Royal Society of Canada, 1942. *Transactions of the Royal Society of Canada*, 3rd series, sec. II, 36:25–32, 12 pl.

Baulig, H.
"Sur la distribution des moyens de transport et de circulation chez les indigènes de l'Amérique du Nord." *Annales de Géographie* 17: 433–456, 1908.

Beauchamp, W. M.
"Indian Corn Stories and Customs." *JAFL* 11: 195–202, 1898.

Belknap, Daniel
"Remarks on the Character of the Indians." *The New York Magazine: or Literary Repository* 4:492–493, Aug. 1793 (NYU).

Bendann, Effie
Death Customs. An Analytical Study of Burial Rites. New York: Alfred A. Knopf, 1930. xiii, 304 pp., bibl. (pp. 285–292).

Berlin, A. F.
"Early Smoking Pipes of the North American Aborgine." *Proceedings and Collections of the Wyoming Historical Society* 9:107–136, 1905.

Birket-Smith, K.
"The Composite Comb in North America." *Ethnos* 2:33–37, 1937.

————.
"Drinking Tube and Tobacco Pipe in North America." *Etnologiska Studier* (Göteberg) 1: 29–39, 1931.

Blumensohn, Jules
"The Fast Among North American Indians." *AA* 35:451–469, 1933. n.s.

Bonnerjea, B.
"Fish-Hooks in North America." *Journ. Indian Anthro. Inst.* 1:69–147, 1938 (Calcutta).

Brickell, John
"John Brickell's Narrative." *The American Pioneer* 1:43–56, Feb., 1842 (NYU).
A narrative of his captivity among the Delaware Indians. Includes observations on manners, customs, and character of the Indian.

Browne, C. A.
"The Chemical Industries of the American Aborigines." *Isis* 23:406–424, 1935.

Buckland, Miss A. W.
"On Tattooing." In: *Journal of Anthropological Institute*, Great Britain and Ireland, XVII. No. 4, 1888.

Bushnell, D. I., Jr.
"The Origin of Wampum." *Journal of the Royal Author Institute of Gt. Britain* 36:172–17, 1906.

————.
"The Various Uses of Buffalo Hair by the North American Indians." *AA* 11:401–425, 1909. n.s.

C.
"Slavery Among the Indians." *Southern Literary Messenger* 28:333–335, May, 1859.
Some account of the slave institutions among the Cherokee, Choctaws, Creeks and Chickasaws and its effect upon Indian civilization.

Carr, Lucien
Dress and Ornaments of Certain American Indians. Worcester: C. Hamilton, 1897. 76 pp. (Reprinted from *American Antiquarian Society*, April, 1897).

———.
"The food of certain American Indians and their methods of preparing it." *American Antiquarian Society Proceedings* vol. X, n.s.: pp. 155–190, 1895.

Catlin, George
"Indian Fop." *N. Y. Mirror* 19:414, Dec. 25, 1841 (NYU).
Extract from Catlin's work on the North American Indians, describing an Indian fop.

———.
Letters and Notes on the Manners, Customs, and Condition of the North American Indians. Written during eight years' travel amongst the wildest tribes of Indians in North America, 1832–1839. New York: Wiley and Putnam, 1841. front., plates, maps (1 fold).

Chamberlain, Alexander F.
"Memorials of the Indian." *JAFL* 15:107–116, 1902.

———.
Mourning Customs. In: *Handbook of the American Indians North of Mexico*, F. W. Hodge, editor. 1:951–953. Bureau of American Ethnology, Bulletin 30. Washington, D. C.: U. S. Government Printing Office, 1907.

Charles, Lucile Hoerr
"The Clown's Function." *JAFL* 58:25–34, 1945.

Chester, J. L.
"Mechanic's Institute." *American Repertory of Arts* 2:352–355, Dec., 1840 (NYU).
Extracts from a lecture delivered by Mr. Chester, before the Mechanic's Institute, Nov. 16, on the subject: "The Aborigines of North America," showing the contrast of appearance and condition of America three centuries and a half ago and its present appearance.

Cohen, Felix S.
Derecho indigena: contribucion Éspanola al sistema legal de los Estados Unidos. Washington, D. C.: Dep't of Interior, 1943. 20 pp., illus.

Cooke, O. F.
"Food Plants of Ancient America." *Annual Reports Smithson. Inst.*, pp. 481–497, 1903.

Cope, Leona
"Calendars of the Indians North of Mexico." *University of California Publications in American Archaeology and Ethnology.* Vol. 16 (No. 4):119–176, 1919. 3 maps, bibl. Berkeley: University of California Press, 1919–1920.

Crawford, M. D. C.
"The Loom in the New World." *Amer. Mus. Jour.* 16:381–387, 1916.

Curtis, Edward S.
The North American Indian; being a series of volumes picturing and describing the Indians of the United States, Dominion of Canada and Alaska. . . . Seattle, Wash.: E. S. Curtis; Cambridge, U. S. A., The University Press, 1907–28. 18 vols., illus., music.

Dall, William Healey
Masks, Labrets, and Certain Aboriginal Customs, With an Inquiry Into the Bearing of Their Geographical Distribution. Washington, D. C.: U. S. Gov't Printing Office, 1885. 202 pp. (Repr. from U. S. Ethnology Bureau, Annual Report, No. 3).

Darusmont, Frances Wright
Views of Society and Manners in America; in a series of letters from that country to a friend in England during the years 1818, 1819, and 1820. By an Englishwoman. London: Longman . . ., 1821. x, 523 pp.

Davenport, C. B.
"The Dietaries of Primitive Peoples." *AA* 47:60–82, 1945. n.s.

Davidson, D. S.
Snowshoes. Memoirs of the American Philosophical Society, No. 6. Philadelphia: 1937. 207 pp.

Dickens, Charles
"The Noble Indian." *The Ladies Repository* 13:415, Sept., 1853 (NYU).
An essay on his unbelief in the "noble savage" and a biting account of the Indians' habits, mode of living and morals.

Douglas, Frederick Huntington
"Types of Indian Masks." *Denver Art Museum Dep't of Indian Art, Leaflet* 67, 1935.

Drake, F. S.
"A Northern Custom." *The American Pioneer* 2:88, Feb., 1843.
Attitude towards killing among the Esquimaux.

Drake, Samuel Gardner
Biography and History of Indians of North America. From its discovery to the present time. Boston: Antiquarian Institution, 1836. 720 pp. reprinted by B. B. Mussey and Co. in 1851.
The lives of all the most distinguished chiefs and counsellors, exploits of warriors, celebrated speeches of orators, etc. Account of their manners, customs, laws, etc.

———.
The Aboriginal Races of North America. Philadelphia: Charles Desilver, 1860. 736 pp.
Biographical sketches of eminent individuals and a historical account of the different tribes, manners, customs, etc.

Edwards, Everett E.
Agriculture of the American Indians: A Classified List of Annotated Historical References, with an Introduction. United States Department of Agriculture, Biological Contributions 23. Washington: U. S. Government Printing Office, 1933. 106 pp.

Ewbank, Thomas
North American Rock-Writing and Other Aboriginal Modes of Recording and Transmitting Thought. Morrisania, New York: Read before the New York Historical Society, March 6, 1866: reprinted from the Historical Magazine for August, September and October, 1866. Pamphlet, 49 pp., illus.

Farabee, W. C.
"The Use of Metals in Prehistoric America."
Mus. Jour. 12:35–42, 1921.

Farrer, James A.
Primitive Manners and Customs. New York:
H. Holtand Company, 1879. xxx, 315 pp.
　　Contents: Some savage myths and beliefs. Savage
　　modes of prayer. Some savage proverbs. Savage
　　moral philosophy. Savage political life. Savage
　　penal laws. Early wedding customs. The fairy-
　　lore of savages. Comparative folklore.

Fletcher, Alice C.
Adornment. In: *Handbook of American In-
dians North of Mexico,* F. W. Hodge, editor.
Vol. I, pp. 16–20. Washington, D. C.: U. S.
Government Printing Office, 1907.

――――――.
Tattooing. In: *Handbook of American Indians.*
Vol. II, pp. 699–701. Bibl. Bureau of American
Ethnology, Bulletin 30. Washington, D. C.:
U. S. Government Printing Office, 1910.

Fletcher, Dr. Robert
"Tattooing Among Civilized People." In:
*Transactions of the Anthropological Society
of Washington,* II, p. 411. Washington: Judd
& Detweiler, 1883. 27 p.

Forster, Georg
*Nathaniel Portlocks und Georg Mortimers
Reisen an die Nordwestküste von Amerika;* ...
Welch eine Beschreibung der Sitten und
Gebräuche der nordamerikanischen Wilden.
. . . Berlin: in der Vossischen Buchhandlung,
1796. viii, 384 pp.
　　Manners and customs of the American Indians
　　of the Old Northwest.

Frazer, James
Garnered Sheaves; essays, addresses, and reviews, by Sir James G. Frazer. London: Macmillan and Co., Ltd., 1931. xi, 538 pp.

Friederici, G.
*Skalpieren und ähnliche Kriegsgebräuche in
Amerika.* Braunschweig: 1906. 170 pp.

――――――.
"Über die Behandlung der Kriegsgefangenen
durch die Indianer Amerikas." *Festschrift
Eduard Seler,* pp. 59–128. Stuttgart: 1922.

――――――.
"Die Wirkung des Indianerbogens." *Globus*
91:325–330, 1907.

Frost, John
Illustrated Historical Sketches of the Indians;
exhibiting their manners and customs on the
battlefield and in the wigwam. With numerous
anecdotes and speeches. ... Hartford: E. Hunt,
1851. viii, 400 pp., illus.

Goldenweiser, A. A.
"The Social Organization of the Indians of
North America." *JAFL* 27:411–436, 1914.

Goodrich, S. G.
*The Manners, Customs and Antiquities of the
Indians of North and South America:* by the
author of Peter Parley's tales. Boston: Bradbury, Soden and Co., 1844. iv, 336 pp., illus.

Grant, Anne
Memoirs of an American Lady, with sketches
of manners and scenes in America as they
existed previous to the revolution. ... New
York: Dodd, Mead and Company, 1901.

Greenman, Emerson F.
"Origin and Development of the Burial
Mound." *AA* 34:286–295, 1932. n.s.

Grinnell, George B.
"Tenure of Land Among the Indians." *AA* 9:
1–12, 1907. n.s.

Groewel, M.
*Haltung und Erziehung des Kindes bei den
nordamerikanischen Indianern.* Hamburg: 1937.
82 pp.
　　On the care and rearing of North American
　　Indian children

Haddon, A. C.
"A Few American String Figures and Tricks."
AA 5:213–223, 1903. n.s.

Harris, J.
"Indian Lore and Customs." *School Arts* 43:
94, Nov., 1943.

Havard, V.
"Drink Plants of the North American Indians."
Bull. of the Torrey Botanical Club 23 (Part
2):33–46, 1896.

――――――.
"Food Plants of the North American Indians."
Bull. of the Torrey Botanical Club 22 (Part
3):98–123, 1895.

Hearne
"Some Account of the Barbarities of the North-
ern Indians." *The New York Magazine: or
Literary Repository* 2:19–22, Jan., 1797. n.s.
(NYU).

Henshaw, Henry W.
"Indian Origin of Maple Sugar." *AA* 3:341–
351, 1890.

――――――.
Sweating and Sweat Houses. In: *Handbook of
American Indians.* Vol. II, pp. 660–662. Bureau
of American Ethnology, Bulletin 30. Washington, D. C.: U. S. Government Printing Office,
1910.
　　"There seems to have been three distinct pur-
　　poses for which sweating was practised. First, it
　　was a purely religious rite or ceremony for the
　　purpose of purifying the body and propitiating
　　spirits. A sweat-bath was always undergone by
　　warriors preparing for war; among many tribes,
　　by boys at the puberty age; and, perhaps gen-
　　erally, before any serious or hazardous under-
　　taking."

Hoebel, E. Adamson
"Primitive Law and Modern." *Transactions
New York Academy of Science* 5:30–41, 1942.

Holmes
"A Widow's Grief." *The American Pioneer* 2: 380, Aug., 1843.
Self-torture of an Indian woman—who tore her hair, drank spirits, beat her breasts to make her tears flow abundantly and grieve sufficiently before taking a new husband.

Holmes, William H.
Ornament. In: *Handbook of American Indians.* Vol. II, (pp. 149–155), illus. Bureau of American Ethnology, Bulletin 30. Washington, D. C.: U. S. Government Printing Office, 1910.

"The Tomahawk." *AA* 10:264–277, 1908. n.s.

Hrdlicka, A.
"The Painting of Human Bones among the Indians." *Annual Reports Smithson. Inst.*, pp. 607–618, 1904.

Hubbard, Ralph
American Indian Crafts, including suggestive outlines and bibliography of Indian lore. New York: Plume Trading & Sales Co., Inc., 1935. 64 pp., bibl., illus.

Humphrey, Norman D.
"The Mock Battle Greeting." *JAFL* 54:186–190, 1941.
European descriptions of military salute among North American Indians.

Hunter, Helen Virginia
The Ethnography of Salt in Aboriginal America. Philadelphia: Clark Printing House, 1940.

Irving, Washington
"Indian Character." *American Turf Register and Sporting Magazine* 7:222, Jan., 1836.
Paragraphs selected from the author's *Indian Sketches.*

J., E. W.
"Letters from the Indian Country." *The Knickerbocker* 20:1–5, July, 1842.
Customs and manners of the Indians of the Northeast.

James, E. O.
"Cremation and Preservation of the Dead in North America." *AA* 30:214–242, 1928. n.s.

Johnson, Sir William
"Extracts of some letters from Sir William Johnson to Arthur Lee, M.D., F.R.S., on the customs, of manners, and languages of the Northern Indians of America." *American Museum* 5:19–21, Jan., 1789.
Discussion of war customs, languages, beliefs, hunts, etc.

Kinietz, W. Vernon
"Notes on the Roached Headdress of Animal Hair Among the North American Indians." *Papers Michigan Academy of Arts and Letters* 24:463–467. Ann Arbor, 1941.

Knortz, Karl
Amerikanische Redensarten und Volksgebräuche. . . . Mit dem Anhang: Folkloristisches in Longfellow's "Evangeline." Leipzig: Teutona Verlag, 1907. 82 pp.
On customs, manners and speech.

Kohler, J.
"Die Rechte der Urvölker Nordamerikas." *Zeit. für Vergl. Rechts.* (Stuttgart) 12:354–426, 1897.
The rights of the North American aborigenes.

Kroeber, A. L.
"Arrow Release Distributions." *Univ. Calif. Publ. Amer. Arch. Ethnol.* 23:283–296, 1927.

La Barre, W.
"Native American Beers." *AA* 40:224–234, 1938. n.s.

Lafitau, Joseph François
Moeurs des Sauvages Amériqains. Comparées aux moeurs des premiers temps. Ouvrage enrichi de figures en tailledouce. Paris: Saugrain l'Aîne, 1724. 2 vols., front., 41 pl., map.
On the customs and manners of the American Indians. Profusely illustrated.

Lang, Andrew
Custom and Myth. New York: Longmans, Green and Co., 1910.

Lasch, R.
"Die Verstümlung der Zähne in Amerika." *Mitteil. Anthro. Gesell.* 31:12–33, 1901.

Le Moine, J. M.
"Les Aborigènes d'Amérique—leurs Rites mortuaires." *Proc. Trans. Royal Soc. Can.* 2 (Part 1):85–96, 1884.
Mortuary ceremonialism among the Indians.

Le Plongeon, Mme.
"Handiwork of Uncivilized Women." *Godey's Lady's Book* 115:384–387, Nov., 1887.
Description how pottery, baskets and clothing are made by various Indian tribes,—the Eskimos, Navajos, and South Central American tribes.

Long, John
John Long's Journal, 1762–1782. Cleveland, O.: The Arthur H. Clark Company, 1904. 329 pp. (Vol. II—Early Western Travels . . . ed. by Reuben G. Thwaites.)
"Describes the manners and customs of the North American Indians, . . . To which is added a vocabulary of the Chippeway language . . . A list of words in the Iroquois, Mohegan, Shawanee, and Esquimaux tongues.

Lucas, Jeannette May
Indian Harvest: Wild Food Plants of the First Americans. Illustrated by Helene Carter. Philadelphia: J. B. Lippincott Co., 1945.
A book for young readers about the wild plant foods the Indians ate.

Marriott, Alice
"When You Go to the Indian Fair." *The Southwest Review* 30:(4):335–338, Summer, 1945.

Martin, P. S.
"The Bow-Drill in North America." *AA* 36: 94–97, 1934. n.s.

McGuire, Joseph Deakins
"Pipes and Smoking Customs of the American Aborigenes Based on Material in the U. S. National Museum." *U. S. National Museum, Annual Report* 1897. (pp. 351–645). Illus. Washington, D. C.: U. S. Gov't Printing Office, 1899.

MacLeod, W. C.
"Economic Aspects of Indigeneous American Slavery." *AA* 30:632–650, 1928. n.s.

Madison, H. L.
Indian Homes. Cleveland: The Cleveland Museum, 1925. 39 pp., illus.

Mangelsdorf, P. C., and Reeves, R. G.
"The Origin of Indian Corn and Its Relatives." *Texas Agricultural Experiment Station Bulletin* 574. 315 pp. 1939.

Mason, O. T.
"Aboriginal American Zootechny." *AA* 1:45–81, 1899. n.s.
On the breeding and domestication of animals.

———.
"Aboriginal Skin-Dressing." *Reports U. S. National Museum*, pp. 553–589, 1889. Washington, D. C.

———.
"Amerindian Arrow Feathering." *AA* 1:583–585, 1899. n.s.

———.
"Cradles of the American Aborigines." *Reports U. S. National Museum*, pp. 161–212, 1887. Washington, D. C.

———.
"North American Bows, Arrows, and Quivers." *Annual Reports Smithson. Inst.*, pp. 631–679, 1893.

———.
"Traps of the American Indians." *Annual Reports Smithson. Inst.*, pp. 461–473, 1901.

———.
"Traps of the Amerinds." *AA* 2:657–675, 1900. n.s.

Messiter, Charles A.
Sport and Adventures Among the North-American Indians. London: R. H. Porter, 1890. xvi, 368 pp.

Moeurs et coutumes des peuples, ou collection de tableaux représentant les usages remarquables ... des diverses nations du monde. Paris: Hocquart, 1811–14. 2 vols. in 1. v, 141 pp.

Mogridge, George
The Book of the Indians of North America; illustrating their manners, customs, and present state. Edited by John Frost. New York: D. Appleton & Co., 1845. x, 283 pp., illus.

Moorehead, Warren King
The Bird Stone Ceremonial. Being an account of some singular prehistoric artifacts found in the U. S. and Canada. Fifty-three illus. Saranac Lake: A. I. Vosburgh, 1899. 31 pp., illus.

———.
Prehistoric Implement. A reference book. . . . Cincinnati, O.: The Robert Clarke Co., 1900. xv, 431 pp., illus.

Morgan, Lewis H.
"Houses and House-Life of the American Aborigines." *Contributions to North American Ethnology.* Vol. IV. Washington, D. C.: Gov't Print. Off., 1881. pp. 1–281.

———.
"The Indian Mode of Bestowing and Changing Names." *Proc. Amer. Antiq. Soc.* 13:340–343, 1859.

———.
"A Study of the Houses of the American Aborigines." *Contributions to North American logical Institute of America* 1:29–80, 1880.

Morse, Jedidah
"Aborigines of America." *Gazette of the United States* 1:16, April 22–25, 1789 (NYU). Excerpt from Morse's Geography enumerating the personal traits of the American Indian.

Murdock, George Peter
"Bifurcate Merging: A Test of Theories." *AA* 49 (No. 1) :56–69, 1947. n.s.

Murray, Hugh
"Courtship Among the Pawnees." *The New Yorker* 8:159, Nov. 23, 1839. Description of the Indian lover's routine and rights of hospitality offered by the girl's father.

Newberry, J. S.
"Food and Fiber Plants of the North American Indians." *Popular Science Monthly* 32:31–46, 1887.

Newell, W. W.
"Primitive Marriage Customs as Preserved in the Game of Children." *JAFL* 5:70–71, 1892.

Nykl, A. R.
"The Quinary-Vigesimal System of Counting in Europe, Asia, and America." *Language* 2: 165–173, 1926.

Palmer, E.
"Food Products of the North American Indians." *Report of the Secretary of Agriculture*, pp. 404–428, 1871.

———.
"Plants Used by the Indians of the United States." *Amer. Natur.* 12:593–606, 645–655, 1878.

Parker, Arthur Caswell
The Indian How Book. New York: George H. Doran Company, 1927. ix, 335 pp., illus.

Parker, Theodore
"The True or False Idea of a Gentleman." *Penn Freeman* 10:4, Jan. 6, 1853. A comparison of values and standards, between the red and white man.

Pellet, Kent
"The Tradition of Indian Democracy." *America Indígena* 3 (No. 4) :345–350, Mexico, D. F., 1943.

Perrot, Nicolas
Mémoire Sur Les Moeurs, Coustumes et Relligion(!) Des Sauvages de L'Amérique Septentrionale.... Leipzig & Paris: A. Franck, 1864. viii, xliii, 341 pp.
On the customs, manners and religious beliefs of the North American Indians.

Pettitt, George A.
Primitive Education in North America. University of California Publications in American Archaelogy and Ethnology. vol. 43, no. 1. pp. 1–182. Berkeley and Los Angeles: University of California Press, 1946.
Includes valuable discussion of effect of symbolism upon emotional nature. A part of the study is devoted to religious training involving "the vision quest and the guardian spirit."

Pogue, Joseph E.
"The Aboriginal Use of Torquoise in North America." *AA* 14:437–467, 1912. n.s.

Randall, S. G.
"The North American Indian." *The Northern Light* 3:12–13, May, 1843.
Sketch of the characteristics of the Indians before and after the coming of the white men.

Rau, C.
"Ancient Aboriginal Trade in North America." *Annual Reports Smithson. Inst.*, pp. 348–394, 1872.

———.
"Die Tauschverhältnisse der eingeborenen Nordamerikas." *Archiv für Anthro.* (Braunschweig) 5:1–43, 1872.

Recueil d'observations curieuses, sur les moeurs, les coutumes, les usages, les différentes langues, le gouvernement, la mythologie, la chronologie, la geographie ancienne & moderne, les cérémonies, la religion, les méchaniques, l'astronomie, la médicine, la physique particuliére, l'histoire naturelle, le commerce, la navigation, les arts & les sciences de différens peuples de l'Asie, de l'Afrique, & de l'Amérique. A. Paris: Chez Prault fils, 1749. 4 vols.

Rogers, S. L.
"The Aboriginal Bow and Arrow of North America and Eastern Asia." *AA* 42:255–269, 1940.

S. S. R.
"Indian Character." *The Oasis* 1:69–71, Dec., 23, 1837 (NYU).
Essay on the character of the North American Indians.

Safford, W. E.
"Food Plants and Textiles of Ancient America." *Proc. Inter. Congr. Amer.* 19:12–30, 1915.

———.
"Narcotic Plants and Stimulants of the Ancient Americans." In: *Smithsonian Report,* 1916. (pp. 387–424) plates Washington, D. C. Washington, D. C.: Government Printing Office, 1916.

Salomon, Julian Harris
The Book of Indian Crafts & Lore; with many illustrations by the author and others. New York: Harper & Brothers, 1928. xvii, 418 pp., illus., bibl., music (pp. 297–327).

Sauer, C.
American Agricultural Origins. In: *Essays in Anthropology Presented to A. L. Kroeber,* pp. 279–297. Berkeley, Cal.: University of California Press, 1936.

Schoolcraft, Henry Rowe
The Indian in His Wigwam, or Characteristics of the Red Race of America.... Buffalo: Derby & Hewson, 1848. 416 pp., illus.

———.
"Travels." *The Cincinnati Literary Gazette* 3 (No. 24) :185–187, June 11, 1825.
Mainly with Indian Customs.

Scott, Leslie M.
"Indian Women as Food Providers and Tribal Counsellors." *Oregon Quarterly* (Portland) 42:208–219, 1941.

Seidel, H.
"Der Schneeschuh und seine geographische Verbreitung." *Globus* 73:155–161, 1898.
Geographic distribution of the snowshoe.

Serfert, E.
"Haus und Dorf bei den Eingeborenen Nordamerikas." *Archive für Anthropologie* 7:119–215, (Braunschweig) 1908.

Setchell, W. A.
"Aboriginal Tobaccos." *AA* 23:397–414, 1921. n.s.

Seton, Julia
The Pulse of the Pueblo; personal glimpses of Indian Life. Santa Fe, N. M.: Seton Village Press, 1939. 249 pp., illus.

Sinclair, A. T.
"Tattooing of the North American Indians." *AA* 11:362–400, 1909. n.s.

Smith, Col. James
"Indian Ceremony." *Ladies Literary Cabinet* 4:52–53, 1851.
An adoption ceremony of a stranger into the tribe.

Smith, H. I.
"Primitive Ways of Working Stone." *So. Workman* 40:88–93, 1911.

Speck, Frank G.
"Land Ownership Among Hunting Peoples in Primitive America and the World's Marginal Areas." *Proceedings of the 22 Session of the International Congress of Americanists* pp. 323–333, 1928, Vol. II.

Spence, Lewis
Calendar. In: *Encyclopedia of Religion and Ethics,* J. Hastings, ed. (New York). Vol. 3, pp. 65–70, 1911.

Spier, Leslie
"The Distribution of Kinship Systems in North America." *Univ. Wash. Publ. in Anthro.* 1:69–88, 1925.

Steele, Rev. S.
"An Incident in Indian History." *The Ladies Repository* 14:554–556, Dec., 1854.
A narrative illustrating Indian custom where father was ransom for son who committed a wrong against a Christian.

Stout, A. B.
"Vegetable Foods of the American Indians." *Journal of the New York Botanical Garden* 15:50–60, 1914.

Swanton, John Reed
"An Indian Social Experiment and Some of Its Lessons." *The Scientific Monthly* 31:368–376, Oct., 1930.

————.
Names and Naming. In: *Handbook of American Indians.* Vol. II, pp. 16–18. Bureau of American Ethnology, Bulletin 30. Washington, D. C.: U. S. Government Printing Office, 1910.

————.
Puberty Customs. In: *Handbook of American Indians.* Vol. II, pp. 314–315. Bureau of American Ethnology, Bulletin 30. Washington, D. C.: U. S. Government Printing Office, 1910.

————.
"The Social Organization of the American Tribes." *AA* 7:663–674, 1905. n.s.

The Indian Sketch Book; containing the narrative of J. D. Hunter, who was captured when four years old, and raised by the Indians. He gives a full account of their manners, customs, travels, adventures, wars, and medicines... tales and romances of the Indians.... Cincinnati: Published & sold by H. S. & J. Applegate, 1852. 384 pp., illus.

Thomas, Cyrus
Mortuary Customs. In: *Handbook of the American Indians North of Mexico,* editor F. W. Hodge. Vol. I, pp. 945–957. Bureau of American Ethnology, Bulletin 30. Washington, D. C.: U. S. Government Printing Office, 1907.

Tijm, J.
Die Stellung der Frau bei den Indianern der Vereinigten Staaten und Canada's. Amsterdam: 1933. 158 pp.

Truesdell, S. E.
"Injun-Giving." *JAFL* 12:240–241, 1899.

Uncle Samuel's Servant.
"Indian Justice." *The Knickerbocker* 44:402, 1854.

Verrill, A. Hyatt
Foods America Gave the World. Boston: L. C. Page & Co., 1937. xvi, 289 pp., illus.
Curious facts and stories of the origin of many of our native foods.

————.
Strange Customs, Manners and Beliefs. Boston: L. C. Page and Company, 1946. 302 pp., illus.
The author deals mainly with primitive people,—large section devoted to the American Indian.

Wakefield, Priscilla
Sketches of Human Manners, delineated in stories intended to illustrate the characters, religion, and singular customs, of the inhabitants of different parts of the world. Philadelphia: Johnson & Warner, 1811. 252 pp.
Contents: The Indian Widow. The North American Warrior. The Russian Peasant. The Convict. The Faithful Spaniards.

Walsh, William Shepard
Curiosities of Popular Customs and of Rites, Ceremonies, Observances, and Miscellaneous Antiquities. Philadelphia: J. B. Lippincott Co., 1925. 1018 pp., illus.

Warale, H. Lewell
"Indian Gifts in Relation to Primitive Law." *Proceedings of the 23rd International Congress of Americanists* pp. 463–470, 1928.

Waterman, T. T.
"North American Indian Dwellings." *Annual Reports Smithson. Inst.,* pp. 461–485, 1924.

Waugh, F. W.
"Canadian Aboriginal Canoes." *Canadian Field Naturalist* (Ottawa) 33:23–33, 1919.

West, George A.
"Tobacco Pipes and Smoking Customs of the American Indians." *Public Museum of the City of Milwaukee, Bulletin 17,* 477 pp., illus. Milwaukee: Public Museum, 1934.

Williams, Rev. John L.
Our Brother in Red. A Synopsis of the Indian life, characteristics, and customs.... Nashville, Tenn.: Publ. House of the M. E. Church, South, 1908. 48 pp.

Williamson, Peter
"Barbarity of American Indians." *Brother Jonathan,* March 4, 1849 (NYU).
An account of the atrocities witnessed by the author while a captive of the Susquehannah Indians. He describes the torture of four white men, put to death.

Wissler, Clark
Indian Costumes in the United States. New York: The Museum of Natural History, 1931. 32 pp., illus. 3rd Ed.

————.
"The Material Culture of North American Indians." *AA* 16:447–505, 1914. n.s.

"Observations on the Face and Teeth of the North American Indians." *Anthropological Papers:* Vol. 33:1931, pp. 1–33. Publications in Anthropology. New York: The American Museum of Natural History.

———.
Riding Gear of the North American Indians. *Anthropological Papers.* Vol. 17:1915, pp. 1–38, 27 figs. Publications in Anthropology. New York: The American Museum of Natural History.

Wood, John G.
The Uncivilized Races of Men in All Countries of the World; being a comprehensive account of their manners and customs, and of their physical, social, mental, moral and religious characteristics. With new designs by Angas, Danby, Wolf, Zwecker. 2 vols. San Francisco: J. A. Brainerd & Co., 1883. Illus. (Eames Indian Collection.)

Yanovsky, Elias
Food Plants of the North American Indian. U. S. Dep't of Agriculture, Miscellaneous Publications 237, 83 pp. Washington, D. C.: U. S. Gov't Printing Office, 1936.

Yarrow, H. C.
"A Further Contribution to the Study of the Mortuary Customs of the North American Indians." *First Annual Report of the Bureau of American Ethnology,* pp. 89–199, figs. 1–47, 1879–1800. Washington, D. C.: U. S. Gov't Printing Office, 1881.
Classification of burial, inhumation, enbalment or mummification, pit burial, cremation, living sepulchres, etc. Funeral rites, mourning sacrifices and feasts, superstitions, etc.

———.
Introduction to the Study of Mortuary Customs Among the North American Indians. Washington, D. C.: 1880. 108 pp.

FOLK POETRY—ART—DRAMA —SPEECH

See: Customs—Manners, pp. 786-95.

A.
"Aboriginal Orator." *The National Register* 3:115, Feb. 22, 1817 (NYU).
Specimen of Indian eloquence. Eulogy on the death of Tecumseh (1786–1813).

Abrahall, John Hoskyns
Western Woods and Waters. Poems and illustrated notes. London: Longman, Green, Longman . . ., 1864. xxxii, 419 pp.

"Addresses of the Five Nations Indian Chiefs." *Gazette of the United States* 3:397, April 11, 1792 (NYU).
Addresses of the two principal chiefs of the Five Nations—Sagoyewatha (Red Jacket) and Agwelonong (Good Peter)—to the Governor of Pennsylvania.

Albee, John
St. Aspenqid of Mt. Agamenticus. An Indian Idyl. Portsmouth: L. W. Brewster, 1879. 24 pp.

Alexander, Hartley Burr
L'art et la philosophie des Indiens de l'Amérique du Nord. . . . Paris: E. Leroux, 1926. 118 pp., illus.

———.
God's Drum and Other Cycles from Indian Lore. Poems by Hartley Alexander; illustrations by Anders John Haugseth. New York: E. P. Dutton & Company, 1927. ix, 231 pp.

———.
The Pictorial and Pictographic Art of the Indians of North America. Denver: 1927.

American Lyceum
"Domestic Correspondence of the American Lyceum, on the Indian Languages." *American Annals of Education* 5:354–359, Aug., 1835.
Copy of a letter from Elisha Loomis on the Ojibway Indian dialect; from Rev. Gardner B. Perry, Bradford, Mass.; on the Essex County Teachers' Association; and from Henry R. Schoolcraft on Indian dialects.

Anon.
"A Pattern for Orators." *The New Yorker* 5: 331, Aug. 11, 1838 (NYU).
Remarks of an Indian chief, containing ten lines, contrasted with Colonel Pepper's three columned Congressional harangue.

———.
"An Indian Talk." *American Museum* 7:20, July, 1786.
Delivered at Fort Pitt, and the answer.

———.
"An Indian's Speech." *The Lady's Magazine and Repository* 2:268–269, May, 1793 (NYU).

———.
"Fulfillment of an Indian Prophecy." *The Telescope* 2:200, May 13, 1826 (NYU).
Address to Washington by a Grand Sachem at a council fire.

———.
"Indian, Creek." *New York Mirror* 4:119, Nov. 5, 1826 (NYU).
Extract of the speech of an Indian chief, as to why he assisted in killing McIntosh, celebrated Indian chief (1775-1825).

———.
"Indian Eloquence." *Niles' Weekly Register* 9:112–113, Oct., 1815 (NYU).
An obituary on Black Buffalo, principal chief of the Teton Tribe who died July 14, 1815 at Portage De Sioux. Big Elk, a Mahan chief delivered an eloquent speech at internment.

———.
"Indian Eloquence." *The Ariel* 5:144, Aug. 20, 1831 (NYU).
In speech and writing.

"Indian Eloquence." *The Ariel* 2:142, Dec. 27, 1828 (NYU).
> Comments on the beauty of the speech of the Indians, from its very simplicity and brevity; with an illustration of a meeting between father and son.

"Indian Eloquence." *The Knickerbocker* 7:385–390, April, 1836.
> Essay on the American Indian's eloquence, as key to their characters and noble monument of their literature. Examples.

"Indian Eloquence." *The New Yorker* 1:52, April 16, 1836 (NYU).
> Eloquence as a key to character, viz.: Tecumseh, Shenandoah, Pushmataha, Sadekanstic, and others.

"Indian Customs." *The National Era* 5:169, Oct. 1851.
> An Indian wedding, and "Walking Thunder's" speech when a storm broke during the festivities.

"Indian Names." *New York Weekly Museum* 5:251, Feb. 15, 1817.

"Indian Oratory." *Universal Asylum* 5:365, Dec., 1790 (NYU).

"Indian Speech." *New York Mirror* 4:119, Nov. 5, 1826 (NYU).
> Extract of the speech of an Indian chief as to why he assisted in killing McIntosh, a celebrated Indian chief.

"Literature." *The Minerva* 1:244–245, Nov. 9, 1822 (NYU).
> An essay on the diversity of languages among the American Indians.

"Logan—the Mingo Chief." *The American Pioneer* 1:7–24, Jan., 1842 (NYU).
> An account of his life, his celebrated speech, which Jefferson defended in his Appendix to *Notes on Virginia*, as to its authenticity, its influence on youth, the Bar, the pulpit, controversy over the genuineness of the speech, extract from Drake's *Indian Biography*.

"Logan's Speech." *National Enquirer* 1:68, Dec. 31, 1836 (NYU).
> Letter with a copy of the speech, from the *Virginia Gazette*, Feb. 4, 1775.

"Obituary and Eulogy." *Niles' Weekly Register* 58:241, June 20, 1840 (NYU).
> Death of Francis Godfrey, chief of the Miami, with the eulogy written by an unnamed friend.

"Pretty Names among the Indians." *American Penny Magazine* 1:432, Aug. 9, 1845.
> A list of the poetical names which the Seneca Indians give their women, such as, Rose-on-the-Bush, Summer-Bird, Shining-Star, Maple-Bud, etc.

"Shenandoah, The Oneida Chief." *Ladies' Literary Cabinet* 5:188, April 20, 1822.
> Anecdotes, specimens of eloquence.

"Speech of Red Jacket." *The American Register* 7:209–212, 1810 (NYU).
> Speech of the Seneca chief to Rev. McCram, of the Boston Missionary Society, giving the Indian's viewpoint towards Christianity.

"Supplementary Notes and Observations on Father Rasle's *Dictionary of the Abnaki Language in North America*." *Memoirs of the American Academy* 1:566–574, 1833, n.s. (NYU).

"Tecumseh." *The American Magazine of Knowledge* 1:78, Sept., 1834 (NYU).
> An account of the Indian Chief's advice to the British when leaving Fort Malden.

"The Indian Character." *Poughkeepsie Casket* 1:148, Sept. 10, 1836 (NYU).
> Essay on the moral characteristics of the Indian, also a few specimens of their intellectual capacities in speeches from various chiefs.

"The Indians." *Parley's Magazine* 1:27–28, Sept. 28, 1833 (NYU).
> A true story of the Choctaw language.

"The Invention of Letters." *Niles' Weekly Register* 44:349, July 20, 1833 (NYU).
> Descriptive account of the invention of the Cherokee alphabet by Sequoyah.

"The Red Swan." *New Yorker* 7:165–167, June 1, 1839 (NYU).
> Folk literature of an Algonquin tribesman in pursuit of this bird. (From Schoolcraft's—*Algic Researches*.)

Astrov, Margot
The Winged Serpent. An Anthology of Indian Prose and Poetry. New York: The John Day Company, 1946. ix, 366 pp., bibl., index.
> Included in the volume are not only songs and tales, but also prayers, formulas, speeches, excerpts from ceremonies and prophecies, as well as anthropological fragments.

Austin, Mary Hunter
The American Rhythm. New York: Harcourt, Brace & Co., 1923. 174 pp.
> Indian Poetry.

Indian Poetry. New York: The Exposition of Indian Tribal Arts, 1931. 5 pp.

Barbeau, Charles Marius
"Backgrounds in North American Folk Arts." *Queens Quarterly* 48:284–294, 1941.

Barnes, Nellie
American Indian Love Lyrics and Other Verse. Foreword by Mary Austin. New York: The Macmillan Company, 1925. 190 pp.

———.
American Indian Verse. Characteristics of
Style. Lawrence: Kansas University Press,
1921. 63 pp. (Kansas University, Bulletin:
Humanistic Studies, V. 2, No. 4.)

Beede, Aaron McGaffey
Toward the Sun. Commentary notes by Melvin
R. Gilmore. Bismark, N. D.: Bismark Tribune
Company, 1916. 199 pp.

Bliss, Robert Woods
Indigenous Art of the Americas. Collection of
Robert Woods Bliss. National Gallery of Art,
Smithsonian Institution. Wash. D. C.: 1947.
159 pp., plates.

Boas, Franz
"Classification of American Indian Languages." *Language* 5:1–7, 1929.

———.
"The Classification of American Languages."
AA 22:367–376, 1920. n.s.

———.
"The Indian Languages of Canada." *Annual
Arch. Report,* pp. 88–106, 1905.

———.
Representative Art of Primitive People. In:
Race, Language and Culture by Franz Boas,
pp. 535–540, reprint (1916). New York: The
Macmillan Co., 1940.

———.
Primitive Art. Cambridge, Mass.: Harvard
University Press, 1927. 376 pp.
"The only full-length book on the subject; not
restricted to Indian art, though about half is
devoted to the best discussion of Northwest Coast
art, literature, music and dance."

———.
Stylistic Aspects of Primitive Literature. In:
Race, Language and Culture by Franz Boas,
pp. 491–502, reprint (1925). New York: The
Macmillan Co., 1940. (*JAFL* 38:329–339,
1925).

———.
The Decorative Art of the North American
Indians. In: *Race, Language and Culture* by
Franz Boas, pp. 546–563, (reprinted 1903,
from *Popular Science Monthly* 63:481–498,
1903). New York: The Macmillan Co., 1940.

Brinton, Daniel Garrison
*Aboriginal American Authors and their Pro-
ductions,* especially those in the native languages. A chapter in the history of literature.
Philadelphia: The Author, 1883. viii, 63 pp.

———.
"Aboriginal American Literature." *Proc. Inter.
Congr. Amer.* 5:56–64, 1884.

Brisbin, James S.
"The Poetry of Indians." *Harper's Magazine*
57:104–108, 1878.

Canfield, Delos L.
"Spanish Literature in Indian Languages of
New Spain." *Spanish Review.* (New York) 2:
9–14, 1935.

Chamberlain, Alexander F.
"American Indian Names of White Men and
Women." *JAFL* 12:24–31, 1899.

———.
"Further Notes on Indian Child Language."
AA 6:321–323, 1893. o.s.

———.
"Notes on Indian Child-Language." *AA* 3:237–
243, 1890.

———.
"Poetry of American Aboriginal Speech."
JAFL 9:43–47, 1896.

———.
"Primitive Woman Poet." *JAFL* 16:205–221,
1903.

———.
"Wisdom of the North American Indians in
Speech and Legend." *Proc. Amer. Antiq. Soc.*
23:63–96, 1913. n.s.

Charles, Lucile Hoerr
"Growing Up Through Drama." *JAFL* 59:247–
262, 1946.
The author explores the role of dramatization
in the adolescent development process as it is
illustrated in puberty rites of primitive peoples.
A number of Indian tribes are included in the
study.

Charency de Hyacinthe, comte
"Noms des points de l'espace dans divers
dialects Américains." *Journ. Société Amér.* 2:
109–178, 1898.

Cook, William
The Cor Felix. Ten Parts. Salem, Mass.: n.p.,
1869–76. 5 parts, illus.

Crawford, M. D. C.
"Design and Color in Ancient Fabrics." *Amer.
Mus. Jour.* 16:417–431, 1916.

Culin, Stewart
"The Origin of Ornament." *Bull. Free Museum
of Science and Art, University of Pennsylvania*
(Philadelphia) 2 (No. 4):235–242, 1900.

Densmore, Frances
"The Poetry of Indian Songs." In: *So Live the
Works of Men; Seventieth Anniversary Volume
Honoring Edgar Lee Hewett.* . . . Albuquerque:
University of New Mexico Press, 1939. 366 pp.,
illus.

———.
"American Indian Poetry." *AA* 28:447–449,
1926.

De Spain, Jay Roderic
Unknown Soldier's Answer. Redlands, Calif.:
The League of Western Writers, 1936. 402 pp.

d'Harnoncourt, Rene
"Living Arts of the Indians." *Magazine of Art* Feb., pp. 72–77. New York: Museum of Modern Art, 1941.

Dixon, R. B.
"Words for Tobacco in American Indian Languages." *AA* 23:19–49, 1921. n.s.

Dougherty, G. H.
"Motives of Indian Speeches and Songs." *Open Court* 40:689–704, 719–733.

Douglas, Frederic H.
"Basketry Construction Technics." *Denv. Art Mus. Ind. Leaf. Ser.* 67:66–68, 1935.

————.
"Basketry Decoration Technics." *Denv. Art Mus. Ind. Leaf. Ser.* 68:70–72, 1935.

————.
"Colors in Indian Arts." *Denv. Art Mus. Ind. Leaf Ser.* 56:22–24, 1933.

————.
"Copper and the Indian." *Denv. Art Mus. Ind. Leaf Ser.* 75–76:98–104, 1936.

————.
"Design Areas in Indian Art." *Denv. Art Mus. Ind. Leaf. Ser.* 62:46–48, 1934.

————.
"Indian Basketry." *Denv. Art Mus. Ind. Leaf. Ser.* 63:30–32, 1933.

————.
"Indian Basketry East of the Rockies." *Denv. Art Mus. Ind. Leaf. Ser.* 87:146–148, 1939.

————.
"Indian Cloth Making." *Denv. Art Mus. Ind. Leaf. Ser.* 59–60:34–40, 1933.

————.
"Indian Linguistic Stocks or Families." *Denv. Art Mus. Ind. Leaf. Ser.* 51–52:2–8, 1933.

————.
"Indian Vegetable Dyes." *Denv. Art Mus. Ind. Leaf. Ser.* 63:50–52; 71:82–84, 1934–1936.

————.
"Types of Indian Masks." *Denv. Art Mus. Ind. Leaf. Ser.* 65–66:58–64, 1935.

————, and d'Harnoncourt, Rene
Indian Art of the United States. New York: Museum of Modern Art, 1941. 220 pp., illus., bibl.

Drummond, T.
"The Canadian Snowshoe." *Proc. Trans. Royal Soc. Can.* (Part 2, Ser. 3) :305–320, 1916.

Eich, L. M.
"The American Indian Plays." *Quarterly Journal of Speech* 30:212–215, 1944.

Emmons, Earl H.
Redskin Rimes. New York: n.p., 1915.

Fletcher, Alice Cunningham
" 'Lazyman' in Indian Folklore." *JAFL* 4:100–104, 1901.

Foster, George E.
"Journalism Among the Cherokee Indians." *Magazine of American History* July, 1887. pp. 65-70.

Gaines, R.
"Books on Indian Arts North of Mexico." *Leaflets of the Exposition of Indian Tribal Arts* (New York). 1931. 15 pp.

Gallatin, Albert, ed.
"Hale's Indians of North-West America and Vocabularies of North America." *Trans. Amer. Ethno. Soc.* Vol. 2, 1848. 130 pp.

Gatschet, A. S.
" 'Real', 'True', or 'Genuine' in Indian Languages." *AA* 1:155–161, 1899. n.s.

Gerard, William R.
"The Term Tomahawk." *AA* 10:277–281, 1908. n.s.

Goddard, Pliny E.
"The Present Condition of Our Knowledge of North American Languages." *AA* 16:555–601, 1914. n.s.

Grossi, Vincenzo
Lingue, Letteratura e Tradizioni Popolari degl' Indigeni d'America. Part I. Genoveva: A. Ciminago, 1890.
Discussion of the language, literature and traditions of the Eskimos, Redskins, and Mexicans.

Haire, Frances Hamilton
The American Costume Book. New York: A. S. Barnes and Co., 1934. xi, 164 pp., illus.

Hale, Horatio
"Indian Migrations as Evidenced by Language." *Reprinted from American Antiquarian* (Chicago) (Jan. and April) 1883.

Harshberger, J. W.
"Phytogeographic Influences in the Arts and Industries of American Aborigines." *Bull. Geog. Soc.* 4 (Part 3) :25–41, 1906.

Hartman, R. B.
"Costumes of the North American Indians." *Wisconsin Archaeologist* (Milwaukee) 18:1–9, 1937. n.s.

Hatt, Gudmund
"Mocassins and Their Relation to Arctic Footwear." *Mem. Amer. Anthro. Assoc.* 3:149–250, 1916.

Hatt, Marcella R.
Basketry of the North American Indian. Bloomfield Hills, Mich.: Cranbrook Institute, 1941. 11pp.

Heath, V. S.
"Dramatic Elements in American Ceremonials." *Nebraska Univ. Studies* 14 (Part 4): 377–415, 1914.

Heckewelder, Rev. John
"Logan, the Mingo Chief." *The American Pioneer* 1:22–24, Jan., 1842 (NYU).
Testimony of the author concerning the speech of Logan, and further information on "Cresap's War."

Henderson, A. C.
"Modern Indian Painting." *Leaflets of the Exposition of Indian Tribal Arts.* (New York) 1931. 11 pp.

Hen-Toh, Wyandot Indian
Yon-doo-shah-we-ah (nubbins). Oklahoma City: Harlow Publishing Co., 1924. 73 pp., illus.

Hensey, George J.
Mighty Manitou; a defense of the brave and noble Red man, as he struggles through the years. And a sincere appreciation to Colorado Springs and Manitou, in their million triumphs for God, country and humanity. Springfield, Illinois: Hartman Printing Company, 1930. viii, 76 pp.

Hewett, Edgar
"On the Revival of Certain Indigenous American Arts." *Proceedings of the 22 Session of the International Congress of Americanists,* pp. 549–561, 1926. Vol. I.
Revival and growth of the ancient skills in their arts and ceremonies encouraged. Outstanding examples of Indian paintings given.

Hoffman, W. J.
"Remarks on Indian Tribal Names." *Proc. Amer. Philo. Soc.* 23:294–303, 1886.

Holmes, William H.
"Art in Shell of the Ancient Americans." *2nd Annual Report: Bureau of American Ethnology,* 1880–1881, pp. 185–267, pts. XXI–LXXVII. Washington, D. C.: U. S. Gov't Printing Office, 1883.

————.
Handbook of Aboriginal American Antiquities, part I. Introductory: the lithic industries. Bureau of American Ethnology, Bulletin 60, 380 pp., 223 figs. Washington, D. C.: U. S. Gov't Printing Office, 1919.

————.
Painting. In: *Handbook of American Indians.* Vol. II, (pp. 185–186). Bureau of American Ethnology, Bulletin 30. Washington, D. C.: U. S. Government Printing Office, 1910.

————.
Pictographs. In: *Handbook of American Indians.* Vol. II, (pp. 242–245), illus. Bureau of American Ethnology, Bulletin 30. Washington, D. C.: U. S. Government Printing Office, 1910.

————.
"A Study of the Textile Art in Its Relation to the Development of Form and Ornament." *Annual Reports Bur. Amer. Ethno.* 6:195–252, 1888.

Hubbard, Ralph
American Indian Crafts, Including suggestive outlines and bibliography of Indian Lore. New York: Plume Trading & Sales Co., 1935. 64 pp., illus., bibl.

Hurst, Ethan Allen
Ad-em-nel-la; an Indian Legendary Love-Story in Verse, and Other Poems. Kansas City: Hudson Press, 1915. 144 pp.

I., J. W.
"Miscellany. Old Names." *Army and Navy Chronicle* 7:231–232, Oct. 11, 1838.
A general discussion of old Indian names.

"Illustrations of the Method of Recording Indian Languages." *1st Annual Report Bureau of American Ethnology,* pp. 581–587, 1879–1880. From the Manuscripts of Messrs. Dorsey, J. D., Gatschet, A. S., and Riggs, S. R. Washington, D. C.: U. S. Gov't Printing Office, 1881.

Ingersoll, E.
"Wampum and Its History." *Amer. Natur.* 17: 467–479, 1883.

Innes, Harry, Hon. Judge
"Logan, the Indian Chief." *The American Pioneer* 1:14–15, Jan., 1842 (NYU).
Extract of a letter from Hon. Judge Innes of Frankfort, Ky., to Thomas Jefferson, dated Ky. near Frankfort, March 2, 1799.

James, George Wharton
Indian Basketry, And how to make Indian and other baskets. New York: H. Malkan, 1903. 274 pp., bibl., illus.

Jayne, C. F.
String Figures. New York: 1906. 407 pp.

Jefferson, Thomas
"Logan, the Mingo Chief." *The American Pioneer* 1:9–12, Jan., 1842 (NYU).
Extract from Jefferson's "Notes on Virginia" (Barton ed., p. 65) praising Logan's speech to Gov. Dumore, 1774.

Johnson, Emily Pauline
Flint and Feather (collected verse), including poem written during her final illness; with introduction by Theodore Watts-Dunton; illustrated by J. R. Seavey. Toronto: Musson Book Co., n.p., 1916. xxx, 166 pp.

Kallay, U. von
"Die zweierlei Farbenortungen einiger Indianer-Stämme Nordamerika's." *Mitteil. Anthro. Gesell.* 69:11–23, 1939.

Keiser, Albert
The Indian in American Literature. New York: Oxford University Press, 1933. vi, 312 pp., bibl.

Kelemen, Pál
Medieval American Art. New York: The Macmillan Co., 1943. 2 vols. xiv, 414 pp., 960 photographs in 306 plates.

Krieger, H. W.
"American Indian Costumes in the United States National Museum." *Annual Reports Smithson. Inst.,* pp. 623–661, 1928.

———.
"Aspects of Original Decorative Art in America." *Annual Reports Smithson. Inst.,* pp. 519–556, 1930.

Kroeber, A. L.
"The Languages of the American Indians." *Scientific Monthly* (New York), pp. 500–515, 1911.

———.
"Noun Composition in American Languages." *Anthropos* 5:204–218, 1910.

Latham, R. G.
"On the Languages of Northern, Western, and Central America." *Trans. Philological Soc.,* pp. 57–115, 1856.

Leechman, D.
"Arts and the Aborigines." *Queens Quarterly* 49:252–260, 1942.
   Canadian Indians.

Lemos, Pedro Joseph
Indian Decorative Design. Worcester, Mass.: The School Arts Magazine, 1926. 4 pp., 28 pl.

Liebler, H. B.
"Christian Concepts and Navaho Words." *Utah Humanities Review* 2 (No. 2):169–175, 1948.
   A study of the impact of European Christian culture upon the Navaho people, and the inevitable linguistic changes brought upon Navaho speech.

Linton, Ralph C.
"Primitive Art." *Kenyon Review* 3:34–51, Jan. 1941.

Logan, John Capt. (Mingo Chief)
"Letter." *The American Pioneer* 1:15, Jan., 1842 (NYU).
   Copy of the letter to Capt. M. Cresap, 1774, asking him why he killed his kin on Yellow Creek.

Lotrich, Victor F.
"Indian Terms for the Cradle and the Cradleboard." *The Colorado Magazine* 28:81–109. Denver: State Museum, 1941.

Ludewig, Hermann Ernst
The Literature of American Aboriginal Languages. London: Trubner and Co., 1858. xxiv, 258 pp.

Mallery, Garrick
"Pictographs of the North American Indians— A Preliminary Paper." In: *The 4th Annual Report of the Bureau of Ethnology* (pp. 3–256). Washington, D. C.: U. S. Government Printing Office, 1886, pl. I–LXXXIII, fig. 1–111, 111a–209.

———.
"Picture-Writing of the American Indians." *10th Annual Report: Bureau of American Ethnology,* 1888–1889, pp. 25–277, pls. I–LIV, figs. 1–1290. Washington, D. C.: U. S. Gov't Printing Office, 1893.
   Petroglyphs; in North America (Canada, U.S.), Mexico, West Indies, etc.; sections, substances of which they are made, their symbolic meaning, etc.

Mason, Bernard S.
The Book of Indian Crafts and Costumes. Illustrated by Frederick H. Koch. New York: A. S. Barnes & Co., 1946. 269 pp., illus.

Mason, Otis T.
"Aboriginal American Basketry." *Report U. S. National Museum,* pp. 171–548. Washington, D. C.: U. S. Government Printing Office, 1902.

———.
"Aboriginal American Harpoons." *Reports U. S. Nat. Mus.* Part 2:193–304, 1900.

———.
"Basket-Work of the North American Aborigines." *Report to Smithsonian Institution,* (Part 2):591–603. Washington, D. C.: U. S. Government Printing Office, 1885.

———.
"Overlaying with Copper by the American Aborigines." *Proc. U. S. Nat. Mus.* 17:475–477, 1894.

———.
"The Technic of Aboriginal American Basketry." *AA* 3:109–128, 1901. n.s.

McGuire, Joseph Deakins
"Anthropological Information in Early American Writings." *Proceedings of the 13th Session of the International Congress of Americanists* pp. 17–27, 1902.

Michelson, Truman
"Remarks on American Indian Languages." *Jour. Wash. Acad. Sci.* (Washington) 7:222–234, 1917.

Moore, J., and Thorpe, H. G.
"How the World Began: A Shadow Play in 2 Acts." *Horn Book* 17:130–141, March, 1941.

Moorehead, Warren King
Stone Ornaments Used by Indians in the United States and Canada. Andover: The Andover Press, 1917. 448 pp., illus.
   A description of charm stones, gorgets, tubes, and bird stones.

Morang, Dorothy
"Modern Designs Inspired by Ancient Indian Arts". *El Palacio* 54(No. 11):270–271, 1947.

Niles, Hezekiah
"Indian Names." *Niles' Weekly Register* 43: 169, Nov. 10, 1832.
   An editorial in which the Editor, after examining and comparing a number of Indian names and English names, concludes that the Indian names are not so bad at all.

Oetteking, B.
"Über die geschichtliche Entwicklung der indianischen Volksdichte." *Zeit. für Rassen.* 3: 171–176, 1936.

Orchard, William C.
"The Technique of Porcupine-Quill Decoration Among the North American Indians." *Contributions of the Museum of the American Indian, Heye Foundation.* Vol. 4, No. 1. New York, 1916. 753 pp.

———.
"Beads and Beadwork of the American Indians." *Contr. Mus. Amer. Ind.* 11:3–140, 1929.

Parker, Arthur Caswell
The Indian How Book. New York: George H. Doran Company, 1927. ix, 335 pp., illus.

Parsons, Elsie Clews
"Riddles and Metaphors Among Indian Peoples." *JAFL* 49:171–174, 1936.

Powell, J. W.
"On the Evolution of Languages." In: *1st Annual Report of Bureau of American Ethnology* (pp. 3–8 1879–1880. Washington, D. C.: U. S. Government Printing Office, 1881.
"The evaluation of languages as exhibited in the specialization of the grammatic processes, the differentiation of the parts of speech, and the integration of the sentence: from a study of Indian Languages."

———.
"Indian Linguistic Families of America North of Mexico." *Annual Reports, Bur. Amer. Ethno.* 7:7–139, 1891. Washington, D. C.

———.
Introduction to the Study of Indian Languages. Washington: 1880. 228 pp.

———.
"Stone Art in America." *AA* 8:1–7, 1895.

Putnam, F. W.
"Conventionalism in American Art." *Bull. Essex Institute* (Salem) 18:155–167, 1887.

Radin, Paul
Literary Aspects of North American Mythology. Geol. Surv. of Can., Anthropol. Ser. No. 16. Ottawa: 1915.

———.
"The Genetic Relationship of the North American Indian Languages." *Univ. Cal. Publ. Amer. Arch. Ethno.* 14:489–502, 1919.

Rau, C.
"Observations on Cup-shaped and Other Lapidarian Sculptures." *Contr. North Amer. Ethno.* 5:1–104, 1881.

Ray, Grace Ernestine
Early Oklahoma Papers. New York: 1923. 76 pp. (NYPL).
Reproductions of a thesis submitted by the School of Journalism in the University of Oklahoma, in 1922. Cites also examples of early Indian literary efforts.

Reade, John
"Aboriginal American Poetry." *Royal Society of Canada. Proceedings and Transactions* (Montreal) 5 (No. 2):9–34, 1888.

Red Jacket (1751-1830).
"Speech." *The Telescope* 1:53–54, Sept. 4, 1824.
In answer to Rev. Alexander, missionary. A specimen of Indian eloquence and sentiment.

Reichard, Gladys A.
"Literary Types and Dissemination of Myths." *JAFL* 34:269–307, 1921.

Renaud, E. B.
"The Tempering of Indian Pottery from the United States." *El Palacio* (Santa Fé) 22: 378–389, 1927.

Rickard, T. A.
"The Use of Native Copper by the Indigenes of North America." *Jour. Anthro. Inst. Gt. Brit.* 64:265–287, 1934.

Riehl, Frank C.
Poems of the Piasa. Alton, Ill.: Melling and Gaskins, 1896. 172 pp.

———.
Runes of the Red Race. Alton, Ill.: Melling and Gaskins, 1899. 190 pp.

Rivet, P.
Langues de l'Amérique du nord. In: *Les Langues du Monde.* (pp. 607–628,) A. Meillet and M. Cohen, eds. Paris: 1924.

Riviere, Georges Henri
Les Arts Ancients de l'Amérique. Paris: Les Éditions G. Van Oest, 1928.

Robinson, Walter Wallace
Mojave Rhymes. Los Angeles, Cal.: The Austin Publishing Co., 1924. 80 pp., illus.

Robinson, William
"Logan, the Indian Chief." *The American Pioneer* 1:15–16, Jan., 1842 (NYU).
The author's declaration concerning Logan's statement to him, while his prisoner, that Capt. Cresap killed his family.

Rollins, A. R.
"Notes on Indian Dolls." *Hobbies* 47:26, 1942.

Roth, H. L.
"American Quillwork: a Possible Clue to Its Origin." *Man* 23:113–116, 1923.

———.
"Mocassins and Their Quill Work." *Jour. Anthro. Inst. Gt. Brit.* 38:47–57, 1908.

Sapir, Edward
"Language and Environment." *AA* 14:226–243, 1912. n.s.

———.
Central and North American Languages. In: *Encyclopedia Brittanica,* 14th Edition. Vol. 5, pp. 138–141, 1929.

"The Problem of Noun Incorporation in American Languages." *AA* 13:250–282, 1911. n.s.

Sapper, K.
"Die Zahl und Volks dichte der indianischen Bevölkerung in Amerika." *Proc. Inter. Congr. Amer.* 21:95–104, 1924.

Sarett, Lew R.
The Box of God. New York: H. Holt & Co., 1935. 89 pp.
Poems on Indian themes.

————.
Many Many Moons; a book of wilderness poems, with an introduction by Carl Sandburg. New York: H. Holt and Company, 1920. xvi, 84 pp.

Schoolcraft, Henry Rowe
Helderbergia or *The Apotheosis of the Heroes of the Antirent War.* Albany: J. Munsell, 1855. 54 pp.
Poem.

————.
"Mohegan Language and Geographical Names." *The Knickerbocker* 10:214–216, Sept., 1837 (NYU).

————, **(translator)**
"Utterances of Alacol, an Indian Poet." *Knickerbocker* 58:112–114, Aug., 1861 (NYU). An allegory of the Wolf and the Dog, the Blue Jay and the Woodpecker, and the Crane and the Beaver.

Sibley
"Indian Opinions." *Niles' Weekly Register* 23: 20, Sept. 14, 1822 (NYU).
Extracts from a letter to Dr. Morse, in which he sets forth the opinion of the "Big Soldier," an Osage, on the white and Indian culture.

Sky, John
"Indian Eloquence." *The Weekly Register* 2: 81–82, April 4, 1812.
Speech delivered at the council of Batavia, N. Y., assuring the inhabitants of that village that the Red Man no longer wants war, but is determined to live in peace and harmony with his white brothers.

Sloan, John, and La Farge, Oliver
Introduction to American Indian Art. Exposition of Indian Tribal Arts, Inc., 1931. 55 pp., 32 plates.

Smith, H. I.
"Primitive Work in Skin." *So. Workman* 40: 515–520, 1911.

Smith, Maurice G.
"American Indian Tribal Names." *AS* 5:114–117, 1929.

Smith, William
Indian Songs of Peace: with a proposal, in a prefatory epistle for erecting Indian schools. And a postscript by the editor, introducing Yariza, an Indian maid's letter, to the principal ladies of the province and city of New York. By the author of the American fables. New York: Printed by J. Parker, and W. Wayman, 1752. 27 pp.

————.
Some Account of the North-American Indians; their genius, characters, customs, and dispositions, toward the French and English nations. To which are added, Indian miscellanies, viz. 1. The Speech of a Creek-Indian against the Immoderate use of Spirituous Liquors; delivered in a national assembly of the Creeks, upon the breaking out of the late war. 2. A Letter from Yariza, an Indian maid of the royal line of the Mohawks, to the principal ladies of New York. 3. Indian Songs of Peace. 4. An American Fable. Collected by a learned and ingenious gentleman in the province of Pennsylvania. London: Printed for R. Griffiths, 1754. viii, 68 pp.

Spencer, Lilian White
Arrowheads. New York: The Parade Publishing Company, 1929. 64 pp., illus.
A book of poems.

————.
"Fine Art and the First Americans." *Leaflets of the Exposition of Indian Tribal Arts* (New York). 1931. 8 pp.

Stearns, R. E. C.
"Ethno-Conchology." *Reports U. S. Nat. Mus.*, pp. 297–334, 1887.

Steward, Julian H.
"Petroglyphs of the United States." *Annual Reports Smithson. Inst.*, pp. 405–425, 1936.

Spinden, Herbert Joseph
"American Indian Poetry." *Natural History* 19:301–308, also in *El Palacio* 7 (2):34–40.

————.
Songs of the Tewa ... preceded by an essay on American Indian poetry, with a selection of outstanding compositions from North and South America; an appendix contains original Tewa texts and explanatory notes. New York: Published Under the Auspices of the Exposition of Indian Tribal Arts, 1933. 125 pp.

"The Indian in Literature."
The Critic 9:313, Dec. 25, 1886 (NYU).

Ten-Kate, Herman F. C.
"The Indian in Literature." *Smithsonian Report* 1921. pp. 507–528. Washington, D. C.: U. S. Government Printing Office, 1921.

————.
"On Paintings of North American Indians and Their Ethnographical Value." *Anthropos* 6: 521–545, 1911.

————.
Introduction to the Study of North American Archaeology. Cincinnati: The Robert Clarke Co., 1898. xiv, 391 pp., illus.

The Four Indian Kings.
Part I. How a beautiful lady conquered one of the Indian Kings. Part II. The Lady's answer. London: n.p., 1710.

Thomas, Cyrus
Catalogue of Prehistoric Works East of the Rocky Mts. Bureau of American Ethnology, Bull. 12, pp. 1–246, pls. 1–17, all maps. Washington, D. C.: U. S. Gov't Printing Office, 1891.

————.
"Report on the Mound Explorations of the Bureau of Ethnology." *12th Annual Report: Bureau of American Ethnology.* 1890–1891. pp. 17–722, plt. I–XLII, figs. 1–344. Washington, D. C.: U. S. Gov't Printing Office, 1894.

W., H. Y.
"Meaning of the Indian names of Penobscot and Kennebec." *The Ladies Repository* 24: 631, Oct., 1864.
Essay on Indian languages, especially the Algonquin group, and numerous dialects.

The Parting and Return of Three Indians, Who Graduated from Dartmouth College. Boston: n.p., 1840.

Uhlenbeck, C. C.
"Zu den einheimischen Sprachen Nord-Amerikas." *Anthropos* 5:779–786, 1910.

Underhill, Ruth M.
"Vocabulary and Style in Indian Language." *AS* 9 (No. 4):279–282, 1934.

United States. American Ethnology Bureau.
Circular of Information Regarding Indian Popular Names. Washington: Gov't Prtg. Off., 1915. 8 pp.

Utzinger, R.
Indianer Kunst. München: 1921.

Vaillant, G. C.
Indian Arts in North America. New York: Harper & Bros., 1939. 63 pp., illus.

Voegelin, C. F.
"Relative Chronology of North American Linguistics." *AA* 47 (No. 2):232–234, 1945.

————, and Harris, Z. S.
"Linguistics in Ethnology." *Southwestern Journal in Anthropology* 1 (No. 4):455–565, 1945.

Walton, Eda Lou, and Waterman, T. T.
"American Indian Poetry." *AA* 27:25–52, 1925. n.s.

Waterman, T. T.
"The Architecture of the American Indians." In: *Source Book in Anthropology,* (pp. 512–524). A. L. Kroeber and T. T. Waterman, eds. New York: Harcourt, Brace & Co., 1931. viii, 571 pp., illus.

Webber, George
The Last of the Aborigines. A poem founded on facts. In four cantos. St. John's, N. F.: Printed at the Office of "The Morning Post," 1851. 40 pp.

Weltfish, Gene
"Prehistoric North American Basketry Techniques and Modern Distribution." *AA* 32:454–495, 1930. n.s.

————.
"Problems in the Study of Ancient and Modern Basket-Makers." *AA* 34:108–117, 1932. n.s.

Westlake, Inez B.
American Indian Designs. Philadelphia: H. C. Perlberg, 1925–30. 2 vols., illus.
Illustrations of prehistoric design, highly valuable and informative.

Whitney, C. F.
Indian Designs and Symbols. Salem, Mass.: Newcomb & Gauss, 1925. 55 pp., illus.

Williams, Roger
A Key into the Language of America. Introduction by Howard M. Chapin. Providence, R. I.: Roger Williams Press; Washington, D. C.: Statesman Press, 1936. 205 pp.
"A reprint from the original edition of 1643, of the first work in English on the Indian language."

Wissler, Clark
"Indian Costumes in the United States." *American Museum of Natural History Guide Leaflet Series* (New York) 43:1–32, 1931.

————.
"A Psycho-Physical Element in Primitive Art." In: *Anthropological Papers. Boas Anniversary Volume* (pp. 189–193). New York: G. E. Stechert & Co., 1906.

————.
"Poetry and Music of Some North American Tribes." *Science* 9:383–385, 1897.

FOLK MEDICINE

Ackerknecht, Erwin H.
"On the Collecting of Data Concerning Primitive Medicine." *AA* 47 (3):427–431, 1945.

————.
"Primitive Autopsies and the History of Anatomy." *Bulletin of the History of Medicine* 13:334–339, 1943.

————.
"Primitive Medicine and Culture Pattern." *Bulletin of the History of Medicine* 12:545–574, 1942.

————.
"Problems of Primitive Medicine" *Bulletin of the History of Medicine* 11:503–521. 1942.
Contains valuable and extensive bibliography on primitive medicine, 518–521.

————.
"Psychopathology, Primitive Medicine and Primitive Culture." *Bulletin of the History of Medicine* 14:30–67, 1943.

"The Development of Our Knowledge of Malaria." *Ciba Symposia* 7(3 & 4) :38–50, 1945. Primitive medicine and cures.

"Medicine Through the Ages. . ." Reprinted from *The Merck Report:* July 1946, Oct. 1946, and Jan. 1947.

"The Treatment and Prevention of Malaria." *Ciba Symposia* 7:(3 & 4) 57–62, 1945. Primitive Cures and Medicines.

"Bibliography of the Peyote Cult" *AA* 40:712–715, 1938. n.s. At end of article, "The Appeal of Peyote," by Richard Evans Schultes.

Black, W. G.
Folk Medicine. London: Folklore Society, 1883.

Brinton, Daniel Garrison
"Nagualism, a Study in Native American Folklore and History." *Proceedings, American Philosophical Society*, Vol. 33, 1894.

Bromberg, W.
"Storm Over Peyote." *Nature* 35:410–412, 1942.

Brown, R.
"A Doctor's Life Among the North American Indians." Illustrated. *The Ladies Repository* 32:114–122, Aug. 1872. An essay on the faith of the Indians in their medicine men.

Clements, Forrest Edward
Primitive Concepts of Disease. Berkeley, Calif.: University of California Press, 1932. 252 pp., illus., bibl., (California University. Publications in American Archaeology and Ethnology. V. 32, No. 2).

Cooper, J. W.
The Experienced Botanist; or, Indian Physician, Being a New System of Practice, Founded on Botany; containing 1. A description of medical plants — their properties, &c., and the method of preparing and using them. 2. A Treatise on the causes, symptoms and cure of diseases . . . For the use of families and practioners. Lancaster, Pa.: Printed for the Author . . . John Bear, printer, 1840. xxi, 303 pp.

Corlett, William Thomas
The Medicine-Man of the American Indian and His Cultural Background. Springfield, Ill.: Charles C. Thomas, 1935. 369 pp., illus.

Coville, Frederick V.
Directions for Collecting Specimens, and Information Illustrating Aboriginal Uses of Plants. Washington: Government Printing Office, 1895. 8 pp., (Smithsonian Institution. Part J. of Bulletin of the U. S. National Museum, No. 39.)

D'Arcy, McNickle
"Peyote and the Indian." *Scientific Monthly* 57 (No. 3) :1943.

Densmore, Frances
"The Study of Indian Medicine." *Smithsonian Report for 1941* pp. 527–550, illus. 1942. Washington, D. C.: U. S. Government Printing Office, 1942.

Diguet, L.
"Le Peyote." *Journal de la Société des Américanistes de Paris.* 4:25, 1907. n.s.

Douglas, F. H., and Marriott, Alice
"Metal Jewelry of the Peyote Cult." *Material Culture Notes* 17:17–82, 1942. (Denver Art Museum.)

Fernberger, Samuel
"Observations on Taking Peyote." *American Journal of Psychology*, Vol. 34, 1923.

"Further Observations on Peyote Intoxication." *Journal of Abnormal and Social Psychology* 26 (No. 4) 1932.

Fletcher, Robert
On Prehistoric Trephining and Cranial Amulets. Washington: U. S. Gov't Prtg. Off., 1882. 32 pp. (In: Contributions to North American Ethnology. v. 5.)

Freeman, L.
"Surgery of the Ancient Inhabitants of America." *Art and Archaeology* (Baltimore) 18:21–36, 1924.

Greene, Reuben
Indianopathy; or, Science of Indian Medicine. Founded upon the "Laws of Nature," the Principles of which were obtained by Dr. Greene in his travels among the Indians. Boston: Publ. by order of the Board of Managers, 1858. 82 pp., illus.

Gusinde, M.
Der Peyote-Kult. In: *Festschrift zum 50 jahrigen Bestandsjubiläum des Missionhaus St. Gabriel*, pp. 401–498. Wien: 1939.

Guttman, Erich
"Artificial Psychoses Produced by Mescaline." *Journal of Mental Science* May, 1936.

Haines, Elijah M.
The American Indian. Chapt. 23. Chicago: The Mas-sin-ná-gan Co., 1888.

Hallowell, A. Irving
"The Bulbed Enema Syringe in North America." *AA* 37:708–710, 1935.

"Primitive Concepts of Disease." *AA* 37:365–368, 1935.

"Psychic Stresses and Culture Patterns." *American Journal of Psychiatry* 92 (No. 6): 1291–1310, May, 1936.

Hollander, A. N. J. den
"De Peyote-Cultus der Noordamerikaansche Indianen." *Mensch en Maatschaapij* 11:17–29, 123–131, 1935.

Hrdlicka, Ales
"Disease Medicine, and Surgery Among the American Aborigines." *Journal of the American Medical Association* 99:1661–1666, 1932.

———.
Medicine and Medicine Men. In: *Handbook of the American Indians North of Mexico*, F. W. Hodge, editor. Vol. I, pp. 836–839. Bureau of American Ethnology, Bulletin 30. Washington, D. C.: U. S. Government Printing Office, 1907.

Humphrey, W. B.
North American Indian Folk-lore; Medicine. New York: The American Indian League, 1911.

Jayne, Walter Addison
The Healing Gods of Ancient Civilization. New Haven: Yale University Press, 1925. xxxix, 569 pp., bibl.

Jenness, Diamond
"An Indian Method of Treating Hysteria." *Primitive Man* 6 (No. 1):13–19, 1933. Catholic Anthro. Conference, Washington, D. C., January, 1933.

Joseph, Alice
"Physician and Patient, with Special Regard to the Relationship between White Physicians and Indian Patients." *Applied Anthropology* 1:1–6, 1942. (Boston)

Karwoski, Theodore
"Psychophysics and Mescal Intoxication." *Journal of Genearl Psychology* 15 (No. 1): 212–220. 1936.

Klüver, Heinrich
Mescal, the "Divine" Plant and its Physiological Effects. London: R. Paul, Trench, Trübner and Company, 1928. viii, 111 pp. Bibl. (pp. 110–111.)

Krogman, W. M.
"Medical Practices and Diseases of the Aboriginal American Indians." *Ciba Symposia* 1:11–18, 1939.

La Barre, Weston
The Peyote Cult. Yale University Publications in Anthropology, 19. New Haven: Yale University Press, 1938. 190 pp.

Leighton, Dorothea C.
"Il Indio y la Medicina." *America Indigena* 3 (No. 2):127–133, 1943.

Loeb, Edwin M.
"Primitive Intoxicants." *Quarterly Journal of Studies on Alchol* 4:387–398, 1943.

Maddox, J. L.
"The Spirit Theory in Early Medicine." *AA* 32:503–521, 1930. n.s.

Millais, Amalia
"Folklore: curanderos indígenes, medicena indígena." *Actividad Medica* (Mexico, D. F.) No. 5:29–30, 1942.

Mooney, James
"Indian Navel-Cord." *JAFL* 17:197, 1904.

———.
"Mescal plant and ceremony." *Therapeutic Gazette* (3rd series): vol. 12.

Munro, Thomas
"Art and Medicine in Ancient and Primitive Cultures." *Medical Library Association. Bulletin* 32:304–317, 1944. illus.

Newberne, Robert E. L.
Peyote: an Abridged Compilation. Washington, D. C.: U. S. Dep't of the Interior, Office of Indian Affairs, 1922. 38 pp.

Pardal, Ramon
"Las Drogas estupefacientes e illusiogenes del indio americano." *Revista Geografica Americana* (Buenos Aires) 6:1–22, 1936. illus.

Part, Louis
Die Medizin der amerikanischen Indianer. Lausanne: Imprimerie Held, 1937. 18 pp., bibl.

Podolsky, E.
"Use of Music as a Healing Agent Among the Indians." *Etude* 52:434, July 1934.

Reagan, Albert B.
"Medicine Songs of George Farmer." *AA* 24:332–369, 1922.

Rouhier, Alexandre
La Plante Qui Fait les Yeux Emerveillés: Le Peyotl (Echinocactus Williamsi Lem.) Préface de M.le Professeur Em. Perrot. Paris: G. Doin et Cie, 1927. xii, 371, illus., includes music, map, bibl. (pp. 359–367).

"Scarification."
In: *Handbook of American Indians* Vol. II, pp. 484–485. Bibl. Bureau of American Ethnology, Bulletin 30. Washington, D. C.: U. S. Government Printing Office, 1910.
Sacrification consists in cutting the skin with any suitable instrument for the purpose of extracting blood producing suffering, or bringing about a scar.... Its objects were (1) medicinal; (2) ceremonial, or emotional; and (3) cosmetic."

Schmiz, Karl
"Die Medizinmanner und ihre besondere Veranlagung." *Deutsche Revue* (Stuttgart) 47:223–231, 1922.

Schultes, Richard Evans
"Peyote—an American Indian Heritage from Mexico." *Mexico Antiguo* 4:199–208, 1938.

———.
"Peyote and Plants Used in the Peyote Ceremony." *Botanical Museum Leaflets*, Harvard University, 4, (No. 8), 1937. pp. 129–152.

———. "The Appeal of Peyote (Lophophora Williamsii) as a Medicine." *AA* 40:698–715, 1938. n.s.

Sharron, J.
The Beauties of the Healing Art, . . . containing numerous medical receipts, which have oft-times, been the means of saving many lives, cures, chiefly performed from the virtues of the vegetable creation. Philadelphia: J. Sharron, 1830. 12 pp.

Smith, Peter
The Indian Doctor's Dispensatory, being Father Smith's advice respecting diseases and their cure. Cincinnati: Browne & Looker, 1813. xxii, 108 pp. (Reprint—Bulletin of the Lloyd Library of Botany. . . . No. 2, 1901.)

Speck, Frank G.
"Notes on the Life of John Wilson: Revealer of Peyote." *General Magazine and Historical Chronicle* Vol. 35, 1933.

Steward, J. D.
"Did the American Indians Use the Cantery in Bone Surgery?" *American Journal of Physical Anthropology* 23:83–88, 1937.

Stone, Eric
Medicine Among the American Indians. New York: P. B. Hoeber. Inc., 1932. xv, 139 pp., illus., bibl.

Taylor, Norma
"Come and Expel the Green Pain; Use of Peyotl and Ololiuqui." *Scientific Monthly* 58:176–184, 1944.

Toner, Joseph Meredith
Address before the Rocky Mountain Medical Association, June 6, 1877, containing some observations on the geological age of the world, the appearance of animal life upon the globe, the antiquity of man, and the archaeological remains of extinct races found on the American continent; with views of the origin and practice of medicine among uncivilized races, more especially the North American Indians. Washington: Pub. for the Association, 1877. 112 pp.

Truesdale, S. E.
"Buffalo-chips as a remedy." *JAFL* 12:295, 1899.

United States. Indian Affairs Office
Peyote. An abridged compilation from the files of the Bureau of Indian Affairs. . . . Washington, D. C.: Gov't. Print. Off., 1922. 38 pp.

Unkalunt, Atalie
The Earth Speaks. New York: Fleming H. Revell Company, 1940. 223 pp., illus.

White, John
"Signification of Hockhocking and Wheeling." *The American Pioneer* 1:38, Jan. 1842 (NYU). Explanation of the Indian words, also cures for a rattlesnake bite.

Whitebread, Charles
The Indian Medical Exhibit of the Division of Medicine in the United States National Museum. Washington: n. p.. 1925. 26 pp., illus., (In: U. S. National Museum. Proceedings. V. 67, Art. 10.).

Wissler, Clark
"The Medicine Pipe." *American Museum Journal* (N. Y.) 11:24–26, 1911.

Wittrack, Marion A. and G. L.
Food and Drug Plants of the North American Indians. New York:Botanical Gardens, 1942.

Youngken, H. W.
"Drugs of the North American Indians." *American Journal of Pharmacy* 96:482–502, 97:158–185, 257–271, 1924–1925.

PROVERBS—RIDDLES

Chamberlain, A. F.
"Race Character and Local Color in Proverbs." *JAFL* 17:28–31, 1904.

Muntsch, Albert
"American Indian Riddles." *JAFL* 54:85, 1941.

Parsons, Elsie Clews
"Riddles and Metaphors Among Indian Peoples." *JAFL* 49:171–174, 1936.

Taylor, Archer
"American Indian Riddles." *JAFL* 57:1–16, 1944.

GAMES

See: Indian Music, pp. 810-18; Indian Dances, pp. 818-19.

Culin, Stewart
"American Indian Games." *JAFL* 11:245–252, 1898.

———. "American Indian Games." *AA* 5: 58–65, 1903 n.s.

———. Indian Games. In: *Handbook of the American Indians North of Mexico,* F. W. Hodge, editor. 1:483–486. Washington, D. C.: U. S. Government Printing Office, 1907.

———. "Games of the North American Indians." *24th Annual Report, Bureau American Ethnology:* 1902–1903, pp. 1–811; pls. 1–21, figs., 1–1112. Washington, D. C.: U. S. Gov't. Printing Office, 1907.

Curtis, Natalie
Games. In: *The Indians' Book,* pp. 7, 158, 161, 162, 201, 202, 332. New York: Harper and Brothers, 1907.

Darlington, H. S.
"The Probable Origin of Some North American Dice Games." *Anthropos* 25:303–310, 1930.

Davis, A. M.
"Indian Games." *Bulletin of the Essex Institute* (Salem) 17:89–144, 1885.

Densmore, Frances
Games. In: *The American Indians and Their Music,* pp. 40–44. New York: The Womans Press, 1936.
See her studies on Indian music for more bibliography on games.

Fletcher, Alice C.
Indian Games and Dances, with native songs, arranged from American Indian Ceremonials and Sports. Boston: C. C. Birchard and Company, 1915. 139 pp., music.

Poast, F. M.
Indian Names, Facts and Games for Campfire Girls. Washington, D. C.: James William Bryan Press, 1916. 78 pp., illus. (1 mounted).

Stow, E.
Boy's Games Among the North American Indians. Illustrated by Hugh Spencer. New York: E. P. Dutton & Co., 1924. x, 126 pp., illus.

INDIAN MUSIC

INDIAN MUSIC

See: Bibliography, pp. 750-53; Serial Publications, pp. 753-54.

BIBLIOGRAPHY

Bibliography.
List of Publications of the Bureau of American Ethnology, with index to authors and titles. Revised to June 30, 1937. Washington, D. C.: U. S. Government Printing Office, 1937.

"Bibliography of music and books, founded on Indian themes and subjects, with list of phonograph records." *Etude* 38: 667–668, 1920.

Conover, H. F.
A Selected List of Books on the Indians of North America. United States Library of Congress, Division of Bibliography. Washington, D. C.: The Library, 1939, 25 pp. (mimeograph).

Densmore, Frances
"Bibliography of Her Work." *The Journal of Musicology* 4 (Nos. 2 and 3):103–109, 1945.
An excellent listing of her writings in and contributions to the field of American Indian music from the year 1901 to 1945.

Gaines, Ruth, comp.
"Books on Indians—1929." *Indian Notes* (New York) 7: 207–236, 1930.

————.
Books on Indian Arts North of Mexico. New York: The Exposition of Indian Tribal Arts, 1931. 15 pp.

Herzog, George
Research in Primitive and Folk Music in the United States. American Council of Learned Societies, Bulletin No. 24 (pp. 33–36). Washington, D. C.: U. S. Government Printing Office, (April) 1936.

Howard, John Tasker
Our American Music; Three Hundred Years of it. New York: Thomas Y. Crowell Company, 1939. 748 pp., illustrated, bibl. (pp. 678–680).

Hubbard, Ralph
American Indian Crafts, Including suggestive outlines and bibliography of Indian lore. New York: Plume Trading & Sales Co., 1935. 64 pp., illus., bibl.

Lesser, Alexander
"Bibliography of American Folklore, 1915–1928" (pp. 2–21, 28–36, 47–52).*JAFL* 41: 1–60, 1928.

Mattfeld, Julius
"Folk Music of the Western Hemisphere Survey List of References in the New York Public Library." *Bulletin of the New York Public Library* (pp. 11–34, 38–46 November, December, 1924.

Toomey, Thomas Noxon
Bibliography of Lesser North American Linguistic Families. St. Louis, Missouri: Hervas Laboratories, 1917, 20 pp.

GENERAL STUDIES AND COLLECTIONS

See: Arrangements below.

Albrecht, Adalbert
"Indianische Musik." *Die Zeit* No. 500, pp. 57–58, 1904.

Alexander, Hartley
"Indian Songs and English Verse." *AS* 1 (No.-11):571–575, 1926.

————.
Manito Masks. Dramatizations with Music, of American Indian Spirit Legends. Illustrated by John Haugseth. New York: Dutton and Co., 1925. 209 pp.

"American Indian Music."
Etude 38: 667–668, 1920.

Anderson, Arthur Olaf
"Geography and Rhythm." *Fine Arts Bulletin* 2: (November 15) 1935. Tucson, Arizona: University of Arizona, Volume I, No. 8.

Armstrong, William
"The American Indian Legend in Music—Its Possibilities." *Music* 16:119–124, 1899.

Austin, Mary
"American Indian Dance Drama." *Yale Review* (Battleboro) 29: 732–745, 1930.

————.
Indian Poetry. In: *Introduction to American Indian Art,* Part 2. New York: Exposition of Tribal Arts, 1931. 5 pp.

————.
"Non-English Writings: Aboriginal." In: *The Cambridge History of American Literature* ed. by Trent, Erskine, Sherman and Van Doren. Vol. III (pp. 610–635). New York: The Macmillan Co., 1917. 3 Vols. Reprinted in 1 Vol. in 1945.
General discussions of Amerindian literature, deals among many other interesting subjects, with Rhythm, Folk tales, Poetry, Poetic forms, Myths, Drama, Rituals, Delight Maker, Night Chant, etc.

————.
"Songs of the American Indian; Re-expressed from the Originals." *Harper Magazine* (New York) 143: 77–80, 1921.

————.
The American Rhythm: Studies and Re-expression of American Indian Songs. Boston: Houghton Mifflin Company, 1930. 174 pp. New and enlarged edition.

Baker, Theodore
Über die Musik der Nordamerikanischen Wilden. Leipzig: Breitkopf and Härtel, 1882.
On the music of the North American Indian. A doctoral dissertation. Among the first scientific attempts to analyze and study Indian music.

Balfour, H.
"Note Upon Musical Bows." *AA* 11: 187, 1898, o. s.

Bancroft, Hubert Howe
Manner of Singing and Dancing. In: *The Native Races of the Pacific States of North America,* Volume III, (Chapter VIII). New York: D. Appleton and Company, 1875.

Barbeau, M.
"Asiatic Survivals in Indian Songs." *Queen's Quarterly* 47(No. I): 67–76, (February) 1940.

"Asiatic Survivals in Indian Songs." *Scientific Monthly* 54: 303–307, 1942.

"Asiatic Survivals in Indian Songs." *MQ* 20: 107–116, 1934.

————, and Melvin, Grace
The Indian Speaks. Toronto: The Macmillan Company, 1943.
The American Indian as he expressed himself in myths, songs and stories.

Barber, Edwin A.
"Indian Music." *American Naturalist* 17: 267–274, 1883.
Mainly with the Indians of Central and South America. Reference to North American Indians also.

Barnes, Nellie
"American Indian Verse; Characteristics of Style." *Humanistic Studies Bulletin* 2(No. 4): 1921, Bibliography pp. 57–61. Lawrence: The University of Kansas.

American Indian Love Lyrics and Other Verses: from the Songs of the North American Indians. Foreword by Mary Austin. New York: The Macmillan Co., 1926. 190 pp.

Boas, Franz
Literature, Music and Dance. In: *General Anthropology,* ed. by Franz Boas. Literature pp. 589. Music, pp. 602. Dance, pp. 605. Boston: D.C. Heath and Co., 1938. xi, 718 pp., illus.

Music and Folk-lore. In: *General Anthropology* (pp. 609–626). Boston: D. C. Heath and Company, 1938.

Primitive Art. Cambridge, Massachusetts: Harvard University Press, Institute for Comparative Culture Research, 1927. 376 pp., Chapter on Primitive Literature, Music and Drama, illustrated.

Boettcher, Dorothea
"Indianer Musik." *Berliner Tageblatt,* 1903, p. 32, no. 193.

Bonner, Aletha M.
"Musical Messages From Many Lands. I. The Indian and His Music." *Music and Youth* 4(No. 8):213, 221, May, 1929.

Botsford, Florence H., comp. and ed.
The Botsford Collection of Folk Songs. New York: G. Schirmer, 1930.
Volume I contains 9 American Indian Songs.

Bourke, John G.
"Song of the Ancient People." *JAFL* 6: 71–72, 1893.

Brinton, Daniel
"Native American Stringed Instruments." *Amer. Antiquarian* 19:19–20, 1897.

Brisbin, James S.
"The Poetry of Indians." *Harper's Magazine* (New York) 57: 104–108, 1878.

Broekhoven, John A. Van
"American Indian Music." *Musical Observer* (New York)5(No. 4): 17–18, 1911.

Bromfield, Louis
"From Tribal Drums and Lover's Flutes Await the American Composer." *Musical America* (New York) 40(No. 21): 5, 19, 1924.

Brown, James Duff
Characteristic Songs and Dances of All Nations. Music arranged for pianoforte by Alfred Moffat. London: Bayley & Ferguson, 1901.

Brown, Mary E. A., and Adams, William
Musical Instruments and their Homes. The whole forming a complete catalogue of the collection of musical instruments now in the possession of Mrs. J. Crosby Brown. New York: Dodd, Mead and Co. 1888, xvii, 380 pp. incl. plates.
Includes a large list of instruments of the Indians of North America.

Burton, Frederick Russell
American Primitive Music; Special Attention to the Songs of the Ojbways. New York: Moffat, Yard and Company, 1909. 284 pp., illus., music.
Twenty-eight Ojibway songs, harmonized and provided with English words, pp. 283–284.

"The Civilizing of Indian Music." *Southern Workman* (Hampton, Virginia) 36: 305–310, 1907.

Cadman, Charles Wakefield
"Anent the Injun Music." *Musical Courier* 60(No. 15):39, 1910.

"The Decadence of the Indian Pow-wow. Tribal Music and Something About It." *Musical Courier* 59(No. 23): 59–60, 1909.

"The 'Idealization' of Indian Music." *MQ* 1: 387–396, 1915.

Cardin, F.
"Our Heritage, the Indian." *Etude* 44: 906, 1926.

Catlin, George
Letters and Notes on the Manners, Customs, and Condition of the North American Indians. London: George Catlin, 1841. 2 volumes, illus.

Chamberlain, Alexander Francis
"Primitive Woman Poet."*JAFL* 16: 205–221, 1903.

"Chinese Words in Indian Songs." *Literary Digest* 115: 28, (February 11), 1933.

Conway, Walker
The Folk Song and Dance. New York: The Caxton Institute, 1926. Fundamentals of Musical Art.—101 pp.
Music of the American Indian (pp. 70-73).

Cringan, Alexander T.
"Indian Music." *Annual Archaeological Report* (pp. 158–161). Ontario: 1905. Toronto: 1906.

Cronyn, George W.
The Path on the Rainbow. Introduction by Mary Austin, illustration by J. B. Platt. New York: Boni and Liveright, 1918 and 1934.
An anthology of songs and chants from the Indians of North America.

Crotch, William
Specimens of Various Styles of Music London: Rt. Birchall, 1808.

Curtis, Edward S.
Indian Days of the Long Ago. Illustrated with photographs by the author and drawings by F. H. Wilson. New York: World Book Company, 1914.

Curtis, Natalie
"A Plea for our Native Art." *MQ* 6(No. 2): 175–188, April, 1920.

"An American Indian Composer." *Harper's Magazine* (New York) 107: 626–632, 1903.

"American Indian Cradle-Songs." *MQ* 7: 549–558, 1921.

"Folk Songs and the American Indian." *Southern Workman* 44(No. 9): 476–480, 1915.

"Indian Folk Music." *Southern Workman* 34–35: 1905–1906.

"Recording for Posterity the Music of Primitive Humanity." *Musical America* (New York) 35(No. 21):3, 38, 1922.

"Saving Indian Music and Legend from Annihilation." *Etude* 38: 666, 1920.

The Indians Book. An Offering by the American Indians of Indian Lore, Musical and Narrative, To Form a Record of the Songs and Legends of their Race. Illustrations from Photographs and from Original Drawings by Indians. New York: Harper and Brothers, 1907. 583 pp., music, illus.

Danckert, Werner
"Musikethnologische Erschliessung der Kulturkreise." *Mitteilungen der Anthropoligischen Gesellschaft in Wien* 67 (Nos. 1–2): 53–57, 1937.

"Musikwissenschaft und Kultur Kreislehre." *Mitteilungen der Anthropoligischen Gesellschaft in Wien* 32(Nos. 1–2) 1–14, 1937.

Dallenbaugh, Frederick Samuel
The North–American of Yesterday. New York: G. P. Putnam's Sons, 1901.

Densmore, Frances
"Field Studies of Indian Music." *Smithsonian Miscellaneous Collection* 78: 240–253, 1927.

"Four Saints and Some Indian Music." *Musical America* 54(No. 13): 12, Aug. 1934.

Handbook of the Collection of Musical Instruments in the United States National Museum. Smithsonian Institution Bulletin 136 Washington, D. C.: U. S. Government Printing Office, 1927. iii, 164 pp. illus.

"How the Indian Seeks Power Through Dream Music." *Musical America* 56(No. 8): 3, 20, June 11, 1927.

Indian Action Songs. Boston: 1921.

"Indian Music." *El Palacio* 10(Nos. 13–14): 3–9.

"La Música de los Indios Northamericanos." *BLAM* 5: 363–368, 1941(Published 1942).

"Musical Composition Among the American Indians." *AS* 2(No. 9):393–394, 1927.

"On 'Expression' in Indian Singing." *AA* 36: 487–488, 1934. n.s.

"Peculiarities in the Singing of the American Indians." *AA* 32: 651–660, 1930.

"Recent Developments in the Study of Indian Music." *Proceedings of the 19th Session of the International Congress of Americanists:* 298–301, 1915.

"Recording Indian Music." *Etude* 61: 15, (January) 1943.

"Rhythm in the Music of the American Indian." *Proceedings of the 20th Session of the International Congress of Americanists* I: 85–90, 1922.

"Scale Formation in Primitive Music." *AA* 11: 1-13, 1909, n.s.

"Some Results of the Study of American Indian Music." *Praktika de l'Academie d'Athens* 3: 347–360, 1928.

"Songs of Indian Soldiers During the World War." *MQ* 20: 419–425, (October) 1934.

The American Indians and Their Music. New York: Woman's Press, 1936. 150 pp. Rev. ed.
Brief discussion of the major characteristics of Indian music, the dances, games, ceremonies, type of songs, musical instruments, and adaptations of Indian music.

"The Influence of Hymns on the Form of Indian Songs." *AA* 40:175–177, 1938, n.s.

"The Music of the American Indian." *Overland Monthly* 45 (series 2): 230–234, 1904.

"Music of the American Indians." *Science* 62:565–566 (December 18), 1925 n.s.

"The Music of the North American Indians." *Proceedings of the 25th Session of the International Congress of Americanists* I: 119–127, 1932.

"Songs of the Indians." *American Mercury* 7: 65–68, (January) 1926.

"The Music of the American Indians." *Overland Monthly* 45:230–234, 1905. n.s.
Discussion, without examples.

"The Music of the American Indians at Public Gatherings." *MQ* 17(No. 4): 464–479, Oct. 1931.

"The Music of the American Indians at Public Gatherings." Abstract. *Journal of the Washington Academy of Sciences* 20:509–510, 1930.

"The Study of the Indian Music." *MQ* 1: 187–197, 1915.

The Study of Indian Music. In: *Smithsonian Institution Annual Report,* 1941 (pp. 527–550). Washington, D. C.: U. S. Government Printing Office, 1942.

"The Study of Indian Music in the Nineteenth Century." *AA* 29:77–86, 1927. n.s.

"The Use of Meaningless Syllables in Indian Song." *AA* 45:160–162, 1943.

"The Use of Music in the Treatment of the Sick by the American Indians." *MQ* 13:555–565, 1927.

"The Use of the Term Tetrachord in Musicology." *Journal of Musicology* 1 (No. 4):16–21, 1940.
"It seems permissible to apply the term to a closely-knit group of tones bounded by four scale degrees, with one or more intermediate tones, occurring in the songs of the American Indian."

"Traces of Foreign Influences in the Music of the American Indians." *AA* 46 (No. 1):106–112, 1944. n.s.
"By sifting, sorting, and examining the old songs as an archeologist examines his specimens, we find traces of foreign influences in the music of the Amecian Indians" (The author).

Dougherty, G. H.
"American Indian Compositions Reflecting the Social and Political Organizations of the Tribes." *Open Court* 41:80–89.

"Motives of Indian Speeches and Songs." *Open Court* 40:689–704, 719–733.

"The Technique of Indian Composition." *Open Court* 41:150–166.

Eames, Henry P.
"The Gamut of Expression in American Indian Music." *Theatre Arts Monthly* 17:611–615 (August) 1933.

Edgerly, Beatrice
From the Hunter's Bow; The History and Romance of Musical Instruments. New York: G. P. Putnam's Sons, 1942.
Chapter VII—Indians of the Americas. D. Tribes of U. S.

Eels, Myron
"Indian Music." *American Antiquarian* 1:249–253, 1878–1879.

Engel, Carl
An Introduction to the Study of National Music. London: Longmans, Green, Reader and Dyes, 1868.

Farwell, Arthur
"Aspects of Indian Music." *Southern Workman* 31:211–217, 1902.

———.
"The Music of the American Indians." *American Art Journal* (New York) 82:386, 1903.

Fillmore, John Comfort
"A Study of Indian Music." *Century* (New York) 47 (new series) 25:616–623, 1893–1894.

———.
"Illustrations of Harmonic Melody in Folk Music." *Music* 5:281–287, 1893. (Chicago).

———.
"Primitive Scales and Rhythms." *Proceedings of the International Congress of Americanists.* (Chicago):158–175, 1894.

———.
"The Forms Spontaneously Assumed by Folk-Songs." *Music* 12:289–294, 1900 (Chicago).

———.
"The Harmonic Structure of Indian Music." *AA* 1:297–318, 1899. n.s.

———.
"What Do Indians Mean When They Sing, and How Far Do They Succeed?" *JAFL* 8:138–142, 1895.

Fletcher, Alice Cunningham
Indian Games and Dances with Native Indian Songs. Boston: C. C. Birchard and Company, 1915. 139 pp. Music.

———.
"Indian Music." *Music* 6:188–199, 1894 (Chicago).

———.
"Indian Songs, Personal Studies of Indian Life." *Century* 47 (new series 25):421–431, 1894.

———.
"Indian Songs and Music." *American Association for the Advancement of Science* 44:281–284, 1895.

———.
"Indian Songs and Music." *JAFL* 11:85–104, 1898.

———.
Indian Story and Song from North America. Boston: Small, Maynard and Company, 1900. 126 pp.

———.
Music and Musical Instruments. In: F. W. Hodge, *Handbook of American Indians North of Mexico* (pp. 958–961). *Bureau of American Ethnology, Bulletin 30* part 1–2. Washington, D. C.: U. S. Government Printing Office, 1907–1910. 2 volumes.

———.
"Music as Found in Certain North American Indian Tribes." *Music* 4:457–467, 1893 (Chicago).

———.
"The Study of Indian Music." *National Academy of Sciences* 1:231–235. Washington, D. C.: U. S. Government Printing Office, 1915.

Fuentes, Eduardo Sanchez de
La Musica Aborigen de America. Discurso leído por su autor en a Solemne session inaugura del curso, de 1938 a 1939, de la misma Corporacíon, celebrada en la noche del 22 de Octobre de 1938. La Habana: Molina Y Cia, 61 pp.
> Includes discussion of songs and dances of the North and South American Indians. Printed under the Auspices of the Academie Nacional de Artes y Letras.

Gagnon, Ernest
"Les Sauvages de l'Amérique et l'Art Musical." *Proceedings of the 15 Session of the International Congress of Americanists* I:179–189, 1906 (Quebec).

Gatschet, Albert S.
"Of the Music of the North American Indians." (Review of "Uber die Musik der Nordamerikanischen Wilden von Theodor Baker, Leipzig, 1882.) *American Naturalist Pamphlet:* 226, 1883.

Gilbert, Henry Franklin Belknap
"Indian Music." *New Indian Review* (New York) 11:56–59, 1911.

———.
"North American Indian Music." *Harvard Musical Review* (Boston) I (No. 6):5–7, 1913.

Gilman, Benjamin I.
"The Science of Exotic Music." *Science* 30:532–535, 1909. n.s.

Goddard, Pliny Earle
A Graphic Method of Recording Songs. In: *Boas Anniversary Volume, Anthropological Papers* (pp. 137–142). New York: G. E. Stechert & Company, 1906.

Goodlander, M. R.
"Primitive Songs and Dances: A Second Grade Assembly." *Elementary School Teacher* 9:65–69 (October) 1908.

Gundlach, Ralph H.
"A Quantitative Analysis of Indian Music." *The American Journal of Psychology* 44:133–145, 1932.

Gustaver, Bror
"On a Peculiar Type of Whistle Found in Ancient American Indian Graves." *AA* 25:305–317, 1923. n.s.

Haines, Elijah Middlebrook
The American Indian. Chicago: The Mas-sin-na-gan Company, 1888.

Harcourt, Raoul, and Marguerite d'
La musique indienne chez les anciens civilisés d'Amerique. In: *Encyclopédie de la musique et dictionnaire du conservatoire*, partie 1, (pp. 3337–3371). Paris: Libraire Delagrave, 1922.

Hare, Maud Cuney
"The Drum in Africa; the Use of Music by a Primitive People." *Musical Observer:* (July) 1918.

Haywood, Charles
The American Scene in Ballad and Song. The growth of American Civilization reflected in its folk songs; the narrative supplied by the voice of the people: letters, diaries, and documents. Illustrated by old prints. New York: Greenberg: Publisher. c. 1950. Illustrated, music.
Contains melodies and texts of various types of songs of representative tribes in the different culture areas of the Indians of North America.

Heinitz, Wilhelm
"Musikwissenschaft und Völkerkunde." *Mitteilungsblatt der Gesellschaft für Völkerkunde* 8:43–54, 1938 (Leipzig).
A study of the relation of music science to folklore.

Herzog, George
"African Influences in North American Indian Music." In: *Papers Read at the International Congress of Musicology* (pp. 130–143). New York: American Musicological Society, 1944. 301 pp.

―――.
"Character of Indian Music." *AA* 36:476–478, 1934. (Review of "Form in Primitive Music" by Helen H. Roberts.)

―――.
"Investigacíon sobre la música primitiva y folklórica en los Estados Unidos." *BLAM* 5: 393–420, 1941 (published 1942).
Reprints of his study in—Bulletin 24 of the American Council of Learned Societies (Washington, D. C.).

―――.
"Music in the Thinking of the American Indian." *Peabody Bulletin:* 1–5, (May) 1938.

―――.
"Musical Styles in North America." *Proceedings of the 23rd International Congress of Americanists* (New York):455–458, 1930.

―――.
"Primitive Music; The Study and Its Problems." In: *Research in Primitive and Folk Music in the United States* (pp. 3–23). American Council of Learned Societies, Bulletin No. 24. Washington, D. C.: U. S. Government Printing Office (April) 1936, 97 pp.

―――.
"Recording Primitive Music in Africa and America." *FSSNE* 8:2–3, 1934.

―――.
"Special Song Types in North American Indian Music." *Zeitschrift für Vergleichende Musikwissenschaft* 3 (1–2):23–33, 1935.

―――.
"Speech-Melody and Primitive Music." *MQ* 20 (No. 4):452–466, 1934.

―――.
"Study of Native Music in America." *PASC 8* 2: (Anthropological Sciences) 203–209, 1942.

―――.
"The Collections of Phonograph Records in North America and Hawaii." *Zeitschrift für Vergleichende Musikwissenschaft* 1 (3):58–62, 1933.

Hofmann, Charles
Aspects of Primitive and Folk Music. American Museum of Natural History (New York), mimeo., n. d.
Outline of lecture series.

―――.
"Frances Densmore and the Music of the American Indian." *JAFL* 59:45–50, 1946.

Hough, Walter
"Indian Music." *The Musician* (Boston) 2 (No. 11):169, 1906.

Howard, John Tasker
Our American Music: Three Hundred Years of It. 2nd Edition revised and enlarged. New York: Crowell and Company, 1939.
Chapter XV: Our Folk Music, Part I—Music of the North American Indian, pp. 404-415.

Hubbard, William Lines
Music of North American Indians. In: *The American History and Encyclopedia of Music* (pp. 39–47). Toledo: Irving Squire, volume 4.

Humphrey, W. B.
North American Indian Folk-Lore Medicine. New York: The American Indian League, 1911.
Words and music of 8 songs.

"Indian Musical and Noise Making Instruments." *Denver Art Museum Leaflet* No. 29, August, 1931. 4 pp.

"Indian Musicians in the Modern World." *Etude* 38:665–666, 1920.

Jeançon, Jean Allard, comp.
"Indian Musical and Noise Making Instruments." *Denver Art Museum Leaflets* 29: (August) 1931.

―――.
Indian Song Book. Denver Art Museum Leaflet. 1924.

"Katherine Burrit and the Songs of the Indians." *Musical Leader* (Chicago) 25:263, 1913.

Kessler, D. E.
"The Indian Influence in Music." *Southern Workman* (Hampton, Virginia) 38:168–170, 1909.

Kinscella, Hazel Gertrude
"Lieurance Traces American Indian Music to Oriental Origins." *Musical America* 27 (No. 24):3–4, 1923.

Krehbiel, Henry Edward
"Folk-music Studies—Songs of the American Indians." *New York Daily Tribune:* (September 24), (October 1, 8), 1899.

Lamkin, Nina B., and Jagendorf, M.
Around America with the Indian. New York:
Samuel French, 1935.
   A book for boys and girls about Indian legends,
   made into plays, Indian village life, ceremonials,
   dance music and games.

Lieurance, Thurlow
"Indian Music." *Southern Workman* (Hampton, Virginia) 42:451–454, 1913.

————.
"The Musical Soul of the American Indian."
Etude (Philadelphia) 38:655–656, 1920.

Lummis, Charles Fletcher
"Catching our Archaeology Alive." *Out-West*
(Los Angeles) 22:35–45, 1905.

Mallery, Garrick
"On the Pictographs of the North American
Indian." In: *4th Annual Report of the United
States Bureau of American Ethnology* (pp. 3–
256), 1882–1883. Washington, D. C.: Government Printing Office, 1886.

————.
"Picture Writing of the American Indians."
In: *10th Annual Report of the United States
Bureau of American Ethnology* (pp. 3–822),
1888–1889. Washington, D. C.: U. S. Government Printing Office, 1893.

Mason, Otis T.
"Geographical Distribution of the Musical
Bow." *AA* 10:377–389, 1897. o.s.

Mathews, William Smythe Babcock
"Indian Music and its Investigation." *Music*
(Chicago) 4:452–456, 1893.

Miller, Dayton C.
"Flutes of the American Indian." *Flutist* 2:
509–512, 1921.

Mindeleff, Cosmos
"Preserving Last Relics of Indian Music
Through Aid of the Phonograph." *Metronome*
24 (No. 6):17, 1908.

Mooney, James
"The Ghost-Dance Religion." In: *The 14th
Annual Report of the Bureau of American
Ethnology,* part 2, 1892–1893. Washington.
D. C.: U. S. Government Printing Office, 1896.

Moorhead, Warren King
The American Indian in the United States—
1850–1914. The present condition of the American Indians, their political history and other
topics. A plea for justice. Andover, Massachusetts: Andover Press, 1914.

"Music From Acorns; Indian Musical Instruments." *Literary Digest* 89:23, (June) 12, 1926.

Myers, Charles S.
"The Ethnological Study of Music." In: *Anthropological Essays,* presented to Howard
Burnett Tylor in honor of his 75th birthday
(pp. 235–253) (October 2, 1907). London:
Oxford—At the Clarendon Press, 1907.

Nevin, Arthur
"Impressions of the Indian Music as Heard in
the Woods, Prairies, Mountains and Wigwams.
A Sketch of the Blackfoot Indian." *Etude*
(Philadelphia) 38:663–664, 1920.

————.
"Two Summers with the Blackfeet Indians
of Montana." *MQ* 2:257–270, April 1916.

Notes and Queries in Anthropology. London:
Royal Anthropological Institute, 1912. (4th
ed.), pp. 214–229.
   Hints to field workers how to record and transcribe non European folksongs. Dated, but still
   valuable. Includes discussion on dancing, drama,
   games and amusements.

Pastor, Willy
"Music of Primitive Peoples and Beginnings
of European Music." In: *Smithsonian Report
of 1912* (pp. 679–700). Washington, D. C.:
U. S. Government Printing Office.

Podolsky, E.
"Use of Music as a Healing Agent Among the
Indians." *Etude* 52:434 (July) 1934.

Pratt, Waldo Selden, and Boyd, Charles N.
"Indian Music." In: *Grove's Dictionary of
Music and Musicians* (pp. 252–253). New
York: The Macmillan Company, 1920, American Supplement, Volume 6.

Putnam, Frederick W.
"Musical Instruments Made of Bones." In: *Report Upon the Archaeological and Ethnological
Collections from the Vicinity of Santa Barbara,
California* (p. 234) (Wheeler's Report, West
100th Meridian, Volume VII). Washington,
D. C.: U. S. Government Printing Office, 1879.

Read, Angelo M.
"The North American Indian and Music."
Musical American (New York) 6 (No. 9):9,
1907.

Reade, John
"Aboriginal American Poetry." *Royal Society
of Canada Proceeding and Transactions* (Montreal) 5 (No. 2):9–34, 1888.

Rivet, Paul
"La Musique Indienne en Amerique." *La
Nature* 69:244–247, 1927.

Riviere, Georges Henri
Les Arts Anciens de l'Amérique. Paris: Les
Editions G. Van Oest, 1928.

Roberts, Helen A.
Form in Primitive Music. New York: American
Library of Musicology, W. W. Sutton and Company, 1933. 180 pp., musical illustrations.
   An analytical and comparative study of the melodic form of some ancient southern Californian
   Indian songs. Special emphasis on the character
   of the music and instruments of the Luiseño.

————.
"Melodic Composition and Scale Foundation
in Primitive Music." *AA* 34:79–107, 1923. n.s.

————*.
Musical Areas in Aboriginal North America.
Yale University Publications in Anthropology
No. 12. New Haven: Yale University Press,
1936. 41 pp.

————*.
New Phases in the Study of Primitive Music.
Menasha, Wisconsin: Banta Press, 1922.

————*.
"The Pattern Phenomenon in Primitive Music."
*Zeitschrift für vergleichende Musik-Wissen-
schaft* 1:49–52, 1933. Music pp. 25–30.

Sachs, Curt
The History of Musical Instruments. New
York: W. W. Norton & Company, 1940. 505
pp., illus., bibl.
> Chapter I—Early Instruments. Chapter IX—
> America.

Salomon, Julian Harris
The Book of Indian Crafts and Indian Lore.
New York: Harper Bros., 1928. 418 pp., illus.,
music (pp. 297–327).

Sanford, David A.
Topics; or Experiences in Indian Missions,
with Selections from Various Sources. New
York: Broadway Publishing Company, 1911.

Schaeffner, André
Origines des Instruments de Musique. Introduction Ethnologique á l'Histoire de la Musique Instrumentale. Paris: Payot, 1936. 405
pp., illustrated.
> On the origin of musical instruments.

Schneider, Marius
Geschicte der Mehrstimmigkeit. Erster Teil:
Die Naturvölker. Berlin: Julius Bard Verlag,
1934.
> Part I—deals with the music of primitive people.

Schoolcraft, Henry Rowe
*Information Respecting the History, Condition
and Prospects of the Indian Tribes of the
U. S.* Collected and prepared under the direc-
tion of the Bureau of Indian Affairs, per act of
Congress of March 3, 1847, by Henry R.
Schoolcraft, L.L.D. Illustrated by S. Eastman,
Capt. of U. S. Army. Published by Authority
of Congress. Philadelphia: Lippincott, Grambo
& Company, 1851–1857.

————*.
Indian Music, Songs and Poetry. In: *Oneota,
or the Red Face of America* (pp. 41). New
York: W. H. Graham, 1844.

Sembrich, Marcella, ed.
My Favorite Folk Songs. Philadelphia: Oliver
Ditson Co., 1918. 138 pp.
> Arranged for voice and piano. Contains two In-
> dian Songs—a Pawnee and Omaha.

"Singing of the American Indian."
JAFL 8:138–142, 1895.

Skilton, Charles Sanford
"Indian Music at Home." *Musician* (Boston)
23:459, 1918.

"Realism in Indian Music." *Musician* (New
York) 24 (No. 2):17, 1919.

————*.
"Realism in Indian Music." *MTNA* 13:106–
115, 1918.

"Songs of the Indian."
Hobbies 45:97, (March) 1940.

Spence, Lewis
Myth and Ritual in Dance, Game and Rhyme.
London: Watts & Co., 1947. x, 202 pp.

Spinden, Herbert J.
Songs of the Tewa. New York: Exposition of
Indian Tribal Arts, 1931. 125 pp.

Starr, F.
"Indian Music and Records of Iroquois Songs."
American Antiquarian (Salem, Massachusetts)
31:29, 1909.

Stone, Mary R. Van
"Songs of the Indians." *El Palacio* 48 (No. 7):
149–154, 1941.
> Includes: Apache Social Dance Song; Santa
> Clara Song of Lasacita; San Juan-Kiowa Love
> Song; and Sioux Soldiers' Dance Song.

Strickland, Anderson Lily
"Aboriginal and Animistic Influences in Indian
Music." *MQ* 15:88, 1929.

Swanton, J. R.
Rattles. In: *Handbook of American Indians.*
Vol. II, pp. 355–356. Bureau of American
Ethnology, Bulletin 30. Washington, D. C.:
U. S. Government Printing Office, 1910.

Tanner, John
*A Narrative of the Captivity and Adventures
of John Tanner,* during 30 years residence
among the Indians in the interior of North
America. Prepared for the press by Edwin
James. London: Baldwin & Cradoch, 1830.

"The Indian in Music."
Music Trade Review (New York) 32 (No. 22):
2, 1901.

"The Rhythm of Indian Songs."
Musician (Boston) 22:257, 1917.

Tiersot, Julien
"Musical Ethnology in America. Music Among
the Indians." *The Musician* (Boston) 12 (No.
2):84–86, 1907.

————*.
*La Musique Chez les Peuples Indigènes de
L'Amérique du Nord. (États-Unis et Canada).*
Paris: Libraire Fischbacher, n.d. 93 pp., bibl.,
music.
> The brochure is a reprint of an article that ap-
> peared in the organ of the *International Society
> of Music,* vol. II, No. 2. The author discusses the
> general musical characteristics of Indian music,
> giving representative examples of various tribes.
> He also includes a discussion, with examples, of
> Negro music.

Titus, M. E.
A Treatise on American Indian Music. Indianapolis: 1920.

W., C. E.
"Miss Densmore and Indian Music." *Music Views* (Chicago) 8 (No. 28):14–15, 1916.

Wallaschek, Richard
Primitive Music. An Inquiry into the Origin and Development of Music, Songs, Instruments, Dances and Pantomines of Savage Races. London: Longman, Green & Company, 1893.
    Chapter I, p. 5—Discusses music of the American Indian.

Wead, Charles Kasson
"Contribution to the History of Musical Scales." In: *Report of the U. S. National Museum for 1900* (pp. 417–463). Washington, D. C.: U. S. Government Printing Office, 1902.

——————.
"Recent Outlooks Upon Music." *Science* (New York) (No. 11):206–215, 1900.

——————.
"The Study of Primitive Music." *AA* 2:75–80, 1900. n.s.

"When the Indian Makes Music."
Mentor 16:65 (September) 1928.

Wielich, L., ed.
"Art and Life in Indian Music,—Ish-Ti-Opi." *Etude* 59:161–162 (March) 1941.

Wissler, Clark
"A Psycho-Physical Element in Primitive Art." In: *Anthropological Papers. Boas Anniversary Volume* (pp. 189–193). New York: G. E. Stechert & Company, 1906.

——————.
The American Indian: An Introduction to the Anthropology of the New World. New York: D. C. Murtrie, 1917.

——————.
"Poetry and Music of Some North American Tribes." *Science* (New York) 9:383–385, 1897.

THE DANCE

GENERAL STUDIES AND COLLECTIONS

Boas, Franz
Literature, Music, and Dance. In: *General Anthropology,* ed. by Franz Boas. Literature pp. 589. Music, pp. 602, Dance, pp. 605. Boston: D. C. Heath and Co., 1938. xi, 718 pp. Illus.

Buckland, A. W.
"The Indian Ghost Dance." *Theological Monthly* 5:122–126, 1891.
    Description, no music.

Butree, Julia M.
The Rhythm of Redman; in song, dance, and decoration. New York: A. S. Barnes Company, 1930.

Casual
"Ceremonial dances of the American Indians." *Nature* 58:490–491, 1898.

"Ceremonial Dances of the American Indians." *Nature* 58:125–127, 1898.
    Review of several books.

"Dancers in Devil's Dance."
JAFL 1:50, 1888; 5:67, 1892; 8:325–326, 1895; 20:17, 1907.

Densmore, Frances
"Imitative Dances Among the American Indians." *JAFL* 60:73–78, 1947.
    Six musical examples: A Menominee Song of the Rabbit Dance, Winnebago Song of the Fish Dance, Seminole Song of the Buzzard Dance, Choctaw Song of the Terrapin Dance, Alabama Song of the Duck Dance, and a Maidu Song of the Grizzly Bear Dance.

Dorsey, Ella Lorraine
"The Forbidden Dance" (Da-H-pi-ke). *Messenger* (New York) 50:466–485, 1908.

Evans, Bessie and M. G.
American Indian Dance Steps. Introduction by Frederick Webb Hodge. Illustrated in color by Poyege, San Ildefonso Indian. New York: A. S. Barnes Company, 1931. xviii, 104 pp., illus., music.
    "Concerned chiefly with elements of the art observed in certain Pueblo tribes of New Mexico— especially those of San Ildefonso, Tesuque, Santa Clara, Cochiti, and Santo Domingo"—Foreword.

Fletcher, Alice C.
Indian Games and Dances, with native songs, arranged from American Indian ceremonials and sports. Boston: C. C. Birchard and Company, 1915. 139 pp., music.

Goodlander, M. R.
"Primitive Songs and Dances: A Second Grade Assembly." *Elementary School Teacher* 9:65–69, October, 1908.

Hartley, Marsden
"Red Man Ceremonials." *Art and Archaeology* 9:7–15, (January) 1920.

Hewitt, J. N. B.
Indian Dance. In: *Handbook of American Indians North of Mexico,* F. W. Hodge, editor. 1:381–382. Bureau of American Ethnology, Bulletin 30. Washington, D. C.: U. S. Government Printing Office, 1907.

Laubin, Reginald and Gladys
"The Indian Dance." *Musical Digest* 30 (No. 3):34–37, 1948. Illus.

Lowie, Robert H.
"Ceremonialism in North America." *AA* 16:602–631, 1914. n.s., (bibliography pp. 629–631).

Lummis, Charles Fletcher
"Catching our Archaeology Alive." *Out-West* 22:35–45, 1905.
    Discussion of collecting Indian songs in the Southwest.

Marriott, Alice
"When You Go to the Indian Fair." *The Southwest Review*, 30 (4):335–338, Summer, 1945.

Mason, Bernard Sterling
Dances and Stories of the American Indian. Photographs by Paul Boris and others, drawings by Frederich H. Koch. New York: A. S. Barnes Company, 1944. 269 pp.

————.
Drums, Tom-Tom, Rattles. Primitive percussion instruments for modern use. Drawings by Frederick H. Koch. New York: A. S. Barnes and Company, 1938. 206 pp., bibl.

Mullins, Cora Phebe
Songs of the Indian Dances. Omaha: 1929.

Nelson, John L.
Rhythm for Rain. Boston: Houghton, Mifflin, 1937. ix, 271 pp.
A work of fiction.

Peck, A. M. and Johnson, E.
"Red Drums of Christmas; Indian Dance that Celebrates the Birth of Jesus." *Pictorial Review* 34:18–19+, November, 1932.

Seton, Ernest Thompson
The War Dance and Fire-Fly Dance. New York: Doubleday Page Company, 1910.

Shafter, Mary Severance
American Indian and Other Folk Dances for Schools, Pageants and Playgrounds. Music arranged by Josephine Condon. New York: A. S. Barnes and Company, 1927. 77 pp., illustrated music.

Tait, W. M.
"Indian Dances." *Overland Monthly* 65:88–92, (January), 1915.

Wissler, Clark
"General Discussion of Shamanistic and Dancing Societies." *Anthropological Papers of the American Museum of Natural History* 11 (part 2)853–856, 1916 (New York).

"Year's Calendar of Indian Dances."
Theatre Arts Monthly 17:663, August, 1933.

ARRANGEMENTS

————: Female Voices

Four American Indian Songs.
Cadman-Harris: White-Smith: SSA, SSAA.

Indian Love Songs (11 Songs).
Lieurance, Thurlow: Presser: SSA.

"Longing."
Stringham, E. J.: Music Publishers Holding Corp.: SSA.

"Ski-Bi-Bi-La" (Indian Spring Bird).
Lieurance, Thurlow: Presser: SSA.

————: Male Voices

Four American Indian Songs.
Cadman-Hearz: White-Smith: TTBB.

————: Mixed Voices

Four American Indian Songs.
Cadman-Hearz: White-Smith: SATB.

Four Choruses on Indian themes.
Farwell, A.: Schirmer: SSAATTBB, a cap.

"Great and Glorious God Antiphon."
(Based on Indian Melody.) Dickinson, Clarence: Gray: SATB.

Hiawatha.
Burton, Frederick R., Cantata

Indian Songs for Mixed Voices.
(10 numbers.) Lieurance, Thurlow: Presser: SATB.

"Medicine Dance."
Lieurance, Thurlow: C. Fischer: SAB or SSAAB with Tom-Toms, Bass Drum, Gong and Piano; also—small orchestra, full orchestra and grand orchestra acompaniment.

"The Father of the Waters."
Cadman, Charles W.: Ditson: SATB.

The Four Winds.
Busch, Carl: Ditson: Cantata.

"The Owl Hoots on a Tepee Pole."
Lieurance, Thurlow: Presser: SATB.

————: Voice and Piano

"Intermezzo."
Farwell, Arthur: Wa-Wan Press: Violin and piano.

American Indian Melodies.
Farwell, Arthur: The Wa-Wan Press.

Four American Indian Songs.
Cadman, Charles Wakefield: White-Smith.

Lyrics of the Red Man.
Opus 76, Book 1–2. Loomis, Harvey Worthington: The Wa-Wan Press: Voice and piano.

Nine Indian Melodies.
Lieurance, Thurlow: Presser: Voice and piano.
Contents: Lullaby; Love Song (Red Willow Pueblo); My Silver Throated Faun (Sioux Love Song); A Crow Maiden's Prayer Song; Aooah (Love Song from the Red Willow Pueblos); Pakoble; Pa-Pup-Ooh; Her Blanket (Navajo). Cycle with descriptive notes; illustrated.

Songs of the North American Indian.
With preface and explanatory notes. Lieurance, Thurlow: Presser: Voice and piano. A cycle of nine songs.

Under Northern Skies.
(3 songs based on Indian themes.) Lieurance, Theodore: Presser: Voice and piano.

——————: *Piano*

From Mesa and Plain.
  Farwell, Arthur: Wa-Wan Press: Piano.

American Indian Melodies.
  Farwell, Arthur: Wa-Wan Press: Piano.
  Contains 10 tunes .

American Indian Rhapsody.
  (By P. W. Orem.) Lieurance, Thurlow:
  Presser.

Dawn: A Development of Indian Melodies. Opus
  2. Farwell, Arthur: G. Schirmer.

Four Indian Themes.
  Miller, Horace Alden: Breitkopf & Hartel.

"*Ichi Buzzhi.*"
  Farwell, Arthur: G. Schirmer.

Idealized Indian Themes.
  Cadman, Charles Wakefield: White-Smith.

"Indian Festival."
  Rolseth, B.: G. Schirmer: Piano (easy).

"Indian Legend."
  Busch, Carl: Schirmer.

"Indian Sketches."
  Gilbert, Henry F.

"Indian Suite."
  Lieurance, Thurlow: Presser.

Lyrics of the Red Man, opus 76.
  Loomis, Harvey W.: Wa-Wan Press.
  Contains 13 compositions—2 books.

Melodic Views of Indian Life.
  Miller, Horace A.: Clayton F. Summy.
  Transcription based on Indian melodies.

"Theme and Variations."
  Miller, Horace A.: Breitkopf & Härtel.

Three Indian Sketches.
  Skilton, Charles S.: Carl Fischer.

——————: *Violin and Piano*

"Deer Dance."
  (By Charles S. Skilton.) Czerwonky, R.: Carl
  Fischer: Violin and piano.

Melodies for Violin and Piano.
  Lieurance, Thurlow: Presser.

——————: *Organ*

"American Indian Fantasie."
  Skilton, Charles S.: J. Fischer & Brothers:
  Organ.

"By the Weeping Waters."
  Lieurance, Thurlow: Presser: Piano, also
  organ.

"From Ghost Dance Canyon."
  Lieurance, Thurlow: Presser: Organ.

"Ghost Pipes."
  Lieurance, Thurlow: Presser: Organ, also violin and piano.

"The Owl Hoots on a Tepee Pole."
  (By Thurlow Lieurance.) Cato, R.: Presser:
  Organ.

——————: *String Quartet*

Indian Sketches.
  Stringfield, L.: MS: flute, string quartet.

Indian Suite.
  (Based on tribal songs of the American In-
  dians.) Pochon, Alfred: Carl Fischer: String
  Quartet.

String Quartet Based on Indian Themes.
  Jacobi, Frederick: Schirmer: String quartet.

Two Sketches for String Quartet.
  (Based on Indian Themes), by Charles Griffes.
  Betti, A.: G. Schirmer.

——————: *Orchestra*

American Indian Fantasie.
  Skilton, Charles S.: MS: Cello, orchestra.

American Symphony.
  Shure, Deane R.: J. Fischer & Brothers:
  Orchestra.
  Based on Anglo-American, Indian, Negro folk
  music.

Amerind Suite.
  Cowell, Henry D.: Axelrod: Chamber orch.

Atala.
  Kroeger, Ernest R.: Overture.

From the Plains.
  Ayres, Frederick: Overture.

Hiawatha.
  Kroger, Ernest R.: Overture.

Hiawatha Overture.
  Goldmark, Rubin: C. Fischer: Orchestra.

Indian Dances.
  Jacobi, Frederick: Universal: Orchestra.

Indian Dances.
  Skilton, Charles S.: C. Fischer.

Indian Legend—Symphonic Poem.
  Stringfield, L.: MS: Orchestra.

"Indian Love Song."
  Lake, M. H.: Carl Fischer.

Indian Pipes.
  Bauer, Marion E.: MS.—for orchestra (orches-
  trated by Martin Bernstein).

Indian Songs and Dances.
  Castelnuovo-Tedesco, Mario: MS: Orchestra.

Indian Suite.
  At Dawn; Dance of the Pumpkin; Love Song;
  At Twilight. Lake, M. H.: Carl Fischer.

Minnehaha's Vision.
Busch, Carl MS: Symphonic Poem.

Second Indian Suite.
MacDowell, Edward: Associated.

"Sipapu."
Hadley, Henry: Carl Fischer.
Ritualistic Indian Dance from the Legend of Hani.

Suite Characteristique.
Schoenfeld, Henry W.: Symphonic Poem.

Suite from "Pocahontas."
Carter, Elliot C.: Kalmus: Orchestra.

Suite Primeval, on Tribal Indian melodies.
Skilton, Charles S.: Carl Fischer. Part I—
1. Deer Dance (Rogue River, Oregon) ; 2. War Dance (Cheyenne). Part II—American Indian Fantasie, Cello and orchestra; 3. Sunrise Song (Winnebago) ; 4. Gambling Song (Rogue River, Oregon) ; 5. Flute Serenade (Sioux, also published separately for full chamber orchestra) ; 6. Moccasin Game (Winnebago).

Three American Indian Songs. Opus 24.
Langstroth, Ivan S.: Gray: SSAA, 2 horns, 2 trumpets, 2 kettle drums.

Thunderbird Suite.
Cadman, Charles W.: Boosey and Co., orchestra.

To A Vanishing Race.
Cadman, Charles W.: John Church Co.: Chamber orchestra.

"Tomahawk Dance," Revised (Seredy).
Herman, A.: Carl Fischer.

Two Indian Dances.
Gaul, Harvey B.: Birchard.

Two Indian Dances—Deer Dance, War Dance.
Skilton, Charles S.: C. Fischer: Orchestra, also for chamber orchestra.

————: *Stage Work*

Feast of the Red Corn.
Bliss, Paul: Willis: Operetta, Women's Voices.

Indian Legends.
Schoenfeld, Henry: Pantomime Ballet.

Machicanta.
Schoenfeld, Henry: Opera.

Indian Love-Charm.
An Amerindian Cantata for Mixed voices. Cadman, Charles Wakefield: Willis.
Within range of Junior and Senior H.S. voices.

Natoma.
Herbert, V.: Schirmer.
An opera in 3 acts.

Pocahontas.
Carter, Elliot C.: MS: Ballet in one act, symphony orchestra.

Shanewis.
Cadman, Charles W.: White-Smith: Opera in 1 act.

The Flaming Arrow.
Indian Intermezzo, 1 Act. Moore, May Carr: Opera.

The Land of Misty Waters.
Cadman, Charles W.: Opera.

The Mound Builders.
American Indian Cantata. Bliss, Paul: Willis: SAB.

The Sun Bride.
1 Act. Skilton, Charles S.: Opera.

RECORDS
STUDIES

"Bibliography of Music and Books, Founded on Indian Themes and Subjects, with List of Phonograph Records." *Etude* 38:667–668, 1920.

Densmore, Frances
"Recording Indian Music." *Etude* 61:15 (Jan.) 1943. *See: AA* 47:637–638, 1945. n.s.

Goddard, Pliny Earle
A Graphic Method of Recording Songs. In: *Anthropological Papers. Boas Anniversary Volume,* pp. 137–143. New York: G. E. Stechert and Company, 1906.

Herzog, George
"The Collections of Phonograph Records in North America and Hawaii." *Zeitschrift für vergleichende Musikwissenschaft* I (3):58–62, 1933.

————.
"Recording Primitive Music in Africa and America." *FSSNE* 8:2–3, 1934.

Mindeleff, Cosmos
"Preserving Last Relics of Indian Music through Aid of the Phonograph." *Metronome* 24 (6):17, 1908.

Starr, F.
"Indian Music and Records of Iroquois Songs." *Amer. Antiquarian* 31:29, 1909.

GENERAL COLLECTIONS

American Indian Songs and Dances.
Recorded on location by Charles Hofmann. 6–10".   DISC–161
Contents: Song of Welcome; Friendship Song; Riding Song; Flag Song; Winnebago's Friend's Song; Winnebago Buffalo Feast Dance Song; Winnebago Mocassin Game Song; Game Song of Decision to Losing Side; Winnebago Morning

Song; Winnebago Love Songs (flute melodies) ; Winnebago Song of the Unfaithful Women; Two Old Winnebago Medicine Songs; Old Medicine Society Song of the Initiation to the Lodge; Opening Song of the Zuni Rain Dance; Zuni Grinding Song; Two Zuni Lullabies; Two Buffalo Feast Dance Songs (Pueblo) ; Acoma Pueblo Wedding Song; Two Old Winnebago War Songs; Two Sun Dance Songs of the Oglala Sioux; Dog Feast Dance of the Oglala Sioux; Sioux Travel Song in Wartime; Sioux War Song.

Herzog, George

"Contents of American Collections of Records of Primitive Music in the United States." *Research in Primitive and Folk Music in the United States;* American Council of Learned Societies, Washington, D. C. Bulletin 24: pp. 25–32, 1936.

_____.

"List of American Depositories of Records of Primitive Music in the United States." *Research in Primitive and Folk Music in United States;* American Council of Learned Societies, Washington, D. C. Bulletin 24: pp. 23–25, 1936.

U. S. Library of Congress. Division of Music. Folklore Section.

Collection of Indian Music. Museum of Anthropology, University of California. 2,000 cylinders.   AAFS–LC

_____.

Folk Music of the United States and Latin America. Combined Catalogue of Phonograph Records. Washington, D. C.: 1948. 47 pp.
Lists 21 albums, with contents of each.
Album 6: Songs from the Iroquois Longhouse.
Album 17: Seneca Songs from Coldspring Longhouse.

_____.

Frances Densmore Collection of Indian Music. Transferred to Library of Congress from National Archives. 3,591 cylinders.   AAFS–LC

_____.

Hopi Indian, Iroquois and Winnebago Songs. Milwaukee Public Museum Duplicating Project.   AAFC–LC

_____.

Recordings in the Archives of American Folksong.
Field recordings in all aspects of American folksong, done by numerous workers and collectors, now (1948) totalling "over 10,000 acetate recordings, with over 40,000 different songs and ballads, fiddle tunes, harmonica and banjo pieces, and other indigenous American folkmusic." This list has been immeasurably enriched by the acquisition of the Densmore Indian recordings, as well as other American Indian collections which are deposited in the Archive of American Folksong, Folksong Section, Division of Music, Library of Congress.

Part Two: Bibliography Of The Various Culture Areas

THE NORTHEASTERN WOODLAND AREA

THE NORTHEASTERN WOODLAND AREA

FOLKLORE

GENERAL STUDIES

Achard, Eugène
Anéatah et Déranah, les Jumelles d'Hochelaga
(légende Indienne). Montreal, Canada: Librairie Générale Canadienne, 1943. 132 pp.
"Hochelaga—a former Iroquoian town, strongly palisaded, situated in 1535 on Montreal id., Canada, about a mile from the mountain first called 'Mont Royal' by Cartier." (J. N. B. Hewitt.)

Anon.
"Indians of America." *Merry's Museum* 4:72–78, Sept., 1843 (NYU).
Chapt. 23 and 24: General resemblance, food, fishing, hunting, houses, dress, manner in training children, anecdote of the missionaries, traditions, superstition.

Armbruster, E. L.
The Indians of New England and New Netherland. New York: 1918. 11pp.

Atwater, C.
Remarks Made on a Tour to Prairie du Chien. Columbus, O.: 1831. 296 pp.

Bailey, Alfred G.
"The Conflict of European and Eastern Algonkian Culture, 1540–1700." *Publication, New Brunswick Museum, Monographic Series 2.* St. Johns, N. B.: 1937. 206 pp.

Bailey, Francis
Journal of a Tour in Unsettled Parts of North America in 1796 and '97. London, Eng.: 1856.

Barbeau, Charles Marius
The Downfall of Temlaham. Illustrated by A. Y. Jackson, E. H. Holgate, V. L. Kihn, E. Carr, and A. D. Savage. Toronto: The Macmillan Company of Canada Ltd., 1928. xii, 253 pp. colored plates.

_____

The Kingdom of Saguenay. Toronto: The Macmillan Company, 1936.

Battey, Thomas C.
Life and Adventures of a Quaker Among the Indians. Boston: Houghton Mifflin Co., 1876.

Beck, Horace P.
"Algonquin Folklore from Maniwaki." *JAFL* 60:259–264, 1947.
A visit to the River Desert Band of Algonquin Indians at Maniwaki, Quebec.

Beauchamp, W. M.
"Indian Nations of the Great Lakes." *Amer. Antiq.* 17:321–325, 1895.

Blair, Emma Helen, ed.
The Indian Tribes of the Upper Mississippi Valley and the Region of the Great Lakes. Cleveland: The Arthur H. Clark Co., 1911. 2 vols.

Bushnell, David, Jr.
Villages of the Algonquins, Siouan and Caddoan Tribes, West of the Mississippi. Bureau American Ethnology, Bulletin 77, pp. 1–211, 55 pls., 12 figs. Washington, D. C.: U. S. Gov't. Printing Office, 1922.

_____

Native Villages and Village Sites East of the Mississippi. Bureau of American Ethnology, Bulletin 69, 111 pp., 17 pls., 12 figs. Washington, D. C.: U. S. Gov't. Printing Office, 1919.

Butler, James D.
"Tay-cho-pe-rah. The Four Lake Country, the First White Footprints There." *Wisconsin Historical Collections,* 10:64–89, 1857–1885.

Carver, Capt. Jonathan
Travels Through the Interior Parts of North America, in the years 1766, 1767, and 1768. Illus. London: Crukshank & Co., 1778. xvi, 982 pp.

Chamberlain, Alexander Francis
"Algonkian Folklore Items." *JAFL* 13:271–277, 1900.

Charlevoix, Pierre François Xavier de
Journal of a Voyage to North America. Undertaken by order of the French King. Containing the geographical description and natural history of that country, particularly Canada. Together with an account of the customs, characters, religion, manners and traditions of the original inhabitants. . . . London: R. and J. Dodsley, 1761. 2 vols.

Cornyn, John Hubert
Around the Wigwam Fire. Boston, Mass.: Little, Brown & Co., 1921.

_____

Glooskap Stories: Related to the traditions of the Algonquin Tribes. Boston, Mass.: Little, Brown & Co., 1923. 223 pp.

_____

When the Camp Fire Burns. Boston, Mass.: Little, Brown & Co., 1923. 223 pp.

Dexter, F.
Extracts from the Itineraries and Other Miscellanies of Ezra Stiles. New Haven: 1916.

Dixon, R. B.
"The Early Migrations of the Indians of New England and the Maritime Provinces." *Proc. Amer. Antiq. Soc.* 24:65–76, 1914. n.s.

Dobbs, A.
An Account of the Countries Adjoining to Hudson's Bay. London: 1744. 211 pp.

Douglas, F. H.
"The New England Tribes." *Denver Art Mus. Ind. Leaf. Ser.* 27–28: 1–8, 1931.

Drake, Samuel G.
Indian Captivities. Auburn: 1850.

Flannery, Regina
"An Analysis of Coastal Algonquian Culture." *The Catholic University of America, Anthropological Series 7,* (pp. 1–219). Washington, D. C.: The Catholic University of America Press, 1939.

Folk-lore and Legends. North American Indian. Philadelphia: J. B. Lippincott Co., 1891. viii, 192 pp.

Forbes, Allan, comp.
Some Indian Events of New England. Boston: State Street Trust Company, 1934.
A collection of interesting incidents in the lives of the early settlers of this country and the Indians. With reproductions of rare prints.

_____
Other Indian Events of New England. Boston: State Street Trust Co., (In Commemoration of its Fiftieth Anniversary) 1941. Vol. II.
A collection of interesting incidents in the lives of the early settlers and the Indians of this country. With reproductions of rare prints and photographs.

Ford, J. A., and Willey, G. R.
"An Introduction to the Prehistory of the United States." *AA* 43:325–363, 1941. n.s.

Foreman, Grant
The Last Trek of the Indians. Chicago: University of Chicago Press, 1946. 382 pp.
"Although Mr. Foreman deals with his subject as an historian, his method of presenting facts incorporates many bits of ethnological material." (Mischa Titiev). The author discusses a Shawnee and Seneca celebration of a "Feast of Death", and a Potawatomi funeral ceremony.

Franklin, Benjamin
"Remarks on the North American Indians." *American Museum* 5:343, April, 1789.

Hamilton, J. C.
"The Algonquin Manabozho and Hiawatha." *JAFL* 16:229–233, 1903.

Henry, Alexander
Travels & Adventures in Canada and the Indian Territories, Between the Years 1760 and 1776 . . . new edition. . . . Toronto: G. N. Morang & Co., Ltd., 1901. xxxv, 347 pp., illus.

Hopkins, William John
The Indian Book. Boston: Houghton, Mifflin Co., 1911. viii, 239 pp.

Hulbert, A. B., and Schwarze, W. N., eds.
"Zeisberger's History of Northern American Indians." *Ohio Arch and Histor. Quart.* 19:1–189, 1910.

Innis, H. A.
The Fur Trade in Canada. Toronto: University of Toronto Library, 1927. 172 pp., bibl.

Jameson, Anna Brownell
Winter Studies and Summer Rambles in Canada. London: Saunders and Otley, 1838. 3 vols.

Jenness, Diamond
Indians of Canada. Bulletins of the Canada Department of Mines, National Museum of Canada. Ottawa, 1932. 446 pp., illus., bibl.

Johnston, John
Account of the Present State of Indian Tribes Inhabiting Ohio. Transactions and Collections of the American Antiquarian Society (Worcester), Vol. 1, 1920.

Judd, M. C.
Wigwam Stories Told by North American Indians. Illustrated by Anjel de Cora. Boston: Ginn and Company, 1901. ix, 276 pp., fronts, illus.

Kellogg, L. P., ed.
Early Narratives of the Northwest. New York: 1917. 382 pp.

Kindail, Edward Augustus
Travels Throughout the Northern Parts of the United States, in the Years 1807 and 1808. New York: I. Riley (Prtg. and Pub.) 1809. 3 vols.

Kittredge, George Lyman
Letters of Samuel Lee and Samuel Sewall Relating to New England and the Indians, The Publications of the Colonial Society of Massachusetts. Cambridge, Mass.: Harvard University Press, 1912.
In the writings of the Colonial fathers one finds much material on the beliefs, myths, superstitions, traditions, legends and customs of the early settlers.

Lacombe, R. P.
"La Génie de la Langue Algonquine." *Proceedings of the 15th Session of the International Congress of Americanists,* 2:225–243, 1906.

Lahontan, Baron
New Voyages to North America. Containing an account of the several nations of that vast continent, etc. (Lord Lieutenant of the French Colony at Placentia in Newfoundland). London: Printed for H. Bonwicke, T. Goodwin, M. Wotton, B. Tooke, and S. Manship, 1703. 2 vols., front. pl. (part. fold.) maps.
Another edition, ed. by R. G. Thwaites, issued in Chicago. 1905.

Lanman, Charles
Haw-ho-noo or Records of a Tourist. Philadelphia: Lippincott, Grambo and Co., 1850. 266 pp.

Laverdière, C. H., ed.
Oeuvres de Champlain. Quebec: 1870. 6 vols.

Long, John
Voyages and Travels of an Indian Interpreter and Trader, describing the manners and customs of the North American Indians; with an account of the posts situated on the St. Lawrence River, Lake Ontario, etc. A vocabulary of the Chippeway language. London: Printed for author, and sold by Robson, 1791. x, 295 pp., fold. map.

Loskiel, G. H.
History of the Mission of the United Brethren Among the Indians of North America. London: 1794.

Mackenzie, Alexander
Voyages from Montreal on the St. Lawrence River, through the Continent of North America to the Frozen and Pacific Oceans, 1789–1793. With a preliminary account of the rise, progress, and present state of the fur trade of that country. Philadelphia: John Morgan, 1802. viii–cxxvi, 392, pp., fold. map.

Margry, Pierre.
Découvertes et establissements des Français dans l'ouest et dans le sud de l'Amérique septentrionale (1614-1754): mémoirs et documents par originaux receuilles et publiés par Pierre Margry, etc. Paris: Impr. D. Jonaust, 1875–1886. 6 vols.

Marquette, J., and Joliet, L.
"An Account of the Discovery of Some New Countries and Nations in North America." *Histor. Coll. of Louisiana* 2:277–297, 1850.

Michelson, Truman
"Algonquian Notes." *International Journal of American Linguistics,* 9:103–116. New York: Columbia University Press, 1939.

Mooney, James
The Siouan Tribes of the East. Bureau of American Ethnology, Bulletin 22, pp. 1–105, 1 map. Washington, D. C.: U. S. Gov't Printing Office, 1894 (1895).

Moorhead, Warren King
"Prehistoric Culture Areas East of the Rocky Mountains." *Proceedings of the 23rd Session of the International Congress of Americanists,* pp. 47–52, 1928.

Parkins, A. E.
"The Indians of the Great Lakes Region and Their Environment." *Georgr. Rev.* 6:504–512, 1918.

Perrot, N.
Mémoire sur les moeurs, coustumes et relligion (!) des sauvages de l'Amérique Septentrionale. Paris: A. Franck, 1864. viii, xlviii, 841 pp.

Pike, Maj. Z. M.
An Account of Expeditions to the Sources of the Mississippi, and through the western parts of Louisiana to the sources of the Arkansas, Kansas, LaPlatte and Pierre Jaun Rivers. Philadelphia: C. and A. Conrad and Company, 1810. v, 277+65+53+87 pp., front, (port) maps (part. fold.), tables (part. fold.).

Potherie, B. de la
"History of the Savage Peoples Who Are Allies of New France." In: *The Indian Tribes of the Upper Mississippi Valley,* ed. by E. H. Blair. Vol. I, pp. 273–372, Vol. II, pp. 13–136, Cleveland. 1911–1912.

Pusey, William Allen
Wilderness Road to Kentucky: Its location and features. New York: George H. Doran Company, 1921. xi+xiii, 131+14 pp., incl. illus., plates, maps, facsims., front 2 fold, maps.

Ritchie, William A.
"Culture Influences from Ohio in New York Archaeology." *American Antiquity 2:* 182–194, 1937.

Silvy, A.
Relation par lettres de l'Amérique Septentrionale, ed. by de Rochemonteix. Paris: 1904. 221 pp.

Skinner, Alanson
"Some Aspects of the Folk-lore of the Central Algonkin." *JAFL* 27:97–100, 1914.

Snelling, William Joseph
Tales of the Northwest; or, Sketches of Indian Life and Character. By a resident beyond the frontier. Boston: Hilliard, Gray, Little, and Wilkins, 1830. viii, 288 pp.

Speck, Frank G.
"Culture Problems on Northeastern North America." *Proceedings American Philosophical Society,* 65:272–311, 1926.

———.
Myths and Folklore of the Timiskaming Algonquin and Timigami Ojibwa. Ottawa: Geological Survey of Canada, Anthropological Series, IX, 1915.

———.
"The Social Structure of the Northern Algonkian." *Publ. Amer. Sociol. Soc.* 12:82–100, 1917.

Spier, Leslie
"The Trenton Argillite Culture." *Anthro. Papers Amer. Mus. Nat. Hist.* 22:167–226, 1918.

Sylvester, Herbert Milton
Indian Wars of New England. Boston: W. B. Clarke Company, 1910. 3 vols.

Terry, F. T.
"Aborigines of the Northwest." *Parkman Club Publications* 4: 59–72, 1896.

Thompson, J. M.
Over Indian and Animal Trails. Eight color illustrations by Paul Bransom. New York: F. A. Stokes Co., 1918. 263 pp.

Thwaites, R. G., ed.
The French Regime in Wisconsin. Annual Reports and Collections of the State Historical Society of Wisconsin. Vols. XVI-XVIII. 1902–1908.

White, Henry
Indian Battles; with Incidents in the Early History of New England. Containing... Narratives of Battles, Captivities, Escapes, Ambuscades, Assaults, Massacres and Depredations of the Indians. The Habits, Customs, and Traits of Character Peculiar to the Indian Race. The Life and Exploits of Capt. Miles Standish. The History of King Phillip's War, and Personal and Historical Incidents of the Revolutionary War. New York: D. W. Evans & Co., 1859. iv, 428 pp.

Wintemberg, W. J.
"Distinguishing Characteristics of Algonkian and Iroquoian Cultures." *Bull. Can. Dept. Mines, Nat. Mus. Can.* 67:65–124, 1931.

MYTHS—FOLKTALES—LEGENDS

Allanson, Winona Blanche
Indian Moons. Illustrations by W. J. Wilwerding. Minneapolis, Minn.: Augsburg Publishing House, 1927. 63 pp., illus.
Legends of the North American Indian.

Alger, Abby Langdon
In Indian Tents. Stories told by Penobscot, Passamaquoddy, and Micmac Indians. Boston: Roberts Brothers, 1897. viii, 139 pp.

Brill, Ethel Claire
The Boy Who Went to the East, and Other Indian Fairy Tales. (Iroquois and Algonquin.) New York: E. P. Dutton & Co., 1917. 296 p.

Brown, William Edgar
Echoes of the Forest, American Indian Legends. Boston: R. G. Badger, 1918. 264 pp., illus., bibl.: pp. 261-264.

Browne, George Waldo
Indian Nights; Famous Indian Legends, illustrated by Alexander Key. New York: Noble and Noble, 1927. vii, 248 pp., illus.

Curtin, Jeremiah
Creation Myths of Primitive America in Relation to the Religious History and Mental Development of Mankind. Boston: Little, Brown and Company, 1898. xxxix, 530 pp.

Dixon, Roland B.
"The Mythology of the Central and Eastern Algonkins." *JAFL* 22 (No. 83):1–9, 1909.

Graves, Merle Dixon
Manitou and the Animals, an Indian Legend. Illustrated by the Author. Albany: L. L. Fuller, 1935. 48 pp., illus.

Hamilton, James Cleland
"Famous Algonquins; Algic Legends." *Canadian Institute Transactions* 6:285–312, 1898–99.

———.
"Two Algonquin Legends. The Loon and the Ka-Kakè." *JAFL* 7:201–204, 1894.

Jones, James Athearn
Traditions of the North American Indians: Being a second and revised edition of "Tales of an Indian Camp." London: H. Colburn & R. Bentley, 1830. 3 vols., illus.

Judson, Katharine Berry
Myths and Legends of the Mississippi Valley and the Great Lakes. Chicago: A. C. McClurg & Co., 1914. xiv, 215 pp.

Krickeberg, Walter
Indianermaerchen aus Nordamerika. Jena: E. Diederichs, 1924. vi, 418 pp., illus., bibl.
North American Indian folktales.

Larned, William Trowbridge
American Indian Fairy Tales. Illustrated by John Roe. New York: P. F. Volland Co., 1921. 93 pp., col. illus.
"With one exception, all the tales in this book are adapted from the legends collected by Henry R. Schoolcraft . . . and published in 1839. With the title "Algic Researches."

Leland, Charles Godfrey
The Algonquin Legends of New England; or, myths and folklore of the Micmac, Passamaquoddy, and Penobscot tribes. Boston: Houghton, Mifflin & Co., 1884. xv, 379 pp., bibl., illus.

Logie, A. E.
Canadian Wonder Tales. (Algonquin). Drawings by Dorothy Hansacre. Chicago: Row Peterson and Company, 1925. v, 228 pp., incl. front., illus.

MacMillan, C.
Canadian Wonder Tales, (Algonquin), with illustrations in color by George Sheringham, and a foreword by Sir William Peterson. London and New York: John Lane, 1918. xvi, 199 pp., col. front, col. plates.

———.
North American Indian Fairy Tales, Folklore and Legend. Illustrated by R. C. Armour. London: Gibbings & Co., 1905. viii, 192 pp., illus.

Schoolcraft, Henry Rowe
Algic Researches, Comprising Inquiries Respecting the Mental Characteristics of the North American Indians. First series. Indian Tales and Legends. New York: Harper & Bros., 1839. 2 vols.

———.
The Myth of Hiawatha, and other Oral Legends, Mythologic and Allegoric, of the North American Indians. Philadelphia: J. B. Lippincott & Co., 1856. xxiv, 343 pp.
An earlier edition, New York 1839, in two volumes, appeared under title: "Algic Researches."

Scott, Robert Graham
Indian Romances. Boston: Meador Publishing Company, 1933. 141 pp., illus.

Skinner, Alanson
"Algonquin and the Thunderbird." *American Museum Journal* (continued as *Natural History*) 14:71–72, 1914.

Speck, Frank G.
"An Algonkian Myth." *University of Penn. Museum Journ.* 1:49–, 1910.

————.
Myths and Folk-lore of the Timiskaming Algonquin and Timigami Ojibwa. Geological Survey of Canada, Anthrop. Ser. 9, Ottawa: 1915. iii, 87 pp.

Spence, Lewis
The Myths of the North American Indians. With plates by Jack, James. London: G. G. Harrap & Co., 1914. xii, 392 pp., illus., bibl.: pp. 363-374.

Wilson, Gilbert L.
Indian Hero Tales. Chicago: American Book Co., 1916. 203 pp.
Abnaki-Algonquian-Micmac tales.

————.
Myths of the Red Children; illustrated by Frederick N. Wilson. Boston: Ginn & Company, 1907. ix, 154 pp., illus.

Young, Egerton Ryerson
Algonquin Indian Tales. New York: Eaton and Mains, 1903. 258 pp., illus.

BELIEFS—WITCHCRAFT—MAGIC

Blinkenberg, Christian
The Thunderweapon in Religion and Folklore. A Study in Comparative Archaeology. Cambridge: University Press, 1911. xii, 122 pp.

Chamberlain, Alexander Francis
"The Maple Amongst the Algonkian Tribes." *AA* 4:39–45, 381–385, 1891.

————.
"The Thunder Bird Among the Algonkians." *AA* 3:51–55, 1890.

————.
"Primitive Nature Study." *Transactions of the Canadian Institute,* (Toronto), 6:330, 1899.

Cooper, John M.
"Field Notes on Nothern Algonkian Magic." *Proceedings of the 23rd Session of the International Congress of Americanists,* pp. 513-519, 1928.

————.
"The Northern Algonquian Supreme Being." *Anthropological Series, Catholic University of America, No. 2.* (78 pp.). Washington, D. C.: Catholic University of America Press, 1934.

Dixon, R. B.
"Mythology of the Central and Eastern Algonkins." *JAFL* 22:1–9, 1909.

Hewitt, J. N. B.
Nanabozho. In: *Handbook of American Indians* Vol. II, pp. 19–23. Bureau of American Ethnology, Bulletin 30. Washington, D. C.: U. S. Government Printing Office, 1910.
"The demiurge of the cosmologic traditions of the Algonquin tribes, known among the various

peoples by several unrelated names, based on some marked characteristic or dominant function of this personage. . . . Nanabozho is apparently the impersonation of life, the active quickening power of life—of life manifested and embodied in the myriad forms of sentient and physical nature."

Jarvis, Rev. Samuel F.
A Discourse on the Religion of the Indian Tribes of North America. Delivered before the New York Historical Society, December 20, 1819. New York: C. Wiley & Co., 1820. 111 pp.

Jones, William
"Algonkin Manitou." *JAFL* 18:183–190, 1905.

Leland, Charles Godfrey
Kulóskap the Master, and other Algonkin poems; translated metrically. New York: Funk & Wagnalls Co., 1902. 370 pp.

Loewenthal, Joel Wulf John
Die Religion der Ostalgonkin. Berlin: W. & S. Loewenthal, 1913. 219 pp., illus., bibl.

MacLeod, W. C.
"The Sun Dials and Other Time-Route Recorders of the Northern Woodlands and the Northwest Coast." *AA* 32:577–578, 1930. n. s.

Smith, Seba
"The Religion and Superstition of the North American Indians-No. II." *The Literary Emporium* 3:97–100, April 1846.
Comments on the beliefs and religious ceremonies of the Chippewas, Sauks and Musquakies.

————.
" The Religion and Superstition of the North American Indians, No. III, IV, V." *The Literary Emporium* 3:129–133; 170–174; 230–233, May, June, Aug. 1846.
Belief and ceremonies for the dead among the Hurons, Iroquois, and Chepewyans, also comments on their beliefs in immortality.

Speck, Frank G.
"Bird Lore of the Northern Indians." *Public Lectures of the University of Pennsylvania Faculty,* 7:349–380, 1920.

————.
"Reptile Lore of the Northern Indians." *JAFL* 36:273–280, 1923.

CUSTOMS

Atwater, Caleb
Indians of the Northwest, their manners, customs, etc., or remarks made on a tour to Prairie du Chien, and thence to Washington City in 1829. Columbus, O.: (No Publisher.), 1850. 269 pp.

Bushnell, David I., Jr.
Burials of the Algonquin, Siouan and Caddoan Tribes, West of the Mississippi. Bureau American Ethnology, Bulletin 77, 103 pp., 37 pl., 3 fig. Washington, D. C.: U. S. Govt. Printing Office, 1927.

————.
Native Cemeteries and Forms of Burial East of the Mississippi. Bureau of American Ethnology, Bulletin 71, 160 pp., 17 pl., 17 figs. Washington, D. C.: U. S. Gov't. Printing Office, 1920.

Chamberlain, L. S.
"Plants Used by the Indians of Eastern North America." *Amer. Natur.* 35:1–10, 1901.

Cooper, John M.
"Snares, Deadfalls, and other Traps of the Northern Athapascans." In: *Anthropological Series I, Catholic Conference of America 5,* (114 pp.). Washington, D. C.: U. S. Government Printing Office, 1938.
Involves discussion of hunting methods.

Douglas, F. H.
"Iroquoian and Algonkian Wampum." *Denver Art Mus. Leaf. Ser.* 31:1–4, 1931.

Hadlock, Wendell S.
"War Among the Northeastern Woodland Indians." *AA* 49(No. 2):204–222, 1947. n.s. bibl.

Hallowell, A. Irving
"Was Cross-Cousin Marriage Practiced by the North-Central Algonkian?" *Proceedings of the 23rd Session of the International Congress of Americanists,* pp. 519–545, 1928.

Hinsdale, W. B.
"Indian Corn Culture in Michigan." *Papers Mich. Acad. Sci Arts. Letters* 8:31–49, 1927.

J., E. W.
"Letters from the Indian Country." *The Knickerbocker* 20:1–5, July 1842.
Customs and manners of the Indians of the Northeast.

Mallery, Col. Garrick
"Sign Language Among Northern Indians." *1st Annual Report: Bureau of American Ethnology, 1879–1880,* pp. 269–550, figs. 61–346. Washington, D. C.: U. S. Government Printing Office, 1881.
Gestures, origin of sign language, gestures of children, deaf mutes, smoke signals, sign language of women, etc.

Merwin, B. W.
"Wampum." *Mus. Journ.* (Univ. Penna.)7: 125–133, 1916.

Michelson, Truman
"Some Algonquian Kinship Terms." *AA* 34:357–359, 1932. n. s.

Philhower, C. A.
"Indian Currency and Its Manufacture." *Proc. New Jersey Hist. Soc.* 13:310–318, 1928. n.s.

————.
"Wampum, Its Use and Value." *Proc. New Jersey Hist. Soc.* 15:216–223, 1930. n.s.

Rogers, Robert
A Concise Account of North America: Containing a description of the several British colonies on that continent including the islands of Newfoundland, Cape Breton, etc. . . . To which is subjoined, an account of the several nations and tribes of Indians residing in those parts, as to their customs, manners, . . . London: Printed for the Author, Sold by J. Millan, 1765. vii, 264 pp.

Speck, Frank G.
The Function of Wampum Among the Eastern Algonkian. Memoir of the American Anthropological Association, No. 6. Lancaster, Pa.: 1919. 71 pp.

————.
"Wampum in Tradition and Currency." *Proceedings of the Numismatic and Antiquarian Society of Philadelphia* 27:121–130, 1916.

————, and Eisley, L. C.
"Significance of Hunting Territory Systems of the Algonkian in Social Theory." *AA* 41:269–280, 1939. n.s.

Strong, J. C.
Wah-kee-nah and her People: The curious Customs, Traditions, and Legends of the North American Indians. New York: G. P. Putnam Sons, 1893.

Strong, W. D.
"Cross-Cousin Marriage and the Culture of the Northeastern Algonkian." *AA* 31:277–288, 1929. n. s.

West, G. A.
"Copper: Its Mining and Use by the Aborigines of the Lake Superior Region." *Bull. Publ. Mus. Milwaukee* 10:1–184, 1929.

————.
"Use of Tobacco and the Calumet by Wisconsin Indians." *Wis. Arch.* 10:5–64, 1911.

Woodward, Ashbel
Wampum; A paper presented to the Numismatic and Antiquarian Society of Philadelphia . . . 2d ed. Albany, N. Y.: Munsell, Printer, 1880. 56 pp.

FOLK MEDICINE

Harris, W. R.
"Practice of Medicine and Surgery by the Canadian Tribes in Champlain's Time." *Ann. Arch. Report* (Toronto), 1915, pp. 35–54.

Speck, Frank G.
"Medicine Practices of the Northeastern Algonquians." *Proceedings of the 19th Session of the International Congress of Americanists,* pp. 303-321, 1915.

————.
"More Algonkian Scapulimancy from the North and the Hunting Territory Question." *Ethnos* 4 (No. 1.):21–28. Stockholm: Bokförlags Aktiebolget Thule, 1939.

FOLK POETRY—ART—SPEECH

Abbott, Charles Conrad
Primitive Industry: or illustrations of the hand-work, in stone, bone and clay, of the native races of the northern Atlantic seaboard of America. Salem, Mass.: G. A. Bates, 1881. vi, 560 pp. illus.

Anon.
"Indian Gods, of Shingaba-Wossins." *American Penny Magazine* 1:261–262, May 31, 1845 (NYU).
> An account of the ability of the native tribes who occupy the borders of the Great Lakes to sculpt loose rocks into idols. Also a description of the various idols—with illustrations.

Barbeau, Charles Marius
"The Origin of Floral and Other Designs Among the Canadian and Neighboring Indians." *Proceedings of the 23rd Session of the International Congress of Americanists*, pp. 512–513, 1928.

Birket-Smith, K.
"Ancient Artifacts from Eastern United States." *Jour. Société Amér.* 12:141–169, 1920. n.s.

Bloomfield, Leonard
"On the Sound System of Central Algonquian." *Language* 1:130–156, 1925.

Campbell, John
"The Affiliation of the Algonquin Languages." *Canadian Institute Proceedings*, New Series, 1(pt.1):15–53, 1879 (Toronto).

——————.
"On the Origin of Some American Indian Tribes." *Montreal National Historical Society Proceedings*, 9:193–212, 1879 (Montreal).

Chamberlain, Alexander Francis
"The Algonkian Linguistic Stock." *Proceedings of the 13th Session of the International Congress of Americanists*, (New York), pp. 5-9, 1902.

——————.
"Algonkian Words in American English." *JAFL* 15:240–267, 1902.

——————.
"Significance of Certain Algonquian Animal-Names." *AA* 3:669–684, 1901. n. s.

Douglas-Lithgow, R. A.
A Dictionary of American Indian Place and Proper Names in New England. Salem, Mass.: 1909. 400 pp.

Griffin, J. B.
"Aboriginal Methods of Pottery Manufacture in Eastern United States." *Penna. Arch.* 5: 19–24, 1935.

Holmes, William Henry
"Aboriginal Pottery of the Eastern United States." *Ann. Report, Bur. Amer. Ethnol.* 20. 201 pp. Washington, D. C.: 1899.

——————.
"Prehistoric Textile Art of Eastern United States." *13th Annual Report: Bureau American Ethnology, 1891–1892.* pp. 9–37, pls.1–9, figs. 1–28. Washington, D. C.: U. S. Government Printing Office, 1896.
> Scope of the work, materials and processes. Products of the art, matting, pliable fabrics, fossil fabrics, etc.

Howes, William J.
"Aboriginal New England Pottery." *Bull. Arch. Soc.* 5(No. 1):1–5, 1943.

Jones, William
"Some Principles of Algonquian Word-formation." *AA* 6:369–413, 1904. n. s.

Kuloskap the master, and other Algonkin Poems. Translated metrically by Leland, C. G. and Prince, J. D. New York: Funk & Wagnalls Co., 1902. 370 pp., illus.

Michelson, Truman
"Some Algonquian Kinship Terms." *AA* 34: 357–359, 1932. n.s.

Müller, F.
"Der grammatische Bau der Algonkin-Sprachen." *Sitzungsberichte der Kaiserlichen Akademie der Wissenschaften.* Philosophisch-Historische Klasse. (Wien) 56:132–154, 1867.

Pilling, J. C.
Bibliography of the Algonquian Languages. Bureau of Amer. Ethnol. Bull. 13. Washington, D. C.: U. S. Gov't. Printing Office, 1891. 614 pp.

——————.
Bibliography of the Iroquoian Languages. Bureau of Amer. Ethnol. Bull. 6. Washington, D. C.: U. S. Gov't Printing Office, 1888. 208 pp.

Sherwin, Reider T.
The Viking and the Red Man: The Old Norse Origin of the Algonquian Language. New York: Funk and Wagnalls Co., 1940. 340 pp.

Speck, Frank G.
"Art Processes in Birchbark of the River Desert Algonquin, a Circumboreal Trait." *Anthropological Papers No. 17, Bureau of American Ethnology*, Bulletin 128:229–274, 13 pls. Washington, D. C.: U. S. Gov't. Printing Office, 1941.

Tooker, W. W.
"Algonquian Names of Some Mountains and Hills." *JAFL* 17:171–179, 1904.

Waugh, F. W.
"Canadian Aboriginal Canoes." *Canad. Field Natur.* (Ottawa) 33:23–33, 1919.

Willoughby, C. C.
"Wooden Bowls of the Algonquian Indians." *AA* 10:423–434 1908. n.s.

GAMES

Anon.
"Jumping Rabbit's Story." *Merry's Museum*
6:20–22, 54–56, 65–68, 118–120, 140–143, 179–
182, July–Dec. 1843.
> A narrative giving a detailed account of games,
> festivities, hunting adventures among the Indians.

—————.
"On Diversions and Holidays." *The Port-Folio*
17(Ser. 5):218–224, March 1824.
> Sports and Games among the Indians. An appeal
> to parents for the need for physical education in
> the schools.

"Algonkin Games."
JAFL 9:275, 1896; 13:272–275, 1900.

Oneota
"Pugasaing, or the Game of Bowl." *The American Eagle Magazine* 1:53–56, 1847.
> Description of the Indian game.

MUSIC

GENERAL STUDIES

Anon.
"Musical Barbarity." *The Musical Review*
2:62, June 15, 1839.
> Description of respect shown to sacred musical
> compositions and their composers; barbaric deeds
> and the role of music.

Barrett, S. A.
"The Dream Dance of the Chippewa and
Menominee Indians of Northern Wisconsin."
Bulletin Milwaukee Museum 1:251–406, 1911.

Shaw, Beatrice M. Hay
"Indians of the Maritimes." *Canadian Magazine* (Toronto) 58:343–350, 1922.
> Contains musical examples.

Skinner, Alanson
"Medicine Ceremony of the Menomini, Iowa
and Wahpeton Dakota." with notes on the ceremony among the Ponca, Bungi, Ojibwa and
Potawatomi. *Indian Notes and Mimeographs,
Museum of the American Indian, Heye Foundation* 4:357 pp., 1920.
> Musical examples.

DANCE

Anon.
"An Indian Dance." *Dwight's American Magazine* 3:520, Aug. 13, 1847.
> An account of the various Indian dances, of
> war and religion, among the different tribes.
> Illustrated.

Hartley, Marsden
"Tribal Esthetics." *The Dial* 45:399–401, 1918.
> The American Indian dances as a means of self-
> expression.

Kool, Jaap
*Tänze der Naturvölker; ein Deutungsversuch
Primitiver Tanzkulte und Kultgebräuche.*
Berlin: A. Fürstner, 1921. 90 pp., illus., bibl.
> A study of primitive dance.

RECORDS

Studies

Herzog, George
North-Eastern Woodlands Area. In: *American
Council of Learned Societies Bulletin No. 24*
(pp. 28–29). Washington, D. C.: U. S. Government Printing Office, 1936.

Individual Titles

"Dirge."
From Indian Suite No. 2, opus 48, (MacDowell,
Edward). Eastman Rochester Orchestra—
Hansen VI–15657. In: Album: *American Music
for Orchestra*   **VM–608**

"Indianisches Tagebuch."
Nos. 1, 2, 3, 4, (Busoni) Egon Petri, Piano.
       CO—69010
> Based on American Indian themes.

"Indian Suite."
No. 2, opus 48, (MacDowell, Edward). CBS
Symphony Orchestra—Barlow   **CM–373**

"Second Sketch Based on Indian Themes."
(Charles T. Griffes).
Flonzaley Quartet.   **VI–545B**

"Suite Primeval."
Part I: Indian War Dance; Suite Primeval.
Part II: Sunrise Dance (Skilton, C.) Eastman-
Rochester Symphony Orchestra.   **VI–11–8302**

"The False-Face Company."
Sung by Joshua Buck and Simeon Gibson at
Six Nations Reserve, Canada, 1941.
1. Marching or Dream Song for the Winds
   (Buck).
2. Onondaga address to the Hunchbacks
   (Gibson).
3. Song of the Hunchbacks or False-faces
   (Buck).
4. Song of the Bush-heads or Husk-faces
   (Buck).
In: Album VI: Library of Congress 1943.
       AAFS528A

"Two Sketches based on Indian Themes."
(Griffes, Charles).
Coolidge Quartet.   **VI–15416N**
In Set: **VM–558**

ABNAKI

See: Penobscot, pp. 877-78.

FOLKLORE

GENERAL STUDIES

Alger, Abby Langdon
In Indian Tents; stories told by Penobscot,
Passamaquoddy and Mimac Indians. Boston:
Roberts Brothers, 1897. x, 139 pp.

Baxter, J. P.
"The Abnakis and their Ethnic Relations."
Collections Maine Hist. Soc., Ser. 2, 3:13–40,
1892.

Burrage, H. S., ed.
Early English and French Voyages, chiefly from Hakluyt, 1534–1608. New York: C. Scribner's Sons, 1906. xxii, 451 pp., illus.

Chamberlain, A. F.
"Indians of the Eastern Provinces of Canada." *Ann. Arch. Report* (Toronto), 1905. pp. 122–136.

Douglas, F. H., comp.
The New England Tribes. Denver Art Museum, Department of Indian Art, Leaflets No. 27 and 28, July 1931.

Kidder, F.
"The Abenaki Indians." *Collections of the Maine Histor. Soc.* 6:229–263, 1859.

Maurault, Joseph Pierre Anselme
Histoire des Abenakis, depuis 1605 jusqu'à nos jours. Sorel. Qué.: Imprimé à l'atelier typographique de la "Gazette de Sorel," 1866. iii, x, 631 pp.

Merlet, Lucien Victor Claude
Histoires des relations des Hurons et des Abnaquis du Canada avec Notre-Dame de Chartres, suivie de documents inédits sur la sainte chemise . . . Chartres: Pétrot-Garnier, 1858. xxiii, 78 pp.

Mooney, J., and Thomas, C.
"Abnaki." *Bur. Amer. Ethnol. Bull.* 30 (Part 1):2–6, 1907.

Nicholar, Joseph
The Life and Traditions of the Red Man. Bangor, Me.: C. H. Glass & Co., 1893. v, 147 pp.

Sabine, L.
"Indian Tribes of New England." *Christian Examiner* 62:27–54, 210–237, 1857.

Speck, Frank G.
"Abnaki Texts." *International Journal of American Linguistics* 11:45–46, 1945.

———.
"Abnaki Clans-Never!" *AA* 37:528–530, 1935. n.s.

———.
"The Eastern Algonkian Wabanaki Confederacy." *AA* 17:492–508, 1915. n.s.

———.
"The Family Hunting Band as the Basis of Algonkian Social Organization." *AA* 17:289–305, 1914. n.s.

———.
"Kinship Terms and the Family Band Among the Northeastern Algonkian." *AA* 20: 143–161, 1918. n.s.

Sylvester, H. M.
Indian Wars of New England. Boston: W. B. Clarke Co., 1910. 3 vols.

Vetromile, Eugene
"The Abanaki Indians." *Collections Maine Hist. Soc.*, 1st ser., 6:203–227, 1859.

———.
The Abanakis and Their History, or, Historical Notices on the Aborigines of Acadia. New York: J. B. Kirker, 1866. xi, 171 pp., illus.

———.
"Acadia and its Aborigines." *Coll. Maine Hist. Soc.*, 1st ser., 7:337–349, 1876.

MYTHS—FOLKTALES—LEGENDS

Brown, Mrs. W. W.
"Wa-bo-nal, or Northern Lights." *JAFL* 3:213–214, 1890.

Eckstorm, Fannie Hardy
"Katahdin Legends." *Appalachia* 16:39–52, 1924. n.s.

Frost, H. K.
"The Abnaki Legends." *JAFL* 25:188–190, 1912.

Mallery, Garrick
"The Fight with the Giant Witch." *AA* 3:65–71, 1890.

Masta, Henry L.
Abenaki Indian Legends, Grammar and Place Names. Victoriaville, P. Q.: La Voix des Bois-Francs, 1932. 110 pp., illus.
Contains tunes and words of two songs, pp. 109-110.

Nicholar, Joseph
The Life and Traditions of the Red Man. Bangor, Me.: C. H. Glass & Co., 1893. v, 147 pp.

Speck, Frank G.
"Wawenock Myth Texts from Maine." *43rd Annual Report: Bureau of American Ethnology*, Smithsonian Institution, 1925. pp. 165–197. Washington, D. C.: U. S. Government Printing Office, 1925.
Wawenoc (Wewenoc)—A tribe of the Abnaki Confederacy that lived on the coast of Maine about the mouth of the Kennebec River, in Lincoln and Sagadanoc Counties.

Stamp, H.
"The Water-Fairies." *JAFL* 28:310–316, 1915.

Tahament, R.
"The Story of the Magic Arrow." *Carlisle Arrow* 8:(No. 2) 4, 1911.

Wilson, Gilbert L.
Indian Hero Tales. Chicago: American Book Co., 1916.

BELIEFS—CUSTOMS

Gatschet, A. S.
"Deities of the Early New England Indians." *JAFL* 12:211–212, 1899.

Hallowell, A. Irving
"Recent Historical Changes in the Kinship Terminology of the St. Francis Abenaki." *Proceedings of the 23rd Session of the International Congress of Americanists*, 2:97–147, 1928.

Willoughby, Charles C.
"Dress and Ornaments of the New England Indians." *AA* 7:499–509, 1905. n. s.

FOLK ART—SPEECH

Eckstorm, Fannie Hardy
"Handicrafts of the Modern Indians of Maine." *Bulletins of the Abbe Museum*, No. 3. 1932. 72 pp.

Laurent, Joseph
New Familiar Abenakis and English Dialogues, the First Ever Published on the Grammatical System . . . Quebec: L. Brousseau, 1884. 230 pp.
　The first vocabulary ever published in the Abanaki language. The work also contains etymology of Indian names, of certain localities, rivers, lakes, etc.

O'Brien, M. C.
"Grammatical Sketch of the Ancient Abnaki." *Coll. Maine Hist. Soc.* 9:259–294, 1887.

Prince, John D.
"The Differentiation Between the Penobscot and the Canadian Abenaki Dialects." *AA* 4: 17–32, 1902. n.s.

——————.
"The Modern Dialect of the Canadian Abenaki." In: *Miscellanea Linguistica in Onore di Graziadio Ascoli*, pp. 343–362. Torino: 1901.

Rasles, S.
"A Dictionary of the Abnaki Language." *Memoirs of the American Academy of Sciences and Arts* 1:375–574, 1833. n.s.

Willis, W.
"The Language of the Abnaquies." *Coll. Maine Hist. Soc.* 4:93–117, 1856.

Willoughby, Charles Clark
"The Adze and Ungrooved Axe of the New England Indians." *AA* 9:296–306, 1907. n.s.

——————.
Antiquities of New England Indians, with notes on ancient cultures of the adjacent territory. Cambridge, Mass.: The Peabody Museum of American Archaeology and Ethnology, Harvard Univ., 1935. 314 pp., illus.

——————.
"Pottery of the New England Indians." In: *Putnam Anniversary Volume*, pp. 83–101. New York: 1909.

——————.
"Textile Fabrics of the New England Indians." *AA* 7:85–93, 1905. n.s.

GAMES

Brown, Mrs. W. W.
"Some Indoor and Outdoor Games of the Wabanaki Indians." *Transactions of the Royal Society of Canada, Section* 6(Part 2):41–46, 1888.

Newell, W. W.
"Wabanaki Counting-out Rhyme." *JAFL* 3:71–73, 1890.

MUSIC
GENERAL STUDIES

Curtis, Natalie
Eastern Indians: Wabanaki. In: *The Indians Book*, pp. 1–31. New York: Harper and Bros., 1907. Texts and Tunes.

Reade, John
"Some Wabanaki Songs." *Proceedings and Transactions of Royal Society of Canada* (Montreal) 5 (sect. 2):1–8, 1888,

BEOTHUK
FOLKLORE
GENERAL STUDIES

Anon.
"Mary May: the Newfoundland Indian." *The Knickerbocker* 23:5–23, June 1844.
　Habits and customs of the Newfoundland aborigines, called "Red Indians."

Blake, E.
"The Beothuks of Newfoundland." *Nineteenth Century* 24:899–918, 1888.

Burrage, H. S., ed.
Early English and French Voyages, Chiefly from Hakluyt, 1534–1608, pp. 4-24. New York: C. Scribner's Son's, 1906. xxii, 451 pp., illus.

Chamberlain, A. F.
"The Beothunks of Newfoundland." *Annual Archaeological Report*, Ontario 1905, Toronto, 1906. pp. 117–122.

Chappell, E.
Voyage of His Majesty's Ship Rosamond to Newfoundland, pp. 69–87. London: 1818.

Gatschet, A. S.
"The Beothuk Indians." *Proceedings of the American Philosophical Society* 23:417–428, 1886.

Hewitt, J. N. B., and Gatschet, A. S.
"Beothukan Family." In: *Bulletin 30* (Part 1): 141–142. *Bureau of Amer. Ethnol.*, 1907.

Howley, James P.
The Beothucks or Red Indians. The Aboriginal Inhabitants of Newfoundland. London: Cambridge University Press, 1915. xx, 348 pp.

Jenness, D.
"Notes on the Beothuk Indians of Newfoundland." *National Museum of Canada*, Bulletin 56:36–40, 1929.

Klittke, M.
"Die Beothuk-Indianer von Neufundland." *Aus Allen Welttheilen* 25:235–247, 1894.

Lloyd, T. G. B.
A Further Account of the Beothucs of New-foundland." *Jour. Royal Anthro. Inst. Gt. Brit.* 5:222–230, 1875.

―――――.
"On the 'Beothucs'." *Jour Royal Anthro. Inst. Gt. Brit.* 4:21–39, 1874.

Macdougall, A.
"The Beothic Indians." *Trans. Can. Inst.* 2: 98–102, 1891.

Patterson, G.
"The Beothiks or Red Indians of Newfound-land." *Proc. Trans. Royal Soc. Can.* 9(Part 2):123–171, 1891.

Pilot, W., and Gray, L. H.
"Beothuks." *Encyclopedia of Religion and Ethics*, J. Hastings, ed. Vol. 2, pp. 501–503. New York: 1910.

Speck, Frank G.
"Beothuk and Micmac." *Indian Notes and Monographs, Museum of the American Indian, Heye Foundation*, misc. ser. 22–187 pp., 1922.

―――――.
"The Beothuks of Newfoundland." *So. Work-man.* 41:559–563, 1913.

Townsend, C. W., ed.
Captain Cartwright and His Labrador Journal. Boston: 1911. (pp. 16–25).

FOLK ART—SPEECH

Patterson, G.
"Beothik Vocabularies." *Proc. Trans Royal Soc. Can.* 10(Part 2):19–32, 1892.

Willoughby, Charles Clark
Antiquities of New England Indians . . . (pp. 11-15). Cambridge, Mass.: The Peabody Museum . . . 1935.

CAYUGA (Iroquois)

FOLKLORE

GENERAL STUDIES

Canniff, William M. D.
History of the Settlement of Upper Canada (Ontario), with Special References to the Bay Quinté. Toronto, Can.: Dudley & Burns, 1869. 671 pp.
"A Cayuga village existing about 1670 on Quinté Bay of Lake Ontario."

Hawley, Charles
Early Chapters of Cayuga History. Auburn, N. Y.: Knapp, Peck & Thomson, 1884. 89 pp.

Mooney, J., and Hewitt, J. N. B.
Cayuga. In: *Bureau Amer. Ethnol. Bull.* 30 (Part 1):223–224, 1907.

Seeber, Edward D.
"Critical Views on Logan's Speech." *JAFL* 60:130–146, 1947.
An exhaustive discussion of Chief Logan's fa-mous speech. It treats of Logan, the man; the delivery of the speech; the language of speech; the "original" and the printed versions. "Among the abundant examples of Indian eloquence, death-songs, letters, speeches, laments, etc.— printed in our early newspapers and literary journals, none gained the lasting fame of the speech said to have been addressed to Lora Dun-more by Chief Logan.

Shoemaker, Henry Wharton
Captain Logan, Blair County's Indian Chief; a Biography. Altoona, Pa.: Altoona Tribune Publishing Co., 1915. 40 pp.

BELIEFS—CUSTOMS

Beauchamp, W. M.
"Cayuga Indian Relics." *Amer. Natur.* 23:401–406, 1889.

Boyle, D.
"The Making of a Cayuga Chief." *Annual Archaeological Report*, Ontario 1905, Toronto, 1906. pp. 56–69.

Fenton, William N.
"An Iroquois Condolence Council for Install-ing Cayuga Chiefs on 1945." *Journal of the Washington Academy of Sciences* 36:(No. 4): 110–127, 1945.

Keppler, J.
"Cayuga Adoption Custom." *Indian Notes* (Heye Foundation, Mus. Amer. Ind.) 3:73–75, 1926.

Speck, Frank G., and Dodge, Ernest S.
"Amphibian and Reptile Lore of the Six Nations Cayuga." *JAFL* 58:306–309, 1945.

Witthoft, John
"Cayuga Midwinter Festival." *NYFQ* 2 (No. 1):24–39, 1946.
The various dances, ceremonies and rites are carefully described.

FOLK MEDICINE

Speck, F. Staniford
"Niagara Falls and Cayuga Indian Medicine." *NYFQ* 1 (No. 4):205–208, 1945.

MUSIC

DANCE

Anon.
"Dancing School Among the Indians." *New York Mirror* 4:285–286, March 31, 1827 (NYU).
Description of a dancing school among the Cayu-gas, in which the teacher, a Frenchmen, was paid for his lessons in animal skins and furs.

RECORDS

"Corn Song."
Sung by George Buck with companion at Six Nations Reserve, Canada, 1941. In:Album VI. Library of Congress, 1943. *AAFS28B*

"War Dances."
1. The Iroquois War Dance (wassá sé) as of 1812.
2. The Scalp Dance, a modern show song, sung with water drum and horn rattle by George and Joshua Buck at Six Nations Reserve, Canada, 1941.
In: Album VI: Library of Congress, 1940. *AAFS29A*

"Women's Shuffle Dance."
Modern social dances. Sung with water drum and horn rattle by George and Joshua Buck at Six Nations Reserve, Canada, 1941. In: Album VI: Library of Congress, 1943. *AAFS30B*

CHIPPEWA (Ojibway)

FOLKLORE

GENERAL STUDIES

Armstrong, H. G.
Early Life Among the Indians. Ashland: 1892. 266 pp.

Babbitt, F. E.
"Illustrative Notes Concerning the Minnesota Odjibways." *Proc. Amer. Assoc. Adv. Sci.* 36: 303–307, 1887.

Bartlett, William W.
History, Tradition and Adventure In the Chippewa Valley. Chippewa Falls, Wisc.: The Chippewa Printery, 1929.

Blackbird, Andrew J.
History of the Ottawa and Chippewa Indians of Michigan. Harbor Springs: Babcock and Darling, 1897. 128 pp.

Blair, Emma Helen, ed.
The Indian Tribes of the Upper Mississippi Valley and the Region of the Great Lakes. Cleveland: The Arthur H. Clark Company, 1911. 2 vols.

Boas, Franz
"Zur Anthropologie der nordamerikanischen Indianer." *Verhandl. Berl. Gesell. Anthro.,* 1895, pp. 367–411.

Brady, Cyrus Townsend
Indian Fights and Fighters. Garden City, N. Y.: Doubleday, Page and Co., 1916.

Calkins, Franklin W.
Two Wilderness Voyagers: A True Tale of Indian Life. Chicago and New York: F. H. Revell Co., 1902.

Carver, J.
Travels Through the Interior Parts of North America. London: 1778. 360 pp.

Chamberlain, A. F.
"Notes on the Ethnology of the Otchipwe of the Lake of the Woods and of Rainy Lake." *Catholic Univ. of America Anthropological Series* 3:1:–29, 1936.

Chippewa Indians.
St. Paul, Minn.: Chippewa Publishing Co., 1941.

Copway, George (Kah-ge-ga-gah-bowh)
Life, History and Travels of Kah-ge-ga-gah-bowh, Indian Chief of the Ojibwa Nation. Albany, N. Y.: Printed by Weed and Parsons, 1847. 224 pp.

———.
Traditional History and Characteristic Sketches of the Ojibway Nation. By Kah-ge-ga-gah-bowh, Chief of the Ojibway Nation. London: C. Gilpin, 1850. 298 pp.

Douglas, F. H., comp.
The Ojibwa or Chippewa Indian. Denver Art Museum, Leaflet 36, (Nov.) 1931.

Ducatel, J. J.
A Fortnight Among the Chippewas of Lake Superior. In: *The Indian Miscellany . . . of the American Aborigines.* W. W. Beach, editor, pp. 361–378. 1877 (Albany).

Eastman, C. A.
"Life and Handicraft of the Northern Ojibways." *Southern Workman* (Hampton, Va.) 40:273–278, 1911.

Flower, F. A.
"The Pillager Indians." *Records of the Past* (Washington) 5:99–103, 1906.

Gilfillan, Joseph Alexander
The Ojibway; a novel of Indian life of the period of the early advance of the civilization in the Northwest. New York: Neale Publishing Company, 1904.

———.
"The Ojibways of Minnesota." *Coll. Minnesota Hist. Soc.* 9:55–128, 1901.

Gilman, Chandler Robbins
Life on the Lakes: Being tales and sketches collected during a trip to the Pictured Rock of Lake Superior. New York: G. Dearborn, 1836. 2 vols.

Greenman, E. F.
"Indian Chiefs of Michigan." *Michigan Historical Museum* 23 (No. 3):247–249, 1939.

Hallowell, A. Irving
"Concordance of Ojibwa Narratives in the Published Works of Henry R. Schoolcraft." *JAFL* 59:136–153, 1946. Bibl.

Hammond, J. H.
"The Ojibwas of Lake Huron and Simcoe."
Annual Archaeological Report 1904; Toronto,
1905, pp. 71–73.

Hilger, M. Inez
A Social Study of One Hundred Fifty Chippewa Indian Families of the White Earth Reservation of Minnesota. Washington, D. C.:
Catholic University of America Press, 1939.

————.
"Some Phases of Chippewa Material Culture."
Anthropology 32 (No. 5, 6):780–782, 1937.

Hind, H. Y.
Narrative of the Canadian Red River Exploring Expedition. London: 1860. 2 vols.

————.
Northwest Territory. Toronto: 1859. 201 pp.

Hoffman, W. J.
"Notes on Ojibwa Folk-lore." *AA* 2:215–225,
1889.

Holling, H. C. and Lucille
Little Buffalo Boy. Illustrated in colors by the
authors. New York: Garden City Publishing
Co. 1939. 42 pp.
A story of the Chippewa Indians.

Hinsdale, Wilbert B.
Distribution of the Aboriginal Population of Michigan. Occasional contributions from Museum of Anthropology, University of Michigan
2. 35 pp. Ann Arbor: University of Michigan
Press, 1932.

————.
First People of Michigan. Ann Arbor: George
Wahr, 1930.

————.
Primitive Man in Michigan. Michigan Handbook Series I. Ann Arbor: University of Michigan Press, 1925.

Hrdlicka, Ales
"Anthropological Work Among the Sioux and
Chippewa." *Smithson. Misc. Coll.* 46 (Part 17):
92–99, 1917.

————.
Anthropology of the Chippewa. In: *Holmes
Anniversary Volume,* pp. 198–227. Washington,
D. C.: 1916.

————.
"A Trip to the Chippewa Indians of Minnesota." *Smithson. Miscel. Coll.* 46 (Part 3):
71–75, 1916.

James, E., ed.
*A Narrative of the Captivity and Adventures
of John Tanner.* New York: 1830. 426 pp.

Jameson, Anna Brownell
*Sketches in Canada, and Rambles Among the
Red Men.* London: Longman, Brown, Green
and Longmans, 1852. 314 pp.

Jenks, Albert Ernest
*The Childhood of Ji-Shib, the Ojibwa, and
Sixty-Four Pen Sketches.* Madison, Wisconsin:
The American Thresherman, 1900. 132 pp.

————.
"The Wild Rice Gatherers of the Upper
Lakes." *19th Annual Report: Bureau of American Ethnology,* 1897–1898, pp. 1013–1137,
pls. LXVI–LXXIX, figs. 47 and 48. Washington, D. C.: U. S. Govt. Printing Office, 1900.

Jenness, Diamond
The Ojibwa Indians of Parry Island. Bulletins
of the Canada Department of Mines, National
Museum of Canada. No. 78 Ottawa: 1935. 115
pp.

Johnson, F.
"Notes on the Ojibwa and Potawatomi of the
Parry Island Reservation." *Indian Notes,* (Museum of the Amer. Indian, Heye Foundation)
6:193–216, 1929.

Johnston, G.
"Ojibwa of St. Mary's." In: *Information Respecting the History, Condition, and Prospects
of the Indian Tribes of the United States,*
H. R. Schoolcraft, ed. Vol. II, pp. 458–469.
Philadelphia: 1852.

Jones, James Athearn
Tales of an Indian Camp. London: Henry Colburn and Richard Bentley, 1829. 3 vols.
In 1830, a second and revised edition was issued
under the title: *Traditions of the North American Indians.*

Jones, Rev. Peter
History of the Ojibway Indians; with special
reference to their conversion to Christianity.
London: A. W. Bennett, 1861. vi, 278 pp.,
front., pl., port.

Jones, W.
"Central Algonkin." *Annual Archaeological
Report,* Ontario, 1905; Toronto, 1906, pp.
136–146.

————.
Ojibwa Texts. Publications of the American
Ethnological Society. No. 7, Part 1, 501 pp.,
Part 2, 771 pp. New York: 1917–1919

Josselin de Jong, J. P. B. de
"Original Odzibwe-Texts." *Baessler-Archiv*
(Berlin), *Beiheft* 5:1–54, 1913.

Kinietz, W. Vernon
Chippewa Village: The story of Katikitegon.
Bloomfield Hills, Mich.: Cranbrook Institute
of Science, 1947. 259 pp.

————.
The Indian Tribes of the Western Great Lakes.
Occasional Contributions from the Museum of
Anthropology of the University of Michigan 10.
Ann Arbor: University of Michigan Press,
1941. 427 pp.

Kohl, J. G.
Kitchi-Gami: Wanderings Around Lake Superior. London: Chapman and Hall, 1860. xii, 428 pp.

Landes, Ruth
Ojibwa Sociology. Columbia University Contributions to Anthropology, No. 29. New York: Columbia University Press, 1937. 144 pp.

————.
The Ojibwa Woman. Columbia University Contributions to Anthropology, No. 31. New York: Columbia University Press. 1938. 247 pp.

————.
"The Personality of the Ojibwa." *Character and Personality* 6:51–60, Sept. 1937.

Larzelere, Claude S.
"The Red Man in Michigan." *Michigan History Magazine* (Lansing) 17:344–376, 1933.

Long, J. K.
Voyages and Travels of an Indian Interpreter and Trader, M. M. Quaife, ed. Chicago: 1922. 238 pp.

Lowie, R. H.
"Ojibwa." In: *Encyclopedia of Religion and Ethics,* John Hastings, ed., Vol. 9, pp. 454–458. New York: 1917.

McKenney, T. L.
Sketches of a Tour of the Lakes. Baltimore: 1827. 493 pp.

Meakins, C.
"Old Albert of Chemung." *Forest and Stream* 91:5–7, 34–38, 64–65, 85–87, 1921.

Mooney, J., and Thomas, C.
"Chippewa." In: *Bureau of Amer. Ethnol. Bull. 30* (Part 1):277–281, 1907.

Montgomery, Henry
"Prehistoric Man in Manitoba and Saskatchewan." *AA* 10:33–41, 1908. n.s.

Moran, G.
"Ojibwa of Saganaw." In: *Information Respecting the History, Condition, and Prospects of the Indian Tribes of the United States,* H. R. Schoolcraft, ed., Vol. II, pp. 458–469, Philadelphia: 1852.

Morse, R. F.
"The Chippewas of Lake Superior." *Coll. State Hist. Soc. Wis.* 3:338–369, 1856.

Neill, Edward
"History of the Ojibway." *Minnesota Historical Collections,* (St. Paul) 5:395–510, 1885.

O'Donnell, S.
"People of the Puckered Moccasin." *So. Workman* 39:439–440, 1910.

Orr, R. B.
"The Chippewa Indians. *Ann. Arch. Report* (Toronto), 1918, pp. 9-23.

Parker, W. T.
"The Muskee-Kee-Win-ni-nee." *Open Court* (Chicago) 15:289–300, 1901.

Radin, Paul
"Ethnological Notes on the Ojibwa of Southeastern Ontario." *AA* 30:659–668, 1928. n.s.

————.
"Ojibwa Ethnological Chit-Chat." *AA* 26:49–530, 1924.

Schoolcraft, Henry Rowe
Historical and Statistical Information Respecting the History, Conditions and Prospects of the Indian Tribes of the United States. Philadelphia: J. B. Lippincott, 1851–1857. xxviii, 6 vols. 756 pp. front., illus.

————.
The American Indians; Their History, Conditions and Prospects, from Original Notes and Manuscript. . . . Together with an Appendix, Containing Thrilling Narratives, Daring Exploits, etc. Buffalo: George H. Derby, 1851, new rev. ed. An identical edition was published at Rochester: Wanger, Foot and Company, 1851.

————.
The Indian in His Wigwam, or, Characteristics of the Red Race of America. Buffalo: Derby and Hewson, 1848. 416 pp.

————.
Narrative of an Expedition Through the Upper Mississippi to Itasca Lake, the Actual Source of this River; Embracing an Exploratory Trip through the St. Croix and Burntwood (or Broule) Rivers; in 1832. New York: Harper and Brothers, 1834. 307 pp.

————.
Personal Memoirs of a Residence of Thirty Years with the Indian Tribes on the American Frontiers: with Brief Notices of Passing Events, Facts, and Opinions, A. D. 1812 to A. D. 1842. Philadelphia: Lippincott, Grambo and Company, 1851. 703 pp.

————.
The Red Race of America. New York: W. H. Graham, 1847. 416 pp.

————.
Travels in the Central Portions of the Mississippi Valley: Comprising Observations on its Mineral Geography, Internal Resources, and Aboriginal Population . . . in the year 1821. New York: Collins and Hannay, 1925.

————.
Western Scenes and Reminiscences: Together with Thrilling Legends and Traditions of the Red Men of the Forest; To Which is Added Several Narratives of Adventures among the Indians. Buffalo: Derby, Orton and Mulligan, 1853. 495 pp.

Reagan, A. B.
"The Bois Fort Chippewa." *Wisconsin Arch.* 3:101–132, 1924. n.s.

—————.
"Rainy Lakes Indians." *Wisconsin Arch.* 2:
140–147, 1923. n.s.

Skinner, Alanson
"A Visit to the Ojibway and Cree of Central
Canada." *American Museum Journal* (New
York) 10:9–18, 1910.

—————.
"Political Organizations, Cults, and Ceremonies of the Plains-Ojibway Indians." *Anthropological Papers:* Vol. 11:1914, pp. 475–542,
10. figs. Publications in Anthropology. New
York: The American Museum of Natural
History.

—————.
"The Cultural Position of the Plains Ojibway."
AA 16:314–319, 1914 n.s.

Smith, H. I.
"Hiawatha's People." *So. Workman* 40:472–
479, 1911.

Stewart, J.
"Rupert's Land Indians in the Olden Times."
Annual Archaeological Report 1904; Toronto,
1905, pp. 89–100.

Swanton, J. R.
"Some Neglected Data Bearing on Cheyenne,
Chippewa and Dakota History." *AA* 32:156–
160, 1930, n.s.

Venne, E.
"Facts About the Chippewas." *Carlisle Arrow*
8 (No. 10):1, 1911.

Warren, William A.
"History of the Ojibway Indians." *Minnesota
Historical Society Collections*, (St. Paul)
5:21–394, 1885.

—————.
"Oral Traditions Respecting the History of
the Ojibwa Nation." In: *Information Respecting History, Condition, and Prospects of the
Indian Tribes of the United States*, H. R.
Schoolcraft, Vol. II, pp. 135–167. Philadelphia:
1852.

Whipple, Henry B.
"Civilization and Christianization of the Ojibways in Minnesota." *Minnesota Historical Collections* (St. Paul) 9:129–142, 1901.

Wilson, E. F.
Missionary Work Among the Ojebway Indians.
London: 1886. 255 pp.

Winchell, N. H.
The Aborigines of Minnesota. A report based
on the collections of Jacob V. Bremer, and on
the field surveys and notes of Alfred T. Hill
and Theodore U. Lewis. St. Paul: Minnesota
Historical Society, 1911. 761 pp., illus.

MYTHS—FOLKTALES—LEGENDS

Anon.
"Shoankah Shahpah." *New England Magazine* 4:187–195, March 1833.
A legend about the extermination of the Kapozah
tribe that lived on the Upper Mississippi River
by the Chippewa Indians.

—————.
"The Indian's Two Souls." *The Ladies Reposi-
tory* 17:712, Dec. 1857.
Legend of the Lake-Algonquins and Chippewa
Indians.

Banér, Johan G. R.
Kitch-iti-ki-pi, the "Big Spring"; wonderfully
beautiful. (Namesakes) The Ojibway and
Chippeway Indian Legends, by Inaqtik Ata-
noqken (Raven Legenbard). Manistique,
Mich.: 1933. 61 pp., illus.

Bell, R.
"Ojibway Legends and Traditions." *JAFL*
6:153–154, 1893.

Burnham, William
The Legend of O-na-wut-a-qut-o; from North
American Indian Folk-lore and Legends.
Orange, Cal.: Sucasa Press, 1903. 5 pp.

Cappel, Jeanne L'Strange
Chippewa Tales, retold by Wa-be-no O-pee-
chee, Jeanne L'Strange Cappel. Los Angeles:
Wetzel Publishing Company, 1928. 64 pp.

Carson, W.
"Ojibwa Tales." *JAFL* 30:491–493, 1917.

Chappel, L.
Chippewa Tales (20 in 1). Los Angeles:
Wetzel Publishing Co., n.d.

Gilman, Chandler R.
Life on the Lakes: being Tales and Sketches
collected during a trip to the pictured rocks of
Lake Superior. . . . New York: G. Dearborn,
1836. 2 vols.

Gordon, Hanford Lennox
Legend of the Northwest. . . . Containing the
Ojibwa legend of the Pictured Rock of Lake
Superior. Minnentonka, St. Paul, Minn.: The
St. Paul Book and Stationery Co., 1881. viii,
143 pp., illus.

Hindley, Rev. John
*Indian Legends. Nanabush, the Ojibbeway
Saviour.* Moosh-kuh-ung, or, The Flood. Barrie,
Ont.: 1885. 22 pp.

Hoffman, Walter
"Notes on Ojibwa Folk-Lore." *AA* 2:215–223,
July, 1889.

James, Edwin, M. D.
"Essay on the Chippewa Language." *American Annals of Education* 3:440–446, Oct. 1833.
Paper read before the American Lyceum, at the
third annual meeting, in the city of New York,
May 3, 1833, explaining not only the language,
but including some Chippewa legends, and a
letter from Thegeid, a chieftain.

Jenks, A. E.
"The Bear Maiden—Ojibwa." *JAFL* 15:33–35, 1902.

Josselin de Jong, J. P. B. de
Original Odjibwe Texts, with English Translations, notes and vocabulary. Leipzig: 1913.

Jones, William
Ojibwa Texts; edited by Truman Michelson. Leyden: E. J. Brill Ltd., 1917–19. 2 vols., illus. (Publications of the American Ethnological Society, edited by Boas, Franz. Vol. III, pt. I–II.)
    Contents: Part I. Nänabushu Tales. Part II. Miscellaneous Tales.

"Ojibwa Tales on the North Shore of Lake Superior." *JAFL* 29:368–391, 1916.

Kane, Mrs. Grace Franks
Myths and Legends of the Mackinacs and the Lake Region. Cincinnati: The Editor Publishing Co., 1897. 159 pp., illus.

Kinnaman, J. O.
"Chippewa Legends." *American Antiquity* 32:96–102, 1910.

Knight, J.
"Ojibwa Tales from Sault Ste. Marie, Michigan." *JAFL* 26:91–96, 1913.

L., G.
"The Spirit of Sacrifice—A Chippewa Legend." *The Literary World* 4:389, May 5, 1849.
    A legend of a terrible plague, how the tribesmen, in order to appease the wrath of the Great Spirit, sacrificed one of their maidens.

Laidlaw, George E.
Ojibwa Myths and Tales. Toronto: Ontario Archaeological Report XXVII–XXX, 1915–18.

Linderman, Frank B. (Co-skee-see-co-cot)
Indian Why Stories; Sparks from the Eagle's Lodge Fire. Illustrated by Charles Russell. New York: C. Scribner's Sons, 1915. xx, 236 pp., col. front, illus. col. pl.

Longfellow, Henry Wadsworth
"Hiawatha," with its Original Indian Legends; compiled, with essays on its authentic background of Lake Superior country and Chippewa Indians, by Osborn, C. S. and Osborn, S. Introduction by Frank Murphy. Lancaster, Pa.: J. Cattell Press, 1944. vii, 225 pp., illus., bibl. (pp. 42–45).

Mathews, Cornelius
The Enchanted Moccasins and other Legends of the American Indians; Compiled from original sources. New York: Putnam's Sons, 1877. 338 pp.

Michelson, Truman
"Ojibwa Tales." *JAFL* 24:249–250, 1911.

Osborn, Chase S. and Stellanova
"Hiawatha" with its Original Indian Legends. Introduction by Frank Murphy. (The Great Lakes Edition.) Lancaster, Pa.: The Jacques Cattel Press, 1944. 255 pp., illus.

Piper, William Samuel
The Eagle of Thunder Cape. New York: The Knickerbocker Press, 1924. x, 235 pp., illus.
    Contents: Introduction. The Lost Mother mine. The legend of Green Mantle. A summer vacation on the north shore of Lake Superior.

Radin, Paul, comp.
Some Myths and Tales of the Ojibwa of Southeastern Ontario. Ottawa: Government Printing Bureau, 1914. 83 pp. (Canada. Geological Survey. Memoir 48, No. 2. Anthropological Series.)

————, and Reagan, A. B.
"Ojibwa Myths and Tales," *JAFL* 41:61–146, 1928.

Reagan, Albert B.
"The Flood Myth of the Chippewas." *Indiana Academy of Sciences.* Proceedings, pp. 347–352, 1919.

"Flood Myths of the Bois Fort Chippewas." *Trans. Kansas Acad. Sci.* 30:437–443, 1921.

Rohr, Jack
Ojibway Trails, by Hotan-Tonka, *"Sound-of-the-Wind-through-the-Pines";* illustrated by Baker, Lillian. Ottawa, Ill.: J. Rohr, 1928. 33 pp., illus.

Schoolcraft, Henry Rowe
Algic Researches, Comprising Inquiries Respecting the Mental Characteristics of the North American Indians. First Series. Indian Tales and Legends. New York: Harper and Brothers, 1839. 2 vols., 248 and 244 pp.

The Indian Fairy Book, from the Original Legends, with illustrations by (John) McLenan, Engraved by (A. V. S.) Anthony. New York: Mason Brothers, 1856. 338 pp.

The Indian Fairy Book, from the Original Legends, with eight illustrations in color by Florence Choate and Elizabeth Curtis. New York: Frederick A. Stokes Company, 1916. 303 pp.

The Myth of Hiawatha, and Other Oral Legends, Mythologic and Allegoric, of the North American Indians. Philadelphia: J. B. Lippincott and Company, 343 pp. London: Trubner and Company, 1856.

"Mythology, Superstitions and Languages of the North American Indians." *New York: Theological Review* 2:96–121, 1835.

Severance, Mary F., comp.
Indian Legends of Minnesota, comp. by Severance, Cordenio A. New York: D. D. Merrill Co., 1893. 184 pp., illus.
    A volume of poems.

Skinner, Alanson
"European Folk Tales from the Plains Ojibway." *JAFL* 29:330–340, 1916.

—————.
"Plains Ojibwa Tales." *JAFL* 32:280–305, 1919.

Smith, Harlan I.
"Monster in the Tree; an Ojibwa Myth." *JAFL* 10:324–325, 1897.

—————.
"Some Ojibwa Myths and Traditions." *JAFL* 19 (No. 14): 215–230, 1906.

—————.
"Scientific Uses for Michigan Folk-Lore." *Michigan Academy of Science*. Annual Report, (2d) 1901, pp. 7-8.

Speck, Frank G.
Myths and Folk-Lore of the Timiskaming Algonquin and Timiskaming Ojibwa. Ottawa: Government Printing Bureau, 1915. iii, 87 pp. (Geological Survey Branch. Memoir 71. Anthropological Series 9.)

Squier, Ephraim G.
"Ne-she-kay-be-nais; or, the "Lone Bird." An Ojibway Legend." *American Review* 2(No. 3) 255–259, 1848.

Warren, William
History of the Ojibways; Based upon Traditions and Oral Statements. St. Paul, Minn.: 1885. (Minnesota Historical Soc. Collections. vol. 5.)

Wright, John Couchois
The Great Myth. Lansing, Mich.: The Michigan Education Company, 1922. v, + xv, 170 pp.

Young, E. R.
Algonquin Indian Tales. New York: 1903. 256 pp.

—————.
Stories from Indian Wigwams and Northern Camp-Fires. New York: 1893. 293 pp.

BELIEFS—CUSTOMS

Anon.
"An Ojibway Funeral." *American Penny Magazine* 2:161–163, April 18, 1846.
    Description of a funeral ceremony for a child.

Babcock, Willoughby M.
"Sioux Versus Chippewa." *Minnesota History* 6:41–45, (March) 1925.
    Discusses customs, habits of dress and intertribal warfare.

Bebean, G.
"The Origin of Thunder." *Red Man* (Carlisle, Pa.) 3:340, 1911.

Bernard, M.
"Religion and Magic Among Cass Lake Ojibwa." *Primitive Man* 2:52–55, 1929.

Bushnell, D. I., Jr.
"An Ojibway Ceremony." *AA* 7:69–74, 1905. n.s.

Chamberlain, A. F.
"Nanibozhu Amongst the Otchipwe, Missisagas, and other Algonkian Tribes." *JAFL* 4:193–213, 1891.

Coleman, Bernard
"The Religion of the Ojibwa of Northern Minnesota." *Primitive Man* 10, (No. 3, 4):33–57, 1937.

Cooper, John M.
"Field Notes on Northern Algonkian Magic." *Proc. Inter. Congr. Amer.* 23:513–518, 1928.

Densmore, Frances
Chippewa Customs. Bureau American Ethnology, Bulletin 86, 204 pp., 90 pl., 27 figs. Washington, D. C.: U. S. Govt. Printing Office, 1929.

—————.
"Material Culture Among the Chippewa." *Smithson. Misc. Coll.* 70(Part 2):114–118, 1919.

—————.
"An Ojibwa Prayer Ceremony." *AA* 9:443–444, 1907. n.s.

—————.
"A Study of Chippewa Material Culture." *Smithson. Misc. Coll.* 68(Part 12):95–100, 1918.

—————.
"Uses of Plants by the Chippewa Indians." *Annual Report, Bureau Amer. Ethnol.* 44: 275–397, 1927.

Hamilton, J. C.
"The Algonquin Manabozho and Hiawatha." *JAFL* 15:229–233, 1903.

Hilger, M. Inez
"Ceremonia para dar nombre a un niño indio Chippewa." *AI* 4:237–242, 1944.
    Naming ceremony of Chippewa Indians .

—————.
"Chippewa Customs." *Primitive Man* 9 (No. 2): 17–24, 1936.

—————.
"Chippewa Interpretations of Natural Phenomena." *Scientific Monthly* 45(No. 2):178–179, 1937.

—————.
"Chippewa Pre-natal Food and Conduct Taboos." *Primitive Man* 9 (No. 3):46–48, 1936.

—————.
"Some Phases of Chippewa Material Culture." *Anthropos* 32:780–782, 1937.

Hoffman, Walter James
"The Midewiwin or 'Grand Medicine Society' of the Ojibwa." *7th Annual Report: Bureau of American Ethnology, 1885–1886.* pp. 149–299, pls. 2–23, figs. 1–39, 1 map. Washington, D.C.: U. S. Government Printing Office, 1891.
    Shamans, Mide Wiwan, Mide Wigân; preparatory instruction, Mide-therapeutics, initiation: first, second, third and fourth degree, etc.

————.
"Pictography and Shamanistic Rites of the Ojibwa." *AA* 1:209–231, 1888.

Hugolin, R. P.
"Lidée spiritualiste et l'idée morale chez les Chippewas." *Proceedings of the 15th Session of the International Congress of Americanists,* 1:329–337, 1906.

Jenness, Diamond
The Ojibwa Indians of Parry Island, Their Social and Religious Life. National Museum of Canada, Bulletin 78. Anthropological Series No. 17, (Ottawa) 1935. 115 pp.

Lips, Julius E.
"Notes on Some Ojibway-Traps (Metagama Band)." *Ethnos* 2, (No. 6):354–360, 1937.

McGee, W. J.
"Ojibwa Feather Symbolism." *AA* 11:177–181, 1898.

McKenney, Thomas L.
Sketches of a Tour to the Lakes; of the character and customs of the Chippeway Indians, and of incidents connected with the Treaty of Fond du Lac. Also, a vocabulary of the Algic, or Chippeway language. Baltimore: F. Lucas, Jr., 1827. viii, 493 pp., front, pl. ports.

Merwin, B. W.
"Some Ojibway Buffalo Robes." *University of Pennsylvania, The Museum Journal* 7:93–96.

Michelson, Truman
"Maiden Sacrifice Among the Ojibwa." *AA* 36:628–629, 1934. n.s.

Radin, Paul
"An Introductive Enquiry in the Study of Ojibwa Religion." *Papers and Records of the Ontario Historical Society* 12:210–218, 1914.

————.
Ojibwa and Ottawa Puberty Dreams. In: *Essays in Anthropology Presented to A. L. Kroeber,* pp. 233–264. Berkeley, Cal.: Univ. of California Press, 1936.

————.
"Some Aspects of Puberty Fasting Among the Ojibwa." *Mus. Bull. Can. Dept. Mines* (Ottawa) 2:69–78, 1914.

Reagan, A. B.
"Plants Used by the Bois Fort Chippewa." *Wisconsin Arch.* 7:230–248, 1928. n.s.

Reid, A. P.
"Religious Beliefs of the Ojibois or Sauteux Indians." *Journ. Royal Anthro. Inst. Gt. Brit.* 3:106–113, 1873.

Skinner, Alanson
Medicine Ceremony of the Menomini, Iowa and Wahpeton Dakota. With notes on the Ceremony among the Ponca, Bungi, Ojibwa and Potawatomi. Indian Notes and Monographs, Museum of the American Indian, Heye Foundation 4:357 pp., 1920.

Smith, H. I.
"Certain Shamanistic Ceremonies Among the Ojibwas." *Amer. Antiq.* 18:282–284, 1896.

Smith, Seba
"The Religion and Superstition of the North American Indians—No. II." *The Literary Emporium* 3:97–100, April 1846.
Comments on the beliefs and religious ceremonies of the Chippewas, Sauks and Musquakies.

FOLK MEDICINE

Densmore, Frances
Uses of Plants by the Chippewa Indians. *44th Annual Report: Bureau of American Ethnology,* 1926–1927, pp. 281–541, pls. 28–63. Washington, D. C.: U. S. Govt. Printing Office, 1928.

Jones, Volney H.
"Some Chippewa and Ottawa Uses of Sweet Grass." *Paper, Michigan Academy of Science, Arts and Letters* 21:21–31, (1935) 1936.

Smith, H. H.
"Botanizing Among the Ojibwe." *Yearbook of the Public Museum of the City of Milwaukee* 3:38–47, 1923.

————.
"Ethnobotany of the Ojibwe Indians." *Bulletin of the Public Museum of Milwaukee* 4:327–525, 1932.

FOLK ART—SPEECH

Adam, L.
"Esquisse d'une grammaire comparée de la langue des Chippeways et de la langue des Crees." *Inter. Congr. Amer.* 1(Part 2):88–148, 1875.

Baraga, F.
A Dictionary of the Otchipwe Language. Montreal: 1878. 422 pp. 2 vols.

Calkins, H.
"Indian Nomenclature of Northern Wisconsin, With a Sketch of the Manners and Customs of the Chippewas." *Coll. State Hist. Soc. Wisconsin* 1:119–126, 1854.

Densmore, Frances
"The Native Art of the Chippewa." *AA* 43:678–681, 1941.

Dustin, Fred
Report on Indian Earthworks in Ogemaw County (Michigan). Cranbrook (Bloomfield Hills, Mich.) 1932. 25 p.

Eastman, C. A.
"Life and Handicraft of the Northern Ojibways." *Southern Workman* (Hampton, Va.) 40:273–278, 1911.

Jones, V. H.
"A Chippewa Method of Manfacturing Wooden Brooms." *Papers Mich. Acad. Sci. Arts and Letters* 20:23–30, 1934.

Merwin, B. W.
"Some Ojibway Buffalo Robes." *Mus. Jour.* 7:93–96, 1916.

Reagan, A. B.
"Picture Writings of the Chippewa Indians." *Wisconsin Arch.* 6:80–83, 1927. n.s.

Speck, F. G.
"Kinship Terms and the Family Bands Among the Northeastern Algonkian." *AA* 20:143–161, 1918. n.s.

Summerfield, J.
Sketch of Grammar of the Chippeway Language. Cazenovia: 1834. 35 pp.

Wilson, E. F.
The Ojebway Language. Toronto: Rowsell and Hutchison, 1874. 412 pp.

GAMES

Brown, Theodore T.
"Plant Games and Toys of Chippewa Children." *Wisconsin Arch.* 9:185–186, 1930. n.s.

Densmore, Frances
"An Explanation of a Trick Performed by Indian Jugglers." *AA* 34:310–314, 1932. n.s.

Highstone, L. S.
"The Indian Play of Hiawatha." *So. Workman* 40:93–99, 1911.

Hoffman, W. J.
"Remarks on Ojibwa Ball Play." *AA* 3:133–137, 1890.

Reagan, A. B.
"Some Games of the Bois Fort Ojibwa." *AA* 21:264–278, 1919. n.s.

MUSIC

GENERAL STUDIES

Burton, Frederick Russell
American Primitive Music, with especial attention to the Songs of Ojibways. New York: Moffat, Yard & Company, 1909.
Many musical examples and analysis presented.

—————.
"Music from the Ojibway Point of View; Art an Unknown Word to These Primitive People and Song Apart of Every Day Living." *Craftsman* (New York) 12:375–381, 1907.

—————.
"Songs of the Ojibways." *Concertgoer* (New York) 209:8–9, 1902.
With music.

—————.
"Songs of the Ojibways." *Strand Magazine* (London) 33:266–271, 1907.
With music.

—————.
"Song of the Ojibways." *Southern Workman* (Hampton, Virginia) 33:12–16, 1904.

Davidson, John F.
"Ojibwa Songs." *JAFL* 58:303–305, 1945.
8 songs with tunes for the first six.

Densmore, Frances
Chippewa Music I. Bureau of American Ethnology, Bull. 45, 216 pp., 12 pl., 8 fig. Washington, D. C.: U. S. Government Printing Office, 1910.
Many musical selections and descriptions of dances, games, and rituals given.

—————.
Chippewa Music II, Bureau of American Ethnology, Bull. 53, pp. 1–335, pls. 1–45, 6 figs., songs listed on pp. 67–305. Washington, D.C.: U. S. Printing Office, 1913.
Report deals with relation of music to tribal life and customs, as well as with a melodic and rhythmic analysis of the songs. Songs of tribal games, dances, individual warriors, etc .

—————.
Indian Action Songs: A Collection of the Chippewa Indians, with directions for pantomimic representation in schools and community assemblies. Boston: C. C. Birchard & Company, 1921. 12 pp.

—————.
"Music of the Winnebago, Chippewa and Pueblo Indians." *Explorations and Field-Work of the Smithson. Inst.,* 1930, pp. 217-224.

—————.
Poems from Sioux and Chippewa Songs. Washington, D. C.: U. S. Government Printing Office, 1917. 23 pp.

—————.
"The Rhythm of Sioux and Chippewa Music." *Art and Arch.* 9:59–67, 1920.

Gagnon, E.
"Les Sauvages de l'Amérique et l'Art Musical." *Proceedings of the 15th Session of the International Congress of Americanists:* 179–188, 1906.
Gives examples of Ojibwa and Huron Songs and Hymns.

Hoffman, W. J.
"The Midewiwin or Grand Medicine Society of the Ojibwa." *7th Annual Report of the Bureau of American Ethnology:* 143–300, 1885–1886. Washington, D. C.: U. S. Government Printing Office, 1891.

Kinsey, Mabel C.
"An Ojibwa Song." *JAFL* 46:416–417, 1933.

Krehbiel, Henry Edward
"Indian Melodies, Interesting Experiments with their settings, primitive tunes, and exotic harmonies—Ojibway Songs." *New York Daily Tribune* (New York): August 31, 1902.

"Ojibway Music—Beauty Discovered in the Indian Themes." *Musical Courier* (New York) 45 (No. 7) : 33, 1902.

Reagan, A. B.
"Medicine Songs of George Farmer." *AA* 24: 332–369.

Watt, Henry J.
"Functions of the Size of Interval in the Songs of Schubert and the Chippewa and Teton Sioux Indians." *British Journal of Psychology* (Cambridge) 14:370–386, 1924.

DANCES

Barrett, S. A.
"The Dream Dance of the Chippewa and Menominee Indians of Northern Wisconsin." *Bulletin of the Public Museum of the City of Milwaukee*, 1 (Art. 4):251–406, (Milwaukee), 1911.

Collier, F. B. M.
"Ojibway Dances." *Dancing Times* (London): 12–15, (April) 1936, illustrated.

Culkin, William E.
"Tribal Dance of the Ojibway Indians." *Minnesota Historical Bulletin* 1 (No. 7):85–93, St. Paul, 1915.

Skinner, Alanson
"The Sun Dance of the Plains Ojibway." *Anthropological Papers*: Vol. 16: 1919, pp. 311–315. Publications in Anthropology. New York. The American Museum of Natural History.

ARRANGEMENTS
————: *Voice and Piano*

"For the Golden Harvest."
Miller, Horace A.: Willis: Voice and piano.

"In the Indian Cradle."
Miller, Horace A.: Willis Music Company: Voice and piano.

"Jibiwanisi Love Song."
Metcalf, John W.: Schmidt: Voice and Piano.

"My Lover Has Departed."
Bimboni, Alberto: G. Schirmer: Voice and Piano.

"Song of the Trees."
Bimboni, Alberto: G. Schirmer: Voice and Piano.

"The Deserted Lodge."
Lemher, Derrick N.: Author: voice, piano and flute.

"The Night Wind's Message." (Chippewa Love Song)
Grant-Shaefer, G. A.: Schmidt: Voice and piano.

"The Night Wind's Message." (Love Song)
Metcalf, John W.: Schmidt: Voice and piano.

Three Ojibway Indian Songs from "The Forest."
Miller, Horace A.: Musicians Publishing Co.: Voice and piano.

————: *Mixed Voices*

"Papoose." (Indian Lullaby)
Dobson, E. Aldrich: Schmidt: SATB, SAB.

————: *Piano*

"Ceremonial Song". In: *Melodic Views of Indian Life.*
Miller, Horace A.: Clayton F. Summy: Piano.

"Eniwube's Vision." (from Four Indian Themes)
Miller, Horace A.: B. & H.: Piano.

"In the Fire's Glow." (from Four Indian Themes)
Miller, Horace A.: B. & H.: Piano.

"Hentanewa." In: *Melodic Views of Indian Life.*
Miller, Horace A.: Clayton F. Sumny: Piano.

"Little Papoose." (From Tales of the Red Man Suite)
Grant-Schaefer, G. A.: Schmidt: Piano.

"The Midewiwin." In: *Melodic Views of Indian Life.*
Miller, Horace A.: C. F. Summy: Piano.

————: *Organ*

"Largo."
Miller, Horace A.: Cornell College: Organ.

————: *String Orchestra*

Four Indian Tribal Melodies.
Busch, Carl: Carl Fischer: String Orchestra.
Contents: 1) Vision (Chippewa); 2) Love Song (Chippewa); 3) Lullaby (Chippewa); 4) Maha Love Song.

"Lullaby." (From Four Indian Tribal Melodies)
Busch, Carl: Carl Fischer: String Orchestra.

"Love Songs." (From Four Indian Tribal Melodies)
Busch, Carl: Carl Fischer: String Orchestra.

"Vision." (From Four Indian Tribal Melodies)
Busch, Carl: Carl Fischer: String Orchestra.

————: *Opera*

Bimboni, Alberto
Winona. An opera based on Chippewa, and Sioux-Dakota tunes. MS.

RECORDS

"By the Weeping Waters." (Lieurance) (Chippewa Mourning Song) Princess Watawaso.
VI–22316

CREE
FOLKLORE
GENERAL STUDIES

Chappell, E.
Narrative of a Voyage to Hudson's Bay. London: J. Mawman, 1817. 279 pp.

Clay, Charles
"Indians As I Know Them." *Canadian Geographical Journal* 8 (No. 1):43–50, (Jan.) 1934.

Cocking, M.
"An Adventurer from Hudson's Bay", Burpee, L. J., ed. *Proc. Trans. Royal Soc. Can.*, ser. 3, 2(Part 2):89–121, 1908.

Faraud, Henri J.
Dix-huit ans chez les sauvages. Bruxelles: R. Ruffet et Cie, 1866. 456 pp.

Fortescue, J.
"Les Indiens Cris de l'Amérique du Nord." *Archives de la Société Américaine de France* 3:31–66, 1883. n.s.

Franklin, John
Narrative of a Journey to the Shores of the Polar Sea. London: J. Murray, 1823.

Godsell, Philip Henry
Red Hunters of the Snows. Toronto: The Ryerson Press, 1938. 324 pp.

Harmon, D. W.
A Journal of Voyages and Travels in the Interior of North America, W. L. Grant, ed., (pp. 269–353). Toronto: 1911.

Henry, A.
Travels and Adventures in Canada, M. M. Quaife, ed., (pp. 339–342). Chicago: 1921.

Leden, C.
"Unter den Indianern Canadas." *Zeit. für Ethnol.* 44:811–831, 1912.

McLean, J.
Notes of a Twenty-five Years' Service in the Hudson's Bay Territory, W. S. Wallace, ed. Publications of the Chaplain Society, No. 19. Toronto: 1932. 402 pp.

Orr, R. B.
"The Crees of New Ontario." *Ann. Arch Report* (Toronto), 1923, pp. 9–24.

Peeso, F. E.
"The Cree Indians." *Museum Journal* 3:50–57, 1912.

Saindon, J. E.
"Mental Disorders Among the James Bay Cree." *Primitive Man* 6 (No. 1):1–12. Washington, D. C.: Catholic Anthropology Conference, (Jan.), 1933.

Skinner, Alanson
"The Cree Indians of Northern Canada." *Southern Workman* (Hampton, Va.) 38:78–83, 1909.

———.
"Notes on the Eastern Cree and Northern Saulteaux." *Anthropological Papers:* Vol. 9, 1911, pp. 1–177, figs. 56, pls. 1–2. Publications in Anthropology. New York: The American Museum of Natural History.

———.
"A Visit to the Ojibway and Cree of Central Canada." *American Museum Journal* (New York) 10:9–18, 1910.

Stewart, J.
"Rupert's Land Indians in the Olden Times." *Annual Archaeological Report 1904;* Toronto, 1905. pp. 89–100.

Swindlehurst, F.
"Folklore of the Cree Indians." *JAFL* 18:139–143, 1905.

MYTHS—FOLKTALES—LEGENDS

Bell, R.
"History of the Che-che-puy-ew-tis, (legend of the Northern Crees)." *JAFL* 10:1–8, 1897.

Boyle, D.
"The Killing of the Wa-sak-apee-quay by Pese-quan, and Others." *Annual Archaeological Report* (Toronto), 1908. pp. 91–121.

Clay, Charles
Swampy Cree Legends, being twenty folk tales from the annals of a primitive, mysterious, fast-disappearing Canadian race, as told to Clay, C. . . . by Kuskapatchees, the Smoky One. Toronto: The Macmillan Company of Canada, 1938. xvii, 95 pp.

Cresswell, J. R.
"Folk-Tales of the Swampy Cree." *JAFL* 36:404–406, 1923.

Linderman, Frank B. (Co-skee-see-co-cot)
Indian Why Stories, Sparks From the Eagles Lodge. Illustrated by Charles M. Russell, (Canne-ta-wah-see-na-e-ket). New York: Charles Scribner's Sons, 1920. 169 pp.

Manitoba Free Press
A Flint and Steel, with the Cree Legend of the Origin of Fire set forth in print for the first time, from a manuscript journal of an officer in the service of the Hudson's Bay Company, dated in the year 1817. Winnipeg: 1905. 24 pp., illus.

———.
A Quill from a Canada Wild Goose, with the Cree Legend of Nih-Ka, the wild goose, set forth for the first time in print. Winnipeg: 1904. 16 pp., illus.

Petitot, Émile Fortuné, S. J.
Essai sur une légende Américaine. Alençon: 1883. 8 pp. (Actes de la Société Philologique. Vol. 12.)

Prud'homme, L. A.
"Carmel, une legende de la Tribu des Cris." Royal Société of Canada. *Proceedings and Transactions.* Series 3, vol. 13:95–100, 1920.

Simms, S. C.
"Myths of the Bungees or Swampy Indians of Lake Winnipeg." *JAFL* 19:334–340, 1906.

Skinner, Alanson
"Notes on the Eastern Cree an Northern Saulteaux." *Anthrop. Papers* of the Amer. Mus. of Nat. Hist. No. 9. New York: The Museum, 1911.
Contains numerous tales.

Young, E. R.
Stories from Indian Wigwams and Northern Camp Fires. New York: 1893. 293 pp.

BELIEFS—CUSTOMS

Bloomfield, Louis
"Sacred Stones of the Sweet Grass Cree." Canada Department of Mines: *National Museum of Canada,* Bulletin 60. Anthropology Series 11.

Cooper, J. M.
"Field Notes on Northern Algonkian Magic." *Inter. Congr. Amer.* 23:513–518, 1928.

————.
"The Northern Algonquian Supreme Being." *Cath. Univ. Anthro. Ser.* 2:1–78, 1934.

Flannery, Regina
"Cross-Cousin Marriage Among the Cree and Montagnais of James Bay." *Primitive Man* 11 (Nos. 1, 2):29–33, 1938.

————.
"The Position of Women Among the Eastern Cree." *Primitive Man* 8(No. 4):81–86, 1935.

Hallowell, A. I.
"Cross-Cousin Marriage in the Lake Winnipeg Area." *Publ. Phila. Anthro. Soc.* 1:95–100, 1937.

————.
"The Incidence, Character and Decline of Polygamy Among Lake Winnipeg Cree and Saulteaux." *AA* 40:235–256, 1938. n.s.

————.
"Kinship Terms and Cross-Cousin Marriage of the Montagnais-Nascapi and the Cree." *AA* 34: 171–199, 1932. n.s.

————.
"Was Cross Cousin Marriage Practiced by the North-Central Algonkian." *Inter. Congr. Amer.* 23:519–544, 1928.

Hind, H. Y.
"Of Some of the Superstitions and Customs Common Among the Indians in the Valley of the Assinboine and Saskatchewan." *Canadian Journal* (Toronto) 22:253–262, 1859. n.s.

Holmes, E. M.
"Medicinal Plants Used by the Cree Indians." *Pharmaceutical Journal and Transactions,* ser. 3, 15:302–304, 1884.

Rossignol, M.
"Cross-Cousin Marriage Among the Saskatchewan Cree." *Primitive Man* 11:26–28, 1938.

————.
"Property Concepts Among the Cree of the Rocks." *Primitive Man* 12: 61–70, 1939.

————.
"The Religion of the Saskatchewan and Western Manitoba Cree." *Primitive Man* 11:67–71, 1939.

Skinner, Alanson
"Bear Customs of the Cree and other Algonkin Indians of Northern Ontario." *Papers and Records of the Ontario Historical Society* 12: 203–209, 1914.

GAMES

"Cree Games."
JAFL 9:275, 1896.

Flannery, R.
"Some Aspects of James Bay Recreative Culture." *Primitive Man* 9:49–56, 1937.

Laidlaw, G. E.
"Gambling Amongst the Crees with Small Sticks." *American Antiquity* 23:275–276, 1901.

MUSIC

GENERAL STUDIES

Skinner, Alanson
Musical Instruments of the Eastern Cree. In: "Notes on the Eastern Cree and Northern Saulteaux" (pp. 41-42). *Anthropological Papers* of the American Museum of Natural History, Volume XI. New York: American Museum, 1911.

DANCES

Goddard, Pliny Earle
"Notes on the Sun Dance of the Cree of Alberta." *Anthorpological Papers:* Vol. 16: 1919, pp. 295–310, 3 figs. Publications in Anthropology. New York: The American Museum of Natural History.

Lane, C.
"The Sun Dance of the Cree Indians." *Canadian Record of Science* 2:22–26, 1887.

DELAWARE (Lenape)

FOLKLORE

GENERAL STUDIES

Adams, R. C.
"History of the Delaware Indians." *Report of the Indians Taxed and Indians not Taxed,* U. S. Dep't of Interior, 11th Census, Wash., D. C., 1890, pp. 297-300.

Alden, Rev. Timothy
An Account of Sundry Missions Performed Among the Senecas and Munsees. (Series of Letters). New York: J. Seymour, 1827.
    Munsee—one of the three principal divisions of the Delawares.

Allinson, S.
"Fragmentary History of the New Jersey Indians." *Proc. New Jersey Hist. Soc.,* ser 2, 4: 33–50, 1875.

Battey, Thomas C.
The Life and Adventures of a Quaker Among the Indians. Boston, Mass.: Lee O. Shepard, 1903. 349 pp.

Brinton, Daniel G.
Folk-Lore of the Modern Lenape. In: *Essays of an Americanist,* (pp. 181–192). Philadelphia: Porter and Coates, 1890. 489 pp., illus.

————.
"Lenape Conversations." *JAFL* 1:37–43, 1888.

Buck, W. J.
"Lappawinzo and Tishcohan, Chiefs of the Lenni Lenape." *Penn. Magazine of History and Biography* 7:215–218, 1883.

Cross, Dorothy
Archaeology of New Jersey I. Trenton: New Jersey State Museum, 1941. 250 pp., illus.

Cummings, R. W.
"Delaware." In: *Information Respecting the History, Condition, and Prospects of the Indian Tribes of the United States,* H. R. Schoolcraft, ed. Vol. 2, pp. 470-481, Philadelphia: 1852.

De Valinger, Leon
Indian Land Sales in Delaware; with addendum: A discussion of the family hunting territory question in Delaware, by C. A. Weslager. Wilmington: Archaeological Society of Delaware, 1941.

Downes, R. C.
Council Fires on the Upper Ohio. Pittsburgh: Univ. Pitt. Press, 1940. 367 pp.

Gifford, A.
"The Aborigines of New Jersey." *Proc. New Jersey Hist. Soc.* 4:165–198, 1850.

Hanna, Charles Augustus
The Wilderness Trail, or the Ventures and Adventures of the Pennsylvania Traders on the Allegheny Path. New York & London: G. P. Putnam Sons, 1911. II vols.

Harrington, M. R.
"The Life of a Lenape Boy." *Penna. Arch.* 3 (Part 4):3–8, 1933.

————.
"A Preliminary Sketch of Lenape Culture." *AA* 15:208–236, 1913. n.s.

Holm, T. C.
"A Short Description of the Province of New Sweden." *Memoirs of the Historical Society of Pennsylvania* 3:112–156, 1834.

Hrdlicka, Alis.
Physical Anthropology of the Lenape or Delawares, and of the Eastern Indians in general. Bureau of American Ethnology, Bulletin 62, 130 pp., 29 pl., 1 fig. Washington, D. C.: U. S. Gov't Printing Office, 1916.

Johnson, Amandus
Geographia Americae, with an account of the Delaware Indians, based on surveys and notes made in 1654–1656 by Peter Lindestrom. Translated from the original manuscript with notes, introduction and an appendix of Indian

Geographical names with their meanings by Amandus Johnson. Philadelphia: Swedish Colonial Society, 1925.

————.
"The Indians and Their Culture as Described in Swedish and Dutch Records." *Inter. Congr. Amer.* 19:277–282, 1915.

Lilly, Eli
Prehistoric Antiquities of Indiana. Indianapolis: Indiana Historical Society, 1937.

McLeod, W. C.
"The Family Hunting Territory and Lenape Political Organization." *AA* 24:448–463, 1922. n.s.

Mooney, James
"Delaware." In: *Bureau of Amer. Ethnol. Bull. 30 (Part 1)*:385–387, 1907.

Meyers, Albert Cook, ed.
Narratives of Early Pennsylvania, Western New Jersey, and Delaware. New York: Charles Scribner's Sons, 1912. 476 pp.

Nelson, William
The Indians of New Jersey, With Some Notice of Indian Place Names. Paterson, N. J.: Press Publishing Co., 1894. 168 pp.

Peet, S. D.
"The Delaware Indians in Ohio." *Amer. Antiq.* 2:132–144, 1879.

Penn, W.
Account of the Lenni Lenape, A. C. Meyers, ed. Moylan, Pa.: 1937. 107 pp.

Philhower, Charles A.
Aboriginal Inhabitants of New Jersey. In: *New Jersey, a History,* I. S. Skull, ed., (pp. 14-53). New York: 1930. 4 vols.

————.
"Some Personal Characteristics of the Lenape Indians." *Proc. New Jersey Hist. Soc.* 16: 138–161, 1931. n.s.

————.
"South Jersey Indians." *Proc. New Jersey Hist. Soc.* 16:1–21, 1931.

Schrabisch, M.
"The Indians of New Jersey." *Americana* 5: 877–887, 1910.

Skinner, Alanson
The Indians of Greater of New York. Cedar Rapids, Iowa: The Torch Press, 1915. 150 pp., bibl.

————.
"The Lenape Indians of Staten Island." *Anthropological Papers, American Museum of Natural History* (New York) 3:1–62, 1910.

Speck, Frank G.
"Indian Life in Bergen County." *Papers and Proceedings of the Bergen County Historical Society* 3:19–28, 1907.

————.
The Nanticoke and Conoy Indians with a review of linguistic material from manuscript and living sources; an historical study. Wilmington: The Historical Society of Delaware, 1927. 77 pp. Papers of the Historical Society of Delaware, new series 1.

The Nanticoke, an Algonquian tribe, "connected linguistically and ethnically with the Delawares and Conoy, notwithstanding the idiomatic variance in the language of the latter."

————.
"The Wapanachki Delawares and the English; their past as viewed by an ethnologist." *Pennsylvania Magazine of History and Biography*, 68:319–344. Philadelphia: Historical Society of Pennsylvania, 1943.

Spier, Leslie
"The Trenton Argillite Culture." *Anthropological Papers:* Vol. 22: 1918, pp. 167–226, 11 figs. Publications in Anthropology. New York: The American Museum of Natural History.

Stiegerwalt, H. J.
"Some Lenape History." *Archaeological Bulletin* 8:3–4, 1917.

Troost, G.
"Extracts from the Voyages of David Pieterszen de Vries." *Coll. N. Y. Hist. Soc.* 1:243–280, 1841. n.s.

Voegelin, C. F.
"Delaware Texts." *International Journal of American Linguistics*, 2(No. 2):2:105–119, (April) 1945.

Wissler, Clark, ed.
"The Indians of Greater New York and the Lower Hudson." *Anthropological Papers:* Vol. 3:1909. Publications in Anthropology. New York: The American Museum of Natural History.

MYTHS—FOLKTALES—LEGENDS

Adams, Richard C.
A Delaware Indian Legend and the Story of their Troubles. Washington: 1899. 72 pp., illus.

————.
Legends of the Delaware Indians and Picture Writing. Washington, D. C.: 1905. 87 pp., illus.

Brinton, Daniel G.
The Lenâpé and their Legends; With the complete text and symbols of the Walam Olum, a new translation, and an inquiry into its authenticity. Philadelphia: D. G. Brinton, 1885. viii, 262 pp., illus. (Vol. V. *Brinton's Library of Aboriginal American Literature.*)

Dunn, Jacob P.
True Indian Stories, with Glossary of Indian Names. Indianapolis: Sentinel Printing Co., 1908.

Leitner, Leander
The Walum-Olum; a legend of the Lenape Indians. Brooklyn: 1941. 11 pp., illus.
"A translation from the picture writing record of the Lenape Indians by Daniel G. Brinton about 1860."

Prime, Rev. Samuel I.
"The Indian's Trance." *Sartain's Union Magazine of Lit. and Art* 5:143–144, Sept., 1849.
Legend of the dream of the chief of the Delawares showing him the sins of his people and his own, and asking him to forsake the evil ways."

Prince, John D.
"A Modern Delaware Tale." *American Philo. Soc. Proc.* 41 (No. 168):20.34, 1902.

Rafinesque, Constantine S.
Wallamolum or Painted Traditions of the Linapi Indians, translated by C. S. Rafinesque Schmaltz, 1833; with a fragment on the history of the Linapi since about 1600 when the Wallamolum closes. Transcript: 1850. 40 pp.

Squier, E. G.
Historical and Mythological Traditions of the Algonquins; with translation of the "Walumolum," or bark record of the Linni-Lenape. New York: 1849. 23 pp.

Stober, A. F.
Indian History and Legends of Pennsylvania's Picturesque Playgrounds. Scranton, Pa.: International Textbook Co., 1936.

BELIEFS—CUSTOMS—FOLK MEDICINE

Abbott, C. C.
"Idols and Idol Worship of the Delaware Indians." *Amer. Nat.* 16:799–802, 1882.

Berlin, A. F.
"Mode of Fishing by the Delaware Indians." *Amer Antiq.* 9:167–169, 1887.

Harrington, M. R.
Religion and Ceremonies of the Lenape. Indian Notes and Monographs. Museum of the American Indian, Heye Foundation. Misc. Ser. 19.

————.
"Some Customs of the Delaware Indians." *Museum Journal* 1:52–60, 1910.

————.
"The Thunder Power of Rumbling-Wings." In: *American Indian Life*, Elsie Clews Parsons, ed., (pp. 107–125). New York: 1925.

————.
"Vestiges of Material Culture Among the Canadian Delawares." *AA* 10:408–418, 1908. n.s.

Heckewelder, John G. E.
History, Manners and Customs of the Indian Nations Who Once Inhabited Pennsylvania and the Neighboring States. Pennsylvania Historical Society Memoirs, Vol. 12. Phila.: Historical Society of Pennsylvania, 1876.

Morgan, Lewis H.
"Systems of Consanguinity and Affinity."
Smithson. Contr. to Knowledge 17:291–382,
1871.

Petrullo, Vincenzo
The Diabolic Root. A Study of Peyotism, the
New Indian Religion Among the Delawares.
Philadelphia: University of Pennsylvania
Press, University Museum, 1934. x, 185 pp.,
illus.

Speck, Frank G.
*Oklahoma Delaware Ceremonies, Feasts and
Dances.* Memoirs, American Philosophical Society, Vol. 7. Philadelphia: University of Pennsylvania Press, 1937. 161 pp., illus.

———.
*A Study of the Delaware Big House Indian
Ceremony.* Publishers of the Pennsylvania Historical Commission, (Harrisburg) Vol. II, 1931.
192 pp., illus.

Tantaquidgeon, Gladys
*A Study of Delaware Indian Medicine Practice
and Folk Beliefs.* Harrisburg: Pennsylvania
Historical Commission, Department of Public
Instruction, 1942. xi, 91 pp.

GAMES

"Lenape Games."
JAFL 1:40, 1888.

FOLK ART—SPEECH

Abbott, C. C.
"The Delaware Indian as an Artist." *Pop.
Sci. Month.* 41:586–594, 1892.

———.
"The Use of Copper by the Delaware Indians."
Amer. Natur. 19:774–777, 1885.

Heckewelder, Rev. John
"Indian Tradition." *American Repository of
Arts, Life and Letters* 4:143–146, 1841.
In a letter dated, Bethlehem, Jan. 26, 1801, the
Reverend discusses the stylistic and grammatical
peculiarities of some of the Indian languages in
Pennsylvania.

———.
"Names which the Lenni Lenape or Delaware
Indians, who once inhabited This Country had
given to Rivers, Streams, Places, etc." *Trans.
Amer. Philo. Soc.* 4:351–396, 1834. n.s.

———.
"Words, Phrases, and Short Dialogues, in the
Language Lenni Lenape of Delaware Indians."
Trans. Hist. Lit. Com. Amer. Philo. Soc. 1:
450–464, 1819.

Nelson, William
Personal Names of Indians of New Jersey:
Being a List of Six Hundred and Fifty Such
Names, Gleaned Mostly from Indian Deeds of
the 17th Century. Paterson, N. J.: The Paterson
Historical Club, 1904. 83 pp.

Prince, J. D.
"An Ancient New Jersey Indian Jargon." *AA*
14:508–525, 1912. n.s.

———.
"Notes on the Modern Minsi-Delaware Dialect." *Amer. Jour. Philol.* 31:295–302, 1900.

Ruttenber, E. M.
Footprints of the Red Men. Newburgh: New
York State Historical Association, 1906. 241 pp.
Indian Geographical Names in the Valley of the
Hudsons' River, the Valley of the Mohawk, and
on the Delaware: their locations and the prob-
able meanings of some of them.

Skinner, Alanson
"Two Lenape Stone Masks." *Ind. Notes and
Monog.* 3:5–7, 1900. n.s.

Wren, C.
"A Study of North Applachian Indian Pottery." *Proc. Coll. Wyoming Hist. Geol. Soc.*
13:131–222, 1914.

Zeisberger, David
Delaware Indian and English Spelling Book.
Philadelphia: Mary Cist, 1806. 179 pp.

———.
"Grammar of the Language of the Lenni
Lenape." *Trans. of the American Philos. So-
ciety* 3:1830. n.s.

———.
Indian Dictionary. Cambridge: 1887. 236 pp.

———.
"Some Remarks and Annotations Concerning
the Traditions, Customs, Languages, etc. of
the Indians of North America." *Olden Time*
1:271–281, 1846.

MUSIC

GENERAL STUDIES

Shoemaker, Henry W.
Indian Folk-Songs of Pennsylvania. Altoona,
Pa.: N. F. McGirr, 1927. 15 pp.

Speck, Frank G.
*Oklahoma-Delaware Ceremonies, Feasts and
Dances.* Memoirs of the American Philosophi-
cal Society, Volume 7. Philadelphia: American
Philosophical Society, 1937. 161 pp., illus-
trated.
Discussion of the dances and music.

FOX (Musquakie)

FOLKLORE

GENERAL STUDIES

Anon.
*Cha kä ta ko si: a Collection of Meskwaki
Manuscripts.* Iowa City: 1907.

Beals, Frank L.
Chief Black Hawk. Chicago: Wheeler Publishing Co., 1943.
Besides being an exciting adventure, the book
deals also with tribal customs, traditions and
beliefs.

Beckwith, H. W.
"The Illinois and Indiana Indians." *Fergus Historical Series.* (Chicago) 27:146–162, 1884.

Bicknell, A. D.
"The Tama County Indians." *Annals of Iowa,* (ser. 3)4:196–208, 1899.

Bond, Beverly W.
The Civilization of the Old Northwest. New York: The Macmillan Co., 1934.

Busby, Allie B.
Two Summers Among the Musquakies. Vinton: Herald Book and Job, 1886.

Davidson, John N.
In Unnamed Wisconsin. Milwaukee: S. Chapman, 1895. 307 pp.

Ferris, I. M.
"The Sauks and Foxes." *Coll. Kansas State Hist. Soc.* 11:333–395, 1910.

Gilbert, J. J.
"Some Notes on the Fox Island Passes." *National Geographic Magazine* 16:427–429, 1905.

Green, O. J.
"The Mesquaki Indians." *Red Man* 5: 47–52, 104–109, 1912.

Indian Tribes of Wisconsin.
U. S. Bureau of American Ethnology, Bulletin 30. Excerpts from the Handbook of American Indians North of Mexico. Washington, D. C.: U. S. Government Printing Office, 1907–1910.

Jenks, A. E.
"The Wild Rice Gatherers of the Upper Lakes." *Annual Report, Bureau Amer. Ethnol.* 19(Part 2):1013–1037, 1898.

Joffe, Natalie Frankel
The Fox. In: *Acculturation in Seven Indian Tribes,* Ralph Linton, ed. New York: D. Appleton-Century, 1940.

————.
The Fox of Iowa. New York: Appleton-Century Co., 1940.

Jones, William
"Algonquian (Fox)." *Bureau Amer. Ethnol. Bull.* 40(Part 1):735–873, 1911.

————.
Ethnography of the Fox Indians. U. S. Bureau of Ethnology, Bulletin 125. Washington, D. C.: U. S. Government Printing Office, 1939. 156 pp., illus.

————.
Fox Texts. Edited by Franz Boas. Publication of the American Ethnological Association. Leiden: Late E. J. Brill, 1907. 383 pp.
    The texts in Fox and English, consist of five historical tales, twelve miscellaneous myths and traditions, twelve parables, seventeen stories of culture hero, and four prayers.

————.
"Notes on the Fox Indians." *JAFL* 24:209–237, 1911.

Kirsch, Mary Moran
"The Indians of Wisconsin." *Wisconsin Blue Book,* pp. 91–112, 1931.

Lawson, P. V.
"The Outagamie Village at West Menasha." *Proc. State Hist. Soc. Wis.* 47:204–211, 1900.

Malin, W. G.
"The Sac and Fox Indians of Iowa." *So. Workman* (Hampton, Va.) 37:481–485, 1908.

Marsh, C.
"Expedition to the Sacs and Foxes." *Coll. State Hist. Soc. Wis.* 15:104–155, 1900.

Michelson, Truman
Contributions to Fox Ethnology. 2. Bureau of American Ethnology, Bulletin 85. Washington, D. C.: U. S. Government Printing Office, 1927. 168 pp., illus.
    Includes notes on ceremonial runners of Fox Indians; Sauk and Fox Sacred Pack; Sacred Pack called A'pena "wa" ha" 'a belonging to Thunder Gens of Fox Indians; Sacred Pack called Sagima 'Kwäwa belonging to Bear Gens of Fox Indians.

————.
Contributions to Fox Ethnology, 2. Bureau of American Ethnology, Bulletin 95. Washington, D. C.: U. S. Government Printing Office, 1930.
    Includes sketch of the Buffalo Dance of the Bear Gens of the Fox Indians; and notes on the Great Sacred Pack of the Thunder Gens of the Fox Indians. Part of the bulletin is given in the Indian text with English translation.

————.
Fox Miscellany. U. S. Bureau of Ethnology, Bulletin 114. Washington, D. C.: U. S. Government Printing Office, 1937. 124 pp., illus.

————.
"Mesa wi'Ka, and Fox Sociology." *AA* 35:397, 1933. n.s.

————.
Miss Owen's "Folklore of the Musquakie Indians." *AA* 38:143–145, 1936. n.s.

————.
"Notes on the Folklore and Mythology of the Fox Indians." *AA* 15:699–700, 1913. n.s.

————.
"Notes on the Fox Society Known as Those Who Worship the Little Spotted Buffalo." *Annual Report, Bureau Amer. Ethnol.* 40: 497–539, 1919.

————.
Notes on the Fox Wapanonowiweni. Bulletin 105. Bureau of American Ethnology, Smithsonian Institution. Washington, D. C.: U. S. Government Printing Office, 1932.

————.
"Notes on the Social Organization of the Fox Indians." *AA* 15:691–693, 1913. n.s.

————.
"Sol Tax on the Social Organization of the Fox Indians." *AA* 40:177–179, 1938. n.s.

————.
"Some General Notes on the Fox Indians—III —Bibliography." *Journal of the Washington Academy of Science* 9:593–596.

————.
"The Autobiography of a Fox Indian Woman." *40th Annual Report: Bureau American Ethnology, 1918–1919.* pp. 295–616. Washington, D. C.: U. S. Government Printing Office, 1925.

————.
"The Traditional Origin of the Fox Society Known as 'The Singing Around Rite'." *40th Annual Report: Bureau of American Ethnology, Smithsonian Institution,* pp. 541–658. Washington, D. C.: U. S. Government Printing Office, 1925.

Mooney, James, and Thomas, Cyrus
"Foxes." In: *Bureau Amer. Ethnol. Bull.* 30 (Part 1):472–474, 1907.

Owen, Mary Alicia
"Algonquins." In: *Encyclopedia of Religion and Ethics,* John Hastings, ed., Vol. I, pp. 319–326. New York: 1908.

————.
Folk-lore of the Musquakie Indians of North America; and catalogue of Musquakie bead-work and other objects in the collections of the Folk-lore Society. London: Published for the Folk-lore Society by D. Nutt, 1904. vii, 147 pp., illus. (Publications of the Folk-lore Society LI).

Radin, Paul
"A Semi-historical Account of the War of the Winnebago and the Foxes." *Wisconsin State Historical Society,* separate 163, 1915.

Rebok, H. M.
"The Last of the Mus-qua-kies." *Iowa Historical Record* 17:305–335, 1901.

Smith, H. H.
"The Red Earth Indians." *Yearbook of the Public Museum of the City of Milwaukee* 3: 27–38, 1923.

Smith, H. I.
"The Prehistoric Ethnology of a Kentucky Site." *Anthropology Papers, American Museum of Natural History,* 6:173–241, 1910. (New York).

Tax, Sol
The Social Organization of the Fox Indians. In: *Social Anthropology of North American Tribes,* F. Eggan, ed., (pp. 241–248). Chicago: 1937.

Ward, D. J. H.
"The Meskwaki People of To-day." *Iowa Jour. Hist. and Pol.* 4:190–219, 1906.

————.
"Meskwakia." *Iowa Jour. Hist. and Pol.* 4: 179–189, 1906.

MYTHS—FOLKTALES—LEGENDS

Ellis, E. W.
"The Raccoon and the Opossum." *Red Man* (Carlisle, Pa.) 3:344, 1911.

Jones, William
"Episodes in the Culture-hero Myth of the Sauks and Foxes." *JAFL* 14:225–239, 1901.

————.
Fox Texts. Leyden: E. J. Brill, 1907. vi, 383 pp. (American Ethnological Society. Publications. Vol. 1.)

————.
"The Heart of the Brave." *Harvard Monthly* 30:99–106, 1900.

Lasley, M.
"Sak and Fox Tales." *JAFL* 15:170–178, 1902.

Michelson, Truman
"Ritualistic Origin Myths of the Fox Indians." *Journal of the Washington Academy of Science* 6:209–211, 1916.

————.
"What Happened to Green Bear Who Was Blessed With a Sacred Pack." *Bureau Amer. Ethnol. Bull. 119* :161–176, 1938.

Owen, Mary A.
Folk-Lore of the Musquakie Indians of North America and catalogue of Musquakie bead-work and other objects in the collection of the Folk-Lore Society. London: D. Nutt, 1904. vii, 147 pp., illus.

————.
"The Mythical Origin of the White Buffalo Dance of the Fox Indians." *Annual Report, Bureau Amer. Ethnol.* 40:23–289, 1919.

————.
"Notes on the Folklore and Mythology of the Fox Indians." *AA* 15:699–700, 1913. n.s.

BELIEFS—CUSTOMS

Burford, C. C.
"Sauk and Fox Ceremonials Attract Large Attendance and Widespread Interest." *Jour. Ill. State Arch. Soc.* 5 (No. 3): 39–41, 1948.

Forsyth, T.
"Account of the Manners and Customs of the Sauk and Fox Nations." In: *The Indian Tribes of the Upper Mississippi Valley,* E. H. Blair, ed., Vol. II, pp. 183-245. Cleveland: 1912.

Harrington, M. R.
"The Algonkin Manitou." *JAFL* 18:183–190, 1905.

————.
"Sacred Bundles of the Sac and Fox." *Univ. Penn. Museum Anthro. Publ.* 4:125–262, 1914.

Jones, William
"Mortuary Observances and the Adoption Rites of the Algonkian Foxes of Iowa." *Proceedings of the 15th Session of the International Congress of Americanists,* 1:263–279, 1906.

Michelson, Truman
"How Meskwaki Children Should Be Brought Up." In: *American Indian Life,* Elsie Clews Parsons, ed., (pp. 81–86). New York: 1925.

————.
"Notes on the Fox Society Known as Those Who Worship the Little Spotted Buffalo." *40th Annual Report: Bureau American Ethnology, 1918–1919.* pp. 501–616, pl. 2, fig. 2. Washington, D. C.: U. S. Government Printing Office, 1925.

————.
"Notes on Fox Mortuary Customs and Beliefs." In: *Annual Report, Bureau Amer. Ethnol.* 40:351–496, 1919.

————.
"Notes on the Social Organizations of the Fox Indians." *AA* 15:691–693, 1913. n.s.

————.
The Owl Sacred Pack of the Fox Indians. Bulletin 72. Bureau of American Ethnology, Smithsonian Institution. Washington, D. C.: U. S. Government Printing Office, 1921. 83 pp., 4 pls.

Smith, H. H.
"Ethnobotany of the Meskwaki Indians." *Bull. Publ. Mus. City Milwaukee* 14:175–326, 1928.

Smith, H. I.
"The Prehistoric Ethnology of a Kentucky Site." *Anthropological Papers of the American Museum of Natural History* (New York) 6: 173–241, 1910.
Includes discussion of games, and dances of the Fox Indians.

Stories of the Indians During the Revolution; with a brief sketch of the customs of the Sauxes and Foxes. New York: Published for the Proprietor, 1836. 31 pp., illus.

Tax, Sol
The Social Organization of the Fox Indians. In: *Social Anthropology of North American Tribes,* F. Eggan, ed., (pp. 241–282). Chicago: 1937.

FOLK ART—SPEECH

Bloomfield, L.
"Notes on the Fox Language." *Inter. Jour. Amer. Ling.* 3:219–232; 4:181–219, 1925–1927.

Flom, G. T.
Syllabus of Vowel an Consonantal Sounds in Meskwaki Indians. Iowa City: 1906.

Harrington, M. R.
"A Bird-Quill Belt of the Sauk and Fox Indians." *Ind. Notes and Monog.* 10.47–50, 1920.

————.
"Old Sauk and Fox Beaded Garters." *Ind. Notes and Monog.* 10:39–41, 1920.

Jones, W.
An Algonquin Syllabary. In: *Boas Anniversary Volume,* (pp. 88–93). New York: 1906.

————.
"Some Principles of Algonquian Word-Formation." *AA* 6:369–411, 1904. n.s.

Michelson, Truman
"Algonquian Linguistic Miscellany." *Jour. Wash. Acad. Sci.* 4:402–409, 1914.

————.
"Fox Linguistic Notes. In: *Festschrift Meinhof,* (pp. 403-408). Hamburg: 1927.

————.
"Notes on Algonquian Languages." *Inter Jour. Amer. Ling.* 1:50–57, 1919.

————.
"The So-Called Stems of Algonquian Verbal Complexes." *Inter. Congr. Amer.* 19:541–544, 1915.

————.
"Vocalic Harmony in Fox." *Amer. Jour. Philol.* 41:181–183, 1920.

Observations on Thunder Dance of Bear Gens of Fox Indians. U. S. Bureau of Ethnology, Bulletin 89. Washington, D. C.: U. S. Government Printing Office, 1929. 73 pp., illus.

GAMES

"Sauk and Fox Games." *JAFL* 24:221–226, 227, 1911.

MUSIC

GENERAL STUDIES—DANCES

Huot, M. C.
"Peyote Songs." *Transition* 24:117–119, 1936.

Michelson, Truman
"The Changing Character of Fox Adoption-Feasts." *Amer. Jour. Sociol.* 34:890–892, 1929.

————.
The Mythical Origin of the White Buffalo Dance of the Fox Indians, together with texts on four minor sacred poets appertaining to this ceremony. U. S. Bureau of American Ethnology, 40th Annual Report. Washington, D. C.: U. S. Government Printing Office, 1918.

————.
Notes on the Buffalo-head Dance of the Thunder Gens of the Fox Indians. Bureau of American Ethnology, Bulletin 87, 94 pp., 1 fig. Washington, D. C.: U. S. Gov't Printing Office, 1928.

————.
"Notes on the Fox Gens Festivals." *Proceedings of the 23rd Session of the International Congress of Americanists,* pp. 545–547, 1928.

HURON (*Including:* Wyandot)

FOLKLORE

GENERAL STUDIES

Anderson, Rev. Joseph
"The Huron Language and Some of the Huron-Iroquois Traditions." *American Philological Association Proceedings 5th Annual Session,* 1873. pp. 23–25. Hartford: 1874.

Biggar, H. P., ed.
The Works of Samuel de Champlain, Vol. III, pp. 114-158. Toronto: 1929.

Boucher, Pierre
Histoire véritable et naturelle des moeurs et productions du pays de la Nouvelle France. Montreal: E. Bastien, 1882. 164 pp.

Brébeuf, J. de
Relations of the Hurons, 1636. In: *The Jesuit Relations and Allied Documents,* R. G. Thwaites, ed. Vol. X, pp. 124-317. Cleveland: A. H. Clark Co., 1897.

Clarke, Peter D.
Origin and Traditional History of the Wyandotts, and Sketches of Other Indian Tribes of North America.... Toronto: Hunter, Rose & Co., 1870. vi, 158 pp.

Connelley, W. E.
"Notes on the Folk-Lore of the Wyandots." *JAFL* 12:116–125, 1899.

———.
Wyandot Folk-Lore. Topeka, Kans.: Crane and Company, 1899. 116 pp.

———.
"The Wyandots." *Annual Arch. Report,* 1899, pp. 92-141.

Downes, Randolph Chandler
Council Fires on the Upper Ohio; a narrative of Indian Affairs in the Upper Ohio Valley until 1795. Pittsburgh: University of Pittsburgh Press, 1940.

Finley, James Bradley
Life Among the Indians; or, Personal Reminiscences and Historical Incidents Illustrative of Indian Life and Character.... Edited by Rev. D. W. Clark. Cincinnati: Methodist Book Concern, 1857. 548 pp., illus.

Gendron, Le Sieur
Quelques particularitez du pays des Hurons. Paris: Denys Bechet, 1640. 26 pp.

Gérin, L.
"The Hurons of Lorette." *Transactions Ottawa Literary and Scientific Society 1899–1900,* pp. 69–92.

Gray, L. H.
"Huron." In: *Encyclopedia of Religion and Ethics,* John Hastings, ed., Vol. VI, pp. 883-886. New York: 1914.

Hale, H.
"Huron Folk-Lore." *JAFL* 1:177–183, 1888; 2:249–254, 1889; 4:289–294, 1891.

Jenness, Diamond
"Indians of Canada." *Bull. Can Dept. Mines* No. 45, pp. 289–299. Ottawa: 1932.

Jones, A. E.
"Huron Indians." In: *Catholic Encyclopedia,* Vol. VII, pp. 565–583. New York: 1910.

Kenton, E., ed.
The Indians of North America, Vol. I, pp. 211–231, 234–312, 498–523; Vol. II, pp. 29–46. New York: Harcourt, Brace Co., 1927.

Kinietz, W. Vernon
The Indians of the Western Great Lakes. Occasional Contributions from the Museum of Anthropology of the University of Michigan, 10. Ann Arbor: University of Michigan Press, 1941. 427 pp.

Lilly, Eli
Prehistoric Antiquities of Indiana. Indianapolis: Indiana Historical Society, 1937.
Contains a valuable bibliography of Indiana archaeology.

Martin, Félix
Hurons et Iroquois. Paris: Téqui, 1898.

Merwin, R. E.
"The Wyandot Indians." *Transactions of the Kansas State Historical Society of Topeka* 9: 73–87, 1906.

Orr, R. B.
"The Hurons." *Annual Arch. Report,* 1921–1922, pp. 9-24.

Powell, J. W.
"Wyandot Government." *1st Annual Report: Bureau of American Ethnology 1879–1880,* pp. 59–68. Washington, D. C.: U. S. Government Printing Office, 1881.
An account of communal life, family, group, etc., and the construction of government—officers, methods of election, etc. The attitude towards murder, theft, treason; the witchcraft, outlawing, etc.

Sagard-Théodat, G.
The Long Journey to the Country of the Hurons, G. M. Wrong, ed. Publications of the Champlain Society, No. 25. Toronto: 1939. 411 pp.
A French earlier version appeared in Paris, in 1865.

Schlup, E.
"The Wyandot Mission." *Ohio State Hist. Arch. Quart.* 15:163–181, 1906.

Wilson, Sir David
"The Huron-Iroquois of Canada. A Typical Race of Aborigines in America." *Proceedings of the Royal Society of Canada,* 1884.

MYTHS—FOLKTALES—LEGENDS

Barbeau, Charles Marius
Huron and Wyandot Mythology. With an appendix containing earlier published records. Ottawa: Gov't Printing Bureau, 1915. xiv, 437 pp. (Geological Survey Branch. Mem. 80. Anthropological Series, No. 11).

————.
"Wyandot Tales, Including Foreign Elements." *JAFL* 28:83–95, 1915.

Connelley, William
Wyandot Folk-Lore. Topeka, Kansas: Crane & Co., 1900. 116 pp. (Twentieth Century Classics and School Readings).

Dunn, Jacob P.
True Indian Stories, with Glossary of Indiana Indian Names. Indianapolis: Sentinel Printing Co., 1908.

Gilman, Chandler Robbins
Legends of a Log Cabin, by a Western Man. New York: G. Dearborn, 1835. 277 pp.
Includes "The Wyandot's story."

Guindon, Arthur
En Mocassins. Montreal: L'Institution des Sourds-Muets, 1920. 240 pp., illus.

Walker, Bertrand, N. O. (Hen-Toh)
Tales of the Bark Lodges, by Hen-Toh, Wyandot. Oklahoma City: Harlow Publishing Company, 1920. vii, 130 pp., illus.

BELIEFS—CUSTOMS—FOLK ART

Barbeau, Charles Marius
"Supernatural Beings of the Huron and Wyandot." *AA* 16:288–314, 1914. n.s.

Brébeuf, J. de.
"Burial Ceremonies of the Hurons." *Annual Report, Bureau Amer. Ethnol.* 5:110–119, 1884.

Bushnell, D. I.
"Native Cemeteries and Forms of Burial East of the Misissippi." *Bull. Bureau Amer. Ethnol.* 71:73–83, 1920.

Carr, L.
"On the Social and Political Position of Woman Among the Huron-Iroquois Tribes." *Reports Peabody Museum Amer. Arch. Ethnol.* 3:207–232, 1887.

Hewitt, J. N. B.
"The Cosmogonic Gods of the Iroquois." *Proc. Amer. Assoc. Adv. Sci.* 44:241–250, 1895.

Hirschfelder, C. A.
"Burial Customs of the Hurons." *Proc. Amer. Assoc. Sci.* 40:363–365, 1891.

Merwin, B. W.
"The Art of Quillwork." *Museum Journal* 9:50–55, 1918.

Perrot, N.
Memoir on the Manners, Customs, and Religion of the Savages of North America. In: *The Indian Tribes of the Upper Mississippi,* E. H. Blair, ed., Vol. I, pp. 25-272. Cleveland: 1911.

Powell, J. W.
"Wyandot Government." *Annual Report, Bureau Amer. Ethnol.* 1:57–69, 1880.

Skinner, Alanson
"Some Wyandot Corn Foods." *Yearbook Public Mus. City Milwaukee* 3:109–112, 1923.

Speck, Frank G.
"Huron Moose Hair Embroidery." *AA* 13:1–15, 1911. n.s.

————.
"Notes on the Material Culture of the Huron." *AA* 13:208–229, 1911. n.s.

————.
"Some Huron Treaty-Belts." *University of Pennsylvania, Museum Journal* (Phila.) 2:26–27, 1911.

Waugh, F. W.
"Notes on Canadian Pottery." *Annual Arch. Report* (Ontario), 1901, pp. 108–115.

Wintemberg, W. J.
"Bone and Horn Harpoon Heads of the Ontario Indians." *Annual Arch. Report* (Ontario), 1905, pp. 33-56.

IROQUOIS

See: Cayuga, Mohawk, Oneida, Onondaga, and Seneca.

FOLKLORE
GENERAL STUDIES

Adams, Spencer L.
The Long House of the Iroquois. Skaneateles, N. Y.: Fairview Farm, 1944. 175 pp.
A history of the Iroquois and European settlements in the Western Hemisphere, with photographs.

Anon.
"An Indian Tradition Concerning the Origin of the Five Nations." *Columbian Magazine* 2:578, Oct., 1788.
Taken from the account of Henry's captivity.

Bartram, J.
Observations on the Inhabitants, Climate, Soil, Rivers, Productions, Animals, and Other Matters Worthy of Notice. London: 1751. 94 pp.

Beauchamp, William Martin
Aboriginal Occupation of New York. New York State Museum Bulletin 32. Albany, N. Y.: State Education Department, 1900. 190 pp., illus.

————.
History of the New York Iroquois. State Museum Bulletin 78. Albany, N. Y.: State Education Department, 1905. 340 pp., illus.

————.
Iroquois Folk Lore Gathered From the Six Nations of New York. Selected and arranged by the Rev. Wm. M. Beauchamp for the Onondaga Historical Association. Syracuse, N. Y.: The Dekler Press, 1922. 247 pp.

————.
"Iroquois Notes." *JAFL* 4:39–46, 1891; 5:223–229, 1892.

————.
"Origin and Antiquity of the New York Iroquois." *Amer. Antiq.* 8:358–366, 1866.

Beaugrand-Champagne, A.
"L'organisation sociale des anciens Iroquois." *Cahiers des Dix* 4:271–289, 1939.

————.
"Le régime politique des anciens Iroquois." *Cahiers des Dix* 5:217–229, 1940.

Boas, Franz
"Zur Anthropologie der nordamerikanischen Indianer." *Verhandl. Berliner Gesell. Anthro. Ethno. Ur.*, 1895, pp. 367-411.

Boyle, D.
"The Iroquois." *Annual Archaeological Report*, Ontario, 1905, Toronto, 1906. pp. 146–158.

Brodhead, J. R.
Wentworth Greenhalgh's Journal of a Tour to the Indians of Western New York. In: *Documents Relative to the Colonial History of the State of New York*, E. B. O'Callaghan, ed., Vol. 3, pp. 250-252. Albany: 1853.

Burtin, Nicolas Victor
Vie de Catherine Tekakwitha, vièrge Iroquoisi decédée en odeur de sainteté à l'ancien village du Sault St. Louis, le 17 Avril, 1680, par le R. P. Burtin. Quebec: Leger Brousseau, 1894. x, 93 pp.
The story of a saintly Iroquois maiden.

Caswell, H. S.
Our Life Among the Iroquois Indians. Boston: 1892. xiii 321 pp.

Chadwick, Edward Marion
The People of the Longhouse. Toronto: The Church of England Publishing Co., 1897. 166 pp., illus.

Chamberlain, A. F.
"Iroquois in Northwestern Canada." *AA* 6: 459–463, 1904, n.s.

Clark, J. V. H.
Lights and Lines of Indian Character. Syracuse: E. H. Babcock, 1854. 375 pp.

Colden, Cadwallader
History of the Five Nations. New York: A. S. Barnes and Company, 1904. 2 vols.

Cusick, D.
Sketches of Ancient History of the Six Nations. Lockport: Cooley & Lothrop, 1848. 35 pp.

Donaldson, T.
"The Six Nations of New York." *Report on Indians Taxed and Indians not Taxed* (Census Office, 11th., Washington, D. C.), 1890, 447–498.

Downes, R. C.
Council Fires on the Upper Ohio. Pittsburgh: 1940. 367 pp.

Fenton, William N.
"Iroquois Suicide: A study in the stability of a cultural pattern." *Anthropological Papers Nos. 13–18. Bureau of American Ethnology*, Bulletin 128, pp. 79-137. Washington, D. C.: 1941.

————.
Problems Arising From the Historic Northeastern Position of the Iroquois. In: *Essays in Historical Anthropology of North America*. Published in honor of John R. Swanton, in celebration of his 40th year with the Smithsonian Institution. Smithsonian Miscellaneous Collection, vol. 100. Washington, D. C.: U. S. Government Printing Office, 1940.

————.
"Simeon Gibson: Iroquois Informant, 1889–1943." *AA* 46:231–235, 1944.

Goldenweiser, A. A.
Hanging Flower, the Iroquois. In: *American Indian Life*, Elsie Clews Parsons, ed., (pp. 99–106). New York: 1925.

Gray, L. H.
"Iroquois." In: *Encyclopedia of Religion and Ethics*, John Hastings, ed., Vol. 7, (pp. 420-422). New York: 1915.

Hale, Horatio Emmons
An Iroquois Condoling Council, a study of aboriginal American Society and Government. Ottawa: J. Durie & Son, 1895. 65 pp., illus. From the Transactions of the Royal Society of Canada, 2nd Ser., 1895–1896. vol. I, sec. 2.

————.
Chief George H. M. Johnson, Onwanonsyshon; his life and work among the Six Nations. New York: A. S. Barnes & Company, 1885. 142 pp., illus.

————.
Hiawatha and the Iroquois Confederation. Salem: 1881. 20 pp.

Harrington, M. R.
"The Story Bag." *Masterkey* 5:147–152, 179–183, 1931–1932.

Heckewelder, John
History, Manners and Customs, of the Indian Nations Who Once Inhabited Pennsylvania and Neighboring States. Historical Society of Pennsylvania, Memoirs No. 12, 1876. 465 pp.

Henning, C. L.
"The Origin of the Confederacy of the Five Nations." *Proc. Amer. Assoc. Adv. Sci.* 47: 477–480, 1898.

Hewitt, J. N. B.
"Era of the Formation of the Historic League of the Iroquois." *AA* 7:61–68, 1894. o.s.

————.
"Ethnological Researches Among the Iroquois and Chippewa." *Smithson. Miscel. Coll.* 88 (Part 6):237–247, 1926.

————.
"Ethnology of the Iroquois." *Smithson. Miscel. Coll.* 68(Part 12):106–107, 1917.

————.
"Field Researches Among the Six Nations of the Iroquois." *Explorations and Field-Work of the Smithsonian Institution* (Wash., D. C.), 1930, pp. 201–206.

————.
"Field Work Among the Iroquois Tribes." *Explorations and Field-Work of the Smithsonian Institution* (Wash., D. C.), 1931, pp. 175-178.

————.
"Field Work Among the Iroquois." *Smithson. Miscel. Coll.* 70(Part 2):103–107, 1911.

————.
"Field Work Among the Iroquois Indians." *Explorations and Field-Work of the Smithsonian Institution* (Wash., D. C.), 1932, pp. 81-84.

————.
"Iroquois." In: *Bull. Bureau Amer. Ethnol.* 30(Part 1):617–620, 1907.

————.
"The League of Nations of the Iroquois Indians of Canada." *Explorations and Field-Work of the Smithsonian Institution* (Wash., D. C.), 1929, pp. 201-206.

————.
"The Requickening Address of the League of the Iroquois." In: *Holmes Anniversary Volume.* . . . Washington: J. W. Bryan, 1916.

————.
"Some Esoteric Aspects of the League of the Iroquois." *Inter. Congr. Amer.* 19:322–326, 1915.

Houghton, F.
"The Indian Inhabitants of the Niagara Frontier." *Journal of American History* 16: 213–228, 1922.

Hunt, George T.
The Wars of the Iroquois; a study in intertribal trade relations. Madison: The University of Wisconsin Press, 1940. 209 pp., maps.

Jenness, Diamond
"Three Iroquois Wampum Records." *Bull. Canad. Dep't. Mines* 70:25–29, 1932.

Kimm, S. C.
The Iroquois. Middleburgh: 1900. 122 pp.

Kraus, Bertram S.
"Acculturation, A New Approach to the Iroquoian Problem." *American Antiquity* 9 (No. 3):302–318, (Menasha), 1944.

Mackenzie, J. B.
The Six-Nations Indians in Canada. Toronto: Hunter, Rose Co., 1896. 151 pp.

Martin, F.
Hurons et Iroquois. Paris: Téqui, 1898.

Mooney, J.
"Cherokee and Iroquois Parallels." *JAFL* 2:67, 1889.

Morgan, L. H.
Ancient Society, Or Researches in the Lines of Human Progress From Savagery Through Barbarism to Civilization. New York: Henry Holt & Co., 1877. 554 pp.
    Chaps. II-V discuss the Iroquois gens, phratry, tribe and confederacy.

————.
League of the Ho-Dé-No-Sau-Nee, or Iroquois. Rochester: Sage and Bros., 1851. New edition, New York: Dodd, Mead and Company, 1901. xviii, 477 pp., col. front., illus., col. plates (1 fold), fold. map.

————.
"Letters on the Iroquois by Skenandoah." *American Review* 5:177–190, 242–257, 447–461; 6:477–490, 623–633, 1847.

Murdock, George Peter
The Iroquois of Northern New York. In: *Our Primitive Contemparies,* Chapt. XI, (pp. 291-324). New York: The Macmillan Company, 1934. 614 pp., illus.

Myrtle, Minnie
The Iroquois, or, the Bright Side of Indian Character. New York: D. Appleton & Co.. 1855. 317 pp.

Neal, Janice
"Wa'n't That Remarkable!" *NYFQ* 1 (No. 4): 209–220, 1945.
    Indian legends (Delawares, Mohawks, Oneidas), tales, remedies, songs (text only), riddles, anecdotes, epitaphs.

O'Callaghan, Dr. E. B., ed.
The Documentary History of the State of New York. New York: D. Appleton and Company, 1849-51. 4 vols., fronts., ports., fold, maps.

Orr, R. B.
"The Iroquois in Canada." *Annual Arch. Report,* 1919, pp. 9-55.

Palmer, R. A.
"The North American Indians." *Smithsonian Scientific Series* 4:70–105, 1929. Washington, D. C.

Parker, Arthur C.
Aboriginal Inhabitants. In: *History of the Genesee Country,* L. R. Doty, ed., Vol. I, pp. 145-165. Chicago: 1925.

"The Amazing Iroquois." *Art and Archaeology* (Baltimore) 23:99–108, 1927.

The Archaeological History of New York. Albany: University of the State of New York, 1922. 2 vol.

The Civilization of the Red Man. In: *History of the State of New York*, A. C. Flick, ed., Vol. I, pp. 99-131. New York: 1933.

The Constitution of the Five Nations. New York State Museum Bulletin 184. Albany: University of the State of New York, 1916. 158 pp.

Influence of the Iroquois on the History and Archaeology of the Wyoming Valley, Pennsylvania. Reprinted from Proceedings of the Wyoming Historical and Geological Society, 11, 36 pp., illus. n.d.

The Iroquois. In: *History of the State of New York*, A. C. Flick, ed., Vol. I, pp. 67–97. New York: 1933.

Rhoades, G. E.
"Prehistoric Iroquois Culture." *Annual Arch. Report*, 1923, pp. 89-95.

Ritchie, W. A.
"The Algonkin Sequence in New York." *AA* 34:406–414, 1932. n.s.

Rousseau, L'Abbe P.
"Les Hochelagas." In: *Proceedings of the 15th Session of the International Congress of Americanists*, 1: pp. 279–297, 1906. (Quebec).
"A former Iroquoian town, strongly palisaded, situated in 1535 on Montreal id., Canada, about a mile from the mountain first called 'Mont Royal' by Cartier." (J. N. B. Hewitt)

Ruttenber, E. M.
History of the Indian Tribes of Hudson's River. Albany: J. Munsell, 1872. v, 415 pp., front., illus.

Schoolcraft, Henry R.
Notes on the Iroquois: or, Contributions to the Statistics, Aboriginal History, Antiquities and General Ethnology of Western New York. New York: Bartlett and Welford, 1846. vii, 285 pp., illus.

Scott, D. C.
"Traditional History of the Confederacy of the Six Nations." *Proc. Trans. Royal Soc. Canada* (ser. 3) 5(No. 2):195–246, 1912.

Scull, G. D., ed.
Voyages of Peter Esprit Radisson. Boston: 1885.

Seaver, J. E.
A Narrative of the Life of Mary Jemison. Howden, Eng.: R. Parkin, 1826.

Skinner, Alanson
The Indians of Greater New York. (Half-title: Little Histories of North American Indians.) Cedar Rapids, Iowa: The Torch Press, 1915. 150 pp., incl. front. (map).

"The Iroquois Indians of Western New York." *So. Workman* (Hampton, Va.) 38:206–211, 1909.
Includes dances.

"Iroquois Material." *Anthropological Papers, American Museum of Natural History,* (New York) 4:278–281, 1910.

Speck, Frank G.
"The Algonkian Influence Upon Iroquois Social Organization." *AA* 25:217–227, 1923. n.s.

The "Jackson-Whites." *So. Workman* 40:104–107, 1911.

Sulte, B.
"The War of the Iroquois." *Annual Arch. Report* 1899, pp. 124-151.

Weer, Paul
Preliminary Notes on the Iroquoian Family. Indiana Historical Society. Prehistory Research Series. Vol. 1, No. 1. Indianapolis, 1937. 24 pp.

Wintemberg, W. J.
"Culture of a Prehistoric Iroquoian Site in Eastern Ontario." *Inter. Congr. Amer.* 19: 37–42, 1915.

Yawger, R. N.
The Indian and the Pioneer. Syracuse: C. W. Bardeen, 1893. 2 vols.

MYTHS—FOLKTALES—LEGENDS

Anon.
"A Tale." *New York Mirror* 4:125–126, Nov. 11, 1826.
A tale of the heroism of an Iroquois girl who married a French officer stationed at the garrison at the junction of the Uswegatchie and St. Lawrence Rivers, and also what befell their son.

Awahyah
Birch Bark Legends of Niagara. Founded on Traditions among the Iroquois, or Six Nations. A Story of the Lunar Bow . . . or, Origin of the Totem of the Wolf. St. Catherines, Ont.: Journal Printing Company, 1884. 56 pp., illus.

Beauchamp, William Martin
"Great Mosquito." *JAFL* 2:284, 1889.
A legend.

"Indian Corn Stories and Customs." *JAFL* 11: 195–202, 1898.

Iroquois Folk-Lore Gathered From the Six Nations of New York . . . for the Onondaga Historical Association. Syracuse, N. Y.: The Dehler Press, 1922. 247 pp.

Bisbee, Ernest E.
The Empire State Scrap Book of Stories and Legends of Old New York: Lancaster, N. H.: The Bisbee Press, 1939. 56 pp., illus.

Brill, E. C.
The Boy Who Went to the East, and Other Indian Fairy Tales. New York: E. P. Dutton & Co., 1917. 296 p.
Iroquois and Algonquin tales.

Canfield, William Walker
The Legends of the Iroquois told by "The Cornplanter." New York: A. Wessels Co., 1902. 211 pp.

"Caughnawaga Legend."
JAFL 19:127–129, 1906.

Converse, Harriet Maxwell Clarke
Myths and Legends of the New York State Iroquois. Edited and annotated by Arthur C. Parker. New York State Museum Bulletin 125. Albany: University of the State of New York, 1908. 195 pp., illus.

Cornplanter, Jesse J.
Legends of the Longhouse. As told to Sah-nee-weh, the White Sister, with an introduction by Carl Carmer, illustrated by the author. Phil.: J. B. Lippincott Co., 1938. 216 pp., illus.

Hamilton, J. C.
"Handsome-Lake." *JAFL* 10:169–180, 1897.

Hewitt, J. N. B.
"Iroquoian Mythologic Notes." *AA* 3:290–291, 1890.

————.
"Legend of the Founding of the Iroquois League." *AA* 5:131–149, 1892.

"Iroquois Myths."
JAFL 2:284, 1889; 13:281–282, 1900; 14:153–159, 1901; 23:473–478, 1910.

Johnson, E.
Legends, Traditions, and Laws of the Iroquois. Lockport: 1881.

M.
"Indian Fragments (Serial I–X), or Traditions of Lake George, The Incantation, Prophet." *The Philadelphia Monthly Magazine* 2:57–60, 120–122, 248–251, 309–310, 1828.
Legends of people and places.

Osborn, Chase and Stellanova
Schoolcraft-Longfellow-Hiawatha. Lancaster, Pa.: The Jacques Cattel Press, 1943.
A study of the work of the student of Indian mythology and of Longfellow's debt to him.

Parker, Arthur C.
"Certain Iroquois Tree Myths and Symbols." *AA* 14:608–621, 1912. n.s.

————.
"Iroquois Sun Myths." *JAFL* 23:473–478, 1910.

————.
The Indian How Book (Gasaso Waneh). New York: George H. Doran, 1927. ix, 335 pp., front., illus.

Peterson, G. W.
Iroquoian Story of the Beginning of the World and Living Things. Torrington, Conn.: The Author, 1937. 69 pp.
The Iroquoian legends of creation.

Powers, M.
Around an Iroquois Story Fire. New York: Frederick H. Stokes Company, 1923. 115 pp.

————. (yeh-sen-noh-wehs)
Stories the Iroquois Tell Their Children. New York, Cincinnati: American Book Company, 1912. 216 pp.

Prince, J. Dyneley
"A Tale in the Hudson River Indian Language." *AA* 7:74–85, 1905. n.s.

Sanborn, J. W.
Indian Stories. Friendship: 1915. 38 pp.

————.
"Myths of the Iroquois." *Amer. Antiq.* 4:31–39, 1882.

Skye, M. L.
Origin of the Green Corn." *Red Man* (Carlisle, Pa.) 4:28–29, 1911.

Smith, Erminie A.
"Myths of the Iroquois." *2nd Annual Report, Bureau of American Ethnology 1880–1881.* pp. 51–112, pls. 12–15. Washington, D. C.: U. S. Government Printing Office, 1883.
Gods and other supernatural beings. Pigmies, practice of sorcery, mythological explanation of phenomena, tales, etc.

Sylvester, Nathaniel B.
Indian Legends of Saratoga and of the Upper Hudson Valley. Troy, N. Y.: N. B. Sylvester & Co., 1884. 47 pp., illus.

Wallace, Paul A.
The White Roots of Peace. Philadelphia: University of Pennsylvania Press, 1946. ix, 57 pp.

Waring, Clare Ingersoll
Faun-Fa: a Story of the Catskill Mountains, in four parts. Detroit: Ostler Prtg. Co., 1889. 147 pp., illus.

BELIEFS—WITCHCRAFT—MAGIC

Beauchamp, William Martin
Civil Religious and Mourning Councils, and Ceremonies of Adoption of the New York Indians. New York State Educational Department Bulletin 402, New York Museum Bulletin 113, (pp. 342-451). Albany: New York State Education Department, 1907.

————.
"Folklore of Stone Implements." *JAFL* 4:166–167, 272, 1891.

"Iroquois Condolence." *JAFL* 8:313–316, 1895.

"Iroquois Dog Feast." *JAFL* 3:244, 1890.

"New Religion of the Iroquois." *JAFL* 10:169–180, 1897.

"The Early Religion of the Iroquois. *Amer. Antiq.* 14:344–349, 1892.

"The Iroquois Book of Rites." *Science* 17:189–190, 1903. n.s.

"The Iroquois White Dog Feast." *Amer. Antiq.* 7:235–239, 1885.

Boyle, D.
"The Paganism of the Civilized Iroquois of Ontario." *Journal Anthropological Institute* (London) 30:263–274, 1900.

Fenstermaker, G. B.
"Iroquois Animal Gods or Hunting Charms." *Penn. Arch.* 6:76–78, 1936.

Fenton, William N.
"Iroquois Suicide." *Bull. Bureau Amer. Ethnol.* 128:80–137, 1941.

"Museum and Field Studies of Iroquois Masks and Ritualism." *Exploration and Field-Work Smithsonian Institution* (Wash., D. C.), 1940, pp. 95-100.

Fletcher, Alice C.
Orenda. In: *Handbook of American Indians.* Vol. II, pp. 147-149. bibl. Bureau of American Ethnology, Bulletin 30. Washington, D. C.: U. S. Government Printing Office, 1910.
"The Iroquois name of the fictive force, principle, or magic power which was assumed by the inchoate reasoning of primitive man to be inherent in every body and being of nature and in every personified attribute, property, or activity, belonging to each of these and conceived to be the cause of force, or dynamic energy, involved in every operation or phenomenon of nature, in any manner affecting or controlling the welfare of man."

Hale, Horatio
"An Iroquois Condoling Council." *Proc. Trans. Royal Soc. Can.* (ser. 2) 1(Part 2):45–65, 1895.

The Iroquois Book of Rites. In: (*Brinton's Library of Aboriginal American Literature,* No. II.) Phila., Pa.: D. G. Brinton, 1883. 222 pp.
Mohawk and Onondaga texts.

The Iroquois Sacrifice of the White Dog. New York, 1885. 14 pp.
Reprinted from the *American Antiquarian* for January, 1885.

Hewitt, J. N. B.
"The Cosmogonic Gods of the Iroquois." *Proc. Amer. Assoc. Adv. Sci.* 44:241–250, 1895.

"Iroquoian Concept of the Soul." *JAFL* 8:107–116, 1895.

"Iroquoian Cosmology." *21st Annual Report: Bureau American Ethnology, 1899–1900.* pp. 133–255, pls. 64–69. Washington, D. C.: U. S. Government Printing Office, 1903.

"Iroquoian Cosmology, 2nd Part," with introduction and notes. *43rd Ethnology Report, 1925–1926,* pp. 449–819. Washington, D. C.: U. S. Government Printing Office, 1927.

"Iroquois Superstitions." *AA* 8:388–389, 1890.

Oyaron. In: *Handbook of American Indians.* Vol. II, (pp. 178–180). Bureau of American Ethnology Bulletin 30. Washington, D. C.: U. S. Government Printing Office, 1910.
"The common Iroquois name of the personal, and sometimes the gentile and tribal, tutelary, guardian genius, or guiding spirit believed to protect and watch over the destiny and welfare of every person or kindred." (J. N. B. H.)

Tawiskaron. In: *Handbook of American Indians.* Vol. II, pp. 707–711. Bibl. Bureau of American Ethnology, Bulletin 30. Washington, D. C.: U. S. Government Printing Office, 1910.
". . . Tawiskaron is the name of the personification of the winter power transfigured into a man-being, a god of winter, whose functions and activities constitute him the mighty frost king, whose breath and magic power blight the verdure of plants and trees and lock lakes and rivers in bonds of ice."

"Sacred Numbers Among the Iroquois." *AA* 2:165–166, 1889.

Teharonhiawagon. In: *Handbook of American Indians.* Vol. II, pp. 718–723. Bureau of American Ethnology, Bulletin 30. Washington, D. C.: U. S. Government Printing Office, 1910.
"An imaginary anthropic being of the cosmogonic philosophy of the Iroquoian and other American mythologies, who for convenience of expression may be called a man-being."

"The Requickening Address of the Iroquois Condolence Council." *Journal of the Washington Academy of Sciences,* 34:65–85, (March 15), 1944.

"The Twin Hai-Hai of Iroquoian Mourning and Condolence Songs." *AA* 7:286–287, 1898.

——————.
White Dog Sacrifice. In: *Handbook of American Indians*. Vol. II, pp. 939–944. Bureau of American Ethnology, Bulletin 30. Washington, D. C.: U. S. Government Printing Office, 1910.

"The annual immolation of the white dog (or dogs) at the New Year ceremony by the Iroquois is the satisfaction or the fulfilment of a dream of Teharonhiawagon, one of their chief gods, who, in the Iroquoian cosmic philosophy, is the impersonation or the embodiment of all faunal and floral life on earth."

——————, and Fenton, William N.
"Some Mnemonic Pictographs Relating to the Iroquois Condolence Council." *Journal of the Washington Academy of Sciences* 35 (No. 10): 301–315, 1945.

Parker, Arthur Caswell
American Indian Freemasonry. Albany, N. Y.: Buffalo Consistory, 1919. 36 pp., illus.
A study in religion and mythology.

Smith, DeCost
"Witchcraft and Demonism of the Modern Iroquois." *JAFL* 1:184–193, 1888.

Smith, Seba
"The Religion and Superstition of the North American Indians, No. III, IV, V." *The Literary Emporium* 3:129–133; 170–174; 230–233. May, June, Aug., 1846.
Belief and ceremonies for the dead among the Hurons, Iroquois and Chepewuans, also comments on their beliefs in immortality.

Speck, Frank G.
"An Ethnologist Speaks for the Pagan Indians." *Crozer Quarterly* 18:213–218, 1941.
Discusses religion, beliefs, traditions, and doctrines of Iroquois.

"Symbolic Ritual of the Iroquois."
Hobbies 45:103–104, (December) 1940.

Witthoft, John, and Hadlock, Wendell S.
"Cherokee-Iroquois Little People." *JAFL* 59: 413–422, 1946.
The authors claim that the "wealth of dwarf lore is of considerable interest when compared with old world traditions," and "that a more thorough study of American belief of this type may reveal that we can readily separate the tales of non-Indian origin and still have a large residuum which is an integral part of indigenous American cultures."

Wolf, Morris
Iroquois Religion and its Relation to their Morals. New York: Columbia University Press, 1919. 111 pp.
Presents an analysis of Iroquois folk beliefs and ethics.

CUSTOMS

Anon.
"Customs and Manners of the American Indian." *The Minerva* 1:76, June 15, 1822.
Warfare customs among the Wyandottes and Iroquois.

Barbeau, Charles Marius
"Iroquoian Clans and Phratries." *AA* 19: 392–405, 1917. n.s.

Beauchamp, William Martin
"Aboriginal Use of Wood in New York." *New York State Mus. Bull.* 89:87–272, 1905.

——————.
Horn and Bone Implements of the New York Indians. Bulletin of the New York State Museum 50. Albany: University of the State of New York, 1902. 100 pp., illus.

——————.
"Indian Corn Stories and Customs." *JAFL* 11: 195–202, 1898.

——————.
Metallic Implements of the New York Indians. Bulletin of the New York State Museum 55. Albany, N. Y., 1902.

Boyle, D.
"Big Corn Feast." *Annual Arch. Report*, 1899, pp. 34-40.

Converse, Harriet Maxwell Clarke
"Induction of Women Into Iroquois Tribes." *JAFL* 6:147–148, 1893.

——————.
"Iroquois Green Corn Festival of 1890." *JAFL* 4:72–78, 1891.

Crowell, S.
The Dog Sacrifice of the Seneca. In: *Indian Miscellany*, W. W. Beach, ed., pp. 323-332. Albany: 1877.

Douglas, F. H.
"Iroquois Foods." *Denver Art Mus. Leaf. Ser.* 26:1–4, 1931.

Hewitt, J. N. B.
"Status of Women in Iroquois Polity Before 1784." *Annual Report Smithson. Inst.*, 1932, pp. 475-488.

——————.
"White Dog Sacrifice." *Bull. Bureau Amer. Ethnol.* 30(Part 2):939–944, 1910.

Keppler, Joseph
Comments on Certain Iroquois Masks. New York: Museum of the American Indians, 1941. 40 pp., illus.

Lafitau, Joseph François
Moeurs des Sauvages Amériquains. Paris: Saugrain l'aîné, 1724. 2 vols.

Lape, Jane M.
"Ticonderoga's Indian Festival." *NYFQ* 1:167-174, 1945.

Morgan, Lewis H.
"The Fabrics of the Iroquois." *Stryker's American Register and Magazine* 4:319–343, July, 1850.
Descriptions of the articles made by the Senecas, detailed illustrations how the moccasin, tomahawk, bow and arrow, musical instruments, clothing, etc., are made.

———.
"Government and Institutions of the Iroquois."
A. C. Parker, ed. *Researches and Transactions of the New York State Archaeological Asociation* (Rochester) 7:5–30, 1928.

———.
"Houses and House-Life of the American Aborigines." *Contr. North Amer. Ethnol.* No. 4, 281 pp. Washington, D. C.: 1881.

———.
"Systems of Consanguinity and Affinity." *Smithson. Contr. Knowledge* 17:150–169, 291–382, 511–514, 1871.

Noyes, James O.
"Logan and the Home of the Iroquois." *Knickerbocker* 57:553–567, June, 1859.
Descriptive account of the natural beauties of Genesee County, N. Y., its group of picturesque lakes, mountains and Indian villages with illustrations.

Parker, Arthur C.
Iroquois Uses of Maize and Other Food Plants. Bulletin 482. Educational Department. Albany: University of the State of New York, 1910. 119 pp., illus.

Perrot, N.
Memoir of the Manners, Customs, and Religion of the Savages of North America. In: *The Indian Tribes of the Upper Mississippi*, E. H. Blair, ed. Vol. I, pp. 25-272. Cleveland: 1911.

Quain, B. H.
The Iroquois. In: *Cooperation and Competition Among Primitive Peoples*, Margaret Mead, ed. pp. 240-281. New York: 1937.

Ritchie, William A.
"A Prehistoric Ceremony of Sacrifice in New York State." *New York History* 28:458–465, (Oct.) 1947.
A brief discussion of the Owasco culture. There is a close identity with Iroquois traits.

Smith, E.
"The Customs and the Language of the Iroquois." *Jour. Royal Anthro. Inst. Gt. Brit. and Ireland* 14:244–253, 1884.

Speck, F. G.
"Algonkian Influence Upon Iroquois Social Organization." *AA* 25:217–227, 1923. n.s.

———.
"The Mutual-aid and Volunteer Company of the Eastern Cherokee: As Recorded in a Book of Minutes in the Sequoyah Syllabary, Compared with Mutual-Aid Societies of the Northern Iroquois." *Journal of the Washington Academy of Sciences*, 35 No. 6):169–179, 1945.

Stites, Sarah H.
Economics of the Iroquois. Bryn Mawr College Monograph Series I, (No. 3), Bryn Mawr, 1905.

Waugh, Frederick Wilkerson
Iroquois Foods and Food Preparation. Ottawa: Government Printing Bureau, 1916. Memoirs of the Canada Dep't. of Mines, No. 86. xxxix plates, 253 pp., bibl. pp. 155-158.

FOLK MEDICINE

Beauchamp, William Martin
"Good Hunter and the Iroquois Medicine." *JAFL* 15:153–159, 1902.

Brant-Sero, J. O.
"O-no-dah, Canadian Iroquois Herb." *JAFL* 24:251, 1911.

Fenton, William N.
"Contacts Between Iroquois Herbalism and Colonial Medicine." *Annual Report of the Smithsonian Institution for 1941*, pp. 503–526. Smithsonian Publication 3651. Washington, D. C.: U. S. Government Printing Office, 1942.

———.
"A Further Quest for Iroquois Medicines." *Explorations and Field-Work Smithsonian Institution* (Wash., D. C.), 1939, pp. 93-96.

———.
"Masked Medicine Societies of the Iroquois." *Smithsonian Report for 1940*, pp. 397–430. Washington, D. C.: U. S. Government Printing Office, 1941.

Loewenthal, J.
"Der Heilbringer in der irokesischen und der algonkinischen Religion." *Zeit. f. Ethnol.* 52–53:171–233, 1920–1921.
The medicine man in Iroquois and Algonquin religion.

Parker, A. C.
"Indian Medicine and Medicine Men." *Annual Arch. Reports*, 1928, pp. 9-17.

GAMES

Beauchamp, William Martin
"Iroquois Games." *JAFL* 9:269–277, 1896.

Cornplanter, Jesse
Iroquois Indian Games and Dances, drawn by Jesse Cornplanter, Seneca Indian boy. Chicago: F. Starr, 1903.

"Iroquois Games."
JAFL 6:76, 1893; 8:212–214, 1895; 9:269–279, 1896; 13:90, 1900.

FOLK ART—SPEECH

Bailey, J. H.
"An Analysis of Iroquoian Ceramic Types." *American Antiquity* 3:333–338, 1938.

Barbeau, Charles Marius
Classification of Iroquoian Radicals, with subjective pronominal prefixes. Ottawa Government Printing Bureau, 1915. 30 pp., plates and tables.

Beauchamp, W. M.
"Aboriginal Chipped Stone Implements of New York." *N. Y. State Mus. Bull.* 16:5–84, 1897.

"Aboriginal Place Names of New York." *N. Y. State Mus. Bull.* 108:5-333, 1907.

"Earthenware of the New York Aborigines." *N. Y. State Mus. Bull.* 22:75–146, 1898.

"Horn and Bone Implements of the New York Indians." *N. Y. State Mus. Bull.* 50:243–350, 1902.

Indian Names in New York. Fayettville: H. C. Beauchamp, 1893. 148 pp.

"Iroquois Pottery and Wampum." *Proc. Coll. Wyoming Hist. Geol. Soc.* 12:55–68, 1912.

"Metallic Implements of the New York Indians." *N. Y. State Mus. Bull.* 83:3–120, 1903.

"Polished Stone Articles Used by the New York Aborigines." *N. Y. State Mus. Bull.* 18:3–102, 1897.

"Wampum and Shell Articles Used by New York Indians." *N. Y. State Mus. Bull.* 41:328–480, 1901.

"Wampum Belts of the Six Nations." *Annual Report Smithson. Inst.*, 1879, pp. 389-390.

Boas, Franz
Notes on the Iroquois Language. In: *Putnam Anniversary Volume*, pp. 427-460. New York: 1909.

Carpenter, Edmund
"Iroquoian Figurines." *American Antiquity* 8:105–113, 1942.

Converse, H. M.
"The Iroquois Silver Brooches." *Annual Reports Regents Univ. State N. Y.* 54(Part 1):231–254, 1900.

Cuoq, Jean André
Études philologique sur quelques langues sauvages de l'Amérique. Montreal: 1866. 160 pp.

Lexique de la Langue Iroquoise. Montreal: J. Chapleau & Fils, 1882. ix, 215 pp.

Forbes, L'Abbé G.
"Étude sur les noms Iroquois." *Proceedings of the 15th Session of the International Congress of Americanists*, 1:301–311, 1906.

Harrington, M. R.
"Iroquois Silverwork." *Anthro. Papers Amer. Mus. Natur. Hist.* 1:351–369, 1908.

"The Last of the Iroquois Potters." *Annual Reports Regents Univ. State N. Y.* 62(Part 1):222–227, 1909.

"The Origin of Iroquois Silversmithing." *AA* 12:349–357, 1910. n.s.

Heye, G. G.
"Wampum Collection." *Indian Notes* 7:320–324, 1930.

Hinsdale, W. B.
"Old Iroquois Needles of Brass." *Indian Notes* 4:174–176, 1927.

Morgan, L. H.
"Report on the Fabrics, Inventions, Implements and Utensils of the Iroquois." *Annual Reports Regents Univ. State of N. Y.* 5:67–117, 1851.

Parker, A. C.
"Additional Notes on Iroquois Silversmithing." *AA* 13:283–293, 1911. n.s.

"The Origin of Iroquois Sivlersmithing." *AA* 12:349–357, 1910. n.s.

Skinner, A.
"An Antique Tobacco-Pouch of the Iroquois." *Ind. Notes Monog.* 2:103–108, 1920.

"An Iroquois Antler Figurine." *Indian Notes Monog.* 2:109–114, 1920.

"Iroquois Falseface Pipe." *Indian Notes* 2:321–322, 1925.

Smith, E. A.
"Comparative Differences in the Iroquois Group of Dialects." *Proc. Amer. Assoc. Adv. Sci.* 30:315–319, 1881.

"The Customs and the Language of the Iroquois." *Jour. Royal Anthro. Inst. Gt. Brit. and Ireland.* 14:244–253, 1884.

"Disputed Points Concerning Iroquois Pronouns." *Proc. Amer. Assoc. Adv. Sci.* 33:606–609, 1884.

"Studies in the Iroquois Concerning the Verb 'to be' and Its Substitutes." *Proc. Amer. Assoc. Adv. Sci.* 32: 399–402, 1883.

Speck, Frank G.
"Northern Elements in Iroquois and New England Art." *Indian Notes* 2:1–13, 1925.

Wren, C.
"A Study of North Appalachian Indian Pottery." *Proc. Coll. Wyoming Hist. Geol. Soc.* 13:131–222, 1914.

"Turtle Shell Rattles and Other Implements from Indian Graves." *Proc. Coll. Wyoming Hist. Geol. Soc.* 10:195–210, 1909.

Zeisberger, D.
Indian Dictionary. Cambridge, Mass.: J. Wilson & Son, 1887. 236 pp.

MUSIC

GENERAL STUDIES

Beauchamp, William Martin
Iroquois Folklore Gathered from the Six Nations of New York. Syracuse: The Dekler Press, 1922. 247 pp.
    Musical examples.

————.
Musical Instruments. In: *The Aboriginal Use of Wood in New York* (pp. 174). Bulletin 89, New York State Museum, Archaeology 11. Albany: New York State Education Department, 1905.

Boyle, David
"Mid-Winter Festival." *Ontario Education Department Archaeological Report* (Toronto): 82–91, 1898.

Burton, Frederick R.
"Hiawatha, the Indian Musical play." *Concert-Goer*, No. 208: 8–9, 1902.

Cringan, Alexander T.
"Iroquois Folk Songs." *Ontario Education Department Archaeological Report:* 137–152, 1902. Toronto: 1903.
    34 tunes given.

————.
"Pagan Dance Songs of the Iroquois." *Archaeological Report, Appendix to the Report of the Minister of Education* (Ontario, Toronto): 166–189, 1899.
    Discussion with music.

————.
"Traditional Songs of the Iroquois Indians." *Musical Times* (London) 41:114, 1900.
    With musical examples.

Fenton, William N.
Songs from the Iroquois Longhouse. Program Notes for an Album of American Indian Music from the Eastern Woodlands, with nine plates. From Records in the Archive of American Folk Song, The Library of Congress Publication 3691, iv, 34 pp. Washington, D. C.: Published by the Smithsonian Institution, 1942.

Hewitt, J. N. B.
"The Term 'haiihaii' of Iroquoian Mourning and Condolence Songs." *AA* 11:286–287, 1898.

Morgan, Lewis H.
League of the Ho-Dé-No-Sau-Nee, or Iroquois. Rochester: Sage and Brother, 1854. xviii, 477 pp., illus.
    Book II, Chapter 4—Musical Performances.

Starr, F.
"Indian Music and Records of Iroquois Songs." *American Antiquarian* (Salem, Massachusetts) 31:29, 1909.

DANCES

Anon.
"Indian War Dance." *North American Review* 1:190, Oct. 27, 1827.
    The author stresses particularly the great energy exerted in the Indian dancing movements.

Boyle, David
"Iroquois Music." *Ontario Archaeological Museum Report.* pp. 143–156, 1898.
    Contains a description of the dances.

Cringan, Alexander T.
Pagan Dance Songs of the Iroquois in Ontario. Educational Department Archaeological Report, (Toronto) 1900, pp. 168-189.

Cornplanter, Jesse
Iroquois Indian Games and Dances, drawn by Jess Cornplanter, Seneca Indian boy. Chicago: F. Starr, 1903.

Harrington, M. R.
"The Dark Dance of the Ji-gé-onh." *Masterkey* 7:76–79, 1933.

"Iroquois Dance in Green Corn Festival." *JAFL* 4:73–75, 1891.

Jameson, Mrs.
"A Red Indian Dance." *Niles' Weekly Register* 56:135, April 27, 1839.
    Extract from *Rambles*, describing an Indian dance, their dress, movements, and music.

Skinner, Alanson
"The Iroquois Indians of Western New York." *Southern Workman* (Hampton, Va.) 38:206–211, 1909.
    Includes discussion of music in dance and ritual.

ARRANGEMENTS

Burke, Carleton
Symphony Iroquoian. A symphonic poem based upon an ancient Iroquois Indian rite and legend.... Rochester, N. Y.: Rochester Museum of Arts and Sciences, 1937. 70 pp., illus.

Cadman, Charles Wakefield
Lelawa, The Maid of Niagara. An Indian Operetta. New York: G. Schirmer. Arranged for mixed voices.

Griffes, Charles T.
"Two Sketches Based on Indian Themes." MS. for String Quartet.

MacDowell, Edward
Second (Indian) Suite, op. 48. Leipzig: Breitkopf & Haertel.
    Perhaps one of the finest examples in American orchestral music showing skilfull utilization of Indian themes.

Macpherson, Stewart
Six Songs Based on Iroquois Melodies. London: J. Williams, Ltd., arranged for voice and piano.

McPhee, Colin
Four Iroquois Dances. New York: New Music: for orchestra.

————.
Iroquois Eclogue. MS.: for full orchestra.

RECORDS

"Records of Iroquois Songs."
American Antiquity 27:103–105, 1905.
Lists 12 songs, sung to phonograph by Ilase Lyon, an Onondaga.

U. S. Library of Congress. Division of Music. Folklore Section
Iroquois Indians of Canada and Six Nations Reserve of Western New York. Recorded by William N. Fenton. AAFS–LC

————.
Seneca Songs from Coldspring Longhouse. Album 17. Folk Music of the United States. . . . Five records. AAFS–81/85
Contents: A. Gane' O'On. The Drum Dance. B. The Drun Dance (con't). AAFS81. I'Yondatha — De'swadenyon (Quavering — Changing-a-Rib). AAFS82. C. Quavering Continued . . . AAFS83. D. De'swadenyon (Changing-a-Rib). AAFS84. E. Bear Society Dance. Fish Dance. AAFS85.

————.
Songs from the Iroquois Longhouse. Album 6. Folk Music of the United States. . . . 5 records. AAFS–26/30
Contents: The Creator's Songs, AAFS26. Medicine Men's Celebration — Onondaga, AAFS27. False Face Company — Six Nations, Canada, AAFS28. War and Peace Songs, AAFS29. Social Dances, AAFS30.

KICKAPOO

FOLKLORE

GENERAL STUDIES

Beckwith, Hiram W.
The Illinois and Indiana Indians. Fergus Historical Series, No. 27. Chicago: Fergus Printing Company, 1884.

Hoad, Louise Green
Kickapoo Indian Trails. Caldwell, Idaho: The Caxton Printers, Ltd., 1944. 129 pp., illus.
This book contains much first-hand information about Indian life and customs before white civilization destroyed the simple dignity of the Indian's existence.

Hunter, J. D.
Memoirs of a Captivity Among the Indians of North America. London: 1823. 447 pp.

Jones, William
"Kickapoo Ethnological Notes." *AA* 15:332-336, 1913. n.s.

Kohl, J. G.
Kitchie-Gami, Wanderings 'Round Lake Superior. Translated by Lascelles Wraxhall, with considerable omissions, from the author's "Kitchie-Gami." London: Chapman and Hall, 1860. xii, 428 pp., illus.
"A tribe living in 1669–70, about Central or S.W. Wisconsin, with the Kickapoo and Mascoutens, with which tribes they were ethnically and linguistically related. . . . After a few brief notices of them . . they drop from history, having probably been absorbed by the Mascoutens or the Kickapoo."

Lilly, Eli
Prehistoric Antiquities of Indiana. Indianapolis: Indiana Historical Society, 1937. 293 pp., illus.

Michelson, Truman
"Algonquian Tribes of Oklahoma and Iowa." *Explorations and Field-Work of the Smithsonian Institution.*" (Wash. D. C.), 1928, pp. 183-188.

————.
"Note on Kickapoo Ethnology." *AA* 36:629, 1934. n.s.

————.
"Studies of the Algonquian Tribes of Iowa and Oklahoma." *Explorations and Field-Work of the Smithsonian Institution* (Wash. D. C.), 1929, pp. 207-212.

Mooney, J. and Jones, W.
"Kickapoo." In: *Bull. Bureau Amer. Ethnol.* 30(Part 1):684–686, 1907.

FOLK TALES—CUSTOMS

Jones, William
Kickapoo Tales. Publications of the American Ethnological Society, No. 9. New York: Columbia University Press, 1915. 142 pp.

Michelson, Truman
"The Punishment of Impudent Children Among the Kickapoo." *AA* 25:281–283, 1923. n.s.

DANCES

Marriott, Alice L.
"Dancing Makes Rain." *TFSP* 19:88–93, 1944.
Description of a rain dance.

MUSIC

ARRANGEMENTS

————: *Piano*

"Indian Dance."
Porter, Addison F.: Schmidt: Piano.

"Kickapoo Social Dance" from *Three Indian Sketches.* Skilton, Charles S.: Carl Fischer: Piano.

MALECITE

See: Passamoquoddy, pp. 876-77

FOLKLORE

GENERAL STUDIES

Mooney, J. and Thomas, C.
"Malecite." In: *Bull. Bureau Amer. Ethnol.* 30(Part 1):793–794, 1907.

Tenesles, N.
The Indian of New England and the North Eastern Provinces. Middletown: 1851. 24 pp.

MYTHS—FOLKTALES—LEGENDS

Jack, E.
"Maliseet Legends." *Jour. Royal Anthro Inst. Gt. Brit. and Ireland* 8:193–208, 1895.

Leland, C. G.
The Algonquin Legends of New England. Boston: 1884. 379 pp.

Mechling, W. H.
Malecite Tales. Ottawa: Gov't Printing Bureau, 1914. vi, 133 pp. (Geological Survey Branch. Mem. 49. Anthropological Series 4.)

————.
"Maliseet Tales." *JAFL* 26:219–258, 1913.

Speck, Frank G.
"Bird Lore of the Northern Indians." *Public Lectures of the University of Pennsylvania Faculty* 7:349–380, 1920.

————.
"Malecite Tales." *JAFL* 30:479–485, 1917.

Stamp, H.
"Adventures of Bukschinskwesk; a Malecite Tale." *JAFL* 28:243–248, 1915.

Wilson, G. L.
Indian Hero Tales. New York: American Book Co., 1906. 203 pp.

MENOMINEE

FOLKLORE

GENERAL STUDIES

Barrett, S. A.
Ancient Aztalan (Wisconsin Culture). Bulletin of the Public Museum of the City of Milwaukee 13. Milwaukee: The Public Museum, 1933. 602 pp., illus.

Biddle, James W.
"Recollections of Green Bay (Wisconsin) in 1816–1817." *Wisconsin Historical Collections* 1:49–63.

Blair, Emma Helen, ed.
The Indian Tribes of the Upper Mississippi Valley and the Region of the Great Lakes. Cleveland: The Arthur H. Clark Company, 1911. 2 vols.

Bloomfield, Leonard
Menomini Texts. American Ethnological Society. Vol. 12. New York: G. E. Stechert & Co., 1928. xiv, 607 pp.

Boas, Franz
"Zur Anthropologie der nordamerikanischen Indianer." *Verhandl. Berliner Gesel. Anthro. Ethno. Ur.,* 1895, pp. 367-411.

Bond, Beverly W., Jr.
The Civilization of the Old Northwest. New York: The Macmillan Company, 1934.

Bruce, W. H.
Menomonee. In: *Information Respecting the History, Condition, and Prospects of the Indian Tribes of the United States.* H. R. Schoolcraft, ed., Vol. II, pp. 470-481. Philadelphia: 1852.

Cooper, L. R.
The Red Cedar River Variant of the Wisconsin Hopewell Culture. Publication of the Museum of the City of Milwaukee, Bulletin 16. Milwaukee: Public Museum, 1933. 62 pp., illus.

Davidson, John N.
In Unnamed Wisconsin. Milwaukee: S. Chapman, 1895. 307 pp.

Doty, James Duane
"Northern Wisconsin in 1820." *Wisconsin Historical Collections* 7:195–206, 1870.

Douglas, F. H.
"The Menomini Indians." *Denv. Art Mus. Leaf. Ser.* 25:1–4, 1931.

Ellis, Albert G.
"Fifty-four years' recollections of men and events in Wisconsin." *Wisconsin Historical Collections* 12: 206–268, 1873–78.

Greenman, Emerson F.
"Indian Chiefs of Michigan." *Michigan Historical Museum* 23 (No. 3):247–249, 1939.

Hoffman, Walter James
"The Menomini Indians." *14th Annual Report, Bureau American Ethnology, 1892–1893:* pp. 11–295, pls. 1–37, figs. 1–55. Washington, D. C.: U. S. Government Printing Office, 1896.

Hinsdale, Wilbert B.
First People of Michigan. Ann Arbor: George Whar, 1930.

————.
Primitive Man in Michigan. Michigan Handbook Series I. Ann Arbor: University of Michigan Press, 1925.

Indian Tribes of Wisconsin
U. S. Bureau of American Ethnology, Bulletin 30. Excerpts from the Handbook of American Indians North of Mexico. Washington, D. C.: U. S. Government Printing Office, 1907–10.

Jenks, A. E.
"The Wild Rice Gathers of the Upper Lakes." *Annual Report Bureau Amer. Ethnol.* 19 (Part 2):1013–1017, 1898.

Keesing, Felix M.
The Menomini Indians of Wisconsin. Memoirs, American Philosophical Society 10. Philadelphia: University of Pennsylvania, 1939. 261 pp., illus.

Kirsch, Mary Moran
"The Indians of Wisconsin." *Wisconsin Blue Book*, pp. 91–112, 1931.

Krautbauer, F. X.
"Short Sketch of the History of the Menominee Indians." *American Catholic Historical Researches* 4:152–158, 1887.

Lapham, Increase A.
The Antiquities of Wisconsin. Smithsonian Institution Publication 70. Washington, D. C.: U. S. Government Printing Office, 1852. 92 pp., 50 pl.

Larzelere, Claude S.
"The Red Man in Michigan." *Michigan History Magazine* (Lansing) 17:344–376, 1933.

Mooney, J., and Thomas, C.
"Menominee." In: *Bull. Bureau Amer. Ethnol.* 30 (Part 1) :842–844, 1907.

Skinner, Alanson
"A Comparative Sketch of the Menominee." *AA* 13:551–566, 1911. n.s.

——————.
"The Menomini Indian." *So. Workman* 40:372–579, 1911.

——————.
"Recollections of an Ethnologist Among the Menomini Indians." *Wis. Arch.* 20:41–74, 1921.

——————, and Satterlee, John V.
"Folklore of the Menominee Indians." *American Museum of Natural History* (New York) *Anthropological Papers*, 13:217–546, 1915. Bibl.

MYTHS—FOLKTALES—LEGENDS

Banér, Johan Gustav Runeskiold
Medicine-Water. Menominee and Chippeway Indian Legends and Myths. Manistigue, Mich.: 1933. 48 pp., illus.

Beck, Walter, comp.
Wisconsin Indian Lore. Madison: 1937. 20 pp., illus., bibl.

Brown, Charles E.
Wigwam Tales. Madison: The Author, 1920.

Davis, Susan B.
Wisconsin Lore for Boys and Girls. Milwaukee: E. M. Hale & Company, 1931. xv, 283 pp., illus.

Federal Writers' Project
Wisconsin Indian Place Legends. Folklore Section, Federal Writers' Project. Madison, Wis.: 1936. 50 pp.

Hoffman, Walter James
"Mythology of the Menomini Indians." *AA* 3:243–259, 1890.

Keshena, E.
"How the Hunter Punished the Snow." *Carlisle Arrow* (Carlisle, Pa.) 7 (No. 37) :4, 1911.

——————.
"Legend of the Catfish." *Red Man* 3:256, 1911.

Michelson, Truman
"Menominee Tales." *AA* 13:68–89, 1911. n. s.

Nichols, Phebe Jewell
Sunrise of the Menominees. Boston, Mass.: Bruce Humphries, 1944. 365 pp.
A story of the Wisconsin Indians.

——————.
Tales from an Old Indian Lodge. Boston, Mass.: Bruce Humphries, 1944. 47 pp.
A collection of Menominee Indian Tales.

Peet, S. D.
"Mythology of the Menominees." *American Antiquarian* (Salem, Mass.) 31:1–14, 1909.

Pletcher, D. E.
"How the Catfish Got His Moose Blanket; Menominee Indian Myth." *Nature Magazine* 25:91 (February), 1935.

Skinner, Alanson
"European Folk Tales. Collected Among the Menomini Indians." *JAFL* 26:64–80, 1913.

Wright, John Couchois
The Crooked Tree. Indian Legends of Northern Michigan. Harbor Springs, Mich.: J. C. Wright, 1917. 148 pp., illus.
Published in 1915 under title: *Stories of the Crooked Tree.*

BELIEFS—CUSTOMS—FOLK MEDICINE

Densmore, Frances
"Tribal Customs of the Menominee Indians." *Explorations and Field-Work of the Smithsonian Institution* (Wash., D. C.), 1929, pp. 217-222.

Morgan, L. H.
"Systems of Consanguinity and Affinity." *Smithson. Contr. Knowledge* 17:291–382, 1871.

——————.
"Little-Wolf Joins the Medicine Lodge. In: *American Indian Life,* Elsie Clews Parsons, ed., pp. 63-73. New York: 1925.

Skinner, Alanson
"Associations and Ceremonies of the Menomini Indians." *Anthropological Papers:* Vol. 13: 1915, pp. 167–215, 2 figs. Publications in Anthropology. New York: The American Museum of Natural History.

——————.
Medicine Ceremony of the Menominee, Iowa, and Wahpeton Dakota, with notes on the ceremony among the Ponca, Bungi, Ojibwa, and Potawatomi. Indian Notes and Monographs, Museum of the American Indian, Heye Foundation 4:357 pp., 1920.

"Social Life and Ceremonial Bundles of the Menomini Indians." *Anthropological Papers, American Museum of Natural History* 13:1–165, 1913. illus.

"War Customs of the Menomini Indians." *AA* 13:299–313, 1911. n. s.

Smith, Huron Herbert
"Ethnobotany of the Menomini Indians." *Bulletin of the Public Museum of the City of Milwaukee,* Vol. 4 (No. 1). Milwaukee, 1923. 173 pp.

GAMES

Skinner, Alanson B.
"The Menomini Game of Lacrosse." *American Museum Journal* (New York) 11:139–141, 1911.

FOLK ART—SPEECH

Bloomfield, Leonard
"Literate and Illiterate Speech." *AS* 2(No. 10):432–439, 1927.
Discussion of Menomini language—emphasizing certain inflections and locutions that convey to the native a feeling of "good" or "bad" speech.

"The Menomini Language." *Inter. Congr. Amer.* 21:336–343, 1924.

Dustin, Fred
Report on Indian Earthworks in Ogemaw County (Michigan). Cranbrook (Bloomfield Hills, Mich.): 1932. 25 pp.

Skinner, Alanson B.
Material Culture of the Menomini. Indian Notes and Monographs, Museum of the American Indian, Heye Foundation, Misc. Ser. 20:478 pp.

"Menomini word 'Häwätûk'." *JAFL* 28:258–261, 1915.

West, George A.
The Aboriginal Pipes of Wisconsin. (Wisconsin Archaeologist). Milwaukee: Wisconsin Archaeologist Society, vol. 4 (No. 3, 4), 1905.

MUSIC

GENERAL STUDIES

Densmore, Frances
Menominee Music. U. S. Bureau of Ethnology, Bulletin 102. Washington, D. C.: U. S. Government Printing Office, 1932, 230 pp., illus.
Discussion of the songs, dances, games, and rituals, and an analysis of the music. As in all her work it is marked by sound and thoro scholarship.

"Music of the Winnebago and Menominee Indians." *Explorations and Field-Work of the Smithsonian Institution,* 1928, pp. 189-198.

"Studies of Indian Music Among the Menominee." *Smithson. Miscel. Coll.* 78(Part 1): 119–125, 1926.

Michelson, Truman
"Further Remarks on the Origin of the So-called Dream Dance of the Central Algonkians." *AA* 26:293–294, 1924. n.s.

Skinner, Alanson B.
Medicine Ceremony of the Menomini Iowa, and Wahpeton Dakota, with notes on the ceremony among Ponca, Bungi, Ojibwa, and Potawatomi. New York: Museum of the American Indian Heye Foundation, 1920.

"Songs of the Menomini Medicine Ceremony." *AA* 27:290–314, 1925.

DANCES

Barrett, S. A.
"The Dream Dance of the Chippewa and Menominee Indians of Northern Wisconsin." *Bulletin of the Public Museum of the City of Milwaukee,* vol. 1(No. 4):251–406. Milwaukee: Public Museum, 1911.

ARRANGEMENTS

————: *Piano*

"Ghost Dance."
by Thurlow Lieurance — Philipp, I.: Presser: Piano.
"Indian Flute Call and Love Song."
Lieurance, Thurlow: Presser: Piano.

MICMAC

FOLKLORE

GENERAL STUDIES

Barbeau, C. Marius
"Gaspésiades." *La Canada Français* 30:725, 1943.
An account of the people of the Gaspé as Barbeau found them when he went to collect folk songs and tales among them. He does not include texts.

Bromley, Walter
A General Description of Nova Scotia. Halifax: Royal Acadian School, 1823.

Campbell, Duncan
Nova Scotia. Montreal: J. Lovell, 1873.

Chamberlain, A. F.
"Indians of the Eastern Provinces of Canada." *Annual Archaeological Report,* Ontario, 1905; Toronto, 1906, pp. 122–136.

Elder, W.
"The Aborigines of Nova Scotia." *North American Review* 112:1–30, 1871.

Fauset, A. H.
"Folklore From the Half-Breeds in Nova Scotia." *JAFL* 38:300–315, 1925.

Gagnon, A.
"Notes sur les Sauvages du Canada." *Proceedings of the 18th Session of the International Congress of Americanists*, pp. 434–440, 1912.

Gilpin, J. B.
"Indians of Nova Scotia." *Proc. Trans. Nova Scotian Inst. Natur. Sci.* 4:260–281, 1877.

Hagar, S.
"A Melange of Micmac Notes." *Proc. Amer. Asoc. Adv. Sci.* 44: 257–258, 1895.

Mooney, J., and Thomas, C.
"Micmac." In: *Bull. Bureau Amer. Ethnol.* 30(Part 1):858–859, 1907.

Pacifique, Père
"Le pays des Micmacs: The Micmac Country." *Bulletin de la Société de Géographie de Québec* 28 (Nos. 1, 2):105–147. (Jan.) 1934.

————.
Quelques traits caracteristiques de la tribu des Micmacs." *Proceedings of the 15th Session of the International Congress of Americanists*, (Quebec) 1:315–329, 1906.

Parsons, Elsie Clews
"Half-Breed." *Scientific Monthly* 18:144–148, 1924.

————.
"Micmac Folklore." *JAFL* 38:55–133, 1925.

————.
"Micmac Notes." *JAFL* 39:460–485, 1926.

Prince, J. Dyneley
"A Micmac Manuscript." *Proceedings of the 15th Session of the International Congress of Americanists* (Quebec) 1:87–125, 1906.

Rand, Rev. Silas Tertius
A First Reading Book in the Micmac Language; comprising the Micmac numerals and the names of the beasts, birds, fishes, trees, etc. Halifax: Nova Scotia Printing Company, 1875. iv, 108 pp.

————.
"The Micmac Indians." *Our Forest Children* (Owen Sound) 2:10–12, 1888.

————.
A Short Statement of Facts Relating to the History, Manners, Customs, Language, and Literature of the Micmac Tribe of Indians. Halifax: 1850. 40 pp.

Shaw, B. H. H.
"The Indians of the Maritimes." *Canadian Magazine* 58:343–350, 1922.

Speck, Frank G.
Beothuk and Micmac. Indian Notes and Monographs, Museum of the American Indian, Heye Foundation, Misc. Ser. 22:187 pp., 1922.

Tenesles, N.
The Indian of New-England and North-Eastern Provinces. Middletown: 1851. 24 pp.

Watson, L. W.
"Origin of Melicities; Prince Edward Island Micmac Tradition." *JAFL* 20:160–162, 1907.

West, J.
A Journal of a Mission to the Indians of the British Provinces of New Brunswick and Nova Scotia. London: 1827. (pp. 235-255).

MYTHS—FOLKTALES—LEGENDS

Hagar, Stansbury
"The Celestial Bear." *JAFL* 13:92–103, 1900.

————.
Weather and the Seasons in Micmac Mythology." *JAFL* 10:101–105, 1897.

Leland, C. G.
Algonquin Legends of New England; or Myths and Folklore of the Micmac, Passamoquoddy and Penobscot Tribes. Boston: Houghton Mifflin and Co., 1884. 379 pp.

Michelson, Truman
"Micmac Tales." *JAFL* 38:33–54, 1925.

Rand, Rev. Silas Tertius
Legends of the Micmacs. In: *Wellesley College Philological Publications.* New York: Longmans, Green & Co., 1894. vi, 452 pp.

————.
"The Legends of the Micmacs." *Amer. Antiq.* 12:3–14, 1890.

Speck, Frank G.
"Micmac Tales from Cape Breton Island." *JAFL* 28:59–69, 1915.

Washburne, M. F.
Indian Legends. Introduction, suggestions to teachers, and bibliography by Alice C. Henderson. Illustrations by Frederick Richardson. Chicago: Rand, McNally and Co., 1915. 144 pp. illus.

Wilson, Gilbert L.
Indian Hero Tales. New York: American Book Co., 1906. 203 pp.

BELIEFS—CUSTOMS—FOLK MEDICINE

Hagar, Stansbury
"Micmac Customs and Traditions." *AA* 8:31–43, 1895.

————.
"Micmac Magic and Medicine." *JAFL* 9:170–177, 1896.

Johnson, Frederick
"Notes on Micmac Shamanism." *Primitive Man* 16 (No. 3, 4):53–80. Washington, D. C.: Catholic Anthropological Conference, 1943.

LeClercq, Father Christian
A New Relation of Gaspesia with the Customs and Religions of the Gaspesian Indians. Toronto: Publication of the Champlain Society, 1910.
> "A name given by early French writers to a part of the Micmac living about Gaspé bay on the Gulf of St. Lawrence, Quebec province." (James Mooney)

Maillard, A. S.
An Account of the Customs and Manners of the Micmakis and Maricheets. London: S. Hooper & A. Morley, 1758. 138 pp.

Morgan, L. H.
"Systems of Consanguinity and Affinity." *Smithson. Contr. Knowledge* 17:291–382, 1871.

Speck, Frank G.
"Bird Lore of the Northern Indians." *Public Lectures of the University of Pennsylvania Faculty* 7:349–380, 1920.

——————.
"The Family Hunting Band as the Basis of Algonkian Social Organization." *AA* 17:289–305, 1914. n.s.

Wallis, W. D.
"Medicines Used by the Micmac Indians." *AA* 24:24–30, 1922, n.s.

FOLK ART—SPEECH

Fewkes, J. W.
"A Pictograph from Nova Scotia." *Amer. Natur.* 24:995–999, 1890.

Ganong, W. F.
"Upon Aboriginal Pictographs from New Brunswick." *Bulletin of the Natural History of New Brunswick*, 1904, pp. 175-178.

Gatschet, A. S.
"Micmac Fans and Games." *Bull. Free Mus. Arts Univ. Penn.* 2:190–194, 1900.

Leland, C. G., and Prince, J. D.
Kulóskap the Master and Other Algonkin Poems. New York: 1902. 370 pp.

Pacifique, Père
"Traité théorique et pratique de la langue Micmaque." *Annales de l'Association Canadienne-française pour l'Avancement des Sciences* 4:213–333; 5:159–276, 1938–1939.

Prince, J. D.
"A Micmac Manuscript." *Inter. Congr. Amer.* 15 (Part 1):87–124, 1906.

——————.
"Notes on the Language of the Eastern Algonquin Tribes." *Amer. Jour. Philol.* 9:310–316, 1888.

Rand, Rev. S. T.
A Dictionary of the Language of the Micmac Indians. Halifax: 1888. 286 pp.

Speck, Frank G.
"Micmac Slate Image." *Indian Notes* 1:153–154, 1924.

GAMES—DANCES

Gatschet, A. S.
"Micmac Fans and Games." *Bull. Free Mus. Arts Univ. Penn.* 2:190–194, 1900.

Shedd, Margaret
"Carib Dance Patterns." *Theatre Arts Monthly* 17:65–77 (January) 1933.

MISSISAUGA

FOLKLORE

GENERAL STUDIES

Orr, R. B.
"The Mississaugas." *Annual Arch. Report,* 1915, pp. 7-18.

MYTHS—FOLKTALES—LEGENDS

Chamberlain, Alexander Francis
"Mississagua Legend of Naniboju." *JAFL* 5:291–292, 1892.

——————.
"Mississagua Tales." *JAFL* 2:141–147, 1890.

——————.
"Nanibozhu Amongst the Otchipwe, Mississagas and Other Algonkian Tribes." *JAFL* 4:193–213, 1891.

BELIEFS—CUSTOMS

Chamberlain, Alexander Francis
"Notes on the History, Customs, and Beliefs of the Mississagua Indians." *JAFL* 1:150–160, 1888.
Includes discussion of music.

MUSIC

DANCES

"Mississagua Dance-Song." *JAFL* 3:152, 1890.

MOHAWK (Iroquois)

FOLKLORE

GENERAL STUDIES

Beauchamp, W. M.
"Mohawk Notes." *JAFL* 8:217–221, 1895.

Chalmers, Harvey
West to the Setting Sun. New York: The Macmillan Company, 1943. 362 pp.
A fictionalized biography of Mohawk Sachem Joseph Brant.

Hewitt, J. N. B.
"Mohawk." In: *Bull. Bureau Amer. Ethnol.* 30(Part 1):921–926, 1907.

Lightall, W. D.
"Hochelagans and Mohawks." *Proc. Trans. Royal Soc. Can.* (ser. 2) 5(Part 2):199–211, 1899.

Lydekker, John Wolfe
The Faithful Mohawks. With a Foreword by the Right Honorable Lora Tweedsmuir. New York: The Macmillan Company, 1938. xvi, 206 pp., illus.

Megapolensis, J.
"Short Sketch of the Mohawk Indians in New Netherlands." *Coll. N. Y. Hist. Soc.* (ser. 2) 3:137–160, 1857.

Smith, E. A.
"Life Among the Mohawks." *Proc. Amer. Assoc. Adv. Sci.* 32:398–399, 1883.

MYTHS—FOLKTALES—LEGENDS

Anon.
"Peabody's Leap." *The Ariel* 4:146–147, Jan. 8, 1831.
An interesting legend of Lake Champlain. Adventures and revenge of Timothy Peabody, whose entire family was massacred by the Indians.

Chamberlain, A. F.
"Mohawk Legend of Adam and Eve." *JAFL* 2:228, 1889.

Holland, Robert E.
The Song of Tekakwitha. New York: Fordham University Press, 1943. illus.
It is a biography in verse that records the story of a seventeenth century Indian Maiden, "The Lily of the Mohawks."

Judson, Edward Zane Carroll
Thayendanegea, the Scourge, or The War-Eagle of the Mohawks. A tale of mystery. New York: F. A. Brady, 1858. 77 pp.

Speck, Frank G.
"The Banished Wife and Maid Without Hands." *NYFQ* 3 (No. 4):312–319, 1947.
"Here we have what many folklorists have found to be amazingly true, as example of folk tale that travelled in colonial times from European hearths to the American wilderness to be recited in an Indian language long after it had ceased to be rehearsed in Celtic, English or French which produced it." (F. G. Speck)

Thompson, Stith
"The Indian Legend of Hiawatha." *PMLA* 37:128–140, 1919.

BELIEFS—CUSTOMS

Beauchamp, W. M.
"Funeral Customs in the Mohawk." *JAFL* 2:70, 1889.

Deserontyon, J.
"A Mohawk Form of Ritual and Condolence." Translated with an introduction by J. N. B. Hewitt. *Indian Notes and Monographs* 10:61–84, 1928.

Ruttenber, E. M.
Footprints of the Red Men. Newburgh: New York State Historical Associations, 1906. 241 pp., illus.
Indian Geographical Names of the Valley of the Hudson's River, the Valley of the Mohawks, and on the Delaware: Their Locations and the Probable Meanings of Some of Them.

Willoughby, C. C.
"A Mohawk (Caughnawaga) Halter for Leading Captives." *AA* 40:49–50, 1938.

FOLK ART—SPEECH

Bruyas, J.
Radical Words of the Mohawk Language with their Derivatives." *Ann. Reports Regents Univ. State N. Y.* 16(Appendix E):1–123, 1863.

Oronhyatekha
"The Mohawk Language." *Canadian Journal* (Toronto) 10:182–194, 1865; 15:1–12, 1876.

Reid, W. M.
"Mohawk Pottery."*Records of the Past* (Washington, D. C.) 3:184–188, 1904.

MOHEGAN (Pequot)

FOLKLORE

GENERAL STUDIES

Anon.
"The Aborigines of New England. Uncas, the Mohegan." *The Knickerbocker* 9:321–328, April 1837.
Historical account, including information on traditions and wild haunts of the Red Man of New England.

Bradshaw, H. C.
The Indians of Connecticut: The Effect of English Colonization. Deep River: 1935. 64 pp.

De Forest, John William
History of the Indians of Conn. from The Earlier and Known Period to 1850. Published with the sanction of the Connecticut Historical Society. Hartford, Conn.: W. J. Hammersley, 1853. xxvi, 509 pp., front., illus.

Douglas, F. H., comp.
The New England Tribes. Denver Art Museum, Department of Indian Art, Leaflets Nos. 27 and 28, 1931.

Holmes, A.
"Additional Memoir of the Mohegans." *Coll. Mass. Hist. Soc.* (ser. 1) 9:75–99, 1804.

Kittredge, G. L., ed.
"Letters of Samuel Lee and Samuel Sewall Relating to New England and the Indians." *Publications of the Colonial Society of Massachusetts* 14:142–186, 1912.

Lossing, B. J.
The Last of the Pequods. In: *Indian Miscellany,* W. W. Beach, ed., (pp. 452-460). Albany: J. Munsell, 1877. viii, 490 pp.

Mooney, J.
"Mohegan." In: *Bull. Bureau Amer. Ethnol.* 30(Part 1):926–927, 1907.

————.
"Pequot." In: *Bull. Bureau Amer. Ethnol.* 30(Part 2):229–231, 1910.

Orr, C.
History of the Pequot War. Cleveland: The Helman Taylor Co., 1897. 149 pp.

Peale, A. L.
Uncas and the Mohegan-Pequot. Boston: Meadow Publishing Company, 1939.

Ray, L.
The Aboriginal Inhabitants of Connecticut. In: *Indian Miscellany,* W. W. Beach, ed., pp 280-302. Albany: J. Munsell, 1877.

Skinner, Alanson B.
An Ancient Algonkian Fishing Village at Cayuga, New York. Indian Notes and Monographs, Heye Foundation, Vol. 2 (No. 2), 1919.

————.
The Indians of Greater New York. Cedar Rapids, Ia.: The Torch Press, 1915. 150 pp., incl. front. (map). Half-title: *Little Histories of North American Indians.*

Speck, Frank G.
"A Modern Mohegan-Pequot Text." *AA* 6: 469–477, 1904. n.s.

————.
"Native Tribes and Dialects of Connecticut. a Mohegan-Pequot Diary." *43rd Ethnological Report, 1925–1926,* pp. 197–287, illus., pls. 14–42. Washington, D. C.: U. S. Government Printing Office.

————.
"Notes on the Mohegan and Niantic Indians." *Anthropological Papers, American Museum of Natural History* 3:181–210, 1909. illus.

Spiess, M.
The Indians of Connecticut. New Haven: Committee on Historical Publications, Tercentenary Commission of the State of Connecticut, 1933. 33 pp.

Sylvester, H. M.
Indian Wars of New England. Boston: W. B. Clarke Company, 1910. 3 vols.

Wheeler, R. A.
The Pequot Wars. Westerly: 1877. 23 pp.

Wilder, H. H.
"Notes on the Indians of Southern Massachusetts." *AA* 25:197–218, 1923. n.s.

Wissler, Clark, ed.
The Indians of Greater New York and the Lower Hudson. Anthropological Papers of the American Museum of Natural History, vol. 3. New York: Hudson-Fulton Publications, 1909. 242 pp., illus.
   Contents: The Lenape Indians of Staten Island," Alanson Skinner; "Aboriginal Remains in Manhattan Island," James K. Finck; "The Indians of Washington Heights," R. P. Bolton; "Archaeology of Manhattan Island," Alanson Skinner; "The Rock Shelters of Armonk, New York," M. R. Harrington; "Indian Rock-Shelters in Northern New Jersey and Southern New York," Max Schrabirch; "Ancient Shell Heaps near New York City," M. R. Harrington; "Notes on the Mohegan and Niantic Indians," F. G. Speck; "Archaeology of the New York Coastal Algonkin," Alanson Skinner.

MYTHS—FOLKTALES—LEGENDS

Speck, Frank G.
"Mohegan-Pequot Legends." *JAFL* 17:183–184, 1904.

————.
"Mohegan Traditions of Muhkeahweesug, 'The Little Men'." *The Papoose* (New York) 1, (No. 7):11–14, 1903.

————.
"Pequot-Mohegan Witchcraft Tale." *JAFL* 16:104–106, 1903.

BELIEFS—CUSTOMS—SPEECH— FOLK ART

Edwards, J.
"Observations on the Mohegan Language." *Coll. Mass. Hist. Soc.* (ser. 2) 10:81–160, 1823.

New England Indian Houses, Forts and Villages, Colonial Period.
Denver Art Museum, Department of Indian Art, Leaflet No. 39, (Jan.) 1932.

Prince, J. D. and Speck, F. G.
"Glossary of the Mohegan-Pequot Language." *AA* 6:18–46, 1904. n.s.

————.
"The Modern Pequots and Their Language." *AA* 5:193–212, 1903. n.s.

Speck, Frank G.
"Decorative Art of the Indian Tribes of Connecticut." *Mem. Can. Dep't Mines* 75: 1–73, 1915.

————.
"Mohegan Beadwork on Birch-Bark." *Indian Notes* 5:295–298, 1928.

————.
"Mohegan Traditions of *Muhkeahweesug,* 'The Little Men'." *Papoose* 1(Part 7):11–14, 1903.

_____.
"Native Tribes and Dialects of Connecticut."
Annual Report Bureau Amer. Ethnol. 43:199–
287, 1926.

MONTAGNAIS

(*Including:* Nascapi)

FOLKLORE

GENERAL STUDIES

Anon.
"Nascapee." *Bull. Bureau Amer. Ethnol.* 30
(Part 2):30–32, 1910.

Beston, Henry
The St. Lawrence (The Rivers of America
Series). Illustrated by A. Y. Jackson. New
York: Farrar and Rinehart, 1942. 274 pp.
"The river, its voyageurs, its fur trade, its folk-
lore, its missionaries, its Catholicism, its French-
Indian intercourse, its chansons, its fisheries, its
little French farms. Farther east its Montagnais
Algonquin Indians."

Burgesse, J. Allan
"Montagnais-Nascapi Nomenclature." *Primi-
tive Man* 16:44–49, 1943. Washington, D. C.:
Catholic Anthropological Conference.

Chamberlain, A. F.
"Indians of the Eastern Provinces of Canada."
Annual Archaeological Report, Ontario 1905;
Toronto, 1906, pp. 122–136.

Comeau, Napoleon Alexander
*Life and Sport on the North Shore of the
Lower St. Lawrence and Gulf,* Containing
chapters on salmon fishing, trapping, the folklore of the Montagnais Indians and tales of
adventure on the fringe of the Labrador Peninsula. Quebec: Daily Telegraph Printing House,
1909. 440 pp., front., plates, ports.

David, R. P. C. E.
"Les Montagnais du Labrador et du Lac St.
Jean." *Proceedings of the 15th Session of the
International Congress of Americanists* (Que-
bec), 1:205–213, 1906.

Davidson, D. S.
"The Family Hunting Territories of the Grand
Lake Victoria Indians." *22nd Session of the
International Congress of Americanists,*
(Rome), 1926.

Grenfell, W. T.
Labrador. New York: Macmillan Co., 1909.

Hind, H. Y.
*Explorations in the Interior of the Labrador
Peninsula.* London: 1863. 2 vols.

Lips, Julius E.
"Notes on Montagnais-Nascapi Economy." *Ethnos* 12(No. 1-2):1–77, 1947.

McLean, J.
"Notes of a Twenty-five Year's Service in the
Hudson's Bay Territory." W. S. Wallace, ed.
Publ. Champlain Soc. 19:258–265, 1932.

Michelson, Truman
"Studies Among the Montagnais-Naskapi Indians of the Northern Shore of the St. Lawrence River." *Exploration and Field Work,
Smithsonian Institution in 1937,* pp. 119–122,
1938.

Mooney, J., and Thomas, C.
"Montagnais." In: *Bull. Bureau Amer. Ethnol.*
30(Part 1):933–934, 1907.

Speck, Frank G.
In Montagnais Country. In: *American Indian
Life,* Elsie Clews Parsons, ed., pp. 87–97. New
York: B. W. Huebsch, 1925.

_____.
"An Incident in Montagnais Winter Life."
Natur. Hist. 26:61–67, 1926.

_____.
"Indian and Eskimo Backgrounds in Southern
Labrador." *General Magazine* (Univ. Penn.)
38:1–17, 143–163, 1935.

_____.
"Mistassini Hunting Territories." *AA* 25:452–
471, 1923. n.s.

_____.
"Mistassini Notes." *Indian Notes* 7:410–457,
1910.

_____.
"Montagnais-Naskapi Bands and Early Distribution in the Labrador Peninsula." *AA* 33:
557–600, 1931. n.s.

_____.
"The Montagnais Indians." *So. Workman*
(Hampton, Va.) 38:148–154, 1909.

_____.
*Naskapi. The Savage Hunters of the Labrador
Peninsula.* Norman, Okla.: University of Okla-
homa Press, 1935. 248 pp., illus.

Stearns, W. A.
Labrador. Boston: 1884. viii, 295 pp.

Townsend, C. W., ed.
*Captain Cartwright and His Labrador Jour-
nal.* Boston: 1911. 385 pp.

Turner, L. M.
"Ethnology of the Ungava District." *Annual
Report Bureau Amer. Ethnol.* 9:159–184,
267–350, 1890.

Wallace, D.
The Long Labrador Trail. New York: The
Outing Publ. Co., 1907. 315 pp.

MYTHS—FOLKTALES—LEGENDS

Davidson, D. S.
"Folk-tales from Grand Lake Victoria, Quebec." *JAFL* 41:275–283, 1928.

Speck, Frank G.
"Mammoth or 'Stiff-Legged Bear'." *AA* 37:
159–163, 1935. n.s.

"Montagnais and Nascapi Tales from the Labrador Peninsula." *JAFL* 38:1–32, 1925.

"Nascapi Myths from Little Whale River." *JAFL* 28:70–77, 1915.

Tremblay, M.
"Contes de Chicoutimi et de la Malbaie." *JAFL* 32:101–112, 1919.

BELIEFS—CUSTOMS—FOLK ART— SPEECH

Cooper, John M.
Northern Algonkin Scrying and Scapulimancy. In: *Festschrift P. W. Schmidt*, (pp. 205-217). Wien: 1928.

"The Northern Algonquian Supreme Being." *Cath. Univ. Anthro. Ser.* 2:1–78, 1934.

"Supreme Being Concept of the Montagnais Speaking People." *Anthropos* 30, (No. 1, 2): 228, (Jan.–April) 1935.

Douglas, F. H.
"A Naskapi Painted Skin Shirt." *Material Culture Notes* (Denver Art Museum) 10:38–42, 1939.

"The Shaking-Tent Rite Among the Montagnais of James Bay." *Primitive Man* 12:11–16, 1939.

Flannery, Regina
"Cross-Cousin Marriage Among the Cree and Montagnais of James Bay." *Primitive Man* 11, (Nos. 1–2):29–33, 1938.

Hallowell, A. I.
"Kinship Terms and Cross-Cousin Marriage of the Montagnais-Nascapi and the Cree." *AA* 34:173–199, 1932. n.s.

Lips, J. E.
"Public Opinion and Mutual Assistance Among the Montagnais-Nascapi." *AA* 39:222–228, 1937. n.s.

Trap Systems Among the Montagnais-Naskapi Indians of Labrador Peninsula. Smarre Meddelanden 13. Stockholm: Statens Ethnografiska Museum, 1936. 38 pp.

Michelson, Truman
"Linguistic Classification of Cree and Montagnais-Naskapi Dialects." *Bull. Bureau Amer. Ethnol.* 123:67–95, 1939.

"Some Linguistic Features of Speck's 'Naskapi'." *AA* 39:370–372, 1937. n.s.

Speck, Frank G.
"Analysis of Eskimo and Indian Skin-dressing Methods in Labrador." *Ethnos* 2:345–353, 1937.

"Central Eskimo and Indian Dot Ornamentation." *Indian Notes* 2:151–172, 1925.

"Ethical Attributes of the Labrador Indians." *AA* 35:559–594, 1933.

"Kinship Terms and the Family Band Among the Northeastern Algonkian." *AA* 20:143–161, 1918. n.s.

"Medicine Practices of the Northeastern Algonquians." *Inter. Congr. Amer.* 19:303–321, 1915.

Montagnais Art in Birchbark, A Circumpolar Trait. Indian Notes and Monographs, vol. 2 (No. 2). New York: Museum of the American Indian, Heye Foundation, 1937.

"More Algonkian Scapulimancy from the North." *Ethnos* 4:21–28, 1939.

"Reptile-Lore of the Northern Indians." *JAFL* 36:273–280, 1923.

"Spiritual Beliefs Among the Labrador Indians." *Inter. Congr. Amer.* 21(Part 1):266–275, 1924.

————, and Heye, G. G.
Hunting Charms of the Montagnais and Mistassini. Indian Notes and Monographs, Museum of the American Indian, Heye Foundation, Misc. Ser. 13:19 pp.

Strong, W. D.
"Cross-Cousin Marriage and the Culture of the Northeastern Algonkian." *AA* 31:277–288, 1929. n.s.

NANTICOKE

See: Piscataway or Conoy, p. 914.

FOLKLORE

GENERAL STUDIES

Babcock, William H.
"The Nanticoke Indians of Indian River, Delaware." *AA* 1:277–283, 1899.

Brinton, D. G.
"Vocabulary of the Nanticoke Dialect." *Proceedings American Philosophical Society* 31: 327, 1893.

Crozier, A.
"The Nanticokes of the Delmarva Peninsula." *Bulletin of the Archaeological Society of Delaware* 1:2–6, 1934.

Marye, W. B.
"The Wiccomiss Indians of Maryland." *Amer. Antiqity* 4(Part 2):146–152, 1938; 5(Part 1): 51–55, 1939.

Mooney, J.
"Indian Tribes of the District of Columbia." *AA* 2:259–266, 1889.

—————, and Thomas, C.
"Conoy." In: *Bull. Bureau Amer. Ethnol.* 30 (Part 1):339–341, 1907.

—————.
"Nanticoke." In: *Bull. Bureau Amer. Ethnol.* 30(Part 2):24–26, 1910.

Murray, W. V.
"Nanticokes." *Trans. Coll. Amer. Antiq. Soc.* 2:305–367, 1836.

Nelson, William
The Indians of New Jersey with Some Notice of Indian Place Names. Paterson: Press Publishing Company, 1894. 168 pp.

Speck, F. G.
Indians of the Eastern Shore of Maryland. Baltimore: 1922. 15 pp.

—————.
"The Nanticoke and Conoy Indians." *Papers of the Historical Society of Delaware* 1:1–77, 1927. n.s.

—————.
The Nanticoke Community of Delaware. Contributions from the Museum of the American Indian, Heye Foundation 2(No. 4):43 pp. 1915.

Weslager, C. A.
Delaware's Forgotten Folk; The Story of the Moors and Nanticokes. Philadelphia: University of Pennsylvania Press, 1943. ix, 215 pp., 4 figs., 8 plates, bibl.
"It is a well-written essay in ethnohistory . . . The second chapter is largely folkloristic in nature and discourse, the "national" legends of the Moors and Nanticokes—their own stories as to time, place, and manner of their origin." (Maurice A. Mook)

—————.
"The Nanticoke Indians in Early Pennsylvania." *The Pennsylvania Magazine of History and Biography* 67, (No. 4):345–355, Philadelphia, 1943.

CUSTOMS—SPEECH

Bushnell, D. I.
"Native Cemeteries and Forms of Burial East of the Mississippi." *Bull. Bureau Amer. Ethnol.* 71:24–26, 1920.

Davidson, D. S.
"Burial Customs in the Delmarva Peninsula and the Question of their Chronology." *Amer. Antiquity* 1:84–97, 1935.

NARRAGANSETT

See: Mohegan, pp. 869–871.

FOLKLORE

GENERAL STUDIES

Chapin, Howard Miller
Sachems of the Narragansetts. Providence: Rhode Island Historical Society, 1931. 117 pp., illus.

Douglas, F. H. comp.
The New England Tribes. Denver Art Museum, Department of Indian Art, Leaflets Nos. 27 and 28, July 1931.

Mooney, J.
"Narragansett." *Bull. Bureau Amer. Ethnol.* 30(Part 2):28–30, 1910.

Rainey, Froelich G.
"A Compilation of Historical Data Contributing to the Ethnobiography of Connecticut and Southern New England." *Bulletin, Archaeological Society of Connecticut* 3:1–89. New Haven, Conn.: Peabody Museum, 1936.

Sedgewick, Catherine Maria
"Hope Leslie; or Early Times in Massachusetts." *North American* 1:121. Sept. 1, 1827.
Legend of the conflict between the Indians and the whites.

Wessel, Bessie Blom
An Ethnic Survey of Woonsocket, Rhode Island. Chicago: University of Chicago Press, 1931. 290 pp.

Willoughby, C. C.
"Houses and Gardens of the New England Indians." *AA* 8:115–133, 1906. n.s.

MYTHS—FOLKTALES—LEGENDS

Anon.
"The Indian Maiden's Revenge." *Lowell Offering* 4:205–207, July 1844.
Legend of the Narraganset Indian girl who killed the white man who broke his promise to her,—then afterward committed suicide.

Gatschet, A. S.
"Deities of the Early New England Indians." *JAFL* 12:211–212, 1899.

FOLK ART—SPEECH

Chapin, H. M.
"Indian Implements Found in Rhode Island." *Rhode Island Historical Society Collections* (Providence) 20:14–32, 1927.

—————.
"Unusual Implements Found in Rhode Island." *Rhode Island Historical Society Collections* (Providence) 19:117–128, 1926.

Parsons, U.
Indian Names of Places in Rhode Island. Providence: 1861. 32 pp.

Willoughby, C. C.
"Dress and Ornaments of New England Indians." *AA* 7:499–508, 1905. n.s.

————.
"Houses and Gardens of the New England Indians." *AA* 8:115–132, 1906. n.s.

————.
"Wooden Bowls of the Algonquian Indians." *AA* 10:423–434, 1908. n.s.

MUSIC
ARRANGEMENTS
—————: *Voice and Piano*

Commuck, Thomas
Indian Melodies by T. C., a Narragansett Indian. Harmonized by T. Hastings. New York: G. Lane and C. B. Tippett, 1845. 114 pp.

NIANTIC

See: Mohegan, pp. 869–871

FOLKLORE
GENERAL STUDIES

De Forest, John Williams
History of the Indians of Connecticut from the Earlier and Known Period to 1850. Hartford, Conn.: W. T. Hamersley, 1852. 509 pp.

Prince, J. D.
"Last Living Ehoes of the Natick." *AA* 9:493–499, 1907. n.s.

Speck, Frank G.
"Notes on the Mohegan and Niantic Indians." *Anthropological Papers, American Museum of Natural History* 3:181–210, 1909. illus.

MYTHS—LEGENDS

Converse, Parker L.
Legends of Woburn, now first written and preserved in collected form . . . to which is added a chrono-indexical history of Woburn. Series 1–2. Woburn, Mass.: Printed for Subscribers Only, 1892–96. 2 vols., illus.

Coxey, Willard D.
Ghosts of old Berkshire. Great Barrington, Mass.: The Berkshire Courier, 1934–35. 253 pp.

Gatschet, A. S.
"Deities of the Early New England Indians." *JAFL* 12:211–212, 1899.

CUSTOMS—SPEECH

Cotton, Josiah
Vocabulary of the Massachusetts (or Natick) Indian Language. Ed. by J. Pickering from manuscript of 1707–1708. Cambridge, Mass.: E. W. Metcalf and Co., 1829. 113 pp.

Willoughby, Charles C.
"Houses and Gardens of the New England Indians." *AA* 8:115–133, 1906. n.s.

ONEIDA (Iroquois)
FOLKLORE
GENERAL STUDIES

Allen, Hope Emily
"An Oneida Tale." *JAFL* 57:280–281, 1944.

Anon.
"Chronicle–1849." *American Quarterly Register and Magazine* 3:375, Dec. 1849.
Description of a religious spectacle, the rite of sacrificing the white dog—observed at Onondaga Castle, Oneida, New York.

————.
"Shenandoah, the Oneida Chief." *Ladies' Literary Cabinet* 5:188, April 20, 1822.
Anecdotes, specimens of eloquence.

Bloomfield, J. K.
The Oneidas. New York: Alden Brothers, 1908. x, vii, 395 pp., illus.

Hewitt, J. N. B.
"Oneida." In: *Bull. Bureau Amer. Ethnol.* 30(Part 2):123–127, 1910.

MUSIC
GENERAL STUDIES

"Music Amongst the Oneidas, of Dutch Creek, Wisconsin." *New York Musical Work* (New York) 14:39–40, 1856.

RECORDS

"The Tracker's Brasting Chant." (Midwinter Festival Chant)
Sung by Simeon Gibson at Six Nations Reserve, Canada, 1941. In: Album VI: Library of Congress, 1943.   AAFS26B31

ONONDAGA (Iroquois)
FOLKLORE
GENERAL STUDIES

Beauchamp, W. M.
"Hi-a-wat-ha." *JAFL* 4:295–306, 1891.

————.
"Onondaga Notes." *JAFL* 8:209–216, 1895.

Hatzan, A. Leon
The True Story of Hiawatha. Toronto, Canada: Mohawk Book and Music Co., 1925.

Hewitt, J. N. B.
"Onondaga." In: *Bull. Bureau Amer. Ethnol.* 30(Part 2):129–135, 1910.

LeFort, Abraham
Hiawatha, or, The Origin of the Onondaga Council-Fire; an Iroquois Tradition. In: *Information Respecting the History, Condition and Prospects of the Indian Tribes of the United States*, by H. R. Schoolcraft. Part 3. 1853.

MYTHS—FOLKTALES—LEGENDS

Beauchamp, W. M.
"Onondaga Tales." *JAFL* 1:44–48, 1888; 2: 261–270, 1889; 6:173–180, 1893; 13:281–282, 1900.

Kunike, H.
"Der verlorene Knabe: ein Märchen der Onondaga Indianer." *Erdball* 3:67–71, 1929.
"The Lost Boy"—a tale.

Osborn, Chase S. and Stellanova
Schoolcraft — Longfellow — Hiawatha. Lancaster, Pa.: The Jacques Cattel Press, 1943.
A study of the work of the student of Indian Mythology and of Longfellow's debt to him.

Thompson, Stith
"The Indian Legend of Hiawatha." *Publications of the Modern Language Association* 37: 128–140, 1919.

BELIEFS—CUSTOMS—WITCHCRAFT

Anon
"Chronicle—Death of an Indian Chief." *Niles' Weekly Register* 57:112, Oct. 12, 1839.
Report of the death of Ondayaka, chief of the Onondagas at the age of ninety-six, with a description of his death, and remarks on his character.

Beauchamp, William M.
"Onondaga Customs." *JAFL* 1:195–203, 1888.

Converse, H. M.
"Festival of the Sacrifice of the White Dog as now practiced at the Onondaga Reservation." *JAFL* 1:83–84, 1888.

Smith, De C.
"Onondaga Hunting Superstitions." *JAFL* 2: 282–283, 1889.

———.
"Onondaga Witchcraft and Hon-do-i." *JAFL* 2:277–281, 1889.

Stephenson, Marion Bailey
"How the World Was Made." *SFQ* 1, (No. 4): 21–25, 1937.

Taft, G. E.
"An Onondaga Festival." *Records of the Past* (Wash., D. C.) 13:101–102, 1914.

SPEECH

Beauchamp, William M.
"Onondaga Names of Months." *JAFL* 2:160–161, 1889.

———.
"Onondaga Plant Names." *JAFL* 15:91–103, 1902.

Zeisberger, D.
"Essay of an Onondaga Grammar." *Pennsylvania Magazine of History and Biography* 11: 442–453, 1887; 12:65–75, 233–239, 325–340, 1888.

MUSIC

DANCES

Beauchamp, W. M.
"Notes on the Onondaga Dances." *JAFL* 6: 181–184, 1895.
No music.

RECORDS

"Dream Song of the Creator at the White Dog Sacrifice."—Onondaga of Canada (Midwinter festival chant). Sung by Chief Joseph Logan with assistance of Simeon Gibson at Six Nations Reserve, Canada. In: Album VI: Library of Congress 1943.   AAFS26B2

"Eagle or Striking Dance" (gane' gwá' e'). A variant of the Calumet dance. Sung with water drum and horn rattle by Chief Joseph Logan at Six Nations Reserve, Canada, 1941. In: Album VI, Library of Congress, 1943.
AAFS29B

"Medicine Men's Celebration." (hadihi' dus) (Onondaga). Sung with sound rattle by Chief Joseph Logan at Six Nations Reserve, Canada, 1941. A—(1) Throwing songs of four individual Medecine Men. (2) Introductory songs of the Medicine Man. B—The Medicine Dance (Selections). (1) Beginning Songs. (2) Dancing Songs. (3) Magic Songs. (4) Ending Songs, as the Steam Settles Down. In: Album VI: Library of Congress, 1943.   AAFS27

OTTAWA

FOLKLORE

GENERAL STUDIES

Blackbird, Andrew J. (Mack-e-te-be-nessy)
History of the Ottawa and Chippewa Indians of Michigan, etc. Ypsilanti, Mich.: The Ypsilantian Job Printing House, 1887. 128 pp.

Blair, E. H.
Indian Tribes of the Upper Mississippi, and the Great Lakes Region. Cleveland: The Arthur Clark Company, 1911. 2 vols.

Hamelin
"Ottawas." *Trans. Coll. Amer. Antiq. Soc.* 2:305–367, 1836.

Hunter, A. F.
"Wampum Records of the Ottawas." *Annual Arch. Report,* 1901, pp. 52–56.

James, E., ed.
A Narrative of the Captivity and Adventures of John Tanner. New York: 1830. 426 pp.

Kinietz, W. Vernon
The Indians of the Western Great Lakes. Occasional Contributions from the Museum of Anthropology of the University of Michigan 10. Ann Arbor: University of Michigan Press, 1941. 427 pp.

Meeker, J.
Ottawa First Book. 1850. 128 pp.

Michelson, Truman
"Notes on the Gentes of the Ottawa." *AA* 13:338, 1911. n.s.

Mooney, J., and Hewitt, J. N. B.
"Ottawa." In: *Bull. Bureau Amer. Ethnol.* 30(Part 2):167–172, 1910.

Orr, R. B.
"The Ottawas." *Annual Arch. Report,* 1916, pp. 7-25.

Parkman, Dr. Francis
The Conspiracy of Pontiac and the Indian War after the Conquest of Canada. Boston: Little Brown and Company, 1886. 2 vols., maps (part. fold.)

Wilson, E. F.
"The Ottawa Indians." *Our Forest Children* (Owen Sound) 3:1–6, 1889.

MYTHS—FOLKTALES—LEGENDS

Edgar, Sir James David
The White Stone Canoe, a Legend of the Ottawas. Illus. by W. D. Blatchly. Toronto: The Toronto News Company, 1885.

Ettawageskik, E.
"The Formation of Gold." *Red Man* (Carlisle, Pa.) 4:27, 1911.

Michelson, Truman
"Three Ottawa Tales." *JAFL* 44:191–196, 1931.

Wright, John Couchois
Chicago-Jig; Legend of the Indian Paradise. Alma, Mich.: Printed by Babcock & Babcock, 1935. 37 pp., illus.

————.
The Crooked Tree, Harbor Springs, Mich.: The Lakeside Press, 1916. 148 pp., illus.

BELIEFS—CUSTOMS

Jones, Volney H.
"Some Chippewa and Ottawa Uses of Sweet Grass." *Papers, Michigan Academy of Science, Arts and Letters* 21:21–31 (1935), 1936.
Studies in Indian medicine.

PASSAMAQUODDY

See: Malecite, p. 864.

FOLKLORE
GENERAL STUDIES

Bateman, L. C.
"The Maine Indians of To-day." *So. Workman* 38:145–152, 1908.

————.
"The Passamaquoddy Indians of Maine." *So. Workman* 39:17–27, 1910.

Fewkes, J. W.
"Contribution to Passamaquoddy Folk-lore." *JAFL* 3:257–280, 1890.

Michelson, Truman
"The Passamoquoddy Indians of Maine." *Explorations and Field Work of the Smithsonian Institution,* 1934, pp. 85-88.

Moorhead, Warren K.
"The Red-Paint People of Maine." *AA* 15:33–48, 1913, n.s.

Prince, John Dyneley
"A Passamaquoddy Aviator." *AA* 11:628–650, 1909. n.s.

————.
"A Passamaquoddy Tobacco Famine." *International Journal of American Linguistics* 1:58–63, 1917.

————.
"Some Passamaquoddy Documents." *Annals of the New York Academy of Science* 11, (No. 15):369–377, 1898.

————.
"The Passamoquoddy Wampum Records." *Proc. Amer. Philo. Soc.* 36:479–495, 1897.

————.
"The Passamoquoddy Wampum Records." *N. Y. State Mus. Bull.* 184:119–125, 1916.

Tenesles, N.
The Indians of New England and the North Eastern Provinces. Middletown: 1851. 24 pp.

Williamson, William D.
The History of the State of Maine. Hallowell: 1832. Vol. I, pp. 453–514.

MYTHS—FOLKTALES—LEGENDS

Fewkes, J. Walter
"The Origin of the Thunderbird." *JAFL* 3:265–266, 1890.

Leland, C. G.
Algonquin Legends of New England; or Myths and Folk-lore of the Micmac, Passamoquoddy and Penobscot Tribes. Boston: Houghton, Mifflin and Company, 1884. 379 pp.

Prince, John Dyneley
Passamaquoddy Texts. New York, G. E.
Stechert & Co., 1921. 85 pp., Publications of
the American Ethnological Society, vol. X.

————————.
"Some Passamoquoddy Witchcraft Tales."
American Philosophical Society. Proceedings
38 (No. 160) : 181–189, 1899.

CUSTOMS—SPEECH

Brown, W. W.
"Chief-Making Among the Passamoquoddy Indians." *JAFL* 5:57–59, 1892.

Prince, John Dyneley
"The Morphology of the Passamoquoddy Language." *Proc. Amer. Philo. Soc.* 53:92–117,
1914.

————————.
"Notes on Passamoquoddy Literature." *Annals
N. Y. Acad. Sci.* 13:381–386, 1901.

Willoughby, Charles C.
"Houses and Gardens of the New England Indians." *AA* 8:115–133, 1906. n.s.

MUSIC
GENERAL STUDIES

Fewkes, J. Walter
"A Contribution to Passamoquoddy Folk-
Lore." *JAFL* 3:257–280, 1890.
Contains 4 tunes.

————————.
"Passamoquoddy—Snake Dance and Song-
Music and Description." *JAFL* 3:261–263,
1890.

PENOBSCOT

See: Abnaki, pp. 831-33

FOLKLORE
BIBLIOGRAPHY

Manuscripts Relating to the History of Maine,
List 1–2, Index. The University of Maine
Studies, Second Series No. 45. *The Maine Bul-
letin,* Vol. 41:1–427, (Aug.) 1938; 42:1–261,
(Aug.) 1939; 43:8–211, (Feb.) 1941. Index.

Williamson, Joseph
A Bibliography of the State of Maine, from
the earliest period to 1891. Portland: The
Thurston Print. 1896. 2 vols., 738 pp., and
669 pp.

GENERAL STUDIES

Eckstorm, Mrs. Fannie (Hardy)
David Libbey, Penobscot woodman and river-
driver. Boston: American Unitarian Association 1907. 109 pp. On Verse of half-title: "The
True American Types," Vol. IV.

————————.
*Old John Neptune and Other Maine Indian
Shamans.* Portland, Maine: The Southworth-
Anthoensen Press, 1945.

————————.
The Penobscot Man. Boston: Houghton Mifflin and Co., 1904. xii, 326 pp., front.

Forbes, Allan
Other Indian Events of New England. Boston:
State Street Trust Company, 1941. 102 pp.,
illus.

Godfrey, J. E.
"The Ancient Penobscot of Panawanskek."
Coll. Proc. Maine Hist. Soc. 7:1–22, 1876.

Mooney, J.
"Penobscot." In: *Bull. Bureau Amer. Ethnol.*
30(Part 2) :226–227, 1910.

Murchie, Guy
St. Croix, Sentinel River. New York: Duell,
Sloan & Pearce, 1946.
History of the Maine-Canada border with much
folk material on the whites and the Indians.

Smith, W. B.
*Indian Remains of the Penobscot Valley and
their Significance.* Orono, Maine: University
Press, 1926. 90 pp., illus. plates.

————————.
The Lost Red Paint People of Maine. A few
things we know about them, and more that we
know we don't. Lafayette National Park Museum, Bulletin II. Bar Harbor: 1930. 43 pp.,
illus.

Speck, Frank G.
"A Visit to the Penobscot Indians." *University
of Pennsylvania (Phila.) Museum Journal* 2:
21–26, 1911.

————————.
"The Penobscot Indians of Maine." *General
Magazine* (Univ. Penn.) 39:396–405, 1937.

————————.
Penobscot Man; the life history of a forest
tribe in Maine. Philadelphia: University of
Pennsylvania Press, 1940. 325 pp., illus. music.
Includes dances.

————————.
Prehistoric Burial Places in Maine. Cambridge, Mass.: Harvard University Press,
1898.

Starbird, Charles Millard
The Indians of the Androscoggin Valley;
tribal history, and their relations with the early
English settlers of Maine. Lewiston, Maine:
Lewiston Journal Printshop, 1928. 108 pp.,
bibl. pp. 107-108.

Sullivan, J.
"The History of the Penobscot Indians." *Coll.
Mass. Hist. Soc.* 9:206–232, 1804.

MYTHS—FOLKTALES—LEGENDS

Alger, Abby Langdon
In Indian Tents; Stories Told by Penobscot, Passamaquoddy and Micmac Indians, x, 139 pp., Boston: Robert Brothers, 1897.

Leland, C. G.
Algonquin Legends of New England; or Myths and Folklore of the Micmac, Passamaquoddy and Penobscot Tribes. Boston: Houghton, Mifflin and Company, 1884. 379 pp.

Speck, Frank G.
"European Folk Tales Among the Penobscot." *JAFL* 26:81–84, 1913.

———.
"Penobscot Tales." *JAFL* 28:52–58, 1915.

———.
"Penobscot Tales and Religious Beliefs." *JAFL* 48:1–107, 1935.

———.
"Penobscot Transformer Tales." *International Journal of American Linguistics,* 1:187–244, 1918.

Stamp, H.
"Water Fairies." (A Penobscot Tale) *JAFL* 28:310–316, 1915.

BELIEFS—CUSTOMS—FOLK ART

Eckstorm, Fannie Hardy
Handicrafts of the Modern Indians of Maine. Bar Harbor: Bulletins of the Abbe Museum, No. 3, 1932. 72 pp.

Gatschet, A. S.
"Deities of the Early New England Indians." *JAFL* 12:211–212, 1899.

Orchard, W. C.
"Notes on Penobscot Houses." *AA* 11:601–607, 1909. n.s.

Speck, Frank G.
"Bird Lore of the Northern Indians." *Public Lectures of the University of Pennsylvania Faculty* 7:349–380, 1920.

———.
"Symbolism in Penobscot Art." *Anthropological Papers:* Vol. 29:1927, pp. 25–80, 44 figs. Publications in Anthropology. New York: The American Museum of Natural History.

Willoughby, Charles C.
"Dress and Ornaments of the New England Indians." *AA* 7:499–509, 1905. n.s.

———.
"Houses and Gardens of the New England Indians." *AA* 8:115–133, 1906. n.s.

———.
Pottery of New England Indians. In: *Holmes Anniversary Volume,* pp. 83-101. Wash. D. C.: James W. Bryan Press, 1916.

Winship, George Parker
"A Maine Indian Ceremony in 1605." *AA* 3: 387–388, 1901. n.s.

SPEECH

Prince, J. D.
"The Differentiation Between the Penobscot and the Canadian Abenaki Dialects." *AA* 4:17–32, 1902. n.s.

———.
"The Penobscot Language of Maine." *AA* 12:183–208, 1910. n.s.

MUSIC

GENERAL STUDIES

Speck, Frank G.
Penobscot Man; the life history of a forest tribe in Maine. Philadelphia; University of Pennsylvania Press, 1940. 325 pp., illus.
Music of Songs and Dances, pp. 167–173, 260–261, 270–300.

SAULTEAUX

FOLKLORE

GENERAL STUDIES

Grant, Peter
The Saulteaux, about 1804. In: Masson, L. R.: *Les bourgeois de la Compagnie du Nord-Ouest.* Quebec: 1890.

Hallowell, A. I.
"Aggresion in Saulteaux Society." *Psychiatry* 3:395–407, 1940.

———.
"The Incidence, Character and Decline of Polygyny Among Lake Winnipeg Cree and Saulteaux." *AA* 40:235–256, 1938. n.s.

———.
"Culture and Mental Disorder." *Journal of Abnormal and Social Psychology 29,* (No. 1): 1–9, (April-June) 1934.

———.
"Fear and Anxiety as Cultural and Individual Variables in a Primitive Society." *Journal of Social Psychology* (Worcester) 9:25–47, 1938.

———.
"Notes on the Material Culture of the Island Lake Saulteaux." *Journal, Société des Americanistes* 30:129–140, 1938.

———.
"Psychic Stresses and Culture Patterns." *American Journal of Psychiatry* 92:291–310, 1936.

———.
"Temporal Orientation in Western Civilization and in the Preliterate Society." *AA* 39:647–670, 1937.

Young, E. R.
By Canoe and Dog-Train Among the Cree and Salteaux Indians. London: 1890. 267 pp.

MYTHS—FOLKTALES—BELIEFS

Hallowell, A. I.
"Freudian Symbolism in the Dream of a Saulteaux Indian." *Man* 38:47–48, 1938.

———.
"Magic: the Role of Conjuring in Salteaux Society. In: *Papers Presented Before the Monday Night Group, 1939-1940*, M. A. May, ed., pp. 94-115. New Haven: 1940.

———.
"Sin, Sex and Sickness in Saulteaux Belief." *British Journal of Medical Psychology* 18: 191–197, 1939.

———.
"Some Empirical Aspects of Northern Saulteaux Religion." *AA* 36:389–404, 1934. n.s.

———.
"Some European Folk Tales of the Berens River Saulteaux." *JAFL* 52:155–179, 1939.

———.
The Role of Conjuring in Saulteaux Society. Publications of the Philadelphia Anthropological Society, vol. 2. Philadelphia: University of Pennsylvania Press, 1942. 96 pp.

———.
"The Passing of the Midewiwin in the Lake Winnipeg Region." *AA* 38:32–51, 1936. n.s.

Reid, A. P.
"Religious Beliefs of the Ojibois or Saulteaux Indians." *Jour. Royal Anthro. Inst. Gt. Brit. and Ireland* 3:106–113, 1873.

MUSIC

GENERAL STUDIES

Skinner, Alanson
Dances and Music of the Northern Saulteaux. In: *Notes on the Eastern Cree and Northern Saulteaux.* Anthropological Papers of the American Museum of Natural History, Volume IX, pp. 142–143. New York: American Museum, 1911.

SAUK

FOLKLORE

GENERAL STUDIES

Armstrong, Perry A.
The Sauks and the Black Hawk War, with biographical sketches, etc. Springfield, Ill.: H. W. Rocker, 1887. 729 pp.

Barrett, S. A.
Ancient Aztalan. Bulletin of the Public Museum of the City of Milwaukee 13. Milwaukee: The Public Museum, 1933. 602 pp., illus.

Beech, Mervyn Worchester Howard
The Suk, their Language and Folklore. Introduction by Charles Eliot. Oxford: The Clarendon Press, 1911. xxiv, 151 pp.

Beckwith, H. W.
"The Illinois and Indiana Indians." *Fergus Historical Series* 27:146–162, 1884.

Black Hawk
Autobiography. St. Louis: 1882. 208 pp.

———.
Life of Black Hawk, Ma-Ka-tai-me-she-Kia-Kiak. Iowa City: State Historical Society of Iowa, 1932.

Blair, E. H.
Indian Tribes of the Upper Mississippi and the Great Lakes Region. Cleveland: The Arthur H. Clark Company, 1911. 2 vols.

Cole, Cyrenues
I am a Man: the Indian Black Hawk. Iowa City: State Historical Society of Iowa, 1938.
"A subordinate chief of the Sauk and Fox Indians and leader of the Black Hawk War of 1832."

Ferris, I. M.
"The Sauk and Foxes." *Coll. Kansas State Hist. Soc.* 11:333–395, 1910.

Fuller, Iola
The Shining Trail. New York: Duell, Sloan and Pearce, 1943.
A fictionalized study of Black Hawk, leader of the Sauk, in the early nineteenth Century.

Hewitt, J. N. B.
"Sauk." In: *Bull. Bureau Amer. Ethnol.* 30 (Part 2):471–480, 1910.

Indian Tribes of Wisconsin.
U. S. Bureau of American Ethnology, Bulletin 30. Excerpts from the *Handbook of American Indians, North of Mexico.* Washington, D. C.: U. S. Government Printing Office, 1907–1910.

Lapham, Increase A.
The Antiquities of Wisconsin. Smithsonian Institution Publication No. 70. Washington, D. C.: U. S. Government Printing Office, 1852. 92 pp., 50 pl.

Lockwood, Myra
Indian Chief. New York: Oxford University Press, 1943.
The story of Keokuk, leader of the Sauks.

Malin, W. G.
"The Sac and Fox Indians of Iowa." *So. Workman* (Hampton, Va.) 37:481–485, 1908.

Marsh, C.
"Expedition to the Sacs and Foxes." *Coll. State Hist. Soc. Wis.* 15:104–155, 1900.

Michelson, T.
"Note on the Hunting Territories of the Sauk and Fox." *AA* 23:238–239, 1921. n.s.

Skinner, Alanson
"Observations on the Ethnology of the Sauk Indians." *Bulletin of the Public Museum of the City of Milwaukee*, Part 1, No. 5 :1–57, 1923; Part II, 5–2:59–95, 1925.

————.
"Sauk War Bundles." *Wis. Arch.* 2:148–150, 1923. n.s.

————.
"A Summer Among the Sauk and Ioway Indians." *Yearbook Publ. Mus. City Milwaukee* 2:6–15. 1922.

West, George A.
The Aboriginal Pipes of Wisconsin. (Wisconsin Archaeologist). Milwaukee: Wisconsin Archaeologist Society, vol. 4, (Nos. 3, 4), 1905.

Wood, E. F. A.
"A Central Basin Manifestation in Eastern Wisconsin." *American Antiquity* 1, (No. 3): 215–219, 1936.

MYTHS—FOLKTALES—LEGENDS

Brown, Charles E.
Wigwam Tales. Madison: The Author, 1920.

Ellis, E. W.
"The Raccoon and the Opossum." *Red Man* (Carlisle, Pa.) 3:344, 1911.

Jones, W.
"Episodes in the Culture Hero Myth of the Sauks and Foxes." *JAFL* 14:225–239, 1901.

Lasley, M.
"Sak and Fox Tales." *JAFL* 15:170–178, 1902.

Michelson, Truman
"What Happened to the Green Bear Who Was Blessed with a Sacred Pack." *Anthropological Papers* 4:161–176, Bulletin 119, *Bureau of American Ethnology.* Washington, D. C.: U. S. Government Printing Office, 1938.

Skinner, Alanson
"Sauk Tales." *JAFL* 41:147–183, 1928.

CUSTOMS—FOLK ART

Forsyth, T.
Account of the Manners and Customs of the Sauk and Fox Nations. In: *The Indian Tribes of the Upper Mississippi Valley,* E. H. Blair, ed., Vol. II, pp. 183-245. Cleveland: 1912.

Harrington, M. R.
"A Bird-Quill Belt of the Sauk and Fox Indians." *Indian Notes and Monographs* 10: 47–50, 1920.

————.
"Old Sauk and Fox Beaded Garters." *Indian Notes and Monographs* 10:39–41, 1920.

GAMES

"Fox and Sauk Games."
JAFL 24:22–226, 227, 1911.

SENECA (Iroquois)
FOLKLORE
GENERAL STUDIES

Alden, Rev. Timothy
An Account of Sundry Missions Performed Among the Senecas and Munsees (Series of Letters). New York: J. Seymour, 1827.

Fenton, William N.
"Fish Drives Among the Cornplanter Seneca." Bulletin, Society for Pennsylvania Archaeology (Harrisburg, Pa.). *Pennsylvania Archaeologist* 12 (No. 3):48–53, 1942.

————.
Last Seneca Pigeon Hunts. Warren County Pennsylvania Almanac 1943, 4–5, 38. Warren, Pa.: Warren Bank and Trust Company, 1943.

————, and Deardorff, Merle H.
"The Last Passenger Pigeon Hunts of the Cornplanter Senecas." *Reprinted from Journal of the Washington Academy of Science* 33: (No. 10):289–315, (Oct. 15) 1943.

Hewitt, J. N. B.
"Seneca." In: *Bull. Bureau Amer. Ethnol.* 30(Part 2):502–508, 1910.

Houghton, F.
"The Migrations of the Seneca Nation." AA 29:241–250, 1927. n.s.

————.
"The Seneca Nation From 1655 to 1687." *Bull. Buffalo Soc. Nat. Sci.* 10:363–476, 1912.

————.
"The Traditional Origin and Naming of the Seneca Nation." *AA* 24:31–43, 1922. n.s.

Meakins, C.
Old Albert of Chemung, Forest and Stream. New York: 1920.
"An Iroquois village, probably of the Seneca, formerly on or near the site of the present Chemung, N. Y." (J. Mooney).

Parker, Arthur Caswell
"Fundamental Factors in Seneca Folk Lore." *N. Y. State Mus. Bull.* 253:49–66, 1924.

————.
History of the Seneca Indians. New York State Archaeological Associaiton, Lewis H. Morgan Chapter, Researches and Transaction, Vol. 6. 1926. 148 pp.

————.
Indian Episodes of New York State; a drama story of the Empire state. A booklet of added information about the pictorial map by this name. Rochester, N. Y.: Rochester Museum of Arts and Sciences, 1935. 35 pp., illus.

————.
The Rise of the Seneca Nation. In: *History of the Genesee Country,* L. R. Doty, ed., pp. 167-189. Chicago: 1925.

—————.
The Senecas in Their Own Homeland. In: *History of the Genesee Country*, L. R. Doty, ed., pp. 192-222. Chicago: 1925.

Schoolcraft, Henry R.
"Aboriginal Nomenclature. Senecas." *The Knickerbocker* 58:109–110, 1861.
On the mystery of the Senecas.

MYTHS—FOLKTALES—LEGENDS

Anon.
"The Legend of the White Canoe." *Merry's Museum* 50:152, May, 1863.
The human sacrifice of the Seneca chief and his daughter to the Spirit of Niagara Falls.

—————.
"The Seneca Indians." *Niles' Weekly Register* 37:19, Sept. 5, 1829.
Anecdotes dealing with their chiefs, Hard Hickory, Comstock, and Seneca John.

Cooper, James Fenimore
The Lake Gun. New York: William Farquar Payson, 1932. 54 pp., illus.
A folk-tale of the Seneca Indians of New York.

Curtin, Jeremiah
Seneca Indian Myths. New York: E. P. Dutton and Company, 1923. xii, 516 pp.

—————, and Hewitt, J. N. B.
"Seneca Fiction, Legends and Myths." *32nd Annual Report: Bureau of American Ethnology, 1910-1911*, pp. 37–815. Washington, D. C.: U. S. Government Printing Office, 1918.

Hillman, L.
"One of the Seneca Stories." *Red Man* (Carlisle, Pa.) 3:251, 1911.

Kennedy, A.
"The Coming of the New Year." *Red Man* 3:454, 1911.

Keppler, Joseph
"Some Seneca Stories." *Museum of the American Indian; Indian Notes* 6:372–376, 1929.

Parker, Arthur Caswell
Rumbling Wings and Other Indian Tales. Illustrated by Will Crawford. Garden City, N. Y.: Doubleday, Doran and Co., 1928. xii, 279 pp., illus.

—————.
Seneca Myths and Folk Tales. Buffalo: Buffalo Historical Society, 1923. xxviii, 465 pp., illus., bibl. Buffalo Historical Society, Publications, V. 27.

—————.
Skunny Wundy, and other Indian Tales. Illustrated by Will Crawford. New York: George H. Doran Co., 1926. xi, 262 pp., illus.

Patterson, S.
"Legend of the Near Star." *Red Man* 4:24, 1911.

Pletcher, D. E.
"Seven Stars of the Dipper; Seneca Indian Myth." *Nature Magazine* 25:42, (Jan.) 1935.

Sanborn, John Wentworth
Day-yu-da-gont; a poem ... and The Hemlock-Bough House. Seneca Indian Legends. Friendship, New York: J. W. Sanborn, 1905. 18 pp.

—————.
"Folklore of the Seneca Indians of North America." *Folk-Lore Journal* (London) 3:196–, 1893.
Various tales presented.

—————.
Indian Stories as Related by the Story-Teller of the Seneca Indians. ... Friendship, N. Y., 1915. 38 pp.
Contents: The man who turned into a bear.— Restored eyes.—Niagara's horseshoe fall.—"Man-with-only-two-feathers-close-together-in-his-cap."

—————.
Legends, Customs and Social Life of the Seneca Indians of Western New York. Gowanda, N. Y.: Horton and Deming, "Enterprise" print, 1878. 76 pp.

Skye, M. L.
"The Seneca Legend of the Seven Stars." *Red Man* 3:235, 1911.

Weitlander, G. W.
"Seneca Tales and Beliefs." *JAFL* 28:309–310, 1915.

BELIEFS—CUSTOMS—SPEECH— FOLK ART

Anon.
"Pretty Names among the Indians." *American Penny Magazine* 1:432, Aug. 9, 1845.
A list of the poetical names which the Seneca Indians gave their women, such as, Rose-on-the-Bush, Summer-Bird, Shining-Star, Maple-Bud, etc.

Converse, Harriet Maxwell
"The Seneca New-Year Ceremony and Other Customs." *Indian Notes, Museum of American Indian, Heye Foundation,* 7:69–89, 1930.

Crowell, S.
The Dog Sacrifice of the Seneca. In: *Indian Miscellany,* W. W. Beach, ed., pp. 323-332. Albany: 1877.

Fenton, William N.
An Outline of Seneca Ceremonies at Coldspring Longhouse. Yale University Publication in Anthropology 9. New Haven: Yale University Press, 1936.

—————.
"The Seneca Society of Faces." *Scientific Monthly* 44:215–238, 1937.

—————.
"Some Social Customs of the Modern Seneca." *Social Welfare Bulletin* 7(Part 1):4–7, 1936.

————.
"Tonawanda Longhouse Ceremonies: Ninety Years After Lewis Henry Morgan." *Bureau of American Ethnology*, Bulletin 128, pp. 140–166. Washington, D. C.: U. S. Government Printing Office, 1941.
The Tonawanda—a Seneca settlement on Tonawanda Creek in Niagara County, N. Y.

Harrington, M. R.
"Some Seneca Corn-Foods and Their Preparation." *AA* 10:575–591, 1908. n.s.

Harris, G. H.
"Root Foods of the Seneca Indians." *Proc. Rochester Acad. Sci.* 1:106–117, 1891.

Lemon, J. S.
"Seneca White Dog Feast." *JAFL* 18:317–319, 1905.

Lismer, Marjorie
"Seneca Splint Basketry." *Indian Handicrafts* No. 4. 39 pp. illus. Chilocco, Okl.

Parker, Arthur Caswell
"Secret Medicine Societies of the Seneca." *AA* 11:161–186, 1909. n.s.

————.
The Code of Handsome Lake, the Seneca Prophet. New York State Museum, Bulletin 163, 1913.

————.
The Indian How Book. New York: George H. Doran Co., 1927. ix, 335 pp.
Customs and traditions.

Seneca Indians; Home Life and Culture.
New York: Conservation Society of York County, 1944. 125 pp., illus.

Skinner, Alanson
"An Old Seneca Warclub." *Indian Notes* 3:45–47, 1926.

————.
"Seneca Charm Canoes." *Indian Notes* 3:36–38, 1926.

————.
"Some Seneca Masks and Their Uses." *Indian Notes* 2:191–207, 1925.

————.
"Some Seneca Tobacco Customs." *Indian Notes* 2:127–130, 1925.

GAMES

Parker, Arthur Caswell
"Snow-Snake as Played by the Seneca-Iroquois." *AA* 11:250–257, 1909. n.s.

MUSIC

DANCES

"Indian Dances: Seneca."
JAFL 18:317–319, 1905.

"Seneca Corn Dance."
JAFL 4:71–78, 1891.

ARRANGEMENTS

"Indian River Song" (Based on Seneca Flute Call). Gaul, Harvey: F. Fischer & Bros.: SSA.

"Seneca Condolence Dirge."
From: "Two Indian Dances." Gaul, Harvey B.: Birchard: Orchestra.

RECORDS

"Dream Song of Our Two Uncles, the Bigheads"—Seneca of Canada (Midwinter Festival Chant). Sung by Joshua Buck at Six Nations Reserve, Canada, 1941. In: Album VI: Library of Congress.   AAFS–26B1

"Individual Thanksgiving Chant."
(Ado'nwen') Seneca (Midwinter Festival Chant). Sung by Chancey Johnny John at Allegany Reservation, New York, 1941. In: Album VI: Library of Congress, 1943.
AFFS–26B4

"The Great Feather Dance" ('osto'we'gowa) (Seneca) The Creator's Songs. Sung with turtle rattle by Chancey Johnny John at Allegany Reservation, New York, 1941. In: Album VI: Library of Congress, 1943.   AAFS–26A

"The Warrior's Stomp Dance" or Trotting Dance (Seneca-Onondaga) Social Dances. Sung by Joshua Buck and Simeon Gibson at Six Nations Reserve, Canada, 1941. In: Album VI: Library of Congress, 1943.   AAFS–30A

U. S. Library of Congress. Division of Music. Folklore Section.
Seneca Songs from Coldspring Longhouse. Album 17. Folk Music of the United States . . . 1948. 5 receords.   AAFS–81/85
For contents see *Records* under Iroquois.

WINNEBAGO

FOLKLORE

GENERAL STUDIES

Barrett, S. A.
Ancient Aztalan (Wisconsin Culture). Bulletin of the Public Museum of the City of Milwaukee 13. Milwaukee: The Public Museum, 1933. 602 pp., illus.

Beckwith, Hiram W.
The Illinois and Indiana Indians. Chicago: Fergus Printing Co., 1884. (Fergus Historical Series, No. 27).

Blair, Emma Helen, ed.
The Indian Tribes of the Upper Mississippi Valley and the Region of the Great Lakes. Cleveland: The Arthur H. Clark Company, 1911. 2 vols.

Boas, Franz, and Swanton, John R.
"Siouan." In: *Bull. Bureau Amer. Ethnol.* 40 (Part 1):875–966, 1911.

Bond, Beverly W., Jr.
The Civilization of the Old Northwest. New York: The Macmillan Company, 1934.

Bowman, J. C.
Winabojo, Master of Life. Racine, Wisc.: Whitman Publishing Company, 1941.

Cooper, L. R.
The Red Cedar River. Variant of the Wisconsin Hopewell Culture. Public Museum of the City of Milwaukee, Bulletin 16, (No. 2). Milwaukee, Public Museum, 1933. 62 pp., illus.

Davidson, John N.
In Unnamed Wisconsin. Milwaukee: S. Chapman, 1895. 307 pp.

Dorsey, J. O.
"Winnebago Folklore Notes." *JAFL* 2:140, 1889.

————, and Radin, P.
"Winnebago." In: *Bull. Bureau Amer. Ethnol.* 30(Part 2):958–961, 1910.

Dustin, Fred
Report on Indian Earthworks in Ogemaw County (Michigan). Cranbrook (Bloomfield Hills, Mich.) 1932. 25 p.

Ellis, Edward S.
The Camp in the Mountains. Deerfoot Series No. 2. Philadelphia: Parter and Coates, 1887. 366 pp. illus.
  Juvenile adventure story of life with the Winnebagoes.

Fletcher, J. E.
Origin and History of the Winnebagoes. In: *Information Respecting the History, Condition, and Prospects of the Indian Tribes of the United States,* H. R. Schoolcraft, Vol. IV, pp. 227-243. Philadelphia: 1854.

Greenman, E. F.
"Indian Chiefs of Michigan" *Michigan Historical Museum* 23 (No. 3):247–249, 1939.

Hinsdale, Wilbert B.
First People of Michigan. Ann Arbor: George Wahr, 1930.

————.
Primitive Man in Michigan. Michigan Handbook Series I. Ann Arbor: University of Michigan Press, 1925.

Indian Tribes of Wisconsin
U. S. Bureau of American Ethnology, Bulletin 30. Excerpts from the Handbook of American Indians North of Mexico. Washington, D. C.: U. S. Government Printing Office, 1907–1910.

Jenks, A. E.
"The Wild Rice Gatherers of the Upper Lake." *Annual Report, Bureau Amer. Ethnol.* 19(Part 2):1013–1137, 1898.

Jipson, N. W.
"Winnebago Villages and Chieftains." *Wis. Arch.* 2:125–139, 1923. n.s.

Kirsch, Mary Moran
"The Indians of Wisconsin." *Wisconsin Blue Book,* pp. 91–112, 1931.

Lapham, Increase A.
The Antiquities of Wisconsin. Smithsonian Institution Publication No. 70. Washington, D. C.: U. S. Government Printing Office, 1852. 92 pp., 50 pl.

Larzelere, Claude S.
"The Red Man in Michigan." *Michigan History Magazine* (Lansing) 17:344–376, 1933.

Lawson, P. V.
"Habitat of the Winnebago, 1632–1832." *Proc. State Hist. Soc. Wis.* 54:144–166, 1906.

————.
"The Winnebago." *Wis. Arch.* 6:78–162, 1907.

Lilly, Eli
Prehistoric Antiquities of Indiana. Indianapolis: Indiana Historical Society, 1937.
  Contains a bibliography on Indian Archaeology.

McGee, W. J.
"The Siouan Indians." *Annual Report, Bureau Amer. Ethnol.* 15:157–204, 1894.

McKern, Will Carleton
"A Hopewell Type of Culture in Wisconsin." *AA* 31:307–312, 1929. n.s.

————.
"Regarding the Origin of Wisconsin Effigy Mounds." *AA* 31:562–564, 1929. n.s.

Michelson, Truman
"Some Notes on Winnebago Social and Political Organization." *AA* 37:446–449, 1935. n.s.

Radin, Paul
Crashing Thunder; the Autobiography of an American Indian. New York, 1926.

————.
A Semi-historical Account of the War of the Winnebago and the Foxes. Wisconsin State Historical Society, Separate 163, 1915.

————.
"The Autobiography of a Winnebago Indian." *University of California Publication in American Archaeology and Ethnology* 16, (No. 7): 381–473, 1920.
  "A representative middle-aged individual of moderate ability discusses his life in relation to the social group in which he had grown up." (P. Radin)

————.
"The Clan Organization of the Winnebago." *AA* 12:209–220, 1910. n.s.

————.
"Personal Reminiscences of a Winnebago Indian." *JAFL* 26:293–318, 1913.

————.
"The Social Organization of the Winnebago Indians." *Mus. Bull. Can. Dept. Mines.* 10:1–40, 1915.

————.
"The Winnebago Tribe." *37th Annual Report: Bureau American Ethnology, 1915–1916*, pp. 47–551, pls. 1–58, figs. 1–38. Washington, D. C.: U. S. Government Printing Office, 1923.

Skinner, Alanson
"The Winnebago Indians of Wisconsin." *So. Workman* (Hampton, Va.) 39:217–221, 1910.

————.
"Wisconsin Winnebago Collections." *Anthropological Papers, American Museum of Natural History* (New York) 4:289–297, 1910.

West, George A.
The Aboriginal Pipes of Wisconsin (Wisconsin Archaeologist). Milwaukee: Wisconsin Archaeological Society, vol. 4, (No. 3, 4), 1905.

MYTHS—FOLKTALES—LEGENDS

Brown, Charles E.
Lake Mendota Indian Legends. Madison: The Author, 1927.

————.
Wigwam Tales. Madison: The Author, 1930. 30 pp.

Dunn, Jacob Piatt
True Indian Stories, with Glossary of Indiana Indian Names. Indianapolis: Sentinel Printing Company, 1908.

Janorin, Mary W.
"The Legend of Starved Rock." *Peterson's Magazine* 30:355–357, Dec. 1856.
A legend of Chief Oronee, who lived in a region adjoining Illinois.

Lilly, Eli
"A Winnebago Myth." *Yearbook, Public Museum* (Milwaukee) 9:215–230, 1929.

McKern, W. C.
"Winnebago Dog Myths." *Yearbook Publ. Mus. City Milwaukee* 10:317–322, 1930.

————.
"A Winnebago Myth." *Yearbook Publ. Mus. City Milwaukee* 9:215–230, 1929.

Radin, Paul
"Personal Reminiscences of a Winnebago Indian." *JAFL* 26:293–318, 1913.

————.
"The Thunderbird Warclub, A Winnebago Tale." *JAFL* 44:143–166, 1931.

————.
"Winnebago Myth Cycles; Their Significance and Function. Part I; The Trickster Cycle." *Primitive Culture*, 1:8–86, 1926.

————.
"Winnebago Tales." *JAFL* 22:288–313, 1909.

BELIEFS—CUSTOMS

Anon.
"Indian Method of Courting." *The Musical Visitor* 3:396, Oct. 8, 1844.
How a brave of the Winnebago tribe courts his love with his flute; he plays of his love instead of speaking about it.

Bergen, F. D.
"Customs and Beliefs of the Winnebago Indians." *JAFL* 9:51–54, 1896.

Densmore, Frances
"Peyote Among the Winnebago" *Bureau of American Ethnology*, Washington, D. C.: U. S. Government Printing Office, 1938.

————.
"Winnebago Beliefs Concerning the Dead." *AA* 33:659–660, 1931. n.s.

Dorsey, J. O.
"A Study of Siouan Cults." *Annual Report, Bureau Amer. Ethnol.* 11:423–430, 1890.

Fletcher, J. E.
Manners and Customs of the Winnebagoes. In: *Information Respecting the History, Condition, and Prospects of the Indian Tribes of the United States*, H. R. Schoolcraft, Vol. IV, pp. 51–59. Philadelphia: 1854.

Lamere, Oliver, and Radin, Paul
"Description of a Winnebago Funeral." *AA* 13:437–445, 1911. n.s.

Radin, Paul
"A Sketch of the Peyote Cult of the Winnebago: A Study in Borrowing." *Journal of Religious Psychology* 3:1–22, 1914.

————.
"Ritual and Significance of the Winnebago Medicine Dance." *JAFL* 24:149–208, 1911.

————.
The Road of Life and Death: A Ritual Drama of The American Indian, with a foreword by Mark Van Doren. New York: Pantheon Books Inc., 1945. xiv, 345 pp. The Bollingen Series 5.

FOLK POETRY—SPEECH—FOLK ART

Carter, B. F.
"The Weaving of Winnebago Bags." *Wis. Arch.* 12:33–47, 1933. n.s.

Hayden, F. V.
"Brief Notes on the Pawnee, Winnebago and Omaha Languages." *Proceedings American Philosophical Society* 10:411–421, 1869.

Radin, Paul
"Literary Aspects of Winnebago Mythology" *JAFL* 39:18–52, 1926.

MUSIC
GENERAL STUDIES

Densmore, Frances
"Music of the Winnebago Indians." *Explorations and Field-Work of the Smithsonian Institution*, 1927, pp. 183–188.

Hofmann, Charles
"American Indian Music in Wisconsin, Summer 1946." *JAFL* 60:289–293, 1947.
The author recorded a number of the songs heard (Disc Records—161).

Radin, Paul
The Winnebago Tribe. In: *37th Annual Report of the U. S. Bureau of American Ethnology* (pp. 35–560), 1915–1916. Washington, D. C.: U. S. Government Printing Office, 1923.
Musical aspects treated.

DANCES

Radin, Paul
"The Ritual and Significance of the Winnebago Medicine Dance." *JAFL* 24:149–208, 1911.

ARRANGEMENTS

"Winnebago Lament"
Lieurance, Thurlow: Presser: Voice and piano.

"From Winnebago Land" — (in *Four Indian Themes*). Miller, H. M.: Breitkopf and Haertel: Piano.

"Winnebago Revel"
(From *Three Indian Sketches*). Skilton, Charles S.: Carl Fischer: Piano

"Moccasin Game" (From "Suite Primeval"). Part II. Skilton, Charles S.: Carl Fischer: Orchestra.

"Sunrise Song" (From "Suite Primeval") Part II. Skilton, Charles S.: Carl Fischer: Orchestra

RECORDS

"Winnebago Love Song."
Thurlow Lieurance and Clement Barone, flute-piano   VI–21972

Winnebago Songs and Dances.
In: *American Indian Songs and Dances.*
                    DISC 161
"Winnebago Friend's Song"; "Winnebago Buffalo Feast Dance Song"; "Winnebago Mocassin Game Song"; "Winnebago Morning Song"; "Winnebago Love Songs" (Flute Melodies); "Winnebago Song of the Unfaithful Women"; "Two Old Winnebago Medicine Songs"; Two old Winnebago War Songs."

OTHER TRIBES

MISCELLANEOUS STUDIES

ABITIBI

Jenkins, William H.
Notes on the Hunting Economy of the Abitibi Indians. The Catholic University of America, Anthropological Series No. 9. Washington, D. C.: Catholic University Press, 1939. 31 pp.

BUNGI

Cadzow, D. A.
"Bark Records of the Bungi Midéwin Society." *Indian Notes* 3:123–134, 1926.

Montgomery, Henry
"Prehistoric Man in Manitoba and Saskatchewan." *AA* 10:33–41, 1908. n.s.

Simms, S. C.
"Metawin Society of the Bungees or Swampy Indians of Lake Winnipeg." *JAFL* 19:330–333, 1906.

———.
"Myths of the Bungees or Swampy Indians." *JAFL* 19:334–340, 1906.

Skinner, Alanson
"Medicine Ceremony of the Menomini, Iowa and Wahpeton Dakota. With Notes on the Ceremony Among the Ponca, Bungi, Ojibwa and Potawatomi." *Indian Notes and Monograhps, Museum of the American Indian, Heye Foundation,* 4:357 pp., 1920.

CHAPPAQUIDDICK

Clough, B. C.
"Legends of Chappaquiddick." *JAFL* 31:553–554, 1918.
A former village on Martha's Vineyard.

ERIE

Banquet, Henry
Relation Historique de l'expedition contre les Indiens de l'Ohio en MDCCIXIV. Par C. G. F. Dumas. Amsterdam: 1769.

Bond, Beverly W., Jr.
The Civilization of the Old Northwest. New York: The Macmillan Co., 1934.

Downes, Randolph C.
Council Fires in the Upper Ohio, a narrative of Indian affairs in the Upper Ohio valley until 1795. Pittsburgh: University of Pittsburgh Press, 1940. 367 pp., illustrated.

Hewitt, J. N. B.
"Erie." *Bureau Amer. Ethnol. Bull.* 30(Part I):430–432, 1907.

Moorhead, Warren K.
"A Study of Primitive Culture in Ohio." Anthropological Essays, In: *Putnam Anniversary Volume.* New York: G. E. Stechert and Co., 1909.

———.
The Indian Tribes of Ohio. *Ohio State Arch. and Histor. Quart.* No. 7, 109 pp. Columbus, O.: 1898.

Parker, Arthur C.
"Excavations in an Erie Indian Village and Burial Site at Ripley, Chautauqua County, New York." *New York State Museum, Bulletin 117,* (Albany) 1907. pp. 457–554, 38 pl.

Stober, A. F.
Indian History and Legend of Pennsylvania's Picturesque Playgrounds. Scranton, Pa.: International Textbook Co., 1936.

Thwaites, R. G., ed.
The Jesuit Relations and Allied Documents. 73 vols. Cleveland, O.: 1896–1901.

Wilcox, Frank Nelson
Ohio Indian Tales. Cleveland: The Gates Press, 1934.

ILLINOIS

(*Including:* Mascouten)

Beckwith, H. W.
"The Illinois and Indiana Indians." *Fergus Historical Series* (Chicago) 27:99–106, 1884.

Carr, L.
"The Mascoutins." *Proc. Amer. Antiq. Soc.* 13:448–462, 1900. n.s.

Hamy, E. T.
"Note sur d'anciennes peintures sur peaux des Indiens Illinois." *Jour. Société des Amér.* 2:185–195, 1897.

Hilder, F. F.
"Cist Burials in Illinois." *AA* 11:46–65, 1898.

Michelson, Truman
"The Identification of the Mascoutens." *AA* 36:226–233, 1934. n.s.

———.
"Once More Mascoutens." *AA* 37:163–164, 1935. n.s.

Mooney, J., and Thomas, C.
"Illinois." *Bull. Bureau Amer. Ethnol.* 30 (Part 1):597–599, 1907.

———.
"Mascoutens." *Bull. Bureau Amer. Ethnol.* 30 (Part 1):810–812, 1907.

Passin, Herbert
"Culture Change in Southern Illinois." *Rural Sociology* 7:303–317, 1942.

Rhinear, T.
"Illinois Indians." *Hobbies* 47:102–103, 1942.

MAHICAN

Bisbee, Ernest E.
The White Mountain Scrap Book of Stories and Legends of the Crystal Hills or White Mountains of New Hampshire. Lancaster, N. H.: The Bisbee Press, 1939. 52 pp., illus.

Bolton, Reginald P.
Indian Paths in the Great Metropolis. Museum of the American Indian, Heye Foundation, (New York) 1922.

———.
Indian Life of Long Ago in the City of New York. New York: Joseph Graham, 1934. 162 pp., illus.

———.
New York City in Indian Possession. Museum of American Indian (New York): 1920.

———.
"The Indians of Washington Heights (New York City)." *Anthropological Papers, American Museum of Natural History* (New York) 3:75–109, 1909.

English, J. S.
Indian Legends of the White Mountains. Boston: Rand Avery Supply Company, 1915.

Finch, J. K.
"Aboriginal Remains on Manhattan Island." *Anthropological Papers, American Museum of Natural History* 3:63–73, 1909.

Hall, Joseph Fred
The Legend of Chocorua; a Story of the Hills of New Hampshire. Norwood, Mass., Printed by Ambrose Brothers, 1915. 23 pp.
    The legend of the last survivor of a small tribe of Indians, who, previous to 1766, inhabited the region about the town of Burton, N. H. Before Chocorua's death he is reported to have cursed the English and their cattle.

Mooney, J., and Thomas, C.
"Mahican." *Bull. Bureau Amer. Ethnol.* 30 (Part 1):786–789, 1907.

Prince, J. D.
"A Tale in the Hudson River Indian Language." *AA* 7:74–84, 1905. n.s.

Rainey, Froelich G.
"A Compilation of Historical Data Contributing to the Ethnobiography of Connecticut and Southern New England." *Bulletin, Archaeological Society of Connecticut* 3:1–89. New Haven, Conn.: Peabody Museum, 1936.

Rhinear, T.
"Religion of the Indians of Connecticut." *Hobbies* 48:103, 1943.

Skinner, Alanson
The Indians of Manhattan Island and Vicinity. Miscellaneous Publications; Guide Leaflet No. 41, 1932, 63 pp., 27 figs. (5th edition.) Publications in Anthropology. New York: American Museum of Natural History.

Speck, Frank G.
Decorative Art of Indian tribes of Connecticut. Ottawa: Government Printing Bureau, 1915. 73 pp., illus. Memoir 75; Anthropological Series, No. 10.

———.
The Legend of Wonalansett; a Tale of the White Hills. Boston: Newtowne Publishing Co., 1914. 28 pp.
    Wonalansett, a son of Passaconaway who succeeded his father as sachem of Pennacook on the Merrimac. The latter are generally classed with the Mahican.

Willoughby, Charles C.
"Dress and Ornaments of the New England Indians." *AA* 7:499–509, 1905. n.s.

MUSIC

"Twas in the Moon of Winter-Time."
(Christmas Carol of the Indians in Manhattan.)
Yon, Pietro: Galaxy Music Corp.: SATB,
TTBB, accompaniment or a cappella.

MASSACHUSET

Bradford, William
History of the Plymouth Plantation. Boston:
Little Brown, & Co., 1856. 476 pp.

Cotton, J.
"Vocabulary of the Massachusetts (or Natick)
Indian Language." *Coll. Mass. Hist. Soc.* (ser.
3) 2:147–257, 1830.

Dwight, T.
Travels in New England and New York. New
Haven: T. Dwight, 1821–22. 4 vols.

Hale, E. E.
"The Language of the Massachusetts Indians."
Records of the Past (Washington, D. C.) 4:
361–363, 1905.

Kittredge, G. L., ed.
"Letters of Samuel Lee and Samuel Sewall
Relating to New England and the Indians."
*Publications of the Colonial Society of Massa-
chusetts* 15:142–186, 1912.

Mooney, J., and Thomas, C.
"Massachuset." *Bull. Bureau Amer. Ethnol.*
30(Part 1):816–817, 1907.

Prince, J. D.
"Last Living Echoes of the Natick." *AA* 9:
493–498, 1907. n.s.

Schoolcraft, H. R.
Massachusetts Indians. In: *Information Re-
specting the History, Condition, and Prospects
of the Indian Tribes of the United States,*
H. R. Schoolcraft, ed., Vol. 1, pp. 284-299.
Philadelphia: 1851.

Trumbull, J. H.
Natick Dictionary. Bulletin 25, Bureau Amer.
Ethnol. 349 pp. 1903. Washington, D. C.

Willoughby, C. C.
"Dress and Ornaments of the New England
Indians." *AA* 7:499–508, 1905. n.s.

———.
"Houses and Gardens of the New England
Indians." *AA* 8:115–132, 1906. n.s.

———.
"Textile Fabrics of the New England Indians."
AA 7:85–93, 1905. n.s.

———.
"Wooden Bowls of the Algonquian Indians."
AA 10:423–434, 1908. n.s.

MIAMI

Beckwith, Hiram W.
The Illinois and Indiana Indians. Fergus Historical Series, No. 17. Chicago: Fergus Printing Co., 1884.

Dillon, J. B.
"The National Decline of the Miami Indians."
Indiana Historical Society Publications 1:121–
143, 1897.

Handy, C. N.
Miami. In: *Information Respecting the History,
Condition, and Prospects of the Indian Tribes
of the United States,* H. R. Schoolcraft, ed.,
Vol. II, pp. 470–481. Philadelphia: 1852.

Kinietz, W. Vernon
The Indians of the Western Great Lakes. Oc-
casional Contributions from the Museum of
Anthropology of the University of Michigan 10.
Ann Arbor: University of Michigan Press, 1941.
427 pp.

Lilly, Eli
Prehistoric Antiquities of Indiana. Indianapolis: Indiana Historical Society, 1937. 293 pp.,
illus.

Mary Celeste, Sister
"The Miami Indians Prior to 1700." *Mid America* 16:225–234, 1934. n.s.

Mooney, J., and Thomas, C.
"Miami." *Bull. Bureau Amer. Ethnol.* 30(Part
1):852–855, 1907.

Robertson, R. S.
"Burial Among the Miamis." *Amer. Antiq.*
2:54–55, 1879.

Smith, G. H.
"Three Miami Tales." *JAFL* 52:194–208, 1939.

Thornton, W.
"Miamis." *Trans. Coll. Amer. Antiq. Soc.* 2:
305–367, 1836.

Trowbridge, C. C. (Vernon Kinietz, ed.)
Meearmeear Traditions. Occasional Contribu-
tions Museum of Anthropology, University of
Michigan. Ann Arbor: 1938. 91 pp.

Voegelin, C. F.
"Shawnee Stems and the Jacob P. Dunn
Miami Dictionary." *Prehistory Research Series,
Indiana Historical Society* (Philadelphia) 1:
63–108, 135–167, 345–406, 409–478, 1938–
1940.

Winger, Otho
The Last of the Miamis. Elgin, Ill.: The Elgin
Press, 1936.

Young, Calvin M.
*Little Turtle, the Great Chief of the Miami
Indian Nation.* Indianapolis: Sentinel Printing
Company, 1917.

MOOR

Weslager, C. A.
*Delaware's Forgotten Folk: the Story of the
Moors and Nanticokes.* Phila., Pa.: University
of Pennsylvania Press, 1943. 215 pp., 22 photographs, 4 figs.
Deals with the people of mixed Indian and white
blood.

NIPMUCK

Mooney, J.
"Nipmuc." *Bull. Bureau Amer. Ethnol.* 30 (Part 2):74–75, 1910.

Speck, Frank G.
"A Note on the Hassanemisco Band of Nipmuc." *Bulletin of the Massachusetts Archaeological Society* (Boston, Mass.) 4:49–56, 1943.

——————.
"Reflections Upon the Past and Present of the Massachusetts Indians." *Bulletin of the Massachusetts Archaeological Society* 4:33–38, 1943.

PENNACOOK

Johnson, Frederick
"The Indians of New Hampshire." *Appalachia* 6(No. 7):3–15, 1940.

Mooney, J., and Thomas, C.
"Pennacook." *Bull. Bureau Amer. Ethnol.* 30 (Part 2):270, 1910.

Schoolcraft, H. R.
Pennacooks. In: *Information Respecting the History, Conditiion, and Prospects of the Indian Tribes of the United States*, H. R. Schoolcraft, ed., Vol. 5, pp. 217-237. Philadelphia: 1852.

PIANKASHAW

Baker, Jessie E.
"Piankishaw Tales." *JAFL* 44:182–191, 1931.

Champney, Stella M.
"Michigan Indian Trails: Legends of Nenaboo-shoo, the Trickster." *Michigan History Magazine* 19 (No. 2) 3:215–229, 1935.

Mooney, J.
"Piankashaw." *Bull. Bureau Amer. Ethnol.* 30 (Part 2):240–241, 1910.

POTAWATOMI

Beckwith, Hiram W.
The Illinois and Indiana Indians. Fergus Printing Series, No. 27. Chicago: Fergus Printing Company, 1884.

Blair, Emma Helen, ed.
The Indian Tribes of the Upper Mississippi Valley and the Region of the Great Lakes. Cleveland: The Arthur H. Clark Company, 1911. 2 vols.

Buechner, C. B.
"The Pokagons." *Indiana Historical Society Publications* 10:281–340, 1933.

Caton, J. D.
"The Last of the Illinois and a Sketch of the Pottawatomies." *Fergus Historical Series* (Chicago) 3:3–30, 1876.

Johnson, F.
"Notes on the Ojibwa and Potawatomi of the Parry Island Reservation." *Indian Notes* 6: 193–216, 1929.

Lawson, P. V.
"The Potawatomi." *Wis. Arch.* 19:41–116, 1920.

Metzdorf, W.
The Potawatomi. In: *The Indian Tribes of the Upper Mississippi Valley*, E. H. Blair, ed. Vol. 2, pp. 287–297. Cleveland: 1912.

Michelson, T.
"The Identification of the Mascoutens." *AA* 36:226–233, 1934. n.s.

——————.
"The Linguistic Classification of the Potawatomi." *Proc. Natl. Acad. Sci.* 1:450–452, 1915.

——————, and Hewitt, J. N. B.
"Potawatomi." *Bull. Bureau. Amer. Ethnol.* 30(Part 2):289–293, 1910.

Quimby, G. I.
"Some Notes on Kinship and Kinship Terminology Among the Potawatomi of the Huron." *Papers Mich. Acad. Sci. Arts and Letters* 25:553–563, 1939.

Smet, P. J. de
Legend of the Potawotomie Indians. In: *Early Western Travels*, R. G. Thwaites, ed. Vol. 29, pp. 373–380. Cleveland: 1906.

Smith, H. H.
"Among the Potawatomi." *Yearbook of the Public Mus. City of Milwaukee* 5:68–76, 1925.

——————.
"Ethnobotany of the Forest Potawatomi Indians." *Bull. Public Mus. City of Milwaukee* 7:1–230, 1933.

Skinner, Alanson
"Mascouten Mythology." *Bulletin of the Public Museum of the City of Milwaukee* 6, No.3: 327–411, 1924.

——————.
Medicine Ceremony of the Menominee, Iowa and Wahpetan Dakota. With notes on the ceremony among the Ponca, Bungi, Ojibwa and Potawatomi. Indian Notes and Monographs, Museum of the American Indian, Heye Foundation 4:357 pp., 1920.

——————.
"The Mascoutens or Prairie Potawatomi Indians. Part I: Social Life and Customs." *Bulletin of the Public Museum of the City of Milwaukee* 6, No. 1:1–262, 1924.

West, George A.
The Aboriginal Pipes of Wisconsin (Wisconsin Archaeologist). Milwaukee: Wisconsin Archaeologist Society, vol. 4 (Nos. 3, 4) 1905.

Winger, Otho
The Potawatomi Indians. Elgin, Ill.: The Elgin Press, 1939.

Wintemberg, W. J.
"Indian Village Sites in the Counties of Oxford and Waterloo, Ontario." *Archaeological Report* 12:37–40, 1900 (1901), Toronto.

———.
"Some Ceremonial Implements from Western Ontario." *Records of the Past* (Washington) 1:150–156, 1902.

SHINNECOCK

Carr, Ensign Lloyd G., and Westey, Carlos
"Surviving Folktales and Herbal Lore Among the Shinnecock Indians of Long Island." *JAFL* 58:113–123, 1945.
Tales of Wandering Ghosts and Spirits, and a list of botanical curatives.

Douglas, F. H.
"Long Island Indian Tribes." *Denver Art Museum Leaflet Series* 49:1–4, 1932.

———.
"Long Island Indian Tribes." *Denver Art Museum Leaflet Series* 49:1–4, 1932.

Harrington, M. R.
"An Ancient Village Site of the Shinnecock Indians." *Anthropological Papers:* Vol. 22: 1924, pp. 227–283, 39 figs. Publications in Anthropology. New York: The American Museum of Natural History.

———.
"Past and Present of the Shinnecock Indians." *Southern Workman* 32:282–289, 1903.

———.
"Shinnecock Notes." *JAFL* 16:37–39, 1903.

Willis, Thomas
The Following Narrative of the Exercise and Experience, Together with a Remarkable Vision of an Indian Woman, yet living on the South Side of Long Island . . . New York: 1820. 7 pp.

SUSQUEHANNOCK (Conestoga)

Alsop, George
A Character of the Province of Maryland. Also a small treatise on the wild and naked Susquehanokes of Maryland. New York: William Gowans, 1869.
Their customs, manners, absurdities and religion.

Eshleman, H. F.
Annals of the Susquehannocks. Lancaster: 1908. 415 pp.

Guss, Abraham L.
Early Indian History on the Susquehanna. Harrisburg: L. S. Hart, 1883. 32 pp.

Heckewelder, John Gottlieb Ernestus
History, Manners and Customs of the Indian Nations who once inhabited Pennsylvania and neighboring states. Phila. Pa.: The Historical Society of Pennsylvania, 1876. 465 pp.

Hewitt, J. N. B.
"Conestoga." *Bull. Bureau Amer. Ethnol.* 30 (Part 1):335–337, 1907.

———.
"Susquehanna." *Bull. Bureau Amer. Ethnol.* 30(Part 2):653–659, 1910.

Landis, D. H.
A Brief Description of Indian Life and Trade of the Susquehannock Indians. Lancaster: 1929. 48 pp.

Murray, E.
"The Noble Savage." *Scientific Monthly* 36: 251–257, 1933.

Murray, Louise Welles
Selected Manuscripts of Gen. John S. Clark Relating to the Aboriginal History of the Susquehanna. Wilkes Barre: Society for Pennsylvania Archaeology I, 1931.

Nelson, William
The Indians of New Jersey with Some Notice of Indian Place Names. Paterson: Press Publishing Company, 1894. 168 pp.

Purdy, Truman H.
Legends of the Susquehanna, and other poems. Philadelphia: J. B. Lippincott Co., 1888. 197 pp., illus.

Stober, A. F.
Indian History and Legends of Pennsylvania's Picturesque Playgrounds. Scranton, Pa.: International Textbook Company, 1936.

Tahament, R.
"The Grasshopper's War." *Carlisle Arrow* 4:29, 1911.

TEMISCAMING

Speck, Frank G.
Myths and folk-lore of the Timiskaming Algonquin and Timiskaming Ojibwa. Ottawa: Gov't. Printing Bureau, 1915. 87 p., illus., Canada Geological Survey, Memoir 71, no. 9.
"Temiscaming—a band of Algonkin, closely related to the Abittibi, formerly living about Temiscaming Lake, Quebec."

TETES DE BOULES

Davidson, D. S.
"Decorative Art of the Tetes de Boule of Quebec." *Indian Notes and Monographs* 10: 115–153, 1928.

———.
"Notes on Tetes de Boule Ethnology." *AA* 30:18–46, 1928. n.s.

————.
"Some Têtes de Boules Tales." *JAFL* 41:262–275, 1928.

Guinard, J. E.
"Witiko Among the Tetes-de-Boule." *Primitive Man* 3:69–71, 1930.

Mooney, J.
"Tetes de Boules." *Bull. Bur. Amer. Ethnol.* 30(Part 2):735–736, 1910.

WAMPANOAG

Anon.
"Origin of Nantucket—An Indian Tradition." *Columbian Magazine* 1:525, July, 1787.
A legend explaining the origin.

Chase, H. E.
"Notes on the Wampanoag Indians."*Annual Reports Board of Regents Smithson. Inst;* 1883, pp. 878-907.

————.
"Origin of Martha's Vineyard Indians." *JAFL* 11:162–164, 1898.

J.
"Indian Tradition." *U. S. Literary Gazette* 4:357–361, Aug. 1826.
A whimsical essay on the origin of Nantucket Island according to the Indian legend.

Knight, W. L.
"Wampanoag Indian Tales." *JAFL* 38:134–137, 1925.
New England Tribe. Narraganset Bay, Nantucket and Martha's Vineyard.

Miller, W. J.
Notes Concerning the Wampanoag Tribe of Indians. Providence: 1880. 148 pp.

Mooney, J.
"Wampanoag." *Bull. Bur. Amer. Ethnol.* 30 (Part 2):903–904, 1910.

Speck, Frank G.
"Mythology of the Wampanoag." *El Palacio* 25:83–86, 1928.

Sylvester, H. M.
Indian Wars of New England. Boston: W. B. Clarke Company, 1910. 3 vols.

Tandaquidgeon, Gladys
"Notes on the Gay Head Indians of Mass." *Indian Notes, Museum of the American Indian* Heye Foundation 7:1–27, 1930.

Weeks, Alvin G.
Massasoit of the Wampanoags. Fall River: The Plimpton Press, 1920. 270 pp.

THE SOUTHEASTERN AREA

THE SOUTHEASTERN AREA
FOLKLORE

GENERAL STUDIES

Abel, Annie Heloise
The Slaveholding Indians. Cleveland: The Arthur H. Clark Co., 1915. 394 pp., bibl.

Adair, James (Trader with the Indians)
The History of the American Indians; particularly those nations adjoining the Mississippi, East and West Florida, Georgia, North Carolina and South Carolina, and Virginia. An account of origin, language, manners, religious and civil customs, punishments, conduct in war and domestic life, etc. London: Printed for E. and C. Dilly, 1775. vi, 464 pp., front. (map).

Bandelier, A. F.
Final Report of Investigations Among the Indians of the Southeastern United States. Carried on mainly in the Years from 1880–1885. Part II, Papers of the Archaeological Institute of America, American Series IV, Cambridge, 1892.

Barcia Carballido y Zúñiga, Andres González de
Ensayo cronológico para la historia general de la Florida. . . Madrid: . . . N. Rodriguez Franco, 1723. 20 pp. + 366 pp.

Berquin-Duvallon, M.
Travels in Louisiana and the Floridas: From the French, with notes by J. Davis. New York: 1806. 181 pp.

Biedma, L. F. de
A Narrative of the Expedition of Hernando de Soto. In: *Historical Collections of Louisiana and Florida,* B. F. French, ed., Vol. 2, pp. 97–109. Philadelphia: 1850.

Brackenridge, Henry Marie
Views of Louisiana, Together With a Voyage Up the Missouri River in 1811. Pittsburgh: Cramer, Spear & Eichbaum. 1814. 304 pp.

Brickell, John
The Natural History of North Carolina. With an account of the trade, manners and customs of the Christian and Indian inhabitants. Dublin, 1737.

Champlain, Samuel de
Voyages of Samuel de Champlain. Trans. from French by Charles Pomeroy Otis. Boston: Prince Society Publications, (3 vols.) vols. 11, 12, 13, 1878–1882.

Charlevoix, Pierre François Xavier de
Historie et Descriptione de la Nouvelle France . . . Paris: Chez Rollin, fils, 1744. 6 vols.

————.
History and General Description of New France. J. M. Shea, ed. New York: J. G. Shea, 1866–1872. 6 vols.

————.
Journal of a Voyage to North America . . . L. P. Kellog, ed. Chicago: The Caxton Club, 1923. 2 vols.

Cotten, Corinne
Reel Foot; or, Indian Blankets and Blue Bonnets in Story Drama; a symphony of words in red and white and blue. Abilene, Texas: Abilene Printing & Stationery Co., 1936. 81 pp., illus.
Chiefly Choctaw and Chikasaw lore.

Coxe, D.
A Description of the English Province of Carolina. In: *Historical Collections of Louisiana and Florida,* B. F. French, ed., Vol. 2, pp. 223–276. Philadelphia: 1850.

Cushman, H. B.
History of the Choctaw, Chickasaw and Natchez Indians. Greenville, Tex.: 1899.

Deuel, T.
"Basic Cultures of the Mississippi Valley." *AA* 37:429–445, 1935. n.s.

Ford, J. A., and Wiley, G. R.
"An Introduction to the Prehistory of the Eastern United States." *AA* 43:325–363, 1941. n.s.

Garcilaso de la Vega
Le Florida del Inca . . . Madrid: N. Rodriguez Franco, 1723. 2 pts. in 1 vol.

Gentleman of Elvas
A Narrative of the Expedition of Hernando de Soto. In: *Historical Collections of Louisiana and Florida,* B. F. French, ed., Vol. 2, pp. 113–120. Philadelphia: 1850.

Gray, L. H.
"Muskhogeans." In: *Encyclopedia of Religion and Ethics,* John Hastings, ed. Vol. 9, pp. 61–62. New York: 1917.

Haas, Mary R.
"Southeastern Indian Folklore." *JAFL* 60:403–406, 1947.

Harpe, B. de la
Historical Journal of the Establishment of the French in Louisiana. In: *Historical Collections of Louisiana and Florida,* B. F. French, ed., Vol. 3, pp. 9–118. Philadelphia: 1851.

Jones, Charles C.
Antiquities of the Southern Indians, Particularly of the Georgia Tribes. New York: 1873.

Joutel, Henri
Joutel's Journal of La Salle's Last Voyage, 1684-7. Albany: J. McDonough, 1906. 258 pp.

La Page du Pratz
Histoire de la Louisiane. Paris: 1758. 3 vols.
Published in an English translation, in London,
in 1763. 2 vols.

Le Moyne, Jacques
Narrative of Le Moyne, an Artist Who Accompanied the French Expedition to Florida under
Laudonnière, 1564. Translated from the Latin
of De Bry. Boston: 1875.

Lorant, Stefan
The New World. The First Pictures of America.
Made by John White and Jacques Le Moyne
and Engraved by Theodore de Bry, with Con-
temporary Narratives of the Huguenot Settle-
ment in Florida, 1562–1565 and the Virginia
Colony, 1585–1590. Edited and Annotated by
Stefan Lorant. New York: Duell, Sloan and
Pearce, 1946. 292 pp.
    The Florida narratives of Le Moyne and Le Chal-
    leux are presented here, together with an infor-
    mative essay by the present editor. And here are
    the more than forty engravings of life in Florida
    made by de Bry. Altogether the volume contains
    eighty engravings in black and white and sixty-
    four plates in color.

Lucius
"A Few Observations on the Western and
Southern Indians." *American Museum* 5:144,
Feb., 1789 (NYU).

Meyer, W. E.
"Indian Trails of the Southwest." *Annual
Report Bureau Amer. Ethnol.* 42:727–857,
1925.

Moorehead, Warren King
"Prehistoric Culture Areas East of the Rocky
Mountains." In: *Proceedings of the 23rd
Session of the International Congress of Ameri-
canists,* pp. 47–52, 1928.

Morgan, Lewis H.
Ancient Society, or Researches in the Lines
of Human Progress From Savagery Through
Barbarism to Civilization. New York: Henry
Holt and Company, 1877. (Part 2, chapt. 6).

Parkman, Francis J.
La Salle and the Discovery of the Great West.
France and England in North America. A
series of historical narratives. Boston: Little,
Brown and Company, 1886. xxv, 483 pp., 2
maps (incl. front.).

Pickett, Albert James
*History of Alabama and Incidentally of Georgia
and Mississippi, from the Earliest Period.* Sheffield, Ala.: R. C. Randolph, 1896. 669 pp., front
(port.), illus., fold. map.

*Proceedings of the Mississippi Valley Histori-
cal Association for the Year 1908–1909,* vol. II,
ed. by Benjamin F. Shambaugh. Cedar Rapids,
Iowa: The Torch Press, 1910. 283 pp.

Rogers, Robert
A Concise Account of North America . . .
London: . . . J. Milan, 1765. vii, 264 pp.

Shetrone, H. C.
The Mound Builders. New York, London: D.
Appleton and Co., 1930.

Shipp, Bernard
The History of Hernando de Soto and Florida;
or Record of Events of Fifty-Six Years, from
1512 to 1568. Philadelphia: Collins, Print.,
1881. xii, 689 pp.

Speck, Frank G.
"Siouan Tribes of the Carolines as Known from
Catawba, Tutelo, and Documentary Sources."
AA 37:201–225, 1935. n.s.

————.
"Some Outlines of Aboriginal Culture in the
Southeastern States." *AA* 9:287–296, 1907, n.s.

Stirling, M. W.
Florida Cultural Affiliations in Relation to
Adjacent Areas. In: *Essays in Anthropology
Presented to A. L. Kroeber,* (pp. 351–357).
Berkeley: University of California Press, 1936.

Swanton, John Reed
"An Indian Social Experiment and Some of its
Lessons." *The Scientific Monthly,* 31:368–376,
October, 1930.

————.
"Aboriginal Culture of the Southeast, and
Indian Trails of the Southeast, by William
Edward Myer." In: *42nd Ethnological Report.
1924–1925,* pp. 673–857, maps. Washington
D. C.: U. S. Gov't. Printing Office, 1928.

————.
Early History of the Eastern Siouan Tribes. In:
*Essays in Anthropology Presented to A. L.
Kroeber,* (pp. 371–381). Berkeley: University
of California Press, 1936.

————.
"Ethnological Value of the de Soto Narratives."
AA 34:570–590, 1932. n. s.

————.
*Indian Tribes of the Lower Mississippi Valley
and Adjacent Coast of the Gulf of Mexico.*
Bureau of American Ethnology Bulletin 43.
Washington D. C.: U. S. Gov't. Printing Office,
1911.

————.
"Notes on the Cultural Province of the Southeast." *AA* 37:373–385, 1935. n. s.

————.
The Indians of the Southeastern United States.
Smithsonian Institute. BAE, Bull. 137. Washington, D. C.: Government Printing Office,
1946. xiii, 943 pp. bibl., index, figures, maps,
107 plates.

————.
"The Relation of the Southwest to General
Cultural Problems of American Pre-History."
*National Research Council, Conference on
Southern Pre-History,* (pp. 60–74). Washing-
ton: 1932.

—————.
"Southeastern Indians of History." *National Research Council, Conference on Southern Pre-History*, (pp. 5–20). Washington: 1932.

—————.
"The Southern Contacts of the Indians North of the Gulf of Mexico." *Inter. Congr. Amer.* 20 (Part 1) :53–59, 1922.

Thruston, Gales Phillips
The Antiquities of Tennessee and the Adjacent State, and the state of the aboriginal society in the scale of civilization represented by them. Cincinnati: R. Clarke Co., 1897. 369 pp., front. illus. places, plates, 2nd ed.

Weer, Paul
Preliminary Notes on the Muskhogean Family. Indianapolis: Indiana Historical Society. Prehistory Research Series, Vol. 1, No. 7, 1939.

Wenhold, L. L.
"A 17th Century Letter of Gabriel Diáz Vara Calderon." *Smithson. Miscel. Coll.* 95 (Part 16) :1–14, 1936.

Willoughby, C. C.
Notes on the History and Symbolism of the Muskhogeans. In: *Etowan Papers*, W. K. Moorehead, ed., (pp. 7–67). New Haven: Yale University Press, 1932.

MYTHS—FOLKTALES—LEGENDS

Brinton, Dr. Daniel Garrison
"The National Legend of the Chahta-Muskogee Tribes." *Historical Magazine* (Second Series) 7:118–126, 1870. (Morrisania, N. Y.).

Speck, Frank G., and Moses, Jesse
The Celestial Bear Comes Down to Earth. Reading Public Museum and Art Gallery, Scientific Publication 7, xiv, 91 pp., pls., figs. Reading, Pa.: Reading Public Museum and Art Gallery, 1945.

Swanton, John R.
"Animal Stories from the Indians of the Muskhogean Stock (Natchez, Alabama, Koasati, Hichiti, and Creek). *JAFL* 26:193–218, 1913.

—————.
Myths and Tales of the Southeastern Indians. Bureau of American Ethnology, Bulletin 88. x, 275 pp. Washington, D. C.: U. S. Gov't. Printing Office, 1929.
Myths and tales of the Creek, Hichiti, Alabama, Koosati, and Natchez Indians.

CUSTOMS—BELIEFS

Bartram, William
Travels through North and South Carolina, Georgia, East and West Florida, the Cherokee Country, the Extensive Territories of the Muscogulges, or Creek Confederacy and the Country of the Choctaws. London: 1792.
An account of the soil and natural production of those regions together with observations on the manners of the Indians.

Battle, H. B.
"The Domestic Use of Oil Among the Southern Aborigines." *AA* 24:171–182, 1922. n.s.

Bushnell, David I., Jr.
Aboriginal Forms of Burial in Eastern United States. In: *Holmes Anniversary Volume*, (pp. 31–43). Washington, D. C.: 1916.

—————.
Native Cemeteries and Forms of Burial East of the Mississippi. Bulletin 71, Bureau of American Ethnology. Washington, D. C.: U. S. Gov't. Printing Office, 1920.

Knowles, N.
"The Torture of Captives by the Indians of Eastern North America." *Proc. Amer. Philo. Soc.* 87:151–225, 1940.

MacLeod, W. C.
"Priests, Temples, and the Practice of Mummification in Southeastern North America." *Inter. Congr. Amer.* 12 (Part 2) :207–230, 1926.

Thomas, Cyrus
"Curious Customs and Strange Freaks of the Mound Builders." *AA* 1:353–355, 1888.

Voegelin, Erminie W.
"Mortuary Customs of the Shawnee and Other Eastern Tribes." In: *Indiana Historical Society, Prehistoric Research Series* 2:227–444, tables. Indianapolis: Indiana Historical Society, 1944.

Waring, A. J., Jr., and Holder, P.
"A Prehistoric Ceremonial Complex in the Southeastern United States." *AA* 47 (No. 1) : 1–34, 1945. n.s.
An analysis of the complex of specific motifs and ceremonial objects.

FOLK MEDICINE

Taylor, Mrs. Lyda Averill (Paz)
Plants Used as Curatives by Certain Southeastern Tribes. Cambridge, Mass.: Botanical Museum of Harvard University, 1940, 75 pp.

FOLK ART—SPEECH—GAMES

Carr, L.
"Dress and Ornaments of Certain American Indians." *Proc. Amer. Antiq. Soc.* 11:381–454, 1897.

Gatschet, A. S.
"The Timucua Language." *Proceedings of the American Philosophical Society* 18:473, 1880.

Griffin, J. B.
"Aboriginal Methods of Pottery Manufacture in the Eastern United States." *Penn. Arch.* 5:19–24, 1935.

Henshaw, Henry W.
"Animal Carvings from the Mounds of the Mississippi Valley." In: *2nd Annual Report: Bureau of American Ethnology 1880–1881,*

pp. 123–166, figs. 4–35. Washington, D. C.: U. S. Gov't. Printing Office, 1883.

Manatee, Taucan,, Paroquet; Knowledge of tropical animals by Mound Builders; skill in sculpture of the Mound Builders; animal mounds, totem poles, etc.

Holmes, W. H.
"Aboriginal Pottery of the Eastern United States." *20th Annual Report: Bureau American Ethnology, 1898–1899,* pp. 15–200: pls. CLXVII, figs. 1–79. Washington, D. C.: U. S. Gov't. Printing Office, 1903.

———.

"Prehistoric Textile Fabrics of the Eastern United States." *Annual Report Bureau Amer. Ethnol.* 13:9–46, 1896.

———.

"Prehistoric Textile Fabrics of the United States." *Annual Report Bureau Amer. Ethnol.* 3:393–425, 1882.

Jones, Charles Colcock
Antiquities of the Southern Indians, particularly of the Georgia Tribes. New York: D. Appleton & Co., 1873. 532 pp.

Nuttal, Zelia
Comparison between Etowan, Mexican, and Mayan Designs. Reprinted from: *The Explorations of the Etowan Site in Georgia,* by Warren King Moorhead (pp. 137–144). New Haven: Yale University Press (for Phillips Academy) 1932.

Pilling, James Constantine
"Bibliography of the Muskhogean Languages." In: *Bureau of American Ethnology Bulletin 1,* pp. 1–114. Washington D. C.: U. S. Gov't. Printing Office, 1899.

Speck, Frank G.
Gourds of the Southeastern Indians; A Prolegomenon on the Lagenaria Gourd in the Culture of the Southeastern Indians. Boston, Mass.: New England Gourd Society, 1941.

———.

"Some Comparative Traits of the Muskogian Languages." *AA* 9:470–484, 1907. n.s.

Swanton, John R.
"A Point of Resemblance Between the Ball Game of the Southeastern Indians and the Ball Games of Mexico and Central America. *Jour. Wash. Acad. Sci.* 19:304–307, 1929.

———.

Unclassified Languages of the Southeast." *Inter. Jour. Amer. Ling.* 1:47–49, 1917.

Thomas, Cyrus
Work in Mound Exploration of the Bureau of Ethnology. Bureau of American Ethnology, Bull. 4, pp. 1–15, 1 fig. Washington, D. C.: U. S. Gov't. Printing Office, 1887.

Toomey, T. N.
"Proper Names from the Muskhogean Languages." *Bulletin of the Hervas Laboratories of American Linguistics* (St. Louis) 3:1–31, 1917.

Voegelin, C. F.
"Internal Relationships of Siouan Languages." *AA* 43:246–249, 1941. n.s.

Willoughby, Charles C.
"Analysis of the Decorations Upon Pottery from the Mississippi Valley." *JAFL* 10:9–20, 1897.

———.

"Antler-Pointed Arrows of the Southeastern Indian." *AA* 3:431–438, 1901. n. s.

MUSIC

GENERAL STUDIES

Bushnell, David I.
Dances and Music. In: *The Choctaws of Bayou Lacomb St. Tammany Parish Louisiana.* Washington, D. C.: U. S. Gov't. Printing Office, 1909.

Densmore, Frances
"The Alabama Indians and Their Music." *TFSP* 13:270–293, 1937.

———.

"A Search for Songs Among the Chitimacha Indians in Louisiana." Bulletin 133. Anthropological Papers, No. 19. of the Bureau of American Ethnology, pp. 5–15, pls. 1–4. Washington, D. C.: U. S. Gov't. Printing Office, 1883.

———.

"A Study of Indian Music in the Gulf States." *AA* 36:386–388, 1934, n. s.

Jones, Charles C.
Music and Musical Instruments. In: *Antiquities of the Southern Indian, Particularly of the Georgia Tribes.* (Chapter IV). New York: D. Appleton & Company, 1873.

MacCauley, Clay
"The Seminole Indians of Florida." *United States Bureau of American Ethnology, 5th Annual Report,* pp. 469–531, 1883–1884. Washington, D. C.: U. S. Gov't. Printing Office, 1887.

Speck, Frank G.
"Ceremonial Songs of the Creek and Yuchi Indians," with music transcribed by Jacob D. Sapir. University of Pennsylvania Museum, Anthropological Publication 1 (No. 1):155–245, 1911. Philadelphia: University Museum, 1911.

———.

"Ethnology of the Yuchi Indians." *University of Pennsylvania Museum Anthropological Publications* 1:1–154. Philadelphia: Published by the University Museum, 1909.

Voegelin, Erminie Wheeler
"Shawnee Musical Instruments." *AA* 44:463–475, 1942.
Discusses rattles and drums.

Wilson, Minnie Moore
The Seminoles of Florida. New York: Moffat, Yard & Company, 1911.
Discussion of music, p. 116.

ARRANGEMENTS

Choral

Bliss, Paul
The Mound Builders. An Indian Cantata. Cincinnati: Willis Music Co. For Chorus, Soprano, and Bass or Baritone.

RECORDS

Herzog, George
"South-Eastern Area." Records Contained in American Collections. *American Council of Learned Societies,* (Washington, D. C.) Bulletin 24:29–30, 1936.

U.S. Library of Congress. Division of Music. Folklore Section.
See Indian Records in the Archives of American Folksong.   AAFS–LC

————.
Tonkawa Indian Music. Recorded by Prof. Martha Lincoln of Phillips University, Enid, Okla.   AAFS–LC

ALIBAMU

FOLKLORE

GENERAL STUDIES

Bludworth, G. T.
"How the Alabamas Came Southward." *TFSP* 13:298–299, 1937.

Densmore, Frances
"The Alabama Indians and Their Music." *TFSP* 13:270–293, 1937.
Historical background of the Alabamas in Big Sandy Village, Texas.

Gatschet, A. S., and Thomas, C.
"Alibamu." *Bull. Bureau Amer. Ethnol.* 30 (Part 1):43–44, 1907.

Harrington, M. R.
"Among Louisiana Indians." *Southern Workman* 37:656–661, 1908.

Smither, H.
"The Alabama Indians of Texas." *Southwestern Hist. Quart.* 36:83–108, 1932.

Swanton, John R.
"Early History of the Creek Indians and Their Neighbors." *Bull. Bureau Amer. Ethnol.* 73:131–141, 191–207, 1922.

Wade, Mary Donaldson
The Alabama Indians of East Texas. Livingston, Tex.: Polk County Enterprise, 1936. 24 pp., illus.

MYTHS—FOLKTALES—LEGENDS

Heard, E.
"Two Tales from the Alabamas." *TFSP* 13:294–297, 1937.

Lusk, Leila Fearn
Chatu-Huchi; or The Painted Rock and other Alabama Legends. Dallas, Texas: The Kaleidograph Press, 1940. 50 pp., illus.
Contents: Chatu-Huchi, or The Painted Rock. Econhutke, or The Silver Mountain. The Bride of Cotaco Falls. Ittachomah, Cave of the Broken Arrows.

Martin, Howard N.
Folktales of the Alabama-Coushata Indians. Livingston, Texas.: Hoeard N. Martin, 1946. viii, 75 pp.

MUSIC

GENERAL STUDIES

Densmore, Frances
"The Alabama Indians and Their Music." *TFSP* 13:270–293, 1937.
Description of their music, dances and musical examples.

CATAWBA

FOLKLORE

GENERAL STUDIES

Ardrey, W. B.
"The Catawba Indians." *Amer. Antiq.* 16:266–269, 1894.

Brickell, John
The Natural History of North Carolina . . . Dublin: James Carson, 1737. xiv, 417 pp. (pp. 277–408).

Briggs, J. E.
"Wisaka." *The Palimpsest* (Iowa State University) 7;97–112.
"Lederer (1672) says they were subject to and might be considered a part of the Catawba."

Green, Edwin Luther
Indians of South Carolina. Columbia, S. C.: University Press, 1920.

Lawson, John
History of Carolina. London: T. Warner and Co., 1718.
Containing the exact description and natural history of the country: together with the present state thereof, and a journal of a thousand miles travelled thro' several nations of Indians, with account of their customs, etc. Reprint: Raleigh, N. C.: O. H. Percy and Co., 1860, 390 pp.

Milling, Chapman J.
Red Carolinians. Chapel Hill: University of North Carolina Press, 1940. 438 pp., illus.

Mooney, James
"Catawba." *Bull. Bureau Amer. Ethnol.* 30 (Part 1):213–216, 1907.

Scaife, H. L.
"History and Condition of the Catawba Indians."*Publications of the Indian Rights Association,* ser. 2, 21:1–24, 1896. (Philadelphia).

Speck, Frank G.
Catawba Hunting, Trapping and Fishing. Joint Publications No. 2 of the University of Pennsylvania, the Philadelphia Anthropological Society. Philadelphia: University Museum, 1946. 42 pp. 34 figures, bibl.

————.
Catawaba Texts. In: *Columbia University Contributions to Anthropology 24.* New York: Columbia University Press, 1934. xvii, 91 pp.

————.
"Catawba Texts and Folklore." *JAFL* 26:319–330, 1913.

————.
"Siouan Tribes of the Carolinas." *AA* 37:201–225, 1935. n.s.

————.
"The Question of Matrilineal Descent in the Southeastern Siouan Area." *AA* 40:1–12, 1938.

Swanton, John R.
"Catawba Notes." *Journal of the Washington Academy of Science* 8:623–629.

FOLKTALES

Speck, Frank G., and Carr, L. G.
"Catawba Folk Tales from Chief Sam Blue." *JAFL* 60:79–84, 1947.

BELIEFS—CUSTOMS—FOLK MEDICINE

Harrington, M. R.
"Catawba Potters and their Work." *AA* 10:399–408, 1908. n.s.

Speck, Frank G.
"Catawba Herbals and Curative Practices." *JAFL* 57:37–51, 1944.

————.
Catawba Medicines and Curative Practices." In: *Twenty-Fifth Anniversary Studies,* D. S. Davidson ed., (pp. 179–197). Publication Philadelphia Anthropological Society, Vol. I, 235 pp. Philadelphia, Pa.: University of Pennsylvania Press, 1937.

————.
"Catawba Religious Beliefs, Mortuary Customs, and Dances." *Primitive Man* (Washington, D. C.) 12 (No. 2):21–57, 1939.

————, and Schaeffer, C. E.
"Catawba Kinship and Social Organization With a Resumé of the Tutelo Kinship Customs." *AA* 44:555–575, 1942.

FOLK ART—SPEECH

Chamberlain, A. F.
The Catawba Langauge. Toronto: Imrie & Graham, 1888. 3pp.

Gatschet, A. S.
"Grammatic Sketch of the Catawba Language." *AA* 2:527–549, 1900. n.s.

Harrington, M. R.
"Catawba Potters and Their Work." *AA* 10:399–407, 1908. n.s.

Pennypacker, S. W.
"A Note on Catawba Ceramics." *Penn. Arch.* 7:55–56, 1937.

CHEROKEE

FOLKLORE

GENERAL STUDIES

Anon.
"Chronicle." *Niles' Weekly Register* 10:16, 127, 1816.
List and origin of names of Cherokee chiefs and officers who served under Gen. Jackson in the War of 1812.

Bartram, William
"Observations on the Creek and Cherokee Indians." *Trans. Amer. Ethnol. Soc.* 3:1–81, 1853.

————.
Travels Through North and South Carolina, Georgia, East and West Florida, the Cherokee Country, The Extensive Territories of the Muscogulges, or Creek Confederacy and the Country of the Choctaws. London: 1792.

Bass, Althea
Cherokee Messenger. Norman, Okla.. University of Oklahoma Press, 1936. 348 pp.

Beckner, Lucien
"Eskippakithiki, Last Indian Town in Kentucky." Louisville, 1932 (Reprint from *Filson Club History Quarterly,* 6:355–382, October, 1932.)

Bloom, L.
"The Cherokee Clan." *AA* 41:266–268, 1939. n.s.

Bunce, William H.
Chula, Son of the Mound Builders. Illustrated by Isaac Hazelton. New York: E. P. Dutton and Company, Inc., 1942. 215 pp.
The story for young readers, of the Indians who inhabited what is now Tennessee.

Coblentz, Catherine Cate
Sequoya. Decorations by Ralph Ray, Jr. New York: Longmans, Green and Co., 1946. 198 pp.

Dale, Edward Everett, and Litton, Gaston, eds.
Cherokee Cavaliers. Norman: University of Oklahoma Press, 1930.

Davidson, Donald
The Tennessee. The Rivers of America Series. Illustrated by Mrs. Davidson. New York: Rinehart and Company, 1946.
The Tennessee might well have been called the river of the Cherokees. The book abounds in life, lore and customs of the Cherokees.

Downing, A.
"The Cherokee Indians and Their Neighbors." *Amer. Antiq.* 17:307–316, 1895.

Eaton, R. C.
John Ross and the Cherokee Indians. Menasha, Wis.: Banta Publishing Co., 1914. 212 pp.

Field, Clark
Fine Root Runner Basketry Among the Oklahoma Cherokee Indians. Tulsa: Philbrook Art Center I, 1943. 10 pp., 3 pls.

Floyd, D. B.
New Yamacraw and the Indian Mound Irene. Savannah, Ga.: Review Printing Co., 1936.

Foreman, Grant
The Five Civilized Tribes. Norman, Okl.: University of Oklahoma Press, 1934. (pp. 281–426).

Indians and Pioneers. Norman, Okl.: University of Oklahoma Press, 1936. 285 pp.

Sequoyah. Norman: University of Oklahoma Press, 1938.

Foster, George E.
Se-quo-yah. Philadelphia: 1885. 244 pp.

Gabriel, Ralph Henry
Elias Boudinot, Cherokee, and His America. Norman: University of Oklahoma Press, 1941. 190 pp.

Gilbert, William Harlen, Jr.
"Eastern Cherokees." In: *Anthropological Papers No. 23: Bulletin 133, Bureau of American Ethnology,* pp. 169–413, pls. 13–17, figs. 36–55, tables 1–9. Washington, D. C.: U. S. Gov't. Printing Office, 1943.

Haywood, John
The Natural and Aboriginal History of Tennessee up to the first settlements therein by the white people in the year 1768. Nashville: Printed by G. Wilson, 1823. 390 pp.

Hollingsworth, Jesse Gentry
A Song from the Cherokee and other poems. New York: H. Harrison, 1941. 63 pp.

Hunter, Anne (Home)
Alknomook, The Death Song of the Cherokee Indians of New York. New York: Printed and Sold by G. Gilfert, 177 Broadway, 1800.

Lanman, C.
Adventures in the Wilds of the United States and British American Provinces. Philadelphia: 1856. Vol. I, pp. 407–430.

Logan, J. H.
A History of the Upper Country of South Carolina. Charleston: 1859. 521 pp.

Milling, Chapman J.
Red Carolinians. Chapel Hill: University of North Carolina Press, 1940. 438 pp., illus.

Mooney, James
"Among the East Cherokee Indians." *Smithson Miscel. Coll.* 63(Part 8):61–64, 1913.

"Cherokee." *Bull. Bureau Amer. Ethnol.* 30 (Part 1):245–249, 1907.

"Cherokee and Iroquois Parallels." *JAFL* 2:67, 1889.

The Swimmer Manuscript, ed. by F. M. Olbrechts. Bulletin 99. Bureau American Ethnology. Washington, D. C.: 1932. 319 pp.

Olbrechts, F. M.
"Two Cherokee Texts." *Inter. Jour. Amer. Ling.* 6:179–184, 1931.

Parker, A. C.
"Aboriginal Culture and Chronology of the Tennessee Country." *Rochester Academy of Science,* Vol. VI, No. 8.

Parker, Thomas Valentine
The Cherokee Indian, with special reference to their relations with the United States Government. New York: Grafton Press, 1907. 116 pp., illus.

Parsons, Elsie Clews
"Folklore of the Cherokee." *JAFL* 32:384–393, 1919.

Phelan, James
History of Tennessee: the Making of a State. Boston: Houghton Mifflin and Company, 1888. vi, 478 pp., (fold. map), Bibl. pp. 446–461.

Putnam, A. W.
History of Middle Tennessee; or, Life and Times of Gen. James Robertson. Nashville: Printed for the Author, 1859. xvi, 17–668 pp., plates, fold. map. 2 fold. plan.

Ramsay, J. G. M.
The Annals of Tennessee to the End of the Eighteenth Century. Philadelphia: Lippincott, Grambo and Company, 1853. viii, 744 pp., front (fold. map) pl.

Royce, Charles C.
"The Cherokee Nation of Indians." *5th Annual Report: Bureau of Ethnology,* 1883–1884, pp. 129–302, pls. 7–9. Washington, D. C.: U. S. Gov't Printing Office, 1887.
Cessions of land-colonial and federal period; Treaty Nov. 28, 1785; material provisions, Treaty July 2, 1791; Treaty Feb. 17, 1792; discontent of Cherokees, Cherokee hostilities, etc.

Setzler, Frank M., and Jennings, Jesse D.
Peachtree Mound and Village Site, Cherokee County, North Carolina. Bureau of American Ethnology, Bulletin 131. Washington, D. C.: U. S. Gov't Printing Office, 1941.

Skinner, Alanson
"Cherokee Collection." *Anthropological Papers, American Museum of Natural History,* Vol. IV:284–289, 1910, New York.

Smith, W. R. L.
The Story of the Cherokees. Cleveland, Tenn.: Church of God Publishing House, 1928.

Speck, Frank G.
"Some Eastern Cherokee Texts." *International Journal of American Linguistics* 4:111–113.

————, and Schaeffer, C. E.
"The Mutual-Aid and Volunteer Company of the Eastern Cherokee: As recorded in a book of minutes in the Sequoyah Syllabary, compared with mutual-aid societies of the Northern Iroquois." In: *Journal of Washington Academy of Sciences* 35 (6):169–179, 1945.

Spence, L.
"Cherokees." In: *Encyclopedia of Religion and Ethics,* John Hastings, ed., Vol. 3, (pp. 503–508). New York: 1911.

Starkey, Marion L.
The Cherokee Nation. New York: Alfred A. Knopf, 1946. xiv, 355 pp., illus., bibl.
A unique study of the remarkable achievements of a primitive people.

Starr, Emmet
Cherokees "West" 1794–1839. Claremore, Oklahoma: Author, 1910. 164 pp.

————.
History of the Cherokee Indians and Their Legends and Folklore. Oklahoma City, Okla.: The Warden Co., 1921. 680 pp., front., illus., maps.

Stuart, John
A Sketch of the Cherokee and Choctaw Indians. Little Rock, Arkansas, 1837.

Thomas, C.
The Cherokees in Pre-Columbian Times. New York: N. D. C. Hodges, 1880. 97 pp.

Timberlake, Henry
Memoirs. London: The Author, 1765. vii, 160 pp.

Tooker, William Wallace
"The Problems of the Rechahecrian Indians of Virginia." *AA* 11:261–271, 1898. o.s.

Walker, Robert Sparks
Torchlight to the Cherokees; The Brainerd Mission. New York: Macmillan and Company, 1931. xi, 339 pp., illus.

Wardell, Morris L.
A Political History of the Cherokee Nation. Norman, Okla.: University of Oklahoma Press, 1938.

MYTHS—FOLKTALES—LEGENDS

Anon.
"The Ancient Cherokee Traditions and Religious Rites." *American Quarterly Register and Magazine* 3:444–450, Dec., 1849.

Bailey, Carolyn
Stories from an Indian Cave; the Cherokee Cave Builders; illustrated by Dash, J. E. Chicago: A. Whitman & Co., 1935. 217 pp., illus.

Capps, Claudius
Indian Legends and Poems. Dalton, Ga.: the A. J. Showalter Co., 1932. 61 pp., illus.

Davis, J. B.
Cherokee Fables. Siloam Springs, Ark.: Bar D Press, 1937. 44 pp.
"These Cherokee fables were gathered from several informants and written out several years ago. Mrs. Eliza Riggs, a Cherokee woman, living near Chelsea, Oklahoma, was my principal informant" —p. 4.

————.
"Some Cherokee Stories." *Annals of Archaeology and Anthropology of the University of Liverpool,* 3:26–49, 1910.

————.
"The Liver Eater: a Cherokee story." *Annals of Archaeology and Anthropology of the University of Liverpool,* 2:134–138, 1909.

Melton, A.
"The Legend of Black Snake." *Carlisle Arrow:* 8 (No. 10):1, 1911.

Mooney, James
"Myths of the Cherokee." *19th Annual Report: Bureau of American Ethnology,* 1897–1898, pp. 11–506, pls. 1–20, figs. 1–2. Washington, D. C.: U. S. Gov't Printing Office, 1900.

————.
"Myths of the Cherokee." *JAFL* 1:97–108, 1888; 12:258, 1899.

Mumblehead, J.
"A Legend of the Cherokee Rose." *Red Man* 4:28, 1911.

Parsons, Elsie Clews
"Folklore of the Cherokee," Robeson County, North Carolina. *JAFL* 32:384–393, 1919.

Pletcher, D. E.
"How the Deer Got His Horns." Cherokee Indian Myth. *Nature Magazine* 25:136, March, 1935.

————.
"How the Rabbit Stole the Otter's Coat," Cherokee Indian Myth. *Nature Magazine,* 25: 205–6, April, 1935.

Saunooke, N.
"Why the Turkey is Bald." *Red Man* 3:255–256, 1911.

Siler, Margaret R.
Cherokee Indian Lore and Smoky Mountain Stories. Pamphlet, Boyson City: Boyson City Times, North Carolina, 1938. Also, the author, Box 234, Franklin, N. C.

Simon, Charlie May (Hogue)
Younger Brother, a Cherokee Indian Tale, illustrated by Howard Simon. New York: E. P. Dutton and Company, Inc., 1942. 182 pp.
A story for younger readers of a little Cherokee Indian boy.

Terrell, J. W.
"Demon of Consumption." *JAFL* 5:125–126, 1892.
A legend.

Witthoft, John, and Hadlock, Wendell S.
"Cherokee—Iroquois Little People." *JAFL* 59: 413–422, 1946.
The authors claim that the "wealth of dwarf lore is of considerable interest when compared with old world traditions", and "that a more thorough study of American belief of this type may reveal that we can readily separate the tales of non-Indian origin and still have a large residuum which is an integral part of indigenous American cultures."

BELIEFS—CUSTOMS—FOLK MEDICINE

Cherokee Nation. Statutes.
Laws of the Cherokee Nation, 1870–72. Tahlequah, 1872. 151 pp.

Davis, J. B.
"Two Cherokee Charms." *Annals of Archaeology and Anthropology* 2:131–133, 1909.

Foreman, Richard
The Cherokee Physician; or, Indian Guide to Health; added, a short dispensatory by J. W. Mahoney. New York: n.p., 1857.

Gilbert, William Harlen, Jr.
Eastern Cherokee Social Organization. In: *Social Anthropology of North American Tribes,* F. Eggan, ed., (pp. 283–338). Chicago: 1937.

Hagar, Stansbury
Cherokee Star Lore. In: Anthropological Papers. *Boas Anniversary Volume.* (pp. 354–367). New York: G. E. Stechert and Co., 1906.

Mackentosh, John
Receipts for the Cure of Most Diseases Incident to the Human Family. By the celebrated Indian doctor John Mackentosh, of the Cherokee Nation; none of which have ever before been communicated to the world. New York: Printed for the Publisher Seth Holderwell, 1827. iv, 12 pp.

Mooney, James
"Cherokee River Cults." *JAFL* 13:1–10, 1900.

————.
"Cherokee Theory and Practice of Medicine." *JAFL* 3:44–50, 1890.

————.
"The Sacred Formulas of the Cherokees." *7th Annual Report: Bureau of Ethnology,* 1885–1886, pp. 307–395, pls. 24–27. Washington, D. C.: U. S. Gov't Printing Office, 1891.
How the formulas were obtained, character of the formulas, myths, medicine, hunting, lore, miscellaneous.

————.
"Two Cherokee Charms." *Annals of Archaeology and Anthropology* 2:131–133, 1909.

————, and Olbrechts, Frans M.
The Swimmer Manuscript, Cherokee Sacred Formulas and Medicinal Prescriptions. Washington: U. S. Gov't Printing Office, 1932. xvii, 319 pp., bibl. (U. S. Bureau of American Ethnology, Bulletin 99.)

Olbrechts, Frans M.
"Cherokee Belief and Practice with Regard to Childbirth." *Anthropos,* 26:1–33, 1931.

————.
"Prophylaxis in Cherokee Medicine." *Janus* 33:18–22, 1929.

————.
"Some Cherokee Methods of Divination." In: *Proceedings of the 23rd Session of the International Congress of Americanists,* pp. 547–553, 1928.

————.
"Some Notes on Cherokee Treatment of Diseases." *Janus* 33:271–280, 1929.

Pickens, S. L.
"Comparison of Cherokee and Pioneer Bird-Nomenclature." *SFQ* 7:213–221, 1943.

Sass, Herbert R.
Hear Me, My Chiefs! New York: W. Morrow & Co., 1940. 256 pp., bibl. 244–251.

GAMES—FOLK ART—SPEECH

Field, Clark
Fine Root Runner Basketry Among the Oklahoma Cherokee Indians. Philbrook Art Center 1. Tulsa: 1943. 10 pp.

Foster, George Everett
"Journalism Among the Cherokee Indians." *Magazine of American History.* July, 1887. pp. 65–70.

Grabelentz, H. G. C. von der
"Kurze Grammatik der tscherokesischen Sprache." *Zeitschrift für die Wissenschaft der Sprache* 3:257–300, 1852.

Gatschet, A. S.
"On the Affinity of the Cheroki to the Iroquois Dialects." *Trans. Philol. Assoc.* 16:xl–xlv, 1886.

Mooney, James
"The Cherokee Ball Play." *AA* 3:105–133, 1890.

Pickering, J.
A Grammar of the Cherokee Language. Boston: Metcalf & Co., 1830. 48 pp.

Speck, F. G.
"Decorative Art and Basketry of the Cherokee." *Bull. Public Mus. City Milwaukee* 2:53–86, 1920.

Thomas, Cyrus
"Burial Mounds of the Northern Sections of the United States." *4th Annual Report: Bureau of Ethnology*, 1883–1884, pp. 9–112, pls. 1–6, figs. 1–49. Washington, D. C.: U. S. Gov't Printing Office, 1887.
> Burial mounds of the Wisconsin districts, burial mounds of the Illinois or upper Missouri, burial mounds of the Ohio district, the Cherokees probably mound builders, etc.

————.
"*The circular, square, and octagonal earthworks of Ohio.*" Bureau of American Ethnology, Bull. 10, pp. 1–35, 11pls., 5 figs. Washington, D. C.: U. S. Gov't. Printing Office, 1889.

————.
The Problem of the Ohio mounds. Bureau of American Ethnology, Bull. 8, pp. 1–54, 8 figs. Washington, D. C.: U. S. Gov't Printing Office, 1889.
> Very likely built by the Cherokee who once inhabited Ohio.

Webster, C. L.
"Prof. D. W. C. Duncan's Analysis of the Cherokee Language." *Amer. Natur.* 23:775–781, 1889.

MUSIC

GENERAL STUDIES

Hunter, Anne
Alknomook—The Death Song of the Cherokee Indians. New York: Printed and sold by G. Gilfert, 1800.

Jones, Charles C.
Music and Musical Instruments. In: *Antiquities of the Southern Indian, Particularly of the Georgia Tribes* (Chapter IV). New York: D. Appleton & Company, 1873.

Mooney, James
"Myths of the Cherokees." *19th Annual Report of the American Bureau of Ethnology*, pp. 3–348, pl. I–XX, fig. 1–2. Washington, D. C.: U. S. Government Printing Office, 1900.
> Discusses music and instruments.

"The Death Song of the Cherokee Indians." *Musical Antiquity* (London) 3:166–170, 1912.

ARRANGEMENTS

"Papoose" (Indian Lullaby).
Dobson, Aldrich E.: Schmidt: SSA, SATB.

"Scalp Dance."
Lake, M. L.: Carl Fischer: Orchestra.

"Sons of Manitou"—Song Cycle—6 songs, 2 keys.
Dobson, Aldrich E.: Schmidt: Voice and piano.
> Mr. Dobson is of Cherokee descent. His music is not based on folk melodies, but is essentially Indian in character.

"Two Cherokee Indian Dances"—separate.
Strickland, Lily: G. Schirmer: Piano.

RECORDS

"Cherokee Maiden."
Wills and Texas Playboys. OK–06568

CHICKASAW

FOLKLORE

GENERAL STUDIES

Cushman, H. B.
History of the Choctaw, Chickasaw and Natchez Indians. Greenville, Tex.: Headlight, 1899. 607 pp.

Foreman, Grant
The Five Civilized Tribes. Norman, Okl.: Oklahoma University Press, 1934. (pp. 97–144).

Gatschet, A. S., and Thomas, C.
"Chickasaw." *Bull. Bureau Amer. Ethnol.* 30 (Part 1):260–262, 1907.

Gosselin, A.
"Les Sauvages du Mississippi (1698–1708) d'après la correspondence des missionaires des missions étrangères de Québec." In: *Proceedings of the 15th Session of the International Congress of Americanists*, Vol. 1:31–53, 1906.

Malone, James H.
The Chickasaw Nation; a Short Sketch of a Noble People. Louisville: J. P. Morton and Company, Inc., 1922. xxx, 537 pp., front., plates, ports, maps.

Nuttall, T.
A Journal of Travels into the Arkansa Territory. Philadelphia: 1821. 296 pp.

Speck, Frank G.
"Chickasaw Ethnology and Folklore." *JAFL* 20:50–58, 1907.

Villiers du Terrage, M. de
"Documents concernant l'historie des Indiens de la région orientale de la Louisiane." *Jour. Société Amér.* 14:127–140, 1922. n.s.

Warren, H.
"Chickasaw Traditions, Customs, etc." *Publ. Miss. Hist. Soc.* 8:543–553, 1904.

————.
"Some Chickasaw Chiefs and Prominent Men." *Publ. Miss. Hist. Soc.* 555–570, 1904.

Williams, Samuel Cole
Beginnings of West Tennessee in the Land of the Chickasaws, 1541–1841. Johnson City: Watauga Press, 1930. 331 pp., front., maps., facsm.

FOLKTALES—LEGENDS

Brinton, Daniel G.
National Legend of the Chahta-Muskokee Tribes. Morrisania: 1870. 13 pp.

Speck, Frank G.
"European Tales Among the Chickasaw Indians." *JAFL* 26:292, 1913.

BELIEFS—CUSTOMS

Swanton, John R.
"Social and Religious Beliefs and Usages of the Chickasaw Indians." *44th Annual Report of the Bureau of American Ethnology, Smithsonian Institution,* pp. 169–273, 1926–1927. fig. 3. Washington, D. C.: U. S. Gov't Printing Office, 1928.

——————.
"Social Organization and Social Usages of the Indians of the Creek Confederacy." *Annual Report Bureau Amer. Ethnol.* 42:23–472, 1925.

Warren, Harry
"Chickasaw Traditions, Customs, etc." *Mississippi Historical Society Publications,* (Oxford) 1904. Vol. 8:543–553.

MUSIC

ARRANGEMENTS
Stage Work

Skilton, Charles
Kalopin. Cincinnati: Willis Music Company: Opera.

CHITIMACHA

FOLKLORE

GENERAL STUDIES

Gatschet, A. S.
"Chitimacha." *Bull. Bureau Amer. Ethnol.* 30 (Part 1):286, 1907.

——————.
"Die Schetimascha-Indianer im Südlichen Luisiana." *Ausland* 57:581–589, 1884.

——————.
"The Shetimasha Indians of St. Mary's Parish." *Trans. Anthro. Soc. Wash.* 2:148–158, 1883.

Haas, M. R.
"Natchez and Chitimacha Clans and Kinship Terminology." *AA* 41:597–610, 1939. n.s.

Harrington, M. R.
"Among Louisiana Indians." *Southern Workman* (Hampton, Va.) 37:656–661, 1908.

MYTHS—FOLKTALES—LEGENDS

Swanton, J. R.
"Chitimacha Myths and Beliefs." *JAFL* 30: 474–478, 1917.

——————.
"Mythology of the Indians of Louisiana and the Texas Coast." *JAFL* 20:285–289, 1907.

FOLK ART—SPEECH

Merwin, B. W.
"Basketry of the Chitimacha Indians." *Museum Journal* 10:29–34, 1919.

Swadesh, Morris
"The Phonetics of Chitimacha." *Language* 10:345–362, 1934.

Swanton, John R.
"A Structural and Lexical Comparison of the Tunica, Chitimacha, and Atakapa Languages." *Bull. Bureau Amer. Ethnol.* 68:1–56, 1919.

Toomey, T. N.
"Relationships of the Chitmachan Linguistic Family." *Bulletin of the Hervas Laboratories of American Linguistics (St. Louis)* 4:1–12, 1914.

MUSIC

GENERAL STUDIES

Densmore, Frances
"A Search for Songs Among the Chitimacha Indians in Louisiana." *Bulletin 133, Anthropological Papers, No. 19 of the Bureau of American Ethnology,* pp. 5–15, pls. 1–4. Washington, D. C.: U. S. Government Printing Office, 1943.
The Chitimacha tribe, field work, reminiscences by Benjamin Paul, beliefs concerning the wild canary and the woodpecker, legends by Benjamin Paul, etc.

CHOCTAW

FOLKLORE

GENERAL STUDIES

Benson, H. C.
Life Among the Choctaw Indians. Cincinnati: Methodist Church, 1860. 314 pp.

——————.
"The Choctaw Indians in the Middle of the Nineteenth Century." *Chronicles of Oklahoma* (Oklahoma City) 10:392–425, 1932.

Bushnell, David I., Jr.
The Choctaw of Bayou Lacomb, St. Tammany Parish, Louisiana. Bureau of American Ethnology, Bull. 48, 37 pp., 22 pl., 1 fig. Washington, D. C.: U. S. Gov't. Printing Office, 1909.

Cushman, H. B.
History of the Choctaw, Chickasaw and Natchez Indians. Greenville, Tex.: Headlight, 1899.

Debo, Angie
The Rise and Fall of the Choctaw Republic. Norman, Okla.: University of Oklahoma Press, 1934. 314 pp.

Edwards, J.
The Choctaws; Their Origin, Language, Manners, Customs . . . Philadelphia: 1887.

Eggan, F.
"Historical Changes in the Choctaw Kinship System." *AA* 39:34–52, 1937. n.s.

Foreman, Grant
The Five Civilized Tribes. Norman, Okl.: Oklahoma University Press, 1934. (pp. 17–94).

Gosselin, A.
"Les Sauvages du Mississippi (1698–1708), d'apres la Correspondence des missionaires des missions étrangères de Québec." In: *Proceedings of the 15th Session of the Internation Congress of Americanists,* Vol. 1:31–53, 1906.

Hodgson, A.
Letters from North America. London: 1824. Vol. I, (pp. 215–224, 240–250).

Lanman, C.
Adventures in the Wilds of the United States and British American Provinces. Philadelphia: 1856. Vol. II, (pp. 429–435).

Lincecum, Gideon
"The Choctaw Traditions: about their Settlements in Mississippi and the Origin of their Mounds." *Mississippi Historical Society Publications* (Oxford) 1904. Vol. 8:521–542.

Ray, Florence R.
Greenwood Leflore. Memphis, Tenn.: Davis, 1935.
An account of the Choctaw chief by his daughter.

Speck, F. G.
"A Social Reconnaissance of the Creole Houma Indian Trappers of the Louisiana Bayous." *AI* 3:135–146; 211–220, 1943.
A Choctaw tribe living during the earlier period of the French colonization of Louisiana.

Spence, L.
"Choctaws." In: *Encyclopedia of Religion and Ethics,* John Hastings, ed., Vol. III, (pp. 567–569). New York: 1911.

Stuart, John
A Sketch of the Cherokee and Choctaw Indians. Little Rock, Ark.: 1837.

Swanton, John R.
"An Early Account of the Choctaw Indians." *Memoirs Amer. Anthro. Assoc.* 5:53–72, 1918.

———.
Source Material for the Social and Ceremonial Life of the Choctaw Indians. Bureau of American Ethnology, Bulletin 103. Washington, D. C.: U. S. Govt. Printing Office, 1931.

———, and Thomas, C.
"Choctaw." *Bull. Bureau Amer. Ethnol.* 30 (Part 1):288–289, 1907.

Villiers du Terrage, M. de
"Notes sur les Chactes." *Jour. Société Amér.* 15:223–250, 1923. n.s.

Watkins, J. A.
"The Choctaws in Mississippi." *Amer. Antiq.* 16:69–77, 1894.

———.
"A Contribution to Choctaw History." *Amer. Antiq.* 16:257–265, 1894.

MYTHS—FOLKTALES—LEGENDS

Brinton, D. G.
National Legend of the Chahta-Muskokee Tribes. Morrisania: 1870. 13 pp.

Bushnell, David I., Jr.
"Myths of the Louisiana Choctaw." *AA* 12:526–536, 1910. n.s.

Halbert, H. S.
"Choctaw Creative Legends." *Mississippi Historical Society Publications,* (Oxford) 1901. Vol. 4:267–270.

———.
"A Choctaw Migration Legend." *Amer. Antiq.* 16:215–216, 1894.

———.
"The Choctaw Robin Goodfellow." *Amer. Antiq.* 17:157, 1895.

Petitot, Émile F. S.
"Six légendes américains." *Les Missions Catholiques* (Lyons) 11:21–22, 32–35, 45–48, 1879.

Pitchlynn, Peter P.
"An Indian Legend." *Atkinson's Casket,* No. 11:505–507, Nov. 1831.
Several legendary tales of the Choctaw Indians.

BELIEFS—CUSTOMS—FOLK MEDICINE

Anon.
"Eagle Dance." *Army and Navy Chronicle* 3:553, May 2, 1844. n.s.
Brief account of an ancient festival of the Choctaw Indians.

———.
"Indian Customs." *Niles' Weekly Register* 39:167–168, Oct. 30, 1830.
A description of a Creek religious custom.

———.
"Missionaries at the Choctaw Nation." *The Telescope* 1:129–130, Jan. 15, 1825.
Information on religious, ceremonialism and customs.

Buckner, H. F.
"Burial Among the Choctaws." *Amer. Antiq.* 2:55–58, 1879.

Bushnell, D. I.
"Native Cemeteries and Forms of Burial East of the Mississippi." *Bull. Bureau Amer. Ethnol.* 71:94–101, 1920.

Catlin, G.
Illustrations of the Manners, Customs and Condition of the North American Indian. Vol. 2, (pp. 122–128). New York: 1841.

Halbert, H. S.
"Courtship and Marriage Among the Choctaws." *Amer. Natur.* 16:222–224, 1882.

———.
"Funeral Customs of the Mississippi Choctaws." *Mississippi Historical Society Publications,* (Oxford) 1900. Vol. 3:353–366.

Swanton, John R.
"Choctaw Moieties." *AA* 34:357, 1932. n.s.

Taylor, L. A.
Plants Used as Curatives by Certain Southeastern Tribes. Cambridge: 1940. 88 pp.

FOLK ART—SPEECH—GAMES

Anon.
"Indian Ball-Player." *Perry's Museum* 9:52, Feb. 1845.
How the Choctaws play at ball, with an illustration.

Byington, C.
A Dictionary of the Choctaw Language. Bureau American Ethnology. Bulletin 46. Washington, D. C.: 1915. 611 pp.

———.
"Grammar of the Choctaw Language," D. G. Brinton, ed. *Proc. Amer. Philo. Soc.* 11:317–367, 1870.

"Choctaw Games." *JAFL* 10:155–156, 1897.

Douglas, F. H.
"A Choctaw Pack Basket." *Material Culture Notes* (Denver Art Museum) 4:15–18, 1937.

Haas, M. R.
"The Choctaw Word for 'Rattlesnake'." *AA* 43:129–132, 1941. n.s.

MUSIC

GENERAL STUDIES

Bushnell, David I.
Dances and Music. In: *The Choctaws of Bayou Lacomb St. Tammany Parish Louisiana.* Washington, D. C.: U. S. Government Printing Office, 1909.

Densmore, Frances
"Choctaw Music." *Anthropological Papers, No. 28, Bulletin 136 Bureau of American Ethnology,* pp. 101–188 pl. 10–21, fig. 3–4. Washington, D. C.: U. S. Government Printing Office, 1943.

CREEK

FOLKLORE

GENERAL STUDIES

Anon.
"Creeks." *Bull. Bureau Amer. Ethnol.* 30 (Part 1):362–365, 1907.

Bartram, William
"Observations on the Creek and Cherokee Indians." *Trans. Amer. Ethnol. Soc.* 3:1–81, 1853.

Bushnell, David I., Jr.
"The Account of Lamhatty." *AA* 10:568–575, 1908. n.s.

Caughey, John Walton
McGillivray of the Creeks. Norman: University of Oklahoma Press, 1938. 385 pp.

Debo, Angie
The Road to Disappearance. Norman: University of Oklahoma Press, 1941.

Eakins, D. W.
Some Information Respecting the Creeks. In: *Information Respecting the History, Condition, and Prospects of the Indian Tribes of the United States,* H. R. Schoolcraft, ed., Vol. I, pp. 265–283. Philadelphia: 1851.

Fowke, Gerard
Antiquities of Central and Southeastern Missouri. Report on explorations made in 1906–7 under the auspices of the Archaelogical Institute of America. Bureau of American Ethnology, Bull. 37, pp. 1–113. Washington, D. C.: U. S. Printing Office, 1910.
Report deals with explorations extending from Missouri River south along the Gasconade and Moreau Creeks, and north from Cedar Creek to Easly southwest to Howard County into Saline County and mounds opposite Kansas City and Pike County.

Hawkins, Benjamin
A Sketch of the Creek Country in 1798 and 1799. Collection Georgia Historical Society, Vol. III. Savannah, Ga.: 1848.

Hewitt, J. N. B.
"Notes on the Creek Indians," J. R. Swanton, ed. *Bull. Bureau Amer. Ethnol.* 123:119–159, 1939.

Hitchcock, Ethan Allen
A Traveler in Indian Territory. (His Journal in 1842). Cedar Rapids. Ia.: The Torch Press, 1930.

Parker, A. C.
"Aboriginal Culture and Chronology of the Tennessee Country." *Rochester Academy of Science,* Vol. VI, No. 8.

Speck, Frank G.
The Creek Indians of Taskigi Town. Memoirs of American Anthropological Association II, pt. 2. Lancaster, Pa.: New Era Printing Co., 1907.
Includes folklore and tales.

———.
"The Negro and the Creek Nation." *Southern Workman* 37:106–110, 1908.

Swanton, John R.
Early History of the Creek Indians and Their Neighbors, Bulletin 73, Bureau of American Ethnology, Smithsonian Institution. Washington, D. C.: U. S. Gov't. Printing Office, 1922.

————.
"A Foreword on the Social Organization of the Creek Indians." *AA* 14:593–600, 1912. n.s.

————.
"Interpretation of Aboriginal Mounds by Means of Creek Indian Customs." In: *Smithsonian Report, 1927.* pp. 495–506, illus. Washington, D. C.: U. S. Gov't. Printing Office.

————.
"Social Organization and Social Usages of the Indians of the Creek Confederacy." *42nd Annual* Report: Bureau of Ethnology, 1924–1925, pp. 23–472, plss. 1–7, figs. 1–107. Washington, D. C.: U. S. Gov't. Printing Office, 1928.
  Native legends dealing with Creek history, social organization, clans, phratries, and moieties, etc.

————.
Tokulki of Tulsa. In: *American Indian Life,* Elsie Clews Parsons, ed., pp. 127–145. New York: B. W. Huebsch, 1925.

Woodward, Thomas S.
Woodward's Reminiscences of the Creek and Muscogee Indians. Montgomery; Barrett and Wimbish, 1859.
  A republication from the original by the Alabama Book Store, Tuscaloosa, and Smith & Hardwick, Birmingham, Alabama, 1939.

MYTHS—FOLKTALES—LEGENDS

Anon.
"The Busk." *Niles' Weekly Register* 25:169, Nov. 15, 1823.
  A description of the religious ceremony of the Creek Indians, with corn, which, when fully ripe, expiates all sins and offenses, except murder.

Gatschet, Albert S.
A Migration Legend of the Creek Indians. Vol. I, Philadelphia, 1884. (Library of Aboriginal American Literature, No. 4) ; vol. II, St. Louis, 1888. (Transactions of the Academy of Science of St. Louis, V, 33–239).
  The author also presents a valuable linguistic, historic, and ethnographic introduction.

————.
Tchikilli's Kasi'hta Legend in the Creek and Hitchiti Languages with a critical commentary and full glossaries to both texts. St. Louis: R. P. Studley & Co., 1888. 207 pp.) (Academy of Science of St. Louis. Transactions vol. 5, No. 1–2. 1886–88, pp. 33–240).

Methvin, J. J.
"Legend of the Tie-Snakes." *Chronicles of Oklahoma.* 5:391–396, 1927.

Schoolcraft, Henry Rowe
Alhalla; or *The Lord of Talladega*—a tale of the Creek war. New York: Wiley, 1843. 116 pp.

Speck, Frank G.
"Mac Henry, the Bad-Man; a Creek Indian's Story." *Red Man:* 4:9–11, 1911.

————.
"Notes on Creek Mythology." *Southern Workman* 38:9–11, 1909.

Swanton, John R.
"Animal Stories from the Indians of the Muskhogean Stock." *JAFL* 26:193–218, 1913.

————.
"Myths and Tales of the Southeastern Indians." *Bull. Bureau Amer. Ethnol.* 88:1–86, 1929.

BELIEFS—FOLK MEDICINE—SPEECH

Read, William A.
Indian Place-Names in Alabama. Baton Rouge, La.: State University Press, 1937.

Swanton, John R.
"The Interpretation of Aboriginal Mounds by Means of Creek Indian Customs." *Annual Reports of the Board of Regents of the Smithsonian Institution* (Wash., D. C.), 1927, pp. 495–506.

————.
"Religious Beliefs and Medical Practices of the Creek Indians." *42nd Annual Report: Bureau of American Ethnology,* 1924–1925, pp. 477–859, pls. 8–13, figs. 108, bibl. Washington, D. C.: U. S. Gov't. Printing Office, 1928.

FOLK ART—SPEECH

Brinton, D. G.
"Contributions to a Grammar of the Muskokee Language." *Proc. Amer. Philo. Soc.* 11:301–309, 1870.

Buckner, H. F., and Herrod, G.
A Grammar of the Maskwke or Creek Language. Marion, Ala.: 1860. 138 pp.

Gatschet, A. S.
"Adjectives of Color in Indian Languages." *Amer. Natur.* 13:475–485, 1879.

Loughridge, R. M., and Hodge, D. M.
English and Muskokee Dictionary. St. Louis: J. T. Smith, 1890. 236 pp.

Swan, C.
Position and State of Manners and Arts of the Creek or Muscogee Nation. In: *Information Respecting the History, Condition, and Prospects of the Indian Tribes of the United States,* H. R. Schoolcraft, ed., Vol. 5, (pp. 251–283). Philadelphia: 1855.

MUSIC

GENERAL STUDIES

"Creek Hymn." Translated by Rev. D. L. Berryhill. *Our Brother in Red,* Vol. 6 (No. 24) pp. 3. Muskogee, Ind.: Feb. 18, 1888.

Densmore, Frances
The Alabama Indians and their Music. In: *Straight Texas*, J. Frank Dobie, and Mody Boatright, editors (pp. 270–293). Austin, Texas: Steck Company, 1937.

Jones, Charles C.
Music and Musical Instruments. In: *Antiquities of the Southern Indians, particularly of the Georgia Tribes* (Chapter IV). New York: D. Appleton & Company, 1873.

Speck, Frank G.
Ceremonial Songs of the Creek and Yuchi Indians, with music transcribed by Jacob D. Sapir. In: *University of Pennsylvania Museum of Anthropology Publications*, Vol. I, (No. 1): 155–245. Philadelphia: Published by the University Museum, 1911.

————.
"The Creek Indians of Taskigi Town" *American Anthropological Association Memoirs* (Lancaster, Pennsylvania) 2:99–164, 1907–1915.

Swanton, John R.
Early History of the Creek Indians and Their Neighbors. Bureau of American Ethnology, Bull. 73, 492 pp. 10 pl. (all maps). Washington, D. C.: U. S. Gov't. Printing Office, 1922.

DANCES

Anon.
"The Pole Cat, or Shell Dance." *Southern Literary Messenger* 3:390–391, June, 1837.
Description of the Pole Cat Dance of the Seminole and Creek Indians.

NATCHEZ

FOLKLORE

GENERAL STUDIES

Bossu, Jean Bernard
Nouveaux voyages aux Indes occidentales. Paris: Le Jay, 1768. Vol. I, (pp. 37–79).

————.
Travels Through that Part of North America Formerly Called Louisiana. London: T. Davies, 1771. Vol. I, pp. 37–67.

Brinton, Dr. Daniel Garrison
"On the Language of the Natchez." *American Philosophical Society Proceedings*, 13:483–499, 1813.
Comparison of Natchez terms with those of Muskoki, Seminole and Choctaw.

————.
"The Natchez of Louisiana, an Offshoot of the Civilized Nations of Central America." *Historical Magazine* (Second Series) Vol. 1: 16–18, 1867 (Morrisania, N. Y.

Cushman, H. B.
History of the Choctaw, Chickasaw and Natchez Indians. Greenville, Tex.: Headlight, 1899. 607 pp.

Harrington, M. R.
"Among Louisiana Indians." *Southern Workman* (Hampton, Va.) 37:656–661, 1908.

Henshaw, H. W., and Swanton, J. R.
"Natchez." *Bull. Bureau Amer. Ethnol.* 30 (Part 2):35–36, 1910.

Josselin de Jong, J. P. B. de
"The Natchez Social Class System." *Proceedings of the 23rd Session of the International Congress of Americanists*, pp. 553–563, 1928.

Kniffen, Fred B.
"The Historic Indian Tribes of Louisiana." *Louisiana Conservation Review*, (July) 1935, Vol. 4, (No. 7): 5–12.

Le Petit, M.
"Relation des Natchez." *Recueil de Voyages au Nord* (Amsterdam) 9:1–79, 1737.

MacLeod, W. C.
"Natchez Political Evolution." *AA* 26:201–229, 1924. n.s.

————.
"On Natchez Culture Origins." *AA* 28:409–413, 1926. n.s.

Mooney, James
"The End of the Natchez." *AA* 1:510–522, 1899. n.s.

Read, William A.
Louisiana Place Names of Indian Origin. Baton Rouge: Louisiana State University Press, 1927.

Swanton, J. R.
"Ethnological Positions of the Natchez Indians." *AA* 9:513–529, 1907, n.s.

————.
"Natchez." In: *Encyclopedia of Religion and Ethics* John Hastings, ed. Vol. 9, (pp. 187–191). New York: 1917.

Walker, Winslow M.
A Reconnaissance of Northern Louisiana Mounds. In: *Explorations and Field Work of the Smithsonian Institution in 1931* (Publication 3134) pp. 169–174. Washington, D. C.: U. S. Government Printing Office, 1931.

CUSTOMS—SPEECH

Haas, M. R.
"Natchez and Chitimacha Clans and Kinship Terminology." *AA* 41:597–610, 1939. n.s.

Swanton, J. R.
"The Muskhogean Connection of the Natchez Language." *Inter. Jour. Amer. Ling.* 3:46–75, 1924.

POWHATAN

FOLKLORE

GENERAL STUDIES

Beverley, Robert
The History and Present State of Virginia, By a Native Inhabitant. London: 1705.

Bushnell, David I., Jr.
Research in Virginia from Tidewater to the Alleghenies. Lancaster, Pa.: New Era Printing Co., 1908. pp. 531–548.
Reprinted from *American Anthropologist.* Historical sketch of Indians from 1716 to 1763.

———.
Native Village and Village Sites East of the Mississippi. Bureau of American Ethnology, Bulletin 69. Washington, D. C.: U. S. Gov't. Printing Office, 1919.

———.
"Research in Virginia from Tidewater to the Alleghenies." *AA* 10:531–549, 1908. n.s.

———.
"Trailing Early Man in Virginia." In: *Explorations and Field Work in the Smithsonian Institutions in 1940,* pp. 75–78, illus. Washington, D. C.: U. S. Gov't. Printing Office, 1941.

———.
"Virginia—From Early Records." *AA* 9:31:45, 1907. n.s.

Criss, Mildred
Pocahontas, Young American Princess. New York: Dodd, Mead & Co., 1943.
For young readers.

Dorsey, Ella Loraine
Pocahontas. Washington, D. C.: The Howard Press, 1906. 58 pp., Second Edition.

Douglas, F. H.
"The Virginia Indian Tribes." *Denv. Art Mus. Leaflet Ser.* 57:1–4, 1933.

Hancock, James E.
"The Indians of the Chesapeake Bay Section." *Maryland Historical Magazine* 22:23–40, 1927.

Hough, W.
"The Indians of the District of Columbia." *Scientific Monthly* 32:537–539, 1931.

Kuhm, H. W.
"The Indians of Virginia." *Wis. Arch.* 11:91–99, 1932. n.s.

Lyman, Dean B.
"Indians in West Virginia." *AS* 11 (no. 1):63, 1936.

Marye, William B.
"Potowmack Above Ye Inhabitants." *Maryland Historical Magazine* 30:1–11, 114–37, 1935.

McDavid, M. O.
Princess Pocahontas. New York: The Neale Publishing Company, 1907. 125 pp.

Mook, Maurice A.
"The Aboriginal Population of Tidewater Virginia." *AA* 46:193–209, 1944, n.s.
Enumerates about thirty tribes of the Powhatan Confederacy.

———.
"The Ethnological Significance of Tindell's Map of Virginia." *William and Mary College, Quarterly Historical Magazine* 33, (No. 4):371–408. map. (Williamsburg) 1943.

Mooney, James
"Indian Tribes of the District of Columbia." *AA* 2:259–266, 1889.

———.
"Powhatan." In: *Bull. Bureau Amer. Ethnol.* 30 (Part 2):299–302, 1910.

———.
"The Powhatan Confederacy—Past and Present." *AA* 9:129–153, 1907. n.s.

———.
The Siouan Tribes of the East. Bureau of American Ethnology, Bulletin 22. Washington, D. C.: U. S. Govt. Printing Office, 1894.

Smith, John
The True Travels, Adventures and Observations of Captain John Smith, etc. From the London edition of 1629. Richmond: Republished at the Franklin Press, 1819.. 2 vols., map.

Speck, F. G.
"Chapters on the Ethnology of the Powhatan Tribes of Virginia." *Indian Notes and Monographs* 1:227–335, 1928. New York: Museum of American Indian, Heye Foundation.

———.
"The Rappahannock Indians of Virginia." *Indian Notes and Monographs* 5:25–83, 1925.

Weslager, C. A.
Delaware's Forgotten Folk. Philadelphia: University of Pennsylvania Press, 1943.
The story of the "Moors and Nanticokes" descendants of Algonkian speaking Indians.

Willoughby, Charles C.
"The Virginia Indians of the 17th Century." *AA* 9:57–87, 1907. n.s.

BELIEFS—CUSTOMS—SPEECH
FOLK ART

Davidson, D. S.
"Some String Figures of the Virginia Indians." *Indian Notes* 4:384–395, 1927.

Gerard, William R.
"The Tapehanek Dialect of Virginia." *AA* 6:313–331, 1904. n.s.
A former tribe of the Powhatan Confederacy on the south bank of the James River in Surry County, Virginia.

———.
"Virginia's Indian Contributions to English." *AA* 9:87–113, 1907. n.s.

Speck, Frank G.
"The Gourd Lamp Among the Virginia Indians." *AA* 43:676–678, 1941.

Swanton, J. R.
"Newly Powhatan Bird Names." *Jour. Wash. Acad. Sci.* 24:96–99, 1934.

Thomas, Cyrus
"Curious Customs and Strange Freaks of the Mound Builders." *AA* 1:353–355, 1888.

Tooker, William Wallace
The Algonquin Names of the Siouan Tribes of Virginia. New York: F. P. Harper, 1901. 83 pp. (Reprinted from the *American Anthropologist.*)

————.
"Some Powhatan Names." *AA* 6:670–695, 1904. n.s.

————.
"The Mystery of the Name Pamunkey." *Amer. Antiq.* 17: 289–293, 1895.

————.
"The Powhatan Name for Virginia." *AA* 8: 23–27, 1906.

Willoughby, Charles C.
"Michabo the Great Hare: A Patron of the Hopewell Mound Settlement." *AA* 37:280–286, 1935. n.s.

SEMINOLE

FOLKLORE

GENERAL STUDIES

Barr, James
A Correct and Authentic Narrative of the Indian War in Florida. New York: 1836.

Brinton, D. G.
Notes on the Floridian Peninsula, its literary history, Indian tribes and antiquities. Philadelphia: J. Sabin, 1859. viii, 202 p.

Ellis, Leonora B.
"The Seminoles of Florida." *Gunton's Magazine* (N. Y.): 25:495–505, 1903.

Foreman, Grant
The Five Civilized Tribes. Norman, Okl.: Oklahoma University Press, 1934. (pp. 223–278).

Greenman, E. F.
"Hopewellian Traits in Florida." *American Antiquity* 3 (No. 4):327–332, 1938.

Laudonnière, Réné
The Second Voyage into Florida. Hakluyt's Collection of the Early Voyages, Travels, and Discoveries of the English Nation. In: *Collection of Voyages,* by Richard Hakluyt, pp. 384–419. London: 1809–1812. Vol. 3.

MacCauley, Clay
"The Seminole Indians of Florida." *5th Annual Report: Bureau of Ethnology,* 1883–1884, pp. 475–529, pl. xix, figs. 60–77. Washington, D. C.: U. S. Gov't. Printing Office, 1887.
Personal characteristics, clothing, adornment, psychical characteristics, Seminole society, myths, tribe, tribal life, religion, etc.

Mooney, James
"Seminole." In: *Bull. Bureau Amer. Ethnol.* 30 (Part 2):500–502, 1910.

Moore-Willson, Minnie
Seminoles of Florida, with introduction by E. S. Martin. New York: Moffat, Yard and Company, 1910. 213 pp., illus.

————.
"Seminoles." In: *Encyclopedia of Religion and Ethics,* John Hastings, ed. Vol. XI, pp. 376–378. New York: 1921.

Nash, R. C.
Survey of the Seminole Indians of Florida. Washington, D. C.: 1931. 88 pp.

Nelson, N. C.
"Chronology in Florida." *Anthropological Papers:* Vol. 22:1918, pp. 75–103, 7 figs. Publications in Anthropology. New York: The American Museum of Natural History.

Romans, Bernard
A Concise Natural History of East and West Florida. Vol. 1: Containing an account of the natural produce of all southern parts of British America, in the three kingdoms of nature, particularly the animal and vegetable. New York: Printed for author, 1775. viii, 342 pp., 8 pl. (incl. front.) 3 maps, fold. tab.

Skinner, Alanson
"The Florida Seminoles." *Southern Workman* (Hampton, Va.) 40:154–163, 1911.

————.
"Notes on the Florida Seminole." *AA* 15:63–78, 1913, n.s.

Spoehr, Alexander
"Camp, Clan and Kin Among the Cow Creek Seminole of Florida." *Anthropological Series* 33, (No. I) 27 pp. Chicago: Field Museum, 1941.

Survey of the Seminole Indians of Florida.
U. S. Office of Indian Affairs. Washington, D. C.: U. S. Gov't. Printing Office, 1931.

Swanton, J. R.
"Early History of the Creek Indians and Their Neighbors." *Bull. Bureau Amer. Ethnol.* 73: 398–414, 1922.

Wenhold, Lucy L.
A 17th Century Letter of Gabriel Diaz Vara Calderón, Bishop of Cuba, describing the Indians and Indian Missions of Florida. Smithsonian Miscellaneous Collections 95, (No. 16), 1936. Washington, D. C.: U. S. Government Printing Office, 1936.

Wilder, Robert
Bright Feather. New York: G. P. Putnam's
Sons, 1948. 408 pp.
A vivid, dramatic chronicle of the merciless bru-
tality of the whites toward the Seminoles.

MYTHS—FOLKTALES—LEGENDS

Bogart, Elizabeth M. M.
Legends of Kan-yuk-sa, illustrated by Fried-
man, K. A. Macon, Ga.: Press of the J. W.
Burke Company 1928. xvii, 141 pp., illus.

Greenlee, Robert F.
"Folk Tales of the Florida Seminole." *JAFL*
58:138–144, 1945.

Sistrunk, Nancy Amelsi Atkinson, comp.
*Heart Poems of Silver Springs and Indian
Legends of Florida*. Ocala, Fla.: Press of Tay-
lor Printing Company, 1917. 56 pp.

Von Hesse, Maxeda Ferguson
Inherit the Wind. New York: William Morrow
and Co., 1944. 282 pp.
Cracker characters against Seminole background,
describes some of the rites of the latter.

CUSTOMS—BELIEFS—FOLK ART
SPEECH

Goggin, John M.
"Silver Work of the Florida Seminole." *El
Palacio* 47:25:32, 1940.

Greenlee, Robert F.
"Medicine and Curing Practices of the Modern
Florida Seminoles." *AA* 46(No. 3):317–329,
1944.

Smith, B.
Comparative Vocabularies of the Seminole and
Mikasuke Tongues. In: *Indian Miscellany*,
W. W. Beach, ed., pp. 120–126. Albany: 1877.

Swanton, John R.
"Religions Beliefs and Medical Practices of
the Creek Indians." *Annual Report Bureau
Amer. Ethnol.* 42:477–672, 1925.

————.
"Social Organization and Social Usages of the
Indians of the Creek Confederacy." *Annual
Report Bureau Amer. Ethnol.* 42:23–472, 1925.

MUSIC
GENERAL STUDIES

Densmore, Frances
"Recording Indian Music." *Exploration and
Field Work of the Smithson. Inst.*, 1931, pp.
183–190.

————.
"Recording Seminole Songs in Florida." *Ex-
ploration and Field Work of the Smithson.
Inst.*, 1932, pp. 93–96.

————.
"Seminole Music Related to Cocopa." *El
Palacio* 32:172–173, 1932.

MacCauley, Clay
"The Seminole Indians of Florida." *United
States Bureau of American Ethnology 5th An-
nual Report:* 469–531, 1883–1884. Washington,
D. C.: U. S. Government Printing Office, 1887.

Moore-Willson, Minnie
The Seminoles of Florida. New York: Moffat,
Yard & Company, 1911.
Brief discussion of music on p. 116.

DANCES

Anon.
"The Pole Cat, or Shell Dance." *Southern Literary Messenger* 3:390–391, June 1837.
Description of the Pole Cat Dance of the Seminole and Creek Indians.

MacCauley, Clay
The Green Corn Dance. In: *The Seminole Indians of Florida. U. S. Bureau of American
Ethnology*. 5th Annual Report: 522–523. Washington, D. C.: U. S. Government Printing Office,
1887.

ARRANGEMENTS

Stage Work

Schoenfeld, Henry
Atala—An Opera in 3 Acts. MS.

SHAWNEE
FOLKLORE
GENERAL STUDIES

Alford, Thomas Wildcat (Florence Drake, ed.)
Civilization. Norman, Okla.: University of
Oklahoma Press, 1936.
Shawnee Culture.

Anon.
"Elkswatawa, the Prophet of the West." *New
York Mirror* 14:10, July 9, 1836.
Extracts form this new novel, bearing above title,
founded on Indian incidents and characters,
manners, traditions and beliefs. The chief characters are Tecumseh and his extraordinary
brother, the Prophet.

Brinton, D. G.
"The Shawnees and Their Migrations." *Historical Magazine* 10 (No. 1): pp. 1–4, 1866.

Butler, R.
"Shawnoes." *Trans. Coll. Amer. Antiq. Soc.*
2:305–367, 1836.

Cummings, R. W.
Shawnee. In: *Information Respecting the
History, Condition, and Prospects of the Indian
Tribes of the United States*, H. R. School-
craft, ed., Vol. 2 (pp. 470–481). Philadelphia:
1852.

Drake, Benjamin
The Life of Tecumseh and of his Brother the Prophet; with a historical sketch of the Shawnee Indians. Cincinnati, O.: H. S. & J. Applegate, 1852. 235 p.

Fowke, Gerard
Archaeological History of Ohio. The Mound Builders and Later Indians. Columbus, O.: Ohio State Archaeological and Historical Society, 1902. 760 pp.

Galloway, William A.
Old Chillicothe, Shawnee and Pioneer History, Conflicts and Romances in the Northwest Territory. Xenia, O.: Buckeye Press, 1934.

Harvey, H.
History of the Shawnee Indians. Cincinnati: E. Morgan & Sons, 1855. 316 pp.

Johnson, F. C.
"Count Zinzendorf and the Moravian and Indian Occupancy of the Wyoming Valley, 1742–1763." *Proceedings and Collections of the Wyoming Historical and Geological Society,* pp. 119–182, 1902–1903. Wilkes Barre, 1904.

Lilly, Eli
Prehistoric Antiquity of Indiana. Indianapolis: Indiana Historical Society, 1937.
    Contains a valuable bibliography on Indiana archaeology.

Mooney, James
"Shawnee." *Bull. Bureau Amer. Ethnol.* 30 (Part 2):530–538, 1910.

Oskison, John M.
Tecumseh and His Times. New York: C. P. Putnam's Sons, 1938. xi, 244 pp.

Rafinesque, C. S.
Ancient History, or, Annals of Kentucky; with a survey of the ancient monuments of North America, and a tabular view of the principal languages and primitive nations of the whole earth. Frankfurt, Ky., Printed for Author, 1824. iv, 39 pp.

Royce, C. C.
"An Inquiry Into the Identity and History of the Shawnee Indians." *Amer. Antiq.* 3:178–189, 1881.

Shetrone, H. C.
The Mound Builders. New York: D. Appleton Co., 1930. xx, 508 pp., illus.

Smith, Harlan I.
"The Prehistoric Ethnology of a Kenutcky Site." *Anthropological Papers of American Museum of Natural History* Vol. 6 (part 2): 173–241, 1910.

Spencer, J.
"Shawnee Folklore." *JAFL* 22:319–326, 1909.

————.
"The Shawnee Indians." *Trans. Kansas State Hist. Soc.* 10:382–402, 1908.

Thomas, Cyrus
"The Story of a Mound; or, The Shawnees in Pre-Columbian Times." *AA* 4:109–161, 237–275, 1891.

Trowbridge, C. C.
Shawnee Tradition. Edited by Vernon Kinietz, and Erminie W. Voegelin. Ann Arbor: University of Michigan Press, 1939.

Voegelin, C. F., and E. W.
"Shawnee Name Groups." *AA* 37:617–635, 1935. n.s.

————, E. W.
"The Place of Agriculture in the Subsistence Economy of the Shawnee." *Papers, Michigan Academy of Arts and Letters* 24:513–520, 1941.

Wilson, William Edward
Shooting Star; the Story of Tecumseh. New York: Farrar and Rinehart Co., 1942.

Young, B. H.
Prehistoric Men of Kentucky. Louisville: Filson Club Publication 25, 1910. 343 pp., illus.

MYTHS—FOLKTALES—BELIEFS
—CUSTOMS

Anon.
"Elkswatawa, the Prophet of the West." *New York Mirror* 14:10, July 9, 1836.

D.
"Tecumseh-Original Tales." *The Cincinnati Literary Gazette* 2 (No. 15):113–115, Oct. 9, 1824; 3 (No. 20):153–154, May 14, 1825.

Dunn, Jacob Piatt
True Indian Stories, with Glossary of Indiana Indian Names. Indianapolis: Sentinel Printing Co., 1908.

Mooney, James
"The Ghost-Dance Religion." *Annual Report Bureau Amer. Ethnol.* 14(Part 2):670–691, 1893.

Voegelin, Charles Frederick
The Shawnee Female Deity. Yale University Publications in Anthropology, No. 10. New Haven: Publication for the Section of Anthropology, Department of the Social Sciences, Yale University, by the Yale University Press. London: H. Milford, Oxford University Press, 1936. 21 pp.

————, and Erminie W.
"The Shawnee Female Deity in Historical Perspective." *AA* 46:370–375, 1944.

————.
"Mortuary Customs of the Shawnee and Other Eastern Tribes." *Indiana Historical Society, Prehistory Research Series* 2:227–444. Tables. Indianapolis: Indiana Historical Society, 1944.

MUSIC

GENERAL STUDIES

Voegelin, Erminie Wheeler
"Shawnee Musical Instruments." *AA* 44:463–475, 1942.
Especially rattles and drums in Oklahoma.

ARRANGEMENTS

"Shawnee Indian Hunting Dance."
Skilton, Charles S.: Carl Fischer: Piano.

"Shawnee Indian Hunting Dance."
Skilton, Charles S.: Carl Fischer: Violin.

RECORDS

"Shawnee Indian Hunting Dance."
Victor Concert Orchestra. VI–22144

TIMUCUA

FOLKLORE

GENERAL STUDIES

Connor, J. T.
"Jean Ribault." *Publ. Florida State Hist. Soc.* 10:1–139, 1927.

Dickinson, Jonathan
Narrative of a Shipwreck in the Gulf of Florida. New York: D. Lawrence, 1803.

Ehrmann, W. W.
"The Timucua Indians of Sixteenth Century Florida." *Florida Hist. Soc. Quart.* 18:168–191, 1940.

Gatschet, A. S.
"Volk und Sprache der Timucua." *Verhandl. Berl. Gesel. Anthro. Ethno. Ur.*, 1877, pp. 245–260.

———, and Grasserie, R. de la
"Textes Timucua." *Revue de Linguistique et de Philologie Comparée (Paris)*. 22:320–346, 1889.

Harrison, B.
"Indian Races of Florida." *Florida Hist. Soc. Quart.* 3:29–37, 1924.

Mooney, J.
"Timucuan Family." *Bull. Bureau Amer. Ethnol.* 30(Part 2):752–754, 1910.

Ribault, J.
"Narrative." *Historical Collections of Louisiana and Florida*, B. F. French, ed., (Ser. 2) 2:170–182, 1875.

Stirling, M. W.
Florida Cultural Affiliations in Relation to Adjacent Areas. In: *Essays in Anthropology Presented to A. L. Kroeber*, (pp. 351–357). Berkeley: University of California Press, 1936.

CUSTOMS—FOLK ART—SPEECH

Bushnell, D. I.
"Drawings by Jacques Lemoyne de Morgues of Saturioua, a Timucua Chief." *Smithson. Miscel. Coll.* 81(Part 4):1–9, 1928.

———.
"Native Cemeteries and Forms of Burial East of the Mississippi." *Bull. Bureau Amer. Ethnol.* 71:116–122, 1920.

Douglass, A. E.
"A Find of Ceremonial Weapons in a Florida Mound." *Proc. Amer. Assoc. Adv. Sci.* 31:585–592, 1882.

Gatschet, A. S.
"The Timucua Language." *Proc. Amer. Philo. Soc.* 16:626–642, 1877; 17:490–504, 1878; 18:465–502, 1879–80.

———.
"Volk und Sprache der Timucua." *Verhandl. Berl. Gesel. Anthro. Ethno. Ur.* 1877, pp. 245–260.

———, and Grasserie, R. de la
"Textes Timucua." *Revue de Linguistique et de Philologie Comparée (Paris)* 22:320–346, 1889.

Pareja, Francisco
Arte de la lengua Timuquana. Paris: Maisonneuves frères, 1886. 132 pp.

Smith, B.
"The Timuquana Language." *Hist. Magaz.* 2:1–3, 1858.

Swanton, J. R.
Terms of Relationship in Timucua. In: *Holmes Anniversary Volume*, (pp. 451–463). Washington: 1916.

TUTELO

FOLKLORE

GENERAL STUDIES

Hale, Horatio
"The Tutelo Tribe and Language." *Proceedings of the American Philosophical Society* 21:1883. 47 pp. (Philadelphia).

Lawson, John
The History of Carolina; containing the exact description and natural history of that country, together with the present state thereof, and a journal of a thousand miles traveled through several nations of Indians; with account of their customs, etc. London: W. Taylor, and F. Baker, 1714. xxix, 259 pp., front. (map) plates.

Milling, Chapman James
Red Carolinians. Chapel Hill: University of North Carolina Press, 1940.

Rights, Douglas L.
The American Indian in North Carolina. Durham, N. C.: Duke University Press, 1947. xvii, 324 pp.

Speck, Frank G.
"Siouan Tribes of the Carolinas as Known from Catawba, Tutelo and Documentary Sources." *AA* 37:201–225, 1935. n.s.

MYTHS—BELIEFS

Speck, Frank G., and Herzog, George
The Tutelo Spirit Adoption Ceremony. Reclothing the living in the name of the dead. Transcription and analysis of Tutelo music. Harrisburg, Pa.: Pennsylvania Historical Commission, 1942. 125 pp., pls., music.
"Horatio Hale, James Mooney, John R. Swanton, and now Frank G. Speck and his collaborators have afforded the Tutelo, a once little known band of Siouan refugees from North Virginia, Piedmont, almost better representation in the literature of ethnology than their Iroquois foster parents, the erstwhile Cayuga of Central New York." (Fenton)

MUSIC
GENERAL STUDIES

Speck, Frank G., and Herzog, George
The Tutelo Spirit Adoption Ceremony. Harrisburg: Pennsylvania Historical Commission, 1942. 125 pp., pls. music.
Analysis of music by Dr. Herzog.

YUCHI
FOLKLORE
GENERAL STUDIES

Speck, Frank G.
Ethnology of the Yuchi Indians. Anthropological Publication of the Museum of the University of Pennsylvania. Philadelphia: University Press, 1909.

———.
"Eggan's Yuchi Kinship Interpretations." *AA* 41:171–172, 1939. n.s.

———.
"Yuchi." *Bull. Bureau Amer. Ethnol.* 30(Part 2):1003–1007, 1910.

Wagner, Günter
Yuchi. In: *Handbook of American Indian Languages,* Franz Boas, ed., Vol. 3, pp. 293–384. Washington. D. C.: 1934.

MYTHS—FOLKTALES

Gatschet, Albert S.
"Mythic Stories of the Yuchi Indians." *AA* 6:279–283, 1893. o.s.

Wagner, Günter
Yuchi Tales. Publications of the American Ethnological Society 13. New York: G. E. Stechert & Co., 1931. x, 357 pp.

MUSIC
GENERAL STUDIES

Jones, Charles C.
Music and Musical Instruments. In: *Antiquities of the Southern Indian, Particularly of the Georgia Tribes* (Chapter IV). New York: D. Appleton & Company, 1873.

Speck, Frank G.
"Ceremonial Songs of the Creek and Yuchi Indians," with music transcribed by Jacob D. Sapir. *University of Pennsylvania Museum, Anthropological Publication I* (No. 1):155–245. Philadelphia: Published by the University Museum, 1911.

———.
"Ethnology of the Yuchi Indians." *University of Pennsylvania Museum Anthropological Publications* 1:1–154. Philadelphia: Published by the University Museum, 1909.

OTHER TRIBES
MISCELLANEOUS STUDIES
ATAKAPA

Dyer, J. O.
The Lake Charles Atakapas. Galveston: 1917.

Gatschet, Albert S., and Swanton, John R.
Dictionary of Atakapa Language Accompanied by Text Material. U. S. Bureau of Ethnology Bulletin 108. Washington, D. C.: U. S. Gov't Printing Office, 1932.

Harrington, M. R.
"Among Louisiana Indians." *Southern Workman* (Hampton, Va.) 37:656–661, 1908.

Hewitt, J. N. B.
"Attacapa." *Bull. Bureau Amer. Ethnol.* 30 (Part 1):114–115, 1907.

Kniffen, Fred B.
"The Historic Indian Tribes of Louisiana." *Louisiana Conservation Review* 4 (No. 7), 5–12, July, 1935.

Swanton, J. R.
"Mythology of the Indians of Louisiana and the Texas Coast." *JAFL* 20:285–289, 1907.

———.
"A Sketch of the Atakapa Language." *Inter. Jour. Amer. Ling.* 5:121–149, 1929.

———.
"A Structural and Lexical Comparison of the Tunica, Chitimacha, and Atakapa Languages." *Bull. Bureau Amer. Ethnol.* 68:1–56, 1919.

BILOXI

Anon.
"Biloxi." *Bull. Bureau Amer. Ethnol.* 30 (Part 1):147–148, 1907.

Dorsey, J. O.
"Biloxi Tales." *JAFL* 6:48–50, 1893.

———.
"The Biloxi Indians of Louisiana." *Proc. Amer. Assoc. Adv. Sci.* 42:267–287, 1893.

———, and Swanton, John R.
Dictionary of Biloxi and Ofo Languages, with 31 Biloxi Texts and Numerous Biloxi Phrases, and Historical Sketches. U. S. Bureau of Ethnology Bulletin 47. Washington, D. C.: U. S. Gov't Printing Office, 1912.

Porter, Kenneth W.
"A Legend of the Biloxi." *JAFL* 59:168–173, 1946.
Gathered from the Seminole Negroes.

Voegelin, C. F.
"Ofo-Biloxi Sound Correspondences." *Proc. Ind. Acad. Sci.* 48:23–26, 1939.

CALUSA

Collins, H. B.
"Burial of the Culusa Indians." *El Palacio* 24:223–224.

———.
"The 'Lost' Calusa Indians." *Explorations and Field-Work of the Smithson. Inst.*, 1928, pp. 151–156.

Fejos, Paul
"Ethnography of the Yagua." *Viking Fund Publications in Anthropology No. 1. New York*: 144 pp., 56 pls., 30 text figs., map, 1943.
A Calusa village on the S.W. coast of Florida, about 1570.

Fewkes, J. W.
"Aboriginal Wooden Objects from Southern Florida." *Smithson. Miscel. Coll.* 80 (Part 9): 1–2, 1928.

Mooney, J.
"Calusa." *Bull. Bureau Amer. Ethnol.* 30 (Part 1):195–196, 1907.

HITCHITI

Gatschet, A. S.
"Hitchiti." *Bull. Bureau Amer. Ethnol.* 30 (Part 1):551, 1907.

———.
"Tchikilli's Kasi'hta Legend in the Creek and Hitchiti Languages." *Trans. Acad. Sci. St. Louis* 5:33–239, 1888.

Swanton, John R.
"Animal Stories from the Indians of the Muskhogean Stock." *JAFL* 26:214–216, 1913.

———.
"Myths and Tales of the Southeastern Indians." *Bull. Bureau Amer. Ethnol.* 88:87–117, 1929.

KAKINONBA

Swanton, J. R.
"The Kaskinampo Indians and their Neighbors." *AA* 32:405–418, 1930. n.s.
Known by the name—*Kakinonba:* A tribe mentioned by several early French writers about the close of the 18th century as living apparently on Tennessee or Cumberland River.

KARANKAWA

Fletcher, A. C.
"Coaque." *Bull. Bureau Amer. Ethnol.* 30 (Part 1):315–316, 1907.

———, and Swanton, J. R.
"Karankawa." *Bull. Bureau Amer. Ethnol.* 30 (Part 1):657–658, 1907.

Gatschet, A. S.
"Die Karankawa-Indianer." *Globus* 49:123–125, 1886.

———.
"The Karankawa-Indians." *Peabody Museum Papers* 1 (Part 2):5–103, 1891.

Jackson, A. T.
Picture Writing of Texas Indians. Anthropological Papers, University of Texas Publication 2. Austin: University of Texas, 1938. 490 pp., illus.

Potter, W. H.
"Ornamentation on the Pottery of the Texas Coastal Tribes." *Bull. Texas Arch. Paleont. Soc.* 2:41–44, 1930.

Swanton, John R.
Linguistic Material from the Tribes of Southern Texas and Northeastern Mexico. Bureau of American Ethnology, Bulletin 127, Smithsonian Institution. Washington, D. C.: U. S. Gov't. Printing Office, 1940.

———.
"Mythology of the Indians of Louisiana and the Texas Coast." *JAFL* 20:285–289, 1907.

MONACAN

Bushnell, David I., Jr.
"The Five Monacan Towns in Virginia, 1607." *Smithsonian Miscellaneous Collections, Vol. 82 (No. 12).* Washington, D. C.: U. S. Gov't Printing Office, 1930.
A confederacy or group of small tribes or bands, possibly Siouan, in north Virginia.

———.
"The Manahoac Tribes in Virginia, 1608." *Smithsonian Miscellaneous Collections, Vol. 94, (No. 8).* Washington, D. C.: U. S. Gov't Printing Office, 1935.

———.
"Native Cemeteries and Forms of Burial East of the Mississippi." *Bull. Bureau Amer. Ethnol.* 71:122–131, 1920.

Douglas, F. H.
"The Virginia Indian Tribes." *Denver Art Mus. Leaf. Ser.* 57:1–4, 1933.

Mooney, J.
"Monacan." *Bull. Bureau Amer. Ethnol.* 30 (Part 1):930–931, 1907.

Speck, F. G.
"The Question of Matrilineal Descent in the Southeastern Siouan Area." *AA* 40:1–12, 1938. n.s.

―――――.
"Siouan Tribes of the Carolinas." *AA* 37: 201–225, 1935. n.s.

PAMUNKEY

Bushnell, David I., Jr.
"Trailing Early Man in Virginia." *Explorations and Field Work in the Smithsonian Institution in 1940.* pp. 75–78, illus. Washington, D. C.: U. S. Gov't Printing Office, 1941.

Mooney, James
"Pamunkey." *Bull. Bureau Amer. Ethnol.* 30 (Part 2):197–199, 1910.

―――――.
The Siouan Tribes of the East. Bureau of American Ethnology, Bulletin 22. Washington, D. C.: U. S. Gov't Printing Office, 1894.

Pollard, J. Garland
The Pamunkey Indians of Virginia preface by W. J. McGee. Bureau of American Ethnology, Bull. 17, pp. 1–19. Washington, D. C.: U. S. Gov't Printing Office, 1894.

Tooker, W. W.
"The Mystery of the Name Pamunkey." *Amer. Antiq.* 17:289–293, 1895.

Rowell, Mary K.
"Pamunkey Indian Games and Amusements." *JAFL* 56:203–207, 1943.

PISCATAWAY (Conoy)

Ferguson, Alice L. L.
Moyaone and the Piscataway Indians. Washington, D. C.: Privately Printed, 1937. 44 pp.
Moyaone—"A tribe living in 1608 on the north bank of the Potomac, about Prince George County, Maryland—they were probably a division of the later Conoy . . . The Piscataway a former Conoy village situated on Piscataway Creek, in Prince George County, Md."

Marye, William B.
"Piscataway." *Maryland Historical Magazine* 30:183–240, 1935.

Semmes, Raphael
"Aboriginal Maryland." *Maryland Historical Magazine* 24:157–172, 196–209, 1929.

RAPPAHANNOCK

Speck, F. G.
The Rappahannock Indians of Virginia. *Indian Notes and Monographs,* 5–3. 83 pp. New York: Museum of the American Indian, Heye Foundation.

―――――, **Hassrick, Royal B., and Carpenter, Edmund S.**
"Rappahannock Herbals, Folk-lore and Science of Cures." *Proceedings of the Delaware County Institute of Science 10, (No. 1),* 55 pp., 1942. Media, Pa.

―――――.
Rappahannock Taking Devices: Traps, Hunting and Fishing. Joint Publications No. 1 Museum of the University of Pennsylvania, the Philadelphia Anthropological Society. Philadelphia: University Museum, 1946. 28 pp. 30 figures.

TAENSA

Brinton, D. G.
"The Taensa Grammar and Dictionary." *Amer. Antiq.* 7:108–113, 1885.

Calhoun, Robert Dabney
"The Taensa Indians." *Louisiana Historical Quarterly:* July, 1934, Vol. 17 (No. 3):411–435; October, 1934, Vol. 17, (No. 4):642–681.
"A tribe related in language and customs to the Natchez, from whom they must have separated shortly before the beginning of the historic period." (J. R. Swanton).

Gatschet, A. S.
"Removal of the Taensa Indians." *Amer. Antiq.* 13:252–254, 1891.

―――――.
"Two Indian Documents." *Amer. Antiq.* 13: 249–254, 1891.

Swanton, J. R.
"The Language of the Taensa." *AA* 10:24–32, 1908. n.s.

―――――.
"Taensa." *Bull. Bureau Amer. Ethnol.* 30 (Part 2):668–669, 1910.

Vinson, J.
"La Langue Taensa." *Revue de Linguistique et Philologie Comparée (Paris)* 19:147–169, 1886.

TONKAWA

Atkinson, M. J.
The Texas Indians. San Antonio: 1935.

Bolton, H. E.
"Tonkawa." *Bull. Bureau Amer. Ethnol.* 30 (Part 2):778–783, 1910.

Gatschet, A. S.
"Remarks Upon the Tónkawa Language."
Proc. Amer. Philo. Soc. 16:318–327, 1876.

————.
"Die Sprache der Tonkawas." *Zeit. für Ethno.*
9:64–73, 1877.

————.
Zwölf Sprachen dem südwesten Nordamerikas.
Weimar: H. Böhlau, 1876. 150 pp.

Hoijer, H.
"Tonkawa." In: *Handbook of American In-
dian Languages,* Franz Boas, ed. New York: J. J.
Augustin, Vol. 3, 1931. 148 pp.

Mooney, J.
"Die Tonkawas." Globus 82:76–79, 1902.

Opler, M. E.
"A Description of a Tonkawa Peyote Meeting."
AA 41:433–439, 1939. n.s.

TUSCARORA

Hewitt, J. N. B.
"Tuscarora." *Bull. Bureau Amer. Ethnol.* 30
(Part 2):842–853, 1910.

Johnson, E.
*Legends, Traditions, and Laws of the Iroquois,
or Six Nations, and History of the Tuscarora
Indians.* Lockport: 1881.

THE PLAINS AREA

THE PLAINS AREA
FOLKLORE

BIBLIOGRAPHY

Campbell, Vera
Myths and Legends of Colorado; a bibliography. Greely, Colo.: Colorado State Teachers College, 1924. 12 pp. (Colorado State Teachers College Bulletin Series XXIV, No. 2. June 1924).

Wissler, Clark
"Publications on the Indians of the Northern Plains." *Science* 32:562–564, 1910. n.s.

GENERAL STUDIES

Belden, G. P.
Belden, The White Chief, or Twelve Years Among the Wild Indians of the Plains, from the diaries and manuscripts of George Belden. Edited by Gen. James S. Brisbin, U. S. A. Cincinnati and New York: C. Z. Vent, 1870. iv, 513 pp., incl. illus., pls., front.

Bennett, John W.
"The Development of Ethnological Theory as Illustrated by Studies of the Plains Sun Dance." *AA* 46:162–182, 1944.

Boyd, George
"Papers of George Boyd, Indian Agent, 1797–1820, 2 vols—1832." *Wisconsin State Historical Society Collections* (Madison) 12:266–298, 1892.

Branch, Edward Douglas
The Hunting of the Buffalo. New York: D. Appleton and Company, 1929. vi. 239 pp.

Burbank, E. A.
Burbank Among the Indians, as told to Ernest Royce. Caldwell, Idaho: Caxton Printers, 1945. 232 pp., illus.
A noted artist records his impression of life and love among many Indian tribes, principally these of the Plains and Southwest.

Chittenden, H. M., and Richardson, A. T., eds.
Life, Letters and Travels of Father Pierre Jean de Smet. New York: 1905. 4 vols.

Custer, General George Armstrong
My Life on the Plains, or Personal Experience With Indians. New York: Sheldon & Co., 1874. 256 pp.

Delano, A.
Life on the Plains and Among the Diggings; Being Scenes and Adventures of an Overland Journey to California. Auburn and Buffalo, 1854.

De Schwirnitz, Bishop Edmund Alexander
The Life and Times of David Zeisberger, the Western Pioneer and Apostle of the Indians. Phila. Pa.: J. B. Lippincott, 1870. 747 pp.

Dodge, Col. Richard Irving
Our Wild Indians. Thirty Three Years' Personal Experience among the Red Men of the Great West. Introduction by General Sherman. Chicago: A. G. Nettleton & Co., 1883. xxxix, 650 pp.

————.
The Plains of the Great West, and Their Inhabitants; being a description of the plains, game, Indians, etc. of the great North American desert. Introduction by Wm. Blackmore. New York: G. P. Putnam's Sons, 1877. lv, 448 pp.

Domenech, Abbe Emmanuel Henri
Seven Year's Residence in the Great Deserts of North America. London: Longman, Green, Longman and Roberts, 1860. illus.

Donaldson, T.
The George Catlin Gallery in the U. S. National Museum. Reports of the United States National Museum. Vol. I. Washington, D. C.: 1885. 939 pp.

Dorsey, J. O.
"Camping Circles of Siouan Tribes." *AA* 2:175–177, 1889.

————.
"The Place of Gentes in Siouan Camping Circles." *AA* 2:375–379, 1889.

Douglas, F. H.
"Plains Indian Tribes." *Denver Art Mus. Leaflet Ser.* 23:1–4, 1931.

Driver, H. E., and Krober, A. L.
"Quantitative Expression of Cultural Relationships." *Univ. Calif. Publ. Amer. Arch. Ethnol.* 31:226–236, 1932.

Eastman, Charles Alexander
Old Indian Days. New York: The McClure Co., 1907. 279 pp.

Farnham, T. J.
Travels in the Great Western Prairies. In: *Early Western Travels,* R. G. Thwaites, ed., Vols. 28–29. Cleveland: 1906.

Foreman, Grant
The Last Trek of the Indians. Chicago: University of Chicago Press, 1946. 382 pp., illus., maps, bibl.

Gass, P.
A Journal of the Voyages and Travels of a Corps of Discovery. Pittsburgh: 1807.

Hafen, LeRoy R., and Rister, Carl C.
Western America: the exploration, settlement, and development of the region beyond the Mississippi. (Prentice Hall books on History). New York: Prentice Hall, 1941.

Hamilton, W. T.
My Sixty Years on the Plains. New York:
Forest and Stream, 1905. 244 pp.

Hanna, Charles S.
The Wilderness Trail. New York: G. P. Putnam's Sons, 1911. 2 vols.

Harmon, Daniel Williams
*Journal of Voyages and Travels in the Interior
of North America (Canada) to the Pacific
Ocean.* New York: Allerton Book Co., 1922.
382 pp.

Harrington, M. R.
"Indian Tribes of the Plains." *Masterkey*
15 (No. 4):6–28, 1941. Los Angeles: Southwest Museum.

Hayden, Ferdinand V.
*Contributions to the Ethnography and Philo-
logy of the Indian Tribes of the Missouri Valley.*
etc. Phila. Pa.: C. Sherman & Sons, Printers,
1862. 461 pp.

————.
"On the Ethnology and Philology of the Indian
Tribes of the Missouri Valley." *Tran. American
Philos. Society* 12: 245+, 1863, n.s. (Phila-
delphia).

Hermant, P.
"Évolution économique et sociale de certaines
peuples de l'Amérique du Nord." *Bulletin de
la Société Royale Belge de Geographie.*
(Bruxelles) 29:5–30, 1905.

Hewitt, J. N. B., ed.
Journal of Rudolph Friedrich Kurz. Bulletin
95. Bureau of American Ethnology Washington, D. C.: 1937. 382 pp.

Hoebel, E. A.
"Associations and the State in the Plains." *AA*
38:433–438, 1926. n. s.

Humfreville, James Lee
Twenty Years Among Our Hostile Indians.
Describing the characteristics, customs, habits,
religion, marriages, dances, and battles, of
the wild Indians. . . . New York: Hunter &
Co., 1903. xxvi, 480 pp., illus.

Humphrey, N. D.
"A Characterization of Certain Plains Associations." *AA* 43:428–436, 1941. n.s.

"Indian History: Scarface Charley, Sitting Bull,
Geronimo."
Hobbies 47: 101, 1942.

James, Edwin
*Narrative of the Captivity and Adventures of
John Tanner, during Thirty Years Residence
Among the Indians in the Interior of North
America.* New York: G. and C. and H. Car-
ville, 1830.

Jameson, Anna Brownell
*Sketches in Canada, and Rambles among
the Red Men.* London: Longman, Brown,
Green and Longmans, 1852. 314 pp.

Jewitt, John Rodgers
A Narrative of Adventures and Sufferings.
Middletown: Loomis and Richards, 1815.

Keim, de Bonneville R.
Sheridan's Troopers on the Borders: A Winter
Campaign on the Plains. Philadelphia: D.
McKay, 1885. viii, 308 pp., front. plates.

Krause, F.
"Zur Besiedelungsgeschichte der nordamerikanischen Prärie." *Korrespondenz-Blatt der
deutschen Gesellschaft für Anthropologie, Ethnologie und Urgeschichte* (Braunschweig) 44:
66–70, 1913.

La Flesche, F.
"The Past Life of the Plains Indians." *So.
Workman* 34:587–594, 1905.

Larpenteur, C.
*Forty Years a Fur Trader on the Upper
Missouri.* E. Coues, ed. New York: F. P. Har-
per, 1898. 2 vols.

Lesser, Alexander
"Some Aspects of Siouan Kinship." *Inter.
Congr. Amer.* 23:563–571, 1928.

Lewis, M., and Clark, W.
Travels. London: Longmans . . . 1815. 3 vols.

Long, Maj. Stephen
*Account of an Expedition from Pittsburg
to the Rocky Mountains in 1819 and 1829.*
"James' Long's Expedition", compiled by Edwin James. Philadelphia: Carey and Lee, 1822.
4 pp., plates, 3 fold. maps.

Lowie, Robert H.
"Plains Indian Age-Societies: Historical and
Comparative Summary." *Anthropological Pa-
pers:* Vol. 11: 1916, pp. 877–984. Publications
in Anthropology. New York: The American
Museum of Natural History.

————.
"Some Problems in Plains Indian Folklore."
JAFL 60:401–403, 1947.

————.
Studies in Plains Indians Folklore. University
of California Publications in American Ethnology, vol. 40, (No. 1), Berkeley and Los
Angeles, 1942.

Lyman, Amy B.
"Indians of the Plains." *Relief Society Maga-
zine* 33:440, 1946.
Tales of Indians and the pioneer trek.

Macgregor, Gordon
*Warriors Without Weapons: A Study of the
Society and Personality Development of the
Pine Ridge Sioux.* Chicago: University of
Chicago Press, 1946. 228 pp.

Möllhausen, B.
*Diary of a Journey from the Mississippi to the
Coasts of the Pacific.* London: 1858. 2 vols.

Moorhead, Warren King
"Prehistoric Culture Areas East of the Rocky Mountains." *Proceedings of the 23rd International Congress of Americanists*, pp. 47–52, 1928.

Paget, Amelia M.
The Peoples of the Plains. Toronto: William Briggs, 1909. 199 pp.

Perrin du Lac, François Marie
Travels Through the Two Louisianas. London: R. Phillips, 1807. 106 pp.

Pike, Z. M.
An Account of Expeditions to the Sources of the Mississippi and through the western parts of Louisiana to the sources of the Arkansas, Kansas, La Platte and Pierre Jaun rivers, performed by order of the U. S. government during the years 1805, 1806, 1807. Illustrated by maps and charts. Philadelphia: 1810.

Pritts, J.
Incidents of Border Life, illustrative of the times and conditions of the first settlements in parts of the middle and western states, etc. Chambersburg, Penna.: J. Pritts, 1839. ix, 491 pp., front, plates (1 fold).

Smet, Pierre Jean de
Letters and Sketches. Philadelphia: 1843.

————.
Voyages aux Montagnes Rocheuses. Lille: L. Lefort, 1873. vii, 268 pp.

Smith, De Cost
Indian Experiences. Caldwell, Idaho: Caxton, Ltd., 1943. 387 pp.

Smith, Marian Wesley
"The War Complex of the Plains Indians." *Proceedings, American Philosophical Society.* 78: 425–464, 1938.

Smith, Maurice G.
"Political Organization of the Plains Indians." *University of Nebraska Publications*, Vol. 24, (Nos. 1, 2). Lincoln: The University of Nebraska Press, 1925.

Snelling, William J.
Tales of the Northwest: Sketches of Indian Life and Character. Boston: 1830.

————.
Tales of Travels West of the Mississippi. Boston: Gray & Brown, 1830.

Strong, William Duncan
From History to Prehistory in the Northern Great Plains. In: Smithsonian Institution. *Essays in Historical Anthropology of North America;* Publication in honor of John R. Swanton in celebration of his fortieth year with the Smithsonian Institution. Washington, D. C.: U. S. Government Printing Office, 1940.

————.
"The Plains Culture Area in the Light of Archaeology." *AA* 35:271–287, 1933. n.s.

Talbot, E.
My People of the Plains. New York: Harper Brothers, 1906. 264 pp.

Thomas, Alfred Barnaby
After Coronado. Norman: University of Oklahoma Press, 1935. 307 pp.

————.
The Plains Indians and New Mexico: 1751–1778; a collection of documents illustrative of the eastern frontier of New Mexico. Coronado Cuarto Centennial Publication, 1540–1940. Albuquerque: University of Mexico Press, 1940.

Thomas, Cyrus
"Catalogue of Prehistoric Works, East of the Rocky Mountains." *Bureau American Ethnology,* Bulletin 12. pp. 7–224, pls. 1–17. Washington, D. C.: U. S. Government Printing Office, 1891.

Truteau, J. B.
"Journal." *Amer. Hist. Rev.* 19:299–333, 1914.

Vestal, Stanley
'*Dobe Walls'*, *A Story of Kit Carson's Southwest.* Boston: Houghton Mifflin Company, 1929. 314 pp.
Excellent characterization of the Plains Indians.

Webb, Walter Prescott
The Great Plains. Boston: Ginn and Company, 1931. 524 pp.

Wedel, Waldo Rudolph
Culture Sequence in the Central Great Plains. In: Smithsonian Institution: *Essays in Historical Anthropology of North America;* published in honor of John R. Swanton, in celebration of his fortieth year with the Smithsonian Institution. Miscellaneous Collection Vol. 100, Washington, D. C.: U. S. Government Printing Office, 1940.

Wellman, Paul I.
Death on the Prairie: The Thirty Years' Struggle for the Western Plains. New York: Macmillan Company, 1934. 298 pp., illus.
"Strong recital of the outstanding features of the Indian struggle to keep their plains. Bibliography." (Dobie)

Wied-Neuwied, Maximillian
Travels in the Interior of North America. Translated by H. Evans Lloyd. London: Ackermann and Company, 1843. x, 520 pp., illus.

Wissler, Clark
"Changes in Population Profiles Among the Northern Plains Indians." *Anthropological Papers:* Vol. 36: 1936, pp. 1–67. Publications in Anthropology. New York: The American Museum of Natural History.

————.
"Diffusion of Culture in the Plains of North America." *Proceedings of the 15th Session of the International Congress of Americanists* (Quebec), 2:39–53, 1906.

————.
"Ethnographical Problems of the Missouri-Saskatchewan Area." *AA* 10: 197–208, 1908, n.s.

————.
North American Indians of the Plains. New York: The American Museum of Natural History, 1934. 172 pp., maps and illus., third edition.

————.
Population Changes Among the Northern Plains Indians. Yale University Publications in Anthropology I. New Haven: Yale University Press, 1936. 20 pp.

MYTHS—FOLKTALES—LEGENDS

Anon.
"The Human Panther." *The Jeffersonian* 1:234, Sept. 1838.
A tale of "Old Meyers" known to the Indians as Panther: a frontiersman of the West, his exploits and amazing deeds.

Benedict, Ruth F.
"The Vision in Plains Culture." *AA* 24:1–23, 1922. n.s.

Borland, Hal
Rocky Mountain Tipi Tales. New York: Doubleday Doran, 1924.

Brown, Charles Edward
Wigwam Tales; thunder birds, water spirits, horned serpents, tie snakes, Wind Bird, Windigos, little Indians, spider men and witches, creation myths, star lore, animal lore, and other Indian folktales. Madison, Wis.: C. E. Brown, 1930. 28 pp.

Davis, A. L.
"American Apostle: Ghost Dance Religion." *American Mercury* 30:219–227 (October) 1933.

Dunlop, G. M.
Tales of the Indians of the Plains. Edmonton, Alberta: Institute of Applied Art, 1934.

Eastman, Charles Alexander, and Eastman, Elaine Goodate
Smokey Day's Wigwam Evenings; Indian Stories Retold. Boston: Little, Brown and Co., 1910. viii, 148 pp., illus.

Fitzgerald, LaVerne H.
Black Feather, Trapper Jim's Fables of Sheepeater Indians in the Yellowstone. Caldwell, Id.: The Caxton Printers, Ltd., 1933. 193 pp., illus.
Legends of the Tukarika Indians.

Fletcher, Alice Cunningham
Wakonda. In: *Handbook of American Indians.* Vol. II, pp. 897–898. Bureau of American Ethnology, Bulletin 30. Washington, D. C.: U. S. Government Printing Office, 1910.
"A term employed by the Omaha, Ponca, Osage, Quapaw, Kansa, Oto, Missouri and Iowa tribes of the Siouan family when the power believed to animate all natural forms is spoken to or spoken of in supplications or rituals."

Gilmore, Melvin R.
Prairie Smoke. New York: Columbia University Press, 1929.

Janes, Mary B.
"Up the Mississippi." *The Ladies Repository* 25:461–464, Aug. 1865.
A description of a trip from Iowa to Minnesota, telling a number of Indian legends.

Judd, M. C.
Wigwam Stories. Boston: Ginn and Co., 1901.

Judson, Katharine Berry, ed.
Myths and Legends of the Great Plains. Chicago: A. C. McClurg & Co., 1913. 204 pp., illus.

————.
Myths and Legends of the Mississippi Valley and the Great Lakes. Chicago: A. C. McClurg and Co., 1914.

Kunike, Hugo
Praerie-Indianer-Maerchen. Berlin: A. Juncker, 1923. 164 pp.
Tales of the Plains Indians.

Larned, William Trowbridge
American Indian Fairy Tales. Illustrated by John Roe. New York: P. F. Volland Co., 1921. 93 pp., illus.
"With one exception, all the tales in this book are adapted from the legends collected by Henry R. Schoolcraft . . . and published in 1893. With the title "Algic Researches"."

Linderman, Frank B.
Indian Why Stories; Sparks From War Eagle's Lodge Fire. (By Co-Skee-see-co-cot.) New York: Charles Scribner's Sons, 1915. xx, 236 pp., illus.

Phillips, Walter Shelley
Indian Tales for Little Folks. Illustrated with eleven full page colored plates reproduced from water color paintings by the author, and further embellished with several hundred little Indian drawings; with explanatory key list so little folks can understand them. New York: The Platt & Peck Co., 1914. 80 pp., illus.

————.
The Sandman: his Indian stories, with many illustrations and decorations by the author. Boston: The Page Co., 1918. xvi, 292 pp.

————.
Teepee Tales by El Comancho. Pictures by Charles Livingston Bull and El Comancho. Chicago: The Reilly & Lee Co., 1927. viii, 208 pp., illus.
Legends and stories of animals.

Reagan, A. B.
Sun God, Moccasin Tales. Provo, Utah: The Author, 1935.

Sturtevant, Mabel
The Good Spirit of Tepee Mountain. Illustrated by Allen Saunders. Crawfordsville, Indiana: Schultz and Schultz, 1926.

Wake, C. S.
"Mythology of the Plains Indians." *American Antiquarian* 27:9–16. 73–80, 823–828, 1905; 28:205–212, 1906.

Wilson, G. L.
Myths of the Red Children. Boston: Ginn and Co., 1907.

BELIEFS—CUSTOMS

Alexander, H. B.
The Horse in American Indian Culture. In: *So Live the Works of Men*, D. D. Brand, and F. E. Harvey, eds., (pp.65–74). Albuquerque: Univ. New Mexico Press, 1939.

Buchanan, James
Sketches of the History, Manners, and Customs of the North American Indians, With a Plan for Their Melioration. Vols. I–II. New York: W. Borradaile, 1824, 1825.

Carr, Lucien
"Food of Certain American Indians." *Proceedings Amer. Antiq. Society*, n.s. *Vol. X*, Worcester, 1895.

Catlin, George
Catalogue of Catlin's Indian Gallery of portraits, landscapes, manners, customs, etc. . . . collected during seven years' travel amongst thirty-eight different tribes, speaking different languages. New York: Piercy & Reed, Printers, 1838. 40 pp.
Numerous editions were issued of this work. Some have slight changes in the title.

———.
Illustrations of the Manners, Customs and Condition of the North American Indians: in a series of letters and notes written during eight years of travel and adventure among the wildest and most remarkable tribes now existing. With three hundred and sixty engravings from the author's original paintings. London: H. G. Bohn, 1845. 2 vols.
Numerous editions of this work appeared, with slight changes in the title.

———.
Letters and Notes on the Manners, Customs, and Condition of the North American Indians. Written during eight years' travel (1832-1839) among the wildest tribes of Indians in North America. New York: Wiley & Putnam, 1841. 2 vols., illus. London: Published by the author; printed by Toswell and Meyers, 1841. Front. (v. 1), plates, ports., 2 maps (1 fold). Many subsequent editions of the same work.

———.
Life Amongst the Indians, A Book for Youth. New York: D. Appleton & Co., 1867. xii, 339 pp., front., illus., plates.

———.
"Missouri." *Waldie's Select Circulating Library*. Part II, No. 27, Dec. 1841.
A description of the Missouri River, also the effect of the steamboat on the Indians.

Clements, F.
"Plains Indian Tribal Correlations with Sun Dance Data." *AA* 33:216–227, 1931. n.s.

Collier, Donald
"The Sun Dance of the Plains Indians." *America Indigena* 3(No. 4):359–364, 1943. Mexico, D.F.

Douglas, F. H.
"Plains Indian Clothing." *Denver Art Mus. Leaflet Ser.* 24:1–4, 1931.

———.
"The Plains Indian Tipi." *Denver Arts Mus. Leaflet Ser.* 19:1–4, 1931.

Farabee, W. C.
"Dress Among the Plains Indian Women." *Museum Journal* 12:239–251, 1921.

Fletcher, A. C.
"The Emblematic Use of the Tree in the Dakotan Group." *Proc. Amer. Assoc. Adv. Sci.* 45:191–209, 1896.

Gilmore, M. R.
"Some Indian Ideas of Property." *Indian Notes* 5:137–144, 1928.

Grinnell, George B.
"Coup and Scalp Among the Plains Indians." *AA* 12:296–349, 1910. n.s.

———.
When the Buffalo Ran. New Haven: Yale University Press, 1920.

Humphrey, N. D.
"A Characterization of Certain Plains Associations." *AA* 43:428–436, 1941. n.s.

Hunter, John Dunn
Manners and Customs of Several Indian Tribes Located West of the Mississippi; including some account of the soil, climate, and vegetable productions, and the Indian materia medica; to which is prefixed the history of the author's life during a residence of several years among them. Philadelphia: J. Maxwell, 1823. viii, 402 pp.
English edition has title *Memoirs of a Captivity*.

Imlay, Gilbert
A Description of the Western Territory of North America; containing a succinct account of its climate, natural history, population, agriculture, manners and customs . . . with an accurate statement of the various tribes of Indians that inhabit the frontier country. Dublin: W. Jones, 1793. xx, 249 pp.

Kroeber, A. L.
"Ceremonial Organization of the Plains Indians of North America." *Proceedings of the 15th Session of the International Congress of Americanists*, 2:53–65, 1906.

Lesser, Alexander
"Cultural Significance of the Ghost Dance." *AA* 35:108–115, 1933. n.s.

Lowie, R. H.
"Marriage and Family Life Among the Plains Indians." *Scientific Monthly* 34:462:464, 1932.

―――――.
"Plains Indian Age-Societies." *Anthro. Papers Amer. Mus. Natur. Hist.* 11:877–992, 1916.

MacLeod, W. C.
"Police and Punishment Among Native American Indians of the Plains." *Journal of Criminal Law* 28:201 (July), 1937.

McGillycuddy, V. T.
The Significance of the Indian Ghost Dance Religion. In: *When People Meet*; A Study in Race and Culture Contacts, edited by Alain Locke and Bernhard J. Stern. (pp. 514–516.) New York: Progressive Education Association, 1942.

Mishkin, Bernard
Rank and Warfare Among the Plains Indians. American Ethnological Society Monographs 3. New York: J. J. Augustin, 1940. 65 pp.

Mooney, James
"The Ghost-Dance Religion and the Sioux Outbreak of 1890." *14th Annual Report of the U. S. Bureau of Ethnology* (pp. 641–1110). Washington, D. C.: U. S. Government Printing Office, 1896.

Muntsch, Albert
"The Relations Between Religion and Morality Among the Plains Indians." *Primitive Man* 4:22–29, 1931.

Olden, Sarah Emilia
Little Slants at Western Life; a notebook of travel and reflection. New York: H. Vinal, Ltd., 1927. 245 pp., bibl.
General observations on life, customs, and Indians.

Parsons, Elsie Clews
"Ritual Parallels in Pueblo and Plains Culture, with a Special Reference to the Pawnee." *AA* 31:642–654, 1929. n.s.

Phister, Lieut. N. P.
"The Indian Messiah." *AA* 4 (No. 2), (April) 1891.

Provinse, John H.
"The Underlying Sanctions of Plains Indian Culture." *Social Organization of North American Tribes,* Fred Eggan, ed., pp. 341–374. Chicago: Chicago University Press, 1937.

Ray, Verne F.
"Historic Backgrounds of the Conjuring Complex in the Plateau and the Plains." *Language, Culture and Personality Essays,* in Memory of Edward Sapir, pp. 204–219. Menasha, Wisc.: Sapir Memorial Publication Fund, 1941.

Roe, F. G.
"From Dogs to Horses Among the Western Indian Tribes." *Proc. Trans. Royal Soc. Can.* (ser. 3)33(Part 2):209–275, 1939.

Smith, M. G.
"Political Organization of the Plains Indians." *Univ. Nebraska Studies* 24:1–84, 1925.

―――――.
"The Distribution and Functions of Tribal Societies Among the Plains Indians." *Proc. Nat. Acad. Sci.* 1:401–403, 1915.

Spier, Leslie
"The Sun Dance of the Plain Indians: Its Development and Diffusion." *Anthropological Papers* (American Museum of Natural History, N. Y.) 16:451–527, 1921. Illus.

Whiting, John W.
"A Glimpse of Indian Warfare." *The Knickerbocker,* 57:599–602, June 1861.
An authentic sketch of a trip through the 'Far West', comprising Illinois, Wisconsin, Iowa, and Minnesota, 1836, accompanied by two trappers and huntsmen.

Wissler, Clark
"Costumes of the Plains Indians." *Anthropological Papers of the American Museum of Natural History,* 17:39–91, 1915.
Part II describes the costumes and adornments of various North American tribes.

―――――.
"Distribution of Moccasin Decorations Among the Plains Tribes." *Anthropological Papers:* Vol. 29, 1927, pp. 1–23, 4 figs. Publications in Anthropology. New York: The American Museum of Natural History.

―――――.
"The Influence of the Horse in the Development of Plains Culture. *AA* 16:1–26, 1914. n.s.

―――――.
"Types of Dwellings and Their Distribution in Central North America." *Proceedings of the 16th Session of the International Congress of Americanists* (Vienna), pp. 477–489, 1908.

FOLK ART—SPEECH

Carr, Lucien
"Dress and Ornaments of Certain American Indians." *Proc. Amer. Antiq. Soc. n.s., vol. XI,* Worcester, 1898.

Clark, W. P.
The Indian Sign Language. Philadelphia: L. R. Hamersley, 1885. 443 pp.

Douglas, F. H.
"An Incised Bison Rawhide Parfleche." *Material Culture Notes* (Denver Art Museum)6: 23–25, 1938.

―――――.
"Plains Beads and Beadwork Designs." *Denver Art Mus. Leaflet Ser.* 73–74:90–96, 1936.

―――――.
"Two Plains Bison Hair Ropes." *Material Culture Notes* (Denver Art Museum) 5:19–22, 1938.

Ewers, J. C.
Plains Indian Painting. Palo Alto: 1939. 84 pp.

Hall, H. U.
"A Buffalo Robe Biography." *Museum Journal*
17:5–35, 1926.

—————.
"Some Shields of the Plains and Southwest."
Museum Journal 17:37–61, 1926.

Mallery, G.
"Sign Language Among North American Indians." *Annual Report Bureau Amer. Ethnol.*
1:263–552, 1880.

—————.
"The Sign Language of the Indians of the
Upper Missouri." *Amer. Antiq.* 2:218–228,
1880.

Matthews, W.
"The Earth Lodge in Art." *AA* 4:1–12, 1902.
n.s.

McAdams, William
*Records of Ancient Races in the Mississippi
Valley,* being an account of some of the pictographs, sculptured hieroglyphics, symbolic devices, emblems, and traditions of the prehistoric race in America. St. Louis: C. R. Barns
Company, 1887. xii, 120 pp., front., illus.

Pilling, J. C.
"Bibliography of the Siouan Languages."
Bull. Bureau Amer. Ethnol. 5:1–87, 1887.

Renaud, E. B.
Indian Petroglyphs of the Plains. In: *So Live
the Works of Men,* D. D. Brand, and F. E.
Harvey, eds. (pp. 295–310). Albuquerque:
1939.

Scott, H. L.
The Sign Language of the Plains Indians.
Archives of the International Folk-Lore Asso-
ciation, Vol. I., 1893. 206 pp.

Spier, Leslie
"An Analysis of Plains Indian Parfleche
Decoration." *Univ. Wash. Publ. Anthro.* 1:89–
112, 1925.

—————.
"Plains Indian Parfleche Designs." *Univ. Wash.
Publ. Anthro.* 4:293–322, 1931.

Tompkins, William
*Universal Indian Sign Language of the Plains
Indians of North America,* together with a
simplified method of study, a list of words in
most general use, a codification of pictographic
symbols of the Sioux and Ojibwa, a dictionary
of synonyms, a history of sign language, chapters on smoke signalling, use of idioms, etc.,
and other important co-related matter. San
Diego, Cal.: Authors' ed., 1941. 106 pp. 8th
edition. First published in 1926.

Vatter, Ernst
"Historienmalerei und heraldische Bilderschrift
der nordamerikanischen Präriestämme" *Ipek*
(Leipzig):46–81, 1927.

Voegelin, C. F.
"Internal Relationships of Siouan Languages."
AA 43:246–249, 1941. n.s.

Wissler, Clark
"Costumes of the Plains Indians." *Anthro.
Papers Amer. Mus. Natur. Hist.*

—————.
"Distribution of Moccasin Decorations Among
the Plains Tribes." *Anthro Papers Amer. Mus.
Natur. Hist.* 29:1–23, 1927.

—————.
Indian Beadwork. New York: The American
Museum of Natural History, 1931. 31 pp., illus.,
second printing.
A description of the technique employed in bead
and quill work from typical Plains Indian beadwork.

—————.
"Riding Gear of the North American Indians."
Anthro. Papers Mus. Natur. Hist. 17:1–38,
1915.

—————.
"Structural Basis to the Decoration of Costumes
Among the Plains Indians." *Anthropological
Papers.* Vol. 17: 1916, pp., 93–114, 12 figs.
Publications in Anthropology. New York: The
American Museum of Natural History.

FOLK MEDICINE

Gilmore, Melvin Randolph
"Uses of Plants by the Indians of the Missouri
River Region." In: *33rd Annual Report:
Bureau American Ethnology, 1911–1912,* pp.
43–154, pls. 1–30. Washington, D. C.: U. S.
Gov't. Printing Office, 1919.

Schonle, R.
"Peyote." *AA* 17:53–75, 1925. n.s.

Wagner, G.
"Entwicklung und Verbreitung des Peyotes-
Kultes." *Baessler-Archiv* (Berlin) 15:59–144,
1932.

MUSIC

GENERAL STUDIES

Anon.
"Item." *The Musical Visitor,* 3:370, Oct. 8,
1844.
According to Catlin, the Indians use the flute as
a messenger of declaration of love.

Bushnell, David Ives
*Villages of the Algonquin, Siouan, and Cad-
don Tribes West of the Mississippi.* Washington, D. C.: U. S. Government Printing Office,
1922.

Curtis, Natalie
The Indians' Book . . . Illustrations from
photographs and from original drawings by
Indians. New York: Harper and Bros., 1907.
(pp. 31–241).
Discussion of legends, myths and ceremonies,
with musical examples.

Dougherty, G. H.
"Songs and Speeches of the Plains." *Open Court*, 41:338–357.

Dodge, Col. Richard Irving
Indian Music and Musicians. In: *Our Wild Indians*; Thirty-three Years' Personal Experiences Among the Red Men of the Great West (Chapter XXVII). Hartford, Connecticut: A. D. Workington & Company, 1885.

Paget, Amelia M.
Poetry and Music. In: *The Peoples of the Plains*, Chapter XII (pp. 160–164). Toronto: William Briggs, 1909.

DANCES

Bennett, John W.
"The Development of Ethnological Theory as Illustrated by Studies of the Plains Sun Dance." *AA* 46:162–182, 1944.

Clements, F.
"Plains Indian Tribal Correlations with Sun Dance Data." *AA* 33:216–227, 1931. n.s.

Collier, Donald
"The Sun Dance of the Plains Indians." *America Indigena* 3(No. 4):359–364 (Mexico, D.F.), 1943.

Davis, A. L.
"American Apostle; Ghost Dance of Religion." *American Mercury*, 30:210–227 (October), 1933.

Dorsey, George A.
Sun Dance. In: *Handbook of American Indians*. Vol. II, pp. 649–652. Bureau of American Ethnology, Bulletin 30. Washington, D. C.: U. S. Government Printing Office, 1910.

E.
"Sketches of Indian Character. The Buffalo Dance." *New World*, 6:461–463, April 22, 1843.
A sympathetic discussion of Indian bravery, fortitude and virtue, with illustrations of the Buffalo dance.

Herzog, George
"Plains Ghost Dance and Great Basin Music." *AA* 37:403–419, 1935, n.s.

Kroeber, A. L.
"The Ceremonial Organization of the Plains Indians." *Inter. Congr. Amer.* 15(Part 2):53–63, 1906.

Lesser, Alexander
"Cultural Significance of the Ghost Dance." *AA* 35:108–115, 1933, n.s.

McGillycuddy, V. T.
The Significance of the Indian Ghost Dance Religion. In: *When Peoples Meet*; A Study in Race and Culture Contacts, edited by Alain Locke and Bernhard J. Stern (pp. 514–516). New York: Progressive Education Association, 1942.

Mooney, James
The Ghost-Dance Religion and the Sioux Outbreak of 1890. In: *The 14th Annual Report of the U. S. Bureau of Ethnology* (pp. 641–1110), pl. LXXXV–CXXXII, fig. 56–104. Washington, D. C.: U. S. Government Printing Office, 1896.

Spier, Leslie
"The Sun Dance of the Plain Indians: Its Development and Diffusion." *Anthropological Papers:* Vol. 16:1921, pp. 451–527, 1 fig. Publications in Anthropology. New York: The American Museum of Natural History.

ARRANGEMENTS

VOICE AND PIANO

"Song of the Wilderness Hosts."
Dobson, Aldrich E.: Schmidt.

PIANO

Tales of the Red Man Suite.
Grant-Schaefer, G. A.: Schmidt: Piano.
Contents: 1. Wooing (Theme from an Indian Love Song; 2. Little Papoose (Chippewa Lullaby); 3. In Her Canoe (In free style—an adaptation); 4. Puk-Wudjes Dance (Teton Sioux Dancing Song); 5. How the Rabbit Lost His Tail; 6. The Old Indian Lament (Free adaptation).

"Indian Drum."
Davis, K.: G. Schirmer: Piano.

"Indian Lullaby."
Williams, J.: G. Schirmer: Piano.

"Indian War Call."
Wright, M.: G. Schirmer: Piano.

"Indian War Dance."
Rolseth, B.: G. Schirmer: Piano.

"The Indian's War Dance."
Belden, L. A.: G. Schirmer: Piano.

STRING QUARTET

Two Indian Dances: Deer Dance, War Dance.
Skilton, Charles Sanford: Carl Fischer: String Quartet.

RECORDS

Herzog, George
"Plains Area: Records Contained in American Collections." *American Council of Learned Societies* (Washington, D. C.), Bulletin 24:28, 1936.

U. S. Library of Congress. Division of Music. Folklore Section.
See: Indian Record Collections in the American Folksong Archive of the Music Division of the Library of Congress.   AAFS–LC
This collection has been immensely enriched by the large Densmore addition.

————.
Indian Songs, by Berry A. Keahtigh, Kiowa; Calvin Solimon, Paguate, Valencia Co., Laguna Pueblo, N. M., and Philip Sheridan Proctor, Piscatawy, Port Tobacco, Md.   AAFS–LC

ARAPAHO

FOLKLORE

GENERAL STUDIES

Beals, Ralph L.
Ethnology of Rocky Mountain Park: the Ute and Arapaho. Berkeley: University of California Press, 1935. 27 pp.

Dorsey, George A., and Kroeber, Alfred L.
Traditions of the Arapaho. Collected under the auspices of the Field Columbian Museum, and of the American Museum of Natural History. Anthropological Series, Vol. 5, No. 81. Chicago: 1903. x, 475 pp.

Elkin, Henry
Northern Arapaho. In: *Acculturation in Seven Indian Tribes.* Ralph Linton, ed. New York: D. Appleton-Century, 1940. (pp. 207–258).

Fisher, M. C.
"On the Arapahoes, Kiowas, and Comanches." *Jour. Ethnol. Soc.* 1:274–287, 1869. n.s.

Hayden, F. V.
"Contributions to the Ethnography and Philology of the Indian Tribes of the Missouri Valley." *Trans. Amer. Philo. Soc.* 12:321–339, 1863. n.s.

Mead, Margaret
"The Mountain Arapaho: I. An Importing Culture." *Anthropological Papers.* Vol. 36:1938, pp. 139–349, 95 figs. Publications in Anthropology. New York: The American Museum of Natural History.

Michelson, Truman
"Narrative of an Arapaho Woman." *AA* 35: 595–610, 1933. n.s.

Mooney, James
"Arapaho." *Bull. Bureau Amer. Ethnol.* 30 (Part 1):72–74, 1907.

Muntsch, Albert
"Notes on Age-Classes Among the Northern Arapahoe." *Primitive Man*, 5(Nos. 2, 3):49–52 (April–July), 1932. Catholic Anthropological Conference Work.

Renaud, E. B.
"The Indians of Colorado", *in Colorado: Short Studies of Past and Present.* Boulder: University of Colorado, 1927.

Scott, H. L.
"The Early History and Names of the Arapaho." *AA* 9:545–560, 1907. n.s.

Seger, John H. (Stanley Vestal, ed.)
Early Days Among the Cheyenne and Arapahoe Indians. Norman: University of Oklahoma Press, 1934.
"While the present volume makes no important direct contribution to Cheyenne and Arapahoe original culture, it does offer materials valuable to the student of frontier history." (Wissler)

Smith, J. S.
Arapahoes. In: *Information Respecting the History, Condition, and Prospects of the Indian Tribes of the United States*, H. R. Schoolcraft, ed., Vol. 3, (pp. 446–459). Philadelphia: 1853.

MYTHS—FOLKTALES—LEGENDS

Harsha, W. J.
"Neatha and the White Man's Bird." *So. Workman* 30:578–586, 1901.

Michelson, Truman
"Narrative of an Arapaho Woman." *AA* 35: 595–610, 1933. n.s.

Voth, H. R.
"Arapaho Tales." *JAFL* 25:43–50, 1912.

BELIEFS—CUSTOMS—FOLK MEDICINE

Carter, John G.
The Northern Arapaho Flat Pipe and the Ceremony of Covering the Pipe. Anthropological Papers 2: Bulletin 119, Bureau of American Ethnology. Washington, D. C.: U. S. Government Printing Office, 1938.

Friday, M.
"Ancient Customs of Araphahoes." *Carlisle Arrow* (Carlisle, Pa.) 7, (No. 39):4, 1911.

Kroeber, Alfred L.
"The Arapaho. III. Ceremonial Organization." *Bulletins:* Vol. 18, Part II: 1904, pp. 151–229, figs. 47–70, pls. 32–37. Publications in Anthropology. New York: American Museum of Natural History.
A systematic discussion of Arapaho ceremonials.

————.
"The Arapaho. IV. Religion." *Bulletins:* Vol. 18, Part IV: 1907, pp. 279–454, figs. 103–180, pls. 57–88. Publications in Anthropology. New York: American Museum of Natural History.

Michelson, Truman
"Some Arapaho Kinship Terms and Social Usages." *AA* 36:137–139, 1934. n.s.

Mooney, James
"The Ghost-Dance Religion." *Annual Report Bureau Amer. Ethnol.* 14 (Part 2):953–1023, 1893.

Pajeken, F. J.
"Religion und religiöse Vorstellungen der Arapahoë-Indianer." *Ausland* 43:1011–1015, 1890.

Voth, H. R.
"Funeral Customs Among the Cheyenne and Arapaho Indians." *Folklorist*, I, 1893.

Wildschut, W.
"Arapaho Medicine Bundle." *Indian Notes* 4:
83–88, 1927.

——————.
"Arapaho Medicine Mirror." *Indian Notes* 4:
252–257, 1927.

FOLK ART—SPEECH

Kroeber, A. L.
"Arapaho Dialects." *University of California
Publications in American Archaeology and
Ethnology*, 12, (No. 3):71–138, 1916. Berkeley:
University of California Press, 1916–1917.
Discusses the dialects of the Arapahoe group
and a sketch of Arapahoe proper.

——————.
"Decorative Symbolism of the Arapaho." *AA*
3:308–337, 1901. n.s.

——————.
"Symbolism of the Arapaho Indian." *Bulletin
American Museum of Natural History*, 13:69–
86, 1900. Illus. (New York).

——————.
"The Arapaho. I. General Description. II.
Decorative Art and Symbolism." *Bulletins*:
Vol. 18, Part I: pp. 1–150, 1902. figs. 1–46, pls.
1–31 (4 coloured). Publications in Anthropology. New York: American Museum of Natural History.

Michelson, Truman
"Phonetic Shifts in Algonquian Languages."
Inter. Jour. Amer. Ling. 8:131–171, 1935.

——————.
"Some Arapaho Kinship Terms and Social
Usages." *AA* 36:137–139, 1934. n.s.

Uhlenbeck, C. C.
"Additional Blackfoot-Arapaho Comparisons."
Inter. Jour. Amer. Ling. 4:227–228, 1927.

GAMES

"Arapaho Games."
JAFL 17:64, 1904.

Culin, Stewart
"Games of the North American Indians." In:
*Twenty-Fourth Annual Report, Bureau Amer-
ican Ethnology*. Washington, D. C.: U. S. Gov't
Printing Office, 1907.

MUSIC
GENERAL STUDIES

Carter, John G.
The Northern Arapaho Flat Pipe and the
Ceremony of Covering the Pipe. In: *Anthropo-
logical Papers 2, Bulletin of U. S. Bureau of
American Ethnology 119*. Washington, D. C.:
U. S. Government Printing Office, 1938.

Curtis, Natalie
The Indians' Book . . . Illustrations from
photographs and from original drawings by
Indians. New York: Harper and Bros., 1907.
(pp. 195–219).

Densmore, Frances
Cheyenne and Arapaho Music. Southwest
Museum Papers. Number 10. Highland, Los
Angeles, Cal.: Southwest Museum, 1936. 111
pp., music, illus., bibl.

DANCES

Dorsey, George A.
*The Arapaho Sun Dance; The Ceremony of
the Offerings Lodge.* Field Columbian Museum,
Publication 75; Anthropology Series, vol. 4.
Chicago: 1903. 228 pp., 137 pl.

"Ghost Dance Song: Arapaho."
Southern Workman (Hampton, Virginia) 36:
111, 1907.

Mooney, James
"The Ghost Dance Religion." *Annual Report
Bureau Amer. Ethnol.* 14(Part 2):953–1023,
1893.

Rogers, F. K.
"The Rain Dance of the Arophahoes and
Cheyennes." *Southern Workman* 29:721–723,
1900.

ARRANGEMENTS

——————: *Piano*

"Father Have Pity."
(In—Melodic Views of Indian Life.) Miller,
Horace A.: Clayton F. Summy: Piano.

"The Song of the Great Spirit."
(In—Melodic Views of Indian Life.) Miller,
Horace A.: Clayton F. Summy: Piano.

"The Seven Venerable Priests."
(In—Melodic Views of Indian Life.) Miller,
Horace A.: Clayton F. Summy: Piano.

ARIKARA
FOLKLORE
GENERAL STUDIES

**Archaeological Survey, Research & Records
Section. WPA.**
Arikara Indians of South Dakota. A brief
history of the Arikara Tribe. . . . South Dakota
Work Projects Administration Vermillion:
University Museum, 1941. ii, 62 pp., illus.

Brownlee, Fred L., and Johnson, Charles S.
The Indians of North and South Dakota. Nashville, Tennessee: Fisk University, 1941. 51 pp.

Denig, Edwin Thompson
"Indian Tribes of the Upper Missouri," edited with notes and biographical sketch by J. N. B. Hewitt. *46th Annual Report: Bureau of American Ethnology, Smithsonian Institution,* pp. 375–628. Washington, D. C.

Dorsey, George A.
Traditions of the Arikara. Carnegie Institution, Publication 17. Washington, D. C., 1904. 202 pp.

Fletcher, A. C.
"Arikara." *Bull. Bureau Amer. Ethnol.* 30 (Part 1):83–86, 1907.

Gilmore, M. R.
"Notes on Arikara Tribal Organization." *Indian Notes* 4:332–350, 1927.

Hayden, F. V.
"Contributions to the Ethnography and Philology of the Canadian Tribes of the Missouri Valley." *Trans. Amer. Philo. Soc.* 12:351–363, 1863. n.s.

Lowie, Robert H.
"Societies of the Arikara Indians." *Anthropological Papers of the American Museum of Natural History* (New York) 11:645–678, 1915.

———.
"Some Problems in the Ethnology of the Crow and Village Indians." *AA* 14:60–71, 1912. n.s.

Smith, G. H.
"J. B. Trudeau's Remarks on the Indians of the Upper Missouri." *AA* 38:565–568, 1936. n.s.

Strong, W. D.
"Studying the Arikara and Their Neighbors." *Explorations and Field Work Smithson. Inst.,* 1932. (pp. 73–76).

Taylor, Joseph Henry
Sketches of Frontier and Indian Lives in the Upper Missouri and Great Plains. Bound with Kaleidoscopic Lives. Valley City: E. P. Getchell, 1932.

Will, George Francis, and Hyde, George E.
Corn Among the Indians of the Upper Missouri. St. Louis, Mo.: William Henry Miner Company, Inc., 1917.

———.
Notes on the Arikara Indians and their Ceremonies. The Old West Series. No. 3. Denver: J. Van Male, 1933.

Wilson, Gilbert L.
Waheenee; An Indian Girl's Story. St. Paul: Webb Publishing Company, 1921.

MYTHS—FOLKTALES—LEGENDS

"Arikara Creation Myth."
JAFL 6:122–128, 1890; 22:90–92, 1909.

Dorsey, G. A.
"An Arikara Story-Telling Contest." *AA* 6: 240–244, 1904. n.s.

Gilmore, Melvin R.
"Arikara Account of the Origin of Tobacco and Catching Eagles." *Indian Notes* 6:26–32, 1929.

———.
"The Arikara Book of Genesis." *Papers. Michigan Academy of Science, Arts and Letters,* 12:95–120, 1929, published 1930.

———.
"Arikara Genesis and its Teachings." *Indian Notes, Museum of the American Indian, Heye Foundation* 3:188–193, 1926.

Hoffman, W. J.
"The Water Babies, an Arickaree Story." *Amer. Antiq.* 14:167–169, 1892.

BELIEFS—CUSTOMS—FOLK MEDICINE

Gilmore, Melvin R.
"Arikara Commerce." *Indian Notes* 3:13–18, 1926.

———.
"Arikara Consolation Ceremony." *Indian Notes* 3:256–274, 1926.

———.
"Arikara Household Shrine to Mother Corn." *Indian Notes* 2:31–34, 1925.

———.
"The Arikara Method of Preparing a Dog for a Feast." *Papers Mich. Acad. Sci.* 19:37–38, 1933.

———.
"Arikara Units of Measure." *Indian Notes* 2: 64–66, 1925.

———.
"The Arikara Tribal Temple." *Paper. Michigan Academy of Science, Arts and Letters* 14: 47–70, 1929, published 1930.

———.
"The Making of a New Head Chief by the Arikara." *Indian Notes* 5:411–418, 1928.

———.
"Months and Seasons of the Arikara Calendar." *Indian Notes* 6:246–250, 1929.

———.
"Notes on Gynecology and Obstetrics of the Arikara Tribe of Indians." *Papers. Michigan Academy of Science, Arts and Letters* 14:71–81, 1930, published 1931.

———.
"Uses of Plants by the Indians of the Missouri River Region." *33rd Annual Report: U. S. Bureau of Ethnology,* 1911–1912, pp. 43–194. Washington, D. C.: U. S. Government Printing Office, 1912.

——————.
"The Sacred Bundles of the Arikaras." *Papers Mich. Acad. Sci.* 16:33–50, 1931.

Goddard, P. E.
"Indian Ceremonies of the Long Ago." *Natur. Hist.* 22:559–564, 1922.

Will, George Francis
"Arikara Ceremonials." *North Dakota Historical Quarterly*, 4:247–263, (July) 1930.

——————.
"Magical and Sleight of Hand Performances by the Arikara." *North Dakota Historical Quarterly* 3:50–65, (Oct.) 1928.

——————.
"Notes on the Arikara Indians and Their Ceremonies." *Old West Series* (Denver) 3: 5–48, 1934.

FOLK ART—GAMES

Gilmore, M. R.
"Arikara Basketry." *Indian Notes* 2:89–95, 1925.

——————.
"Arikara Uses of Clay and of Other Earth Products." *Indian Notes* 2:283–289, 1925.

——————.
"The Cattail Game of Arikara Children." *Indian Notes* 5:316–318, 1928.

——————.
"Glass Bead Making by the Arikara." *Indian Notes* 1:20–21, 1924.

——————.
"Some Games of the Arikara Children." *Indian Notes* (Museum of the American Indian Heye Foundation) 3:9–12, 1926.

Morgan, L. H.
"The Stone and Bone Implements of the Arickarees." *Annual Reports Regents Univ. State N. Y.* 21:25–46, 1871.

ASSINIBOIN

FOLKLORE

GENERAL STUDIES

"Assiniboin Gentes." *JAFL* 4:263, 264, 1891.

Barbeau, Charles M.
Indian Days in the Canadian Rockies. Toronto: The Macmillan Co., 1923. 208 pp.

Breton, A. C.
"The Stoney Indians." *Man* 20:65–67, 1920.

Denig, E. T.
Assiniboine. In: *Information Respecting the History, Condition, and Prospects of the Indian Tribes of the United States*, H. R. Schoolcraft, ed., Vol. 4, pp. 416–431. Philadelphia: 1854.

Doughty, A. G., and Martin, C., eds.
The Kelsey Papers. Ottawa: 1929.

Hayden, F. V.
"Contributions to the Ethnography and Philology of the Indian Tribes of the Missouri Valley." *Trans. Amer. Philo. Soc.* 12:379–391, 1863. n.s.

Henry, A.
Travels and Adventures, M. M. Quaife, ed., (pp. 266–297). Chicago: 1921.

Hind, Henry Youle
Narrative of the Canadian Red River Exploring Expedition of 1857, and of the Assiniboine and Saskatchewan Exploring Expeditions of 1858. London: Longman, Green, Longman, and Roberts, 1860. 2 vols.

Lowie, Robert H.
"The Assiniboine." *American Museum of Natural History, Anthropological Papers* 4:1–270, New York, 1909. Illus.

Matson, G. A.
"Blood Groups and Ageusia in Indians of Montana and Alberta." *Amer. Jour. Phys. Anthro.* 24:81–89, 1938.

McGee, W. J.
"The Siouan Indians." *Annual Report Bureau Amer. Ethnol.* 15:157–204, 1894.

Mooney, J., and Thomas, C.
"Assiniboin." *Bull. Bureau Amer. Ethnol.* 30 (Part 1):102–105, 1907.

Moorhead, Warren King
"Prehistoric Cultural Areas East of the Rocky Mountains." *Proceedings of the 23rd International Congress of Americanists*, pp. 47–52, 1928.

Montgomery, Henry
"Prehistoric Man in Manitoba and Saskatchewan." *AA* 10:33–41, 1908. n.s.

Rodnick, David
The Fort Belknap Assiniboine of Montana: A Study in Culture Change. New Haven: The Author, 1938. 125 pp.

——————.
"Political Structure and Status Among the Assiniboine Indians." *AA* 39:408–416, 1937. n.s.

Wied-Neuwied, M. zu
"Travels in the Interior of North America." In: *Early Western Travels*, R. G. Thwaites, Vol. 22, pp. 370–371, Vol. 23, pp. 14–24, Vol. 24, pp. 215–217. Cleveland: 1906.

MYTHS—FOLKTALES—LEGENDS

Potts, W. J.
"Creation Myth of the Assiniboin." *JAFL* 5: 72–73, 1892.

Reagan, Albert B.
The Sun God Moccasin Tales. Provo, Utah: Graham Printing Company, 1935. 44 pp.

————.
The Sun God Moccasin Tales. II—Some Flood Myths of the Indians. Provo, Utah: M. H. Graham Printing Company, 1936.

MUSIC
GENERAL STUDIES

Lowie, Robert H.
"Music of the Assiniboine." *Anthropological Papers of the American Museum of Natural History* IV (Part I):26. New York: Published by the Order of Trustees, 1909.

BLACKFOOT
(*Including:* Piegan)

FOLKLORE
GENERAL STUDIES

Bradley, J. H.
"Characteristics, Habits, and Customs of the Blackfeet Indians." *Contributions to the Historical Society of Montana* 9:255–287, 1923.

Brown, John M.
"Traditions of the Blackfeet." *The Galaxy* 3: 157: 164, 1867.

Burpee, L. J., ed.
"An Adventurer From Hudson Bay." *Proc. Trans. Royal Soc. Can.* (ser. 3)2(Part 2): 109–112, 1908.

Coues, E., ed.
Manuscript Journals of Alexander Henry and of David Thompson. New York: 1897. 3 vols.

Doty, James
"Reports on the Indian Tribes of the Blackfoot Nation." *Pacific Railroad Reports,* Vol. I, pp. 441–446, Washington, 1855.

Douglas, F. H.
"The Blackfoot Indians." *Denver Art Museum, Department of Indian Art,* Leaflets No. 37, 38:1–8. Denver, (Dec.) 1931.

Goldfrank, Esther S.
Changing Configurations in the Social Organization of a Blackfoot Tribe during the Reserve Period. American Ethnological Society, Vol. VIII. New York: J. J. Augustin, 1945. vii, 273 pp., illus.

Grinnell, George Bird
"Early Blackfoot History." *AA* 5:153–174, 582–583, 1892.

————.
"The Lodges of the Blackfeet." *AA* 3:650–669, 1901. n.s.

Hale, H.
"Report on the Blackfoot Tribes." *Report 55th Meeting British Assoc. Adv. Sci.,* pp. 696–708, 1885.

Hanks, L. M., and Richardson, Jane
Observation on Northern Blackfoot Kinship. American Ethnological Society, Vol. IX. New York: J. J. Augustin, 1945. v, 31 pp.

Hyde, G. E.
"The Early Blackfeet and Their Neighbors." *Old West Series* (Denver) 2:5–45, 1933.

Josselin de Jong, J. P. B. de, ed.
Blackfoot Texts from Southern Peigans, Blackfoot Reservation Teton County, Montana with the help of Black-Horse-Rider collected and published with an English translation. Amsterdam: J. Müller, 1914. iv, 153 pp.

————.
"Prof. C. C. Uhlenbeck's Latest Contribution to Blackfoot Ethnology." *Inter. Archiv für Ethno.* 21:105–115, 1913.

————.
"Social Organization of the Southern Peigans." *Inter. Archiv für Ethno.* 20:191–197, 1912.

Linderman, F. B.
Blackfeet Indians. St. Paul: 1935. 65 pp.

Long Lance, Chief Buffalo Child
Long Lance. New York: Cosmopolitan Book Corp., 1928. xv, 278 pp.
  "Profoundly moving autobiography of a Blackfoot Indian representing his people and all natural life of the Plain." (Dobie)

McClintock, Walter
"The Blackfoot." *Masterkey* 10:85–96, 1936.

————.
"Blackfoot Warrior Societies." *The Masterkey* 11, (No. 5):148–160, 1937. Los Angeles: Southwest Museum.

————.
The Old North Trail. London: 1910. 532 pp.

————.
"The Thunderbird Motive in Blackfoot Art." *Masterkey* 15, (No. 4):129–134. Los Angeles: Museum of the Southwest, 1941.

————.
The Tragedy of the Blackfoot. Los Angeles: Publication of the Southwest Museum, No. 3, 1930. 53 pp., illus.

McLean, J.
Canadian Savage Folk. Toronto: 1896.

————.
The Indians of Canada. London: 1892. 351 pp.

Mooney, James
"Siksika." *Bull. Bureau Amer. Ethnol.* 30 (Part 2):570–571, 1910.

Palliser, J.
Further Papers. London: 1960. 325 pp.

Petitot, Émile F. S.
"Traditions indiennes du Canada nord-ouest." *Les Litteratures Populaires de Toutes les Nations,* Vol. 23, (pp. 489–507). Paris: 1886.

Schultz, James Willard
Apank, Caller of the Buffalo. Boston: Houghton Mifflin Co., 1916. 226 pp., illus.
  The story of the youth of a Pilgan Indian, told to the author in the winter of 1879-1880. Pilgan, or Piegan, is one of the three tribes of the Siksika or Blackfoot Confederacy.

—————.
Boy Trapper in the Rockies. Illustrations by George Varian and Patten Wilson. London: G. G. Harrap & Co., 1914. ix, 284 pp.
  The first half of the book was published in 1912 by Houghton Mifflin under the title: "With the Indians of the Rockies." The Author's works, although mainly fiction, make extensive use of folklore data.

—————.
Friends of My Life as an Indian. Boston: Houghton Mifflin Co., 1923.

—————.
In the Great Apache Forest, the story of a lone Boy Scout. Boston: Houghton Mifflin Co., 1920. 224 pp.

—————.
Lone Bull's Mistake: A Lodge Pole Chief story. Illustrations by George Varian. Boston: Houghton Mifflin Co., 1918. 207 pp.

—————.
My Life as an Indian; the story of a red woman and a white man in the lodges of the Blackfeet. Illustrated from photographs, mostly by George Bird Grinnell. New York: Doubleday, Page & Co., 1907. x, 326 pp.

—————.
Red Crow's Brother; Hugh Monroe's Story of his second year on the plains. Illustrations by Frank E. Schoonover. Boston: Houghton Mifflin Co., 1927. 208 pp.

—————.
Rising Wolf, the White Blackfoot; Hugh Monroe's story of his first year on the plains. Illustrations by Frank E. Schoonover. Boston: Houghton Mifflin Co., 1919. ix, 252 pp.

—————.
Running Eagle, the warrior girl. Boston: Houghton Mifflin Co., 1919. 311 pp.

—————.
Sahtaki and I. Boston: Houghton Mifflin Co., 1924. 305 pp.

—————.
Seizer of Eagles. Illustrated by Frank E. Schoonover. Boston: Houghton Mifflin Co., 1922. 229 pp.

—————.
Short Bow's Big Medicine. Illustrated by Stockton Mulford. Boston: Houghton Mifflin Co., 1940. 201 pp.

—————.
Signposts of Adventure; Glacier National Park As the Indians Know it. Boston: Houghton Mifflin Co., 1926. vii, 224 pp.

—————.
Sinopah, the Indian Boy. Illustrated by E. Boyd Smith. Boston: Houghton Mifflin Co., 1913. 154 pp.
  "The Story of Sinopah, a Blackfoot Indian boy; he who afterward became the great chief Pitamakan."

—————.
Skull Head. Illustrated by Frank E. Schoonover. Boston: Houghton Mifflin Co., 1929. 207 pp.

—————.
Stained Gold. Illustrations by Frank E. Schoonover. Boston: Houghton Mifflin Co., 1937. 217 pp.

—————.
Sun Woman; a novel. Boston: Houghton Mifflin Co., 1926. 244 pp.

—————.
The Dreadful River Cave; Chief Black Elk's Story. Illustrations by Harold Cue. Boston: Houghton Mifflin Co., 1920. v, 243 pp.

—————.
The War-Trail Fort; Further Adventures of Thomas Fox and Pitamakan. Illustrations by George Varian. Boston: Houghton Mifflin Co., 1921. 192 pp.

—————.
The White Beaver; illustrated by Rodney Thompson. Boston: Houghton Mifflin Co., 1930. 271 pp.

—————.
The White Buffalo Robe; Illustrations by Frank E. Schoonover. Boston: Houghton Mifflin Co., 1936. 220 pp.

—————.
With the Indians of the Rockies; Illustrated by George Varian. Boston: Houghton Mifflin Co., 1912, 1925. viii, 252 pp.

—————, **Donaldson, Jessie Louise**
The Sun God's Children. Portraits by Winold Reiss. Boston: Houghton Mifflin Co., 1930. vii, 254 pp.
  "The life of the Blackfeet tribes in the days of the buffalo . . . and their ceremonials of the present time."—Pref.

Stanley, J. M.
"Visit to the Piegan Camp." *Reports of Explorations and Surveys* 1:447–449, 1855.

Tyrrell, J. B., ed.
"David Thompson's Narrative of Explorations in Western America." *Publ. Champlain Soc.* (Toronto) 12:345–371, 1916.

Uhlenbeck, Christianus Cornelius
"Blackfoot Notes." *International Journal of American Linguistics* 5:119–120, 1929.

—————.
"A New Series of Blackfoot Texts." *Verhandelingen der Koninklijke Akademie van Wetenschappen, Afdeeling Letterkunde* (Amsterdam) 13(Part 1):1–264, 1912. n.s.

————.
Original Blackfoot Texts for the Southern Piegans Blackfoot Reservation, Teton County, Montana, With the help of Joseph Tatsey. *Verh. d. Kon. Akad. van Wetenschappen Amsterdam, Afd. Letterk.* n.r.d. 12 (No. 1): 1–106, 1911.

Wilson, E. F.
"Report on the Blackfoot Tribes." *Report 57th Meeting British Assoc. Adv. Sci.*, pp. 183–200, 1887.

Wissler, Clark
"The Blackfoot Indians." *Annual Arch. Report*, pp. 162–178, 1905.

MYTHS—FOLKTALES—LEGENDS

Anon.
"Indian Affection." *The Telescope* 2:142–143, Feb. 4, 1826.
The story of a Blackfoot's Indian devotion and help.

Grinnell, George Bird
Blackfoot Indian Stories. New York: C. Scribner's Sons, 1913. viii, 214 pp.

————.
Blackfoot Lodge Tales; the Story of a Prairie People. New York: C. Scribner's Sons, 1920. xv, 310 pp.

————.
"Blackfoot Sun and Moon Myth." *JAFL* 6:44–47, 1893.

Knox, R. H.
"Blackfoot Version of the Magic Flight." *JAFL* 36:401–403, 1923.

Kunike, H.
"Der Werwolf: Ein Märchen der Blackfoot Indianer." *Erdball* 4:469–471, 1930.

Linderman, F. B.
Indian Why Stories. New York: 1915. 236 pp.

McClintock, Walter
"Blackfoot Legends: The Twin Brothers: The Story of Belly Fat." As related by Bull Plume, of the Northern Piegan, to Walter McClintock in 1903. *Masterkey* 1933. March, pp. 41–46; May, pp. 70–73.

————.
"Bräuche und Legenden der Schwarzfuss-Indianer." *Zeit. für Ethnol.* 40:606–614, 1908.

————.
The Old North Trail: or, Life, Legends and Religion of the Blackfeet Indians. London: Macmillan & Co., 1910. xxvi, 539 pp., illus.

McLean, J.
"Blackfoot Indian Legends." *JAFL* 3:297–298, 1890.

————.
"Blackfoot Mythology." *JAFL* 6:165–172, 1893.

Michelson, Truman
"Piegan Tales." *JAFL* 24:238–248, 1911; 29: 408–409, 1916.
One of the three tribes of the Siksika or Blackfoot Confederacy.

Mitchell, D. D.
"The White Antelop, or Indian Lover." *Southern Literary Messenger* 1:393–395, April, 1835.
A Blackfoot Indian tale.

Schultz, James Willard
Blackfeet Tales of Glacier National Park. Boston: Houghton Mifflin Co., 1916. ix, 241 pp., illus.

Uhlenbeck, C. C.
"A New Series of Blackfoot Texts." *Verhandelingen der Koninklijke Akademie van Wetenschappen, Afdeeling Letterkunde* (Amsterdam) 13(Part 1):1–264, 1912. n.s.

————.
"Original Blackfoot Texts." *Verhandelingen der Koninklijke Akademie van Wetenschappen, Afdeeling Letterkunde* (Amsterdam) 12(Part 1):1–106, 1911. n.s.

Wilson, R. N.
"Blackfoot Star Myths." *Amer. Antiq.* 15: 149–150, 200–203, 1893.

Wissler, Clark
Star Legends Among the American Indians. New York: The American Museum of Natural History, 1936. 29 pp.

————, **Duvall, D. C.**
"Mythology of the Blackfoot Indians." *American Museum of Natural History, Anthropological Papers* 2:1–163, New York, 1908.

BELIEFS—CUSTOMS—FOLK MEDICINE

Barrett, S. A.
"The Blackfoot Iniskim or Buffalo Bundle." *Yearbook Publ. Mus. City Milwaukee* 1:80–84, 1921.

————.
"The Blackfoot Sweat Lodge." *Yearbook Publ. Mus. City Milwaukee* 1:73–80, 1921.

Bradley, J. H.
"Characteristics, Habits, and Customs of the Blackfeet Indians." *Contributions to the Historical Society of Montana* 9:255–287, 1923.

Brown, John M.
Indian Medicine. In: *Indian Miscellany*, W. W. Beach, ed., pp. 74–85. Albany. 1877.

Catlin, George
Letters and Notes on the Manners, Customs, and Condition of the North American Indians . . . New York: Wiley & Putnam, 1841. 2 vols.

Ewers, John C.
"Food Rationing is Nothing New to the Blackfoot." *The Masterkey* 18:(No. 3):73–80, 1944.

————.
"The Blackfoot War Lodge: Its Construction and Use." *AA* 46:182–193, 1944.

Grinnell, George B.
"The Butterfly and the Spider Among the Blackfeet." *AA* 1:194–196, 1899. n.s.

——.
"The Lodges of the Blackfeet." *AA* 3:650–668, 1901.

——.
The Punishment of the Stingy. New York: Harper & Bros., 1901. (pp. 127–235).

Knox, R. H.
"A Blackfoot Version of the Magic Flight." *JAFL* 36:401–403, 1923.

L'Heureux, J.
"Ethnological Notes on the Astronomical Customs and Religious Ideas of the Chokitapia or Blackfeet Indians." *Jour. Royal Anthro. Inst. Gt. Brit. and Ireland* 15:301–304, 1885.

Lincoln, J. S.
The Dream in Primitive Cultures. London: The Cresset Press, 1935. 359 pp.

McAllister, David
"Water as a Disciplinary Agent Among the Crow and Blackfoot." *AA* 43:593–604, 1941.

McClintock, Walter
"Blackfoot Warrior Societies." *Masterkey* 11: 148–158, 198–204, 1937; 12:11–23, 1938.

——.
"Medizinal—und Nutzpflanzen der Schwarzfuss —Indianer." *Zeitschrift für Ethnologie* 41:273–279, 1909.
Medical practices and use of plants by the Blackfoot Indians.

——.
"The Blackfoot Beaver Bundle." *The Masterkey* 9, (No. 3):77–84. Los Angeles: Southwest Museum, (May) 1935.

——.
The Blackfoot Beaver Bundle—I and II. Los Angeles, Cal.: Publication of the Southwest Museum, Leaflets No. 2 and 3.

——.
The Old North Trail: Life, Legends and Religion of the Blackfeet Indians. London: The Macmillan Company, 1910. 95 pp., illus.

——.
"Saitsiko, Blackfoot Doctor." *Masterkey* 15 (No. 3):80–86, 1941.

McClean, J.
"The Mortuary Customs of the Blackfeet Indians." *Proc. Can. Inst.* (ser. 3) 5:20–24, 1887.

——.
"Social Organization of the Blackfoot Indians." *Trans. Royal Can. Inst.* 4:249–260, 1895.

Richardson, Jane, and Hanks, L. M., Jr.
"Water Discipline and Water Imagery Among the Blackfoot." *American Anthropologist* 44: 331–333, 1942.

Townsend, J.
"Letters from Columbia River." *Waldie's Journal of Belles Lettres* Part 2, No. 3, July 19, 1836.
Extract from a letter from Fort Vancouver, Columbia River. Description of a now extinct tribe of Indians. Attack of the Potameos Indians on some white visitors, also description of an attack by the Blackfoot tribe.

Uhlenbeck, C. C.
The Origin of the Otter-Lodge. In: *Festschrift Vilhelm Thomsen*, pp. 74–77. Leipzig: 1912.

Wildschut, William
"Blackfoot Beaver Bundle." *Indian Notes* 1: 138–141, 1924.

——.
"Blackfoot Pipe Bundles." *Indian Notes* 5: 419–433, 1928.

Wilson, R. N.
"The Sacrificial Rite of the Blackfoot." *Proc. Trans. Royal. Soc. Can.* (ser. 3), 3(Part 2): 3–21, 1909.

Wissler, Clark
"Ceremonial Bundles of the Blackfoot Indians." *Anthropological Papers:* Vol. 7, 1912. pp. 1–64, figs. 35. Publications in Anthropology. New York: The American Museum of Natural History.

——.
"Material Culture of the Blackfoot Indians." *Anthropological Papers of the American Museum of Natural History*, 5 (Part 1):175 pp., illus. New York: Published by Order of Trustees, 1910.

——.
Smoking Star, a Blackfoot Shaman. In: *American Indian Life*, Elsie Clews Parsons, ed., pp 45–62. New York: B. W. Huebsch, 1925.

——.
"The Social Life of the Blackfoot Indians." *Anthropological Papers of the American Museum of Natural History*, Vol. 7 (Part 1). New York, 1911. 64 pp.

——.
"Societies and Dance Associations of the Blackfoot Indians." *Anthro. Papers Amer. Mus. Natur. Hist.* 11:359–460, 1913.

FOLK ART—SPEECH

Barrett, S. A.
"The Painted Lodge or Ceremonial Tipi of the Blackfoot." *Yearly Publ. Mus. City Milwaukee* 1:85–88, 1921.

Lanning, C. M.
A Grammar and Vocabulary of the Blackfoot Language. Fort Benton: 1882. 143 pp.

McClintock, Walter
"The Blackfoot Language." *Trans. Royal Can. Inst.* 5:128–165, 1898.

———.
"Painted Tipis and Picture-writing of the
Blackfoot Indians." *Masterkey* 10, (No. 4):
121–133, 169–179, 1936.

———.
"The Blackfoot Tipi." *Masterkey* 10, (No. 3):
85–96, 1936. Los Angeles: Southwest Museum.

McLean, J.
"Picture-Writing of the Blackfeet." *Trans.
Royal Can. Inst.* 5:114–120, 1898.

Michelson, T.
"Notes on Some Word-Comparisons Between
Blackfoot and Other Algonquian Languages."
Inter. Jour. Amer. Ling. 3:233–235, 1925.

Petitot, Émile F. S.
"Vocabulaire piéganie." *Actes de la Société
Philologique* 14:170–198, 1885.

Spier, Leslie
"Blackfoot Relationship Terms." *AA* 17:603–
607, 1915. n.s.

Tims, J. W.
*Grammar and Dictionary of the Blackfoot
Language in the Dominion of Canada.* London:
1889. xii, 191 pp.

Uhlenbeck, C. C.
"Additional Blackfoot-Arapaho Comparisons."
Inter. Jour. Amer. Ling. 4:227–228, 1927.

———.
A Concise Blackfoot Grammar. Verhandelingen der Koninklijke Akademie van Wetenschappen, Afdeeling Letterkunde. Vol. 41.
Amsterdam: 1938. n.s. 240 pp.

———.
"Flexion of Substantives in Blackfoot." *Verhandelingen der Koninklijke Akademie van
Wetenschappen, Afdeeling Letterkunde* (Amsterdam) 14 (Part 1):1–40, 1913, n.s.

———.
"Some General Aspects of Blackfoot Morphology." *Verhandelingen der Koninklijke Akademie van Wetenschappen, Afdeeling Letterkunde* (Amsterdam) 14(Part 5):1–61, 1914.
n.s.

———.
"Some Word-Comparisons Between Blackfoot
and Other Algonquian Languages." *Inter.
Jour. Amer. Ling.* 3:103–108, 1924.

Wissler, Clark
"Material Culture of the Blackfoot Indians."
*Anthoropological Papers of the American Mu-
seum of Natural History* (New York). Vol. 5,
pt. 1, 1910.

GAMES

Ewers, John C.
"Some Winter Sports of Blackfoot Indian
Children." *Masterkey* 18:180–187, 1944, illus-
trated.

McLean, J.
"Blackfoot Amusements." *American Antiquity*
23:163–169, 1901.

MUSIC
GENERAL STUDIES

"Blackfoot and Navaho Songs." *El Palacio* 20
(No. 5):104–106.

McClintock, Walter
The Old North Trail: Life, Legends and Religion of the Blackfeet Indians. London: Macmillan & Company, 1910.
Includes 9 tunes.

Nevin, Arthur
"Two Summers with the Blackfeet Indians of
Montana." *MQ* 2:257–270, 1916.

Uhlenbeck, C. C.
"Some Blackfoot Song Texts." *Internationales
Archiv für Ethnographie* (Leiden) Band 23:
241–242, 1916.

Wissler, Clark
"Material Culture of the Blackfoot Indian."
*Anthropological Papers of the American Mu-
seum of Natural History* 5:84. New York:
Published by the Order of Trustees, 1910.
Music.

DANCES

Laidlaw, G. E.
"The Sun Dance Among the Blackfeet." *Amer.
Antiq.* 8:169–170, 1886.

McClintock, Walter
"Dances of the Blackfoot Indians." *Masterkey*
11, (No. 3) :77–86, 111–121, 1937.

McLean, J.
"Blackfoot Amusements." *American Antiquity*
23:163–169, 1901.

———.
"The Blackfoot Sun-Dance." *Canadian Institute
Proceedings.* Series 3, (Toronto) 6:231–237,
1889.

McQuesten, C.
"The Sun Dance of the Blackfoot." *Rod and
Gun in Canada* 13:1169–1177, 1912.

Wissler, Clark
"The Social Life of the Blackfoot Indians."
Anthropological Papers: Vol. 7: 1911, pp. 1–64,
figs. 15. Publications in Anthropology. New
York: The American Museum of Natural
History.

———.
"Societies and Dance Associations of the Blackfoot Indian." *Anthropological Papers, American Museum of Natural History* 11:363–460,
1913.

"The Sun Dance of the Blackfoot Indians."
Anthropological Papers of the American Museum of Natural History 16 (part 3):223–270.
New York: The Trustee, 1918.

ARRANGEMENTS

——: *Voice and Piano*

"From Ghost Dance Canyon."
Lieurance, Thurlow: Presser: Voice and piano.

"The Spirit of Wanna."
Lieurance, Thurlow: Presser: Voice and piano.

"Waste, Wala Ka Kelo."
Lieurance, Thurlow: Presser: Voice and piano.

CADDO

FOLKLORE

GENERAL STUDIES

Bolton, H. E.
"Nebedache." *Bull. Bureau Amer. Ethnol.* 30 (Part 2):1–4, 1910.

——.
"Nacogdoche." *Bull. Bureau Amer. Ethnol.* 30 (Part 2):6–8, 1910.

——.
"Neche." *Bull. Bureau Amer. Ethnol.* 30 (Part 2):49–50, 1910.

——.
"Xinesi." *Bull. Bureau Amer. Ethnol.* 30 (Part 2):981, 1910.

Bushnell, David I.
Villages of the Algonquian, Siouan, and Caddoan Tribes West of the Mississippi. Bureau of American Ethnology, Bulletin 77. Washington, D. C.: U. S. Government Printing Office, 1922.

Dorsey, George Amos
Traditions of the Caddo. Carnegie Institution, Publicaiton 41. Washington, 1905. 136 pp.

Fletcher, A. C.
"Caddo." *Bull. Bureau Amer. Ethnol.* 30 (Part 1):179–182, 1907.

Foreman, Grant
Indians and Pioneers. New Haven: Yale University Press, 1930.
Deals mainly with the Indians of Arkansas.

——, ed.
A Traveler in Indiana Territory. Cedar Rapids, Iowa: The Torch Press, 1930.
Ethan Allen Hitchcock's Journal during his investigation of Indian mistreatment by contractors and Government agents. Deals mainly with Indian tribes of Arkansas Territory.

Gallaher, Ruth A.
"The Tama Indians." *Palimpsest,* 7:44–53, (February) 1926.
The native name of one of the administrative functionaries of the Hasinai (Caddo).

Glover, William Bonny
"A History of the Caddo Indians." *Louisiana Historical Quarterly* 18, (No. 4):872–946, (Oct.) 1935.

Harby, Mrs. L. C.
"The Tejas." *Annual Report, American Historical Association,* 1894, (pp. 63–82).

Hatcher, M. A.
"Descriptions of the Tejas or Asinai Indians." *Southwestern Hist. Quart.* 30:206–218, 283–304; 31:50–62, 150–180, 1927.

Jackson, A. T.
"Fire In East Texas Burial Rites." *Bulletin, Texas Archaeological and Paleontological Society* 10:77–113, Abilene, 1938.

Parsons, Elsie Clews
"Notes on the Caddo." *Memoirs of the American Anthropological Association* No. 57. Supplement to American Anthropologist Vol. 43 (No. 3), Part 2. Menasha, Wisc.: 1941.

Shetrone, Henry Clyde
The Mound Builders. New York: D. Appleton and Company, 1930.
Indians of Arkansas.

Swanton, John R.
"The Caddo Social Organization and Its Possible Historical Significance." *Jour. Wash. Acad. Sci.* 21:203–206, 1931.

——.
Source Material on the History and Ethnology of the Caddo Indians. Bureau of American Ethnology, Bulletin 132. Washington, D. C.: U. S. Government Printing Office, 1942. 332 pp., illus.
Origin legends 25-29; religious and medical beliefs and ceremonies 210-234.

Weer, Paul
Preliminary Notes on the Caddoan Family. Indiana Historical Society. Prehistory Research Series. Vol. 1, No. 4. Indianapolis, 1938.

Weltfish, Gene
Caddoan Texts; Pawnee, South Bend Dialect. Publication, American Ethnological Society, 17. New York: J. J. Augustin, 1937. 251 pp.

MYTHS—FOLKTALES—LEGENDS

"Bibliography of Caddoan Mythology."
JAFL 8:114–115, 1895.

Castañeda, C. E.
"Myths and Customs of the Tejas Indians." *TFSP* 9:167–174, 1931.
The name was applied to the Hasinai (Caddo) tribes of Angelina and Upper Neches Valleys, Texas; also designated by other names; *Tayas, Teixa, Texas, Teyas,* and others.

Hatcher, M. A.
"Myths of the Tejas Indians." *TFSP* 6:107–118, 1927.

Hilder, F. F.
"A Texas Indian Myth." *AA* 1:592–594, 1899. n.s.

Peck, William McCarthy
Caddolina, A Story of the Caddo Tribe. Denison, Texas: Privately Printed, 1917. 45 pp.
Legends told in verse.

BELIEFS—CUSTOMS

Castañeda, C. E.
"Myths and Customs of the Tejas Indians." *TFSP* 9:167–174, 1931.

Dorsey, George Amos
"Caddo Customs of Childhood." *JAFL* 18:226–228, 1905.

Douglas, F. H.
"The Grass House of the Wichita and Caddo." *Denver Art Mus. Leaflet Ser.* 1(Part 42): 1–4, 1932.

Hungate, M.
"Religious Beliefs of the Nebraska Indian." *Nebraska History Magazine* 14(Part 3):207–226, 1938.

Jackson, A. T.
"Fire in East Texas Burial Rites." *Bull. Texas Arch. Ethnol. Soc.* 10:77–113, 1938.

Mooney, James
"The Ghost-Dance Religion." *Annual Report Bureau Amer. Ethnol.* 14(Part 2):1092–1102, 1893.

Zavala, A. de
"Religious Beliefs of the Tejas or Hasanias Indians." *TFSP* 1:39–43, 1916.

FOLK ART—SPEECH

Dormon, C.
"Caddo Pottery." *Art and Arch.* 35:59–68, 1934.

Lesser, Alexander, and Weltfish, Gene
"Composition of the Caddoan and Linguistic Stock." *Smithson. Miscel. Coll.* 87(Part 6): 1–15, 1932.

Spier, Leslie
"Wichita and Caddo Relationship Terms." *AA* 26:258–263, 1924. n.s.

Walker, W. M.
"A Variety of Caddo Pottery from Louisiana." *Jour. Wash. Acad. Sci.* 24:99–104, 1934.

MUSIC
GENERAL STUDIES

Parsons, Elsie Clews
Notes on the Caddo. Memoir of the American Anthropological Association No. 57. Menasha,

Wisconsin: American Anthropological Association, 1941, 76 pp., illustrated.
Also deals with dances and games.

ARRANGEMENTS
————: *Piano*

"The Reveille."
(In—Melodic Views of Indian Life.) Miller, Horace Alden: Clayton F. Summy: Piano.

CHEYENNE
FOLKLORE
GENERAL STUDIES

Bonnerjea, Biren
"Reminiscences of a Cheyenne Indian." *Journal, Société des Américanistes de Paris:* 27: 129–143, 1935. n.s.

Brininstool, Earl Alonzo
Dull Knife (a Cheyenne Napoleon). The story of a wrong and outraged Indian tribe, and the most masterful and stubborn resistance in the history of the American Indian. Hollywood, Cal.: Privately Published, 1935. 31 pp.

Dodge, Col. Richard I.
Our Wild Indians. Hartford, Conn.: N. D. Worthington and Company, 1882. 653 pp.

Dorsey, George Amos
The Cheyenne—Part 1–2. Field Columbian Museum Publications 99–103. Anthropological Series, Vol. 9 (No. 1–2). Chicago: 1905. 2 Vols., illus.

Gilder, Robert F.
"Indians Sites Near Frederick, Wyoming." *Records of the Past* 7:179–182, 1908.

Grinnell, George Bird
By Cheyenne Campfires; with photographs by Elizabeth Grinnell. New Haven: Yale University Press, 1926. xviii, 305 pp., illus.

————.
"Social Organization of the Cheyennes." *Proceedings of the 13th Session of the International Congress of Americanists,* pp. 135–147, 1902 (New York).

————.
The Cheyenne Indians; their history and ways of life. New Haven: Yale University Press, 1923. 2 vols.

————.
The Fighting Cheyennes. New York: Charles Scribner's Sons, 1915. 431 pp., maps.

————.
When Buffalo Ran. New Haven: Yale University Press, 1920. 114 pp.

Hebard, Grace Raymond
Washakie; an Account of Indian Resistance of the Covered Wagon and Union Pacific Invasion of their Territory. Cleveland: Arthur H. Clark Company, 1930. 337 pp.

Hoebel, E. A., and Llewellyn, K. N.
The Cheyenne Way. Conflict and Case Law in Primitive Jurispudence. Norman: University of Oklahoma Press, 1941. 360 pp.
". . . A study of a number of legal disputes among the Cheyenne Indians, occurring primarily between the years 1820-1880, with a description of the methods used by the Indian tribes for the settling of disputes." (O. P. Field)

Keith, Marshall
The Story of Chief Washakie, an Indian Odyssey. Caldwell: Caxton Printers, Ltd. 1935. 218 pp.

Marquis, T. B.
A Warrior Who Fought Custer. Minneapolis: Midwest Co., 1931. 384 pp.

Michelson, Truman
"The Narrative of a Southern Cheyenne Woman." *Smithsonian Miscellaneous Collection,* 87, (No. 5) :13. Washington, D. C.: U. S. Government Printing Office, 1932.

Mooney, J., and Petter, R.
"The Cheyenne Indians." *Memoirs, American Anthropological Association 1,* Part 6. Lancaster, Pa.: New Era Publishing Company, 1907. 135 pp., illus.

Renaud, E. B.
"The Indians of Colorado." In *Colorado: Short Studies of Past and Present.* Boulder: University of Colorado Press, 1927.

Seger, John H.
Early Days Among the Cheyenne and Arapahoe Indians. Edited by Stanley Vestal. Norman, Okla.: University of Oklahoma Press, 1934. 155 pp., illus.
"While the present volume makes no important direct contribution to Cheyenne and Arapahoe original culture, it does offer materials valuable to the student of frontier history." (Wissler)

Smith, J. S.
Cheyennes. In: *Information Respecting the History, Condition, and Prospects of the Indian Tribes of the United States,* H. R. Schoolcraft, ed., Vol. 3, pp. 446–459. Philadelphia: 1853.

Spence, L.
"Cheyenne." In: *Encyclopedia of Religion and Ethics,* John Hastings, ed., Vol. 3, pp. 513–514. New York: 1911.

Swanton, John R.
"Some Neglected Data Bearing on Cheyenne, Chippewa, and Dakota History." *AA* 32:156–160, 1930. n.s.

Vestal, Stanley
Happy Hunting Ground. Chicago: Lyons and Carnahan, 1928.
Story of Mandan and Cheyenne warfare.

MYTHS—FOLKTALES—LEGENDS

Campbell, S.
"Two Cheyenne Stories." *JAFL* 29:406–408, 1916.

"Cheyenne Tales."
JAFL 13:161–190, 1900; 16:108–115, 1903; 20:164–194, 1907; 21:269–320, 1908; 29:406–408, 1916; 34:308–315, 1921.

Dorsey, George Amos
"How the Pawnee Captured the Cheyenne Medicine Arrows." *AA* 5:644–659, 1903. n.s.

Grinnell, George Bird
"Cheyenne Obstacle Myth." *JAFL* 16:108–115, 1903.

———.
"Early Cheyenne Tales." *JAFL* 20:169–194, 1907; 21:269–320, 1908.

———.
"Falling Star" (Cheyenne Tale). *JAFL* 34:308–315, 1921.

———.
"The Great Mysteries of the Cheyenne." *AA* 12:542–576, 1910. n.s.

Kroeber, Alfred L.
"Cheyenne Tales." *JAFL* 13(No. 50) :161–190, 1900.

Randolf, Richard
Sweet Medicine and other Stories of the Cheyenne Indians, as told to Randolf, R; illustrated by Hall, R. H. Caldwell, Id.: the Caxton Printers, Ltd., 1937. 196 pp., illus.

Smith, Louise H.
The Indian Story of the Creation and the Flood; being the first of the Myths and Legends of Colorado done into Tales. Illustrated by Robert Paley. Denver: 1906. 23 pp., illus.

BELIEFS—CUSTOMS—SPEECH

Dorsey, George A.
The Cheyenne. Part I. Ceremonial Organization. Part II. The Sun Dance. Field Columbian Museum Publications, Anthropological Series, Vol. 9(Nos. 1 and 2). Chicago, 1905. 2 vols. Illus.

Grinnell, George Bird
"Account of Northern Cheyennes Concerning the Messiah Superstition." *JAFL* 4:61–69, 1891.

———.
"Cheyenne Stream Names." *AA* 8:15–23, 1906. n.s.

———.
"Cheyenne Woman Customs." *AA* 4:13–17, 1902. n.s.

———.
"Coup and Scalp Among the Plains Indians." *AA* 12:296–310, 1910. n.s.

Llewellyn, K. N. and Hoebel, E. Adamson
The Cheyenne Way. Conflict and Case Law in Primitive Jurispudence. Norman, Okla.: University of Oklahoma Press, 1941. 360pp.

Mooney, J.
"A Cheyenne Tree Burial." *So. Workman* 36: 95–97, 1907.

—————.
"The Ghost-Dance Religion." *Annual Report Bureau Amer. Ethnol.* 14(Part 2):1023–1042, 1893.

Potter, R.
"Sketch of the Cheyenne Grammar." *Mem. Amer. Anthro. Assoc.* 1:443–478, 1907.

Seger, J. H.
"Cheyenne Marriage Customs." *JAFL* 11:298–301, 1898.

Voth, H. R.
"Funeral Customs Among the Cheyenne and Arapaho Indians." *Folklorist*, Vol. I, 1893.

Will, G. F.
Corn Among the Indians of the Upper Missouri. St. Louis: 1917. 317 pp.

FOLK MEDICINE

Goggin, John M.
"Note on Cheyenne Peyote." *New Mexico Anthropologist* 3, (No. 2):26–30. Albuquerque: University of New Mexico, 1939.

Grinnell, George Bird
"Some Cheyenne Plant Medicines." *AA* 7:37–44, 1905.

—————.
"The Cheyenne Medicine Lodge." *AA* 16:245–257, 1914. n.s.

FOLK ART—GAMES

"Cheyenne Games." *JAFL* 20:189, 1907.

Culin, Stewart
Games of the North American Indians. 24th Report. Bureau of American Ethnology, Washington, D.C.: U. S. Gov't. Printing Office, 1907.

Densmore, Frances
Cheyenne and Arapaho Music. Southwest Museum Papers, No. 10. Los Angeles, Cal.; Publication of the Southwest Museum, 1936. 111 pp. illus. music.
Discussion of games, songs and dances.

Douglas, F. H.
"A Cheyenne Peyote Fan." *Material Culture Notes* (Denver Art Museum) 12:47–52, 1939.

Wildschut, W.
"Cheyenne Medicine Blanket." *Indian Notes* 3:33–36, 1926.

MUSIC
GENERAL STUDIES

Curtis, Natalie
The Indians' Book . . . Illustrated. New York: Harper and Bros., 1907.
Music and Texts.

Densmore, Frances
Cheyenne and Arapaho Music. Southwest Museum Papers, No. 10. Los Angeles, California: Publication of the Southwest Museum, 1936, 111 pp., 8 illustrations, 72 songs.
As in all her work the author includes, in addition to discussion of the music, song, dance and games, much information on mythology, ritual, customs, legends and medical practices.

Dorsey, George Amos
"The Cheyenne" Part I–2. Field Columbian Museum Publication 99, 103. *Anthropos Series* 9:1–2. Chicago: 1905, 2 volumes, illustrated.

Grinnell, George Bird
"Notes on Some Cheyenne Songs." *AA* 5:312–323, 1903, n.s.
Text only.

DANCES

Densmore, Frances
See above.

Dorsey, George A.
"The Sun Dance." Part II, of *The Cheyenne*. Field Columbian Museum Anthropological Series, Vol. IX, No. 2. Chicago, 1905.

Rogers, F. K.
"The Rain Dance of the Arapahoes and Cheyennes." *Southern Workman* 29:721–733, 1900.

ARRANGEMENTS

—————: *Voice and Piano*

"Chief Washakie's Son."
Boothroyd, Frederick: Coolidge Publishing Co.: Voice and piano

"Dying Moon Flower."
Lieurance, Thurlow: Presser: Voice and piano.

"My Lark, My Love."
Lieurance, Thurlow: Presser: Voice and piano.

"O'er the Indian Cradle."
Lieurance, Thurlow: Presser: Voice and piano.

"Pakoble (Flute Song).
Lieurance, Thurlow: Presser: Voice and piano.

"Wild Bird."
Lieurance, Thurlow: Presser: Voice and piano.

—————: *Piano*

"To the Sacred Bow" (In—Four Indian Themes).
Miller, Horace Alden: Breitkopf & Härtel: Piano.

"War Dance."
Skilton, Charles S.: Carl Fischer: Piano

———: *Orchestra—Band*

Two Indian Dances.
1. Deer Dance. 2. War Dance. Skilton, Charles
S.: Carl Fischer: Band

"War Dance." (From—Suite Primeval)
Skilton, Charles S.: Carl Fischer: Orchestra.

RECORDS

**U. S. Library of Congress. Division of Music.
Folklore Section.**
Densmore Recordings of Indian Music.
AAFS-LC.
With the acquisition of this great collector's
records, the Archive of American Folksong, in
the Library of Congress is thereby tremendously
enriched in Indian lore and music. It affords
great opportunity to students and scholars.

"Cheyenne War Dance" (Skilton)
Victor Concert Orchestra.   VI–22144

"Love With Tears."
Thurlow Lieurance and Clement Barone, flute-
piano   VI–21972

"War Dance."
Victor Concert Orchestra.   VI–22144

COMANCHE

FOLKLORE

GENERAL STUDIES

Atkinson, Mary Jordan
The Texas Indians. San Antonio: Naylor Company, 1935. bibl.

Austin, Mary
The Trail Book. Boston: Houghton Mifflin Company, 1918. xi, 304 pp., illus.

Bollaert, W.
"Observations on the Indian Tribes in Texas."
Jour. Ethnol. Soc. 2:262–283, 1850.

Buckelew, F. M.
Buckelew, the Indian Captive; or, The life
Story of F. M. Buckelew, while a captive among
the Lipan Indians in the western wilds of fron-
tier Texas, as related by himself—Written by
S. E. Banta. Mason, Texas: Printed by the
Mason Herald, 1911, 112 pp.

Burnet, D. G.
The Comanches and Other Tribes of Texas.
In: *Information Respecting the History,
Condition, and Prospects of the Indian Tribes
of the United States,* H. R. Schoolcraft, ed.,
Vol. 1, pp. 229–241. Philadelphia: 1851.

Cessac, L. de
"Renseignements ethnographique sur les Comanches." *Revue d'Ethnographie* (Paris) 1:94–
118, 1882.

Espinosa, Aurelio M., ed.
Los Comanches. University of New Mexico
Bulletin, Language, Series I, Part 1. Albuquer-
que, New Mexico: 1907. 46 pp.

Eastman, Edwin
*Seven and Nine Years Among the Camanches
and Apaches.* Jersey City, 1874.

Fisher, M. C.
"On the Arapahoes, Kiowas, and Comanches."
Jour. Ethnol. Soc. 1:274–287, 1869. n.s.

Humfreville, J. L.
Twenty Years Among Our Savage Indians . . .
Hartford: 1897. 674 pp.

Hyde, George E.
Rangers and Regulars. Denver, Col.: J. Van
Male, 1933. 47 pp.

Jones, J. H.
*A Condensed History of the Apache and Co-
manche Indian Tribes.* San Antonio: 1899.

Ten-Kate, H. F. C.
"Notes ethnographiques sur les Comanches."
Revue d'Ethnographie (Paris) 4:120–136,
1885.

Kendall, G. W.
Narrative of the Texan Santa Fé Expedition:
comprising a description of a tour through
Texas, and across the great southwestern
prairies, the Comanche and Caygüa hunting
grounds, with an account of the sufferings from
want of food, losses from hostile Indians and
final capture of the Texans, and their march as
prisoners to the city of Mexico. London: 1884.

Lee, Nelson
Three Years Among the Comanches, The Narrative of Nelson Lee, the Texas ranger, containing a detailed account of his captivity
among the Indians, his singular escape through
the instrumentality of his watch, and fully illustrating Indian life as it is on the war path and
in the camp. Albany: B. Taylor, 1859. xii,
224 pp.

Lehmann, H.
Nine Years Among the Indians. Austin: Von
Boeckmann-Jones Co., 1927. 235 pp.

Marcy, R. B.
Thirty Years of Army Life on the Border. New
York: Harper & Bros., 1866. 442 p.

Mooney, James
"Comanche." *Bull. Bureau Amer. Ethnol.* 30
(Part 1): 327–329, 1907.

Nye, W. S.
Carbine and Lance: The Story of Old Fort Sill.
Norman, Okla.: University of Oklahoma Press,
1937.

Opler, M. K.
"Origins of Comanche and Ute." *AA* 45:155–158, Jan. 1943.

Pettis, George H.
Kit Carson's Fight with the Comanche and Kiowa Indians at the Adobe Walls on the Canadian river, Nov. 25, 1864. Pamphlet, 44 pp. Providence: 1878.

Richardson, Rupert Norval
The Comanche Barrier to the South Plains Settlements; a century of savage resistance to the advancing white frontiers. Glendale, California: The Arthur H. Clark Co., 1933. 424 pp. illus.

————.
"The Culture of the Comanche Indians." *Bull. Texas Arch. Ethnol. Soc.* 1:58–73, 1929.

Setzler, F. M.
"A Prehistoric Cave Culture in Southwestern Texas." *AA* 37:104–110, 1937. n.s.

Sowell, A. J.
Early Settlers and Indian Fighters of Southwest Texas. Austin, Texas: B. C. Jones & Co., 1900. 844 pp.

Thomas, A. B.
"An Eighteenth Century Comanche Document." *AA* 31:289–298, 1929. n.s.

Tilghman, Z. A.
Quanah, The Eagle of the Comanches. Oklahoma City: Harlow Publ. 1938. 196 pp.

Wilbarger, I. W.
Indian Depredations in Texas, Austin, Texas 1899. Austin: Steck Company, (reprinted 1936.)

MYTHS—FOLKTALES—LEGENDS

Austin, Mary
One Smoke Stories. Boston: Houghton Mifflin Company, 1934. xiv, 294 pp., illus.

Lowie, R. H. and St. Clair, H. H.
"Shoshone and Comanche Tales." *JAFL* 22: 265–282, 1909.

Opler, Marvin K.
"The Origins of Comanche and Ute." *AA* 45: 155–158, 1943.

Reed, Mrs. Bruce
"An Indian Legend of the Blue Bonnet." *TFSP* 3:197–200, 1924.

BELIEFS—CUSTOMS—FOLK ART

Anon.
"Arab and Comanche Horsemen." *Grahams American Monthly Mag.* 40:550–554, May 1852.
Interesting account with extracts from various writers relative to the skill of the Arab and American Indian horsemen.

Carlson, G. A., and Jones, V. H.
"Some Notes on Uses of Plants by the Comanche Indians." *Papers Mich. Acad. Sci.* 25: 517–542, 1939.

Cumins, H., and Goldstein, M. S.
"Dermatoglyphics in Comanche Indians." *Amer. Jour. Phys. Anthro.* 17:229–235, 1932.

Dunlop
"Instruments en pierre de Texas." *Bulletin Société d'Anthropologie de Paris,* 10:56–57, 1909.

Hoebel, Edward Adamson
"The Comanche Sun Dance and Messianic Outbreak of 1873." *AA* 43:301–303, 1941.

————.
The Political Organization and Law-Ways of the Comanche Indians. Memoirs. Contribution from the Laboratory of Anthropology, 54. Menasha, Wisc.: American Anthropological Association, 1940. 149 pp.

Jackson, A. T.
Picture-Writing of Texas Indians. Anthropological Papers, University of Texas, Publications 2. Austin: University of Texas, 1938. 490 pp., illus.

Peters, J. H.
Dyeing, Spinning and Weaving by the Comanches, Navajoes, and Other Indians of New Mexico. In: *Indian Miscellany,* W. W. Beach, ed., (pp. 352–360). Albany: 1877.

Smith, Victor J.
"Indian Pictographs of the Big Bend Indians." *TFSP* 2:18–30, 1923. 12 illus.

DANCES

Hoebel, E. A.
"The Comanche Sun Dance and Messianic Outbreak of 1873." *AA* 43:301–303, 1941. n.s.

Linton, Ralph
"The Commanche Sun Dance." *AA* 37: 420–428, 1935, n.s.

CREE (Plains Cree)

FOLKLORE

GENERAL STUDIES

An Interesting Account of the Voyages and Travels of Captains Lewis and Clark, in the years 1804, 1805, and 1806. Giving a faithful description of the river Missouri and its source—of the various tribes of Indians which they passed —manners and customs—soil—climate—commerce—gold and silver mines—animal and vegetable productions . . . To which is added a complete dictionary of the Indian tongue. By William Fisher, esq. Baltimore: Printed by Anthony Miltenberger, 1812. xv, 326 pp.

Beardsley, Gretchen
"Notes on Cree Medicine Based on a Collection Made by Cowie in 1892." *Papers Mich. Acad.* 27(Pt. 4):483–496, 1942.

Bloomfield, Leonard, coll.
Plains Cree Texts. New York: G. E. Stechert & Co., 1934. viii, 309 pp. (American Ethnological Society—Publications. vol. 16).

Cooper, John M.
"The Cree Witiko Psychosis." *Primitive Man* 6, (No. 1):20–24, 1933.

"Cree Folklore"
JAFL 15:16–62, 1902; 18:139–143, 1905.

Montgomery, Henry
"Prehistoric Man in Manitoba and Saskatchewan." *AA* 10:33–41, 1908. n.s.

Skinner, Alanson
"Notes on the Plains Cree." *AA* 16:68–88, 1914. n.s.

————.
"Political Organizations, Cults, and Ceremonies of the Plains—Cree Indians." *Anthropological Papers of the American Museum of Natural History* 2:475–542, 1914. Illus.

FOLKTALES

Abenakew, Rev. E.
"Cree Trickster Tales." *JAFL* 42:309–354, 1929.

Bloomfield, Leonard
"The Story of the Bad Owl." *Proceedings of the 22nd Session of the International Congress of Americanists* 2:23–35, 1928.

Skinner, Alanson
"Plains Cree Tales." *JAFL* 29:341–367, 1913.

Teit, J. A.
"Plains Cree Tales." *JAFL* 34:320–321, 1921.

BELIEFS—CUSTOMS—SPEECH

Bloomfield, Leonard
"The Plains Cree Language." *Proceedings of the 22nd Session of the International Congress of Americanists* 2:427–433, 1928.

Michelson, Truman
"Plains Cree Kinship Terms." *AA* 40:531–532, 1938. n.s.

Rossignol, M.
"Cross-Cousin Marriage Among the Saskatchewan Cree." *Primitive Man* 11, (No. 1, 2):26–28, 1938.

————.
"The Religion of the Saskatchewan and Western Manitoba Cree." *Primitive Man* 11, (No. 3, 4):67–71. Washington, D. C.: Catholic Anthropological Society, 1939.

DANCES—GAMES

"Cree Games."
JAFL 9:275, 1896.

Skinner, Alanson
"The Sun Dance of the Plains Cree." *Anthropological Papers of the American Museum of Natural History* (New York) 16:283–293, 1919. illus.

CROW

FOLKLORE

GENERAL STUDIES

Anon.
"Crows." *Bull. Bureau Amer. Ethnol.* 30 (Part 1):367–369, 1907.

Bonner, T. D.
The Life and Adventures of James P. Beckwourth, Mountaineer, Scout, and Pioneer, and Chief of the Crow Nation of Indians. London: 1856. Republished in New York by Alfred A. Knopf, 1931.

Bradley, J. H.
"Indian Traditions." *Contributions to the Historical Society of Montana* 9: 288–299, 1923.

Coolidge, Grace
Tepee Neighbors. Boston: Over Seas Publishing Company, 1917. 325 pp.

Dodge, Col. Richard I.
Our Wild Indians. Hartford, Conn.: A. D. Worthington and Company 1833, 653 pp.

Gilder, Robert F.
"Indian Sites Near Frederick, Wyoming." *Records of the Past,* 7:179–182, 1908.

Goldenweiser, A. A.
"Remarks on the Social Organization of the Crow Indians." *AA* 15:281–295, 1913. n.s.

Laroque, F. A.
"Journal." *Publications of the Canadian Archives* 3: 55–70, 1910.

Leonard, Z.
Narrative of the Adventures of Zenas Leonard. Edited by M. M. Quaife. Chicago: Lakeside Press, 1934.

Linderman, Frank Bird
American: The Life Story of a Great Indian, Plenty Coups, Chief the Crow. New York: John Day Company, 1930.

————.
Old Man Coyote. New York: John Day Company, 1931. 254 pp.

————.
Red Mother. New York: John Day Company, 1933. 256 pp.
An autobiography of a Crow woman, Pretty-Shield, of the Sore-Lip Clan.

Lowie, Robert H.
"Some Problems in the Ethnology of the Crow and Village Indians." *AA* 14:60–72, 1912. n.s.

———.
"Societies of the Crow." *Anthropological Papers:* Vol. 11:1913, pp. 143–358, 18 figs. Publications in Anthropology. New York: The American Museum of Natural History.

———.
The Crow Indians. New York: Farrar and Rinehart, 1935. 350 pp., illus.
Describes also the elaborate ritualistic ceremonies of the Bear Dance, Sacred Pipe, Tobacco Society and Sun Dance, as well as presenting a selection of tales, description of rituals and festivals, and the kind of music and dance used.

———.
"The Crow Indians of Montana." *American Museum Journal* 11:179–181, 1911. (New York).

———.
"The Omaha and Crow Kinship Terminologies" *Proceedings of the 24th Session of the International Congress of Americanists,* pp. 102–109, 1930.

———.
"The Material Culture of the Crow Indians." *Anthropological Papers:* Vol. 21: 1922, pp. 201–270, 19 figs. Publications in Anthropology. New York: The American Museum of Natural History.

———.
Takes-the-Pipe, A Crow Warrior. In: *American Indian Life,* Elsie Clews Parsons, ed., (pp. 17–33). New York: 1925.

———.
"The Tobacco Society of the Crow Indians." *Anthropological Papers:* Vol. 21: 1920, pp. 101–200, 13 figs. Publications in Anthropology. New York: The American Museum of Natural History.

Marquis, Dr. Thomas B.
Memoirs of a White Crow Indian. New York and London: The Century Company, 1928. 356 pp.

Mason, J. A.
"A Collection from the Crow Indians." *Museum Journal* 17: 393–413, 1926.

Murdock, George Peter
The Crows of Western New York. In: *Our Primitive Contemporaries,* Chapter 10. New York: The Macmillan Company, 1936.

Quaife, M. M., ed.
Narratives of the Adventures of Zenas Leonard. Chicago: Lakeside Press, 1934.

Simms, Stephen C.
"Traditions of the Crows." *Field Columbian Museum. Publication No. 85. Anthropological Series.* 2 (No. 6):281–324, 1903.

Spring, Agnes W.
Caspar Collins. (Indian Fighter of the 60's.) New York: Columbia University Press, 1927. 187 pp., illus.

Wagner, Glendolin Damon, and Allen, William A.
Blankets and Moccasins. Caldwell, Idaho: Caxton Printers, Ltd., 1933. 304 pp.
Mainly concerned with the career of the Crow Chief Plenty-Coups.

Wildschut, W.
Buffalo Days and Danger Trails: Biography of Two Leggings, Chief of the River Crows. Ms. 1942.

MYTHS—FOLKTALES—LEGENDS

Dobie, J. Frank
"Greatest of all the Grizzlies." *CFQ* 3:12–15, 1944.

Ehrlich, Clara
"Tribal Culture in Crow Mythology." *JAFL* 50:307–409, 1937. Bibl.

Hoffman, W. J.
"An Absaroka Myth." *Jour. Royal Anthro. Inst. Gt. Brit. and Ireland* 10: 239–240, 1880.
The Absaroka—another name for the Crow.

Judson, Katharine Berry
Old Crow Stories, Illustrations by Charles Livingston Bull. Boston: Little, Brown and Co., 1917. vi, 163 pp., illus.

Linderman, Frank B.
Old Man Coyote; illustrated by Stoops, H. M. New York: John Day Company, 1931. 254 pp., illus.
Collection of folk tales of the Crow Chief Plenty-Coups.

———.
Red Mother, illustrated by Stoops, M. H. New York: The John Day Company, 1932. 256 pp., illus.

Lowie, Robert H.
"A Crow Text." *Univ. Calif. Publ. Amer. Arch. Ethnol.* 29: 155–175, 1930.

———.
A Crow Woman's Tale. In: *American Indian Life,* Elsie Clews Parsons, ed., pp. 35–40. New York: B. W. Huebsch, 1925.

———.
"Myths and Traditions of the Crow Indians." *American Museum of Natural History, Anthropological Papers* 25:1–308, 1918. (New York).

Reagan, A. B.
Sun God, Moccasin Tales. Provo, Utah: The Author, 1935.

Simms, Stephen Chapman
Traditions of the Crows. Field Museum of Natural History, Anthrop. Series, No. 2. Chicago: The Museum, 1903.
A number of characteristic tales are recounted.

Voegelin, E. W.
"Kiowa-Crow Mythological Affiliations." *AA* 35:470–474, 1933. n.s.

BELIEFS—CUSTOMS

Campbell, W. S.
"The Tipis of the Crow Indians." *AA* 29: 87–104, 1927. n.s.

Catlin, George
Illustrations of the Manners, Customs, and Condition of the North American Indian. Vol. I, pp. 42–51. New York: Wiley & Putnam, 1841.

Lowie, Robert H.
"Crow Prayers." *AA* 35:433–442, 1933. n.s.

————.
"Indian Theologians." *El Palacio* 35:217–231, 1933.

————.
"The Kinship Systems of the Crow and Hidasta." *Inter. Congr. Amer.* 19:340–343, 1915.

————.
"Military Societies of the Crow Indians." *Anthro. Papers Amer. Mus. Natur. Hist.* 11:143–217, 1913.

————.
"Minor Ceremonies of the Crow Indians." *Anthropological Papers:* Vol. 21: 1924, pp. 323–365. Publications in Anthropology. New York: The American Museum of Natural History.

————.
"Notes on the Social Organization and Customs of the Crow Indians." *Anthropological Papers:* Vol. 21: 1917, pp. 1–99. Publications in Anthropology. New York: The American Museum of Natural History.

————.
Primitive Religion. New York: Boni & Liveright, 1925. 346 pp., illus. (pp. 2–32).

————.
"The Religion of the Crow Indians." *American Museum of Natural History. Anthropological Papers* 25:309–444, 1922. Illus.

————.
"Supplementary Notes on the Social Life of the Crow." *Anthro. Papers Amer. Mus. Natur. Hist.* 21:53–99, 1917.

————.
A Trial of Shamans. In: *American Indian Life,* Elsie Clews Parsons, ed., (pp. 41–43). New York: B. W. Huebsch, 1925.

McAllister, David
"Water as a Disciplinary Agent Among the Crow and Blackfoot." *AA* 43:593–604, 1941.

Simms, S. C.
"Crow Indian Hermaphrodites." *AA* 5:580–581, 1903. n.s.

————.
"A Crow Monument to Shame." *AA* 5:374–375, 1903. n.s.

FOLK MEDICINE

Lowie, Robert H.
"Crow Indian Medicine." *AA* 35:207, 1933. n.s. See the author's comprehensive study of *The Crow Indians,* listed above, for further discussion of medical practices.

Simms, S. C.
"The Cultivation of 'Medicine Tobacco' by the Crows." *AA* 6:331–369, 1904. n.s.

Wildschut, W.
"Crow Love Medicine." *Indian Notes* 2:211–214, 1925. n.s.

————.
"The Crow Skull Medicine Bundle." *Indian Notes* 2:119–122, 1925.

FOLK ART—PROVERBS—GAMES

"Crow Games." *JAFL* 27:330–331, 1914.

Douglas, F. H.
"A Crow Beaded Horse Collar." *Material Culture Notes* (Denver Art Museum) 2:5–8, 1937.

Lowie, Robert H.
"Crow Indian Art." *Anthropological Papers.* 21:271–322, 1922. Illus. Publications in Anthropology. New York: The American Museum of Natural History.

————.
"Proverbial Expressions Among the Crow Indians." *AA* 34:739–740, 1931. n.s.

Wagner, G. D., and Allen, W. A.
Blankets and Moccasins. Caldwell, Id.: Caxton Printers, Ltd., 1933. 304 pp.

Wildschut, W.
"A Crow Pictograph Robe." *Indian Notes* 3:28–32, 1926.

————.
"A Crow Shield." *Indian Notes* 2:315–320, 1925.

————.
"Moccasin-Bundle of the Crows." *Indian Notes* 3:201–205, 1926.

MUSIC
GENERAL STUDIES

Lowie, Robert Heinrich
"Social Life of the Crow Indians." *American Museum of Natural History Anthropological Papers* (New York) 9:179–253, 1912.

————.
The Crow Indians. New York: Farrar and Rinehart, 1935. 350 pp., illus.
Contains discussion of songs and dances.

DANCES

Lowie, R. H.
"Crow Sun Dance." *JAFL* 27:94–97, 1914.

——.
"The Crow Tobacco Dance." *Carlisle Arrow* (Carlisle, Pa.) 8, (No. 9):8, 1911.

——.
"The Sun Dance." *American Museum of Natural History Anthropological Papers* (New York) 16:1–50, 1915. Illus.

Nixon, A. L.
"Crow Indian Dance in Miniature." *Hobbies* 48:116–117, 1943.

ARRANGEMENTS

"A Crow Maiden's Prayer."
(In—*Nine Indian Songs*.) Lieurance, Thurlow: Presser: Voice and piano.

"Prayer to the Rain God."
(By Thurlow Lieurance.) Philipp, I.: Presser: Piano.

"The Weaver."
Lieurance, Thurlow: Presser: Voice and piano.

GROS VENTRE
FOLKLORE
GENERAL STUDIES

Flannery, Regina
"The Dearly-Loved Child Among the Gros Ventres of Montana." *Primitive Man* 14, (No. 3):33–38, Catholic Anthropological Conference, Washington, 1941.

——.
"The Changing Form and Functions of the Gros Ventre Dance." *Prim. Man* 20(No. 3): 39–70, 1947.

Grinnell, George Bird
"Some Indian Stream Names." *AA* 15:327–332, 1913. n.s.

Kroeber, A. L.
"Notes on Gros Ventre." *University of California Publications of American Archaeology and Ethnology* 12, (No. 3):131–137, 1916. Berkeley: University of California Press, 1916–1917.
Linguistic study.

——.
"The Ethnology of the Gros Ventre." *American Museum of Natural History, Anthropological Papers* 1:141–281, 1908. Illus.

Mooney, J.
"Atsina." *Bull. Bureau Amer. Ethnol.* 30 (Part 1): 113, 1907.
The Atsina—another name for the Gros Ventre.

Terrell, John Upton
Plume Rouge: A Novel of the Pathfinders. New York: Viking Press, 1942. 498 pp.
Lends insight into the life and manners of the Gros Ventre.

MYTHS—FOLKTALES—LEGENDS

Kroeber, A. L.
"Gros Ventre Myths and Tales." *American Museum of Natural History* (New York), *Anthropological Papers* 1 (Part 3):55–140, 1907.

HIDATSA
FOLKLORE
GENERAL STUDIES

Brownlee, Fred L., and Johnson, Charles S.
The Indians of North and South Dakota. Fisk University, 1941. 51 pp.

Catlin, George
Illustrations of the Manners, Customs, and Condition of the North American Indians, with letters and notes written during eight years' travel and adventure (engraved by author). 10th edition. London: Chatto & Windus, 1866. 2 vols., illus. First Edition: New York: Wiley and Putnam, 1841.

Denig, Edwin Thompson
"Indian Tribes of the Upper Missouri." Edited with notes and biographical sketch by J. N. B. Hewitt. *46th Annual Report: Bureau of American Ethnology. Smithsonian Institution,* pp. 375–628. Washington, D. C.

Libby, O. G.
"Typical Villages of the Mandans, Arikara, and Hidatsa." *Collections of the State Historical Society of North Dakota* 2:498–508, 1908.

Matthews, Washington
Ethnography and Philology of the Hidatsa Indians. U. S. Geologic and Geographic Survey, Miscellaneous Publications, No. 7. Washington, D. C.: U. S. Government Printing Office, 1877. 239 pp.

Mooney, James
"Hidatsa." *Bull. Bureau Amer. Ethnol.* 30 (Part 1): 547–549, 1907.

Thwaites, Reuben Gold, ed.
"Lewis and Clark, original Journals of the Lewis and Clark Expedition, 1804–1806." 7 *Volumes,* Vol. 1:208–276 (Oct. 17, 1804–March 17, 1805.) New York, 1904.

Wilson, G. L.
Goodbird, the Indian. New York: 1914. 80 pp.

MYTHS—FOLKTALES—LEGENDS

Beckwith, Martha Warren, coll.
"Mandan and Hidatsa Tales." *Publications of the Folklore Foundation* (Poughkeepsie: Vassar College) 14:269–320, 1934.

———. "Myths and Ceremonies of the Mandan and Hidatsa." *Publications of the Folklore Foundation* (Poughkeepsie: Vassar College) 12: 117–267, 1932.

———. *Myths and Hunting Stories of the Mandan and Hidatsa Sioux.* Vassar College Field Work in Folklore, 1930. 116 pp.

———. *Mandan-Hidatsa Myths and Ceremonies.* Memoir of the American Folklore Society, No. 32. Philadelphia: American Folklore Society, 1938.

Lowie, Robert H.
"Hidatsa Texts." *Prehistory Research Series* (Indiana Historical Society, Indianapolis) 1: 173–239, 1939.

———. "Studies in Plains Indians Folklore." *University of California Publications in American Archaeology and Ethnology* 40, (No. 1):1–28, 1942. Berkeley: University of California Press, 1942.
> The Hidatsa Grandson Myth is given in full, followed by analysis of variation resulting when formulas or tales are repeated by the same Indian, or at least by Indian of the same local group.

Will, G. F.
"Some Hidatsa and Mandas Tales." *JAFL* 25: 93–94, 1912.

BELIEFS—CUSTOMS—SPEECH

Catlin, George
Illustrations of the Manners, Customs, and Condition of the North American Indians. Vol. I, pp. 185–202. New York: Wiley & Putnam, 1841.

Dorsey, J. O.
"A Study of Siouan Cults." *Annual Report Bureau Amer. Ethnol.* 11:513–518, 1890.

———. "Siouan Sociology." *Annual Report Bureau Amer. Ethnol.* 15:242–243, 1894.

Lowie, Robert H.
"The Kinship System of the Crow and Hidatsa." *Inter. Congr. Amer.* 19:340–343, 1915.

———. "Notes on the Social Organization and Customs of the Hidatsa Indians." *American Museum of Natural History Anthropological Papers* 21:1–99, 1917. (New York).

———. "Societies of the Hidatsa and Mandan Indians." *American Museum of Natural History Anthropological Papers* 11:143–358, 1913. Illus. (New York).

———. "Social Life of the Hidatsa." *Anthro. Papers Amer. Mus. Natur. Hist.* 21:17–52, 1917.

Matthews, Washington
Ethnography and Philology of the Hidatsa Indians. U. S. Geological and Geographical Survey of the Rocky Mountain Region. Miscellaneous Publications No. 7. Washington, D. C.: U. S. Government Printing Office, 1877.

———. *Grammar and Dictionary of the Language of the Hidatsa.* New York: 1874. 169 pp.

Pepper, George H., and Wilson, Gilbert L.
"An Hidatsa Shrine and the Beliefs Respecting It." *Memoirs American Anthropological Association* 2, (Part 4):275–328. Lancaster, Pa.: 1908. Illus.

Wilson, Gilbert Livingstone
"Agriculture of the Hidatsa Indians." *University of Minnesota Studies in the Social Sciences* 9. St. Paul: University of Minnesota Press, 1917. 129 pp.

———. "Hidatsa Eagle Trapping." *American Museum of Natural History, Anthropological Papers* 30:99–245, (New York) 1928. Illus.

———. "The Hidatsa Earth Lodge." Edited by Bella Weitzner. *American Museum of Natural History, Anthropological Paper* 33, (Part 5):341–420, 1934.

———. "The Horse and the Dog in Hidatsa Culture." *American Museum of Natural History. Anthropological Papers* 15:125–311, 1924. (New York).

DANCES

Lowie, Robert H.
"The Sun Dance of the Hidatsa." *American Museum of Natural History Anthropological Papers* (New York) 16:387–431, 1919. Illus.

MUSIC
GENERAL STUDIES

Densmore, Frances
Mandan and Hidatsa Music. Bulletin of American Ethnology, Bulletin 80. Washington, D. C.: U. S. Government Printing Office, 1923. 192 pp.
> Classification of the songs and dances, the rituals and ceremonies connected with them, as well as legends and myths.

IOWA
FOLKLORE
GENERAL STUDIES

Adams, Ephraim
The Iowa Band. Boston: The Pilgrim Press, 1902. xx, 240 pp., illus., map.

Black Hawk
Life of Black Hawk, Ma-Ka-tai-me-she-Kia-Kiak. Iowa City: State Historical Society of Iowa, 1932.

Catlin, George
Notice sur les Indiens Ioway. Paris: Imprimerie de Wittersheim, 1845. 24 pp.

Cole, Cyrenus
I Am A Man—The Indian Black Hawk. Iowa City: State Historical Society of Iowa, 1938.

Dorsey, J. O., and Thomas, C.
"Iowa." *Bull. Bureau Amer. Ethnol.* 30 (Part 1): 612–614, 1907.

Fulton, A. R.
The Red Men of Iowa. Des Moines, 1882.

Irvin, S. M., and Hamilton, W.
Iowa and Sac Tribes. In: *Information Respecting the History, Condition, and Prospects of the Indian Tribes of the United States*, H. R. Schoolcraft, ed. Vol. 3, pp. 259–277. Philadelphia: 1853.

Miner, William Harvey
The Iowa. A reprint from The Indian Record, as originally published by Thomas Foster, with introduction and elucidation through text. Cedar Rapids, Ia.: The Torch Press, 1911. 100 pp., illus.

Plank, P.
"The Iowa, Sac and Fox Mission." *Trans. Kansas State Hist. Soc.* 10:312–325, 1908.

Skinner, Alanson
"A Summer Among the Sauk and Ioway Indians." *Yearbook Publ. Mus. City Milwaukee* 2:16–22, 1922.

————.
"Ethnology of the Ioway Indians." *Public Museum, City of Milwaukee*, Bulletin 5:181–354, 1926.

————.
"Societies of Iowa, Kansa, and Ponca Indians." *Anthropological Papers of the American Museum of Natural History* (New York) 11:679–801, 1915.

————.
"Traditions of the Iowa Indians." *JAFL* 38:425–506, 1925.

Stout, E. J.
Folklore from Iowa. Memoirs of the American Folklore Society, No. 29. Phila.: American Folklore Society, 1936.

MYTHS—BELIEFS—FOLK MEDICINE

Irvin, S. M.
The Waw-ru-haw-a; the Decline and Fall of Indian Superstitions. Philadelphia: 1871.

Skinner, Alanson
Medicine Ceremony of the Menomini, Iowa and Wahpeton, Dakota. With notes on the ceremony among the Ponca, Bungi, Ojibwa and Potawatomi. Indian Notes and Monographs, Museum of the American Indian, Heye Foundation No. 4, 357 pp., 1920.

————.
"The Iowa Origin Myth." *Museum of the American Indian, Indian Notes and Monographs* (New York) 4:189–192, 1920.

SPEECH—GAMES—DANCES

Hamilton, William, and Irvin, S. M.
An Ioway Grammar, Illustrating the principles of the Language Used by the Ioway, Otoe, and Missouri Indians. Ioway and Sac Mission Press, 1848.

Marriott, Alice L.
"Dancing Makes Fun." *TFSP* 19:82–87, 1944. A dance and game of the Iowa Indians of Oklahoma.

KIOWA

FOLKLORE

GENERAL STUDIES

Fisher, M. C.
"On the Arapahoes, Kiowas, and Comanches." *Jour. Ethnol. Soc.* 1:274–287, 1869. n.s.

Gatschet, A. S.
"Sinti, der erste Mensch." *Ausland* 63:901–904, 1890.

Harrington, John P.
Kiowa Memories of the Northland. In: *So Live the Works of Men*, D. D. Brand, and F. E. Harvey, eds., (pp. 162–176). Albuquerque: Univ. New Mexico Press, 1939.

————.
"Three Kiowa Texts." *International Journal of American Linguistics* 12, October, 1946.

Historical Sketches. A series of Kiowa and Comanche articles published in a small religious leaflet called the "Day Star," Nos. 58–66, 1890 and 1891. Mount Vernon, Iowa.

La Barre, Weston
"Kiowa Folk Sciences." *JAFL* 60:105–114, 1947.
The author discusses four major aspects: ethnobotany, ethnobiology, folk physiology, and folk anthropology. He cautions the reader to "discover the obvious, that his (primitive man's) original motives and meanings are clearly not those we impute to him in our inveterate attempt to rationalize them into motives and meanings which are intellectually more comfortable and familiar to us. The motives of primitive man are his own."

Lowie, Robert H.
"Societies of the Kiowa." *Anthropological Papers:* Vol. 11: 1916, pp. 837–876. Publications in Anthropology. New York: The American Museum of Natural History.

Marriott, Alice L.
The Ten Grandmothers. Norman, Okla.: University of Oklahoma Press, 1945. xiv, 306 pp., illus., bibl.
The author builds a saga of a prominent family for almost a hundred years.

Methvin, J. J.
Andele, or the Mexican-Kiowa Captive. Louisville, Ky.: Pentecostal Press, 1899.

Mooney, James
"Calendar History of the Kiowa Indians." *7th Annual Report: Bureau of American Ethnology.* 1895–1896. pp. 141–447, pls. LVII–LXXXI, figs. 43–229, 1 map. Washington, D. C.: U. S. Gov't Printing Office, 1898.

————.
"Field-Work Among the Kiowa." *Smithson. Miscel. Coll.* 70 (Part 2):99–103, 1919.

————.
"Kiowa." *Bull. Bureau Amer. Ethnol.* 30 (Part 1):699–701, 1907.

Wharton, Clarence
Santana, the Great Chief of the Kiowas and his People. Dallas: Upshaw and Company, 1935. 239 pp., illus.
Sun Dance, pp. 130, Burial Ceremony, pp. 183–184.

MYTHS—FOLKTALES—LEGENDS

Marriott, Alice
Winter-Telling Tales. Illustrated by Roland Whitehorse. New York: William Sloan Associates, 1947. 84 pp.
"Tales about Kiowa trickster-hero, Sayndaym, told with sly humor and reserve—and in print for the first time. These are variants of stories in other trickster cycles but have utterly different individual touches. Recommended for 8–12 year olds and for adults as well." (Elaine L. Lewis)

Parsons, Elsie Clews
Kiowa Tales. Memoir of the American Folklore Society, No. 22. Phila.: American Folklore Society, 1929. 151 pp.

Voegelin, E. W.
"Kiowa-Crow Mythological Affiliations." *AA* 35:470–474, 1933. n.s.

BELIEFS—CUSTOMS—FOLK ART

Jackson, A. T.
Picture-Writing of Texas Indians. Anthropological Papers, University of Texas Publications 2. Austin: University of Texas, 1938. 490 pp., ill.

Mooney, James
"The Ghost-Dance Religion." *Annual Report Bureau Amer. Ethnol.* 14 (Part 2):1078–1091, 1893.

————.
"Indian Shield Heraldry." *South. Workman* 30:500–504, 1901.

————.
"The Kiowa Peyote Rite." *Der Urquell* (Leyden) Vol. 50, 1897.

Richardson, Jane
Law and Status Among the Kiowa Indians. Monographs of the American Ethnological Society 1. New York: J. J. Augustin, 1940. 136 pp.
The author's central thesis is "that each behavior pattern was generally correlated with a specific status level or status relationship of the opponents."

SPEECH—DANCES—GAMES

Harrington, John Peabody
Vocabulary of the Kiowa Language. Bulletin 84. Bureau Amer. Ethnol. Washington, D. C.: 1928. 255 pp.

————.
"Kiowa Games."
JAFL 6:216, 1893.

Lowie, Robert H.
"A Note on Kiowa Kinship Terms and Usages." *AA* 25:279–281, 1923. n.s.

Mooney, James
"A Kiowa Mescal Rattle," *AA* 5:64–67, 1892.

————.
Kiowa Sun Dance. In: *Calendar History of the Kiowa Indians* (pp. 237, 243–244). U. S. Bureau of American Ethnology 17th Report. Washington, D. C.: U. S. Government Printing Office, 1898.

Nye, Wilbur J.
"The Annual Sun Dance of the Kiowa Indians." *Chronicles of Oklahoma* (Oklahoma City) 12:340–358, 1934.

Scott, Hugh Lenox
"Notes on the Kado or Sun Dance of the Kiowa." *AA* 13:345–380, 1911. n.s. Illus.

Spier, Leslie
"Notes on the Kiowa Sun Dance." *Anthropological Papers of the American Museum of Natural History* (New York) 16 (part 7):451–527, 1921.

Watkins, F. E.
"Kiowa Woman's Ghost-Dance Dress." *Masterkey* 18:118–119, 1944.

MUSIC

ARRANGEMENTS

————: *Piano*

"Ghost Dance."
(In—*Melodic Views of Indian Life.*) Miller, Horace A.: Clayton F. Summy: Piano.

Kiowa-Apache War Dance. For pianoforte. Wa-Wan Press, Series of American Compositions, Vol. 6, (No. 45), Part 2. Troyer, Carlos: Newton Center, Mass.: The Wa-Wan Press, 1907.

MANDAN

FOLKLORE

GENERAL STUDIES

Brownlee, Fred L., and Johnson, Charles S.
The Indians of North and South Dakota. Nashville, Tenn.: Fisk University, 1941. 51 pp.

Denig, Edwin Thompson
"Indian Tribes of the Upper Missouri." Edited with notes and biographical sketch by J. N. B. Hewitt. *46th Annual Report: Bureau of American Ethnology, Smithsonian Institution,* pp. 375–628. Washington: U. S. Government Printing Office, 1930.

Dorsey, J. O., and Thomas, C.
"Mandan." *Bull. Bureau Amer. Ethnol.* 30 (Part 1): 796–799, 1907.

Hayden, F. V.
"Contributions to the Ethnography and Philology of the Indian Tribes of the Missouri Valley." *Trans. Amer. Philo. Soc.* 12:426–444, 1863, n.s.

——.
"A Sketch of the Mandan Indians." *American Journal of Science and Arts* 34:57–66, 1862.

Hopkins, William John
The Indian Book. Boston: Houghton, Mifflin Company, 1911. vii, 239 pp., illus.

Kipp, J.
Mandan. In: *Information Respecting the History, Condition, and Prospects of the Indian Tribes of the United States.* H. R. Schoolcraft, ed. Vol. 3, pp. 446–459. Philadelphia: 1853.

Libby, O. G.
"Typical Villages of the Mandans, Arikara, and Hidatsa." *Collections of the State Historical Society of North Dakota* 2: 498–508, 1908.

Lowie, Robert H.
"Plains Indians Age-Societies; Historical and Comparative Summary." *American Museum of Natural History, Anthropological Papers* 11: 877–1031, 1916. (New York).

——.
"Social Life of the Mandan." *Anthro. Papers Amer. Mus. Natur. Hist.* 21:7–16, 1917.

——.
"Societies of the Crow, Hidatsa, and Mandan Indians." *American Museum of Natural History* (New York), *Anthropological Papers* 11: 145–358, 1913. Illus.

——.
"Some Problems in the Ethnology of the Crow and Village Indians." *AA* 14:60–71, 1912. n.s.

Lyons, T. D.
"Mandan; Sioux and Mandan Indians in the Northwest." *Commonweal* 37:164–166, 1942.

Matthews, W.
"Two Mandan Chiefs." *Amer. Antiq.* 10:269–272, 1888.

Mayer, Frank Blackwell
With Pen and Pencil on the Frontier in 1851. Diary and sketches. Edited by Bertha L. Heilbros. Minnesota Historical Society Narratives and Documents, Vol. 1, St. Paul, 1932.

Maximilian, Prince of Wied
Travels in the Interior of North America, 1832–1934. Translated from the German by Hannibal Evans Lloyd. Edited by Reuben Gold Thwaites. (3 vols.) Cleveland: 1905. Vol. 2:252–385; Vol. 3:11–83.

Neill, E. D.
"Life Among the Mandans Eighty Years Ago." *Amer. Antiq.* 6:248–253, 377–384, 1884.

Thwaites, Reuben Gold, ed.
"Lewis and Clark, Original Journals of the Lewis and Clark Expedition. 1804–1806." *7 Volumes,* Vol. 1:208–276 (October 17, 1804—March 17, 1805). New York, 1904.

Vestal, Stanley
Happy Hunting Ground. Chicago: Lyons and Carnahan, 1928.
Story of Mandan and Cheyenne warfare.

Will, George Francis
"The Mandans." *North Dakota Historical Society* 5:38–48, 1930. (A revision and condensation of an earlier article written for the Peabody Museum of American Archaeology and Ethnology.)

——, **and Hyde, George E.**
Corn Among the Indians of the Upper Missouri. St. Louis, Mo.: William Henry Miner Company, Inc., 1917.

——, **and Spinden, H. J.**
"The Mandans." *Peabody Museum of American Archaeology and Ethnology,* 3:81–219. Cambridge, Mass.: Harvard University, 1906.

MYTHS—FOLKTALES—LEGENDS

Beckwith, Martha Warren
"Mandan and Hidatsa Tales." Publications of the Folk-Lore Foundation (Poughkeepsie; Vassar College) 14:269–320, 1934.

——.
Mandan—Hidatsa Myths and Ceremonies. New York: The American Folk-Lore Society, G. E. Stechert & Co., 1938. xviii, 327 pp., illus. (Memoirs of the American Folk-Lore Society, Vol. XXXII.)

——.
Myths and Ceremonies of the Mandan and Hidatsa. (Second Series). Publications of the Folk Lore Foundation 12:117–267, 1932.

——.
Myths and Hunting Stories of the Mandan and Hidatsa. Vassar College Publications in Folklore No. 10. Poughkeepsie: 1930, 116 pp.

Hopkins, W. J.
The Indian Book. Boston: Houghton Mifflin Company, 1911. vii, 239 pp., illus.

"Mandan Tales."
JAFL 25:93–94, 1912; 26:331–337, 1913; 39:402–406, 1926.

McCowan, S. M.
"The Story of Mah-to-th-pa, Second Chief of the Mandans." *So. Workman* 30:200–205, 1901.

Mitchell, D. D.
"Remarkable Dream and Prediction." *Southern Literary Magazine* 1:658–660, Aug. 1835.
A descriptive account of the dream of an old Mandan Chief to avenge the death of his son, and also of the prediction of an Indian prophet of the death of one of the wives of the Menominie's tribe.

Will, George Francis
"No-Tongue, a Mandan Tale." *JAFL* 26:331–337, 1913.

————.
"Some Hidatsa and Mandan Tales." *JAFL* 25:93–94, 1912.

————.
"Story of No-Tongue, a Mandan Tale." *JAFL* 29:402–406, 1916.

BELIEFS—CUSTOMS

Catlin, George
An Account of An Annual Religious Ceremony Practised by the Mandan Tribe of the North American Indians. London: Privately printed, 1865. 67 pp.

————.
North American Indians; being letters and notes on their manners, customs and conditions written during eight years' travel amongst the wildest tribes of Indians in North America, 1832–1839. London: The Author, 1841. 2 vols., illus. New York: Wiley and Putnam, 1841.

————.
O-Kee-pa: A Religious Ceremony; and Other Customs of the Mandans. With thirteen colored illustrations. Philadelphia: J. B. Lippincott and Company, 1867. iv, 52 pp., col. pl.

Dorsey, J. O.
"A Study of Siouan Cults." *Annual Report Bureau Amer. Ethnol.* 11:501–513, 1890.

Gilmore, Melvin R.
"Uses of Plants by the Indians of the Missouri River Region." *33rd Annual Report: Bureau of American Ethnology, 1911–1912*, pp. 43–194. Washington, D. C.: U. S. Government Printing Office, 1912.

Lowie, Robert H.
"Notes on the Social Organization and Customs of the Mandan, Hidatsa and Crow Indians." *American Museum of Natural History* (New York), *Anthropological Papers* 21:1–99, 1917.

————.
"Societies of the Hidatsa and Mandan Indians." *Anthro. Papers Amer. Mus. Natur. Hist.* 11:294–358, 1913.

MUSIC

GENERAL STUDIES

Densmore, Frances
Mandan and Hidatsa Music. Bureau of American Ethnology, Bulletin 80, 192 pp., 19 pls., 6 figs. Music. Washington, D. C.: U. S. Govt. Printing Office, 1923.

ARRANGEMENTS

Organ

"Barbaric Splendor."
Miller, Horace A.: Cornell College: Organ

RECORDS

U. S. Library of Congress. Division of Music. Folklore Section.
Mandan Indians' Tribal Songs, recorded by Mark Mahto, Elbowoods, N. D. AAFS–LC

OMAHA

FOLKLORE

BIBLIOGRAPHY

La Flesche, Francis
"Bibliography of His Works: 1855–1932." *AA* 35:330–331, 1933.

GENERAL STUDIES

Allis, Rev. Samuel
Forty Years Among the Indians and on the Eastern Borders of Nebraska. Transactions and Reports of the Nebraska State Historical Society, Lincoln, Nebraska, 1887.

Dorsey, J. Owen
"Omaha Sociology." *3rd Annual Report: Bureau of Ethnology*, 1881–1882, pp. 211–368, pls. XXX–XXXIII, figs. 12–42. Washington, D. C.: U. S. Gov't. Printing Office, 1884.
Early and subsequent migrations of the Omahas, the state, state classes, the Gentile system, tribal circles, sacred tents, laws of membership, domestic life, visiting customs, industrial occupations, songs and dances, etc.

————.
"Omaha Folklore Notes." *JAFL* 1:213–214, 1888; 2:190, 1889.

————.
"Omaha and Ponka Letters." *American Bureau of Ethnology*, Bulletin 11, pp. 5–121. Washington, D. C.: U. S. Government Printing Office, 1891.

The Dhegiha Language. U. S. Geographical and Geological Survey of the Rocky Mountain Region. Contributions to North American Ethnology, Vol. 6. Washington, D. C.: U. S. Government Printing Office, 1890.

————.
"Siouan Folk-Lore and Mythologic Notes." *Amer. Antiq.* 6:174–176, 1884; 7:105–108, 1885.

————, and Thomas, C.
"Omaha." *Bull. Bureau Amer. Ethnol.* 30 (Part 2):119–121, 1910.

Fletcher, Alice C.
Historical Sketch of the Omaha Tribe. Washington, D. C. 1885. 12 pp.

————.
"Home Life Among the Indians." *Century Magazine* 54:252–263, 1897.

————.
Indian Story and Song from North America. Boston: C. C. Birchard and Co., 1900. 126 pp.

————.
Tribal Structure: A Study of the Omaha and Cognate Tribes. Putnam Anniversary Volume: Anthropological Papers. New York: G. E. Stechert and Company, 1909.

————, and La Flesche, Francis
"The Omaha Tribe." *27th Annual Report: Bureau American Ethnology, 1905–1906,* pp. 15–655, pls. 1–65, figs. 1–132. Washington. D. C.: U. S. Government Printing Office, 1911.

Fontenelle, H.
"History of the Omaha Indians." *Trans. Reports Neb. State Hist. Soc.* 1:76–83, 1885.

Giffin, Fannie Reed
Oa-Mah-Ha-Ta-Wa-Tha (Omaha City). With illustrations by S. La Flesche Tibbles (Bright Eyes). Lincoln, Nebr.: Published by the Author, 1898.

Hayden, F. V.
"Brief Notes on the Pawnee, Winnebago, and Omaha Language." *Proceedings American Philosophical Society* 10:393–, 1869.

Kobelt, W.
"Das Volk der Omaha." *Globus* 50:347–351, 1886.

La Flesche, Francis
Middle Five; Indian Boys at School Boston: Small, Maynard and Company, 1900. xvii, 227 pp.

————.
"Omaha and Osage Traditions of Separation." *Proceedings of the 19th Session of the International Congress of Americanists,* pp. 459–462, 1915.

————, and Fletcher, Alice C.
"The Omaha Tribe." *27 Annual Report: Bureau of American Ethnology,* 1905–1906, pp. 15–672. Washington, D. C.: U. S. Government Printing Office, 1911.

Lowie, R. H.
"The Omaha and Crow Kinship Terminologies." *Proceedings of the 24th Session of the International Congress of Americanists,* pp. 102–109, 1930.

Mead, Margaret
The Changing Culture of an Indian Tribe. New York: Columbia University Press, 1932. 313 pp.
"A signal contribution to our knowledge of the reactions of a typical Indian tribe to the impact of white civilization." (Goldenweiser)

Strong, William Duncan
"An Introduction to Nebraska Archaeology." *Smithsonian Institution, Miscellaneous Collections* Vol. 93 (No. 10). Washington, D. C., 1935.

MYTHS—FOLKTALES—LEGENDS

Dorsey, James Owen
"Abstracts of Omaha and Ponka Myths." *JAFL* 1:74–78, 204–208, 1888.

————.
"How the Rabbit Caught the Sun in a Trap." *Annual Report Bureau Amer. Ethnol.* 1:581–583, 1880.

————.
"How the Rabbit Killed the (Male) Winter." *Amer. Antiq.* 2-128–132, 1879.

Kercheval, G. T.
"An Otoe and an Omaha Tale." *JAFL* 6:199–204, 1893.

Indian Place Legends.
Nebraska Folklore Pamphlets 2. Federal Writers' Project in Nebraska. Lincoln: (May 29) 1937.

Indian Ghost Legends.
Nebraska Folklore Pamphlets, 12. Federal Writers' Project in Nebraska. Lincoln: (Nov. 15) 1937.

La Flesche, Francis
"Wakondagi." *AA* 14:106–109, 1912. n. s.
"Wakonda" is the name given by the Omaha, Ponca, Osage, Quapaw, Kansa, Oto, Missouri and Iowa tribes of the Siouan family "to the mysterious all pervading and life-giving power to which certain anthropomorphic aspects are attributed. The word is also applied to objects or phenomena regarded as sacred or mysterious" . . . Wagondagi denotes the power of possession or "belonging to or of the power denominated."

————.
"The Laughing Bird, the Wren." *So. Workman* 29:554–556, 1900.

"The Story of a Vision." *So. Workman* 30:106–109, 1901.

BELIEFS—CUSTOMS—FOLK MEDICINE

Dorsey, J. O.
"Omaha Clothing and Personal Ornaments." *AA* 3:71–105, 1890.

———.
"Omaha Dwellings, Furniture and Implements." *13th Annual Report: Bureau of American Ethnology, 1891–1892.* pp. 263-288, figs. 306–327. Washington, D. C.: U. S. Government Printing Office 1896. illus.
Dwellings, earth lodges, bark, tents, etc. Furniture, fireplaces, beds, cradles, children's swings, pottery, etc. Musical instruments, weapons, firearms, etc.

———.
"On the Gentile System of the Omahas." *Amer. Antiq.* 5:312–318, 1883.

———.
"The Religion of the Omahas and Ponkas." *Amer. Antiq.* 5:271–275, 1883.

———.
"A Study of Siouan Cults." *Annual Report Bureau Amer. Ethnol.* 11:361–422, 1890.

Fletcher, Alice Cunningham
"The Child and the Tribe." *Proc. Nat. Acad. Sci.* 1:569–574, 1915.

———.
"The Emblematic Use of the Tree in the Dakota Group." *Proc. Amer. Assoc. Adv. Sci.* 45:191–209, 1896.

———.
"The Emblematic Use of the Tree in the Dakotan Group." *Science* 4:475–487, 1896. n.s.

———.
"Glimpses of Child-Life Among the Omaha Tribe of Indians." *JAFL* 1:115–123, 1888.

———.
"Hae-Thu-Ska Society of the Omaha Tribe." *JAFL* 5:135–144, 1892.

———.
"Häusliches Leben bei den Indianern." *Globus* 73:252–259, 1898.

———.
"Home Life Among the Indians." *Century Magazine* 54:252–263, 1897.

———.
"The Indian and Nature," *Proc. Nat. Acad. Sci.* 1:467–473, 1915.

———.
"Leaves From My Omaha Notebook. Courtship and Marriage." *JAFL* 2:219–226, 1889.

———.
"Nature and the Indian Tribe." *Art Arch.* 4:291–296, 1916.

———.
"Observations on the Laws and Privileges of the Gens in Indian Society." *Proc. Amer. Assoc. Adv. Sci.* 32:395–396, 1883.

———.
"Observations on the Usage, Symbolism and Influence of the Sacred Pipes of Fellowship Among the Omahas." *Proc. Amer. Assoc. Adv. Sci.* 33:615–617, 1884.

———.
"The Sacred Pole of the Omaha Tribe." *Proc. Amer. Assoc. Adv. Sci.* 44:270–280, 1895.

———.
"Sacred Pole of the Omaha Tribe." *JAFL* 8:249–250, 1895.

———.
"The Significance of the Scalp-Lock." *Jour. Royal Anthro. Inst. Gt. Brit. and Ireland* 27:436–450, 1897.

———.
"A Study of the Omaha Tribe: the Import of the Totem." *Proc. Amer. Assoc. Adv. Sci.* 46:325–334, 1897.

Fortune, R. W.
Omaha Secret Societies. Columbia University Contributions to Anthropology 14. New York: Columbia University Press, 1932. 193 pp.
Dances and ceremonials also discussed.

Gilmore, M. R.
"The Mescal Society Among the Omaha Indians." *Publications of the Nebraska State Historical Society* 19:163–167, 1919.

———.
"Teokanha's Sacred Bundle." *Indian Notes* 1:52–62, 1924.

———.
"Uses of Plants by the Indians of the Missouri River Region." *Annual Report Bureau Amer. Ethnol.* 33:43–154, 1912.

Gleason, F. D.
"Social Life Among the Indians." *So. Workman* 29:565–568, 1900; 30:156–159, 1901.

La Flesche, Francis
"Death and Funeral Customs Among the Omaha." *JAFL* 2:3–11, 1889.

———.
"Omaha and Osage Traditions of Separation." *Inter. Congr. Amer.* 19:459–462, 1915.

———.
"Omaha Buffalo Medicine-Men." *JAFL* 3:215–221, 1890.

Wardle, H. N.
"Indian Gifts in Relation to Primitive Law." *Inter. Congr. Amer.* 23:463–469, 1928.

GAMES—SPEECH—FOLK ART

See: Music and Dances below.

Dorsey, J. O.
"Indian Personal Names." *Proc. Amer. Assoc. Adv. Sci.* 34:393–399, 1886.

"Omaha Clothing and Personal Ornaments."
AA 3:71–78, 1890.

"Omaha Dwellings, Furniture, and Implements." *Annual Report Bureau Amer. Ethnol.*
13:263–288, 1892.

Hayden, F. V.
"Brief Notes on the Pawnee, Winnebago, and
Omaha Languages." *Proc. Amer. Philo. Soc.*
10:406–411, 1868.

La Flesche, Francis
"The ˙ Sacred Pipes of Friendship." *Proc.
Amer. Assoc. Adv. Sci.* 33:613–615, 1884.

"Omaha Games."
JAFL 1:118–119, 1888; 3:215–216, 1890.

Culin, Stewart
Games of the North American Indians. 24th
Report. Bureau of American Ethnology. Washington, D. C.: U. S. Gov't. Printing Office,
1907.

MUSIC
GENERAL STUDIES

Cady, Calvin B.
"A Study of Omaha Indian Music." by Alice
C. Fletcher (a review). *Music Review* 3:53–57,
1893.

Densmore, Frances
"The Survival of Omaha Songs." *AA* 46:418–
420, 1944. n.s.

Dorsey, James Owen
"Dance Songs of the Omaha." *JAFL* 2:273–
276, 1889.

"Omaha Sociology." *3rd Annual Report of the
U. S. Bureau of American Ethnology*, 1881–
1882 (pp. 205–370). Washington, D. C.: U. S.
Government Printing Office, 1885.

"Omaha Songs."*JAFL* 1: 209–213, 1888.

"Ponka and Omaha Songs." *JAFL* 2: 271–276,
1889.

"Songs of the Hecucka Society." *JAFL* 1: 65–
68, 1888.

Fletcher, Alice C.
"A Study of Omaha Indian Music—aided by
Francis La Flesche, with a report on the
Structural Pecularities of the Music of John
Fillmore." *Archaeological and Ethnological
Papers of the Peabody Museum*, 1 (No. 5).
Cambridge: Harvard University, 1893. 152 pp.

"Glimpses of Child-Life Among the Omaha
Tribes of Indians." *JAFL* 1: 115–123, 1888.

Love Songs of the Omaha. In: *The Memoirs
of the International Congress of Anthropology*, edited by Charles Staniland Wake
(pp. 153–157) ; Chicago: 1894.

————, **and La Flesche, Francis**
"The Omaha Tribe." *The 27th Annual Report
of the U. S. Bureau of American Ethnology*,
1905–1906 (pp. 17–672). Washington, D. C.:
U. S. Government Printing Office, 1911.

La Flesche, Francis
"Death and Funeral Customs Among the
Omahas." *JAFL* 2: 3–11, 1889.

"The Omaha Buffalo Medicine Man; An
Account of their Method of Practice." *JAFL*
3: 215–221, 1890.

DANCES

Dorsey, James Owen
"Dance-Songs of the Omaha." *JAFL* 2:273–
276, 1889.

Fletcher, Alice Cunningham
"The 'Wawan' or Pipe Dance of the Omahas."
*Harvard University. Peabody Museum of
American Archaeology and Ethnology.* Annual
Report 3, (No. 3, 4) :308–333, Cambridge,
1884.

"The Wa-Wan, or the Pipe Dance of the
Omahas." *Music* (Chicago) 4: 468–477, 1893.

————, **and La Flesche, Francis**
The Omaha Tribe. *27th Annual Report of the
Bureau of American Ethnology, 1906–1906.*
Washington, D. C.: U. S. Government Printing Office, 1911.

ARRANGEMENTS
————: *Voice and Piano*

"Little Papoose."
Loomis, Harvey W.: Ditson: Voice and piano.

Three Songs—for a Low Voice.
Farwell, Arthur: G. Schirmer: Voice and
piano.
    Contents: 1) Song of the Deathless Voice; 2)
    Inketungas Thunder Song, based on Omaha
    Tribe Melodies; 3) The Old Man's Love Song.

————: *Piano*

"From Blackbird Hills" (Omaha Tribal Dances).
Beach, Mrs. H. A.: Schmidt: Piano.

"How the Rabbit Lost His Tail,"
(From—*Tales of the Red Man Suite*) Grant-
Schaefer, G. A.: Schmidt: Piano.

"Impressions of the Wa-Wan Ceremony." Farwell, Arthur: G. Schirmer: Piano.

"Thunderhead Suite."
Cadman, Charles Wakefield: White-Smith:
Piano.

————: *Orchestra*

Busch, Carl
Omaha Love Song. (From Four Tribal Melodies). New York: Carl Fischer: String Orchestra.

Cadman, Charles Wakefield
American Suite. New York: The Composer's Press. For String Orchestra.
Three Movements: 1st—Indian (Omaha); 2nd —Negro (spirituals); 3rd—Old Fiddle (Dance Tunes).

————.
Thunderbird Suite. Cincinnati: White-Smith: Orchestra.

Farwell, Arthur
Dawn—Omaha Indian Themes.
MS. For Chamber Orchestra: 18 instruments, piano ad lib.

RECORDS

"Dance Song."
Victor Orchestra.   VI–22174

"Omaha Ceremonial"
Thurlow Lieurance and Clement Barone, flute-piano.   VI–21972

OSAGE

FOLKLORE

GENERAL STUDIES

Barrett, Stephen Melvil
Shinkah, the Osage Indian. Oklahoma City: Harlow Publishing Co., 1916. 113 pp., col. front, illus., col. pl.

Bradbury, J.
Travels in the Interior of America. In: *Early Western Travels*, R. G. Thwaites, Vol. 5. Cleveland: A. H. Clark Co., 1904. 320 pp.

Dorsey, George Amos
"Traditions of the Osage", *Field Columbian Museum*, Chicago. *Publication No. 88. Anthropological Series*, vol. 7, no. 1, 9–60 pp., 1904.

Dorsey, J. Owen
"Osage Traditions." *6th Annual Report: Bureau of Ethnology*, 1884–1885, pp. 377–396, figs. 389. Washington, D. C.: U. S. Gov't. Printing Office, 1888.
Traditions of the elders, etc.

Foreman, Grant
Indians and Pioneers. Norman, Okl.: Oklahoma University Press, 1936. 285 pp.

Gatschet, A. S.
"Die Osageindianer." *Globus* 73:349–355, 1898.

Hunter, J. D.
Memoirs of a Captivity Among the Indians of North America. London: 1823. 447 pp.

La Flesche, Francis
"Bibliography of His Works."*AA* 35:330–331, 1933.

————.
"Ethnology of the Osage Indians." *Smithson. Miscel. Coll.* 76 (Part 10):104–107, 1924.

————.
"The Osage Tribe." *Annual Report Bureau Amer. Ethnol.* 36:35–604, 1921; 39:31–630, 1925; 43:23–164, 1928; 45:529–833, 1930.

————.
"Researches Among the Osage." *Smithson. Miscel. Coll.* 70 (Part 2):110–113, 1919.

————.
"Work Among the Osage Indians." *Smithson. Miscel. Coll.* 66 (Part 17):118–121, 1917.

Mathews, John Joseph
Talking to the Moon. Chicago: University of Chicago Press, 1945. 244 pp.
"He records dozens of acute glimpses into the lives of his prairie companions —." (Devoe)

McDermott, J. F., ed.
Tixier's Travels on the Osage Prairies. Norman, Okl.: Oklahoma University Press, 1940. 309 pp.

Nuttall, T.
A Journal of Travels Into the Arkansa Territory. Philadelphia: 1821. 296 pp.

Speck, Frank G.
"Notes on the Ethnology of the Osage Indians." *Transactions of the Department of Archeology, University of Pennsylvania* 2:159–171, 1907.
Includes discussion of dances: The "green corn dance."

Swanton, John R.
"Osage." *Bull. Bureau Amer. Ethnol.* 30 (Part 2):156–158, 1910.

Will, George F.
"Archaeology of the Missouri Valley." *Anthropological Papers of the American Museum of Natural History*, Vol. 22 (Part 6). New York: Museum Press, 1924. 59 pp.

MYTHS—LEGENDS—BELIEFS

Anon.
"The Three Friends—An Osage Legend." *The Illustrated Family Magazine* 3:125–129, March 1846.

Dorsey, George A.
"The Osage Mourning-War Ceremony." *AA* 4:404–412, 1904. n. s.

————.
"A Study of Siouan Cults." *Annual Report Bureau Amer. Ethnol.* 11:361–422, 1890.

La Flesche, Francis
"The Osage Tribe: Two versions of the Child-naming Rite." *43rd Annual Report: Bureau of American Ethnology,* 1925–1926, pp. 23–164, pls. 1–12, figs. 1–8. Washington, D. C.: U. S. Gov't. Printing Office, 1928.

————.
"Right and Left in Osage Ceremonies." *Holmes Anniversary Volume,* pp. 278–287. Washington, D. C.: James W. Bryan Press, 1916.

————.
"Osage Tribal Rites." *Smithson. Miscel. Coll.* 72 (Part 1):71–73, 1920.

————.
"The Osage Tribe, Rite of the Chiefs; Sayings of the Ancient Men." *36th Annual Report: Bureau of American Ethnology 1914–1915,* pp. 43–599, pls. 1–23, figs. 1–15, 2 maps. Washington, D. C.: U. S. Government Printing Office, 1921.

————.
"The Osage Tribe: Rite of Vigil." *39th Annual Report: Bureau American Ethnology 1916–1917,* pp. 31–631, pls. 17, figs. 4. Washington, D. C.: U. S. Government Printing Office, 1925. Music in text.

————.
"The Osage Tribe: Rite of the Wa-xó-be." *45th Annual Report: Bureau of American Ethnology, Smithsonian Institution,* pp. 523–833. Washington, D. S.: U. S. Government Printing Office, 1930.

————.
"The Symbolic Man of the Osage Tribe." *Art and Archaeology* (Washington, D. C.) 9:68–72, 1920.

————.
"Tribal Rites of Osage Indians." *Smithson. Miscel. Coll.* 68 (Part 12):84–90, 1918.

Mathews, John Joseph
Wah-Kon-Tah An interpretation of the Osage spirit, based on notes kept by Laban J. Miles, U. S. Agent to the tribe. Norman: University of Oklahoma Press, 1932. 259 pp.

Neihardt, John G.
Indian Tales and Others. New York: The Macmillan Company, 1926.

CUSTOMS—SPEECH
Dorsey, J. O.
"An Account of the War Customs of the Osages." *Amer. Natur.* 18:113–133, 1884.

La Flesche, Francis
Dictionary of Osage Language. U. S. Bureau of Ethnology, Bulletin 109. Washington, D. C.: U. S. Government Printing Office, 1932.

————.
"Omaha and Osage Traditions of Separation." *Proceedings of the 19th Session of the International Congress of Americanists* 459–462, 1915.

————.
"Osage Marriage Customs." *AA* 14:127–131, 1912. n. s.

War Ceremony and Peace Ceremony of the Osage Indians. U. S. Bureau of Ethnology, Bulletin 101. Washington, D. C.: U. S. Government Printing Office, 1939.

MacRitchie, D.
"A Red Indian Coiffure." *Man* 17:7–9, 1917.

MUSIC
GENERAL STUDIES
Dorsey, Rev. J. Owen
"Osage Songs and Rituals." *Smithson. Miscel. Coll.* 65 (Part 6):78–81, 1915.

————.
Osage Traditions. In: *Sixth Annual Report of the U. S. Bureau of Ethnology, fig. 389* (pp. 373–389). Washington, D. C.: U. S. Government Printing Office, 1888.

La Flesche, Francis
"The Osage Tribe: Rite of the Chiefs, Sayings of Ancient Men." *36th Annual Report of the Bureau of American Ethnology,* 1914–1915. Washington, D. C.: U. S. Government Printing Office, 1921.

————.
"The Osage Tribe: The Rite of Vigil." *39th Annual Report of the Bureau of American Ethnology,* 1917–1918. Washington. D. C.: U. S. Government Printing Office, 1925.

————.
"The Osage Tribe: Rite of Wa-xó-be." *45th Annual Report of the U. S. Bureau of Ethnology,* 1927–1928 (pp. 523–833). Washington, D. C.: U. S. Government Printing Office, 1930. illustrated, includes music.

————.
"War Ceremony and Peace Ceremony of the Osage Indians." *Bureau of American Ethnology,* No. 101. Washington, D. C.: U. S. Government Printing Office, 1939. vii, 280 pp. illustrated.

Sebbelov, G.
"The Osage War Dance." *Museum Journal* 2:71–74, 1911.

PAWNEE
FOLKLORE
GENERAL STUDIES
Barrett, Stephen Melvil
Beaver, the Pawnee Indian. Oklahoma City: Harlow Publishing Co., 1916. 92 pp., front., illus.

Carleton, Lieut. J. Henry
The Prairie Logbooks. Edited with an introduction by Louis Pelzer. Chicago: The Caxton Club, 350 E. 22nd St., 1944. 295 pp. Limited edition.
An account of the dragoon campaigns to the Pawnee Villages in 1844 and the Rocky Mountains in 1845.

Clayton, William, ed.
William Clayton's Journal. Salt Lake City: The Deseret News, 1921. 376 pp.

Dorsey, George A.
"Traditions of the Skidi Pawnee." *JAFL* 17:189–196, 1904.

———.
Traditions of the Skidi Pawnee. With Introduction, Notes, and Illustrations. Memoirs of the American Folklore Society, vol. 8, Boston: Houghton Mifflin & Co., 1904. xxvi, 366 pp.

———, **and Murie, J. R.**
"Notes on Skidi Pawnee Society." *Field Columbian Museum of Natural History, Anthropological Series* (Chicago) 27:67–119, 1940.

Dunbar, John Brown
"The Pawnee Indians." *Magazine of American History* 4:241–281; 5:320–345, 1880; 8 (Part 2):734–754, 1882.

———.
"The Pawnee Indians. Their History and Ethnology." *Magazine of American History*, (New York and Chicago) 1883. 90 pp.

———.
The Pawnee Indians, a sketch. (Articles reprinted from the Magazine of American History). Morrisania, N. Y.: The Author, 1882.

Fletcher, Alice C.
"Pawnee." *Bull. Bureau Amer. Ethnol.* 30 (Part 2):213–216, 1910.

———.
"Pawnee." In: *Encyclopedia of Religion and Ethics,* John Hastings, ed. Vol. 9, pp. 698–700. New York: 1917.

———.
"Skidi." *Bull. Bureau Amer. Ethnol.* 30 (Part 2):589–591, 1910.

Gilder, Robert F.
The Nebraska Culture Men. Omaha: H. F. Kieser, 1926. 32 pp., illus.

Hazen, R. W.
History of the Pawnee Indians. Fremont, Neb.: Fremont Tribune, 1893. 80 pp., illus.

Hyde, G. E.
"The Pawnee Indians." *Old West Series* (Denver) 4:5–54, 5:3–50, 1934.

Irving, John Treat, Jr.
Indian Sketches, taken during an expedition to the Pawnee tribes. Philadelphia: Carey, Lea and Blanchard, 1835. London: J. Murray, 1835. 2 vols.

Judson, Edward Zane Carroll (Ned Buntline)
Texas Jack, the White King of the Pawnees. New York: Street & Smith, 1891. 210 pp.

Murie, J. R.
"Pawnee Indian Societies." *Anthro. Papers Amer. Mus. Natur. Hist.* 11:543–644, 1914.

Murray, Sir Charles Augustus
Travels in North America; including a summer residence with the Pawnee tribe of Indians, in the remote parts of Missouri. . . . London: R. Bentley, 1854. 2 vols.

Platt, E. G.
"Reminiscences of a Teacher Among the Nebraska Indians." *Trans. Reports Nebr. State Hist. Soc.* 3:125–143, 1892.

———.
"Some Experiences as a Teacher Among the Pawnees." *Coll. Kansas State Hist. Soc.* 14:784–794, 1918.

Shine, Father Michael A.
"The Nebraska Aborigines as they Appeared in the 18th Century. *Nebraska Academy of Science,* Publication 9, (No. 1), Lincoln, 1914.

Strong, William Duncan
"An Introduction to Nebraska Archaeology." *Smithsonian Institution. Miscellaneous Collections* Vol. 93 (No. 10). Washington, D. C.: U. S. Government Printing Office, 1935.

Weltfish, Gene
Caddoan Texts: Pawnee, South Bend Dialect. Publications, American Ethnological Society 17. New York: J. J. Augustin, 1937.

Zimmerman, Mark E.
"The Pawnee American." *Collections of the Kansas State Historical Society, 1923–1925* (Topeka), 16:463–475, 1925.

———.
"The Ground-House Indians and Stone-Cist Grave Builders of Kansas and Nebraska." *Collections of Kansas State Historical Society* (Topeka), 14:471–487, 1918.

MYTHS—FOLKTALES—LEGENDS

Dorsey, George A.
"Pawnee War Tales." *AA* 8:337–346, 1906. n.s.

———.
"The Pawnee: Mythology (Part I)." Collected under the auspices of the *Carnegie Institute of Washington,* Publication 59:5–546. Washington, D. C.: Carnegie Institute of Washington, 1906.

Grinnell, George Bird
"Development of a Pawnee Myth." *JAFL* 5:127–134, 1892.

———.
Pawnee Hero Stories and Folk Tales, with notes on the origin, customs and character of the Pawnee people. To which is added a chapter on the Pawnee language by John B. Dunbar. New York: Forest & Stream Publishing Co., 1889. xxi, 417 pp., illus. Reprinted by Scribner's Sons, N. Y., 1904, 1920.

"Pawnee Mythology." *JAFL* 6:113–130, 1893.

"Pawnee Star Myth." *JAFL* 7:197–200, 1894.

Indian Ghost Legends.
Nebraska Folklore Pamphlets, 12. Federal Writers' Project in Nebraska. Lincoln: (Nov. 15) 1937.

Indian Place Legends.
Nebraska Folklore Pamphlets 2. Federal Writers' Project in Nebraska. Lincoln: (May 29) 1937.

Judson, Katharine B.
Myths and Legends of the Great Plains. Chicago: A. C. McClurg & Co., 1913. 204 pp. Pawnee myths, tales, beliefs, pp. 92-94.

Weltfish, Gene
"The Vision Story of a Fox-Boy, a South Bend Pawnee Text." *International Journal of American Linguistics* 9, (No. 1):44–76, 1936.

BELIEFS—CUSTOMS

Alexander, H. B.
The Mystery of Life. A Poetization of "The Hako"—a Pawnee Ceremony. Chicago: 1913. Illus.

Buckstaff, R. N.
"Stars and Constellations of a Pawnee Sky Map." *AA* 29:279–285, 1927. n.s.

Dangel, R.
"Tirawa, der höchste Gott der Pawnee." *Archiv für Religionswissenschaft* (Leipzig) 27:113–144, 1929.

Dorsey, George A.
"Notes on Skidi Pawnee Society." *Anthropological Series, Field Museum* 27, (No. 2):71–119, (Chicago) 1940.

"One of the Sacred Altars of the Pawnee." *Proceedings of the 13th Session of the International Congress of Americanists,* pp. 167–175, 1902.

A Pawnee Ritual of Instruction. In: *Boas Anniversary Volume,* pp. 350–353. New York: Columbia University Press, 1906.

"Skidi Rite of Human Sacrifice." *Proceedings of the 15th Session of the International Congress of Americanists,* 2:65–77, 1906.
Skidi—"One of the tribes of the Pawnee Confederacy sometimes called Wolf Pawnee, and by the French Pawnee Loup." (A. C. Fletcher)

Fletcher, Alice Cunningham
"A Pawnee Ritual, When Changing a Man's Name." *AA* 1:82–98, 1899. n.s.

" 'Giving Thanks', a Pawnee Ceremony." *JAFL* 13:261–266, 1900.

"Pawnee Star Lore." *JAFL* 16:10–15, 1903.

"Star Cult Among the Pawnee." *AA* 4:730–737, 1904, n.s.

"The Hako: a Pawnee Ceremony." By A. C. Fletcher, assisted by James R. Murie. Music transcribed by Edwin S. Tracy. *22nd Annual Report: Bureau of American Ethnology.* 1900–1901. Part 2, pp. 5–368. Washington, D. C.: 1904.

Grinnell, George Bird
"Marriage Among the Pawnees." *AA* 4:275–301, 1891.

Hocart, A. M.
"Covenants." *Man* 35, (No. 164), (Oct.) 1935. Contrast of the Pawnee 'Hako' and an Azande ritual.

Hungate, M.
"Religious Beliefs of the Nebraska Indian." *Nebraska History Magazine* 14 (Part 3): 207–226, 1938.

Lesser, Alexander
"Cultural Significance of the Ghost Dance." *AA* 35:108–115, 1933. n.s.

"Levirate and Fraternal Polyandry Among the Pawnees." *Man* 30:98–101, 1930.

The Pawnee Ghost Dance Hand Game. A Study of Cultural Change. Columbia University Contributions to Anthropology 16. New York: Columbia University Press, 1933. 377 pp., illus.

Linton, Ralph
"Origin of the Skidi Pawnee Sacrifice to the Morning Star." *AA* 28:457–466, 1926. n.s.

"Purification of the Sacred Bundles." *Field Museum Natur. Hist.* 7:1–11, 1923.

"The Sacrifice to the Morning Star by the Skidi Pawnee." *Field Mus. Natur. Hist.* 6:1–18, 1922.

"The Thunder Ceremony of the Pawnee." *Field Museum Natur. Hist.* 5:1–19, 1922.

Murray, Hugh
"Courtship Among the Pawnees." *The New Yorker* 8:159, Nov. 23, 1839.
Description of the Indian lover's routine and rights of hospitality offered by the girl's father.

Parsons, Elsie Clews
"Ritual Parallels in Pueblo and Plains Cultures, with a special reference to the Pawnee." *AA* 31:642–654, 1929. n.s.

Wissler, Clark
"Comparative Study of Pawnee and Blackfoot Rituals." *Inter. Congr. Amer.* 19:335–339, 1915.

———.
"The Sacred Bundles of the Pawnee." *Natur. Hist.* 20:569–571, 1920.

———, **and Spinden, H. J.**
"The Pawnee Human Sacrifice to the Morning Star." *Amer. Mus. Jour.* 16:49–55, 1916.

FOLK MEDICINE—SPEECH

Dorsey, George A.
"A Pawnee Personal Medicine Shrine." *AA* 7:496–499, 1905. n.s.

———.
"How the Pawnee Captured the Cheyenne Medicine Arrows." *AA* 5:644–659, 1903. n.s.

Hayden, F. V.
"Brief Notes on the Pawnee, Winnebago and Omaha Language." *Proceedings American Philosophical Society* 10:393–406, 1869.

Linton, George
Annual Ceremony of the Pawnee Medicine Men. Chicago: Field Museum of Natural History, 1923. 20 pp., (Field Museum of Natural History. Anthropology, Dept. of Leaflet, No. 8).

MUSIC

GENERAL STUDIES

Densmore, Frances
Pawnee Music. U. S. Bureau of American Ethnology, Bulletin 93. Washington, D. C.: U. S. Government Printing Office, 1929.

Fletcher, Alice Cunningham
The Hako: A Pawnee Ceremony. Assisted by James R. Murie, music transcribed by Edwin S. Tracy. *22nd Annual Report of the U. S. Bureau of American Ethnology*, 1900–1901 (pp. 5–372). Washington, D. C.: U. S. Government Printing Office, 1904. Illustrated, includes music.

———.
Indian Story and Song From North America. Boston: C. C. Birchard and Co., 1900. 126 pp.

DANCES

Grinnell, George B.
"The Young Dog's Dance." *JAFL* 4:307–313, 1891.

Lesser, Alexander
The Pawnee Ghost Dance Hand Game. A Study of Cultural Change. Columbia University Contributions to Anthropology 16. New York: Columbia University Press, 1933. 377 pp., illus.

ARRANGEMENTS

"Laughing Water."
Loomis, Harvey W.: Ditson: Voice and piano.

"Pawnee Horses."
Farwell, Arthur: G. Schirmer: Piano.

"Victory Song."
Burlin, N.: G. Schirmer: SSAATTBB, a cap.

PONCA

FOLKLORE

GENERAL STUDIES

Dorsey, James Owen
"Omaha and Ponca Letters." *American Bureau of Ethnology*, Bulletin 11, pp. 5–121. Washington, D. C.: U. S. Government Printing Office, 1891.

———, **and Thomas, C.**
"Ponka." *Bull. Bureau Amer. Ethnol.* 30 (Part 2): 278–279, 1910.

McGee, W. J.
"The Siouan Indians." *Annual Report Bureau Amer. Ethnol.* 15:157–204, 1894.

Skinner, Alanson
"Societies of Iowa, Kansa and Ponca Indians." *Anthropological Papers of the American Museum of Natural History* (New York) 11:679–801, 1915.

Whitman, William
"Xube, a Ponca Autobiography." *JAFL* 52:180–193, 1939.

MYTHS—FOLKTALES

Dorsey, James Owen
"Abstracts of Omaha and Ponka Myths." *JAFL* 1:74–78, 204–208, 1888.

———.
"The Myths of the Raccoon and the Crawfish." *Amer. Antiq.* 6:237–240, 184.

———.
"Ponka Stories." *JAFL* 1:73, 1888.

BELIEFS—CUSTOMS—FOLK MEDICINE

Dorsey, J. O.
"The Religion of the Omahas and Ponkas." *Amer. Antiq.* 5:271–275, 1883.

McGee, W. J.
"Ponka Feather Symbolism." *AA* 11:156–165, 1898. o.s.

Skinner, Alanson
Medicine Ceremony of the Menomini, Iowa and Wahpeton Dakota. With notes on the ceremony among the Ponca, Bungi, Ojibwa and Potawatomi. Indian Notes and Monographs, Museum of the American Indian, Heye Foundation 4:357 pp., 1920.

MUSIC
GENERAL STUDIES

Dorsey, J. O.
"Ponka and Omaha Songs." *JAFL* 2:271–276, 1889.

DANCES

Dorsey, G. A.
"The Ponka Sun Dance." *Field Columbian Museum, Anthropology Series* 7:62–88, 1905. Illus.

Skinner, Alanson
"Ponca Societies and Dances." *Anthro. Papers Amer. Mus. Natur. Hist.* 11:777–801, 1915.

SARSI
FOLKLORE
GENERAL STUDIES

Dorsey, J. O., and Goddard, P. E.
"Sarsi." *Bull. Bureau Amer. Ethnol.* 30 (Part 2): 467–468, 1910.

Goddard, Pliny Earle
"Sarsi Texts." *University of California Publications in American Archaeology and Ethnology* vol. 11 (No. 3):189–277, 1915. Berkeley: University of California Press, 1911–1916.
Medicine bundle rituals and narratives.

Jenness, Diamond
"The Sarcee Indians of Alberta." *Bull. and Annual Reports Can. Dept. Mines* 90:1–98, 1938.

Simms, S. C.
"Traditions of the Sarcee Indians." *JAFL* 17: 180–182, 1904.

Wilson, E. F.
"Report on the Sarcee Indians." *Report 58th Meeting Brit. Assoc. Adv. Sci.*, pp. 242–245, 1888.

——————.
"The Sarcee Indians." *Our Forest Children* (Owen Sound) 3:97–102, 1889.

DANCES—FOLK ART—SPEECH

Goddard, Pliny Earle
"Dancing Societies of the Sarsi Indians." *Anthropological Papers of the American Museum of Natural History.* New York: 11, (No. 5): 461–474, 1914.

——————.
"Notes on the Sun Dance of the Sarsi." *Anthropological Papers of the American Museum of Natural History* (New York) 16:271–282, 1919.

Sapir, Edward
"A Note on Sarcee Pottery." *AA* 25:247–253, 1923, n.s.

——————.
"Personal Names Among the Sarcee Indians." *AA* 26:109–119, 1924. n.s.

Shaw, A. C.
"A Sun Dance Among the Sarcees." *Canadian Magazine* (Toronto) 3:10–17, 1894.

SHOSHONI
(*See also:* Shoshoni, pp. 1055–56)

FOLKLORE
GENERAL STUDIES

Brackett, A. G.
"The Shoshonis." *Annual Reports Smithson. Inst.*, 1879, pp. 328–333.

Churchill, Claire Warner
South of the Sunset, an interpretation of Sacajawea, the Indian girl that accompanied Lewis and Clark. New York: R. R. Wilson, Inc., 1936. vii, 287 pp.

Emmons, Della Gould
Sacajawea of the Shoshones. Portland, Oregon: Binfords & Mort Publishers, 1943. 316 pp.
The life story of the Lewis and Clark guide, told in novel form.

Hebard, Grace R.
Sacajawea. A scholarly treatment of the printed and unprinted material, relating to Sacajawea. Glendale, California: 1933.

Henshaw, H. W.
"Shoshoni." *Bull. Bureau Amer. Ethnol.* 30 (Part 2):556–558, 1910.

Keith, Marshall
The Story of Chief Washakie, an Indian Odyssey. Caldwell, Idaho: Caxton Printers, Ltd., 1935. 218 pp.

Lowie, Robert H.
"Notes on the Shoshonean Ethnography." *Anthropological Papers of the American Museum of Natural History* (New York) 20:185–314, 1924. Illus.

——————.
"The Northern Shoshone." *Anthropological Papers of the Ameriacn Museum of Natural History* (New York) 2 (Part 2):163–306, 1909. Illus.

McGuire, A. J.
Sacajewea, the Indian Girl Who Led Lewis and Clark. Portland, Oregon: 1905.

Olden, S. E.
Shoshone Folk Lore. Milwaukee: 1923. 97 pp.

O'Malley, Richard Lynott
Wyoming and Indian Melodies, and other poems. Philadelphia: Ketterlinus Prtg. House, 1891. 120 pp.

Roberts, Edwards
Shoshone and Other Western Wonders. With a preface by Charles Francis Adams. New York: Harper and Brothers, 1888. xvi, 275 pp., illus.

Schultz, James Willard
Bird Woman (Sacajawea) the guide of Lewis and Clark; her own story now given to the world. Boston: Houghton Mifflin Co., 1918. 234 pp.

Shimkin, D. B.
Childhood and Development Among the Wind River Shoshone. Anthropological Records, 5:5. Berkeley: University of California Press, 1947. v, 325 pp., illus., bibl.

Williams, P. L.
"Personal Recollections of Wash-a-kie." *Utah Hist. Quart.* 1:101–106, 1928.

Wilson, E. N.
The White Indian Boy, H. R. Driggs, ed. Yonkers: N. Y. World Book Co., 1919.

MYTHS—FOLKTALES—LEGENDS

Lowie, Robert H.
"Shoshonean Tales." *JAFL* 37:1–242, 1924.

——————, and St. Clair, H. H.
"Shoshone and Comanche Tales." *JAFL* 22: 265–282, 1909.

Olden, Sarah Emilia
Shoshone Folk Lore. Milwaukee: 1923. 97 pp.

CUSTOMS—GAMES

Dibble, Charles E.
"Here's Spit in Your Ear." *Utah Humanities Review* 1 (No. 2):186, 1947.
The practice of the Shoshoni of spitting in each other's ear as an Indian ritual meaning friendship and loyalty.

Dorsey, G. A.
"The Shoshonean Game of Na-wá-ta-pi." *JAFL* 14:24–25, 1901.

MUSIC

GENERAL STUDIES

Lowie, Robert H.
"The Northern Shoshone." *Anthropological Papers of the American Museum of Natural History* II (part 2):206. Discussion of Music. New York: Published by Order of Trustees, 1909.
The author includes a discussion and description of Shoshonean music, and dances.

DANCES

Hoebel, E. Adamson
"The Sun Dance of the Hedankika Shoshone." *AA* 37:570–81, 1935. Illustrated.

Lowie, Robert H.
"Dances and Societies of the Plains Shoshone." *Anthropological Papers of the American Museum of Natural History* (New York) 11 (Part 10):803–835, 1915.

——————.
"Sun Dance of the Shoshoni." *Anthropological Papers of the American Museum of Natural History* (New York) 16:387–431, 1919. Illus.

SIOUX (Dakota)

(Including: the Oglala and Teton Divisions)

FOLKLORE

GENERAL STUDIES

Anon.
"Dakota." *Bull. Bureau Amer. Ethnol.* 30 (Part 1):376–380, 1907.

——————.
"Wahpeton." *Bull. Bureau Amer. Ethnol.* 30 (Part 2):891–893, 1910.

Barrett, Stephen Melvil
Hoistah, an Indian Girl. New York: Duffield and Co., 1913. 136 pp., front., plates.

——————.
Mocco, an Indian Boy. New York: Duffield and Co., 1911. 191 pp., front, plates.

Boas, Franz, and Swanton, John R.
"Siouan." *Bull. Bureau Amer. Ethnol.* 40 (Part 1):875–966, 1911.

Bradley, J. H.
"Indian Traditions." *Historical Society of Montana Contributions* 9:29–140, 1923.

Brady, Cyrus Townsend
Indian Fights and Fighters. Garden City, N. Y.: Doubleday, Page and Company, 1916.

Brininstool, Earl Alonzo
Fighting Red Cloud's Warriors; true tales of Indian days when the West was young. Columbus, Ohio: The Hunter-Trades-Trapper Co., 1926. 241 pp., illus. ("The Frontier Series," Vol. II.)

Brownlee, Fred L., and Johnson, Charles S.
The Indians of North and South Dakota. Nashville, Tenn.: Fisk University, 1941. 51 pp.

Bryant, Charles S., and Murch, Abel B.
History of the Great Massacre by the Sioux Indians. St. Peter, Minn., 1872.

Burdick, Usher L.
Last Battle of the Sioux Nation. Stevens Point, Wisc.: Worzalla Publishing Company, 1929.

Bushnell, David I.
Villages of the Algonquian, Siouan, and Caddoan Tribes West of the Mississippi. Bureau of American Ethnology, Bulletin 77. Washington, D. C.: U. S. Government Publishing Office, 1922.

Byrne, Patrick E.
Soldiers of the Plain. New York: Minton, Balch and Company, 1928. xi, 260 pp.

Catlin, George
Last Rambles Among the Indians of the Rocky Mountains and the Andes. New York: D. Appleton and Co., 1867. 361 pp., front, illus., plates.

Colby, Gen. L. W.
"The Sioux Indian War of 1890–1891." *Transactions and Reports of the Nebraska State Historical Society,* (Fremont, Nebr.) 1892.

"Dakota, Teton Folklore Notes."
JAFL 2:133–139, 1889.

De Land, Charles Edmund
"The Aborigines of South Dakota." *South Dakota Historical Collections* 3:267–586, 4:275–730.

———.
"The Sioux Wars." *South Dakota Historical Collections* 15:9–730, 16:175–552.

Deloria, Ella
Dakota Texts. Publications of the American Ethnologocial Society, Vol. 14. New York: G. E. Stechert and Company, 1932. xvi, 279 pp.

Dorsey, James Owen
"Siouan Sociology." *15th Annual Report: Bureau of American Ethnology,* 1893–1894, pp. 213–244, figs. 30–38. Washington, D. C.: U. S. Gov't Printing Office, 1897.
General features of organization, the Dakota tribes, tribal divisions, social customs, etc.

———.
"Teton Folk-Lore." *AA* 2:143–158, 1889.

———.
"Teton Folk-Lore Notes." *JAFL* 2:133–139, 1889.

———, and Thomas, C.
"Oglala." *Bull. Bureau Amer. Ethnol.* 30 (Part 2):109–111, 1910.

Douglas, F. H.
"The Sioux or Dakota Indians." *Denver Art Mus. Leaflet Ser.* 41:1–4, 1932.

Eastman, Charles Alexander (Ohiyesa)
Aus dem Leben der Prärie-Indianer. Berlin: Allstein, 1925. 153 pp., Half title: "Wege zum Wissen," 48.
Life among the Prairie Indians.

———.
From the Deep Woods to Civilization; chapters in the autobiography of an Indian. Boston: Little, Brown and Co., 1916. x, 206 pp., front, plates, ports.

———.
Indian Boyhood; with illustrations by E. L. Blumenschein. New York: McClure Phillips & Co., 1902. viii, 289 pp.

———.
Indian Child Life. Illustrated by George Varian. Boston: Little, Brown and Co., 1913. vii, 160 pp.
Contents: My Indian Childhood. Stories of Real Indians.

———.
Indian Heroes and Great Chieftains. Illustrated with photographs, Boston: Little, Brown and Co., 1918. iv, 241 pp.
Contents: Red Cloud, Spotted Tail, Little Crow, Tamakay, Gall, Crazy Horse, Sitting Bull, Rain-in-the-Face, Two Strike, American Horse, Dull Knife, Roman Nose, Chief Joseph, Little Wolf, Hole-in-the-Day.

———.
Indian Scout Talks; a Guide for Boy Scouts and Campfire Girls. Boston: Little, Brown and Co., 1914. x, 190 pp., illus.
A great deal on social life and customs.

———.
Old Indian Days; illustrated in color by Dan Sayre Groesbeck. New York: The Macmillan Co., 1907. v, 279 pp., col. front.
Reprinted from various periodicals.

———.
Red Hunters and the Animal People. New York: Harper & Brothers, 1904. viii, 248 pp.

Ewers, John C.
Teton Dakota Ethnology and History. Berkeley: National Park Service, 1937. 108 pp.

Finert, John F.
War-Path and Bivouac, or the Conquest of the Sioux. Chicago: Donohue, 1890. 460 pp., illus.

Fiske, Frank B.
The Taming of the Sioux. Bismarck: Tribune Publishing Company, 1917. 186 pp., illus.

Gardner, W. H.
"Ethnology of the Indians of the Valley of the Red River." *Annual Report Smithson. Inst.,* 1870, pp. 369–373.

Garst, Doris Shannon
Sitting Bull. Illustrated by Elton C. Fax. New York: Julian Messner, 1946. 183 pp.

Gavreau, Emile
"Les Dakotas, Religion, Moeurs, Costumes." *Proceedings of the 15th Session of the International Congress of Americanists* (Quebec), 2:311–315, 1906.

Goldfrank, Esther S.
"Historic Change and Social Character: A Study of the Teton Dakota." *AA* 45:67–84, 1943. n.s.

Hans, Frederic Malon
The Great Sioux Nation. Chicago: M. A. Dono-hue and Company, 1907. 575 pp., illus.
A complete history of Indian life and warfare in America. The Indians as nature made them. Graphic description of the social life, religious superstitions, habits, traits, customs, and manners.

Hassrick, Royal B.
"Teton Dakota Kinship System." *AA* 46(No. 3):338–348, 1944.

Heard, Isaac, V. D.
History of the Sioux War and Massacres of 1862 and 1863. New York: Harper and Brothers, 1864. x, 354 pp., illus.

Hilliard, J. N.
"Sitting Bull's Capture and the Messiah Craze." *Southern Workman* 39:545–551, 1910.

Holley, F. C.
Once Their Home: or, Our Legacy from the Dah Kotahs. Historical, biographical and incidental material. Chicago: Donohue and Henneberry, 1890. 423 pp., illus.

Hyde, George E.
Red Cloud's Folk: A History of the Oglala Sioux Indians. Norman, Okla.: University of Oklahoma Press, 1937. 331 pp.

Kelly, Mrs. Fannie
Narrative of My Captivity Among the Sioux Indians. Chicago: Donnelly Gassette and Lloyd, 1880.

Lange, Dietrich
The Threat of Sitting Bull. Boston: Lothrop, 1920. 370 pp., front.

Larimer, Sarah L.
Capture and Escape; or, Life Among the Sioux. Philadelphia: 1870. xii, 252 pp.

Lesser, Alexander
"Some Aspects of Siouan Kinship." *Proceedings of the 23rd Session of the International Congress of Americanists,* pp. 563–572, 1928.

McGee, W. J.
"The Siouan Indians." *15th Annual Report: Bureau of American Ethnology,* 1893–1894, pp. 157–199. Washington, D. C.: U. S. Gov't Printing Office, 1897.
The Siouan stock, habitat, organization, history, some features of Indian sociology, etc.

McLaughlin, James
My Friend the Indian. Boston: Houghton, Mifflin Company, 1910, 1926. 417 pp., illus.

Meacham, A. B.
Wigwam and Warpath; or the Royal Chief in Chains. Boston: J. P. Dale & Co., 1875

Mekeel, H. Scudder
"A Short History of the Teton Dakota." *North Dakota Historical Quarterly* 10, (No. 3):137–205, 1943.

————.
"A Discussion of Culture Change as Illustrated by Material from a Teton-Dakota Community." *AA* 34:274–285, 1932. n.s.

————.
The Economy of a Modern Teton Dakota Community. Yale University Publications in Anthropology 6. New Haven: Yale University Press, 1936. 14 pp.

Montgomery, Henry
"Remains of the Prehistoric Man in the Dakotas." *AA* 8:640–652, 1906. n.s.

Neihardt, John G.
Black Elk Speaks, Being the Life Story of a Holy Man of the Oglala Sioux. New York: Morrow, 1932. 280 pp., illus.

Newson, Thomas McLean
Thrilling Scenes Among the Indians. With a graphic description of Custer's last fight with Sitting Bull. Chicago: Belford, Clarke & Co., 1884. 241 pp., illus.

Olden, Sarah Emilia
The People of Tipi Sapa (the Dakotas) Tipi Sapa Mitaoyate Kin. Foreword by Hugh Latimer Burleson. Milwaukee, Wis.: Morehouse Publishing House, 1918. xxiii, 158 pp., illus.

Pond, Samuel W.
"The Dakotas or Sioux in Minnesota as They Were in 1834." *Minnesota Historical Collections* (St. Paul) 12:319–350, 1908.

Poole, De Witt Clinton
Among the Sioux of Dakota. Eighteen Months Experience as an Indian Agent. New York: D. Van Nostrand, 1881. 235 pp.

Riggs, Stephen Return
May and I:—Forty Years with the Sioux. Chicago: W. G. Holmes, 1880. 338 pp., illus.

————, and Dorsey, James Owen
Dakota Grammar, Texts and Ethnography. U. S. Geographical and Geological Survey of the Rocky Mountain Region. Contributions to North American Ethnology, Vol. 9. Washington, D. C.: U. S. Government Printing Office, 1893.

Robinson, D.
"A History of the Dakota or Sioux Indians." *South Dakota Historical Collections* 2:1–523, 1904.

Saint-Paul, C.
"Die Dakotahs oder Sioux." *Ausland* 64:121–126, 1891.

Sandoz, Mari
Crazy Horse, the Strange Man of the Oglalas. New York: Alfred A. Knopf, 1943.
The exciting tale of the Sioux chief who defeated Custer and his men.

Sheldon, A. E.
"Some Indian Fire-Places in South Dakota Bad-Lands." *AA* 7:44–49, 1905. n.s.

Shetrone, Henry Clyde
The Mound Builders. New York: Appleton and Company, 1930. 580 pp., illus.

Smith, H. I.
"Minnehaha's People." *So. Workman* 40:336–344, 1911.

Standing Bear, Luther
My People the Sioux. Boston: Houghton Mifflin Company, 1928.

Sullivan, Louis R.
"Anthropometry of the Siouan Tribes." *Anthropological Papers of the American Museum of Natural History* (New York) 23:81–174, 1920. illus.

Swanton, John R.
"Some Neglected Data Bearing on Cheyenne, Chippewa and Dakota History." *AA* 32:156–160, 1930. n.s.

──────.
"Siouan Tribes and the Ohio Valley." *AA* 45:49–67, 1943. n.s.

Tallent, Annie D.
The Black Hills, the Last Hunting Ground of the Dakotahs. St. Louis: Nixon, 1899. 713 pp., illus.

The Sioux or Dakota Nations.
Denver Art Museum, Department of Indian Art, Leaflet 41, (Feb.) 1932.

Thomas, Cyrus
"Teton." *Bull. Bureau Amer. Ethnol.* 30 (Part 2):736–737, 1910.

Useem, John, Macgregor, Gordon, and Useem, Ruth Hill
"Wartime Employment and Cultural Adjustments of the Rosebud Sioux." *Applied Anthropology* 2, (No. 2)1–9, 1943.

Vestal, Stanley
New Sources of Indian History, 1850–1891; the ghost dance—the prairie Sioux; a miscellany. Norman: University of Oklahoma Press, 1934. xix, 351 pp.

──────.
Sitting Bull, Champion of the Sioux. Boston: Houghton, Mifflin Company, 1932. xvi, 350 pp., illus., bibl.
A biography.

──────.
Warpath. Boston: Houghton, Mifflin Company, 1934. xv, 291 pp., illus., bibl.
The true story of the fighting Sioux told in a biography of Chief White Bull.

Welsh, Herbert
"The Meaning of the Dakota Outbreak." *Scribner's Magazine,* 9, (No. 4):429–452, (April) 1891.

Wemett, William Marks
The Indians of North Dakota. Fargo: Northern School Supply, 1927.
Written for school children.

Wissler, Clark
"Distribution of Deaths Among American Indians (Dakota)." *Human Biology* 8, (No. 2): 223–231, 1936.

MYTHS—FOLKTALES—LEGENDS

Beckwith, Martha Warren
"Mythology of the Oglala Dakota." *JAFL* 43:339–442, 1930.

Bonnin, G. (Zitkala-Sa)
American Indians Stories. Washington, D. C.: Hayworth Publ. Co., 1921.

Bushotter, G.
"Teton-Dakota Ghost Story." *JAFL* 1:68–71, 1888.

Cloud, B.
"How the Great Spirit Taught the Dakotas to Pray." *Carlisle Arrow* (Carlisle, Pa.) 8: (No. 12):4, 1911.

"Dakota Legend."
JAFL 2:65, 1889.

"Dakota Mythology Number Four."
JAFL 20:204–205, 1907.

"Dakota, Teton, Folklore Notes."
JAFL 2:133–139, 1889.

Dorsey, G. A.
"Legend of the Teton-Sioux Medicine Pipe." *JAFL* 19:326–329, 1906.

Dorsey, James Owen
"A Study of Siouan Cults." *11th Annual Report: Bureau American Ethnology 1889–1890;* pp. 361–554, pls. 44–50, figs. 156–200. Washington, D. C.: U. S. Government Printing Office, 1894.
Siouan family, alphabet, etc. Cults of the Omaha, Ponka, Kansa and Osage, Leiwere and Winnebago cults, traditions, folklore, etc.

──────.
"Nanibozhu in Siouan Mythology." *JAFL* 5:293–304, 1892.

──────.
"Teton Folklore." *AA* 2:143–159, 1889.

──────.
"Teton Folklore Notes." *JAFL* 2:133–139, 1889.

Eastman, Charles Alexander
Red Hunters and Animal People. New York: Harper and Bros., 1904. vii, 248 pp., col. front.
Contents: The Great Cat's Nursery; On Wolf Mountain; The Dance of the Little People; Wecah, the Provider; The Mustering of the Herds; The Sky Warrior; A Founder of Ten Towns; The Gray Chieftain; Hootay of the Little Rosebud; The River People; The Challenge; Wild Animals from the Indian Standpoint; Glossary of Indian Words and Phrases.

──────.
The Soul of the Indian; an interpretation. Boston: Houghton, Mifflin Co., 1911. xiii, 170 pp.
Mainly on religion and mythology.

——, and Eastman, E. G.
Wigwam Evenings. Sioux Folk Tales Retold.
Illustrated by Deming, E. W. Boston: Little,
Brown & Co., 1909. xvi, 253 pp., illus.

——.
Wigwam Evenings; Animal Tales. Boston:
Little, Brown and Company, 1930. 250 pp.,
illus.

Eastman, Mrs. Mary (Henderson)
*Dahcotah; or, Life and Legends of the Sioux
Around Fort Snelling.* Preface by Mrs. C. M.
Kirkland. Illustrated from drawings by Cap-
tain Eastman. New York: J. Wiley, 1849. xxxi,
268 pp. illus.

Federal Writers' Project.
Indian Ghost Legends. Nebraska Folklore
Pamphlets 12. Federal Writers' Project in
Nebraska. Lincoln: (Nov. 15) 1937.

——.
Indian Place Legends. Nebraska Folklore
Pamphlets 2. Federal Writers' Project in Ne-
braska. Lincoln: (May 29) 1937.

——.
Legends of the Mighty Sioux, compiled by
workers of the South Dakota Writers' Project,
Works Projects Administration, illustrated by
Sioux Indian artists. Chicago: A. Whitman &
Company, 1941. 158 pp., illus.

——.
Santee-Sioux Indian Legends. Nebraska Folklore Pamphlets 21, 23. Federal Writers' Project
in Nebraska. Lincoln: May, 1939; October,
1939.

Gilmore, Melvin R.
*Prairie Smoke, a Collection of Lore of the
Prairies.* Bismarck: Tribune Printing, 1922.
80 pp., illus.

Gordon, Hanford Lennox
Legends of the Northwest. Containing: Prelude—The Mississippi. The Feast of the Virgins, a legend of the Dakotas. The legend of
the falls, a legend of the Dakotas. Winona, a
legend of the Dakotas. The sea gull, the Ojibwa
legend of the Pictured Rocks of Lake Superior. Minnetonka. St. Paul, Minn.: The St.
Paul Book and Stationery Co., 1881. viii, 143
pp., illus.
   In verse.

——.
Indian Legends. Salem, Mass.: The Salem
Press Company, 1910.

Indians of South Dakota.
Brookings: South Dakota State Planning
Board, 1937. 97 pp.

Legends of the Pipestone Quarries.
Pipestone City, Minn.: Close Bros. & Co.,
188-. 10 pp.
   Poetry of the Dakota Indians.

Linderman, Frank Bird
Indian Old War Stories; More Sparks from
War Eagle's Lodge-fire. New York: Charles
Scribner's Sons, 1920.

Mathews, John Joseph
Wah'Kon'-tah. Norman: University of Oklahoma Press, 1932. 360 pp., illus.

McLaughlin, Marie
Myths and Legends of the Sioux; with illustra-
tions from original drawings. Bismarck, N. D.:
Bismarck Tribune Co., 1916. 200 pp., illus.

Meeker, L. L.
"Siouan Mythological Tales." *JAFL* 14:161–
164, 1901.

——.
"White Man" (Siouan Myth). *JAFL* 15:84–87,
1902.

Newell, W. W.
"Dakota Legend of the Head of Gold." *JAFL*
14:138–139, 1901.

Price, Samuel G.
Black Hills, the Land of Legend; illustrations
by Gutshall, C., drawings made from actual
photographs of the period indicated. Los Angeles, Cal.: De Vorss & Co., 1935. 139 pp., illus.

Riggs, S. R.
"Mythology of the Dakotas." *Amer. Antiq.*
5:147–149, 1883.

——.
"The Theogony of the Sioux." *Amer. Antiq.*
2:265–270, 1880.

Skinner, Alanson
"Wahpeton Dakota Origin Myths." *Museum
of the American Indians (New York), Indian
Notes and Monographs,* 4:273–278, 1920.

Snelling, W. J.
Tales of the North-West. Boston: 1830. 288 pp.

Standing Bear, Luther
Stories of the Sioux. Boston: Houghton, Mifflin Company, 1934.

Thorson, Alice O.
*The Tribe of Pezhekee; a Legend of Minne-
sota.* Minneapolis: Heywood Manufacturing
Co., 1901. 232 pp., illus.

Wallis, W. D.
"Beliefs and Tales of the Canadian Dakota."
JAFL 36:36–101, 1923.

Wilson, T.
"Dakota Legend of the Head of Gold." *JAFL*
13:294–296, 1900.

Wissler, Clark
"Dakota Myths." *JAFL* 20:120–131, 195–206,
1907.

——.
"Whirlwind and the Elk in Dakota Mythology."
JAFL 18:257–268, 1905.

Zitkala-Sa
Old Indian Legends. New York: Ginn and Co., 1901. 165 pp., illus.

BELIEFS—CUSTOMS

Babcock, Willoughby M.
"Sioux Versus Chippewa." *Minnesota History,* 6:41–45, (March) 1925.
Discusses customs, habits of dress, and intertribal warfare.

Beckwith, P.
"Notes on the Customs of the Dakotahs." *Annual Report Smithson. Inst.,* 1886, pp. 245–257.

Blish, H. H.
"The Ceremony of the Sacred Bow of the Oglala Dakota." *AA* 36:160–1687, 1934. n.s.

Bushotter, G.
"Oath-Taking Among the Dakota." *Indian Notes* 4:81–83, 1927.

Bushnell, David I.
Burials of the Algonquian, Siouan and Caddoan Tribes West of the Mississippi. Bureau of American Ethnology, Bulletin 83. Smithsonian Institution. Washington, D. C.: U. S. Government Printing Office, 1927.

Clericus
"Sioux Indians." *The National Register* 3:297, May 8, 1819.
A letter describing their religious beliefs, in comparing them to the Christian doctrines, the author finds those of the Indians, in many respects, far superior to the Christian religion.

"Dakota Courtship."
JAFL 18:266–267, 1905.

Dorsey, James Owen
A Study of Siouan Cults. Eleventh Report. Bureau of American Ethnology. Washington, D. C.: U. S. Government Printing Office, 1894.

Erikson, E. H.
"Observations on Sioux Education." *Journal of Psychology* 7:101–156, 1939.

Fletcher, Alice C.
"The Elk Mystery or Festival. Ogalala Sioux." *Harvard University. Peabody Museum of Archaelogy and Ethnology, Annual Report* 3 (No. 3, 4):267–288, Cambridge, 1884.

———.
"The Religious Ceremony of the Four Winds or Quarters, As Observed by the Santee Sioux." *Reports Peabody Museum* 16–17:289–295, 1883.

———.
"The White Buffalo Festival of the Uncapas." *Reports Peabody Museum* 16–17:260–275, 1883.

Gilmore, Melvin R.
"The Dakota Ceremony of Hunka." *Indian Notes* 6:75–78, 1929.

———.
"The Dakota Ceremony of Presenting a Pipe." *Papers Mich. Acad. Sci.* 18:15–21, 1932.

———.
"Dakota Mourning Customs." *Indian Notes* 3:295–296, 1926.

———.
"Oath-Taking Among the Dakota." *Indian Notes* 4:81–83, 1927.

———.
"The Old-Time Method of Rearing a Dakota Boy." *Museum of the American Indian, Indian Notes* 6:367–371, 1929.

———.
"Pasque Flower, Bloom of Dakota Folklore." *Nature Magazine* 21:17, (January) 1933.

———.
"Uses of Plants by the Indians of the Missouri River Region." *Annual Report Bureau Amer. Ethnol.* 33:43–154, 1912.

Haeckel, Josef
"Totemismus und Zeiklassen-System bei den Sioux-Indianern." *Anthropos* 32 (No. 1, 2): 210–238; (No. 3, 4):450–501, 1937.

Hulsizer, Allan
Region and Culture in the Curriculums of the Navaho and Dakota. Federalsburg, Va.: J. W. Howell, 1940.

Lynd, James W.
"The Religion of the Dakotas." *Collections of the Minnesota Historical Society* (St. Paul) 2:63–84, 1864.

Mirsky, J.
The Dakota. In: *Cooperation and Competition Among Primitive Peoples,* Margaret Mead, ed., pp. 382–427. New York: 1937.

Mooney, James
The Ghost-Dance Religion and the Sioux Outbreak of 1890. Fourteenth Report, Bureau of American Ethnology, Part 2. Washington, D. C.: U. S. Gov't Printing Office, 1896.

Moorehead, W. K.
"The Indian Messiah and the Ghost Dance." *Amer. Antiq.* 13:161–167, 1891.

———.
"Sioux Women at Home." *Illustrated American* 5:481–484, 1891.

Neill, E. D.
"Dakota Land and Dakota Life." *Coll. Minn. Hist. Soc.* 1:254–294, 1872.

Pond, G. H.
"Dakota Superstitions." *Coll. Minn. Hist. Soc.* 2:32–62, 1867.

Prescott, P.
Contributions to the History, Customs and Opinions of the Dacota Tribe. In: *Information Respecting the History, Condition, and Prospects of the Indian Tribes of the United States,* H. R. Schoolcraft, ed., Vol. 2, pp. 168–199, 1852; Vol. 3, pp. 225–246, 1853; Vol. 4, pp. 59–72, 1854. Philadelphia: 1854.

Riggs, Stephen R.
Tah-koo, Wah-kan; or The Gospel Among the Dakotas. Boston: 1869. xxxvi, 491 pp., illus.

Robinson, Doane
Sioux Indian Courts. An Address Delivered Before the South Dakota Bar Association at Pierre, South Dakota, January 12, 1909. 14 pp.

Speck, Frank G.
"The Question of Matrilineal Descent in the Southeastern Siouan Area." *AA* 40:1–12, 1938. n.s.

Walker, James R.
"Oglala Kinship Terms." *AA* 16:96–109, 1914. n.s.

Wallis, W. D.
"Beliefs and Tales of the Canadian Dakota." *JAFL* 36:36–101, 1923.

Weygold, F.
"Die Hunkazeremonie." *Archiv für Anthropologie* (Braunschweig) 39:145–160, 1912.

Wissler, Clark
"Societies and Ceremonial Associations in the Oglala Divisions of the Teton-Dakota." *Anthropological Papers of the American Museum of Natural History* (New York) 11:1–99, 1912. illus.

––––––. "Some Protective Designs of the Dakota." *Anthropological Papers of the American Museum of Natural History* 1:19–53, 1907.

FOLK MEDICINE—FOLK POETRY —ART—SPEECH

Boas, Franz
"Some Traits of the Dakota Language." *Language* 13:137–141, 1937.

––––––, and Deloria, E.
"Notes on the Dakota-Teton Dialect." *Inter. Jour. Amer. Ling.* 7:97–121, 1933.

Densmore, Frances
Poems from Sioux and Chippewa Songs. Washington, D. C.: U. S. Gov't Printing Office, 1917. 23 pp.

Dorsey, James Owen
"Siouan Onomatopes." *AA* 5:1–8, 1892. o.s.

Gatschet, A. S.
"Adjectives of Color in Indian Languages." *Amer. Natur.* 13:475–485, 1879.

Lewis, T. H.
"Stone Monuments from Southern Dakota." *AA* 2:159–167, 1889.

Mooney, James
"Mescal Plant and Ceremony." *Therapeutic Magazine*, 3rd Ser., Vol. xii, Detroit, 1896.

Montgomery, Guy
A Method of Studying the Structure of Primitive Verse Applied to the Songs of the Teton Sioux. In: *The Charles Mills Gayley Anniversary Papers*, (pp. 267–283). University of California Publications in Modern Philology, No. 9. Berkeley, Cal., 1922.

Pond, G. H.
Power and Influence of Dakota Medicine Men. In: *Information Respecting the History, Condition, and Prospects of the Indian Tribes of the United States*, H. R. Schoolcraft, ed., Vol. 4, pp. 641–651. Philadelphia: 1854.

Riggs, S. R.
A Dakota-English Dictionary. Contributions to North American Ethnology, Vol. 7. Washington, D. C.: Department of Interior, U. S. Geographical and Geological Survey of the Rocky Mountain Region, 1890. 665 pp.

––––––. *Grammar and Dictionary of the Dakota Language.* Smithsonian Institution Contributions to Knowledge, No. 4. Washington, D. C.: 1852. 338 pp.

Skinner, Alanson
Medicine Ceremony of the Menomini, Iowa and Wahpeton Dakota. With notes on the Ceremony Among the Ponca, Bungi, Ojibwa, and Potawatomi. Indian Notes and Monographs, Museum of the American Indian, Heye Foundation 4:357 pp., 1920.

Speck, Frank G.
"Notes on the Functional Basis of Decoration and the Feather Technique of the Oglala Sioux." *Indian Notes* 5:1–42, 1928.

Thomas, Sidney J.
"A Sioux Medicine Bundle." *AA* 43:605, 609, 1941.

Walker, J. R.
"Oglala Kinship Terms." *AA* 16:96–109, 1914. n.s.

Wissler, Clark
"Decorative Art of the Sioux Indians." *Bulletins of the American Museum of Natural History (New York), Publications in Anthropology* 18 (Part 3):231–277, 1904. figs. 71–102, pls. 38–56.

––––––. "Some Protective Designs of the Dakota." *Anthro. Papers Amer. Mus. Natur. Hist.* 1:21–53, 1907.

––––––. "Symbolism in the Decorative Art of the Sioux." *Proceedings of the 13th Session of the International Congress of Americanists*, pp. 339–345, 1902.

GAMES

Dorsey, J. Owen
"Games of Teton Dakota Children." *AA* 4: 329–347, 1891.

Fletcher, A. C.
Indian Games and Dances with Native Songs;
arranged from American Indian Ceremonials
and Sports. Boston: Birchard & Company, 1915.
Music.

Meeker, L. L.
"Ogalala Games." *Bulletin Free Museum of
Science and Art* (Phila.) 3:23–46, 1901.

Walker, J. R.
"Sioux Games." *JAFL* 18:277–290, 1905; 19:
29–36, 1906.

Wissler, Clark
"Sioux Hoop Game." *JAFL* 18:281–283, 1905.

MUSIC

GENERAL STUDIES

Boas, Franz
"Review of: *Teton-Sioux Music* by Frances
Densmore." *JAFL* 38:319–324, 1927.

Catlin, George
Instruments of Music of the Teton River
(Sioux). In: *Illustrations of the Manners, Cus-
toms and Conditions of the North American
Indians* Volume I (p. 241). London: Chatto
& Windus, 1876.

Colby, Leonard Wright
"Wanagi olawaukui—The Ghost Songs of the
Dakotas." *Proceedings of the Nebraska State
Historical Society* I, series 2:131–150, 1894
(Nebraska, Lincoln).

Densmore, Frances
Music in Relation to the Religious Thought of
the Teton Sioux. In: *Holmes Anniversary Volume* (pp. 667–679). Washington, D. C.: James
Bryan Press, 1916.

———.
Poems from Sioux and Chippewa Songs. Washington, D. C.: U. S. Government Printing Office, 1917. 23 pp.

———.
Teton Sioux Music. Bureau of American
Ethnology, Bulletin 61, 561 pp., 82 pl., 43 figs.
Washington, D. C.: U. S. Gov't Printing Office,
1918.
Analysis and description of the songs, the rituals
and ceremonies connected with them, as well as
discussion of myths, legends, traditions, dances
and games.

———.
"The Rhythm of Sioux and Chippewa Music."
Art and Archaeology (Washington) 9:59–67,
1920.

McGee, W. J.
"The Siouan Indians; A Preliminary Sketch."
*Fifteenth Annual Report of the Bureau of
Ethnology* (pp. 153–204). Washington, D. C.:
U. S. Government Printing Office, 1897.

Montgomery, Guy
A Method of Studying the Structure of Primitive Verse Applied to the Songs of the Teton
Sioux. In: *The Charles Mills Gayley Anniversary Papers* (pp. 267–283). *University of California Publications in Modern Philology*
(Berkeley, California) 9:1922.

Moorhead, Warren King
"The Sioux Messiah." *Archaeologist* (Water-
loo, Indiana) 2:146–149, 168–170, 1894.
With musical discussion and examples.

Watt, Henry J.
"Functions of the Size of the Interval in the
Songs of Schubert and the Chippewa and
Teton-Sioux Indians." *British Journal of Psy-
chology* (Cambridge) 14:370–386, 1924.

DANCES

Blish, Helen
"Drama of the Sioux Sun Dance." *Theatre
Arts Monthly* 17:629–634, (August) 1933.

———.
The Sun Dance. In: *Ethical Conception of the
Oglala Dakota* (pp. 95–105). Lincoln, Ne-
braska: Univ. Press, 1926.

Deloria, Ella
"The Sun Dance of the Oglala Sioux." *JAFL*
42:354–412, 1929.

Fletcher, Alice Cunningham
Indian Games and Dances with Native Songs;
Arranged from American Indian Ceremonials
and Sports. Boston: Birchard and Company,
1915.

———.
"The Elk Mystery or Festival—Ogalala Sioux."
*Annual Report of the Peabody Museum of
Archaeology and Ethnology* 3 (No. 3–4):276–
288. Cambridge: Harvard University, 1884.

Lowie, Robert H.
"Dance Associations of the Eastern Dakota."
*Anthropological Papers of the American Mu-
seum of Natural History* (New York) II (part
2):101–142, 1913.

Parker, A. Z.
"Ghost Dance at Pine Ridge." *JAFL* 4:160–
162, 1891.

Scoville, Annie B.
"Ogalala Day Schools." *So. Workman* 30:646–
649, 1901.
Includes discussion of dances.

Skinner, Alanson
"Notes on the Sun Dance of the Sisseton
Dakota." *Anthropological Papers of the American Museum of Natural History* (New York)
16:381–385, 1919.

Walker, J. R.
"The Sun Dance and Other Ceremonies of the
Oglala Division of the Teton Dakota." *Amer-
ican Museum of Natural History* (New York),
Anthropological Papers 16:51–221, 1917.

Wallis, W. D.
"The Sun Dance of the Canadian Dakota." *Anthropological Papers of the American Museum of Natural History* (New York) 16:319–380, 1919.

Williamson, T. S.
"Dakota Scalp Dance." *Collection of Minnesota Historical Society.* (St. Paul, Minnesota) 6:409–416, 1894.

ARRANGEMENTS

————: *Voice and Piano*

"A Sioux Serenade."
Lieurance, Thurlow: Presser: Voice and piano.

"By the Waters of Minnetonka."
Lieurance, Thurlow: Presser: Voice and piano. Sioux Love Song, published in concert edition, with violin or flute obligato, also duet.

"By the Weeping Waters."
Lieurance, Thurlow: Presser: Voice and piano.

"In Mirrored Waters."
(In *Songs of the North American Indian.*)
Lieurance, Thurlow: Presser: Voice and piano.

"In the Lodges of the Sioux."
Grunn, Homer: Ditson: Voice and piano.

"My Heart is Sad."
Boothroyd, Frederick: Coolidge Publishing Company: Voice and piano.

"My Silver Throated Fawn."
(In *Nine Indian Songs.*) Lieurance, Thurlow: Presser: Voice and piano.

"Rainbow Land."
Lieurance, Thurlow: Presser: Voice and piano.

"Red Day."
Bimboni, Alberto: G. Schirmer: Voice and piano.

"Sa-Ma-Wee-No."
Lieurance, Thurlow: Presser: Voice and piano.

"Ski-Bi-Bi-La" (Indian Spring Bird).
(In *Songs of the North American Indian.*)
Lieurance, Thurlow: Presser: Voice and piano.

"Song of the Sun Dance."
Bimboni, Alberto: G. Schirmer: Voice and piano.

"Songs of the American Indian."
Bimboni, Alberto: G. Schirmer: Voice and piano.
Consists of two Chippewa, and two Sioux tunes, taken from Densmore's study.

"The Sacrifice."
Lieurance, Thurlow: Presser: Voice and piano.

————: *Choral*

"By the Waters of Minnetonka."
(Sioux Love Song.) Lieurance, Thurlow: Presser: SA (violin obligato), SSA.

"By the Waters of Minnetonka."
(Sioux Love Song.) Lieurance, Thurlow: Presser: TTBB.

"By the Waters of Minnetonka."
(Sioux Love Song.) Lieurance, Thurlow: Presser: SAB, SATB.

"Stars Lead Us Ever On."
Gaul, Harvey: Ditson: SSA, accomp.

"Stars Lead Us Ever On" (Sioux Tribal Carol).
Gaul, Harvey: Ditson: SATB.

"The Sun-Friend."
Miller, Horace Alden: Schmidt: SSA.

————: *Piano*

"By the Waters of Minnetonka" (Sioux Love Song). Lieurance, Thurlow: Presser: Piano concert version—medium—easy; also organ, violin and piano.

"Puk-Wudjies Dance."
(From—"Tales of the Red Man" Suite.)
Grant-Schaefer, G. A.: Schmidt: Piano.

"Sioux Flute Serenade."
(From *Three Indian Sketches.*) Skilton, Charles S.: Carl Fischer: Piano.

"Sioux Scalp Dance."
Oren, Preston Ware: Presser: Piano 4 hands.

————: *Violin and Piano (and for other instruments with piano)*

"By the Waters of Minnetonka."
Lieurance, Thurlow: Presser: Flute or Cello and piano; also Cornet and piano.

"Sioux Flute Serenade."
Skilton-Czerwonky, R.: Fischer: Violin and piano.

"Sioux Indian Fantasie."
Lieurance, Thurlow: Presser: Violin and piano.

"The Gods of the Mountain."
Farwell, A.: MS: Violin, cello, piano.

————: *Orchestra—Band*

"By the Waters of Minnetonka."
(By Thurlow Lieurance.) Lake, M. L.: Carl Fischer: Band.

"By the Waters of Minnetonka."
Lieurance, Thurlow: Carl Fischer: Orchestra.

"Flute Serenade" from (*Suite Primeval* Part II).
Skilton, Charles S.: Carl Fischer: Orchestra.

"Sad Moon of Falling Leaf."
Lieurance, Thurlow: Carl Fischer: Orchestra.

"Scalp Dance."
Kinscella, H. G.: Carl Fischer: Orchestra.

"Sioux Flute Serenade."
Skilton, Charles S.: C. Fischer: Chamber orchestra.

"The Gods of the Mountain-Suite."
Farwell, Arthur: MS: Orchestra.

————: *Stage Work*

Bimboni, Alberto
Winona. MS. An opera. Based on Chippewa
and Sioux-Dakota Tunes.

Converse, Frederick S.
The Peace Pipe—Cantata. New York: Birchard: For SATB, baritone solo, and orchestra.

De Leone, F. B.
Aglala. New York: Schirmer: Opera.

Hanson, W. F.
The Sun Dance. MS. Opera, in 5 Acts.

RECORDS

"By the Waters of Minnetonka."
Frances Alda, soprano.   VI–1268

"By the Waters of Minnetonka."
Renée Chemet, violin.   VI–1228

"By the Waters of Minnetonka."
Nelson Eddy, baritone.   VI–4366

"By the Waters of Minnetonka."
Thurlow Lieurance and Clement Barone, flute-
piano.   VI–21972

"By the Waters of Minnetonka."
Malneck Orchestra.   DE–2616

"By the Waters of Minnetonka."
Ray Noble and Orchestra.   BB–8247

"By the Waters of Minnetonka."
Schumann-Heink, contralto.   VI–1198

"Dog Feast Dance of the Oglala Sioux."
In: *American Indian Songs and Dances*.
                                      DISC–161

"From the Land of the Sky Blue Water."
André Kostelanetz, and his orchestra.
                                      CO–7569–M

"From the Land of the Sky Blue Waters."
Fritz Kreisler, violin-piano.   VI–1115

"From the Land of the Sky Blue Water."
Mary Lewis, soprano.   VI–1140

"From the Land of the Sky Blue Water."
Jeanette MacDonald, Soprano.   VI–2055

"Shuffling Feet."
Victor Orchestra.   VI–22174

"Sioux Travel Song in Wartime."
In: *American Indian Songs and Dances*.
                                      DISC–161

"Sioux War Song."
In: *American Indian Songs and Dances*.
                                      DISC–161

"Two Sun Dance Songs of the Oglala Sioux."
In: *American Indian Songs and Dances*.
                                      DISC–161

**U. S. Library of Congress. Division of Music.
Folklore Section.**
Indian Songs—in the Densmore and Other
Collections—in the Archive of American Folk
Song.   AAFS–LC

WICHITA
(*Including:* Kichai)
FOLKLORE
GENERAL STUDIES

Bolton, Herbert Eugene
The Jumano Indians of Texas, 1650–1771.
Austin, Tex.: Texas State Historical Associ-
ation, 1911. Peprint from the *Quarterly of the
Texas State Historical Association*, vol. xv, no.
1 (pp. 68–84).
> "A tribe of unknown affinity, first seen,—about
> the beginning of 1536 by Cabeza de Vaca and his
> companions in the vicinity of the junction of the
> Conchos with the Rio Grande, or northward to
> about the southern boundary of New Mexico."
> (F. W. Hodge). The author cites a statement by
> Cabello that "the Taguayazes (Wichita) are
> known in New Mexico by the name of Jumanes
> also."

Debo, Angie
And Still the Waters Run. Princeton, N. J.:
Princeton University Press, 1940.

Douglas, F. H.
*The Wichita Indians, and Allied Tribes Waco,
Towakoni, and Kichai*. Denver Art Museum,
Department of Indian Art, Leaflet 40, (Jan.)
1932.

Fletcher, Alice C.
"Kichai." *Bull. Bureau Amer. Ethnol.* 30
(Part 1):682–683, 1907.

Foreman, Grant
The Five Civilized Tribes. Norman: University of Oklahoma Press, 1934. 455 pp., illus.

Gatschet, A. S.
"Two Indian Documents." *Amer. Antiq.* 13:
249–254, 1891.

Hodge, F. W.
"The Jumano Indians." *Proceedings of American Antiquity Society*. 20:249–268, Worcester,
1910. n. s.

Jackson, A. T.
"Fire in East Texas Burial Rites." *Bulletin
Texas Archaeological and Paleontological So-
ciety* 10:77–113, 1938.
> "A Caddoan tribe whose language is more
> closely allied to the Pawnee than to the other
> Caddoan groups . . . since 1858 they joined the
> Wichita with whom they have since been
> associated, and whom they resemble in their
> agriculture, house-building, and general cus-
> toms." (Fletcher, A. C.)

Michelson, Truman
"Studies of the Algonquin Tribes of Iowa and Oklahoma." *Exploration and Field Work of Smithsonian Institution in 1929.*:207–212, 1930.

Mooney, J.
"Wichita." *Bull. Bureau Amer. Ethnol.* 30 (Part 2):947–950, 1910.

MYTHS—FOLKTALES—LEGENDS

Dale, Edward E.
Tales of the Teepee. Boston: D. C. Heath & Company, 1920. v, 119 pp., illus.

Dorsey, George A.
The Mythology of the Wichita. Collected under the auspices of the Carnegie Institution of Washington, D. C.: Carnegie Institution, 1904. 351 pp.

———.
"Wichita Tales." *JAFL* 12:215–239, 1899; 16:160–179, 1903; 17:153–160, 1904.

Hunter, J. M.
"Legend of the Valley of Paint." *TFSP* 18:126–128, 1943.

BELIEFS

Harrington, M. R.
"Peyote Outfit." *Masterkey* 18:143–144, 1944. illus.
Objects used in Peyote ceremony from Oklahoma Indians.

Hungate, M.
"Religious Beliefs of the Nebraska Indians." *Nebraska History Magazine* 14 (Part 3):207–226, 1938.

SPEECH—DANCES—GAMES

Dorsey, G. A.
"Hand or Guessing Game Among the Wichita." *American Antiquity* 23:363–370, 1901.

Eagle, Acee Blue
"Oklahoma Plains Indian Dances." *School Arts* 40:327–329, (June) 1941.

Lawrence, D. H.
"The Dance of the Sprouting Corn." *Theatre Arts Monthly* (New York) 8: 447–457, 1924, illustrated.

Payne, J. H.
"The Green Corn Dance." *Chronicles of Oklahoma* (Oklahoma City) 10: 170–195, 1932.

Spier, Leslie
"Wichita and Caddo Relationship Terms." *AA* 26:258–263, 1924. n.s.

Tilghman, Z. A.
"Origin of the Name Wichita," *AA* 43:488–489, 1941. n.s.

Vestal, Stanley
"They Dance in Oklahoma." *Southwest Review* (Dallas) 20: 336–340, 1935.

OTHER TRIBES
MISCELLANEOUS STUDIES
KANSA

Anon.
"Kansa." *Bull. Bureau Amer. Ethnol.* 30 (Part 1):653–656, 1907.

Campbell, C. E.
"Down Among the Red Men." *Collection of the Kansas State Historical Society (Topeka),* 7:623–691, 1928.

Dorsey, J. O.
"Mourning and War Customs of the Kansas." *Amer. Natur.* 19:671–680, 1885.

Jones, Paul A.
Quivira. Wichita: McCormick-Armstrong, 1929.

Morehouse, G. P.
"History of the Kansa or Kaw Indians." *Trans Kansas State Hist. Soc.* 10:327–368, 1908.

Skinner, Alanson
"Societies of the Iowa, Kansa and Ponca Indians." *Anthropological Papers of the American Museum of Natural History* (New York) 11:679–801, 1915.

Spencer, J.
"The Kaw or Kansas Indians." *Trans. Kansas State Hist. Soc.* 10:373–382, 1908.

Udden, John August
An Old Indian Village. Rock Island, Illinois,— Published by authority of the Board of Directors of Augustaner College and Theological Seminary, 1900. 80 pp.

Zimmerman, Mark E.
"The Ground-House Indians and Stone-Cist Grave Builders of Kansas and Nebraska." *Collections of the Kansas State Historical Society* (Topeka), 14:471–487, 1918.

MISSOURI

Berry, J. Brewton
"The Missouri Indians." *Southwestern Social Science Quarterly* 17, (No. 2), 1936.

Burrill, Alfred C.
Missouri Caves Yield Up Their Secrets. Missouri State Museum, Bulletin No. 5. (Feb. 1934). Jefferson City, Mo.: 1934.

Dellinger, S. C.
"Baby Cradles of the Ozark Bluff Dwellers." *American Antiquity* 1:193–196, 1936.

Dorsey, J. O., and Thomas, C.
"Missouri." *Bull. Bureau Amer. Ethnol.* 30 (Part 1):911–912, 1907.

OTO

Allis, Rev. Samuel
"Forty Years Among the Indians and on the Eastern Borders of Nebraska. *Transactions and Reports of the Nebraska State Historical Society* (Lincoln, Nebr.) 1887.

Harrington, M. R.
"A Visit to the Otoe Indians" *Museum Journal* 4:107–113, 1913.

Hayden, F. V.
"Brief Notes on the Present Condition of the Otoe Indians." *Annual Reports U. S. Geological and Geographical Survey of the Territories (Washington, D. C.)* 1:32–35, 1867.

Kercheval, G. T.
"An Otoe and Omaha Tale." *JAFL* 6:199–204, 1893.

Shunatona, R.
"Otoe Indian Lore." *Nebraska History and Record of Pioneer Days.* 5:60–64. 1922.

Skinner, Alanson
"Remarkable Oto Necklace." *Indian Notes* 2: 36–38, 1925.

Whitman, William
"Origin Legends of the Oto." *JAFL* 51:173–205, 1938.

The Oto. Columbia University Contributions to Anthropology, No. 28. New York: Columbia University Press, 1937. 132 pp.

QUAPAW (Arkansa)

Dorsey, J. O.
"Kwapa Folk-Lore." *JAFL* 8:130–131, 1895.

Foreman, Grant
Indians and Pioneers. New Haven: Yale University Press, 1930.
> Concerned mainly with Indians of Arkansas. Quapaw—"A southwestern Siouan tribe, forming one of the two divisions of the Ohegiha group of Dorsey."

————, ed.
A Traveler in Indian Territory. Cedar Rapids, Ia.: The Torch Press, 1930.
> Ethan Allen Hitchcock's Journal during his investigations of Indian mistreatment by contractors and Government agents. Deals mainly with Indian Tribes of Arkansas.

Nuttall, T.
A Journal of Travels Into the Arkansa Territory. Philadelphia: 1821. 296 pp.

Shetrone, Henry Clyde
The Mound Builders. New York: D. Appleton and Co., 1930.
> Deals mainly with Indian Tribes of Arkansas.

Thomas, C.
"Quapaw." *Bull. Bureau Amer. Ethnol.* 30 (Part 2):333–336, 1910.

WACO

Bolton, H. E.
"Waco." *Bull. Bureau Amer. Ethnol.* 30 (Part 2):887–888, 1910.

Douglas, F. H.
The Wichita Indians and Allied Tribes Waco, Towakoni, and Kichai. Denver Art Museum, Department of Indian Art, Leaflet 40. (Jan.) 1932.

Harrington, M. R.
"Fresh from Oklahoma." *Masterkey* 18:90–93, 1944.
> Indian pottery from Le Flore County, Oklahoma.

Jackson, A. T.
Picture-Writing of Texas Indians. Anthropological Papers, University of Texas, Publications 2. Austin: University of Texas, 1938. 490 pp., illus.

Scarborough, Dorothy
"Traditions of the Waco Indians." *TFSP* 1:50–54, 1916.

YANKTON

Belden, G. P.
Belden, the White Chief . . . Cincinnati: C. Z. Vent, 1870. 513 pp.

McGee, W. J.
"The Siouan Indians." *Annual Reports Bureau Amer. Ethnol.* 15:157–204, 1894.

Olden, S. E.
The People of Tipi Sapa . . . Milwaukee: Morehouse Publishing Co., 1918. xxiii, 158 pp., illus.

Thomas, C.
"Yankton." *Bull. Bureau Amer. Ethnol.* 30 (Part 2):988–990, 1910.

————.
"Yanktonai." *Bull. Bureau Amer. Ethnol.* 30 (Part 2):990–991, 1910.

THE SOUTHWESTERN AREA

THE SOUTHWESTERN AREA

FOLKLORE

BIBLIOGRAPHY

See: Bibliography of the Folklore of the North American Indian, pp. 750–53.

Alliot, Hector
Bibliography of Arizona; being the record of literature collected by Joseph Amoso Munk and donated by him to The Southwest Museum of Los Angeles, California. Los Angeles: The Southwest Museum, 1914.
Folklore, music and Indian bibliography.

Anonymous
"Bibliography of New Mexican Ethnology and Ethnography." *New Mexico Anthropologist* 2: 52–62, 1938.

————.
"Bibliography of New Mexico Archaeology, 1936–1937. With Resumé of Field Work." *New Mexico Anthropologist* 2, (No. 2) :36–37, (Albuquerque), 1937.

Baldwin, Gordon C.
"Bibliography on Southwest—Emphasis on Basket Maker III Sandals in Arizona." *AA* 41: 243–244, 1939.
In article: "Basket Maker III Sandals from Arizona" by Gordon C. Baldwin.

Chapman, Charles Edward
Catalogue of Materials in the Archives General de Indias for the History of the Pacific Coast and the American Southwest. Berkeley: University of California Press, 1919. University of California Publications in History, v. 8.

Chapman, Kenneth M., comp.
Decorative Art of the Indians of the Southwest: a list of publications containing illustrations from basketry, costumes, and ornaments, pottery, textiles, etc., of special value in the study of design. Laboratory of Anthropology, General Series, Bulletin 1. Santa Fe: University Press, 1934.

Dobie, J. Frank
Guide to Life and Literature of the Southwest. With a few observations. Illustrated. Austin, Texas: The University of Texas Press, 1943. 111 pp.
Chapters 2 and 4 list books on Indians of the Southwest.

Grammer, Maurine
Indians of the Southwest. No. 27 (Revised) Teacher's Lesson Unit Series. This unit lesson plan is intended for Grade 4. New York: Teachers College: Bureau of Publications, Columbia University, 1932–1937.
Good bibliography, mainly of children's books on Indian life in the Southwest.

Hargrett, Lester
A Bibliography of the Constitutions and Laws of the American Indians. Cambridge: Harvard University Press, 1948.

Saunders, Lyle, comp.
A Guide to Materials Bearing on Cultural Relations in New Mexico. Albuquerque, New Mexico: The University of New Mexico Press, 1944. 528 pp.
A comprehensive bibliography — including a number of entries on folklore and folksong of the Spanish-speaking population, the Indians; Pueblos, Navahos and Apaches, and the American frontier.

————.
"A Guide to the Literature of the Southwest." *New Mexico Quarterly Review* 18:121, Spring, 1948.

"Southwestern Archaeology: Bibliography." *AA* 37:33–35, 1935.
Part of article on Southwestern Archaeology by Frank H. H. Roberts, Jr.

Tucker, Mary
Books of the Southwest. New York: J. J. Augustin, 1937.
A general bibliography: deals with Indians of the Southwest, Spain in the Southwest, American Pioneer History, the Southwest country, and the Southwest in literature.

PERIODICALS

See: Periodicals of the Folklore of the North American Indians, pp. 753–55.

The Kiva.
Tucson: Arizona Archaeological and Historical Society, 1936.

The Masterkey
A popular magazine devoted chiefly to the work of the Southwest Museum in American Archaeology and Ethnology. Volume I to IV consist each of eight monthly issues. Volume V and subsequent volumes comprise six issues each, published bi-monthly. Los Angeles.

El Palacio.
Santa Fe Museum of New Mexico and the School of American Research, Santa Fe, N. M. No. 1, 1913–

Southwestern Lore
Gunnison, Colorado. V. 1, No. 1, June 1935–

Southwest Museum Leaflets
Highland Park, Los Angeles, Calif.: Southwest Museum.
Devoted mainly to American anthropology.

Southwestern Journal of Anthropology.
A Joint Publication of the University of New Mexico and the Laboratory of Anthropology, 1944. Spier, Leslie, ed.
An outlet for professional papers in addition to the existing periodicals in folklore and anthropology.

Texas Folklore Society Publications.
Editor: J. F. Dobie, Austin, Texas. I (1916), II (1923). Since then about a volume every year.

GENERAL STUDIES

Antevs, Ernst
"Dating Records of Early Man in the Southwest." *American Naturalist* 70:332–336, 1937.

Aubry, F. X.
"Aubry's Journey from California to New Mexico." *The Western Journal and Civilian* 11 (No. 5) 2: 84–96, 1853.

Austin, Mary Hunter
The Trail Book. New York: Houghton, Mifflin & Co., 1918. 304 pp.

Bailey, Philip A.
Golden Mirages. New York: The Macmillan Company, 1941. 353 pp.
"An authoritative book on the legends, tall tales, customs, language and manners of the wild region stretching from San Diego in the west to Maricopa and Pima Counties (Arizona) in the east and centering in the area around the Salton Sea." (D. Emrich.)

Baldwin, Gordon C.
"Indian Tribes of Arizona: Part I" *The Kiva 3,* No. 5:17–20. Tucson: Arizona Archaeological and Historical Society, 1938.

Bandelier, Adolph Francis Alphonse
The Delight Makers. Introduction by Charles F. Lummis. New York: Dodd, Mead and Co., 1916. xvii, 490 pp. 2nd ed.

——————.
The Gilded Man (El Dorado) and Other Pictures of the Spanish Occupancy of America. New York: D. Appleton and Co., 1893. iv, 302 pp.

——————.
Final Report of Investigations Among the Indians of the Southwestern United States, carried on mainly in the years from 1880 to 1885. Cambridge, Mass.: J. Wilson and Son, 1890–1892. 2 vols. (Papers of the Archaeological Institute of America. American Series III–IV.)

——————, **Hewett, Edgar L.**
Indians of the Rio Grande Valley. Publication of the University and the School of American Research. Albuquerque: University of New Mexico Press, 1937. 274 pp.

Bartlett, John Russell
Personal Narrative of Explorations and Incidents in Texas, New Mexico, Sonora, and Chihuahua, connected with the United States and Mexican Boundary Commission, during 1850, 1851, 1852, and 1853. New York and London: D. Appleton and Company, 1854. 2 vols., folded front, illus., plates, folded map.

Beals, Ralph L.
Preliminary Report on the Ethnography of the Southwest. Berkeley: National Park Service, 1935. 120 pp.

Benedict, Ruth
"Some Psychological Types in the Cultures of the Southwest." *Proceedings of the 23rd Session of the International Congress of Americanists,* pp. 572–582, 1928.

Bernard, R. B.
"Tribal Notes from the West." *Hobbies* 47:102, 1942.

Blake, William P.
"The Racial Unity of the Historic and Prehistoric Aboriginal People of Arizona and New Mexico." *Proceedings of the 13th Session of the International Congress of Americanists,* pp. 203–205, 1902.

Bloom, L. B.
"Bourke on the Southwest." *New Mexico Hist. Rev.* 8:1–30, 1933; 9:33–77, 159–183, 273–289, 373–435, 1934; 10:1–35, 271–322, 195; 11:77–122, 188–207, 217–282, 1935; 12: 41–77, 337–379, 1936; 13:192–238, 1937.

Bolton, Herbert Eugene
Spanish Exploration in the Southwest. 1542–1706. New York: C. Scribner's Sons, 1916. 487 pp.

Burbank, E. A.
Burbank Among the Indians, as Told to Ernest Royce. Caldwell, Idaho: Caxton Printers, 1945. 232 pp., illus.
A noted artist records his impressions of life and lore among many Indian tribes, principally those of the Plains and Southwest.

Carroll, H. Bailey, and Haggard, J. Villasana (translators and editors)
Three New Mexico Chronicles. Albuquerque, N. M.: The Quivira Society, 1942. 342 pp.
Mainly concerned with the white population, with treatment of the Comanches, Apaches, Navajos and Utes included.

Castañeda de Haçera, Pedro de
"Relacion de la jornado de Cibola." In: *The Coronado Expedition,* by G. P. Winship, (pp. 413–546), with translation. U. S. Bureau of Ethnology. 14th Annual Report. Washington: U. S. Gov't Printing Office, 1892-93.
The story of a journey undertaken in 1540,—discusses, among other things, the customs and manners of the natives.

Colton, Harold S.
"Names of the Four Culture Roots in the Southwest." *Science* 87, (No. 2268):551-552, 1938.

Coolidge, Mrs. Mary Elizabeth Burroughs (Roberts) Smith
The Rain-makers; Indians of Arizona and New Mexico. Boston: Houghton Mifflin Company, 1929. xiii, 326 pp., front., plates, port., bibl. (pp. 309–313).

Crane, Leo
Indians of the Enchanted Desert. Boston: Little, Brown Company, 1925. x, 364 pp.

Crimmins, M. L.
"The Aztec Influence on the Primitive Culture of the Southwest." *Texas Archaeological and Paleontological Society*, Bulletin 4:32–39, (Abilene), (Sept.) 1932.

Dorsey, G. A.
Indians of the Southwest. Published by the Santa Fe Railway, 1903. 223 pp., illus., bibl.

Douglass, A. E.
"The Secret of the Southwest Solved by Talkative Tree Rings." *National Geographic Magazine*, (Dec.) 1929.

Dutton, Bertha P.
"The New Hall of Ethnology." *El Palacio* 48 (No. 8):178–188, 1941.

Foreman, Grant
Indians and Pioneers. Norman: University of Oklahoma Press, 1936. xvi, 348 pp.

Forrest, Earle Robert
Missions and Pueblos of the Old Southwest; their myths, legends, fiestas and ceremonies, with some account of the Indian tribes and dances, and of the penitentes. Cleveland: A. H. Clark Company, 1925. 2 vols.

Franciscan Fathers
"The Franciscan Missions of the Southwest." *Fathers of Saint Michaels*, (Arizona), Nos. 1–10, 1913–1922.

Gillmor, Frances and others
"Opportunities in Arizona Folk-Lore." *Arizona University General Bulletin.* No. 9:1–55, (Tucson) 1945.

Gladwin, Harold S.
"The Archaeology of the Southwest and its Relation to the Cultures of Texas." *Bulletin, Texas Archaeological and Paleontological Society* 6:19–37, (Sept.) 1934.

Goddard, Pliny Earle
Indians of the Southwest. New York: The American Museum of Natural History, 1931. 205 pp., maps, illus., 4th edition.

Goodwin, Grenville
"The Characteristics and Function of Clan in a Southern Athapascan Culture." *AA* 39:394–407, 1937. n.s.

―――――
"The Southern Ashapascans." *The Kiva* 4: No. 2. Tucson: Arizona Archaeological and Historical Society, 1938.

Haeckel, Josef
"Das Mutterrecht bei den Indianerstämmen im südwestlichen Nordamerika und seine kulturhistorische Stellung." *Zeitschrift für Ethnologie* 68 (No. 1–3):227–249, 1936.
Mother-right among the Indians of the Southwest.

Hafen, LeRoy R., and Rister, Carl C.
Western America: the exploration, settlement of the region beyond the Mississippi. Prentice Hall Books on History. New York: Prentice Hall, 1941. xxvi, 698 pp., bibl.

Hall, Edward Twitchell, Jr.
"Recent Clues to Athapascan Prehistory in the Southwest." *AA* 46 (No. 1):98–105, 1944.
Based mainly on archaeological investigation.

Halseth, O. S.
"The Acculturation of the Pueblo Indians." *El Palacio* 18:254–268, 1925.

―――――
"The Pueblo Indians." *El Palacio* 22:238–251, 1927.

Hammond, George P., and Rey, Agapito
"The Rodriguez Expedition to New Mexico, 1581–1582." *New Mexico Historical Review* (Santa Fe, New Mexico) 2:239–268, 334–362, 1927.

Hewett, Edgar Lee
Ancient Life in the American Southwest. Indianapolis: Bobbs-Merrill Company, 1930.
Archaeological study.

―――――
Les Communautés anciennes dans le désert Amèricain. Recherches archeologiques sur la distribution et l'organisation sociale, des anciennes populations au sud-ouest des États-Unis et au Nord du Mexique. Géneve: Libraire Kündig, 1908. 107 pp., 17 pl. 20 fig.

Hurt, Wesley
"Indian Influence at Manzano." *El Palacio* (Santa Fe, New Mexico), 46:245–254, 1939.

Ickes, Anna Wilmarth
Mesa Land: the history and romance of the American Southwest. New York: Houghton Mifflin Company, 1933. ix, 285 pp., bibl.

James, George Wharton
The Indians of the Painted Desert Region; Hopis, Navahoes, Wallapais, Havasupais. Boston: Little, Brown and Company, 1903. 268 pp., 65 pl.

Judd, Neil Merton
Progress in the Southwest. In: *Essays in Historical Anthropology of North America.* Published in honor of John R. Swanton, in celebration of his 40th year with the Smithsonian Institution. Smithsonian Miscellaneous Collection, V. 100. Washington, D. C.: U. S. Government Printing Office, 1940.

Ker, Henry
Travels Through the Western Interior of the United States, from the year 1808 up to the year 1816.... Containing a particular account of thirteen different tribes of Indians.... Elizabethtown, N. J.: The Author, 1816. viii, 376 pp.

Keyes, E. T.
Featherbed Flute. Rancho Santa Fe, Calif.: Langford Press, 1941. 61 pp.

Kluckhohn, Clyde
Beyond the Rainbow. Boston: The Christopher Publishing House, 1933. 271 pp. map.
Description of travels, customs of the Southwest, Colorado River, the Hopi and Navaho Indians.

————.
To the Foot of the Rainbow; a tale of twenty-five hundred miles of wandering on horseback through the Southwest enchanted land. New York: The Century Co., 1927. xiii, 276 pp.

La Farge, Oliver
The Changing Indian. Norman: University of Oklahoma Press. 1942. x, 184 pp.
Conditions of American Indian life today.

Lummis, C. F.
Mesa, Canyon, and Pueblo; our wonderland of the Southwest, its marvels of nature, its pageant of earth building, its strange peoples, its centuried romance. Illustrated with nearly 100 rare photographs. New York: The Century Company, 1925. xvi, 517 pp.
Based on the authors, "Some Strange Corners of Our Country." Bibl. pp. 485-495.

————.
Some Strange Corners of Our Country. The Wonderland of the Southwest. New York: The Century Company, 1908. xi, 270 pp., incl. illus., plates, facisms., col. front.

Malouf, Carling
"Prehistoric Exchange in the Northern Periphery of the Southwest." *American Antiquity* (Menasha) 6, (No. 2):115–122, 1940.

Parsons, Elsie Clews
"Relations Between Ethnology and Archaeology in the Southwest." *American Antiquity* 5:214–220, 1940.

Pearce, Thomas M.
"Some Anthropological Terms Used in the Southwest." *El Palacio* 50:130–141, 1943.
Relating to Indian folklore.

Peters, Mary Eleanor
"Texas Trails." *Proceedings Mississippi Valley Historical Association (Cedar Rapids), 1913–1914.* 7:56–66, 1914.

Postlethwaite, W. W.
"Indians and Spaniards in the Southwest." *Southwestern Lore* (Gunnison) 8:48–52, 1943.

Reichard, Gladys A.
"A Few Instances of Cultural Resistance in Southwest North America." *Proceedings of the 22nd Session of the International Congress of Americanists*, 2:289–297, 1928.

Rogers, Malcolm J.
"Aboriginal Culture Relations between Southern California and the Southwest." *San Diego Museum Bulletin* 5, (No. 3):1–6, 1941.

Schmitt, Martin F., and Brown, Dee
Fighting Indians of the West. With 270 illustrations. New York: Charles Scribner's Sons, 1948. 362 pp.
A collection of photographs, supplemented by a number of drawings, arranged in context with a running commentary.

Steward, Julian H.
"Ecological Aspects of Southwestern Society." *Anthropos* 32, (Nos. 1–2):87–104, 1937.

Strong, W. D.
"An Analysis of Southwestern Society." *AA* 29:1–61, 1917. n.s.

The New Trail: A Book of Creative Writing by Indian Students. Phoenix, Ariz.: Printed at the Pheonix Indian School, 1941. 158 pp., bibl., illus.
"A beautiful panorama of the Indian way of life from the standpoint of the Indians themselves—presents culture and modern contemporary life of Papago, Pima, Maricopa, Colorado River, Apache and Hopi Tribes." (G. H. Shinn).

Tobin, Samuel J.
"Culture Sequence in the Southwest." *Southwestern Lore* 12:55, March, 1948.

Wagner, Henry Raup
The Spanish Southwest, 1542–1794; An annotated bibliography. Berkeley: 1924. 302 pp., illus.

Waterman, T. T.
"Culture Horizons in the Southwest." *AA* 31:367–400, 1929. n.s.

MYTHS—FOLKTALES—LEGENDS

Applegate, Frank G.
Native Tales of New Mexico; introduction by Mary Austin; with illustrations in color by the author. Philadelphia: J. B. Lippincott Company, 1932. 263 pp., illus.

Butterfield, Marguerite, and Brown, Dorothy Lathrop
Morning Star. New York: Lyons and Carnahan, 1943.
Stories for young children of the Indians of the Southwest.

De Huff, Elizabeth
Say The Bells of Old Missions; Legends of old New Mexico Churches. St. Louis, Mo.: B. Herder Book Co., 1943. viii, 168 p., illus.

Evans, Will
"How Jackrabbit Got His Long Ears." *Southwestern Lore* 13:41, Dec. 1947.

————.
"The White-faced One Wrestles with Hostien Bear: A Navajo Folk Story." *Southwestern Lore* 12:53, March, 1948.

Fergusson, Erna
Dancing Gods. Indian Ceremonials of New Mexico and Arizona. New York: Alfred A. Knopf, 1931. xxvi, 276 pp., illus.

Hough, W.
"Sacred Springs of the Southwest." *Records of the Past* (Washington) 5:163–169, 1906.

James, H. C.
"Halikasai." El Centro,: Desert Magazine (Calif.):1940. 28 pp., illus.

Judson, Katharine B.
Myths and Legends of California and the Old Southwest. Chicago: A. C. McClury and Co., 1912. xvi, 193 pp., illus.

McKee, Louise, and Summers, Richard
Dusty Desert Tales. Illustrated with photographs and with drawings by J. Powell Scott. Caldwell, Idaho: The Caxton Printers, Ltd., 1941. 191 pp., illus.
    Contains retold myths from Pima, Apache, Yuma and Hopi.

Reagan, A. B.
The Sun God, Moccasin Tales. Provo, Utah: The Author, 1935.

Roberts, Mrs. Elizabeth (Judson)
Indian Stories of the Southwest. Ilustrations by Ben Ward. San Franciso: Harr Wagner Publishing Co., 1917. 258 pp., illus.

BELIEFS—CUSTOMS

Hewett, Edgar Lee
"From Barter to World Trade." *El Palacio* (Santa Fe, N. M.) 49:219–224, 1942.
    Observations on Southwestern Indian barter customs.

Hodge, Gene Meany
The Kachinas Are Coming. Los Angeles: Steller Millar, 1937. xvii, 129 pp.

Loeb, Edwin M.
"A Note on Two Far-Travelled Kachinas." *JAFL* 56:192–199, 1943.
    Treats with Kachina diffusion from Hopi-Zuni to the Tewa and Navaho, and influence of the eastern Apache.

Michael, Dorothy Jean
"Grave Decoration." *TFSP* 18:129–136, 1943.
    Discusses these customs among Negroes, Whites, Mexicans and Indians in Texas.

Opler, Morris Edward
"Examples of the Ceremonial Interchanges Among Southwest Tribes." *The Masterkey* 16–3:77–80, (May) 1942.

Spinden, Herbert J.
"Sun Worship." *Smithsonian Annual Report for 1939:* pp. 447–469. Washington, D. C.: U. S. Government Printing Office, 1940.

Steece, H. M.
"Corn Culture Among the Indians of the Southwest." *Natur. Hist.* 21:414–424, 1921.

Stevenson, P.
"Fire Magic in the Southwest." *Travel* 65:18–22, (June) 1935.

FOLK MEDICINE

Bell, William H., and Castetter, Edward F.
"Ethnobiological Studies in the American Southwest: V. The Utilization of Mesquite and Screwbean by the Aborigines in the American Southwest." *Bulletin, University of New Mexico, Biological Series* 5, (No.2), 1937.

Castetter, Edward F.
Ethnobiological Studies in the Southwest: IV. The Aboriginal Utilization of Tall Cacti in the American Southwest." *Bulletin, University of New Mexico* 307. *Biological Series 5,* 1937. 48 pp.

——————.
"Ethnobiological Studies in the American Southwest: I. Uncultivated Plants Used as Sources of Food." *University of New Mexico Bulletin 266, Biological Series 4,* (No. 1), 1935.

——————.
"Early Tobacco Utilization and Cultivation in the American Southwest." *AA* 45:320–325, 1943. n.s.

Hrdlicka, Ales
Physiological and Medical Observations Among the Indians of the Southwestern United States and Northern Mexico. Bureau of American Ethnology, Bulletin 34. pp. 1–460, 28 pls., 2. figs. Washington, D. C.: U. S. Government Printing Office, 1908. 425 pp., illus.

Jones, Volney H.
"A Native Southwestern Tea Plant." *El Palacio* 49:272–280, 1942.

Petrullo, Vincenzo
The Diabolic Root. Philadelphia: University of Pennsylvania Press, 1934.
    "A study both humanistic and scientific of that highly interesting form of plant life of the Southwest, the peyote. Bibliography." (Dobie)

FOLK ART—SPEECH

Amsden, Charles
"Arts and Crafts of the Southwestern Indians." *Masterkey* 15, (No. 3):74–80, 1941.

Austin, Mary
"Folk Plays of the Southwest." *Theatre Arts Monthly* 17:599–610, August, 1933.

Canfield, Delos L.
"Spanish Literature in Indian Language of New Spain." *Spanish Review* 2:9–14, 1935.

Chapman, K. M.
"Decorative Art of the Indians of the Southwest." *Bulletin of the Laboratory of Anthropology, General Series* 1:1–11, 1934.

Cummings, Byron
"Prehistoric Pottery of the Southwest." *The Kiva* 1. (No. 2). *Arizona Archaeological and Historical Society,* (Oct.) 1935.

Douglas, Frederic H.
Pottery of the Southwestern Tribes. Denver Art Museum, Department of Indian Art, Leaflet 71, 1936.

Germann, F. E. E.
"Ceramic Pigments of the Indians of the Southwest." *El Palacio* 20:222–226, 1926.

Gifford, E. W.
"Pottery-Making in the Southwest." *AA* 37:535, 1935. n.s.

Goddard, Pliny Earle
Pottery of the Southwestern Indians. New York: The American Museum of Natural History, 1931. 30 pp., illus.

Haeberlin, H. K.
"Das Flachenornament in der Keramik der alten Pueblo-Kultur." *Baessler-Archiv* (Berlin) 6:1–35, 1922.

Hargrave, Lyndon L.
"Concerning the Names of the Southwest Pottery Types." *Southwestern Lore* 1:17–23, 1935.

Haury, E. W.
"The Age of Head Glaze Decorated Pottery in the Southwest." *AA* 34:418–425, 1932. n.s.

Hodge, F. W.
"Coral Among Early Southwestern Indians." *Masterkey* (Southwest Museum, Highland Park, Los Angeles, California) 18:99–102, 1943.

Indian Sand-Painting; Tribes, Techniques and Uses.
Denver Art Museum, Department of Indian Art, Leaflets 43 and 44, (March) 1932.

Kelemen, Pál
Medieval American Art. New York: The Macmillan Company, 1943. 2 Vols. Vol. I, xiv, 414 pp., Vol. 2, 33 pp. 306 pls.
The author selects five regions as especially notable for the artistic achievements of their inhabitants, the North American Southwest, Mexico, the Maya area, the interlying zone between Costa Rica and Ecuador, and the Andean region.

McGregor, John Charles
Southwestern Archaeology. New York: Wiley and Sons, 1941.

Morris, Ann Axtell
Digging in the Southwest. Garden City, N. Y.: Doubleday, Doran, 1933. xviii, 301 pp.

Oglesby, Catherine
Modern Primitive Arts of Mexico, Guatemala and the Southwest. New York: McGraw-Hill, 1939. 236 pp., illus., bibl.

Parsons, Elsie Clews
"Masks in the Southwest of the United States." *Mexican Folk-Ways* 5:152, 1929.

Pepper, G. H.
"The Throwing-Stick of the Prehistoric People of the Southwest." *Proceedings of the 13th Session of the International Congress of Americanists,* (New York), pp. 107–131, 1902.
"This implement, also known as a throwing board, dart sling, and atlatl, is an apparatus for hurling a lance, spear, or harpoon at birds and aquatic animals."

Renaud, E. B.
"Fabrication de la céramique Indiennes du sud-ouest des États-Unis." *Jour. Société Amér.* 17:85–117, 1925. n.s.

Sides, Dorothy Smith
Decorative Art of the Southwestern Indian. Santa Ana: Fine Arts Press, 1936. 8 pp., 50 pl.

Smith, Victor J.
"The Relation of the Southwestern Basket Maker to the Dry Shelter Culture of the Big Bend." *Texas Archaeological and Paleontological Society* (Abilene), Bulletin 4:55–62, 1932.

Waterman, T. T.
"Ornamental Designs in Southwestern Pottery." *Indian Notes* 7:497–522, 1930.

Watkins, Frances E.
"The Frederick Hastings Rindge Memorial Collection." *Masterkey* 18:15–20, 1944.
5,477 specimens of Spanish Californian and American Indian artifacs in the Southwest Museum.

White, L. A.
"Masks in the Southwest." *AA* 36:626–628, 1934. n.s.

Woodward, Arthur
"Ancient Artists of the Southwest." *Quart. Los Angeles County Mus.* 6(No. 1):3–6, 1947.

GAMES

Chard, Chester S.
"Distribution and Significance of Ball Courts in the Southwest." *Papers of the Excavator's Club,* 1, (No. 2): 18, (Cambridge), 1941.

Culin, Stewart
Games of the North American Indians. 24th Report, Bureau of American Ethnology. Washington, D. C.: U. S. Gov't. Printing Office, 1907.

MUSIC

GENERAL STUDIES

Bourke, John G.
"The Miracle Play of the Rio Grande." *JAFL* 6:89–95, 1893.

Chesky, Jane
"Indian Music of the Southwest." *The Kiva* 7 (No. 3):9–12, 1941.

Curtis, Natalie
The Indian's Book. New York: Harper and Brothers, 1907. 583 pp., illus., music.

Densmore, Frances
The American Indians and their Music. New York: The Womans Press, 1936. 150 pp., music.

Fletcher, Alice C.
Indian Games and Dances with Native Songs. Arranged from American Indian Ceremonials and Sports. Boston: C. C. Birchard & Company, 1915. vi, 139 pp., music.

Jeançon, Jean Allard
Indian Song Book. (Ute, Hopi, Navajo, Tewa) Denver, 1924.

Parsons, Elsie Clews
"The Humpbacked Flute Player of the Southwest." *AA* 40:337–338, 1938. n.s.

Roberts, Helen H.
"Indian Music from the Southwest." *Natural History* 27:257–265, 1927.

DANCES

Alexander, Hartley
"The Fiesta Theatre in Santa Fe." *Theatre Arts Monthly* 11:27–34, (Jan.) 1927.

Austin, Mary
"Sekala Ka'ajma: An interpretive dance drama of the Southwest." *Theatre Arts Monthly* 13:267–278, (April) 1929.

———.
"Folk Plays of the Southwest." *Theatre Arts Monthly* 17:599–610, (August) 1933.

Carnac, Levin
"The Snake-Dancers of Arizona." *Pearson's Magazine* 8:324–328, 1899.

Cushing, Frank H.
"Pueblo Myths and Ceremonial Dances." *Amer. Assoc. for the Advancement of Science, Proceedings,* 41:296, 1892.

Draper, W. H.
"Indian Dances of the Southwest." *Outing* (No. 37):659–666, (March) 1901.

Evans, Bessie and M. G.
American Indian Dance Steps. New York: A. S. Barnes, 1931. xviii, 104 pp., music.

Fergusson, Erna
"Laughing Priests." *Theatre Arts Monthly,* pp. 657–662, (Aug.) 1933.

———.
Dancing Gods. Indian Ceremonials of New Mexico and Arizona. New York: Alfred Knopf, 1931. illus.

"Ghost Dances of the West."
Illustrated America (New York) 5, (No. 48): 327–333, 1891.
Origin and development of the messiah craze and the ghost-dance.

Hodge, Gene Meany
The Kachinas Are Coming. Los Angeles: Steller Millar, 1937. xvii, 129 pp.

La Farge, Oliver
"Plastic Prayer Dances of the Southwestern Indians." *Theatre Arts Monthly* (New York) 12:218–224, 1930. illus.

Loeb, Edwin M.
"A Note on Two Far-Traveled Kachinas." *JAFL* 56:192–199, 1943.
Treats with Kachina diffusion from Hopi-Zuni to the Tewa and Navaho, and influence of the eastern Apache.

Spinden, Herbert J.
"Indian Dances of the Southwest; Ceremonies Symbolic of Daily Life." *Scientific American,* Supplement No. 83:8–9, (Jan.) 1917.

RECORDS

Herzog, George
Southwestern Area: Records Contained in American Collections. American Council of Learned Societies, Bulletin 24:29. Washington, D. C.: 1936.

Indian Music of the Southwest.
Recorded by Laura C. Bolton. Tribes included: Zuni, Navajo, Taos, San Ildefonso, Santa Ana, Mohave, Papago, Pima and Apache. 3–10"
VP–49

The Charles F. Lummis Collection of Spanish California and Indian Songs in the Southwest Museum, Los Angeles.
Has 131 Indian songs.

U. S. Library of Congress. Division of Music. Folklore Section.
The American Folksong Archive, now under the direction of Dr. Duncan Emrich, has a great number of Indian recordings, more recently enriched by the Frances Densmore collection.
AAFS–LC

———.
University of Arizona Recording Project.
AAFS–LC

———.
University of New Mexico Recording Project.
AAFS–LC

APACHE

(Includes: Chiricahua, Jicarilla, Lipan, Mescalero, San Carlos, White Mountain)

FOLKLORE

GENERAL STUDIES

Arnold, Elliott
Blood Brother. New York: Duell, Sloan and Pearce, 1947. 558 pp.
"His two most important figures in the book are an Indian and a White Man, the Apache Chieftain Cochise and the American General Oliver Otis Howard. Cochise was the greatest of all the Apache leaders in their struggle to survive against American treachery, cruelty and deceit . . . no one will finish the book without a deeper understanding of the background of Southwestern life." (T. M. Pearce)

Atkinson, Mary Jordan
The Texas Indians. San Antonio: Naylor Company, 1935. 345 pp., illus. bibl.

Austin, Mary
The Trail Book. Boston: Houghton Mifflin Company, 1918. 304 pp.

Barrett, S. M.
Geronimo's Story of His Life, taken down and edited by S. M. B. New York: Duffield and Company, 1906. 216 pp., illus.
He was of the Chiricahua-Apaches.

Bourke, John Gregory
"Gentile Organizations of the Apache of Arizona." *JAFL* 3:111–126, 1890.

———.
On the Border with Crook. New York: Charles Scribner's Sons, 1892. xiii, 49 pp., illus.
"A great book on both Apaches and Arizona frontier." (Dobie)

Buckelew, F. M.
F. M. Buckelew, the Indian Captive; or, the Life Story of F. M. Buckelew (sic) while a captive among the Lipan Indians in the western wilds of frontier Texas, as related by himself. Written by S. E. Banta. Mason, Texas: The Mason Herald, 1911. 112 pp., illus.

"Chiricahua-Apache Social Organizations."
JAFL 3:115–116, 1890.

Clum, Woodworth
Apache Agent. Boston: Houghton Mifflin Company, 1936. xiv, 29 pp.
"Worthy autobiography of a noble understander of the Apache people." (Dobie)

Comfort, Will Levington
Apache. New York: E. P. Dutton and Company, 1931. 274 pp.
"The most moving and incisive piece of writing on the Indians of the Southwest." (Dobie)

Cremony, John C.
Life Among the Apaches. New York: A. Roman and Company, 1868. 322 pp.

Davis, Britton
The Truth about Geronimo. New Haven: Yale University Press, 1929.
"Davis helped run Geronimo down." (Dobie)

Davis, William Watts Hart
El Gringo, or New Mexico and Her People. New York: Harper Bros., 1857. 332 pp.

De Shields, James T.
Cynthia Ann Parker. St. Louis: 1886 Reprinted in San Antonio by the Naylor Company, in 1934. vii, 80 pp.
"Good narrative of noted woman captive." (Dobie)

Forrest, E. R., and Hill, E. B.
Lone War Trail of Apache Kid. Illustrated by Charlie Russell. Pasadena, Calif.: Trails End Publishing Co., 1947. 143 pp., illus.
Life of a famous Indian in Arizona.

Goddard, Pliny Earle
"Apache Tribes of the Southwest." *Southern Workman* (Hampton, Va.) 39:481–485, 1910.

———.
"Jicarilla Apache Texts." *Anthropological Papers American Museum of Natural History* (New York) 8:1–276, 1911.

———.
"White Mountain Apache Texts." *Anthropological Papers American Museum of Natural History* 24, (Part 4):369–527, 1920.
"The name is now applied to all the Apache under Ft. Apache Agency, Arizona, consisting of Arivaipa, Tsiltaden or Chilion, Chiricahua, Coyotero, Mimbreno, and Mogollon."

Goodwin, Grenville
"Clans of the Western Apache." *New Mexico Historical Review* 8, (No. 3):176–182, (July) 1933.

———.
"The Social Divisions and Economic Life of the Western Apache." *AA* 37:55–64 1935. n. s.

———.
The Social Organization of the Western Apache. Chicago: University of Chicago Press, 1942. xx, 701 pp., 10 pls.

Haury, Emil W.
The Mogollón Culture of Southwestern New Mexico. Globe, Arizona: Priv. Print. For the Medallion, 1936. IX, Medallion Papers, No. XX. bibl. (pp.137–141).
"A subdivision of the Apache that formerly ranged over the Mogollon Mesa and Mts. in West New Mexico and East Arizona." (Frederick W. Hodge)

Hodge, F. Webb
"The Early Navajo and Apache." *AA* 8:223–241, 1895. o. s.

Hoijer, Harry
Chiricahua and Mescalero Apache Texts. University of Chicago Publications in Anthropology, Linguistic Series. Chicago: University of Chicago Press, 1938. 219 pp.

Hooker, Forrestine Cooper
When Geronimo Rode. Garden City, N. Y.: Doubleday Page, 1924. xv, 325 pp.

Hrdlicka, Ales
"Notes on the San Carlos Apache." *AA* 7:425–480, 1905. n. s.

Lambert, Elizabeth
There Go the Apaches. Portland, Ore.: Binfords and Mort, 1941.
Juvenile story—adventures of an Indian boy in Arizona.

Lehmann, Herman
Nine Years with the Indians. Bandera, Texas: Frontier Times, 1927. x, 325 pp.
Best captive narrative of the Southwest." (Dobie)

Lewis, Alfred Henry
The Apaches of New York. New York: G. W. Dillingham Co., 1912. 272 pp.

Lockwood, Francis Cummings
The Apache Indians. New York: The Macmillan Co., 1938. xvi, 384 pp., plates.

Lummis, Charles F.
The Land of Poco Tiempo. New York: Charles Scribner's Sons, 1925. xii, 310 pp., music.

Opler, Morris Edward
"A Summary of Jicarilla Apache Culture." *AA* 38:202–223, 1936. n. s.

——————.
An Apache Way of Life. Chicago: University of Chicago Press, 1941. xviii, 500 pp., illus.

——————.
"Apache Data Concerning the Relation of Kinship Terminology and Social Classication." *AA* 39:201–212, 1937. n. s.

Reagan, A. B.
"Notes on the Indians of the Fort Apache Region." *American Museum of Natural History, Anthropological Papers* 31:288–345, 1930.

Reed, Erik K.
"Implications of the Mogollon Concept." *American Antiquity* 8:27–32, 1942.

Rinaldo, John
"Conjectures in the Independent Development of the Mogollon Culture." *American Antiquity* 7, (No. 1):5–20, 1941.

Rister, Carl C.
Border Captives. Norman, Okla.: University of Oklahoma Press, 1940. xi, 220 pp.

Santee, Ross
Apache Land. New York: Charles Scribner's Sons, 1947. vii, 216 pp., illus.
  The Apache Indian, past and present, by a man who lived on their reservation and shared their customs.

Smith, C. L., and J. D.
The Boy Captives. Bandera, Texas: Frontier Times, 1927.

Wellman, Paul I.
Death in the Desert. New York: The Macmillan Company, 1935. xiv, 294 pp.
  "A graphic review of the conflict between whites and Indians, mostly Apaches, in the Southwest. Bibliography." (Dobie)

MYTHS—FOLKTALES—LEGENDS

Bourke, John Gregory
"Apache Mythology." *JAFL* 3:209–212, 1890.

Caldwell, James Ralston
"A Tale Actualized in a Game." *JAFL* 58:50, 1945.
  The author shows how a tale of the Chiricahua Apache Indians recorded by Opler was acutally the same as a game of "Snatchgrab" played by Wisconsin youngsters.

Dobie, J. Frank
Apache Gold and Yaqui Silver. Boston: Little, Brown and Company, 1939. xvii, 366 pp.

Goddard, Pliny Earle
"Myths and Tales from the San Carlos Apache." *Anthropological Papers of the American Museum of Natural History* 14:1–87, 1918 (New York).

——————.
"Myths and Tales from the White Mountain Apache." *Anthropological Papers of the American Museum of Natural History* (New York) 14:87–139, 1919.

——————.
"San Carlos Apache Texts." *Anthropological Papers American Museum of Natural History* 24:141–367, 1919 (New York).

Goodwin, Grenville
Myths and Tales of the White Mountain Apache. Memoir of the American Folklore Society, No. 33. Phila.: American Folklore Society, 1939. xviii, 223 pp.

McKee, Louise, and Summers, Richard
Dusty Desert Tales. Caldwell, Idaho: Caxton Printers, Ltd. 1941. 191 pp., illus.

Mooney, James
"The Jicarilla Genesis." *AA* 11:197–229, 1898. o.s.

Opler, Morris Edward
Dirty Boy: a Jicarilla Tale of Raid and War. American Anthropological Association, Memoir 52. Menasha, Wisc.: George Banta Publishing Company, 1938. 80 pp.

——————.
"Mythology and Folk Belief in the Maintenance of Jicarilla Apache Tribal Endogamy." *JAFL* 60:126–129, 1947.
  "Although marriages between Jicarrilla Apache and members of neighboring tribes sometimes occur, strong social pressure is exerted to maintain tribal endogamy. Alien peoples are separated according to mythological origin and are associated with particular animals and birds. Anyone who marries or has sexual relations with an outsider dooms his ghost to become, at death, or even before, the animal or bird which his partner's group represents."

——————.
Myths and Tales of the Chiricahua Apache Indians. Appendix of Apache and Navaho. Comparative References by David French. Memoir of the American Folklore Society, No. 37. Phila.: American Folklore Society, 1942. xiv, 101 pp.

——————.
Myths and Tales of the Jicarilla Apache Indians. Memoir of the American Folklore Society, No. 31. Phila.: American Folklore Society, 1938. xxiii, 406 pp.

——————.
Myths and Legends of the Lipan Apache Indians. Memoir 36 of the American Folklore Society. Phila.: American Folklore Society, 1940. x, 296 pp., bibl.

Three Types of Variation and Their Relation to Culture Change. In: *Language, Culture and Personality*. Menasha, Wisc.: Sapir Memorial Publication Fund, 1941. pp. 146–157.
Variation in Chiricahua Apache myths.

Russell, F.
"Myths of the Jicarilla Apache." *JAFL* 11:253–271, 1898.

Storm, Joe
"Sons of the Devil." *TFSP* 12:190–193, 1935.
An Apache tale.

BELIEFS—CUSTOMS—FOLK MEDICINE

Bourke, John G.
"The Medicine-Men of the Apache." *9th Annual Report: Bureau of Ethnology*, 1887–1888, pp. 451–596, pls. III–VIII, figs. 429–448. Washington, D. C.: U. S. Gov't. Printing Office, 1892.
Medicine-men, their modes of treating disease, their superstitions, paraphernalia, etc.

Castetter, Edward F., and Opler, M. E.
"Ethnological Studies in the American Southwest. III. The Ethnobiography of the Chiricahua and Mescalero Apache. A. The Use of Plants for Food, Beverages and Narcotics." *Bulletin, University of New Mexico*, Biological Series 4, (No. 5), 1936.

Flannery, Regina
"The Position of Woman Among the Mescalero Apache." *Primitive Man* 5:(Nos. 2–3):26–32. Washington, D. C.: Catholic Anthropological Conference, (April–July) 1932.

Goddard, P. E.
A Mescalero Apache Ceremony. In: *Putnam Anniversary Volume*, Anthropological Papers. New York: S. E. Stechert and Company, 1909.

Goodwin, Grenville
"White Mountain Apache Religion." *AA* 40:24–37, 1938. n. s.

Opler, Morris Edward
"Adolescence Rite of the Jicarilla." *El Palacio* 49:25–38, 1942.

————.
"Navaho Shamanistic Practice Among the Jicarillo Apache." *New Mexico Anthropologist* (Albuquerque) 6–7, (No. 1):13–18, 1943.

————.
"The Concept of Supernatural Power Among the Chiricahua and Mescalero Apaches." *AA* 37:65–70, 1935. n. s.

————.
"The Creative Role of Shamanism in Mescalero Apache Mythology." *JAFL* 59:268–281, 1946. bibl.

————.
"The Influence of Aboriginal Patterns and White Contact in a Recently Introduced Ceremony, the Mescalero Peyote Rite." *JAFL* 49:143–167, 1936.

————.
"The Jicarilla Apache Ceremonial Relay Race." *AA* 46:75–98, 1944. n. s. illus.

————.
"The Sacred Clowns of the Chiricahua and Mascalero Indians." *El Palacio* 44:75–79, 1938.

————.
"The Use of Peyote by the Carrizo and Lipan Apache Tribes." *AA* 40:271–285, 1938. n. s.

Reagan, A. B.
"Some Notes on the Occult and Hypnotic Ceremonies of Indians." *Proceedings, Utah Academy of Sciences, Arts and Letters* 11:65–71, 1934.

RIDDLES—FOLK ART

Carter, Isabel Gordon
"Mountain White Riddles." *JAFL* 47:76–81, 1934.

Mera, H. P.
Outline of Ceramic Developments in Southern and Southeastern New Mexico. Santa Fe, N. M.:Laboratory of Anthropology, 1943. 20 pp.

Opler, Morris Edward
"The Mescalero Apache Bow-Drill." *AA* 37:370, 1935. n.s.

Roberts, Helen H.
"Basketry of the San Carlos Apache." *Anthropological Papers of the American Museum of Natural History* (New York) 31:121–218, 1929. illus.

MUSIC

GENERAL STUDIES

Bourke, John G.
"The Medicine-Men of the Apache." *9th Annual Report: Bureau of Ethnology*, pp. 443–603, pl. 3–8, fig. 1–428. Washington, D. C.: U. S. Government Printing Office, 1892.
Presents discussion of the music, songs and dances associated with the ceremonies.

DANCE

Goddard, P. E.
"The Masked Dancers of the Apache." In: *Holmes Anniversary Volume. . . .* Washington: J. W. Bryan, 1916.

Opler, Morris Edward
"A Jicarilla Apache Expedition and Scalp Dance." *JAFL* 54:10–23, 1941.

————.
"The Jicarilla Apache Ceremonial Relay Race." *AA* 46 (No. 1):75–97, 1944.

Russell, Frank
"An Apache Medicine Dance." *AA* 11:367–373, 1898. o.s.

ARRANGEMENTS

"Apache Medicine Chant."
Troyer, Carlos: Presser. Voice and Piano.
"Indian Fire Song, 'Uru Kuru'."
Troyer, C.: Wa-Wan Press: Voice and Piano.
"Scalp Dance."
Lake, M. L.: Carl Fischer: Orchestra.

RECORDS

"Crown Dance." (Apaches, N. Mex.) Laura
Boulton.
In: *Indian Music of the Southwest.*   VP-49

HOPI (Pueblo)

(*Includes:* Hano, Mishongopowi, Oraibi, Shongopowi, Walpi)

FOLKLORE

GENERAL STUDIES

Bartlett, Katherine
"Spanish Contacts with the Hopi, 1540–1823."
Museum Notes 6, (No. 12):55–60. Flagstaff,
Ariz.: Museum of Northern Arizona, (June)
1934.

"Hopi History, No. 2. The Navajo Wars: 1823–
1870." *Museum Notes* 8, (No. 7) (Flagstaff,
Ariz.:) Museum of Northern Arizona, (Jan.)
1936.

Beaglehole, Ernest
Notes on Hopi Economic Life. Yale University
Publications in Anthropology 15. New Haven:
Yale University Press, 1936. 90 pp.

De Huff, Elizabeth Willis
Two Little Hopi. Illustrated by Gerald Cassidy.
New York, Chicago: Mentzner, Bush and Com-
pany, 1936. 224 pp., illus.
A story for young readers.

Dennis, Wayne
The Hopi Child. Monograph 26 of the Univer-
sity of Virginia. Institute for Research in the
Social Studies. New York: D. Appleton-Century
Company, 1940. 209 pp., illus.

Donaldson, Thomas
*The Moqui Indians of Arizona and Pueblo In-
dians of New Mexico.* Eleventh Census, U. S.
(Extra Census Bulletin). Washington, D. C.:
U. S. Gov't. Printing Office, 1893.

Federal Writers' Project
The Hopi. Federal Writers' Project, of the
Works Progress Adminstration for the State
of Arizona. *Arizona State Teacher's College,
Flagstaff Bulletin,* Vol. 18 (No. 2) (Sept.)
1937.

Fewkes, J. W.
"Hopi." *Bull. Bureau Amer. Ethnol.* 30 (Part
1):560–568, 1907.

"The Kinship of the Tusayan Villages." *AA*
7:394–418, 1894. o.s.

"The Sun's Influence on the Form of Hopi
Pueblos." *AA* 8:88–101, 1906. n.s.

"Tusayan Migration Traditions." *19th Annual
Report: Bureau of American Ethnology,* 1897–
1898, pp. 577–633. Washington, D. C.: U. S.
Gov't. Printing Office, 1900.
The Hopi pueblos, clans living or extinct in
Walpi and Sichumovi, chronological sequence
of the advent of clans, clans from Tokonabi,
religious societies at Walpi, etc.

Garland, Hamlin
"Among the Moqui Indians." *Harper's Weekly:*
August 15, 1896. Illustrated by Langren.

Hack, John T.
"The Changing Physical Environment of the
Hopi Indians of Arizona." *Reports of the Awa-
tovi Expedition,* Report No. 1. Papers of the
Peabody Museum of American Archaeology
and Ethnology, Harvard University, Vol. 35,
(No. 1), (Cambridge) 1942. 85 pp., illus.

Hargrave, Lyndon L.
"Sikyatki; Were the Inhabitants Hopi?" *Museum Notes* 9, (No. 12):63–66. Flagstaff, Ariz.:
Northern Arizona Society of Science and Art,
1937.

Hough, Walter
"The Hopi in Relation to their Plant Environment." *AA* 10:33–45, 1897. o.s.

The Hopi Indians. Little Histories of North
American Indians, No. 4. Cedar Rapids, Ia.:
The Torch Press, 1915.

Lowie, Robert H.
"Notes on Hopi Clans." *American Museum of
Natural History* (New York) *Anthropological
Papers* 30:303–360, 1929.

"Hopi Kinships." *American Museum of Natural
History* (New York) *Anthropological Papers*
30:361–388, 1929.

Mindeleff, Cosmos
"Localization of Tusayan Clans." *19th Annual
Report: Bureau of American Ethnology,* 1897–
1898, pp. 635–653, pls. XXI–XXVIII, 3 figs.
Washington, D. C.: U. S. Gov't Printing Office,
1900.

Navajo and Hopi Directory for Arizona.
Utah, and New Mexico, 1941.

Nelson, J. L.
Rhythm for Rain: the Drama and Ancient
Culture of the Hopi Indians. Boston: Hough-
ton Mifflin Company, 1937. 272 pp., illus.

Nequatewa, Edmund
Truth of a Hopi. Flagstaff, Arizona: Museum
of Northern Arizona, 1936. 113 pp.

Parsons, Elsie Clews
"Review: Notes on 'Hopi Clans and Hopi Kinship', by Robert H. Lowie." *AA* 33:232–236, 1931.

"Review: *The Hopi Child*, by Wayne Dennis." *JAFL* 54:221–223, 1941.

"Early Relations Between Hopi and Keres." *AA* 38:554–560, 1936. n.s.

Hopi Journal of Alexander M. Stephen. New York: Columbia University Press, 1936.
The work is devoted mainly to the towns of the first mesa: the Hopi Pueblo of Walpi, and the Tewa form of Ham. Excellent descriptive accounts of the major Hopi ceremonies, as well as information on other subjects.

Po-Lin-Gay-Si (Mrs. Elizabeth White)
The Sun Girl. Berkeley, Calif.: The Gillick Press, 1941.
(Juvenile) The story of a Hopi Indian child.

Rust, H. N.
"Through Arizona's Wonderland." *Inter Ocean* (Chicago): July 26, 1896.

Simmons, Leo W., ed.
Sun Chief: The Autobiography of a Hopi Indian. New Haven: Yale University Press, 1942. 460 pp.
"It is a comprehensive case history, reported in the first person, for those who are interested in the development of personality in relation to society and culture." (L. W. Simmons)

Smith, Dama Margaret
Hopi Girl. Stamford University, Cal.: Stamford University Press, 1931.

Stephen, Alexander MacGregor
"Hopi Indians of Arizona V." *Masterkey* 14, (No. 5):170–179. Los Angeles: Southwest Museum, 1940.

Hopi Journal, edited by Elsie Clews Parsons. New York: Columbia University Press, 1936. 2 vol., front. (port) illus., XXV col. plates, 12 fold. maps.

Thompson, Laura, and Joseph, Alice
The Hopi Way. Chicago: University of Chicago Press, 1945. 151 pp. tables, plates, bibl.
In some 35 pages, comprising the first part, one finds "the best available summary of the very voluminous and often quite involved literature on Hopi archaeology, history, social organization, and ceremonial life. The next part the 'journey from birth to death' sets the background for the special studies by sketching the development of the individual in Hopi culture—childhood, youth, adulthood and old age. The third and fourth parts contain the distinctive contribution of 'the Hopi Way.' The authors use the concepts and methods of educational and developmental psychology, but not of psychoanalysis. . . . The conclusion is that the Hopi way of life has a durable quality, a stable, organic interrelation of man,

nature and culture, that has enabled it to maintain its integrity in the past, despite a series of readjustments, and will presumably enable it to survive in the future in the face of economic, educational, and other acculturating influences." (Julian H. Steward)

Titiev, Mischa
Old Oraibi. Cambridge, Mass.: Peabody Museum of American Archaeology and Ethnology, Vol. XXII, No. 1. 1944. xi, 277 pp.
A study of the Hopi Indians of the Third Mesa.

Underhill, Ruth M.
First Penthouse Dwellers of America. New York: J. J. Augustin, 1938.

Voth, Henry R.
The Traditions of the Hopi. The Stanley McCormick Hopi Expedition. Chicago: 1905. vii, 319 pp. (Field Museum of Natural History. Publications No. 96.)

Yount, George C.
"A Sketch of the Hopi in 1942." *Masterkey* (Los Angeles) 16:193–199, 1942.

MYTHS—FOLKTALES—LEGENDS

Applegate, F. G.
Indian Stories from the Pueblos, foreword by Bynner, W., illustrations from original Pueblo Indian paintings. Philadelphia: J. B. Lippincott Company, 1929. 178 pp., illus.

De Huff, Mrs. Elizabeth (Willis)
Tatay's Memories, collected and retold. Illustrations by Fred Kabotie. New York: Harcourt, Brace and Company, 1924. ix, 255 pp., illus.

Taytay's Tales, illustrations by Fred Kabotie and Otis Poleolonema. New York: Harcourt, Brace and Company, 1922. xiii, 213 pp., illus.

Fewkes, J. W.
"A-wá-to-bi: An Archaeological Verification of a Tusayan Legend." *AA* 6:363–377, 1893. o.s.

"Hopi-Moquis Legend of the Snake Order." *JAFL* 1:109–114, 165, 1888; 5:246, 1892.

"Hopi Myths." *JAFL* 1:109–114, 1888; 8:132–137, 1895; 36: 163–170, 1923.

James, Harry Clebourne
Haliksai! A Book of Hopi Legends of the Grand Canyon Country as told to H. C. James. El Centro, Calif.: The Desert Magazine, 1940. 28 pp., illus.

McKee, Louise, and Summers, Richard
Dusty Desert Tales. Caldwell, Idaho: Caxton Printers, Ltd., 1941. 191 pp., illus.

Milford, Stanley J.
"Why the Coyote Has a Black Spot On His Tail." *El Palacio* 48, (No. 4):83–84, 1941.

Nequatewa, Edmund
Truth of a Hopi and the Clan Stories of Shungopovi. Museum of Northern Arizona, Bulletin 8. Flagstaff, Ariz.: Northern Arizona Society of Science and Art, 1936. 114 pp., illus.

Nusbaum, M. A. B.
"Another Tower of Babel." *El Palacio* 18 (No. 1) :9–12, 1925.

Parsons, Elsie Clews
"Origin Myth from Oraibi." *JAFL* 36:163–170, 1923.

Rollins, W. E.
"Story of the Sacred Stone." *El Palacio* 6, (No. 3) :37–39.

Stephen, Alexander
"Hopi Tales." *JAFL* 42:1–85, 1929.

"Legend of the Snake Order of the Moqui." *JAFL* 1:109–114, 165, 1888.

Titiev, Mischa
"The Story of Kokopele." *AA* 41:93, 1939, and footnote 10.
A Hopi tale.

"Two Hopi Myths and Rites." *JAFL* 61:31–43, 1948.
"— the present article is designed to demonstrate the likelihood that two other Hopi rites are in some degree dramatizations of myths."

"Two Hopi Tales from Oraibi." *Papers of the Michigan Academy of Science, Art and Letters* 29:425–437, 1943. Published 1944.

Wallis, Wilson D.
"Folk Tales from Shumopovi, Second Mesa." *JAFL* 49:1–68, 1936.
Also called Shongopovi, — "A Hopi pueblo of the middle mesa of Tusayan, N.E. Arizona, built probably about 1680." (Frederick W. Hodge)

————, and Titiev, Mischa
"Hopi Notes from Chimopovy." *Papers of the Michigan Academy of Science, Arts and Letters* 30:523–555, 1945. Illus.
Folk tales, pp. 547–553.

BELIEFS—CUSTOMS

Barrett, S. A.
"An Observation on Hopi Child Burial." *AA* 39:562–564, 1937. n.s.

Beaglehole, Ernest
Hopi Hunting and Hunting Ritual. Yale University Publications in Anthropology No. 4. New Haven: Yale University Press, 1936. 26 pp.
A discussion of the ritual that accompanies each stage of the hunting cycle.

Bourke, John G.
"The Snake Ceremonials at Walpi." *AA:* 8: 192–196, April, 1895.

Colton, Harold S.
A Brief Survey of Hopi Common Law. Museum Notes, No. 5. Flagstaff, Ariz.: (Dec.) 1934.

"Hopi Number Systems." *Plateau* 14 (No. 2) : 33–36, 1941.

De Huff, Elizabeth Willis
Five Little Katchinas. Illustrated by Fred Kabotie. Boston: Houghton Mifflin Company, 1930. iv, 86 pp., illus.

Fewkes, Jesse Walter
"A Comparison of Sia and Tusayan Snake Ceremonials." *AA* 8:118–142, 1895. o.s.

"A Study of Summer Ceremonials at Zuni and Moqui Pueblos." *Essex Institute Bulletin* 22, (Nos. 7–9), (Salem), 1890.

"A Theatrical Performance at Walpi." *Proceedings Washington Academy of Science* 2: 605–629, 1900.

"Ancestor Worship of Hopi Indians." *Smithsonian Report,* pp. 485–506, illus. Washington, D. C.: U. S. Government Printing Office, 1921.

"Destruction of the Tusayan Monsters." *JAFL* 8:132–137, 1895.

"Fire Worship of Hopi Indians." *Smithsonian Report,* pp. 589–610, illus. Washington, D. C.: U. S. Government Printing Office, 1920.

"Growth of the Hopi Ritual." *JAFL* 11:173–194, 1898.

"Hopi Ceremonial Frames from Cañon de Chelly, Arizona." *AA* 8:664–671, 1906. n.s.

"Hopi-Walpi Initiation Ceremony." *JAFL* 5:189–221, 1892.

"Interpretations of Katchina Worship." *JAFL* 14:81–94, 1901.

"Oraibi Flute Altar." *JAFL* 8:265–282, 1895.

"Property-Right in Eagles Among the Hopi." *AA* 2:690–708, 1900. n.s.

"Sacrificial Element in Hopi Worship." *JAFL* 10:187–201, 1897.

"Sky-God Personations in Hopi Worship." *JAFL* 15:14–32, 1902.

"Snake Ceremonies at Walpi." *Journal of American Ethnology and Archaeology,* (Boston and New York) 4:1–126, 1894.

"Sun Worship of Hopi Indians." *Smithsonian Report*, pp. 493–562, illus. Washington, D. C.: U. S. Government Printing Office, 1918.

"The Alósaka Cult of the Hopi." *AA* 1:522–545, 1899. n.s.

"The Butterfly in Hopi Myth and Ritual." *AA* 12:576–595, 1910. n.s.

"The Feather Symbol in Ancient Hopi Designs." *AA* 11:1–15, 1898. o.s.

"Hopi Snake Washing." *AA* 11:313–325, 1898. o.s.

"The Lesser New-Fire Ceremony at Walpi." *AA* 3 (No. 3):438–453, 1901. n.s.

"The Mam-zraú-ti: A Hopi Tusayan Ceremony." *AA* 5:217–247, 1892.

"The Mishongnovi Flute Altars." *JAFL* 9:241–255, 1896.

"The New-Fire Ceremony at Walpi." *AA* 2 (No. 1):80–138, 1900. n.s.

"The Oraibi White Altar." *JAFL* 8 (No. 31): 265–282, Oct.–Dec., 1895.

"The Owakü Hi Altar at Sichomovi Pueblo." *AA* 3:211–227, 1901. n.s.

"Tusayan Flute and Snake Ceremonies." *19th Annual Report: Bureau of American Ethnology*, pp. 853–955, 955–1011, fig. 23–41. Washington, D. C.: U. S. Government Printing Office, 1900.
See also the 16th Annual Report, 1894–1895, pp. 273–312.

"Tusayan Katcinas." *15th Annual Report: Bureau of American Ethnology*, 1893–1894, pp. 251–304, pls. CIV–CXI, figs. 39–48. Washington, D. C.: U. S. Gov't Printing Office, 1897.
Tabular view of the sequence of Tusayan celebrations, names of months and corresponding ceremonials, classification of ceremonials, Katcina dances in Cibola and Tusyan, etc.

"Tusayan Migration Traditions." *U. S. Bureau of Ethnology. 19th Annual Report*, pp. 573–633, 1897–98. In two parts—part 2. Washington, D. C.: U. S. Gov't Printing Office, 1900.

"Tusayan Totemic Signatures." *AA* 10:1–13, 1897. o.s.

"Use of Idols in Hopi Worship." *Smithsonian Report*, pp. 377–397. Washington, D. C.: U. S. Government Printing Office, 1922.

"Walpi Flute Observance." *JAFL* 7:265–287, 1896.

———, and Stephen, A. M.
"Pá-lü-koñ-ti: a Tusayan Ceremony." *JAFL* 5: 189–221, 1892.

"Na-áo-nai-ya: a Tusayan Initiation Ceremony." *JAFL* 5:189–221, 1892.

Forde, C. D.
"Hopi Agriculture and Land Ownership." *Journal of Royal Anthropological Institute* (London) 61:357–406, 1931.

"Hideous Rites."
Globe (Utica): Oct. 10, 1896.

"Hopi Ceremonial Circuit."
JAFL 5:33–42, 1892.

"Hopi Ceremonies."
JAFL 4:129–138, 1891; 5:33–42, 188–221, 1892; 6:269–284, 1893; 7:265–287, 1894; 11: 173–194, 1898.

"Hopi, Moquis Legend of the Snake Order."
JAFL 1:109–114, 165, 1888; 5:246, 1892.

Hough, Walter
"A Collection of Hopi Ceremonial Pigments." *Report of the U. S. National Museum*, pp. 463–471. Washington, D. C.: U. S. Government Printing Office, 1900 (1902).

Jenkins, C. Francis
"The Moki Bread." *Popular Science* (New York), pp. 6, (Jan.) 1900.

Kennard, E. A.
"Hopi Reactions to Death." *AA* 39:491–496, 1937. n.s.

Parsons, Elsie Clews
"A Hopi Ceremonial." *Century* 101:177–180, 1920.

"Hopi Mothers and Children." *Man* (London) 21:98–104, 1921.

"The Hopi Wöwöchim Ceremony in 1920." *AA* 25:156–187, 1923.

"Hopi and Zuni Ceremonialism." *Memoir of the American Anthropological Association*, No. 39. 1933.

Senter, D., and Hawley, F.
"Hopi and Navaho Child Burials." *AA* 39:131–134, 1937. n.s.

Steward, J. H.
"Notes on Hopi Ceremonies in their Initiatory Form in 1927–1928." *AA* 35:56–79, 1933. n.s.

Titiev, Mischa
"A Hopi Visit to the Afterworld." *Papers, Michigan Academy of Arts and Letters,* (Ann Arbor) 24:495–564, 1941.

———.
"Hopi Snake Handling." *The Scientific Monthly* 57:44–51, 1943.

———.
"The Problem of Cross-Cousin Marriage Among the Hopi." *AA* 40:105–111, 1938. n.s.

———.
"The Use of Kinship Terms in Hopi Ritual." *Museum Notes* 10, (No. 3):9–11. Flagstaff, Ariz.: Northern Arizona Society of Science and Art, 1937.

Voth, H. R.
"Oraibi Marriage Customs." *AA* 2:238–247, 1900.

———.
"The Oraibi Oáqöl Ceremony." *Field Columbian Museum, Anthropological Series* 6:1–46, 1903.

———.
"The Oraibi Powamu Ceremony." *Field Columbian Museum,* Publication No. 61. Anthropology Series Vol. III, (No. 2). The Stanley McCormick Hopi Expedition, Chicago, 1901. 97 pp., 37 plates.

———.
"Oraibi Summer Snake Ceremony." Field Museum of Natural History. *Anthropol. Papers,* No. 3. Chicago: The Museum, 1902.

Whiting, Alfred F.
"Hopi Indian Agriculture. I: Background." *Museum Notes,* Flagstaff, Ariz.: 8, (No. 10): 51–53, 1936.

———.
"Hopi Indian Agriculture. II: Seed Source and Distribution." *Museum Notes, Museum of Northern Arizona* 10, (No. 5):13–16, 1937.

FOLK MEDICINE

Coleman, G. E.
Rattlesnake Venom Antidote of the Hopi Indians. Bulletin of the Antovenin Institute of America, Vol. 1, (Jan.) 1928. Glenolden, Pa.: 1928.

MacLeish, Kenneth
"Notes on Folk Medicine in the Hopi Village of Moenkopi." *JAFL* 56:62–68, 1943.

Rollins, W. E.
"The Medicine of Machetto." *El Palacio* 11, (No. 11):144–147.

FOLK ART

Earle, Edwin
Hopi Kachinas. New York: J. J. Augustin, 1938. 40 pp., 28 col. pl.

Fewkes, Jesse Walter
"Casa Grande, Arizona." In: *28th Annual Report: Bureau of American Ethnology, 1906–1907.* pp. 25–180, pls. 1–78, figs. 1–54. Washington, D. C.: U. S. Gov't Printing Office, 1912.
It would seem more probable that these remains are due to some of the clans of the present Hopi or Zuni Pueblos, one at least of the former tribe tracing its origin to the "land of the giant cactus." (Frederick W. Hodge)

———.
"Designs on Prehistoric Hopi Pattern." *33rd Annual Report: Bureau of American Ethnology, 1911–1912,* pp. 215–284, pls. 76–90, figs. 12–112. Washington, D. C.: U. S. Government Printing Office, 1919.

———.
"Hopi Katchinas." Drawn by native artists. *21st Annual Report, Bureau of American Ethnology,* 1899–1900, pp. 13–126, pls. 2–63. Washington, D. C.: U. S. Gov't Printing Office, 1903.

———.
"The Feather Symbol in Ancient Hopi Designs." *AA* 11:1–15, 1898. o.s.

Lockett, Hattie Green
"The Unwritten Literature of the Hopi." *University of Arizona,* Bulletin 4, (No. 4): Tucson: University of Arizona, 1933. 101 pp.

Mindeleff, Cosmos
"Casa Grande Ruin." *13th Annual Report: Bureau of American Ethnology, 1891–1892,* pp. 295–318, figs. 328–330, pls. 52–60, 1 map. Washington, D. C.: U. S. Government Printing Office, 1896.
Location and character, history and literature, description, etc.

GAMES

Watkins, Frances E.
"Indians at Play; I: Hopi Parchesi." *Masterkey* 18:139–141, 1944.
Description of a game from the Hopi Indian pueblo of Oraibi.

MUSIC

GENERAL STUDIES

Curtis, Natalie
"An American Indian Composer." *Harper's Magazine* 107:626–632, 1903.
With music of the Hopi Indians.

Fewkes, Jesse Walter
"The Oraibi Flute Altar." *JAFL* 8:265–282, 1895.

———.
"Tusayan Flute and Snake Ceremonies." *19th Annual Report: Bureau of American Ethnology,* (part 2):957–1011. Washington, D. C.: U. S. Government Printing Office, 1902.

Gilman, Benjamin I.
Hopi Songs. Journal of American Ethnology and Archaeology 5, 1908. 226 pp.

Hough, Walter
"Music of the Hopi Flute Ceremony." In: *The Hopi in Relation to Their Plant Environment*, pp. 45–46. *AA* 10:33–46, 1897.

MacLeish, Kenneth
"A Few Hopi Songs from Moenkopi." *Masterkey* 15, (No. 5):178–184. Los Angeles: Southwest Museum, 1941.

Stephen, Alexander MacGregor
"Hopi Indians of Arizona." *Masterkey* 13 (No. 6):197–204, 1939; 14 (No. 1):3–6, 20, 102, 143, 170, 207, 1940.
  Many references to music and musical instruments and dances (Snake Dance).

Voth, Henry R.
Brief Miscellaneous Hopi Papers. The Stanley McCormick Hopi Expeditions, Chicago, 1912. Field Columbian Museum, Publications 157, *Anthropological Series* 7, (No. 2).

———

"Powamu Ceremony." The Stanley McCormick Hopi Expedition. *Field Museum Publications 61* (Chicago), *Anthropological Series*, Vol. 3 (No. 2), 1901.

DANCES

"A Moqui Snake Dance."
Bulletin (San Francisco): Sept. 3, 1895.
Evening Sun (Baltimore): Sept. 14, 1895.

"Amid Ancient Moqui Ruins." The Famous Snake Dance. *Times* (Washington): Sept. 28, 1896.

"An Indian Snake Dance."
Register (New Haven): Sept. 22, 1895.

Anonymous
"The Snake Dance of the Moqui Indians; a religious drama and a prayer for rain." *Times-Herald* (Chicago): Oct. 13, 1895.

Baxter, Rupert H.
"The Moqui Snake Dance." *Amer. Antiquarian* 17:205–207, 1895.
  A description, without music.

Beckwith, M. W.
"Dance Forms of the Moquis and Kwakiutl Indians." *Proceedings of the 15th Session of the International Congress of Americanists* (Quebec), 2:79–114, 1907.

Bourke, John Gregory
The Snake-Dance of the Moquis of Arizona; being a narrative of a journey from Santa Fe, New Mexico to the villages of the Moqui Indians of Arizona, with a description of the manners and customs, and especially of the revolting religious rite, the snake-dance; to which is added a brief dissertation upon serpent-worship in general, with an account of the tablet dance of the Pueblo of Santo Domingo,

New Mexico. New York: Charles Scribner's Sons, 1884. xiv, 371 pp., illus.

Carnac, Levin
"The Snake-Dance of Arizona." *Pearson's Magazine* 8:324–328, 1899.
  A description, without music.

Coe, Curtis P.
"Moqui Snake Dance." *Moqui Mission Messenger* 1 (Nos. 8, 9).

Collier, F. B. M.
"The Rattlesnake Dance." *Dancing Times* (London), pp. 27–28 (Oct.) 1938. Illus.

De Huff, Elizabeth Willis
Five Little Katchinas. Illustrations by Fred Kabotie. Boston: Houghton Mifflin Company, 1930. iv, 86 pp., col. front., col. illus.

Dorsey, G. A.
"Mishongnovi Antelope, Snake Ceremonies." *Nature* (London) 58:111–113, 1903.

Earle, Edwin
Hopi Kachinas. New York: J. J. Augustin, 1938. 40 pp., 28 col. pl.

Fewkes, Jesse Walter
"A Comparison of Sia and Tusayan Snake Ceremonies." *AA* (No. 2): April, 1895.

———

"Hopi Basket Dances." *JAFL* 12:81–96, 1899.

———

"Hopi Katcinas." Drawn by native artists. *21st Annual Report: Bureau of American Ethnology*, 1899–1900, pp. 13–126, pls. 2–63. Washington, D. C.: U. S. Government Printing Office, 1903.

———

"Minor Hopi Festivals." *AA* 4:482–564, 1904. n.s.

———

"The Walpi Flute Observance." A study of primitive dramatization. *JAFL* 7:275–287, 1894.

———

"Tusayan Flute and Snake Ceremonies." *19th Annual Report: Bureau of American Ethnology*, 1897–1898, pp. 957–1011, pls. XLV–LXV, figs. 42–46. Washington, D. C.: U. S. Gov't Printing Office, 1900.
  Snake dance at Mishongnovi in 1897, snake dance at Walpi in 1897, snake whips, washing the reptiles, public antelope and snake dances, flute ceremony at Mishongnovi in 1897, etc.

———

"Tusayan Katchinas." *15th Annual Report, Bureau of American Ethnology*, 1893–1894, pp. 251–304. Illus. Washington, D. C.: U. S. Gov't Printing Office, 1897.

———

"Tusayan Snake Ceremonies." *16th Annual Report: Bureau of American Ethnology*, 1894–1895, pp. 273–312, pls. LXX–LXXXI. Washington, D. C.: U. S. Gov't Printing Office, 1897.
  The Cipaulori snake ceremony, antelope altar, snake race, totokya, snake dance, etc. The Cunopari snake ceremony, the Oraibi snake ceremony, etc.

————, and Owen, J. G.
"The Là-là-Kŏn-ta: A Tusayan Dance." *AA* 5: 105–131, 1892.

Forrest, Karl R.
"The Hopi Flute Dance." *Archaeological Bulletin* (Madison, Ind.) 4:33–39, 1916.

"Hideous Rites."
Globe (Utica): Oct. 10, 1896.

"Hopi Dances."
JAFL 4:129–138, 1891; 12:81–96, 1899.

"Hopi Katchina Worship."
JAFL 14:81–94, 1901.

Hough, Walter
Snake Dance. In: *Handbook of American Indians*. Vol. II, pp. 604–606. Bibl. Bureau of American Ethnology, Bulletin 30. Washington, D. C.: U. S. Government Printing Office, 1910.

James, George W.
"The Hopi Snake Dance." *Outlook* (No. 36): 302–310, (June) 1900.

Klauber, L. M.
A Herpetological Review of the Hopi Snake Dance. Zoological Society of San Diego, Bulletin 9, (Jan. 25) 1932. 92 pp.

Masillon, C.
"Les Indians Moki et leur danse de serpent." *Nature* (Paris): vol. 24, 1896.
Moki snake dance.

McLaughlin, Ruth
"The Hopi Snake Dance." *Overland Monthly* (San Francisco) 64:419–426, 1914. Illus.

Mindeleff, Cosmos
"Ghost Dance." *Scientific American* (New York), Supp. 46: 19071–19074, 1898.

Momsen, Frederick
"Festivals of the Hopi: Religion, the inspiration, and dancing an expression in all their national ceremonies." *The Craftsman*, (No. 12):269–286, (June) 1907.

Monroe, Harriet
"To the Snake Dance." *Fortnightly Review*, (No. 84):665–678, (Oct.) 1905.

"Moqui Snake Dances."
Scimitar (Memphis): Oct. 21, 1896.

Nelson, John L.
Rhythm for Rain. Boston: Houghton, Mifflin Co., 1937. 272 pp., 54 pl.

Oliver, M. L.
"The Snake Dance." *National Geographic Magazine* (Washington) 22:107–137, 1911. Illus.

Parsons, Elsie Clews
"The Hopi Buffalo Dance." *Man* 23:21–26, 1923.

Politzer, J. H.
"Among the Moquis." *Daily Traveller* (Boston): Nov. 7, 1894.
Describes Oraibi snake dance.

————.
"Mouthfuls of Rattlesnakes." *Examiner* (San Francisco): Oct. 21, 1894.

————.
"Snake Dance of the Moqui." *Herald* (New York): Nov. 11, 1894.

————.
"The Moqui Serpent Dance." *Republic* (St. Louis): Nov. 7, 1894.

Roosevelt, Theodore
"The Hopi Snake Dance." *Outlook*, (No. 105): 365–374, (Oct.) 1913. Illus.

Rust, H. N.
"The Moqui Snake Dance." *Land of Sunshine* (Los Angeles): Jan., 1896.
Illustrated account of Walpi Snake Dance of 1895.

Sheldon, Charles M.
"The Hopi Snake Dance." *Independent*, (No. 57):1026–1031, (Nov.) 1933.

"Snake Dance of the Moquis of Arizona."
JAFL 1:165, 1888; 4:129, 1891.

"Snake Dance Secret Bared."
Scientific American 156:237, 1937. Illus.

Stephen, A. M.
"Clowns in Hopi Ceremonial Dances." *Nature* 139:888, (May 22) 1937.

Stirling, M. W.
"Snake Bites and the Hopi Snake Dance." *Annual Report of the Smithsonian Institution*, pp. 551–555. *Smithsonian Publication 3651*. Washington, D. C.: U. S. Government Printing Office, 1942.

"The Moquis Snake Dances."
Sun (New York): Oct. 4, 1896.

"The Snake Dance."
Journal (Boston): Aug. 28, 1895.

Teters, Sue Ellen
"The Moqui Snake Dance." *Godey's Magazine* 127–565–568, June, 1896.
An account of the annual rattlesnake worship in the Southwest, with illustrations.

Townshend, R. B.
"The Snake Dancers of Mishongnovi." *Nineteenth Century* (London) 429–443, 1904.

"Weird Arizona Snake Dance."
Evening Gazette (Boston): Oct. 10, 1896. Reprinted from the World, N. Y.

"With the Snake Dancers."
Call (San Francisco): Jan. 31, 1896.

ARRANGEMENTS

—————: *Voice and Piano*

"Grinding Song"
Lemher, D. N.: Author: voice, piano and flute.

"Hopi Indian Cradle Song"
Guion, D.: Boosey and Company. Text by Louis Untermeyer.
An idealized version of a Hopi melody.

"The Scalp Dance"
Loomis, H. W.: Ditson. Voice and Piano·

—————: *Choral*

"Hopi Indian Cradle Song"
Guion, D.: Boosey and Company: SSA

"Hopi Indian Cradle Song"
Guion, D.: Boosey and Company: TTBB.

"Hopi Indian Cradle Song"
Guion, D.: Boosey and Company: SATB.

"Hopi Indian Dance—Op. 16, No. 2."
Grunn, H.: Ditson: SATB.

—————: *Piano*

"Moqui Indian Dance"
Bilbro, M.: Schirmer: piano (8 hands)

RECORDS

"American Indian Songs"
Hopi Chanters   VI–20093

"Butterfly Dance"
Victor Dance Orchestra   VI–22174

"Chant of the Eagle Dancers"
Hopi Indian Chanters   VI–20043

"Chant of the Snake Dancers"
Hopi Indian Chanters.   VI–20043

"Chant of the Snake Dancers"
Hopi Indian Chanters   VI–500A — VI–20043

"Mudhead Kachina"
Recorded by Laura Boulton. In: *Indian Music of the Southwest*   Set V–P49

NAVAHO

FOLKLORE

BIBLIOGRAPHY

Kluckhohn, Clyde, and Spencer, Katharine
A Bibliography of the Navaho Indians. New York: J. J. Augustin, 1940. xiv, 93 pp.

Navajo and Hopi Directory for Arizona, Utah, New Mexico. 1941.

GENERAL STUDIES

Armer, Mrs. Laura (Adams)
The Traders' Children; With illustrations from photographs by the author; decorations by Sidney Armer. New York: Longmans, Green & Co., 1937. ix, 241 pp.

Backus, E.
An Account of the Navajoes of New Mexico. In: Schoolcraft—*Information Respecting the History, Condition and Prospects of the Indian Tribes of the United States,* part iv, (pp. 209–215). Philadelphia: Lippincott, Grambo and Co., 1854.

Bartlett, Katherine
"Hopi History, No. 2. The Navajo Wars—1823–1870." *Museum Notes 8,* (No. 7) :33–37, *Museum of Northern Arizona,* (Jan.) 1936.

Bourke, J. G.
"Navaho Gentes." *JAFL* 3:102, 1890.

Coolidge, Dane
Under the Sun: A Novel of the Navajo Exile in 1863–1868. New York: E. P. Dutton and Company, 1927.

—————, and Coolidge, Mary Roberts
The Navajo Indians. Boston: Houghton Mifflin Company, 1930. 316 pp., illus. bibl.
Gives text of many songs, but no music.

Dyk, Walter
Son of Old Man Hat, a Navaho Autobiography. New York: Harcourt, Brace and Company, 1938. 378 pp.

Elim, Zay
"A Night With the Navajos." *Forest and Stream* 23:282–283, (New York, November 6) 1884.

Evans, Trader
"The Navaho." Federal Writers' Project, nison, Colo.) 1 (No. 1) :10–16, (June) 1935.

Farmer, Malcolm F.
"The Growth of Navaho Culture." *San Diego Museum Bulletin* 4, (No. 1) :8–16, 1941.

Federal Writers' Project.
"The Navaho." Federal Writer's Project, W. P. A. of the State of Arizona. *Arizona State Teachers College, Flagstaff Bulletin* 18, (No. 4), 1937.

Fergusson, Erna
"Navajos: Whose Problem?" *New Mexico Quarterly Review* 18:25, Spring, 1948.

Fitzpatrick, George
"Fall and Rise of the Navajo." *Rotarian* 70:33–35, March, 1947.

Gillmore, Frances, and Wetherell, Louise Wade
Traders to the Navajos. Boston: Houghton Mifflin Co., 1934. 265 pp.
"A book both realistic and sympathetic." (Dobie)

Goddard, Pliny Earle
"Navajo Texts." *American Museum of Natural History, Anthropological Papers* 34, 1933. 179 pp.

Gregory, Herbert E.
The Navajo Country, 1916. A geographic and hydrographic reconnaissance of parts of Arizona. New Mexico and Utah: U. S. Geological Survey, 1916. bibl.

Hargrave, Lyndon L.
"The Tsegi Country (Arizona)." *Museum Notes* 6, No. 11. Flagstaff, Ariz.: Northern Arizona Society of Science and Art, May 1934. "A canyon on the Navaho reservation, Northeast Arizona in which are numerous ancient cliff-dwellings."

Hassell, Sanford W.
"A Trader Views the Navaho." *El Palacio* 48: 146–147, 1941.

Hayes, Florence
Hosh-Ki, the Navajo. New York: Random House, 1943. 250 pp.
A juvenile story of a Navajo Indian boy of today. "The Indians' own ways and thought are so well portrayed that nine to twelve year-old readers will fully grasp Hosh-Ki's first fear and bewilderment, while they will learn too, much about a life which has its own dignity." (Ellen Lewis Buell)

Hill, Faith, and Rice, Mabel F.
Ashkee of Sunshine Water, a Navaho Indian boy. Illustrated by Bull Ulreich. Evanston, Ill.: Row, Peterson and Co., 1941. 39 pp., illus.
A work of fiction utlizing folk lore.

Hill, W. W.
"Some Aspects of Navajo Political Structure." *Plateau* (Flagstaff) 13, (No. 2):23–28, 1940.

Hodge, F. Webb
"The Early Navajo and Apache." *AA* 8:22 3–241, 1895. o.s.

Hogner, D. C.
Navajo Winter Nights. New York: Thomas Nelson and Sons, 1938. xii, 180 pp.

Hollister, U. S.
The Navajo and His Blanket. Denver, Colo.: Roy, 1903. 144 pp., 10 col. pl., 25 fig. and pl.

Hulsizer, Allan
Region and Culture in the Curriculum of the Navaho and Dakota. Federalsburg, Va.: J. W. Stowell, 1940. xxv, 334 pp.

Keur, Dorothy Louise
Big Bear Mesa; An Archaeological Study of Navaho Acculturation 1745–1812. Memoir of the Society of American Archaeology No. 1. Menasha, Wisc.: 1941.

Kimball, Solon T., and Provinse, John H.
"Navajo Social Organization in Land Use Planning." *Applied Anthropology* 1:18–25, 1942.

Kimball, Spencer W.
"The Navajo — His Predicament." *Improvement Era* 51: Feb., March, and April, 1948.

Kluckhohn, Clyde
"A Navaho Personal Document with a Brief Paretian Analysis." *Southwestern Journal of Anthropology* 1 (No. 2):260–283, 1945.

————.
Patterning as Exemplified in Navaho Culture. In: *Language, Culture and Personality* edited by Leslie Spier. Menasha, Wisconsin: Sapir Memorial Publication Fund, 1941.

————, and Leighton, Dorothea
The Navaho. Cambridge, Mass.: Harvard University Press, 1946. 258 pp.

La Farge, Oliver
As Long as the Grass Shall Grow. New York: Alliance Book Corporation, 1940. 140 pp., illus.

————.
Laughing Boy. Boston: Houghton Mifflin Company, 1929. viii, 302 pp.
"The Navajo in fiction." (Dobie)

Lauritzen, Jonreed
Arrows in the Sun. New York: Alfred A. Knopf, 1943. 311 pp.
A novel set against the background of Navajo hunting grounds, Mormon pioneers and vignettes of the west.

Leighton, Alenander H. and Dorothea C., M. D.
"Some Types of Uneasiness and Fear in a Navaho Indian Community." *AA* 44, (No. 2): 194–210, 1942.

————.
The Navaho Door. Cambridge, Mass.: Harvard University Press, 1944. 149 pp., illus.
"The discussion of the importance of careful selection and training of an interpreter, of the method of working with one, of their patterning of linguistic expression, and the concrete examples of conversations with patients, couched in 'interpreter English,' are useful for anyone who has to approach a native through an interpreter. It is here that the folk-lorist will find hints of practical value in field work." (Leland C. Wyman)

Letherman, Jonathan
Sketch of the Navajo Tribe of Indians, New Mexico. Smithsonian Institution Report, 1855.

Lipps, Oscar Hiram
A Little History of the Navajos. Cedar Rapids: The Torch Press, 1909. 136 pp., illus.

————.
"The Evolution of the Navaho and His Blanket." *So. Workman* 35:14–24, 1906.

Long, Haniel
Piñon Country (American Folkways Series.) New York: Duell, Sloan and Pearce, 1941.
Discusses among other interesting items the Navajo and Pueblos.

Luomala, Katherine
Navaho Life of Yesterday and Today. Berkeley, Calif.: National Park Service, 1938. 115 pp.

Matthews, Washington
"The Gentile System of the Navajo Indian." *JAFL* 3(No. 9):89–110, 1890.

——.
"Navaho." *Bull. Bureau Amer. Ethnol.* 30 (Part 2):41–45, 1910.

Means, Florence C.
The Navajos. Illustrated by Lorence Bjorklund. Boston: Houghton Mifflin Company, 1942. 227 pp.
A finely wrought story for young readers.

Newton, E. E.
"Impressions of the Navahos." *So. Workman* 34:600–615, 1905.

Ostermann, L.
"The Navajo Indians of New Mexico and Arizona." *Anthropos* (Wien) 3:857–869, 1908.

Pepper, G. H.
"The Navaho." *So. Workman* 29:639–644, 1900.

Reichard, Gladys A.
Dezba, Woman of the Desert, with 56 photographs, by Lillian J. Reichard. New York: J. J. Augustin, 1939. 161 pp.

——.
Social Life of the Navajo Indians, with some Attention to Minor Ceremonies. Columbia University Contributions to Anthropology, 7. New York: Columbia University Press, 1928. vii, 239 pp., illus.

——.
Spider Woman. A Story of Navajo Weavers and Chanters. New York: Macmillan Company, 1934. 287 pp., illus.

Sapir, Edward
Navaho Texts. With Supplementary Texts by Harry Hoijer. Edited by Harry Hoijer. William Dwight Whitney Linguistic Series, No. 8. Iowa City, Ia.: Published by Yale University for the Linguistic Society of America, 1942. 543 pp.

Schultz, J. W.
A Son of the Navahoes. Boston: Houghton Mifflin Co., 1927. 200 pp.
Fiction.

Simpson, Lieut. James H.
Journal of a Military Reconaissance from Santa Fe, New Mexico to the Navajo Country in 1849. Philadelphia: Lippincott, Grambo and Company, 1852. 140 pp., illus., 75 pl. (part. col. incl. front., ports.) fold. map.

Steele, J. N.
"Navajo Notes." *Assembly Herald* (Phila.) 15: 71–75, 1909.

Stephen, A. M.
"The Navajo." *AA* 6:345–363, 1893. o.s.

Sullivan, Belle Shafer
The Unvanishing Navajos. Philadelhia: Dorrance and Company, 1938. 141 pp.

Telford, Emma P.
"Among the Navahos." *So. Workman* 32:329–335, 1903.

Underhill, Ruth
"Men with Ears Down to Their Ankles: A Chapter in Navajo History." *New Mexico Quarterly Review* 18:39, Spring, 1948.

Watkins, Frances E.
"The Navaho." *Masterkey* 17:77–81, 1943. (Southwest Museum Leaflets 17. Los Angeles.)

——.
"Navaho Indians, I." *The Masterkey* 16:109–118, (July) 1942.

——.
"The Navaho, II, III." *Masterkey,* (Los Angeles) 16:149, 156, 210, 214, 1942.

Weber, Anselm O. F. M.
The Navajo Indians: a Statement of Facts. Saint Michaels, Ariz.: 1914. 29 pp.

Wyman, Leland C., and Bailey, Flora L.
"Idea and Action Patterns in Navaho Flintway." *Southwestern Journal of Anthropology* 1:357, 1935.

Yanh-na-ba (Elma Smith)
"Navajo Sketches." *TFSP* 15:142–145, 1939.

MYTHS—FOLKTALES—LEGENDS

Aberle, David F.
"Mythology of the Navaho Stick-Dice." *JAFL* 55:144–155, 1942.

Boas, Franz
"Northern Elements in the Mythology of the Navaho." *AA* 10:371–376, 1897. o.s.

Buxton, L. H. Dudley
"Some Navajo Folktales and Customs." *Folk-Lore* (London) 34:239–313, 1923.

Cassidy, Perlina (Sizer) Davis
How Fire was Brought to the Navajo Indians; as told by Chee Nez, the medicine man, and retold by Ina Sizer Cassidy; etchings by Gerald Cassidy. Vienna: Sesame Pub. Co., 1927. 15 pp., illus.

Chapin, Gretchen
"A Navajo Myth from the Chaco Canyon." *New Mexico Anthropologist* 4, (No. 4):63–67, 1940.

Cotten, C. C.
Reelfoot; or, Indian Blankets and Blue Bonnets in Story and Drama; a symphony of words in red and white and blue. Abilene, Tex.: Abilene Printing & Stationery Co., 1936. 81 pp., illus.

"Day and Night, Navaho Tradition." *JAFL* 3:31, 1890.

De Huff, Elizabeth Willis
"Navajo Creation Myths." TFSP 14:127–144, 1938.

Doxbury, William Crocker
"A Legend of the Navajo." *The Cosmopolitan*, pp. 73, (Nov.) 1896.

Gillmore, Frances, and Wetherill, L. W.
Traders to the Navajos; the story of the Wetherills of Kayenta. Boston: Houghton Mifflin Company, 1934. 265 pp., bibl. (pp. 257–260).

Goddard, Pliny Earle, ed.
"Navaho Myths, Prayers and Songs, with Texts and Translations, by Washington Matthews." *University of California Publications in American Archaeology and Ethnology*, 5, (No. 2): 21–63, (no tunes). Berkeley: The University Press, 1907.

Haile, Berard
Origin Legend of the Navaho Enemy Way: Text and Translation. Yale University Publications in Anthropology 17. New Haven: Yale University Press, 1938. 320 pp. Illus.

_____.
Origin Legend of the Navaho Flintway; Text and Translation. Publications in Anthropology, Linguistic Series. Chicago: University of Chicago Press, 1943. xi, 319 pp., 8 drawings.

Hill, W. W., and Dorothy W.
"Navaho Coyote Tales and Their Position in the Southern Athabascan Group." *JAFL* 58: 317–343, 1945. bibl.

_____.
Navaho Humor. General Series in Anthropology (Menasha) 9, 1943. 28 pp.

King, Jeff (Medicine Man)
Where the Two Came to their Father; A Navaho War Ceremonial. Given by Jeff King. Text and paintings recorded by Maud Oakes, commentary by Joseph Campbell. With portfolio of eighteen paintings. The Bollingen Series I. New York: Pantheon Books, 1943. 84 pp.

The ceremonial text is essentially the creation myth—despite the subtitle. This particular myth is more of a blessing ceremony than a war ceremony.

Klah, Hasteen
Navajo Creation Myth; the story of the emergence; recorded by Mary C. Wheelright. Sante Fe, New Mexico: Museum of Navajo Ceremonial Art, 1942. 239 pp., illus. Navajo Religion Series, Vol. I.

Matthews, Washington
"A Part of the Navajo Mythology." *American Antiquarian* 5 (no. 3):207–224, 1883.

_____.
"Mythic dry-painting of the Navajos." *American Naturalist* 19(no. 10):931–939, 1885.

_____.
Navaho Legends. With introduction, notes, illustrations, texts interlinear translations, and melodies. Memoirs of the American Folklore Society, vol. 5. Boston: Houghton Mifflin and Company, 1897. 299 pp., illus., map, music, bibl.

_____.
Navajo Myths, Prayers, and Songs, with Text and Translations, edited by Pliny Earl Goddard. University of California Publications in American Arachaeology and Ethnology, Vol 5. 63 pp. Berkeley: University Press, 1907.

_____.
"Navajo Rite-Myths." *JAFL* 7:249–250, 1894.

_____.
"Noquoilpi, the gambler: A Navajo Myth." *JAFL* 2(no. 2):89–94, 1889.

_____.
"Part of Navajo Mythology." *American Antiquarian* 5, (No. 3): 207–224, 1883.

_____.
"Some Deities and Demons of the Navajos." *American Naturalist* 20:841–850, 1886.

_____.
Some Illustrations of the Connections Between Myth and Ceremony. Memoirs of the International Congress of Anthropology (Chicago) 1894. pp. 246–251.

_____.
"The Mountain Chant: A Navajo Ceremony." *5th Annual Report: Bureau of Ethnology*, 1883–1884, pp. 385–467, pls. 10–18, figs. 50–59. Washington, D. C.: U. S. Gov't. Printing Office, 1887.

Myths, ceremonies, original texts and translations of songs, dances, etc.

_____.
The Night Chant. A Navaho Ceremony. Edited by Pliny Earl Goddard. Memoirs of the American Museum of Natural History (New York), Vol. VI, Anthropology Vol. V. Publication of the Hyde Southwestern Expedition, 1902. 332 pp., 8 plates, **9 figs.**

_____.
"The Origin of the Utes, a Navajo Myth." *American Antiquarian* 7:271–274, 1885.

Morgan, William
Human-Wolves Among the Navajo. London: Oxford University Press, 1936. 43 pp. (Yale University Publications in Anthropology, No. 11).

_____.
"The Organization of a Story and Tale." with a preface by Alfred North Whitehead. *JAFL* 58:169–194, 1945.

Newcomb, Franc Johnson
"Origin Legend of the Navajo Eagle Chant." *JAFL* 53: 50–77, 1940.

Newell, W. W.
"Navajo Legend." *JAFL* 9:211–218, 1896.

Oakes, Maud
Where Two Came to Their Father: A Navaho War Ceremonial. Bollingen Series I. New York: Pantheon Books, 1943. 100 pp., 18 pls. in color.

Packard, R. L.
"A Navaho Myth." *Transactions of the Anthropological Society of Washington* 1:84, 1882 (Washington, D. C.)

Parsons, Elsie Clews
"Navajo Folk Tales." *JAFL* 36:368–375, 1923.

Pepper, G. H.
"Ah-jih-lee-hah-heh, A Navajo Legend." *JAFL* 21:178–183, 1908.

Pousma, Richard H.
He-Who-Always-Wins, and other Navajo Campfire stories. Grand Rapids, Michigan: W. B. Eerdmans Publishing Co., 1934. 147 pp.

Reichard, Gladys A.
"Individualism and Mythological Style." *JAFL* 57:16–26, 1944.
> The author suggests thru the study of Navaho ritual how the internal evidence of myth furnishes clues to the individual character of the narrator, and reciprocally, how his control of the ritualistic medium affects his own literary treatment.

————.
"Good Character in Myth: The Navaho Sun God." *JAFL* 56:141–143, 1943.

————.
Myth of the Chant-of-Waning-Endurance Text, Manuscript. (Columbia University, N. Y.)

————.
Myth of the Male Shooting Chant Evil Text, Manuscript. (Columbia University, N. Y.)

————.
Navajo Medicine Man; Sandpaintings and Legends of Miguelito. New York: J. J. Augustin, 1939. xvi, 83 pp., illus.

————.
The Legend of the Big Star Chant. Text, Manuscript. (Columbia University, N. Y.).

Richardson, Toney
"Trees That Died of Fear." *Desert Magazine* 10:19–21, March, 1947.
> The Indian story of the dead trees in the Navajo country.

Schevill, Margaret Erwin
In the Garden of the Home God. A Retelling of a Navajo Tale. Plates by Louie Ewing after drawings of the author. Santa Fe, N. M.: Santa Fe Press, 1944. 25 pp. illus.

Spencer, Katherine
Reflection of Social Life in the Navaho Origin Myth. University of New Mexico Publications in Anthropology, No. 3. Albuquerque, New Mexico, 1947. 140 pp., bibl.

Stephen, A. M.
"Navajo Origin Legend." *JAFL* 43:88–105, 1930.

Valkenburgh, Richard Van
"Wolf Men of the Navajo." *Desert Magazine* 11:4, Jan. 1947.

Van Vleet, T. Stanton
"Legendary Evolution of the Navajo Indians." *American Naturalist* 27:69–79, 1893.

Washburne, M. F.
Indian Legends. With an introduction, suggestions to teachers and a bibliography by Alice Corbin Henderson; illustrations by Frederick Richardson. Chicago: Rand McNally Company, 1915. 144 pp., illus.

Wetherill, L. W., and Cummings, B.
"A Navaho Tale of Pueblo Bonito." *Art and Archaeology* (Washington) 14:132–136, 1922.

Wheelwright, Mary C.
Navajo Creation Myth; the Story of the Emergence, by Hasteen Klah. Recorded by M. C. W. Navajo Religion Series, Vol. I. Museum of Navajo Ceremonial Art. Santa Fe, N. M.: The Rydal Press, 1942. 237 pp., 17 col. illus. of sandpaintings.
> Also contains translations of thirty songs. "Since they are selected so as to cover the entire myth, they afford invaluable material for determining the relation between songs used in ceremonials and specific events in the accompanying mythology." (L. C. Wyman)

Whitman, William
Navajo Tales, with illustrations by John P. Heins. Boston: Houghton Mifflin Co., 1925. viii, 217 pp., illus.

Wyman, Leland C.
"Origin Legends of Navaho Divinatory Rites." *JAFL* 49:134–143, 1936.

————.
"The Female Shooting Life Chant; a Minor Navaho Ceremony." *AA* 38:634–653, 1936. n.s.

BELIEFS—WITCHCRAFT—MAGIC

Armer, Mrs. Laura (Adams)
Waterless Mountain; illustrated by Sidney Armer and Laura Adams Armer. New York: Longmans, Green & Co., 1931. xi, 212 pp.
> A study for children of Navaho magic and mystery.

Dutton, Bertha P.
"The Navaho Wind Way Ceremonial." *El Palacio* 48, (No. 4):73–82, 1941.

Haile, Berard
"Navaho Chantways and Ceremonials." *AA* 40:639–652, 1938. n.s.

————.
"Reichard's Chant of Waning Endurance (Navaho)." *AA* 45:306–311, 1943. n.s.

Star Lore Among the Navajos. Sante Fe, New Mexico. Museum of Navajo Ceremonial Art, Inc., 1948. 44 pp., illus.
Contains three plates in colour of sandpaintings and several star charts.

————.
"Why the Navaho Hogan?" *Primitive Man* 15, (Nos. 3–4):39–56, 1942.

Hall, B. P.
"Sand Magic of the Navaho." *Overland* 87: 137, (May) 1929. n.s.

Kluckhohn, Clyde
Navaho Witchcraft. (Papers of the Peabody Museum of American Archaeology and Ethnology. Vol. 22, No. 2. Cambridge, Mass., Harvard University Press, 1944. ix, 149 pp.
According to Dr. Gladys Reichard—Dr. Kluckhorn continues in this volume his study of Navaho behaviorism in the realm of witchcraft which he uses as an overall term for Navaho idea and action patterns concerned with the influencing of events by supernatural techniques that are socially disapproved.

————.
"Some Personal and Social Aspects of Navaho Ceremonial Practice." *Harvard Theological Review* 32, (No. 1):52–82, 1939.

————, and Wyman, Leland Clifton
An Introduction to Navaho Chant Practice, with an account of the behaviors observed in four chants. Memoirs of the American Anthropological Association, No. 53. Menasha, Wisc.: American Anthropological Association, 1940. 204 pp.

Liebler, H. B.
"Christian Concepts and Navaho Words." *Utah Humanities Review* 2 (No. 2):169–175, 1948.

Matthews, Washington
"A Navajo Initiation." *Land of Sunshine* 15: 353–356, 1901.

————.
"A Vigil of the Gods—a Navajo Ceremony." *AA* 9 (No. 2):50–57, 1896. n.s.

————.
"Navajo Night Chant." *JAFL* 14:12–19, 1901.

————.
"Prayer of the Navajo Shaman." *JAFL* 1:166–167, 1888.

————.
"Serpent Worship Among the Navajos." *Land of Sunshine* 9:228–235, 1895.

————.
"The Prayer of a Navajo Shaman." *American Antiquarian* 1 (No. 2):149–170, 1888.

Morgan, William
Human-Wolves Among the Navaho. Yale University Publications in Anthropology No. 11. New Haven: Yale University Press, 1936.

————.
"Navaho Dreams." *AA* 34:390–405, 1932. n.s.

Newcomb, Franc J.
"How the Navajo Adopt Rites." *El Palacio* (Santa Fe, N. M.) 46:25–27, 1939.

————, and Reichard, Gladys A.
Sandpaintings of the Navajo Shooting Chant. New York: J. J. Augustin, 1937. 80 pp., illus.

Peet, S. D.
"The Swastika and Fire Worship in America." *American Antiquity* 26:185–192, 1904.

Reichard, Gladys A.
"Distinctive Features of Navaho Religion." *Southwestern Journal of Anthropology* 1 (No. 2):199–220, 1945.

————.
Prayer: The Compulsive Word. (Monograph of the American Ethnological Society, Vol. 7). New York: J. J. Augustin, 1944. x, 97 pp., illus., bibl.
A detailed study of Navaho prayer, part of a larger study on Navaho religion.

————.
"The Nature of Man as Conceived by the Navajo Indians." *The Review of Religion* 7: 357–360, 1943.

————.
The Story of the Navajo Hail Chant. New York: Gladys A. Reichard, 1944. xii, 155 drawings.
Navaho text and English translation. Photolithograph.

————, and Bittany, Adolph Dodge
Agentive and Causative Elements in Navajo. New York: J. J. Augustin, 1940. 22 pp.

Stevenson, James
"Ceremonial of Hasjelti Dailjis and Mythical Sand Painting of the Navajo Indians." *8th Annual Report: Bureau of American Ethnology,* 1886–7, pp. 235–284, pls. CXII–CXXIII, figs. 115–118. Washington, D. C.: U. S. Gov't Printing Office, 1891.
Construction of the Medicine Lodge, 1, 2, 3, 4, 5, ceremonies, Song of the Esthelte, Myths of the Navajo.

Tozzer, A. M.
"A Navajo Sand Picture of the Vain Gods and its Attendant Ceremony." *Proceedings of the 13th Session of the International Congress of Americanists* (New York), pp. 147–157, 1902.

————.
Notes on Religious Ceremonials of the Navaho. *Putnam Anniversary Volume, Anthropological Papers.* New York: G. E. Stechert and Company, 1909.

————.
"Star Lore Among the Navajo." *JAFL* 21:28–32, 1908.

Valkenburgh, Richard Van
"We Saw the Devil Chant of the Navajo." *Desert Magazine* 10:5–8, March, 1947.

Voth, H. R.
"The Oraibi Powamu Ceremony." *Publications, Anthropological Series, Field Museum of Natural History* 3:118, 1901–1903.

Wheelwright, Mary C.
Hail Chant and Water Chant. Commentary by Dr. Phyllis Ackerman. Illustrated with 24 sand paintings and ritual objects reproduced in serigraph color plates by Louie Ewing. Santa Fe, New Mexico: Museum of Navajo Ceremonial Art, 1946. 244 pp., illus.
> This is the second volume in the Navajo Religion Series. They are not only a major record of Amerindian literature and art, but also primary documents in the religion of the Navajos, an important phase of Amerindian religious thought and ritual, and likewise in the general history of myth and cosmology.

Wyman, Leland C., and Bailey, Flora L.
"Navajo Upward-Reaching Way: Objective Behavior, Rationale and Sanction." *University of New Mexico* (Albuquerque), Bulletin 4, (No. 2), 1943. 47 pp .

————.
"Navaho Girl's Puberty Rite." *New Mexico Anthropologist* 6–7, (No. 1):3–12, 1943.

————, **and Hill, W. W., Osani, Iva**
Navajo Eschatology. University of New Mexico, (Albuquerque) Bulletin 337, 1942.

FOLK MEDICINE

Elmore, Francis H.
Ethnobotany of the Navajo. New Mexico University, Monograph Series, No. 7. Albuquerque, N. M., 1944.

Gillmore, Frances
Windsinger, Story of a Navajo Medicine Man. New York: Minton, Balch Company, 1930.

Leighton, Dorothea C.
"El Indio y la Medicina." *America Indigena* (Mexico, D. F.) 3:127–135, 1943.
> The role of the Witch Doctor, the "Singing Healers" among the Navahos of Arizona and New Mexico, and their attitude towards the white doctors.

Morgan, William
"Navaho Treatment of Sickness: Diagnosticians." *AA* 33:390–402, 1931. n.s.

Pepper, G. H.
"An Unusual Navaho Medicine Ceremony." *So. Workman* 34:228–235, 1905.
> Ceremony for cure of sore throat, said to be caused by nightly visits of eagle.

Reichard, Gladys A.
Navajo Medicine Man, Sandpainting and Legends of Miguelito. Sandpaintings from the John Frederick Huckel Collections, Ltd. Ed. 500 copies. New York: J. J. Augustin, 1939. xvi, 83 pp., illus.

Wyman, Leland C.
"Navajo Diagnosticians." *AA* 38:236–246, 1936. n.s.

————, **and Harris, Stuart Kimball**
"Navajo Indian Medical Ethnobotany." *University of New Mexico Bulletin, Anthropological Series,* Vol. 3, (No. 5, whole No. 366). Albuquerque: University of New Mexico Press, 1941.

CUSTOMS—FOLK ART—SPEECH

Armer, Laura Adams
Sand-painting of the Navaho Indians. Exposition of Indian Tribal Arts. New York: Longmans, Green and Co., 1921.

————.
Southwest. Illustrated from paintings by the author. New York: Longmans, Green and Co., 1935. xiii, 224 pp.

Bailey, Flora L.
"Navaho Foods and Cooking Methods." *AA* 42:270–290, 1940.

————.
"Navaho Motor Habits." *American Anthropologist* 44, (No. 2):210–235, 1942.

Buxton, L. H. Dudley
"Some Navajo Folktales and Customs." *Folk-Lore* (London) 34:239–313, 1923.

Curtis, W. E.
"Education and Morals Among the Navajos and Pueblos." *American Antiquity* 27:259–264, 1905.

Fewkes, J. Walter
Antiquities of the Mesa Verde National Park: Spruce Tree House. Bureau of American Ethnology, Bull. 41, 57 pp., 21 pls., 37 figs. Washington, D. C.: U. S. Gov't Printing Office, 1909.

————.
Antiquities of the Mesa Verde National Park: Cliff Palace. Bureau of American Ethnology, Bull. 51, 82 pp., 35 pl., 4 figs. Washington, D. C.: U. S. Gov't Printing Office, 1911.

————.
Preliminary Report on a Visit to the Navaho National Monument, Arizona. Bureau of American Ethnology, Bull. 50, 35 pp., 22 pl., 3 figs. Washington, D. C.: U. S. Gov't Printing Office, 1911.

Franciscan Fathers
An Ethnologic Dictionary of the Navaho Language. St. Michaels, Ariz.: The Franciscan Fathers, 1910. 536 pp.

————.
A Vocabulary of the Navajo Language. Saint Michaels, Ariz.: The Franciscan Fathers, 1912. 2 vols.

Fryer, E. R.
"Navajo Social Organization and Land Use Adjustment." *Christian Science Monthly* 55: 408–422, 1942.

Hill, W. W.
Navaho Humor. General Series in Anthropology 9. Menasha, Wisconsin: 1943. 28 pp.

————.

"Navajo Use of Jimson Weed." *New Mexico Anthropologist* 3, (No. 2):19–21, 1939.

————.

Navaho Warfare. Yale University Publications in Anthropology, No. 5. New Haven: Yale University Press, 1936. 19 pp.
A descriptive account of the formalized pattern of warfare and its relation to the Squaw or War Dance and the Natc'it.

————.

The Agricultural and Hunting Methods of the Navaho Indians. Yale University Publications in Anthropology No. 18. New Haven: Yale University Press, 1938.

————.

"The Status of the Hermaphrodite and Transvestite in Navaho Culture." *AA* 37:263–269, 1935. n.s.

Matthews, Washington
"A Study in Butts and Tips." *AA* 5 (No. 4): 345–350, 1892.

————.

"A Two-Faced Navaho Blanket." *AA* 2:638–643, 1900. n.s.

————.

"Marriage Prohibitions on the Father's Side Among the Navajos." *JAFL* 4:78–79, 1891.

————.

"Mythic Dry-Painting of the Navajos." *American Naturalist* 19 (No. 1):931–939, 1885.

————.

"Navajo Names for Plants." *American Naturalist* 20:767–777, 1886.

————.

"Navajo Weavers." *3rd Annual Report: Bureau of American Ethnology,* 1881–1882, pp. 371–420, pls. 34–38, figs. 42–59. Washington, D. C.: U. S. Gov't Printing Office, 1884.

————.

"The Basket Drum." *AA* 7:202–233, 1894.

Mera, Harry Percival
Navajo Twilled Weaving. General Series, Bulletin 4. Santa Fe, N. Mex.: Laboratory of Anthropology, 1943.

Mindeleff, Cosmos
"Navaho Houses." *17th Annual Report: Bureau of American Ethnology,* 1895–1896, pp. 475–514. pls. LXXXII–LXXXIX, figs. 230–244. Washington, D. C.: U. S. Gov't Printing Office, 1898.
Description of the country, habits of the people, legendary and actual winter hogans, sweat houses, etc.

Neumann, David L.
"Navaho Silversmithing Survives." *El Palacio* 50:6–8, 1943.

Newcomb, Franc J., and Reichard, Gladys A.
Sandpaintings of the Navajo Shooting Chant. New York: J. J. Augustin, 1937. 80 pp., illus.

Parsons, Elsie Clews
"Naming Practices in Arizona." *AA* 39:561–562, 1937. n.s.

Reichard, Gladys A.
Navajo Shepherd and Weaver. New York: J. J. Augustin, 1936. xvii, 222 pp., illus. xv pl.
Navajo weaving and fabric work.

Senter, D., and Hawley, F.
"Hopi and Navaho Child Burials." *AA* 39:131–134, 1937. n.s.

Shufeldt, R. W.
"Mortuary Customs of the Navajo Indians." *American Naturalist* 25:303–306, 1891.

————.

"The Evolution of House-Building Among the Navajo Indians." *Proceedings of the U. S. National Museum.* 15:279–282, 1892.

Stephen, A. M.
"Navajo Shoemaker." *Proc. U. S. National Museum.* Smithsonian Institution Vol. 11: 131–136, Washington, D. C.: U. S. Government Printing Office, 1888.

Swan, A. M.
"Some Navajo Traditions and Customs." *The Southwest Magazine,* pp. 36, (Feb.) 1896.

Tschopik, H., Jr.
"Navaho Basketry: Study of Culture Change." *AA* 42:444–462, 1940. n.s.

————.

"Navaho Pottery Making; an inquiry into the affinities of Navaho Painted Pottery." *Papers,* Vol. 17, (No. 1). Howard N. Peabody Museum of American Archaeology and Ethnology, (Cambridge, Mass.), 1941.

————.

"Taboo as a Possible Factor Involved in the Obsolescence of Navaho Pottery and Basketry." *AA* 40:257–260, 1938. n.s.

Vabre, Cyp.
"The Swastika." *The Catholic Pioneer,* pp. 12, (Dec.) 1905.

Valkenburgh, Richard F. Van
"Navajo Common Law, I. Notes on Political Organization, Property and Inheritance." *Museum Notes, Museum of Northern Arizona* 9, (No. 4):17–22, 51–54, 1936.

————.

"Navajo Common Law, III." *Museum Notes, Museum of Northern Arizona* 10, (No. 12): 39–45, (June) 1938.

Walton, Eda Lou
"Navaho Poetry; an Interpretation." *Texas Review* 7:198–210, 1922.

———.
"Navajo Song Patterning." *JAFL* 43:105–129, 1930.

———.
"Navaho Verse Rythms." *Poetry* 24:40–44, 1924.

Young, Robert, and Morgan, William
The Navajo Language. Phoenix, Ariz.: U. S. Department of the Interior, Office of Indian Affairs, Education Division, 1943.

GAMES

Haile, Berard
"Navaho Games of Chance and Taboo." *Primitive Man* 6, (No. 2) :35–40. Washington, D. C.: Catholic Anthropological Conference, 1933.

Matthews, Washington
"Navajo Gambling Songs." *AA* 2:1–21, 1889. Text only.

"Navaho Games."
JAFL 2:91–93, 1889; 3:30–31, 1890.

Reagan, A. B.
"Navajo Sports." *Primitive Man* 5, (No. 4): 68–70. Washington, D. C.: Catholic Anthropological Conference, (Oct.) 1932.

Telford, Emma P.
"Navaho Games and Handicrafts." *Southern Workman* 32:369–375, 1903.

MUSIC

GENERAL STUDIES

Anonymous
"Navaho Goat Song." *The Masterkey* 8, (No. 6) :188. Los Angeles: The Southwest Museum, 1934.
Text only.

"Blackfoot and Navaho Songs." *El Palacio* 20 (No. 5) :104–106.

Fillmore, John Comfort
"Songs of the Navajos. From the Musicians Point of View." *Land of Sunshine* (Los Angeles) 5:238–241, 1896.

Haile, Berard
"Navaho Chantways and Ceremonials." *AA* 40:639–652, 1938. n.s.

Kluckhohn, Clyde
"Great Chants of the Navajo." *Theatre Arts Monthly* 17:639–645, (Aug.) 1933.

Marshall, L. R.
"Drum for the Navajo Chorus." *Etude* 59:126, (February) 1941.

Matthews, Washington
"Navajo Gambling Songs." *American Antiquarian* 2 (No. 1) :1–19, 1889.

———.
Navaho Legends; collected and translated by W. Matthews. With introduction, notes, illustration texts, interlinear translations, and melodies. American Folklore Society Memoirs, Vol. 5. Boston: Houghton, Mifflin and Company, 1897. 31 pp.

"Navaho Melodies." *Memoirs of the American Folklore Society*, 5:279–291. Boston: Houghton, Mifflin Company, 1897.

"Navajo Myths, Prayers and Songs, with Text and Translations," edited by Pliny Earl Goddard. *University of California Publication of American Archaeology and Ethnology* (Berkeley), 5:21–63, 1907.

———.
"Navaho Night Chant." *JAFL* 14:12–19, 1901.

———.
"Songs of the Navajos." *Land of Sunshine* (Los Angeles) 5:197–201, 1896.

"Songs of Sequence of the Navajos." *JAFL* 7: 185–194, 1894.

———.
"Study of Ceremony." *JAFL* 10:257–263, 1897.

"The Mountain Chant: a Navajo Ceremony." *5th Annual Report: Bureau of American Ethnology*, pp. 379–467, pl. 10–18, fig. 50–59. Washington, D. C.: U. S. Government Printing Office, 1887.

———.
The Night Chant: a Navaho Ceremony. American Museum of Natural History Memoirs, Vol. 6. New York: Knickerbocker Press, 1902. 332 pp., illus.

Pepper, G. H.
"An Unusual Navaho Medicine Ceremony." *So. Workman* 34:228–235, 1905.
Ceremony for cure of sore throat, said to be caused by nightly visits of eagle.

Walton, Eda Lou
"Navaho Poetry: an Interpretation." *Texas Review* (Austin, Texas) 7:198–210, 1922.

"Navajo Song Patterning." *JAFL* 43:105–129, 1930.

Wyman, L. C., and Kluckhohn, C.
Navaho Classification of Their Song Ceremonials. American Museum of Natural History, Memoir No. 50. New York: American Anthropological Association, 1938. 38 pp.

DANCES

See: See the various entries involving ritual and ceremony under *myths* and *beliefs* (religious) above.

Haile, Father Berard
Navaho Fire Dance or Corral Dance. St. Michaels, Arizona: St. Michaels, 1948.

Reagan, A. B.
"A Navaho Fire Dance." *AA* 36:434–437, 1934. n.s.

Spencer, Lilian W.
"Navajo Indian Fire-Dance." *Southwest Lore* 2:17–19, 1936.

ARRANGEMENTS

Grunn, Homer
From Desert and Pueblo: Five authentic Navajo and Tewa Indian songs. The lyrics based on Indian text by Elizabeth Willis De Huff; the Indian melodies transcribed and harmonized by Homer Grunn. Boston: Ditson Music Company, 1924.

"Her Blanket."
Lieurance, T.: Presser: Voice and piano.

"Navajo War Dance."
Farwell, A.: Schirmer: Piano.

"Navajo War Dance."
Farwell, Arthur: Schirmer: Chamber orchestra (18 instruments).

"The Waving Blanket" (Navaho).
Treharne, B.: Willis: SA.

RECORDS

"Funeral Song."
Chief Os-ko-mon, with tom-tom.   DE–20496

"Her Blanket."
Princess Watawaso.   VI–22316

"Navajo War Dance," opus 20 (Farwell, A.).
Jeanne Behrend, piano. In: *Album of Piano Music by American Composers.*   VM–764

"Night Chant."
Laura Boulton. In: *Indian Music of the Southwest.*   VP–49

"Squaw Dance."
Laura Boulton. In: *Indian Music of the Southwest.*   VP–49

"Sun Dance."
Chief Os-ko-mon with tom-tom.   DE–20496

"War Song."
Chief Os-ko-mon with tom-tom.   DE–20496

U. S. Library of Congress. Division of Music. Folklore Section.
Indian Recordings—by various collectors, individuals and institutions, have deposited their disks in the Archive of American Folksong. Many Navaho tunes and ceremonies included.   AAFS–LC

PIMA (Piman)
(*Including:* Papago)

FOLKLORE
GENERAL STUDIES

Gaillard, D. D.
"The Papago of Arizona and Sonora." *AA* 7: 293–297, 1894.

Hodge, Frederick W.
"Pima." *Bull. Bureau Amer. Ethnol.* 30(Part 2):251–253, 1910.

————.
"Papago." *Bull. Bureau Amer. Ethnol.* 30 (Part 2):200–201, 1910.

Hoover, J. W.
"The Generic Descent of the Papago Villages." *AA* 37:257–264, 1935. n.s.

————, Kroeber, Henriette R.
"Traditions of the Papago Indians." *JAFL* 25: 95–105, 1912.

Hrdlicka, Ales
"Notes on the Pima of Arizona." *AA* 8:39–47, 1906. n.s.

Lolorias, J. M.
"As an Indian Sees It." (Papago). *So. Workman* 31:476–480, 1902.

Lumholtz, C.
"Indiens Papagos." *Journal de la Société des Américanistes de Paris* 7:331–332, 1910 (1911). n.s.

————.
New Trails in Mexico. New York: Charles Scribner's Sons, 1912. 411 pp.
Lore and life of the Papagos.

Russell, Frank
"Pima Annals." *AA* 5:76–81, 1903. n.s.

————.
"The Pima Indians." *26th Annual Report: Bureau of American Ethnology, 1904–1905.* pp. 3–390, pls. 1–47, figs. 1–102. Washington, D. C.: U. S. Government Printing Office, 1908.

O'Neale, Lila M., and Dolores, Juan
"Notes on Papago Color Designations." *AA* 45:387–397, 1943. n.s.

Spicer, Edward
"The Papago Indians." *The Kiva* 6, (No. 6): 21–24, 1941. Tucson: Arizona State Museum.

Spier, Leslie
Cultural Relations of the Gila River and Lower Colorado Tribes. Yale University Publications in Anthropology No. 3. New Haven: Yale University Press, 1936. 22 pp.
Discusses the culture elements peculiar to the Maricopa, the Pima-Papago, and the Lower Colorado Tribes.

Underhill, Ruth M.
Hawk Over Whirpools. New York: J. J. Augustin, 1940. 255 pp.
About the Papagos.

———.

Papagos. With fifty full page photographic reproductions. New York: J. J. Augustin, 1940.

———.

Social Organization of the Papago Indians. Columbia University Contributions to Anthropology 30. New York: J. J. Augustin, 1937.

———.

The Autobiography of a Papago Woman. Memoirs No. 46. Menasha, Wisc.: American Anthropological Association, 1936. 64 pp.

MYTHS—FOLKTALES—LEGENDS

Antonio, Hal
"Pima Story of the Deluge." *Native American,* pp. 53, (February 18) 1905.

Azul, J.
"How the Earth Was Made: An Indian Legend." *Assembly Herald* (Phila.) 15:70–71, 1909.

Juillard, George T.
"Legends of the Papago Indians." *The Catholic Pioneer,* pp. 14, (Nov.) 1905.

Kroeber, Henriette Rotschild
"Papago Coyote Tales." *JAFL* 22:339–342, 1909.

———.

"Pima Tales." *AA* 10:231–236, 1908. n.s.

Lloyd, J. William
Aw-aw-tam Indian Nights. Being the Myths and Legends of the Pimas of Arizona, as received by J. William Lloyd from Comalk-hawk-Kih (their Buckskin), thru the interpretation of Edward Hubert Wood. Westfield, N. J.: The Lloyd Group, 1911. 241 pp.

Mason, J. Alden
"Papago Migration Legend." *JAFL* 34:254–268, 1921.

McKee, Louise, and Summers, Richard
Dusty Desert Tales. Caldwell, Idaho: Caxton Printers, Ltd., 1941. 191 pp., illus.

Neff, M. L.
"Pima and Papago Legends." *JAFL* 25:51–55, 1912.

Osterman, L.
"Legend of the Papago Indians." *Catholic Pioneer,* (December) 1905.

Russell, Frank
"Myths of the Pimas." *Outwest,* (May, June, July, Sept., Nov.) 1909.

Wright, Harold Bell
Long Ago Told (Huh-Kew Ah-Kah); Legends of the Papago Indians, illustrated by Mrs. Katherine F. Kitt. xvii, 289 pp., illus., New York: D. Appleton & Co., 1929.

BELIEFS—CUSTOMS

Brown, Herbert
"A Pima-Maricopa Ceremony." *AA* 8:688–691, 1906. n.s.

Castetter, Edward F., and Underhill, Ruth M.
"Ethnobiological Studies in the American Southwest II: Ethnobiology of the Papago Indians." *University of New Mexico, Bulletin 275, Biological Series 4,* (No. 3):3–84, 1935.

———, **and Bell, Willis H.**
Pima and Papago Indian Agriculture. Inter-Americana Studies I. Albuquerque, N. M.: University of New Mexico Press, 1942. 245 pp., illus.

Hayden, Julian, and Steen, Charlie R.
"The Vikita Ceremony of the Papago." *South-Western Monuments Monthly Report,* pp. 263–283, (April) 1937.

Herzog, George
"Note on Pima Moieties." *AA* 38:520–521, 1936. n.s.

Hill, W. W.
"Notes on Pima Land Law and Tenure." *AA* 38:586–589, 1936. n.s.

———.

"Note on the Pima Berdache." *AA* 40:338–340, 1938. n.s.

Mason, J. Alden
"The Papago Harvest Festival." *AA* 22:13–25, 1920.
Includes songs.

Parsons, Elsie Clews
"Review: *Singing for Power;* the Song Magic of the Papago Indians of Southern Arizona, by R. M. Underhill." *AA* 41:482–483, 1939.

Pinkley, E. T.
"The Shrine of the Children." *El Palacio* 20: 119–122.

Russell, Frank
"Pima Constitution." *JAFL* 16:222–229, 1903.

Underhill, Ruth M.
Hawk Over Whirlpools. New York: J. J. Augustin, 1940. 255 pp.

———.

"Note on Easter Devils at Kawori'k on the Papago Reservation." *AA* 36:515–516, 1934. n.s.

———.

Papago Indian Religion. New York: Columbia University Press, 1946. vii. 359 pp., bibl.
The author presents a great deal of material on ritual songs, prayers and formalized orations, as well as valuable information on ritual and ceremonialism, shamanism and curative practices.

———.

Singing for Power: The Song Magic of the Papago Indians of Southern Arizona. Berkeley: University of California Press, 1938. 158 pp.

GAMES—FOLK ART—SPEECH

Dolores, Juan
"Papago Nicknames." *Essays in Anthropology, Presented to A. L. Kroeber.* pp.45–47. Berkeley: University of California Press, 1936.

————.
"Papago Nominal Stems." *Univ. Cal. Publ. Amer. Arch. Ethnol.* 20:19–31, 1923.

————.
"Papago Verb Stems." *Univ. Cal. Publ. Amer. Arch. Ethnol.* 10:241–263, 1913.

Kissell, Mary Lois
"Basketry of the Papago and Pima." *Anthropological Papers of the American Museum of Natural History* (New York) 17:115–264, 1916. Illus.

"Papago-Pima Games."
JAFL 25:60, 1912.

MUSIC

GENERAL STUDIES

Brown, Herbert
"A Pima-Maricopa Ceremony." *AA* 8:688–691, 1906. n.s.

Herzog, George
"A Comparison of Pueblo and Pima Musical Styles." *JAFL* 49:284–417, 1936.
Musical analyses and comparisons. A comprehensive study.

Mason, John Alden
"The Papago Harvest Festival." *AA* 22:13–25, 1920.

Russell, Frank
"The Pima Indians." *26th Annual Report: Bureau of American Ethnology,* 1904–1905, pp. 3–389. Washington, D. C.: U. S. Government Printing Office, 1908.

Schinhan, Jan Philip
Die Musik der Papago und Yurok. (Dissertation) University of Vienna, 1937.

Stricklen, E. G.
"Notes on Eight Papago Songs." *University of California Publications in American Archaeology and Ethnology* 20:361–366. Berkeley: The University Press, 1923.

Underhill, Ruth M.
Singing for Power: The Song Magic of the Papago Indians of Southern Arizona. Berkeley: University of California Press, 1938.

ARRANGEMENTS

————: *Organ*

"The Indian Flute." (Papago).
Miller, H. A.: Cornell College.

PUEBLO

[*Including:* **Acoma, Cochiti, Hopi** (see above), **Isleta, Jemez, Laguna, Picuris, San Felipe, Santa Ana, Santa Domingo, Sia, Taos, Tewa** (**San Ildefonso, Santa Clara**), **Zuni** (see below)]

Keresan Family: Acoma, Cochiti, Laguna, San Felipe, Santa Ana, Santo Domingo, Sia.

FOLKLORE

GENERAL STUDIES

Abeita, A.
"The Pueblo Indians." *So. Workman* (Hampton, Va.) 38:477–478, 1909.

Bandelier, Adolph Francis
The Delight Makers. New York: Dodd, Mead and Co., 1890. iv, 490 pp. New and revised edition issued in 1946, with an introduction by Charles F. Lummis.
"Historical fiction on acient Pueblo life." (Dobie)

————.
The Unpublished Letters of ——, concerning the writing and publication of "The Delight Makers", with an introduction by Paul Radin. El Paso: Carl Hertzog, 1942. 33 pp.

Barber, E. A.
"On the Ancient and Modern Pueblo Tribes." *Amer. Naturalist* 11:591–599, 1877.

Bartlett, Katherine A.
"Life in Pueblo II (Ca. 700–1000 A. D.)." *Museum of Northern Arizona* (Flagstaff), *Museum Notes* 6, (No. 3):13–18, (Sept.) 1933.

————.
The Material Culture of Pueblo II in the San Francisco Mountains. Museum of Northern Arizona, Bulletin No. 7. Flagstaff, Ariz.: Northern Arizona Society of Science and Art, (August) 1934.

Baum, H. M.
"Pueblo and Cliff Dwellers of the Southwest." *Records of the Past* (Washington) 1:357–361, 1902.

Beckwith, F.
"A Day in Acoma." *El Palacio* 35:201–210, 1933.

Boas, Franz
Keresan Texts. New York: American Ethnological Society., 1926–28. 2 vols. (American Ethnological Society Publ. vol. 8, part 1–2).

————.
"Further Notes on San Felipe." *JAFL* 41:592, 1928.

————.
"The Emergence (San Felipe)" *JAFL* 41:288–290, 1928.

Burrows, E. D.
"The Pueblos of America." *So. Workman* 35:78–87, 1906.

"Cochiti Gentes."
JAFL 3:117, 1890.

Colton, Harold Sellers
Pueblo II in the San Francisco Mountains. Museum of Northern Arizona (Flagstaff, Ariz.)', Buletin 4, 1933.

Crane, Leo
Desert Drums: the Pueblo Indians of New Mexico, 1540–1928. New Jersey: Explorer's Book Service, 1928. x, 393 pp., illus.

Davis, W. H. H.
El Gringo; or New Mexico and her People. New York: Harper and Bros., 1857. 332 pp.

Dumarest, Father Noel
Notes on Cochiti, New Mexico. Translated and edited by Elsie Clews Parsons, Memoir of the American Anthropological Association, Vol. 6, (No. 3):137–236. Lancaster, Pa.: American Anthropological Society, 1919.

Espinosa, Aurelio Macedonio
"Miscellaneous Materials from the Pueblo Indians of New Mexico." *Philological Quarterly* 21:121–127, 1942.

Fewkes, Jesse Walter
"Prehistoric Mesa Verde Pueblo and its People." *Smithsonian Report,* pp. 461–488. Washington, D. C.: U. S. Government Printing Office, 1916.

"The Pueblo Settlements near El Paso, Texas." *AA* 4:57–76, 1902. n.s.

"Two Summer's Work in Pueblo Ruins." *22nd Annual Report: Bureau of American Ethnology, 1900–1901,* pp. 17–193, pls. 1–19, figs. 1–122. Washington, D. C.: U. S. Government Printing Office, 1904.

Fynn, A. J.
The American Indian as a Product of Environment. With special reference to the Pueblos. Boston: Little, Brown and Company, 1907. 275 pp., 8 pl.

Goldfrank, E. S.
The Social and Ceremonial Organization of Cochiti. Memoirs of the American Anthropological Association 33, 1927. Menasha, Wis.: The Anthropological Association. 129 pp.

Gunn, John Malcolm
"History, Traditions, and Narratives of the Queres Pueblos of Laguna and Acoma." *Records of the Past* (Wash.) 3:291–310, 323–344, 1904.

Schat-chen; History, Traditions and Narratives of the Queres Indians of Laguna and Acoma. Albuquerque, N. M.: Albright and Anderson, 1917. 222 pp., illus. by Queres Indians.

Hawley, F. M.
"Kokopelli, of the Prehistoric Southwestern Pueblo Pantheon." *AA* 39:644–646, 1937. n. s.

"Pueblo Social Organization as a Lead to Pueblo History." *AA* 39:504–522, 1937. n.s.

Hewett, Edgar L.
Antiquities of the Jemez Plateau, New Mexico. Bureau of American Ethnology, Bulletin 32. pp. 1–55. 17 pls. (incl. map), 31 figs. Washington, D. C.: U. S. Gov't. Printing Office, 1906.

Hodge, F. W.
"Acoma." *Bull. Bureau Amer. Ethnol.* 30 (Part 1):10–11, 1907.

"Cochiti." *Bull. Bureau Amer. Ethnol.* 30 (Part 1):317–318, 1907.

"Isleta." *Bull. Bureau Amer. Ethnol.* 30 (Part 1):622–624, 1907.

"Jemez." *Bull. Bureau Amer. Ethnol.* 30 (Part 1):629–631, 1907.

"Laguna." *Bull. Bureau Amer. Ethnol.* 30 (Part 1):752–753, 1907.

"Pueblo Indian Clans." *AA* 9:345–353, 1896. o.s.

"Pueblos." *Bull. Bureau Amer. Ethnol.* 30 (Part 2):318–324, 1910.

"San Felipe." *Bull. Bureau Amer. Ethnol.* 30 (Part 2):432–433, 1910.

"San Ildefonso." *Bull. Bureau Amer. Ethnol.* 30 (Part 2):440–441, 1910.

"Santa Ana." *Bull. Bureau Amer. Ethnol.* 30 (Part 2):454, 1910.

"Santa Clara." *Bull. Bureau Amer. Ethnol.* 30 (Part 2):456–457, 1910.

"Santa Domingo." *Bull. Bureau Amer. Ethnol.* 30 (Part 2):462, 1910.

"Sia." *Bull. Bureau Amer. Ethnol.* 30 (Part 2): 562–563, 1910.

"Tewa." *Bull. Bureau Amer. Ethnol.* 30 (Part 2) :737–738, 1910.

"Tigua." *Bull. Bureau Amer. Ethnol.* 30 (Part 2) :747–749, 1910.

Holmes, W. H.
"Notes on the Antiquities of Jemez Valley, New Mexico." *AA* 7:198–213, 1905. n.s.

Hooton, E. A.
The Indians of Pecos Pueblo. New Haven: Yale University Press, 1930. 391 pp.

Hough Walter
"Ancient Pueblo Subsistance." *Proceedings of the 23rd Session of the International Congress of Americanists,* pp. 67–70, 1928.

————.
Culture of the Ancient Pueblos of the Upper Gila River Region. U. S. Government Printing Office, 1914. xiv, 139 pp., illus.

Hurt, Wesley R.
"Notes on the Santa Ana Indians." *El Palacio* 48 (No. 6) :131–143, 1941.

Krause, F.
Die Pueblo Indianer. Halle: 1907. 226 pp.

Lewis, Frances W.
"Life Among the Pueblos." *So. Workman* 30:757–760, 1901.

————.
"The Pueblo Home." *So. Workman* 30:316–320, 1901.

Long, Haniel
Piñon Country. (American Folkways Series.) New York: Duell, Sloan and Pearce, 1941. Discusses among other interesting items, the Navajo and Pueblos.

Martinez, I.
"The Pueblo of Taos." *So. Workman* (Hampton, Va.) 37:500–503, 1909.

Parsons, Elsie Clews
A Pueblo Indian Journal, 1920–1921. Memoirs, American Anthropological Society 32, 1925.

————.
A Pueblo of Jemez. Department of Archaeology, Phillips Academy, (Andover, Mass.). New Haven: Yale University Press, 1925.

————.
"Early Relations Between Hopi and Keres." *AA* 38:554–560, 1936. n.s.

————.
"Hidden Bull on First Mesa Arizona." *Man* 22:89–91, 1922.

————.
"Isleta, New Mexico." *47th Annual Report: Bureau of American Ethnology,* 1929–1930, pp. 201–465, pls. 17–20, figs. 1–26, 1 map. Washington, D. C.: U. S. Gov't. Printing Office, 1932.

————.
"Laguna Genealogies." *Anthropological Papers, American Museum of Natural History* 19:133–292, 1923.

————.
"Mothers and Children at Laguna." *Man* 19:34–38, 1919.

————.
"Pueblo Indian Clan in Folklore." *JAFL* 34:209–216, 1921.

————.
Social Organization of the Tewa of New Mexico. Memoirs No. 36 of the American Anthropological Association, 1929. Menasha, Wis: Anthropological Society, 1929.

————.
"Some Aztec and Pueblo Parallels." *AA* 35:611–631, 1933. n.s.

————.
Taos Pueblo. General Series in Anthropology 2. Menasha, Wisc.: George Banta Publishing Company, 1936. 121 pp., illus.

————.
"The Kinship Nomenclature of the Pueblo Indians." *AA* 34:377–389, 1932. n.s.

Pepper, George H.
"Pueblo Bonito." *Anthropological Papers of the American Museum of Natural History* (New York). 27:1–398, 1920., illus.

Pericot y Garcia, Luis
La Historia de America La America Indigena: Vol. I, Historia de America y los Pueblos Americanos. Barcelona: Salvat Edetores, 1935. 732 pp., 8 color plates, 341 figures, maps, etc.

Reagan, Albert B.
Don Diego, or, The Pueblo Indian Uprising of 1680. New York: The Alice Harriman Company, 1914. ix, 352 pp., illus.

————.
"The Jemez Indians." *El Palacio* 4, (No. 2) :24–72.

Reed, Erik
"The Abandonment of the San Juan Region." *El Palacio* 51:61–74, 1944.

Roberts, H. H.
"The Reason for the Departure of the Pecos Indians for Jemez Pueblo." *AA* 34:359–360, 1932. n.s.

Sedgwick, M. K.
Acoma, the City Sky; A Study in Pueblo-Indian History and Civilization. Cambridge: Harvard University Press, 1927. xiv, 318 pp., illus., bibl. 301–309.

Seton, Julia
The Pulse of the Pueblo; personal glimpses of Indian life. Santa Fe, N. M.: Seton Village Press, 1939. 249 pp., illus.

Smith, Jeanette
Tula; a Little Pueblo Girl. Bloomington, Ill.: McKnight Publishing Company 1940. 96 pp.

Stallings, W. S., Jr.
"A Tree-Ring Chronology for the Rio Grande Drainage in Northern New Mexico." *National Academy of Science, Proceedings 19,* (No. 9) :803–806. Washington, D. C.: U. S. Government Printing Office, 1933.

————.
"Notes on the Pueblo Culture in South Central New Mexico and in the Vicinity of El Paso, Texas." *AA* 34:67–78, 1932. n.s.

Stevenson, Matilda C.
"The Sia." *11th Annual Report: Bureau of American Ethnology, 1889–1890.* pp. 9–157, pls. 1–35; figs., 1–20. Washington, D. C.: U. S. Government Printing Office, 1894. ,

Thomas, Alfred B.
After Coronado. Norman, Okla.: University of Oklahoma Press, 1935. 307 pp.

Underhill, Ruth M.
First Penthouse Dwellers of America. Santa Fe, New Mex.: Laboratory of Anthropology, 1946. 161 pp., illus., bibl., rev. ed.

Waters, Frank
The Man Who Killed the Deer. New York: Farrar & Rinehart, 1942. 311 pp.
A novel built around Pueblo life, customs and traditions.

White, Leslie
"New Material from Acoma." *Bureau of American Ethnology, Anthropological Papers 32,* Bulletin 136, pp. 301–360, pl. 29–327, fig. 5, pls. index. Washington, D. C.: U. S. Government Printing Office, 1943.
Emphasis on ceremonialism and social order.

————.
"Punche: Tobacco in New Mexico History." *New Mexico Historical Review 18,* (No. 4) :386–393, 1943.

————.
"The Acoma Indians." *47th Annual Report: Bureau of American Ethnology,* 1929–1930, pp. 17–192, pls. 1–16, figs. 1–6. Washington, D. C.: U. S. Gov't. Printing Office, 1932.

————.
"The Pueblo of Santa Ana, New Mexico." *Memoirs of the American Anthropological Association 60,* Vol. 44:(No. 4, Part 2):360 pp., 7 pls. 54 figs. Menasha, Wisc.: George Banta, for the American Anthropological Association, 1942.

————.
"The Pueblo of San Felipe." *Memoirs of the American Anthropological Associatiion 38.* Menasha, Wis.: George F. Banta. 1932. 69 pp.

————.
"The Pueblo of Santo Domingo, New Mexico." *Memoirs of the American Anthropological Association 43.* Menasha, Wisc.: George F. Banta. 1935. 210 pp.

Whitman, William
Pueblo Indians of San Ildefonso: A Changing Culture. New York: Columbia University Press, 1947. vii, 164 pp., illus.

————.
The San Ildefonso. In: *Acculturation in Seven Indian Tribes.* Ralph Linton, ed. New York: D. Appleton-Century, 1940.

Whittaker, Milo Lee
Pathbreakers and Pioneers of the Pueblo Region. Pueblo: Franklin Press, 1917. 160 pp.

MYTHS—FOLKTALES—LEGENDS

"A Laguna Folk-Tale." *So. Workman* (Hampton, Va.) 39:618–619, 1910.

Applegate, Frank Guy
Indian Stories from the Pueblos. foreword by Witter Bynner; illustrations from original Pueblo Indian Paintings. Phil.: J. B. Lippincott Company, 1929. 178 pp., illus.

————.
Native Tales of New Mexico. Philadelphia: J. B. Lippincott Company, 1932. 263 pp.

Bayliss, C. K.
"Tewa Sun Myth." *JAFL* 22:333–335, 1909.

Benedict, Ruth
"Eight Stories from Acoma." *JAFL* 43:59–88, 1930.

————.
Tales of the Cochiti Indians. Bureau of American Ethnology, Bulletin 98. Smithsonian Institution. Washington, D. C.: U. S. Government Printing Office, 1931. x, 256 pp.

Boas, Franz
"Abstract Characteristics of Keresan Folk Tales." *Inter. Congr. Amer.* 20(Part 1):223–224, 1922.

————, **and Parsons, Elsie Clews**
"Spanish Tales from Laguna and Zuni, New Mexico." *JAFL* 33:47–72, 1924.

Chase, Mrs. Amanda (Mathews)
From the Old Pueblo and Other Tales. Los Angeles: No Publisher, 1902.
Tales of early day life, customs.

Cloutier, J. E. A.
"Anecdotes de d'Islet." *JAFL* 33:273–294, 1920.

De Huff, Elizabeth Willis
"More Pueblo Tales." *El Palacio* 11, (No. 11) :140–144, 1921.

————.
"Myths told by the Pueblos." *El Palacio* 11, (No. 7) :86–92; (No. 8) :98–99, 1921.

————.
"Pueblo Versions of Old World Tales." *TFSP* 14:104–126, 1938.
Tales of San Juan.

Taytay's Memories. Illustrations by Fred Kabotie. New York: Harcourt, Brace and Company, 1924. 255 pp., illus.

Taytay's Tales. Illustrations by Fred Kabotie and Otis Polelonema. New York: Harcourt, Brace and Company, 1922. 213 pp., illus.

Espinosa, Aurelio Macedonia
"All Soul's Day at Zuni, Acoma and Laguna." *JAFL* 31:550–552, 1918.

"Pueblo Indian Folk Tales." *JAFL* 4:69–134, 1936.

Forde, C. D.
"A Creation Myth from Acoma." *Folk-Lore* (London) 41:370–387, 1930.

Gatschet, Albert S.
"A Mythic Tale of the Isleta Indians, New Mexico." *Proceedings of the American Philosophical Society*, 29:208–217, 1891.

Harrington, J. P., and Roberts, Helen H.
"Picuris Children's Stories, With Texts and Songs." *43rd Annual Report: Bureau of American Ethnology*, Smithsonian Institution, pp. 289–447. Washington, D. C.: U. S. Government Printing Office, 1928.

Hodge, Gene Meany
The Kachinas are Coming. Pueblo Indian kachina dolls with related folktales; foreword by Dr. Frederick Webb Hodge . . . with eighteen color plates of kachina dolls from original drawings by the author. L. A., Calif.: Steller-Millar, 1936. 129 pp., illus.

James, Ahlee
Tewa Firelight Tales; with illustrations by Awa Tsireh and others. New York: Longmans, Green and Company, 1927. 247 pp., illus.

Lee, F. H., ed.
Folk Tales of All Nations. New York: Tudor Publishing Company, 1946. 947 pp.
Pueblo Tales, pp. 98–105.

Lummis, Charles Fletcher
The Man Who Married the Moon, and other Pueblo Indian folk-stories. New York: The Century Co., 1894. x, 239 pp., illus.

A New Mexico David. New York: Charles Scribner's Sons, 1891. ix, 217 pp.

"Pueblo Indian Folk Stories." *Drake's Magazine*, pp. 1, (April) 1891.

Pueblo Indian Folk Stories. New York: The Century Co., 1910. x, 257 pp., illus.
Published in 1894 under the title: "The Man who Married the Moon."

"Pueblo Rabbit-Hunt." *JAFL* 9:72, 1896.

Parsons, Elsie Clews
"Acoma Tales." *JAFL* 31:216–255, 1918.

"All Souls Day at Zuni, Acoma, and Laguna." *JAFL* 30:495–496, 1917.

"Der spanische Einflus auf die Märchen der Pueblo-Indianer." *Zeitschrift für Ethnologie* 58:16–28, 1926.
Spanish influence on Pueblo tales.

"Laguna Tales." *JAFL* 44:137–143, 1931.

"Nativity Myth at Laguna and Zuni." *JAFL* 31:256–263, 1918.

"On the Travels of Folk Tales, and One Tale from the State of Puebla." *Mexican Folkways* 5:71–77, 1929.

"Pueblo Indian Folk Tales, Probably of Spanish Provenience." (Zuni, Acoma, Laguna) *JAFL* 31:216–255, 1918.

Taos Tales. Memoirs of the American Folklore Society, No. 34. Philadelphia: American Folklore Society, 1940. vii, 185 pp., illus., bibl.

Tewa Tales. Memoir of the American Folklore Society, No. 19. Philadelphia: American Folklore Society, 1928. 304 pp., bibl.

"The Antelope Clan in Keresan Custom and Myth." *Man* 17:190–193, 1918.

——, and Boas, Franz
"Spanish Tales from Laguna and Zuni." *JAFL* 33:47–72, 1920.

Pletcher, D. E.
"Coyote Scatters the Stars; Cochiti Pueblo Indian Myth." *Nature Magazine* 24:280 (December) 1934.

"Two Little Doves and the Drought; a Picuris Pueblo Indian Myth." *Nature Magazine* 25:336, (June) 1935.

Pradt, G. H.
"Shakoh and Miochin: Origin of Summer and Winter." (Acoma and Laguna). *JAFL* 15:88–90, 1902.

Stirling, Matthew W.
Origin Myth of Acoma and Other Records. Bureau of American Ethnology, Bulletin 135. Washington, D. C.: U. S. Government Printing Office, 1942. vii, 123 pp., illus. 17 plates, 8 text figures, bibl.

Tichy, Marjorie Ferguson
"Six Pieces from Otowi." *El Palacio* 48:1-6, 1941.

Waters, Frank
The Man Who Killed the Deer. New York: Farrar and Rinehart, 1942.
Story of the Pueblo Indians.

Wittfogel, Karl A., and Goldfrank, Esther S.
"Some Aspects of Pueblo Mythology and Society." *JAFL* 56:17-30, 1943.

BELIEFS—WITCHCRAFT

Bartlett, Katherine A.
"A Unique Pueblo II Bird Fetish." *AA* 34:315-319, 1932. n.s.

Bunzel, Ruth L.
"Notes on the Katchina Cult in San Felipe." *JAFL* 41:290-292, 1928.

Espinosa, A. M.
"All Soul's Day at Zuni, Acoma, and Laguna." *JAFL* 31: 550-552, 1918.

Fewkes, J. Walter
"A Comparison of Sia and Tusayan Snake Ceremonials." *AA* 8:118-142, 1895. o.s.

Goggin, John M.
"Calendar of Eastern Pueblo Festivals, September and December." *New Mexico Anthropologist* (Albuquerque) 2, (No. 1):21-23, 1937.

Goldfrank, E. S.
"Notes on Two Pueblo Feasts." *AA* 25:188-196, 1923. n.s.

Haeberlin, H. K.
"The Idea of Fertilization in the Culture of the Pueblo Indians." *Memoirs of the American Anthropological Association* 3:1-55, 1916.

Hodge, F. W.
"Pueblo Snake Ceremonials." *AA* 9:133-151, 1896. o.s.

Jones, Volney H.
"Ceremonial Cigarettes." *Southwestern Monuments Monthly Report*, Supplement, pp. 287-291, (Oct.) 1935.

Laswell, Harold D.
"Collective Autism as a Consequence of Culture Contact: Notes on Religious Training and the Peyote Cult at Taos." *Zeitschrift für Socialforschung* (Paris) 4:232-247, 1935.

Parsons, Elsie Clews
"All Soul's Day at Zuni, Acoma, and Laguna." *JAFL* 30:495-496, 1917.

————.
"Notes on Ceremonialism at Laguna." *Anthropological Papers of the American Museum of Natural History* (New York) 19:85-131, 1920. illus.

————.
"Ceremonial Tewa du Nouveau Mexique et en Arizona." *Journal de la Société des Americanistes de Paris* 18:9-14, 1926.

————.
Pueblo Indian Religion. Chicago University Publications in Anthropology. Ethnological Series. Chicago: University of Chicago Press, 1939. 2 vols. xviii, 1275 pp.
"This is a monumental work of classic calibre. The two volumes bring together rich materials from one of the most intensively worked of ethnological areas." (Mandebaum)

————.
"Ritual Parallels in Pueblo and Plains Cultures, with a Special Reference to the Pawnee." *AA* 31:642-654, 1929. n.s.

————.
"Spanish Elements in the Kachina Cult of the Pueblos." *Proceedings of the 23rd Session of the International Congress of Americanists*, (New York), pp. 582-603, 1930.

————.
"The Religion of the Pueblo Indians." *Proceedings of the 21st Session of the International Congress of Americanists*, I:140-161, 1924.

————.
"Witchcraft Among the Pueblos, Indian or Spanish." *Man* 27:106-112, 125-128, 1927.

————, and Beals, R. L.
"The Sacred Clowns of the Pueblo and Maya-Yaqui Indians." *AA* 36:491-514, 1934. n.s.

Robbins, William J.
"Some Aspects of Pueblo Indian Religion." *Harvard Theological Review* 34:25-49, 1941.

White Leslie A.
"A Ceremonial Vocabulary Among the Pueblos." *International Journal of Linguistics* 10:161-167, 1944.

————.
"The Impersonation of Saints Among the Pueblos." *Papers of the Michigan Academy of Science, Arts and Letters* 27:559-564, 1941. (Published 1942.)

FOLK MEDICINE

Harrington, John Peabody
"The Ethnography of the Tewa Indians." *29th Annual Report: Bureau of American Ethnology, 1907-1908.* pp. 29-619, pls. 1-21, maps 1-29. Washington, D. C.: U. S. Government Printing Office, 1916.

————, Henderson, Junius
Ethnozoology of the Tewa Indians. Bureau of American Ethnology, Bull. 56, 76 pp. Washington, D. C.: U. S. Gov't Printing Office, 1914.

Judd, Neil M.
"When the Jemez Medicine Men Came to Zuni." *JAFL* 60:182-184, 1947.
Notes on a Jemez curing ceremony held for the benefit of Zuni.

Robbins, Wilfred William; Harrington, John Peabody; Marrico-Freire, Barbara
Ethnobotany of the Tewa Indians. Bureau of American Ethnology, Bull. 55, 124 pp., 9 pl., 7 fig. Washington, D. C.: U. S. Gov't Printing Office, 1916.

White, Leslie A.
"A Comparative Study of Keresan Medicine Societies." *Proceedings of the 23rd International Congress of Americanists,* pp. 604–619, 1928.

> Keresan—"A linguistic family of Pueblo Indians including the inhabitants of several villages on the Rio Grande, in North Central New Mexico, between the Rito de los Frijoles . . . and the Rio Jemez, as well as on the latter stream from the Pueblo Sia to its mouth." (Frederick W. Hodge)

CUSTOMS—FOLK POETRY—FOLK ART

Adam, L.
Primitive Art. London: Allen Lane Penguin Books, 1940. 160 pp., illus.

Alexander, H. B.
Pueblo Indian Painting. Nice: 1932.

Barber, E. A.
"Pueblo Pottery." *Amer. Natur.* 15:453–462, 1881.

Baumann, G.
Frijoles Canyon Pictographs. Sante Fe: Writers' Editions Inc., 1939. 43 pp.

Bloom, L. B.
"Early Weaving in New Mexico." *New Mexico Hist. Rev.* 2:228–238, 1927.

Boas, Franz
The Pueblo Potter. A Study of Creative Imagination in Primitive Art. Columbia University Contributions to Anthropology, Vol. 8. New York: Columbia University Press, 1929.

Chapman, K. M.
"Life Forms in Pueblo Pottery Decoration." *Art and Arch.* 13:120–122, 1922.

————.
"Pueblo Indian Pottery of the Post-Spanish Period." *Bull. Laboratory of Anthro. General Series* 4:1–4, 1938.

Clark, Ann Nolan
In My Mother's House. Illustrated by Velino Herrara. New York: The Viking Press, 1941. (First published May, 1941). 56 pp.
> An account of life among the Tewa Indian children.

Colton, H. S., and Hargrave, L. L.
"Handbook of Northern Arizona Pottery Wares." *Bull. Mus. North. Arizona* 11:1–267, 1937.

Cummings, Byron
"Kiwas of the San Juan Drainage." *AA* 17: 272–282, 1915. n.s.

Curtis, N.
"Pueblo Poetry." *El Palacio* 12, (No. 7): 95–99, 1922.

Curtis, W. E.
"Education and Morals Among the Navajos and Pueblos." *American Antiquity* 27:259–264, 1905.

Dennis, W., and M. G.
"Cradles and Cradling Practices of the Pueblo Indians." *AA* 42:107–115, 1940.

Fewkes, Jesse Walter
"Winter Solstice Altars at Hano Pueblo." *AA* 2 (No. 1):80–138, 1900.

Gilmore, Melvin R.
"An Interesting Vegetal Artifact from the Pecos Region of Texas." *Bulletin, University of Texas, Anthropological Papers* 1, (No. 5): 21–26, 1937.

Harrington, John Peabody
"Tewa Relationship of Terms." *AA* 14:472–499, 1912. n.s.

Hewett, E. L.
"Native American Artists." *Art and Arch.* 13: 103–113, 1922.

Hodge, F. W.
"Pueblo Names in the Onate Documents." *New Mex. Hist. Rev.* 10:36–47, 1935.

Holmes, William H.
"Pottery of the Ancient Pueblos." *4th Annual Report: Bureau of Ethnology,* 1882–1883, pp. 265–358, figs. 210–360. Washington, D. C.: U. S. Gov't Printing Office, 1886.
> Pueblo art (distribution, character, treatment). ceramic age, coil-made ware, illustrations of vessels, plain and painted ware, districts of the Rio San Juan, districts of the Colorado Chiquito, etc.

Jeançon, J. A.
"Pueblo Beads and Inlay." *Denver Art Mus. Leaf. Ser.* 30 (Part 1), 1931.

Keech, R. A.
"Pueblo Dwelling Architecture." *El Palacio* 36:49–53, 1934.

Kidder, Alfred Vincent
The Artifacts of Pecos. New Haven: Yale University Press for Phillips Academy, 1932.

Lemos, P. J.
"Marvelous Acoma and Its Craftsmen." *El Palacio* 24:234–244, 1928.

Mera, H. P.
Pueblo Indian Embroidery; drawings by the author. Memoirs of the Laboratory of Anthropology 4. Santa Fe: Laboratory of Anthropology, 1943. 73 pp., 26 pls.

————.
The Rain Bird: A Study in Pueblo Design. Memoirs, Laboratory of Anthropology 2. Santa Fe: Laboratory of Anthropology, 1937. 113 pp., illus.

Mindeleff, Victor
"A Study of Pueblo Architecture, Tusayan and Cibola." *8th Annual Report: Bureau of Ethnology*, 1886–7, pp. 13–223, pls. I–CXI, figs. 1–114, 1 map. Washington, D. C.: U. S. Gov't Printing Office, 1891.
   Traditionary history of Tusayan ruins and villages, ruins and inhabited villages of Cibola, physical features of the province, architecture, Kivas, etc.

Nordenskiöld, G.
The Cliff Dwellers of the Mesa Verde, Southwestern Colorado, their pottery and implements. Translated by D. Lloyd Morgan. Stockholm: P. A. Norstedt and Soner, 1893. xi, 174 pp., 6 maps.

Parsons, Elsie Clews
"Tewa Mothers and Children." *Man* 24:148–151, 1924.

Pepper, George H.
"Ceremonial Objects and Ornaments from Pueblo Bonito, New Mexico." *AA* 7:183–198, 1905. n.s.

―――――.
Ceremonial Deposits Found in an Ancient Pueblo Estufa in Northern New Mexico, U. S. A. New York: 1899. 6 pp., illus.

Pillsbury, D. L.
"Drums of Christmas: Pueblo Indians Celebrate." *Christian Science Monitor*, Dec. 20, 1947. p. 5.

Roediger, Virginia More
Ceremonial Costumes of the Pueblo Indians; their evolution, fabrication and significance in the prayer drama. Berkeley: University of California Press, 1941. xvii, 234 pp., bibl.

Smith, A. S.
"Primitive Work in Clay." *So. Workman* 40:143–154, 1911.

Spencer, F. C.
Education of the Pueblo Child. New York: The Macmillan Co., 1899. vi, 97 pp.

Spencer, J. E.
"Pueblo Sites of Southwestern Utah." *AA* 36:70–80, 1934. n.s.

Steward, Julian H.
"Pueblo Material Culture in Western Utah." *University of New Mexico Bulletin, Anthropological Series* I, (No. 3):1–64. Albuquerque, N. M.: University of New Mexico Press, 1936.

Trager, G. L.
"The Language of the Pueblo of Taos." *Le Maître Phonétique*, troisième serie, no. 56:59–62, Oct.–Dec., 1936.

Underhill, Ruth M.
Pueblo Crafts. Denver, Colo.: Educational Division, United States Indian Service, 1944. 147 pp.

White, Leslie A.
"Further Data on the Cultivation of Tobacco Among the Pueblo Indians." *Science* 96:59–60, 1942.

―――――.
"Keresan Indian Color Terms." *Papers of the Michigan Academy of Science, Arts and Letters* 28:559–563, 1943.

―――――.
"Nicotiana Ustica Cultivated by Pueblo Indians." *Science* 94:64–65, 1941.

GAMES

See: Music Studies Listed Below.

Harrington, John P.
"The Tewa Indian Game of Canute." *AA* 14:243–287, 1912. n.s.
   Music on pp. 263.

MUSIC

GENERAL STUDIES

Cowell, Henry
"La Musica entre los Pueblos primitivos." *BLAM* 5:105–108, 1941. (pub. 1942.)

Curtis, Natalie
The Indian's Book. . . . Illustrations from Photographs and from Original Drawings by Indians. New York: Harper and Brothers, 1907. 583 pp.
   Music, legends, and rituals of the Pueblo Indians —(pp. 423-533).

Densmore, Frances
"A Resemblance between Yuman and Pueblo Songs." *AA* 34:694–700, 1932. n.s.

―――――.
Music of the Santo Domingo Pueblo, New Mexico. Southwest Museum Papers, No. 12. Los Angeles: Southwest Museum, 1938. 186 pp., illus., music, bibl.
   Discusses, with numerous examples and illustrations, musical instruments, songs medicine societies, games, and rituals.

―――――.
The American Indians and Their Music. New York: The Womans Press, 1936. 150 pp.

Espinosa, Aurelio M.
Romances españoles tradicionales que cantan y recitan los Indios de los pueblos de Nuevo Mejico. Santander: 1932.
   Spanish traditional songs sung by the Pueblo Indians of New Mexico.

Freire-Marreco, Barbara
"New Mexican Spanish Folklore." *JAFL* 29 (No. 114):536–546, 1916.
   Texts of 3 songs as sung by the Pueblo Indians.

Harrington, John Peabody, and Roberts, Helen H.
"Picuris Children's Stories with Texts and Songs." *43rd Annual Report: Bureau of American Ethnology*, 1925–1926, pp. 289–447. Washington, D. C.: U. S. Government Printing Office, 1928.

Herzog, George
"A Comparison of Pueblo and Pima Musical Styles." *JAFL* 49:284–417, 1936.
A comparative study of melodic structure and contour, numerous examples carefully analyzed and discussed. Excellent musicological study.

Roberts, Helen H.
"Analysis of Picuris Songs," in: J. P. Harrington, *Picuris Children's Stories. 43rd Annual Report: Bureau of American Ethnology, 1925–1926,* pp. 339–447. Washington, D. C.: U. S. Government Printing Office, 1928.

————.
"Chakwena Songs of Zuni and Laguna." *JAFL* 36:177–184, 1923.

Spinden, Herbert Joseph. ed. and tr.
Songs of the Tewa. Preceded by an essay on American Indian poetry, with a selection of outstanding compositions from North and South America; an appendix contains original Tewa texts and explanatory notes. New York: Pub. under the Auspices of the Exposition of Indian Tribal Arts, 1933. 125 pp.

DANCES

See: Music studies listed above.

Bailey, F. M.
"Some Plays and Dances of the Taos Indians." *Natural History* 24:85–95, 1924.

Craig, E. L.
"Basket Dance." *School Arts* 40:99–100, (Nov.) 1940.

Freire-Marreco, Barbara
"Two American Indian Dances." *Sociological Review* (London) 4:324–337, 1911.

Harrington, J. P., and Roberts, Helen H.
"Picuris Children's Stories, with texts and songs." *Forty-third Annual Report of the Bureau of American Ethnology.* Smithsonian Institute. Washington, D. C.: Government Printing Office, 1928. pp. 289–447.

Henderson, Alice
"The Dance-Rituals of the Pueblo Indians." *Theatre Arts Monthly* (New York) 7:109–115, 1922.

Hodge, F. W.
"Pueblo Snake Ceremonials." *AA* 9:133–136, 1896.

Huebner, H.
"The Green Corn Dance at Santo Domingo." *El Palacio,* pp. 1–17, (July 6), 1938.

Pancoast, C. L.
"Last Dance of the Picuris." *American Museum Journal* (New York) 8:309–311, 1918.

"The Ritual Dances of the Pueblo Indians." *Denver Art Museum (Denver, Colo.), Cooke Daniels Foundation, Lectures* No. 1, pp. 7–18, 1927.

Thompson, Gilbert
"An Indian Dance at Jemez, New Mexico." *AA* 2:351–355, 1889.

Wolfe, E. F.
"The Oldest Dance in America. A close-up of the Pueblo Indian ritual ceremonies." *Dance Magazine* (New York) 14:19–48, 1930.

ARRANGEMENTS
————: *Voice and Piano*

"A oo ah—(Love Song of Red Willow Pueblo)." In: *Nine Indian Songs.* Lieurance, T.: Presser: Voice and piano.

"At the Sundown" (Red Willow Pueblo). Lieurance, T.: Presser: Voice and piano.

Curtis, Natalie
Songs of Ancient America. New York: G. Schirmer, 1905.
2 Pueblo Indian Corn-grinding Songs.

Grunn, Homer
From Desert and Pueblo: Five authentic Navajo and Tewa Indian songs; the lyrics based on Indian text by Elizabeth Willis De Huff; the Indian melodies transcribed and harmonized by Homer Grunn. Boston: Ditson Music Company, 1924. Voice and piano.

"Love Song" (Red Willow Pueblo). Lieurance, T. Presser: Voice and piano.

"Pa-Pup-Ooh" (Red Willow Pueblo). Lieurance, T. Presser: Voice and piano.

"Rue" (A Pueblo Love Song). Lieurance, T. Presser: Voice and piano.

"Wi-um Lullaby." Lieurance, T. Presser: Voice and piano.

————: *Female Voices*

"Longing" (Tewa). Stringham, E. J.: Witmark and Sons: SSA, with optional Flute obbligato. Text freely adapted by E. J. S.

"Love Song" (from the Red River Pueblo). Lieurance, T.: Presser: SSA.

"Pa-Pup-Ooh" (Deerflower — Red Willow Pueblo). Lieurance, T.: Presser: SSA (flute obbl.)

"Pueblo's Basket Dance." Vene, R.: Ricordi: SA.

"Rue" (Pueblo Spring Song). Lieurance, T.: Presser: SSA.

"Wi-um" (Pueblo Lullaby). Lieurance, T.: Presser: SSA.

————: *Mixed Voices*

"Chant of the Corn Grinders" (Pueblo). Lieurance, T.: Presser: SATB.

"Love Song" (From the Red Willow Pueblo).
Lieurance, T.: Presser: SATB.

"Rue" (Pueblo Spring Song).
Lieurance, T.: Presser: SATB.

"Wi-um" (Pueblo Lullaby).
Lieurance, T.: Presser: SATB.

————: *Piano—Organ*

"Four Impressions Based on Pueblo Indian Themes." Grunn, H.: Sam Fox: Piano.

"Wi-um" (Pueblo—Indian Lullaby).
Lieurance, T.: Presser: Organ.

————: *Orchestra*

Grunn, Homer, and Tobani, T. M., arr.
Desert Suite. Five Tone Pictures based on Pueblo Indian Themes. New York: Carl Fischer: Orchestra.
Contents: At Sunrise; Choya Dance; On the Mesa; Mirage; At Twilight.

Saminsky, Lazar
Pueblo—A Moon Rhapsody. MS. Orchestra.

————

Pueblo—Ballet. MS. Stage Work.

RECORDS

"Acoma Pueblo Wedding Song."
In: *American Indian Songs and Dances.*
DISC–161

"A-oo-ah" (Pueblo Indian Love Song).
Princess Watawaso.   VI–22316

"Pueblo Lullaby."
Thurlow Lieurance and Clement Barone, flute-piano.   VI–21972

U. S. Library of Congress. Division of Music. Folklore Section.
Indian Songs—in the Record Collection in the Archive of American Folksong. AAFS–LC

YUMA (Yuman)

(*Including:* Cocopa, Havasupai, Maricopa, Mohave, Walapai, Yavapai)

FOLKLORE

GENERAL STUDIES

Anon.
"An excursion of the Coco-Maricopa Indians Upon the River Gila." *The Ladies Repository* 40:15–16, Jan., 1855.
A description of these people, their customs, the journey through the wilderness to visit them, mentions other tribes of American Indians.

————

"Yuma." *Bull. Bureau Amer. Ethnol.* 30 (Part 2): 1010–1011, 1910.

Corbusier, W. H.
"Apache-Yumas and Apache-Mohaves." *American Antiquarian and Oriental Journal* 8:338, 1886.

Corle, Edwin
Listen, Bright Angel. New York: Duell, Sloan and Pearce, 1946. 312 pp., illus.
A dramatic narrative of the Southwest, in which the Grand Canyon is highlighted. The life of the Havasupai is colorfully sketched.

Coues, Elliott, trans. and ed.
On the Trail of a Spanish Pioneer. The Diary and Itinerary of Francisco Garcés, 1775–1776, 2 vols. New York: Francis P. Harper, 1900.

Douglas, F. H. comp.
The Havasupai Indians. Denver Art Museum, Leaflet 33, (Oct.) 1931.
"A small isolated tribe of the Yuman stock (the nucleus of which is believed to have descended from the Walapai) who occupy Cataract Canyon of the Rio Colorado in north-west Arizona." (H. W. Henshaw)

Fischel, Hans E.
"Folsom and Yuma Culture Finds." *American Antiquity* 4, (No. 2):24–26, 1939.

Gifford, E. W.
"Cultural Relations of the Gila River and Lower Colorado Tribes." *AA* 38:679–682, 1936. n.s.

————

"The Cocopa." *University of California Publications in American Archaeology and Ethnology* 31, (No. 5):257–334. Berkeley: University of California Press, 1933. Illus.

————

"The Northeastern and Western Yavapai." *University of California Publications in American Archaeology and Ethnology,* Vol. 34, (No. 4). Berkeley: University of California Press, 1936. Illus.
Appendix A relates thirteen Northeastern Yavapai war tales.

————

"The Southeastern Yavapai." *University of California Publications in American Archaeology and Ethnology* 29: (No. 3):177–252. Berkeley: University of California Press, 1932.
The Yavapai are popularly known as Apache Mohave and Mohave Apache.

Koch, J.
"A Visit to the Yuma Indian Reservation." *So. Workman* 35:593–597, 1906.
Lists important dances and games.

Kroeber, A. L.
Earth Tongue, a Mohave. In: *American Indian Life,* ed. E. C. Parsons, (pp. 189–202). New York: Huebsch, 1922.

————

"Preliminary Sketch of the Mohave Indians." *AA* 4:276–286, 1904. n.s.

———.
Walapai Ethnography. Memoir American Anthropological Association, No. 42. Lancaster, Pa.: 1935. 239 pp.

———.
"Yuman Tribes of the Lower Colorado." *University of California, Publications in American Archaeology and Ethnology* 16, (No. 8):475–485, 1920.
"Beside the Mohave and Yuma, only the Cocopa and Kamia retain their identity. The others are extinct or merged." (A. L. K.)

Nichols, Charles L.
Crazy Weather. New York: The Macmillan Company, 1944. 195 pp.
"The contrast in this book between Indian and white ways of facing the physical universe is interesting. Havek, the Mohave lad, lives in the present. Even when he is dreaming of his ghosts, and of the great days of the Mohave past, it is without a thought that his gods or his tradition might be invoked to alter his fate. But even when he is most obviously loafing, South Boy is wondering how to use his will power and his ingenuity to build himself a future." (John Chamberlain)

Schaffhausen, J. F.
"Indian Shangri-La." *Saturday Evening Post* 215:20–21, (Dec. 5), 1942.

Spier, Leslie
Comparative Vocabularies and Parallel Texts in Two Languages of Arizona. University of New Mexico Publications in Anthropology 2. Albuquerque, New Mexico: University of New Mexico Press, 1946. 150 pp.

———.
Cultural Relations of the Gila River and Lower Colorado Tribes. Yale University Publications in Anthropology 3. New Haven: Yale University Press, 1936. 22 pp.

———.
"Havasupai Ethnography." *American Museum of Natural History, Anthropological Papers* 29:81–392, 1928. Illus.

———.
"Havasupai (Yuman) Texts." *International Journal of American Linguistics,* 3:109–116.

———.
"Problems Arising from the Cultural Position of the Havasupai." *AA* 31:212–213, 1929. n.s.

———.
Yuman Tribes of the Gila River. Chicago: University of Chicago Press, 1933. 433 pp., illus.
The music is discussed by George Herzog.

Walapai Papers, Historical Reports, Documents, and Extracts from Publications, Relating to the Walapai Indians of Arizona. Senate Document 273 (Washington) 1936.

White, Helen C.
Duel on the King's Highway. New York: The Macmillan Co., 1947.
Includes observations on conditions, traditions, and customs of the Yuma Indians.

MYTHS—FOLKTALES—LEGENDS

Curtis, Natalie
"Creation Myths of the Cochans (Yuma Indians)." *Craftsman,* 16:559.

Devereux, George
"Mohave Coyote Tales." *JAFL* 61:233–255, 1948.

DuBois, Constance Goddard
"Diegueño Myths and their Connections with the Mohave." *Proceedings of the 15th Session of the International Congress of Americanists* (Quebec) 2:129–135, 1906.

Gifford, E. W.
"Northeastern and Western Yavapai Myths." *JAFL* 46:347–415, 1933.

Gould, M. K.
"Two Legends of the Mojave-Apache." *JAFL* 34:319–320, 1921.

Harrington, J. P.
"Yuma Account of Origins." *JAFL* 21:324–348, 1908.

Kroeber, A. L.
Seven Mohave Myths. University of California Anthropological Records, Vol. 9, No. 3. (in press). Los Angeles: University of California Press, 1948.

McKee, Louise, and Summers, Richard
Dusty Desert Tales. Caldwell, Idaho: Caxton Printers, 1941.

Perkins, Mrs. Edna (Brush)
The White Heart of Mohave. New York: Boni and Liveright, 1922. 229 pp.
Desert tales.

BELIEFS—CUSTOMS

Bourke, J. G.
"Cosmogony and Theogony of the Mojave Indians of the Rio Colorado, Arizona." *JAFL* 2:169–189, 1889.

Brown, Herbert
"A Pima-Maricopa Ceremony." *AA* 8:688–691, 1906. n.s.

Devereux, George
"Der Begriff der Vaterschaft bei den Mohave Indianerin." *Zeitschrift für Ethnologie* 69, (Nos. 1–3):72–78, 1937.
The status of father by the Mohave Indians.

———.
"Funeral Suicide and the Mohave Social Structure." *Bulletin of the History of Medicine* 11:522–542, 1942.

———.
"Institutionalized Homosexuality of the Mohave Indians." *Human Biology* 9, (No. 4):498–527, 1938.

———.
"Mohave Beliefs Concerning Twins." *AA* 43:573–592, 1941.

_____.
Sexual Life of the Mohave Indians. Los Angeles: University of California, 1936. Unpublished Ph.D. thesis.

Fewkes, J. W.
"Ceremonial Circuit Among the Village Indians of Northwestern Arizona." *JAFL* 5:33–42, 1892.

Gifford, E. W.
"Yuma Dreams and Omens." *JAFL* 39:58–69, 1926.

Gould, M. K.
"Mohave Soul Concepts." *AA* 39:417–422, 1937. n.s.

Putnam, G. R.
"A Yuma Creation." *AA* 8:264–267, 1895.

Wallace, W. J.
"The Dream in Mohave Life." *JAFL* 60:252–258, 1947.
Discussion of power-bestowing dreams, and individual dreams.

FOLK ART—GAMES—SPEECH

Fewkes, J. Walter
"A Fictitious Ruin in Gila Valley, Arizona." *AA* 9:510–513, 1907. n.s.

Hawley, F. M.
"Prehistoric Pottery and Culture Relations in the Middle Gila." *AA* 32:522–536, 1930. n.s., 34:548–550, 1932.

Hough, Walter
"Antiquities of the Upper Gila and Salt Rivers in Arizona and New Mexico." *Read Before the National Academy of Science,* No. 20, pp. 219–239, 1907. Washington, D. C.: U. S. Government Printing Office, 1908.

Kroeber, A. L.
"Phonetic Elements of the Mohave Language." *University of California Publications in American Archaeology and Ethnology* 10, (No. 3): 45–96, 1911. plates 6–20. Berkeley: The University Press, 1911–1914.

"Mohave Games."
JAFL 2:170–171, 1889.

Schmidt, Erich F.
"Time-Relations of Prehistoric Pottery Types." *Anthropological Papers of the American Museum of Natural History* (New York) 30:247–302, 1928. Illus.

Watkins, Frances E.
"Another County Heard From. A 'Yuma Type' Dart Point from Southwestern Oregon." *The Masterkey* 8, (No. 3):73, 76. Los Angeles: Southwest Museum, (May) 1934.

MUSIC
GENERAL STUDIES

Brown, Herbert
"A Pima-Maricopa Ceremony." *AA* 8:688–691, 1906. n.s.

Densmore, Frances
"A Resemblance Between Yuman and Pueblo Songs." *AA* 34:694–700, 1932. n. s.

_____.
Yuman and Yaqui Music. U. S. Bureau of Ethnology, Bulletin 110. Washington, D. C.: U. S. Government Printing Office, 1932. 216 pp., music, illus., bibl.
Contains a comparison of Yuman and Yaqui songs with Chippewa, Sioux, Ute, Mandan, Hidasta, Papago, Pawnee and Menominee songs. Also, Yuman legends, dances, medicine songs, games, children songs, and a melodic analysis of the tunes.

Herzog, George
Maricopa Music. In: *Yuman Tribes of the Gila River,* by L. Spier, pp. 272–279. Chicago: University of Chicago Press, 1933. 433 pp., illus.

_____.
"The Yuman Musical Style." *JAFL* 41:183–231, 1928.
An analysis and comparative study with numerous examples.

Koch, J.
"A Visit to the Yuma Reservation." *So. Workman* 35:593–597, 1906.
Lists important dances and games.

Spier, Leslie
Yuman Tribes of the Gila River. Chicago: University of Chicago Press, 1933. 433 pp., illus.
The music is discussed by George Herzog.

ARRANGEMENTS
Orchestra

McDonald, Harl
Mojave-Symphonic Fantasy MS—for Orchestra.

ZUNI (Pueblo)
FOLKLORE
GENERAL STUDIES

Bandelier, A. F.
An Outline of the Documentary History of the Zuni Tribe. Papers of the Hemenway Southwestern Archaeological Expedition. Journal of American Ethnology and Archaeology (Cambridge), Vol. III, 1892.

Bunzel, Ruth L.
Zuni Texts. Publication of American Ethnological Society No. 15. New York: G. E. Stechert and Company, 1933. vii, 285 pp.

Coolidge, Mary R.
The Rainmakers. Boston: Houghton, Mifflin Company, 1929. xiii, 326 pp., illus.

Cushing, Frank Hamilton
My Adventures in Zuni. Sante Fe, N. M.: The Peripatetic Press, 1941. 178 pp., illus.

Davis, W. W. H.
El Gringo, or New Mexico and Her People.
New York: Harper and Bros., 1857. 332 pp.

Hodge, Frederick Webb
*History of Hawikuh, New Mexico: One of the
So-called Cities of Cibola.* Publications, Fred-
erick Webb Hodge Anniversary Publication
Fund, Vol. I. Los Angeles: Southwest Museum,
1937. 155 pp., illus.
> A former pueblo of the Zuni and one of the Seven
> Cities of Cibola of early Spanish times.

————.
"Zuni." *Bull. Bureau Amer. Ethnol* 30 (Part
2) : 1015–1020, 1910.

Kroeber, A. L.
"Zuni Kin and Clan." *Anthropological Papers
of the American Museum of Natural History*
(New York) 18:39–204, 1917. illus.

Parsons, Elsie Clews
"Mothers and Children at Zuni." *Man* 19:168–
173, 1919.

————.
"Notes on Zuni, Parts I, II." *Memoirs of the
American Anthropological Association* 4:151–
225, 229–337, 1917.

————.
"Reasoning from Analogy at Zuni." *Scientific
Monthly* 4:365–368, 1917.

MYTHS—FOLKTALES—LEGENDS

Applegate, Frank G.
Native Tales of New Mexico. Introduction by
Mary Austin. Illustrated in color by author.
London and Phila.: J. B. Lippincott Company,
1932. **263 pp.**

Benedict, Ruth
Zuni Mythology. Columbia University Contributions to Anthropology 21. 2 vols. New York:
Columbia University Press, 1935. Part 1—342
pp.; Part II—345 pp.

Boas, Franz
"Tales of Spanish Provenience from Zuni."
JAFL 35:62–98, 1922.

————, **and Parsons, E. C.**
"Spanish Tales from Laguna and Zuni, New
Mexico." *JAFL* 33:47–72, 1924.

Bunzel, Ruth L.
"Introduction to Zuni Ceremonialism, Zuni
Origin Myths, Zuni Ritual Poetry, Zuni Katcinas." *47th Annual Report: Bureau of American Ethnology,* pp. 467–1086. Washington,
D. C.: U. S. Government Printing Office, 1930.
illus.

————.
"Zuni Origin Myths." *47th Annual Report: Bureau of American Ethnology, Smithsonian Institution,* pp. 545–609. Washington, D. C.: U. S.
Government Printing Office, 1932.

Cushing, Frank Hamilton
"A Zuñi Folktale of the Underworld." *JAFL*
5(No. 16) : 49–56, 1892.

————.
"Outlines of Zuni Creation Myths." *13th Annual Report: Bureau American Ethnology
1891–1892,* pp. 325–446. Washington, D. C.:
U. S. Government Printing Office, 1896.

————.
"The Giant Cloud-Swallower." A Zuñi tale of
the Cañonde Chelly. *Archaeologist* 1:241–244,
1893.

————.
Zuñi Breadstuff. New York: Museum of the
American Indian, Heye Foundation, 1920. 673
pp., illus. (Indian notes and monographs, vol.
8).

————.
"Zuñi Fetishes." *Ann. Rep. Bur. Amer. Ethnol.*
2:9–45, 1883.

————.
Zuni Folk Tales. Recorded and Translated by
F. Hamilton, with an Introduction by J. W.
Powell. London and New York: G. P. Putnam's
Sons, 1901. xxix, 474 pp., Reprinted in New
York by Alfred A. Knopf in 1931. illus.

————.
"Zuni Social, Mythic and Religious Systems."
Popular Science Monthly 21 :186–192, 1882.

Gatschet, A. S.
"Frank Hamilton Cushing und die Mythen und
Märchen der Zuñi-Indianer." *Globus* 81(Nr.
23) : 361–364, 1902.

Handy, Edward L.
"Zuni Tales." *JAFL* 31:451–471, 1918.

Hodge, Frederick Webb
"A Zuni Folktale of the Maximilian Jay."
Masterkey 2, (No. 3) :89, 1937.

Matthews, Washington
"Myths of Gestation and Parturition." *AA*
4:734–743, 1904. n.s.

Myers, S.
"Giant Who Swallowed the Clouds; Zuni Folk
Tale Dramatized in One Act." *School Arts
Magazine* 34:436–441, (March) 1935.

Nusbaum, Mrs. Mary Aileen
The Seven Cities of Cibola, with pictures by
Margaret Finnan. New York: G. P. Putnam's
Sons, 1926. xi, 167 pp., illus.
> Zuni tales and legends. The same book also ap-
> peared under the title: 'Zuni Indian Tales.'

Parsons, Elsie Clews
"Nativity Myth at Laguna and Zuni." *JAFL*
31:256–263, 1918.

————.
"Origin Myth from Zuni." *JAFL* 36:135–162,
1923.

"Review: *Zuni Mythology* by Ruth Benedict and *Zuni Texts* by Ruth Bunzel." *JAFL* 50: 107–109, 1937.

———.
"Zuni Tales." *JAFL* 43:1–59, 1930.

Risser, Anna
"Seven Zuni Folk Tales. *El Palacio* 48:215–226, 1941.

Wetherell, Betty
"A Zuni Legend." *Masterkey* 12, (No. 5): 196–198, 1938.

"Why There Are No More Giants; Indian Fairy Tale from New Mexico." *Pan American Magazine* 42:359, (February) 1930.

BELIEFS—MAGIC—CUSTOMS

Bunzel, Ruth L.
"Introduction to Zuni Ceremonialism." *47th Annual Report: Bureau of American Ethnology, Smithsonian Institution*, pp. 467–544. Washington, D. C.: U. S. Government Printing Office, 1932.

———.
"Zuni Katcinas: an Analytical Study." *47th Annual Report: Bureau of American Ethnology, Smithsonian Institution*, pp. 837–1086. Washington, D. C.: U. S. Government Printing Office.

Cushing, Frank Hamilton
"Zuni Fetiches." *2nd Annual Report: Bureau American Ethnology, 1880–1881*. pp. 9–44, pls. 1–11, figs. 1–3. Washington, D. C.: U. S. Government Printing Office, 1883.
Zuni philosophy: worship of animals, origin of Zuni fetiches, Zuni Iliad, prey gods of the six regions, of the hunt worship rites, prey gods of the priesthood of the bow, etc.

———.
"Zuni Breadstuff." *Indian Notes and Monographs*, Museum of the American Indian, Heye Foundation, 8, 1920. 642 pp. New Ed.

Espinosa, A. M.
"All Soul's Day at Zuni, Acoma and Laguna." *JAFL* 31:550–552, 1918.

Fewkes, Jesse Walter
"A Study of Summer Ceremonials at Zuni and Moqui Pueblos." *Essex Institute Bulletin*, Vol. 22, (Nos. 7–9) :89–113, (Salem) 1890.

———.
"Zuni Summer Ceremonials." *JAFL* 4:80–82, 1891.

Kirk, Ruth F.
"Introduction to Zuni Fetishism." *El Palacio* 50:117–129, 146–159, 183–198, 206–219, 235–245, illus.

Kroeber, A. L.
"Thoughts on Zuñi Religion." In: *Holmes Anniversary Volume. . . .* Washington: J. W. Bryan, 1916.

Parsons, Elsie Clews
"A Few Zuni Death Beliefs and Practices." *AA* 18:245–256, 1916. n.s.

———.
"All Soul's Day at Zuni, Acoma and Laguna." *JAFL* 30:495–496, 1917.

———.
"A Zuni Detective" *Man* 16:99–100, 1916. (London)

———.
"Holding Back in Crisis Ceremonialism." *AA* 18:41–52, 1916. n.s.

———.
Hopi and Zuni Ceremonialism. Memoirs American Anthropological Association, No. 39. Menasha, Wis.: The American Anthropological Association, 1933.

———.
"Increase by Magic; a Zuni Pattern." *AA* 21:279–286, 1919.

———.
"Spring Days in Zuni, New Mexico." *Scientific Monthly* 36:49–54, 1933.

———.
"Teshlativa at Zuni." *Journal of Philosophy, Psychology and Scientific Methods* 16:272–273, 1919.

———.
"The Favorite Number of the Zuni." *Scientific Monthly* 3:285–288, 1916.

———.
The Scalp Ceremonial of Zuni. Memoirs American Anthropological Association No. 31. Menasha, Wis.: The American Anthropological Association, 1924.

———.
"The Zuni Adoshle and Suuke." *AA* 18:338–347, 1916. n.s.

———.
"The Zuni Lamana." *AA* 18:521–528, 1916.

———.
"Waiyautitsa of Zuni, New Mexico." *Scientific Monthly* 9:443–457, 1919.

———.
"Zuni Conception and Pregnancy Beliefs." *Proceedings of the 19th Session of the International Congress of Americanists*, pp. 379–383, 1917.

———.
"Zuni Mo'lawia (Shalako)." *JAFL* 29:392–399, 1916.

———.
"Zuni Names and Naming Practices." *JAFL* 36:171–176, 1923.

Stevenson, Matilda Coxe
"Zuni Ancestral Gods and Masks." *AA* 11: 33–41, 1898. o.s.

——————.
"The Zuni Indians: Their Mythology, Esoteric Societies, and Ceremonies." *23rd Annual Report: Bureau of American Ethnology, 1901–1902.* pp. 13–578, pls. 1–129, figs. 1–34. Washington, D. C.: U. S. Government Printing Office, 1904.

——————.
"The Religious Life of the Zuñi Child." *5th Annual Report: Bureau of Ethnology, 1883–1884,* pp. 539–557, figs. 69–77. Washington, D. C.: U. S. Gov't. Printing Office, 1887.
Brief account of Zuñi mythology, birth customs, involuntary and voluntary initiation into the kak-ko.

GAMES

Hodge, Frederick Webb
"A Zuni Foot-Race." *AA* 3:227–233, 1890.

Klett, Francis
"The Cachina, a Dance at the Pueblo of Zuni." *U. S. Engineers Bureau Report of U. S. Geographical Survey* (Washington) 7:332–336, 1879.

Stevenson, Matilda Coxe
Zuni Games. *AA* 5:468–498, 1903 n.s.

FOLK POETRY—ART—MEDICINE

Bunzel, Ruth L.
"Zuni Ritual Poetry." *47th Annual Report: Bureau of American Ethnology, Smithsonian Institution,* pp. 611–835. Washington, D. C.: U. S. Government Printing Office, 1932.

Cushing, Frank Hamilton
"A Study of Pueblo Pottery as Illustrative of Zuñi Culture Growth." *4th Annual Report: Bureau of Ethnology, 1882–1883,* pp. 473–510, figs. 490–564. Washington, D. C.: U. S. Gov't. Printing Office, 1886.
Habitations affected by environment, pottery affected by environment, evolution of forms, evolution of decoration, decorative symbolism, etc.

Kroeber, A. L.
"Zuni Potsherds." *Anthropological Papers of the American Museum of Natural History* (New York) 18:1–37, 1916. illus.

Roberts, Frank H. H., J.
The Village of the Great Kivas on the Zuni Reservation, New Mexico. Bulletin 111. Bureau of American Ethnology, Smithsonian Institution. Washington, D. C.: U. S. Government Printing Office, 1932.

Ruins at Kiatuthlanna, Eastern Arizona.
Bureau of American Ethnology, Bulletin 100. Washington, D. C.: U. S. Government Printing Office, 1931. 195 pp., illus., map.
Covers house remains of Zuni Indians, objects of culture, basketry, stone objects, humans remains, etc.

Shufeldt, R. W.
"Examples of Unusual Zuni Pottery." *Records of the Past* (Washington) 9:208–212, 1910.

Spier, Leslie
"An Outline for a Chronology of Zuni Ruins." *Anthropological Papers of the American Museum of Natural History* (New York) 18:207–331, 1917. illus.

Stevenson, Matilda Coxe
"Ethnobotany of the Zuni Indians." *30th Annual Report: Bureau of American Ethnology, 1908–1909,* pp. 31–102, pls. 1–3. Washington, D. C.: U. S. Government Printing Office, 1915.

MUSIC

GENERAL STUDIES

Bunzel, Ruth Leah
"Singing and Dancing." In: *Introduction to Zuni Ceremonialism. 47th Annual Report, Bureau of American Ethnology,* pp. 494–498. Washington, D. C.: U. S. Government Printing Office, 1932.

Curtis, Natalie
"A Bit of American Folk Music. Two Pueblo Indian Grinding Songs." *Craftsman* 7:35–41, 1904–05.
Includes the music.

——————.
The Indians' Book . . . New York: Harper and Brothers, 1907.
Contains Zuni melodies, texts, legends, myths, and rituals.

Cushing, Frank Hamilton
"Outlines of Zuni Creation Myths." *13th Annual Report, Bureau of American Ethnology,* pp. 321–447; index. pp. 449–462. Washington, D. C.: U. S. Government Printing Office, 1896.

——————.
"Zuni Fetishes." *2nd Annual Report: Bureau of American Ethnology to the Secretary of the Smithsonian Institution,* pp. 3–45; pl. 1–11; fig. 1–3. Washington, D. C.: U. S. Government Printing Office, 1883.

Fillmore, John Comfort
"The Zuni Music, as translated by Mr. Benjamin Ives Gilman." *Music* (Chicago) 5:39–46, 1893–1894.

Gilman, Benjamin I.
"Zuni Melodies." *Journal of American Ethnology and Archaeology* 1:63–92, 1891.

"Music of the Zuni Indians of New Mexico." *Musical Courier* (New York) 37, (No. 1):19, 1898.

Roberts, Helen H.
"Chakwena Songs of Zuni and Laguna." *JAFL* 36:177–184, 1923.

Stacey, Reid
"Some Zuni Ceremonies and Melodies." *The Music Lovers' Calendar* (Urbana, Ill.) 2:54–61, 1907.

Troyer, Carlos
Indian Music Lecture: The Zuni Indians and their Music. An address designed for reading at musical gatherings, describing the lives, customs, religions, occult practices, and the surprising musical development of the cliff dwellers of the Southwest. Philadelphia: Theodore Presser Company, 1913. vii, 44 pp.

DANCES

Bourke, John Gregory
The Urine Dance of the Zuni Indians of New Mexico—from ethnological notes collected by J. G. B. under the direction of Lt. Gen. P. H. Sheridan in 1881. Read at the Annual Meeting of the *American Association for the Advancement of Science*, Ann Arbor Michigan, 1885. Vol. 34, pp. 400–403.

————.
"The Wine Dance of the Zuñis." *American Association for the Advancement of Science.* 34th Meeting held at Ann Arbor, Michigan, 1885. Salem, 1896).

Fewkes, Jesse Walter
"A Study of Summer Ceremonials at Zuñi and Moqui Pueblos." *Essex Institute Bulletin,* Vol. 22 (nos. 7–9):89–113, (Salem), 1890.

L'Allemand, G.
"Pageantry on the Mesa; Masked Kachina Butterfly Dance." *Travel* 61:15–17, (June) 1933.

Parsons, Elsie Clews
"Winter and Summer Dance Series in Zuni in 1918." *University Publications in American Archaeology and Ethnology,* 17:(No. 3): 171–216. Berkeley: University of California Press, 1922.

ARRANGEMENTS

————: *Voice and Piano*

"Hunting Song of the Cliff-dwellers." (Song and Dance). Troyer, C.: Presser.

"Hymn to the Sun." Troyer, C.: Presser.

"Incantation Upon a Sleeping Infant (Lullaby). Troyer, C.: Presser.

"Indian Fire Drill Song" Troyer, C.: Presser.

"Inketunga's Thunder Song" Farwell, A.: Schirmer.

"Invocation to the Sun God" (Lullaby) Troyer, C.: Presser.

"Sunset Song" Troyer, C.: Presser.

"The Coming of Montezuma" (With Great Drum Reveille). Troyer, C.: Presser.

"The Festive Sun Dance of the Zunis." Troyer, C.: Presser.

"The Great Rain Dance of the Zunis" Troyer, C.: Presser.

"The Sunrise Call, or Echo Song" Troyer, C.: Presser.

Traditional Songs of the Zunis
Troyer, Carlos: Newton Center, Mass.: Wa-Wan Press, 1904. 2nd series.

"Two Zunian Melodies"
Troyer, C.: Presser. *Contents:* Awakening at Dawn (a Processional chant); Recall of the Tribal Hunters.

"Zuni Lover's Wooing, or Blanket Song" Troyer, C.: Presser.

————: *Choral*

"Incantation Upon a Sleeping Infant." Matthews, A. H.: Presser: SATB a cap.

"Invocation to the Sun God" (Zuni) Matthews, A. H.: Presser: SATB a cap.

"Montezuma Comes" Loomis, H. W.: Birchard: SSA.

"Montezuma Comes" Loomis, H. W.: Birchard: SATB.

"The Sun Worshippers" (Zuni) Loomis, H. W.: Birchard: SATB, SAB.

————: *Piano*

"Ghost Dance of the Zunis" Troyer, C.: Schirmer and Presser: with violin and obbl.

"Zunian ("Kor-Kok-Shi") Clown Dance" Troyer, C.: Presser.

Zuni Impressions. An Indian Suite, Opus 27, with descriptive foreword by Homer Grunn. Grunn, Homer: Boston Music Company.

————: *Orchestra*

Grunn, Homer
Zuni Impressions. An Indian Suite. New York: Carl Fischer.

RECORDS

"Harvest Dance Song"
Laura Boulton. In: *Indian Music of the Southwest.* Set V–P49

"Zuni Songs and Dances." In: *American Indian Songs and Dances.* DISC 161
Contents: Opening Song of the Zuni Rain Dance; Zuni Corn Grinding Song; Two Zuni Lullabies.

U. S. Library of Congress. Division of Music. Folklore Section.
Indian Music—Among the many records, collected by individuals and institutions and deposited in The Archives of American Folksong are many discs of the Southwestern tribes, the Pueblos, and others.

AAFS–LC

THE CALIFORNIA AREA

THE CALIFORNIA AREA

FOLKLORE
GENERAL STUDIES

Atkins, Elizabeth H.
Little Wolf's Brother. New York: Frederick A. Stokes Company, 1939. 195 pp.
A story of the California Indians, for young readers.

Bancroft, Hubert Howe
The Native Races of the Pacific States of North America. San Francisco: A. L. Bancroft and Co., 1874–75. 5 vols., illus.
Contents: 1. Wild Tribes. 2. Civilized Nations. 3. Myths and Languages. 4. Antiquities. 5. Primitive History.

Boller, Henry A.
Among the Indians. Eight Years in the Far West. 1858–1866. Phila., Pa.: T. E. Zell Co., 1868. 428 pp.

Burbank, E. A.
Burbank Among the Indians, as Told to Ernest Royce. Caldwell, Idaho: Caxton Printers, Ltd., 1945. 232 pp., illus.
A noted artist records his impressions of life and lore among many Indian tribes, principally those of the Plains and Southwest.

"California Indian Folklore."
JAFL 19:141–144, 322–325, 1906.

Carson, Kit
Kit Carson's Life and Adventures from Facts Narrated by Himself. Hartford, Conn.: Dustin, Gilman and Company, 1873. 604 pp., illus.
Embracing events in the life-time of America's greatest trapper, scout and guide, including vivid accounts of the every day life, inner character, and peculiar customs of all Indian tribes of the far west. Edited by Dewitt C. Peters.

Caughey, John W.
California. (Prentice-Hall Books on History.) New York: Prentice-Hall, 1940. xiv, 680 pp.

Chever, E. E.
"The Indians of California." *American Naturalist* 4:129–148, 1870.

Coyner, David H.
The Lost Trappers: A Collection of Interesting Scenes and Events in the Rocky Mountains; Together with a Short Description of California. Cincinnati, 1847. xv, 255 pp.

Dalton, O. M.
"Notes on an Ethnographical Collection from the West Coast of North America." *Internationales Archiv für Ethnographie* (Leyden) 10: 225–245, 1897.

Dixon, Roland B., Kroeber, A. L.
"Linguistic Families of California." *University of California Publications in American Archae-*

ology and Ethnology, 16, (No. 3):47–118, 1919. map, 1 figure in text. Berkeley: University of California Press, 1919–1920.

Drucker, Philip
"Culture Element Distribution: V—Southern California." *Anthropological Records. University of California* 1, (No. 1):52 pp., 1937.

Duflot de Mofras, E.
Exploration du territoire de l'Orégon, des Californies, et de la mer Vermeille, exécutée pendant les années 1840, 1841 et 1842. Tomes I–II. Paris: A. Bertrand, 1844.

Engelhardt, Zephyrin
The Franciscans in California. Harbor Springs, Mich.: 1897. xvi, 516 pp.

————.
The Missions and Missionaries of California. San Francisco: 1908–15. 4 vols.

Fages, P.
"Diary." *Publications of the Academy of Pacific Coast History* 2:141–159, 1911.

————.
A Historical, Political, and Natural Description of California. Berkeley: 1937. 83 pp.

Farnham, Thomas J.
Travels in the Californias and Scenes in the Pacific Ocean. New York: 1844. iv, 416 pp.

Forbes, Alexander
California; a History of Upper and Lower California from their First Discovery to the Present Time. London: 1839.

Frémont, John C.
Geographical Memoir Upon Upper California. Washington: Wendell & Benthuysen, 1848.

————.
The Exploring Expedition to the Rocky Mountains, Oregon and California. To which is added a physical description of California. Auburn and Buffalo: 1854. 456 pp.

Frignet, Ernest
La Californie, Histoire des Progrès de l'un des États-Unis de L'Amérique et des Institutions Qui Font sa Prosperité. Paris: 1867.
A history of California. General observations on Indian tribes, customs, and lore.

Gibbs, George
"Journal of the Expedition of Colonel Redick M'kee." In: *Information Respecting the History, Condition, and Prospects of the Indian Tribes of the United States.* Henry Rowe Schoolcraft, ed. Vol. 3, pp. 99–177. Philadelphia, 1853.

Gifford, Edward Winslow
"California Indian Types." *Natural History* (New York) 26:50–60, 1926.

————, and Harris, Gwendoline Block, comps.
California Indian Nights Entertainments. Glendale, Calif.: The Arthur H. Clark Company, 1930. 323 pp., illus.
> Stories of the creation of the world, of man, of fire, of the sun, of thunder, etc.: of coyote, the land of the dead, the sky land, monsters, animal people, etc.

Haeckel, Josef
"Das Männerhaus in nordlichen Kalifornien." *Mitteilungen der Anthropologischen Gesellschafft* (Wien) 70 (No. 2):144–259, 1940.
> The male house in northern California.

Hafen, Le Roy R., and Rister, Carl C.
Western America: the exploration, settlement of the region beyond the Mississippi. (Prentice Hall Books on History.) New York: Prentice Hall, 1941. xxiv, 698 pp.
> General discussion on the Plains Indians, as well as those of the Southwest and California.

Hastings, Lansford W.
The Emigrant's Guide to Oregon and California. Cincinnati: G. Conclin, 1845. 152 pp.

Henshaw, H. W.
Introductory Note to the Account by the Pilot Ferrel of the Voyage of Cabrillo along the West Coast of North America in 1542. Wheeler Survey Reports, Vol. 7, pt. 1. Washington, D. C.: 1879.

Hittell, Theodore H.
History of California. Vols. I–IV. San Francisco: 1885–1897.
> Vol. 1-2: Pacific Press Publishing House and Occidental Co., 1885. Vol. 3-4: N. J. Store & Co., 1897.

Hoffman, Walter J.
Miscellaneous Enthnographic Observations on Indians Inhabiting Nevada, California and Arizona. Tenth Annual Report, Hayden Survey, Washington, D. C.: 1878.

Holmes, William H.
"Anthropological Studies in California." *National Museum Report,* pp. 155–187, 1900. Illus.

Jackson, H. M. H., and Kinney, A.
Report on the Condition and Needs of the Mission Indians. Washington, D. C.: U. S. Gov't. Printing Office, 1883. 35 pp.

Klimek, Stanislaw
"Culture Element Distributions, I. The Structure of California Indian Culture." *University of California Publicaitons in American Archaeology and Ethnology* 37, (No. 1):70 pp. Berkeley: University of California Press, 1935.

Kotzebue, Otto von
Voyage of Discovery Into the South Sea and Behrings Straits. For the Purpose of Exploring a North-East Passage, in 1815–1818. Translated by H. E. Lloyd. Vols. I–III. London: 1821.

Krause, F.
"Die Kultur der kalifornischen Indianer in ihrer Bedeutung für die Ethnologie und die nordamerikanische Völkerkunde." In: *Festschrift Eduard Seler....* Stuttgart: Strecker und Schroeder, 1922, vi, 654 pp., illus.
> A study of the culture elements among the California Indians and their relation to the Ethnology of North America.

Kroeber, A. L.
"A Mission Record of the California Indians." *University of California Publications in American Archaeology and Ethnology* 8:1–27, 1908.

Anthropology: Race, Language, Culture, Psychology, Pre-History. New York: Harcourt, Brace Co., 1948. New ed., rev. xii, 856 pp., illus., bibl.

"Area and Climax." *Univ. of Cal. Publ. in Amer. Arch. and Ethnol.* 37:101–116, 1936.

"California." In: *Encyclopedia of Religion and Ethics.* J. Hastings, ed. Vol. 3, pp. 141–145. New York: 1911.

"California Culture Provinces." *Univ. of Cal. Publ. in Amer. Arch. and Ethnol.* 17:151–169, 1920.

"California Folklore Notes." *JAFL* 19:142–143, 1906.

"California Kinship Systems." *University of California Publications in American Archaeology and Ethnology,* 12, (No. 9):339–396, 1917. Berkeley: University of California Press, 1916–1917.
> Tribes discussed: Mohave, Luiseño, Yokuts, Miwok, Northern Paiute, Wappo, Tubatulabal and Kawaiisu, Shoshone, Wintun, Pomo, Yuki, Yurok.

"Elements of Culture in Native California." *Univ. of Cal. Publ. in Amer. Arch. and Ethnol.* 13:259–328, 1922.

"Earthquake in California Folklore." *JAFL* 19:322–323, 1906.

"Elements of Culture in Native Calfiornia." *University of California Publications in American Archaeology and Ethnology,* 13, (No. 8): 259–328, 1922. 4. maps, (one on ghost dances), Berkeley: University of California Press, 1917–1923.
> Discussion of arts of life, society, religion and knowledge.

Handbook of the Indians of California. Bureau of American Ethnology, Bulletin 78, 995 pp., 83 pl., map. 78 figs. Washington, D. C.: U. S. Gov't. Printing Office, 1925.

————.
"Prospects in California Prehistory." *American Antiquity* 2, (No. 2):108–116, 1936.

————.
"Serian, Techquistlatecan, and Hokan." *Univ. of Cal. Publ. in Amer. Arch. and Ethnol.* 11 No. 4 :270–290, 1915. Berkeley: University of California Press, 1911–1915.
> Review and Criticism of Brinton's classification, and compared with those made by Dixon and A.L.K.

————.
"The Anthropology of California." *Science* 27: 281–290, 1908. n.s.

————.
"The History of Native Culture in California." *Univ. of Cal. Publ. in Amer. Arch. and Ethnol.* 20:125–142, 1923.

————.
"Types of Indian Culture in California." *Univ. of Cal. Publ. in Amer. Arch. and Ethnol.* 2 (No. 3) :81–103. Berkeley: The University Press, 1904.

Lamotte, A. V.
"The Californian Indian." *Overland Monthly* (San Francisco) 37:831–837, 1901.

Latta, Frank F.
California Indian Folklore. Shafter, Calif.: The Author, 1936.

Loew, Oscar
Notes on the Ethnology of Southern California and Adjacent Regions. U. S. War Department, Annual Report, Chief of Engineers for 1876. Washington, D. C.: 1876.

Lowie, Robert H.
"The Cultural Connection of Californian and Plateau Shoshonean Tribes." *Univ. of Cal. Publ. in Amer. Arch. and Ethnol.* 20:145–156, 1923.

Manhattan
"Indian Tribes of the Far West." *Niles' Weekly Register* 66:393, Aug. 10, 1844.
> Description of a tour by Major Harvey, Sup't of Indian affairs visiting the various western Indian tribes, relative to their progress, prospect of improvement in education, agriculture, and mechanic arts.

Merriam, Clinton Hart
"Distribution of Indian Tribes in the Southern Sierra and Adjacent Parts of the San Joaquin Valley, California." *Science* 19:912–917, 1904. n.s.

————.
"The Indian Population of California." *AA* 7: 594–607, 1905. n.s.

Milet de Mureau, Marie L. A., ed.
Voyage de la Pérouse Autour du Monde. Paris: Chez Plassan . . ., 1798. 4 vols.

North, A. W.
"The Native Tribes of Lower California." *AA* 10:236–250, 1908. n.s.

Powers, Stephen
Tribes of California. Vol. III. Contributions to North American Ethnology; U. S. Geographical and Geological Survey of the Rocky Mountain Region. Washington, D. C.: U. S. Government Printing Office, 1877.

————.
"Northern California Indians." *Overland Monthly* (San Francisco), Vol. VIII, 1872; Vol. XII, 1874.

Radcliffe-Brown, A. R.
"Kinship Terminologies in California." *AA* 37:530–535, 1935. n.s.

Ray, Verne F.
"Far Western Indian Folklore." *JAFL* 60:406–416, 1947.

Reid, Hugo
The Indians of Los Angeles County. "Los Angeles Star" (1852) republished by A. Taylor in "California Farmer" 14, (Jan. 11–Feb. 8), 1861, and abridged by W. J. Hoffman in "Bulletin Essex Institute," Salem, 1885.

Robinson, A.
Life in California, During a Residence of Several Years in that Territory, Comprising a Description of the Country and the Missionary Establishments. New York: Wiley & Putnam, 1846. xii, 341 pp.
> To which is annexed a historical account of the origin, customs and traditions of the Indians of Alta—California.

Rogers, Malcolm J.
"Aboriginal Culture Relations between Southern California and the Southwest." *San Diego Museum Bulletin* 5 (No. 3):1–6, 1941.

Sage, Rufus B.
Scenes in the Rocky Mountains, and in Oregon, California, New Mexico, Texas, and the Grand Prairies. Philadelphia: Carey & Hart, 1846. xii, 303 pp.

Schmidt, W.
"Die Altstämme Nordamerikas." In: *Festschrift Eduard Seler,* pp. 471–502. Stuttgart: Strecker und Schroder, 1922.

Strong, W. D.
"An Analysis of Southwestern Society." *AA* 29:1–61, 1927. n.s.

Taylor, Alexander S.
"The Indianology of California." *California Farmer and Journal of Useful Sciences* (San Francisco), Vol. XIII (No. 3), Feb. 22, 1860 to Vol. XX (No. 12), October 30, 1863.

Venegas, Miguel
A National and Civil History of California. Translated from the Original Spanish, Madrid, 1758. Vols. I–II. London: 1759.

Voegelin, Erminie W.
"Culture Elements Distributions XX. Northeast California." *Anthropological Records* (Berkeley) 7, (No. 2):251 pp., 1942.

Walker, E. F.
"Indians of Southern California." *Masterkey* 11:184–194; 12:24–29, 1937–1938.

Washington, F. B.
"Notes on California Folklore." *JAFL* 19:141–144, 1906.

Wilkes, Charles
Western America, Including California and Oregon, with Maps of those Regions and of the Sacramento Valley. Philadelphia: Lea & Blanchard, 1849. 130 pp.

MYTHS—FOLKTALES—LEGENDS

Bancroft, Hubert Howe
The Native Races of the Pacific States of North America. San Francisco: A. L. Bancroft and Company, 1874–1882. 5 vols., illus., bibl.
Vol. III—Myths and languages.

Caldwell, George W.
Legends of Southern California. Illustrated by Flippin, J. J. San Francisco, Cal.: Phillips & Van Orden Co., 1919. 101 pp., illus.
Legends of the Soboda Indians of Southern California. *Contents:* The Lights of Elsinore. The Stepping Stones. The Echo. Arrowhead Hot Springs. The blue lizard of San Jacinto. The rumblings of Tarquitz. The Prince of Plenty. How the road runner won his red feather.

"California Indian Creation Myth."
JAFL 5:73–74, 1892.

"California, San Joaquin Myth."
JAFL 15:104–106, 1902.
San Joaquin—A collective name for the Costanoan, Moquelumnan, and Yokuts tribes on San Joaquin River, California.

Demetracopoulou, D.
"The Loon Woman Myth." *JAFL* 46:101–128, 1933.

Gayton, A. H.
"Areal Affiliations of California Folktales." *AA* 37:582–599, 1935. n.s.

Gifford, Edward W.
California Indian Nights Entertainments; stories of the Creation of the World, of Man, of Fire, of the Sun, of Thunder, etc.; of coyote, the land of the dead, the sky land, monsters, animal, people, etc., compiled by Gifford, E. W. and Block, G. H. Glendale, Calif.: The Arthur H. Clark Company, 1930. 323 pp., illus.

Graves, Charles S.
Before the White Man Came. Yreka, Calif.: The Siskiyou News, 1934. 99 pp., illus.

Judson, Katharine Berry
Myths and Legends of California and the Old Southwest. Chicago: A. C. McClurg & Co., 1912. xvi, 193 pp.

Kroeber, A. L.
"Indian Myths of South Central California." *University of California Publications in American Archaeology and Ethnology* 4, (No. 4): 167–250. Berkeley: The University Press, 1907.
Compares the mythologies of North and South Central California. Quotes myths of the Costanoan, Miwok, Yokuts and Shoshonean myths.

Latta, Frank F.
California Indian Folklore.... Shafter, Calif.: The Author, 1936. 209 pp., illus.

Morrison, Frederick
"An Indian Legend and Modern Tradition." *CFQ* 2:47, 1943.

Powers, Stephen
"North American Indian Legends and Fables of the California Indians." *Folk-Lore Record.* (London) V. 5: 1882. 51 pp.

Schmidt, Wilhelm
Zwei Mythen Kalifornischer Indianer; Uber die Entstehung der Welt und über den Ursprung des Todes. Düsseldorf: L. Schwann, 1926. 42 pp.
Two origin myths—of the earth and death.

BELIEFS—CUSTOMS—FOLK MEDICINE

"California Indian Method of Challenge."
JAFL 5:62, 1892.

Chestnut, V. K.
"Plants Used by the Indians of Mendocino County, California." *Contribution U. S. National Herbarium* Vol. VII, No. 3. Washington, D. C., 1902.

————.
Principal Poisonous Plants of the United States. U. S. Department of Agriculture. Division of Botany. Bulletin 20. Washington, D. C.: U. S. Gov't Printing Office, 1898.

Dixon, Roland B.
"Shamans of Northern California." *JAFL* 17:23–27, 1904.

Driver, Harold E.
"Girls' Puberty Rites in Western North American Culture. Element Distribution XVI." *Anthropological Records* 6, (No. 2):90 pp., illus. Berkeley: University of California Press, 1941.

Du Bois, Constance G.
"The 1870 Ghost Dance." *Anthropological Records* (Berkeley) 3:1–151, 1939.

Essig, E. O.
"The Value of Insects to the California Indians." *Scienctific Monthly* 38, (No. 2):181–186, (Feb.) 1934.

Heizer, R. F., and Hewes, G. W.
"Animal Ceremonialism in Central California in the Light of Archaeology." *AA* 42:587–603, 1940. n.s.

Kroeber, A. L.
"California Kinship Systems." *Univ. of Cal. Publ. in Amer. Arch. and Ethnol.* 12:339–396, 1917.

———.
"Salt, Dogs, Tobacco." *Anthropological Records* (Berkeley) 6:1–20, 1941.

———.
"Stepdaughter Marriage." *AA* 42:562–570, 1940. n.s.

———.
The Growth of a Primitive Religion. In: *The Making of Man,* an Outline of Anthropology, edited by V. F. Calverton, pp. 714–744. New York: The Modern Library, 1931.
The author places special emphasis on the tribes of California.

———.
"The Religion of the Indians of California." *Univ. of Cal. Publ. in Amer. Arch. and Ethnol.,* 4, (No. 6): 319–356. Berkeley: The University Press, 1905.

Loeb, E. M.
"The Religious Organization of North Central California and Tierra del Fuego." *AA* 33:517–556, 1931. n.s.

MacLeod, W. C.
"On California Mortuaries." *AA* 31:722–776, 1929. n.s.

Merriam, Clinton Hart
"Totemism in California." *AA* 10:558–563, 1908. n.s.

———.
"Transmigration in California." *JAFL* 22:433–434, 1909.

Park, W. Z.
"Shamanism in Western North America." *Northwestern University Studies in the Social Sciences* 2:1–166, 1938.

Voegelin, E. W.
"Suicide in Northeastern California." *AA* 39:445–456, 1937. n.s.

W., J. J.
"The Eagle Feast of the California Indians." *CFQ* 3:155–157, 1944.

Washington, F. B.
"Customs of the Indians of Western Tehama County (California)." *JAFL* 19:144, 1906.

FOLK ART—SPEECH—GAMES

Alliot, Hector
Primitive Art in Southern California. San Francisco: R. L. Bernier, 1916.

Buschmann, J. C. E.
"Die Spuren der aztekischen Sprache im nördlichen Mexico und höheren amerikanischen Norden." *Abhandlungen der Königlichen Akademie der Wissenschaften* (Berlin). Supplement—Band 2:455–511, 1854.

Burnett, E. K.
Inlaid Stone and Bone Artifacts from Southern California. New York: Contributions of the Museum of the American Indian, Heye Foundation 13. 16 pp., illus. 1944.
"While consideration of archaeological material has little place in these pages (JAFL), it may be permitted entry if the artistic or technical excellence of the materials stands as an expression of primitive folk art. . ." (A. H. Gayton)

Campbell, Elizabeth W. Crozer, and Amsden, Charles
"The Eagle Mountain Site (Southern California)." *The Masterkey* 8, (No. 6):170–173. Los Angeles: Southwest Museum, (Nov.) 1934.

Cody, Bertha Parker
"California Indian Baby Cradles." *Masterkey* 14:89–96, 1940.

Dixon, Roland B.
"Basketry Designs of the Indians of Northern California." The Huntington California Expedition. *Bulletin American Museum of Natural History* (New York), 17, (Part 1):25 pp., 1902. 37 pl.

———.
"Numerical Systems of the Languages of California." *AA* 9:663–691, 1907. n.s.

———, and Kroeber, A. L.
"Linguistic Families of California." *Univ. of Cal. Publ. in Amer. Arch. and Ethnol.* 16:47–118, 1919.

———.
"New Linguistic Families in California." *AA* 15:647–655, 1913. n.s.

———.
"The Native Languages of California." *AA* 5:1–26, 1903. n.s.

Douglas, F. H.
"The Main Divisions of California Indian Basketry." *Denver Art Museum, Indian Leaflet Series.* 88:130–136, 1937.

Gatschet, A. S.
"Indian Languages of the Pacific States and Territories." *Magazine of American History* (Mt. Vernon, N. Y.) 1:145–171, 1877.

Gibbs, George
"Vocabularies of Indian Languages in Northwest California." In: *Information Respecting the History, Condition, and Prospects of the Indian Tribes of the United States.* Henry Rowe Schoolcraft, ed. Vol. 3, pp. 428–445. Philadelphia: 1853.

Heizer, R.
"Baked-Clay Objects of the Lower Sacramento Valley." *American Antiquity* 3:34–50, 1937.

————, and Hewes, G. W.
"Animal Ceremonialism in Central California in the Light of Archaeology." *AA* 42:587–603, 1940. n.s.

Henshaw, Henry
Perforated Stones from California. Bureau of American Ethnology, Bull. 2. pp. 1–34, 16 figs. Washington, D. C.: U. S. Gov't. Printing Office, 1887.

Inverarity, R. B.
Movable Masks and Figures of the Pacific Coast Indians. Bloomfield Hills, Mich.: Cranbook Institute of Science,, 4 pp. 18 col. pl. 1941.

Kelly, Isabel T.
"The Carver's Art of the Indians of Northwestern California." *University of California Publications in Archaeology and Ethnology* 24:343–360, 1930.

Kroeber, A. L.
"Basket Designs of the Indians of Northwestern California." *University of California Publications in Archaeology and Ethnology* 2, (No. 4):105–164, plates 15–21. Berkeley: The University Press, 1904–1907.

————
"Basket Designs of the Mission Indians." *Anthropological Papers of the American Museum of Natural History* (New York) 20:149–183, 1922.

————
"Basketry Designs of the Mission Indians." *American Museum of Natural History, Guide Leaflets* 55:1–10, 1926.

————
"California Basketry and the Pomo." *AA* 11: 233–249, 1909. n.s.

————
"California Place Names of Indian Origin" *University of California Publications in American Archaeology and Ethnology*, 12, (No. 2): 31–69, 1916. Berkeley: University of California Press, 1916–1917.

————
"Games of the California Indians." *AA* 22: 272–27, 920. n.s.

————
"Notes on the Shoshonean Dialects of Southern California." *University of California Publications in American Archaeology and Ethnology* 8, (No. 5):235–269. Berkeley: The University Press, 1909.
Comparative study of the dialects of the Cahuilla, Agua Caliente, San Juan Capistrano, Gabrielino, Chemehuevi Tribes.

————
"Phonetic Constituents of the Native Languages of California." *University of California Publications in American Archaeology and Ethnology* 10, (No. 1):1–12, 1911. Berkeley: The University Press, 1911–1914.

————
"Shoshonean Dialects of California." *University of California Publications in American Archaeology and Ethnology* 4, (No. 3):65–166. Berkeley: The University Press, 1905.

————
"The Languages of the Coast of California North of San Francisco." *University of California Publications in American Archaeology and Ethnology* 9, (No. 3):273–435, 1911. Berkeley: The University Press, 1911.
Discussion of the Miwok, Pomo, Yuki, Wiyot, Yurok, Karok Dialects.

————
"The Languages of the Coast of California South of San Francisco." *University of California Publications in American Archaeology and Ethnology* 2, (No. 2):29–80, with map. Berkeley: The University Press, 1904.

McNary, Laura Kelly
California Spanish and Indian Place Names Los Angeles: Wetzel, 1932. 77 pp.

Merriam, John C.
"Recent Cave Excavations in California." *AA* 8:221–229, 1906. n.s.

Merrill, R. E.
"Plants Used in Basketry by the California Indians." *Univ. of Cal. Publ. in Amer. Arch. and Ethnol.* 20:215–242, 1923.

Pope, Saxton T.
"A Study of Bows and Arrows." *Univ. of Cal. Publ. in Amer. Arch. and Ethnol.* 13, (No. 9) :329–414, 1923, plates 45–64. Berkeley: University of California Press, 1917–1923.
Most of the bows were selected from the Museum of Anthropology of the University of California.

Sanchez, Nellie van de Grift
Spanish and Indian Place Names of California. Their Meaning and Their Romance. San Francisco: 1914.

Schumacher, Paul
"Ancient Graves and Shell Heaps in California." *Smithsonian Report* for 1874. Washington, D. C.: U. S. Gov't. Printing Office, 1875.

————
"Methods of Making Stone Weapons." *Bulletin of the Geologic and Geographic Survey of the Territories*, vol. 3, No. 3. Washington, D. C. 1877.

————
"The Method of Manufacturing Pottery and Baskets Among Indians of Southern California." *12th Report, Peabody Museum of American Archaeology and Ethnology* (Cambridge, Mass.) 1880.

Yates, Lorenzo G.
"Aboriginal Weapons of California." *Overland Monthly* (San Francisco), (Ser. 2), 27: 337–342, 1896.

————.
Archaeology of California. Prehistoric Implements, W. K. Moorhead, ed., (pp. 230–252). Cincinnati: 1900.

MUSIC

GENERAL STUDIES

Angulo, Jaime de, et d'Harcourt, Béclard
"La Musique des Indiens de la Californie du Nord." *Journal de la Société des Américanistes* 23: 189–217, 1931. n.s.
Music of the Northern California Indian.

Dixon, R. B.
"The Musical Bow in California." *Science* 13: 274–275, 1901. n.s.

Kroeber, A. L.
"A Mission Record of the California Indians." *University of California Publications in American Archaeology and Ethnology* 8:1–27, 1908.
Discussion of music, dances and ceremonies included.

Powers, Stephen
Tribes of California. Department of the Interior, Georgraphical and Geological Survey. Rocky Mountain Region, Contributions to North American Ethnology, Vol. 3. Washington, D. C.: U. S. Government Printing Office, 1877.

Steward, H. J., and Dunn, Allan
Legends of the Yosemite, Yosemite Valley, California. (Folklore of the Ah-Wah-Nee-Chee Indians). Boston: White-Smith Publishing Company, 1910. 40 pp., illus.
5 songs with legends.

Waterman, T. T.
"Native Musical Instruments of California." *Out West* 28:276–286, 1908.

DANCES

Gayton, Anna H.
"The Ghost Dance of 1870 in South-Central California." *University of California Publications in American Archaeology and Ethnology* 28:57–82, 1930.

"Ghost Dance"
JAFL 5:65–69, 1892.

Kessler, D. E.
"The Passing of the Old Ceremonial Dances of the Southern California Indians." *Southern Workman* (Hampton, Va.), 38:527–638, 1908.

Kroeber, A. L.
"Ghost Dance in California." *JAFL* 17:32–35, 1904.

Lamotte, A. V.
"The Californian Indians." *Overland Monthly* (San Francisco) 37:831–837, 1901.

Reagan, A. B.
"The Klukwalle Dance of the West Coast Indians." *Frontier Magazine* (Missoula) 12: 67–71, (Nov.) 1931.

Rukeyser, Muriel
"Indian Dancing Fiesta: Southern California." *Nation* 144:616–617, 1937.

Sachs, Curt
World History of the Dance. New York: W. W. Norton and Company, 1937. 469 pp., bibl.
Chapter II: Themes and types (pp. 49-139). Deals with primitive dance. California Dance p. 103.

Watkins, Frances E.
"Indians at Play." *California History Nugget,* 7:187–193, 1933.

RECORDS

Herzog, George
California Area: Records Contained in American Collection. American Council of Learned Societies, (Washington, D. C.) Bulletin 24:27, 1936.

Lehmer, N. Lehmer
Collection of Recordings of Indian Songs. Berkeley, California: University of California.

U. S. Library of Congress. Division of Music. Folklore Section.
Indian Recordings—A great many discs deposited in the Archive of American Folksong, by individuals and institutions. Recently the whole Frances Densmore Indian recording collection has been deposited in the Archive. Many of these discs are from California Indian tribes.
AAFS-LC.

CHIMARIKO

FOLKLORE

GENERAL STUDIES

Dixon, Roland B.
"The Chimariko Indians and Language." *University of California Publications in American Archaeology and Ethnology* 5:293–380. Berkeley: The University Press, 1910.
"In general culture the Chimariko were much like their neighbors to the northwest, the Hupa, though they are said to have lacked canoes, and did not practice the Deerskin Dance of the Hupa and Yurok." (A. L. Kroeber)

Driver, H. E.
"Northwest California." *Anthropological Records* (Berkeley) 1:297–433, 1939.

Kroeber, A. L.
"Chimariko." In: *Bureau of American Ethnology, Bulletin 30,* Part I, pp. 270, 1907.

————.
"The Chimariko." In: *Handbook of the Indians of California.* Bureau of American Ethnology, Bulletin 78, (pp. 109–112). Washington, D. C.: U. S. Gov't Printing Office, 1925.

Merriam, C. H.
"The New River Indians of Tlo'-hom-tah'-hoi."
AA 32:280–293, 1930. n.s.
A tribe in North-West California, near the Chemareko and Hupa.

Powers, S.
"Tribes of California." *Contributions to North American Ethnology, Department of the Interior, United States Geographical and Geological Survey of the Rocky Mountain Region.* (Washington, D. C.), 3:474–477, 1877.

COSTANO
(Including: Mutsun)

FOLKLORE

GENERAL STUDIES

Anonymous
"Costanoan Family." In: *Bureau of American Ethnology, Bulletin 30.* Part I, p. 351, 1907.

Kroeber, A. L.
"Costanoan." In: *Handbook of the Indians of California.* Bureau of American Ethnology, Bulletin 78, pp. 462–473. Washington, D. C.: U. S. Government Printing Office, 1925.

————.
"A Mission Record of the California Indians." *Univ. of Cal. Publ. in Amer. Arch. and Ethnol.* 8:20–27, 1908.

MYTHS

"California, San Joaquin Myth."
JAFL 15:104–106, 1902.
San Joaquin—"A collective name for the Costanoan, Moquelumnan, and Yokuts tribes on San Joaquin River, California."

Kroeber, A. L.
"Indian Myths of South Central California." *Univ. of Cal. Publ. in Amer. Arch. and Ethnol.* 4:167–250, 1907.

SPEECH

Arroyo de la Cuesta, F.
Grammar of the Mutsun Language. Vol. 4, in— The Library of American Linguistics. New York: 1861. 48 pp.

————.
A Vocabulary or Phrase-Book of the Mutsun Language of Alta California. Vol. 8, in—The Library of American Linguistics. New York: 1862. 96 pp.

Gatschet, A. S.
"Specimen of the Chúmeto Language." *American Antiquarian and Oriental Journal* (Chicago) 5:71–73, 173–180, 1883.

Kroeber, A. L.
"The Chumash and Costanoan Languages." *Univ. of Cal. Publ. in Amer. Arch. and Ethnol.* 9, (No. 2) :237–271, 1910. Berkeley: The University Press, 1910–1911.

————.
"The Languages of the Coast of California South of San Francisco." *Univ. of Cal. Publ. in Amer. Arch. and Ethnol.* 2:29–80, 1904.

Mason, J. Alden
"The Mutsun Dialect of Costanoan Based on the Vocabulary of De La Cuesta." *Univ. of Cal. Publ. in Amer. Arch. and Ethnol.* 11, (No. 7) :399–472, 1916. Berkeley: University of California Press, 1911–1916.

DIEGUEÑO
(Mission Indians)

FOLKLORE

GENERAL STUDIES

Kroeber, A. L.
"Diegueño." In: *Handbook of the Indians of California.* Bureau of American Ethnology, Bulletin 78, pp. 709–725, 1925.

Lummis, C. F.
"The Exiles of Cupa; Two Days at Mesa Grande." *Out West* 16:465–479, 602–612, 1902.

Miller, Joaquin
Songs of the Sierras. Boston: Roberts Brothers, 1871. 299 pp.

Woodward, A.
"Notes on the Indians of San Diego County." *Masterkey* 8:140–150, 1934.

MYTHS—FOLKTALES—LEGENDS

"Diegueño Mythology."
JAFL 14:181–185, 1901; 17:217–242, 1904; 19:145–164, 1906; 21:40–42, 228–236, 1908.

"Diegueño Yuma Creation Myth Told by Diegueños." *JAFL* 21:236, 1908.

Du Bois, Constance Goddard
"Diegueño Myths and Their Connections with the Mohave, and Two Types or Styles of Diegueño Religious Dancing." *Proceedings of the 15th Session of the International Congress of Americanists,* 2:129–134, 135–138, 1907. (Quebec).

————.
"Mythology of the Diegueños." *JAFL* 14:181–185, 1901.

————.
"Religious Ceremonies and Myths of the Mission Indians." *AA* 7:620–629, 1905. n.s.

—————.
"Story of the Chaup; a Myth of the Diegue-ños." *JAFL* 17:217–242, 1904.

—————.
"The Mythology of the Diegueños. Mission Indians of the San Diego County, California, as proving their status to be higher than is generally believed." *Proceedings of the 13th Session of the International Congress of Americanists*, pp. 101–107, 1905.

Waterman, T. T.
"Analysis of the Mission Indian Creation Story." *AA* 11:41–55, 1909. n.s.

BELIEFS—CUSTOMS—SPEECH

Davis, E. H.
"The Diegueño Ceremony of the Death Images." *Contributions from the Museum of the American Indian, Heye Foundation* (New York) 5 (Part 2):7–33, 1919.

—————.
"Early Cremation Ceremonies of the Luiseño and Diegueño Indians of Southern California." *Heye Foundation, Indian Notes and Monographs* 7:93–110, 1921.

Du Bois, Constance Goddard
"Ceremonies and Traditions of the Diegueño Indians." *JAFL* 21:228–236, 1908.

—————.
"Diegueño Mortuary Ollas." *AA* 9:484–487, 1907. n.s.

—————.
"Two Types or Styles of Diegueño Religious Dancing. The Old and the New in Southern California." *Proceedings of the 15th Session of the International Congress of Americanists* (Quebec) 2:135–139, 1907.

Kessler, D. E.
"El Capitan Blanco—the White Chief of Mesa Grande." *So. Workman* 38:655–671, 1909.
Gives a brief account of the adoption ceremony.

—————.
"The Lighting of the Graves." *So. Workman* 37:86–89, 1908.

Kroeber, A. L., and Harrington, J. P.
"Phonetic Elements of the Diegueño Language." *University of California Publications in American Archaeology and Ethnology* 11, (No. 2):177–188, 1914. Berkeley: University of California Press, 1911–1916.

Rust, H. N.
"A Puberty Ceremony of the Mission Indians." *AA* 8:28–32, 1906. n.s.

Spier, Leslie
"Southern Diegueño Customs." *University of California Publications in American Archaeology and Ethnology* 20:298–358, 1923. Berkeley: The University Press, 1923.

Taffelmeier, Gertrude, and Luomala, Katherine
"Dreams and Dream Interpretations of the Diegueño Indians of Southern California." *Psychoanalytic Quarterly* 5, (No. 2):195–225, 1936.

Waterman, T. T.
"The Religious Practices of the Diegueño Indians." *University of California Publications in American Archaeology and Ethnology* 8 (No. 6):271–358, pls. 21–28. Berkeley: The University Press, 1910.

—————.
"Diegueño Identification of Color with the Cardinal Points." *JAFL* 21:40–42, 1908.

GAMES—FOLK ART

Davis, E. H.
"Modern Pottery Vessels from San Diego County." *Indian Notes, Museum of the American Indian, Heye Foundation* (New York) 5: 93–97, 1928.

Du Bois, Constance Goddard
"Games, Arts and Industries of the Diegueños and Luiseños." *University of California Publications in American Archaeology and Ethnology* 8 (No. 3):167–173. Berkeley: The University Press, 1908–1910.

—————.
"Diegueño Games."
JAFL 17:299, 1904.

Kroeber, A. L.
"Basket Designs of the Mission Indians." *Anthropological Papers of the American Museum of Natural History* (New York) 20:149–183, 1922.

Lee, M. L.
"The Ancient House of the San Diegueno Indians." *Art and Archaeology* 25:100–105, 108, 1928.

MUSIC

GENERAL STUDIES

Waterman, T. T.
"The Religious Practices of the Diegueño Indians." *University of California Publications in American Archaeology and Ethnology* (Berkeley) 8:271–358, 1910.
Includes discussion of the music.

DANCES

Du Bois, Constance Goddard
"Two Types of Styles of Diegueño Religious Dancing. The old and the new in Southern California." *Proceedings of the 15th Session of the International Congress of Americanists* (Quebec) 2:135–139, 1906.

HUPA

FOLKLORE

GENERAL STUDIES

Culin, Stewart
"A Summer Trip Among the Western Indians."
Bulletin of the Free Museum of Science and Arts, University of Pennsylvania (Phila). 3:
102–117, 1901.

Driver, H. E.
"Northwest California." *Anthropological Records* (Berkeley) 1:297–433, 1939.

Goddard, Pliny Earle
"Athapascan (Hupa)." *Bureau of American Ethnology, Bulletin 40*, (Part 1) :85–158, 1911.
(Washington, D. C.)

————.
"Hupa." In: *Bureau of American Ethnology, Bulletin 30 (Part 1):* 581–584, 1907.

————.
"Hupa." *Encyclopedia of Religion and Ethics*, Hastings, ed., New York, vol. 6:880–883, 1914.

————.
"Hupa Texts." *University of California Publications in American Archaeology and Ethnology* 1, (No. 2) :96–378. Berkeley: The University Press, 1903–1904.

————.
"Life and Culture of the Hupa." *University of California Publications in American Archaeology and Ethnology* 1, (No. 1) : 3–87, with 30 plates and map. Berkeley: The University Press, 1903–1904.

Kroeber, A. L.
"Hupa." In: *Handbook of the Indians of California*. Bureau of American Ethnology, Bulletin 78, pp. 128–141. Washington, D. C.: U. S. Government Printing Office, 1925.

Powers, S.
"The Northern California Indians." *Overland Monthly* 9:155–164, 1872.

CUSTOMS—SPEECH

Goddard, Pliny Earle
"The Morphology of the Hupa Language."
Univ. of Cal. Publ. in Amer. Arch. and Ethnol.
3:7–344. Berkeley: The University Press, 1905.

————.
"The Phonology of the Hupa Language; Part I. The Individual Sounds." *Univ. of Cal. Publ. in Amer. Arch. and Ethnol.* 5, (No. 1) :20. plates 1–8. Berkeley: The University Press, 1907.

————.
"Pitch Accent in Hupa." *Univ. of Cal. Publ. in Amer. Arch. and Ethnol.* 23:333–338, 1928.

Kroeber, A. L.
"Yurok and Neighboring Kin Term Systems."
Univ. of Cal. Publ. in Amer. Arch and Ethol.
35:15–22, 1934.

Sapir, Edward
"Hupa Tattooing." *Essays in Anthropology, Presented to A. L. Kroeber.* pp. 273–277.
Berkeley: University of California Press, 1936.

FOLK ART

Kelly, I. T.
"The Carver's Art of the Indians of Northwestern California." *Univ. of Cal. Publ. in Amer. Arch. and Ethnol.* 24:343–360, 1936.

Kroeber, A. L.
"Basket Designs of the Indians of Northwestern California." *Univ. of Cal. Publ. in Amer. Arch. and Ethnol.* 2:105–164, 1905.

Ray, P. H.
"Manufacture of Bows and Arrows among the Natano (Hupa) and Kenuck (Klamath) Indians." *American Naturalist* 20:832–833, 1886.

MUSIC

DANCES

Goddard, Pliny Earle
"Hon-sitch-a-til-ya." *Bulletin of the Free Museum of Science and Arts, University of Pennsylvania* (Phila.) 3:117–122, 1901.

Goldschmidt, Walter R., and Driver, Harold Edson
"The Hupa White Deerskin Dance." *Univ. of Cal. Publ. in Amer. Arch. and Ethnol.* 35.
(No. 8) :103–142. Berkeley: University of California Press, 1940.

Woodruff, Chase E.
"Dances of the Hupa Indians." *AA* 5:53–63, 1892.

KAROK

FOLKLORE

GENERAL STUDIES

Anon.
"Karok." In: *Bureau of American Ethnology, Bulletin 30* (Part 1) :659, 1907. (Washington, D. C.).

Angulo, Jaime de, and Freeland, Lucy S.
"Karok Texts." *International Journal of American Linguistics.* 6:194–226, 1931.

Gifford, Edward W.
"Karok Texts." *International Journal of American Linguistics* 6:121–161, 194–226, 1930–1931.

————.
"The Karok Tribe." *El Palacio* 26:316–319, 1929.

Kroeber, A. L.
"Karok." In: *Handbook of the Indians of California.* Bureau of American Ethnology, Buletin 78, pp. 98–108. Washington, D. C.: U. S. Gov't. Printing Office, 1925.

———.
"Karok Towns." *Univ. of Cal. Publ. in Amer. Arch and Ethnol.* 25:29–38, 1936.

Powers, S.
"The Northern California Indians." *Overland Monthly* 8:325–333, 425–435, 1872.

MYTHS—FOLKTALES—LEGENDS

Denny, M. B.
"Orleans Indian Legends." *Out West* (Los Angeles) 25:37–40, 161–166, 268–271, 373–375, 452–454; 26:73–80, 168–170, 267–268, 1906–1907.
Orleans Indians—Karok.

Harrington, John P.
Karuk Indian Myths. U. S. Bureau of Ethnology, Bulletin 107, Smithsonian Institution. Washington, D. C.: U. S. Government Printing Office, 1932. v, 34 pp.

Kroeber, A. L.
"A Karok Orpheus Myth." *JAFL* 59:13–19, 1946.

Olden, Sarah Emilia
Karoc Indian Stories. San Francisco, Calif.: Harr Wagner Publishing Co., 1923. iii, 191 pp., illus.

BELIEFS—CUSTOMS

Drucker, Philip
"A Karuk World-Renewal Ceremony at Panaminik." *University of California Publications in American Archaeology and Ethnology* 35, (No. 3):23–28. Berkeley: University of California Press, 1936.

Gifford, Edward W.
"Tobacco Among the Karuk Indians." *Bureau of American Ethnology, Bulletin 94*, pp. 1–284, 1932.

Harrington, J. P.
"Chainfern and Maidenhair, Adornment Materials of Northwestern California Basketry." In: *So Live the Works of Men;* D. D. Brand, and F. E. Harvey, eds., pp. 159–162. Albuquerque: 1939.

Kroeber, A. L.
"A Ghost-Dance in California." *JAFL* 17:32–35, 1904.

———.
"Yurok and Neighboring Kin Term Systems." *Univ. of Cal. Publ. in Amer. Arch. and Ethnol.* 35:15–22, 1934.

Roberts, Helen H.
"The First Salmon Ceremony of the Karuk Indians." *AA* 34:426–440, 1932. n. s.

FOLK ART

Kelly, I. T.
"The Carver's Art of the Indians of Northwestern California." *Univ. of Cal. Publ. in Amer. Arch. and Ethnol.* 24:343–360, 1936.

Kroeber, A. L.
"Basket Designs of the Indians of Northwestern California." *Univ. of Cal. Publ. in Amer. Arch. and Ethnol.* 2:105–164, 1905.

O'Neale, L. M.
"Yurok-Karok Basket Weavers." *Univ. of Cal. Publ. in Amer. Arch. and Ethnol.* 32:1–184, 1932.

MUSIC
GENERAL STUDIES

Angulo, Jaime de, and d'Harcourt, B.
"La musique des Indiens de la Californie du Nord." *Journal de la Société des Américanistes* 13:189–228, 1931. n. s.

DANCES

Kroeber, A. L.
"California Ghost Dance." *JAFL* 17:32–35, 1904.

Roberts, Helen H.
"The First Salmon Ceremony of the Karuk Indians." *AA* 34:426–440, 1932. n. s.
Discussion of the dance and music.

Woodward, A.
"Karok Dance Paraphernalia." *Indian Notes, Museum of the American Indian, Heye Foundation* (New York) 4:257–271, 1927.

KLAMATH
FOLKLORE
GENERAL STUDIES

Barrett, S. A.
"The Material Culture of the Klamath Lake and Modoc Indians of Northwestern California and Southern Oregon." *Univ. of Cal. Publ. in Amer. Arch. and Ethnol.* 5 (No. 4):239–292, pl. 10–25. Berkeley: The University Press, 1907.

Cressman, L. S., Williams, H., and Krieger, A. D.
"Early Man in Oregon." *Studies in Anthropology,* No. 3., pp. 1–78, 1940. University of Oregon Monographs.

Douglas, F. H.
"The Klamath Indians." *Denver Art Museum Indian Leaflet Series* 48:1–3, 1932. (Denver).

Gatschet, Albert Samuel
"Oregonian Folklore." *JAFL* 4:139–143, 1891.

———.
"Sketch of the Klamath Language." *American Antiquarian* 1:81–84, 1878.

———.
The Klamath Indians of Southwestern Oregon.
Contributions to North American Ethnology.
2 Parts. vol. II. Department of the Interior.
Washington, D. C.: U. S. Government Printing Office, 1890.

———.
"Volk und Sprache der Máklaks." *Globus*
35:167–171, 187–189, 1879.
 The people and language of the Luthuamian
 family.

Hale, Horatio
"The Klamath Nation." *Science* 19:6–7, 20–
21, 29–31, 1892.

Hedrick, Helen
The Blood Remembers. New York: Alfred A.
Knopf, 1941. 288 pp.
 A regional novel, showing good knowledge of
 the Indian country and its mores.

Howard, O. O.
*My Life and Experiences Among Our Hostile
Indians.* A record of personal observations, adventures, and campaigns among the Indians
of the Great West, with some account of their
life, habits, traits, religion, ceremonies, dress,
savage instincts, and customs in peace and
war . . . Hartford: A. D. Worthington & Company, 1907. 570 pp.

Kroeber, A. L.
"The Klamath Indians." In: *Handbook of the
Indians of California.* Bureau of American
Ethnology, Bulletin 78, pp. 318–335. Washington, D. C.: U. S. Gov't. Printing Office,
1925.

Meacham, A. B.
*Wi-Ne-Ma. (The Woman Chief and Her
People.)* Hartford: American Publishing Co.,
1876. vi, 168 pp.

Powers, S.
"The California Indians." *Overland Monthly*
10:535–545, 1873.

Spier, Leslie
"Klamath Ethnography." *Univ. of Cal. Publ.
in Amer. Arch. and Ethnol.* 30:1–338, 1930.

Thompson, L.
To the American Indian. Eureka: Press of
the Times, 1916. 214 pp.

MYTHS—FOLKTALES—LEGENDS

Gatschet, Albert S.
"Mythologic Text in the Klamath Language."
American Antiquarian 1:161–166, 1879.

Graves, C. S.
*Lore and Legends of the Klamath River
Indians.* Eureka, Calif.: Press of the Times,
1929. 157 pp. illus.

BELIEFS—CUSTOMS

Colville, Frederick V.
"Notes on the Plants Used by the Klamath
Indians of Oregon." *Contributions U. S.
National Herbarium*, vol. 5, no. 2. Washington,
D. C., 1897.

———.
"Wokas, a Primitive Food of the Klamath
Indians." *Report, U. S. National Museum*,
1902. Washington D. C., 1904.

Nash, Philleo
The Place of Religious Revivalism in the
Formation of the Intercultural Community in
Klamath Reservations. In: *Social Organization
of North American Tribes.* Fred Eggan editor,
pp. 377–442. Chicago: University of Chicago
Press, 1937.

FOLK ART—SPEECH

Gatschet, A. S.
"Adjectives of Color in Indian Languages."
American Naturalist 13:475–485, 1879.

———.
"The Numerical Adjective in the Klamath
Language." *American Antiquarian* 2:210–217,
1880.

Ray, P. H.
"Manufacture of Bows and Arrows Among
the Natano and Kenuck Indians." *American
Naturalist* 20:832–833, 1886.
 Natano is another name for the Hupa, and Kenuck
 is for the Klamath.

GAMES

Dorsey, George A.
"Certain Gambling Games of the Klamath
Indians." *AA* 3:14–28, 1901 n. s.

MUSIC

Angulo, Jaime de, and d'Harcourt, B.
"La Musique des Indies de la Californie du
Nord." *Journal de la Société des Américanistes*
23:189–228, 1931. n. s.

DANCES

Arnold, Mary E., and Reed, Mabel
"An Indian New Year." *Southern Workman*
(Hampton, Va.) 38:24–27, 1909.
 Discussion and description of dance.

Putnam, Edna Hildebrand
"Ah-Pura-Way: The Dance of the White Deerskin and other Klamath Indian Worship
Dances." *Cleveland Monthly* 69:276–283,
(April) 1917.

Spier, Leslie
"The Ghost Dance of 1870 Among the Klamath
of Oregon." *University Publications in Anthropology*, 2, (No. 2):43–55. Seattle: University
of Washington Press, 1927.

LUISEÑO
(Mission Indians)

FOLKLORE
GENERAL STUDIES

Benedict, Ruth
Patterns of Culture. New York: Houghton Mifflin Co., 1934. 272 pp.
Mission Indians—adolescent rite, p. 94; proverb, p. 19; the place of warfare, p. 28.

Caballeria y Collell, Juan
History of San Bernardino Valley, 1810–1851. San Bernardino, Cal.: Times-Index Press, 1902. 130 pp., illus.

Drucker, P.
"Southern California." *Anthropological Records* (Berkeley) 1:1–52, 1937.

Du Bois, Constance Goddard
The Condition of the Mission Indians of Southern California. Philadelphia: Office of the Indian Rights Association, 1901, 16, pp.

Engelhardt, Zephyrin
The Franciscans in California. Harbor Springs, Mich.: Holy Childhood Indian School, 1897. xvi; 516 pp.

Foote, K.
"Mission Indians." Report on Indians Taxed and Indians not Taxed, United States Department of the Interior, Census Office, 11th Census. Washington, D. C.

Gifford, Edward Winslow
"Clans and Moieties in Southern California." *University of California Publications in American Archaeology and Ethnology*, 14, (No. 2): 155–219, 1918. 1 figure in text. Berkeley: University of California Press, 1918–1919.
Clans discussed: Yuman (Colorado River and Diegueño), Piman Shoshonean (Serrano, Cahuilla Cupeno, Luiseño).

Harrington, John P.
"A New Original Version of Boscana's Historical Account of the San Jaun Capistrano Indians of Southern California." *Smithsonian Institution, Miscellaneous Collections* 92, (No. 4), Publication 3255, 1934.

Hayes, Benjamin
"Notes on the Indians of San Diego County (California)." *The Masterkey* 8, No. 5:140–150. Los Angeles: Southwest Museum, Sept. 1934.

Jackson, Helen M. H., and Kinney, Abbott
Report on the Condition and Needs of the Mission Indians of California to the Commissioner of Indian Affairs. Washington, D. C.: 1883.

Kroeber, A. L.
"Luiseño." In: *Handbook of the Indians of California.* Bureau of American Ethnology, Bulletin 78, pp. 636–667. Washington, D. C.: U. S. Gov't. Printing Office, 1925.

"A Mission Record of the California Indians. From a Manuscript in the Public Library." *University of California Publications in American Archaeology and Ethnology* 8, (No. 1): 1–27. Berkeley: The University Press, 1908.

"Notes on the Luiseños." *University of California Publications in American Archaeology and Ethnology* 8, (No. 3):174–186, illus. Berkeley: The University Press, 1908–1910.
Discussion of girl's and boy's puberty ceremonies, mourning ceremonies, customs and beliefs, and houses and implements.

North, Arthur W.
The Mother of California. Being an historical sketch of the little known land of Baja California, from the days of Cortez to the present time, depicting the ancient missions therein established, etc., together with an extensive bibliography. San Francisco: Paul Elder and Company, 1908. 169 pp., 32 pl., map.

"The Native Tribes of Lower California." *AA* 10:236–251, 1908. n. s.

Sparkman, Philip Stedman
"The Culture of the Luiseño Indians." *University of California Publications in American Archaeology and Ethnology* 8, (No. 4):187–234, pl. 20. Berkeley: The University Press, 1908–1910.

Strong, W. D.
"Aboriginal Society in Southern California." *University of California Publications in American Archaeology and Ethnology* 26:1–358. Berkeley: University of California Press, 1929.

Walker, Edwin F.
"Indians of Southern California." *Masterkey* 17, (No.6):201–216, 9 figs. Los Angeles: Southwest Museum, 1943.

MYTHS—FOLKTALES—LEGENDS

Caldwell, George Walter
Legends of Southern California. Illustrated by Jane Jefferson Flippin. San Francisco, Californina: Phillips & Van Orden Co., 1919. vi, 101 pp., front.
"The following stories are founded on legends of the Saboba Indians of Southern California." Introd.

"California Mission Indian Myths." *JAFL* 19:309–321, 1906; 21:35–42, 237–245, 1908.

Du Bois, Constance Goddard
"Across the Purple Sea. An Indian Tale." *So. Workman* 37:101–106, 1908.

"Mission Indian Religion: a myth in the making." *So. Workman* 33:353, 1904.

"Mythology of the Mission Indians, San Luiseño." *JAFL* 17:183–188, 1904; 19:52–60, 145–164, 1906.

"Religious Ceremonies and Myths of the Mission Indians." *AA* 7:620–630, 1905. n.s.

"The Religion of the Luiseño Indians of Southern California." *University of California Publications in American Archaeology and Ethnology* 8, (No. 3):69–186, pl. 16–19, 5 text figures. Berkeley: The University Press, 1908–1910.
> Contents: Initiation Ceremonies, Mourning Ceremonies, Ceremonial Song (with music). Various Myths and Traditional Knowledge.

James, G. W.
"Saboba Origin Myth." *JAFL* 15:36–39, 1902. "A Luiseño village, said to have been the principal one of San Jacinto Res., Cal. . . . They are said to have a noticeable strain of Mexican blood."

"Saboba Legend of Tauquitch and Algoot." *JAFL* 16:153–159, 1903.

Kroeber, A. L.
"Mission Indian (Luiseño) Myths." *JAFL* 19: 309–321, 1906.

Sparkman, Philip Stedman
"Luiseño Tale." *JAFL* 21:35–36, 1908.

Waterman, Thomas
"Analysis of the Mission Indian Creation Story." *AA* 11:41–56, 1909. n.s.

BELIEFS—CUSTOMS

Davis, E. H.
"Early Cremation Ceremonies of the Luiseño and Diegueño Indians of Southern California." *Indian Notes and Monographs, Museum of the American Indian, Heye Foundation* 7:93–110, 1927.

"Survivals of Pagan Beliefs Among the Indians of South California." *Nature* (London) 79:295–296, 1909.

Rust, Horatio N.
"A Puberty Ceremony of the Mission Indians." *AA* 8:28–33, 1906. n.s.

FOLK ART—GAMES—SPEECH

Du Bois, Constance Goddard
"Games, Arts and Industries of the Diguenos and Luiseños." *University of California Publications in American Archaeology and Ethnology.* 8 (No. 3):167–173. Berkeley: The University Press, 1908–1910.

Kroeber, A. L.
"Basket Designs of the Mission Indians of California." *Anthropological Papers of the American Museum of Natural History* (New York) 20:149–183, 1922., illus.

Basketry Design of the Mission Indians. Guide Leaflet No. 55, Miscellaneous Publications in Anthropology. New York: The American Museum of Natural History, 1932. 20 pp., illus. 3rd ed.

Schumacher, P.
"The Methods of Manufacturing Pottery and Baskets Among the Indians of Southern California." *Reports of the Peabody Museum in American Archaeology and Ethnology* 2:521–525, 1880.

Sparkman, P. S.
"A Sketch of the Grammar of the Luiseño—Language." *AA* 7:656–662, 1905. n.s.

Tagliavini, C.
"L'evangelizzazione e i costumi degli Indi Luisenos." *Proceedings of the International Congress of Americanists* 23:633–648, 1928. Religion and customs of the Luiseños.

"Frammento d'un dizionarietto Luiseño—Spagnuolo." *Proceedings of the International Congress of Americanists* 23:905–917, 1928. Fragment of a Luiseño-Spanish dictionary.

MUSIC
GENERAL STUDIES

Du Bois, Constance Goddard
"The Religion of the Luiseño Indians of Southern California." *University of California Publications in Archaeology and Ethnology* 8, (No. 3):69–186, pl. 16–19, 5 text fig. Berkeley: The University Press, 1908–1910.
> Contents: Initiation Ceremonies, Mourning Ceremonies, Ceremonial Songs (with music). Various Myths and Traditional Knowledge.

Roberts, Helen A.
Form in Primtive Music. An analytical and comparative study of the melodic form of some ancient Southern Californian Indian songs. New York: American Library of Musicology, (W. W. Norton and Company) 1933. 180 pp., music.
Special emphasis on the character of the music and instruments of the Luiseño.

MAIDU
(Including: Nissenan)
FOLKLORE
GENERAL STUDIES

Beals, R. L.
"Ethnology of the Nisenan." *Univ. of Cal. Publ. in Amer. Arch. and Ethnol.* 31:335–410, 1933.
Nisenan (Nishinam)—"The southern branch of the Maidu, occupying the valley of Bear River, Cal. While this portion of the Maidu is in some ways distinct from the northern branches, all of this family are so similar in every respect that even without the fact of the complete linguistic unity which they represent it would seem illogical to separate them." (Roland B. Dixon)

Dixon, Roland B.
"Maidu." In: *Bureau of American Ethnology, Bulletin* 40, (Part 1) :679–734, 1911.

——. *Maidu Texts.* Leyden: Late E. J. Brill, 1912. 241 pp. Publications of the American Ethnological Society, vol. IV.
Maidu texts and English translations on opposite pages.

——. "The Northern Maidu." *Bulletins of the American Museum of Natural History* (New York) 17 (Part 3) :119–346, 1905. Illus.

——. "Pujunan Family." In: *Bureau of American Ethnology, Bulletin 30* (Part 2) :326–327, 1910.
Pujunan family—"a linquistic family named by Powell (7th Rep. B.A.E., 99, 1891) from a former Nishinam settlement properly called Pusune, between American and Sacramento Rivers, Cal. As the family includes only a single group, known as Maidu, a description of the tribal group serves also for the family." (Roland B. Dixon).

Fassin, A. G.
"The Con-Cow Indians." *Overland Monthly,* (Ser. 2) 4:7–14, 1884.

Faye, P. L.
"Notes on the Southern Maidu." *Univ. of Cal. Publ. in Amer. Arch. and Ethnol.* 20:35–53, 1923.

Gifford, Edward Winslow
"Dichotomous Social Organization in South Central California." *Univ. of Cal. Publ. in Amer. Arch. and Ethnol.,* 11, (No. 5) :291–296, 1916. Berkeley: University of California Press, 1911–1916.
Tribes visited: Miwok, Yokuts, Mono, Shoshones.

Kroeber, A. L.
"The Maidu." In: *Handbook of the Indians of California.* Bureau of American Ethnology, Bulletin 78, pp. 391–441. Washington, D. C.: U. S. Gov't Printing Office, 1925.

——. "The Patwin and Their Neighbors." *Univ. of Cal. Publ. in Amer. Arch. and Ethnol.* 29:375–391, 1932.

——. "The Valley Nissenan." *Univ. of Cal. Publ. in Amer. Arch. and Ethnol.* 24:253–290, 1929.

Miller, M. L.
"The So-called California 'Diggers'." *Popular Science Monthly* 50:201–214, 1896.

——. "Der Untergang der Maidu oder Digger-Indianer." *Globus* 72:111–113, 1897.
On the disappearance of the Maidu or Digger Indians.

Powers, Stephen
"The California Indians." *Overland Monthly* 12:21–31, 420–424, 1874.

Tribes of California. Vol. III. Contributions to North American Ethnology. U. S. Geographical and Geological Survey of the Rocky Mountain Region. Washington, D. C.: U. S. Gov't Printing Office, 1877.

Spencer, D. L.
"Notes on the Maidu Indians of Butte County, California." *JAFL* 21:242–245, 1908.

MYTHS—FOLKTALES—LEGENDS

Cody, Bertha Parker
"A Maidu Myth of the Creation of Indian Women." *Masterkey* 13, (No. 2) :83, 1939.

Dixon, Roland Burrage
"Coyote Stories from the Maidu Indians of California." *JAFL* 13:267–270, 1900.

——. "Maidu Myths." *Bulletin of the American Museum of Natural History* (New York) 17 (Part 2) :33–118, 1902. (The Huntington California Expedition.)

——. *Maidu Texts.* Leyden: E. J. Brill, 1912. 241 pp. (American Ethnological Society Publications. Vol. 4.)

——. "System and Sequence in Maidu Mythology." *JAFL* 16:32–36, 1904.

Fassin, A. G.
"Un-Koi-to, the Savior." *Overland Monthly* (Ser. 2) 4:141–150, 1884.

Kroeber, A. L.
"Indian Myths of South Central California." *Univ. of Cal. Publ. in Amer. Arch. and Ethnol.* 4:167–250, 1907.

BELIEFS—CUSTOMS

Dixon, Roland B.
"Some Shamans of Northern California." *JAFL* 17:23–27, 1904.

Gifford, Edward W.
"Southern Maidu Religious Ceremonies." *AA* 29:214–257, 1927. n.s.

Powers, Stephen
"Aboriginal Botany." *Proceedings of the California Academy of Science* 5:373–379, 1874.

Thurston, B. P.
"A Night in a Maidu Shaman's House." *Masterkey* 7:111–115, 1933.

FOLK MEDICINE—FOLK ART—SPEECH

Dixon, Roland Burrage
"Basketry Designs of the Maidu Indians of California." *AA* 2:266–277, 1900. n.s.

——. "Basketry Designs of the Indians of Northern California." *Bulletin of the American Museum of Natural History* (New York) 17:2–14, 1902.

Gatschet, Albert S.
"Adjectives of Color in Indian Languages."
American Naturalist 13:475–485, 1879.

Thurston, Bertha Parker
"How a Maidu Medicine Man Lost His Power."
The Masterkey 9:28–29. Los Angeles: Southwest Museum, (Jan.) 1935.

_____
"A Night in a Maidu Shaman's House." *The Masterkey* 7, (No. 4):111–115. Los Angeles: Southwest Museum.

Willoughby, C. C.
"Feather Mantles of California." *AA* 24:432–437, 1922. n.s.

GAMES

Stearns, R. E. C.
"On the Nishinam Game of 'Ha' and the Boston Game of 'Props'." *AA* 3:353–359, 1890.

MUSIC

GENERAL STUDIES

Densmore, Frances
"Musical Instruments of the Maidu Indians."
AA 41:113–118, 1939. n.s.

Dixon, Roland B.
"The Musical Bow in California." *Science* 13:274–275, 1901. n.s.

_____
"The Northern Maidu." *Bulletin of the American Museum of Natural History,* 17 (Part 3):119–346. New York: American Museum, 1905. Music, pp. 221-222.

MIWOK

FOLKLORE

GENERAL STUDIES

Clark, Galem
Indians of the Yosemite Valley and Vicinity, their history, customs, and traditions. Yosemite Valley: Cal. G. Clark, 1904. xviii, 110 pp., illus.

Gifford, Edward Winslow
"Miwok Moieties." *University of California Publications in American Archaeology and Ethnology* 12, (No. 4):139–194, 1916. Berkeley: University of California Press, 1916–1917.

Henshaw, H. W., and Kroeber, A. L.
"Moquelumnan Family." In: *Bureau of American Ethnology, Bulletin 30* (Part 1):941–942, 1907.
A linquistic family . . . consisting of three divisions, the Miwok, the so-called Olamentke, and the Northern or Lake County Moquelumnan."

Hittell, John S.
Yosemite; its Wonders and its Beauties. San Francisco: H. H. Bancroft & Company, 1868. vi, 59 pp., illus.

Hutchings, J. M.
In the Heart of the Sierras. The Yosemite Valley both historical and descriptive. Oakland: Pacific Press Publishing House, 1886. 496 pp.

Kroeber, A. L.
"The Miwok"—In: *Handbook of the Indians of California.* Bureau of American Ethnology, Bulletin 78, pp. 442–461. Washington, D. C.: U. S. Gov't Printing Office, 1925.

_____
"On the Evidences of the Occupation of Certain Regions by the Miwok." *University of California Publications in American Archaeology and Ethnology* 6 (No. 3):369–380. Berkeley: The University Press, 1908.

Merriam, Clinton Hart
"Distribution and Classification of the Mewan Stock of California." *AA* 9:338–358, 1907. n.s.

Mooney, J.
"Notes on the Cosumnes Tribes of California."
AA 3:259–263, 1890.
"A tribe, probably Moquelumnan, formerly residing on or near Cosumnes River, San Joaquin County, California."

Wilson, Herbert E.
The Lore and Lure of the Yosemite; The Indians, their customs, legends and beliefs, big trees, geology, and the story of Yosemite. Los Angeles: Wolfer Printing Co., 1928. 135 pp., illus.

MYTHS—FOLKTALES—LEGENDS

Angulo, J. de, and Freeland, L. S.
"Miwok and Pomo Myths." *JAFL* 41:232–253, 1928.

Barrett, S. A.
"Myths of the Southern Sierra Miwok." *University of California Publications in American Archaeology and Ethnology* 16 (No. 1):1–28, 1919. Berkeley: University of California Press, 1919–1920.
"Myths of the Yosemite Valley," (pp. 21-23).

Gifford, Edward Winslow
"Miwok Myths." *University of California Publications in American Archaeology and Ethnology* 12, (No. 8):283–338, 1917. Berkeley: University of California Press, 1916–1917.
Contains fourteen stories given by two narrators.

Kroeber, A. L.
"Indian Myths of South Central California."
Univ. of Cal. Publ. in Amer. Arch. and Ethnol. 4:167–250, 1907.

Lehmer, D. N.
"First People; Miwok Indian Myths." *Overland* 87:378–379, (Dec.) 1929. n.s.

Merriam, Clinton Hart
The Dawn of the World; Myths and Weird Tales Told by the Mewan Indians of California. Cleveland: The Arthur H. Clark Co., 1910. 273 pp., illus.
    Bibliography of California mythology, pp. 243-246.

Smith, Bertha
Yosemite Legends. With drawings by F. Lundborg. San Francisco: P. Elder & Co., 1904. 64 pp., illus.

Smith, Elinor
Po-ho-no and the Legends of Yosemite, including "In the far beginning of years," primitive myths of the Yosemite Indians; illustrated by Wallace, Moira and Dickinson, E. Monterey, Calif.: Peninsula Printing Co., 1927. 39 pp., illus.

Stewart, Humphrey J., and Dunn, Allan
Legends of the Yosemite: Five songs with legends. Boston: White Smith Publishing Company, 1910. 40 pp., illus.
    Folklore of the Ah-wah-nee-chee Indians of the Yosemite Valley, California.

Vivian, C. A.
"Yosemite Legends." *Overland Monthly* (San Francisco) 37:1068–1075, 1901.
    Idealized version of five Indian Legends. Yosemite (Awani) is a division of the Miwok living in Yosemite Valley.

BELIEFS—CUSTOMS—FOLK ART

Barrett, S. A.
"The Geography and Dialects of the Miwok Indians." *University of California Publications in American Archaeology and Ethnology* 6, (No. 2):333–368, map 3. Berkeley: The University Press, 1908.

——.
"Totemism Among the Miwok Indians." *JAFL* 21:237, 1908.

——, **and Gifford, E. W.**
"Miwok Material Culture." *Milwaukee Public Museum, Bulletin* 2, (No. 4):117–376, 1933. Illus.

Gifford, Edward Winslow
"Californian Kinship Terminologies." *Univ. of Cal. Publ. in Amer. Arch. and Ethnol.* 18:86–94, 1922.

——.
"Miwok Cults." *Univ. of Cal. Publ. in Amer. Arch. and Ethnol.* 18, (No. 3). Berkeley: University of California Press, 1926.

——.
"Miwok Lineages and the Political Unit in Aboriginal California." *AA* 28:389–401, 1926. n.s.

Kroeber, A. L.
"The Dialectic Divisions of the Moquelumnan Family." *AA* 8:652–663, 1906. n.s.

——.
"The Languages of the Coast of California North of San Francisco." *Univ. of Cal. Publ. in Amer. Arch. and Ethnol.* 9:278–291, 1911.

Merriam, Clinton Hart
"Totemism in California." *AA* 10:558–562, 1908. n.s.

MUSIC
GENERAL STUDIES

Angulo, Jaime de, and d'Harcourt, B.
"La musique des Indiens de la Californie du Nord." *Journal de la Société des Américanistes* 23:189–228, 1931. n.s.

ARRANGEMENTS

"Down the Stream."
    Lemher, N. D.: Published by author, 2736 Regent St., Berkeley, Calif., 1927: Voice and piano.

"Song of the Sun."
    In: H. & M. Auditorium Series, No. 26. Olds, W. B.: Hall & McCreary: TTBB.

MODOC
FOLKLORE
GENERAL STUDIES

Meacham, A. B.
Wigwam and Warpath; or, The Royal Chief in Chains. Boston: J. P. Dale and Company, 1875. 2d. and rev. ed., xxiii, 700 pp.

Miller, Joaquin
Life Among the Modocs, London: R. Bentley & Sons, 1873. viii, 400 pp.

Payne, Doris Palmer
Captain Jack, Modoc Renegade. Portland: Binfort and Mort., 1938. vi, 259 pp., pl., port., bibl. pp. 257–259.

Turner, W. M.
"Scraps of Modoc History." *Overland Monthly* 11:21–25, 1873.

MYTHS—FOLKTALES

Curtin, Jeremiah
Myths of the Modocs. Boston: Little, Brown and Company, 1912. xii, 389 pp.

Gatschet, Albert S.
"Modoc Tales." *JAFL* 4:139–141, 1891.

——.
"Die Windhose: ein Mythus der Modoc Indianer." *Am Urquell* 2:1–3, 1891.

Merriam, Clinton Hart
An-nik-a-del, the History of the Universe as told by the Modés-se Indians of California. Boston: The Stratford Co., 1928. xi, 166 pp.

BELIEFS—FOLK MEDICINE—FOLK ART

Barrett, S. A.
"The Material Culture of the Klamath Lake and Modoc Indians of Northeastern California and Southern Oregon." *University of California Publications in American Archaeology and Ethnology* 5, (No. 4):239–292. plates 10–25. Berkeley: The University Press, 1907.

Franks, A. W.
"A Bow and Two Arrows of the Modoc." *Journal of the Royal Anthropological Institute of Great Britain and Ireland* (London) 3:204–205, 1873.

"Modoc Animism."
JAFL 2:236–237, 1889.

"Modoc Medicine Arrows."
JAFL 6:111–112, 1893.

MUSIC

GENERAL STUDIES

Angulo, Jaime de, and d'Harcourt, B.
"La Musique des Indiens de la Californie du Nord." *Journal de la Société des Américanistes* 23:189–228, 1931. n.s.

Gatschet, Albert S.
"Songs of the Modoc Indians." *AA* 7:26–32, 1894. o.s.
Text only.

Specimen of Songs of the Modoc Indians. Washington, D. C.: Judd and Detweiler, 1894. Reprinted: American Anthropologist, Washington, D. C.: 1894, vol. 7.

DANCES

"Modoc Ghost Dance."
JAFL 19:141–142, 1906.

POMO

FOLKLORE

GENERAL STUDIES

Aginsky, B. W.
"Population Control in the Shanel (Pomo) Tribe." *American Sociological Review* 4, (No. 21):209–216, 1939.

"Psychopathic Trends in Culture." *Character and Personality* 7:331–343, 1939.

Angulo, Jaime de
"Textes en langue Pomo." *Journal de la Société des Américanistes* 19:129–144, 1927. n.s.

Barrett, S. A.
"The Ethno-Geography of the Pomo and Neighboring Indians." *University of California Publications in American Archaeology and Ethnology* 5, (No. 1):1–332, map.
The tribes discussed: Pomo, Yuki, Athapascan, Wintun, Moquelumnan.

"Pomo." In: *Bureau of American Ethnology, Bulletin 30* (Part 2):276–277, 1910.

Gifford, Edward W.
"Clear Lake Pomo Society." *Univ. of Cal. Publ. in Amer. Arch. and Ethnol.* 18:287–390, 1926.

"Notes on Central Pomo and Northern Yana Society." *AA* 30:675–684, 1928. n.s.

———, and Kroeber, A. L.
"Culture Element Distributions. IV. Pomo." *University of California Publications in American Archaeology and Ethnology* 37 (No. 4): 117–254. Berkeley: University of California Press, 1937.

Kroeber, A. L.
"California Kinship Systems." *Univ. of Calif. Publ. in Amer. Arch. and Ethnol.* 12:370–372, 1917.

"Pomo." In: *Handbook of the Indians of California.* Bureau of American Ethnology, Bulletin 78, pp. 222–271. Washington, D. C.: U. S. Gov't Printing Office, 1925.

Loeb, Edwin M.
"Pomo Folkways." *University of California Publications of American Archaeology and Ethnology* 19:149–405, 1926.

Menefee, Campbell Augustus
Historical and Descriptive Sketch Book of Napa, Sonoma Lake, and Mendocino. Napa City: Reporter Publishing House, 1873. 356 pp., illus.

Powers, Stephen
"The Northern California Indians." *Overland Monthly* 9:498–507, 1872.

Stewart, Omer C.
"Notes on Pomo Ethnogeography." *University of California Publications in American Archaeology and Ethnology* 40, (No. 2):29–62, map. Berkeley and Los Angeles: University of California Press, 1943.

MYTHS—FOLKTALES—LEGENDS

Angulo, Jaime de
"Pomo Creation Myth." *JAFL* 48:203–263, 1935.

———, and Benson, William R.
"The Creation Myth of the Pomo Indians." *Anthropos* 27:261–274, 1932.

————, and Freeland, L. S.
"Miwok and Pomo Myths." *JAFL* 41:232–253, 1928.

Barrett, Samuel Alfred
"Composite Myth of the Pomo Indians." *JAFL* 19:37–51, 1907.

————.
Pomo Myths. Bulletin of the Public Museum of the City of Milwaukee. Milwaukee, Wis.: Published by Order of the Board of Trustees, 1933. 608 pp., bibl. (pp. 549–553).

BELIEFS—CUSTOMS

Aginsky, B. W.
"An Indian's Soliloquy." *American Journal of Sociology* 46:43–44, 1940.

————.
"The Mechanics of Kinship." *AA* 37:450–457, 1935. n.s.

————.
"The Socio-Psychological Significance of Death among the Pomo Indians." *American Imago* 1 (Part 3):1–18, 1940.

Barrett, S. A.
The Army Worm: a Food of the Pomo Indians. In: *Essays in Anthropology Presented to A. L. Kroeber,* pp. 1–5. Berkeley: University of California Press, 1936.

————.
"Ceremonies of the Pomo Indians." *University of California Publications in American Archaeology and Ethnology* 12, (No. 10):397–441, 1917. 8 text figures. Berkeley: University of California Press, 1916–1917.
Discussion of the Ghost Ceremony, the Guksu Ceremony, Dances, and the Messiah Cult.

————.
"Pomo Bear Doctors." *University of California Publications in American Archaeology and Ethnology* 12, (No. 11):443–465, 1917. plate 7. Berkeley: University of California Press, 1916–1917.
Also comparison with Yuki and Miwok beliefs.

————.
Pomo Buildings. In: *Holmes Anniversary Volume,* pp. 1–17. Washington, D. C.: 1916.

Chestnut, V. K.
"Plants Used by the Indians of Mendocino County, California." United States Department of Agriculture, Division of Botany. *Contributions from the U. S. National Herbarium* 7, (No. 3), 1902.

Cody, B. P.
"Pomo Bear Impersonators." *Masterkey* 14: 132–137, 1940.

Freeland, Lucy Shepard
"Pomo Doctors and Poisoners." *Univ. of Cal. Publ. in Amer. Arch. and Ethnol.* 20:55–73, 1923. (In: Phoebe Apperson Hearst Memorial Volume.)

Loeb, Edwin M.
"The Creator Concept Among the Indians of North Central California." *AA* 28:467–493, 1926.

————.
"The Western Kuksu Cult." *Univ. of Cal. Publ. in Amer. Arch. and Ethnol.* 33:3–13, 101–105, 125–131, 1932.

Orchard, W. C.
"A Pomo Headress." *Indian Notes, Museum of the American Indian, Heye Foundation,* (New York) 4:170–175, 1927.

FOLK ART—FOLK MEDICINE—SPEECH

Barrett, S. A.
"Basket Designs of the Pomo Indians." *AA* 7: 648–653, 1905. n.s.

————.
"Pomo Bear Doctors." *Univ. of Cal. Publ. in Amer. Arch. and Ethnol.* 12 (No. 11):443–465, 1917. Illus.
Also comparison with Yuki and Miwok beliefs.

————.
"Pomo Indian Basketry." *Univ. of Cal. Publ. in Amer. Arch. and Ethnol.,* 7, No. 3):134–308, plates 15–31, text figures 231. Berkeley: The University Press, 1908.

Gifford, Edward W.
"Californian Kinship Terminologies." *Univ. of Cal. Publ. in Amer. Arch. and Ethnol.* 18:104–115, 1922.

Harrington, M. R.
"A Glimpse of Pomo Archaeology." *The Masterkey* 17:9–12. Los Angeles: Southwest Museum, 1942.

Hudson, J. W.
"Pomo Basket Makers." *Overland Monthly* 21:561–578, 1893. n.s.

————.
"Pomo Wampum Makers." *Overland Monthly* 30:101–108, 1897. n.s.

Kroeber, A. L.
"California Basketry and the Pomo." *AA* 11: 233–249, 1909. n.s.

Orchard, W. C.
"An Unusual Pomo Basket." *Indian Notes, Museum of the American Indian, Heye Foundation* (New York) 2:102–109, 1925.

Purdy, C.
"The 'Dau' in Pomo Basketry." *Out West* (Los Angeles) 18:317–325, 1903.

————.
"The Pomo Indian Baskets and Their Makers." *Out West* (Los Angeles) 15:438–449,; 16: 9–19, 151–158, 262–273, 1901–1902.

MUSIC

GENERAL STUDIES

Angulo, Jaime de, and d'Harcourt, B.
"La musique des Indiens de la Californie du Nord." *Journal de la Société des Américanistes* 23:189–228, 1931. n.s.

DANCE

Gorringe, Katherine
"The Ukiah Big-Time." *Dial* 86:580–585, July, 1929.
Description of a party, dance and festivities among the Pomo Indians.

ARRANGEMENTS

————: *Voice and Piano*

"Pomo Love Song."
Lemher, D. N.: Author: Voice, piano and flute.

SHASTA

FOLKLORE

GENERAL STUDIES

Dixon, Roland B.
"The Shasta." *Bulletin of the American Museum of Natural History* (New York) 17 (Part 5):381–498, 1907. Illus.

————.
"Shasta." In: *Bureau of American Ethnology, Bulleton 30 (Part 2)*:527–528, 1905. (Washington, D. C.)

————.
"The Shasta-Achomawi: A New Linguistic Stock, with Four New Dialects." *AA* 7:213–218, 1905. n.s.

Kroeber, A. L.
"Shasta." In: *Handbook of the Indians of California*. Bureau of American Ethnology, Bulletin 78, pp. 279–304. Washington, D. C.: U. S. Gov't Printing Office, 1925.

MYTHS—FOLKTALES—LEGENDS

Burns, L. M.
"Digger Indian Legends." Part I–IV. *Land of Sunshine* 14:130–134, 223–226, 310–314, 397, 402, 1901.
The author presents English versions of six Shasta myths.

Dixon, Roland B.
"Shasta Myths." *JAFL* 23:8–37, 364–370, 1910.

————.
"The Mythology of the Shasta-Achomawi." *AA* 7:607–613, 1905. n.s.

Farrand, L., and Frachtenberg, L. J.
"Shasta and Athapascan Myths from Oregon." *JAFL* 28:207–223, 1915.

Voegelin, Erminie W.
"Three Shasta Myths, Including 'Orpheus'." *JAFL* 60:52–58, 1947. Bibl.

BELIEFS—SPEECH

Dixon, Roland B.
"Linguistic Relationships Within the Shasta-Achomawi Stock." *Proceedings of the International Congress of Americanists* 15 (Part 2): 255–263, 1906.

————.
"Some Shamans of Northern California." *JAFL* 17:23–27, 1904.

MUSIC

GENERAL STUDIES

Angulo, Jaime de, and d'Harcourt, B.
"La musique des Indiens de la Californie du Nord." *Journal de la Société Américanistes* 23:189–228, 1931. n.s.

Dixon, Roland B.
"The Shasta." *Bulletin of the American Museum of Natural History*. New York: 17 (part 5):381–498. Music, pp. 449–550, 1907.
The author includes a discussion of the music, ritual, and dance.

TAKELMA

FOLKLORE

GENERAL STUDIES

Sapir, Edward
"Notes on the Takelma Indians of Southwestern Oregon." *AA* 9:261–276, 1907. n.s.
"Culturally the Takelma Indians were closely allied to the Shasta of north California, with whom they frequently intermarried. . . . In clothing and personal adornment the Takelma differed but little from the tribes of northern California, red-headed-woodpecker scalps and the basket caps of the women being perhaps the most characteristic articles." (E. S.)

————.
Takelma Texts. Anthropological Publications of the Pennsylvania Museum vol. 2, no. 1. Philadelphia: University of Pennsylvania Press, 1910. 263 pp.

BELIEFS

Sapir, Edward
"Religious Ideas of the Takelma Indians of Southwestern Oregon." *JAFL* 20:33–49; 455–472, 1907.

————.
"Takelma Dreams."
JAFL 20:49, 1907.

MUSIC
GENERAL STUDIES

Sapir, Edward
"Religious Ideas of the Takelma Indians of Southwestern Oregon." *JAFL* 20:455–472, 1907.
Contains discussion of songs.

WAILAKI
(*Including*: Kato, Lassik, and Sinkyone)

FOLKLORE
GENERAL STUDIES

Driver, H. E.
"Northwest California." *Anthropological Records* 1:297–433, 1939.

Emeneau, M. B.
"Kato Texts. Part I." *University of California Publications in Linguistics* 2: (No. 1) vii+ 199 pp. Berkeley: University of California Press, 1944.
"A Kuneste tribe or band formerly living in Cahto and Long Valleys, Mendocino, California ...closely related to the Wailaki, although they resemble the Pomo in culture." (P. E. Goddard)

————.
"Kato Texts: Part Two." *University of California Publications in Linguistics* 2 (No. 2): 193–390, 1946. Berkeley and Los Angeles: University of California Press.

Goddard, Pliny Earle
"Kato Texts." *University of California Publications in American Archaeology and Ethnology* 5 (No. 3):65–238, 1909. Illus.

————.
"Wailaki Texts." *International Journal of American Linguistics* 2:77–135, 1923.

————.
"Lassik." In: *Bureau of American Ethnology, Bulletin 30* (Part 1):761, 1907. (Washington, D. C.)

————.
"Wailaki." In: *Bureau of American Ethnology, Bulletin 30*, (Part 2) :893–894, 1910. Washington, D. C.)

Kroeber, A. L.
A Kato War. In: *Festschrift Publication d'Hommage offerte au P .W. Schmidt*, (pp. 394–400). Wien: 1928.

Nomland, Gladys Ayer
"Bear River Ethnography." *Anthropological Records* 2:91–123, 1938.

————.
"Sinkyone Notes." *Univ. of Cal. Publ. in Amer. Arch. and Ethnol.*, 35 (No. 2), 29 pp. Berkeley: University of California Press, 1935.

FOLKTALES

Goddard, Pliny Earle
"Lassik Tales." *JAFL* 19:133–140, 1906.
A people of the Athapascan family, neighbors of the Wintun and Hupa. Their dialect resembles the Hupa in its morphology and the Wailaki in its phonology.

Kroeber, A. L.
"Sinkyone Tales." *JAFL* 32:346–351, 1919.
This tribe belongs to the Athapsacan group formerly living on the lower part of the South Fork of Eel River, Humboldt County, California.

BELIEFS—CUSTOMS

Foster, G. M.
"String-Figure Divination." *AA* 43:126–127, 1941. n.s.

Goddard, Pliny Earle
"Habitat of the Pitch Indians." *Univ. of Cal. Publ. in Amer. Arch. and Ethnol.* 17:217–225, 1924.

————.
"Habitat of the Wailaki." *Univ. of Cal. Publ. in Amer. Arch. and Ethnol.* 20:95–109, 1923.

Loeb, E. M.
"The Western Kuksu Cult." *Univ. of Cal. Publ. in Amer. Arch. and Ethnol.* 33:14–54, 73–95, 1932.

Nomland, G. A.
"A Bear River Shaman's Curative Dance." *AA* 33:38–41, 1931. n.s.

DANCE—SPEECH

Goddard, Pliny Earle
"The Bear River Dialect of Athapascan." *Univ. of Cal. Publ. in Amer. Arch. and Ethnol.* 24: 291–324, 1929.

————.
"Elements of the Kato Language." *Univ. of Cal. Publ. in Amer. Arch. and Ethnol.*, 11, (No. 1) :1–176, 1912. pls. 1–45. Berkeley: University of California Press, 1911–1916.

Nomland, G. A.
"A Bear River Shaman's Curative Dance." *AA* 33:38–41, 1931. n.s.

WINTUN
(*Including*: Patwin)

FOLKLORE
GENERAL STUDIES

Anonymous
"Patwin." *Bureau of American Ethnology, Bulletin 30* (Part 2):211, 1910. Washington, D. C.

DuBois, C.
"Wintu Ethnography." *Univ. of Cal. Publ. in Amer. Arch. and Ethnol.* 36:1–148, 1935.

Kroeber, A. L.
"Wintun." In: *Handbook of the Indians of California.* Bureau of American Ethnology, 78, pp. 351–390. Washington, D. C.: U. S. Gov't Printing Office, 1925.

Menefee, Campbell Augustus
Historical and Descriptive Sketch Book of Napa, Sonoma Lake, and Mendocino. Napa City: Reporter Publishing House, 1873. 356 pp., illus.

Washington, F. B.
"Notes on the Northern Wintun Indians." *JAFL* 22:92–95, 1909.

MYTHS—FOLKTALES

DuBois, Cora, and Demetracopoulou, Dorothy
"Wintu Myths." *University of California Publications in American Archaeology and Ethnology* 28:279–403, 1931. Bibl. Berkeley: The University Press, 1931.

————.
"A Study of Wintu Mythology." *JAFL* 45:373–500, 1932.

Goldschmidt, Walter, Foster, George, and Essene, Frank
"War Stories from Two Enemy Tribes." *JAFL* 52:141–154, 1939.

BELIEFS—CUSTOMS

Barrett, Samuel Alfred
"The Wintun Hesi Ceremony." *Univ of Cal. Publ. in Amer. Arch. and Ethnol.*, 14 (No. 4) :437–488, 1919. plates 22–23, 3 figs. in text. Berkeley: University of California Press, 1918–1919.
The object of the Hesi (and of all ceremonies) was to insure plentiful wild harvests and secondarily to secure the health and general prosperity of the people.

Kroeber, A. L.
"California Kinship Systems." *Univ. of Cal. Publ. in Amer. Arch. and Ethnol.* 12:368–370, 1917.

Lee, D. Demetracopoulou
"A Wintu Girl's Puberty Ceremony." *New Mexico Anthropologist* 5 (No. 4) :57–60, 1940.

McKern, W. C.
"Patwin Houses." *Univ. of Cal. Publ. in Amer. Arch. and Ethnol.* 20:159–171, 1923.

Voegelin, Erminie W.
"Suicide in Northeastern California." 39:445–456, 1937. n.s.

FOLK ART—SPEECH

Dixon, R. B.
Outlines of Wintun Grammar. In: *Putnam Anniversary Volume,* (pp. 461–476.) New York: 1909.

Kroeber, A. L.
"Basket Designs of the Indians of Northwestern California." *Univ. of Cal. Publ. in Amer. Arch. and Ethnol.* 2:105–164, 1905.

Lee, D. Demetracopoulou
"Linguistic Reflection of Wintu Thought." *International Journal of Linguistics* (Indiana University, Bloomington, Ind.) 10:181–187, 1944.

————.
"The Place of Kinship Terms in Wintu Speech." *AA* 43:604–616, 1940. n.s.

MUSIC
GENERAL STUDIES

Angulo, Jaime de, and d'Harcourt, B.
"La musique des Indiens de la Californie du Nord." *Journal de la Société des Américanistes* 33:189–228, 1931. n.s.

Demetracopoulou, D.
"Wintu Songs." *Anthropos* 30 (Nos. 3–4): 483–494, 1935.

WIYOT
(*Including:* Wishosk)
FOLKLORE
GENERAL STUDIES

Kroeber, A. L.
"Wishosk." In: *Bureau of American Ethnology, Bulletin 30* (Part 2) :964, 1910.
"The word (Wishosk) seems to be a misapplication of their own name for their Athapascan neighbors, *Wishashk.* Wiyot, which has sometimes been used as an equivalent, is therefore probably a better term than Wishosk, though not entirely exact. . . . In general culture the Wishosk resembled the tribes of the lower Klamath and Trinity. . . . Similar in all essentials to those of the Yurok, Karok, and Hupa."

————.
"Wiyot." In: *Handbook of the Indians of California.* Bureau of American Ethnology, Bulletin 78, pp. 112–120. Washington, D. C.: U. S. Gov't Printing Office, 1925.

————.
"Wiyot Folklore." *JAFL* 21:37–39, 1908.

Nomland, Gladys Ayer, and Kroeber, A. L.
"Wiyot Towns." *University of California Publications in American Archaeology and Ethnology* 35, (No. 5) :39–48. Berkeley: University of California Press, 1936.

Reichard, Gladys A.
Wiyot Grammar and Texts. Berkeley, Calif.; University of California Press, 1925. 215 pp. (University of California Publications in American Archaeology and Ethnology. vol. 22, no. 1.)

MYTHS

Kroeber, A. L.
"Wishosk Myths." *JAFL* 18:85–107, 1905.

FOLK ART—SPEECH

Kroeber, A. L.
"Yurok and Neighboring Kin Term Systems." *Univ. of Cal. Publ. in Amer. Arch. and Ethnol.* 35:15–22, 1934.

Loud, Llewellyn L.
"Ethnogeography and Archaeology of the Wiyot Territory." *Univ. of Cal. Publ. in Amer. Arch. and Ethnol.* 14, (No. 3) :221–436, 1918. plates 1–21, 5 text figs. Berkeley: University of California Press, 1918–1919.

Reichard, Gladys A.
"Wiyot: An Indian Language of Northern California." *AS* 1 (No. 12) :654–658, 1926.

Sapir, Edward
"The Algonkin Affinity of Yurok and Wiyot Kinship Terms." *Journal de la Société des Américanistes* (Paris) 15:37–74, 1923. n.s.

————.
"Wiyot and Yurok, Algonkin Languages of California." *AA* 15:617–646, 1913. n.s.

Uhlenbeck, C. C.
"Algonkisch-klinkende woorden in her Wiyot." *Mededeelingen der Koninklijke Akademie van Wetenschappen, Afdeeling Letterkunde* (Amsterdam) 63 (Part 9) :233–258, 1927.

YANA

FOLKLORE

GENERAL STUDIES

Gifford, E. W., and Klimek, Stanislaw
"Culture Element Distributions: II. Yana." *University of California Publications in American Archaeology and Ethnology* 37 (No. 2): 71–100, 1936. Berkeley: The University Press.

————, **and Spier, Leslie**
"Notes on the Culture of the Yana." *Anthropological Records* 3 (No. 3) :239–297, 6 pls. 5 figs. Berkeley and Los Angeles: University of California Press, 1943.

Kroeber, A. L.
"Yana." In: *Handbook of the Indians of California.* Bureau of American Ethnology, Bulletin 78, (pp. 336–346). Washington, D. C.: U. S. Gov't Printing Office, 1925.

————, **and Spier, Leslie**
"Notes on the Culture of the Yana." *Anthropological Records 3 (No. 3):* 239–297, 1943. Berkeley and Los Angeles: University of California Press, 1943. Illus.

Sapir, Edward, and Dixon, Roland B.
"Yana Texts, Together with Yana Myths Collected by Roland B. Dixon." *University of California Publications in American Archaeology and Ethnology* 9:1–235, 1910. Berkeley: The University Press, 1910–1911.

Waterman, T. T.
"The Yana Indians." *University of California Publications in American Archaeology and Ethnology* 13, (No. 2) :35–102, 1918. plates 1–20. Berkeley: University of California Press, 1917–1923.
More of a historical study.

MYTHS

Sapir, Edward, and Dixon, Roland B.
"Yana Texts, Together with Yana Myths Collected by Roland B. Dixon." *University of California Publications in American Archaeology and Ethnology* 9:1–235, 1910. Berkeley: The University Press, 1910–1911.

BELIEFS—FOLK MEDICINE—CUSTOMS

Pope, Saxton T.
"The Medical History of Ishi." *University of California Publications in American Archaeology and Ethnology* 13 (No. 5) :175–213, 1920. plates 38–44, 8 text figures. Berkeley: University of California Press, 1917–1923.
Ishi was the last remaining survivor of the Yahi tribe. Died March 25, 1916.

Sapir, Edward
"Luck Stones Among the Yana." *JAFL* 21:42, 1908.

FOLK ART—SPEECH

Pope, Saxon T.
"Yahi Archery." *University of California Publications in American Archaeology and Ethnology* 13, (No. 3) :103–152, 1918. pls. 21–37. Berkeley: University of California Press, 1917–1923.
The Yahi or Deer Creek Indians is the most southerly division of the Yanan stock.

Sapir, Edward
"Male and Female Form of Speech in Yana." In: *Donum Natalicium Schrijnen*, St. W. J. Teeuven, ed., pp. 79–85. Nijmegen-Utrecht, 1929.

————.
"Text Analyses of Three Yana Dialects." *Univ. of Cal. Publ. in Amer. Arch. and Ethnol.* 20: 263–294, 1923.

————.
"The Fundamental Elements of Northern Yana." *University of California Publications in American Archaeology and Ethnology* 13, (No. 6) :215–234, 1922. Berkeley: University of California Press, 1917–1923.
Linguistic study.

————.
"The Position of Yana in the Hokan Stock."
University of California Publications in American Archaeology and Ethnology 13, (No. 1): 1–34, 1917. Berkeley: University of California Press, 1917–1923.

The Hokan languages the author recognizes are: Shasta-Achomawi, Chimariko, Karok, Yana, Pomo, Esselen, Yuman, Salinan, Chumash, Seri, and Chontal.

————.
"Yana Terms of Relationship." *Univ. of Cal. Publ. in Amer. Arch. and Ethnol.* 13:153–173, 1918.

YOKUTS

FOLKLORE

GENERAL STUDIES

Anon.
"Mariposan Family." In: *Bureau of American Ethnology, Bulletin 30* (Part 1):807–808, 1907. Washington, D. C.

The name applied by Powell to a linguistic stock of Indians, generally known as Yokuts, in San Joaquin Valley, Cal."

Driver, H. E.
"Southern Sierra Nevada." *Anthropological Records* (Berkeley) 1:53–154, 1937.

Latta, F. F., ed.
Uncle Jeff's Story; A Tale of a San Joaquin Valley Pioneer and his Life with the Yokuts Indians. Tulane, California: Tulane Times Press, 1929. 88 pp.

————.
California Indian Folklore. Shafter, Calif.: The Shafter Press, 1936.

Most of the stories are from the Yokuts Tribe, and a few from the neighboring Miwoks.

Menefee, Campbell Augustus
Historical and Descriptive Sketch Book of Napa, Sonoma Lake, and Mendocino. Napa City: Reporter Publishing House, 1873. 356 pp., illus.

Stewart, G. W.
"The Yokut Indians of the Kaweah Region." *Sierra Club Bulletin* 12:385–400, 1927.

————.
"Yokuts Traditions." *JAFL* 21:237–239, 1908.

MYTHS

Gayton, A. H., and Newman, Stanley S.
"Yokuts and Western Mono Myths." *Anthropological Records* 5, (No. 1):1–109, 2 maps, bibl. (pp. 105–108). Berkeley and Los Angeles: University of California Press, 1940.

Hudson, J. W.
"Indian Myths of the San Joaquin Basin." *JAFL* 15:104–106, 1901.

A collective name for the Costanoan, Moquelumnan and Yokuts tribes of San Joaquin River, California.

Kroeber, A. L.
"Indian Myths of South Central California." *Univ. of Cal. Publ. in Amer. Arch. and Ethnol.* 4:167–250, 1907.

Potts, W. J.
"Creation Myth of the California Indians." *JAFL* 5:73–74, 1892.

Rogers, Barbara Thrall, and Gayton, A. H.
"Twenty-seven Chuckchansi Yokuts Myths." *JAFL* 57:190–207, 1944.

Stewart, G. W.
"Yokuts Creation Myth." *JAFL* 19:322, 1906.

BELIEFS—CUSTOMS

Gayton, A. H.
Estudillo Among the Yokuts. In: *Essays in Anthropology Presented to A. L. Kroeber.* pp. 67–85. Berkeley: University of California Press, 1936.

————.
"The Ghost Dance of 1870." *Univ. of Cal. Publ. in Amer. Arch. and Ethnol.* 28:57–82, 1930.

————.
"Yokuts-Mono Chiefs and Shamans." *Univ. of Cal. Publ. in Amer. Arch. and Ethnol.* 24:361–420, 1930.

Kroeber, A. L.
"California Kinship Systems." *Univ. of Cal. Publ. in Amer. Arch. and Ethnol.* 12:352–358, 1917.

————.
"Yokuts Ceremony." *JAFL* 21:40, 1908.

Walker, Edwin F.
"Yukuts Cemetery at Elk Hills." *The Masterkey* 9, (No. 5):145–150. Los Angeles: Southwest Museum, (Sept.) 1935.

FOLK ART—SPEECH

Gayton, A. H.
"Yokuts and Western Mono Pottery Making." *Univ. of Cal. Publ. in Amer. Arch. and Ethnol.* 24:239–251, 1929.

Harris, Zellig S.
"Yokuts Structure and Newman's Grammar." *International Journal of Linguistics* (Indiana University, Bloomington, Ind.) 10:196–211, 1944.

Kroeber, A. L.
"The Yokuts Language of South Central California." *Univ. of Cal. Publ. in Amer. Arch. and Ethnol.* 2 (No. 5):165–377. Berkeley: The University Press, 1904–1907.

The author discusses the Yaudanchi and the Yauelmani Dialects.

————.
The Yokuts and Yuki Languages. In: *Boas Anniversary Volume,* pp. 64–79. New York: G. E. Stechert and Company, 1906.

"Yokuts Names." *JAFL* 19:142–143, 1906.

Newman, Stanley S.
"The Yawelmani Dialect of Yokuts." *International Jouranl of Linguistics* (New York). 7:85–89, 1932.

———.
Yokutus Language of California. Viking Fund Publications in Anthropology 2: 247 pp. New York: The Viking Fund, Inc., 10 Rockefeller Plaza, 1944.

DANCE

Gayton, A. H.
"The Ghost Dance of 1870." *Univ. of Cal. Publ. in Amer. Arch. and Ethnol.* 28:57–82, 1930.

YUKI

(*Including:* Wappo)

FOLKLORE

GENERAL STUDIES

Driver, Harold E.
"Wappo Ethnography." *University of California Publications in American Archaeology and Ethnology* 36 (No. 3):179–220, Berkeley: University of California Press, 1936.
"A small detached portion of the Yukian family of north California, separated from the Huchnom, the nearest Yuki division, by 30 or 40 miles of Pomo territory."

Gifford, E. W.
"The Coast Yuki." *Anthropos* (Wien-Mödling) 34 (Nos. 1–3):292–375, 1939.

Kroeber, A. L.
"The Coast Yuki of California." *AA* 5:729–730, 1903. n. s.

———.
"Wappo." In: *Handbook of the Indians of California.* Bureau of American Ethnology, Bulletin 78, pp. 217–221. Washington, D. C.: U. S. Gov't. Printing Office, 1925.

———.
"Yuki." In: *Handbook of the Indians of California.* Bureau of American Ethnology. Bulletin 78, pp. 159–216. Washington, D. C.: U. S. Gov't. Printing Office, 1925.

Radin, Paul
"Wappo Texts." *University of California Publications in American Archaeology and Ethnology* 19:1–147, 1924. Berkeley: The University Press, 1924.

MYTHS—FOLKTALES

Gifford, E. W.
"Coast Yuki Myths." *JAFL* 50:115–173, 1937.

Goldschmidt, Walter, Foster, George, and Essene, Frank
" War Stories from Two Enemy Tribes." *JAFL* 52:141–154, 1939.
The Yuki and Nomlaki.

Kroeber, A. L.
"Yuki Myths." *Anthropos* 27:905–940, 1932.
"In their mode of life, habits, and beliefs the Yuki generally resemble the better known Pomo, though the Yuki proper show the closest resemblances to the neighboring Athapascan Wailaki."

———, H. R.
"Wappo Myths." *JAFL* 21:321–323, 1908.

BELIEFS—CUSTOM

Chestnut, V. K.
"Plants Used by the Indians of Mendocino County." *Contributions from the U. S. National Herbarium* 7:295–408, 1902.

Kroeber, A. L.
"Yukian Family." *Bureau of American Ethnology, Bulletin* 30(Part 2):1008–1009, 1910. (Washington, D. C.).

Loeb, E. M.
"The Western Kuksu Cult." *Univ. of Cal. Publ. in Amer. Arch. and Ethnol.* 33:106–112, 1932.

Schmidt, W.
Donner und Regenbogen beim höchsten Wesen der Yuki. In: *Essays in Anthropology Presented to A. L. Kroeber,* pp. 299–308. Berkeley: University of California Press, 1936.
Thunder and rainbow in Yuki belief.

FOLK ART—SPEECH

Kelly, I. T.
"Yuki Basketry." *Univ. of Cal. Publ. in Amer. Arch. and Ethnol.* 24:421–444, 1930.

Kroeber, A. L.
"The Languages of the Coast of California North of San Francisco." *Univ. of Cal. Publ. in Amer. Arch. and Ethnol.* 9:348–383, 1911.

———.
The Yokuts and the Yuki Language. In: *Boas Anniversary Volume,* pp. 64–79. New York: G. E. Stechert & Co., 1906.

Radin, Paul
"A Grammar of the Wappo Language." *Univ. of Cal. Publ. in Amer. Arch. and Ethnol.* 27:1–94, 1929.

YUROK

FOLKLORE

GENERAL STUDIES

Anon.
"Yurok." In: *Bureau of American Ethnology, Bulletin* 30 (Part 2):1012–1014, 1910. (Washington, D. C.).

Kroeber, A. L.
"Yurok." In: *Handbook of the Indians of California.* Bureau of American Ethnology, Bulletin 78, pp. 1–97. Washington, D. C.: U. S. Gov't. Printing Office, 1925.

Spott, Robert, and Kroeber, A. L.
"Yurok Narratives." *University of California Publications in American Archaeology and Ethnology* 35, (No. 9) :143–156, 1942.
"This publication is of significant interest to anthropologists from every approach—the cultural, the psychological, the historical, the folkloristic." (A. H. Gayton)

Waterman, T. T.
All Is Trouble Along the Klamoth. In: *American Indian Life.* Elsie Clews Parsons, ed., (pp. 289–296). New York: Huebsch, 1925.

FOLKTALES

Cody, Bertha Parker
"Yurok Tales." *The Masterkey* 15, (No. 6): 228–231. Los Angeles: Southwest Museum, 1941.

Sapir, Jean
"Yurok Tales." *JAFL* 41:253–262, 1928.

BELIEFS—CUSTOMS

Cody, Bertha Parker
"Some Yurok Customs and Beliefs." *Masterkey* (Los Angeles) 14:157–162, 1942; 17:81–87, 1943.

Erikson, Erik Homburger
"Observations on the Yurok: Childhood and World Image." *University of California Publications in American Archaeology and Ethnology* 35 (No. 10) :257–302. Berkeley and Los Angeles: University of California Press, 1943.

Kroeber, A. L.
"Law of the Yurok Indians." *Proceedings of the 22nd Session of the International Congress of Americanists* 2:511–517, 1928.

————.
"Yurok and Neighboring Kin Term Systems." *University of California Publications in American Archaeology and Ethnology* 35, (No 2) :8, 1934.

Waterman, T. T., and Kroeber, A. L.
"Yurok Marriages." *University of California Publications in American Archaeology and Ethnology* 35, (No. 1) :14, 1934. Berkeley: The University Press.

FOLK ART—SPEECH

Heye, G. G.
"Objects Illustrating Yurok Ethnology." *Indian Notes, Museum of the American Indian, Heye Foundation* (New York) 1:91–93, 1924.

Kelly, I. T.
"The Carver's Art of the Indians of Northwestern California." *Univ. of Cal. Publ. in Amer. Arch. and Ethnol.* 24:343–360, 1936.

O'Neale, L. M.
"Yurok-Karok Basket Weavers." *Univ. of Cal. Publ. in Amer. Arch. and Ethnol.* 32:1–184, 1932.

Sapir, Edward
"The Algonkin Affinity of Yurok and Wiyot Kinship Terms." *Journal de la Société des Américanistes* 15:37–74, 1923. n. s.

————.
"Wiyot and Yurok," Algonkin Languages of California." *AA* 15:617–646, 1913. n.s.

MUSIC
GENERAL STUDIES

Schinhan, Jan Philip
Die Musik der Papago und Yurok. (Dissertation) University of Vienna, 1937.

DANCES

"California Ghost Dance." *JAFL* 17:32–35, 1904.

Cody, Bertha Parker
"Yurok Fish-Dam Dance." Told by Jane Van Strahlen. *The Masterkey* 16 (No. 3) : 3:81–86, (May) 1942.

ARRANGEMENTS

————: *Voice and Piano*

"The Song of the Lonely Trail."
Lemher, D. N.: Author: voice, piano and flute.

OTHER TRIBES
MISCELLANEOUS STUDIES
ACHOMAWI

(Including: Atsugewi)

Angulo, Jaime de
"The Background of the Religious Feeling in a Primitive Tribe." *AA* 28:352–360, 1926. n.s.

————.
"La Psychologie Religieuse des Achomawi." *Anthropos* 23:141–166, 561–589, 1928.

————.
"Two Achumawi Tales." *JAFL* 44:125–137, 1931.

————, and Freeland, L. S.
"The Achumawi Language." *International Journal of American Linguistics* (New York) 6:77–120, 1930.

Curtin, J., and Dixon, R. B.
"Achomawi Myths." *JAFL* 22:283–287, 1909.

Dixon, Roland B.
"Achomawi and Atsugewi Tales." *JAFL* 21: 159–177, 1908.

————.
"Linguistic Relationships Within the Shasta-Achomawi Stock." *Proceedings of the International Congress of Americanists* 15 (Part 2) 255–263, 1906.

————.
"Notes on the Achomawi and Atsugewi Indians of Northern California." AA 10:208–220, 1908. n.s.

————.
"Some Shamans of Northern California." *JAFL* 17:23–27, 1904.

————.
"The Shasta-Achomawi; a New Linguistic Stock, with Four New Dialects." *AA* 7:213–218, 1905. n.s.

————.
"The Mythology of the Shasta-Achomawi." *AA* 7:607–613, 1905. n.s.

Gifford, Edward Winslow
"Californian Kinship Terminologies." *Univ. of Cal. Publ. in Amer. Arch. and Ethnol.* 18:35–37, 1922.

Kroeber, A. L.
"The Achomawi Indians." In: *Handbook of the Indians of California.* Bureau of American Ethnology, Bulletin 78, (pp. 305–317). Washington, D. C.: U. S. Gov't. Printing Office, 1925.

Uldall, H. J.
"A Sketch of Achomawi Phonetics." *International Journal of American Linguistics* 8:73–77, 1933.

CAHUILLA

(Mission Indians)

Barrows, David Prescott
"Ethno-botany of the Coahuilla Indians of Southern California." *University of Chicago, Department of Anthropology,* Chicago, 1900.

————.
"Some Coahuia Songs." *Land of Sunshine* (Los Angeles) 4:38–41, 1895.

————.
"The Desert of Colorado." *Land of Sunshine* (Los Angeles) 13:312–322, 1900.
Reference to Coahuia, (Kawia) Indians. "The name, of uncertain derivation, of a Shoshonean division in southern California, affiliated linguistically with the Aguas Calientes, Juaneños, and Luiseños.

Caballeria y Collell, Juan
History of San Bernardino Valley. San Bernardino, 1902.

Davis, E. H.
"Early Cremation Ceremonies." *Indian Notes and Monographs, Museum of the American Indian, Heye Foundation* (New York) 7:93–110, 1921.

Drucker, P.
"Southern California." *Anthropological Records* (Berkeley) 1:1–52, 1937.

Faye, P. L.
"Christmas Fiestas of the Cupeno." *AA* 30:651–658, 1928. n.s.

Foote, K.
"Mission Indians." *Report on the Indians Taxed and Indians Not Taxed, United States Department of the Interior,* Census Office, Eleventh Census (Washington, D. C.).

Gifford, Edward W.
"Californian Kinship Terminologies." *Univ. of Cal. Publ. in Amer. Arch. and Ethnol.* 18:56–60, 1922.

————.
"Clans and Moieties in Southern California." *Univ. of Cal. Publ. in Amer. Arch. and Ethnol.* 14:186–201, 1918.

Hooper, Lucille
"The Cahuilla Indians." *Univ. of Cal. Publ. in Amer. Arch. and Ethnol.* 16, (No. 6) :315–380. Berkeley: University Press, 1920.
Discussion of religious life, social life, industries and knowledge, tales and beliefs. Bibliography.

Kroeber, A. L.
"The Ethnobiography of the Cahuilla Indians." *Univ. of Cal. Publ. in Amer. Arch and Ethnol.,* 8, (No. 2) :29–68, plates 1–15. Berkeley: The University Press, 1908–1910.

Patencio, Francisco
Stories and Legends of the Palm Springs Indians, as told to Margaret Boynton. Palm Springs, Cal.: Mrs. C. S. Snyder, Box 1289, 1943. xiv, 132 pp.
Known as the Sechi, a Kawia village in Cahuilla Valley, Southern California.

Riley, J. H.
"Vocabulary of the Kah-we'-yak and Kah-so'-wah Indians." *Historical Magazine* (Ser. 3) 3:238–240, 1868.

Rush, E. M.
"The Indians of the Coachella Valley Celebrate." *El Palacio* 32:1–19, 1932.

Strong, W. D.
"Aboriginal Society in Southern California." *Univ. of Cal. Publ. in Amer. Arch. and Ethnol.* 26:36–273, 1929.

Woolsey, D. J.
"Coahuilla Tales." *JAFL* 21:239–240, 1908.

CHILULA

Goddard, Pliny Earle
"Chilula Texts." *University of California Publications in American Archaeology and Ethnology,* 10, (No. 7):289–379, 1914. Berkeley: The University Press, 1911–1914.
Tales, myths, medicines, etc.

——————.
"Notes on the Chilula Indians of Northwestern California." *University of California Publications in American Archaeology and Ethnology* 10, (No. 6):265–288, 1914. pls. 38–41. Berkeley: The University Press, 1911–14.
Includes discussion of their culture.

Lowie, R. H.
"Selk'nam Kinship Terms." *AA* 35:546–548, 1933. n.s.

CHUMASH

(Mission Indians)

Bowers, S.
"Santa Rosa Island." *Annual Reports of the Board of Regents of the Smithsonian Institution* (Washington, D. C.) 1877, pp. 316–320.

Costanso, M.
"Early California History." *Land of Sunshine* 14:486–496; 15:38–49, 1901.

Eisen, G.
"An Account of the Indians of the Santa Barbara Islands." *Sitzungsberichte der Königlichen Böhmischen Gesellschaft der Wissenschaften, Mathematisch — Naturwissenschaftliche Classe,* (Prag), (Part 1):1–30, 1904.

Harrington, J. P.
"The Mission Indians." *Explorations and Field Work of the Smithsonian Institution* (Washington, D. C.), 1927, pp. 173–178; 1928, pp. 169–178.

Henshaw, H. W., and Kroeber, A. L.
"Chumashan Family." In: *Bureau of American Ethnology, Bulletin 30* (Part 1):296–297, 1907.

Kroeber, A. L.
"Basket Designs of the Mission Indians." *Anthropological Papers of the American Museum of Natural History* (New York) 20:149–183, 1922.

——————.
"The Chumash," In: *Handbook of the Indians of California.* Bureau of American Ethnology, Bulletin 78, pp. 550–568. Washington, D. C.: U. S. Gov't. Printing Office, 1925.

——————.
"The Chumash and Costanoan Language." *University of California Publications in American Archaeology and Ethnology* 9, (No. 2): 237–271, 1910. Berkeley: The University Press, 1910–1911.
The Chumash—"a linguistic family on the coast of Southern California, known also as Santa Barbara Indians."

Nelson, N. C.
Notes on the Santa Barbara Culture. In: *Essays in Anthropology Presented to A. L. Kroeber,* pp. 199–209. Berkeley: University of California Press, 1936.

Robinson, Eugene
"Plank Canoes of the Chumash." *Masterkey* 17:13–19, 1942. Los Angeles: Southwest Museum.

Rogers, David Banks
Prehistoric Man of the Santa Barbara Coast. Santa Barbara: Museum of Natural History, 1929.

Woodward, Arthur
"An Early Account of the Chumash." *The Masterkey* 8, (No. 4):118–123. Los Angeles: Southwest Museum, (Sept.) 1934.
Navaho textile.

GABRIELEÑOS

(Mission Indians)

Kroeber, A. L.
"Gabrielino." In: *Handbook of the Indians of California.* Bureau of American Ethnology, Bulletin 78, pp. 620–635. Washington, D. C.: U. S. Gov't. Printing Office, 1925.
See the author's numerous articles on the Mission Indians listed above.

Reid, H.
"An Account of the Indians of Los Angeles County." *Bulletin of the Essex Institute* (Salem) 17:1–33, 1885.

Roberts, Helen H.
Form in Primitive Music. New York: American Musicological Society, 1933. 180 pp.

Walker, Edwin F. A.
"A Ceremonial Site at Porter Ranch, San Fernando." *Masterkey* 10, No. 3:98–104. Los Angeles: Southwest Museum, 1936.
"The Indians in the neighborhood of San Fernando belong to the Shoshonean stock and have been included under the name Gabrieleños. . . ."

MONO

Chalfant, W. A.
"Medicine Men of the Eastern Mono." *Masterkey* 5:50–54, 1931.

Coville, Frederick Vernon
"The Panamint Indians of California." *AA* 5:351–363, 1892.
"It is uncertain whether their affinities are with the Ute-Chemehuevi or Mono-Paviotso group of Shoshoneans. . . ." (H. W. Henshaw)

Gayton, A. H., and Newman, Stanley S.
"Yokuts and Western Mono Myths." *Anthropological Records* 5, (No. 1):1–109. Berkeley: University of California Press, 1940.

Gifford, Edward Winslow
"Western Mono Myths." *JAFL* 36:301–367, 1924.

Noble, W. B.
"A Day with the Mono Indians." *Out West* 20:413–421, 1904.

PATWIN

Kroeber, A. L.
"The Patwin and Their Neighbors." *University of California Publications in American Archaeology and Ethnology* 29 (No. 4) 253–423. Berkeley: University of California Press, 1932.

> "A name adopted by Powers to designate a division of the Copehan family. They occupied the area extending from Stony Creek, Colusa County, to Suisun Bay, Solano County. Cal., and from Sacramento River to the boundary of the Kulanapan family on the west but excluding the so-called Coyote Valley Indians on the headwaters of Putah Creek in the southern part of Lake County, determined by Barrett to be Moquelumnan and not Copehan." *(Handbook of American Indians,* F. W. Hodge, ed. Vol. II, pp. 211)

McKern, W. C.
"Functional Families of the Patwin." *University of California Publications in American Archaeology and Ethnology* 13, (No. 7) :235–258, 1922. Berkeley: University of California Press, 1917–1923.

> These Indians belonged to the Central and Southeastern Wintun Provinces.

SALINA

Henshaw, H. W., and Kroeber, A. L.
"Salinan Family." In: *Bureau of American Ethnology, Bulletin* 30 (Part 2) :415, 1910.

Mason, J. Alden
"The Ethnology of the Salinan Indians." *University of California Publications in Archaeology and Ethnology* 10, (No. 4) :97–240, pls. 21–37, 1912. Berkeley: The University Press, 1911–1914.

> Includes discussion of mythology, religion and music (no tunes).

———.
"The Language of the Salinan Indians." *University of California Publications in American Archaeology and Ethnology* 14, (No. 1) : 1–154, 1918. Berkeley: University of California Press, 1918–1919.

> The Salinan language comprises the two surviving dialects of the Missions of San Antonio and San Miguel. General discussion of Phonology, Morphology, Texts and Vocabulary.

Sapir, Edward
"A Supplementary Note on Salinan and Washo." *International Journal of American Linguistics* 2:68–72, 1921.

SERRANO

Anon.
"Serranos." *Bull. Bureau Amer. Ethnol.* 30 (Part 2) :512–513, 1910.

Benedict, Ruth
"A Brief Sketch of Serrano Culture." *AA* 26:366–392, 1924. n. s.

———.
"Serrano Tales." *JAFL* 39:1–17, 1926. In San Bernardino Mountains, South California.

> The Serranos formed part of the Indians brought under San Gabriel and San Fernando Mission.

Gabriel, C.
"Stories of the Serrano." *Red Man* 4:82, 1911. Folklore concerning bear, eagle, horn toad.

———.
"The Fiestas of the Serrano Indians." *Red Man* (Carlisle, Pa.) 4:25–26, 1911.

Hoffman, Walter J.
"Hugo Ried's Account of the Indians of Los Angeles County, California." *Bulletin, Essex Institute* vol. XVII, (Salem, Mass.), 1885.

Kroeber, A. L.
"Indian Myths of South Central California." *Univ. of Cal. Publ. in Amer. Arch. and Ethnol.* 4:167–250, 1907.

Mott, Emma
Legends and Lore of the Long Ago (Ventura County, California). Los Angeles, Calif: Wetzel Publishing Co., 1929. 223 pp., illus.

TOLOWA

See: pp. 1107–09, for more correct location.

Drucker, Philip
The Tolowa and Their Southwest Oregon Kin. University of California Publications American Archaeology and Ethnology 36, (No. 4) 80 pp. Berkeley: University of California Press, 1937.

> "In culture they resemble the Hupa and Yurok, the chief difference being in their folklore and religion. They have been greatly influenced by the sea."

DuBois, Constance Goddard
"Tolowa Tales." *AA* 34:248–262, 1932. n.s.

TÜBATULABAL

(Including: Kawaiisu)

Gifford, Edward Winslow
"Tübatulabal and Kawaiisu Kinship Terms." *University of California Publications in American Archaeology and Ethnology* 12, (No.6) : 219–248, 1917. Berkeley: University of California Press, 1916–1917.

> Both belong to the Shoshonean Group of California.

———.
"Tübatulabal." In: *Handbook of the Indians of California.* Bureau of American Ethnology, Bulletin 78, pp. 605–610. Washington, D. C.: U. S. Gov't. Printing Office, 1925.

Kroeber, A. L.
"Kawaiisu." In: *Handbook of the Indians of California.* Bureau of American Ethnology, Bulletin 78, pp. 601–605. Washington, D. C.: U. S. Gov't. Printing Office, 1925.

Voegelin, Erminie W.
"Tübatulabal Ethnography." *Anthropological Records* (Berkeley) 2:1–84, 1938.

————.
"Tübatulabal Grammar." *Univ. of Cal. Publ. in Amer. Arch. and Ethnol.* 34:55–190, 1935.

————.
"Tübatulabal Texts." *Univ. of Cal. Publ. in Amer. Arch. and Ethnol.* 34:191–246, 1935.

Whorf, B. L.
"Notes on the Tübatulabal Language." *AA* 38:341–344, 1936. n.s.

Zigmond, M. L.
"Kawaiisu Territory." *AA* 40:634–638, 1938. n.s.

THE GREAT BASIN AREA

THE GREAT BASIN AREA

FOLKLORE
GENERAL STUDIES

Goddard, Pliny Earle
"The Cultural and Somatic Correlations of Uto-Aztecan." *AA* 22:244–247, 1920. n.s.
The tribes of the Basin Area (with the exception of the Washo) belong to the Shoshonean branch of the Uto-Aztekan linguistic stock.

Lowie, R. H.
"The Cultural Connection of Californian and Plateau Shoshonean Tribes." *Univ. of Cal. Publ. in Amer. Arch. and Ethnol.* 20:145–156, 1923.

Mack, E. M.
Nevada. Glendale: The Arthur H. Clark Company, 1936.

Park, Willard Z.
Culture Succession in the Great Basin. In: *Language, Culture and Personality*, Essays in Memory of Edward Sapir. (pp. 180–204). Menasha, Wis: Sapir Memorial Education Fund, 1946.

Simpson, J. H.
Report of Explorations across the Great Basin. Washington, D. C.: U. S. Gov't. Printing Office, 1876.

Stegner, Wallace
Mormon Country. New York: Duell, Sloane and Pearce, 1942. x, 362 pp. index.
Excellent chapter on folklore and myth.

Steward, Julian Haynes
Basin—Plateau Aboriginal Socio-Political Groups. Bureau of American Ethnology: Bulletin 120 Washington, D. C.: U. S. Government Printing Office, 1938. 330 pp.

————.
"Changes in Shoshonean Indian Culture." *Scientific Monthly* 49:524–537, 1939.

————.
"Linguistic Distribution and Political Groups of the Great Basin Shoshoneans." *AA* 39:625–634, 1937. n.s.

————.
Native culture of the Inter-montane (Great Basin) area. In: *Essays in Historical Anthropology of North America*; published in honor of John R. Swanton, in celebration of his 40th year with the Smithsonian Institute. (Smithsonian Miscellaneous Collection V.: 100). Washington, D. C.: U. S. Government Printing Office, 1940.

————.
"Some Observations on Shoshonean Distributions." *AA* 41:261–265, 1939. n. s.

Strong, W. D.
"An Analysis of Southwestern Society." *AA* 29:1–61, 1927. n.s.

Wyeth, N. J.
"Indian Tribes of the South Pass of the Rocky Mountains, the Salt Lake Basin, the Valley of the Great Säaptin, or Lewis' River, and the Pacific Coasts of Oregon." In: *Information Respecting the History, Condition and Prospects of the Indian Tribes of the United States*, Henry Rowe Schoolcraft, ed. Philadelphia 1851. Vol. I, pp. 204–228.

Zingg, R. M.
"A Reconstruction of Uto-Aztecan History." *University of Denver Contributions to Ethnography* 2:1–274, 1939.

————.
"The Ute Indians in Historical Relation to Proto-Azteco-Tanoan Culture." *Colorado Magazine* 15:134–152, 1938.

MYTHS

Cooke, Anne M.
An Analysis of Basin Mythology. (To be published as a Memoir of the American Folklore Society). Philadelphia: American Folklore Society.

BELIEFS—CUSTOMS

DuBois, Constance G.
"The 1870 Ghost Dance." *Anthropological Records* (Berkeley) 3:1–151, 1939.

Kroeber, A. L.
"Salt, Dogs, Tobacco." *Anthropological Records* 6:1–20, 1941.

————.
"Stepdaughter Marriage." *AA* 42: 562–570, 1940. n.s.

Lesser, Alexander
"Cultural Significance of the Ghost Dance." *AA* 35: 108–115, 1933. n.s.
"A ceremonial religious dance connected with the Messiah doctrine, which originated among the Paviotso in Nevada about 1888, and spread among other tribes until it numbered among its adherents nearly all the Indians of the interior basin, from Missouri River to or beyond the Rockies. The Prophet of the religion was a young Paiute Indian, Wovoka, also called by the whites, Jack Wilson." (John Mooney)

Mooney, John
"The Ghost-Dance Religion." *14th Annual Report, Bureau of American Ethnology.* pp. 641–1110. Washington, D. C.: U. S. Gov't. Printing Office, 1896.

Park, W. Z.
"Shamanism in Western North America." *Northwestern University Studies in the Social Sciences*, 2:1–166, 1938.

Scott, Capt. A. L.
The Messiah Dance in the Indian Territory. Essay for the Fort Sill Lyceum, March, 1892. (Manuscript.)

Shimkin, D. B.
"The Uto-Aztecan System of Kinship Terminology." *AA* 43:223–245, 1941. n.s.

SPEECH

Kroeber, A. L.
"Shoshonean Dialects of California." *Univ. of Cal. Publ. in Amer. Arch. and Ethnol.* 4:65–165, 1906.

Whorf, B. L.
"The Comparative Linguistics of Uto-Aztecan." *AA* 37:600–608, 1935. n.s.

MUSIC

GENERAL STUDIES

Herzog, George
"Plains Ghost Dance and Great Basin Music." *AA* 37:403–419, 1935. n.s.

RECORDS

Herzog, George
Great Basin Area: Records Contained in American Collections. American Council of Learned Societies, (Washington, D. C.) Bulletin 24:28, 1936.

U. S. Library of Congress. Division of Music. Folklore Section.
Indian Records—in the Archive of American Folksong.   AAFS–LC

BANNOCK

FOLKLORE

GENERAL STUDIES

Brimlow, George F.
The Bannock Indian War of 1878. Caldwell, Idaho: Caxton Printers Ltd., 1938. 231 pp.

Henshaw, G. F., and Thomas, C.
"Bannock." *Bureau of American Ethnology.* Bulletin 30, pp. 129–130. Washington, D. C.: U. S. Government Printing Office, 1907.

Hoffman, W. J.
"Die Shoshoni—und Banak-Indianer." *Globus* 69:57–60, 1896.

Jones, Daniel W.
Forty Years Among the Indians. Salt Lake City: Juvenile Instructor Office, 1890. iii, 400 pp.

Steward, Julian H.
"Basin Plateau Aboriginal Socio-political Groups." *Bureau of American Ethnology*, Bulletin 120, pp. 1–346. Washington, D. C.: U. S. Government Printing Office, 1938.

CUSTOMS—SPEECH

Hoffman, W. J.
"Remarks on Indian Tribal Names." *Proceedings of the American Philosophical Society* 23: 298–299, 1886.

Kroeber, A. L.
"The Bannock and Shoshoni Languages." *AA* 11:266–277, 1909. n.s.

Lowie, R. H.
"The Kinship Terminology of the Bannock Indians." *AA* 32:294–299, 1930. n.s.

GOSIUTE

FOLKLORE

GENERAL STUDIES

Anonymous
"Gosiute." *Bureau of American Enthnology, Bulletin 30*, pp. 496–497. Washington, D. C.: 1907.

Malouf, Carling
The Gosiute Indians. In: *Archaeology and Ethnology Papers* 3. Salt Lake City: University of Utah, 1940.
A Shoshonean tribe,—they affiliate themselves largely with the Paiute.

Reagan, Albert B.
"The Gosiute (Goshute) or Shoshoni-Goship Indians of the Deep Creek Region in Western Utah." *Proceedings of the Utah Academy of Sciences, Art and Letters* 11:43–54, 1934.

————.
"The Shoshoni-Goship Indians." *Transactions of the Kansas Academy of Science* 28:227–232, 1918.

Steward, Julian H.
Early Inhabitants of Western Utah. University of Utah, Bulletin 23, (No. 7):34 pp. Salt Lake City: 1933. Illus.

MYTHS

Malouf, Carling, and Smith, Elmer R.
"Some Gosiute Mythological Characters and Concepts." *Utah Humanities Review* 1 (No. 4):369–377, 1947.
"The mythology of the Gosiute Indians of Western Utah is important to an understanding of the basic 'survival values' held by these people in the midst of a very hostile environment. Their myths were, to the Gosiute, the vocalizations of things hoped for and things realized. The mythologies became for them at once stories for entertainment and teaching of 'facts' and moral values recognized in their culture." (the authors)

BELIEFS—CUSTOMS—SPEECH

Chamberlain, R. V.
"Animal Names and Anatomical Terms of the Goshiute Indians. *Proceedings of the Academy of Natural Science, pp.* 74–103, 1908.

———.
"Place and Personal Names of the Gosiute Indians of Utah." *Proceedings of the American Philosophical Society* 3 (No. 208):8–, Jan.–April, 1913.

———.
"The Ethno-Botany of the Gosiute Indians." *Memoirs of the American Anthropological Association* 2:329–405, 1911. (Lancaster, Penna.)

Hayes, Alden
"Peyote Cult on the Goshiute Reservation at Deep Creek." *New Mexico Anthropologist* 4 (No. 2):34–36, 1940.

Malouf, Carling
"Gosiute Peyotism." *AA* 44:93–103, 1942.

Reagan, Albert B.
"Some Notes on the History of the Uintah Basin, in Northeastern Utah, to 1850." *Proceedings of the Utah Academy of Sciences, Arts and Letters* 11:55–64, 1934.

PAIUTE
(Northern and Southern, Including Chemuhevi)

FOLKLORE

GENERAL STUDIES

Alter, J. C.
"Father Escalante and the Utah Indians." *Utah Historical Quarterly* (Salt Lake City) 1:75–86, 106–113; 2:18–25, 46–54, 1928–1929.

———.
"Some Useful Early Utah Indian References." *Utah Historical Quarterly* (Salt Lake City) 1:26–32, 52–56, 1928.

Angulo, J. de, and Freeland, L. S.
"Notes on the Northern Paiute of California." *Journal de la Société des Américanistes* (Paris) 21:313–335, 1929. n.s.

Blyth, B.
"Northern Paiute Bands in Oregon." *AA* 40:402–405, 1938. n.s.

Dellenbaugh, F. S.
A Canyon Voyage. New York: G. P. Putnam's Sons, 1908. xx, 277 pp., illus.

Driver, H. E.
"Southern Sierra Nevada." *Anthropological Records* (Berkeley) 1:53–154, 1937.

Drucker, P.
"Southern California." *Anthropological Records* 1:1–52, 1937.

Ellison, W. H.
Adventures of George Nidever. New Spain and the Anglo-American West, ed. by C. W. Hackett, and others. Los Angeles: 1932. Vol. 2, pp. 21–45.

Gifford, E. W.
"Tübatulabal and Kawaiisu Kinship Terms." *University of California Publication in American Archaeology and Ethnology* 12:219–248, 1917.
> Kawaiisu—"The most westerly subdivision of the Ute—Chemuhevi linguistic division of the Shoshonean family."

Henshaw, H. W., and Kroeber, A. L.
"Chemuhevi." *Bureau of American Ethnology, Bulletin* 30:242–243, 1907. (Washington, D. C.)

———, and Mooney, J.
"Paiute." *Bureau of American Ethnology, Bulletin 30:* 186–188, 1910. (Washington, D. C.)

Hopkins, Sara Winnemucca
Life Among the Paiutes. Edited by Mrs. Horace Mann. New York: G. P. Putnam's Sons, 1883.

Jones, D. W.
Forty Years Among the Indians. Salt Lake City: Juvenile Instructor Office, 1890. 400 pp.

Kelly, Isabel T.
"Band Organization of the Southern Paiute." *AA* 40:633–634, 1938. n.s.

———.
"Ethnography of the Surprise Valley Paiute." *Univ. of Cal. Publ. in Amer. Arch. and Ethnol.* 31:67–210, 1932.

———.
"Southern Paiute Bands." *AA* 36:548–560, 1934. n.s.

Kroeber, A. L.
"Origin Tradition of the Chemuhuevi Indians." *JAFL* 21:240–242, 1908.
> "A Shoshonean tribe, apparently an offshoot of the Paiute, formerly inhabiting the east bank of the Rio Colorado from Bill Williams Fork to the Needles and extending westward as far as Providence Mts., California."

———.
Handbook of the Indians of California. Bureau of American Ethnology, Bulletin 78, 995 pp., illus. Washington, D. C.: U. S. Gov't Printing Office, 1925.

Loew, Oscar
Notes on the Ethnology of Southern California and Adjacent Regions. U. S. War Department, Annual Report, Chief of Engineers for 1876. Washington, D. C.: 1876.

Loud, L. L.
"Notes on the Northern Paiute." *Univ. of Cal. Publ. in Amer. Arch. and Ethnol.* 25:152–164, 1929.

Lowie, R. H.
"Notes on Shoshonean Ethnography." *Anthropological Papers of the American Museum of Natural History* 20:185–314, 1924.

Marsden, W. L.
"The Northern Paiute Language of Oregon." *University of California, Publications in American Archaeology and Ethnology,* 20:175–191. Berkeley: University of California Press.

Murdock, George Peter
"Notes on the Tenino, Molala, and Paiute of Oregon." *AA* 40:395–402, 1938. n.s.

Palmer, William R.
"Pahute Indian Homelands." *Utah Historical Quarterly 6,* (No. 3):88–102, 1933.
Tribal Distributions in Central Utah with map.

—————.
"Utah Indians Past and Present." *Utah Historical Quarterly* 1:35–52, 1928.

Sapir, Edward
"Southern Paiute." *Proceedings of the American Academy of Arts and Sciences* 65:1–296, 1930.

—————.
"Southern Paiute and Nahuatl." *AA* 17:98–120, 306–328, 1915. n.s.

—————.
"Southern Paiute and Nahuatl." *Journal de la Société des Américanistes* (Paris) 10:379–425; 11:443–488, 1913–1919.

—————.
"Texts of the Kaibab Paiutes and Uintah Utes." *Proceedings of the American Academy of Arts and Sciences* (Boston) 65:297–535, 1930.

Steward, Julian H.
"Ethnography of the Owens Valley Paiute." *University of California Publication in American Archaeology and Ethnology* 33:233–350, 1933. Berkeley: The University Press, 1933.

—————.
"Panatübiji, An Owen Valley Paiute." *Anthropological Papers 6, Bulletin of American Ethnology, 119.* Washington, D. C.: U. S. Government Printing Office, 1938.

—————.
"Two Paiute Autobiographies." *University of California Publication in American Archaeology and Ethnology* 33, (No. 5):423–438, 1934. Berkeley: The University Press.

Stewart, Omer Call
"Northern Paiute Culture Element Distribution XIV." *Anthropological Records 4,* (No. 3): 361–446, 1941. Berkeley: University of California Press, 1941.

—————.
"The Northern Paiute Bands." *Anthropological Records* (Berkeley) 2:127–149, 1939.

MYTHS—FOLKTALES—LEGENDS

Barnes, L. M.
"Digger Indian Legends." *Land of Sunshine* (Los Angeles) 14:130–134, 310–314, 397–402, 1901.
"It was the only Paiute tribe practicing agriculture, hence the original significance of the name 'Digger'."

—————.
"Digger Indian Legends." *Land of Sunshine,* 16:130, 223, 310, 397, 1909.

Kelly, Isabel T.
"Northern Paiute Tales." *JAFL* 51:363–438, 1939.

Lowie, R. H.
"Shoshonean Tales." *JAFL* 37:92–200, 1924.

Palmer, William R.
Pahute Indian Legends. Salt Lake City: Deseret Book Company, 1946. 134 pp.
A collection of tales from the Southern Paiute. "These tales in general conform to the pattern of Basin mythology. They are concerned with the doings of animal named characters in a pre-human world, with Coyote and Wolf the favorite characters." (Anne M. Smith)

Rush, Emmy Matt
"Legends of the Paiutes of the Owens River Valley in California," *El Palacio* (Santa Fe) March, 1930. pp. 72–87. Illus.

Sapir, Edward
"Song Recitative in Paiute Mythology." *JAFL* 23:455–472, 1910.

—————.
"Two Paiute Myths." *Museum Journal of University of Pennsylvania* 1:15–18, 1910.

Steward, Julian Haynes
"Myths of the Owens Valley Paiute," *California University. Publications in American Archaeology and Ethnology,* v. 34, no. 5, illus., 439 pp. Berkeley, Calif.: University of California Press, 1936.

BELIEFS—CUSTOMS—FOLK MEDICINE

Fletcher, A. C.
"Indian Messiah." *JAFL* 4:57–60, 1891.

Hart, C. P.
"Piute Herbalists." *Proceedings of the American Association for the Advancement of Science* 35:330–331, 1886.

Hoffman, W. J.
"Pah-Ute Cremation." *Proceedings of the American Philosophical Society* (Philadelphia) 14:297–298, 1874.

Kelly, Isabel T.
Chemehuevi Shamanism. In: *Essays in Honor of Alfred L. Kroeber* (pp. 129–142). Berkeley: University of California Press, 1936.

—————.
"Southern Paiute Shamanism." *Anthropological Records* (Berkeley) 2:151–167, 1939.

Kroeber, A. L.
"California Kinship Systems." *University of California Publications in American Archaeology and Anthropology* 12:366–368. 1917. Berkeley: University of California Press.

Lyman, A. R.
"Pahute Biscuits." *Utah Historical Quarterly* (Salt Lake City) 3:118–120, 1930.

Mooney, John
"The Ghost-Dance Religion." *Annual Reports of the American Bureau of Ethnology* (Washington, D. C.) 14:764–791, 1048–1057, 1893.

Phister, Nat P.
"The Indian Messiah." *AA* 4:105–109, 1891.

Stewart, Omer C.
"Northern Paiute Polyandry." *AA* 39:368–369, 1937. n.s.

—————.
"Washo-Northern Paiute Peyotism; a study in acculturation." *University of California Publications in American Archaeology and Ethnology*, 40 (No. 3) :63–141. Berkeley: University of California Press, 1944.

Thompson, A. H.
"Oral Information Concerning the Religious Ferment Among the Paiute of Utah in 1815." *U. S. Geological Survey.*

FOLK ART—SPEECH

Duffield, M. S.
"Aboriginal Remains in Nevada and Utah." *AA* 6:148–197, 1904. n.s.

Kroeber, A. L.
"Notes on the Shoshonean Dialects of Southern California." *University of California Publications in American Archaeology and Ethnology* 8:256–262, 1909.

Marsden, W. L.
"The Northern Paiute Language of Oregon." *University of Calif. Publ. in Amer. Arch. and Ethnol.* 20:175–191, 1923.

Natches, Gilbert
"Northern Paiute Verbs," In: *Phoebe Apperson Hearst Memorial Volume.* California University Publications American Archaeology and Ethnology, vol. 20. 243–259 pp., Berkeley, 1923.

Palmer, W. R.
"Pahute Indian Government and Laws." *Utah Historical Quarterly* (Salt Lake City) 2:35–42, 1929.

—————.
"Pahute Indian Homelands." *Utah Historical Quarterly* (Salt Lake City) 6:88–102, 1933.

Sapir, Edward
"A Note on Reciprocal Terms of Relationship." *AA* 15:132–138, 1913. n.s.

—————.
"Southern Paiute Dictionary." *Proceedings of the American Academy of Arts and Sciences* 65:537–730, 1931.

Stewart, Omer C.
"Navaho Basketry as Made by Ute and Paiute." *AA* 40:758–759, 1938. n.s.

Waterman, T. T.
"The Phonetic Elements of the Northern Paiute Language." *University of California Publications in American Archaeology and Ethnology* 10 (No. 2) :13–44, pls. 1–5, 1911. Berkeley: The University of California Press, 1911–1914.

MUSIC

GENERAL STUDIES

Sapir, Edward
"Songs Recitative in Paiute Mythology." *JAFL* 23:455–472, 1910.

Steward, Julian H.
"Ethnography of the Owens Valley Paiute." *University of California Publications in American Archaeology and Ethnology*, 33:279–285. Berkeley: The University Press, 1933.
Discussion of music in song, dance and ritual.

ARRANGEMENTS

"Gambling Song."
In: *Melodic Views of Indian Life.* Miller, H. A.: Clayton F. Summy: Piano.

"Paiute Cradle Song."
Landau, V.: Hall and McCreary: SSATB.

PAVIOTSO

See: Paiute (Northern) pp. 1052–54; and Shoshoni, pp. 958–59, 1055–56.

FOLKLORE

GENERAL STUDIES

Berreman, J. V.
"Tribal Distribution in Oregon." *Memoirs of the American Anthropological Association* 47: 7–65, 1937.

Fry, W. S.
"Humboldt Indians." *Out West* (Los Angeles) 21:503–514, 1904.

Hoffman, W. J.
"Miscellaneous Ethnographic Observations." *Annual Reports of the United States Geological and Geographical Survey of the Territories* (Washington, D. C.) 10:461–478, 1876.

BELIEFS—CUSTOMS

Harrington, M. R.
"A Cat-tail Eater." *Masterkey* 7:147–149, 1933.

Park, W. Z.
"Paviotoso Polyandry." *AA* 39:366–368, 1937. n.s.

————.
"Paviotso Shamanism." *AA* 35:98–113, 1933. n.s.

————.
"The Organization and Habitat of Paviotso Bands." *AA* 40:622–626, 1938. n.s.

SHOSHONI

See: Shoshoni, pp. 958-59.

FOLKLORE

GENERAL STUDIES

Emmons, Della Gould
Sacajawea of the Shoshones. Portland: Binfords and Mort. Publishers, 1943. 316 pp.
The life story of the Lewis and Clark guide told in novel form.

Farnham, Thomas J.
Travels in the Great Western Prairies. New York: Killey and Lossing, 1843. 197 pp.

Harris, Jack Sargent
"Western Shoshoni." *AA* 40:407–410, 1938. n.s.

————.
White Knife Shoshoni. In: *Acculturation in Seven Indian Tribes.* Ralph Linton, editor, (pp. 39–118). New York: D. Appleton-Century Company, 1940.

Hebard, Grace Raymond
Sacajawea, A Guide and Interpreter of the Lewis and Clark Expedition; with an account of the travels of Toussaint Charbonneau, and of Jean Baptiste, the Expedition Papoose. Glendale, California: Arthur H. Clark and Co., 1933. 430 pp.

Henshaw, H. W.
"Shoshoni." *Bureau of American Ethnology, Bulletin 30,* (Part 2): 556–558, 1910.

Hoebel, E. A.
"Bands and Distributions of the Eastern Shoshoni." *AA* 40:410–413, 1938. n.s.

Hoffman, W. J.
"Die Shoshoni-und Banak-Indianer." *Globus* 69:57–60, 1896.

Leonard, Z. (M. M. Quaife, editor)
Narrative of the Adventures of Zenas Leonard. Chicago: Lakeside Press, 1934.

Lowie, Robert H.
"Notes on Shoshonean Ethnography." *Anthropological Papers of the American Museum of Natural History* (New York) 20:185–314, 1924.

————.
"The Northern Shoshoni." *Anthropological Papers of the American Museum of Natural History* 2:165–306, 1909. Illus.

Reagan, Albert B.
"Shoshoni-Goship Indians and the Deep Creek Region, Utah." *Improvement Era* 22 (No. 18): 1041–, Oct., 1919.

Schultz, James W.
Bird Woman: Sacajawea's Story. Illustrated by Hart M. Schultz. Boston: Houghton Mifflin Company, 1918. 234 pp.

Shinn, G. Hazen
Shoshonean Days. Glendale: The Arthur H. Clark Company, 1941. 183 pp.
"The book should be of interest to students who specialize in these Indians because of the first-hand observations of customs and characters of which little is known today." F. H. Douglas.

Steward, Julian H.
"Changes in Shoshone Culture." *Scientific Monthly,* 49:524–537, Dec. 1939.

————.
"Nevada Shoshone." *Anthropological Records* (Berkeley) 4:209–259, 1941.

Wellman, Paul I.
Death on Horseback. New York: J. B. Lippincott Co., 1947. 484 pp., 32 pages of photos, 4 maps.
"It is one of the very few popular books dealing with American Indian wars to present an understanding approach to the Indians' reasons for fighting to protect their land and their way of life from the encroachment of a foreign people and culture." (Elmer R. Smith)

Wilson, Elijah Nicholas
Among the Shoshones. Salt Lake City: Skelton Publishing Company, 1910. 222 pp.

Wyeth, N. J.
"Indian Tribes of the South Pass of the Rocky Mountains." In: *Information Respecting the History, Condition, and Prospects of the Indian Tribes of the United States,* ed. by H. R. Schoolcraft. (pp. 204–228). Philadelphia, 1851.

MYTHS—FOLKTALES—LEGENDS

Lowie, Robert H.
"Shoshonean Tales." *JAFL* 37:1–242, 1924.

Merriam, C. H.
"The Em'-tim'-bitch, a Shoshonean tribe." *AA* 32:496–499, 1930. n.s.

Olden, Sarah Emelia
Shoshone Folklore, as discovered from the Rev. John Roberts, a hidden hero, on the Wind River Indian Reservation in Wyoming. Milwaukee, Wis.: Morehouse Publishing Co., 1923. 197 pp., illus.

Richards, C. E.
"Indian Legends of Colorado." *American Library Association,* Bulletin 14:203–210, 1920.

CUSTOMS—GAMES—SPEECH

Dorsey, G. A.
"Shoshonean Game of Ha-wa-ta-pi." *JAFL* 14:24–25, 1901.

Hoebel, E. A.
"Comanche and Hekandika Shoshone Relationship Systems." *AA* 41:440–457, 1939. n.s.

Hoffman, W. J.
"Remarks on Indian Tribal Names." *Proceedings of the American Philosophical Society* (Philadelphia) 23:296–298, 1886.

Kroeber, A. L.
"The Bannock and Shoshoni Languages." *AA* 11:266–277, 1909. n.s.

————, Steward, Julian H.
"Lemhi Shoshoni Physical Therapy." *Anthropological Papers 5*, Bulletin of American Ethnology 119. Washington, D. C.: U. S. Government Printing Office, 1938.

————.
"Shoshoni Polyandry." *AA* 38:561-564, 1936. n. s.

DANCES

Hoebel, E. A.
"The Sun Dance of the Hekandika Shoshone." *AA* 37:570–581, 1935. n.s.

UTE

FOLKLORE

GENERAL STUDIES

Alter, J. C.
"Father Escalante and the Utah Indians." *Utah Historical Quarterly* 1:75–86, 106–113; 2:18–25, 46–54, 1928–1929.

Anonymous
"Ute." *Bureau of American Ethnology, Bulletin 30* (Part 2):874–876, 1910.

Beals, R. L.
Ethnology of Rocky Mountain Park: the Ute and Arapaho. Berkeley: University of California Press, 1935. 27 pp.

Boas, Franz
"Zur Anthropologie der nordamerikanischen Indianer." *Verhandlungen der Berliner Gesellschaft für Anthropologie, Ethnologie, und Urgeschichte* (Berlin), pp. 367–411, 1895.

Burton, Richard F.
The City of Saints, and Across the Rocky Mountains to California. London: Longman, Green Longman and Roberts. 1861. x, 707 pp., illus.

Cooke, A. M.
"The Northern Ute." *AA* 40:627–630, 1938. n.s.

Douglas, F. H.
"The Ute Indians." *Denver Art Museum, Indian Leaflet Series* (Denver) 10:1–4, 1930.

Gilbertson, A. N.
"Negro-Ute Métis." *AA* 15:363–364, 1913.

Haskell, Thomas N.
The Indian Question: Young Konkaput the King of Utes, a Legend of Twin Lakes and occasional Poems. Denver: 1889. 257 pp., illus.

Hrdlicka, Ales
"Southern Ute." *Bureau of American Ethnology, Bulletin* 30, pp. 619–620, 1910.

Humfreville, J. L.
Twenty Years Among our Savage Indians. Hartford: A. D. Worthington & Co., 1889. lxiv, 674 pp.

Hunter, Milton R.
Utah Indian Stories. Springville, Utah: Art City Publishing Co., 1946. illus.
Besides information on Indian and white relationship, customs and traditions, a number of tales are included.

Jones, D. W.
Forty Years Among the Indians. Salt Lake City: Juvenile Instructor Office, 1890. 400 pp.

Kelly, Charles
"In-Nip-E-Gaut, the Crazy Ute." *Utah Magazine* 9:26, Feb., 1947.

Mason, J. A.
"Myths of the Uintah Ute." *JAFL* 23:299–363, 1910.

Matthews, Washington
"The Origin of the Utes, A Navajo Myth." *American Antiquarian* 7 (No. 5):271–274, 1885.

Meeker, N. C.
"The Utes of Colorado." *American Antiquarian* (Chicago) 1:224–226, 1879.

Opler, Marvin K.
"Origins of Comanche and Ute." *AA* 45:155–158, Jan., 1943.

————.
Southern Ute. In: *Acculturation in Seven Indian Tribes.* Ralph Linton, editor, (pp. 119–206). New York: D. Appleton-Century Company, 1940.

————.
"The Southern Ute." *AA* 40:632–633, 1938. n.s.

Palmer, W. R.
"Utah Indians Past and Present." *Utah Historical Quarterly* 1:35–52, 1928.

Reagan, A. B.
The Sun God Mocassin Tales. Provo: M. H. Graham Printing Co., 1935. 35 pp.

Sapir, Edward
"Texts of Kaibab Paiutes and Uintah Utes."
*Proceedings of the American Academy of Arts
and Sciences* 65:297–535, 1930.

Stewart, Omer C.
"Culture Element Distributions: XVIII, Ute-
Southern Paiute." *Anthropological Records*
4:3; 6:4. Berkeley: University of California
Press, 1941, 1942.

Zingg, Robert M.
"The Ute Indian in Historical Relation to
Proto-Azteco-Tanoan Culture." *Colorado Maga-
zine*, 1–19, July 1938.

MYTHS—FOLKTALES—LEGENDS

Gibbs, J. F.
"Moshoquop the Avenger as Loyal Friend."
Utah Historical Quarterly 2 (No. 1) : 3–8, 1929.

Haskell, Thomas N.
The Indian Question: Young Konkaput the
King of the Utes, a Legend of Twin Lakes
and occasional Poems. Denver: Collier and
Cleaveland, 1889, xiv, 257 pp., illus.

Kroeber, A. L.
"Ute Tales." *JAFL* 14:252–285, 1901.

Schmerler, Henriette
"Trickster Marries His Daughter." *JAFL*
44:196–208, 1931.

Smith, Louise H.
The Indian Story of the Creation and Flood;
being the first of the Myths Legends of Colorado done into Tales. Illustrations by Robert
Paley. Denver: 1906. 23 pp., illus.

Turenne, L. de
"Une légende indienne." *Journal de la Société
des Américanistes* (Paris) 1:61–71, 1896.

"Ute Legend of Creation."
El Palacio 14, (no. 7) :104–105, 1924.

BELIEFS—CUSTOMS

Reagan, A. B.
"Mortuary Customs of the Ouray Utes." *El
Palacio* 31:411–413, 1931.

FOLK ART—SPEECH

Boyd, H. H.
"Saguache Antelope Traps." *Southwestern Lore*
6:28–34, 1940.

Barber, E. A.
"Language and Utensils of the Modern Utes."
*Bulletin of the United States Geological and
Geographical Survey of the Territories* (Wash-
ington, D. C.) 2:71–76, 1876.

Chamberlain, Alexander F.
"Some Plant Names of the Ute Indians." *AA*
11:27–41, 1909. n.s.

Fewkes, J. Walter
*Prehistoric Villages, Castles, and Towers of
Southwestern Colorado.* Bureau of American
Ethnology, Bulletin 70, 79 pp., 33 pls., 18 figs.
Washington, D. C.: 1919.

Harrington, J. P.
"The Phonetic System of the Ute Language."
University of Colorado Studies, No. 8, pp. 199–
222, 1910.

Hurst, C. T.
"A Ute Shelter." *Southwestern Lore* 5:57–64,
1939.

Jackson, Wm. H.
Ancient Ruins in Southwestern Colorado. In:
*8th Annual Report: U. S. Geological and
Geographical Survey. (Hayden Survey) 1874.*
pp. 369–381. Washington, D. C.: 1876.

Kroeber, A. L.
"Notes on the Ute Language." *AA* 10:74–88,
1908. n.s.

Opler, M. K.
"Southern Ute Pottery Types." *Masterkey*
13:161–163, 1939.

Reagan, Albert B.
"Some Names of the Ute Indians of Utah,
followed by a Selected List of Words Used
by the Indians of the State." *Utah Academy
of Sciences, Arts and Letters* 12:1–39, 1935.

"Ute Dwellings." *El Palacio* 31:410–411, 1931.

Sapir, Edward
"A Note on Reciprocal Terms of Relationship."
AA 15:132–138, 1913. n.s.

"Some Fundamental Characteristics of the
Ute Language." *Science* 31:350–352, 1910. n.s.

Steward, Julian H.
Ancient Caves of the Great Salt Lake Region.
Bureau of American Ethnology, Bulletin 116.
Washington. D. C.: 1937.

Stewart, Omer C.
"Navaho Basketry as Made by Ute and Paiute."
AA 40:758–759, 1938. n. s.

FOLK MEDICINE

Hrdlicka, Ales
*Physiological and Medical Observations among
the Indians of Southwestern United States
and Northern Mexico.* Bureau of American
Ethnology, Bulletin 34. 425 pp. 1908.

Opler, M. K.
"The Character and History of the Southern
Ute Peyote Rite." *AA* 42:463–478, 1940. n.s.

"Fact and Fancy in Ute Peyotism." *AA* 44:
151–159, 1942. n.s.

Stewart, Omer C.
"The Southern Ute Peyote Cult." *AA* 43:303–
308, 1941. n.s.

GAMES

Barber, E. A.
"Gaming Among the Utah Indians." *American Naturalist* (Salem) 11:351–353, 1877.

Reagan, Albert B.
"Some Games Played by the Northern Utes." *Northwest Science* 8:12–16, March 1934. Bibl.

MUSIC

GENERAL STUDIES

Densmore, Frances
Northern Ute Music. Bureau of American Ethnology, Bulletin 75. Washington, D. C.: U. S. Government Printing Office, 1922. 213 pp., illus., music.
> Includes discussion of habitat, language, food and industries, as well as the songs, dances, and games.

———.
"Preservation of Indian Music." *Smithsonian Miscellaneous Collections* (Washington, D. C.) 65:81–85, 1915.

———.
"Study of Indian Music." *Smithsonian Miscellaneous Collections* (Washington, D. C.) 66:108–111, 1917.

Miller, Dayton Clarence
Analytical Study of Photographs taken with Phonodeik. In:*Northern Ute Music*, by Frances Densmore. Washington, D. C.: U. S. Government Printing Office: 1922.

DANCES

Lowie, R. H.
"Ute Dances." *Anthropological Papers American Museum of Natural History* (New York) 11:823–835, 1915.

———.
"Sun Dance of the Ute." *Anthropological Papers of the American Museum of Natural History* (New York 3) 16:387–431, 1919. Illus.

———.
"The Sun Dance of the Wind River Shoshoni and Ute." *Anthropological Papers of the American Museum of Natural History* (New York) 16:405–410, 1919.

Opler, Marvin K.
"A Colorado Ute Indian Bear Dance." *Southwestern Lore* 7(No.2):21–30, 1941.

———.
"Integration of the Sun Dance in Ute Religion." *AA* 43:550–572, 1941.

———.
"The Southern Ute Dog-Dance and Its Reported Transmission to Taos." *New Mexico Anthropologist* (Albuquerque) 3:66–72, 1939.

Reagan, A. B.
"The Bear Dance of the Ouray Utes." *Wisconsin Archaeologist* (Milwaukee) 9:148–150, 1929. n.s.

Reed, Verner Z.
"The Ute Bear Dance." *AA* 9:237–263, 1896. o.s.

Steward, Julian H.
"A Uintah Ute Bear Dance." *AA* 34:263–273, 1932, n.s.

WASHO

FOLKLORE

GENERAL STUDIES

Barrett, Samuel A.
The Washo Indians. Bulletin of the Public Museum of the City of Milwaukee. Vol. 2., No. 1. Milwaukee, Wis.: Published by Order of the Board of Trustees, 1917. 52 pp., illus.
> "A small tribe, forming a distinct linguistic family, the Washoan, which when first known to Americans, occupied Truckee River, Nevada, as far down as the Meadows."

Dangberg, G.
"Washo Texts." *Univ of Cal. Publ. in Amer. Arch. and Ethnol.* 22:391–443, 1927.

Kroeber, A. L.
Handbook of the Indians of California. Bureau of American Ethnology. Bulletin 78, pp. 362–365. Washington, D. C.: U. S. Gov't. Printing Office, 1907.

Lowie, Robert H.
"Ethnographic Notes on the Washo." *Univ. of Cal. Publ. in Amer. Arch. and Ethnol.* 36:301–352, 1939. (Berkeley: Univ. of Cal. Press).

Sapir, Edward
"A Supplementary Note on Salinan and Washo." *International Journal of American Linguistics* (New York) 2:68–72, 1921.

Siskin, E. E.
"Washo Territory." *AA* 40:626–627, 1938. n.s.

BELIEFS—CUSTOMS

Kroeber, A. L.
"California Kinship Systems." *Univ. of Cal. Publ. in Amer. Arch. and Ethnol.* 12:362–365, 1917.

Stewart, Omer C.
"Washo-Northern Paiute Peyotism; A Study in Acculturation." *Univ. of Cal. Publ. in Amer. Arch. and Ethnol.* 40 (No. 3) :vi, 63–142, illus. Berkeley and Los Angeles: University of California Press, 1944.

FOLK ART—SPEECH

Cohn, C. A.
"Arts and Crafts of the Nevada Indians." *Nevada Historical Society Biennial Reports* 1: 75–79, 1909.

Kroeber, A. L.
"The Washo Language of East Central California." *Univ. of Cal. Publ. in Amer. Arch. and Ethnol.* 4 (No. 5) :251–318. Berkeley: The University Press, 1905.

Schellbach, L.
"A Bone Implement of the Washo." *Indian Notes, Museum of the American Indian, Heye Foundation* (New York) 4:400–403, 1927.

THE PLATEAU AREA

THE PLATEAU AREA

FOLKLORE

GENERAL STUDIES

Alvord, B.
Concerning the Manners and Customs, Superstitions...of the Indians of Oregon. In: *Information Respecting the History, Condition and Prospects of the Indian Tribes of the United States.* Henry Rowe Schoolcraft, ed., Vol. V, pp. 651–657, Philadelphia: 1855.

Bancroft, Hubert Howe
The Native Races of the Pacific States of North America. San Francisco: A. L. Bancroft and Co., 1874–1882. 5 vols., illus., bibl.
Vol. 3—Myths and languages.

Barbeau, Charles Marius
Indian Days in the Canadian Rockies. Illustrated by W. Langdon Kuhn. Toronto: The Macmillan Company, Ltd., 1923. 207 pp., illus., bibl.

Barry, J. N.
"The Indians of Oregon." *Oregon Historical Society Quarterly* 28:49–61, 1927.

Berreman, Joel V.
"Tribal Distribution in Oregon." *Memoirs of the Amer. Anthrop. Association* 47:1–67, 1937.

Boas, Franz
"The Salish Tribes of the Interior of British Columbia." *Annual Archaeological Report...of the Minister of Education* (Ontario, Toronto), pp. 219–225, 1905.

———.
"Zur Anthropologie der nordamerikanischen Indianer." *Verhandlungen der Berliner Gesellschaft für Anthropologie, Ethnologie und Urgeschichte* (Berlin), pp. 367–411, 1895.

Charnay, M.
"Sur la disparition des Cliff-dwellers." *Proceedings of the 10th Session of the International Congress of Americanists,* pp. 52–57, 1894.
On the disappearance of the Cliff-Dwellers.

Chittenden, H. M., and Richardson, A. T., eds.
Life, Letters and Travels of Father Pierre-Jean de Smet. New York: F. P. Harper, 1905. 4 vols.

Churchill, Claire Warner
Slave Wives of Nehalem. Portland: Metropolitan Press, 1933. 104 pp.
"A Salish tribe formerly living on or near Nehalem R. in N.W. Oregon, but now on Grande Ronde Res."

Coues, E., ed.
Manuscript Journals of Alexander Henry and David Thompson. New York: 1897. 3 vols.

Cox, Ross
Adventures on the Columbia River. London: H. Colburn and R. Bentley, 1831. 2 vols.

Eels, M.
"Aboriginal Geographic Names in the State of Washington." *AA* 5:27–35, 1892.

Franchère, G.
"Narrative of a Voyage to the Northwest Coast of America." In: *Early Western Travels.* R. G. Thwaites, ed. Vol. 6, pp. 167–410, Cleveland, 1904.

Fraser, S.
"Journal of a Voyage from the Rocky Mountains to the Pacific Coast." In: *Les Bourgeois de la Compagnie du Nord-Ouest,* L. F. R. Masson, ed. Vol. 1, pp. 156–221, Quebec, 1889.

Gass, P.
A Journal of the Voyage and Travels of a Corps of Discovery. Pittsburgh: David M'Keehan, 1808. iv, 381 pp.

Hafen, LeRoy R., and Rister, Carl C.
Western America; the exploration, settlement and development of the region beyond the Mississippi. (Prentice Hall Books on History.) New York: Prentice Hall, 1941.

Hale, H.
Ethnology and Philology. In: *Narrative of the United States Exploring Expedition* by C. Wilkes. Vol. 6. Philadelphia: C. Sherman, 1846. 5 vols., illus.

———.
"Indians of North-West America." *Transactions of the American Ethnological Society,* Vol. 2, pp. 1–24, 1848.

Hill-Tout, Charles
British North America: The Far West, The Home of the Salish and the Déné. London: A. Constable and Co., 1907. xiv, 263 pp.

Kane, P.
Wanderings of an Artist Among the Indians of North America, from Canada to Vancouver's Island, and Oregon and Hudson's Bay Territory and Back Again. London: Longman, Brown, Green, Longmans and Roberts, 1859. xvii, 455 pp., illus.

Lewis, Albert Buell
"Tribes of the Columbia Valley and the Coast of Washington and Oregon." *Memoirs of the American Anthropological Association,* Vol. I, pp. 147–209, 1906.

Lewis, Meriwether, and Clarke, Capt.
Travels to the Source of the Missouri River, etc., and across the American Continent to the Pacific Ocean. London: Longman, Hurst, Rees, Orme and Browne, 1814. xxiv, 663 pp., fold. front., maps.

Mackenzie, Alexander
Voyages from Montreal on the St. Lawrence River, Through the Continent of North America to the Frozen and Pacific Oceans, 1789 and 1793. London: 1801.

Mayne, R. C.
Four Years in British Columbia and Vancouver Island. London: J. Murray, 1862. xi, 468 pp.

Murdock, George Peter
"Notes on the Tenino, Molala, and Paiute of Oregon." *AA* 40:395–402, 1938. n.s.

Parker, Samuel
Journal of an Exploring Tour Beyond the Rocky Mountains . . . Containing description . . . of the manners and customs of the natives . . . Ithaca: The Author, 1938. xii, 371 pp.

Peet, Stephen D.
"The Great Plateau and its Inhabitants." *American Antiquarian* 22:1–16, 1900.

Prudden, T. Mitchell
On the Great American Plateau. Wanderings among Canyons and Buttes, in the land of the Cliff-Dwellers, and the Indians of today. New York: G. P. Putnam's Sons, 1906. 243 pp., illus.

Ray, Verne Frederick
"Culture Elements Distributions: XXII Plateau." *Anthropological Records* (Berkeley) 8: 99–257, 1942.

————.
"Cultural Relations in the Plateau of Northwestern America." *Publications of the Frederick Webb Hodge Anniversary Publication Fund Southwest Museum* (Los Angeles), Vol. 3, pp. 1–154, 1939.

————.
"Native Villages and Groupings of the Columbia Basin." *Pacific Northwest Quarterly* 27 (No. 2):99–152, 1936.

————.
"Tribal Distribution in Northeastern Oregon." *AA* 40:384–395, 1938. n.s.

Ross, A.
The Fur Hunters of the Far West. M. M. Quaife, ed. Chicago: R. R. Donnelly & Sons Co., 1924. xxxix, 371 pp.

Scouler, J.
"Observations on the Indigenous Tribes of the N. W. Coast of America." *Journal of the Royal Geographical Society* (London) 11:215–250, 1841.

Smet, Pierre Jean de
New Indian Sketches. New York: D. & J. Sadlier & Co., 1863. 175 pp., bibl.
Contains a vocabulary of the Kootenay tribe, and the use of the catechism among the Flatheads, Kalispels, Pends-d' Oreilles, and other Rocky Mountain Indians.

————.
Western Missions and Missionaries. New York: J. B. Kirker, 1863. 532 pp.

Steward, Julian H.
Basin - Plateau Aboriginal Socio - Political Groups. Bureau of American Ethnology, Bulletin 120, 330 pp. Washington, D. C.: U. S. Government Printing Office, 1938.

Swanton, John R.
"Salish." In: *Encyclopedia of Religion and Ethics.* J. Hastings, ed. (New York). Vol. 11, pp. 97–100, 1921.

Teit, James A.
"Indian Tribes of the Interior." In: *Canada and Its Provinces,* No. 21, pp. 283–312, (Toronto), 1914.

————.
"The Middle Columbia Salish." *University of Washington Publications in Anthropology* (Seattle) 2:98–108, 1928.

————, (ed. Franz Boas)
The Salishan Tribes of the Western Plateaus. *45th Annual Report: Bureau of American Ethnology,* 1927–1928, pp. 23–396, pls. 1–4, figs. 1–39. Washington, D. C.: U. S. Gov't Printing Office, 1930.

Thwaites, Reuben G., ed.
Original Journals of the Lewis and Clark Expedition. Cleveland: The A. H. Clark Co., 1904–1905. 7 vols.

Townsend, J. K.
Narrative of a Journey Across the Rocky Mountains to the Columbia River. In: *Early Western Travels,* R. G. Thwaites, ed. Vol. 21, pp. 111–369, Cleveland: 1905.

Tyrrell, J. B., ed.
"David Thompson's Narrative of His Explorations in Western America." *Publications of the Champlain Society* (Ontario) 12:1–582, 1916.

Wellman, Paul I.
Death on Horseback. New York: J. B. Lippincott Co., 1947. 484 pp., 32 pages of photos, and 4 maps.
"It is one of the very few popular books dealing with American Indian wars to present an understanding approach to the Indians' reasons for fighting to protect their land and their way of life from the encroachment of a foreign people and culture." (Elmer R. Smith)

Whitman, Mrs. M.
"Letters Written by Mrs. Whitman from Oregon to Her Relations in New York." *Transactions of the Oregon Pioneer Association* 19: 79–179; 21:53–219, 1891–1893.

Young, F. G., ed.
The Correspondence and Journal of Captain Nathaniel J. Wyeth. In: *Sources of the History of Oregon.* Vol. I, pp. 1–256, Eugene: University of Oregon Press, 1899.

MYTHS—FOLKTALES—LEGENDS

Farrand, Livingston
"Sahaptin Tales." In: *Memoirs of the American Folklore Society.* No. 11, pp. 135–179, 1917. Lancaster, Pa.

Lyman, William Denison
"Indian Myths of the Northwest." *Proceedings of the American Antiquarian Society* (Worcester) 25:375–395, 1915. n.s.

―――.
"Myths and Superstitions of the Oregon Indians." *Proceedings of the American Antiquarian Society* 16:221–251, 1904. n.s.

Teit, James A., Gould, Marian K., Farrand, Livingston, and Spinden, Herbert J., colls
Folk-Tales of Salishan and Sahaptin Tribes. Edited by Franz Boas. Memoirs of the American Folklore Society, vol. 11. Lancaster, Pa.: The American Folklore Society, 1917. xi, 201 pp.
> *Salishan Tribes:* 1. Thompson Tales, by James A. Teit (pp. 1-64), 2. Okanagon Tales, by James A. Teit (pp. 65-98), also by Marian Gould (pp. 98-101), 3. Sanpoil Tales, by Marian K. Gould (pp. 101-114), 4. Pend d'Oreille Tales, by James A. Teit (pp. 114-119), 5. Coeur d'Alène Tales, by James A. Teit (pp. 119-128), 6. Tales from the Lower Fraser River, by James A Teit (pp. 129-135) (Uta'mqt).
> *Sahaptin Tribes:* 1. Sahaptin Tales, by Livingston Farrand (pp. 135-180), 2. Nez Percé Tales, by Herbert J. Spinden (pp. 180-201).

BELIEFS—CUSTOMS

DuBois, Cora
"The Feather Cult of the Middle Columbia." *General Series in Anthropology* (Menasha) 7: 1–45, 1938.

Gunther, E.
"An Analysis of the First Salmon Ceremony." *AA* 28:605–617, 1926. n.s.

―――.
"A Further Analysis of the First Salmon Ceremony." *University of Washington Publications in Anthropology* (Seattle) 2:129–173, 1928.

Huggins, E. L.
"Smohalla, the Prophet of the Priest Rapids." *Overland Monthly* (ser. 2) 17:208–215, 1891.

Kroeber, A. L.
"Salt, Dogs, Tobacco." *Anthropological Records* 6:1–20, 1941.

Leighton, Caroline C.
Life at Puget Sound. Boston: Lee & Shepard, 1884. ix, 258 pp.

MacMurray, J. W.
"The 'Dreamers' of the Columbia River Valley." *Transactions of the Albany Institute* 11: 241–248, 1887.

Mooney, James
"The Ghost-Dance Religion." *14th Annual Report of the American Bureau of Ethnology* (Part 2) 641–1110, 1896. Washington, D. C.: U. S. Gov't Printing Office, 1896.

Olson, R. L.
"Adze, Canoe, and House Types of the Northwest Coast." *University of Washington Publications in Anthropology* (Seattle) 2:1–38, 1927.

Park, W. Z.
"Shamanism in Western North America." *Northwestern University Studies in the Social Sciences* 2:1–166, 1938.

Ray, Verne Frederick
Historic Backgrounds of the Conjuring Complex in the Plateau and the Plains. In: *Language, Culture and Personality, Essays in Memory of Edward Sapir* (pp. 204–216). Menasha, Wisconsin: Sapir Memorial Publication Fund, 1941.

―――.
"The Kolaskin Cult." *AA* 38:67–75, 1936. n.s.

FOLK ART—SPEECH

Boas, Franz
"Comparative Vocabulary of Eighteen Languages Spoken in British Columbia." *Report of the 40th Meeting of the British Association for the Advancement of Science* 40:692–715, 1890.

―――.
"Die Verbreitung der Indianer-Sprachen in British-Columbia." *Petermanns Mitteilungen aus Justus Perthes Geographischer Anstalt* (Gotha) 42:21, 1896.

―――, and Haeberlin, H. K.
"Sound Shifts in Salishan Dialects." *International Journal of American Linguistics* 4:117–136, 1927.

Haeberlin, H. K.
"Types of Reduplication in the Salish Dialects." *International Journal of Linguistics* 1: 154–174, 1918.

―――, Teit, J. K., and Roberts, H. H.
"Coiled Basketry in British Columbia and Surrounding Regions." *41st Annual Report of the Bureau of American Ethnology*, pp. 119–484, 1928.

Hill-Tout, Charles
"Some Features of the Language and Culture of the Salish." *AA* 7:674–687, 1905. n.s.

Jacobs, M.
"Historic Perspectives in Indian Languages of Oregon and Washington." *Pacific Northwest Quarterly*, pp. 55–74, 1937.

Jenness, D.
"Indians of Canada." Bulletins of the Canada Department of Mines, National Museum of Canada (Ottawa). Vol. 65, pp. 351–358, 1932.

Kissell, M. L.
"Organized Salish Blanket Pattern." *AA* 31: 85–88, 1929, n.s.

Meany, E. S.
Origin of Washington Geographic Names. Seattle, Wash.: University of Washington Press, 1923. 357 pp.

Ray, Vern Frederick
"Pottery in the Middle Columbia." *AA* 34: 127–133, 1932. n.s.

Rogers, M. J.
"The Stone Art of the San Dieguito Plateau."
AA 31:454–467, 1929. n.s.

Smith, D. A., and Spier, Leslie
"The Dot and Circle Design in Northwestern
America." *Journal de la Société des Améri-
canistes* 19:47–55, 1927. n.s.

Smith, Harlan I., and Fowke, Gerard
"Cairns of British Columbia and Washington."
Memoirs: Jesup North Pacific Expedition:
Vol. 2:1901, pp. 55–75, figs. 1–9, pls. 1–5, 1
map. *Publications in Anthropology.* New York:
The American Museum of Natural History.

Spier, Leslie
"An Analysis of Plains Indian Parfleche
Decoration." *University of Washington Publications in Anthropology* (Seattle) 1:89–112,
1925.

Wardle, H. N.
"Certain Rare West-Coast Baskets." *AA* 14:
287–313, 1912. n.s.

MUSIC
DANCES

Mooney, James
"The Ghost-Dance Religion." *14th Annual Re-
port of the American Bureau of Ethnology*
(Part 2):641–1110, 1896. Washington, D. C.:
U. S. Gov't Printing Office, 1896.

Ray, Vern F.
"Bluejay Character in the Plateau Spirit
Dance." *AA* 39:593–601, 1937. Bibl.

Spier, Leslie
"The Prophet Dance of the Northwest and Its
Derivatives." *General Series in Anthropology*
(Menasha) 1:1–74, 1935.

Turney-High, H. H.
"The Blue-Jay Dance." *AA* 35:103–107, 1933.
n.s.

RECORDS

Herzog, George
*Plateau Areas: Records Contained in Amer-
ican Collections.* American Council of Learned
Societies (Washington, D. C.) Bulletin 24 :26
1936.

**U. S. Library of Congress, Division of Music.
Folklore Section.**
Indian Recordings. Various Regions and Tribes
are represented in the great collection of
American Indian music deposited in the Archive of American Folksong. The collection
was recently immeasurably increased by the
Frances Densmore recordings of some 5000
discs of Indian music.   AAFS–LC

COEUR D'ALENE
FOLKLORE
GENERAL STUDIES

Manring, Benjamin F.
*The Conquest of the Coeur d'Alenes, Spokanes
and Palouses.* Spokane: Inland Printing Co.,
1912, 280 pp.

McGeorge, Alice Sutton
Kamaiwea: The Coeur d'Alène. Kansas City,
Mo.: Burton Publishing Company, 1939.
A tale of the Idaho gold rush, with some insights
into the life and lore of the Indian tribe.

Reichard, Gladys A.
"Coeur d'Alene." In: *Handbook of American
Indian Languages,* Franz Boas, ed. Vol. 3, pp.
517–707. New York: J. J. Augustin, 1938.

Teit, James A.
"The Salishan Tribes of the Western Plateaus;
The Coeur d'Alène." *45th Ethnological Report. pp. 37–97. 1928.* Illus. Washington,
D. C.: U. S. Government Printing Office.
Covers habitat, boundaries and migration; manufacturers, houses and households, clothing and
ornaments, subsistence, travel, transportation and
trade; warfare, games and pastimes, sign-lan-
guage; festivals, childhood, marriage and death,
religion and ceremonials, etc.

MYTHS—FOLKTALES—LEGENDS

Phillips, E. M.
"Columbia River Tales." *The Idaho Farmer.*
August 7, 14; September 18, 1930.

Reichard, Gladys A.
An Analysis of Coeur D'Alene Indian Myths.
With a comparison by Adele Froelich. MAFS
41. Philadelphia: American Folklore Society,
1947. 216 pp.
The author discusses the style of and the cultural
reflections in Coeur d'Alene mythology; the diffusion and mythological process, and presents 48
myths and tales. The latter are divided into
four categories: chief child of the root (transformer); coyote cycle; myths not in the coyote
cycle; and tales with historical elements.

————.
"The Style of Coeur d'Alène Mythology." *Proceedings of the 24th Session of the International Congress of Americanists,* 243–253, 1930.

Teit, J. A.
"Coeur d'Alene Tales." In: *Memoir of the
American Folklore Society,* 11:119–128, 1917.
(Lancaster, Pa.)

SPEECH

Reichard, Gladys A.
"Imagery in an Indian Vocabulary." *AS* 18:
96–102, 1943.

————.
"Stem-List of the Coeur d'Alene Language."
International Journal of American Linguistics
10:92–108, 1939.

FLATHEAD
(Salish)

FOLKLORE

GENERAL STUDIES

Cox, Ross
Adventures on the Columbia River. New York: H. Colburn and R. Bentley, 1832. 2 vols.

Curtis, E. S.
Indian Days of Long Ago. Illustrated with photographs by author, and drawings by F. N. Wilson. Yonkers: World Book Company, 1914. x, 221 pp., incl. front, illus. pl.
Indian life and Indian lore.

Mengarini, G.
"Indians of Oregon." *Journal of the Anthropological Institute of New York* 1:81–88, 1871–1872.

Ogden, Peter S.
Traits of American-Indian Life and Character. London: Smith, Elder and Co., 1853. xiv, 218 pp.

Palladino, L. B.
Indian and White in the Northwest. Baltimore: J. Murphy & Co., 1894. xxv, 411 pp.

Ronan, Peter
History of the Flathead Indians, Their Wars and Hunts, 1813–1890. Helena, Mont.: Journal Publishing Company, 1890.

Schaeffer, Claude
"The First Jesuit Mission to the Flathead, 1840–1850: a Study of Cultural Conflict." *Pacific Northwest Quarterly* 28:227–250, 1937.

Schultz, James
My Life as an Indian; edited by George Bird Grinnell. New York: Doubleday, Page and Company, 1907.

Smet, Pierre Jean de
Life, Letters and Travels . . . ed. by H. M. Chittenden, and A. T. Richardson. New York: F. P. Harper, 1904. First published in 1843.

————.
Oregon Missions and Travels Over the Rocky Mountains. New York: 1847.
In Thwaites: *Early Western Travels,* Vol. 29.

————.
Voyages Aux Montagnes Rocheuses. Lille: Lefort, 1875. vi, 229 pp.

————.
Western Missions and Missionaries. New York: J. B. Kirker, 1863. 532 pp.

Teit, James A.
"The Salishan Tribes of the Western Plateaus; The Flathead Group." *45th Ethnological Re-*

port, pp. 295–395, illus. Washington, D. C.: U. S. Government Printing Office, 1928.

Turney-High, H. H.
The Flathead Indians of Montana. American Anthropological Association Memoir 48. Menasha, Wis.: The Anthropological Association, 1937. 161 pp.

MYTHS

Altman, George J.
"Guardian-Spirit of the Salish." *The Masterkey* 21(No. 5):155–160, 1947.

Hoffman, W. J.
"Selish Myths." *Bulletin of the Essex Institute* (Salem) 15:24–40, 1883.

McDermott, L.
"Folklore of the Flathead Indians of Idaho. Adventures of Coyote." *JAFL* 14:240–251, 1901.

CUSTOMS—FOLK ART—SPEECH

Elrod, M. J.
"Pictured Rocks. Indian Writings on the Rock Cliffs of Flathead Lake, Montana." *Bulletin University of Montana (No. 46)* (Missoula) 1908. Biological Series (No. 14) 10 pp. 9 pl. 4 fig.

Hoffman, W. J.
"Vocabulary of the Selish Language." *Proceedings of the American Philosophical Society* (Philadelphia) 23:361–371, 1886.

Hunter, J. D.
Manners and Customs of Several Indian Tribes. . . . Philadelphia: J. Maxwell, 1823. viii, 402 pp.

Mengarini, Gregory
A Selish or Flat-head Grammar. New York: Cramoisy Press, 1861. 122 pp.

————.
"Vocabulary of the Selish Proper." *Contributions to North American Ethnology,* Department of the Interior, United States Geographical and Geological Survey of the Rocky Mountain Region (Washington). Vol. I, pp. 267–282, 1877.

Turney-High, H. H.
"Cooking Camas and Bitter Root." *Scientific Monthly* 36:262–263, 1933.

MUSIC
DANCE

Turney-High, H. H.
"The Bluejay Dance." *AA* 35:103–107, 1933. n.s.

KALISPEL
(*Including:* Pend d'Oreilles)
FOLKLORE
GENERAL STUDIES

Smalley, E. V.
"The Kalispel Country." *Century Illustrated Magazine* 29:447–455, 1885.

Teit, James A.
"The Salishan Tribes of the Western Plateaus." *45th Annual Report of the Bureau of American Ethnology*, pp. 295–396, 1930. (Washington, D. C.)

FOLKTALES

Teit, James A.
Pend D'Oreilles Tales. In: *Folk-Tales of Salishan and Sahaptin Tribes*, (pp. 114–119). Memoirs of the American Folklore Society No. 11. Lancaster, Pa.: The American Folklore Society, 1917. xi, 201 pp.
The tribe is also known as Kalispel.

CUSTOMS—SPEECH

Boas, Franz
"Terms of Relationship of the Salish Languages." *Report of the 60th Meeting of the British Association for the Advancement of Science* (London), pp. 688–692, 1890.

Gibbs, G.
"Vocabulary of the Kalispelm." *Contributions to North American Ethnology, Department of the Interior, United States Geographical and Geological Survey of the Rocky Mountain Region* (Washington, D. C.) Vol. I, pp. 267–282, 1877.

Giorda, Joseph
A Dictionary of the Kalispel or Flat-head Indian Language. St. Ignatius Mission: St. Ignatius Printer, 1877–1879. 644 pp.

Tolmie, W. F.
"Vocabulary of the Kulleespelm." *Contributions to North American Ethnology, Department of the Interior, Unitde States Georgraphical and Geological Survey of the Rocky Mountain Region* (Washington, D. C.), Vol. I, pp. 267–282, 1877.

————, and Dawson, G. M.
Comparative Vocabularies of the Indian Tribes of British Columbia. Montreal: Dawson Bros. 1884.

Vogt, H.
The Kalispel Language. Oslo: J. Dybwad, 1940. 178 pp.

KLIKITAT
FOLKLORE
GENERAL STUDIES

Farrand, Livingston
"Klikitat." In: *Handbook of the American Indians.* Bureau of American Ethnology, Bulletin 30 (Part 1), pp. 713–714. Washington, D. C.: U. S. Gov't. Printing Office, 1907.

Gibbs, G.
"Tribes of Western Washington and Northwestern Oregon." *Contributions to North American Ethnology, Department of Interior, United States Geographical and Geological Survey of the Rocky Mountain Region* (Washington, D. C.). Vol. I, pp. 157–241, 1877.

Jacobs, M.
"Northwest Sahaptin Texts." *University of Washington Publications in Anthropology* 2: 175–244, 1929.

————.
Northwest Sahaptin Texts. Columbia University Contributions to Anthropology, No. 19. New York: Columbia University Press, 1934.

Parker, Samuel
Journal of an Exploring Tour Beyond the Rocky Mountains in the Years 1835–37. Ithaca: The Author, 1838. xii, 371 pp.

Scouler, J.
"On the Indian Tribes Inhabiting the North-West Coast of America." *Journal of the Ethnological Society* (London) 1:228–252, 1848.

MYTHS—FOLKTALES—LEGENDS

Ballard, A. C.
"Mythology of the Southern Puget Sound." *University of Washington Publications in Anthropology* 3:31–150, 1929.

Bunnell, Clarence O.
Legends of the Klickitats, A Klickitat Version of the Story of the Bridge of the Gods. Portland, Ore.: Metropolitan Press, 1933. 64 pp., illus.

Lyman, W. D.
"Myths and Superstitions of the Oregon Indian." *Proceedings of the American Antiquarian Society* 16:221–251, 1904. n.s.

BELIEFS—FOLK ART—SPEECH

Du Bois, Cora
"The Feather Cult of the Middle Columbia." *General Series in Anthropology (No. 7).* Menasha, Wis.: George Banta, 1938.

Haeberlin, H. K., Teit, J. A., and Roberts, H. H.
"Coiled Basketry in British Columbia and Surrounding Regions." *41st Annual Report of the Bureau of American Ethnology*, pp. 119–484, 1928. Washington, D. C.: U. S. Gov't Printing Office.

Jacobs, M.
"Northern Sahaptin Kinship Terms." *AA* 34:
688–693, 1932. n.s.
The Sahaptin tribes in the Plateau Area are:
Klikitat, Nez Perce, Tenino, Umatilla, Walla-
walla, and Yakima.

———.
"A Sketch of Northern Sahaptin Grammar."
*University of Washington Publications in An-
thropology* 4:85–292, 1931.

Tolmie, W. F., and Dawson, G. M.
*Comparative Vocabularies of the Indian Tribes
of British Columbia.* Montreal: Dawson Bros.
1884.

KOOTENAY

FOLKLORE

GENERAL STUDIES

Baillie-Grohman, W. A.
"The Kootenay Country." *Geographical Journal* (London) 52:44–51, 1918.

Boas, Franz
"Additional Notes on the Kutenai Language."
International Journal of American Linguistics
4:85–104, 1927.

———.
"First General Report on the Indians of British
Columbia." *Report of the 59th Meeting of the
British Association for the Advancement of
Science,* pp. 801–900, 1889.

———.
"Kutonáqua." *Report of the 59th Meeting of
the British Association for the Advancement of
Science,* pp. 889–893, 1889.

Chamberlain, Alexander F.
"The Kootenay Indians." *Annual Archaeological Report* (Ontario, Toronto), pp. 178–187,
1905.

———.
"Kutenai." In: *Handbook of the American Indians.* Bureau of American Ethnology, Bulletin
30 (Part 1), pp. 740–742. Washington, D. C.:
U. S. Gov't Printing Office, 1907.

———.
"Note sur l'association des idées chez un peuple
primitif." *Bulletin de la Société d'Anthropologie* (Paris), (Ser. 5), 10:132–134, 1909.
Association of ideas among primitive people.

———.
"Notes on the Kootenay Indians." *American
Antiquarian* 15:292–294; 16:271–274; 17:68–
72, 1893–1895.

———.
"Report on the Kootenay Indians." *Report of
the 62nd Meeting of the British Association for
the Advancement of Science,* pp. 549–617, 1892.

Teit, James A.
"Traditions and Information Regarding the
Tonáxa." *AA* 32:625–632, 1930. .n.s.
Related to Kootenay and Flatheads.

Turney-High, Harry Holbert
Ethnography of the Kutenai. Memoirs of the
American Anthropological Association, No. 56.
Supplement to the American Anthropologist
Vol. 43, No. 2, Part 2. Menasha, Wis.: The
Anthropological Association, 1941.

Wilson, E. F.
"Kootenay Indians." *JAFL* 3:10–12, 1890.

———.
"The Kootenay Indians." *Our Forest Children*
(Owen Sound) 3 (Part 13), 1890.

MYTHS—FOLKTALES—LEGENDS

Boas, Franz
"Einige Sagen der Kootenay." *Verhandlungen
der Berliner Gesellschaft für Anthropologie,
Ethnologie und Urgeschichte* (Berlin), pp.
161–162, 1891.
Kutenay Tales.

———.
Kutenai Tales (together with texts collected
by Alexander Francis Chamberlain). Bureau
of American Ethnology, Bull. 59, xii, 387 pp.
Washington, D. C.: U. S. Gov't Printing Office,
1918.

Chamberlain, Alexander F.
"The Coyote and the Owl." *Memoirs of the
International Congress of Anthropologists*
(Chicago), pp. 282–284, 1893.

———.
"Kootenay Legend; Coyote and the Mountain
Spirit." *JAFL* 7:195–196, 1894.

———.
"Mythology and Folk-lore of the Kootenay Indians." *American Antiquarian,* 17:68, 1887.

———.
"Sagen vom Ursprung der Fliegen und Moski-
ten." *Am Urquell* 4:129–131, 1893.
Tales of the origin of flies and mosquitoes.

Linderman, F. B.
Kootenai Why Stories. New York: Charles
Scribner's Sons, 1926. xx, 168 pp.

Schaeffer, Claude
"The Bear Foster Parent Tale: A Kutenai
Version." *JAFL* 60:286–288, 1947.

Smyth, Fred J.
Tales of the Kootenays, with historical sketches
by the author and others. Cranbrook, B. C.:
Printed in the Office of the Courier, 1938. 205
pp., illus.

BELIEFS—CUSTOMS

Chamberlain, Alexander F.
"Beitrag zur Pflanzenkunde der Naturvölker
Amerika's." *Verhandlungen der Berliner
Gesellschaft für Anthropologie, Ethnologie und
Urgeschichte* (Berlin), pp. 551–556, 1895.
A study of ethnobotany.

"Der 'Kartensinn' der Kitonaqua Indianer."
Globus 95:270–271, 1909.

"Kootenay Medicine Men." *JAFL* 14:95–99,
1901.

"Der Wettlauf." *Am Urquell* 3:212–213, 1892.
The foot race—sport and game.

Morgan, Lewis H.
"Systems of Consanguinity and Affinity."
Smithsonian Institution Contribution to Education (Washington, D. C.) 17:291–382, 1871.

Sperlin, O. B.
"Two Kootenay Women Masquerading as
Men." *Washington Historical Quarterly*
(Seattle) 21:120–130, 1930.

FOLK ART—SPEECH

Boas, Franz
"Kinship Terms of the Kutenai Indians." *AA*
21:98–101, 1919. n.s.

Campbell, J.
"The Kootenay and Tsimshian Languages."
Proceedings and Transactions of the Royal Society of Canada (Ottawa), (Ser. 2) 4 (Part
2):23–42, 1898.

Canestrelli, P.,
"Earlier and Later Kootenay Onomatology."
AA 4:229–236, 1902. n.s.

"Geographic Terms of Kootenay Origin." *AA*
4:348–350, 1902. n.s.

"Grammar of the Kutenai Language." *International Journal of American Linguistics* 4:1–
84, 1927.

"Incorporation in the Kootenay Language."
*Proceedings of the American Association for
the Advancement of Science* 43:346–348, 1894.

Chamberlain, Alexander F.
"Kootenai Group Drawings." *AA* 3:248–251,
1901. n.s.

"Kootenay Indian Drawings." *Report of the
67th Meeting of the British Association for the
Advancement of Science*, pp. 792–793, 1897.

"Kutenai Basketry." *AA* 11:318–319, 1909. n.s.

"Kutenaian and Shoshonean." *AA* 11:535–536,
1909. n.s.

"Some Kutenai Linguistic Material." *AA* 11:
13–26, 1909. n.s.

Terms for the Body, Its Parts, Organs, etc., in
the Language of the Kootenay Indians. In:
Boas Anniversary Volume, pp. 94–107. New
York: G. E. Stechert and Company, 1906.

"Über Personennamen der Kitonaqua-Indianer." *Zeitschrift für Ethnologie* (Berlin)
41:378–380, 1909.
On personal names of the Kutenai.

"Word-Formation in the Kootenay Language."
*Proceedings of the American Association for
the Advancement of Science* 44:259–260, 1895.

"Words Expressive of Cries and Noises in the
Kootenay Language." *AA* 7:68–71, 1894.

Kissell, M. L.
"A Kutenai Berry-Basket." *AA* 11:529–531,
1909. n.s.

Mason, O. T.
"Pointed Bark Canoes of the Kutenai and
Amur." *Reports of the United States National
Museum*, pp. 523–537, 1899.

Sapir, Edward
"Kinship Terms of the Kootenay Indians." *AA*
20:414–418, 1918. n.s.

Tolmie, W. F., and Dawson, G. M.
*Comparative Vocabularies of the Indian Tribes
of British Columbia*. Montreal: Dawson Bros.
1884.

MUSIC
GENERAL STUDIES

Turney-High, Harry Holbert
Ethnography of the Kutenai. Memoirs of the
American Anthropology Association, No. 56.
Menasha, Wisc.: American Anthropological
Association, 1941. 201 pp., illus.
Lists 9 songs.

LILLOOET
FOLKLORE
GENERAL STUDIES

Hill-Tout, Charles
"Report on the Ethnology of the Sí'ciatl of
British Columbia." *Journal of Anthropological
Institute of Great Britain and Ireland*, 34:33–
34, 1904.
"A Salish tribe on Jervis and Seechelt Inlets,
Nelson Island, and the southern part of Texada
Island, British Columbia. They speak a distinct
dialect, and are thought by Hill-Tout on physical
grounds to be related to the Lilloet." (J. R.
Swanton)

".
"Report on the Ethnology of the StlatlumH of British Columbia." *Journal of Anthropological Institute of Great Britain and Ireland*, 35: 126–128, 1906.

Teit, James A.
"The Lillooet Indians." *Memoirs of the American Museum of Natural History*. No. 4, pp. 193–300, illus., edited by Franz Boas. New York: The Museum, 1906.

".
"Traditions of the Lillooet Indians of British Columbia." *JAFL* 25:287–371, 1912.

MYTHS—FOLKTALES

Elliott, W. C.
"Lake Lillooet Tales." *JAFL* 44:166–182, 1939. Anderson and Seton Lake Indians.

GAMES—SPEECH

Gibbs, G.
"Vocabulary of the Lilowat." *Contributions to North American Ethnology, Department of Interior, U. S. Geographical and Geological Survey of the Rocky Mountain Region* (Washington, D. C.) ,Vol. I, pp. 268–283, 1877.

Teit, James A.
"Lillooet Games." *JAFL* 25:317, 338, 339, 1912.

Tolmie, W. F., and Dawson, G. M.
Comparative Vocabularies of the Indian Tribes of British Columbia. Montreal: Dawson Bros. 1884.

NEZ PERCÉ
(Sahaptin)
FOLKLORE
GENERAL STUDIES

Burbank, E. A.
Burbank Among the Indians. As told to Ernest Royce. Caldwell, Idaho: Caxton Printers, Ltd., 1944.
Reminiscences of the artist who spent ten years painting portraits among the Navaho, Hopi, Zuni, Crow, Ute, and Nez Percé Indians.

Farrand, Livingston
"Notes on the Nez Percé Indians." *AA* 23:244–246, 1921. n.s.

Fee, Chester A.
Chief Joseph: The Biography of a Great Indian. With a foreword by Col. Charles Erskine Scott Wood. New York: Wilson-Erickson, Inc., 1936. xiii, 346 pp., front., pl., ports, maps. Bibl. (pp. 313–318.)

Haines, Francis
Red Eagle of the Northwest; the Story of Chief Joseph and his People. Portland, Oregon: Scholastic Press, 1939.

Henshaw, H. W., and Farrand, L.
"Nez Percés." In: *Handbook of the American Indian.* Bureau of American Ethnology, Bulletin 30 (Part 2), pp. 65–68. Washington, D. C.: U. S. Gov't Printing Office, 1910.

Howard, Gen. Oliver Otis
My Life and Experience Among Our Hostile Indians. Hartford: A. D. Worthington & Company, 1907. 570 pp.

".
Nez Percé Joseph; an account of his ancestors, his lands, his confederates, his enemies, his murders, his war, his pursuits, and capture. Boston: Lee & Shepard, 1881. 274 pp.

Howard, Helen Addison
War Chief Joseph. Caldwell, Idaho: Caxton Printer Ltd., 1941.

Hunter, J. D.
Manners and Customs of Several Indian Tribes, located west of the Mississippi; including some account of the soil, climate, and vegetable productions, and the Indian's materia medica: to which is prefixed the history of the author's life during a residence of several years among them. Philadelphia: J. Maxwell, 1823. viii, 402 pp.

Irving, Washington
The Adventures of Captain Bonneville. New York: G. P. Putnam, 1850. xvii, 428 pp., new ed.

Jacobs, Melville
"Northern Sahaptin Kinship Terms." *AA* 34: 688–693, 1932. n.s.

".
Northwest Sahaptin Texts. Seattle: University of Washington Press, 1929. University of Washington Publications in Anthropology 2 (No. 6):175–244, 1929.

".
Northwest Sahaptin Texts. Columbia University Contributions to Anthropology 19:3–291. New York: Columbia University Press, 1934.

McBerth, Kate C.
The Nez Percés Since Lewis and Clark. Introduction by Alice C. Fletcher. New York: Fleming H. Revell Company, 1908. 272 pp.

McWhorter, Lucullus V.
Yellow Wolf; His Own Story. Caldwell, Idaho: Caxton Printer Ltd., 1940.

Parker, Samuel
Journal of an Exploring Tour Beyond the Rocky Mountains, 1835–37. Ithaca: The Author, 1838. xii, 371 pp.

Phinney, Archie
Nez Percé Texts. New York: Columbia University Press, 1934. xii, 497 pp. (Columbia University Contributions to Anthropology. Vol. XXV.)

Scouler, J.
"On the Indian Tribes Inhabiting the North-West Coast of America." *Journal of the Ethnological Society* (London) 1:228–252, 1848.

Smet, Pierre Jean de
Life, Letters and Travels of Father Pierre Jean de Smet, S. J. Edited by H. M. Chittenden, and A. T. Richardson. New York: F. P. Harper, 1904.

————.
New Indian Sketches. New York: D. & J. Sadlier and Company, 1865. 175 pp., incl. front., pl.

Spinden, Herbert Joseph
The Nez Percé Indians. Memoirs of the American Archaeological Association vol. II (part 3), pp. 165–274. Lancaster, Pa.: The New Era Publishing Company, 1908.

Sutherland, T. A.
Howard's Campaign Against the Nez Percé Indians. Portland, Oregon, 1878. Pamphlet.

MYTHS—FOLKTALES—LEGENDS

Bailey, Robert G.
Hell's Canyon, a Story of the Deepest Canyon on the North American Continent, together with historical sketches of Idaho, interesting information of the state, Indian wars and mythology, poetry and stories. Lewiston: R. G. Bailey Printing Co., 1943. 575 pp., illus.

Butterfield, Grace, and Horner, J. H.
"Romantic Tale of the Nez Percés." *Oregon Historical Quarterly* (Portland, O.) 48:150–159, 1942.

Farrand, Livingston
"Sahaptin Tales." *New York American Folk Lore Society Memoirs* 11:135–179, 1917. Ed. by Teit, Gould, Farrand and Spinden. Philadelphia: American Folklore Society, 1917.

Melançon, C.
"Légendes de Percé." *Proceedings and Transactions of the Royal Society of Canada,* 16 (No. 1):113–120.

Packard, R. L.
"Mythology and Religion of the Nez Percé." *JAFL* 4:327–330, 1891.

Spinden, Herbert Joseph
"Myths of the Nez Percé Indians." *JAFL* 21: 13–23, 149–158, 1908.

————.
"Nez Percé Tales." *Memoir of the American Folklore Society* 11: 180–201, 1917.

BELIEFS—CUSTOMS

Alvord, B.
Concerning the Manners and Customs, the Superstitions ... of the Indians of Oregon. In: *Information Respecting the History, Condition, and Prospects of the Indian Tribes of the United States,* Henry Rowe Schoolcraft, ed., Vol. 5, pp. 651–657. Philadelphia: 1855.

Carter, C.
"Christmas Among the Nez Percés." *Red Man* (Carlisle, Pa.) 3:252–254, 1910.
Description of ceremonials.

————.
"How the Nez Percé Trained for Long Distance Running." *Red Man* (Carlisle, Pa.) 4:15–16, 1911.

Huggins, E. L.
"Smohalla, the Prophet of Priest Rapids." *Overland Monthly,* (Feb.) 1891; 17, (No. 98): 208–215, second series.
"He belonged to the Sokulk, a small tribe cognate to the Nez Percés and centering about Priest Rapids on the Columbia in E. Washington." (James Mooney).

Packard, R. L.
"Mythology and Religion of the Nez Percé." *JAFL* 4:327–330, 1891.

FOLK ART—SPEECH

Ainslie, G.
"Notes on the Grammar of the Nez Percés Language." *Bulletin of the United States Geological and Geographical Survey of Territories* (Washington, D. C.), Vol. 2, pp. 271–277, 1876.

Erwin, Richard P.
"Indian Rock Writing in Idaho." *Twelfth Biennial Report of the State Historical Society,* 1929–1930.

Gatschet, A. S.
"Adjectives of Color in Indian Languages." *American Naturalist* 13:475–485, 1879.

Morvillo, Anthony
A Numipu or Nez Percé Grammar. Desmet: Typis Puerorum Indorum, 1891. iv, 255 pp.

————.
A Dictionary of the Numípu or Nez Percé Language. n.p.: St. Ignatius Mission Printing, 1895. x, 242 pp.

Smith, Elmer R.
"An Indian Burial. A Barbed Bone Projectile Point and Accompanying Artifacts from Bear Lake, Idaho." *Archaeological and Ethnological Papers 6.* 6 pp., 1942. Salt Lake City.

Wyman, Anne
"Cornhusk Bags of the Nez Percé Indians." *Masterkey* 9:89–95, 1935.

MUSIC

GENERAL STUDIES

Spinden, Herbert Joseph
Musical Instruments. In: *The Nez Percé Indians. Memoirs of the American Archaeological Association,* Vol. 2, (Part 3). Lancaster, Pa.: The New Era Printing Company, 1908.

Wyman, L.
"Songs from Percé." *JAFL* 33:321–335, 1920.

OKANAGON

FOLKLORE

GENERAL STUDIES

Allison, S. S.
"Account of the Similkameen Indians." *Journal of the Royal Anthropological Institute of Great Britain and Ireland (London)* 21:305–318, 1892.
"Similkameen—the local name for several bands of Okinagan on a river of the same name, a n.w. tributary of the Okanagan, Brit. Col."

Cline, W., Commons, R. S., Mandelbaum, M., Post, R. H., and Walters, L. V. W.
The Sinkaietk or Southern Okanagon of Washington. Leslie Spier, ed. General Series in Anthropology. Vol. VI. Menasha, Wis.: Anthropological Society, 1938. 262 pp.

Hill-Tout, Charles
"Report on the Ethnology of the Okanaken of British Columbia, an Interior Division of the Salish Stock." *Journal of the Royal Anthropological Institute* 41:130–161, 1911.

Ross, A.
Adventures of the First Settlers on the Oregon or Columbia River. London: Smith, Elder & Co., 1849. xv, 352 pp.

Teit, James A.
"The Salishan Tribes of the Western Plateaus; The Okanagon." *Forty-fifth Annual Report,* pp. 198–294. Bureau of American Ethnology. Washington, D. C.: U. S. Gov't Printing Office, 1928.
Covers history, habitat and boundaries; manufactures, houses and house-holds, clothing and ornaments; war-fare, games and pastimes, social oragnizations; birth, childhood, marriage and death, religion, medicines and current beliefs.

Wade, M. S.
The Thompson Country. Kamloops, B. C.: Inland Sentinel Print., 1907. 136 pp.

MYTHS—FOLKTALES—LEGENDS

Teit, James A.
Okanagan Tales. In: *Folk-Tales of Salishan and Sahaptin Tribes,* (pp. 65–98). by Teit, J. A.; Gould, M. K.; Farrand, L.; Spinden, H. J. Memoirs of the American Folklore Society 11. Lancaster, Pa.: The American Folklore Society, 1917. xi, 201 pp.

SPEECH

Boas, Franz
"Terms of Relationship of the Salish Languages." *Report of the 55th Meeting of the British Association for the Advancement of Science,* pp. 688–692, 1890.

Gibbs, G.
"Vocabulary of the Okinaken." *Contributions to North American Ethnology, Department of the Interior, United Staes Geographical and*

Geological Survey of the Rocky Mounain Region (Washington, D. C.), Vol. I, pp. 248–264, 1877.

Tolmie, W. F.
"Vocabulary of the Wa-ky-na-kaine." *Contributions to North American Ethnology, Department of Interior....* (Washington, D. C.), Vol. I, pp. 248–265, 1877.

SANPOIL
(*Including:* Colville, Nespelem)

FOLKLORE

GENERAL STUDIES

Gwydir, R. D.
"A Record of the San Poil Indians." *Washington Historical Quarterly* (Seattle) 8:243–250, 1917.

Ray, Verne F.
The Sanpoil and Nespelem. The University of Washington Publications in American Anthropology, No. 5. Seattle, Wash.: University of Washington Press, 1932. 237 pp.

Teit, James A.
"The Salishan Tribes of the Western Plateaus." In: *45th Annual Report of the Bureau of American Ethnology,* pp. 37–396. Washington, D. C.: U. S. Gov't Printing Office, 1930.

MYTHS—FOLKTALES—LEGENDS

Gould, Marian K.
Sanpoil Tales. In: *Folk Tales of Salishan and Sahaptin Tribes,* (pp. 101–114) by Teit, J. A.; Gould, M. K.; Farrand, L.; Spinden, H. J. Memoirs of the American Folklore Society, 11. Lancaster: The American Folklore Society, 1917. xi, 201 pp.
Sanpoil—"A body of Salish on Sans Poil River and on the Columbia below Big Bend, Washington. Gibbs classed them as one of the eight bands of Spokan and also as one of the six bands of Okinagan, they being claimed by both tribes." (Handbook of American Indians, Vol. II, pp. 451–452).

Ray, Verne F.
"Sanpoil Folk Tales." *JAFL* 46:129–201, 1933.

Runnels, L.
"The Struggle Against Darkness." *Red Man* 4:27, 1911.

BELIEFS—FOLK ART—SPEECH

Gibbs, G.
"Vocabulary of the Shwoyelpi." *Contributions to North American Ethnology, Department of Interior, . . .* Vol. I, pp. 248–265, 1877.
Shwoyelpi—also known by the name of Colville, —"a division of Salish between Kettle Falls and Spokane River, east Washington," said by the author to have been one of the largest of the Salish Tribes." (BBAE 30, I, 326.)

Mengarini, G.
"Vocabulary of the Skoylpeli." *Contributions to North American Ethnology, Department of Interior....* Vol. I, pp. 248–265, 1877.

Ray, Verne F.
"The Kolaskin Cult." *AA* 38:67–75, 1936. n.s.

————.
"Pottery of the Middle Columbia." *AA* 34:127–133, 1932. n.s.

SHUSWAP

FOLKLORE

GENERAL STUDIES

Boas, Franz
"The Shuswap." *Report of the 60th Meeting of the British Association for the Advancement of Science,* pp. 632–647, 1890.

————.
"Zur Anthropologie der nordamerikanischen Indianer." *Verhandlungen der Berliner Gesellschaft für Anthropologie, Ethnologie und Urgeschichte,* pp. 367–411, 1895.

Dawson, Dr. George M.
"Notes on the Shouswap of British Columbia." *Proceedings and Transactions of Royal Society of Canada* (Section II), pp. 3–44, 1891.

Mackenzie, A.
Voyages from Montreal . . . London: T. Cadwell and W. Davies, 1801, cxxxii, 412 pp.

Smith, H. I.
"Some Indians of British Columbia." *Southern Workman* 41:477–483, 1912.

Teit, James. (Edited by Franz Boas)
"The Shuswap." *Memoirs: Jesup North Pacific Expedition:* Vol. 2:1909, pp. 443–789, figs. 199–281, pls. 13–14. *Publications in Anthropology.* New York: The American Museum of Natural History.

Wade, M. S.
The Thompson Country. Kamploops, B. C.: Inland Sentinel Print, 1907. 136 pp.

MYTHS—FOLKTALES

Boas, Franz
"Sagen aus Britisch-Columbien." *Verhandlungen der Berliner Gesellschaft für Anthropologie, Ethnologie und Urgeschichte* (Berlin), pp. 532–546, 1891.

SPEECH

Boas, Franz
"Terms of Relationship of the Salish Languages." *Report of the 60th Meeting of the British Association for the Advancement of Science,* pp. 688–692, 1890.

Gibbs, G.
"Vocabulary of the Shihwapmukh." *Contributions to North America Ethnology, Department of Interior....* (Washington, D. C.) Vol. I, pp. 247–264, 1877.

Tolmie, W. F.
"Vocabularly of the Shooswaap." *Contributions to North American Ethnology, Department of Interior....* (Washington, D. C.), Vol. I, pp. 247–264, 1877.

THOMPSON
(Nitlakapamuk)

FOLKLORE

GENERAL STUDIES

Boas, Franz
Introduction, to *Traditions of the Thompson River Indians of British Columbia,* by J. A. Teit. 18 pp., Boston: Amer. Folk-Lore Society, 1896. Memoirs. vol. 6.

————.
"The NtlakyápamuQ." *Report of the 68th Meeting of the British Association for the Advancement of Science,* pp. 654–662, 1898.

Hill-Tout, Charles
"Sqaktktquaclt' or The Benign Faced, the Oaunes of the N'tlakápamuQ, British Columbia." *Folklore* (London) 10:195, 1899.
The tribe is one of the four great Salish tribes inhabiting the interior of British Columbia and popularly called Thompson Indians, from the river on which a large part of them live.

Smith, Harlan I.
"The Thompson Indians." *Southern Workman* 40:23–36, 1911.

Teit, James A.
"The Thompson Indians of British Columbia. (edited by Franz Boas)." *Memoirs: Jesup (North Pacific) Expedition.* Vol. 1:1900, pp. 163–392, figs. 118–315, pls. 14–20, 1 map. *Publications in Anthropology.* New York: The American Museum of Natural History.

————.
"Tradition of the Thompson River Indians of British Columbia." *JAFL* 11:67–73, 1898.

————.
Traditions of the Thompson River Indians of British Columbia. Memoirs of the American Folklore Society, No. 6. Philadelphia: American Folklore Society, 1898. x, 437 pp.

Wade, M. S.
The Thompson Country. Kamloops: 1907. 136 pp.

1074 BIBLIOGRAPHY OF THE NORTH AMERICAN INDIAN

MYTHS—FOLKTALES—LEGENDS

Boas, Franz
"Sagen aus Britisch Columbien. *Verhandl. Berl. Gesel. Anthro. Ethnol. und Ur.*, pp. 546–549, 1891.

Teit, James Alexander
"European Tales from the Upper Thompson Indians." *JAFL* 29:301–329, 1916.

————.
"More Thompson Indian Myths." *JAFL* 50: 173–191, 1937.

————.
"Mythology of Thompson Indians." *Memoirs (Jesup North Pacific Expedition):* Vol. 8: 1912. pp. 199–416. *Publications in Anthropology.* New York: American Museum of Natural History.

————.
Thompson Tales. In: *Folk-Tales of Salishan and Sahaptin Tribes*, (pp. 1–64). by Teit, J. A.; Gould, M. K.; Farrand, L.; and Spinden, H. J. Memoirs of the American Folklore Society, Vol. 11. Lancaster, Pa.: The American Folklore Society, 1917. xi, 201 pp.

————.
Traditions of the Thompson River Indians of British Columbia, collected and annotated by J. Teit, with introduction by F. Boas. Boston: Houghton, Mittlin & Co., 1898. vii, 137 pp. (Amer. Folk-Lore Soc., Memoirs, vol. 6.)

CUSTOMS—FOLK ART

Smith, Harlan I.
"Archaeology of the Thompson River Region, British Columbia." *Memoirs: Jesup North Pacific Expedition:* Vol. 1:1900, pp. 401–442, figs. 331–380, pls. 24–26. *Publications in Anthropology.* New York: The American Museum of Natural History.

Steedman, Elsie Viault ed. (based on notes by Teit, James A.)
"Enthnobotany of the Thompson Indians of British Columbia." *45th Annual Report: Bureau of American Ethnology*, 1927–1928, pp. 447–519. Washington, D. C.: U. S. Gov't. Printing Office, 1930.

Teit, James (ed. from notes of collector, by Franz Boas)
"A Rock Painting of the Thompson River Indians, British Columbia." *Bulletins:* Vol. 8, Art. 12:1896, pp. 227–230, 28 figs. *Publications in Anthropology.* New York: American Museum of Natural History.

————, (ed. Franz Boas)
"Tattooing and Face and Body Painting of the Thompson Indians of British Columbia." *45th Annual Report: Bureau of American Ethnology*, 1927–1928, pp. 403–439, pls. 5–13, figs. 40–47. Washington, D. C.: U. S. Gov't Printing Office, 1930.

WISHRAM

FOLKLORE

GENERAL STUDIES

Alvord, B.
Concerning the Manners and Customs, the Superstitions, . . . of the Indians of Oregon. In: *Information Respecting the History, Condition, and Prospects of the Indian Tribes of the United States*, Henry Rowe Schoolcraft, ed. Vol. 5, pp. 651–657. Philadelphia: 1855.

Biddle, H. T.
"Wishram." *Oregon Historical Quarterly* 27:113–130, 1926.

Boas, Franz
"Chinook." *Bureau of American Ethnology, Bulletin 40* (Part 2):638–645, 650–654, 1911. (Washington, D. C.).

Lee, Daniel, and Frost, J. H.
Ten Years in Oregon. New York: J. Collord, 1844. 344 pp.

Sapir, Edward, and Curtin, Jeremiah
Wishram Texts, Together with Wasco Tales and Myths, collected by Jeremiah Curtin. American Ethnological Society Publications v. 2. Leyden: Brill, 1909. xv, 314 pp.
Wishram—"Formerly the principal village of the Tlakluit, and now their chief fishing settlement; situated on Columbia River."

Spier, Leslie, and Sapir, Edward
"Wishram Ethnography." *University of Washington Publications in Anthropology* 3:151–300, 1930.

MYTHS—SPEECH

Sapir, Edward
"A Chinookian Phonetic Law." *International Journal of American Linguistics* 4:105–110, 1926.

————.
"Preliminary Report on the Language and Mythology of the Upper Chinook." *AA* 9:533–544, 1907. n. s.

————.
"Terms of Relationship and the Levirate." *AA* 18:327–337, 1916. n. s.

YAKIMA

FOLKLORE

GENERAL STUDIES

McWhorter, L. V.
The Crime Against the Yakimas. North Yakima, Wash.: Republic Printer, 1913. 56 pp., illus.

Mooney, James
"Yakima." In: *Handbook of American Indians.* Bureau of American Ethnology, Bulletin 30 (Part 2), pp. 983–984, 1910. Washington, D. C.: U. S. Gov't. Printing Office, 1910.

Splawn, A. J.
Ka-mi-akin, the Lost Hero of the Yakimas. Portland, Oregon: Kilham Printing Co., 1917. 438 pp., illus.
"Little is known of the particular customs of the Yakima, but there is no reason to suppose that their life differed greatly from that of the Nez Percés and other Shahaptian peoples." (James Mooney)

MYTHS—BELIEFS

Lyman, W. D.
"Myths and Superstitions of the Oregon Indians." *Proceedings of the American Antiquarian Society* 16:221–251, 1904. n. s.

Mooney, James
"The Ghost-Dance Religion." In: *14th Annual Report of the Bureau of American Ethnology* (Part 2):708–745, 1893. Washington, D. C.: U. S. Gov't. Printing Office, 1893.

FOLK ART—SPEECH

Pandosy, Marie C.
Grammar and Dictionary of the Yakama Language. London: Trübner & Co., 1862. 59 pp.

Smith, Harlan I.
"The Archaeology of the Yakima Valley." *Anthropological Papers of the American Museum of Natural History* (New York)6:1–171, 1910.

——.
"A Costumed Human Figure from Tampico." *Bulletin of the American Museum of Natural History* (New York) 20:195–203, 1904.

Steward, Julian H.
"A Peculiar Type of Stone Implement." *AA* 30:314–316, 1928. n. s.

OTHER TRIBES

MISCELLANEOUS STUDIES

NICOLA

Anon.
"Stuichamuk." In: *Handbook of the American Indians.* Bureau of American Ethnology, Bul-letin 30 (Part 2), pp. 645. Washington, D. C.: U. S. Gov't. Printing Office, 1910.
"An Athapascan tribe, now absorbed into the surrounding Salishan tribes, that inhabited Nicola Valley, Brit. Col."

Boas, Franz
"The Tinneh Tribe of Nicola Valley." *Report of the 65th Meeting of the British Association for the Advancement of Science,* pp. 551–555, 1895.

——.
"Vocabulary of the Athabascan Tribe of Nicola Valley." *International Journal of American Linguistics* 3:36–38, 1924.

SPOKAN

Gibbs, G.
"Vocabulary of the Spokan." *Contributions to North American Ethnology, Department of Interior . . .* (Washington, D. C.), Vol. I, pp. 249–265, 1877.

Gwydir, R. D.
"Prehistoric Spokane . . . an Indian Legend." *Washington Historical Quarterly* (Seattle) 1:136–137, 1907.

Teit, James A.
"The Salishan Tribes of the Western Plateaus." *45th Annual Report of the Bureau of American Ethnology,* pp. 295–396. Washington, D. C.: U. S. Gov't. Printing Office, 1930.

WASCO

Lewis, N. M.
"Sunlight Legend of the Warm Spring Indians." *So. Workman* 38:685–686, 1909.
The chief tribes of the reservation are the Wasco, Paiute, Tenino, and Tyigh.

——.
"The Warm Spring Indian Legend of the Fox and the Spirits." *So. Workman* 39:94–98, 1910.

Sapir, Edward
"Wasco." In: *Handbook of American Indians.* Bureau of American Ethnology, Bulletin 30 (Part 2):917–918, 1910. (Washington, D. C.).

——.
Wishram Texts; together with Wasco tales and myths, collected by Jeremiah Curtin and ed. by Edward Sapir. Leyden: Late E. J. Brill, 1909. xiv, 314 pp. (Publications of the American Ethnological Society. Vol. II.).

THE NORTHWEST COAST

THE NORTHWEST COAST

(*Including:* Tribes of the Oregon Seaboard)

FOLKLORE
BIBLIOGRAPHY

Appleton, John Bargate, comp.
The Pacific Northwest: A selected bibliography; 1930–1939. Portland, Ore.: Northwest Regional Council, 1939. 455 pp.

Smith, Charles W.
Pacific Northwest Americana. New York: H. W. Wilson Co., 1921. 329 pp.

GENERAL STUDIES

Armstrong, Sir Alexander
A Personal Narrative of the Discovery of the Northwest Passage; with numerous incidents of travel and adventure during nearly five years. London. Eng.: Hurst & Blackett, 1857. xxii, 616 pp.

Armstrong, A. N.
Oregon: comprising a brief history of the territories of Oregon and Washington, embracing the cities, towns, rivers, etc. Description of the Indian tribes, manners, customs, etc. Chicago: Chas. Scott and Company, 1857.

Bancroft, Hubert Howe
The Native Races of the Pacific States of North America. San Francisco: A. L. Bancroft and Co., 1874–1882. Five vols., illus., bibl.
Vol. 3—myths and languages.

Barbeau, Charles Marius
"Asiatic Migrations into America." *Canadian Historical Review* 13:403–417, 1932.

————.
"The Bearing of Heraldry of the Indians of the North-West Coast of America Upon Their Social Organization." *Man* 12:83–90, 1912.

————.
Indian Days in the Canadian Rockies. Illustrated by W. Langdon Kuhn. Toronto: The Macmillan Company of Canada, Ltd., 1923. 207 pp., col. plates, and maps. Sources and references, pp. 205–208.

————.
The Kingdom of Saguenay. Illustrated by A. Y. Jackson, G. Pepper, K. Daly. Toronto: The Macmillan Company of Canada, Ltd., 1936. 167 pp., illus.

————.
"Parallel Between the Northwest Coast and Iroquoian Clans and Phratries." *AA* 19:403–405, 1917. n. s.

————.
"The Siberian Origin of our Northwest Indians." *Proceedings of the Fifth Pacific Scientific Congress of Canada* 4:2777–2789, 1933. Toronto, University of Toronto Press, 1934.

Barry, J. N.
"The Indians of Oregon." *Oregon Historical Quarterly* 28:49–61, 1927.

Bastian, A. ed.
Amerikas Nordwestküste. Berlin: 1893.

Berreman, J. V.
"Tribal Distribution in Oregon." *Memoirs, American Anthropological Association,* No. 47, pp. 7–65, 1937.

Boas, Franz
"First General Report of the Indians of British Columbia." *59th Meeting British Association Advancement Science,* 801–899, 1899.

————.
"The Development of Culture of North West America." *Science* 12:194–196, 1888.

————.
"Fifth Report on the Indians of British Columbia." *65th Meeting British Association Advancement Science,* pp. 522–592, 1895.

————.
"The Indians of British Columbia." *Proceedings and Transactions of the Royal Society of Canada,* (Ser. 1) 6(Part 2):47–57, 1889.

————.
"The Jesup North Pacific Expedition." *International Congress of Anthropology* 13:91–100, 1902.

————.
"Preliminary Notes on the Indians of British Columbia." *Report of the 58th meeting of the British Association for the Advancement of Science,* pp. 236–242, 1888.

————.
"Report on the Northwestern Tribes of the Dominion of Canada." *Report to the 59th Annual Meeting of the British Association for the Advancement of Science,* London, 1889.

————.
"Die Resultate der Jesup-Expedition." *International Congress of Anthropology* 16:3–18, 1908.
Results and achievements of the Jesup expedition.

————.
"Salishan Texts." *Proceedings of the American Philosophical Society,* 34:31–48, 1895.

————.
The Social Organization of the Tribes of the Northwest Coast In: *Race, Language and Culture* (pp. 370–378). New York: The Macmillan Company, 1940.
First appeared in *AA* 26: 323–332, 1924. n. s.

————.
"Summary of Work of the Committee in British Columbia." *Report of the 68th Meeting of the British Assoc. for the Advanc. of Science*, pp. 667–683, 1898.

————.
"The Tribes of the North Pacific Coast." *Annual Archaeological Report*, pp. 235–249. Ontario 1905, Toronto 1906.

————.
"Zur Ethnologie von Britisch-Kolumbiens." *Petermanns Mitteilungen aus Justus Perthtes Geographischer Anstalt* (Gotha). 33:129–133, 1887.

Bogoras, Waldemar G.
The Folklore of Northwestern Asia, as compared with that of Northwestern America. New York: G. P. Putnam Sons, 1902. 577–683 pp. Reprinted from Amer. Anthro. vol. 4, n. s.

Buschmann, J. C. E.
"Die Völker und Sprachen Neu-Mexico's und der Westseite des britischen Nordamerika's." *Abhandlungen der Königlichen Akademie der Wissenschaften* (Berlin), pp. 209–404, 1857.
Tribes and languages of New Mexico and British North-America.

Carr, Emily
Klee Wyck: (Story of the Northwest Indian-Canada). New York: Farrar and Rinehart, 1942. xiii, 174 pp., illus.

Chamberlain, Alexander
"Iroquois in Northwestern Canada." *AA* 6:459–464, 1904. n. s.

Chandler, Katherine
In the Reign of Coyote, folklore from the Pacific Coast . . . drawings by J. W. Ferguson Kennedy. Boston, New York: Ginn & Co., 1905. xii, 161 pp., illus.

Davidson, D. S.
"Family Hunting Territories in Northwestern North America." *Indian Notes and Monographs* no. 46: pp. 1–34, 1928. Heye Foundation, New York.

Defenbach, Byron
Red Heroines of the Northwest. Caldwell, Idaho: The Caxton Printers, Ltd., 1929.

Douglas, F. H.
"Northwest Coast Indians." *Denver Art Museum, Indian Leaflet Series* 1:1–3, 1930.

————.
"The Northwest Coast Tribes." *Denver Art Museum, Department of Indian Art Leaflet 72,* 1936.

Dunn, John
History of the Oregon Territory, and British North-American Fur Trade. London: Edwards & Hughes, 1846. 359 pp.

Eells, Myron
History of Indian Missions on the Pacific Coast—Oregon, Washington and Idaho. Phila., and New York: American Sunday School Union, 1882. 270 pp.

"Ethnographical Album of the North Pacific Coast of America and Asia."
Miscellaneous Publications of the American Museum of Natural History (New York) Part 1, pp. 1–5, 1900., illus.

Franchère, G.
Narrative of a Voyage to the Northwest Coast of America. In: *Early Western Travels,* R. G. Thwaites, ed. Vol. 6, pp. 167–410. Cleveland: 1904.

Fraser, S.
"Journal of a Voyage from the Rocky Mountains to the Pacific Coast." In: *Les Bourgeois de la Compagnie du Nord-Ouest.* L. F. R. Masson, ed. Quebec. Impr. Générale A. Coté et Cie, Vol. 1, pp. 156–221, 1889.

Gallatin, Albert
"Hale's Indians of Northwest America." *Transactions of the American Ethnological Society* 2: 13, 1848.

Gibbs, George, M.D.
Journal of the Expedition of Colonel Redick M'Kee. In: *Information Respecting the History, Condition, and Prospects of the Indian Tribes of the United States.* Henry Rowe Schoolcraft, ed. Vol. 3, pp. 99–177. Philadelphia, 1853.

————.
"Report on the Indian Tribes of the Territory of Washington." *Reports of Explorations and Surveys* (Washington, D. C.) 1:402–436, 1855.

————.
"Tribes of Western Washington and Northwestern Oregon." *Contributions to North American Ethnology, Department of the Interior* (pp. 157–241) vol. I. Washingtton, D. C.: U. S. Government Printing Office, 1877.

Goddard, Pliny Earle
"Assimilation to Environment as Illustrated by Athapascan Peoples." *Proceedings of the 15th Session of the International Congress of Americanists* (Quebec), Vol. 5: 337–362, 1906.

————.
"Indians of the Northwest Coast." *Miscellaneous Publications of the American Museum of Natural History* (New York) 10. 1934. 175 pp. illus.

Hafen, Le Roy R., and Rister, Carl C.
Western America; the exploration and settlement of the region beyond the Mississippi (Prentice Hall Books on History). New York: Prentice Hall, 1941.

Hale, H.
Ethnology and Philology. In: *Narrative of the United States Exploring Expedition*, by C. Wilkes. Vol. I. Philadelphia: C. Sherman, 1844. 5 vols., illus.

————.
"Remarks on the Ethnology of British Columbia." *Report of the 60th Meeting of the British Association for the Advancement of Science*, pp. 553–562, 1890.

Hall, Christopher
The First Voyage of Master Martin Frobisher, made to the west and northwest regions in the year 1577. With a description of the country and people. In: *Collection of Voyages*, by Richard Haklyut. vol. 3, pp. 52–65. London: R. H. Evans and Company, 1589.

Hatt, Gudmund
"North American and Eurasian Culture Connection." *Proceedings of the Fifth Pacific Scientific Congress*, 4:2755–2765, 1933. Toronto: University of Toronto Press, 1934.

Hill-Tout, Charles
British North America: The Far West, the Home of the Salish and the Déné. London: A. Constable Co., 1907. xiv, 263 pp.

————.
"Some Feature of the Language and Culture of the Salish." *AA* 7:674–687, 1905. n.s.

Jenness, Diamond
Indians of Canada. Bulletins of the Canada Department of Mines, National Museum of Canada, No. 65, 446 pp. Ottawa: 1932.

Jochelson, Waldemar
"The Ancient and Present Kamchadal and the Similarity of their Culture to that of the Northwestern American Indians." *Proceedings of the 23rd International Congress of Americanists* pp. 451–455, 1928.

Kane, Paul
Wanderings of an Artist Among the Indians of North America, from Canada to Vancouver's Island, and Oregon through Hudson's Bay Company Territory and back again. London: Longman, Brown, Green, Longmans and Roberts, 1859. xvii, 455 pp., col. front., illus. col. plates, map.

Kelley, Hall J.
A Geographical Sketch of that Part of North America Called Oregon. Boston: J. Howe, 80 pp. 1830.

Kroeber, A. L.
"American Culture and the Northwest Coast." *AA* 25:1–20, 1923. n.s.

————.
"The Tribes of the Pacific Coast of North America." *Proc. Inter. Congr. Amer.* 19:385–401, 1915.

Lapérouse, J. F. de G. de
A Voyage Round the World in the Years 1785, 1786, 1787, and 1788 . . . Edinburgh: J. Moir, 1798, 3 vols.

Lewis, Albert Buell
Tribes of the Columbia Valley and the Coast of Washington and Oregon. Memoirs of the American Anthropological Association, Vol. I, part 2. Lancaster, Pa.: The New Era Printing Company, 1906. 56 pp.

Macfie, M.
Vancouver Island and British Columbia. London: Longman, Green, Longman, Roberts & Green, 1865. xxi, 574 pp., illus.

Mackay, Isabel E.
Indian Nights. Toronto: McClelland & Stewart, Ltd., 1930. 198 pp., illus.

Mackenzie, Alexander
Voyages from Montreal on the St. Lawrence River,—Through the Continent of North America to the Frozen and Pacific Oceans, 1789–93. London: 1801. Other subsequent editions.

MacLeod, W. C.
"Certain Aspects of the Social Organization of the Northwest Coast and of the Algonkian." *Proc. Inter. Congr. Amer.* 21 (Part 1): 253–265, 1924.

Mayne, Richard C.
Four Years in British Columbia and Vancouver Island. London: J. Murray, 1862. xi, 468 pp.

Meares, J.
Voyages Made in the Years 1788 and 1789. London: Logographic Press, 1791. 2 vols.

Milet de Mureau, M. L. A., ed.
Voyage de la Pérouse Autour du Monde. Paris: Chez Plassan, 1797. 4 vols.

Morice, A. G.
"The Great Déné Race." *Anthropos* 1:229–277, 483–508, 695–730; 2:1–34, 181–196; 4:582–606; 5:113–142, 419–443, 643–653, 969–990, 1906–1910.

Newcombe, C. F., ed.
Menzies' Journal of Vancouver's Voyage. Archives of British Columbia, Memoir 5. 171 pp. 1923.

Niblack, Ensign Albert, U.S.N.
"The Coast Indians of Southern Alaska and Northern British Columbia." *Report to the U. S. National Museum*, 1887–1888, pp. 225–368. Washington, D. C.: U. S. Government Printing Office, 1890.

Olson, Ronald L.
"The Indians of the Northwest Coast." *Natural History* 35(no. 3):182–197, 1935.

————.
"The Possible Middle American Origin of Northwest Coast Weaving." *AA* 31:114–119, 1929. n.s.

Osgood, C.
"Tanaina Culture." *AA* 35:695–717, 1933. n.s.

Petitot, Émile Fortuné, S. J.
Traditions Indiennes du Canada Nord-ouest.
Paris: Maisonneuve frères et C. Leclerc, 1886.
xvii, 521 pp.

Portlock, N.
A Voyage Round the World, but more particularly to the North-West coast of America
. . . London: J. S. Stockdale, and G. Goulding,
1789. xii, 384 pp.

Ravenhill, Alice
The Native Tribes of British Columbia. Victoria, B. C.: C. R. Banfield, 1938. 142 pp.

Russell, Frank
Explorations in the Far North. Iowa City:
University of Iowa Publications, 1898. vii, 290
pp.

Sapir, Edward
Indian Tribes of the Coast. In: *Canada and Its
Provinces.* A. Shortt and A. G. Doughty, eds.,
No. 21, pp. 315–346. Toronto: 1914.

————.
"The Social Organization of the West Coast
Tribes." *Proc. Trans. Royal Soc. Can.* (ser. 3)
9 (Part 2):355–374, 1915.

Schoolcraft, Henry Rowe
*Narrative Journal of Travels Through the
Northwestern Regions of the United States.*
Albany: E. and E. Hosford, 1821. xiv, 419 pp.

Scouler, J.
"Observations on the Indigenous Tribes of the
N. W. Coast of America." *Journ. Royal Geogr.
Soc.* 11:215–250, 1871.

————.
"On the Indian Tribes Inhabiting the North-
West Coast of America." *Journ. Ethnol. Soc.*
1:228-252, 1848.

Shotridge, L. and F.
"Indians of the Northwest." *Museum Journal*
4:71-99, 1913.

Simpson, Thomas
*Narrative of the Discoveries of the North
Coast of America during 1836–1839.* London:
R. Bentley, 1843. xix, 419 pp., 2 fold. maps.

Smith, H. I.
"A Visit to the Indian Tribes of the Northwest
Coast." *American Museum Journal* (New
York) 10:31–42, 1910.

Smith, H. W.
"Anthropology and Northwestern Folklore."
JAFL 5:162–165, 1892.

Spier, Leslie
Tribal Distribution in Washington. *General
Series in Anthropology No. 3.* Menasha, Wisc.:
George Banta Publishing Co., 1936.

Sullivan, M. S.
The Travels of Jebediah Smith. Santa Ana:
The Fine Arts Press, 1934. 195 pp.

Swan, James G.
*The Northwestern Coast; or, Three Years'
Residence in Washington Territory.* New York:
Harper and Brothers, 1857. Illus.

Swanton, John R.
"Salish." *Encyclopedia of Religion and Ethics.*
J. Hastings, ed. Vol. 11, pp. 97–100, New
York: 1921.

Underhill, Ruth
Indians of the Pacific Northwest. Indian Life
and Customs Series No. 5. Education Division
of United States Office of Indian Affairs. River-
dale, Calif.: Sherman Press, 1945. 232 pp.,
pls., map, figs., bibl.
Bibliography—North Pacific Coast Mythology,
pp. 230–231.

Vancouver, G.
*Voyage of Discovery to the North Pacific
Ocean and Round the World, 1790–1795.* Lon-
don: G. G. and J. Robinson, 1801. 6 vols.

Victor, Frances F.
"The Oregon Indians." *Overland Monthly* 3,
October 1871.

Wagner, Henry R. (trans. and ed.)
"Journal of Tomás de Suría of his Voyage
with Malaspina to the Northwest Coast of
America in 1791." *Pacific Historical Review*
5, (no. 3): 234–276, 1936.

Wells, Philip F.
"Ninety-Six Years Among the Indians of the
Northwest." *North Dakota Hist.* 15 (No. 2):85–
133; 15 (No. 3):169–215, 1948.

Wickersham, James
"Notes on the Indians of Washington." *American Antiquarian* 21: 369–375, 1899.

Woldt, A.
*Captain Jacobsen's Reise an der Nordwest-
küste Amerikas.* Leipzig: M. Spohr, 1884.
viii, 431 pp.

MYTHS—FOLKTALES—LEGENDS

Adamson, Thelma
Folk Tales of the Coast Salish. Memoirs Ameri-
can Folklore Society 27. New York: G. E.
Stechert and Company, 1934. 430. pp.

Bagley, Clarence B.
Indian Myths of the Northwest. Seattle, Wash.:
Lowman & Hanford Co., 1930.

Barbeau, Charles Marius
"Bear Mother." *JAFL* 59:1–12, 1946. Illus.
An exhaustive treatment of this myth among the
North American Indian, particularly those of the
Northwest coast.

Boas, Franz
"The Growth of American Mythologies." *JAFL*
9:1–11, 1896.

————.
*Indianische Sagen von der Nord-Pacifischen
Küste Amerikas.* Berlin: A. Asher and Co.,
1895. vi, 363 pp.
Indian tales of the Northwest coast.

——————.
"Die Mythologie der nordwest-amerikanischen Küstenvölker." *Globus* 53:121–127, 153–157, 299–302; 54:10–14, 1888.

Brinton, Daniel Garrison
*The Myths of the New World; a treatise on the symbolism and mythology of the red race of America. New York: Leypoldt & Holt, 1868. viii, 307 pp.

Carmichael, Alfred
Indian Legends of Vancouver Island, illustrated by Semeyn, J. Toronto: The Musson Book Co., Ltd., 1922. 97 pp., illus.

Chandler, Katherine
In the Reign of Coyote: Folklore from the Pacific Coast. Drawings by J. W. Ferguson Kennedy. Boston: Ginn & Co., 1905. xii, 161 pp., illus.

Crane, W. E.
Totem Tales. New York: Fleming H. Revell Company, 1932. 95 pp.

Deans, James
"The Raven in the Mythology of Northwest America." *American Antiquarian,* 1888–89, pp. 109–114, 273–278, 297–301, 368–369, 383.

Dubé, Dollard
"Légendes Indiennes du St. Maurice." *Pages Trifluviennes.* Sér. C., No. 3:1–78, Les Trois-Rivieres: 1933.

Dugas, George
Légendes du Nord-Ouest. Montreal: Librairie Beauchemin, 1904. 142 pp.

Erkes, E.
"Chinesisch-amerikanische Mythenparallelen." *T'oung Pao* 24:32–53, 1926.
Similarities in Chinese and American myths.

Farrand, L., and Frachtenberg, L. J.
"Shasta and Athapascan Myths from Oregon." *JAFL* 28:207–242, 1915.

Getchell, Alice
Bibliography of Oregon Indian Myths. Salem: 1924. 3 pp. Reprinted from *Oregon Sunday Journal* July 27, 1924.

Gordon, H. L.
Legends of the Northwest, St. Paul: St. Paul Book and Stationery Co., 1881. Re-printed in Salem, Mass., 1910.

Gridley, Marion E.
Indian Legends of American Scenes, with eleven full color illustrations.... Chicago: M. A. Donohue & Company, 1939. 127 pp., illus.

Griffin, George H.
Legends of the Evergreen Coast. Vancouver, B. C.: Clark & Stuart Co., 1935. 141 pp., illus.

Hoebel, E. A.
"The Asiatic Origin of a Myth of the Northwest Coast." *JAFL* 54:1–9, 1941.

Johnson, Emily Pauline
Legends of Vancouver. Toronto: McClelland & Stewart, 1920. xvi, 165 pp., illus.

Judson, Katharine Berry
Myths and Legends of the Pacific Northwest, especially of Washington and Oregon. 50 illustrations from photographs. Chicago: A. C. McClurg and Company, 1910. xvi, 144 pp., front. pl.

Linderman, Frank B.
Indian Why Stories, Sparks from the Eagle's Lodge Fires. Illustrated by Charles M. Russell. New York: Charles Scribner's Sons, 1915. 236 pp.

Lyman, William Denison
"Indian Myths of the Northwest." In: *American Antiquarian Society Proceedings.* Worcester, Mass., 1915. n.s. 25:375–395. Bibl.

Mowrning Dore (Humishuma)
Coyote Stories, Caldwell, Idaho: Caxton Printers, Ltd., 1933.

Neihart, John G.
Song of the Indian Wars. New York: The Macmillan Company, 1925. 231 pp., illus.

Phillips, Walter Shelley
Indian Fairy Tales; folklore, legends, myths, totem tales as told by the Indians, gathered in the Pacific Northwest—with a glossary of words, customs and history of the Indians; fully illustrated by the author. Chicago: Star Publishing Co., 1902. xvii, 326 pp., illus.

——————.
Totem Tales; Indian Stories Indians Told, Gathered in the Pacific Northwest. Fully illustrated by the author. Chicago: Star Publishing Co., 1896. xvii, 326 pp., illus.

Sampson, Martin J.
The Swinomish Totem Pole; Tribal Legends. As told by Sampson, M. J. to Whitney, R. M. Bellingham, Washington: Union Printing Co., 1938. 38 pp., illus.

Spence, Lewis
The Myths of the North American Indians. With ... plates ... by James Jack. London: G. G. Harrap & Co., 1914. xii, 392 pp., illus., bibl. (pp. 363–374).

Thompson, William
Wigwam Wonder Tales; illustrated by Carle Michel Boog. New York: C. Scribner's Sons, 1925. xii, 156 pp., illus.

Wardle, H. Newell
"The Sedna Cycle: A Study in Myth Evolution." *AA* 2:568–603, 1900. n.s.

Webber, William L.
The Thunderbird "Tootooch" Legends; folk tales of the Indian Tribes of the Pacific Northwest coast Indians. Seattle, Wash.: Ace Printing Company, 1936. xxi, 38 pp., illus.
"These legends are the key to the most important single objects carved on totem poles and used in decorative arts by the Indian tribes of the Pacific Northwest."

Wilson, Gilbert Livingstone
Myths of the Red Children.... Illustrated by
Frederick N. Wilson. Boston: Ginn & Company,
1907. ix, 154 pp., illus.

Wood, Charles Erskine Scott
A Book of Indian Tales. New York: The Vanguard Press, 1929. 165 pp.

BELIEFS

Barbeau, Charles Marius
"How Totem Poles Originated." *Queens Quarterly* 46, No. 3:304–311, August, 1939.

————.
The Modern Growth of the Totem Pole on the
North-West Coast. In: *Custom Is King;* essays
presented to R. R. Marett on his seventieth
birthday... edited by L. H. Dudley Buxton, pp.
85–94. London: Hutchinson's Scientific and
Technical Publ., 1936. xiii, 325 pp.

————.
"The Modern Growth of the Totem Pole on
the Northwest Coast." *Smithsonian Institution
Annual Report* (pp. 491–498), 1939. Washington. D. C.: U. S. Gov't. Printing Office, 1940. 5
plates.

————.
"The Modern Growth of the Totem Pole in
Northwest." *Proceedings of the Twenty-third
International Congress of Americanists,* pp.
505–512, 1928.

————.
"Totemism, A Modern Growth on the North
Pacific Coast." *JAFL* 57:59, 1944.

————.
"Totem Poles; A By-product of the Fur Trade,"
Scientific Monthly 55:507–514, 1942.

————.
"Totem Poles, Recent Native Art of the Northwest Coast of America." *Smithsonian Institution Annual Report for 1931:* pp. 559–570.
Washington, D. C.: U. S. Gov't Printing Office,
1932.

Gunther, E.
"An Analysis of the First Salmon Ceremony."
AA 28:605–617, 1926. n.s.

————.
"A Further Analysis of the First Salmon Ceremony." *Univ. of Wash. Publ. in Anthro.* 2:129–
173, 1928.

Lang, Andrew
The Secret of the Totem. London: Longmans,
Green and Company, 1905. 225 pp.
General discussion of the various theories of the
origin, refutation and enunciation of author's
theory.

Lantis, M.
"The Alaskan Whale Cult and Its Affinities."
AA 40:438–464, 1938. n.s.

McDonald, Lucille
Bering's Potlatch. New York: Oxford Univer-
sity Press, 1944. 232 pp.
A story (juvenile) about the explorations of
Vitus Bering in the Northern Pacific.

MacLeod, W. C.
"Mortuary and Sacrificial Anthropophagy on
the Northwest Coast of North America and its
Culture-Historical Sources." *Journal de la
Société des Américanistes de Paris* 25:335–
366, 1933.

————.
"The Sun Dials and other time-Ronte Recorders of the Northern Woodlands and the Northwest Coast." *AA* 32:577–578, 1930. n.s.

MacMurray, Major J. W.
"The Dreamers of the Columbia River Valley
in Washington Territory." A revised Manuscript copy, with notes and other additions of
an article originally read before the Albany
Institute, January 19, 1886, and published in
the *Transaction of the Albany Institute,* 11:
240–248, 1887 (Albany, N. Y.).

Park, Willard Z.
"Shamanism in Western North America."
Northwestern Studies in the Social Sciences 2.
(Evanston, Ill.), 1938. 116 pp.

Sarat, Chandra Nitra
"The Bear in Asiatic and American Ritual."
Journal of the Asiatic Society of Bombay 7:467.

Seler, E.
"Die Lichtbringer bei den Indianerstämmen
der Nordwestküste." *Globus* 61:195–198, 212–
216, 230–235, 243–246, 1892.

Shelton, William
The Story of the Totem Pole. Everett, Washington: Kane and Harcus Company, 1923. 80 pp.,
illus.

Smith, H. I.
"Totem Poles of the North Pacific Coast."
American Museum Journal 11:77–82, 1911.

Spier, Leslie
"Tribal Distribution in Washington." *General
Series in Anthropology* 3:1–43, 1936.

Swanton, John R.
"Explanation of the Seattle Totem Pole."
JAFL 8:108–110, 1895.

Willoughby, Charles C.
"A New Type of Ceremonial Blanket of the
Northwest Coast." *AA* 12:1–11, 1910. n.s.

Young, Kimball, and Cutsforth, T. D.
"Hunting Superstitions in the Cow Creek
Region of Southern Oregon." *JAFL* 41:283–
297, 1928.

CUSTOMS

Adam, Leonard
Potlatch. In: *Festschrift Eduard Seler,* pp. 27–
45. Stuttgart: 1922.

Averkieva, U. P.
Rabstvo i plemen severo-zapadnovo pober-ezh'ia Sev. Ameriki." *Sovetskaia Etnografia* (Part 4) :40–61, 1935.
Slavery in Northwest coast Indian tribes.

Barnett, H. G.
"The Nature of the Potlatch." *AA* 40:349–358, 1938. n.s.
"The great winter ceremonials among the tribes of the North Pacific coast from Oregon to Alaska. . . . Although varying considerably in different parts of the coast these potlaches were mainly marked . . . by the giving away of quantities of goods . . ."

———.
"Facial Paintings of the Indians of Northern British Columbia." *Memoir of the American Museum of Natural History* (New York) 2:13–24, 1900.

Cressman, L. S.
"Aboriginal Burials in Southwestern Oregon." *AA* 35:116–130, 1933. n.s.

Dall, W. H.
"On Masks, Labrets and Certain Aboriginal Customs." *3rd Annual Report, Bureau of American Ethnology*, pp. 106–120, 1884. Washington, D. C.

Dixon, Roland B.
"Tobacco Chewing on the Northwest Coast." *AA* 35:146–150, 1933. n.s.

Drucker, P.
"Rank, Wealth and Kinship in Northwest Coast Society." *AA* 41:55–65, Jan., 1939.

Halliday, W. M.
Potlatch and Totem and the Recollection of an Indian Agent. London: Dent and Company, 1935. 240 pp.

Hill-Tout, Charles
"Communal Houses in British Columbia." *American Antiquarian* 24:107, 1902.

———.
"Curious and Interesting Marriage Customs of Some of the Aboriginal Tribes of British Columbia." *American Antiquity* 24:85–87, 1902.

Kroeber, A. L.
"Salt, Dogs, Tobacco." *Anthro. Rec. Amer. Mus. Nat. Hist.* 6:1–20, 1941.

———.
"Stepdaughter Marriage." *AA* 42:562–570, 1940. n.s.

Large, R. W.
"Mortuary Customs in British Columbia." *Annual Archaeological Report*, pp. 100–101, 1904. Toronto, 1905.

MacLeod, W. C.
"Certain Mortuary Aspects of Northwest Coast Culture." *AA* 27:122–148, 1925. n.s.

———.
"Marriage, Divorce and Illegitimacy in a Primitive Pecuniary Culture." *Social Forces* (Chapel Hill) 5:109–117, 1926.

———.
"Mortuary and Sacrificial Anthropophagy of the Northwest Coast." *Journ. Société Amér.* 25:335–366, 1933. n.s.

———.
"The Origin of Servile Labor Groups." *AA* 31: 89–113, 1929. n.s.

———.
"Some Social Aspects of Aboriginal American Slavery." *Journ. Société Amér.* 19:123–128, 1927. n.s.

Reagan, A. B.
"Whaling of the Olympic Peninsules Indians of Washington." *Natural History* 25:25–32, 1945.

Rickard, T. A.
"The Use of Iron and Copper by the Indians of British Columbia." *British Columbia Historical Quarterly* 3:25–50, 1939.

Smith, De Cost
"Jean François Millet's Drawings of American Indians." *Century Magazine* (New York) 80: 78–84, 1910.
These paintings of Indian and frontier life were inspired by Bodmer, the Swiss artist who had been in America among the Indians of the Canadian Northwest.

Smith, S. B.
"Primitive Customs and Beliefs of the Indians of the Pacific Northwest Coast." *Oregon Historical Quarterly* 2:255–265, 1901.

Stanner, W. E. H.
"Aboriginal Modes of Address and Reference in the Northwest of the Northern Territory." *Oceania* 7 (No. 3):300–315, 1937.

Swanton, John R.
"The Development of the Clan System and of the Secret Societies among the Northwestern Tribes." *AA* 6:477–486, 1904. n.s.

FOLK MEDICINE

Darby, George E.
"Indian Medicine in British Columbia." *Canadian Medical Association Journal* 28, No. 4: 433–438, 1933.

Reagan, Albert B.
"Various Uses of Plants by West Coast Indians." *Wash. Hist. Quart.* 25:133–137, 1934.

FOLK ART—SPEECH

Adam, Leonard
Nordwest-Amerikanische Indianerkunst. Berlin: E. Wasmuth, 1923. 44 pp.

———.
"North-West American Indian Art and Its Early Chinese Parallels." *Man* 36:8–11, 1936.

Boas, Franz
"A Bronze Figurine from British Columbia." *Bulletin of the Amer. Mus. of Nat. Hist.* 14: 51–52, 1901.

―――――.
"Classification of the Languages of the North Pacific Coast." *Memoirs of the International Congress of Anthropology* 1:339–346, 1894.

―――――.
"Comparative Vocabulary of Eighteen Languages Spoken in British Columbia." *Report of the 60th Meeting of the British Association for the Advancement of Science*, Vol. I, pp. 339–346, 1894.

―――――.
"Facial Paintings of the Indians of Northern British Columbia." *Memoir of the American Museum of Natural History* 2:13–24, 1900.

―――――.
"The Decorative Art of the Indians of the North Pacific Coast." *Bulletin of the American Museum of Natural History* (New York) 9: 123–176, 1897. Illus.

―――――.
Primitive Art. Oslo: Aschehoug & Co., 1927. (pp. 183–298).

―――――.
"Die Verbreitung der Indianer-Sprachen in British Columbien." *Petermanns Mitteilungen aus Justus Perthes Geographischer Anstalt* (Gotha) 42:21, 1896.

―――――, and Haeberlin, H. K.
"Sound Shifts in Salishan Dialects." *Intern. Journ. of Amer. Ling.* 4:117–136, 1927.

Cressman, Luther
"Contributions to the Archaeology of Oregon; Final Report on the Gold Hill Burial Site." *University of Oregon Studies in Anthropology*, Vol. 1, Bulletin 1, pp. 1–24. Oregon: 1933.

―――――.
Petroglyphs of Oregon. University of Oregon Monographs, Studies in Anthropology, No. 2. 78 pp., 1937.

Deans, James
"Antiquities of British Columbia." *American Antiquarian* vol. 14:41–44, 1892.

Douglas, F. H.
"Main Types of Basketry in Washington and Northwestern Oregon." *Denver Art Museum, Indian Leaflet Series* 98:190–192, 1940.

Eells, M.
"Aboriginal Geographic Names in the State of Washington." *AA* 5:27–35, 1892.

Emmons, George T.
"The Art of the Northwest Coast Indians." *Natural History* 30:282–292, 1930.

―――――.
"Jade in British Columbia and Alaska." *Indian Notes and Monographs* (Ser. 2) 35:11–53, 1923.

―――――.
"Portraiture Among the North Pacific Coast Tribes." *AA* 16:59–68, 1914. n.s.

Ernst, Alice Henson
"Masks of the Northwest Coast." *Theatre Arts Monthly* 646–656, August, 1933.

Farrand, Livingston
"Basketry Designs of the Salish Indians." *Memoirs of the American Museum of Natural History* (New York) 1:393–399, 1900. Illus.

Gatschet, A. S.
"Indian Languages of the Pacific States." *Magazine of American History* 1:145–171, 1877.

―――――.
"Indian Languages of the Pacific States and Territories." *Magazine of American History* 8: 254–263, 1882.

Gibbs, G.
Vocabularies of Indian Languages of Northwest California. In: *Information Respecting the History, Condition, and Prospects of the Indian Tribes of the United States.* Henry Rowe Schoolcraft, ed., Vol. 3, pp. 428–445. Philadelphia: 1853.

Goddard, Pliny Earle
"Wayside Shrines in Northwestern California." *AA* 15:702–703, 1913. n.s.

Grasserie, R. de la
"Renseignements sur les noms de parenté dans plusieurs langues américaine." *Journ. de la Société des Amér.* 2:333–338, 1905. n.s.
    On kinship terms among many tribes—mainly those of the Northwest.

Haeberlin, H. K.
"Principles of Esthetic Form in the Art of the North Pacific Coast." *AA* 20:258–264, 1918. n.s.

―――――.
"Types of Reduplication in the Salish Dialects." *Int. Jour. of Amer. Ling.* 1:154–174, 1918.

―――――, Teit, J. A., Roberts, H. H. (directed by Franz Boas)
"Coiled Basketry in British Columbia and Surrounding Region." *41st Annual Report, Bureau of American Ethnology*, 1919–1924. pp. 131–483, 94 pls., 122 figs., 1 map. Washington, D. C.: U. S. Government Printing Office, 1928.

Howay, F. W.
"The Dog's Hair Blankets of the Coast Salish." *Wash. Histor. Quart.* 9:83–92, 1918.

―――――.
"The Early Literature of the Northwest Coast." *Proc. and Trans. of the Royal Soc. of Can.* (Ser. 3) 18 (Part 2):1–31, 1924.

Inverarity, Robert Bruce
Movable Masks and Figures of the North Pacific Coast Indians. Introduction by Erna Gunther. Bloomfield Hills, Mich.: Cranbook Institute of Science, 1941. 4 pp., 18 col. pl.

Jacobs, M.
"Historic Perspectives in Indian Languages of Oregon and Washington." *Pacific Northwest Quarterly*, pp. 55–74, 1937.

Jochelson, Waldemar
"Past and Present Subterranean Dwellings of the Tribes of North Eastern Asia and North Western America." *Proc. Intern. Congr. Amer.* 15 (Part 2) :115–128, 1907.

Kissell, M. L.
"Organized Salish Blanket Pattern." *AA* 31: 85–88, 1929. n.s.

Krickeberg, W.
"Malereien auf ledernen Zeremonialkleidern der Nordwest-amerikaner." *Ipek*, pp. 140–150, 1925.
Paintings on leather ceremonial clothes.

Krieger, H. W.
"Some Aspects of Northwest Coast Indian Art." *Scientific Monthly* 23:211–219, 1926.

Kroeber, A. L.
"Athabascan Kin Term Systems." *AA* 39:602– 609, 1937. n.s.

Latham, R. G.
"On the Languages of the Oregon Territory." *Journal of the Ethnol. Soc.* 1:154–166, 1848.

Meany, E. S.
Origin of Washington Geographic Names. Seattle: University of Washington Press, 1923. 357 pp.

Olson, R. L.
"Adze, Canoe, and House Types of the North- west Coast." *Univ. Wash. Publ. Anthro.* 2:1– 38, 1927.

Pilling, J. C.
"Bibliography of the Salishan Languages." *Bureau of American Ethnology, Bulletin* 16, pp. 1–86, 1893. (Washington, D. C.)

Smith, D. A., and Spier, Leslie
"The Dot and Circle Design in Northwestern America." *Journ. Société Amér.* 19:47–55, 1927. n.s.

Smith, H. I.
"Archaeological Investigations on the North Pacific Coast." *AA* 2:563–567, 1900. n.s.

———.
"Kitchen-Middens of the Pacific Coast of Canada." *Bulletins of the Canada Department of Mines* (Ottawa) 56:42–46, 1929.

———.
"Noteworthy Archaeological Specimens from the Lower Columbia Valley." *AA* 8:298–307, 1906. n.s.

———.
"Recent Archaeological Discoveries in North- Western America." *Bulletin of the American Geographical Society* 38:287–295, 1906.

———.
"Stone Hammers or Pestles of the Northwest Coast." *AA* 1:363–368, 1899. n.s.

Steward, Julian H.
"A New Type of Carving from Columbia Val- ley." *AA* 29:255–261, 1927. n.s.

Waterman, T. T.
"Native Houses of Western North America." *Indian Notes and Monographs* (Ser. 2) 11:1– 97, 1921.

———.
"Some Conundrums in Northwest Coast Art." *AA* 25:435–451, 1923. n.s.

———, and Coffin, G.
"Types of Canoes of Puget Sound." *Indian Notes and Monographs* 5:1–43, 1920. n.s.

———, and Greiner, R.
"Indian Houses of Puget Sound." *Indian Notes and Monographs* 9:7–59, 1921. n.s.

Willoughby, C. C.
"A New Type of Ceremonial Blanket from the Northwest Coast." *AA* 12:1–10, 1910. n.s.

MUSIC

GENERAL STUDIES

Barbeau, Charles Marius
"Songs of the Northwest." *MQ* 19:101–111, 1933.

———.
"The Siberian Origin of Our Northwestern Indians." *Pacific Science Congress, 5th, Vic- toria and Vancouver, B. C., 1933. Proceedings.* Vol. 4, pp. 2777–2789.
Contains music of native songs.

Casual
"Music of the Vancouver Indians." *Music* 4: 490–491, 1893.
Discussion only, without the music.

Davis, C. B.
Songs of the Totem. Juneau, Alaska: Box 516, The Compiler, 1939.

Densmore, Frances
"Music of the Indians of British Columbia." *Anthropological Papers* 27:1–100 in *Anthro- pological Papers Nos. 27–32, Bulletin 136, Bureau of American Ethnology*, 359 pp., pls., index. Washington, D. C.: U. S. Government Printing Office, 1943.

Edgerly, Beatrice
From the Hunter's Bow. The History and Romance of Musical Instruments. New York: G. P. Putnam's Sons, 1942.
Chapter VII: Indians of America. C: Northwest.

Galpin, F. W.
"The Whistles and Reed Instruments of the Northwest Coast." *Proceedings of the Musical Association* 29:115–138, 1903.

Herzog, George
Appendix: Songs. In: *Folk Tales of the Coast Salish*, T. Adamson. Memoirs of the American Folklore Society 27, pp. 422–430, 1934.

Niblack, Albert P.
Singing Drums, Rattles and Whistles. In: *The Coast Indians of Southern Alaska and Northern British Columbia*, Part 7. Report of the National Museum, 1888. Washington, D. C.: U. S. Government Printing Office, 1888.

Swan, James G.
Music of the Indians of the Northwest Coast. In: *The Northwest Coast; or, Three Year's Residence in Washington Territory*, pp. 200. New York: Harper and Bros., 1857.

DANCES

Ernst, Alice Henson
"Northwest Coast Animal Dances." *Theatre Arts Monthly* 23:661–672, (Sept.) 1939.

Laguna, Frederick de
"Indian Masks from the Lower Yukon." *AA* 38:569–585, 1936.
Indian dances.

Spier, Leslie
"The Prophet Dance of the Northwest and its Derivatives; The Dance one of the Ghost Dance." *General Series in Anthropology, No. 1.* Menasha, Wisconsin: George Banta Publishing Co., 1935.

ARRANGEMENTS

Orchestra

Along the Columbia River-Suite.
Saar, Louis V.: MS: Orchestra.

Suite on Northwest Indian Songs and Dances.
McKay, George F.: MS: Orchestra.

RECORDS

Abraham, Otto, and Hornbostel, Erich M. von
Phonographierte Indianer—Melodien aus Britisch Columbia. In: *Boas Anniversary Volume.* pp. 447–474, New York: G. E. Stechert and Co., 1906.

Herzog, George
Northwest Coast Area: Records Contained in American Collections. American Council of Learned Societies, (Washington, D. C.) Bulletin 24:25–26, 1936.

U. S. Library of Congress. Division of Music. Folklore Section.
Indian Recordings—Songs and Dances. A large collection representing many regions, tribes, and areas. AAFS–LC

ALSEA

FOLKLORE

GENERAL STUDIES

Barnett, H. G.
"Oregon Coast." *Anthropol. Records* 1:155–204, 1937.

Drucker, P.
"Contributions to Alsea Ethnography." *Univ. Cal. Publ. Amer. Arch. and Ethnol.* 35:81–102, 1939.

Farrand, Livingston
"Notes on the Alsea Indians." *AA* 3:239–248, 1900. n.s.

MYTHS—FOLKTALES—LEGENDS

Frachtenberg, Leo J.
Alsea Texts and Myths. Bulletin 67. Bureau of American Ethnology. Washington, D. C.: U. S. Government Printing Office, 1920. 304 pp.

"Myths of the Alsea Indians." *Inter. Journ. Amer. Ling.* 1:64–75, 1917.

BELLA BELLA

FOLKLORE

See: Kwakiutl, pp. 1097–99.

GENERAL STUDIES

Adam, L.
"Stammesorganisation und Häuptlingstum der Wakashstämme." *Zeitschrift für Vergleichende Rechtswissenschaft* (Stuttgart) 35:105–158, 1918.

Boas, Franz
"First General Report on the Indians of British Columbia." *Report of the 59th Meeting of the British Association for the Advancement of Science*, pp. 801–900, 1889.

"The Social Organization of the Tribes of the North Pacific Coast." *AA* 26:323–332, 1924. n.s.

Swanton, John R.
"Bellabella." In: *Handbook of American Indians.* Bureau of American Ethnology, Bulletin 30, (Part 1), pp. 140–141. Washington, D. C.: U. S. Gov't Printing Office, 1907.

MYTHS—FOLKTALES—LEGENDS

Boas, Franz
Bella Bella Tales. Memoirs of the American Folklore Society, vol. 25. New York: G. E. Stechert and Co., 1932. xiii, 178 pp.
Tales of Creation, Raven Tales, Mink Tales, Ancestor Tales, etc., etc.

——————.
Bella Bella Texts. New York: Columbia University Press, 1928. ix, 291 pp. Columbia University contributions to Anthropology. Vol. V.

——————.
"Sagen aus Britisch-Columbien." *Verhandlungen der Berliner Gesellschaft für Anthropologie, Ethnologie und Urgeschichte* (Berlin), pp. 444–477, 1893.

Farrand, L.
"Myths of the Bellabella." In: *31st Annual Report of the Bureau of American Ethnology,* pp. 883–888. Washington, D. C.: U. S. Gov't Printing Office, 1916.

SPEECH

Gibbs, G.
"Vocabulary of the Ha-ilt'-zukh." *Contributions to North American Ethnology.... Department of Interior* (Washington, D. C.) 1:144–150, 1877.
 Heiltsuk—"a dialect of Kwakiutl embracing the Bellabella (after whose name it is called), the China Hat, Somehulitk, Nohunitk, and Wikeno."

Tolmie, W. F., and Dawson, G. M.
Comparative Vocabularies of the Indian Tribes of British Columbia. Montreal: Dawson Bros. 1884.

BELLA COOLA

FOLKLORE

GENERAL STUDIES

Boas, Franz
"The Bilqula." *Report of the 61st Meeting of the British Association for the Advancement of Science,* pp. 408–424, 1891.

——————.
"The Bi'lxula." *Reports of the U. S. National Museum,* pp. 645–651, 1895.

——————.
"Mitteilungen uber die Vilxûla-Indianer." *Original Mitteilungen aus der Ethnologischen Abteilung der Königlichen Museum* (Berlin), 1:177–182, 1886.

——————.
The Social Organization of the Tribes of the North Pacific Coast. In: *Race, Language and Culture,* by Franz Boas, (pp. 370–378). New York: The Macmillan Company, 1940.

——————.
"Zur Anthropologie der nord-amerikanischen Indianer." *Verhandlungen der Berliner Gesellschaft für Anthropologie, Ethnologie, und Urgeschichte* (Berlin), pp. 367–411, 1895.

Swanton, John R.
"Bellacoola." In: *Handbook of American Indians.* Bureau of American Ethnology, Bulletin 30 (Part 1), pp. 141. Washington, D. C.: U. S. Gov't Printing Office, 1907.

Virchow, Rudolph
"Die anthropologische Untersuchung der Bella-Coola." *Verhandlungen der Berliner Gesellschaft für Anthropol., Ethnol., und Urgeschichte,* pp. 206–215, 1886.

MYTHS—FOLKTALES—LEGENDS

Boas, Franz
"Mythology of the Bella Coola Indians." *Anthropological Papers of the American Museum of Natural History,* 2:25–127, 1898.

——————.
"Sagen Aus Britisch-Columbien." *Verhandlungen der Berliner Gesellschaft für Anthropologie, Ethnologie, und Urgeschichte* (Berlin), pp. 281–306, 1894; 189–195, 1895.

——————.
"Salishan Texts." *Proc. Amer. Philo. Soc.* 34: 31–48, 1895.

Jacobsen, J. A.
"Bella-Coola Sagen." *Ausland* 65:437–441, 1892.
 Folk tales.

BELIEFS—WITCHCRAFT

Goeken
"Das religiöse Leben der Bella Coola Indianer."*Original Mitteilungen aus der Ethnologischen Abtheilung der Königlichen Museen,* 1:183–186, 1886.

Jacobsen, J. A.
"Geheimbünde der Küstenbewohner Nordwest-America's." *Verhandlungen der Berliner Gesellschaft für Anthropologie, Ethnologie, und Urgeschichte,* pp. 383–395, 1891.
 Secret societies of the Northwest coast Indians.

——————.
"Der Kosiyut-Bund der Bella-Coola-Indianer." *Ausland* 65:437–441, 1890.

McIlwraith, T. F.
"Certain Beliefs of the Bella Coola Indians Concerning Animals." *Annual Archaeological Report* (Ontario, Toronto), pp. 17–27, 1924–1925.

Smith, H. I.
"Sympathetic Magic and Witchcraft among the Bella Coola." *AA* 27:116–121, 1914.

FOLK MEDICINE—CUSTOMS

Smith, H. I.
"Entomology Among the Bellacoola and Carrier Indians." *AA* 27:436–440, 1925. n.s.

——————.
"Materia Medica of the Bella Coola and Neighboring Tribes of British Columbia." *Bulletin* 56:47–69, 1929. National Museum of Canada.

FOLK ART—SPEECH

Boas, Franz
"The Language of the Bilhoola in British Columbia." *Science* (ser. 1) 7:218, 1886.

————.
"Sprache der Bella-Coola Indianer." *Verhandlungen der Berliner Gesellschaft für Anthropologie, Ethnologie, und Urgeschichte (Berlin)*, pp. 202–206, 1886.

————.
"Terms of Relationship of the Salish Languages." *Report of the 60th Meeting of the British Association for the Advancement of Science*, pp. 688–692, 1890.

————.
"The Use of Masks and Head Ornaments on the North-West Coast." *Internationales Archiv für Ethnographie* (Leiden) 3:7–15, 1890.

Gibbs, G.
"Vocabulary of the Belhoola." *Contributions to North American Ethnology . . . Department of Interior* (Washington, D. C.), Vol. I, pp. 267–283, 1877.

Tolmie, W. F., and Dawson, G. M.
Comparative Vocabularies of the Indian Tribes of British Columbia. Montreal: Dawson Bros. 1884.

DANCE

Jacobsen, F.
"Sissauch-dansen." *Ymer* 15:1–23, 1895.

CHEHALIS

FOLKLORE

GENERAL STUDIES

Barnett, H. G.
"The Coast Salish of Canada." *AA* 40:118–141, 1938 n.s.

Eells, M.
"The Indians of Puget Sound." *American Antiquarian* 8:40–41; 9:1–9, 97–104, 211–219, 271–276; 10:26–36, 174–178, 1886–1888.

Gibbs, George
"Report on the Indian Tribes of the Territory of Washington." *Reports of Explorations and Surveys* Vol. I, pp. 428–433, 1855.

————.
"Tribes of Western Washington and Northwestern Oregon." *Geological Survey, Rocky Mountain Region, Contributions to American Ethnology* 1 (part 2):213. Washington, D. C.: U. S. Government Printing Office, 1887.

Hill-Tout, Charles
"Report on the Sts Eélis and Sk'aúlits Tribes of the HalkomélEm Division of the Salish of British Columbia." *Journal of Anthropological Institute of Great Britain and Ireland*, 34:311–376, 1905.
Cowichan tribes living along the middle course of Harrison River, British Columbia. Article also includes a discussion and description of dances.

————.
"The Salish Tribes of the Coast and Lower Fraser Delta." *Annual Archaeological Report, Ontario, 1905*, pp. 225–235. Toronto: 1906.

Lee, Daniel, and Frost, J. H.
Ten Years in Oregon. New York: J. Collord, 1844. 344 pp.

Swan, James G.
The Northwest Coast; or, Three Years Residence in Washington Territory. New York: Harper & Bros., 1857. xiv, 435 pp., illus.

MYTHS—FOLKTALES—LEGENDS

Adamson, Thelma, ed.
Folk-Tales of the Coast Salish. Memoirs of the American Folklore Society, Vol. 28. Lancaster, Pa.: The Folklore Society, 1934. 350 pp.

Boas, Franz
"A Chehalis Text." *International Journal of American Linguistics* 8 (No. 2):103–110, 1934.

————.
"Zur Mythologie der Indianer von Washington und Oregon." *Globus* 63:154–157, 172–175, 190–193, 1893.

Hoffman, Walter James
Selish Myths. Salem, Mass., 1884. 20 pp.

Palmer, Katherine E.
Honne, the Spirit of the Chehalis; the Indian Interpretation of the origin of the People and Animals—as narrated by George Saunders. Geneva, N. Y.: Press of W. F. Humphrey, 1925. 204 pp., illus.

BELIEFS

Barbeau, Marius
Totem Poles of the Gitskan, Upper Skeena River, British Columbia. National Museum of Canada, 209 pp., ill. n.d.

Haeberlin, H. K.
"Sbetedaq, A Shamanistic Performance of the Coast Salish." *AA* 20:249–257, 1907.

SPEECH

Hill-Tout, Charles
"Some Features of the Language and Customs of the Salish." *AA* 7:674–688, 1905. n.s.

Tolmie, W. F., and Dawson, G. M.
Comparative Vocabularies of the Indian Tribes of British Columbia. Montreal: Dawson Bros. 1884.

CHINOOK

FOLKLORE

GENERAL STUDIES

Boas, Franz
Chinook Texts. Bureau of American Ethnology, Bulletin 20, pp. 1–278, 1 pl. Washington, D. C.: U. S. Gov't Printing Office, 1895.

————.
Kathlamet Texts. Bureau of American Ethnology, Bull. 26, pp. 1–261, 1 pl. Washington, D. C.: U. S. Gov't Printing Office, 1901.
"A Chinookan tribe formerly residing on the south bank of Columbia River near its mouth, in Oregon."

Corney, P.
Voyages in the Northern Pacific. Honolulu: T. G. Thrum, 1896. x, 138 pp.

Coues, Elliott, ed.
Manuscript Journals of Alexander Henry and David Thompson. New York: 1897. 3 vols.

Cox, Ross
Adventures on the Columbia River. London: H. Colburn and R. Bentley, 1831. 2 vols.

Dunn, John
History of the Oregon Territory and British North American Fur Trade. London: Edwards & Hughes, 1846. viii, 359 pp.

Emmons, George T.
Replies to Inquiries Respecting the Indian Tribes of Oregon and Washington. In: *Information Respecting the History, Condition, and Prospects of the Indian Tribes of the United States.* Henry Rowe Schoolcraft, ed. Vol. 3, pp. 200–225. Philadelphia: 1853.

Farrand, Livingston
"Chinookian Family." In: *Bureau of American Ethnology, Bulletin 30* (Part 1):273–274, 1907. (Washington, D. C.)

Gass, Patrick
Journal of the Voyages and Travels of a Corps of Discovery, Under Command of Lewis and Clarke. Pittsburgh: 1807. iv, 381 pp.

Gibbs, George
"Report on the Indian Tribes of the Territory of Washington." *Reports of Explorations and Surveys . . .* 1:402–436, 1855.

————.
"Tribes of Western Washington and Northwestern Oregon." *U. S. Geologic Survey,* Rocky Mountain Region. Contributions to American Ethnology 1 (part 2):213 pp. Washington, D. C.: U. S. Government Printing Office, 1887.

Jacobs, Melville
"Texts in Chinook Jargon." *University of Washington Publications in Anthropology* 7, (No. 1):1–120. Seattle, Wash., 1936.

Kane, Paul
"The Chinook Indians." *Canadian Journal* (Toronto) 3:273–279, 1855.

McInnes, T. R. E.
Chinook Days. Nine drawings by J. H. Smith. Vancouver: Sun Publishing Company, 1926. 206 pp., illus.

Meany, E. S., ed.
"Diary of Dr. W. F. Tolmie." *Washington Historical Quarterly* 23:205–227, 1931.

Palmer, J.
Journal of Travels Over the Rocky Mountains to the Columbia River. Cincinnati: J. A. and U. P. James, 1847. iv, 189 pp.

Ray, Verne F.
Lower Chinook Ethnographic Notes. In: *University of Washington Publications in Anthropology* 7, (No. 2):137 pp., illus. Seattle: University of Washington Press, 1938.

————.
"The Historical Position of the Lower Chinook in the Native Culture of the Northwest." *Pacific Northwest Quarterly* 28, (No. 4):363–372, 1937.

Rollins, P. A., ed.
The Discovery of the Oregon Trail. New York: Charles Scribner's Sons, 1935.

Ross, A.
Adventures of the First Settlers on the Oregon or Columbia River. London: Smith, Elder and Co., 1849. xv, 352 pp.

Spence, L.
"Chinooks." *Encyclopedia of Religion and Ethics.* J. Hastings, ed. Vol. 3, pp. 560–563. New York: 1911.

Strong, T. N.
Cathlamet on the Columbia. Portland, Or.: The Holly Press, 1906. 119 pp.

Swan, James G.
The Northwest Coast. New York: Harper & Bros., 1857. xiv, 435 pp.

Thomas, Edward H.
Chinook, A History and Dictionary. Portland, Oregon: Metropolitan Press, 1925. 179 pp.

Thwaites, R. G., ed.
Original Journals of the Lewis and Clark Expedition. Cleveland: The A. H. Clark Co., 1904–1905. 7 vols.

Townsend, J. K.
Narrative of a Journey Across the Rocky Mountains to the Columbia River. Philadelphia: H. Perkins 1839. viii, 352 pp.

Victor, Frances Fuller
The Early Indian Wars of Oregon. Salem: F. C. Baker Company, 1894. 719 pp.

MYTHS—FOLKTALES—LEGENDS

"Chinook Mythology, Bibliographical."
JAFL 18:115, 1905.

Boas, Franz
"Zur Mythologie der Indianer von Washington und Oregon." *Globus* 63:154–157, 172–175, 190–193, 1893.

Colbert, Mildred
Kutkos. Chinook Tyee. Boston: D. C. Heath and Company, 1943.
A story for young readers based on the myths and legends of the Chinook Indians.

Lyman, W. D.
"Myths and Superstitions of the Oregon Indians." *Proceedings of the American Antiquarian Society* 16:221–251, 1904. n.s.

Sapir, Edward
"Preliminary Report on the Language and Mythology of the Upper Chinook." *AA* 9:533–545, 1907. n.s.

BELIEFS—CUSTOMS

Anon.
"Customs Among the Oregon Indians." *American Penny Magazine* 1:63, 1845.
Burial ceremony among the Chinook tribe.

Boas, Franz
"Doctrine of Souls and Disease among the Chinook Indians." *JAFL* 6:39–43, 1893.

Gatschet, A. S.
"Medicine Arrows of the Oregon Indians." *JAFL* 6:111–112, 1893.

SPEECH

Boas, Franz
"Notes on the Chinook Language." *AA* 6:55–63, 1893.

————.
"The Vocabulary of the Chinook Language." *AA* 6:118–148, 1904. n.s.

Frachtenberg, L. J.
"Comparative Studies in Takelman, Kalapuyan and Chinookan Lexicography." *Intern. Journ. Amer. Ling.* 1:175–182, 1918.

Gibbs, George
Alphabetical Vocabulary of the Chinook Language. New York: Cramoisy Press, 1863. viii, 23 pp.

————.
A Dictionary of the Chinook Jargon. New York: Cramoisy Press, 1863. xiv, 43 pp.

Grant, Rena V.
"Alphonse Pinart and the Chinook Jargon." *CFQ* 5:277–297, 1946.

————.
"Chinook Jargon." *International Journal of Linguistics* 11:225–233, 1946.

————.
"The Chinook Jargons, Past and Present." *CFQ* 3:259–276, 1944.

Jacobs, Melville
"Notes on the Structure of Chinook Jargon." *Language* 8:27–50, 1932.

Leechman, Douglas
"The Chinook Jargon." *AS* 1 (No. 10):531–534, 1926.

Phillips, Walter Shelley
The Chinook Book; a descriptive analysis of the Chinook jargon in plain words, giving instructions for pronunciation, construction, expression and proper speaking of Chinook with all the various shaded meanings of the words. Seattle: R. L. Davis Printing Co., 1913. 118 pp.

Pilling, J. C.
"Bibliography of the Chinookian Languages." *Bureau of American Ethnology, Bulletin 15,* pp. 1–81, 1893. (Washington, D. C.)

Sapir, E.
"A Chinookian Phonetic Law." *Inter. Journ. Amer. Ling.* 4:105–110, 1927.

Swanton, John R.
"Morphology of the Chinook Verb." *AA* 2:199–237, 1900. n.s.

Thomas, Edward Harper
"The Chinook Jargon." *AS* 2 (No. 9):377–384, 1927.

MUSIC

GENERAL STUDIES

Boas, Franz
"Chinook Songs." *JAFL* 1:220–226, 1888.

ARRANGEMENTS

"Deer Dance."
Skilton, C. S.: Carl Fischer.: Piano.

"Deer Dance."
In: *Suite Primeval*, by Charles S. Skilton. Skilton, C. S.: Carl Fischer: Full orchestra.

"Gambling Song."
In: *Suite Primeval*, Part II, by Charles S. Skilton. Skilton, C. S.: Carl Fischer: Full orchestra.

COMOX

FOLKLORE

SPECIAL STUDIES

Barnett, H. G.
"The Coast Salish of Canada." *AA* 40:118–141, 1938. n.s.

————.
"Gulf of Georgia Salish." *Anthro. Records* 1:221–295, 1939.

Hill-Tout, Charles
"Notes on the Sk-qo'mic of British Columbia."
70th Meeting of British Association for Advancement of Science, pp. 472–549, 1900.

——.
"Report on the Ethnology of the Síciatl of British Columbia." *Journ. Anthro. Inst. Gt. Brit.* 34:20–91, 1904.

MYTHS

Boas, Franz
"The Mythologies of the Indians." *International Quarterly* 12:157–173, 1905.

——.
"Myths and Legends of the Çatloltq of Vancouver Island." *Amer. Antiq.* 10:201–211, 366–373, 1888.

——.
"Sagen aus Britisch-Columbien." *Verhandl. Berl. Gesel. Anthro. Ethnol. Ur.,* pp. 639–643, 1891; 32–66, 1892.

Hill-Tout, Charles
"Notes on the Cosmogony and History of the Squamish Indians." *Proc. Trans. Royal Soc. Can.* Ser. 2, 3 (Part 2) :85–90, 1897.

SPEECH

Boas, Franz
"Terms of Relationship of the Salish Language." *60th Meeting of British Assoc. for Advancement of Science,* pp. 688–692, 1890.

Gibbs, George
"Vocabulary of the Ko-mookhs." *Contr. North Amer. Ethnol.* 1:269–283, 1877.

Tolmie, W. F., and Dawson, G. M.
Comparative Vocabularies of the Indian Tribes of British Columbia. Montreal: Dawson Bros. 1884.

MUSIC

GENERAL STUDIES

Sapir, Edward
"Songs for a Comox Dancing Mask." *Ethnos* 4 (Part 2) :49–55, 1939.

COOS

FOLKLORE

GENERAL STUDIES

Barnett, H. G.
"Oregon Coast." *Anthropol. Records* 1:155–204, 1937.

Dorsey, J. O.
"Gentile System of the Siletz Tribes." *JAFL* 3:227–237, 1890.

Farrand, Livingston
"Kusan Family." In: *Handbook of American Indians.* Bureau of American Ethnology, Bulletin 30 (Part 1) :737, 1922. Washington, D. C.

Frachtenberg, L. J.
"Coos." *Bureau of American Ethnology, Bulletin 40* (Part 2) :279–430, 1922. (Washington, D. C.)

Gatschet, A. S.
"Volk und Sprache der Máklaks." *Globus* 35: 167–171, 187–189, 1879.
    The Maklaks—character of the people and its language.

St. Clair, H. H., and Frachtenberg, L. J.
"Traditions of the Coos Indians." *JAFL* 22: 25–41, 1909.

MYTHS—FOLKTALES—LEGENDS

Frachtenberg, Leo J.
Coos Texts. Columbia University Contributions to Anthropology 1. New York: Columbia University Press, 1913.

——.
Lower Umqua Texts and Notes on the Kusan Dialects. Columbia University Contributions to Anthropology, No. 4. New York: Columbia University Press, 1914. 156 pp.

Jacobs, Melville
"Coos Myth Texts." *Univ. Wash. Publ. Anthro.* 8, (No. 2) :127–260. Seattle: University of Washington Press, 1940.

——.
"Coos Narrative and Ethnologic Texts." *Univ. Wash. Publ. Anthro.* 8:1–125, 1939.

COWICHAN

FOLKLORE

GENERAL STUDIES

Barnett, H. G.
"The Coast Salish of Canada." *AA* 40:118–141, 1938. n.s.

——.
"Gulf of Georgia Salish." *Anthro. Records* 1: 221–295, 1939.

Boas, Franz
"The Indian Tribes of the Lower Fraser River." *64th Meeting of the British Association for the Advancement of Science,* pp. 454–463, 1894.

——.
"Notes on the Snanaimuq." *AA* 2:231–328, 1889.

Crosby, T.
Among the An-ko-me-nums. Toronto: W. Briggs, 1907. vii, 243 pp.

Grant, W. C.
"Description of Vancouver Island." *Journ. Royal Geogr. Soc.* 27:268–320, 1857.

Harris, Martha D.
History and Folklore of the Cowichan Indians. Cover and illustrations by Maclure, Margaret. Victoria, B. C.: The Colonist Printing and Publishing Company, 1901. 89 pp., illus.

Hill-Tout, Charles
"Ethnological Report of the Sts Eélis and Sk.aúlits Tribes of the HalkomélEm Division of the Salish." *Journ. Royal Anthro. Inst. Gt. Brit.* 34:311–376, 1904.

——.
"Ethnological Studies of the Mainland Halko-mélem." *72nd Meeting of the British Association for the Advancement of Science*, pp. 355–490, 1902.

——.
"The Salish Tribes of the Coast and Lower Fraser Delta." *Annual Arch. Report* (Ontario) 1905. pp. 225–235.

Weber, E. R. C.
"An Old Kwanthum Village." *Amer. Antiq.* 21:309–314, 1899.

Wilson, E. F.
"Report on the Indian Tribes." *Trans. Ethnol. Soc.* 4:275–292, 1866. n.s.

MYTHS—FOLKTALES

Boas, Franz
"Sagen aus Britisch Columbien." *Verhandl. Berl. Gesel. Anthro. Ethno. Ur.*, pp. 546–576, 628–638, 1891.

Teit, James A.
"Tales from the Lower Frazer River." *Memoirs of the American Folklore Society*, No. 11, pp. 129–134. New York: Folklore Society, 1917.

FOLK ART—SPEECH

Gibbs, G., Tolmie, W. F., and Mengarini, G.
"Comparative Vocabularies." *Contr. to North Amer. Ethnol.* 1:268–283, 1877.

Kissell, M. L.
"A New Type of Spinning in North America." *AA* 18:264–270, 1916. n.s.

Orchard, W. C.
"Technique of the Salish Blanket." *Leaflets of the Museum of the Amer. Indian*, 5:7–15, 1926.

HAIDA

FOLKLORE

GENERAL STUDIES

Anon.
"Die Haida-Indianer." *Ausland* 57:792–797, 1884.

Bastian, A.
"Die Haidas." *Verhandlungen der Berliner Gesellschaft für Anthropologie, Ethnologie und Urgeschichte*, pp. 278–298, 1882.

Boas, Franz
"Haida." *Report of the 59th Meeting of the British Association for the Advancement of Science*, pp. 867–877, 1889.

——.
"The Social Organization of the Haida." *Report of the 68th Meeting of the British Association for the Advancement of Science.* pp. 648–654, 1899.

Campbell, J.
"The Origin of the Haidas." *Proc. Trans. Royal Soc. Can.* (Ser. 2), 3(Part 2):91–112, 1897.

Chamberlain, Alexander F.
"Haida." In: *Encyclopedia of Religion and Ethics*, J. Hastings, ed., Vol. 6, pp. 469–474. New York: 1914.

Dawson, G. M.
"The Haidas." *Harper's Monthly Magazine* 65:401–408, 1882.

Harrison, Rev. Charles
Ancient Warriors of the North Pacific: the Haidas, their customs, laws and legends, with some historical account of the Queen Charlotte Islands. London: H. F. and G. Witherby, 1925. ii, 222 pp., front, pl. fold. map.

Krause, Aurel
Die Tlinkit-Indianer. Jena: H. Constable, 1885. xvi, 420 pp., illus.

Leighton, Margaret W.
"The Haida Indians." *Overland Monthly* (San Francisco) 37:1083–1086, 1901.

Murdock, George Peter
"Kinship and Social Organization among the Haida." *AA* 36:355–385, 1934. n. s.

Newcombe, C. F.
"The Haida Indians." *Proceedings of the 15th Session of the International Congress of Americanists* (Quebec) pp. 135–149, 1906. Vol. 1.

Swan, James G.
"The Haidah Indians of Queen Charlotte's Islands." *Smithsonian Institution Contributions to Knowledge* (Washington, D. C.) 21(Part 4):1–15, 1874.

Swanton, John Reed
"Contributions to the Ethnology of the Haida." *Publications of the Jesup North Pacific Expedition, V, part 1.* Leiden: E. J. Brill, Ltd. New York: G. E. Stechert, 1905. 300 pp.

——.
"Haida." In: *Handbook of American Indians.* Bureau of American Ethnology, Bulletin 30 (Part 1):520–523, 1907. (Washington, D. C.).

"Haida Texts, Masset Dialect." *Publications of the Jesup North Pacific Expedition, X.* Leiden: E. J. Brill, Ltd. New York: G. E. Stechert and Co., 1908, 812 pp. (American Museum of Natural History).

"Social Organizations of the Haida." *Proceedings of the 13th International Congress of Americanists* pp. 327–335, 1902.

Tribes of North America, with Synonymy. Skittagetan family. Bureau of American Ethnology Smithsonian Institution. Washington, D. C.: U. S. Government Printing Office, 1890.

MYTHS—FOLKTALES—LEGENDS

Boas, Franz
"Sagen aus Britisch-Columbien." *Verhandlungen der Berliner Gesellschaft für Anthropologie, Ethnologie, und Urgeschichte,* pp. 217–222, 1895.
Folktales.

Bouche, L'Abbé Pierre
"Contes Nagos." *Melusine,* Vol. II, 1884–5.
"A town of the Hagi-lanas family of the Haida on an inlet on the S.W. coast of Moresby Island, Queen Charlotte Islands, British Columbia."

Deans, James
"Legend of the Finn-back Whale Crest of the Haidas." *JAFL* 5:43–47, 1892.

"Story of the Bear and his Indian Wife." *JAFL* 2:255–260, 1889.

Tales from the Totems of the Hidery. Edited by O. L. Triggs. Chicago: 1899. 96 pp., illus. (International Folk-Lore Association, Archives, vol. 2).

"What Befell the Slave Seekers." *JAFL* 1:123–124, 1888.

Griffin, George H.
Legends of the Evergreen Coast. Vancouver: Clark & Stuart Co., Ltd., 1934. 141 pp., illus.

Hill-Tout, C.
"Haida Stories and Beliefs." *Report of the 68th Meeting of the British Association for the Advancement of Science,* pp. 700–708, 1898.

Jacobsen, J. A.
"Die Sintflutsage bei den Haida-Indianer." *Ausland* 65:170–172, 184–188, 1892.
Tale of the flood.

Swanton, John R.
Haida Texts and Myths. Bureau of American Ethnology, Bull. 29, pp. 1–448, 5 figs. Washington, D. C.: U. S. Gov't. Printing Office, 1905.

"Types of Haida and Tlingit Myths." *AA* 7:94–104, 1905, n. s.

BELIEFS—CUSTOM

Adam, L.
"Stammesorganisation und Häuptlingstum der Haida und Tsimshian." *Zeitsch. für Vergleich. Rechsts.* 30:161–268, 1913.
On tribal organization and chiefs.

Boas, Franz
"Tattooing Among the Indians of British Columbia." *Trans. N. Y. Acad. Sci.* 8:115–116, 1888.

"The Social Organization of the Haida." *68 Meeting Brit. Assoc. Adv. Sci.* 648–654, 1899.

Deans, James
"Carved Columns or Totem Posts of the Haidas." *Amer. Antiq.* 13:282–287, 1891.

"Hidery Prayers." *Amer. Antiq.* 22:31–32, 1900.

"The Huida-kwul-ra or Native Tobacco of the Queen Charlotte Haidas." *Amer. Antiq.* 12:48–50, 1890.

"Inside View of a Huidah Dwelling." *Amer. Antiq.* 9:309–310, 1887.

"The Moon Symbol on the Totem Posts on the Northwest Coast." *Amer. Antiq.* 13:341–346, 1891.

"On the Copper Images of the Haidah Tribes." *Proceedings of the Numismatic and Antiquarian Society of Philadelphia,* pp. 14–17, 1885.

"A Strange Way of Preserving Peace Amongst Neighbors." *Amer. Antiq.* 10:42–43, 1888.

"Totem Posts at the World's Fair." *Amer. Antiq.* 15:281–286, 1893.

"When Potlatches Are Observed." *Amer. Antiq.* 18:329–331, 1896.

Durlach, Theresa M.
"The Relationship Systems of the Tlingit, Haida, and Tsimshian." *Publications of the American Ethnological Society of New York* 11:1–177, 1928.

Harrison, Charles
"Family Life of the Haidas." *Journal of the Royal Anthropol. Institute of Great Britain and Ireland* 21:470–476, 1892.

"Religion and family among the Haidas." *Journal of the Royal Anthropol. Institute of Great Britain and Ireland* 21:14–29, 1892.

Hill-Tout, C.

"Haida Stories and Beliefs." *Report of the 68th Meeting of the British Association for the Advancement of Science.* pp. 700–708, 1898.

Murdock, George Peter

Rank and Potlatch Among the Haida. Yale University Publications in Anthropology no. 13. New Haven: Yale University Press, 1936.

Nieuwenhuis, A. W.

"The Differences Between the Conception of Soul (animus) and of Spirit (spiritus) among the American Indians." *Proc. Inter. Congr. Amer.* 21(Part 1):125–139, 1927.

Swanton, John R.

"The Haida Calendar." *AA* 5:331–385, 1903 n.s.

————.
"A Haida Food Plant." *AA* 15:543–544, 1913. n.s.

Tylor, E. B.

"Note on the Haida Totem-Post Lately Erected in the Pitt Rivers Museum." *Man* 2:1–3, 1902.

————.
"On the Totem-Post from the Haida Village of Masset." *Journal Royal Anthropol. Institute of Great Britain and Ireland* 28:133–135, 1899.

Watkins, Frances E.

"Potlatches and a Haida Potlatch Hat." *Masterkey* (Los Angeles: Southwest Museum) 13, no. 1:11–17, 1939.

FOLK ART—SPEECH

Balfour, H.

"Haida Portrait Mask." *Man* 7:1–2, 1907.

Beasley, H. G.

"A Memorial Figure of a Haida Shaman." *Man* 35:113, August 1935.

Boas, Franz

"Vocabularies from the Northwest Coast of America." *Publ. Amer. Sociol. Soc.* 26:200–202, 1916. n. s.

————.
"Vocabularies of the Tlingit, Haida and Tsimshian Languages." *Proc. Amer. Philo. Soc.* 29:183–193, 1891.

Emmons, G. T.

" 'Wings' of Haida Ceremonial Canoes." *Indian Notes* 5:298–302, 1928.

Hamy, M. E. T.

"Sculptures Haida." *Proc. Intern. Congr. Amer.* 12:109–114, 1900.

Harrison, Charles

"Haida Grammar." *Proceedings and Transactions of the Royal Society of Canada,* 2 (Part 1) 128, 1895.

Hoffman, W. J.

"Die Kunst Unter den Haida-Indianer." *Ausland* 58:701–704, 1885.
Haida art.

————.
"Remarks on Aboriginal Art in California and Queen Charlotte Island." *Proceedings of the Davenport Academy of Sciences,* 4:105–122, 1886.

Krieger, H. W.

"Archaeological and Ethnological Studies in Southeast Alaska." *Smithsonian Miscellaneous Collections* (Washington, D. C.) 78(Part 7): 174–187, 1927.

————.
"Some Aspects of the Northwest Coast Indian Art." *Scientific Monthly* 23:211–219, 1926.

Orchard, W. C.

"A Chilkat Blanket and a Haida 'Copper'." *Indian Notes* 4:33–40, 1927.

Ridgeway, W.

"Note on the Motives Carved on some Haida Totem Spoons and Pipes." *Man* (London), 1906, pp. 145–148.

Swanton, John R.

"Notes on the Haida Language." *AA* 4:392–403, 1902. n. s.

Waterman, T. T.

"Observations Among the Ancient Indian Monuments of Southeastern Alaska." *Smithsonian Institution Miscel. Coll.* 74(Part 5): 115–133, 1925 (Washington, D. C.).

MUSIC

GENERAL STUDIES

Deans, James

"A Weird Mourning Song of the Haidas." *Amer. Antiquarian* 13:52–54, 1891.
Without the music.

Swanton, John R.

Haida Songs. Reprinted from Publications of the American Ethnological Society, Vol. 3. New York: G. E. Stechert and Company, 1910. 63 pp.
Texts only, English translation.

KALAPUYA

FOLKLORE

GENERAL STUDIES

Farrand, Livingston

"Kalapooian Family." In: *Handbook of American Indians.* Bureau of American Ethnology, Bulletin 30(Part 1):645–646, 1907. (Washington, D. C.).

Frachtenberg, L. J.

"Ethnological Researches among the Kalapuya Indians." *Smithson. Inst. Misc. Coll.* 65 (Part 6):85–89, 1916.

Gatschet, A. S.

"The Kalapuya People." *JAFL* 12:212–214, 1899.

"Oregonian Folk-Lore." *JAFL* 4:139–143, 1891.

Gibbs, George
"Tribes of Western Washington and North-western Oregon." *U. S. Geological Survey, Rocky Mountain Region Contributions to American Ethnology* 1 (pt. 2) 213. Washington, D. C.: U. S. Government Printing Office, 1887.

Jacobs, Melville
"Texts in Chinook Jargon." *Univ. Wash. Publ. Anthro.* 7:14–19, 1936.

————, **Frachtenberg, L. J., and Gatschet, A. S.**
Kalapuya Texts. Seattle: University of Washington Press, 1945.
Part I: Santiam Kalapuya Ethnologic Texts by Jacobs, Melville; Part II: Santiam Kalapuya Myth Texts by Melville Jacobs; Part III: Kalapuya Texts by L. J. Frachtenberg, A. S. Gatschet, and Melville Jacobs.

SPEECH

Frachtenberg, L. J.
"Comparative Studies in Takelman Kalapuyan and Chinookan Lexicography." *Inter. Journ. Amer. Ling.* 1:175–182, 1918.

Gatschet, A. S.
"Adjectives of Color in Indian Languages." *Amer. Nat.* 13:475–485, 1879.

DANCE

De Angullo, J. A.
"Atfalati Dance-Song in Parts." *AA* 31:496–498, 1929, n. s.
A divison of the Kalapooian family.

KLALLAM
(*Including:* Lumi, Nootsak, and Songish)
FOLKLORE
GENERAL STUDIES

Boas, Franz
"The Lkúngen." *60th Meeting of British Association for the Advancement of Science* (London). pp. 563–582, 1890.
A Salish tribe, called Songish, about Victoria, Vancouver, and on the west shore of San Juan.

"The Lkúngen." *Rep. U. S. Nat. Mus.* pp. 644–646, 1895.

Eells, M.
"The Indians of Puget Sound." *Amer. Antiq.* 8:40–41; 9:1–9, 97–104, 211–219, 271–276; 10:26–36, 174–178, 1886–1888.

Ten Years of Missionary Work Among the Indians at Skokomish. Boston: Congregational Sunday-School and Publishing Society, 1886. x, 271 pp.

"The Twana, Chemakum, and Klallam Indians." *Ann. Rep. Regents Smithson. Inst.,* 1887, pp. 605–681.

Gunther, Erna
"Klallam Ethnography." *Univ. Wash. Publ. Anthro.* (Seattle) 1:171–314, 1927.

Hill-Tout, Charles
"Report on the Ethnology of the South-Eastern Tribes of Vancouver Island." *Journ. Anthro. Inst. Gt. Brit.* 37:306–374, 1907.

Reagan, A. B.
"Some Notes on the Lumminooksack Indians." *Trans. Kansas Acad. Sci.* 30:429–437, 1921.

Stern, Bernhard J.
The Lummi Indians of Northwest Washington. Columbia University Contributions to Anthropology 17. New York: Columbia University Press, 1934. 127 pp., illus.

MYTHS—FOLKTALES—LEGENDS

Boas, Franz
"Sagen aus Britisch Columbien." *Verhandl. Berl. Gesel. Anthro. Ethnol. Ur.,* pp. 643–645, 1891.

Eells, M.
"Myths of the Puget Sound Indians." *Amer. Antiq.* 12:160–165, 1890.

Gunther, Erna
"Klallam Folk Tales." *Univ. Wash. Publ. Anthro.* 1:113–169, 1925.

BELIEFS—CUSTOMS

Douglas, F. H.
"Puget Sound Indian Houses." *Denver Art Mus. Ind. Leaflet Series* 34:1–3, 1931.

Eells, M.
"The Religion of the Clallam and Twana Indians." *Amer. Antiq.* 2:8–14, 1879.

"The Religion of the Indians of Puget Sound." *Amer. Antiq.* 12:69–84, 1890.

Reagan, Albert B.
"Some Notes on the Occult and Hypnotic Ceremonies of Indians." *Proceedings of the Utah Academy of Sciences, Arts and Letters* 11:65–71, 1934.

FOLK ART—SPEECH

Gibbs, George
Alphabetical Vocabularies of the Clallam and Lummi. New York: Clamoisy Press, 1863. vii, 40 pp.

Smith, Harlan I.
"Archaeology of the Gulf of Georgia and Puget Sound." *Memoirs Amer. Museum Nat. Hist.* 2:301–441, 1907. illus.

"The Cairns or Stone Sepulchres of British Columbia and Washington." *Records of the Past* (Washington, D. C.) 3:243–254, 1904.

————, **and Fowke, G.**
"Cairns of British Columbia and Washington." *Memoirs Amer. Mus. Nat. Hist.* 4(Part 1): 55–75, 1901.

Tolmie, W. F., and Dawson, G. M.
Comparative Vocabularies of the Indian Tribes of British Columbia. Montreal: Dawson Bros. 1884.

MUSIC
GENERAL STUDIES

Eells, M.
"Indian Music." *Amer. Antiq.* 6:35–38, 1884.

KWAKIUTL
FOLKLORE
GENERAL STUDIES

Barrett-Lennard, C. E.
Travels in British Columbia. London: Hurst & Blackett, 1862. xii, 307 pp.

Benedict, Ruth
Patterns of Culture. An Analysis of Our Social Structure as Related to Primitive Civilizations. New York: Penguin Books, 1946. 272 pp. Reprint.
  Chapt. VI—The Northwest Coast of America. Life, lore and customs of the Kwakiutls.

Boas, Franz
Contributions to the Ethnology of the Kwakiutl. Columbia University Contributions to Anthropology, Vol. 3. New York: Columbia University Press, 1925. 357 pp.

"Der Einfluss der Sozialen Gliederung der Kwakiutl auf deren Kultur." *Proceedings of the 14th Session of the International Congress of Americanists,* pp. 141–148, 1904, 1906.

"The Indians of British Columbia." *Proc. Trans. Royal Soc. Can.,* ser. 1, 6(Part 2): 47–57, 1889.

"The Indians of British Columbia." *Journ. Amer. Geog. Soc.* 28:229–243, 1896.

"Kwakiutl." *Bureau of American Ethnology, Bulletin* 40(Part 1):423–558, 1911.

"The Kwakiutl." *60th Meeting British Association for the Advancement of Science,* pp. 604–632, 655–658, 1890.

"The Kwakiutl of Vancouver Island." *Memoir Amer. Mus. Nat. Hist.* 5:301–522, 1909. illus.

"Notes on the Kwakiutl." *66th Meeting, British Association for the Advancement of Science,* pp. 569–580, 1896.

The Social Organization of the Kwakiutl In: *Race, Language, and Culture,* by Franz Boas (pp. 356–369), reprint. 1920. New York: The Macmillan Company, 1940. Reprinted from *AA* 22:111–126, 1920. n.s.

————, **and Hunt, George**
"Ethnology of the Kwakiutl." *35th Annual Report of the Bureau of American Ethnology.* Smithsonian Institution. Part I pp. 43–794; Part II pp. 795–1473. Washington, D. C.: U. S. Government Printing Office, 1921.

Kwakiutl Texts. Memoirs of the American Museum of Natural History vol. V. Jesup North Pacific Expedition. New York: The Museum of Natural History, 1902. 270 pp.

Kwakiutl Texts-Second Series. Publications of the Jesup North Pacific Expedition, vol. X, part I. 1906. 269 pp. New York.

Dawson, G. M.
"Notes and Observations on the Kwakiool People." *Proc. Trans. Royal Soc. Can.* 5(Part 2):63–98, 1888.

Ford, Clellan S.
Smoke from Their Fires; The Life of a Kwakiutl Chief. New Haven: Yale University Press, 1941. 248 pp., illus.

Hayward, V.
"The Indians of Alert Bay." *Canadian Magazine* 51:371–382, 1918.

Henshaw, Henry W.
"Kwakiool Indians." *AA* 1:184–186, 1888. n. s.

Jenness, Diamond
"Fading Scenes on Quatsino Inlet." *Canadian Geographical Journal* 8, (no. 2):88–97, 1934.

Shotridge, L., and F.
"Indians of the Northwest." *Museum Journal* 4:71–99, 1913.

MYTHS—FOLKTALES—LEGENDS

Bayliss, C. K.
"A Kwakiutl Fragment." *JAFL* 22:335, 1909.

Boas, Franz
Kwakiutl Culture as Reflected in Mythology.
Memoirs of the American Folklore Society,
No. 28. Philadelphia: American Folklore
Society, 1935. 190 pp.

Kwakiutl Tales. Columbia University Contributions to Anthropology, vol. 2. New York:
Columbia University Press, 1910. 496 pp.

Kwakiutl Tales. New Series. New York: Columbia University Press, 1936. Vol. 26.

"Sagen aus Britisch-Columbien." *Verhandl.
Berl. Gesel. Anthro. Ethno. Ur.,* pp. 383–410,
1892; 228–265, 430–444, 1893.

"Tsimshian Mythology." *31st Annual Report,
Bureau of American Ethnology,* pp. 494–495,
1916.

Carmichael, A.
Indian Legends of Vancouver Island. Toronto:
The Musson Book Company, 1922. 97 pp.

Deans, J.
"The Thunder Bird." *Amer. Antiq.* 7:357–358,
1885.

Grant, Rena V.
"The Koni Killah. A Kwakiutl Tale." *JAFL*
59:194–196, 1946.

Hunt, George
"The Rival Chiefs; A Kwakiutl Story." *Anthropological Papers, Boas Anniversary Volume,*
pp. 108–137. New York: G. E. Stechert and
Company, 1906.

Leeson, B. W.
"A Quatsino Legend." *Canadian Geographical
Journal* 7, (no.1):23–39, July 1933.

"Wakashan Mythology."
JAFL 8:121–122, 1895.

BELIEFS—CUSTOMS

Boas, Franz
Die Ausdrücke für einige religiöse Begriffe
der Kwakiutl Indianer. In: *Festschrift Meinhof,*
pp. 386–392. Hamburg: 1927.
Religious expressions.

"Current Beliefs of the Kwakiutl Indians."
JAFL 45:177–277, 1932.

Die Entwicklung der Geheimbünde der Kwakiutl-Indianer. In: *Festschrift Adolph Bastian,*
pp. 435–444. Berlin, 1896.

The Growth of the Secret Societies of the
Kwakiutl. In: *Race, Language, and Culture,*
by Franz Boas, (pp. 379–383) reprint. 1896.
New York: The Macmillan Company, 1940.

The Houses of the Kwakiutl Indians. U. S.
National Museum. Washington, D. C.: U. S.
Government Printing Office, 1888.

The Religion of the Kwakiutl Indians. Columbia University Press, 1930. 2 vols. 284 pp.,
288 pp.

Religious Terminology of the Kwakiutl. In:
Race, Language and Culture, by Franz Boas.
(pp. 612–618) reprint. 1927. New York: The
Macmillan Company, 1940.

"The Social Organization and the Secret Societies of the Kwakiutl Indians." *The Annual
Report of the U. S. Natural Museum,* pp. 311–
738. Washington, D. C.: U. S. Government
Printing Office, 1895.

"The Use of Masks and Head Ornaments on
the North-West Coast." *Inter. Archiv. Ethno.*
3:7–15, 1890.

Dawson, G. M.
"Customs and Arts of the Kwakiool." *Popular
Science Monthly* 33:345–352, 1888.

Goldman, I.
The Kwakiutl Indians of Vancouver. In:
Cooperation and Competition Among Primitive Peoples, Margaret Mead, ed., pp. 180–
209. New York: McGraw-Hill, 1937. xii, 531
pp.

Hunt, George
The Rival Chiefs. In: *Boas Anniversary Volume,* pp. 108–136. New York: G. E. Stechert
and Company, 1906.

Jacobsen, J. A.
"Geheimbünde der Küstenbewohner Nordwest-
Amerika's." *Verhandl. Berl. Gesel. Anthro.
Ethno. Ur.,* pp. 383–395, 1891.

Lincoln, J. S.
The Dream in Primitive Cultures. London:
The Cresset Press, 1935. xii, 359 pp.

Lindblom, G.
"A Kwakiutl Totem Pole in Stockholm."
Ethnos 1:137–141, 1936.

Locher, G. W.
*The Serpent in Kwakiutl Religion; A Study in
Primitive Culture.* Leiden: E. G. Brill, Ltd.,
1932. 118 pp., illus.

Teall, G. C.
"The Salmon Wife." *Amer. Antiq.* 16:140–
142, 1894.

Wardle, H. N.
"Indian Gifts in Relation to Primitive Law."
Proc. Inter. Congr. Amer. 23:463–469, 1928.

FOLK ART—SPEECH

Boas, Franz
Geographical Names of the Kwakiutl Indians.
Columbia University Contributions to Anthropology, vol. 20. New York: Columbia University Press, 1934.

———.
Metaphorical Expression in the Language of the Kwakiutl Indians. In: *Race, Language and Culture*, pp. 232–239. New York: 1940.

———.
"Notes on Some Recent Changes in the Kwakiutl Language." *Inter. Journ. Amer. Ling.* 7: 90–93, 1932.

———.
"Notes on the Kwakiutl Vocabulary." *Inter. Journ. Amer. Ling.* 6:163–178, 1931.

———.
"Vocabulary of the Kwakiutl Language." *Proc. Amer. Philo. Soc.* 31:34–82, 1893.

Dawson, G. M.
"Customs and Arts of the Kwakiool." *Popular Science Monthly* 33:345–352, 1888.

Gibbs, George
"Vocabulary of the Kwa'kiutl." *Contributions to North American Ethnology* (Washington, D. C.) Vol. I, pp. 144–150, 1877.

Hall, A. J.
"A Grammar of the Kwagiutl Language." *Proc. Trans. Royal Soc. Can.* 6 (Part 2):59–105, 1888.

Hodge, F. W.
"Kwakiutl Sword." *Indian Notes* 1:200–204, 1924.

La Grasserie, R. de
Cinq Langues de la Colombie Brittannique.
Paris: J. Maisonneuve, 1902. 530 pp.

Pilling, J. C.
"Bibliography of the Wakashan Languages."
Bureau of American Ethnology, Bulletin 29, pp. 1–70, 1894.

Tolmie, W. F., and Dawson, G. M.
Comparative Vocabularies of the Indian Tribes of British Columbia. Montreal: Dawson Bros., 1884.

Zeh, L. E.
"Grotesque Indian Masks." *South. Workman* 41:473–477, 1912.

MUSIC

GENERAL STUDIES

Abraham, O., and Hornbostel, E. M.
Phonographirte indianer Melodien aus British Columbia. In: *Anthropological Papers, Boas Anniversary Volume*, pp. 447–475. New York: G. E. Stechert and Company, 1906.

Beckwith, M. W.
"Dance Forms of the Moqui and Kwakiutl Indians. Bibliography." *Proceedings of the 15th Session of the International Congress of Americanists* 2:79–111, 1906.

Boas, Franz
"On Certain Songs and Dances of the Kwakiutl." *JAFL* 1:49–64, 1888.

———.
"Songs of the Kwakiutl Indians." *Internationales Archiv für Ethnographie* 9:1–9, 1896. Leiden: E. J. Brill.

———.
"The Social Organization and the Secret Societies of the Kwakiutl Indians." *U. S. National Museum Report for 1895* (Washington, D. C.), pp. 311–738, 1897.
    Discussion of music, with examples, pp. 325–327, 412, 487, 587, 671, 686–733.

Fillmore, John Comfort
"A Woman's Song of the Kwakiutl Indians."
JAFL 6:285–290, 1893.

Salt, A. E. W.
"The Lost Song." *Cornhill Magazine* 141, (No. 893):545–549, (May) 1934.

DANCES

Beckwith, Martha Warren
"Dance Forms of the Moqui and Kwakiutl Indians." Bibliography. *Proceedings of the 15th Session of the International Congress of Americanists*, vol. 2:79–111, 1906.

Drucker, Philip
"Kwakiutl Dancing Societies." *Anthropological Records* 2 (No. 6):201–230. Berkeley: University of California Press, 1940.

NOOTKA

(*Including:* Makah)

FOLKLORE

GENERAL STUDIES

Barrett-Lennard, Charles E.
Travels in British Columbia, With the Narrative of a Yacht Voyage Round Vancouver Island. London: Hurst & Blackett, 1862. xii, 307 pp.

Boas, Franz
"The Nootka." *Bureau Amer. Ethnol. Bull. 40*, pp. 582–604, 668–679, 1911.

Brabant, A. J.
Vancouver Island and Its Missions. New York: Messenger of the Sacred Heart Press, 1900.

Cook, James
A Voyage to the Pacific Ocean. Philadelphia: J. Maxwell, 1818.

Culin, S.
"A Summer Trip Among Western Indians."
Bulletin of the Free Museum of Science and Arts, Univ. of Pennsylvania 3:143–152, 1901.

Giglioli, E. H.
"Appunti interno ad una collezione etnografica fatta durante il terzo viaggio di Cook." *Archivio per l'Antropologia e l'Etnologia* (Firenze) 23: 102–123, 1895.
Discussion of the ethnographic collection made during Cook's third journey to the Pacific Ocean.

Grant, W. C.
"Description of Vancouver Island." *Journ. Royal Geogr. Soc.* 27:268–320, 1857.

Gunther, Erna
A Preliminary Report on the Zoological Knowledge of the Makah. In: *Essays in Anthropology Presented to A. L. Kroeber,* pp. 105–118. Berkeley: University of California Press, 1936.

Hill-Tout, Charles
"Report on the Ethnology of the Southeastern Tribes of Vancouver Island, British Columbia." *Journal of the Royal Anthropological Institute of Great Britain and Ireland,* 37:306–374, 1908.

Jewitt, John Rodgers
A Journal Kept at Nootka Sound. Boston: C. E. Goodspeed & Co., 1931. xxiv, 91 pp.

————.
A Narrative of the Adventures and Sufferings of John R. Jewitt. Middletown, Conn.: S. Richards. 1815. 204 pp.

Koppert, Vincent A.
"Contributions to Clayoquot Ethnology." *Cath. Univ. Anthro. Ser.* 1:1–124, 1930.

Moser, Charles
Reminiscences of the West Coast of Vancouver Island. Victoria, B .C.: Acme Press, Ltd., 1926. 192 pp.

Mozino, José M.
Noticias de Nutka. Mexico: Impr. de la Secretaria de fomento, 1913. 117 pp.
A general ethnographic study.

Sapir, Edward A.
"Anthropological Division Report." *Summary Report of the Geological Survey.* British Department of Mines, 1910, Ottawa, 1911. pp. 284–285.
67 songs recorded on phonograph.

————.
"Life of a Nootka Indian." *Queen's Quarterly* 28:232–243, 351–367, 1921.

————.
"Some Aspects of Nootka Language and Culture." *AA* 13:15–29, 1911. n.s.

————.
"Vancouver Island Indians." *Encyclopedia of Religion and Ethics.* J. Hastings, ed. Vol. 12, pp. 591–595. New York: 1922.

————, and Swadesh, Morris, ed.
Nootka Texts; Tales and Ethnological Narratives, with Grammatical Notes and Lexical Materials. Philadelphia: Linguistic Society of America, University of Pennsylvania, 1939. 334 pp., illus.

Sproat, Gilbert M.
Scenes and Studies of Savage Life. London: Smith, Elder & Co., 1868. xii, 317 pp.

————.
"The West Coast Indians of Vancouver Island." *Trans. Ethnol. Soc.* 5:243–254, 1867. n.s.

Strange, James
Journal and Narrative of the Commercial Expedition from Bombay to the North-West Coast of America. Madras: Sup't. Gov't. Press, 1928. 63 pp.

Swan, J. G.
The Indians of Cape Flattery, at the Entrance to the Strait of Fuca, Washington Territory. Smithsonian Institution, Contribution to Knowledge. Vol. 16, 1868. Washington, D. C. 106 pp.

MYTHS—FOLKTALES—LEGENDS

Boas, Franz
"Sagen aus Britisch-Columbien." *Verhandl. Berl. Gesel. Anthro. Ethnol. Ur.,* pp. 314–344, 1892.

————.
"Tsimshian Mythology." *31st Annual Report Bureau Amer. Ethnol.,* pp. 888–935, 1916. Washington, D. C.

Carmichael, A.
Indian Legends of Vancouver Island. Illustrated by J. Semyn. Toronto: The Musson Book Company, 1922. 97 pp., incl. front illus.

Hunt, George
"Myths of the Nootka." *31st Annual Report of the Amer. Bureau of Ethnol.,* pp. 888–935, 1916.

Johnson, E. P. (Tekahionwake)
Legends of Vancouver. Vancouver, B. C.: G. S. Forsyth and Company, 1912. 2nd ed. x, 89 pp.

Sapir, Edward A.
"A Flood Legend of the Nootka Indian of Vancouver Island." *JAFL* 32:351–355, 1919.

————.
"The Rival Whalers, A Nitinat Story." *International Journal of American Linguistics* 3: 76–102.
NITINAT—"A Nootka tribe on a tidal lake of the same name, near the Southwest coast of Vancouver Island."

————, and Swadesh, Morris
Nootka Texts; Tales and Ethnological Narratives. Philadelphia: Linguistic Society of America, 1939. 334 pp.

Swadesh, Morris, and Swadesh, Mary Haas
"Nitinat Texts" (Nootka). *International Journal of American Linguistics* 7:195–208, 1933.

BELIEFS—CUSTOMS

Bushnell, D. I.
"Drawings by John Webster of Natives of the Northwest Coast." *Smithson. Miscel. Coll.* No. 80 (Part 10):1–12, 1928.

Densmore, Frances
"Conscious Effort Toward Physical Perfection Among the Makah Indians." *AA* 25:564–567, 1923. n.s.

Jacobsen, J. A.
"Geheimbünde der Küstenbewohner Nordwest-Amerika's." *Verhandl. Berl. Gesel. Anthro. Ethno. Ur.,* pp. 383–395, 1891.

Koppert, Vincent A.
"The Nootka Family." *Primitive Man* 3:49–55, 1930.

Sapir, Edward
"A Girl's Puberty Ceremony Among the Nootka Indians." *Proc. Trans. Royal Soc. Can.* Ser. 3, 7 (Part 2):67–80, 1913.

————.
Sayach'apis, A Nootka Trader. In: *American Indian Life,* Elsie Clews Parsons, ed., pp. 297–323. New York: B. W. Huebsch, 1925. 419 pp.

Waterman, T. T.
"The Whaling Equipment of the Makah Indians." *Univ. Wash. Publ. Anthro.* 1:1–67, 1920.

Wickersham, J.
"Pueblos of the Northwest Coast." *Amer. Antiq.* 18:21–24, 1896.

Willoughby, C. C.
"Hats from the Nootka Sound Region." *Amer. Natur.* 37:65–68, 1903.

FOLK ART—SPEECH

Boas, Franz
"Vocabularies from the Northwest Coast of America." *Proc. Amer. Antiq. Soc.* 26:186–200, 1916. n.s.

Deans, James
"Burial Mounds of Vancouver Islands." *American Antiquarian* 13:171–172, 1891.

Densmore, Frances
"The Language of the Makah Indians." *AS* 2 (No. 5):237, 1927.
"The southernmost tribe of the Wakashan stock, the only one within the United States. They belong to the Nootka branch."

Hodge. F. W.
"A Nootka Basketry Hat." *Indian Notes* 6:254–248, 1929.

Knipe, C.
Some Account of the Tahkant Language. London: 1868. Hatchard and Co., 80 pp.

La Grasserie, R. de
Cinq Langues de la Colombie Brittannique. Paris: J. Maisonneuve, 1902. 530 pp.

Pilling, J. C.
"Bibliography of the Wakashan Languages." *Bureau Amer. Ethnol. Bull. 19,* pp. 1–70, 1894.

Sapir, Edward
"Abnormal Types of Speech in Nootka." *Memoirs of the Canada Department of Mines, Geological Survey* (Ottawa) 62:1–21, 1915.

————.
"Nootka Baby Words." *Inter. Journ. Amer. Ling.* 5:118–119, 1929.

————.
"Some Aspects of Nootka Language and Culture." *AA* 13:15–28, 1911. n.s.

Thomas, C.
"On Certain Stone Images." *AA* 10:376–377, 1897.

Tolmie, W. F., and Dawson, G. M.
Comparative Vocabularies of the Indian Tribes of British Columbia. Montreal: Dawson Bros., 1884.

GAMES

Dorsey, G. A.
"Games of the Makah Indians of Neah Bay." *American Antiquity* 23:69–73, 1901.

MUSIC

GENERAL STUDIES

Densmore, Frances
"Field Studies of Indian Music." *Smithson. Miscel. Coll.* No. 76 (No. 10):119–127; 78 (Part 7):247–254, 1925–1927.

————.
Nootka and Quileute Music. Bureau of American Ethnology, Bulletin 124. Washington, D. C.: U. S. Government Printing Office, 1939.

Sapir, E.
"Anthropological Division. Report." *Summary Report, Geological Survey. British Department of Mines 1910;* Ottawa, 1911. pp. 284–285.
67 songs recorded on phonograph.

ARRANGEMENTS

"Huvakan the West Wind."
Loomis, H. W.: Birchard: SSA.

QUILEUTE
(Including: Hoh)

FOLKLORE

GENERAL STUDIES

Andrade, Manuel J.
"Quileute." In: *Handbook of American Indian Languages.* Franz Boas, ed. Vol. 3, pp. 151–292, New York: J. J. Augustin, 1933.

———.
Quileute Texts. Columbia Univ. Contributions to Anthropology. No. 12. New York: Columbia University Press, 1931. 211 pp.

Barnett, H. G.
Culture Element Distributions: VII Oregon Coast. *Anthropological Records, University of California,* No. 3:155–204. Berkeley: University of California Press, 1937.

Farrand, Livingston
"Quileute." In: *Handbook of American Indians.* Bureau Amer. Ethnol. Bull. 30 (Part 2):340–341, 1910.

Frachtenberg, L. J.
"Ethnological Researches in Oregon and Washington." *Smithson. Miscel. Coll.* 66 (Part 17):111–117, 1917.

Hobucket, H.
"Quillayute Indian Traditions." *Wash. Hist. Quart.* 25:49–59, 1934.

Reagan, Albert B.
"Traditions of the Hoh and Quillayute Indians." *Washington Historical Quarterly:* 20 (No. 3):178–189, 1929.

MYTHS—FOLKTALES—LEGENDS

Farrand, Livingston, and Mayer, T.
"Quileute Tales." *JAFL* 32:251–279, 1919.

Reagan, Albert B.
"Some Myths of the Hoh and Quillayute Indians." *Transactions, Kansas Academy of Science* 38:43–85, 1935.

———, **and Walters, L. V. M.**
"Tales from the Hoh and Quileute." *JAFL* 46:297–347, 1933.

BELIEFS—CUSTOMS

Frachtenberg, Leo J.
"The Ceremonial Societies of the Quileute Indians." *AA* 23:320–352, 1921. n.s.

———.
"Eschatology of the Quileute Indians." *AA* 22:330–340, 1920. n.s.

Reagan, Albert B.
"Hunting and Fishing of Various Tribes of Indians." *Trans. Kansas Acad. Sci.* 30:443–438, 1921.

———.
"Plants Used by the Hoh and Quillayute Indians." *Transactions, Kansas Academy of Science* 37: 55–70, 1934.
Hoh—a band of the Quileute.

———.
"Sketches of Indian Life and Character." *Trans. Kansas Acad. Sci.* 23:141–149, 1911.

———.
"Some Notes on the Occult and Hypnotic Ceremonies of Indians." *Proceedings of the Utah Academy of Sciences, Arts and Letters* 11:65–71, 1934.

———.
"Various Uses of Plants by West Coast Indians." *Wash. Hist. Quart.* 25:133–137, 1934.

———.
"Whaling of the Olympic Peninsula Indians." *Natural History* 25:25–32, 1925.

Swan, J. G.
"The Surf-Smelt of the Northwest Coast and the Method of Taking Them by the Quillehute Indians." *Proc. U. S. Nat. Mus.* 3:43–46, 1880.

SPEECH

Frachtenberg, L. J.
"Abnormal Types of Speech in Quileute." *Inter. Journ. Amer. Ling.* 1:295–299, 1920.

MUSIC

GENERAL STUDIES

Densmore, Frances
Nootka and Quileute Music. U. S. Bureau of Ethnology, Bulletin 124. Washington, D. C.: U. S. Government Printing Office, 1939. 358 pp., illus., music.
Besides valuable information on music and musical instruments, with numerous examples, there is also much on customs, beliefs, rituals, legends, dances, folk medicine, ethnobotany, and game songs.

QUINAULT

FOLKLORE

GENERAL STUDIES

Conard, L. M.
"A Visit to Quinault Indian Graves." *Open Court* 19:737–744, 1905.

Farrand, Livingston, and Kahnweiler, W. S.
"Traditions of the Quinault Indians." *Memoirs Amer. Mus. Natur. Hist.* 4:77–132, 1902.

Olson, Ronald
The Quinault Indians. Univ. of Washington Publications in Anthropology 6, n. 1. Seattle: Univ. of Washington Press, 1936. 190 pp., illus.

Willoughby, C.
"Indians of the Quinaielt Agency." *Ann. Reports Board Regents Smithson. Inst.,* pp. 267–283, 1886.

CUSTOMS—FOLK ART

Farrand, Livingston
"Basketry Designs of the Salish Indians." *Memoirs Amer. Mus. Natur. Hist.* 2:391–399, 1900.

Reagan, Albert B.
"Ancient Sites and Burial Grounds in the Vicinity of Queets." *El Palacio* 25:296–299, 1928.

SNUQUALMI

(*Including*: Dwamish, Nisqualli, Puyallup and Snohomish)

FOLKLORE

GENERAL STUDIES

Anderson, Eva Greenslit.
Chief Seattle. Caldwell, Idaho: The Caxton Printers, 1943. 390 pp.

Denny, Emily I.
Blazing the Way. Seattle: Ranier Printing Co., 1909. 503 pp.

Douglas, F. H. comp.
"The Puget Sound Indians." *Denver Art Museum, Leaflet 32*, Sept., 1931.

Eells, M.
"The Indians of Puget Sound." *Amer. Antiq.* 8:40–41; 9:1–9, 97–104, 211–219, 271–276; 10:26–36, 174–178, 1886–1888.

Haeberlin, H. K., and Gunther, E.
"The Indians of the Puget Sound." *University of Wash. Publications in Anthropolgy* 4:1–84, 1930.

———, **and Gunther, E.**
"Ethnographische Notizen über die Indianerstämme des Puget-Sundes." *Zeit. f. Ethno.* 56: 1–74, 1924.

Rakestraw, C. D.
"The Shaker Indian of Puget Sound." *Southern Workman* 29:703–709, 1900.

Smith, Marian Wesley
"The Coast Salish of Puget Sound." *AA* 43: 197–211, 1941. n.s.

———
The Puyallup. In: *Acculturation in Seven Indian Tribes*, Ralph Linton, editor. New York: D. Appleton-Century Co., 1940.

———
The Puyallup-Nisqually. Columbia Univ. Contributions to Anthropology. Vol. 32. New York: Columbia University Press, 1940.

MYTHS—FOLKTALES—LEGENDS

Adamson, Thelma
Folk-Tales of the Coast Salish. Memoirs of the American Folklore Society, No. 27, pp. 351–360. New York: G. E. Stechert Co., 1934.

Ballard, Arthur C.
"Mythology of Southern Puget Sound." *University of Washington Publications in Anthropology* 3:31–150, 1929.

———
"Some Tales of the Southern Puget Sound Salish." *University of Washington Publications in Anthropology* 2(No. 3):77–81, 1927.

Boas, Franz
"Zur Mythologie der Indianer von Washington und Oregon." *Globus* 63:154–157, 172–175, 190–193, 1893.

Calhoun, Francy
"Four Puget Sound Folktales." *JAFL* 59:40–44, 1946.

Codere, Helen
"The Swai'xwe Myth of the Middle Fraser River: The Integration of Two Northwest Coast Cultural Ideas." *JAFL* 61:1–17, 1948.
After presenting three versions of the myth, the author draws these conclusions: "Such analysis demonstrates that the crest idea which is a cultural idea emphasized in Kwakiutl and northern Northwest Coast and the power idea which is emphasized in Puyallup—Nisqually and southern Northwest Coast are integrally combined in the Middle Fraser River swai-xwe myth."

Haeberlin, H. K.
"Mythology of Puget Sound." *JAFL* 37:371–438, 1924.

Wickersham, J.
"Nusqually Mythology." *Overland Monthly* 32:345–351, 1898. n.s.

BELIEFS—CUSTOMS

Dorsey, G. A.
"The Dwamish Indian Spirit Boat and Its Use." *Bull. Free Museum Sci. and Arts* 3:227–238, 1902.

Eells, M.
"The Religion of the Indians of Puget Sound." *Amer. Antiq.* 12:69–84, 1890.

Haeberlin, H. K.
"SbEtStdáq, a Shamanistic Performance of the Coast Salish." *AA* 20:249–257, 1918. n.s.

Mooney, James
"The Ghost Dance Religion." *14th Annual Report Bureau Amer. Ethnol.* (Part 2):746–763, 1893.

Waterman, T. T.
"The Paraphernalia of the Duwamish 'Spirit-Canoe' Ceremony." *Indian Notes* 7:129–148, 295–312, 535–561, 1930.

———
"The Shake Religion of Puget Sound." *Ann. Reports Board Regents Smithson. Inst.*, 1922. pp. 499–507.

FOLK MEDICINE—SPEECH

Ballard, A. C.
"Southern Puget Sound Salish Kinship Terms." *AA* 48:111–116, 1935.

Buchanan, C. M.
"Some Medical Customs, Beliefs and Practices of the Snokomish Indians." *St. Louis Courier of Medicine* 21:277, 355, 1889.

Gibbs, George
"Dictionary of the Niskwalli." *Contr. North Amer. Ethnol.* 1:285–361, 1877.

Tolmie, W. F., and Dawson, G. M.
Comparative Vocabularies of the Indian Tribes of British Columbia. Montreal: Dawson Bros., 1884.

MUSIC

GENERAL STUDIES

Roberts, Helen H., and Haeberlin, H. K.
"Some Songs of the Puget Sound Salish." *JAFL* 31:496–520, 1918.

TAKELMA

FOLKLORE

GENERAL STUDIES

Dorsey, J. O.
"Gentile System of the Siletz Tribes." *JAFL* 3: 227–237, 1890.

Drucker, P.
"The Tolowa and Their Southwest Oregon Kin." *Univ. Cal. Publ. Amer. Arch. and Ethno.* 36:221–300, 1936.

Sapir, Edward
"Notes on the Takelma Indians." *AA* 9:251–275, 1907. n.s.

—————.
"Takelma." In: *Handbook of American Indians. Bureau Amer. Ethnol.* Bull. 30 (Part 2):673–674, 1910.

—————.
Takelma Texts. Univ. Penn. Museum Anthro. Publ. No. 2. Philadelphia: University of Pennsylvania Press, 1909. 267 pp.

—————.
"Upper Takelma." In: *Handbook of American Indians.* Bureau of American Ethnol., Bull. 30 (Part 2):872, 1910.

Spier, Leslie
"Tribal Distribution in Southwestern Oregon." *Oregon Historical Quarterly* 28:358–365, 1927.

BELIEFS—SPEECH

Frachtenberg, Leo J.
"Comparative Studies in Takelman, Kalapuyan and Chinookan Lexicography." *Inter. Journ. Amer. Ling.* 1:175–182, 1918.

Sapir, Edward
"Religious Ideas of the Takelma Indians." *JAFL* 20:33–49, 1907.

"The Takelma Language." *Bureau Amer. Ethnol. Bull. 40* (Part 2):1–296, 1922.

TILLAMOOK

FOLKLORE

GENERAL STUDIES

Barnett, H. G.
"Oregon Coast." *Anthropol. Records* 1:155–204, 1937.

Boas, Franz
"Notes on the Tillamook." *Univ. of Cal. Publications in American Archaelogy and Ethnology* 20:3–16, 1923. Berkeley: The University Press.

—————.
"Traditions of the Tillamook." *JAFL* 11:23–38, 133–150, 1898.

Dorsey, J. Owen
"Indians of the Siletz Reservation, Oregon." *AA* 2:55–63, 1889.

Edel, May M.
"Stability in Tillamook Folklore." *JAFL* 57: 116–128, 1944.
The Tillamook were a Salish-speaking people who lived on the coast of Oregon, south of the Chinook. There are few survivors today.

Gibbs, George
"Tribes of Western Washington and Northwestern Oregon." *U. S. Geological Survey, Rocky Mountain Region, Contributions to American Ethnology* 1 (Part 2):213. Washington, D. C.: U. S. Government Printing Office, 1887.

Lee, Daniel, and Frost, J. H.
Ten Years in Oregon. New York: J. Collord, 1844. 344 pp.

MYTHS—FOLKTALES—LEGENDS

Boas, Franz
"Zur Mythologie der Indianer von Washington und Oregon." *Globus* 63:154–157, 172–175, 190–193, 1893.

CUSTOMS—SPEECH

Dorsey, J. Owen
"The Gentile System of the Siletz Tribes." *JAFL* 3:227–237, 1890.

Edel, M. M.
"The Tillamook Language." *Inter. Journ. Amer. Ling.* 10:1–57, 1939.

Frachtenberg, Leo J.
"A Siletz Vocabulary." *Inter. Journ. Amer. Ling.* 1:45–46, 1917.

TLINGIT
(Kolosh)

FOLKLORE

GENERAL STUDIES

Boas, Franz
"Tlingit." *59th Meeting, British Association Advancement of Science,* pp. 856–867, 1889.

Bugbee, A. M.
"The Thlinkets of Alaska." *Overland Monthly* 22:185–196, 1893. n.s.

Chase, W. G.
"Notes from Alaska." *JAFL* 6:57–53, 1893.

Cross, J. F.
"Cape Prince of Wales and its People." *Southern Workman* 35:535–539, 1906.

Dall, William H.
Alaska and Its Resources. Boston: Lee & Shepard, 1870. xii, 627 pp., illus.

Dixon, G.
A Voyage Round thhe World. London: Geo. Goulding, 1789. xxix, 360 pp.

Dorsey, G. A.
"A Cruise Among Haida and Tlingit Villages." *Popular Science Monthly* 53:160–174, 1898.

Durlach, Theresa
"The Relationship Systems of the Tlingit, Haida, and Tsimshian." *Publications of The American Ethnological Society of New York* 11:1–177, 1928.

Erman, A.
"Ethnographische Wahrnemungen und Erfahrungen an den Küsten des Berings-Meeres." *Zeit.f.Ethno.* 2:295–327, 369–393; 3:149–159, 1870–1871.
Ethnographic observations and experiences on the Bering Sea coasts.

Fernhelm, H.
"Notes on the Natives of Alaska." *Contr. North Amer. Ethnol.* 1:111–116, 1877.

Garfield, Viola E.
"Historical Aspects of Tlingit Clans in Angoon, Alaska." *AA* 49:438–452, 1947. n.s.

Gatschet, A.
"Alaska und seine Bewohner." *Allen Weltt-heilen* 6:195–204, 1875.

Grinnell, G. B.
The Natives of the Alaska Coast Region. In: *Harriman Alaska Expedition* Vol 1, pp. 137–164, New York: Doubleday, Page & Co., 1901.

Henshaw, H. W., and Swanton, J. R.
"Tlingit." In: *Handbook of American Indians.* Bureau of American Ethnology, Bulletin 30 (Part 2):764–765, 1910.

Holmberg, H. J.
"Ethnographische Skizzen über die Völker des russischen Amerika." *Acta Societatis Scientarium Fennicae* (Helsingfors) 4:289–354, 1856.

Jackson, S.
Alaska and Missions on the North Pacific Coast. New York: Dodd, Mead & Co., 1880. ix, 327 pp.

Jones, Livingston F.
A Study of the Tlingit of Alaska. New York: Fleming H. Revell Company, 1914.

Keithahn, Edward L.
Monuments in Cedar. Ketchikan, Alaska: Roy Anderson, 1945. 160 pp.
"It contains a good deal of accurate and interesting information about the art, religion, customs, social organization, and oral literature of the Tlingit and Haida Indians." (H. V. Velten).

Knapp, Frances, and Childe, R. L.
The Thlinkets of Southeastern Alaska. Chicago: Stone & Kimball, 1896. vi, 197 pp.

Krieger, H. W.
"Indian Villages of Southeast Alaska." *Annual Reports Board of Regents Smithson. Inst.* 82 (Part 1):467–494, 1928.

Krause, Aurel
Die Tzlinkit-Indianer. Ergebnisse einer reise nach der nordwest-küste von Amerika nach der Beringstrasse, ausgeführt mit auftrage der Bremer geographischen Gesellschaft in den jahren 1880–1881 durch die doktoren Arthur und Aurel Krause. Jena: H. Constenoble, 1885. xvi, 420 pp., illus., 4 pl., fold. map, tables.
Description, incidents and customs of the Tlinkit.

Langsdorff, Georg H. von
Voyages and Travels in Various Parts of the World, During the Years 1803, 1804, 1805, 1806, and 1807. Parts I–II. London: 1813–14.

Lisiansky, Urey Feodorovich
Voyage Round the World in the Years 1803–1806. London: J. Booth, 1814. xxi, 388 pp.

Lutke, Feodor P.
Voyage Autour Du Monde. Parts I–III. Translated from Russian by F. Boyé. Paris: 1835–36.

Miner. L. R.
"With the Thlingets in Alaska." *South. Workman* 28:130–133, 218–220, 428–429, 1899.

Niblack, A. P.
"The Coast Indians of Southern Alaska and Northern British Columbia." *Reports U.S. National Museum* (Washington, D. C.), pp. 225–286, 1888–1890.

Pinart, A. L.
"Notes sur les Koloches." *Bull. Société d'Anthro.* (ser. 2)7:788–811, 1872.

Schwatka, F.
A Summer in Alaska. Philadelphia: I. Y. Huber & Co., 1891. 418 pp.

Shotridge, L.
"My Northland Revisited." *Museum Journ.* 8: 105–115, 1917.

————, and F.
"Indians of the Northwest." *Museum Journ.* 4:71–99, 1913.

Swanton, John R.
"Social Conditions, Beliefs, and Linguistic Relationship of the Tlingit Indians." *26th Annual Report, Bureau of American Ethnology*, 1904–1905, pp. 395–472, figs. 103–117. Washington, D. C.: U. S. Government Printing Office, 1908.

————.
"Tlingit." *Bureau of Amer. Ethnol. Bull. 40 (Part 2):* 159–204, 1911.

————.
"Tlingit." In: *Encyclopedia of Religion and Ethics.* J. Hastings, ed. Vol. 12, pp. 351–353. New York: 1922.

Thorne, James F.
In the Time That Was. Seattle: The Raven, 1909. 30 pp.

Wood, C. E. S.
"Among the Thlinkits in Alaska." *Century Magazine* 24:323–339, 1882.

MYTHS—FOLKTALES—LEGENDS

Boas, Franz
"Einige Mythen der Tlingit." *Zeit. Gesel.f.Erd.* 23:159–172, 1888.

————.
"The Mythologies of the Indians." *International Quarterly* 12:157–173, 1905.

————.
"Sagen aus British-Columbien." *Verhandl. Berl. Gesel. Anthro. Ethno. Ur.* 1895. pp. 222–234.

Golder, F. A.
"Tlingit Myths." *JAFL* 20:290–295, 1907.

BELIEFS—CUSTOMS

Adam, L.
"Stammesorganisation und Häuptlingstum der Tlinkitindianer Nordwestamerikas." *Zeit. f. Vergleich. Rechts.* 29:86–120, 1913.

Anon.
"Cremation Among the Sitka Indians." *Amer. Natur.* 11:372–374, 1877.

Corser, H. P.
"Intellectual Life of the Thlinket Indians." *Alaska-Yukon Magazine* 13:151–158, 1912.

Davidson, D. S.
"Family Hunting Territories in Northwestern North America." *Indian Notes and Monogr.* 46:5–34, 1928.

Emmons, George T.
"The Potlatch of the North Pacific Coast." *American Museum Journal* 10:229–234, (New York). 1910.

————.
"The Use of the Chilcat Blanket." *Journal of the American Museum* 8:65–72, 1908. New York.

————.
"The Whale House of the Chilkat." *Anthropol. Papers Amer Mus. Natur. Hist.* 19:1–36, 1916. illus.

"In the Land of Shakes; revival of potlatch feast among the Tlingit Indians of Southeastern Alaska." *Christian Science Monitor*, pp. 14, July 27, 1940.

Jones, Livingston F.
Indian Vengeance. Boston: The Stratford Co., 1920. 68 pp.

Oberg, K.
"Crime and Punishment in Tlingit Society." *AA* 36:145–156, 1934. n.s.

————.
"A Comparison of Three Systems of Primitive Economic Organizations." *AA* 45:572–587, 1943. n.s.

Olson, R. L.
Some Trading Customs of the Chilkat Tlingit. In: *Essays in Anthropology Presented to A. L. Kroeber*, (pp. 211–214). Berkeley: University of California Press, 1936.

Shotridge, F.
"The Life of a Chilkat Indian Girl." *Museum Journ.* 4:101–103, 1913.

————, L.
"The Bride of Tongas." *Museum Journ.* 20:131–156, 1929.
Tongas—a Tlingit tribe at the mouth of Portland Canal, Alaska.

————.
"The Emblems of the Tlingit Culture." *Museum Journ.* 19:350–377, 1928.

Swanton, John R.
"Explanation of the Seattle Totem Pole." *JAFL* 18:108–110, 1905.

FOLK ART—SPEECH

Boas, Franz
"Grammatical Notes on the Language of the Tlingit Indians." *Univ. Penn. Mus. Anthro. Publ.* 8:1–179, 1917.

————.
"Vocabularies of the Tlingit, Haida and Tsimshian Languages." *Proc. Amer. Philo. Soc.* 29: 174–183, 1891.

Douglas, F. H.
"A Tlinkit Stone Mortar." *Material Culture Notes* (Denver Art Museum) 8:31–33, 1938.

"Copper Neck-Rings of Southern Alaska." *AA* 10:644–649, 1908. n.s.

Emmons, George T.
"Basketry of the Tlingit." *Memoirs Amer. Museum Natur. Hist.* 1:229–277, 1903. illus.

———.
"The Chilkat Blanket." With notes on the blanket designs by Franz Boas. *Memoirs Amer. Museum Natur. Hist.* 3:329–401, 1907.

———.
"Native Account of the Meeting between La Perouse and the Tinglit." *AA* 13:294–298, 1911. n.s.

———.
"Petroglyphs in Southeastern Alaska." *AA* 10:221–230, 1908. n.s.

Gibbs, George, and Dall, W. H.
"Comparative Vocabularies." *Contr. North Amer. Ethnol.* 1:121–142, 1877.

Keithahn, E. L.
"The Petroglyphs of Southeastern Alaska." *Amer. Antiq.* 6:123–132, 1940.

Kissell, M. L.
"The Early Geometric Patterned Chilkat." *AA* 30:116–120, 1928. n.s.

Krieger, H. W.
"Some Aspects of the Northwest Coast Indian Art." *Scientific Monthly* 23:211–219, 1926.

Krusenstern, A. J. von
Wörter-Sammlungen aus den Sprachen einiger Völker des östlichen Asien und der Nordwest-Küste von Amerika. St. Petersburg, Druckerey der Admiralität, 1813. 69 pp.

La Grasserie, R. de
Cinq Langues d la Colombie Brittanique. Paris: J. Maisonneuve, 1902. 530 pp.

Meany, E. S.
"Attu and Yakutat Basketry." *Scientific Monthly* 10:211–219, 1903.

Orchard, W. C.
A Chilkat Blanket and a Haida "Copper." *Indian Notes* 4:33–40, 1927.

Pfizmaier, A.
"Aufklärungen über die Sprache der Koloschen." *Sitzungsberichte der Kaiserlichen Akademie der Wissenschaften, Philosophisch— Historische Klasse* (Wien) 105:169–234, 1883.

Sapir, Edward
"The Na-dene Languages." *AA* 17:535–538, 1915. n.s.

Schott, W.
"Etwas über die Sprache der Koloschen." *Archiv für Wissenschaftliche Kunde von Russland* (Berlin) 3:349–445, 1843.

Shotridge, L.
"Tlingit Woman's Root Basket." *Museum Journ.* 12:162–178, 1921.

"War Helmets and Clan Hats of the Tlingit Indians." *Museum Journ.* 10:43–48, 1919.

———, and F.
"Chilkat Houses." *Museum Journ.* 4:81–100, 1913.

Tolmie, W. F., and Dawson, G. M.
Comparative Vocabularies of the Indian Tribes of British Columbia. Montreal: 1884.

Wardle, H. N.
"Certain Rare-West Coast Baskets." *AA* 14:287–313, 1912 n.s.

Waterman, T. T.
"Observations Among the Ancient Indian Monuments of Southeastern Alaska." *Smithson. Inst. Misc. Coll.* 74(Part 5):115–133, 1925.

MUSIC

GENERAL STUDIES

Jones, Livingston F.
A Study of the Thlingets of Alaska. New York: Fleming H. Revell Company, 1914.
Chapter XX: Discusses music and ceremonial.

TOLOWA

FOLKLORE

GENERAL STUDIES

Barnett, H. G.
"Oregon Coast." *Anthro. Records* 1:155–204, 1937.

Driver, H. E.
"Northwest California." *Anthro. Records* 1:297–433, 1939.

Drucker, P.
"The Tolowa and Their Southwest Oregon Kin." *Univ. Cal. Publ. Amer. Arch. Ethnol.* 36:221–300, 1936.

Du Bois, Cora
"Tolowa Notes." *AA* 34:248–262, 1932. n.s.

Kroeber, A. L.
"Tolowa." In: *Handbook of the Indians of of California.* Bureau Amer. Ethnol. Bull. 78, pp. 121–127. Washington, D. C., 1925.

Powers, S.
"Tribes of California.' *Contr. North Amer. Ethnol.* 3:65–71, 1877.

CUSTOMS—FOLK ART—SPEECH

Dorsey, J. O.
"The Gentile System of the Siletz Tribes." *JAFL* 3:227–237, 1890.

Du Bois, Cora
The Wealth Concept as an Integrative Factor in Tolowa-Tututni Culture. In: *Essays in Anthropology Presented to A. L. Kroeber,* pp. 49–65. Berkeley: University of California Press, 1936.

Gifford, E. W.
"Californian Kinship Terminologies." *Univ. Cal. Publ. Amer. Arch. Ethnol.* 18:15–17, 1922.

Harrington, E.
"The Driftwood Witch and the Tolowa Adze Handle." *Masterkey* 14:13–16, 1940.

Kroeber, A. L.
"Yurok and Neighboring Kin Term Systems." *Univ. Cal. Publ. Amer. Arch. Ethnol.* 35:12–22, 1934.

Woodward, A.
"Some Tolowa Specimens." *Indian Notes* 4:137–150, 1927.

TSIMSHIAN
(*Including:* Gitksan, and Niska)
FOLKLORE
GENERAL STUDIES

Benyon, W.
"The Tsimshians of Metlakatka." *AA* 43:83–88, 1941. n.s.

Boas, Franz
"The Nass River Indians." *65th Meeting. British Association for the Advancement of Science* pp. 569–592, 1895.

———.
"Niská." *66th Meeting. British Association for the Advancement of Science.* pp. 586–591, 1896.

———.
"Tsimshian." *59th Meeting. British Association for the Advancement of Science,* pp. 877–889, 1889.

———.
"Tsimshian." In: *Bureau of Amer. Ethnol. Bull. 40 (Part 1):* 283–422, 1911.

———.
"Die Tsimshian." *Zeit f. Ethno.* 20:231–247, 398–405, 1888.

———.
Tsimshian Texts. Bureau of American Ethnology, Bull. 27, pp. 1–244. Washington, D. C.: U. S. Gov't. Printing Office, 1902.

———.
"Tsimshian Texts." (New Series). *Publ. Amer. Ethnol. Soc.* 3:65–284, 1912.

Dorsey, G. A.
"Up the Skeena River to the Home of the Tsimshians." *Popular Science Monthly* 54:181–193, 1898.

Emmons, George E.
"The Kitselas of British Columbia." *AA* 14:467–472, 1912. n.s.
A Tsimshian division.

———.
"Niska." In: *Handbook of American Indians, Bull. 30 (Part 2):*75–76, 1910. (Washington, D. C.).

Mayne, Richard C.
Four Years in British Columbia and Vancouver Island. London: J. Murray, 1862. xi, 468 pp.

McCullagh, J. B.
Red Indians I Have Known. London: 1919. 47 pp.

Niblack, A. P.
"The Coast Indians of Southern Alaska and Northern British Columbia." *Reports U. S. Nat. Museum,* 1888, pp. 225–386.

Shotridge, L.
"A Visit to the Tsimshian Indianer." *Museum Journ.* 10:49–67, 117–148, 1919.

Swanton, John R.
"Chimmesyan Family." In: *Handbook of American Indians.* Bureau of Amer. Ethnol. Bull. 30 (Part 1):270–271, 1907. Washington, D. C.

Wellcome, Henry S.
The Story of Metlakahtla. New York: Saxon & Co., 1887. xx, 483 pp.
A Tsimshian town 15 miles south of Port Simpson, British Columbia.

MYTHS—FOLKTALES—LEGENDS

Boas, Franz
"Eine Sonnensage der Tsimshian." *Zeitschrift für Ethnologie* Heft 5:776–797, 1908.

———.
"Sagen aus Britisch-Columbien." *Verhandl. Berl. Gesel. Anthro. Ethno. Ur.,* pp. 195–216, 1895.

———.
Tsimshian Mythology. Based on Texts and Reports by Henry W. Tate. 31st Annual Report. Bureau of American Ethnology, pp. 43–881, illus., bibl. Washington, D. C.: U. S. Government Printing Office, 1916.

Deans, James
"Creation Myth of the Tsimshian of Northwest British Columbia." *JAFL* 4:34, 1891.

———.
"The Daughter of the Sun." *JAFL* 4:32–33, 1891.
A legend.

Emmons, G. T.
"Tsimshian Stories in Carved Wood." *American Museum Journal* 15:363–366.

Gordon, G. B.
"Legends of the Kit-selas." *Museum Journ.* 9:39–49, 1918.

Hillyer, William H.
The Box of Daylight, and with drawings by Erick Berry. New York: A. A. Knopf, 1931. vii–xv, 179 pp., illus.
An Indian hero story of Tchamsem the Raven, based on "Tsimshian mythology" by Franz Boas.

Krappe, Alexander H.
"A Solomon Legend Among the Indians of the North Pacific." *JAFL* 59:309–314, 1946.

Martin, Fredericka
"A Tlingit Legend." In: *The Hunting of the Silver Fleece. Epic of the Fur Seal.* (pp. 291–294). New York: Greenberg: Publisher, 1946. 328 pp., photos.

Shotridge, L.
"Ghost of Courageous Adventurer." *Museum Journ.* 11:11–26, 1920.

——.
"How Ats-ha followed the Hide of His Comrade to Yek Land." *Museum Journ.* 21:215–226, 1930.

——.
"Keyt-Gooshe." *Museum Journ.* 10:213–216, 1919.

——.
"Land Otter-Man." *Museum Journ.* 13:55–59, 1922.

Swanton, John R.
Tlingit Myths and Texts. Bureau American Ethnology, Bulletin 39. Washington, D. C.: U. S. Government Printing Office, 1909. viii, 451 pp.

——.
"Types of Haida and Tlingit Myths." *AA* 7:94–104, 1905. n.s.

Velten, H. V.
"Three Tlingit Stories." *International Journal of Linguistics* (Indiana University, Bloomington, Indiana) 10:168–180, 1944.

——.
"Two Southern Tlingit Tales." *International Journal of American Linguistics* 10:65–74, 1939.

BELIEFS—CUSTOMS—FOLK MEDICINE

Adam, L.
"Stammesorganisation und Häuptlingstun der Haida und Tsimshian." *Zeit. f. Vergleich. Recht.* 30:161–268, 1913.

Barbeau, Charles Marius
"Growth and Federation of the Tsimshian Phratries." *Proc. Inter. Congr. Amer.* 19:402–408, 1915.

——.
"Totem Poles of the Gitskan Upper Skeena River."*Anthropological Series No. 12, Bulletin 61.* Ottawa: F. A. Acland, 1929. vi, 275 pp., 32 plates, map.

Boas, Franz
"The Houses of the Tsimshian and Niská." *66th Meeting. British Association for the Advancement of Science.* pp. 580–583, 1896.

Breton, A. C.
"Tsimshian Crest Poles at Hazleton and Kishpiox." *Man* 17:137–139, 1917.

Durlach, Theresa M.
"The Relationship Systems of the Tlingit, Haida and Tsimshian." *Publications of the American Ethnological Society of New York* 11:1–177, 1928.

Emmons, G. T.
"The Kitikshan and Their Totem Poles." *Natur. Hist.* 25:33–48, 1925.

——.
"Some Kitksan Totem Poles." *Amer. Museum Journ.* 13:362–369, 1913.

Garfield, V.
"Tsimshian Clan and Society." *University of Washington Publications in Anthropology* 7, no. 3:167–340. Seattle: University of Washington Press, 1939.

Halliday, William M.
Potlatch and Totem. London: J. M. Dent & Sons, 1935. xvi, 240 pp.

Kerr, R.
"A Totem-Pole from the Nass River." *Man* 31:20–21, 1931.

Ogden, Peter S.
Traits of American-Indian Life and Character. London: Smith, Elder & Co., 1853. xiv, 218 pp.

Sapir, Edward
"A Sketch of the Social Organization of the Nass River Indians." *Museum Bull. Can. Dep't. Mines.* 19:1–30, 1915.

Smith, H. I.
"Materia Medica of the Bella Coola and Neighboring Tribes." *Bull. Can. Dep't. Mines* 56:47–68, 1927.

FOLK ART—SPEECH

Boas, Franz
"Vocabularies of the Tlingit, Haida and Tsimshian Languages." *Proc. Amer. Philo. Soc.* 29:193–208, 1891.

Emmons, G. T.
"Slate Mirrors of the Tsimshian." *Indian Notes Monogr.* 15:5–21, 1921. n.s.

Gibbs, G.
"Notes on the Use of Numerals Among the T'sim Si-an'." *Contr. North Amer. Ethnol.* 1:155–156, 1877.

——, and Dall, W. H.
"Comparative Vocabularies." *Contr. North Amer. Ethnol.* 1:143–150, 1877.

Hamy, E. T.
"Note sur un masque en pierre des Indiens sur la rivière Nass." *Journ. Société Amér.* 1:167–170, 1897.

La Grasserie, R. de
Cinq Langues de la Colombie Brittannique. Paris: J. Maisonneuve, 1902. 530 pp.

Sapir, Edward
"A Haida Kinship Term Among the Tsimshian." *AA* 23:233–234,1921. n.s.

—————.
"Nass River Terms of Relationship." *AA* 22:261–271, 1920. n.s.

Schulenburg, Albrecht C.
Die Sprache der Zimshian-Indianer in Nordwest Amerika. Braunschweig: 1894. viii, 372 pp.

Tolmie, W. F., and Dawson, G. M.
Comparative Vocabularies of the Indian Tribes of British Columbia. Montreal: 1884.

PROVERBS

Barbeau, Charles Marius
"Totem Poles." *Geographical Review* (N. Y.) 20:258–272, 1930.

Morison, O.
"Tsimshian Proverbs." *JAFL* 2:285–286, 1889.

MUSIC—DANCE
GENERAL STUDIES

Barbeau, Charles Marius
"Songs of the Northwest." *MQ* 19:101–111, 1933.

Drucker, P.
"Kwakiutl Dancing Societies." *Anthro. Records* 2:221–223, 1940.

TWANA (Skokomish)
(*Including:* Chemakum)
FOLKLORE
GENERAL STUDIES

Eells, Rev. M.
"The Indians of Puget Sound." *Amer. Antiq.* 8:40–41; 9:1–9, 97–104, 211–219, 271–276; 10:26–26, 174–178, 1886–1888.

—————.
Ten Years of Missionary Work Among the Indians at Skokomish. Boston: Congregational Sunday School & Publishing Society, 1886. x, 271 pp.

—————.
"The Twana, Chemakum, and Klallam Indians." *Ann. Reports Board of Regents Smithson. Inst.*, 1887, pp. 605–681.

—————.
"Twana Indians of the Skokomish Reservation in Washington Territory." *Bulletin, U. S. Geological Survey*, 3:57–114. Washington, D. C.: U. S. Government Printing Office, 1877.

Quimby, L. W.
"Among the Skokomish Indians." *South. Workman* 30:511–513, 1901.

Squier, Emma L.
Children of the Twilight. New York: Cosmopolitan Book Corp., 1926. 257 pp.

MYTHS—FOLKTALES—LEGENDS

Adamson, Thelma
"Folk-Tales of the Coast Salish." *Memoirs of the American Folklore Society*, No. 27, pp. 364–378. New York: Folklore Society, 1934.

Eells, M.
"Do-ki-batt, or the God of the Puget Sound Indians." *Amer. Antiq.* 6:389–393, 1884.

—————.
"Myths of the Puget Sound Indians." *Amer. Antiq.* 12:160–165, 1890.

Shelton, William
The Story of the Totem Pole; Early Indian Legends as handed down from generation to generation, are herewith recorded. Everett, Washington: Kane & Harcus Co., 1923. 80 pp., illus.

Legends of the Tulalip Indians, "one of the three divisions of the Twana, a Salish tribe on the west side of Hood Canal, Washington."

BELIEFS—CUSTOMS

Eells, M.
"The Potlatches of Puget Sound." *Amer. Antiq.* 5:135–147, 1883.

—————.
"The Religion of the Clallam and Twana Indians." *Amer. Antiq.* 2:8–14, 1879.

—————.
"The Religion of the Indians of Puget Sound." *Amer. Antiq.* 12:69–84, 1890.

FOLK ART—SPEECH

Boas, Franz
"Notes on the Chemakum Language." *AA* 5:37–44, 1892.

Eells, M.
"The Chemakum Language." *Amer. Antiq.* 3:52–54, 1880.

—————.
"The Twana Language." *Amer Antiq.* 3:296–303, 1880.

MUSIC

GENERAL STUDIES

Eells, M.
"Indian Music." *Amer. Antiq.* 1:249–253, 1878.

UMPQUA

(*Including:* Chastacosta and Tututni)

FOLKLORE

GENERAL STUDIES

Anon.
"Umpqua." In: *Handbook of American Indians.* Bureau Amer. Ethnol. Bull. 30 (Part 2):866, 1910.

Dorsey, J. O.
"Tututni." In: *Handbook of American Indians.* Bureau Amer. Ethnol. Bull. 30 (Part 2):857–858, 1910.

Frachtenberg, L. J.
Lower Umpqua Texts, and Notes on the Kusan Dialects. New York: Columbia University Press, 1914. vi, 156 pp. (Columbia University Contributions to Anthropology. vol. 4.).

Goddard, Pliny Earle
"Chastacosta." In: *Handbook of American Indians.* Bureau Amer. Ethnol. Bull. 30 (Part 1):236, 1907.

Hines, G.
Wild Life in Oregon. New York: Hurst & Co., 1881. viii, 437 pp.

Spier, Leslie
"Tribal Distributions in Southwestern Oregon." *Oregon Historical Quarterly* 28:358–365, 1927.

MYTHS—SUPERSTITION

Farrand, Livingston
"Shasta and Athapascan Myths from Oregon." JAFL 28:224–242, 1915.

Young, K., and Cutsforth, T. D.
"Hunting Superstitions in the Cow Creek Region." *JAFL* 41:293–295, 1928.

CUSTOMS—SPEECH

Cressman, L. S.
"Aboriginal Burials in Southwestern Oregon." *AA* 35:116–130, 1933. n.s.

Morice, A. G.
"Chasta Costa and the Déné Languages of the North." *AA* 17:599–572, 1915. n.s.

Sapir, Edward
Notes on Chasta Costa Phonology and Morphology." *Univ. Penn Mus. Anthro. Publ.* 2:273–340, 1914.

THE MACKENZIE–YUKON AREA

FOLKLORE

BIBLIOGRAPHY

Bibliography of the Indians of Canada. In: *The Indians of Canada*, by Diamond Jenness, pp. 430–436. Ottawa: National Museum of Canada, (Bulletin 65), 1932.

GENERAL STUDIES

Anderson, A. A.
"Notes on the Indian Tribes of British North America." *Histor. Mag.* 7:73–81, 1863.

Bailey, Alfred G.
"The Indian Problem in Early Canada." *America Indigena* 2:35–39, 1942.

Barbeau, Charles Marius
Alaska Beckons, illustrated by Arthur Price. Caldwell, Id.: The Caxton Printers, Ltd., 1947. 343 pp., illus., bibl: 331–343.

————.
"The Folklore Movement in Canada." *JAFL* 56:166–168, 1943.

————, **and Melvin, Grace**
The Indian Speaks. Caldwell, Idaho: Caxton Printers, 1943. 117 pp., 40 illus.
Myths, legends, traditions, tales and songs of Canadian Indians.

Beaugrand, Honoré
New Studies of Canadian Folk Lore. Montreal: E. M. Renouf, 1904. 130 pp., illus.

Boas, Franz
"Ethnological Problems in Canada." *Proceedings of the 15th Session of the International Congress of Americanists* 1:151–161, 1906.

Bompas, William C.
Diocese of Mackenzie River. London: Society for Promoting Christian Knowledge, 1888. 108 pp.

Chapman, Rev. J. W.
"Athapascan Tradition from the Lower Yukon." *JAFL* 16:180–185, 1903.

————.
"Notes on the Tinneh Tribe of Anvik, Alaska." *Proceedings of the 15th Session of the International Congress of Americanists* (Quebec), 2:39, 1906.
Contents: 1. Traditions; 2. Notes on Shamanism; 3. Ceremonies; 4. Festival of Masks; 5. Potlach Dance and Feast; 6. A Potlach at Anvik.

Dall, William H.
"The Native Tribes of Alaska." *Proc. Amer. Assoc. Adv. Sci.* 34:363–379, 1885.

Duchaussois, Pierre J. B.
Mid Snow and Ice. London: Geo. E. J. Coldwell, 1937. xvi, 386 pp.

Franklin, John
Narrative of a Journey to the Shores of the Polar Sea. London: J. Murray, 1829.

Fraser, S.
"Journal of a Voyage from the Rocky Mountains to the Pacific Coast." *Les Bourgeois de la Compagnie du Nord Ouest* (L. F. R. Masson, ed., Quebec) 1:156–221, 1889.

Gibbs, G.
"Notes on the Tinneh or Chepewyan Indians." *Ann. Reports Board Regents Smithson. Inst.* 1866. pp. 303–327.

Goddard, Pliny Earle
"Assimilation to Environment as Illustrated by Athapascan Peoples." *Proc. Inter. Congr. Amer.* 15 (Part 1):337–359, 1906.

————.
"Similarities and Diversities Within Athapascan Linguistic Stocks." *Proc. Inter. Congr. Amer.* 22 (Part 2):489–494, 1926.

————, **and Swanton, John R.**
"Athapascan Family." In: *Handbook of American Indians*. Bureau of American Ethnol. Bull. 30 (Part 1):108–111, 1907. (Washington, D. C.)

Goodsell, P. H.
Red Hunters of the Snows. Toronto: 1938. 324 pp.

Henry, Alexander
Travels and Adventures in Canada and the Indian Territories between the years 1760 and 1776. Boston, Mass.: Little, Brown & Co., 1901. 347 p. Re-print of edition of 1809.

Hermant, P.
"Evolution économique et sociale de certaines peuplades de l'Amérique du nord." *Bulletin de la Société Royale Belge de Géographie (Bruxelles)* 28:341–357, 1904.

Hill-Tout, Charles
British North America. London: Arnold Constable & Co., 1907. 263 pp.

Hooper, William Hulme (Lieut.)
Ten Months Among the Tents of the Tuski, with incidents of an Arctic boat expedition in search of Sir John Franklin, as far as the Mackenzie River and Cape Bathurst. London: J. Murray, 1853. 417 pp.

Huscher, Betty H., and Harold A.
"Athapascan Migration via the Intermontane Region." *American Antiquity* 8:80–88, 1942.

Innis, Harold A.
The Fur Trade in Canada. Toronto: University of Toronto Library, 1927. 172 pp.

Jameson, Anna Brownell
Winter Studies and Summer Rambles in Canada. London: Saunders and Otley, 1838. 3 vols.

Jenness, Diamond
"The Indian Background of Canadian History." *Bulletin, National Museum of Canada* (Ottawa) 86, 1937. 46 pp., illus.

The Indians of Canada. Ottawa: Bulletin 65, National Museum of Canada, Department of Mines, 1932. 446 pp., illus., bibl.

"Notes and Traditions from Northern Alaska, The Mackenzie Delta and Coronation Gulf." *Report of the Canadian Arctic Expedition, Southern Party,* 13:1–90, 1913–1916. (Ottawa, 1924).

The Prehistory of the Canadian Indians. In: *Custom Is King;* essays presented to R. R. Marett on his seventieth birthday ... edited by L. H. Dudley Buxton. London: Hutchinson's Scientific and Technical Publ., 1936. xiii, 325 pp.

Kirchoff, Paul
"Versuch einer Gliederung der Südgruppe des des Athapaskischen." *Proceedings of the 24th Session of the International Congress of Americanists.* pp. 258–263, 1930.

Latham, R. G.
"On the Ethnography of Russian America." *Journ. Ethnol. Soc.* 1:182–191, 1848.

Mackenzie, Alexander
Voyages from Montreal on the St. Lawrence River, Through the Continent of North America to the Frozen and Pacific Oceans, 1789 and 1793. London: T. Cadell and W. Davies, 1802. 2 vols.

Maclean, John
Canadian Savage Folk: The Native Tribes of Canada. Toronto: W. Briggs, 1896. viii, 641 pp.

McLean, J.
"Notes of a Twenty-Five Years' Service in the Hudson's Bay Territory." *Publications of the Champlain Society* (Toronto) 19:1–402, 1932.

"The Canadian Dénés." *Annual Archaeological Report* (Toronto), pp. 187–219, 1906.

Mason, Michael H.
The Arctic Forests. London: Hodder & Stoughton, 1924. viii, 320 pp.

Morice, Adrien G.
Au pays de l'ours noir. Paris: Delhomme et Briguet, 1897. viii, 305 pp., illus.

"Dénés." In: *Catholic Encyclopedia* 4:717–719.

"Dénés." In: *Encyclopedia of Religion and Ethics.* J. Hastings, ed. Vol. 4, pp. 636–641. New York: 1912.

"Les Dénés du Nord." *Bulletin de la Société de Geographie* (Quebec) 22:146–190, 1928.

"The Great Déné Race." *Anthropos* 1:229–277, 483–508, 695–730; 2:1–34, 181–196; 4:582–606; 5:113–142, 419–443, 643–653, 969–990, 1906–1910.

"Northwestern Dénés and Northeastern Asiatics." *Trans. Royal Can. Inst.* 10:131–193, 1914.

"Notes on the Western Déné." *Transactions of the Canadian Institute,* Vol. 4, 1894.

Osgood, Cornelius
The Distribution of the Northern Athapascan Indians. Yale University Publications in Anthropology 7. New Haven: Yale University Press, 1936. 23 pp.

Petitot, Émile F. S.
"Les Déné-Dindjiés." *Proc. Inter. Congr. Amer.* 1 (Part 2):13–37, 1875.

"Étude sur la Nation Montagnaise ou Tchipewayne." *Les Missions Catholique* (Lyons) 1: 135–136, 144, 151–152, 159–160, 168, 183–184, 199–200, 206–208, 215–216, 1868.

Explorations de la Région du Grand Lac des Ours. Paris: Téqui, 1893. vi, 488 pp.

Monographie des Déné-Dindjié. Paris: 1876. 109 pp.

"On the Athabascan District of the Canadian North-West Territory." *Proc. Royal Geogr. Soc.* 5:633–635, 1883 n.s.

Quinze Ans sous le Cercle Polaire. Paris: E. Dentu, 1889. xxi, 322 pp.

"Traditions Indiennes du Canada Nordouest." *Actes de la Société Philologique* 16–17:169–614, 1888.

Roe, F. G.
"Buffalo and Snow." *Canadian Historical Review* 17, (No. 2):125–146, 1936.

Sapir, Edward
"An Anthropological Survey of Canada." *Science* 34:789–793, 1911. n.s.

Sniffen, M. K.
"Canada and Her Indians." *Southern Workman* 40:165–168, 1911.

Stewart, E.
"The Mackenzie River Basin." *Transactions of the Ottawa Literary and Scientific Society* pp. 31–48, 1907.

Taché, Joseph C.
Esquisse sur le nord-ouest de l'Amérique. Montreal: Librairie Saint Joseph 1869.

———.
Forestiers et voyageurs, moeurs, et légendes Canadiennes. Montréal: Librairie Saint Joseph, 1844. 240 pp.

Teit, J. A.
Indian Tribes of the Interior. In: *Canada and Its Provinces,* Vol. 21, pp. 283–312. Toronto: 1914.

Thomas, C.
"Historical Account of the Indians of Canada." *Annual Archaeological Report,* Ontario, 1905; Toronto, 1906. pp. 71–83.

Wissler, C.
"Culture of the North American Indians Occupying the Caribou Area." *Proc. Nat. Acad. Sci.* 1:51–54, 1915.

MYTHS—FOLKTALES—LEGENDS

Brown, Abbie Farwell
Tales of the Red Children, by Brown, A. F. and Bell, J. M. New York: D. Appleton & Company, 1909. 125 pp., illus.
Contents: Why the white bear lives alone. Crow Feet. The story of Ithenhiela. The cleft mountain. Why there is but one moon. How Summer came. The wandering star. The unhappy son. The monster fish. The great flood. The adventures of Jahkarpasse.

Jenness, Diamond
"Myths and Traditions from Northern Alaska, the Mackenzie Delta and Coronation Gulf." *Report of the Canadian Arctic Expedition, 1913–1918,* 1924.

Judson, Katharine Berry
Myths and Legends of Alaska. Chicago: A. C. McClurg & Co., 1911. 148 pp., illus.

———.
Myths and Legends of British North America. Chicago: A. C. McClurg, 1917. vii, 211 pp., front, plates.

Logie, Alfred Ernest
Canadian Wonder Tales; drawings by Dorothy Hansacre. Chicago: Row, Peterson and Company, 1925. v, 228 pp., illus.

Macmillan, Cyrus
Canadian Fairy Tales; with an introduction by John Grier Hibben. Toronto: The Macmillan Co. of Canada, Ltd., 1928. xiv, 234 pp.

———.
Canadian Wonder Tales; with illustrations in color by George Sheringham and a foreword by Sir William Peterson. London: John Lane Company, 1918. xvi, 199 pp., illus.

Petitot, É. F. S.
Accord des mythologie dans la cosmogonie des Danites arctiques. Paris: 1890. 493 pp.

Rossiter, Harriet
Indian Legends from the Land of Al-ay-ek-sa, published by E. C. Howard. Ketchikan, Alaska: Ketchikan Alaska Chronicle, 1925. 30 pp., illus.

Smith, Laura R.
Fifty Indian Legends. Chicago: Albert Whitman Co., 1924. 128 pp., illus.

Taschereau-Fortier, Marie
Fées de la Terre Canadienne. Montreal: Librarie d'Action Canadienne-Français, 1928. 209 pp., illus.

BELIEFS—CUSTOMS

Beatrix, Ernest
Chez les Sauvages; illustrations de M. Jean-Paul Lemieux. Montreal: A. Lévesque, 1931. 172 pp., illus.
Contains about one hundred anecdotes dealing with the speech, customs, and manners of the Canadian Indians.

Morice, A. G.
"La femme chez les Dénés." *Proceedings of the 15th Session of the International Congress of Americanists.* pp. 361–394, 1906.

———.
"Smoking and Tobacco Among the Northern Dénés." *AA* 23:482–488, 1921. n.s.

Olson, R. L.
"Adze, Canoe, and House Types of the Northwest Coast." *Univ. Wash. Publ. Anthro.* 2: 1–38, 1927.

Roy, J. Edmond
"Principes de Government chez les Indiens du Canada." *Proceedings of the 15th Session of the International Congress of Americanists* 1: 161–179, 1906.

Schmitter, Ferdinand
Upper Yukon Native Customs and Folklore. Smithson. Miscel. Coll. No. 56. Washington, D. C.: U. S. Government Printing Office, 1910.

Swanton, John R.
"The Development of the Clan System and of Secret Societies Among the Northwestern Indians." *AA* 6:477–485, 1904. n.s.

FOLK ART—SPEECH

Boas, Franz
"Die Verbreitung der Indianer-Sprachen in British-Columbien." *Publ. Mus. Journ. Univ. Penn.* 42:21, 1896.

Brinton, Daniel G.
"On the Affinities of the Otomi Language with Athapascan Dialects." *Proceedings of the 10th Session of the International Congress of Americanists,* pp. 151–163, 1894.

Buschmann, J. C. E.
"Der athapaskische Sprachstamm." *Abhandlungen der Königlichen Akademie der Wissenschaften* (Berlin), pp. 149–319, 1855.

————.
"Systematische Worttafel des athapaskischen Sprachstamms." *Abhandlungen der Königlichen Akademie der Wissenschaften (Berlin)* (Part 3), pp. 501–586, 1859.

————.
"Die Verwandschafts-Verhältnisse der athapaskischen Sprachen." *Abhandlungen der Königlichen Akademie der Wissenschaften (Berlin)*, (Part 2), pp. 195–252, 1862.

————.
"Die Völker und Sprachen im Innern des britischen Nordamerika's." *Monatsberichte der Königlichen Preussischen Akademie der Wissenschaften zu Berlin.* 1858. pp. 465–486.

Cooper, John M.
Snares, Deadfalls, and Other Traps of the Northern Algonquians and Northern Athapaskans. Anthropological Series, Catholic Conference of Americanists, No. 5. Washington, D. C.: Catholic University Press, 1938. 114 pp.
The author discusses hunting methods.

Kroeber, A. L.
"Athabascan Kin Term Systems." *AA* 39:602–608, 1937. n.s.

Leechman, D.
"Arts and the Aborigines." *Queens Quarterly* 49:353–360, 1942.

Morice, A. G.
"The Déné Languages." *Trans. Royal Can. Inst.* 1:170–212, 1889.

————.
"Déné Roots." *Trans. Royal Can. Inst.* 3:145–164, 1891.

————.
"The Unity of Speech Among the Northern and the Southern Déné." *AA* 9:720–737, 1907. n.s.

Petitot, Émile F. S.
Outils en Pierre et en os du Mackenzie. In: *Matériaux pour l'Histoire Primitive et Naturelle de l'Homme*, pp. 398–405. Paris: 1875.

Pilling, J. C.
"Bibliography of the Athapascan Languages." *Bureau of American Ethnol., Bull.* 14, pp. 1–125, 1892.

Sapir, Edward
"The Na-dene Languages." *AA* 17:535–538, 1915. n.s.

Waugh, F. W.
"Canadian Aboriginal Canoes." *Canadian Field-Naturalist* (Ottawa) 33:23–33, 1919.

MUSIC

GENERAL STUDIES

Sargent, Margaret
The Native and Primitive Music of Canada. Mimeographed. 41 pp. Texts and music. Columbia University Music Library. n.d., bibl.
Contents: Classification of Various Aboriginal Races of Canada (after Jenness). The Recording and Transcribing of Primitive Canadian Music. Instruments. Migratory Tribes of the Eastern Woodlands. Agricultural Tribes of the Eastern Woodlands. Plains' Tribes, Tribes of the Cordillera, Tribes of the Mackenzie and Yukon River Basins. Tribes of the Pacific Coast, and the Eskimo.

RECORDS

Herzog, George
Mackenzie Area: Records Contained in American Collection. American Council of Learned Societies (Washington, D. C.) Bulletin 24:25, 1936.

AHTENA

(*Including:* Eyak)

FOLKLORE

GENERAL STUDIES

Abercrombie, William R.
A Military Reconnaissance of the Copper River Valley. In: *Compilation of Narratives of Explorations in Alaska.* Washington: U. S. Gov't. Printing Office, 1900. 464 pp.

Allen, H. T.
"Atnatanas." *Ann. Reports Board of Regents Smithson. Inst.*, 1886. pp. 258–266.

————.
Report of an Expedition to the Copper Tanana, and Koyukuk Rivers. Washington: 1887.

Birket-Smith, Kaj. and de Laguna, Frederica
The Eyak Indians of the Copper River Delta, Alaska. (Kungl. danske videnskabernes selskab. Publications.) Philadelphia: University of Pennsylvania Press; Copenhagen: Munksgaard, 1938. 591 pp.

Corser, Harry Prosper
Totem Lore of the Alaska Indian and the Land of the Totem. Wrangel, Alaska: W. C. Waters, 1940. New ed. rev., 116 pp., illus.

de Laguna, Frederica
"A Preliminary Sketch of the Eyak Indians." *Publ. Phila. Anthro. Soc.* 1:63–75, 1937.

Galitzin, E.
"Observations recueillis par l'Admiral Wrangell." *Nouvelles Annales de Voyage* (Paris) 137:195–221, 1853.

Huntington, F.
"Ahtena." In: *Handbook of American Indians.* Bureau of American Ethnol. Bull. 30 (Part 1):30–31, 1907.

Learnard, H. G.
A Trip from Portage Bay to Turnagain Arm and up the Sushitna. In: *Compilation of Narratives of Explorations in Alaska,* pp. 648–677. Washington: 1900.

Pinart, A. L.
"A Few Words on the Alaska Déné." *Anthropos* 1:907–913, 1906.

"Sur les Atnahs." *Revue de Philologie et d'Etnographie* 2:1–8, 1875.

BEAVER (Tsattine)

FOLKLORE

GENERAL STUDIES

Anon.
"Tsattine." In: *Handbook of American Indians.* Bureau Amer. Ethnol. Bull. 30 (Part 2): 822, 1910.

Barbeau, Charles Marius
Indian Days in the Canadian Rockies. Toronto, Can.: The Macmillan Co. of Canada, Ltd., 1923. 207 pp.

Faraud, H. J.
Dix-huit ans chez les sauvages. Paris: R. Ruffet et Cie, 1866. xvi, 456 pp.

Goddard, Pliny Earle
"The Beaver Indians." *Anthro. Papers. Amer. Mus. Nat. Hist.* 10:201–293, 1916.

"The Beaver Indians." *Anthropological Papers of the American Museum of Natural History* 24:1–87, 1924.

"Beaver Texts." *Anthro. Papers Amer. Mus. Nat. Hist.* 10:295–397, 1916.
Contains myths and legends.

SPEECH

Garrioch, A. C.
A Vocabulary of the Beaver Indian Language. London: 1885. 138 pp.

Goddard, Pliny Earle
"Beaver Dialect." *Anthro. Papers Amer. Mus. Nat. Hist.* 10:399–517, 1917.

CARRIER (Takulli)

FOLKLORE

GENERAL STUDIES

Anon.
"Takulli." In: *Handbook of American Indians.* Bureau Amer. Ethnol. Bull. 30 (Part 2), pp. 675–666, 1910.

Barbeau, Charles Marius
Indian Days in the Canadian Rockies. Toronto: The Macmillan Company, 1923. 208 pp.

Boas, Franz
"Summary of the Work of the Committee in British Columbia." *68th Meeting. British Association for the Advancement of Science,* pp. 667–683, 1898.

Cox, R.
Adventures on the Columbia River. New York: H. Colburn and R. Bentley, 1831. 2 vols.

Goldman, I.
The Alkatcho Carrier of British Columbia. In: *Acculturation in Seven American Indian Tribes.* Ralph Linton, ed., pp. 333–389. New York: Appleton Company, 1940.

"The Alkatcho Carrier: Historical Background of Crest Prerogatives." *AA* 43:396–418, 1941. n.s.

Harmon, D. W.
A Journal of Voyages and Travels in the Interior of North America. Andover: Flagg and Gould, 1820. xxiii, 432 pp.

Hill-Tout, Charles
British North America. Toronto: A. Constable and Co., 1907. 263 pp.

Mackenzie, Alexander
Voyages from Montreal on the river St. Lawrence, Through the Continent of North America, to the Frozen and Pacific Oceans; in the years 1789 and 1793. London: 1801.

McLean, J.
"Notes of a Twenty-Five Years Service in the Hudson's Bay Territory." W. S. Wallace, ed. *Publications of the Champlain Society* (Toronto) 19:176–184, 1932.

Morice, A. G.
"Carrier Indians." In: *Encyclopedia of Religion and Ethics,* J. Hastings, ed. Vol. 3, pp. 229–230. New York: 1911.

"The Great Déné Race." *Anthropos* 1:229–277, 483–508, 695–730; 2:1–34, 181–196; 4:582–606; 5:113–142, 416–443, 643–653, 969–990, 1906–1910.

The History of the Northern Interior of British Columbia. Toronto: W. Briggs, 1904. xi, 349 pp.

"Notes Archaeological, Industrial, and Sociological on the Western Déné." *Trans. Royal Canad. Inst.* 4:1–222, 1893.

"Two Points of Western Déné Ethnography." *AA* 27:478–482, 1925. n.s.

"The Western Dénés." *Proc. Can. Inst.,* ser. 3, 7:109–174, 1889.

Ogden, P. S.
Traits of American-Indian Life and Character.
San Francisco: The Grabhorn Press, 1933. 107
pp.

MYTHS—FOLKTALES—LEGENDS

Jenness, Diamond
"Myths of the Carrier Indians of British
Columbia." *JAFL* 47:97–269, 1934.

Morice, A. G.
"Are the Carrier Sociology and Mythology
Indigenous or Exotic." *Proc. Trans. Royal Soc.
Can.*, ser. 1, 10 (Part 2):109–126, 1892.

———.
"Three Carrier Myths." *Trans. Royal Can.
Inst.* 5:1–36, 1895.

BELIEFS—CUSTOMS

Hamilton, G.
"Customs of the New Caledonian Women Be-
longing to the Nancausky Tine or Stuart's
Lake Indians, Natotin Tine or Babine's and
Nantley Tine or Fraser Lake Tribes." *Journ.
Royal Anthro. Soc. Gt. Brit.* 7:206–208, 1878.

Jenness, Diamond
"The Ancient Education of a Carrier Indian."
Bull. Can. Dept. Mines 62:22–27, 1929.

———.
"The Carrier Indians of the Bulkley River;
Their Social and Religious Life." *Bureau of
American Ethnology* 133 (No. 25):469–587,
illus. Washington, D. C.: U. S. Government
Printing Office, 1943.

Morice, A. G.
"Carriers and Ainos at Home." *American Antiquity* 24:88–93, 1902.

———.
"Smoking and Tobacco Among the Northern
Dénés." *AA* 23:482–488, 1921. n.s.

SPEECH

Morice, A. G.
"L'abstraction dans la langue des Porteurs."
Proc. Inter. Congr. Amer. 21 (Part 1):323–
335, 1924.

———.
The Carrier Language. Winnipeg, Man.: The
Author, 1932. 2 vols.

———.
"Carrier Onomatology." *AA* 35:632–658, 1933.
n.s.

———.
"The Déné Languages." *Trans. Royal Can.
Inst.* 1:170–212, 1891.

Tolmie, W. F., and Dawson, G. M.
*Comparative Vocabularies of the Indian Tribes
of British Columbia.* Montreal: Dawson Bros.,
1884.

FOLK MEDICINE

Jenness, Diamond
"An Indian Method of Treating Hysteria."
Primitive Man (Wash., D. C.) 6:13–20, 1933.

Morice, A. G.
"Déné Surgery." *Trans. Royal Can. Inst.* 7:15–
27, 1901.

Smith, H. I.
"Materia Medica of the Bella Coola and Neighboring Tribes." *Bull. Can. Dept. Mines.* 56:47–
68, 1929.

MUSIC
GENERAL STUDIES

Barbeau, Charles Marius
"Songs of the Northwest." *MQ* 19:101–111,
1933.

CHILCOTIN
FOLKLORE
GENERAL STUDIES

Boas, Franz
"Summary of the Work of the Committee in
British America." *68th Meeting of the British
Society for the Advancement of Science*, pp.
667–683, 1898.

Farrand, Livingston
"The Chilcotin." *68th Meeting of the British
Association for the Advancement of Science*,
pp. 645–648, 1898.

———.
"Traditions of the Chilcotin Indians." *Memoirs
Amer. Mus. Nat. Hist.* 4:1–54, 1900.

———.
"Tsilkotin." In: *Handbook of American Indians.* Bureau of Amer. Ethnol. Bull. 30 (Part
2): 826, 1910.

Morice, A. G.
"The Great Déné Race." *Anthropos* 1:229–277,
483–508, 695–730; 2:1–34, 181–196; 4:582–
606; 5:113–142, 419–443, 643–653, 969–990,
1906–1910.

———.
*The History of the Northern Interior of British
Columbia.* Toronto: W. Briggs, 1904. xi, 349
pp.

———.
"The Western Dénés." *Proc. Can. Inst.*, ser. 3,
7:109–174, 1889.

Teit, J. A.
"Notes on the Chilcotin Indians." *Memoirs
Amer. Mus. Nat. Hist.* 4:759–789, 1907.

FOLK ART—SPEECH

**Haeberlin, H. K., and Teit, J. A., and Roberts,
H. H.**
"Coiled Basketry in British Columbia and Surrounding Regions." *41st Annual Report Bureau Amer. Ethnol.*, pp. 119–484, 1928.

Tolmie, W. F., and Dawson, G. M.
Comparative Vocabularies of the Indian Tribes of British Columbia. Montreal: Dawson Bros., 1884.

CHIPPEWYAN

FOLKLORE

GENERAL STUDIES

Anon.
"Chipewyan." In: *Handbook of American Indians.* Bureau Amer. Ethnol. Bull. 30 (Part 1):275–276, 1907.

————.
"Indian Tradition." *The Athaneum* Second ser. 9:486, Sept. 15, 1828.
Legend, history and tradition of the Chapewee and Chipewyans.

————.
"Thilanottine." In: *Handbook of American Indians.* Bureau Amer. Ethnol. Bull. 30 (Part 2):742–743, 1910.

Back, George
Narrative of the Arctic Land Expedition. London: Y. Murray, 1836. x, 663 pp.

Birket-Smith, Kaj.
Contributions to Chippewyan Ethnology. Copenhagen: Gyldendalske Boghandel, Nordisk Forlag, 1930. 113 pp.

————.
"The Cultural Position of the Chippewyan within the Circumpolar Culture Region." *Proceedings of the 24th Session of the International Congress of Americanists* pp. 97–102, 1930.

Dobbs, Arthur
An Account of the Countries Adjoining to Hudson's Bay. London: Y. Robinson, 1744. ii, 211 pp.

Dunn, John
History of the Oregon Territory. London: Edwards and Hughes, 1846. viii, 359 pp.

Faraud, H. J.
Dix-huit Ans Chez les Sauvages. Paris: R. Ruffet et Cie, 1866. 456 pp.

Franklin, J.
Narrative of a Journey to the Shores of the Polar Sea. London: J. Murray, 1829.

Goddard, Pliny Earle
"Chipewyan Texts." *Anthro. Papers Amer. Mus. Nat. Hist.* 10:1–65, 1912.

Hearne, S.
"A Journey from Prince of Wale's Fort in Hudson's Bay to the Northern Ocean." J. B. Tyrrell, ed. *Publications Champlain Society* (Toronto) 6:1–437, 1911.

Henry, Alexander
Travels and Adventures in Canada. New York: I. Riley, 1809. vi, 330 pp.

King, Richard
Narrative of a Journey to the Shores of the Arctic Ocean. London: R. Bentley, 1836. 2 vols.

Lowie, R. H.
"The Chipewyans of Canada." *South. Workman* 38:278–283, 1909.

————.
"An Ethnological Trip to Lake Athabasca." *Amer. Mus. Journ.* 9:10–15, 1909.

Petitot, E. F. S.
Autour du Grand Lac des Esclaves. Paris: A.Savine, 1891. 369 pp.

————.
"On the Athabascan District." *Record of Science* 1:27–53, 1884.

————.
"Traditions Indiennes du Canada Nord-ouest." *Les Litteratures Populaires de Toutes les Nations* (Paris) 23:345–442, 1886.

Robson, Joseph
An Account of Six Years Residence in Hudson's Bay. London: J. Payne and J. Bouquet, 1752. vi, 84 pp.

Ross, B. R.
"The Eastern Tinneh." *Ann. Reports Board Regents Smithson. Inst.*, 1886. pp. 304–311.

Rourke, Louise
The Land of Frozen Tide. London: Hutchinson & Co., 1924. 352 pp., illus.

Seton, Ernest T.
The Arctic Prairies. New York: Charles Scribner's Sons, 1917. xii, 308 pp., illus.

Tyrrell, J. B., ed.
"David Thompson's Narrative of His Explorations in Western America." *Publications of the Champlain Society* (Toronto) 12:1–582, 1916.

West, J.
The Substance of a Journal During a Residence at the Red River Colony. London: L. B. Seeley & Son, 1827. xvi, 210 pp.

Whitney, C.
On Snow-Shoes to the Barren Grounds. New York: Harper & Brother, 1896. x, 324 pp.

MYTHS—FOLKTALES—LEGENDS

Bell, J. M.
"Fireside Stories of the Chippewyans." *JAFL* 16:73–84, 1903.

Lofthouse, J.
"Chipewyan Stories." *Trans. Royal Can. Inst.* 10:43–51, 1913.

Lowie, R. H.
"Chipewyan Tales." *Anthro. Papers Amer. Mus. Nat. Hist.* 10:171–200, 1912.

———.
Windigo, a Chipewyan Story. In: *American Indian Life*. Elsie Clews Parsons, pp. 325–336. New York: B. W. Huebsch, 1925. 419 pp.

Petitot, E. F. S.
"La femme au serpent." *Mélusine* 2:19–20, 1884.

CUSTOMS—BELIEFS—SPEECH

Goddard, Pliny Earle
"Analysis of Cold Lake Dialect Chipewyan." *Anthro. Papers Amer. Mus. Nat. Hist.* 10:67–168, 1912.

Legoff, Laurent
Grammaire de la Langue Montagnaise. Montreal: 1889. 351 pp.

Mackenzie, Sir Alexander
"Mackenzie's Travels." *Port-Folio* 2:148–149, May 15, 1802.
Brief excerpt from Mackenzie's *Voyages from Montreal*, describing the traditional beliefs of the Chipewyan tribe.

Morgan, Lewis H.
"Systems of Consanguinity and Affinity." *Smithson. Inst. Contr. Knowledge* 17:291–382, 1871.

Pénard, J. M.
"Land Ownership and Chieftaincy among the Chippewyan and Caribou Eaters." *Primitive Man* 2:20–24, 1929.

DOGRIB
FOLKLORE
GENERAL STUDIES

Anon.
"Thlingschadinne." In: *Handbook of American Indians.* Bureau of Amer. Ethnol. Bull. 30 (Part 2):744–745, 1910.

Franklin, J.
Narrative of a Second Expedition to the Shores of the Polar Sea. London: J. Murray, 1828.

Jérémie, N.
Account of Hudson Strait and Bay. R. Douglas and J. N. Wallace. eds. Ottawa: Thorburn and Abbott, 1926. 42 pp.

Osgood, C.
"The Ethnography of the Great Lake Indians." *Bull. Can. Dept. Mines* 70:31–92, 1931.

Petitot, E. F. S.
Autour du Grand Lac des Esclaves. Paris: 1891. 369 pp.

———.
"Traditions Indiennes du Canada nord-ouest." *Les Litteratures Populaires de Toutes les Nations* (Paris) 23:307–344, 1886.

Russell, F.
Explorations in the Far North. Iowa City: The University, 1898. vii, 290 pp.

CUSTOMS

Wheeler, D. E.
"The Dog-Rib Indian and His Home." *Bulletin of the Geographical Society of Philadelphia* 12 (Part 2):1914.

HARE (Kawochodinne)
[Including: Satudene (Great Bear Lake Indians)]

FOLKLORE
GENERAL STUDIES

Anon.
"Kawchodinne." In: *Handbook of American Indians.* Bureau Amer. Ethnol. Bull. 30 (Part 1):667, 1907.

Franklin, John
Narrative of a Second Expedition to the Shores of the Polar Sea, 1825–27. London: J. Murray, 1828.

Keith, G.
"Letters to Mr. Roderic McKenzie." *Les Bourgeois de la Compagnie du Nord-Ouest*, L. F. R. Masson, ed. (Quebec), Vol. 2, pp. 111–123, 1890.

Morice, A. G.
"Hare Indians." In: *Catholic Encyclopedia*, Vol. 7, pp. 136–137, 1910.

Osgood, C.
"The Ethnography of the Great Bear Lake Indians." *Bull. Can. Dep't Mines* 70:31–92, 1931.

Petitot, Émile F. S.
Exploration du Grand Lac des Ours. Paris: 1893.

———.
"Traditions indiennes du Canada nord-ouest." *Les Littératures Populaires de Toutes les Nations* (Paris) 23:103–306, 1886.

Richardson, John
Arctic Searching Expedition: A Journal of a Boat-Voyage Through Rupert's Land and the Arctic Sea. 2 vols. London: Longman, Brown, Green, and Longmans, 1851. 2 vols.

Ross, B. R.
"The Eastern Tinneh." *Ann. Reports Board Regents Smithson. Inst.* 1886. pp. 304–311.

Simpson, Thomas
Narratives of the Discoveries on the North Coast of America; Effected by Officers of the Hudson's Bay Company During the Years 1836–39. London: R. Bentley, 1843. xix, 419 pp.

MYTHS—FOLKTALES—LEGENDS

Bell, J. M.
"Fireside Stories of the Chippewyans." *JAFL*
16:73–84, 1903.

CUSTOMS—SPEECH

Morgan, Lewis H.
"Systems of Consanguinity and Affinity."
Smithson. Contr. Knowledge 17:29–382, 1871.

Petitot, Émile F. S.
Dictionnaire de la langue Déné-Dindjié. Paris:
É. Leroux, 1876.

KASKA (Eastern Nahane)

FOLKLORE

GENERAL STUDIES

Allard, E.
"Notes on the Kaska and Upper Liard Indians." *Primitive Man* 2:24–26, 1929.

Chamberlain, Alexander F.
"Kaska." In: *Handbook of American Indians.*
Bureau Amer. Ethnol. Bull. 30 (Part 1), pp.
661, 1907.

Dawson, G. M.
"Notes on the Indian Tribes of the Yukon
District and Adjacent Northern Portion of
British Columbia." *Annual Reports Canadian
Geological Survey (Montreal)* 3:199B–201B,
1888. n.s.

Honigman, John J.
"Witch-Fear in Post-Contact Kaska Society."
AA 49:222–243, 1947. n.s., bibl.

————, and Irma
"A Kaska Oracle." *Man* 47 (Art. 159) :139–
140, 1947.

Morice, A. G.
"The Western Dénés." *Proc. Can. Inst.* (ser.
3) 7:109–174, 1889.

Swanton, John R.
"Nahane." In: *Handbook of American Indians.*
Bureau of Amer. Ethnol. Bull. 30 (Part 2), pp.
10, 1910.

Underwood, F. W., and Honigman, I.
"A Comparison of Civilization and Personality
in Two Simple Societies." *AA* 49:557–577,
1947.

FOLKTALES

Teit, J. A.
"Kaska Tales." *JAFL* 30:427–473, 1917.

SPEECH

Morice, A. G.
"The Nah-ane and their Language." *Trans.
Royal Can. Inst.* 7:517–534, 1903.

KHOTANA

(Including: **Coyukon, Ingalik, Nebesna,
Tanana, and Ten'a)**

FOLKLORE

GENERAL STUDIES

Allen, H. T.
*Report of an Expedition to the Copper, Tananá,
and Kóyakuk Rivers.* Washington: U. S. Gov't.
Print. Office, 1887. 172 pp.

Anon.
"Kaiyukhotana." In: *Handbook of American
Indians.* Bureau Amer. Ethnol. Bull. 30 (Part
1) :643–644, 1907.

————.
"Koyukukhotana." In: *Handbook of American
Indians.* Bureau Amer. Ethnol. Bull. 30 (Part
1) :729–730, 1907.

————.
"Tenankutchin." In: *Handbook of American
Indians.* Bureau Amer. Ethnol. Bull. 30 (Part
2), pp. 727–728, 1910.

Chapman, John Wright
"Athapascan Traditions from the Lower
Yukon." *JAFL* 16:180–185, 1903.

————.
"Happy-hunting-ground of the Ten'a." *JAFL*
25:66–71, 1912.
Contains an Athapascan tale, burial customs and
beliefs.

————.
"Notes on the Tinneh Tribes of Anvik." *Proc.
Inter. Congr. Amer.* 15 (Part 2) :7–38, 1907.

————.
"Ten'a Texts and Tales from Anvik." *Publ.
Amer. Ethnol. Soc.* 6:1–230, 1914.

Dall, W. H.
Alaska and Its Resources. Boston: Lee and
Shepard, 1897. xii, 627 pp.

————, and Dawson, G. M., and Ogilvie, W.
The Yukon Territory. London. Downey & Co.,
1898. xiv, 438 pp.

Erman, A.
"Ueber die Reise und Entdeckungen des Lieutenant L. Sagoskin im russischen Amerika."
*Archiv für Wissenschaftliche Kunde von Russ-
land* (Berlin) 6:499–522, 613–672; 7:429–512,
1848–1850.

Galitzin, E.
"Observations recueillies par l'Admiral Wrangell sur les habitants des côtes nord-ouest de
l'Amérique." *Nouvelles Annales des Voyages*
(Paris) 137:195–221, 1853.

Gordon, George Byron
In the Alaskan Wilderness. Philadelphia:
John C. Winston Co., 1917. 247 pp.

Hrdlicka, A.
"The Ancient and Modern Inhabitants of the Yukon." *Explorations and Field-Work of the Smithsonian Institution* (Washington), 1929. pp. 137–146.

———.
"Anthropological Survey of Alaska." *46th Ann. Report Bureau Amer. Ethnol.*, pp. 19–374, 1930.

Jetté, J.
"On Ten'a Folk-Lore." *Journ. Royal Anthro. Inst. Gt. Brit.* 38:298–367; 29:460–505, 1908–1909.

Krieger, H. W.
"Tinne Indians of the Lower Yukon River Valley." *Explorations and Field-Work of the Smithsonian Institution* (Washington) 1927. pp. 125–132.

Murray, A. H.
"Journal of the Yukon." *Publications of the Canadian Archives* 4:1–125, 1910.

Osgood, Cornelius
Ingalik Material Culture. Yale University Publications in Anthropology, Vol. 22. New Haven: Yale University Press, 1940. 500 pp.

Schott, W.
"Ueber ethnographische Ergebnisse der Sagoskinschen Reise." *Archiv für Wissenschaftliche Kunde von Russland (Berlin)* 7:480–512, 1849.

Schwatka, Frederick
Report of a Military Reconnaissance made in Alaska in 1883 Washington: U. S. Gov't. Printing Office, 1885.

———.
The Children of the Cold. New York: Educational Publishing Co., 1899. vi, 212 pp.

Sniffen, M. K., and Carrington, T. S.
"The Indians of Yukon and Tanana Valleys." *Publications of the Indian Rights Association,* Ser. 2, 98:3–35, 1914.

Whymper, Frederick
"A Journey from Norton Sound, Bering Sea, to Fort Yukon." *Journ. Royal Geogr. Soc.* 38: 219–237, 1868.

———.
"Russian America." *Trans. Ethnol. Soc.* 7: 167–185, 1869. n.s.

———.
Travel and Adventure in the Territory of Alaska. London: J. Murray, 1868. xix, 331 pp., illus.

Woldt, A.
Capitain Jacobsen's Reise an der Nordwestküste Amerikas Leipzig: M. Spohr, 1884. viii, 431 pp.

Zagoskin, L. A.
Pyeshkodnaya opis chastyi ruskikh vladenyi v'Amerike. St. Petersburg: Karla Kraya, 1847–48. 2 vols.
"Account of Pedestrian Journeys in Russian Possessions in America."

———.
"Resumé des journaux de l'expedition executée dans l'interieur de l'Amerique russe." E. Galitzin, ed. *Nouvelles Annales des Voyages* (Paris) 125:5–16, 216–229, 249–284; 126:170–186; 241–268, 1850.

MYTHS—FOLKTALES—LEGENDS

Chapman, John Wright
Ten'a Texts and Tales from Anvik, Alaska... with a vocabulary by Pliny Earle Goddard. Leyden: E. J. Brill, Ltd., 1914. vi, 230 pp. Publications of the American Ethnological Society. Vol. VI.

Parsons, Elsie Clews
"A Narrative of the Ten'a of Anvik, Alaska." *Anthropos* 17:51–71, 1921–1922.

CUSTOMS—BELIEFS—FOLK MEDICINE

Chapman, John Wright
"Athapascan Ten'a Tale, Burial Customs, and Beliefs." *JAFL* 25:66–71, 1912.

———.
"Tinneh Animism." *AA* 23:298–310, 1921. n.s.

Jetté, J.
"On the Medicine-Men of the Ten'a." *Journ. Royal Anthro. Inst. Gt. Brit.* 37:157–188, 1907.

———.
"On the Superstitions of the Ten'a Indians." *Anthropos* 6:95–108, 241–259, 602–615, 699–723, 1911.

———.
"L'organisation sociale des Ten'as." *Inter. Congr. Amer.* 15 (Part 1):395–409, 1906.

Reed, T. B., and Parsons, E. C.
Cries-for-Salmon, a Ten'a Woman. In: *American Indian Life,* Elsie Clew Parsons, ed., pp. 337–361. New York: B. W. Huebsch, 1925. 419 pp.

Schmitter, Ferdinand
Upper Yukon Native Customs and Folk-Lore. Washington: 1910. 30 pp. (Smithsonian Institution. Miscellaneous Collections. Vol. 54, No. 4.)

Sullivan, Rev. Robert J.
The Ten'a Food Quest. Catholic University of America Anthropological Series XI. Washington, D. C.: 1942.

———.
"Temporal Concepts of Ten'a." *Primitive Man* 15(3 and 4):57–65, 1942.

FOLK ART—SPEECH—RIDDLES

de Laguna, Frederica
"Indian Masks from the Lower Yukon." *AA* 38:569–585, 1936. n.s.

Disselhoff, H. D.
"Bemerkungen zu einigen Eskimo-Masken." *Baessler Archiv* (Berlin) 18:130–137, 1935. Remarks on some Eskimo masks.

Jetté, J.
"On the Language of the Ten'a." *Man* 7:51–56; 8:72–73; 9:21–25; 1907–1909.

————.
"Riddles of the Ten'a Indians." *Anthropos* 8: 181–201, 630–651, 1913.

KUTCHIN (Loucheux)

(*Including*: Han, and Tutchone)

FOLKLORE

GENERAL STUDIES

Anon.
"Handkutchin." In: *Handbook of American Indians*. Bureau of Amer. Ethnol. Bull. 30 (Part 1) :531, 1907.
"A Kutchin tribe on upper Yukon River below Klondike River, Alaska."

————.
"Kutchin." In: *Handbook of American Indians*. Bureau Amer. Ethnol. Bull. 30 (Part 1) :739–740, 1907.

————.
"Tenakutchin." In: *Handbook of American Indians*. Bureau Amer. Ethnol. Bull. 30 (Part 1), pp. 727–728, 1907.
Another name for the Mountain Indians.

————.
"Tutchonekutchin." In: *Handbook of American Indians*. Bureau Amer. Ethnol. Bull. 30 (Part 2), pp. 855, 1910.
"A Kutchin tribe on Yukon River from Deer River to Ft. Selkirk, Yukon Territory, Canada. They number about 1,100 and differ but little from their Kutchin neighbors below."

————.
"Vantakutchin." In: *Handbook of American Indians*. Bureau Amer. Ethnol. Bull. 30 (Part 2) :882–884, 1910.
"A Kutchin tribe, now greatly modified by contact with whites, occupying the country north of Porcupine River, Alaska, as far as the Eskimo territory on the Arctic Coast."

Bompas, W. C.
Diocese of Mackenzie River. London: 1922. 108 pp.

Dall, W. H.
Alaska and Its Resources. Boston: Lee and Shepard, 1897. xii, 627 pp.

Dawson, G. M.
"Notes on the Indian Tribes of the Yukon District and Adjacent Northern Portion of British Columbia." *Ann. Reports Can. Geol. Survey* 3:191–213, 1888. n.s.

————.
"Report on an Exploration in the Yukon District." *Annual Reports Can. Geol. Survey* 3 (Part 1) 7B–277B, 1889. n.s.

Franklin, J.
Narrative of a Second Expedition to the Shores of the Polar Sea. London: J. Murray, 1828.

Hardisty, William
"The Loucheux Indians." *Ann. Reports Smithson. Inst.*, 1866. pp. 311–320.

Hooper, William H.
Ten Months Among the Tents of the Tuski. London: J. Murray, 1853. xv, 417 pp.

Jones, Strachan
"The Kutchin Tribes." *Ann. Reports Smithson. Inst.*, 1866. pp. 320–327.

Kirby, W. W.
"A Journey to the Youcan." *Ann. Reports Smithson. Inst.*, 1864. pp. 416–420.

Mackenzie, Alexander
Voyages from Montreal on the River St. Lawrence, Through the Continent of North America, to the Frozen and Pacific Oceans, in the Years 1789 and 1793. London: 1801. New ed. New York: 1902. 2 vols.

Mason, M. H.
The Arctic Forests. London: Hodder and Stoughton, 1924. xiii, 320 pp.

McKennan, R.
"Anent the Kutchin Tribes." *AA* 37:369, 1935. n.s.

Morice, A. G.
"Loucheux." In: *Catholic Encyclopedia*, Vol. 9, pp. 367–368. New York: 1910.

Murray, A. H.
"Journal of the Yukon." *Publications of the Canadian Archives* 4:1–125, 1910.

Osgood, Cornelius
Contributions to the Ethnography of the Kutchins. Yale University Publications in Anthropology, No. 14. New Haven: Yale University Press, 1936. 189 pp.

————.
"Kutchin Tribal Distribution and Synonymy." *AA* 36:168–179, 1934. n.s.

Petroff, Ivan
The Population and Resources of Alaska. In: *Compilation of Narratives and Explorations in Alaska*; pp. 258–263. Washington: 1900.

Richardson, John
Arctic Searching Expedition: A Journal of a Boat-Voyage Through Rupert's Land and the Arctic Sea. London: Longman, Brown, Green, and Longman, 1851. 2 vols.

Schwatka, Frederick
Along Alaska's Great River. New York: Cassel & Co., 1885. 360 pp.

Simpson, Thomas
Narrative of the Discoveries on the North Coast of America; Effected by the Officers of the Hudson's Bay Company During the Years 1836–1839. London: R. Bentley, 1843. xix, 419 pp.

Whymper, Frederick
"A Journey from Norton Sound, Bering Sea, to Fort Youkon (Junction of Porcupine and Youkon Rivers)." *Journ. Royal Geogr. Soc.* 38:219–237, 1868.

―――.
Travel and Adventure in the Territory of Alaska, Formerly Russian America. London: 1868. xix, 353 pp.

MYTHS—FOLKTALES—LEGENDS

Barbeau, C. M., and Camsel, C.
"Loucheux Myths." *JAFL* 28:249–257, 1915.

Petitot, Émile F. S.
"Six Légendes Américaines." *Les Missions Catholiques* (Lyon) 10:605–607, 616–620, 1878.

Russell, F.
"Athapascan Myths" (Loucheux and Slavey). *JAFL* 13:11–18, 1900.

CUSTOMS—BELIEFS—SPEECH

Adney, T.
"Moose Hunting with the Tro-chu-tin." *Harper's Monthly Magazine* 100:495–507, 1900.

Cadzow, D. A.
"Habitat of Loucheux Bands." *Indian Notes* 2:172–177, 1925.

―――.
"Old Loucheux Clothing." *Indian Notes* 2:292–295, 1925.

Isbester, J. A.
"On a Short Vocabulary of the Loucheux Language." *Proceedings of the Philological Society* 4:184–185, 1850.

Morgan, Lewis H.
"System of Consanguinity and Affinity." *Smithson. Inst. Contr. Knowledge* 17:293–382, 1871.

Petitot, Émile F. S.
Dictionnaire de la langue Déné-Dindjié dialectes Montagnais ou Chippéwyan, Peaux de Lièvre et Loucheux renfermant en outre un grand nombre de termes propres à sept autres dialectes de la même langue précédé d'une monographie des Déné-Dindjié d'une grammaire et de tableaux synoptiques des conjugaisons. Bibliothèque de Linguistique et d'Ethnographie Américaines, tome II, Paris: 1876.

Schmitter, F.
"Upper Yukon Native Customs." *Smithson. Inst. Misc. Coll.* 56 (Part 4):1–30, 1910.

SEKANI
FOLKLORE
GENERAL STUDIES

Anon.
"Sekani." In: *Handbook of American Indians.* Bureau Amer. Ethnol. Bull. 30 (Part 2), pp. 498–499, 1910.

Hill-Tout, Charles
British North America. Toronto: A. Constable & Co., 1907. 263 pp.

Jenness, Diamond
"Indians of Canada." *Bull. Can. Dept. Mines* 65:377–382, 1932.

―――.
"The Sekani Indians of British Columbia." *Proc. Trans. Royal Soc. Can.,* ser. 3, 25 (Part 2):21–34, 1931.

―――.
"The Sekani Indian of British Columbia." *Bulletin 84, National Museum of Canada,* 82 pp., illus. Ottawa, 1937.

Morice, A. G.
"The Great Déné Race." *Anthropos* 1:229–277, 483–508, 695–730; 2:1–34, 181–196; 4:582–606; 5:113–142, 419–443, 643–653, 969–990, 1906–1910.

―――.
The History of the Northern Interior of British Columbia. Toronto: W. Briggs, 1904. xi, 349 pp.

―――.
"The Western Dénés." *Proc. Can. Inst.* ser. 3, 7:109–174, 1889.

CUSTOMS—BELIEFS—FOLK MEDICINE

Morice, A. G.
"About Cremation." *AA* 27:576–577, 1925. n.s.

―――.
"Déné Surgery." *Trans. Royal Can. Inst.* 7:15–27, 1901.

SLAVEY
FOLKLORE
GENERAL STUDIES

Anon.
"Etchareottine." In: *Handbook of American Indians.* Bureau Amer. Ethnol. Bull. 30 (Part 1), pp. 439–440, 1907.
"They were a timid, pacific people, called 'the people sheltered by willows' by the Chipewyan, indicating a riparian fisher folk. Their Cree neighbors, who harried, and plundered them and carried them off into bondage, called them Awokanak, 'slaves,' an epithet which in its French and English forms came to be the name under which they are best known."

Honigman, John J.
Ethnography and Acculturation of the Fort Nelson Slave. Yale Univer. Publ. Anthro. No. 33. Yale Univ. Press. 1946.

Jenness, Diamond
"Indians of Canada." *Bull. Can. Dept. Mines* 65:389–392, 1932.

Osgood, C.
"The Ethnography of the Great Bear Lake Indians." *Bull. Can. Dept. Mines* 70:31–92, 1931.

Petitot, Émile F. S.
Autour du Grand Lac des Esclaves. Paris: 1891. 369 pp.

——.
"Traditions Indiennes du Canada nord-ouest." *Les Litteratures Populaires de Toutes les Nations* (Paris), Vol. 23, pp. 307–344, 1886.

Ross, B. R.
"The Eastern Tinneh." *Ann. Reports Board of Regents Smithson. Inst.*, 1866. pp. 304–311.

MYTHS—LEGENDS

Bell, R.
"Legends of the Slavey Indians of the Mackenzie River." *JAFL* 14:26–29, 1901.

Russell, F.
"Slavey Myths." *JAFL* 13:11–18, 1900.

TAHLTAN (Western Nahane)

(*Including:* Tsetsaut)

FOLKLORE

GENERAL STUDIES

Anon.
"Nahane." In: *Handbook of American Indians.* Bureau Amer. Ethnol. Bull. 30 (Part 2), pp. 10, 1910.

——.
"Tsetsaut." In: *Handbook of American Indians.* Bureau Amer. Ethnol. Bull. 30 (Part 2), pp. 825, 1910.
"An Athapascan band long settled among the Niska on Portland Canal, Alaska, reduced in 1895 to 12 individuals. They are a branch of the western Nahane, speaking a dialect similar to the Tahltan."

Boas, Franz
"The Tinneh Tribe of Portland Inlet." *65th Meeting of the British Association for the Advancement of Science,* pp. 555–569, 587–592, 1895.

——.
"Traditions of the Ts'ets'aut." *JAFL* 9:257–268, 1896; 10:35–48, 1897.

——.
"Ts'ets'aut." *Inter. Journ. Amer. Ling.* 3:1–35, 1924.

Callbreath, J. C.
"Notes on the Tahl-tan Indians." *Ann. Reports Can. Geol. Survey* 3:195B–199B, 1888. n.s.

Dennis, Alfred Pierce
"Life on a Yukon Trail." *National Geographic Magazine* 10:377–391, 457–466, 1899.
Includes popular description of Tahltan Indians.

Emmons, G. T.
"Tahltan." In: *Handbook of American Indians.* Bureau Amer. Ethnol. Bull. 30 (Part 2), pp. 670–671, 1910.

——.
"The Tahltan Indians." *Univ Penna. Museum Anthro. Publ.*, No. 4. 120 pp. Phila: Univ. of Penna. Press, 1911.

Jenness, Diamond
"Indians of Canada." *Bull. Can Dept. Mines* 65:370–376, 1932.

Morice, A. G.
"The Great Déné Race." *Anthropos* 1:229–277, 483–508, 695–730; 2:1–34, 181–196; 4:582–606; 5:113–142, 419–443, 643–653, 969–990, 1906–1910.

——.
The History of the Northern Interior of British Columbia. Toronto: W. Briggs, 1904. xi, 349 pp.

——.
"The Nah-ane and their Language." *Trans. Can. Inst.* 7:517–534, 1903.

——.
"Nahanes." In: *Catholic Encyclopedia.* Vol. 10, pp. 669–670, New York: 1911.

——.
"The Western Déné." *Proc. Can. Inst.* (ser 3,) 7:109–174, 1889.

Teit, James A.
"Notes on the Tahltan Indians of British Columbia." *Anthropological Papers, Boas Anniversary Volume* pp. 337–350. New York: G. E. Stechert and Co., 1906.

——.
"On Tahltan (Athabascan) Work." *Summary Reports of the Geological Survey of Canada* (Ottawa) 1912, pp. 484–487.

——.
"Two Tahltan Traditions." *JAFL* 22:314–318, 1909.

MYTHS—FOLKTALES—LEGENDS

Teit, James A.
"Tahltan Tales." *JAFL* 22:314–318, 1909; 32:198–250, 1919; 34:223–253, 335–356, 1921.

MUSIC

GENERAL STUDIES

Barbeau, Charles Marius
"Songs of the Northwest." *MQ* 19:101–111, 1933.

TANAINA
(Kenai and Knaiakhotana)
FOLKLORE
GENERAL STUDIES

Abercrombie, W. R.
A Military Reconnaisance of the Copper River Valley. In: *Compilation of Narratives of Explorations in Alaska*, pp.563–591. Washington: U. S. Gov't. Printing Office, 1900. 464 pp.

Anon.
"Knaiakhotana." In: *Handbook of American Indians*. Bureau Amer. Ethnol. Bull. 30 (Part 1), pp. 715–717, 1907.

———.
"Ueber die Kinaivölker im äussersten Nordwesten Amerikas." *Globus* 26:87–88, 1874.

Castner, J. C.
A Story of Hardship and Suffering in Alaska. In: *Compilation of Narratives of Explorations in Alaska*, pp. 686–709. Washington: 1900.

Cook, F. A.
To the Top of the Continent. New York: Doubleday, Page & Co., 1908. xxi, 321 pp., illus.

Galitzin, E.
"Observations recueillies par l'Admiral Wrangell sur les habitants des côtes nord-ouest de l'Amérique." *Nouvelles Annales des Voyage* (Paris) 137:195–221, 1853.

Glenn, E. F.
Explorations in and about Cooks Inlet. In: *Compilation of Narratives of Explorations in Alaska*, pp. 713–724. Washington: 1900.

Herron, J. S.
Explorations in Alaska, 1899, for All-American Overland Route from Cook Inlet, Pacific Ocean, to the Yukon. Washington: 1901. 77 pp.

Learnard, H. G.
A Trip from Portage Bay to Turnagain Arm and up the Sushitna. In: *Compilation of Narratives of Explorations in Alaska*, pp. 648–677. Washington: 1900.

Lisiansky, U.
A Voyage Round the World in the Years 1803–1806. London: 1814.

Osgood, Cornelius
The Ethnography of the Tanaina. Yale University Publications in Anthropology, No. 16. New Haven: Yale University Press, 1937. 230 pp., illus.

———.
"Tanaina Culture." *AA* 35:695–717, 1933. n.s.

Richardson, John
Arctic Searching Expedition: a Journal of a Boat-Voyage Through Rupert's Land and the Artic Sea. London: Longman, Brown, Green, and Longman, 1851. 2 vols.

Woldt, A.
Capitain Jacobsen's Reise an der Nordwestküste Amerikas. Leipzig: M. Spohr, 1884. viii, 431 pp.

Wrangell, F. P. von
"Obitatyeli syevero-zapadykh Beryegov Ameriki." *Syin Otyechestva* 7:51–82, 1839. (St. Petersburg).

———.
"Statistische und Ethnographische Nachrichten an der Nordwestküste von Amerika." *Beiträge zur Kenntnis der Russischen Reiches (und Angränzenden Länder Asiens)* (St. Petersburg) 1:103–116, 1838.

FOLK ART—SPEECH

Krusenstern, A. J. von
Wörter-Sammlungen aus den Sprachen einiger Völker des östlichen Asien und der Nordwest-Küste von Amerika. St. Petersburg: Druckery der Admiralität, 1813. 69 pp.

Mason, J. A.
"A Remarkable Stone Lamp from Alaska." *Museum Journ.* 19:170–194, 1928.

Radloff, L.
"Einige kritische Bemerkungen über Hrn. Buschmann's Behandlung der Kinai-Sprache." *Académie Impériale des Sciences, Mélanges Russes,* 3:364–399, 1857.
Critical observations on Buschmann's work on the Kinai language.

———.
"Wörterbuch der Kinaisprache." *Mémoires de l'Académie Impériale des Sciences de St. Petersbourg,* (ser. 7), 21(Part 8):1–33, 1874.
Dictionary of the Kinai language.

YELLOWKNIFE
FOLKLORE
GENERAL STUDIES

Anon.
"Tatsanottine." In: *Handbook of American Indians*. Bureau Amer. Ethnol. Bull. 30 (Part 2), pp. 698–699, 1910.

Franklin, John
Narrative of a Journey to the Shores of the Polar Sea in the Years 1819, 20, 21, and 22. London: J. Murray, 1829.

———.
Narrative of a Second Expedition to the Polar Sea, 1825–27. London: 1828.

Hearne, S.
"A Journey from Prince of Wale's Fort in Hudson's Bay to the Northern Ocean." J. B. Tyrrell, ed. *Publications of the Champlain Society* (Toronto) 6:1–437, 1911.

King, Richard
Narrative of a Journey to the Shores of the Arctic Ocean in 1833, 1834, and 1835. London: R. Bentley, 1836. 2 vols.

Morice, A. G.
"Yellow-Knives." In: *Catholic Encyclopedia.* Vol. 15, p. 733, New York: 1912.

Pike, W. M.
The Barren Ground of Northern Canada. London: The Macmillan Company, 1892, ix, 300 pp.

Ross, B. R.
"The Eastern Tinneh." *Ann. Reports Board of Regents Smithson. Inst.,* 1866, pp. 304–311.

MYTHS

Petitot, Émile F. S.
La femme aux métaux. Meaux: E. Marguerith-Dupré, 1888. 24 pp.
    Origin myth of the Yellowknife.

THE ARCTIC COAST (Eskimo)

THE ARCTIC COAST (Eskimo)

FOLKLORE

BIBLIOGRAPHY

Farrell, James, ed.
Annotated Bibliography of the Polar Regions:
Series B. Selected List of Bibliographies of
the Polar Regions; Part 1. New York: United
States Works Progress Administration, 1938.
41 pp.

GENERAL STUDIES

Back, Sir George
*Narrative of the Arctic Land Expedition to the
Mouth of the Great Fish River, and along the
shores of the Arctic Ocean.* 1833, 4, 5. Philadelphia, Pa.: E. L. Carey, 1836. 456 pp.

Beechey, Frederick William
*Narrative of a Voyage to the Pacific & Beer-
ing's Straits* to cooperate with the polar expeditions. London, Eng.: H. Colburn & R. Bentley,
1831.

Birket-Smith, Kaj.
Eskimo Cultures and Their Bearing Upon the
Prehistoric Cultures of North America and
Eurasia. In: *Early Man,* G. G. MacCurdy, ed.,
pp. 293–302. Philadelphia: 1937.

———.
The Eskimos. New York: E. P. Dutton, 1926.
250 pp., illus.

———.
"Folk Wanderings and Culture Drifts in Northern North America." *Proceedings of the 22nd
Session of the International Congress of Americanists.* pp. 1–32, 1930.

———.
"On the Origin of Eskimo Culture." *Proceed-
ings of the 23rd Session of the International
Congress of Americanists* pp. 470–477, 1928.

———.
"Preliminary Report of the Fifth Thule Expedition." *Proceedings of the International Congress of Americanists.* (Paris) 21 (Part 2):
190–205, 1924.

———.
"The Question of the Origin of Eskimo Culture; a Rejoinder." *AA* 32:608–624, 1930. n.s.

———.
"Spørgsmaalet om Eskimo-Kulturens Oprin-
delse." *Geografisk Tidsskrift* (Kjøbenhavn)
32:222–239, 33:161–168, 1929–30.

———.
"Über die Herkunft der Eskimos und ihre
Stellung in der Zirkumpolaren Kulturentwick-
lung." *Anthropos* 25:3–24, 1930.

Boas, Franz
"The Eskimo." *Annual Archaeological Report.*
(Ontario, Toronto) pp. 107–116, 1905.

———.
The Folk-Lore of the Eskimos. In: *Race,
Language and Culture,* by Franz Boas, (pp.
503–516). New York: The Macmillan Com-
pany, 1940.
Reprint of an article that originally appeared in
JAFL 17:1-13, 1904.

———.
"Über die Ehemalige Verbreitung der Eskimos." *Zeitschrift der Gesellschaft für Erdkunde.* (Berlin) 18:118–136, 1883.

Bogoras, W. G.
"Elements in the Culture of the Circumpolar
Zone." *AA* 31:579–601, 1929. n.s.

———.
"The Folklore of Northeastern Asia, as Compared with that of Northwestern America." *AA*
4:577–683, 1902. n.s.

———.
"New Problems of Ethnographical Research in
Polar Countries." *Proceedings of the Interna-
tional Congress of Americanists* (Paris) 21
(Part 1):226–246, 1924.

Bolles, T. D.
"A Preliminary Catalogue of the Eskimo Collection in the U. S. National Museum." *Reports
of the United States National Museum.* (Washington) Part 2:335–365, 1887.

Brown, R.
"The Origin of the Eskimo." *Archaeological
Review* 1:237–253, 1888.

Brown, R. N. R.
"Some Problems of Polar Geography." *Annual
Reports of the Board of Regents of the Smithsonian Institution.* (Washington) pp. 349–375,
1928.

Byhan, A.
Die Polarvölker. Leipzig: Quelle & Meyer,
1909. 148 pp.

Caamaño, Jacinto
"The Journal of Jacinto Caamaño." Translated
by Capt. Harold Grenfell, R. N. Edited with
introduction and notes by Henry R. Wagner
and W. A. Newcombe. *British Columbia Historical Quarterly* 2:189–222, 265–301, 1938.

Collins, H. B.
"Eskimo Archaeology and Somatology." *AA*
36:309–313, 1934. n.s.

———.
"Outline of Eskimo Prehistory." *Smithsonian
(Institution) Miscellaneous Collections.* (Wash-
ington) 100:533–592, 1940.

Driggs, John B.
Short Sketches from Oldest America. Philadelphia: George W. Jacobs and Company, 1905. 163 pp.
Notes on the ethnology and folk-lore of the Eskimo of the Arctic Coast by a physician and missionary among the natives of Point Hope.

Faustini, Arnaldo
Gli Eschimesi. Torino: Fratelli Bocca, 1912. 204 pp.

Flaherty, Robert J. in collaboration with Frances Hubbard Flaherty.
My Eskimo Friends—Nanook of the North. New York: Doubleday, Page and Company, 1924. 170 pp., illus.

Freuchen, Peter
Eskimo. New York: Horace Liveright, 1930.
A novel of exceptional beauty of Eskimo life and character.

Gessain, R.
Les Esquimaux du Groëland d'Alaska. Paris: Bourrelier, 1947. 124 pp.

Gilder, William H.
Schwatka's Search. Sledging in the Arctic in quest of the Franklin records. New York: Charles Scribner's Sons, 1881. 316 pp.

Godsell, Philip Henry
Red Hunters of the Snows; an account of thirty years' experience with the primitive Indian and Eskimo tribes of the Canadian Northwest and Arctic Coast, with a brief history of the early contact between white fur traders and the aborigines. Toronto: Ryerson Press, 1938. 324 pp.

Hall, Capt. Charles Francis
Arctic Researches and Life Among the Eskimo. (Narrative of an expedition in search of Sir John Franklin) 1860, 1861, 1862. New York: Harper & Bros., 1865. 595 pp.

Narrative of the Second Arctic Expedition. Washington: Government Printing Office, 1879. 644 pp.

Hassert, K.
"Die Völkerwanderung der Eskimos." *Geographische Zeitschrift* 1:302–322, 1895.

Hatt, Gudmund
"North American and Eurasian Culture Connections." *Proceedings of the (Fifth) Pacific Science Congress.* (Toronto) 5 (Part 4):2755–2765, 1934.

Hayes, Florence
The Eskimo Hunter. Illustrated by Kurt Wiese. New York: Random House, 1945. 275 pp.
The author provides "abundant local color, and gives a vividly accurate picture of Eskimo life and customs in Northern Alaska."

Henshaw, H. W., and Swanton, J. R.
"Eskimo." *Bulletins of the Bureau of American Ethnology.* (Washington) 30 (Part 1):433–437, 1907.

Jenness, Diamond
"Ethnological Problems of Arctic America." *American Geographical Society Special Publications.* (New York) 7:167–75, 1928.

"Indians of Canada." *Bulletins (and Annual Reports) of the Canada Department of Mines, National Museum of Canada.* (Ottawa) 65:405–423, 1932.

"Prehistoric Culture Waves from Asia to America." *Journal of the Washington Academy of Sciences.* (Washington) 30:1–15, 1940.

"The Problem of the Eskimo." In: *The American Aborigines,* D. Jenness, ed., pp. 373–396. Toronto: 1933.

Jochelson, W.
"The Ethnological Problems of Bering Sea." *Natural History* (New York) 26:90–95, 1926.

König, H.
"Gedanken zur Frage nach der Urheimat der Eskimo." *Proceedings of the International Congress of Americanists.* (Paris) 21:256–262, 1924.

Kumlien, Ludwig
Contributions to the Natural History of Arctic America, made in connection with the Howgate polar expedition, 1877–78. Bull. 15, U. S. National Museum. Washington, D. C.: U. S. Gov't Printing Office, 1879.

Mathiassen, Therkel
Ancient Eskimo Settlements in the Kangamuit Area. Copenhagen: Meddelelser om Grønland, Bd. 91, (No. 1) 1931.

"Preliminary Report of the Fifth Thule Expedition." *Proceedings of the International Congress of Americanists.* (Paris) 21:206–215, 1924.

"The Question of the Origin of Eskimo Culture." *AA* 32:591–607, 1930. n.s.

Murdoch, John
"Dr. Rink's 'Eskimo Tribes'." *AA* 1:125–133, 1888.

Nippgen, M. J.
"Le Folklore des Eskimos; ses caractères généraux." *Revue d'éthnographie et des traditions populaires* 4:189–192, 1923.

"Les Resultats Ethnographiques de L'Expedition Danoise dans L'Amérique Arctique." *Revue Anthropologique* 36:411–426, 1926.

Poncins, Gontram de
Kabloona. Written in collaboration with Lewis Galantiere. Illustrated by the author. Garden City, N. Y.: Garden City Publishing Company, 1941. 339 pp.

Radin, P., and Gray, L. H.
"Eskimos." *Encyclopedia of Religion and Ethics.* J. Hastings, ed., (New York) 5:391–395, 1912.

Rae, Dr. John
Narrative of an Expedition to the Shores of the Arctic Sea in 1846 and 1847. London: T. and W. Boone, 1850. viii, 247 pp., front, map.

Rainey, Froelich G.
"A New Form of Culture on the Arctic Coast." *Proceedings of the National Academy of Science* 27:141–144, 1941.

———. "Eskimo Chronology." *Proceedings, National Academy of Science* 22, (No. 6):357–362, 1936.

———. "Native Economy and Survival in Arctic Alaska." *Applied Anthropology* 1(No. 1):9–14, 1941.
An açount of the reindeer experiment.

Rasmussen, Knud
Across Arctic America. New York: G. P. Putnam's Sons, 1927. xx, 388 pp.

———. "Adjustment of the Eskimos to European Civilization." *Proceedings of the (Fifth) Pacific Science Congress.* (Toronto) 5 (Part 4):2889–2896, 1934.

———. "Eskimos and Stone Age Peoples." *Proceedings of the Fifth Pacific Science Congress* (Canada) 4:2762–2772, 1933. Toronto: University of Toronto Press, 1934.

———. "Tasks for the Future Research in Eskimo Culture." *American Geographical Society Special Publications.* (New York) 7:177–187, 1928.

Richardson, Sir John
Arctic-Searching Expedition: A journal of a boat voyage through Rupert's Land and the Arctic Sea, in search of the discovery ships under Sir John Franklin. London: Longman, Brown, Greene and Longman, 1851. col. fronts., plates, fold. map.

———. *The Polar Regions.* Edinburgh: A. & C. Black, 1861. ix, 400 pp.

Riedel, F.
Die Polarvölker. Halle: C. A. Kaemmerer & Co., 1902. 71 pp.

Rink, Henry
"The Eskimo Tribes." *Meddelelser om Grønland.* (Kjøbenhavn) 11:1–163, 1887.

———. "The Migrations of the Eskimo." *Journal of the (Royal) Anthropological Institute of Great Britain and Ireland.* (London) 17:68–74, 1887.

———. "On a Safe Conclusion Concerning the Origin of the Eskimo." *Journal of the (Royal) Anthropological Institute of Great Britain and Ireland.* (London) 19:452–458, 1890.

———. *Tales and Traditions of the Eskimo.* With a sketch of their habits, religion, language, and other peculiarities. Translated from Danish by the author. Edited by Dr. Robert Brown. Numerous illustrations drawn and engraved by Eskimo. Edinburgh: W. Blackwood and Sons, 1875. xii, 472 pp., fold. front., illus.

Ross, John
Appendix to the Narrative of a Second Voyage in search of a Northwest Passage, and of a Residence in the Arctic Regions during the Years 1829, 1830, 1831, 1832, 1833. London: A. W. Webster, 1835. 2 vols., front., (port. v. 2), plates (part. col.), maps (part. fold.), col. plan.

Shapiro, H. L.
"The Alaskan Eskimo." *Anthropological Papers of the American Museum of Natural History.* (New York) 31:347–384, 1931

———. "Some Observations on the Origin of the Eskimos." *Proceedings of the (Fifth) Pacific Science Congress.* (Toronto) 5 (Part 4):2723–2732, 1933.

Simmons, H. Q.
"Eskimaernas Forna och Nutida Utbredning Samt Deras Vandringsväger." *Ymer.* 25:173–192, 1905.

Simpson, John, Dr.
"Observations on the Western Eskimo, and the Country they Inhabit; from Notes Taken During Two Years at Point Barrow." *Reprinted and Presented to the Arctic Expedition of 1875 by the Royal Geographical Society,* pp. 233–275, 1875 (London).

Steensby, H. P.
"An Anthropological Study of the Origin of Eskimo Culture." *Meddelelser om Grønland.* (Kjøbenhavn) 53:39–228, 1917.

———. *Om Eskimokulturens Oprindelse.* Kjøbenhavn: 1905. 219 pp.

Stefansson, Vilhjalmur
"The Eskimo and Civilization." *American Museum Journal.* (New York) 12:195–204, 1912.

———. "Eskimos." *In: Encyclopedia Britannica.* 14th Edition, 8:708–710, 1937.

———. "Prehistoric and Present Commerce among the Arctic Coast Eskimo." *Museum Bulletins of the Canada Department of Mines, Geological Survey.* (Ottawa) 6:1–29, 1914.

Sutherland, P. C., Dr.
"On the Eskimo." *Journal of the Ethnological Society of London.* (London) 4:193–214, 1856.

Thalbitzer, W.
"Eskimo." *Bulletins of the Bureau of American Ethnology.* (Washington) 40 (Part 1):967–1069, 1911.

——.
"Der Ethnographische Zusammenhang der Eskimo Grönlands mit denen der Hudsonbai." *Baessler-Archiv.* (Berlin) 2:32–44, 1912.

Uhlenbeck, C. C.
"Eskimo en Oer-Indogermannsch." *Mededeelingen der Koniklijke Akademie van Wetenschappen, Afdeeling Letterkunde.* (Amsterdam) 77A (Part 6):179–196, 1935.

——.
"Ontwerp van Eene Vergelijkende Vormleer der Eskimo-Talen." *Verhandelingen der Koninklijke Akademie van Wetenschappen, Afdeeling Letterkunde.* (Amsterdam) 8 (Part 3):1–76, 1907. n.s.

——.
"Opmerkingen Over Het Eskimo-Problem." *Jaarboek der Koninklijke Akademie van Wetenschappen te Amsterdam.* pp. 1–14, 1936.

Van Valin, W. B.
Eskimo Land Speaks. Caldwell, Idaho: The Caxton Press, Ltd., 1941.

Victor, Paul Émile
My Eskimo Life. Translated from the French by Jocelyn Godefido. London: H. Hamilton, 1938. v, 349 pp., illus., maps, diagrs.

Weyer, Edward Moffat
The Eskimos: Their Environment and Folkways. New Haven: Yale University Press, 1932. 483 pp.
Has the best treatment of religion among the Eskimos.

Whittaker, C. R.
Arctic Eskimo. A Record of Fifty Years' Experience and Observation among the Eskimo. London: Seeley Service and Company, Ltd. 1927. 259 pp., illus., map.
Chapter on folklore.

Wissler, C., ed.
"Notes Concerning New Collections." *Anthropological Papers of the American Museum of Natural History.* (New York) 2:314–320, 1909.

Zolotarev, A.
"On the Question of the Origin of the Eskimo." *Anthropological Journal* 1, (Moscow), 1937. In Russian, English resumé.

MYTHS—FOLKTALES—LEGENDS

"Bibliography of Eskimo Mythology." *JAFL* 8:116–117, 1895.

Bayliss, C. K.
Treasury of Eskimo Tales. Illustrated in color by George Carlson. New York: Thomas Y. Crowell and Company, 1922. vii, 135 pp., col. front., col. pls.

Boas, Franz
"Eskimo Tales and Songs." *JAFL* 7:45–50, 1894; 10:109–115, 1897.

——.
"Folk-lore of the Eskimo." *JAFL* 17:1–13, 1904.

Bogoras, W. G.
"Le mythe de l'animal-dieux mourant et ressuscitant." *Proceedings of the International Congress of Americanists.* (Paris) 22 (Part 2):35–52, 1928.

Burrows, E.
"Eskimo Tales." *JAFL* 39:79–81, 1926.

"Eskimo Animal Tales."
JAFL 4:16–19, 1891; 12:17–23, 1899.

Eskimo Märchen; übersezt von Paul Sock. Berlin: Axel Juncker, 1924. 183 pp.
Eskimo folk tales.

"Eskimo Tales" (and songs).
JAFL 2:123–131, 1889; 7:45–50, 1894; 10:109–115, 1897.

Golder, F. A.
"Eskimo and Aleut Stories from Alaska." *JAFL* 22:10–24, 1909.

Kroeber, A. L.
"Animal Tales of the Eskimo." *JAFL* 12:17–23, 1899.

Lee, F. H., ed.
Folk Tales of All Nations. New York: Tudor Publishing Company, 1946. 947 pp.
Eskimo Tales, pp. 53-60.

Morrison, A. D.
"Tales the Eskimos Tell." *School Aids,* 1944.

Munn, T. H.
"Tales of the Eskimo." *Chambers Journal,* (London) pp. 425–428, 534–537, 553–555, 668–672, 681–683, 1922.

Murdoch, John
"A Few Legendary Fragments from the Point Barrow Eskimos." *American Naturalist* 19:594, (July) 1886.

Rasmussen, Knud, and Worster, W. W.
Eskimo Folk-Tales. London: Glydenal, 1921.

Riggs, R. C.
Animal Stories from Eskimo Land, adapted from the original Eskimo stories, collected by Dr. Daniel S. Neumann, with illustrations and decorations by George W. Hood. New York: Frederick A. Stokes Company, 1923. vi, 113 pp., col. front., col. illus.

Rink, Signe
"A Comparative Study of the Indian and Eskimo Legends." *Proceedings of the 13th Session of the International Congress of Americanists,* pp. 279–305, 1902.

———.
"The Girl and the Dogs—An Eskimo Tale with Comments." *AA* 11:181–187, 1898. o.s.

Róheim, G.
"Die Sedna Sage." *Imago* 10:159–177, 1924.

Smith, H. I.
"Notes on Eskimo Tradition." *JAFL* 7:209–216, 1894.

Wardle, H. N.
"The Sedna Cycle." *AA* 2:568–580, 1900. n.s.

Worster, W. W.
"Eskimo Folklore and Myths." *Edinburgh Review* 242:94–107.

BELIEFS—CUSTOMS—MAGIC

Anon.
"A Group of Esquimaux Indians." *The American Magazine of Knowledge* 2:145, Dec., 1835.
Description of habits, manner of dress, and customs of the Esquimos of America and Asia.

———.
"Indians of America." *Merry's Museum* 4:141–143, Nov., 1842.
Chapt. XXV: The Esquimaux—Personal appearance, houses, food, fishing, females, dress, children, character, beliefs.

Birket-Smith, K.
"Det eskimoiske slaegtskabssystem." *Geografisk Tidsskrift* (Kjøbenhavn) 30:96–111, 1927.

Cross, J. F.
"Eskimo Children." *Southern Workman* (Hampton, Va.) 37:433–437, 1908.

Drake, F. S.
"A Northern Custom." *The American Pioneer* 2:88, Feb., 1843.
Attitude towards killing among the Esquimaux.

"Eskimo Ceremonies of Initiation."
JAFL 7:213–214, 1894.

"Eskimo Customs."
JAFL 3:65–67, 1890.

Felstead, Edwin
"Eskimo Sorcerers." *Occult Review* (London) 55:98–101, 1932.

Giffen, N. M.
The Rôles of Men and Women in Eskimo Culture. Chicago: University of Chicago Press, 1930. 114 pp.

Gilbertson, A. N.
"Some Ethical Phases of Eskimo Culture." *Journal of Religious Psychology.* 6:321–374, 7:45–74, 1913–1914.

Hawkes, E. W.
"Eskimo Magic." *Wide World Magazine* (London) 61:141–145, 1928.

Hermant, P.
"Evolution Economique et Sociale de Certaines Peuplades de l'Amérique du Nord." *Bulletin de la Société Royale Belge de Géographie.* (Bruxelles) 28:321–341, 1904.

Hoebel, E. Adamson
"Law-ways of the Primitive Eskimos." *Journal of Criminal Law and Criminology* 31, (No. 6): 663–683, 1941.

Hough, W.
"The Lamp of the Eskimo." *Reports of the United States National Museum.* (Washington) pp. 1025–1057, 1896.

König, H.
"Das Recht der Polarvölker." *Anthropos* 22: 689–746, 24:87–143, 621–664, 1927–1929.

———.
"Das Rechtsbruch und sein Ausgleich bei den Eskimo." *Anthropos.* 18–19:484–515, 771–792, 20:276–315, 1923–1925.

Lantis, M.
"The Alaskan Whale Cult and Its Affinities." *AA* 40:438–464, 1938. n.s.

———.
"The Social Structure of the Nunivak Eskimo." *Transaction of the American Philosophical Society,* n.s. 35 (No. 3):152–323, 1946. Bibl., index.

Laufer, B.
"The Eskimo Screw as a Culture-Historical Problem." *AA* 17:396–406, 1915. n.s.

Marderner, J.
"Das Gemeinschaftsleben der Eskimo." *Mitteilungen der Anthropologischen Gesellschaft.* (Wien) 69:273–348, 1940.

Mason, O. T.
"Aboriginal American Harpoons." *Reports of the United States National Museum.* (Washington) Part 2:193–304, 1900.

———.
"Throwing-Sticks in the National Museum." *Reports of the United States National Museum.* (Washington) pp. 279–289, 1884.

———.
"The Ulu or Woman's Knife of the Eskimo." *Reports of the United States National Museum.* (Washington) Part 2:411–416, 1890.

Mathiassen, T.
"Notes on Knud Rasmussen's Archaeological Collections from the Western Eskimo." *Proceedings of the International Congress of Americanists.* (Paris) 23:395–399, 1928.

———.
"The Present Stage of Eskimo Archaeology." *Acta Archaeologica* 2:185–199, 1931.

"Det Vingede Naalhaus." *Geografisk Tidsskrift.* (Kjøbenhavn) 32:15–22, 1929.

Mauss, M., and Beuchat, M. H.
"Essai sur les Variations Saisonnières des Sociétés Eskimos." *L'Année Sociologique* 9: 39–130, 1906.

Murdoch, John
"On the Siberian Origin of Some Customs of the Western Eskimo." *AA* 1:325–335, 1888.

"Sinew-Backed Bow of the Eskimo." *Smithsonian (Institution) Miscellaneous Collections.* (Washington) 34 (Part 2):168–171, 1893.

"A Study of the Eskimo Bows in the U. S. Museum." *Reports of the United States National Museum.* (Washington) Part 2:207–216, 1884.

Porsild, M. P.
"The Principle of the Screw in the Technique of the Eskimo." *AA* 17:1–16, 1915. n.s.

Soper, J. D.
"Eskimo Dogs of the Canadian Arctic." *Canadian Geographical Journal* 20:96–108, 1940.

Thalbitzer, William
"The Cultic Deities of the Innuit." *Proceedings of the International Congress of Americanists.* (Paris) 22 (Part 2):367–393, 1926.

"Die Kultischen Gottheiten der Eskimos." *Archiv für Religions-wissenschaft.* (Leipzig) 26:364–430, 1928.

"Les Magiciens Esquimaux, leurs Conceptions du monde, de l'Ame et de la vie." *Proceedings of the 22nd Session of the International Congress of Americanists* pp. 73–106, 1930.

Turquetil, Arséne
"Have the Eskimo the Concept of a Supreme Being?" *Primitive Man* 9 (No. 3):33–38, 1936.

GAMES

"Eskimo Games."
JAFL 36:281–294, 1923.

SPEECH

Birket-Smith, K.
"Five Hundred Eskimo Words." *Report of the Fifth Thule Expedition.* (Copenhagen) 3 (Part 3):5–64, 1928.

Chamberlain, A. F.
"The Eskimo Race and Language." *Proceedings of the Canadian Institute.* (Toronto) (Ser. 3) 6:261–337, 1887–1888.

Pilling, J. C.
Bibliography of the Eskimo Language. *Bulletins of the Bureau of American Ethnology.* (Washington) 1:1–112, 1887.

Rink, H.
"The Eskimo Dialects." *Journal of the (Royal) Anthropological Institute of Great Britain and Ireland.* (London) 15:239–245, 1886.

"Om de Eskimoiske Dialekter." *Aarbøger for Nordisk Oldkyndighed og Historie.* (Kjøbenhavn) 20:219–260, 1885.

Thalbitzer, William
"Eskimo as a Linguistic Type." *Proceedings of the International Congress of Americanists.* (Paris) 23:895–904, 1928.

"Eskimo Dialects and Wanderings." *Proceedings of the International Congress of Americanists.* (Paris) 14:107–118, 1904.

"Eskimo Language." In: *Encyclopedia Britannica.* 14th Edition. 8:707–708, 1937.

"The Eskimo Numerals." *Journal de la Société Finno-Ougrienne.* 25 (Part 2):1–25, 1908.

"Is There Any Connection Between the Eskimo Language and the Uralian?" *Proceedings of the International Congress of Americanists.* (Paris) 22 (Part 2):551–567, 1926.

A Phonetical Study of the Eskimo Language, based on observations made on a journey in North Greenland 1900–1901; with a historical introduction about the east Eskimo, a comparison of the Eskimo dialects, a new collection of Greenlandic folk-tales, songs, and music, and a map of the Eskimo territories. Copenhagen: Printed by B. Luno, 1904. xvii, 405 pp., illus. Melodies of the Songs: (pp. 375–387).

Uhlenbeck, C. C.
"Uralische Anklänge in den Eskimosprachen." *Zeitschrift der Deutschen Morgenländischen Gesellschaft.* (Leipzig) 59:757–765, 1905.

Wells, R., and Kelly, J. W.
"English-Eskimo and Eskimo-English Vocabularies. *U. S. Bureau of Education, Circular of Information.* Part 2:1–72, 1890.

FOLK ART

Anon.
Art of the Arctic. The Living Museum, Vol. 9, No. 3. Springfield: Illinois State Museum, 1947. 210 pp.

Boas, Franz
"Decorative Designs of Alaskan Needle Cases." *Proceedings of the United States National Museum,* 34:321–344. Washington, D. C.: U. S. Government Printing Office, 1908.

Hoffman, W. J.
"The Graphic Art of the Eskimos." *Reports of the United States National Museum.* (Washington) pp. 739–968, 1895.

Laguna, F. de
"A Comparison of Eskimo and Palaeolithic Art." *American Journal of Archaeology* 36: 477–508, 37:77–107, 1932–1933.

Simpson J. Clarence
"Eskimo Art in Ivory." *Masterkey* 22:183–188, 1948.

Speck, F. G.
"Central Eskimo and Indian Dot Ornamentation." *Indian Notes.* 2:151–172, 1925.

MUSIC
GENERAL STUDIES

Boas, Franz
"Eskimo Tales and Songs." *JAFL* 7:45–50, 1894; 10:109–115, 1897.

————, **and Rink, H.**
"Eskimo Tales and Songs." *JAFL* 2:123–131, 1889.

Edgerly, Beatrice
From the Hunter's Bow. The History and Romance of Musical Instruments. New York: G. P. Putnam's Sons, 1942.

"Eskimo Songs."
JAFL 2:123–131, 1889; 7:45–50, 1894; 10: 109–115, 1897; 28:96–98, 1915.

Hague, Eleanor
"Eskimo Songs." *JAFL* 28:96–98, 1915.

Nansen, Fridtjof
Eskimoliv. Kristiana: H. Aschehoug and Company, 1891. viii, 293 pp.
   Chapter XII: Discusses Eskimo Music.

Sargent, Margaret
The Native and Primitive Music of Canada. Mimeographed, 41 pp. Texts and music. In the Columbia University (New York) Music Library, n.d., bibl.
   Chapter 8: "The Eskimo." The author draws the information from *On Eskimo Music* by Thuren and Thalbitzer.

Thalbitzer, William
A Phonetical Study of the Eskimo Language. ... Copenhagen: B. Luno, 1904.
   See entry above, contains discussion and songs, (pp. 375–387).

Whittaker, C. E.
Arctic Eskimo. A Record of Fifty Year's Experience and Observation Among the Eskimo. With 60 illustrations and map. London: Seeley, Service and Company, Ltd., n.d.
   Excellent chapter on folklore, games, songs and dances.

ARRANGEMENTS
————: *Band*

"Animal Magic."
   Cowell, H.: Leeds Music Corp.
   A fantasy on Eskimo Indian names.

RECORDS

Herzog, George
Eskimo. Records Contained in American Collections. American Council of Learned Societies (Washington, D. C.) Bulletin 24:25, 1936.

U. S. Library of Congress. Division of Music. Folklore Section.
Eskimo Recordings—made by individuals and institutions deposited in the Archive of American Folksong.   AAFS–LC

ALEUT
FOLKLORE
GENERAL STUDIES

Anderson, H. D., and Eells, W. C.
Alaska Natives. Stanford: Stanford University Press, 1935. 472 pp.

Anonymous
"Aleut." *Bulletins of the Bureau of American Ethnology.* (Washington) 30 (Part 1):36–37, 1907.

Bancroft, H. H.
The Native Races of the Pacific States. Vol. I, pp. 87–94. New York: A. L. Bancroft and Co., 1875.

Barbeau, Charles Marius
"The Aleutian Route of Migration into America." *The Geographical Review* 35 (3): 424–443, 1945.

Berg, L.
"On the Origin of the Aleut." *Proceedings of the (Fifth) Pacific Science Congress.* (Toronto) 5 (Part 4):2773–2775, 1934.

Bushnell, D. I.
"Drawings by John Webber of Natives of the Northwest Coast." *Smithsonian (Institution) Miscellaneous Collection.* (Washington) 80 (Part 10):1–12, 1928.

Chamberlain, A. F.
"Aleuts." In: *Encyclopedia of Religion and Ethics.* J. Hastings, ed. (New York) 1:303–305, 1908.

Coxe, William
Account of the Russian Discoveries Between Asia and America. London: T. Caddell, 1787. xxviii, 454 pp.

Dall, W. H.
Alaska and Its Resources. Boston: Lee and Shepard, 1897. xii, 627 pp.

"On the Distribution and Nomenclature of the Native Tribes of Alaska." *Contributions to North American Ethnology, Department of the Interior, United States Geographical and Geological Survey of the Rocky Mountain Region.* (Washington) 1:7–40, 1877.

"On the Distribution of the Native Tribes of Alaska." *Proceedings of the American Association for the Advancement of Science.* (Philadelphia) 18:263–273, 1869.

Desmond, Alice Curtis
The Sea Cats. Illustrations by Wilfred Bronson. New York: The Macmillan Company, 1944. 216 pp.
A book for young readers, of life among the Aleuts.

Eells, W. C.
"Mental Ability of the Native Races of Alaska." *Journal of Applied Psychology.* (Worcester, Bloomington) 17:417–438, 1933.

Erman, A.
"Ethnographische Wahrnehmungen und Erfahrungen an den Küsten des Berings-Meeres." *Zeitschrift für Ethnologie.* (Berlin) 2:295–327, 369–393, 3:149–175, 205–219, 1870–1871.

Hellwald, F. von
"Das Volk der Aleuten." *Ausland* 54:789–793, 1881.

Hrdlicka, A.
"Anthropological Explorations on the Aleutian and Commander Islands." *Explorations and Field-Work of the Smithsonian Institution.* (Washington) pp. 87–94, 1937.

"Exploration in the Aleutian and the Commander Islands." *Explorations and Field-Work of the Smithsonian Institute.* (Washington) pp. 79–86, 1938.

Jacobi, A.
"Carl Heinrich Mercks Ethnographische Beobachtungen über die Völker des Beringsmeers." *Baessler-Archiv.* (Berlin) 20:113–137, 1937.

Jochelson, Waldemar
History, Ethnology and Anthropology of the Aleut. Carnegie Institute Publication 432. Washington, D. C.: Carnegie Institute, 1933. 91 pp., illus., bibl.

"People of the Foggy Seas." *Natural History.* (New York) 28:413–424, 1928.

"Scientific Results of the Ethnological Section of the Riabouschinsky Expedition." *Proceedings of the International Congress of Americanists.* (Paris) 18:334–343, 1912.

Langsdorff, G. H. von
Voyages and Travels in Various Parts of the World, London: H. Colburn, 1813–1814. 2 vols., illus., music.

Löwe, F.
"Wenjaminow über die aleutischen Inseln und deren Bewohner." *Archiv für Wissenschaftliche Kunde von Russland.* (Berlin) 2:459–495, 1842.

Lütké, F.
Voyage Autour du Monde. Paris: 1835. 3 vols.

Muir, J.
The Cruise of the Corwin. Boston: Houghton Mifflin Co., 1917. xxxi, 278 pp.

Petroff, I.
"The Limit of the Innuit Tribes on the Alaskan Coast." *American Naturalist.* (Salem) 16:567–575, 1882.

The Population and Resources of Alaska. Compilations of Narratives of Explorations in Alaska. pp. 239–257. Washington: 1900.

Pinart, A.
"Les Aléoutes et leur origine." *Mémoirs de la Société d'Ethnographie* 11:155–165, 1872.

Schwatka, F.
Report of a Military Reconnaissance made in Alaska in 1883, pp. 323–362. Washington: 1900.

Veniaminov, Ivan
"Charakterzüge der Aleuten." *Beiträge zur Kenntnis des Russischen Reiches (und Angränzenden Lander Asiens).* (St. Petersburg) 1:177–225, 1839.

"Les Iles Aléoutes et leurs habitants." *Nouvelles Annales des Voyages.* (Paris) 112:66–82, 124:112–148, 1849.

Zapiski ob Ostrovakh Unalashkinskavo Otdyela. St. Petersburg: Roseskoye Akademi, 1840. 3 vols.

MYTHS—FOLKTALES—LEGENDS

Golder, F. A.
"Aleutian Stories." *JAFL* 18:215–222, 1905.

"Eskimo and Aleut Stories from Alaska." *JAFL* 22:10–24, 1909.

"Songs and Stories of the Aleuts, with transcriptions from Veniaminov." *JAFL* 20:132–142, 1907.

Lavrischeff, T. I.
"Two Aleut Tales." *AA* 30:121–124, 1928. n.s.

Ransom, Jay Ellis
"Stories, Myths and Superstitions of Fox Island Aleut Children." *JAFL* 60:62–72, 1947.

BELIEFS—CUSTOMS

Dall, W. H.
"Alaskan Mummies." *American Naturalist.* (Salem) 9:433–440, 1875.

Elliott, C. P.
"Salmon Fishing Grounds and Canneries."
*Compilation of Narratives of Explorations in
Alaska.* pp. 738–741, Washington: 1900.

Heizer, Robert F.
"Aconite Poison Whaling in Asia and Amer-
ica; an Aleutian Transfer to the New World."
*Anthropological Papers No. 24, Bulletin 133,
Bureau of American Ethnology,* pp. 415–468,
pl. 18–23A, fig. 56–60. Washington, D. C.: U. S.
Government Printing Office, 1943.

> Describes whaling methods from Japan, Kam-
> chatka, Kurile, Eskimo, Aleut to Vancouver,
> Washington Northwest.

——————.
"A Pacific Eskimo Invention in Whale Hunting
in Historic Times." *AA* 45:120–122, 1943. n.s.

Hrdlicka, A.
"Exploration of Mummy Caves in the Aleutian
Islands." *Scientific Monthly.* (New York) 52:
5–23, 113–130, 1941.

Ransom, Jay Ellis
"About Religious Beliefs: Veniamonov's Account." *JAFL* 58:346–349, 1945.

——————.
"Aleut Natural Food Economy." *AA* 48:607–
623, 1946. n.s.
> Practices, techniques and ceremonies of hunting
> and of food preparation of the Fox Island
> Aleuts.

Weyer, Edward Moffat, Jr.
"An Aleutian Burial." *Anthropological Papers
of the American Museum of Natural History.*
(New York) 31:219–238, 1929.

FOLK ART—SPEECH

Buynitsky, S. N.
English-Aleutian Dictionary. San Francisco:
1871. 13 pp.

Geoghegan, Richard Henry
*The Aleut Language: The Elements of Aleut
Grammar with a Dictionary in Two Parts Con-
taining Basic Vocabularies of Aleut and Eng-
lish.* Washington, D. C.: U. S. Government
Printing Office, 1944. 169 pp.

Henry, V.
*Esquisse d'une Grammaire Raisonnée de la
Langue Aléoute.* Paris: Maisonneuve et cie,
1879. 73 pp.

Ivanov, S. V.
"Aleut Hunting Headgear and Its Ornamentation." *Proceedings of the International Congress of Americanists.* (Paris) 23:477–504,
1928.

Jochelson, W.
"The Aleut Language and Its Relation to the
Eskimo Dialects." *Proceedings of the International Congress of Americanists.* (Paris) 18:
96–104, 1912.

Kissell, M.
"An Aleutian Basket." *American Museum
Journal.* (New York) 7:133–136, 1907.

Schott, W.
"Ueber die Sprachen des Russischen Amerika
nach Wenjaminow." *Archiv für Wissenschaftliche Kunde von Russland.* (Berlin) 7:126–
143, 1849.

Thalbitzer, W.
"The Aleutian Language compared with
Greenlandic." *International Journal of Amer-
ican Linguistics.* (New York) 2:40–57, 1921.

GAMES

Ransom, Jay Ellis
"Children's Games Among the Aleut." *JAFL*
59:196–198, 1946.

MUSIC
GENERAL STUDIES

Eells, W. C.
"Mechanical, Physical, and Musical Ability of
the Native Races of Alaska." *Journal of Applied Psychology.* (Worcester, Bloomington)
17:493–506, 1933.

Golder, F. A.
"Songs and Stories of the Aleuts, with Transcriptions from Veniaminov." *JAFL* 20:132–
142, 1907.

BAFFINLAND ESKIMO
FOLKLORE
GENERAL STUDIES

Abbes, H.
"Die Eskimos des Cumberland-Sundes."
Globus 46:198–201, 213–218, 1884.

Bilby, Julian W.
Among Unknown Eskimo. London: S. Service
& Co., 1923. 280 pp.

——————.
Nanook of the North. London: Arrowsmith,
1925. 318 pp., illus.

Birket-Smith, Kaj.
"Anthropological Observations on the Central
Eskimos." *Report of the Fifth Thule Expedi-
tion 1921–1924, Danish Expedition to Arctic
North America* 3. (No. 1). Copenhagen: 1940.
121 pp., illus.

Boas, Franz
"Baffin-Land." *Petermanns Mitteilungen, Er-
gänzungshefte.* (Gotha) 17 (Part 5):1–100,
1885.

"The Central Eskimo." *6th Annual Report: Bureau of Ethnology*, 1884–1885. pp. 409–667, pls. 2–10, figs. 390–546. Washington, D. C.: U. S. Gov't Printing Office, 1888.

Geography of Northeastern America, distribution of the tribes, Baffin Land, Western Shore of Hudson Bay, Barthia Felix and Back River, Smith Sound, etc.: trade and intercourse between the tribes, influence of geographical conditions on distribution of settlements, etc.

——————.
"Cumberland Sound and Its Eskimos." *Popular Science Monthly*. (New York) 26:768–779, 1885.

——————.
"The Eskimo of Baffin Land and Hudson Bay." *Bulletin of the American Museum of Natural History*. (New York) 15:1–570, 1901–1907.

——————.
"The Eskimo of Baffin Land." *Smithsonian (Institution) Miscellaneous Collection*. (Washington) 34 (Part 2):95–102, 1893.

From notes collected by Capt. G. Comer, Capt. J. S. Mutch and Rev. E. J. Peck.

——————.
"An Eskimo Winter." *American Indian Life*. E. C. Parsons, ed., pp. 363–378. New York: B. W. Huebsch, 1925. 419 pp.

——————.
"Second Report on the Eskimo of Baffin Land and Hudson Bay." From notes collected by Captain George Carver, Captain James S. Mutch, and Rev. E. J. Peck. *Bulletin, American Museum of Natural History*. (New York) 15, (Part 2):371–570, 1907. Illus.

——————.
"A Year Among the Eskimo." *Journal of the American Geographical Society*. (New York) 19:383–402, 1887.

Chappell, E. (Lieut. R. N.)
Narrative of a Voyage to Hudson's Bay in His Majesty's ship Rosamund, containing some account of the northeastern coast of America, and of the tribes inhabiting that remote region. London, Eng.: 1817.

Dobbs, Arthur
An Account of the Countries Adjoining to Hudson's Bay in the North-west Part of America. London, Eng.: J. Robinson, 1784. 211 pp.

Ellis, Henry
A Voyage to Hudson's Bay, by the Dobbs Galley and California, in the years 1746 and 1747 for discovering a northwest passage. London: H. Whitridge, 1748. 336 pp.

Hall, C. F.
Arctic Researches and Life with the Esquimaux. New York: Harper & Brother, 1865. xxviii, 595 pp., illus.

Jenness, Diamond
"A New Eskimo Culture in Hudson Bay." *Geographical Review*. (New York) 15:428–437, 1925.

Kumlien, L.
"Fragmentary Notes on the Eskimo of Cumberland Sound." *Bull. U. S. Nat. Mus.* 15:1–171, 1879.

Manning, Mrs. Tom
Igloo for the Night. Toronto: Univ. of Toronto Press, 1947. 234 pp., illus.

Markham, C. R., ed.
The Voyages of William Baffin. London: Hakluyt Society, 1881. 192 pp.

Oetteking, B.
"A Contribution to the Physical Anthropology of Baffin Land." *American Journal of Physical Anthropology*. (Washington) 15:421–468, 1931.

Parry, W.
Journal of a Voyage for the Discovery of a North-West Passage. London: J. Murray, 1821. xxix, 310 pp.

MYTHS—FOLKTALES—LEGENDS

Boas, Franz
"Eskimo Tales and Songs." *JAFL* 2:123–131, 7:45–50, 10:109–115, 1889–1897.

——————.
"Die Sagen der Baffin-Land Eskimos." *Verhandlungen der Berliner Gesellschaft für Anthropologie, Ethnologie und Urgeschichte*. (Berlin) pp. 161–166, 1885.

BELIEFS—CUSTOMS—SPEECH

Boas, Franz
"Der Eskimo Dialekt des Cumberland-Sundes." *Mitteilungen der Anthropologischen Gesellschaft*. (Wien) 24:97–114, 1894.

——————.
"Religious Beliefs of the Central Eskimo." *Popular Science Monthly*. (New York) 57:624–631, 1900.

——————.
"Die religiösen Vorstellungen und einige Gebräuche der zentralen Eskimos." *Petermanns Mitteilungen aus Justus Perthes Geographischer Anstalt*. (Gotha) 33:302–316, 1887.

Heinbecker, P., and Pauli, R. H.
"Blood Grouping of Baffin Island Eskimos." *Journal of Immunology* 15:407–409, 1928.

Morgan, L. H.
"Systems of Consanguinity and Affinity." *Smithsonian (Institution) Contributions to Knowledge*. (Washington) 17:291–382, 1871.

Munn, H. T.
"The Economic Life of the Baffin Island Eskimo." *Geographical Journal.* (London) 59: 269–273, 1922.

Speck, F. G.
"Eskimo Collections from Baffin Land and Ellesmere Land." *Indian Notes.* (New York) 1:143–149, 1924.

CARIBOU ESKIMO

FOLKLORE

GENERAL STUDIES

Barbeau, Marius
Mountain Cloud. Caldwell, Idaho: Caxton Printers, Ltd., 1944.
A novel of Indian life in Canada's Hudson Bay region.

Birket-Smith, Kaj.
"The Caribou Eskimos. Material and Social Life and their Cultural Position. I, II." *Report, Fifth Thule Expedition 1921–1924,* 5:1–307, 1929; 5:1–420, 1929. (Copenhagen).

Boas, Franz
"The Eskimo of Baffin Land and Hudson Bay." *Bull. Amer. Mus. Nat. Hist.* (New York) 15: 1–570, 1901–1907.

Breynat, Gabriel
Cinquante ans au pays des neiges. Vol. I, Chez les mangeurs de caribou. Montréal: Fides, 1945. 347 pp., illus.

Gabus, Jean
"Les Mouvements Migratoires chez les Esqui-maux-Caribous." *Anthropos* (Freiburg) 35–36:221–238, 1942.

Gilder, W. H.
Schwatka's Search. Sledging in the Arctic in Quest of the Franklin Records. New York: Charles Scribner's Sons, 1881. xvi, 316 pp., illus.

Hanbury, D. T.
Sport and Travel in the Northland of Canada. London: E. Arnold, 1904. 319 pp.

Mathiassen, T.
"Spørgsmaalet om Eskimokulturens Oprin-delse." *Geografisk Tidsskrift.* (Kjøbenhavn) 32:116–126, 33:65–74, 1929–1930.

Rasmussen, Knud
"Iglulik and Caribou Eskimo Texts." *Report of the Fifth Thule Expedition.* (Copenhagen) 7 (Part 3):1–160, 1930.

———.
Intellectual Culture of the Hudson Bay Eski-mos. Report of the Fifth Thule Expedition 1921–1924. Vol. VII. Copenhagen: Gyldenhal, 1930. 3 vols. in 1, plates, ports., maps.
Discussion and texts of the Iglulik and Caribou Eskimos.

Turquetil, A.
"Notes sur les Esquimaux de Baie Hudson." *Anthropos* 21:419–434, 1926.

Tyrrell, J. B.
Across the Sub-Arctics of Canada. Toronto: T. F. Unwin, 1897. vi, 280 pp., illus.

CUSTOMS—BELIEFS

Manning, T. H.
"Pipestems of the Caribou Eskimos." *AA* 50:162–163, 1948.

Turquetil, A.
"Have the Eskimo the Concept of a Supreme Being?" *Primitive Man.* (Washington) 9:33–38, 1936.

———.
"Le Mariage chez les Esquimaux." *Revue de l'Université d'Ottawa,* Section Spéciale. 4:125–137, 197–237, 1935.

———.
"The Religion of the Central Eskimo." *Primitive Man.* (Washington) 2:57–64, 1929.

COPPER ESKIMO

FOLKLORE

GENERAL STUDIES

Collinson, R.
Journal of H. M. S. Enterprise. London: S. Low, Marston, Searle & Rivington, 1889. xi, 531 pp.

Finnie, R.
Lure of the North. Philadelphia: David McKay Company, 1940. 227 pp.

Hanbury, D. T.
Sport and Travel in the Northland of Canada. London: E. Arnold, 1904. xxxii, 319 pp., illus.

Hearne, S.
A Journey from Fort Prince of Wales in Hudson's Bay to the Northern Ocean. London: A. Strahan and T. Cadell, 1795. xliv, 458 pp., illus.

Jenness, Diamond
"The 'Blond' Eskimos." *AA* 23:257–267, 1921. n.s.

———.
"The Copper Eskimo." *Geographical Review.* (New York) 4:81–91, 1917.

———.
"The Cultural Transformation of the Copper Eskimo." *Geographical Review.* (New York) 11:541–550, 1921.

———.
"The Life of the Copper Eskimo." *Report of the Canadian Arctic Expedition.* (Ottawa) 12: 1–277, 1922.

———.
"The Origin of the Copper Eskimos and their Copper Culture." *Geographical Review.* (New York) 8:540–551, 1923.

The People of the Twilight. New York: The Macmillan Company, 1928. xii, 247 pp., illus.

Merwin, B. W.
"The Copper Eskimo." *Museum Journal, University of Pennsylvania.* (Philadelphia) 6:163–168, 1915.

Rasmussen, Knud
Intellectual Culture of the Copper Eskimos. Report of the Fifth Thule Expedition 1922–1924. Vol. 9. Danish Expedition to Arctic North America in charge of Knud Rasmussen. Copenhagen: Gyldendalske Boghandel, Nordisk, Forlag, (AN), 1932. 350 pp.

Richardson, J.
Arctic Searching Expedition. London: Longman, Brown, Green, and Longman, 1851. 2 vols.

Rickard, T. A.
"The Chalcolithic Eskimos." *Man* 38:191–192, 1938.

Stefansson, Vilhjálmur
The Friendly Arctic. New York: The Macmillan Co., 1921. xxxi, 784 pp., illus.

————.
My Life with the Eskimo. New York: The Macmillan Company, 1913. ix, 538 pp.

————.
Hunters of the Great North. London: G. G. Harrap & Co., 1923. 287 pp., illus.

————,and Irwin, Violet
Kak, the Copper Eskimo. New York: The Macmillan Co., 1924. vii, 253 pp., illus.

Sullivan, L.
"The 'Blond' Eskimo." *AA* 24:225–228, 1922. n.s.

Whittaker, C. E.
Arctic Eskimo. London: Seely Service and Company, Ltd., 1927. 259 pp.

MYTHS—FOLKTALES—LEGENDS

Jenness, D.
"Myths and Traditions from Northern Alaska, the Mackenzie Delta and Coronation Gulf." *Report of the Canadian Arctic Expedition.* (Ottawa) 13 (Part A):1–90, 1924.

CUSTOMS—FOLK ART—SPEECH

Cadzow, D. A.
"Eskimo Lamps and Cooking Vessels." *Indian Notes.* (New York) 1:26–28, 1924.

————.
"Native Copper Objects of the Copper Eskimo." *Ind. Notes and Monogr.* (New York) 8 (Ser. 2):1–22, 1920.

————.
"Unusual Eskimo Snow Shovel." *Indian Notes.* (New York) 1:150–152, 1924.

Jenness, Diamond
"Eskimo String Figures." *Report of the Canadian Arctic Expedition.* (Ottawa) 13 (Part B):1–192, 1924.

————.
"Comparative Vocabulary of the Western Eskimo Dialects." *Report of the Canadian Arctic Expedition.* (Ottawa) 15 (Part A):1–134, 1928.

MUSIC
GENERAL STUDIES

Béclard-d'Harcourt, Marguerite
"Le Systeme Pentaphone dans les Chants des Copper-Eskimos." *Proceedings of the 22nd Session of the International Congress of Americanists,* 2:15–23, 1928.

Roberts, Helen H., and Jenness, Diamond
Songs of the Copper Eskimos. Report of the Canadian Arctic Expedition, 1913–1918. Volume XIV: *Eskimo Songs.* (Southern Party 1913–1916.) Ottawa: F. A. Acland, 1925. 506 pp.

EAST GREENLAND ESKIMO
FOLKLORE
GENERAL STUDIES

Amdrup, G.
"The Former Eskimo Settlements on the East Coast of Greenland." *Meddelelser om Grønland.* (Kjøbenhavn) 28:285–328, 1909.

Birket-Smith, K.
"Ethnographie Problemer i Grønland." *Geografisk Tidsskrift.* (Kjøbenhavn) 25:179–197, 1920.

————.
"The Greenlanders of the Present Day." *Greenland* 2:1–207, 1928.

Boas, Franz
"The Relationships of the Eskimos of East Greenland." *Science* 30:535–536, 1909. n.s.

Clavering, D. C.
"Journal of a Voyage to Spitzbergen and the East Coast of Greenland." *Edinburgh New Philosophical Journal* 9:1–30, 1830.

Dumbrava, C.
"Une Année au Milieu des Esquimaux." *La Geographie* 51:14–23, 1929.

Glob, P.
"Eskimo Settlements in Kempe Fjord and King Oscar Fjord." *Meddelelser om Grønland.* 102 (Part 2):1–97, 1935.

Graah, W. A.
Narrative of an Expedition to the East Coast of Greenland, London: J. W. Parker, 1837. xvi, 199 pp.

Hansen, S.
"Bidrag Til Østgrønlaendernes Anthropologi."
Meddelelser om Grønland. (Kjøbenhavn) 10:
1–41, 1886.

———.
"Contributions to the Anthropology of the East
Greenlanders." *Meddelelser om Grønland.*
(Kjøbenhavn) 39:149–179, 1911.

Henshaw, H. W.
"East Greenlanders." *Bulletins of the Bureau
of American Ethnology.* (Washington) 30
(Part 1):411–412, 1907.

Holm, G.
"Ethnological Sketch of the Angmagsalik
Eskimo." *Meddelelser om Grønland.* (Kjøben-
havn) 39:1–147, 1911.

———.
"Ethnologisk Skizze af Angmagsalikerne."
Meddelelser om Grønland. (Kjøbenhavn) 10:
43–182, 1887.

———.
"Konebaads-Expeditionen Til Grønlands Øst-
kyst." *Geografisk Tidsskrift.* (Kjøbenhavn)
8:79–98, 1886.

Johnson, D. M.
"Observations on the Eskimo Remains on the
East Coast of Greenland." *Meddelelser om
Grønland.* (Kjøbenhavn) 92 (Part 6):1–69,
1933.

Kruuse, C.
"Angmagsalikerne." *Geografisk Tidsskrift.*
(Kjøbenhavn) 16:211–217, 1902.

Larsen, H.
"Dødemandsbugten: an Eskimo Settlement
on Clavering Island." *Meddelelser om Grønland.* (Kjøbenhavn) 102 (Part 1):1–185, 1934.

Markham, C. R.
Franklin's Footsteps; A Sketch of Greenland.
London: Chapman and Hall, 1853. vii, 143 pp.

———.
"Papers on the Greenland Eskimos." *Arctic
Geography and Ethnology.* pp. 163–229. Lon-
don: 1875.

Mathiassen, T.
"The Archaeological Collection of the Cambridge East Greenland Expedition." *Meddelelser om Grønland.* (Kjøbenhavn) 74:137–166,
1929.

———.
"Bidrag til Angmagssalik-Eskimoernes Forhis-
torie." *Geografisk Tidsskrift.* (Kjøbenhavn)
35:129–136, 1932.

———.
"The Prehistory of the Angmagssalik Eskimos." *Meddelelser om Grønland.* (Kjøbenhavn) 92:1–158, 1933.

Mikkelson, E.
"The Eskimo of East Greenland." *Man* 38:188–
189, 1938.

Mirsky, J.
The Eskimo of Greenland. In: *Cooperation
and Competition Among Primitive Peoples,*
Margaret Mead, ed., pp. 51–86, New York:
McGraw-Hill, 1937.

Murdoch, John
"The East Greenlanders." *American Naturalist.*
21:133–138, 1887.

Nippgen, J.
"Le Folklore des Eskimos." *Revue d'Ethnographie et des Traditions Populaires.* 4:189–
192, 1923.

Normann, C.
"En Rejse Langs Grønlands Ostkyst i Aaret
1777." *Geografisk Tidsskrift.* (Kjøbenhavn)
2:49–63, 1878.

Paterson, T. T.
"Anthropogeographical Studies in Greenland."
*Journal of the (Royal) Anthropological Insti-
tute of Great Britain and Ireland.* (London)
69:45–76, 1936.

Peters, H.
"Anthropologie und Enthnographie." *Wissenschaftliche Ergebnisse der Deutschen Grönland Expedition Alfred Wegener.* 6:1–172,
1934.

Rasmussen, Knud
"South East Greenland." *Geografisk Tidsskrift.*
(Kjøbenhavn) 35:169–197, 1932.

Rink, H.
"Østgrønlaenderne i Deres Forhold Til Vest-
grønlaenderne og de Ørrige Eskimostammer."
Geografisk. Tidsskrift. (Kjøbenhavn) 8:139–
45, 1886.

———.
"Die Ostgrönlander." *Deutsche Geographische
Blätter.* 9(Part 3):228–239, 1886.

Roberts, B.
"The Cambridge Expedition to Scoresby
Sound." *Geographical Journal.* (London) 85:
234–251, 1935.

Ryder, C. H.
"Om den Tidligere Eskimoiske Bebyggelse
af Scoresby Sund." *Meddelelser om Grønland.*
(Kjøbenhavn 17:281–343, 1895.

Schell, O.
"Die Ostgrönlander."*Globus.* 94:85–88, 1908.

Schultz-Lorentzen, C. W.
"Eskimoernes Invandring i Grønland." *Meddelelser om Grønland.* (Kjøbenhavn) 26:289–
330, 1904.

———.
"Intellectual Culture of the Greenlanders."
Greenland. 2:209–270, 1928.

Stolpe, H.
"Über die Forschungsergebnisse der Schwedi-
schen Grönland-Expedition." *Proc. Intern.
Congr. Amer.* (Paris) 14:101–105, 1904.

Thalbitzer, William
The Ammasalik Eskimo; Contributions to the ethnology of the East Greenland natives. Copenhagen: Luno, 1914–1923. Vol. 1–2; Illus. plates, music, bibl.

"The Ammassalik Eskimo." *Meddelelser om Grønland.* (Kjøbenhavn) 53:435–481, 1917.

Eskimoiske Digte Fra Ostgrønland. Kjøbenhavn: Aschehoug and Co.,, 1920.

"Eskimokulturen ved Angmagssalik." *Geografisk Tidsskrift.* 19:56–69, 1907.

"Ethnographical Collections from East Greenland." *Meddelelser om Grønland.* (Kjøbenhavn) 39:319–755, 1912.

"Ethnological Description of the Amdrup Collection from East Greenland." *Meddelelser om Grønland.* (Kjøbenhavn) 28:329–542, 1909.

Fra Grønlands forskningens første dage. Kjøbenhavn: B. Lunos, 1932. 107 pp. illus.

Thomsen, T.
"The Angmagsalik Eskimo." *Meddelelser om Grønland.* (Kjøbenhavn) 53:379–434, 1917.

Thostrup, C. B.
"Ethnographic Description of the Eskimo Settlements and Stone Remains in North-East Greenland." *Meddelelser om Grønland.* (Kjøbenhavn) 44:177–355, 1917.

Victor, Paul E.
My Eskimo Life. London: H. Hamilton, 1938. 349 pp.

MYTHS—FOLKTALES—LEGENDS

Holm, G.
"Legends and Tales from Angmagsalik." *Meddelelser om Grønland.* (Kjøbenhavn) 39: 225–305, 1912.

"Sagn og Foretaellinger Fra Angmasalik." *Meddelelser om Grønland.* (Kjøbenhavn) 10:235–334, 1888.

Rasmussen, Knud
Eskimo Folk-Tales. W. Worster, ed., London: Gyldendal, 1921. 156 pp.

Myster og Sagn Fra Grønland. Kjøbenhavn: 1921. 382 pp.

Rink, H.
"Bemaerkninger til G. Holmes Samling af Sagn og Fortaellinger Fra Angmagsalik." *Meddelelser om Grønland.* (Kjøbenhavn) 10:335–345, 1887.

"Notes to G. Holm's Collection of Legends and Tales from Angmagsalik." *Meddelelser om Grønland.* (Kjøbenhavn) 39:307–317, 1912.

Thalbitzer, W.
Grønlandske Sagn om Eskimoernes Fortid. Stockholm: 1913.

Légendes et Chants Esquimaux du Groenland. Paris: Libraire Ernest Leroux, 1929. 188 pp.

BELIEFS—CUSTOMS

Birket-Smith, K.
"The Greenland Bow." *Meddelelser om Grønland.* 56:1–28, 1918.

Nippgen, J.
"Les Prêtres Payens du Groenland Oriental." *L'Ethnographie.* 3:55–65, 1914. n.s.

Ostermann, H.
"Knud Rasmussen's Posthumous Notes on the Life and Doings of the East Greenlanders." *Meddelelser om Grønland.* (Kjøbenhavn) 59 (Part 1):1–212, 1938.

Sollas, W. J.
"On Some Eskimos' Bone Implements from the East Coast of Greenland." *Journal of the (Royal) Anthropological Institute of Great Britain and Ireland.* (London) 9:329–336, 1880.

Thalbitzer, William
"The Heathen Priests of East Greenland." *Proc. Intern. Congr. Amer.* (Paris) 16:447–464, 1908.

"Les Magiciens Esquimaux, Leurs Conceptions du Monde, de l'ame et de la Vie." *Journal de la Société des Américanistes.* (Paris) 22:73–106, 1930. n.s.

FOLK ART—SPEECH

Rink, H.
"The East Greenland Dialect." *Meddelelser om Grønland.* (Kjøbenhavn) 39:203–223, 1911.

"Den Østgrønlandske Dialect." *Meddelelser om Grønland.* (Kjøbenhavn) 10:207–234, 1887.

Thomsen, T.
"Implements and Artifacts of the North-East Greenlanders." *Meddelelser om Grønland.* (Kjøbenhavn) 44:357–492, 1917.

Vibaek, P.
"Contributions to the Study of the Eskimo Language in Greenland." *Meddelelser om Grønland.* (Kjøbenhavn) 33:9–60, 1907.

GAMES

Thalbitzer, William
"Cultic Games and Festivals in Greenland."
Proc. Intern. Congr. Amer. (Paris) 21(Part
2):236–255, 1924.

Victor, P. E.
"Le Bilboquet chez les Eskimo d'Angmags-salik." *Journal de la Société des Américanistes.*
(Paris) 30:299–331, 1938. n.s.

—————.
"Les Jeux de Ficelle chez les Eskimo d'Ang-magssalik." *Journal de la Société des Améri-canistes.* (Paris) 29:387–395, 1937. n.s.

MUSIC

GENERAL STUDIES

Thalbitzer, William
Légends et Chants Esquimaux du Groenland.
Paris: Libraire Ernest Leroux, 1929. 188 pp.

—————.
Eskimo-Liederen van Oost-Groenland. Nether-lands: N. V. Vitgeverif vh. C. A. Meer, 1933.

—————, and Thuren, Hjalmar
"Melodies from East Greenland, with a Supple-ment Containing Melodies from North-West
Greenland." In: *The Ammassalik Eskimo,* by
W. Thalbitzer and Hj. Thuren (pp. 47–112).
Copenhagen: Bianco Lunis Bogtrykkeri, 1911.
music, illus. Meddelesler om Grønland vol. 40.

Thuren, H.
"On Eskimo Music of Greenland." *Meddelelser
om Grønland.* (Kjøbenhavn) 40:1–45, 1911.

DANCE

Thalbitzer, W., and Thuren, H.
"Dans i Grønland." *Fästkrift till F. H. Feil-berg.* pp. 77–97, Stockholm: 1911.

IGLULIK ESKIMO

FOLKLORE

GENERAL STUDIES

Boas, Franz
"The Eskimo of Baffin Land and Hudson Bay."
Bull. Amer. Mus. Nat. Hist. (New York) 15:1–570, 1901–1907.

Comer, G.
"Notes on the Natives of the Northwestern
Shores of Hudson Bay." *AA* 23:243–244, 1921.
n.s.

Gilder, William H.
Schwatka's Search. Sledging in the Arctic
in Quest of the Franklin Records. New York:
Charles Scribner's Sons, 1881. xvi, 316 pp.
illus.

Hall, C. F.
Narrative of the Second Artic Expedition.
Washington: U. S. Gov't. Print. Office, 1879.
644 pp.

Hearne, Samuel
*A Journey from Prince of Wale's Fort in
Hudson's Bay to the Northern Ocean.* London:
A. Strahan & T. Cadell, 1795. xliv, 458 pp.

Lyon, G. F.
*The Private Journal of Captain G. F. Lyon
of H. M. S. Hecla.* London: J. Murray, 1824.
xiii, 468 pp.
"Principally devoted to the narration of the
peculiarities of the aborigines of the Arctic
region." (Sabine)

Mathiassen, T.
"Archaeology of the Central Eskimos." *Report
of the Fifth Thule Expedition.* (Copenhagen)
4(Part 1–2):533 pp., 1927.

—————.
"Material Culture of the Iglulik Eskimos."
Report of the Fifth Thule Expedition. (Copen-hagen) 6(Part 1):1–242, 1928.

—————.
"Traek of Iglulik-Eskimoernes Materielle Kul-tur." *Geografisk Tidsskrift.* (Kjøbenhavn)
30:72–88, 1927.

Parry, W. E.
*Journal of a Second Voyage for the Discovery
of a North West Passage.* New York: F. Duyck-nick, 1824. vii, 464 pp.

Rae, J.
"On the Esquimaux." *Trans. Ethnol. Soc.*
4:138–153, 1866. n.s.

Rasmussen, Knud
"Iglulik and Caribou Eskimo Texts." *Report
of the Fifth Thule Expedition.* (Copenhagen)
7(Part 3):1–160, 1930.

—————.
"Intellectual Culture of the Iglulik Eskimos."
Report of the Fifth Thule Expedition. (Copen-hagen) 7(Part 1)1–304, 1929.

Speck, F. G.
"Eskimo Collection From Baffin Land and
Ellesmere Land. *Indian Notes.* 1:143–149,
1924.

Sutton, G. M.
Eskimo Year. New York: The Macmillan
Company, 1934. 321 pp.

Waterman, T. T.
"Hudson Bay Eskimo." R. H. Lowie, ed.
Anthro. Papers. Amer. Mus. Nat. Hist. (New
York) 4:299–307, 1910.

SPEECH

Dall, W. H.
"On Some Peculiarities of the Eskimo Dialect."
*Proceedings of the American Association for
the Advancement of Science.* (Philadelphia)
19:332–349, 1870.

MUSIC
GENERAL STUDIES

Hague, Eleanor
"Eskimo Songs." *JAFL* 28:96–98, 1915.

LABRADOR ESKIMO
FOLKLORE
GENERAL STUDIES

Anonymous
Suhinimiut." *Bureau Amer. Ethnol. Bull.* 30 (Part 2) :647, 1910.

Cadzow, D. A.
"Archaeological Work with the Putnam Baffin Island Expedition." *Indian Notes.* 5:98–106, 1928.

Cartwright, George
A Journal of Transactions and Events During a Residence of Nearly Sixteen Years on the Coast of Labrador. London: Allen and Ridge, 1792. 3 vols.

Comeau, Napoleon Alexander
Life and Sport on the North Shore of the Lower St. Lawrence and Gulf. Containing chapters on salmon fishing, trapping, the folk-lore of the Montagnais Indians and tales of adventure on the fringe of the Labrador Peninsula. Quebec: Daily Telegraph Printing House, 1909. 440 pp., front., plates, ports.

Curtis, H.
"Fragments sur les Eskimaux." *Nouvelles Annales des Voyages.* (Paris) Part 4:329-339, 1838.

Davies, W. H. A.
"Notes on Ungava Bay and Its Vicinity." *Transactions of the Literary and Historical Society.* (Quebec) 4:119–137, 1854.

Duckworth, W. L. H., and Pain, B. H.
"An Account of Some Eskimo from Labrador." *Proceedings of the Cambridge Philosophical Society.* 10:286–291, 1900.

Flaherty, R. J.
My Eskimo Friends, Nanook of the North, New York: Doubleday, Page and Co., 1924. 170 pp. illus.

Gathorne-Hardy, G. M.
"A Recent Journey to Northern Labrador." *Geographical Journal.* (London) 59:153–169, 1922.

Gosling, William G.
Labrador. Its Discovery, Explorations, and Development, New York: John Lane Company, 1911. xii, 574 pp.

Grenfell, W. T.
Labrador. New York: The Macmillan Co., 1909. xii, 497 pp., illus.

———.
Down North on the Labrador. New York: Fleming H. Revell Co., 1911. 229 pp.

———.
Down to the Sea; Yarns from the Labrador. New York: Fleming H. Revell Co., 1910. 226 pp.

———.
Labrador Days; Tales of the Sea of Toilers. Boston: Houghton Mifflin Co., 1919. 230 pp.

———.
Northern Neighbors; Stories of the Labrador People. Boston: Houghton Mifflin Co., 1923. 332 pp.

———.
Off the Rocks; Stories of the deep sea fisher folk of Labrador. Philadelphia: The Sunday School Times Co., 1906. xi, 203 pp.

———.
Tales of the Labrador. Boston: Houghton Mifflin Co., 1916. 239 pp.

Hanzsch, B.
"Beiträge zur Kenntnis des Nordöstlichen Labradors." *Mitteilungen des Vereins für Erdkunde zu Dresden.* 1(Part 9):245–320, 1909.

Hawkes, E. W.
"The Labrador Eskimo." *Memoirs of the Canada Department of Mines, Geological Survey.* (Ottawa) 91:1–165, 1916.

Hind, Henry Youle
Explorations in the Interior of the Labrador Peninsula. London: Longman, Green, Longman, Roberts and Green 18863. 2 vols.

Hutton, M. W.
Among the Eskimos of Labrador. Philadelphia: 1912.

———.
An Eskimo Village. London: 1929.

Leith, C. H., and A. T.
A Summer and Winter in Hudson Bay. Madison: Cartwell Printing Co., 1912. 203 pp.

Low, A. P.
"Report on Explorations in the Labrador Peninsula." *Annual Reports of the Canada Geological (and Natural History) Survey.* (Montreal) 8:1–387, 1896. n.s.

McLean, J.
"Notes of a Twenty-Five Years' Service in the Hudson's Bay Territory." W. S. Wallace, ed. *Publications of the Champlain Society.* (Toronto) 19:1–402, 1932.
  Contains vocabulary of the principal Indian dialects in use among the tribes in Hudson's Bay Territory.

Markham, C. R., ed.
The Voyages of William Baffin. London: Hakluyt Society, 1881. 192 pp.

Packard, A. S.
The Esquimaux of Labrador. *Indian Miscellany*. W. W. Beach, ed., pp. 65–73, Albany, 1877.

———.
The Labrador Coast. New York: 1891.

Payne, F. F.
"Eskimo of Hudson's Strait." *Proceedings of the Canadian Institute*. (Toronto) 6(Ser. 3): 213–230, 1899.

Pittard, E.
"Contribution à l'étude Anthropologique des Esquimaux du Labrador et de la Baie d'Hudson." *Bulletin de la Société Neuchateloise de Géographie*. 13:158–176, 1901.

Quimby, G. I.
"The Manitunik Eskimo Culture of East Hudson's Bay." *American Antiquity*. 6:148–165, 1940.

Silvy, A.
Relation par lettres de l'Amerique Septentrionale. C. de Rochemonteix. ed., pp. 42–60. Paris: A. Picard et fils, 1904.

Smith, H. I.
"Notes on Eskimo Traditions." *JAFL* 7:209–216, 1894.

Speck, F. G.
"Indian and Eskimo Backgrounds in Southern Labrador." *General Magazine, University of Pennsylvania*. (Philadelphia). 38:1–17, 143–163, 1935.

———.
Inland Eskimo Bands of Labrador. In: *Essays in Anthropology*. Presented to A. L. Kroeber, pp. 313–330, Berkeley: University of California Press, 1936.

Strong, William Duncan
"A Stone Culture from Northern Labrador and its Relation to the Eskimo-like Cultures of the Northeast." *AA* 32:126–144, 1930. n.s. Bibliography, pp. 142–144.

Stupart, R. F.
"The Eskimo of Stupart Bay." *Proceedings of the Canadian Institute*. (Toronto) 4(Ser. 3) 95–114, 1887.

Turner, Lucien M.
Ethnology of the Ungava District, Hudson Bay Territory. Washington: U.S. Government Printing Office, 1894.

———.
"On the Indians and Eskimos of the Ungava District." *Proceedings and Transactions of the Royal Society of Canada*. (Ottawa) 5(Part 2):99–119, 1887.

Virchow, R.
"Eskimos von Labrador. *Verhandl. Berl. Gesel. Anthro. Ethnol. Ur*. pp. 253–274, 1880.

Waldmann, S.
"Les Esquimaux du Nord du Labrador." *Bulletin de la Société Neuchateloise de Géographie*. 20:430–441, 1910.

Wallace, D.
The Long Labrador Trail, New York: The Outing Publishing Co., 1907. xii, 315 pp.

Wheeler, E. P.
"Journeys About Nain." *Geographical Review*. (New York) 20:454–468, 1930.

BELIEFS—CUSTOMS

Hanzsch, B.
"Eskimo Stone Graves in North Eastern Labrador." *Canadian Field-Naturalist*. (Ottawa) 44:180–182, 1930.

Hutton, M. W.
By Eskimo Dog-Sled and Kayak. London: 1919. 219 pp.

Junek, Oscar Waldemar
Isolated Communities; a Study of a Labrador Fishing Village. American Sociology Series. New York: American Book Company, 1937. 130 pp., illus.

Speck, F. G.
"Analysis of Eskimo and Indian Skin-Dressing Methods in Labrador." *Ethnos*. 2:345–353, 1937.

———.
"Labrador Eskimo Mask and Clown." *General Magazine* Univ. of Pennsylvania (Philadelphia) 37:159–173, 1935.
lin: 1851. 182 pp.

———.
"Spiritual beliefs among the Labrador Indians." *Proceedings of the 21st Session of the International Congress of Americanists 1:* 266–275, 1924.

Wintemberg, W. J.
"Eskimo Sites of the Dorset Culture in Newfoundland." *American Antiquity*. 5:83–102, 1939.

FOLK ART—SPEECH—RIDDLES

Boas, Franz
"Two Eskimo Riddles from Labrador." *JAFL* 39:486, 1926.

Bourquin, T.
Grammatik der Eskimo-Sprache. London: Moravian Mission Agency, 1891.

Erdmann, J.
Eskimoisches Wörterbuch gesammelt von den Missionaren in Labrador. Budissin: E. M. Monse, 1864. 2 vols.

Kleinschmidt, Samuel Petrus
Grammatik der Grönlandischen Sprache. Ber-

König, H.
"Die Eskimo-Mundarten von Nord-und Nordost-Labrador." *Anthropos.* 32:595–632, 1937.

Speck, F. G.
"Collections from Labrador Eskimo." *Indian Notes.* 1:211–217, 1924.

———
"Eskimo Carved Ivories from Northern Labrador." *Indian Notes.* 4:309–314, 1927.

MACKENZIE ESKIMO

FOLKLORE

GENERAL STUDIES

Bompas, W. C.
Diocese of Mackenzie River. London: 1888. 108 pp.

Cameron, A. D.
The New North; Being Some Account of a Woman's Journey Through Canada to the Arctic. New York: D. Appleton and Co., 1910. xix, 398 pp., illus.

Franklin, J.
Narrative of a Second Expedition to the Shores of the Polar Sea. London: J. Murray, 1828.

Mackenzie, A.
Voyages from Montreal through the Continent of North America to the Frozen and Pacific Oceans. London: T. Cadell and W. Davies, 1801.

Mathiassen, T.
"Archaeological Collections from the Western Eskimos." *Report of the Fifth Thule Expedition.* (Copenhagen) 10:1–98, 1930.

Mayor, J.
"The Eskimo of the Mackenzie River." *University of Misserion,* (Toronto) 8:142–145, 1908.

Petitot, E. F. S.
"Die Eskimos am Mackenzie und Anderson." *Globus.* 31:103–105, 1877.

———
Les Grands Esquimaux. Paris: E. Plon, Nourrit, 1887. vi, 307 pp.

———
Monographie des Esquimaux Tchiglit du Mackenzie et de l'Anderson. Paris: 1876.

———
Quinze ans sous le Cercle Polaire. Paris: E. Dentu, 1889. xxi, 332 pp.

———
Traditions Indiennes du Canada Nordouest. Paris: Maisonneuve frères et C. Leclerc, 1886. xvii, 521 pp.

Richardson, J.
Arctic Searching Expedition. London: Longman, Brown, Green, and Longman, 1851. 2 vols.

Simpson, T.
Narrative of the Discoveries on the North Coast of America. London: R. Bentley, 1843. 419 pp.

Stefansson, V.
The Friendly Arctic. New York: The Macmillan Co., 1921. xxxi, 784 pp.

———
Hunters of the Great North. New York: Harcourt Brace and Co., 1922. vii, 301 pp.

———
My Life with the Eskimo. New York: The Macmillan Co., 1913. ix, 538 pp.

———
"The Stefansson-Anderson Arctic Expedition." *Anthro. Papers Amer. Mus. Nat. Hist.* 14:1–395, 1914.

MYTHS—BELIEFS

Jenness, Diamond
"Myths and Traditions from the Northern Alaska, the Mackenzie Delta and Coronation Gulf." *Report of the Canadian Artic Expedition.* (Ottawa) 13 (Part A):1–90, 1924.

Stefansson, V.
"Religious Beliefs of the Eskimo." *Harper's (New) Monthly Magazine.* (New York) 127: 869–878, 1913.

FOLK ART—SPEECH

Jenness, Diamond
"Comparative Vocabulary of the Western Eskimo Dialects." *Report of the Canadian Arctic Expedition.* (Ottawa) 15 (Part A):1–134, 1928.

———
"Eskimo String Figures." *Report of the Canadian Arctic Expedition.* 13 (Part B) :1–192, 1924.

Petitot, E. F. S.
Vocabulaire Français-Esquimaux. Paris: É. Leroux, 1876. lxiv, 76 pp.

FOLK MEDICINE

Stefansson, V.
"Theory and Treatment of Disease among the Mackenzie River Eskimo." *JAFL* 21:43–45, 1908.

NETSILIK ESKIMO

FOLKLORE

GENERAL STUDIES

Amundsen, R.
Nordvestpassagen. Kristiania: H. Aschehoug & Co., 1908. xv, 511 pp. illus.

The North West Passage. London: 1908. 2 vols.

Gilder, W. H.
Schwatka's Search . . . New York: Charles Scribner's Sons, 1881. xvi, 316 pp., illus.

Hall, C. F.
Narrative of the Second Arctic Expedition. Washington: U. S. Gov't. Print. Office, 1879. 644 pp.

Hanbury, D. T.
Sport and Travel in the Northland of Canada. London: E. Arnold, 1904. xxxii, 319 pp., illus.

Poncins, G. de
Kabloona. New York: Reynal & Hitchcock, 1941. 339 pp.

Rae, J.
Narrative of an Expedition to the Shores of the Arctic Sea. London: T. W. Boone, 1850. viii, 247 pp.

Rasmussen, K.
"The Netsilik Eskimos." *Report of the Fifth Thule Expedition.* 8:1–542, 1931.

Ross, J.
Narrative of a Second Voyage in Search of a North West Passage. London: A. W. Webster, 1835. 2 vols.

Schwatka, F.
"The Netschilluk Innuits." *Science.* 4:543–545, 1884.

CUSTOMS

Boas, Franz
"Über die Wohnsitze der Neitchillik Eskimos." *Zeitschrift der Gessellschaft für Erdkunde.* (Berlin) 18:222–233, 1883.

Schwatka, F.
"The Implements of the Igloo." *Science.* 4:81–85, 1884.

NORTH ALASKA ESKIMO

FOLKLORE

GENERAL STUDIES

Anderson, H. D., and Eells, W. C.
Alaska Natives. A Study of Their Sociological and Educational Status, Stanford: Stanford University Press, 1935. 472 pp.

Collins, H. B.
"Archaeological Investigation at Point Barrow." *Explorations and Field-Work of the Smithsonian Institution.* (Washington) 1932: 45–48, 1933.

Giddings, J. L., Jr.
Dendrochronology in Northern Alaska. Laboratory of Tree-Ring Research Bulletin 1. University of Alaska, and University of Arizona, 1942. 107 pp., illus.

"Ethnographic Notes. Kobuk River Region." *Kiva* 6:25–28, 1941.

Hooper, W. H.
Ten Months among the Tents of the Tuski. London: J. Murray, 1853. xv, 417 pp.

Hrdlicka, Ales
"Anthropological Survey of Alaska." *Annual Reports of the Bureau of American Ethnology.* (Washington) 46:19–374, 1930.

"Anthropological Work in Alaska." *Smithson. Misc. Coll. Part* 7:137–58, 1927.

Jenness, Diamond
"The Eskimos of Northern Alaska." *Geographical Review.* (New York) 5:89–101, 1918.

"Notes and Traditions from Northern Alaska, the Mackenzie Delta, and Coronation Gulf." Ottawa: *Report of the Canadian Arctic Expedition, Southern Party, 1913–16,* Vol. XIII, part A, pp. 1–90a. 1924.

Murdoch, John
"Ethnological Results of the Point Barrow Expedition." *9th Annual Report: Bureau of Ethnology,* 1887–1888, pp. 19–434, pls. 1–8, figs. 1–428, 1 map. Washington, D. C.: U. S. Gov't Printing Office, 1892.
Situation and surroundings, climate, people, physical characteristics, tribal phenomena, social surroundings, culture, clothing, means of subsistence, etc.

Ray, Patrick Henry, Lt.
Report of the International Polar Expedition to Point Barrow, Alaska. Washington, D. C.: Government Printing Office, 1885. pp. 35–87.
Contains an ethnographic sketch of the natives.

Simpson, J.
"Observations on the Western Eskimo and the Country they Inhabit." *Arctic Geography and Ethnology.* pp. 233–275. London: 1875.

Simpson, T.
Narrative of the Discoveries on the North Coast of America. London: 1843. 419 pp.

Stefansson, V.
My Life With The Eskimo. New York: 1913.

Stockton, C. H.
"The Arctic Cruise of the U.S.S. Thetis." *National Geographic Magazine* 2:171–198, 1890.

MYTHS—FOLKTALES—LEGENDS

Jenness, Diamond
"Myths and Traditions from Northern Alaska." *Report of the Canadian Arctic Expedition.* (Ottawa) 13 (Part A):1–90, 1924.

Murdoch, John
"A Few Legendary Fragments from Point Barrow Eskimos." *American Naturalist.* (Salem) 20:593–599, 1886.

Rasmussen, Knud
The Eagle's Gift: Alaska Eskimo Tales, translated by Isobel Hutchinson. Illustrated by Ernst Hansen. New York (Garden City): Doubleday, Doran Inc., 1932. xiv, 255 pp., incl. pl. map. col. front, col. plates.

BELIEFS—CUSTOMS

Boas, Franz
"Property Marks of the Alaskan Eskimo." *AA* 1:601–613, 1899. n.s.

Ford, J. A.
"Eskimo Burial Customs." *El Palacio.* (Santa Fe) 33:198–199, 1932.

Gould, I.
"Customs of the Alaskans." *Carlisle Arrow* 8, (No. 4):1, 1911.

Murdoch, John
"The Animals Known to the Eskimos of Northwestern Alaska." *American Naturalist.* (Salem) 32:719–734, 1898.

"Notes on the Counting and Measuring among the Eskimo of Point Barrow." *AA* 3:37–43, 1890.

"The Retrieving Harpoon." *American Naturalist.* (Salem) 19:423–425, 1885.

"Seal Catching at Point Barrow." *Smithson. Misc. Coll.* 34 (Part 2):102–108, 1893.

Smith, M.
"Superstitions of the Eskimo." *The White World.* R. Kersting, ed., pp. 113–130. New York: Lewis, Scribner & Co., 1902. 386 pp.

FOLK ART—SPEECH

Douglas, John M.
"Alaskan Eskimo Labret Exhibit." *Museum Record* (Milwaukee)3(No. 24):27, 1947.

Jenness, Diamond
"Comparative Vocabulary of the Western Eskimo Dialects." *Report of the Canadian Arctic Expedition.* (Ottawa) 15 (Part A):1–134, 1928.

"Eskimo String Figures." *Report of the Canadian Arctic Expedition.* (Ottawa) 13 (Part B):1–192, 1924.

MacCurdy, G. G.
"An Example of Eskimo Art." *AA* 23:384–385, 1921. n.s.

Mason, J. A.
"Eskimo Pictorial Art." *Museum Journal (University of Pennsylvania).* (Philadelphia) 18:248–283, 1927.

Wells, R., and Kelly, J. W.
"English-Eskimo and Eskimo-English Vocabularies." *Bureau of Education, Circular of Information.* 2:1–72. Washington: 1890.

Wissler, Clark
"Harpoons and Darts in the Stefansson Collection." *Anthro. Papers Amer. Mus. Nat. Hist.* 14:397–443, 1916.

MUSIC
GENERAL STUDIES

Jenness, Diamond
"Eskimo Music in Northern Alaska." *Musical Quarterly* 8:377–383, 1922.

POLAR ESKIMO
FOLKLORE
GENERAL STUDIES

Astrup, Eivind
Blandt Nordpolens Naboer. Khristiania: H. Aschehoug & Co., 1895. vi, 319 pp.

With Peary Near the Pole. London: C. A. Pearsen, Ltd., 1898. 362 pp.

Bessels, Emil
Die Amerikanische Nordpol-Expedition. pp. 350–373. Leipzig: W. Engelmann, 1879. xx, 647 pp., illus.

"Einige Worte Uber die Innuit (Eskimo) des Smithsundes." *Archiv für Anthropologie.* (Braunschweig) 8:107–122, 1873.

Birket-Smith, K.
"The Greenlanders of the Present Day." *Greenland* 2:1–207, 1928.

Bryant, H. G.
"Notes on the Most Northern Eskimos." *Report of the Sixth International Geographical Congress* pp. 677–683, 1895.

Ekblaw, W. Elmer
"Significance of Movement Among Polar Eskimo." *Bull. Mass. Arch. Soc.* (Andover) 10 (No. 1):1–4, 1948.

Freuchen, Peter
Arctic Adventure. New York: Farrar & Rinehart, 1935. iv, 467 pp., illus.

Ivalu, the Eskimo Wife. New York: L. Furman, 1935. 332 pp.

Haig-Thomas, D.
Tracks in the Snow. London: Hodder & Stoughton, 1939. x, 292 pp.

Hayes, I. I.
The Open Polar Sea. New York: Hurd & Houghton, 1867. xxiv, 454 pp.

Kane, E. K.
Arctic Explorations. Philadelphia: Childs & Peterson, 1856. 2 vols.

Koch, L.
"Ethnographical Observations from the Southern Coast of Washington Land." *AA* 24:484–487, 1922. n.s.

Kroeber, A. L.
"The Eskimo of Smith Sound." *Bull. Amer. Mus. Nat. Hist.* 12:265–327, 1899.

Markham, C. R.
"The Arctic Highlanders." *Transactions of the Ethnologocial Society.* (London) 4:125–137, 1866. n.s.

———.
"Papers on the Greenland Eskimos." *Arctic Geography and Ethnology.* pp. 163–229. London: 1875.

Murdock, George Peter
Our Primitive Contemporaries. New York: The Macmillan Company, 1934. (pp. 192–218).

Mylius-Erichsen, L., and Moltke, H.
Grønland. Kjøbenhavn: Gyldendal, 1906. vi, 628 pp., illus.

Nares, G. S.
Narrative of a Voyage to the Polar Sea. London: S. Low, Marston, Searle & Rivington, 1878. 2 vols.

Paterson, T. T.
"Anthropogeographical Studies in Greenland." *Journ. Royal Anthro. Inst. Gt. Brit.* 69:45–76, 1936.

Peary, J. D.
My Arctic Journal. New York: The Contemporary Publishing Co., 1893. 240 pp.

Peary, R. E.
Nearest the Pole. New York: Doubleday, Page & Co., 1907.

———.
Northward Over the "Great Ice." New York: F. A. Stoke Co., 1898. 2 vols.

Petersen, C.
Erindringer fra Polarlandene. Kjøbenhavn: 1857.

Preuss, K. T.
"Die Ethnographische Veränderung der Eskimo des Smith-Sundes." *Ethnologisches Notizblatt* 2 (Part 1):38–43, 1899.

Rasmussen, Knud
Greenland by the Polar Sea. London: W. Heinemann, 1921. xxiii, 326 pp.

———.
The People of the Polar North. London: K. Paul, Trench, Trübner & Co., 1908. 358 pp.

———.
Under Nordenvindens Svøbe. Kjøbenhavn: Gyldendal, 1906. 202 pp.

Ross, J.
A Voyage of Discovery. London: J. Murray, 1819. xxxix, 252 pp.

Steensby, H. P.
"Contributions to the Ethnology and Anthropogeography of the Polar Eskimos." *Meddelelser om Grønland.* (Kjøbenhavn) 34:253–405, 1910.

Thomsen, T.
"Eskimo Archaeology." *Greenland* 2:271–329, 1928.

Wissler, Clark
"Archaeology of the Polar Eskimo." *Anthro. Papers Amer. Mus. Nat. Hist.* 22:105–166, 1918.

MYTHS—FOLKTALES—LEGENDS

Kroeber, A. L.
"Tales of the Smith Sound Eskimo." *JAFL* 12:166–182, 1899.

Rasmussen, Knud
Myter og Sagn fra Grønland. Kjøbenhavn: Gyldendal, 1925. 340 pp.

CUSTOMS—SPEECH

Birket-Smith, K.
"The Greenland Bow." *Meddelelser om Grønland.* (Kjøbenhavn) 56 (Part 1):1–28, 1918.

Ekblaw, W. E.
"Eskimo Dogs." *Natural History.* (New York) 37:173–184, 1936.

———.
"The Food Birds of the Smith Sound Eskimos." *Wilson Bulletin* 31:1–5, 1919.

———.
"The Material Response of the Polar Eskimo to Their Environment." *Annals of the Association of American Geographers* 17:147–198, 18:1–24, 1927–1928.

Hovey, E. O.
"Child-Life Among the Smith Sound Eskimo." *American Museum Journal.* (New York) 18:361–371, 1918.

MacMillan, D. B.
"Food Supply of the Smith Sound Eskimo." *American Museum Journal.* (New York) 18:161–192, 1918.

Paterson, T. T.
"Eskimo 'Cats' Cradles'." *Geographical Magazine* 9:85–91, 1939.

Schultz-Lorentzen, C. W.
"Intellectual Culture of the Greenlanders." *Greenland* 2:209–270, 1928.

Stein, R.
"Geographische Nomenklatur bei den Eskimos des Smith-Sundes." *Petermanns Mitteilunge aus Justus Perthes Geographischer Anstalt.* (Gotha) 48:195–201, 1902.

Whitaker, W. L.
"The Question of Season Sterility Among the Eskimos." *Science* 88:214–215, 1938.

MUSIC
GENERAL STUDIES

Leden, C.
"Musik und Tänze der Grönländischen Eskimos." *Zeitschrift für Ethnologie.* (Berlin) 43: 260–270, 1911.
Discussion, with examples, of music and dance of the Greenland Eskimos.

Stein, R.
"Eskimo Music." *The White World.* R. Kersting, ed., pp. 337–356. New York: Lewis, Scribner & Co., 1902. 386 pp.

SOUTH ALASKA ESKIMO
FOLKLORE
GENERAL STUDIES

Anderson, H. D., and Eells, W. C.
Alaska Natives. Stanford: 1935. 472 pp.

Birket-Smith, K.
"Foreløbig Beretning om den Dansk-Amerikanske Ekspedition til Alaska." *Geografisk Tidsskrift.* (Kjøbenhavn) 37:187–227, 1934.

Collins, H. B.
"Archeology of the Bering Sea Region." *Proceedings of the (Fifth) Pacific Science Congress.* (Toronto) 5 (Part 4):2825–2839, 1934.

Cook, J.
A Voyage to the Pacific Ocean. London: G. Nicol & J. Cadell, 1785. 3 vols.

Coxe, W.
Account of the Russian Discoveries Between Asia and America. London: J. Cadell, 1787. xxviii, 454 pp.

Dall, W. H.
"The Native Tribes of Alaska." *Proc. Amer. Assoc. Adv. Sci.* 34:363–379, 1885.

"On the Distribution and Nomenclature of the Native Tribes of Alaska." *Contr. North Amer. Ethnol.* 1:7–40, 1877.

"On the Distribution of the Native Tribes of Alaska." *Proc. Amer. Assoc. Adv. Sci.* 18:263–273, 1869.

Erman, A.
"Ueber die Reise und Entdeckungen des Lieutenant L. Sagoskin." *Archiv für Wissenschaftliche Kunde von Russland.* (Berlin) 6:499–522, 613–672, 7:429–512, 1848–1849.

Holmberg, H. J.
"Ethnographische Skizzen über die Völker des Russischen Amerika." *Acta Societatis Scientiarum Fennicae.* (Helsingfors) 4:355–421, 1856.

Hrdlicka, Ales
Alaska Diary. Lancaster, Pa.: Jacques Cattell Press, 1943. 407 pp.
Among many interesting scientific observations the author also relates some strange tales of medicine men, and other lore.

"Anthropological Explorations on Kodiak Island." *Explor. Field Work Smithson. Inst.* pp. 41–44, 1932.

"Anthropological Work in Alaska." *Explor. Field Work Smithson. Inst.* pp. 91–102, 1931.

"Archaeological Excavations on Kodiak Island." *Explor. Field Work Smithson. Inst.* pp. 47–52, 1934.

Jacobi, A.
"Carl Heinrich Mercks Ethnographische Beobactungen Uber Die Völker des Beringsmeers." *Baessler-Archiv.* (Berlin) 20:113–137, 1937.

Laguna, F. de
The Archaeology of Cook Inlet. Philadelphia: University of Pennsylvania Press, 1934. 263 pp.

Langsdorff, G. H. von
Voyages and Travels in Various Parts of the World. London: H. Colburn, 1813.

Lantis, Margaret
Alaskan Eskimo Ceremonialism.
Monographs American Ethnol. Soc. XI. New York: J. J. Augustin, 1947. 127 pp.

The Social Culture of the Nunivak Eskimo. Transactions of the American Philosophical Society, Volume 35. Phila., Pa.: The American Philosophical Society, 1946. 171 pp. 84 fig., 2 maps.
The work is divided into two parts, the first dealing with "Non-material Culture"—natural environment and economic factors, ceremonialism, religion, recreation, life crises, social organization, followed by a summary. The second part, "Mythology," contains translations of mythical tales which were related to the author by the Eskimos. The translations are followed by an analysis and summary of the tales.

Petroff, I.
"The Limit of the Innuit Tribes on the Alaskan Coast." *Amer. Natur.* 16:567–575, 1882.

Portlock, N.
A Voyage Round the World. London: J. Stockdale, and G. Goulding, 1789. xii, 384 pp.

Schott, W.
"Ueber Ethnographische Ergebnisse der Sagoskinschen Reise." *Archiv für Wissenschaftliche Kunde von Russland.* (Berlin) 7:480–512, 1849.

Woldt, A., ed.
Capitain Jacobsen's Reise an der Nordwestküste Amerikas. Leipzig: M. Spohr, 1884. viii, 431 pp.

Wrangell, F. P. von
"Statistische und Ethnographische Nachrichten über die Russischen Besitzungen an der Nordwestküste von Amerika." *Beiträge zur Kenntnis des Russischen Reiches (und Angränzenden Lander Asiens.)* (St. Petersburg) 1:1–332, 1839.

MYTHS—FOLKTALES—LEGENDS

Deans, J.
"Doom of the Katt-a-quins." (Stickeen, Southern Alaska.) *JAFL* 5:232–235, 1892.

Golder, F. A.
"Eskimo and Aleut Stories from Alaska." *JAFL* 22:10–24, 1909.

—————.
"A Kodiak Island Story." *JAFL* 20:296–299, 1907.

—————.
"Tales from Kodiak Island." *JAFL* 16:16–31, 85–103, 1903.

Lantis, Margaret
"The Mythology of Kodiak Island." *JAFL* 51: 123–172, 1938.

BELIEFS—CUSTOMS

Dall, W. H.
"Alaskan Mummies." *American Naturalist.* (Salem) 9:433–440, 1875.

Elliott, C. P.
"Salmon Fishing Grounds and Canneries." *Compilation of Narratives of Explorations in Alaska.* pp. 738–741. Washington: U. S. Gov't. Print. Off., 1900.

Gordon, G. B.
"The Double Axe and Some Other Symbols." *Museum Journ.* 7:46–68, 1916.

Krieger, Herbert W.
"Indian Village of Southeast Alaska." *Smithsonian Report 1927*, pp. 467–494. Washington, D. C.: U. S. Government Printing Office. Illus.

Lantis, Margaret
"The Alaskan Whale Cult and its Affinities." *AA* 40:438–464, 1938. n.s.

FOLK ART—SPEECH

Disselhoff, H.
"Bemerkungen zu Einigen Eskimo-Masken." *Baessler-Archiv.* (Berlin) 18:130–137, 1935.

Emmons, G. T.
"Jade in British Columbia and Alaska." *Indian Notes and Monogr.* 35:11–53, 1923.

Himmelheber, H.
Eskimokünstler. Stuttgart: Strecker und Schröder, 1938. 111 pp.

Laguna, F. de
"Eskimo Lamp and Pots." *Jour. Royal Anthro. Inst.* 70(Pt. 2):53–76, 1940.

—————.
"Peintures Rupestres Eskimo." *Journ. Société Amer.* 25:17–30, 1933. n.s.

—————.
"A Pottery Vessel from Kodiak Island." *American Antiquity* 4:334–343, 1939.

Mason, J. A.
"Eskimo Pictorial Art." *Museum Journ.* 18: 248–283, 1927.

—————.
"A Remarkable Stone Lamp from Alaska." *Museum Journ.* 19:170–194, 1928.

Radloff, L.
"Ueber die Sprache der Ugalachmut." *Bulletin de l'Académie Impériale des Sciences de St. Pétersbourg, Classe Historico-Philologique* 15: 26–38, 48–63, 126–39, 1858.

SOUTHAMPTON ESKIMO

FOLKLORE

GENERAL STUDIES

Boas, Franz
"The Eskimo of Baffin Land and Hudson Bay." *Bull. Amer. Mus. Nat. Hist.* 15:1–570, 1901–1907.

Comer, G.
"Notes on the Natives of the Northwestern Shores of Hudson Bay." *AA* 23:243–244, 1921.

Hrdlicka, Ales
"Contribution to the Anthropology of Central and Smith Sound Eskimo." *Anthro. Papers Amer. Mus. Nat. Hist.* 5:177–280, 1910.

Lyon, G. F.
A Brief Narrative of an Unsuccessful Attempt to Reach Repulse Bay. London: J. Murray, 1825. xvi, 198 pp.

Mathiassen, T.
"Archaelogy of the Central Eskimos." *Report of the Fifth Thule Expedition.* (Copenhagen) 4:1–533, 1927.

—————.
"Southampton Island og dens Oprindelige Beboere." *Geografisk Tidsskrift.* (Kjøbenhavn) 30:39–56, 1927.

Sutton, George Miksch
Eskimo Year. A Naturalist's Adventure in the Far North. Illustrated with drawings and photographs by the author and with photographs by several men of the North Country. New York: The Macmillan Company, 1934. 321 pp.
  This is the story of a year with the AIVILIKMIUT, the walrus-hunting Eskimos of Southampton Island, Hudson Bay. Included are also a number of Aivilik tribal stories.

Waterman, T. T.
"Hudson Bay Eskimo." *Anthro. Papers Amer. Mus. Nat. Hist.* R. H. Lowie, ed., 4:299–307, 1910.

CUSTOMS

Ferguson, R.
Arctic Harpooner. L. D. Stair, ed. Philadelphia: 1938. 216 pp.

WEST ALASKA ESKIMO

FOLKLORE

BIBLIOGRAPHY

Wickersham, James
Alaskan Literature, a Bibliography of 1724–1924. Containing the titles of all Histories, Travels, Voyages, Newspapers, Periodicals, Public Documents, etc. printed in English, Russian, German, French, Spanish, etc. relating to, descriptive of, or published in Russia, America, or Alaska, from 1724 to and including 1924. Fairbanks, Alaska: Alaska Agricultural College and School of Mines, 1927.

GENERAL STUDIES

Anderson, H. Dewey, and Fells, Walter Crosby
Alaska Natives. A Survey of their Sociological and Educational Status. Stanford University: Stanford University Press. 1935. 472 pp., illus.

Bancroft, H. H.
The Native Races of the Pacific States. Vol. I, pp. 37–94, New York: A. L. Bancroft and Co., 1875.

Bartels, P.
"Kasuistische Mitteilung über den Mongolenfleck bei Eskimo." *Zeitschrift für Ethnologie.* (Berlin) 41:721–725, 1909.

Beechey, F. W.
Narrative of a Voyage to the Pacific and Berring's Strait. Philadelphia: Carey & Lea, 1832. xi, 493 pp.

Boas, Franz
"Notes on the Eskimo of Port Clarence." *JAFL.* 7:205–208, 1894.

Colby, Merle, ed.
Alaska, Last American Frontier. American Guide Series, Federal Works Project. New York: Duell, Sloan & Pearce, 1939. 580 pp.

Collins, H. B.
"Archaeological Excavations at Bering Strait." *Explor. Field Work Smithson. Inst.* pp. 63–68, 1936.

————.
"Culture Migrations and Contacts in the Bering Sea Region." *AA.* 39375–384, 1937.

Collison, William H.
In the Wake of the War Canoe. New York: E. P. Dutton & Co. 1916. 351 pp.

Coxe, W.
Account of the Russian Discoveries between Asia and America. London: J. Cadell, 1787. xxviii, 454 pp.

Curtis, E. S.
The North American Indian. Vol. 20, Norwood: The Plimpton Press, 1930. 320 pp.

Dall, W. H.
Alaska and Its Resources. Boston: Lee and Shepard, 1897. vii, 627 pp.

————.
"The Native Tribes of Alaska." *Proc. Amer. Assoc. Adv. Sci.* 34:363–379, 1885.

————.
"On the Distribution and Nomenclature of the Native Tribes of Alaska." *Contr. North Amer. Ethnol.* 1:7–40, 1877.

————.
"On the Distribution of Native Tribes of Alaska." *Proc. Amer. Assoc. Adv. Sci.* 18:263–273, 1869.

————, **and Dawson, G. M., and Ogilvie, W.**
The Yukon Territory. London: Downey & Co., 1898. xiv, 438 pp.

Erman, A.
"Ueber die Reise und Entdeckungen des Lieutenant L. Sagoskin im Russischen Amerika." *Archiv für Wissenschaftliche Kunde von Russland.* (Berlin) 6:499–522, 613,–672, 7:429–512, 1848–1849.

Gordon, George Byron
In the Alaskan Wilderness. Philadelphia: John C. Winston Co., 1917. 247 pp.

————.
"Notes on the Western Eskimo." *Trans. Free Mus. Sci. Art.* 2:69–101, 1906.

Hrdlicka, Ales
"The Ancient and Modern Inhabitants of the Yukon." *Explor. Field-Work Smithson. Inst.* pp. 137–146, 1929.

————.
"Anthropological Survey of Alaska." *Annual Reports Bur. Amer. Ethnol.* 46:19–374, 1930.

————.
"Anthropological Work in Alaska." *Smithson. Inst. Miscell. Coll.* 78 (Part 7) :137–158, 1927.

"Anthropological Work on the Kuskokwim River." *Explor. Field-Work Smithson. Inst.* pp. 123–134, 1930.

"The Eskimo of Kuskokwim." *Amer. Journ. Phys. Anthro.* 18:93–145, 1933.

Jenness, Diamond
"Archaeological Investigations in Bering Strait." *Bull. Can. Dep't. Mines.* 50:71–80, 1926.

Muir, J.
The Cruise of the Corwin. Boston: Houghton Mifflin Co., 1917. xxxi, 278 pp.

Nelson, Edward William
The Eskimo About Bering Strait. *18th Annual Report: Bureau of American Ethnology*, 1896–1897, pp. 19–517, pls. I–CVII, figs. 1–165. Washington, D. C.: U. S. Gov't. Printing Office, 1899.
Sketch of the western Eskimo, personal adornment, utensils and implements, hunting and hunting implements, trade, feasts and festivals, customs, etc.

Nordenskiöld, A. E.
The Voyage of the Vega. New York: The Macmillan Co., 1882. xxvi, 756 pp.

Petroff, I.
"The Population and Resources of Alaska." *Compilation of Narratives of Explorations in Alaska.* pp. 210–239, Washington:1900.

"Report on the Population, Industries, and Resources of Alaska." *United States Department of the Interior. Tenth Census.* 8:124–146, 1881.

Richet, E.
"Les Esquimaux de l'Alaska." *Bulletin de la Société Royale Géographique d'Anvers.* 41:5–51, 103–153, 197–245, 42:5–50, 182–231, 1921–1922.

Schott, W.
"Ueber Ethnographische Ergebnisse der Sagoskinschen Reise." *Arch. Wissen. Kunde Russl.* 1:480–512, 1849.

Schwatka, F.
Report of a Military Reconnaissance Made in Alaska in 1883. pp. 323–362, Washington: U. S. Gov't. Print. Off., 1900.

Shapiro, H. A.
"The Alaskan Eskimo." *Anthro. Papers Amer. Mus. Nat. Hist.* 31:347–384, 1931.

Simpson, John
"Observations on the Western Esquimaux and the Country They Inhabit." In: *Further Papers to the Recent Arctic Expedition in*

Search of Dr. John Franklin. London: 1855.
Customs, traditions, beliefs and tales mentioned.

Thornton, H. R.
Among the Eskimos of Wales, Alaska. Baltimore: The John Hopkins Press, 1931. xxxviii, 235 pp.

Whymper, F.
"Russian America." *Trans. Ethnol. Soc.* 7:167–185, 1869. n.s.

Woldt, A., ed.
Captain Jacobsen's Reise an der Nordwestküste Amerikas. Leipzig: M. Spohr, 1884. viii, 431 pp.

Zagoskin, L. A.
Peshkhodnaya Opis Chastyi Russkikh Vladenyi v' Amerike. St. Petersburg: 1847–1848.

MYTHS—FOLKTALES—LEGENDS

"Eskimo Alaskan."
JAFL 1:215–219, 1888; 7:205–208, 1894; 22:10–24, 1909; 26:191–192, 1913.
Tales, myths and legends.

Garber, Clark McKinley
Stories and Legends of the Bering Strait Eskimo. Boston: The Christopher Publishing House, 1940. 260 pp.

Gillham, Arthur
Beyond the Clapping Mountains; Eskimo Stories from Alaska. Illustrated by Chanimun. New York: The Macmillan Company, 1943. 134 pp.

Judson, Katharine B.
Myths and Legends of Alaska. Chicago, Ill.: A. C. McClurg & Co., 1910.

Lantis, Margaret
"The Mythology of Kodiak Island, Alaska." *JAFL* 51: 123–172, 1938.

Oliver, Nola Nance
Alaskan Indian Legends. New York: House of Field, Inc., 69 pp.

Rossiter, H.
"Indian Legends from the Land of Al-ay-ek-sa." *Ketchikan Alaska Chronicle*, 1926.

CUSTOMS—BELIEFS

Boas, Franz
"Property Marks of the Alaskan Eskimo." *AA* 1:601–613, 1899. n.s.

Cross, J. F.
"Eskimo Children." *Southern Workman.* (Hampton) 37:433–437, 1908.

Dall, W. H.
"Social Life Among Our Aborigines." *Amer. Natur.* 12:1–10, 1878.

Garber, C. M.
"Eating with Eskimos." *Hygeia.* 16:242–245, 272, 278–279, 1938.

———.
"Marriage and Sex Customs of the Western Eskimos." *Scientific Monthly.* New York: 41:215–227, 1935.

———.
"Some Mortuary Customs of the Western Alaska Eskimos." *Scientific Monthly* 39:203–220, 1934.

Giraux, L.
"Gravures Colorées sur Dents de Morse des Esquimaux de l'Alaska." *Journ. Société Amer.* 18:91–102, 1926. n.s.

Gordon, G. B.
"The Double Axe and other Symbols." *Mus. Journ.* 7:46–68, 1916.

Hrdlicka, Ales
"Fecundity of Eskimo Women." *Amer Journ. Phys. Anthro.* 22:91–95, 1936.

———.
"Puberty in Eskimo Girls." *Proceedings of the National Academy of Science.* (Washington) 22:355–357, 1936.

Jacobsen, J. A.
"Leben und Treiben der Eskimo." *Ausland.* 44:593–598, 636–639, 656–658, 1891.

Krause, E.
"Die Schraube, eine Eskimo-Erfindung?" *Globus.* 79:8–9, 1901.
The screw—an Eskimo invention?

Murdoch, John
"On the Siberian Origin of Some Customs of the Western Eskimo." *AA* 1:325–336, 1888.

Steinen, K. von den
"Die Schraube keine Eskimo-Erfindung." *Globus.* 79:125–127, 1901.
The author claims that the screw is not an Eskimo invention.

FOLK ART—SPEECH

Barnum, F.
Grammatical Fundamentals of the Innuit Language. Boston: Ginn & Co., 1901. 384 pp.

Boas, Franz
"Decorative Designs of Alaskan Needlecases." *Proc. U. S. Nat. Mus.* 34:321–344, 1908.

Collins, H. B.
"Check-Stamped Pottery from Alaska." *Journal of the Washington Academy of Sciences.* (Washington) 18:254–256, 1928.

Disselhoff, H. D.
"Bemerkungen zu einigen Eskimo-Masken." *Baessler-Archiv.* (Berlin) 18:130–137, 1935.

Himmelheber, H.
Eskimokünstler. Stuttgart: Strecker und Schröder, 1938. 111 pp.

Jenness, Diamond
"Notes on the Phonology of the Eskimo Dialect of Cape Prince of Wales." *International Journal of American Linguistics.* (Washington) 4:168–180, 1927.

Mason, J. A.
"Eskimo Pictorial Art." *Mus. Journ.* 18:248–283, 1927.

Mathiassen, T.
"Some Specimens from the Bering Sea Culture." *Indian Notes.* 61:33–56, 1929.

Murie, M. E.
"Modern Eskimo Art." *Natural History.* (New York) 44:49–52, 1939.

Orchard, W. C.
"Present-Day Pictography." *Indian Notes.* 1:70–73, 1924.

Schultze, A.
A Brief Grammar and Vocabulary of the Eskimo Language. Bethlehem: The Comenius Press. 1889. 21 pp.

DANCE

Hawkes, E. W.
"The Dance Festivals of the Alaskan Eskimo." *Trans. Free Mus. Sci. Art.* 6 (Part 2) :41 pp., 1914.

———.
"The 'Inviting-In' Feast of the Alaskan Eskimo." *Mem. Can. Dept. Mines.* 45:1–20, 1913.

WEST GREENLAND ESKIMO

FOLKLORE

BIBLIOGRAPHY

Lauridsen, P.
"Bibliographia Groenlandica." *Medd. Grønl.* 12:137–161, 199–217, 1890.

GENERAL STUDIES

Behrens, W.
Ethnografisk Beskrivelse Over Nord Grønland. Kjøbenhavn: 1860. 46 pp.

Birket-Smith, K.
"Ethnografiske Problemer i Grønland." *Geog. Tidssk.* 25:179–197, 1920.

———.
"Ethnography of the Egesminde District." *Meddelelser om Grønland.* (Kjøbenhavn) 66:1–484, 1924.

———.
"Foreløbigt Bidrag til Kap Farvel-Distrikternes Kulturhistorie." *Medd. Gronl.* 53:1–38, 1917.

———.
"The Greenlanders of the Present Day." *Greenland.* 2:1–207, 1928.

Bruun, D.
"Arkaeologiske Undersogelser i Julianehaabs Distrikt." *Medd. Grønl.* 16:171–461, 1896.

Carmichael, D. M.
"Psychology and Ethnology. The Cambridge Expedition to West Greenland, by H. I. Drever." *Geographical Journal.* (London) 94:398–401, 1939.

Cranz, David
The History of Greenland. London: Longman, Hurst, Reese, 1767. 2 vols.

Egede, H. P.
Ausführliche und Wahrhafte Nachricht vom Anfange und Fortgange der Grönländischen Mission. Hamburg: 1740.

————.
Description et Historie Naturelle du Groenland. Copenhague: C. & A. Philibert, 1763. xxviii, 171 pp.

————.
A Description of Greenland. London: C. Hitch, 1745. xvi, 220 pp.

————.
Omstaendelig og Udførlig Relation Angaaende den Grølandske Missions Begyndelse og Fortsaettelse. Kjøbenhavn: 1738.

————.
"Relationer fra Grønland." *Medd. Grønl.* 64: 1–304, 1925.

Egede, P.
Continuation af Relationerne Betreffende den Grønlandske Missions Tilstand og Beskaffenhed. Kjøbenhavn: 1741. 184 pp.

————.
Efterretninger om Grønland. Kjøbenhavn: Trykt at H. C. Schrøder, 1788. 284 pp.

————.
Nachrichten von Grönland. Kopenhagen: 1790.

Elgstrom, Ossian
Moderna Eskimaer. Stockholm: A. Bonnier, 1916. 431 pp. illus.

Fabricius, O.
Den Grønlandske Ordbog. Kjøbenhavn: C. F. Schubert, 1804. viii, 795 pp.

————.
"Udførlig Beskrivelse over de Grønlandske Saele." *Skrivter af Naturhistorie-Selskabet.* 50 (Part 1) :79–157, 1790.

Fries, Theodor Magnus
Grönland, dess Natur och Innevanare. Upsala: E. Berling, 1872.

Glahn, H. C.
Anmaerkninger Over de tre Første Bøger af Hr. David Crantzes Historie om Grønland. Kjøbenhavn: 1771.

Gosch, C. C. A., ed.
Danish Arctic Expeditions 1605 to 1620. London: Printed for the Hakluyt Society, 1897. 2 vols.

Haan, L. F.
Beschryving van de Stratt Davids. Amsterdam: G. van Keulen, 1720. 40 pp.

Hansen, S.
"Bidtrag til Vestgrønlaendernes Anthropologi." *Medd. Grønl.* 7:163–248, 1893.

Holm, G.
"Beskrivelse af Ruiner i Julianehaabs Distrikt." *Medd. Grønl.* 6:57–145, 1894.

Kjer, J., and Rasmussen, C.
Dansk-Grønlandsk Ordbog. Kjøbenhavn: 1893.

Markham, A. H., ed.
The Voyages and Works of John Davis the Navigator. London: 1880. 373 pp.

Mathiassen, T.
"Ancient Eskimo Settlements in the Kangamiut Area." *Medd. Grønl.* 91:1–150, 1931.

————.
"Contributions to the Archaeology of Disko Bay." *Medd. Grønl.* 93 (Part 2) :1–192, 1934.

————.
"The Eskimo Archaeology of Greenland." *Annual Reports Smithson. Inst.* pp. 397–404, 1936.

————.
"Eskimo Finds from the Kangerdlugssuaq Region." *Medd. Grønl.* 104 (Part 9) :1–25. 1934.

————.
"Inugsuk, a Mediaeval Eskimo Settlement." *Medd. Grønl.* 77:145–340, 1930.

————, and Holtved, E.
"The Eskimo Archaeology of Julianhaab District." *Medd. Grønl.* 118 (Part 1) :1–141, 1936.

Nansen, Fridjof,
Eskimo Life. London: Longmans, Green & Co., 1893. xvi, 350 pp.

Paterson, T. T.
"Anthropological Studies in Greenland." *Journ. Anthro. Inst. Gt. Brit.* 69:45–76, 1939.

Poincy, L. de
"The Eskimos of Davis Straits in 1656." *Scottish Geographical Magazine.* 28:281–294, 1912.

Porsild, M. P.
"Studies on the Material Culture of the Eskimo in West Greenland." *Medd. Grønl.* 51:113–250. 1915.

Rasmussen, K.
The People of the Polar North. London: 1908.

Rink, H.
Danish Greenland. London: H. S. King & Co., 1877. xvii, 468 pp.

————.
"Om Grønlaedernes Gamle tro-og Hvad der af Samme er Bevaret under Kristendommen." *Aarbøger for Nordisk Oldkyndighed og Historie.* (Kjøbenhaven) 3:192–256, 1868.

Ryberg, C.
Dansk: Grønlandsk Folk. Kjøbenhavn: 1891.

————.
"Om Erhvervs-og Befolkningsforholdene i Grønland." *Geog. Tidssk.* 17:69–92, 1904.

Saabye, H. E.
Brudstykker af en Dagbog Holden i Grønland. Odense: S. Hempel, 1816. x, 144 pp.

————.
Fragmenter af en Dagboek. Stockholm: Wybe Wouters, 1817.

————.
Greenland. London: Boosey & Sons, 1818.

Schultz-Lorentzen, C. W.
"Eskimoernes Invandring i Grønland. *Medd. Grønl.* 26:289–330, 1904.

————.
"Intellectual Culture of the Greenlanders." *Greenland.* 2:209–270, 1928.

Steensby, H. P.
"Ethnografiske og Anthropogeografiske Rejes-tudier i Nord-Grønland." *Medd. Grønl.* 50:133–173, 1912.

Steenstrup, K. J. V.
"Beretning om Undersøgelsesrejserne i Nord-Grønland." *Medd. Grønl.* 5:1–41, 1893.

Stefansson, Vilhjalmur
Greenland. Illustrated by photographs and drawings. New York: Doubleday, Doran and Company, 1942. 338 pp.

————, ed.
The Three Voyages of Martin Frobisher. London: 1938. 2 vols.

Thorhallesen, E.
"Beskrivelse Over Missionerne i Grønlands Søndre Distrikt." L. Bobe, ed. *Grønlandske Selskabs Skrifter.* 1, 1914.

Trebitsch, R.
Bei den Eskimos in Westgrönland. Berlin: 1909.

Tylor, E. B.
"Old Scandinavian Civilisation among the Modern Esquimaux." *Journ. Anthro. Inst. Gt Brit.* 13:348–357, 1884.

MYTHS—FOLKTALES—LEGENDS

Grøndlanske Folgesagn, opskrevne og med-deelte af Indfødte, med dansk Oversaettelse. Godthaab, 1859.
Tales of Greenland Eskimo, text in Eskimo, Danish translation.

Morillot, l'abbé
Mythtologie et Légendes des Esquimaux du Groenland. n.p.: Alençon, 1874. 74 pp.

Rasmussen, Knud Johan Victor
Myter Og Sagn Fra Grønland. Kjøbenhavn; Gyldendal, Nordisk forlag, 1921. vol. 1, plates, map.
Myths and legends.

Rink, H.
Eskimoiske Eventyr og Sang. Kjøbenhavn: C. A. Reitzel, 1866–1871. 2 vols.

————.
Tales and Traditions of the Eskimo. Edinburgh: W. Blackwood & Sons, 1875. 472 pp.

Thalbitzer, W.
"Folklore from West Greenland." *Medd Grønl.* 40:496–564, 1921.

Worster, W. W.
"Eskimo Folklore and Myths." *Edinburgh Review.* 242:94–107, 1925.

BELIEFS—CUSTOMS—FOLK MEDICINE

Bartels, M.
"Geräthe der Eskimo aus Neu-Herrnhut bei Godhaab." *Verhandl. Berl. Gesel. Anthro. Ethno. Ur.* pp. 542–543, 1900.

Bertelsen, A.
Folkemedicinen i Grønland i Aeldre og Nyere Tid. Grølandske Selskabs Aarsskrift: 1914.

Birket-Smith, K.
"Det Eskimoiske Slaegtskabssystem." *Geog. Tidssk.* 30:96–111, 1927.

————.
"The Greenland Bow." *Medd. Grønl.* 56 (Part 1):1–28, 1918.

Bistrup, A.
"Eskimo Women in Greenland." *Century Magazine.* 82:668–674, 1911.

Glahn, H. C.
Om den Grønlandske Hund." *Nye Samling af Det Kgl. Norske Videnskabers Selskabs Skrifter.* 1:485–496, 1874.

Morgan, L. H.
"Systems of Consanguinity and Affinity." *Smithson. Inst. Contrib. Knowl.* 17:291–382, 1871.

Porsild, M. P.
"On Eskimo Stone Rows in Greenland." *Geog. Rev.* 6:297–309, 1918.

————.
"Uber Einige Geräte der Eskimo." *Zeitschrift für Ethnologie.* (Berlin) 44:600–623, 1912.

Swenander, G.
"Harpun-, Kastpil-och Lansspetsar Fran Väst-Grönland." *Kungliga Svenska Vetenskapsakademiens Handlingar.* 40 (Part 3):1–45, 1906.

Trebitsch, R.
"Die 'Blauen Geburtsflecke' bei den Eskimos in Westgrönland." *Archiv für Anthropologie.* (Braunschweig) 34:237–242, 1907.

Whitaker, W. L.
"The Question of Season Sterility among the Eskimos." *Science.* 88:214–215, 1938.

SPEECH

Bertelsen, A.
"Navnegivning i Grønland." *Medd. Grønl.* 56:221–287, 1918.

Finck, F. N.
"Die Grundbedeutung des Grönländischen Subjektivs." *Sitzungsberichte der Berliner Akademie.* Part 1:280–287, 1905.

Kleinschmidt, S.
Grammatik der Grönländischen Sprache. Berlin: 1851, 182 pp.

————.
Den Grønlandske. Ordbog. Kjøbenhavn: 1871.

Rasmussen, C.
Grønlandsk Sproglaere. Kjøbenhavn: 1888. 201 pp.

Schultz-Lorentzen, C. W.
"Dictionary of the West Greenland Eskimo Language." *Medd. Grønl.* 69:1–303, 1927.

Thalbitzer, W.
"The Aleutian Language Compared with Greenlandic." *International Journal of American Linguistics.* (New York) 2:40–57, 1921.

————.
"A Phonetical Study of the Eskimo Language." *Medd. Grønl.* 31:1–405, 1904.

GAMES

Thalbitzer, W.
"Cultic Games and Festivals in Greenland." *Pro·. Intern. Congr. Amer.* 3 (Part 2):236–255, 1924.

MUSIC

GENERAL STUDIES

Hollatz-Bretagne, Mme.
Légendes et chants esquimaux du Groenland. Libraire Leroux, 45. 1929. 188 pp.

Leden, C.
"Musik und Tänze der Grönländischen Eskimos und die Verwandschaft der Musik der Polareskimos mit der Indianer." *Zeitschrift für Ethnologie* (Berlin) 43:261–270, 1911.
Specimens of songs (Melody and Text), are given from Eskimo of Umanatsiak (west); North Star Bay (polar); Cape Dan (east); with American Indian songs (Thompson R., Hopi) for comparison.

Stiasny, G.
"Volkslieder und Sagen der Westgrönländischen Eskimo." *Mitteilungen der Kaiser-Königlichen Geographischen Gesellschaft in Wien.* 51:327–335, 1908.

Thalbitzer, W.
Inuit Sange og Danse Fra Grønland. Kjøbenhavn: E. Munksgaard, 1939. 75 pp.

Thuren, H.
"On the Eskimo Music of Greenland." *Medd. Grønl.* 40:1–45, 1911.

YUIT

FOLKLORE

GENERAL STUDIES

Bogoras, W. G.
"The Chukchee." *Mem. Amer. Mus. Nat. Hist.* 11, 1904–1909. 2 vols.

————.
"The Eskimo of Siberia." *Mem. Amer. Mus. Nat Hist.* 12:417–456, 1910.

Collins, H. B.
"Ancient Culture of St. Lawrence Island." *Explor. Field-Work Smithson. Inst.* pp. 135–144, 1930.

————.
"The Ancient Eskimo Culture of Northwestern Alaska." *Explor. Field-Work Smithson. Inst.* pp. 141–150, 1928.

————.
"Prehistoric Eskimo Culture of Alaska." *Explor. Field-Work Smithson. Inst.* pp. 147–156, 1929.

Coxe, William
Account of the Russian Discoveries Between Asia and America. London: J. Cadell, 1787. xxviii, 454 pp.

Dall, W. H.
Alaska and Its Resources. pp 378–385, Boston: Lee and Shepard, 1897. xii, 627 pp.

————.
"The Native Tribes of Alaska. *Proc. Amer. Assoc. Adv. Sci.* 34:363–379, 1885.

Geist, O. W., and Rainey, F. G.
"Archaeological Excavations at Kukulik." *Miscellaneous Publications of the University of Alaska.* 2:1–391, 1936.

Gerland, G.
"Zur Ethnographie des Aussersten Nordostens von Asien." *Zeitschrift der Gesellschaft für Erdkunde.* (Berlin) 18:194–222, 1883.

Grinnell, G. B.
"The Natives of the Alaska Coast Region."
Harriman Alaska Expedition. 1:171–178, New
York: 1901.

Hooper, W. H.
Ten Months Among the Tents of the Tuski.
London: J. Murray, 1853. xv, 417 pp.

Lütke, F.
"Die Tschuktschen." *Arch. Wissen. Kunde
Russl.* 3:446–464, 1843.

Mathiassen, T.
"Archaeological Collections from the Western
Eskimos." *Report of the Fifth Thule Expedi-
tion,* (Copenhagen) 10:1–98, 1930.

Muir, J.
The Cruise of the Corwin. Boston: Houghton
Mifflin Co., 1917. xxxi, 278 pp.

Nelson, E. W.
"The Eskimo About Bering Strait." *Ann.
Reports Bur. Amer. Ethnol.* 18 (Part 1):3–
518, 1899.

Nordenskiöld, A. E.
*The Voyage of the Vega Round Asia and
Europe.* New York: The Macmillan Co., 1882.

Rainey, F. G.
"Eskimo Chronology." *Proceedings of the
National Academy of Sciences.* (Washington)
22:357–362, 1936.

CUSTOMS—FOLK ART—SPEECH

Cadzow, D. A.
"Objects from St. Lawrence Island." *Indian
Notes.* 2:122–125, 1925.

Collins, H. B.
"Prehistoric Art of the Alaskan Eskimo."
Smithson. Inst. Miscell. Coll. 81 (Part 14):1–
52, 1929.

Friedman, H.
"Bird Bones from Eskimo Ruins on St. Lawrence Island." *Journal of the Washington
Academy of Sciences.* (Washington) 24:83–
96, 1934.

Moore, R. D.
"Social Life of the Eskimo of St. Lawrence
Island." *AA.* 25:339–375, 1923. n.s.

Wells, R., and Kelly, J. W.
"English-Eskimo and Eskimo-English Vocabu-
laries." *Bureau of Education, Circular of
Information.* 2:1–72, Washington: 1890.

Index

Index

1161

Agricultural College, South Dakota, 416a

Agriculture: British comments, 50a; Indians, 751a, 755-56, 787a, 793b; *California*, 1020a; *Chitimacha*, 902b; corn, 829a; *Digger*, 1053b; *Hidatsa*, 945b; *Hopi*, 985b, 986a; *Maya*, 762a; *Michigan*, 829a; *Navaho*, 996a; *Paiute*, 1053b; *Papago*, 999b; *Pima*, 999b; *Plains*, 922b; *Shawnee*, 910b; *Wisconsin*, 829a; Louisiana, 578b; Northeast, 177b; Pennsylvania Dutch, 587a; slang, 46b; Southeast, 902b; threshing, 322b; West, 701b. *See also* Farms

Agua Caliente Indians, 1023a, 1044a

Agwelonong (Indian chief), 795a

"Ah! No, No, I Never Will Marry," 103a

"Ah, Suzette, Chère," 547b, 548a, 549a

Ahrend, Evelyn R., 424

Ahtena Indians, 1117-18

Ah-Wah-Nee-Chee Indians, 1024a, 1034a

Aiken, Albert W., 693

Aiken, Janet R., 41

Aiken, South Carolina, 434a

Aikin, J., 80

Aikman, Duncan, 409, 415

Ailing Gods 775a

Aimes, Hubert H. S., 552

Ainslie, G., 1071

"Ain't Dat Good News," 468b

"Ain't Gonna Ring No More," 169a, 490a

"Ain't Goin' Down to the Well No Mo'," 485b

"Ain't Goin' to Study War No More," 461b, 468b

"Ain't Got No Place to Hang my Haid," 666a

"Ain't It A Sin To Steal On Sunday," 473b

"Ain't No Grave Can Hold My Body Down," 476a

"Ain't No More Cane On This Brazos," 485b

"Ain't You Glad," 485b

Aitken, B., 771

Aivilik Eskimo. *See* Eskimos

Alabama, 247-49, 272b; geography, 236a; humor, 25b, 31a; Indians, 893a, 905b. *See also* Alibamu Indians; Negroes, 432b, 436-40, 445b, 447ab, 452a: *social songs*, 488b; *spirituals*, 455b, 457b; *work songs*, 488b; nursery rhymes, 165b; placenames, 905b; political life, 190b; printing, 248a; shape note singing, 457b; social life, 190b

"Alabama," 745a

"Alabama Bound," 485b, 500a

"Alabama Gal," 148b

Alabama Historical Society, 248a

Alabama Indians. *See* Alibamu Indians

Alabama University. Library, 262

Alacol (Indian poet), 802a

Alamance, North Carolina, 161a

Alamo, The (Franciscan mission), San Antonio, Texas, 344b, 346b; Crockett, Davy, 693b, 694b; Houston, Sam, 695a; legends, 348b; Mexicans, 695a; siege, 675b; stories, 351b

"Alas, To Whom Dare I Complain?", 122a

Alaska, 404a, 417-19; animals known to Eskimos, 1149a; anthropology, 1123a, 1148b, 1151b, 1153b; archaeology, 1095b, 1148a, 1151b, 1158b, *see also* mummies; art, 1135b, 1159b; characters, 419b, 706b; Danish-American expedition, 1151a; dendochronology, 1148a; documents (1724-1924), 1153a; Eskimos, 1131-33, 1135b, 1148-49, 1151-55: *Aleut*, 1133b, 1136b, 1152ab; *Copper*, 1141a; *Innuit tribes*, 1137b; *Mackenzie*, 1147b; *Yuit*, 1159b; gold, 706b; histories (1724-1924), 1153a; humor, 26a, 418b; Indians, 757b, 1080b, 1108b, 1114-16, 1152a: *Ahtena*, 1117b; *Déné*, 1118a; *Haida*, 1095b; *Kutchin*, 1124-25; *legends*, 1154b; *Northwest Coast*, 1083ab, 1085a, 1086-87; *Tanaina*, 1127ab; *Ten'a*, 1114a, 1122b, 1123b; *Tlingit*, 750b, 1105-7; industries, 1154a; jade, 1152b; legends, 1154b; literature (1724-1924), 1153a; military reconnaissance (1883), 1137b; missions, 1105b; mummies, 1137b; myths, 1154b; place-name, 52b, 55a, 419b; population, 1137b; pottery, 1155a; resources, 1137b, 1153b; stone lamps, 1152b; whale cult, 1134b, 1152a

Albain, W., 527

Albany County, N. Y., 213a, 217a

Albee, John, 795

Albemarle County, Va., 281b, 282b, 285b

Alberta, Canada, 422a, 435ab; characters, 423b; Hickock, James Butler ("Wild Bill"), 705a; Indians, 845b, 929b, 958a; place names, 425ab; skipping rhymes, 426b

"Alberta," 500a, 666a

Albertson, Catherine Seyton, 269

Albrecht, Adalbert, 810

Albrecht, Henry F., 220

Alcott, Frances Jenkins, 755

Alden, Carroll Storrs, 658

Alden, Rev. Timothy, 182, 845

Alderson, Nannie G., 410

Alderson William, 650-51

Aldrich, Jonathan, 736

Aldrich, Richard, 70

Aldrich, Thomas Bailey, 208

Aldridge, Reginald, 610

Alert Bay, Canada, 1097b

Aleut language, 1158a

Aleutian Islands, 1137ab, 1138a

Aleuts, 1136-38

Alexander, Arthur, 84

Alexander, Frances, 358

Alexander, Hartley Burr: Indians, 768, 795, 810: *Plains area*, 922, 956; *Southwestern area*, 978, 1006

Alexander, Henry, 41, 206

Alexander, Joseph, 187

"Alexander and Rosine," 96b

Alexandria, Va., 281a

Alfonse, Jean, 425a

Alford, Thomas (Wildcat), 909

Alger, Abby Langdon, 827

Alger, Horatio, Jr., 374

Algic languages. *See* Algonquian languages

Algic legends. *See* Algonquian Indians—legends

Algic Society, 765a

Algonkin Indians: bear customs, 845b; birchbark, 830b; games, 831a; lore, 824a; New York State, 856a; poems, 830b; St. Lawrence River, 871a; Siouan tribe names, 908a; tales, 827a, 796b; Timiskaming Algonquins, 826b, 840a

Algonquian Indians, 824b, 826b; animal names, 830a; art, 830b; beliefs, 773a, 776a, 872a, 840b, 850a; burial customs, 828b; California, 776a; Canada, 566a, 824a, 827b; Central, 826b, 829a, 836b; Coastal, 825a; culture, 824a, 827a; dream dance, 866b; family band, 832a; Hunting Territory Systems, 829b, 832a; Iowa, 969a; kinship terms, 829a, 832a; Lake, 838b; legends, 827ab, 838b; magic, 180b, 828a, 829b, 872a; marriage customs, 845a, 872b; medicine, 829b, 872b; medicine man, 860b; mental characteristics, 827b; Mississippi, West of, 828b; myths, 826-28, 840b, 847b; Oklahoma, 969a; place-names, 55a, 426a; River Desert Band, 824a, 830b; scapulimancy, *see* magic; social organization, 868a, 1080b; speech, 825b; 826a, 868a, 1040a: *affiliations*, 830a; *American-English words*, 44a; *Blackfoot language, comparison*, 834a; *kinship terms*, 829a; *name meanings*, 803a; *phonetic shifts*, 927a; *vocabulary*, 44a, 841a; *word-formation principles*, 851b; Staten Island, 215b; tales, 828a, 840a, 857a; traditions, 824b; villages, 824b; Wabanaki Confederacy, 832a; wampum, 829ab; wooden bowls, 887a. *See also* Abitibi Indians; Abnaki Indians; Algonkin Indians; Arapaho Indians; Cheyenne Indians; Chippewa Indians; Conoy Indians; Cree Indians; Delaware Indians; Fox Indians; Illinois Indians; Kickapoo Indians; Mahican Indians; Malecite Indians; Mascouten Indians; Massachuset Indians; Menominee Indians; Mi-

Barrett, Samuel Alfred: Indians, 772: *California area*, 1028, 1033-36, 1039; *Great Basin area*, 1058; *Northeastern area*, 831, 864; *Plains area*, 932-33; *Southwestern area*, 984
Barrett, Stephen Melvil, 756, 953-54, 959, 979
Barrett, William Alexander, 81, 454
Barrett-Lennard, C. E., 1099
Barroso, Gustavo, 6
Barrow, Rube, 685a
Barrows, Charles Henry, 207
Barrows, David C., 255-56
Barrows, David Prescott, 1044
Barrows, H. D., 383
Barrows, John R., 404
Barrows, Mary, 186
Barrows, William, 369
Barry, J. M., 84
Barry, J. Nielson, 1078
Barry, James Buckner, 352
Barry, John S., 198
Barry, Phillips: ballads and songs, 70, 96-98, 104-12, 118: *Midwest*, 304; *Northeast*, 186, 194-95, 207, 220; *Southern Highlands*, 242, 259; dance, 136; non-English speaking groups, 569, 592, 607; Shakers, 731
Barry, Theodore A., 383
Barry, William E., 192
Barstow, Marjorie Latta, 443
Bartels, M., 1157
Bartels, P., 1153
Barter customs, **976a**
Barthelson, Joyce, 122
Bartlett, Arthur, 183
Bartlett, Frederic Charles, 22, 778
Bartlett, John Henry, 179
Bartlett, John Russell, 43, 228, 973
Bartlett, Katherine, 982, 989, 1000, 1005
Bartlett, Stanley Foss, 630
Bartlett, William W., 324, 630
Barton, Benjamin Smith, 756
Barton, Henry W., 348
Barton, William Eleazar, 256, 443-44, 454
Bartram, John, 252, 853
Bartram, William, 894, 897
Bary, Helen Valeska, 383
Barzee, Clark Louis, 412
Bascom, Louise Rand, 711
Baseball terminology, 46ab, 50a
Basel, Edmund, 778
"Bashful Thames, The," 123a
"Basin Street Blues," 500-01
Basket dances, 987b, 1008ab
Basket drum, 996a
Baskets and basket-making. *See* Indians
Basques in Oregon, 413a
Bass, Althea, 897
Bass, Robert Duncan, 444
Bass, Sam, 674a, 685a, 709b
Bassett, Fletcher Stewart, 658
Bassett, Sara Ware, 198
Bastian, Adolph, 6, 1078, 1093
Batavia, N. Y., 802a
Batchelder, Eugene, 26

Batchelder, Samuel F., 659
Bateman, L. C., 876
Bates, Albert Carlos, 187
Bates, Barnabas, 727
Bates, Mrs. D. B., 383
Bates, Ernest S., 6
Bates, Paulina, 727
Bates, William C., 546
Batie, Russell V., 650
Battey, Thomas C., 824
Battle, H. B., 894
Battle, J. H., 703
Battle, Kemp Plummer, 270
"Battle Ax and the Devil, The," 131b
Battle ballads, 227b
Battle cries, 221a
"Battle Cry of Freedom," 722a
"Battle Hymn of the Republic, The," 723a
"Battle of Jericho, The," 468b, 476b
"Battle of Roslin, The," 103b
"Battle of Waterloo, The," 103b
Battles. *See* Wars
"Battleship Connecticut," 666b
Batty, Joseph, 369
Bauer, Marion, 75, 195, 210
Baughman, Abraham J., 677
Baughman, Ernest W., 26, 302
Baulig, H., 788
Baum, H. M., 1000
Baum, P. F., 106, 778
Baumann, Gustav, 1006
Bax, Arnold E., 84, 122
Baxter, J. P., 831
Baxter, Rupert H., 987
Bay, Jens Christian, 360
Bay State. *See* Massachusetts
Bayard, Samuel Preston, 75, 106, 225, 227, 285
Bayer, Henry G., 52
Bayley, Charles, 636
Baylies, Francis, 185
Bayliss, Clara Kern, 772, 778, 1003, 1097, 1133
Bayly, George, 654
Bayou ballads, 547b
Bayou Lacomb, St. Tammany Parish, La., 902b
"Be Ready When My Jesus Comes," 469a
Beach, Joseph Warren, 43
Beach, R. F., 174
Beach, S. B., 778
Beach, William Wallace, 756
Beach Hills, South Dakota, 416a
Beadle, Erastus Flavius, 319
Beadle, John Hanson, 360
Beads and beadwork. *See* Art, Indian
Beaglehole, Ernest, 982, 984
Beale, Edward Fitzgerald, 375b
Beale Street, Memphis, Tenn., 493a
"Beale Street Blues," 494b, 495b, 500a, 501a
Beall, Thomas E., 141
Beals, Carlton, 593
Beals, Frank L., 636, 686, 693, 848
Beals, Katharine (McMillan), 37
Beals, Ralph L.: Indians, 756:

Beals, Ralph L.—*cont.*
California area, 1031; *Great Basin area*, 1056; *Plains area*, 926; *Southwestern area*, 973, 1005
Bean, L. L., 183a
Bean, Roy, 674a, 675ab, 685ab, 709b
"Bean Porridge Hot," 169b
"Bean Setting," 146b
Bear gens, Fox Indians, 894b, 851
Bear Lake, Idaho, 1071b
"Bear Mash Blues," 501a
Bear Mother, 1081b
Bear River Indians, 1038ab
Bear River Valley, California, 1031b
"Bear Society Dance," 863a
"Bear the Burden," 461a, 466a, 469a, 474b
"Bear Trap Blues," 501a
Beard, Daniel Carter, 164, 677
Beard, George M., 202
Beards, 225b
Beardsley, Gretchen, 941
Beardsley, Richard K., 16
Bears: California, 376a; ceremonial, 774a; Crockett, Davy, 695b; customs, 845b; dance, 942, 1058ab; Fink, Mike, 700b; Glass, Hugh, 329a, 704a; grizzly, 330-31, 334a, 367b; humor, 33a; hunting, 369b, 395b; Indians, 771a, 778a, 783a, 785b: *California area*, 1036ab, 1046b; *Navaho*, 975b; *Northwestern area*, 1081b, 1083b; *Plateau area*, 1068b; Rocky Mountains, 369b; stories, 179b, 333b, 408b, 795b
Beasley, Delilah Liontium, 430
Beasley, Gladys, 274
Beasley, H. G., 1095
Beasley, Norman, 292
Beason, George D., 249
Beath, Paul Robert, 43, 319
"Beatin' up Sandy," 148b
Beatrix, Ernest, 1116
Beattie, John W., 87, 89
Beatty, Arthur, 22
Beaty, John O., 344
Beauce, Canada, 566b, 567a
Beauchamp, William Martin, 16; Canada, 423; Indians, 778, 788: *Northeastern area*, 824, 834, 853-54 856-62, 868-69; Northeast, 219
Beauchat, M. H., 1135
Beaugrand Honoré, 369, 566, 1114
Beaugrand-Champagne, A., 854
"Beautiful Katie," 103b
Beaver, Tony, 674b, 676a, 685b
Beaver Bundle, 933ab
"Beaver Creek," 624a
Beaver Indians, 1118a
Beazley, Julia, 706, 710
Bebean, G., 840
Bechdolt, Frederick Ritchie, 369, 375, 674, 699
Bechstein, Ludwig, 582
Bechtel, John Hendricks, 39
Beck, Earl Clifton: ballads, 105; characters, 689; French-Cana-

England—*cont.*
57-58, 182a
Englekirk, John Eugene, 340
English, J. S., 209
English ballads and songs, 98b, 107a, 534b; American versions, 101a, 103a; Appalachian Mountains, 242a, 244a, 245b; Canada, 427a; Cumberland Mountains, 243b; Illinois, 301a; Jamaica, 553a, 557b; Kentucky, 110a; Maine, 102b, 118a; New England, 96b, 186b; Nova Scotia, 427a; Ozark Mountains, 288b; school songs, 81a; Tennessee, 276b; Texas, 357b; Virginia, 283a
English dances. *See* Dancing
English Folk Dance and Song Society, 136a
Enigmas. *See* Riddles
Enigmatic songs, 484a
"Eniwube's Vision," 843b
Eno, Clara B., 250
Eno, Joel N., 45, 59, 211, 219, 227
Enterprise, H. M. S., 1140b
Entwistle, William J., 98
Epigrams, 5b, 55b, 80a. *See also* Aphorisms and apothegms
Epiphany, 598b
Epitaphs, 39a, 40a, 48b, 59b; Indian, 216a, 855b; New England, 178a, 182b, 184a, 206a, 230a; New York, 218a
Epler, Blanch N., 240
Epler, William, 701
Eppert, Carl, 642
"Eppie Adair," 123b
"Epping Forest," 150b
Eppse, Mere R., 431
Erdmann, J., 1146
Erich, Oswald Adolf, 582
Erichsen, H., 679
Ericksen, Mabel N., 690
Ericson, Eton Everett, 45, 236, 268, 270, 318
"E-r-i-e," 667a
Erie Canal, New York, 217b, 663a; children, 218a; colloquialisms, 297b; songs, 662a
"Erie Canal," 92b, 126a, 168b, 222a, 665ab
Erie County, N. Y., 217a, 218a, 223a
Erie Indians, 885-86
Erikson, Erik Homburger, 964, 1043
Erkes, E., 1082
"Erlinton," 105a
Erman, A., 1105, 1122
Ermine, Will, 400
Ernest-Beatrix, frère, 566
Ernst, Alice Henson, 405, 1085, 1087
Eros, 10b
Errett, Russell, 53
Ersine, Noel, 45
Erskine, Clara, 771
Erskine, Mrs. Gladys (Shaw), 362
Erskine, John, 45, 75
Ertz Susan, 396
Erwin, Richard P., 1071
Esarey, Logan, 301

Escalante, Father, 1052a
Eshleman, Henry F., 889
Eskimo language, 780a, 1132b, 1135b, 1152b, 1157a; Alaska, 1149ab, 1152b, 1155ab; Aleuts, 1138ab; Baffinland, 1139b; Caribou, 1140a; dialects, 1135b, 1144a, 1147b: *Cape Prince of Wales,* 1155b; *Copper,* 1141b; *Cumberland Sound,* 1139b; *Greenland,* 1143b; dictionaries, 1138a, 1146b, 1158a; grammars, 1155b: *Aleut,* 1138a; *Greenland,* 1146b, 1158a; *Innuit,* 1155a; *Labrador,* 1146b; *Greenland,* 1138b, 1143b, 1158a; *Iglulik,* 1144b; Labrador, 1146-47; *Mackenzie,* 1147b; nomenclature of tribes, 1153b; numerals, 1135b; phonetics, 1135b; place-names, 1150b; Polar, 1150b; Ugalakmiut, 1152b; Uralian language, 1135b; vocabularies, 1138a, 1149ab, 1155b; words, 791, 1135a; Yuit, 1159
Eskimos: Alaska, 1131-32, 1148-49, 1151-52; Aleut, 1136-38; Angmagssalik, 1142a, 1143a; animals, 1149a, *see also* birds; dogs; seals; walrus; whales; Aivilik, 1153a; archaeology, 1130b, 1134b, 1142a, 1144b, 1148a; Baffinland, 1138-40; beliefs, 1134a, 1154b, *see also* religion; Bering Sea, 1131b; birds, 1150b; blond, 1140b, 1141a; blood-grouping, 1139ab; bows, 1135a; Canadian northwest, 1131ab; canneries, 1152a; Caribou, 1140; cats' cradles, 1150b; ceremonial life, 1140a; Chalcolithic, 1141a; characteristics, 1131b, 1137b; children, 1134a, 1137-38, 1150b, 1154b; chronology, 1132a; Chukchee, 1158b; civilization and, 1132b; clowns, 1146b; commerce, 1132b; Copper, 1140-41; costume and adornment, 1134a, 1148b; counting, 1149a; community-life, 1134b; Cumberland Sound, 1138-39; customs. *See* Customs, Eskimo; dances, 1151a, 1155b; dendochronology, 1148a; disease, 1147b; distribution, tribal, 1137a, 1139a; dogs, 1134a, 1135a, 1150b, 1157b; dwellings, 1134a, 1137b; economic life, 1140a; ethics, 1134a; European civilization, adjustment, 1132a; feasts, 1154a; festivals, 1154a; fishing, 1134a, 1145b; food, 1134a, 1138a, 1148b, 1150b, 1155a; girls' puberty, 1155a; gods, 1133b, 1135a, 1140b; graves, 1146b; Greenland, 1141-44, 1155-58; history, 1137a; Hudson Bay, 1139ab; hunters and hunting, 1147b, 1153a, 1154a; Iglulik, 1144-45; implements, 1143b, 1152a, 1154a; Innuit, 1135a, 1137b, 1148-49, 1151b, 1158b; Kangamuit area, 1131b; killing, attitude toward,

Eskimos—*cont.*
1134a; Labrador, 1145-47; lamps, 1134b, 1141a; language. *See* Eskimo language; law-ways, 1134b; Mackenzie, 1147; magic, 1134b; Manitunik, 1146a; masks, 1146b; measuring, 1149a; medicine, 1157b; medicine men, 1151b; mental ability, 1137a; migrations, 1132a: *Aleut,* 1136b; *Bering Sea region,* 1135b; *Caribou,* 1140a; *Polar,* 1149a; mummies, 1137b, 1138a; Netsilik, 1147-48; Nunivak, 1134b, 1151b; origin, 1130-33, 1136b, 1140b; pipe-stems, 1140b; place-names, 1150b; Polar, 1149-51; priests, 1143b; property marks, 1149a; recreation, 1151b; relationships, 1141b; religion, 1132b, 1138a, 1139b, 1151b, *see also* beliefs; riddles, 1146b; rites and ceremonies, 1134a, 1151b; Scandinavian civilization, 1157a; screws, 1134-35, 1155a; seals and seal-catching, 1149a; Sedna cycle, 1134a; settlements, 1141-43, 1145-46; snow-shovel, 1141a; social life, 1159b; social organization, 1151b; somatology, 1130b; songs, 1133b, 1136ab, 1141ab, 1144-45, 1158ab; sorcerers, 1134a; Southampton, 1152-53; sterility, 1151a; Stone Age peoples and, 1132a; stone rows, 1157b; string-figures, 1141b, *see also* cats' cradles; symbols, 1152a; trade, 1139a, 1154a; tribes, 1148b; Tuski, 1159a; utensils, 1154a: *cooking vessels,* 1141a; weapons: *darts,* 1149b; *harpoons,* 1134b, 1149ab, 1157b; *javelins,* 1157b; *knife, woman's,* 1134b; *lances,* 1157b; *throwing sticks,* 1134b; whale cult, 1134b; whaling, 1138a; women, 1134a, 1155a, 1157b; Yuit, 1158-59
Eskippakithiki, Kentucky, 897b
Espenshade, A. Henry, 227
"Esperanzo-Barn Dance," 150b
Espinel, Luisa, 602
Espinet, Charles S., 558
Espinosa, Aurelio Macedonio, 23; Indians: *Comanche,* 939; *Pueblo,* 1001, 1005, 1007; Spanish-Americans, 594, 597: *ballads,* 602; *games,* 605; *language,* 600; *legend,* 596; *riddles,* 599; *tales,* 596
Espinosa, José Manuel, 596
Esquemeling, Joseph, 198
Esselen language, 1041a
Essene, Frank, 1042
Essex County, New York, 213a
Essig, E. O., 1021
Estabrooke, Horace Melvyn, 194
Esterby, J. H., 272
Estes, George, 650
Estill, Julia, 349, 353
Estudillo, 1041b
Estufa pueblo, 1007a
Etagotine Indians. *See* Kaska Indians

Hot Springs, Alaska, 1138a
Hottes, A. C., 680
Houck, Louis, 316
Hough, Donald, 400
Hough, Emerson, 613, 675, 693, 702
Hough, Walter, 760, 770, 774; Eskimos, 1134; Indians: *music*, 815; *Powhatan*, 907; *Southwestern area*, 976, 982, 985, 987-88, 1002, 1011
Houghton, F., 855, 880
Housatonic River, 188b
House, Boyce, 346, 350, 354, 596, 647
House, Dorothy E., 46
"House Carpenter, The," 106a, 126a, 129b, 132b, 247a
"House Done Built Without Hands," 478a
"House of the Rising Sun," 93a, 127a, 666a
Household words, 39b
Houses. *See* Dwellings
Houston, Margaret Bell, 346
Houston, Samuel, 675a, 695a
Houston, Texas, 347b
Hovey, E. O., 1150
How, Louis, 166, 221
"How Could I Be So Mean," 508b
"How Long," 478a
"How Much I Owe," 478b
"How Should I Your True Love Know?," 121a
"How Summer came," 1116a
"How the Raven Stole the Sun," 567a
Howard, Clarence J., 40
Howard, E. B., 760
Howard, Guy, 286
Howard, Helen Addison, 1070
Howard, John Tasker, 68, 72, 76; ballads, 99; cowboys, 618; Indian music, 810, 815; lumberjacks, 633; Negroes, 443, 446, 524; spirituals, White, 735; wars, 717
Howard, Joseph Kinsey, 410
Howard, Leon, 31
Howard, Oliver Otis, 1029, 1070
Howay, F. W., 408, 1085
Howe, Edgar Watson, 308, 309, 371
Howe, Elias J., 140, 533
Howe, Henry: circuit riders, 324; history: *Midwest*, 292; *Ohio*, 322, 702; *West*, 363
Howe, M. A. D., 488
Howe, Martin, 495
Howe, Mary, 143
Howe, Octavius Thorndike, 638
Howe, R. Wilson, 446
Howells, William Cooper, 323
Howells, William Dean, 322, 323, 707, 729
Howells, William White, 760, 774
"Howell's Railroad," 486a
Howes, Frank, 72
Howes, William J., 830
Howgate polar expedition (1877-78), 1131b
Howland, Russell, 709
Howley, James P., 833
Hoy, William J., 562

Hoyt, Henry F., 341
Hrdlicka, Ales, 760, 791, 805; Eskimos, 1137-38, 1148, 1151-55; Indians: *Khotana*, 1123; *Northeastern area*, 836, 846; *Southwestern area*, 976, 979, 998; *Ute*, 1056
Hubbard, Bernard Rosecrans, 418
Hubbard, Frank McKinney, 31
Hubbard, Freeman H., 651, 704, 705
Hubbard, Lester A., 399
Hubbard, Lucius Lee, 194
Hubbard, Margaret Ann, 410
Hubbard, Ralph, 799
Hubbard, Stephen, 533
Hubbard, William Lines, 76, 446, 815
Hubbell, Jay Broadus, 277
Hubbs, James, 363
Hubert, P. M., 736
Huckel (John Frederick) Collections, 995a
Hucks, J. Jenkins, 442
Huddle, Franklin P., 46
Huddleston murder, 216b
Hudson, Arthur Palmer: Negroes, 442; songs and ballads, 99-100: *Mississippi*, 109, 267, *South*, 242; South, 240, 266-67, 275
Hudson, J. W., 1036, 1041
Hudson Bay and Hudson Bay Territory, 825a, 843b, 844a, 1121a; Eskimos, 1133a, 1139b, 1146a, 1153a: *Baffinland*, 1139a; *Caribou*, 1140a; *Iglulik*, 1144ab; *Southampton*, 1152b; Indians, 1145b: *Carrier*, 1118b; *Chipewyan*, 1120a; *Dogrib*, 1121a; *Montagnais*, 871a
Hudson River and Hudson River Valley: Dutch folklore, 214a, 219a; ghost lore, 217a; Indian tribes, 856a, 886b; landings, 214b; legends and stories, 212b, 215ab, 216ab; place names, 869b; superstitions, 217b, 218b; songs, 221b, 222ab
Hudson River Legend (ballet), 222a
Hudson Strait, Can., 1121a, 1146a
Hudson's Bay Company, 1121b
Huebner, H., 1008
Hueston, Ethel, 705
Huffman, O. H., 385
Hufford, David Andrew, 363
Huger, Alfred, 457
Huggins, E. L., 1071
Hughes, Dan de Lara, 338
Hughes, Herbert L., 85, 265
Hughes, Josiah, 284
Hughes, L., 495
Hughes, Robert, 233
Hughs, Fannie May, 350
Hugolin, R. P., 841
Huguenots, 280a, 893a
Huida Indians. *See* Haida Indians
Huida-kwul-ra (native tobacco), 1094b
Hulbert, Archer Butler: California trail, 638; Indians, 825; Ohio River, 702; Santa Fe trail, 335; Wilderness Road, 257

Hulbert, F. Randolph, 533
Hulbert, W., 760
Hull, A. E., 72
Hull, Eleanor, 57, 63
Hull, Isaac, 537a
Hull, Myra E., 108, 309
"Hullabaloo Belay," 92b, 126a, 666b, 667ab
Hulley, Lincoln, 253
"Hull's Victory," 146ab, 152a
Hulme, Frederick Edward, 14, 37
Hulsizer, Allan, 990
Human sacrifice. *See* Rites and ceremonies, Indian
"Humble," 466b
Humboldt Indians, 1054b
Humboldt River, Nevada, 394b
Hume, Edgar Erskine, 260
Humfreville, James Lee, 761, 939
Hum-ishu-ma, Okinaqan Indian, 780
Hummel, Lynn E., 288
Humor, 4a, 25-35, 676ab, 691b, 701b; Alaska, 418b; almanacs, 696b, 697a; Arkansas, 250b; ballads, 59a, 108a, 113b, 357b. *See also* Humorous songs; California, 377b, 379a, 383a; characters, 348b, 685a, 691a, 695b, 706b, 707a; college, 179a; Colorado, 393a; Cornish, 310a; cowboy, 610b, 613b, 614b, 615b; epitaphs, 218a; Finnish, 310a; Forty-Niners, 639b; French, 310a; French Canada, 565b, 566b, 567b; Haiti, 555a; heroes, 674a; Indians, 784-85, 786a, 992a, 996a; Italian, 310a; Jews, 578ab; Kentucky, 258b, 259a; logging camps, 689b; Louisiana, 335b; lumberjacks, 630a; Maine, 192b, 193b; Maryland, 196b; Massachusetts, 199a; Michigan, 310a; Midwest, 296b; Minnesota, 313b; Mississippi, 266a; Mormons, 397a; music, 87b. *See also* Humorous songs; Negro minstrelsy, 523ab, 527a, 528b, 529b, 531b; Negroes, 437a, 442b, 541a; New England, 175ab, 176a; New Mexico, 339a; New York State, 212b, 213a, 215b; newspapers, 13a; Northeast, 179b, 180a, 181ab, 184a; Pennsylvania Germans, 587b; Prince Edward Island, 424b; railroaders, 13b, 650a; sailormen, 655b; Scotland, 60a; South, 237b, 239a, 334a; Southwest, 333a; Swedish, 310a; tales, 24b, 299a, 300b; Tennessee, 275a; Texas, 345a, 346a, 350-52, 355b, 596b; Utah, 397a; Virginia, 278b, 280b; weather lore, 184a; West, 365b, 369b, 397a; Wisconsin, 324a; World War I, 716a; Yankees, 176a, 177a, 180b. *See also* Anecdotes; Children—anecdotes; Parody
"Humoresque, Banjo Song," 143b
Humorous songs: Arkansas, 251b; England, 78b, 82b; Irish, 534b;